BUDDHIST HYBRID SANSKRIT GRAMMAR

VOLUME II: DICTIONAR

BUDDHIST HYBRID SANSKRIT GRAMMAR AND DICTIONARY

FRANKLIN EDGERTON
Sterling Professor of Sanskrit and Comparative Philology, Yale University

VOLUME II: DICTIONARY

MOTILAL BANARSIDASS PUBLISHERS
PRIVATE LIMITED • DELHI

First Edition: New Haven, 1953
Reprint: Delhi, 1970, 1972, 1977, 1985, 1993, 1998, 2004

(By arrangement with Yale University Press, New Haven)

ISBN: 81-208-0999-8 (Vol. II)
ISBN: 81-208-0997-1 (Set)

Also available at:

MOTILAL BANARSIDASS
41 U.A. Bungalow Road, Jawahar Nagar, Delhi 110 007
8 Mahalaxmi Chamber, 22 Bhulabhai Desai Road, Mumbai 400 026
236, 9th Main III Block, Jayanagar, Bangalore 560 011
120 Royapettah High Road, Mylapore, Chennai 600 004
Sanas Plaza, 1302 Baji Rao Road, Pune 411 002
8 Camac Street, Kolkata 700 017
Ashok Rajpath, Patna 800 004
Chowk, Varanasi 221 001

Printed in India
BY JAINENDRA PRAKASH JAIN AT SHRI JAINENDRA PRESS,
A-45 NARAINA, PHASE-I, NEW DELHI 110 028
AND PUBLISHED BY NARENDRA PRAKASH JAIN FOR
MOTILAL BANARSIDASS PUBLISHERS PRIVATE LIMITED,
BUNGALOW ROAD, DELHI 110 007

WILLIAM DWIGHT WHITNEY LINGUISTIC SERIES

Edited by

BERNARD BLOCH FRANKLIN EDGERTON

ISIDORE DYEN ALBRECHT GOETZE

KONSTANTIN REICHARDT

of the Department of Linguistics in Yale University

CONTENTS OF VOLUME TWO

A

a-, an-, negative prefix: (**1**) prefixed to finite verbs, as rarely in Skt. (Renou p. 175) but rather often in Pali (CPD s.v., 7); here not common: apaśyanti SP 324.2; anatikramāmo Mv ii.80.8; anicchiyati (?) Mv iii.295.18; see § 23.17; (**2**) in sense described for Pali in CPD s.v. 2, a cpd. in a- following the same word without a-, and preceding a form of kṛ: samitim asamitiṃ kṛtvā Divy 41.10, lit. *making the assembly no assembly*, i. e. *quitting the assembly*; tasya vacanam avacanaṃ kṛtvā Divy 41.28, *disregarding his advice*. See **an-a-**.

1 **aṃśa**, m., (**1**) (= Pali aṃsa, only in comp.) (*part*, and so) *time* (as past, present, future): Mv i.160.8, 9 (prose) atīte aṃśe ... anāgate aṃśe ... pratyutpanne aṃśe (in sense of usual adhvani, see **adhvan**, which is used in Sūtrāl. xx–xxi.57 and Mvy 151–153 in parallel to this passage, on the 18 **āveṇika** buddha-dharma); atīte aṃśe Mv i.161.6; atītāṃśagatā (= Pali atītaṃsa-) Mvy 6438; (**2**) *portion*, in **maitra aṃśa** *portion of affection*, virtually = *love* (so Pali cpd. mettaṃsa, It. 22.4, not adj. with PTSD but noun *love*, °so sabbabhūtesu veraṃ tassa na kenaci, *he has love for all creatures, has no enmity with anyone*); maitreṇāṃśena sphuritvā, *having suffused with love* Divy 60.24 (so with mss.); 61.12 (here mss. and ed. maitreyāṃśena, a corruption due to repeated occurrence of name Maitreya in the context); 66.18 (here kept in ed. with mss.); see **sphurati**; a variant form, in comp. with maitra or **maitrā**, seems to occur in **maitrāsa-ṭā**, q.v.—See **aṣṭāṃśa**.

[2 **aṃśa-dhātrī**, see **aṃsa-**].

-aṃśika (cf. 1 **aṃśa**, 2), ifc., *belonging to the part of*; *pertaining to*; sometimes with vṛddhi of first syllable of prior member of cpd.: maraṇāṃśika Mvy 5345, upapattyaṃśika 5346, *belonging to* (*the part of*) *death, birth*; Tib. char gtogs pa, *included in the division of* (Das); aupapattyaṃśika = upa° Śikṣ 226.7 ff. (Śāl 87.10 ff.); 253.3, 5. Equivalent to -aṃśika are **-antika** in māraṇāntika Śikṣ 226.7 ff. (same passage Śāl) and **-aṅgika** in aupapattyaṅgika Laṅk 277.6 (said of citta). It is natural to suspect that corruption of tradition is responsible for one or two of these. But (1) all can be plausibly explained as of independent origin; (2) -aṃśika is well authenticated, while -antika is supported by Pali (māraṇantika Miln. 48.11).

aṃśu (= Skt. aṃśuka), *cloth*, or *garment* (less probably *thread*, a meaning recorded for Skt. aṃśu and for Pali aṃsu): -kāśikāṃśu-kṣomakādyāḥ Divy 316.27.

aṃsa-dhātrī, also written **aṃśa-**, and in mss. atsa-, lit. *'shoulder nurse'*, one who carries a baby; usual substitute for **aṅka-dh°**, q.v.: Divy 3.13; 26.9; 58.11; 99.25; 271.18; 441.22; MSV i.132.20; iii.134.7; Av i.15.11 and often. App. secondary to **aṅka-**, yet supported by MSV iii.134.12 dhātry-aṃsa-gato niṣaṇṇo.

akaṇa, adj. (= Pali id., see **kaṇa, niṣkaṇa**), *free from the red coating under the husk* (of rice): (śāli) Mv i.342.1, 7; iii.72.19.

akaṇaka = prec.: -śālim akaṇakam Divy 120.2.

Akaṇṭaka, nt., n. of a Buddhakṣetra: Mv i.123.12.

akati-gāthā (cf. Pkt. akai, *unnumbered, infinite*), *having numberless* (a-kati) *verses*, or *an infinite(ly numerous) verse*; of the sāvitrī stanza, Divy 638.2. In an examination on Vedic lore: paṭhatu bhavān sāvitrīṃ. (Answer:) akatigāthā. — katyakṣarā sāvitrī, katigaṇḍā, katipadā. (Answer:) caturviṃśatyakṣarā, trigaṇḍā, aṣṭākṣarapadā.

akaniṣṭha (= Pali akaniṭṭha; see also **aghaniṣṭha**), (**1**) n. of the fifth and highest class of the Śuddhāvāsakāyika gods (see **deva**), and (**2**) sg., n. of the region where they live (Bbh 61.4 yāvad akaniṣṭhād; but more normally yāvad akaniṣṭhabhavanam, Divy 162.16, or the like). They dwell brahmaloke SP 359.1. Often mentioned alone as the highest of the 'form' (**rūpāvacara**) gods, as also in the lists of classes of gods: Mvy 3106; Dharmas 128; LV 47.1; 150.11; 227.2; 266.8; 342.18; Mv i.266.3, 7; ii.314.3, 9; 319.7; 349.2; iii.139.3; Divy 68.17; 367.14; Av i.5.4; ii.105.11; RP 6.16; Mmk 19.10; 69.7; Bbh 69.19; 360.26; Sukh 64.11. Sometimes in sg. of a single member of the class, LV 44.13.

akaniṣṭhika (prec. plus -ika), adj. with deva, *belonging to the akaniṣṭha class*: °ikādibhir devaiḥ Karmav 157.2.

Akampitasāgara, n. of a Bodhisattva: Gv 443.3.

akampiya, adj. (= Pali id., Skt. °pya), *unshakable*: Gv 25.21 (vs).

Akampya, m., so read with v.l. in Mironov for Ākampya, n. of a Bodhisattva-samādhi: Mvy 739; Tib. mi (b)sgul pa = a-kampya.

Akampyanetra, n. of a Bodhisattva: Gv 443.8.

Akardama, nt., n. of a Buddhakṣetra: Mv i.124.1.

akalpika, adj. (Pali akappiya), *improper*; cf. **kalpika**, and next: MSV i.234.5; **-dāna**, *gift of something that is improper*, Śikṣ 271.7; Bbh 123.8; **-pradāna** Karmav 44.17.

a-kalpya, adj. (= prec., and Pali akappiya; not in Skt., nor is **kalpya**, q.v., there recorded in a corresponding sense), *improper*: Laṅk 249.13, of māṃsarudhirāhāra.

akalmāṣa, adj. (= Pali akammāsa), *pure* (lit. *not variegated*; in this sense once in ŚB., otherwise in Skt. only as n. pr.): Mv i.211.11 = ii.15.10, along with pariśuddha, of brahmacarya; i.239.5–6, of ceto-praṇidhāna; iii.343.2, of Buddha's voice.

akākolīna, ?(said of water): °ne jātīkusumānāṃ pānīye juhuyāt Mmk 313.26; °ne pānīyakumbhaṃ nivedayet 320.1, *he shall offer a jar of water in* (water that is?) *ak°*; possibly *free from* (the plant) *kākolī* (?).

akāca, adj. (= Pali id.; etym. uncertain; PTSD *not glass*, originally of jewels; it is once applied to jewels, along with vimala and suddha, in DN ii.244.10 = Jāt. ii.418.20; another theory in Senart i note 508), *free from blemish or impurity*: achidram akācam avraṇaṃ anāśravam te caraṇaṃ Mv i.164.7.

akāmaka, adj. (= Pali id.; Skt. akāma), *unwilling*; *in spite of (adverse) desire*: °kānāṃ mātāpitṝṇām Mv ii.68.20 and 117.18; °kā(ḥ) iii.92.6; °kena Śikṣ 19.21.

a-kāmakāmin, adj. (= Pali id.; Skt. kāma°, BhG. 2.70), *not lusting after lusts*: sthitalapā (see this) °naś ca bhavanti Mv i.134.10 (wrongly Senart); **°mi-tva**, *state of being ak°*, Mv i.153.11.

akāmam, adv., *whether he likes or not*, (*even*) *unwillingly, willy-nilly*: Prāt 496.14.

akāyikā (or **°ka**, n. pl. **°kā**), *a kind of toy* (Index wrongly *a game*): krīḍāpanikāni bhavanti, tad yathā, akāyikā ... Divy 475.18 (cf. **sakāyikā**).

akāryopaka, see **upaka**.

a-kāla (m.?, neg. of 2 **kāla** 1, *day*, q.v.; cf. Skt. vikāla), *night*: akālāt kālībhūtam Divy 336.14, *from night it became day*; akālībhūtam, *it became night*, Divy 335.17; 337.11 (kālād akā°).

akālaka, (1) nt. (from **akāla**), *food (delicacies) suitable for eating at other than meal times* (= **akālakhādyaka,** q.v.): śālīnām odanavidhim akālakam (so Senart em., mss. odanaṃ viditakālakaṃ, or °kārakaṃ) anekavyañjana-m-upetaṃ Mv i.306.13 (vs; otherwise Senart); tair °kāni sajjīkṛtāni Divy 130.22; (**2**) adj. (cf. Pali akāla-cīvara), of monks' robes, *provided at extraordinary times:* (akā)lakaiś cīvaraiḥ MPS 40.54.

akāla-kaumudī, *an irregular festival,* i. e. one not held at any fixed time: puṇyāni kriyatām °mudī ca kriyatām Divy 514.17 ff.

akālakhādyaka, nt. (cf. **khādyaka**) = **akālaka (1),** q.v.: °kāni śīghraṃ sajjīkuruteti Divy 130.21 (consisting of ghṛta-guḍa-śarkarā-pānakāni, 130.20).

Akāladarśana, n. of a mountain: Kv 91.17.

akālika, adj. (= Pali id.; ep. of dhamma; also BHS **āk**°, q.v.), *immediate, not dependent on lapse of time* (said of dharma-vinaya): Mv iii.200.10, see s.v. **ehipaśyika.**

akilāntaka, adj. (for **a-klāntaka**), *unwearied*: °kā LV 359.20 (vs), voc. sg., m.c.; to Buddha.

a-kilāsi-tā (to next), *non-indolence, non-weariness*: °tayā, *without weariness,* AsP 104.21.

a-kilāsin, adj. (Pali akilāsu; see **kilāsin**), *unwearied, not indolent*: (of a kalyāṇamitra) pratisaṃkhyānabahulaḥ °sī . . . dharmadeśanāyai Bbh 238.11; saṃharṣakaś cā °si (m.c. for °sī) nityaṃ SP 204.10 (vs).

a-kisara-lābhin, adj., and °**bhi-tā,** abstr.; also in Skt. form as **a-kṛcchra**°, *(state of) obtaining without difficulty*: akṛcchra-lābhī (n. sg.) Mvy 2432 = dkaḥ pa med par thob pa, and akisara-l° 2433 = tshegs med par°, or, ṅan ṅon ma yin par°; akṛcchrākisaralābhi-tā Bbh 388.13 = (acc. to note) Tib. ṅan ṅon ma yin par thob pa daṅ tshegs med par thob pa. The three Tib. translations are synonymous; it is striking that both the MIndic and the Sktized forms are recorded together in both Mvy and Bbh. Pali has both akasiralābhi(n) and akiccha°; otherwise the cpd. is not recorded. Even akṛcchra is not recorded in Skt. except for akṛcchra-laṅghya in pw 5.240 (from Rājat.; perhaps due to Buddhist influence?). See **kisara**; it appears that in Pali, too, kasira and kiccha, both historically from kṛcchra, came to be understood as different words. This suggests that BHS a-kṛcchra-lābhin may be a Sktization of an older MIndic a-kiccha° (= Pali and Pkt. id.), specifically, and not of BHS **kisara,** which maintained an independent existence for a time, tho ultimately it was crowded out by the Sktized kṛcchra.

Akutobhaya, n. of a former Buddha: Mv iii.237.10.

-akumbha, *best of its kind* (lit. *no pot, no commonplace thing*), ifc.: avataṃsakṛtākumbhaṃ kretum icchati kaḥ kumbham Jm 101.14 (vs; with word-play), *who wants to buy this jar which is a no-jar made into a crown*?; 186.16, see s.v. **sātman.**

Akulika, n. of a nāga king: Mmk 18.10. Follows (in a list of nāga kings) immediately after Kulika (Skt.), and evidently fashioned on that.

? **akulejyeṣṭhāpacāyaka,** m.: Divy 293.26 °kaiḥ, *not honoring the elders of the family*; neg. of kulajyeṣṭhā°, see s.v. **apacāyaka**; prob. read akula°, tho a loc. in a tatpuruṣa cpd. kulejyeṣṭha would not be impossible (*eldest in the family*).

akuśala, nt. (= Pali °sala), *sin, evil*; ten (3 of body, 4 of speech, 3 of thought): Mvy 1681–4 (not named); Dharmas 56 (named; opposites of the 10 **kuśala,** q.v.).

akuśalamūla, nt. (= Pali akus°), *root of demerit*, opp. of **kuśalamūla**: three (lobha, moha, dveṣa, as in Pali which has dosa for dveṣa): Dharmas 139.

a-kuśīda-vartin, adj. (cf. **kusīda**), *not living slothfully*: Mv i.357.13 °**vartī,** n. sg. m., in same vs as Pali Sn 68 akusītavuttī.

a-kūhaka, see **kūhaka.**

a-kṛcchra-lābhin, see **a-kisara**°.

akṛtaka, adj. (see **kṛtaka**; cf. Pali akata as ep. of nibbāna, and **akṛtajña** 1), *not created, unfashioned, intangible, immaterial,* in Laṅk standardly as epithet of ākāśa, nirvāṇa, nirodha. Often mistranslated as if active by Suzuki, *no doer, not working,* or the like: Laṅk 60.6; 72.5; 77.1, etc. Also more generally: sarvaṃ . . . kṛtakam, or sarvam . . . akṛtakam Laṅk 176.11 and 13, *all is created* or *all is uncreated,* as doctrines of two materialistic schools; the question is raised Laṅk 187.9 whether the Tathāgata is *uncreated* (akṛtakaḥ) or *created* (kṛtakaḥ).

akṛtajña (in mg. 1 = Pali akataññu), (**1**) adj., *knowing the uncreated* (i. e. nirvāṇa; cf. **akṛtaka**) : Ud xxix.33 = Pali Dhp. 97; (**2**) (Skt., also Pali akataññu, adj., *ungrateful*) n. of a prince, brother of **Kṛtajña**: RP 25.5.

akṛpaṇam, adv., *not poorly, very well*: SP 79.12 (Skt. kṛpaṇam and Pali kapaṇaṃ are used as adverbs, *miserably*).

akoṭi or °**ṭī,** see **bhūtakoṭi.**

akopya, adj. (= Pali akuppa, used with cetovimutti; cf. **avikopita**), *immovable, steadfast, fixed, sure*; *not to be violated* (of a command): cetovimukti or cetomukti LV 418.17; Mv ii.139.6; iii.333.13, 16; dharma LV 426.20 (akopyadharma-deśaka); Mv iii.200.15; Divy 617.13 (akopya-dharmā, said of a bhikṣuṇī); (dharma-)cakra LV 422.17; ājñā (śāstur) Divy 185.8.

akausīdya, see **kausīdya.**

akrudhyana-tā (a plus **krudhyana** = Pali kujjhana, °nā; to Skt. krudhyati with -ana, -anā, plus -tā), *state of not being angry*: °**tayā** Śikṣ 35.9.

aklāntaka, see **akilāntaka.**

Aklinnagātra, n. of a former Buddha: Mv i.141.9.

a-kliṣṭa, see **kliśyati.**

akṣaṇa, m. or nt. (= Pali akkhaṇa), *inopportune birth, birth under such circumstances that one cannot learn from a Buddha.* There are eight such in Pali, DN iii.287.12 ff.; AN iv.225.19 ff. (9 in DN iii.263.31 ff.), viz.: (at a time when a Buddha is living) one is born (1) in a hell, (2) as an animal, (3) as a preta, (4) as one of the 'long-lived gods', (5) in border countries or barbarian regions, (6) with perverted, heretical mentality, (7) dull, stupid, incapable of distinguishing the gospel from what is inconsistent with it; or (8) he is born capable of profiting from the gospel but at a time when no Buddha exists to teach it. (DN iii.263 ff. adds as 9th, after No. 3, birth as an asura.) These same 8, transposing 6 and 7, are briefly listed Mvy 2299–2306: (1) narakāḥ, (2) tiryañcaḥ, (3) pretāḥ, (4) dīrghāyuṣo devāḥ, (5) pratyantajanapadam, (6) indriyavaikalyam, (7) mithyādarśanam, (8) tathāgatānām anutpādaḥ. In Dharmas 134 No. 5 is put before 4, otherwise 1–7 as in Mvy, but 8 (obviously by a secondary change) is wholly different: (1) narakopapattis, (2) tiryagupapattir, (3) yamalokopapattiḥ, (4) pratyantajanapadopapattir, (5) dīrghāyuṣadevopapattir, (6) indriyavikalatā, (7) mithyādṛṣṭiś, (8) cittotpādavirāgitatā (seems to be a different version of 6, which corresponds to Pali 7, while 8 of the others is omitted). As opposed to these there is only one **kṣaṇa,** *opportune birth*; see s.v. Eight akṣaṇa Mv ii.363.3; LV 412.14; Śikṣ 2.4; 114.14; Gv 116.16; Suv 41.13. The word never means *misfortune* in general, but only *unfavorable birth,* and in most cases clearly in just the sense described above. So Śikṣ 147.14 akṣaṇagatiṃ na gacchaty anyatra sattvaparipākāt, (a Bodhisattva) *is not born in an inopportune birth, except to mature creatures* (the transl. misunderstands); LV 278.22 akṣaṇāni pithitāny abhūvan, and 279.19 akṣaṇāḥ pithitāḥ, are explained by Gv 112.19 sarvākṣaṇadvārakapāṭāni pithayiṣyati (or with text pithapayiṣ°, see Chap. 43, s.v.) *he will close the door-panels (opening into) all the inopportune births.* The akṣaṇa are śodhita, *purified,* LV 53.6; 357.5, or made śūnya, *empty,* LV 358.13. Others: LV 12.3; 34.22; 275.21; 327.13; 364.7; Mv ii.358.5; 371.12; 392.5 = Śikṣ 306.1; Av i.291.12; RP 35.19; Śikṣ 69.5; Sukh 23.9; Gv 54.9 (preta-tiryaṅ-narakākṣaṇe-gatāḥ); cf. Lévi, Sūtrāl. 17.26. On SP 163.8 akṣaṇāḥ saṃvṛtā cf. Senart's note Mv i.405 f.; it is (as Senart says) certainly secondary, the original being aghā(ḥ) aghasaṃvṛtā(ḥ), *miseries, surrounded by miseries* (in apposition with **lokāntarikā,** q.v., sc. narakāḥ or nirayāḥ); akṣaṇāḥ in SP was, in my opinion as in Senart's (if I understand him), a noun and a near-synonym of aghā(ḥ), *(constituting) unfavorable births,* see **agha** (2). Perhaps akṣaṇasaṃvṛtā(ḥ) was originally read after it(?). In Dbh.g. 7(343).4 read probably akṣaṇāḥ for text akṣalāḥ: sarve ti pāpapatitā 'kṣalāḥ (text) prabhonti.

akṣaṇa-vedha, *the art of piercing the target (unerringly)*; first member hyper-Skt. for Pali akkhaṇa (-vedhin; see **akṣaṇa-vedhin**), which really derives from Skt. ākhaṇa, *target,* see BR 5 App. s.v., and Coomaraswamy, Ars Islamica X (1943). 109, n. 9. Cf. **śabda-vedha, vāla-vedhin.** The mss. in Divy read akṣuṇa-, or akṣūṇa-; ed. always akṣuṇṇa-: (read) akṣaṇavedhe Divy 58.27; 100.12; 442.8, in lists of martial arts; °vedhaḥ Mvy 4994 (text akṣuṇṇa°, v.l. akṣuṇa°; Mironov 217.22 akṣūṇa° by em.).

akṣaṇavedhi-tva, nt., *state or art of being an akṣaṇavedhin:* °tve LV 156.13, where text akṣuṇṇa°, most mss. akṣuṇa°; none apparently have the correct akṣaṇa°.

akṣaṇa-vedhin (= Pali akkhaṇa°), *having the art of hitting the bull's-eye,* **akṣaṇa-vedha,** q.v. Implied in LV 181.7, where text kālākṣuṇṇadharmavedhī; best ms. °kṣaṇa°; read vālākṣaṇa°, *an archer-in-religion who can split a hair as target,* cf. **vālavedhin.**

Akṣatabuddhi, n. of a former Buddha: Mv i.138.4.

a-kṣamaṇa, see **kṣamaṇa.**

akṣamātra, *reaching up to the axle (of a chariot)*; with dhārā, *as deep as a chariot's axle (from the ground)*: Mv ii.349.17 °mātrāhi dhārāhi buddhakṣetraṃ phalī, (the gods) *filled this Buddha-field with streams* (of flowers rained down) *to the depth of a chariot's axle*; Mvy 7151 °mātrābhir dhārābhiḥ (same phrase, Sktized); °mātrābhir vāridhārābhir MSV i.40.4.

akṣaya (**1**) a high number, m. in Mvy 7793, nt. in Gv 134.2 and Mvy 7922 (cited from Gv); gender ambiguous (°asya, gen.) Gv 106.5, 18, in both of which read sattvākṣaya- for sattva-kṣaya-; (**2**) m., n. of a samādhi: Mvy 547; ŚsP 1418.15.

Akṣayakaraṇḍa (in Mvy var. °**ḍaka**), m., n. of a samādhi: Mvy 603; ŚsP 1424.12.

Akṣayakaraṇḍā, n. of a Bodhisattva-dhāraṇī: Mvy 750.

akṣayanikā (printed so, with n; cf. Skt. -kṣayaṇa), in °**kā-dāna** Bbh 233.26, *gift of something inexhaustible* (acc. to Chin., *wealth*: Tib. zad mi śes pa [= akṣaya, Das] can).

Akṣayabuddhavaṃśanirdeśā, n. of a lokadhātu: Gv 15.18.

Akṣayabuddhavaṃśavyūha, n. of a samādhi: Gv 206.7.

Akṣayamati, n. of a Bodhisattva: SP 3.8; 438.2 ff.; Mvy 702; RP 2.1; Mmk 311.14; 312.5; 461.6.

Akṣayamati-nirdeśa, n. of a work: Mvy 1344; (°**śa-mahāyānasūtra**) Śikṣ 278.4; cf. °**mati-sūtra.**

Akṣayamati-paripṛcchā, n. of a work, apparently not the same as prec.: Mvy 1400.

Akṣayamati-sūtra, n. of a work, = °**mati-nirdeśa**: Śikṣ 11.8 and often (on 190.4 Transl. Kṣayamati°!).

akṣayamukta, n. of a high number: Gv 106.5 (°tasya, gen.).

Akṣarāpagata, m., n. of a samādhi: Mvy 572; ŚsP 1421.3.

[**akṣala**: Dbh.g. 7(343).4 'kṣalāḥ; read probably (a)kṣaṇāḥ; see **akṣaṇa.**]

[**akṣuṇa, aksuṇṇa,** wrong readings for **akṣaṇa** (**-vedha, -vedhin,** qq.v.).]

[**akṣuṇṇa**(**-vyākaraṇa**), wrong reading for **akṣūṇa,** q.v.]

a-kṣudra, *not mean, not petty, i. e. excellent, superior.* In **akṣudrāvakāśa,** q.v.; also akṣudrāvacara (see ibidem); and akṣudrānulepana, *having fine ointments,* Mv ii.102.2; 104.13; for LV 23.12 see next.

akṣudrāvakāśa (= Pali akkhuddāvakāsa), *of fine (not inferior) appearance.* Almost always follows prāsādika and darśanīya; all virtual synonyms, applied to women and less often to men and children: Mv i.196.20; 352.15; ii.422.1, 7 (boy); 432.14; iii.35.18 (man); 153.16 (here prāsādika is lacking); 218.11; 377.12; 404.17 (an infant boy). In Mv i.197.16 (not accompanied by the other adj.) said of the family (kulam) in which a Bodhisattva is born; but perhaps this is an erroneous reading, or if correct means rather *possessing no small scope, range, sphere of activity or opportunity* (with the meaning of **avakāśa** normal in Skt., Pali, and BHS). This latter, at least, is clearly meant by Mv ii.1.7, a parallel passage, which reads akṣudrāvacaraṃ instead of this. A third parallel, LV 23.12, reads akṣudrānupaghāti, which surely means *not petty and not injurious* (so Tib., phran tshegs med ciṅ gnod par byed pa med pa yin), not *ne frappe pas ceux qui ne sont pas méchants* (Foucaux).

a-kṣūṇa, adj. (neg. of **kṣuṇa,** q.v.), *not faulty*: (kāyasaṃdarśanam) akṣūṇam avandhyaṃ ca sattvaparipākavinayāya Dbh 69.10; for Mvy 6463, text akṣuṇṇa-vyākaraṇa, read with v.l. of Index and Mironov (by em., 245.61) akṣūṇa- (confirmed by kṣūṇa-vyākaraṇa, see **kṣūṇa**). On the other hand, the em. akṣūṇa-vedhaḥ in Mironov 217.22, for Mvy 4994 akṣuṇṇa°, v.l. akṣuṇa°, is not correct; read **akṣaṇa-vedha,** q.v.

akṣobhiṇī (= Pali akkhohiṇī), a high number: LV 151.4 (vs). Cf. **akṣobhya** 3, the usual term in BHS, but not recorded in Pali.

Akṣobhya, (**1**) m., n. of a Buddha; the 2d of the 5 ('transcendent') Buddhas: Dharmas 3; Mvy 83; Sādh 16.9; (**2**) m., n. of a Buddha dwelling in an eastern region: SP 184.7; Suv 7.11; 120.5; Sukh 97.1; his lokadhātu is Abhirati, SP loc. cit., and (direction unspecified) Gv 82.9; AsP 366.14; see also **Akṣobhyarāja**; direction unspecified, in some cases at least doubtless the same personage, Mv i.139.5; Suv 152.15; RP 58.1; Śikṣ 14.13 ff.; see P. Mus, Barabudur, p. 578 ff.; (**3**) nt. (or m.), a high number (cf. **akṣobhiṇī**): in LV 147.22 = Mvy 7959, a hundred vivaras or viṃvaras; other, or unspecified, values SP 409.6; Mvy 8008 (here masc.); Sukh 31.1; Mmk 262.13.

Akṣobhyarāja, n. of a Buddha, probably = **Akṣobhya** (**2**): Suv 2.4 (in the east, like Akṣobhya); LV 172.11.

akṣobhyendriya, a kind of perfume: Gv 153.17 (-gandharāja).

akhaṇḍa-cārin (cf. Pali akhaṇḍa-kārī), *of perfect (unbroken) conduct*: LV 223.13, of the Bodhisattva.

a-khalita, see 2 **khalita.**

a-khinna-vacana (cf. Pali a-khīṇa-vacana, see CPD; somewhat problematic; the two words are probably connected, one being a distortion of the other; cf. §§ 3.2, 4 a), *unwearied in speech*: Mv i.134.8 °nāḥ, of Bodhisattvas.

1 **akhila** (opp. of, and perh. back-formation from, 1 **sakhila,** q.v.), *ungentle,* = paruṣa, of speech: Mv i.202.7 = ii.6.4, read both times: akhilavacanāc ca narapati viramāmi tathaiva paiśunyāt; same line i.145.10 has paruṣa° for akhila°, and in the next line anṛtavacanāc ca, which should be read in i.202.8 and ii.6.5 instead of paruṣa° (which duplicates akhila°, and leaves 'lying' unmentioned).

2 **a-khila** (= Pali id.), *free from harshness, hardness*

(of mind, **khila**): Mv iii.124.12 saṃvakpramuktam akhilaṃ anāśravaṃ.

agaṇanīya, nt., a high number: Gv 134.10; = **agaṇeya**, q.v.

agaṇanīya-parivarta, nt., *square* of the preceding: Gv 134.11; = **agaṇeya-pari°**, q.v.

agaṇiya (= Skt. agaṇya), *incalculable*: SP 192.7 (vs).

agaṇeya (in Skt. as adj., BR s.v. gaṇeya), nt., a high number: Gv 106.23; Mvy 7810 and (cited from Gv) 7942; = **agaṇanīya**, which is read in Gv 134.10, the passage from which Mvy usually cites.

agaṇeya-parivarta, m., *square* of the preceding: Gv 106.23; Mvy 7811; 7943.

agaṇya (cf. **agaṇiya**), a high number: Sukh 31.2.

a-gatika, *not subject to passing away*, see **gatika**.

[?**agalita**, *fluent*, of voice; see **galita**.]

agava, nt., var. for **ārāva**, q.v. Also: Gv 133.25, in lieu of **magava**, q.v.; in position corresponds to **kamara**, q.v.

agasti-harītakī, a kind of plant or tree: Mvy 5781; Tib. a-gas (partial transliteration). In Mironov agasti and harītakī are presented as separate items, perhaps correctly; **agasti** is recorded as n. of a plant or tree in Skt. But the Kyōtō ed. interprets **Agasti-** in the cpd. as the ṛṣi-name.

agāra, nt., a high number: Mvy 7705 = Tib. yid yal, which also renders **āgāra**, q.v.

agārastha, adj. (= AMg. agārattha; not in Pali), *dwelling in houses* (before retiring from the world): Mv i.104.8 (prose).

a-gāha, see **gāha**.

a-guru (= Pali agaru), *not offensive, not troublesome*: yadi te aguru Av i.94.3 (Pali sace te agaru); saced . . . asty aguru i.229.6 and 230.1, 9; saced . . . (gen. of person) aguru, ii.90.12, *if you don't mind*.

agocara (= Pali id.), *improper behavior*; underlies **agocarī-karoti** *acts improperly, does wrong*, and **-bhavati**, *wrong behavior takes place*: nāgarājau yadi Sūrpārakaṃ nagaram āgamiṣyato 'gocarīkariṣyataḥ Divy 50.23; samanvāharata nāgendrau Sūrpārakaṃ nagaraṃ mā 'gocarībhaviṣyati 51.1–2, *take heed for the city of S. that no wrong behavior* (i. e. *injury to the inhabitants*, 51.3–5) *takes place*.

Agni, n. of a yakṣa leader: Māy 236.17.

agni-karṣu, or °**ṣū** (cf. Pali aṅgāra-kāsu, °sū), *fire-pit*: sarpaśiro-'gnikarṣu-sadṛśāḥ (kāmāḥ) LV 329.9 (vs); Tib. me mur, according to Jäschke and Das = me mdag, *burning embers*; ye kāma varjenti yathāgnikarṣūṃ Śikṣ 193.7 (vs, cited from Samādh).

agni-khadā (see s.v. **-khadā**), *fire-pit*: Mvy 6622 = Tib. me mur gyi ḥobs, *oven, fire-pit*, or doṅ, *pit*; SP 448.5 °khadāya (loc.); LV 174.1; Av i.220.13; 264.1; Suv 157.4; RP 19.11 (text °khadhāṃ, read °khadāṃ); Kv 9.21; 10.12; 37.4 (in Kv associated with hells); Gv 116.14; 184.21 (°dāyām api prapatito na dahyate); Dbh 33.17; Bbh 337.1 (sacen mahatyām °dāyām ātmānaṃ prakṣipasi).

Agnighaṭa, n. of a hell: Kv 18.13 (misprinted °vaṭa); 98.2; pl. Kv 66.17. Not likely to be a MIndic corruption of **agnikhadā** (altho this is associated with hells in Kv), which occurs Kv 98.5 just after agnighaṭa.

agnijuha(?), see s.v. **agnihuta**.

Agnidatta, n. of a king: Divy 620.13; (the same? at Vairambhya) MSV i.25.16 ff.

agninya, distorted Sktization of Pali aggañña, *primeval* (derived from Skt. agra, perhaps with -jña?), see CPD and Senart Mv i note 617: Mv i.340.17 (taṃ eva) paurāṇam akṣaram °nyaṃ upanipate, arthaṃ cāsya na vibhāvayetsuḥ; similarly 341.10; 342.6, 16; iii.206.13; always epithet of akṣara, and in all but the last associated with paurāṇa; Pali also combines porāṇa and aggañña as ep. of akkhara, *ancient primeval formula*, in similar phrase; in BHS always subject of upanipate, *came in, occurred, was mentioned* (in Pali the phrase is object of anupatanti or anupadanti, *they repeat*; CPD s.v. akkhara 2).

Agniprabhā, n. of a 'gandharva maid': Kv 5.15.

agni-bala(-ratna), n. of a jewel: Mvy 5962; cited under one heading with agnivarṇa-ratna, and both translated literally in Tib. Mironov reads only **agnivarṇa**, without v.l.

Agnibhāṇḍa, n. of a people, among whom Buddha made a 'descent from the gods'; this event is otherwise always located at **Sāṃkāśya**, q.v., which is mentioned two lines above in Mmk but seems to be definitely not the place meant here: (bahutīrthāyatanāṃ sthānāṃ saṃpratoṣya tadā punaḥ,) Agnibhāṇḍe jane kṛtvā devāvataraṇaṃ śubham Mmk 582.(25–)26.

Agnimālin (Pali Aggimāli), n. of a mythical sea: Jm 91.14.

Agnimukha, n. of a nāga: Divy 119.26; 122.27.

Agnirakṣitikā, n. of a piśācī: Māy 239.23.

agni-varṇa(-ratna), n. of a jewel: Mvy 5962; see s.v. **agni-bala.**

?**agnivalukā(-bhayātaḥ)**: Māy 248.6, in a list of dangers from which freedom is sought: nirmuktā garuḍabhayātaḥ, agni°yātaḥ, dharaṇīkampabhayātaḥ. Should we read vālukā°? But what would *fire-sand* mean? Obscure.

Agniveśya, pl., n. of a brahmanical school: Divy 635.18. (Sg. as n. of a teacher, Mbh. crit. ed. 1.158.27; and cf. Skt. āgniveśya).

Agnivaiśyāyana (= Pali Aggivessāna, n. of Dīghanakha; cf. AMg. Aggivesāyaṇa), surname of **Dīrghanakha**: Av ii.187.10 ff.

Agniśrī, n. of a Bodhisattva: Gv 442.7.

agni-huta, *fire-offering, agnihotra*: °hutaṃ (or v.l. agnijuhaṃ, mss.) tasya pratiṣṭhato mama (*as I am setting about to sacrifice* . . .), prabhaṃkaro lokatamonudo yathā, āditya lokasmiṃ tatheva īryasi . . . Mv ii.55.10 (vs); one of these forms (or agnī° m.c.) should doubtless be read (Senart em. wrongly); cf. Pali aggihutta and aggijuhana, °jūh°, both = agnihotra.

agnihotrika (= Pkt. aggihottiya; not in Pali; cf. Skt. agnihotrin, and āgnihotrika, Schmidt s.v.), *cultivating the agnihotra*: Av i.208.9 ṛṣiḥ . . . °kaḥ; ii.28.3; 65.17 (Corrigenda).

Agnīśvara, n. of a former Buddha: Samādh p. 57 line 9.

[**agneya, Agneyī**, read **Āg°**, q.v.]

agra, (1) adj. (in Skt. only Lex.; replaces Skt. agrya; = Pali agga), *first, chief, prime, foremost, best*: Mvy 2521; ye brāhmavimāna agrās SP 190.16 (vs); sūtram agram 385.2 (vs); lokasyāgro LV 162.2, *best of the world*; dhyāyina agrā 169.5 (vs); jñānaṃ cāgraṃ 371.14; agraṃ ca . . . ojaḥ 387.1; bhavān ihāgras tribhave 398.21; agro prajñāye Mv i.44.9, *first in wisdom*; 113.6 (food); 248.17, 18; ii.208.13; 259.9; iii.63.17–18; Divy 61.29; 349.14; 385.8; Śikṣ 129.4; 311.14 f.; Bbh 94.17; etc., common. As prior member of cpds.: agra-gaṇikā, *leading harlot* Mv iii.35.17 ff.; agra-pudgala, *foremost person*, a Buddha, Mv i.47.2 (mss. mostly °puṅgala); agrapura, *leading city*, Mv i.4.6; agrabala, *having prime powers* Divy 99.20; agrabalin, MSV ii.78.4; agraśrāvakā, *leading disciples*, Mv i.307.4; others, see the following entries; also (like vara) at the end of cpds. in same sense, see **rasāgra**; **(2)** nt. of the preceding used as substantive: (a) *the best of its class*, used particularly as predicate to ākhyāyate (°ti), with a personal subject (so in Pali, tathāgato tesam aggaṃ akkhāyati, CPD s.v. akkhāyati): (sā . . .) agram ākhyāyati Mv iii.390.6; samyaksaṃbuddhas teṣām agram ākhyātaḥ Av i.50.1 (so ms.; Speyer em. agra(ḥ); to be sure agra(ḥ) is printed in the text of the same phrase, without report of v.l., in Av i.329.16, but Mv and Pali support agram of ms. in i.50.1); (b) *first-class gift*, as if for agra-dāna (cf. Pali agga-dāna and CPD s.v. agga 2, c), agraṃ abhiharāmi te Mv iii.211.10; the same vs in Pali DN ii.240.17 has aggha twice in text but v.l. once agga, and cf. Jāt. v. 377.19 aggaṃ in same sense.

agrakulika (= Pali agga°), *of very prominent family*: agrakulika-putra, Divy 366.6; Karmav 70.5. In Divy contrasted with the milder kulika-putra, see **kulika.**

agrataḥ sthāpayitvā seems to mean hardly more than *beginning with, including* (as the most prominent or important of the group), = -ādi in comp.: (sarvāvān bodhisattva-gaṇo maitreyaṃ ...) agrataḥ sthāpayitvā SP 315.6 (prose).

Agratā-sūtra, n. of a work (probably = Pali Etadagga-vagga, AN 1.23 ff.): Karmav 155.14; 157.10; 161.20; see Lévi's notes.

agrapada (= Pali aggapada, cf. **pada**), pl., *the highest, most sublime subjects* (or *utterances*?): (padena padaṃ vyañjanena vyañjanaṃ saṃsyandate sameti) yad utāgrapadaiḥ Av ii.142.17; 143.6, *and that too with . . .*

Agrapuruṣa, n. of a former Buddha: Mv i.141.5; as common noun, *leading personage*, Mv i.3.9.

agra-prajñapti (= Pali agga-paññatti; in AN ii.17.12 list of four, relating to Rāhu, Mandhātar, Māra, and the Tathāgata), *proclamation of superiority*, statement that some person or thing is supreme in his or its class: Av i.49.10 ff. and 329.13 ff. (three, relating to Buddha, dharma, and saṃgha).

Agramaticitracūḍa, n. of a serpent king: Mvy 3428.

agrayāna, (1) *best vehicle*, = **mahāyāna**: Vaj 30.6; also °nin, see **-yānin**; **(2)** n. of a Bodhisattva: Gv 442.11.

Agravīrabāhu, n. of a yakṣa: Mvy 3373.

Agrasānumati, n. of a Bodhisattva: Gv 443.5.

agrasārā, a high number, or method of calculation (gaṇanā): LV 148.19; Mvy 7986 (cited from LV).

Agrāṭavika (cf. Pali Aggāḷava, adj.), n. of a wood at **Āṭavikā**: °ke dāve MSV ii.51.9.

agrāsanika, adj. (= Pali aggāsanika), *having a chief seat, occupying a high position*: brāhmaṇo ... rājño 'grāsanikaḥ Av i.105.6, *a brahman who occupied the chief seat (position) with the king*. In line 11 he says to a Buddha, niṣīdatu bhagavān agrāsane.

a-grāha, m. (neg. to **-grāha**), (*no-belief*) *false belief, attachment to an erroneous view*: Vaj 42.13; 45.5 (cited s.v. **-grāha,** q.v.).

agre, postpos. with abl., *from* (of time): ito ... agre Mv i.165.16, *from this point* (of time). Cf. Pali agge, only in cpds.; and **-agreṇa,** in cpds., in same meaning and much more commonly. Cf. also Skt. agre, used (see pw s.v. agra) in much the same way but apparently recorded only in ŚB.

-agreṇa, postpos., (beginning) *from*, of time. (In Pali it seems that only agge is used in this sense, not aggena as PTSD says; CPD seems to be right in saying that aggena means only *according to*.) tadagreṇa, *from that* (time) *on*, LV 19.4; 265.9; 407.10; adyāgreṇa, *from now on*, SP 107.3; 467.12; Mv i.365.13; Av i.89.7; ii.13.2; Divy 7.10; 32.8; 53.8; 72.2; 187.21, etc.; Bhīk 24b.4.

Agrodaka, n. of a town: Māy 18, 70 (cf. Lévi p. 65).

Agrodikā, n. of a piśācī: Māy 239.22.

agha, m. (= Pali id.), **(1)** *sky, atmosphere*; only in **aghaniṣṭha,** q.v.; **(2)** in the **lokāntarikā** (q.v.) passage, aghā aghasaṃvṛtā(ḥ) or aghasphuṭā(ḥ) (or other cpd.) means *miseries* (? *miserable*) *and enclosed by* (*full of*, or the like) *miseries*; so essentially Senart, Mv i note 405 f. We could perhaps recognize the first agha as an adj. (so in RV and once in BhāgP.); but it seems more likely that it is the more familiar noun, which esp. in Pali often means *misery*. In the Pali version (CPD s.v. ²agha, end) we should read aghā aghasaṃvutā, as Senart perceived (texts asaṃvutā, a very old corruption); or at least, that must have been the original version. The CPD assumes an otherwise unknown adj. agha, *aerial, without support*, which is inappropriate and implausible.

aghaniṣṭha, doubtless understood as *sky-based* (see **agha,** 1), a class of gods: Mvy 3107, where it follows **akaniṣṭha,** of which it is surely nothing but a folk-etymological distortion. So Wogihara, Lex. It occurs in no other of my texts unless in Bbh; Wogihara reads so in 62.6 and 68.5; actually it is read only in the latter place by one of the two mss. (which reads aniṣṭha in the former place), while the other ms. reads akaniṣṭha both times. Wogihara's suggested interpretation, and those he quotes from Yaśomitra and Chin., seem to me fantastic and worthless. Cf. **lokaniṣṭha.**

agharikā, or °**ka,** n. pl. °kā(ḥ), a kind of toy: Divy 475.19. Etym.?

aghāvin (= Pali id., see § 22.51), *sinful*: Ud v.10 (= Pali Ud ii.7), read aghāvinaḥ (text aghādinaḥ; Pali aghāvino); in Ud ix.16 ms. aghātinaḥ, for which Chakravarti would read aghāvinaḥ (the line is fragmentary).

aṅka-dhātrī, *nurse who carries a baby on her hip*: Mvy 9478; Divy 475.12, defined 13–14: aṅkadhātrīty ucyate yā dārakam aṅkena parikarṣayaty aṅgapratyaṅgāni ca saṃsthāpayati. Tib. on Mvy paṅ na = aṅka, which it seems must be the orig. form, since in India babies are carried on the hip. Yet in all other cases the word is written **aṃsa-dh°** (or aṃśa-, in mss. also atsa-), and this seems to have had real currency, as shown s.v. For the cliché see s.v. **kṣīra-dhātrī.**

aṅkula (= Skt. °ra), *sprout*: ratnāṅkulāḥ LV 76.15, *jewelled sprouts* (no v.l. in mss.; Calc. °rāḥ); -bhaiṣajāṅkula-, śraddhāṅkulānāṃ LV 352.12 and 13 (both edd. °ra°, but in 12 best mss., in 13 all mss. °la°).

aṅkuśagraha, m. (in Pali aṅkusaggaha is one who practices the art, and so Skt. °śagraha, a rare word; the art in Pali is aṅkusagayha), *the art of handling an (elephant-) goad*: Mvy 4981; LV 156.11 (one of the arts mastered by the young Bodhisattva); Divy 442.6.

aṅga, (1) *member, part* (as in Skt. and Pali, where it is recorded as nt. only), m. (at least modified by two m. adj.), sarve bhavāṅga ... niruddhāḥ LV 420.14 (so all mss., Lefm. °dhā); **(2)** *attribute, quality, characteristic*, like the Skt. guṇa (so Pali, CPD s.v., 4, where it is shown that Pali uses it 'mostly with numbers', and often in dependence on samannāgata, cf. below); the 60 *qualities* (aṅga) of the Buddha's voice, Mvy 444, listed 445–504, cf. Sūtrāl. xii.9; same mg. in cpds., see **aṣṭāṅga** (2), **āprāṇyāṅga, svarāṅga**; also kulaṃ (the family in which the Bodhisattva is born in his last existence) ṣaṣṭīhi aṅgehi samanvāgataṃ bhavati Mv i.197.14 (there follows a list of the 60 'qualities'). In the LV parallel, 23.10 ff., catuḥṣaṣṭy-ākārair ... saṃpannakulaṃ bhavati. Repetition Mv ii.1.6, also with list following. Both Pali and BHS further refer to five *bad qualities* as pañcāṅga (Pali °aṅga): pañcāṅga-viprahīṇa (124.15 -viprahīna), of Buddhas, Divy 95.17; 124.15; 264.30; acc. to Vism. 146.5–6 they are the nīvaraṇāni. On the other hand, there are five *good qualities* referred to by Pali pañcaṅga in Vism. 146.25 ff.; and a different set, characteristic of kings or brahmans, *'gentlemanly qualities'*, PTSD s.v.; cf. s.v. **pañcāṅgika,** esp. 3; the Buddha speaks pañcāṅgena svareṇa, MSV i.220.20. The line between meanings 1 and 2 is not always easy to draw. E. g. Mvy 424 describes the Tathāgata as ṣaḍaṅgasamanvāgataḥ, referring to the six aṅgas (*'qualities'*? or *members, parts*?) of **upekṣā,** cf. chaḷaṅgasamannāgata DN iii.269.19 (list follows; consists of indifference to the objects of each of six senses), and Vism. 160.9 ff. (chaḷaṅgupekkhā is the first of ten upekkhā).

aṅgaṇa, nt. =Pali id.), *spot, blemish, depravity, evil*: Mvy 2157 °ṇam. Common in compounds **anaṅgaṇa, nir-a°, sāṅgaṇa,** qq.v., which are often spelled with °na in BHS.

aṅgadāha, m., *body-burn*, a disease: Mvy 9523; Bhīk 17 a.2.

Aṅgadikā, n. of a city: MSV i.66.2, 13.

Aṅgadinna, n. of a king of Videha: Jm 192.12. The Pali form is Aṅgati (Jāt. 544, which is the same story).

aṅga-nāḍikā, acc. to Tib. (pa car, see Das) *loin-cloth*: °kāṃ ... āgārikadharmas tarhy ... yad utāṅganāḍi(kā) MSV ii.94.15–17, in a list of garments forbidden to monks; abbreviated aṅga in the uddāna ii.91.17; Pali Vin. i.306.8 has instead akkanāla, supposed to be for Skt. arka-; see CPD.

aṅgabheda, m., a disease (perhaps something like *rheumatism*): thrice in AV, where it is not entirely clear whether it is an epithet of yakṣma or an independent disease; Mvy 9510 = Tib. yan lag tu zug pa, *pain in the limbs*. Not noted in Pali or Pkt.

aṅga-maṇi(-vidyā), *(science of) bodily marks*: Mvy 5055 = śa mtshan (-gyi dpyad).

aṅga-lipi, *script of the Aṅgas*, a kind of writing: LV 125.20 (Tib. also aṅga-).

aṅgānusārin (= Pali id.), *attendant on, attached or conforming to, the limbs* (of the body); with vāyu, one of the winds pervading the body: pl. °riṇo vāyava(ḥ) Śikṣ 248.13, rendered by Bendall and Rouse as *rheumatism*, for reasons not evident to me.

aṅgārin (= Pali id.), (apparently) *red* (like coals, aṅgāra); only in the verse Therag. 527 = Jāt. i.87.1 = Mv iii.93.10 aṅgāriṇo, of trees (in the Pali; in Mv hopelessly corrupt, the noun being omitted).

-aṅgika, see **-aṃśika.**

Aṅgiras (= Pali °rasa), nom. sg. °rāḥ, n. of a king (in Pali of the race of Mahāsaṃmata): Mvy 3572 (in a list of cakravartins headed by Mahāsaṃmata, 3552).

Aṅgīrajva (?), n. of a ṛṣi: Aṅgīrajvă (so!) nāma maharṣiḥ Māy 256.18. Note that Aṅgirasa (also in Skt.; = Aṅgiras) is mentioned just before this.

Aṅgīrasa (= Pali id. in mg. 1; regular Skt. would be **Āṅgirasa**, q.v.), (**1**) ep. of the Buddha: Mv iii.109.20; (**2**) n. of a former Buddha: Mv iii.239.5 f.

aṅgulikā, (**1**) (Pali id., = Skt. aṅguli) *finger*; only in ekāṅgulikayā or pl. °kābhis, (pointing) *with single finger(s)*: sg. LV 49.3; 67.12; pl. LV 290.17; (**2**) = Skt. aṅgulīya(ka), *finger-ring*; both times with v.l. aṅgulīkā, probably read so (MIndic reduction, § 3.118, of **aṅgulīyakā**, q.v.), Mv ii.73.1; 102.16.

Aṅgulimāla (= Pali id.), n. of a brigand converted by Buddha: Av i.148.9.

Aṅgulimālika, n. of a work: Laṅk 258.4 (nirvāṇāṅgul°, v.l. nirmāṇāṅgul°, presumed to be dvandva by Bendall-Rouse and Suzuki), presumably = next; quoted Śikṣ 133.4 (here ms. °laka).

Aṅgulimālīya, nt., n. of a work, presumably = prec.: Mvy 1398.

aṅgulīkā, see **aṅgulikā** (2).

aṅgulīphaṇahastaka, *having a hand with fingers* (round and awkward) *like a snake's hood*: Mvy 8776 (Chin. *round-fingered*); MSV iv.68.6 (read with ms.). Corresponds to Pali phaṇa-hatthaka Vin.i.91.11, interpreted SBE 13.225 as *having hands like a snake's hood*; comm. 1027.1 yassa vaggulipakkhakā (*bat's wings*) viya aṅguliyo saṃbaddhā honti.

aṅgulīyakā, fem., *finger-ring*; nowhere else recorded in this form and gender; but cf. **aṅgulīkā** (°**ikā**): aṅgulīyakā ... patitā Mv ii.110.4; sā aṅgulīyakā dṛṣṭā parijñātā 5; aṅgulīyakā ... patitā 13.

aṅgulīya-lipi, a kind of script: LV 125.20; Tib. *finger* (sor mo paḥi) *writing*.

aṅguṣṭha-vibhedika, nt., *thumb-separater*, presumably a *glove* or *mitten* with separate hole for thumb but not for the other fingers: °kāny anyāni ca vividhāni vastrāṇi Kv 78.21.

Aṅgottama, n. of a former Buddha: Mv iii.233.2 f.

Acaraṭarkirāja, one of the 10 krodha: Dharmas 11; = **Acalaṭakkirāja**, q.v.

Acala, m., (**1**) n. of a samādhi: Mvy 580; ŚsP 1421.19; (**2**) n. of a future Buddha: Av i.53.18; (**3**) one of the krodha (cf. next): Sādh 137.13.

Acalaṭakkirāja, n. of one of the krodha: Sādh 418.6; both **Acala** and **Ṭakkirāja** are thus used, alone; and see **Acaraṭarkirāja.**

Acaladeva, n. of a Bodhisattva: Gv 443.6–7.

Acalamati, n. of a son of Māra (favorable to the Bodhisattva): LV 313.15.

Acalaśrī, n. of a kiṃnara maid: Kv 6.2.

Acalaskandha, n. of a Bodhisattva: Gv 443.5.

acalā, (**1**) n. of the 8th Bodhisattva bhūmi: Mvy 893; Dharmas 64; Laṅk 15.5; 221.19; Dbh 5.10 etc.; Bbh 353.3; (**2**) n. of a rākṣasī: SP 400.6; Māy 243.26; (**3**) n. of a female-lay-disciple: Gv 170.13; 172.1 ff.; **Acalopāsikāvimokṣa** (so read for text vācanopās°), Śikṣ 36.4, refers to Gv 170–179, dealing with Acalā's instruction to Sudhana; Śikṣ 36.5–8, cited from Gv 171.21–26.

acalācala, *immovable* (acala) *as a mountain* (acala): acalācalam (niścayaṃ) LV 216.15 (vs).

Acalitasumana(s), n. of a former Buddha: Mv i.141.16 (°naḥ, n.sg.).

Acalendrarāja, n. of a Bodhisattva: Gv 4.7.

Acalopāsikāvimokṣa, see **Acalā** (3).

acāra, probably m.c. for Skt. acara, *unchanging, constant*: acāra-cārikāṃ, *unchanging* (constant) *course* (of the Buddha, for countless aeons) RP 5.13 (vs). To be sure there is a Skt. noun cāra, *movement*, of which this might be a compound with a-; but no such cpd. is recorded in Skt. or MIndic.

acinti(ṣu) for Skt. acintya, see § 3.115.

acintia, see **acintiya.**

acintika (perhaps MIndic for **acintyaka**, q.v.? or hyper-Skt. for **acintiya** = Skt. acintya?), *unthinkable, incomprehensible*: Mvy 733 (Tib. bsam gyis mi khyab pa, *impenetrable by thought*); Mmk 559.20 (vs) caryā bodhim acintikā (in line 25 below note acintyaka); kalpām acintikām Mmk 587.2 (= kalpān acintyakān, *for unthinkable aeons*).

Acintikamadhyabuddhivikrīḍita, n. of a Bodhisattva: Mvy 733; see prec. Tib. bsam gyis mi khyab paḥi dkyil ḥkhor la blo gros rnam par rol pa, *sporting in enlightenment in*(to) *a circle* (dkyil alone generally = madhya) *that is incomprehensible by thought.*

acintiya, adj. (= Pali id., Skt. acintya), *unthinkable*: examples § 3.103. Once written **acintia**: dāna-acintia-tyāga-mukhena Śikṣ 328.2 (vs; wrongly divided in ed.), *by means of inconceivable giving of gifts.*

acintya, nt., a very high number: Mvy 7814; 7946 (here cited from Gv); 8047; Sukh 31.3; Gv 106.24; 134.13.

acintyaka (= Skt. acintya), *unthinkable*; cf. **acintika** (°tikā occurs Mmk 559.20): Mmk 559.25 (vs).

Acintyaguṇānuttaradharmagocara, n. of a Bodhisattva: Gv 443.9.

acintyaparivarta, m. (or, in Gv 134.13, nt.), *square of* **acintya**: Mvy 7815; 7947 (here cited from Gv); Gv 106.24; 134.13.

Acintyaśrī, n. of a Bodhisattva: Gv 443.7.

acira-cira-cireṇā (m.c. for °ṇa; no v.l.; as one word? so text): LV 78.5 (vs). Rendered by Foucaux *for a long time.* Māyā speaks to the King: deva śṛṇu hi mahyaṃ bhāṣato yaṃ mataṃ me; acira-cira-cireṇā jāta udyāna-buddhiḥ, ... *for a long time I have conceived the thought of* (going to) *the pleasure-park.* Could acira(ṃ?) be taken separately, with preceding line? Tib. seems to have nothing for acira; it says yun riṅ riṅ po ḥdas nas, *for a long, long time past.*

acirayānasaṃprasthita, = **nava-yāna**°, q.v.: AsP 286.6.

a-cirasthitika-tā, see **cirasthitika**, and s.v. **sthitaka** (4).

[**acīrṇa-daṇḍatā**, var. for **ācīrṇa°**, q.v.]

acela (= Pali id.) m., a member of a sect of naked ascetics: Mvy 8467 (-dānam; cf. Pali Vin. iv.92.3–5); Śikṣ 331.12.

acelaka (= Pali id.), = prec.: Mvy 3528; Prāt 511.10.

acchaṭa, nt. (only Mmk 159.23; in Pali acchara as stem in comp. beside °rā) = **acchaṭā**, q.v.

acchaṭā, also **acchaṭā-saṃghāta** (= Pali and AMg. accharā, Pali also accharā-saṃghāta), once **ac-chaṭā-saṃhāta** (see **saṃhāta**); cf. **ricchaṭā** (for ṛcch-aṭā? which could be the original of acchaṭā), (**1**) *snap of the fingers*: ekācchatā ye (so read with WT) ca karonti śabdam SP 392.6; acchaṭā-śabdena Divy 555.21; °śabdaḥ Mvy 2802; °śabdam akārṣīt, *snapped his fingers*, Gv 510.22; °saṃghāta-śabdaḥ SP 388.8; (**2**) as n. of a small unit of time, *instant, jiffy*: °ṭā (printed °ṭāṃ in 160.7, wrongly) tvaritā gatiḥ Mmk 160.7; 279.23; once as nt. (see **acchaṭa**), °ṭam Mmk 159.23; various adverbs, *in a jiffy*, acchaṭāmātreṇa Mmk 79.27; °ṭā-saṃghāta-mātram Mvy 8226; Divy 142.11; °ṭā-pada-mātram Mmk 268.18; ekācchaṭāsaṃhātamātram Śikṣ 214.11; as adj., *having* or *characterized by the measure of a finger-snap*, i. e. *in a jiffy*, agreeing with personal subject, (Mañjuśrīḥ . . .) °ṭāsaṃghātamātro . . . vikurvaṇaṃ . . . samāpadyata Mmk 3.27.

acchati (= Pali id., Pkt. acchai), *sits*: acchā drume tuva LV 343.2 (vs) *sit at the tree!*; [(pīṭhe) acchati Mv ii.379.5 (vs), but this is surely an error for acchambhī of Śikṣ 303.3, which meter requires;] kausīdyaṃ acchati Śikṣ 298.4 (could be *sits in sloth*, but might also be *goes to sloth* as Bendall assumes following Pischel 480; in LV this is impossible).

acchandagāmin, adj., probably *not going after whims or desires*, of the family of the Bodhisattva: °gāminaṃ LV 24.1 n.sg.; °gāmi Mv i.197.20; ii.1.10 (all same passage).

acchambhita, adj. (neg. of **chambhita**, and cf. next; Pali has acchambhitatta), *not frightened*: Gv 37.1; 40.20, etc.; 452.24; adv. °taṃ, *without consternation*, Mv ii.281.15 (parallel with abhītaṃ, asamvignaṃ, asaṃtra-staṃ).

acchambhin, adj. (= Pali id.; cf. **astambhin**; neg. of **chambhin**; cf. prec., and **chambati, chambhita**, etc.; on etymology see under **chambati**), *not paralyzed with fear, not frightened*: acchambhī, n. sg. m. (in LV 284.18, and possibly 285.9, voc.) LV 284.18 (vs); 285.9 (vs); Mvy 1821; Mv ii.269.20; 270.1, 18; 278.21; 281.13; read ac-chambhī Mv ii.379.5, with the parallel Śikṣ 303.3, for text **acchati**; acchambhi, n. sg. m. Gv 364.20 (vs); accham-bhinam (! n. sg. m.; -m 'hiatus-bridger'?) amaṅkubhūtaḥ Mmk 93.24 (prose).

acchindati (= Pali id., for Skt. ācchinatti; Senart always emends to ācch°), (**1**) *takes away, removes*, with gen. of person, acc. of thing: acchinditvā Mv ii.434.3, 9 (teṣāṃ bhrātṛṇāṃ); iii.7.17 (gulikām); in Mv iii.403.12, 14, read ahaṃ na (14 . . . naiva) kasyaci demi nāpi acchindāmi (with mss., misinterpreted by Senart), *I do not give to anyone nor take away from anyone*; (**2**) *abolishes, puts away*: acchet(t)va (tṛṣṇāṃ) Mv iii.285.6, 9 (= Pali acchejja, acchijja, same vs, SN i.127.3, 6).

Acchinnadhāra, n. of a rain-deity: Śikṣ 247.8.

Acchila, n. of a nāga-king: Māy 247.34.

Acyuta, (**1**) n. of a Bodhisattva cakravartin: Mv i.113.14; (**2**) n. of a nāga-king: Mvy 3292; Māy 247.34; (**3**) pl., n. of a class of gods (as in Pali accuta): Mahāsamāj. Waldschmidt, Kl. Skt. Texte 4, 185.18.

Ajakarṇa, n. of a disciple of Buddha: Mv i.76.1.

ajanya (cf. Pali ajañña), prob. *ignoble, debased*: ajanyasya brāhmaṇasya putro Mv i.319.12; 321.16; 323.7; said of Jyotipāla; since he was a friend of a potter's son, his father may have been an outcaste brahman. Senart assumes mg. *noble*, on grounds which I find unconvincing The mg. I assume fits the Pali ajañña, Jāt, ii.437.17 In Mv iii.119.23 prob. read with v.l. anajanyarathā, *not ignoble chariots*, for ajanya° of text. (Meter is bad in either case.) In Kv 42.10 for na jatyeṣu read perhaps nājanyeṣu, *not among ignoble people*; see s.v. **jatya.**

ajapadaka-daṇḍa, m. (= Pali ajapada-daṇḍa), *staff* (cleft) *like a goat's hoof*: Mvy 9045; **ajapādaka-daṇḍaka**, id., MSV iv.75.5.

Ajapāla-nyagrodha (= Pali °nigrodha), *the Goat-herd's Banyan*, under which Buddha spent some time (the 6th week, according to Mv) shortly after enlight-enment: Mv iii.302.21; 313.18. Story of how it got its name, Mv iii.301.8 ff. (apparently does not occur in Pali; doubtless a late invention based on the name); ajapālasya nya° iii.302.21; 425.18, 23; 436.19, 22.

Ajayā, n. of a goddess: Sādh 502.10.

aja-r-eḍakā (cf. Pali ajeḷaka, Skt. Gr. ajaiḍaka), voc. °ke, *O female of the goats-and-sheep!* (cf. § 4.63): MSV iv.228.16 (vs). Addressed to a ewe; use of the dvandva cpd. is peculiar but hardly questionable; cf. § 23.3. Confirmed by nom. (sā) 'ja-r-eḍikā 228.21 (prose).

ajava, perhaps to be read for **java**, a high number, in Gv 106.13; see s.v. **ayava.**

a-jātaka, adj. (=Skt. ajāta), *unborn*: ajātakāś ca (v.l. ajāta sarve) SP 281.9 (vs), m.c.

Ajātaśatru (= Pali Ajātasattu), n. of a king of Magadha, son of Bimbisāra: SP 5.5 (attends the Buddha); Divy 55.17; 279.20 ff.; 369.9; 380.18; 545.8; Av i.54.6 ff.; 83.6; 88.7; 308.5 ff.; ii.182.1 ff.; Śikṣ 274.3–4 (from Tathā-gataguhya-sūtra); Mmk 590.2 (in the sequel repeatedly referred to as Ajātākhya, e. g. ajātākhyo nṛpottamaḥ 592.7); Karmav 45.3; 49.20 (summary of his story), et alibi.

Ajātaśatrukaukṛtyavinodana, m., n. of a work: Mvy 1358.

Ajātākhya, see **Ajātaśatru.**

ajānaka, adj., *foolish*, see **jānaka.**

ajānanaka, adj., = prec., see **jānanaka.**

Ajita, (**1**) (= Pali id.) epithet of **Maitreya**; mostly voc. in direct address, the name Maitreya being otherwise used in same context; but other forms occur (ajitasya Karmav 40.1): SP 18.4; 308.1, 2; 309.2 ff.; 327.3; 332.6 ff.; 345.7 ff., etc.; Mv i.51.6; Śikṣ 97.8; (an unidentified Bodhisattva, prob. Maitreya) Sukh 64.7 ff.; 92.10; (**2**) n. of a future Buddha, but seemingly distinguished from Maitreya: Mv iii.330.8; (**3**) n. of an attendant on the Bodhisattva (Śākyamuni) in a previous birth: Jm 3.4 (query: to be identified with Maitreya?).

Ajita Keśakambala, or °lin (= Pali Ajita Kesakam-bala, or °lī, °lin), n. of one of the six heretical teachers of Buddha's time (see s.v. **Pūraṇa Kāśyapa**), named with the others: °laḥ Mvy 3548 (Ajita-keś°, as cpd.; so also Mironov); Divy 143.11; Av i.231.4 (ms. Kesa°); °lasya Mv i.253.14; °lī, nom. sg. Mv i.256.20; iii.383.16.

Ajitacakra, n. of a former Buddha: Mv i.137.12.

Ajitaṃjaya, (**1**) n. of a Bodhisattva: Mmk 41.17; (**2**) n. of a locality: Māy 27; 69.

Ajitapuṣya (? Senart with v.l. °**puṣyala**), n. of a former Buddha: Mv i.137.13; see **puṣyala.**

Ajitabala, n. of a former Buddha: Mv i.140.2.

ajitavatigandha, a (mythical?) kind of jewel: (-maṇirāja-) Gv 101.8; cf. **ajitāvati.**

Ajitasena, n. of a householder: Gv 453.18, 26, etc.

? **Ajitasenarājan** (mss. Ajinasenah Rājā), n. of a former Buddha: Mv i.140.11.

Ajitā, n. of one of the four **Kumārī**, q.v., or **Bhaginī**: Mmk 537.8; 539.25; 543.9 et alibi; prob. the same, a yakṣiṇī, 573.14.

ajitāvati, a kind of perfume (cf. **ajitavatigandha**): ajitāvati(gandharāja-) Gv 153.15.

ajinaka (= Skt. °na plus -ka svārthe), *deerskin*: °kena Mv iii.144.9; 154.11 (both prose).

? **ajina-khipa** (or, Sktized, °kṣipa; m. or nt.; = Pali °kkhipa), *deerskin dress* (of an ascetic): °khipena, so I em. Mv ii.147.7, for mss. jana-kapilena, -karitena. The vs was puṣpitāgrā; Senart fails badly on it, but some of my guesses, too, are far from certain: kaṣayapaṭa-(m.c. for kaṣāyapaṭā-) -valambitaprakarṣī ajinakhipena vistīrṇa aindramārge, bhūrikamalajāvakīrṇagātro śaraṇavare gata eka cakravākaḥ. See my Reader, *Four Sights* (Mv), end.

Ajiravatī (Skt. Gr.: = Pali Aciravatī; see also **Āryavatī**), n. of a river at Śrāvastī: Av i.63.5 ff.; ii.69.3; MSV ii.85.20.

ajihma-kukṣi = **abhugna** (q.v.) -kukṣi.

a-jihmīkaraṇa, see **jihmī°**.

ajīvika: Śikṣ 332.1 (vs), probably only m.c. for **āj°** (despite note p. 414).

Ajeya, m., n. of a samādhi: Mvy 548 (not in ŚsP).

Ajñānavidhvaṃsana, n. of a former Buddha: Sukh 6.12.

a-ñāna (nt.; Pali aññāṇa; MIndic for ajñāna, § 2.15), *ignorance*: jñānaṃ na kalpeti, añānu (n. sg.) no bhavet MadhK 157.1 (vs; no v.l.).

[**añja** (**añjas**?), cf. Skt. añjas, *quickly*; exclamation used in Pali (Jāt. i.192.5, 29) in urging a draft-animal to go (*gee*! *get up*! *go ahead*!), *come up*! In LV 394.18 (vs) tad añja is Lefm.'s em. for tad-anya of all mss. and Calc. which seems to make no sense. Addressed by Brahmā to the Buddha, urging him to preach the law; presumed to mean perhaps *come on*! But Tib. seems to have had a quite different reading: kha ḥbyed pa, *mouth open* (Foucaux, *ouvre ta bouche*; but the form is not given as impv. by Jä.). Should we read **ud-añca**, 2 sg. impv., for Skt. ud-añcaya, *ertönen lassen* (pw)? Graphic confusion of *u* and *ta* occurs in some Indian alphabets, e. g. in **Śāradā**.]

añjati (= Pali id., Skt. anakti), *anoints*, ppp. añjita: añjitehi akṣīhi Mv ii.234.17.

1 **Añjana** or °**na-ka**, n. of a king of Benares, father of Puṇyavant(a): Mv iii.33.12 (°nako, n. sg.), 15 (°nasya, gen.).

(2 **añjana**: mṛgo . . . raktehi khurehi añjanehi akṣīhi prabhāsvarehi darśanīyehi Mv i.363.18. No v.l.; but there is no authority for añjana as adj. [PTSD quotes 3 Jāt. passages for this, all erroneous.] Senart suggests sāñjanehi or equivalent. But perhaps render: *with red hoofs and eyes bright and beautiful* (as if?) *with collyrium*.)

añjanīya or °**yā** (so Senart with one ms.), or **añjanaka** or °**kā** (v.l.), acc. to Senart *box for holding collyrium*; cf. Pali añjanī, AMg añjaṇiyā (for °kā), id.: °nīyā (v.l. °nakā; n. pl.) pi Mv ii.473.10, listed among products of a **śaṅkha-valayakāra**, q.v.

Añjalipriya, n. of a yakṣa: Māy 49.

Añjalimālādhārin, n. of a former Buddha: Mv i.140.3.

? **añjiṣṭha**: ŚsP 1561.6, 7 nā 'ñjiṣṭham, in a list of color words. Perhaps error (haplogr.) for (na) māñjiṣṭhaṃ? Otherwise may be identified with Skt. Gr. (Uṇādi) añjiṣṭha, Pali (according to Maung Tin, cited CPD) añjiṭṭha, *the sun* (to Vedic añji); in that case perhaps *bright-colored*.

aññāya, so Senart (with the Pali version, SN i.126.27) for mss. **anyāya** = Skt. ājñāya, ger. of ā-jñā, *knowing*: °ya dharmaṃ Mv iii.284.4 (vs).

Aṭakāvatī (var. **Ala°**; Mironov **Aṭaka°**, no v.l.), n. of a place: Mvy 4137; presumably = **Aḍakavatī**, q.v., = Skt. Alakā.

aṭakkara, m., apparently *pathologically ravenous appetite*: Mvy 9515, according to Tib. bkres ṅa ba (ed. suggests rṅab, misprinted rñab, ba) and Chin.; in a list of diseases. See **āṭakkara**.

aṭaṭa, m. (= Pali id.), n. of a hell (cold, acc. to Dharmas and Tib. Mvy): Mvy 4931; Dharmas 122; Divy 67.23; 138.7; Av i.4.9 etc.; Mmk 635.22.

aṭanin (Skt. aṭana plus -in), *wandering* (adj.): paśyathā katham aṭany akhedavān Gv 481.24 (vs), *see how, wandering, he is not wearied*.

Aṭavaka (cf. **Āṭavaka**), n. of a nāga king: Māy 247.22.

Aṭavī (= Pali Āḷavī), n. of a town: Māy 15, 90. Lévi identifies the first with the Pali city-name but thinks the second a different locality.

Aṭavīsaṃbhavā, n. of a pond: Suv 184.6 ff. (note especially 188.2).

aṭṭa, m. (v.l. **atta**; so Mironov), a high number: Mvy 8067; Tib. phyor, which Das gives as = anta (read atta?), n. of a number. Cf. also **iṭṭā**.

[**aṭṭahā(ḥ)**: Mmk 19.10, read abṛhā(ḥ) or **avṛ°**, q.v. a class of gods.]

? **aṭṭiyānika** or °**vānika**, pl. °kā, so mss. at Mv iii.442.15, corresponding to **āgrīvanīya** at iii.113.10; Senart em. aṭṭavāṇijā, which is quite implausible and not really easier to interpret. In a list of designations of various tradesmen or artisans.

Aṭṭeśvara, n. of a **suparṇin**, previous birth of **Virūpākṣa**: MSV i.260.19 ff.

Aḍakavatī (=Skt. Alakā; see **Aṭakā°**, **Ala°**), n. of the capital of the yakṣas: LV 202.13; Suv 116.1 °vatyāṃ (Nobel em. Aḍakā°, needlessly); Māy 106; 228.21.

aḍḍhatiya (= Pali id., acc. to CPD by haplol. for aḍḍhatatiya = Skt. ardhatṛtīya), or **aḍḍhā°**, *two and a half*. Senart's Index cites only aḍḍhātiya, which is read in text Mv iii.72.12 (mss. āvṛttiya) and 13 (mss. aṭṭātiya or āṭṭā°), while aḍḍhatiya is read in text Mv ii.312.10 (mss. aṭṭāti, omitting ya) and iii.75.7 (mss. aṭṭatiya).

Aṇāla (so Lefm. with some mss.) or Anāla (so Calc. with best mss.), n. of a town: LV 406.20 (prose) °lam, acc. sg.

aṇu, *grain of sand* (nowhere recorded in this sense): gaṅgāṇubhiḥ saṃmitāḥ LV 360.17.

aṇu-phala, m., lit. *having minute fruit*, *millet* (Tib. tsi tsi, tsi tse): Mvy 5657.

(**aṇḍa**, *cupola*, the bulb-shaped part on the top of a stūpa: Divy 244.10, 11. See P. K. Acharya, Dict. Hindu Arch. 16, and pw 1.284.)

aṇḍakāṣṭha: Divy 384.24, acc. to Burnouf Intr. 376 *eggshell*; doubtful; see s.v. **hirodaka**.

Aṇḍabha, n. of a yakṣa: Māy 51.

Aṇḍāyana, pl., n. of a brahmanical gotra: Divy 635.19.

aṇvati, rarely °**te** (derived by Senart, note on Mv i.15.10, from Skt. ṛṇvati), *goes*: aṇvati LV 192.7 (text 'nveti, unmetr.; cf. vv. ll. 'ṇvata, 'ṇtata); Mv i.264.12; ii.101.18 (mss.); 211.2 (mss.), 3; 457.15; iii.28.8; 144.17 ff; 154.17; 155.3, 9, etc.; °te SP 111.4 (Kashgar rec.; text haṃce); aṇvanti Mv i.15.10; ii.211.7; aṇvāmi Mv ii.226.14; aṇvāma (pl. for dual) Mv iii.310.10; aṇvāmas (v.l., text añcāmas) SP 168.9; aṇvantehi (em.; pres. pple.) Mv i.356.5; °ntena Mv ii.83.21; °nto Mv ii.212.16; 217.5; iii.28.9 (mss. °ati); 35.17; aṇvatī (text °ntī; n. sg. fem.) Mv iii.12.10; aṇvamānā Mv ii.441.6; aṇvi (aor., *went*; read °karmāṇvi, cf. WT who cite their ms. as °ñvi!) SP 258.10; ppp. aṇvitaḥ Mv ii.210.15 (pādehi, *went on foot*); iii.144.15; °tā (em.) Mv i.356.10; ger. aṇviya Mv iii.145.1; inf. aṇvitu-kāmā(ḥ) Mv ii.211.10; gdve. bhikṣā aṇvitavyā Mv iii.178.7 *one must go a-begging*.

atapa, once **atapas**, the second of the śuddhāvāsa, and (usually pl.) the class-name of the gods who dwell there; in Pali atappa: Mvy 3103; Dharmas 128; LV 150.10; Mv ii.314.9; 319.7; 349.1; 360.22; Divy 68.16; 367.14; Av i.5.3; Mmk 19.10; 43.21 (text anaya); 69.6 (here sg. of an individual member of the class); atapas (s-stem, in comp.) Gv 249.10. Others, see s.v. **deva**.

atara, m. (cf. next), a high number: Mvy 7777 (°raḥ); Gv 106.14 (°rasya).

ataru (cf. prec.), a high number: Mvy 7906 (°ruḥ; cited from Gv); Gv 133.25 (°rum, n. sg. nt.!).

a-tarkika, adj. (Pali atakkika, see CPD; cf. **tarka**), *free from (sophistical) ratiocination*: °kaṃ sūkṣmam anāsravaṃ ca jñānaṃ ... SP 62.12 (vs).

[**atarṣaka**: Śikṣ 255.8 °kā(ḥ), followed by atṛptikarāḥ; read atarpakāḥ, *not satisfying*; of the viṣayas.]

[**atarṣaṇīya**: Śikṣ 255.8 °yāni, after atṛptāni; read atarpaṇīyāni, *insatiable*; of the indriyas.]

[**Ati**, read Atri, n. of a Prajāpati: Māy 257.18.]

[**ati tvāṃ**: LV 253.8 (vs), so text, but most mss. atīva, and so Tib. (śin tu); read atīvā (m.c.).]

atikāla (= Pali id.), *too early time*; cf. **ativikāla**; na cātikāle (v.l. °laṃ) na cātivikāle (v.l. °laṃ) Mv iii.255.14, *not too early and not too late*; iii.414.5 (mss. nānyātikāle).

atikrānta, adj. (ppp.), *surpassing, wonderful*, (specifically of appearance) *beautiful*: atikrāntā (so mss., Senart abhi°) ca mānuṣāḥ Mv iii.96.19; 100.20; °ta-varṇa, *of beautiful appearance*, LV 396.17; Mv iii.316.13; 317.11; also Mv ii.257.9; 258.7; iii.197.15; 302.10 (in these four Senart em. abhikrānta°). The equivalent Pali is regularly abhikkanta (-vaṇṇa), but atikkanta also occurs in the same sense (CPD s.v.). In BHS, in this sense, abhikrānta occurs, if at all, only in LV 398.11 °ta varṇa, see **abhikrānta** 2. Since t and bh are easily confused, it may be that graphic confusion is here concerned. On the other hand, atikrānta is erroneously read, e. g. in Divy 462.13, for **abhikrānta** (1), which is correctly read in the same passage in MSV i.70.3, and elsewhere in that text.

atikrānta-mānuṣyaka, *surpassing human powers* or *nature*: Mv ii.283.15 (cakṣuṣā viśuddhena) °ṣyakena (*transcending human sight*).

atikṣuṇaka, adj. (var. atikhuntannaka-, corrupt; read °kṣuṇṇaka, *broken*?), *over-small*: nāti°kair ālopaiḥ (sc. paribhokṣyāmaḥ) Mvy 8572; so Tib. ha caṅ chuṅ ba. See **kṣuṇa**. (Mironov as text.)

aticirayati (= Pali aticirāyati; cf. Skt. cirayati), *delays excessively*: Divy 175.20.

atijalpati, *talks too much*: Mvy 7024 °lpet.

atitti-(ga-) ? (= Pali id., Skt. atṛpti); assumed by Senart at Mv i.133.12 (prose) atittigāś (no ms. reads quite so, yet the variants seem indeed to tend in this direction), *ils ne tendent pas à la satisfaction de leurs sens, ils ne sont pas esclaves de leurs sens*. It seems to me, however, that the general use of derivatives of tṛp would suggest just the opposite meaning, which would not fit here (ep. of Bodhisattvas): *they never reach satiety*.

atināmayati, atināmeti (= Pali atināmeti), *causes* (time) *to pass, spends* (time): kumārabhūmīm atināmayitvā SP 68.7 (vs), *having spent his childhood period (stage)*; rātriṃdivāny SP 61.1; kālaṃ LV 384.14; Mv i.192.14 (atināmenti); Śikṣ 40.5; Bbh 172.7; (saptāhapūraṃ ...) atināmesi Mv ii.348.16, *spent a full week*; saptāham Divy 443.6; rātriṃdivasam Divy 82.29; rātridivasāny Suv 113.2; ahorātram Jm 36.4; divasam Divy 304.4; rātrir ... atināmitā Av ii.153.14; also used absolutely, without a word for (period of) *time*, yan nv ahaṃ tūṣṇībhāvenātināmayeyam RP 39.14, *suppose I spend (my time) in silence*; similarly Dbh 5.26–7 tūṣṇīṃbhāvenātināmayati; suciram (prob. adv., *for a long while*) atināmayām āsa Gv 342.5 (*spent the time*; or is suciraṃ a noun, object of the verb?). See also **abhināmayati** (4), **adhinām°**, **vyatināmayati** (**vīti°**).

atiniryāti, *goes all the way thru*: (in hell, dhūmo ... asthiṃ) bhittvā asthimarjaṃ mānsādy °yāti Mv i.20.2 (some mss. °jāti).

atipaścāt, see **abhipaścāt**.

Atipuruṣa, n. of a former Buddha: Mv i.138.13.

atiprathate, *spreads abroad exceedingly, becomes very well known*: °thante ... cariteṣv atikramāḥ Jm 188.21 (mss., Kern em. abhi°, hardly necessarily).

ati-pravaṇṇa, see **pravaṇṇa**.

atiprāgas, adv., *too early*, see under next, and cf. Pali atippāgo (ending analogical to forms like bhūyas): °gas tāvad ... piṇḍāya carituṃ Mv i.54.12; 56.6.

atiprāg eva, adv. (see prec.), *too early, very early*, cf. Skt. atiprage and prāk (Lex. = prabhāte), Pali atippageva: °eva ... piṇḍāya carituṃ Mv i.34.16, *it is too early to go begging food*.

Atibalavīryaparākrama, n. of a future Buddha (= **Nanda** 8, 'the lazy'): Av i.22.3.

atimanyanā (= Pali °maññanā; Vedic atimanyate plus -anā), *despising, contempt*: an-a° sarvasattveṣu KP 18.3; Tib. mi brñas pa.

atimāna (= Pali id.), *self-conceit, excessive pride*; see also **mānātimāna**: Mv iii.214.9; an-atimāna-tayā, Gv 464.5.

Atimāyā, n. of a sister of Māyā: Mv i.355.17.

atimukta (m. or nt.; Skt. Lex., = Skt. atimuktaka, Pali atimutta beside °taka), a kind of shrub and its flower: SP 342.8 (vs); °ta-kadalī- Divy 619.18 (prose).

Atimuktaka (= Pali Atimuttaka-susāna; presumably named from the creeper atim°), n. of a cemetery near Benares: °ke (Senart em. °ka-) śmaśāne Mv ii.168.8; °kaṃ (Senart em. °ka-) śmaśānaṃ id. 11.

Atimuktakamalā (v.l. Abhi°), n. of a village chief's daughter: LV 265.5.

atiyātrā, *passage-fee*: Divy 92.27. Probably about the same as ativāhika in Kauṭ. Arth., cited s.v. **gulma**, q.v.

atiriktaka, adj., *completely (miserably?) empty*; in this sense (ati plus rikta, *empty*) nowhere recorded, either with or without suffixal -ka (pejorative?). Otherwise Skt. atirikta, and Pali atiritta(ka), are pples. of ati plus ric- and mean *left over, excessive, superfluous* or the like: Kāśyapo ca Pūraṇo 'tiriktakena pātreṇa nirdhāvati Mv ii.207.2 (whereas the Bodhisattva received a bowl full of delicacies).

ati-r-iva (= Pali id., Skt. atīva, § 4.61), *in excess*; noted only in Mv: prose, i.302.19; iii.60.8; 147.3, 11; 258.9; 302.2; 334.2; 341.5; verses, i.129.6 (read tvayā atirivāpi, with v.l., *even in a manner surpassing you*; Senart em. wrongly; v.l. atiriccāpi, which would be possible if tvayā were construed as acc.); 266.14; ii.37.10; 227.7; iii.109.17; 246.6.

atireka-, *excess(-ive)*, as prior member of cpd. (so in Pali, but in Skt. app. only as final member): atireka-pūjā, *exceedingly great respect*, Mv i.89.16 (prose); same cpd. in Pali, MN i.220.11–12; read Mv 1.89.15 f., yataś ca bodhisattvacaritabhūmiṃ prāpnuvanti, taṃ (so mss.!) na pūjayanti atirekapūjāye (correct punctuation!), *and from whom they obtain the stage of Bodhisattva-course-of-conduct, him they do not (as they should) honor with exceeding great respect*; atireka-lābha, *extra allowance*, Bhīk 22b.3–4; 23a. 2, 5; °ka-cīvara (Pali id.), *extra robe*, MSV ii.91.11 f.

atilakṣa, nt., *a million*: Mvy 7995.

atilīyate (cf. Pali atilīna), *becomes slack*: nātilīyase MSV i.9.12.

ativatta, in ativattākṣa Mvy 8833; Tib. (mig) ha caṅ che ba, (having) *very large* (eyes). There is a v.l. ativantā°, and Mironov reads ativatrā° without v.l. Seems to be MIndic, for ati plus either Skt. vṛtta (Pali vaṭṭa), *round*, or vyātta (Pali vatta), *wide-open* (in Skt. and Pali only recorded of the *mouth*).

ativākya (= Pali id. [so, ā and ky! Sanskritic]; cf. Skt. ati-vac), *blame, abuse*: Ud xix.6 (°kyaṃ titikṣati; = Pali Dhp. 321); xxix.31 (°kyaṃ titikṣāmi); MSV i.11.17.

ativāha (= Pali id.), *guide, conductor*; only in sārthātivāha (-sadṛśa) = sārthavāha (and perhaps m.c.), *caravan-leader, merchant*: Gv 474.14 (vs).

ativikāla (= Pali id.), *too late a time*: Mv iii.255.14 (see s.v. **atikāla**); °kāle 414.5.

ati-viśvasta, adj. (Pali ativissattha), *exceedingly intimate*: me bhagavāṃ ... ativiśvasto Mv i.327.20; 329.5.

ativiṣa (1) adj. (= Pali ativisa), *very poisonous*: Jm 229.17; (2) nt., a plant, according to Tib. boṅ ṅa dkar po, said to mean *white wolfsbane*; cf. Pali ativisa, a medicinal plant, and Skt. ativiṣā, identified as one or more varieties of Aconitum: Mvy 5821.

ativistṛta (cf. Pali ativitthāra, °ārita), *too expanded, too diffuse*: Bbh 264.24 (applied to śāstras; opposed to saṃkṣipta).

[(**a**)**tisaṃlayana**, doubtless error for prati°, *privacy*: Divy 204.4 sāyāhne 'tisaṃlayanād vyutthāya; this phrase regularly has **pratisaṃlayanād** (q.v.), and there seems little doubt that the syllable pra has been accidentally lost from the text.]

atisadṛśa, see **anati°**.

atisamṛddha, m., n. of a muhūrta: Divy 643.10 (text here °ddhir); 644.14 (°ddhaḥ).

atisarati, *transgresses, goes too far* (in Pali also *sins*; since it follows, and is parallel with, nātijalpet in Mvy, it seems not likely to mean that here; but cf. **atisāra**): nātisaret Mvy 7025 = Tib. ha caṅ ḥphro bar mi bya (byed), *not make going too far*; acc. to Chin., in speech.

? **atisarjana**, nt., see **abhiṣajjana**.

atisāra (= Pali id.), *sin*, in sātisāra (= Pali id.), *sinful, guilty*: Mvy 9336 = Tib. ḥgal tshabs can. Here, and seemingly always, used in nom. with bhavati, *becomes guilty of a sin*. So Divy 275.18; 330.1; Śikṣ 63.8; Bbh 160.24; °rā (fem.) Bhīk 10a.3–4.

-atisārin (to prec.; cf. Pali id.), *transgressing*: vinayātisāriṇīr duṣṭhulā āpattīr deśayitvā MSV iii.79.5; similarly 86.12 etc.

[**Atisūrya**, Senart's em. for mss. **Abhisūrya**: Mv iii.330.13.]

? **atisvāra**, in Divy 304.28 tasyātisvāreṇa gacchato 'nupadaṃ gacchanti. The word seems certainly corrupt; read atitvareṇa, *with very great speed*? This at least would make good sense, and tvareṇa, *with speed*, is recorded.

atīcchā, *excessive desire*: Śikṣ 255.16. Cf. Pali aticchā, aticchatā, and atricchā.

atītaka = Skt. atīta, *past* (opposed to *present* and *future*): RP 6,5; Bhad 13; Gv 384.6. In all may be m.c.

atītārtha (= Pali atītattha, atīta-m-attha), *having missed one's aim, object*, or *profit*: (na ...) nirvṛtāḥ puruṣaśreṣṭhā atītārthe (so all mss.; n. pl.; or loc. abs., *when their aim is missed*?) jinātmajā Mv i.122.18 (vs), *Buddhas and Bodhisattvas never die leaving uncompleted their aims.*

atīśaya (m.c. for Skt. ati°), *abundance*: Mv i.100.10 (vs).

atula (1) (-gandharāja), some kind of perfume: Gv 153.14; (2) m. (Pali id.), n. of a nāga-king, previous incarnation of Śākyamuni: Mv i.249.18; 251.12; [(3) a high number: in Gv 105.25 text sattvatulasya, read certainly sattvā°; but possibly sattvātulyasya (see **atulya**).]

Atulaprabha, n. of a kalpa: Gv 447.1.

atuliya, adj. (= Pali id., Skt. atulya), *incomparable*: Mv ii.300.8, 9 (vss); 362.11 (prose).

atulya (cf. **atula**, 3), nt., a high number: Mvy 7812; 7944 (cited from Gv), 8045; Gv 106.23; 134.12; Sukh 31.2.

atulyaparivarta, m. (in Gv 134.12 nt.), square of **atulya**: Mvy 7813; 7945 (cited from Gv as °taḥ, n. sg.); Gv 106.24; 134.12 (°tam, n. sg.).

atṛtīya, adj., *with no third* (of two individuals); nowhere recorded, but cf. Skt. advitīya: ubhaye atṛtīyā Mv ii.171.16, *the two of them* (alone) *without a third.*

atta, see **aṭṭa**.

-attamanas, adj. (= Pali id., BHS **ātta°**), in an-atta° *not glad*, Gv 411.8. Possibly retention of MIndic short a- before consonant cluster; § 3.32; but may be mere corruption for **-ātta°**.

attāttamīya (= Pali attattanīya; semi-MIndic for ātmātmīya, § 3.34), *the self, and what pertains to the self*: -vigatās Dbh.g. 16(352).6. The same cpd. in prose as ātmātmīya-vigata Dbh 43.13; ātmātmīya-rahita Dbh 50.29.

attīyati (Pali aṭṭīyati), see **ar(t)tiyati**: attīyate, °yantā.

attīyanā (to prec. plus -anā), *aversion*, with ablative: dharmebhyo 'ttīyanā (so mss., text artī°) jugupsanā MadhK 297.4; see **ar(t)tiyati.**

atma, semi-MIndic for ātmā, *self*: LV 419.8 (vs); see § 3.35.

atyatīta, nt., *what is beyond death*: in cliché of wish for a son (s.v. **ādiśati**, 2, 3), asmākaṃ cātyatītakālagatānām, Divy 2.15, *and when we have died* (and so entered) *into the postmortal state*; same 440.28–29; Av i.14.15; ii.73.10 (so ms. in these); read so Av i.197.2; 277.1; ii.180.13 (Speyer reads always cāpy atīta°, sometimes with ms. support); in same cliché, asmākaṃ cātyatītaṃ kālagatānām uddiśya Divy 99.6, *and with reference to the postmortal state of us after we have died.*

atyantakāle, adv. (cf. AMg. accantakālassa, Ratnach.), *for a very long time*: Mv i.103.9, read yadā (mss., Senart omits this) preteṣu, atyantakāle (mss. reported °kāye, Senart em. °kāyeṣu; perh. read °kālena?) nopapadyanti, *if* (*they are born*) *among pretas, they are not born* (*so*) *for a very long time.*

Atyantacandramas, n. of a Bodhisattva: Gv 443.5.

atyantatā, instr. °tayā, *absolutely*, with neg., *not at all*: °tayā hi bhagavan svapnāntare (254.5 svapne) ... na saṃvidyate Śikṣ 252.8; 254.5.

[**atyantarībhūta**, error for **abhyant°**, q.v.]

atyaya, m., (once nt., Av ii.151.3), *sin* = Pali accaya (hardly in this sense in Skt.; Manu 8.243 is close to it but apparently isolated); with paśyati, dṛś-, *recognize as a sin*; with deśayati (rarely pratideśayati, āviṣkaroti) *confess as a sin*; with **pratigṛhṇāti** (rarely jānāti), *accept* (*a confession of*) *a sin* = *forgive, absolve* it; with kṣamāpayati (rare), *ask forgiveness for a sin*. Often atyayam atyayato instead of the simple atyayam, with all these expressions, in the same meanings. Pali uses accayam accayato, and verbs passati, deseti, paṭigaṇhāti, as in BHS; also khamati, *forgives*: atyayo me Divy 617.17, *I have sinned*; atyayam atyayataḥ paśyāmi Divy 617.20; ° °dṛṣṭvā deśayāmi, ° °āviskaromi (so!) id. 20–21; atyayam atyayato dṛṣṭvā pratideśayati LV 379.13; °yaṃ deśayanti LV 409.22; °yo deśito Av i.149.12–13; °yaṃ deśitavān 272.13; °yam °yato deśitam (as if nt.!) ii.151.3; °yam °yato deśaya, *confess as a sin!*, Śikṣ 58.15; Divy 5.5; 55.1; 567.29–30 (read deśayāpy for °yāmy); 570.23; °yaṃ ... deśayāmo SP 210.1; deśemahe atyayu SP 212.7; °yam °yato deśayāmy Gv 122.8; atyayaṃ no bhagavān pratigṛhṇātu LV 379.6; bhagavān atyayam atyayato jānātu pratigṛhṇātu Divy 617.22–3; atyayaṃ pratigṛhṇantu (subject the Buddhas) Suv 30.8; sā tenātyayam atyayato kṣamāpitā Divy 5.6, *he asked her to pardon his offense.* Once, atyayam atyayato āgamā(ḥ; aor.) MSV i.43.5, *you have arrived at* (*been guilty of*) *a sin.*

atyaya-deśana, nt., *confession of sin*: Karmav 49.24; °**nā**, f., id., RP 34.11; Jm 127.13.

[**atyayika**, read **ātyayika**, q.v.]

aty-avaśyam, adv., *quite certainly*: Mv ii.491.7, 8; iii.263.16; 265.7, 10.

[**atyavahāra**, read abhyavahāra, which is Skt., pw 7.306, (digestible) *food*, Gv 401.6.]

-atyastam, ifc. adv. (cf. Pāṇ. 2.1.24), *when ... has passed, after ...*: anekajanmātyastam Laṅk 251.9.

atyastikā, a certain posture, presumably of the hands: Stein ms. fragments 1.3b, 4a, La Vallée Poussin JRAS 1913.844; adjoins **vinyastikā**; cf. also **udvyastikā, vyastikā.**

[**atyākhyāya** (tāṃ te gatiṃ gamiṣyanti), by em., LV 88.22 (prose). But Lefm. misedits and misunderstands the passage, and Weller ignores it. Foucaux is practically right. Read with most and best mss. vyākhyāyatām te tām; all mss. have vyā°. not tyā°. Render *What is the fate of those who expound the Buddhas past, present, and future, while yet ignoring* (or *concealing*) *the enlightenment of the Buddhas, — to that fate will they go.*]

aty-ārabdha, (=Pali accāraddha), *too greatly exerted*, adj. with vīrya (so in Pali, with viriya): Śikṣ 51.2.

? **atyāhata**, *afflicted* (but probably error for Skt. abhyāhata): Divy 460.7, text duḥkhenātyāhato.

Atyuccagāmin, n. of a former Buddha (spelled Abhy° in Gv; in mss. of Mv iii.245.6; 247.6; 248.9; and in v.l. at LV 172.3, where Tib. rab ḥthor gśegs; Foucaux interprets rab = abhi, but it may = ati, see Das s.v. rab-ḥkhrugs; Tib. for LV 5.6 śin tu . . . = aty-): Mv i.137.11; iii.240.2 f.; 243.5, 6; 244.1; 245.6; 247.6; 248.9; LV 5.6; 172.3; Gv (see above) 204.26; 205.2, 10.

Atyuccadeva, n. of a Bodhisattva: Gv 443.9 (text Abhy°, cf. prec.).

Atyuttama, n. of a former Buddha: Mv iii.239.2.

[**atyutsāhatā**, Divy 547.26, or **°hanā**, Divy 549.7, read **abhyut°**.]

atyudgacchati, and ppp. **atyudgata**, sometimes in texts and oftener in mss. (frequently as v.l.) for **abhyud°** in meaning *rises* (ppp. *risen*) *above*. Graphic confusion is certainly concerned here, at least in part; except as under **atyudgata**, q.v., all occurrences are grouped under **abhyud°**, q.v. For the most part Pali abbhuggacchati and derivatives support this classification. Note however (aside from Pali accuggata, apparently only used as adjective, often with specialized meanings) Pali accuggamma, ger., used of water-plants, *having grown out above* (the water, acc. or abl.); but BHS uses (only) abhyudgacchati in this sense, according to unanimous tradition, tho perhaps this tradition may be erroneous. Contrariwise, there is even in Pali tradition some confusion between abbhugg- and accugg- in this group; see CPD s.v. abbhuggata (a var. accuggata occurs with subject yaso).

atyudgata, m.: Mvy 7734, or nt.: Mvy 7862, a high number, = Tib. zaṅ(s) yag; in 7862 cited from Gv, text of which reads **abhyud°**, q.v.

atyunnamayya (cf. Skt. unnamayati), ger., *raising* or *stretching up very high*: Divy 36.10; 120.5; Av i.276.16; in all pūrva- (or °vaṃ) kāyam aty°, preparatory to expressing an udāna. Perhaps only graphic error for abhyu°; Skt. has abhyunnata, ppp.; and see **abhyunnāmya**.

atramantrā, a high number: Gv 106.7; seems to be a corrupt substitute for **bhramantra**, q.v.

atrāṇa, adj. *defenseless* (= Pali atāṇa and attāṇa; only Buddh.; a- plus Skt. trāṇa): Mv i.22.14 (prose) atrāṇā(ḥ). To be read metrically atāṇām, though written atrāṇām, Gv 474.23. Cf. next.

atrāṇya = prec.: °yāḥ Suv 53.1 (vs; v.l. atrāṇāḥ).

Atri, see **Ati**.

atha, followed by **khalu, tarhi**, or **evaṃ** (= Pali atha, and atha kho; seems not used in this sense in Skt.), after a negative clause: atha khalu (not . . .) *but rather*, Ger. *sondern* Mv ii.161.15, 18; 162.1, 3; atha tarhi, id., LV 19.11, 16, 20; 20.3; atha evaṃ anyatra Mv iii.66.8 and 15 (see s.v. **anyatra**, 1), *but rather, on the contrary*. . . .

atharvaṇa, nt., *Atharvanic practices, sorcery, black magic*: Divy 629.16 (mss.; ed. em. āth°). Pali (Sn 927) has v.l. athabbaṇa for edd. āth°; Skt. has atharvaṇa also but apparently not in precisely this sense.

atharvaṇika, *a member of a school of the AV*: Divy 633.10 ff.

adattādāyika (= Skt. °yin, Manu 8.340; also BHS, Gv 159.13; 228.13), *thief*: Divy 301.23; 418.28.

adattādāsyatha, 2 pl. fut., mādattā°, *do not steal*: LV 15.9; see § 28.53.

Adana, n. of a nāga king: Māy 246.25.

Adarśamukha, n. of a nāga king: Māy 247.36; cf. **Ādarśamukha**, for which this is probably a misprint or error.

adānta-damaka (= Pali adanta°), *tamer of the untamed*, epithet of Buddha (cf. **puruṣadamyasārathi**). Reference lost.

adinna, adj. (= Pali id.), *not given*: Mv i.346.10 ff.; abbreviated expression for **adinnādāna**, q.v., Mv i.145.9 = 202.6 = ii.6.3 (vs) viramāmi cāpy adinnā(d), *and I abstain also from* (taking) *what is not given*, i. e. from theft.

adinnādāna, nt. or m. (= Pali, nt.; MIndic for Skt. adattādāna, nt., see pw s.v.), *theft*: °naṃ (n. sg.) Mv i.347.13; adinnādāno adharmo adattādānavairamaṇo dharmo Mv ii.99.6.

Adīnakusuma, n. of a Bodhisattva: Gv 443.2.

Adīnagāmin (mss. mostly Adīva°), n. of a former Buddha: Mv i.141.12.

Aduka, n. of a nāga king: Māy 247.27.

adūṣin, adj., in Divy printed **aduṣin**, prob. by error, *doing no wrong* (Skt. -dūṣin); in adūṣy-anapakārin (in Divy wrongly printed -anayakārin), *doing no wrong and not offending*: °kārī, n. sg. m., Divy 574.11; 581.18; MSV i.215.13; °kāriṇo, n. pl., ii.78.21.

adṛśyā (not recorded in this sense), probably to be read for text ādṛśyā, n. of a magic herb (which makes invisible): Gv 498.1, 2; in line 2 could be either a- or ā-, in saṃdhi; but the stem, in composition, is printed as ending in -a, for which probably read -ā; in line 1 text asty ādṛśyā nāmauṣadhiḥ.

adekṣiya (hyper Skt. for Pkt. *a-dekkhiya, to dekkhai, on which see J. Bloch, Fest. Wackernagel, 143 ff.; blend of dakkhai and pekkhai = prekṣati; cf. **adrākṣaṇīya**), *ugly*: (śobhano rājā . . . chattradhāro punar) °yo Mv iii.10.15.

adbhuta (in Mvy Kyoto ed. always adbhūta, 1277, 5043, 7164; but Mironov adbhuta without v.l.), (**1**) adj. *amazed, wonder-struck* (in Skt. only *astonishing*, and so usually Pali abbhuta, but see Ap 109.24, CPD s.v.) āścaryabhūtā sma tathādbhutāś ca SP 110.12, *we are amazed and astonished*; (**2**) nt., also adbhuta-dharma, m. (Pali abbhuta, °ta-dhamma), one of the divisions or types of literature in the Buddhist canon, *marvel(s)*, itivṛttakaṃ jātakam adbhutaṃ ca SP 45.7; adbhutadharmaḥ Mvy 1277; °dharma, Dharmas 62, one of the nine pravacana. (Not in this sense, adbhutānāṃ ca dharmāṇāṃ viśuddhir upalabhyate Mv i.175.17, *of marvelous conditions or states*.)

adyatve, loc. = adya, *today, in the present time* (so Skt. Gr., BR 5.968): LV 155.20 (prose); **adyatvena**, instr., id.: MSV i.89.20; ii.186.15.

adyāgre, Karmav 158.4 (much more commonly adyāgreṇa, see s.v. **-agreṇa**), and **adyād-agre** Karmav 158.3, *from now on*: = Pali ajjatagge, ajjadagge (but not °aggena!), derived by CPD from *ajjato agge, a theory perhaps supported by adyād (abl.?) agre (but *adya-d-agre, with hiatus-bridging d, see § 4.64, might have been secondarily reinterpreted as adyād-).

adyād-agre, see prec.

?**adrākṣaṇīya**, Senart's em. at Mv ii.152.14; explained in note as hyper-Skt. for Pkt. *a-dakkhaniya, read °ṇiya, *ugly*, = **adekṣiya**, q.v.; in description of the sick man as seen by the young Bodhisattva; Senart, °ṇīyo saṃvegakārako; mss. adrākṣāṇī (v.l. ayakṣāni)-ṣoḍaśa-vegakārako. Uncertain.

(**adruta-lipi**, see **anudruta°**.)

advaya, nt., *non-duality*, as designation of the Buddhist doctrine. In Mvy 1717 advayam (Tib. gñis su med pa, *non-duality*) is listed among paramārtha-paryāyāḥ, *synonyms for the true doctrine*; advayasaṃjñā udapāsi Mv i.237.14, *consciousness of non-duality arose in him* (so that he resolved to become a Buddha).

Advayavajra, n. of an author: Sādh 48.18, etc.

advaya-vādin, *preaching non-duality,* ep. of Buddha: Mvy 23; Divy 95.13.

[**adha,** text in Sukh 22.8 (vs) -adha nānaprabhūta-, erroneously; read adhanāna (= °nānāṃ) prabhūta-.]

Adhaūrdhvadigjñānāvabhāsa, n. of a Buddha: Gv 309.18.

a-dhandha (see **dhandha**), *not slow*: Bbh 9.19; 15.22.

adhandhāyamāna, see **dhandhāyati, °te.**

adha-m-ūrdhva, with 'Hiatus-bridging' m, for *adha-ūrdhva (adhas plus ū°), *upside down*: adhamūrdhva-lokadhātu Gv 518.4 (prose), (follows vyatyasta-lokadhātu-); in Laṅk 28.1, text adhamūrdhāś ca, read adha-m-ūrdhvāś ca (after vyatyastā[ḥ]).

-adharaka, fem. **-ikā** (= Skt. adhara), in Bhvr. cpd., *lower lip,* endearing diminutive (§ 22.34): bimba-supakvanibhādharikā[ḥ], LV 322.14 (vs), of daughters of Māra.

adhara-tas, adv. (Skt. Gr. id.), *downward, sinking*: asthicarmāvaśeṣaḥ samantād gātreṇādharataḥ MSV ii.32.11.

adharima, adj. (§ 22.15), *lowest*: ep. of bhūmi, *ground,* in the cliché on birth of children, avatarantī(m) °māṃ bhūmim Divy 99.15; 167.12; 441.5; Av i.15.6 (elsewhere adhara in same cliché, Speyer, Av Index); °me skandhe MSV ii.6.17 ff.

adhar-diś (**-dik**) (= Skt. adho-diś, recorded in comm. on Hem. Abhidh., BR; also, without citation, in Apte), *the nadir*; acc. to Kern, SP Preface vi, in Kashgar rec. of SP, for Nep. adhodik.

adharṣikatā, *state of not violating* or *disturbing*: Śikṣ 3.7 (vs).

adhasta, adj. (= Skt. adhastana; cf. Skt. adhastāt adv.), *below*: adhastāyāṃ diśi, *in the nadir*: SP 240.12; 243.11 (here Kashgar rec. heṣṭimāyāṃ); Sukh 98.7.

adhikaraṇa (= Pali id., in both senses), nt., (**1**) *matter of contention* or *dispute,* especially among monks: saṃghe kalahabhaṇḍanavigrahavivādaṃ adhikaraṇaṃ kaukṛtyaṃ utpādetsuḥ Mv iii.48.(13–)14; adhikaraṇa na tasya jātu bhotī Śikṣ 195.10; °ṇa-kuśala MSV i.55.13; adhikaraṇa-vastu Mvy 9115 = Tib. rtsod paḥi gzhi, *ground of dispute*; **adhikaraṇa-śamatha** Mvy 8630 (= Pali °samatha), *the* (7 rules for) *quieting of disputes,* a part of the Prātimokṣa; they are listed 8631–7, mostly as in Pali, **saṃmukha-vinayaḥ, smṛti-vinayaḥ, amūḍha-vinayaḥ, yadbhū-yasikīyaḥ, tatsvabhāvaiṣīyaḥ, tṛṇaprastārakaḥ, pratijñākārakaḥ,** qq.v.; (**2**) -adhikaraṇaṃ, ifc. adv., *by reason of*: yato-adhikaraṇaṃ, conj. (= Pali yatvādhika-raṇaṃ) Mv iii.52.7, *because,* lit. *by reason of which*; also stem in comp., pramādādhikaraṇahetor MPS 4.7 ff., *because of negligence* (Pali pamādādhikaraṇaṃ, adv.; elsewhere -adhikaraṇa-hetu, CPD).

adhikāra, m., (= Pali id.), *service, respectful duty performed towards another,* usually a superior (and esp. a Buddha); Senart Mv i.402, note on i.37.11–12, renders *offrande,* and so Suzuki on Laṅk 6.3 *offerings.* No doubt the 'service' often included or consisted of offerings; but that this was not necessarily so is proved by SP 111.12 bahūhi kāryehi kṛtādhikārāḥ, said of merchants (vāṇijāḥ) employed by a wealthy capitalist. who *do service* (to him) *with many business-operations* (certainly not *offerings,* kāryehi!). The cpd. **kṛtādhikāra** (Pali katā°) is very common and in BHS most often refers to *services* performed for present or past Buddhas: SP 49.13; Laṅk 6.3 (kṛtādhikārā buddheṣu kariṣyanty adhunā ca vai); Mv ii.288.8; iii.263.12; purima-jina-kṛtādhikāra LV 393.6; Mv ii.312.5; sumahantā adhikārā mayā kṛtā (to former Buddhas) Mv iii.241.12; (bhagavato . . .) adhikāraṃ kartuṃ Mv i.37.12; . . . kṛtvā Mv i.44.14; prasannādhikāra, *service tendered by one who is kindly disposed,* i. e. *service of friendship,* Divy 305.7; 308.20 ff.

-adhikārika, ifc. adj., f. **°kī,** (= Pali id.), *referring to, concerned with*: -pratyaṅgaśīrṣachedādhikārikāś ca duḥkhās Gv 159.21; kiṃcid evālpaṃ vā prabhūtaṃ vā pūjādhikārikam akṛtvā Bbh 160.19, *without doing at least something, be it little or much, that relates to homage*; dharmā-dhikārikī kathā MSV i.162.14. In MPS 45.2 and 6 (prose) yasya vayaṃ pūjādhikārikām autsukyaṃ na samāpannāḥ, I cannot explain the ā in °kām (reported 3 times from 2 mss.); I should expect °kam; a fem. substantive °kā seems implausible.

adhikālam, adv., Sukh 8.1 (vs), (reading uncertain, several vv.ll.) ato 'dhikālam, *in reference to time hereafter,* i. e. *for all future time* (? adhi as in **adhicittam,** governing the noun with which it is compounded).

adhigama, m., also (even after consonants) **dhigama** (q.v.), *spiritual realization*; *attainment of religious goal*; used in senses very close to this in Skt. (BR and pw), as well as in Pali; seems nearly equivalent to **abhisamaya,** q.v.: (bhagavantaṃ . . .) adhigamabuddhir yadyogināṃ yogābhisamayakāle samādhisukhe (so with Tib. for °mukhe, note in ed., and Suzuki) samāptānām adhigamo bhavati, tasya cādhigamād yogināṃ yogaśabdo nipātyate adhigamaneneti Laṅk 11.17–12.3, *of whose* (viz. Buddha's) *yogins the will to spiritual-realization becomes spiritual-realization when they have attained perfection* (samāpta) *in the bliss of trance at the time of spiritual-realization* (attainment, abhisamaya) *of yoga*; *and thru realization* (attainment) *of him* (tasya = bhagavataḥ) *on the part of* (his) *yogins the word yoga is* (rightly) *applied, by reason of* (this) *realization* (attainment, that comes thru it); yasyāṃ ca rātryāṃ dhigamo, Laṅk 144.10 = 324.5, referring to the night of Buddha's attainment of enlightenment, cf. 142.17; Bbh 81.24; Mvy 134; punar bodhisattvaḥ adhigamajñāne sāradarśī bhavati, na śruta-cintā-dharmārtha-vijñāna-mātrake Bbh 257.16, referring to Mvy 1548 jñāna-pratisaraṇena bhavitavyam, na vijñāna-pratisaraṇena.

adhigamana = °**gama,** *spiritual realization*; so Pali (both forms): ye me bhaṇanti varṇaṃ samādhito ca śīlato ca prajñāto ca adhigamanato ca . . . Mv i.270.4; for Laṅk 12.3 see s.v. **adhigama.**

adhicitta, nt. (Pali id.), *superior mind, intellect*; also adj., and °**cittaṃ,** °**citte,** adv., *relating to intellect*; see s.v. **śikṣā**.

adhitanaya, m., *supreme offspring*: śākyarājādhita-nayaḥ (of Buddha) Mmk 230.1.

adhitapta (error for Skt. abhi°?), *inflamed*: skandhā adhitaptā Mv iii.345.5.

adhitiṣṭhati, also **adhiṣṭhahati,** °**ṣṭhihati** (and noun **adhiṣṭhāna,** q.v.; Pali adhitiṭṭhati, adhiṭṭhāna, in general in same meanings; previous translations of BHS vary widely and are hardly worth systematic quotation; very common is *bless,* which I think should be deleted, see below): (**1**) *masters, controls,* in normal Skt. (BR sthā with adhi 3, 4) and also BHS (exx. La Vallée Poussin, AbhidhK. vii.119 note 2, b); in BHS particularly *takes possession* or *control of,* MSV i.248.20 (sāptāhikaṃ), and ff.; Bhīk 15a.1 (the newly initiated nun says to her instructress) samanvāhara upādhyāyike, aham . . . idaṃ cīvaraṃ saṃghātīm adhitiṣṭhāmi, *I take* (formal) *possession of my nun's garments* (similarly with other implements, below: Ridding p. 124 calls this rite *benediction* of the garments, etc.; but the nun is the only speaker; she would not 'bless' her own belongings!); in BHS (**2**) the power or control is usually *supernatural* or *magical*: adhitiṣṭhantu buddhā bhagavanto idaṃ paṭasūtram Mmk 56.12, *let the Lord Buddhas exercize their supernatural power over* (assume control of) *this thread* (Lalou, Iconographie p 20, *occupent*); in the sequel, favorable sounds show the performer that, adhiṣṭhitaṃ me buddhair . . . tat paṭasūtraṃ (17); he reflects, buddhānāṃ . . . adhiṣṭhā-nam etat (24), *this is the controlling power of the B.*; Laṅk

100.6 ff., Bodhisattvas may be adhiṣṭhānadvayādhiṣṭhitāḥ, *controlled by two supernatural powers* (of Buddhas, cf. 11 buddhādhiṣṭhānādhiṣṭhitāḥ); these are (9) samādhisamāpattyadhiṣṭhāna; *the control that gives attainment of samādhis* (cf. 12 samādhiṃ samāpadyante; to this verb **samāpatti,** q.v., is merely a noun of action; wrongly Suzuki), and sarvakāyamukhapāṇyabhiṣekādhiṣṭhāna, *the control that comes from sprinkling by* (the Buddha's) *hands of the whole body and face* (cf. 101.10–11); persons are said to be adhiṣṭhita, *supernaturally controlled* by Buddhas (may often be rendered *inspired*) SP 231.1; 238.2; 420.4; LV 275.2; Laṅk 4.13; cf. **adhiṣṭhāna**; this *control* often involves (**3**) *magic transformation*, and even the *creation of magic appearances*; not easily separated from the preceding; transitional is sarvabuddhādhiṣṭhito 'yaṃ . . . dharmaparyāyaḥ SP 288.13, *it is under the supernatural control of all the Buddhas* (hence marvelous effects for one who preaches it, as related above), with this cf. tasmāt tarhi . . . adhitiṣṭhāmīmaṃ dharmaparyāyaṃ asmiñ jambudvīpe SP 421.2, *therefore I* (lit. *exercize supernatural power over this Dh.*, which however here seems to mean) *make this Dh. appear in this J.* (with magical effects, some mentioned above, some in the next sentence); from such passages as this and SP 384.3, below, La Vallée Poussin, AbhidhK., Index, and esp. vii.119, note 2, derives the supposed meaning *faire durer*, but in iii.31, note 2, quoting the vyākhyā, he translates adhitiṣṭhati *bénit*, whereas it means *takes under control, assumes control of*; the meaning *bless*, assumed by Burnouf and many others, rests on Tib. byin kyi rlabs, which to be sure often means *bless*, but acc. to Jäschke also *create, change into*; this kind of change by magical mastery or control need not be a *blessing*, cf. (tā jarājarjarā) adhyatiṣṭhat LV 378.17, *he changed them* (the daughters of Māra, by magic control) *so as to be decrepit with age*, and later, buddhasya yo hy adhiṣṭhānaṃ śaknuyāt kartum anyathā 379.3, (I see no one) *who could alter a magic transformation of the Buddha*; mahābrahmā imaṃ . . . lokadhātuṃ tat kṣaṇaṃ samam adhyatiṣṭhat, pāṇitalajātam . . . tṛṇair imaṃ . . . lokadhātuṃ saṃchāditam adhyatiṣṭhat LV 276.19 ff., *the Great Brahmā magically mastered* (and thereby changed) *this entire world* (so as to be) *even*, etc., . . . *covered with grass*; in SP 384.3 (as he was about to die, Sadāparibhūta heard this sūtra; then, not dying after all,) adhiṣṭhihitvā ca sudīrgham āyuḥ, *and having mastered, acquired, assumed by magic, very long life* (he proceeded to proclaim this sūtra; similar passages are taken by La Vallée Poussin l.c. to mean *faire durer*); (Bhagavān . . .) jīvitasaṃskārān adhiṣṭhāya āyuḥsaṃskārān utsraṣṭum ārabdhaḥ. samanantarādhiṣṭhiteṣu jīvitasaṃskāreṣu (omens occurred) Divy 203.7–8 (in this phrase LaV-P, AbhidhK. ii.122, renders *stabilisé*; note the term vaśitva in the comm., l.c. 124 line 1; render *controlling*), see **saṃskāra** 2; buddhā bhagavantaḥ taṃ pṛthivipradeśaṃ vajramayam adhitiṣṭhanti sma LV 86.16–17, . . . *magically made this spot of ground* (where the young Bodhisattva took seven steps) *hard as a diamond*, so that it did not sink under his feet (N.B. they did not literally *stand upon* it; they were located, sthitāḥ line 16, in the ten quarters); tatrāpi cātmānam adhiṣṭhahāmi, sarvāṃś ca sattvān ah[am] adhiṣṭhihāmi (so read, § 8.99) SP 323.13, *there* (having made it appear that I entered nirvāṇa, tho I did not) *I make myself appear* (create myself magically, cf. 316.1, s.v. adhiṣṭhāna 3), *and I control all creatures* (in next line, *men of perverted minds were deluded and did not see me, tho I was standing right there*); with SP 384.3 cf. Dbh 91.28 sarvasattvāṃś ca ākāṅkṣan yathābhiprāyaṃ rūpāśrayālaṃkṛtān adhitiṣṭhati; in this section adhitiṣṭhati occurs many times, beginning with 90.21–22 saṃkṣiptāyā lokadhātor vistīrṇatām adhitiṣṭhati, and means always (a Bodhisattva in the tenth stage) *makes appear magically*, either by transformation or creation; cf. in Pali Therag. 1131 satthā ca me lokam imaṃ adhiṭṭhahi (aor.) aniccato... *the Teacher made this world appear to me as impermanent* (by his supernatural power, but this time without the usual connotation of magic or illusion); catvāri pātrāṇi pratigṛhyaikaṃ pātram adhitiṣṭheyam LV 384.4–5, *accepting the four bowls I will change them magically into a single bowl*, which he does; pratigṛhya caikaṃ pātram adhitiṣṭhati sma, adhimuktibalena 385.4 (see **adhimukti** 2 which in such passages = adhiṣṭhāna).

[**adhināmayati,** prob. error for **ati-** or **abhi-nām°**, qq.v., *spends* (time): saptāham °yāmi MSV i.134.15 = Divy 443.6 ati-nām°, in same story.]

adhipati (as in Pali) used in figurative sense, *controller, dominant influence* or *factor*: **adhipati-pratyaya,** *relation of dominance* (CPD), Mvy 2270, fourth of 4 kinds of **pratyaya** (1), q.v.; adhipatinā (sc. pratyayena) Śikṣ 253.2; Bbh 14.4, 10 etc.; 80.22; defined as upāya-hetu, 99.2–3; etc. (common in Bbh); the four pratyaya listed also ŚsP 80.4, but there seems to be a corruption in place of adhipati: ālambanāmateya-samanantara-hetu-pratyayatām (text °tā; amateya or ām° instead of adhipati!); the other three are as in Mvy; **°ti-phalam,** *dominant fruition*, one of the 5 **phala** (acc. to Sūtrāl. of karuṇā), Mvy 2273, 'because it is the seed of supreme enlightenment', Sūtrāl xvii.31, comm.; but in more general sense Bbh 102.18, expl. 103.5 ff., cakṣurvijñānaṃ cakṣurindriyasyādhipatiphalam, . . . (etc. with all senses,) svena-svenādhipatyena yat phalaṃ nirvartate, tad adhipatiphalaṃ.

adhipatya (nt., = Pali adhipacca, adhipatiya, cf. Skt. ādhipatya), *overlordship*: °tyena Sukh 42.15 (prose).

adhipālayati, *protects*: °lentu LV 388.7 (vs), repeated 11, 14, etc.

adhiprajñā (Pali adhipaññā), *superior wisdom*; adv. **adhiprajñaṃ,** and stem in comp. adhiprajña, *relating to wisdom*, see s.v. **śikṣā.**

adhibhāṣati, °te (cf. **sam-adhi°**), recorded only in augmented forms, both presents (as adhyabhāṣati, § 32.8) and preterites; so also in Pali ajjhabhāsi etc.; *addressed, spoke to* (always with acc. of person; pw 4.263 also *aussprechen, hersagen*, citing LV (Calc.) 111.2, but for this Lefm. 97.4 reads abhyabhāṣatām): adhyabhāṣat LV 130.1; 302.20; °ṣata LV 132.6; Mv i.101.5; RP 42.10; 46.2, 6, 12; °ṣanta LV 56.4; 205.19; 378.5; aor., °bhāṣi Mv i.35.13; °bhāṣasi Mv i.55.6; °bhāṣe Mv i.108.6, etc.

adhimanyati, °te (not in Pali; cf. **adhimāna**), *despises, shows haughtiness*: °yanti KP 18.9 (in corresponding prose 18.3 an-atimanyanā, noun); kutaḥ punar adhikaṃ yenādhimanyeta evam adhimānaḥ parivarjayitavyaḥ ŚsP 1465.1–2.

Adhimātrakāruṇika, n. of a Mahābrahmā: SP 167.15–16.

adhimāna, m. (= Pali id.; Skt. abhimāna; cf. **adhimānika, °nin, ādhimānika**), *pride, arrogance, haughtiness, overbearing behavior*: SP 13.5; 57.8; 481.5; Mvy 1947; ŚsP 1465.2 (see **adhimanyati**); Karmav 47.5 (follows māna and abhimāna); **niradhimāna-tā** (see this). Also occurs as v.l. for text abhimāna, e.g. SP 37.1, 5; 38.14; 44.7.

adhimānika, adj. (Pali id.; to prec. plus -ika, or next plus -ka), *haughty, arrogant, conceited*: SP 234.1; 267.5; 377.10.

adhimānin = prec.: SP 272.1; 279.3.

adhimukta (Pali adhimutta), ppp. of **adhimucyate,** (**1**) *zealous about, actively interested in or devoted to* (a) non-religious objects (loc., or in cpds.): yathādhimuktavāṇijāṃ Mv iii.289.12, referring to 15 ff. tatra ye rūpādhimuktā vāṇijā (*the merchants whose interests were centered in forms*, i. e. the objects of sight) te rūpehi lobhitā, ye śabdādhimuktā vāṇijā te manojñagītavāditaśabdehi lobhitā (etc., with other objects of sense); kimadhimuktā jaṭilā? jaṭilā khalu jaṭilādhimuktā Mv iii.424.4, *what do jaṭila-ascetics* *like? They like jaṭila-ascetics, of course* (with this thought Buddha surrounds himself with 1000 magically created jaṭila-ascetics and visits the jaṭila Uruvilvā-Kāśyapa); the family into which a Bodhisattva must be born in his last existence must be kriyādhimuktaṃ . . . tyāgādhimuktaṃ *fond of activity, of liberality* LV 24.5–6; Mv i.198.3; ii.1.13 (LV adds dānādhimuktaṃ; Mv i.198.3 adds vratādhimuktaṃ); (b) religious objects (with loc., or perh. acc.): devā ca namasyanti yo yādṛśam asmiṃ adhimukto Mv iii.77.19 (read with ms. B), *and they worship the gods, whosoever which* (god), *being devoted to him*; śūnyatam adhimukta-m (corr. adhimukta, prob. so read, or take m as hiatus-bridger) ānimittaṃ (corr. °ttāṃ) vicarati RP 16.13 (vs), *he lives with his mind centered on emptiness, causelessness*; usually in cpds., -dharmādhimukta *zealously devoted to dharma* Mvy 854; śraddhādhi° Divy 49.18 (= Pali saddhādhimutta, both of Vakkali); pravrajyādhi° Divy 302.23 ff.; pradānādhi° Jm 23.6; -buddhadharmādhi° Samādh 19.3; often modifying sattva, *creatures*, yathādhimukta-sattva-, *creatures according to their inclinations*, LV 35.8; creatures are often described as nānādhimukta, *having inclinations towards various objects*, SP 71.8; 318.1; the Bodhisattva is śubhādhimukta, *inclining towards excellent things*, LV 141.8; common folk are hīnādhimukta SP 113.9; 114.4; or lūhādhimukta LV 264.4 (of certain gods; misrendered by Foucaux *devoted to* (the Bodhisattva) *in wretched condition*, but it means *having inclinations to petty things*; these gods tried to persuade the Bodhisattva to let them restore his strength magically); Av i.285.5 (of evil monks); (**2**) ppp. periphrastic, (was) *changed magically*, Divy 393.18, see under **adhimucyate** (2).

[**-adhimuktaka,** see **°tika.**]

adhimukti, f. (= Pali adhimutti; to **adhimucyate**), (**1**) *strong inclination, attachment; earnest, zealous application*; Tib. mos pa (Jäschke, *to be pleased*, la *with*; *to wish, to have a mind; to take pleasure in, to rejoice at*; as substantive *pleasure, satisfaction, esteem*; also *to respect, to esteem, to respect with devotion, to revere, to adore*); La V-P. AbhidhK. Index = ruci; cf. Bbh 95.12–13 kathaṃ ca bodhisattvo 'dhimuktibahulo bhavati? iha bodhisattvo 'ṣṭavidhe 'dhimuktyadhiṣṭhāne śraddhāprasādapūrvakeṇa niścayena *rucyā* samanvāgato bhavati. (Other alleged meanings, as *croyance* Lévi Sūtrāl. i.13 note 1; *confiance*, Burnouf; *good will*, Kern, in translation of SP; etc., are not supported by BHS usage, except as under 2, below.) It may be (but rarely is) applied to (a) non-religious objects: sa ca puruṣas (the father) teṣāṃ kumārakāṇām (his ignorant sons) āśayajño bhaved, adhimuktiṃ ca vijānīyāt, SP 73.14–15, . . . *and he understands their inclinations, what they are interested in.* But usually the object is related to (b) a religious aim. It may be specified, syntactically (in the loc.), as in yaṃ . . . sugataḥ prabhāṣate, adhimuktisaṃpanna bhavāhi tatra SP 32.15, *what the Buddha says, be perfect in zealous application to that.* Usually it is not so specifically stated, tho the context is apt to suggest that it is *zealous cultivation* (study or propagation) of sacred texts or religious instruction that is meant (note that the object of the verb **adhimucyate** is commonly something of this sort); cf. e. g. -lokaṃ yathādhimuktyā (*according to their* [varying types or degrees of] *zeal or application*) subhāṣitena saṃtoṣayantam LV 160.17; adhimuktisāro yo syād . . . saḥ, puṇyaṃ labheta yo etaṃ (most mss.) sūtraṃ vācel likheta vā SP 342.3–4. And this is probably meant as a rule when the context gives no special clue, as in many of the following: SP 6.13; 31.6; 93.9; 125.8; 235.10; 274.10; LV 10.11; 182.20; 432.8; Mvy 856; Samādh 22.43; RP 20.5; Bhad 7, 48; Bbh 195.12; anadhimukti, *lack of* (religious) *zeal* RP 19.18; 35.4; various gods in Mv ii.309.14 ff. see the bodhi-tree svakāye adhmuktiye, *according to their tastes, inclinations, interests* (Senart *suivant l'inclination de chacun*) as made of various precious materials; one of the ten bala of a tathāgata is nānādhimuktijñānabala Mvy 122 (and cf. Mv i.159.15 adhimuktinānātvaṃ vetti, as one of the ten bala); adhimuktivaśitā Mvy 776, one of the 10 vaśitā of a Bodhisattva; yathādhimuktyā, adv., LV 160.17 (above) and 179.17; hīnādhimukti, *attachment to low ends*, SP 115.12 (cf. hīnādhimukta, °tika, s.vv. **adhimukta, °tika**); (in LV 294.4 for vidyādhimuktiprabhaḥ read probably vidyāvimukti°, *having the splendor of* (true) *knowledge and emancipation*, so Tib., rnam par grol ba = vimukti); (**2**) *magic transformation*, in adhimukti-balena LV 385.5, see s.v. **adhimucyate** (2), and **adhitiṣṭhati,** end.

-adhimuktika (once °taka, probably by error; to prec. plus -ka; = Pali -adhimuttika; in both Pali and BHS used only ifc. Bhvr.), *having a zealous interest* (adhimukti) *in* . . .: hīnādhi° (generally with sattvāḥ) Mvy 2448; SP 109.2; 110.7; LV 248.14; 289.10; Sukh 71.14; lūkhādhi° (= hīnādhi°) Mv ii.313.9; adharmādhi° LV 257.21; nānādhi° Mv iii.321.1; anekādhi° 2; udārādhi° LV 439.3; Gv 94.17 (text °muktak°, corr. 2d ed.); Sukh 7.5; audārādhi° Gv 534.20 (see **audāra**); -buddhadharmādhi° Samādh 19.2 (°muktikena, v.l. °muktena).

-adhimuktika-tā (= Pali °muttikatā), abstr. from preceding, *state of having zealous interest*: hīnādhi° SP 105.1; 109.6.

adhimukticaryā, *course of conduct determined by* (religious) *zeal*, Sūtrāl. i.13 (Lévi note 1, *conduite par croyance*, see s.v. **adhimukti**): °bhūmi, *stage of zealous conduct*, Mvy 896–901 (five such listed); the first of a list of six bodhisattva-bhūmis Bbh 84.23, or the second of seven, 367.4 (see s.v. **bhūmi** 4, end).

Adhimuktitejas, form used in verse of the n. of a Buddha = **Vipuladharmādhimuktisaṃbhavateja(s), Vipulādhimukti°**: Gv 428.10 (vs).

adhimucyate, °ti (= Pali adhimuccati; cf. prec. and foll. items), (**1**) *is actively interested in, zealous for, earnestly devoted to, intent upon* (with acc.); see under **adhimukti** for Tib. rendering, and discussion of meanings, which on the whole parallel those of the verb; see also **adhimukta, adhimokṣa,** and other derivatives. The object is generally religious, and most commonly religious knowledge or sacred texts (see especially **adhimukta** for non-religious applications): eṣāṃ . . . nirvāṇaṃ bhāṣate yad adhimucyante, SP 187.2–3, *preaches to them nirvāṇa* (the Hīnayāna goal), *to which they zealously apply themselves*; adhimucyante SP 288.3 (upāyakauśalyaṃ saṃdhābhāṣitaṃ); (jñāna[m]) 302.7; KP 140.9; °yanti SP 232.9 (dharmaparyāyaṃ); KP 139.6; adhimucyami Bhad 3, 7 (pūja sarvajinānāṃ); adhimucye (1 sg.) Bhad 6[3]; adhimucyed (opt.) SP 255.2 (idaṃ sūtraṃ); 336.4; adhimokṣyate (fut.) SP 260.8 (saddharmapuṇḍarīkaṃ); °kṣyanti LV 89.8 (sūtrāntān); adhimucyamāna (pres. pple.) RP 4.15; an-adhimucyamāna (preceded by hiatus-bridging m-) KP 139.3, 5, *not showing inclination towards* (instruction); sa maitrīsahagatena cittena . . . ekāṃ diśam adhimucya (Tib. mos te; *zealously concentrating on one direction*) sphāritvopasaṃpadya viharati Mvy 1508 (and so on, until finally he does the same with sarvāvantam imaṃ lokam, 1509); adhimoktum (inf.) Gv 5.10 (tathāgatajñānaṃ); adhimucyitum KP 39.9; (**2**) rarely, used in the sense defined by CPD under adhimuccati (d) as *to make a* (*magical*) *act of volition*; but a better definition would be *changes* (something, acc.) *by magic into* (something else, acc.), as in Vin. iii.250.25–26 pāsādaṃ suvaṇṇaṃ ti adhimucci, so ahosi sabbasovaṇṇamayo (comm. sovaṇṇamayo hotū ti adhiṭṭhāsi). Doubtless the original or literal meaning was, *he concentrated his interest on the palace, with the thought* — (it is to be) *gold!* — *and it became entirely made of gold.* In BHS the word (i)ti is omitted: Bbh 60.5 pṛthivīm apo 'dhimucyate, *changes* (magically) *earth into water*, and a series of like clauses in the sequel. So in the miracle of turning four bowls into one: catvāri śailamayāni pātrāṇi grahāyaikaṃ pātram adhimuktam Divy 393.17–18, (by the Buddha) *taking the four stone bowls, a single bowl was made by magic*; cf. pratigṛhya caikaṃ pātram adhitiṣṭhati sma, adhimuktibalena LV 385.4–5, *and having accepted* (the four bowls) *he changed* (them) *magically* (see s.v. **adhitiṣṭhati**) *into a single bowl, by his power of magic transformation.*

adhimucyana-tā (= Pali adhimuccana, nt.) = **adhimukti,** *zealous application, interest,* with gen., ŚsP 615.11 (prajñāpāramitāyāḥ, but with an intervening parallel noun; perhaps rather loc. understood). Cf. next.

adhimucyanā = prec., q.v.: Sūtrāl. xi.61.

[**adhimuṣyanti,** SP 351.6, for which WT read adhiśuṣyanti with their ms. K′; both are wrong. See **dhi** = dhik.]

adhimūrchita (= Pali °mucchita), *clinging* (to); also **-tva,** *state of* ...: an-adhimūrchito Mv ii.139.11 ff.; iii.201.5; an-adhimūrchitatvāt Jm 35.4, *because he was unattached, had no clinging* (Speyer fails to observe special Buddhist sense).

adhimokṣa (= Pali °mokkha), = **adhimukti,** *zealous application*: Mvy 1929; Dharmas 30; śūnyatādhi° Bbh 40.5, *zealous adherence to* (the theory of) *nullity*; with loc. Bbh 282.7 (arthe); neg. an-adhi° *lack of interest* Bbh 174.12 (in profound and difficult text-passages); (buddhadharmeṣu) yo 'dhimoksah Bbh 313.5, part of definition of **adhyāśaya,** q.v.

adhimokṣati, or °**kṣayati,** denom. from **adhimokṣa,** = **adhimucyate,** *applies oneself zealously to,* with acc.; adhimokṣanti Laṅk 193.12 (-pāṭham); adhimuktā adhimokṣayiṣyanti adhimokṣayanti ca AsP 148.5 (dharmam, understood from preceding dharme śikṣitāḥ etc.).

-adhimoca, °**cya,** only in **dur-adhi°,** q.v.

adhirūḍhaka, adj. (= Skt. °ḍha), *mounted*: Divy 565.5 (vs, may be m.c.).

adhiropayati, *attributes, imputes* (to, loc.): nārhasi mayy adhiropayituṃ ... kapirājavadham Jm 150.20.

adhilaya, *objection, refutation, opposition in argument*: MadhK 159.15; 499.4, 10; in 10 comm., glossed adhikṣepa, nirākaraṇa, pratikṣepa; Tib. smod pa (so ed. on 159.15; on 499.10 printed erroneously smoṅ pa). On 159.15 vv.ll. adhiraya, adhirepa.

adhivacana, nt. (= Pali id.), *designation, appellation, name, term* (of, for, gen.): Mvy 6333; Mv i.161.2; tathatā tathateti ... śūnyatāyā etad adhivacanam Śikṣ 263.1, *tathatā is a name for nullity*; KP 71.9, 10; bhūtatathatāyā etad adhivacanam Vaj 37.3; AsP 342.1; kasyaitad adhivacanaṃ yad uta nirvāṇam iti Laṅk 182.9, *of what is this a designation, viz. the word nirvāṇa*?; anāyavyaya ity anutpādasyaitad adhivacanam Laṅk 175.18; katamasyaitad dharmasyādhivacanaṃ samādhir iti Samādh p. 13 lines 19–20, *of what matter is this a designation, the word samādhi*?

Adhivacanapraveśa, m., n. of a samādhi: Mvy 523 = **Adhivacanasaṃpraveśa** ŚsP 1416.17; in 1416.16 (by error) Vacanasaṃpraveśa.

adhivartati (= Pali °vattati), *comes to, falls to the lot of,* with acc. of person: dāyakam adhivartati Mv i.269.15 (one ms. **adhivattati,** the Pali form, probably to be adopted in text).

adhivāsa?: Mv i.253.4, 5, and 6 (prose): app. adj. with rogajāta, defined as *a kind of disease which carries off a region or country* (pradeśaṃ harati). Opp. **maṇḍalaka,** q.v. Perhaps *enduring*? See s.v. **ārddha.**

adhivāsana, nt., also °**natā** or °**nā,** f. (to next; = Pali °na, °nā; the nt. very rare in Pali), (**1**) (a) *endurance* (of suffering): °na, duḥkhādhiv° Bbh 250.25; °na-jātīya, *characterized by patience,* Sukh 25.15; sthāvarādhivāsanajātya, Śikṣ 23.9; -duścintitādhiv°, -pīḍādhiv° Gv 248.2, 3; °nā, duḥkhādhiv° Bbh 189.10; 192.10 (here v.l. °na); (b), *toleration* (of an evil or sin, wrongfully), see s.v. **adhivāsayati** 1, b: kleśādhivāsanatā KP 114.1; kleśāsevādhivāsanatā Bbh 288.26; (**2**) *consent*: °na, LV 7.13; Mv i.116.3; Mvy 9381; °nā (the common form) LV 6.3; 395.13; 400. 20; Mv i.114.2; 230.20; 263.4; 285.4; 324.2; ii.258.1; iii.93.1; 255.5; Divy 66.1 (here text em. °naṃ); 306.20; Av i.42.5.

adhivāsayati, °**seti** (= Pali °seti, both mgs.), (**1**) (a) *endures, puts up with*: °sayati Mvy 7041, Tib. daṅ du len (pa); Bbh 192.22 (duḥkham); duḥkham adhivāsya Bbh 132.5; adhivāsitā duḥkhānī LV 354.4 (vs); misc. forms SP 271.10 (fut. °vāsiṣyāma); Mv i.285.2; Av ii.199.8; Śikṣ 177.6; Gv 244.1; (b) *tolerates* (an evil or sin, wrongfully, instead of fighting it), Bbh 161.6; 168.23 (here keep adhivāsayati of mss., despite Corrig. p. 5; with Tib. as cited there cf. Mvy 7041, above); (**2**) *consents,* especially *agrees to, accepts* (an invitation), with gen. of person: sacāsya (= sace[t] asya) ... adhivāsayati Mv i.323.21, *if ... consents to him* (Senart's note wrong); teṣāṃ pi nādhivāseti Mv iii.103.4, *did not consent to them, either*; in acceptance of an invitation, regularly with tūṣṇībhāvena or tūṣṇīṃ, which may precede the verb (so Mvy 6451; SP 39.2; 167.9; 171.3; Mv i.263.4; LV 416.13), or the sentence may begin adhivāsayati, then subject nom., then gen. of person, then tūṣṇībhāvena (so LV 6.1, 19; 395.11; Mv i.230.19; ii.257.17; iii.92.18; Divy 19.27; 151.10; Av i.42.4); if object of invitation is expressed it is regularly acc. as in Pali (adhivāsayatu ... bhojanavidhānam Mv i.116.2), or nom. in passive expressions (kasya bhagavatā śuve āgāram adhivāsitam Mv i.271.11, *whose house has been accepted by the Bh. for tomorrow* [to visit]?); but once instr., adhivāsayatu bhagavān asmākaṃ nagare śvo bhaktena (then the usual adhivāsayati plus nom. plus gen. plus tūṣṇībhāvena) RP 56.6; misc. passages LV 408.5; 412.8; Laṅk 6.15; Mv i.113.5; 189.12; iii.255.4 (°vāsaye, aor.).

adhivāsitatā (from °vāsita, ppp. of **adhivāsayati,** q.v.), *state of having been endured:* Dbh 75.24.

[**adhiviśuddha,** Gv 231.9, read ati°, *very pure,* with 2d ed.]

adhiśīla, nt. (Pali adhisīla), *superior morality*; adj., and °laṃ adv., *relating to morality*: see s.v. **śikṣā.**

adhiṣṭa, see **adhīṣṭa.**

adhiṣṭha, f. °**ṣṭhā,** *resident, permanently abiding*: devate adhiṣṭhā bhava, ihaiva tiṣṭheti Divy 578.8. [In LV 442.21 (prose) Lefm. adhiṣṭhamāno, which is impossible; v.l. atiṣṭhamāno, *not stopping,* which is certainly right.]

adhiṣṭhahati = **adhitiṣṭhati,** q.v.

adhiṣṭhāna, (regularly) nt. (= Pali adhiṭṭhāna; see 6 below for forms of other genders; from **adhitiṣṭhati,** q.v.), (**1**) *basis,* as in Skt. (BR s.v.1); special usage, SP 405.8–9 (a Buddha of old preached the SP at length) Sarvasattvapriyadarśanaṃ bodhisattvaṃ ... adhiṣṭhānaṃ kṛtvā, *making* (his disciple) *the Bodhisattva S. the basis,* i. e. with special regard to him, or for his special benefit; (**2**) (mental) *firm basis* = *determination, resolve, resolution, vow,* = Pali (cetaso) adhiṭṭhāna (see CPD); rare in BHS: (a Bodhisattva is about to burn his body to honor the SP and the Buddha who revealed it to him; having purified, adorned, and scented his body) svakam adhiṣṭhānam akarot SP 407.6, *he made his resolution, firm mental determination*; followed by svakam adhiṣṭhānaṃ kṛtvā svaṃ kāyaṃ prajvālayām āsa; buddhān bhagavataḥ sākṣiṇaḥ kṛtvā teṣāṃ purataḥ satyādhiṣṭhānaṃ (q.v.) karomi: yena satyena etc., SP 413.7–8, ... *I make a truthful resolve* ... and he proceeds with an 'act of truth', see **satyavacana**; (?) LV 423.5–6 akṣaṇasattvavinayādhiṣṭhānāpratyudāvartyacakraṃ (said of the dharmacakra; text °dhiṣṭhānapraty°, but see s.v. **apratyudāvartya**), *wheel that cannot be turned back because of* (the Buddha's) *fixed determination to discipline creatures that are subject to bad births* (? or possibly *because of the Buddha's supernatural power to discipline* etc.; otherwise, implausibly, Foucaux); here perhaps also the 'four adhiṣṭhāna' (*firm resolves*?) of Mvy 1580–84 (satya-, tyāga-, upaśama-, prajñā-) = Pali four adhiṭṭhāna, DN iii.229.18 (paññā-,sacca-, cāga-,upasama-); (**3**) in Skt. (BR s.v. 2) *mastery, power*; in BHS *control*, e. g. of a monk's own robes (cf. **adhitiṣṭhati** 1), MSV ii.91.12 tricīvarādhiṣṭhānena; oftener *supernatural, magic power*: puṇyavipākādhiṣṭhānādhiṣṭhitās LV 48.21 (Apsarases) *empowered* (controlled) *by the power of the ripening of merit* (which enables them to disappear from their heavenly home and appear in Kapilavastu); -devatādhiṣṭhānāt LV 381.12, *by the magic power of the ... deity* (the merchants' wagons were stopped and could not be moved); usually a Buddha's or Bodhisattva's; it may be his *supernatural control* over his own destiny, SP 64.13, where bodhisattvādhiṣṭhānena goes closely with tat paurvakaṃ caryāpraṇidhānam, see s.v. **saṃmantrita**; but it is usually *control* over another person, a Bodhisattva or disciple: Maitreyasya bodhisattvasyādhiṣṭhānabalena sarveṣu teṣu kūṭāgāreṣv abhyantarapraviṣṭam ātmānaṃ saṃjānīte sma, Gv 512.13–14, *by the force of the supernatural power of Maitreya* (Sudhana) *fancied that he had entered into each one of those palaces*; buddhānāṃ ... adhiṣṭhānena LV 163.9–10 (text adhisthān°; when the women were making music for the Bodhisattva) *by the supernatural power of the Buddhas* verses of exhortation to him came forth (in 163.14 **āveśa**, q.v., or v.l. ādeśa, replaces adhi°); similarly 182.3; adhiṣṭhānena buddhānām anubhāvād (another near-synonym) vikurvitaiḥ Samādh 22.19 (the body of the Buddha can be seen); other like cases Laṅk 2.10; LV 31.3, 6; 237.18; 368.12; in 415.16, the dharmacakra is sarvabuddhādhiṣṭhānāvilopitam, *unbroken thru the supernatural power* (influence) *of all the Buddhas*; for Laṅk 100.6 and Mmk 56.24 see s.v. **adhitiṣṭhati** (2); etaṃ ... samādhiṃ samāpannasyādhiṣṭhānam: lokadhātuvijñaptiṣu adhiṣṭhānam, etc., long series of locs. each with adhi° repeated, stating the spheres of the *mastery* obtained, Gv 98.15 ff.; mamādhiṣṭhānabalādhānam SP 316.1, *my assumption of the force of supernatural* (magic) *power* (here causes people to believe that the earthly life of Śākyamuni, which was unreal, is real); but the corresponding verse, 323.13, has adhiṣṭhahāmi in the sense of *I make appear by magic* (see **adhitiṣṭhati** 3), and possibly adhiṣṭhāna may be concrete here (and in sadādhiṣṭhānaṃ mama etad īdṛśaṃ SP 324.11, resuming the same subject), *exhibition of supernatural* (magic) *power* = *magical appearance* or *transformation*; this latter is certainly the meaning in LV 379.3, see **adhitiṣṭhati** (3), and perhaps in Prabhūtaratnasya tathāgatasya ... etad adhiṣṭhānam abhūt SP 241.8, *this was the adhiṣṭhāna of the Tathāgata P.* (there follows a quotation of his words: *Let this stūpa of my remains appear whenever the SP is preached*). Does *this adhiṣṭhāna* mean *this exhibition of supernatural power*, viz, the making of the stūpa to appear? Or is it *this fixed determination, resolution* (2, above)? Near synonyms are **āveśa**, (Skt.) anubhāva, **adhimukti**; cf. also Laṅk 292.13 and 15, where one of the sources of abhijñā is 'from adhiṣṭhāna' (adhiṣṭhānān, so read in 13 for text °nāṃ, abl., before n-), which means *from the controlling power of the Buddhas* and is paraphrased in 15 by buddhaprasādataḥ, *from the grace of the Buddhas*. Suzuki, Transl. of Laṅk passim, renders *sustaining power*; I think rather *controlling power*. Even Bodhisattvas are at times dependent on Buddhas and need their control; (**4**) in architecture, Skt. (see Acharya, Dict. Hindu Arch. s.v.), *basement, foundation* of building or *base* of a pillar. Here in Mvy 5591 = Tib. lan kan gyi rten ma, *prop* (i. e. base) *of a railing*; so Chin. Whatever it means here is certainly meant also in Divy 221.9, 10 adhiṣṭhānaṃ, and Mv i.195.1 ff.; iii.227.8 ff., adhiṣṭhānakam, where the context is the same as in Mvy 5591; see **sūcī, sūcikā**; (**5**) see **pādādhiṣṭhāna**; (**6**) m., n. of a (mythical) samādhi: Gv 451.26. In this curious passage, 451.25–452.6, the word adhiṣṭhāna is further used predicatively in a series of equational sentences, varying in gender like an adjective with different subjects. Bhadrottamā says to Sudhana: ahaṃ kulaputrā 'nālayamaṇḍalaṃ nāma dharmaparyāyaṃ jānāmi deśayāmy, adhiṣṭhānaś ca me samādhiḥ pratilabdho; na tatra samādhau kasyacid dharmasyā 'dhiṣṭhānam; adhiṣṭhānaṃ tatra sarvajñatācakṣuḥ pravartate, 'dhiṣṭhānaṃ sarvajñatāśrotram, adhiṣṭhānaṃ sarvajñatāghrāṇam, adhiṣṭhānā sarvajñatājihvā, 'dhiṣṭhānaḥ sarvajñatākāyo, 'dhiṣṭhānaṃ tatra sarvajñatāmanaḥ pravartate, 'dhiṣṭhānā sarvajñatormir, adhiṣṭhānā sarvajñatāvidyud, adhiṣṭhānāḥ sarvajñatāvegāḥ pravartante jagadrocanāmaṇḍalāḥ; etam ahaṃ kulaputrā 'nālayamaṇḍalaṃ dharmaparyāyaṃ jānāmi. (Punctuation introduced by me.) There is no further light from the context. I am not sure what meaning the author attributed to the word adhiṣṭhāna: presumably something like either *basis* or *controlling power*.

adhiṣṭhānaka, nt., see **adhiṣṭhāna** (4).

adhiṣṭhāyika, m. (Pali adhiṭṭhāyika, beside °yaka; Skt. °yaka), *supervisor, superintendent*: MSV i.70.15 ff. (in same passage Divy 462.26 ff. always °yaka); prose.

adhiṣṭhita, ppp. of **adhitiṣṭhati**, q.v.

adhiṣṭhihati = **adhitiṣṭhati**, q.v.

adhisevā (no *adhi-sev- recorded), *service, attendance*: kṣāntyādhiseve 'ti ca durbaleṣu KP 20.10 (vs; cf. durbaleṣu sattveṣu kṣāntyā sevanatā 20.3, prose).

[**adhisthāna** is read for **adhiṣṭhāna**, q.v., in LV 163.10 (acc. to Lefm. with all mss.) and 182.3 (here v.l. -ṣṭh-).]

adhīṣṭa (in Skt., e. g. Pāṇ. 5.1.80, but very rare), ppp. of **adhyeṣati**, *requested* (for instruction); cf. Pali ajjhiṭṭha, used with ajjhesita as ppp. to ajjhesati: tena adhīṣṭu (= °ṭo) LV 393.14; yais tathāgato 'dhīṣṭo 'bhūd asya dharmaparyāyasya saṃprakāśanāya 438.15; Mv iii.403.14 (prob. read with mss. adhiṣṭo); yādhīṣṭā bhavati tayāsau bhikṣuṇī praṣṭavyā Bhīk 10a.3; anadhīṣṭa *not requested for instruction*, Divy 329.21 ff.

Adhovāṇa, or (MSV) **Adhunāna**, m., n. of a mountain: Divy 450.11; 455.30; MSV i.144.17 (ms. here Avevāṇa, ed. em.); 152.13.

adhyabhāṣati, see **adhibhāṣati**.

? **-adhyayitā**, in sarvaśāstrādhya°, Mv i.78.16 (prose), without v.l. or note; seems clearly intended for -adhyāyi-tā, from Skt. adhyāyin (Pali -ajjhāyi); *state of being a reader or student*.

Adhyardhaśataka, n. of a sūtra (unidentified): °ke sūtre, Karmav 63.3 (see Lévi's note).

adhyavakirati, adhyok° (= Pali ajjhokirati, in mg. 1), (**1**) *bestrews* (with acc. and instr.): puṣpais taṃ ratnastūpam avakiranty adhyavakiranty abhiprakiranti SP 240.2; okiresi adhyokiresi prakiresi, okiritvā adhyokiritvā abhiprakiritvā ... Mv i.38.9–10; candanacūrṇa-adhyokirṇo Mv ii.309.8, *bestrewn with ...*; adhyokiritvā (mss. adhyā°) Mv i.212.4; (**2**) *introduces* (food, into the pores of the skin), (devatā ...) romakūpavivarehi divyām ojām adhyokiretsuḥ (Senart °ensuḥ; v.l. adhyak°) Mv ii.131.6; in the like phrase above, line 3, the verb was adhyohariṣyāmaḥ; possibly read a form of this verb in line 6?

[***adhyavagacchati**: °gacchan in Lefm. LV 239.5 (prose), pres. pple.; an otherwise unknown form. Required is adhyagaccham, *I studied*; so read; several mss. adhyagacchan, before sākṣād-akārṣam; cf. lines 8–9 below, dharmaḥ sākṣātkṛto 'dhigataḥ.]

adhyavasāna, nt., and once **°sāna-tā** (= Pali ajjhosāna, see **adhyavasyati**), *clinging to, grasping, coveting* (regularly *desires* or *worldly things*, loc. or in comp.), once adhyavasāna-tā, id. (LV 246.13 kāmeṣv adh°natā; below, 246.22, in same formula, °nam); in similar passage kāmādhyavasānā (pl.) Mv ii.121.4; 122.7; kāyādhy° Av ii.191.7; kāyajīvitādhy° Samādh 22.2; adhy° (kāyi, jīviti, locs.) 4, 5, 6 (vss); without dependent noun Mvy 2197–8; Av ii.188.10; 189.4; RP 17.10 (°na-parāḥ); 34.3 (°ne bahulāḥ, of evil monks); Śikṣ 19.18; others Śikṣ 222.6 (vedanādhyavasānaṃ tṛṣṇā, *thirst is clinging to sensa-*

tions; wrongly Bendall and Rouse); Laṅk 251.1 (tṛṣṇādhy°); Bhīk 24a.3 (kāmādhy°); Bbh 222.4; RP 17.5; anadhy°, *not grasping* (Pali anajjhosāna) Bbh 411.18 (svasukhānadhy°); as synonym of rāga MadhK 457.3 (see s.v. **dūṣaṇa**).

adhyavasāya, m. or nt. = °**sāna**, *grasping, clinging, devotion* (to something deprecated; cf. **adhyavasita**): Divy 534.19; adhyavasāye tiṣṭhati, cited from Mādhyamikā-vṛtti in note 4 on Śikṣ 223.8. (On adhyavasāya, ger., see **adhyavasyati**.)

adhyavasita (Pali ajjhosita, in mgs. 1 and 2, and neg. an-ajjh°, cited CPD only in sense 1), ppp. of °**syati**, q.v., (**1**) of things, *grasped, coveted* (in BHS less common than the following): an-adhy° *not coveted* Dbh 13.23; Śikṣ 23.12, 16; (**2**) of persons, *attached* (with loc. or in comp.), *grasping, coveting* (the usual BHS meaning): SP 78.12; LV 207.7 (Lefm. °śita with mss.); Mvy 2196; Divy 534.19; Av i.271.15; 289.11; 296.1; RP 35.6 (kulādhy°); Laṅk 253.15; an-adhy° *not attached, not covetous* Mv ii.139.10; iii.201.5; Samādh 22.1 (kāyajīvite cānadhy°), 3 (kāyajīvitānadhy°); Śikṣ 269.8 (sv-anadhy°); Bbh 274.18 (kāmeṣv anadhy°); Laṅk 250.9; (**3**) *accepted, agreed to* (a proposal, offer): MSV ii.10.5–6.

adhyavasyati (cf. **adhyavasāna**, °**sāya**; Pali *ajjhosati, fut. °sissati etc.; not exactly in this sense in Skt.), *clings to* (something deprecated), *covets*: °syati Śikṣ 223.8; °syaty adhyavasāya (ger.) tiṣṭhati Divy 37.23; ppp. **adhyavasita**, q.v.

adhyākramaṇa, *stepping, marching upon*: mad-°ṇe viśaṅkā niśritya māṃ svasti gatāḥ Jm 180.8.

adhyāgacchati (nowhere recorded in this sense), = **deśayati** (2), *recognizes* (a sin), *confesses*: atyayam atyayato 'dhyāgamad (aor.) Divy 617.25.

[**adhyācara**, °rā: LV 395.9, see **adhyāvara**.]

adhyācaraṇa, *behavior* (but used of *good* behavior, in contrast with **adhyācarati**, °**cāra**, qq.v.): prasādenādhyācaraṇād Bbh 30.11.

adhyācarati (= Pali ajjhāc°), *performs, does*, only in bad sense (as in Pali), *commits* (a sin; so **adhyācāra**; but cf. **adhyācaraṇa**): °caranti (-duścaritam) Bbh 302.7, 8; akuśalaṃ karmādhyācarati Śikṣ 160.7; madyapānaṃ ca nādhyācaranti MSV iii.130.8.

adhyācāra, m. (to prec.; = Pali ajjhācāra, regularly in bad and 'especially in an erotical sense', CPD), *performance, commission* (of evil, sin), (sinful) *behavior* (with gen. of the sin, or in comp.): punar anadhyācārāya Bbh 181.12, *so as not to sin again*; sāvadyasya ca dānādikasya kuśalasyādhyācāraḥ 289.11; āpatty-anadhyācāra- 289.22; anadhyācāre adhyācāravairamaṇyāṃ tīvraś ... yogaḥ karaṇīyaḥ Bhīk 27b.4, *serious discipline in not sinning, ceasing from sin, must be undertaken*; for this, which seems the correct reading, Bhīk 24b.5; 28a.1, 4; 28b.2 (by error?) °anadhyācāravairamaṇyāṃ°; but also in MSV iii.8.10 anadhyācāram ācarate, *engages in sinful behavior*, implies adhyācāra = *good behavior*; Tib. also has a neg., spyad par bya ba ma yin pa spyod pa; but the text is pretty surely wrong, since in 9.10 the opposite is na adhyācāram ācarate, *engages in no sinful behavior*.

[? **adhyāpaṭyati**, Śikṣ 171.16, acc. to note, p. 408, tāṃ ca °paṭyet, *should violate her* (a mother or arhantī). But read adhyāpadyet, cf. next but one. I question such a form from root paṭ. The meaning would be the same and is supported by Tib. de la log par spyad pa.]

adhyāpatti, f. (in Pali only neg. an-ajjhāpatti; see **anadhyāpatti**), *commission* (of a sin, or of an offense against a moral principle, cf. under **adhyāpadyate**): pāpakarmādhyāpatti- Gv 264.19–20; sahādhyāpat(t)yā Bhīk 23b.4; 24a.1, *with the commission* (of an offense against a moral principle).

adhyāpadyate (= Pali ajjhāpajjati), (**1**) *incurs* (guilt), *commits* (a sin, acc.): duścaritam adhyāpadyamānaḥ Bbh 117.21; pārājayikādhyāpannaḥ 159.22; (daśākuśalān [so read for text daśa-kuśalān, which makes nonsense with the following na samudācarati] karmapathān...) nādhyāpadyate AsP 325.9; (**2**) *violates* (a moral principle, acc.): anyatamānyatamaṃ dharmam adhyāpadya Bbh 159.4; (pārājayikasthānīyaṃ dharmam) adhyāpanno bhavati id. 181.1; gurudharmādhyāpannayā (mss. °nāya) Bhīk 5b.4, *by one who has violated an important rule* (so Pali garudhammaṃ with ajjhāpanna, q.v. in CPD); adhyāpadya (ger.) Bhīk 23b.4; 24a.1; adhyāpatsyase, °patsye (fut.) 24b.5, all with (anyatamat) sthānam, *some point* or *item* (of the moral code); (**3**) *violates* (a woman): °dyet, see **adhyāpaṭyati**; [(**4**) in Gv 531.14 adhyāpanna would be used in a good sense, if the text were sound: (sarvabuddhakṣetrāṇi viśudhyanti sma sarvasattva-)-dhātv -anyonya-maitra-hita-citrādhyāpanna-citta-saṃsthānatayā; but read with 2d ed. °citrāvyāpanna°.]

adhyārāma-, *in the park* (stem form representing Pali adverb ajjhārāme, q.v. CPD): -gataṃ (ratnaṃ) Prāt 516.13.

adhyārohati (= Pali ajjhārūhati), *acts in a tyrannical* or *bullying way*: krudhyetādhyārohet Bbh 171.6.

adhyālamba = °**bana**, (mentally) *seizing, grasping*: udārabuddhadharmamativipulādhyālambena Dbh 29.18.

1 **adhyālambate** (cf. Pali ajjholambati), *hangs down upon* (of shadows, at evening; so Tib., grib so cher babs pa): Mvy 6922 (same context in Pali, see **abhipralambate**).

2 **adhyālambati**, °**te** (not in Pali or Pkt.; Skt. ālambati, °te), *grasps, takes hold of*, (**1**) literally and physically: taṃ daridrapuruṣam adhyālambeyuḥ SP 104.3; sumeruṃ yaś ca hastena adhyālambitva ... SP 253.5 (vs); (pāṇinā ... dakṣiṇahasteṣv, em.) adhyālambya SP 484.4, and similarly 8; adhyālambamānāḥ (sc. utensils for worship) LV 77.2; (phalakam ...) adhyālambante AsP 286.11; (tam ... pārśvābhyāṃ) svadhyālambitam (so with v.l. for text svā°) adhyālambya suparigṛhītaṃ parigṛhya 291.6; (**2**) metaphorically, *grasps* = *reaches, attains*: -jñānabhūmir adhyālambitā (so read, text °batā) Gv 18.18; (bodhisattvacaryā ...) katham adhyālambitavyā Gv 59.19.

adhyālambana (n. act. to prec.), (act of) *grasping*, in metaphoric use, *acquiring* (cf. prec., 2; this noun has not been recorded in the literal and physical sense, possibly by oversight): Mvy 6991; -kuśalamūlādhyālambana-tvād LV 429.14–15; buddhadharmādhyālambana- Gv 72.9; tathāgatasukhādhyālambanaiḥ Gv 321.26; buddhadharmādhyālambanāya Dbh 3.18; -praṇidhānādhyālambanena Dbh 57.29.

adhyālambanatā = °**bana**, q.v.: buddhajñānādhyālambanatā Mvy 186; daśatathāgatabalādhyālambanatayā Śikṣ 123.1; -praṇidhānādhyālambanatāyai Gv 279.21.

adhyāvara, m. (= Pali ajjhāvara), *associate, attendant, member of retinue*: adhyāvarā (acc. pl.; so all mss., Lefm. em. °carā) kṛtvana sarvadevān LV 395.9 (vs), *having made all gods my associates*. CPD and PTSD suggest emending the Pali form, also, to ajjhācara. But the two forms confirm each other and must surely be kept, whatever the etymology of this rare and obscure word may be.

adhyāvāsa-gata, adj., *in the dwelling*: Prāt 517.1 (cf. **adhyārāma**, and Pali ajjhāvasathe, adv.).

adhyāviśati, *attacks, strikes down*: MSV iv.120.12, 18; 121.9; Tib. ḥbab par byed, *make fall*.

[**adhyāśana**, (probably error) for Skt. adhyāsana: samādhibhāvanādhyāśanatayā Gv 494.8–9, *because it is the basis for realization* (bringing into being) *of samādhi*(s).]

adhyāśaya, m. (= Pali ajjhāsaya), (**1**) commonly *mental disposition*; (strong) *purpose, intent, determination* (esp. religious); clearly understood as a more intensive near-synonym of **āśaya**, which is used often in substantially the same sense in BHS as already in Skt. (so far as I can see there is no difference between Skt. and BHS āśaya except for the adverbial uses of forms of the latter, q.v.): adhyāśayaḥ Mvy 7116 = Tib. lhag paḥi bsam pa, *superior* (adhi) *thought, will, inclination* or the like (āśaya = Tib. bsam pa Mvy 7117); āśayena adhyāśayena LV 182.18; āśayo LV 34.18, as a dharmālokamukha, immediately followed by adhyāśayo, used in the same way. Definition: Bbh 313.4 ff. śraddhāpūrvo dharmavicayapūrvakaś ca buddhadharmeṣu yo 'dhimokṣaḥ... bodhisattvasya so 'dhyāśaya ity ucyate. te punar adhyāśayā bodhisattvasya ... pañcadaśa veditavyāḥ. katame pañcadaśa: agryāśayaḥ vratāśayaḥ etc., all cpds. of āśaya. With adj. dṛḍha, *firm determination*, SP 97.10; or **vajraka** (= dṛḍha), LV 216.4; bracketed with gaurava, adhyāśayena gauraveṇa, *with resolution and with earnestness*, SP 286.2; LV 203.4; adhyāśayena *with one's whole heart, wholeheartedly*, SP 337.10 (adhimucyate); 389.9; (dharmārthiko, *seeking the dharma*) LV 179.10; RP 14.7; adhyāśayena LV 180.12, *with resolve* (see s.v. **anarthika**); tadadhyāśaya- Mv i.128.7, *intent on that*; adhyāśayena saṃpannāḥ SP 337.1, *perfected in disposition*; adhyāśaya-saṃpannā(ḥ) Mv ii.288.14; list of adhyāśaya, *mental dispositions*, which a Bodhisattva in the 2d bhūmi cherishes, Mv i.85.3 ff.; adhyāśaya-bala, one of the 10 bala of a Bodhisattva, Mvy 761; dvāv imau ... bodhisattvasya sattveṣu kalyāṇādhyāśayau (*excellent intentions towards creatures*) pravartete, hitādhyāśayaś ca sukhādhyāśayaś ca Bbh 18.16–18; a Tathāgata knows the adhy°, *mental dispositions*, of all creatures SP 163.3; 180.15; adhyāśayaṃ (with dependent gen.) viditvā Samādh 8.14; RP 56.3; °śayaṃ (of others) parīkṣanti (Buddhas) Mv i.192.19; a Tathāgata is sarvadharmārthavaśitāprāptaḥ sarvadharmādhyāśayaprāptaḥ SP 121.8, *arrived at control of the meaning of all dharma, attained to* (an understanding of) *the intent* (purpose) *of all dharma*; durbalādhyāśayāś ca Mv i.79.13, *and feeble in determination*; bodhisattvasyādhyāśayaśuddhitām Av i.221.4, cf. adhyāśayāś ca pariśuddhāḥ Mv i.102.5; similarly Dbh 63.23; miscellaneous, Mv i.77.6; 153.10 (kalyāṇa-, cf. Bbh 18.16–18 above); RP 10.7 (corrupt; read yad uta tāraṇādhyāśayapratipattyā, *determination to save*, cf. 10.13 tāraṇārtha); Jm 41.2–3 (jagatparitrāṇādhyāśayaḥ, cf. prec.); 45.24; 68.6; Gv 143.3; Bbh 242.8 ff.; (**2**) in looser sense of *mentality, mind* in general, upahatādhyāśayatvāt Jm 186.13, *because his mind was affected*.

adhyāśayati (rare; doubtless denom. from **adhyāśaya,** q.v.; Pali only ppp. ajjhāsita *intent upon*, rare and only in cpds.), *is intent upon*, with loc.: bodhisattvo 'dhyāśayaty anuttarāyāṃ samyaksaṃbodhau Śikṣ 17.21. In LV 18.8 the good ms. A reads adhyāśayati for text °sayati (mahāpṛthivīṃ ... abhinirjityādhyāsayati), *is firmly fixed upon, occupies*, with acc.; but probably text is right; Skt. adhyāste is used in this sense, and the LV form is only an aya extension of this; the meaning and construction do not fit adhyāśayati.

adhyāśayana (to prec.), = **adhyāśaya**: °naṃ mārg(ay)itvā MSV iv.109.18; 110.9, etc.

Adhyāśayasaṃcodana-sūtra, n. of a work: Śikṣ 15.13; 97.19; 104.9; 351.1.

adhyāhāriṇī-lipi, a kind of script: LV 126.9; so read for Lefm. madhyā° (after -lipiṃ), allegedly with all mss.; Calc. adhyā-, supported by Tib. bla (*superior*) thabs su bsnan pa (? *augmentation to a higher means*?), which suggests a form containing adhi; but I do not understand the meaning of either the Tib. or the BHS form, unless the latter means *suppletive script* (a term which might conceivably have been applied e.g. to writing of consonants alone, without vowels).

adhyupekṣaṇa (= Pali ajjhupekkhaṇa), *impartiality*: yathākālāvavādānuśāsanādhyupekṣaṇa-guhyaṃ (tathāgatānām) Dbh 87.8, *impartiality in the timely imparting of admonition and instruction*. See next two.

adhyupekṣati or °**te** (= Pali ajjhupekkhati), *ignores, disregards, is indifferent to*: Divy 25.6 (svāminam), 16, 18; 127.12; 185.23, 27; Bbh 40.11; 116.18; 173.15; 179.25; 254.24 (sattvaṃ ... nādhyupekṣate); 268.20.

adhyupekṣā (cf. Pali ajjhupekkhaṇā), *disregard, disesteem*: vimānayed bhūpatir °kṣayā Jm 154.14; anadhy° Bbh 81.10, *non-disregard*.

adhyuṣṭa (var. ardhuṣṭa, so Mironov), m., (= Pali aḍḍhuḍḍha, AMg. addhuṭṭha; false Skt. instead of ardhacaturtha), *three and a half*: Mvy 8172.

adhyeṣaka, m. (to **adhyeṣati** with -aka; = Pali ajjhesaka, in cpds.), *one who seeks instruction*: °ṣako 'haṃ LV 395.9 (vs).

adhyeṣaṇa, nt., °**ṇā,** f. (to next with -ana; Skt. °ṇa recorded once, Kull. on Manu 1.2; °ṇā Lex.; Pali ajjhesanā), *request* (for instruction): °ṇa Mvy 861 (-buddhādhyeṣaṇa-); Bhad 12 (vs); °ṇā SP 38.8 (all Nep. mss. °ṇa); 178.15; 315.11; 404.9; LV 7.13; 395.17; Bbh 75.6 (saddharmadeśanāyai); Dharmas 14; Sādh 64.7. The fem. is much commoner than the nt. In LV 53.11 and 178.19 (vss) text kileśa-dhyeṣaṇā(t); read kileśadharṣaṇā(t); some mss. -dhyaṣaṇāt, dhyāṣaṇā.

adhyeṣati, °**te,** °**ṣayati,** °**ṣyati** (= Pali ajjhesati; in Skt. only ppp. **adhīṣṭa,** q.v., rare; cf. prec. and next items), *requests* (in general): adhyeṣya Mv i.254.14; adhyeṣiṣyaṃ ii.108.5; in SP 116.3 asmāṃś ca adhyeṣati lokanātho, *the Buddha requests us* (to instruct creatures); in Av i.75.10 someone *requests* the Buddha to cause rain to fall in a drought; most commonly, however, *requests* (a teacher, generally Buddha, acc.) for instruction (may also be acc., Divy 160.20; Dbh 7.17; or quasi-infinitival dative, dharmacakrapravartanatāyai SP 162.9, and similarly Bhad 10; LV 394.2, 7; 396.12; 397.5;) dharmabhāṇakān adhyeṣayeyuḥ asya ... sūtrendrarājasya saṃprakāśanārthāya Suv 123.9; adhyeṣate, °se SP 36.4; 37.6; 38.9; Divy 160.20; °sati SP 116.3; °ṣante SP 162.9; °ṣanti Laṅk 7.10; °ṣāmas SP 167.8; °ṣāma LV 50.14; °ṣāmi Bhad 10; adhyeṣi (aor.) LV 416.3; °ṣya (ger.) Laṅk 2.15; Mv i.254.14; °ṣitum (inf.) LV 396.12; Av i.75.10; °ṣṭavyā (gdve.) Bhīk 10a.3; °ṣita (ppp.) SP 174.4; 178.12 (for ppp. **adhyeṣṭa, adhīṣṭa,** see these); adhyeṣayeyam (caus. opt.) LV 415.22 saṃbodhiprāptu ahu dharmu adh° (the Bodhisattva speaks in a praṇidhi), *having attained enlightenment, I would cause* (others) *to ask* (me) *for* (instruction in) *the law*; but usually non-caus., adhyeṣayāmi Laṅk 7.13, 15, like adhyeṣanti 7.10; adhyeṣayasi Divy 329.3, 7; dharmabhāṇakam adhyeṣayet (read °yed) dharmaśravaṇāya Mmk 38.14; also Suv 123.9, above; also adhyeṣyeyaṃ (opt.) LV 394.2, and adhyeṣyemahi 7 (but LV 397.5 adhyeṣyante is passive, *are asked for instruction*); adhyeṣanti Mv i.106.12 (vs; Senart em. °ṣyanti), in passive mg., § 37.32.

adhyeṣā (to prec.), *request* (for instruction): adhyeṣayā, instr., Av i.87.9. But perhaps read adhyeṣaṇayā; see **adhyeṣaṇā.**

adhyeṣṭa, ppp. of **adhyeṣati,** *applied to, besought* (for instruction): (of Buddha) adhyeṣṭu brāhmaṇayutebhi (no v.l.; Calc. id., interpreting as m.c. for °ṇāyutebhi, i. e. °ṇa-ayu°; read brahma-nayu°?) LV 48.11 (vs); (of Buddha) adhyeṣṭo LV 412.7 (vs).

adhyo-, see also **adhyava-.**

adhyoharati (for adhyava-h°; = Pali ajjho°), *puts in, inserts* (food): divyām ojām adhyohariṣyāmaḥ (romakūpavivarāntareṣu) Mv ii.131.3. The verb, and noun °hāra, m., are used of food in Pali. In line 6 Mv uses adhyokiretsuḥ (see **adhyavakirati**), perhaps by error for °haretsuḥ.

adhvagata (= Pali addha°; cf. **adhvan**), *that has reached old age; old*: °taḥ Mvy 7658; adhvagatavayam anuprāptaḥ Mv ii.151.2, *who has arrived at an advanced age*.

adhvan, m. (= Pali addha[n], addhāna), *time*. (Cf. 1 **aṃśa,** 1.). The three adhvānaḥ listed Dharmas 86 (atīto, anāgato, pratyutpanno 'dhvā). Very common are atīte and anāgate (less common pratyutpanne, SP 42.1) 'dhvani *in past (future, present) time* SP 17.8; 40.16; 41.10; LV 87.11; 88.13; Mv i.1.8; 39.9; Divy 60.13; 62.7; Av i.32.8; Suv 97.3; atītānāgatapratyutpanneṣv adhvasu LV 263.7; 435.4; adhvasu triṣu RP 6.11; also acc., in dating, ahaṃ pi bhaveyaṃ anāgatam adhvānaṃ tathāgato... Mv i.238.14, *may I also in future time become*...; 335.14; but acc. generally of extent of time, ciraṃ dīrgham adhvānaṃ *for a very long time* Mv i.52.3; 244.19 (suciraṃ°); ii.424.10; Ud v.7 (omits ciraṃ); tr(i)yadhva-, *past, present and future* LV 151.12; 435.5; Bhad 1 etc.; Śikṣ 17.13; Dbh 55.22; trayo adhvānaḥ Gv 478.9; yasmin-yasmin adhvani Gv 82.14, *in whatever time*; dīrghasyādhvano 'tyayena Mv i.338.14, *with the lapse of a long time.*

adhva-mārga, Prāt 497.9, and v.l. 519.10; **adhvāna-mārga** Prāt 510.4; Suv 72.11 (=Pali addhāna-magga), *travel-road, highroad*: in Prāt 497.9 and Suv 72.11 cpd. with -pratipanna, *when on a journey.*

adhvānīya (better adhvaniya; Pali addhaniya), *fit for a journey*: some such form seems clearly intended by mss. at Mv iii.93.19; they read (nātyātiśītaṃ nātyātiuṣṇaṃ) ṛtusukhaṃ adhvānīyaṃ (v.l. adhyā°) taṃ bhagavantaṃ (read bhavantaṃ, or bhadanta, m.c.; object of paśyantu, next line, or voc.). They are clearly corrupt, but Senart's emendations are proved wrong by the Pali parallel Therag. 529; divide ṛtu (ṛtuṃ? ṛtū?) sukhaṃ, *the season is pleasant and fit for travel.*

an-a-, double neg. prefix, = a(n)-, as in Pali (CPD). In Mv i.14.10 (gambhīro) 'nasamuttaro (see **samuttara**; Senart assumes na used in comp.); **anaparāmṛśant** (q.v.); and Mmk 53.21 an-a-patnīkam, *one who has no wife* (after this a word has been lost from the text; it must have named the place where the appropriate ceremony, to get a wife, was performed, as in the surrounding parallel phrases).

anagārikā; **anagāriya**, nt.; **anāgāra** (nt.); **anāgārikā** (= Pali anagāriya or anā°, generally nt.; anagāra nt. only once, Sn 376, otherwise m. and personal, also °rika, adj. and m. subst., personal; °rikā not in Pali), *homeless* (ascetic) *life*. In most texts anagārikā (LV 18.8; 101.19; 103.20; Divy 17.17; 37.12; 141.1; Samādh 8.15, etc.; rare in Mv, ii.69.1 with v.l. °riya), or anāgārikā (Av i.136.6, so best ms., text ana°; i.234.1, no v.l.; Bbh 26.12; °kāṃ pravrajyāṃ Bhīk 10b.1), are the regular forms, but in Mv it is almost always anagāriya as in Pali; this has not been noted elsewhere. Regularly in acc. sg. °rikāṃ, °riyaṃ (only once anāgāraṃ [mss., Senart ana°] upetasya Mv iii.387.1) depending on a form of pra-vraj (rarely of abhi-niṣ-kram, Mv ii.161.5 ff.), and preceded by abl. (or in Mv gen.) of agāra, *retire from the home to the homeless life*. In this phrase the preceding form is always agārād in all texts other than Mv, and sometimes there (ii.161.5 ff.; iii.408.2); in Mv also agārato iii.378.4; agārāto iii.176.2; agārebhyo i.128.10; read agārasmā, the Pali form, for agārasthā i.104.8; but most commonly the gen. agārasya i.322.15; 323.1; ii.117.18, 20; 140.3; 271.8; iii.50.11–12; 213.2–3.

Anagha, n. of a Bodhisattva: Mmk 62.13.

Anaṅga, n. of a nāga king: Māy 247.1.

anaṅgaṇa, (**1**) adj. (= Pali id.; often written °na), *spotless, free from blemish* or *evil* (**aṅgaṇa**): LV 344.6; 345.19; Mvy 2607 (Tib. ñon moṅs pa med pa, *without evil*); Mv i.228.11, 15; 229.6; 316.8; ii.132.14; 359.16; iii.396.6; Sukh 59.13; Dbh 7.6; 35.19; Ud xvi.3; (**2**) m., n. of a śreṣṭhin in Bandhumatī in the time of the Buddha Vipaśyin (later reincarnate as **Jyotiṣka**): Mv ii.271.13 ff.; Divy 283.1 ff. (here called a gṛhapati).

an-ativara (not in Pali, AMg. aṇaivara, see Sheth, not in Ratnachandra), *having no superior; supreme*, ep. of Buddha: Mv i.206.8, 10 = ii.10.2, 4; i.220.8, 14, 16; ii.22.9, 15; iii.110.19. The AMg. form confirms Senart's choice of this reading; the mss. vary between it and anabhivara, °cara, anaticara.

anatisadṛśa, *who has none superior to him*: śīlenānatisadṛśu LV 164.4 (vs); the only v.l. is °śa for °śu.

anatīta (= Pali id.), *not having got over, not free from*, with loc.; in Pali app. with acc. only (and so atīta in Skt.): (jarādharmā) jarādharmatāyām (so both mss.) anatītāḥ Mv ii.151.7, *subject to old age, not passed over in reference to old age.*

an-adhimūrchita (**-tva**), see **adhi°**.

an-adhimokṣa, see **adhi°**.

[**anadhiṣṭhāpada-**: Laṅk 180.17, corrupt; read **aniṣṭhāpada-**, q.v., with Suzuki, Transl. 156. note 1.]

an-adhyavasāna, see **adhy°**.

an-adhyavasita, see **adhy°**.

an-adhyācāra, see **adhy°**.

an-adhyāpatti, f. (= Pali anajjhāpatti), neg. of **adhyāpatti**, *non-transgression*: āpatty-anāpatty-anadhyāpatti-tām upādāya ŚsP 56.5, ... *state of sin, non-sin, and non-transgression.*

anadhyupekṣā, see **adhyu°**.

an-anuyukta (= Pali °yutta), neg. of **anuy°**, *not devoted to, experienced* or *practised in*, with acc.: jāgarikāyogam ananuyuktāye (parṣāye) Mv iii.48.17–18 and 49.4–5; mss. both times anuyuktāye but sense requires neg. (haplography). In Pali also used with jāgariyā.

an-anuyujya, or °**yuñjitvā**, neg. ger., *without having interrogated* (an accused person), or *made inquiry* (into an accusation), (Skt. anu-yuj-; cf. anuyuñjati, b, CPD): in Mv i.96.7, read (aparādhaṃ ca) an-anuyujya for °yā; in Mv iii.160.6 text °yujitvā, read doubtless °yuṃj° (°yuñj°) with text in 165.11; 170.7, 8 (in these no expressed object).

an-anuśruta, see **anuśruta.**

anantaka, nt. (= Pali id., also nantaka), *rag, worn-out cloth*: °kāni prāvṛtya Divy 175.19.

Anantakośa (? all but 1 ms. Antakośa), n. of a former Buddha: Mv i.141.11.

Anantagupta, n. of a former Buddha: Mv i.138.8.

Anantaghoṣa, n. of a Bodhisattva: Gv 442.3.

Anantacāritra, n. of a Bodhisattva: SP 300.13.

Anantachattra, n. of a former Buddha: Mv i.138.13.

Anantajñānottara, pl., n. of a group of Buddhas: Samādh p. 66, line 21.

Anantanirdeśapratiṣṭhāna, n. of a samādhi: SP 19.14; in the verse account 23.12 Anantanirdeśa (divide: anantanirdeśa varaṃ samādhiṃ).

Anantanemi, n. of a king: Mvy 3646.

Anantaparikarasāgarameghavyūhatejomaṇḍala-chattrākārarāja, n. of a nāga king: Megh 292.8 ff.

Anantapīlu, n. of a piśāca: Mmk 18.5.

Anantapratibhāna, m., n. of a samādhi: Mvy 585; ŚsP 1422.11.

Anantaprabha, m., (**1**) n. of a samādhi: Mvy 541; ŚsP 1417.22; (**2**) n. of a Tathāgata: Śikṣ 9.3.

Anantabalavighuṣṭanināditaśrīsaṃbhavamati, n. of a Buddha: Gv 358.20.

Anantabuddhi, n. of a former Buddha: Mv i.140.9.

Anantamati, (**1**) n. of one of the sons of the Buddha Candrasūryapradīpa: SP 19.3; (**2**) n. of a Bodhisattva: RP 1.12.

an-anta-madhya, lit. *without extremes or middle*, = *infinitely numerous or varied*, as adj. modifying, or in composition with, various nouns: °ya-dharmadhātu- LV 423.3; °yāṃ bodhisattvacaryāṃ Gv 387.21; in Gv 349.9–17 a series of typical instances, °ya-kāyavarṇasaṃsthānatāṃ 9; °yān varṇasamudrān (*seas*, i. e. *masses of colors*) 10; °yān raśmimeghān 11; °yān buddhakṣetrapratibhāsān 11–12; °yān tathāgatotpādān 12–13; °yāni vikurvitāni (of Tathāgatas) 13; °yaṃ sattvadhātum 17. The word occurs often in Gv, rarely elsewhere.

Anantamāyā, n. of a sister of Māyā: Mv i.355.17.

Anantamukhadevāsuranetrāsura, n. of a kumbhāṇḍa: Mvy 3446.

Anantamukhanirhāradhāraṇī, n. of a work: Śikṣ 18.15.

Anantayaśas, n. of a cakravartin: Śikṣ 255.8 ff.

Anantaraśmidharmadhātusamalaṃkṛtadharmarāja, n. of a former Buddha: Gv 150.4.

anantarāyika, adj. (= Pali id., neg. of **antar**°), *not connected with* (causing, or subject to?) *hindrances*: °ka-vaiśāradyam (of Bodhisattvas) Mvy 784.

anantariya, subst. nt. = ān°, *crime bearing immediate fruition, deadly sin* (one of five): °riyāṇi (pañca) Bhad 51. Cf. **ānantarīya**, and °**tarya**; in Bhad -i- could be m.c., but is regular in Pali. The initial short a- may also be m.c.; but CPD lists it as adj.

(**anantarya**, adj., *immediately successive*, in) **anantarya-tā**, *state of being* ...: °rya-tayā, Gv 104.22, instr. (= Skt. ānantarya, used only as noun, and BHS **ānantarya**, also adj., q.v.)

[**Anantaryasamādhi**, misprint in Mvy 901 for **Ānant**°, q.v.; corrected in Index.]

anantava(t), (= Pali id.; cf. BR 1.172), *infinite*, in anantav' udagro (mss. °grāḥ) Mv i.83.8, which Senart em. °ūdagro, m.c., understanding ananta + vūd°. Probably cpd., *infinitely delighted*; in any case -v- must be taken as belonging to anantav(at); § 18.52.

anantavarṇa-ratna, some kind of a jewel: Mvy 5967. Tib. translates literally.

Anantavarṇā, n. of a Bodhisattva-dhāraṇī: Mvy 757.

Anantavikrāmin, v.l. °kramin, °krama, n. of a Bodhisattva: SP 3.7.

Anantavīrya, (**1**) n. of a Buddha in the south: Sukh 97.9; (**2**) n. of a Bodhisattva: ŚsP 6.18.

Anantaśira (for °ras), n. of a rākṣasa king: Mmk 18.2.

Anantaśubhanayanakesarin, n. of a kumbhāṇḍa: Mvy 3445.

Anantāvabhāsarājendra, n. of a Tathāgata: Mmk 7.12.

Anantāvarta, n. of a dhāraṇī: Gv 66.14.

Anantāvartā, n. of a Bodhisattva-dhāraṇī: Mvy 751.

Anantāsana, n. of a Bodhisattva: Gv 443.4.

Anantaujas, n. of a Buddha: Śikṣ 169.11.

Ananyagāmin, n. of a Bodhisattva: Gv 215.17 ff.

an-anyatha (adj., based on adv. ananyathā), *unfailing, sure*: girām ananyathām SP 152.2 (here v.l. ananyathā, Kashgar rec. only); 308.8 (no v.l.).

ananyadeva, m., *having no other god* (beside him), i.e. *sole god*, ep. of Buddha: LV 18.9; so Lefm.; Burnouf, Lotus 581, followed by BR, *not having* (recognizing) *other gods* (implausible).

ananyaneya (= Pali anaññaneyya), *not to be led by others*, ep. of Buddha: Mv i.118.14 (em.); 208.5 (em.) = ii.12.14; iii.110.12; 123.21; Mvy 2399; of a Buddhist convert, MSV ii.46.18. Cf. **aneya**.

ananyapakṣika, see **anya**°.

an-a-patnīka, see under **an-a-**.

anapatrāpya, nt. (= Pali anottappa; neg. to **apa**°, q.v.), *indecency, lack of modesty and delicacy*; associated with **āhrīkya**: °pyam Mvy 1972; stem °pya- Śikṣ 105.8; Bbh 14.25; 223.12.

an-a-parāmṛśant (Pali a-parāmasanta, CPD), *not paying any attention, unconcerned*: read anaparāmṛśantaṃ Mv i.131.14 (see **an-a-**, double neg. prefix) for mss. anaparaśyantaṃ (or °sya°), Senart aparipaśyantaṃ.

Anapaviddhakarṇa (v.l. Anupraviddha°), n. of a former Buddha: Mv i.140.4.

Anapekṣa, pl., n. of a brahmanical school: Divy 635.18.

an-abhidrohin (from Skt. an-abhidroha), *not injuring*: Bbh 29.2; 363.5.

an-abhidhyālu, see **abhidhyālu**.

(**an-abhinirvṛtta**, neg. of ppp. (Skt., see pw 5 App.; Pali anabhinibbatta), *not* (really) *come into existence*: °ttān sarvadharmān Śikṣ 203.5, *all states of being*; preceded by svalakṣaṇaśūnyān asaṃbhūtān aniṣpannān.)

an-abhiniviṣṭi, adj. Bhvr. (from **abhiniviśati**, q.v.), *having no devotion* or *attachment* (to evil things, loc.): bodhisattvo ... 'nabhiniviṣṭiḥ sarvadharmeṣu ŚsP 381.16.

an-abhinivṛtti-tā (cf. **abhinivṛtta**), *state of having no cessation* or *ending*: Dbh 64.1 (opp. to apravṛttitā).

an-abhiniveśana = **an-abhiniviṣṭi**, but as Karmadh., cf. **abhi**°; °**na-tā**, in ātmānabhiniveśanatāyai, dat., LV 32.6, *unto* (resulting in) *the state of having no* (unworthy) *devotion to oneself*; or perhaps better, *of having no attachment to the heresy that there is a self*, cf. **abhiniveśa**; sarvadharmānabhiniveśanatām AsP 206.10, 18, *state of not being* (reprehensibly) *attached to* (? or, *of not believing in the reality of*) *all states of being*.

Anabhibhūtamakuṭa, n. of a Bodhisattva: Gv 3.7.

Anabhibhūtayaśas, n. of a former Buddha: Mv i.141.10 (mss. °yaśāḥ, so read, n.sg.; Senart em. °yaśa-ḥ).

anabhiramya = **nirabhi**°, *unpleasing*: Samādh 19.20 (m.c. ānabhi°).

Anabhilakṣita, m., n. of a samādhi: Mvy 601; ŚsP 1424.4.

an-abhilapanīya (see next), *not capable of being expressed in words*: Śikṣ 251.11.

an-abhilapya = prec. (cf. also next): Vaj 24.8 (said of tathāgatena dharmo ... deśito); syn. of **avyavahāra**, q.v., Vaj 45.6. Elsewhere **anabhilāpya** is the normal form.

anabhilāpya (not in Pali; AMg. aṇabhilappa, as adj.; cf. preceding two, **abhilāpya**, and **nirabhi**°), (**1**) adj., *inexpressible, that cannot be put in words*, of the dharma LV 392.14; 434.12; of the (dharma-)cakra LV 423.4; syn. of **avyavahāra** (like **anabhilapya**, q.v.) Śikṣ 251.11; with suggestion of large numbers or quantities, Mv ii.362.12 (of tathāgate pratiṣṭhāpitā dakṣiṇā); Śikṣ 178.5; Gv 7.14 ff., Dbh 55.20; Sukh 25.11; (**2**) subst. nt. (cf. the following entries), a very high number: Mvy 7818; 7950 (cited from Gv); 8048; Gv 106.26; 134.15.

anabhilāpyaparivarta, m. (in Gv nt.), *square* of the preceding (2): Mvy 7819; 7951 (cited from Gv, but m.); Gv 106.26; 134.15. Cf. next.

anabhilāpyānabhilāpya, nt., a still higher number than the preceding: Mvy 7952 (cited from Gv); Gv 106.26; 134.16; quite common in Gv, and occurs elsewhere, e. g. Dbh 2.23; 70.8; read (a)nabhilāpyānabhilāpya- in Bhad Introduction, line 2, with v.l. and Gv 543.6, for Watanabe (a)bhilāpyānabhilāpya-. See next.

anabhilāpyānabhilāpyaparivarta, m. (in text of Gv nt.), *square* of the preceding: Mvy 7953 (cited from Gv); Gv 107.1; 134.17. Cf. next.

anabhilāpyānabhilāpyaparivartanirdeśa, m., a very high number (cf. the preceding; in its own list follows **anabhilāpyaparivarta**): Mvy 7820.

Anabhilāpyodgata, n. of a Bodhisattva: Gv 442.25.

an-abhisaṃskāra, neg. of **abhi**°, (**1**) (m.,) *non-accumulation* (of karman), as Karmadhāraya, Gv 70.7, see s.v. **vipratilambha**; generally as bahuvrīhi, adj., *having* or *characterized by no accumulation* (of karman): LV 422.21 (-cakram, of the dharmacakra); Mvy 173 (°rāḥ sarvadharmāḥ); 799; Śikṣ 190.16; LV 428.10 sarvaprasthānāliptatvād anabhisaṃskāragocara ity ucyate (tathāgataḥ), *he is out of range of the accumulation* (of karman), *because he is unstained by any setting-out* (to do or get anything); anabhisaṃskāragatir bodhisattvānām Gv 525.10, *the course of B's is free from accumulation* (of karman); (**2**) adj., *without proper mental preparation*: Mvy 1018 °ra-parinirvāyī (contrast sābhi° pari° 1017).

anabhisaṃskārikā (cf. **ābhisaṃskārika**), fem. adj.

and subst. (from °**skāra**), with or sc. ṛddhi, (magic potency) *of non-accumulation* (of karman): °skārikāyā ṛddher anubhāvena Gv 70.8; as subst., understand ṛddhi, Gv 180.6 abhāvapratiṣṭhitayā (*which is established in non-becoming*, see Gv 70.7, preceding the above, s.v. **vipratilambha**) 'ryānabhisaṃskārikayā *by the* (magic potency of) *non-accumulation* (of karman).

an-abhisaṃskṛta (neg. of **abhi°**, q.v.; Pali °saṃkhata, see below), *not* (specially) *prepared*, of food: Laṅk 196.12, said of rice offered to infants without proper boiling (and seasoning?); *not affected* (by some outside influence), avikopitair indriyair anabhisaṃskṛtair gātrair LV 323.16, in description of the Bodhisattva's indifference to the daughters of Māra, *with senses undisturbed, with body-members unaffected*. So Tib., lus (*body*) ma bcos pa, lit. *not made* (up), see Jäschke s.v. bcos-pa, '3. *made or contrived by art, artificial* (so Pali abhisaṃkhata is sometimes used, CPD) ... ma bcos, *artless, unaffected, genuine*; it also seems to denote an absence of mental activity (see s.v. **abhisaṃskāra**) or a forbearance of exercising such activity, in short that indifference to the world, which is so highly valued by the Buddhist.'

an-abhisaraṇa, adj. Bhvr. (*abhiśaraṇa, °saraṇa = śaraṇa; cf. Pali an-abhisara), *without refuge*: atrāṇā anabhisaraṇā Mv i.22.14.

an-abhyasūyikayā, adv. (instr. sg. f. of neg. of Skt. abhyasūyaka), *in a not-unfriendly way*: (**anuparigrāhikayā**, see this) anabhya° dharmaṃ deśayati SP 283.3. So read with Kashgar rec.; Nep. mss. quoted as ananyasūcanayā; KN em. anabhyasūyayā, kept by WT without note.

anabhraka, m., *unclouded*, n. of the first (but omitted in Pali and the Mv lists) of the classes of rūpāvacara gods in the 4th dhyāna-bhūmi; see **deva**: LV 150.8; Divy 68.16; Av i.5.3; Gv 249.12; Mvy 3098; Dharmas 128; etc.

anayaka, adj., f. °**ikā** (from anaya, *misfortune*; not recorded), *unfortunate, unhappy*: anāyikeyaṃ praja sarvaduḥkhitā SP 162.1 (vs). I interpret with Kern (Transl.) except that he derives from an-āya; I regard ā as m.c. for a. Burnouf *without protector*, a-nāyaka.

anaya-vyasana, nt. (=Pali id.; as cpd. seems not to occur in Skt.), *misfortune and disaster*: SP 73.7, 13; Mv ii.493.2.

anarghyeya, *priceless*: -maṇiratnam Gv 499.26. Perhaps error for anargheya (also with maṇiratna SP 210.10), which occurs in Skt. (BR 5.1042, s.v. argheya).

an-arthika, adj. (= Pali anatthika; not in Skt.; see **arthika** and next), *not desirous* (of: instr., rarely loc. or abl.), (a) with instr.: anarthikāś ca te śrāmaṇyena bhaviṣyanti LV 88.18, *and they will not be anxious for monkhood* (duty of monks), so read with Foucaux's ms. A, see his Notes p. 113 (Lefm. śrāmaṇyo na); saṃskṛtenādhyāśayenānarthikaḥ sarvopādānaparigrahair anarthiko LV 180.12, *with his resolve not desirous of the conditioned* (see **saṃskṛta** and **adhyāśaya**, which are not to be construed together), *and not desirous of all grasping and possessions*; RP 15.1 (lābhena); 34.10 (dharmaśravaṇena); 43.12 (kāmabhogaiḥ); KP 125.2, 4, 6; sv-anarthiko Śikṣ 113.9 (guṇaiḥ), *very undesirous of virtues* (wrongly Bendall and Rouse); (b) with loc.: anarthiko sarvakāmabhogeṣu Mv iii.104.17; (c) with abl.: saṃsārād anarthikaḥ Divy 2.1, *averse from the saṃsāra.*

anarthika-tā (to preceding), *state of not desiring*, in comp.: saṃsāropakaraṇānarthikatayā Gv 391.11 (1st ed. misprinted °rdhika°; corr. 2d ed.)

Anala, n. of a king: Gv 154.20; 155.12 ff.

analpaka, adj. (= Pali anappaka), *not insignificant, distinguished, excellent* (in ..., loc.): akṣarapadavyākaraṇe analpako (of a brahman) Mv ii.77.10.

anavakāra, adj. (= Pali id.; cf. **avakāra**), *without elimination*; *not partial, complete, absolute*, ep. of śūnyatā, *absolute void*; °ra-śūnyatā Mvy 944; ŚsP 191.21; 642.16, etc. (common in this text). Cf. **ākārānavakāra.**

anavakāśa, m. (once nt., Laṅk 198.9; = Pali anavakāsa; in Skt. Gr., see pw s.v.), *what is out of the question, an impossibility*, only noted in phrase asthānam (etad) anavakāśo (regularly followed by yat-clause): Gv 498.5 etc. (see s.v. **asthāna**). Cf. **anokāśa.**

anavakīrṇa, see **ava°**.

Anavatapta (= Pali Anotatta, in meaning 1), (**1**) n. of a lake: LV 332.12; Divy 150.23; 152.23; 153.4; 344.13; 399.14; Śikṣ 247.12; Dbh 95.17; Karmav 62.1; °ta-kāyikā devatāḥ, *the deities inhabiting Lake A*, Divy 153.7 ff.; (**2**) n. of a nāga-king: Mvy 3239; SP 4.12; LV 204.10; 219.9 (here anāva°, m.c.); Suv 85.4; 91.19; 158.14; 162.8; Kv 2.14; 68.5; Gv 196.13; Māy 221.20; 247.9.

Anavataptanāgarāja-paripṛcchā (cf. prec., 2), n. of a work: Mvy 1389.

an-avatāra (neg. of Skt. avatāra, mg. 2 in pw), *non-appearance, the not coming into existence*: Śikṣ 157.16 tasya (sc. ayoniśo-manaskārasya) anavatāre yatnaḥ kāryaḥ *one must strive to avoid the occurrence* (appearance, coming into existence) *of this.*

Anavadya, n. of a Bodhisattva: Gv 442.24.

[**anavadya-bhīru**, wrong reading for **avadya-bhīru,** q.v.]

anavadhīṣṭha, or (in footnote) °**dhiṣṭha**, sarvasattvānavadhīṣṭhakalyāṇamitrasya Dbh 29.21; prob. contains anavadhi = Pali anodhi, *without limits, not making any distinction, indiscriminate, absolute* (is the syllable -ṣṭha the root-adj. of sthā? *abiding in no limitation?*). Acc. to Rahder, footnote, Tib. (and Mongol) suggest mg. akṛtrima, *not faked, sincere, genuine* (ma bcos pa, also for **an-abhisaṃskṛta** q.v.).

an-avanamana, see **ava°**.

Anavanāmitavaijayantī, n. of the lokadhātu of the future Buddha Sāgaravaradharabuddhivikrīḍitābhijña: SP 216.10 (no v.l.; so also WT). In the verse form 217.11 analyzed into Anonatā Dhvajavaijayantī (loc. °tāyāṃ °ntyām).

anavamardanīya, *not to be crushed*: AsP 401.1. Cf. the next items.

Anavamardabalaketu, n. of a Tathāgata: Gv 360.14. Cf. prec. and next items.

anavamardya, *not to be crushed*: Śikṣ 32.11 (°dya-kāyabala-); ŚsP 283.6; read so for text anavamadya(-lakṣaṇā) ŚsP 1410.16. Cf. prec. two and next items.

[**anavamūḍhyatā**, wrong reading in LV 34.3 for **anavamṛdyatā**,q.v.]

anavamṛdya, *not to be crushed*: Gv 146.8 (-bala); ŚsP 311.20 (-pāramitā); AsP 205.3 (id.). Cf. prec. items and next.

anavamṛdya-tā, *state of being uncrushable* (from prec.): LV 34.3 (read °mṛdyatāyai with most mss. for Lefm. °mūḍhya°); Dbh 4.5 (-balānava°); Śikṣ 183.5 (cittasya); Gv 430.18.

anavarāgra, adj. (corresp. to Pali anamatagga, AMg. aṇavadagga, aṇavayagga, and prob. hyper-Skt. for the latter; see CPD for theories about this doubtful word), probably understood as *without end or beginning*; Tib. thog ma daṅ tha ma med pa, interpreted CPD as *without top and bottom*, but it may, and probably does, mean *without beginning and end*; commonly ep. of saṃsāra and its constituents: °grasmiṃ saṃsāre Mv i.282.6; ii.94.1; 188.13; 237.9; iii.26.10; 90.2; °gro saṃsāro Divy 197.15; °gre jātisaṃsāre Śikṣ 170.2; mayā 'navarāgrasya jātijarāmaraṇaduḥkhasyāntaḥ kṛta iti LV 351.17; 377.3, 6; anavarāgra-jātijarāmaraṇa-saṃsāra- Mv i.34.7; in Mv ii.419.7 mss. anavarāgre (as subst.? Senart em. °gra-, perhaps rightly) jātijarāmaraṇasaṃsāra-; as separate adj. with similar cpds. Mv iii.67.10; 281.6; cpd. with śūnyatā, Mvy 943; Dharmas 41.

anavarāgra-tā, from prec., *state of being without end or beginning*: °tāṃ Dbh 75.19.

anavalīna, anolīna, adj. (= Pali anolīna), *not shrinking, not downcast* (so CPD), *not despondent*; ano° SP 279.10; Śikṣ 100.17 (ms., wrongly em. to anālīnaḥ; Tib. cited as zhum pa med, *not faint-hearted*); parallel with viśārada *confident* SP 278.9; 354.13; aprakampyo 'navalīno 'navadīrṇo LV 323.17; anavalīna-citta *with not downcast mind* SP 324.11; Gv 202.5.

anavalīna-tā, from prec., *state of being not downcast*: Śikṣ 183.5.

an-avalīyana-tā (cf. Pali olīyanā, I think wrongly defined in PTSD, and BHS 2 **avalīyate, avalīna**), *state of not being downcast*: Samādh p. 5 line 20 (prose; or read **an-avalīna-tā**?).

an-avaśruta (= Pali anavassuta; see **avaśruta**), *free from lust and moral defilement* (CPD): Mv i.88.7 (vs) parānnāny avaśrutā, mss. (Senart em. °srutā), metr. deficient; meter and sense both require em. anavaśrutā (a sort of haplography has occurred, na lost after nya).

anavīkaroti, pple. **anavīkṛta** (in Skt. with different mg., pw), *made not fresh*, i. e. *stained, spoiled* (with dust; of a silk cloth): Divy 576.30 (pāṃśubhir).

anasamuttara, see under **an-a-**, and **samuttara.**

Anākṛtsnagatā (?), n. of a nāga maid: Kv 4.4.

an-āgatika, Bhvr., *having no coming into existence* (āgati): sarvadharmā(ḥ) . . . anāgatikā agatikā(ḥ) AsP 162.2; saṃskṛta-gatīkam (see s.v. **gatika**) anāgatīkaṃ (ī m.c.) Dbh.g. 11(347).2; °kā hi te tathāgatāḥ svabhāvasaṃbhūtatvāt Gv 238.7, *without origination* (they are self-existent); but 2d ed. svabhāvāsaṃbhūtatvāt (*because by nature they have not originated*).

anāgāmin, f. **°nī** (= Pali id.), *one who is destined no more to return to this world*: Mvy 5135–6; Av i.286.7; f. °nī (pl. °nyo) Divy 533.26; °mi-phala, *the fruit of attaining this condition*, Divy 18.6; 48.14; 50.9; Av i.65.1 etc. See s.v. **srota-āpanna.**

anāgāra, nt. = **anagārikā**, q.v. Only Mv iii.387.1 (Senart em. ana°).

anāgārikā = **anagārikā**, q.v.

anāgṛha?: anāgṛhābhāsarvajagatparāṅmukhavarṇā Gv 348.10; doubtless corrupt; read anāgrahā°?

anāgṛhīta (= Pali anaggahīta, neg. of **āgṛhīta**, q.v.), *not niggardly*: in Mv ii.376.6, text anāgrahītaḥ (with one ms., v.l. anogṛhīto), read anāgṛhītaḥ.

anācāryaka (= Pali anācariyaka), see **ācāryaka.**

an-āchindana, see **āchi°.**

anāchedya (neg. gdve. of Skt. ā-chid), *that cannot be cut off, destroyed*; **-tā**, *state of being . . .*: anāchedyapratibhānaḥ Mvy 851 (of Bodhisattvas); mārgānāchedyatā Dbh 57.12 (of Bodhisattvas).

anājñātam ājñāsyāmī 'ndriyam (Pali anaññātaññassāmītindriyam), *the mental faculty of resolving to come to know something unknown* (CPD): Mvy 2078.

an-ātmanīya, adj. (neg. of **ātmanīya**, q.v.) = next: Mv iii.447.12.

an-ātmīya, adj. (not in this sense in Skt.; cf. **ātmīya**), *not characterized by a self*; (what is) *without self*: nāpi ye dharmā anātmīyā te ātmato deśayāmi Mv i.173.4; anātmīye ātmīyasaṃjñāyā KP 94.8.

Anāthapiṇḍada (once **°piṇḍika**, q.v., as in Pali), n. of a rich layman (gṛhapati), owner of the grove (ārāma) in Jetavana at Śrāvastī where Buddha often stayed: LV 1.5; Mv i.4.13 (5 of 6 mss. read here °piṇḍasya); iii.224.11 (here Senart °piṇḍasya with 1 ms., v.l. °piṇḍādasya); Mvy 4111; Divy 1.2; 35.11; 77.27; 80.12; 168.5; 172.27; 429.8; 466.23, etc.; Av i.13.5 etc., common; title af Av chap. 39 (i.223.1), see also Av i.313.6 ff.; Kv 1.5; Karmav 21.13 etc.; 71.19; MSV iii.135.22 (his life, as **Sudatta**, more fully than in Pali).

Anāthapiṇḍika (= Pali id.) = **°piṇḍada**, q.v.: °ko Mv iii.375.6 (no v.l.).

Anādarśaka, n. of a mountain: Kv 91.14.

Anādarśanā, n. of a 'gandharva maid': Kv 4.16.

an-ādāna, see **ādāna.**

an-ādikarmika, see **ādik°.**

anādikālika, adj. from (Pali) anādikāla, *of beginningless time, from everlasting*: °liko Bbh 3.4.

anādeya-vākya, see **ādeya-.**

anāpatti, f. (noun, = Pali id.; neg. of **āpatti**, q.v.) *no offense; unpunishableness*: Divy 330.1 (read with mss. anāpattis, or °ttiḥ, followed by punctuation: *there is no offense*); similarly 544.17, 19; Śikṣ 11.8; anāpattiḥ kṣiptacetasaḥ, °ttiḥ śuddhāśayabhūmipraviṣṭasya Bbh 160.27; ŚsP 56.5 (see s.v. **anadhyāpatti**). The Index to Divy renders *guiltless*, as if Bhvr., but wrongly; as in Pali, the word is always a Karmadh.

anāpattika, adj. (= Pali id.; to -āpatti with -ka Bhvr.; cf. **sāpattika**), *free from offense*: °kasya sato deveṣūpapattir bhaviṣyati Divy 303.3.

anāpanna, see s.v. **āpanna.**

anābhāsa, (**1**) m., (lit. *non-appearance*,) *disappearance, vanishing*: Mvy 6654 = Tib. mi snaṅ ba, *vanishing* (Das); ihāśravo niravaśeṣam anābhāsam astaṃgacchatīti LV 349.1 (repeated in sequel); ucchinnamūlaṃ tālamastakavad anābhāsagatam āyatyām anutpādadharmi Samy. Āg. 1.1 ff., cf. Pali Vin. iii.2.18, where instead of this anabhāvaṃ gatā (or, var., anabhāva-katā, see CPD s.v.); Pali anabhāva, *annihilation* = our word; (**2**) adj. (Bhvr., an- plus **ābhāsa**, q.v.), *having no range or scope* (of action), i. e. *substantially inactive*, of the mind: °sa-citta Gv 279.10; also (**3**) as subst., neg. of **ābhāsa** in same sense: Śikṣ 129.3 anābhāsagatāḥ sattvā(ḥ), *not coming into range.*

anābhibhū, adj. Bhvr. (for an-a°, with ā m.c., § 3.11), *having no superior*: bhagavān °bhūḥ SP 128.4; 190.7 (vss).

anābhibhūta, neg. ppp. (= Skt. anabhi°, § 3.11), *unconquered*: SP 69.4.

an-ābhoga (see **ābhoga** and **sābhoga**), (**1**) adj., *effortless*: crucial is Dbh 67.10 ff., where a boat, before it reaches the open sea, is sābhoga-vāhana, *traveling with* (human) *effort*; when it reaches the open sea it is anābhogavāhano vātamaṇḍalīpraṇīto, *traveling without effort, borne along by a tornado*, and goes in a single day farther than it could go in a hundred years by all effortful traveling (sarvasābhogavāhanatayā, i. e. by rowing etc.). So, by the knowledge of the Omniscient (sarvajñajñānena), because this knowledge is *effortless* (automatic, spontaneous: jñānānābhogatayā), a Bodhisattva gets in a single moment farther than he could get in 100,000 kalpas by his former effortful activity (pūrvakeṇa sābhogakarmaṇā). Again, in Sūtrālaṃkāra ix.18–19, a Buddha's activities proceed without ābhoga, *effortlessly, spontaneously*, like music from instruments that are not being played, or jewels that shine without labor. So understand anābhogabuddhakāryāpratiprasrabdaḥ Mvy 411, (a Tathāgata is) *never ceasing from spontaneous* (Tib. lhun grub pa, *self-created; not contrived by human labor*, Jäschke) *Buddha-activities*, and the same cpd. prefixed to -cakram LV 423.3 (see **apratipraśrabdha**); *automatic* Śikṣ 7.15; °ga-vāhanaḥ Bbh 260.18, *bringing automatically*; mahākaruṇopāyakauśalyānābhogagatena prayogena Laṅk 42.8, *by praxis that effortlessly* (spontaneously) *arrives at great compassion and skill in devices*; sometimes best rendered by *impassive* (not involving or subject to any effort), anābhogaprekṣikayā *with impassive look* Śikṣ 268.1; (see s.v. **ābhoga** for Dbh 64.16;) prob. *impassive* in Bbh 317.3, and 350.12 bodhisattvānām anābhogo nirnimitto vihāraḥ, which is contrasted with (and higher than) their **sābhoga** (*effortful*) vihāra (346.14); cf. Lévi, Sūtrāl. i.7 n.7; (**2**) subst. m., *non-effort, impassivity*: anābhoge tathā siddhiḥ Mmk

116.24; svabhāvānābhogābhyām ca vigacchanti Dbh 48.21, *and they pass away by natural process and without effort* (na caiṣām kaścid vigamayitā, *and no one makes them pass away*); as one of the samādhy-āvaraṇāni, Dharmas 118, see s.v. **ābhoga**; (3) adverbs, *without effort, effortlessly,* anābhogataḥ Dbh 56.19; Śikṣ 12.1; anābhogena pariniṣpadyante, *are automatically perfected*, Dbh 58.9; (4) m., n. of a yakṣa: Māy 52.

a-nāmana-tā (see **nāmanā**), *not changing, not disturbing* or *transgressing*: (pūrṇacandrasamacittena) kālākālānāmanatayā Gv 464.1, *because of not infringing right and wrong times.*

an-āmantraṇaka, see **āmantraṇaka.**

? **anāyaka,** f. **-ikā,** acc. to Burnouf *without any protector* (Buddha): SP 162.1; but see s.v. **anayaka.**

an-āyatana (nt.; neg. of **āyatana** (3) q.v., in sense of Skt. pātra; = Pali id.), *an unworthy object*: mā tvam anāyatane (sc. heretics) prasādam utpādaya, api tu buddhadharmasamghe ... Divy 419.22.

Anāyāsa, n. of a yakṣa: Māy 66.

anāyikā: SP 162.1, m.c. for **anayikā**, see **anayaka.**

an-āyūha, adj. (Pali id.; see also **anāvyūha**), *effortless; free from exertion or striving*; usually cpd. with **a-niryūha,** *without abandonment, riddance, giving up*; the two terms together seem clearly to be opposites, and to mean about the same as a-pravṛtti, a-nivṛtti, *without activity or abstention from it* (so Suzuki, 'neither taking birth nor ... going out', on Laṅk 115.11–12; 196.3). However, Tib. (e. g. on LV 423.4 and on Laṅk) renders an-āyūha by blaṅ ba med pa, or the like, and aniryūha by dor ba med pa, which seem most naturally to mean *without* (intellectual) *acceptance* or *rejection* respectively; La Vallée Poussin, note on MadhK 517.20, see **āvyūhati,** gives his Tib. versions as mi len and mi ḥdor (which are equivalent to the above), and equates ā(v)yūha and nir(v)yūha with Skt. samāropa and apavāda. I find no support in BHS texts for this interpretation; whether the Tib. terms must necessarily be so understood I do not venture to say. Without aniryūha the word occurs Gv 17.13 anāyūha-sarvajñatā-bhūmi-gagana-vīryāḥ (of Bodhisattvas); anāyūhān 25.19 (id.), *effortless, unstriving* (in complimentary sense, like **anābhoga**; substantially *unparticipating, impassive*); anāyūhaviyūho (read with 2d ed. °viyūha-, cpd. with next, if not niryūha-)-gatir bodhisattvānām kāyacittāsampravaṇatayā (see **asampravaṇa**) 525.11, *the course of B.'s is free from effort and striving, because they are not interested in* (their own) *bodies or minds*; anāyūhāniryūha- LV 423.4 (-cakram); °ham aniryūham (dharmacakram) LV 436.13; apratiṣṭhānāyūhāniryūha(ḥ) LV 424.7–8 (tathāgataḥ); anāyūhāniryūhāḥ (sarvadharmāḥ) Laṅk 115.11–12; °hāniryūha-tā (sc. sarvadharmāṇām) ŚsP 283.3 (text by error °niyūhatā).

anārabdha (cf. Pali an-ārambha, *free from damage or trouble*, CPD, and cf. BHS and Pali **ārambha,** *slaughter*, Pali ārabhati, *slaughters* (an animal); but our word has a less drastic mg.): *uninjured*, said of the womb of the Bodhisattva's mother after his birth (rendered so by his magic power), sampratijāte ... bodhisattve bodhisattvamātuḥ kukṣi pratipūrṇā yeva abhūṣi anārabdhā (v.l. °labdhā) ca bodhisattvasyaiva tejena Mv i.221.4–5.

anārja (= Skt. anārya; perhaps semi-Skt. based on MIndic aṇajja [AMg., beside aṇāriya]; possibly influenced by confusion with ārjava?), (adj., *ignoble, base, evil*;) subst., *wickedness*: sarve anārjam parivarjayāmaḥ Mv ii.79.3 (text °jeyāmaḥ, formally possible, § 29.33, but metrically bad, unless *e* be short, § 3.65); the corresponding Pali has anariyam (Jāt. iv.53.8 °yam parivajjemu sabbam).

Anārthikā, n. of a rākṣasī: Māy 241.31.

Anāla, see **Aṇāla.**

anālabdha?, *uninjured*, see **anārabdha.**

Anālambha, n. of a former Buddha: Mv i.138.10.

an-ālaya, adj., *without* **ālaya** (in two senses): (1) *without base, foundation, firm footing*; of states of being (dharma), anālayā dharmā (ā)kāśasvabhāvalakṣaṇāḥ LV 177.20 (like ether); °yāḥ sarvadharmāḥ Mvy 161, Tib. gzhi med pa, *without gzhi*, usually more fully kun gzhi = *basis, ground, foundation*, (also) *abode, home*; dharmi anālaye Gv 256.21; so even dharma in the other sense, the *profound* (gambhīra) dh. realized and preached by the Buddha, is anālaya, which we might take in sense (2) as *without attachment*, but acc. to Tib. on LV 392.12 anālayaḥ = kun gzhi med pa, and likewise the (dharma-) cakra LV 422.19 anālaya-cakram (Tib. same). But (2) *without attachment* must surely be the mg. in niṣprapañcān anālayān Gv 25.19 (of Bodhisattvas).

Anālayamaṇḍala, n. of a (mythical) dharmaparyāya: Gv 451.25; 452.5, see s.v. **adhiṣṭhāna** (6).

Anālayav(i)yūha, n. of a kalpa: Gv 259.13 (vs).

[**anālasa,** in SP 200.5 aklānto dharmadeśanayā, anālasasya dharmasyākhyātā, corrupt: read with WT alam asya dharm°; so Tib., nus pa, *capable.*]

an-ālīḍha, see **ālīḍha.**

anālokiya, ? ep. of Buddhas: tato anālokiyā lokabāndhavā Mv i.162.16; Senart's note may be consulted but I find it hardly helpful.

Anāvatapta, m.c. for **Anava°** (2), q.v.: LV 219.9.

anāvaraṇa, (1) nt., *non-obstruction* (neg. of **āvaraṇa,** q.v.): °ṇa-gatimgata Mvy 356, of Tathāgatas, *having attained freedom from the obstructions*; ākāśadhātur bījasyānāvaraṇa-kṛtyam karoti Śāl 74.16; (2) (much commoner; = Pali id.) adj., *free from the obstructions*, of jñāna (cf. jñeyāvaraṇa, s.v. **āvaraṇa**) KP 22.1; Gv 473.25; LV 8.4 (read with v.l. -āsaṅgānāvaraṇajñāna-, confirmed by Tib.); 424.18; Bbh 88.7; Mvy 832 (-jñānī); vimokṣa LV 435.6; (buddha-vimokṣa) RP 4.15; darśana LV 433.18; prajñācakṣus Dbh 28.10; pratibhāna Bhad 6[2]; pratisamvid LV 426.5; (dharma-)cakra LV 423.2; nirvāṇa Dbh 29.9; a road (mārga; here literal), -anāvaraṇa-tā Gv 186.7; (3) substantivized as n. of a samādhi: anāvaraṇam nāma mahākaruṇāsamādhim Śikṣ 236.8.

Anāvaraṇajñānaviśuddhigarbha, n. of a Bodhisattva: Dbh 2.11.

Anāvaraṇadarśin, n. of a Bodhisattva: Gv 443.2.

Anāvaraṇadharmagaganaprabha, n. of a Tathāgata: Gv 311.25.

Anāvaraṇamati, n. of a Bodhisattva: ŚsP 6.15.

Anāvaraṇasvaramaṇḍalamadhuranirghoṣagarbha, n. of a Bodhisattva: Dbh 2.18.

anāvartika-dharma (= Pali anāvatti-dhamma), *characterized by no more returning* (to rebirth): °mā, acc. pl., asmim loke Mv i.33.7, of śuddhāvāsakāyika gods. Cf. **anāvṛttika-dharmin.**

Anāviddhavarṇa, em. for **Anivi°,** q.v.

anāvila-samkalpa (= Pali °samkappa, DN iii.270.14, of bhikkhus), *of not impure resolve*: Mvy 434, of Tathāgatas.

anāvṛta (1) (= Pali anāvaṭa) = **anāvaraṇa** (adj.), *free from the obstructions*: Gv 473.11; darśayāmi ti (= te) anāvṛtām diśam 480.22; (2) neg. of BHS **āvṛta,** q.v., and = Pali an-ovaṭa (q.v. in CPD), *not forbidden*: Bhīk 5b.1.

anāvṛttika-dharmin, adj., fem. °iṇī, *having a nature characterized by no return* (into the round of existences): Divy 533.26 (followed by dependent accusative imam lokam, *into this world*). Cf. **anāvartika-dharma** and next.

anāvṛttidharman = prec.: °māṇaḥ (ms. °maṇaḥ; n. pl.) MPS 9.14.

anāvyūha = **anāyūha,** q.v., in sarvadharmānāvyūhānirvyūha-samatayā Dbh 47.13 (= the usual anāyūhāniryūha-).

anāścarya, nt. (cf. Pali anacchariya; not cited for Skt. except in MW, without ref., *not wonderful*), *a natural, spontaneous quality*: Bbh 285.2, 12 etc. (a Bodhisattva has five such, listed here in detail).

anāśrava, see **āsrava.**

anāśvāsa (?) = **anāśvāsika,** *unreliable*: asāram itvaraṃ ca lokaṃ anāśvāsam (so I would read for Finot anāśvāsan; ms. anāsvāsan) apriyasamavadhānaṃ etc. RP 39.12 (prose).

anāśvāsika, adj. (= Pali anassāsika), *unreliable*: (anityā ... sarvasaṃskārā) adhruvā anā° Divy 207.23; anityeṣu ... dharmeṣv adhruveṣv anāśvāsikeṣv (by em.) Śikṣ 150.9; °ka-tā, *unreliability*, Dbh 31.3 (anityatāṃ ca sarvasaṃskāragatasya ...) aśubhatāṃ cānāśvāsikatāṃ ca.

anāsrava, see **āsrava.**

anāharaṇā (an- plus n. act. to āharati with anā; cf. Skt., Pali anāhāra), *the not taking food, fasting*: te 'nāharaṇāṃ (text nāh°) pratipannāḥ MSV i.58.5.

Aniketa, n. of a Bodhisattva: Gv 442.3.

Aniketacārin, m., n. of a samādhi: Mvy 577; ŚsP 1421.12.

Aniketasthita, m., n. of a samādhi: Mvy 538; ŚsP 1417.16.

anikṣipta-dhura, (**1**) adj. (= Pali anikkhittadhura), *not laying down the burden, persevering*: Bbh 203.21; Gv 514.18; °**ra-tā,** *state of being persevering*, AsP 287.15 etc.; (**2**) n. of a Bodhisattva: Mvy 719; SP 3.5; Kv 1.11 (text °dhūra); Sukh 92.12.

anikṣipta-bhāra = °**ta-dhura** (1), adj., q.v.: Mv i.95.10.

anigha, adj. (= Pali id., also anīgha), *free from evil* (? see **nigha, nīgha**); occurs chiefly (in Pali literature, aside from commentarial etymologies, only) in the neg. form; ep. of Buddha, or at least of perfected saints. In Pali often rendered *calm, unperturbed*, but it seems that *free from evil* (whether *sin*, pāpa, or *misery*, duḥkha) will suffice in all Pali and BHS occurrences. Regularly in lists of formulaic epithets which give little clue to a more precise mg.: LV 358.5; Mv ii.397.16; iii.400.2 (same vs in Pali Sn 534 with anigha); 418.14; Ud xxix.34; Gv 284.6.

an-icchantika-tā(-mokṣa), (salvation that consists in) *the state of not being* **icchantika** (q.v.): Laṅk 65.17.

aniñja = **aniñjya,** q.v.: sthito 'niñja-prāptena (but Kashgar rec. 'niñjya°) ca cittena SP 5.10; in ŚsP this is the spelling regularly found in ed., e.g. aniñjo nāma samādhiḥ 1418.22.

aniñjana, adj. (see **iñjana**; Pali id. only as noun, *immobility*, CPD), *immovable*: LV 250.16, of the 4th dhyāna (see under **aniñjya**): °na-cittā (n. sg. f.) Gv 279.9; °na-tā, *immobility*, AsP 206.2 °tām upādāya (referring to prajñāpāramitā).

an-iñjita, adj. (= Pali id.), *without vacillation* (see **iñjita**): °tā manyana-varjitāś ca (of dharmas) SP 282.1.

aniñjya: variants **āniñja, an°, āniñjya, ānijya, āneñj(y)a, an°,** qq.v. The nasalless ānijya occurs without v.l. only once and may be an accidental corruption (anusvāra omitted); but see § 2.73. The omission of y after j is called 'une orthographe prâcritisante' by Senart, Mv i.399; at any rate it occurs frequently in the mss. In Pali the same word is written ānejja, ānañja, āneñja, and with short initial a- (stigmatized as wrong reading in CPD); forms with i in the penult are very rare in Pali, but CPD records aniñja-ppatta once; this surely cannot be separated from the common āneñja- (ānejja-, ānañja-)-ppatta. BHS has no ānañj- or ānejj-, which are not infrequent in Pali. The wild variety of spellings in Pali itself shows that it early became an obscure word in the tradition. BHS occurrences of the spelling aniñjya include SP 161.10; Mvy 554, Śikṣ 237.1 (and 223.3, 4 in the ms.); perhaps Mv i.133.13 (Senart āniñjya, em., mss. mostly anīca [*not low*?], one animca, perhaps intending aniñj[y]a); either an- or ān- (uncertain because of saṃdhi) Mv i.228.11, 15; 229.6; ii.132.15 (here v.l. °nijya-). For examples of the other spellings see s.vv. There seems to be no difference in mg. between the various spellings; any of them may be an adj., *immobile, immovable*, or a nt. n., *immovability*. As adj., ānimjehi vihārehi Mv i.34.11; ii.419.11, *in immovable conditions*; ep. of citta Mv i.133.13 (see above on form); oftener °niñjyaprāpta, of citta, LV 344.6; Mv i.228.11, 15; 229.6; ii.132.15; aniñja-prāpta, of citta, SP 5.10; aniñjya-bhūta, of citta, SP 161.10; ānijyāṃ śāntim Av ii.199.5; aniñjyo (ŚsP aniñjo) nāma samādhiḥ Mvy 554; ŚsP 1418.22; virajasko (a)neñjyaś ca Mmk 476.14; clearly noun, āniñjyam Mvy 6387 = Tib. mi gyo ba, *not moving*; doubtless noun also in cpds. with -prāpta (Pali -ppatta) and -bhūta, above; apparently primarily adj. as third of a triad, the first two members of which are puṇya and apuṇya, or kuśala and akuśala; all three are applied to *deeds* (karman), or the *performance* or *accumulation* thereof (**abhisaṃskāra,** q.v.), or the *underlying conditions* (saṃskāra; cf. Śāl 81.5, abhisaṃskārārthena saṃskārāḥ), or finally the *states of existence* (dharmāḥ) to which such various acts lead as fruit. The first two, meritorious and demeritorious, relate to good and bad deeds as leading to rebirth in the kāmāvacara and (only good deeds) in the rūpāvacara states, or to these resulting states; the word aniñj(y)a, aneñj(y)a, or ā°, refers to deeds leading to rebirth in the arūpāvacara states, or to those states themselves (the dhyāna states), cf. Bbh 90.16 āniñjya-caturtha-dhyāna-vihāraḥ; on the subject in Pali see Warren, B. in Tr. 179 f. (from Vism.), and in general La Vallée-Poussin, note on MadhK 334.8; a good Pali passage is DN iii.217.25 tayo saṃkhārā, puññābhisaṃkhāro, apuññā°, āñanjā° (see Comm. iii.998.29). In BHS, Śāl 82.3–4 (cited Śikṣ 222.11–223.1) evam avidyāyāṃ satyāṃ trividhāḥ saṃskārā abhinivartante, puṇyopagā apuṇyo° āneñjyo° (Śikṣ āniñjyo°); Dbh 48.7 puṇyāpuṇyāneñjyān abhisaṃskārān; karmāṇi kuśalākuśalāneñjāni MadhK 334.7–8 (cf. 543.1 with note); (dharmāḥ) kuśalā vā 'kuśalā vā aniñjyā vā Śikṣ 237.1.

anidhārya, nt., Mvy 5206, a variant for **avivārya,** q.v. No Tib. or Chin. given; om. Mironov; Jap. *not to be repressed*. Doubtless a corruption.

Aninditā, n. of a pond: Gv 336.21, 25.

anibaddha-vacana (see pw s.v. anibaddha), *disconnected* (idle, frivolous) *talk*, as a sin: Mv i.145.9 = 202.6 = ii.6.3 viramāmi ... °nāc ca.

(**animitta,** adj., = Skt.; for technical Buddhist use see **śūnyatā, apraṇihita,** and **ānimitta.**)

Animiṣa, m., n. of a samādhi, acc. to Mvy 537 (same in Mironov); but Tib. tshol ba med pa, *not seeking*, shows that this is an error for **Aneṣa,** q.v., which is correctly read in the ŚsP version of this very list (taken from the 'Prajñāpāramitā' acc. to Mvy 505).

animiṣa-tā (= Pali °sa-tā), *condition of not winking*: indrasyānimiṣatena (instr.!) Divy 222.22 (prose).

Animiṣā, n. of a lokadhātu: Laṅk 105.9.

aniyata, m., (**1**) with or sc. dharma (= Pali id., with dhamma), one of the two sorts of possible transgressions of monks which are *undetermined* as to type of offense and consequent punishment, i. e. of which the punishment depends on circumstances (Pali Vin. iii.187–194; SBE 13.16 f.): dvāv aniyatau (sc. dharmau) Mvy 8382; dharmau Prāt 488.7; (**2**) aniyata-gotra, or aniyataikatara-g°, see s.v. **gotra** (1). See also s.v. **rāśi.**

Aniyavanta, n. of a brother of Mālinī and son of Kṛkin: °vanto nāma kumāro Mv i.313.1 (prose).

[**aniyūha,** error for **aniryūha**; see s.v. **anāyūha,** ŚsP 283.3.]

Aniruddha (rarely **Anu°**, q.v.; Pali only Anu°), one of Buddha's chief disciples, mentioned frequently with his brothers **Mahānāma(n)** and **Bhadrika** (**Bhaṭṭika**), as e.g. LV 229.13; Mvy 3608. Other occurrences: Mvy 1038; SP 2.3; 207.4 (v.l. Anu°); LV 1.15; Mv i.66.4; 75.1; Divy 182.21; 361.18; Jm 115.23; Av ii.67.9 ff.;

112.4; 134 1.12;99.3; Mmk 589.10; 595.23; Sukh 2.8; 92.8; Karmav 66.19; 76.17; 102.14; 154.16.

anirmuktaka (m. or nt.), one of a list of plant names (in a cpd.): Kv 8.5. Might be supposed to be a corruption for atimuktaka, but for the following, which seems a kind of confirmation.

anirmuktā (cf. prec.), n. of an herb (oṣadhi): °tā . . . tayā gṛhītayā sarvaparopakramabhayāni na bhavanti Gv 496.26.

aniryāṇa (cf. Pali aniyyāna, °nika), *not arriving at*, neg. of **niryāṇa**, q.v. (2): -anyayānāniryāṇa- Mvy 785 = Tib. (theg pa gzhan gyis) mi ḥgyur ba(r).

aniryūha, *without abandonment, riddance, withdrawal, giving up*; only in comp. with its opposite **anāyūha**, q.v. for references. See also **anirvyūha** and **niryūha**.

a-nirvāha, (1) m., *no 'exporting', giving* (of a girl) *in marriage* outside the clan: MSV ii.7.4 (kanyāyā) °haḥ; (2) Bhvr., *not subject to* this: ib. ii.17.7 kanyā anirvāhā.

anirvṛttamūlā, or °la, a kind of medicament (mahābhaiṣajyajāti) which is said to stimulate the growth of trees: Gv 497.16 (°lā nāma mahābhaiṣajyajātir), 18 (°la-mahābhaiṣajya-). Cf. **anivṛttamūla**.

anirvyūha = **aniryūha**: Dbh 47.13; see under **anāvyūha**, and cf. **nirvyūhati**.

Anilanama (!), n. of a Bodhisattva: Gv 443.3 (corrupt? read Anila-gamana?).

[**anilapaka**, see **nirlapaka**.]

a-nilambha (as if from an unrecorded ni-lambh), (1) adj., *independent* (Tib. on Mvy 619 brten pa med pa); as such, except in the next following cpds., only noted in Gv; sarvabhavānilambha-jñāna-gocarāḥ Gv 17.13; jñāne . . . anilambhe nirālaye 30.20; others 37.11, etc.; (2) as subst., n. of a samādhi, °bha-samādhi-pratilabdho SP 424.3, for which Tib. strangely: rluṅ (*wind, air*) lha buḥi (= devaputrasya), (samādhi) *of the wind-devaputra*, or *devaputra-wind*, as if cpd. of anila! (with what?); (3) n. of a kalpa: Gv 446.25. Cf. the following cpds.

Anilambhacakṣurvairocana, n. of a Tathāgata: Gv 81.10.

Anilambhacakṣus, n. of a Tathāgata: Gv 11.23 (as line numbers are printed; actually 24; 2d ed. line 22).

Anilambhaniketanirata, m., n. of a samādhi: Mvy 619; ŚsP 1425.22.

Anilambhamati, n. of a Bodhisattva: Gv 443.1.

Anilambhasunirmita, n. of a Bodhisattva: Gv 81.11.

Anilayajñāna, n. of a Bodhisattva: Gv 443.4.

Anilavegaś(i)rī, n. of a Buddha: Gv 285.11 (vs).

Anilaśrī, n. of a Bodhisattva: Gv 442.10.

anivarta, adj. (see s.v. **anivartiya**), *not liable to turning back*: Mv i.85.8 anivartādhyāśayāś, of Bodhisattvas in 2d bhūmi; resumed 87.10, 12 by anivart(i)ya-; °tayā śraddhayā Gv 367.2; samādhim anivartam LV 374.8 (vs; acc. to Foucaux, Notes 194, Tib., in a passage omitted in his ed. of Tib., gives equivalent of animittam, which he would adopt).

anivartana-caryā, *the course* or *stage* (of a Bodhisattva's development in which he is) *incapable of backsliding*, see **caryā**: Mv i.1.3; 2.1. See also **avivarta-**, and s.v. **anivart(i)ya**.

anivartika (= Pali anivattika; also = **anivartiya**, q.v. for other equivalents), *not liable to turning back*: Mv i.174.9 (vs) cakraṃ (i. e. dharma-c°) pravartesi anivartike (so mss., one °ko; Senart em. °kaṃ; perhaps keep the loc., *on the* (way) *that has no turning back*?). Cf. next.

Anivartikabala, n. of a former Buddha: Mv i.138.13. Cf. prec.

Anivartin, n. of a son of Māra (unfavorable to the Bodhisattva): LV 312.3. In Mv i.87.12 mss. anivartiyas or anavartayas (adhyāśayās), n. pl., which may indicate a stem anivarti(n) = Pali anivatti(n); Senart em. anivartiyās, n. pl. of **anivartiya**, q.v.

anivartiya, anivartya (= Pali anivattiya; in BHS the form in -tiya may be only m.c. for °tya, which mss. give in a prose occurrence; see also **anivarta**, **°tin**, **°tika**, and s.vv. **avivart(i)ya**, **avinivartya**, **avaivartika**, all equivalent in mg.), *not liable to turning back*: anivartyādhyāśayā Mv i.87.10 (prose; all mss.; Senart em. °tiyā°), of Bodhisattvas in 2d bhūmi; resumes anivartādhyāśayāś (see **anivarta**) of 85.8, and cf. 87.12, next passage; anivartiyās Mv i.87.12 (vs; Senart's em. for °tiyas, °tayas; see s.v. **anivartin**; n. pl., with adhyāśayāḥ); anivartiyā(ḥ) Mv i.102.6; 105.16 (both vss), of Bodhisattvas in 8th and succeeding bhūmis; Dbh.g. 10(346).17, of Bodhisattvas in 3d bhūmi; in prose Dbh 30.29 **avinivarta-**, q.v.; in Gv 331.3 read -yācanakasaṃtarpaṇānivartya-vīryavegaḥ or with 2d ed. °tarpaṇāvivartya° (1st ed. °paṇāni vartya°, °vegā).

Anividdhavarṇa (so some mss.; Senart em. Anāviddha°), n. of a former Buddha: Mv i.140.5. Most mss. read -ni-, none -nā-.

anivṛttamūla, n. of a medicament: °la-mahābhaiṣajya-rāja-bhūtaṃ Gv 494.26. Cf. **anirvṛttamūlā**.

[**aniścara**, *unswerving, steady*: so 'niścareṇa hṛdayena suniścitena kṣipraṃ prayātu Divy 130.1. But Mr. D. R. S. Bailey kindly informs me that Tib. reads ḥjigs med = nirbhayena.]

aniśrita (= Pali anissita), *unattached, free, independent, emancipated* (esp. from worldly things): Mvy 2352 = Tib. mi gnas pa, *without fixed abode*, or, mi brten pa, *without dependence, independent*. (Regularly misunderstood by older interpreters; correctly Senart Mv i note 456 *détaché*; *sans attache aux choses terrestres*.) SP 92.7; 276.7, 10; 279.10; Mv i.167.11 (of Buddha); LV 250.17 (of dhyāna); RP 16.3 (of Bodhisattvas); Dbh 24.14 (cited Śikṣ 126.11) of the speech of Bodhisattvas (so also of speech in Pali, *unworldly* CPD: SN ii.280.8 = AN ii.51.17 anissitāya, AN comm. iii.90.10 vaṭṭaṃ anissitāya, *independent of the world*); Bbh 303.15 aniśrita-dānatā; Gv 472.8 sarvopapatty-aniśrita-vihāriṇaś ca; Gv 473.10; in Mv i.165.20, a corrupt and difficult passage, read aniśritā(ḥ) with mss.

aniṣṭhā-pada, apparently intended at Laṅk 180.17 (text anadhiṣṭhāpada) and 227.4 (text aṣṭāpada); Tib. thug pa med paḥi gnas. Suzuki transl. *inexhaustible vows*; rather, *unlimited terms*; S. uses the same transl. for **niṣṭhā-pada**, q.v. It seems, indeed, that these two formally opposite expressions, *unlimited term* and *fundamental term*, are virtual synonyms. Cf. Dbh 17.9, where each of the 10 niṣṭhā is specifically said to be aniṣṭhā (the trick seems to lie in different uses of niṣṭhā: the *fundament, basis* is said to be *without end or limit, end* being also a mg. of niṣṭhā).

a-niḥsaraṇa, adj. and subst. (cf. Pali a-nissaraṇa; see **niḥs°**), *not being* (or as Bhvr. *not having*; sc. a means of) *salvation*: sarve te bhavā aniḥsaraṇā (so mss., Senart ś for s) ti vademi Mv ii.418.8; aniḥsaraṇa-niḥsaraṇa-saṃjñino Dbh 28.17 *imagining what is not* (a means of) *salvation to be one*; similarly, aniḥśaraṇe niḥśaraṇabuddhiḥ Laṅk 145.6; °ṇa-tā, *state* or *fact of not being* or *having* (a means of) *salvation*, LV 244.5.

aniḥsṛta (= Pali anissaṭa; cf. **a-niḥsaraṇa**), *not freed* (religiously, from the bonds of existence): Mv iii.345.6 °tā asārā ca (skandhāḥ).

Anihata, n. of a Buddha: Mv i.123.17.

Anihatatejas (text Nihata°, after -o), n. of a Bodhisattva: Gv 443.6.

Anihatamalla, n. of a Bodhisattva: Gv 442.6.

Anihatavarṇa (? mss. mostly Anihita°), n. of a former Buddha: Mv i.141.5.

Anihitamati (read Anihata°? but cf. prec.), n. of a Bodhisattva: Gv 443.1.

Anihīnārtha, n. of a Bodhisattva: Gv 443.2.

an-ītika (= Pali id.; from īti), *free from evils* (cf. Skt. nirītika): °kām, acc. sg. f., Gv 418.16.

an-īrṣu (cf. next; Skt. īrṣu, considered by BR error for īrṣyu), *not jealous*: Mv ii.368.2.

an-īrṣuka (= prec.; cf. Pali anissuki-n, id.), *not jealous*: Mv ii.363.7; SP 284.11; 285.6; LV 26.19 (prose); 28.14.

1 **anu**, indecl. in noun and verb cpds.; (a) in distributive (? or intensive) noun cpds., as in Pali, CPD s.v. anu (g); also in JM, e.g. gāmāṇugāmaṃ Jacobi Erz. 13.2; rare in Skt., 'typical in Buddh.', Renou, Gr. scte. p. 94: divasānudivasaṃ, adv., *day after day*, Av i.208.10; 261.14; see **kālānukālam, kṣudrānukṣudra, kṣudrakānukṣudraka, anucāra, anudharma**; but the usage is not always clear and the last-named, at least, prob. does not belong here; (b) in verb cpds. used in many cases which have no parallels in Skt., nor (often) even in Pali or Pkt.; usually before other preverbs. See the following entries in this work. Very often it is hard to see any definite meaning which anu adds; Tib. in its wooden way renders by rjes su, *after*, which as Jäschke says 'is often not to be translated'.

2 **anu** = Skt. aṇu, *subtle*; subst. *atom*. So often spelled in Pali; acc. to CPD false reading. Cf. LV 261.18 anumātraṃ, all mss., only Calc. aṇu°, = Pali Sn 431 aṇumattena (v.l. anu°), adv., *even the least bit.*

[**anukampa**, read °pya, *to be pitied*: Laṅk 6.14 anukampo (read °pyo) 'si... sugatānāṃ, *you have the compassion of the Sugatas* (Suzuki).]

anukuṭṭaka, *abusing, reviling*: °kāḥ SP 272.12 (v.l. **parikuṭṭ°**, q.v.).

anukūla-yajña, adj. Bhvr. (Pali °yañña), *presenting an appropriate* or *agreeable offering* (to monks): MSV iv.139.3. Pali also anukula°, acc. to CPD the correct form; but Tib. mthun ba = anukūla.

anukūle, adv. (= Pali id.; Skt. and Pali anukūlam), plus gen., *on the bank*: yasyā (nadyā) anukūle Karmav 34.15.

anukṣamati, *endures, puts up with*: °masva Jm 165.12; caus. °kṣamāpayati, *asks forgiveness*: °payiṣyaṃ, 1 sg. fut., Mv ii.213.16; °petvā iii.44.6; °pito ppp. iii.363.11; °pitā id. f. iii.27.13.

(**anukhanati**,) **anukhaneti** (Pali anukhaṇe, opt.), *digs near* or the like: nyagrodhapotaṃ... anukhaneti Mv iii.301.16.

anugantī? Divy 507.15 Panthakasyānugantī moktavyā; Index *message*, suggesting reading anugantrī.

anugaveṣate (AMg. aṇugavesai), *searches for* (acc.): °ṣamāṇaḥ (bhikṣum) Gv 59.8.

anugīta-, adj., ppp. (Skt. and Pali id., not recorded in this sense), *sung in conformity with* (a preceding passage): anugīta-gāthā Mv i.42.5 (repeating an episode just told in prose).

anuguṇin, adj. (= Skt. and Pali °ṇa), *appropriate, conformable*: f. °ṇinī, Divy 592.1.

anuguṇya, nt. (cf. Skt. ānu°), *conformability, compatibility*: Mvy 2673 = Tib. rjes su mthun pa.

Anugravarṇakṣemagupta, n. of a former Buddha: Mv i.140.10 (prose; to be read as two names?).

Anugrahacandra, n. of a Bodhisattva: Gv 443.5.

Anugrahamati, n. of a Bodhisattva: Gv 443.5.

anucaṅkramyati, °te, more commonly **°kramati, °te** (= Pali anucaṅkamati; cf. **caṅkramati**), *wanders along*: °myamāṇa, pres. pple., LV 128.18; 248.7; °mati, Suv 184.3; 186.4 (here best ms. °myati); °māmi SP 55.1; °manti SP 84.8; pres. pple., n. m. °manto SP 61.10; Mv i.353.12; ii.45.5; 457.15; f. °mantī Mv ii.452.3; 454.10; acc. °mantaṃ Mv iii.117.6; n.m. °man Suv 185.2; n. pl. °māṇā(ḥ) Sukh 58.11; aor. 3 pl. °metsuḥ Mv iii.283.1, 6; ger. °mitvā Mv ii.455.16; 456.21.

anucalati, *follows, cleaves to*, ppp. °lita: satkāyadṛṣṭir asyānucalitā bhavati KP 134.8, *is attached, cleaves to him.*

anucāra? only in cārānucāra-prayoga-nimittāni, Dbh 45.28, in a list of signs and omens, perhaps *omens derived from various manners of walking* (cāra), see 1 **anu**, distributive cpd.?

anucālin, adj. (cf. **anucalati** and Pali anucārin), *following after*: °libhir Laṅk 11.3.

anucira, adj., *continuously* or *successively long* (time): read with mss. in Mv i.126.7 nanu anucireṇa kālena sarvasattvān parinirvāpayiṣyanti, (if as you say many Buddhas all bring countless creatures to nirvāṇa,) *in the course of continued time they will bring all creatures to it.* Senart em. acireṇa, *in a short time*; but the text means rather *in a sufficiently long time.*

anucīrṇa, ppp. (= Pali anuciṇṇa, act. and pass.), *following, having followed* or *practised*; (pass.) *followed, practised*: Mv ii.401.1 (act., śākyottamaṃ): 403.9 (pass., caritāṃ, mss., Senart em. cariyāṃ... anucīrṇāṃ, v.l. °ṇaṃ).

an-uccalana- (nt.; Skt. uccalana, see Schmidt, Nachtr., not in this sense), *non-departure*: Gv 242.12 anuccalanāgamana-vikramaṃ kalyāṇamitropasaṃkramaṇam adhyatiṣṭhat; 525.11 sarvatathāgata-pāda-mūlānuccalana-tayā.

an-uccāvaca, adj. (= Pali id.), *not various*; *unvarying, unchanging, equable*: Mv i.176.6 °ca-darśanā(ḥ), of Buddhas.

anujava (m.? cf. **anujavati, °vana**), (swift) *pursuit; swift motion, swiftness, speed*: Śikṣ 28.4 °va-saṃpannān, of horses; Gv 222.22–23 cittakṣaṇa-dharmadhātu-spharaṇānujavānāṃ (bodhisattvānāṃ), *possessing swiftness in penetrating the dharma-element in a moment of thought.*

anujavati (= Pali id.; Chap. 43, s.v. ju), *runs after, pursues* (cf. **anujava, °vana**): mṛgam °vati Mv ii.212.17; °vanto n. sg. m. pres. pple., ii.217.6; °vitvā i.321.6; °vitum, inf., Gv 400.7 (prose).

anujavana, (nt.? cf. **anujava, anujavati**), *pursuit, chasing after*, in śvaloṣṭv-anujavana-sadṛśa, *like a dog's chasing a clod* (thrown at him, instead of the thrower), KP 105.2 (text °loṣṭvānu°, by error), 3 (here text °loṣṭānu°, which could be kept, with Skt. loṣṭa for loṣṭu); 106.8; 107.1, 5; the simile is clearly explained in KP 105; also (sarvadiksamudra)-prasarānujavanena Gv 242.19.

an-ujjuka, adj. (= Pali id.; cf. **ujju, ujjuka**), *crooked, perverted*: read anujjuko in Mv ii.481.1 (mss. antarjjuko) = iii.16.9 (mss. anujjako, anurjjako); proved by Pali form of the same vs, Jāt. v.293.22, which reads anujjubhūtena (comm. anujjukena cittena).

-anujñā, in **lokānujñā** Mv i.78.17, one of the 8 **samudācāra** (q.v., 1) of Bodhisattvas in the 1st bhūmi. Senart p. xxvii *l'adieu au monde.* But if I am right in relating this list to the 10 bhūmipariśodhakā dharmāḥ of Dbh p. 19 (sec. UU), see esp. lines 20–23, it must correspond to lokajñatā, see Dbh 19.12–15; *knowledge of* (the varying traits of) *people.* The Mv may even contain a corruption of lokajñatā; equally bad corruptions occur often in its mss.

anujñātāvin (§ 22.51), *having understood*: durvijñeyadharmānujñātāvinaḥ SP 29.6.

anutaṭa (in Skt. °ṭam, adv., and °ṭa- in comp., *along the bank*), pl., *parts along the slope* (of a mountain): girivarasya (himavataḥ) anutaṭehi gatā Mv ii.107.9 (Senart's reading; conjectural but fairly plausible).

anutapyana, nt. (= Pali anutappana), or **°nā**, f., *regretting, repenting*, in Bhvr. cpd. an-anutapyanākāraṃ Śikṣ 191.2.

anutapyanīya, adj. or nt. subst., (a matter that is) *to be regretted* or *lamented*, (a) *lamentable* (thing); could be considered gdve. of anutapyate; cf. also **anutapyana**: tato °yaṃ bhavet Mv iii.74.4.

anutarṣa (Skt. Lex.), *desire, longing*: pradānānutarṣa-Jm 39.18.

anutāpya, gdve., *to be repented*: an-anutāpya-dāyī Bbh 274.20, *giving* (things) *which he is not going to repent.*

an-utkarṣaṇa-tā, see **utkarṣaṇa**.

anuttara, adj. (= Pali id.; cf. **sottara**; Skt. in this sense only Lex., replaced by anuttama, which has had its ending assimilated to superlatives owing to the mg. of the word), *having no superior, highest, supreme*: AsP 266.13, of cittāni; Gv 244.7 °rāṃ tathāgatavarṇaviśuddhiṃ; LV 24.13 °ra-parivāraṃ (kulaṃ); 85.2 anuttaro bhaviṣyāmi sarvasattvānām; Divy 144.5 anuttare-manuṣyadharme (see s.v. **uttari-**, end); esp. epithet of samyaksaṃbodhi, SP 100.3; AsP 293.10; Vaj 24.2; LV 183.17; Laṅk 148.3 etc., etc., extremely common (see under **abhisaṃbudhyate**); m. as epithet of a Buddha, Mvy 9; as n. of a samādhi, Kv 52.3; f. with ellipsis of samyaksaṃbodhi (see above), SP 216.8 (prose) °rāṃ samyaksaṃbuddhaḥ samāno, *being enlightened unto supreme* (enlightenment); normally the noun samyaksaṃbodhiṃ follows anuttarāṃ in this common phrase; has it dropped out by haplography? (WT same text).

Anuttararāja, n. of a Bodhisattva: Gv 443.7.

Anuttaraśrī, n. of a Bodhisattva: Gv 443.8.

[**anuttarāyo**, LV 219.22 (vs), both edd. without v.l., but can only be corruption for anantarāyo, *without obstacle*; so Foucaux, with Tib. (bar chad with negative).]

an-uttarika, opposite of **uttarika**, q.v.

anuttarya, nt. (= Pali °riya; also ān°; CPD regards an° as w.r. for ān°), *excellence, supremacy*; they number six, Mvy 1573–79: darśana, śravaṇa, lābha, śikṣā, paricaryā, **anusmṛti** (each cpd. with anut°). A corresponding list in Pali, see PTSD s.v. anuttariya. A different one is nivāsānuttarya, Mv iii.320.5, see s.v. **nivāsa**; here ānutt° may have been intended.

an-u(t)traṣṭa, neg. ppp. (= Skt. °sta), *not frightened*: °ṣṭāḥ LV 12.16 (both edd., no v.l.; § 2.61).

an-uttrāsa, adj. (= Pali anutrāsa; see **uttrāsa**), *without fear, not frightened*: Śikṣ 176.5.

an-uttrāsita, neg. ppp., *not frightened*: °sitāsaṃtrastā Mv i.177.4.

anutpattika-dharma-kṣānti, *intellectual receptivity* (see **kṣānti**) *to the truth that states of existence have no origination* (utpatti); also **anutpāda-kṣānti**, q.v.: SP 136.10 (read with v.l. °ttika- for °ttikīṃ dh° of both edd.); 266.1; 327.4; 419.6; 437.1; LV 35.21; 440.21; Dbh 47.21; 64.5; Śikṣ 212.13–14; Bbh 348.18; Sukh 55.13; Laṅk 12.9; anutpattika-kṣānti, omitting dharma, Gv 525.25; the cpd. is analyzed as anutpattikeṣu dharmeṣu kṣānti(-pratilambho 'bhūt) LV 36.9, °ttikeṣu dharmeṣu kṣāntir AsP 408.8. The expression was misunderstood by older interpreters, e.g. Burnouf and Kern on SP 136.10.

anutpāda (m., Skt., and Pali anuppāda), *non-origination*: anutpāde kṣāntiḥ Laṅk 203.11, and cpd. **anutpāda-kṣānti-** LV 33.10, = prec., q.v.; anutpāda-jñāna, *knowledge of the non-origination* (of the states of being), the 10th of the ten jñāna: Mvy 1243; Dharmas 93.

anutsada, adj., substantially = **anutsanna** (neg. of Skt. utsanna, *lofty*; Pali anussada not defined in this sense), *not excessive, not over-full*: Mv iii.343.4, of Buddha's voice (immediately follows anutsanna); Bbh 252.16–17 niṣkaṣāyānutsadakaṣāya-kāla-tāṃ *state of times that are free from impurities, or have moderate* (not excessive) *impurities*.

anutsanna, neg. ppp. (= Pali anussanna; cf. prec., **utsadana** 2, and Skt. utsanna, *stärker als normal*, pw s.v. ud-sad), *not excessive* (in extent, number, or the like; cf. **anutsada**): Mv iii.343.4 °naś ca, of the Buddha's voice, *not excessive(ly loud), not too full*; Mv ii.43.12, read anutsanna-gātrā (mss. quoted anusanta; Senart em. anusandhi), *limbs not excessive* (too many), one (29th in my list) of the **anuvyañjana**, q.v.; corresponding to Pali anussannāsannasabbagattatā (CPD), *condition of having all his limbs not too many nor deficient*.

an-utsṛjana-tā (see **utsṛjana**), *non-abandonment, not getting rid* (of, gen.): Śikṣ 183.9, dharmachandasya.

anudadhyamāna (? v.l. anubadhy°; irregular pres. pple. of pass. of *anu-dadhati = anudadhāti, not recorded in this mg.), *being presented* (Tib. dus kyis bstabs pa [see Das], which seems to mean *given in timely manner*): Bbh 163.2. Very doubtful; § 37.37.

anudarśa (? v.l. °śī, i. e., n. sg. of °śin), *viewing, consideration*, in kāyānu°-smṛtyupasthāna (see this), and vedanānu°, cittānu°, dharmānu°: Dharmas 44 (replacing the usual **anupaśyanā**, or °paśyī to °**paśyin**).

an-udāhāra, see **udāhāra**.

anudeśana (nt., = Skt. anudeśa, rare), *instruction*: Mmk 133.2 (vs) dattadharmānudeśanam.

an-uddhata (= Pali id.; *not violent or rough*, or *not agitated*, or, as in Skt., *not haughty*), *calm, gentle*, particularly of speech, as also in Pali: Mv i.166.3 anuddhatāṃ ... girā (acc.; Senart em. girāṃ); Mv iii.280.17 acapalā anuddhatā ca, of speech (read so in same line Mv ii.356.11; Pali also associates acapala with this word); Bbh 239.1 anuddhatācapala-kāya-vāṅ-manaḥ-karmānta-pracāraḥ. See **anuddhṛta**.

an-uddhṛta (= prec., q.v., for which this appears to be a hyper-Sktism), (**1**) adj. *calm, gentle*, or *not proud, not haughty*: Gv 484.26 (vs) bodhimārga (acc.) ... tvaṃ anuddhṛto mārgase dṛḍhamate atandritaḥ; (**2**) nt., n. of a buddhakṣetra: Mv i.124.9 (vs; mss. unmetr. anudhṛtaṃ).

anudrakṣi, 3 sg. aor., *looked at*: Mv ii.54.3. See Chap. 43, s.v. dṛś (3).

anudruta(-lipi), v.l. anupadruta-, read perhaps an uddruta-, or adruta-, *not hurried* (?), a kind of writing: LV 126.6. Tib. riṅs med, *not hurried, not speedy*.

anudhanvana (nt., n. act. in -ana from anu-dhanvati, recorded only RV 2.5.3), *pursuit, running after*: Śikṣ 33.4 -anudhanvana-tayā.

anudharma (= Pali anudhamma). Acc. to PTSD, Pali dhammānudhamma is used as a distributive or intensive cpd., see under 1 **anu**, *the Law in all its parts*; while Childers understands anudh° as *lesser or inferior dhamma* (against which see Lévi on Sūtrāl. xiii.1 comm.). Acc. to CPD anudhamma means (*right*) *method* and is a 'hypostasis of anu-dhammaṃ' (adv., *in accordance with dhamma*). In BHS (as also in Pali, e.g. Dhp. 20) there is some evidence suggesting that dharmānudharma is equivalent to dharmasya anu°, perhaps *the true method of the law* or the like: Bbh 284.1 na pratipadyante dharmasyānudharmam, *they do not attain* (? *practise*) *the anudh° of the dh°*; 197.16 dharmasyānudharmaṃ pratipadyamānasya (sc. Bodhisattvasya; not agreeing with dharmasya, which depends on anudh°); Gv 383.5 dharmasya cānudharmaṃ pratipadye, *and I attain* (? *practise*) *the anudh° of the dh°*. Without dharma in the context, we find anudharma-cārin Divy 617.16 (°riṇī, f.), anudharma-praticārin Mvy 1123 (°rī). So we should probably interpret all cpds. of dharmānudharma-, which usually parallel the like cpds. in Pali: dharmānudharma-cārin Dbh 32.21; °rma-pratipatti, *attainment* (? *practice*) *of the anudh° of the dh°* Mvy 1801 (mss. erroneously omit dharma after anu; em. Kyoto ed.); Dbh 33.29; Bbh 204.7; KP 9.2; LV 32.16; °rma-pratipanna Bbh 84.4; LV 179.12; 377.14; Mvy 1124. In Mvy 9321 are mentioned ṣaḍ anudharmāḥ, after 9320 ṣaḍ dharmāḥ; so also Bhīk 16b.4 ṣaṭsu dharmeṣu ṣaṭsv anudharmeṣu śikṣā; in neither place do I find any clue to what the six anudharma (or dharma) are. I have not noted any adv. anudharmaṃ (parallel to Pali anudhammaṃ).

Anudharmamati, n. of a Bodhisattva: Gv 443.8.

?**anudharmya**, adj. (cf. Pkt. anudhammiya; not in Pali), *conformable to religion*: Bbh 61.23, v.l. anudharmyayā (for text ānudhārmyā, see **ānudhārma**) kathayā, instr.

-anudhāra, adj., f. -ī, *bearing, holding* (*in attendance*? anu): Divy 513.25 -vilepanānudhārī (f.).

anudhārayati (cf. Pali °dhāreti), *upholds, maintains*: Gv 484.11 buddhavaṃśam anudhārayiṣyasi.

-anudhārin, adj., *keeping, holding fast to*: Gv 222.22 sarvabuddhakathānudhāriṇāṃ (gen. pl.).

anudhyāpita, ppp. of caus. of Skt. anu-dhyā, lit. *caused to think on* or *long for* = *made interested in, concerned with*, with loc.: Mv iii.119.(18–)19 (na cīvare śayane bhojane vā) anudhyāpitā bhonti jinā.

anudhvaṃsana, nt. (= Pali anuddhaṃ°), *false charge* or *accusation* (see next two): Mvy 9404 = Tib. (b)skur, *abuse.*

anudhvaṃsayati, °**seti** (= Pali anuddhaṃseti; see prec. and next), *falsely accuses* (with, on the ground of, instr.): abhūtenābrahmacaryaṃvādena (mss.) *with a false charge of unchastity* Mv i.36.13 °seti; 37.7 °sito, ppp.; pārājikena dharmeṇa °sayet Prāt 481.7; (amūlakena ... dharmeṇa) °sayet 519.8.

anudhvaṃsayitar (cf. prec. two), (false) *accuser*: Prāt 481.9 °tā, n. sg.

anunaya, m. (= Pali id.; also Skt. in mg. *propitiation, das Geneigtmachen*; *friendliness, affection*, in favorable or at least neutral sense), *love, attachment*; *ingratiation*, in BHS almost invariably in a bad sense (a rare exception is Divy 510.4, of innocent *attachment, affection*). Very often contrasted with **pratigha,** q.v.; the pair may replace rāga and dveṣa, as feelings to be avoided; so in dvandva cpd. anunaya-pratigha- (Pali also anunaya-paṭigha), LV 10.1; 33.7; 275.6–7; 374.3, (read) ihānunaya-pratighānāṃ kalvahaivādaprahāṇaparyantaḥ prāpto mayā, *here I have got to the end—which consists of abandonment of quarrels and disputes—of attachment and repugnance*; 442.5; Divy 240.24; KP 101.1; Mmk 13.22; Dbh 29.6; also, less commonly, pratighānunaya (Pali also paṭi°) Sādh 115.15; Gv 245.24; without pratigha, anunaya (undesirable) *attachment* or *lust* is contrasted with maitrī, (desirable) *affection*, (pure) *love* in Gv 472.3–4 ye te maitrīvihāriṇaś ca na kvacid anunayavihāriṇaḥ; in Gv 351.24 perhaps contrasted with **pratighāta,** q.v. (viṣaya-raty-)anunayo vā pratighātacittatā vā; Divy 257.20 anunaya-vacanair, *with words of* (impure sexual) *love* (spoken by a mother to her son with whom she had incestuous relations); LV 319.21 (yadi) tāvac chakyetāyam anunayenotthāpayitum, (Māra speaks:) *whether he can be moved by lust* (for women; M. is sending his daughters to tempt the Bodhisattva); anunayāsaṃdhukṣaṇatā (Mvy °saṃdhukṣ°, v.l. and Mironov °saṃpṛkṣ°), *state of not being inflamed with* (sexual) *lust* Mvy 2594; LV 32.7; anunaya-nimittaṃ SP 277.1 *a cause* (or motive) *for ingratiating oneself* (with women; should be avoided by a Bodhisattva); Mvy 2131 = Tib. rjes su chags pa, *affection towards*; visabhāgasattvānunayāt Śikṣ 193.17, see **visabhāga.**

Anunaya-gātra (! perhaps corrupt), n. of a Bodhisattva: Gv 443.8.

Anunaya-vigata, n. of a Bodhisattva: Gv 443.1.

anunāthanā (to anunāthayati, see BR 5.1541; the verb also occurs in Sādh 199.12; 231.3; 493.5), *entreaty*: Sādh 446.7.

anunāma (m.?; n. act. from *anu-nāmayati), (lit. *bending, bringing under control,*) *training*: AsP 54.11 paridamanāya ... anunāmāya bodhisattvānāṃ.

anuniścara, adj. (to *anu-niś-carati), *coming forth successively*: LV 13.4 (vs) saṃgīti-ravānuniścarā gāthā (so more likely than °ravānu = °ravānāṃ, gen. pl., which would give a forced construction).

anunīya-tā, *state of needing to be conciliated* (based on gdve. of anu-nī; cf. Whitney 963b,2); SP 128.9 (vs) °tā mahya na kācid asti, *and there is no need of conciliating me.*

anunīyate, *follows upon*: ... vijñānaṃ nānuśete tan (acc.) nānunīyate Samy. Āg. 1.3.1 (and ff.).

an-unnaḍa, an-unnata, an-unnamana, an-unnahana-tā, see **unn°.**

an-upakruṣṭa, adj. (= Pali anupakkuṭṭha; cf. Skt. upakruṣṭa, *a low-caste man*; *a carpenter*), *blameless*: Mv i.133.17 anupakruṣṭa-vṛtti-dvārāḥ, *means of* (instruments of attaining) *blameless livelihood*, of Bodhisattvas; i.177.2 °ṣṭa-cāraṇā; Gv 526.14 jātigotreṇa anupakruṣṭo bhavati (bodhisattvaḥ).

Anupagamanāman, n. of a Bodhisattva: Gv 443.6.

an-upaghātya, adj. (neither this nor upa° recorded in Skt., Pali, or Pkt.), *invulnerable*: °tya-śarīro Gv 505.13.

an-upacchinna, neg. ppp. (= Pali id.; cf. **upacchinatti**), *uninterrupted*: Mv i.171.10 (of Buddha's speech).

Anupacchinnālambha, n. of a former Buddha: Mv i.141.10.

an-upaccheda (m.; = Pali id.; cf. **upaccheda, anupacchinna**), *the not cutting off*: LV 34.17 triratnavaṃśānupa°; 137.3 cakravartivaṃśasya; Gv 260.19 buddhavaṃśānupacchedāya.

an-upacchedana (nt.), cf. **upa°**, *the not cutting off*: LV 5.22 triratnavaṃśasyānupacchedanārthaṃ. See prec. and next.

an-upacchedana-tā = prec.: LV 440.21 (triratnavaṃś-)ānupa°; Mmk 23.2 (paramantrānup°), 9 (triratnaprasādānup°), etc.; Gv 280.2 (bodhisattvacaryānup°).

anupadruta-lipi? see **anudruta-.**

an-upadhi-śeṣa, adj. (= **nir-upadhi°**, q.v.; = Pali an-upādi-sesa), *free from upadhi* = *skandha*, ep. of nirvāṇa(-dhātu), i. e. *absolute, complete*: °śeṣa- (ŚsP 1264.16, misprinted anupari°) or °śeṣe (SP 21.9; 411.5; ŚsP 1450.4; AsP 152.8, here misprinted anupavi°) nirvāṇadhātau.

an-upadhīka (= Pali id.; in both ī m.c.), *free from the* **upadhi,** q.v., or *bonds attaching to existence*: °kaṃ Mv iii.445.2 (em.) = (same vs in Pali) Vin. i.36.26.

an-upanāha, see **upanāha.**

anupanthake, adv. (= Pali anupanthe), *along the road*: Mv ii.423.13 (a)nupanthake viya drumo (mss.); iii.184.5 (a var. of same vs), mss. °kā (or °ka) viya drumā (°kā could be kept as n. pl. of adjective).

anupamacitta, adj. or subst. m., *person of matchless mind*; sixty such, of whom Mañjuśrī is the first, attend on the Buddha: RP 2.2.

Anupamamati, (**1**) n. of a **satpuruṣa,** q.v.: SP 4.1; (**2**) n. of a Bodhisattva: ŚsP 6.21.

Anupamarakṣita, n. of a sthavira and author: Sādh 62.6; 206.22.

Anupamā, n. of the daughter of Mākandika (in Pali called Māgandiyā): Divy 515.22 ff.

anuparikṣipta, ppp., *surrounded*, as with strings of jewels, rows of trees, walls: LV 278.16; RP 39.18; Gv 161.17, 19; 163.8; Sukh 36.3.

anuparigaṇikā, instr. °kayā, adverbially used, *with successive enumeration*, going around the whole circle (of the order of nuns): Bhīk 10a.4.

anuparigṛhṇīte (cf. **anuparigraha,** °**grāhikayā**; no such cpd. in Skt. or Pali, but substantially = pari-g° in various senses; forms noted are °gṛhṇīte, ger. °gṛhya, ppp. °gṛhīta, gdve. °grahītavya): (**1**) *surrounds in attendance, closely waits upon*, LV 82.2 anuparigṛhītā (Māyā, by soldiers etc.); AsP 34.(13–)14 (asmābhir api bodhisattvā) ... anuparigrahītavyā anuparivārayitavyāś ca (similarly in line 16 anuparigṛhītāḥ); (**2**) *holds in the arms, embraces closely*, LV 103.9 kumāram ubhābhyāṃ pāṇibhyāṃ sādhu ca suṣṭhu cānuparigṛhya; Śikṣ 155.2 glānaṃ bhikṣuṃ sādhu ca suṣṭhu cānuparigṛhya bahirdhā nīharitvā (see this) snāpayet; Divy 116.11 sarvāṅgair anuparigṛhya; 387.5 and 388.13 sarvāṅgenānuparigṛhya; (**3**) *cultivates, devotes oneself to, tends, favors*, AsP 463.9–10 (yo ... prajñāpāramitāṃ) pralujyamānām anuparigṛhṇīte .. buddhānāṃ ... tena bodhir anuparigṛhītā bhavati;

Gv 356.8–9 samanvāhṛtāḥ (see this) smaḥ tathāgatena, anuparigṛhītāḥ smaḥ sugatena (said to a Tathāgata in welcome on his arrival), *the T. has turned his attention to us, the S. has bestowed his gracious favor on us.*

anuparigraha (m.; see prec.), (**1**) *the embracing* (*in one whole*), *uniting*: Śāl 77.17 f. yaḥ kāyasyānuparigraha-kṛtyaṃ karoty ayam ucyate 'b-dhātuḥ, *what does the work of embracing-in-a-unit the body is called the element water,* and so 78.14 (these are cited Śikṣ 220.14, where text °parigrahaṃ kṛtyaṃ, and 221.6; Tib. lus sdud pa, *body-uniting*); (**2**) *tending, cultivating, favoring*: LV 5.(21–)22 (saddharmasya) cānuparigrahārthaṃ, triratnavaṃśasy-ānuparigrahārthaṃ.

anuparigrāhikayā, adv. (instr. sg. f. of *anuparigrāhaka, *helping,* to °**gṛhṇīte,** q.v., mg. 3), *in a favoring, gracious way*: SP 283.2 °kayā **anabhyasūyikayā** (q.v.) dharmaṃ deśayati. So read with WT and their ms. K′; KN °hikā without v.l.

anuparicarati, *follows in attendance*: ger. °caritvā Mv iii.155.16.

anuparindanā (to °**dāmi**; cf. **parindanā**), *the giving over, presenting*: °nārthaṃ LV 443.11; Dbh.g. 56(82).25 (prose, not vs). See also **anuparīndanā.**

anuparindāmi (= **pari**°, q.v.), *I present, hand over*: °āmi SP 420.12; 484.5; LV 91.8; 443.9; Dbh.g. 56(82).5 (prose, not vs); fut. °iṣyāmo LV 90.22. Also **anuparīn**°, q.v.

anuparipāṭikayā, adv. (instr. sg. f. of *°ṭikā, cf. Skt. anuparipāṭi-krama, pw s.v.), *in regular order, in turn*: Av ii.11.1; Bbh 92.26.

anuparipālayati, *protects*: Mvy 7386; AsP 275.2.

anuparimārjati (or °**jayati**?), *touches lightly*: aor. °mārje Mv ii.282.6–7 (pāṇinā ... śiram); ger. °mārjya (mukhatuṇḍakena ca pādāv anu°, in token of profound respect) Divy 387.7; 400.18–19.

anuparivartati, °**te** (= Pali °vattati), *moves along, after,* or *according to*; *follows* (with or without acc.): °tanti (so read with 2 mss., Senart °tayanti) Mv i.25.9; brāhmaṇapariṣāya kriyā °titavyā Mv i.310.6, and kriyām °tantasya 8; (bodhisattvam) °tetsuḥ (aor.) Mv ii.264.18 f.; 400.4 ff.; (utsaṅgenotsaṅgam, acc. to Tib. *from lap to lap,* paṅ ba nas paṅ ba dag tu, in the harem) °tamānāḥ (devadārakāḥ) LV (76.20–)77.1; in LV 278.16 for Lefm. anuparivṛtair read, with the only mss. which have the word at all, (ratnasūtraiḥ samantād) anuparivṛttaiḥ (°ttair) anuparikṣiptaṃ (bodhivṛkṣam), *surrounded by strings of jewels that passed all around it* (ppp. with active meaning as regularly with intrans. verbs of motion).

anuparivartana, adj., f. °**nī** (Pali °vattana, nt., n. act.; from prec.), *moving after* or *according to, following*: Dbh 75.1; satyānuparivartanī (vāc) Gv 455.1 (possibly read °tinī, in agreement with LV 440.3; Mv ii.197.10, see next).

-anuparivartin, adj. in comp. (= Pali °vattin; from °vartati), *moving after* or *according to, following*: jñānānuparivarti(n) (= Pali ñāṇānuparivatti-n) LV 435.3–4; id., in list of āveṇika buddhadharmāḥ, Mv i.160.10 f.; Mvy 148–150; ŚsP 1450.10 f.; cittānu° (= Pali °vatti-n) Mvy 2168; satyānuparivarti-vāk- LV 440.3; °vartinyā ... girā Mv ii.197.10; perhaps read °vartinī (vāc) Gv 455.1, see prec.; dīrghānuparivartin (of Buddha) *who has long followed* (the proper course) LV 8.7; Mvy 2161; similarly sadānu° Mvy 2162.

anuparivārayati, °**reti** (= Pali °reti; cf. also **anuparivṛta**), *encircles, surrounds,* (**1**) of things, Mv i.227.19 °ritam, ppp. (padmaṃ, aparehi padmasahasrehi); Mv i.238.3 °retvā, ger. (mukhamaṇḍalam); Gv 326.1 tāṃ (a city) anuparivārya, ger.; (**2**) of persons, generally *surrounds* = *attends, waits on,* ger. °rya Dbh 84.33; Divy 464.2; °ritvā Mv ii.211.9; °retvā Mv iii.145.4; ppp. °ritaḥ Divy 7.22 (here by pretas); gdve. °rayitavyāḥ (asmābhir bodhisattvāḥ) AsP 34.14; (**3**) of abstractions, *attends* = *devotes oneself to, furthers, promotes*; fut. °rayiṣyati (prajñāpāramitām), parallel with anugrahīṣyati, anuvartiṣyate, AsP 286.8; °rayati (bodhisattvānām ... utsāham) AsP 134.4; (**4**) with caus. mg., *causes to be attended,* ger. °rya LV 61.21 (deva ... sahasraiḥ); perf. °rayām āsa Gv 444.16.

anuparivṛta, ppp. (cf. °**vārayati,** and Skt. parivṛta beside °vārita, both in same mg.), *surrounded, attended*: Divy 361.20 (prose). In LV 278.16 (prose) for Lefm. anuparivṛtair read °vṛttair (see **anuparivartati**).

anupariśoṣita, ppp., *continually* or *gradually dried up*: Śikṣ 212.3 vātānu°.

anuparītaka, m., for °**parīttaka** = °**parītta,** q.v., with specifying -ka (§ 22.39), *one that has been handed over*: Divy 332.16 (prose; parallel **anupradattaka,** q.v. for citation). Cf. parīta = °tta, BR s.v. i with pari, 3, end; twice in Mbh. In one of these, i.8437 Calc., Sukthankar i.224.9 reads parīttāś ca, tho no ms. reads so; N mss. all parītāś ca; but S mss. (with a further change) paridattāś ca, supporting the em. The other passage has not yet been edited.

anuparītta, ppp. (cf. Skt. parītta, prec., and next two), *handed over, delivered*: Mv ii.77.16 (so ... tasya) brāhmaṇasya anuparītto, vedān adhyāpehīti (last word an em., but plausible).

anuparīndanā = **anuparin**°, given in KN (with the colophon of a single ms.; and kept without note in WT) as title of SP chap. 27; but in the text only (anu-)parind°, with short i, occurs.

anuparīndāmi (= **anuparin**°, **parīn**°, **parin**°), *I give over, present*: AsP 460.14; 461.12.

anuparyavanaddha (= **paryava**°), *covered over*: kudṛṣṭi-viṣama-jālānu° Dbh 28.15.

anupalabdhi, f. or adj. (Bhvr.), = **an-upalambha,** q.v.: (the being) *not to be grasped or conceived* (mentally): °dhi-hetuḥ Mvy 4461 (as term in logic); atyantānupalabdhi-cakraṃ (sc. dharma-c°) LV 423.4, *completely ungraspable*; gambhīraṃ ... dharmacakraṃ grāhānupalabdhi-tvāt LV 422.11 *profound ... because it cannot be grasped by* (mental) *grasping*; °dhi-tvāt (also) KP 148.3; Laṅk 162.13.

anupalabdhika, adj. (Bhvr.) = °**bdhi**: yāvad anupalabdhikaṃ kuryāt Sādh 258.16, *until he makes it beyond the power of thought to grasp.*

anupalambha, m.c. also **anopa**°, m., or adj. (Bhvr.), *inconceivability*; *inconceivable* (see s.v. **upalambha**); often substantially *non-reality* or *without reality*: °bha-dharma-kṣānti RP 12.2; opposed to the heresy (dṛṣṭi) of upalambha; anopalambha dharma śrutva kāṅkṣa nāsya vidyate, niḥsattva eti sattvadharma nātra ātma vidyate RP 12.10; °bha-śūnyatā Mvy 948, *emptiness that consists in inconceivability* (unreality, of everything); śūnyatānupalambheṣu dharmeṣu KP 97.3, *in regard to states of being which because of voidness* (so Tib., stoṅ pa ñid kyis) *are inconceivable* (unreal); śūnyatānupalambhā(ṃ)ś (here noun, Tatpur.) ca dharmeṣu śrutvā KP 123.6; of dharma as the 'law' preached by the Buddha, śūnyatānupalambhas, *inconceivable because of voidness* LV 395.22 and (Lefm.) 392.16 (here most mss. °tānupacchedaḥ, also interpretable); anupalambha-vihāra-vihāriṇāṃ Gv 471.8 (parallel: niḥprapañca-vih°); anupalambha-yogena bhāvayati Mvy 971 (opp. of upalambha-yogena, s.v. **upalambha**); anopalambhaṃ āryāṇa gotraṃ KP 137.11 (vs).

an-upalipta, (**1**) adj. (= Pali °litta; also **an-ūpa**°, **an-opa**°; Skt. has upalipta), *undefiled*: Mv i.134.6; LV 3.2; etc. (common); (**2**) n. of a Bodhisattva: Mvy 687; (**3**) n. of a former Buddha: Sukh 5.11.

Anupavadya, n. of a former Buddha: Mv i.136.14 (mss. anopravadya; cf. **upavadati,** and Pali anupavajja).

Anupaśānta, n. of a son of Māra, unfavorable to the Bodhisattva: LV 312.16.

anupaśyanā (= Pali °passanā), *viewing, considera-*

tion: Śikṣ 232.7; 236.13; KP 95.2 ff.; Bbh 259.21 ff.; in all these in statements of the **smṛtyupasthāna,** q.v.

anupaśyin, adj. (= Pali °passin), *regarding, looking upon, considering*: °paśyī, n. sg., KP 95.2 ff.; cittānupaśyī Laṅk 360.15; duḥkhānupaśyinā ... anityānupaśyinā, instr. sg., Mv iii.266.1; in KP in a statement of the **smṛtyupasthāna,** q.v.; prob. so meant in Laṅk and Mv also.

an-upasaṃpanna, adj. (= Pali id.; neg. of **upa°**, q.v.), *unordained*: Mvy 8478; yaḥ punar bhikṣur anupasaṃpannena pudgalena sārdhaṃ padaśo dharmaṃ vācayet pātayantikā Prāt 503.9.

(**anupasthita,** Skt., *not present*; -tva, *the not being present*; spṛhānupasthitatvāt Mv i.153.11, *because desire is not present in him.* Wrongly Senart n. 497.)

Anupahatamati, n. of a Bodhisattva: Mvy 720.

anupāṭa (m.?; cf. next; no cpd. of anu-paṭ-is recorded), presumably *rending* or the like, one of the torments of hell, in comp. with **utpāṭa**: Divy 301.26.

anupāṭana (nt.?) = prec., in the same cpd.: Divy 299.2, 20; 303.19.

anupāta, m., perh. *trimming around the edge* (of the border of a monk's robe): MSV ii.51.2, 3 (Tib. mthaḥ skor, *circumference*).

anupādā (= Pali id., 'mostly used before nouns ... while anupādāya ... is preferred before finite verb forms', CPD), abbreviated form of ger. **anupādāya,** q.v., *not clinging* (to existence): Mv ii.293.13 anupādāśravebhyaś cittāni vimuktāni (same phrase with anupādāya, q.v.); in Mv i.69.15 read anupāda (m.c. for °dā; mss. °dāya, unmetr.; Senart em. °di, wrongly) vimukti, cf. Pali anupādā vimutto (CPD s.v.).

an-upādāna, see **upādāna.**

anupādāya, indecl. (ger.; = Pali id.; also °**dā,** q.v.; formally neg. to **upādāya,** which however seems not recorded in Pali or BHS in mg. corresponding to this; but cf. **upādiyati**), *not clinging* (to existence): anupādāyāśravebhyaś (or °āsrav°) cittāni vimuktāni, *not clinging, their thoughts were freed from the depravities*, SP 179.17; Mv i.329.19; iii.67.1; 337.4 (cittaṃ vimuktaṃ); 338.20; RP 59.19; KP 138.2; 145.2; (cf. Pali yāva me anupādāya āsavehi cittaṃ vimuccati, Dhp. comm. i.86.7;) anupādāya parinirvṛto Mv i.302.12; 357.16 (°vṛtā); cf. Pali °dāya nibbuto, e. g. Dhp. 414.

anupāna-paṭṭaka, nt. (v.l. anupāra°, so Mironov; v.l. in both edd. antupāra°), °kam Mvy 9030, acc. to Chin. *a dish, bowl or saucer, that has a standard*; Tib. phul baḥi btuṅ phor (or gtaṅ phor); this cpd., reading btuṅ phor, seems to mean *drinking-cup for presentation*; it is recorded in Das, s.v. phul ba, transl. by the BHS word here treated and by Eng. *a drinking plate.*

an-upāyāsa, see **upāyāsa.**

anupārśva (as adj. in MW without reference; not in BR, pw, or Schmidt, nor in Pali or Pkt.), °śvena, adv., *along the sides*, with gen.: tasyā anu° Divy 240.5.

anupālanā (= Pali id.; Skt. only °na, nt.), *the keeping, maintaining*, with loc.: śikṣāpadeṣv anu° Bbh 81.20.

-anupīḍana, f. °ī, as final in cpd. adj. (Bhvr.? cf. next; cf. Pali anupīḷita; no cpd. of anu-pīḍ- in Skt.), *oppressing*: Mmk 114.15 (vs) parasattvānupīḍanīm (sc. pūjām). A possible, but less likely, analysis would be parasattvānu (gen. pl., m.c., = °nāṃ) pī°.

-anupīḍin, adj. (see prec.), *oppressing*: Mmk 151.1 (vs) parasattvānupīdinaḥ, with mantrā(ḥ); for a less likely analysis cf. prec.

anupūrva, adj. (cf. Pali anupubba; Skt. anupūrva hardly in the following senses), (**1**) *tapering*, Tib. (Mvy 273 etc.) byin gyis phra ba, *becoming* (gradually) *smaller* (Jäschke s.v. byin po, *by degrees, more and more fine*); so in Pali Jāt. v.155.22, of thighs (ūrū), *tapering* (not *regularly formed* with CPD, PTSD): SP 338.8 yāvad brahmalokam uccaistvena, anupūrvapariṇāhena, *reaching to Brahmaloka in height, tapering in circumference* (i. e. each smaller than the next lower); anupūrvāṅguli *with tapering* (so Burnouf correctly, *effilés*) *fingers*, Pali anupubbaṅguli, one of the **anuvyañjana,** Mvy 273; Dharmas 84; (anupūrvacitrāṅguli) LV 106.12; Mv ii.43.9; anupūrvapāṇilekha, *with tapering lines of the hand*, another anuvyañjana, LV 106.15; Mv ii.43.14 (other versions read āyata *long* instead of anupūrva); anupūrva-daṃṣṭra, *with tapering* (so Tib.) *teeth*, another anuvyañjana LV 107.6; Mvy 325; Dharmas 84 (not in Pali); anupūrva-sujāta-skandho Mv ii.71.16, of a lion, *with tapering, well-formed shoulders*; anupūrvapravaṇam anupūrvaprāgbhāram Divy 113.5, of a mountain, *with tapering slopes and sides* (getting smaller as they rise); in 113.15 same, preceded by anupūrvanimnam; anupūrvonnatāni (padmapuṣpāṇi) Mmk 62.5 *taperingly lofty*, i. e. placed one above another, each smaller than the one below; °va-grīvā LV 27.6 *with tapering neck*; here Tib. mgul rim bzhin du ḥdug pa, *neck made in regular stages* or the like (not the usual expression); anupūrva-samudgate, of the shanks (jaṅghe) of the mahāpuruṣa, Gv 400.6, in explaining the epithet **aiṇeya-jaṅgha**; (**2**) *made according to regular order or arrangement*, Tib. on Mvy 288 rim par ḥtsham pa, *according to regular order*: °va-gātra, one of the **anuvyañjana,** *whose limbs are all as they should be in arrangement*, LV 106.21; Mv ii.44.3; Mvy 288; Dharmas 84 (Pali anupubba-gatta, and anupubba-rucira-gatta); anupūrva (so with v.l.) -surucirāṅgo (cf. the Pali just cited) Mv iii.85.9, said of the horse Valāha; (**3**) noun, m. (cf. Pali anupubba, nt., Skt. ānupūrva, nt., and ānupurvī, f.), *regular order*; *serial process*: Śikṣ 108.3 anupūrva eṣo iha śāsanasya, naikena janmena labheta bodhim, *this serial* (successive) *process applies to the teaching in this world*; *one cannot get enlightenment in a single birth.* See the following entries.

anupūrvam, adv. (= Pali anupubbaṃ; app. not in this sense in Skt.), *in the course of time*: anupūrva, m.c. for °vam, SP 203.11; 384.7 (in the last ed. prints as if cpd. with puṇyena, which is less likely than taking it as separate adv.).

anupūrvaka, f. °**ikā** (= Pali anupubbaka, ānupubbika; also ānupubbi-kathā), *graduated, arranged step by step*: °vikāṃ kathāṃ kṛtvā Divy 355.17.

anupūrva-vihāra-samāpatti, f. (= Pali anupubba°; also **anupūrva-(samādhi-)samāpatti,** q.v.), *the attainments of* (nine) *successive stages*: navānu° (see **samāpatti**) Mvy 1498; ŚsP 58.8. They consist of the four dhyāna, the four ārūpya stages, and (**saṃjñā-vedayita-)nirodha**-samā°. So also in Pali, e. g. AN iv.410.1 ff. (list of the nine anupubbavihāra) and 23 ff., list and detailed description of the nine samāpatti; both consist of four jhāna, four formless states, āruppa, and saññāvedayitanirodha (or their 'attainments').

anupūrvaśas, adv. (= Pali °pubbaso), *in due course*: SP 112.7; Mv ii.240.2 (°saḥ).

anupūrva-samāpatti (= Pali anupubba°), = **anupūrva-vihāra-samāpatti**: Divy 95.21–22 navānup°; also **anupūrva-samādhi-samāpatti,** Dharmas 82.

Anupūrvasamudgata-parivarta, m., n. of a (? part of a) work: Śikṣ 313.1.

anupūrvī (= Pali °pubbī, beside ānupubbi; Skt. only ānu°), *succession, regular series*: °vī-bandham Laṅk 255.1, cited Śikṣ 135.5 (wrongly em. in ed.).

anupūrvīya, adj., *following a regular order*: °vīya-dharmadeśanā Mv iii.257.11, 12 (= Pali anupubbi-kathā, ānu°).

anupūrveṇa, adv. (= Pali °pubbena), *in due course*: SP 102.14; LV 157.5; 159.17; 238.12; 406.22; Mv i.354.15; ii.90.8, 11; 131.10; 210.14; 442.5; 461.14; 485.10; iii.73.4; 256.10; Divy 20.3; 42.26; 94.18; 213.8; Kv 58.23; etc., common.

anu-prajñāpti (f., cf. Pali anuppaññatti), *supple-*

mentary prajñāpti, Mvy 9214; follows prajñāpti 9213, q.v. Lack of clear context leaves precise mg. uncertain.

anupraṇidhi (not in Pali), = **praṇidhi**, *vow* (to persist towards enlightenment); commoner than the verb anupraṇidheti and often object of praṇidheti, e. g. Mv i.112.15; 113.7; 114.3; 115.5; 116.12; 117.8; 118.13; used after anupraṇidheti Mv i.119.15 (mss., Senart wrongly praṇidhiṃ for anu°, presumably m.c., but meter is defensible with anu); °dhiḥ, without either verb, Mv i.336.14.

anu-praṇidheti (not in Pali), = **praṇidheti**, *makes a vow* (to persist towards enlightenment); °dheti Mv i.119.15; °dhemi (mss. anuparidehi) 323.1; °dhesi, aor., 335.11; °hitaṃ, ppp., i.63.3. See **anupraṇidhi**, which is commoner than the verb. If there is any difference between this and praṇi° without anu, it does not appear clearly; anu does not necessarily imply *after* (a gift or meritorious act), tho this often precedes; in Mv i.323.1 however none is mentioned.

anu-pratipanna (ppp. of *anu-prati-padyati, Aśokan anupaṭipa(j)jati, and in the Pali adj. anu-paṭipajjanaka; cf. next), *following after*: tathatvānupratipannaḥ Dbh 42.11.

anu-pratipādayate (caus. of *anu-prati-padyati, see prec.), *causes to follow*: -mārgam °yamānaḥ Jm 143.8.

anu-pratiṣṭha, adj. (anu plus pratiṣṭhā, Bhvr.), *having a corresponding basis*: Śikṣ 42.13 (cited s.v. **upanikṣipati** 2).

anu-pradakṣiṇīkaroti, = Skt. pradakṣ°, *passes around to the right*: °rontā, pres. p. Mv ii.400.4 ff.; °ronto Mv iii.74.20.

anu-pradattaka, m. (ppp. with specifying ka), *one that has been handed over, entrusted*: (Ārya-saṃgharakṣito...) -śāriputreṇānupradattako bhagavatānuparītakaḥ (23 °nupradattakaḥ) Divy 332.15, 23; f. °ikā, *given* (in marriage): MSV i.105.9.

anu-pradadāti (= Pali anu(p)padeti), *gives, presents*: pres. opt. °dadyām Av i.17.1; fut. °dāsyāmi etc. SP 106.12, 13; Mvy 2868; 7307; Divy 61.6; Suv 103.1; Kv 27.19; Gv 327.24; aor. °pradāsi Mv iii.159.8; perf. °dadau Av i.245.3; ppp. °datta Divy 22.12; 94.23; 117.8; 234.25; gdve. °deya SP 338.6; °dātavya Av i.314.3; pass. °dīyante RP 56.16.

anu-pra-darśita (ppp. of *anu-pra-darśayati), *pointed out, shown*: Jm 94.20.

anu-pradāna, nt. (1) (= Pali anuppa°; to **anupradadāti**), *act of giving, presentation*: LV 429.19, 22; 430.4, etc.; Mv ii.221.5; iii.322.5; dharmāṇām, *of religious instruction* (= **upasaṃhāra**, 1) Bbh 82.4; Dbh 15.4; (2) *encouragement*: Dbh 24.4 (na saṃhitān bhinatti,) na bhinnānām anupradānaṃ karoti, *he does not divide* (cause dissension among) *those that are united, nor give encouragement to those that are divided* (i. e. schismatics; cf. CPD s.v. anuppadātar).

-anuprapūra, adj. ifc., *fulfilling* (cf. next): °pūre, voc. sg. f.: sattvārthasamantā-(mss. °matā-, °matvā-, em. Nobel)-nuprapūre Suv 117.8 (so nearly all mss.; text °pure with 1 ms.).

[**anu-prapūrayati**, *fulfills* (cf. prec.): LV 46.5 (vs) sarvajñajñānam anuprāpuritum, inf., could be m.c. for °prapūr(ay)itum, which Calc. reads; but see **anuprāpunati**.]

anu-prabadhnāti (or °**bandhati**; = Pali anuppabandhati), *keeps continually on* or *after*: pres. p. (praṇidhiviṣayam) °bandhan Gv 99.26–100.1.

anuprabandha (m.; = Pali anuppa°; to °**badhnāti**), (1) *continuity, continuation*: Śāl 75.15; 76.6 f. (cited Śikṣ 226.6; 227.2 f.); Dbh 77.9 (°dhānupacchedatāṃ dharmāṇāṃ); (2) *constant pursuit of, devotion to*, dharma-naya-samudrānuprabandheṣu Gv 344.15.

anu-prayacchati (once in TS, see BR; not in Pali, yet seems to be a Buddh. word) *gives, presents*: Divy 7.25 etc. (common, see Index); Av i.18.8; Kv 27.12 etc. (see pw); Bbh 4.22; 5.4 etc.; vācam anu° Divy 338.17, *gives a word, says anything, makes answer*; apavādam anu° Divy 578.23, *offers insult* (to, gen.); pārśvam anu° Bbh 193.20, see **pārśva**.

anupravartaka, adj. (Pali anup(p)avattaka, of one that *keeps rolling* the dhamma-cakka), *that keeps providing or furnishing* (pra-vartayati): (bhāṇḍopaskarāṇām) °kaṃ dhyānam Bbh 210.15.

anupravartana (nt.; = Pali anuppavattana), *pursuit, following, proceeding along*: Gv 37.8 (see **āvart(t)i**).

anupravartayati (= Pali anupavatteti), *keeps moving*: dharmacakram ... °yataḥ MSV iii.54.4.

anu-pravārita, adj. (ppp.), *completely covered over, enclosed* (?): narako āyasehi śūlehi santaptehi samantato hi anupravārito (v.l. °vāl°, one ms. °vās°) Mv i.25.5.

Anupraviddhakarṇa, see **Anapaviddha°**.

anu-praviśati, app. *accompanies* (? a musical instrument): (salīlaṃ vīṇām) anupraviśya gāthābhir gītair anugāyati sma Laṅk 3.9.

anupraveśaka, adj., *penetrating*: sattva-cittānupraveśakair nirmāṇavigrahaiś Laṅk 43.10.

anupravrajati (= Pali anupabbajati; the single Skt. quotation in BR, from Rām., can hardly be said to have this mg.), *follows* (another) *into the ascetic life*: LV 10.12; Mv i.336.14; 337.19; iii.50.16; 222.18; Divy 61.17; Bhīk 11b. 3; Jm 110.13.

anupravrajana (nt.; to prec.), *the following* (another) *into ascetic life*: °ne Jm 120.24.

anu-prasarati (only caus. and intens. in RV; not in Pali), *spreads over, penetrates*, with acc.: °ranti Gv 432.10 (subject, raśmijālāni); ppp. °sṛta- Gv 365.2 (1 in 2d ed.); 438.3.

anu-praskandati (= Pali anupakkhandati), *encroaches, intrudes upon*: °skandya, ger. Prāt 506.2 (°ya śayyāṃ kalpayed, where another was located); 511.6 (text here °skadya; the Pali ger. is always anupakhajja); Mvy 8437; 9447 (balena).

anu-prākāram and °**re**, adv. (= Pali anupākāre, and stem in comp. °ra-), *along* or *near a wall*: (nagarasya) °ram Mv ii.429.16; °re Mv iii.5.20.

anu-prāpaṇa (from next, or Skt. °prāpnoti), *attainment*: Dbh.g. 20(356).18 °ṇārthī; Mmk 107.16.

anuprāpunati, °**ṇati** (= Pali anupāpuṇāti, Skt. anuprāpnoti), *obtains*: pres. opt. °neyāma SP 163.2 (so read with Kashgar rec.); aor. °ṇe Mv iii.67.2, 4; ger. °ṇitvā SP 291.13; inf. °nitum LV 46.5 (so prob. read for text °puritum; see s.v. **anuprapūrayati**); gdve. °ṇitavya Mv iii.287.17; in Mv ii.415.16 (vs) read -vaśitānuprāpuṇe for mss. °tāni prāpuṇe (Senart em. wrongly); with Pkt. v for p, anuprāvetsuḥ Mv iii.52.8.

anuprārthayate, *seeks after*: °yamāna, pple. pres., Bhad 48.

anuprekṣaṇa (nt.; to Skt. anu-pra-īkṣ- plus -ana), *examination, investigation*: deśānu° MSV ii.170.19. Cf. next.

-anuprekṣin (Pali -anupekkhin; see prec.), *examining, investigating*: deśānu° MSV ii.170.11.

anuplava (m.), n. act. (not in Pali; in Skt. only as n. ag., *follower*), *following, pursuit*: nāma-nimittānuplavena Laṅk 225.16–17.

[**anubadha**, Śikṣ 271.13, read doubtless anubandha, *consequence*. See s.v. **gurula**.]

anubuddhi (f.; to Skt. anu-budh-; cf. next, and **anubodha**, °**dhana**), *an awakening, enlightenment, making up of the mind*, with infin.: adyāvaboddhum amṛtaṃ anubuddhi śāstā LV 299.12 (vs), last word by em., best ms. śāstar, others vary; read śāstur, gen. sg., *today the teacher makes up his mind to win knowledge of what is deathless*; anubuddhi, n. sg. With Lefm.'s em., anubuddhi could be 3 sg. aor. of anu-budh (Chap. 43, s.v. budh 2).

anubudhyana (nt.; to Skt. anubudhyate plus -ana;

= Pali anubujjhana; cf. prec.), *the understanding, becoming aware of*: pratītyasamutpādānubudhyana-tā, Hoernle MR 118, last line (from Ratnarāśi Sūtra).

anubṛṃhaṇa-tā, °ṇā (= Pali anubrūhana, °nā; to next with -ana-tā, -anā), *strengthening, making to increase*: Bbh 18.25 °ṇā (hitasukhādhyāśayasya); 203.6 (-vīryānubṛṃhaṇatayā), 25 (-praṇidhānānubṛṃhaṇatayā).

anubṛṃhayati (= Pali anubrūheti), *strengthens, makes to increase; devotes oneself to*: °hayati Bbh 394.15 (śubhāṃ cādhimuktim); °hayant, pple. pres., Bbh 93.10; °hayiṣyati Mmk 154.7; °hita, ppp., Bbh 93.7; °hayet, pres. opt. Ud xiii.6 *should devote oneself to* (vivekam; so Pali, Dhp. 75, vivekam anubrūhaye).

anubodha (m.; = Pali id.; cited once from comm. on ĀpŚ. in pw 4.292; cf. next, **dur-anubodha**, and **anubuddhi**), *comprehension*: SP 64.14; tenāsmi buddho jagatānubodhāt SP 47.6, *therefore I am a Buddha, because of* (my) *understanding of the world* (otherwise Burnouf and Kern); SP 80.9; -jñāna-bala-vaiśāradyānubodhāya 81.3; sarva-arthānubodhā RP 47.6, of Buddha's speech, *having* or *yielding comprehension of all meanings*; ekakṣaṇatryadhvānubodhaṃ (buddhānāṃ) Dbh 55.22; 67.7; -balajñānānubodhāya Gv 345.17.

anubodhana (nt.; = Pali id.; not in BR, pw; cited in MW without reference; cf. under prec.), *comprehension*: Dbh 26.3; sarvākārānu° Dbh.g. 55(81).6; °na-vaineyānāṃ Gv 349.1, *of persons convertible by* (logical) *comprehension, by reason*; **°na-tā**, at end of cpds., *state of having comprehension of* . . . LV 34.12; bodhisattva-śikṣānubodhana-tayā Gv 463.14.

[**anubhartsyanti**, AsP 246.17, 18, 20; 247.9; 248.1, is apparently a strange error or misprint for anuvartsyanti, *will follow*. It is certainly a fut. and cannot be connected with root bharts.]

anubhavati (in this sense = Pali anubhoti; cf. **pratyanubhavati** and **abhisaṃbhuṇati**), *suffices for, is sufficient to produce*: ābhayāpy ābhāṃ nānubhavato (candrasūryau) SP 163.10; Pali equivalent nānubhonti, DN ii.12.13 etc., see CPD s.v. anubhavati, and cf. passage cited s.v. **lokāntarikā**; in Mv parallels abhisaṃbhuṇanti; in Divy pratyanubhavatas. Cf. **anubhūta**.

-anubhavana-tā (cf. Pali anubhavana, same mg.): lokānubhavanatayā LV 157.7 (prose), of the Bodhisattva, *by way of experiencing worldly life*: substantially = lokānuvartanā, see **anuvartanā**.

anubhāsati, *shines thru*: śobhati lokam imaṃ tv anubhāsan RP 3.7.

anubhūta, in Gv 402.13 °tāḥ, of the hair of a mahāpuruṣa, after sujātamūlāḥ and before niṣpīḍitāḥ (*pressed down firmly*?). The meaning is obscure (*lying in an ordered way*?); perhaps corrupt.

anubhoktar, *enjoyer*: °tā, n. sg., Mmk 157.23.

anubhokti (f.; expected would be anubhukti, which is also not recorded; perhaps corrupt), *enjoyment*: °ti-kriyā LV 45.12.

? **anubhrama**, *conduit*: perhaps in Divy 538.10, see s.v. **bhrama**.

anubhramati, *strays after*: °mitum, inf. Jm 222.24; °manti 226.22.

anumajjhima, adj. (MIndic for Skt. Gr. °madhyama, § 22.16; mg. assigned it in Kāś. seems not the same as in BHS; cf. also **anumadhya** and **madhyima**), (located) *in the middle*: Mv ii.262.14, contrasted with **pratyantika**, q.v.

anumadhya (= Pali anumajjha), *middling; between small and great*: °dhyāto madhyimaṃ (sc. dadyāt) Mv ii.49.20 (= Pali °jjhato, in same vs, Jāt. v.387.19).

anumārga, adj. or (°gaṃ) adv. (cf. Skt. anumārgeṇa, with gen.; Pali anumagga in cpds., °ge, °gaṃ, advs.), *following along*: sarvamārga-anumārga (one word; either °ga m.c. for °gaṃ, adv., or stem in comp. with the next word) susthitaḥ Gv 488.17 (vs), *firmly fixed in pursuit of the whole* (religious) *path*.

anumārjati (= Pali anumajjati; not in this mg. in Skt.), *considers, ponders thoroughly*: °jan, pres. pple., Gv 63.2; 84.12.

anumodanā (Pali id.; cf. Skt. °na, nt., rare; in Pali °na, nt., is much commoner than °nā, which is very common in BHS; cf. next), (expression of) *thanks, gratification*, or *approval*: Mv i.297.18 imāye °nāye (of foll. vss); 298.19; iii.426.6 (of foll. vss); SP 346.5 (°nā-sahagatam); Śikṣ 9.18; Mmk 79.5, etc.; Dharmas 14, one of seven forms of worship.

anumodanī = **°nā**, q.v.: LV 200.10 (vs); so both edd. and all but one ms. (which has °nā).

anuyukta (= Pali anuyutta; see also **an-anu°**) (**1**) *devoted* or *addicted to, practising* (with acc.): anuyogam (see next) anu° LV 264.20; Mv i.96.5; KP 105.9; (jāgarikā-, bhāvanā-, etc.) -yogam Mv iii.383.9; Kv 73.5; Śikṣ 104.15; Samādh 8.15; other objects Mv iii.201.1 (see **ekārāma**); Ud xv.8 (see **jāgarya**); (**2**) in Mvy 7665 = Tib. brgal ba (see s.vv. **pratyanuyukta, samanuyujyate**; ppp. to Pali anuyuñjati in sense b of CPD). *examined, questioned*; see next (2).

anuyoga (cf. prec.), m., (**1**) *devotion, addiction, application to* (so Pali id.; not Skt. in this sense): sukhallikānu° (see **sukhallikā**); kāmasukhallikātmaklamathānu° Bbh 187.11–12; (ātma)kāya-klamathānu° LV 416.20; -dyūtakrīḍānu° Mv i.96.5; ākalanānu°, see **ākalana**; (**2**) *questioning, examination* (Pali id., esp. °gaṃ dadāti, *passes an examination*; Skt. also *questioning*; BR 5.990): anuyogo ca dinno Mv iii.57.1, *and he passed an examination*; anuyogaṃ deti 383.2 (after a course of Vedic study).

-anuyogin (= Pali id., only ifc.), *characterized by devotion* (anuyoga): satatānuyogī Mv i.357.12 (same cpd. in Pali, Pv iii.7.10, where ed. sattānuyogino, but see comm. 206.7).

anuyojya (gdve. of anu-yuj, caus.; Skt. not in this sense), *capable of being made to be devoted* (to, loc.): (eteṣu, sc. tri-yāneṣu) tatrānuyojyaḥ Laṅk 65.3. Cf. **anuyoga, °yukta.**

Anuraktarāṣṭra, n. of a former Buddha: Mv i.141.14.

-anurakṣaṇa-tā, ifc. (see next), *state of protecting* . . .: ātmaparānurakṣaṇa-tāyai LV 32.19; bahujanacittānurakṣaṇa-tayā Laṅk 247.8, 16.

anurakṣaṇā (= Pali anurakkhaṇā and °ṇa; MW cites Skt. °ṇa, nt., without reference; not in BR, pw, Schmidt), *guarding, protection*: °ṇā-prayogena Bbh 288.2, 6.

anurakṣā (= Pali anurakkhā), *protection, guarding, keeping; sparing*: guṇānu° Jm 189.2, *preserving virtue*; Śikṣ 124.17; sarvasattvānu° 127.7; mama cittānurakṣayā Divy 82.22, 26, *by way of sparing my thoughts = so as not to hurt my feelings*; similarly, tāsām anurakṣayā MSV ii.144.10.

anuracita, prob. *provided, endowed with*: (bodhimaṇḍavṛkṣaḥ . . . sarvatathāgataviṣayavikurvitanir)ghoṣānuracitaḥ Gv 270.10, *provided with the sound* (*report, renown*?) *of the miracles* . . .; cf. next, where the precise mg. is not clear.

anuracitagandhagarbha, a kind of jewel supposed to emit a perfume (see s.v. **vibodhana**): Gv 101.9 (cf. prec.).

anuraṇati (cf. Skt. anuraṇana), *sounds in response*: LV 318.22; 319.1; °ṇe, aor., Mv ii.282.10; 412.8.

-anuravaṇa (nt.; Pali °ṇā), *resounding*: Dbh 83.17; Gv 247.10; °ṇa-tā, Gv 82.23.

anuravita (ppp. to anuravati, Pali, rare in Skt. for °ruvati, °rauti; cf. **°ravaṇa**), *resonant, resounding thruout*: Gv 511.20 (-manojñarutānuravitālaṃkāram, sc. kūṭāgāram); Mvy 503 and Sūtrāl. xii.9, comm., sarva-pariṣad-(Sūtrāl. °parṣad)-anuravitā, of Buddha's voice, *sounding thruout all assemblies*; so Tib.

anurāgaṇa (nt.; to Skt. anu-rañj-, cf. anurāga), °**ṇā**, and ifc. f. °**ṇī**, *gratification*: °ṇam Guhyasamāja 152.13; °ṇā Mvy 4302; °ṇī (as f. to °ṇa), *causing gratification* (in adj. cpd.), Mvy 4316.

anurāgataṃ (= AMg. aṇurāgayaṃ), *welcome!*, exclamation of greeting following svāgataṃ (see § 4.63): Mv i.35.6; 152.2; 225.18; 273.8; ii.28.19; 38.9; iii.169.18; 181.17; 329.8.

anu-rāśi, m., *continuous heap*: MSV ii.103.6 matsyānāṃ mahānurāśiḥ saṃvṛttaḥ.

Anuruddha (so Pali) = **Ani°**, q.v.: Mv iii.177.2 ff.; son of Amṛtodana and brother of Mahānāma and Bhaṭṭika (= Bhadrika); also v.l. for Ani° SP 207.4.

Anurūpagātra, n. of a former Buddha: Mv i.140.4.

Anurūpasvara, n. of a Bodhisattva: Gv 443.9.

anu-rūpe (carati), (moves along) *in* (or, *upon*) *form*; ŚsP 765.2. Not from anurūpa; anu governs the loc., as in Pali anu-tīre etc. (CPD s.v. anu, b, δ). In the parallel passages below locs. are used without anu: vedanāyāṃ 765.11; saṃjñāyāṃ 765.20, etc.

anurodha-virodha (= Pali id.), *compliance and aversion* (dvandva; one of the pairs of opposites from which the perfected are freed): °dhāpagataḥ Śikṣ 203.4; °vipramuktaḥ Mvy 425 (= Pali °vippamutto), of a Tathāgata (mss. erroneously an-anu°, kept in Mironov's ed.; Tib. bsñen confirms anu°, without neg. an-).

Anurodhāpratirodha, m., n. of a samādhi: Mvy 608; ŚsP 1424.21.

anu-lagnati, °**nayati** (see **lagnati**), *clings on behind*: Mv iii.73.4 °niṣyati, and in prec. line 3 read doubtless (aṅgajāte . . . parasparasya) anulagnayiṣyanti with one ms. (or °niṣyanti) instead of Senart's avalambiṣyati.

anu-liṅgin, adj., *according to one's characteristic marks*: yathāveṣānuliṅginam Mmk 133.7 (of a painted image of a Buddha).

anuliptaka, adj. (**1**) = Skt. anulipta, *anointed*: candanānuliptakagātro Mv iii.412.12 (prose); (**2**) mg. not clear to me in Mmk 322.12 (of a magic formula) asahyaṃ sarvabhūtānāṃ, sarvalokānuliptakam, adhṛṣyaṃ sarvalokānāṃ, bhavamārgaviśodhakam.

anuloma-caryā (see s.v. **caryā**), *course of conduct conforming* (to a Bodhisattva's vow to attain bodhi): Mv i.1.3; 46.7; 63.11.

-anulomana-tā (abstr. from Skt. °na, adj.), *the acting conformably to*: dharmānu° LV 35.20.

anuloma-praṇidhāna, see **praṇidhāna**.

Anulomapratiloma, n. of an ocean and of a mountain, Divy 102.27; 103.3–23; also of certain winds, 103.5, 14. In first occurrence Anulomapratilomadvayam, as if two names compounded in a dvandva; but below only one name is clearly meant in each case.

anuloma-lipi, a kind of script: LV 125.22 (confirmed in Tib.).

anulomika, adj., f. °**kī** (= Pali id. = **ānu°**, q.v.), *conformable* (to the continuation of religious development): °kīṃ (-kṣāntim) Sukh 55.13 = ānu° kṣā°.

an-ullokita- (ppp. of **ullokayati**, q.v.), in anullokitamūrdhnāni surehi asurehi ca Mv ii.307.5, of Buddhas, *gods and asuras cannot look up* (reach by vision) *to their heads* (? v.l. anulokita-).

anuvarga (m.? = Pali °vagga, see below), some part or accessory of a city gate: dvinnāṃ varṇānāṃ anuvargā abhunsuḥ (sc. teṣāṃ dvārāṇāṃ) Mv i.195.(11–)12. Cf. Pali Bv i.14 tulā saṃghāṭānuvaggā sovaṇṇaphalakatthatā. CPD interprets anuvaggā as adj., citing comm., = anurūpā. But this is proved wrong by Mv; like tulā, which occurs in the prec. line of Mv, it must be a part of a structure. See Senart's note for a conjectural attempt at interpretation.

anuvartaka, adj. (= Pali °vattaka), *conforming to, imitating; following, cleaving to*: lokānuvartaka LV 425.5, of Buddha, see s.v. **anuvartanā**; samanta-bhadra-kāyena hīnānāṃ cānuvartakaḥ 438.6, *with completely excellent body, and* (yet) *conforming to* (the physical life of) *the vulgar*; utkṣiptānuvartakaṃ (vacanapatham), Bhīk 29 b. 1, *following, cleaving to a suspended* (monk); teṣa . . . pathe 'nuvartakaḥ RP 39.4; tadanuvartakaḥ Mvy 8379, *one who adheres to him* (sc. to a monk who causes dissension; this is a saṃghāvaśeṣa sin, cf. Prāt 483.9 ff., with anuvartino); see s.v. **anuvartita**.

anuvartanatā = °**tanā**, q.v., *conformity to*, with gen. or loc.: °natā (caturṇām āryavaṃśānām) RP 13.18 (prose); Śikṣ 183.17 (saṃrañjanīyadharmeṣu); loki (m.c. for loke) anuvartanatāṃ karoti LV 48.5; janasya °natāṃ karoti 124.19.

anuvartanā (Skt. °na, nt., Pali °vattana, nt.; see also °**vartanatā**), *conformity to, imitation of*, with gen. or in comp.: (dharmāṇām) Bbh 107.24; 108.2; lokānu°, said of the Buddha, LV 238.3 °nām upādāya; 392.8 °nāṃ (so with best mss., edd. °tināṃ) praty; 119.7 °na (m.c. for °nāṃ) pratī (m.c. for prati); acc. to the Lokottaravādin school, this *conformity to worldly life* on the part of the Buddha is a mere 'imitation' or 'reflection', as in a mirror, bimbe kanakabimbābhe eṣā °tanā Mv i.168.15; this passage is a locus classicus for this doctrine; in 168.8–9 lokānuvartanāṃ buddhā anuvartaṇti laukikīṃ, prajñaptim anuvartanti yathā lokottarāṃ api; in what follows, Buddhas are said to imitate worldly actions (the care of the body, etc.), tho they have no need to, since everything about them is lokottara, *transcending the world*.

anuvartita- (stem in comp.; ppp.; seemingly used as noun), in tasyānu°, the saṃghāvaśeṣa sin mentioned s.v. **anuvartaka**: MSV iii.88.3.

? **anuvarṣa** (m.? cf. Vedic anu-varṣati), *the raining upon*: (megho . . .) [śa]syānuvarṣeṇa karoti tṛptim KP 44.6 (vs); so ed.; but śasyānu may be gen. pl., for śasyānāṃ (Tib. lo tog, *crops*), § 8.125.

-anuvāhin, adj., ifc., *carried along by*, lit. *having . . . as that which carries along*: saṃsārasroto-'nuvāhin (read as one cpd.) Dbh 28.23 (°hinas); 31.23 (°hi); Dbh.g. 11(347).17 (m.c. °srota-anuvāhina).

anuvikṣepa, (m.,) *scattering, dispersal* (cf. Pali anuvikkhitta-), i. e. *gradual abandonment* (?): (yatra samādhau sthitvā sarva-)samādhīnām (i. e. of all other sam°?) °pam ekāgratām upalabhate, ayam ucyate **Samādhisamatā** (AdP °taḥ) nāma samādhiḥ ŚsP 1425.16; AdP Konow MASI 69,27.32. (Or, *gradual extension* = *merging in each other*?)

anuvicaraṇa (nt.), *the roaming thru*: sarvalokadhātv-anu° Gv 149.18; Dbh 16.3.

anuvicarati (= Pali id.; rarely in RV. and once in Skt. acc. to BR), *roams along, thru*; often follows **anucaṅkramati**, q.v.: pres. p. °ran(to) etc. Mv i.353.12; ii.452.3; 454.10; 457.15; Suv 185.3; Sukh 58.12; Jm 106.5; 130.22; 135.1; 155.23; ger. °ritvā Mv ii.455.16; otherwise, °rāmi Gv 165.14; °ret Bbh 170.4; KP 129.1; °cacāra, perf., Jm 185.24; -rita, ppp., Jm 163.17; Gv 226.8.

anuvicāraṇā (cf. next), *meditation* (on, with gen.): (dharmasya) anuvitarkaṇā anuvicāraṇā Bbh 30.13.

anuvicārayati, °**te** (= Pali °reti), *meditates on, thinks on*: RP 4.12 (buddhagocaram) °rayamāṇaḥ; ppp. °rita Bbh 39.15; 396.7, following (manasā) anuvitarkita; °rayanti LV 219.18 (vs), apparent object naiṣkramyaśabdo, (the sun and moon, at the abhiniṣkramaṇa) *meditate on the word* (sound?) *of* (the Bodhisattva's) *departure from the world* (?). Either °śabdo is acc. sg. (§ 8.36), or read °śabdā (acc. pl.) with Calc. against all Lefm.'s mss.; or there is some other corruption in °śabdo, which is not found in Tib.: mṅon par ḥbyuṅ (= abhiniṣkramaṇa) la rjes su rtog par byed, *make careful consideration of the* (*world-*)*renunciation*.

anuvicintayati (= Pali id.), *reflects on, considers*:

°tayanti Kv 65.9; opt. °tayet SP 72.10; °tayeyuḥ SP 31.10; °taye(ḥ) Laṅk 11.13; impv. °tayata Kv 25.6; pres. p. °tayatā (instr.) Divy 412.15; °tayamānaḥ SP 108.4 (prose); ppp. °tita SP 76.13; ger. °tya SP 215.2, 3; LV 405.1; Divy 94.6; 109.3; Kv 13.19; ppp. of caus. °cintayitāḥ SP 109.2 (prose) *caused to consider*, see § 34.9.

anuvitarkaṇā (cf. next), *study, reflection* (on, with gen.): Bbh 30.13, see **anuvicāraṇā.**

anuvitarkayati (= Pali °takketi), *ponders, reflects on*: ppp. °tarkita Mvy 6684; (foll. by anuvicārita) Bbh 39.14; 396.7; periphrastic fut. tāny anuvitarkayitā bhavati, *he is to reflect on them*, Dbh 25.6.

anuvidita, adj. (= Pali id., Sn 528, 530), *experienced, 'who has come to thorough understanding, well-informed'* (CPD): Mv iii.397.13; 398.4 (vss), = Pali Sn (above).

anuvidiś, f. (blend of Skt. vidiś and Pali anudisā), *supplementary direction, semi-cardinal point*, = vidiś, in Bcṭ 328.11 (= Śikṣ 245.18, where text na tu vidiśam); in Śikṣ 252.15 text correctly nānuvidiśaṃ (acc. sg.); in these adhaḥ and ūrdhvam are separately mentioned, as in AsP 481.18–19 mordhvaṃ mādho mā cānuvidiśam avalokayan gāḥ; but for this fact, Sukh 36.11 could easily be taken to prove that anu° means specifically the nadir and zenith, since, after the 4 cardinal points (°paścimottarāsu dikṣu), it follows with adha ūrdhvam anuvidikṣu. But the above passages show that adha ūrdhvam in Sukh must not be taken with anu°, which must apparently mean instead *the semicardinal points* (not otherwise mentioned here).

anuvirājita, adj., *resplendent*: °śarīro (mss. °rā): Mv i.38.14.

anuvilokana (nt.; = Pali id.), *looking over thoroughly, examination*: buddhadharmadeśanānu° Gv 98.23.

anuvilokayati (= Pali °keti, in sense 1), (**1**) *looks over, views completely*: °kayati LV 62.6; °kayanti LV 62.21; Jm 92.16; °kayann (pres. p.) LV 101.6; (**2**) metaphorically, *considers, ponders*: cintayann anuvilokayan (Mañjuśriyam, who was not present) Gv 529.4.

Anuvaineya, n. of a settlement (nigama) of the **Maineya** people: LV 225.6. Tib. rjes su dpag pa, acc. to Das = anumāna, *to weigh, deliberate upon*. No v.l.; but it is hard to doubt phonetic variation or corruption between m and v here (§ 2.30).

anuvyañjana, nt. (= Pali id.), erroneously written °cana SP 62.3 (WT em.), *minor or secondary characteristic*, of things in general, associated with **nimitta,** q.v.; the Buddha (or a Bodhisattva) is neither nimitta-grāhin nor anuvyañjana-grāhin (Pali °gāhi), Mv iii.52.6, 12; Śikṣ 357.2; also, specifically, one of the 80 *minor marks* or *characteristics* of a mahāpuruṣa, esp. a Buddha: SP 259.4; 264.3; LV 34.21; 100.2; 103.12; 270.17–18; 428.4; Mv i.38. 14; 50.3; 237.8; 335.12; ii.38.16; Divy 46.29; 75.3; Av i.18.1. Lists are given LV 106.11 ff.; Mv ii.43.8 ff.; Mvy 268 ff.; Dharmas 84; a Pali list cited by Burnouf, Lotus App. VIII, 2, from the Dharmapradīpikā; this I have been able to use only at second-hand, from Burnouf. (In Bbh 376.11 ff. a wholly discordant list which consists simply of 80 parts of the body.) From the five lists above mentioned I have tried to reconstruct, as well as possible, what may have been the original list; some items are conjectural. In order, the Pali list is quite close to Mvy and Dharmas; Mv is not too remote from it; LV is radically shifted in order. In my list I cite adjectival forms (applied to the Buddha), as in Mvy; some texts add -tā, making abstract nouns: 1. (ā)tāmra-nakha; 2. snigdha-n°; 3. tuṅga-n°; 4. vṛttāṅguli; 5. anupūrvāṅguli; 6. citāṅguli; 7. (ni-)gūḍha-śira (*veins*); 8. nirgranthi-ś°; 9. gūḍha-gulpha; 10. aviṣama-pāda; 11 siṃha-vikrānta-gāmin; 12. nāga-v°-g°; 13. haṃsa-v°-g°; 14. vṛṣabha-v°-g°; 15. pradakṣiṇāvarta-gāmin; 16. cāru-g°; 17. avakra-g°; 18. vṛtta-gātra; 19. mṛṣṭa-g°; 20. anupūrva-g°; 21. śuci-g°; 22. mṛdu-g°; 23. viśuddha-g°; 24. paripūrṇa-vyañjana (*sex organs complete*); 25. pṛthu-cāru-jānu-maṇḍala; 26. sama-krama; 27. sukumāra-gātra; 28. adīna-g°; 29. (?) anutsanna-g°; 30. susaṃhata-g°; 31. suvibhaktāṅga-pratyaṅga; 32. (?) vitimira-viśuddhāloka; 33. vṛtta-kukṣi; 34. mṛṣṭa-k°; 35. abhugna-k°; 36. (?) kṣāmodara; 37. gambhīra-nābhi; 38. (pra-)dakṣiṇāvarta-nābhi; 39. samanta-prāsādika; 40. śuci-samācāra; 41. vyapagata-tila-kālaka-gātra; 42. tūla-(?)sadṛśa-sukumāra-pāṇi; 43. snigdha-pāṇilekha; 44. gambhīra-p°; 45. āyata-p°; 46. (? bimba-prati)-bimboṣṭha; 47. nātyāyata-vadana; 48. mṛdu-jihva; 49. tanu-j°; 50. rakta-j°; 51. gaja-garjita-(?)jīmūta-ghoṣa; 52. madhura-(?)cāru-mañju-svara; 53. vṛtta-daṃṣṭra; 54. tīkṣṇa-d°; 55. śukla-d°; 56. sama-d°; 57. anupūrva-d°; 58. tuṅga-nāsa; 59. śuci-n°; 60. viśuddha-netra; 61. viśāla-n°; 62. citra-pakṣma; 63. sitāsita-kamala-dala-(? śakala-) nayana; 64. (?) āyata(asita?)-bhrū; 65. ślakṣṇa-bhrū; 66. (?) anuloma-bhrū; 67. snigdha-bhrū; 68. pīnāyata-karṇa; 69. (?) sama (or, aviṣama)-k°; 70. (?) anupahata-karṇendriya; 71. (?) supariṇata-lalāṭa; 72. pṛthu-l°; 73. (su-)paripūrṇottamāṅga; 74. (?) asita-(or, bhramara-sadṛśa)-keśa; 75. (?) cita (Tib. on Mvy stug pa, *thick*) -keśa; 76. ślakṣṇa-keśa; 77. asaṃlulita-keśa; 78. aparuṣa-keśa; 79. surabhi-keśa; 80. śrīvatsa-svastika-nandyāvarta-vardhamāna-(? or, lalita-)pāṇipāda. There are of course variants for many of these, but except as indicated by question-marks and parentheses, I believe the list is substantially original.

anuvyavalokita, *continuously gazed at* (by, in comp.): sarvabodhisattvānu° Gv 533.11.

anu-vyavaharati, *operates according* (to something else): Bbh 174.(14-)15 me . . . andhasyācakṣuṣmataḥ tathāgatacakṣuṣaivānuvyavaharataḥ, *of me who am blind, sightless, and who only by the eye of the Tathāgata carry on according* (to it). Cf. next.

anu-vyavahāra (m.), *regular, successive* (in stages), or *corresponding* (anu) *process, operation*, or *business*: °ra-hetuḥ Bbh 97.10, 16; 99.15; 100.14; laukikārthānu°ra-taḥ 140.18. Cf. prec.

anu-vyākṛta (cf. **vyākaroti** 2), *prophesied afterwards* (anu): Mv i.2.2, 3, 7.

anuvraja (m.?), *the following after*: (sc. mama) °jamātreṇa Gv 540.24, *by merely following* (*me*). Cf. Skt. anuvrajana (Schmidt's Nachträge); should we emend to this? The parallel nouns are -ana formations.

anuśaṃsa, m.; **°sā,** f.; also **ānuśaṃsa** **°sā**; and **ānṛśaṃsa,** Buddhacarita 6.12, mss. (Johnston em. anuśaṃsa; Tib. supports anu° or ānu°, rjes-su); acc. to Kern SBE 21.336 note 1, ānṛśaṃsa in title of SP chap. 18, but KN ed. has °nu° (quantity of preceding a- obscured by saṃdhi); La Vallée-Poussin, Bodhicaryāvatārapañjikā 22 n. 3, assumes ānṛ° as orig. form; Pali only ānisaṃsa; BHS mss. often °saṃś° for °śaṃs°; *benefit, blessing, advantage, profit*, as derived from virtuous actions of various kinds; Pali lists five (PTSD; other lists occur), and five are often mentioned in BHS, but they are different for different works of merit, and other numbers (as 10, 18) also occur; I have not found the PTSD list in BHS. Forms: anuśaṃsa, m., Mv ii.81.2 eṣo 'nuśaṃso dharme sucīrṇe; Sūtrāl. i.3, comm.; Divy 437.25; Śikṣ 16.8; 124.2; Bbh 196.6; 304.12 ye . . . anuśaṃsā(ḥ); Karmav 40.22 (note katame following; here the five are those of Pali AN iii.244.8 ff., only the first two being named in Karmav); anuśaṃsā, f., Mvy 2626 (Tib. phan yan, read phan yon); Bbh 42.12 imā(ḥ) . . . anuśaṃsā(ḥ); anuśaṃsa or °sā, m. or f., Mmk 658.27 (n. pl.); Dbh 32.6 °sānugata-; ānuśaṃsa, m., SP 296.1 ānuśaṃsāś ca . . . ye; 391.1 bahūn ānuśaṃsān; Mv ii.324.9 (vs), mss. anuśaṃsa, but meter requires ānu°; form app. acc. sg.; Senart em. ānisaṃsaṃ; ii.372.16 (mss. ānuśaṃso, Senart em. °saṃ); Av i.213.12 ime . . . ānuśaṃsāḥ; Śikṣ 121.2 ānuśaṃsa(ḥ); ānuśaṃsa or °sā, m. or f., SP 373.8, 12 (°sāḥ, n. pl.); on ānṛśaṃsa see above; ānuśaṃsa or ānu°, m. (initial vowel obscured by saṃdhi), SP 420.11 (prose) °sā(ḥ), with ime; Bbh 296.21 °sāḥ, n. pl., with m.

pronouns; Divy 92.25 °sā(ḥ), n. pl. (note following katame); 302.22 pañcānuśaṃsān; 436.17 °so; Samādh 19.1 °sa-, in comp.; anuśaṃsā or ānu°, f., Mv iii.357.13 (prose) naiṣkramyānuśaṃsā-vyavadānaṃ; Mv ii.373.18 -sā(ḥ), mss., acc. pl. (Senart em. °sāṃ); title of SP chap. 18 °sā-parivartaḥ; anu° or ānu°, m. or f., SP 421.10; Divy 567.7; Karmav 31.15 ff. (all n. pl.); Bhvr. adjective, -anu° or -ānu°, mahānu° Mv iii.221.5; LV 439.6; Divy 228.17; Av ii.108.1; alpānu° Mv iii.221.3.

-anuśaṃsaka (or **-ānu°**), = **anuśaṃsa**, q.v., in Bhvr. adj. cpd.: mahānu° Divy 200.14, *of great advantage.*

anuśakya? Mv i.23.11, mss. °kyā or nānuśakyā; Senart em. anuśakyaṃ (not explained); I suggest anusak(k)ya or nānu°, ger., *following*, see Chap. 43, s.v. sakk; note avasakkanti in preceding line.

anuśaya, m. (= Pali anusaya; see pw s.v. for rare Skt. occurrences with similar mg.; essentially a Buddhist word), *propensity* (usually to evil), (innate) *proclivity* (inherited from former births), *disposition* (to do something, usually evil); the whole of ch. v of AbhidhK (La Vallée Poussin vol. 4, p. 1–118) deals with them; they are identified or associated with **kleśa, paryavasthāna,** and **āsrava,** and they are the 'root' of bhava, renewed or continued existence, l. c. p. 1. They number 7 in Pali: (kāma-)rāga, paṭigha, diṭṭhi, vicikicchā, māna, bhavarāga, avijjā (CPD); and in BHS 7 or (the two rāgas being taken together) 6: (kāma-)rāga, pratigha, (bhavarāga), māna, avidyā, dṛṣṭi, vicikitsā or vimati (l. c. 2, 3); or (ibid. 9), dividing dṛṣṭi in five, ten anuśaya; or (ibidem) by further classification, 98 (acc. to Yogācāras, ib. 21 n. 1, 128); on the 98 cf. Sūtrāl. xiv. 46, Lévi's note; LV 372.13. Clearly of evil *propensities* LV 351.8 (udghāṭitā) anuśayā(ḥ); 363.4 purimam (from former births) anuśayaṃ; 371.16, read sānuśaya-mūlajālā with v.l. for text °jātā; 373.9 mūlakleśāḥ sānuśayāḥ; 373.17 anuśaya-paṭalā(ḥ) *masses of anuśaya,* compared to clouds; Gv 387.4 bandhanānuśaya-paryavasthāna-vaśagatāḥ; Mvy 862 nānādṛṣṭy-anuśaya-; 2136 (follows bandhanam); Laṅk 140.7; Divy 210.5; 314.21; Śikṣ 19.18 tṛṣṇānuśayaḥ; 50.9; 232.12; Bbh 202.20; 388.8; Dbh 75.7 so 'nuśayānām āśaya-sahaja-citta-sahaja-tāṃ ca yathābhūtaṃ prajānāti, *the fact that the anu° are born with intention and thought,* and see ff. (75.7–13); in Pali āsaya and anusaya, *disposition* (or *intention,* **āśaya**) *and propensity,* are often mentioned together as parallels, and are compounded; so BHS āśayānuśaya, Divy 46.23; 47.9; 48.12; 49.11; 209.12 etc.; Av i.64.12 etc.; in these the cpd. usually refers to the mental condition of persons ripe for conversion; Speyer, Index to Av, renders *inclination of the heart,* as if a tatpuruṣa, but this seems clearly wrong; it is a dvandva. In Av i.169.14 āśayānuśayam is parallel with, and follows, **nidānam** (q.v. 2).

anu-śalya-samābṛṃhaṇa-tā (cf. **samābṛṃhaṇa**), *state of the continuous* (constant, anu) *plucking out of thorns* (i. e. evils): °tāyai, dat., Gv 491.22.

anuśākṣyate (°**ti**), ? fut. of anu-śās, see § 31.25.

anuśāsanā (= °**nī,** q.v.), *instruction:* Mvy 1439; [Jm 29.5 °nāṃ, ed. by em., all mss. °nīṃ].

anuśāsanī (= Pali anusāsanī, commoner than °na, as in BHS; cf. also °**nā**; in Skt. only °na, nt.), *instruction, admonition;* hard to distinguish from **avavāda,** q.v., with which it is often compounded; LV 432.18 -mitrānu°; Mv i.277.12 = 279.21 = 281.19; 282.2; iii.51.17; 128.17; Gv 179.11; 223.16 sarvabodhisattvānuśāsanīṣu; 464.10 (cited Śikṣ 36.2); Śikṣ 2.6; 73.12 °nī-gāthāṃ; 184.3; 286.4 (Transl. *for those who admonish;* rather, *admonitions* or *instructions*); Jm 29.5, see prec.; anuśāsanī-prātihārya, one of three kinds of miracles performed by Buddhas (see **prātihārya**), Mvy (232–)234; Mv i.238.5; iii.137.17; 321.13; Dharmas 133; Gv 537.8 (in Pali also anusāsanī-pāṭihāriya).

anuśāsti, f. (cited once in Skt., BR 5.992, on Max Müller's authority; = Pali anusatthi, AMg. aṇusaṭṭhi; cf. **anuśāsanī,** and **ānuśāsti**), *instruction:* LV 364.4 (vs) na ca chidyati sā anuśāsti; Bbh 210.5 °ti-prātihārya = the more usual **anuśāsanī-**prā°.

anuśikṣaṇa (nt.; to prec.), *imitation:* Śikṣ 215.13 °ṇa-cetasaḥ; Bbh 138.13 °ṇataś ca; Gv 318.25 tathāgatānuśikṣaṇena.

anu-śikṣati, °**te,** °**śikṣayati,** °**te** (= Pali anusikkhati; not in this mg. in Skt.), *imitates,* with gen. of person, and usually loc. (rarely acc.) of thing: foll. by virtual synonyms anuvidhīyate, anukaroti Mvy 8705 °ṣe anuvidhīye anukaromi; Bhīk 10a.1 teṣām ... śikṣāyām (see **śikṣā,** 2) °ṣe etc., as prec.; SP 55.14 °ṣase lokavināyakānām; Mv ii.315.2 mama ca anuśikṣitvā, *and imitating me;* RP 57.14 tasya cānuśikṣitvā, 15 puṇyaraśmer anuśikṣamāṇaḥ, *imitating P.;* Śikṣ 14.6 buddhānām °ṣiṣye, 17 tathāgatasyānuśikṣitavyam, *one must imitate the T.;* 40.5 bodhisattvasyānuśikṣamāṇāni; Gv 462.10 kalyāṇamitrānuśikṣitā(ḥ), ppp. with active mg., *having imitated ...;* 481.22 °ṣatho, 2 pl. impv. m.c. for °tha; with acc. of thing, LV 422.5 (vs) anuśikṣi (ger.) tasyā mune(r) vīrya sthāmodgataṃ, *imitating this sage in regard to exalted heroism and power;* forms in -aya-: LV 138.6 (vs) anuśikṣayi (= °ye, 1 sg.) ahaṃ pi guṇeṣu teṣām, *I too* (will) *imitate them in virtues;* Bhad 17 sarvajinān' (for °nānām) anuśikṣayamāṇo, *imitating all the Jinas;* Bhad 55 teṣu (v.l. teṣa; gen. pl.) aham anuśikṣayamāṇo. These -aya- forms could all be m.c.

anuśikṣā (to **anuśikṣati**), *imitation:* SP 304.8 ye 'nuśikṣā-sahāyakāḥ, *who are companions in imitation* (text uncertain, see notes in KN and WT): Jm 117.23 °kṣayā; Divy 263.29 śamānuśikṣās (Bhvr. adj. cpd.).

anuśṛṇoti, *hears* (religious instruction, dharma; regarded by pw as sufficiently different from normal Skt. usage to deserve separate record, tho I question this), with antike or sakāśāt plus gen. of the instructor: Kv 63.16; 95.24.

anuśete (cf. Pali anuseti), *follows upon:* Samy. Āg. 1.3.1 ff., see **anunīyate.**

anuśraya (the only recorded derivative of Skt. anu-śri is °śrita, app. *followed, attended,* BR s.v. śri with anu, once only), *following, attendance?:* Gv 243.17 sarvalokānuśraya-tāṃ (saṃdarśayamānān), *displaying the condition of having the attendance* (following) *of all people*(?).

anuśrava (= Pali anussava; in Skt. mg. *tradition,* cf. Schmidt, Nachträge), *report, hearsay:* anuśraveṇāpi śrutvā Bbh 238.25.

anuśrāvaṇa, nt., and °**ṇā** (to next plus -ana; = Pali anussāvana, °nā), *public proclamation:* °ṇam MSV ii.206.13 ff.; °ṇā Prāt 475.7.

anuśrāvayati (= Pali anussāveti), **(1)** *makes to resound:* jayavṛddhiśabdam LV 96.18; jayavṛddhir anuśrāvitā LV 112.19; śabdam LV 101.4; 401.2; Mv i.40.11; 239.20; 336.13; iii.303.17; 319.14; Gv 85.20; **(2)** *proclaims:* **ghoṣam** (q.v.) SP 123.1; LV 266.1; Samādh 8.10; Śikṣ 38.1; nāmagotrāṇi Mv iii.443.20; Divy 619.3 (*announces*); *proclaims* a condemned criminal, i. e. announces his crime and sentence (publicly, as he is being led to execution), Av i.102.8 anuśrāvyamāṇa, pass., *being* (thus) *proclaimed;* ii.182.6 anuśrāvya, ger.; **(3)** *plays* (a musical instrument): Av i.95.12 vīṇām anuśrāvitum, inf.

anuśruta (= Pali [an-]anussuta; ppp. of Skt. anu-śru; is this used in the same sense? cf. anuśrava), *traditionally handed down:* (darśanam) anuśrutaṃ purā Mv i.165.12, *repeatedly heard* (or *handed down*) *from olden times;* Senart misunderstands; pūrve ananuśrutehi dharmehi iii.332.13, *by principles unrecorded in traditional doctrine.*

anuśrotaṃ, so prob. read with v.l. for °śrotraṃ Mv ii.161.2, adv., = Skt. anusrotas, Pali anusotaṃ, (*with the current* =) *in a conforming manner:* (kaṇṭhaka)jātānugāmī anuśrotaṃ **pelavako** (q.v.) ca niṣkrānto, *and pelavaka* (whatever this means) *went forth in a way conforming* (to K.), *he who was born with and attendant on Kaṇṭhaka* (?).

anuśliṣṭa (ppp. of anu-śliṣ, which seems unrecorded anywhere), *clinging to, leaning on,* with gen.: prākārasya anuśliṣṭaṃ uccaṃ śirīṣavṛkṣaṃ paśyati Mv iii.71.14.

anuṣkṛta (ppp. of anu-kṛ; but there is no record of this mg., nor of s prefixed to kṛ after anu), *permitted, given leave*: mātā-pitṛ-anuṣkṛtā Mmk 56.3 (prose), *given leave by her mother and father.*

anu-saṃvarṇayati (not recorded, but cf. Skt. saṃvarṇayati, Pali saṃvaṇṇeti, the latter especially used in both mgs.), (**1**) *mentions, describes*: Laṅk 139.9 **deśanāpāṭhe** (q.v.) 'nusaṃvarṇitāni; (**2**) *sanctions, approves, recommends*: Divy 196.3 bhāṣitam; 263.11; MSV i.47.7; Prāt 478.1 maraṇaṃ... anusaṃvarṇayet, *should recommend (speak well of) death,* i. e. prompt someone to seek it.

[?**anusaṃśaya,** in Gv 472.(4–)5 ye te karuṇāvihāriṇaś ca na kvacid anusaṃśaya-darśana-vihāriṇaḥ, seems pretty surely corrupt; prob. read **anuśaya-,** q.v.]

[**anusaṃsārya,** ed., Divy 211.27; 212.13, 22; mss. corrupt the first and third time; in all three read anusaṃyāya, *having toured* (janapadān). This verb is so used in Skt. and Pali.]

anusaṃsīdati, (gradually) *sinks down, becomes discouraged*: °danti Gv 144.13.

anusak(k)ya, see **anuśakya.**

anusaṃjñapti, f., *explanation*: °tir dattā Divy 29.11.

anusaṃdhi (m., = Pali id., in mg. 2), (**1**) (literal, physical) *connexion*: Gv 268.5 lokadhātoḥ ... cakravāḍānusaṃdhau, *in connexion with the cakravāḍa mountain-range of the lokadhātu* (? or possibly to mg. 3, *in the serial line of the...*?); (**2**) (logical) *connexion* (esp. of a text); *application*: SP 394.1 (vs) anusaṃdhi sūtrāṇa sadā prajānati, *he knows the logical connexion,* or *application, of the sūtras always*; Dbh 42.22; 43.3; 51.21; Mvy 2176 = Tib. ḥtshams sbyor ba, *conforming conjunction*; Laṅk 143.7 svapratyātmadharmatānusaṃdhiḥ katamat (! note gender), *what thing is the application* (logical connexion; virtually = meaning) *of* (the term) *sva°*?; vāsanānusaṃdhi- LV 433.19; 442.8; Gv 108.14; (**3**) *serial line, series*; Suv 169.7 tasya tathāgatasyānusaṃdhau, *in that T.'s line* (of spiritual transmission, from one T. to another); Gv 206.13 buddhadarśanānusaṃdhau buddhaparaṃparānupacchedena; Laṅk 59.7 bhūmikramānusaṃdhau, *in the serial line of steps of the* (ten) *Stages* (of bodhisattvas); 211.3 -nirodhakramānusaṃdhi-, *serial line or succession* (of steps) *in* (the development of) *nirodha*; (**4**) adv. °dhiṃ, Mv iii.394.19 (repeated 395.4, 9; 396.13), following anupūrvam, anulomam, and preceding anudharmam; perhaps prepositional cpd. (anu governing saṃdhi), *according to the totality* (or *profound essence,* see **saṃdhi** 5), but possibly rather with mg. 3, *seriatim*; the same adverb (or anusaṃdhi) should be read for °dhiḥ in Bbh 107.15, after anupūrvam, and before **anusahitaṃ,** q.v.

anusaṃbandha, *connexion, association*: (bodhisattvo) mahāsattvānu° ŚsP 1298.15, 19 (Bhvr. adj.).

? **anusaṃbuddha** (ppp. of *anu-saṃ-budh, nowhere recorded), *illumined* or *realized*: Mv iii.331.8 °dhā (madhyamā pratipadā, sc. tathāgatena, which read in prec. line, cf. lines 10, 14); but in repetitions, lines 10, 14, abhisaṃbuddhā, which Pali has in the corresponding formula. Perhaps read abhisaṃ°?

***anu-sahāya,** *a follower-after* (cf. Skt. Gr. anusahāyībhāva, Patañjali, see BR 7 App., 1695), in anusahāyībhūtā(ḥ), *become followers*: SP 380.3.

anu-sahita, adj. (cpd. of anu and sahita, from saha), *attended, joined*: Mvy 2169 = Tib. rjes su ḥbrel ba; adv. °taṃ Bbh 107.15, after **anusaṃdhi(ḥ)** (q.v. 4). Cf. Pali anu-sahagata.

anusādhaka, m. (cf. sarvārthānusādhin, adj., cited Lex., see BR 7.835; otherwise no form of anu-sādh seems to be recorded in any dialect; see next), *assistant* (in a magic rite): °kena Mmk 39.17; 40.1; 48.26.

anusādhi? (cf. prec.), *accomplishment*: in Mmk 59.24 kṣiprakāryānusādhy-arthaṃ, *in order to the speedy successful completion of the performance.* Or should we read °sādhyārthaṃ (°sādhya-)? This seems implausible. Or possibly °siddhy-arthaṃ? No *anusiddhi has been found.

anu-sārayati, *modulates* (?), of music, or *plays* (?): Laṅk 3.8 -gītasvara-grāma-mūrchanādi-yuktenānusārya (ger.; for continuation see **anupraviśati**).

anusīvana (reading uncertain; cf. **anusyūti,** Pali anusibbati, and Skt. anusyūta), *sewing to one another, patching, mending*: (śāṇapāṃśukūlaṃ...) śilāpaṭṭena (mss.) bhagavato °vanam (mss. corrupt; Senart em. otherwise) āpadye (aor.) Mv iii.313.5.

anu-sukham, adv., *according to pleasure, as much as one likes*: Mv ii.131.8; Sukh 38.16.

anustanayati (mss. sometimes °stanāy°; anu with Skt. stanayati; cf. Pali anutthunāti), *mourns, laments*: Mv i.341.8, 9, 11; 342.4, 5; all aor. 3 pl. °yetsu(ḥ).

anusmṛti, f. (= Pali anussati; virtually non-existent in Skt., cf. BR 5.993), *mindfulness*: there are six anu°: buddhānu°, dharmānu°, saṃghānu°, śīlānu°, tyāgānu°, devatānu° (Dharmas devānu°), all listed in Pali forms in Vism. (CPD), and in BHS, Mvy 1148–54; Dharmas 54; LV 31.18–22 (each is a dharmālokamukham); four others later named in Vism. (CPD), the first three usually compounded with sati instead of anussati: maraṇa(-sati, or °ṇānussati), kāyagatā sati, ānāpāna-sati, upasamānussati; these, with the other six, form a list of ten in ŚsP 1443.6 ff., the last four being ānāpānānusmṛti (prob. read so with ŚsP 60.8 for text ānāpānusmṛtir, which could also be a corruption for **ānāpāna,** q.v.,-smṛtir), udvegānu° (instead of Pali upasamānu°), maraṇānu°, and kāyagatānu°. Of all these the only one often found elsewhere, apart from the lists, is buddhānusmṛti Divy 352.21; Av i.82.3; Suv 7.3; Gv 61.7; cf. anusmṛti buddha (loc.) abhedyā Śikṣ 4.17, 18 (vss). Other occurrences Mvy 860; 1579 (see **anuttarya**); LV 182.21, read anusmṛtī bhāvanu; Gv 36.9.

anusyūti, f. (cf. s.v. **anusīvana**; Skt. anusyūta-tva), (lit. *the being sewn together*;) *close connexion, logical dependence*: Mvy 7505 = Tib. rjes su ḥbrel ba. The next phrase is: asmin satīdaṃ bhavati; this makes the mg. of anusyūti evident, and the Tib. confirms it.

anuhiṇḍate, *wanders thru* or *after*: SP 102.6 (prose), Kashgar rec., anuhiṇḍamānaḥ (Nep. mss. paryeṣamāṇo; ed. paryaṭamāno, with Foucaux only); Divy 574.9 pṛṣṭhato 'nuhiṇḍya, ger. Cf. **anvāhiṇḍati.**

anuhimavanta, adj. or (nt.?) subst., (*the region*) *near the Himālaya,* common in Mv, not noted elsewhere: °tā, abl., Mv i.232.3; °te, loc., Mv i.253.1; 272.3; 284.8; 350.14; 351.5; 355.3; °taṃ (acc.) praviṣṭaḥ ii.96.13, *entered the* (region) *near the H.*; °te pratyuddeśe iii.29.9, °ta-pratyuddeśe 10.

-anūccalita, ppp. of *anu-uc-cal, *pursuing, following*: Gv 72.23–24 -praṇidhy-anūc°.

anūnaka, adj. (= Pali and Skt. Lex. id., Skt. anūna; only noted in vss, may be m.c.), *not deficient, not less*: SP 44.8 pañc' anūnakāḥ; 83.3 pañcāna anūnakānāṃ; 111.4 pañcāśad anūnakāni; Mv ii.369.11 pañca anūnakā.

anūpabṛṃhayati, *steadily increases* (with object acc.): Bbh 153.16 °hayatā (cittaprasādam), instr. sg. pres. pple.

anūpalipta (= Pali °litta) m.c. for **anupa°,** see also **anopa°,** *unstained*: SP 313.3 (vs).

an-ūhata (= an-uddhṛta), see **ūhata.**

anṛtaṃvada, *speaking falsehood*: Ud xi.13.

anṛtaka, adj. or subst. m. (= anṛta; in vs, perhaps

m.c.), *lying* or *a liar*: Ud xx.19 satyenānṛtakaṃ jayet, *one should conquer a liar* (not *le mensonge* with Chakravarti; Pali alīkavādinaṃ; all the parallel words in the vs should also be taken as personal) *by truth.*

aneñja, or **ān°**, = **aniñjya,** q.v.; adj.: MadhK 334.8 karmāṇi kuśalākuśalāneñjāni.

aneñjya = **aniñjya,** q.v.; adj.: Mmk 476.14 virajasko [a]neñjyaś ca (meter requires the a- which is elided in writing); a- or ā- (uncertain because of saṃdhi) Dbh 48.7 puṇyāpuṇyāneñjyān abhisaṃskārān; and mss. at MadhK 543.1 kuśalākuśalāneñjyādi-.

aneḍa, anela, nela, adj. (= Pali aneḷa, °la, nela, see CPD s.v. anela-gala, of speech or voice; presumed to represent Skt. an-enas; cf. **aneḍaka, anel°**), *pure,* perhaps *perfect*; acc. to Tib. on Mvy 454 mi tsugs pa, *not injurious*; recorded only in application to sounds, and chiefly to the Buddha's voice: LV 286.9–10, read: aneḍā kalaikavarṇasukhā (i.e. kalā eka°), cf. CPD s.v. anela-gala, and Lévi Sūtrāl. Transl. page 143 n. 2, anelā kalā; of Buddha's voice; the em. is further confirmed by Mvy 454 anelā, of Buddha's voice, foll. in 455 by kalā; also in Mv iii.322.2 prob. read anela-kalāye (for mss. °katāye; Senart em. anelakāye), of Buddha's speech; anelā, of human speech, Mmk 244.20; 330.16; °laḥ, of a sound (nirghoṣa), Sukh 38.5; nelā (vāk) Dbh 24.13 (follows hitakaraṇī); nelavarṇā (buddhasya girā) Mv i.314.14; nelayā pūrṇayā vācā (of Buddha) MSV i.273.7 (vs).

aneḍaka, anelaka, f. **°ikā,** adj. (= Pali aneḷaka, °laka, of honey; cf. **aneḍa, °la**), *pure*; (a) of Buddha's voice, like **aneḍa** etc., Mv i.255.21 (vs) anelikāṃ (with girāṃ, in prec. line; misunderstood by Senart); on Mv iii.322.2, Senart anelakāye (of Buddha's speech), see s.v. **aneḍa** (read prob. anela-kalāye); (b) of honey: aneḍakam (madhu, or a synonym) Mvy 5729; Mv i.339.8; 340.13 (°ko); Av i.187.7; 243.1; Bbh 75.11; Karmav 45.14; anelakam Dbh 6.8; in Mv i.341.7 Senart aneḷakaṃ, but mss. °ḍakaṃ or °lakaṃ (of honey); see also **nīḍaka.**

aneya, adj., hyper-Skt. (or Pkt. dial., Pischel 236) for MIndic (Pali) aneja (Pkt. aṇeja), *immovable,* or *free from desire*; ep. of Buddha, Mv ii.35.6; iii.93.7; 121.5; (not of Buddha; text fragmentary; app. *firm, hard to move*) Mahāsamājasūtra, Waldschmidt, Kl. Skt. Texte 4 p. 159, last line. Interpretation correct in Waldschmidt; Senart thinks = **ananyaneya,** q.v., but there is no support for this in Pali or elsewhere. The Pali parallel to the Mahāsamāj. verse, DN ii.254.18, actually reads anejā, proving our interpretation.

anela and **anelaka** = **aneḍa, °ḍaka,** qq.v.

Aneṣa, m., n. of a samādhi, *not seeking*: ŚsP 1417.14 f. (defined: yatra samādhau sthitvā na kaṃcid dharmam eṣate). The Mvy has erroneously **Animiṣa,** q.v., in place of this.

anairyānika, adj. (cf. Pali aniyyānika; opp. of **nairy°**) *not conducive to deliverance*: Bbh 13.14 and Dbh 69.32, see **nairy°** for both.

a-naiṣpeṣikatā, see **naiṣ°.**

anokāśa, adj. Bhvr. (= Pali anokāsa; for **an-avakāśa**), *having no sufficient space, crowded*: Mv i.175.12 °śā kṛtā svargā, *the heavenly worlds are made crowded* (by Buddha's appearance, which leads many to heaven). Most mss. read anākāśā, but there can be little doubt that Senart's text is correct.

Anotaptagātra, n. of two former Buddhas in the same list: Mv i.141.10, 15. (Cf. **Anavatapta.**)

anotrapa, adj. (see next), *shameless, indecent*: Mv iii.11.4 °po. The short penultimate vowel may well be m.c.; see **otrapa.**

anotrāpin, adj. (= Pali anottāpin; cf. prec., **otrapa, otrapya, avatrāpya**), *shameless, indecent*: Mv i.110.8 (prose) °piṇaś ca; in Ud xx.5 prob. read anotrāpī (or °apī?) for what ed. doubtfully records as anotrapū.

an-odaka (= Pali id., besides an-ud°, an-ūd°; in Pali usually adj., but also noun), (*waterless*;) as subst. *a waterless place*: Mv ii.263.1 °ke *in a waterless place.* The passage is prose; o cannot be m.c.

anopa (m.? = Skt. anūpa), *marsh*: Mv iii.326.21; the mss. are corrupt but Senart's em., pauṇḍarīkaṃ yathā varṇaṃ anope na pralipyate, seems plausible; Pali has anopā, f. (CPD).

an-opapanna, ppp. (m.c. for an-upa°), *not born*: Gv 334.3.

an-opama, f. **°mī,** adj. (= Pali id.; for Skt. an-upama; in BHS prob. only m.c.), *matchless*: Mv i.166.12 (°mī); 207.18 = ii.12.8; ii.379.19; iii.110.14. All vss; so far as meter and text-readings are clear, m.c.

anopalambha, m.c. for **anupa°**, q.v.: RP 12.10; KP 137.11.

an-opalipta, neg. ppp. (= **an-upa°**; Pali has **an-ūpa°** in vss, and so also BHS; in BHS not exclusively m.c., see § 3.71), *not defiled*: Mv ii.419.4 (prose); Śikṣ 46.16 (so ms.; vs but not m.c.); may be m.c. in Mv iii.118.9 = 326.6; SP 14.6 (vs); LV 224.15; Samādh p. 59 l. 9 f.

Anomiya, nt. (cf. Pali Anomā, n. of a river, see CPD; plays the same rôle in the Buddha's life-history), n. of a place (adhiṣṭhāna) in the Malla country, south of Kapilavastu, to which the Bodhisattva went first after leaving home: it was near the hermitage of the ṛṣi **Vasiṣṭha** (2), q.v.: °yaṃ Mv ii.164.18; 207.12; iii.189.9; °yāto, abl., Mv ii.166.11; 189.1. (Mss. corrupt in first occurrences.)

anolīna, see **anavalīna.**

an-osāna (for Skt. an-avasāna), *without end*: anutpannā °nā(ḥ) Mv i.314.17 (vs), of Buddhas.

anaupamya (nt.?), a high number: °yasya Gv 105.21. See s.v. **poma** for correspondents.

an-aupaśamika, adj. (neg. of **aupa°**, q.v.), *not tending to tranquillity*: Jm 181.19 °kaṃ (gṛhavāsam; mss. gṛhā°).

anta, m. (= Pali id., see CPD 3), *contrasting principle or opinion*: anta-samudāhāraḥ MSV i.221.8 (here, discussion as to whether Buddha and his order were greedy or not).

antaḥ-kalpa, see **antara-k°.**

antaḥ-pūti, adj. (= Pali anto-pūti), *rotten inside*: Mvy 9138; ed. antarpūty-avasrutaḥ, as cpd., but Mironov anta-pūti (so Kyoto ed. v.l.) and avasrutaḥ as separate words; in MSV i.50.7 (antaḥpūtir), and in Pali, where the same cliché of which this word forms a part occurs repeatedly (see CPD), this and avassuta (= BHS avasruta) are separate words. Applied to a bad monk; on the orig. literal meaning see **avasruta.** Also antaḥpūtī-bhāva, m., MSV i.49.3, 11; 50.6.

antaka, adj. (or subst.; = Pali id., anta [cf. **ānta**], Skt. antya; a MIndic form; not *destructions* with Senart), *low, vile* (person or thing): Mv iii.186.2–3 na ātapo tāpayati, antakā tāpayanti māṃ; antakāś ca . . . te tāpenti na ātapo. Cf. line 4 itvaraṃ khu ayaṃ tāpo; see **itvara,** which is the clue to the mg. of antaka.

? **antakoṭa,** nt. (Senart's em.; mss. amba°, ava°, ata°), n. of some product of the carpenter's craft: Mv ii.465.2 °ṭāni, 13 °ṭā.

? **Antakośa,** see **Anantakośa.**

Anta-giri (= **Antarā-giri**; neither form in Pali; perh. cf. Antargiri, n. of a people, Kirfel, Kosm. 74, 77), n. of a mountain near Rājagṛha, seat of **yaṣṭīvana**: °girismiṃ, loc., Mv iii.441.15 (v.l. Antar-g°); 442.3; 443.14.

antagrāha-dṛṣṭi, f. (Pali anta(g)gāhaka-diṭṭhi), *the heresy of holding extreme views* (see CPD): Mvy 1956; Dharmas 68; Gv 469.9; in AbhidhK. LaV-P. v. 17 f. paraphrased by dhruvoccheda(d°), *belief in permanence or annihilation.*

anta-jana, m.c. for **antar-jana,** q.v.

antatas, adv. (= **antaśas, antamaśas,** qq.v.), (*even*) *so much as*, Ger. *sogar*; (once) *in fact*: LV 72.6 (prose; v.l. antaśo); 257.1; Divy 142.11; 191.3; Av ii.130.4; Kv 27.15; Mmk 74.11; Bbh 39.15 antato yāvan nirvāṇam iti vā, *or, in fact, up to nirvāṇa*; 156.19 *even so much as*; Prāt 519.10 et alibi; Bhīk 24b.1.

anta-pūti, see **antaḥ-pūti.**

antamaśato (°**sato**), adv. (blend of **antamaśas** and **antatas**, qq.v.), *so much as*, Ger. *sogar*: (Mv i.7.10, Senart °masato, but mss. indicate rather **antaśas**;) Mv i.211.13 = ii.15.12 °masato (vv.ll. °śato, antamato); iii.92.14 °sato; in Mv i.211.5 Senart antamaśato, mss. corruptly anasato; parallel ii.15.5 antaso.

antamaśas, adv. (= Pali antamaso; BHS also **antaśas, antatas, antamaśato**, °**sato**), (*even*) *so much as*, Ger. *sogar*: KP 4.4 (prose; cited Śikṣ 52.18 as antaśas); 21.3 (prose); Lüders ap. Hoernle MR 146 antamaśas for SP 263.11 antaśas, both edd.

anta-yugika, adj., *of the last age*: Bbh 14.23.

antara (**1**) nt. (= Pali id., defined by kāraṇa; see CPD s.v. [2]antara, A, 3, kim antaraṃ = kiṃ kāraṇaṃ, *what's the matter?*, not well defined in Dictt.), *state of the case, circumstance, matter, reason*: Mv i.360.11 ko jānāti kim atra antaraṃ, *who knows what is the matter (reason, circumstance) in this?*; ii.66.15 na paribudhyāmi kim atra antaraṃ, *I do not understand what is the matter here*; (**2**) nt. and m. (essentially = Skt. id., nt., noted here as somewhat peculiar idiom), *interval, space between*: Mv ii.101.13 (janapadasya) antaraṃ nāsti, *there was no interval of* (space between) *people*, i. e., they were closely crowded together; Mv ii.113.9 antaro janasya nāsti; (**3**) see **triy-antara.**

antara-kalpa, m. (= Pali °kappa), *internal* (subdivision of a) *kalpa* or *aeon*, or *intermediate kalpa* (period between major kalpas). In AbhidhK. iii.181 the var. antaḥkalpa is recorded, along with this; it seems to point to the first definition above, and La Vallée Poussin, ad loc., considers this the only correct definition; there are 80 in a mahākalpa, op. cit. 187 (in Pali 64, CPD). On the other hand Mvy 8281 renders antara-(kalpa) by Tib. bar gyi, *intermediate*, and similarly śastrāntara-, rogāntara-, durbhikṣāntara-k° 8282–4; these suggest that antara-kalpas are periods of destruction or disaster for people, cf. CPD s.v. °kappa, *a* (short) *intermediate period* (of destruction of mankind). CPD recognizes both the above meanings, and this seems provisionally probable. It is often not clear which appears in specific cases; in Gv 325.15 perhaps the second: dvādaśānām antarakalpānām atyayena SP 67.1; prabhāṣate taj jina agradharmān ... antarakalpaṣaṣṭim SP 25.8; cf. Dharmas 87 (see s.v. **kalpa** 4); SP 159.3 ff.; Mmk 295.9 (°paṃ jīvati). In SP 68.10 text manujānam abhyantara-kalpa (= antara°), but prob. read °jān' apī antara° (see WT).

antara-dvīpa (m.; = Pali °dīpa; Skt. *antar-dvīpa). *island in the midst* (of a body of water): Mv i.221.6 = ii.23.11 (prose).

antara-dhāyati (= Pali id., to Skt. antar-dhatte, -dhīyate; see Chap. 43, s.v. dhā (8); also **antara-hāyate** and ff.), *disappears*: °dhāyiṣuḥ (v.l. °ṣu), aor., LV 397.21; ppp. antara-hita Mv i.50.14 (cf. antarhita in similar phrase 51.10); i.206.6 = ii.9.22; i.340.14; ii.101.8; 179.8; iii.116.2 ff.; Gv 325.16 (prose!) °hiteṣu. Cf. also **antardhita.**

antara-hāpayati (sometimes **antar-h**°; cf. Pali antara-dhāpeti; caus. to °**hāyate**, °**ti**, q.v.), *causes to disappear*: impv. °hāpaya Mv i.75.14, so Senart, app. with 1 inferior ms.; most mss. °hāyanā or °ṇā; fut. °hāpayiṣyanti RP 17.15; ger. °hāpayitvā Mv ii.431.1 (and see Mv iii.6.9, under °hāyate); antarhāpayitvā (semi- Skt.) Divy 329.12; ppp., read °hāpitam for antara-hāyitam (v.l. antarhāy°) *caused to disappear* Mv iii.424.16.

antara-hāyate, °ti, antar-hā° (= **antara-dhāyati**, q.v.; except the ppp. °hita, for which see **antara-dhāyati**, no form of this verb with h for dh seems to be recorded outside of BHS), *disappears*: Mv i.175.9 °hāyate or (unmetr.) °ante (mss., Senart em. °yatu); °hāyati Mv iii.410.12 (prose); impv. °hāyatu Mv iii.346.21; aor. antarhāyetsu, v.l. antarahāyetsuḥ Mv i.231.2 (prose); antarahāye i.339.18; 340.11; °hāyi ii.256.11 (prose); °hāyithā (3 sg.; v.l. °tha) ii.240.17; °hāyetsuḥ (3 pl.; cf. above) ii.258.3; 259.2; iii.93.2; °hāyiṣu (3 pl.) Suv 158.1; inf. °hāyituṃ Mv ii.97.10, 20; ger., apparently in caus.sense, *concealing*, iii.6.9 antarahāyitvā (brāhmaṇaveṣam, *his brahman's garb*; but the mss. are reported as reading °hāyatvā; prob. -ya- is an error or misreading for -pa-, and the true reading is °hāpayitvā; see °hāpayati); see also next two.

antara-hāyita, *caused to disappear*, Mv iii.424.16; read °hāpita, see °**hāpayati.**

antara-hīyati (for °te, equivalent to Skt. antardhīyate, pass. to antar-dhā; cf. **antara-hāyate**), pres. pple. °hīyanto *being covered over* (in a basket) Mv ii.178.3 (mss. °nti, °ntī).

antarā (= Skt. and Pali id.; see also **antarāt**) *between*, with acc. and gen., once app. nom. (!); repeated (usually with ca after antarā both times) with each of two nouns; so Pali, but not Skt.; Lat. inter may be thus used twice, with each noun; after the double phrase, atrāntarā (°rāt, or °re) is often added: gen., Mv ii.264.5 an° ca bodhiyaṣṭīye an° ca nadīye, *between the Bodhi tree and the river*; acc., Jm 19.21 an° ca taṃ bhadantaṃ an° ca dvāradehalīṃ; foll. by atrānt°, Divy 94.1 an° ca śrāvastīm an° ca rājagṛham atrāntarāt; 151.5, 7 an° bhadanta (in 7 an° ca) śrāvastīm an° ca jetavanam atrāntarāt; 275.26 an° ca rājagṛham an° ca campām atrāntare; Av i.256.6 an° ca rājagṛham an° ca veṇuvanam atrāntare; nom. (?) Divy 514.11 an° ca vārāṇasī (but read °sīṃ?) an° codyānam atrāntarā.

antarā-kathā (= Pali id.), *mutual talk, conversation* (CPD thinks antarā should be treated as a separate word, and so Divy 143.14 is printed, but it seems to me difficult to take it otherwise than as a cpd.): Av i.230.12 ānandasya subhadreṇa parivrājakena sārdham antarākathāṃ (mss. °thā) viprakṛtām (mss. °tā; Pali also uses vippakatā with this word, see CPD) aśrauṣīd; antarā-kathā-samudāhāra, m., ibid., Divy 143.14; Av i.230.15; Pischel, SBBA 1904 p. 818, fol. 173a; MSV i.37.9.

Antarā-giri = **Anta-giri**, q.v.: °girismiṃ Mv iii.60.1.

antarāt (= Skt. Pali antarā; prob. false hyper-Skt. for this, interpreted as MIndic abl.), (**1**) adv., *in the meantime*: SP 159.6 (prose); 161.9 (vs; here ed. em. °rā; Nep. mss. quoted 'ntarān (before k-), read doubtless °rāt; Kashgar rec. °re); (**2**) prep. with gen. and loc., *between*: atha gayāyāṃ bodhimaṇḍasya cāntarād LV 405.3, *between Gayā and the Bodhimaṇḍa*; also follows yāvac ca ... yāvac ca ..., *from ... to*, Divy 386.9–10, see **yāvat** (3); repeated, like **antarā**, with both nouns, and both times followed by ca, antarāc ca rājagṛhasyāntarāc ca gayāyā(ḥ) LV 246.3 (read, however, gayāyāṃ as in 405.3 above, with all mss. and Calc.); with **antare** instead of the first antarāt, antare ca mucilindabhavanasyāntarāc cājapālasya, *between M.'s dwelling and A.'s* (fig-tree), LV 380.11; (**3**) *after*, with gen. (not in Pali; cf. Skt. nimiṣāntarāt *after a moment*, pw s.v. antara, 2 g); SP 67.3 (prose), mss. mamāntarād (so read) or °raṃ, *after me*; KN em. mamāt-antaram, intending mamānan°; WT em. mamottaram; Tib. cited by WT as (ṅaḥi) ḥog tu, *after* (*me*).

antarāntaram (?), °**rāt**, °**rā** (?), adverbs (= Skt. °rā, see pw s.v. antarā; Pali antarantarā, in temporal sense), (**1**) *from time to time, now and then*: SP 323.3 (prose), text °ram, vv.ll. (apparently) °rā and °ra (or does the note intend °rām?); I would read °rā, possibly with 'hiatus-bridging' -m added; (**2**) local, *here and there*: °rāt Divy 155.25. Cf. **antarāt** (= Skt. antarā).

antar-āpatti, f. (= Pali id.), *a* (repeated) *offense performed during probation* (**parivāsa**) and concealed: MSV iii.34.15 °tiṃ pūrvāpattipratirūpāṃ praticchannāṃ; 35.2, 5 etc. This leads to **mūlaparivāsa.**

antarā-parinirvāyin, adj. (= Pali °nibbāyī), acc. to Tib. on Mvy 1015 (bar ma dor, for antarā) *attaining nirvāṇa in the intermediate state* (between death and rebirth; i. e. before the soul can be reborn in a new existence); Dharmas 103; Mv i.33.6. Acc. to CPD, rather *entering nirvāṇa before the term*, i. e. *before having passed the first half of life* (in the middle of life). This seems to be the orthodox Pali interpretation, but the Tib. interpretation was also known (cf. CPD s.v. antarābhava); it is refuted in Kathāvatthu viii.2 (Transl. pp. 212–3).

antarā-pūrṇa-tā, *state of being full in the middle*: Gv 64.12 (mahāsāgarasya).

antarā-bhava, m. (= Pali and Skt. Lex. id.), *intermediate state of existence* (between death and rebirth; in standard Pali rejected as a heresy, see **antarāparinirvāyin**): Mvy 7680; Bbh 390.19 ff. (discussion); Laṅk 160.5; 177.4; 370.14. See MadhK p. 286 note 1, and next; AbhidhK. LaV-P. Index s.v.; Sūtrāl. xviii.84–88, comm.

antarābhavika, adj., *of* or *belonging to the intermediate state* (between death and rebirth; see **antarābhava**): Laṅk 355.13; 370.13. See also **āntarābhavika**, which MadhK 286.9 reads by em., but mss. antar°.

antarā-marśana (nt.), *stroking inside* (the garments; of a woman, by a man); Bhīk 28a.1 yā . . . adhaś cakṣuṣor ūrdhvaṃ jānvor °naṃ (text °marṣaṇaṃ) parāmarśanaṃ (text °marṣaṇaṃ) svīkuryād. (Perhaps less specifically *intimate stroking*?).

antarāya, nt. (only m. in Skt. and Pali), *hindrance*: LV 111.6 (vs) na cāntarāyam iha. (Could perhaps be analyzed as °rāya-m-iha, with 'hiatus-bridging' m.).

[**antarāyaṇa**, nt., often in AsP (e. g. 495.5) erroneously for antarāpaṇa, *market*.]

antarāyika, adj. (= Pali id.; also **āntar°**, and neg. **an-antar°**, qq.v.), *connected with hindrances*; *causing obstacles* or *obstruction*, regularly with dharma, *obstructive conditions* (so in Pali with dhamma): °ka-dharma Mvy 133; 9324; °kā dharmās Prāt 514.5 ff.

? **antarāvāsa** (m.?), *interval*: Mv i.258.20 (prose), ardhayojanikenāntarāvāsena, *at intervals of half a yojana* (but mss. °āntarvās°, °āntavās°; em. Senart). Cf. Pali antarāvāsa, Dīp. 5.80 Tambapaṇṇi-antar°, apparently *interval of time*; *interregnum* (so Oldenberg, CPD).

antarika, adj. (to Skt. antara), *neighboring*, *situated near*: Mvy 8593, 8594.

antarikā (= Pali id.; in Skt. cited from Kauṭ.A., see Schmidt, Nachträge; cf. **āntarikā**; see also **lokāntarikā**, separately), *space between*, *interval*, *interstice*; in some of the following ānt° may be intended, saṃdhi ambiguous: Mv i.13.12 teṣām (sc. parvatānām) antarikāṃ (all mss.; Senart em. °kaṃ!) . . . praveśitāḥ (so read); i.21.1 parvatāntarikaṃ (all mss., perhaps to be kept as adv. from cpd., *in between the mountains*; Senart em. °ka-); i.21.3 parvatāntarikaṃ (so Senart with most mss., but C, one of the best, °kā; read °kā or °kāṃ) praviśanti; ii.300.19 sapta parvatā dvīpāntarikā (cpd. adj.), *the 7 mountains between the continents*; Dbh 58.13 bodhisattvacaryāntarikā, of the dividing line between the various bhūmi; ŚsP 1442.20 prathamasya dhyānasya dvitīyasya dhyānasyāntarikā, *the interval between the 1st and 2nd dhyāna.*

antarikṣa, adj. (= Skt. ānt°), *of the atmosphere*, *atmospheric*, of a class of gods, see **deva**; also **antarīkṣa**, and under **antarīkṣecara**, q.v.: LV 367.7 (devās); Av i.109.7 (devāsura . . . mahoragāḥ; Speyer em. ānt°).

[**antarī**, implied in LV 28.18 kuto ntarī; should be read kutottarī, i. e. -uttarī, *how much less* (a woman) *superior* (to Māyā); see § 11.3.]

antarīkṣa, adj. (= **antarikṣa**; Skt. ānt°), *of the atmosphere*, a class of gods, see **deva**: LV 266.1, 4; 396.14; 401.1. As noun, antarīkṣa also occurs in Skt., but much more commonly in BHS (= antarikṣa): e. g. SP 23.14; 69.10; LV 75.7; 218.18; Mv i.31.4; 33.5; 179.10; Divy 324.28; 340.5; Suv 84.9; RP 45.20; Gv 117.15.

antarīkṣadevalipi, a kind of script: LV 126.4.

antarīkṣecara, adj. m. (with deva; cf. Pali antalikkhacara, which seems not to be recorded of any class or category of gods), *moving* or *living in the atmosphere*, n. of a class of gods, see **deva**; = **antarikṣa**, **°īkṣa**, **āntarikṣavāsin**: Mv i.40.14; 229.15; 240.4; ii.138.12; 348.16; in all after bhūmya deva, and before other classes of kāmāvacara gods.

-antarīya (**1**) adj. ifc. (from Skt. antara), *belonging to a different* . . ., see **gotrāntarīya**, and cf. **-antarīyaka**; [(**2**)? nt. (= Skt. Lex. and Pali Lex. id., Pkt. antarijja; once in Skt. literature, see Schmidt, Nachträge), *undergarment*: SP 212.12; 213.2 baddhvā (mss. in 212.12 baddho) 'ntarīye. But WT cite ms. K' both times as baddhvottarīye, supported by Tib. bla gos, *upper garment* (Skt. uttarīya); doubtless read so.]

-antarīyaka, adj. ifc., = **-antarīya**, adj.; see **jātyantarīyaka.**

antare (= Skt., BR s.v. antara, 2e), prep. with gen., *between*; paralleled by antarāt before the second noun, LV 380.11, see s.v. **antarāt.**

antareṇa, instr. of n. used as adv. and prep. (in this sense nowhere recorded in Skt. or MIndic), (*at a*) *later time* (orig. *interval*): yena antareṇa ahaṃ prasūtā bhaviṣyaṃ tato gamiṣyaṃ Mv i.365.3, *at what later time*, *after what interval*, *when* (later) . . .; adv., *afterwards*, *after* (this) Mv ii.362.8 (with no dependent noun; Senart wrongly *in the interval*); atrāntareṇa *after this* Mv i.96.6 (so mss., to be kept, Senart em. wrongly); mamāntareṇa *after me* SP 26.4 (vs); LV 39.4 (prose); yo (e)tasya (mss.) mṛgīye antareṇa Mv i.362.5, 7, *who* (comes) *after this doe* (here Senart correctly recognizes the mg., referring to Burnouf on SP 26.4, where the right interpretation is already given). (In Mv ii.209.6 mamāntareṇa means *with reference to me*; Senart misunderstands. Skt. uses antareṇa in this sense with acc. and also with gen., see BR 5.997.)

antaroddāna, nt. (see **uddāna**), *internal*, *inserted summary of details of contents* (in the midst of a story, referring to an episode), Tib. bar sdom (bar = antarā, °ra-): Mvy 1475; Divy 102.27 (a mark of punctuation should be put before and after °dānam; what follows is a tabulation of the proper names occurring in the following episode); MSV i.69.16 (referring to a minor part of the story).

[**antargata**, Skt., see **antogata.**]

antar-jana, m. (once **antajana**, m.c.; = Pali antojana), *people of the inside*, *family*, *household*: LV 135.4 antajanaṃ (m.c.; v.l. antarj°, unmetr.); otherwise always antarj°: LV 157.11, 14; 302.18; Mvy 3916; Divy 301.12; 312.5.

antardhāni (f.?; cf. Skt. °dhāna, Pali antaradhāna; more particularly cf. AMg. antaddhāṇī, *the art of making oneself invisible*; and see next), *disappearance*: Bbh 14.13, 21 saddharmāntardhānim (acc. sg.).

antardhānika, adj. (to prec., q.v.), *causing to disappear* (by magic), ep. of mantras, cf. Pali antaradhāna-manta: Mmk 151.20 °ka-mantrā(ḥ); usually as subst. without expression of mantra, *a magic charm having this effect*, Mmk 670.2 °kaṃ (sc. mantraṃ) bhavati; 705.29; sarvāntardhānikānāṃ rājā (696.10 prabhur) bhavati, *he becomes master of all* (charms) *that cause invisibility*, Mmk 291.24; 295.8, 14; 696.10; 719.2.

antar-dhita, ppp. (hyper-Skt. = Skt. antar-hita, BHS antara-hita; see **antara-dhāyati**), *concealed*: Gv 444.13 (prose).

antar-pūti, see **antaḥ-pūti.**

antarmukha, adj. (pendant to Skt. bahirmukha), *turned towards* (loc.): antarmukho nirvāṇe bahirmukhaḥ saṃsārād MSV iv.22.6; this (perh. with MIndic antemukho or antomukho?) was surely the orig. reading in Divy 1.18 (delete na; construe bahirmukhaḥ with the abl. as regularly).

antarvartinī (? possibly cf. Skt. antarvatnī, f. to °vant, Pāṇ. 4.1.32; but the word has the aspect of a cpd. of Skt. antar with -vartin), *pregnant*: patnī antarvartinī saṃvṛttā Divy 234.17.

antarvarṣā, or **°ṣa,** m. (= Pali antaravassa, antovassa), *the rainy season*: °ṣā Mvy 9424; °ṣa MSV iii.27.16, 17; 28.3, 4.

(**antarvāsika,** m. [prob. = Skt. id., rare, see pw s.v.; elsewhere Skt. antarvaṃśika], *superintendent of the inner apartments* (harem): Mvy 3690 = Tib. naṅ paḥi bla.)

antar-hāpayati, °hāyati, °te, see **antara-hā°.**

antavāsin (= Skt. Lex. id., for the usual antevāsin), *pupil*: Sukh 3.5 karmārāntavāsinā, instr.

antaśalya-, see **antaḥśalya-.**

antaśas, adv. (= **antatas, antamaśas,** etc., qq.v.), *so much as*, Ger. *sogar*: Mvy 6331 = Tib. tha na; SP 108.3; 224.6 ff. antaśa ekāpi gāthā, *so much as a single stanza*; 263.11 (Kashgar rec. antamaśaḥ, q.v.); 277.6 nāntaśo dharmasaṃrāgeṇāpi, *not even with passion for the Law*; 277.7; 286.3; 349.4; 372.2; Mv i.104.6; ii.15.5 (see s.v. **antamaśatas**); Divy 161.24; Av i.314.6 (kecit suvarṇaṃ kecid antaśaḥ kārṣāpaṇam, *some gold, some as much as,* i. e. *at least, a kārṣāpaṇa*); Suv 6.12; 89.5 (foll. by **prāg eva,** *not to speak of*...); 125.10; 129.2, 5; 132.9; RP 57.12; Śikṣ 16.13 etc.; Gv 160.3–4; 175.20; Dbh 23.14; Sukh 71.14 etc.; Laṅk 255.3 tato 'ntaśaḥ (so read with citation Śikṣ 135.6 for text daśa-) prakṛtimṛtāny api; Vaj 25.2 etc.

antaścālin, *going within* (to the heart, reality, of matters): Laṅk 10.7 °cālinā, na bāhyārthadṛṣṭyabhiniviṣṭena.

antaḥśalya- (once in ŚB, once Cl. Skt., see BR, pw), *inner dart*, fig. *internal torment, anguish*: only noted in cpd. antaḥśalyaparidāghajāta (also antaś°, antoś°) *afflicted with the anguish of internal torment* Mv i.42.3 = 230.11 = 240.20; ii.163.2; 268.9, 12; 276.16.

-antika, adj. (from anta; = Pali id.), *ending in*...: abhisamayāntika, *ending in* **abhisamaya,** q.v. (1): °kaṃ kuśalamūlam Mvy 1208; °kaḥ (without noun, context not clear; sc. mārgaḥ?) Mvy 6891; *belonging to, related to, connected with, occasioned by,* (prakramaṇa-, etc.; corresp. to Pali list Vin. i.256.20 ff.) MSV ii.161.16 ff. For other cpds. see s.v. **-aṃśika,** and **śākhāntika.**

antikāt, adv., postpos. (**1**) *than*, with gen.: mamāntikād abhirūpatara Divy 75.1, 6; pūrvikānām antikād Divy 115.14; 117.14, 28; tavāntikāt Divy 85.29; (asya ...) puṇyaskandhasyāntikād asau paurvakaḥ puṇyaskandhaḥ śatatamīm api kalāṃ nopaiti Vaj 35.7, *in comparison with this*...; (**2**) *on the part of*, with gen., substantially = *by*: SP 109.5 tathāgatasyāntikād eṣu dharmeṣv abhiyuktā(ḥ), *charged, employed in these* (inferior) *conditions of life on the part of* (i. e. *by*) *the T.*; wrongly Burnouf and Kern.

antikāvacara, m. (= Pali santikāvacara, DN i.206.2), (one who lives near, i. e.) *companion, close associate*: Mv i.67.20 °kaḥ kāśyapas.

antike, adv., postpos., *in reference to*, with gen.: SP 107.4–5 daridrapuruṣas tasya gṛhapater antike pitṛsaṃjñām utpādayet, *would conceive the notion of father in reference to that householder*, i. e. would think of him as his father; similarly SP 286.1; also LV 244.1 naiṣa mamāntike viśiṣṭasaṃjño bhaven (see **saṃjñā** 5); Mv i.30.9 devānām ... antike cittāni pradūṣayitvā, *because they conceived evil thoughts in reference to the gods*; Divy 212.2 sattvānām antike ... anukampā; Av i.264.10 bhagavato 'ntike cittaṃ prasādayām āsuḥ, *in reference to the Blessed One*; Av i.287.1 arhato 'ntike.

antiṣṭha-, in Mv ii.390.1, Senart antiṣṭha-guptām (but mss. °guptaṃ or °uptaṃ) bahuśālimadhye, apparently epithet of rājadhānīm, *capital city*. The following word, *in the midst of much rice*, suggests that a form of upta, *sown*, may be the true reading, with v.l.; antiṣṭha- could be superl. to Pali anti(ṃ), *close by, near* (Ved. anti): *sown very close* (up to the city-limits), *in the midst of abundant rice*?

ante, adv. (= Pali id., Skt. antar), *within* (cf. also next), contrasted with bahis; ante nidhiḥ bahir nidhiḥ etc. Mv ii.436.8–9, repeated 437.4 etc.

ante-pura (nt., = Pali id., Skt. antaḥp°; cf. prec.), *inner apartments, harem*: Mv ii.159.11 °pure (v.l. antaḥpure).

antevāsika, m. (= Pali id.; Skt. antevāsin), *pupil*: Gv 464.19 (prose); Laṅk 48.8 (vs).

antogata, adj. (= Pali id., Skt. antargata), *turned inward*, of the indriyas (so in Pali): Mv i.237.10 antogatehi indriyehi abahirgatamānasena (of a Buddha).

antodaka, adj. (for anta(r) or Pali anto, *within*, plus (u)daka *water*, prepos. cpd.), *within the water*: Mv iii.318.7 (prose) antodakāni (utpalāni etc.); in Mv ii.121.9 antodake, perhaps *in* (a place that is within the) *water*; this could be two words, = Skt. antar udake, but the parallel suggests that it too is a cpd.

antośalya-, see **antaḥś°.**

antra-guṇa, m., nt. (= Pali anta-guṇa, nt.; cf. **guṇa** 2), *intestinal tract, mesentery*: Mvy 4025 °guṇa, = Tib. gñe ma *the twisted part of the colon or great gut* (Jäschke); *the coiled intestine* (Zam. ap. Das); Mv i.8.8; Divy 375.14 °guṇān; Śikṣ 81.13 (read with mss. antrāṇy antraguṇaṃ; n. sg.); 209.9 antrāṇy antraguṇa(ḥ); Gv 328.19 °guṇa-, stem. See also **āntraguṇa.** In BHS seems to be masc. except in Śikṣ 81.13, and sometimes pl.

antrā (**1**) (Skt. and Pali only nt. antra, anta) *intestines*: antrāyāṃ, loc., Divy 409.15; (**2**) a high number: Gv 106.7 (could also intend āntrā).

andhakāra-tamisrā (= Pali °timissā), *deep (blinding) darkness*, in the passage treated s.v. **lokāntarikā,** q.v.: SP 163.8; LV 410.14 (in 51.11 andhakārās tamisrā; prob. haplog. for °kārā andhakāra-tamisrā both times); Divy 204.23 (and repetitions); ŚsP 102.17.

andhakāra-tamisrita (ppp. denom. from prec.), *made completely dark*: °taṃ Mv ii.266.9; so I would emend; mss. corrupt; Senart's em. surely wrong.

andhakārāpita-tva, nt. (abstr. from caus. pple. to denom. verb from andhakāra, *darkness*), *state of being darkened*; so (or, possibly, andhakārāyita-tva, from noncaus. denom. pple.) I would read at Mv i.41.5; 229.20; 240.9; ii.162.9; iii.334.7; 341.12. The mss. are corrupt in the entire passage (see **lokāntarikā**) and particularly at this point; Senart reads °kārārpitā, but there is no support for the -r- in the mss. The Mv seems to have read andhakārā andhakārāpitatvā (? °yitatvā), tamisrā **tamisrāyitatvā** (q.v.), *darknesses, darkenednesses, glooms, begloomednesses.* Only Mv has the second member of each pair (the derivatives of denom. pples.); the other parallel passages point to something like andhakārā **andhakāratamisrāḥ,** q.v.

andhakāla (m. or nt.), (**1**) *time of being blind*: Kv 59.4, said of a son by his parents, (jarākāle yaṣṭibhūto) andhakāle mārgasyopadarśakaḥ (so read for text °opamardakaḥ; foll. by maraṇakāle piṇḍadātā); (**2**) n. of a hell: Kv 18.14 (read Andhakāra? but this is not recorded as n. of a hell).

andhala, adj. (to andha; recorded only as Pkt. in Hem. 2.173), *blind*: Mvy 8873.

andhāra (m. or nt.; § 3.118; = AMg. id., Skt. and Pali andhakāra), *darkness*: Mmk 61.3 saṃsārāndhāra-cārake, and 66.25 °cāriṇām (both vss, may be m.c.). Cf. next two.

Andhāravāsinī, n. of a yakṣiṇī: Mmk 567.10. Cf. prec. and next.

Andhārasundarī, n. of a yakṣiṇī (= **Tama(ḥ)-sundarī**, q.v.): Mmk 567.5. Cf. prec. two.

anyajānmika, adj. (from Skt. anyajanman), *belonging to another birth*: Bbh 100.19, 25.

anyatama, adj. (**1**) (in this sense not precisely paralleled; cf. BR 7.1697, with śrī, *another, a second Śrī*), *other*, = anya: Av i.95.13 rājā prasenajid anyatamaś ca mahājanakāyaḥ, *King P. and the other people, a great multitude*; (**2**) at end of cpd., in (devo vā) devānyatamo vā MSV i.50.5, = Pali devo vā devaññataro vā, acc. to PTSD (*a god or*) *one of the retinue of a god*. Neither the context nor the Pali citations give any clue; it would seem to mean lit. *some one of the gods*.

anyatamaka, adj. (to **anyatama**), *belonging to another*: Sukh 58.15 (nāsti teṣām) anyatamaka-saṃjñā nāsti svaka-saṃjñā, *they have no notion of what is another's nor of what is their own.*

anyatamānyatama, adj., = **anyatarānyatara**: MSV ii.99.3.

anyatara, adj., like Pali aññatara (and cf. **katara**, q.v.) is very commonly used without its Skt. limitation to *one of two*; rather, as equivalent of Skt. anyatama (which is also used in BHS in the same way, notably in Divy and Av), and chiefly (**1**) in the mg. *a certain*; (an unspecified) *one* (*of many*): Mv i.36.10 (here could be interpreted in mg. 2); 343.4; ii.31.19; 65.1; 96.15; 145.4; 171.9; 461.14; iii.15.7; 53.13; Divy 102.8; 226.19; 227.26; 254.6; Av i.137.11; 208.8; 235.6; 244.3; Suv 214.4; RP 39.16; Śikṣ 39.1 (wrongly rendered *another* by Bendall and Rouse); Gv 84.17; Karmav 32.12; 35.16; Laṅk 176.8; (**2**) much more rarely, *another, any other* (of an unlimited number); so possibly (but not probably) Mv i.36.10, above; and RP 56.19 sarvathānapekṣo 'bhūt kāye jīvite ca, prāg evānyatarasmin bāhyavastuni, . . . *how much less* (not to speak of) *in regard to any other external matter*; (**3**) *some* (one or other), *one or another*, substantially = **anyatarānyatara**, q.v.: Mmk 304.16 anyatareṇa śucinā celakhaṇḍena.

[**anyatarāgra-**, read **abhyantarāgram**; see this.]

anyatarānyatara, adj. (= Pali aññataraññatara), *one or another* (of many, or more than two)· Mv ii.362.9 °tareṇa yānena, *by one or other of the* (three) *vehicles*; Mv iii.73.2 °tare vā aṅgajāte, *or to one or another sort of member* (of the horse's body); 74.4 (pañcānāṃ vāṇijaka-śatānāṃ) °taro vāṇijako; Śikṣ 98.20; Vaj 28.16; MSV ii.199.13.

anya-tīrthika (cf. Pali añña-titthiya), see **tīrthika.**

anyatra, adv., (**1**) *on the contrary* (this mg. seems exclusively peculiar to BHS); always after negative expressions: SP 73.10 anyatra tena tenaiva dhāvanti, (they pay no attention and do not understand;) *on the contrary, they run this way and that*; 102.9 na kasyacid ācakṣed anyatraika evātmanādhyātmaṃ saṃtapyed, *he would not speak of it to anyone*; *on the contrary, he would all alone be grieving himself by himself*; 284.9; 378.4; LV 71.6 (Māyā felt no heaviness of body, gurukāyatāṃ;) anyatra laghutām eva, *on the contrary, nothing but lightness*; 259.16; 260.8; 268.15; Mv iii.66.8 and 15 (there is no soul nor anything resembling a soul;) atha evaṃ anyatra karma caiva karmavipākaṃ ca hetuś (first time, hetuṃ) caiva hetusamutpannā ca dharmā(ḥ), *but rather, on the contrary, only action* etc. (see under **atha**); Laṅk 9.7 (see s.v. **vikalpa**; wrongly Suzuki); 39.7 anyatra kāraṇataḥ, *on the contrary, from a cause* (wrongly Suzuki); 119.6 (place daṇḍa between evam and anyatra); 152.1; RP 42.4; Samādh 22.39 (wrongly Régamey); Śikṣ 147.3 (and several times in Śikṣ followed by **yāvad eva,** *just simply*, q.v.); the negative may be repeated just before anyatra, but only as resuming the neg. of the preceding clause, not negating the clause containing anyatra: Bbh 121.(19)21 (a Bodhisattva does not give a petitioner the trouble of asking repeatedly before he gives him a gift;) nānyatra yācitamātra eva, *no; on the contrary*, (he gives) *the very moment he is asked*; (**2**) *except*; in Skt. and Pali hardly used except as preposition (with abl. in Skt., Pali aññatra also with instr. and gen.); in Skt. very rarely as adverb, the noun being construed with other words in the sentence (see BR 1.266 and pw 3.251). In BHS I have noted a single case, not wholly certain, of anyatra as preposition with instr. (as in Pali, instead of abl. as in Skt.): RP 40.4 rātriṃdivaṃ bhavantībhir nānyā kathā kāryā, anyatra nṛttagītavāditena, *you are to say nothing else, except dance, song, and instrumental music* (?). But the adverbial use in this mg., so rare in Skt. and not recorded for Pali, is well established in BHS; in the following cases the form and construction of other words in the clause is totally unaffected by anyatra; often it may be translated as if it were a conjunction, *except that* . . . It almost always follows a negative expression (or interrogative, rhetorically equivalent to neg.); and this is sometimes resumed by an additional na before anyatra (as in the last case under 1, above): Divy 6.28 sārthaṃ na paśyati nānyatra gardabhayānam eva, *he didn't see the caravan, not except only a donkey-cart*; and with anyatra as quasi-conjunction, Mv ii.90.14–15 nāsti anyo upāyo nānyatra etaṃ samudraṃ utsicāmi, *there is no other means, not* (any) *except* (that) *I bale out* (exhaust) *this sea*. In the next the na before anyatra goes with the main verb (or rather ppp.): SP 318.4 nānyatra sattvānāṃ paripācanārtham avatāraṇārtham ete dharma-paryāyā bhāṣitāḥ, *these dharmaparyāya are not spoken except* (i.e. are spoken only) *to mature creatures and make them arrive at comprehension*. Otherwise, after negs.: LV 149.1 (nānyaḥ . . . saṃvidyate ya etāṃ gaṇanāṃ prajānāty) anyatrāhaṃ vā yo vā syān mādṛśaḥ, *except* (it be) *I or someone like me*; SP 276.6–7 na ca taiḥ sārdhaṃ saṃstavaṃ karoty anyatropasaṃkrāntānāṃ ... dharmaṃ bhāṣate, *and he has no association with them, except that . . . he preaches the Law to them when they come to him*; similarly 276.9–10; 324.8 yūyaṃ ca śabdaṃ na śṛṇotha mahyaṃ, anyatra so nirvṛtu lokanāthaḥ, *and you do* (would) *not listen to my words, except* (i. e. *unless*; sc. you believed that) *the Lord of the World has entered nirvāṇa*; Sukh 42.(10–)11 (na ca . . . nānātvam asty) anyatra . . . saṃkhyāṃ gacchanti, *except that* . . .; Laṅk 19.8 (a passage badly misunderstood by Suzuki; e. g. in 7 read 'dharmā = adharmāḥ) na lakṣaṇataḥ kalpyāḥ (delete daṇḍa) te 'nyatra saṃvyavahārārthā abhidhīyante, *they* (impossibilities like the son of a barren woman) *are not conceivable by way of characteristic marks, except that* (? or possibly *on the contrary*, to 1) *they are spoken of as terms of common use* (they have existence only as words); Laṅk 20.1 anyatra . . . vibhāvyate, *except that it is discussed* . . . (after neg.); after interrog., Av ii.121.4 kānyā putrasya gatir anyatra mātāpitarāv eva, *what other recourse could there be for a son* (i. e. there could be none), *except his parents*; no negative (except by vague implication), Divy 293.(15–)16 (annādyaṃ parikṣīṇam) anyatra . . . ekā māṇikā . . . avaśiṣṭā, (edible things were destroyed, i. e. there were none), *except that . . . one m. was left;* Gv 206.5 (see s.v. **upādāya** 1 d).

anyathātva, nt. (= Pali aññathatta; Pali adv. aññathā is correspondingly used; neither used in this mg. in Skt.), (*change for the worse*,) *depression, distress, disturbed* (mental) *state*: Divy 49.22 apareṣāṃ bhaviṣyaty °tvaṃ, *the others will be distressed*; 51.11; Sukh 4.13 na mukhavarṇasyānyathātvaṃ bhaven (? may perhaps be rendered simply *alteration*, but certainly *for the worse* is implied).

anyathībhāva (m.; in Skt. and Pali only anyathā-bhāva, añña°), *alteration, altered state or condition*: LV 423.11–12 -ananyathībhāvaṃ (Bhvr. cpd.); Bbh 243.8 °bhāvād; Ud iii.12 °bhāvo (Bhvr. cpd.; v.l. -anyathā°); and in Mv ii.146.14–15 read, na vipariṇāmānyathībhāvo bhaveyā (mss. °mānyarthī°; Senart em. °mānyārtī°).

anyapakṣikāṃ, mss., Mv ii.80.17; Senart em. ananyapakṣikā (with jñātayo), perhaps rightly (better meter, and a n. pl. seems required); Senart *harmonious*; better *not adhering to other* (heretical) *sects*?

anyamanya, adj. or pron. (= Pali aññamañña, in both mgs.; cf. **anyonya**), (**1**) *one another*; as pron., adj., or adv. (°nyaṃ) or in comp., *mutual, reciprocal* (= anyonya): SP 209.5 (vs) paraṃparā eva tathānyamanyaṃ te vyākariṣyanti; 359.2 (vs) ye cānyamanyasya karonti ghoṣān; LV 176.9 (vs) anyamanyopacayena, *by mutual assistance*; Suv 16.12 (vs) anyamanyānukūlena; RP 38.11 (vs). In prose of most texts replaced by anyonya; but Mv has it often in prose. Note anyonya SP 163.11, 12; LV 51.16; 410.19, 20; while in the same passage (prose) anyamanya is used in Mv i.41.8 = 230.3 = iii.334.11 = 341.15 (but in i.240.13 anyonya). Inflected like anyonya in Skt.: °nyaṃ, acc., Mv i.10.12 (here adv.); 13.8; ii.436.16, 17; iii.453.7; °nyasya i.27.7; 266.1; °nyasmiṃ i.16.10; (**2**) like Pali aññamañña and like **anyonya** in BHS, also *various, different*, with no reciprocal sense: SP 125.14 (vs) °nyehi arthehi; 358.11 (vs) ghoṣāṃs tatha cānyamanyān; in this mg. also replaced by anyonya in prose generally, but in Mv retained in prose: iii.390.5 °nyāhi parivrājikāhi.

anyavāda- (m.?; cf. Pali aññavādaka, adj. and n. nt.), *talking about something else, shuffling and evading the question* (CPD); in anyavāda-viheṭhana, nt., (a monk's) *causing annoyance* (to the community) *by doing this*, v.l. in Kyoto ed. of Mvy for 8433, text ājñā-viheṭhanam (so Mironov without v.l.; Tib., Chin. and Jap. *violation of commands*; for the v.l. the Jap. editor gives the correct interpretation, as above); Prāt 505.1, text anyā-vāda (-viheṭhanāt), which Finot would em. to anya°; Chin 'si un bhikṣu ennuie les autres en donnant des réponses à côté' (= anya°). The corresp. Pali, Vin. iv.36.3, 18, 37 etc., has añña-vādaka, which certainly means what is stated above (the context proves it clearly). Mvy ājñā-(-vāda) is evidently an ignorant and secondary hyper-Sktism, based on a MIndic form of anya- interpreted as = ājñā- (cf. § 2.15). It is, however, very curious that the text of Prāt reads anyā- with long stem-final ā!

anyātaka, adj. (§ 2.15; = Pali aññāta, °taka; AMg. aṇṇāya; from Skt. ajñāta, in MIndic *stranger*), *belonging to another* or *others*; the word was unhistorically Sktized by association with anya, *other*: Mv i.346.11 ff. (repeatedly), e. g. adinnam anyātakaṃ śālim, *rice belonging to others and not given* (by them). In MSV iv.107.11 spelled **anyādakam** (ed. em. ajñātakaṃ); Tib. (Dutt, 108 n. 1) gzan gi, *of another* (anya!).

anyāya, see **aññāya.**

anyāvāda, see **anyavāda.**

anyāsi (representing Pali aññāsi? quasi-MIndic for semi-MIndic ajñāsi, which Senart reads by em., or āj°), aor. of jñā-, *knew*: Mv iii.386.18 (vs); § 2.15.

anyena, adv. (**1**) *elsewhere, to another place*: Mv iii.425.13 aho punar me āśramāto ... anyena prakrameyā, *but I wish he would depart elsewhere, away from my hermitage*; (**2**) anyena ... anyena (= Pali aññena ... aññena), *by one way ... by another*: Mv iii.59.18 anyena śāriputro ... anyena maudgalyāyano.

anyonya, adj. (generally used as in Skt.; but also) *various, different* (= **anyamanya**, 2, and Pali aññamañña); replaces anyamanya in prose of most texts: SP 132.3 (prose) na santi ... trīṇi yānāni, kevalam anyonya-caritāḥ sattvāḥ, *there are not three vehicles, only creatures with different courses of action*; 134.6 (prose) anyonya-dravyasaṃyuktāṃ, *mixed with various substances*; 137.13 (prose); 221.7 (prose) anyonyāsu lokadhātuṣu; 242.8 (prose) °nyeṣu buddhakṣetreṣu ... °nya-nāmadheyās (Bhvr., *of various names*); Mv i.62.8 (vs) sugatānāṃ anyonya-nāmadheyānāṃ (as in SP 242.8); in the prose corresp. to this, i.58.16, we should surely read nānā-nāma° (mss. corruptly nānāṃ-nāma°; one ms. by haplogr. nā-nāma°; Senart em. anyonya-nāma°).

anvardhamāsam, adv. (= Pali anvaḍḍha°, anvaddha°), *every half month*: Av ii.21.12; Prāt 476.7; Bhīk 5a.1; 5b.5, etc.

anvādiśati (cf. AMg. aṇṇāiṭṭha, ppp., Ratnachandra v. 4; otherwise not in this mg.), *commands*; Jm 117.25 svaṃ puruṣam anvādideśa; 133.4.

anvāvartayati (caus. of anu-ā-vṛt; not recorded in this sense), *converts* (so in all the following; wrongly Divy, Index): °yati Divy 128.1; 263.2; °yiṣyati 128.2 (nānvā°, question, *will he not convert*?); 164.18; °titaḥ MSV i.211.5.

anvāhiṇḍati, °te, rarely **°hiṇḍayati, °hiṇḍyate** (= Pali °ti; cf. **anuhiṇḍati**), *roams thru*: °ti Divy 249.11; °nti Mmk 139.19 (so read for text aṇḍā hi°); 249.10; °ḍate Av ii.116.10; °ḍyante Divy 175.12, 15; pres. p. °ḍantā, n. pl. m., Mv i.20.3; °ḍatā, instr. sg., Divy 237.24; °ḍamāna Av i.242.6; ger. °hiṇḍya LV 16.4; Mvy 5116; Divy 68.23; 139.3; Av i.5.10; °hiṇḍayitvā Mvy 6942.

(**anveṣati**, *seeks*, occurs in Epic and perhaps other Skt., see pw, which associates this with iṣyati, but see s.v. **eṣati**: Mv ii.179.2 (prose) taṃ nāgarājam anveṣiya (ger.), etc.)

anvodahana, nt. (cf. Pali odahana; to *anv-o(ava)-dahati, as in Pali for -dadhati, -dadhāti; cf. **samodahana**), *penetrating consideration*: Mvy 7474 °nam = Tib. rjes su rab tu rtog pa.

? **apakara**, false Skt. or (more probably) error for Skt. avakara, *rubbish*: Mmk 131.21; see **saṃkāra** (1).

apakarṣa, in mūlāpa°, see **mūla.**

-apakarṣaṇa-tā (Skt. °ṇa), *state of removing*: LV 32.3 (prose).

apakarṣaṇā (Skt. only °ṇa, nt.), *removal*: Śikṣ 183.5.

apakarṣikā (cf. Pali avakaḍḍhati, *is depressed, downcast*; perhaps read ava°?), *depression, lowering* (with implication of grief): LV 227.9 (prose) śīrṣopakarṣikayā (rudanti), *with bowing of the head* (v.l. śiro-pa-, more regular), see **śīrṣas.**

apakarṣitaka, adj. (ppp. of Skt. apakarṣayati plus specifying -ka, § 22.39), *which had been removed*: Mv i.353.15.

-apakarṣin, adj., *removing*: LV 281.11 (prose) sarvakleśāpakarṣiṇyā (prabhayā).

[**apakubjaka**, adj., text in Mv ii.126.6; 283.1, but read **avak°** with v.l. both times.]

[**apakoṭana**, var. for **ākoṭana**, q.v.]

[**apakkā, °kvā**, or with final -ă, see s.v. **ayakvā, °va.**]

[**apakrānta**, text in Divy 272.16, 21, acc. to Index *abused*. But read (tathā) pra° with all mss. in 16 and one in 21: *treated, behaved towards*.]

***apakrāntaka**, see **avakrāntaka.**

[? **apakṣaṇa**, m., acc. to Kyoto ed. °ṇaḥ in Mvy 7069, and alleged (l.c.) to be indicated by Chinese versions instead of apakṣāla(ḥ) Śikṣ 145.6; but Mironov has **apakṣālaḥ**, with v.l. of Kyoto ed., and this (q.v.) seems prob. the true form.]

apakṣāla, m., *fault, defect, failing, sin*: Bbh 351.17 (catvāraḥ) °lāḥ, te prahīṇā bhavanti (they are then listed; as a result of the riddance, the vihāra becomes supariśuddha, line 21); 352.23 sarvāpakṣālāpagata-; cf. Wogihara, Lex. 17; in Mvy 7069 v.l. for Kyoto ed. **apakṣaṇa**, q.v. (Mironov reads apakṣālaḥ, with v.l. only avakṣayaḥ);

Tib. skyon, regularly = doṣa; Chin. *transgression, evil*; Jap. *evil, calamity*; Śikṣ 145.6 ata evodārakuśalapakṣavivarjanatā 'pakṣāla ity ucyate (Bendall and Rouse *throwing away*, but the above meaning would fit well; Tib. ma bsruṅs pa, could mean *non-observance*); but acc. to the Kyoto ed. of Mvy (above), Chinese versions of Śikṣ prove that its text had a form of -kṣaṇ- (which is said to be phonetically reproduced in the Chin.). Bendall and Rouse compare Pali khalayati, in Jāt. iv.205.13 (correct their ref.) khalayātha; comm. khalīkāraṃ pāpetvā niddhamatha. Cf. also Pali avakkhalita, *mistake, offense* (CPD), which is connected with Skt. skhal-. Is apakṣāla an unhistorical back-formation from a MIndic word related to this latter? Despite the alleged Chinese support for apakṣaṇa, it seems a questionable reading, and apakṣāla should prob. be read, with Mironov in Mvy (as well as in Śikṣ, for which no v.l. is recorded).

? **apakṣya**, adj. (cf. Skt. pakṣya, *adherent of a party*, as deva-p°), *having no adherents*: doubtful reading, LV 301.4 (vs), Lefm. apakṣyapakṣyo, but many mss. apakṣapakṣo; we must read certainly pakṣo, and before it as a separate word apakṣya or apakṣa (n. sg. m.), *your* (Māra's) *party is without adherents*. The form apakṣa occurs in Skt. (Mbh. Crit. ed. 1.134.24) and in LV 273.3 saṃsārapakṣāpakṣa-karaṇa-gatiḥ, *with the gait of one who makes partisanless the party of the saṃsāra*; LV 302.13 (Māraḥ) svapakṣaṃ cāpakṣam apaśyat, *saw his party without adherents* (i.e. *annihilated*); also in Pali as apakkha (which however could of course = apakṣya); whereas apakṣya has not been noted elsewhere.

apagata-kālaka, adj. (= Pali °kāḷaka; cf. **kālaka** 2), *having no black spots*, of a garment: Divy 617.8 vastram apa° (in Pali also vatthaṃ apa°); MSV iii.142.19 id.; also (as in Pali) *free from moral guilt* (a delinquent monk attains this state when *all* his penitential rites have been correctly performed), MSV iii.76.18; 79.1.

apa-ghāṭayati, *closes, shuts*: LV 186.18 °yanti (kapāṭam).

apacaya (m., = Pali id.), in good sense, *diminution* (sc. of karman, or worldliness; in Pali sometimes virtually = nirvāṇa): Av ii.188.10; 189.6 °yāya, dat.; see **saṃcaya.**

[***apacayati** = **apacāyati**, *honors*: in Mv iii.138.8 (prose) ger. apacayitvā, so printed without v.l. or note. But elsewhere, as i.44.12, apacāyitvā is printed in the same phrase, and this should probably be read here. Misprint?]

[**apacaraka**, m., v.l. for **ava°**, q.v.: Mvy 3807. Mironov ava° without v.l.; apa° mere error.]

-apacāyaka (to next), *honoring, one who honors*, in kulajyeṣṭhāpa° Mv i.46.9; 198.6 = ii.2.3; Bbh 252.22; in Divy 293.26 text **akulejyeṣṭh°**, q.v.

apacāyati (only in Ved. and Br. language and in Pali id.), *reveres, honors*: °yanti Mv ii.259.10; 260.3; °yet AsP 57.9; °yiṣyanti Mv iii.424.14; °yitvā Mv i.44.12 (= iii.138.8 where text °**cay**°, q.v.); °yanīyaḥ AsP 57.2; apacāhi Mv ii.335.12 (vs), so mss. (§ 28.54); Senart em. apacinohi, metr. impossible; object smṛtiṃ; addressed to Māra: *respect, have regard for* (proper) *mindfulness* (wrongly Senart). For ppp. **apacāyita** see s.v.; Class. Skt. has apacita.

apacāyanā (= Pali id.), *the paying of respect, honoring*: SP 144.3; 148.6; 151.5; 161.3; Mvy 1758; AsP 59.3.

apacāyita, ppp. of °**cāyati**, q.v. (Pali id.; cf. Pāṇ. 7.2.30 and Kāś.), *honored*: SP 5.8; 22.8; Mv ii.139.10, 12; Śikṣ 147.11 (all prose).

apacitā, *honor, respect*: Mv ii.259.9 paramāya apacitāya, and 260.3 °māye °tāye, both instr. sg. I do not find the stem (= °citi) so natural as Senart does (ii.544), and it seems to be unrecorded elsewhere; but there seems no doubt of its reality. Cf., perhaps, § 10.142.

apaṇyī-jāta, adj., Divy 170.1; and **-bhūta**, 172.20; 174.17: *become unmerchandisable* (to Skt. apaṇya).

apatāna (m. or nt.; in Skt. apatānaka, m.), *cramp* (due to famine): na sukaram °ne pragrahaṇe (*in the cramp-convulsions of hunger*, ed. p. 710) yāpayitum Divy 471.4 (cited by misprint as 171.4 in pw 7.302, and copied as such in Schmidt, Nachträge).

a-pattana (nt.), lit. *no* (proper) *city*: Divy 276.14, 16; 277.13 ff. (ghoṣayatī), *proclaims a disgraceful town*.

[**apatthadāyin**, see **aparipanthadāyin.**]

apatrapitavya, gdve. to apa-trap-, *of which one should feel abashed*: Bbh 223.12 °vyeṣu (sthāneṣu).

apatrāpya (once, Mv iii.53.1, °trapya, Senart, but v.l. contains -āpya-; if correct, short -a- must be MIndic in nature), nt. (= Pali ottappa, otappa; see under **an-apa°**, **otrapa**, **an-o°**, **an-otrāpin**), *modesty, bashfulness, shame* (rarely *shame* in the other sense which the word now commonly has in English; so Av i.216.10; Śikṣ 12.1); Av ii.167.4 (read °pya-parigṛhītaṃ as cpd.); almost always associated with its virtual synonym hrī, Mv iii.53.1 hrī cāpatrapyaṃ (cf. above) ca; Mvy 1569 (fourth of the **dhana**, q.v., hrī being the third); and usually compounded with it, hry-apatrāpya- LV 25.14; 27.2; 430.1; Gv 146.23; Dbh 13.18; 19.15, etc.; or **hrīr-apatrāpya** (q.v. for explanation of the form) Śikṣ 136.1 (prose; here as a reason for wearing a loin-cloth); 192.1; Karmav 89.3; RP 28.17 (read with ms. hrīr-apatrāpya-śīla-). Cf. also **vyapatrāpya.**

apada, adj. (= Pali id.; not in Skt. in this mg.), *trackless, that cannot be traced*: Mv iii.91.20 (= Dhp. 179 id.) buddhaṃ . . . apadaṃ; AsP 306.7, of the (Buddha's) dharma.

[**apadarśayati**, misprint or error for upa°: Śikṣ 57.7 gṛhītvāpadarśayanti, read °tvopa°.]

apadeśa, m. (= Pali °sa; hardly Skt. in this sense), *expression*: Mvy 7619 kāpa°, 7620 yāpa°, *the interrogative* (*relative*) *pronoun* (*-expression*); Bbh 403.7, 9 bodhisattvāpadeśaḥ, *the expression Bodhisattva*. See also **kālāpadeśa.**

[**apadruta**, wrongly assumed by Calc. 214 n. 5 as contained in kleśapadrutāṃ LV 178.22 (vs), which Calc. interprets as for kleśāpa°; but it stands for kleśopadrutāṃ, *afflicted* (upadruta) *with depravities*; § 4.16.]

apanāmayati (= Pali apanāmeti), *removes, takes off or away*: °yati Mv i.181.9; ratnajālikām apanāmya, ger., LV 209.13 (prose), so read with ms. A, proved right by Mv and Pali; both edd. with other mss. avanāmya.

apanāya, nt. (cf. AMg. avaṇaya, *censure, abuse*), *rebuke* (?): RP 40.6 (prose) na ca kasyacit sattvasyāpanāyaṃ vaktavyam.

apanīta, ppp. of apa-nī, as adj., epithet of dhyāna, prob. *removed, remote, abstract*: LV 250.16. Tib. sems pa med, rendered by Foucaux *sans vitalité*, but it seems rather to mean *without thought*, or possibly *without consciousness*.

[**apanthadāyin**, see **aparipanthadāyin.**]

apapa, m., n. of a (cold) hell: Dharmas 122 (replaces **hahava**, q.v., of other lists.)

apapravrājana (nt.; presumably = Skt. pravrājana; perhaps formed ad hoc, m.c.), *banishment*: Śikṣ 66.19 (vs) °nena ca (of a member of the order; Bendall and Rouse understand expulsion from the order, but this is supported by nothing in the context and is unlikely; parallel are such things as stealing his robe, beating, and putting him in prison).

apabādha (m. or nt.), *pressure, oppressive influence*: pūrvakarmāpabādhena MSV i.60.2.

? **a-pabbhāra** (MIndic, intended by mss.?), see **a-prāgbhāra.**

apa-matsara, adj., *unenvious*: Jm 128.23.

-apamardana, nt. (= Skt. ava°, Pali avamaddana), *crushing, ruin, destruction*: rāṣṭrāpa° Divy 63.1; 548.9.

apamārgaka (m.; from Skt. °ga, *wrong way*), *adherent of a wrong way*, or perhaps *wrong way*: Mv i.176.8

(prose) apamārgaka (mss. °kā)-kutsakā, said of Buddhas, *contemners of* . . .

apara, adj. (used like **anyatara 1**, q.v.), *a certain*: Mv ii.234.19 aparo ca nīlako nāma lubdhako, *and there was a certain hunter named N.* (no hunter has been mentioned, only a deer); 244.6 apara-mālākārasya, *of a certain garland-maker*; 251.2 aparo śakuntako.

aparakīya, adj. (from *aparaka, nowhere recorded, = Skt. apara, with suffix īya), *belonging to outsiders, foreign*: Av ii.196.1.

? **aparakṣa**, adj., (cf. AMg. aparaccha; for Skt. a-parokṣa; ending influenced by pratyakṣa; [stealing] *in the presence of the owner or others when inattentive*, Ratnach.; cf. also Sheth s.v. aparaccha), *manifest*, ep. of dhana, *wealth*: Gv 407.2 (vs) mā te (')parakṣeṣu dhaneṣv abhidhyā, *have no covetousness for property in the presence of the owner.* But perhaps better parakṣeṣu, *when* (the owner) *is absent*, tho this is not recorded. In any case a MIndic form, for **(a-)parokṣa**, q.v.

Apara-gayā, n. of a place, *the other* (further, or western) *Gayā* (qy: = Buddha-gayā?): Mv iii.324.21 (gayāto) aparagayāṃ gacchati.

Aparagodānīya (usually m., rarely nt., Divy 214.24 ff.; no °godāna, corresp. to Pali °goyāna, occurs; other variant forms, see below, and cf. **Godānīya**), one of the 4 Buddhist continents, see **dvīpa**. The regular form is °dānīya, while only °yāna occurs in Pali (but also Goyānīya, without Apara); for occurrences see s.v. **dvīpa**. Of the passages there listed, the following show variant forms, aside from **Godānīya**, q.v.: avara-go° MSV i.94.4; aparagoḍānī-lipi LV 126.5 (v.l. °nīya-lipi; apparently all mss. ḍ!); °dānika Mv ii.158.18; iii.378.2; aparagodānir (n. sg. m.) Dharmas 120.

Apara-cāmara (cf. **Cāmara**), n. of a country or part of the world: Mvy 3053.

aparajjukāto, adv. (cf. Pali aparajju = Skt. aparedyus), *on the next day*: Mv ii.456.9 (no v.l.); in iii.255.14 v.l. for **aparejjukāto**, q.v.

Aparapuraṃjaya, n. of a yakṣa: Māy 62.

a-para-pratyaya, adj. (= Pali a-para-(p)paccaya, given as a masc. noun in CPD, but occurs only in adverbial forms, instr. and abl.; prob. really adj., as certainly in BHS), *not dependent on others*: Mvy 2396; Divy 617.15; LV 275.1; MSV ii.46.18.

apara-mātar, f. (lit. *other mother*: nowhere recorded), *step-mother, father's second wife*: Mv i.244.7, 8; MSV ii.40.15 ff.

Apara-rājāvavādaka-sūtra, nt., n. of a work: Śikṣ 9.12; see **Rājāvavādaka**.

Apara-śaila, m. pl. (= Pali Apara-seliya, m. pl.; cf. **Pūrva-ś°**), n. of a (heretical) school: Mvy 9091.

? **apara-svara** (m.), perh. *different, strange sound*, said of the distressed cry of a very sick person: °ram akārṣīt MSV ii.128.14 = Tib. skad (*voice, sound*) na (*sick*?) bton pa (*emitted*); his words are then quoted.

Aparājita, (**1**) n. of a Bodhisattva cakravartin: Mv i.112.11; (**2**) n. of a former Buddha: Mv iii.230.10 f.; (**3**) n. of a yakṣa: Māy 1; (**4**) (m. or nt.?) n. of a medicament (-bhaiṣajya; cf. aparājitā, n. of plants in Pali and Skt.): Gv 497.5 (prose).

Aparājitajñānasthāma, n. of a Tathāgata: Gv 421.20.

Aparājitatejas, n. of a Bodhisattva: Mvy 732.

Aparājitadhvaja, (**1**) n. of a former Buddha: Mv i.1.4; (**2**) n. of a Bodhisattva (? hardly the same as 1): Gv 115.9.

Aparājitadhvajabala, n. of a Buddha: Gv 285.20.

Aparājitameru, n. of a Bodhisattva: Gv 443.3.

Aparājitavratadhvaja, n. of a Buddha: Gv 284.26.

Aparājitā, (**1**) n. of a devakumārikā in the eastern quarter: LV 388.9 = Mv iii.306.8; (**2**) n. of a goddess: Mmk 312.6 (here text by error Āryăparājitā); 318.12; 396.1 f.; Sādh 352.6 et alibi (a different personage?); (**3**) n. of one of the four **Kumārī**, q.v., or **Bhaginī** (hardly to be identified with 2): Mmk 537.9; 540.5; 543.19 et alibi.

a-parājita, adj. (m.c. for °jita), *unconquered*: Gv 57.18 (vs).

aparādhika, adj. (= Pali id., and Skt. id. acc. to pw but with wrong reference; cf. **sāparādhika**), *guilty of offense*: Av i.102.7; ii.171.1 (by em.); 182.5; Bbh 255.14.

aparādhyati (cf. AMg. avarajjhati (2), *to be destroyed, to be ruined*, Ratnach., naṣṭa honā, Sheth; naśyati often means *disappear*!), *disappears*: Mv ii.137.9 (śakuntā . . .) aparādhyetsuḥ, aor.; so mss., Senart em. apavidhyinsuḥ, but this could only mean *were thrown away*, which is completely inappropriate; in Mv ii.139.4, in identical context, mss. aparijhiṃsuḥ (°nsuḥ), Senart em. °vijhinsuḥ; read perhaps MIndic aparajjhiṃsuḥ, cf. AMg. above; in any case some form related to apa-rādh, aor., *disappeared*.

aparānta, m. (= Pali aparanta; sometimes contrasted with **pūrvānta**, q.v.), *the future*: °ntaḥ, n. sg., Mvy 8307; RP 4.17 aparānta-kalpa-koṭibhir api nāsti buddhānāṃ . . . guṇaparyantaḥ; Śāl 98.2 °ntaṃ, acc. (adv.?), cited Śikṣ 227.8; Gv 37.17, 18; 49.25 (read pūrvāntāparānta-); 242.16 aparānta-kalpa-; 242.19 same, 1st ed. misprinted aparanta°; corr. 2d ed.; Dbh 31.5. See **aparānta-koṭi**.

aparāntaka, f. °**ikā**, adj. *of the western border, or of the country called Aparānta*; used of cloth or garments, also as nt. noun, (cloth or garments) *of Aparānta* Mvy 9179; °ka- in cpd. Divy 316.26, of garments (adj. or noun?). In Divy 20.22–23 perhaps read aparāntikayā guptikayā *in the style of Aparānta* (? see **guptikā**); text asmāt parānti°. In Divy 1.3; 18.6; 19.16, 19, 23; 21.2, 12 the mss. read corruptly, and with much variation, a text discussed by the editors on p. 703; they read asmāt parāntaka- and interpret as a synonym of **pratyantima**, except in 19.19 where they read asmākam aparāntaka-, interpreting (with privative a-) as the opposite, *not distant, near*. The forms are troublesome; without much confidence I suggest that forms of aparāntaka may have been found in all, meaning something like *of the western border* (if not specifically *of the country Aparānta*). But Tib. (Bailey, JRAS 1950.172) on 19.19 points to **Aśmāparāntaka**, q.v.; and this seems to have been the regular Tib. form acc. to Schiefner, cited Divy p. 703.

aparānta-koṭi, f., esp. acc. sg. adv. (see **koṭi**, and cf. **pūrva-koṭi**, of which this is the opposite; corresp. to Pali pacchima-koṭi, *the farthest* (*future*) *end*, in Pali as here of the saṃsāra), *the future end, the utmost limit* (of existence, saṃsāra); Śikṣ 14.8 aparāntakoṭiṃ (adv., so read with ms.) sthāsyāmi sattvasyaikasya kāraṇāt, *I will remain* (in existence) *to the utmost limit for the sake of a single creature*; 167.16 aparāntakoṭiḥ saṃsaritavyā sattvānāṃ paripācanahetor iti, *one must subject himself to the round of existences to the uttermost end in order to bring creatures to maturity*; 186.12 sacet punar mamaite sarvasattvā aparāntakoṭiṃ chindyur . . ., *but if all these creatures should split me, up to the end of time* (adv.; Bendall's note on 14.8 and Transl. misunderstand the word); -aparānta-koṭi-niṣṭha, Mvy 372 (ep. of a Tathāgata).

aparāpara, adj., (= Pali id.; cf. Skt. aparāparotpatti, pw), *one after another, other and other, various*: Mv ii.434.16 sarvaśilpāyatanehi aparāparehi; Mv iii.402.3 aparāpare, n. pl., *various, ever other, people*; Gv 184.15 aparāpara-krimiko (vyādhir), (disease) *due to one or another worm, to various worms*; 521.10 °rair ākārair, *with various forms*.

a-parāmṛṣṭa (neg. of **parā°**, q.v.; = Pali °maṭṭha), *unaffected* (by anything unfavorable), *uninfected, untarnished*: Mvy 1625; 7032; AsP 292.18 and 293.5 (cited s.v. **parāmṛśati**).

a-parikāṅkṣin, see **pari°**.

a-parikhinna (neg. of Skt. pari°, ppp. of pari-khid),

unwearied: Dbh 19.11 (see next); SP 77.9 °na-mānasaḥ *of unwearied mind* (wrongly Burnouf and Kern); °tā, *state of being*..., Gv 464.6 nausamacittena gamanāgamanāparikhinna-tayā (so read for text °na-pari°), *with mind like a ship, because it is unwearied in coming and going.*

a-parikheda, m. (neg. of Skt. pari°; cf. prec. and next); *non-lassitude*: Mv i.78.16 (one of the 8 **samudācāra**, 1, q.v.): Dbh 19.10 f. aparikheda-cittam (here apari° may, but need not, be a Bhvr. adj.) utpādayati; evam asyāparikhedaḥ (here certainly n.) saṃbhavati.

a-parikhedana- (nt.? cf. prec. two; only in comp., and in next), *non-lassitude*: LV 432.19 (prose; but v.l. a-parikheda-).

a-parikhedana-tā = prec.: ŚsP 1462.8.

? **a-paritamana-(tā)**, in Gv 463.25 dhātrīsamacittena sarvakleśāparitamanatayā, *with mind like a nurse, because of not being oppressed by all impurities.* BR record pari-tam once in Suśr. as *beklommen werden*, which yields a possible sense. Yet I suspect a graphic corruption for **a-paritasana-**, q.v.

a-paritarṣaṇā (if neg. to BHS **paritarṣaṇā**, q.v.), *not craving* (so Bendall and Rouse): Śikṣ 183.5 cittasyānavalīnatā 'navamṛdyatā 'paritarṣaṇā. There is no doubt that BHS paritarṣaṇā means *desire.* But CPD derives Pali (a)paritassanā from root tras (while noting that comms. derive from tṛṣ), and this seems to get some support from the two preceding and parallel nouns in Śikṣ; perhaps, then, after all, *the not being wearied, depressed, or anxious.* Cf. **paritasyati.**

a-paritasana- (nt.; = next, q.v.), *the not being wearied* or *exhausted*: Bbh 143.21 duḥkhasahiṣṇur aparitasana-jātīyaḥ; see also s.v. **a-paritamana**, and **paritasana**, to which I have (with hesitation) attributed a different mg.

a-paritasyana (or °**nā**), °**na-tā** (= prec.; neg. of n. act. to **paritasyati**, q.v. with discussion and references; cf. Pali aparitassana, °nā), *non-exhaustion, lack of discouragement, not being wearied* or *troubled in spirit*: aparitasyanābhimukhenākhedacittotpādena (so ms., ed. em. aparitrasya°) Śikṣ 25.7, *not turned towards weariness* (note a-kheda-); aparitasyanatayā, ms. at Śikṣ 35.6 for apariṇamanatayā which ed. reads with Gv 463.21 (the source of the citation; see **pariṇamana**); nausamacittena gamanāgamanāparitasyanatayā (so mss., ed. em. °trasya°, without good reason) Śikṣ 35.9, *with mind like a ship because unwearied in going and coming*; this is cited from Gv 464.6 which reads parikhinnatayā, certainly an error for **aparikh°**, a synonym of aparitasyana(tā), cf. akheda- above on Śikṣ 25.7, and s.vv. **paritasyati, °tras°.** Wogihara, Lex. 32 note 1, assumes that the original form of these nouns contained °tasy° and that (a-)paritasana (prec.) is a 'purism'. This can hardly be assumed in view of Pali paritasati beside °tassati, and BHS **paritrasati** beside °**syati.**

Aparitṛṣita (cf. **paritṛṣita**), n. of a former Buddha: Mv i.141.13.

a-paripantha-dāyin, adj., *not causing fear or danger, not a source of alarm* (to anyone? to himself?), said of a successful performer of certain magic rites (cf. Skt. bhayadāyin, and BHS **paripantha** which as in Pali is a near-synonym of bhaya): so read in Mmk 291.13 (text apanthadāyī, n. sg.); 297.28 (text apatthadāyī); 299.3 (text aparipatthadāyī).

Aparibhinna, n. of a former Buddha: Mv i.137.4.

aparimāṇa, nt. or m., a high number, Mvy 7804 (m.); 7936 (nt., cited from Gv); 8044, (nt.); Gv 106.21 (°ṇasya); 134.7 (nt.).

aparimāṇa-parivarta, m. or nt., *square* of prec., Mvy 7937 (m., cited from Gv); 7805 (m.); Gv 106.21 (°tasya); 134.8 (nt.).

a-parimāṇavant, adj. (Pali aparimāṇa), opp. of **pari°**, q.v.

aparimita, nt., a high number: Mvy 8043.

Aparimitaguṇadharma, n. of a Bodhisattva: Gv 442.2.

Apariśrotavāhana, n. of a former Buddha: Mv i.139.6.

a-parisrāva, see **pari°.**

a-parihāṇīya, adj. (= Pali id.), *not connected with loss* (CPD): with sapta ... dharma, as in Pali (satta ... dhamma), (seven) *conditions of welfare* (CPD), MPS 1.14 ff.; listed 2.5 ff., several lists.

aparejjukāto (but v.l. **aparajju°**, q.v.), adv., *on the next day*: Mv iii.255.14.

aparokṣa (= Skt.) in °kṣa-vijñāna LV 403.5, 9 (of Rudraka Rāmaputra) and °kṣa-jātīya Mv iii.322.11, 14 (of Udraka Rāmaputra) or -jātika Mv iii.415.10, all Bhvr. adj., *of manifest, open understanding* (LV), or *manifest, open* (? *not obscure*? precise mg. not very clear) *in nature* (Mv). Tib. renders LV rnam par śes pa (= vijñāna) lkog tu ma gyur pa, (having) *not secret intelligence* (wrongly Foucaux). Cf. **aparakṣa.**

[**aparodha** (m.?), *trouble*, acc. to KN in SP 321.2 (asmād ātmano) 'parodhād garād vā viṣād vā, with no v.l. But WT with their ms. K' (asmākam asmād) ātmoparodhād etc., which is supported by Tib. (uparodha = lus ḥjig par byed pa); even avarodha, for which apa° might be regarded as a hyper-Sktism, is hardly used in this sense in Skt., and certainly not in Pali.]

aparyanta, m. or nt., a high number: Mvy (m.) 7806, 7938 (here cited from Gv); Gv 106.21; 134.8 (here nt.). (On LV 147.2 see s.v. **paryanta** 3.)

aparyanta-parivarta, m. or nt., *square* of prec.: Mvy (m.) 7807, 7939 (here cited from Gv); Gv 106.22; 134.9 (here nt.).

Aparyantabhadra, n. of a Bodhisattva: Gv 443.9.

a-paryātta, a-paryādatta, and **a-paryādinna** (all ppp. to pary-ā-dā with neg. a-; = Pali apariyādinna; cf. **paryādadāti, paryādāna**), *not overcome, not mastered* (by disturbing or hostile elements or entities); *not exhausted*; in the latter sense (**1**) Gv 502.15 aparyādatta, said of a light which is *not exhausted* by the lighting of many other lights from it (see s.v. **niryāṇa**); but (**2**) regularly applied to citta or equivalent (so also in Pali), *with mind* (thoughts, or the like) *not overcome* (by deleterious influences): aparyādinnādhyāśaya Mv i.85.6; 86.12 (defined 86.13–14, where in 13 °dinna-citta is included in the definition); °dinna-citta Mv i.133.10; °datta-citta KP 161.2; Gv 202.3; °datta-cetana Gv 151.20; °datta- (with citta in later part of cpd.) Gv 246.19 (1st ed corruptly °danta-; corr. 2d. ed.); aparyātta-vedita-citta Śikṣ 24.11 (see s.v. **vedita**).

apalakṣaṇa, adj. (Bhvr.; = Pali avalakkhaṇa; not noun, as it is stated to be used in pw), *having inauspicious marks*: Jm 82.5, 18. Cf. **avalakṣaṇa.**

Apalāla (= Pali id. or °lāla), n. of a nāga king: Mvy 3273; Divy 348.20; 385.3; Mmk 18.12; Āṭānāṭiya Sūtra, Hoernle MR 27.3; Samādh p. 42 line 27; Māy 221.24; 247.3, MSV i.2.6.

[**apava**, m., Mvy 7903, is doubtless a false reading for **ayava**, q.v., a high number.]

apaviJjhati (MIndic for Skt. apavidhyati), *throws away, rejects*: ger. apavijjhiyāna Mv ii.104.4 (rājyaṃ). Acc. to Senart, apavijjhati or °vidhyati would also mean *disappears*; see **aparādhyati.**

apa-vivāra, adj., *not characterized by wide opening of the mouth passage in speech* (see vivāra in BR): Gv 401.4 °raḥ, said of the Buddha as possessing the lakṣaṇa siṃhahanutā; in the same passage he is called su-**niṣpīḍihanuḥ**, see **niṣpīḍin**, which confirms the mg. as stated. Evidently his speech was *tight*, not *loose.*

apaścimaka, adj., (**1**) *having no later, last* (so Skt. apaścima): Divy 209.1 (vs, but not m.c., in fact -ka spoils meter!), 4 (prose); MSV i.112.18; (**2**) perhaps = aśeṣa, *complete* (? or *at the least, not containing less than the number stated*?): Bhīk 18b.5 sarvabhikṣusaṃghe ... apaścimake vā bhikṣūṇāṃ daśavarge maṇḍalake, sarvabhikṣuṇīsaṃghe ... (19a.1) apaścimake vā bhikṣuṇīnāṃ dvādaśavarge maṇḍalake; MSV iii.94.15 °kena bhikṣuṇā parivāso deyaś caturvargamaṇḍalakena.

a-paśyanā (neg. n. act. to paśyati, cf. **paśyana, anupaśyanā**), *the not-seeing*: SP 137.12 °nayā, *by not-seeing*; Kern *as if he were not seeing*, not quite rightly; Burnouf is farther from the truth. 'Sight' is false, illusory; one must *not-see* to truly see. Confirmed by verse version SP 143.2; and cf. Laṅk 9.8 ye paśyanti yathādṛṣṭaṃ na te paśyanti nāyakam.

a-paśyanīya, adj. (neg. gdve. to paśyati), *hideous* (lit. *not to be looked at*): Mv ii.447.9; 491.18.

? **apaśraya-** (m.? cf. Pali apassaya, Skt. apāśraya; Ved. apaśrayaḥ, AV 15.3.8, BR *Kopfpolster*, but Whitney *support*?), *support*: LV 430.20 (prose; in comp.). But good mss. support apāśraya-, which should probably be adopted.

apasaṃharati, *beguiles, seduces*: SP 476.8 (prose) na ca nāryo 'pasaṃhariṣyanti, *and women will not distract* (*seduce*) *them* (preachers protected by certain dhāraṇīs). But Kashgar rec. na ca nārībhiḥ saṃhriyate.

apa-savyakam, adv. (= Skt. and Pali °vyam, which in Skt. means *to* or *on the right*, also *to* or *on the left*, see BR 1.296, 5.1009; in Pali only the latter, except for a lexical citation borrowed from a Skt. lexicon, CPD), in Mmk 125.13 kṛtvā vā apasavyakam, (if I understand the passage rightly, can only mean) *keeping on the right*, i. e. showing respect, not disrespect. Cf. next.

apasavyī-karoti (cf. prec.; Pali °vyaṃ karoti), *keeps on the left*, to show disrespect: °ti Mv iii.325.3.

apa-sṛjati (in Skt. rare and perhaps questionable, possibly to be em. to the usual ava-s°; not in Pali), *drops, abandons*: Av ii.184.11 apasṛjya, text, with supralineal correction in one ms. only, for apasṛtya, which the other mss. read; perh. read ava-s°.

apaspṛṣṭa (ppp. of *apa-spṛś; cf. AMg. avapuṭṭha *touched*, by moonbeams), *smitten* (with affection): Gv 326.7 °ṭāḥ, parallel to upadrutāḥ.

apasphoṭana, nt. (or **ava°**, see below), apparently *shrugging off* (an argument or opinion), *rejection*: Mvy 7560 = Tib. sprugs bsigs, seemingly *shrugging* or the like; Das gives for this word avasphoṭana, which Mironov reads for apa° in Mvy. See **ava°**.

apasmāra, m., also **°rī,** f. (Skt. and Pali °ra, also Pali apamāra, *epilepsy*, see below), a sort of demon or supernatural evil being: Laṅk 261.10 °raḥ and °rī; Mvy 4762 °raḥ = Tib. brjed byed, *epilepsy*; Māy 219.10 etc., °rā(ḥ).

apasmāraka, m. = prec.: SP 401.5 (prose; in a list of demons).

apasvāpana, nt. (no form or derivative of apa-svap is otherwise recorded; perhaps hyper-Skt. for ava-svāpana, see **o-svāpana** and **ava-svāpayati**), *going to sleep* or *sleeping*: Mvy 6639 = Tib. gñid kyis log pa; LV 217.7 °nam akurutām, (two gods) *caused a going-to-sleep* (of the people of Kapilavastu). We should expect a caus. mg., *putting to sleep*; and this may be the mg. in the LV passage (*made a putting to sleep*); but the Tib. is very definitely non-caus., and Das cites apasvāpana for the same Tib.

apaharaṇa- (nt.?), in Jm 88.10, see s.v. **āharaṇa**; perhaps *piloting* (a ship) *out* (of harbor)?

apaharati (in this sense not recorded), *captivates*: °hriyante, pass. Divy 443.4; °hṛto 445.12.

-apahārakam, adv. (quasi-ger.), in gallāpa° Mvy 8584, *not stuffing* (the cheeks); so Tib., ḥkhur ba (= mkhur ba) [mi] sbo; same mg. seems assured for Pali ava-gaṇḍakārakaṃ Vin. iv.196.11 (SBE 13 p. 64 line 16 and n. 2); a Stein fragment of BHS, La Vallée Poussin JRAS 1913 p. 846 line 1, has corruptly gṛṣma-hārakam.

apahārika? see **upahārika.**

apahṛta-bhāra, adj. (= Pali ohita-bh°; so also in BHS, see s.v., but not in the passages cited PTSD s.v. ohita, which quotes LV apahṛta as apahita; Pali also panna-bh°), *having laid aside one's burden(s)*, in Pali said of arahats, and so of arhants in BHS, SP 1.7; also of Buddha, LV 425.20; of śrāvakas, Mvy 1084 (and ohita° of Bodhisattvas). Probably **ohita-** in this cpd. in Pali (and in BHS) historically represents apahṛta, *removed* (so Tib. on Mvy khur bor ba, *having laid off the burden*); ava-dhā does not have this mg. in either Skt. or Pali, and apa-dhā is exclusively Rigvedic and rare even there.

a-pāniya, adj. Bhvr., *without water* (pānīya; m.c.): °yā ca SP 195.8 (vs).

apāya (= Pali id., also Skt. but not in this technical application), *evil state*, = **durgati,** q.v. There are three such (see s.v. **gati**): in hells, as animals, as ghosts. In Pali this group of three is rare; usually there are four, life as asuras being added: LV 32.12 try-apāya; 89.14 muktāś ca te tribhyo 'pāyebhyo; 92.15 (vs) triṣu apāyi (= °ye!); 196.8 trīṇy apy apāyāḥ; 300.21 (vs) apāya trayo (acc. pl.); 357.4 (vs) trīṇi śāntā apāyāḥ; Mv i.61.4 apāya-pratipūraka, *filling* (= crowding into) *the* (3) *evil states of existence*; ii.215.10 apāyeṣu apāyaṃ gamiṣyati, *he will go to an evil existence in the* (3) *evil states*; apāya-patha, ibid., LV 46.7; 117.9; °bhūmi, virtually = *hell*, more specifically (so also apāya in Pali), Suv 23.11 (vs) ye sattva tiṣṭhanti apāyabhūmau, ādīptasaṃprajvalitāg-nigātrāḥ; LV 178.7 (and 9, read with Tib. ṅan soṅ gsum, tri-apāya-, or tri-r-a°, for nirayāya).

Apāya-jaha, n. of a Bodhisattva: Mmk 40.13; 63.5; 111.8; 425.19.

Apāyapramathana (so 2d ed., 1st ed. Upā°), n. of a Bodhisattva: Gv 443.1.

apāya-sthāna, nt., in ṣaḍ bhogānām °nāni Mvy 2504 (Tib. loṅs spyod, *enjoyment*, ḥbri baḥi, *of diminution*, gnas, *place*, drug [là], *six*), *six occasions for evil on the part of enjoyments*. They are listed 2505–10, madyapānam, dyūtam, vikāla-caryā, pāpamitratā, samājadarśanam, ālasyam.

a-pārājikīya, °kiya, adj. (neg. of *pārājikīya, °kiya, not in Pali, from **pārājika,** q.v.), *not guilty of a pārājika offense*: Prāt 481.6 °kīya; 482.2 °kiya.

a-pārima, adj. (neg. of **pārima,** q.v.), *not further*, i. e. *hither* (bank), always in contrast with pārima: Mv ii.259.7, 17 °māto (tīrāto) pārimaṃ tīraṃ; Av i.148.14 °māt tīrāt pārime tīre; Gv 351.2 °me tīre (contrast pārime, next line).

apāvaraṇī (to Skt. apavṛṇoti), *key* (so Tib., lde mig): MSV ii.128.10.

apāvurīyati, *is opened*, pass. to *apāvurati = Pali apāpurati; see Chap. 43, s.v. 1 vṛ (3): Mv ii.158.1 °yati, and pres. pple. °yantasya. Cf. ii.161.3 apāvṛtam, the regular Skt. ppp.

apāśrayaṇa (nt.), in catur-a°, adj. (= Pali apassena, catur-āpas°), (*possessing the four*) *base(s), support(s)*, of a Tathāgata (*modes of observance*, CPD): Mvy 430 catur-apāśrayaṇaḥ. CPD gives the Pali list, which is not found in Mvy.

api, indecl., (**1**) *if*: SP 229.4 (vs) apy ekavāraṃ pi vadeta sūtram, *if he should recite the sūtra even* (pi) *once*; (**2**) after negative expressions, *but*, Ger. *sondern* (Skt. api tu; cf. CPD s.v. api A, 1, a, 4): Mv ii.109.16 (na adya kiṃcit parvo na utsavo,) api drumasya ... dhītā ... āgatā, *it is no holiday or festival today, but the daughter of Druma ... has arrived*; 110.12, na me svayaṃ dṛṣṭo nāpi parato śruto, api me ... aṅgulīyakā utsaṅge patitā, *I have not seen him myself nor yet heard of him from another, but ... his ring fell in my lap*; 248.12 na ca kiṃci śarīrapīḍā āsi, api me samudrapāraṃ gatvā āgatvā, *and I have no bodily disease, but as I am going to the other side of the sea and* *coming back* — (sentence unfinished); (**3**) api ... api, *either ... or*; in Skt. apparently only api vā, or vāpi, are so used; but in Pali pi ... pi, see CPD s.v. api, B (l): SP 321.12 (prose) varṇenāpi na rocate gandhenāpi rasenāpi na rocate, *is not pleasing by reason of either color or smell or taste*; [(**4**) in api nāma tvaṃ ... adinnam ... ādiyasi Mv i.346.13, api nāma apparently means *surely! most certainly!* in a strong asseveration. But exactly the same expression is repeated twice below, 346.20 and 347.8, with asti (nāma) instead of api, and this is the true reading; see s.v. 1 **asti** (1);] (**5**) apy eva nāma (= api nāma, *perhaps*, in Skt. BR s.v. api 13; in Pali, both api nāma and app' eva nāma, *perhaps*, CPD s.v. api, A, 1, c), (**a**) *perhaps* SP 228.1; 459.8; Śikṣ 58.16; Bbh 15.7; (**b**) *if only*, in strong wish (so Skt. api nāma, e.g. Śākuntala, Pischel[2], HOS 16, 1.20.30), Mv iii.272.8 apy eva nāma āryaputraḥ agāram adhyāvaseyā, *if only my dear lord would take up domestic life!* This mg. is recognized for api alone, BR s.v. 11. See **apy-ekatya.**

a-piḍita, neg. ppp. (m.c. for °pīḍ°), *not harrassed*: LV 361.16 (vs).

a-pitṛjña, *not honoring one's father*, see under **a-mātṛjña.**

apidheti, see **pidh°.**

[**apimanya,** erroneously implied in text of LV 259.9; see **manyanā** 1.]

apiśliṣṭa, ppp. (if correct, to api-śliṣ, otherwise unknown; perhaps read āśliṣṭa, cf. the v.l.), *clinging to*: Mv iii.76.10 vālam (of the supernatural horse) apiśliṣṭā(ḥ); but v.l. aśli° (intending āśli°?).

a-punaḥ-pratyudāvartya = **a-pratyudāvartya,** *not to be turned back*: Bbh 225.14.

a-punāgamana, nt. (= Pali id.; cf. Skt. punarāgamana), *non-return, not coming again*: LV 175.8 (vs).

a-punāvarta (m.? for °nar-āv°, cf. Skt. apunarāvartana and °vṛtti), *not returning again* (noun): Mv i.142.4 (prose), read with mss. °varta (= °varte) evam-.

apūrveṇa, adv., *extraordinarily, in high degree* (Divy Index, *suddenly*; pw 7.304 *vor Allem*): Divv 36.8 °ṇa ... icchāmi ... bhikṣubhāvam.

apotsṛjati, *abandons*; Divy 203.16 bhavasaṃskāram (see **saṃskāra** 2) °jan, pres. pple. In same vs Pali Ud 64.29 avassajji.

a-poṣadhika, *not keeping the 'sabbath'*: Mmk 76.26 (see s.v. **poṣadhika**).

Apkṛtsna, n. of a samādhi: SP 424.8; °snāyatana (= Pali Āpo-kasiṇ°), one of the 10 **kṛtsnāyatanāni,** q.v., Mvy 1534.

appeti (= Pali id., = Skt. arpayati), *delivers*: appehi Mv iii.295.2 (vs).

apy-ekatya (properly two words; = Pali app-ekacca), see **ekatya** (7).

Aprakāra, m., n. of a samādhi: Mvy 574; ŚsP 1421.10.

[**Aprakṛṣṭa,** see **Aprākṛṣu.**]

apragalbhāyate (or, with one ms., °bhayate; denom. to apragalbha), *is not proud. is humble*: Divy 615.3 pres. pple., °yamāna-rūpo.

a-praṇidhi, adj. or subst. (= **a-praṇihita,** q.v.), *(the state) that is free from desire, longing,* or *purpose*: LV 296.8 (vs), read: śūnyānimittapraṇidhīrava muñcamānāḥ (understand -animitta-apraṇidhi-; m.c. a for ā), *emitting a sound* (concerning) *the void, causeless, purposeless (state,* i. e. mokṣa, or nirvāṇa); cf. Śikṣ 6.15, s.v. **apraṇihita.**

a-praṇihita, adj. and subst. (= **apraṇidhi,** q.v., and Pali appaṇihita, CPD *aimless, not bent on anything*; in Pali as in BHS parallel to suññatā, °ta, the latter being used as adj. in Pali!, and animitta (ān°); as epithet of samādhi [suññato ... animitto ... appaṇihito samādhi SN iv.360.17 = DN iii.219.22] and of vimokkha, nibbāna, also as substitute for the latter), *(state that is) free from desire, longing,* or *purpose*; often in cpds. it is hard to say whether it would be better to call it adj. or subst.; śūnyatānimittāpraṇihitam SP 101.1 (adj. or subst.?); 136.13 (subst.; with nirvāṇadvāraṃ as fourth member of cpd., but this is unique; there are four herbs in the preceding parable; in 137.1–2 the three alone are named as vimokṣa-mukhāni); Śikṣ 6.15 śūnyatānimittāpraṇihita-rutam = buddha-rutam (see LV 296.8, s.v. **apraṇidhi**); LV 374.4, read apraṇihita-samādhim with v.l. for text apratihata-; 422.21 apraṇihita-cakram (Lefm. with all mss. aprani°), parallel to preceding śūnyatā-, animitta-c°; 428.9–10 °ta-vihārī, parallel to śūnyatā-, ānimitta-v°; KP 94.5 and 125.3, both parallel to śūnyatā, ānimitta; AsP 256.13 (subst.) et passim.

a-pratikāṅkṣaṇa(-tā), see **prati°.**

a-pratikāṅkṣa-tā (see **pratikāṅkṣā**), *non-expectation*: RP 15.11 sarvasvaparityāgino vipākāpratikāṅkṣatā.

a-pratikāṅkṣin, see s.v. **parikāṅkṣin.**

a-pratigrāhita-, see **prati°.**

a-pratighāta, see **pratighāta.**

a-praticodya, see **praticodayati.**

a-pratipudgala, adj. (= Pali appaṭipuggala; cf. **prati°**; in mss. of LV, Mv, Av, and in Lefmann's ed. of LV, written °puṃgala, see **pudgala**; the var. °puṅgava also occurs in mss. of Mv), *matchless, unequalled*, ep. of Buddha: SP 69.15; LV 126.22; 313.17; 358.7; Mv i.219.9; ii.141.12; Divy 393.13; Mvy 42; Av ii.199.1.

a-pratipraśrabdha (neg. of **prati°**, q.v.; also written °srabdha), *not quieted, not ceased, not abandoned* (regularly with passive force, but also active, *that has not ceased*): Mvy 411 anābhogabuddhakāryāpratiprasrabdhaḥ, of a Tathāgata, *unceasing in the effortless activities of a Buddha*; same cpd. in LV 423.3, ending °śrabdha-cakram (read with nearly all mss. and Tib. °kāryāpra°, for Lefm. °kārya-pra°); Mvy 815 apratipraśradbha-mārga, *having (keeping) the Way uninterrupted*, of Bodhisattvas; Dbh 1.11 °dha-gocara, 45.1 °dha-vīrya, both of Bodhisattvas, *of uninterrupted scope, of unabated vigor*; Divy 133.19 yāvan mayā prayoga(ḥ) °dha(ḥ), *not finished*; Gv 246.9 tathāgata - bala - praveśāpratipraśrabdha - tāṃ; 246.20 -adhiṣṭhānāpratipraśrabdhaṃ; adv. °dham *unceasingly* Gv 351.2.

a-pratipraśrabdhi, f. (or °**srabdhi**; neg. of **prati°**, q.v.), *the non-ceasing; permanence*: Dbh 42.13 °srabdhitas; Divy 134.3, read (a)pratipraśrabdhi(r), mss. °bdhi, n. sg.; Śikṣ 214.7 °bdhaye; Gv 175.17–18 sarvabuddhadarśanābhilāṣāpratipraśrabdhaye; 217.22 (paripākavinaya-) prayogāpratipraśrabdhaye, so read with 2d ed. for 1st ed. °yoga-prati°; 245.26 f. °śrabdhiṃ.

a-pratipraśrambhaṇa, nt. (neg. of **prati°**, q.v.), *the not ceasing*: Gv 371.8 sattvadhātunayāprati°.

Apratimā, n. of a queen, previous incarnation of Yaśodharā: Mv i.128.13 ff.

a-prativacana, adj. (neither this nor its opposite prati° seems recorded in this sense in Skt. or MIndic), *not going back on his word, dependable*: Mv i.349.5, followed by synonym satyavādī.

aprati-varṇanīya, in LV 411.10, *incomparably worthy of praise*, in a list of complimentary epithets of sounds (śabda), after nirvarṇanīya, *praiseworthy*. I believe that aprati- must be recognized as used in Skt. as prior element in cpds. in this sense, as e. g. in aprati-cakra (pw) and aprati-karman (commonly analyzed as a-pratikarman; but there is no record of any *pratikarman in the sense of *a corresponding action*, and the immediate constituents seem to me clearly aprati and karman). Tib. zla med pa, *matchless*, for aprati.

a-prativartiya (semi-MIndic for °tya; = Pali appaṭivattiya), *not to be turned back* (by any creature; said of the dharmacakra, once set in motion by a Buddha): Mv iii.327.7 (vs, no v.l.); in Mv i.330.4 (prose) doubtless read so with 1 ms., the other pravartayaṃ, Senart em. apravartiyaṃ; in Mv i.331.4 Senart with mss. apravartiyaṃ, in 332.7 apravartitaṃ, which is read in the same formula SP 179.1 (prose, no v.l.); in Mv i.332.21 aparivartitaṃ, in 333.12 apravartiyaṃ, v.l. aparivartiya. In Pali apparently only appaṭi° occurs, and I believe this must have been the original reading. No being could *turn back* the wheel started by the Buddha. But evidently in BHS tradition this became confused with forms (ppp. as well as gdve.) of pra-, pari-vṛt-, which of course also yield a tolerable sense: *which had never been set in motion* or *could not be set in motion* by any (other) being.

a-prativāṇi, f. (also nt.? neg. of **prati°**, q.v.; Pali appaṭivāni, °nī, °na, also spelled with ṇ; Pali also has paṭivāna acc. to CPD s.v. appaṭi°, but no paṭivāni), *non-aversion, non-opposition* (to religious teaching or the like): °ṇiḥ, n. sg., Divy 654.27; 655.2 (to understanding, abhisamaya, of the four noble truths; parallel with **utsāhanī, ūti,** qq.v., and see **saṃprajanya** for the rest of the passage); °ṇi Mvy 7649 (so also Mironov, no v.l.) = Tib. phyir mi nur ba, *non-aversion*; as to the form, see s.v. **prativāṇi.**

a-prativāṇīya, adj. (to °ṇi; cf. Pali appaṭivāniya), *not repellent, not causing aversion*: Mv iii.343.1, of Buddha's voice.

a-prativinīta (neg. of **prati°**, q.v.), *not removed*: Mv ii.121.5, of kāmādhyavasāna and the like.

aprativirata, see **prati°.**

aprativīryārambha, adj., *without energy sufficient for* (any) *undertaking:* SP 100.9 (prose; formed in imitation of apratibala, which precedes).

a-pratiśaraṇa, adj. (= Pali appaṭisaraṇa; Bhvr., from **pratiśaraṇa**), *without resource* or *refuge, helpless*: LV 189.12; Gv 534.16.

apratiṣṭhā-dhyāna-vartanin, *abiding in a trance* (or nirvāṇa?) *which is not* (permanent) *fixation* (cf. under **apratiṣṭhita**): °nī, n. sg., Mvy 437, ep. of a Tathāgata; Tib. bsam gtan gyi ḥjug pa la gnas pa mi mṅaḥ ba, *not being fixed in entrance into trance?*

a-pratiṣṭhita, *not permanently fixed*: °to nirvāṇe, of a Tathāgata, Mvy 406; °ta-nirvāṇa Mvy 1728, *nirvāṇa qui n'est pas l'arrêt*, Lévi, Sūtrāl. Transl. iii.3 note 4, which see on this term; it is the Mahāyānistic nirvāṇa in which the Tathāgata returns to worldly life to save creatures, tho remaining incapable of personal involvement in it. Cf. **apratiṣṭhā-.**

a-pratisaṃvidita, ppp. (in senses 1 and 2 = Pali appaṭi°; BHS **pratisaṃvidita** is not recorded in the first sense), **(1)** *unannounced*: Divy 557.16; **(2)** *not known* or *not* (fully) *comprehended*: Bbh 217.16 °viditātmavṛddhikānāṃ sattvānāṃ; **(3)** °taṃ, adv., *unawares* (*unknownwise*): Bhīk 11a.5.

a-pratisaṃveda (m.; cf. **pratisaṃvedayati**), *lack of perception, realization,* or *recognition*: Bbh 175.5 °dataḥ glānaḥ syād apratibalaḥ, (he is not guilty if he does this thing) *thru inadvertence, or if he is sick or incapable* (of doing his duty); °**vedaka,** see **prati°.**

a-pratisaṃvedanā = preceding (cf. **prati°**): Bbh 75.6.

a-pratisaṃhārya, adj. (cf. **pratisaṃharaṇa,** 1), *not to be restored* (exile; i. e. irrevocable banishment): Bbh 83.22 yā punar apratisaṃhāryā pravāsanā (ed. wrongly punar-aprati°, as if cpd.); so Tib., slar mi dgug par.

a-pratisaṃkhyā- (= Pali appaṭisaṃkhā, regarded by CPD as abstracted from the ger. which in Pali occurs as °khā beside °khāya; BHS has the word only in cpds., where it could be understood as ger.; so also **pratisaṃkhyā,** q.v., and cf. the parallel forms in °**khyāya**), *no careful consideration*, or (if ger.) *not after careful consideration*: LV 434.18 °khyā-samupekṣaka-tvād *from the state of being one that shows indifference without consideration* (i. e. without giving careful thought to it); cf. Lévi, Sūtrāl. xx.57 *sans calcul respectif*; usually in °khyā-nirodha, *suppression not as a result of consideration or knowledge,* one of the 3 **asaṃskṛta** (q.v.), Dharmas 32; Mvy 2186; Laṅk 177.3; 197.12; see Suzuki, Stud. 264 note 1, and especially La Vallée Poussin, AbhidhK. i.10.

a-pratisaṃkhyāya, ger. (cf. **prati°, a-prati-saṃkhyā,** and Pali appaṭisaṃkhāya), *without deliberation* or *reflection*: Mvy 141 °khyāyopekṣā; Mv i.160.15 nāsti aprati° upekṣā, *he has no unpremeditated* (without reflection or deliberation) *indifference,* one of the 18 **āveṇika** Buddha-dharma.

a-pratisama, adj. Bhvr. (= Pali appaṭi°; neg. of Skt. pratisama), *having no equal, incomparable*: Mv i.135.13; RP 51.1; Bbh 89.20, 23; Mvy 2530; -tā, *state of being . . .,* Mv ii.260.14; 261.16.

Apratihataguṇakīrtivimokṣaprabharāja, n. of a Tathāgata: Gv 81.25.

Apratihatanetra, n. of a devaputra, one of the 16 guardians of the bodhimaṇḍa: LV 277.14.

apratihataprabha, m. or nt., a kind of gem: Mv ii.310.18.

Apratihatavega, nt., n. of the *disk-jewel* of a cakravartin: Gv 418.6.

a-pratīśa, adj. (= Pali appaṭissa, °tissa; etym. obscure; see CPD s.v. and Senart, Mv i note 516, who suggests relation to pratīkṣ-; Childers s.v. paṭissā; cf. **sa-pra°, su-pra°**), *disrespectful*: Divy 333.23, 27; Bbh 163.24.

a-pratyanīya, adj. (nonce-form, = **vipratyanīka** or °**nīya-ka,** qq.v.; based on wrong analysis of the latter as containing negative vi-, for which a- is then substituted; this is all that is implied by Tib. cited in Burnouf, Lotus 323 f.; in Pali a-paccanīka is recorded only in the expected sense of *not opposed, not hostile,* CPD), *antipathetic, hostile, unwelcome*: SP 95.7 (vs) apratyanīyāś ca bhavanti loke, pūtī mukhāt teṣa pravāti gandhaḥ. (One ms. °nīkāś.)

a-pratyaya (m.; = Pali appaccaya; not in this sense in Skt.; cf. Pali paccaya = pīti, Jāt. ii.241.10), *discontent, ill-will*: Mv i.30.5 kopaṃ ca roṣaṃ ca apratyayaṃ ca āviṣkaronti.

a-pratyudāvarta, Bhvr. adj. (not in Pali, nor is *paccudāvatta recorded), *that does not turn back*: °tāṃ pratipadam Bbh 219.12.

a-pratyudāvartana- (nt.; neg. of **praty°**, q.v.), *not turning back*: Gv 105.6 bodhisattvamārgāpratyudāvartanatayā; in Śikṣ 296.8 read **praty°**, q.v., instead of apraty°.

a-pratyudāvartanīya = °**vartya**: Mvy 5099; AsP 329.8 pratyekabuddhayānikaiś cāpratyudāvartanīyadharmā (bodhisattvaḥ); Dbh 42.15 °ya-manasikāro; 45.19 °ya-kuśalamūlaprayogo; Gv 402.10 °ya-romā, here in physical sense, of the body-hairs of a mahāpuruṣa.

a-pratyudāvartya (also **a-punaḥ-praty°,** q.v.; neg. gdve. of **pratyudāvartate,** q.v.), *not to be turned back,* regularly from a religiously desirable course: LV 181.15 °tya-smṛtimān, *irreversibly intent upon . . .*; 423.6, read -adhiṣṭhānāpratyudāvartya-cakram, for °na-praty° of both edd. with no v.l., but Tib. has neg. (ldog pa med pa) and sense requires this (see **adhiṣṭhāna** 2); 439.19 °vartya- (one, sc. a Bodhisattva) *who is not to be turned back*; Mvy 357 °tya-dharma; Dbh 19.17 °tya-balādhānaprāpta; 38.9; Bbh 225.27, of persons under the training of Bodhisattvas; Gv 246.20 °tyādhiṣṭhāna.

apratyuddhārya, see **pratyu°.**

a-pradharṣya, adj. (= Skt. apradhṛṣya; neg. gdve. of pra-dhṛṣ), *not to be violated*: Mv ii.2.4 (v.l. °dharṣa).

a-pranihita = **a-praṇihita,** q.v.

a-prapañca, see **prapañca.**

a-prapata, adj., *not conducive to falling down*: Jm 102.14 deśeṣv aprapateṣv api prapatito (in a vs; m.c. for a-prapāta?; but see **prapata**).

apramāṇa, nt. (in mg. 1 = Pali appamaññā, f.; see CPD s.v.), (**1**) *infinitude*, as n. for **brahmavihāra** (q.v.), of which there are four, maitrī (**maitrā**), karuṇā, muditā, upekṣā: listed as apramāṇāni Sūtrāl. xvii.17, cf. xx–xxi.43; AbhidhK. LaV-P. viii.196; Mvy 1503–7; Bbh 241.15–16; LV 297.12 (vs) maitrī-upekṣa-karuṇā-muditā-pramāṇāḥ (read °ṇā? hardly Bhvr.); mentioned without list, Gv 471.18 catur-apramāṇa-vihāra-; Śikṣ 105.16; LV 45.16 catur-apramāṇa-prabha-teja-dharaḥ; 341.1 catur-apramāṇa (wrongly printed catura pramāṇa); (**2**) a high number: Mvy 7934 (cited from Gv); 8041; Gv 134.7.

Apramāṇaguṇasāgaraprabha, n. of a Tathāgata: Gv 81.19.

apramāṇaparivarta, m., *square* of **apramāṇa** (2): Mvy 7935; cited from Gv, where it is (certainly by accident) omitted in the text 134.7; by analogy of parallel forms it would be nt. there.

apramāṇa-śubha, m. pl. (= Pali appamāṇa-subha), *of limitless magnificence*, n. of one (usually the 2d) of the classes of **rūpāvacara** gods in the 3d dhyāna-bhūmi (see s.v. **deva**): Mvy 3095; Mv ii.314.8; 349.1; LV 150.7; Av i.5.3; Divy 68.15; 138.22; 367.12; 568.27; Gv 249.13; Bbh 62.4.

apramāṇābha, m. pl. (= Pali appa°), *of limitless splendor*, n. of one (usually the 2d) of the classes of **rūpāvacara** gods in the 2d dhyāna-bhūmi (see s.v. **deva**): Mvy 3091; Dharmas 128; Mv ii.348.19; 360.18; LV 150.6; Av i.5.2; Divy 68.14; 138.21; 367.12; 568.27; Gv 249.14; Bbh 62.3.

apramāṇābhāsvara, m. pl., n. of a class of gods (see **deva**): Divy 367.12, mss.; text by em. **ābhāsvara**, q.v.

a-pramādya (nt.; neither this nor pra° appears to be recorded in Skt., Pali, or Pkt.), *non-heedlessness*: Divy 426.3 °yena.

aprameya (Skt. as adj.), (**1**) m. *unmeasurable thing* (there are five such, all cpds. of -dhātu): Bbh 294.21 ff.; 296.9 ff.; (**2**) nt., a high number: Mvy 8042; Sukh 31.2.

a-pravyāhāra, see **pravyāhāra**.

a-prasāda (m.; = Pali appasāda; neg. of **prasāda**, q.v.), *unbelief*: Mv iii.63.10 alam arthikasya (see **arthika** 2) aprasādena. To be sure, prasāda, *faith*, is normally accompanied by the loc.; here gen., *lack of belief in the Buddha*.

a-prasūti, f., *a woman who has not borne children*; *a young but mature woman*, contrasted with kumārī, *girl*, and **madhyastrī**, q.v.: LV 321.8 (prose) °ti-rūpāṇi.

? **Aprākṛṣu** or **Aprāptiṣu**, mss., n. of a former Buddha: Mv i.141.15; what was meant is not clear to me, but Senart's em. Aprakṛṣṭa is not plausible.

? **aprāgbhāra** (see **prāg°**), adj., Mv iii.343.2 (so Senart; mss. apabhāra, apadbhāra, intending Pali form?), of the Buddha's voice, perhaps *level, even, without descents or drops*? Pali apabbhāra is used of a body of water, *having even* or *smooth banks, without steep slopes*.

aprāpta-kāya, adj. (nowhere recorded), something like *faint, feeble, overcome*: Divy 334.2 f.; 571.11; MSV i.i.11; parallel with kṛśāluka, durbalaka, mlāna(ka).

a-prāptika, adj. (cf. Pali apattika, Dhp. comm. i.270.23, also pattika = *prāptika 271.1), *having no share in profit* (Skt. prāpti), so, *unprofitable*: Śikṣ 251.11, of states of being (dharma); Bendall and Rouse *powerless*.

Aprāptiṣu, see **Aprākṛṣu**.

a-prāpya, adj. (neg. of **prāpya**, q.v.), *not easy, difficult*: Mv i.89.17 (bhāra; see s.v. **prāpya**).

a-prāsādika, adj. (= Pali a-pā°; see **prā°**), *inauspicious, improper*: °kam (sc. karma) akārṣīḥ MSV iii.53.15; °kaṃ kṛtam 18.

Apriyākhya, n. of a yakṣa: Divy 41.4.

apriyākhyāyin, m., *reporter of bad news*: Divy 529.11 f.; 534.29; 535.2.

a-phāṣa, adj. (neg. of **phāṣa**, q.v.), *unpleasant, disagreeable*: Prāt 518.4 °ṣaṃ (n. sg., *something unpleasant*) bhaved.

abaddhapralāpa, m., = **saṃbhinna-pralāpa**, q.v.: °po (so read with mss.), Mv i.107.15, in list of the 10 akuśala karmapatha.

Abala, n. of a nāga king: Mvy 3254; Māy 246.22.

abalaṃkartar, *one who makes powerless*: LV 316.16 (vs) °kartā namucipakṣāṃ (= °ān).

a-bahumāna, (**1**) nt. *disesteem, lack of respect*: Mv i.309.15 mālinīye brāhmaṇānāṃ mūle abahumānam utpannam; (**2**) adj. Bhvr. (in Pali only *disregarded*, CPD.), *showing no regard* or *respect* (with loc.): Jm 234.22 (guṇeṣv, *for virtues*).

abṛha(t), a class of gods, see **avṛha**.

a-bodhi-ka (cf. AMg. abohiya, *ignorant, unenlightened*), *unconscious*; *fainting*: Māy 219.33.

abrajas, nt., *a particle of water* (as a small unit of measure): Mvy 8193; see **truṭi**.

abrahmacaryaṃ-vāda, *report* or *accusation of unchastity*: Mv i.36.13; 37.6 (mss. both times; Senart em. °carya-vāda).

a-brāhmaṇya, adj. (neg. of **brāh°**), *not devoted to brahmans*, regularly after **amātṛjña, apitṛjña, aśrāmaṇya**; see s.v. **amātṛjña** for references; in Mvy 2459 °yam, nt., perhaps *the group of those not devoted to brahmans*, see s.v. **aśrāmaṇya** Mvy 2460.

Abhaya, m. (**1**) n. of a king of Kaliṅga, converted by Buddha: Mv i.178.11; 180.6, 9; (**2**) n. of a sārthavāha: Mv ii.2.11; (**3**) n. of a former Buddha: Mv iii.237.1 f.; (**4**) n. of a people (? cf. Kirfel, Kosm. 76); sc. lipi, the script used by them: Mv i.135.7, read ramaṭhābhaya- for text ramaṭha-bhaya- (v.l. cama°); (**5**) n. of a son of King Bimbisāra and Āmrapālī (not corresponding exactly to Pali Abhaya, either 2 or 3 in DPPN, but perhaps a confusion of the two): MSV ii.22.20 ff.

Abhayagirivāsin, m. pl., n. of a school: Mvy 9098.

Abhayaṃkarā, n. of a lokadhātu: Gv 398.20.

Abhayadeva, n. of a former Buddha: Mv i.140.13.

abhayaṃdada, adj. and subst. m. (cf. **-dada**), (**1**) (= Pali id.) *giving security*: Śikṣ 176.5, ep. of Bodhisattvas; (**2**) n. of a supernatural ray emitted by Bodhisattvas: Śikṣ 338.9; (**3**) ep. of Avalokiteśvara specifically: SP 441.2; etymologically explained 445.9.

Abhayapurā, or °**ra**, n. of a capital of the former Buddha Supātra: Mv iii.234.8 and 236.2 °rā, n. sg.; 234.20 °rasmiṃ, loc.

abhayā, (**1**) n. of an herb, presumably Terminalia chebula as in Skt. and Pali: Gv 496.21; (**2**) n. of a goddess, to whom the infant Śākyamuni is presented to worship: Mv ii.26.4 ff.

Abhayākaragupta, n. of an author: Sādh 579.12.

a-bhavya, adj. (= Pali abhabba; neg. of **bhavya**; not in this sense Skt.), *unable*, with inf. or dat., sometimes absolute: (**a**) inf., LV 19.19; 246.15 (sākṣātkartum; see below), 18; 247.8, 9; Mv i.316.17 (ājānituṃ); iii.263.12; 318.10; Bbh 291.1; (**b**) dat., Mv i.292.9 abhavya so tasya nigūhanāya (so Senart em., mss. taṃ nigūhanāpi), *he is unable to conceal that* (fault); ii.121.6, same passage as LV 246.15, but here datives: abhavyā eva te . . . jñānāye darśanāye saṃbodhāye (same passage in Pali MN i.241.8 abhabbā va te ñāṇāya etc.); Bbh 159.5; Ud vi.7 (parihāṇāya, ms. °nāya, *incapable of loss*); haritatvāya Mvy 9135 (so with v.l. and Mironov, text haritvāya); Bhīk 23b.5; (**c**) absolute, *incapable, impotent*, LV 407.22 (delete following daṇḍa); Śiks 209.12; Mmk 5.26.

abhavya-tā (to prec.), *inability, incapacity*: Mv i.292.10.

abhājana-bhūta, adj. (= Pali id.; Skt. abhājana in same mg.), *no proper vessel, unworthy*: Mvy 2457 -sattva. Cf. next.

abhājanī-bhavati (cf. prec. and Skt. bhājanī-bhūta), *becomes no proper vessel*: MSV ii.73.12.

Abhāvasamudgata, n. of a former Buddha: Samādh 8.8, 10 etc.

abhikiraṇa (nt.), *bestrewing* (to Skt. abhi-kirati): LV 430.13 suvarṇacūrṇābhikiraṇa-.

abhikīrṇīkṛta, adj. (to Skt. abhikīrṇa, ppp. of abhikirati), *made to be bestrewn*: LV 82.10 divyapuṣpābhikīrṇīkṛtaṃ (lumbinīvanam).

abhikīrtana (nt.; to Pali abhikitteti), *recitation*: RP 30.17 corakathābhikīrtanaratāś ca.

abhikrānta (= Pali abhikkanta; on confusion with ati°, partly no doubt graphic, see **atikrānta**), (**1**) adj., *advanced, eminent, successful*: Divy 311.5 f. abhikrānto 'haṃ bhadanta (note p. 707 would read ati°, but Pali abhikkanta is used in mgs. very close to this; instead, read abhikr° for atikr° Divy 462.13); MSV i.54.5; 58.16, etc.; (**2**) adj., *fine, beautiful*, of color (Pali abhikkanta, also with vaṇṇa): prob. read in LV 398.11 abhikrāntena varṇena; Lefm. em. abhisaṃkrāntena v°; most mss. abhisaṃskāreṇa (seems senseless); v.l. atisaṃkrāntena; Calc. atikrāntena, which is the usual BHS form in this mg. and may be right; (**3**) n., *approach*: °ta-pratikrānta, *approach and recession*, Mv i.301.5 (mss. ati°); iii.60.5; 182.12 (mss. ati°); °tena pratikrāntena Mv iii.171.2; atikrāntābhikrāntaḥ Divy 47.16 (? so mss., ed. em. atikrāntātikrāntaḥ), perhaps *having passed over the approach* (to the religious goal)?

a-bhikṣuka, adj. (= Pali abhikkhuka; -ka Bhvr.) *containing no monks*: °ke āvāse (so in Pali) MSV ii.96.10. Cf. **sa-bhi°**

abhigīta, in gāthābhigīta, (ppp.) subst. (in Skt. as ppp., rare; Pali only in the same cpd., gāthābhi°, but its meaning is disputed, see CPD; in any case it certainly does not have the mg. it has in BHS), either dvandva, *verses and songs* (so Burnouf and Kern on SP 191.3), or (more likely) tatpuruṣa, *recitation of verses* (so apparently B. and K. on SP 303.2, and Régamey on Samādh); only in instr. °gītena (in SP 191.3 v.l. °gītebhi), *with recitation of (a) verse(s)*; in every case except SP 191.3 followed by one or more stanzas, to which this noun clearly refers: SP 191.3 °tena abhistaviṃsu (sc. Buddhaṃ); 303.2 °tenaitam evārthaṃ paripṛcchati sma; Gv 275.25 buddhadarśanaṃ °tena saṃvarṇayām āsa; Divy 83.9; Samādh 8.20; MSV ii.104.14.

? **abhigṛhṇati** (°āti; Pali abhigaṇhāti, *overcomes*, once, see CPD which suggests em. to adhi°), *excels, surpasses*: Mv ii.307.6, mss. abhigṛhṇanti (buddhā, raśmibhiḥ), Senart em. ati° (but ati-grah- in this sense is rare and doubtful in Skt. and does not occur in Pali); in next line 7 Senart reads atigṛhyate with one ms., the other reads abhigṛhniṣu; a pass. seems required but perhaps abhigṛhyate is to be read.

abhigrasta, ppp. (occurs in Amarak. as gloss for abhipanna; otherwise no abhi-gras is recorded), *overcome, scorched*: agninā abhigrastā Mv ii.458.3.

abhigrahaṇa (nt.; Skt. Lex.; not in Pali), *seizing, grasping*: Laṅk 18.8 viṣayābhigrahaṇapravṛttānām (vijñānānām).

abhighoṣa (m. ? no form of abhi-ghuṣ recorded), *renown*: Mv ii.1.14 abhighoṣa-ghuṣṭaṃ (kulam; not found in parallel passages Mv i.198 and LV 24). Precedes **abhidevādighoṣa°**, q.v.

abhichāda, nt. (to **abhichādayati**, q.v.), *present, honorarium*: Mv iii.193.8 (hiraṇyasya suvarṇasya ca vastrābharaṇānāṃ ca mahāntam rāśim kṛtvā . . .) idam te abhichādaṃ bhavatu.

abhichādana (nt.), = prec.: Mv iii.127.17 tasya vipulaṃ abhichādanaṃ (*a liberal reward*) dadeyam.

abhichādayati (nowhere recorded in this sense; orig., *clothes*, trans.), *presents*, with instr. of the thing given, acc. of recipient; the gift may be garments but very often is not: AsP 518.16–17 °yati (svakena ca kāyena . . . bodhisattvaṃ); Mv ii.367.17 (vs) daridra sattva paśyitvā dhanena abhichādaye; pres. pple., Megh 288.16–17 mahatā gurugauravacitrīkāreṇa bhagavantam abhichādayantaḥ, *presenting . . . with homage* etc. (wrongly Bendall); perf., Gv 332.21–22 sa tān . . . sarvavastuparityāgair °yām āsa; 415.3–4 mahāmaṇiratnapadmaśatasahasraiḥ taṃ bhagavantam °yām āsa; ger. °chādya LV 108.2–3; 159.14; ppp. °dita, SP 76.10 jīvitena, *presented with life*; Mv i.61.1 (with garments); iii.278.13 dhanena; Śikṣ 33.7 guṇajñānābhichāditā(ḥ), *presented with knowledge of virtues* (wrongly Bendall and Rouse).

abhijānāti (= Pali id.), (**1**) *knows by* **abhijñā**, q.v. The technical Buddhist meaning of the noun is certainly at times associated with the verb, which in Skt. means *knows* in a very general way. The extent to which the special Buddhist sense is present in the verb is often doubtful; I list a few cases where it seems pretty clear: abhijānāmi SP 200.8 (Burnouf and Kern, *remember*, I think wrongly); Mv i.57.7, 12; Gv 446.14; Vaj 34.20. The translation *remember*, also given CPD, is due to the fact that events of the past are often referred to; but I think the Buddha (the usual subject in such cases) *knows* them by *supernatural knowledge* or so-called *intuition* (**abhijñā**, q.v.), not by *memory*; (**2**) *recognizes* (as a duty), *takes upon oneself* (a vow or undertaking); so also in Pali, e. g. MN i.80.5 (definitions in Pali dictionaries including CPD hardly do justice to this mg.): LV 254.2 abhijānāmy ahaṃ . . . ekaṃ evādvitīyaṃ kolam āhāram āhartum, *I undertake to allow myself to eat only a single kola as food*; similarly LV 255.8, 15.

Abhiji(t), (**1**) n. of a former incarnation of Śākyamuni: Mv i.2.3 °ji, n. sg.; 5 °ji-, stem in comp.; (**2**) n. of a former Tathāgata: Mv iii.236.13 °jitaṃ, acc. sg.; 14 °ji, n. sg.

abhijīvin (cf. Pali abhijīvati), *living*: Mmk 614.7 dīrghakālābhijīvī, n. sg.

abhijñā (= Pali abhiññā), *higher or supernatural knowledge; intuition* (CPD). There are 5 or 6, in both Pali and BHS, agreeing in essence tho the order and precise forms of the names vary. In Dharmas 20, five: divyacakṣus, divyaśrotra, paracittajñāna, pūrvanivāsānusmṛti, ṛddhi; in Mvy 201–209 six, same order, with variant forms, (parasya) **cetaḥ-**(citta-)-**paryāya-**(q.v.)-jñāna, for the third; the sixth is āśravakṣayajñāna, as in Pali and elsewhere when 6 are named; the fifth is ṛddhividhijñāna in Mvy 208; SP 134.11 lists 5, practically as in Dharmas except that the fifth is ṛddhivimokṣakriyā, an unusual phrase, for which no v.l. is given in KN or WT; Burnouf (Lotus App. XIV, p. 821) cites his ms. as reading ṛddhisākṣātkriyā, which is much more plausible. Twenty abhijñā-karmāṇi are set forth in detail Mvy 210–230. In Laṅk 292.13–16 the abhijñā, collectively, are classified as to their origin in four ways (in l. 16 read with Suzuki Transl. 242 n. 1 te 'bhijñā na vipākajāḥ). References to *five* abhijñā: SP 12.4; 141.9; 254.14; Mv i.284.3; ii.33.11; in ii.96.1 attributed to brahmanical, non-Buddhist *ṛṣis*; Divy 321.3; Śikṣ 243.13 (read pañco, see p. 412, note) etc.; *six*, SP 90.7; 129.10; 150.2; 155.2; 255.4; 272.6; Mv iii.55.5 ff.; Divy 399.27, etc.; note Mv i.165.12 where 'by abhijñā' (abhijñāye) the Buddha attains knowledge of the Doctrine taught of old by other Buddhas; this certainly does not mean *memory*, cf. s.v. **abhijānāti**, which is commonly but wrongly rendered *remembers* in similar contexts; mahābhijñā- SP 66.8.

Abhijñāketu, n. of a Bodhisattva: Gv 3.18.

Abhijñājñānābhibhū, only in vs, = **Mahābhi°**, n. of a former Buddha: SP 157.11 (vs).

abhijñāta, adj. (= Pali abhiññāta), *well-known, celebrated, distinguished*: LV 23.11 (kulam) = Mv i.197.15 = ii.1.6; LV 99.8; Mv i.197.17 = ii.1.8 abhijñāta-pūrva-

(ii.1.8 adds puruṣa-) yugasaṃpannaṃ-(kulam); here LV parallel 23.15 has abhijāta-(*noble*)-puruṣayuga-(*generations*, wrongly Foucaux)-saṃpannam; Mv ii.263.2 (pṛthivīpradeśo); SP 1.9 abhijñānābhijñātair, *renowned for knowledge* (or, with v.l., *for the abhijñā*, abhijñābhijñātair, cf. Burnouf, note, p. 291).

abhijñāvatī (once written °vati) is apparently used in same mg. as **abhijñā**, q.v., in cpds. in Gv 40.5 (text °vati); 44.24 (1st ed. corruptly °jñānāvatī; corr. 2d ed.), 25, 26; 45.1, 2; see § 22.50.

abhitunna, and **abhitūrṇa** (= Pali abhitunna, also written °ṇṇa; etym., see below), *afflicted*: Mv i.156.10 (vs) tasya ... vacābhitunno ... rudanto (subject Chandaka: *afflicted by his words*); iii.284.13 śokābhitunna (so Pali sokābhi°). The form abhitūrṇa is read by KN in SP 320.9 duḥkhābhir vedanābhir abhi°, with Kashgar rec.; in 321.3 Kashgar rec. also vedanābhitūrṇān, but KN this time °bhibhūtān. Kern cites Pāṇ. 6.4.21 for tūrṇa (not recorded in literature) as ppp. of turvati, *overcomes*. Neither this root nor tud is recorded with abhi, except for the Pali form cited, which CPD derives from tud, but Kern (see PTSD) from turv, doubtless because of BHS abhitūrṇa. The BHS °tunna could be a MIndicism; but contrariwise, perhaps, °tūrṇa could be an unhistoric hyper-Sktism. All that seems certain is that the two belong together and with Pali abhitunna.

abhitūrṇa, see **abhitunna.**

abhitvaraṇa-tā (cf. Skt. abhi-tvarati), *state of hastening towards*, with loc.: Bbh 203.10 (samyaksaṃbodhāv) °tayā.

abhidakṣiṇati, or **°ṇīyati** (denom. from Skt. abhidakṣiṇam, Pali abhi-dakkhiṇa), *goes around keeping on the right, in homage*: Mv ii.416.11 devarājam °ṇetsuḥ, or °ṇīyetsuḥ, aor. 3 pl.; so mss., Senart em. °ṇiyensuḥ. In vs, but meter obscure to me.

abhidarśanīya, adj. (not recorded, but cf. Skt. abhidarśayati, °darśana), *beautiful*: SP 89.7; 128.5.

abhidaśati, *bites*: Jm 229.12 °śanti.

abhidṛḍha, adj., *firm*: LV 278.17 (pṛthivīpradeśaḥ ...) °ḍhaḥ.

abhidevaghoṣaghuṣṭa Mv i.198.3, or **abhidevādighoṣaghuṣṭa** (v.l. °devābhigho°), ii.1.14, °ṭaṃ (kulam), of the family in which the Bodhisattva is born for the last time, *renowned in a manner surpassing the renown of the gods (and their like)*. In the parallel LV 24.11 daśadigvighuṣṭaśabdam, *having its renown bruited about all ten directions*. Cf. **abhighoṣa.**

abhidyotana (nt.; to **°dyotayati**), (intellectual) *illumination, making clear, explanation*: Laṅk 108.13 padasyā-(of a sentence, expression)-bhidyotanārtham; Gv 243.5 -pāramitācaryābhidyotana-meghān.

abhidyotayati, °te (= Pali abhijotayati, with object atthaṃ = artham), *illumines, makes clear, explains* (in applied, intellectual sense; object artha, *a meaning*, or the nature of some religious truth etc.): pres. p. °tayantī Gv 371.19 (-artham); °tayamāna Mvy 6372 (artham); Gv 245.13; 543.7 = Bhad, prose Introduction (kalpān kalpaprasarān); ppp. °titaṃ (-niryāṇaṃ) Bbh 258.3.

Abhidharma, m. (= Pali Abhidhamma), n. of the third section of the Buddhist canon: Mvy 1413; Laṅk 290.8; Karmav 94.7; 102.1; 103.6; 155.1.

Abhidharma-saṃyukta, pl. (°teṣu, loc.), n. of a text or class of texts (otherwise unknown, Lévi p. 12), in which some schools are said to have included the Karmav: Karmav 167.12.

abhidhārayati (= Pali id. or °reti), *supports, upholds, assists*: opt. °rayet Mv i.275.13 (rāṣṭraṃ), 15 (parijanaṃ); with aor. mg., Mv i.250.6 (vs; dharmolkāṃ; = Pali Jāt. i.34.15 dhammokkam abhidhārayi; Senart wrongly em. abhijvālayet); inf. °rayituṃ LV 100.15 (Mahāprajāpatī ... samarthā ...)rājānaṃ ... abhidhārayitum.

(**abhidhyā** (= Pali abhijjhā), *covetousness*, occurs in Skt., BR 5.1019, tho commoner in Buddhist literature; as one of the 3 akuśala **karmapatha** (see this) of the mind: Mv i.107.15; LV 31.17, etc.)

abhi-dhyāyati (§ 2.14; to **dhyāyati,** q.v., = Pali jhāyati), *burns*, intrans.: °yati Mv iii.341.6, three times; subject, the earth; follows kampe and vedhe (portents which followed the dharmacakrapravartana).

abhidhyālu, adj. (= Pali abhijjhālu; to abhidhyā, imitating īrṣyālu to īrṣyā), *covetous*: Divy 301.24; Gv 157.4; 228.15; AsP 427.8; an-abhi°, *not covetous*, Divy 302.9.

abhinada-tā, *condition of resounding, reverberation*: Bbh 76.23 (prose) devadundubhīnām °tā.

abhinadita, ppp. (m.c. for °nādita), *made to sound*: LV 80.21 (vs).

(**abhinandati,** *desires*; this mg. exists in Skt., BR, tho the Pali Dictt. do not recognize it; it is very clear in BHS, as in SP 442.1 yo dārikām abhinandati, *who wants* (to have) *a daughter*; with inf., Mv ii.65.14 abhinandati bhoktum, *wants to eat*. Note that a native Pali lex. gives taṇhā as a meaning of the verb, CPD.)

abhinandana, nt., **°nā,** and **°na-tā** (= Pali °na, °nā), (**1**) *welcome, joyous greeting*: Śikṣ 183.7; (**2**) *delight* (in an evil sense), *lust*: Av ii.188.10 °nāya, dat.; Dbh 48.15 °nā, n. sg. f., and 16 °na-taḥ, abl.; KP 125.5 traidhātukābhinandanatayā, instr. sg. (Both mgs. in Pali.)

abhinamana (to Skt. abhi-nam- plus -ana), nt., *respectful salutation*: Mvy 1770.

Abhinamitā, n. of a gandharva maid: Kv 4.22.

abhināmayati, (**1**) *inclines* (trans.), *makes* (the heart) *incline* (to something, dat.); cittam abhināmayati LV 394.6, 12; cittam abhināmayitum (nivāsāya, *towards remaining*) Jm 132.11; (**2**) *turns away* (trans.), *distorts*: dharmabhāṇakasyārthāny akathām abhināmayati Śikṣ 96.10, *distorts the preacher's meaning into a wrong statement*; (**3**) *prepares* (food): khādyabhojyam abhināmayet Mv i.325.8; (**4**) *causes to pass, passes, spends* (time), = atināmayati, q.v., for which this may be only a graphic corruption (t and bh often confused): LV 369.11 (a week, saptarātraṃ); kausīdenābhināmitaṃ Divy 464.20, 25, (time, or life: subject unexpressed) *was spent in idleness*, cf. the absolute use of **atināmayati,** q.v.; MSV i.18.16; but i.72.18 and 73.3 (same passage as Divy above) °tināmitam.

abhinikūjati (= Pali id., rare), *warbles*: pakṣiṇo °janti MSV i.93.16. Cf. next.

abhinikūjita, ppp. to prec. (= Pali id.), *made to resound indistinctly* (Skt. nikūjita): Divy 221.17 (puṣkiriṇyaḥ ... śakunakair ...) °tāḥ; in Mvy 5238 read with Mironov śaikṣābhinikūjitam for text śaikṣābhir ni°.

abhinigūḍha, ppp., *hidden* or *protected*: Av ii.115.8 prākāra-parikhā-dvāra-stūpābhinigūḍhaḥ.

abhinigṛhṇati (= Pali abhiniggaṇhati), *holds fast, restrains, controls*: Mv ii.124.2 °hṇe (cetas), aor.; 126.6 °hṇe (pṛṣṭhimakaṃ, sc. kāyam), prob. 1 sg. pres. mid., *hold under control* (?); Bbh 161.12 mānābhinigṛhīta, *restrained by pride*; auddhatyābhi° (cetas) 169.3.

abhinipatati (not recorded in these mgs. in Skt. or Pali): (**1**) *falls down* (in respectful salutation): LV 413.21 (vs) jinasya krame 'bhinipatya (so read for kramebhi nipatya), *falling at the feet of the Jina*; (**2**) *falls upon, attacks*: LV 153.1 (prose) (bodhisattvam) °titāḥ; (**3**) *falls on* (a couch): MSV iv.196.4; (**4**) caus. °pātayati, ppp. °pātita, (words) *hurled upon*: Jm 125.16 °pātitākṣara.

abhinimna, adj. (in sense of **nimna,** q.v.), *inclined to, bent upon*: LV 402.12 (vs) dharmābhinimnaḥ.

abhinirūpaṇā (= Pali °ropanā; see next), *fixation of thought*: Mvy 7457 = Tib. mṅon par rtog pa.

abhinirūpayati (= Pali °ropeti, cf. prec.; assumed to be from caus. of ruh with abhi-ni; in BHS perhaps influenced in form by Skt. nirūpayati), *concentrates* (with the mind, instr.): Śikṣ 16.6 cittenābhinirūpayed.

abhinirghoṣa (m.), (vocal) *sound*: Kv 89.5 kalaviṅkarutasvarābhinirghoṣeṇa bhagavān ārocayati.

abhinir-jayati, °jiṇati (Skt. °jita, ppp., recorded only Mbh 14.2220 Calc. = 14.76.26 Bomb.; not in Pali), *conquers*: in BHS only ppp. °jitaḥ Mvy 5247, and gerunds, °jitya Mvy 3636; LV 101.19; Divy 60.22; Bbh 126.12; °jitvā Mv iii.378.3; °jiṇitvā or °jinitvā Mv i.52.9; 193.20.

abhinirṇāmayati (= Pali abhininnāmeti; see also **nirṇāmayati**), *bends, inclines* (the mind; only with cittam, and dat. of remoter object, *to*...): LV 344.8 and 345.22 (-sākṣātkriyāyai cittam) °yati; similarly Mv ii.132.6, 16; °ye (aor.) 283.14. Always follows a parallel form of **abhinirharati,** q.v.

abhinirbhidya, ger., and **-bhinna,** ppp. (Pali abhinibbhijjati, virtually if not exclusively limited to mg. *hatches out*, of eggs, cf. **abhinirbheda**), *penetrating, piercing; penetrated*: LV 155.16 (subject, an arrow) abhinirbhidya (the target); Sukh 63.5 (mountains, buildings, etc.) tayā prabhayābhinirbhinnāni, *penetrated.*

abhinirbheda (Pali abhinibbhidā; see under prec.), *hatching out* (of eggs): Mv i.272.19 °dāya, dat.; 273.2 °daṃ gacchanti, (eggs) *hatch out.*

abhinirmiṇoti, °ṇati (also with dental n), and **°mimīte, °mimāti** (= Pali abhinimmināti, °nati; Skt. abhi-nir-mita, ppp., and abhi-nir-māya, ger., in mg. *create, fashion*, without implication of magic; cf. **nirminoti** etc.), *creates by magic*: (**A**) forms implying presents in nirmin(ṇ)-: °ṇoti Divy 251.19; °ṇvanti LV 350.19; opt. °ṇeyam SP 196.7, 9; aor. °ṇe Mv i.183.10; 266.5; °ṇi 185.4; ger. °miṇitvā SP 63.6 (°nitvā); Mv ii.49.11; 164.1; 256.2; 275.1; 301.17; iii.116.1; 282.10; 410.11; °miṇīya (§ 35.15) Mv ii.411.10; (**B**) forms of pres. abhinirmimīte, °māti, and others from Skt. root mā: °mīte SP 189.3; LV 70.20; 293.2; Divy 166.6; opt. °mīyāt SP 188.1; perf. °nirmame Jm 19.22; ger. °nirmāya LV 77.20; 386.13; Divy 83.22; 361.16; 473.4; Av i.85.3; 298.12; Jm 8.13; RP 50.5; °nirmimīya (§ 35.14) Bbh 152.2; pres. pass. pple. with active ending, abhinirmimīyantaṃ *being magically created*, Gv 444.15 (§ 37.15); (**C**) ppp. °nirmita LV 191.14; 273.18; Laṅk 8.9; Mv ii.150.18.

abhinirvarjya, ger. of °varjayati (Pali abhinibbajjeti, see CPD; commoner is abhinivajjeti), *putting off, discarding, abandoning*: Bbh 408.13.

abhinirvartaka (to Skt. °vartayati plus -aka; cf. next and **°vṛtta**), adj., *producing, productive*: Mvy 7416; Mmk 55.8, 9.

abhinirvartana, or **°nā** (nt. or f.; cf. under prec.; = Pali abhinibbattana, nt.), *production*: (tejasya) °tanāye, dat., Mv ii.121.9 (mss. abhinirvanatāye); 122.5 and 123.2 (in both mss. abhinivarttanāye; cf. under **abhinivartate,** also error for abhinir°; note that 121.9 has °nirv° tho otherwise corrupt.)

abhinirvāṇa (cf. next and Pali abhinibbuta), *complete serenity* or *passionlessness*: Mv iii.395.12.

abhinirvṛti (f.), = prec., or *complete extinction*: Gv 17.7.

(**abhinirvṛtta,** ppp. Skt., also Pali °nibbatta; cf. **°vartaka, °vartana, an-abhi°**; *come into being*: to be read with ed. Divy 71.6 (mahānyagrodhavṛkṣo) 'bhi° (most mss. °vṛtaḥ), and with Senart's note on Mv i.168.7 °vṛttaṃ dharmaṃ deśenti nāyakāḥ. Senart does not indicate that this is an em., altho both his text and the crit. app. read °vṛtaṃ; this however seems uninterpretable in the context. Senart understands *attained to* (repeated) *existence* (with different Buddhas). Cf. under **abhinivartate.**)

abhinirharaṇa (nt.; = Pali abhinīharaṇa), = **abhinirhāra,** 1 (much rarer than this): Śāl 74.15 vāyudhātur bījasyābhinirharaṇa-kṛtyaṃ karoti, *does the work of the development* (lit. *realization, effectuation*) *of the seed*; Śikṣ 123.7 -sarvākuśaladharma-pratipakṣābhinirharaṇa-tayā, *production, establishment* (above in line 4 **abhinirhāra,** see s.v.).

abhinirharati (= Pali abhinīharati, the definitions of which in the Pali Dictt. do not fit BHS usage; cf. **abhinirhāra,** more rarely **°haraṇa,** n. act. to this verb, with about the same range of mgs.; one or two passages containing the verb, cited there, are not repeated here), (**1**) *produces, accomplishes, effects, realizes* (commonly something in oneself); na ca tāvad divyaṃ śrotram abhinirharati SP 357.4–5 and 8, *and yet he does not realize* (*effect, produce in himself*) *a divine ear* (despite the fact that he has certain marvelous powers of hearing); SP 141.11 ff. sarvajñatvaṃ prārthayase yady abhijñā 'bhinirhareḥ, taṃ cābhijñābhinirhāram araṇyastho vicintaya, dharmaṃ viśuddhaṃ tena tvam abhijñāḥ pratilapsyase, *if thou seekest omniscience, produce* (realize, in thyself) *the abhijñā, and meditate on that realization of the abhijñā, abiding in the forest*; *by this means thou shalt win the pure law* (and) *the abhijñā* (or, possibly, dharmaṃ viśuddham may be a second object of vicintaya); LV 180.6 praṇidhānabalaṃ cābhinirharati sma, *and he brought to realization the power of his* (former) *vow*; 415.15 pūrvapraṇidhānābhinirhṛtaṃ (so read with v.l. for text °nihṛtaṃ; sc. dharmacakram) *produced* (realized) *as a result of a former vow*; ṛddhiś cābhinirhṛtā *and power of magic was produced* Divy 48.15; 49.13; (dharmadeśanām, *a preaching of the law*) abhinirhṛtya, *having accomplished*, Gv 52.9; an-abhinirhṛta-sarvajñatājñānair, *not having accomplished the knowledge of omniscience*, Gv 19.21; abhinirhari, aor., *produced, effected* (kṣetraviyūha) Bhad 34; abhinirhṛta (pūjā), *accomplished*, Bhad 6[2]; ppp. nt. used absolutely, without expression of noun, abhinirhṛtaṃ mantrayate sma Divy 542.19, apparently *he* (Buddha) *considered* (reflected on) *what he had undertaken* (? produced, realized? or initiated, taken upon himself?); but in parallel passage MSV ii.128.3 and 180.5 abhinirhṛta-piṇḍapātaḥ evidently means, *when alms-food had been produced* (entertainment provided by a layman), and I suspect a corruption in mantrayate of Divy, see s.v. **aupadhika** (2); with cittam as direct object and a dat. of remoter object, LV 344.7 -vidyā-sākṣātkriyāyai cittam abhinirharati sma, **abhinirnāmayati** (q.v.) sma, *effected* (realized, produced in himself) *a thought* (mind) *tending to realization of wisdom* (etc.) *and bent* (inclined) *it in that direction*; so 345.22; similarly Mv i.228.12 (parallel to LV 344.7) abhinirharesi, aor.; ii.132.16 °harāmi; 283.14 °hare, aor.; (**2**) *takes* (a corpse) *out to cremation* or *burial* (so Skt. nirharati and once abhinir°, see pw 7.257; apparently Pali abhinīharati is not so used; cf. **abhinirhāra** 2): Divy 264.16, 23 abhinirhṛtā, ppp.; MSV ii.126.20 °haratha; 127.3 ff.

abhinirhāra, m. (= Pali abhinīhāra; acc. to CPD generally *earnest wish*, synonym of paṇidhāna, patthanā; BHS shows no such usage; even when associated with praṇidhi or °dhāna it is clearly different in mg.; cf. **abhinirharati,** under which will be found another case or two of this noun); (**1**) *production, accomplishment, effectuation, undertaking, realization* (particularly of something in oneself); Lévi, Sūtrāl. iv.12, *production, réalisation* (Chin. *accomplishing*). Rarely used of *production* of physical things, as in Sukh 27.15 ff. of garments, flowers, etc., also music. That it is not, in BHS, equivalent to praṇidhāna is illustrated by Gv 5.20 pūrva-bodhisattva-praṇidhānābhinirhāraṃ ca saṃdarśayet, *and shall exhibit the accomplishment* (*performance*) *of former B. vows*; followed in 22 by pūrva-bodhisattva-caryā-maṇḍalābhinirhāra-paripūriṃ ca saṃdarśayet, and other similar cpds.; Dbh 14.10 evaṃrūpāṇi mahāpraṇidhānāni mahāvyavasāyān mahābhinirhārān abhinirharati, *he undertakes such great vows, resolutions, undertakings*; *accomplishment* or *production* of samādhi, Bbh 141.23 (teṣām, sc. samādhīnām, abhi°); 175.11 (samādhy-abhi°); of a course of conduct, caryā, Dbh 17.15; Mmk 23.5; SP 68.5; of mental states such as compassion, Dbh 13.17; of preaching, (dharma-)deśanā, SP 186.8 (here dharmadeśanābhi° virtually = a kind of **upāyakauśalya**); 317.13 (preceded in comp. by upāyakauśalya); upāyakauśalya-parigrahābhi° Laṅk 15.11, *realization of the possession of skillful devices*; upāyakauśalya-jñānābhi° SP 82.10 *production of (effectuation, setting in motion of) knowledge of skillful devices*; kṛtasaṃmodanakathāsatkārāsanābhinirhāraś ca Jm 147.24–25, *and after making the accomplishment of return greetings* etc.; gāthābhi° *production* (= *recitation*) *of verses* SP 329.9; Samādh 19.37 (see Régamey's transl. and note); nānābhinirhāra-, *various undertakings* (accomplishments, initiations of activities for religious purposes) SP 41.2, 12; 54.2, 4; 71.7; citta-nagara-duryodhana-durāsadatābhi- (text erroneously °bhir)-nirhāra-prayukta Śikṣ 123.4, *zealous to produce* (effect) *the state of impregnability and inviolability in the city of the mind*; in Dbh 55.11 ff., repeatedly, -abhinirhāraṃ cābhinirharati, *produces the effect* (accomplishes the accomplishment) *of* (various religiously desirable ends); Mvy 593 ākārābhi°, as n. of a samādhi, *effectuation of forms*; 758 buddhakāya-varṇa-pariniṣpatty-abhinirhāra, adj., as n. of a dhāraṇī; in Dbh 45.17 read maharddhi-vikurvaṇābhinirhāra-nānopacāra- (text °ṇānopa°) -kriyāprayogair, *production of great magic (and?) miracles*; (**2**) *funeral obsequies* (cf. **abhinirharati**, 2; not in this sense in Pali): Av i.272.1 śarīrābhi°.

abhinirhāraka, adj. (to °harati), *who produces, serves* (almsfood): piṇḍapātābhi°ko bhikṣuḥ MSV ii.180.12.

abhinilīnaka, adj. (to ppp. of abhi-ni-lī, see BR; Pali °līyati, *hides*), *lurked in* (by crows, kākābhi°), of an old house: MSV i.82.12 (= **abhilīnaka**).

[**abhinivartate**, error for Skt. abhinirvartate, see **abhinirvṛtta** etc., *comes into existence (as), becomes*: Divy 111.20, 29; 112.13; 227.1; ed., apparently with mss., always °niv°, but °nirv° must surely be read. Cf. under **abhinirvartana**; mss. at Mv ii.122.5; 123.2 also read °niv° for °nirv°.]

abhinivasati (= Pali id.), *dwells, has a habitation*: RP 31.14 °santi, with loc. prānta-vane; caus. (not in Pali) ppp. abhinivāsita, *taken for a dwelling*, LV 82.22 °taḥ (pūrvajina-janetryā).

abhiniviśati, °te (Skt. id., Pali °visati), *adheres to, is attached to*: yasyāṃ dārikāyāṃ kumārasya cakṣur abhiniveṣyati (for °kṣyati; perh. thru °khyati, § 2.26) LV 141.11, *on whatever girl the prince's eye becomes fixed* (Tib. mṅon par chags par gyur pa de); especially of adherence to disapproved objects (in Skt. similarly used but not so prevailingly); more specifically with object dṛṣṭi (= Pali diṭṭhi, similarly with abhinivisati), *heretical view*, or the like, e. g. Bbh 228.1 dṛṣṭigatāny an-abhiniviśya; Jm 146.7 yathābhiniviṣṭāni dṛṣṭigatāni; MSV iii.113.20. Hence, apparently, *cleaves to* (belief in), *holds fast to, takes for real* or *true* (things which are false or fanciful): Śikṣ 254.4 yo 'sau svapnāntare śatrum abhiniviśet, *who should insist upon* (Bendall and Rouse 234 *believe in*) *his enemy* (seen) *in a dream*; similarly 254.8 rūpāṇi dṛṣṭvā daurmanasyasthānīyāny (misprinted °syāsthān°) abhiniviśate; Laṅk 14.3. Cf. **an-abhiniviṣṭi, abhiniveśa.**

abhiniviṣṭi, see **an-abhi°**.

abhinivṛtta, ppp. (not in Skt. in this sense; not in Pali), *ceased, departed*: Laṅk 51.7 māyāviṣayābhinivṛttaṃ (tathāgatakāyam), *ceased, departed from the realm of māyā* (wrongly Suzuki); 152.5, read ātmātmīyābhinivṛtta-dṛṣṭayaḥ (so all mss. but one, text °bhivinivṛtta°).

abhinivṛtti (not in Skt. or Pali), see **an-abhinivṛtti-tā.**

abhiniveśa (m.; to **abhiniviśati**, q.v.; in Skt. *strong attachment*; in Pali and BHS usually to something evil; Pali abhinivesa also *false opinion, superstition*, CPD), (**1**) as in Pali abhinivesa, sometimes *false belief, insistence on an erroneous opinion*, as in Śikṣ 198.21 ātmābhi° *the heretical belief that there is a self*; this mg. may be found in some of the following, which however can be interpreted as *evil propensity, adherence to something bad*: Bbh 339.17; 340.21 (see **iñjita**); Gv 188.23; Laṅk 174.12 (see **āya, dṛṣta** 2); Śikṣ 180.16; Divy 210.5; 314.21; (**2**) *diameter*, either *length* (horizontally) or *width*, contrasted with uccatva or **udvedha**, *height*: Mv i.61.2 (yojanaṃ °śena); 196.18; iii.229.14; 232.11 (catvāri yojanāni °śaṃ; acc. sg. adv.).

abhiniveśana (nt.; = Skt. id. in different sense, see **an-abhiniveśana-tā**), *ingress*, in the sense of *point of attack*, = **avatāra** (4), q.v.: Mv ii.241.6 (Māro) alabhanto abhiniveśanam (against the Bodhisattva).

abhiniveṣyati, see **abhiniviśati.**

abhiniścaya (m.; not in Pali; cf. Skt. abhiniścita), *determination*: LV 182.11 prabhedārthābhiniścaya-jñāna-.

abhiniṣīdati (in Skt. rare and only Vedic; = Pali °sīdati), *sits down*: Mv i.223.5 (kīdṛśena) yānena kumāro °dati, *in what vehicle does the prince* (= is he to) *sit?*; aor. °ṣīdi, Senart em. °ṣīde (m.c.) Mv i.202.18; in LV 39.6 ger. abhiniṣadya in caus. sense, *having seated* (or with Foucaux *consacré*), bodhisattvo maitreyaṃ . . . tuṣitabhavane 'bhiniṣadya (to take his own place after his descent to earth); abhiniṣaṇṇaḥ, *sat down*, MSV ii.22.17.

abhiniṣkramaṇa, nt. (= Pali abhinikkhamaṇa; to next), *departure from worldly life, entrance into ascetic life*: LV 36.2; 183.16; Mv i.142.8; 154.4; iii.263.17 f.; Gv 247.25, etc., common.

abhiniṣkramati (= Pali abhinikkhamati), *enters ascetic life*: LV 136.14; 186.5; Mv i.154.5; ii.141.1, 2; 158.3, 6; 161.5, 7, 8; iii.178.11, etc., common. (Also as in Skt., *goes forth*, in any secular sense, as udyānabhūmim *to a pleasure park*, Mv i.262.2, 4; udyānam ii.150.10.)

abhiniṣpadyate (not in Skt. in this sense; in Pali, in this sense, only caus. abhinipphādeti), *gets, secures, obtains*: Prāt 495.7 ff. °dyeta (cīvaraṃ); 10 °dyamāna(ḥ), *in (while) obtaining* (trying to obtain, sc. a robe); ppp. abhiniṣpanne cīvare Prāt 493.19; 495.12.

abhiniṣpīḍayati (= Pali abhinippīḷeti), ppp. °pīḍita-, *squeezed out, got out with difficulty*: °ta-spaṣṭapadām Jm 168.7 (human speech, by a deer).

abhiniṣpeṣayati (caus. of *abhi-niṣ-piṣ-), *crushes utterly*: °yan, pres. pple., MSV ii.75.1; Tib. cited as phye mar (*into powder*) glog ciṅ (? glog cited only as noun, *lightning*; here it seems to mean *crush*); same Tib. for niṣpīṣanto 76.7.

abhiniṣyandana (nt.; cf. Skt. abhiniṣyandate, very rare), *irrigation, infiltration* (as) *with moisture*: Gv 430.19 cittanagarābhiniṣyandanaprayuktena te . . . bhavitavyaṃ sarvatathāgatadharmameghasaṃpratīcchanatayā.

abhinīra, adj., = **abhinīla**: Gv 401.20, of eyes, one of the 32 lakṣaṇa. But 2d ed. °nīla.

abhinīla, adj. (= Pali id.; once in Skt., Schmidt, Nachtr.), *very dark*, of eyes (29th of the 32 **lakṣaṇa**, q.v.) and hair: (eyes) LV 105.16; 432.4; Mv i.119.1; ii.306.15; Mvy 240 (here °netra-gopakṣmā, see **gopakṣman**); Gv 404.11; Dharmas 83; (hair) LV 105.13; Gv 404.12.

[**abhinda-sroto**, read abhindan (pres. pple.) sroto, *not breaking the* (surface of the) *water*: MSV iv.214.16, repeated; cf. CPD s.v. abhijjamāna.]

a-bhinna, adj. (cf. BR bhid, 8), *not seduced, not won* (amorously, of a woman, by a man): Mv ii.105.9 (vs) kā tuhyam abhinna (so mss.; Senart em. abhukta, which is right in sense) varteyā, *what woman could you not seduce?*

Abhinnaparivārā, n. of a nāga maid: Kv 4.7.

Abhinnarāṣṭra, n. of a former Buddha: Mv i.137.5.

Abhinnābha, n. of a future Buddha: Mv iii.330.13.

? **abhipaścāt**, adv. *after* (others), *last* (of all), or temporally, *too late*, LV 142.14 tvam abhi° āgatā. But probably read with v.l. **atipaścāt** = Pali atipacchā (graphic confusion of t and bh).

Abhipaśya, nt., n. of a cetiya (caitya) in the south: Mv iii.307.17; in the parellel LV 389.10 **Padma** (6).

Abhipāraga (= Pali Ahipāraka), n. of a minister: Jm 82.11 ff.

abhipūjana or °**nā** (to Skt. abhipūjayati), *the paying of homage*: LV 219.10, 12 °nārtham.

abhiprakirati (= Pali abhippa°; once in Skt., pw 6.299), *bestrews* (often after **adhyavakirati**, q.v., or abhyava°): °kirati RP 50.6; °kiranti SP 169.6; 172.9; 240.2; Mvy 6137; Sukh 43.16; ger. °kiritvā Mv i.38.10; 212.4; ppp. °kīrṇa LV 162.18.

abhipraṇamati; ppp. °ṇata, *stretched out towards*: Jm 176.1 (śākhā . . . nimnagām abhipraṇatābhavat); caus. abhipraṇamayati, *extends, holds out* (= **praṇāmayati**, q.v., cf. also **praṇamati**, °**mayati**): Mv i.65.18 (vs) abhiprāṇamayetsuḥ, aor. (burning brands, towards a pyre); ā perh. m.c. (or augment?).

abhipradakṣiṇī-karoti (cf. Skt. pradakṣiṇī-karoti and abhipradakṣiṇam karoti), *passes around keeping on the right* (respectfully): pres. p. n. pl. °karontā Mv ii.264. 18 ff.; ger. °kṛtvā id. 17.

abhipradarśayati, *points to*: Jm 144.20 (with acc.).

abhiprapūraṇa, nt. (cf. Skt. abhiprapūryate, once), *filling*: SP 16.12 (prose) -śaṅkhābhiprapūraṇam.

abhipramodana, m., or °**nā** (cf. Pali abhippamoda), *great joy*: Gv 193.17 (prose) °nān, acc. pl.; Bbh 30.11 (prose) °nā, n. sg.

abhiprayojana (nt.; cf. abhiprayuṅkte, Vedic only), *possession*: °nāya, dat., Suv 13.6.

abhipralamba (m.; cf. next), *hanging down* (noun): Gv 270.8 (prose) samabhāgābhipralamba-racita-śākhaḥ (of a tree).

abhipralambate (= Pali abhippalambati), *hangs down* (intrans.): °te Mvy 6130; 6923, here with ālambate and **adhyāl**°, of lengthening shadows falling on earth at evening (same context in Pali abhippal° MN iii.164.30, subject chāyā, with loc. paṭhaviyā); pres. pple. °bamānāni LV 77.14; ppp. °bita, *hanging down*, Sukh 54.5 (aṣṭau yojanaśatāny) abhipralambita-śākhāpattrapalāśaḥ (bodhivṛkṣaḥ); *behung* (*with*), *having . . . suspended upon them*, at end of cpds. preceded by names of articles suspended, SP 75.6; 103.4; LV 30.13; 82.18; 162.15; 187.17; Gv 162.24 (in this mg. perhaps derived from caus.?); caus. °bayanti *they hang* (trans.), *cause to be suspended* (acc., *from*, abl.), LV 124.6 (gaganatalāt puṣpapaṭṭadāmāni); 294.16 (puṣpadāmāni); pres. pple. °bayantyo LV 295.5.

abhipravarṣaṇa (nt.; to Skt. °varṣati), *act of raining down*: Gv 100.14 -vṛṣṭy-abhi°; 169.2; SP 16.11 dharmavṛṣṭy-abhi°; Dbh 90.9; Sukh 60.7 dharmasalilābhipravarṣaṇa-tayā, *because of state-of-raining-down the flood of dharma*.

abhipravarṣayitar (cf. prec.), *one who causes to rain down*: Gv 463.8 °tāro dharmaśravaṇameghānām.

abhipravādayati, *makes resound* or *play* (musical instruments) *in honor of someone*: devadundubhim °dayām āsus tasya . . . satkārārtham SP 160.3; AsP 158.21 (divyāni vādyāni).

abhiprasanna (ppp. of °**sīdati**, q.v.: Pali abhippa°), *favorably disposed*, with gen., loc. with or without antike, or at end of cpds.; in Pali and BHS also *believing in*, religiously, see esp. Divy 53.8; *croyant parfaitement*, AbhidhK. LaV-P. iv.74; the two mgs. often hardly distinguishable: SP 459.3 (brāhmaṇeṣv); LV 308.16 (ye Māraputrā bodhisattve); Mv i.36.7, 11 (bhikṣūṇām, bhikṣusya); 294.23; 301.9; 302.8; 309.9 (brāhmaṇeṣu); 311.13 (śramaṇānām); ii.108.4 (mama, sc. a hermit); iii.413.4 °na-citta (see s.v. °**sīdati**); 424.9 (asmākam); Mvy 8353, and an-abhi° 8352; Divy 23.13; 40.7; 53.8 (śaraṇaṃ gatām °sannām); 75.19; 137.1 (bhagavato 'ntike cittam °sannam); Av i.47.7 (buddhe); Gv 414.26 (bhagavantam . . . dṛṣṭvā cāsya cittam °sannam); Bbh 14.9; buddhadharmasaṃghābhi° Kv 65.16; but also lūhābhi°, with lūhādhimukta, *inclined to what is mean* or *base*, Mv ii.131.5.

abhiprasarati (in this sense app. not recorded), *sets out towards*: Mv ii.104.6 himavantam abhiprasaresi (aor.); ppp. °sṛta *having come into*, Jm 97.9 °sṛtair . . . salilapravāhair (*that had flowed in*).

abhiprasāda (m., to next, or its caus.; cf. **abhiprasanna**; Pali abhipassāda, said to mean only *faith, belief*), either *the making well-disposed*, or *the making to believe*: Mvy 8352 an-abhiprasannānām abhiprasādāya; Divy 423.8 buddhaśāsanābhiprasādārtham, *in order to make well-disposed*, or *believing* (in).

abhiprasīdati (= Pali abhippa°; in Skt. only caus. °sādayati, *makes well disposed*), *favors, is well disposed* (to), *conceives faith* (in, gen. or acc.): (sarvajanakāyo etasya) ṛṣisya (viz. the Buddha) sahasraparivārasya . . . °diṣyati Mv iii.424.12; (bodhisattvapiṭakam . . . śrutvā ca) punar °dati Bbh 14.9; caus., *makes well disposed to*, or *makes to believe in*, °sādayanti Yaśodasya mātāpitarau bhagavato santike cittam Mv iii.413.3, . . . *made their hearts favorable to* (prob. = *believing in*) *the Bh*. Cf. **abhiprasanna**, °**sāda**.

abhiprāya, m., *difference*: Divy 222.20 (na . . .) kaścid viśeṣo vā 'bhiprāyo vā nānākaraṇam vā. Based on use of Pali adhippāya (= Skt. abhiprāya) *intention*, but also *difference*; on the latter mg. see CPD s.v. The old Buddhist word adhippāya was Sktized, keeping this new mg. in addition to its normal Skt. mg. Compare with Divy passage the Pali, ko viseso ko adhippāyo kiṃ nānākaraṇam MN i.64.23–24.

abhipriya, adj. (intensifying to priya; cf. BR s.v. abhi 1, d), *quite agreeable*: Mv i.310.13 yathā brāhmaṇapariṣāye abhipriyan (Senart em. abhiprāyan; but for this °prāyas, °prāyo would be expected) tathā bhavatu.

abhibudhyati (for °te, pass.; no cpd. of abhi-budh is recorded in Skt. or Pali, except rarely the noun abhibuddhi, on which see BR 5.1021), *becomes enlightened*: LV 185.12 (vs; no v.l.) drakṣyāmy abhibudhyato bodhim, *I shall behold the enlightenment of him as he is becoming enlightened*.

abhibhakṣaṇa, nt., *feeding upon* (to Pali abhibhakkhayitvā); so prob. read with 1 ms. in Mv i.361.9 ekam mṛgam visarjayiṣyāmaḥ, mahārājasya ca mṛgamānsena abhibhakṣaṇam (v.l. avikṣaṇam; Senart em. avibhakṣaṇam, supposed to mean *non-cessation de nourriture*; implausible) bhaviṣyati, ime ca mṛgā evam anayavyasanam nopapadyiṣyanti, *we will let go one deer* (every day), *and the king will feed on deer-meat, and* (*at the same time*) *thus these deer will not get into serious trouble*. Less likely is the v.l. avikṣaṇam = AMg. avikkhaṇa (by false Sktization) = Pali (an-)apekkhana, Skt. (rare) apekṣaṇa = apekṣā *desire* (*at the same time the king will crave deer-meat, and these deer . . .*).

abhibhavati (not recorded in this physical sense; Skt. and Pali only *overcomes* and the like), *mounts, climbs upon* or *over*; *passes over*: LV 197.4 (vs) (mīḍhamgirī . . .) abhibhūya caṅkramati tatra ca nopalipto; LV 198.16 (vs) kuḍyā ca vṛkṣa abhibhūya, (the Buddha's radiance, ābhā) *passing over walls and trees* (leaves no shadow).

abhibhāna (cf. Skt. abhibhāti), perhaps *appearance*, in yathābhibhānam, adj. (or adv.?), something like *immediately evident*?: °nam ca na duḥpṛcchayā . . . pratiṣṭhitam Suv 1.12 (textually uncertain).

abhibhāvana, adj. or subst. (to Skt. abhibhavati), *overcoming*: ananta-pariṣad-abhibhāvanaḥ Mvy 852, ep. of Bodhisattvas (Bhvr.? or Tatpur.? in the latter case is abhi° adj. or n. ag.?); °**na-tā**, *state of overcoming*, LV 32.1 (prose).

abhibhāṣati, ppp. °ṣita (in this sense not recorded), *promise(d)*: SP 88.8 (vs) dadāhi nas tāta yathābhibhāṣitaṃ (no v.l.) ... yānāni, *give us, father, as* (you) *promised, cars*, etc.

abhibhinatti (not in Pali; in Skt. once pass. abhibhidya-, BR 5.1658), *splits*: Māy 259.30 °bhindyāt, opt.

abhibhū (f.; not in this sense in Pali; = **abhibhv-āyatana**, q.v.), *supremacy*: abhibhuvas ... aṣṭau Sūtrāl. vii.9 (comm. abhibhvāyatana); sarvalokābhibhū (Bhvr.), xx–xxi.44.

? **Abhibhūyayaśa(s)**, n. of a future Buddha: n. sg. °yaśo Mv iii.330.14 (so mss.; Senart em. °bhūyaśo, perhaps rightly).

abhibhv-āyatana, nt. (= Pali abhibhāyatana), *sphere of sovereignty, one of the eight stages of mastery over the senses* (in jhāna, CPD); also called **abhibhū**, q.v., in BHS: Mvy 1519 (listed in 1520–27); Sūtrāl. vii.9, comm.; xx–xxi.44, comm.

[**abhimanyatā**, see **abhimanyanatā**.]

abhimanyati, with acc. or dat. (loc.?), in Mv ii.440.15–17, used four times of the attitude of a husband or wife towards a very ugly spouse; perhaps *is hostile towards* (as in Skt.), but *despises, contemns*, or perhaps *loathes* would seem more natural: (14) anyam-anyam (15) °yanti, ... patiṃ °yati, (16) ... patiḥ pāparūpāye bhāryāye abhimanyati, (17) ... yā te putra nābhimanyiṣyati. Cf. next.

abhimanyanatā (to Skt. °manyate, BHS °ti), *injuriousness, seeking to do harm*: RP 19.16 jñānenā 'bhi° (prose); could be em. to avamany°, cf. 20.2 avamanyatī, 20.11 mss. atimanyanatā, Finot em. ava°. But cf. LV 32.14 where probably read parānabhimanyanatāyai for Lefm. parābhimanyatāyai (by em.; mss. parābhigamanyatāyai, parāgamanatāyai; Calc. as Lefm.).

abhimānika, adj. (from Skt. and Pali abhimāna, in two different mgs.; cf. **ābhi°**), (1) *proud, conceited*: SP 380.1 (prose); KP 118.2 (prose), 5 (vs); Mvy 2446; (2) *holding an erroneous view*: Laṅk 146.13 (could be interpreted as ābhi°) nāsty-asti-tvābhimānikasya.

abhimānikā (cf. Skt. and Pali °māna), *pride*: Gv 527.10 jāty-abhimānikā-nirabhimānatāyai, *to make prideless their pride of birth.*

Abhimukhī, n. of the 6th of the 10 Bodhisattva-bhūmi: Mvy 891; Dharmas 64; Bbh 346.10; Dbh 5.9 etc.

Abhiya, n. of a monk of old (previous incarnation of Śākyamuni): Mv i.35.13 ff. (A transl. of his story, Mv i.34–45, by R. Otto Franke, in Königsberger Beiträge, 1929, pp. 115–124).

abhiyaśa(s), adj., *glorious*: LV 12.22 (vs) °śā, voc. sg. (before k-).

abhiyācanā (to Skt. abhiyācati; cf. Skt. satyābhiyācana, adj., *making requests true*, BR s.v.), *entreaty*: Mv iii.318.14 °nāṃ viditvā; in satyābhiyācanayā Divy 154.5 *with appeal to truth* = **satya-vacana**, q.v., Pali saccakiriyā, solemn declaration by the truth of something (in Divy spoken by Buddha in effecting a miracle; see 154.25).

abhiyuktaka, adj.-ppp. (= Skt. °yukta), *zealous, intent*, (mentally) *applied*: RP 10.10 āśayena ... abhiyuktakā(ḥ). May be m.c.

abhiyujyate (also °ti; orig. pass. of Skt. abhi-yuj), (is yoked;) *yokes oneself*; fig. *applies oneself* (to, loc.; or absolutely): SP 79.11 (prose) abhiyujyadhve, *you are yoked, harnessed* (to the vehicles just mentioned; wrongly Burnouf and Kern); 80.5, 7 (tathāgataśāsane) 'bhiyujyante, *apply themselves*; LV 203.4 abhiyujyatha (gauraveṇa), *apply yourselves!*

abhiraktaka, f. °ikā, adj. (= Pali abhiratta; Skt. °rakta not in this sense), (very) *red*: Mmk 156.24 (vs) tālukā cā 'bhiraktikā (perhaps m.c.).

abhiraṅga (m.?), of unknown mg.: Mv ii.86.7 yena saptābhiraṅgā ca. The whole passage is obscure.

abhiracita, ppp. of *abhiracayati: *prepared, arranged, fixed up*: RP 42.13 (vs) mayābhiracitam yad idam tvadarthe.

Abhirati, n. of a lokadhātu, where dwells the Buddha Akṣobhya: SP 184.7 (located in the east); Gv 82.9; AsP 366.15.

abhiramya (Pali allegedly abhiramma, Maung Tin, see CPD; Ap. ahiramma, Jacobi, Bhav.; see **an-, nir-abhi°**), *pleasing*: LV 187.10–11 sarvamanāpāni copasaṃhartavyāni viṣayābhiramyāṇi; Tib. yul ñams dgaḥ ba thams cad ni sbyor cig, apparently making viṣaya (yul) subject of upasaṃhartavyāni, and not translating abhi°. The sense must apparently be *all-mind-charming and pleasing objects of sense are to be collected* (prepared, for the prince to enjoy); yathābhiramyam (= Pali yathābhirantam), adv., *as long as is agreeable*: MSV ii.87.19.

[? **abhirādha** (m.? to Skt. abhi-rādh-; cf. next two), *winning*: Gv 171.22 (prose) ... bodhisattvasya buddhā(ḥ) ... abhirādhacittā bhavanti: but prob. read abhirāddha- (Skt.) with citation of the passage Śikṣ 36.6, *the Buddhas have minds favorably disposed towards* ...]

abhirādhanā (cf. prec. and next; Skt. °dhana, Pali an-abhirādhana), *winning favor, conciliation*: Mvy 2944.

abhirādhya, adj. (gdve. to Pali abhirādheti = sādhayati, see CPD; Skt. abhirādhayati, only *propitiates, wins the favor of*; cf. prec. two), *to be won, attained*: Jm 119.8 -abhirādhyā guṇavibhūtis.

Abhirāmavartā, n. of a girl attendant on **Subhadrā** (1): Gv 52.2.

Abhirāmaśrīvaktrā, n. of an actor's daughter: Gv 283.3.

-abhirucitaka, adj. (= Skt. and Pali °ta), in yathābhirucitakam, adv., *as one pleases*: Mmk 76.19 (prose; not dimin.).

abhirudati (in Skt. only ppp. °rudita; not in Pali), *laments*: ger. °rudya Divy 323.25.

Abhirūpa, n. of a former Buddha: Mv i.139.14.

abhirūha (so Senart with 1 ms.) or °**hana** (so v.l.; = Pali abhirūhana; cf. **abhirohaṇa**; to Skt. abhirohati), *mounting, ascent*: Mv ii.289.8 abhirūha(na)saṃpannāḥ (sattvāḥ, sc. Bodhisattvas; in Pali lit. or fig. of *mounting* as on a ship, esp. by a gangplank; so presumably here, fig. furnishing a gangplank to salvation).

abhirocate (= Pali °ti; not in this sense in Skt.), *surpasses* (lit. *outshines*): Śikṣ 43.2 (sumeruḥ parvatarājaḥ sarvān kulaparvatān abhibhavann) abhirocate ca samabhirocate coccatvena vipulatvena ca.

abhirocana (nt.; to prec.), *surpassing brilliance, splendor*: Dbh.g. 20(356).21; Gv 243.4, in adj. cpd. (sarva-) sattvābhirocanāṃ, *having the splendor of all beings*, or, *illuminating all beings* (of a divinity); 345.14 (prose) °nasabhāgatām.

abhirohaṇa (nt.; Sktized form of **abhirūhana**, see **abhirūha**), *mounting* (on a ship or other vehicle): Gv 494.7 yānabhūtaṃ sarvabodhisattvābhirohaṇatayā, *because all Bodhisattvas mount upon it.*

abhi-lakṣaṇa, adj. (app. cpd. of abhi, intensive, with lakṣaṇa; Bhvr.), *having superior appearance, fine looking* (of grass growing on the place of bodhi): Mv ii.263.11.

abhilakṣita (orig. ppp. of Skt. abhi-lakṣ-; = Pali abhilakkhita, see CPD), *distinguished*; in Pali often with abhiññāta *renowned*, and so in BHS with abhijñāta Mv ii.263.3, of the place of bodhi; Mv ii.441.18, of a king (mss. abhirakṣito, em. Senart); LV 23.16 °ta-puruṣa-, *distinguished men*; 25.8 °tāyā(ḥ), and Mv ii.9.1 °tāyāṃ (with mss.), of the mother of a Bodhisattva in his last rebirth; Mvy 2887; Jm 188.21 abhilakṣitātmanām, *of distinguished persons.*

-abhilagna (only in **śakrābhi°**, q.v.), *fixed upon, worn by* (Tib. on Mvy 5960 thogs pa, presumably to ḥdogs pa, *tie* or *fasten on*).

abhilapanatā, Mvy 2795 = Tib. mṅon par brjod pa, *full expression, elucidation* (Das); not *Geschwätzigkeit* (pw 7.306).

abhilāpya (rare except in neg. **anabhi°**, **nirabhi°**, qq.v.), *expressible, that can be put in words*: Bbh 265 16 °pya-vastu; 20 °pyāḥ svabhāvā dharmāṇām. In the prose Introduction to Bhad, line 2, Watanabe reads paraṃparābhilāpyānabhilāpya-buddhakṣetra-, but the true reading is paraṃparānabhilāpyānabhi° with v.l. and Gv 543.6; see **anabhilāpyānabhilāpya.**

abhilāṣa, nt. (in Skt. m.), *desire*: Mv ii.65.13 °ṣam utpannam.

abhilāṣika, adj. (= Skt. °ṣin, Pali °si), *desirous, wishful*: Gv 233.4 (prose) °keṇa cittotpādena.

abhilikhati (not elsewhere recorded in this sense), *touches lightly, grazes*, with acc.: LV 76.19 (elephants abhilikhanti the feet of Śuddhodana with the tips of their trunks).

abhilīnaka, adj. (= Skt. °līna; cf. **abhinilīnaka**), *lived in* (by birds): Divy 83.21 (prose) kākābhi°, of an old house; perhaps pejorative -ka.

abhilīyati (abhi with Skt. ḍī), *flies thither*: °yathā (mss., Senart em. °ta) Mv ii.21.5 (= i.219.3, where ni-lī° is read, see **nilīyati**).

-abhilokana, ifc. (adj.? or n. act., in Bhvr. cpd.? to Skt. abhi-lokayati), *seeing*: LV 179.2 (vs) bahudharmaśatābhilokane... cakṣuṣi (nt. acc. dual).

abhivatsala, adj. (abhi, intensive, with Skt. vatsala), *very affectionate*: Mv ii.206.11.

-abhivarṣika, adj. (= Skt. °varṣin, Pali °vassi), *raining, pouring down*: Gv 481.9 (vs) amṛtābhivarṣikāḥ, n. pl. m. (-ka m.c.?).

abhivādanā (in Skt. and Pali only °na, nt.), *salutation*: Bbh 139.7 (prose) °nā-vandana-.

abhivāhayati (Skt. in this sense only non-caus. °vahati, chiefly Vedic; Pali abhivāheti, *removes, puts away*), *causes to be brought near*: Gv 54.20 (vs), read, śūra bhūta abhivāhayāhi me, *cause true heroes to be brought to me*; 56.8 (vs) dharmayānam °yāhi me.

abhi-vicitrita, adj. (abhi, intensive, and Skt. vicitrita), *highly embellished*: SP 151.9 and 153.12 (prose) ratnavṛkṣābhi°; Sukh 54.12 (prose) -ratnavastuśatābhi°.

abhi-vi-jinati (= Pali °jināti, °jinati, °jeti), ger. °jinitvā, *conquers*: Mv ii.159.2.

abhivijñāpayati and **°jñapayati** (Pali abhiviññāpeti only Vin iii.18.32, object methunaṃ dhammaṃ, *makes manifest = consummates*; Skt. only non-caus. abhivijānāti, *perceives*), (**1**) lit. *makes perceptible* (by sound), and so *makes to resound*, with acc. object and instr. svareṇa (śabdena); the common mg. in BHS: SP 122.10 (prose) lokaṃ svareṇābhivijñāpayati; 369.1 (vs) lokadhātuṃ svareṇa... abhivijñāpeyā (opt.); LV 85.9 lokadhātuḥ svareṇābhivijñāpto 'bhūd; 155.3 mahānagaraṃ śabdenābhivijñāptam abhūt; Mv ii.160.8 svareṇa abhivijñāpitam; Mvy 2785 svareṇa abhivijñāpayati; Samādh 8.9 lokadhātuḥ svareṇābhivijñāpto (Régamey wrongly *instructed*); Sukh 64.15 buddhasvareṇābhivijñāpayantam (pres. pple.); (**2**) *makes perceptible* (visually), *makes manifest*: pres. pass. pple. abhivijñāpyamānāni, *being manifested*, Gv 537.5 (sarvārambaṇāni), 6 (sarvabodhisattvaparṣanmaṇḍalāni).

abhivinayati, °neti (not in Pali; Skt. only ppp. °nīta), *trains completely*: fut. pple. °neṣyan Jm 216.8; ger. °netvā (mss., Senart em. °neti) Mv i.297.17.

abhivilokanā (to next), *close examination*: °nāpūrvaṃgamehi dharmehi Mv ii.259.8; 260.1.

abhivilokayati, °keti (not in Pali or Pkt.; Skt. once °lokya, ger., Haravijaya 42.31, see Schmidt, Nachtr.), *gazes intently at, examines closely* (with acc.): °kayati Mv ii.447.5; °keti ii.259.7; 260.1; pres. pple. °kayanto iii.318.1; °kento ii.398.2; °kayan Gv 99.21; ger. °ketvā Mv i.317.8, 10, 14; all prose except Mv ii.398.2. Cf. prec.

abhiviśrāṇayati (abhi with Skt. viśrā°), *gives away in largess*: pass. LV 123.19, read abhyavakīryante (best mss.) smābhiviśrāṇyante (certainly intended, tho acc. to Lefm. not supported in mss.; text °śrāmyante which is nonsense); so Tib., mṅon par- (= abhi) byin no (*give*).

?**abhivusta**, doubtful reading, LV 185.11 (vs); if correct, must mean *dwelling*; *who dwelt*, Skt. abhyuṣita, to otherwise unrecorded *abhi-vasati: devata °ta bodhimaṇḍesmin.

abhivṛṣṭa, nt. (substantivized ppp. of Skt. abhivṛṣ), *what is rained* (upon); *rain*: SP 127.6 meghābhivṛṣṭena, *by reason of the rain of the clouds upon* (them).

abhivedana or **°nā** (in comp.; to Pali abhivedeti), *experience, suffering* (of pain): Bbh 180.11 (prose) duḥkhābhivedanābhinunnasya.

(**abhivyūhayati**,) **abhivyūhita**, ppp. (to abhi with denom. *vyūhayati to Skt. vyūha), *festively adorned*: LV 273.17 (prose) mārgo 'bhivyūhito 'bhūt.

abhiśraddadhāti, °dadhati, rarely **°dhayati** (?), (= Pali abhisaddahati, always with single s, pointing to a new MIndic prefixation of abhi; not in Skt.), *believes*, with gen. of person, acc. of thing (as in Pali): °dadhāti Mv ii.209.5; 219.15; KP 16.2; °dadhāsi Divy 305.20 (bhagavataḥ); °dadhāmi Mv ii.184.17 (etaṃ); °dadhati (3 pl.) Sukh 66.6; °dadhasi Divy 538.3 (bhagavataḥ); °dadhanti SP 80.4 (prose; tathāgatasya); °dhayanti Suv 192.8 (prose; v.l. °dadhanti); opt. °dadheta SP 93.4 (sūtram); impv. °dadhadhvam SP 315.2 (tathāgatasya); fut. °dadhāsyati Divy 7.29; °dadhāsyanti Divy 14.24; Vaj 41.7; Kv 23.14; °dadhāsye (1 sg. mid.) Divy 8.1; °dadhiṣyanti Mv iii.76.9; ppp. °dadhāta Divy 16.5; gdve. °dadhitavya Mv iii.76.6.

abhiśraddadhāna-tā (n. act. from prec., with suffix ana plus -tā, § 22.42; not from Sanskritic pres. mid. pple. -dadhāna), *state of believing*: SP 332.7; ŚsP 615.10 (both prose).

abhiṣakta, adj. (ppp. of Skt. abhi-ṣajati, Pali abhisajati, both *offend, give offense to*; *afflict*; cf. **abhiṣajyate**; wrongly defined in BR s.v. sañj with abhi; Mbh. Crit. ed. 3.30.26 [Nīl. tāpito, tāpayet for abhiṣakto, abhiṣajet] and 4.4.9 [Rāmakṛṣṇa paraphrases using abhiṣaṅga, glossed parābhava], which are the only two passages cited in BR; pw adds one other from Caraka, abhiṣakta, defined correctly *heimgesucht*), (**1**) lit. *offended*, hence *angered, wrathful* (so the cognate Pali abhisaṅgin is used; Pali abhisatta, in most occurrences, = Skt. abhiśapta *cursed*, but see below), always followed by synonyms kupita, caṇḍībhūta (or in Prāt caṇḍīkṛta): Divy 622.11; Karmav 26.5 (here krodhābhiṣakta); 27.13; Prāt 500.8; 512.9 et alibi; (**2**) in Mvy 2965 abhiṣaktaḥ defined by Tib. (ṅan ba) and Chin. as simply *bad, wicked*; the Jap. has three alternative renderings, all obviously based on etymological guesswork; one means *vituperated*. Occurs in a section entitled krodhakārāḥ, and containing mostly words for *anger, angry* etc., and perhaps to be interpreted precisely in this sense; in that case belonging with (1). However, Pali abhisattarūpa occurs once (Vv.chap. 84 vs. 5; p. 78 line 8) as ep. of bhūmippadesa, a *region*, described as desolate, barren wilderness; the comm. and modern interpreters take it as meaning *accursed*, identifying it with the usual Pali abhisatta (=°śapta, above); but the Vv.context contains no evidence for this; possibly it = Skt. abhiṣakta, orig. *heimgesucht* (as in Caraka, above), *afflicted, evil.* In that case abhiṣakta of Mvy might mean what Tib. and Chin. say, simply *wicked*, which would be not a difficult development from *afflicted.*

? **abhiṣajjana**, nt. (to Skt. abhi with saj or sañj, in a sense not recorded in Skt., but cf. Pali abhisajjati, a, CPD), perh. *sticking fast* (together), said of the teeth during the process of eating: Gv 401.10 (asyāhāraṃ paribhuñjānasya na)... paryavanāho (q.v.) vābhiṣajjanaṃ (printed vā bhi°) vā; but 2d ed. vātisarjanaṃ; what **atisarjana** would mean in this context is obscure; *excessive emission* (spitting out of food)?

abhiṣajyate (pass. of Skt. abhiṣajati, Pali °sajati; = Pali abhisajjati, b, CPD; cf. **abhiṣakta** and **abhisañjanī**), *gets angry* (lit. *is offended*): Av i.286.4.

abhiṣaṇṇa (ppp. of Skt. abhiṣīdati, in different mg., only Vedic and Kāś. on Pāṇ. 8.3.118 f.), apparently *seated*: Sukh 67.8 sa tatra tadābhiṣaṇṇo vābhisampanno vā bhavet (Müller, SBE 49, Part 2, 64: *there he might then be either sitting or resting*).

abhiṣūyate (= Skt. abhyasū°; in vs but not m.c.; § 3.115), *complains*: na cābhiṣūyase MSV i.10.6; i.12.1.

abhiṣeka, n. of the tenth (bodhisattva-) bhūmi in one list (not the ordinary one, see **bhūmi** 4; see also next): Mv i.76.18 daśamī tv abhiṣekāto; 124.20 °ka-bhūmi-prāptānāṃ; Gv 472.25 °ka-bhūmi-sthita, said of Maitreya; Gv 514.7 ekajāti-pratibaddhānām abhiṣekaprāptānāṃ.

abhiṣekavatī = prec.: °tī nāma daśamā bhūmiḥ Mv i.193.6, in a colophon.

Abhiṣecanī (v.l. °cavatī), n. of a Bodhisattva-dhāraṇī: Mvy 747.

abhiṣṇam, see **abhīṣṇam.**

abhiṣyaṇṇa (ppp. of Skt. abhi-ṣyandati, *overflows*), (lit. *overflowing*;) *over-exuberant, excessive*, of the bodily humors (dhātu); so Pali abhis(s)anna is used, of the bodily humors (dosa): Mv iii.143.16 °ṇā **vātātapā** (see this); 144.6 °ṇehi dhātūhi, and same (but with mss. reading abhiṣyandehi, em. Senart) 153.11 and 154.8. See the following entries.

abhiṣyanda, m. (in Skt. used of a pathological eye-condition; cf. prec. and next), *flux, ulceration* of the teeth: Gv 401.9.

abhiṣyandati (cf. prec. and following entries), (**1**) *overflows* with evil emotion, specifically anger or malice: Mv i.30.5 (asurāḥ) kupyanti vyāpadyanti abhiṣyandanti; (**2**) some form or derivative of this verb is intended in Mv iii.311.1, which Senart misunderstands; the mg. must be *becoming inflated* (with evil bodily humors), cf. **abhiṣyaṇṇa**; this condition of the Buddha's body resulted from his first meal after the seven-weeks fast. The next sentence says that Śakra brought harītakī, a purgative medicine, so that *his humors might become pacified, restored to ease*, dhātūnāṃ sukhaṃ (em. to mukhaṃ by Senart!) bhaviṣyati. The exact reading in 1 is uncertain; possibly tathā abhiṣyanditam, impersonal, *inflation, over-exuberance* (of humors) *was caused.*

abhiṣyandana (nt.; = Pali abhisandana; cf. prec. and next), (over-)*flowing*: -mahākaruṇābhiṣyandana-tavā Gv 294.15, *because it is full to overflowing with great compassion.*

abhiṣyandayati, °deti (= Pali abhisandeti; caus. to °**ṣyandati**), *drenches, saturates, irrigates*, (**a**) lit. of plants etc., Mv iii.301.17 vāriṇā °deti **pariṣyandeti** (q.v.); ppp. °dita, SP 122.8 (plants and seeds); Mvy 6584 (= Tib. brlan pa, sbaṅs pa, *drenched, wet*); fig. of kuśalamūlāni, *roots of merit*, °dayiṣyati, fut., Gv 457.18; (**b**) of mental organs or states, °dita-niścita-citto Gv 151.13; -karuṇā-snehābhiṣyandita-saṃtāno 189.9; in yoga practice, °dayati *softens, makes supple* (one's own person), as in Pali (CPD), Mvy 1646 = Tib. mṅon du mñen par byed pa, *makes very supple*; here too followed by **pariṣyandayati.**

abhiṣvakta (ppp. of Skt. abhi-ṣvaj), *attached* (to, acc.): Suv 209.9 (prose) jīvitaśarīrāṇy abhiṣvaktānām (Nobel em. °śarīrābhi°).

abhisaṃyujyate (pass. of Skt. abhi-sam-yuj), *applies oneself to* (acc.): SP 124.4 ye . . . tathāgatasya dharmaṃ bhāṣamāṇasya śṛṇvanti dhārayanty abhisaṃyujyante, *who . . . apply themselves to the law of the T. as he declares it.*

abhisaṃrādhayati (cf. Skt. abhisaṃrādhana, BR 5.1025, once in Bhāg. P., defined *wohl das Befriedigen, Zufriedenstellen*), *applauds*: pres. pple. °dhayan Jm 97.16; ger. °dhya Jm 13.15; 26.16; 27.5; 235.8.

abhisaṃskaroti (= Pali °saṃkharoti; recorded in Vedic (ŚB) as *zurechtmachen, bilden*, BR; see **abhisaṃkaroti, °skṛta, °saṃskāra**, etc.), *accomplishes, performs, does, fashions*; often governs acc. of cognate **abhisaṃskāra**, q.v., in various shades of its meaning; Av i.68.1 prāsādam abhisaṃskṛtavantaḥ, *built a palace*; Śikṣ 252.12 karmābhisaṃskaroti, *performs action*; with cittam, *makes up, fixes* (the mind, thought), Bbh 12.5 cittam °roti; Dbh.g. 44(70).13 (bhūmidharma) °ronti, (Bodhisattvas in 9th bhūmi) *fully realize* (in their minds, the conditions or laws of the bhūmi); without object cittam (cf. abhisaṃskāra without citta-, *mental determination*) LV 254.20–21 uttiṣṭhāmīti cābhisaṃskurvaṃs, *making up my mind* (Tib. sñam na, *thinking*) *that I would arise* (I fell down), cf. Mv ii.126.7 s.v. **abhisaṃskāra** (the situation is the same); but in the parallel LV 256.3 uttiṣṭhāmīti gātrāṇy abhisaṃskurvann, *preparing* (making ready, fixing) *my limbs with the intent to arise.*

abhisaṃskāra, m. (cited from Skt. only BR 7.1700, from Caraka; essentially a Buddhist word; = Pali abhisaṃkhāra; see **°skaroti, °skṛta**), *performance, accomplishment*: SP 226.9 (udāraṃ dharmābhi°, *noble performance of dharma*); in all meanings often made object of the cognate verb **°skaroti**, as Dbh 55.8–9 pāramitābhisaṃskāraṃ cābhisaṃskaroti, *and accomplishes the accomplishment of the Pāramitās*; Dbh 22.23 *performances*; Bbh 256.25 na vyañjanābhisaṃskārārthī, *not seeking the accomplishment of the letter* (but of the spirit, the true esoteric meaning, arthārthī); often ṛddhyabhi° (= Pali iddhābhi°) *performance of magic*, SP 300.9; 388.6; Divy 161.11; 190.22; 340.11; Jm 11.6; 153.2; object of the verb °skaroti, *perform a magic performance*, LV 182.14; 290.13 f.; Samādh 19.14–15; Av i.24.3; *performance* of action, Samādh 22.2 (here specified as karmābhi°), generally with special reference to its fruits, good or bad, esp. when modified by, or cpd. with, words like puṇya, apuṇya, kuśala, pāpa(ka), the Pali equivalents of which are similarly used; here abhi° often may be rendered *accumulation, piling up* (of merit or demerit), and abhisaṃskaroti *accumulates*; cf. LV 88.17 pāpakān abhisaṃskārān abhisaṃskariṣyanti with Dbh 48.7 puṇyāpuṇyāneñjyān abhisaṃskārān upacinvanti, (ignorant persons) *accumulate* (upa-ci, unambiguous!) *performances* (or accumulations, of karman) *that are meritorious, demeritorious*, or *leading to immovable states* (see **aneñjya**), suggesting that the LV passage means really *will accumulate evil accumulations* (of karman); so also LV 398.18 duḥkhābhisaṃskāra-mala- *impurity due to the accumulation* (hardly *performance*!) *of miseries* (thru karman); puṇyābhi° and kuśalābhi°, together, SP 333.3; 348.11; Suv 83.3; puṇyābhi° also SP 337.4; 414.13; AsP 346.8; apuṇyābhi° LV 88.10; kuśalābhi° Śikṣ 190.16; cittābhisaṃskāra, *accomplishment of* (proper) *thoughts* or *state of mind, right mental make up*, Divy 90.26 ayaṃ pradīpas tayā dārikayā mahatā cittābhisaṃskāreṇa prajvalito (this gives the flame magic power of persistence); same without citta, Mv iii.391.8–9 parivrājikā . . . visṛṣṭena svareṇābhisaṃskāreṇa (*with mental preparation* or *concentration, application of mind, fixed determination*) svādhyāyaṃ karontī; Mv ii.126.7 sādhu ca suṣṭhu ca abhisaṃskāreṇa, *with careful mental preparation, application, determination* (here, to rise up after having fallen down; and so ii.127.11; 128.16; 130.1–2; the situation is the same as in LV 254.21 where abhisaṃskurvaṃs occurs, see **°skaroti**); see **sābhisaṃskāra**, in which abhi° comes close to this shade of mg.

abhisaṃskārika, see **ābhi°**, and **an-abhisaṃskārikā.**

abhisaṃskṛta (= Pali °saṃkhata), ppp. of **°skaroti**; see also **an-abhi°**; *accomplished, effected, formed*: KP 79.2

(°taṃ, jñānaṃ bodhisattvasya), 5; Divy 78.5 and 467.1 (cetasā cittam °tam, *the thought was mentally formed*; same omitting cetasā, Divy 78.25; 467.26); of action, good or bad, with reference to its necessary fruit, *accomplished, done, accumulated, stored up*, SP 27.11 °tena (karmaṇā); Mv i.26.7 °taṃ (pāpakaṃ karma, pūrve, *previously*); in Śikṣ 252.13 tac ca karmābhisaṃskṛtam, merely *that action that has been performed.*

abhisaṃsphuṭati, *bursts* (intrans.): LV 309.4 (vs) °ṭanti (subject hṛdayāni).

abhisaṃhāra (m.), *abandonment* (Tib. bskyur ba; opp. to **abhinirhāra**): (tatrāyam) °ra-samkocaḥ, tatrāyam abhinirhāra-vistaraḥ MSV iv.90.15.

abhisaṃkaroti (cf. **abhisaṃskaroti**), app. *honors, treats with respect*: śreṣṭhidārakam abhisaṃkurvanti, jayatu jayatu . . . śreṣṭhidārako etc. Suv 183.3; Tib. mṅon par du byed do (literal; cf. Mvy 1017, 1018); lit. perhaps *makes up properly.*

abhisaṃkṣipati (= Pali °saṃkhipati; in Skt. recorded only in mg. *compress*, by magic into a small size; so used also in BHS, e. g. Bbh 61.11), *subsumes, collects, puts together under one heading*: Śikṣ 9.18 sarvakuśalamūlāny abhisaṃkṣipya tulayitvā piṇḍayitvā; esp. with aikadhyam (so in Skt. aikadhyaṃ saṃsṛjya, and synonyms; in Pali ekajjhaṃ . . . abhisaṃkhipitvā), Bbh 22.3; 25.16–17; 203.12 et alibi; AsP 138.4.

abhisaṃkṣepa (m.; only in the lex. Trik. in definition of the Buddhist term **middha,** q.v.), *compression, summary statement*: Mmk 471.7 tān aham abhisaṃkṣepād vakṣye.

abhisaṃkṣepaṇa-tā (to **abhisaṃkṣipati**), *compression, contraction*: Bbh 264.24 ativistṛtānām cā 'bhisaṃkṣepaṇatayā.

[**abhisaṃkṣepika,** see **ābhi°**.]

abhisañjanī, fem. to °na, adj. (to Pali abhisajati, Skt. °ṣajati, see **abhiṣajyate, abhiṣakta**; cf. Pali parābhisajjanī, CPD s.v. abhisajjanī, used with vācā, *offending*), *offending*: Dbh 24.8, read parābhisañjany (°nī), with vāk, *giving offense to others*, for text parābhisaṃjanany (which is uninterpretable).

abhisaṃdarśayati, *manifests, shows*: ger. °darśya LV 122.10 (prose; audārikam ātmabhāvam abhi°).

abhisamaya, m. (= Pali id., in both mgs.; to **abhisameti,** q.v.), (**1**) *comprehension, clear understanding*; (spiritual) *realization, intuitive grasp* (of religious verities), in Pali especially *grasp* of the Law (dhamma) or the four noble truths (sacca); Tib. mṅon par rtogs pa, *clear comprehension*; cf. Stcherbatskoy, Abhisamayālaṃkāra (Bibl. Bu. 23), p. iii, 'abhisamaya means direct intuition of the Absolute. Here it means the Path of attaining that intuition . . . a synonym of mārga;' often in comp. with that which is comprehended: dharmābhi° Mv i.261.19; SP 328.11; Sukh 42.16; satyābhi° (as in Pali, above) Bbh 38.12; Divy 340.8 and 355.20 (in these two saha, preceding satyā°, should be taken as a separate word); Ud xx.2; āryasatyānām abhisamayāya Divy 654.26; jñānābhi° RP 34.12; prāpty-abhi° ŚsP 615.17 ff. (on prāpti cf. AbhidhK. La V-P. ii.179 et passim); yogābhi° Laṅk 12.1; mārgābhi° LV 38.5 (*realization, intuitive comprehension, of the Path*); (śrāvaka-, pratyekabuddha-, and tathāgata-) yānābhi° Mvy 1261-3 (*comprehension of the vehicles*); of the inferior *intuitions* or *realizations* of śrāvakas and pratyekabuddhas Gv 505.15; Dbh 62.19; 96.28–29; used absolutely, something like *enlightenment* or *spiritual realization* in general, Laṅk 10.12; Dbh 63.13; Dbh.g. 54(80).10; listed among synonyms of nirvāṇa Mvy 1731; abhisamayāntika (see **antika**), *ending in abhi°* (realization? enlightenment? nirvāṇa?) Mvy 1208; 6891; abhisamayādhigamajñāna-Laṅk 218.6, 7 (Suzuki *enlightenment = an intuitive understanding*, for abhisamaya); (**2**) any of the three *collective conversions* of crowds of disciples, accomplished by Buddha; so (and also dhammābhi°) in Pali, see CPD: Mv i.250.16; 251.2.

abhisamayati, see **abhisameti.**

abhisamāgacchati (= Pali id.; = **abhisameti**; in Skt. only in literal sense, *comes to*), *arrives at understanding of* (with acc.): Bbh 38.11 āryasatyāni pravicinvato 'bhisamāgacchato (gen. sg. pres. pple.) 'bhisamāgateṣu ca tajjñānam utpadyate.

abhisamitavant (cf. **abhisameti, abhisamaya,** and next), *having perfectly* (intuitively) *comprehended*: Bbh 248.10 duḥkhasatyam °tavata(ḥ), gen. sg.

abhisamitāvin (see § 22.51; Pali abhisametāvin, also samitāvin), = prec., q.v.: Mvy 2884 °vī, n. sg.

abhisamūḍha, ppp., Senart's plausible em. for mss. abhisaṃmūḍha, in an identical passage Mv iii.217.16 = 218.3 = 222.5; to *abhi-sam-vah: *collected, brought together.* See **abhisāhita.**

abhisameti, also (hyper-Skt.? or denom. to abhisamaya?) °**samayati** (= Pali °meti; CPD identifies this with Skt. both abhi-sam-i and abhi-sam-ā-i, but neither of these is used in any such mg. in Skt.), *realizes* (intuitively), *understands perfectly* (cf. s.v. **abhisamaya,** to which this is the verb, but the noun is commoner): °meti Mv i.312.10 (dharme, acc. pl.); ger. (satyā) °metiya (Senart's em. m.c., mss. °metya) Mv i.165.11; in Mv iii.382.3 mss. abhisame (aor.?) catasro satyāṃ (i.e. the Four Noble Truths); Senart em. abhisamita (evidently as n. pl. of ppp.) catasro satyā; Laṅk 139.5 abhisamita-dharmaḥ, *one who has grasped the dharma*; Divy 617.11 abhisamayati (caturāryasatyāni).

abhisaṃpanna (ppp. of Skt. abhisaṃpadyate, not in this sense), apparently *in a comfortable state*: Sukh 67.9 (see under **abhiṣaṇṇa**; Müller, *resting*).

abhisaṃparāya, m. (= Pali id.; based on the adv. Pali °rāyaṃ, prepos. cpd., see CPD; cf. **saṃparāya**), *future state*: LV 88.20 (kā . . . gatir . . .) ko 'bhisaṃparāyaḥ (in Pali also correlated with gati); Divy 187.16 and 200.5 kā gātiḥ kā upapattiḥ ko °yaḥ; in Bbh 25.16 and 28.1 dṛṣṭe dharme abhisaṃparāye vā (ca) *in the present state or* (and) *in a future one* (in this last phrase Pali uses instead the adv. °rāyaṃ, see CPD: diṭṭhe c' eva dhamme abhisaṃparāyaṃ ca DN iii.83.19 etc.).

abhisaṃpratyaya, m. (nowhere recorded), *complete confidence*: Mvy 2097 °yaḥ = Tib. mṅon par yid ches (-śes) pa, *superior belief*; Divy 309.3 bhagavadvacanābhisaṃpratyayāt, *thru reliance on what the Lord said*; Bbh 81.24.

-abhisaṃpravarṣaṇa-tā (no cpd. abhi-sam-pra-vṛṣ is recorded), *state of raining down* (abundantly): Gv 74.22 -meghābhi°.

abhisaṃprasthita (ppp. of abhi-sam-pra-sthā, unrecorded), *set out towards* (with acc. or loc.): samyaksaṃbodhim (Gv 489.16 °dhāv) abhi° SP 19.9; Gv 489.16; 492.25.

abhisaṃprārthayate (not recorded), *strives for*: Mv i.57.15 saṃbodhim abhisaṃprārthayamānena.

-abhisaṃbuddhana (nt.; n. act. in -ana from **abhisaṃbuddhati** = °**budhyati,** q.v.), *the becoming perfectly enlightened*: Bbh 328.22, in cpd., (praṇidhānam...) anuttarasamyaksaṃbodhy-abhisaṃbuddhana-tāyai.

abhisaṃbudhyate, °**ti,** °**bodhati,** °**budhati** (?), °**buddhati** (on the last two see Chap. 43, s.v. budh; = Pali °bujjhati; very rare in Skt., recorded BR and pw only once, ppp. °buddhaḥ, with atra, *well skilled, learned, enlightened* on this matter, Mbh. Crit. ed. 3.178.27; the pres. °bodhati implied in ger. °bodhitvā), (**1**) *becomes enlightened, attains complete enlightenment* (i. e. becomes a Buddha); the common meaning in BHS. Used absolutely: °budhyati (v.l. °buddhati) Mvy 6907; fut. °bhotsyate Mvy 6905; ppp. °buddho bhagavān LV 350.15; gdve. °boddhavyam *one ought to become enlightened* Mv i.8.13; 229.10;

ii.133.11. Much more often with 'cognate' acc., regularly anuttarāṃ samyaksaṃbodhim, *unto supreme perfect enlightenment*, the subject being a Buddha or other person: °budhyate SP 159.4; LV 85.11; opt. °budhyeyam Sukh 11.10–11; °buddheyam Sādh 225.8; fut. °bhotsyasi SP 216.7; 220.7; °se LV 39.4–5; °sye (1 sg.) Av i.171.15; °syante SP 207.2; 221.8; Suv 97.3; °budhiṣyam (sic!) Mv ii.265.6; °buddhiṣyati Mv ii.313.11; °ṣyasi ii.400.14; °ṣyāmi ii.314.16; aor. °buddhe Mv ii.285.3; ppp. °buddha, still with acc. of complement (anuttarāṃ samyak°), °buddho Mv i.229.11; ii.133.12; °buddho bhaviṣyati Kv 37.25; °buddhaḥ with complement bodhim Mvy 6906; saṃbodhim an-abhisaṃbuddho Mv ii.136.14; (on the same ppp. in passive sense see below;) ger. °buddhitvā (anuttarāṃ samyak°) Mv iii.111.17; 272.18; 349.6; °bodhitvā Mv i.312.18; ii.348.15 (here v.l. °buddhitvā); inf. °boddhukāmena Samādh 8.1; instead of acc., loc. of same complement, opt. °buddheyaṃ (anuttarāyāṃ samyaksaṃbodhau) LV 38.18, and ppp. °buddhaḥ Mvy 6355; the pres. °budhyate, the ppp., and the gdve., are also used passively, subject being anuttarā samyaksaṃbodhiḥ, and the person put in the instr.: Vaj 37.8–9 (tathāgatena...) an°rā samy°dhir abhisaṃbuddhā, *supreme enlightenment was attained, realized*; so also SP 218.11–12; LV 377.2; Divy 393.9; pres. °budhyate Vaj 41.19; gdve. °boddhavyā Kv 18.18; note also the cpd. abhisaṃbuddha-bodhis (tathāgataḥ) LV 377.1, *the T. having attained enlightenment*; (**2**) the verb is however also used (as in the isolated Skt. occurrence noted above) in the sense of *learns thoroughly, becomes skilled in, comprehends perfectly*: SP 210.3–4 asmābhir ... tathāgatajñāne abhisaṃboddhavye (loc. abs.), *when the T. knowledge ought to have been realized* (thoroly learned) *by us*; Ud xviii.18 (kāyaṃ) marīcidharmaṃ °budhānaḥ (so oldest ms., with Pali Dhp. 46; later mss. paribudhya caiva, see **paribudhyati**), *learning to know* (realizing) *the body as having the nature of a mirage*; LV 263.21 nāsau mārgaḥ śakya evaṃ... °boddhum, *that Way cannot be realized* (made the object of enlightened understanding) *in this manner*; Bhīk 22b.5 kaccid evaṃrūpaṃ sthānam abhisaṃbhotsyase? abhisaṃbhotsye, *you will learn perfectly such-and-such a point* (of duty), *won't you? I will*; (**3**) when the subject is dharma, and perhaps in some other cases, it may not be clear whether the verb means *understands* or *illumines, makes clear*; in Mv iii.314.1 dharmaḥ abhisaṃbuddho (said by the Buddha shortly after his enlightenment) probably means *the Law that I have perfectly comprehended*, but possibly *made clear* (to myself); in Mv iii.331.10, 14 tathāgatenāryasmiṃ dharmavinaye madhyamā pratipadā abhisaṃbuddhā, apparently *the middle course of conduct, perfectly illumined* (made clear) *by the T. in the noble dharma* (i. e. sūtras) *and vinaya*; Vaj 32.13 yas tathāgatena dharmo 'bhisaṃbuddho deśito nidhyāto; Vaj 37.11–12 yaś ca ... tathāgatena dharmo 'bhisaṃbuddho deśito vā, *realized* (? *made clear*) *or taught*; and (**4**) we even find, in a few curious passages in Vaj, the complement anuttarāṃ (or °rā) samyaksaṃbodhim (or °dhir), as in (1) above, with dharmaḥ ... abhisaṃbuddhaḥ; the precise meaning is not too clear: Vaj 36.8–9 asti sa kaścid dharmo yas tathāgatena dīpaṃkarasya ... antikād anuttarāṃ samy° °bodhim abhisaṃbuddhaḥ (repeated below), *is there any principle which has been realized (comprehended? made clear?), unto supreme perfect enlightenment, by the T.* (taking it) *from D.?* (the transl. in SBE 49 pt. 2, p. 132 is very loose); Vaj 37.10–11 nāsti ... dharmo yas tathāgatenānuttarāṃ samy° °bodhim °buddhaḥ: and with nom. of complement, Vaj 24.2–3 asti sa kaścid dharmo yas tathāgatenānuttarā samy° °bodhir ity abhisaṃbuddhaḥ, ... *any principle which was realized as* (?) ... (SBE 49 pt. 2, p. 118 *known under the name of*); perhaps the nom. of the complement (apparently isolated) is a corruption for the acc., used at least twice in such a phrase.

abhisaṃbodha, m. (to prec.; = Pali id.; cf. next two), (**1**) *perfect enlightenment*: sukhābhisaṃbodhāya Śikṣ 122.9; mahābodher abhisaṃbodhaḥ Bbh 75.4; (**2**) *perfect comprehension*; *learning perfectly*: LV 428.9; cpd. durabhisaṃbodha, *hard to learn perfectly*, with inf., durabhisaṃbodhāny araṇyavanaprasthāni ... adhyāvastum Av ii.119.11, ... *hard to learn to dwell in*.

abhisaṃbodhana (nt.; = prec.), *perfect enlightenment*: bodhy-a° LV 44.18; 128.5 (sarvajña-jñā)nābhisaṃbodhanaśabda; 357.16, colophon, title of chap. 22; SP 185.9 samyaksaṃbodher abhisaṃbodhanāya; in Dbh 26.2 read as cpd. svayam-abhisaṃbodhana-tayā, *because he* (a follower of the pratyekabuddha-yāna) *is enlightening himself*.

abhisaṃbodhi (= Pali id.) = prec., *perfect enlightenment*; *perfect comprehension*: LV 367.7 °dheḥ, gen.; Gv 36.16 and 38.17 °dhi-vikurvita-; 37.13 -buddhakṣetrābhi°; 370.26.

-abhisaṃbhava, see **dur-abhi°**.

abhisaṃbhāvayati (= Skt. and Pali °bhavati; caus. recorded only once in Bhāg. P. in mg. *salute*, and not in Pali; cf. **abhisaṃbhuṇati**), *attains, brings to realization*: only in formula, bhagavān samyaksaṃbuddho yadarthaṃ samudāgato tadarthaṃ (or tam ar°) abhisaṃbhāvayitvā, common in Mv, e.g. i.4.12; 34.1; ii.115.6; iii.90.18; 382.8.

abhisaṃbhinna, adj. (ppp. of abhi-sam-bhid, nowhere recorded), *brought together, collected, joined, united, associated*: Gv 36.3 (twice); 273.22; °nnā bodhisattvena dharmameghāḥ saṃpratyeṣṭavyāḥ 460.5.

-abhisaṃbhuṇa (to next), see **dur-abhi°**.

abhisaṃbhuṇati (°ṇoti, also **saṃbhuṇati**; = Pali °ṇāti; on formation see Chap. 43, s.v. bhū, 5; = **abhisaṃbhāvayati**, q.v.), *attains*; *reaches to*; *suffices, is adequate for*; in formula (see s.v. **lokāntarikā**) in which the orig. form seems to have read nānubhavanti or °bhonti: ābhāṃ nābhisaṃbhuṇanti, prob. *suffice, are adequate for light* (see **anubhavati**) Mv i.41.6 (by em.); 230.2; 240.11; iii.334.9; 341.13; gatiṃ ... °bhuṇema iii.374.7 and °bhuṇetha 12, opt.; tenāpi abhisaṃbhuṇitvā (Senart em. °ṇitaṃ) tad vayaṃ nābhisaṃbhuṇiṣyāmaḥ iii.265.3; in iii.206.7–10 abhisaṃbhuṇoti four times, the first two with object karmāntāni, acc. to Senart *carries out*, perhaps more lit. *is capable of*; in the last two, with object arthārthaṃ, the mg. *attains* is possible, but it may also mean *is adequate for*.

abhisaṃmodayati, *greets* in the sense of *confronts*, something unpleasant, viz. the evil deeds of former births: Mv i.26.7 taṃ pūrve manuṣyabhūtehi abhisaṃskṛtaṃ abhisaṃmodayitaṃ (so most mss., but one °dayitvā, prob. read so!) niyataṃ vedanīyaṃ, *that which they formerly accomplished* (or *accumulated*) *while men, having confronted, must assuredly be suffered* (in hell). Senart em. and renders otherwise.

abhisaraṇa, see **an-abhi°**.

abhisāra, m. (nowhere recorded; corresponds to Pali abhihāra, also BHS, see s.v., which in Pali is cpd. with bhatta-, cf. bhaktābhisāra below; abhi-harati has a mg. appropriate to this in Skt., and abhi-sarati does not; only in Divy, MPS, and MSV; var. twice atisāra), *gift, present, honorarium*: Divy 6.18, 20 (here given to a bringer of good tidings); usually of food offered to the Buddha and or his monks, Divy 187.23, and almost always in the cpd. bhaktābhi° *offering of food*, MPS 6.8; Divy 43.22 (mss. °āti°); 65.2; 81.16; 85.16; 97.3 (ed. °saras); 177.26 (mss. °āti°); 183.21; 285.2–3; 286.26; of a physician's fee, MSV i.218.10 f.; ii.25.20.

abhisāhita, ppp., prob. to be read in Mv iii.217.16 = 218.2 = 222.5 for Senart's em. abhisāhṛta; doubtless = AMg. sāhiya (which Ratnach. derives from Skt. sv-āhita, rendering *well got*), *acquired, collected*; for abhisaṃhita, which is used in Skt. in substantially this sense; see § 3.3. The mss. read: ... prabhūtā mānuṣyakā bhogā dhārmikā dharmalabdhā dhārmikena balena abhisāhitā (218.2 abhyāhṛtā) abhisaṃmūḍhā (Senart em. **abhisamūḍhā**, q.v.).

Abhisūrya (v.l. Abhibhūya; Senart em. Atisūrya), n. of a future Buddha: Mv iii.330.13.

abhistanita (nt.; orig. ppp. of abhi-stanati or °stanayati, in Skt. only Ved. and very rare; Pali abhitthanati or °nayati), *thunder*: LV 106.16–17 (prose) gajagarjitābhistanita-meghasvara-madhura-mañjughoṣaś, one of the 80 anuvyañjana.

abhistavati (= Pali abhitthavati; Skt. abhiṣṭauti, abhiṣṭuvate), *praises*: °vati Mv ii.157.10; °vanti SP 12.6 (vs); aor. °ve Mv ii.403.4; iii.343.14; 3 pl. °viṃsu SP 191.3 (vs); °vetsuḥ Mv ii.187.6; ppp. °stuto Mv ii.157.18; also **abhistuvati** (cf. § 28.7) in LV 185.11 (vs) read abhistuva, 3 sg. imperf. (§ 32.115).

abhisthiti (f.; from abhi-sthā), *lasting* (noun), *permanence*: Mmk 104.11 (śakaṭasya) cirakālābhisthityartham, *in order that* (the cart) *may last long*; cf. next line sthitaye.

[**abhisvara**, see **avisvara**.]

abhihāra (m.; to Skt. abhiharati; = Pali id., not recorded in this sense in Skt.; cf. **abhisāra**), *offering, gift, present*: Mv iii.387.18; (gandhamālyādy)abhihāreṇa Jm 207.17.

abhīkṣṇāpattika, adj., Bhvr. (abhīkṣṇa plus āpatti, with -ka, Bhvr.; = Pali abhiṇhāpattika), *constantly sinning*: MSV iii.11.15 ff.; Bbh 182.21 nābhīkṣṇāpattiko vivṛtapāpaś ca bhavati. Cf. abhīkṣṇāpatti- KP 119.2, s.v. **āpatti.**

[**abhīrā**, see **āpīrā**.]

a-bhīṣaṇa, adj. (neg. of Skt. bhīṣaṇa), *not terrifying*, with gen.: Mv ii.295.13 (prose) °ṇa sattvānāṃ, *who does not terrify creatures* (said of Bodhisattva); so mss. (one corruptly om. a-); Senart em.

abhīṣṇam, adv. (false Skt. for Pali abhiṇhaṃ = Skt. abhīkṣṇam), *constantly*: LV 397.15; all mss. (a)bhīṣṇaṃ or °bhi°; Lefm. and Calc. abhīkṣṇaṃ.

a-bhugna, adj. (neg. of Skt. bhugna), in °na-kukṣi, adj., *having a belly that is not crooked*, one of the anuvyañjana: Mvy 303; Dharmas 84 (°tā); in Mv ii.44.3 doubtless read abhugnodara for abhagno°; cf. the synonym ajihmakukṣi LV 107.4.

a-bhūta, adj. (neg. of **bhūta**, q.v.; rare in Skt. in this sense), *not true, false*: Ud viii.1 abhūta-vādī(r) *speaking falsehood*; Suv 58.1; Karmav 44.12; Bhīk 16a.2; Jm 116.3; Mv i.36.13 (abrahmacaryavāda); 44.13 (**abhyākhyāna**, q.v.).

abhūtvā-śraddhā (cpd.; ed. prints as two words), *belief in* (coming into existence of something) *after not having been*: yadi . . . °ddhā (*if one accepts* that *belief*), vijñānānāṃ . . . utpattir abhaviṣyad Laṅk 41.6; in Laṅk 40.14 read (ye kecin . . . śramaṇā vā brāhmaṇā) vā bhūtvāśraddhā(ḥ), as Bhvr. cpd., *who cherish a belief in* (existence of something) *after having been*, i. e. *in persistence of* (real) *existence* (text °vābhūtvā śr°, i. e. vā abh°, and so Suzuki).

? **a-bhūmi**, adj. (or read or understand a-bhūmyam, neg. of **bhūmya**, q.v.?), *non-terrestrial*, i. e. *celestial, supernal*: Mv i.72.9 (vs) vartayiṣyi varacakram abhūmi, *I shall start turning the celestial excellent wheel* (of the Law). So one ms.; the rest abhūṣi (which makes no sense); Senart em. adbhutaṃ, which is violent, and metrically impossible. PTSD alleges a Pali abhumma, *groundless, unfounded, unsubstantial*, Jāt v.178.11; vi.495.23; but CPD rejects this word and reads abhuṃ me in both passages.

abhaiṣajya, nt. (= Pali abhesajja, Vin. i.270.18, in parallel to MSV ii.28), *what is not a medicinal remedy*: MSV ii.28.11 ff.

? **abhauti-**, in Laṅk 17.5, text abhauti-bhautikānām; Suzuki *things created and uncreated*; the mss. are very confused; some simply abhautikānāṃ; perhaps read abhautika-bhaut° (and perhaps render rather *of things non-elemental and elemental*). Surely no stem abhauti should be recognized. See **bhautika** (2); one possible reading for the above passage might be bhūta-bhautikānām, *of gross elements and* (subsidiary elements or) *sense-objects*.

abhyaṅga(ya)ti, °**geti** (denom. to Skt. abhyaṅga; = AMg. abbhaṅgai, °gei), *anoints*: tailena °geti Mv iii.154.14; 156.7 (here v.l. °gi, ger.?); ger. °gitvā or °getvā (mss.; Senart em. abhyañcitvā, intending °jitvā?) Mv iii.23.16 (tailehi).

? **abhyadbhuta**, adj. (abhi plus adbhuta), *very wonderful*: SP 23.15. No v.l. in KN; but WT atyad° with ms. K′; perhaps read so (Skt. atyadbhuta).

abhyanumodana, nt. (= Pali abbhanu°; to Skt. °moda(ya)ti), or °**nā**, *approval, applause, approbation*: Jm 49.16; Karmav 37.13; 39.5; fem., MPS 6.11.

[**abhyanta-**, read **atyanta-**, *complete*: Gv 243.21; Śikṣ 296.9.]

abhyantara-kalpa, see **antara-k°**.

abhyantarā, adv.-prep. (cf. Skt. abhyantara, adj., °raṃ, °re, Pali abbha°; and **antarā**), *within*, with gen.: Mv iii.57.17 °rā varṣaśatasya, *in the space of 100 years.*

abhyantarāgra, adj., *with tips* (directed) *inward* (and roots outward), said of the grass ground-cover spread by the Bodhisattva for himself at the Bodhi-tree: LV 289.12 °graṃ bahirmūlaṃ . . . tṛṇasaṃstaraṇaṃ saṃstīrya; in the corresponding passages Mv ii.131.14 and 268.2 read abhyantarāgraṃ (in the first Senart anyatarāgra, reportedly with one ms., v.l. °graṃ; in the second Senart abhyantarāgre, with mss.; in both the following noun is tṛṇasaṃstaraṃ; has bahirmūlaṃ been accidentally lost in the Mv text?).

abhyantarita, ppp. (cf., in diff. mg., Pali abbha°, acc. to CPD ppp. of abhi plus antar plus i, but rather denom. pple. to abbhantara = Skt. abhyantara), *located within*: (sarṣapasya) ākāśa-m °to parittaṃ (so read) KP 78.5 (vs), *the space within a mustard-seed is a small thing.*

abhyantarima, adj. (= Pali abbha°; § 22.15), *interior; that is within*: Mv i.308.18 °me catuḥśāle.

abhyantarimaka, adj. (= prec.), *that is within*: Mv iii.72.15 °makānāṃ vāṇijakānāṃ; 73.17 °makehi (mss. °taramakehi) vāṇijakehi.

abhyantarībhūta, ppp. (cf. Skt. abhyantarī-kṛ), *included, contained* (in, with instr.): Gv 524.19, read na kāyena cittenābhyantarībhūtaṃ (1st ed. by error °tyantarī°; corr. 2d ed.).

abhyantaroṣṭha, adj. (or ābhy°; saṃdhi makes ambiguity), lit. *having a lip in between* (the two halves of a cleft lip), referring to an extreme form of hare-lip in which a flap hangs down between the two halves of the cleft lip: SP 350.8 nābhyantaroṣṭho . . . bhavati.

abhyabhistutya, ger. (with intensive repetition of abhi, not recorded for this preverb; cf. Pāṇ. 8.1.7, adhyadhi etc.), *having greatly praised*: LV 319.10 (prose), so Lefm. with best mss.; v.l. abhyarcya stutvā; Tib. bstod de, *having praised*, not rendering even one preverb.

[**abhyaya** (m.), in Samādh 8.17, read atyaya, *passage, lapse* (of time): kalpakoṭīnām abhyayena, read atyayena. Not noticed by Régamey.]

abhyavakāśa (m.? or nt. = Pali abbhokāsa, m.; in Skt. only Kauś. 46.55 °śe), *the outdoors, free space, the open air*: twice in a formula = Pali sambādho ('yaṃ) gharāvāso (rajāpatho) abbhokāso (ca) pabbajjā (see CPD), Mv ii.117.16 = iii.50.9–10 saṃbādho punar ayaṃ gṛhāvāso (ii.117.16 gṛhavāso; iii.50.9–10 adds, rajasām āvāso) abhyavakāśaṃ (in ii.117.16 mss. °śā, prob. intending °śo, but Senart reads °śam both times) pravrajyā, *the household life is confinement* (PTSD takes sambādho as adj., but it is prob. a noun), *mendicant's life is open space, free room*; °kāśe, *in the open air, outdoors*, Divy 278.10; Av i.228.9;

Śikṣ 65.14; Mmk 88.26; Laṅk 308.10; Prāt 508.8; °kāśa-prakṛtitas Dbh 64.5 (Tib. nam mkhaḥi, *sky, heaven*).

abhyavakāśika, adj. and subst. m. and (?) nt. (from prec.; = Pali abbhokāsika; BHS also **ābhy°**, q.v.; cf. also Skt. abhrāvakāśika, which in MIndic would have the same form, and which CPD suggests may be the historic original, BHS having hyper-Skt. forms; but cf. **abhyavakāśa,** for which no Skt. *abhrā° is recorded), (an ascetic) *living in the open air*, one of the **dhūtaguṇa**: AsP 387.8; Śikṣ 137.1 (contrasted with one who lives in a monastery); °kam, n. sg. nt., Mvy 7477, *the practice of living as a monk in the open air* (but see **ābhy°**, which prob. read).

abhyavakīrati (= Skt. °kirati; § 28.34; Pali abhikīrati is used not only as pass., cf. Geiger 175.2, but also, by the side of °kirati, as active, CPD), *strews* (upon): pres. pple. °kīramāṇā, with active mg., *strewing* (flowers), Gv 430.3 (prose); ppp. °kīrita, *bestrewn*, Mmk 63.25 (prose).

abhyavagāhya, ger. (to Skt. abhy-ava-gāh), Divy 130.13 tāṃ parṣadam abhy°, perhaps *having ripened, matured*, cf. abhyavagāḍha = pariṇata, *completed* (of time of life; see Schmidt, Nachtr., s.v. gāh with abhy-ava); or possibly *having occupied himself with*, cf. -avagāhin in pw s.v.

? **abhyākirati** (not recorded), *strews* (upon): Dbh.g. 6(342).5 °ranti. Note also Dbh.g. 14(350).4, where text abhyokiranti with one of Susa's mss. only; the other, and Rahder's text, abhyā°. Should abhyo° (= abhyava°) be read in the first passage also?

abhyākhyāna, nt. (in Mv once app. m. (or f.?); = Pali abbhakkhāna, nt.; Skt. Lex. and Jain, Hem. Yogaś., BR 7.1700; the ppp. °khyāta is recorded twice in BR s.v. khyā with abhy-ā, and occurs also in BHS, Śikṣ 95.13; the noun seems to be a Bu., also Jain, term; cf. **abhyācikṣati**), *false accusation, slander*: often modified by **abhūta,** *false*, as Mv i.44.13 abhūto abhyākhyāno (v.l. °nā) dinno (v.l. °nā); 45.11 °naṃ (acc. sg.); abhūtābhy° Karmav 44.12; Laṅk 254.1; °na-bahula, *given to false accusations*, Śikṣ 69.5; °la-tā Dbh 26.22; other passages Mvy 5233; 8494 (amūlakābhy°); Śikṣ 171.16; KP 5.5; Laṅk 66.3 (read °naṃ for °nāṃ).

abhyācikṣati (= Pali abbhācikkhati, see s.v. **ācikṣati**; cf. prec. and Skt. abhyākhyāta), *accuses falsely*: Mv i.45.1, opt. °ṣeyaṃ, with abhyākhyānena (see prec.), *may I accuse him with a false accusation*; ppp. °ṣita iii.27.18 (em., but certain).

abhyānandya, ger., *having greeted with approval* or *gratitude*: °dyānumodya Divy 147.20; 462.18 (here mss. abhyan°).

[**abhyāyata,** adj. (error for atyāyata, which is read in other texts), in Mv ii.43.15 nābhyāyata-vacanā ca, one (No. 47) of the **anuvyañjana** (q.v.). For °vacana the orig. certainly had °vadana (so Mvy 314 etc., and Pali āyata-vadana, Burnouf, Lotus 589); yet other versions show the same substitution, and LV 106.16 has a further rationalizing change, to be read with v.l. noccaśabdavacana (for Lefm. noccavacanaśabda). The orig. = *with not too long face* or the like.]

abhyāvasati, *indulges in* (laughter and conversation); cf. Skt. (adhy-)āvasati, *enters into* (a state or condition). In Mv i.214.10 read mātā (Senart em. mātāṃ) . . . abhyāvasati hāsyaṃ ca kathāṃ (Senart with v.l. abhyābhavati and kathā) ca; in repetition ii.17.8–9 both mss. mātā and kathāṃ, omitting the verb altogether; Senart reads as in the first passage.

abhyāsanna, adj. (orig. ppp. of Skt. abhyāsīdati, *reaches, attains*, a rare word; cf. next three), *near*: Śikṣ 349.19.

abhyāsannī-bhavati (from prec.), *becomes* or *comes near* (to, with gen.): °bhavati AsP 348.18, and ppp. °bhūta, *brought near*, SP 232.5, both with anuttarāyāḥ samyaksaṃbodheḥ.

abhyāsāda (cf. prec. and next), *attainment*: Jm 116.5 anekaśāstrābhyāsādā-.

abhyāsādeti (°dayati; cf. prec. three), *presses* (too) *close to* (? so Senart), with acc.: tathāgataṃ °deti Mv iii.179.12; impv. °dehi 13.

abhyāsī-bhavati (= Skt. Gr. abhyāśī°; to Skt. abhyāśa, °sa), *comes near* (to, with gen. or comp.): ŚsP 681.11 sarvākārajñatāyā(ḥ) °vati; caus. ppp. LV 9.8 -vaiśāradyābhyāsībhāvitabalasya; see also **svabh(y)āsībhavati.**

Abhyuccagāmin, occurs in mss. of Mv, in Gv, and as v.l. in LV, for **Atyucca°**, q.v.

Abhyuccadeva, text of Gv, read doubtless **Aty°**, q.v.

abhyutkṣipati, (**1**) *picks up, raises, lifts up* or *out*: LV 67.12 (of Bodhisattva) pāṇim abhyutkṣipya, *raising his hand* (most mss. aty°); 72.7 (tṛṇagulmakam api dharaṇitalād) °pya, *picking up even a handful of grass from the ground*; 83.16 °pya (the gods, *picking up* the new-born Bodhisattva); 305.14 sāgarād °pya (most mss. aty°); Sukh 31.12 (samudrāt . . .) udakabindum °pet; Mv ii.315.9 °peyā, opt.; 329.2 °pitvāna, ger. (mss. corrupt); Śikṣ 306.11 (vs) °pitvā, ger. (nirmālya śuṣkaṃ, so separate); (**2**) *picks out, selects*: Dbh 97.26 °ptaṃ, ppp. (of a jewel, *picked out* in preference to others).

abhyutsada, adj. (cf. **utsada** 3, *abundant*; abhi intensive), *highly excessive*: Gv 335.22 °sade pañcakaṣāyakāle.

abhyutsāha, m. (= Pali abbhussāha; see next two), *energy*: Mvy 1813; Bbh 200.3, 14; vīryam abhyutsāho Bbh 204.15.

abhyutsāha-tā, or **°sāhanā** (so read for atyut° of text; to prec. plus -tā, or to next plus -anā; cf. Pali abbhussahana, °sahanatā, °sāha), *energy, energizing, instigation, encouragement*: (iyaṃ abhyupapattir) iyaṃ śikṣā iyaṃ lokasaṃvṛttir iyam °sāhatā Divy 547.26; similarly, idaṃ kim? °sāhanā 549.7.

abhyutsāhayati (Pali ppp. abbhussāhita; see prec. two), *encourages*: rājānam °sāhayan, pres. pple., Av i.185.9; 191.10.

abhyudīraṇa (nt.; to Skt. abhyudīrayati), *lifting up* (the voice), *uttering*: LV 399.20, read sugirābhyudīraṇe for pratilābhy-ud° (supported by Tib. and both parts found in some mss.).

abhyudgacchati (for which atyud° often occurs in the tradition, either as v.l. or in all mss.; see under **atyudgacchati**; in most meanings Pali abbhuggacchati and derivs. support this reading), (**1**) *arises*, of the sun: sūrye 'bhyudgate Vaj 32.17; *rises* in the air, often with vaihāyasam (as in Pali, vehāsaṃ) or the like, vaihāyasam abhyudgamya Divy 223.12; Mv i.55.2; 239.18 (mss. atyu°); iii.425.17, 23; vaih° abhyudgacchanti (v.l. atyu°) Mv i.21.7; parṣanmaṇḍalamadhyād abhyudgamyopary antarīkṣe vaihāyasaṃ (mss. °se) sthitvā SP 241.15; vihāyasam abhyudgataḥ Divy 223.13; kālo nāgarājā . . . svakāto bhavanāto (i. e. from the nether world) abhyudgamitvā (v.l. atyu°) Mv ii.302.14; vihāyasā saptatālamātram abhyudgamya (both edd. atyu°, no v.l.) LV 18.16; so also Samādh 8.9 (antarīkṣe saptatālamātram atyudgamya); yāvad brahmakāyaṃ ghoṣam (n. sg.) abhyudgacchet (preterite; mss. atyu°, em. Senart) Mv i.229.16, *the sound rose up as far as the company of Brahman*; similarly Mv i.240.5 (mss. atyudgame) and 333.7 (yāvad brahmakāyikā devanikāyā, *as far as the divine abode of the companions of B.*, ghoṣam atyudgacchet, Senart em. abhyu°); also Mv i.231.4 śāram (mss., see s.v. **śāra**) abhyudgato (mss. atyudgataṃ); fig. sarvalokābhyudgato LV 60.14, *risen above the whole world* (of Buddha); fig. *advances, prospers*, bhogair abhyudgacchati Divy 237.19; (**2**) of water-plants, which *rise above* the water (in this sense Pali seems to use only accuggamma = atyudgamya! but BHS tradition abhyud°): LV 76.11 -puṇḍarīkāny abhyudgatāni (puṣkariṇīṣu; in next line 12, puṣpaphalavṛkṣā dharaṇītalād abhyudgamya, confirming the reading of all mss.); Mv iii.318.8 udakāto abhyudgatāni (contrasted with other water-plants which are antodakāni or samodakāni, *under the water* or *level with it*), parallel to LV 400.5 udakābhyudgatāni (contrasted with udakāntargatāni and udakasamāni); (**3**) *arises* = *sets out upon* an undertaking: lokahitārtham (*the welfare of people*) abhyudgatasya Divy 102.7, cf. abhyudgamya (ger.) 103.11; (**4**) *arrives at, comes to, gets*: naivaṃ tṛptim abhyudgacchate Divy 235.21, *does not by this means become satiated.* See also next.

abhyudgata (**1**), nt., a high number: Gv 106.1; 133.10; = **atyudgata**, which is cited from Gv in Mvy 7862. Either might be original; see the two verbs, and cf. Pali accuggata and abbhuggata; (**2**) m., n. of a Buddha: Gv 284.12.

Abhyudgatakarman, n. of a Bodhisattva: Gv 443.8.

Abhyudgataprabhaś(i)rī, n. of a Buddha: Gv 285.2 (vs).

Abhyudgatarāja, n. of a kalpa: SP 469.8.

Abhyudgatābha, n. of a Buddha: Gv 285.10.

Abhyudgatoṣṇīṣa, n. of one of the 8 Uṣṇīṣarājānaḥ (see **Uṣṇīṣa** 3): Mmk 41.10.

abhyudgamana, (**1**) *rising* in respectful salutation (so Skt. Lex.): kumārasyābhyudgamanaṃ kariṣyāmi Mv iii.111.18, *I will cause* (people) *to rise and salute the prince*; (**2**) *rising* of the sun: Divy 334.28 (sūryasyābhyudgamanasamaye); LV 16.12 (°na-velāyāṃ; here v.l. °tyudgam°).

abhyuddidhīrṣā (from desid. of abhy-ud-dhṛ, not recorded; cf. Skt. ud-didhīrṣati, and the foll. items), *desire of lifting up* or *rescuing*: Sādh 97.6 jagatām abhy°.

Abhyuddhara, n. of a Bodhisattva: Gv 443.5.

abhyuddharaṇa (nt., = Pali id.; cf. prec. and next two), *pulling out*, with implication of rescue: Śikṣ 6.5–6 (cited from Gv but not in the pertinent passage, Gv 495) baḍisabhūtaṃ (sc. bodhicittaṃ) saṃsārajalacarābhyuddharaṇa-tayā, *it is like a fishhook, because it pulls out people moving* (like fish) *in the water of the round of existences* (otherwise Bendall and Rouse Transl. p. 6). See especially **abhyuddhāraṇa**.

abhyuddhāra, m. (cf. prec. items, and next), *rescue, deliverance*: °ro Divy 192.6.

abhyuddhāraṇa (nt., cf. prec. items, esp. **abhyuddharaṇa**), = prec.: Gv 143.22 sarva-sattva-saṃsāra-sāgarābhyuddhāraṇa-tāyai.

abhyunnata (ppp. of abhy-un-nam; Skt. id. and Pali abbhuṇṇata, °unnata, as adj.), (*risen up, erect*;) as periphrastic past, *arose*: Mv i.187.15, mss. abhyunnato or aty°; Senart em. abhyudgato.

abhyunnāmya, ger. (to Pali abbhunnāmeti, caus. of Skt. abhy-un-nam; Skt. only **abhyunnata**, q.v.), *having lifted, raised up*: LV 319.6 (prose). Cf. **atyunnamayya.**

? **abhyupakāla**, adj., apparently something like *competent*: Mv i.134.3 (prose), mss. kleśavyupasame (vv.ll. °vyayasame, °vyapasame; understand °śame) 'bhyupakālāś (2 of 6 mss. 'tyupa°) ca kuśalāś (1 ms. °pakāla-kuśalāś) ca bhavanti (Senart reads by em.: kleśavyaya-śamābhyupakāra-kuśalāś ca bha°; there is no record of any abhyupakāra, any more than of °kāla).

(**abhyupekṣya**, ger. [of °kṣati, once in Skt. °kṣitavān Mbh 16.160 = 16.6.13, same mg. as here], *ignoring, overlooking, putting up with* (cf. **upekṣā**): Divy 168.24.)

abhyuhya, ger. (read prob. abhyūhya; to Skt. abhy-ūh; cf. next), *having deduced by reasoning*: Bbh 156.4.

abhyūhanā (= Skt. abhyūha; cf. prec.), *reasoning, logical deduction, inference*: Bbh 83.6.

? **abhrati** (Skt. Dhātup. only, with artificial occurrences in Bhaṭṭikāvya; Pali abbhati, also only Gr.), *goes*: perhaps read (a)bhritvā, or MIndic (a)bbhitvā, ger., *having gone*, Mv i.187.7 (vs; after final -o, -ā, or -e); mss. bhyatvā or bhyotvā (one tyotvā, one datvā); Senart em. bhūtvā, which I think is clearly wrong; a verb of motion seems required.

amaṅku-bhūta, see **maṅku.**

amata, adj. (MIndic for Skt. amṛta), *immortal*: LV 261.20 (vs), read with best ms. naivāhaṃ amataṃ (ma)-nye; cf. Mv ii.238.19 (same line) nāhaṃ amaro ti manyāmi; so Tib. mi ḥchi sñam du ṅa mi sems.

[**amateya**? ŚsP 80.4, see s.v. **adhipati.**]

amatsyamāṃsaka, adj. or subst., (an ascetic practice) *involving eating no fish or meat*: LV 248.17 (prose) °kair (sc. ātāpana-paritāpanaiḥ).

a-madgu, adj. (neg. of **madgu**, s.v. **maṅku**), *not annoyed*: Bbh 125.26 °gur (so mss., one possibly a-maṅgur; ed. wrongly em. a-maṅkur).

a-madhyama, adj. (not recorded in this sense), *immoderate, extreme*: LV 416.19 °mā pratipad, viz. *extreme asceticism*, opp. to the middle course, madhyamā pratipad.

a-manaāpa, see **a-manāpa.**

a-manasikāra, m. (= Pali id.; neg. of **manasi°**, q.v.), *lack of attention*; *inattention*: Bbh 240.19 (pañca-sthāneṣv) amanasikāraṃ kṛtvā; 20, 25, etc.

a-manāpa (less often **a-manaāpa**), adj. (= Pali id.; neg. of **man°**; cf. next), *unpleasant*: Mv ii.150.6, 10; Gv 157.10 (text amān°, misprint?); Bbh 186.2, 6; LV 71.11; amanaāpa Dbh 24.10.

a-manāpika, adj. (neg. of Pali manāpika = °pa), = prec.: Mv ii.150.5, mss. amanāpikāni, Senart em. amān°; to be sure **mānāpikāni** (see this) occurs in the same line; but next line has amanāpaṃ, and in view of the Pali form no em. is necessary.

amanuṣya, subst. m. and adj. (cf. next and **amānuṣa**; as subst. = Pali amanussa; in Skt. only Lex. and Pāṇ. 2.4.23), (**1**) subst. *spirit, demon*; SP 83.9; in lists of kinds of creatures, in cpd. SP 169.2 deva-nāga-yakṣa-gandharvāsura-garuḍa-kiṃnara-mahoraga-manuṣyāmanuṣyais; SP 69.5–6; same list as separate words Gv 141.24 devān . . . manuṣyān amanuṣyān; Mv ii.107.13, read with mss. anyā kiṃnarīṇāṃ gatiḥ, amanuṣyāṇām, *different is the path of the k°, who are demons* (or, as adj., *superhuman*); amanuṣya-vyādhi, *disease caused by a demon or spirit*, Mv i.253.11 ff.; 284.6 ff.; 287.5; amanuṣya-upasarga (so prob. read, as cpd., with one ms.), id., Mv i.287.17; °ṣyābhisṛṣṭa Bbh 63.6; (**2**) adj., *superhuman*: Mv ii.30.16 °ṣyāṇi ca gītavādyaśabdāni (so with mss.; Senart amānu°).

amanuṣyaka, subst. m. = prec.: °kā(ḥ) palānā(ḥ), *the demons fled*, (or, *were put to flight*; often with instr. of agent) Mv i.270.11 (bhagavatā); 283.7 ff.; 288.9–12; amanuṣyakāḥ Divy 451.3 (vs, bad meter; in same vs 456.21 amānuṣāḥ, correct meter; of beings who evidently resemble kiṃnaras).

Amanoratha (cf. **Manoratha**), n. of a piśāca: Mmk 18.5.

amantra, nt., or **amantrā**, f., a high number: °tram Gv 133.17; Mvy 7880, cited from Gv, Tib. gzal yas, implying **amātra**, q.v.; amantrā Gv 106.7.

a-manyana-tā (cf. **manyana**, **°nā**), *the not being proud*: Śikṣ 192.3 svaguṇair a°.

amama, m. or nt., a high number: °maḥ Mvy 7795; °maṃ Mvy 7924, cited from Gv 134.3, where text mamamaṃ (read amamaṃ); Gv 106.18 sattva-mamasya, text, read sattvāmamasya.

Amaradeva, n. of a former Buddha: Mv i.137.4.

Amaraparpaṭa, nt. (or m.), n. of a town: Māy 18 °ṭe; cf. Lévi p. 66.

Amarā, (**1**) n. of a smith's daughter (= later Yaśodharā), who married Mahauṣadha; heroine of a Jātaka which = the Pali Sūci-j., No. 387: Mv ii.83.19 ff.; colophon 89.11 Amarāye karmāradhītāye jātakam. In the Sūci-j. the characters are unnamed; but (Pali) Mahosadha is the hero of the Mahāummagga-j., No. 546, and Amarā is his wife. This has misled both CPD and DPPN into identifying *this* Pali Jātaka with the story of Mv. Actually the stories are quite different, and Mv agrees with the Sūci-j., which, to be sure, acc. to the Story of the Present, belongs to the same occasion as the Mahāummagga; hence doubtless the transfer of the names of the hero and heroine from one to the other. Which was the original? (**2**) n. of a river: Māy 253.6; in a list between Viśvāmitrā and Tāmarā; not in Kirfel; perhaps read Amalā? (but this also is not recorded as a river-name).

Amalagarbha, n. of a Bodhisattva: Mvy 710; Dbh 2.12.

Amalā, n. of a rākṣasī: Māy 243.26.

a-mātṛjña (neg. of **mā°**, q.v.), *not honoring one's mother*, regularly followed by apitṛjña, aśrāmaṇya, abrāhmaṇya, *not honoring fathers, monks, brahmans*: Mv iii.363.8; Divy 293.25; Gv 228.15; 353.3; Bbh 252.21; SP 429.7; amātāpitṛjña-tā, aśrāmaṇya-tā, abrāhmaṇya-tā Karmav 40.10.

amātya-prekṣita, Mv ii.1.9 (mss.), or **amātyāvekṣita**, LV 23.20, *watched (guarded) by ministers*, nt. adj., epithet of the family in which the Bodhisattva is to be born; to be taken closely with foll. phrase, Mv taṃ kulaṃ bhogāṃ bhuṃjati, LV tat kulaṃ bhavati bhogān paribhunakti, *it eats its meals* (or, *enjoys its wealth*) *under the guardianship of ministers*; so Tib. blon pos blta zhiṅ loṅs spyod la spyod pa yin. In Mv the mss. have °preṣitaṃ, which Senart emends rightly; but he also, wrongly, em. amānya for amātya. The parallel Mv i.197.19 is different and doubtless corrupt.

amātra, m., a high number: Mvy 7752a. So read with v.l. for **sumātra**, m., which is read by Mironov without v.l. But Tib. gzhal yas, *without measure*. Cf. **amantra**.

a-mātrajña, adj. (neg. of **mā°**; = Pali amattaññu; cf. next), *immoderate* (in eating): Ud xxix.15.

a-mātrajña-ta, adj., f. **°tā** (or, in mss., °jña°; see under **mātrajñatā**), Bhvr. cpd., *which has no moderation* (in eating): Mv iii.48.17; 49.4 (parṣāye...) bhojane amātrajñatāye (so Senart; it seems to me necessary to read °jñatāye, with v.l. 48.17).

amānuṣa, m. (**1**) = **amanuṣya(ka)**, subst.: Divy 456.21 (see s.v. **amanuṣyaka**); LV 75.15; (**2**) n. of a nāga king: Māy 247.26.

amāpya, amāpiya (not in Pali or Skt.; neg. gdve. to caus. of root mā), (**1**) adj. *immeasurable*: °pya SP 66.4; Vaj 34.2; °piya Mv ii.362.11 (prose): (**2**) subst. nt., a high number: Mvy 7948 (cited from Gv); 8046; Gv 106.25; 134.14 (all °pya).

amāpya-parivarta, m. (Mvy) or nt. (Gv 134.14), *square of* prec. (2): Mvy 7949 °taḥ (cited from Gv); Gv 106.25 (gen.); 134.14 °tam, n. sg.

amita, ppp. (to root am; recorded only in Skt. Gr.), *sick*: Mv ii.430.3, mss. varaṃ te amito (Senart em. ramito, implausibly) ahaṃ, *sick as I am, I am a better choice for you.*

Amitateja(s), n. of a former Buddha: Mv i.136.16.

Amita-tosala (nt. or m.; cf. **Tosala**), n. of a country in the south: Gv 179.3 °le.

Amitadhvaja, n. of a Buddha in the west: Sukh 97.15.

Amitanātha, another name for **Amitābha**: Sādh 360.4; 363.13.

Amitaprabha, (**1**) another name for **Amitābha**: Sukh 50.6 (vs); 53.15 (vs); 62.13–14 (prose), here one of three names for the same personage, Amitābham Amitaprabham Amitāyuṣaṃ (tathāgatam etc.); (**2**) n. of a different (future) Buddha: Sukh 70.6.

Amitalocana, n. of a former Buddha: Mv i.138.11.

Amitavyūhavatī, n. of the lokadhātu of Amitāyurjñānaviniścayarājendra: Mmk 303.24.

Amitaskandha, n. of a Buddha in the west: Sukh 97.14.

Amitā, n. of a sister of Śuddhodana: Mv i.352.14; 355.20.

Amitābha, (**1**) n. of the Buddha who presides over the western paradise **Sukhāvatī** (lokadhātu); also known as **Amitāyu(s)**, **Amitaprabha**, **Amitanātha**, and doubtless intended by the Mmk names **Amitāyu(rjñāna)-viniścayarājendra** (or the like), even tho he is once depicted separately in a painting centering about that personage (Mmk 305.12–13, cf. 304.25). See these names separately. The two commonest names are Amitābha and Amitāyus, and they are as a rule quite equivalent and interchangeable; see notably Sukh 62.13–14; 95.15 and 20. Often Sukhāvatī is mentioned with him. He is the fourth of the 'transcendent' Buddhas, Dharmas 3; Mvy 85. Other occurrences: Suv 2.5; Bhad 49, 57, 59, 62; Śikṣ 175.6; Kv 18.7; 21.8 etc.; Mmk 42.16; 426.7; Gv 82.5; Laṅk 283.7; Sukh 1.6; 28.10 etc.; Sādh 16.10 etc.; (**2**) n. of a Bodhisattva: Gv 442.22 (one of a long list, and hardly to be identified with the Buddha A.).

Amitāyu (or **°yus**; n. sg. always °yus), another name for **Amitābha**, q.v.: SP 184.13; 419.3 (one ms. °tābha); Suv 8.2; 120.6; RP 57.21; Sukh 32.13; 49.4; (in the 'Smaller Sukh' mentioned before, and oftener than, Amitābha: 93.3; 95.15 etc.).

Amitāyurjñānaviniścayarāja, Mmk 7.12, or **°rājan**, id. 301.20, n. of a Tathāgata, presumably = **Amitābha** (**°tāyu**); see the following items.

Amitāyurjñānaviniścayarājendra, Mmk 301.15; 303.23; 426.8; or **°viniścayendra** 365.16, = prec.

Amitāyurvatī, n. of the lokadhātu of **Amitāyuviniścayarājendra**: Mmk 304.21 f.

Amitāyuviniścayarājendra = **Amitāyurjñānaviniścayarāja** etc.: Mmk 304.25.

Amitāyus, see **°yu.**

Amitauja(s; n. sg.), n. of a former Buddha: Mv i.138.1.

amitraka (cited for Skt. by Galanos [pw]; = Skt. amitra, with -ka, perh. specifying), *(one that is) an enemy*: MSV ii.20.7; 21.3.

amila (v.l. **āmila**, q.v.), m. (AMg. amila, *'a cloth made in the Amila country; a woollen cloth'*, Ratnach.; there is no country called Amila in Kirfel; cf. also Pali āmilāka, a certain kind of woolen cloth), Mvy 9172 = Tib. beḥu ras yug chen, which seems to mean about what the Chin. means, viz.. *large cloth of calf's hair.*

a-milāna, see s.v. **milāyati.**

a-mukhara, adj. (= Pali id.; neg. of Skt. mukhara), either *not garrulous*, or (acc. to CPD for Pali equivalent, used in parallel formula) *not scurrilous* (cf. also **mukhara**): Mv ii.356.12 = iii.280.18, with **avikīrṇa-vāca**, q.v.

[**amuñciyaṃ**, Senart's em. at Mv i.184.9, apparently understood as neg. gdve. from muñcati, *not to be escaped from.* But mss. a-muñciya (one °yaḥ; at end of line of vs), and this is prob. to be kept, as neg. ger.: *not having got rid of*, i. e. *if one does not get rid of* (this evil thought).]

amūḍha-vinaya, m. or nt. (= Pali amūḷha°, see CPD; described MN ii.248.5 ff.), *disciplinary procedure for one not* (any longer) *insane* (and forgiven sins committed during past insanity), one of the **adhikaranaśamatha**: Mvy 8633; nt. MSV ii.207.12.

a-mūlaka, f. **°ikā** (= Pali id., as adj.), *groundless, baseless* (of an accusation): Mvy 8494 amūlakābhyākhyānam; Prāt 519.7 amūlakena saṃghāvaśeṣeṇa dharmeṇānudhvaṃsayet; MSV iii.108.19 ff.; as subst. nt., *groundless accusation*: °kam Mvy 8376, a **saṃghāvaśeṣa** offense, described Prāt 481.6–10 and in Pali Vin. iii.163.21 ff. (a monk falsely accuses another monk of a **pārājika** sin, then of his own accord repents and confesses); MSV iii.88.1.

amūlā (hardly identifiable with Skt. amūlā, BR 1.378; cf. Pali amūlā latā, amūla(ka)-vallī), a kind of tree (?): Gv 508.3 °lā nāma vṛkṣajātiḥ; but the context suggests a parasitic woody vine.

amūlyaka, f. °**kā** (Skt. °ya plus -ka), *priceless*: °kayā śraddhayā MSV iv.225.16; so ms., ed. amūlakayā, with Tib., but this gives an impossible mg.

Amṛta, n. of a nāga: Mvy 3319.

Amṛtakuṇḍalī, n. of a deity: Mvy 4330.

Amṛtaparvataprabhāteja(s), n. of a Tathāgata: Gv 422.9 °jas, n. sg.

Amṛtaphala, n. of a former Buddha: Mv i.141.3.

Amṛtavindu (= °bindu), n. of an apsaras: Kv 3.11

amṛtāśmagarbha (m.; cf. amṛtāśma, Kāś. on Pāṇ. 5.4.94), n. of gem: Mv ii.310.12.

Amṛtodana (= Pali Amito°, brother of Suddhodana and father of Anuruddha and Mahānāma), n. of a Śākyan aristocrat, brother of Śuddhodana: Mv i.352.13; 355.20; father of Anuruddha, Mahānāma, and Bhaṭṭika, Mv iii.177.2; mentioned Mvy 3602; Av ii.111.8.

ameya, nt. (Skt. adj. *immeasurable*), a high number: Mvy 7816.

ameya-parivarta, m., *square* of the prec.: Mvy 7817.

Amoghacaṇḍa, n. of a deity: Sādh 3.4 et alibi.

Amoghadarśana, n. of a nāga: Mvy 3332.

Amoghadarśin, (**1**) n. of a **satpuruṣa**, q.v.: SP 3.12; (**2**) n. of a former Buddha: LV 171.9; Śikṣ 169.9; (**3**) n. of a Bodhisattva: Mvy 717; Samādh p. 36 line 2.

Amogharāja, (**1**) n. of a disciple of Buddha: LV 2.1; Sukh 2.10; (**2**) = **Amoghasiddhi**: Sādh 16.10.

Amoghasiddhi, n. of the 5th of the ('transcendent') Buddhas of Dharmas 3; Mvy 86; Sādh 13.6 et alibi. Cf. **Amogharāja** (2).

Amohadharmeśvara, n. of a Bodhisattva: Gv 442.23 (text Moha°, without avagraha, after -o).

amoham, adv. (= AMg.id., Skt. and Pali amogham; cf. **moham**), *not in vain*: Mv iii.254.14 ff.

ambakā (= Pali id.; cf. Skt. ambā), *a* (*poor*, CPD) *woman*: MPS 11.25, of Āmrapālī.

? **ambakoṭa**, see **antakoṭa.**

ambara, (**1**) m., *garment* (recorded only as nt. in Skt. and Pali): LV 92.16 (vs) ambarān, acc. pl.; (**2**) m., n. of a Buddha: Mv i.124.4. See also **dravyāmbara.**

? **ambāsanaka** (or **āmb**°), in Divy 221.29, mss. prāsādāmbāsanakā; some part, or accompaniment, of a palace; ed. em. prāsādā svāsanakā, which is implausible.

Ambulima (m. or nt.), n. of a locality: Māy 92 (cf. Lévi p. 103).

ambhīrya, v.l. for **āmbhirya**, q.v.

Amrapālī, see **Āmra**°.

ayakva, or **ayakka**, or **apa**°, or with stem-final ā, Mv ii.465.2, 13, some product of the carpenter's craft; the mss. vary as indicated; the form ends in -ā and is n. pl.

a-yathāvata, adj. (cf. Skt. a-yathāvat, adv.; Pali yathāva and a-yāthāva, adj.), *not normal, not 'comme il faut'*: Gv 436.13 (prose) °vatena rūpeṇa. (Read a-yāth°? Cf. **yāthāvatas.**)

[**ayamaka**, in Bbh 152.10, ep. of prātihārya, read **yamaka**, q.v.]

ayava, m. or nt., a high number, Mvy 7774 (m.; so also Mironov); Gv 133.24 (nt.), cited in Mvy 7903 apparently in mss. as apavaḥ, but Kyoto ed. in paren. adds (as em.?) ayavam, and Tib. rendering is clearly meant to be identical with that for ayava 7774. Altho Mironov reads apavaḥ without v.l. in 7903, further confirmation of stem ayava is prob. furnished by Gv 106.13 where for text sattvajavasya we should doubtless understand sattvāj°, that is -ajava = ayava (or even read sattvāyavasya?).

Ayaskīla, m., n. of a mountain; **Ayaskīlā**, n. of a river: (both) Divy 106.25.

ayas-prapāṭikā, see **prapāṭikā.**

Ayātī-vana, n. of a forest: Māy 59.

ayukta-yogin, *one who has not practised discipline*: SP 93.11 (vs) °gīna, gen. pl.; Kern, *yogins who are not self-restrained*, and similarly Burnouf; this seems to me inaccurate.

ayuta, nt. (m. in Skt. only Mbh. Crit. ed. 3.21.24; in BHS noted as m. Mvy 7998), in Skt. only defined as 10,000; so also Mvy 8054 = Tib. khri; but oftener = 100 koṭis or 1,000,000,000 = Tib. ther ḥbum, so defined LV 147.20 (cited Mvy 7955), also Mvy 7998, and presumably also 7701, 7827 (in these at least higher than koṭi, and between this and niyuta); in Sukh 31.1 a very much higher number, listed between nayuta and akṣobhya.

ayoniśa, adj. (abstracted from ayoniśo-manasikāraḥ, cpd., see next, secondarily analyzed as °śo (n. sg.) manasikāraḥ; hence nonce-form °śena, instr.), *not fundamental* or *thoroughgoing, superficial*: LV 419.17 (vs) saṃkalpakalpajanitena ayoniśena (so best mss., Lefm. °sena; sc. manasikāreṇa?; no noun expressed, unless **saṃkalpa,** q.v., be taken as a separate instr.) bhavate avidyā etc.

a-yoniśas (neg. of **yoniśas**, and similarly used; = Pali ayoniso; for usage see **yoniśas**), *not in a fundamental or thoroughgoing way; superficially*: (a) adv., Bbh 46.10 °śo vikalpya; (b) in comp., °śo-manasikāra Dbh 48.6 (prose); °manaskāra Divy 445.2; Gv 495.7 (cited Śikṣ 6.4, where read ayoniśo-man°); Śikṣ 157.14; °śaś-citta (so Pali °so-citta) Suv 61.12; RP 48.10 (here could only be a cpd.); °śo-vikalpena, *by superficial* (false) *imagination*, Laṅk 265.15.

ayyaka, m. (= Pali id.; MIndic for Skt. āryaka), *grandfather*: Mv ii.426.16; iii.264.2. Cf. **aryaka, payyaka.**

Araktapravāḍa, n. of a former Buddha: Mv i.140.5.

arakṣya (written also arakṣa, ārakṣa, °ṣya in mss.), nt. (= Pali arakkheyya or ār°), *point that does not need to be guarded*; the Tathāgata has three or four, in Pali and BHS; viz., his conduct is completely and automatically pure, so that he does not need to be on guard, in body, speech, and mind (kāya, vāc, manas); when the fourth is added it is manner of livelihood (ājīva). True reading a-rakṣya; Tib. bsruṅ pa med pa (Mvy 191; note on Bbh 375.6), and so Chin. acc. to Lévi, Sūtrāl. Transl. p. 303 note. Three (as in Pali DN iii.217.8 ff.): Sūtrāl. xx.53; Bbh (mss. sometimes corrupt) 89.6; 230.13 (ed. ārakṣyāṇi, ms. ārakṣāṇi); 375.6; 403.23; no number, 408.4; four (as in Pali AN iv.82.15 ff.) Mvy 191–195; in 195 read ājīva for jīva; in 191 Mironov ārakṣāṇi, but Kyoto ed. correctly arakṣyāṇi without v.l.

araṅgaṇa, some kind of flower: Mmk 668.8 (prose) °ṇa-puṣpāṇām.

Arajottarīya, n. of a former Buddha: Mv i.140.9.

Arajovirajonayayukta, m., n. of a samādhi: Mvy 616. Not in the list ŚsP 1425.17 (where it should be inserted), but in corresponding list 1414.16 (misprinted °rajonayukto).

a-raṇa, adj. and subst. nt., also **araṇā** subst. f. (= Pali a-raṇa, adj. and subst. nt.; araṇā not in Pali unless, by em. m.c., in Pv iv.1.33 for text araṇa-vihārī, see CPD s.v.; neg. of Pali, BHS **raṇa**, q.v., = **kleśa,** Pali kilesa), (**1**) adj., *free from depravity, passion, impurity*, = Tib. ñon moṅs pa (also = **kleśa**) med pa: Divy 395.30 parvataguhānilayam araṇaṃ vairaparāṅmukhaṃ praśamayuktam; on Av ii.130.2 see s.v. **araṇya**; RP 16.3 (vs), text araṇya-vividhaprānta sevamāno, read araṇa (required by meter; for °ṇaṃ) vivi°; in some cpds. seemingly adjectival, as araṇāśaya- (misprinted araṇaśaya), *passionless heart*, Dbh.g. 7(343).7, which suggests that for the corrupt text maitrapeśi raṇvanāśayo (!) ghanaḥ Gv 482.25 (vs) we must read maitra peśir araṇāśayo (°aṇva° is unmetr.!) ghanaḥ; prob. also Mvy 617 araṇa-samavasaraṇa, n. of a samādhi, cited from ŚsP 1414.17 where **saraṇa** is added after araṇa; Mvy 618, cited from same place; also araṇa-samādhi, *passionless samādhi,* Mv i.164.15, or *having* . . . (Bhvr.), Mvy 1125 (note that Pali uses araṇa as adj. with samādhi); (**2**) °ṇa, subst. nt., *freedom from passion* or *depravity, non-passion,* etc. Mv i.165.5 (vs) sukhaṃ samādhiṃ araṇāni sevato; in cpds., araṇa-bhāvanayā Samādh 19.4 (prose; cf. 3, below), *by bringing to pass freedom from kleśas*; araṇavihārin (= Pali id.), *dwelling in a passionless state,* Mvy 6366 (here araṇā-vihārin, below, seems to indicate that araṇa is substantival in force); (**3**) araṇā, subst. f. (on Pali see above), in BHS seems = araṇa nt.; as separate word, in AbhidhK, see below, and Bbh 89.1 yā ca tathāgatasyāraṇā; in comp., araṇā-vihārin = araṇa-v°, above; sometimes ā could be m.c., as Divy 401.4; but in prose in the rest; Subhūti is the first of araṇāvihārin, AsP 20.8; Vaj 26.12; Av ii.131.5–6; AdP, Konow MASI 69, 13.33; other cpds., pratisamvid-araṇā-praṇidhi-jñānādīnāṃ (contains a four-member dvandva) guṇānāṃ Bbh 207.22; araṇā-bhāvanayā Samādh 8.16 (prose, = araṇa-bh°, above, in a closely parallel passage); araṇā-sampannā(ḥ) Mv ii.292.17; in LV 428.13 read with v.l. araṇā-dharma-supratilabdha for text araṇya°. La Vallée-Poussin, AbhidhK vii.86–88 defines araṇā as *le pouvoir d'empêcher la naissance de la passion d'autrui*; but in my texts it seems to be much less complicated, a simple equivalent of araṇa. Did it start in verses, m.c. (cf. Pali, above, Pv iv.1.33), and somehow come thence into prose? Or (more likely) was araṇā orig. adj. (to 1, above) with a fem. noun (samāpatti? cf. AbhidhK LaV.-P. iv. 121; or maitrā, Pali mettā?). See also Renou, JA 1939, 369 note 1.

Araṇasamavasaraṇa, m., n. of a samādhi, Mvy 617; cited from ŚsP 1414.17; 1425.17 where saraṇa is added after araṇa-; Tib. supports the BHS in Mvy. See **araṇa.**

Araṇasaraṇasarvasamavasaraṇa, m., n. of a samādhi, Mvy 618; cited from ŚsP 1414.17; 1425.19 (here °śaraṇa).

araṇā, see **araṇa.**

Araṇemi (°min, °mī?), m. (= Pali id.; also °**nemi,** q.v.), n. of a brahmanical sage: °ṇemī-Gautamau, dual dvandva, Divy 632.12; °mī (n. sg.) Gautamo (two words, but the same person) 651.7; °miś ca Gautamo (one person) 653.12. Cf. next. Probably the dual cpd. is a mere error.

Araṇemika, m. pl., n. of a brahmanical school (of the Chandogas): Divy 632.23. Cf. prec.

? **araṇya,** adj.: in Av ii.130.1–2 ms. so 'raṇyaṃ pratipadaṃ samādāya vartate; Speyer em. 'raṇya-prati°, interpreting *the rules of forest-life* (see his note). But prob. read araṇāṃ pratipadaṃ, *the passionless* (kleśa-less) *course of conduct* or *path*; see s.vv. **araṇa** and **pratipad**; this would be paleographically close to the reading attributed to the ms.; a similar error in RP 16.3, s.v. **araṇa.**

araṇyaka, m. (= Pali araññaka), = **ār°**, one of the **dhūtaguṇa**: Divy 141.21.

Arati (in Mv Aratī), (**1**) n. of a daughter of Māra: LV 378.4 °tiś ca; Mv iii.281.15 (mss. Aparatī); 284.12, 17; 285.5; 286.6; (**2**) n. of one of the 'armies' (senā) of Māra: LV 262.14 (see **Ārati,** which Mv reads in the same vs). See also **ārāti.**

Aranemi = °**ṇemi,** q.v. (= Pali id.), n. of a brahmanical ṛṣi: Mvy 3472.

Arapacana, a name of Mañjuśrī: Sādh 94.15 et alibi.

Aravāḍa (= Pali °vāla, °vāḷa), n. of a nāga-king: Mvy 3282; see next.

Aravāla = prec.: Māy 247.29.

araha, adj. (= Pali id., Skt. arha), *worthy*: nigrahārahaṃ, pragrahārahaṃ Mv i.347.18 (prose).

arahant (= Pali id. = Skt. and BHS **arhant,** q.v.,), see § 3.100.

Arāḍa = **Ārāḍa,** q.v.: Mv ii.200.13 (vs; ă here required by meter), in dvandva cpd. with -udraka; Buddhacarita (Johnston) vii.54; xi.69; xii.1 ff. (in 2 kālāma). Pali also has Alāra, but only of a different person.

arāva, nt., Mironov's reading for **ārāva,** q.v.

Arigupta, n. of a Bodhisattva: Gv 442.11.

ariñcana (nt.; neg. of riñcana = Pali id., to riñcati), *the not abandoning*: Gv 456.25 sattvaparipākāriñcanatāyai, *so as not to abandon the maturation of creatures.*

[**aritīyate,** read **artī°**: Bbh 282.7–8.]

Arinihantar, n. of a former Buddha: Mv i.140.13.

Arindama (= Pali id.), n. of an ancient king (previous incarnation of Śreṇiya Bimbisāra; but in the Pali version, Jāt. 529, of the Bodhisattva): Mv iii.449.17 ff. (one or both mss. often cited as reading Anindama).

Arimardana, n. of two former Buddhas: Mv i.137.4; 139.8 (here v.l. avi°).

ariya, adj. (= Pali id.; MIndic for Skt. ārya), *noble*: Mv iii.400.6 ariyo (both mss., Senart em. āryo) tāyi (so with Senart, mss. tāpi).

Ariṣṭa, (**1**) n. of a former Buddha: Mv iii.231.1; (**2**) perhaps to be read for **Ṛṣṭa,** q.v.; (**3**) n. of a monk (= Pali Ariṭṭha, see Vin. ii.25.12 ff.), punished for heresy by the **utkṣepaṇīya**: MSV iii.30.4 ff.

Ariṣṭanemi, n. of a former Buddha: Mv i.140.5.

Ariṣṭā, n. of a devakumārī in the western quarter: Mv iii.308.8; cf. next.

Ariṣṭikā, n. of a goddess: Mahāsamāj. 185.15, identified by Waldschmidt with prec.; the Pali (DN) correspondent Ariṭṭhakā appears to be m. pl., a class of gods (see CPD s.v.).

Arisūdana, n. of a Buddha, Mv i.124.10 (regarded by Senart as adj. epithet: he takes **Mahābhāga** as the name, Index).

Aruṇa, n. of a nāga king (note the nāga priest Aruṇa Āṭa in PBr, see BR s.v. 2 g): Māy 246.19.

aruṇavati, some kind of perfume: Gv 153.15 (prose) °vati-gandharāja-.

Aruṇā, n. of a devakumārikā in the western quarter: LV 390.5.

aruṇodghāṭa- (Mv), or **aruṇodghāṭana-** (LV), *break of dawn* (= Skt. aruṇodaya), cpd. with -kāla-samaye (kāla once omitted): Mv i.229.7 (here Senart em. °ṇopagh°, wrongly); ii.133.7; 284.16; 415.18; 422.6; 431.11; LV 345.20; 350.8. The stems udghāṭa and °ṭana both occur in Skt. in mg. *opening,* but do not seem to be used of the dawn.

? **aruṣya,** adj. (to Skt. arus, *wound, sore*), *characterized by sores*: LV 189.14 (vs) kiṃ sārathe puruṣa ruṣya-vivarṇa-gātraḥ, where ruṣya could well stand for aruṣya: *with limbs full of sores and discolored.* Cf. Pali aru-gatta, *with limbs full of sores.* Tib. rtsub, which otherwise = paruṣa; and accordingly Foucaux *rude* (rough). But connexion with rūkṣa is scarcely possible, unless by hyper-Sktism (AMg. rukkha).

arūpāvacara, m. (= Pali id.; but in BHS usually **ārūpyāv°**, q.v., or simply ārūpyā(ḥ) devāḥ, see **ārūpya**), *belonging to the sphere of the formless,* ep. of a group of (4) classes of gods, Dharmas 129; see also next, and s.v. **deva.**

arūpin, adj. (= **ārūpya,** adj., °**pyāvacara, arūpāvacara**), *formless*: Mmk 45.7 °piṇaś ca devā(ḥ). (Pali arūpin, not in this sense).

a-rūha, mss. at Mv ii.65.12, Senart em. **a-lūha,** q.v.

Arka, n. of a king (previous incarnation of Śākyamuni): Mv i.54.5.

argaḍa, m. (= Skt. °la, Pali °ḷa or °la; once in ŚB Mādhy., ŚBK. reading °la, see BR), *bolt, bar*: Mv ii.115.12 (read) nivātāni sparśitārgaḍāni (kūṭāgārāṇi), see **sparśita;** Mvy 5581; Prāt 506.11; SP acc. to KN Preface vi, in Nep. (Kashgar rec. °ṭa).

argalaka (nt.? = Pali aggala), *patch* (on garments, here sandals): MSV iv.203.11.

argalapāśa, m. (= Pali aggaḷa-pāsaka or aggala°, AMg. aggalapāsaga), *receptacle* or *latch in which the bolt fits,* a part of a city gate: Mv i.195.19 (prose).

-arghyeya, see **an-a°**.

Arciketu, n. of a former Buddha: LV 172.10.

(**arcita**, ppp. [= Skt., used, tho rarely, in this sense, pw s.v. arc; cf. BR 5.1042], [decorated,] *beset, studded* [with jewels]: Mvy 6056, defined as = the preceding khacita [and cf. the following racita].)

Arcitanama (read Arcitamana, for °manas?), n. of a Bodhisattva: Gv 443.6 (prose) °masya, gen.

Arcinetrādhipati, n. of a yakṣa: Mvy 3371.

Arcimant (°**mat**, °**ma**), (**1**) n. of a legendary cakravartin who became the father of **Dīpaṃkara**: Mv i.193.14 °māṃ (v.l. °mo; n. sg.); 198.16 °mo, etc.; (**2**) n. of a previous incarnation of Śākyamuni: LV 170.17. See also **Arciṣmant.**

Arcimahendra, n. of a Bodhisattva: Gv 442.15 (prose) °rasya, gen.

Arcirmaṇḍalagātra, n. of a Tathāgata: Gv 422.18 (prose).

Arciśiri (semi-MIndic = *Arciḥśrī), n. of a Tathāgata: Gv 259.8 (vs) °riś, n. sg.

Arciścandra (see s.v. **Kuṇḍaśriyārciścandra**), n. of a Bodhisattva: Gv 443.1.

Arciṣmatī, n. of the 4th (bodhisattva-) bhūmi: Dbh 5.8 etc.; Mvy 889; Dharmas 64; Bbh 341.2.

Arciṣmant, (**1**) n. of a Tathāgata: Śikṣ 9.3; (**2**) n. of a Bodhisattva: Gv 442.11; (**3**) n. of an ancient king, a previous incarnation of Amitāyus, and father of Puṇyaraśmi: RP 36.18 ff. Cf. also **Arcimant.**

Arciḥsamudramukhavegapradīpa, n. of a Tathāgata: Gv 422.20.

Arjuna, (**1**) n. of a king of Hastināpura (= Pali Ajjuna; identified with Arjuna Kārtavīrya of Skt. epic), character in the **Śarabhaṅga** (q.v.) Jātaka: Mv iii.361.4 ff.; 368.15; (**2**) n. of a yakṣa: Māy 23; (**3**) n. of a Śākyan mathematician: LV 146.9 ff.

Arjunāvana (ā for a m.c.), n. of a locality (pertaining to Arjuna 2, above): Māy 23.

artita, *distressed*: pple. of next.

ar(t)tiyati or °**tīyati**, °**te**; in one doubtful passage perhaps ārtī°, otherwise always art° when not fused in saṃdhi with preceding vowel; forms occurring include ar(t)tīyati, °yanti, °tīyate, °tiyante, °tīyanto and °taṃ (pres. pple.), aritīyeran (! read art°), artita (ppp.); also ārtīyate (? v.l. attī°); attīyantā (and probably attīyate for prec.); ṛtīyate, °yante, °yamāna (pres. pple.; for ṛt° we usually find rit° written); ardīyamāna (pres. pple.); āstīryati; and noun **attīyanā**. The corresp. Pali (see CPD) is written aṭṭīyati, aṭṭhī°, aḍḍhī°, addiyati. Despite all this confusion, there is no doubt that we are dealing with essentially one word, with modifications due to diverse influences, including popular etymology and hyper-Sktism. Wogihara, ZDMG 58.454, gives the 'correct form' as ṛtīyate (which, or rather usually rit°, is customary in Bbh, but I believe occurs nowhere else), and the mg. as *er schämt sich*; both statements are wrong, I believe. As to mg., Wogihara was evidently influenced by the fact that the word is often associated in Pali with harāyati, jigucchati, and in BHS with jehrīyate, (vi)jugupsati, or equivalents. But it is also often used where *shame* cannot be involved. Most likely the MIndic word is a denominative from ārti (for which arti, with semi-MIndic shortening, is recorded even in Skt.). All forms are included here since the word is clearly a unit, but they are also entered under the several headings: (**1**) *is grieved, perturbed, distressed*: Mv i.219.17 = ii.21.19 kecit saṃsārapāśena arttiyante (ii.21.19 saṃsāracāreṇa artīyanti) yathā aham (said by the infant Bodhisattva), *are distressed*; Mv ii.161.7 bodhisattvo jātīye arttīyanto, *being pained by* (or, *on account of*) *birth*, 11–12 . . . maraṇena artt°, 13 śokehi attī°; Mv ii.242.13 arttīyati (Senart em. attī°); Mv i.89.18 (ākīrṇavihāreṇa) nārtīyanti; Mv ii.480.7 śokārtita; LV 174.14 jarārtita; Bbh 166.11 ṛtīyamānaḥ (of a Bodhisattva); Bbh 171.9 ritīyamānaṃ. (**2**) In some transitional cases, leading over to the next group, the additional note of *aversion, revulsion* seems more or less clearly present: Bbh 282.7–8 tena pūrvakeṇādhimokṣeṇāritīyeran (read °ṇārtīyeran; but in same phrase line 23 °mokṣeṇa ritīyante), *they would be annoyed by, sick of, disgusted with their former enthusiasm*; Bbh 168.23 ritīyate; Mvy 1830 nārtīyate (no context); (**3**) like preceding but accompanied by parallel forms of hrī-, jugups-, or the like: SP 108.6 daridracintayārtīyantaṃ jehrīyamāṇaṃ jugupsamānaṃ, *distressed, ashamed, disgusted by the thought of being poor*; Mv i.343.1 (tena adharmeṇa) attīyantā (Senart em. artī°) vijigupsantā or °satā (mss. °satāṃ, evidently pres. pple., Senart em. wrongly °sitā) *distressed and disgusted by this immorality*; Karmav 47.26 āstīryati jihreti vigarhati vijugupsati, *is distressed, ashamed, offended, disgusted* (by acts he has done); 49.2; Divy 39.7 ye 'nena pūtikāyenārdīyamānā jehrīyante vijugupsamānāḥ, *being distressed, are ashamed, disgusted*; (**4**) with abl., *feels aversion* (from): MadhK 297.2, text ārtīyate (ebhyo dharmebhyo), but v.l. attīyate, so prob. read; followed by jehrīyate vitarati vijugupsate; in line 4 below (see note 1) mss. dharmebhyo attīyanā (text artī°) vijugupsanā (nouns).

[**artīyanā**, read **attīyanā**, q.v.]

artha, nt. (as in RV generally; in later Skt. only m.), *aim, goal*, etc.: idam eva cārthaṃ (acc.) SP 97.5 (vs); paramārtham etat (acc.) 8,10 (vss); yad arthaṃ samudāgato tad artham abhisaṃbhāvayitvā Mv i.4.12, formula repeated i.34.1 etc.; in these two occurrences all mss. yad, tad. (As one of the four **pratisaṃvid**, see this.)

arthakriyā, *action for the benefit* (of others), one of the four **saṃgraha-vastu** (q.v.), but only in LV (instead of the usual **arthacaryā**, q.v.): LV 38.17; 160.6; 182.6; 429.13.

artha-cara, adj. (= Pali attha°), *helpful, rendering service*: Jm 2.8. Cf. next.

artha-caryā (= Pali attha-cariyā; cf. prec.), *conduct for the benefit* or *profit* (of, gen. or comp.): devānāṃ (Mv iii.91.1, 3 deva-) manuṣyāṇāṃ (i.231.6 adds ca) °ryāṃ caramāṇo (or caranto) Mv i.231.6–7; iii.91.1, 3; svāmyarth° Jm 85.1; parārth° Jm 95.8, etc.; technically as one of the **saṃgraha-vastu** (q.v.; in LV replaced by **arthakriyā**, q.v.), *conduct for the religious benefit of others*, viz., inspiring them to act for their own religious profit, as explained Bbh 220.25 ff.; in lists of the 4 saṃgra°, Mv i.3.12; ii.395.8; Mvy 927; Dharmas 19.

Arthadarśi(n), (**1**) n. of a former Buddha: Mv iii.236.9; (**2**) n. of another former Buddha, in the same list, iii.240.4 f.; 241.15; 243.10; 244.2; 245.12 f.; 247.8; 248.16.

artha-darśimant (= Pali attha-dassima(nt), cf. **darśimant**), *having insight into meanings*: Mv iii.345.7 tattvārthadarśimāṃ (v.l. sattvā°).

artha-dhāraṇī, see **dhāraṇī.**

arthanatā (= Skt. arthanā, Pali atthanā; § 22.41), *request, prayer*: LV 393.13 (vs).

Arthavacanaśrī, n. of a Buddha: Gv 259.2.

Arthavargīya, nt. pl., n. of certain Buddhist sūtras (= Pali aṭṭhaka-vaggika, or °iya, = Sn sect. 4, see CPD s.v.; acc. to Lévi, JAs. 1915, I, p. 413, the BHS form points to the true interpretation of the Pali), Divy 20.24; 35.1 (in both, mss. °vadgīya); Bbh 48.23 (citing a vs = Sn 897, in the above section).

artha-vaśa, nt. (? = Pali attha-vasa, see CPD, '-vasa . . . little more than a suffix'; called masc. by CPD, but idam, kim, are used with it), *reason, motive, purpose* (virtually = artha): LV 244.8 idam arthavaśam adhikṛtya; Mv iii.48.5 (kati), 10 (dve) arthavaśāṃ, acc. pl.; kimarthavaśaṃ samanupaśyantī MSV ii.84.19; 85.3 etc. (same phrase with kim-artham 84.15; Pali uses kim with atthavasaṃ).

Arthaviniścaya, m., n. of a work: Mvy 1405.

Arthasiddhi, n. of a king, former incarnation of Śākyamuni: RP 24.12.

arthika (Pali atthika; very rare in Skt., see BR 5.1048, and pw s.v.; essentially a Buddhist word; cf. **anarthika**), (**1**) *desirous* (of, instr. or in comp.): with instr., LV 111.13 (kāmaguṇebhir); 242.2 (id.); Mv i.327.2 (tehi bhājanehi); ii.354.2, and 355.1, 3 (buddhajñānena); ii.426.8 (striyāya arthiko, *wanting a woman*); iii.391.14 ahaṃ tvayā arthiko, 15 ahaṃ tvayā arthikā, *I am in love with you, I want you*; Divy 616.8 arthikāsi... Ānandena, *are you in love with Ā.?*; Divy 345.7 (puṇyena); RP 19.7 (buddhajñānena); Śikṣ 38.1 (kaḥ puruṣenārthikaḥ, *who wants a man?*); 342.20; in comp., LV 139.22 (na...) kulārthiko na gotrārthiko, guṇārthika eva; 179.10 dharmārthiko, 431.22 sarvarasārthikebhyaś; Mv ii.121.8 jyotiarthiko jyotigaveṣī; ii.124.1 prahāṇārthikasya (with v.l., see **prahāṇa** 1; Pali padhānatthikassa MN i.167.6); ii.183.5 and 238.16 puṇyārthika; as subst., *petitioner*, RP 17.1; *aiming at* (in comp.), vighātārthika *aiming at prevention* (of evil), Bbh 114.5, 14, etc. (common in Bbh, see Wogihara's Index); (**2**) ep. of a Buddha, or in the first passage of the Bodhisattva at the moment of his attaining Buddhahood; this usage seems unknown in Pali and I have not seen it noted previously; perhaps it means *in possession of, having attained* (his proper, i. e. the supreme religious) *aim*: Mv ii.284.19 (in a long list of epithets of the Enlightened One); Mv iii.63.10 alam arthikasya aprasādena, *away with disbelief in the One* (Buddha) *who has attained the goal!* (see s.v. **aprasāda**; misunderstood by Senart); (**3**) see **pratyarthika.**

ardīyate, pple. °yamāna, see **ar(t)tiyati**: Divy 39.7.

Ardravalika, n. of a nāga king: Māy 246.29.

(**ardha-kāya** [= Skt. id., recorded only from the Yogayātrā 6.7, I.St. 14.327; Pali aḍḍha-kāya, also rare], *half the body; the bust*: Gv 519.15 ff.)

ardhakāyika, adj. (from prec.; cf. Pali aḍḍhakāyika), *with half the body* (visible): LV 124.5 (°kā gaganatalāt... abhipralambayanti); 295.2; 367.9 (all prose).

ardhagallī (cf. **gallī**), some kind of vehicle: Mv ii.434.8 (prose; v.l. agallī).

ardhacandra, m. (? or nt.; in Skt. *half-moon, crescent,* etc.), (**1**) a kind of (presumably crescent-shaped) personal ornament (also °**draka,** q.v.): LV 201.19; Mv ii.317.7 (here hung on the bodhi-tree); (**2**) as in Skt. acc. to Schmidt, Nachtr., s.v., from Haravijaya, *a* (crescent-shaped) *decoration on a building* (Schmidt *Torbogenschmuck*): Gv 167.16 °drā(ḥ), n. pl.; 154.4, 202.23 (all prose).

ardhacandraka (m. or nt.; = °**dra,** 1), a kind of ornament: LV 367.10 °kaiś.

ardha-cola, m. (Skt. Lex. °colaka; otherwise unrecorded), *short jacket*: Mvy 5847.

Ardha-nārāyaṇa (m.), *a 'half-*Nārāyaṇa' (q.v.), whose power is used as a unit of strength: MPS 31.21; LV 229.14, see s.v. **saṃghaṭana.**

ardha-paryaṅka (m.; = Pali aḍḍha-pallaṅka), *half-paryaṅka position* (with only one leg bent under): LV 155.1 (°kaṃ kṛtvā).

ardhaparyaṅkin, adj. (from prec. plus -in; cf. **paryaṅkin**), *sitting in the ardha-paryaṅka position*: °kinaṃ, acc. sg., Sādh 64.14 et alibi.

ardha-rātri (f. or) nt. (= Pali aḍḍha-ratti, f., rarely; usually °ratta, m. = Skt. ardha-rātra; cf. Skt. rātri), *midnight*: LV 210.2 (prose) °triṃ ca samayaṃ saṃprāptaṃ. dṛṣṭvā ca... (best punctuated so with Lefm.), *and the time* (of) *midnight was arrived. And seeing* (all this)... (Foucaux takes °triṃ and samayaṃ as objects of dṛṣṭvā; the two ca's are against it); LV 217.9 (prose) °tri-samayaṃ (acc.).

[**ardhāpayati,** read **vardh°.**]

ardhuṣṭa, see **adhyuṣṭa.**

arpaṇā (cf. also **vyarpaṇā**; prob. = Pali appanā; in Skt. only °ṇa, nt., not in this mg.), *'fixing of thought ... application of mind,* esp. in jhāna = *complete concentration, ecstasy'* (CPD): Mvy 7428; Tib. ḥbul ba, gtod, etymolog. renderings, *giving, delivering.*

Arbuda, m. (nt. in Ud? = Pali Abbuda), n. of a hell, acc. to Mvy and Dharmas a cold one (so in Pali, CPD): Mvy 4929; Dharmas 122; Divy 67.22; 138.7; Av i.4.9 etc.; Ud viii.5 arbudāni, gender app. influenced by sahasrāṇi of prec. line, which as Chakravarti assumes may be understood here, i. e. arbudāni short for °da-sahasrāṇi?

aryaka, m. (= **ayyaka,** q.v.; semi-MIndic for Skt. āryaka), *grandfather*: Mv iii.265.9 (Senart em. āry°).

[**arśāṅgi** (some mss. add kuṣṭam; Mironov arśā), *hemorrhoids*; Mvy 9518. Read arśāṃsi, pl. of Skt. arśas (also arśa); cf. Bhīk 17a.1, in parallel passage, arśānsi.]

arhaṭa-ghaṭī-cakra (Mironov arhad-gh°; cf. Skt. araghaṭṭa, Pali arahattha- (once v.l. °haṭa, see CPD) -ghaṭī-yanta), *Persian* (well-)*wheel*: Mvy 2833.

arhati, *ought*, is normally construed with inf. as in Skt. In Mv ii.491.11–12, by a curious blend construction, it is followed by an opt.: arhasi putrī (mss.) ... bhartāraṃ ... upasthihesi (2 sg. opt. § 29.21), *you, daughter, ought—you should serve your husband,* etc.

arhant, also (MIndic) **arahant,** q.v., the ideal personage in Hīnayāna Buddhism, fourth and last stage in religious development (see **srota-āpanna**), SP 1.6 et passim. In Mvy 1, 5138, etymologically rendered Tib. dgra bcom pa, *having conquered the enemy,* as if ari plus root han! Fem. arhantī Av ii.4.12; Śikṣ 171.16; arhantinī MSV i.22.9 (prose); abstract arhattva, nt., Mvy 5137 etc.

arhavant = **arhant** (§ 22.50; not otherwise recorded; m.c.?): LV 283.7, repeated 19 (vss), bhāvi (read bhāvī m.c.) tvam adyārhavān, *thou shalt become an arhat today* (no v.l.).

? **Alaṃvarṣā,** see **Alambuṣā.**

Alaka, n. of a yakṣa (prob. really a generic name, *an inhabitant of Alakā* or °**kā-pura,** q.v.; pl. so used in Skt.): Māy 103.

Alakaśīrṣa, n. of a nāga king: Māy 246.27.

Alakā-pura (nt.), *the city Alakā,* capital of Kubera and home of the yakṣas (= next, etc.): Māy 103. Lévi p. 115 very strangely calls it a *ville inconnue.*

Alakāvatī, v.l. for **Aṭa°,** q.v.

Alakuṇḍalabhaṭṭiya, n. of a disciple of Buddha: Mv i.75.1.

alakṣaṇa, adj., *without characteristic mark* (so Skt.); ep. of dharma, *undefinable, absolute*: Mvy 353.

alakṣaṇaka, adj., with Buddha, (a Buddha) *without the* (32) *marks* (so Burnouf Intr. 378, note 1), i. e. a substitute for a Buddha, a 'near-Buddha' (not actually a Buddha but a saint living in the absence of a B. and 'Buddha-work', buddha-kārya), said of Upagupta: Divy 348.24; 350.28; 356.20; 357.24; 385.8; MSV i.4.3.

alaṃkaraṇīya, adj., °yena, adv. (corresponds to Pali alaṃkammaṇiya, used in same mg. and context), *in a suitable or convenient situation* (for the undertaking in question; here, as in Pali, specifically for sexual relations): Prāt 488.10 °ṇīyena, adv. (in Pali, Vin. iii.187.19, °ṇiye, adj. with āsane, *the seat* occupied by the accused monk).

Alaṃkārabhūṣita, n. of a gandharva king: Kv 2.20.

Alaṃkāra-śubha (m.), n. of a samādhi: SP 458.3 (one ms. °sūra for °śubha; so Burnouf and Kern Transl.).

-alaṃkārika, adj. ifc. (cf. pw 7.309), in tad-alaṃkārikaṃ (read as cpd.) Divy 247.24, *pertaining to that* (or *those*) *ornament(s).*

Alaṃkṛta, n. of a former Buddha: Mv i.137.2.

alaṃkṛtaka, f. °**ikā,** = Skt. °ta, *adorned,* with endearing diminutive flavor: LV 322.5 (vs) su-laṃkṛtikā (= *sv-alaṃkṛtikāḥ), said by the daughters of Māra of themselves; §§ 4.11; 22.34.

alajjita (nt.), *shamelessness, impudence*: MSV ii.188.4 (see s.v. **vaitarika**).

a-lajjitavya (= Pali °tabba), see **lajjitavya.**

a-lajjin (cf. **lajjin**; = Pali id.), *not ashamed*: Ud xvi.4 °naḥ, n. pl. (? text °na, but oldest ms. alajjitā, for °tāḥ); *shameless*, MSV ii.210.12; °ji-saṃgha MSV iii.116.18, 20.

alam-ārya, adj. (= Pali alam-ariya), *truly noble*: of dharma LV 392.11; jñāna LV 407.21; 409.4; Bhīk 26a.3 (°ya-viśeṣādhigamaṃ jñānam . . .); anta LV 416.17 and Mv iii.331.4 (same passage) nālamāryo.

alambu, or **āl°**, or **alāmbu,** or **āl°** (= Skt. and Pali alābu, Skt. Lex. ālābu), *bottle-gourd*: Mv ii.126.4; 127.8; 128.13; 129.15 (in all these tiktāl°); 232.3; °bu-śreṇi, *row of gourds* (used as a raft), Mv iii.68.6 (°iyaṃ, acc. sg.); 78.3 (°iyo, acc. pl.). Initial ā in one ms. iii.68.6; short a iii.78.3, and Senart with v.l. 68.6 (tiktalāmbu mss. ii.129. 15); otherwise saṃdhi makes quantity undetermined. In second syllable mss. regularly -āmb-; -amb- only ii.232.3; -āb- in one ms. only ii.126.4; iii.68.6; Senart usually prints -āb-.

Alambuṣā, n. of a devakumārikā in the western quarter: Mv iii.308.8 (mss. Alaṃvarṣā, em. Senart) = LV 390.5 (Lefm. with all mss. °śā).

a-layana, adj. (= Pali alena), *without refuge*: Gv 534.16.

a-lavaṇaka, f. **°ikā,** adj. (also aloṇaka, q.v.; = Pali aloṇaka), *unsalted*: f. Divy 87.1, 9; 88.8 ff.; = MSV i.86.12 ff.

alātacakra, nt. (= Skt., pw 7.310, *wheel of fire*, of a firebrand whirled in the air), used as symbol of something transitory and illusory (so Pali °cakka, CPD); Laṅk 9.3 (vs; separate alātacakra = °kraṃ from dhūmo); Mvy 2832; MadhK 173.3; as symbol of restless, unceasing motion, LV 205.13 °kra-samārūḍhasya (lokasya), of persons living in the saṃsāra.

alāmbu, see **alambu.**

alika, (1) adj. (= Pali id., Skt. alīka; see § 3.40), *false*: LV 174.7 (vs); Mv ii.70.2 (prose); 71.2 (vs); **(2)** n. of a nāga king: Mvy 3275; Māy 247.22.

alinda, nt. (= AMg. id., rendered by Hindi kūṃṛā and Eng. *a round tub-like vessel*; cf. also next), a kind of dish (v.l. sometimes aliṇḍa): Mv ii.461.21 mahāntam alindam odanasya (dinnam); similarly 462.3, 12, 13 (in the last two read alindam odanasya instead of Senart's reading). Regularly a receptacle for soft food, esp. odana, *gruel*.

alindā, (1) = prec. (v.l. °ṇḍā): mahatī ca alindā bhaktasya (q.v.) Mv iii.15.9; (odanasya mahatī) alindā ibid. 13; **(2)** n. of a queen, wife of Ikṣvāku and mother of Kuśa (in the Pali version named Sīlavatī): Mv ii.425.2 ff.; iii.2.20 ff.

Alimanmatha, n. of a form of Mañjuśrī: Sādh 146.1 et alibi.

a-līna, adj. (= Pali id.; neg. of **līna,** q.v.), *not dispirited* or *faint-hearted; intrepid*: Mvy 491 = Tib. ma zhum pa; often assoc. with adīna: LV 23.14, 18 (in 18 adīnālīnaṃ); 284.19 alīnā adīnā; 318.12 adīno 'līnaḥ (of the Bodhisattva); 415.6 -vīrya alīnu; Mv ii.354.1 °nakāya-mānasāḥ; alīna-vikrāntaṃ (cognate acc.) vikramanto Mv ii.267.17, or . . . vikrame (aor.) 399.12, *marching (striding) an intrepid march (stride)*, or *he marched* etc.

a-luḍita (= Pali aluḷita; neg. of **luḍita,** q.v.), *not agitated, unperturbed; calm, imperturbable*: LV 318.13 (of the Bodhisattva); 361.16 (of Buddha); °ta-citta LV 181.12; Sukh 59.1; °ta-gati LV 272.12.

a-lūkha, adj. (= Pali id., of the pupil of the eye; neg. of **lūkha,** q.v., and cf. next), *not coarse*, of food, Mv iii.120.22; *not harsh*, i. e. *comfortable*, of the householder's life (**gṛhāvāsa,** q.v.; v.l. gṛha°), Mv iii.50.12.

a-lūha, adj. (= prec.; neg. of **lūha,** q.v.), *not coarse*, of food, Mv ii.65.12, but mss. **(a)rūha,** q.v.; *not harsh, comfortable*, of gṛhavāsa: Mv ii.69.1; 117.19.

alena, see **lena.**

aloka, m., a high number: Mvy 7869 (cited from Gv) = Tib. śugs sbyoṅ, or śugs ḥphyo (the latter also renders **heluga,** q.v.); in Gv 133.13 āloka, m.; but in Gv 106.3 sattva-lokasya, for which certainly read sattvālokasya.

aloṇaka, adj. (= Pali id.; also **alavaṇaka,** q.v.), *unsalted*: Mv iii.120.21 °kaṃ (food).

alohinī (f. to Vedic a-lohita; cf. Pali alohitā, same mg.), (a woman) *who does not menstruate*: Mvy 8929.

alpa-kisareṇa (mss. often ś for s, l for r, n for ṇ; = Pali appa-kasireṇa; Sktized as °kṛcchreṇa, a form not recorded in Skt., Mvy 6370; SP 103.9, and elsewhere, also in Mv, see Senart i note p. 580; no correspondent recorded in Pkt.; the only Pkt. resultant of kṛcchra is kiccha), *with little difficulty*: Mv i.270.8 (here Senart wrongly em. °kisaraṃ); ii.216.6, 9; 227.5; 286.9; 418.3; iii.31.13; 318.6. See **kisara.**

alpa-guṇa, adj. (= Pali appa°), *insignificant*: Mv i.89.18 °ṇa-parituṣṭa, *content with insignificant* (worldly) *things*.

alpa-jñāta, adj. (seems = Pali appaññāta, which acc. to CPD = Skt. aprajñāta), *little known, not celebrated*: MSV ii.124.12; bhikṣur bāḍhaglānaḥ alpajñātaḥ sve mūtrapurīṣe nimagno 128.13; yaḥ parṣadvinirmukto 'lpajñātaś ca 131.13. Is our form hyper-Skt., or the true orig. of the Pali?

alpataraka, adj. comparative (= °tara; nowhere recorded), *less numerous*: AsP 430.8, 9. In 430.2 **bahutaraka,** q.v.; in vicinity alpaka, and alpatama (without ka); the suffix has no special force that I can detect; the whole passage is prose.

alpabhikṣuka, nt. (cf. Pali appabhikkhuka, adj., *having few monks*), *a state of having few monks*: (parāntakeṣu) janapadeṣv °kaṃ, kṛcchreṇa daśavargo gaṇaḥ paripūryate Divy 18.7.

alpamanyate (= Pali appamaññati, pendant to bahu manyate, two words in Skt., may be one in Pali), *thinks little of* (gen.): nālpamanyeta puṇyasya Ud xvii.6.

alparajaska, adj. Bhvr. (= Pali apparajakkha), *of slight passion, free from passion*, in °ka-jātīya (= Pali °jātika), see **-jātīya,** Mv iii.322.16 (prose).

alpātaṅka, adj. (and subst. m.? = Pali appā°, acc. to CPD subst. as well as adj.; see below), (almost) *free from illness*, following **alpābādha,** q.v. for occurrences; in Av i.325.13 text °taṅkaṃ (acc. sg.), after alpābādhatāṃ, seemingly subst., (relative) *freedom from disease*; but in the same cliché ii.90.14; 93.15 °ka-tāṃ is read, matching °bādhatāṃ. See next.

alpātaṅka-tā (= Pali appā°), *state of being* (almost) *free from illness*, abstr. to prec.; usually follows **alpābādhatā,** q.v. for occurrences (as in Pali). But also without that word, Kv 18.8. In Av i.325.13 read prob. °taṅkatāṃ for °taṅkaṃ, see prec.

alpābādha, adj. (= Pali appā°, acc. to CPD noun, = °dha-tā, as well as adj.), (almost) *free from disease*, often followed by **alpātaṅka,** as in Pali by appātaṅka: so Mv i.211.6 = ii.15.5; Av i.168.8; but also without this, Divy 396.5; Suv 182.15; Bbh 20.1. See next.

alpābādha-tā (= Pali appā°), *state of being* (almost) *free from disease*, abstr. to prec.; usually followed (as in Pali) by **alpātaṅkatā**: so Mv i.323.20; Mvy 6284; Divy 156.13; Kv 89.12; Av i.325.13 (see **alpātaṅka**); ii.90.13; 93.15; in Divy 21.4 no alpātaṅkatā occurs but it may have been included in what is understood by the abbreviation yāvat.

alpāyuṣka, adj. (= Pali appāyuka; cf. Skt. alpāyus), *short-lived*: Mv i.199.1 = ii.2.19; i.200.2 = ii.3.18; ii.208.16; Av i.296.4; 316.2 (all prose). Cf. next.

alpāyuṣka-tā, abstr. to prec.: Dbh 26.19 (prose).

alpārtha, adj. (= Pali appaṭṭha), *wanting little, undemanding, modest,* ep. of proper monks: MSV iii.96.14.

alpāsvāda, adj. (subst.? = Pali appassāda), *affording little pleasure,* in Mv i.121.4 perhaps subst., a sort of kenning for kāma (the Pali word is often an epithet of kāma, and sometimes seems to be a substitute for it). The Mv line (vs) is corrupt; perhaps alpāsvāda-nibaddho (or read °dhā?) means kāma-nibaddho; in the second half line surely lokā vartenti dāruṇāḥ is intended, rather than Senart's em.; as adj., e. g. Divy 41.26 (mahāsamudro) 'lpāsvādo bahvādīnavas.

alpeśākhya, adj. (= Pali appesakkha), opp. of the much commoner **maheśākhya** (q.v.), with which it is contrasted Mvy 6412; Karmav 29.26, *insignificant, petty*: of persons Mv i.28.7; Mmk 74.15; of a caitya Divy 243.2, 5.

alpeśākhya-tva, abstract from prec.: Av ii.177.6.

alpotsuka (= Pali appossuka, °kka), *indifferent, unconcerned, undisturbed, unworried*: Mv ii.427.4; Divy 41.23 ff.; LV 396.2 °ka-vihāreṇaiva vihareyam (in contrast with preaching the Law; Buddha speaks); Ud xiv.16 (= Pali appossukko Dhp. 330); Av i.89.1 °kas tvam ... bhava, *don't worry,* and similarly 93.10; 331.10 etc.

alpotsuka-tā (= Pali appossukka-tā), abstr. to prec.: LV 393.21–394.1 alpotsukatāyai bhagavataś cittam abhinatam na dharmadeśanāyām, *the mind of the Lord inclined to being unconcerned* (with the fate of the world), *not to teaching the Law*; similarly 394.5; 396.7; 398.1; *freedom from desires,* Bbh 219.24.

alpotsuka-tva, nt., = prec., Mv i.170.10 (in the sense of LV 393.21 etc.).

allāpayati, allīna, allīpayati, see next.

allīyati (only in Mv; Pali id., in different mg.; AMg. allīai, *resorts to*; to Skt. ālīyate; see §§ 3.4a; 38.66, 67), *comes* (to), *approaches,* with gen., loc., or acc.: °yati (gen.) Mv ii.210.19; 480.8; °yanti Mv ii.252.6 (with form in -ehi, intended as loc.), 10; 253.12 (with loc. in -eṣu); iii.127.8 (gen.); °yatha, 2 pl. impv., Mv iii.24.5 (acc.); allīṣyatha (fut. with mā[atra], *don't go there!*) Mv ii.253.5, 7 (in 7 v.l. allīyiṣyatha); with caus. mg., *bring, put, place,* Mv ii.190.5 ff. allīyanti, five times; iii.127.17 mss. allīyeya (-ḥ, or -n), opt., *should bring* (Senart em. allīpeya); see also Mv iii.144.12 under causative below; ppp. allīna, (a) commonly *went to,* as periphrasis for past tense, with acc., gen., or loc.: Mv ii.32.1; 48.8, 11 ff.; 64.5, 6; 70.4, 9; 107.8; 172.12; 198.1; 200.8; 463.1; 464.1, 19; 470.6; iii.16.1; 69.9; 362.2; 365.23; (b) *attached* (in love) *to* (gen.; Pali id.): kumārasya allīnā (kiṃnarī) Mv ii.100.1; caus. (1) *allāpayati; ppp. allāpita (see § 38.66), *brought, caused to come* (to, gen.) Mv iii.362.3; (2) allīpayati, usually *brings, causes to come,* but occasionally *causes to be brought,* and on the other hand sometimes apparently intrans., *approaches* (these exceptional meanings will be noted; the former may be based on the trans. use of allīyati, *brings*): °payati Mv ii.435.14 *causes to be brought*; (°peti, Senart's em. Mv iii.144.12, mss. °yeti, °yanti, read prob. °yati, as trans., *brings*;) ppp. °pita i.311.2; ii.107.5 (*were caused to be brought*); 471.1; 472.11; iii.24.4; 408.4; 421.8; passive °piyanti iii.68.11; 405.15; °pīyati iii.127.4; gdve. allīpitavyam, intrans. *to be approached,* Mv iii.288.9–10 (or em. to allīyitavyam?).

Alluka, n. of a nāga king: Māy 247.28.

ava, as neg. prefix with nouns (so also in Pali): see **ava-kāma-sevā.**

ava-kaṭṭati (mss.: Senart em. ava-kaḍḍhati), see **o-kaṭṭati.**

avakara, m., prob. read with Index and Mironov **avakāra,** rendered by Tib. ḥgod pa, perhaps *arrangement, placement, ordering,* or the like: Mvy 571 samākṣarāvakaro (°kāro) nāma samādhiḥ. No v.l. in either ed. But ŚsP 1421.3 (from which, or an allied text, Mvy cites) reads samākṣarākāro, explaining: sarvasamādhīnāṃ samākṣaratāṃ pratilabhate. This seems to fit the reading °kṣarākāra, and definitely does not fit the apparent meaning of **avakāra,** q.v. Yet in another list ŚsP 1413.15 reads °kṣarāvakāra.

avakarṣati (corresponds to Pali apakassati, used in same passage SN ii.198.1–5, see CPD s.v.), *holds back, keeps under control*: ger. avakṛṣya (kāyam, cittam), Candropama Sūtra, Hoernle, MR 42.11 (43.5, 9); see s.v. **jarodapāna.**

avakalpanatā = next, *the putting faith or confidence in*: abhiśraddadhānatāvakalp° ŚsP 615.10.

avakalpanā = prec. (= Pali okappanā; to next): Dbh 13.17 (substantially = śraddhā, adhimukti, in prec. line); Mvy 7289 = Tib. ṅes par (also legs par) rtog pa, the former of which is rendered avakalpanā in Das, whose English rendering is not quite in accord with BHS usage; the Tib. could, it seems, mean *considering certain.*

avakalpayati, °te (= Pali okappati, °peti), *has confidence in, puts faith in,* synonym of śrad-dhā, as also in Pali, with gen. of person, acc. of thing: SP 44.3 śraddadhādhvaṃ me ... pattīyatāvakalpayata; 315.1 avakalpayadhvaṃ me ... abhiśraddadhadhvaṃ tathāgatasya; LV 88.8 (ṛddhiprātihāryam api ...) nāvakalpayiṣyanti; Gv 171.2 °yantaṃ, pres. pple., perhaps *putting trust in, relying on,* object bodhisattvaparivārasaṃpatpariśuddhim.

***ava-kas-?** see **okasta.**

ava-kāma-sevā (see **ava**), *no practice of love*: LV 28.22 (vs; wrongly divided in ed.) dvātriṃśa māsām (= māsān, acc. pl.) avakāmaseva (= °vā, n. sg.) hi, *for she abstained from love-making for 32 months*; so Tib. renders. There is a v.l. akāma for avakāma but it is metrically impossible.

avakāra, m. (1) see **avakara**; (2) okāraṃ acc. sg. (= Pali okāra, in phrase kāmānaṃ ādīnavo okāro saṃkileso; cf. Pali anavakāra), perhaps *elimination, getting rid* (sc. of desires): Mv iii.357.13 kāmeṣu bhayaṃ okāraṃ (mss. okara-) saṃkileśaṃ, *in regard to desires* (he preached) *the danger of them, the elimination of them, their impurity.* Senart's em. seems confirmed by the Pali.

avakāśa, (1) in Skt. mg., *room, space,* but nt. instead of m., LV 367.20 (vs) nābhūd °śam asmin; RP 31.4 teṣv °śam asti (or assume m as 'Hiatus-bridger'?); see also **an-avakāśa**; (2) *appearance,* in **akṣudrāvakāśa,** q.v.; (3) see **an-avakāśa, an-okāśa.**

avakāśati (ms. °sati; denom. to avakāśa), *gets a chance at, works upon,* with loc.: Av ii.183.13 nāgniḥ kāye 'vakāśati; caus. °śayati, gdve. °śayitavyaḥ, *to be given a chance to work* (in a certain function), MSV ii.154.12, where prob. read a negative before it; this is read by em. in text in line 18, where, it seems to me, the neg. is *not* wanted.

avakāsayati (caus. to Pali avakassati, apak°, apakāsati; cf. Skt. kas-), *removes, dismisses*: °yitavyaḥ MSV iv.77.13 ff.

avakīrṇa, *confused, mixed up* (of speech): LV 158.16 sadānavakīrṇavācaḥ, *always of unconfused speech*; so Tib., tshig ḥchal med gyur la.

avakīrṇakusuma, n. of a group of (predicted) future Buddhas: AsP 458.9.

avakuṇṭhita, adj. (ppp.; cited in MW as Skt. Lex., but not in BR or pw; cf. Skt. avakuṇṭhana), *covered, clothed*: Mmk 290.10 śuklavastrāvak°.

avakubja and **°jaka,** adj. (= Pali avakujja, cf. AMg. avaujjiya, denom. ppp.; from ava and kubja), *prone, flat on the face on the ground*: in Mv i.213.7 = ii.16.11 na ca avakubjako (ii.16.11 mss. avakubjaṃ, may be kept as adv.; sc. tiṣṭhati; said of the Bodhisattva in his mother's womb); otherwise only with a form of prapatati, *falls,* and only as adj.: °ja LV 254.21; 256.3; Mv i.28.13; °jaka

Mv ii.126.6; 127.11; 128.15; 130.1; 283.1; 412.16. In two of these Senart erroneously apa° with one of his two mss.; read ava° with the other.

? **avakoṭa**, see **antakoṭa.**

avakoṭimaka, adj. (= Pali okoṭ°), *deformed, misshapen*; so Tib. acc. to Speyer, byad (on i.280.3 byed) ṅan po; the precise mg. in Pali is disputed; Av i.280.3 and ii.152.10, in phrase durvarṇo durdarśano ava°; in Pali only in corresp. phrase dubbaṇṇa duddas(s)ika oko°. But mss. of Av avahoṭimako or °ḍimako, and in ii.152.10 Speyer adopts the latter, stating that it is also written so in the Ratnāvadānamālā version of the same story. It seems that it should be the same as the Pali word, which is well attested. Yet I think the form with h is supported by Laṅk 27.4, mss. uhātrimā, ed. em. uhoḍimā, and 33.15, text ahoḍimā, most mss. uho°; both initially in anuṣṭubh lines, where avaho° could be read as a standard hypermetric type, or u- could stand for ava- (cf. § 3.55, **ukirati**); Tib. cited as ṅan paḥi mi, *miserable man*, in Suzuki, Index, which attributes to Wogihara the interpretation ūnendriya (fitting our word).

avakramaṇa, okramaṇa, nt. (= Pali avakkamana, okka°), *entrance* (into the womb): ava° LV 36.2 = garbhāvakrānti; garbhokramaṇaṃ, Mv ii.18.1 (vs, = i.215.4 where read so; mss. corrupt, Senart garbhāvakramaṇaṃ).

avakramati, see **°krāmati.**

-avakrāntaka, also **°ika**, f. °ikā, only in tīrthikāv°, *one who has gone over to heretics, a renegade Buddhist*: Mvy 8759 °takaḥ; Bhīk 16b.2 °tikā. The corresp. Pali, Vin. i.89.35, has titthiya-pakkantaka, apparently = prakrānta(ka); but I suspect that the true original of both this and avakr° was *apakrāntaka; Pali apakkamati and apakkanta are used in mgs. very close to this, and neither ava- nor pra-kram- seems so appropriate.

avakrānti, f. (= Skt. id., in garbhāva°, Caraka, pw 2.159; Pali avakkanti, okk°), *entrance*; common in garbhāva° *entrance into the womb* (as in Skt.), LV 87.15, 21 etc.; tathāgatadivasāvakrānti-vijñapti-vyūhānāṃ (bodhisattvānāṃ) Gv 114.18, *having supernal manifestations* (or, *a mass*?) *of knowledge of the coming in* (? *occurrence*) *of the day of the T.* (or, *the T.'s entrance into the light of day*?).

-avakrāntika = **°taka**: tīrthikāv° MSV ii.204.10.

-avakrāma (to avakrāmati), *entrance* (into a way or course; so Pali avakkanti, with niyāma): Gv 460.3 dur-avakrāmo bodhisattvaniyāmo 'vakramitavyaḥ.

avakrāmati, °kramati, °krāmayati, o-kr°, ukr°, § 3.54 (Pali avakkamati, okk°; in Skt. in this sense only of *entering* the womb, conception; so Caraka, pw 2.111; so LV 39.8 kukṣāv avakrāmeyaṃ; Mv i.205.5 etc.), *enters* (a condition or state): Gv 460.3 (see s.v. **-avakrāma**) gdve. avakramitavyaḥ; LV 180.6 sattveṣu ca mahākaruṇām avakrāmati sma; in Mv i.51.3 (prose) okrami (aor.) has as its subject, not goal, mahākāruṇaṃ (sattveṣu), *great compassion entered into him* (gen.); yakṣagraho ukrami (§ 3.54) teṣa kāye SP 95.8 (vs); *enters into, realizes* (dharma, true religion; cf. Pali dhammassa avakkanti, see CPD), dharmam avakrāntaḥ MSV iii.62.11; middham (*sleep*) avakrānto Divy 579.20; avakrāmayati, formally caus., could by a forced interpretation be taken to mean *allows* (e. g. compassion, or sluggishness) *to enter* (into himself), but prob. more realistically to be taken as meaning the same as the simplex, *enters into* (a state): LV 400.14 (prose) mahākaruṇām avakrāmayati, and in same context Mv iii.318.15 °ṇāṃ okrāmetvā; RP 56.17 styānamiddhaṃ nāvakrāmitavān, and similarly 57.11; note close resemblance to passages using the simplex, above.

ava-kṣapayati, see **o-kṣap°.**

avakṣipta, ppp. (Skt.), (**1**) °ta-cakṣuṣ(a) = Pali avakkhittacakkhu (or okkhi°), *with downcast eyes*, of a monk: LV 191.15, read avakṣipta-cakṣuṣaṃ (acc. sg.), for text avi° (confirmed by Tib. phab ba); (**2**) svedamalāvakṣiptaḥ (sc. bhogaḥ?) Mvy 7055, *acquired* (Tib. bsgrubs pa) *by sweat-stain*, i. e. *by the sweat of one's brow*, cf. Pali AN ii.67.27 (bhogehi bāhābalaparicitehi) sedāvakkhittehi; comm. iii.99.4 = avakkhittasedehi, sedaṃ muñcitvā vāyāmena payogena saṃhatehi ti attho.

avaga, nt., a high number, Mvy 7713 = Tib. rig(s) sdom; see s.v. ārāva, for which prob. read this; in Mvy 7839 ārāva (Tib. id.) is cited from Gv, but Gv 133.3 reads avagaṃ; avaga should also be read for **vaga**, q.v., in Gv 105.22.

avagīta, ppp. (lit. *sung down*), *reduced, diminished*: °ta-pratanūbhūtāntaḥpura-. . . śokasya (Bhvr.) Jm 11.21.

? **avaguṇṭhikā** (Skt. Lex.), *veil*: LV 321.5 (prose) kāścid (daughters of Māra) avaguṇṭhikayā vadanāni chādayanti sma. But the mss. are said to read avaguṇṭitakāyā (ṭ for ṭh), or °ta-kayā (°ta-yā? not clear).

avagūhayati (cf. **gūhati, gūhayati**; perhaps related to Pali ogumpheti; -umph- yielding -ūph-, then -ūh-?), *winds* (garlands): Mv i.304.15 dīrghamālāṃ (but v.l. °mālā) vagūhayet (aor.); see § 4.7.

avagrahaṇa (nt.; Skt. only Lex. in different mgs.; not in Pali; seems = AMg. uggahaṇa, equated with avagrahaṇa by Ratnach. and defined *general perception, perception of broad outlines*), *perception*, (sensual or mental) *grasping*: Dbh 75.19 traidhātukāvagrahaṇa-saṃjñāniṣkarṣaṇa-tāṃ, *state of getting rid of notions based on perception of the triple universe.*

avaghoṣaṇa, nt., and **°ṇā**, f., *proclamation, public announcement*: udghoṣaṇāvaghoṣaṇaṃ kṛtvā Divy 502.27 (dvandva? or *public proclamation of an announcement*?); āhvānāvaghoṣaṇāyāṃ, loc. sg., Jm 8.9; very commonly ghaṇṭāvaghoṣaṇa or °ṇā, *proclamation by bell-ringing*: °ṇam, n. sg., Mvy 9263; Divy (usually with kṛtam or kāritam) 4.11; 34.10; 118.28; 274.22; 285.22; 317.19; 320.2; 501.22; 524.7; 540.4; 556.16; Av i.48.2; 58.4 etc.; °ṇaṃ acc. sg., Divy 242.13; Av i.18.11; ii.2.11, etc.; Gv 327.23; °ṇena, instr. sg. Av i.366.2; °ṇāṃ, acc. sg. LV 187.8; Divy 122.6; 317.21 (śrutvā; two lines after °ṇam, n. sg.); in Divy 134.28 mss. °ṇāṃ kāritaṃ, rightly em. in ed. to °ṇaṃ.

a-vaṅka, adj. (= Pali id.; see **vaṅka**), *not crooked* (fig.), *not dishonest*: LV 8.8.

a-vaṅka-tā, subst. from prec., *non-dishonesty*: AsP 327.6 cittāvaṅkatāṃ.

avacanīkaroti (cf. Skt. and Pali avacana-kara), *disobeys, does not agree to* (words): tasya vacanam °kṛtya MSV iii.24.1.

-avacara (= Pali id.; orig. noun, cf. Senart Mv i.397, but only used at end of Bhvr. cpds., *having* . . *as scope*; f. **°rī**; called 'ts.' by CPD, but clearly a Buddhist word, as stated in pw s.v.; found virtually only in Bu. works and Lexx. in Skt.; otherwise occurs once in Rājat.(?), and, to be sure, yajñāvacará in MS., see pw s.v.; despite these rare Skt. occurrences belongs fundamentally to Pali and BHS, where it is very common); *scope, sphere, range of activity or existence*: antarīkṣāv° *who live in the atmosphere* SP 288.10 (devatāḥ); Mv i.33.5 (śuddhāvāsakāyika deva); dakṣiṇāvacara, vāmāv°, *having the right* (*left*; viz. part of the womb) *as his abiding-place* LV 55.5, 6; buddhaśāsanāv° Śikṣ 214.10 *within the scope of the Buddha's commands* (wrongly Bendall); saṃsārāvacarīṃ . . . samyagdṛṣṭim Śikṣ 316.16, *true views regarding the saṃsāra*; saṃskṛtāv° Gv 496.6, *things in the realm of the conditioned*; traidhātukāv° Bbh 246.25, *belonging to the sphere of the trai°*; caturbhir mārāv° Dbh 54.17, with Rahder, citing a Jap. source, *things belonging to the four Māra-domains*, i. e. *the domains* of the four **Māra**, q.v.; atarkāv° Mv iii.314.2, *not within the scope of reasoning* (of dharma; so Pali atakkāv°, of dhamma); akṣudrāv° Mv ii.9.1 (of the Bodhisattva's mother); ii.1.7 (of the family where the

Bodhisattva is born); antaḥpurāv° Jm 185.24, *whose business was the harem*: turagāv° Buddhac. v. 68, *groom*; esp. in **kāmāv°, rūpāv°, arūpāv°** (or **ārūpyāv°**), of classes of gods, see under these entries. See also **tāḍāvacara.**

avacaraka (1) m. (= Pali id.), *messenger*, (secret) *agent*: Mvy 3807 = Tib. bya ma rta, *courier* (v.l. apa°, but Mironov ava° without v.l.); Divy 32.25; 127.26; 287.3; **(2)** (m.?) in Gv 522.1 tac ca gṛhaṃ vā avacarakaṃ vā vipulaṃ paśyet, *and he would see* (in his dream) *that house or locality* (? the preceding sentence is our only clue to the mg. and it is so general that it gives little help) *as vast*. Is it a ka-derivative of avacara (physical) *domain*? Or an otherwise unrecorded word for some kind of building? Ratnach. records AMg.ocāra (=avacāra), *a granary or store-house of grain*, which does not fit our context.

avacarati (cf. Pali id. or ocarati, similarly used), *busies* or *occupies oneself with* (intellectually): °ti Gv 252.20, may perhaps be rendered *investigates*, see s.v. **vyavacārayati**; ppp. °rita, *frequented* (physically), *occupied, besetzt*: Divy 102.11 mahāpattano 'manuṣyāvacarito, and similarly 103.13; 110.8; 119.22 etc.; neg. an-avacarita, Divy 103.4 mahāsamudre manuṣyānavacarite.

avacāraka, adj. or subst m., perhaps *slinking off*: muktahastāvacārakaḥ Divy 165.19. See also **ekāvacāraka.**

avacīra-vicīraka, adj., in Divy 83.21 epithet of a (dilapidated) house, acc. to Index, *tumbledown*; perh. cf. Pali ocīraka, said of a tree, *stripped of its bark*, to be read with PTSD for odīraka in SN iv.193.30; same passage MSV i.82.11 **cīra-cīra-cīvaraka.**

avacodayati, ppp. dita, *instructed* (religiously): MSV i.266.7, 13, 17; 267.10–12, 18, 20. One is tempted to emend to avavādita, which fits, at any rate.

avajāta, adj. (= Pali id., cf. Skt. apajāta), *misbegotten, unworthy* (offspring), only in phrase jāto me syān nāvajātaḥ (sc. putraḥ) Divy 2.13; 440.27; Av i.14.14 etc.

avajīryati, *wastes away*: °yatu, impv., Mv ii.239.4 mānsāni lohitaṃ caiva ava°.

[**ava-ḍīyati**, see **ava-lī°**.]

avataṃsaka, m. or nt., fig. *a large number, collection*: buddhāva° Divy 162.26; 401.14; Av i.87.9.

avataraṇa, n. act., **(1)** *overpowering, subduing*, in dur-avataraṇa-, *hard to overcome*: Gv 242.6 -vīrya-karma-; **(2)** *taking off, clipping* (of hair), in keśāvataraṇaṃ (of a prospective monk) kṛtvā MSV ii.140.2.

avatarati, otarati (see also **avatīrṇa, avatārayati**), *penetrates* (intellectually), *comprehends*: SP 125.2 (saṃdhābhāṣitaṃ tathāgatasya) avataritum; 232.9 (dharmaparyāyaṃ . . .) avataranti vijānanti; Gv 253.18 (vs) buddha-bala-naya-praveśān otarasi; RP 4.16 avataramāṇāḥ, and 17 avataran, both *penetrating, comprehending*; Dbh 56.2 ff.; buddha-sarasvatim otari (opt.) Bhad 30. See also **uttarati.**

avatāra, m. (= Pali otāra, esp. in mg. 4) [**(1)** as in Skt., *descent, appearance* (on earth), e. g. Mv ii.263.6 °raṃ gacchati, *appears, is born*;] **(2)** *entrance into, attainment of* (a moral state), LV 182.10 -mahākaruṇāvatāra-tāṃ, *state of attainment of great compassion*; so, perhaps (or to 3), pratisaṃvid-avatāro and pratiśaraṇāvatāro, LV 35.16 and 17; Samādh 19.6 mahākaruṇāvatārābhimukhāni cittāni, *thoughts tending to attainment of great compassion*; **(3)** *intellectual penetration, comprehension* (cf. **avatarati**): LV 423.2 and 11 and Gv 469.9 pratītyāvatāra-, *penetration, comprehension of* (origination by) *dependence*, see **pratītya**; LV 423.5 ekaviṣaya-sarvadharma-samatāvatāra-cakraṃ *wheel of the comprehension of the equality of all substantial states as belonging to one sphere*; followed in cpd. by (-jñāna)-kuśala or -kauśalya, *clever(-ness) in* (the knowledge of) *the penetration of* . . . (Tib. ḥjug pa, *entrance*), -avatāra-kuśala Mvy 856, 858; -kauśalya RP 8.10; -avatāra-jñāna-kuśala LV 8.13; Mvy 835; -svabhāvāvatāra(-tā) RP 4.13, 15; in Mv i.47.6 = 81.15 meter (supported by some readings of mss.) indicates reading jñānasāgar'avatāra nāyakā(ḥ), the cpd. agreeing with preceding mānasaṃ, (a mind) *that penetrates into the ocean of knowledge*; avatāreṇa, *by penetration*, Gv 40.2; yathāsvaṃ avatāraiḥ (so read) Gv 253.19; avatārataḥ Bbh 80.4; avatāraḥ Bbh 80.22; 81.6; -sukhopāyāvatāra-dharmadeśanatā Bbh 82.18, *preaching doctrines that are capable of comprehension by easy means*; mahāyāna-samudayāvatāra-nirdeśanāṃ avatarati Dbh 56.14–15; **(4)** (way of) *entrance, ingress* in the sense of *opportunity for hostile approach*; *weak spot*, often as object of a form of labh or adhi-gam, *find, obtain*, the subject often being Māra the Evil One, so SP 145.3 (na ca tatra māraḥ pāpīyān) avatāraṃ lapsyate (om. WT with v.l.); esp. often in cpds. avatāra-prekṣin (cf. Pali otārāpekkha), avatāra- (or raṃ)-gaveṣin, *looking for, seeking a point of attack*, these two often together and esp. with Māra as subject; SP 474.6 and 7 na . . . avatāraprekṣy avatāragaveṣy avatāraṃ lapsyate; SP 398.1 na . . . °raprekṣy . . . avatāraṃ lapsyate; LV 47.10 (vs) yasyāvatāra (acc. sg.; so divide) labhate na manaḥ praduṣṭam; LV 260.18 avatāraprekṣī avatāragaveṣī (māraḥ, bodhisattvasya) . . . (19) na . . . avatāram adhyagacchat; Mv iii.298.16 °ram adhigantum; avatārārthī (= °ra-prekṣī) avatāraṃgaveṣī, of Māra, with reference to the Bodhisattva, Mv ii.241.5; of the daughters of Māra Mv iii.286.10; 299.4; avatāraprekṣī skhalitāṃ gaveṣī RP 18.10; avatāraprekṣin also Mvy 5357; Divy 322.7; Śikṣ 152.9; śatruvad avatāraprekṣī 230.14; avatāragaveṣin Divy 322.7; (Māraḥ . . .) avatāraṃ labhiṣyati Samādh 22.35.

avatāraka, adj. **(1)** *one who causes to penetrate* (intellectually) or *comprehend* (cf. **avatāra** 3): SP 40.12 tathāgatajñāna-darśanāvatāraka evāhaṃ; 121.9 sarvajñajñānāvatārakaḥ (of Buddha); 183.6 buddhajñānāvat°; **(2)** f. °ikā, *one who cuts off* (hair; cf. **avatārayati** 2): Bhīk 10b.5 keśāvatārikā bhikṣuṇī.

avatāraṇa, nt. (to avatārayati, mg. 1), *the causing to penetrate* (intellectually), *bringing to comprehension*, usually in comp., preceded by the thing taught (or with loc.): tathāgatajñānāvatāraṇa- SP 3.2 (-kuśalair); 40.5 (-hetunimittaṃ); avatāraṇārthaṃ (sattvānāṃ; sc. regarding enlightenment) 318.4; karmakriyāvatāraṇārthaṃ LV 251. 1–2; with loc., avatāraṇaṃ buddhaviṣaye LV 423.13; avatāraṇāya *to make them penetrate* (religious knowledge) Bbh 308.11.

Avatāraprekṣin (see s.v. **avatāra** 4), n. of a son of Māra (ill-disposed to the Bodhisattva): LV 311.16.

avatārayati, otāreti (caus. to **avatarati**; in mg. 1, associated with **avatāra** 3), **(1)** *causes to penetrate intellectually, to comprehend*; *initiates into, introduces to*, with acc. or (oftener) loc. of what is taught or explained: SP 49.7 (vs) sarve ca te darśayi ekayānam ekaṃ ca yānaṃ avatārayanti; 182.11 (anuttarāyāṃ samyaksaṃbodhau . . .) avatāritavān; 347.8 (dharmavinaye) 'vatārayeyam; with (buddha-)śāsane, Bbh 222.26; 261.26 (here buddhaśāsane or °nam implied from prec.); Av i.112.8; with tasyāṃ (pratipadi) Bbh 262.17; **(2)** *removes* (hair, keśa, or also beard), of a barber's activity, esp. with reference to monks and nuns, cf. **avatāraka** (2): keśāni otāreti Mv iii.179.10, 11, 12 (in 9 °reṣyati by em.); keśāny otāretvā (mss. otāritā, avat°) iii.268.18; keśān avatārya Bhīk 10b.1; Jm 122.11; keśaśmaśrūṇy avatārya Divy 35.8; 37.11; 556.6; Samādh 8.15; keśaśmaśru avatārya Av i.136.6; 234.1; an-avatāritakeśā, *with hair unshorn* Bhīk 10a.5; with causative mg., keśaśmaśrūṇy avatārayitvā, *having had the hair and beard cut, caused it to be cut* Mv iii.222.17 (in the same passage in Pali, DN ii.249.20, the form used is ohāretvā); object unexpressed, avatāraya MSV i.280.18; °rayitum id.; °rita, ppp., 281.1, 2.

avatīrṇa, ppp. of **avatarati,** q.v., *that has penetrated* (intellectually), *comprehended*: avatīrṇasya pudgalasya Bbh 81.8 (cf. avatāra 3, q.v., 81.6); avatīrṇānāṃ paripācanāya

Bbh 308.12 (follows madhyasthānām avatāraṇāya, see **avatāraṇa**); -dharmanayāvatīrṇaḥ LV 181.21.

avatrāpin, adj. (= Pali ottāpin; cf. Aśokan avatrapeyu, Skt. apa-trap-), *modest*: (with hrīmant) MPS 1.21.

avada, nt., a high number: Mvy 7925 (cited from Gv) = Tib. gsal yas, or bsal yas (cf. **avānta**); Gv 106.19, read sattvāvadasyā°; 134.3 avadam (avadānām), n. sg.

avadadhati, odhāya (ger.), **avahita** (ppp.), cf. also under **odahana** (= Pali avadahati, with sotaṃ, *give ear attentively*; cf. Skt. avadhīyate *attention is paid*, avahita *attentive*), with **śrota** (q.v.), *gives ear attentively*: śrotam avadadhata LV 409.10, *pay heed closely!*; avahita-śrotaḥ LV 442.1–2 (so read with Weller 39; Pali ohita-sota); °śrotā, n. sg. f., Mv i.158.3; in Mv i.10.8 for śrotum ādāya read śrotam odhāya (satkṛtya śṛṇotha mama bhāṣataḥ).

? **avadarpita**, in LV 275.8 sv-avadarpita-vimala-buddhir; textually uncertain; mss. vary greatly on ava°; many omit vimala; Tib. śin tu (= su) dkar baḥi (*white*, often = avadāta) blo (= buddhi) daṅ ldan pa (*having*), apparently omitting vimala, and suggesting that it is based on avadāta, *white*, i. e., *bright*, instead of avadarpita, which is nowhere recorded and seems senseless, as do the alternative readings of the other BHS mss.

Avadātakeśā, n. of a goddess: Mahāsamāj. Waldschmidt Kl. Skt. Texte 4.187.3; confirmed by Tib. ibid. 204.20. In the Pali correspondent DN ii.260.23 the name Odātagayhā, v.l. Odātavhayā, is taken as n. pl. masc. by DPPN.

avadāna, nt. (= Pali apadāna), n. of a part, or parts, of the Buddhist canon (and of other Buddhist works): Mvy 1273; colophons of Divy, Av, etc. See also **sāvadānam**. The word avadāna occurs in Skt.; its exact mg. is much disputed; see e. g. Speyer, Av Preface p. I ff.

avadya-bhīru, *dreading* (and shunning) *reproach* (blame, evil, sin), ep. of the family into which a Bodhisattva is born in his last existence: Mv i.198.1; ii.1.11; LV 24.4. All these are forms of the same passage; in LV text anavadya-, with v.l. avadya-; in Mv ii.1.11 Senart reads anavadya, tho he recognizes at i p. 532 that the corrupt mss. point rather to avadya-, which he reads with mss. at i.198.1. The reading avadya- is confirmed by Tib. on LV kha na ma tho bas (= avadya, see Das s.v.) ḥjigs pa (= bhīru). Note the noun avadya-bhī RV 10.107.3 (isolated).

? **avadraga**, m., acc. to N. Dutt's interpretation of Tib., *dinner*: °go nāsti; tayā vṛṣo darśitaḥ, etaṃ praghātayata MSV ii.79.7. Tib. sa (*ground*, etc.) ḥdzar ba (for which Das gives a mg. *taking dinner at midday*). Acc. to Skt. Lex. avadraṅga (cf. next) or v.l. avaḍaṅga = *market* (BR 1.473); avadraga could be an error for avadraṃga, and *there was no market* (where meat could be bought) would be a possible mg.; I do not understand Tib.

avadraṅga, m. or nt., *deposit* (on a business transaction); *earnest*: Divy 32.22 tisro lakṣā avadraṅgaṃ (so one ms.; v.l. draṅgaṃ) gṛhṇīta; 33.1, 2, 6 (no v.l.) avadraṅge dattaṃ, *given in* (by way of) *deposit*. Can this be somehow related to Niya Pkt. draṅga, *'taxation depot or office in general'*, said to be an Iranian loanword (Burrow, BSOS 7.509 f.)?

avadvārāpayati (ava plus caus. to denom. from dvāra), *shuts off* (a gate): Mv ii.490.1 nagaradvāram avadvārāpayitvā (v.l. avaddhār°), *having had the city gate closed*.

[**avadhārin**? in MSV i.63.20 vraṇapūyotkīrṇair aṅgapratyaṅgāvadhāribhiḥ paṭṭakopanibaddhaiḥ, of a sick man; -avadhāribhiḥ seems to conceal a substantive, perhaps a cpd. of avayava, *member* of the body; parallels accessible to me have failed to clear up the apparent corruption.]

? **avadhika**, adv. °kam (cf. Pali -odhika, in yathodh°; from Skt. avadhi, *limit*), *to the limit*; *in an extreme degree*: LV 29.8 paśyeta evāvadhikaṃ guṇānvitā, dayāsutā sā janani ca māyā. So Lefm.; but the text is uncertain at more than one place; Tib. also apparently confused; Foucaux's text (see his transl. 35 n. 3) reads mchog, *superior*, modifying yon tan = guṇa. I suspect that originally the text had adhikam, *exceedingly*.

avadhūta (cf. BR 5.1527, dhū with ava, ppp., glossed malina), in a list of evil (magic) powers and influences: Māy 220.19; 245.19; 259.13. Not in the similar list Mvy 4372–87.

avadhūtī, f., n. of an artery, vein, or canal (nāḍī) in the body: Sādh 366.15 °tī-randhreṇa; 383.13 °tī-mārgeṇa; 448.11 nāḍyo lalanārasanāvadhūtayaḥ; 14 avadhūtī madhyadeśe tu mahāsukhādhārarūpiṇī; 16 avadhūty amitanāthasya ādhārabhāvinī sadā. Cf. **rasanā, lalanā.**

-avadhūnakam, adv., *accompanied by shaking*: Prāt 534.3 na hastāvadhūnakaṃ (piṇḍapātaṃ paribhokṣyāmaḥ), *not with waving of the hands*. Corresponds to **-saṃdhunakam**, q.v.

? **avadhya**, adj., ep. of śilpa, *art*, in LV 23.21 avadhya-śilpa-niveśanaṃ (kulam, in which the Bodhisattva is reborn for the last time); so all Lefm.'s mss., but he translates *nützlichen (freien) Künsten zugetan*, prob. following Tib. don yod pa (which once renders amogha, *unfailing*, see Das), *useful, successful*. Calc. reads abandhya (i. e. avandhya, *not barren*); I suspect that this should be adopted. But cf. next but one.

ava-dhyati or °**dhyāti** (cf. Pali avajjhāyati, apa°; to Skt. dhyāti with ava, in Skt. with different mg.), *ponders, meditates on*: Mv i.9.4 (vs), read with mss. avadhyanto saphalatāṃ karmaṇāṃ (n. sg. m. pres. pple.; v.l. °ntā; Senart wrongly em. āvajjanto). Skt. pres. dhyāti = dhyāyati; in ava-dhyanto the short a of the penult may be MIndic, before a consonant cluster, cf. § 3.34.

Avadhyaparamabuddhi, n. of a former Buddha: Mv i.137.13 (or should Avadhya(ḥ) be taken as a separate name? there is no v.l.; see s.v. **avadhya**).

avadhyāna, nt. (to Skt. ava-dhyā-; cited once from Bhāg.P. as mg. *Geringachtung*, BR 5.1059; cf. AMg. avajjhāṇa, *painful and revengeful meditation*, Ratnach.), *ill-feeling, censoriousness, abusiveness*: Mvy 8432, 8594 = ḥphya ba, ḥphyas (by Das rendered avadhyāyana; *blame, censure; abuse, deride*); Prāt 504.12 avadhyānakṣepaṇāt (Chin. si un bhikṣu blâme irrespectueusement).

avana, nt., a high number: Mvy 7854 (cited from Gv); Gv 105.25 (read sattvāvanasya for text sattvavanasya); 133.8 avanam.

avanatā (cf. Pali avana, *free from lust*, CPD, and see **vanatā**), *freedom from desire*: ŚsP 633.18 °tām upādāya.

avanamana (nt.) and **onamanā**, f. (= Pali onamana), *bending*: Gv 400.22 an-avanamanena ... pāṇibhyāṃ jānumaṇḍale parimārjati, *he touches his knees with his hands without bending* (because his arms are so long); usually of *bowing, bending* in humility, a sign of absence of pride: Śikṣ 153.18 (here text by error avanama) and 19 avanamana-praṇamanatāyām (sarvasattveṣu, in 19 defines nirmānatā, *freedom from pride*); LV 182.20 (vs) nirmāṇatā onamanā gurūṇāṃ; LV 430.22 (prose) -avanamana-praṇamana- (in a long cpd.), *bowing and bending* (in humility before persons worthy of deference).

avanādayati, onādeti, *makes resound*: Mv i.237.4 (vs) onādenti (v.l. onādyanti) puravaraṃ (mss. puna, or punaḥ, varaṃ). No ava-nad- recorded. Read unnād°?

avanāma (not in Pali or Pkt.; in Skt. only of (reverential) *bowing*), *depression* (of spirits), opposite of **unnāma**, and only in comp. with that word, q.v. for citations.

avanāmana = prec., LV 33.7; see s.v. **unnāma.**

avanāha, m. (Pali onāha; cf. Pali Vin. iv.169.28 pīṭhaṃ vā tūlonaddhaṃ kārāpeyya), *covering, upholstering* (of a seat; a sin for a monk): Mvy 8513.

Avantaka, m. pl., n. of a school: Mvy 9087 (v.l. Āv°; so Mironov).

avapāṭana (nt., = AMg. ovāḍaṇa, Sheth; to Skt. ava-pāṭ- plus -ana), *rending, tearing*: aṅgāvapāṭana-samarjana- (q.v.) Kalpanā-maṇḍitikā (Lüders, Kl. Skt. Texte 2) 44 V 1 (p. 143).

***avapunati**, °**punāpayati**, see **o-pu°**.

Avapura, see **Opura**.

avapṛcchati, *asks permission* (not recorded); neg. ger. an-avapṛcchya (santaṃ bhikṣuṃ) Prāt 521.10; 522.2, *without asking permission of; disregarding* (corresponds to Pali anāpucchā).

avapṛṣṭhīkṛta, adj. (see s.v. **pṛṣṭhībhavati**), *with back turned away* (from the world): Divy 326.11, see s.v. **Maitrīya**.

avapravrajati (unrecorded), *withdraws from ascetic life*: Kalpanāmaṇḍitikā 114 V 2 (Lüders, Kl. Skt. Texte 2 p. 45) °jatu, impv.

? **avabodhi**, see **samyaġ-ava°**.

avabhā (unrecorded), (illusory) *appearance* (to Skt. avabhāti; cf. next): Gv 69.26 nāsti me sarvasattva-citta-(so 2d ed.) -caritāvabhāsu saṅgaḥ, *I have no attachment to the appearances of thoughts and actions of all creatures.*

avabhāna (unrecorded), *appearance* or *sheen* (cf. prec.): Gv 29.21 samantāvabhāno loke (buddhakāyaḥ).

avabhāsa, m. (in Skt. *sheen; appearance; manifestation*, and so also in BHS; in mg. 1 = Pali obhāsa), (**1**) *hint* given in words by a monk as to something he desires (a sinful act); cf. Childers 298; Vism. i.23.17 and 41.1 ff., where it as well as **nimitta**, 3, *suggestion*, and **parikathā**, qq.v., are briefly explained: Śikṣ 131.3 nāvabhāsa-kareṇa bhavitavyam, *one should not be a maker of hints*; 4 katamo 'vabhāsaḥ (in the following example a monk says things designed to get tasty food from donors); 6 avabhāsa-nimittaṃ; see **avabhāsa-tā**; (**2**) *range*, = **ābhāsa**, q.v., used in similar cpds.: (aham ...) bālānāṃ śravaṇāvabhāsam āgacchāmi Laṅk 192.10; bodhisattvasya ... dharma-śabdā (text °dhā) śrotrāvabhāsam āgacchanti, Bhadrapāda Sūtra, Thomas ap. Hoernle MR 89.13; rūpaśabdagandhara-sasparśāvabhāsam āgacchanti KP 105.8 (prose).

Avabhāsakara, n. of a devaputra, one of the 16 guardians of the bodhimaṇḍa: LV 277.13.

avabhāsa-tā, *state of* (making) *hints* (see **avabhāsa** 1): Śikṣ 140.6 °tāṃ ca pratilabdhukāmena, *by one who* (is sinful in that he) *wants to attain this state* (misunderstood by Bendall and Rouse, Transl.).

Avabhāsanaśikhin, n. of a nāga, Mvy 3357; of a nāga-king, Megh 308.9 (here with the epithet saptaśīrṣa; see **Saptaśīrṣaka**, apparently the same personage).

Avabhāsaprabha, n. of a devaputra: SP 4.4.

Avabhāsaprāptā, n. of the lokadhātu in which Kāśyapa is to appear as a Buddha: SP 144.4.

Avabhāsamakuṭa, n. of a Tathāgata: Gv 361.7.

Obhāsayanta- (for Avabhāsayat-)-**prabharājan**, n. of a Buddha: Gv 259.7 (vs; n. sg. °jā).

avabhāsayitar, *one who makes to shine*: Gv 463.8 °tāro dharmālokamukhānām.

(**Avabhās°**) **Obhāsarāja**, n. of a Buddha: Gv 256.19 (vs).

Avabhāsarāja-prabhaketuś(i)rī, n. of a Buddha: Gv 284.16 (vs). Perhaps two separate names (cf. prec.); see s.v. **Citrārtha**.

(**Avabhās°**) **Obhāsasāgaraviyūha**, n. of a Buddha: Gv 257.24 (vs; read °haḥ for °haṃ).

[**avabhāsya**, *brilliance*: LV 16.20 (antaḥpuram) avabhāsyena sphuṭaṃ bhavati. Read probably avabhāsena, as in 17.2, tho here all mss. °syena acc. to Lefm.]

avabhūṣita, *adorned*: nāgarājānau saptasphaṭāvabhūṣitau Mmk 76.6.

avamanyana-tā = next: RP 20.11 (prose; mss. parātimanyanatā; cf. 20.16).

avamanyanā, and (?) °**na**, nt. (to avamanyate; = Pali avamaññanā, °na), *contempt*: Śikṣ 9.7 (prose; text °yatā, see Corr.); 52.9; 271.5; KP 22.3; Bbh 104.20; 145.15. In these always °nā, f.; in RP 21.4 (vs) avamanyana-manyana (acc. sg.) tyaktvā, apparently nt., but could be m.c. for °nā (or °nāṃ).

(**avamardita-cittam**, SP 108.5, rendered by Kern *mentally developed*; similarly Burnouf. But Skt. avamardati and Pali omaddati mean only *distress* or the like. The form means *having his spirit depressed, crushed*; note that it *follows* viditvā; it is not parallel with the words preceding viditvā, but is modified by the following udārasaṃjñayā; the phrase is explained by what follows.)

Avamūrdha, m. (adj., *with head downward, upside down*; cf. next, and Skt. Gr. avamūrdhaśaya), n. of a lokadhātu, associated with **Vyatyasta** (lokadhātu), q.v.: °dhaḥ Mvy 3068 (followed by Vyatyastaḥ); Gv 126.2 (after Vyatyasta-lokadhātu-mukham) Avamūrdha-hāra-mukham (hāra seems to be corrupt; should we read lokadhātu for it?); Dbh 15.14 -vyatyastāvamūrdha- (in long cpd., beginning niravaśeṣasarvalokadhātu-); Avamūrdha-lipi, a kind of script, *the script of the Avamūrdha lokadhātu*, LV 125.22 (cf. **Vyatyasta**-lipī Mv i.135.6).

avamūrdhaka (also **omūrdhaka, omuddhaka**, qq.v., and s.v. **-mūrdhaka**; see preceding), *with head downwards, upside down*: Mvy 6800; Divy 9.24; 505.16.

avayāna (nt. or m.), *retreat* (of an army), one of the arts mastered by the Bodhisattva as prince: LV 156.12 °ne, loc. = Tib. bzur ba, *giving way*.

avara, m., a high number: Mvy 7708, or nt. 7834, in the latter cited from Gv; Gv 105.20, text sattva-varasya, read sattvāvarasya (gen.). In Gv 133.2 the item seems to be omitted (in a list which generally corresponds better to Mvy).

avaraka, adj. (= Pali oraka; -ka prob. pejorative), *wretchedly poor, inferior, mean*: °keṇa kuśalamūlena SP 456.3; LV 89.22; AsP 79.12 (all prose); °kam, quasi-substantive (?) nt., Mvy 2701 = Tib. ṅan ṅon *sordid*, etc. (Das). In some cases the mss. of Divy and Av read avaraka for **avavaraka**, q.v., which Mironov reads for Mvy 2701.

Avara-godānīya, see **Apara°**.

avarabhāgīya, adj. (Pali orambhāgiya), (*binding*) *to lower states* (viz. to the kāmadhātu), only said of the first five **saṃyojana** (q.v.): Mvy 2156 (without mention of saṃyojana); Divy 533.24; MSV ii.87.7. They cause rebirth in a *state of desire* (kāmabhave) also in Pali, MN comm. iii.143.21; in Pugg. 22.11–12 called *personal, internal* (ajjhatta). See **ūrdhvabhāgīya**.

[**avaruṇḍa**? see **oruṇḍa**.]

avarupta, also **orupta**, quasi ppp., analogical back-formation to avaropita (ppp. of **avaropayati**, q.v.), on some model like gopayati (gopita): gupta; *planted*, literally of a tree: Gv 278.22 taddivasāvaruptasya sālakalyāṇavṛkṣasya; oftener fig., of (roots of) *merit*, (kuśala-)mūla; Mv ii.314.11 avarupta-kuśalamūlā(ḥ), v.l. avalupta°; iii.406.11 avarupta-kuśalamūlo, v.l. anavarupta°, which could be interpreted as *not cut off* (see **avaropayati**, 2); avarupta (of kuśalamūla) Suv 91.8; 103.7; 113.5; 114.1 etc.; acc. to Kern, SP Preface vi, in Kashgar rec. for Nep. avaropita; orupta (kuśalamūla) Mv iii.104.18; 432.9; orupta-kuśaleṣu Mv iii.155.6.

(**avarūpayati**,) **orūpayati**, *cuts off* (hair): Mv i.169.14 (vs) keśāṃ ca orūpayanti. On the form see Chap. 43, s.v. ruh- (5).

avaropaṇa, nt. (to **avaropayati**; in Skt. in mg. *planting*), (**1**) *cutting off* (hair) (in this sense = Pali oropaṇa): LV 432.15 -keśāvaropaṇa-; (**2**) *depositing* (of relics, in a stūpa): dhātv-avaropaṇa Kv 20.2 (text dhyānāva°); 40.24; 41.1; 77.3 (in all three text dhātvāva°); (**3**) *discrediting, lowering in estimation*: Śikṣ 126.4 na mukhasākṣy-avaropaṇa-vacano bhavati, *he is not one to speak to the discredit of a direct witness.*

Avaropanarāja (text has n, not ṇ), n. of a Bodhisattva: Gv 442.7.

avaropayati (caus. to ava-ruh; Skt. in sense 1; in sense 2 = Pali oropeti; cf. **avarūpayati, orūp°**), (**1**) *plants* (so Skt., of planting trees); here very commonly of *planting roots of merit, kuśalamūla* (not in Pali in either literal or fig. sense); cf. **avarupta, °ropaṇa**: kuśalamūlāny avaropayāmi Divy 95.25; avaropayitum, inf., Sukh 16.4; °lāny avaropitāni Mv i.1.5; 57.7; Suv 81.15 (here most mss. avaruptāni); avaropitakuśalamūla- *that has* (*have*) *planted r. of m.* Mvy 7417; Vaj 22.20; 23.1; Gv 47.12; kuśalam avaropitaṃ Mv i.136.10; avaropitaṃ cittabījaṃ Dbh 48.8; (**2**) *cuts off* (hair, beard): -avaropitakeśaśmaśrur Divy 37.2; -avaropitair iva keśair Av i.284.8; (evil conditions) buddhāvaropitānām (so read with mss.) akuśalānāṃ dharmāṇāṃ Divy 359.26, *that are* (= are to be,can be) *cut off* (= obliterated) *by a Buddha.*

? **avarṇa**, adj., in Mv iii.343.1 °ṇaś ca, epithet of the Buddha's voice (svara); hence must be complimentary; but Skt. id. and Pali avaṇṇa are normally uncomplimentary. Senart has no v.l. or note and does not list the word in his Index. Perhaps semi-MIndic for Skt. avarṇya (or read this?), *indescribable*; cf. Pali avaṇṇanīya.

avalakṣaṇa (nt.; cf. **apala°** and Pali avalakkhaṇa, Bhvr. adj.), *evil, inauspicious, bodily mark*: aṣṭādaśabhir °ṇaiḥ MSV i.100.9; 106.3.

-avalambaka, m., and **°ikā**, f., see **nagarāvalambaka, °ikā.**

avalambanā (= Skt. °na, nt.), *dependence*: Divy 199.19 tau Buddha-dharma-saṃghāvalambanayā smṛtyā kālagatau . . . deveṣūpapannau.

Avalambā, see **Olambā.**

avalava, m. (v.l. avalapa; so Mironov), *harvest*: Mvy 5314 °vaś ca na prajñāyate = Tib. bṅas sar (v.l. par) yaṅ mi mṅon.

avalīna, see 2 **avalīyate.**

1 **avalīyati, olīyati** (= ava-ḍī°; Skt. avalīna, said of birds, BR 6.550; cf. Skt. avaḍīna, n., pw 2.292), *flies down*: gaganapathagatā olīyanti (mss. khagapatha°) Mv i.216.5; in the parallel ii.19.2 gaganapathagatā pralīyanti (mss.; better meter; Senart praḍī°).

2 **avalīyate** (Skt. avalīyate, not quite in this mg.; = Pali olīyati, ppp. olīna; wrongly defined PTSD; cf. CPD s.v. an-olīna, *not shrinking, not downcast*, and °vuttika, *not sluggish in one's duties*), *is depressed, downcast*: cittaṃ nāvalīyate AsP 5.6 etc.; ŚsP 1643.20; ppp. avalīna, *downcast, despondent*: Śikṣ 126.1 nāvalīna-vacano, *not despondent in his talk*; Śikṣ 309.17 na cāvalīna-saṃtatayo bhavanti (see s.v. **saṃtati**); the opposite is udāra-saṃtatikāś, following.

avalīyana, see **an-avalīyana-tā.**

?**avalupta**, *planted*, v.l. for **avarupta**, q.v.: Mv ii.314.11, Senart avarupta-kuśalamūlā(ḥ), v.l. avalupta°. Also elsewhere as v.l.

-avalehakam, adv. (Skt. °ka, adj., *one who licks*, BR 5.1063; so, hastāvalehakā(ḥ) abudhāḥ, *foolish hand-lickers*, said of certain ascetics, LV 258.5), *in a manner accompanied by licking* (of the hands or bowl; said of the eating process): Prāt 533.10 (Mvy 8587) na hastāvalehakaṃ piṇḍapātaṃ paribhokṣyāmaḥ, and Prāt 533.11 (Mvy 8588) na pātrāvalehakam . . . The Pali equivalent (Vin. iv.198.5, 11) is -nillehakaṃ; but hatthāpalekhana also occurs (PTSD).

avalokanaka (gender? = **olok°, ullok°**, qq.v.), *window*: Divy 221.29 °nakā (for °kāḥ? or °kāni? followed by s-; n. pl., in a list of structures and their accessories).

Avalokana-sūtra, or **Avalokanā-sūtra**, nt., n. of a work: Śikṣ 297.10 and 89.15 respectively. It is a variant form of the **Avalokitaṃ** (nāma sūtraṃ, or vyākaraṇaṃ), q.v., in the second Mv version. On the language and meter see §§ 1.47.48.

avalokanīya, adj., *pleasant*, of sounds: prasādanīyā avalokanīyāḥ prahlādanīyāḥ (śabdāḥ) LV 52.6; 411.9; of persons, *worthy of* (admiring) *contemplation*: Mv i.103.5 ullokanīyāś cāvalokanīyāś cābhivandanīyāś cādeyavākyāś ca. (All prose.) Cf. **ullokanīya.**

avalokayati (= Pali apaloketi), (**1**) *asks permission of* (acc.): Bhīk 3b.5 yāvad ahaṃ bhagavantam avalokayāmi, *until I ask the Lord's permission* (for the admission of nuns); Divy 331.18 nāhaṃ svādhīna upādhyāyam avalokayata; 331.23; 511.10 rājānam avalokya; 439.22, 23 mātāpitarāv avalokya, *having asked permission of my parents*; (**2**, cf. Skt. āpṛcchate) *takes leave of, says farewell to* (acc.): Divy 4.26 gacchāmi avalokitā bhava, *I am going; be greeted in farewell!*; 128.2; 580.26; °to bhava MSV i.41.6; -bāndhavān avalokya Divy 281.17; 524.14; (**3**) *entrusts* (acc.) with a function (cf. Pali apaloketi, d, in CPD, *consult*): bhikṣum avalokayitvā (Tib. bcol nas, *entrusted to one's charge*) gantavyaṁ yo 'sya lābhaṃ gṛhṇāti MSV ii.97.8 (and ff.); avalokayasi (perh. *do you consult*? as in Pali) tvaṃ . . . Upanandaṃ MSV ii.119.2 and f.

avalokita (**1**) nt., and once **°tā**, f. (= Pali °ta, oftener apalokita, nt.), *act of looking; a look, gaze*: fem. only LV 227.9–10 anyonya-mukhāvalokitayā rudanti sma, *they wept with a gazing look at each other's faces*; nt. LV 84.5 siṃhāvalokitaṃ mahāpuruṣāvalokitaṃ vyavalokayati sma; LV 191.17 (prāsādikena) avalokita-vyavalokitena (see s.v. **vyavalokita**), acc. to Tib., *looking forward*; Śikṣ 215.10 -prasāritāvalokita-vilokita-supta-jāgarita-svaśarīragatopasthānaṃ; elsewhere in a similar cliché **ālokita**-(instead of ava°)-**vilokita**, q.v.; esp. nāgāvalokita (= Pali id., oftener °palokita), *the gaze of an elephant* (turning the whole body), Mv iii.55.18 sarvāvantena kāyena (so read with v.l. for text kālena) nāgāvalokitena; Divy 208.16–17 sarvakāyena nāgāvalokitena; Gv 48.15 nāgāvalokitena **pratyudāvṛtya** (q.v.); MSV i.62.17; (**2**) nt., n. of a work (called a vyākaraṇaṃ Mv ii.257.13; 259.4; but a sūtraṃ in the colophons, 293.15; 397.7) imbedded in the Mv in two forms, following one another, ii.257.6–293.15, and 293.16–397.7. The second of these, under the name **Avalokana-** (or **°nā-)sūtra**, q.v., was used (in a rather widely variant form) as one of the sources of Śikṣ. (**3**) m., said to be used for **Avalokiteśvara**, q.v.: Burnouf, Introd. 224 (and Skt. Lex.).

Avalokitanetra, n. of a Bodhisattva: Gv 3.2

avalokita-mūrdhi-tā (suffix tā added to stem in -in from *avalokita-mūrdhan), *state of having his head gazed upon* (revered) by others, said of a Tathāgata: Gv 65.18.

Avalokitalakṣmī, n. of a kiṃnara-maid: Kv 6.3.

Avalokiteśvara (on the name cf. Mironov, JRAS 1927.241 ff., suggesting that the original form was Avalokita-svara), n. of a celebrated Bodhisattva: first in lists of Bodhisattvas, SP 3.4; Mvy 645; cf. also Kv 1.2; lives on Mt. Potalaka Gv 208.8; subject of ch. 24 of SP (named 438.4 ff.), where he has the epithet **Samantamukha**, q.v.; other occurrences Śikṣ 286.7; Samādh p. 36 l. 1; Kv 1.16; 8.19 etc.; Mmk 62.24 etc.; Sukh 52.4; 56.7–8; Sādh 42.10 etc.

Avalokiteśvaravimokṣa, n. of a work: Śikṣ 296.2.

avavadati, ovadati (= Pali ovadati), *admonishes, instructs*; regularly followed by parallel anuśās(a)ti, as also in Pali: samyag avavadati samyag anuśāsti Divy 299.10; avavadāmy anuśāsmi, yathā mayā samyag avavaditāḥ samyag avaśiṣṭā(ḥ) LV 409.11; taṃ bhagavāṃ ovadatu anuśāsatu Mv i.321.17; ovadatu me bhavāṃ . . . anuśāsatu me Mv iii.206.2–3; ovadeyaṃ SP 351.6; ppp. avavadita SP 70.13; 101.4; gdve. avavaditavya Divy 492.29; kevarūpeṇa ovādena ovadanti Mv i.104.9.

avavaraka (also **avaraka**? m. or nt.; = Pali ovaraka, Skt. apavaraka, which is read also in mss. of Divy), *a secret apartment* or *chamber*; acc. to Speyer Av ii.158.10 n., *a subterranean room*. Several times mss. (of Av, Divy) present avaraka, which might be regarded as a case of haplology or haplography; but twice, at least, Pali seems to read (a)varaka instead of ovaraka: jāto (')varake Jāt. i.391.21 and Vv comm. 158.14 (PTSD would understand jāt' ovarake; both prose): KP 71.1 (prose) gṛhe vā layane vā avavarake vā; Mmk 519.27 (prose) guhye pradeśe avavarake vā; 534.10 (vs) prachanne ... svagṛhe vāvavarake 'pi ca (meter corrupt); Av ii.54.5 avarakaṃ praviṣṭā udbandhanahetoḥ (to hang herself); here text with ms. avara°; 55.7 avavarakam (so ms., text avara°) avabhāsamānā; 158.10 avavarakaṃ praviśa, and °kaṃ praviṣṭā; Divy 471.8 apavarakaṃ (no v.l.) prāviśat; avavarake (or avarake) strī prasūtā Divy 471.9 (text apav°, but no ms. has -p-; they point to avarake or avavarake); 479.25 (text apav°, but all mss. avarake), 26–27 (text apav° with 1 ms., 2 mss. (a)varake, actually varake after -e).

avavahati (not in Skt.; in Pali only pass. ovuyhati *is carried off* by a river, Itiv. 114.1, 3), *carries, bears* (a burden): Śikṣ 13.13 -dhuram avavoḍhum (inf.).

avavāda, ovāda (so regularly Mv, otherwise ava°; to **avavadati**) m. (= Pali ovāda), *admonition, instruction*: SP 202.10 sattvāvavāda-kuśalānāṃ; LV 244.16 datto 'vavādo 'bhūt, *the admonition (instruction) was granted*; Mv i.104.9 ovādena ovadanti; 307.10; iii.53.8, 10; Mvy 1440; 6534; 7600; 8442–4; Divy 240.17; 281.28; bodhisattvāvavāda, SP 65.1 et alibi, epithet of Mahāvaipulya sūtras such as SP (for this Kashgar rec. regularly reads bodhisattvotpāda, KN note to l. c.); parallel with the virtual synonym **anuśāsanī**, q.v., Mv iii.51.16–17 karaṇīyo ovādo karaṇīyā anuśāsanī; these two often compounded as avavādānuśāsanī (Mv ovādānu°), dvandva, but regularly sg. with fem. gender (§ 23.3): LV 244.15 (read with mss. avavādānuśāsanī, or °nīm, asya; the reading of both edd. is impossible), *admonition and instruction*: Divy 318.24; 340.28 = 567.9; Mv iii.60.16; 206.4; Bbh 178.17; 224.16; Bhīk 5a.1.

avavādaka, adj. (to **avavadati**; = Pali ovādaka), *instructing, admonishing*; m., *instructor* (in religion); nt. also used of a text: Divy 48.26 yas teṣāṃ ṛṣir avavādakaḥ; 385.8 °kānām agro; 493.5 (ko 'smākam) avavādaka ājñaptaḥ; 254.10 kulāvavādako, *a family* (religious) *instructor*, of a rich man; Gv 171.14 mahāyānasyāvavādakāni (*are instructors in the Mahāyāna*) mama kalyāṇamitrāṇi; nt., of a work, **Rājāvavādakam**, see this.

avavād(ay)ati, ovā° = **avavadati**; noted only in iminā ovādena ovādito Mv iii.53.8 and ... ovāditvā 10; prob. denom. to **ovāda (ava°)**.

avavāditar (n. ag. to **avavadati**, or to prec.?), *one who instructs* or *admonishes*: Gv 463.3 °tāraḥ pāramitāsu.

ava-vāyati, see **o-vā°**.

[**-avavicārād** Śikṣ 271.13, seeming text, but only by misprint; see **gurula.**]

ava-vidhyana, see **ovidhyana-khā**.

[**avaśaṃsyati** Mvy 2637, read avamaṃsyati, fut. of ava-manyate, with var. in Kyoto ed., and with Mironov's text without v.l. No ava-śaṃs is recorded anywhere, if we except the AV noun avaśas, ἅπ. λεγ. Moreover no ya-present to śaṃs is known.]

avaśayati (nowhere recorded), *lies down*: Divy 559.14 (vs) paryaṅke 'vaśayitvā (ger.). Cf. **avaśāyita.**

avaśākha, or **ośākha**, only in °kha-praśākha, adj., *having down-hanging twigs* or *branches*, said of several kinds of trees: ośākha-praśākhaṃ (nyagrodhapotaṃ) Mv iii.302.1; °kho (kakubho nāma vṛkṣo) 313.9; avaśākha-praśākhā (harītakī) 311.4.

avaśāyita, ppp. (cf. **avaśayati**; this form could be m.c. for avaśayita), *lying, resting, bedded*: Mv ii.351.19 (vs) dārikā dārakā caiva śayyāsanāvaśāyitāḥ (Senart; mss. śayyāyāṃ avaś°, śayyāsanaśāyitā, the latter metrically bad).

avaśāvaśam, adv. (āmreḍita cpd.; avaśam, adv. from Skt. avaśa), *quite certainly*: Mv iii.88.18.

avaśirati, ośirati, °**reti** (also spelled with ṣ, s for ś, and mss. sometimes show a for i after the sibilant, **oṣarati**, (2) **osarati**; see **avasarati**; cf. Pkt. Lex. osiraṇa = vyutsarjana, parityāga, Sheth; etym. obscure, cf. Senart Mv i note 380, noting semantic correspondence with Skt. ava-sṛj): (**1**) *clears away*: LV 240.15 (vs) vīthi racita ratnavastra-dhāryai(r) (Foucaux °dhānyair, *grain*, with Tib. ḥbrus) avaśiriyā (ger.), *having cleared the streets which were adorned* etc. (before the Bodhisattva); (**2**) *sends off, throws* (into prison): osiranti Mv i.24.1 (see Senart's note, 389); (**3**) *sends forth, emits* (light, sound, breath): Mv ii.315.6 mukhavātam (so with v.l. for Senart °vāṭam) osireyā, (if the Bodhisattva) *should send forth the breath of his mouth*; Mv ii.344.15, read prob. avaśiri *sent forth* (a ray of light; mss. avaśiti, avati; Senart em. avasṛjati); LV 357.3 (should be read) °sahasrāṃś c'ośarī(r) ātmabhāvā, probably (Buddha) *sent forth from his body* (hundreds of) *thousands* (of rays), see § 8.85; Gv 255.14 (vs) raśmisamudra ośiratu (n. sg. m. pres. pple.); in Gv 254.26 (vs) 1st ed. eṣiriṣū jinaḥ, read osiri pūjitaḥ (see 2d ed.); Mv ii.383.7 osire (v.l. ośire) *would send forth* (svaraṃ, *a sound*); (**4**) *throws down* (fragrant powder, flowers; said of gods, upon the Bodhisattva or Buddha; = avakirati, which Senart reads by em. in Mv ii.343.19 and 349.16): Mv ii.343.19 avaśire (or °sire, mss.) cūrṇadhārāṃ ... varacandanasya; iii.273.16 ratanacūrṇaṃ antarikṣāto osire (v.l. ośire; here kept by Senart); ii.349.16 puṣpavarṣāṇi antarīkṣeṇa ośiri (mss.); also of *throwing down* missiles, SP 449.3 (vs) vajrāmayaparvatā-śani (i. e. aśanī; v.l. yadi, so WT, emending to °parvato; acc.) ghatanārthāya ca (WT hi) mūrdhi (better with v.l. °dha, loc.; WT °dhni) oṣaret, *if one should hurl down on his head to kill him* ... (for WT's interpretation see **avasarati** 1); (**5**) *lets loose, releases*: Mv ii.452.16 (devīm) ośiritvā (after violently seizing her); ii.459.15 yadi me na osariṣyasi (so mss., Senart em. osir°) ... ātmānaṃ mārayiṣyaṃ; *lets go* (women from a harem), *gives license to*: ośiritavyā (Senart em. °yaṃ) Mv ii.424.20; (note ośiṣṭā, v.l. ośiriṣṭā, 425.3, not osṛṣṭa as quoted from this place by Senart i note 380; text seems to intend pple. of ava-śiṣ, *left alone*, and so *abandoned*;) the subject is strīkāgāraṃ (v.l. strīyāg°), *the women of the harem must be turned loose* (to carry on affairs with other men); so 425.16 (istriyāgāraṃ, v.l. stryā°) ośiritavyā (Senart em. °yaṃ); 426.7 striyāgāraṃ (mss.) ośirati (mss. °riti); in another version of the same story, iii.1.4, mss. osare(yaṃ) (Senart em. osir°), but 1.6 and 2.11 ośirati (stryāgāram); but on the borderline between this and the next, or belonging perhaps to the next, are (in the same story) Mv ii.426.17–18 mā hevaṃ māṃ imasya brāhmaṇasya upasthānaparicaryāye osiriṣyati (Senart; mss. ośiri°, osari°), *I'm afraid he will hand me over to serve and wait on this brahman* (spoken by the chief queen); 427.10 na me ... eṣo brāhmaṇo ośiriṣyati, ... *will not give me up*; (**6**) *abandons, throws out* or *away, renounces* (cf. the last two citations): Mv iii.165.12 padumāvatīṃ vadhyām avasirasi, *you abandon P. to be killed*; ośiritvā kāmaratiṃ, *abandoning the pleasure of desire* Mv i.143.13, repeated i.200.9 where mss. osaritvā (Senart ośir°) and ii.4.6 where mss. okiritvā (Senart ośir°); Mv ii.272.13 ośirāhi (v.l. ośirehi) bhagavato traimāsaṃ bhaktam, *give up* (*renounce, resign the right to*); ii.298.6 (vs) divya ośiritvā (so 1 ms., v.l. okiritvā, Senart wrongly em. otaritvā) *giving up heavenly things*; Mv ii.367.19 vasudhāṃ sarvāṃ osiritvā (so 1 ms., v.l. osar°), *abandoning the whole earth*; 367.22 ośiritvāna (one's family, to lead a religious life); ii.334.22 suvarṇaniṣkāṃ ... ośiritvā, *throwing away gold coins*; ii.335.4, mss. manuṣya-pātraṃ (read madhusya p°? Senart amṛtasya p°, bad metrically and otherwise) ... ośiritvā viṣasya pātraṃ pibed bālabuddhiḥ.

avaśeṣa, adj. (= Pali avasesa), *left over, remaining*: Mv i.7.6 yaṃ teṣām asthīni avaśeṣāṇi (but so only 1 ms., the other 5 avaśeṣanti) bhūyo 'pi mānsachavi(?) ... upajāyati, *when* (only) *their bones are left, flesh and skin is produced again.* See also **kalpāvaśeṣam, niravaśeṣa, saṃghāvaśeṣa, sāvaśeṣa.**

avaśya, osa (m. or nt.; = AMg. osa; Skt. avaśyāya, once Lex. avaśyā, f.), *hoarfrost*, as symbol of transitoriness, used of life or worldly things: LV 214.8 (vs) osavindūpamā ... śūnyasvabhāvā(ḥ), *like drops of hoarfrost* (fleeting and vain); Samādh 22.6 jīviti svapnanibhe cali 'vaśye (Régamey's note states that Tib. renders *hoarfrost*, which he unwisely abandons); Śikṣ 18.12 (vs, cited from Candrapradīpa Sūtra = Samādh, but not the same vs) jīvite cañcale 'vaśye māyāsvapnanibhopame. In the LV osa could be m.c. for osā = Skt. (Lex.) avaśyā; but the loc. (a)vaśye in the others points to a m. or nt. stem; AMg. osa is given by Ratnach. as m.

avaśyāyati (denom. from prec.), *turns into hoarfrost*: LV 251.8 (prose) (svedāḥ ...) bhūmau nipatanti sma, avaśyāyanta ūṣmāyanto ...

avaśyāya-paṭṭa or **-paṭa**, m., lit. *frost-cloth*, a fine silk fabric, allegedly 'used for protection against frost' (Das) = Tib. dar-la (which also renders paṭṭāṃśu Mvy 5881 and aṃśuka 9166): Mvy 5880 °paṭṭaḥ (v.l. °paṭaḥ: Mironov °paṭṭaḥ, no v.l.); LV 162.17 (prose) avaśyāyapaṭa-vitata-vitāne.

avaśruta, f. **°tā** (= Pali avassuta; cf. **an-ava°**; derived from Skt. root sru, for which even Skt. texts often read śru), (sexually) *lustful*: Bhīk 27b.5 bhikṣuṇī avaśrutā avaśrutena puruṣeṇa ...; 28a.3 (see s.v. **saṃcagghati**).

avaṣaṅga, m., some part of a building: Mvy 5570 = Tib. ya phubs (? *top roof*?). Prof. Lo Ch'ang-pei informs me that the Chin. translation now means *grand, huge* or *empty*, but that the 'radical' of the sign suggests a possible original meaning *roof*. In MPS 34.61 acc. to Tib. *large beam*, gduṅ bo che.

avaṣṭabhya, ger. (cf. BR s.v. stabh with ava, 4), *embracing, enveloping*: Laṅk 16.5 bhagavantaṃ bodhisattvāṃś ca ratnajālenāva°, *embracing, enclosing in a* (? magic) *network* (? *mass*) *of jewels.*

ava-sakkati, o-sa° (= Pali o-sa°; see s.v. **-sakkati**), *withdraws, retreats*: Mv i.23.10 (apy ekatyāḥ palāyanti) apy ekatyā na palāyanti apy ekatyā kutrāpi avasakkanti (mss. °sappanti, one °sarppanti) apy ekatyā na avasakkanti (so 2 mss.; others °sarkkanti, °śakyanti, °sappanti); i.353.14 so dāni vyāghro taṃ ṛṣiṃ dṛṣṭvā osakkito (no v.l. in Critical App., but note p. 626 indicates that mss. read osaṃkito); ii.83.2 (vs) yadi si na maritukāmo, osakka (2 sg. impv.) mama rājyato.

(**avasanna**, see **osanna.**)

avasarati, (1) **osarati**, once **oṣar**°(?); on forms with -sār- see below, but also caus. s.v. 1 **osarati** (cf. Pali avasarati, osarati, *to enter, to arrive*, CPD), (**1**) *approaches, arrives*: Mv i.13.6 (vs) tasmiṃ narake osaranti, *they arrive at this hell* (otherwise Senart); osarantasya Mv ii.108.7, 9, 11, and °nto 10 (pres. pple.), *approaching, drawing near*; aor. avasāri or °riṃ, 1st or 3d sg., in phrase yena ... tad avasāri(ṃ), *arrived at, went to where ... was* (on the long ā see § 38.23; the corresponding Pali phrase is tad avasari, e. g. Vin. iii.11.30) Mv i.319.14, 16, 20; 323.13, 16 (in 16 mss. anusāri); ii.117.20; 119.6; 120.17; 123.16; iii.47.12; aor. with short ă, osare Mv ii.222.1 (mṛgābhimukhaṃ, *approched, went up* in the direction of the deer, in hunting); iii.364.19 vanāto so osare rājadhānīṃ; iii.453.3 (= Pali Jāt. v.252.20), read: na te koṣṭhesmiṃ osaranti (*go to, resort to*; Pali upenti) na kumbhe na kalopiyaṃ (see s.v. **kalopī**); Gv 241.13 ekaromi sugatasya osarī (3 pl. aor.), *settled, lodged*; osari Śikṣ 336.3 (read) prajñapradīpa ya osari, and 15; 337.3, 17; oṣaret (opt.) SP 449.3, see **avaśirati** 4, WT vajrāmaya-parvato yadi ghatanārthāya hi mūrdhni oṣaret, *should alight, fall upon his head*, which is perhaps possible; (**2**) **osarati** and its forms also are written for ośirati (**avaśirati**, q.v.); in my opinion this set of forms must be wholly unrelated to the above (despite Senart i note 380). Perhaps ośir° (or osir°) should always be read by em. when osar° occurs in the mss. in the meanings of avaśirati. Note especially Mv iii.1.4 osare(yaṃ), mss. (Senart osir°), but in 1.6 and 2.11 mss. ośirati in precisely similar context.

avasavya, adj. (Skt. and Pali apasavya; Pkt. avasavvaya, cf. AMg. avasavva, *a particular kind of the motions of the planets*), *not left, right* (-hand): °vyaṃ Sādh 20.5; °vyena (adv.) *on the right* 20.10; utsaṅgasthitāvasavyahastaṃ 24.10.

avasāda, m. (to **avasādayati**), *abuse*: Mvy 2636 = Tib. smad pa, or spyo ba.

avasādana (to **avasādayati**), (**1**) adj., f. **°nī**, *censuring, rebuking*: Bbh 220.3 (kuśale sthāne pratiṣṭhāpanārthaṃ...) -saṃcodanāvasādanī priyavāditā; (**2**) **°nā**, subst. f. *censure, rebuke*: Bbh 83.18 avasādanā madhyame vyatikrame, *censure* (is appropriate) *in case of a transgression* (of) *middling* (gravity); 179.18, see s.v. **avasādayati**; 295.21 avasādanāsādhyaḥ, *to be perfected by censure*; Jm 217.8 tām avasādanām amṛṣyamāṇaḥ, *impatient of this rebuke*; Divy 490.5, 6 avasādanāvineyaḥ, *to be converted* (substantially = °nā-sādhyaḥ, above) *by rebuke* (which is applied in 7 in the words tvaṃ tāvac cūḍaḥ etc.; ed. Index *discouragement*, not quite rightly; the opposite is utsahanā-vineya, see **utsahanā**); in LV 70.11 (saṃcārya) vicāryāvasādanākāreṇa pāṇiṃ saṃcārayati sma (subject, the Bodhisattva in his mother's womb); Foucaux, 'en l'étendant pour le signal du départ' (sc. for the attendant gods), but avasādanā can hardly mean this. Tib. had a quite different reading, containing smṛtaḥ saṃprajānan as in l. 15 (dran zhiṅ śes bzhin du, both times). I cannot solve the passage but think it probably corrupt, despite the lack of variants. Perhaps follow the lead of Tib.

avasādanikā, *censure, rebuke*: Bbh 150.22, see prec. and s.v. **avasādayati**; similarly 151.3, 4.

avasādayati (= Pali apasādayati, in both mgs.; cf. prec. two), (**1**) *rejects, repulses*: Mv iii.184.11 tāye māṇavikāye ... avasādito, *rejected by this girl* (with whom he was in love); (**2**) *censures, rebukes*: Bbh 150.22 (mṛdvaparādhaṃ mṛdu-vyatikramaṃ...) mṛdvyā (text mṛdhvyā) avasādanikayā avasādayati; so also 151.3; Bbh 107.16 toṣayatā utsāhayatā anavasādayatā, *by him gratifying, enthusing, not reproaching*; Bbh 179.18–20 bodhisattvaḥ avasādanārhān ... pravāsanārhān kliṣṭacitto nāvasādayati, avasādayati vā na ca daṇḍakarmaṇā samanuśāsti; °yitavyaḥ MSV iii.53.11.

avasāraṇa, nt. (seemingly = **osāraṇā**, q.v.), *restitution* (of a monk that has been suspended from the order): °ṇam Mvy 9306 = Tib. bzod par gsol ba, *request for forgiveness*; so also Chin.

avasirati, see **avaśirati.**

avasṛjana, nt. (to Skt. avasṛjati), *emission, pouring forth*: Gv 18.9 (prose) bodhisattvanirmitameghāvasṛjanaṃ.

avasevita-vant (no ava-sev is recorded), *having cultivated, devoted oneself to*: LV 10.5–6 pañcavidhapuṇyakriyāvastv-avasevitavatas (bodhisattvasya); Calc. 11.1 reads upasev° for avasev°, unsupported by any of Lefm.'s mss.

avaskandanā (cf. Skt. avaskandana, nt., *accusation, legal attack*; to ava-skand-, *attack*, usually in military sense), (verbal) *attack*; *injurious speech*; °skandanā is read for **°sphaṇḍanam** in a text parallel to Śikṣ 172.1 idam agraṃ pāruṣyāṇāṃ yad utāryāṇāṃ avasphaṇḍanam, see Bendall's note p. 408; Tib. gnod pa, *injure.*

avaskhalita, adj. (ppp. of Skt. skhal, not cpd. with ava in Skt.; cf. Pali avakkhalita, n., *offense*), *guilty, at fault; having offended*: Divy 359.26 (tvaṃ hi) bhagavaty asakṛd-asakṛd avaskhalito.

avastabdha, ppp. (= Pali avaṭṭhaddha, also with dental ttha; Skt. avaṣṭabdha, ppp. to ava-stambh), *founded* (upon), *supported* (by), in comp.: Divy 45.4 tīrthikāvastabdhaṃ tan nagaraṃ.

avasphaṇḍaka (to next but one with -aka), *one who addresses contemptuously*: bhikṣor gṛhapater °kasya MSV iii.24.10, *of a monk who speaks contemptuously to a householder*.

avasphaṇḍana, in Bbh °**spa**°, nt. (n. act. to next, q.v.), *ridicule* or *contemptuous treatment*: Bbh 238.8 (kṣamaś) ca bhavati parato 'vamānānām avahasanāvaspaṇḍana-durukta-durāgatādīnām . . . vacanapathānāṃ; Śikṣ 172.1, see **avaskandanā**.

avasphaṇḍayati, in Bbh °**spa**° (cf. Skt. Dhātup. sphaṇḍ, parihāse; see prec. two) *ridicules* or *treats with contempt*: Bbh 123.10 (na ca bodhisattvo) yācanakam avahasati nāvaspaṇḍ°; 150.4 (na ca . . . bodhisattvaḥ param avahasati) nāvaspaṇḍ°; 175.16 avahasati avaspaṇḍ°; mayā . . . gṛhapatir °ḍitaḥ MSV iii.24.7; Tib. bṅas thabs gyiso (gyis so?), *acted contemptuously* (towards).

avasphoṭana, nt. (Skt. id., *snapping of the fingers*, pw; possibly the same word, applied to 'casual rejection' of an argument?), reading of Mironov in Mvy and of Das s.v. Tib. sphrugs bsigs instead of **apasphoṭana**, q.v.

avasyandana (? the same word recorded in Pāṇ.'s gaṇa gahādi? cf. Skt. avasyandita), *changing the meaning of one's own words*: Śikṣ 126.1 nāvasyandanavacanaḥ.

avasruta, adj. (= Pali avassuta), *wet, dripping*, and so *foul, rotten*, orig. of a tree the inside of which is rotten, Pali AN iv.171.9 (rukkhāni) antopūtīni avassutāni kasambujātāni; fig., usually in Pali, and in BHS, of evil monks: Mvy 9138 antarpūty (read as separate word, see antaḥpūti) avasrutaḥ; foll. by kaṣambaka-jātaḥ (see **kaśambaka**); MSV i.50.7 antaḥpūtir °taḥ kaṣambaka-jātaḥ.

avasvapati, °**pana**, see **osopati**, °**pana**.

avasvāpana, see **osvāpana**, **apa**°.

(**avasvāpayati**,) ppp. avasvāpita, osvā° (caus. to ava-svap-, in Skt. recorded only in ppp. avasupta, *asleep*, Rām.; but see **osopati**; note also Jain Skt. (Hem.) avasvāpanikā and °panī, pw 2.292), *put to sleep, asleep*: LV 220.10 (vs) te cāpy avasvāpitāḥ (so Lefm. em., confirmed by Tib. ñal; mss. avasthāpitāḥ, avasaṃsthitāḥ); 221.5 **śayavatī** (q.v., read prob. yaśavatī) osvāpitā devataiḥ, and 10 puravaraṃ osvāpitaṃ devataiḥ, . . . *put to sleep by the gods*. Cf. also **apasvāpana**, **osvāpana**.

avahoṭimaka (or °ḍimaka), see **avakoṭimaka**.

avānta, m., a high number: Mvy 7796 = Tib. bsam yas, or bsal yas (cf. **avada**).

avārṣika, adj. (or subst.?), (**1**) (an ascetic practice) *that consists of not going abroad in the rainy season*: LV 248.18 avārṣikair (sc. ātāpanaparitāpanaiḥ, l. 15); Tib. dbyar mi byuṅ ba; (**2**) (a monk) *who does not observe the* (rule for not wandering during the) *rains*: MSV ii.154.12; read so with v.l. and Mironov in Mvy 9426 (Tib. dbyar gnas su ma zhugs pa).

avāśiro, adj. n. sg. m. (or could be adv., acc. sg. nt.; = Pali avaṃsira(s), avasira(s), Skt. avākśiras), *head downwards, headlong*: Mv iii.454.6 = 457.4 atha (457.4 mā; so Senart; mss. apparently lack any such word, except that one reads nā in 457.4) ghorarūpaṃ narakaṃ prapatiṣye avāśiro (so clearly the mss. read or intend; vv. ll. avāraśiro, avaśiro, unmetr.; Senart em. ~~avākśiro~~).

avāśruta, ppp. (to Skt. ava-ā-sru-, not recorded; cf. Pali avassuta, taken by CPD as from ava plus Skt. sru-), *descending in floods*: Divy 608.19 (vs, printed as prose) payomucaḥ . . . avāśrutāmbhaso.

avikampana-tā (cf. **vika**°; = Pali avikampana, nt.), *the not-wavering* (from . . ., in comp.): Bbh 251.1 samyakprayogāvikampanatā.

Avikāra, m., n. of a samādhi: Mvy 575; ŚsP 1413.17; 1421.8.

avikīrṇa-vāca, adj. (= Pali avikiṇṇa-vāca), *not loose, not uncontrolled, in speech*: Mv ii.356.12 = iii.280.18 (in both read: amukharā (ca?) abhū avikīrṇavācā; in prec. line acapalā, anuddhatā; these four adj. associated formulaically in Pali).

a-vikopana (nt.; = Pali id.), *the not disturbing, non-confusion*: LV 423.1 bhūtakoṭy-avikopana-cakraṃ; 3 -dharmadhātv-avikopana-cakraṃ; Dbh 71.16 parāvikopana-tvāt, *because of the fact that it is not subject to disturbance by others* (or, *by foes*).

a-vikopita (neg. ppp. of **vikopayati**, q.v.), *unperturbed, undisturbed, unmoved*: avikopitayā caryā (instr.) LV 259.14; -avikopitajñāna- LV 428.11; avikopita (**asthisaṃghāta**, q.v.) Divy 61.22, 24; 76.27; 465.25; replaced by **avigopita**, Bhagavataḥ śarīram °taṃ MPS 48.3; 49.15 (Tib. ma ñams pa, *undisturbed*; but in 49.15 occurs vigopayati, *opens*, Tib. kha phye, see **vigopita**).

(**avikṣaṇa**, nt.; see s.v. **abhibhakṣaṇa**).

Avikṣiptāṃśa, n. of a former Buddha: Mv i.137.6.

avikhinna, see **vikh**°.

avigopita, see **avikopita**.

Avigraha, nt., n. of a Buddhakṣetra: Mv i.124.3.

avijahanatā, see **vija**°.

avijugupsanatā, see **viju**°.

avijñaptika, see **vijña**°.

avitarka(-dhyāyin), (= Pali avitakka-jhāyī, SN i.126.27), (devoted to the [2d] stage of dhyāna) *in which there is no ratiocination*: Mv iii.284.4, Senart avitarka-(mss. avitakāyaṃ, avitarkaṃ kāyaṃ)-dhyāyī (mss. -dhyāyino, which is possible in sense and meter and should perhaps be kept, despite the Pali parallel -jhāyī).

avitṛpti, f. (neg. to *vitṛpti, nowhere recorded; to vi-tṛp-), *insatiableness*: Dbh 49.15 vedayato 'vitṛptis tṛṣṇā.

avidu, see **vidu** (1).

aviddasu, adj. (= Pali id.; see **avidvasu**), *ignorant*: °**su**, n. sg. (or perhaps °sū, cf. ms. B in l. 16 abhiddaśū) is plausibly conjectured by Senart for corrupt readings of mss. Mv ii.369.5 and 16.

avidyatā, *ignorance* (= avidyā): LV 420.13 (vs) °tāyāḥ.

avidyā, *ignorance*, occurs in Mv ii.99.10 (text without v.l.) in the place of abhidhyā in a list of the 10 karmapatha; certainly in some sense secondary and perhaps a mere textual corruption for **abhidhyā**, *covetousness*.

Avidyāndhakāravidhvamsanakara, n. of a former Buddha: Sukh 6.1.

? **avidvala**, v.l. for next, q.v.

avidvasu, adj. (Sktized form of **aviddasu**, q.v.; Geiger 100.2 records but does not explain the Pali form, which seems to be a curious blend of Pali avidvā = Skt. a-vidvān with **a-vidu**, the s due to Skt. viduṣ-, cf. **viduṣaka**), *ignorant*: °sū, nom. pl., SP 45.9; 55.2 (Kashgar rec. avidvalāś); 56.2; 204.6; °sūnāṃ, gen. pl., 57.8 (all vss).

avidhaṃ, avidhā, interj. (always repeated; most often followed by (i)ti; = Pkt. avihā, cf. avidā, avida, *exclamation of sorrow*, Sheth), exclamation of disapproval or dismay; only noted in Mv; mss. sometimes abhi- for avi-, occasionally -dhāṃ for -dhaṃ or -dhā: avidhā avidhā ii.450.5; avidhāvidhaṃ (ti; so mss.) ii.450.7; avidhāvidhā (usually followed by ti) i.301.19; iii.73.17; 86.16; °dhāṃ (mss.) ii.452.11; °dheti i.303.21 (mss.); °dhaṃ or °dhan (ti) i.301.20; 302.1; 303.19; ii.452.8 (mss.); 462.15; iii.15.15; 189.10, 11. Rarely ā- is written in mss. for initial a-.

avinipāta-dharman, adj. (= Pali °dhamma), *not liable to fall* (to evil existences): Sukh 56.16 °dharmāṇaḥ, n. pl. m.

avinipāta-dharmin, adj. = prec.: Divy 534.4 °rmiṇyo, n. pl. f.

avinirbhāga (m.; corresponds to Pali avinibbhoga; see also **vinirbhāga**; note AbhidhK. La V-P. vii.122 avinirbhūta = avinirbhāgena avasthita; acc. to CPD s.v. avinibbhutta, avinirbhūta = this Pali form 'through confusion with a-vinā-bhūta'), *non-differentiation, non-distinction, confusion*: Dbh 18.7; 74.8 (kleśānāṃ...) sahajāvinirbhāga-tāṃ, *innate* (natural) *confusion*; Dbh 53.4, see **vinirbhāga**; Laṅk 63.9; Mvy 6569, text avinirbhāva, v.l. °bhāga, which read with Mironov without v.l. (-varti, *abiding in non-discrimination*) = Tib. tha (so Tib. Index, misprinted thad in text) dad du mi ḥjug pa (or, gnas pa), *not differing, not admitting of differentiation*, Das.

(**avinirbhāva**, read **avinirbhāga**, q.v.; but cf. **avinirbhūta**, cited there.)

avinivarta (see s.v. °**tya**), *not liable to turning back*: Dbh 30.29 °ta-cittāśayamanaskārair, of Bodhisattvas in 3d bhūmi; in vs Dbh.g. 10(346).17 replaced by **anivartiya**, q.v.

avinivartanīya, *incapable of turning back* (= **avinivartya**, q.v., etc.), of persons destined for enlightenment, commonly with the word Bodhisattva, often (e. g. SP 260.5; 265.11; Sukh 99.4) with dependent phrase anuttarāyāṃ samyaksaṃbodhau: SP 260.5; 265.11; Śikṣ 313.20; Sukh 99.4; AsP 323.1 ff.; Gv 514.6; as subst. m., n. of a Bodhisattva-samādhi: Mvy 740.

avinivartin (Skt. *not fleeing in battle*, Yājñ., see pw s.v.; here = **avinivartya, anivart(i)ya, avivart(i)ya**, qq.v., etc.), *not liable to turning back* (religiously): SP 263.5 bodhicittāvinivartinī (of a woman).

avinivartya (= ° **ta**, °**tin**, °**tanīya**; also **avivart(i)ya, anivart(i)ya, avaivartika**, qq.v.; in Pali only forms of anivatt- seem to be recorded), *not liable to turning back*: Śikṣ 317.15 (prose).

a-vipañcita, see **vip°**.

a-viparokṣa(-tā), see **vi-parokṣa**.

avipratisāra, m. (neg. of **vi°**, q.v.; = Pali avippaṭisāra), *absence of regret* or *remorse*; *contentment*: Bbh 72.15 °raḥ prāmodyaṃ; Divy 78.7 and 467.3 °ra-saṃjananārthaṃ (in 467.3 text °saṃjanārthaṃ). See the next entries.

avipratisāri-tā, abstr. to next, *state of non-discontent, absence of regrets*: Śikṣ 20.3 prītiṃ prāmodyam avipratisāritāṃ ca janayiṣyati (said of an act of giving).

avipratisārin, adj. (= Pali avippaṭi°; cf. **viprati°** and **avipratisāra**), *unregretful* (esp. about something one has given away): Śikṣ 21.14 aśocann avipratisārī avipākapratikāṅkṣī parityakṣyāmi; Bbh 72.2 dattvā cāvipratisārī; same Bbh 123.1; Dbh 57.7 yā 'vipratisāryavisṛtamārga-tā, *state of being not regretful and of not turning aside from the Path* (lit. *having un-turned-aside-from Path*, see **avisṛta**).

Avipranaṣṭarāṣṭra, n. of a former Buddha: Mv i.138.6.

aviprapañca, adj.: n. sg. m. °caḥ Mvy 2926, following aprapañcaḥ and niṣprapañcaḥ, and evidently substantially a synonym of these; all occur in a list of synonyms of gambhīra, most of which mean something like *hard to comprehend*. See s.v. **prapañca**.

a-vipravāsa, m., see **vipra°**.

a-vimardana-tā (cf. Skt. vimardana), *non-destruction*: śraddhabalaṃ °natāyai Śikṣ 3.6 (vs), *the power of faith tends to non-destruction* (of the indriyas).

Aviraktarāṣṭra, n. of a former Buddha: Mv i.140.2.

avi-rajas, nt., = **eḍaka-rajas**, q.v.: Mvy 8195.

Avirasa, n. of a former Buddha: Mv i.141.7.

a-virāgaṇa (nt.; neg. of n. act. to **virāgayati**, q.v.), *non-displeasing*: -ārāgaṇāvirāgaṇa- Gv 529.23.

a-virāgayati, neg. of **virāgayati**, q.v., *is not averse to, does not turn away from*: Dbh 52.20 (na cātyantopaśamaṃ...) avirāgayiṣyāmaḥ, *and we shall not fail to be averse to complete cessation* (of sentient existence, until all creatures are matured).

a-vilomana (nt.; neg. n. act. to **vilomayati**, q.v.; cf. Pali vilomana), *the not going contrary to*: Gv 463.23 śiṣyasamacittena, sarvābhijñāvilomana-tayā (i. e.- bhijñā-avil°; better with 2d ed. sarvājñā°), *by reason of not going contrary to all the abhijñā* (rather, *to all commands*); Bcṭ 284.5.

Avivarta (see under **avivartya**), m., n. of a samādhi: ŚsP 1419.3; cited as **Avaivarta**, q.v., from this list in Mvy 553. Orig. adj., *not liable to turning back*; see next.

avivarta-caryā (= **avaivarta-, anivartana-caryā**), *course that is not liable to turning back* (backsliding): Mv i.63.13. The text explains by vivartanti saṃsaranti vivartacaryā (cf. **vivarta**, *world-evolution*); but I agree with Senart, note on i.1.3, that this is mere fantasy and wholly misleading.

avivartika = **avivartya**, q.v.; see also **avaivartika**: of Bodhisattvas SP 32.11; 90.8 (v.l. avaiv°, unmetr.); 93.2; Mv i.83.12 (prose); prob. also Bodhisattvas are meant in Śikṣ 3.16, 17; °ka-tā, *state of being...*, Mv i.101.2 °katāye (instr. or loc. sg.; of Bodhisattvas).

avivartiya = next, in Mv i.80.4 (prose); Bodhisattvas in 2d bhūmi may be either **vivartiya**, q.v., or a-vi°; (vss) SP 294.8; 330.3.

avivartya (= °**tiya**, °**tika**, °**ta**; for other forms of same mg. see under **anivart(i)ya, avinivartya, avaivartika**; Pali has only forms of anivatt-), *not liable to turning back*: SP 149.13 -(dharma-)cakra; RP 10.10 bodhimārga-avivartya-mānasā (so mss.; as one word, *with minds that are not to be turned back on the path of enlightenment*); Gv 104.10 °tyāḥ; avivartyāpratyudāvartya- Gv 246.20; Dbh 19.17; jñānāvivartya-tvāt Dbh 71.12.

Avivartyadharmadhātunirghoṣa, n. of a Buddha: Gv 296.12.

avivārya, nt., Mvy 5205 = Tib. mi zlogs pa, *what can not be repulsed* or *diverted, turned away*; of this **anidhārya**, q.v., is a var. Are both corruptions of anivārya? Mironov only avivārya.

Aviśuṣkamūla, n. of a former Buddha: Mv i.141.13.

Aviṣahya (corresponds to Pali Visayha, which may be an error for Avisayha, cf. Speyer, transl. of Jm, p. 30, n. 3), n. of a śreṣṭhin: Jm 22.15.

a-visaṃvādana-tā (Pali id.; Skt. a- °na), *keeping one's word*: (devama)nuṣyāvisaṃ°tāyai LV 32.10.

a-visabhāga, see **visa°**.

a-visaraṇā, *non-relaxation, non-distraction, not turning aside* (of thoughts): Bbh 109.27 (cittasyācalanaṃ...) saṃgraho 'visaraṇā. Cf. next.

a-visṛta (neg. ppp. of vi-sṛ; = Pali visaṭa, visata, for the mg. of which cf. CPD s.v. anuvisaṭa), *undistracted, not turned aside*: Dbh 57.7 (see s.v. **avipratisārin**); in Mmk 92.20 text dharmameghavisṛta-samanupraveśanatāyai, read °meghāvisṛta? *for penetration without being turned aside*... Cf. prec.

avistara, adj. (Bhvr. cpd. of a- and vistara), *not diffuse*; *compact, full*, of sound: Mv i.171.7 (vs) avistara-piṇḍita-ravā, *having a full and compact* (cf. **piṇḍita**) *sound*. Cf. Pali avisaṭa (=Skt. avisṛta), used in the same way as synonym of piṇḍita applied to a sound, Jāt. ii.439.8 (comm.) bindussaro ti bindunā avisaṭena piṇḍitena sarena. Wrongly Senart's note.

a-vismaraṇa (nt.; neg. of Skt. vismaraṇa), *non-forgetting*: -dharmāvi° Mvy 784.

(**a-visvara**, adj. (cf. Skt. visvara, and adv. avisvaram, BR s.v. visvara), *not discordant*: read avisvara-rutā, *of not discordant note*, Mv i.172.3 (of Buddha's voice); so half the mss.; Senart abhisvara°.)

avīci, m. or f. (in Skt. only m.; rarely also f. in Pali, see CPD s.v.), n. of a hell (= Skt. and Pali id.), a hot hell acc. to Mvy 4927 and Dharmas 121; passim. Fem. e. g. RP 30.16 (vs) dāruṇam (short -a- m.c.) avīcim (end of line). Most forms, of course, are ambiguous as to gender. Cf. **āvīci**.

avīcika, adj., *pertaining to the hell Avīci*: Dbh.g. 12(348).18 dukham avīcikam utsahāmi; Gv 160.2–3 āparāntikāvīcikaduḥkhena (2d ed. °khe); m., *an inhabitant of Avīci*, Laṅk 138.4 kulaputro vā kuladuhitā vāvīciko bhavati. In the last two āvīcika might be intended; it is clearly read (as adj.) in MSV iv.251.9.

[**avustaṃ** LV 388.13 (vs), both edd., no v.l.; read **āvustaṃ,** q.v.]

avṛha, or **abṛha,** rarely **abṛhat** (= Pali aviha; Tib. on Mvy mi che ba *not great*, abṛhat noted only Gv 249.10 abṛhac [chuddhāvāsa-]; this interpretation could be due to popular etymology; however, no other etym. is known for the Pali, and as the lowest of the five Śu. classes these gods may have been called [relatively] *not great*; cf. s.v. **bṛhatphala,** which gives some confirmation of the etymology), n. of a heavenly world, the first of the five śuddhāvāsa, and of a class of gods who inhabit it, see s.v. **deva**: usually spelled avṛha, Mvy 3102; Dharmas 128; Mv ii.314.8; 349.1; 360.22; LV 150.10; Divy 568.28; Mmk 43.21 (in 19.10 corruptly aṭṭaha); abṛha Divy 68.16; 138.23; 367.14; Av i.5.3; Bbh 62.5; **abṛhat,** see above.

avekṣavant, adj., n. sg. m. °vān (from Skt. avekṣā with -vant; Pali apekkhavant, with the same shortening of ā m.c.), *attentive* (to, loc.): Ud xiii.9, 10, 11; in 10 and 11 text unmetrically avekṣāvāṃ; same vss in Pali, Therag. 228–230, apekkhavā.

Avekṣita, nt., n. of a Buddhakṣetra: Mv i.123.14 °taṃ (Senart's em.; mss. °kṣataṃ).

avetya-prasāda, m. (= Pali avecca-ppasāda), *serenity based on trusting faith* (cf. Wogihara, Lex. 17): °daḥ Mvy 6823; buddhe 'vetya-prasādena AsP 59.20, and similarly in foll. (in Pali also with buddhe etc., loc.); °dalābhī Bbh 161.2, and °da-prāptaḥ 327.2.

a-vaira (adj., = Pali avera), *without enmity*; -tā, *state of being* . . .: śāmyanti vairāṇi °tābhiḥ MSV ii.184.8 (vs; so ms., ed. em. avairi°, needlessly). In Jm 127.17 avaira prob. noun, *non-enmity*, with pw 7.312.

Avaivarta, m., n. of a samādhi: Mvy 553, cited from Prajñāpāramitā; the list occurs in ŚsP where **Avivarta,** q.v., is read for this, 1419.3. Cf. next two.

avaivarta-caryā = **avivarta°, anivartana°,** qq.v.: Mv i.63.14 (mss.; Senart em. avivarta°).

avaivarta-varṇa, *with color not subject to passing away*(?): Gv 347.6 °ṇā, of a rātri-devatā.

avaivartika (perhaps the commonest BHS form of many equivalents; see also **avaivarta, °tya,** and s.vv. **anivart(i)ya, avivart(i)ya, avinivartya**), *not liable to turning back*: regularly of Bodhisattvas (usually this word being used; if not, of persons firmly set on the road to enlightenment, which is the same thing): SP 2.11; 264.12; 383.2; LV 23.2; 39.14; 181.6; 370.2; Mv i.82.8; 102.13; 104.8; 107.9, 12; 128.2, 6; Suv 81.8; 89.9; RP 56.4; Gv 104.3; 308.8 etc.; Dbh 1.8; Sukh 21.13 etc.; °ka-bhūmi Kv 82.10; Bbh 235.17–18; °ka-dharma LV 424.14 (here of the Tathāgata); Mv i.124.19; °ka-kṣāntipratilabdha SP 259.13 (see **kṣānti**); °ka-dharmacakra-SP 270.9.

Avaivartikacakra, nt., n. of a work: Mvy 1371.

avaivartika-tā, state of being **avaivartika**: Mv i.81.1; **-tva,** id., LV 432.10.

avaivartiya = °**tika**: Mv i.63.13 (but 3 mss. out of 6 °tika); 82.19 (v.l. °tika). Both prose.

avaivartya = °**tika**: SP 2.12 (of dharmacakra); LV 277.16 (-kṣāntipratilabdhāḥ); RP 59.18; Gv 287.12. All prose.

[**avoditāḥ** is kept in ed. with mss. at Divy 300.2. Instead, some form of the n. pl. m. of ppp. of ava-vad should be read; possibly ovaditāḥ or ovāditāḥ, if not avavad° or avavād°.]

avyakta, adj. (= Pali avyatta; neg. of **vyakta,** q.v.), (**1**) *ignorant*: SP 210.3 °tā akuśalā; LV 264.20 °to bālo; Divy 301.2 °tān apy akuśalān api; 617.18; (**2**) (cf. Skt. id., Pali avyatta) *obscure*: avyaktendriyaḥ Karmav 31.12, see s.v. **jihma.**

avyayaṃ, adv., *permanently*: LV 186.7 (prose) na khalv avyayaṃ kumāreṇa kadācid udyānabhūmim abhinirgantavyam, *the prince must never, as a permanent rule, go forth to the park.*

a-vyavakīrṇa, adj. (neg. of **vyava°,** q.v.; = Pali abbokiṇṇa), *uninterrupted*: ŚsP 1333.1, 3, etc. °ṇaiḥ . . . manasikāraiḥ.

avyavacāra, m., (neg. of **vyavacāra,** q.v.), *non-consideration, contempt, despising* (Tib. khyad du gsod pa, *despise*): Mvy 8510, in śikṣāpadadravyatāvyavacāraḥ, which I analyze °dravyatā-avyavacāraḥ, as the Tib. and the sense seem to require (the situation is that of Vin. iv.143.16–19; the Pali equivalent is vivaṇṇaka, line 19). It seems hardly possible that **vyavacāra,** without a neg., should have this mg.

a-vyavahāra, adj., *not capable of discussion* (mention in words, see BR s.v. vyavahāra 8); followed by syn. **anabhilapya,** Vaj 45.6, or **anabhilāpya,** Śikṣ 251.11.

?**avyaṣṭa,** in Mmk 51.7 (sarvamantramudrāsādhaneṣu ca) avyaṣṭo bhavati (read abhyasto, *practised, exercised*?).

avyākṛta, adj. (= Pali avyākata, *indeterminate*), *indistinct, neutral, median* (neither good nor bad): kuśalākuśalāvyākṛta- *good, bad, and indifferent*, Dbh 73.18; 74.14; 75.23; kuśalāś ca dharm' akuśalāś ca avyākṛtāś ca Dbh.g. 44(70).7.

a-vyāpanna, adj. (= Pali id.; neg. of **vyāpanna,** q.v., and cf. next), *unmalicious*: °na-citta Divy 302.9; Dbh 25.1; Gv 531.14 (with 2d ed. for 1st ed. adhyā°); °nena cittena Divy 105.18; °na-manaskāra SP 339.17; all *having unmalicious mind* or *thoughts.*

avyāpāda, m. (= Pali id.; neg. of **vyāpāda,** q.v.), *non-malice*: LV 32.22, see s.v. **vyāpāda**; Mvy 1597, see id.; Ud xv.18, read avyāpāde for text tyāpāde with initial syllable missing. (Tib. ḥchi ba med, *non-death* or *non-killing*, is due to false rendering of vyāpāda, in accord with regular Skt. usage.)

a-vyābadhya or °**vadhya,** adj. and nt. subst. (see next, and cf. Pali avyāpajjha, as mentioned there), (**1**) adj., *that cannot be injured* or *disturbed, inviolable*: Mv ii.259.15 °dhyaṃ (ms.) . . . dharmaṃ deśayiṣyati; 279.9 °dhyaṃ arthaṃ prārthayamāno; in both of these spelled avyāvadhyaṃ, and associated with asādhāraṇaṃ; (**2**) apparently subst., *not doing harm* (so Tib., gnod pa mi byed): LV 380.17 avyābadhyaṃ (Foucaux *la mansuétude*) sukhaṃ loke. There is a v.l., in mss. usually regarded as the best, adhyāvadhya; one might conjecture a-vyāvadhya, or °bādhya, ger., *not committing injury.* But the context suggests that a nom. sg. noun is intended, sukhaṃ being apparently predicate (Foucaux *douce*); so Tib. takes it. In all of these forms the root vadh may have been felt to be concerned; or the short a of the root may be semi-MIndic (based on forms of bādh which are certainly commoner).

a-vyābādha, also written °**vādha,** in MSV i.97.19 wrongly °vāda, adj. (cf. prec. and next, also **vyābādha** etc.; corresponds to Pali avyāpajjha, avyābajjha), apparently usually *free from injury, inviolable, secure,* but possibly in some passages *free from injuriousness,* i. e. *not given to injuring others, kindly*; the Pali equivalent appears to be interpreted in the same two ways, but it is not easy to distinguish them clearly: Mvy 1508 maitrīsahagatena cittenā 'vaireṇā 'sapatnenā 'vyābādhena; to this passage corresponds Mv iii.213.13 (cetasā . . .) avaireṇā 'vyābādhena (so Senart em., mss. 'vyābaddhena or °rddhena); also Dbh 34.(18–)19 (maitrīsahagatena cittena . . .) avaireṇā 'sapatnenā 'nāvaraṇenā 'vyābādhena; and in Pali DN ii.242.11 (cetasā . . .)averena avyāpajjhena; the mg.

uninjurious, kindly might be assumed in SP 288.8 (prose) (bodhisattvo . . .) avyāvādho bhavati, but Kern *unmolested*, and similarly Burnouf. Cf. avyābādhya, said of a Bodhisattva, Bbh 73.21.

a-vyābādhya, adj. (cf. prec.), *that cannot be injured, inviolable, undisturbed*: said of puṇya Bbh 19.21, 22; 20.24, 26; of sukha, 25.13; 26.9 (there are four avyā° su°, listed as naiṣkramya-, praviveka-, upaśama-, and saṃbodhi-su°); 27.2, 6; of a Bodhisattva, 73.21 (cf. avyābādha SP 288.8).

avyāvadhya, see **avyābadhya.**

a-vyoṣita, adj., ppp. (neg. of Skt. vyavasita; but actually Sktization of Pali a-v(y)osita, acc. to CPD *who has not reached his place of rest*, i. e. *final emancipation*), *restless, unsteady, activated by desires* (for, loc.): pāpeccha (text pāye°) vyoṣita (read avyo°) pātra-cīvare Samādh p. 53 line 4 (vs); kūleṣu (read ku°?) cāvyoṣita lābhakāmāḥ 5 (vs); bhonti utsukāḥ, pāneṣu cāvyoṣita teṣu lajjāḥ (? doubtless corrupt; lagnāḥ?) 12 (vs).

a-vraṇa, see **vraṇa.**

(**aśate**,) **asate**, 1 sg. ase (to Skt. aś-nāti), *I eat* (cf. Pali *asati, pres. pple. asamāna, etc.): Mv ii.56.10 amṛtaṃ pi no ase (so with mss.), *I do not eat even nectar*; the corresponding Pali vs, Jāt. v.397.29, has udakaṃ pi nāsmiye (asmiye, *I* [*would*] *eat*, see CPD s.v.).

[**Aśanī**? see **As°**.]

aśabala, adj. (= Pali asabala, in same sense and associated with akammāsa, DN ii.80.24), *unspotted, pure*, of brahmacarya (together with **akalmāṣa**, q.v.): Mv i.211.11 = ii.15.10; of śīla, MPS 2.34.

aśāta, also **asāta**, adj. (and subst. nt.?) (= Pali asāta; neg. of **śāta**, q.v.), *unpleasant, disagreeable*: asātā vedanā (acc. pl.), *disagreeable pains* (same phrase in Pali) Mv i.5.9; asātānubhavanaṃ (Śikṣ aśāt°) duḥkhaṃ Śāl 81.2; Śikṣ 222.9 anandāsātakāntārāṇi AsP 367.19; *displeased, averse, offended*: Mv iii.16.4 sudarśanāpi . . . asātā vāreti. Cf. also **viśāta.**

aśāśvatam (after anucchedam) in LV 423.10 (prose), applied to the (dharma-)cakra, is misunderstood by Foucaux (*non immobile*). Like everything in the universe acc. to the śūnyavāda, it is *neither annihilable nor eternal*; neither of these attributes, nor any attribute contrastable with an opposite, can be predicated of anything. Tib. rtag pa med pa, *not eternal*. See **śāśvatoccheda** and references there to Laṅk.

aśitaka, aśita(ka) = **āśītakī**, q.v.

Aśucikuṇapa, (prob.) m., n. of a hell (*of impure corpses*): °pam, acc. sg., Jm 197.5.

aśubhata-saṃjñi(n), *engaging in contemplation of the offensiveness* (of corpses; see **aśubha-bhāvanā, -saṃjñā**), Śikṣ 328.10 (vs). I take aśubhata- as = aśubhatā (m.c.), *offensive-ness*, so substantially = aśubha (-saṃjñā, with suffix -in). Bendall assumes the adverbial suffix -ta(s).

aśubha-bhāvanā, f. pl. °nāḥ Mvy 1155; Bbh 98.18 (read aśubha-bhāvanā for ed. aśubhā-bh°); or **aśubhasaṃjñā**, Bhīk 27a.2 (= Pali asubha-bhāvanā or -saññā), see **saṃjñā**, *contemplation of offensive things*, specifically of human corpses in various states of disintegration; there are nine (in Pali, Vism. i.110.29–31 ten) such monkish disciplines, elsewhere called simply nava saṃjñāḥ, *the nine concepts* (of offensive things), ŚsP 59.1; 1258.5; a less schematized passage of the same sort in older Pali, MN i.58.9 ff. In Mvy 1156–64 they are listed, each cpd. with -saṃjñā: (1) **vinīlaka-**, (2) **vipūyaka-** (so read), (3) **vipaḍumaka-**, (4) **vyādhmātaka-**, (5) **vilohitaka-**, (6) **vikhāditaka-**, (7) **vikṣiptaka-**, (8) **vidagdhaka-**, (9) **asthi-saṃjñā** (see each of these). Bhīk 27a.2–3 agrees except that it transposes Nos. 5 and 6 and accidentally omits 8 (which perhaps should be put after 9; only Mvy has it before 9). There are three lists (one incomplete, one very corrupt) in ŚsP 59.1 ff., 1258.5 ff., 1431.19 ff. (six items only; cited from the last, with only four items one of which is not in this ŚsP list, in Śikṣ 211.1). Barring corruptions, the ŚsP lists agree with Mvy and Bhīk except in order of the terms, in which they show some (slight) resemblance to the Pali (Vism.) arrangement. ŚsP 1 (Śikṣ 1) = Vism 1 = Mvy 4; ŚsP^{3} (= 1431.19 ff.) 2 = Śikṣ 2 = Vism 2 = ŚsP^{1} (= 59.1 ff.) and ^{2} (= 1258.5 ff.) 5 = Mvy 1; ŚsP and Śikṣ 3 = Vism 3 = Mvy 2; Śikṣ 4 (not in ŚsP^{3}) = ŚsP^{1} and ^{2} 2 = Vism 9 = Mvy 3; ŚsP^{1} and ^{2} 4 = ŚsP^{3} 5 = Vism 8 = Mvy 5 (Bhīk 6); ŚsP^{1} and ^{2} 6 = ŚsP^{3} 4 = Vism 5 = Mvy 6 (Bhīk 5); ŚsP^{1} and ^{2}, Mvy 7 = ŚsP^{3}, Vism 6; ŚsP^{1} and ^{2} 8 = Vism 10 = Mvy 9; ŚsP^{1} and ^{2} 9 = Mvy 8 (omitted in Bhīk; Vism 4 has a different term, vicchiddaka, *fissured* Pe Maung Tin; Vism 7 hata-vikkhittaka is a variation on Vism 7 vikkhittaka = Mvy 7). On the meanings, as well as the variants and corruptions, see the terms as listed above from Mvy.

aśeṣa, nt., a high number: Mmk 343.26 (= 10 **gharā**; see **mahāśeṣa**).

aśaikṣa, m. (= Pali asekha, asekkha; neg. of **śaikṣa**, q.v.), *one who no longer needs religious training*, being in the 8th stage (see Childers s.v. sekho); = **arhant**: °ṣaḥ Mvy 1734; °ṣa-mārgaḥ Mvy 1320, the third parivarta of the dharmacakra, in which 'misery is known, its origin abandoned, its suppression attained, the way leading to its suppression realized' (1321–24). Often in cpd. śaikṣāśaikṣa, or bracketed with śaikṣa as separate word; see **śaikṣa**; its place may be taken by arhant, e. g. Mv i.158.7; Divy 399.24. Written aśaiṣya in LV 250.18, see s.v. **śaiṣya.**

Aśoka, n. pr.: (**1**) name of a former Buddha, Mv iii.238.6, 7; (**2**) name of a nephew and disciple of the Buddha Kāśyapa, Av i.237.14 ff.; (**3**) name of a king who lived in the time of the Buddha Krakucchanda, Divy 418.26 f.; (**4**) name of a yakṣa, Māy 68; (**5**) name of an uncle of King Mahāpraṇāda, and previous incarnation of **Bhaddālin**, q.v., Divy 59.20; 60.10; (**6**) name of the historic emperor, Mvy 3653; Mmk 606.14; Karmav 154.14; was given the epithet **Dharmāśoka**, q.v.; his family name was **Maurya**, q.v.; he lived 100 years after Buddha's death acc. to Av ii.200.7; in Divy 364.17 ff. is told first his previous life as **Jaya**, in which he gave some dust (this is the pāṃśu-pradāna) to the Buddha, made a **praṇidhāna**, and hence became later the emperor Aśoka, 368.26 ff.; his birth and life as emperor, 370.10 ff.

aśoka-bhāṇḍa, nt., LV 141.13; Mv ii.48.4; and **-bhāṇḍaka**, nt., LV 141.10, 16; 142.3, 5, 6, 11 (but many mss. -bhāṇḍa in some of these), perhaps lit. *good-luck* (no-sorrow) *articles-of-value*; *gifts of largess*, said of presents (of gold, silver, and jewels, LV 141.14) provided by Śuddhodana for Prince Siddhārtha to give to the maidens who appeared before him as possible brides. Acc. to pw, *present to an affianced bride*; but note that the prince gives them to *all* the girls who present themselves, LV 142.4–5.

Aśokavarṇa, n. of a future cakravartin who is to become a pratyekabuddha: Divy 140.21; 141.2.

Aśokaviraja, m., n. of a kalpa: Gv 233.14.

Aśokaśrī, (**1**) m., name of a Buddha: Śikṣ 169.12; (in the south) ŚsP 32.1 (misprinted Aśīka°); (**2**) f., n. of a deity of the bodhisattva-saṃgīti-prāsāda in Kapilavastu: Gv 385.19.

Aśokasattva, n. of a former Buddha: Mv i.141.4.

Aśokā (= Pali Asokā), n. of a leading female laydisciple under Maṅgala Buddha: Mv i.248.19; 252.8.

(**aśokāhvaya**,) with 'hiatus-bridging m' (m.c.) aśokam-āhvaya, adj., *of auspicious name*: voc. °ya Mv i.68.3 (vs); so mss., addressed by Kāśyapa to Aniruddha; for this mg. of aśoka cf. **aśoka-bhāṇḍa(ka)**. Senart em. aśeṣam āhvaya, but does not indicate how he interprets āhvaya, which in both Skt. and Pali (avhaya) is used chiefly at the end of cpds. meaning *having* . . . (as) *name.*

aśmagarbha (mss. sometimes asma°), m. or nt. (only Lex. in Skt. except once in a Jain work, pw 7 Add.; recorded nowhere else; popular etym. based on [aśma-] marakata?), *emerald*: n. sg. °bham Mvy 5957; °bho, °bhaḥ Divy 51.24; 229.7; 502.7; Av i.205.3; other forms SP 50.5; 151.2; 153.3–4; 239.7; 256.12; LV 383.2; Mv ii.302.9; 309.16; 310.8; Mvy 6245; Divy 115.3; 297.25; Mmk 63.19; 436.11; Gv 52.15.

aśmantaka, m. or nt. (Skt. Lex.; whether it occurs in this sense in Skt. literature seems doubtful, cf. BR 5.1071), *stove*: Karmav 22.3, 5.

Aśmāparāntaka, MSV iv.186.7, f. °**tikā**, 188.8 *belonging to the country* (janapada, 186.7) called by that name, which is supported by regular Tib. tradition; see **aparāntaka.**

a-śraddadhāna-tā (§ 22.42), *state of not believing, infidelity*: RP 18.1–2.

a-śraddadhānīya, adj., *incredible*, SP Kashgar rec., for a-śraddheya acc. to Kern, Preface, p. vii.

a-śraddha, adj. (neg. of **śraddha**; = Pali a(s)saddha), (**1**) *not credulous* (in good sense; Pali saddha sometimes *credulous*, in bad sense), °dhaś cākṛtajñaś ca Ud xxix.33 = Pali Dhp. 97; (**2**) *unbelieving, not having* (true) *faith*, Av i.83.7 (ms.; ed. em. aśrā°).

? **aśraddhya**, var. for **āśraddhya**, q.v.

[**a-śrāddha**, adj., *unbelieving, not having* (true) *faith*: Av i.83.7, ed. by em.; but ms. **a-śraddha**, q.v.]

a-śrāddhya, nt. (= **āśraddhya**, q.v.; Pali assaddhiya), *disbelief, lack of* (true) *faith*: Dharmas 30,69.

a-śrāmaṇaka, adj. (= Pali assām°; cf. **śrām**°), *unseemly for monks*: °kāni karmāṇi MSV iii.16.1.

a-śrāmaṇya, adj. (= Pali asāmañña), *not devoted to monks*; regularly with amātṛjña, apitṛjña, and abrāhmāṇya, see s.v. **amātṛjña** for references; in Mvy 2460 °yam, nt., following abrāhmaṇyam, also nt., but just before apitṛjñāḥ, amātṛjñāḥ, m. pl.; perhaps collective, *the group of those who are not devoted to monks*?

aśruka, nt. (= Pali assuka; Skt. aśru), *tear*: °kāni Mv i.326.4 (prose).

a-śreṇika, adj. (neg. of **śreṇika**), with parivrājakaḥ ŚsP 615.9, an uncomplimentary epithet of a wandering mendicant, *not a* **śreṇika** (q.v.).

aśleṣa, m., *non-binding, disconnection, freedom*: AsP 294.18–19 yaḥ . . . rūpasyāsaṃbandhaḥ sa rūpasyāśleṣaḥ . . . sa rūpasyānutpādo 'nirodhaḥ.

aśleṣaka, adj., applied to colors: °kai raṅgaiḥ Mmk 61.14; 68.8; 74.22; °kair varṇaiḥ id. 289.11; 304.15; 699.17; 702.6; °kair varṇakaiḥ 318.7; 322.20; 567.25; perhaps *not bound or mixed* (with foreign substances), *pure*; so apparently Lalou, Iconographie p. 30, l. 3, *couleurs franches*; she cites Tib. (78.24) as chon (read surely tshon) ma ḥdres, *unmixed color.*

a-śloka (m.; = Pali a-siloka), *dispraise, ill-repute, blame*: aśloka-bhaya- *fear of blame or ill-repute*, Śikṣ 296.6; Dbh 13.6.

-aśva, see **gajāśva.**

aśvaka, m., (**1**) (= Pali assaka) *toy-horse*: °kāḥ Jm 63.10; (**2**) n. of one of the **Ṣaḍvārgika** (q.v.) monks, Mvy 9475; = Pali Assaji, one of the chabbaggiya monks; with **Punarvasuka** disciplined for immoral conduct, MSV iii.15.21 ff.; cf. **Aśvaki(n)** = **Aśvajit** as one of the bhadravargīya monks; Aśvaka was later incarnate as a nāga, MSV i.xviii.5.

Aśvakarṇa, m. (= Pali Assakaṇṇa), n. of one of the 7 mountains surrounding Sumeru (Kirfel, Kosm. 186): ~~Mv~~ ii.300.18; Mvy 4141; Divy 217.6, 7; Dbh 96.4; (with Sumeru eight,) Dharmas 125.

Aśvaki(n), = **Aśvajit**, q.v., in Mv only: Mv iii.328.20 (°kī, nom.); °kī also iii.139.5; °ki (m.c., nom.) 13; °kinā (instr.) 8; °kisya (gen.) iii.337.5; 339.1.

Aśvagupta, n. of a son of Gupta the perfumer: Divy 351.14.

Aśvaghoṣa, n. of a teacher (and author): Mvy 3480.

Aśvajit (= Pali Assaji, one of the pañcavaggiyā bhikkhū; cf. **Aśvaki[n]**), n. of one of the five monks (see **bhadravargīya**, with variants): SP 1.10; LV 1.7; Mvy 1037; Divy 268.6; Sukh 2.3.

Aśvatīrthika, var. °**aka**, n. of a nāga: Divy 184.5 ff.

(**aśvapṛṣṭha**, m., is not exclusively BHS, though not clearly defined in BR (s.v. pṛṣṭha) or pw (s.v. aśvap°); cf. Pali assapiṭṭha; *the art of riding horseback*: °thaḥ Mvy 5003 = Tib. rta la gzhon pa, *riding on a horse*; LV 156.10, in list of arts mastered by Prince Siddhārtha; Divy 58.24; 100.10; 442.6.)

? **Aśvara**, read prob. Aśvala, n. of a ṛṣi: Mmk 18.18.

Aśvaśīrṣa, n. of a nāga king: Māy 246.28.

Aśvastha, n. of a mountain: Māy 253.35.

aṣṭa, ppp. of aśnoti (Vedic -aṣṭa in cpds.), *obtained*: LV 390.9 (vs) aṣṭam arthaṃ. A word-play is clearly intended; see **Aṣṭaṃga.** (Calc. reads iṣṭam, without support of any of Lefm.'s mss.)

Aṣṭaka (= Pali Aṭṭhaka), n. of a king: Mv iii.375.7 (vs); he is otherwise in Mv always called **Aṣṭamaka**, q.v.

aṣṭaka-rātri, in LV 251.6 (prose) haimantikāsv aṣṭakarātriṣu (read aṣṭakā°?), *the nights between the eighth days after the full moon of the two winter months*, see CPD s.vv. aṭṭhakā, antaraṭṭhaka.

Aṣṭaṃga, m. (for *Astaṃga = Pali Atthaṃga; Skt. Asta; ṣṭ for st seems arbitrarily used for the sake of word-play with aṣṭam in the next line, § 2.61, see **aṣṭa**), n. of the western (sunset) mountain: LV 390.8 aṣṭaṃgo nāma parvataḥ . . . aṣṭam arthaṃ dadātu vaḥ. (Some mss. aṣṭamo, so Calc.; all have ṣṭ.)

Aṣṭabhaginī, n. of the gotra of the nakṣatra Revatī: Divy 641.11.

aṣṭamaka, (**1**) adj. or subst. m. (= Pali aṭṭhamaka, see CPD s.v.), *one who is in the eighth* (and lowest) *stage of* (Hīnayāna) *religious development*, = **srotaāpanna**-phala-pratipannaka (Dharmas 102; for the Pali see Childers, cited s.v. **śaikṣa**): Mv i.120.9 (prose) aṣṭamake dhutā vedanāgṛddhā bhāvanān (so with all mss.; or read °nām; Senart em. °nā) uttrasanti, said of backsliding Bodhisattvas, *being eager for the sensations which are* (or should be) *destroyed* (even) *in a person in the lowest stage of religious development, they shrink from self-cultivation* (bhāvanā); Senart fails to understand; Mv i.159.8 aṣṭamakādikā pudgalā yāvad arhatpudgalā (mss. puṃgalā both times), *from the srotāpanna to the arhat*; aṣṭamaka-bhūmi, here the third of the (seven) bhūmi of a śrāvaka, Mvy 1143; ŚsP 1473.12 et alibi, see **bhūmi** 4; aṣṭamaka-dharma, *the conditions* (or religious principles) *of a person in this stage*, ŚsP 1555.11; (**2**) m., n. of the king otherwise called **Aṣṭaka**, q.v.: Mv iii.364.7; 365.18; 366.7; 373.23; (**3**) n. of a nāga king: Māy 246.22; (**4**) n. of a maharṣi: Māy 256.13.

Aṣṭamahābhaya-tārā, Sādh 208.6, or **-tāriṇī**, 207.1, n. of a goddess, a form of Tārā.

aṣṭamika, nt. (also **āṣṭa**°, q.v.), *food given away on the feast of the eighth lunar day*: Mvy 5758.

aṣṭavat-, in cpd., seems = aṣṭa, *eight* (§ 22.50): prāsādā uccaistvenāṣṭavat-talāḥ SP 341.10 (vs), *palaces eight floors in height*; so Tib. brgyad brtseg.

Aṣṭasāhasrikā-prajñāpāramitā, n. of a work (= AsP): Mvy 1328; referred to Śikṣ 37.13 as Prajñāpāramitā Aṣṭasāhasrikā.

aṣṭāṃśa, adj. (= Pali aṭṭhaṃsa; for Skt. aṣṭāśri, perhaps by confusion with Skt. aṃśa), *eight-edged*, of the jewel (maṇi-ratna) of a cakravartin: MSV i.36.5.

aṣṭāṅga (Pali aṭṭhaṅga), (**1**) *having 8 members or parts*; so often of the 8-fold way, e. g. Mv iii.332.10 āryāṣṭāṅgo mārgo; Gv 521.5 aṣṭāṅga-poṣadhe (see **poṣadha**;

Pali aṭṭhaṅguposatha; = *observance of the sabbath maintaining the* 8 [first of the 10] *precepts*, sīla, see CPD s.v.); prob. this is meant by °ga-samanvāgataṃ vrataṃ Av i.170.13 and °ga-samanvāgata upavāsa 339.7 ff.; (**2**) either alone, as Bhvr., or aṣṭāṅgopeta, *having 8* (unspecified good) *qualities*, substantially = *excellent, fine, supreme*, so Pali aṭṭhaṅga (-samannāgata, etc.), said of food, fields, men, a voice; in BHS I have recorded it only of water (! with never any indication of any specific 8 qualities): Mv ii.365.7 aṣṭāṅga-jala (mss., confirmed by quotation Śikṣ 299.13); 386.20 (vs) aṣṭāṅgupetāṃ (but prob. read with v.l. °taṃ, and jala as separate word) jala (text cpds. with next) śobhamānāṃ ... puṣkiriṇyo; Av ii.84.15 aṣṭāṅgopetaṃ pānīyaṃ; Śikṣ 350.8 aṣṭāṅgopetapānīya-; aṣṭāṅgopeta-, also of water, Kv 8.1; 60.11; Mmk 105.20; Gv 100.25 (misprinted °pata); 163.10; 193.20; 202.20; AsP 363.5; Sukh 93.16; aṣṭāṅga-vāriparipūrṇā Kv 12.20; aṣṭāṅga-saliladhārābhiḥ Mmk 444.3; aṣṭāṅga sad-vāri Gv 336.7 (vs); °ga-saṃmitam (mss. °mataṃ, read so?) Mv iii.94.5 (vs), ep. of **sopānīya(ṃ)**, q.v.

aṣṭāṅgika, adj. (= Pali aṭṭhaṅgika), *of 8 members*, said of the *way* (mārga) to the release from misery (more commonly **aṣṭāṅga**): LV 183.7; 414.13; Mv iii.456.21; Ud xii.4 (these all vss); Dharmas 50 (here the 8 stages are listed).

Aṣṭādaśavakra, m., n. of a mountain: Divy 103.2; 106.26, 28.

Aṣṭādaśavakrikā, n. of a river: Divy 106.28; 107.1.

[**aṣṭuñcaka**, nt., var. for **ākañcuka**, q.v.]

a-saṃvara (m.; Pali id.; neg. of **saṃvara**, q.v.), instr. °reṇa KP 130.1–2, 3, 4, 8, or abl. °rato 130.6, *not according to prescription* or *rule*: 130.1–2 bheṣajyam (= bhai°) upayujyāsaṃvareṇa kālaṃ kuryāt, *using medicine not in the way prescribed, he would die*. Tib. renders cho ga, usually = vidhi or ācāra, but later sdom pa (= saṃvara, Mvy 1608 etc.); (in the more usual sense of saṃvara) KP 103.3 tatra na saṃvaro (*restraint*) nāsaṃvaraḥ.

a-saṃvaraṇa, adj. (neg. of Skt. saṃvaraṇa), *free from obstruction*: Mv i.204.5 = ii.7.20 sarvadiśā (or °śāṃ) kurutha asaṃvaraṇā (or °ṇāṃ), *make all directions free from obstruction* (for him).

a-saṃvāsika, m., and f. °**kā** (cf. next, and Pali id. and asaṃvāsa, same mg.), (a monk or nun) *that is denied the right of living with the order*; *one expelled from the monastic community*: °kaḥ Mvy 8758; MSV ii.204.11; °kā Bhīk 16b.2.

a-saṃvāsya, and f. °**yā** (cf. Pali asaṃvāsiya; see PTSD s.v. saṃvāsiya), = prec.: °yaḥ, °yo Prāt 477.2; Bbh 46.19; °yā Bhīk 28b.1.

asaṃvidita, perhaps *unperceived, not consciously grasped*: in Mv i.41.5 and iii.334.8 (both somewhat corrupt, prob. intending) asaṃviditā asaṃviditapūrvā (lokāntarikā, sc. nirayā or narakā); in Mv ii.162.10 Senart also reads asaṃviditapūrvā, mss. (aghā)-saṃvidhipūrvā. The three other Mv versions of this formulaic passage have (aghā) aghasaṃbhūtapūrvā, or (aghā) asaṃbhūtā asaṃbhūtapūrvā. All these are corruptions of an original prob. to be reconstructed as aghā aghasaṃvṛtā; the Pali has aghā asaṃvutā (brilliantly corrected by Senart, Mv i n. 405–6, to aghā aghasaṃvutā); LV and ŚsP aghā aghasphuṭā (*full of misery*, substantially = aghasaṃvṛtā *enwrapped in misery*). See discussion of the passage s.v. **lokāntarikā**.

[**asaṃvivāda-**, *not breaking one's word*, in °daparamatā: Gv 89.3; apparently error for Skt. a-visaṃvāda; curiously the same error is recorded once in Skt. a-saṃvivādi-tā, see BR 7.473, for a-visaṃvādi-tā, 6.1270.]

asaṃvṛta, (**1**) adj. (= Pali asaṃvuta; apparently not in this sense in Skt., tho saṃvṛta *restrained* occurs), *uncontrolled, unrestrained* (cf. **saṃvara, saṃvṛti**): LV 87.13; 138.13; vācā asaṃ° MSV ii.210.14; (**2**) subst. nt.: LV 372.7 (vs) ṣoḍaśa asaṃvṛtānī *the 16 uncontrolled things* (... chinnāni mayeha saṃsthena; said by the Buddha at the Bodhimaṇḍa). I have no clue to what is meant and have found no parallel. The passage is omitted in Foucaux's Tib.; his transl. of Skt. says *omissions*. Cf. asaṃvara, '*indiscipline*', AbhidhK. LaV-P. iv. 57 (?).

asaṃskṛta, adj. and subst. nt. (= Pali asaṃkhata, ep. of nibbāna, perh. as *uncreated by a combination of factors*, but see CPD), *unconditioned*; as nt., one of three *unconditioned things*. The adj. occurs e. g. Laṅk 189.14. The three asaṃskṛtāni are ākāśa, pratisaṃkhyā-nirodha (which = nirvāṇa), aprati° (see **pratisaṃkhyā** and **aprati°**), Dharmas 32; in Mvy 2184 °tam, but 2185–6 name only the 2d and 3d, not ākāśa; without mention of the term asaṃskṛta, and with substitution of nirvāṇa-(-dhātu) for pratisaṃkhyānirodha, the three are named Laṅk 177.3; 197.12; see also AbhidhK. La V-P. i.7.8.

a-saṃkathya, adj. (neg. gdve. of Skt. saṃkathayati), *not fit to be talked with*; *to be avoided in social relations*: Laṅk 61.13; 331.10 °yāḥ.

Asaṃkīrṇa, n. of a former Buddha: Mv i.139.1.

asaṃkrānti-tā, *condition of not passing* (into another state): Dbh 36.25 sa sarvadharmāṇām asaṃkrāntitāṃ cāvināśitāṃ ... vyavalokayati.

a-saṃkliṣṭa (= Pali asaṃkiliṭṭha), *not impure*, see **saṃkliśyati**.

asaṃkhya, nt., a high number: Mvy 8040.

? **asaṃkhyaya**, adj., *innumerable*, occurs repeatedly (instead of regular asaṃkhyeya) in mss. of LV, and is sometimes adopted by Lefm. in the text: 86.15 (vv. ll. asaṃkhya, asaṃkhyeya); 112.4 (with most mss., v.l. °khyeya). Weller 23 would read asaṃkhyeya always, perhaps rightly; but the frequent occurrence of °khyaya in the mss. is strange. Like Weller I am unable to understand the long ā in asaṃkhyayā-kalpakoṭi- 86.15; probably read °ya- as in 112.4. Instr. of a-saṃkhyā unlikely.

asaṃkhyeya, (**1**) adj. (= Skt. id., Pali asaṃkheyya), *innumerable*. In Pali (see Childers s.v. kappo) as an adj., applied to kappa (see BHS **kalpa**), denotes a world-age of a certain extent; in some definitions at least, of a length intermediate between a mahā- and an antara-k°. Acc. to La Vallée Poussin, AbhidhK iii.188, asaṃkhyeya kalpa means here *le temps que durent un nombre asaṃkhyeya* (10 à la 59me puissance) *de mahākalpas*. I have not noted the Pali usage in the texts excerpted by me (but see Przyluski, Açoka, 408). Typical of their use of this adjective with kalpa is SP 17.8 asaṃkhyeyaiḥ kalpair asaṃkhyeyatarair vipulair aprameyair acintyair etc., in which asaṃkhyeya has its normal Skt. mg. of *innumerable*; (**2**) nt., a very high number: Mvy 7802; 7932 (cited from Gv); Gv 106.20; 134.5; SP 316.7; Sukh 31.2; Divy 245.11 tribhir asaṃkhyeyair; 246.2; 254.3.

asaṃkhyeya-parivarta, m. (Mvy) or nt. (Gv 134.6), *square of* prec. (2): Mvy 7803; 7933 (cited from Gv): Gv 106.20 (gen.); 134.6 °tam, n. sg.

Asaṅga, (**1**) n. of an author: Sādh 325.4 (= 3?); (**2**) n. of a yakṣa: Māy 43; (**3**) see **Āryāsaṅga**.

Asaṅgakāyaraśmitejomati, n. of a Bodhisattva: Gv 81.20.

Asaṅgacitta, n. of a Bodhisattva: Gv 81.6.

Asaṅgajñānaketudhvaja, n. of a Tathāgata: Gv 14.24.

Asaṅgadhāraṇī, n. of a samādhi: Mvy 811.

Asaṅgadhvaja, n. of a Bodhisattva: Gv 2.18.

Asaṅganetra, n. of a Bodhisattva: Gv 3.1.

asaṅga-pratibhāna, nt. and adj. (see **pratibhāna**), *unobstructed confidence* or *readiness* (in speaking): SP 330.4 (vs) °bhāni (so read with WT, for °bhāne; KN °bhāṇi) sthitā (read with WT °tāś ca) kecit; as adj., *possessing this faculty*, Mv i.119.16; asaṅga-pratibhāna-tā- (one ms. omits -tā, perhaps correctly, °bhāna being then a subst. as in SP 330.4) -pratilambho SP 327.6 (prose), *attainment of the state of possessing this faculty.*

Asaṅgabaladhārin, n. of a Buddha: Gv 257.20.

Asaṅgabalavīryamati, n. of a Bodhisattva: Gv 81.26.

Asaṅgabuddhi, n. of a Bodhisattva: Gv 4.13.

Asaṅgamati, n. of a Buddha: Gv 285.21.

Asaṅgamaticandra, n. of a Buddha: Gv 256.8.

Asaṅgamukha, n. of a method of 'Bodhisattva-salvation' (Bodhisattva-vimokṣa): Gv 69.22 ff.

Asaṅgamukhapraveśā, n. of a Bodhisattva-dhāraṇī: Mvy 754.

Asaṅgavyūha (m.?), n. of a method of 'Tathāgata-salvation' (T°-vimokṣa): Gv 80.23; 83.12.

Asaṅgaśrīgarbharāja: Gv 27.1, or (corruption) **Asaṅgaśrīrāja**: Gv 11.5 (corrected 2d ed.), n. of a Bodhisattva.

Asaṅgasvara, n. of a Bodhisattva: Gv 4.8.

Asaṅgottarajñānin, n. of a Bodhisattva: Gv 2.14.

asaṃgrāha, see **saṃgrāha.**

asaṃjñā-samāpatti, f., a kind of **samāpatti,** q.v.: Mvy 1502 = **asaṃjñi-samāpatti,** q.v.

[**asaṃjñika,** read **āsaṃjñika,** q.v.]

asaṃjñin (= Pali asaññi-n), *unconscious,* only noted in the cpds. which follow; cf. also āsaṃjñika.

asaṃjñi-sattva (= Pali asañña-satta), *having a nature that is free from consciousness,* or acc. to CPD *Unconscious Beings,* n. of a class of gods (see s.v. **deva**), one (in Dharmas and LV the 4th) of the classes of rūpāvacara gods of the 4th dhyāna-bhūmi (missing in the other standard lists of gods, but required to make up the standard count of 18 classes of gods in BHS or 16 in Pali): Dharmas 128; LV 150.9; Divy 505.23 (see s.v. **āsaṃjñika**); in Mvy 2297 mentioned as an example of dwellers in the 9th and highest **sattvāvāsa,** but this is certainly an error; they belong in the 5th sattvāvāsa, see this word. This is confirmed AbhidhK. LaV-P. ii.199. f., where the name is discussed, and it is said that they dwell in (a specially high part of) the **bṛhatphala** heaven.

asaṃjñi-samāpatti, f., also **asaṃjñā°,** q.v., *attainment of the state of those who are without consciousness* (**asaṃjñin,** q.v.), or *unconscious state of attainment*: Mvy 1987; AbhidhK. LaV-P. ii.200 f., with notes (it is lower than nirodha-samā°). See also **āsaṃjñika.**

Asadṛśaguṇakīrtidhvaja, n. of a Tathāgata: Gv 422.22.

a-saddadhāna, pres. m. pple. (MIndic for a-śradda°, which is a v.l. here), *not believing*: °no Mv ii.338.10.

asadha, read **asaḍha**? (see s.v. **śaḍha**), *not tricky*: in Mv ii.63.15 (vs) read prob. asaḍh' (mss. cited as asadh') ṛjjubhūto.

Asanī (read Aśanī, *devouring one*?), n. of a piśācī: Māy 239.6; n. of a rākṣasī: Māy 243.19.

asantaka, adj. (a-santa-ka, cf. **santaka**; ka-extension of a-extension of Skt. asa(n)t), *unreal*: SP 281.9 (vs) asantakā dharma ime.

a-saṃdhi, in Laṅk 160.11 ff. *non-attachment* = parimocana, *release*; neg. of **saṃdhi,** q.v., in the unusual sense of *attachment, binding,* which it has in this passage.

a-saṃdhūkṣaṇa-tā, see **saṃ°.**

asamanta, m. (Mvy) or nt. (Gv 134.9), a high number: Mvy 7808; 7940 (here cited from Gv); Gv 106.22 (gen.); 134.9 °tam (n. sg.).

asamanta-parivarta, m. (Mvy) or nt. (Gv 134.10), *square* of prec.: Mvy 7809; 7941 (here cited from Gv); Gv 106.22 (gen.); 134.10 °tam (n. sg.).

a-samanvāharitvā (neg. ger. of **samanvāharati**; cf. °**vāhṛtya**), *without giving thought to the matter; negligently*: Mv ii.97.10.

a-samanvāhāra, m. (cf. Pali asamannāhāra; neg. of **samanvāhāra,** q.v.), *lack of concentration* (with additional connotation of *heedlessness, negligence*): Divy 190.28 f.

a-samanvāhṛtya (neg. ger. of **samanvāharati,** q.v.: cf. °vāharitvā), *without having concentrated the mind* (by a special effort); in the phrase asamanvāhṛtyā 'rhatāṃ (or, 'rhacchrāvakapratyekabuddhānāṃ; or, śrāvakapratyekabuddhānāṃ) jñānadarśanaṃ na pravartate, *without having concentrated the mind* (by a special effort), *the insight-into-truth of arhats* (etc.) *does not operate*: Divy 84.6; 190.8; 313.10 etc.; Av i.244.16; 255.5.

asamaya-vimukta, adj. (= Pali °vimutta; opp. of **samaya-vi°,** q.v., with references), *released finally, without term, absolutely*: Mvy 1026.

asama-sama, adj. (= Pali id.), *without a peer, unequalled, supreme* (lit. having no equal like him? Müller, in Transl. of Sukh 9.16, *equal to the unequalled*): Mvy 6379; usually ep. of Buddhas or Bodhisattvas, LV 100.2; RP 4.12; Śikṣ 139.5; Sukh 9.16; of the five groups (**skandha,** 3) of factors in the development of dharma, Mvy 103; as n. of a former Buddha, Mv iii.231.3 f.; as n. of a samādhi, Mvy 587 (text asamasamā, but Index °mo, and so Mironov) = ŚsP 1422.13 (°mo).

asaṃprakampin, adj. (= Pali asaṃpak°; to sampra-kamp-; cf. **saṃprakampana**), *not subject to shaking*: Mv i.292.15 caturbhi vātehi asaṃprakampi.

a-saṃprakhyāna, nt. (neg. of **saṃ°,** q.v.), *lack of clarity, obscurity, confusion*: Mvy 2672 (follows saṃ°); 2478 = Tib. mi gsal ba (in a list of vices and faults). Note that **saṃprakhyāna,** q.v., is equated with **a-saṃmoṣa,** *non-confusion,* implying synonymity of saṃmoṣa and asaṃprakhyāna.

a-saṃprajanya, (**1**) nt. (neg. of **saṃ°,** q.v.; = Pali asaṃpajañña), *lack of intelligence* or *mindfulness* (CPD, *want of consideration* or *self-control*): Dharmas 69 (one of the upakleśa); Mvy 1978; Śikṣ 82.21 °nyācārin, *behaving with . . .*; 123.14 °nya-paratantra, *subject to . . .*; (**2**) adj. (Bahuvrīhi), *lacking in saṃprajanya*: Śikṣ 108.8 muṣitaśrutiś cāpi asaṃprajanyo; °-tā, *state of being . . .*: KP 95.10 (cittavikṣepa-)asaṃprajanyatā-duṣprajñatā-.

asaṃprajñāna, nt. (neg. to an unrecorded saṃprajñāna, from Skt. sam-pra-jñā-), *lack of perfect knowledge*: Mvy 6893 = Tib. śes bzhin ma yin pa.

a-saṃprabhīta, adv. °tam (neg. of ppp. of *sampra-bhī-, unrecorded), *in an unterrified manner*: Mv ii.281.3 °taṃ ca viloketi (mss. °kesi).

a-saṃpramuṣita (neg. of ppp. of **saṃpramuṣyate**) (**1**) *not deprived* (of what is expressed by preceding member of cpd.): Mvy 803 -cittāsaṃpramuṣitāḥ; LV 275.6 sarvadharma-dhāraṇy-asaṃpramuṣitaḥ; (**2**) *not taken away* or *not lost*: Gv 521.17 asaṃpramuṣitena smṛtibalādhānena.

Asaṃpramoṣa, m., n. of a samādhi: Mvy 526; ŚsP 1416.22 (misprinted °modho); 1417.2. Cf. **Bodhicittāsaṃpramoṣa.** As common noun (neg. of Skt. saṃpramoṣa, *disappearance, loss,* see s.v. **saṃpramuṣyate**) the word hardly needs recording; it means *non-disappearance, non-deprivation, non-loss,* e. g. Mvy 785; 961; etc.

a-saṃpramoṣaṇa (nt.; cf. prec. two), *the non-loss*: Suv 103.6 smṛty-asaṃpramoṣaṇāya, *unto non-loss of memory or mindfulness.*

a-saṃpravaṇa-tā (? neg. of sam plus pravaṇa, Pali poṇa), (state of being) *not devoted to, bent upon* (in comp.): Gv 525.12 kāyacittāsaṃpravaṇatayā (see s.v. **anāyūha**).

a-saṃpravedhana (nt.; to **saṃpravedhati,** q.v.), *non-shaking, non-perturbation*: Gv 463.22, cited Śikṣ 35.7 sarvaduḥkhāsaṃpravedhana-tayā, *because of the state of not being subject to perturbation by any sorrow.*

a-saṃpravedhin, adj. (= Pali asaṃpa°; as prec.), *not subject to shaking or perturbation*: Mv ii.300.5 (vs) acalo asaṃpravedhi (n. sg. m.); 383.22 °vedhī (n. sg. m.).

a-saṃbhinna, a-saṃbhedana, see **saṃ°.**

Asaṃbhrāntavacana, n. of a former Buddha: Mv i.141.12.

asaṃmoṣa (m.; prob. Sktized from Pali asammosa, neg. of sammosa, to mussati, historically connected with Skt. mṛṣyati; but acc. to CPD to Skt. root muṣ), *non-confusion* (synonym of **saṃprakhyāna,** *clarity,* q.v.): asaṃmoṣa-dharmāṇo Buddhā Bhagavantaḥ Divy 49.10; 50.21; 154.15; 178.6; 190.11; -jñāna-praveśāsaṃmoṣa-smṛti-vyūha-gato (2d ed. °garbho) nāma eṣa vimokṣaḥ Gv 524.12. Cf. next.

a-saṃmoṣaṇa-tā (cf. prec. and Pali asammosana-rasa, CPD), *state of having no* (mental) *confusion*: LV 440.17 (smṛti-nidhānaṃ, sc. pratilapsyate) asaṃmoṣaṇa-tayā.

a-sahita, adj. (= Pali id.), *not sensible,* see **sahita** (1).

a-sahya, (1) adj. (in Skt. *unendurable, insupportable; irresistible*), *that cannot be supported,* and so *in hopeless state, lost,* of a ship doomed to destruction: Divy 229.17 asahyaṃ vahanam; 502.14; (2) subst. (nt.), (what is insupportable,) *ill-health* or *bad luck* (cf. **sahya**): Divy 258.16 sahyāsahyaṃ pṛṣṭvā, *having asked about good or bad health* (fortune); (3) m., n. of a former Buddha (*irresistible*): Mv iii.237.8.

asahya-sāhin, adj. (only m. as epithet of a Buddha; = Pali asayha-sāhin, also so used), prob. *enduring* (or *sustaining, accomplishing*) *what cannot be endured* (*accomplished,* sc. by others); so the Pali comms. (e. g. on Pv ii.9.22) seem to take it; cf. Senart i n. 571, suggesting also the possibility *conquering the unconquerable* (but preferring the other): Mv i.255.16; 256.1 °sāhi (n. sg.), of Buddha; in Mv iii.109.19 read buddhasya asahyasāhino (for text °tāyino), with same verse in Pali Therag. 536 (asayhasā°).

asāta = **aśāta,** q.v.

asādiśa, see **sādṛśa.**

a-sāṃpreya, adj. (neg. of **sāṃ°,** q.v.; = Pali asappāya), *unfit, improper*: Prāt 526.15, as quasi-subst., *an improper thing*: (garhaṇīyam . . . sthānam āpanno 'smy) asāṃpreyaṃ pratideśanīyam (in a formula of confession).

asāraka, adj. (= Pali id., Skt. asāra), *unsubstantial, empty, worthless* (see synonyms below): LV 242.15 and Suv 57.14, of the body (kāya); SP 282.1, read with WT asārakā for KN na sārakā, of conditions of existence (dharmāḥ); Mv ii.145.19 (sarvadharmaṃ) riktakaṃ tucchakaṃ asārakaṃ, *empty, vain, unsubstantial*; AsP 346.(9–)10 (puṇyābhisaṃskāro bodhisattvasya . . . śūnyaka . . . riktaka) . . . tucchaka . . . asāraka ity evākhyāyate; śāstrāṇi . . . °kāni (so, with n) Mv i.79.5 (vs), *worthless* (false) *sciences* (of the world). In some or all of these pejorative force may reside in the suffix -ka.

Asiccheda, n. of a hell (cf. Asipattra): Kv 50.3 °de mahānarake.

asita, (1) adj. (*black,* and hence) *inauspicious, offensive*; so AMg. asiya = aśubha, Sheth, Ratnach.; not in Skt. or Pali: LV 327.8 (vs) na ca jara asitā, *and* (while) *there is no offensive old age* (so Tib, mi śis, normally = aśubha); (2) adj. (= Pali id.; a-sita), *unfettered, free*: of Buddha, MPS 12.9; MSV i.12.14; (3) m. (= Pali id.), n. of a well-known sage, 'the Buddhist Simeon': LV 101.1 ff. (his story told); 253.1, 15; Mv ii.30.13 ff. (his story; in 37.13 called **Kāla** (5), q.v., if Senart is right); 144.8; 151.12; he was the maternal uncle of **Nālaka,** q.v., Mv iii.382.16; Divy 391.6; (4) n. of a Bodhisattva: Gv 442.18; (5) m. or nt., n. of a plant, as var. in mss. for **āśītakī,** q.v.

Asitabhānu, n. of a former Buddha: Mv i.139.5.

Asidharā, n. of a rākṣasī: Māy 241.33.

(**asipattra,** occurs as n. of a hell in Skt., see Schmidt's Nachträge, and in Mmk 115.1 °ttre; presumably = the commoner asipattravana = Skt. id., Pali °patta°, *sword-leaf-wood,* e. g. Mmk 635.23; in this the trees have swords as leaves, which the wind blows down on those who live in it, Mv i.7.8.)

Asimuśaladharā, n. of a rākṣasī: Māy 243.32.

Asurakā, n. of a pool near Nirati, the city of the Kiṃnaras: Mv ii.111.5.

Asuradeva, n. of a former Buddha: Mv i.141.2.

Asuranemin, n. of a maharṣi: Māy 256.29. Cf. **Suranemin.**

Asuraprāmbhāra (! read °prāgbhāra?), n. of a mountain: Māy 253.34.

Asura-lipi, n. of a kind of script: LV 126.3 (confirmed by Tib. lha ma yin = asura).

Asurendrā, n. of a kiṃnara-maid: Kv 6.21.

asecana, adj. (Pali id., CPD; = next; partly m.c.? § 22.24), *delightful, blissful*: (of salvation) Mv iii.421.19 adhigacchati (mss. °anti) padaṃ śāntaṃ asecanaṃ ca mocanaṃ (°nakaṃ would be unmetrical); manāpāsecana-Mv iii.66.4–5 (prose).

asecanaka, adj. (= Pali id.; in BHS also **asecanīya, asecana,** and **āsec°,** qq.v.; etym. uncertain, cf. Tib. below), *charming, pleasing,* almost always, as in Pali, of sights (particularly of the appearance of persons, notably a Buddha) or sounds: Mvy 392 asecanako rūpeṇa (of Tathāgatas) = Tib. sku byad blta bas chog mi śes pa (chog śes pa = *content*), *having beauty of form which one cannot be satiated with looking at,* perhaps analyzing a-plus a form of secayati *cause to drip, saturate,* and so *satiate*; but I find no such meaning recorded for secayati or any relative. See CPD on Pali exegesis. Often associated with apratikūla, *not repulsive,* of both sights and sounds: asecanaka-darśana, *of lovely aspect,* of Buddhas LV 427.20; Mv iii.259.17; Divy 226.27; 251.21; 547.12; of a stūpa Divy 23.13; of the ocean, as compared to a park Gv 194.21 (mahodyānam . . . mahāsāgaram iva . . .) asecanaka-darśanam (1st ed. asevanaka°); foll. by apratikūla, darśanāye (or °ya), *fair and lovely to see,* of Buddhas Mv iii.64.10; 379.9; 407.8; 425.8; °nako (both edd. °kā-) rūpeṇa, of an emperor Gv 333.19; pañcā 'secanakā darśanena, hastī nāgaś ca rājā ca sāgaraś ca śiloccayo 'secanakā darśanena, Buddhaś ca bhagavatāṃ vara iti Divy 334.15–16; of sounds, (ghoṣo . . .) manojñaḥ asecanakaḥ apratikūlaḥ śravaṇāya Mv iii.226.17; 229.3; almost the same Sukh 36.1; 38.6; asecanakaś ca . . . apratikūlaś ca, of Buddha's voice Mv iii.343.1; (mahāpṛthivī . . . kampe, or kampayati . . .) ullokanīyaṃ ca asecanakaṃ (so, or **asecanīyaṃ,** q.v., mss.; Senart sometimes em. āsec°) ca apratikūlaṃ ca (adverbs: *in an admirable, charming, unrepellent way*) Mv i.207.1 = ii.10.11; iii.341.8 (of the quaking of the earth).

asecanīya, adj. (= **asecanaka,** q.v.), *charming, pleasing,* of sounds (śabdāḥ) LV 52.7; 411.10 (here several mss. asecanakā); and v.l. (one ms.) °yaṃ for asecanakaṃ, adv., Mv i.207.1 = ii.10.11.

Askhalitapravarāgra, n. of a former Buddha: Mv i.137.8.

astaṃgama (m.; = Pali atthaṃgama, used as synonym of nirodha, as in LV; not in Skt., which has astaṃgamana, *setting,* of heavenly bodies), *disappearance, cessation*: LV 263.(12–)13 jātijarāmaraṇasaṃbhavānām astaṃgamāya (v.l. °gamanāya).

astambhin, adj. (= BHS and Pali **acchambhin,** q.v.), *not paralyzed with fear, not frightened*: LV 84.14 asaṃtrastaḥ, astambhī; 318.12 anuttrasto 'stambhī adīno 'līnaḥ.

1 asti, (there, it) *is*: (1) alone or with nāma, in strong asseverations: Mv ii.145.15 (also 18, etc.), in response to a question, *I hope you don't see any bodily affliction,* etc.: asti tāta śarīre pratipīḍāṃ paśyāmi, *I do indeed* (*I certainly do*) *see affliction in the body*! etc.; iii.440.7 (without preceding question) asti nāma tvaṃ mohapuruṣo, *you are most certainly a man of delusion*!; (in response to a question, as in Mv ii.145.15) Jm 17.12 asti deva kiṃcid aham api . . . samanusmarāmi, *O yes indeed, my lord, I too have some remembrance* . . .!; Mv i.346.20 and 347.8

(and i.346.13 where text erroneously api for asti) asti nāma tvaṃ... adinnam anyātakaṃ śālim ādiyasi, *you most certainly are taking*...!; (**2**) in Divy 424.27 asti khalu me (printed as a complete sentence): ?perhaps *I have it*! = *I know what I have to do*! (followed by: pūrvaṃ rājño 'śokasya gṛhadvāram anuprāptaḥ); (**3**) as prior member of noun cpds. (Pali also atthi-dhamma, -bhāva, and natthi°): asti-dharma, m., *condition of being*, and asti-nāsti-bhāva, *condition of being and not being*: LV 393.7 (vs) na ca punar iha kaścid astidharmaḥ, so 'pi na vidyati yasya nāstibhāvāḥ, (8)... tasya na bhot' iha asti-nāsti-bhāvāḥ.

2 asti, noun (f.?), *property, goods*, only in comp. with parityāga or °gin: Gv 332.21 sarvāstiparityāgatayā, *by the process of giving away all property* (to beggars); 333.24 sarvāstiparityāgī; 540.6 sarvāstiparityāgena.

?**astopaka** or **astomaka,** see **āst°.**

asthāna, nt. (= Pali aṭṭhāna), opp. **sthāna** (4, 5), q.v., (**1**) *an impossibility*, generally followed by a clause introduced by yat: LV 232.17 asthānam etad... yat kumāro aprāpya bodhiṃ punar iha āgameyā, *it is impossible that the prince should return here without having attained enlightenment*; Av ii.4.6; often followed by the synonym **anavakāśo** (yat...), as in Pali aṭṭhānaṃ (etaṃ) anavakāso: Gv 498.5; Divy 174.1; 207.9; 264.5; 270.13–14; Dbh 25.14; Laṅk 198.9 asthānam anavakāśaṃ coktaṃ; in cpd. sthānāsthāna, *possibilities and impossibilities, sound and unsound propositions or conclusions*, Bbh 4.8; Mv i.134.12 sarvakarmeṣu nānāsthānāsthānakuśalāḥ *clever in regard to various sound and unsound conclusions* (or, *possibilities and impossibilities*) *in dealing with all actions*; sthānāsthāna-jñāna (Pali ṭhānaṭṭhāna-ñāṇa), *knowledge of*..., the first of the 10 bala of a Tathāgata, Mvy 120; Dharmas 76; LV 433.4; (**2**) *impropriety* (this is closer to Skt. usage, BR and pw): in Mv i.101.7 read asthānato for mss. asthānanto (Senart em. asthānatāye, unmetr.) *from* (because of) *non-place, non-propriety, impropriety*, see s.v. **asthānatā.**

asthāna-tā, *impropriety* (cf. **asthāna** 2): Mv i.101.2 kevattakāni karmāṇi asthānatāye na samupacaranti, *what actions do they refrain from performing, because* (such actions) *are improper*? Senart omits na, which mss. read, and so misunderstands the sentence (pp. xxx and 455). Below in l. 7 read asthānato, see **asthāna.**

asthi-bheda, m., acc. to pw 7 App., *Knochenbruch*; but rather *pain in the bones*, n. of a kind of disease: in lists of diseases, Bhīk 17a.2; Mvy 9525 = Tib. rus pa la zug pa, or, rus pa zugs pa; Chin. also *bone-pain*.

asthi-yantra, *skeleton*, in phrase asthiyantravad ucchrita-, of pretas: Divy 7.20; 8.19; MSV i.59.20; Av i.243.9 (Féer *se dressant comme un squelette*).

asthi-śakalā, °śaṅkalā, °saṃkalikā, °śakalīkṛta, °saṃkalībhūta (Pali aṭṭhi-saṃkhalā, °likā, see CPD), (*made, become*) *a skeleton*: °śaṅkalā, thrice in Kalpanāmaṇḍitikā, see Lüders, Kl. Skt. Texte 2, 42; °saṃkalikā Mv i.21.9 (°kāḥ, v.l. sakal°, parivarjyanti nirmānsā snāyusaṃyuktāḥ); 22.2 (°kāyo, mss. °kāyā, n. pl.); 24.9 (nirmānsā °kā); Śikṣ 211.9 (°kāṃ māṃsaśoṇitamrakṣitāṃ snāyuvinibaddhāṃ); °śakalā Divy 239.29; 240.3, 11; Divy Index takes śakalā as *skin*, against which see Lüders, who does not cite the Pali equivalent, which conclusively proves his and my interpretation; °śakalīkṛtaḥ, *made into a skeleton*, Divy 476.20 (preceded by nirmāṃso); °saṃkalībhūtāni (mṛtaśarīrāṇi) Śikṣ 211.11, *turned to skeletons*; CPD cites 'Skt.' asthi-śṛṅkhalī, which is a Lex. word said to be n. of a plant, only; but whether Senart is right in separating this (and Pali aṭṭhi-saṃkhalikā) from Skt. śṛṅkhalā (also °la), Pali saṅkhalā, °likā, *chain*, is doubtful; Senart assumes secondary influence in Pali of the latter on an orig. (aṭṭhi-)saṃkalā, °likā; but in AMg. the words for *chain*, saṃkala, °lā, °liyā (surely related to Skt. śṛṅkhalā) have k for kh, presumably by influence of AMg. saṃkalia = Skt. saṃkalita, *united* etc. (cf. also Pkt. saṃkalaṇa, Skt. °na), and the BHS words here treated might have a like origin. It is significant that BHS, like AMg., seems clearly to have **śaṅkalā** and **saṃkalā,** qq.v., *chain*.

asthi-saṃghāta, m. (= Pali aṭṭhi-saṃ°), *heap of bones, skeleton*: Divy 61.21 yatra kāśyapasya bhikṣor asthisaṃghāto 'vikopitas tiṣṭhati; 61.24; 76.27; 465.25.

asthi-saṃjñā (= Pali aṭṭhika-saññā), (contemplation of) *the notion of a skeleton*; one of the **aśubha-bhāvanā** or **-saṃjñā,** q.v.: Mvy 1164; Bhīk 27a.3; ŚsP 59.15; 1258.7 (here corruptly asmi-).

Asthisena (= Pali Aṭṭhisena; the 'correct' Skt. form prob. **Ārṣṭiṣeṇa,** cf. CPD), n. of a purohita's son, previous incarnation of the Buddha: Mv iii.418.19 ff. (called a **vanīpaka).**

Asthisenasya jātakaṃ (colophon), see prec., n. of a jātaka (= Pali Jāt. 403): Mv iii.420.5.

asthīkṛtya, ger. (= Pali atthikatvā, °tvāna), *paying careful heed to*: Mvy 1809. The Pali form is taken by comm. and modern exegetes as for arthīkṛtvā. Our form might be a false Sktization of this. But Tib. rus śiṅ ltar ḥdzin pa, *taking hold in persevering* (rus śiṅ; but lit. *bone-like*? rus pa, *bone*) *fashion* (alternatively, ched cher ḥdzin pa, *taking hold more and more, with intensity*). Is the resemblance of rus śiṅ to rus (pa) *bone* a mere coincidence? There is, however, a v.l. āsthī°, which suggests derivation from a form of ā-sthā-; cf. **āsthiti.**

a-sparśa-vihāra, m. (cf. **sparśa-vihāra-tā;** = Pali aphāsu-vihāra), *discomfort*: AsP 253.9 na cāsyā asparśavihāra amanaāpaḥ kāye utpadyeta.

a-spharaṇīya, neg. gdve. (to **spharati,** q.v.), *not to be pervaded* or *penetrated*: Śikṣ 249.5, 8 asphuṭam aspharaṇīyaṃ (in 5, tvaṅmānsaśoṇitena; of the elements in the body constituting the ādhyātmika ākāśadhātuḥ, line 3).

asmākīna, adj. (see s.v. **āsmākīna**), *our*: °nāṃ karmaplotiṃ Av i.242.9; 257.8 etc.

asmimāna, m. (= Pali id.), *self-conceit, egotism*: °naḥ Mvy 1949; Karmav 47.6; stem in comp. Mvy 1601; Divy 210.5; 314.21; Dbh 28.26; 48.11.

[**asmi-saṃjñā,** ŚsP 1258.7, read **asthi-saṃjñā,** q.v.]

asya, also **sya,** apparently particle of emphasis; acc. to Senart on Mv i.45.1, = Skt. svid, Pali su (also assu). (Note that PTSD s.v. su³ derives this not only from Skt. svid but also from Skt. sma, for which it there states that Pali also has sa and assa; but neither of these forms is cited in their proper places in PTSD; Andersen, Reader, Glossary s.v. sudaṃ, also mentions sa and assa as occurring for Skt. sma but does not list them; PTSD s.v. assu cites once assa as v.l. for assu; otherwise I have no record of Pali (as)sa as a particle.) In mss. of Mv anya or anyaṃ is sometimes read for asya: evam asya syāt Mv i.45.1, 5, 9, 12; kim asya nāma i.343.4; tasya sya dharmā i.292.1; kiṃ sya nāma, and kena sya nāma, i.346.8 and 9, 15 and 16; 347.3.

?**aha,** interj. of grief or objurgation (such a form may have existed in Pali, see PTSD s.v.; cf. Skt. and Pali ahaha and aho), *oh*! *fie*!: prob. read aha bhoḥ Mv i.8.1 (Senart em. ahaha bhoḥ).

ahaṃghāta, m., in Kv 94.23 apparently *self-slayer, suicide*; text seems corrupt: ye mātāpitṛghātakā ahaṃghāta stūpabhedakā-s (so printed); ahaṃghāta can hardly be part of the cpd. stūpabhedakās; should we read ahaṃghātakāḥ, assuming accidental omission of the syllable kāḥ?

a-hasita-keśa, adj. Bhvr. (a-hasita, neg. of Pali hasita = Skt. hṛṣita, of hair), *with hair not standing on end*; so read with mss. Mv ii.44.10 (Senart em. sahitakeśa); one of the **anuvyañjana** of the Buddha.

ahārya-hāriṇī, said of a river, acc. to Speyer *carrying away rocks or boulders*: Av i.235.11 sā ca nadī ah° śīghrasrotās te ca mṛgā durbalāḥ. Perhaps rather, (*capa-*

ble of) carrying away a mountain; in Skt. ahārya (as adj. *what cannot be carried away*) seems to be used as subst., *mountain*, not only in Lex. (BR) but in literature (Schmidt, Nachträge).

ahituṇḍika (also °aka?), m. (Skt. Lex. °ika, but in literature only āhituṇḍika recorded; Pali ahi°, see CPD s.v. ahi-guṇṭhika), (**1**) *snake-charmer* (the spelling °aka only Mv ii.178.1, and with v.l. °ika 178.11; 179.12): Mv i.92.3; 131.5; ii.178.1, 2, 3, 11, 14; 179.3, 5, 9, 12, 13; 183.14, 18; 188.20; Divy 436.28; 437.3, 9; 497.12; (**2**) n. of a brahman of Śuśumāragiri: Divy 188.11.

Ahibhānurāga, n. of a former Buddha: Mv i.141.7.

ahirī(ka), see **ahrīka.**

[**ahirodaka**, Divy 384.24, read **hirodaka**, q,v.]

ahu, m.c., rarely for Skt. aho, interj.: ahu vañcito 'smi SP 62.4 (vs), *alas*! (so Tib., kye ma; and cf. aho 61.12) *I am deceived*. But in 62.16 ahu = aham, as very commonly (§ 20.7).

? **ahṛsvara**, m. or nt., or adj., *(making) a piteous sound, lament(ing)*; in Mv iii.43.3, 6; 45.17 the mss. almost unanimously read ahṛsvaraṃ (or °rā; once one ms. ahiś-varā) krandamānā(ḥ), *crying piteously*, of hell-inhabitants. I cannot explain the form (it could be an adverb); but Senart's violent em. bhīṣmasvaram is unconvincing, even to himself (see his note).

a-heṭhaka, adj. (neg. of **heṭhaka**, q.v.), *not doing harm*, or as subst. *a non-injurious person*: Mv i.364.6 °kā . . . tṛṇāni bhakṣayanti; 365.10 sattvaratnānām aheṭhakānāṃ; ii.213.10 vayaṃ aheṭhakā adūṣakā anaparādhino; 215.11; 217.14; iii.363.9; aheṭhakā(ḥ) Ud xxx.48.

ahoḍima, read prob. **uhoḍima** or **avaho°**, see s.v. **avakoṭimaka.**

aho nāma, interj. (the combination has not been found recorded), *Oh, I say*!: SP 102.12 (prose) aho nāmāhaṃ nirvṛtiprāpto bhaveyaṃ yadi me sa putra imaṃ dhanaskandhaṃ paribhuñjīta, *Oh, I say*! *I would be blissfully happy if this son of mine could enjoy this mass of wealth*!

[**Aholūkhalamekhalā**, see **Maholū°**.]

(**ahirī**,) **ahrīka, ahirīka**, adj. (= Pali ahirīka; neg. to hrī plus -ka; in Skt. Lex. ahrīka only = *a Buddhist*!), *shameless*: ahirīkāś (mss. ahīrikāś) ca bhavanti Mv i.110.8 (prose); ahrīkeṇa Jm 98.19 (prose); ahirīko anotrapo Mv iii.11.4 (vs; here used of a very ugly man, without other evident cause for the epithet); in Ud xx.5 oldest ms. ahirī (Bhvr.), later ms. ahrīko (Sktizing).

Ā

ākañcuka, nt. (v.l. aṣṭuñcaka, nt.; so Mironov), Mvy 8996; context indicates reference to something worn at the waist; Tib. rgya caṅ (or rgya lcaṅ), *a kind of girdle*, Jä., *narrow, long money-bag made of net and securely joined to the sash*, Das; Chin. *belt* or *sash*. The var. aṣṭuñcaka seems probably a corruption.

ākaṭṭati (cf. **ākaḍḍhana**, and see s.v. **kaṭṭati**), *pulls, draws*: Mv ii.429.12 (prose), mss. (incorrectly) devī . . . brāhmaṇena . . . ākaṭṭati (passive is required; read ākaṭṭīyati or ākaṭṭyati? v.l. ākatti, cited with dental tt!) kaṭṭāṃkriyati (q.v.); below, line 15, (rājagṛhāto) kaṭṭīyamānī, confirming the sense and approximate form I assume; *draws hither, attracts, summons*: Megh 306.17 (in a charm for rain invoking serpent deities, nāgas) (sarvanāgahṛdayāni saṃcodayāmi) ākaṭṭāmi, *I incite, I draw hither the hearts of all nāgas*; there follow magic formulas (sara 2 hara 2, etc.), then, sarvakṣetrāṇi āpūrayatha sarvaśasyāni varṣatha, etc. Bendall renders āk° *I murmur*.

ākaḍḍhana (cf. **ākaṭṭati**, and see under **kaṭṭati**), acc. to KN Preface p. vii read in Kashgar rec. of SP for ākarṣaṇa.

Ākampya Mvy 739, see **Akampya.**

-ākara, see **-ākāra.**

ākarṣaṇā, °**ṇa-tā**, and °**ṇī** (cf. Skt. ākarṣaṇa, nt., *attraction*), (a Buddha's) *power of attraction* (of men, to himself and his doctrine): Mv i.314.2–3 (prose) ākarṣaṇā eṣā buddhānāṃ; bhagavatā vaineyasattvānāṃ ākarṣaṇatāyai (instr.! for °ye; here perhaps rather *by the exercize of that power*) . . .; Mvy 4315 sarvatathāgatākarṣaṇī.

ākalana (not in Pali, very rare in Skt., see pw 5 and 6 App.), in Bbh 251.8 paravādibhir ākalanānuyogo, an activity of Bodhisattvas, perhaps *regular practice* (see **anuyoga**) *of investigation* (? *careful consideration*) *by reason of* (? *under the stimulus of*) *opposing teachers.*

ākaluṣa, adj. *somewhat turbid*: Jm 145.14 °ṣā kṛśā ca (arthasiddhiḥ).

ākalpa (m.), probably = Pali ākappa in sense of *behavior, deportment* (PTSD): Gv 22.20 (prose) vividhākalperyāpathānāṃ . . . manuṣyāṇāṃ, *men of various deportment and behavior* (see **īryāpatha** 4); and 22.24 nāneryāpathākalpavihāriṇaṃ (janakāyaṃ). (The meaning *adornment* attributed to this word in Skt surely does not fit.)

ākāṅkṣati, °**te** (cf. **kāṅkṣati, kāṅkṣā**; in Skt. only *desires*, and so app. Pali ākaṅkhati), *doubts*: Mv i.165.3 ākāṅkṣamāṇā . . . vipaṇḍitā sattvā na jānanti . . . sukhaṃ samādhiṃ, *creatures that are doubting and ignorant do not know bliss or concentration*; perhaps Laṅk 14.19 (pracalitamaulin) yad-yad evākāṅkṣasi ahaṃ te tasya-tasyaiva praśnasya vyākaraṇena, (O chief of confused ones,) *whatever you are doubtful about, by explaining every such question to you I* (etc.) (otherwise Suzuki); Sukh 99.6 is interpreted by the ed. as mākāṅkṣayatha (i. e. mā āk°) mama ca teṣāṃ ca buddhānāṃ . . . *and have no doubt both of me and of these Buddhas*; but it could as well be mā kāṅkṣayatha (= kāṅkṣatha). (Also *desires* as in Skt., e. g. Mv i.158.14.)

Ākāṅkṣitamukha, m. pl., n. of a group of Bodhisattvas in Sukhāvatī: Kv 13.23.

-ākāra, *disposition* (as in Pali, much more clearly than in Skt.), in svākāra, durāk°, *of good* (bad) *disposition*: Mv iii.318.2–3 adrākṣīt sattvā durākārā durvineyā durviśodheyā, adrākṣīt sattvā svākārāṃ suvineyāṃ suviśodheyāṃ; LV 393.16 (vs) santi vijānaka sattva svākarāś (ă m.c.) ca; 394.14 (prose) santi sattvāḥ svākārāḥ suvijñāpakāḥ etc.; 399.22 f. svākārān suviśodhakān durākārān durviśodhakān (sattvān); 403.4, 9 (sattvaḥ) śuddhaḥ svākāraḥ (suvineyaḥ) suvijñāpakaḥ . . .

ākāra-parivitarka, see **pari°**.

ākārayati (denom. from Skt. ākāra, *external sign*; so in Pali), *makes known by a gesture* or *sign*: Divy 403.10 (tenā 'ṅgulidvayam utkṣiptaṃ na tu vāg bhāṣitā;) dviguṇaṃ tv ahaṃ pradāsyāmī 'ty ākārayati.

ākārānavakāra (wrongly °pakāra in Mvy), m., n. of a samādhi (cf. **anavakāra**), *complete* or *absolute in form*: ŚsP 1423.11; Mvy 595, text °pakāro (so also Mironov, but one ms. °vak°).

ākārābhinirhāra, m., n. of a samādhi, *visible-accomplishment* or *effectuation in form*: Mvy 593; ŚsP 1423.5.

ākālika, adj. (= BHS and Pali **akālika**; Skt. only adv. akālikam; so in Mbh.Cr. ed. 1.99.42 °kam for Calc. Bomb. °kaḥ), *immediate, not dependent on any lapse of time*, ep. of dharma: Mvy 1294; Śikṣ 323.6. In a like context ak° occurs.

[**ākāleyaṃ**, 1 sg. opt., Mv ii.253.17; so Senart; mss. akāleyam, akāreyaṃ; read ākāreyaṃ, to Skt. ākārayati, *invites, causes to approach* (here, birds into a net).]

ākāśa (m.), (**1**) *region, place*: Mv ii.49.3–4 kahiṃ ... ākāśe pravṛttajīvo ti mṛto ti, *in what region* (lit. under what sky?) *is his life taking place, or is he dead*?; (**2**) in SP 124.11 acc. to Kern *voidness*: (dharmam) ākāśagatikam, *placed in voidness* (as if synonym of śūnyatā; but Burnouf *qui a pour étendue l'espace*); cf. under **dhātu** 1 b, where it is made clear that ākāśa, as the fifth of six *elements* (dhātu), means absolutely *empty space*; (**3**) short for ākāśānantya, in cpd. ākāśa-vijñānā° (etc.), Bbh 49.17–18, see s.v. **naivasaṃjñānāsaṃjñāyatana**; (**4**) *emptiness*, implying *vanity* (? cf. 2 above): KP 111.1 dvāv imau ... pravrajitasyākāśapaligodhau (see **paligodha**, and **godha**); katamau dvau? lokāyatamantraparyeṣṭitā ca, utsadapātracīvaradhāraṇatayā (read °tā?) ca. In vs, l. 6: ākāśabodhe (see 2 **bodha**) imi dve pratiṣṭhite.

Ākāśagarbha, m. (**1**) n. of a Bodhisattva: Mvy 647; Śikṣ 64.14 ff.; Kv 1.10; Mmk 312.4; 405.24; (**2**) n. of a work: Mvy 1342; °sūtra, Śikṣ 10.14; 11.1; 59.10.

Ākāśajñānārthapradīpa, n. of a Buddha: Gv 422.25.

Ākāśadhātuvipula, m., n. of a samādhi: Dbh 82.13.

Ākāśapratiṣṭhita, n. of a Buddha in a southern lokadhātu: SP 184.10.

Ākāśaplavā, n. of a kiṃnara maid: Kv 5.24.

ākāśamātar(ā), pl., n. of a class of malevolent supernatural beings; also mahākāśa°: Mmk 17.7 ākāśamātarā mahākāśamātarāḥ.

Ākāśarakṣitā, n. of a kiṃnara maid: Kv 6.8.

Ākāśaspharaṇa, m., n. of a samādhi: Mvy 528, = **Ākāśasphuraṇa**: ŚsP 1417.5.

ākāśānantya, m. pl., *the gods dwelling in* **ākāśānantyāyatana**: Mmk 19.11.

ākāśānantyāyatana (= Pali ākāsānañcāy°), (**1**) nt., *stage of the infinity of space*; as first of the stages of arūpāvacara gods (see **deva**), Mvy 3110; Dbh 34.11; as first of four **ārūpya samāpatti** (q.v.), Mvy 1492; Karmav 47.21; as condition of the 4th **vimokṣa**, Mvy 1514; as condition of the 7th **abhibhvāyatana**, Mvy 1526; as fifth **sattvāvāsa**, Mvy 2293; (**2**) m. pl., = next: Suv 86.11; cf. ākāśānantya.

ākāśānantyāyatanopaga, m. pl., *the gods dwelling in* **ākāśānantyāyatana**: Dharmas 129.

Ākāśāsaṅgavimuktinirupalepa, m., n. of a samādhi: Mvy 623; ŚsP 1426.12.

ākiṃcanya, m. sg., *one who is in the stage called* **ākiṃcanyāyatana**: Buddhacarita xii.63 (wrongly queried by Johnston); pl., *the gods who are in that stage*, Mmk 19.10. In Bbh 49.17–18 āyatana, at the end of the cpd. ākāśavijñānākiṃcanya-naivasaṃjñānāsaṃjñāyatanam, is to be taken with each of the four members, including this.

ākiṃcanyānantyāyatana, nt. = next: Karmav 47.22 (as 3d of the four **ārūpya samāpatti**). Nonce-form, in which ānantya is carried over from the preceding ākāśānantyāyatana and vijñānānantyāy°.

ākiṃcanyāyatana (= Pali ākiṃcaññāy°), nt., *stage of nothingness*; as 3d stage of the **arūpāvacara** gods, Mvy 3112; Dbh 34.14; as 3d of the **ārūpya samāpatti**, Mvy 1494; as condition of the 6th **vimokṣa**, Mvy 1516; as 7th of the **sattvāvāsa**, Mvy 2295; **Ārāḍa Kālāma** (**Kālāpa**) taught the goal of association with this stage, LV 238.16 = Mv ii.118.3 °tana- (Mv corrupt, Senart **āśaṅkitavya**, q.v.) -sahavratāyai dharmaṃ deśayati.

ākiṃcanyāyatanopaga, m. pl., *the gods who are in the stage* of the prec.: Dharmas 129.

ākiṃcityāyatana, m. pl., *the gods who are in the stage* (otherwise called) **ākiṃcanyāyatana**: Suv 86.12. Nonce-form, based on a-kiṃcit instead of a-kiṃcana.

ākirati (= Pali id.; in Skt. only Vedic, except ppp. ākīrṇa and cpds. with other preverbs), *spreads out*: pṛthivyām ākirata MSV i.44.9.

ākīrṇa-vihāra, m., *dwelling in crowds* (opp. to solitary, monastic life): Mv i.89.17 °reṇa ca nārtīyanti (a cause of backsliding with Bodhisattvas). Cf. Pali ākiṇṇo viharāmi, DN ii.30.16.

ākīrṇa-vihārin, adj. (to prec.), *dwelling 'in a crowd', not alone*: Divy 201.26; MPS 15.17.

ākūtana (= Skt. ākūta; § 22.7), *wish, purpose*: Bbh 125.22 yācanakam ākūtana-nimitta-mātrakeṇaiva jñātvā yathākāmaṃ deyadharmaiḥ pratipādayati.

ākṛṣṭimant, adj., *quick at learning*: Mvy 2908. So Tib. (lobs skyen pa, or ldob rkyen pa), confirmed by surrounding words.

ākoṭana, nt. (cf. **ākoṭayati**), *beating* (of clothes): Mvy 9257; cf. ākoṭayet 9260. In Kyoto ed. there is a v.l. apakoṭana, but Mironov records no such reading and it is surely to be rejected.

ākoṭayati (= Pali ākoṭeti; cf. **koṭayati**), *beats*: a drum, LV 299.10 (ke cāgatā grahiya bheri yathaiva merur, so read) ākoṭyamānu (pres. pass. pple., n. sg. m., with merur) gagaṇe sumanojñaghoṣāṃ, ... *taking a drum, as if Mt. Meru* (were) *being beaten*, (a drum) *producing very pleasing sounds in the sky*; Suv 22.2; a gong, gaṇḍir (gaṇḍy) ākoṭitā Divy 335.13; 336.11; 337.9; ākoṭyatāṃ gaṇḍī Av i.258.9, and similarly ii.87.2; Kv 13.8 (read dharmagaṇḍikām ākoṭayanti); 36.17 dharmagaṇḍī-m-ākoṭyamānā śrutā; *hits, knocks on*, a stick, Av i.18.8 yaṣṭim ākoṭaya; a door, Divy 117.26 dvāraṃ trir ākoṭayati (*knocks*; Index wrongly *breaks*); MSV ii.80.9 kapālam ākoṭya (cf. **kapāla-koṭanī**); *beats* (clothes, in washing, cf. Pali ākoṭita-paccākoṭita, of robes, misinterpreted PTSD), Prāt 491.8 (purāṇacīvaraṃ ...) ākoṭayed (text ākoṭh°); suraktākoṭitaṃ (... paṭaṃ) Laṅk 363.9; Mvy 9260 ākoṭayet *would beat* (clothes, in washing; follows rañjayet *would dye*); *beats* or *presses* (earth) *down hard* (cf. Pali Jāt. i.264.20), Mmk 37.21 (pṛthivīpradeśaṃ ...) pūrayitvā ca sv-ākoṭitaṃ samatalaṃ ... kārayet; *caulks* (a ship), AsP 288.10 nāvam anākoṭitām aparikarmakṛtāṃ cirabandhanabaddhām, of an unseaworthy ship, *that was not caulked or repaired, tied to its moorings a long time*; 289.7 (nāvaṃ subaddhāṃ bandhayitvā) sv-ākoṭitām ākoṭayitvā, *having caulked it so as to be well caulked*; in Śikṣ 66.5 figuratively, of erring Bodhisattvas, te tatrākoṭitāḥ svanāmagrahaṇadarśanād bhayotpādanārthaṃ, *they are then disciplined* (perhaps originally physically *beaten*? then, *punished*; Bendall and Rouse, *struck at*) *by seeing their names mentioned* (publicly, in accusation), *in order to make* (them) *afraid*.

-ākramaṇatā = Skt. °ṇa (§ 22.42), *the walking upon* or *according to, moving in*: LV 31.20 and 34.10 nyāyākramaṇatāyai saṃvartate, *conduces to observance of the rules* (of conduct).

ākramati (in Skt. *treads on, tramples*, and so Pali akkamati; see **ākrāmayati**), *buries*: Mv iii.365.1 so taṃ ṛṣiṃ pāṃśunā ăkrametsuḥ (mss.; perh. MIndic ă; Senart em. ākrameti); 369.2 ṛṣī (acc. sg.!) yaṃ ca (mss. paṃca) vatsā (acc. sg.) ākrami ... daṇḍakī (n. sg.), *and since he buried the ṛṣi Vatsa* (perhaps em. ṛṣiṃ, Vatsaṃ); in 363.9 tena (sc. daṇḍakinā) so vatso ṛṣī dṛṣtvā paṃśunā ākramāyito (or ākrāmamāpito, mss.; prob. read ākramāpito with Senart, or ākrāmāpito, caus.), ... *was caused to be buried with dirt*.

ākramyati, °te = Skt. ākramati, °te, or ākrāmati, *approaches*: Divy 399.25 (prose) ākramyate; LV 163.21 (vs) ākramyā (2 sg. impv., rather than ger.).

ākrāmayati, Mvy 6914, app. caus. to **ākramati**; *causes to be buried* (? or, *trodden upon, oppressed*?) = Tib. gnon par (may mean *press down, cover with earth, overcome, oppress*) byed pa.

(**ākrośana**, *abuse, scolding*; rare in Skt., noted only JB, Whitney, JAOS 11.cxlv; Pali akkosana is less rare:

Bbh 122.22 (na . . .) °nāya . . . dānaṃ dadāti, *not in order to rebuke others.*)

[**ākhāyita,** at Mv iii.72.12 °tā, read khāditā with v.l. or khāyitā, see s.v. **khāyati.**]

ākhyāta, see **dur-ā°.**

ākhyāyati (= Skt. ākhyāti; in Skt. only °yate, as pass., and so regularly Pali akkhāyati, but once akkhāyantassa Jāt. iii.106.6 (comm.), active, gen. sg. pres. pple. In Pkt. Sheth cites gdve. akkhāiyavva = *ākhyāyitavya, implying pres. ākhyāyati), *tells, relates*: Mv ii.437.3 ākhyāyatha *relate!*, 2 pl. impv.

āgacchati (cf. **āgama, āgamayati**), (1) *is recorded, is handed down by tradition*: LV 39.15 yathā brāhmaṇānāṃ mantravedaśāstrapāṭheṣv āgacchati, tādṛśenaiva rūpeṇa etc.; 105.8 yathā hy asmākaṃ . . . mantravedaśāstreṣv āgacchati, nārhati . . . kumāro 'gāram adhyāvasitum; (2) *seeks, hunts for*: Av ii.150.5 paścācchramaṇam (q.v.) āgacchati na ca pratilabhate, *seeks . . . and does not find.*

āgataka, f. **°ikā,** adj. (to Skt. and Pali āgata), (*one that has*) *arrived*: -ka perhaps m.c., Divy 603.9 (vs) °kasya; endearing dim. (§ 22.34) LV 321.19 suvasantake . . . āgatake; 322.6 °tikā(ḥ); 323.14 read with v.l. °tikāṃ (acc. sg. f.; ed. °tiko) na hi bhuñjasi kāminikāṃ; specifying -ka (§ 22.39), Mv i.232.7 yaṃ nūnāhaṃ āgatako yena dīpavatī rājadhānī cakravartipuraṃ . . . paśyeyaṃ ti, *suppose I, as a returner* (one characterized by having returned) *to Dīpavatī, behold the Cakravartin's city*; Senart, note 557, assumes wrongly that the suffix has mg. of fut.

-āgatika (= Skt. āgati, at end of Bahuvrīhis), see **an-āgatika.**

āgati-gati, nt. dvandva, *coming and going* (in successive births): Mv i.4.7 (prose), read sattvānām āgatigati (so one ms., the rest °gami; Senart em. °gatiṃ) vividhaṃ (so, or °dha, all mss.; Senart em. °dhāṃ) bhagavāṃ abhijñāsi. Cf. Mv i.9.2 (vs) sattvānām āgatiṃ gatiṃ (here āgatiṃ, rather than °ti, is required by meter). The two words are often collocated in this sense in Pali; this use of each of them individually is, however, not foreign to Skt.

āgama, (1) m. (= Skt., as general term), *traditional* or *canonical text*; esp. applied to the four collections called in Pali nikāya, see **Ekottarika, Dīrghāgama, Madhyamāgama, Saṃyuktāgama**; (2) in āgama-vastu Mv i.318.7, mg. obscure; see **vastu.**

āgamana (nt.; = Skt. and Pali āgama), *traditional* or *authoritative doctrine*: Mv i.218.20 = ii.21.2 (vs) atra āgamanaṃ śṛṇu, *on this point hear what the doctrine is.*

Āgamanagamanā, n. of a 'gandharva maid': Kv 5.15.

āgamayati = āgacchati, *comes*: see § 38.21.

āgamika, m., (a monk) *that arrives at* (or, returns to) *a monastery*; *visitor, guest, arrival.* Not in Pali, which uses āgantuka (= Skt.) instead as pendant to **gamika** (q.v.): Mvy 8748, Tib. ḥoṅs pa, *arrival.* Note that 8746 also has āgantuka, defined Tib. blo bur du ḥoṅs pa, *sudden arrival.*

āgamya (orig. ger. of ā-gam; = Pali āgamma, in both mgs.), with acc., *with reference to*, patnīm ā° Divy 269.16; (much more commonly) *owing to, because of, on account of, thanks to*, (kalyāṇamitrāṇy) ā° Mv i.243.13; kalyāṇamitram Av i.210.11; 211.14; Mālinīm Mv i.313.5; Bhagavantam Divy 95.10; 97.18; 309.29; -bodhisattvam Śikṣ 91.6; Devadattam SP 259.3, 6; tau śrāmaṇerāv Divy 404.25; tat sarvam imaṃ markaṭam āgamya Divy 350.17 *all that is owing to this ape* (so mss., ed. wrongly em. āgamyāt); yam Divy 173.16; 175.25; -svāgatam Divy 188.6; tam Divy 514.23; tvām Divy 129.25; 549.21; tava (as acc.!) Mv i.365.12; yuṣmākam (acc.) Divy 405.10; mamāgamya *owing to me* (mama, acc.) Av ii.96.8 (ms.); i.321.13 (ms.); in Av i.239.6 ms. haplog. māgamya, prob. intending mamāg° (Speyer em. mām āg°, which is of course possible); bhikṣākavṛttam ā° Bbh 194.17; tāṃ protsāhanām āg° SP 350.3 *owing to this instigation*; MSV iii.22.14 (prose) corrupt, read perh., kiṃ mamāgamya? na tvayā-(as acc.)-m-āgamya, *for my sake? not for your sake*; ib. 24.5, read tvām (text tvam) āgamya, *owing to you.*

āgāḍha-tara, adj. compv. (to Pali āgāḷha; cf. next, and **samāgāḍha-tara**), *more serious* (of evils): SP 227.6–7 °taraṃ pāpakaṃ karma; *very serious* SP 483.2 (same phrase).

āgāḍhī-karoti, fut. °kariṣyāmi (cf. prec. and Pali āgāḷha), *I will make firm* or *strong*: Mvy 6997 = Tib. dam por (or, sra bar) byed pa; the alternative Tib. renderings daṅ por (or, dra bar) byed pa seem to be corruptions.

āgāmika, adj. (Skt. Lex.; no literary occurrence found, tho not marked * in pw; cf. Skt. āgāmin, *future*) *of* or *pertaining to the future* (opp. to **sāṃdṛṣṭika,** q.v.): Mv ii.405.16 (vs) mā āgāmike vihanyāhi hitvā sāṃdṛṣṭikaṃ phalam, *do not be subject to disappointment in regard to future* (fruit), *abandoning visible* (actual, of the present life) *fruit* (reward). Senart's note is wrong.

āgāra, (1) m., a high number: °raḥ Mvy 7831 = Tib. yid yal; cited from Gv, but Gv 133.1 reads **magara**; see also **agāra**; (2) see **stry-āgāra.**

āgārika (m., perh. also adj.; = Pali id., see CPD s.v. agārika, a form not noted in BHS), *householder, one living in worldly life*: Divy 275.17 na bhikṣuṇā āgārikasya purastād ṛddhir vidarśayitavyā; MSV i.248.19; in Bbh 26.13, in comp., pravrajitasya āgārika-vicitra-vyāsaṅga-duḥkha-nirmokṣāt, could be either n., *householder*, or adj., *of the householder's life.*

āgilāyati, see **āglā°.**

Āguhyakādhipati, m. = (and prob. wrong reading for) **Guhyakādhipati,** q.v., ep. of Vajrapāṇi and styled lord of yakṣas (yakṣendra): Mmk 25.12 evam ukta Āguh° patinā.

āgṛhīta (= Pali aggahīta; cf. **an-āg°** and **āgraha**), *held back* = *niggardly*; āgṛhītena cetasā (cf. Pali anaggahīta-citta) Divy 291.3; 298.11; Av i.173.12; 174.7; nāgṛhī-tacittatayāvasṛjan Śikṣ 28.7, *releasing* (gifts) *without niggardliness of heart*; āgṛhīta-pariṣkāra, *having utensils held back, stingy with objects*, Divy 302.3; Av i.250.16; and repeatedly in a cliché with matsarin and **kuṭukuñcaka,** see the latter for references.

āgneya, (1) nt., *fiery* (jewel), n. of a kind of gem: Mv ii.296.8 (vs) āgneyamaṇīnāṃ (mss. agneya°) yā ābhā gagane vidyutāna vā; Gv 499.23 (prose) āgneyaṃ nāma mahāmaṇiratnaṃ sarvatamo'ndhakāraṃ vidhamati; (2) m., with jaṭila (cf. Pali aggika), *fire-worshiping*, a kind of ascetic: MPS 40.51 (v. l. ag°).

Āgneyī, so doubtless read for text Agneyī, n. of a mātar, the śakti of Agni: Māy 242.19.

āgrathita, perh. ppp. to Skt. ā with gra(n)th, *wrapped up* (?): Mmk 145.(22-)23 khadirakāṣṭhair agniṃ prajvālya, paṭasyāgrataś caturhastapramāṇam āgrathitaḥ āhutiṃ sahasrāṣṭam (read °ṭāṃ?) juhuyāt (etc.).

āgraha (presumably m.; cf. **āgṛhīta**), *niggardliness, holding back* (from giving): SP 257.1 (after long description of how the Bodhisattva gave away everything, even his life) na ca me kadācid āgrahacittam utpannam, *and I never conceived a thought of holding back* (wrongly Burnouf and Kern); Av i.174.5 (vs; after 4 nādattvā paribhuñjīran na syur matsariṇas tathā,) na caiṣām āgrahe cittam utpadyeta kadācana, *and there would never arise for them a thought of holding back* (from giving). As Speyer points out in his Index to Av, KSS 90.22 probably contains the word āgraheṇa *with niggardliness, holding back from giving*; but this mg. has not been recognized; the ordinary Skt. usage is not quite the same.

? **āgrīvanīya,** pl. °yā, represents some word for a tradesman or artisan; so Senart with mss. at Mv iii.113.10; corresponds to **aṭṭiyānika** or **°vānika** (q.v.) at 442.15.

āglāyati, āgilāy° (= Pali āgilāyati), *gets weary*: Mv iii.206.3 mā . . . āgilāyatu (mss. āgirā°; Senart em. cirāyatu, clearly wrongly). See also **āvilāyati.**

āghaṭana, equated by Tib. with nimitta, *mark, sign*, as boundary: teṣām °nānām MSV iv.93.4 ff.

āghaṭṭana (presumably nt.; cf. Skt. āghaṭṭanā), *scraping, running aground upon* (submarine rocks, of a ship), with gen.: Divy 229.24 antarjalagatānāṃ parvatānām āghaṭṭana-bhayam (said in reference to ships).

āghatana, prob. m.c. for **āghātana** (= Pali āghātana, in same sense, Skt. id. *slaughter-house*, so also in Pali), *place of execution* (of criminals): SP 449.7 (vs) saci āghatane (2 mss. āghātane, unmetr.) upasthito. In LV 207.3 ed. āghātana, but see s.v. **āghātin.**

āgharate (Skt. Dhātup. only, gharati; Vedic jigharti, with ā- in different mg.), *drips*: Śikṣ 82.6 (vs) kakṣāsv āgharate svedo. Tib. cited as ḥdzag, *drip*.

āghāta, m. (= Pali id.), *malicious feeling, anger, hatred*: Mvy 2104 (Tib. kun nas mnar sems pa, inaccurately, *very tormented spirit*); Mv i.79.15 āghāta-bahulāś ca bhavanti (a cause of backsliding of Bodhisattvas); Av ii.129.3 yo 'bhūt sattveṣv āghātaḥ sa prativigataḥ (anger had characterized the person referred to); Bbh 161.12 āghāta-cittaḥ pratigha-citto vā; Karmav 27.17 mā te bhaviṣyati āghātaś cākṣāntiś ca.

āghātana, see **āghatana**; in this sense MSV iv.64.2.

āghātayati (°**teti**; denom. from **āghāta,** q.v.; = Pali āghāteti, with cittaṃ and loc.), with cittam, *hardens one's heart against, cherishes hatred for*, with loc.: Mv iii.56.3 mahākāśyape cittam āghātetvā; Śikṣ 188.9–10 cittaṃ nāghātayitavyam (no loc.).

āghātin, adj.-subst. (from āghāta *slaying* with -in), *murderous* (person), *murderer*: LV 207.3 (vs) āghātina (so read with all mss. but one which omits the syllable ti; Lefm. em. °tana, wrongly) iva vadhyāḥ, *like murderers to be executed*. In Ud ix.16 ms. aghātinaḥ could possibly stand for āghātinaḥ, but more likely read aghāvinaḥ with Chakravarti.

Āṅgirasa (cf. **Aṅgīrasa**), ep. of Buddha: Mvy 77 = Tib. ñi maḥi rgyud, (of the) *family of the sun*; MSV i.274.4.

ācariya, m. (= Pali id.; MIndic for Skt. ācārya), *teacher*; only in vss of most texts, but in prose Mv ii.87.12 °riyo; in vss, m.c., ācariya(ḥ) LV 125.5; lokācariyāṇa (gen. pl.) SP 59.5; °riyaḥ 118.1; °riyehi 374.3 (note below in 374.7, vs, ācārya-bhūmau).

ācāryaka, f. °**ikā** (as subst. = Pali ācariyaka, *teacher*; Skt. ācārya plus -ka), (**1**) adj. *of a teacher*: °ryakaṃ padam avāpa, *attained the station of a teacher* Jm 2.5–6 (sakalāsu kalāsv); 142.16 (teṣv, sc. dharmaśāstreṣu); (**2**) subst. *teacher*, esp. in Bhvr. cpds., as SP 81.1 (prose) svayaṃbhujñānam anācāryakaṃ jñānam, . . . *that needs no teacher*; LV 377.14 svayam-ācāryakaṃ jñānaṃ, *that is self-instructing, acts itself as teacher*; Av i.193.8 sācāryakāṇi tāni kulāni; but also as separate word Bhīk 10b.3 ācāryike (voc.) and 4 °yikām (acc.), both fem.; ācāryakatvam Bbh 226.16 (prose) *teacherhood, state of being a teacher* (bodhisattvamārge).

ācārya-muṣṭi, m. or f. (= Pali ācariya-muṭṭhi), *close-fistedness of a teacher, keeping things* (particularly instruction) *back from pupils*: Mvy 6525 = Tib. slob dpon gyi dpe mkhyud (so also Tib. on KP) *a teacher's refusing to lend books*; LV 179.12 °ṭi-vigato (preceded by: dharmadānenāmatsaraḥ); KP 1.4 dharmācāryamuṣṭim, cf. 1.11 (vs) ācāryamuṣṭiṃ . . . dharme; Bbh 41.28 na ca pareṣām °ṭiṃ karoti; 106.18 nācāryamuṣṭiṃ dharmeṣu karoti; 363.14.

ācikṣati (cf. also **abhy-ā°**; hyper-Skt. based on Pali ācikkhati, AMg āikkhai, under influence of Epic Skt. ācakṣati; the Pali forms are ignored in Geiger's Index; Pischel 492 considers the Pkt. forms redupl. from Skt. root khyā, while Ratnach. derives āikkhai from ā-cakṣ, abbhāikkhai from both -khyā and -cakṣ. There is no doubt that BHS abhy-ā-cikṣ- is associated with the noun abhyākhyāna; Pali has equivalents of both; and I believe with Pischel that the whole group is based primarily on khyā; but at least in BHS it is blended with cakṣ; Skt. ā-cakṣ and ā-khyā are synonyms), *tells, says*, only in Mv: °ati i.243.6; 244.6 (em.); ii.408.7; 463.19; 464.17; 486.14; iii.74.16; 125.17; 132.16; 149.10; 164.15, etc.; °anti ii.132.3; impv. °a ii.57.17; 58.15; °āhi iii.192.13; °atha iii.72.16; fut. °iṣyāmi iii.74.3 (em.), 8; °iṣyaṃ iii.258.13 ff.; °iṣyati iii.256.12; °iṣyanti i.272.5; ppp. °ita i.355.2, 5; ii.73.14; 178.6; iii.40.4; gdve. °itavya ii.73.13; iii.256.12. Note ācikṣanti Mv ii.132.3, in a passage where all other texts incl. Mv i.228.7 have ācakṣate; but Pali ācikkhanti.

ācinati (= Pali id.) = Skt. ācinoti, *accumulates*: Ud xvii.5, pūryati bālo pāpena stokastokaṃ pi ācinaṃ (= ācinan; text unmetr. ācīnaṃ; Pali Dhp. 121 correctly ācinaṃ; n. sg. m. pres. pple.).

ācīrṇa-daṇḍa-tā (v.l. acīrṇa°, so Mironov without v.l., but a- seems impossible), *practise* (or *occupation*) *of wielding a club*: Mvy 3812 = Tib. dbyug pa gcod pa, app. *wielding a club*; Chin. seems to mean *use by a horseback-rider or messenger of a stick in driving his horse.* The next word in Mvy is dūtaḥ, *messenger.*

ācūṣayati (cf. Skt. cūṣayati and ācūṣaṇa), *sucks up* or *in*: °yanti Sādh 125.12 (svarān); 149.14 (makarandam).

āchāda, m. (cf. the following items), *gift, present* (not necessarily a garment!): Mv ii.98.3 lubdhakena vipulo āchādo (*a rich reward*) labdho; iii.128.10 vipulo āchādo dinno; 162.16 teṣām āchādam dāsyāmi (here gold minted and unminted, and garments, lines 14, 15); food, bhaktāchādena (Speyer em. °chādanena; not *food and dress* but *a gift of food*) paripālanaṃ kariṣyati Av ii.112.7; dharmāchāda, *a pious* or *religious gift*, SP 445.12 (dāsyāmo . . . avalokiteśvarāya . . .) dharmaprābhṛtaṃ dharmāchādam (note āchāda as synonym of prābhṛta! the gift given was a necklace, muktāhāra, 446.1, again called dharmāchāda 446.2); LV 352.5 f. dharmāchādāṃś ca saṃpreṣayanti sma (by which, yair dharmāchādair, the universe became covered with many jewelled parasols).

āchādana, nt. = prec. (cf. next), *gift, present* (not necessarily clothes): LV 58.2 āchādanāni codgṛhya; this vs deals with the same events described in prose 58.6 saṃpravāryāchādanāni ca dattvā (clothes might, but need not necessarily, be meant); Mv iii.177.16 -pauruṣeyā veṣṭetavyā (see **veṣṭeti**) bhojanāchādanena sarvehi ca utsavehi samanvāharitavyā; Bbh 115.7 kaścit pareṣāṃ bhaktāchādanahetoḥ dāsabhāvam upagacchet; 269.24 tasyāham ucitaṃ vā bhaktāchādanaṃ samucchetsyāmi . . ., *I will deprive him of his customary gift of food*; bhaktāchādana MSV i.51.22. (Some take bhojanāch°, bhaktāch° as dvandvas, *food and clothing*; while perhaps not impossible, this seems to me unlikely.)

āchādayati (Skt. id. and Pali acchādeti used of *presenting* with clothes, only, so far as appears; in BHS also used of presents of clothes, but extended to other kinds of gifts; see **āchāda,** °**dana**), *presents*, with instr., rarely acc., of thing given, which may be garments, Divy 29.6, 9 (vastrair āchāditaḥ); 89.18 (bhikṣuḥ . . . vastreṇāchāditaḥ); 254.23 (navena paṭenāchāditā); Av i.32.5 (vastreṇāchādya); 43.2 (vastreṇāchāditaḥ); or the price of a garment, Prāt 492.14 (cīvara-cetanakair . . .) bhikṣum āchādayiṣyāmi; but also gold, Mv iii.38.12 prabhūtaṃ ca hiraṇyasuvarṇam āchādayanti (recipient not mentioned); life, Divy 136.18–19 ko mā . . . aśaraṇam iṣṭena jīvitenāchādayed iti; 137.12, 13 jīvitenāchādaya, °dayitum; Av i.236.10 jīvitenāchādita(ḥ); 300.17 °ditaḥ; a gift of villages, Divy 445.9 (sa ca lubdhaḥ) pañcagrāmavareṇāchāditaḥ.

āchāya, m. (Prakritic for **āchāda,** q.v.), *gift, present*: Mv iii.449.12 vipulo (mss. vipulena, but see the same phrase s.v. **āchāda**) āchāyo dinno.

āchindana(-tā), (cf. Pali acchindana), *breaking, violation*, in an-ā°, *non-violation*: Śikṣ 126.15 guruvacanānavamardanatayā paravacanānāchindanatayā cādeyagrāhyavacano bhavati.

āchoḍita (?), ppp. (for āchorita, cf. Skt. āchurita, KSS, *scratched, drawn*?), *set, inlaid* (with strings of jewels): SP 151.9 (prose) suvarṇasūtrāchoḍitaṃ (buddhakṣetraṃ). So both edd., but with only 1 ms. (KN); the others °āchāditaṃ *covered*. However, Tib. bris pa (acc. to WT), *scratched, drawn, inscribed* (if connected with ḥbri ba), would seem to support this reading.

ājanya, also **ājaniya, ājānya, ājāniya, ājāneya**, adj. (= Pali ājañña, ājāniya, ājānīya, ājāneyya), *of noble race, blooded*, primarily of animals, esp. horses; by extension used of men, esp. Buddhas and Bodhisattvas, and very rarely (meaning *noble*) of other, inanimate entities. Tib. (e.g. Mvy 1080, 4769, etc.) regularly renders caṅ śes (pa), *omniscient*, falsely interpreting the word as derived from jñā *know*. In composition, the word in all its forms regularly (not always) follows the noun, e. g. aśvājāneya, *a blooded horse* (orig. perhaps *a thoroughbred of a horse*?), below. As separate word: of animals, yo aśvavaraṃ damayed ājāneyan (= °yaṃ) va saindhavaṃ Ud xix.7; ājāneyā hayottamāḥ Mv ii.487.20; iii.22.11; cf. yuktāni ājānyarathāni Mv iii.441.10 *chariots of* (drawn by) *blooded* (horses), *all hitched up*; ājāneyau dvau balīvardhāv LV 381.7; ājăniyo hastipoto Mv iii.130.7 (prose, no v.l.); of men, ājāneyānāṃ sattvānāṃ Gv 322.8; °neyaḥ Mvy 1080, of śrāvakas; °neya ity ucyate LV 425.19, of the Tathāgata; ājāneyo kahin ti nāma (so Senart em., mss. kāma) bhoti Mv iii.397.14, answered by ... ājāneyo (v.l. °ya) tam (Senart em. ti tam) āhu bhūriprajñā (mss. °jño) 398.12; voc. ājanya, addressed to Buddha, namas te muktāyājanya Mmk 4.22; cf. Divy 617.16 ājāneya-mānā, *paying reverence to the Noble One* (the Buddha); in KP 9.5 and 10.5 dāntājāneya-prāpta; 9.14; 10.17 and 20 ājanya-prāpta, all of Bodhisattvas (cf. 10.1 ājāneyā bodhisattvāḥ), *become noble* (steeds), see s.v. **prāpta**; the figure of a horse is surely intended here, since there is contrast with KP 9.1 bodhisattva-khaḍuṅkāḥ, the latter (q.v.) being a term pertaining in its literal sense to horses; here may also belong Mv ii.264.14 ājāneya-vikrāntaṃ vikramantam, said of the Bodhisattva, *striding with the stride of a blooded horse*, or *of a noble person* (cf. the next following mahāpuruṣavikrāntaṃ vikr°), but possibly *striding with a noble stride* (cf. the preceding aparājitavikrāntaṃ vikr°), as in the next example; as prior member of karmadhāraya cpds. or bahuvrīhis based on them, occasionally *noble, distinguished*, in application to other than animate beings: catasra imā ... ājāneya-gatayo bodhisattvenānugantavyāḥ RP 14.13, *noble procedures* (listed as sugatipratilābha, guruśuśrūṣaṇā, prāntaśayyāsanābhirati, pratibhānapratilābha; is the literal meaning *gaits of a blooded horse*?); ājāneya-svaraḥ Mv iii.343.5 could, then, also be taken as *having a noble sound* (ep. of the Buddha's voice), but in view of the preceding vṛṣabhasvaraḥ and the following krauñcasvaraḥ it probably means *having the sound of a blooded* (*horse*) and belongs above; once, at least, this adj. precedes in composition the name of the animal to which it is applied, ājāneya-hasty-upetān Śikṣ 26.14; but regularly this order is reversed (as in such cpds. as nara-śārdūla) and we find aśvājāneya, m. (lit. *thoroughbred of a horse*) Mvy 4773 (misunderstood pw s.v. ājāneya); Divy 510.21, 22; 511.1 ff.; Mv ii.270.11 (mss.); Gv 400.13; Śikṣ 28.3 (ms. aśvāyāneyān); bhadrāśvājāneya- Sukh 60.8–9; hastyājāneya Mvy 4771; Gv 400.12; Śikṣ 27.21; siṃhājāneya Mvy 4769; and (cf. above, and Pali purisājāneyya) by extension puruṣājāneya (the corruptions puruṣājāneya and °ṣajāna occur in mss. and sometimes in edd.) LV 350.11, corresponds to Mv i.229.8; Mv ii.133.8; 284.18; in Mv i.316.4 ed. em. puruṣājāniyam, mss. corrupt, reading doubtful; puruṣājanya Mv iii.109.5 (vs); Bbh 50.6 (voc., to the Buddha).

ājavaṃjava (m. or nt.), *coming and going, moving to and fro* (in the saṃsāra): Mvy 5393 °va- (Mironov ājāvaṃ°, but v.l. text) samāpannaḥ = Tib. ḥoṅ ba daṅ ḥgro bar (*coming and going*) gyur ba; LV 205.12 (lokasya, *people*) ... ājavaṃjavasamāpannasyāsmāl lokāt paraṃ lokaṃ paralokād imaṃ lokaṃ saṃdhāvataḥ saṃsarataḥ. See next two items. The word contains double forms of java or at least the root ju but its precise formation is not clear to me; is ājava *moving swiftly hither*, and java *hastening away*? For the preceding part of this cliché see s.v. **guṇāvaguṇṭhitabhūta**; but the Pali correspondent does not contain ājavaṃjava°, at least in most of its occurrences.

ājavaṃjava-tā = prec.: Buddhacarita xii.41 °tāṃ hitvā prāpnoti padam akṣaram (Johnston's *rushing torrent of birth and death* seems to me not quite accurate, but obviously the saṃsāra is meant).

ājavaṃjavībhāva, m. (see prec. two), *state of moving restlessly to and fro* (in the saṃsāra): MadhK 218.4 °bhāvena janmamaraṇaparaṃparayā saṃsaraṇaṃ syāt; 529.1 ya ājavaṃjavībhāva upādāya pratītya vā.

ājāniya, ājāneya, ājānya, see **ājanya**.

ājāvaṃjava-, see **ājavaṃjava-**.

ājīva, m., = next: MSV ii.50.1 (prose).

ājīvaka, m. (= Pali id.), a member of a heretical ascetic sect: SP 276.3 (to be avoided by Bodhisattvas); LV 405.4, and repeatedly in the sequel; MSV ii.49.4 ff. See next (1).

ājīvika, (**1**) m. (= Pali id.) = prec.: MSV ii.83.19; LV 380.12 (v.l. °aka); Divy 393.20; 427.7, 8 (here identified with nirgrantha, 9); ajīvika, with a- m.c., Śikṣ 332.1 (vs); (**2**) nt. (= Pali id., Skt. ājīva), (means of) *livelihood, profession*: °bhayam (= Pali id.), *danger due to profession* or *means of livelihood*, Dharmas 71; (**3**) °**ikā**, f. (= Pali id.) = (2): °bhaya- (as under prec.), Gv 264.9; Śikṣ 296.5; Dbh.g. 2(338).10 °kā-maraṇa-'kīrty (dvandva); -bhaya is understood from prec. line with all three items).

-ājñaka = Skt. ājñā at end of adj. cpd.; see **yathājñaka.**

ājñā (= Pali aññā; in Skt. only *command*, which in Pali is always āṇā), *perfect, esoteric knowledge*, identified with *arhatship*: as object of ārādhayati, *gets perfect knowledge*, LV 238.22, or of **ārāgayati**, id., Mvy 7602; ārāgaye, aor., Mv iii.53.9; ārāgayiṣyasi Divy 302.20; ājñā-citta (in Pali nt. subst., *a mind disposed to perfect knowledge*), in Bbh 105.7 ājñācitta ekāgracittaḥ, Bhvr., *having* (*such*) *a mind*; in Mvy 7259 °cittena, not clear whether Bhvr. or Karmadh.; samyag-ājñā-vimukta (= Pali sammad-aññā-vimutta), *freed thru perfect knowledge*, Mv i.59.7, 9, 12 (arhantānāṃ) ... °muktānāṃ; Ud vi.19; xx.17,20; °suvimukta-cittaiḥ Sukh 1.14. See also **ājñendriya.**

ājñākṛta, adj. (ppp.), *made subject to*, with gen.: Mv i.311.4 brāhmaṇānām ājñākṛtā (mss. °to, but f.; Senart queries whether ājñīkṛtā is intended).

Ājñāta-kauṇḍinya (= Pali Aññāta-koṇḍañña, also Aññā-k°; see **Kauṇḍinya**), n. of the first of the **bhadravargīya** monks; corruptly Ājñāna° LV 408.5, or Jñāna° LV 1.6, v.l. both times (Ā)jñāta°; Mv iii.328.20; 333.19; 337.4; 338.20; 345.3; 347.14; 348.8; 349.6, 7; SP 1.9; 33.5; 212.3; Mvy 1030; Divy 182.21; 268.5; Av ii.134.12; Sukh 2.2; °nyasya jātakam, colophon, Mv iii.349.3, and again (a different story) 353.13.

ājñātar (= Pali aññātar), *knower*: LV 397.11 deśaya tvaṃ mune dharmaṃ ājñātāro bhaviṣyanti.

ājñātāvin, adj. (= Pali aññātāvi-n; § 22.51), *possessed of perfect knowledge*: Ud vi.12, read °tāvī for text °tāpī; °tāvīndriya (= Pali aññātāvindriya), nt., *the faculty of an ājñātāvin*, °yam Mvy 2080; ŚsP 64.3 f.; Bhvr. *possessing that faculty*, Sukh 56.12 °yā(ḥ).

ājñāna (nt.; neither Skt. id. nor Pali aññāṇa is recorded in this sense), *authority*, substantially = Skt. ājñā, Pali āṇā: Gv 493.2 kalyāṇamitrājñānaṃ na vilomayanti. In LV 3.13 -asaṅgājñāna-, read -asaṅga-jñāna- with best ms. A; so also LV 4.6; see **Pūrvabuddhānusmṛty-asa°**.

ājñāpana, f. **°nī**, adj., *giving orders* or *instructions, authoritative*: LV 286.9 yāsau (sc. bodhisattvasya) vāg ājñāpanī vijñāpanī . . . (long series of adjectives).

ājñendriya, nt. (= Pali aññindriya), *the faculty of perfect knowledge* (**ājñā**, q.v.): Mvy 2079. (Tib. renders ma śes paḥi dbaṅ po, as if a-jñe°, with neg. a-!)

ājñeya, f. **°yā**, adj. (= Pali aññeya, of dhamma), *understandable, comprehensible*: Mv i.172.14 °yā vijñeyā..., of Buddha's voice (vācā); iii.342.16 °yaś ca hṛdayaṃgamaś ca . . ., of Buddha's voice (svaraḥ). The opposite is dur-ājñeya (-vihāra-vihāriṇāṃ) Gv 471.6, *incomprehensible*.

āṭakkara, m., = **aṭ°**, q.v.: Bhīk 17a.2, in list of diseases.

Āṭavaka (cf. **Aṭ°**; = Pali Āḷavaka), n. of a yakṣa: Mvy 3377; Māy 15; Suv 161.13 (here saṃdhi permits interpretation as Aṭ°); doubtless read so (or Aṭ°) for Aṭhavaka, Samādh p. 43 line 19; and for Ārṭavaka Māy 237.1.

Āṭavikā (= Pali Āḷavī, cf. **Agrāṭavika**), n. of a city in Magadha, and of a river near it: MSV ii.51.8, 9.

Āṭānāti, acc. to Hoernle n. of a yakṣa, but rather (with Hoffmann, Kl. Skt. Texte 5.8–10) n. of a magic charm, contained or dealt with in the Āṭānāṭika sūtra (see next): °ṭi, n. sg., and °ṭisya, gen. sg., Hoernle MR 26.15 and 19.

Āṭānāṭika (sūtra), (= Pali Āṭānāṭiya-suttanta; cf. prec.), n. of a work: Mahāsamāj. Waldschmidt Kl. Skt. Texte 4, p. 175.2; fragments, containing the name as above, publ. by Hoffmann, Kl. Skt. Texte 5; on the name see pp. 8–10. Hoernle, MR 26 f., publishes a fragment from what he calls by its Pali name the Āṭānāṭiya (Sūtra).

?**āṭhya**; if not an error, can only represent āḍhya, *rich*: SP 72.3 āṭhyo; WT print āḍhyo, with their ms. K′.

āṇatta, ppp. (= Pali, AMg. id., Skt. ājñapta; cf. the following items), *commanded* (very common in Mv, not noted elsewhere): Mv i.258.7, 16; 272.9; 273.5; 356.1; 362.7; 364.12; ii.26.3; 32.2; 72.17; 101.6; 103.7; 111.4; 112.6; 150.2; 156.5; 167.9, 11; 174.9; 180.4; iii.126.17; 127.16, etc.

āṇatti, f. (= Pali, AMg. id., Skt. ājñapti; cf. prec. and foll. items), *command* (not noted outside of Mv): āṇatti (ii.95.8 °ttī, mss. °ntī) dinnā *a command was given* Mv i.360.10; ii.95.8; 153.13; āṇatti-karāḥ *doers of the bidding* (of, gen.) ii.112.6; rājāṇattīye, instr., *by the king's command*, i.274.2; 350.2; ii.48.6; 101.7; 167.11 (mss. rājā-āṇ°, Senart em. rāja-āṇ°); iii.132.2 (v.l. rājā-āṇ°). All prose.

āṇattikā (= **°tti**; AMg. °ttiyā), *command* (only noted in Mv): n. sg. °kā Mv ii.436.18; 451.7; 453.13; 479.11; iii.266.3; acc. sg. °kā śrutvā (so with v.l.; text °kāye) ii.453.16; °kāṃ deti ii.455.1; °kaṃ kartuṃ (so both mss., with MIndic shortening of ā) iii.126.8; instr. rāja-āṇattikāye (mss. rājā-āṇ°) ii.470.6. All prose.

āṇapaka, m. (to **āṇapeti**, with suffix aka), *one who orders* or *gives instructions*: Mv i.361.21; 362.4, 6; 363.2, 3, 5, 12. Senart reads āṇāpaka in each case; the mss. are corrupt but invariably show short -a- in the second syllable (altho Pali has only āṇāpaka).

āṇapeti (for Skt. ājñāpayati, rarely ājñap°(?); § 2.15; Pali only āṇāpeti, q.v. in BHS; Pkt. āṇāvei and āṇa°) *commands* (only noted in Mv; cf. prec. and foll. items); commoner than āṇāpeti, but sometimes wrongly replaced by the latter in Senart's text: pres. °peti Mv iii.125.21 (mss.); 264.2; °pesi, 2 sg. ii.490.8, 16; impv. °pehi ii.108.15; 247.6 (mss. °yehi); in i.223.4 = ii.25.15 mss. ānayasi (sic) or āṇayati (v.l. °tti), 3 sg. *orders*, Senart em. āṇāpesi or °ti, read prob. āṇapati or at best āṇapeti; in i.362.2, 5 read with mss. āṇapehi (v.l. °yehi) for Senart āṇāpehi (impv.); in i.362.17 Senart āṇāpiyanti, and in 364.20, 365.4 and 5, Senart āṇāpyati, all passives, and all to be read with short a, as the mss. clearly indicate tho with more or less corruption; read respectively āṇapiyanti and āṇapyati (passives to āṇapeti).

āṇā (= Pali id., Skt. ājñā), *command*: Mv iii.7.16 yā me (so Senart em.; mss. corrupt, one maṃ, perhaps read mam-) āṇā (so one ms., acc. sg.; v.l. [pr]āṇā; Senart em. āṇāṃ, unnecessarily) pratikrośe . . .

[**āṇāpaka**, see **āṇapaka**.]

āṇāpeti (= Pali id., Pkt. āṇāvei; see **āṇapeti**, which must be read for Senart's āṇā° in several cases), *commands* (only noted in Mv): impv. °pehi Mv iii.125.19; 3 sg. impv. pass. āṇāpīyatu or °piyatu, *be it commanded*, i.310.14.

Āṇinetra, n. of a Bodhisattva: Gv 442.4 (text Āni°).

Āṇinema, n. of a Bodhisattva: Gv 442.3–4 (text Āni°).

āṇī-pratyāṇī-nirhāra-yoga, instr. **°yogena**, *by homosexual procedure*: Mvy 6865 = Tib. khye ḥus khye ḥu ḥbyuṅ baḥi tshul du, *by way of the manner* (lit. *happening, procedure*) *of boy with boy*; similarly Chin. (The Index reads āṇi°.) From āṇī or (Skt.) āṇi, *axle-pin*, and pratyāṇī, otherwise unrecorded, *that in which the axle-pin fits* (both in obscene sense). For such practices and their punishments cf. Śikṣ 75.13 f.

ātakṣati (recorded only RV and not in this sense), *carves, chops in pieces*: ger. ātakṣya (. . . gātrāṇi) Jm 196.3.

ātapa, m. or nt., in ṣaṣṭeḥ kārṣāpaṇānām arthāyātape dhāritaḥ Divy 33.13, and ātape vidhāritaḥ 16, apparently *was assessed a fine* (in the amount of 60 kārṣāpaṇas). Perhaps corrupt; I find it hard to understand connexion with ātapa *heat* (kept on a hot spot?). The Index omits the word.

ātapta-kārin, adj., *acting zealously*: °rī Mvy 1806 = Tib. brtun ciṅ byed pa; °riṇa(s), n. pl., Mahāsamāj. 195.1; Waldschmidt, Kl. Skt. Texte 4 p. 5, regards ātapta as hyper-Skt. for Pali ātappa, nt., *zeal*, which PTSD derives from Skt. *ātāpya, to (Pali, not Skt.!) ātāpa, a much rarer form than ātappa in Pali; but cf. **ātāpin**, which is common also in Pali.

? **Ātaptarāṣṭra**, perh. to be read as n. of a former Buddha, Mv i.139.13–14; closer to mss. (Āttapta° or Attapta°) than Senart's em. **Uttapta°**, q.v.

(**ātasya**, adj. [Skt. id., rare, see Schmidt, Nachtr.], *made of the atasī plant, flaxen*: Mmk 131.22 [paṭe . . .] ātasye vālkalai [read °le] caiva śuddhe . . .)

ātāna, nt., *warp*: Mvy 7519 = Tib. rgyu. In Vedic used in a closely related way, e. g. Ait. Br. 8.12, *lengthwise ropes* (Keith) used in constructing the seat of a throne. Contrasted with **vitāna**, q.v.

ātāpana-, noted only in cpd. °na-**paritāpana**, which occurs in Pali too, (self-)*castigation* and (self-)*torture* (in ascetic practice): LV 211.12 anekavidhāni kāyasyātāpanaparitāpanāni samutsahante; 248.15 nānāvidhaiś cātāpanaparitāpanaiḥ kāyaśuddhiṃ paryeṣante; Gv 229.23 śarīrātāpanaparitāpanaprayuktānāṃ.

ātāpayati (denom. to Pali ātāpa, cf. **ātāpin**), *is zealous, shows energy*: (aśucimrakṣitāni) śayanāsanāni śocayanty ātāpayanti praviśajanti MSV ii.88.2 (and ff.).

ātāpin, adj. (= Pali id., from Pali ātāpa, oftener ātappa, *zeal*, with suffix -in; neither occurs in Skt.), *zealous*: °pī, n. sg. Mvy 1805; LV 239.4 (apramatta ātāpī); same passage Mv ii.118.11 and 120.3; similar phrase ii.285.1, also Divy 37.10, MSV i.50.14 etc., and fem. (apramattā) °pinī Divy 618.3; Ud xix.1 (aśvaḥ . . .) ātāpinaḥ, n. sg. (*ardent, spirited*); Śikṣ 31.3 āhāraprajñātāpino, n. pl., *diligent in making proper distinction in food* (Bendall and Rouse).

ātāla (m. or nt.), prob. *watchtower*: LV 193.18 (vs) prāsādeṣu gavākṣatoraṇavareṣv ātāla-mañceṣu ca (all parts of a building). Apparently = Skt. aṭṭāla (also aṭṭa); Tib. LV yaṅ thog, which Das defines by *the highest storey of a house*, also . . . *a dome*, and which in Mvy 5522 renders aṭṭa = aṭṭāla.

ātiyāntrika? prob. corrupt; Śikṣ 361.7 (vs) vajrapāṇy-ātiyāntrikaiḥ, adj. with buddhakiṃkaraiḥ (*servants of Buddha*); acc. to Bendall's note, Tib. *choice charms* (sel mchog; sc. of) *Vajrapāṇi*; but Bendall and Rouse Transl. *with Vajrapāṇi as their supreme chief* (p. 317, without note).

ātireka (m.c. for Skt. ati°), *excess*: aṅga manorama divya-ātirekāḥ LV 49.15 (vs), *his members are charming beyond divine ones.*

ātīkṣṇendriya, adj. (ā-tīkṣṇa-indriya; cf. **tīkṣṇendriya**), *of rather keen senses* or *faculties*: AsP 387.2 sacet prakṣyaty, ātīkṣṇendriyo bhaviṣyati, tatas tam evaṃ vakṣyati, pūrvam api tvaṃ tīkṣṇendriyo 'bhūḥ.

[**ātīrī,** acc. to Tib. (phyugs rdzi bud med) *cowherdess*: °rya(ḥ) MSV iv.198.10. Read ābhī°.]

āttamana(s), adj. (= Pali attamana(s), which is also, but less often, represented by **āptamana(s)**, q.v., on which cf. CPD s.v. attamanas, which fails to note occurrence of āpta° in BHS), *glad at heart, delighted*; esp. in certain formulas; applied to the audience at the end of a discourse by Buddha, e. g. Mv i.61.8 idam avocad bhagavān, āttamano (n. sg. m.) āyuṣmān Mahāmaudgalyāyano bhagavato bhāṣitam abhyanandat; Divy 197.26 idam avocad bhagavān, āttamanasas te bhikṣavo 'bhyanandan; often in a series of synonyms, as tuṣṭa udagra āttamanāḥ pramuditaḥ prītisaumanasyajātaḥ Gv 99.15; Suv 9.7–8; plurals of the same words SP 209.9–10; and variations, as hṛṣṭā tuṣṭā āttamanā (n. pl. m.) pramudita-prītisaumanasyajātā Mv i.230.20; more briefly, tuṣṭo āttamano abhūt Mv ii.195.10; tuṣṭo āttamanā (n. sg. m.) imaṃ udānam udānaye (aor.) i.351.13; dātāraṃ ca dṛṣṭvā āttamanā bhavati sumanaskaḥ Bbh 4.24; sattvā āttamanaso 'bhūvan RP 37.8–9; Indra āttamanā (n. sg. m.) tasyāṃ velāyāṃ . . . Divy 195.24; dṛṣṭvā ca bhavati (bhoti) āttamanā (n. sg. f.) Mv i.213.13 = ii.16.16; doubled (intensive āmreḍita), sā 'ttamanāttamanā(ḥ) *she, greatly delighted*, Divy 2.8; Av i.14.11; so 'py āttamanāttamanā(ḥ) Divy 2.11; Av i.14.13; similarly Divy 440.24; neg. an-āttamanā(ḥ) Karmav 22.10 (follows atiśayitaroṣaś caṇḍībhūto). Once printed **attamanas,** q.v. This word is to be analyzed as a cpd. of Skt. ātta, ppp. of ā-dā, with manas. The alternant **āptamanas** is analyzable as āpta, ppp. of āp (cf. **manaāpa, manāpa**) plus manas. Pali attamana(s) could represent both; both may be Sktizations of that MIndic form.

āttamanaska, adj. = **āttamanas**: °kaḥ SP 103.13; fem., (pramodāmi) °kā bhavāmi Gv 290.3; comp. °kataro 'bhūn Gv 331.6; abstr. n. °ka-tā *state of being delighted* Karmav 37.16.

-āttamīya (or **-attamīya**), semi-MIndic for -ātmīya, in **attāttamīya,** q.v.

-ātmaka, false Sktization of a MIndic form (§ 2.33), if not merely error, for Skt. ātmaja, *son*, in nṛpātmakaiḥ KP 115.7; Tib. rgyal sras rnams kyis, *by kings' sons.*

ātma-grāha (m.: = Pali atta-gāha), *belief in the* (existence of a) *self*; see **-grāha.**

ātmadīya, adj. (analog. to yuṣmadīya etc.), *(one's) own*: MSV i.27.1 (so mss.; ed. em. ātmīy-).

ātma-dhāraṇī, see **dhāraṇī.**

Ātmana (! n. sg. °no), n. of a nāga king: Māy 247.34.

ātmanīya, adj., also subst. nt. (= Pali attaniya), *own, one's own* (= sva, adj., or ātmanaḥ, gen.): LV 301.21 (prose) °yāś ca duhitrīr (acc. pl.; § 13.15), *his own daughters*; usually quasi-subst., *what pertains to the self, what is of the nature of the self* (the existence of which is denied): LV 205.8 (see under **-grāha**); 340.1 (vs) cakṣur na istri puruṣo na pi cātmanīyaṃ; RP 14.6 (vs) strī neha nāsti ca pumān na ca ātmanīyaṃ; KP 137.3 (vs) yasyeha ātmā (read nātmā? Tib. and Chin. render the neg. twice) na ca ātmanīyam (so read, text °yām); Mv iii.66.8 and 14–15 naivātmā naivātmanīyā śūnyā ātmena vā ātmanīyena vā (so Senart, prob. rightly; mss. corrupt, esp. in 8); iii.447.12–13 śūnyā an-ātmanīyā (Bhvr., *having nothing that pertains to the self*) ātmena vā ātmanīyena vā.

ātmapuruṣa, m., *attendant, servant*: Divy 223.2 °ṣā ānayantu bhavanto dhanuḥ.

ātmapūrvāpara, adj., perhaps *having continuity with itself*: Mv ii.1.13–14 °raṃ ca taṃ kulaṃ bhavati, of the family in which the Bodhisattva is born. Corresponds to **labdha-pūrvāpara** Mv i.198.3; not in corresponding passage LV p. 24. Senart keeps the form with mss., but in his note suggests that it is false Sktization of MIndic atta- = ātta- (synonym of labdha-).

ātmabhāva, m. (rarely nt.), (= Pali attabhāva, listed by Pali Lex. among words denoting body, CPD), *body*, synonym of śarīra: SP 11.7 śirāṃsi kecin nayanāni kecid dadanti kecit pravarātmabhāvān; 55.12 darśinsu te mahya tadātmabhāvaṃ; 76.10 ātmabhāvapratilambhenaiva bhagavan sarvakrīḍanakāni labdhāni bhavanti, *only by rescuing their own bodies* . . .; 95.2 dīrghātmabhāvā hi bhavanti, *of long bodies*; 95.5 puruṣātmabhāvaṃ ca yadā labhante, *and when they get a human body*; 236.13; 237.9; 240.11 -stūpe tathāgatasyātmabhāvas tiṣṭhaty ekaghanas . . .; 303.6 mahātmabhāvā rūpeṇa, *great-bodied in form*; 324.1; 406.13 ātmabhāvaparityāgena, *by sacrifice of one's body*; LV 48.20–21 divyamanomayātmabhāvapratilabdhāḥ; 66.16 mātuḥ-kukṣigatasyātmabhāvo 'bhinirvṛtto 'bhūt; 219.19; 306.9 -kākagṛdhro- (mss. gṛddho-; Lefm. gṛdho-, misprint?) -lūkagaruḍādisadṛśātmabhāvāḥ, *having bodies like* . . .; Mv i.245.2–3 āyāmato bahuyojanaśatikena ātmabhāvena; ii.297.5–6 abhedyo siṃhārdhapūrvo bhagavato ātmabhāvo; 326.3 (pūyaṃ yakṛdvṛkkaphusphasehi) gūthaṃ ca anyaṃ anugatam ātmabhāve; 326.14 asīhi chinnā bahuvidham ātmabhāvā; 343.9 te nirmiṇitvā vikṛtātmabhāvāṃ, *distorted bodies*; 369.7, 8, 10; Divy 62.1; 70.3 °va-pratilambhe, *attainment of a body, reincarnation*; same 140.20; 230.23 ff. yojanaśatikā ātmabhāvā, and the like; °va-pratilambhe (as above) Av i.162.5; same cpd. Suv 81.14; as nt., perhaps by attraction to associated form of śarīra, Suv 75.13 yuṣmākam etāny ātmabhāvāni saṃtarpayed mahataujasā yuṣmākam etāni divyāni śarīrāṇi vivardhayet; Suv 225.7 (vs) tyaktā maya ātmabhāvāḥ; Dbh 19.4 (cpd. with list of bodily members, ending) -hṛdaya-sarvātmabhāva-parityāgo; others, Av i.171.15; Samādh 22.44; Suv 83.4; Śikṣ 21.21; 44.19; Gv 8.9; 218.21; 220.7; 537.4; Dbh 31.10; 91.6; Bbh 42.21; Vaj 29.20; Sukh 27.15; Sādh 64.6–7; could be indefinitely extended (very common in most texts). The fact has not been recognized sufficiently clearly that this is a quite plain and simple synonym of śarīra, *body*. The same is in general true of Pali, tho I am not prepared to say that it always has that mg. there. The Pali dictionaries (even CPD) do not bring this out clearly.

[**ātmabhāvatā,** Senart's em. Mv ii.301.11 (prose) sarvatra bodhisattvasya °tāṃ anuprāptāṃ saṃjānanti; should mean *embodiment*, from ātmabhāva plus -tā. But the occasion is the approach to his enlightenment (not his conception or birth), which is signalized by miracles and cosmic portents. The mss. read °bhāvanām, which is doubtless right: *they recognize on all sides that the Bodhisattva's self-realization* (ātma-bhāvanā) *is at hand.*]

ātma-vṛṣabhitā (see **vṛṣa°**), *lordliness of person*: °tām, acc. sg., Mv ii.261.5; 262.6 (in the latter v.l. °bhatāṃ; in the former mss. are corrupt but read °bhi°). This is one of the qualities attained by Bodhisattvas when they have acquired perfection of powers.

ātmātmīya, *the self and what pertains to the self*: Dbh 43.13; 50.29 (see **attāttamīya**). Cf. Bbh 276.17–18 asad ātmā vā ātmīyaṃ vā (contrasted with: saṃskṛtam asaṃskṛtaṃ ca sat).

ātmīya (hardly in this sense in Skt.; cf. **anātmīya**), *characterized by a self*; (*what is*) *possessed of a self*: Mv i.173.4–5 nāpi ye dharmā ātmīyās te anātmato deśayāmi; KP 94.8 °ya-saṃjñā, *false notion of something as being concerned with the self*.

ātmopanāyika, see **upanāyika.**

ātmya (nt.), *self-ness, the having a self* or *doctrine that there is a self*, opp. **nairātmya**: LV 436.21 (vs) asti-nāsti-vinirmuktam ātmyanairātmya-varjitaṃ (... dharmacakram).

ātyayika, adj. (from atyaya; in Divy quantity of initial -a- ambiguous in saṃdhi, taken as aty° by Burnouf and Divy Index; on mg. see Burnouf, Introduction 628), *transcending, exceptional, irregular, overstepping normal procedure*: -piṇḍapāta, Divy 50.25, 26 tathāgatasyātyayika-piṇḍapātam ... pañca me Maudgalyāyanātyayikapiṇḍapātāḥ ... āgantukasya, gamikasya, glānasya, glānopasthāyakasyo, 'padhivārikasya ca; Śikṣ 17.19 sarvasattvānām ātyayikaṃ parigṛhyaitad api me varjayan niṣīdāmi (so a Bodhisattva should ponder); perh. *transcendent, very important* (matter); cf. Aśoka, Rock Ed. 6, line 7 (Girnar); Kauṭ. Arth. Sham.[1] 29.12. Bendall and Rouse *troubles.*

Ātreya, (**1**) name assumed by **Kuśa** (2) as physician: MSV i.104.3; (**2**) n. of a distinguished physician of Taxila: MSV ii.26.7 ff.; note that this is the name of a great physician in Skt.

ādapana, acc. to Kern SP Preface p. vii, in Kashgar rec. of SP for Nep. ādāpana.

ādarśa-jñāna, nt., *mirror-like knowledge* (one of the 5 jñāna of a Tathāgata; = **ādarśana-j°**, q.v.): Mvy 111. (See **jñāna.**) Tib. me loṅ lta buḥi (*like a mirror*) ye śes.

ādarśana (nt.), *mirror* (≐ Skt. ādarśa): Suv 106.5 (vs) °na-padādyaś ca ... niyojayet (see Nobel's note). Cf. next.

ādarśana-jñāna, nt., = **ādarśa-j°**, q.v.: Dharmas 94. Cf. prec.

Ādarśamaṇḍalanirbhāsā, n. of a lokadhātu: Gv 82.10.

Ādarśamukha, (**1**) n. of a prince (= Pali Ādāsamukha): MSV i.114.9 ff.; (**2**) n. of a nāga king: Mvy 3297. Cf. **Adarśamukha.**

ādāna (= Pali id.; from Skt. ā-dā, suffix -ana), *grasping, clinging* (to existence or to worldly things): Mvy 2018 ādāna-vijñānam (follows **ālaya-vij°**, q.v.): an-ād°, neg. Bhvr., Ud iii.18 (= Pali Sn 741) vītatṛṣṇo hy anādānaḥ ... parivrajet.

[**ādāye,** in Mv i.10.2 (vs) ekaiko yojanaśataṃ ādāye saṃprabhāsati: read ābhāye with same line Mv iii.454.18: *each one shines with radiance* (ābhā) *for 100 yojanas.*]

?**ādārita,** adj. (ppp.) perh. to be read in Mv i.187.8 (vs) where all mss. mūrdhnā (one ms. adds ca) dārito bhūmau (one syllable short, without ca); if we read ādārito (or ādarito; ppp. denom. from ādara?) meter would be correct; it should mean *prostrated in respectful salutation with the head on the ground.* (Senart em. violently: mūrdhinā patito.) Uncertain.

ādi, *beginning* (= Skt.): **ādiṃ**, acc. (= Pali ādiṃ katvā, with acc. object) and ādau, loc., with following kṛtvā, and preceding acc. (once gen.), lit. *putting ... first*; so *beginning with, starting with, from ... on* (the loc. ādau used precisely like the acc. ādiṃ; *putting at the beginning* = *making the beginning*; loc. only in Mv): tuṣitabhavanavāsam ādiṃ kṛtvā, *beginning with* (the Bodhisattva's) *dwelling in the Tuṣita-heaven* (= *from then on*) Śikṣ 292.5 = Dbh 14.21, cf. tuṣitabhavanam ādau kṛtvā sarveṣāṃ bodhisattvānāṃ ... Mv i.147.15; āvīcim ādiṃ kṛtvā sarvanairayikāṇāṃ sattvānāṃ ... LV 86.11, *of all hell-inhabitants from Avīci on*; mātuḥ kukṣim ādau kṛtvā bodhisattvānāṃ yāvat parinirvṛtā Mv i.145.2, *beginning with the mother's womb, of Bodhisattvas, until they have entered complete nirvāṇa*; bhartāraṃ ādau kṛtvā Mv i.147.8 (no man has any carnal desire for the destined mothers of Buddhas) *from their husbands on*; bodhisattvasya garbhāvakrāntim ādau kṛtvā Mv i.157.15; śākyamuniṃ samyaksaṃbuddhaṃ ādau kṛtvā daśa bhūmayo deśitā Mv i.161.7, *beginning from* (*the time of*) *Śākyamuni the Buddha, the Ten Stages have been taught* (not before! so, I think, the parallels require us to interpret, contrary to Senart n. 506); with gen. of the dependent noun (rather than acc.), evidently construed as modifier of ādiṃ: tṛṣṇāyāḥ paunarbhavikyā ādiṃ kṛtvā Laṅk 180.10, *beginning with* (*starting from*; lit. *making a beginning of*) *desire for rebirth.* Cf. Mbh. Crit. ed. 2.52.17d saha strībhir draupadīm ādi-kṛtvā, *along with the women, beginning with Draupadī* (i. e. *D. and the others*). This seems to be unparalleled in Skt. See also s.v. **ādīkaroti.**

ādika, adj. (= Pali id., see Childers; Mahāvaṃsa 12.21 phalaṃ ... ādikaṃ), *first, initial*: Śikṣ 356.6.

ādikarmika, adj. and subst. (= Pali ādikammika; cf. next; wrongly defined in pw 7.317 following Divy Index), *beginner*, (*one who is*) *inexperienced*: Mvy 387 (tathāgataḥ) sārthavāha ādikarmikāṇām; Divy 544.19–20 anāpattir ādikarmikasya, *for a beginner*, (the actions described are) *not a sin*; RP 5.1 navakair ādikarmikair acirapravrajitair (sc. bhikṣubhiḥ); Śikṣ 11.6 °ka-bodhisattvena (misprinted °tvane); 20.5–6 °ko mahāyāne, *a beginner in the M.*; 60.11 °kā mahāyānasaṃprasthitāḥ; Bbh 205.2 iha bodhisattvo na ādikarmika-tat-prathamakarmika-vīryeṇa samanvāgato bhavati; 205.7–8 °ka eva (*while still a beginner*) sa bodhisattvaḥ ...; 394.24 (bodhisattvam) °kaṃ tatprathamakarmikaṃ (see this); 395.2; Gv 503.9 sarvādikarmika-bodhisattvasiṃhapotāḥ puṣyanti buddha-dharmaiḥ ...; an-ādi°, *not inexperienced*, SP 66.7 °kāś ca te bodhisattvā bhaviṣyanti, ciracaritakuśalamūlā ...

ādikarmin, adj. and subst., = prec. (which replaces this two lines below): Śikṣ 60.9 °miṇāṃ mahāyānasaṃprasthitānāṃ kulaputrāṇāṃ ...

Āditya, m. (**1**) the gotra name of Śākyamuni's family (= Pali Ādicca): Mv ii.199.16 = Pali Sn 423; (**2**) n. of a former Buddha: Mv iii.237.3, 4.

Ādityagarbha, n. of a Bodhisattva: Mvy 708; Dbh 2.6.

Ādityagarbhaprabhameghārāja, nt., n. of the 'gem-jewel' of a cakravartin: Gv 418.9.

Ādityateja(s), n. of a former Buddha: Gv 258.17 (vs).

Ādityadatta, n. of a former Buddha: Mv i.138.5.

Ādityasaṃbhava, n. of a Buddha in the south: Sukh 98.1.

ādiyati, or **ādīyati** (formally looks like passive to ā-dā; = Pali ādiyati, only with short i; cf. **upād°, paryād°, samād°**; all these regularly used with active mg., except paryādīyante KP 5.2 [and this is uncertain; Śikṣ 148.9 cites it as parihīyante]; in Pali also active mg., except sometimes pariyādiyati, pass., PTSD; Geiger 175.1 calls these forms 'passive with middle meaning'; I prefer the term 'active'), *takes; takes on, assumes*: Mv i.346.10 (yaṃ nūnāhaṃ) adinnaṃ anyātakaṃ (q.v.) śālim ādiyeyaṃ (v.l. ādī°), opt., and (11) ādiyeya (v.l. °yaṃ, ādī°) 3 sg. pret., also (12) ādiyantaṃ (v.l. ādī°), acc. sg. pres. pple.; iii.93.16 (vs) puṣpaṃ tyajitvā phalam ādiyante (mss. °nta, to be kept as imperf.?); 217.17 (bhavān ...) dhanam ādiyatu (v.l. ādī°); 218.12 (bhavān ...) striyaḥ ādiyatu; 447.12 (yo imāṃ saṃskārāṃ) ādīyati (no v.l.) vā nikṣipati vā.

ādiśati, (**1**) (cf. Hindi ādes *salutation*, late Skt. ādeśa id., Edgerton, JAOS 38.206 f.), *salutes, greets*: °śitavya, gdve., Mv iii.420.11 (na bhikṣavo) yuṣmābhir ādiśitavyaṃ bhikṣāyāṃ labdhāyāṃ, *monks, you must not salute* (the donor) *when you have received alms*; (**2**) (= Pali ādisati, obj. dakkhinaṃ, dānaṃ), *assigns* (the profit from a meritorious act, ordinarily a gift of alms to the Buddha and his monks; object dakṣiṇām, once dakṣiṇādeśanām; this profit is, at the desire of the donor, often assigned by the recipient, ordinarily the Buddha, to the credit of someone else, e. g. a tormented preta, or the deceased father of the donor): Divy 85.28–30 bhagavatābhihitaḥ: mahārāja, kasya nāmnā dakṣiṇām ādiśāmi, kiṃ tavāho svid yena tavāntikāt prabhūtataraṃ puṇyaṃ prasūtam iti (similarly 86.3, 4, 7, etc.), *the Lord said: O King, in whose name shall I assign the profit of your gift? yours, or that of one who has produced more merit than you?*; Av i.258.13 tato bhagavān ... dakṣiṇām ādiśati (in a verse, 259.1–2, assigning it to the benefit of pretas); 264.12 bhagavāṃś ca ... dakṣiṇādeśanām ādiśati (as prec.); 272.13 tato bhagavatā pretasya nāmnā dakṣiṇā ādiṣṭā; but the same ādiśati may be used when the subject is the donor, as in a frequent cliché in which a man hopes to have a son who will assign to him after death the profit of gifts and works of merit: Divy 99.6–8 asmākaṃ ca (see **atyatīta**) ... dānāni dattvā puṇyāni kṛtvā nāmnā dakṣiṇām ādiśed, ... *he would assign the profit* (of the gifts and virtuous acts) *in my name*; virtually the same Divy 440.30 ādekṣyati; Av i.15.1 and 197.3 etc. ādekṣyate; but elsewhere, (**3**) when the donor (not the Buddha) is the subject, the caus. ādeśayati is used; so in the same cliché just mentioned, Divy 2.(15–)16 ... dakṣiṇām ādeśayiṣyati, (my son ...) *will cause the profit to be assigned* (to me); Av i.264.2–3 putraka ... mama nāmnā buddhapramukhaṃ bhikṣusaṃghaṃ bhojaya dakṣiṇām ādeśaya ...; Divy 10.28 (asmākaṃ) ca nāmnā dakṣiṇām ādeśaya (also addressed by a father to his son). See s.v. **dakṣiṇādeśanā.**

ādīkaroti (see s.v. **ādi**), *starts from* (acc.), *makes the starting point*: ger. °kariyāṇa, SP 192.1 (vs) avidya (acc.) ādīkariyāṇa cakṣumān, prabhāṣate maraṇam anantaduḥkham (so apparently mss., combining the note to KN ed. with that to Kern's Transl. SBE 21.185), *starting with ignorance, the Enlightened One expounded death and infinite misery*. This reading is perfect in meter and sense. Possibly ādī is to be taken as a separate word, = ādiṃ; certainly it means the same as ādiṃ kṛ-.

ādīnava, m. or (rarely) nt., once perh. adj., (= Pali id.; clearly Buddhist word, despite rare occurrences in late Skt., and despite ādīnava-darśa in Vedic, see Schmidt Nachtr., s.v. ādīnava, and Renou, JA 1939 p. 391), *misery, evil, danger, mishap, wretchedness*: nt. noted only Mv iii.297.12 tāye atra mahādīnavaṃ utpāditaṃ; m. (unambiguously) Mvy 7309 °vaḥ; Divy 9.21 and 335.12 °vo (*mishap*) 'tra bhaviṣyati; Divy 190.25–26 ime cānye ādīnavā madyapāne; 224.24–25 kṛtā kāmeṣv ādīnavakathā, gṛhāśramapadasyādīnavo bhāṣitas; 329.21 yaḥ kaścid ādīnavo, *any disaster whatever* (may occur); same, MSV i.44.19; Karmav 33.14 tathā daśādīnavā Nandikasūtra uktāḥ prāṇātipātasya; 42.6 pañcatriṃśad ādīnavāḥ surāmaireyamadyapramādasthāne; often with loc. of that in, or in connection with, which the evil is manifested, as, kāmeṣu ādīnavaṃ dṛṣṭvā Mv i.283.19; iii.193.1; 418.20; 450.8; mitreṣu ādīnavaṃ (read °va, m.c.) saṃmṛśanto Mv i.359.2 (vs); taṃ tiryagyoniṣu mahantaṃ ādīnavaṃ dṛṣṭvā Mv i.27.11, similarly 29.13; 30.11; dṛṣṭvā ādīnavaṃ loke Mv ii.166.6; other locs. above and below; but occasionally gen. instead, kāyasyādīnavaṃ saṃpaśyan LV 208.9; prāṇātipātasya Karmav 33.14 (above); or prior member in comp., saṃsāra-doṣādīnava-niḥśaraṇa-(= niḥsa°)-kuśalaḥ LV 180.15; lokādīnavaṃ lokaniḥsaraṇaṃ api deśayāmi Gv 191.25; in contrast with āsvāda, āsvādādīnaveṣu Mv i.134.1 *in enjoyments and miseries*; kāmāna āsvādaṃ ... ādīnavaṃ ca kāmānāṃ bhāṣate puruṣottamaḥ Mv i.184.13–14 (vs); others, miscellaneous, ahaṃ ca ādīnava (acc.) tatra darśayīṃ (WT °yī) SP 90.3 (vs); taṃ kampille mahāntam ādīnavaṃ dṛṣṭvā Mv i.284.8; etam ādīnavaṃ ācikṣiṣyāmi Mv iii.74.8; ādīnavadarśāvī (= Pali °dassāvi-n) *perceiving the misery or danger*, n. sg. of °vin, kāmeṣu Mv i.283.18–19; ii.144.16 (here text °darśī, v.l. °darśāvī); without dependent noun, °śāvī, followed by niḥsaraṇa- (or niḥśa°; delete final -ḥ in the first passage) -prajñaḥ (or -prājño) Mv iii.52.5; 201.5; °va-darśin = °va-darśāvin, tatrādīnavadarśinaḥ Bbh 29.20 (tatra = strīṣu); in Bhvr. cpds., (kāmāḥ) sabhayāḥ saraṇāḥ sādīnavāḥ sadoṣā iti LV 213.1; anantādīnavā mārṣa kāmāḥ Jm 114.15; bahvādīnavaś ca gṛhāvāso RP 48.2–3; once apparently ādīnava alone, uncompounded, used as adj., *wretched, evil, miserable*, Mv i.33.11 (vs) sarvaṃ ādīnavaṃ lokaṃ (parallel with ādīpitaṃ, prajvalitaṃ, prakampitaṃ, in same vs applied to lokaṃ).

ādīptaka, adj. (= Skt. ādīpta plus -ka), *ablaze, on fire*: SP 88.5 (vs) °ke jvālasahasrapūrṇe (sc. gṛhe); perhaps ka m.c.

ādīptaśiraścailopama (in Mvy °celop°), adj., and °ma-tā, subst., (state of being) *like one whose head or clothes are on fire* (i. e. who is in extreme danger and needs nirvāpaṇa, *the putting out* of the flames; applied to one leading a worldly life; in Pali ādittasīsa and ādittacela occur as separate cpds., AN iv.320.26, cf. also SN v.440.7): °maḥ Mvy 1802; Śikṣ 54.3–4 kusīdo 'haṃ bodhiś cādīptaśiraścailopamena bahūn kalpān ... samudānetavyā; 191.8–9 parākramasaṃpannatā ādīptaśiraścailopamatā jñānaparyeṣṭyā (here *state of realizing, being aware, that one's head and clothes are on fire*, and so in next); Gv 493.2 īdṛśyādīpta° °pamatayā (text separates īdṛśyā dīpta°) kalyāṇamitrājñānaṃ na vilomayanti. Bendall and Rouse in Śikṣ Transl. misunderstand the word.

ādīyaka, m. (to **ādīyati, ādi°**, with -aka), *one who takes (up, or on), assumes* (the **saṃskāras**): Mv iii.447.16 ahaṃ so atra kārako vā kārāpako vā utthāpako vā ādīyako vā nikṣepako vā (sc. of the saṃskāras; such things are not to be said); similarly 448.5.

ādīyati = **ādiyati,** q.v.

Ādumā (Pali Ātumā), n. of a (Malla?) village: MPS 28.24 (Tib. a-du-ma).

[**ādṛśyā,** Gv 498.1, see **adṛśyā.**]

ādeya-vacana, adj. Bhvr. (= Pali ādeyya-vacana, also -vāca Vin. ii.158.17; in PTSD defined as Karmadh., but actually Bhvr. in all citations traced [Jāt. vi.243 seems to be an error]); also °**na-tā,** abstr. *state of being* ... (this); *of welcome, acceptable*, i. e. *pleasing, agreeable speech*: Bbh 29.(16–)17 satyavacano 'piśunāparuṣāsaṃbhinnapralāpābhyāsaḥ ādeyavacanatāyā hetuḥ; 31.15–17 °cano bodhisattvaḥ priyavāditayā arthacaryayā samānārthatayā ca sattvāṃ saṃgṛhṇāti paripācayati, idam ādeyavacanatāyā ... phalaṃ ...; Mv i.270.6 °canā ca bhavanti kīrtanīyā ca bahujanasya (of devotees of Buddha); Suv 80.11; Śikṣ 351.7. Cf. next.

ādeya-vākya, adj. Bhvr., = prec.: Mv i.103.5 °yāś (of Boddhisattvas); Karmav 29.27 an-ādeyavākyā api ādeyavākyā api (Lévi *qui ont la parole antipathique ou sympathique*).

ādeśanā, (**1**) (= Pali ādesanā-, cpd. with pāṭihāriya), *reading of the mind*: Bbh 264.21 sa ṛddhyā cittādeśanayā ... (sattvān vinayati); usually in cpd. ādeśanā-prātihārya, *trick* or *marvelous ability of mind-reading, reading other people's thoughts*, see s.v. **prātihārya**; (**2**) in **dakṣiṇādeśanā** (once °**na**), *assignment of profit of good deeds*, see that cpd.

ādeśayati, *causes* (dakṣiṇā, the profit from gifts or works of merit) *to be assigned* (to someone else); see s.v. **ādiśati** (3), of which this is the caus.

-ādharṣaka, see **sv-ā°.**

-ādhāra, see **śrutādhāra.**

-ādhāraka, see **śastrādhāraka.**

ādhāraṇa-tā (= Pali id., wrongly defined in PTSD;

ādhāraṇa only doubtfully in Nirukta 7.11, where Sarup reads rasa-dhāraṇam), *holding firm, maintenance*: LV 35.18 dhāraṇīpratilambho ... sarvabuddhabhāṣitādhāraṇatāyai saṃvartate.

Ādhāraṇamudrā, n. of a samādhi: Mvy 525; = **Ādhāramudrā**, q.v.

Ādhāraṇī, n. of a goddess: Mvy 4288.

Ādhāramudrā = prec. but one: ŚsP 1416.20.

ādhārayati, with object śastram (cf. **śastrādhāraka**, which makes the mg. unmistakable), *wields, plies* (a knife): Divy 39.(6–)7 (santi ... śrāvakā ye 'nena pūtikāyenārdīyamānā ... śastram) apy ādhārayanti viṣam api bhakṣayanti ... *there are disciples who, afflicted by this stinking body, even wield a knife* (here, against themselves!), *even eat poison* ... (or kill themselves in other ways).

ādhāvana (nt.; Pali id.), in comp. with following **paridhāvana**, *running around, to and fro, this way and that*: Śikṣ 268.(12–)13 lābhahetor lābhanidānam ādhāvanaparidhāvanaṃ dauḥśīlyasamudācaraṇaṃ ca. (In Pali the verbs ādhāvati and paridhāvati are frequently used together in this sense.)

ādhikaraṇika, adj. (not in this sense elsewhere; from **adhikaraṇa**, q.v., with suffix ika), *given to disputes*: Bbh 171.5 sacet prakṛtyā kalahakāraḥ syād ādhikaraṇikaḥ; MSV ii.188.2; iii.5.9.

ādhipateya, nt. (anomalously m. Mvy 7192 °yaḥ = Tib. bdaṅ du ḥgyur ba (or bya ba), so also Mironov; = Pali ādhipateyya, see below; from adhipati, roughly = Skt. ādhipatya, which is used in AbhidhK., see Index, in ways not closely parallel to the Pali usage), *control, influence, mastery, prime motivation* (lit. *overlordship*). In Pali esp. used of one of three influences leading to virtue, attādhi° (q.v. CPD), lokādhi°, dhammādhi°, see Childers s.v. ādhipateyya and Vism. i.14.1 ff. (*the influence of oneself*, i. e. *conscience* or *self-respect*; *the influence of the world* or *public opinion*; *the influence of dhamma* or *regard for moral principles* as authoritatively laid down). In BHS little evidence is found for the existence of these, tho Speyer (Transl. 114) renders Jm 80.14 (hrīvarṇapratisaṃyukteṣu) lokādhipateyeṣu ca (sc. upaneyam) by ... *the regard of public opinion*, perhaps rightly. On the other hand, lokādhipateya-prāpta LV 425.5 can only mean *arrived at the overlordship of the world*; it is one of a long list of epithets of the Buddha as the one that has 'turned the wheel of the Law'; it is preceded by lokagurur ... lokārthakara ... lokānuvartaka ... lokavid ity ucyate, and it would be absurd to interpret it as *under the control of public opinion*. (See also LV 179.20–21 s.v. **ādhipateyatā**.) Mv i.16.12 = 18.5, 15 = 19.5 = 20.10 (evaṃ khalu) punaḥ ādhipateya-mātram etaṃ tatropatteḥ, *but this, of course, is only the principal cause* (controlling influence) *of rebirth there* (viz. in one of various hells); Gv 19.8 na tad balaṃ na tad ādhipateyaṃ ... (saṃvidyate), *that* (sort of) *power* or *controlling influence* (is not found); oftener at the end of Bhvr. cpds., Śikṣ 117.3 mahākaruṇādhipateyam, (any action of Bodhisattvas is ...) *controlled* (influenced) *by supreme compassion*; Śikṣ 250.5 cakṣurindriyādhipateyā rūpārambaṇaprativijñaptiḥ, *recognition of the sense-object form, which* (recognition) *is controlled by* (= dependent on) *the sense of sight*; Dbh 11.20 (tac cittam utpadyate bodhisattvānāṃ) mahākaruṇāpūrvaṃgamaṃ prajñājñānādhipateyaṃ ...; Śikṣ 322.15 dharmādhipateya, of Buddhas. See next.

ādhipateya-tā (from prec.), (1) *state of overlordship or control*; (2) at the end of Bhvr. cpds. ending in °teya-, *state of being under the control of* ... (lit. *state of having ... as controlling influence*); (**1**) LV 204.(17–)18 (pūrvaṃ mayā svayaṃbhuvām) ādhipateyatām abhilaṣatā, *of old by me* (Buddha) *desiring supremacy over* (first place among) *Self-existent Ones*; LV 179.20–21 -puṇyasaṃbhārabalaviśeṣaṇāsadṛśī- (better would seem to be °sadṛśīṃ, which is read by Calc. but none of Lefm.'s mss.) -lokādhipateyatāṃ saṃdarśya, (said of the Bodhisattva) *manifesting an unexampled state of mastery over the world thru ...*; (**2**) Gv 17.25 buddhādhipateyatāṃ, *state of being under the control of the Buddhas*; 68.18 supratiṣṭhitasya bhikṣor maitryādhipateyatayā, ... *because he is under the influence of love*; KP 99.6–7 cittam ... rājasadṛśaṃ sarvadharmādhipateyatayā (so read for text °pateyā, uninterpretable), (in a passage decrying the vanity of cittam,) *citta is like a king, because it is controlled by all the states of* (conditioned, transitory) *existence*; at least, this mg. seems more consistent with the context than *because it is the ruler of all states* ..., but this latter is what Tib. means (chos thams cad la dbaṅ byed paḥi phyir); in that case to 1.

? **ādhimānika**, adj. (**adhimāna** plus -ika), *proud*: so v.l. for text **ābhimānika** in SP 38.12; 39.4.

ādhimokṣika, adj. (to **adhimokṣa** plus -ika), *of zealous application*: °kaṃ samādhiṃ MSV iv.237.7.

ādhiṣṭhānika, m. (to Skt. adhiṣṭhāna, *capital, seat of government*, plus -ika), pl. *people of the capital*, or perhaps *government men*: °kāś ca chattraṃ paṭṭaṃ mukuṭaṃ cādāya ... āgatāḥ MSV i.68.14.

ādhyātmika (= Pali ajjhattika), *internal*: ādhy° **āyatana**, q.v., *the sense organs* or *powers*, in contrast with bāhira **āyatana**, *the objects of sense*, Mv iii.66.3. See also **ābhāsa**.

āna, *breath* (so Skt. Lex.); in Pali and BHS apparently replaces Skt. prāṇa in cpd. **ānāpāna**, q.v. Pali seems not to have the cpd. *pāṇāpāna.

-ānanaka, f. °**nikā**, = Skt. ānana, *face*, at the end of Bhvr. cpds., with endearing dim. connotation (§ 22.34): LV 322.10 pattra-vibodhita-ānanikā(ḥ); 11 sulepana-ānanikā(ḥ); 13 paripūrita-candra-nibhānanikā(ḥ); all in vss, all applied to the daughters of Māra.

[**ānanta-paṭṭikā**, given by Das for Tib. mthaḥ skor which in Mvy 9191 = **ānanda-paṭṭika**, q.v.]

[**ānantarīya**, nt., °yāṇi, Mvy 2323; but prob. read with Mironov **ānantarya**, q.v. Cf. however next.]

ānantarīyaka, adj. (cf. prec. and **ānantarya**), in prayatnānantarīyakaḥ (so correctly Index, and Mironov), *immediately occurring* (as a result of effort): Mvy 4493.

ānantarya, adj. and subst. nt. (in Skt. as subst. nt., *unmittelbare Folge*, BR, or *unmittelbares Darauf*, ... *Nachher*, pw; cf. °**rīya**, **anantariya**, and next, also **upānantarīya**); as subst. nt., not limited to evil connotation and much as in Skt., Gv 250.25 bodhicitto- (1st ed. °catto-; corr. 2d ed.)-tpādapraśaṃsāparaṃparānantaryāṇi, *enlightenment-thought-production-laudation-series-immediacies*, and a long series of terms ending likewise in °paraṃparānantaryāṇi, *actions or events succeeding one another immediately*, ending in 251.18–20 bodhisattvasusūkṣmajñānapraveśaparaṃparānantaryāṇi, tāny asyāḥ sarvaromavivarebhyo nirmāṇakāyameghān niścaritvā sattvebhyo dharmaṃ deśayamānān (read °mānāny?) apaśyat; Gv 522.13 upapatty-ānantarya-citte (but here perhaps as adj.) *the mental state which immediately precedes rebirth* (see **upapatti**); perhaps in same sense Mvy 1206 ānantarya-mārgaḥ, of the 8-fold noble path as *characterized by immediate succession* (of its stages, one after another) or *causing immediate results*, as below; the latter surely in Śikṣ 17.20 pañcemāni ... ānantaryāṇi yair ānantaryaiḥ samanvāgatā bodhisattvāḥ kṣipram anuttarā (read °rāṃ) samyaksaṃbodhim abhisaṃbudhyate (read °yante?); here Bendall and Rouse 19 translate *continuities*, but better *procedures bringing immediate, speedy* (desirable) *results* (note kṣipram; the five are listed in what follows); see also **ānantaryasamādhi**; otherwise the word has been noted only as adj. with karman, or subst. nt. without karman; (evil) *action bringing immediate retribution, deadly sin* (= Pali ānantariya or °rika, with or sc. kamma, see Childers s.v. pañcānantariyakammaṃ); there are five such, viz. killing of mother, father, or an arhant, causing dissension in the order of monks, and deliberately causing a Tathāgata's blood to flow (same list in Pali): pañcānantaryāṇi Mvy 2323 (Kyoto ed. °tarīyāṇi but Mironov °taryāṇi; list of 5 given 2324–28); Dharmas 60 (with list); Mv i.243.18 °ryāṇi kṛtāni (listed and described in the following, down to) 244.17 etāni pañcānantaryāṇi karmāṇi kṛtvā mahānarakeṣūpapanno; Śikṣ 257.11, 12 and Laṅk 138.2, 3, 8 (without karmāṇi); Mmk 57.2 pañcānantaryakariṇasyāpi, *even of a doer of* . . .; Śikṣ 60.5 (after a list of the five crimes) ebhiḥ pañcabhir ānantaryaiḥ karmabhir . . .; two or three of the list mentioned, Divy 260.5–8 yadā tasya trīṇy ānantaryāṇi paripūrṇāni . . . pāpa eṣa pitṛghātako 'rhadghātako mātṛghātakaś ca, trīṇy anenānantaryāṇi narakakarmasaṃvartanīyāni karmāṇi kṛtāny upacitāni; Divy 567.27 dve tvayā ānantarye karmaṇī kṛte (killing of father and of an arhant bhikṣu); others, Gv 228.21–22 °rya-karma-kāriṇāṃ . . . sattvānāṃ; Bbh 166.8 °ryam karma kṛtvā; Sukh 15.4 °rya-kāriṇaḥ . . . sattvān.

Ānantaryasamādhi, the fifth of the **adhimukticaryā**-bhūmi, Mvy 901. (Printed Anant°; correct in Index and in Mironov.) See **ānantarya.** In Sūtrāl. xiv.26, comm., identified with **laukikāgra-dharma,** q.v., 4th and highest of **nirvedha(-bhaga),** q.v.; ib. 27 explains that it is called this, yato grāhakavikṣepo hīyate tadanantaram, *because the 'dispersion'* (confusion) *of the Subject* (grāhaka) *is abandoned immediately after* (attainment of) *it.* Lit., then, *immediate concentration* or *concentration of immediacy.* In Dharmas 101 occurs as the 4th of four **samādhi** (q.v.). Mv i.291.11 (vs) yam āhu ānantariyaṃ (mss. āhuḥ an°, meter demands Senart's em.) samādhiṃ, samādhino tasya samo na vidyate.

Ānanda (= Pali id.), (**1**) n. of a well-known disciple of the Buddha, a Śākyan: son of Śuklodana Mv iii.176.14, and of Mṛgī Mv ii.157.9; iii.176.15; called *servant* (upasthāyaka) of Buddha Divy 90.7–8; 396.15–18; 612.1–2; called Ānanda-sthavira Mv ii.114.9, Ānanda-bhadra SP 217.8; 218.12; in Mv iii.47.10 ff. story of how his followers among the monks proved imperfect, and how he was rebuked and instructed by Mahākāśyapa; called a śaikṣa SP 2.8; a few (out of many) other occurrences are Mv i.77.16; iii.225.10 ff.; SP 215.1; 216.3; 221.3; Divy 20.6; 56.2; 69.9; 72.17; 76.10 (= 465.11); 91.21; LV 2.4; 60.12; 73.2; 87.3; 443.7; Suv 202.5, 6; Sukh 2.11; 92.7; Karmav 155.2; Bhīk 3b.2; (**2**) n. of a Śākyan youth (perhaps = prec.?): LV 152.12; 153.21; (**3**) n. of a cakravarti-rājan (listed among other names ordinarily applied to disciples of Buddha): Mvy 3609; (**4**) n. of a devaputra: LV 6.12 (but omitted in some mss. and prob. not original); (**5**) n. of a yakṣa: Māy 18; (**6**) n. of a king (prob. not = 3): MSV i.114.7.

Ānandacandra, n. of a former Buddha: Mv i.139.9.

ānanda-paṭṭika, m. (nom. °kaḥ), Mvy 9191 (so also Mironov) = mthaḥ skor, defined in Das by Skt. ānantapaṭṭikā, Eng. *all round; . . . the whole circumference, the perimeter.* So also Chin. *circumference* (*edge going all around*). Context seems to indicate *circumference* (of a robe); perhaps *hem*? Cf. **ānandā.**

Ānanda-bhadra, see **Ānanda** (1).

Ānandamāla, n. of a former Buddha: Mv i.139.9.

ānandā, app. *hem* (or *fringe*?), around a cushioned seat, cf. **ānanda-paṭṭika**: MSV iv.75.10.

?**ānandika,** a kind of ascetic: Mv iii.412.7, see s.v. **tredaṇḍika.**

Ānandita, n. of Māra's doorkeeper: LV 302.11.

ānandī, *joy*: Divy 37.24 °dyā nandīsaumanasyaṃ bhavati. Acc. to PTSD, this stem occurs in Pali, Jāt. vi.589.11, where ānandi-cittā should be read for °di vittā.

ān-abhiramya, adj., m.c. for **an°**, q.v.

ānāpāna (= Pali id.), *breath* (see below): °na-bhāvanā-vidhiḥ Mvy 1165; °na-smṛti (= Pali °na-sati), *mindfulness of breathing,* Mvy 1166; Bbh 110.24; 204.26; 396.22; Ud xv.1; °nānusmṛti, id., ŚsP 60.8; on this and ŚsP 1443.8 (where text ānāpā-nusmṛtir) see s.v. **anusmṛti.** The word is an old dvandva; āna (= prāṇa) plus apāna (cf. Skt. prāṇāpāna, on which see G. W. Brown, JAOS 39.104 ff.). In Pali commentarial diction replaced by assāsa-passāsa (= **āśvāsa-praśvāsa,** q.v.). Tib. on Mvy 1166 ānāpāna (-smṛtiḥ) renders dbugs rṅub pa daṅ ḥbyuṅ ba, *breathing in and out*; the same or related terms are used for āśvāsa and praśvāsa. It is clear that Tib. understands āna = āśvāsa as *inbreathing,* apāna = praśvāsa as *outbreathing.* There is BHS evidence supporting this interpretation of **āśvāsa-praśvāsa,** q.v.

ānāpeti (= Pali id.), caus. to ā-nī, see § 38.55.

ānāha (m.; Skt. Lex. id., not in Pali or Pkt.), *height* (of a man): Divy 546.12 kīdṛśas tasya rājño ānāhapariṇāhaḥ. Usually **āroha** (which read?).

ānijya = **aniñjya,** q.v.: adj., Av ii.199.5 ānijyāṃ śāntiṃ; in Mv ii.132.15 there is a v.l. anijya- or ān- for °niñjya- of text.

āniñja = **aniñjya,** q.v. (Mv i.34.11; ii.419.11).

āniñjya = **aniñjya,** q.v.

Āninetra, Āninema, see **Āṇi°.**

ānimitta, adj. and subst. nt. (from Skt. animitta plus suffix -a), *causeless(ness)*; usually parallel with **śūnyatā** and **apraṇihita,** qq.v.; as in the case of apraṇihita, it is often hard to be sure whether adj. or subst. is intended, but sometimes certainly the latter; sometimes preceded by śūnyatā in comp. so that an- or ān- would be equally possible, see **śūnyatā**; clearly subst. nt. Dbh.g. 29(55).6 bhavate idam ānimittaṃ; AsP 204.12 (nāpi) ānimittaṃ pravartate; 256.13 na ca . . . ānimittaṃ vā apraṇihitaṃ vā anabhisaṃskāro vā (and other noms. masc.) . . . lujyate; Bbh 317.3 dve ānimitte (the only noun which could be understood is vihāra, masc.); more or less clearly adj. Bbh 276.10 ānimittaḥ samādhiḥ (in 2 śūnyatā-samādhiḥ, 5 apraṇihitaḥ sa°); KP 125.3 śūnyatā ānimittā apraṇihitāś (all seemingly acc. pl.!) ca dharmāṃ śrutvā; other cases, LV 428.9 ānimitta-vihārī; KP 94.4 (prose) °tta (read °ttaṃ? prob. subst.) cikitsā; Laṅk 274.4 yogī ānimitta-pratiṣṭhitaḥ; AsP 298.6 °tta-gatikā(ḥ) . . . sarvadharmās (cf. parallel 5 śūnyatā-gatikā); Dbh.g. 29(55).14 °tta-varadaṃ; śūnyatam . . . ānimittaṃ (corr. °ttāṃ, which would make the form adj.) RP 16.13 (see s.v. **adhimukta**).

?**āniṣada** (= Pali ānisada, nt.), *sit-down, rump, buttocks*: Mv ii.125.13 (prose), mss. evam evā (me) anuśīdana (Senart em., 'desperately' as he says, parśukā) abhūnsuḥ. True approximate reading proved by Pali parallel, MN i.80.14 = 245.29, ānisadaṃ hoti. In Mv pl. verb seems to indicate that the noun was pl. (for dual); the stem may have been āniṣīdana, or the like.

ānucchavika, adj. (= Pali anu°), *suitable, conformable, appropriate*: Mvy 7175; 7019; Bbh 145.22 °kair aupayikaiḥ pratirūpaiḥ . . . °saṃbhāraiḥ.

ānuttarya (?) see **anuttarya.**

ānudhārma, f. **°ī,** adj., *conformable to religion*: Bbh 61.23 ānudhārmyā (v.l. anudharmyayā, see **anudharmya**) kathayā, instr.

ānupathika, adj. or subst. m. (to Skt. anupatham with -ika), (person) *along the road*: °kair dṛṣṭās MSV i.52.8.

ānupūrvā (= Skt. °va, nt., and °vī, f.; perhaps read °vī here?), *regular order*: Mv ii.224.(11–)12 (jātena jīvaloke sarveṇa avaśyaṃ, for which read °ya m.c., martavyaṃ) eṣā kilānupūrvā.

ānubhāva, m. (= Pali id., Skt. anu°) *dignity, power, greatness*: SP 175.8 (vs) upapannu tasyo ayam ānubhāvo. Here ā could be m.c., but it is regular in Pali in prose as well as vs (see CPD s.v. anubhāva); the explanations in PTSD s.v. and Geiger 24 do not satisfy me.

ānulomika, adj., f. **°kā** or (oftener) **°kī** (= Skt. Gr.

id.; rarely **anu°**, q.v., the only form recorded in Pali), *conformable, suitable*: m. and nt. °kaiḥ (padavyañjanaiḥ) Mvy 7018; (-bhaiṣajyāny) °kāni Divy 109.26; °kair bhaiṣajyair Bbh 283.1; śṛṇoti dharma nāyakāna śāntam °kam RP 12.8 (vs); °kair . . . aṅgasaṃbhāraiḥ Bbh 145.22; °kena ca kāyavākkarmaṇā Bbh 255.1; °ko . . . upāyaḥ Bbh 264.8, and bodhisattvasyānulomika upāyaḥ 10; f. °kā, abhijña pañca . . . labdha °kā (n. pl.) LV 172.20 (vs); °kām api kṣāntim RP 34.13 (prose); f. °kī, with kṣānti (q.v.; cf. prec.) Mvy 6571; Dbh 53.24; °kī (so mss., Lefm. em. °ka-) dharmakṣānti (read °tir) dharmālokamukhaṃ LV 35.20 (prose); °kīṃ dharmadeśanāṃ Kv 49.10; °kīṃ śraddhāṃ Gv 239.12; °kī (no noun) Mvy 2678; with **caryā**, q.v. (also **anuloma-caryā**), caryāṃ caritvā tada ānulomikīm SP 27.2 (vs), *carrying along the true religious course, that which leads to continued religious progress*; cīrṇā ca caryā vara ānulomikī SP 27.13 (vs); cariṣyate carya tadānulomikīṃ SP 149.8 (vs).

ānuśaṃsa, m., and **°sā**, f., = **anu°**, q.v.; **ānuśaṃsaka**, see **-anu°**.

ānuśāsti, f. (= **anu°**; acc. to CPD, Pali also -ānusatthi, ifc.), *instruction*: Mv ii.323.21 (vs) ānuśāstiṃ; the ā could be m.c.

ānṛśaṃsa = **anu°**, **ānu°**, see s.v. **anuśaṃsa**.

āneñja, see **aneñja**.

āneñjya = **aniñjya**, q.v.: Śāl 82.4, 7 °jyopaga (of saṃskāras; cited Śikṣ 223.1 as āniñjy°, 3 and 4 as aniñjy° in ms.); see under **aneñjya** for cases where saṃdhi makes initial quantity obscure.

ānta, adj. (cited in MW without reference; not in BR or pw or Schmidt; Skt. back-formation, or error, based on Pali anta = Skt. antya; cf. **antakā**), *ultimate, final, extreme, supreme*: Kv 89.6 āntas tvaṃ kulaputra kṛtas te sattvaparīpākaḥ, *you are a supreme one* . . . (it would seem more natural, if only tvaṃ were omitted, to make āntas agree with sattvaparīpākaḥ; perhaps the passage is corrupt).

āntaḥpura, f. **°rī**, adj. or subst. (cf. Skt. āntaḥpurikā), (women) *of the harem*: LV 211.7 (vs) vijahya-m-āntaḥpuri (acc. pl.; most mss. °raṃ, unmetr.), *abandoning the women of the harem*.

āntarābhavika, adj. (= **antarā°**, q.v.), *of or belonging to* (or *existing in*) *the intermediate state* (**antarābhava**, q.v.): °kaḥ Bbh 295.24 *one who is living in* . . .; in a list, following divyamānuṣyakaḥ; of vipāka, AbhidhK. LaV-P. iv.129; °ka-skandha-saṃbhavāt MadhK 286.9, so text by em., but read antar° with mss.

āntarāyika (= **ant°**, q.v.), *causing obstacles; obstructive*: like **ant°** and Pali ant°, regularly of dharmas, Bhīk 9a.2 °kān dharmān pṛṣṭvā, *after inquiring* (whether there are) *obstructive conditions*; LV 434.2 (in saṃdhi, could be ant°) °ka-dharma-; Bbh 402.11 °kā dharmāḥ; MSV iii.30.6; also with hetu, Bbh 98.6 utpattāv āntarāyiko hetur virodhahetuḥ.

āntarikā (= **ant°**, q.v.; some cases there cited may belong here), *space between, interval, interstice*: LV 254.11 gopānasy-āntarikāś (n. pl.), *interstices of the roof-frame*; Gv 268.18 ekaikasyāṃ ca nady-āntarikāyāṃ, and *in each interval between the rivers*.

āntarikṣa-vāsin (so Mironov; Kyoto ed. indicates both this and āntarī° as var. readings), m. pl. °naḥ, *dwelling in the atmosphere*, n. of a class of gods: Mvy 3077; = **antarikṣa**, **°rīkṣa**, **°rīkṣecara**, qq.v.; see also **deva**.

āntra-guṇa, m. (pl.), = **antra-guṇa**, q.v.: ŚsP 1430.21; 1431.11; read in both (āntraṃ) āntraguṇā(ḥ). (In Gv 328.19 could be intended as well as antra°.)

āpa (= Pali id., thematization of Skt. āp, ap), *water*; clear cases noted only in cpd. āpa-skandha *mass of water*, SP 126.7 (vs) sa caiva sama muñceta āpaskandham analpakam; with adhaḥ or heṣṭā, heṣṭi, of subterranean mass of water, LV 64.12 adha-āpaskandham; 298.20 (vs) heṣṭāpaskandha (acc. sg.; so divide) caraṇaiḥ pratigrāhyamāṇāḥ, *being caused to receive with their feet the mass of water underneath* (the earth); 368.19 (vs) heṣṭi śatasahasraṃ yāvataś cāpaskandho (contrasted with dharaṇitalu, next line). In Mv ii.92.5 (vs) āpaṃ, acc. sg., could be referred to this stem, or regarded as belonging to the Skt. stem āp, ap, transferred to the sing. (cf. Wackernagel-Debrunner 3.240 f.).

Āpajjura, n. of a grove at **Sāṃkāśya**: Av ii.94.8, 14.

-āpaṇika, in comp. (= Pali id.; rare in Skt., see Schmidt, Nachträge), *dealer, shopkeeper*: Av i.198.12 pitā te gāndhikāpaṇika āsīd, *perfume-shopkeeper*.

āpatti, f. (= Pali and Skt. Lex. id.), *sin* (see also **anāpatti**, **mūlāpatti**): °tiḥ Mvy 9222; naiḥsargikāpattiḥ (so correctly Index and Mironov; see **naiḥsargika**) Mvy 9309; °tyā **codayati**, see this; duṣṭhulām (q.v.) āpattim Prāt 504.1; abhīkṣṇāpatti-āpadyana-tā KP 119.2 *state of constantly committing sins* (cf. **abhīkṣṇāpattika**); (bodhisattvasy)āpattir api veditavyā Bbh 160.11; °ty-anadhyācāra-vyutthāne Bbh 289.22; (see s.v. **anadhyāpatti**) ŚsP 56.5; five groups of sins to which monks may be subject, Sūtrāl. xi.4 comm., see Lévi Transl. p. 100 n.1.

-āpatti-ka = **āpatti** in Bhvr. cpd.; see **an-ā°**, **abhīkṣṇāpattika**, **sāpattika**.

āpadā (Pali and Skt. Lex. id., Skt. āpad; cf. § 15.9), *disaster*: āpadāsu MSV iv.115.14; 116.1, 7.

āpadyana, also **°na-tā** (from āpadyate, °ti, with suffix ana, n. act.), *the getting into*, or *commission* (of a sin): KP 119.2 (prose) abhīkṣṇāpatti-āpadyana-tā, see s.v. **āpatti**; Mmk 202.24 (vs) na te bheje devamukhyānāṃ (bad meter!) tarjanyāpadyanālaye (?obscure; app. tarjanī, or a case-form of it, compounded with or followed by cpd. of āpadyana and ālaya).

āpanna, ppp.-adj. (to **āpatti**), *guilty of a sin* (is Pali āpanna so used without complement?): yad uta, āpanna iti vā anāpanna iti vā MSV ii.176.6.

Āpannaka, n. of a yakṣa: MSV i.xvii.10.

āparāntika, f. **°kī**, adj. (from **aparānta**, q.v., plus ika), *future, of the future*: Gv 160.2 (prose) āparāntikāvicikaduḥkhena (2d ed. °khe); Dbh 51.3 (cited Śikṣ 228.2) eṣāparāntiky apekṣā.

āpaśyati (recorded once in AV.), *beholds*: LV 344.18 (prose) sattvān āpaśyati sma (so Lefm. with best mss.); doubtful; in parallel 344.10 all mss. and both edd. paśyati, with v.l. here.

?**āpas-kara**, m., *action of water*: Mv ii.366.13 (na tasya caurā rājāno dhanaskandha [so one ms., Senart with v.l. °dhaṃ] parāmṛṣe) agnir vā āpaskaro (read °kāro?) vā (one ms. om. vā; Senart em. apaskaroti, very implausibly) pūjāṃ kṛtvā tathāgate.

?**āpāya**, adj. = **āpāyika** (apāya with suffix -a), in Śikṣ 46.6 paścaināṃś codayiṣyāmo bhūtam āpāya-gocarān, *and afterwards we will incite them who are veritably in a sphere-of-existence characterized by evil fate*. So if text be kept; note states that Tib. (sdig med) points to apāpa-, and Bendall and Rouse p. 47 translate with this, *so that they may . . . be beyond the sphere of sin*.

āpāyaka (cf. **āpāyita**, **āpyāyaka**), *giving to drink, nourishing*: °kaṃ poṣakaṃ saṃvardhakaṃ Bbh 118.28.

āpāyika, f. **°kī**, adj. and subst. (= Pali id.; from **apāya** with suffix ika), *pertaining or leading to an evil fate* (such as existence in hell); subst., *one doomed to*, or *suffering, such an existence*: Gv 407.14 °ke karmaṇi ca pravṛttā; Jm 192.21–22 tena dṛṣṭivyasanopanipātenāpāyikena lokānarthākarabhūtena; Bbh 10.14 tīvrām āpāyikīṃ duḥkhāṃ vedanām; 245.10 āyatyām āpāyikaṃ duḥkham pratyanubhavati; 356.17 °ka-kleśa-pakṣyasya; 368.1 °kaṃ karma; subst., Mv iii.214.6, 13 (vs) āpāyikā nirvṛtā brahmalokaṃ (cf. Pali DN ii.242.18); Divy 165.19 (vs) āpāyiko nairayiko.

āpāyita, ppp. (cf. **āpāyaka**; to ā-pā-, caus.), *given* *to drink, nourished*: °tā poṣitā saṃvardhitā MSV ii.17.5. This and āpāyaka together forbid em. to āpyāy-. The same three ppp. stems MSV ii.25.3; 80.6.

āpīḍaka (= Skt. āpīḍa, *chaplet, wreath*), only in °ka-jāta *hung with wreaths*, noted only as ep. of trees: °ka-jātam Mvy 6061 (context suggests that it was prob. epithet of a tree, or at least referred to trees); °ka-jātān (vṛkṣān) Divy 215.25, 27; 216.1; °ka-jātāḥ (phalavṛkṣāḥ) Divy 221.14 (so certainly read as suggested in note; text with mss. āpīnaka-).

?**āpīrā**, in (-hūṇ)āpīrā (sc. lipi), n. of some kind of writing: Mv i.135.7 (v.l. °āpirā or °ro). Senart would understand abhīrā (preferably the regular Skt. ābhīrā).

āptamanas (also °**nas-ka**, MPS 32.29) = **āttamanas**, q.v.: Hoernle MR 26, Obv. 3 idam avocat bhagavān, āptamanas (read °manasas) te bhikṣavo . . .; 39 Rev. 5, same phrase, reading °manasas; cf. 26 n. 2 and 198 (erroneously rendered *with receptive mind*); Stönner, SBBA 1904 p. 1283, line 30; Ud xiv.13 āptamanā, n. sg. m.; neg. anāptamanā(ḥ), n. sg. m., Prāt 500.8 abhiṣaktaḥ kupitaḥ caṇḍīkṛto 'nāpta°; 505.7 abhiṣakta-kupitaś caṇḍīkṛto 'nāpta°.

āpya, nt. (gdve. of āp-), *what can be received* (of food), *one's fill*: (ghṛtasya madhunaś) cāpyaṃ pūrayitvā MSV ii.24.10, *having given* (the infant) *all he could eat of ghee and honey*; so app. Tib. de ḥdraṅs par bsñod nas.

āpyāyaka, adj. or subst. (m.), *nourishing, nourisher*: Divy 51.20 putrasya mātāpitarāv āpyāyakau poṣakau . . . Cf. **āpāyaka** (which perh. read?).

āprāṇya, adj. (possibly read apr°? corresp. to Pali apaṇṇa-ka, q.v. in CPD; cf. apaṇṇakaṅga, CPD *unique* or *universal factor*; etymology unknown), *perfect*, in āprāṇyāṅga, *of perfect qualities*: Mmk 57.(15–)16 (see Lalou, Iconographie, p. 22) (nihitaṃ tu tato kṛtvā dhūpayet karpūradhūpanaiḥ; read with Lalou) āprāṇyāṅga-samutthaṃ vā (Lalou, *où avec un produit sans parcelles vivantes*, etymologizing as from a-prāṇa) kuṅkumacandanādibhiḥ. The evident correspondence between our word and Pali apaṇṇa(ka) makes Lalou's interpretation hardly possible. Our word is a secondary hyper-Sktism, but the history of it remains quite unknown.

ābaddhaka, adj. or subst. (Skt. ābaddha, with suffix ka, perhaps specifying, § 22.39), (something that is) *tied on* (as an ornament): Mv ii.68.5 (prose) tasyāpi rājño śatasahasramūlyo hāro ābaddhako, tasya ca hārasya . . .; 72.19 (prose) yo kumārasya hāro ābaddhako mahāraho śatasahasramūlyo, so hāro . . .; ii.352.9 = iii.276.11 (vs) ābaddhakā manuṣyāṇāṃ (apparently agreeing with words in prec. line which Senart reads by em. hārā and niṣkāni [sic, °ni]; the mss. are very corrupt).

ābaddha-parikara, adj., lit. *having tied one's girdle*, i. e. *girded one's loins*, or freely, *vigorously setting out upon action*: °raḥ Mvy 6428; Tib. renders approximately *going out without being touched at all*; Chin. (*walking*) *without leaning on others* (or, *without help of others*).

ābandhya, adj. (from Skt. ābandha with suffix ya), *serving* or *intended for binding, capturing* (animals): Divy 583.1 mamāmī kūṭāḥ pāśālepāś cābandhyāḥ (said by a hunter).

ābādhika, adj. (= Pali id.; from Skt. ābādha with suffix ika), *sick, ailing*: Mv iii.348.9 tasya pratyekabuddhasya pittābādhikasya (v.l. °dhitasya); Bbh 268.6 ābādhikānāṃ sattvānāṃ vyādhitānāṃ; Samy Āg 13 verse 1 bhikṣur ābādhiko duḥkhito; Samādh p. 52 line 21, read ābādhiko for text ābodhiko. See also **vāyv-ābādhika**.

ābūḍha, see **ābṛḍha**.

ābṛṃhaṇa (cf. Pali abbāhana, abbūhana, nom. act.), *instrument for extraction* (of thorns, splinters, etc.): Gv 495.13 (prose) ābṛṃhaṇabhūtaṃ satkāyaśalyasamābṛṃhaṇatayā. Said of bodhicitta.

ābṛṃhita, see **āvṛṃhita**.

ābṛḍha-, ppp. of **ābṛhati**, in ābṛḍha-śalya (= Pali abbūḷha-salla), *having the sting* (of craving) *pulled out*: Mvy 7216 (v.l. ābrīḍha°, so Mironov, with v.l. āvṛta°) = Tib. (zug-rṅu) byuṅ ba; cf. āvrīḍha, to **āvarhati**, MSV iii.74.6 ff. This word, in some form, is certainly intended by the corrupt āpraṭṭa-śalya of Samādh p. 28 line 14; and by text (vicikitsā-kathaṃkathā-śalyaḥ samūla) ārūḍho Divy 84.10, where presumably read ābūḍho, see Pali above; MSV i.83.9 (same passage) āvṛḍho.

ābṛhati (and āvṛhati; see also **āvṛṃhati**) both occur in Skt. in mg. *extracts, draws out*, and in Pali as abbahati, abbuhati, abbū°, abbāheti, id. (as, thorns); both are so used also in BHS; but in BHS they both (oftener, it seems, spelled with v) have also the meaning exclusively noted for **āvarhati**, *restores* (a monk to good standing), which in Pali is abbheti (noun, abbhāna), apparently from Skt. āhvayati. I shall record such mgs., even where texts read āb°, under **āvarhati**; in BHS the two groups are not clearly distinguishable. They may even be identical in origin, as N. Dutt holds, MSV iii.74 n. 3 (*withdrawal of offences* committed by the monk implies restoration to good standing); so also in essence, tho doubtfully, Finot, Prāt 488 n. 1. But on this theory it is hard to explain Pali abbheti (abbhāna), and I incline to believe that BHS has a secondary and confused blend, in which a form close to the Pali, meaning *recall*, was adapted to the word meaning *extract, remove*.

ābrahitavya, see **āvarhati**.

ābrīḍha, see **ābṛḍha-**.

ābha, m. pl. (= Pali id., misprinted once Abha, see CPD s.v. Abhā), n. of a class of rūpāvacara gods of the 2d dhyāna-bhūmi, see **deva** (only in a few lists): Mv ii.314.7 ābhā devā(ḥ); 348.19 ābhā (v.l. ābhāś) ca (sc. devāḥ); 360.15 ābhāṃ (acc. pl.; v.l. ābhā) paśyati devatāṃ (v.l. °tāḥ).

ābhakṣaṇa, only in comp. with **saṃbhakṣaṇa**, q.v., and associated with other social activities; perhaps *feasting* (in groups); distinction from saṃbhakṣaṇa is not clear: Bbh 7.7 āvāha-vivāhābhakṣaṇa-saṃbhakṣaṇeṣv evaṃbhāgīyeṣu (sc. parakṛtyeṣu, 7.2) sahāyībhāvaṃ gacchati; 267.13 (after āvāha-vivāhārthikānāṃ) ābhakṣaṇa-saṃbhakṣaṇārthikānāṃ kṛtyasahāyārthikānāṃ ca sattvānāṃ . . . Neither word is known in this use outside BHS.

ābharaṇa, *ornament*, as m. (recorded only as nt. in Skt., Pali, and Pkt.): SP 362.12 (vs) ye (so, or ye hy, all mss.; ed. em. yā) ābharaṇā bhavanti . . . vicitrarūpāḥ (so all Nep. mss.; ed. °pā); LV 194.17 (vs) sarve ābharaṇā vikīrṇa patitā muhyanti te vāriṇā, and 18 (with mss.) bhartuś cābharaṇā (acc. pl.; with adṛśi 15) savastramukuṭāṃ śayyāgatāṃ vyākulāṃ (Lefm. omits the three anusvāras).

Ābharaṇachattranirghoṣa, n. of a Tathāgata: Gv 422.3.

Ābharaṇa-puṣkariṇī, n. of the pool into which the Bodhisattva's ornaments were cast: LV 229.19.

[**Ābhaśiri**, see **Samantābhaśrī**.]

ābhasvara = **ābhāsvara**, a class of gods: Ud xxx.49.

ābhāṣati, *addresses insultingly*: (kulastrī . . .) ākruṣṭā bhavaty ābhāṣṭā(ḥ) parāmṛṣṭā vā MSV iv.119.10; Tib. kha ṅan smras, *bad-mouth-speak*.

ābhāsa, m. (in Pali only in the Skt. meaning of *light, radiance*; so also in BHS, e. g. Mv i.83.5), *appearance* and hence *range, scope*, of sense organs: Mv iii.66.4 ff., where each of the external (bāhirāṇi) āyatanāni (i. e. the objects of sense) *comes into the range* of the corresponding internal (ādhyātmikāni) āyatanāni (i. e. the sense organs or powers), e. g. rūpo ca bāhiraṃ āyatanaṃ cakṣuṣaḥ ābhāsam āgataṃ bhavati. In a similar Pali passage, MN i.190.21 ff., āpātha takes the place of our ābhāsa. Similarly Mv i.6.3 manuṣyāṇāṃ śrotābhāsam āgacchati, *comes within the range of men's hearing*; Śikṣ 128.13 cakṣuṣa ābhāsam āgacchanti;

129.3 santy anābhāsagatāḥ (see **anābhāsa**) sattvā ye mama cakṣuṣa ābhāsaṃ nāgacchanti; 151.10 śrotendriyasyābhāsam āgacchanti; Sukh 55.2 cakṣuṣa ābhāsam āgacchati. In same mg. **avabhāsa**, q.v. 2.

ābhāsībhavati (see **ābhāsa**), *comes into range, into play; becomes perceptible*: Dbh 64.27 ... nimitta-samudācāro vā nābhāsībhavati.

ābhāsvara, m., generally pl. (= Pali ābhassara; cf. **ābhasvara**), *one* (usually the 3d) *of the classes of rūpāvacara gods in the 2d dhyāna-bhūmi* (see **deva**): sing. of one of the class, LV 44.12 (see **Prabhāvyūha**); Mmk 19.9 mahābrahmā °raḥ prabhāsvaraḥ śuddhābhaḥ etc.; in Mmk 69.7 also sg. in a list of sg. deities; ābhāsvare devanikāye Divy 327.21–22, as a place of happy rebirth, in this class of gods (or in their dwelling-place); several times in Mv this place or state of existence is mentioned as the abode of creatures in general, or of a Buddha and his disciples, in interim periods between world aeons, after destruction and before re-creation of the world, so Mv i.52.4 ābhāsvare devanikāye upapadyanti, and 6–7 °rād devanikāyato cyavitvā; similarly 63.7; 338.15 ff.; pl. of the class as a whole, Mvy 3092; Dharmas 128; SP 359.1; 365.3; LV 150.7; 315.5; 359.3; 396.15; Mv ii.314.7; 319.4; 348.19; Divy 68.15; 367.12; Av i.5.2, etc.; in Mvy 2291 named as an example of creatures in the third **sattvāvāsa** (q.v.), characterized as ekatvakāyā nānātvasaṃjñinas.

ābhicāruka, adj. and subst., repeatedly in Mmk = Skt. ābhicārika, *pertaining to* (hostile, black) *magic* or as subst. (perh. by ellipsis of karman) *a performance or practice of* (hostile, black) *magic*: Mmk 25.19; 33.24 °keṣu sarveṣu (subst.); 124.18 °ka-kāṣṭhāni; 174.7 ardharātre sthite candre kuryāt karmābhicārukam; 174.11, 17; 178.9; 189.10 °ka-karmāṇi; 320.10 (aśeṣaṃ karma) karoti, varjayitvā kāmopasaṃhitam, ābhicārukaṃ ca; in 465.8–9 contrasted with śāntika, *pacifying* (performance), as antonym, ābhicāruke mahāmāṃsena, śāntike mṛgaromāṇi ... Many other occurrences, but not noted outside of Mmk. One might be tempted to emend to °rika, were the cases not so numerous.

[**ābhiprāyāś** in evam-ā° LV 160.11, uncorrected misprint for (evam-)abhiprāyāś, with Calc.]

ābhiprāyika, adj. (from Skt. abhiprāya with suffix ika; once in Skt. in Sāmav. Br., BR 7 App., *nach Belieben geschehend, beliebig*, with karman), (*specially, esoterically*) *intentional, intended*: Bbh 265.5 (gambhīrāṇāṃ tathāgatabhāṣitānāṃ ... sūtrāntānām) °kaṃ tathāgatānām artham avijñāya; 303.26–304.1 °ka-nigūḍha-dharma-saṃjñārthavibhāvanatā. See s.v. **saṃdhā**.

ābhimānika, adj. (= **abhi°** 1; once in Skt. in different mg., pw 7.318), *proud*: SP 38.12 and 39.4 (prose; both times v.l. ādhi° or adhi°); 43.13 (prose, no v.l.); Śikṣ 126.8 (prose) °ka-vyākaraṇa-vacanā; KP 1.6 (prose) °kaś ca bhavaty ātmotkarṣī.

ābhirūpya (nt.; from Skt. abhirūpa, *beautiful*, with suffix ya; once Lex. in Skt., BR 5 App.), *beauty*: Bbh 245.21 °pya-kāmasya cākāmaṃ vairūpyataḥ.

ābhisaṃskārika, f. °**kī** (cf. **an-abhisaṃskārikā**, and Pali abhisaṃkhārika; Suzuki Index records abhi°, but 211.15 has ā- while 361.17 could intend either ā- or a-), *characterized by accumulation* (of karman; **abhisaṃskāra**): Laṅk 211.15 ābhisaṃskārikī ... nirodhasamāpattiḥ; Laṅk 361.17 nābhisaṃskārikair buddhā lakṣaṇair lakṣaṇānvitāḥ.

ābhisaṃkṣepika (adj.), °kam, adv. (to **abhisaṃkṣepa**, q.v.), app. *in a manner produced by compression, condensation*: Mvy 7476 (so also Mironov; pw 7.306 abhi°) = Tib. bsdus pa las gyur pa; but the real meaning of this seemingly technical term escapes me. The next word is **abhyavakāśikam** (ābhy°), q.v.

ābhīkṣṇaka, adj. (from Skt. abhīkṣṇam; cf. Skt. Lex. ābhīkṣṇa, nt.), *recurring, repeated, constant*: Bbh 142.1 yam ābhīkṣṇakaṃ vipratisāram ādīnavadarśanam āgamya...

? **ābhīra**, see **āpīrā**.

ābhujati, or also **ābhuñjati**, recorded only in ger. forms with object paryaṅkam (= Pali pallaṅkam ābhuj-; Skt. seems to have used badhnāti instead, but BR, pw record only noun cpds. such as paryaṅka-bandha; BHS also uses forms of bandhati, as paryaṅka bandhitvā SP 23.11 (vs); a theory of the orig. mg. in BR which is not repeated in pw; for other theories see PTSD s.vv. ābhujati, pallaṅka), *having assumed a sitting posture with the legs doubled under the buttocks*; in prose of all texts except Mv, only paryaṅkam ābhujya: Mvy 6283; SP 5.9 (here Kashgar rec. baddhvā, cf. above); 19.13; 409.9; LV 59.22; 244.18; 251.4; 289.16; 410.8; Divy 20.17; 162.12; 294.3, etc.; in vss, °kam ābhujiya LV 133.20; °kam ābhujitvā 259.5; in prose of Mv °kam ābhuñjitvā i.144.11; ii.131.15, also v.l. ii.268.4 where Senart ābhujitvā; the latter is a v.l. for text ābhuṃj° ii.16.12 (= i.213.8, mss. corrupt); ābhuṃjitvāna mss. at iii.245.2 (vs, bad meter).

ābhoga, m. (derived by Leumann, Das nordarische Lehrgedicht des Buddhismus, AKM 20.1, p. 68, from bhuj *bend*, as *Anbiegung* = *Anlehnung*; an-ā°, *ohne Anlehnung d.h. ohne Rückhalt oder Stützpunkt*. Some Pali interpreters also derive from this root, see PTSD. Whatever the etymology, the primary mg. in BHS is clearly *effort*; so some Skt. lexx., = yatna. This also fits at least many Pali occurrences of ābhoga, but in Pali the word needs more study; dict. definitions are all unsatisfactory; it is often bracketed or equated with manasikāra, esp. with cetaso or cittassa, DN comm. i.122.6–7, perhaps as (mental) *effort*, e. g. Miln. 97.10), *effort, earnest application* (directed towards, loc.): Mvy 2092 = Tib. sgrim pa, ḥjug pa, bzo (gzo) ba, *endeavor*; *setting about*; *work*; śīle ābhogaṃ kṛtvāna, *having made effort for* (in regard to) *morality* Mv ii.358.7; 360.9; ekāntaśukleṣv eva karmasv ābhogaḥ karaṇīyaḥ, *one must strive for* ... Divy 23.30–24.1; 55.12; 193.15; 289.23; sarvābhogavigato 'nābhogadharmatāprāptaḥ kāyavākcittautsukyāpagataḥ Dbh 64.15–16, *rid of all* (interested) *effort, arrived at a state of effortless* (*impassive*, see **anābhoga**) *condition, free of bodily, vocal, mental desires* (said of the Bodhisattva); in Dharmas 118, list of six 'hindrances' (**āvaraṇa**) to samādhi: kausīdya, māna, śāṭhya, auddhatya, anābhoga, satyābhoga; here anābhoga *lack of effort* has a bad sense, not a good one as in Dbh 64.16; satyābhoga is obscure (saty-ābhoga, *effort directed towards something concretely existing* as distinguished from abstract goals? if satya-ābhoga, as cpd., I do not understand what it could mean as a *hindrance to samādhi*). See **anābhoga, sābhoga**, both clearly supporting mg. *effort*.

ābhyantaroṣṭha, see **abhy°**.

ābhyavakāśika, adj. and subst. m. or nt. (as m. = **abhy°**, q.v.), (an ascetic) *living in the open air* (one of the 12 **dhūta-guṇa**): Mvy 1136 = Tib. bla gab med pa (see Das); Dharmas 63; nt. °kam, *the practice of living as such an ascetic*, Mvy 7477 (Kyoto ed. abhy°, but Index also ābhy°, and Mironov ābhy°) = Tib. mṅon par skabs yod pa (see Das).

1 āma, interj. (= Pali, Pkt. id., once in Jain Skt., pw 2 App.; cf. Skt. ām), *yes* (giving consent or approval): Mv ii.107.8; 154.16; Av i.36.11 sa kathayaty āmeti.

2 āma, m., defined in ŚsP as = *religious longings* (lit. *thirsts*; could the word be connected with Skt. Lex. āma, m., *disease*? i. e. *pathological state*?): ŚsP 486.4–5 ... mahāsattvasyāmaḥ; 7 āmaḥ, dharmatṛṣṇāḥ; 14–15, 22, etc., dharmatṛṣṇā āmaḥ. See s.v. **mūdhāma**.

āmagandha, m. (see also **nir-āma°**; = Pali id.; defined DN comm. ii.665.10 by vissa-gandha, and cf. 665.35–666.1 sāmagandhā [so read with v.l.] glossed by sa-kuṇapagandhā pūtigandhā), *the odor of carrion*; (more loosely) *stench, evil odor*: literally, SP 96.16 (vs) (kāye ...) kuṣṭhaṃ kilāsaṃ tatha āmagandhaḥ; Mv i.75.14 (after 13 vividhagandhapuṣpāś ca upavāyantu sarvataḥ) mānuṣā-ṇām āmagandhāś (Senart em. °dhā) ca śīghram antarahāpaya (5 mss. °hāpanā or °ṇā); fig. of the *stench* of immorality, opp. of the *odor of sanctity*, Mv iii.214.3 ke āmagandhā manujeṣu brahma, and 11 (after a list of vices) te āmagandhā manujeṣu brahma (corresp. to Pali DN ii.242.15 and 243.5). This is the basis of the usually fig. meaning of **nirāmagandha.**

[**āmateya**? ŚsP 80.4, see s.v. **adhipati.**]

āmatha (m. or nt.; from Skt. ā-math-), *agitation, violent stirring*, or perhaps concretely *eddy, whirlpool*: Dbh 28.22 mahaughormy-āmathair nimagnā vateme sattvāḥ...

-āmantraṇaka, in **an-āma°**, adj. (neg. Bhvr. to Skt. āmantraṇa, Pali āmantaṇa or °na; in Pali āmantanikā is recorded in a concrete, personal application), *having no conversation, characterized by not talking with people*: of ascetic practices, (ātāpana-paritāpanaiḥ . . .) anāmantraṇakair LV 248.17 (prose).

? **āmanyate** (only Vedic and very rare; not recorded in MIndic), *desires, intends, longs*: Mv ii.194.13 (vs) eṣo cāham api āmaṃsye (1 sg. fut.; v.l. āmaṃsa) vanditum puruṣottamam. But I suspect a corruption.

āmārjayati (formally caus. to Skt. āmārṣṭi, āmṛjati), *purifies* (a **maṇḍalaka,** 3, q.v.): Divy 333.18 bhagavato maṇḍalakam āmārjaya; 345.22–23 tayor (gen.) dve te āsanaprajñaptī kṛtau (sic!) dvau maṇḍalakāv āmārjitau.

āmila, m. (= **amila,** q.v., for which var. āmila occurs), presumably the same kind of cloth called amila: Bhīk 22b.4 °lā(ḥ), n. pl.

āmilāta, ppp. (MIndic for Skt. āmlāna; cf. Pali milāta = Vedic mlāta), *withered*; āmilātam (bhavati) sammilātaṃ sampuṭa(ka)jātaṃ Mv ii.126.4, 5; 127.8, 9; 128.13, 14; 129.15, 16, all prose, in modulations of the same phrase; the corresponding passage LV 254.14 has the regular Skt. āmlāna.

āmiṣa, nt. (except for the strange āmiṣā Mvy 6753; the BHS word also has its Skt. meanings, as well as those listed here, in which it = Pali āmisa; even in Skt. a few occurrences approach this sphere of use, cf. BR s.v., *Alles worüber man mit Gier herfällt*), lit. or orig. (the) *flesh* (contrasting with dharma, as in Pali with dhamma, *the spirit*); *worldly things, possessions*, or *enjoyments*, as contrasted with religious or spiritual ones (dharma): Mvy 6753 āmiṣā (! so also Mironov) = Tib. zaṅ ziṅ, *matter, object, goods; external goods, earthly possessions* (contrasted with internal, spiritual gifts); also śa, *meat*, and zas, *food*; **sāmiṣaḥ,** q.v., Mvy 6751, and **nirāmiṣaḥ,** q.v., Mvy 6752 (here āmiṣa = Tib. zaṅ ziṅ, only); dual dvandva dharmāmiṣa, *spiritual and worldly things*, °ṣābhyāṃ yathāśaktyā saṃgrāhakaś ca Bbh 254.21; °ṣābhyāṃ dāne 'matsariṇo Sukh 61.5; atha dharmāmiṣam iti bhagavan kaḥ padārthaḥ Laṅk 179.17; āmiṣam Laṅk 180.6, defined at length in 6–13 as including what leads to longing (tṛṣṇā, 10) and rebirth, away from the religious goal; cf. āmiṣasaṃgraho bhavati na dharmasaṃgraha iti 179.16; lokāmiṣasaṃgraho bhavati na dharmasaṃgraha iti 173.5; lokāmiṣa-phalābhilāṣiṇo (gen. sg.) vā punaḥ lokāmiṣanimittaṃ tathāgatacaityapūjā Bbh 22.25–26; dharmasaṃbhoga āmiṣasaṃbhogo Divy 93.1 *spiritual and worldly enjoyment*; in Mv iii.55.1, 3 Mahākāśyapa is described as the Lord's dharmajo dharmanirmito dharmadāyādo na āmiṣadāyādo, *spiritually born, spiritually fashioned spiritual heir, not physical* (or *worldly*) *heir* (Pali also uses dhamma- and āmisa-dāyāda); āmiṣalolupaḥ puṅgalo . . . bodhisattvena na sevitavyaḥ RP 19.1; apy oṣitā āmiṣapātracīvare (so prob. divide, see **oṣita**) RP 19.10; āmiṣa-priyāś RP 34.2 *fond of worldly things*; āmiṣa-gurukasya RP 35.2 *devoted to . . .*; nāmiṣaprakṣiptayā samtatyā Śikṣ 128.7, *with mental disposition* (see **saṃtati**) *not intent on worldly* (or *material*) *things*; āmiṣa-kiṃcitka, see **kiṃcitka;** na labhyaṃ bhikṣavas tenāmiṣeṇāmiṣakṛtyaṃ kartum MSV i.249.12, *it is not allowable to pursue enjoyment with this worldly enjoyment* (sugar added to food).

[? **āmukta,** ppp., f. **°tā,** acc. to Divy Index *jewel*, in Divy 2.28 (ratnapratyuptikayā) karṇikayā āmuktayālaṃkṛtaḥ; 3.7 koṭimūlyayā ratnapratyuptikayā āmuktayā jātaḥ; and see **āmuktaka, °ikā.** I doubt this mg.; in 2.28 it seems a normal ppp. = Skt. āmukta, °ā: *adorned with a jewel-set earring fastened on him* (cf. also Divy 614.17 āmuktamālyābharaṇā, *with garlands and ornaments fastened on*); this is a regular mg. of āmuñcati. In 3.7, to be sure, no noun is expressed; the same karṇikā of 2.28 is however clearly meant; possibly here ratna-pratyuptikayā may be understood as a subst., with specifying ka (§ 22.39): *with a jewel-studded thing fastened on.*]

āmuktaka, f. **°ikā** (= Skt. āmukta, ppp.), *fastened on*: Divy 23.7 tasya ratnakarṇikā karṇe āmuktikā. (Taken by Index as noun, *jewel*; see s.v. **āmukta.**) I see no meaning in the suffix ka (§ 22.29).

āmukha, adj., (presenting itself) *before one's face; present, at hand*: Jm 92.24 mṛtyor mukham ivāmukham (. . . vaḍabāmukham); Bhad 58 āmukhi (m.c. for °khe; one ms. °kha) sarvi bhaveyu samagrāḥ, *may they all be present* (to me; āmukhi prob. loc. sg., adverbial, rather than n. pl. with pronominal ending); Gv 54.20 (vs) māramaṇḍalaraṇasmi āmukhe (loc. abs.), *when the battle . . . is at hand*; Bbh 14.13 -saddharmāntardhānim āmukhām upagatāṃ paśyati; Bbh 251.1 (bhayabhairavair) āmukhaiḥ. Cf. the following items, and s.v. **poṣadha.**

āmukhayati (denom. from prec.), *presents, puts before one*: Sādh 548.14 śūnyaṃ jagad akhilam āmukhayet.

āmukhī-karaṇa (n. act. to next), *the making present, realization, manifestation*: LV 432.22 -bodhicittāmukhīkaraṇa-; 441.6 -samāpatty-āmukhīkaraṇa-tayā (instr. of -tā); Śikṣ 33.15 (cf. note p. 399); 276.6 punar-āmukhīkaraṇena.

āmukhī-karoti (see **āmukha,** and cf. prec.), *makes present* (regularly in oneself), *realizes, manifests*: -karoti LV 180.5 (buddhadharmān); 182.5 (dharmamukhāni; cf. also id. 7, 9, etc.); Bbh 126.10 (śilpakarmasthānam); -kṛtya, ger. LV 137.18 (-upāyakauśalyam); Divy 350.14 (bodhipakṣān dharmān); Śikṣ 355.11; Gv 179.10 (Acalām upāsikām; *keeping present in his mind*); Sādh 24.4 (śūnyatām); 58.12 (pariśuddhatām).

āmukhī-pravṛtta (= -bhūta, see next), (which have) *come to be present to one's mind, realized*: Divy 491.18 (tasya . . . tisro) gāthā ā° °ttā jātāḥ, *three verses occurred to him, were presented to his mind.*

āmukhī-bhavati (see **āmukha,** and cf. prec. and foll. items), *becomes present* (to oneself, to one's mind), *is realized, is manifest*: °vati KP 4.2 (bodhicittam); Dbh 52.24 (prajñāpāramitāvihāra); °vanti SP 159.2 na ca tāvat tasya te dharmā ā° (so both edd., but most mss. abhimukhī-bha°); LV 204.17 (pūrvapraṇidhānapadāny); 244.21–22 (samāpattiśatāny); ppp.-bhūto Mv i.245.17 (dīpaṃkarabuddhaśabdo . . .); -bhūtam Divy 180.19 (nīlakṛtsnam); 411.16 (sthavirāṇāṃ vacanam).

āmukhī-sthita, ppp. (cf. prec. items and especially **āmukha**), *situated facing* or *in the presence of* (with acc.): Gv 241.11 (vs) tathāgataḥ sattva sarvi (acc. pl.) samam āmukhīsthitaḥ, *facing* (or *in the presence of*) *all creatures at once.* (Perhaps *in the minds of*, but in the sense that he knows their minds.)

āmutrika, adj. (Skt. amutra with suffix ika), *of a future life* or *other world*: aihikaḥ āmutrikaḥ Bbh 22.16; 24.13.

āmṛduka, adj. (ā plus **mṛduka,** q.v.), *rather mild*: AsP 387.1 °ko bhaviṣyati.

āmṛśa, nt., *touching, enjoyment*; only as etymologizing substitute for, and interpretation of, **āmiṣa,** q.v.: Laṅk 180.7 (in definition of āmiṣa) āmiṣam āmṛśam . . .

āmodanīya, adj., gdve. to next, *subject of rejoicing, to be rejoiced over*: Mv ii.259.10 (and ff.) śuddhāvāsā ca devā aṣṭādaśa āmodanīyāṃ dharmān pratilabhanti (listed in sequel).

āmodayati (= Pali °deti; prob. denom. to āmoda), *gratifies*: °dayitvā (so read, text āmohayitvā) MSV iv.130.1, 2–3.

? **āmbāsanaka**, see **amb°**.

? **āmbhirya**, (m. or nt.) °rye LV 156.21 (prose), one of the arts (kalā); from the context (after bārhaspatye and before āsurye) perhaps a philosophic system; v.l. ambhīrye (also ācīrye, asvīrye, but Tib. chuḥi lugs, *way*, or *system, of water* indicates that the orig. began ambh- or āmbh-, tho it does not give much further help).

Āmratīrtha, = next: °tho nāgarājā Mvy 3272.

Āmratīrthika (= Pali Ambatitthaka), n. of a nāga: Māy 247.17.

Āmrapālikā = next: Mv i.261.15.

Āmrapālī (also °**likā**; = Pali Ambapālī, °likā; in Pali and in MSV she was a courtesan), n. of a Licchavi woman, who donated her mango grove to the Buddha: Mv i.300.16; in Mv ii.293.16 Buddha is dwelling at Vaiśālī in this grove, Āmrapālī-vane; her miraculous origin, MSV ii.16.15 ff.; in mss. of MPS, e. g. 11.1, regularly written **Amra°** (semi-MIndic).

āmreḍayati, perh. *gears up, makes work* (a machine): MSV iv.247.18, 20 (Tib. sbyar, *put together, prepare*).

āmlavetasa, m. (= Skt. amla°, and lex. āmla°), n. of a plant, a kind of sorrel, *Rumex vesicarius*: Mvy 5780 = Tib. star bu, acc. to Jäschke *Hippophae rhamnoides*, but 'acc. to a *Lex.* also a kind of sorrel in India.'

(**āmlāta**, see **āmilāta**).

āmlāyati, caus. to ā-mlā (in Skt. only in āmlāna, caus. of mlā in Skt. is mlāpayati), *causes to wither*: fut. medio-passive (pass. force) LV 335.5 āmlāyiṣyase ... bodhisattvena, *you shall be made to wither by the B.* (said to Māra).

āya, m. (in Skt., and usually in Pali, only *income*, opp. to vyaya *expense*; rarely in Vedic and Up. something like *arrival*; see BR, and so in Pali e. g. MN i.277.1 udakass' āya-mukham, acc. to comm. ii.322.14 = āgamana-maggo; see also **āya-dvāra**), *coming, arrival*, esp. *coming into existence, origination, source*: KP 46.6, 7, 8 (vs), replacing āyadvāraṃ, q.v., of prose above, karṣāpaṇāyo ... bhoti, saṃbodhicittasya ca yatra āyo, āyo bahū tatra ca śrāvakāṇām; same comparison KP 92.7, 9 (vs), āyu and āyo again replacing āyadvāraṃ of prose; āyaḥ Mvy 2654 = Tib. ḥbuṅ ba (meaning?), or, ḥdu ba, *coming together*; associated or cpd. with vyaya, (in Skt. *income* and *outlay*, but) here *origination, coming into being*, and *passing away* (belief in which is a false opinion), Laṅk 174.12 āya-vyaya-dṛṣṭābhiniveśena; 175.14–176.1 nāhaṃ mahāmate lokāyataṃ deśayāmi, na cāyavyayam, kiṃ tu mahāmate anāyavyayaṃ deśayāmi. tatrāyo nāma mahāmate utpādarāśiḥ samūhāgamā utpadyante (read °gamād utpadyate with Tib. acc. to note). tatra vyayo nāma ... vināśaḥ. an-āyavyaya ity an-utpādasyaitad adhivacanam; Laṅk 182.3 āyaṃ kāryārthanirvṛttiṃ (accs. sg., obj. of paśyate, prec. line), and 4 āyavyaya-parijñānād; Gv 470.3 sarvāyāśrayaniśrita-vihāra-vihāriṇām (does āya here mean *cause, basis, origin*?).

āyatana, nt. (in Skt. *seat, abiding-place, home*; the following senses seem hardly, if at all, to occur in Skt., but most of them apparently in Pali), (**1**) *department, field* (of art): in śilpāyatana (= Pali sippāy°), Mv ii.434.16 sarvaśilpāyatanehi ... kuśo kumāro viśiṣyati, *Prince Kuśa excelled in all departments of art*; but the same word is also used (**2**) personally, applying to practitioners of the arts (perhaps *as vessels*, pātra, of the arts, cf. 3 below): Mv iii.113.12 sarve ca kapilavāstavyā śilpāyatanā (as masc.? one ms. °nāḥ!), tad yathā lohakārakā etc. (list of artisans), *all the artisans of Kapilavastu, such as ...*; similarly iii.442.17 śilpāyatanā (no v.l.), tad yathā lohakārakā etc.; in the same way tīrthyāyatana (*vessel of heresy*?) is used of heretical teachers Av i.231.3 yānīmāni ... pṛthag loke tīrthyāyatanāni, tad yathā, Pūraṇaḥ Kāśyapo Māskarī etc. (all persons); Pali has titthāyatana, nt., only as *heretical school* or *doctrine* (acc. to Ledi Sadaw JPTS 1913.117 *harbours of error*), or at least, it seems, never clearly of persons (some passages are ambiguous and might be so interpreted); Pali sippāyatana also does not seem to be applied to artisans, but only to crafts; (**3**) *a worthy object* (cf. **an-āy°**), = Skt. pātra: Divy 419.(22–)23 (api tu Buddhadharmasaṃghe) prasādam utpādaya, eṣa āyatanagataḥ prasāda iti, ... *this is favor bestowed on a worthy object*; (**4**) *stage* of ecstasy or trance (four such), see **ākāśānantyāyat°, vijñānānantyāyat°, ākiṃcanyāyat°, naivasaṃjñānāsaṃjñāyat°**: listed Mvy 3110–3113; also 1492–5 in list of **samāpatti**, q.v.; Dharmas 129; see also s.v. **deva**; (**5**) *sense; organ of sense* (six in number), distinguished as ādhyātmika āy° (= Pali ajjhattika āy°) or as sparśāy° (= Pali phassāy°); likewise *object of sense* (also six), distinguished as **bāhira** (= Pali id.) or bāhya āy°: Mvy 2027 dvādaśāyatanāni, listed 2028–2039 in pairs, each cpd. with āyatanam (cakṣur-āy° etc.); the standard list contains six of each category, viz. cakṣus and rūpa, śrotra and śabda, ghrāṇa and gandha, jihvā and rasa, kāya and **spraṣṭavya** (q.v.), manas and **dharma** (2); Dharmas 24 lists each group of six as a (dvandva) cpd. concluded by -āyatanāni (with sparśa in lieu of spraṣṭavya); Śikṣ 244.15 ṣaḍ imāni ... sparśāyatanāni, katamāni ṣaṭ, cakṣuḥ sparśāyatanaṃ rūpāṇāṃ darśanāya, etc., including kāya (read kāyaḥ) sparśāy° spraṣṭavyānāṃ sparśanāya, manaḥ sparśāy° dharmāṇāṃ vijñānāya; adhyatmikam āy° and bāhiram āy° Mv iii.66.3 ff. (parallel passage in Pali, MN i.190.20 ff.); ṣaḍ-āyatanam, *the six senses* (sense-organs and their respective objects, each pair regarded as a unit), one of the steps in the **pratītya-samutpāda** (= Pali saḷāyatana), Mvy 2246; Mv ii.285.9 f.; LV 347.2, 4; etc., cf. Lévi, Sūtrāl. xi.30, Transl. n. 2; actions are *rooted* in them, LV 374.13 (vs) iha me karmavidhānā ... ṣaḍāyatanamūlā, chinnā drumendramūle (i. e. by attaining Buddhahood); compounded or associated with **skandha**, q.v., and **dhātu** (*element*, q.v.), the total being an expression for states of physical existence, LV 420.17 (vs) na skandha āyatana dhātu (better as dvandva cpd.?) vademi buddhaṃ, *I do not call ... the Buddha*; LV 177.5 (cited Śikṣ 240.5; vs) skandhadhātvāyatanāni (prob. read with Śikṣ skandhāyatanāni, better meter; so also Tib.) dhātavaḥ; Laṅk 18.6 skandha-dhātv-āyatanopagānāṃ sarvadharmāṇām; (**6**) **abhibhv-āyatana**, see s.v.; (**7**) **kṛtsnāyatana**, q.v., s.v. **kṛtsna**.

-āyatanika, ifc. adj. (**āyatana** 5 with suffix ika), in dharmāyatanikam Mvy 7565, prob. *having to do with* or *based on the 'sphere' of dharmas* (as objects of manas, see āyatana 5), i. e. 'objects of ideation' (PTSD s.v. dhamma, cpd. dhammāyatana). In Pali, -āyatanika is recorded PTSD only in phassāyatanikā nāma nirayā, and ... saggā, SN iv.126.4–5 and 17–18, *hells* or *heavens based on the 'contact fields'* or *senses* (cf. sparśāyatana s.v. āyatana 5), with unpleasant or pleasant sensations respectively.

āyatiṃ, adv. (Pali id.; acc. of Skt. āyati, *the future*, but not recorded there as adv.), *in the future*: °tiṃ saṃbodhim abhisaṃprārthayamānena Mv i.57.15, or bodhiṃ prārthayamānena 58.5.

āya-dvāra, nt. (see **āya**), (**1**) *cause* or *means* (lit. *door*) *of arrival* or *origin*: of rain, jewels, money, flowers, KP 43.1–3 tad yathāpi ... vyabhre deve vigatavalāhake nāsti varṣasyāyadvāraṃ, evam eva ... alpaśrutasya bodhisattvasyāntikā (read °kān) nāsti saddharmavṛṣṭer āyadvāraṃ: 46.1–4 tad yathāpi ... yatra maṇiratnāyadvāraṃ bhavati, bahūnāṃ tatra karṣāpaṇaśatasahasrāṇām āyadvāraṃ bhavati; evam eva ... yatra bodhisattvasyāyadvāraṃ bhavati, bahūnāṃ tatra śrāvakapratyekabuddhaśatasahasrāṇām āyadvāraṃ bhavati (in lines 6, 7, vs, āyo replaces āyadvāraṃ; same comparison KP

92.2, 4, āyadvāraṃ, replaced in vs by āyu 7, āyo 9); Gv 501.17 bahūnāṃ puṣpaśatasahasrāṇām āyadvāraṃ bhaviṣyatīti; of dharma, Bbh 19.4 (dve ime ... bodhisattvasya) mahatī kuśaladharmāyadvāre (dual); Gv 495.24 sarvadharmāyadvāra-tayā; others, Gv 466.5-6 kalyāṇamitrāyadvārāḥ, *having good friends as their origin* or *cause* (agrees with series of nouns ending sarvabuddhadharmapratilambhapariniṣpattayaḥ, l. 4); āyadvārārthena ṣaḍāyatanam Śāl 81.7 and MadhK 564.2 (cf. 552.9 with note: *la porte d'arrivée, la porte de naissance*); (**2**) *source of income* (cf. Skt. āya, *income*), substantially = karmānta: Bbh 5.15–16 udāreṣu ca karmānteṣv adhimukto bhavati, na parīttāyadvāreṣu; perhaps in this sense Mvy 2333 saṃghāyadvāraharaṇam, *depriving the assembly* (of monks) *of sources of income* (?in a list of sins; Tib. is literal and not helpful).

āyācana (nt., = Pali id., to Skt. and Pali āyācati), *supplication* (of a deity): Divy 1.10 āyācanahetoḥ putrā jāyante; 231.25 °nena.

āyācñā (to Skt. āyācati, cf. Skt. yācñā), *entreaty*: Jm 120.6 (prose) -parisamāpty-āyācñayā, *with entreaty to complete* ... Crit. app. suggests em. to °pti-yācñayā, but the formation seems quite possible (to āyācati as yācñā to yācati).

āyātrika, m., *guard* or *attendant on a journey*: kimartham vayam °kāṇāṃ bhṛtim anuprayacchāmaḥ MSV iv.62.12.

āyāpita, ppp. (of Skt. āyāpayati, not in this mg.), *reared, brought up*: (tvaṃ mayā ...) svahastabalenāyāpitaḥ poṣitaḥ saṃvardhitaḥ Divy 499.9.

[**āyāsa**, m., °saḥ Divy 82.13, read ācāmaḥ with Tib. (letter from Mr. D.R.S. Bailey) and same passage MSV i.80.18, cf. Divy 82.17 etc.]

[**āyika**? LV 34.6, see **samādhyāyika-tā**.]

Āyudhiṣṭhira(?), n. of a Bodhisattva: Gv 443.4. Uncertain reading; initial in saṃdhi with preceding -a, permitting analysis as Ayudhi°, which seems scarcely possible; perhaps the long ā is an error or misprint, and we should understand Yudhiṣṭhira.

Āyurdadā (see **-dada**), n. of a kiṃnara-maid: Kv 6.12.

-āyuṣika, adj. ifc. (from āyus with suffix ika), *aged*...: Kv 48.13 (prose) (jīrṇo vṛddho mahallakaḥ ...) anekavarṣaśatasahasrāyuṣikaḥ.

āyuṣmaṃ, i. e. Skt. āyuṣman, functions like Pali āvuso (see **āvusa** and **āyuṣmaṃvāda**), and like it (see Childers s.v.) may be adressed to more than one person, *sirs* (usually to equals or inferiors): Mv i.328.16 (prose) (te bhikṣū ... kumbhakārasya mātāpitarau etad uvāca), yatra āyuṣmaṃ bhikṣū (n. pl., so read with mss., Senart wrongly em. bhikṣūṇāṃ) ... tṛṇā na saṃbhuṇanti ...

āyuṣmaṃvāda (m.; = Pali āvusovāda, DN ii.154.9, 12; cf. **āyuṣmaṃ**), *address using the term āyuṣmaṃ* (āyuṣman): Mv iii.329.10 (mā bhikṣavo ...) tathāgataṃ āyuṣmaṃvādena samudācaratha (in corresponding passage LV 409.6 āyuṣmadvādena, regular Skt.).

Āyustejas, n. of a former Buddha: LV 5.14.

āyuḥ-saṃskāra, see s.v. **saṃskāra** (2).

āyūha (Pali id.), *effort, striving*, chiefly in neg. **an-āyūha** (also **anāvyūha**), q.v. for discussion of mg.; cf. also **āyūhati**: āyūhaniryūha-vigata (= anāyūhāniryūha) Laṅk 80.7 °tam (traidhātukam); 115.15 °tāḥ (sarvadharmāḥ); in Gv 40.11 āyūha-sarvadharma-vimāna-pratiṣṭhānāṃ (bodhisattvānāṃ), prob. error for anāyūha-.

āyūhati (= Pali id.), cf. (**an**)**āyūha**, *exerts oneself, strives* (for, acc.): Gv 69.24 (bodhisattvavimokṣam; similarly in the rest); 80.24, 25; 83.12; 199.24 (in all these followed by corresp. form of **niryūhati**, q.v.); 222.15 °hantī, followed by viyūhantī; passive, Laṅk 115.13 āyūhyamānaṃ nāyūhyate, niryūhyamānaṃ na niryūhyate, ata etasmāt kāraṇān ... sarvadharmā āyūhaniryūhavigatāḥ, *being striven after it is not attained* (or [successfully] *striven after*), *being renounced it is not got rid of; that is why all states of existence are without either acquisition or riddance* (Suzuki, *neither taking birth nor ... going out*).

āyoga, m. (= Pali id.; in sense 1 Skt. Lex., and acc. to BR once in Rām., but acc. to pw bhramarāyoga there means *Bienenschwarm*), (**1**) *practice* (of), *application* (to), with loc. or as posterior in cpd.: sukhallikāyoga, *addiction to pleasures* (otherwise °kānuyoga, which alone seems to be known in Pali), see s.v. **sukhallikā**, LV 407.22; 416.16; adhicitte ca āyoga(ḥ) Ud xxxii.27(32) (= Pali Dhp. 185, same text); (**2**) in SP 102.4 (prose) (dhanikaḥ) syād āyogaprayoga-kṛṣi-vaṇijya-prabhūtaś ca bhavet, and in corresponding vs 111.9 prayoga āyoga ...; here both āyoga and prayoga apparently mean different kinds of business activity; acc. to Tib. it seems that āyoga = ḥdu ba, *accumulation* (of wealth), prayoga = ḥphel ba, *increase* (qy: by usury?), but acc. to Das also *accumulation, collection, excess*.

āra, nt., *the hither* or *nearer side* or *part*, in contrast to pāra: Mvy 2662 = Tib.tshu rol, *this side* (2663 pāraṃ); ŚsP 1360.9 (kasyacid dharmasyotpādaṃ vā nirodhaṃ vā ...) āraṃ vā pāraṃ vopalabhate. (Cf. AMg. āra, nt., *this world, this life, this existence*. Doubtless the stem from which is derived the Skt. adverb ārāt *near*, see Edgerton, Mīmāṃsā Nyāya Prakāśa, Gloss. Ind. s.v. ārād-upakāraka.)

[**ārakṣa**, m.: LV 192.18, text ārakṣān sthāpayati sma, *he establishes guards*. But v.l. rakṣā; read either this or ārakṣāṃ; in any case the stem is fem. (in -ā); cf. 193.15 ārakṣāṃ prakarotha. In Bbh 230.13 ms. ārakṣāṇi, ed. ārakṣyāṇi; read arakṣyāṇi, see **arakṣya**.]

ārakṣaṇa-tā (cf. °ṇa, Schmidt, Nachträge), *the being on guard*: °tā vipratipanneṣu Śikṣ 286.3 (prose).

ārakṣitar, *one who guards* (from, with abl.): °tāraḥ pranāśapathebhyo Gv 463.7.

(**ārakṣya**, see **arakṣya**.)

āraṅga, m. or nt. (associated with **ārāgayati**, q.v.; root raj, rañj, cf. Skt. raṅga etc.), *acquisition, attainment*: LV 35.3 (prose) sarvakuśalamūladharmāraṅgottāraṇāya, *to the bringing over into acquisition of* ... Tib. brtsams, *accomplishment*.

āraṇyaka, m. (Skt. id., *forest dweller*, not in technical sense; = Pali āraññaka, also **ara**° in both BHS and Pali), *dwelling in the forest*, one of the **dhūtaguṇa**: Mvy 1134; Dharmas 63; AsP 387.3; MSV iii.122.4.

āraṇya-dhuta, see s.v. **dhuta**.

āra-tas, adv. (= Skt. ārāt), *at a distance, afar* (from, with gen.): Gv 488.7 (vs) tasya sarvi sugatā na durlabhā, tasya sarvi jinaputra nārataḥ.

Ārati, f., n. of one of the 'armies' (senā) of Māra: Mv ii.240.3 (vs) kāmā te prathamā senā dvitīyā ārati vuccati. The meter is indifferent as to a- or ā- initially, and LV in the same vs has **Arati**, q.v. It is hard to be sure what meaning was attributed to the word. Foucaux (*mécontentement*) and Tib. (mi dgaḥ ba) understand LV as a-(neg.)-rati.

-ārabdha, *injured*, in **an-ārabdha**, q.v.

ārabhya, ger., postpos. with acc. (= Pali ārabbha), *referring to, having to do with*: SP 21.1 (taṃ varaprabhaṃ bodhisattvam) ārabhya ... dharmaparyāyaṃ saṃprakāśayām āsa (practically = *revealed to the bodhisattva V.*); 71.9 samyaksaṃbodhim ārabhya ... bodhisattvayānam eva samādāpayati; 109.10; LV 400.13 (prose) sattvān ārabhya mahākaruṇām avakrāmayati sma (= 180.6 sattveṣu ca mahākaruṇām avakrāmati sma); Mv i.319.3–4 ... śrotuṃ imam eva mārakaraṇḍaṃ nigamam ārabhya (*about*); iii.212.5 ... pṛccheyaṃ dṛṣṭadhārmikaṃ artham ārabhya utāho sāmparāyikaṃ; 7 pañca kāmaguṇān ārabhya; 318.13 (aniyataṃ) rāśim ārabhya; 412.14 yaśodaṃ śreṣṭhiputram ārabhya imam udānam udānaye; Divy 98.8; 348.17 sthaviropaguptam ārabhya; 619.8 bhikṣuṇyāḥ pūrvanivāsam ārabhya bhikṣūn āmantrayate sma (repetitions below); Jm 172.17 (vs) ... tad brūhi kam ārabhyeti bhāṣase; Bbh 37.1–2 yathāvadbhāvikatāṃ dharmāṇām ārabhya yā bhūtatā; 49.15–16 Saṃthakātyāyanam ārabhya; 223.2 hīnayāna-niḥsṛtiṃ cārabhya mahāyāna-niḥsṛtiṃ vā; etc.

ārambaṇa, nt. (= Pali ārammaṇa; in mg. 1 = Skt. **ālambana**; in BHS this, q.v., is also used in mg. 3), (**1**) *basis, support, point d'appui; basis, reason,* (logical) *ground*; in Bhvr. cpds., *having ... as basis, based on ...*: SP 6.13 (see s.v. **āśravaṇa**); 71.7 -vividha-hetu-kāraṇa-nidarśanārambaṇa-niruktyupāyakauśalyair; 318.6–7 yāṃ ca ... tathāgataḥ ... vācaṃ bhāṣata ātmopadarśanena (add with WT vā paropadarśanena) vātmārambaṇena vā parārambaṇena vā ..., either *on his own authority* (Kern) *or that of others*, or *on the basis of* (presentation of) *himself* (in visible form) *or of others* (so essentially Burnouf; perhaps more exactly, *on the basis of* giving an account, a description, sc. of himself, *by himself or by others*); 318.14 vividhair ārambaṇair, *with various bases* or *authorities*; 319.12 tad ārambaṇaṃ kṛtvā, probably *making that my reason* or *basis*; 320.3 tathāgatārambaṇa-manaskārakuśalamūlāni, *roots of merit* (due to) *attentiveness based upon the T.*; LV 244.5 (dhyānagocarāṇāṃ) ca samāpattyārambaṇānāṃ laukikasamādhīnām; Mv ii.260.15 mahantānāṃ varṇānām ārambaṇam ... (16) bhūtānāṃ ca varṇānām ārambaṇam anuprāpnuvanti (Bodhisattvas), apparently *basis of great castes ... and of bygone castes** (so Senart, but he disclaims understanding what is meant); Gv 18.21 -bodhy-ārambaṇa- (1st ed. misprinted; corr. 2d ed.) -kuśalamūla-; 64.8 and 116.5 ārambaṇīkṛtya, *making a basis, object of attention* (with acc.); in Śikṣ 253.3 ārambaṇena = ālambanapratyayena (cf. Mvy 2269; Pali ārammaṇapaccaya), the third of the four **pratyaya**, q.v.; (**2**) *physical basis, location* (= Skt. viṣaya): Gv 82.14 yasmin yasminn adhvani (*time*, i. e. present, past, or future) yasmin yasminn ārambaṇe (*cosmic location*, of a Tathāgata) ... tathāgataṃ draṣṭuṃ ākāṅkṣāmi; Gv 512.4–5 ābhāsam agamann ekasminn ārambaṇe yathā caikasminn ārambaṇe tathāśeṣasarvārambaṇeṣu, *location(s)*, of the palatial structures presided over by Maitreya; (**3**) like Pali ārammaṇa, also = Skt. viṣaya in sense of *sense-object*, of which in Pali there are six (the 6th being dhamma, object of manas); Śikṣ 250.5 cakṣurindriyādhipateyā rūpārambaṇa-prativijñaptiḥ, *recognition of the sense-object form, dependent on the sense-organ eye* (sight); Mv i.120.11, read with mss. ārambaṇārambaṇacittaṃ hetuno parikarmenti, ... *the thought as it grasps the sense-objects* (here perhaps more particularly the objects of the manas, *ideas*, to which Pali ārammaṇa is sometimes restrictedly applied). —*(Mv ii.260.15–16) Better, *basis of great and true renown*, or *qualities*, or (physical) *appearance*? (Addition in proof.)

ārambaṇaka, nt., = **ālambana(ka)** as architectural term: Mvy 5589 = Tib. gdaṅ bu, *peg, nail*, or *step* (*of a ladder*); Chin. *staircase* or *step of a ladder*. Associated with 5586 **vedikā**, 5587 **sūcakaḥ**, 5588 śaṅkuḥ, 5590 **sūcikā**, 5591 **adhiṣṭhānam**; cf. s.v. **ālambana**.

Ārambaṇachedana, m., n. of a samādhi: Mvy 573; ŚsP 1421.6.

ārambaṇīya, adj., *pertaining to the objects of sense* (see **ārambaṇa**, 3): Gv 83.(7–)8 (svacittam eva pariśodhayitavyaṃ) ārambaṇīya-dharmebhyaḥ, substantially (*must be purified*) *from physical conditions.*

ārambha (Skt. Lex., see pw 5 App., which follows Zachariae in calling this an error for ālambha, but Pali and BHS support it; = Pali id., in mahārambha, = our word, SN i.76.21; not recorded in PTSD, except in nir-ā°, or Childers), (sacrificial) *slaughter* (of animals), substantially = yajña: Bbh 118.2 (kṣudrayajñeṣu ca) mahārambheṣu ca yeṣu bahavaḥ prāṇinaḥ ... jīvitād vyaparopyante. Cf. also **anārabdha.**

ārāgaṇa, nt., °**ṇā**(?), and °**ṇa-tā** (to **ārāgayati**), (**1**) *attainment*: Mv iii.57.14 āryadharmāṇāṃ ārāgaṇāye (so mss.; Senart em. ārādha°); KP 17.2 and Bbh 287.14–15 buddhotpādārāgaṇatā, *attainment of the production of Buddhas*, i. e. of the privilege of being born when a Buddha is living; see under **ārāgayati** (1); paraphrased in KP 17.6 (vs) buddhānam ārāgaṇa sarvajātiṣu; (**2**) *propitiation, pleasing, winning the favor* (of): Gv 529.23 sarvakalyāṇamitrārāgaṇāvirāgaṇabuddhiḥ, *with a mind to please and not displease all excellent friends*; Gv 84.1 kalyāṇamitrārāgaṇābhimukhaḥ; 107.11 naikabuddhārāgaṇatāyai ... (12) yaduṭārāgaṇābhirādhanapūjopasthānatāyai; 247.22 kalyāṇamitrārāgaṇaprayogāḥ.

ārāgayati (peculiar to BHS, except for ppp. āräiaṃ Deśīn. 1.70 = gṛhītam, āsāditam ity anye; quasi-denom. to an unrecorded *ārāga, cf. **āraṅga** and **ārāgaṇa**, but prob. actually formed as a pendant and opposite to **virāgayati**, q.v., with which it is often associated; used extensively as substitute for ārādhayati, which is often, e. g. in the Kashgar rec. of SP, recorded as v.l. for this; Senart Mv i.458 emended ārāg- to ārādh-, but on iii.472 recognized that this was indefensible; Skt. vi-rādh- is used, tho not often, in ways approaching **virāgayati**; see also **saṃrāgayati** and **saṃrādhayati** for a third confusion of these two roots): (**1**) *attains, gets, acquires*: object **ājñām**, q.v. (perfect knowledge) Mvy 7602; Mv iii.53.9; Divy 302.20; kuśalāṃ dharmāṃ (so interpret ārādhyate ... dharmo Jm 106.19, as in Skt., BR s.v. rādh with ā 2; pw 7.371 *befolgen, vollführen*) Mv ii.118.9 °yet, 120.1 °ye (opt.; Senart em. ārādh°); nirvāṇam ārāgayiṣyatīti LV 434.6 and 7; °yiṣyanti mamāgrabodhim SP 222.2; ārāgeti (Śikṣ °gayaty) ... buddhotpādaṃ Mv ii.363.4 = Śikṣ 298.2 (see under **ārāgaṇa**, 1); saced yūyaṃ yācanakam ārāgayatha Bbh 124.23, *if you get* (*come upon, meet*) *a petitioner* (i. e. an opportunity to show generosity); oṣadhīr ārāgayed ārāgya ca ... SP 134.3, *would get the herbs, and having got them* ...; food, Divy 173.4, 29 °gayati; (āhāram) 236.10 °gayāmi; in Divy 314.17; 328.17 na tv eva pitṛmaraṇam ārāgitavantau, (they entered nirvāṇa, or died,) *but did not attain* (wait for) *their father's death* (i. e., they predeceased him); so mss. in these places, while acc. to ed. in 314.23 and 315.3 mss. have āgamitavantau, *waited for*, which is the essential meaning in any case, but prob. a lect. fac.; (**2**) *propitiates, gratifies, pleases*; object (or subject of passive forms) almost always Buddha(s): °gayati Mvy 2394; °yanti SP 184.2; RP 15.4; °yeyam, opt. Mv ii.276.12; Divy 23.20; 131.5; 133.15; 192.16; Av i.287.9; °ye Mv ii.393.1 = °yed Śikṣ 306.12; °yema Bbh 271.5; °yiṣyasi, fut. Suv 91.3; °yiṣyati SP 153.1; ārāgayī, aor. SP 27.12; 384.6; ārāgita, ppp. (various forms; subject Buddhas) SP 22.7; 70.10; 184.2; 290.11; 393.5; Suv 81.10; Gv 104.17; °gitavān SP 380.10; °gayām āsa Samādh 8.16; °gayitvā, ger. SP 385.6; Mv i.104.8 (Senart em. ārādh°); °getvā Mv iii.415.4; °gayitu-kāma Śikṣ 244.3; °gayitavyā, gdve. (subject a human instructress) Bhīk 31b.3.

ārājaka, nt. (secondary deriv., with vṛddhi, from arāja or °jaka), *state of kinglessness*: Mv ii.70.13 (vs, but quantity of initial indifferent) °kam idam asmākam.

Ārāḍa (also **Arāḍa**, q.v., and see next; = Pali Āḷāra), n. of a sage under whom Śākyamuni studied for a time; in a dvandva cpd. Ārāḍodraka (-Udraka) Divy 392.1 (see also under **Arāḍa** and **Ārāḍaka**); generally surnamed Kālāma (= Pali id.): °ḍa-Kāl° as one word Mvy 3515, but regularly two words: Mv ii.118.1 ff.; 198.1; iii.322.15, 17; in LV 238.14, 19 f.; 239.6, 12; 403.20; 404.2–3, 3–4, Lefmann reads the surname always Kālāpa; the mss. generally vary, in 404.3 all have Kālāma. However, there seems to have been some support in northern tradition for the ending -pa, for Tib. on Mvy and LV renders sgyu rtsal śes (byed), *knowing arts*, which seems to point to analysis into kalā plus a form of root āp-.

Ārāḍaka = prec.: Divy 392.3 (vs), in a dvandva, Udrakārāḍakā (see under prec. and **Arāḍa**); the -ka is probably m.c.

ārāti, m.c. for **arati**, *displeasure* (in this mg. Skt. arati), by em. (required by meter) in LV 325.11, where word-division should be: ārātīya ratīya (both instr. sg.) saṃvase na ca sārdhaṃ, *and I do not dwell together with displeasure or pleasure.*

[**ārāmatha**, *grove*, = ārāma, acc. to KN in SP 61.10 ārāmatha vṛkṣamūlam; but read ārām' atha.]

ārāmika, m. (in sense 1 once in Rājat., pw; in Pali apparently only in sense 2, and so usually in BHS), (**1**) *gardener*: Av i.36.10 ff.; 120.14; 124.6, et alibi; (**2**) *an attendant* in a Buddhist ārāma, i. e. a grove used by monks: Mvy 3843; Mv i.325.19 °ka-sahasrāṇi upasthāpayiṣyanti (in a grove for monks); Divy 43.20 (here Tib. khim pa zhig, Bailey, JRAS 1950.180; **āgārika**?); 155.13; 157.25, 27 et alibi; Bbh 166.25; Prāt 494.10; Laṅk 308.6.

ārāva, nt., a high number: Mvy 7839 = Tib.rig(s) sdom; cited from Gv; var. **agava**, q.v. But Gv 133.3 reads **avaga** (nt.), which has the same Tib. rendering Mvy 7713 and is probably to be read for ārāva. Mironov reads arāvam, noting vv.ll. agavam, aravam. In Gv 105.21 replaced by **vipāsa.**

ārāvita, ppp. (of denom. to Skt. and Pali ārāva, *cry*, not to caus. of ā-ru which is unrecorded), *made resonant*: Mv ii.215.13 (sarvaṃ vanakhaṇḍaṃ . . . nināditaṃ mṛgapakṣiravehi) ca ārāvitaṃ (mss. °pitaṃ).

ārītīyate, see **ar(t)tiyati.**

(**āruta**, in Jm 123.18, *cry* (noun), not ppp. of ā-ru as stated in pw 7.371. The noun is Skt.: BR 6.355, s.v. ā-ru.)

[**ārūḍha**, Divy 84.10, see s.v. **ābṛḍha.**]

[**ārūḍha-cīvara**, see **rūḍha-cīvara.**]

ārūḍhayati (denom. to ārūḍha, *mounted*), *makes mounted, causes to mount*: Mv iii.146.14 aśvarathe ārūḍhayitvā (ger.).

ārūpa, nt. (= **ārūpya**; cf. **ārūpin**), *formlessness*: Laṅk 312.8(–9) ārūpya-rūpaṃ hy ārūpair . . . (9) rūpaṃ darśyanti sattvānāṃ.

ārūpayati (= Skt. āropayati; for ū cf. Pali rūhati and ārūha = āroha; see Chap. 43, s.v. ruh), *causes to mount*: ppp. ārūpitā Mv iii.68.19; ger. ārūpiya Mv i.352.20; ārūpetvā iii.160.7 (so em. Senart, plausibly); tridaṇḍaṃ ārūpayitvā Mv iii.393.18, *having caused* (her) *to take up* (the triple staff, as brahman pupil).

ārūpin, adj. (from **ārūpa**, q.v., plus -in), (something) *characterized by formlessness*: catvāra ārūpinaḥ skandhā(ḥ) Laṅk 113.9; ŚsP 382.(15–)16 (tat kiṃ manyase) subhūte ārūpi bodhisattva iti, *so what think you, S.? is a Bodhisattva something characterized by formlessness?*

ārūpya, adj. and subst. nt. (=Pali āruppa, both), *formless* (state), *formlessness*; there are, as in Pali, four such, listed s.v. **deva**, end: °pyā ca samāpattir Laṅk 24.10; °pya-samāpatti LV 442.6; Bbh 90.11 (four); Dharmas 82 (four); Karmav 47.21 ff. (four, listed); Gv 471.20 ye te catur-ārūpya-samāpatti-vihāra-vihāriṇaś ca na cārūpya-dhātu-gatiṃ gacchanti, mahākaruṇāparigṛhītatvāt; °pyāś ca samādhayaḥ Laṅk 65.15; ārūpya as adj. with or sc. deva (= **ārūpyāvacara, arūpāv°**, qq.v.) Mmk 103.28; 473.24; 474.1 etc.; ārupye nāvatiṣṭhati Laṅk 355.8; in comp. with dhātu (perhaps as adj., as with samāpatti above, but parallel cpds. with kāma-, rūpa- suggest subst.), parallel or cpd. with **kāma-dh°, rūpa-dh°**, LV 428.20; Mvy 2149 (here the stem dhātu is omitted); KP 94.5; alone, KP 27.9. In Mv ii.123.18 ārūpyāṇi is an error for sārūpyāṇi, see **sārūpya.**

ārūpyāvacara, m. (see s.v. **ārūpya**), = **arūpāvacara**, q.v.: Mmk 419.8; Karmav 30.14.

ārogyayati (denom. to ārogya), (**1**) *salutes* (personally and directly): °yayitvā, ger. Divy 259.11; MSV i.42.1; (**2**) *sends a greeting to*, Ger. *lässt grüssen* (= caus.): Divy 129.5 and 273.25 °yayati; 273.19 °yaya, impv.; MSV i.42.3 °yayati; (**3**) caus. ārogyāpayati, = (2): Divy 128.25 °paya, impv. (but MSV i.245.14, same passage, °gyaya).

ārocaka, f. °**ikā**, adj. (to **ārocayati** with -aka), *announcing, making known*: preṣyadārikayā kālārocikayā MSV ii.83.16; °cakaḥ 84.5.

ārocana, nt., or °**na-tā** (not recorded in Pali, except CPD an-ārocanā; n. act. to ārocayati), *saying, statement, declaration*: °naṃ Mvy 8424–5; 9295; sarvasattveṣu bodhicittārocanatā KP 20.3; anārocanatā paraskhaliteṣu Śikṣ 286.3.

ārocayati, (rarely) **āroceti** (= Pali id., usually °ceti), *declares, announces, tells*: usually with acc. of thing and gen. or dat. of person, but sometimes with acc. of person, Mv i.226.14 = ii.29.17 rājānam ārocenti; ārocentā, pres. pple., Mv iii.345.4, 12; caus. (kālam) ārocāpitaṃ Mv i.307.13, *the time was caused to be announced*; otherwise the following are formally standard Skt.; ārocayāmi vo (te) . . . (voc. usually here) prativedayāmi (te, SP 269.8, but usually no repetition of pronoun), in formal pronouncements (usually) by a Buddha, SP 144.1; 259.6; 269.8; 309.2; 395.10; Sukh 71.15–16; LV 90.21 (ca instead of vo or te); kālam ārocayati Av i.9.5 *announces* (that) *the time* (has arrived); object prakṛtim, (this) *circumstance*, LV 137.11; 200.16; 386.6; 407.8; Mv i.246.11; Suv 187.11; 190.8; or artham, *the matter*, LV 141.6; 404.1; Sukh 3.15; (chandaṃ ca tais tathāgatair) . . . ārocitaṃ viditvā SP 248.(12–)13, *and knowing that these Tathāgatas had announced their consent*; yan nv aham anena saha vādam ārocayeyam Av i.94.1, *suppose now I propose a contest* (in music) *with him*; miscellaneous, LV 18.11; Mv i.8.11; 197.1; ii.112.3; 167.10; 178.20; iii.402.15; Divy 2.9; 6.9; 260.6; Av i.14.11; Kv 55.23; etc., common in most texts.

ārodana (nt.; = Pali id.), *weeping, lamentation*: Mv ii.215.9 mahāntaṃ ārodanaṃ karetsuḥ (Senart karensuḥ); MSV i.64.11 °na-śabdaṃ.

āropayati (unrecorded in this sense; cf. Skt. id. *plants*?), *buries*: Divy 484.13 atha kālaṃ karoti, tatraivāropayitavyaḥ, *but if he dies, he is to be buried right there*; 485.18 atha kālaṃ karoti, tatraivāropayitvāgaccha.

āroha, m. (= Pali id., regularly with pariṇāha; cf. **ānāha**), *height* or *length* (of persons, animals, trees, etc.); usually cpd. or associated with pariṇāha, *circumference*: āroha-pariṇāhaṃ, dvandva, Divy 57.1; °ṇāho, id. masc. sg., Divy 222.21 (mss.; see s.v. **gupti**); °ṇāhaḥ Bbh 61.19; other cases, °ṇāhena etc., Samādh 22.20; Gv 45.18; Sukh 40.17; tulyārohapariṇāhau (Bhvr., dual, with nau, pronoun) Jm 136.7; ārohapariṇāha-saṃpanna Mvy 2684; of the bodhi-tree LV 278.12; of the Bodhisattva's mother, LV 25.9 (analyzed in Mv i.205.7 = ii.9.3 into āroha-saṃpannāyāṃ pariṇāha-saṃpannāyāṃ, of the same); ārohaḥ Mvy 2685 (pariṇāhaḥ 2686); without juxtaposition to pariṇāha, Śikṣ 28.4 āroha-saṃpannān, said of horses, *perfect as to height* (mistranslated Bendall and Rouse).

ārjanā (to **ārjayati**), *winning, acquisition*: Bbh 35.9 (prose) bhogānām ārjanā.

ārjayati, *wins*: LV 203.7 (vs) puṇyam ārjayāmo (meter requires short penult; °yamo? all mss. ārj°) bahuṃ. Cf. **ārjanā**, supporting ā (preverb); BR 5.1043 cite samārjita (sam-ā-arj-) once from Mbh 13.5551.

Ārjava, n. of a cakravartin: Mv i.154.1.

[**Ārtavaka**, see **Āṭa°**.]

ārṇava, adj. (perh. = Pali aṇṇava as ep. of saraṃ, see CPD), *of the ocean*: °vaṃ saraḥ MPS 7.9; Ud xvii.7.

[**ārtībhāva**, m., *state of distress*, Senart's em. at Mv ii.146.15; but read anyathībhāva, q.v.]

ārtīyate, see **ar(t)tiyati.**

ārddha(?), Mv i.253.4, Senart rogajātā ārddhā, but mss. °jātānāddhe or °nārddhe; text and mg. obscure; Senart's note takes ār° as adj. from ṛddhi, (diseases) *produced by magic*, which does not seem to me plausible. But

I have no interpretation to propose. Followed by maṇḍalako ca adhivāso ca, qq.v.

Ārdravallipratirūpa, n. of a former Buddha: Mv i.141.5.

Āryaka, n. of a cakravartin: SP 160.14 mahārājñā cakravartināryakeṇa mahākośena. Burnouf and Kern take this word as an adj. and Cakravartin as the king's name, which I think unlikely.

āryakā (= Pali ayyakā), *grandmother*: MSV ii.70.2 f.

Āryadeva, n. of a teacher: Mvy 3476.

āryapakṣa, m., *group of noble persons*, designation of a list of 500 Tathāgatas (divided into two halves, and each half into two hundred plus fifty — approximately): Mv i.137.9; 138.8; 140.6; 141.8. See Senart's note, p. 485.

āryapuṅgala, m. (= Pali ariya-puggala), *a model human personality*: LV 423.13 parijñātam (so read with v.l. for text °nam) āryapuṅgalair (said of the dharmacakra). Prob. refers to persons in the eight stages of (Hīnayāna) religious development, Dharmas 102; see **aṣṭamaka, śaikṣa.**

Āryabhṛkuṭī, n. of a goddess, Mvy 4282; certainly the same as **Bhṛkuṭī**, q.v.

ārya-mahāsiṃha-ukkāsita, nt. (MIndic for °utkāsita), *Exalted-Great-Lion's-throat-clearing*: Mv ii.281.12 (here ārya is accidentally omitted), 14, 16, 18 (bodhisattvo . . . caturvidhaṃ) °sitaṃ ukkāsi. Cf. next two. The four ways are listed.

ārya-mahāsiṃha-vijṛmbhita, nt., *Exalted-Great-Lion's-yawn*: Mv ii.281.7–11 (bodhisattvo . . . caturvidhaṃ) °bhitaṃ vijṛmbheti. Cf. prec. and next. The four ways are listed.

ārya-mahāsiṃha-vilokita, nt., *Exalted-Great-Lion's gaze*: Mv ii.281.1–5 (bodhisattvo . . . caturvidhaṃ) °kitaṃ viloketi. Cf. prec. two. The four ways are listed.

ārya-māna, m. or nt., *exalted pride*: Mv ii.279.1 ff. (bodhisattvo . . . dvātriṃśatākārasamanvāgataṃ) °naṃ pragṛhṇe. The 32 forms are then listed. On dvātriṃśatasee § 19.34.

āryavaṃśa (m.; = Pali ariyavaṃsa, see CPD s.v.), *the* (fourfold) *attitudes* (lit. 'stocks', sources) *of the Buddhist saint*, listed AbhidhK. LaV-P. vi.146 ff.: RP 13.17–18 caturṇām °śānām anuvartanatā; 14.7 caturāryavaṃśaniratā; KP 6.17 (vs) ājīvaśuddho sthita āryavaṃśe; 123.3 saṃtuṣṭaḥ caturbhir āryavaṃśair (the first three are *contentment* with garments, food, seat-and-bed of monks; acc. to AbhidhK. the fourth is devotion to the way to release, by appropriate behavior); 126.7 (vs) °vaṃśehi samanvito 'pi; Śikṣ 105.8 caturāryavaṃśaparivarjanatayā (due to lābhasatkāra; misunderstood by Bendall and Rouse); 191.10 °vaṃśa-saṃtuṣṭi (cf. above).

Āryavaṃśaketu, n. of a former Buddha: Mv i.141.6.

Āryavatī, n. of a river: Karmav 162.14; prob. false Sktization for Pali Aciravatī = BHS **Ajiravatī**, q.v., (thru a MIndic *Ayiravaī, *Ariyavaī); cf. Lévi's note, which states that it is the same river as the **Hiraṇyavatī** (q.v.; on what evidence I do not know).

Āryaśūra, n. of a teacher: Mvy 3479.

ārya-satya, nt. (= Pali ariya-sacca), (the four) *noble truth*(s): listed, Mvy 1310 ff.; Dharmas 21 (duḥkham, samudayaḥ, nirodhaḥ, mārgaḥ); SP 179.2–3; Mv ii.138.4; Bbh 38.9 (as in Dharmas); full statements of all four, Mv iii.331.17 ff.; LV 417.2 ff. The standard names are duḥkham, duḥkhasamudayaḥ, duḥkhanirodhaḥ, duḥkhanirodhagāminī pratipat.

Āryasatyaka Parivarta (m.), n. of a work, or part of a work (cf. Bendall 407, note): Śikṣ 165.17.

Āryasaṃmatīya, m. pl., n. of a school: Mvy 9085.

Ārya-sarvāstivāda, m. pl., n. of a school: Mvy 9077 °vādāḥ; Śikṣ 148.13 °vādānāṃ (so ed. with ms.; Bendall's note suggests reading °vādināṃ) ca paṭhyate (a quotation follows).

Ārya-sthāvira, m. pl., n. of a school: Mvy 9095 (printed °sthaviraḥ, both a's short, but Index °sthāvirāḥ, and so Mironov).

Āryasthāvirīya Nikāya, n. of a work belonging to that (prec.) school, from which Jm xvi vss 2–3 are quoted: Jm 98.24. The verses occur in the Pali Dhp.

ārya-smita (nt.), *Exalted-smile* or *smile of an Exalted One* (or saint): Mv ii.280.15 ff. (Bodhisattvo . . . pañcavidhaṃ) āryasmitaṃ prādurkare. The five kinds are then listed.

Āryā, n. of a yakṣiṇī: Sādh 561.1, 11; 562.5.

Āryākṣa (? mss. Āryakṣa), n. of a former Buddha: Mv i.137.14.

Āryāsaṅga, n. of a teacher: Mvy 3477. Cf. **Asaṅga.**

āryikā (Skt. Gr. and lex.; f. to Skt. āryaka), *a venerable woman*, used of Buddhist nuns: °kā-saṃghaḥ (read as cpd.) Bhīk 17b.1 and ff.

[**ārṣa**, corruption for **ārṣabha**, adj., q.v.: Bbh 385.17; Gv 401.8.]

ārṣabha, adj. (= Pali āsabha; °bhaṃ, often written °bhaṇ-, ṭhānaṃ paṭijānāti MN i.69.32; SN ii.27.26 etc., cf. below), *of the first rank* (esp. religiously), *prime, worthy of admiration*: udāram ārṣabhaṃ sthānaṃ pratijānāti Dbs 209.10; 211.4 etc.; . . . pratijānīte Av ii.105.15; . . . prajānāmi (read pratijā°?) ŚsP 1448.12; . . . draṣṭavyam Bbh 386.13; in Bbh 385.17 (after 15 nirvāṇam udāram ity ucyate, cf. the above phrase), read ārṣabham (text ārṣam; refers to nirvāṇa; meaning supported by Tib. and Chin.) ity ucyate; of the teeth of a mahāpuruṣa, in a list of the lakṣaṇa, Gv 401.(7–)8 (aviralā) aviṣamārṣā (read aviṣamārṣabhā, for °mā ārṣabhā; same corruption as in Bbh 385.17 above) asya dantā abhūvan.

Ārṣṭiṣeṇa, m. pl. (cf. **Asthisena**), n. of a brahmanical school, of the chandogas: Divy 637.27.

(**Ārhata**, m., a member of some heretical sect: Mvy 3531. Perhaps, as in Skt., a Jain; but Nirgrantha occurs separately in 3529.)

ālakṣya (nt.? in Skt. as adj., *wahrzunehmen, sichtbar*), *visible sign, emblem*: Divy 118.24 (idam . . . maṇiratnam . . .) cihnabhūtam ālakṣyabhūtaṃ maṇḍanabhūtaṃ ca.

ālaptaka, m., *one with whom one talks familiarly*: Mvy 2711. In section entitled mitrakāryam; pw 7.319 *gesprächig, leutselig*. Tib. gtam ḥdres pa, defined by Das ālaptakā (so!), *mixed-up stories, garbled accounts*, which cannot be the mg.; MSV ii.131.11 ālaptakenālaptakasya (sc. upasthānaṃ, *waiting on when sick*, karaṇīyam), which makes the mg. certain; cf. **saṃlaptaka.**

ālabdha, ppp., in Mv ii.479.10 mālā ca se ālabdhā, *and a garland was hung on him.* As Senart's note indicates, this seems to require ālambitā, and to imply confusion of roots labh and lamb; note pw 5.217 ālalambhe Rājat. 2.212 'fehlerhaft für ālalambe'.

-ālambaka = Skt. ālamba, *support*, at end of Bhvr. cpd.: Bbh 242.3 dharmālambaka-maitrī, *love* (benevolence) *that is based on dharma.*

ālambana, nt. (in mg. 1, essentially = Skt. id.; in mg. 2 = **ārambaṇa**, q.v.), (**1**) *basis, ground, reason* (= Skt. id.); ālambana-pratyaya, third of four **pratyaya**, q.v., cf. **ārambaṇa**, 1, end: Mvy 2269; (**2**) *object of sense* (= **ārambaṇa**, 3): LV 392.15 sarvālambana-samatikrāntaḥ (dharmaḥ); Bbh 384.8 (see s.v. **saṃprakhyāna**); Sūtrāl. iv.1 (see Lévi's note in Transl.; seems restricted to correspondence with citta = manas(?), at least acc. to Tib.); (**3**) architectural term, part of a railing or balustrade; *bar, crossbar* (functioning as *support*), esp. of a **vedikā**(-jāla), q.v., one of the *cross-pieces* of a balustrade or railing; = **ārambaṇaka**, q.v.; associated with **adhiṣṭhāna** (q.v., 4) or °**naka** (q.v.); repeatedly a **sūcī** (**sūcikā**) is stated to function as ālambana to the upright pillars (**pādaka**) of a **vedikā**-jāla (Mv), or simply to a vedikā (Divy): Mv i.195.1 sūcikā ālambanam adhiṣṭhānakaṃ ca abhūṣi; iii.227.7 ff. sūcikā ālambanaṃ adhiṣṭhānakaṃ ca (in some repetitions below, abhūṣi is added); Divy 221.9 sūcī ālambanam adhiṣṭhānam (sc. āsīt); see next.

ālambanaka, nt., = **ālambana** (3); varies with °bana in repetitions of Mv iii.227.7, above, viz. in 9, 10, 11, 12, 13 (in some v.l. °banam).

ālambu = **alambu**, q.v.

?**ālambuṣa** (m. or nt.?), n. of a plant: Mmk 82.18 ālambuṣa-mūlaṃ kṣīreṇa saha pīṣayitvā. Prose; perhaps error for alambuṣā, which is the only form recorded in literary Skt. (Lex alambuṣa; no āl° is recorded anywhere).

ālambya, adj. (gdve.) or subst., *thing to be supported*: Laṅk 153.6 ālambālambyavigatam... saṃskrtam, *free from support and from anything to be supported*; 169.5 and 170.9 yadā tv ālambyam arthaṃ nopalabhate jñānam, *but when knowledge finds no object which can be supported* (by it); see also **nir-ālambya**.

ālaya, m., rarely nt. (in Skt. 'home', also in BHS; Pali id., same mgs. as BHS): (**1**) (*habitation*, hence) *firm basis, fundamental base*, in **an-ālaya, ālaya-vijñāna**, qq.v. for Tib.; also Laṅk 374.3 mano hy ālayasaṃbhūtam, 4 ālayāt sarvacittāni pravartanti taraṅgavat (in both of these substantially = ālaya-vijñāna); perhaps here also Av ii.175.2-3 tatas tena bhagavato 'ntike cittaṃ prasāditaṃ teṣāṃ ca mahāśrāvakāṇām ālayasamāpannānām (*arrived at the fundamental basis, the proper mental state*?); (**2**) *attachment, clinging*: Mvy 5382 kāmālayaḥ, *attachment* (Tib. zhen pa) *to desires* (Tib. ḥdod pa la); Mv iii.314.2 (mss. corrupt, ed. incorrect; read) ālayārāmā... ālayaratā ālayasamuditā (prajā), *mankind takes pleasure, joy, delight in attachment* (to lusts; see **samudita**, and Pali parallels SN i.136.11 ff.; Vin. i.4.35 ff.); Mv iii.400.3 hitvā ālayāni (em., from Pali Sn 535; mss. ālepati); Ud xii.18 ālayāṃs trīn (= the three **tṛṣṇā** 2 = Pali taṇhā; cf. Sn 635 ālayā, comm. taṇhā); Mv iii.200.11 ālayasamudghāto, *rooting out of attachment*, cf. Pali AN ii.34.24; Vism. 293.9, 25 f. See also **nirālaya.**

ālayana (= Skt. ālaya; Deśīn. 1.66 and 8.58 ālayaṇam, vāsagṛham), or (v.l.) **ālayaka**, nt., *dwelling, nest, lair* (of animals): SP 84.3 (vs) nikṣipanti te potakāny ālayanāni (v.l. °kāni) kṛtvā.

ālaya-vijñāna (see **ālaya**, 1) *connaissance-réceptacle* (E. Lamotte, L'Ālayavijñāna [Le Réceptacle] dans le Mahāyāna-saṃgraha, Mél. chin. et boud., vol. 3, Brussels, 1935, 169 ff.), or *basic, fundamental, underlying vijñāna*: Mvy 2017, where **ālaya** = kun gzhi, *ultimate basis*, identified sometimes with citta (Lévi, Sūtrāl. i.18, n. 2 in Transl.), and opp. to manas. Frequent in Laṅk; notably 2.13 (samudrataraṅgān avaloky)ālaya-vijñānodadhipravṛttivijñānapavanaviṣaye preritāṃs... cittāny avalokya, *looking on the waves of the sea, stirred in the range* (viṣaye) *of the wind of the active vijñāna and the ocean of the basal vij., and looking on the minds* (of the people there; ālaya-vi° is the ocean, pravṛtti-vi° the wind which stirs it; see under **ālaya** 1).

[**-ālāpaka**, read **-ālopaka**, q.v.: LV 248.21, 22.]

[**ālāpana**, nt., in bālālāpanam Dbh 43.6, read bālollāp°; see **ullāpana.**]

ālāmbu = **alambu**, q.v.

āli, f. (m.? nom. āliḥ), (**1**) *small ditch* (for water): Mvy 4177 = Tib. yur phran; cf. the Pali (and Skt. Lex.) meaning *dike*; (**2**) *a-series* (i. e. a plus āli), name for a series of syllables (chiefly vowels and combinations of a or ā with semivowels), used as a magic formula in Sādh, and defined there 478.7 ff. Cf. **kāli.**

Ālikāvendā, n. of a yakṣiṇī: MSV i.17.7. Foll. by **Maghā** (perh. part of same name?).

ālikhana (nt.?; cf. Skt. likhana and ālekhana), *painting, depiction, delineation*: Mmk 67.6 (vs) paṭa-m-ālikhanād (cpd.; m is hiatus-bridger); 524.12 (vs) maṇḍalālikhane.

āliṅga (m. or nt.; cf. next; = Pali, AMg., Skt. Lex. id.), *a kind of drum*: Mv ii.159.7 (prose) kācid āliṅgaṃ (in a series of mus. instruments); iii.70.14 (prose) mṛdaṅgavādyeṣu āliṅgavādyeṣu; 82.3 (vs; mss. slightly corrupt).

āliṅgikā (to prec.; prob. dim. -ka), *a kind of drum*: Mv iii.407.20 (prose) kācit mṛdaṅgaṃ kācid āliṅgikāṃ (mss. ăliṅgikā).

ālīḍha, ppp. of ā-lih, in an-ālīḍha Laṅk 14.13; 172.12 (Suzuki *not tasted*, prob. rather) *not 'licked' = not grazed, not* (even) *lightly touched* (by sectarian or heretical theorists); applied to questions or doctrines to be expounded.

ālu, m. (or f.; Skt. Lex. nt., and Skt. āluka, nt.; Pali ālu, nt. acc. to PTSD; but AMg. ālu, m. acc. to Ratnach., Pkt. m. and nt. acc. to Sheth), *a certain edible tuber*: Mvy 5730 āluḥ.

ālekhya, or (v.l.) **ālekha**, m., Mvy 5234, defined Tib. and Chin. as synonym of vipratisāra, kaukṛtya, and **vilekha, vilekhya**, qq.v.

āloka, m. (once nt.), *light*, as in Skt.; (**1**) fig., see **dharmāloka**(-mukha); like this, -jñānālokamukha Gv 169.24, *introduction to the light of knowledge*; -pratibhānālokamukha Gv 174.13–14; (prajñā udapāsi) ālokaṃ (n. sg. nt.) prādur-abhūṣi Mv iii.332.15 *illumination* (of the mind) *became manifested* (virtually = *enlightenment, true knowledge*); (**2**) m., a high number: Gv 133.13 (= **aloka**, q.v.). See the following items.

Ālokakara, m., n. of a samādhi: Mvy 557; ŚsP 1419.11.

ālokati (hardly = ālokayati or the rare Skt. ālokate, *sees, perceives*; not even in the 'sens moral' suggested by Senart; rather denom. to **āloka**, q.v.), *furnishes light*: Mv i.165.7 (vs, addressed to Buddha) yadā ca ālokasi nāgagāmi, yadā ca āgata maraṇāya pāraṃ, *when you provide illumination* (for creatures lost in the darkness of ignorance, l. 3 ff.)... *and when you have arrived at the shore beyond death* (? readings here uncertain),... (then the earth is shaken etc.)

Ālokamaṇḍalaprabha, n. of a Buddha: Gv 285.6.

āloka-lābha, m. (so read for edd. °labdha; see Lévi Sūtrāl. n. 1 on xiv.24), *attainment of illumination*, one of the **adhimukti-caryā**-bhūmi: Mvy 898.

āloka-vṛddhi, f., *increase of illumination*, one of the **adhimukti-caryā**-bhūmi: Mvy 899.

āloka-saṃdhi (m. or f.; = Pali id.), *light-joint, opening for light, window*: Jm 113.23 °dhiṃ divasaiḥ karotu. Prob. read this for āloka-saṃta-(-bhūmi, then lacuna), which seems corrupt, in Prāt 506.11; Chin. mentions *windows*. On the passage see **dvāra-kośa.**

Ālokasuvegadhvaja, n. of a serpent king: Mvy 3431.

ālokita-vilokita (nt., dvandva; on Pali see below), *look and gaze*; in a cliché, (prāsādikena...) °kitena Mv i.301.6; iii.60.6; 182.12; in other forms of the same cliché **avalokita** and **vyavalokita** are substituted; see these on the Tib. interpretation of the difference of mg. between them, to which I do not attach much importance (it sounds etymologizing). However, acc. to Pali DN comm. i.193.17 these two words mean *looking ahead* and *looking all around*, which substantially = Tib.

Ālokinī, acc. to printed text also **Lokinī**, n. of a yakṣiṇī: Mmk 566.13 ālokinyā mantraḥ: oṃ lokini lokavati svāhā (seeming to use both forms as equivalents). Mmk 564.26 probably contained a form of this name originally, but is hopelessly corrupt and unusable.

ālopa, m. (= Pali id.), *mouthful* (of food); cf. next: Mv i.339.13 ālopa-kāram (ger., see §§ 22.5; 35.3, 5) āhāram āharesi (so with v.l.), and 16 ālopa-kārakam (ger.) āhāram āharetsuḥ, *making a mouthful of it, took food*; Mvy 5766; 8572; 8574–6; Prāt 533.1–6 (= Mvy 8572–6); Divy

290.23 carama ālopas; 470.17; 481.9; Av i.341.13 °pam anuprayacchati; Śikṣ 84.3; 138.5; 215.16; Bbh 76.19 (na) cāvaśiṣṭam bhavati yāvad dvitīyam ālopam prakṣipati.

-ālopaka, m. or nt. (from prec. plus suffix ka), in ekālop° and saptālop°, *the practice of eating only* (one, or seven) *mouthful(s) of almsfood*: LV 248.21, 22, ekālopakair, and saptālopakaiḥ; so read for °lāp° of both edd., no v.l.; cf. Pali ekālopika, sattālopika, DN i.166.11 and 12, *one who adheres to these respective practices*. Confirmed by Tib. kham.

āvaḍi (f.; = Skt. āvali, °lī), *row, line*: SP 340.14 chattrāvaḍibhir anvitāḥ.

Āvantaka, m. pl., v.l. (read by Mironov) for **Avantaka,** q.v.: Mvy 9087.

āvaraṇa, nt. (= Pali id.; see also **an-āv°** and **āvṛti**), *hindrance, obstruction* (= pratighātaḥ Bbh 38.19; in Tib. standardly rendered sgrib pa, *darkness, obscuration*, hence *sin*); Lévi, Sūtrāl. i.6, note. Two kinds, kleśāv° (moral faults) and jñeyāv° (intellectual faults); gotra of śrāvakas and pratyekabuddhas free from the former, that of bodhisattvas, only, free also from the latter, Bbh 3.13 ff.; the two kinds mentioned also Bbh 37.6 f.; 88.3; Dharmas 115; āvaraṇa-dvayam Laṅk 140.16; karmāv°, *obstruction due to past actions*, Mvy 845; 1383; Av ii.155.9; Śikṣ 68.14; six obstacles to samādhi, samādhy-āv° Dharmas 118 (kausīdyam mānam śāṭhyam auddhatyam anābhogaḥ satyābhogaś ceti); general, Mvy 814; 6512; Bhad 57 āvaraṇām (acc. pl.) vinivartiya sarvām; Mvy 814 sarvāvaraṇa-vivaraṇa-; Gv 107.22, 24 -āvaraṇāya (see s.v. **vimātratā**), etc., common.

āvaraṇīya, adj., *pertaining to* (causing) *obstruction* (āvaraṇa, q.v.): of karman Śikṣ 280.3; Gv 20.5; of dharma *conditions, states of being* LV 424.18; Bbh 193.18; of thoughts (citta) Bhad 19; as quasi-subst., without noun, *things that cause obstruction*, Gv 462.19 viśodhakāni ... āvaraṇīyānām.

āvarjana, nt. (to **āvarjayati,** q.v.; see also **āvarjanā**; substantially as in Skt., once, *das Sich-geneigt-Machen, Gewinnen*, BR 5.1123), wrongly defined for LV and Divy in pw; *attraction, winning to oneself*: LV 250.(7–)8 (dhyānagocarāṇām ca rūpāvacarāṇām) ca devānām dhyānaviśeṣopadarśanād āvarjanam kuryām (by performing severe austerities; said by the Bodhisattva); 250.22 devānām cāvarjanārtham; Mv ii.423.18 āvarjana-sampanno (Senart *doué de bonne grâce, d'affabilité*; i. e. *gifted with winning ways*; followed by mārdavasampanno aparuṣo); especially (cf. **āvarjayati**) *conversion*: Bbh 180.5–6 āvarjanārhāṇām sattvānām āvarjanāya (contrasts with preceding uttrāsanārhāṇām sattvānām uttrāsanāya); often this is accomplished by miracles, because, as Divy 133.9 says, āśu pṛthagjanāvarjanakarī ṛddhiḥ, *magic converts the vulgar quickly*; virtually the same words 192.8; 313.15; 539.5; Bbh 80.6 and 82.5 ṛddhy-āvarjanatā, *process of conversion by* (exhibitions of) *magic*; Av i.9.12 tad atyadbhutam devamanuṣyāvarjanakaram prātihāryam dṛṣṭvā; the same ii.4.4–5 etc.

āvarjanā = **āvarjana,** *winning to oneself, the making kindly disposed*: in LV 245.14–15 read: bodhisattvo rudrakasya rāmaputrasya saśiṣyasyāvarjanām (so 2 mss. incl. the best; ed. °janī-) kṛtvā ... prakrāmad. (The gen. requires noun āvarjanām.) Tib. ḥdun par byas nas, which is wrongly rendered by Foucaux; it appears to mean lit. *having made reconciled* or *desirous*, i. e. having made to be, of good will (towards himself, the Bodhisattva).

[**āvarjanīkṛtvā,** see prec.]

āvarjayati (Skt., *sich Jmd geneigt machen, für sich gewinnen*, BR), in BHS specifically *converts*; cf. prec. two (Pali āvajjeti not recognized in this sense; but acc. to PTSD often rendered in comms. by pariṇāmeti, which could surely mean *brings to* religious *maturity*): Mv i.34.9 (bhagavān ... nirvāṇe pratiṣṭhāpayanto) āvarjayitvā aṅgamagadhām etc. (long list of peoples), *having converted*...; closely similar is ii.419.8; Divy 355.14 Vāsavadattā saṃsārād udvignā buddhaguṇānusmaraṇāc cāvarjitahṛdayo-vāca, ... *her heart converted, turned* (to religion); Bbh 180.7 nāvarjayati, *does not convert* (people); often this is done by miracles, Av i.3.4 yan nv aham Pūrṇa-brāhmaṇam ṛddhiprātihāryeṇāvarjayeyam; Divy 365.19 prātihāryair āvarjitāḥ; Bbh 82.10 (prātihāryeṇ-)āvarjitamānasā(ḥ); Mvy 2429 āvarjitamānasaḥ; see under **āvarjana.**

Āvarta, m., n. of a sea and of a mountain: Divy 102.28; 103.23–104.20. Note: as common noun, āvarta seems to me to have only meanings which it has in Skt., as *turn, turning, turning-place* (dhāraṇyāvartām ... dhāraṇīm SP 475.8 etc.); *eddy, whirlpool* (Mvy 7037); etc.; in LV 126.7, several times, probably of *turns* (curves, or the like) of alphabetic signs; see **utkṣepa-lipi.**

āvartana, nt., (**1**) *wandering, straying about* (= Pali āvattana; in Skt. not after RV.): Mvy 6868 (= skor ba; followed by parivartanam); Divy 194.6 adrākṣīc Chakro ... tam devaputram atyartham pṛthivyām āvartanam parivartantam; (**2**) *devious winding*, with implication of deceptive, wily movements (= Pali āvaṭṭana): Dbh 72.1 sarvamārapathāvartana-vivartanajñānānugataḥ, *pursuing knowledge of all the devious windings and turnings-back of the paths of Māra.*

āvar(t)ti, seems = **āvartana,** q.v., *wandering, (re-)turn*, in Gv 37.8 sarvalokāvarty-anupravartana-karuṇāgarbha, n. of samādhi, *full of the compassion* (born of) *following the wanderings* (rebirths) *of all* (the) *world*(s).

avarhaṇa, nt. (to next with -ana; cf. Pali abbāhana, *extraction*, as of thorns; but the real Pali equivalent is abbhāna), *removal, freeing* (of a monk from certain penances): Mvy 8656 = Tib. dbyuṅ ba, *removal*, also *freeing*; MSV ii.203.16, 18 ff. (requires a quorum of twenty monks); iii.51.9; 53.4.

āvarhati, ābṛhati, also **ābrah-** (on origin and Pali relations see s.v. **ābṛhati**), *frees* a monk from religious disabilities (cf. prec.): ābrahitavya, gdve., Prāt 488.1; ābṛhyāt, prec., 2; ābṛhita, ppp., 3; āvarhata MSV iii.49.11; °hatu 51.9; °het 53.10; āvarhitavya, gdve., 49.17; °hitum, inf., 57.2; ppp. āvarhitaḥ 57.4; 58.18; āvṛīḍhaḥ 74.6, 16; 75.10, 20, etc. (cf. ābrīḍha to ābṛhati, *extracted*, s.v. **ābṛḍha-**).

āvasānika (from avasāna plus -ika), *of the end, final*: Bbh 97.24 tatra bījam āvasānikasya svaphalasyākṣepahetuḥ.

āvāra- (m.; rare in Skt. except in cpds., cf. durāvāra, BR), *guard*, in °ra-nibandhana, nt., *imprisonment under guard*: Mv i.188.17 (vs) kṛtvāvāranibandhanam, *making* (i. e. applying to his victims) ... (so mss., possibly intending vāra°, but this word is hardly used except at the end of cpds.; āvāra occurs also in Pali; Senart emends to kārā-nib°).

āvārī (once acc. °rim, otherwise all unambiguous forms show ā- and -ī; Skt. Lex. āvārī; Deśin. 1.12 avārī and avāra), *shop, bazaar*, only noted in Divy: °ryām vyāpāram kuru 27.3; 28.7; °rī-samutthitam dravyam 27.8; kāśikavastrāvārī 29.4–5, 7, and other cpds. in °rī 29.7, 12, etc.; °rī-gatam kṣetragatam ca śasyādidhanajātam tad apy agninā dagdham 169.28; bhāṇḍāvārīm (in 15 °rim) gatvā 256.15, 27.

āvāsaśuddha, m. pl., a class of gods, = **śuddhāvāsa,** q.v.; only in vs, presumably m.c.: Mv ii.346.15 °ddhā upagatā devaputrāḥ.

āvāsika, adj. (= Pali id.), *resident*? (in a monastery; said of a monk) or possibly *servant*, see s.v. **navakarmika**: Av i.286.8–9 sa cāvāsiko bhikṣus tatra nāsīt ... bhakte sajjīkṛte āvāsiko bhikṣur āgataḥ (in 286.4 and 287.1 called **naivāsika,** q.v.); Jm 113.22 °kaḥ so 'stu mahāvihāre; āvāsika-naivāsikair bhikṣubhir MSV iv.84.7.

āvāsin (Skt. ifc.), *dweller* (*with, near, in the confines of*;

with gen.): brāhmaṇagṛhapatayaḥ (sc. varṣāḥ, see 109.17) upagatakānām (sc. bhikṣūṇām) āvāsī (n. pl.) . . . anuprayacchanti MSV ii.110.2, and ff., *brahmans and householders living (in the confines settled upon) for (the monks) that have entered into residence* (for the rains) . . .

āvāha, m. (= Pali id.), *taking in marriage, taking to wife*; as in Pali, compounded or associated with **vivāha** (q.v. in PTSD) *giving* (a girl) *in marriage*: Mvy 9465 = Tib. bag mar blaṅ(s) pa (vivāha 9466 = bag mar btaṅ ba); āvāha-vivāha-, cpd., Bbh 7.7; 267.12, *taking and giving in marriage*; often rendered, approximately, *marriage of a son and of a daughter*; āvāho vā vivāho vā MSV ii.119.3; iii.138.9. Skt. vivāha *marriage* seems usually to have no such limitation of meaning, but perhaps āvāha and vivāha have the BHS mgs. in Mbh 13.3232 (otherwise BR 5.1124).

āvāhaka, f. **°ikā**, adj. (to Skt. ā-vah-), *bringing in, introductive, inductive*: Bbh 97.12 āvāhaka-hetuḥ (one of 10 kinds of hetu); 98.1 (tat punar bījanirvṛttam) phalam uttarasya bījākṣiptaphalasyāvāhakahetuḥ; 99.26 (. . . tasyāḥ sasyaniṣpatteḥ sasya-)-paripākasyāvāhakahetuḥ; AsP 203.10 (sā . . . prajñāpāramitā na kasyacit dharmasyāveśikā) vā . . . āvāhikā vā nirvāhikā vā.

? **āvigalita**, perhaps *slightly* (ā) *fallen down* (see **vigalita**): Mv i.154.12, a corrupt and dubious line of vs: kiṃ dāni āvigalitā (mss. °to) vara- (mss. vana-)-keśa- (so 5 mss., Senart with 1 ms. kośa-)-bhārā (mss. °ro) vāṣpaughasaṃstaragatā madanābhibhūtā; said of the harem-women's expected reaction to the Bodhisattva's impending departure. If -keśa- be adopted, possibly *with their beautiful masses of hair somewhat loosened* (dishevelled).

[**āviddha**, ppp. of ā-vyadh, in Av i.87.5 vihāraḥ . . . āviddhaprākāratorаṇo, prob. (with walls and arched gateways) *fastened on, attached*, or possibly *pierced*. Acc. to Speyer *curved, crooked*; he refers to LV 207.16, but here the word is applied to a potter's wheel and means *whirled, set in motion, made to revolve*.]

? **āviddhaka**, m., in Mv iii.113.10 (prose) °kā(ḥ), n. pl., n. of some kind of tradesman or artisan; in a long list of such. Senart also reads so by em. at iii.442.15, where mss. ācambika or āvambikā. In both followed by guḍapācakāḥ. Obscure and prob. corrupt.

? **āvilāyati**, *is tired* or *aches* (Tib. mi bde, *not well*), only in pṛṣṭhī me °ti MPS 30.5 = Pali piṭṭhī me āgilāyati (stock phrase). The seeming denom. from Skt. āvila is prob. a corruption or rationalization for **āgilāyati**, q.v. (MIndic form, perh. deliberately made over).

āvīci = **avīci**, n. of a hell: °cim ādiṃ kṛtvā LV 86.11 (prose), so both edd. without v.l.; but Lefm.'s Index reads avīci, referring to this passage.

āvīcika, see **avīcika**.

āvus = **āyus**, *life*? (§ 2.31) So acc. to Senart, Mv i.176.7 (prose) samaye ca āvusā (one ms. āyusā, dental s) dayanto (mss. °nte), presumed to mean *and on occasion giving alms with their lives*. Doubtful.

āvusa, and other forms based on Pali āvuso, *brother*! (see s.v. **āyuṣmaṃ**): āvusa, as if voc. to a stem of that form, is used repeatedly as an address in AdP, e. g. 13.4, 10, 22, etc. In Mv i.91.6 (vs) Senart reads āvuso; meter needs — ⏑ ×; mss. āyuṣaḥ (note that no form of āyuṣmant is metrically possible), ānuṣaḥ, onuṣaḥ, ānuṣa; in SP 378.1 (prose) Kashgar rec. āvusāho (for ed. āyuṣmanto), certainly to be read (voc. pl. of a stem āvusa, as in AdP, with ending āho, § 8.88); in Mv i.317.15, 16 (prose) āvusāvo seems to be found in the same sense (mss. unanimous on -vo; see § 8.89; in 16 mss. ānusāvo or anu°, but no v.l. in 15).

āvustaṃ, ppp. of ā-vas (= Pali āvuttha), *inhabited*: so read for avustaṃ (both edd., no v.l.) LV 388.13 (vs; meter indifferent).

āvṛṃhati (see **ābṛhati, ābṛṃhaṇa**, etc.), *removes, tears away*: Mv i.18.12 (prose) teṣām āvṛṃhitaṃ (v.l. āvṛh°) tac chavimānsalohitaṃ vyavadahyati; in Mv i.13.2 read with mss. āvṛṃhato (pres. pple.) chavimānsarudhiraṃ vā prasāraye, *tearing off the very skin, flesh, and blood, would remove them*.

āvṛta, ppp. (corresp. to Pali ovaṭa, as Vin. ii.255.23), *forbidden* (also **an-ā°**, q.v.): Bhīk 5a.5 āvṛtam ānanda bhikṣuṇyā bhikṣuṃ codayituṃ (5b.1) . . . anāvṛtaṃ bhikṣor bhikṣuṇīṃ codayituṃ . . ., *it is forbidden for a nun to warn a monk, not for a monk to warn a nun*.

āvṛti, f. = **āvaraṇa**, q.v.: Gv 32.23 (vs) kṣapayaty āvṛtī sarvā(ḥ); cited Śikṣ 311.3 with āvṛtīḥ; Tib. sgrib pa, regularly = āvaraṇa.

? **āveṭhita**, ppp. (= Pali id.; see **veṭhayati**), *put around*: Mv iii.225.6 (prose) āveṭhita- (but only by em.; mss. āveṭī-)prākārā, fig. of Buddhas, *having encircling* (moral) *walls*. Could āveṭhī be defended, as a noun, from the same root?

āveṇika, adj. (= Pali id. or °ṇiya; etym. obscure; see also **āveṇīya, āvedanika**, and Konow, Avhandl. Norske Viden. Akad. 1941, II. Hist.-Fil. Kl., p. 41), *peculiar, individual, particular, special*: Divy 2.3 (a cliché, practically identical with Av i.14.7 etc.) pañcāveṇikā dharmā ekatye paṇḍitajātīye mātṛgrāme, *there are five peculiar characteristics in every intelligent woman* (listed in the sequel); Divy 302.24 °kā ime svārthā anuprāpto bhaviṣyāmi, *I shall have attained these special purposes of mine* (iti saṃpaśyatā paṇḍitenālam eva pravrajyādhimuktena bhavitum); Mv iii.320.6 ye te sattvā āveṇikā bhavanti, evaṃrūpāḥ sattvā (sc. Buddhas, *special creatures*) āryadharmacakraṃ pravartenti; there are three āveṇika **smṛtyupasthāna** (q.v.) in a Buddha, Divy 182.20; Av i.7.5; listed Mvy 187–190; (referred to without the adjective āveṇika, Sūtrāl. xx.53; AbhidhK. La V-P. vii.76;) especially used of the 18 āveṇika buddhadharma of a Buddha, listed Mvy 135–153 (Tib. ma ḥdres pa, *unmixed, unadulterated, pure*); the list here is, (1) nāsti tathāgatasya skhalitam, (2) nāsti ravitam, (3) nāsti muṣitasmṛtitā (or °tiḥ), (4) nāsty asamāhitacittam, (5) nāsti nānātvasaṃjñā, (6) nāsty apratisaṃkhyāyopekṣā, (7) nāsti chandasya hāniḥ, (8) nāsti vīryasya hāniḥ, (9) nāsti smṛtihāniḥ, (10) nāsti samādhihāniḥ, (11) nāsti prajñāyā hāniḥ, (12) nāsti vimuktihāniḥ, (13) sarva-kāya-karma jñānāpūrvaṃgamaṃ jñānānuparivarti, (14 and 15) id. with vāk, manaḥ, for kāya, (16–18) atīte (17 anāgate, 18 pratyutpanne) 'dhvany asaṅgam apratihataṃ jñānadarśanaṃ pravartate; similarly Mv i.160.8 ff. (here they constitute the 5th **cakṣuḥ**, q.v., viz. buddha-c°); Mvy 1–6 = Mv 13-16, 18, 17; Mvy 7–12 = Mv 7–12; Mvy 13–15 = Mv 4–6; Mvy 16–18 = Mv 1–3; Dharmas 79 (substantially as in Mvy; two obvious errors); in Sūtrāl. xx.57 comm. (before the vs called āveṇika guṇa, but after it āv° buddhadharma) divided into groups, called six cāra-saṃgṛhīta āv° bu° (= Mvy 1–6), six adhigama-saṃgṛhīta (= Mvy 7–12), three jñāna-saṃgṛhīta (= Mvy 16–18), three karma-saṃgṛhīta (= Mvy 13–15); Burnouf, Lotus Appendice IX, cites a late Pali list from the Jinālaṃkāra, which substantially agrees in order with that of Mv (but the category is unknown to older and genuine Pali Buddhism, cf. Konow, l. c. above); references to the 18 āv°(bu°)dh°, SP 62.4; 259.5; LV 160.15; 275.10–11 (text corrupt, see Weller and Foucaux); 403.2; 428.6; Mv i.38.14; 50.4; 237.9; 335.13; iii.64.4; 138.12; 407.3; āveṇika bu° dh° (no number given) SP 77.7; Divy 148.23; Dbh 13.26; 63.22; eighteen āveṇika (no noun expressed) LV 438.8; āveṇika, without number or noun but obviously meaning the same 18, SP 29.11; LV 343.4; acc. to Bbh 88.27 ff. and 375.3 ff., 140 āveṇika buddhadharma, listed (incl. the 32 lakṣaṇa, 80 anuvyañjana, etc., but not the 18 usually recognized); in Mvy 786–804 a totally different list of 18 āveṇika bodhisattva-dharma.

āveṇīya, adj. = **āveṇika**, q.v.: Divy 98.22 and 440.16

pañcāveṇīyā dharmā ihaikatye paṇḍitajātīye mātṛgrāme, see the same cliché under **āveṇika.**

āvedanika, adj., used in AdP for **āveṇika,** by false Sktization (Konow MASI 69 p. 11, and loc. cit. s.v. āveṇika; for MIndic (Pali) āveṇiya, 'analyzed as āveyaṇiya from āvedanika'): 13.38–39 aṣṭādaśasv āvedanikeṣu buddhadharmeṣu; 14.19 etc., regularly; yet in 35.16 āveṇika (still in text of AdP).

āvedha, (**1**) (m.?; not in this sense Skt. or Pali; not in Pkt.), *depth* (of a sea or river; lit. *penetration?* cf. **udvedha**): Sukh 31.10 mahāsamudrāc caturāśītiyojana-sahasrāṇy āvedhena tiryag-aprameyāt, *from the great ocean, 84,000 yojanas in depth and immeasurable across*; 37.18 (santi yāvad...) -pañcāśadyojanavistārā (sc. mahānadyo) yāvad dvādaśayojanāvedhāḥ, (there are great rivers, up to) 50 *yojanas in width, up to 12 yojanas in depth*; (**2**) m., *continuing force,* as of an arrow that has been shot, or as of the shoot of a plant growing forth, and fig. of the *continuative force* of life which manifests itself in the **skandha,** see AbhidhK. LaV-P. ii.217; pūrvāvedhāt = pūrvābhyāsāt iii.118, *from the continuing force of past activity*: nikāya-sabhāgasyāvedhaḥ Mvy 7004, *the continuative force of the common element in the class* (of living beings, sattva; see **sabhāga** 2), which causes rebirth; Tib. ḥphen pa, something like *projection.* So also āvedhaḥ Mvy 7535 = Tib. ḥphen pa, or śugs, *inherent power, energy* (Jä.). In Mvy 6857 āvedhaḥ (between ākṣepaḥ and prasabham), physical *projection, penetration* (cf. Pali id.); Tib. also ḥphen pa.

āveśa, in LV 163.14 (vs) āveśād (but best ms. ādeśād)... jinottamānām, equivalent to buddhānām ... adhiṣṭhānena (q.v.: *by the supernatural power of the Buddhas*) in 9–10 above. Our phrase, as in text, could mean *because of entrance, possession, on the part of the Buddhas* (BR s.v. 2 and 3); or, reading ādeśād, *by command* of them. Tib. mthu, *power* (esp. of magic).

(**āveśaka**) f. **°ikā,** adj., *introducing, bringing in; one who or that which introduces*: AsP 203.9 (sā) khalu punar iyaṃ subhūte prajñāpāramitā na kasyacid dharmasyāveśikā vā niveśikā vā...

āvyūhati = **āyūhati,** *exerts oneself towards, carries out, performs,* with acc.: MadhK 298.13; 517.20 sa na kaṃcid dharmam āvyūhati nirvyūhati tasyaivam anāvyūhato 'nirvyūhatas traidhātuke cittaṃ na sajjati. Is nirvyūhati a near-synonym of āvyūhati, as niryūhati certainly is of āyūhati in Gv? Or is it (as assumed by Tib. and La Vallée-Poussin) an antonym of āvyūhati, as **niryūhati** is of **āyūhati** in Laṅk, and as (a)niryūha is of (an)āyūha? See s.vv **anāyūha, anāvyūha, anirvyūha.**

āvrīḍha, ppp. to **āvarhati,** q.v.

āśa = aṃśa, see **maitrāsa-tā.**

[**āśaṅkitavya**(-sahavratā), Mv ii.118.3 (mss. āśaṅkitavyaṃ or āsakitavyaṃ sahavratāyai), is certainly a corruption for **ākiṃcanyāyatana**-(sahavratā), q.v., as in LV 238.16; cf. Mv ii.119.9 f. = LV 243.17.]

āśa-pātrī, *food-bowl*: in Divy 246.18 (cf. note p. 707) read sauvarṇāśapātrī (= °ṇā āśa°), for text °ṇā sapātrī.

āśaya, as in Skt., and Pali āsaya, *mental disposition, intent* (La Vallée-Poussin, AbhidhK. iv.24 *intention*); common, but not specifically Buddhist, except the adverbs āśayena *heartily, earnestly* RP 12.9 (ms. āśrayena; cf. adhyāśayena), and āśayataḥ ibid. Mvy 7119; Divy 281.4, 10; Av ii.151.2; Dbh.g. 16(352).11. The mgs. *abode, basis* etc. are also standard Skt. Cf. **adhyāśaya,** which is specifically Buddhist. If Senart is right in keeping āsayāni in Mv iii.400.3, it would have to be understood as = āśayāni, (evil) *intentions* or *inclinations*; but see **āsaya.** Often cpd. with **anuśaya,** q.v.

Āśā, (**1**) n. of one of four daughters of Indra: Mv ii.58.22 ff.; all four are among eight devakumārikā in the northern quarter, Mv iii 309.9 = LV 391.4; (**2**) n. of a female lay-disciple (upāsikā): Gv 99.12 ff. In mg. 1 certainly a personification of āśā *hope*: the other three are **Śraddhā, Śrī,** and **Hrī,** qq.v.

[**āśāṭavī,** conjectured (Index to Divy) to mean *great wood*: Divy 7.5 yāvad anyatamāśāṭavī praviṣṭā (mss. °ṭāḥ). Tib., cited by Bailey, JRAS 1950.169, shows true reading, °tamā śālāṭavī.]

āśātikā (dental t; = Pali āsāṭikā), *egg of a fly or other insect; nit* (Childers compares Marathi āsāḍī); as vermin afflicting cattle, Kalpanāmaṇḍitikā 196.V.2 (Lüders Kl. Skt. Texte 2 p. 177, cf. pp. 43, 63, with comparison of corresponding Pali text).

āśāsti, f. (once in Skt., pw 3.256 *Gebet*; from ā-śās, *wish, desire*), *desire*: Ud xxx.29 sarvā hy āśāstaya(ś) chit(t)vā, = Pali (Vin. ii.156.27 et alibi) āsattiyo, but this Pali word = Skt. āsakti, *attachment,* and so substantially the same as *longing, desire.* Is āśāsti false Skt. for Pali āsatti (used in the Pali form of the same verse where it occurs in Ud)?

[**āśivrate,** LV 275.20 (vs), Lefm.'s em.; read with most mss. (some āsā-) āśāvrate, *in the solemn-undertaking of his aspiration* (āśā, proved by Tib. bsam pa). Cf LV 285.15 (vs) prapūrṇā ti āsā (= āśā).]

āśītakī, or **ās°,** also written aśītaka, aśīta, aśitaka, asita, the a-stems being prob. m. (Mv ii.231.13); the Pali equivalent is āsītika, m. (not °kā, f., as stated in PTSD), n. of some plant; occurs, regularly in comp. with -parvāṇi (as in Pali with -pabbāni, MN i.80.11 = 245.27), in the account of the Bodhisattva's emaciated state after his long fast, his members being compared to the joints of this plant. The reading asita(ka) is prob. due to popular etymology, association with asita *black*; **kāla,** q.v., occurs in the context, and note kālāśītako (perhaps read °ke with v.l.) Mv ii.231.13. Other cases, all in comp. with -parvāṇi: LV 254.7 āsītakī-; 255.21 āśītakī- (all mss.; Lefm. inexplicably reads āsitakī- here!); Mv ii.126.18 aśītaka- (v.l. asita-); in 125.12 Senart omits the word with one ms., but the other ms. has aśita-parvāṇi; 128.5 aśītaka- (one ms., the other omits, Senart em. aśītaka-); 129.7 aśīta- (v.l. asita-). The evidence points, on the whole, to āśītaka- or °kī- as the original form.

āśīviṣa, m. (in Skt., and Pali-Pkt. āsīvisa, only *serpent*; so also here, even in LV, e. g. 317.9; 339.2), *serpent-venom,* repeatedly in LV: °ṣān vamanti sma 305.13, °ṣān ... bhakṣayanti sma 14; °ṣān niścārayanti sma 306.13, ... vamanto 21. In 306.18 āśīviṣapariveṣṭitaśarīrāḥ is taken by Foucaux in this sense, *le corps enduit de venin de serpent*; but surely it is rather *having bodies entwined by serpents,* despite neighboring passages showing the other mg. See **sumbhalikā.**

Āśīviṣa-nadī, f. pl., n. of certain rivers: Divy 107.23 °nadīnāṃ tīre śālmalīvanam. See **Saptāśīviṣa-,** and next.

Āśīviṣā, n. of a river: °ṣāyāṃ, loc., Divy 451.6, 10; 456.24, 28. See under prec.

[**āśu**: Johnston, notes on Saundarān. vi.9 and Buddhac. vi.64, assumes use as 'expletive', 'to strengthen the force of the verb,' 'in epic and Buddhist Skt.,' and suggests relation to the Pali particle assu. He so interprets āśu in Manu 4.171. I disagree on all this; it seems to me that there is no reason to assume any āśu except the adj. and adverb, *quick(ly)*. Tib. renders *quickly* at Buddhac. vi.64.]

Āśukāri(n), n. of a former Buddha: Mv i.136.16 (n. sg., mss. °rīḥ or °riḥ, Senart em. °rī; prose, followed by dh-).

Āśuketu, n. of a king, former incarnation of Buddha: RP 24.14.

Āśugandha, n. of a Bodhisattva: Mvy 714.

āśraddhya, nt. (also **aśrāddhya,** q.v.; = Pali assaddhiya), *disbelief, lack of* (true) *faith*: Bbh 15.1; Mvy 1973 acc. to text of Kyoto ed. and v.l. of Mironov; text of Mironov aśraddhya; Index to Kyoto ed. cites both.

āśraya, m. (Skt., *basis* etc.), (**1**) in Laṅk., acc. to Suzuki, the **ālaya-vijñāna** (q.v.) as *basis* of all vijñānas; one must make it *converted, in revulsion* (parāvṛtta, cf. Laṅk 9.11 parāvṛttāśraya); Laṅk 10.5 anyathā dṛśyamāna ucchedam āśraye (so read with v.l. for °yo, text °yaḥ), *if the basis is otherwise regarded* (loc. abs.), (there is) *destruction* (it is fatal to the holder of such a view); (**2**) acc. to citation in Burnouf Introd. 449, six āśraya = the six sense organs (as one of the three groups constituting the 18 dhātu); this is said to be attributed to the Yogācāras in 'le commentaire de L'Abhidharma'; it does not seem to occur in AbhidhK. and I have not noted precisely this usage in any text, but cf. next; (**3**) acc. to AbhidhK. LaV-P. iii.126, *le corps muni d'organes, qui est le point d'appui* (āśraya) *de ce qui est appuyé* (āśrita) *sur lui: à savoir de la pensèe et des mentaux* (cittacaitta). Is the obscure passage Mv ii.153.1–2 somehow concerned here? It reads, in a verse (see my Reader, *Four Sights* [Mv], n. 40) describing disease (vyādhi): ... śokānāṃ prabhavo rativyupasamo (i. e. °śamo) cittāśrayāṇāṃ nidhi, dharmasyopaśamaḥ (lacuna of 6 syllables) gātrāśritānāṃ gṛhaṃ, yo lokaṃ pibate vapuś ca grasate etc. I should be inclined to emend to cittāśravāṇāṃ (cf. LV 345.21, below), but for the phrase gātrāśritānāṃ gṛhaṃ, which implies support for āśraya; Senart refers to Burnouf (l. c.), but finds it hard to apply āśraya and āśrita as used in that passage; (**4**) commonly, *body* (cf. prec.): LV 324.16 (vs) subhato (= śu°) kalpayamāna āśrayaṃ vitathena, *falsely imagining the body to be handsome*; RP 6.13 lakṣaṇaiś ca pratimaṇḍitāśrayo; 23.1 me jvalita āśrayaḥ, *my body was burned*; 25.7 me tyakta varāśrayaḥ; 26.8; 27.16; Dbh 16.10; Av i.175.4 pretāśrayasadṛśāḥ; 264.9 pretīṃ vikṛtāśrayāṃ; 272.3; 291.17; 332.9; 356.7; 361.2; ii.172.9; see also **cañcitāśraya**; [in LV 345.21 āśraya(-kṣaya-jñāna-) without v.l., but Tib. translates āśrava, which must be adopted: *knowledge leading to destruction of the impurities*, not ... *of the body*]. See next.

-āśrayaka, at end of Bhvr. cpd. = āśraya, *body*: LV 153.14 (vs) ko vismayo manuja-āśrayake asāre, ... *in a weak possessor-of-a-human-body*.

āśrava, a very common (perhaps prevalent) reading for **āsrava**, q.v.

?**āśravaṇa-**, prob. *lesson* (so Kern; otherwise Burnouf): SP 6.13 anekavividhāśravaṇārambaṇādhimuktihetukāraṇair upāyakauśalyair, *with skillful devices which had as causes and reasons their* (Bodhisattvas') *zeal for the fundamental bases of many various lessons* (in the law). However, WT °vividha-śravaṇā° with ms. K′; perh. read so.

āśrāvayati (caus. of ā-śru, unrecorded in this sense), *plays* (a mus. instrument): Av i.96.1 vīṇām āśrāvitavān.

āśrita (ppp. of ā-śri); see s.v. **āśraya** 2, 3; acc. to Burnouf, there cited, the 6 āśritas are *la connaissance produite par la vue et par les autres sens* ...; acc. to AbhidhK iii.126, = citta-caitta; what gātrāśritānāṃ gṛhaṃ means (Mv ii.153.2), as applied to vyādhi, is not clear.

āśvāsa, see **āśvāsa-praśvāsa.**

āśvāsaka, m. (**1**) (= Pkt. āsāsaa, Sheth; Skt. āśvāsa), *chapter, section* (in a book): Mvy 1468; (**2**) (= Pali assāsaka), *desire, aspiration*: MSV ii.6.8.

Āśvāsanī, n. of a kiṃnara maid: Kv 6.16.

āśvāsa-praśvāsa (Pali assāsa-passāsa), m. dual or pl., *breath*; usually used without clear indication of difference between the two terms, like **ānāpāna**, q.v.: LV 251.15–16 nāsikātaś cāśvāsapraśvāsāv uparuddhāv abhūtāṃ; 252.3 °sā ūrdhvaṃ śiraḥkapālam upanighnanti sma; as separate words, 259.7 āśvāsaviprahīnaḥ praśvāsavarjitu; Mv ii.124.10 (and ff.) mukhato nāsikāśrotrehi ca āśvāsapraśvāsā uparundhi (1 sg. aor.); Mv iii.179.19 °sehi tathāgataṃ upahanati; Śāl 78.3, 17 kāyasyāśvāsapraśvāsakṛtyaṃ; Sādh 61.19 °sādikam; the verb **uśvasati**, q.v., corresponds to āśvāsa in Mv ii.208.3–4 āśvāsapraśvāsā uparuddhā ... no pi uśvasati na praśvasati (the two verbs repeated twice in lines 8, 9), cf. LV 189.12 ucchvasantam praśvasantam, rendered by Tib. dbugs dbyuṅ zhiṅ rṅub *breathing out and in*, but in line 15 below praśvasantaḥ is rendered dbugs dbyuṅ, *breathing out* (implying that ucchvasantaṃ was understood as *breathing in*); **ucchvāsa-praśvāso** (sg.) also occurs, seemingly = āśvāsa-pra°, Śikṣ 42.5; in Sādh 146.17 ff. it is entirely certain that praśvāsa is understood as *outbreathing* and āśvāsa *inbreathing*, tadanu tan mithunaṃ praśvāsavāyurathārūḍhaṃ nāsikāvivareṇa niḥsṛtya ... sattvānāṃ kāyavākcittāni viśodhya gṛhītvā ca punar āśvāsavāyum āruhya tenaiva pathā svahṛtkamalakarṇikāyāṃ praviśet; consistent with this is AMg. ussāsa (and relatives), which BHS usage would clearly have associated with āśvāsa, and which acc. to Ratnach. means *breathing in*; Pali tradition is indeterminate, see Vism i.272.1 which states that Vin. comm. defines assāsa as *outgoing*, passāsa as *incoming* breath, but that in Sutta comms. (Suttantaṭṭhakathāsu) the reverse is taught (the passage is misunderstood by PTSD and Pe Maung Tin; uppaṭipāṭiyā = Pkt. upparivāḍi, *inverted, transposed*). Tib. regularly āśvasati = dbugs brṅubs (or cognate) *breathe in* Mvy 1173, 1175, etc., praśvasati = dbugs phyuṅ (or cognate) *breathe out* Mvy 1174, 1176, etc.; it therefore supports Sādh 146.17 ff., and incidentally the equation of āśvāsa with āna and praśvāsa with apāna (see **ānāpāna**). How old this interpretation is remains uncertain, esp. in view of the fact that in Pali the comms. differed; Buddhaghosa himself, in the Vism. passage cited, declines to arbitrate between the two opposing views. Whatever may have been the meaning of the two terms, it seems clear that the cpd. (like **ānāpāna**) was commonly used in the sense of *breath*, collectively and as a whole.

Āśvāsahasta, n. of a Bodhisattva: Kv 2.2.

Āṣāḍha, n. of a householder: Av i.338.6.

āṣṭamika, nt. = **aṣṭamika**, q.v., Bhīk 23a.3 naityakaṃ vā nimantraṇakaṃ vā āṣṭamikaṃ vā cāturdaśikaṃ vā ...

Āṣṭhiyana, m. pl., n. of a brahmanical gotra: Divy 635.11.

āsa, m. (only known in Vedic cpd. sv-āsa-stha), *seat*: Gv 474.18 (vs) śūrāṇa teṣam ayam āsu (n. sg.) sudurjayānām, *this is the seat of those heroes* ... Meter does not permit emendation to āvāsa, which is used in parallel lines 2, 10, etc.; other parallels vihāra; all three are virtual synonyms. Prakritic contraction of āvāsa to āsa is improbable. For āsa = aṃśa see **maitrāsa-tā.**

āsaṃjñika, nt. (to **asaṃjñin**, q.v.), *unconsciousness*: Mvy 1989; Dharmas 31; Divy 505.22 sa tatrāsaṃjñikam (i. e. tatra-āsaṃjñikam; Index wrongly asaṃj°) utpādyāsaṃjñisattveṣu (see **asaṃjñisattva**) deveṣūpapannaḥ; similarly AbhidhK. LaV-P. ii.199. (In Divy, this state is deliberately induced by dhyāna.)

āsattvasthāyin, adj., *abiding until* (ā) *the* (coming into) *existence of* (gen.): ŚsP 300.3–4 ime bodhisattvā mahāsattvāḥ buddhānāṃ bhagavatām āsattvasthāyino (here misprinted °syāyino) bhaviṣyanti, ime nāsattvasthāyinaḥ.

āsanaka, nt. (= Pali id., Vv 1.5, taken by comm. 24.16–17 as dim.), *seat* (= Skt. āsana), here certainly not dim.: Av i.321.10 (rājā ...) Bhagavato rthena āsanakāni prajñapya, *having provided seats for the Lord's use*; MSV i.79.14.

āsana-tā (= Skt. āsana as nom. act.), *seating, the giving a seat* (to someone, as a courtesy): Mv i.298.18 pratyutthānam (mss. paryut°) āsanatāṃ tato ca (... mahājano prīto karoti); ŚsP 1470.1 (?not clear).

āsannaka, adj. (= Skt. āsanna; perhaps m.c.), *near*: Śikṣ 305.11 (vs) °ko bhavati tathāgatānām (= Mv ii.388.18 with different and secondary meter, reading āsannaprāpto).

āsannībhavati (āsanna with bhū), *comes near, approaches* (with gen.): AsP 11.7–8 evaṃ carata(ḥ)... bodhisattvasya... sarvajñatā āsannībhavati; ŚsP 825.5–6 āsannībhavaty ayaṃ bodhisattvo... sarvākārajñatāyā iti; ppp. °bhūtaḥ Mvy 5109.

āsamudācārika, adj., with dharma, (rule) *applying to customary behavior* (**samudācāra** 1): Bhīk 11a.1 keśāvatārikāyā ahaṃ... bhikṣuṇyā āsamudācārikān dharmān prajñapayāmi...(2) keśāvatārikā bhikṣuṇī yathāprajñaptān āsamudācārikān dharmān asamādāya vartate, sātisārā bhavati; MSV i.vi.9, 13; vii.15 etc.

? **āsaya**, nt., in Mv iii.400.3 hitvā ālayāni (see **ālaya**) āsayāni (v.l. āsanāni); the Pali parallel Sn 535 reads āsavāni = BHS āśravāṇi, ās°, which must probably be read, since **āśaya** (q.v.) seems not to be used in a pejorative sense, and no other interpretation for āsaya seems possible.

āsarita, nt., and **niḥsarita**, nt.; °taṃ Gv 351.18, 19 respectively: the first two of ten 'bodily conditions' (śarīrasthā dharmāḥ), the other 8 being cold, heat, hunger, thirst, delight, anger, birth-old-age-diesase-and-death, and pain (pīḍā). Context throws no further light. Interpretation of these two terms obscure. Are they somehow related to āsario = saṃmukhāgataḥ Deśīn. 1.69, and ṇissariaṃ = srastam ibid. 4.40? Something like *slack condition, slumped-down state* might be intended by niḥsarita; would āsarita be its opposite, a state *arrived* at the right point?

āsādana (nt.) or **°nā**, n. act. to **āsādayati** (not in PTSD, but occurs in Pali Vin. iv.84.16 āsādanāpekkho, same passage as Prāt 510.1; could be °na or °nā), *annoyance*: Prāt 510.1 (bhuṅkṣvety) āsādanaprekṣī, *seeking to annoy* (him); Jm 199.24 evam āsādanām api... pratinudanti.

āsādayati (= Pali āsādeti, not in Skt. in this sense; cf. prec.), *annoys, troubles, disturbs*: ppp. Prāt 510.2 (kaccid eṣa bhikṣur muhūrtam apy) āsāditaḥ syād, *should (might) be annoyed.*

āsītakī, see **āśī°**.

āsīyati Mv iii.86.3 (vs), apparently 3 sg. pass. of ās, impersonal, *it is sat, one sits*; but the passage is obscure to me.

[**āsīvaka**, m., app. only by em. for **āsevaka**, q.v.]

āsupta, ppp. of ***āsvapati** (cf. **āsvāpana**), *gone to sleep*: Mv i.227.16 (prose) kilāntaṃ antaḥpuram āsuptam.

āsurya (nt.?), n. of some art or philosophy or science, in a list: °ye LV 156.21 (prose), after **āmbhirye**; Tib. lha ma yin gyi lugs, *way or system of the asuras.*

āsecanaka, adj. (= **asecanaka**, q.v.), *charming, pleasing*, of sights and sounds: darśanīyo °ko apratikūlo Mv i.237.13, of the appearance of a Buddha; darśayanti ca ātmānaṃ āsecanakavigrahaṃ Sādh 16.8, and sarvāṅgapratyaṅgāsecanakavigrahaṃ (here could be asecanaka) 22.15, both said of Buddhas; of sound, (ghoṣo...) manojñaḥ °ko apratikūlo śravaṇāya Mv i.194.13, 14; 196.8, 10. (In Mv i.207.1 = ii.10.11 read with mss. asecanaka or asecanīya.)

āsevaka, or **°kā**, some kind of garment: SP 283.9 (vs), cited Śikṣ 352.13, āsevaka (unmetr.! one ms. and Śikṣ °kaṃ; WT with most mss. °kāṃ; Kashgar rec. °kā) kṛṣṇa tathādaditvā. Tib. acc. to Bendall rdul gzan, *dust garment* (Jä. *cloak*, against dust on a journey), but acc. to WT, and my own copy of Tib. SP, rṅul gzan, which = **saṃkakṣikā**, q.v.; Burnouf and Kern *woolen garment*; note that Tib. rdul and rṅul are very easily confused in writing; in MSV ii.52.5 āsevaka (ms., ed. em. āsīvaka) seems to mean *patch* (so Tib., lhan thabs kyis klan pa); in the next line, 6, sevakaṃ (ms., ed. em. sīv°) dattvā dhāraya, seems to show the same mg., and in 11 below, text āsīvakāṃs (by em.? ms. āsev° as before?) tu dattvā dhārayitvayam, confirms this mg. (reference is to materials unsuitable for making robes).

āsevanā (= Pali id.; Skt. only °na, nt., recorded), *cultivation* (of), *devotion* (to), at end of cpd.: Bbh 35.28 (bhogātmabhāvasaṃpado) hetv-āsevanā.

āstīryati = **ar(t)tiyati**, q.v.: Karmav 47.26; 49.2.

? **āstopaka**, or (v.l.) āstomaka, āstoka (could also be understood as having initial ă-), in LV 249.2–3 ārdrapaṭāstopaka-jāla-śayanaiś ca (in list of ascetic practices); this part of cpd. in Tib. rendered stegs buḥi steṅ, *top surface of a board*, which makes sense (*lying or sleeping in wet clothes, ... or in water*; read jala for jāla, as Tib. proves). This word is prob. corrupt, and in fact the mss. vary greatly; the best ones °maka.

āsthiti (f.; not recorded, but see below), *perseverance, persistence*: in °ti-kriyā, *acting with*..., Mvy 1797; = Pali aṭṭhita-kiriyatā, id. (CPD), which would be *āsthitakriyatā. See s.v. **asthīkṛtya.**

[**āsparśa**, supposedly *contact*, assumed by Senart in a cpd. Mv ii.115.12; but see **sparśita.**]

āspharaṇaka-samādhi, name of a dhyāna: n. sg. °dhiḥ Mvy 1487; Tib. mkhaḥ khyab, *expanse of heaven*; cf. under **āsphānaka.**

āsphāṭayati, *tears, rends*: ger. āsphāṭya Divy 375.25; 376.5 (santi sattvā... yān narakapālā... ayomayena sūtreṇa... āsphāṭya...).

āsphānaka, nt. (= Pali appānaka, °ṇaka; etym. and lit. mg. obscure; doubtless = **āspharaṇaka** (-samādhi), q.v.; CPD conjectures relation to (ā-)sphāyate, *swells, grows*; LV seems to think of forms of spharati, but this may be etymological fancy, despite the Mvy āspharaṇaka-), n. of a kind of dhyāna (either alone, or in cpd. °ka-dhyāna): LV 250.14 °ka-dhyānaṃ samāpadyate... °nakam iti; explained lines 19–20 ākāśam aspharaṇam akaraṇaṃ avikaraṇaṃ tac ca sarvaṃ spharatīti hy ākāśasamaṃ tad dhyānaṃ (cf. Tib. on **āspharaṇaka-**) tenocyate āsphānakam iti; °kaṃ dhyānaṃ dhyāyeyaṃ (or other form of this verb) Mv ii.208.2; LV 251.14 f., 21; 259.1, 8, 10 (ākāśadhātuspharaṇaṃ dhyāyaty āsphānakaṃ dhyānaṃ, *he meditates the ā° meditation which agitates the ether-element*), and ff.; Mv ii.124.9, 15 °nakaṃ (in 9 v.l. °nakadhyānaṃ; in 15 mss. °nakaṃ dhyānaṃ, or āsphārakaṃ) dhyāyeyaṃ.

[**āsphāra**, *tearing*, acc. to Senart, Mv i.9.16, in a corrupt line of vs; ed. em. sadāyasaphālāsphārā, see note p. 377. But Senart failed to note that the passage i.9.8–12.14 is repeated in iii.454.7–456.20. This line occurs iii.454.15, reading kadaryatapanā ghorā, which disproves at least part of Senart's em. and is close enough to the reading of the mss. at i.9.16 to make it acceptable as a whole.]

? **āsphuṭa**, adj., *clear, clarified, illumined*: LV 17.3 (prose) tenāvabhāsenāsphuṭa-samānā(ḥ), *being illumined by that light.* The mg. is certain, and acc. to Lefm. all mss. read so; but not only is āsphuṭa suspicious in itself; composition with samānāḥ is also difficult. The expected reading is °bhāsena sphuṭāḥ samānāḥ.

āsmākīna, adj. (prescribed Pāṇ. 4.3.2), *our*: Av i.327.4; so best ms., v.l. asm°, which is the form regularly recorded in Av (see **asmākīna**) and which Speyer adopts in the text here; but in ii p. 210 he withdraws that reading in favor of āsm°. There is no record of either form, nor of any MIndic equivalent, elsewhere.

āsrava (perhaps oftener written āśrava), m. (= Pali āsava), *evil influence, depravity, evil, sin, misery*; CPD s.v. anāsava, *intoxicants*, i. e. ... *passions*; Lévi, Sūtrāl. ix.23 n.1, L'écoulement (āsrava) est le mouvement qui porte la pensée à se répandre, comme une eau qui fuit, vers les choses du dehors; Johnston, Saundarān. xvi.3, Transl., note: the influences which attach a man to the saṃsāra; hence sāsrava and laukika are equivalent, as are anāsrava and lokottara; Tib. (e. g. on Mvy 2141 āśravaḥ) zag pa, *misery*, also *sin*: anupādāyāsravebhyaś cittāni vimuktāni, see **anupādāya**; āśravakṣayajñāna is the sixth **abhijñā**, q.v.; śuṣkā āśravā na puna śravanti LV 351.1 (with play on etym., root sru), *the āśravas, dried up, flow no more*; getting rid of them is arhatship, prāptaṃ mayārhatvaṃ kṣīṇā me āśravā(ḥ) LV 376.11; jinā ... ye prāptā āśravakṣayam LV 406.6; arhantānāṃ kṣīṇāśravāṇām Mv i.59.7 ff.; the Buddha is sarvāśravāntakaraṇam Mv i.203.16 = ii.7.12; prahīnasarvāśravabandhanasya Buddhasya Divy 379.12; kṣīṇāśrava (or °srava), said of a bhikṣu, Divy 542.21, of a muni Jm 17.16; equivalent to duḥkha, in formula of 4 noble truths: (after idaṃ duḥkham) ayam āśravasamudayo 'yam āśravanirodha iyam āśravanirodhagāminī pratipad LV 348.19 f.; in Mv ii.285.5, after statement of all four truths as usual with duḥkha, they are repeated with āśravāḥ (pl.), ime āśravāḥ, imo (mss. ime) āśravasamudayo ayaṃ āśravanirodho etc.; nirvāsyanti anāśravāḥ Mv ii.66.6; there are four āśrava (also = **ogha, yoga**), listed LV 348.21–22, viz. kāma-, bhava-, avidyā-, dṛṣṭi- (so also in Pali, kāma, bhava, avijjā, diṭṭhi, but also a list of only three, omitting diṭṭhi); very common is anāsrava (= kṣīṇā° above), *free from the depravities* or *from evil*; *pure* (less commonly nirāśrava, LV 405.21, of Buddha), sometimes contrasted with its opposite sāśrava: nāpi ye dharmā anāśravāḥ te sāśravā ti deśayāmi (and vice versa) Mv i.173.8–9; sāsravānāsravāḥ (dharmāḥ) SP 142.10; devamanuṣyasarvaśrāvakapratyekabuddhakuśalāni sāsravāṇy anāsravāṇi vā (all of little value) Gv 500.14; anāsrava (or °śrava), of persons, SP 34.13 (read here adya me with mss. for adyeme); LV 242.11; jñānaṃ vipulaṃ anāsravam SP 15.7; anāśravaṃ te caraṇaṃ Mv i.164.8, *thy conduct is pure*; āśravāṇāṃ kṣayād anāśravāṃ cetovimuktiṃ (acc. sg.) Mv iii.321.9–10; anāśravasadṛśaṃ prathamadhyānaṃ Divy 391.16; sāśravaṃ cittaṃ Mv ii.403.13; sāśravānāṃ (dental n) ... dhyānasamādhisamāpattīnāṃ (of the false teacher Rudraka) doṣo LV 244.2–3; unlike **anuśaya,** with which it is sometimes associated or even equated (AbhidhK. LaV-P. v.79), it is always used with evil connotation; in Gv 461.3–4 kalyāṇamitrādhīnāḥ ... bodhisattvānāṃ sarvabodhisattvacaryāśravāḥ, the last cpd. contains -bodhisattvacaryā plus śravāḥ (= sravāḥ, *streams*; cf. -praṇidhāna-śrotāṃsi, line 6), not -āśravāḥ.

***āsvapati,** nowhere recorded except in BHS ppp. **āsupta,** and caus. adj. or nom. act. **āsvāpana,** qq.v.; must have meant *goes to sleep* (caus. *puts to sleep*).

āsvādanīya, (**1**) adj. (gdve.) *enjoyable, pleasant* (of sounds): Mvy 391 °nīyo ghoṣeṇa (of Tathāgata); (**2**) subst. (also **svādanīya,** q.v., in same use) only noted in triple dvandva cpd. khādanīya-bhojanīyāsvādanīya (Mv i.38.7 °bhojanīya-āsvādanīyena), in which this third element (after *hard food* and *soft food*) may perhaps mean *condiments*, or *savories*; Tib. on LV 2.22 myaṅ ba, *to be tasted*: LV 2.22 (text corrupt); 58.5–6; Mv i.38.7; Śikṣ 208.2 (Bendall and Rouse *to relish*). The gdve. assādanīya exists in Pali and assāyaṇijja in AMg. (*tasteful; full of relish*, Ratnach.), but no equivalent of the word seems to be recorded elsewhere in the BHS meanings.

āsvāpana, nt. (adj. or nom. act. to caus. of ***āsvapati,** q.v.), *sleeping potion* or *charm* (lit. *putting to sleep*): Divy 526.23, 25 rājñaḥ sāntaḥpurasyāsvāpanaṃ dattvā (25 dattam).

āha, interj. (only in Skt. Lex., 1. *des Vorwurfs*, 2. *des Befehls*, 3. dṛḍhasaṃbhāvanāyām, BR): Jm 222.12 āha! (between two verses; in mg. 1, I think, tho acc. to Speyer, Av i.244 n. 6, mg. 3; the Bodhisattva is rebuking a king who eats human flesh); Av i.244.15 sa pratyekabuddha uktaḥ: āha re (so Speyer em., ms. ra) bhikṣo ... (said by an evil, malicious person; mg. 2, but doubtless colored by mg. 1).

āhataka, adj. (to ppp. āhata, with specifying ka, § 22.39), *the ones that were wounded*: yattakā(ni) āhatakā(ni) Mv i.359.22; 360.2; 361.4, *as many* (deer) *as were wounded*.

āharaṇa- (nt.?), in Jm 88.10 āharaṇāpaharaṇakuśalatvād, some kind of operation in handling a ship, perhaps *towing*, see **āhāra(ka)**-. Otherwise Speyer Transl. 125 with n. 1.

āharaṇatā = Skt. āharaṇa, *winning, getting*: dat. °tāyai, °tāye, quasi-infin., Mv ii.279.11 ff. tasya arthasya °tāyai bodhisattvo āryamānaṃ pragṛhṇe, *for the attainment of this purpose (goal)* ...; ii.399.7, 15 anuttarasya amṛtasya °tāye.

āhavanīya, adj. (= Pali id., cf. Vism. i.220.6; more usually Pali āhuneyya; mg. prob. influenced by Pali pāhuneyya, see s.v. **prāhavanīya**; both these forms in -havanīya prob. due to popular etym., tho found in Pali and BHS), *worthy of receiving offerings* (respectful gifts): Mvy 1772 (in section named mānanā-paryāyāḥ); Av i.193.10 °yāni tāni kulāni yeṣu kuleṣu mātāpitarau samyaṅ mānyete.

āhāra, m. (**1**) some member of a ship's crew, mentioned with nāvika and others Av i.200.5; ii.61.9; evidently = **āhāraka,** q.v.; perhaps *tower*, cf. Pali Jāt. iv.159.16 (nāvaṃ) āharitvā gāmato, apparently *having towed away from the village*; cf. also **āharaṇa**; (**2**) in Mvy 798 = Tib. rgyud, usually = tantra; perhaps *a mystic technique* in general, or possibly *bringing in* in a more specific sense, see s.v. **yamaka**; (**3**) *district, province*: Māy 28; see Hultzsch, Aśoka, 163 n. 11; (**4**) āhāra, nt. = Skt. āhāra, m. *food*: Divy 13.7 °raṃ, n. sg.; same MSV iii.22.10. On āhāra-kṛtya see s.v. **kṛtya** (2).

āhāraka, m., in Mvy 3851, acc. to Tib. sñod ciṅ stobs pa, which seems to mean someone concerned with food; so also Chin. Prob. this is etymological guesswork (Skt. āhāra). Certainly it refers to some member of a ship's crew; see **āhāra, āharaṇa**; perhaps *one who tows* (or otherwise propels?) *a boat*, as in Pali āharitvā (nāvaṃ) Jāt. iv.159.16.

āhārika, nt. (from āhāra with ika), *bringer, that which brings*: °kaṃ sarvajñajñānasya Samādh p. 6 line 15 (said of a kind of samādhi).

āhārya-pādaka, adj. (or subst.; = Pali āhacca-p°, apparently based on *āhṛtya-p°), (a couch or seat) *having removable* (or more literally *insertable*?) *legs*: Mvy 8438 °dakārohī (ārohin, *one who mounts* or *sits upon*...); Prāt 506.6 °ke pīṭhe vā mañce vā balena niṣīded ...

āhiṇḍati, °te, also **°ḍyate,** (= Pali °ti; see **hiṇḍati**), *wanders*: °ḍati Māy 242.31; °ḍase Divy 165.3; °ḍyamāna, pres. pple., Divy 141.22.

(**āhṛtaka,**) f. °ikā (doubtless = Pali āhataka, m., Vin. iv.224.34, where kammakāro is glossed by bhaṭako āhatako, in contrast with dāsa = antojāto dhanakkīto karamarānīto), perhaps *hired servant* (of some particular kind): Bhīk 16a.4 (the candidate for initiation is asked) māsi dāsī? ... mā āhṛtikā mā vikrītikā etc. PTSD derives āhataka from Skt. āhata, implausibly.

āhṛṣṭa, ppp. (cf. Skt. āhṛṣyat-, once), *bristling*: (romakūpa) MSV iii.138.21.

āhetuka, adj. (from ahetu(ka), vṛddhi deriv.; cf. **nairhetuka**), *arising from no cause*: °kaṃ (sc. rūpam), na cāsty arthaḥ kaścid āhetukaḥ kva cit MadhK p. 24 line 11 (so mss.); p. 123 line 13.

āhrīkya, nt. (cf. Pali ahirika, °īka, adj., and sometimes nt. noun), *immodesty, shamelessness*; associated with **anapatrāpya**; Mvy 1971 °yam; stem °ya- Śikṣ 105.8; Bbh 14.25; 223.10, 11.

āhvaya (m.?: same mg. Pali avhāna), *begging aloud, vocally asking for alms*: Mv iii.387.18 (vs, = Pali Sn 710, where avhānaṃ) °yaṃ nābhinandeyā (Senart °ya).

āhvānana, nt. (n. act. in ana from denom. āhvānayati *summons*, in Skt. recorded only in legal sense, but e. g. in Mmk 48.3 [mañjuśriyam ...] āhvānayet): *summoning* (a deity), *invocation*: °na-mantrā Mmk 27.3, 8, 17–18 (see s.v. **mantrā**); 53.19 °na-visarjanaṃ kuryād; 94.13 °na-visarjana-; 126.16, 18; 358.6 aṣṭamaṃ °naṃ proktaṃ.

I

ikṣu-kuṭṭitikam, adv. (see note in Śikṣ p. 409), with kuṭṭyamānasya, *by* (the torture of) *being crushed like sugar-cane*: Śikṣ 182.1.

ikṣu-dvādaśī, n. of a festival, *sugarcane-twelfth* (a day on which presents of sugarcane are made): Karmav 68.19.

Ikṣvāku (= Pali Okkāka 2, DPPN), n. of a legendary king, son of Subandhu and father of Kuśa, named from his birth from a sugar-cane plant: Mv ii.422.20 ff.; iii.1.1 ff.

?**iṅkhika** (or **īnkh°**), adj., with śirā = sirā, *vein*, of unknown mg.: pañceṅkhikāḥ śirā mocayitvā rudhiraṃ pāyitā (sc. devī) MSV ii.15.8; pañceṅkhika-śirāvedha 133.9.

iṅgā, a large number or method of computation: LV 148.15; no v.l., but Mvy 7982, citing this LV passage, iṭṭā; Tib. for both gtan la ḥbebs pa (v.l. in Mvy gdan for gtan), which regularly = viniścaya; is it intended here to render the root iṅg in the sense of *separation*? Cf. the phonetic-grammatical use of the root, esp. s.v. iṅgya in BR.

icchatva = (and prob. false reading for) **itthatva,** q.v. However, if Wogihara were right in his interpretation of **icchantika,** q.v., this would support derivation of icchatva from itthatva.

icchantika, adj. or subst. m., acc. to Suzuki (Studies, 219 n. 1, and 391), *one destitute of Buddha-nature*: Mvy 2210, 2223 = Tib. ḥdod chen (po), (subject to) *great desire* (somehow based on pres. pple. of icchati); Laṅk 27.5 katham °ko bhavet; 65.17 °kānāṃ ... anicchantikatā-mokṣam (read as one cpd. word) kena pravartate; and often in Laṅk. Wogihara, as cited by Suzuki l. c., thought that the word was derived from *itthaṃtvika (cf. **itthatva**), *worldly*; Tib. does not support this.

(**icchitavya**, gdve., *to be accepted, recognized* (as in Skt. icchati): Mv iii.406.8–10 na khalv ayaṃ gharāvāso vā icchitavyo yasyedṛśo upabhogaparibhogo; niḥsaṃśayaṃ ayaṃ kumāro ... kṛtādhikāro icchitavyo ... Acc. to Senart, MIndic for īkṣitavya, *to be regarded.* But in Pali and Pkt. icchati and derivs. seem always to represent Skt. iṣ, *desire* [except that Sheth derives some forms from īps, *seek*], while only ikkh- seems to represent īkṣ-.)

[**icchu**, see **ucchu**.]

ijita, m.c. for **iñjita**, q.v.

iñcati = **iñjati**, which perhaps should be read: Mahāsamāj. Kl. Skt. Texte 4, 195.4 tasya romāṇi neñcati; Pali equivalent na saṃ lomaṃ pi iñjayuṃ DN ii.262.12.

iñjate or **°ti** (= Pali iñjati, iñjamāna), *moves, stirs* (intrans.); caus. iñjayati, *moves, disturbs* (trans.); frequently spelled in mss. and edd. iñjya-, also ijya- (esp. in Av, often kept by Speyer, as in i.253.9–10 anijjyamānair indriyaiḥ, but elsewhere, as i.187.7; 250.1 he reads with mss. aniñja- in the same cliché; these readings are probably only corruptions, but see s.vv. **aniñja, aniñjya,** and other forms there referred to: na ceñjate balavān LV 259.7 (of Bodhisattva); na ca iñjate bhramati vā 259.20 (id.); an-iñjamānāś ca SP 24.15 (Bodhisattvas); an-iñjamānam (bhikṣum) Gv 84.18; romaṃ na iṃjeya (opt.) Mv ii.408.5, *a hair would not be moved* (or caus., *it would not move a hair*; mss. iccheya, but em. proved by ii.411.8); an-iñjamānena kāyena sthito 'niñja- (v.l. 'niñjya-, q.v.) -prāptena ca cittena SP 5.10, and so read (omitting ca; see critical note) 19.14; an-iñjamānena cittena SP 159.6; an-iñjyamānena (see above; vv.ll. °iñja°, °ijya°) kāyena LV 131.2; an-iñjamānair (text sometimes an-ijya°, see above) indriyais Av i.187.7; 250.1; 253.9–10, etc. (in a cliché, see Index); caus., inf., ... me te romāpi neñjayituṃ samarthāḥ syuḥ Divy 185.10, *they would not be able to move even my hairs*; also iñjitum (caus. inf.), na ca samarthā mama romam iṃjituṃ Mv ii.340.13 = 341.11 (and cf. 340.17); cf. s.v. **iñjitatva.** See also next entries.

iñjana, nt., or **°nā**, f. (both = Pali id.; cf. **an-i°**, prec., and next), *motion, wavering, vacillation* (of mind; body; hair, as a very small and delicate part of the body): LV 259.9 (vs) na ceñjanaṃ nāpi manyana-pracāraṃ (so read, see s.v. **manyanā**); Av i.88.7 (prose) na ca śakitaṃ bhagavato romeñjanam api kartuṃ; Gv 128.6 (prose) sarveñjana-manyana-(read so with 2d ed.) -spandana-prapañcanāpagatacittam; Gv 253.14 (vs) na ca tubhya iñjana (could be nt. or f.) ... manyana-spandanā na ca prapañcā; (the rest are fem.) LV 366.3 (vs) no ca kāyeñjanā (n. sg.); Mv ii.414.19 (vs) na sattvasārasya karonti iñjanā (acc. sg.; Senart em. °nāṃ); RP 12.15 (vs) citta-iñjanā (read as cpd.); 13.14 (vs) citteñjanā; KP 136.8 (vs) sarveñjanā-manyana-vipramuktaḥ; Dbh.g. 26(52).4 bhāvi tatha abhāve iñjanā nāsti kācit.

iñjita (= Pali id.), (**1**) primarily ppp. of **iñjate,** q.v.; see **iñjita-tva**; (**2**) subst. nt., *motion, movement* (literal and physical): Mv i.305.21 (vs) prāsādiken' iṃjitena (read **ijitena**; § 2.73; cf. ijya- forms s.v. **iñjate**) praviśantāṃ (buddhasya śrāvakān), *entering with serene walk*; (**3**) subst. nt., *mobility, vacillation, unsteadiness*; = **iñjana** or **°nā**, and like these often associated with **manyanā** (or **manyita**), **spandita** (miswritten sya°), and other qualities deprecated in religious life: Mvy 7218 °tam = Tib. gyo ba, foll. by syanditam; SP 336.3 (vs) varjitvā iñjitā (v.l. °tān) manyitāni ca; 372.7 (prose) iñjita-manyita-prapañcitāni jñāsyati; Dbh 64.13 sarveñjita-manyanā-syandita-vikalpāpagato bhavati; Bbh 339.18 (prose) (**-abhiniveśa-**, q.v.) -sarveñjitāni ... prahīyante; 340.21 sarvābhiniveśeñjitaprahāṇataś ca. See also **an-iñjita.**

iñjita-tva, nt. (to prec.), *state of being moved*: Mv ii.411.(7–)8 (nāpi bodhisattvasya) romasyāpi iñjitatvam, *and not so much as a hair of the B. was moved.*

iṭṭā, Mvy 7982, prob. error for **iṅgā**, q.v.; cf. however **aṭṭa.**

(**itara**, adj., *commonplace, low, vulgar*, = Pali itara and ittara, but also Skt. itara, BR 5.1139; hence not a specifically Buddhist word; doubtless specialized semantic development of itara, *other*: e. g. LV 88.11 itara-jātīyāḥ, *commonplace, vulgar people.* No *ittara has been recorded, but see **itvara,** which is presumed to be its Skt. original.)

itaretara, adj. (= Pali itarītara; the Skt. word not in this sense but only reciprocal, cf. Wackernagel II.1 § 60a, note), *any sort of, this or that, any at all, miscellaneous, hit-or-miss*: Mvy 2216 netaretareṇa saṃtuṣṭiḥ; Mv iii.348.4 °reṇa ca piṇḍapātreṇa saṃtuṣṭo bhaveyaṃ; RP 13.9 alpecchā itaretarair abhiratā(ḥ), *pleased* (*satisfied*) *with anything at all*; 16.5 bhavati ca itaretareṇa tuṣṭaḥ.

itivṛtta (nt. or m.), = next (rarely): nidānetivṛtta-Kv 81.21 (prose), in list of canonical writings.

itivṛttaka, nt. (in Bbh m.; = **ityukta, °taka,** qq.v., = Pali itivuttaka, which seems clearly based on iti vuttaṃ = ity uktam, but in BHS has been blended formally, by Hypersanskritism, with Skt. itivṛtta, nt., see BR; Tib., see below, proves that at least for Tib. translators the word was connected with vṛtta rather than ukta), n. of a canonical work or type of literature, *story of past events* (associated with jātaka): Mvy 1274 = Tib. (de lta bu) byuṅ ba (-ḥi sde), *story, history* (root ḥbyuṅ, *happen, take place,* = vṛt); here itivṛttakam is foll. by jātakam; SP 45.7 (vs) sūtrāṇi (or, with v.l., sūtrānta) bhāṣāmi tathaiva gāthā itivṛttakaṃ jātakam adbhutaṃ ca; Bbh 67.20 (wrongly punctuated) ... prakāśayati (comma, or no punctuation) itivṛttakāṃś ca pūrvayogapratisaṃyuktāṃ (= °tān; end of sentence!); Bbh 397.12–13 tathāgataḥ pūrvānte itivṛttakāṃś ca jātakāṃś ca smṛtvā... Cf. **vṛttaka.**

itihāsaka, nt. (! = Skt. itihāsa, m.), *history, story, legend*: Mvy 4971 °kam, n. sg. (follows purāṇaṃ; gender influenced by this?).

itthatva, nt. (= Pali itthatta), *the being in this world*: Mv iii.447.8 (kṣīṇā me jātir ...) noparim itthatvam iti prajānāti. Recorded as icchatva Mv i.52.7 devanikāyato cyavitvā icchatvam āgacchanti, and in similar phrases 52.8; 338.18; ii.133.4. Senart allows icchatva to stand, regarding it as a genuine phonetic alternative form (i.417); and all mss. read so in these passages. But in view of iii.447.8 it seems to me likely that icchatva is a mere graphic corruption, § 2.22. See however **icchatva.**

ityukta (nt.), cited by Burnouf, Intr. 60 f., and Kern, SBE 21.45 n. 4; not noted in texts; = next.

ityuktaka (nt.; cf. prec.; = **itivṛttaka,** q.v.; a more historical Sktization of Pali itivuttaka), *sayings* (sc. of the Buddha), n. of a canonical work or type of literature: ŚsP 1460.5 gāthoddānanidānatyuktaka- (read °nidānetyuktaka-)-jātaka-.

itvara, adj. (= Pali ittara; Skt. Lex., rare and late in lit., see pw; cf. **itara,** which in Pali is commonly treated as the same word but seems to be unrelated in origin; possibly secondary blending has occurred between the two words), *slight, small, trivial, unimportant; brief, momentary* (of time): Mvy 2699 °ram (n. sg.); Mv iii.186.4 °raṃ khu ayaṃ tāpo, *this* (sun's) *heat is a trivial thing*; LV 123.4 (vs) kiṃ tasyābharaṇebhir (so, as one word) itvaraiḥ, *what need has he of trivial* (ordinary, worthless) *ornaments*?; RP 39.12 asāram itvaraṃ ca lokam (acc. sg.); Śikṣ 167.8 mahākāruṇyacittotpādenetvareṇa kāmopasaṃhitena, *by an impulse of pity, tho vile* (? better *trivial, slight*), *and full of desire* (Bendall-Rouse); of virtue, merit, etc., Gv 529.9 itvara-guṇa-saṃtuṣṭair, *satisfied with slight virtues*; LV 271.3 (vs) itvarapuṇya devamanujā; Gv 508.24 itvara-kuśalamūlānāṃ devamanuṣyāṇāṃ (of those who do not follow the Mahāyāna); Śikṣ 60.14 itvara-kuśalamūlāḥ; of time, Bbh 87.4 itvarakālābhyāsāt (*short*), contrasted with dīrghakālābhyāsāt line 3; vijñāyate netvaradarśanena Ud xxix.11 = Pali SN i.79.17 (*momentary, fleeting glance*); of gifts, Divy 317.8 kiṃ punar me itvareṇa dānena pradattena.

idaṃpratyaya, adj. (= Pali idappaccaya, e. g. Vism. 518.30), *having this* (or *that*) *as its cause*: Dbh 26.3 ... gambhīredaṃpratyayānubodhanena pratyekabuddhayānaṃ saṃvartayanti.

idaṃpratyaya-tā (= Pali idappaccayatā; abstr. from prec.), *state of having this* (or *that*) *as its cause*; generally in comp. with pratītya-samutpāda, *dependent origination owing to the state of* (etc.); so also the Pali equivalent is usually cpd. with paṭiccasamuppāda (or °panna), tho the editions wrongly separate the words, as in Vin. i.5.1: idaṃpratyayatā-pratītyasamutpādam Gv 89.13; Bbh 204.25; 396.21; °pādena Bbh 110.23; °pādānulomāḥ Bbh 303.22.

idāni (MIndic for °nīm; cf. **dāni**), *now*: Mv i.154.15 (vs, m.c.); 247.20 (vs, m.c.; v.l. idānī, unmetr.)

iddhi (= Pali-Pkt. id.; MIndic for ṛddhi), *magic power*: Mv ii.322.1 (vs; read) marūṇa rājā vaśir iddhiprāpto (or perhaps vaśi **riddhi°**, see this; text divides wrongly, va śiriddhi°).

idha, adv. (= Pali id., Skt. iha, § 2.36), *here*: Mv i.19.10 (all mss. but one); 20.6 (4 of 6 mss.); iii.134.20 (no v.l.).

indra, m. (**1**) as in Pali (Sakko devānaṃ indo), the deva who in Skt. is named Indra (but frequently also called Śakra) is in BHS often called Śakra, devānām indra, *Śakra king of the gods*, the word indra being clearly a common, not a proper, noun; so SP 69.8; LV 62.14; 66.4; etc., passim; this is specially clear when the n. pr. Śakra is omitted but the gen. devānām retained, as in LV 62.15, 18 devānām indra, *O king of the gods*! (**2**) a high number: Mvy 8022 indraḥ = Tib. dbaṅ po, *lord* (regularly = indra); (**3**) n. of a yakṣa: Māy 29; 236.25; (**4**) n. of a brahman: Divy 74.17 ff.; (**5**) n. of a king: Mmk 625.21.

-indraka (= Pali -indaka), at end of Bhvr. cpds., = indra (either as n. pr. or in the sense of *lord, king*): LV 54.13 (vs) devadānavagaṇāḥ sa-indrakāḥ; 391.14 (vs) devāḥ sa-indrakās; Mv ii.260.4 (prose) sendrakā devā.

indrakīla, m. (= Pali inda°, also °khīla; not recorded in this sense in Skt., where it appears to mean *bar, bolt* to a gate or door; AMg. indakhīla, said to mean *a portion of a city gate; a door bolt*..., Ratnach.; qy: was the 'bolt' fastened *under* the door, in the pavement? cf. Meyer, Kauṭ. 71, 689), *threshold slab*, a stone imbedded in the ground at the entrance to a city gate, or to a palace, house, or apartment: Mvy 5582 °laḥ = Tib. ḥkor gtan, lit. *circle bar*, or Tib. sgoḥi them pa, *threshold of a door*; Das cites both these Tib. phrases as synonymous renderings of indrakīla, and defines them as *steps at the threshold* or *at the entrance of a house*; cf. Divy 544.7, three indrakīlas, viz. nagare indrakīlo, rājakule ..., and antaḥpure ..., *thresholds to a city, a royal palace, and a harem*; this passage is a comm. on Divy 543.22 (yaḥ ... bhikṣur ...) rājñaḥ ... indrakīlaṃ vā indrakīla-sāmantaṃ vā samatikrāmed, *if any monk crosses a king's threshold or its environs*; generally referred to as located at a city gate; in entering the city one steps upon it: Mv i.308.7 samanantaraṃ indrakīlaṃ pādena cokramati (= ca-avakr°), *and as soon as he* (Buddha, entering a city) *stepped on the i° with his foot*; Divy 250.20 (Bhagavatā) **sābhisaṃskāra** (q.v.) indrakīle pādo vyavasthāpitaḥ (in entering a city); 365.1 (Buddhā ...) indrakīle pādau vyavasthāpayanti (in entering a city by the gate); Av i.109.1 yadā ca bhagavatā indrakīle pādo nyastaḥ (in entering a city; the gate is not mentioned); Gv 205.3 rājadhānīṃ praviśata indrakīlam ākrāmataḥ, *as* (a Buddha) *was entering the capital, as he stepped upon the threshold* (pres. pples., gen. sg.); Mv ii.396.3 (vs) so indrakīle (mss. °kīlo) sthita, *standing on the threshold*, apparently of the city (rājadhānī) mentioned line 2; used in comparisons as type of immobility, recommended in religious life: Mv i.292.14 yathendrakīlo pṛthivīsaṃniśrito syā ... asaṃprakampi, *as an i° should be fixed in the earth*, (so ...) *immovable*; Ud xvii.12 indrakīlopamā; in this sense applied to the mind or thoughts of a Buddha or Bodhisattva, Mv ii.261.3 and 262.5 (Bodhisattvas) indrakīlopamacittatāṃ ca anuprāpnuvanti; iii.225.5 indrakīlopamacittā (of Buddha); Av i.223.12 bhagavān ... indrakīla iva (here physically and literally motionless, like a threshold-stone) tasmin pradeśe sthitaḥ.

indrakīlaka, m. = prec., q.v.: Mv i.195.16 (prose) teṣāṃ ... dvārāṇāṃ caturṇāṃ varṇānāṃ indrakīlakā abhunsu, *these gates* (of a city) *had threshold-stones of four colors.*

Indrakuśa, n. of a brother of Kuśa: Mv ii.433.16.

Indraketu, (**1**) n. of a samādhi: Mvy 531 (not in ŚsP); (**2**) n. of a former Buddha: LV 172.5; (**3**) n. of a yakṣa: Samādh p. 43 line 21.

Indraketudhvajarāja, n. of a Buddha: Śikṣ 169.13; (the same?) of a Buddha in the zenith: Sukh 98.15.

indragopa, or **°paka,** in comp. with śiras or śīrṣa(n), *redheaded*, said of (miraculous) elephants: LV 55.3–4 (prose) indragopaka-śirāḥ, n. sg., of the Bodhisattva in the form of a small elephant, about to enter his mother's womb (in vs line 7 replaced by suraktaśīrṣaḥ); Mv iii.411.4 (prose) indragopa-śīrṣam, of another magically created elephant. The words °pa and °paka denote a red insect in Skt. and Pali; acc. to BR the cochineal insect.

Indracūrṇa, n. of a former Buddha: Mv i.139.7.

Indrajālin, n. of a Bodhisattva: LV 291.18.

Indratapanā, n. of a capital of the former Buddha Indradhvaja: Mv iii.226.6 ff.

Indrateja(s), n. of a former Buddha: Mv i.136.14 °jaḥ, n. sg.

Indradatta, n. of a 'virtuous man' (**satpuruṣa**, q.v.): SP 3.11.

Indradamana, n. of a former Buddha: Av i.86.8 ff.

Indradeva, n. of a Bodhisattva: ŚsP 6.10.

Indradhvaja, (**1**) n. of various former Buddhas: Mv i.138.4; iii.226.6 (with capital Indratapanā); Av i.105.3 ff.; 84,000 former Buddhas of this name, Mv i.58.14; 62.4; a Buddha in the southwest quarter, SP 184.11; (**2**) n. of a nāga: Mvy 3363.

Indradhvajaketu, n. of a Tathāgata: Gv 281.7; same as **Candradhvajaśrīketu** 280.12.

indra-paṭa, nt., acc. to pw 2.294, *Luftgewand*, so v.a. *Nacktheit*: °ṭaṃ śvetapaṭaṃ dhyuṣitapaṭaṃ Kv 81.6–7; but can indra- have this mg. (=*sky, air*, as in digambara)? I find no basis for the theory. All the context shows is that persons dressed in these garbs should not be consecrated (dīkṣ). What the *garb of Indra* (? *of a prince*) means is not clear. It is true that śveta-paṭa is recorded as used of the Jain sect otherwise called śvetāmbara; doubtless this was the reason for Boehtlingk's conjecture, based on the assumption that this word equals digambara; but I doubt that this is sufficient to support it. That a real sort of cloth is meant is suggested by nānā-paṭeṣu, line 6.

Indrapura, n. of a town: Māy 29.

Indrabhūti, n. of an author: Sādh 353.11.

Indramaghaśrī, n. of a gandharva-maid: Kv 5.9.

Indramati, n. of a Buddhist monk: Gv 47.10.

indra-yaṣṭi, f. (nowhere recorded in this sense, which = Skt. indra-cāpa etc.), (**1**) *rainbow*: LV 296.17 (vs) ke cāgatā vimalaketu yathendrayaṣṭyaḥ, *bright-colored as rainbows*; Śikṣ 258.9 (vs) yatha naru iha indrayaṣṭi (Tib. ḥjaḥ, *rainbow*) dṛṣṭvā vimṛśati aṅgaśu (= °śas) niḥsvabhāva śūnyam; (**2**) n. of a nāga: Mvy 3358.

(**Indraśaila**, as n. of a mountain, recorded in BR, pw only as Buddhist, but occurs in Skt., see Kirfel Kosm. 99; noted by me in Māy 253.30; and see next.)

Indraśailaguhā, n. of a locality (cf. prec.): Mvy 4124 °guhā, n. sg.

Indraśrī, (**1**) m., n. of a Buddha: Gv 284.15 (vs) °śiri, n. sg.; but see s.v. **Citrārtha**; (**2**) m., n. of a Bodhisattva: Gv 442.6 °śriyo, gen. sg.; (**3**) f., n. of a gandharva maid: Kv 5.9.

Indrasena, n. of a nāga: Mvy 3310.

indrahasta, m. (°taḥ, n. sg.), Mvy 5823, or °**stā**, f. (n. sg.), Suv 104.7; Tib. in both dbaṅ poḥi lag (pa), a literal rendering of the Skt., which Das says means 'a plant the viscid aromatic root of which resembles the human arm in shape'; in both Mvy and Suv one item in lists of herbs, oṣadhi (Suv auṣadhayo, n. pl.). Mvy has other Tib. renderings, apparently foreign words and not in Dictt., ḥab śaṅ tse ḥu (which also renders prativiṣam, Mvy 5822) and ḥa ba śa tshe ḥu.

Indrāyudhaśikhin, n. of a nāga: Mvy 3356.

indriya, (**1**) nt. (Pali also uses the word of this group, see PTSD s.v., B, Nos. 15–19), one of the five moral *faculties* (śraddhā, vīrya, smṛti, samādhi, prajñā), to which correspond five *powers* (bala) with the same names: listed Mvy 976–981; Sūtrāl. xviii.55 (and cf. xi.12, Transl. 106, n. 10); Dharmas 47; each treated as a dharmālokamukha, LV 33.17–20; mentioned, with balas, but not listed, SP 47.2; 80.1; (**2**) a high number, Gv 106.3 sattvendriyasya.

Indriyeśvara, n. of a boy: Gv 131.5 ff.

imaṃhi, loc. sg. of idam, = iha, *here*; repeatedly in Mv, e. g. ii.107.6; 478.7; see § 21.66.

iyaṃtata, adj., *of such an extent, so great*, or (here) *so small*: Sukh 32.1 (prose) tad yathā sa ekavindur iyaṃtataḥ sa prathamasaṃnipāto (see **saṃnipāta**) 'bhūt. Could this be an error for iyantaḥ = Skt. iyān, n. sg. m. of iyant? But I have not noted such MIndic morphology in the prose of Sukh. Emendation to iyattakaḥ (Vedic only and rare) is not attractive.

iyaṃduḥkha, adj., *having torments to this extent* (iyaṃ for Skt. iyat, see § 18.54): Divy 375.15, 21; 376.1, 9 °khā hi bhikṣavo nārakāḥ (or narakāḥ).

iranta(ḥ), n. pl. pres. pple. = Skt. īrayantaḥ (§ 3.38), *setting in motion*: Gv 372.13 (vs) paripācayanti jagu dharmaprabhām iranta (imu . . .) Cf. **iryati.**

iriyāpatha, MIndic for **īryā**°, q.v.

iryati (= Pali iriyati; cf. Vedic īrte), *wanders*: Mv iii.118.18 vanād vanaṃ iryasi (so mss., Senart em. īr°) caṃkramanto. The ya-present formation is doubtless due to influence of the noun iryā (see **īryā**), commonly in the cpd. **īryāpatha** or **iryā**°.

iryā, iryāpatha, iryāvant, iryavant, semi-MIndic spelling for **īry**°, q.v.

irṣyā = Skt. īrṣyā, *jealousy*: all mss. at LV 52.13; 372.17. Weller 20 would em. to īrṣyā; but this may be only Sktization of semi-MIndic ir°, cf. **iryā**- etc. As Weller notes, irṣyā is found as v.l. in some mss. of Mv (i.37.6; 44.13, four of six mss.; iii.27.17; 164.19); tho in all these cases at least one ms. has īr°, the form ir° may have been original.

Ilā devī, n. of a devakumārikā in the northern quarter: Mv iii.309.8 = LV 391.3.

Iśādhāra, n. of a nāga: Mvy 3333 (but Mironov Īśā°); Tib. gśol mdaḥ ḥdzin, *plow-holder* (implying Īṣā°).

Iṣaṃdhara, m., n. of one of the seven mountains (or mountain ranges) surrounding Sumeru, = **Īṣādhara**, q.v.; read so at Mv ii.300.18 where the only ms. reads iyaṃdharā (Senart em. iṣāṃdharo).

Iṣāṇa, m., n. of a region, in the south: Gv 115.1 dakṣiṇāpatha °ṇo nāma janapadas; 116.3.

Iṣādhāra, v.l. in Mironov for Mvy 4144 **Īṣādhara**, q.v., n. of a mountain. See also **Īṣādhāra** (2).

Iṣāṃdhara, see **Iṣaṃdhara.**

iṣika, nt., or **iṣikā**, f. (perhaps also iṣika, nt.; cf. Pali esika, °kā, interpreted in Dictt. as *pillar, post*), *sign-post*: Mvy 7048 iṣikā māpitā bhavanti (Tib. śiṅ-rtags, *tree* (or *wood*) *sign*; Chin. app. *sign-post* or the like): Mv i.196.1 and iii.228.12 dvārāṇāṃ purato iṣikāni (iii.228.12 iṣī°, v.l. iṣi°) māpitāni abhūnsuḥ; Śikṣ 173.16 iṣikā-padaṃ vā dadyāt, *or should present a sign-post* (at the caitya of a past Buddha, marking the holy spot; otherwise but implausibly Bendall and Rouse).

Iṣidatta (= Pali Isi°; semi-MIndic for **Ṛṣidatta**, q.v., also Riṣi°), n. of a sthapati of King Prasenajit of Śrāvastī (Kosala): Divy 77.27; 466.23, in both read, substantially with mss., (gṛhapatir) Iṣidattaḥ Purāṇaḥ sthapatī (dual).

iṣu, nt. (in Skt. only m., f.), *arrow*: Mv ii.82.4 and 5 iṣu kṣiptaṃ (n. sg.).

Iṣṭaka, m. pl., n. of a brahmanical gotra: Divy 635.17.

Iṣṭarūpa, n. of a former Buddha: Mv i.139.11.

iṣṭā (cf. AMg. iṭṭā, with non-aspirate, beside iṭṭayā = Skt. iṣṭakā), *brick*: SP 50.9 (vs) iṣṭā-mayā (ed. em. °yān) . . . stūpān. Perhaps loss of suffixal ka m.c.; § 22.24.

iṣṭikā (= **iṣṭī, istrikā, istrī, iṣṭiyā**, all semi-MIndic forms of strī; for i- see § 3.113; cf. Pali itthikā, AMg. itthiyā, etc.; no MIndic *iṭṭhī or *iṭṭhikā, with domal stops, seems recorded), *woman*: LV 43.5 (vs) puruṣa-iṣṭika- (m.c. for °kā-) dārakāś ca; 79.20 (vs) iṣṭikān (acc.

pl.) evam āha; Mv i.244.5 (prose) iṣṭikāye (gen. sg.), v.l. for text istrikāye; ii.384.22 (vs) iṣṭikāsu (no v.l.).

iṣṭiyā, v.l. for text istriyā and °yo at Mv ii.70.1, see s.v. **istrī**. If iṣṭiyā is correct, it corresponds to **iṣṭī**, q.v., as **striyā** (n. sg.), q.v., does to strī. It would be n. sg. (while istriyo, at least, is n. pl.).

iṣṭī, iṣṭi (Pali itthi, itthī), = **iṣṭikā, istrī**, qq.v., *woman*: LV 74.15 (vs) ye ca iṣṭidārakā suduḥkhitā (Lefm. wrongly °dārakāsu duḥ°), *and what women and boys*...; LV 235.15 (vs), perhaps read ima iṣṭi°, cf. ms. A imeṣṭikāmaratiṃ (= imām plus iṣṭi°), for Lefm. ima istri°; Mv ii.299.14 (vs) iṣṭibhāvaṃ, *state of (existence as) a woman*; other instances as v.l. for forms of **istrī**, q.v.

iṣyate, °ti (= Skt. icchati; acc. to Wh. Roots, used in certain cpds. E +), *seeks*: Divy 476.16 (na) mama ... kiṃcid evam iṣye (1 sg.); 560.7–8 (vs) yadi tvaṃ prītim iṣyasi.

istrikā = **istrī, istri**, q.v., *woman*: LV 220.5 (vs) istrika (n. pl., or stem in comp. with foll.) dārakāś ca; Mv i.244.5 (prose) istrikāye (v.l. iṣṭikāye), gen. sg.

istrigāra, istriyāgāra, see **stryāgāra**.

istrī, istri (= Aśokan id. [Shāh., Mān.]; Skt. strī; see s.v. **iṣṭikā, iṣṭī**), *woman*: SP 358.6; 455.3; LV 42.17; 80.10; 193.14 (istriya gen. pl., = striyām); 195.16; 242.17; 330.14, 18; 340.1; Mv i.303.20; 304.4; all the prec. vss; Mv ii.70.1 (prose) istriyā (instr. sg.; v.l. **iṣṭiyā**) sma parājitā, na ca kahiṃcit istriyo (n. pl.; v.l. iṣṭiyā, q.v.) rājā, sarvatra puruṣo (Senart °ṣā) rājā; 71.1 istriye (instr. sg., v.l. iṣṭiye); 321.23 istrī- (v.l. iṣṭī-) sahasraiḥ; iii.26.21 istriye (oblique case); 84.8, 14 istrīhi (instr. pl.); Śikṣ 242.13 (vs) istriṇāṃ (gen. pl.); Gv 254.16 (vs) istri-koṭi; 255.18 (vs) istri-gaṇaś ca.

ihatra, adv. (iha plus the suffix of amutra, which is the next word in Mvy; cf. AMg. ihaiṃ, from iha plus another loc. ending), *here, in this world*: Mvy 2975 (foll. by amutra).

Ī

?**īṅkhaka, °ikā**, see **iṅkh°**.

īdṛśika, f. **°kī**, adj. (cf. Skt. īdṛśaka; no form in °ika seems recorded), *such*: SP 325.11 (vs) kriyām īdṛśikīm (no v.l.).

***īryati**, see **iryati**.

īryā or **iryā** (chiefly the latter, semi-MIndic, has been noted; = Pali and AMg. iriyā) = the much commoner **īryā-patha** (or iryā°), *deportment, behavior*, particularly *good, dignified, proper deportment*: Mv i.302.10 iryaṃ (mss., Senart īryāṃ) paśyitvā (of a Pratyekabuddha); iii.60.9 (kalyāṇā) punar iyaṃ pravrajitasya iryā (Senart īryā); 92.10 iryā (Senart īryā); LV 115.2 (vs) teṣa (gods) yathā ca iryā; 116.7 (vs) yatha irya netra vimalāprabha, *since he possesses proper deportment and an eye of pure splendor* (so better than taking irya-netra as cpd. with Foucaux); 330.12 (vs) īryāṃ (no v.l. in mss.) caryāṃ ca prekṣate, *he* (Bodhisattva) *regards* (considers duly) *proper deportment and conduct*; MSV ii.186.10 (prose) tayā īryayā caryayā.

īryā-patha, m. (= Pali iriyā-patha, AMg. iriyāvaha; in mss., esp. of Mv and LV, often written **iryā°** or **iryyā°**, semi-MIndic, which Lefm. usually keeps but Senart emends to īryā°; once, at least, iriyā-patha, as in Pali, Mv ii.157.1, prose, kept by Senart; also **airyāpatha**, q.v.; see prec. and next), much commoner than the synonymous **īryā**, (**1**) *movement* (of physical movements of any sort): Mv i.22.11 (prose) chinna-iryāpathā (all mss., Sen. em. °īryā°) gacchanti (mss. gacchati), sinners in hell, confined in huts (gharakehi oruddhā), *go with (freedom of) movement cut off*, i. e. *suffer restraint of movement* (but possibly more specifically, *suffer restraint of posture*, see 4 below, e. g. are not allowed to sit or lie down); (**2**) applied to any particular course of religious, esp. ascetic, performance, and specifically to disapproved ascetic practices of heretics, such as the 'five-fire' practice (mentioned in the prec.): Divy 350.7 (sa) teṣāṃ-teṣām (of heretical ascetics) īryāpathān vikopayitum ārabdhaḥ; (**3**) generally less specific, *behavior, deportment*, good or bad, of people in general; but esp. of the approved deportment of pious Buddhists, of monks, or of Bodhisattvas or Buddhas; most commonly with favorable implication; but this may be made clear by an adjective, esp. prāsādika, *gracious*, (religiously) *attractive*: Mv iii.27.3–4 prāsādikena īryāpathena (v.l. iryyā°), of a Pratyekabuddha; in Śikṣ 348.6 prāsādika and aprāsādika īryā°, *good* and *bad deportment*, contrasted; Divy 82.14 śānteneryāpathena, of Mahākāśyapa; LV 427.18 praśānteryāpathaḥ, and 19 sarveryāpathacaryāviśeṣasamanvāgataḥ, *attended by all excellent deportment and behavior*, of the Tathāgata; creatures in general vary in deportment, LV 35.8 yathādhimukta-sattveryāpatha- (v.l. cited °iryyā°)-saṃdarśanāya; Gv 527.3–4 sarvasattvādhimuktisamair īryāpathaiḥ; specifically *good deportment*, SP 282.3 (vs) °pathaṃ yo mama rakṣamāṇo bhaveta bhikṣū...; LV 29.4 (vs) iryāpathe-ṣṭhā, *abiding in*...; 179.17 (bodhisattvo ... sarvāntaḥpurasya ...) īryāpatham upadarśya, *having displayed proper behavior to all the harem* (so Tib.); 220.6 īryāpathebhyaś (most mss. iry°) cyutāḥ, *fallen away from right behavior*; Dbh 71.19 tathāgateryāpathacaryācāritrānugato; Mv ii.157.1 (prose) iriyāpathasaṃpanno, *perfect in deportment*, of a monk; 390.8 (vs) īryāpathena su-upeta (with mss.) satvā, (there are no evil-doers here;) *creatures are well endowed with proper deportment*; Av ii.130.4 (corrupt); Mv i.174.11 (vs) īryāpathe (3 mss. iry°) ca vīrye ca dhyāne jñāne śame dame; iii.346.6 iryāpathe (so mss.) ca vīrye ca dhyāne jñāne tathaiva ca; often it is said that a newly-initiated person (of superior character) shows the īryāpatha, *deportment*, of a monk of long standing, LV 409.19–20 tad yathāpi nāma varṣaśatopapannasya bhikṣor īryāpathaḥ saṃvṛtto 'bhūt; Mv iii.65.5 iryāpatho (Senart em. īry°) sānaṃ saṃsthihe sayyathāpi nāma varṣaśatopasaṃpannānāṃ bhikṣūṇāṃ; similarly Mv ii.234.5; iii.92.10 (iryā instead of iryāpatho); 180.15; 181.7; 329.12; 413.13; Divy 37.3 (varṣaśatopasaṃpannasya) bhikṣor īryāpathenāvasthitaḥ; Av i.284.9 (dvādaśavarṣopasaṃpannasyeva) bhikṣor īryāpathena ... avasthitaḥ; (**4**) as in Pali iriyāpatha, also used of *four postures* or *bodily attitudes*, that is *modes of physical behavior*, viz. walking, standing, sitting, and lying down: Mvy 212 vihāyasābhyudgamya caturvidham īryāpathaṃ kalpayati, *mounting in the air, displays the four* ... (one of the abhijñākarmāṇi); Mv i.168.10 (vs) īryāpathāṃ (3 mss. iry°) darśayanti catvāraḥ puruṣottamāḥ, no ca pariśramas teṣām..., *Buddhas display the four modes of behavior* (like other men), *and yet they are never weary* (i. e. do not need to sit or lie down); AsP 520.12 dvābhyām everyāpathābhyāṃ sthitvā, sthānena caṅkrameṇa ca (only standing and walking; he vows not to sit or lie down) kālam atināmayeyaṃ, repeated (var.) 521.6, which is cited Śikṣ 40.5 dvābhyām everyāpathābhyāṃ...; Gv 22.20 ff., īryāpatha repeatedly of physical movements (walking, standing, and sitting, line 22) of ordinary (not religious) men; LV 9.8 caturīryāpatha-vinayanopavana-(so read, text °naupavana-)-suvardhita-taror (Tib. lus, *body*, for -taror, implying -tanor), (of the Bodhisattva) *who possessed a 'tree' (body?) well-raised in the grove of (by?) exercise of the four modes of behavior*; LV 256.18 (ṣaḍvarṣā bodhisattvo yathā niṣaṇṇa evāsthāt paryaṅkena) na ca īryāpathāc (all mss. ca iry° or cery°) cyavate sma, *and did not abandon the posture* (of sitting cross-legged); Mv i.236.14 (here mss. iry°) = 241.8 (vs) īryāpathaṃ ... sarvābhibhuno (mss. °to) na vijahante (i. e. they walk and stand still when he does, see prec. line); only three, tribhir īryāpathair ... sthānena caṅkrameṇa niṣadyayā RP 45.18.

īryāvant, adj. (recorded only in semi-MIndic form iryavant, with short a m.c.; from **īryā**), *characterized by proper deportment*: LV 113.20 and 114.7 (vss) iryavantaḥ, n. pl. (of gods); 240.10 (vs) iryavanto, n. sg. (of the Bodhisattva).

īrṣī, or **īrṣi** = Skt. īrṣyā, *envy* (see § 3.115): LV 75.10 (vs) kāmachandu naiva tasya īrṣi (some mss. īrṣyā, unmetr., while īrṣya would be possible; v.l. also irṣu) naiva hiṃsitā.

īrṣu, īrṣuka, see **an-ī°**.

(**īrṣyāyate, °ti**, *is jealous, is envious*: Mv ii.480.5 (prose) °yase; Śikṣ 62.2 (prose) te pareṣām īrṣyāyanti. Must have existed in Skt. since the ppp. īrṣyāyita, as nt. nom. act., is recorded; see pw. Denom. from īrṣyā.)

īrṣyāluka, adj. (= Skt. īrṣyālu), *jealous, envious*: SP 429.6 (prose) mā ... sattvā īrṣyālukā mā matsariṇo ...; Samādh p. 53, line 5 (vs; here -ka could be m.c.).

Īśādhara, m., n. of a mountain: Dharmas 125; Mironov for Mvy 4144 (with v.l. **Iśādhāra**). See under **Īṣādhara.**

Īśādhāra, (1) n. of a nāga, Mironov's reading for **Iśā°** Mvy 3333; (2) m. pl., n. of a range of mountains (= Īṣā°; see under **Īṣādhara**): Śikṣ 246.4 °rā(ḥ).

Īśvara, (1) n. of a rich householder's son in Campā: Karmav 66.9; (2) n. of a Bodhisattva: Gv 442.9.

Īśvaraguṇāparājitadhvaja, n. of a Tathāgata: Gv 380.22; later, in vs, called Īśvarājitaguṇadhvaja, 383.14.

Īśvaragupta, n. of a former Buddha: Mv i.141.4.

Īśvaradeva, n. of (apparently) two Bodhisattvas (in the same list! is one an error?): Gv 442.8, 10.

Īśvarājitaguṇadhvaja, see **Īśvaraguṇāparājitadhvaja.**

īśvarīya, nt. (= Pali issariya, AMg. id. or īsariya; penultimate ī may be m.c.), *sovereignty*: Mv ii.395.6 (vs) na tasya ko pi (by em.; one ms. vī) jane īśvarīyam The Śikṣ parallel, 308.4, has īśvaratvam.

Īṣādhara, m. (= Pali Īsadhara), n. of a mountain (one of the seven ranges surrounding Sumeru; Kirfel, Kosm. 186): Mvy 4144 (but Mironov Īśā°, with v.l. Iṣādhāra). Cf. next, **Iṣāṃdhara** (**Iṣaṃ°**), **Īśādhāra**, Īśādhara. Kyoto ed. text Īsā°, Index 'Īṣā° (Īśā°)'.

Īṣādhāra, m. (see under prec.), (1) n. of a mountain or mountain-range: Divy 217.12, 14; MSV i.94.6; (2) n. of a deity (giving rain): Śikṣ 247.7 (or may be Iṣā°; samdhi ambiguous); (3) implied by Tib. instead of **Iśādhāra**, q.v.

īṣi, īṣit, adv. (= AMg. īsi; Skt. īṣat; form lacking -t noted only in vss, but regularly in metr. indifferent positions, hence not m.c.), *a little, slightly*; only noted in Mmk, but common there: īṣismitamukhaṃ 133.3; 135.2; °mukhā 236.11; 239.21; īṣitkāyāvanāmitam 133.6; mahātmā ... īṣi dṛśyati tatkṣaṇāt 240.1; īṣit pracoditā 363.25; in prose, īṣitprahasitavadanaḥ 41.22; īṣid avanāmayet 391.2; others 388.3; 390.22; etc

U

?**ukara-** (v.l. udakara-, utkara-; cf. **ugra-lipi**), in Mv i.135.6 (prose) ukara-madhura-darada-cīṇa- (etc.), sc. lipi, a list of various kinds of writing. Senart would em. ukaramadhura to uttara-kuru, very implausibly; the parallel LV passage has **ugra-lipi** which surely represents the same original as this word.

ukirati (m.c. for o-k° = ava-k°; § 3.55), *scatters, throws down* upon (acc.): °ranti naranāyakottamaṃ Sukh 49.7 (all mss. uk°); 50.3 (mss. ok°, unmetr.; Müller ok° both times).

ukkaṭṭati, see **utkaṭṭati.**

ukkarikā (= Skt. utk°), a kind of sweetmeat: Divy 500.23, 24, 26 ukkarikāpaṇaḥ (and acc. °ṇam). Cf. **ukkārika.**

Ukkala, nt. (presumably = Skt. Utkala, *Orissa*; cf. Pali Ukkalā), n. of a locality (adhiṣṭhāna), where **Trapuṣa** and **Bhallika** originated; when they visited Buddha they were journeying from the south (Mv iii.303.6), presumably homeward bound (so also in LV 381.4–6, where they are described as uttarāpathakau): Mv iii.303.4 uttarāpathe ukkalaṃ nāmādhiṣṭhānaṃ. tato ukkalāto ... trapuṣo ca bhalliko ca ...

ukkārika, nt. (cf. **ukkarikā**), some kind of sweetmeat or delicacy: Mv ii.190.6 (prose) anye nānāprakārāṇi khajjakāni allīyanti, anye ukkārikāni allīyanti, anye modakāni allīyanti; iii.158.9, 12 (modakāni ca) ukkārikāni ca. (In line 12 v.l. ukvāritāni.)

ukkāsati (MIndic for Skt. utkā°; = Pali id.), *coughs, clears the throat*: Mv ii.281.13, 18 ukkāsi, 14, 15 ukkāse (both aor.). See next two.

ukkāsana (nt.; = Skt. utkā°; cf. prec. and next), *a cough*, or *clearing of the throat*: Mv ii.418.16 °na-śabdena māro ... bhagno; 419.16, 18.

ukkāsita (nt.; = Pali id.), = prec.: Mv ii.281.13 (mahāsiṃha-) ukkāsitāṃ ukkāsi (repetitions in sequel); 410.4 (bodhisattvena ca) ukkāsitaśabdena bhagno (sc. māro).

[**uktamuṣṭivat** LV 176.4, error for **rikta°**; see Śikṣ 238.2 (citation from LV) and Bendall's note.]

ukramati (for o- = ava-k° § 3.54), see **avakrāmati.**

ukṣa, m. (false Skt. for Pali, AMg. ukkhā, each recorded once, cf. Pischel 194, or for Skt. ukhā), *pot, vessel*: LV 324.13 (vs) udaro mūtrapurīṣasaṃcayo asucokṣaḥ, *the belly is a heap of urine and dung, a vessel of impurities.* Is the masc. gender due to assimilation to udara, in this isolated occurrence?

Uggata, see **Udgata.**

uggam-, uggir- (or **uggur-**), MIndic for Skt. ud-g°, see § 2.9.

Ugra, (1) n. of a nāga king, previous incarnation of Buddha: Mv i.131.5; (2) n. of a householder (gṛhapati; prob. = Pali Ugga, in DPPN no. 5), character in the **Ugrasūtra**, q.v.: Karmav 162.6, 10. See Lévi's note, and Pali AN iii.51.

Ugratejas, (1) n. of a former Buddha: LV 5.11 (2) n. of a god (devaputra): LV 39.13 (prose; °tejo, n. sg.); (3) n. of a son of Māra, unfavorable to the Bodhisattva: LV 310.9 °tejā(s), n. sg.

Ugradattaparipṛcchā, n. of a work, = next: Śikṣ 18.18; 37.7; 78.7; 180.1, 14; 192.11; 193.3; 196.7; 198.1; 290.1.

Ugraparipṛcchā, = prec.: Mvy 1396; Śikṣ 11.2;

120.3; 131.10; 315.14; called Ugraparipṛcchā-sūtra (cf. **Ugrasūtra**?), Śikṣ 136.1.

Ugra-lipi, a kind of writing: LV 125.22. Tib. drag śul can confirms ugra-; cf. under **ukara-**.

Ugra-sūtra, n. of a work: Karmav 162.6; see s.v. **Ugra** (2), and Lévi's note. The passage here cited does not occur among the Śikṣ citations from the **Ugraparipṛcchā(sūtra)**, which may or may not be a different work.

Ugrasena (= Pali Uggasena), n. of a king of Benares, in story of the nāga Campaka (Pali Campeyya Jātaka): Mv ii.177.9 ff.

ucita, nt., *merit*: Karmav 26.23 yathā hy ucitaṃ nikṣiptam, evam ... gacchanti durgatim, *for as their merit has been thrown away* (laid down), *so they go to an evil fate.* Contrasts with duritam, *sin*, in 29.14 yathā duritaṃ nikṣiptam, evam ... gacchanti sadgatim. (This specialized use of ucita seems nowhere recorded.)

[**uccaka**, wrongly suggested Divy p. 705, note on 40.10, as contained in vṛṣikoccaka-; read vṛṣi-kocava-, see **kocava**.]

uccagghati, also °**ghayati** (= Pali ujjagghati; cf. **saṃcagghati**; sometimes written °caghati, doubtless by mere error; c for j is surely secondary but unexplained, cf. Pischel 190, 191, and Wogihara, Lex. 41), *laughs at, mocks, sneers at, derides*; often with forms of **ul-lap-** (**-lāp-**), q.v.: SP 382.12 ye te taṃ bodhisattvaṃ ... ullāpitavanta uccaghitavantaḥ (WT uccaggh°), *who yelled derisively and laughed at that B.*; Śikṣ 12.15 uccagghantaḥ prakrāmeyuḥ, *would depart sneering* (at not receiving promised food); 13.1 devatā uccagghanti vivādayanti (a Bodhisattva who fails in his duty); 49.12 (prose) evaṃ vijṛmbhamāṇā uccagghanto; AsP 232.(12–)13 (te vijṛmbhamānā) hasanta uccagghayanto likhiṣyanti; 18 parasparam uccagghayamānā (v.l. °yanto) likhiṣyanti; 385.13 anyān ... avamaṃsyate uccagghayiṣyati ullāpayiṣyati kutsayiṣyati paṃsayiṣyati; 388.19.

uccagghana, nt., and °**nā** (to prec.; sometimes written with gh for ggh), *mocking, laughing at*: Mvy 5226 °nam (followed by **ullāpanam**); SP 482.6 (ya evaṃ) sūtrāntalekhakānām uccagghanaṃ kariṣyanty ullapiṣyanti; LV 431.18 hāsyoccagghanavivarjana- (so read for Lefm. °occaṭyana°); Śikṣ 45.7 uccagghanāṃ tarjanāṃ ca; 185.1 uccaghanāṃ (read -ggh-) sahate, unmananāṃ kutsanāṃ sahate; 271.6 nāsty uccagghanollāpana-dānam, *there is no giving with sneers and derisive yells.*

uccaṃgama, m. (uccaṃ, adv., = Pali id., see Childers, plus gama, *going aloft*), a kind of bird: Divy 476.10 ff.; 480.11.

[**uccaṭyana**, LV 431.18, error for **uccagghana**, q.v.]

uccataraka, adj. (cf. Pali uccatara, see PTSD s.v. ucca; Skt. uccaistara), *higher*: Mvy 8603 na nīcatarake niṣaṇṇā uccatarake āsane niṣaṇṇāyāglānāya dharmaṃ deśayiṣyāmaḥ.

uccati, MIndic for Skt. ucyate, *is said*: Mv ii.101.2.

Uccadhvaja, nt., n. of a palace in the Tuṣita heaven: LV 29.14 °jaṃ nāma tuṣitālaye mahāvimānaṃ.

uccandra-bhakta, adj., *eating at night* (? *in the last part of the night*, if Skt. Lex. definition of uccandra cited in BR is correct; rather, *when the moon has risen*?): °tāḥ MSV i.15.1 (as an **ādīnava**).

uccalana, see **an-ucc°**.

uccā- (adv., Vedic), as in Pali in cpds., *aloft, on high, high(ly)*: uccā-pragṛhītān SP 75.6 (most mss.; ed. uccān pra° with 1 ms.).

uccāvaca-tā (to Skt. uccāvaca), *state of being greater or less*; *variation*: Mv i.59.5 antarā ca °tā āyuṣaḥ (sc. manuṣyāṇām), *and between them there was variation of* (length of) *life*.

ucchaṅkha-, ucchaṅga-, utsaṅga-, cpd. with -pāda (or -caraṇa), (= Pali ussaṅkha-pāda,) ep. of a mahāpuruṣa (esp. Buddha), no. 7 of the 32 lakṣaṇa; orig. form, etym., and mg. obscure; acc. to Pali DN comm. ii.446.28 ff. it means that the soles of the feet can be seen as they walk, because 'the ankles are fixed high'; if from utsaṅga, *having feet characterized by a 'lap'* (an up-curve under the foot, making the sole visible?). Tib. on Mvy 260 says *having the ankle-bone* (or, *joint of the ankle-bone*) *not visible* (so one Chin. version, and Jap.); but Tib. on Bbh 375.14, cited by Wogihara, *having feet not uneven*; another Chin. gloss (also cited in Mvy 260, and elsewhere, Burnouf infra) refers the epithet to the *knees*; Gv 399.24 glosses suvyaktaparamopaśobhitopari-pādacchavikusumagarbhātirekaprabhāsvarā (not very clear or specific). These northern interpretations make the impression of floundering in a morass of ignorance. See Burnouf, Lotus, 573. Forms: utsaṅga-pāda Mvy 260 (but Mironov ucchaṅkha-); LV 106.1; Dharmas 83 (v.l. utsaṅkha-); utsaṅga-caraṇa Bbh 375.14; 378.19; 379.9; 381.10; ucchaṅga-pāda LV 429.13–14; ucchaṅkha-pāda, Mironov Mvy (see above); Mv i.226.16; ii.29.19; 304.19 (the mss. clearly intend this all three times! correct Senart's text); Gv 399.24 (note also v.l. utsaṅkha- in Dharmas 83, above). This form ucchaṅkha is closest to the Pali; the very obscurity of its etymology may argue for its originality.

ucchaṅga, nt. = 2 **utsaṅga**, q.v.; and see prec.

[**ucchata**, Mmk 371.24, 25; 372.13; read ucchrita, or possibly **ucchṛta**, q.v., cf. 373.12, 21.]

ucchada- (**1**) (= Pali ussada; = **ucchādana**, q.v.), *shampooing, rubbing down*: KP 152.2 ucchada-snapana-parimardana-bhedana-vikiraṇa-vidhvaṃsana-dharmaḥ (of the body); (**2**) in Śikṣ 208.11 -sāntarocchada-paṭikobhaya-kṛtopadhāneṣu paryaṅkeṣu śayitvā; Bendall and Rouse app. understand ucchada as some kind of *cloth* (cf. **ucchadaka**); but the preceding sāntara, which certainly goes closely with what follows it, is hard to interpret on that theory, and suggests em. to **sāntarottara** (q.v.), a cpd. known to Pali; it might mean here ... *having cushions made on both sides with woolen cloths inside and outside*; (**3**) in Av i.354.10 Speyer's em. is certainly wrong. The ms. is quoted as prāptaucchadakāyaś ca; certainly ucchada = **utsada** (1), Pali ussada, *elevation* on the 7 parts of the body which show this feature in a mahāpuruṣa; Tib. mtho ba confirms this. Acc. to Speyer, Tib. has mdun, *fore-part*, before that word; but surely Tib. read, or intended, bdun, *seven*, and we must read sapto- for prāptau-; the cpd. means *with a body possessing the 7 high places* or *protuberances* (see under utsada (1), and cf. Bbh 375.20 saptotsadakāyaḥ). — Add to (**2**): my suggestion on Śikṣ 208.11 is made dubious by sottarocchada-paṭa (ms.; ed. em. sottaracch°), adj., MPS 34.68 and 69.

ucchadaka, m. (? cf. **ucchada, utsada**, Pali ussada), only noted SP 341.14 (vs) bahu-ucchadakāś caiva bahurūpavicitritāḥ (dattāḥ, viz. to monasteries); Burnouf *coussins*; Kern *elegant objects*; Tib. for the pāda reads kun dgaḥ dag dad ḥchag sa byin, in which I cannot discern a rendering of anything which ucchadaka could represent; ḥchag sa = caṅkrama, *place of promenade* (for monks); neither *high places* nor *cloths* seem to fit here.

uccharkara, adj. (subst.? n. sg. °raḥ; so Mironov; Kyoto ed.ucchargara, ucchakara, var. ucarkara, and in Index ucakara, uccharkara; evidently from ud plus śarkarā), *stony* (*stony ground*?): Mvy 9338–9 = (ḥ)gram sa, gram pa; Das cites gram sa, *stony*, = uccharkara.

ucchava, MIndic (AMg. id., cf. Pali ussava) for utsava, *festival, festivity*: Śikṣ 365.7.

ucchahati, °**te**, MIndic (cf. Pali ussahati and Pkt. ucchāha = utsāha) for Skt. utsahate, *can, is able*: °hate Av ii.21.15; °hanti Mv i.27.10, 13.

ucchādaka, m. (cf. next), *shampooer, rubber-down*: Bbh 379.12 °kaḥ snāpakaś ca.

ucchādana (= Pali id., also Skt., but see below),

in Mv ii.269.15 and 278.1, ucchādana-(in 278.1 Senart em. āchādana-)-parimardana-svapna- (278.1 supana-) -bhedana-vikiraṇa-vidhvaṃsana-dharma, ep. of the body; corresp. to Pali anicc'ucchādana-parimaddana-bhedana-viddhaṃsana-dhammo, e. g. DN i.76.18, of which I believe the true interpretation was given by Rhys Davids, Dialogues 1 (1899), p. 87 and note; ucchādana and parimardana are primarily shampooers' terms, *shampooing and rubbing down* (so Skt.), but with double entente (not recognized in Pali comms.) also *destruction and wiping out*; BR suggested that Skt. ucchādana was MIndic for utsādana, which means both *rubbing down* and *destruction*; Skt. śātayati, *cuts off, destroys* (n. act. śātana), and root śad-, *fall* (n. act. śādana, *das Ausfallen*), may also be concerned, at least in part; see **śatana,** used in a cpd. very similar to that of Mv above; parimardana is noted in Skt. and MIndic only of shampooing (so also Mvy 6779), but the verb Skt. parimardati means also *crushes, destroys*. In KP 152.2 **ucchada** (q.v.) must have been limited to its shampooers' mg., since snapana follows. But in some BHS texts **śatana,** q.v., is substituted, eliminating that mg. and bringing in exclusively what I (with Rh.D.) regard as the secondary, punning mg. of the Pali cpd. Rhys Davids renders *erasion, abrasion,* admitting that the pun is untranslatable. In American gangsters' jargon, *to rub out* means *to obliterate, kill*. We might render Mv: (the body) *which is characterized by rubbing down* (*'off'*), *wiping away* (*'out'*), *sleep* (or *dreams*, often symbol of impermanence; here, too, a sort of word-play), *breaking up, scattering, destruction.*

ucchādita, ppp. (to Pali ucchādeti = Skt. utsādayati, see s.v. **ucchādana**; ger. ucchādya recorded in Skt., BR s.v. ucchādana), *shampooed, anointed*: Mv i.213.10 = ii.16.14 (prose) ucchādita-snāpita-viśada-gātro; i.217.14 °gātraṃ.

ucchādya, ger. (to *ucchādayati, MIndic for avachād°, § 3.54, cf. AMg. ucchāiya, *covered*, Ratnach., = avachādita), *covering*: LV 227.11 (prose) svavadanāni vastrair ucchādya (all mss.; only Calc. āchādya).

ucchitya? seemingly ger.; so mss., Divy 103.22 ... unmādam api prāpnoty ucchitya vā kālaṃ karoti. Ed. em. ucchritya, which seems to make no sense; it means *having lifted, raised up*, trans., and there is no object here; even if intrans., *having risen*, I do not see that it makes sense. There is some corruption, but I see no good em.

(**ucchinna,** ppp. (Skt.), *cut off*: SP 43.12 (prose) ucchinno 'smi buddhayānād iti vaded, *would say 'I am cut off from the Buddha-vehicle'*. Mss. vary and text has been questioned (Kern, Transl., adopts another reading), but it is supported by Tib. ṅa ni saṅs rgyas kyi theg pa bcad pa ḥo.)

ucchiraska, adj. (= Skt. ucchiras; Skt. has -śiraska in other cpds., but this form may have -ka m.c.), *with head uplifted*: Jm 119.21 (vs) krodhocchiraskān iva kṛṣṇasarpān.

[**ucchihitvā,** in Mv ii.127.12; 128.16; 130.2 (sādhu ca suṣṭhu ca abhisaṃskāreṇa) uc°, is a mere graphic corruption for utthihitvā (ger. of utthihati = uttiṣṭhati); cf. LV 254.21 and 256.4 utthito, in a parallel passage, and § 2.22. Senart doubtfully assumes that it is 'equivalent' to utthihitvā; this form should rather be put into the text.]

ucchu (m.; = Pali id., Skt. ikṣu), *sugar-cane*: Mv i.241.11 (vs) ucchusamavarṇaṃ (of Dīpaṃkara), *of color like sugar-cane*. So read also with Senart in same vs i.236.17 (mss. corrupt). And in RP 59.5 (vs) jñānaṃ tatra utpādaye cchu ivātra, we may understand utpādaye(t) (u)cchu, or possibly (i)cchu, as in Pkt.

ucchurita, ppp. (to ud plus Skt. churayati), *beset, bestrewn*: Divy 594.28 (vs) jvālākalāpocchuritormicakram (samudram).

Ucchuṣma, n. of a deity: Mvy 4332.

ucchṛta, ppp. (hyper-Skt., if not corruption, for Skt. ucchrita; cf. **utsṛta**), *raised*: SP 235.14 (vs) śuṣkapāṃsur itocchṛtaḥ (both edd., no v.l.), for ita(s) ucch°; also Mmk 373.12 (= ucchrita 21), see **ucchata.**

uccheda, nt. (m. in Skt.), *cutting off, destruction*: Laṅk 10.5 f. (prose) anyathā dṛśyamāna (= °ne) ucchedam (n. sg.; or for uccheda plus m, Hiatusbridger?) āśraye (so read with v.l. for °yaḥ), *if the basis* (of the universe, or of consciousness) *is viewed otherwise*, (it is) *destruction* (acc. to Chin. cited in note, *of insight*; or, perhaps, simply *ruin, fatal consequences*?). Suzuki *nihilism* (see **śāśvatoccheda**), but this seems hardly appropriate to this context.

ucchedana; f. °**nī,** adj. (= Pali id.; in Skt. nt. subst.), *cutting off, destroying*, or *destroyer*: Jm 103.10 °nī vittavatāṃ kulānāṃ (surā). Same line in Pali Jāt. v.16.27.

[?**uccheṣṭum,** v.l. ucchreṣṭum, infin., *to send forth, emit, hurl out*: Divy 186.5 (nāgo 'ṅgāravarṣam) ucch° ārabdhaḥ (against a monk). But ud plus śiṣ can hardly have the required meaning, and the v.l., tho nonsensical, seems to point in the right direction: read utsraṣṭum, from ud plus sṛj (or a MIndic or false hyper-Skt. form thereof).]

(**ucchoṣa,** (m.; Skt., see Schmidt, Nachtr.), *drying up, extirpation*: Mmk 495.15 (vs) read, sarva (or sarve) ucchoṣam (text sarvecchoṣam) āyānti (meter is thus corrected).)

ucchraya (m.; = **samucchraya,** q.v.), *body, bodily existence*: SP 145.12 (vs) sa paścime cocchrayi ... (Also used as in Skt. in sense of *height*, e. g. SP 159.9, prose.)

ucchrāpayati (= Pali ussāpeti; VS 23.26 ucchrāpaya, isolated; caus. to ud plus śri; see also **ucchrāyayati, ucchrepayati**), *raises, sets up*: LV 193.6 (vs) prākāra ucchrāpitā(ḥ); Mv i.176.6 (vs) ucchrāpita-dharmadhvajā; ii.112.18 patākān ucchrāpayanti; 343.22 (vs) (dhvajāna koṭinayutāsahasrā) ucchrāpayetsu (aor.); Av i.384.10 patākāḥ ... ucchrāpitā(ḥ).

ucchrāyayati (caus. to ud plus śri; = **ucchrāpayati,** q.v.), *raises, sets up*: Divy 76.6 (yaṣṭir) ucchrāyitā; 77.20; 466.16, 20 śarīrasaṃghāta ucchrāyitaḥ (in 76.6; 77.20 ed. em. ucchrāpi°).

ucchrepana (nt.; nom. act. to next), *the lifting up*: Bbh 379.1 (bhaiṣajyaṃ ca) dattvā vyādhy-avanatocchrepanān mātrāśī ca ...

ucchrepayati, °**te** (= **ucchrāpayati,** q.v.; cf. prec.; on form see § 38.65), *raises, sets up*: LV 213.18 °pitaṃ vaijayantāsamaṃ; 351.7 °pito dharmadhvaja(ḥ); 394.22 (vs) °payasva mahadharmayūpaṃ; 399.19 (vs) °paya ... tathāgatadhvajaṃ; 413.17 (prose) °paya mahādharmadhvajam; Suv 62.8 (vs) °pitaṃ dharmadhvajam (note in prose 90.11 ucchrayiṣyasi, v.l. ucchrāpayiṣyasi).

ucchvāsa-praśvāsa, m., = **āśvāsa-praśvāsa,** q.v.: Śikṣ 42.5.

ucyati (only Vedic, and not quite in this sense; here perhaps back-formation from ppp. ucita, the only form known in Skt. and MIndic), *suits, is pleasing*: Mv i.348.18 (prose) tad yuṣmākaṃ kiṃ varam ucyati, *so what boon seems good to you?*

ujjaṅkikā, some kind of attitude or behavior which monks must avoid in begging food: Mvy 8546 nojjaṅkikayā (instr.). Tib. ḥjol thabs su (? perhaps *with robe dragging*, sc. on the ground?); Chin. (here) apparently *pulling at clothes while walking*; elsewhere, acc. to Wogihara, Lex. 41, Chin. *walking on tiptoe*, and so Jap. on Mvy. The pw 7.322 says the 'correct' reading would be ujjakṣikā, and Wogihara, Lex. 41, suggests that the corresponding Pali is ujjhaggikā (or rather, by em. ujjagghikā), Vin. iv.187.16, which means *laughing, derision*, see **uccagghati**; this seems indeed quite possible.

ujjaṅgala, adj. (= Pali id.; defined DN comm. ii.586.22 by visama, Vv comm. 335.15 by jaṅgalaṃ, lūkhadhūsaro anudako bhūmippadeso ... jaṅgalato pi ukkaṃsena jaṅgalaṃ, on Vv 84.5), *desert, waste* (land): SP 233.2 °le pṛthivīpradeśe; AsP 429.4 (pṛthivīpradeśā ya) ūṣarā ujjaṅgalā(ḥ); Mv ii.207.5, 8 (vss) ujjaṅgalo ca jaṅgalo (Senart, Index, treats ujj° as n. pr.).

ujjighrant, pres. pple. (cf. Skt. Gr. ujjighra; otherwise no form of ud plus ghrā seems to be recorded), *sniffing, smelling* (at food): Prāt 533.8 nojjighrantaḥ piṇḍapātaṃ paribhokṣyāmaḥ. (Same passage cited from a Stein ms. fragment, La Vallée Poussin JRAS 1913.846, top.)

Ujjitapara (mss. mostly Ujita°; Senart Ujjhita°, which seems implausible), n. of a former Buddha: Mv i.141.2.

ujju, adj. (= Pali id., beside uju; Skt. ṛju; cf. next, **ṛjju,** and **anujjuka**), *straight, right*; usually in vss where jj could be m.c., but once in prose in Mv iii.225.1 ujjucittā; the rest in vss: Mv iii.436.3 °gateṣu; LV 133.20 ujju karitva kāyaṃ; 138.20 ujju-bhraṣṭā; 295.8 sadojjupraṣṭho (so read; = sadā ujju°).

ujjuka (= prec., q.v.; also **ṛjuka**; Pali id., beside ujuka): SP 125.14 (vs) dṛṣṭiṃ kurvāmi ujjukām; in SP 324.2 ms. K′ indicates ujjuka for text -rjuka (ṛj°).

[**Ujjhitapara,** see **Ujjita°.**]

Ujjhebhaka Toṇehāraka, n. of a king: Mv iii.382.10–11 (prose); called **Toṇehāra** 386.9 (vs).

-ujña-ka, ifc. Bhvr. (to *ujñā = Pali uññā for Skt. avajñā; see § 3.55), *contempt*, in a-śaṭh'-ūjñakāś ca (ū may be in saṃdhi for a-u), *free from deceitfulness and contempt*: Dbh.g. 6(342).21.

uṭṭaṅkikā, some kind of attitude or behavior which monks must avoid in begging food: Mvy 8545 noṭṭaṅkikayā (instr.). Tib. braṅ bas (? braṅ *breast*; also *dwelling*); Chin. (here), perhaps *walking with the palm of the foot* (? or, *with hands touching* the feet?); acc. to Wogihara, Lex. 41, another Chin. renders *limping* (*das Hinken*); Jap. *squatting* (at the entrance of a house).

uḍaya (m. or nt.; = AMg. id., Skt. uṭaja), *hut*: Mmk 37.3 ekānte uḍayaṃ kṛtvā prativastavyam; 83.5; 106.21; 113.18; 121.20; 145.19; 524.19; 573.18.

uḍigalla (or oḍi°?), only in **gūthoḍi°**, q.v. See Lévi's note, Karmav (22-) 25 f., where Dravidian origin is suggested: Telugu oḍagala-vādu (= Hindi -wāla), *sweeper* (in the Indian sense, cleaner of toilets); Tamil oḍugāl, *conduite d'eau.*

uḍḍara-, in °ra-dharma-vihāriṇam (acc. sg.), Thomas, ap. Hoernle MR 119, cf. 121 note 22 (from Ratnarāśi Sūtra), conjecturally rendered (*practising*) *heretical* (*principles*).

Uḍḍiyāna = **Oḍḍiyāna**: Sādh 361.16.

Uḍḍiyānaka = prec.: Māy 97 (see Lévi p. 105 ff.).

? **utacchiyam,** Ud xviii.22, is prob. a mere corruption: yo rāgam utacchiyam aśeṣaṃ = Pali Sn 2, yo rāgam udacchidā asesaṃ, *who has cut off passion without remainder.* If a substitute for ud-acchidat is intended (which should end in a long syllable; °yaṃ?), it would seem to show t for d (by hyper-Sktism? § 2.29) and y for the second d (Pktic). I do not understand Chakravarti's note.

utapta(vant), m.c. for Skt. utta°, *glowing* etc.: utapta Dbh.g. 41(67).10; °ta-vatī Śikṣ 337.12 (= uttap° 7, where meter also requires uta°).

utittira, onomat., a sound said to be uttered exceptionally by a tittira bird; see MSV i.118.10; 120.18. (Tib. says only *a different sound.*)

utkaca, adj. (in Skt. rare and doubtful in mg.), *with hair standing up*: Mvy 9197; Bhīk 28b.4; MSV iii.7.14 (see s.v. **prakaca**).

Utkaṭa, m., nt., or °**ṭā,** f., n. of a town (**droṇamukha,** °**khya,** q.v.): Mvy 5285 °ṭo nāma droṇamukham; Divy 620.12 °ṭaṃ nāma droṇa° (acc.), 28 utkaṭadroṇamukhyaṃ; 621.10 yenotkaṭaṃ droṇamukhaṃ (nom., nt.), 19 °ṭān (abl.); fem. 620.21 °ṭāṃ nāma droṇamukhaṃ (acc.), °ṭā 26. From a verbally close Pali parallel DN i.87.6 it appears that the town called in Pali Ukkaṭṭhā (see DPPN) is the same; see **Puṣkarasārin.**

utkaṭṭati, or (MIndic) **ukka°** (see s.v. **kaṭṭati**), *takes out*: Mv iii.158.13 yamalakāto (see **yamalaka**) modakaṃ ukkaṭṭetvā; 431.7 taṃ bhāṇḍaṃ sarvaṃ ukkaṭṭitaṃ (sc. from a river); in Mv ii.249.11 read mama hṛdayo udumbare utkaṭṭito sthapito (Senart with one ms. utkaṇṭhito, v.l. utkarito; in the other two passages above Senart em. ukkaḍḍh-).

utkaṇṭhati, and ppp. utkaṇṭhita (cf. next; in Skt. only *longs for*; *longing*; but Pali ukkaṇṭhati also *is annoyed,* °ṭhita *annoyed*), *is annoyed*; *annoyed*; the ppp. in Mv ii.272.7 rājā śrutvā utkaṇṭhito evaṃ jāto, *the king, hearing* (this), *became annoyed, as follows* (here certainly not *desirous*!); similarly ii.274.11 so utkaṇṭhito (context makes *desirous* impossible). In Bbh 193.6 (tair bodhisattvaḥ lūhaiḥ stokair asatkṛtya dhandhaṃ) ca labdhair notkaṇṭhyate na paritasyati, prob. *is not made annoyed* (pass. of caus.). There may be other cases; many are ambiguous.

utkaṇṭhā (see prec.; Pali ukkaṇṭhā), possibly *annoyance, mental distress*: AsP 494.8, see s.v. **paritasana.**

Utkarika, n. of a merchant: Divy 227.26 tatrānyataraś cotkariko nāma baṇig ... Cf. **Otkarika** (the same person as Utk°). There seems to be no reason to connect this n. pr. with aukarika (okkarika), qq.v., as has been assumed by Feer, Speyer (on Av, Index, s.v. okkarika) and Cowell and Neil (Index to Divy). But perhaps we should read cautk° in 227.26 and assume Otk° as the name.

utkarṣaṇa (nt.), °**ṇā,** and °**ṇa-tā** (= Pali (att-)-ukkaṃsana, °nā; cf. next), *praise, laudation, exaltation* (regularly of oneself, or one's own): LV 32.14–15 ātmān-utkarṣaṇa-tā (i. e. ātma-an-utk°); KP 1.15 (vs) ātmotkarṣaṇi (loc.); 135.6–7 (prose) ātmaśīlotkarṣaṇā; Bbh 158.4 ātmotkarṣaṇā; Śikṣ 126.6 svapakṣotkarṣaṇa-(vacana).

utkarṣayati (cf. prec.; not in this sense Skt.; = Pali ukkaṃsati, °seti), *exalts*, i. e. *praises*: gdve., Śikṣ 197.10 sacec cañcalendriyo (rājā) bhavati, utkarṣayitavyaṃ (sc. bhikṣuṇā), *if* (the king) *is flighty* (unstable), *praise must be bestowed* (saying: It is very meritorious on your part that your kingdom contains so many worthy monks and brahmans who live undisturbed by thieves etc.). Acc. to Bendall, Tib. has bstan par bya ḥo, and accordingly Transl. renders 'the Brother should admonish him' (more exactly, the Tib. means *elucidate, make intelligible*). But I do not see how the BHS word can mean this. The mg. of the Pali word is appropriate here; by encouraging flattery the king is to be strengthened in a good course.

utkārika, m., *the expression evam*: Mvy 7618 = Tib. de bzhin no zhes bya ba (Chin. similarly). There is a var. udgārikaḥ (cf. Skt. udgāra, *sound, utterance*?), but Mironov utkā° without v.l. I do not understand the etym. (ut-kṛ, °karoti, or °kirati?).

***utkāreti** (°rayati, °rati?), ger. °ritvā, *having emptied*: Mv i.327.3 (prose) (bhājanāni ...) pūretvā utkāritvā, *having filled and emptied the pots.* The mg. is clear; etym.? to utkirati? Senart em. utkiritvā, without good reason.

utkāśa, m., see next. Perhaps utkāśaḥ, alone, is to be read in this sense for text utkāsaḥ in Gv 307.23 (prose); after a Tathāgata's parinirvāṇa, by a follower of his, udvegasaṃjananārthaṃ dhārmika utkāsaḥ (i. e. °śaḥ?) kṛto 'bhūt: aho bateyaṃ ... mahādharmolkāntardhāsyatīti saṃvegajananīyā kathā kṛtā. But cf. **utkāsa.**

utkāśana-śabda, m. (ud plus kāś; cf. next), *conspicuous, vigorous pronouncement* (so Tib. on Mvy): Mvy 2799; Divy 517.25 bhagavatotkāśaśabdaḥ kṛtaḥ ... parivrājako (26) bhagavata utkāśanaśabdaṃ śuśrāva; also 27.

utkāśa-śabda, m. = prec., q.v.: Divy 517.25. See also utkāśa, m., perhaps used in this same sense.

utkāsa, (**1**) (m.), *clearing of the throat* (= Skt. utkāsana): LV 416.11 (vs) utkāsaśabdu napi śrūyati tanmuhūrtaṃ (mss. vary greatly, but Tib. lud paḥi sgra confirms this form and mg.); (**2**) m. utkāsaḥ, see s.v. **utkāśa**; if the theory there stated be rejected, the word would have to be classed with (1) and would seem to mean something like *hemming and hawing*, or rather *ominous sound* (calling attention to the future disappearance of the dharma), in Gv 307.23.

-utkira, m. (in Skt. adj., *aufhäufend*), *heap, something thrown* or *dug up*, in mūṣī-utkira, see s.v. **mūṣī**.

Utkīlaka, m., n. of a mountain: Divy 450.9, 11; 455.28, 29.

(**utkīlayati** (= Skt., pw 7.322, also 1.220 utkīlita; wrongly defined in Divy Index and for Divy passage in pw 7.322), *opens*: Divy 528.9, 11 nagaram (a stronghold of ogresses) utkīlayitvānyatra gacchatha (11 gatvāvasthitāḥ), *having opened up the city*...; Mmk 395.19 sādhakecchayā utkīlayati mocayati yathāvyavasthāyām upasthāpayati, *opens, frees*, etc.)

utkuṭa (?reading stated in note to be 'not clear'; cf. utkuṭuka?), seems to designate some kind of entertainer: Śikṣ 330.16 (vs; after naṭa-nartaka jhallaka-mallāḥ) utkuṭa-śobhika-hāraka (qq.v.)... (Tib. cited as bzhugs; not clear to me.)

utkuṭa-sthāyin (cf. prec. and next), lit. *remaining in a squatting position*(?), designation of certain ascetics, app. Ājīvikas (cf. note in ed., and 332.1): °yina ekacarāṇāṃ Śikṣ 332.7.

utkuṭuka, adj. (cf. **utkuṭa-**; acc. to BR, occurs in Skt. (Suśruta) only as utkaṭuka or utkuṭaka; the Pali form is app. only ukkuṭika; AMg. usually ukkuḍua, °ḍuga, °ḍuyā, but also ukkaḍuya), *squatting* on the heels (see PTSD s.v. ukkuṭika for detailed description); as adj. applied to persons, to postures, also in comp. either adjectivally or adverbially; adv. utkuṭukaṃ(?), °kena, *in squatting posture*: °kā niṣaṇṇā (n. sg. f.) Av i.315.11; °kāṃ niṣādayitvā Bhīk 16a.1 *having made her sit squatting*, but in 10b.3 °ṭukena niṣadya, *sitting in a squatting posture* (adv.); in 10a.4 °ṭukāṃ niṣādya, in sense = 16a.1, °kaṃ either adv., or MIndic (or corruption?) for °kāṃ; °kena adv. also Mv i.144.10 (na...) bodhisattvā mātuḥ kukṣigatā utkuṭukena (so read, Senart °ṭakena, mss. utkutumbakeṇa) pārśvena vā yathā kathaṃcid vā sthitā bhavanti (but paryaṅkam ābhumjitvā); in i.213.7; ii.16.11 situation is the same, but adj. is used, na utkuṭuko (so Senart with both mss. ii.16.11; in i.213.7 Senart °ṭiko, but one ms. has -uko); in cpds., Mvy 6709 °kāsanam, Tib. tsog tsog por; 9275 °ka-sthaḥ, Tib. cog (read tsog) bur; see next; °ka-**prahāṇam** (see this), an ascetic exercise, = Pali ukkuṭika-(p)padhāṇaṃ, Mv iii.412.17 (vs) = Divy 339.24 = Pali Dhp. 141; °ka-sthaṇḍila-śayanaiś ca LV 249.4, *and by sleeping in a squatting posture or on bare ground*; 258.15 (vs) utkuṭuka-dhyāyi (so read with best mss., metr. superior to Lefm.'s reading utkuṭa-dh°), *meditating in a squatting posture*; °ṭuka-sthitena, adv., *while sitting in a squatting posture*, Bbh 153.12; 181.20.

utkuṭukikā (to prec.), *squatting posture*: Mvy 8548 notkuṭukikayā (instr.); Tib. rtsog (read tsog?) bus ma yin. (Jäschke and Das record tsog pu, *squatting*; the French Catholic Dict. tsog pu or °bu; see prec.)

utkubjāpayati, caus. (to Pali denom. ukkujjati), *causes to be set* (*right side*) *up*: °yiṣyatha MSV iv.140.15.

utkumbhati, prob. *rears* (of a balky horse; so guessed from context): KP 108.2 (yatra...) aśva(ḥ) skhalati utkumbhati vā khaḍunka- (q.v.)-kriyā vā karoti, *when a horse stumbles or rears or acts viciously*. Tib. seems to have no correspondent for this word; the several Chin. versions, likewise, fail to clarify it; they seem to have only two verbal expressions for three of the BHS.

utkūla, adj., *high, rising*; only with nikūla, *low, descending*, and usually in cpd. utkūla-nikūla (cf. Pali ukkūla-vikūla, interpreted as *high and low*, AN comm. ii.35.21), *high and low*, hence *uneven*: Mvy 2708 °lam, and 2709 nikūlam (the Tib. definitions, śaṅ ṅam śoṅ 2708, ḥbar ḥbur ram mtho dman 2709, seem to refer confusedly to the pair of words together, and mean *uneven, high-and-low*); LV 77.17 utkūlanikūlāś ca pṛthivīpradeśāḥ samāḥ samavasthitāḥ, *and the high-and-low* (*uneven*) *places became even*; 272.17 utkūla-nikūla-sama-kara-caraṇa-gatiḥ (of the Bodhisattva's gait), ... *making even places that were uneven*; MSV i.14.19 (as an ādīnava). The cpd. utkūla-nikūla occurs VS 30.14, where it is unexplained in comm. and not definable by context; utkūla occurs once or twice besides; nikūla is hardly recorded otherwise, and seems to be unknown in MIndic (Pali has vikūla instead, above).

Utkūlaka, m., n. of a mountain (= **Kūlaka**, q.v.): Divy 450.10. Cf. preceding.

utkṛṣṭataraka, adj. (compv. of utkṛṣṭa plus ka), *rather superior*: Bbh 16.8 (prose) utkṛṣṭatarakebhyo guṇebhyo na vicchandya ... nihīnatarakeṣu guṇeṣu samādāpayati.

utkṛṣṭikā, prob. *cocking* or *throwing back* or *up* (of the head): Mvy 8541 notkṛṣṭikayā; Tib. (mgo mi gyog, *head not covered*; or) mgo mi brdze (= our def.); °kā-kṛta, *one who has adopted the above attitude*: Mvy 8607 °kṛtāya (Tib. only brdzes, or rdzes, pa, as above); Prāt 536.4 °kṛtasya (but here Chin. is said to mean *qui a la poitrine découverte*).

utkoṭana, nt. (see below), or (var. in Kyoto ed.; and Mironov without v.l.) khoṭana, nt.: °nam Mvy 8423. Both form and mg. obscure; occurs between bhikṣupaiśunyam and duṣṭhulārocanam. Tib. skyo sṅogs (var. brṅogs) byed pa, *causing quarrels*; Chin. *disturbing the saṃgha*; Jap. *raising questions about a matter already decided*. The last implies derivation from **utkoṭayati**, q.v. Skt. has nothing helpful on either reading. Pali ukkoṭana-ka, Vin. ii.94.7, means *reopening a settled question* (wrongly PTSD), just as the verb ukkoṭeti seems always so used. But ukkoṭana is defined by DN comm. i.79.30 as *taking bribes* (to obstruct justice), which finds support in AMg. ukkoḍā, *bribery* (Ratnach.), and seems to fit better the Pali occurrences; it is always found in a list of instances of trickery and deceit (typical is DN i.5.22 ukkoṭana-vañcana-nikati-sāciyogā paṭivirato); cf. the Skt. root kuṭ. If khoṭana (Skt. Gr., *limping*) is the true reading, I know of no plausible interpretation.

utkoṭayati (= Pali ukkoṭeti; cf. prec.), *reopens a question already legally settled*: Prāt 503.4 (yaḥ punar bhikṣur jānaṃ saṃghena yathādharmaṃ) nikṣiptam adhikaraṇaṃ punaḥ karmaṇy utkoṭayet, pātayantikā.

utkrośa, m. (to ut-kruś; nowhere recorded except as n. of a bird), *outcry*: LV 230.5 (vs) utkrosu (n. sg.) mukto, and 8 utkrosu (acc. sg.) kṛtvā aho mama ekaputro!; 232.20 (vs) utkrosu (mss. utkrāsu, utkāsu) kṛtvā dharaṇitale nirasto; Gv 326.6 mahāntam ārtasvaram utkrośam akārṣuḥ. Uncertain is Divy 453.21 (in a list of five individuals who sleep little at night) utkrośa (v.l. utkoṇa) ṛṇī; possibly *a debtor in case of an outcry* (made against him by his creditor? understanding utkrośe). But Tib., as translated in the note p. 709, is said to render utkrośaḥ *the red duck* (see below; in Skt. a bird, *Seeadler*), and seems to omit ṛṇī; probably read for this prāṇī (below). Divy Index *watchman*(?); implausible; PTSD compares this word with Pali ukkusa, a bird, apparently *osprey* (= kurara). Lacuna in this story MSV i.149.10; N. Dutt, on basis of Tib. srog chags (*living being*) ṅur pa (*red duck*), conjectures utkruśa-prāṇī. Should not Tib. be corrected to ṅu ba, *weep*(*ing*), = ut-kruś-?

utkrośate (not recorded in this sense), *cries for, demands* (alms): Divy 473.11 (Śakro...) dvāri sthitvā bhaikṣyam utkrośate.

utkrośana (nt.; = **utkrośa,** q.v.), *outcry*: Gv 326.21 mahāntam ārtasvaram utkrośana-śabdaṃ śrutvā.

utkrośayati (denom. to AMg. ukkosa, see below), *exalts, magnifies*: AsP 419.4 ātmānam utkrośayati parān paṃsayati. The AMg. ukkosa is derived by Sheth and Ratnach. from utkarṣa (or utkṛṣṭa) and defined as adj., *highest, supreme*, or, as n., *pride*. If this is the true etym., our word would be a hyper-Sktism, by false etym. Possibly, however, the AMg. word may really represent a Skt. *utkrośa, which, like Eng. *a crying-up*, could conceivably have meant *glorification*. To be sure I find no record, otherwise, of such a mg. in any deriv. of ut-kruś.

utkṣipaṇa (nt.; from ut-kṣip plus -ana, but new MIndic formation, like Pali ukkhipana; cf. Skt. utkṣepaṇa), *lifting up*, nom. act.: LV 114.10 (vs) caraṇotkṣipaṇe, *in the lifting of their feet*.

utkṣipati (Skt. in mg. *lifts up*, etc.), (**1**) *lets up* in sense of *permits to ascend*, opp. **nikṣipati**: LV 186.(12–)13f. ekaikasya ca prāsādasya sopānān: pañca-pañca puruṣa-śatāny utkṣipanti sma nikṣipanti sma (*let go up and down*); teṣāṃ tathotkṣipyamāṇānāṃ nikṣipyamāṇānāṃ ca śabdo 'rdhayojane śrūyate sma; (**2**) (= Pali ukkhipati) *suspends* (from the order of monks); ppp. utkṣipta: Bhīk 29b.1 utkṣiptānuvartaka (see **anuvartaka**); similarly Mvy 8480 utkṣiptānuvṛttiḥ, *the following* (*cleaving to*) *a suspended* (monk), so Tib. spaṅs paḥi...; (**3**) *averts* (the senses, particularly the eyes, from forbidden objects): Divy 278.29 indriyāṇy utkṣipati, and in the following lines; indriyāṇy utkṣipyāvasthitāḥ MSV iii.18.11, *stood averting their eyes* (in embarrassment); in this sense = Pali (indriyāni) okkhipati from avakṣipati, see **avakṣipta**; apparently BHS utkṣ° is false Skt. for MIndic okkh°; acc. to Chin. (*eyes not cast to one side*), anutkṣiptacakṣuṣo Prāt 529.10 would belong here; curiously the Pali equivalent, Vin. iv.186.29 okkhittacakkhu (note lack of negative!), appears to mean *with downcast eyes*, which the old comm. interprets by observing that it is a sin to enter a house or sit down *looking around at this or that* (tahaṃ tahaṃ olokento), so that okkhitta-, as opposite of this, would mean essentially the same as BHS an-utkṣipta- as interpreted by Chin. But for this evidence, an-utkṣipta- might be interpreted, in accordance with Skt. usage, as *not lifted up* (thus in another way = okkhitta-).

utkṣiptaka, m. (°pta, see prec. 2, plus specifying -ka; = Pali ukkhittaka), (a monk) *that has been suspended*: MSV ii.113.12, 15, etc. Read this for utkṣepaka(-tva) MSV iii.67.11, 12; cf. 69.6.

utkṣepaka, m. (= Pali ukkhepaka, Vin. i.338.24 ff.; to **utkṣipati** 2 with -aka), *one who moves suspension* (of a monk): MSV ii.177.6 ff.; 191.7 ff. See prec. for MSV iii.67.11, 12.

utkṣepaṇīya, adj. (gdve., to **utkṣipati,** 2; = Pali ukkhepanīya, with kamma), with karman, (*ceremony*) *of suspension* (from the order): Mvy 8646 °ṇīyam (doubtless supply karma); Divy 329.10 kurutāsyotkṣepanīyaṃ (so text) karma; Bhīk 28b.4 yasya bhikṣoḥ samagreṇa bhikṣusaṃghenotkṣepaṇīyaṃ karma kṛtam; MSV ii.176.4; 201.13; penalty for refusal to recognize or correct sins, MSV iii.28.10 ff. (as in Pali Vin. ii.21.21 ff.), or for heresy, ib. 30.9 ff.

utkṣepa-lipi, n. of a kind of script: LV 126.5; followed by **nikṣepa°, vikṣepa°**, and (6) **prakṣepa-lipi**; also, line 7, utkṣepāvarta-lipi, and (in some mss., supported by Tib.) nikṣepāvarta-lipi. All these terms seem to be intended to refer to the shape of the letters, rather than to the countries where they are used. It is hardly possible to guess what the author meant by them, and the woodenly literal Tib. translations give little help; Tib. renders utkṣepa, gdeg pa, *elevation* (and āvarta, skor ba, *turn*); nikṣepa, bzhag pa or bzhog pa, *putting down*; vikṣepa (which Tib. transposes to the point in line 6 where Lefm.'s ms. A has it), rnam ḥthor, *scattering*; prakṣepa, bsnan pa, *addition, increase*.

utkhalati, see **utskhalati.**

Utkhalin, m., n. of one of the 16 devaputra guardians of the Bodhimaṇḍa: LV 277.12. (Tib. ut-ka-li.) Cf. next.

Utkhalī, or (v.l. supported as to vocalism by Tib. u-khu-li) Utkhurī, n. of a goddess, attendant on the Bodhisattva in his mother's womb: LV 66.8. Cf. prec.

utkhāṭayitar, m. (cf. Dhātup. khāḍayati = bhedane? is there some confused relation to Pali ukkheṭita, Vin. iii.97.21, *abandoned*?), *one who causes to depart from* (abl.), *to abandon*: Gv 462.23 (kalyāṇamitrāṇi) ... °tāro lokaniketāt (sc. for a Bodhisattva).

Utkhurī, see **Utkhalī.**

[**utta,** implied in (duḥkhena) cotto LV 133.16; read either cātto = ca-ātto, with ms. A, or cārto = ca-ārto (one ms. cited as cortto); Foucaux *affecté par la douleur*, which must be substantially the meaning.]

-uttaka, adj. ifc., perhaps *made, produced*: Mv ii.457.14 (prose) hastiśālāya paṭalāni ghanāni mahantāni bahujana-uttakāni, (when a fire had broken out in the elephant-stables)... *the thatches of the elephant stable, thick, great, made by many people*... This assumes a ka-extension of AMg. -utta in deva-utta, bambha-utta, *produced* (*created*) *by* (*the*) *god*(*s*), *by Brahmā* (see citation in Sheth s.v. utta). The origin of the word is obscure; Sheth and Ratnach. regard it as identical with Skt. upta, *sown*. Senart has no suggestion as to mg. or etym.

uttanūruha, adj. (ut plus tanū°), *with hair erect* (thru joy): Jm 204.18 mudottanūruhāḥ.

uttapta, ppp. (to Skt. uttapati, cf. BHS uttāpayati), orig. (and in Skt.) *purified by fire* (of metals; so also BHS, suvarṇam uttaptam Mv i.165.2); here fig., *purified, pure*, of food: uttaptottaptair upakaraṇa-viśeṣair MSV iii.19.20; 134.10; of mental and abstract qualities, Mv i.106.1 uttapta- (so mss., Senart em. °taṃ) jñānaṃ teṣāṃ pravartate; LV 8.2 smṛti-mati-gati-dhṛty-uttapta-vipula-buddheḥ, *of vast enlightenment purified by*...; 11.6 -prāmodyottapta-vipula-smṛti-saṃjanane; uttapta-kuśalamūlās te Suv 5.4; °ta-kuśalamūlena 159.6; 167.9; 171.12; °taṃ (mss. uptaṃ, but Tib. and Chin. render uttaptaṃ) kuśalamūlaṃ 172.11; °mūlānām Gv 268.3; uttaptaḥ Mvy 1816, where context suggests *earnest, strenuous*, and one of three Tib. renderings, sbyaṅs pa, means primarily *purified*, but also *exercised, trained*; **uttapta-tā,** abstr., *state of being purified*, LV 422.1 (vs) tena hitakareṇa uttaptatā-prāpta (so read, as cpd.) bodhiḥ śivā, ... *attained thru being purified*.

?**Uttaptarāṣṭra,** Senart's em. at Mv i.139.13–14 for mss. Āttapta°, Attapta°, see s.v. **Ātapta°**. But the em. may be right: *having a pure rule* or *kingdom*, see **uttapta.**

Uttaptavīrya, n. of a previous incarnation of Buddha: RP 22.20.

Uttaptavaiḍūryanirbhāsa, n. of a former Buddha: Sukh 5.19.

Uttaptaśrī, n. of a kalpa: Gv 447.3.

uttama (**1**) (nt.?), *top part* (of a building), *roof* or *top story*: Divy 321.17 (yuvatayo) rodanti veśmottame; (**2**) (m. or nt.; = Pali id., see PTSD s.v. kāsika), *upper garment*: kāśikottama-dhāriṇaḥ (mss. °vāriṇaḥ) Mv i.296.4. In Pali also, apparently, only after kāsika; (**3**) m., n. of a nāga king: Māy 247.27.

Uttara, m. (and nt., see 8) (**1**) n. of a former Buddha: Mv iii.239.2 f.; (**2**) n. of a follower of the Buddha Kāśyapa, who later became Śākyamuni: Av i.239.7; ii.23.5; 51.8; 88.1; referred to MSV i.217.13 as if concerned in the story of (**Nandīpāla**) **Ghaṭīkāra**; also MSV i.261.20; (**3**) n. of a maharṣi (perhaps = 1 or 2?): Śikṣ 189.9; (**4**) n. of a brother of Nālaka Kātyāyana: Mv iii.382.14; 383.1; (**5**) n. of a youthful (māṇava) follower of King Prasenajit (cf. DPPN Uttara 10): Divy 156.10 ff.; (**6**) n. of a merchant of Rājagṛha who became a Buddhist disciple and whose mother became a pretī (cf. DPPN Uttara 7): Av i.261.11; a like story of an Uttara of Śrāvastī, MSV iii.19.18 ff.; (7) n. of a nāga king (cf. **Uttaraka**): Mvy 3261; (8) nt., n. of the Buddha Maṅgala's city (= DPPN Uttara 19): Mv i.249.2; described in the following.

Uttaraka, n. of a nāga king (cf. **Uttara** 7): Māy 247.27.

uttarakalā, app. *further, higher art*: Jm 208.2 sottarakalānāṃ kalānāṃ. No clue has been found as to precisely what is meant.

Uttarakuru, if Senart's text is right, in Mv i.103.10 designates an *inferior* region or people in which successful Bodhisattvas are *not* reborn: °ruṣu nopapadyanti (along with pretas, asuras, and animals). But mss. all vary: utte ca kuruṣu, uttame ca kuleṣu, (one only) uttara ca kuruṣu. Doubtful. As n. of one of the dvīpas, see **dvīpa.**

uttarakuru-dvīpa-lipi, a kind of script: LV 126.4 (Tib. indicates omission of dvīpa).

Uttarakururāja, n. of a former Buddha: Mv i.140.3.

Uttarakaurava, adj. with manuṣya, *inhabiting* (the dvīpa) *Uttarakuru*: Divy 215.28 ff.

(**uttaraṇa**, nt. [as in Skt., e. g. saṃsāra-samudrottarāṇa, BR s.v. uttaraṇa], *rescue, salvation*: listed Mvy 1751 as one of the synonyms of śaraṇam, esp. as applied to the Buddha [follows tārakaḥ, followed by paritrātā].)

uttarati, false-Skt. for MIndic (Pali) otarati = **avatarati** (§ 3.54), *arrives at*: SP 302.7 (vs) śrutvā ca (sc. jñānam) adhimucyante uttaranti ca ... (one ms. only cited as otaranti; WT utt° without v.l.).

Uttaradatta, n. of a Bodhisattva: Gv 443.4.

uttaram, see s.v. **uttari.**

Uttaramati, (1) n. of a **satpuruṣa**, q.v.: SP 3.12; (2) n. of a Bodhisattva: RP 1.12; ŚsP 6.12.

uttara-manuṣyadharma, see s.v. **uttari.**

Uttaramantrin, m. pl., n. of a people: Mvy 3056.

Uttaramānuṣa, n. of a nāga king: Māy 247.26.

uttaraṃ-manuṣyadharma, see s.v. **uttari.**

Uttaraśrī, n. of a gandharva maid: Kv 5.18.

Uttarā, n. of a girl, servant of **Sujātā**: LV 268.7 ff.

uttarāgamana (nt., or m.; uttara plus āg°), *subsequent arrival* (in the world), i. e. *rebirth*; *future incarnation*: Mv i.189.1 (vs) °ne (*in a new incarnation*) kulavā maheśākhyo ... so copapadyate.

uttarāpathaka, adj. (or subst.; from °patha plus -ka), *of the north country*; *one who lives in it*: LV 381.4 (prose) °pathakau dvau bhrātarau trapuṣa-bhallikanāmakau; Mv ii.175.4 °pathakaṃ bhāṣyaṃ, *northern dialect*; 6 °pathakā vayam. (They came from Taxila, 7 takṣaśilāto.)

uttari (apparently the usual form; also **uttarī**, chiefly if not wholly m.c.; **uttariṃ**, once **uttarīṃ**; **uttare**, **°reṇa**; possibly **uttaraṃ**, but use of this as separate adv. uncertain; in prior part of cpds. uttari-, °re-, °raṃ-, besides normal Skt. uttara-; Pali apparently only uttariṃ as separate word, uttari- in prior part of cpds, besides uttara-) adv., and prep. or postposition with abl. or gen., *further, beyond*, of time, space, number, etc.; synonym of bhūyas; all the forms enumerated seem to be equivalent and interchangeable to the extent indicated above; none seem recorded in these uses in Skt. or Pkt. acc. to the dictionaries; once uttarī may be intended as n. sg. m. of an adj., Bbh 102.15 (prose) na ebhya uttarī na ebhyo bhūyān anyo hetur vidyate, *no other cause is found beyond these, greater than these* (cf. the next passages); with dependent abl., usually atas, tatas: nāsty ata uttari nāsty ato bhūyaḥ (cf. prec.) Bbh 25.17 (prose); nāta uttari nāto bhūyaḥ 36.18; (cf., without dependent, kutaḥ punar uttari kuto bhūyaḥ 297.22;) tatottarī (m.c.?) agaṇiyu tasya āsīt saṃghas ... SP 192.7 (vs; for tata uttari), *beyond that* (number), *incalculable was his assembly*; ataś ca bhūya uttari viśiṣṭatarāṃ (both edd. as cpd. uttari-vi°) ... pūjāṃ kariṣyāmi SP 412.3 (prose); tata uttari (of time) SP 160.4 (prose); ato 'py uttari (of serial numbers) LV 148.12 (prose, and repeatedly in sequel); tatottari LV 154.7 (prose! for tata ut°); tata uttarīṃ (this form is isolated) bahukalpaṃ Dbh.g. 17(353).17, *many kalpas beyond this*; ata uttari Gv 104.25; LV 239.15 (both prose; to LV corresponds Mv ii.119.5 and 120.16 where uttari has no dependent form); ato ca uttari Mv iii.55.15 (prose); tato vottari tiṣṭhet Sukh 4.12 (prose), *or should remain* (a time) *beyond that*; ato bahū uttari lokadhātu Sukh 46.1 (vs); varṣaśataṃ vā tato vottari Gv 522.6 (prose); tata uttare Dbh 48.15 (prose); atottareṇa LV 172.21 (vs; for ata ut°); uttari manuṣyadharmād ... jñānadarśanaviśeṣaṃ sākṣātkartum (263.11 °śeṣaḥ sākṣātkṛto) LV 246.16; 263.11 (both prose; cf. the cpd. uttari-manuṣya° below), ... *beyond human conditions*; with dependent gen., mama uttari yo (ed. uttariyo) viśiṣṭo LV 119.3 (vs), *who is distinguished beyond me*; naitasya (ed. ne°) ācariya uttari LV 125.5 (vs), *there is no teacher higher than he*; tasyottareṇa Mv i.2.2, Senart em., but read with mss. **pratyot°**, q.v.; i.250.5 (śloka vs) dīpaṃkarasya **ottareṇa** (see this; bad meter), prob. read °karasyottareṇa, which may mean °sya-ut°, *after Dīpaṃkara*; uttareṇa Vairambhasya mahāsamudrasya Divy 105.29 (prose) *beyond ...*; adv., without dependent: form uttari, uttari cābhyanumodayiṣyanti SP 338.3 (prose), *and further they will ...*; yad uttary arhattve pratiṣṭhāpayet 348.2 (prose), *if further he should establish them in arhatship*; dānanisargaḥ punar uttari pravartate sma LV 95.7 (prose); (tathā) cottari paryeṣate LV 245.20 (prose); uttari senām āmantrayate sma 319.19 (prose), (Māra) *further addressed his host*; Mv ii.119.5 and 120.16 (parallel to LV 239.15, above, where ata uttari); uttari viśeṣaṃ (Senart °ri-viś° as cpd.) ārabheyam Mv iii.173.4 (prose), *may I attain further* (exceptional) *distinction* (as compared with the retinue, who were now his equals); Mv iii.396.9 (prose; parallel to Pali Sn prose after 517, where uttariṃ, v.l. uttari); Sukh 10.12 (prose); RP 4.3 (vs); Śikṣ 16.14 (prose); Dbh.g. 20(356).17; 23(359).2; in some of the preceding uttari occurs in situations where we should except an adjective, which seems even more called for in the next, where, however, f. or m. gender would be demanded: (na sā strī ... saṃvidyate) yā tasyā rūpeṇa samā kutaḥ punar uttari Gv 172.21 (prose) ... *no one who would be equal to her in beauty, how much less beyond* (superior to) *her*!, and parallels in the sequel with masc. for fem., but always uttari, 172.23, 26, etc.; uttarī (prob. m.c., but cf. Bbh 102.15 above), na uttarī prārthayi (ger., or aor.?) SP 213.10, *not asking* (or, *we did not ask*) *further*; uttariṃ (not m.c., tho in vss!), Dbh.g. 6(342).9; te kalpakoṭīm athavāpi cottariṃ ... Sukh 45.6; uttare, sometimes, as in the first two, interpretable as n. sg. m. of uttara (§ 8.25), but so closely parallel in use to uttari that it is better taken as adv.: jātyā ca so viṃśatir uttare vā SP 313.8 (vs); sadṛśo 'sti na te kutottare LV 364.18 (Lefm. with mss. kutontare, Foucaux cites kutottare from a ms., and this is certainly meant); na me 'sty ato 'rtha(ḥ), ata uttare gaṇana apratimasya jñānam (so read) LV 151.4–5 (vs); kaścid uttare naivasaṃjñānāsaṃjñāyatanasamāpatter mārgaḥ LV 245.3 (prose); uttare vai nānāmiṣeṇa saṃtarpya Gv 146.3, similarly 146.16; 152.15 (all prose); te kalpakoṭir athavāpi uttare Sukh 74.17 (cf. 45.6, above; vs but end of pāda), *they, for crores of kalpas or even further ...*; in LV 119.6 (vs) reading uncertain, kuta uttaraṃ (so Lefm. with ms. A, other mss. °ri, unmetr.; Calc. °rī, perhaps rightly) vā, *how could there be one higher* (prob. adverb); [in Mv ii.243.7 (prose) ed. tasya pañjarasya uttariṃ sthitvā, but read with v.l. upari, *on top of the cage*; this mg. is not found for uttari(ṃ);] in composition, uttari-jñāna-viśeṣasūcanatāyai Gv 191.11 (prose; apparently substantially = uttara); note esp.

uttarottari-(v.l. °ra-)-viśiṣṭatara-kuśalamūla- LV 429.14 (prose), *more and more exceedingly superior roots of merit*; (ekam pudgalam sthāpayitvā) śaikṣapratipady uttarikaraṇīyam Sukh 2.13 (prose), (except one person) *who had something left to do in the śaikṣa course* (the rest all being arhats); note that Pali has the same cpd. uttari-karaṇīya, but acc. to PTSD only as a karmadharaya, *an additional duty*, not as a bahuvrīhi as here; in some of the above it is not certain whether uttari- is compounded with the following word or a separate adverb; in LV 246.16; 263.11, above, uttari must be prep., governing manuṣyadharmād; to these passages correspond Mv ii.121.7, 12; 122.2 uttari-manuṣyadharmasya jñānāye darśanāye saṃbodhāye; Senart takes the word as a cpd., depending on jñānāye etc., prob. rightly, tho the gen. manuṣyadharmasya might be dependent on prep. uttari; the latter construction is impossible, and a cpd. (= Pali uttarimanussadhamma, *superhuman faculties* or *conditions*; the analysis of the Pali comm. cited by Childers is inconsistent with that indicated by LV 246.16 and 263.11) must be assumed in Mv ii.130.12 kaṃcid uttarimanuṣyadharmaṃ; Divy 145.21, 28 and 146.16 uttarimanuṣyadharme (so with mss., ed. wrongly em. uttare man°); Śikṣ 62.4 uttarimanuṣyadharmair; besides this, the same cpd. is recorded in BHS (not in Pali) as uttara-manuṣyadharma-(-pralāpa, m.), Mvy 8367, *declaring* (falsely the possession of) *superhuman faculties* (one of the **parajika** sins); also uttaram-man° Divy 144.4, 28; 145.18 (mss., in 144.4 ed. em. °re); Bhīk 26a.3; uttare-man° Divy 144.9, 13, 21, 23, 27; 145.3, 11, 13, 17; 146.8, 25 (in all these read as cpd.; ed. takes uttare as separate adj., misled by the fact that the cpd. is a loc., ending °dharme; see above for evidence that uttare = uttari as adv. and prep.); in Divy 144.5 apparently anuttare is used as synonym of uttare in this cpd. (taken by ed. as separate adj.), yady ekaṃ śramaṇo Gautamo 'nuttare-manuṣyadharme riddhiprātihāryaṃ vidarśayiṣyati vayaṃ dve (see **anuttara**; but this word does not fit and must be either a corruption, or a sign of misunderstanding by the author of the passage; elsewhere in the same passage only forms of uttara-, uttari- etc. are used).

uttarika (Pali, see below), in Śikṣ 332.1 (vs) ājīvikadharma-carāṇāṃ uttarikāṇa anuttarikāṇāṃ, *of Ājīvika-sectarians, superior and not superior*(?); acc. to Bendall and Rouse, Transl., *those who have or those who have not the higher aim*, which is hardly illuminating. See Bendall's note in Text p. 414 for report of a Chin. interpretation, for which I find no basis in Indic. In Pali uttarika is reported only Nett. 50.10 °kānaṃ phalānaṃ pattiyā; obviously *superior* or the like. Pali has no anuttarika.

uttari-karaṇīya, see s.v. **uttari.**

uttarikā (to Skt. uttara), *superiority*, in bhaktottarikā, *superiority of food*: Divy 284.24 yo °rikayā jeṣyati...; 285.15 na kvacid °kayā parājayati; 285.20.

uttarim, see s.v. **uttari**; **uttari-manuṣyadharma**, and other cpds. of **uttari-**, see id.

uttarī, uttarīm, uttare, uttareṇa, and their cpds., see s.v. **uttari.**

1 **uttarya**, nt., and °**ryā**, f. (cf. Skt. and Pali uttarīya, AMg. uttariya; perhaps a hyper-Skt. form for the latter?), apparently *a covering* (for a part of the body: hands, ears, or back), but cf. 2 **uttarya**: karṇa-pṛṣṭhottaryāṇi stambhāni (!?) maṇiratnakaṭakakeyūrakāṇi pralambitāni saṃdṛśyante sma Kv 7.20; in Kv 30.12 in a long cpd. describing ornaments and clothes of girls, keyūra-... kaṭimekhalā-hastottaryā-karṇapṛṣṭhottaryā-hastāṅgulīya-samāyuktānāṃ (kumārīṇāṃ); in Kv 78.(20–)21 at end of a long cpd., list of ornaments and garments, maulīkuṇḍala- ... ratnahāra-skandhopariṣvajānika-(corrupt?) -pṛṣṭhottaryāṇy anguṣṭha-vibhedikāny (q.v.) anyāni ca vividhāni vastrāṇi.

2 **uttarya**, ger., in Kv 32.17 vāmanakarūpam abhinirmāya, mṛgājinenottarya, veṇudaṇḍam upagṛhya..., evidently *covering* (with a deerskin). Cf. 1 **uttarya.** As a ger. the form seems inexplicable, unless as an extension of the Skt. usage with ut-thā-, ut-tambh-; is a MIndic uttharya intended (to utstarati, see s.v. **uttharati,** = stṛṇoti; or to Skt. ava plus stṛ-)? Note that Kv is also the only text where 1 uttarya is recorded; has the noun influenced the form of the gerund?

uttāna, adj. (= Pali id.; in this sense hardly Skt., but see pw for approximations; cf. **uttānī-karoti**), *open*: of the face, in uttāna-mukha-varṇa (= Pali uttāna-mukha, wrongly defined PTSD), *of open* (frank) *countenance* (suggesting accessibility, friendliness; so Pali DN comm., contrary to PTSD), Bbh 123.11; 217.9 (in both foll. by smitapūrvamgama); *clear, manifest*, of dharma, Mvy 1304; Av ii.106.11 (with vivṛta); uttāna-kriyām āgamya Bbh 81.11, *coming to manifestation*; °nāṃ dharmadeśanām, °nām avavādānuśāsanīm Bbh 224.15; te (sc. doṣāḥ) ... uttānā viśaditāḥ prakāśitāḥ Bbh 45.20; of doctrines that are *obvious* and so *simple, easily comprehensible*, in contrast with such as are profound (gambhīra) and hence comprehensible only to superior minds, Bbh 82.18; 283.19.

uttānaka, adj. (= Pali id., Skt. uttāna), *supine, on the back*; *upturned* (with back down): Mv i.213.7 (prose; parallel **ottānako**, q.v.) na uttānako (tiṣṭhati; the Bodhisattva in his mother's womb); °kā prapatetsuḥ Mv ii.283.1; 412.15; (bhūmāv ...) °kān pratiṣṭhāpya Divy 375.10 (these all prose); °kān kṛtva ... bhūmau SP 84.9 (vs); hastau ... °kāvasthitau Mmk 407.3 (prose; the hands upside down, in a mudrā); °kaḥ Mmk 362.23 (vs).

uttānī-karoti (= Pali id.; to **uttāna**; in Skt. mukham °nīkṛtya, *opening the mouth*, see pw), *publishes, makes known*: Mv iii.408.18 (āryasatyaṃ...) °roti prakāśayati; Mvy 2771 °kariṣyati (sc. dharmam); Av i.287.5 karma ... prakāśitam uttānīkṛtam; ii.151.3 atyayam ... vivṛtam uttānīkṛtam; Gv 48.3 vibhajaty °roti; 67.3 (dharmaparyāyam ...) °romi vivarami; 149.2 °kurvatām, gen. pl. pres. pple.

uttānī-karman (= Pali °kamma; to prec.), *publication, proclaiming, making known*: Bbh 408.14 tesām (sc. dharmāṇāṃ) samākhyānaṃ vivaraṇā °karma.

Uttāpanarājamati, n. of a Bodhisattva: Gv 442.8 (read °rājasyottāpana° for °rājasyāttāpana°).

uttāpayati (caus. of Skt. ut-tapati; on mg. see uttapta; Skt. caus. not recorded in this sense, even of metals), *purifies* (orig. of metals; here fig.): Gv 385.17 (bodhisattvavimokṣam ...) uttāpayan, *purifying.*

uttāraṇa (nt.; in this sense not Skt. or Pali; see **uttarayati**), *carrying out* (of a promise): Sikṣ 126.7 pratijñottāraṇavacanā vā; a neg. is needed; either delete preceding punctuation and understand a-prati°, in samdhi with preceding vā; or read with ms. of Bodhicaryav. pañjikā on 5.54 (ed. 124.3, with note) pratijñānuttāraṇavacanā; in either case, *not carrying out one's promise.* La Vallée Poussin erroneously corrects to the reading of Bendall's text of Śikṣ.

uttārayati (in this sense not recorded), *carries out, fulfils*: LV 184.14 (vs) °raya pratijñāṃ, *fulfil your promise*; or rather, with Corrigenda (and metrical requirements) pratikāṅkṣāṃ, *carry out the expectation* (of people, i. e. what they hope from you). Cf. prec. and **samuttāraṇa.**

uttārayitar, m. (in this sense not recorded; to Skt. uttārayati), *one who brings forth, rescues*: Gv 462.25 °tāro bhavaughebhyaḥ.

? **uttiṇī-karoti,** see **uttṛṇī°.**

uttima, adj. (= Pkt. id., Sheth, and Pischel 101; in AMg. uttimaṅga = uttamāṅga, Pischel l. c.; Skt. and Pali uttama; see § 22.16), *highest, supreme*: Mv iii.268.1 °ma-yasaṃ, mss. (Senart em. uttama-yaśaṃ).

Uttiya, n. of a śreṣṭhin: Mv i.36.3 ff.

uttiṣṭhate (special use of Skt. sthā plus ud, q.v. in BR s.v. 3), *arises = is being built*, of a house: Divy 304.12 (anyatarasya gṛhapater gṛham) °te.

uttṛṇī-karoti (= Pali uttiṇaṃ karoti; implies adj. *uttṛṇa, *deprived of thatch*), *makes* (a building) *roofless*, object āveśana-mālām (so read with mss., see s.v. **mālā**): °kṛtvā Mv i.328.10, 14, 20; 329.1 (in the last two read with mss. °mālām ut°kṛtvā); °karetsu (v.l. °suḥ) i.328.12 (here one ms. uttīni-k°, apparently intending the MIndic uttiṇī°).

uttrāsa, m. (Skt. Lex.; = Pali uttāsa, utrāsa; cf. **an-u°**, **nir-u°**), *fear*: Mv i.79.13 °sa-bahulā(ḥ); Śikṣ 83.8 sūkarasyeva uttrāso; Gv 351.5 na cāsyāpārime tīre uttrāso bhavati; MadhK 264.4 śrotṛṇām uttrāsaparivarjanārthaṃ.

uttrāsana, n. (and adj.?) (once in Skt., Dhātup., pw 2.295, as n. act.; not in Pali; cf. AMg. uttāsaṇaa, °ṇaga, adj., *terrifying*), *the act of frightening*: Bbh 146.13 uttrāsanāvarjanena (dvandva), *by frightening and propitiation*; 180.5 uttrāsanārhāṇāṃ sattvānām uttrāsanāya; (adj., or ifc. Bhvr.?) Divy 604.2 -paramabhīṣaṇanirṇādaṃ sakalajanottrāsanam, *terrifying all people*. Cf. next.

Uttrāsanī (to prec.), n. of a rākṣasī: Māy 243.20.

utthapeti (cf. Skt. ut-thāpayati, *ermuntern*, BR s.v. 5), *raises up, exalts = cheers, refreshes*: fut., eṣā me utthapeṣyati Mv iii.3.16 (vs).

? **uttharati**, cf. AMg. uttharanta, pres. pple.; seemingly implied by ger. uttharya, if this is to be read for 2 **uttarya**, q.v., Kv 32.17.

utthala (adj., or subst. m. or nt.: = AMg. id., *a sandhill, a sandy down*; Skt. *ut-sthala), (*a*) *dry, sandy* (*place*): Śikṣ 249.13 puruṣa utthale deśe udapānaṃ ... khānayet.

(**utthāpana**, f. **°nī**, adj. [= Skt. utthāpanī, sc. ṛc, Kauś., BR s.v. 2], *concluding* [verse]: n. pl. °nīye [mss.; Senart em. °nīyā] gāthā Mv ii.26.13, prose.)

utpattati (ger. °ttitvā(na), ppp. °ttita; app. blend of utpatati with a quasi-denom. from utpatti, or modification of utpatati by confusion with utpatti; Senart i.374 n.), *springs up, goes forth, flies up*: °tvā Mv i.6.8 ff. (prose), six times, subject *rays of light*, arci(s), as also with ppp. °tā Mv i.26.3 (prose; in same line nipatitāyo, *fallen down*); °tvā Mv ii.243.11 (prose), subject śakuntako, hence clearly to root pat, *fly*; ger. °tvāna, Mv iii.456.5, subject inhabitants of hell; in parallel to this, i.11.15, Senart reads utpatitvāna, but mss. (upetitvāna or upentitvāna) are equally favorable to utpatti°; the mg. could be *having gone (flown?) forth*, or perhaps *having originated, been (re-)born*.

utpatti, f. (= Pali uppatti, see esp. aṭṭhuppatti, CPD; cf. Skt. utpatti in pw, 4), orig. *occurrence*, and so *occasion*: asyām utpattau Mvy 9209, *on this occasion*, see **nidāna** 6.

-utpattika, ifc. Bhvr. = **utpatti**, see **sotpattika**.

ut-pattra, adj., *with leaves fully out*: Jm 129.20 °traiḥ (drumaiḥ).

utpathājīva, adj. m., *one who makes his living on by-paths*: MSV i.52.7, see **pathājīva**; ii.146.12.

utpathika, adj. (°i(n) plus -ka), = next; in Mv iii.179.7 (prose) read na utpathiko āryadharmāṇāṃ, *not going astray from Aryan principles*; one ms. na utpatiko; Senart with v.l. **navutpattiko**, q.v.

utpathin, adj. (Skt. utpatha plus -in; cf. prec.), *going on a wrong course*: LV 325.6 (vs) (yo nara ...) śīle utpathi (n. sg.) dhyāna (so read with ms. A for ed. dhyāyi) utpathī (so read, as required by meter, for °thi; n. sg.) matihīno.

utpadyati, (**1**) *arises in one's mind, appears or occurs to one*: kathaṃ tava utpadyati Mv iii.393.1, *how does it strike you? what do you think of it* (the proposal of an opponent in debate)?; ppp., teṣāṃ .... utpannaṃ Mv i.311.11, *it occurred to them* (foll. by direct quotation; so also in the next two); rājño utpanno (read °nnam?) Mv ii.64.17; teṣāṃ dāni utpannaṃ ii.69.14; (**2**) in mg. of Skt. caus. utpādayati, *produces, causes*: ye ... heṭhām utpadyema Mv i.365.10, *who (= if we) should cause injury*.

utpadyana (nt.; = Pali uppajjana; MIndic -ana formation to utpadyate), *production, origination*: Gv 48.5 (prose), read: harṣa-utpadyana-saṃtānāni (see s.v. **saṃtāna** 2).

utpanna, see **utpadyati**.

utpala, (**1**) m., Mvy 7797, or nt., Mvy 7926 (cited from Gv) and Gv 106.19; 134.3, a high number; (**2**) m., n. of a former Buddha: Mv iii.235.16; (**3**) m. (= Pali uppala, °laka), n. of a (cold, Dharmas, Tib. Mvy) hell: Mvy 4934; Dharmas 122; Divy 67.23; 138.7; Av i.4.9 etc.; (**4**) m., n. of a kalpa: see **Upala** (and cf. **Utpalaka** 3).

Utpalaka, m. (**1**) n. of a hunter: Mv ii.102.1; 104.8*; 105.18; 114.6*, 7* (in passages marked * Senart prints Uppalaka with one ms.); (**2**) n. of a nāga: Mvy 3287; SP 4.12 (Burnouf, and hence BR, Utpala); Māy 247.30; (**3**) n. of a kalpa (cf. prec. and **Upala**): Gv 446.14.

utpala-gandhika (in Skt. Lex. as n. of a kind of sandal), see s.v. **gandhika**.

Utpalanetra, (**1**) n. of a king, former incarnation of the Buddha: RP 24.4; (**2**) n. of a Bodhisattva (the same as 1? but represented as contemporary with the Buddha): Gv 3.2.

Utpalapadmanetra, n. of a former Buddha: Mv i.138.13.

Utpalabhūti, n. of a perfume-dealer: Gv 182.10.

Utpalavaktra, n. of a cakravartin: Thomas ap. Hoernle MR 101, from Mahāsaṃnipāta Sūtra.

Utpalavarṇā (= Pali Uppalavaṇṇā, called Therī), n. of a follower of the Buddha, referred to as a śrāvikā Mvy 1072; Mv i.251.21; as a bhikṣuṇī Divy 160.7; 401.24; Karmav 159.18 (see Lévi's note on her story). See also **Utpalāvarṇā**.

Utpalaśrīgarbha, n. of a Boddhisattva: Dbh 2.10.

Utpalā, n. of a rākṣasī: Māy 243.15.

Utpalāvatī, f., Divy 471.1 ff.; 476.21; or **Utpalāvata**, nt., Divy 479.19, n. of a city.

Utpalāvarṇā, n. of a Buddhist disciple, doubtless = **Utpalavarṇā**, Jm 115.24 (vs; but °lā° does not seem to be m.c.).

(**utpāṭa**, [m.], *the act of plucking out*, cf. pw 2, App.: Divy 299.2, 20; 301.26; 303.19. [In Divy 517.18 utpāṭam, epithet of padam, *foot*(print), prob. corrupt; the same vs in Pali, Dhp. comm. i.201.5, reads ukkuṭikaṃ, v.l. ukka°.])

utpāṭaka, adj. (cf. Pali uppāṭaka; in Skt. only as n. of a disease), *plucking out*: Śikṣ 69.18 dantotpāṭakā(ḥ), n. pl.

utpāṇḍūtpāṇḍu, or **°ḍuka**, adj. (āmreḍita, ut plus pāṇḍu, with or without -ka which may have pitying dim. force; = Pali uppaṇḍuppaṇḍuka-jāta), *very pale*: °ḍukaḥ kṛśāluko durbalako Divy 334.1, 3; °ḍuḥ kṛśāluko durbal-(ak)o 571.18, 20; °ḍuko bhavāmi kṛśāluko durbalako 571.21; °ḍukāni sphuṭitapāṇipadāni 463.8; °kā(ḥ) MSV i.i.10 etc.

utpāta, m. (or °taka, m., or **upādu**, m.; = Skt. utpātaka, Mbh 18.44, AMg. uppāyaga, Ratnach. 5.15; cf. Pali uppāṭaka, an insect), *flea*; three variants, upāduḥ Mvy 4858, utpātaḥ 4859, °takaḥ 4860; Mironov utpātakaḥ, v.l. utpātaḥ only; Tib. lji ba, or khyi śig, both *flea*. With the form upādu may be compared Skt. Lex. (Trik.) upādika, some sort of insect.

utpāda, m. (Skt. id., *production* etc.; so in **cittotpāda**, q.v.), (**1**) in bodhisattvotpāda, Kashgar rec. for bodhisattvāvavāda, SP 65.1 et alibi, see **avavāda** (of which this seems to be a secondary distortion); (**2**) (= Pali uppāda, for Skt. utpāta), *portent, omen*: Mv iii.386.10 °deṣu vidyāyukto (of a brahman purohita); prob. in this mg. utpāda-gaṇḍa-piṭakāni MSV ii.82.17, (bad) *omens*.

boils and abscesses, or *boils and abscesses due to the* (above-described) *omens*; but Tib., if I understand it, fails to interpret the word. Senart, Mv ii.549, note on ii.279.20, assumes this mg. also in pūrvotpāda-saṃpanno bodhisattvo, which however seems to me to mean simply *perfect in* (or, *as a result of*) *previous births*; so agrotpāda-saṃpanno ii.279.21; and cf. ii.259.12 ff., also of bodhisattvas, pūrvotpāda-saṃpanno ... kalyāṇotpāda° agrotpāda° jyeṣṭhotpāda° śreṣṭhotpāda° praṇidhi-pūrvotpāda°; a very similar list ii.291.12 ff. If I am right, utpāda here has its normal Skt. mg; (**3**) *calamity* (due to bad omens; development of 2): °dam āpadyeyur MPS 31.63 (otherwise Waldschmidt).

utpādayati, with object citta, saṃjñā, manasikāra, or the like, *produces an intention, resolution* (cf. **cittotpāda**): cittam, Mv i.38.10; 80.4 (to become a Buddha); iii.138.8; Kv 12.16; 27.12 (read -cittam utpādayanti); 59.20; ppp., spṛhācittam utpāditam abhūt SP 101.5; manasikāram, SP 72.15, duḥkhamanasikārasaṃjñām, SP 78.5; bhūtasaṃjñām, Vaj 22.10, 18.

utpādika, adj. (cf. also **cittotpādika**), *productive*: Kv 80.6 prajāmaṇḍalasyotpādikāḥ (kleśāḥ).

utpika, v.l. for **utphikā**, q.v.

utpiṇḍa, nt., *condiment, relish* (going with food): Mvy 5765. So, apparently, Chin. and Jap., also BR, *Zuspeise*; Tib. sbags pa, or nos pa, which are not clear to me.

(**utprāsayati**, *mocks*; rare in Skt., see pw 7.386 s.v. root as plus ut-pra; but cf. Skt. utprāsa, utprāsana: Divy 17.11 (prose) tvam apy asmākam utprāsayasi; Śikṣ 266.10 utprāsyamānasya, pres. pple. pass., *of one that is mocked*.)

utplava, m. (cf. Pali uplavati, uppilavati; and see the foll. items), *joy*: Mvy 7693 (Mironov utyavaḥ, clearly nonsense; Tib. dgaḥ yal yal, *extreme joy* (?); Chin. and Jap. *joy*); Śikṣ 183.6 manasa utplavaḥ, in a list of synonyms for joy and gladness.

utplāva (m.; = Pali ubbilāpa, v.l. uppilāva, 'which is probably the correct reading,' PTSD; cf. prec. and next three), *joy*: Śikṣ 126.12 mana-utplāva-karī (vāc).

utplāvaka, adj. (to **utplāvayati**, q.v.), *deceiving*: Bbh 23.2 pareṣām utplāvakaṃ vicitrābhūtaguṇākhyānam.

utplāvana (nt.) and °**nā** (connected with **utplava, utplāva**, qq.v.), *joy*: Dbh 12.9 prīti-bahula utplāvanā-bahula; 24.16 manautplāvana-karī manaḥprahlādanakarī.

utplāvayati (cf. **utplāvaka**; in this sense seems unrecorded except in BHS; perhaps caus. to Pali uplavati, uppilavati, *rejoices* [cf. **utplava, utplāva**, and prec.], caus. *makes happy* [for insufficient reasons], so *wheedles*; or else belongs to Pali uplāpeti, *immerses, ducks* in water, and so *tricks, gets the better of*), *seduces, leads astray*: SP 111.1 (vs) yathāpi bālaḥ puruṣo bhaveta utplāvito bālajanena santaḥ, in parable of the prodigal son; Kern *seduced*, confirmed by Tib. bslus.

? **utpharati** (cf. Skt. utphalati, recorded in this sense, pw), *jumps up*: Mv ii.249.16 (prose) (tato vānaro tasya śuśumārasya) grīvāto utphāritvā (so, or uṣphār°, mss.; Senart upphār°; but not causative; prob. read utpharitvā, or upphar°?) taṃ udumbaraṃ prakrānto.

utphikā, Mvy 9542 (so Mironov), or **utpika** (m. or nt.?), 9541 (and v.l. Mironov), n. of a disease; Tib. either glo baḥi (*of the lungs*), or mgoḥi (*of the head*), glog pa (on which see **rajata**; *ulcer*? *cancer*?). Chin. apparently *a disease characterized by insanity*. See also **uvyadha.**

utsaktikā, perhaps *attitude of head thrown back* or *held up stiffly*: Mvy 8542 notsaktikayā, instr. (of monk's behavior); °kā-kṛta, *one who is in that attitude*, Mvy 8608. In the former, Tib. mgo mi (g)zar, *with the head not stiff* or *abruptly straight*, so also in the latter except that mgo, *head*, is lacking; Chin. acc. to Ting's Dict. *with robe inside-out.*

1 **utsaṅga-** (-pāda, or -caraṇa), see **ucchaṅkha-**.

2 **utsaṅga**, nt. or m. (var. ucchaṅga), a high number = 100 vivāhas: LV 76.20 f. utsaṅgenotsaṅgam, *by myriads*; 148.1 °gam, n. sg., cited from LV by Mvy 7961 as ucchaṅgaṃ; but Mvy 8012 utsaṅgaḥ (Mironov same both times); Tib. phaṅ, or paṅ, steṅ = *lap-top*; Mv ii.421.16 (hiranya)-suvarṇasya utsaṅgāṃ kṛtvā; iii.405.6 °varṇasya utsaṅga-śatāni dattvā. Cf. **mahotsaṅga.**

utsajati (if not a misprint, MIndic for utsṛjati; cf. **sajati** which supports this), *abandons*: Gv 481.25 (vs) utsajitva (ger.; final a m.c.) amaropamaṃ gṛham.

utsada, m., and adj. (see also **ucchada**, °**daka**; = Pali ussada, used in all mgs. here recorded), (**1**) *elevation, prominence, protuberance, swelling*, esp. one of 7 such on the hands, feet, shoulders, and back of the neck of a mahāpuruṣa, constituting the 16th of the 32 **lakṣaṇa**, q.v. (and cf. Pali sattussada): Bbh 375.20 saptotsadakāyaḥ (Bhvr.), saptāsyotsadāḥ kāye jātāḥ, dvau hastayor dvau pādayoḥ dvāv aṃsayor eko grīvāyām; cf. the list Gv 400.9–11, ... two aṃsakūṭayoḥ, one pṛṣṭhato grīvāyām; Mv i.226.19 utsadāḥ, subst.; in Bhvr. cpd. saptotsadaḥ Gv 400.8; Mvy 250; LV 105.18; 430.18; °daṃ; acc., Gv 128.1; saptotsadāṅga RP 47.9; and in other lists of **lakṣaṇa**, q.v.; (**2**) *addition, supplement*, in connection or composition with naraka, *hell*, one of the 16 *supplementary hells* which belong to each major hell (mahānaraka; = Pali ussada-niraya, not well defined PTSD): Mv i.5.1 aṣṭasu mahānarakeṣu pratyeka-ṣoḍaśotsadeṣu; 1.7.3 kuṇapāto muktā (n. pl.) narakotsadā (abl. sg.); i.8.12 aṣṭasu mahānarakeṣu ṣoḍaśotsadeṣu, and i.244.19 same; i.9.11 pratyekaṣoḍaśotsadā; iii.454.10 (aṣṭa mahānarakā ...) pratyekaṃ ṣoḍaśotsadā; (**3**) adj., *abundant*, and n. *abundance* (distinction between the two often not clear; generally used in prior or posterior part of cpds. where either could be assumed); certainly adj. in Bbh 379.19 prabhūtenotsadena viśadenānnapānena (3 synonymous adj., see **viśada**); Divy 646.16 utsadānnapāno bhavati, *has abundant food and drink*; MSV i.36.18 nāty-utsadamāṃsā tanugātrī, *of not excessive flesh, slender-bodied*; KP 111.2 (prose) utsada-pātracīvaradhāraṇatayā (an [ākāśa-] **-paligodha**, q.v., for an ascetic); 111.5 (vs) tatotsadaṃ cīvarapātra-dhāraṇaṃ (Tib. lhag par, *surpassing*, modifying dhāraṇaṃ); Śikṣ 56.6 yadi ... lābha utsado bhavet, *if the profit should be abundant* (but Bendall and Rouse, *should amount to a surplus*); doubtless subst. in Gv 495.16 (bodhicittaṃ ...) utsadabhūtam akṣayajñānatayā, *it is an abundant store* ...; but 2d ed. utsa-bhūtam, *spring, source*; in most of the rest adj. seems simpler, but subst. possible: Mv ii.319.21 (vs) utsada-prāptaṃ (here perhaps better subst., *attained to abundance*, sc. of creatures, viz. of the followers of Māra, as following mārāṇa koṭī ... shows; not reduction of utsadakuśalaprāptaṃ with Senart i.372 note); utsada-kuśala-saṃcayo Mv i.249.18; 251.12; ii.177.14; abstract in -tva, Śikṣ 248.5 (yasya, sc. tejodhātoḥ) cotsadatvāj jvarito jvarita iti saṃkhyāṃ gacchati, *and thru the abundance of which a feverish man comes to be called feverish*; Śikṣ 107.1 (vs) pradoṣa vardhenti vitarka utsadā (adj. with vitarka, or subst. in comp. with it? Bendall and Rouse the latter, but text prints as two words!); Bbh 252.16 kaṣāyotsada-kāla-tāṃ, *condition of time abundant in kaṣāya*; 16–17 niṣkaṣāyānutsadakaṣāya-kāla-tām (... *free from, or not abundant in, kaṣāya*); Mv i.61.3–4 (sattvā ...) utsadalolā (so Senart em., mss. all corrupt; but read °lobhā, proved by Vism.) utsadadoṣā utsadamohā, cf. Pali Vism. i.103.19 (sattā ...) lobhussadā dosussadā mohussadā, *having abundant* (Pali, *abundant in*, or *having abundance of*) *lobha, doṣa, moha*; SP 170.1 (vs) apāya-bhūmīs (so all Nep. mss.) tada utsadāsi, *the stages of misfortune were then superabundant*; LV 276.21 utsada-maṇimuktivaiḍūryaśaṅkhaśilāpravāḍarajatajātarūpyaṃ (? v.l. °rūpaṃ; sc. lokadhātuṃ); RP 35.11 (vs) asaṃyatā uddhata unnatāś ca, agauravā mānina lābha-utsadā (cpd.) . . . sudūra te tādṛśa agrabodhaye (either *abounding in profit* or *having abundance of profit*). Peculiar is saptotsada in Divy 620.13 (Utkaṭaṃ nāma droṇamukhaṃ paribhuṅkte sma) saptotsadaṃ satṛṇakāṣṭhodakaṃ dhānyasahagataṃ . . . brahmadeyaṃ, and 620.28–621.1, similarly, with sa-saptotsadam; a close parallel in Pali, DN i.87.(6–)7 Ukkaṭṭhaṃ ajjhāvasati sattussadaṃ (comm. i.245.20 sattehi ussadaṃ, ussannaṃ bahujanaṃ ākiṇṇamanussaṃ . . . anekasattasamākiṇṇaṃ ca) satiṇakaṭṭhodakaṃ sadhaññaṃ . . . brahmadeyyaṃ; cf. also Pv comm. 221.11 sattussadan ti pāpakārīhi sattehi ussannaṃ (this, in line 16, = uparūpari nicitaṃ). It seems clear that *this* sattussada in Pali = Skt. *sattvotsada, *abounding in living creatures*. It seems to have been falsely Sktized in Divy (which, or its source, obviously followed closely a MIndic original very close to the Pali of DN) to saptotsada, because the adapter knew familiarly this cpd. as one of the 32 lakṣaṇa (above, 1). Presumably he thought it meant here *containing seven elevations* of some sort, but I see no use in speculating further as to his intentions.

utsadana, nt. (= **utsīdana**; with mg. 1 cf. Skt. utsīdati; with mg. 2 cf. prec. and **an-utsanna**), (**1**) *coming to grief, ruin*: sthale utsadanam MSV i.49.10, 17 (in 2 above read utsatsyati for utpat°); (**2**) *superfluous abundance, excess*, in °na-dharmakaṃ (bhaktaṃ) Divy 307.23, 27, of food offered to monks and not fully used by them, *of the nature of excess* (pw 7.323 *zum Wegräumen bestimmt*). For Mvy 6781 utsādanam = Tib. dril ba (*rolling*, in sense of *rubbing down, massage*; so Skt.), Minayev and Mironov read utsadanam, apparently a faulty reading.

utsanna (= Pali ussanna), *excessive*; see **an-u°**. Cf. prec. 2.

utsaraṇa, nt., *ascent, marching up*, in Mvy 4485 pipīlikotsaraṇam = Tib. grog ma gyen du ḥdzeg pa, *ants marching up hill* (a term used in logic).

utsarpita, adj. (ppp. of ud plus sṛp, caus.), app. *laid by as balance, left over* (from a sum of money): Divy 23.11 aparam utsarpitam; 16 (nāsmābhiḥ kiṃcid uddharīkṛtaṃ) kiṃ tv aparam utsarpitaṃ tiṣṭhati, (*we have not incurred any debt,*) *but the rest remains put aside as left over*.

utsaryati (semi-MIndic for utsāryate, § 3.34, pass. of **utsārayati**, also Skt., q.v.), *is put aside, is violated*: Mv ii.92.18 kathaṃ tu utsaryati dharmaśāstram.

utsavika, adj. (Skt. utsava plus ika), *pertaining to festivals*: Mv ii.84.20 vastrā ca utsavikā, *holiday clothes*; iii.177.17 vyayakarmeṇa (em.) utsavikena, *matters of expense due to festivals*.

utsahana-tā (to Skt. utsahati; cf. next), *fortitude, persistent energy, endurance*: ŚsP 1461.11 (a Bodhisattva resolves to endure infinite torments in hells to bring creatures to enlightenment: evaṃ yāvat sarvasattvānāṃ) kṛte yāty utsahanatā aparikhedaḥ (are the two last words a cpd.? *lack of weariness in fortitude, endurance*?).

utsahanā (to Skt. utsahati; but perhaps better read **utsāhanā**, to caus. utsāhayati, *encouragement*), *enthusiasm, energy* (?): Divy 490.5 kiṃ nv ayam utsahanā-vineyaḥ āhosvid **avasādanā**-(q.v.)-vineyaḥ.

utsāraka, m. or f. pl., n. of a class of malevolent superhuman beings: Mmk 17.5; foll. by mahotsārakā(ḥ); in a long list of demons etc.

utsāraṇa, nt. (to next with -ana), acc. to N. Dutt (Introd. xxii) = **āvarhaṇa**; it seems, at any rate, to mean *removal* of religious disabilities from a monk, cf. the following **osāraṇa** (206.16): MSV ii.206.12, 14.

utsārayati (specialized mg. of caus. of Skt. utsarati; see also **utsaryati**), *frees* (from religious disabilities), see prec.: MSV ii.206.13–16; Tib. seems to be cited as smoṅ (zhig), which I cannot interpret; ib. 113.13 (see Corrigenda), cf. osāray° 115.2 etc. See **(v)osārayati.**

utsāhana (nt.; cf. **utsahanā**, and next), *inspiration, the making energetic*: in title of SP chap. 26, samantabhadrotsāhana-parivarta, SP 483.5, 7.

utsāhanī (cf. prec. and next), in Divy 654.27 either noun, *energy*, or adj. with ūtir, *energetic* or *inspired, inspiring*: °ny ūtir aprativāṇiḥ (qq.v.) smṛtyā saṃprajanyenāpramādato (see **saṃprajanya**) yogaḥ karaṇīyaḥ.

utsāhayati (caus. to utsahati), (**1**) *considers* (lit. *makes*) *capable*: LV 100.16 (prose) te sarve . . . mahāprajāpatīṃ gautamīm utsāhayanti sma, *they all considered M.G. capable* (of tending the Bodhisattva); (**2**) *tests the capacity of*: Bhīk 15b.2 karmakārikayā . . . utsāhayitavyā: utsahase tvam, etc., *she is to be tested as to her capacity by the* karmakārikā (nun, saying): *Are you capable . . .*

utsicati (Skt. utsiñcati not in this sense; = Pali ussiñcati; § 28.12), *bales out, exhausts*: Mv ii.90.15 (prose) etaṃ samudraṃ utsicāmi (mss., Senart em. utsiñcāmi), 17 (prose) utsicāmi (kept by Senart) mahodadhiṃ; 91.1 (prose) utsicituṃ (inf.; mss. unsic°, Senart em. utsiñc°); 92.6 (vs) mss. unsici, °ciṃ (opt. 1 sg.; Senart em. utsiṃci, which this time seems required by meter) mahāsamudraṃ.

utsiṣṭa, ppp. (hyper-Skt. for ucchiṣṭa, § 2.19), (something) *left over*: Śikṣ 125.4 raha utsiṣṭaṃ kṛtvānutsiṣṭāhāreṣv adadataḥ pretagatiḥ paṭhyate; 139.14 utsiṣṭasyāpy aśucer na doṣaḥ.

utsīdana (nt., quasi-MIndic formation from utsīdati plus ana; unrecorded; = **utsadana** 1 and 2; cf. **saṃsīdana**), (**1**) *destruction* (of a ship, on land, sthale, i. e. by running aground in shipwreck): Divy 229.23 sthala utsīdanabhayaṃ; (**2**) °na-dharma = (2) utsadana-dharmaka, *of the nature of superfluity*: MPS 7.2.

[**utsukya**, error for aut°, in Divy 601.21 gamanāyotsukyamanā, read °yaut°.]

?**utsukha** = Skt. utsuka, *longing, desirous*: Gv 330.25 ity utsukheṣu (so also 2d ed.). Perhaps error; but cf. Geiger 40.1; Pischel p. 148, middle.

utsūḍhi (f.?), n. sg. °ḍhiḥ, (**1**) Mvy 1789 = Tib. spro ba, *joy*; so Mironov (v.l. both edd. utsṛcitaḥ); (**2**) Mvy 7683 = Tib. mthan pa (?not in Tib. Dictt.; perhaps = ḥthan pa, *firmness*, but Chin. *obscurity, confusion*, hence Mvy Kyoto ed. suggests em. unmūḍhiḥ). Probably = **utsoḍhi**, q.v.; both *firmness* and *joy* are meanings of Skt. utsāha, from the same root.

[**utsṛcita**? v.l. for **utsūḍhi**, q.v.: °taḥ Mvy 1789.]

utsṛjana (cf. Skt. utsarjana; semi-MIndic formation in -ana on the pres. Skt. utsṛjati), *letting loose, letting fly* (pennants, in the wind): Gv 163.3 utsṛjana-nānāratnadhvaja-patākam, *with various . . . pennants for flying* (in the wind). See also **anutsṛjanatā.**

utsṛjyate = Skt. utsṛjati, *abandons*: Mvy 2558 = Tib. gtoṅ ba.

utsṛta, adj. (hyper-Skt., § 2.19, for Pali ussita, Skt. ucchrita, for which utsṛta is recorded rarely, at least as v.l., in Skt.; cf. **ucchṛta**), *high*: Mv ii.239.18 °ta-dhvajāṃ (note in 240.8 ucchrita-dhvajā, of the same entity); Mmk 407.9, read dvau-m-utsṛtāu (text °mṛsṛtau), and 419.12 dvi-m-utsṛtai(ḥ) . . . tri-m-utsṛtaiḥ (in all with hiatus-bridging m).

utsoḍhi, f. (?m.; = Pali ussoḷhi; cf. also **utsūḍhi**; in mg. = Skt. utsāha), *exertion, strenuosity*: Gv 109.11 (prose) bodhisattvānām °ḍhir ājāyate.

utskhalati, or (semi-MIndic) **utkhalati**, *trips, stumbles*: ppp. °lita, as active, Mv iii.223.19 (prose) brāhmaṇagṛhapatikā nigamajānapadā utkhalitā (so Senart with 1 ms.; v.l. uskha°, intending utskha°).

utstīrya (ger. to *ut-stṛ), *wiping away* (tears): MPS 31.71 (see Waldschmidt's n. 3).

[**Udaka**, see **Uddaka.**]

udaka-candra, m., (**1**) *the moon in water*, as symbol of deceptive and unsubstantial things: Mvy 2814 (among synonyms for māyā); also **uda-candra, daka(-candra)**, qq.v.; no such form noted elsewhere; (**2**) n. of a former Buddha: Sukh 6.1.

Udakaniśrita, m. pl., n. or ep. of a class of nāgas, who are wardens (rakṣa) of the Trayastriṃśa gods: Divy 218.8 ff.

udakaprasāda (nt.? cf. next), a kind of jewel: Gv 495.1 (prose) °da-maṇiratna-.

udakaprasādaka, nt., = prec.: °ka-maṇiratna- Gv 53.2, 3; °kaṃ (n. sg.) mahāmaṇiratnam 498.14.

Udakaplotika, n. of an upāsaka at Kiṭāgiri: MSV iii.18.12 f.

udaka-bhrama, m. (cf. Skt. bhrama, perhaps *a conduit*, Schmidt, Nachtr.), *gutter for waste water* (from a bathroom): Mvy 9290 = Tib. gtor (stor) khuṅ; Mv ii.167.5 udakabhrameṇa vārāṇasīṃ nagaraṃ praviśitvā. Cf. Lévi, Karmav p. 269.

udaka-maṇi, m. (= Pali °maṇika), *water-pot*: °maṇīn pratiṣṭhāpya Divy 64.26; 81.12; 183.16; 284.27; 507.8; MSV i.79.14; °maṇayaḥ pratiṣṭhāpitāḥ Divy 306.23.

udaka-rākṣasa, m. (Pali °rakkhasa), *water-ogre*, who lives in water and devours bathers: tatra ca udakahrade udakarākṣaso (mss. °sa) prativasati punar-punaḥ janaṃ snapayantaṃ māreti Mv ii.77.17 (and in foll. lines); satkāyadṛṣṭy-udakarākṣasa-gṛhītāḥ Dbh 28.25. Also **dakarākṣasa**; see s.v. **daka.**

udaka-vāha (= Pali °vāhaka), *flood*: Mv iii.303.10 °ha-bhayaṃ vā, in a list of dangers to a caravan.

udaka-śāṭikā (= Pali °sāṭikā), *water-garment*, to be worn while bathing (= **varṣā-śāṭī**): MSV ii.84.11; 85.19 ff.

udaka-saṃvāsa, n. of a gem which keeps people from dying in the water: Gv 498.16 tad yathā kulaputrodakasaṃvāsamaṇiratnāvabaddhe (read °ddho?) kaivarta udake na mṛyate (so text).

udaka-hāra, m., °hārī, f.; °hāri(ṃ), see under 2 **hāra, -hāri,** and cf. **uda-hāraka.**

udagra, (**1**) adj. (= Pali udagga; not in this sense in Skt. or Pkt.), *joyful, delighted*: esp. often in formula, tuṣṭa udagra āttamanāḥ pramuditaḥ prītisaumanasyajātaḥ, SP 60.1; Mvy 2929–33 (udagraḥ 2930); RP 47.18; Suv 9.7; Gv 99.15, etc.; plurals, SP 69.7; also with variations, hṛṣṭatuṣṭaḥ udagra etc. Divy 297.15; hṛṣṭā abhūṣi udagrā pramuditā prītisaumanasyajātā Mv ii.163.19; in Av (e. g. i.4.1) repeatedly in the form (hṛṣṭatuṣṭapramudita) udagraprītisaumanasyajāta; (hṛṣṭa-)tuṣṭodgraprītisaumanasyajāta Karmav 28.27; (tuṣṭa) udagraḥ Suv 191.3; hṛṣṭā udagrāḥ SP 190.8 (vs); miscellaneous, SP 214.4; LV 41.17; 47.15; 271.19; 361.8; Mv i.83.7; 219.7 = ii.21.9; ii.397.18; iii.143.1; Dbh.g. 18(354).3; udagra-citta SP 56.6; 197.3; LV 392.3; Mv i.247.6; (**2**) noun, prob. nt. (cf. Pali odagya), *joy*: Mv ii.171.1 na ca te paśyāmi abhiratiṃ (so read with mss.; Senart em. °taṃ) na udagraṃ; Mv ii.147.5 and 148.5 udagram anubhavāhi, *experience joy! = farewell!*; cf. also **udagrī.** The adj. also occurs in senses recorded in Skt.; *intense*, Bbh 11.11 udagra-pratatavīrya-samanvāgataḥ.

[**Udagragāmin,** read **Udayagāmin,** q.v.]

udagrī (cf. **udagra**), *joy*, in °grī-bahula Dbh 12.10, preceded by prāmodya-, prasāda-, prīti-, utplāvanābahula, and foll. by **uśī-** (q.v.), utsāha-b°. Is the fem. form due to attraction to the surrounding fem. stems?

uda-candra = **udaka-c°** and **daka-c°**, qq.v.: °drasamā imi kāmaguṇāḥ LV 174.5 (vs), cited Śikṣ 204.15, reading dakacandranibhā.

?**ud-añcati** (= Skt. °cayati), *makes* (voice) *resound*: perh. to be read in LV 394.18, see s.v. **añja(s).**

udapāsi, aor. 3 sg., *originated, was produced*, for Skt. ud-apādi, Mv i.248.7 etc. (only in Mv; see § 32.60 for list of occurrences; sometimes written udupāsi in mss.).

udaya (m., as in Skt.), (**1**) with vyaya (cf. Pali khandhānaṃ udayavyaya or udayabbaya, as cpd.; see also **samudayāstaṃgama**), *arising and passing away* (of skandhas): SP 69.16 (vs) (dharmacakram...) skandhānām udayaṃ vyayam, (the wheel of the law...) *which is* (consists of) *the* (doctrine of the) *arising and passing away of the skandhas* (wrongly Burnouf, not quite rightly Kern); (**2**) n. of a mleccha king: Mmk 622.1.

Udayagāmi(n), n. of a former Buddha: n. sg. °miḥ, Mv i.138.7 (so Index; text Udagra°, apparently misprint).

Udayana, (**1**) n. of Śuddhodana's purohita (father of **Udāyin** 1): LV 121.1; (**2**) n. of nāga: Mvy 3324. (Also n. of the well-known king of Vatsa, as in Skt., Mv ii.2.12; cf. next.)

Udayanavatsarājaparipṛcchā, n. of a work: Śikṣ 80.13.

Udayin, see **Udāyin.**

Udayibhadra (in Pali Udāyibhadda), n. of a son of Ajātaśatru: Divy 369.10. In the same line he is called **Udāyin** (n. sg. °yī); prob. read Udāyibhadra.

Udaryā, n. of a yakṣiṇī: MSV i.xviii.17.

[**udaśvin,** read udaśvit (Skt., see BR), *a mixture of buttermilk and water*: MSV ii.34.8; 35.1.]

uda-hāraka, adj. or subst. m. (= Pali id.; Skt. uda-hāra; see s.v. **hāraka**), *carrying* (*one who carries*) *water*: Av ii.69.10.

Udāgata (v.l. **Udāragata**) n. of a former Buddha: Mv i.137.8.

Udāttakīrti (v.l. Udānta°), n. of a former Buddha: Mv i.138.11.

Udāttavarṇa (by em.; mss. Udānta°), n. of a former Buddha: Mv i.137.15.

Udāttavastra (v.l. Udānta°), n. of a former Buddha: Mv i.139.13.

udāna, m. or nt. (= Pali id.; with acc. pron. usually imam, sometimes idam), *a solemn but joyous utterance* (acc. to PTSD sometimes a sorrowful one in Pali), usually but not always having religious bearings; almost always in modulation of phrase imam (less often idam, as LV 350.21; Mv ii.286.1; or omitted) udānam udānayati (usually with sma after verb), very common: LV 103.13; 159.14; 380.15; Laṅk 2.15; Mv iii.254.13; Divy 558.1; 3 pl. udānayanti LV 31.5; Divy 163.28; aor. udānaye Mv i.351.13; ii.417.8, 13; iii.412.14; udānesi ii.286.1; udān' udānayī (3 sg. aor.) Gv 489.11 (vs); perf. udānayām āsa Suv 193.2; °āsuḥ LV 278.8; udānitavān Karmav 155.18; in non-religious connexions, udānam udānayati Divy 2.11; Av i.14.13; udānayetsu (3 pl. aor.) Mv i.340.14; udānesi (3 sg. aor.) iii.162.7; nt. udānam, as n. of a type or class of Buddh. literature, one of the 12 (Mvy) or 9 (Dharmas) pravacanāni, Mvy 1271; Dharmas 62; Udāna-varga, n. of a specific work (abbreviated Ud).

udānayati, denom., *utters an udāna*: used virtually always with object **udānam,** q.v. for forms and passages; used absolutely, without object, Mv iii.111.8 (vs) trikhuttam udānayati sulabdhā lābhā (so Senart, but mss. lābhā sulabdhā; meter is bad in either case).

[**Udānta-,** in proper names, see **Udātta-.**]

Udāyin (or Udayin? below), (**1**) = **Kālodāyin** (also appears as °dayin), q.v. (in Pali he is also called Udāyī): Mvy 1056, in text (also Mironov) printed Udayī, but Index Udāyin; Mv ii.234.8; iii.91.8; 93.3; LV 121.1 (son of the purohita Udayana); (**2**) one of the **ṣaḍvārgika** monks: Mvy 9476. (Tho not named in Pali as one of the Chabbaggiya monks, 2. Udāyī in DPPN seems to have had a character deserving this reproach and is doubtless the same person as ours.) Named Divy 543.24 as type of a monk who might commit a sin; subjected to **parivāsa** and succeeding penances, MSV iii.32.14 ff. (in Divy and MSV not identified with the ṣaḍvārgika); (**3**) n. of a son of Ajātaśatru and ancestor of Aśoka (= Pali Udāyibhadda): Divy 369.10; in the same line called, acc. to text, **Udayibhadra**; MSV ii.42.11 ff.

udāra, adj. (= **audāra**, °**rika**; neither Skt. udāra nor Pali udāra, uḷāra, seems so used), *coarse*: Samādh 22.26 (vs) yasya codāra saṃjñādi nāmarūpasmi vartate, visabhāgāya saṃjñāya udāraṃ citta jāyate, *if in the nāma-rūpa of someone there works a coarse saṃjñā etc., then, since this saṃjñā is not homogeneous* [with the pure mind], *the mind becomes coarse too* (Régamey).

Udāragata, v.l. for **Udāgata**, q.v.

Udāragupta, n. of a former Buddha: Mv i.138.12.

udārataraka, adj. (compv. of udāra plus ka), *more exalted*: AsP 373.5.

Udāradeva, n. of a Bodhisattva: Gv 442.14.

udārika, adj. = **audārika 2** (if reading is correct), *exalted, abundant*: SP 164.3 mahataś codārikasyāvabhāsasya (both edd., no v.l., but perhaps read caudār°) loke prādurbhāvo 'bhūt.

[**Udālin**, error or variant for **Upālin**, q.v.]

udāhāra, m. (= Pali id.; Skt. Lex.), *lifting up* (of the voice); *utterance*; often in comp. with vacana or another word denoting *voice* or some form of utterance: ekavacanodāhāreṇa, *with one voice (-utterance)*, Mvy 2792; LV 147.1 (śākyakumāraśatāny) ekavacanodāhāreṇāpūrvacaritaṃ samuddiśanti sma; Samādh 19.9 (devāḥ . . .) evaṃ caikodāhārasvareṇa (*with the sound of a single utterance*) vāco bhāṣante sma; in ŚsP 567.6–7 read ekodāhāreṣu na sthātavyaṃ pṛthagudāhāreṣu (or °hāre) na sthātavyaṃ vyudāhāre na sthātavyaṃ, and in 615.7–8 read ekodāhāro (text °haro) nimittaṃ vyudāhāro (text °haro) nimittaṃ pṛthagudāhāro (text °haro) nimittaṃ (see the several cpds.); ghoṣodāhāra- *utterance of sound* (in speech), Dbh 56.9 buddhānāṃ bhagavatāṃ ghoṣodāhārasattvasaṃtoṣaṇam; Gv 543.2 ghoṣodāhāra-samatāṃ (. . . anuprāptaḥ); Gv 390.22 ayaṃ praśnodāhāraḥ, *this utterance of a question*; SP 18.4 etena paraṃparodāhāreṇa *by this successive expression (utterance*; here substantially the same as *word, name*; of a succession of Tathāgatas all bearing the same name); **an-udāhāra**, adj., *without utterance, not capable of being spoken*, LV 392.15 (a-ruto 'ghoṣo) 'nudāhāraḥ, said of the Buddha's dharma; KP 59.3 (yo 'syānta-dvayasyānugamo) 'nudāhāro 'pravyāhāra(ḥ).

udikṣati (for udīkṣ°, § 3.38), *looks (up)*: 3 pl. aor. udikṣiṣu twice, in bah(u) ud° LV 364.11 (vs; Tib. sdod, *wait*); and sarva udikṣiṣu prāñjalibhūtāḥ Śikṣ 343.18 (vs; Bendall wrongly; the Tib. he cites as lha zhiṅ must surely be read lta zhiṅ).

Udiyāna, n. of a country: Mmk 325.10 °ne, loc. sg. See s.v. **Kāviśa**.

udu-pāna (= Aśokan id.), m. or nt., for Skt. uda°, *well, spring*: so repeatedly mss. of Mv, kept by Senart, who suggests (note on i.220.20) assimilation to initial u- (so Hultzsch, Inscr. Aśoka, lxx): i.220.20 (here one ms. uda°; in the rest no v.l.) = ii.23.5; i.308.5; ii.39.5; 438.6, 7; iii.380.13. It may be noted that the Mv mss. often write udupāsi for **udapāsi**, q.v.

Udumā, n. of a city, home of **Kaineya**: MSV i.255.14ff. Identified by N. Dutt with Pali Ātumā; but the corresponding story is located in Āpaṇa in Pali.

Udumbara (= Pali id., n. of a village? cf. also Lévi p. 94), n. of a town: Māy 51 (°re, loc.).

udūḍha, adj. (ppp.; Skt. Lex. = sthūla, pīvara), *coarse*, or *gross, swollen*(?): Divy 83.22 udūḍha-śiraskaḥ śaṇaśāṭikā-nivāsitaḥ (mss. saṇa°) sphaṭitapāṇipādo; same passage MSV i.82.13 uddhūta°, which seems not to fit.

udga, adj. (cf. uga, cited as Ap. from Piṅg. in Sheth, = udgata, udita), *arising, arisen*: Gv 266.16 (vs) tada saukhyam udgu (n. sg. nt.) mam' udāram abhūt.

Udgata, (**1**) (= Pali Uggata) n. of a king of Dantapura in Kaliṅga: Mv iii.364.3 (here ed. with one ms. Uggata, v.l. Udg°); 365.19; 366.8; 374.1; (**2**) n. of a maharṣi: Māy 256.23.

udgataka, f. °**ikā** (§ 22.34) = udgata, *high, elevated*: LV 322.17 (vs) kaṭhinapīnapayodhara-udgatikām, of the daughters of Māra.

udgamayati, with aruṇam, lit. *makes the dawn arise*: tatra (sc. in or on heresy) cāruṇam °yati MSV iv.53.16; i. e., prob., either (1) *and attaches great importance* to it (cf. Eng. *he thinks the sun rises and sets on* . . .), or (2) *spends all his nights* (in meditating) on it; said of a tīrthikāvakrāntaka (see **avakrāntaka**). Tib. translates literally.

udgārika, v.l. for **utkārika**, q.v.

udgīraṇa (?) see **udguraṇa**.

udguṇṭhikā (cf. Skt. Lex. avaguṇṭhikā, and Pali oguṇṭheti, °ṭhita), *veil, head-covering*: nodguṇṭhikayā Mvy 8540; -kṛta, *(one) having the head covered* (so Tib.), Mvy 8606 nodguṇṭhikākṛtāyāglānāya dharmaṃ deśayiṣyāmaḥ; similarly Bbh 106.12.

udguraṇa, or **udgūr°**, or **udgīr°**, nt. (ud plus gṛ [girati? or gurate?]; Skt. records udgoraṇa once), *brandishing* (of weapons): Mvy 8472 udguraṇam (Mironov udgūr°, v.l. udgur°) = Tib. gzas pa, *brandishing* (Das); SP 271.9 (vs) daṇḍa-udgūraṇāni, by em., kept without note in WT; mss. udgīr° (except Kashgar rec. which is altered).

udgṛhṇāti (**1**) (= Pali uggaṇhāti), *acquires (knowledge of truth), learns, comprehends*: ger. often followed by paryavāpya, Divy 18.12 uddeśayogamanasikārān udgṛhya paryavāpya; 77.21 udgṛhṇīta bhikṣavo nimittam antardhāsyati, antarhitaḥ; 207.27 te (dharmāḥ) bhikṣubhir udgṛhya paryavāpya . . . dhārayitavyā(ḥ) etc.; Mvy 784 sadodgṛhīta-dharmāvismaraṇa-; Samādh 8.15 imaṃ samādhim udgṛhītavān, udgṛhya paryavāpya dhārayitvā . . .; 19.4 samādhiṃ śroṣyati śrutvā codgrahīṣyati dhārayiṣyati . . .; 22.39 na sukaraṃ . . . kāyasya pramāṇam udgrahītum; Dbh 80.14 (sarvasattvarutapadavyañjanam) udgṛhṇīyād udgṛhya ca . . .; Karmav 28.11 atha śuko . . . bhagavatā bhāṣitam udgṛhya paryavāpya . . .; RP 42.3, 4 na jātu rūpanimittam udgṛhītavān . . . na sparśanimittam udgṛhītavān; Kv 28.6, 11; 29.11 udgṛhītum (so text each time); (**2**) *holds fast to, keeps hold of*, so AMg. uggiṇhati, = dhār rakhnā, Ratnach.): Mv i.52.1 so loko udgṛhīto sarvehi, *all* (the monks attendant on the Buddha Samitāvin) *held fast to this world* (i. e. imitated him in determining to remain until a new Buddha arose).

udgraha (m. or nt.; to prec.; cf. Pali uggaha, not in this mg.), *taking hold* (sc. of a woman's person), a saṃghāvaśeṣa sin (= **kāyasaṃsarga**): MSV iii.87.16.

udgrahaṇa, nt. (= Pali uggahaṇa; to **udgṛhṇāti**; cf. **ogrāhaka**), *grasping* (intellectually), *comprehension*: Mvy 908 = Tib. ḥdzin pa (id.); 782; Gv 496.9–10 sarvabuddhadharmodgrahaṇatayā; Dbh 79.21–22 (na tv eva) mahābāhuśrutyaprāptaḥ śrāvakaḥ śrutodgrahaṇadhāraṇīpratilabdhaḥ kalpaśatasahasrodgrahaṇādhiṣṭhānena.

udghaṭaka, m. (see also **udghāṭaka, ghaṭaka**; twice recorded udghaṭṭaka in mss.), lit. *one who opens* or *reveals*, i. e. *explains* (science or techniques; so Leumann, cited by Wogihara, Lex. 19); in cliché (aṣṭāsu parīkṣāsu, not in 100.5) udghaṭako vācakaḥ paṇḍitaḥ paṭupracāraḥ (. . .) saṃvṛttaḥ Divy 3.19; 26.14; 58.20; 100.5 (in the last two udghaṭṭakaḥ); same cliché reading ghaṭako for udgh° Divy 442.1; 523.25; and with udghāṭako MSV i.133.3; iii.20.2; *he became an expounder, explainer, scholar, one of skillful performance* (in the 'eight testings' of valuable things).

udghaṭita-jña, adj. or subst. m. (= Pali ugghaṭitaññu; see Wogihara, Lex. 19: 'das Geöffnete kennend' = 'sich auf das Offenliegende d.h. auf eine kurze Darstellung verstehend'), *understanding* (by) *a condensed statement*, opp. to **vipañcitajña, vyañjitajña**, qq.v., *understanding* (by) *a full, detailed explanation*: udghaṭitajñān (so with v.l., for text udghāṭ°) vipañcitajñān LV 400.1 (in a list of creatures, sattvān, of all kinds); same passage Mv iii.318.3 (read as in LV, or possibly °jñā for °jñān, but accs. pl.); Mvy 2384 °jñāḥ (Mironov udghaṭṭita°),

2385 vipañcitajñāḥ (Tib. on 2384 mgo smos pas go pa, *understanding by mention of chief points*); AsP 243.19 nodghaṭitajño (so two mss.; text °ghaṭṭ°) vā na vā vipañcitajño 'nabhijño vā bhaviṣyati; Bbh 295.15 vyañjitajñaḥ (q.v.) udghaṭitajñaḥ; implies high intellectual capacity, Mv iii.382.15 nipuṇo medhāvī udghaṭitajño (so read) tīkṣṇabuddhiko; other passages Mv iii.270.9; SP 473.7 (here most mss. udghā°).

udghaṭṭayati (note spelling udghaṭṭaka for **udghaṭaka**, q.v., and cf. sam plus ud plus ghaṭṭ-, BR 5.1400), *opens, loosens, undoes*: pāśāv udghaṭṭayām āsa Jm 135.2; phuṭṭakavastrāvārī udghaṭṭitā Divy 29.12, mss. (ed. em. udghāṭitā with 29.8); for udghaṭita-jñāḥ (see this) Mvy 2384, Mironov udghaṭṭita°. Cf. **ghaṭṭita**.

udghāṭa, see **aruṇodghāṭa**.

udghāṭaka, m. (adj.?), = **udghaṭaka**, q.v., *one who reveals* or *expounds*: Divy 329.20 śāsanakoṭim udghāṭako, *one who explains the height of the religious doctrine*; MSV i.133.3; iii.20.2.

udghātikā (v.l. °ṭikā; to ud plus han), in vāsodgh°, lit. perh. *interruption of, intervals between* (or, *postponement of*) *lodging*, i. e. spending the nights (on a journey) in different places in succession: Divy 173.20 tvaṃ paścād vāsodghātikayā gaccha, ahaṃ tavārthe āhāraṃ sthāpayāmi; 24 so 'pi vāsodghātikayā gantum ārabdhaḥ (the other person places caches of food for him at various points).

Uddaka, the Pali form of **Udraka**, q.v., varies with the latter (and Udaka) in mss. and ed. of Mv ii.120.10, 11; in Mv ii.207.15 ed. prints Udaka (not in Index; by misprint for Udraka?) with v.l. Uddaka; the latter also v.l. in Mv iii.322.11, 13.

uddahati (= Pali uḍḍahati), *burns up*: ger. uddahitvā Śikṣ 324.15 (vs); ppp. uddagdha daṇḍakavanaṃ LV 316.2 (vs); pass. Mv ii.262.12 (saṃvartamāne ... loke...) pṛthivīpradeśo uddahyati, *is burnt up*. See also Waldschmidt, Kl. Skt. Texte 3.117, note 2. Cf. **uddāha**, **°hana**.

uddāna, nt. (= Pali id.; see also **antaroddāna**, **piṇḍodd°**), *summary, brief statement*, esp. of the contents of a longer literary work or passage: Mvy 1476 = Tib. sdom, *summary*; Gv 496.10, cited Śikṣ 6.6, uddānabhūtaṃ sarvabodhisattvacaryāpraṇidhāna-saṃgrahaṇatayā, *it is like a summary, because it comprises all*...; Ud xx.23 uddānaṃ, applied to the following verse, which lists simply the titles of ten chapters of Ud; Karmav 82.8 asyoddānam, *this is a summary of it* (viz. of the results of a certain kind of good action; there follows in 5–6 lines the summary statement); Bbh 22.9 (refers to the following verse summarizing seven points listed just before); similarly 114.1; 137.1; 189.1; 200.1 etc.; MSV i.66.1; catvārīmāni dharmoddānāni Bbh 277.5 (and ff.), *four summary statements of doctrine*, which are then listed: (1) anityāḥ sarvasaṃskārāḥ, (2) duḥkhāḥ sarva°, (3) anātmānaḥ sarva°, (4) śāntaṃ nirvāṇam; ŚsP 1460.5, here by error for **udāna**, q.v., and see s.v. **ityuktaka**.

ud-dāyāda, adj., (one) *who has no heir*: Mvy 6972 = Tib. rabs chad pa, *having lineage cut off*; MSV i.99.14.

uddāha (m.; cf. **uddahati** and next; = AMg. id., also uḍḍāha; not noted in Pali; once in Skt., pw 7.386), *consumption by fire*, particularly in kalpoddāha, *the world-conflagration*: Śikṣ 177.14 kalpoddāhāgnibhūtaṃ (sc. bodhicittaṃ) sarvaduṣkṛtanirdahanatayā; 324.15; Laṅk 231.18 pṛthivī kalpoddāhe dahyamānā; Gv 389.4 kalpoddāhe (misprinted kulp°) yathā vahniḥ.

uddāhana (nt.? cf. prec.), in kalpodd°, (world-) *conflagration*: Gv 494.25 kalpoddāhanabhūtaṃ (sc. bodhicittaṃ) sarvaduṣkṛtanirdahanatayā (cf. Śikṣ 177.14, s.v. **uddāha**, cited from Maitreyavimokṣa; our passage is from the Maitreya chapter of Gv, extracts from which, not including this one, are cited from Gv by name in Śikṣ 5.20 ff.; the two seem not to be identical).

uddiśati, *poses, proposes* (a mathematical problem; Tib. rtsis mgo phogs, *set the beginning of a calculation*): LV 146.12 tatra bodhisattvaś coddiśati, ekaś ca śākyakumāro nikṣipati (*figures, works out* the problem) sma; na ca pariprāpayati sma bodhisattvasyaikadvau ... yāvat pañcāpi śākyakumāraśatāni yugapatkāle nikṣipanti sma, na ca pariprāpayanti sma; tato bodhisattva āha: uddiśata yūyam, ahaṃ nikṣepsyāmīti... (19) pañcāpi śākyakumāraśatāni yugapad uddiśanti sma, na ca paripṛāpayanti sma bodhisattvasya nikṣipataḥ; 146.22; in 147.1 samuddiśanti, same mg. The Tib. renders nikṣipati by brtsis (brtsi, fut.), rtsis, *calculate, figure*. In same sense, uddiśati sma Mvy 6657 = Tib. sbaṅs (? sbyaṅs?) pa, or luṅ phog pa (?); Chin. uses the word used for BHS **vyākaraṇa** (3).

uddiśana (nt.? to **uddiśati**), *prescription, order*: RP 31.11 (vs) śayyāsanoddiśana (n. sg.) teṣāṃ naiva bhaviṣyate 'pi ca kadācit (no *order* for them is needed; they are provided without it).

uddiśyati (= **uddiśati**; not recorded in this sense), *recognizes*: Divy 191.3 (māṃ ...) śāstāram uddiśyadbhir madyam apeyam, *those who recognize me as teacher must not drink liquor*.

uddiṣṭaka (ppp. of uddiśati plus -ka, perhaps specifying, § 22.39; cf. AMg. uddiṭṭha [*food etc.*] *specially prepared for an ascetic*, Ratnach.), (one who or that which has been) *appointed, specified, prescribed*; only in saṃghoddiṣṭaka,... *by the brotherhood*: Mmk 291.15 °kāṃ bhikṣāṃ bhojayitvā, *having fed them the food prescribed by the brotherhood*; same, with bhikṣām understood, 294.7; in 701.20 saṃghoddiṣṭaka-bhikṣavo (*monks* [as] *directed by the assembly*) bhojayitavyā(ḥ); 711.24 prabhāte saṃghoddiṣṭakā bhikṣavo (n. pl.) bhojayitavyā(ḥ); °kān bhikṣūn MSV iii.20.14.

(**uddeśa**, m. [= Pali uddesa; the Skt. use, see BR s.v. 2, is perhaps close enough to justify calling it the same mg.], *exposition, explanation, setting forth* (of a doctrine): Bbh 68.15 °śaḥ svādhyāyo viniścayaḥ...; 264.25 °śa-dānena; 297.3 °śa-svādhyāya-saṃpratipatti-pāraṃparya-yogena; 410.3. See **śramaṇoddeśa**, **°śikā**.)

-uddeśaka, m. (= Pali uddesaka), *director, manager*: Mvy 9056 vihāroddeś°; 9057 bhaktoddeś° (= Pali bhattoddes°).

-uddeśika, adj. (= Pali uddesika), *intended for*, in ātmodde° *intended for oneself*: Prāt 480.8 °kaṃ (kuṭiṃ, *hut*), in parallel to Pali Vin. iii.149.11, where attuddesaṃ (sc. kuṭiṃ).

uddhanana, see **uddhānana**.

uddhara (m.? only in comp.; to Skt. ud with hṛ; also **an-uddhara-tā** below), *neglect, ignoring*: LV 342.8 (vs) evaṃ hi teṣa bhavate guru-uddharāṇāṃ (so best mss. and ed.), *for so it happens to those who ignore* (the words of) *the Master*; RP 37.14 na karmakriyoddhareṇa (bhavitavyam), *one must not ignore, neglect*...; an-ud° *non-neglect*, LV 432.18 -ānuśāsany-anuddhara-, *non-neglect of instruction*; in LV 440.4 (prose), for ed. anuddharatayā, read anuddhuratayā (anuddhara-tā, abstr.; grāhyavacanatām, sc. pratilapsyate), (*he will attain a state of having his words accepted*) *because* (they) *will not be ignored*, lit. *by reason of non-ignored-ness*. (Possibly read with some mss. anuddharaṇa-tayā, which would mean the same.)

uddharati (special mg. of Skt. id.; Pali has ppp. ubbhata, of kathina, Vin. i.255.19, = BHS uddhṛta), *suspends, stops, cancels* (the **kaṭhina** ceremony); cf. Pali (kaṭhin)uddhāra: uddhṛte kaṭhine Prāt 490.10 and ff. (Chin. as rendered by Finot otherwise); MSV ii.157.9 (the kaṭhināstāraka speaks, in ending the ceremony) śva āyuṣmantaḥ kaṭhinam uddhariṣyāmi, yūyaṃ svakasvakāni cīvarāṇy adhitiṣṭhata (*take possession of*...); 158.7 (corair muṣitakānāṃ) bhikṣūṇām arthāya kaṭhinam (which had been concluded) uddhartavyam (*must be suspended*); 158.19 uddhṛtam saṃghena coramuṣitakānām bhikṣūṇām arthāya; 159.1–2 bhājite yasyābhipretaṃ tena svakāt pratyaṃśāt coramuṣitakānāṃ bhikṣūṇāṃ saṃvibhāgaḥ kartavyaḥ.

[**uddhartya** MSV iii.137.8, *having lifted up*, read prob. udvartya, cf. parallel ii.129.15 udvartitaḥ; uddhṛtya would also be possible.]

uddhava (m.? cf. Deśīn. i.106 uddhava [comm. uddhavaa] = utkṣipta), perhaps *pride, arrogance* (so pw 7.324); or *excitement* (so pw 6.298; in some passages the context seems more favorable to this): in a verse found twice in Divy (69.13; 72.22) and repeatedly in Av (i.6.8; 12.4 etc.), vigatoddhavā dainyamadaprahīṇā buddhā(ḥ); otherwise recorded only in Jm: 70.22 avinaya-ślāghānu-vṛtty-uddhavāt; 74.15 yuddhoddhavābhimukhatāṃ; 124.15 darpoddhavād apratisaṃkhyayā vā; 141.15 amarṣa-darpoddhava-karkaśāni; 200.20 naṣṭa-harṣoddhava-dravaḥ; 227.11 vyāvṛtta-pramododdhavena manasā; 233.4 durjanaḥ paṭutarāvalepoddhavaḥ.

uddhānana, or (v.l., and Mironov's text, with v.l. uddhā°) **uddhanana**, nt., *rude behavior*: Mvy 5193 = Tib. rgod byed (which probably has this meaning, despite Das); so one Chin. interpretation. Cf. **samuddhānana** (°**dhanana**).

uddhāra (m.?), (**1**) some branch of mathematics, perhaps *subtraction* (or *debits*? accounting of debts, cf. 2), in a cliché, list of subjects studied by youths, mudrāyām uddhāre nyāse nikṣepe ... Divy 3.18; 26.12; 58.17; 100.1; 441.28; MSV iii.20.1; seems to be replaced in Mv by **dhāraṇa**, °**ṇā**, q.v.; (**2**) (= Pali id., and once in Skt., Kāty. Dharmaś., acc. to Stenzler cited in pw) *debt*, in uddhārīkṛtam, Divy 23.15 kiṃcid ud° *has anything been incurred as a debt*?; (**3**) kaṭhinoddhāra (see **uddharati**; Pali uddhāra and ubbhāra), *suspension, cancellation*: MSV ii.161.14 ff.

uddhāraka (m. or nt.), *act of lifting*, in pādoddhārakeṇa, instr., *with lifting up of the feet*: Divy 211.26 yadā teṣāṃ ṛṣikopena pakṣāṇi śīrṇāni tatas te pādod° prasthitāḥ; 211.27, 28.

[**uddhura**, in anuddhuratayā LV 440.4, read **uddhara**, q.v.]

? **uddhya** (m.? so Skt. Lex., once in literature, BR), perhaps *river, stream* (suspected by BR of being only n. pr. of a river); in LV 274.12 (prose) (mahatā) puṣpāḍhyena (pravarṣatā), should mean *with a great stream of flowers raining down*. Both edd. puṣpāḍhyena, which can only be understood if a noun for *stream* or *rain* is supplied; nearly all mss. puṣpodyena; udya is recorded as v.l. in a Hindu Lex. for uddhya, see BR; perhaps read puṣpod-dhyena, or even puṣpodyena with mss.? Tib. me tog maṅ poḥi char chen po ni ḥbebs, *a great rain of many flowers rained down*.

uddhvasyate (pass. to Skt. ud-dhvaṃs-), and caus. °**syāpayati**, *is* (*causes to be*) *insulted* or *mocked*; so read in Śikṣ 57.6, 8, see s.v. **udvaśyate**.

udbilya, udvilya, nt. (= **audbilya**, q.v.), *joy, pleasurable excitement*: prabhayā kāyacittodbilyasaṃjananyā LV 41.5 (cf. under audbilya, also with prabhā); (prabhayā ...) kāyacittaprahlādodbilyajananyā LV 281.11 (so most mss., Lefm. °daudbilya°); (vāk ...) kāyacittodbilyakaraṇī LV 286.12; kāyacittodbilyakaraṇatayā (of speech) LV 440.6; udvilya-(mss. udvīla, °ra)-harṣā hāhākāraṃ udīretsuḥ Mv i.266.14; cittodbilya-karī (of Buddha's voice; n. sg. f.) Mvy 462; cittodvilyaṃ pratilabhante Sukh 58.3; cittodvilyasamanvāgatāḥ Sukh 61.13.

udbhāvaka, f. °**ikā**, adj. (cf. next), *manifesting, declaring, setting forth*: dharmaparyāyodbhāvikā priyavāditā Bbh 219.20, and similarly in foll. lines.

udbhāvana, nt., and °**nā**, f. (= AMg. °ṇā; °na recorded in this mg. once in Skt., pw 1.298), (laudatory) *manifestation, making known, declaration*: LV 5.19 mahāyānodbhāvanārthaṃ; 5.20 sarvabodhisattvānāṃ codbhāvanārtham; otherwise noted only in cpd. guṇodbhāvanā, rarely °na, *manifestation* or *making known, proclamation of virtues*: Divy 184.21 Svāgatasya guṇodbhāvanāṃ kartukāmaḥ; 492.23 °nāsya kartavyā; Kv 14.17 (śrutā ...) āryāvalokiteśvarasya guṇ°nā; same 14.19, 20; 15.12; 16.2; āryāvalokiteśvarasya guṇ°nāṃ kurute (in words then quoted) 18.10; nt., vikurvitāni śrūyante guṇodbhāvanāni ca 24.10, but 24.13 guṇodbhāvanāṃ śṛṇu; 48.17 °nāṃ bhāṣitum ārabdhaḥ.

udbhida, m. (= Pali, in cpd. ubbhidodaka; Skt. udbhid, acc. to pw fem.), *spring, fountain*: Mvy 4176 = Tib. chu mig.

–**udbhuta** (m.c. for udbhūta), *manifested, appeared*: LV 282.2 (vs); read gātrodbhutā (= gātrā ud°) with mss. and Tib.

udbhūta-vastuka, adj., *for which the site* (vastu) *is visible*: (**kalpika-śālā** ...) °tukā MSV i.235.5; glossed in 14 by prahīṇa-vastukā, *the site for which has been abandoned* (i. e. not in use otherwise); seems to correspond to Pali gahapati (°tī?) Vin. i.240.2 (see comm. 1099.17 ff.), *one offered by a layman*.

? **udya**, in puṣpodya (mss.), see **uddhya**.

Udyataka (m.?), n. of an ocean (samudra) in which the nāḍikerī tree grows: Gv 501.26.

udyāna (in Skt. nt., *park*, and so Pali uyyāna), (**1**) *park*, as m. (? with m. form of pron.): udyāna sarve (n. pl.) LV 231.1 (vs); (**2**) *advance* (of an army), one of the arts mastered by the young Bodhisattva: LV 156.12 udyāne (Tib. mdun du bsnur ba, *moving forward*) niryāṇe avayāne ...; (**3**) in Dbh.g. 20(356).11 divide, probably, udyāna (for °naṃ) dhāraṇ' (for °ṇīnām! § 10.207) ita (= itaḥ) pañcamim (sc. bhūmim) ākramanti, *for this reason* (so Chin.) *they enter the fifth* (stage), *a garden of dhāraṇīs* (so Chin.). Were it not for the Chin. translation, I should be tempted to understand udyāna-dhāraṇ(am)..., *they proceed to maintenance of progress* (in general; an extension of 2, above) *from this point to the fifth* (stage). It may, however, be noted that in the prose of Dbh, 5th Bhūmi, the words udyāna (in mg. *park*) and dhāraṇī occur, not to be sure together, but in 45.24 and 46.12 respectively.

udyāma, m. (cf. Vedic id., the mg. of which in some places, ŚB 8.5.1.13, is not clear), in sūtrodyāmaḥ Divy 643.1 = 644.9, perhaps *extension, drawing out* (of thread), see s.v. **tatkṣaṇa**; but the precise meaning of the phrase excapes me. It may mean *effort, exertion* (Skt. udyama), as in Aśokan u(y)yāma, Rock Ed. (Kalsi) 13.18. In this sense probably read nir-udyāmā, as suggested by Kashgar rec., SP 100.9 (prose).

udyūthikā, f. subst. (adj.?), (cf. Pali uyyodhika, Vin. iv.107.26, old comm. = yattha sampahāro dissati, the correspondent of our word, which seems to have been Sktized by association with yūtha, prob. unhistorically; root yudh is doubtless the true source; but mg. is rather obscure, see Childers, who guesses *sham fight*), perhaps some sort of military exercise, such as *sham battle*; in Mvy 8470 °kā-gamanam = Tib. gyul bśams pa ḥkhrug tu (ḥgro ba), (going to) *an army prepared for battle*? or *a battle-prepared combat* (i. e. a military maneuver)?; in Prāt 512.6 seemingly adj. with senā, udyūthikāṃ senāṃ darśanāya (Chin. *regarder les manœuvres*, Finot); in accord with this possibly udyūthikā in Mvy may imply senā, meaning (an army) *ready for military operations* (?).

Udyogapāla, n. of a yakṣa-leader: Māy 235.31.

? **udyojayati** (see also s.v. **udyotita**), acc. to Bendall and Rouse, Śikṣ Transl. 57 note 1, = Pali uyyojeti, *dismisses, sends away*: Śikṣ 56.2 yāvad dharmaśravaṇikāś codyojayitavyāḥ parṣanmaṇḍalaṃ parisaṃsthāpayitavyam; but Tib. brtson par ḥgyur, = (to be) *made zealous*, the regular Skt. mg.; yāvad can be understood as *up to the point* (in the text where it is said –), thus fitting this mg., and B. and R.'s interpretation seems implausible.

They assume the same mg. for Mv iii.141.12 (bhagavān .... asuranayutāni ... samyaksaṃbodhīye vyākaritvā bahūni ca prāṇisahasrāṇi āryadharmeṣu pratiṣṭhāpayitvā rājānaṃ śuddhodanaṃ ca) saparivāraṃ ca udyojaye; but here too this verb (mss. udyojeya or °yaṃ) may well mean *aroused, inspired*, as regularly in Skt.; this accords well with the preceding parts of the sentence, and seems more natural than *dismissed* (tho Ś. and his followers did in fact depart, as the next sentence says).

? **udyoṭita,** in Prāt 513.7 eṣa bhikṣu(r) muhūrtam apy udyoṭitaḥ syād, acc. to Chin. (Finot) would seem to mean (*may this monk be*) *annoyed* (if only for a moment). But for this, I should assume a substitute for udyojitaḥ, *dismissed, sent away* (ppp. to **udyojayati,** q.v., in mg. of Pali uyyojeti). Cf. AMg. joḍiya (= yojita, Ratnach.), *united*; Hindi joṛnā; Skt. Dhātup. juṭ, juḍ, *join*.

Udraka Rāmaputra (= Pali Uddaka, which also occurs in mss. of Mv, see s.v., Rāmaputta; see also **Rudraka**), n. of a teacher with whom the Bodhisattva studied for a time: Mv ii.119.8 ff.; 200.13; iii.322.11, 13; Mvy 3516; Udraka (alone), associated with **Ārāḍa,** q.v., Divy 392.1, 3; Mv ii.200.8; and with Devadatta (as persons of bad conduct), Śikṣ 105.17. Udraka also Buddhacarita 12.84 ff. Tib. lhag spyod (*superior conduct*) for Udraka (Mvy) and **Rudraka** (LV 243.15 ff.).

Udrāyaṇa, (**1**) n. of a disciple of Śākyamuni (= Pali DPPN 2 Udena?): Mvy 1060; (**2**) another form of **Rudrāyaṇa,** q.v., a king of Roruka: Divy 565.30 (prose; mss.); 567.20 (vs; here Rudr° would be metrically impossible; nevertheless the same pāda is repeated 570.4 with the unmetrical reading Rudr°!).

(**udvartayati** [= Pali ubbaṭṭeti; in Skt. rare and chiefly ppp. udvartita], *rubs down, anoints*, or the like: Mv ii.423.7 (kumāraṃ) ... udvarteti supeti; so 433.12; °teti ca snāpeti ca iii.405.7.)

[**udvaśyate,** Śikṣ 57.8 °yamānas, and caus. Śikṣ 57.6 udvaśyāpayitvā, for which Tib. mtho brtsams la is cited, 57.6, read **uddhvasyate,** pass. of Skt. ud-dhvaṃs-, *is mocked*, and caus. uddhvasyāp° (§ 38.13).]

udvahana (nt.; perhaps Sktization of Pali *ubbahana, to ubbahati *pluck out, destroy*, prob. from Skt. ud-vṛh-), *removal, destruction*: duḥkhodvahanacittāś ca Bbh 248.8; saṃsāre sarva-duḥkhodvahanāya bhavati 249.6.

? **udvighāṭana,** *opening* (?); see **vighāṭana.**

udviciya, ger. (perhaps to otherwise unrecorded ud-vi-ci-, *pluck, gather*): Mv ii.244.7 (prose) puṣpāṇi udviciya, *gathering flowers* (v.l. uddhiricya).

udvilya, see **udbilya.**

udvīkṣya, adj. (gdve., to ud-vi-īkṣ-), (*worthy to be gazed at,*) *beautiful*: Mv iii.69.16 bhavanāni (*houses, palaces*) ... udvīkṣyāṇi.

udvetana (m. or nt.), a high number: Gv 106.17; corresponds to **upavarta,** q.v.

udvedha (m.? = Pali ubbedha, defined as *height*; AMg. uvveha, defined by Ratnach. only as *depth*; Pkt. uvveha, acc. to Sheth *height* or *depth*, also zamīn-ka avagāha, *penetration of the ground* [?]), *height* (so surely in most cases): Śikṣ 246.5 lokadhātuḥ saṃtiṣṭhate, caturaśītiryojanasahasrāṇy udvedhena; Mv i.196.17; iii.229.14; 232.10 (yaṣṭi, or yaṣṭī ...) dvādaśayojanāni udvedhena; Mv i.196.2 (iṣikāni, so text ...) dvādaśapauruṣā udvedhena; here preceded by figures relating to *depth* (extent of penetration of the ground), see **naikhanya,** and *circumference* (? see **parigohya**); in a close parallel, Mv iii.228.13, (iṣīkāni ...) dvādaśapuruṣa-udvedhena (mss. udvehena, uddehena) is preceded by the statement of depth (**naikhanya**) and by a form read by Senart tripauruṣoccāni, which would refer to *height* and so be inconsistent with -udvedhena (which, however, if it meant *depth*, would be inconsistent with the preceding form containing naikhanya); it seems that Senart should have assumed -parigohya (as in i.196.2; or some form relating to *circumference*) instead of -ucca (mss. read -pauruṣaroccāni or -puruṣaroddhā, perhaps showing, in the syllable -ro-, a faint trace of that original). Senart himself saw this in his note on i.196.2, but overlooked it on iii.228.13. Cf. **āvedha, pravedha.**

udveṣṭayati, *tears apart, destroys*: (tadāsya gṛhād ekaikāṃ) śilām °yāma iti MSV i.229.5; = Tib. bkogs te gzhig go, *pulling apart we will destroy*.

udvyastikā, *a posture with hands joined at the back of the neck*: Mvy 8543; so Tib. (gñaḥ goṅ du [mi = Skt. na] bsnol) and Chin.; = **vyastikā** (-kṛta); cf. also **vinyastikā, atyastikā,** one of which probably = this.

unnaḍa, adj. (= Pali unnaḷa; doubtless dial. form of next), *haughty, arrogant*: Śikṣ 120.4 an-un°, foll. by parallel anuddhata.

unnata, (**1**) adj. (ppp.; cf. prec. and next; not recorded in this evil sense), *arrogant*: Mv i.305.15 uddhatāṃ unnatāṃ dṛṣṭvā capalāṃ ...; Śikṣ 158.5 bodhisattvo 'n-unnatavīryo bhavati; (**2**) n. of a former Buddha: LV 5.8; Mv i.137.12 (here of course in the good sense recorded in Skt. and Pali, *lofty*).

unnati, f. (not recorded in this evil sense; cf. prec. and **unnamana**), *pride, arrogance*: Śikṣ 157.14 °tiṃ varjayet sadā.

Unnatoṣṇīṣa, n. of one of the 8 Uṣṇīṣa-rājānaḥ (see **uṣṇīṣa** 3): Mmk 41.11.

unnamana (nt.), or °**nā** (= **unnati,** q.v.), *pride, arrogance*: Bbh 201.18 (vigatamānaṃ) tena vīryārambheṇānunnamanāt (neg. an-un°); Sukh 7.20 (vs) tenonnamanā na cāsti śāstuḥ.

unnayati (not recorded in this sense), *brings up* = *raises* (a child); pass. unnīyate (°ti): Mv ii.210.14 tahiṃ āśramapade so māṇavako unnīyati, *in this hermitage-place the boy was brought up*.

(**an-**)**unnahana**(**-tā**), (cf. Skt. unnaddha, *haughty*), (*state of absence of*) *pride*: Śikṣ 119.5.

unnāma (AMg. uṇṇāma, unnāma, *elation, pride*; in Skt. one doubtful occurrence where, if correct, it means [physical] *elevation*; not in Pali), *elevation* (of spirits), *elation*; usually in comp. with its opposite **avanāma** or °**mana,** once with **nāma,** also of opposite mg.: Gv 244.3 an-unnāmāvanāma-tāṃ, *state of not being elated* or *depressed*; Śikṣ 105.5 lābhālābhatayā unnāmāvanāma-karo, *causing elation or depression by getting or not getting*; Śikṣ 108.12 (vs) unnāma-nāmāni bahūni gacchatī, *goes to many fits of elation and depression*, see s.v. **nāma** = avanāma; Śikṣ 150.6 nonnāmajāto bhavati; LV 33.7, text an-unnāmāvanāmana-tāyai, *unto being not subject to elation or depression* (mss. vary greatly).

-unnodana(**-tā,** in comp.; nom. act. to ud-nud-, no form or deriv. of which is otherwise recorded), *thrusting forth* (from), *driving out* (of): Gv 491.19–20 sarvālayanilayonnodanatāyai, said of activities of a candidate for Bodhisattvahood.

unmatti, f. (= Skt. unmāda), *madness*: Mmk 567.5 (prose) (yadi gacchen) maraṇonmattiṃ vā prayacchante.

Unmada, m., n. of a demon that causes madness: Mvy 4760 = Tib. smyo byed. Cf. **Unmāda,** in similar list of demons.

unmananā, *disrespect, contemptuous treatment*: Śikṣ 185.1 °nāṃ kutsanāṃ sahate. No *un-man- seems recorded.

unmardana (m.), n. or epithet of some hostile (magic or supernatural) power: Māy 237.27 °nātaḥ, abl.; follows huvanātaḥ, see **huvana**; followed by bhūtātaḥ vetāḍātaḥ etc.

Unmāda, n. of a class of demons (causing madness), = **Unmada,** which occurs in a similar list: Māy 219.9 etc.

Unmādayantī, n. of a woman: Jm 81.8. In Pali version of same story called Ummadantī; see DPPN.

unmijitakā (?), *a turning sideways*: in śīrṣonmijitakayā, instr., LV 62.21 (prose), *with a turning of their heads to one side* (they gazed at the Blessed One); of gods. So apparently Tib. mgo byol nas. Is the word somehow related to un-miñj- (see the foll. words)? The only v.l. is A śirṣāmiñjitakāyā; I have thought of śirsāniñjitakāyā(ḥ), *with bodies unmoved as to the heads* (see **aniñjita**). But Tib. clearly had no such reading (and no word for *body*).

unmiñja, m. (to ud-miñj, cf. under **miñj-**; and next), apparently lit. *opening*, and so *starting, initial development, initiation* of something: Dbh 18.17 sattveṣu mahākaruṇonmiñjaḥ saṃbhavati, and 19 mahāmaitryunmiñjaḥ, of Bodhisattvas; Sukh 4.4 (udāraḥ khalu ta) unmiñjo bhadrikā mīmāṃsā kalyāṇaṃ pratibhānaṃ. Müller (SBE 49 Pt. 2, p. 4) translates *question*, stating that 'all the Chinese translators' translate so.

unmiñjita, nt. and adj. (see s.v. **miñj-**, and cf. prec. two), (**1**) nt. *opening*, as of the mouth (so Mvy 6303): Mvy 2670; 6303 (in both Tib. phye ba); AsP 268.19 ff. parapudgalānām unmiñjita-nimiñjitāni, lit. *openings and closings of* (or, *things opened and closed by* = *beginnings and endings, starts and finishes, of*) *other individuals*; Gv 84.21, of an ascetic, tasya ... śāntasya nirunmiñjitasya (*without initiation* of anything) nirālambasya; (**2**) adj. *opened* = *initiated, begun*: Dbh 39.22 °tāni nimiñjitāni vicintitāni vitarkitāni... (see **kelāyati**) niketasthānāni tāni sarvāṇi vigatāni bhavanti sma; (**3**) nt. *mouthful* (lit. *opening*, sc. of the mouth, as in Mvy 6303) Śikṣ 215.16 (śvasv api...) ekaudanonmiñjitam ekālopaṃ vā parityajati, *throws even to dogs ... a single mouthful of porridge or a single bit of food.*

unmūḍha, adj. (ppp. to ud-muh-; = Pkt. ummūḍha), *infatuated*: Śikṣ 185.4 °ḍha-cittaṃ nigṛhṇāti.

? **unmūḍhi**, suggested em. for **utsūḍhi**, q.v.: Mvy 7683.

unmūrdhaka, f. °**ikā**, adj. (= unmūrdhan, *mit aufgerichtetem Kopfe*, pw 5.250), *with head thrown back*: Mv ii.452.6 (rājā) kuśo... sudarśanāye devīye unmūrdhikāye (i. e. trying to escape from his violent embrace) āliṅgito (the king, whom the queen did not recognize, was hideously ugly).

(-)**upaka**, (**1**) at end of cpds. (= Pali -upaka, -ūpaka, °ikā f.; BHS also has equivalent **-upaga**, q.v.), *pertaining, belonging to* ...; *suitable, appropriate* (to)...; *fit* (for)...; *like*: Vaj. fragment in Pargiter ap. Hoernle MR 180.3–4 naivasaṃjñānopakā(ḥ), haplog. for naivasaṃjñānāsaṃjñāyatanopakāḥ, which read, *belonging to the* ... (= °yatanopagāḥ Dharmas 129, see **-upaga**; Vaj. ed. 20.18–19 reads naivasaṃjñino nāsaṃjñino, a secondary recast); kulopaka (= Pali kulūpaka), lit. *belonging to a family*, = *family associate*, said of a monk who is regularly supported by a certain family, Mv i.244.12 (tasya yo mātāpitṛṇāṃ, so mss., Senart em. °tṝṇāṃ) bhikṣu kulopako āsi; (in Av ii.67.9 replaced by **kulopagata**, q.v.; in Mv iii.453.3 wrongly read by em. in text, see s.v. **kalopī**;) also, by extension, said of the houses visited by such monks, Divy 307.2 kulopaka- (mss. kulopa-) gṛheṣu gatvā, and 3 te kulopakagṛhāṇy upasaṃkrāntāḥ; prob. by analogy with this word Mv iii.372.16 prajñopaka (em. for ājñop°, ājñāp°; context makes em. seem quite certain), *dependent on prajñā*, (śīlaṃ śirim [so mss.] caiva kṛtajñatā ca) prajñopakā tu pravarā bhavanti, *but* (the virtues of) *morality, majesty, and gratitude are excellent* (but) *subordinate to prajñā*; akāryopaka, *not fit for use*, KP 131.2 anarghaṃ vaiḍūryamahāmaṇiratnam uccāre patitam akāryopakaṃ bhavati; yathopakam, adv., *according to what is fitting*, Mv iii.257.6; 272.4 (after a seat of honor has been provided for the Buddha) °kaṃ ca bhikṣusaṃghasya, *and* (seats) *for the assembly of monks according to propriety* (i. e. relative rank); nirupaka, apparently adj., *without a correspondent* or *match, peerless, unequalled*, Gv 301.11 (vs) dharmaś ca me nirupakāyu (i. e. nirupaka = °kaḥ plus ayu = ayaṃ) śrutaḥ; (**2**) (= Pali id.) n. of a Ājīvaka, with whom Buddha conversed while going to Benares to deliver his First Sermon: Mv iii.325.12 ff. (note esp. 326.20 tasmād ahaṃ upaka jino, a line which elsewhere contains the form **Upaga**, q.v.); (**3**) n. of a purohita's son in the Upāli-Gaṅgapāla Jātaka: Mv iii.184.1 ff.; corresponds to the character Aḍḍhamāsaka in the Pali Gaṅgamāla Jāt., see DPPN.

upakaṇṭhaka (nt.? = Skt. °ṭha), *vicinity*: Divy 174.3 (prose) udapānopakaṇṭhake viśrāntaḥ.

Upakambala, n. of a nāga king: Mmk 18.9.

upakara, adj. (and subst. m.?; to Skt. upa-kṛ), *beneficent*: Bbh 218.1 vāg upakarā; 218.6, 16 upakarāṃ (in 16 text °kārāṃ, erroneously) vācam; Śakrapraśnasūtra, Waldschmidt, Kl. Skt. Texte 4,113.2–4 upakaras tvaṃ tāta pañcaśikhāsmāka(m u)pakaraś ca yo hi nāma...; MSV i.287.13.

upakaraṇa, = bhoga, *food*: Bbh 246.24 upakaraṇavaikalya-jaṃ (duḥkham), one of 5 kinds of duḥkha, clearly = 293.10 bhoga-vaikalya-duḥkha-, *pain due to defects in food*; prob. in this mg. Bbh 11.1 upakaraṇavikalasya jīvikāpekṣāyaṃ caturtha upakleśaḥ; MSV iii.19.20; 134.10. Cf. **upakāraṇa**.

-upakarṣikā, acc. to Tib. *dishevelled state* (of the hair of the head): LV 227.9 (prose; of the harem women mourning the loss of the Bodhisattva) kāścic chīrṣopakarṣikayā ... rudanti sma (Tib. mgo ḥbal lo, *had their heads dishevelled*).

Upakāṇa, n. of a nāga king: Māy 247.24.

? **upakāraṇa** (cf. AMg. uvagāraṇa = Skt. upakāra? or for Skt. and Pali upakaraṇa?), in Mmk 48.10 evaṃ laḍḍukāgarbhoktārakaviśeṣān (? seems corrupt) pūpopakāraṇān sarvadevabhūtagaṇān sarvasattvāṃś ca mantropetān vidhinā niryātayet. We seem to need dat. instead of acc. forms for °gaṇān and °sattvāṃś (as in the following parallel sentence); with that change, pūpopakāraṇān might mean *benefactions consisting of cakes*, or *instruments* (cf. upakaraṇa) *of* (making) *cakes*; or, with a mg. characteristic of upakaraṇa in Pali rather than Skt., *commodities consisting of cakes*; or finally, if = BHS **upakaraṇa** in Bbh 246.24 (see s.v.), *food consisting of cakes.*

Upakāla (= next; associated in both mgs. with **Kāla**, q.v.), (**1**) n. of a nāga king: Mvy 3252; (**2**) n. of a yakṣa leader: Māy 236.10 (prose).

Upakālaka (= prec.), (**1**) n. of a nāga king: Māy 247.4 (prose); (**2**) n. of a yakṣa: Māy 7 (vs; cpd. Kālopakālakau).

upakileśa = **upakleśa**, q.v.

upakīrṇaka (cf. Skt. upakīrṇa, *covered, bestrewn*), in Rājopakīrṇaka (sūtra), q.v.; mg. not clear, but the subject of the story suggests *falling, reverting* (to the king; of the property of one who dies without heirs), or *that which has reverted* etc.

Upakuśa, n. of a cakravartin king: Mvy 3567.

Upakeśinī, n. of a Buddhist deity or yakṣiṇī, always associated with **Keśinī**, q.v.: Sādh 118.18; 120.4; 121.19; 131.18 (all prose). See next.

Upakeśī, once for **Upakeśinī** in vs (doubtless m.c.): Sādh 113.19.

upakrama, m. (= Pali upakkama; to **upakramati**; see also **upasaṃkrama**), *violence, doing violence to*..., *attack* (by violence): LV 258.2 (vs) kāyopakrama-karaṇai(r) manyante bāliśāḥ śuddhiṃ; Mv ii.448.12 °meṇa ātmānaṃ māreyā; 492.1 ātmānaṃ ca upakrameṇa māritukāmaḥ; similarly 493.20; Divy 235.9 sa evaṃvidha upakramaḥ kṛtaḥ; Bbh 244.6 ātmopakrama-duḥkham, and 7 paropakrama-duḥkham, ... *thru violence by oneself* and *by others.*

upakramaṇa (nt.? = Pali upakkamana), = **upakrama**, *violent attack*: Gv 244.1 sarvasattvakāyotpīḍanopakramaṇādhivāsayamānān, *enduring ... violent attacks.*

upakramati, also °**meti** (= Pali upakkamati; Skt.

upakrāmati in this sense once, Mbh 13.6716; cf. **upakrama, °maṇa, °mika, aupakramika**), *attacks, does violence to*: Mv ii.459.16 upakramemi ātmānaṃ mārayiṣyaṃ; 492.(7–)8 mātmānam (mss.) upakramāhi; iii.25.2 ātmānaṃ upakramiṣyāmi, and 4 °nam upakramitukāmaḥ; Divy 264.12 upakrāntā, ppp., see s.v. **upasaṃkrama.**

-upakramika, adj. (also **aupa°**, q.v.; upakrama plus ika: = Pali opakkamika), *due to, caused by violence, violent attack*: Gv 152.6 (vyādhīn...) amanuṣyavaikārikān api viṣayaparopakramikān api (cf. Bbh 63.5 s. v. **aupakramika**); (ābādho...) ātmopakramiko vā paropakramiko vā MSV ii.45.8; otherwise recorded only in a cliché, ātmopakramikāṃ (*due to self-inflicted violence*) śarīropatāpikāṃ duḥkhāṃ tīvrāṃ kharāṃ kaṭukām amanāpāṃ (te added once) vedanāṃ vedayanti LV 246.14 (vedayante); 263.7; (in Mv amanāpāṃ omitted) Mv ii.121.5, 10–11; 122.1, 8, 16; 123.5; 130.7–8, 10. A shorter Pali form MN i.241.10 opakkamikā dukkhā tippā kaṭukā vedanā vediyanti (Pali has no *attopakkamika). In Mv vedanā is usually recorded instead of °nāṃ.

upakliśyate (cf. Pali ppp. upakkiliṭṭha; and **upakleśa**), *is stained*: Bbh 10.8 (caturbhir upakleśair...) upakliṣṭo bhavati; Śikṣ 234.8 (prose) āgantukaiḥ kleśair upakliśyate, in passage cited from 'Ratnakūṭa' = KP 99.2, of which however text reads ... upakleśe (read °śaiḥ) saṃkliśyate.

upakleda, m. (cf. Skt. upaklinna, *rotten*), *putrefaction*: Gv 401.9 nābhūt ... upakledo (of the teeth, of the mahāpuruṣa).

upakleśa, m. (also semi-MIndic °**kileśa**; cf. **upakliśyate**; = Pali upakkilesa, of which 5, 10, or 18 are enumerated; evidently there was no definitively fixed list), (*minor, secondary*) *impurity, stain, depravity*; in most texts no very clear distinction is made between them and the **kleśa** in principle, but AbhidhK. La V-P. v.88 ff. (see esp. 89 of Transl. note 2) insists on the fundamental distinction, and comm. cites a list of 21 upa°; they 'proceed from' kleśa, 91; a list of 24 in Dharmas 69, whereas in 67 the 6 kleśa have been listed; 4 upak° listed Bbh 10.7 (caturbhir upakleśair ... upakliṣṭo bhavati) and 22 ff. (no relation to Dharmas list); Mvy 2138, following saṃyojana, bandhana, anuśaya, paryutthāna, and followed by paryavasthāna (so read); cf. Bbh 202.20 saṃyojana-bandhanānuśayopakleśa-paryavasthānānām; Śikṣ 222.10 (defining upāyāsa) (ye cānya evamādaya) upakleśās ta upāyāsāḥ; cf. KP 93.3 sopadravaḥ sopakleśa(ḥ) sopāyāso; KP 99.2, see s.v. **upakliśyate**; Mv i.228.11, 15 vigatopakileśena; SP 318.2 (sattvānām alpakuśalamūlānāṃ) bahūpakleśānām; Laṅk 358.11 (vs) upakleśair manādibhiḥ (see s.v. **mana**, app. m.c. for māna, which however is standardly one of the kleśa); 369.4 °śair na lipyate. The word seems likely to have been originally a noun cpd., upa plus **kleśa**; the rare verb upakliśyate may be a back-formation from it; yet the ppp. upakkiliṭṭha occurs in canonical Pali.

upakṣetra, nt., *subordinate* (Buddha-)*field*: Mv i.121.9, 12, stated to be four times the size of a (Buddha-)kṣetra; the implication seems to be that the environs of the kṣetra constitute the upakṣetra. But no other reference has been noted.

(-)**upaga**, (1) at end of cpds. = **-upaka** (1); with MIndic g for k, partly induced by secondary association with upa-ga(m)-; cf. Aśokan chāyopagāni, *concerned with* (i. e. *providing*) *shade*; *belonging to*: Dharmas 129 ākāśānantyāyatanopagāḥ, and three others of the same group incl. **naivasaṃjñānāsaṃjñāyatanopagāḥ** (q.v. for other occurrences; see -upaka; Pali has °yatanūpaga); Mvy 6050 hastopagaḥ, 6051 pādopagaḥ, lit. doubtless *belonging to the hands* or *feet*, of ornaments placed there (Tib. rgyan = *ornament*); Pali has hatthupaga and pādupaga, Vv. comm. 12.5, as epithets of ornaments; (2) n. of an Ājīvaka, = **Upaka** (2), q.v.: Divy 393.20 (so mss., wrongly em. in ed. to Upagaṇa); LV 406.7 (vs), same as Ud xxi.5, in both Upaga for Upaka of Pali correspondent and Mv iii.326.20 (LV tenopaga jino hy ahaṃ; Ud tato 'ham upaga jino; LV alone corrects the meter by transposing Upaga; Pali Vin. i.8.29 tasmāham upaka jino).

upagataka, also **an-upa°** (to Skt. °ta with specifying -ka), pl., *those that have* (or, *have not*) *entered* (here, to residence for rains): MSV ii.110.2 ff., see **āvāsin**; in 114.14 Tib. cited as dam bcas pa, *entered upon a vow*.

upagama, m., Mvy 7801, or nt., id. 7929, cited from Gv 134.5, a high number (in Gv 106.20 text **upāgama-**, q.v.)

upaguṇṭhita, ppp. (of upa-guṇṭh-, not noted elsewhere), *entwined, encircled*: Mmk 63.1 (prose) hārārdhahāropaguṇṭhitadehaṃ.

Upagupta, n. of an **alakṣaṇaka** (q.v.) Buddha: Divy 348.24 ff.; converts Māra, 357.3 ff.; 385.7 ff.; 428.4; Av ii.203.1 (here called Sthavira-Upa°) ff.; MSV i.4.2 ff.; see next.

Upaguptaka = prec.: Divy 359.9 (prose; neither dim. nor pejorative force perceptible).

upagūḍhaka, adj. (Skt. °ḍha plus -ka, pejor.?), *embraced* (wrongly): pāpamitropa° MSV iv.223.1 (so the repentent Ajātaśatru, of himself; Buddha, repeating his words, uses upagūḍha, 223.6, 224.2).

[**upagṛṇīte**, *approves, recommends*: Jm 143.24 (dayānuvṛttyā ca nāma te kṛtya-pakṣam) āśvāsanavidhinopagṛṇīte. So ed., but mss. (u)pagṛhṇīte, *wins over*, which seems better.]

[**upaghāṭa**, wrong em. in ed. Mv i.229.7; see **aruṇodghāṭa.**]

upaghātika, adj. (cf. Skt. °tin, °taka; Pali °tika but as noun, *injury*, Vin. ii.13.31, contrary to PTSD), *injuring* ... (end of cpd.): Mmk 559.6 atikrūras tvaṃ vajrapāṇeḥ (read °ṇe) yas tvaṃ sarvasattvānāṃ sattvopaghātikaṃ kāmopasaṃhitaṃ ca mantratantrāṃ (= °trān) bhāṣayase.

upacaraṇa, nt., in piṇḍopacaraṇam Karmav 21.15, *begging-round* (= Pali piṇḍa-cāra; upacaraṇa not in Pali, in Skt. only in sūpa°, see BR).

upacāyaka, adj. (cf. Skt. upacāyin; to root cāy), *revering*: kulajyeṣṭhopacāyakaḥ Mvy 2434 (Tib. ri mor byed pa, *revering*).

upacāra, m. (= Pali id.; see also s.v. **tāḍāvacara**), (1) *environs, neighborhood*: Gv 151.18 deśapradeśopacāreṣu nimnonnata-samaviṣameṣv; Dbh 81.24 (mahābrahmā ...) lokadhātau gahananimnopacārān avabhāsayati; (2) *access* (for Pali cf. PTSD s.v. 7, with references): Bbh 44.14 (see **prajñapti** 4).

Upacāru, n. of a cakravartin king: Mvy 3560. Seems to correspond to Pali Upacara, Mahāv. ii.2. Cf. **Cāru.**

upacita, adj.-ppp. (Skt., *heaped up*), (1) technically applied to karman, *piled up*; *aggravé* (Lévi): Karmav 30.14 ff.; 47.25 ff. (as explained here, acts may be kṛta, *done*, or *not done*, and both kinds may be upacita or not; see AbhidhK. La V-P. iv.114 n., 242); (2) *honored* (perhaps error for apacita): Mv ii.416.14 tasya (sc. Buddhasya) devamanujopacitasya (read °jāpacitasya?) añjaliṃ kurutha.

Upacitaskandha, n. of a Bodhisattva: Gv 443.1.

Upacitahanu, n. of a former Buddha: Mv i.141.16.

upacitra, °traka, adj. (in Skt. °tra only as n. of a meter), (*somewhat*) *variegated*: citropacitro Mv i.363.18 (of the deer-king); citropacitrāṇi pratyāstaraṇāni MSV ii.90.8. The cpd. seems to be intensive. Also, citropacitrako vatso MSV iv.196.15.

Upacelā, n. of a daughter of **Siṃha** (8): MSV ii.8.12 (cf. **Celā**).

upaceṣṭita, ppp. (to upa-ceṣṭ-, unrecorded), *performed*: Mmk 152.21 (vs) kriyā ... sattvopaceṣṭitā.

upacchinatti (= Pali upacchindati; Skt. has no cpd. of upa and chid; cf. **upaccheda(-na)** etc., **an-upacchinna**), *cuts off, interrupts*: AsP 177.4 kathāṃ nopacchinatti.

upaccheda, m. (= Pali id.; see **upacchinatti, an-upaccheda,** etc.), *cutting off, severance, destroying*: dharmopa° *the cutting off of the states of existence, of conditioned existence,* in a formulaic list, followed usually by tṛṣṇākṣayo virāgo nirodho nirvāṇam: Mv ii.285.20; iii.200.11; 314.5; LV 392.16 (separate from prec., for which mss. samartho); in LV 395.22 text sarvatamopacchedaḥ, no v.l., read perh. (sarva-?)dharmopa°; āhāropa° Mv iii.65.18; -dāridryopa° Śikṣ 190.19; yamalokopa° Śikṣ 215.2; vṛttyupa° Karmav 41.8; vaiśāradyopa° Karmav 41.26.

upacchedana (nt.), *cutting off*: vaṭṭopacchedana- LV 127.17, see **vaṭṭa.** See also **upacchinatti,** and **an-upacchedana(-tā).**

upajanayati, also °jān° (see under **janayati,** and Senart n. on Mv i.248.2), *conceives* (lit. *produces*) a thought or feeling, in oneself: Mv i.248.2 dullabhasaṃjñām upajanetvā, *conceiving the thought that it is hard to get*; ii.135.4 (vs) upajānaya tvaṃ sukhāni, *rejoice!*; in LV 36.20 (vs) Lefm. gauravam upajenitvā (best mss. °janitvā; read °jānitvā, as meter requires long initial syllable?), *conceiving veneration.*

upajīvita, nt. (to Skt. and Pali upajīvati; cf. Skt. upajīvana), *dependence, living a subject life*: LV 262.10 (vs) varaṃ mṛtyu (most mss. °yuḥ) prāṇaharo dhig grāmyaṃ nopajīvitam, *better death that takes away life; fie! is not dependence vulgar?*

[**upajenitvā,** see **upajanayati.**]

upa-tarati, ger. °tīrya, *having crossed over* (the saṃsāra), *become saved*: LV 329.18 (vs) svām' (see **svāmam**) upatīrya tāraya jagad, *yourself having crossed* (being saved), *make to cross* (i. e. save) *the world*; Tib. ñid rgal nas . . .

Upatiṣya (= Pali Upatissa; cf. **Tiṣya** 6–9), the given name of **Śāriputra**: Mv iii.56.11 ff. (story of his conversion); 269.11; 271.7; in Mvy 1047 mentioned in a list of śrāvakas, following Tiṣya, but not juxtaposed with Śāriputra (who occurs in 1032 in the same list).

upadarśayati, °**śeti,** (**1**) *exhibits* (in words) *as a future prospect; promises, predicts* (for someone): trīṇi yānāny upadarśayitvā SP 76.6; 79.5–6 (°darśayati); 82.4, 7, *having held out a prospect of* (promised) *three vehicles*; kusumāyāṃ (loc., so read with mss.) mahāvīcim upadarśeti nāyakaḥ Mv i.184.4 (vs), *the Leader holds out for Kusumā the prospect of* (predicts, prophesies) *the* (hell called) *Great Avīci* (as recompense for sin); (**2**) as in normal Skt., *exhibits, displays* (e. g. an art or skill: LV 143.22 śakyasi . . . śilpam upadarśayitum, *can you exhibit an art?*); in LV 143.20 mayā sārdhaṃ samarthaḥ śilpena śilpam upadarśayitum, lit. *able to display art for art with me,* i. e. *to vie with me* in such displays.

upadiśyati (semi-MIndic for Skt. °dṛś°), *appears,* perh. to be read in Mv i.50.15 and 51.11, see § 31.1 s.v. pad.

Upadukura, n. of a nāga king: Mmk 18.11.

Upadundubhi, n. of a nāga king: Māy 247.16.

upadeśa, m., n. of a type of Buddhist literature, one of the pravacana (last in both lists, ninth in Dharmas, twelfth in Mvy), lit. *instruction*: Dharmas 62; Mvy 1278. App. not so used in Pali. See Burnouf, Intr. 65 f.

upadeśeti (°**śayati**), *exhibits, displays*: Mv i.169.16 jarāṃ ca upadeśenti, na caiṣāṃ vidyate jarā; and 19, ārabdham (? mss. alabdhi) upadeśenti eṣā lokānuvartanā (see **anuvartanā**). Similarly 170.2 (they are not born or begotten, yet) mātāpitṛñ ca deśenti eṣā lokānuvartanā; 170.10 alpotsukatvaṃ pradeśenti eṣā°. The mg. is regular for Skt. deśayati and for upadiśati, pradiśati, but not recorded for the causatives of the two latter. Nevertheless it seems necessary to keep the mss. readings, rather than read (upa-, pra-)darśenti, as Senart in his note was tempted to do (and that altho forms of darśayati are similarly used in the context, e. g. 170.4, 6).

upadrotar (to Skt. upa-dru-), *oppressor, aggressor*: Mvy 2959 °tāraḥ (n. pl.? or intended as n. sg.? cf. § 13.19; all other nouns in the section are sg.).

Upadharma, n. of one of the brothers of Śāriputra: Mv iii.56.11.

upadhāna, (**1**) nt. (= Pali id., Dhp. 291 paradukkhūpadhānena yo attano sukham icchati, *on the basis of, by means of, pain to others . . .*, cf. Senart Mv i.464, n. on i.112.3), *basis, what causes* or *is needful for . . .*, usually in comp. with sukha-: SP 284.10 (vs), read, evaṃ (or, etan) mamo sarvasukhopadhānaṃ saddharma . . ., *the Good Law which is the basis of all happiness for me*; 339.4 sarvasukhopadhāna-pratimaṇḍitāḥ; 348.2 sattvānāṃ sarvasukhopadhānaṃ dadyāt; Jm 18.12 dānaṃ naikasukhopadhānasumukhaṃ; Mvy 6140 sukhopadhānam = Tib. bde baḥi yo byad, *what is needful for happiness*; sarvasukhopadhānena Mv i.302.6; Suv 67.11 (sukhitān kuryāt); 114.3; Kv 28.7; °dhānair Śikṣ 173.14; sukhopadhānaiḥ (preceding word missing) KP 159.3; manuṣyasukhopadhānena Suv 113.10; upadhānasaṃpanno Mv ii.259.14, ep. of Buddha, *possessed of the basis* (sc. of happiness, presumably short for sukhopa°); also cpd. with hita-, Mv i.112.3 (vs) sarvaṃ hitopadhānaṃ, *all the basis of welfare*; with duḥkha- (as in Pali, above), Gv 354.16 yat teṣāṃ sattvānāṃ duḥkhopadhānaṃ tad utsṛjya; Mmk 110.20–21, see s.v. **śatana**; (**2**) ifc. Bhvr., *base, rest, support* (lit. and physical): Karmav 22.3, 5 and 27.9 aśmantakopadhānāyāṃ (*resting on a stove*) kāṃsyapātryāṃ (in 22.5 °kopādh°, misprint); (**3**) **piṇḍopadhāna,** see this; (**4**) m., n. pr., in Mv iii.176.14, a cousin of the Buddha, son of Śuklodana and brother of Ānanda and Devadatta; perh. distortion of some other name (Upananda?).

upadhānī, some part of a lute, perhaps *bridge* (as the *support* on which the strings rest)?: AsP 515.19 droṇīṃ ca pratītya carma ca pratītya tantrīś ca pra° daṇḍaṃ ca pra° upadhānīś ca pra° koṇaṃ ca pra° . . . vīṇāyāḥ śabdo niścarati.

upadhi (m.; = Pali upadhi, and also Pali upādi), (**1**) *substratum* of continued existence; *attachment, bond* uniting one to existence. Acc. to Childers upādi means the khandhas alone, while upadhi includes also kilesa (with which PTSD makes it 'almost synonymous'), kāma, and kamma; but acc. to PTSD upadhi is sometimes equated with the pañca-kkhandnā. In Pali, upādi is, acc. to PTSD, used only in comp. with -sesa, in cpds. usually beginning sa- or an- and regularly epithets of nibbāna (-dhātu); these are represented in BHS by **anupadhiśeṣa, nirupa°, sopa°,** qq.v. But BHS also has upadhi and **nir-up°** (m.c. **niropadhi**) = Pali (nir-)upadhi. The passages here listed belong exclusively to this latter class, = Pali upadhi. (But it seems that even in Pali, upadhi and upādi are not always clearly distinguished.) upadhī-kṣīṇā LV 358.18 (vs); sarvopadhi-pratiniḥsarga *the getting rid of all up°* LV 31.21; Mv ii.285.20; iii.314.4; sarvopadhi-niḥsarga (Bhvr., with dharma) LV 392.11; 395.21; sarvopadhikṣaya- Mv i.115.8; cf. ii.418.10 upadhi (mss., Senart em. °dhiṃ) pratītya duḥkhasya saṃbhavo sarvaśopadhikṣayato (mss., Senart em. sarvopa°) . . . nāsti duḥkhasya saṃbhavo; Mv iii.282.6 upadhi-saṃkṣaye; Divy 224.20 śalyam upadhiṃ viditvā; Ud ii.20 upadhiṃ hi loke śalyam iti matvā, *l'attachement . . . c'est la misère . . .* Others s.v. **niropadhi.** In Mvy 6499 upadhi has three Tib. definitions; the first, phuṅ po, regularly = **skandha** (as Pali upādi = khandha); the third, ñon moṅs pa, regularly = **kleśa** (as Pali upadhi, 'almost syn. with kilesa,' PTSD); while the second, rdzas, *thing, substance, matter,* belongs to a meaning of the word app. unknown to Pali, viz. (**2**) *material thing, 'chose matérielle'* (Lévi, = Tib. dṅos, which also = Skt. vastu), Sūtrāl. xvii.3 (n. 1 in Transl.); see also LaVallée Poussin, AbhidhK. iv.15 with n. 1: 'Par upadhi, il faut entendre la chose (ārāma, vihāra, etc.) donnée à un moine ou au Saṃgha: le mérite qui procède (tadbhava) de cet upadhi s'appelle aupadhika' (q.v.). Hence, (3) in Divy 50.28 bhagavān upadhau vartate, *the Lord was acting in regard to material things* (of the assembly of monks), i. e. in the function of an **upadhi-vārika**, q.v. (= **aupadhike** Divy 542.17). (See also s.v. **plotikā**.)

upadhika, adj. = **aupadhika**, q.v.: LV 32.1 (prose) sarvopadhika-puṇyakriyāvastv-abhibhāvanatāyai (no v.l.). Weller 18 assumes sarv' opadhika-, MIndic for aup°, which seems less plausible than assumption of the form lacking vṛddhi.

upadhi-vāra, m., *guardianship of material objects*, the office of an **upadhi-vārika**, q.v.: Divy 54.17 anyatamasyārhata upadhivāraḥ prāptaḥ; 21 kasya dāsīputrasyopadhivāra iti. (Divy Index wrongly treats this as equivalent to °**vārika**.)

upadhi-vāraka (only Divy 542.21), regularly °**vārika**, m. (from prec.; see **upadhi** 3), lit. *guardian of material objects*; *beadle* or *provost* of a monastery, in charge of physical properties: Mvy 9067 = Tib. dge skos (Jä. dge bskos, Das dge skyos or bskyos), lit. *virtue* (or *welfare*, or *alms*) *commissioner*; see AbhidhK. LaV-P. iv.237 note 1; Divy 50.27 upadhivārikasya; 81.27 (= MSV i.80.5) °kaḥ pṛṣṭaḥ; 237.16 (Dharmarucir) vihāre °ko vyavasthāpitaḥ; 237.24; 542.21 °vārakasya, but 543.17, repeating the substance of 542.21, °vārikasya; Av ii.87.2 tata upadhivārikeṇa gaṇḍīr ākoṭitā; he announced the day of the half-month to the monks, MSV iii.98.8–9. Acc. to Das, this officer was 'a supervisor or director of monks ... a sort of provost-sergeant ... who keeps strict order and punishes transgressors.' This fits well the usual mg. of Tib. dge ba (*virtue*).

upadhyāyati, *blames, finds fault with, thinks* (or *speaks*) *ill of*: LV 157.11 (prose) te tām upadhyāyanti.

Upananda, (1) n. of a monk, disciple of the Buddha: SP 2.6; one of the ṣaḍvārgika or ṣaḍvargīya group, Mvy 9472 (with **Nanda**, 9471; cf. **Nandopananda**); MSV ii.99.4 ff.; 117.6 ff.; 199.14 ff.; (2) n. of a nāga-king, always associated and almost always compounded with **Nanda**, 2, q.v. for references.

Upanandaka (= prec., 2), n. of a nāga-king: Suv 162.9; Mmk 437.2 (both vss, prob. m.c.; in cpd. Nandopa°).

Upanara, n. of a nāga-king: Mvy 3266. Cf. next (doubtless the same).

Upanala, n. of a nāga-king: Māy 246.18. Cf. prec.

upa-naśyati, *perishes*: Sukh 4.13 (na ca tathāgatasyendriyāṇy) upanaśyeyur.

(**upanahyati** = Skt. id., Pali upanayhati; in Dhp. 3,4 PTSD defines (ye taṃ) upanayhanti by *bear enmity towards*; but most interpreters take it in the usual sense, ye taṃ upanayhanti, *who are attached to this* (thought). The same vss Ud xiv.9, 10; MSV ii.184.2, 4 read atra ye copanahyanti (Ud 10, MSV 4 nopa°; MSV 2 ye upa°); here atra, loc., depends on the verb: *who are* (not) *attached to this* (thought). However, note the BHS and Pali **upanāha**, q.v.)

upanāmayati, °**te**, °**nāmeti** (= Pali upanāmeti, *brings, presents*; once in Skt., GobhGS. 2.1.7 (piṇḍān) kumāryā upanāmayet, *he shall offer* [tender, hold out] *to the girl*); most mgs. classifiable under the two headings *brings* (to a person or place), and *presents, offers*; but the two shade into each other, and there are aberrant cases; in practically all, the thing (or person) *brought* or *presented* is acc., or nom. in passive expressions; the goal or recipient is sometimes acc., rarely loc., but much more commonly gen., rarely dat., with both act. and pass. expressions; very rarely nom., subject of a pass., the thing *presented* being then acc., LV 386.17 (vs), read with best mss. āhāram upanāmye 'yaṃ (for °yet-ayaṃ; Lefm. °yeta), *let him be tendered food*; (1) *brings*, physically (to): Mv ii.159.13 and 160.2 upanāmehi me (chandaka aśvaṃ) kaṇṭhakaṃ, *bring me* ...; Mv i.156.11 (vs); Av i.341.11 (prose) pañca haṃsaśatāny upanāmitāni, *were brought* (physically; here not 'presented') *to the king*; LV 83.17 (prose) (yasmiṃś ca kūṭāgāre bodhisattvo mātuḥ kukṣigato 'sthāt, taṃ brahmā ... brahmakāyikāś ca devaputrā abhyutkṣipya brahmalokaṃ ...) pūjārthaṃ copanāmayām āsuḥ, *transported* (the apartment) *to the brahma-heaven*; LV 103.10 (kumāram ... asitasya maharṣer) antikam upanāmayati sma, *brought into the presence of* ...; LV 118.8 upanāmyantāṃ maṅgalāni, *let auspicious objects be brought*; 118.11 (text upā°); also *brings* to enlightenment, SP 326.12 (vs) kathaṃ nu bodhāv upanāmayeyaṃ (sc. sattvān); in SP 195.2 (vs) supply tān, (ye cāpi saṃśrāvitakā tadāsī te śrāvakā teṣa jināna sarve,) imam (most mss. idam) eva bodhiṃ upanāmayanti, *they bring* (them) *to enlightenment* (subject the Jinas, not the disciples as Burnouf and Kern assume); (2) *delivers*, as a letter, or the like: LV 140.20 sa tasyās taṃ lekham upanāmayati sma; Mv ii.90.8 (prose) tena taṃ lekhaṃ tasya sārthavāhasya upanāmitaṃ; Divy 546.1 (prose) (sā ratnapeṭā rājño Bimbi)sārasyopanāmitā lekhaś ca; Suv 205.5 (prose) tāny asthīny ādāya bhagavate Buddhāyopanāmayām āsa; (3) *presents* (*introduces, shows, makes known*) a person to another (usually gen. but may be acc., as in) LV 115.21 (vs) (kumāram ...) upanāmayan suravarām (for °rān), cf. Mv i.226.11 = ii.29.14 (vs) vādicandraṃ upanāmayati suravarāṇām (and cf. upanayati in similar context Mv i.152.17); Mv ii.32.2 upanāmetha kumāraṃ ṛṣisya, and 3 (kumāro) ṛṣisya upanāmito; SP 108.7 (prose) taṃ daridrapuruṣam ānāyya (or ānayitvā) mahato jñātisaṃghasyopanāmayitvā, ... *to a great crowd of his kinsfolk*; Mv ii.38.12 upanāmayi (aor.); Divy 405.26 (kumāro rājño) 'śokasyopanāmitaḥ; (4) *hands over* an arrested person (criminal, etc.) to the king: Mv ii.168.6 (prose) (sa ...) rājño upanāmayito (!ppp.; v.l. °nāmito); iii.39.18 so ... rājño ... upanāmito; 352.6 kāśirājño upanāmehi; and similarly, of a snake subdued and confined, Mv iii.429.8 (bhagavāṃ taṃ nāgaṃ ...) uruvilvākāśyapasyopanāmayati; (5) *presents, offers, tenders, gives* (e. g. food and drink, medicine, etc.): LV 386.17 (above); Mv i.306.14 (vs) (odanavidhim ...) svahastam upanāmayate, *offered them* (food) *with her own hand*; Mv ii.38.1 (vs) phalāni upanāmaye (aor.); ii.96.18 (prose) (tasya lubdhakasya) phalodakam upanāmitaṃ; ii.170.9 (prose) tena so bhojano tasya vadhyasya upanāmito; ii.211.15 (prose) mātāpitṝṇāṃ upanāmeti; iii.111.4 (vs) upanāmaye (aor.) piṇḍapātraṃ jinasya; Divy 14.3 asmākaṃ lūhāny (sc. **praheṇakāni**, q.v.) upanāmayasi; 349.25 (teṣāṃ ... mūlaphalāni) copanāmayati; Sukh 67.10 (prose) (bahu cāsya ...) pānabhojanaṃ tatropanāmyeta (pass., *would be provided there* for him); LV 265.7 (prose) bodhisattvāya ... tā yūṣavidhāḥ kṛtvopanāmitā abhūvan; KP 87.9 (vs) yatropanāmyanti (pass., sc. bheṣajā), *and wherever* (the medicines) *are given*; in prose, 87.3 (yatra ca punar vyādhyā) vyupanāmyante (q.v.); Tib. (both times) btaṅ, *give* (medicine; in line 3 nad gaṅ la, *for whatever disease*); SP 321.11 (prose) tac ca bhaiṣajyam upanāmitaṃ na pibeyuḥ, and 12 upanāmitam; (jewels, ornaments, etc.) SP 227.13 (prose) ratnarāśayas tasya dharmabhāṇakasyopanāmayitavyāḥ; Mv ii.66.9 sarvaṃ devīye upanāmeti, 10 tāni devīya upanāmayati; ii.463.10 sudarśanāye upanāmiyanti (pass.); (bowls) LV 382.20 tathāgatasyopanāmayanti; 383.13, 14; 384.8; (a seat) LV 408.18; (garments) LV 267.11 (bodhi)sattvāyopanāmayati sma; (a car) Laṅk 6.16 yāne rāvaṇenopanāmite; (a celestial palace; for residence) LV 59.16 (vs) upanāmayiṣye (sc. madvimānaṃ; a god speaks); (water for bathing) Mv iii.135.13 upanāmemi (could also be rendered *bring*); (flowers) Kv 18.6 bhagavatas tāni padmāny upanāmayati sma; (a putative son) Mv iii.291.9 sārthavāhasya upanāmeti (dārakaṃ); (taxes) Divy 22.14 tasya ... karapratyayā upanāmitāḥ (also 16); (a bow) LV 154.11 (prose) (bodhisattvasya) yad-yad eva dhanur upanāmyate (could also be rendered *was handed to, provided for*) sma, tat-tad eva vichidyate sma; (6) *presents = proclaims, makes known* (a religious text or 'door to salvation'): Suv 67.3 (where monks shall preach this sūtra) sūtrendrarājaḥ teṣu viṣayeṣu upanāmito bhaviṣyati; Gv 54.26 (vs) mokṣadvāram upanāmayāhi me (addressed to Mañjuśrī); (7) (orig. *brings*, and so) *places, locates*: Suv 190.10 (prose) tad bhojanaṁ hastipṛṣṭham (acc. of goal) upanāmya, *having placed that food on the elephant's back.*

-upanāyika, f. °**ikā**, (1) adj. (= Pali id., see below), only in cpds., *introducing to, functioning as introduction to, having reference to, relating to*: ātmopanāyika (= Pali attūpa°, often ep. of dhamma or the like, as spoken) *introducing oneself, relating to oneself*, LV 438.21 (Lalitavistaro nāma dharmaparyāyasūtrānto ...) ātmopanāyikas tathāgatena bhāṣitas ...; Jm 13.25 °kaṃ dharmaṃ deśayām āsa; -jñānopanāyika-, *constituting an introduction to knowledge*, Gv 41.23 sarvajagaj-jñānopanāyika-dharmacakrapravartanā-; other cpds., Gv 44.22 -jagadupasaṃkramaṇopanāyika-sarvajñatā-; 348.15 yathāvaināyikopanāyika-varṇā (n. sg. f.), *having a color* (aspect) *that acts as introduction to that which is in accord with Buddhism* (see **vaināyika**); (2) f., in varṣopanāyikā, subst. (= Pali vassūpa°), *the first day of* (i. e. serving as introduction to) *the rainy season*: °kā Mvy 8681; °kāyāṃ, loc. sg., Divy 18.10; 489.10; Av i.182.7.

upanāha, m. (= Pali id.), *hatred, malice*; follows krodha: Mvy 1962 = Tib. (ḥ)khon du ḥdzin pa (after krodha, before mrakṣa); Dharmas 30 (one of 40 cittasaṃprayuktasaṃskārāḥ); 69, list of 24 upakleśa begins krodha, upanāha, mrakṣa; these three also listed Karmav 37.19; kleśopakleśāṃ (for °śān) krodhopanāhādīn Bbh 144.5; krodhopanāha as cpd. also Mv ii.56.1; Dbh 18.3; 25.3; neg. anupanāho (= Pali id.; *non-hatred*) dharmālokamukhaṃ LV 32.19.

upanāhin, adj. (or subst.; = Pali id.; to prec.), *malicious (person)*: Bbh 156.16 (na krodha)nasyopanāhinaḥ akṣāntibahulasya ...

upanikṣipati (not recorded in either mg., cf. next), (1) *lays down, establishes* (dharma): SP 121.5–7 yaṃ ca kāśyapa tathāgato dharmaṃ yatropanikṣipati sa tathaiva bhavati; sarvadharmāṃś ca kāśyapa tathāgato yuktyopadiśaty (WT om. upadiśaty with v.l.) upanikṣipati; tathāgatajñānenopanikṣipati ...; (2) *includes*: Śikṣ 42.13 ... praṇidhānāni, tāny ekasmin mahāpraṇidhāne upanikṣiptāny antargatāny anupratiṣṭhāni.

upanikṣepaka, m. (to prec., q.v.), *establisher*: SP 121.9 sarvajñajñānopanikṣepakaḥ ... tathāgato.

upanikṣepaṇa (nt.; cf. Pali upanikkhepana, not noted in this mg.), *laying aside, putting down, leaving off*: saṃghāṭyā pañcopanikṣepaṇakalpā(ḥ) MSV ii.96.18 (cf. Pali Vin. i.298.20 ff.).

upa-ni-dadhāti (in Pali only ger., see 2 below; in Skt. used of *secretly depositing, caching* treasures, not in mg. 2), (1) *hides, secretes*: Prāt 518.13 (yaḥ punar bhikṣur bhikṣoḥ ...) jīvitapariṣkāram upanida [-dhyād upanidhāpayed vā ...], confirmed by Chin. as to mg.; but Pali equivalent, Vin. iv.123.13, has apa-ni-dheyya vā °dhāpeyya vā, and this cpd. is regular in Skt. and Pali in this mg.; perhaps read apa- for upa- in Prāt; (2) ger. upanidhāya (= Pali id.), *comparing, making comparison with* (acc.): Bbh 137.19, 21: (18–22) tatra parataḥ śīlasamādānād bodhisattvasya param upanidhāya śikṣāvyatikrame vyapatrāpyam utpadyate. suviśuddhāśayatayā śīleṣu bodhisattvasyātmānam upanidhāya śikṣāvyatikrame hrīr utpadyate.

upanidhyāti, see **upanidhyāyati.**

upanidhyāna (and °dhyāyana?), nt. (to next; = Pali °nijjhāna and °nijjhāyana), *reflection (upon)*: Bbh 8.22 dharmārthopanidhyāne; 17.2 paṇḍito bhavati samyagupanidhyāna-śīlaḥ; 209.10 sva-parārtha-samyag-upanidhyānāya dhyānam; in ŚsP 1325.3 text corruptly, uparidhyāyatanatā (the complement is teṣāṃ manasikārāṇāṃ, line 1), for which read either upanidhyāna-tā or (rather more likely) upanidhyāyana-tā, cf. the second Pali form above.

upanidhyāyati, or (less often) °**dhyāti** (Skt. has both presents to dhyā but does not use this cpd.; = Pali upanijjhāyati; cf. prec.), *thinks, reflects upon* (acc.): LV 131.3 te bodhisattvam upanidhyāya (ger.) gāthābhir abhituṣṭuvuḥ; Śikṣ 187.14 ... bhūtaśāntatāṃ ca kāyasyopanidhyāyati; Gv 19.2 (tathāgatavikurvitaṃ ...) na nidhyāyanti nopanidhyāyanti; 66.5 -dharmaparyāyam ... upanidhyāyāmi (so read for text °dhāyāmi); similar context 80.20 upanidhyāyati; Mvy 7459 upanidhyātavyaḥ (follows vyavacārayitavyaḥ); Bhīk 24a.4 tvam (read tvayā, with note) ... saṃraktacittayā puruṣaś cakṣuṣā cakṣur upanidhyāyatyā (pr. pple., instr. sg. fem.) na vyavalokayitavyaḥ; Mv i.342.10 raktacittā anyonyaṃ upanidhyāyetsu (of the two sexes), repeated in 11 in dubious form °dhyāyeta or °dhyāyet, mss., Senart em. °dhyāya (ger.) te ... (the forms of mss. could be used as aor. but seem repetitious in that sense); upanidhyāti only noted in ŚsP 642.4 and 652.7 evam (as described in preceding) upanidhyāti; but in 652.7 followed in same line by evam upanidhyāyataś, gen. sg. pres. pple.

upanidhyāyana-tā, see under **upanidhyāna.**

upanipātita, ppp. to °pātayati (caus. to Skt. upa-nipat, or denom. to upanipāta?), in °ta-tva, *state of being made to appear*, or the like: Dbh 42.(27–)28 (cittaśarīrapra)pīḍanopanipātitatvād vastusatyaṃ prajānāti.

upa-ni-pīḍayati (in Skt. ppp. °pīḍita, only in fig. sense, *afflicted, heimgesucht*), *presses down upon* (lit. and physically): Mv i.65.14 (vs) (caraṇau mahāmune) mūrdhinā upanipīḍya (v.l. upari pīḍya) vanditum, *to revere the feet of the Great Seer, pressing with his head upon them.*

upa-ni-badhnāti (cf. next; Pali °bandhati, *binds to, attaches*; Skt. *writes, composes*, except once ppp. *haftend an*, pw 4.207), *fastens, attaches*: Śikṣ 230.6 sarvasattvakāyāṃs tatra svakāya upanibadhnāti, *connects the bodies of all creatures with his own body*; Gv 99.24 (guṇān ... na vijahan, manasā āgamayann,) upanibadhnan, *making fast, attaching* (to oneself); yeṣu kuleṣu piṇḍakā upanibaddhās (*attached to, fixed for, himself*) teṣu bhoktuṃ preṣayati (sc. his guest-monks) MSV ii.199.8; SP 211.2 maṇiratnaṃ vastrānta upanibaddhaṃ, *fastened on* (lit. and physically); MSV i.119.9 balīvardā nopanibaddhāḥ, *not tied up.*

upanibandha, m. (= Pali id.; Skt. not in this mg.; cf. prec.), *connexion, dependence* (of effect on cause): Śāl 76.13 pratītyasamutpādasya hetūpanibandhaḥ katamah (and repeatedly in the sequel), cited Śikṣ 220.1.

[**upanirbaddha**, ppp., *written, recorded*; surely error for Skt. upanibaddha: Divy 274.14 sthavirair api sūtrānta °ddham.]

upaniśā = **upaniṣā**, see **upaniṣad.**

upaniśraya, m. (cf. Pali upanissaya, but the usual Pali mg. does not seem to be quite paralleled here), (1) *dependence, reliance*: Śikṣ 32.4 sarvasatvā buddhopaniśrayavihāriṇo (*dwelling in reliance on the Buddha*) bhavantu; Gv 462.17 kalyāṇamitropaniśraye vihāriṇo bodhisattvā(ḥ); 470.24 ye te sarvakalyāṇamitropaniśraya-vihāra-vihāriṇaś ca; (2) in Mvy 9194 °yaḥ, *residence for a little while, temporary residence*, acc. to Tib. re zhig gnas bcaḥ ba, and Chin.

upaniśrāya, ger., postposition (= Pali upanissāya; § 35.20; also Sktized as **upaniśritya**, q.v.), *near*, with acc.: SP 309.11 (prose) naite ... devamanuṣyān upaniśrāya viharanti, *they do not dwell near* (in the company of) *gods or men*; Mv iii.223.16 (yaṃ ...) grāmaṃ vā nigamaṃ vā upaniśrāya viharati.

upaniśrita, ppp. (= Pali upanissita; cf. prec. two and next), *dependent on, reliant* or *based upon*, once with instr.: Ud xxx.50 satkāyenopaniśritāḥ (text erroneously

°niḥśritā; see s.v. **satkāya**); Mv i.304.16 (vs), Senart reads (with several em.) mahyam mālā citrā upaniśritā, which (if correct) I would interpret *bright garland that depends on me* (*for which I am responsible*; otherwise Senart's note).

upaniśritya, ger., postposition (to Skt. upa-ni-śri-, but actually a Sktization of **upaniśrāya,** q.v.; in mss. often written upanisṛtya, sometimes °śṛtya, which is undoubtedly an error, Speyer Av Introd. CIX, Weller p. 29), *near,* with acc.: LV 2.17 śrāvastīṃ mahānagarīm upaśritya viharati sma; so regularly foll. by viharati, nagarīm upa° vi° Divy 54.15; Av i.237.13; 248.1 etc.; caityam upa° viharanti Divy 207.11; pūrvāṃ diśam upaniśrityāsthāt LV 217.19, *took a stand near the eastern quarter,* and so 218.3, 8, 14; examples of spelling °sṛtya in mss. (and Lefm.'s text of LV), vaiśālīm upanisṛtya prativasati sma LV 238.14; mahānagaram upanisṛtya viharati sma LV 243.16 (one ms. °śṛtya); rājadhānīm upanisṛtya (Speyer em. °śritya) viharati Av i.349.5 etc.

upaniṣaṇṇa, ppp. (to upa-ni-ṣīdati, only Vedic and not in this sense; cf. Pali upanisīdati), *seated*: Bbh 59.20 sukhopaniṣaṇṇa-, *comfortably seated.* Cf. next.

upaniṣaṇṇaka, m. (= prec. plus 'specifying ka'), *the one that is seated*: Mv ii.447.1 kuśadrumaṃ kumāraṃ rājāsane upaniṣaṇṇakaṃ upadarśayati, *showed K. the prince, who was seated on the throne* (not the real king).

upaniṣad, f., **upaniṣā,** also written **°śā, °sā, °sad** (= Pali upanisā, in mgs. 1 and 2; on relation to Skt. upaniṣad see Schayer, RO 3.57 (1926), *magic correspondence*; Renou, in C. Kunhan Raja Presentation Volume, orig. *connexion,* from upa-ni-sad- *approcher . . . être ou mettre en regard, confronter*), (**1**) *cause, basis*: AbhidhK ii.106 duḥkhopaniṣac chraddhā, *la foi nait de la souffrance* (LaV-P.); ii.245 hetu, pratyaya, nidāna, kāraṇa, nimitta, liṅga, upaniṣad are synonyms (Vyākhyā); ib. Index, referring to v.40, mokṣadharmopaniṣad ucchedaḥ; Sūtrāl. xi.9 (*base causale,* Lévi); Bbh 2.26 (ādhāra ity ucyate,) upastambho hetur niśraya upaniṣat pūrvaṃgamo nilaya (cf. the synonym-list above, AbhidhK.Vy.) ity ucyate; Ud xiii.5 anyā hi lābhopaniṣad anyā nirvāṇagāminī, *for the cause* (basis) *of gain is one thing, that which leads to nirvāṇa is another* (same vs in Dhp. 75, with lābhūpanisā); see also under (3) below, and s.v. **candropaniṣad**; (**2**) *likeness, comparison* (so Pāṇ. 1.4.79), chiefly in a frequent cliché, found SP 333.7; 349.3; Mvy 5087; RP 59.16; KP 159.17; Sukh 31.9; Vaj 35.10; 42.7; Gv 542.3; AsP 72.4; 98.11; Śikṣ 187.1; 312.12, 21; Dbh 66.26; Bbh 104.9; 236.22; usually a long formula, ending kalām api gaṇanām apy upamām apy upaniṣadam (or °ṣām, etc.) api na kṣamate (or, nopaiti); sometimes abbreviated by yāvad (e. g. Vaj 42.7; Śikṣ, all 3 times) or vistareṇa yāvad (Bbh 236.22) or without any such phrase indicating abbreviation (e. g. Bbh 104.9); on the other hand, additional terms may be added, esp. at the end (before na . . .), as **dhṛtipadam** (q.v.) api RP, aupamyam api Vaj 35.10; AsP (both times but before upani°); Dbh. The forms of our word, besides the regular upaniṣadam, are: upaniṣām SP 333.7 (ed., but most mss. °ṣadam; one °sām api °ṣadam api); RP; KP; °sām AsP both times, and see SP 333.7 above; °śām Sukh; Gv; Dbh; in AsP (both times), as in one ms. of SP 333.7 (above), the item is duplicated, reading upaniśām apy upaniṣadam (72.4 °sadam) api; for the verb, na kṣamate (or pl. °nte) and nopaiti are equally common, while Sukh has the isolated na gaṇito bhavet. Tib. (on Mvy, and acc. to Bendall on Śikṣ 187.1) renders upaniṣad in this passage by rgyu, *cause,* but this clearly makes no sense. A sort of modulation of this cliché, with nom. sg. forms, in SP 299.13 na teṣāṃ saṃkhyā vā gaṇanā vopamā vopaniṣad vopalabhyate; also Dbh 66.8 (yeṣāṃ saṃkhyā nāsti) gaṇanā pramāṇam upaniṣad aupamyaṃ nāsti. [(**3**) acc. to Wogihāra, ZDMG 58.454, and Index to Bbh s.v., where Dharmarakṣa is cited as authority, the word also means *step, degree* (*Grad, Stufe*), and W. finds this mg. in Bbh 144.21 f. This passage reads (18–23) tasyaibhir daśabhir ākāraiḥ kuśaladharmasaṃgrāhakaśīlavyavasthitasya kṣipram eva kuśalasaṃgraho bhavati, sarvākārasaṃgrahaś ca: yad uta, dānopaniṣadā śīlopaniṣadā kṣāntyupaniṣadā vīryopaniṣadā dhyānopaniṣadā pañcākārayā ca prajñayā. Clearly the 10 ākāra = the 10 pāramitā (Mvy 913 ff.), the last five being 'forms' of prajñā. But I doubt that upaniṣad here means *degree, step,* or *stage*; rather as in 1 above, *by the cause of* dāna etc., *on the basis of . . ., by means of . . .* (**4**) In Divy 530.21 for (tayā) svopaniṣad (uktā) read prob. svā pariṣad, *her retinue,* with note.]

[**upanisṛtya,** written for **upaniśritya,** q.v.]

upanisevin, adj., f. **°nī** (= Pali id.; to Skt. upaniṣevate, Pali °sevati), *serving, waiting upon*: read akṣudrasattvopanisevinī sadā, in Mv ii.57.3; 59.23, with Pali Jāt. v.399.2 (same vs) apāpasattūpanisev°. The mss. read °sattvopari° or °sattva-pari°, unmetr.; Senart em. °sattvā pari° in 57.3, °sattva-prati° in 59.23. But ri for ni is an easy corruption, and the -o- (required by meter), together with the Pali, confirms our reading.

upanīta, ppp. (= Pali id., Jāt. v.375.23 upanītasmiṃ jīvite; also upanīyati *is brought to an end,* MN ii.68.18), *ended, finished*: LV 56.11 (vs) māya (= māyāṃ) . . . mānadarpopanītāṃ, *done with* (= free from; lit. finished as to) *arrogance and pride.*

[**upanetrī,** Lefm. LV 168.18 (vs); read vadhakāṃ (= °kān) sa tavā upanetī (= upanayati); all mss. but one panetī.]

upaneya, gdve. of Skt. upa-nī, (it is) *to be applied, used* (for edification): Jm 80.13; 108.22; 142.7; 155.7–8; 175.9; 181.16.

upanyasta, ppp. defined in Divy Index by *educated in*; but it means primarily *entrusted to,* with gen. or dat., as in BR s.v. 2 as plus upa-ni, 2; so Divy 99.24 dārako 'ṣṭābhyo dhātrībhyo upanyasto; 170.13 (tayā sa lipyakṣarācāryasyākṣarāṇi śikṣayitum) upanyastaḥ. The Index refers to Divy 3.18 (lipyām) upanyastaḥ saṃkhyāyāṃ gaṇanāyāṃ etc. (so also 100.1; 485.5; MSV iii.20.1), where there is ellipsis of the person to whom the boy was *entrusted*; it might be rendered *enrolled* (i. e. handed over, sc. to a teacher) *in. . .*

Upapañcaka, n. of a yakṣa: Māy 236.28.

upapatti, f. (= Pali id.; cf. next three, and **upapāda**; specialization of Skt. id., cf. pw s.v., 7.324), (*re-*)*birth, state of existence* (past or future or present): SP 228.10 (vs) °tiṃ śubhāṃ tyaktvā, *giving up a glorious state of existence* (in a heavenly world, to be reborn on earth); Mv i.282.18 upapattiyā (loc. sg.) . . . vaśitāṃ gato (see **°tti-vaśitā**); Divy 187.16 kā upapattiḥ (*future state*) ko **'bhisaṃparāya** (q.v.) iti; 194.20 (tiryagyony-)upapattibhayabhīto; Dbh 75.14 °tti-nānātva-tāṃ; KP 102.7 na cyutir nopapattiḥ; Bbh 359.1 bodhisattvānāṃ pancavidhā upapattiḥ; Gv 522.13 upapatty-ānantarya-citte pratyupasthite, said of a man at the point of death, *when the mental state which immediately precedes rebirth has arrived* (he becomes aware, by sight, hearing, etc., of the state in which he is about to be reborn by the power of karma); upapatti-**pratilambhika,** or **°prātilambhika,** qq.v.

-upapattika (cf. Skt. aupapattika, and see s.v. **aupapatti**; from upapatti plus (i)ka), *spontaneously produced,* or perhaps merely *of* (various) *origins* (nānopa°): Gv 244.10 nānopapattika-sarvakāyanirmāṇameghān niścarya.

upapatti-vaśitā, *supernatural power of choosing rebirth* (Senart i, note 586 conjectures, of choosing the family he is to be born in; perhaps too limited), one of the **vaśitā,** q.v.: Mvy 775; Dbh 70.13, defined sarvalokadhātūpapattisaṃdarśana(-tayā); cf. SP 260 11–12, s.v. **aupapāduka**; in SP 228.12 (vs) read upapatti-vaśītāsya

= °vaśitā (ī m.c.) asya, which mss. clearly intend; ed. has false em. See also under **upapatti**, Mv i.282.18.

upapatty-aṃśika, see **-aṃśika**, and cf. **aupapatty°**.

[**upapaddha**? apparently error (misprint?) for upapanna, in ŚsP 1349.1 tiryagyoni-yamalokopapaddhānāṃ sattvānāṃ and 3 °paddhāṃ (! read °āḥ) sattvās (n. pl.). Certainly means *reborn in* (states of animals or of Yama's world), and is associated with upa-pad-, cf. 7 upapadyante.]

(**upapadyate, °ti** [= Pali upapajjati, also Skt. °yate but rarely, see BR s.v. upa-pad- 8], *is* (re-)*born* [cf. **upapatti**; one or two cases are here cited]: SP 260.11 upapatsyate, see s.v. **aupapāduka**; Divy 194.14 saptame divase ... sūkaryāḥ kukṣāv upapatsyāmi; 194.25 (Tuṣite) devanikāye upapannaḥ. For upapadiṣyati, Senart, Mv i.50.15; 51.11, read upadṛśyati or °diśyati, see § 31.1.)

upaparīkṣaka, m. (cf. next two), *investigator, advisor* (of a king): rājño ... amātyāś cintakās tulakā upaparīkṣakāś cintayitvā tulayitvopaparīkṣya ... ime tulakā upaparīkṣakā iti Divy 212.9–11.

upaparīkṣaṇa, nt., and **°ṇā** (= Pali °rikkhaṇa; cf. prec. and next), *investigation, examination*: Mvy 7456 °ṇam; Bbh 193.26 (dharmāṇām ... samyak-cintanā) tulanā upaparīkṣaṇā.

upaparīkṣate, rarely **°kṣyate** and **°kṣyati** (ya-present? or possibly phonetic corruption? cf. **parīkṣy°**, **nirīkṣy°**; = Pali upaparikkhati; not in Skt., but Nir. has noun upaparīkṣā, BR s.v.; cf. prec. two), *investigates, gives consideration to* (acc.): saṃsāram upaparīkṣate sma LV 180.8; (yoniśa, Mv °śo; KP evam) upaparīkṣitavyam, *must be carefully considered*, Mvy 7454 (so v.l., Index, and Mironov; Kyoto text upalakṣitavyam); Mv iii.339.10; KP 96.7; °kṣya, ger., Divy 212.10 (see s.v. **upaparīkṣaka**); (kācamaṇayo ratnasadṛśās te) bhavadbhir upaparīkṣyopaparīkṣya (in 230.9 °kṣya-m-upa°, with 'hiatus-bridging' m) Divy 230.9; 503.6; °kṣyopaparīkṣya also Divy 5.13 (jewels); (vastu ...) cintayitvā tulayitvā upaparīkṣya Bbh 37.20; (mantrapadānām artham cintayati) tulayaty upaparīkṣate 273.13; dharmāṇām artham upaparīkṣate 288.10; tad evaṃ ... samyag upaparīkṣamāṇena Jm 195.1; present forms in ya, upaparīkṣyeta Laṅk 214.13 (prose); arthaṃ ca dharmaṃ ca cintayanti tulayanty upaparīkṣyanti Divy 220.9, 15.

upapāda (m.; in this sense not in Skt.; cf. **upapāduka, aupa°**; corresp. to Pali upapāta, in cutūpapāta or cutup° Vin. iii.4.38; SN iv.59.13; and AMg. uvavāa, °vāya, *birth*, derived by Ratnach. from upapāta, but could as well represent upapāda; cf. also **upapatti**, same mg., from upa-pad-yate), *birth, incarnation*: SP 24.2 (vs) darśeti sattvāna cyutopapādam (= cyuty-upa°, Pali cutūpapāta, above; dvandva, *fall* from one existence and *rebirth* in another); Mv ii.359.12 (vs) cyutopapādaṃ jānāti sarvasattvāna nāyako. Knowledge of this constitutes one of the three vidyā (see **traividya**) and is a product of divyacakṣus as one of the abhijñā, AbhidhK. LaV-P. vii.106.

upapāduka = **aupapāduka**, q.v.; used in exactly the same ways, often in the same texts which elsewhere use aup°, and by me grouped under the occurrences of that form; note esp. Av ii.89.1 aupapādukaḥ as title of the story, but in the text itself always upa°, ii.94.17 ff.; other occurrences of upa° are Mvy 2282; Mv i.212.7; Dharmas 90; Mmk 16.14; Gv 254.12; 264.24; 339.4; SP 205.14; 455.4; Mv i.145.4; Divy 533.25; Śikṣ 175.8. In some the v.l. aupa° is recorded.

Upapīlu, n. of a piśāca: Mmk 18.5.

upapeta, adj., quasi-ppp. (= AMg. uvavea, upaveya; correctly explained by Senart Mv i.628 n. as = upeta blended with upapanna, which replaces it in Pali, below), *provided* (with), *possessed* (of), at end of cpds., and only in vss, apparently used m.c.: LV 29.4 āryaguṇopapetā; 80.20 patrapuṣpopapetāḥ; Mv i.357.14 vīryabalopapetā (same vs in Pali, Sn 68, thāmabalūpapanno); ii.63.15 śīlopapeto; 135.5 kuśalopapetaṃ; 182.2 balopapeto; 328.20 puṇyopapete (mss. °pamete); 330.14 varṇopapetaṃ (v.l. varṇopetaṃ, metr. inferior); iii.134.14 lakṣaṇopapeto (mss., Senart em. °ṇupa°); Dbh.g. 1(337).16 sumatopapeta-; 17(353).15 vīryopapeta; 27(53).5 jñānabalopapetāḥ; 29(55).21 jñānapathopapetā(ḥ); 38(64).15 kuśalopapetā(ḥ); Ud xii.19 dhyānabalopapetaḥ.

upapravahati, *flows* (trans., makes to flow) *towards* or *for* (gen.): Kv 41.6 (gāthāṃ) śṛṇvatāṃ puṇyaughapravāham upapravahasi.

Upabindu, n. of a nāga king: Māy 247.21.

Upamadā, n. of a piśācī: Māy 239.6.

upamarda, m., *disturbance, threshing about*: (tayā ...) hrade mahān °daḥ kṛto MSV i.135.2; prob. read so in same passage Divy 443.15, see **mahātapamanda.**

[**-upamardaka**, Kv 59.4, corruption for -upadarśaka; see s.v. **andhakāla.**]

Upamāna (Pali Upavāṇa), n. of a monk: MPS 35.1.

[**upamāna**(-vardhana), see **uyate.**]

upamopanyāsa (m.; Skt. upamā plus Skt. upanyāsa), *use of comparisons* (in disquisitions): LV 422.15 sūkṣmaṃ (text śū°) tac cakram an-upamopanyāsa-vigatatvāt, ... *because it is not* (to be) *separated from the use of comparisons*; KP 29.1 upamopanyāsa-nirdeśās (read °śāms?) te ... nirdekṣyāmi.

upamya, m., a high number: Mvy 7931; cited from Gv which reads aupamya, nt., q.v.

upayika, adj. (to Pali upaya, cf. Skt. and BHS upāya, plus -ika), *serving as an approach* or *means*: only in cpd. sādhanopayika (-karma-, or -visaraḥ), in colophons: Mmk 80.9 (here sādhanaup°); 84.19; 117.23; 144.25.

-upayogika, adj. (Skt. °ga plus -ika), *to be used* (for ...): pratimopa° MSV ii.142.10.

uparikoṣṭhaka, m. or nt., *upper storeroom, loft*? or *cupboard* for storing food? (Senart p. lvi *grenier*): Mv i.327.12 uparikoṣṭhake sūpaś ca odanaś ca (and repeatedly in sequel).

? **upari-garbholika**, see **garbholika.**

uparim, adv., postp. (= Skt. upari; 3 times in prose of Mv, otherwise in vss), (**1**) adv. *on high, above*: SP 190.5 uparim ca khe dundubhayo vineduḥ; 325.3 u° ca devā 'bhihananti tūryān; 331.5; 364.7; Mv ii.62.8 (vs) heṣṭā ... uparim ca; (**2**) adv., *further*: Mv iii.447.8 (prose) noparim itthatvam (q.v.); (**3**) postp. with gen., *above, on top of*: Mv ii.137.11 (prose) mīḍhaparvatasya uparim anupalipyamāno caṃkramaṃ cakrame (mss., Senart em. caṃkrame); Mv ii.15.4–5 (prose) bodhisattvamātur na kvacid uparim (so mss.!) uparimena gacchati, *does not pass aloft anywhere above the bodhisattva's mother.* (Senart's em. is bad.)

uparima, adj., and **uparimeṇa**, adv.-postp. (Pali uparima, id.), (**1**) adj. *upper, higher*: °maḥ kāyaḥ, *upper* (part of the) *body*, Mvy 213, and various case-forms of same phrase Mv iii.115.19, 20; 410.6; Divy 161.8; Bbh 59.12; °maṃ prāvaraṇam, *upper garment* (cloak), Divy 256.23; °mā diśā, *the zenith*, Mv ii.163.6, and so °mā dik, Kashgar rec. of SP acc. to Kern p. vii for ūrdhvā dik; uparimaṃ dakaskandham (so read; falsely edited) Divy 231.1, *a higher* (or, *the highest*) *mass of water*; (**2**) °meṇa (dental n in Mv text), adv., *above, on high*, sc. in the air: Mv i.211.4 na kiṃcid uparimena gacchati (also in parallel ii.15.5, for which see s.v. uparim, occurs uparimena as adv.); postp. with gen., Rājagṛhasyoparimeṇa, (in the air) *above Rājagṛha*, Karmav 45.1–2.

Upariṣṭa, once recorded for **Upāriṣṭa**, q.v.

upariṣṭā, semi-MIndic for Skt. °ṭāt, postp., *above*, with gen.: Mmk 41.7 teṣām apy upariṣṭā aṣṭau uṣṇīṣarājānaḥ (in 41.5 note teṣām upariṣṭāt); 63.9 teṣāṃ copariṣṭā ...; 63.14 āryamañjuśriyasyopariṣṭāḥ (read °ṭā) anekaratnoparacitaṃ ... vimānamaṇḍalaṃ ... abhilikhet; 68.23 teṣāṃ copariṣṭā ...; 132.5 (vs) parvatasyopariṣṭā vai kuryād ratnamālakām. (Impossible to construe the form as n. pl. of adj. upariṣṭa = Pali upariṭṭha, n. pr., see prec.)

upariṣṭima, adj. (= Pali upariṭṭhima; cf. Skt. upariṣṭāt and § 22.15) = **uparima**, *upper, aloft*: noted only in °ṭimāyāṃ, sc. diśāyām, SP 191.6 (vs), *in the zenith.*

uparodha-śīla, adj., *whose character is subject to importunity*: Mvy 2440 = Tib. ṅo mi chod pa (or, mi zlog pa), defined Das p. 356 *one who listens to or does a thing to please another which he would not otherwise have done.* The cpd. is not otherwise known, but Skt. uparodha may mean *importunity*, KSS 54.173 (inaccurately defined *Rücksicht* in BR 5.1192); Vikramacarita JR 4.2.1.

-uparodhaka, f. **°ikā**, adj. (Skt. upa-rudh plus aka), *interfering with...*, in dharmoparodhikāyāṃ vedanāyāṃ vartamānāyāṃ Av i.234.8.

uparddha, regularly written in Mv for **upārdha**, q.v.; and see next.

Uparddha-kāśikā (mss., Senart em. Upārdha-), n. of a harlot: Mv iii.375.18, sister of **Kāśikā**, q.v.; so called because she was worth a fee of half a thousand (**kāśi**, q.v.), 376.1. Cf. Pali Aḍḍhakāsī, °sikā (CPD, DPPN).

Upala (prob. represents, m.c., MIndic Uppala = Skt. Utpala; § 2.88; cf. **Utpala** 4, **Utpalaka** 3, and **Padma** 4, id.), n. of a mythical kalpa, in which lived successively 300 former Buddhas termed Kauṇḍinya-gotra: Mv iii.233.17 (vs) ekatra kalpe upalāhvayasmiṃ.

upala-kuṇḍaka (m. or nt.), *chamber-pot* (lit. stone pot): °ke saśukraṃ prasrāvaṃ kṛtaṃ Mv iii.143.16; 144.7; 153.11; 154.8; tato °kāto tam ṛṣisya saśukraṃ prasrāvaṃ pītaṃ 153.12.

upalagna, ppp. (= JM. Ap. uvalagga), *attached, clinging*: Mmk 62.26 (prose) (daśa)balajaṭāntopalagnopaviṣṭaṃ.

upalabdha, ppp. (in specialized mg., which I have failed to find elsewhere), *won over, persuaded to one's wishes*: (tayā ta) upalabdhā uktāś ca MSV ii.22.8.

upalabhyate, °ti (in mg. 1 = Pali upalabbhati, pass. of upa-labh, much commoner than the act.): (**1**) *is found, occurs*, like Skt. vidyate. This mg. seems probable in KP 98.1, where for corrupt text read prob. nobhayayor antarāle upalabhyate, or perh. with the quotation Śikṣ 234.2 nobhayam antareṇopa°; and KP 102.1–2 yan na labhyate tan nopalabhyate, *what is not found, does not occur* (*exist*?); it must however be noted that Tib. renders mi dmigs pa, *is not conceived mentally, fancied* (see under **upalambha**); (**2**) *is upbraided, reproached*: Mv iii.291.16 °yati; 295.13 °yamāno; no v.l., but as Senart notes, this is the regular mg. of Skt. upālabhyate; perhaps read upā°, but note the curious fact that Das cites a Tib. dmigs paḥi (regularly = upa-labh and derivatives!) smra (*speech*), defined by *execration, revilling* (apavāda)!

upalambha (cf. Skt. id.; not recorded in Pali; cf. prec., **an-upa°**, **an-upalabdhi**, the next items, and **aupalambhika**), acc. to standard interpretation, *mental perception* or *apperception, realization by the intellect*; Sūtrāl. xviii.92 comm. buddhyā pratipattiḥ; Tib. dmigs (-pa) *thought, fancy, imagination*; *to construe in one's mind*, etc.; see also La Vallée-Poussin, AbhidhK. Index s.v. upalabdhi. Were it not for this persistent tradition, some occurrences, esp. of the neg. forms (**an-upalambha, °labdhi**), could easily be interpreted as related to upalabhyate (1) and mg. (non-)*occurrence*, (non-)*existence*. These mgs. are attributed by CPD to an-upaladdhi, °labbhana; and tho not recognized in PTSD, *occurrence, existence* seems to me the probable mg. of upaladdhi in the two passages cited for it, Miln. 268.7 and Vv. comm. 279.10. In many BHS places *inconceivability* or *non-occurrence, non-reality* would make equally good sense for an-upa°. I do not, however, venture to abandon what seems to have been the standard tradition. Reliance on upalambha, *mental perception, fancy*, is an error, stigmatized as upalambha-dṛṣṭi, *the heresy that relies on upalambha*, LV 35.6 (or as Bhvr., *one who adheres to that heresy*, SP 383.12); see also °dṛṣṭika. Similarly upalambha-saṃjñin Śikṣ 315.1, *having the* (false) *notion of upalambha*; upalambha-yogena, *by the* (erroneous) *method of upalambha*, ŚsP 1042.16, repeated formulaically (cf. anupalambha-yogena s.v. **anupalambha**).

upalambha-dṛṣṭika (see prec.) *one who holds the heretical view of reliance on mental perception* or *imagination* (see **upalambha**): RP 18.18 °ko ... bodhisattvena na sevitavyaḥ; KP 123.6; 134.14.

upalambhika? see **aupa°, opa°**.

upalāḍana (nt., = Skt. upalālana; to next), *coddling, amusing, spoiling*: Bbh 302.13 ātmopalāḍana-parāḥ, *bent on amusing themselves* (with shows and other amusements).

upalāḍayati (= Skt. upalālayati), *caresses, coddles, treats affectionately*: Prāt 516.10 upasthāpayed vā upalāḍayed vā; Divy 114.26 tās tvām atyartham upalāḍayanti; 230.11–12 (see note p. 707); 503.9. Cf. prec.

upalāpana, nt. (= Pali id.; to next), *wheedling, cajoling, humbugging*: Śikṣ 261.8 bālopalāpanaṃ (... *of fools*, or *children*) mūrkhasaṃmohanam. The more usual term is bālollāpana, see **ullāpana**.

upalāpayati (cf. Pali upalāpeti, and prec.), *flatters, cheers up*: pass. pres. pple., Jm 113.11 strīnṛttagītair upalāpyamānaḥ.

Upalāla, n. of a nāga king: Kv 2.9.

upa-vatsati, or (v.l.) **upa-vatsayati** (denom. to vatsa; as to preverb, cf. **upalāḍayati**), *treats affectionately*: Bbh 362.23 kālena ca kālaṃ vaiśeṣikeṇa lābhena priyavāditayā copavatsati (v.l. °tsayati), na caiṣu dāsīdāsa-saṃjñāṃ karoti (sc. a bodhisattva, in dealing with servants and dependents).

upavadati (= Pali id.; also Vedic, but not Cl. Skt. in this mg.; cf. **Anupavadya, nirupavadya**), *blames, reproaches*: Mv i.70.2 (vs) te hi no upavadeyur (so 4 mss.; Senart with v.l. upapadeyur, but this form is bad, it should be °padyeyur) anudagrā (mss.), *they would blame us as ignoble* (or, if anudagrā is nom., *being displeased, distressed*; this is perhaps more likely).

upavarga (m. or nt.; cf. JM. uvavajjana = Skt. *upavarjana, *abandonment*), *abandonmen* : Gv 364.16 (vs) svargopavargair viniveśya sattvān sarvajñabhūmim pravidarśayanti.

upavarta, m. Mvy 7791, or nt. id. 7920; Gv 134.1: *a high number.* In Mvy 7920 cited from Gv, which in the source of the quotation, 134.1, has the same, but in a corresponding list 106.17 **udvetana**, q.v.

upavartana (nt.; Pali Upavattana, see below; Skt. upavartana, nt., *country*, Lex., and once Śukasaptati text. orn. p. 340 (24), line 32, virāṭopavartane), *land, country* (? in Pali, at least later, n. of a locality in the Malla country or of the śāl-grove there where Buddha entered nirvāṇa): Divy 208.25, 209.3 (tathāgato ... pari)nirvāṇāya gamiṣyati Mallānām upavartanaṃ Yamakaśālavanaṃ; Av i.227.6 (viharati sma Mallānām) upavartane (ms. °tate) Yamakaśālavane; virtually the same Av ii.197.5; Mmk 580.9(–10) (vss) Mallānām upavartane (text °te), Yamakaśālakavane madhye nirvāṇaṃ me bhaviṣyati; 580.17 (vs) Yamakaśālakavane tatra Mallānām upavartane (so read for text upadartate!); 598.22–24 (vss) Yamakaśālavane vane caitye makuṭabandhe tu (cf. 580.11 caitye makuṭavardhane) Mallānām upavartane, parinirvṛte (? read °to or °taś) ca tatrāhaṃ ... Occurs in Pali and BHS only in reference to the place of the Buddha's parinirvāṇa. In the canonical Pali texts, e. g. DN ii.137.3 (cf. comm. ii.572–573) yena Kusinārā upavattanaṃ Mallānaṃ sālavanaṃ ten(a)..., and cf. esp. Dpv. 15.70 Kusinārāyaṃ bhagavā Mallānaṃ upavattane, it could be understood as *the country* (of the Mallas); but the comms. seem to have taken it as a place-name, specifically the name of the śāl-grove where the Buddha died. And this is perhaps confirmed by one passage, Dpv. 6.19 yadā ca parinibbāyi saṃbuddho Upavattane, where the gen. Mallānaṃ is not found, and Upa° most naturally would be a n. of a place (but see below). In Akanuma's Dictionary of the Proper Names of Indian Buddhism the word is misquoted as Upavattava = Skt. °vartava (but the Chinese transcriptions quoted end consistently in -tan, supporting °vartana); the Chin. translations seem regularly to interpret it as a common noun, *uncultivated land* (the word for *land* usually rendering bhūmi, *land, country*). This may be interpreted as support for use as a common noun, as it is used (rarely) in Skt. Note that in BHS the name of the grove is clearly **Yamakaśāla(ka)vana,** q.v.; not so in Pali. Modern editors and interpreters seem unanimously to take Pali Upavattana as n. of the grove (see DPPN s.v. for some other references; but the important Dpv. 6.19 is not cited there). On the other hand, Divy ed. prints upavartanaṃ with a small initial letter; it fails to record the word in Index or Notes. I am inclined, with some dubiety, to understand the BHS word as a common noun, *country*. Even the Pali word may have had that meaning originally, and in the canonical passages still. Later, the Pali comms. seem clearly to have understood it as the n. of the śāl-grove; and in Dpv. 6.19 it looks like a place name. Yet, if the Chin. translation *uncultivated* (waste, barren) *land* be accepted, perhaps upavattane might be understood in this sense in that passage.

upavarṣita, ppp., *rained down* (upon): Divy 357.6 (prose) muktāhāram ca varṣopavarṣitam, ... *rained down in a shower.*

upavāyati (= Pali id.; also Vedic, not recorded for Cl. Skt.), *blows near* (intrans.): Mv i.7.8 (prose) vātāni upavāyanti yais tāni asipattrāṇi patanti; iii.367.12, 17 (ṛṣīṇāṃ gandho ...) upavāyati erito mārutena.

upavāsaka, °sika, see **śvāsopav°.**

upavāsita, adj., ppp. (= Pali id.; to *upa-vāsayati, unrecorded otherwise), *perfumed*: LV 59.15 (vs) divyagandhopavāsitaṃ; 97.17 (vs) divya°tāḥ; Mv ii.180.12 (prose) nānāprakārehi ca mālyehi upavāsitaṃ.

upavicarati (= Pali id., not in Childers or PTSD, but occurs MN iii.239.30 ff.; cf. next two), *ranges over, occupies oneself with*: Śikṣ 244.20 (see s.v. **upavicāra**); 251.17 (atra hi manaś) carati, upavicarati, tasmān manogocarā ity ucyante; Gv 390.12 (sarva)lokagatiṣu copavicaranti.

upavicāra, m. (to prec.; in mg. 2 = Pali id., badly defined in PTSD), (**1**) *environs*: Mvy 5505 (Tib. ñe ḥkhor) grāmopavicāraḥ; Gv 161.4 (yena suprabhasya) mahānagarasyopavicāras tenopasaṃkramya; kṣetrāṇi samāni samopavicārāṇi MSV ii.50.9; (**2**) *range, scope*; substantially = Skt. gocara, see Śikṣ 251.17 s.v. **upavicarati**: Divy 19.25 udakastabdhikā manuṣyāḥ snānopavicārāḥ (text snāto°), ... *devoted to bathing* (lit. *having bathing as their range of interest;* cf. note p. 704, where this word is wrongly interpreted); Bhīk 15a.5 tataḥ paścāc (not cpd. with the following as note suggests!) chravaṇopavicāraṃ vijahayya darśanopavicāre kāyam avanāmya ..., *after that, causing her to leave the range of hearing* (of the assembly of nuns, but still) *in the range of* (their) *sight, having made her bow down her body*, etc. (what follows is a private examination of the initiate by a specially designated nun; it is to be held in sight of the assembly but out of their hearing); Bbh 37.13 (pāne yāne) vastre alaṃkāropavicāre bhāṇḍopaskare ..., *in regard to the sphere of ornaments* (i. e. things that fall under the head of ornaments); Śikṣ 244.12 aṣṭādaśamana-upavicāraḥ (Bhvr.), *having 18 spheres of mental activity* (said of man; cf. Pali aṭṭhādasamanopa° MN iii.239.28), listed in Śikṣ 244.18 ff. aṣṭādaśeme ... mana-upavicārāḥ ... cakṣuṣā rūpāṇi dṛṣṭvā saumanasyadaurmanasyopekṣāsthānīyāny upavicarati, *on seeing forms with the eye he ranges over* (*experiences*) *such* (forms) *as give rise to pleasure, pain,* or *indifference*; (20) evaṃ śrotrādiṣu vācyam (with the other five senses, incl. manas), so that there are 6 times 3 = 18 in all.

upavicārayati (otherwise unrecorded; formally caus. to **upavicarati,** q.v., but seems to be used in same mg.; possibly denom. to **upavicāra,** q.v.), *occupies oneself with, dwells on* (mentally): Gv 83.25 muktakasya ... guṇān udānayann upavicārayann abhilaṣan ...

upavicinoti, *accumulates, heaps up*: SP 136.1 (prose) avidyāndhāś ca saṃskārān upavicinvanti.

? **upavitarka** (m.?), in Mv ii.74.3 °keṣu vā, at the end of a list of arts and exercises (in Mv almost wholly martial; LV p. 156 in corresponding passage includes many non-martial) in which the Bodhisattva challenges the other Śākya youths; preceded by rathasmiṃ vā dhanusmiṃ vā tharusmiṃ vā, which does not fit well with any intellectual exercise (*reasoning* or the like) such as the apparent etymology suggests.

-upaviśeṣa, adj., at end of cpds., lit. *forming a subordinate variety* (of ...), *a kind* or *sort, variety* (of ...): LV 44.3 (vs) devy-upaviśeṣa marutsnuṣeva, *a kind of goddess* ... (said of Māyā); Mmk 73.7 (bodhisattvānāṃ upāyakauśalyatā ... nirvāṇoparigāminī) vartmopaviśeṣā, *a particular kind of way* ...

upavistīrṇa, adj., ppp. of *upa-vi-stṛ-, or cpd. of upa- plus vistīrṇa (?), *extended,* or *rather extended*: Gv 400.17, in explaining siṃhapūrvārdhakāyaḥ (one of the 32 lakṣaṇa), (anupūrvodgataśarīra) upavistīrṇavṛtorasko.

upavusta, adj. (= Pali upavuttha, MIndic ppp. = Skt. upoṣita, to upa-vas), *having fasted*: Mv iii.216.5 (vs) sarvato yaṣṭukāmasya upavustasya (mss. opa°; no metr. reason for o- instead of u-; Senart em.) me sataḥ; the same vs in Pali, DN ii.244.3, has upavutthassa.

Upaśamavant, n. of a Bodhisattva: Gv 442.15.

upaśamika, adj. (= AMg. uvasamiya), *peaceful, characterized by tranquillity*: LV 205.14 (prose) °kaṃ (Lefm. with all mss. upasamikaṃ) ... dharmaṃ saṃprakāśayeyam. See **aupaśamika.**

? **upaśayana** (m. or nt.), perhaps *a small bed, cot*; or, *surface of a bed*: Suv 195.12 (prose) tena ... samayena Jalavāhanaḥ śreṣṭhidāraka upaśayane (but reading uncertain; 3 mss. om. upa; one ms. upasamane) śayitaḥ.

Upaśānta, n. of a former Buddha: Mv iii.237.11 f.

Upaśāntā, n. of a lokadhātu: ŚsP 34.11.

? **upaśiṣṭa,** ppp. of *upa-śiṣ-, *taught*: Senart's em., Mv i.135.(1–)2 yāni ca bhaiṣajyāni loke pracaranti sattvānaṃ hitasukhārthaṃ sarvāṇi tāni bodhisattvebhyaḥ upaśiṣṭāni (mss. upariṣṭāni or °sthāni; like Senart I find it hard to interpret either form; but the absence of record of any upa-śiṣ- or equivalent in Skt. or MIndic makes the em. dubious; cf. however Skt. upa-śikṣ-).

Upaśuklaka, n. of two nāga kings: Māy 248.1.

upaśrambhayati, *confirms, strengthens, encourages*: Gv 321.14 (sarvāryadhana-)pratilambhair upaśrambhayām āsa (sc. sattvān).

upaśrava- (m. or nt.; = Skt. upaśruti, Pali upassuti; cf. next), *listening secretly, eavesdropping*: Mvy 8501 °vagatam.

upaśrutika, adj. or subst. m. (= Pali upassutika; from Skt. upaśruti, see prec.), *an eavesdropper,* or (adj.) *engaging in eavesdropping*: Prāt 521.6 tūṣṇīm upaśrutikas tiṣṭhed, yad ete bhikṣavo vakṣyanti tad ahaṃ (śrut)yāvāpya dhārayiṣyāmīti. Cf. Pali Vin. iv.150.20 upassutiṃ tiṭṭheyya.

upasaṃvarayati, *causes* (a man) *to choose, take to himself* (a woman, as wife): Divy 525.6 tad arhasi taṃ mamopasaṃvarayitum, *so please make him take me as wife* (said to a merchant by an ogress pretending to be the deserted bride of another merchant).

upasaṃhata, ppp. of *upa-sam-han-, *struck, played* (of mus. instruments): Divy 459.4 daivatyopasaṃhatena vāditraviśeṣeṇa.

upasaṃharaṇa (nt.; = Pali id.; to next), *provision, production*: Gv 463.12 pitṛbhūtāni kalyāṇamitrāṇi vipulahitopasaṃharaṇa-tayā, *good friends are like fathers, because they provide many salutary things*; Bbh 18.21 sattvānāṃ kliṣṭavarjitānugrāhakavastūpasaṃharaṇa-kāmatā.

upasaṃharati, rarely °te (cf. prec. and °**hāra**; use in Pali needs more careful definition than Dictt. have given; the only Skt. use pertinent to BHS uses here cited seems to be *collect*, as in Mbh. Cr. ed. 1.186.4 dravyāṇy anekāny upasaṃjahāra, *collected many things of value*; we begin with passages closest to this), (**1**) *collects* (as in Skt., above), annajātam upasaṃhṛtya Jm 31.7; (**2**) *brings together, provides for someone*: (pañca cāsya kāmaguṇān asadṛśān) upasaṃharati sma LV 186.20, *and he* (Śuddhodana) *provided for him* (the Bodhisattva; pw, strangely, *als Beispiel herbeiholen*) *incomparable* (specimens of the) *five objects of sense*; sarvaratikrīḍāś copasaṃhartavyā(ḥ) LV 193.1 (same situation); (glānopasthāna...)-kriyayā premagauravaprasādopasaṃhṛtayā Bbh 239.22, *provided (tendered) with affection* etc.; kiṃcid eva mātram upasaṃhariṣyāmaḥ Prāt 500.2 (and upasaṃharet 4), *we will provide a little something* (recompense, present) *for you*; dṛṣṭibandhanabaddhānāṃ prajñāśastram upasaṃhartukāmaḥ Gv 492.8, *wishing to furnish the knife of knowledge for those bound in the bonds of heresy*; this shades over into (**3**) *produces, effects, brings about*, often as in prec. with gen., *for*...: Bbh 27.(9–)10 (tatra bodhisattvo yad eva hitapakṣyaṃ sukhaṃ, tad eva) sattvānām upasaṃharet, na tv ahitapakṣyam; Gv 459.16 apramāṇāni sattvasukhāny upasaṃhartavyāni, *must be effected* (here, instead of gen., sattva- as prior member of cpd.); Bbh 15.24 na pramādasthānam asyopasaṃharati, *and he does not produce* (cause, make) *for him any occasion for heedlessness*; Bbh 123.11 (na madgubhāvam, so read with ms.) asyopasaṃharati, *and he does not cause any annoyance to him* (a petitioner, beggar); SP 285.9 and 11 (na...) kaukṛtyam upasaṃharati, (a Bodhisattva) *does not produce* (cause) *regret* (remorse, troubled feelings, see **kaukṛtya**; sc. in others); similarly KP 3.6 (vs) pareṣu kaukṛty' upasaṃharanti; Tib. renders verb by ñer (= *near*, rendering preverb upa) sgrub (*produce*); Suv 102.17 (ahaṃ ... Sarasvatī ... dharmabhāṇakabhikṣor) ... pratibhāṇam upasaṃhariṣyāmi; Dbh 72.(10–)11 (pūjayati sarvākāra-)pūjābhinirhāraṃ copasaṃharati, ... *and makes an accomplishment of homage of all forms* (to Buddhas); (**4**) esp. with the object something said, *produces* (stories, sacred utterances, etc.), *tells*: SP 123.8 (tathāgato ... tāṃs-) tān dharmaparyāyān upasaṃharati, tāṃ-tāṃ dharmakathāṃ kathayati...; SP 283.13 (subj. a preacher) upasaṃharec citrakathāṃ (so, or kathān, mss.); in Mvy 6272 vividhasaṃmodanakathām upasaṃhṛtya, so prob. read with v.l. in both edd., text of both upasaṃskṛtya; Tib. byas nas, *having made*; *produces* or *presents* (orally), *recites* (as, a sacred stanza), Divy 489.8 te upasaṃharanti (sc. the verse cited above, 2–5); Gv 251.22 (dharmaṃ deśayamānān ... vijñāpayamānān) upasaṃharamāṇān (mid. = act., *proclaiming*) apaśyat; (**5**) *adduces* (verbally), *mentions, describes, brings up, refers to*: Sukh 4.8 (tathāgateṣu...) jñānadarśanam upasaṃharet, *one might adduce* (*describe*; but Müller, *pile up*); Divy 359.18 (katham...) tathāgatamāhātmyeṣu śrāvakam upasaṃharasi, *how can you speak of* (*adduce*) *a disciple*?; Śikṣ 211.2 (after contemplation of decomposed corpses; sa imam eva kāyaṃ) tatropasaṃharati, ayam api kāya evaṃdharmā evaṃsvabhāvaḥ, *he speaks of* (*adduces*) *this very* (living) *body in this connection, saying, this body too is of the same nature.*

upasaṃharṣī, f. (to *upa-saṃ-harṣayati, unrecorded), *one who causes joy* or *exhilaration, augmentation* (to, gen.): (jīvitasya dhanasya ca) prajñayā °ṣī MSV ii.69.18.

upasaṃhāra, m. (to °**harati**; Pali cited PTSD only Miln. 298.7, where devatūpasaṃhārato (supinaṃ passati) prob. means not '*being seized or possessed by a god*' but *thru providing, procurement, causation of*, i. e. *by, a god*), (**1**) (cf. **upasaṃharati** 1 and 2) *collection* or *provision*, esp. of food and drink: Divy 237.7 (also 9) bhikṣubhir upasaṃhāra ārabdhaḥ kartum; Av i.113.3 (kriyatām asya gṛhapater) upasaṃhāra iti; Bbh 80.6 and 81.27 āmiṣopasaṃhāra, defined 81.28 as bhojanapānādivikalānāṃ bhojanapānādyupasaṃhāraḥ; Bbh 209.26, 27; also *furnishing, providing* of other things, Bbh 80.6 and 82.3 dharmopasaṃhāra, defined 82.4 as dharmāṇām **anupradānam**, q.v.; Bbh 208.4 upakaraṇavikalānām upakaraṇopasaṃhāraṃ karoti; Bbh 19.2 hitasukhopasaṃhāra-prayogaḥ; 23.24 (dharma, as above); 27.20 (hita); 210.8 (naṣṭapratibhānānāṃ) sattvānāṃ pratibhānopasaṃhārāya, cf. Suv 102.17, s.v. **upasaṃharati** 3; Dbh 65.7 (tasya ... bodhisattvasya ... buddhā) bhagavantas ... tathāgatajñānopasaṃhāraṃ kurvanti, *the Blessed Buddhas make* (for this Bodhisattva) *a providing of Tathāgata-knowledge*; Gv 144.17 mayaite poṣitāḥ pāramitopasaṃhārair, ... *by providing for them the perfections*; Suv 68.14 (sarvasattvānāṃ) sarvahitopasaṃhārābhiyuktāḥ; Av ii.129.14 mayātīva evaṃvidho dveṣapratyayopasaṃhāraḥ kṛto, *by me such an excessive collection of causes of hatred was made*; so the ms., Speyer em. to °opasaṃbhāraḥ, and in fact in the next line (15) the ms. reads dveṣopasaṃbhāro, but upasaṃbhāra seems otherwise unknown and should prob. be emended to upasaṃhāra, rather than vice versa; one alternative Tib. rendering of upasaṃhāraḥ at Mvy 6395 is ñe bar (*near*, a lit. rendering of upa) bsgrub pa (*make, provide, supply*), cf. KP 3.6 s.v. **upasaṃharati** 3; (**2**) *production, the act or process of producing or causing*: in Tib. the usual rendering seems to be ñe bar (= upa) sbyor (or sbyar) ba (*produce, compose*), as in Mvy 4407 and 4414 (see below), and in one alternative at 6395 (see just above), while at 4457 it is lti bar sbyor ba (I cannot find what lti means); another word meaning *produce*, bskyed pa, is used in 8487 for kaukṛtyopasaṃhāraḥ, *the causing of disturbance of mind or conscience, remorse* (see **kaukṛtya** and **upasaṃharati** 3; the corresp. Pali passage, Vin. iv.149.9, has kukkuccaṃ upadaheyya); on Mvy 8502 see below; Dbh 72.12 dharmālokopasaṃhāraṃ pratīcchati (here the mg. *production*, viz. of *the light of the law*, is guaranteed by the verb **upasaṃharati** just before, see that word, 3); (**3**) (cf. **upasaṃharati** 4, 5) specialized as *production in words, presentation* (orally), *statement, declaration, proclamation*, esp. of something of religious nature: Mvy 8502 śikṣopasaṃhārapratikṣepaḥ, *rejection of a statement of instruction* (prob. refers to the case of Pali Vin. iv.143.16, Minayeff, 17.20 ff.); here Tib. ñe bar (= upa) ḥjog pa (*put, place, arrange*); Mvy 4407, 4414 -dṛṣṭāntopasaṃhāra-, *presentation* or *statement of a comparison*; Śikṣ 2.6 durlabho bhūtanayānuśāsany-upasaṃhāraḥ; 11.8–9 dānakāle śīlopasaṃhārasyāpekṣā (acc. to note in Transl. of Bendall and Rouse, read °syopekṣā).

upasaṃhāraṇa (nt.; = prec.), *provision, furnishing*: Bbh 270.12–13 priyāpriya-saṃyogaviyogopasaṃhāraṇatayā, *by the fact of provision* (for creatures in need) *of association or dissociation with pleasant or unpleasant things* (respectively), i. e. by the fact that he (the Bodhisattva) sees to it that creatures are thus looked out for.

upasaṃkrama (m.; to **upasaṃkramati**), *violent attack*, = **upakrama**; Mv ii.492.2 ātmānaṃ upasaṃkrameṇa māritukāmo (in prec. line same phrase with upakrameṇa); Divy 264.11 na śakyam asyā atropasaṃkramaṃ kartum araṇyaṃ nayāmīti; sā tenāraṇyaṃ nītvā tathopakrāntā yathā kālagatā (otherwise Index and pw 7.325).

upasaṃkramaṇa (nt.; = Pali °kamaṇa; in Skt. only Gr.; to °**kramati**), (**1**) *act of approaching, approach*: Mv i.255.5 (bhagavantaṃ) darśanāya upasaṃkramaṇāya paryupāsanāya (quasi-infinitives); LV 36.2 -bodhimaṇḍopasaṃkramaṇa-; 430.15 paṇḍitopasaṃkramaṇa-; Gv 44.21 sarvatathāgatopasaṃkramaṇa-, 22 -jagadupasaṃkramaṇa-; 242.5 -kalyāṇamitropasaṃkramaṇam adhyatiṣṭhat; Bbh 31.26 sarvasattva-sarvakālopasaṃkramaṇa-saṃbhāṣaṇa-saṃvāsa- (etc.); 240.5 upasaṃkramaṇa-paryupāsana- (etc.); (**2**) *approaching* (a man, sexually): (girls) nṛttakuśalāḥ hasitakuśalāḥ puruṣopasaṃkramaṇa-kuśalā(ḥ) RP 41.17.

upasaṃkramati (cf. **upasaṃkrama**, °**maṇa**; in Skt. *approaches*, and so also BHS, e. g. Mv iii.94.6; Divy 129.10), *violently attacks*: Mv ii.174.3 and 4 ātmānam (aham) upasaṃkrameyaṃ, *I would do violence to* (= *kill*) *myself*; 492.4 ātmānam upasaṃkramitukāmaḥ; iii.25.15 ātmānam eva upasaṃkramitukāmo; Śikṣ 355.12.

upasaṃjaneti (for °nayati; Skt. upa-saṃ-jan-, mid. intrans., *appears, presents oneself*), *produces, establishes*: Mv ii.223.3 karaṇaṃ upasaṃjanetvā (so with mss.) imāṃ girām abhyudīremi (mss. °retsuḥ, °ransuḥ).

upasaṃdarśayati, *manifests*: LV 244.4 (prose) tathārūpam upāyam upasaṃdarśayeyaṃ, yenaite ca pratyakṣā bhaveyuḥ.

upasamanvāhṛta, ppp. (to *upa-sam-anv-ā-har-; note that samanvāhṛta (see **samanvāharati** 3) is used in this same sense, but only once, in the near vicinity of this word, Divy 288.16), *collected* (of food): Divy 286.18 trailokyaguror anurūpa āhāra upasamanvāhṛtaḥ.

upasamika, see **upaśamika.**

upasaṃpad, and °**padā**, f. (cf. the next items; = Pali upasaṃpadā, in both mgs.; the form °padā is regular, perhaps universal, in Mv, but has been noted elsewhere only in Kv 96.7, other texts having °pad), (**1**) *attainment*: Mv iii.420.12 (vs, = Pali Dhp. 183) kuśalasyopasaṃpadā (Dhp. kusalassa upasaṃpadā); (**2**) *ordination* (as monk or nun): four kinds Mv i.2.15 f., **svāma-up°**, **ehibhikṣukāya** (instr.) up°, **daśavargena** (so!) gaṇena up°, **pañcavargena** gaṇena up° (see the several terms); °padābhāvam icchanti Kv 96.7; usually in standing formula preceded by pravrajyā, and followed by bhikṣubhāvaḥ (or bhikṣuṇī-bh°); so (°padā) Mv ii.234.7; iii.65.7; 92.11; 180.16; 329.14; 376.15; 379.17; only pravrajyā and upasaṃpadā Mv ii.271.2; iii.386.16; pravrajyā upasaṃpad bhikṣubhāvaḥ Bbh 193.2; similarly LV 409.20; and (bhikṣuṇībhāvaḥ) Bhīk 4a.2; pravrajyām upasaṃpadam (acc.) bhikṣubhāvam Divy 15.19; 340.(14–)15; 551.11; Av i.233.10; (bhikṣuṇībhāvam) Bhīk 3a.1; 4a.1.

upasaṃpanna, adj. (ppp.; = Pali id.; cf. **an-upa°**, and the prec. and foll. items), *ordained* (as a monk): Mvy 8715; sūpasaṃpannaḥ (of śrāvakas) Mvy 1093; varṣaśatopasaṃpannasya bhikṣusya Mv iii.180.16; °nnānāṃ bhikṣūṇāṃ Mv iii.329.13; 379.16; °nnasya bhikṣor LV 409.19.

upasaṃpannaka, m. (prec. plus specifying -ka), *one that has been ordained* (with gen. of ordainer): sarvasyopasaṃpannako MSV iii.124.13, ... *by anybody*.

upasaṃpādana, nt. (to next; not in Pali Dictt.), *ordination, act of ordaining* (a monk): Mvy 8498 unaviṃśavarṣopasaṃpādanam.

upasaṃpādayati, °deti (= Pali °deti; cf. prec. items), *ordains, receives into the order of monks*: Kv 96.13 duḥśīlena bhikṣuṇā nopasaṃpādayitavyaṃ; regularly preceded by a parallel form of pravrājayati, °jeti: Mv i.323.7 pravrājetu upasaṃpādetu, similarly Mv iii.65.1; 180.11; °pādetha Mv i.323.8; (pravrājehi...)upasaṃpādehi Mv iii.379.12; ppp. upasaṃpādita, regularly used when the actual ordination ceremony is in mind, thus slightly differing from **upasaṃpanna**, q.v., which means (*one that has been*) *ordained*; regularly preceded by pravrājita (in Divy 180.21 text pravrajita); nom. of various numbers, Mv iii.376.14; 377.5; 401.16; Divy 180.21; 331.7; 551.13 (dual); Av i.104.4.

[**upasaṃbhāra**, *collection, accumulation*: Av ii.129.15, read prob. **upasaṃhāra**, q.v. (1).]

-upasargin (to Skt. upasarga), *having... as an affliction, afflicted by...*: Mmk 144.1 (vs), read prob. mahāmāry-upasargiṇaḥ (text -opusargiṇaḥ!), gen., *of one afflicted by a great pestilence.*

Upasāgara, n. of a nāga king: Mmk 18.13 (follows **Sāgara**, q.v.).

Upasiṃha, n. of a yakṣa leader: Māy 235.18.

?**upasṛṣṭa**, in sopasṛṣṭāmbaravasanā MSV ii.23.7, would seem to mean *she* (a wife whose husband had gone away), *abandoning the wearing of* (*fine*) *garments* (kleśair bādhitum ārabdhā). But Tib. seems to have been different; it is cited as de yaṅ (should = sāpi) kha zas zhim po daṅ (= *with well-tasting food*).

Upasena (identity of 1, 2, and 3, and of any of them with one of the Pali personages of this name, not certain), (**1**) n. of a monk who converted Śāriputra: Mv iii.60.3; (**2**, possibly = 1) n. of a nephew of the three Kāśyapas, who became a follower of Buddha: Mv iii.431.1; doubtless the same iii.103.2 (named after Nadī-Kāśyapa and Gayā-Kāśyapa) and Mvy 1053 (named shortly after Uruvilvā-Kāśyapa and Nadī-K°); (**3**) **Upasena Balāntīputra** (perh. = Pali U. Vaṅgantaputta? Instead of Balāntī- Tib., gar mkhan ma, points to Nartakī-), n. of an evidently important Buddhist elder, who had a retinue of 500 monks: MSV iii.21.12 ff.; (**4**) n. of a former Buddha: Mv i.138.9.

upaskṛta, ppp. (cf. Skt. an-upaskṛta, nir-upa°; apparently Skt. literature knows no other forms of upa-(s)kar- in this sense), *corrupted*: Mv i.132.7 deśikena sārthacaurair upaskṛtena, *by a guide who had been corrupted* (bribed) *by caravan-thieves.*

upastabdha, ppp. (to Skt. upa-stambh-; in BHS, = Pali upatthaddha, used in ways apparently not closely paralleled in Skt.), *based upon, supported by, resting* or *relying on*, with instr., or in comp.: Mv i.5.9, repeated 12 and 6.6, karmopastabdhatvāt, *because of the fact that it* (the body, or bodily existence) *is based on karma* (kept going by it); ii.255.13–14 paṇḍito buddhimanto sukuśalamūlapuṇya-upastabdho; ii.280.16–17 pañcavidhaṃ āryasmitaṃ prādur-akare, sayyathīdaṃ: chandopastabdhaṃ, vīryopastabdhaṃ, smṛtyupa°, samādhyupa°, prajñopa° (*based on...*); SP 463.5 paramapuṇyopastabdhā (*as a consequence of supreme merit*) vayam īdṛśe pravacana upapannāḥ; Gv 392.6 (vs) upastabdha (= °dhāḥ, n. pl.) ye (text °bdhaye) guṇamahodadhibhiḥ sumedhāḥ; 493.23 tvaṃ... sūpastabdhaś ca śukladharmaiḥ (*well supported by, firmly based on...*).

upasthapeti, see **upasthāpayati.**

upasthāka, m. (= Pali upaṭṭhāka; for the usual BHS **upasthāyaka**, q.v.), *servant*: Mv i.252.9 (vs) °ko (v.l. upasthāyako, which is metr. impossible).

upasthāna-kāri (f.), **-kārikā**, (a woman) *serving, doing service to* (a man, sexually; said of a courtesan): Mv iii.37.5 and 8 (°kāri), 12 (°kārikā). Both mss. in 5, and one in 12, read upasthāna; Senart upasthāpana- with v.l. in 8 and 12 (one ms. in 8 °sthapana-); see **upasthāpana.** See also **smṛty-upasthāna.**

upasthāna-śālā (= Skt. °na-gṛha, Pali upaṭṭhāna-sālā), *hall of meeting* (for monks): Divy 207.12 ff.

[**upasthānāni**, Divy 561.10, read apāstāni, *cast away*, with Pali Dhp. 149 apatthāni.]

[**upasthāpaka**, m., read °**yaka**, q.v., *servant*: Mv ii.159.12 (bodhisattvena...) chandako... upasthāpako (so text, no v.l. cited) upasthāpito upanāmehi me chandaka aśvaṃ kaṇṭhakaṃ. In view of the following upasthāpito, p for y in the preceding noun is a particularly easy error, possibly made by Senart.]

[**upasthāpana-**, see **upasthāna-kāri**; read **upas-**

thāna-. To be sure PTSD defines Pali upaṭṭhāpana by *attendance, service*; but in the only passage cited, Vin. iv.291.13, cf. the comm. 27, it certainly is causative: *causing* (someone else) *to attend, wait upon*. That meaning is impossible in Mv iii.37.5, 8, 12.]

Upasthāpanaka-sūtra, n. of a work: Karmav 161.6.

upasthāpayati, °peti, upasthapeti (cf. Skt. caus. of upa-sthā-; Pali upaṭṭhapeti, °ṭṭhāpeti, only partly corresponding in mg.), (**1**) (substantially as in Skt.) *provides, furnishes*: Mv ii.95.11 ye kecij jalacarā prāṇāḥ, te na (i. e. te = tān, naḥ? or read tāni? Senart tena, which I cannot interpret) upasthapetha (*provide them for us?*), sarvabhūtehi yajñaṃ yajiṣyāmi; in SP 88.12 (vs) reading doubtful, Nep. mss. upasthāna anekavidhānayānān (or °yānaṃ), which is metr. and otherwise impossible; Kashgar rec. upasthape sya neka°, metr. bad; KN em. upasthāyakā neka°; prob. read, nearly with WT and K', upasthape (or °pesy? cf. Kashgar rec. above) ekavidhāṃ sa yānān, *he provided vehicles of a single kind*; (**2**) *produces* a mental state, idea, or emotion, in oneself: Mv iii.265.18 mātṛsaṃjñā upasthāpayitavyā, *the notion must be formed that* (other women) *are as a mother*; LV 54.15 (vs) premagauravam upasthapitvanā (ger., so read with v.l. for text °pisva nā), *having formed* (in oneself) *love and respect* (for the Bodhisattva); with object smṛtim (cf. Pali parimukhaṃ satiṃ upaṭṭhapetvā or °ṭṭhāp°, MN iii.89.12, Vin. i.24.34–35, *surrounding oneself with heedfulness* or *'watchfulness of mind'*, PTSD), LV 289.17 abhimukhāṃ smṛtim upasthāpya; same with pratimukhīṃ (v.l. abhimukhāṃ) Vaj 19.10; with abhimukhaḥ (read °khāṃ?) Kv 85.8; smṛtim upasthāpayati Divy 542.22; (**3**) *causes to wait upon* (someone), *commands attendance* (as caus. to Skt. upatiṣṭhati, *waits upon*): Mv ii.159.12 (bodhisattvena . . .) chandako . . . upasthāyako (text °pako) upasthāpito, upanāmehi me chandaka aśvaṃ kaṇṭhakam, *the Bodhisattva summoned-into-attendance his servant Ch.* (*saying*): *Bring me* . . .; (**4**) sometimes such forms seem used in the sense of the simplex upatiṣṭhati, *waits upon* (§ 38.58): LV 100.13 naitāḥ samarthā bodhisattvaṃ kālena kālam upasthāpayitum; Mv ii.220.18 (vs) mātāpitṛṣu vīro upasthapetvā tīvraṃ paricarati, *in regard to his parents* (the loc. is strange; acc. is to be expected), *the hero served* (them) *sedulously, looking after their needs*; (**5**) *treats* (medically), *cures*: Mv ii.218.4–6 vayan taṃ ṛṣikumāraṃ satyavākyena upasthāpeṣyāmaḥ, satyavākyena ca taṃ mṛgaviṣaṃ haniṣyāma. tasya rājño bhavati: . . . pratibalā ete tam upasthāpayitum; ibid. (15–)16 (taṃ karoma satyavacanaṃ yenāsya mṛgaviṣaṃ haniṣyāmaḥ jīvitaṃ) ca upasthapeṣyāmaḥ (v.l. °sthāpayiṣyāmaḥ); Mv iii.131.7 kena te upakaranena vaikalyaṃ upasthāpayiṣyāmi.

upasthāyaka, m., f. **°ikā**; rarely (Divy 426.27; MSV i.30.10; 90.7) m. °ika (once also **upasthāka**, q.v.; Skt. seems to have m. °ika very rarely, see pw, but no °aka; Pali only upaṭṭhāka recorded), *servant, attendant*: SP 95.9 (vs) °kā nitya parasya; 215.6 bhagavataś caite putrā bhagavataś copasthāyakā(ḥ); 245.1 te buddhā bhagavanta upasthāyakadvitīyā upasthāyakatṛtīyā(ḥ); 293.4; LV 91.17 (vs) upasthāyikās (f.) te vayaṃ, and 19; 421.18 (vs), read, teṣa munina ye (ed. muninaye) upasthāyakāḥ; Mv i.249.1 °yako; 251.22 Ānando . . . upasthāyako (sc. of Śākyamuni) bhaviṣyati; 322.18 teṣāṃ (of aged parents) nāsty anyo upasthāyako, and similarly ii.214.5; i.326.5 ff. °yako, *attendant* of a Buddha (like Ānanda, above); f. °yikā ii.433.14; °yikāye (so read with v.l. for °yakāye) 467.3; (chandako . . . bhagavato kumārabhūtasya) upasthāyako iii.91.8; vaidyabhaiṣajyopasthāyaka- . . . pratyayasaṃpadam Gv 328.8; upasthāyaka Divy 35.25; 50.27 (glānopa°); 90.13 (buddhānāṃ); 612.2 (Ānando nāma śramaṇagautamasya); in 426.27 upasthāyikāś, n. pl. m., all mss., while in 29 below all have vaidyopasthāyakāś ca visarjitāḥ, of the same persons.

Upasthūṇa or **°ṇaka**, m., n. of a brahman-village in the west, only in dvandva cpd. with **Sthūṇa**, q.v.: Mvy 4117 °ṇa-; Divy 22.1 (prose) °ṇaka-.

-upahatya (°**tyā**?), *damage, harm*, in Bhvr. cpd. nir-upahatyaṃ nirupadravaṃ bhavet Mmk 37.16 (prose) Cf. Skt. upahati, and (once in AV.) upahatyā.

upahāra, m. (nt. once; = Skt., Pali, Pkt. id.), fundamentally *gift*, (loving) *present*, in BHS as elsewhere; e. g. (with change of gender) Av i.378.2 (prose) sarvopahārāṇi copaḍhaukitāni. In a Mv passage beginning i.177.13 used repeatedly in a somewhat peculiar way which misled Senart, who in two notes (i.518 f., 523 f.) offers three different interpretations, all wrong (the passage cited 519 from SP contains a false reading; the SP ed. 476.5–6 does not contain the word cited by Senart, not even as a v.l.). In this Mv passage, the word applies to various acts by which the Buddha miraculously intervenes to save someone from an intended grievous sin or to convert him from a dangerously false heresy. It should be rendered by something like (kindly or compassionate) *favor, gift, beneficial service*: Mv i.177.13–15 introduces the detailed stories of specific acts called upahāra thus: paropahārāṃś ca . . . upaharanti (*they present beneficial favors to others*) samyaksaṃbuddhāḥ sattvānām anugrahārthaṃ. tad yathā, kaliṅgarājñaḥ kusumāye devyā paropahāraṃ bhagavāṃ vṛttavāṃ, dhruvasya śreṣṭhino vacanopahāraṃ (*a benefit by spoken words*) bhagavāṃ vṛttavāṃ; the cpd. paropa° also 178.5; 180.12; vacanopa° also 178.2. Other occurrences: 178.7–8 (vs) etāṃ sarvāṃ pravakṣyāmi upahārāṃ manoramāṃ, tasya sattvapradhānasya śṛṇu vikrīḍitaṃ śubhaṃ; 184.(17–)18 (vs) (koṭiyo dvādaśa muniḥ) mānuṣāṇāṃ vinayati, upahāro ayaṃ iti; 185.3 upahāro vidhātavyo (to prevent Dhruva from burning his parents); 188.(10–)11 (vs) (yat tasya parikarma tat . . .) tam āhur upahāro ti; 192.(10–)11 (vs) (ye tatra nirmitā bhiksūḥ na caite bhikṣuṇo matā,) upahāraṃ vadanty etaṃ jinā śāstraviśāradāḥ.

[**upahārika**, adj., in cpd.; Mmk 153.17 (vs) sarvavighnopahārikaḥ, *removing* (all obstacles). But since no form or deriv. of upa-har- has any such mg. (BR upa-har- 6 *vernichten* is an error), we must doubtless read °ghnāpahārikaḥ, or perhaps °rakaḥ (i. e. **apahār°**).]

[**upahṛta**, MSV ii.96.11 saṃghāṭy °tā, *spoiled, destroyed*; prob. error, or possibly hyper-Sktism, for upahatā; § 3.95; in Mbh. Calc. 2.861 = Crit. ed. 2.20.7 upahṛta = *imprisoned*, not *destroyed* (BR).]

upa-hṛdaya, nt., *subordinate* or *secondary 'heart'* or *core* (of a mantra): Mmk 3.9 upahṛdayaṃ cātra vākye hūṃ (contrasted with 3.8 paramahṛdayam); 26.18; 29.16, etc.; 397.9.

upāgama (m. or nt.; = **upagama**, q.v., which should perhaps be read), a high number: Gv 106.20.

upātidhāvati (= Pali id.), *runs over* or *transgresses into* (an evil state): Ud xxix.5 °vanti hi sārabuddhyā navaṃ navaṃ bandhanam ādadantaḥ (same vs, with varr., in Pali Ud vi.9, with same verb form).

upātivṛtta, ppp. (to *upa-ati-vṛt-; = Pali upātivatta, which seems to govern only acc.), *passed beyond, escaped from*, with acc. or abl.: Mv i.306.5 (vs) rāgā (mss. nāgā or nāgām; conceivably abl. sg., but looks more like acc. pl.) upātivṛttā . . . (buddhasya śrāvakā); iii.281.14 (prose; Māra speaks) śramaṇo me gautamo viṣayāto (abl.) upātivṛtto; jātīmaraṇaṃ upātivṛtto 397.1 (vs), by em., confirmed by Pali Sn 520.

upādātar, m. (nom. ag. to upa-ā-dā-, pendant to **upādāna**, q.v.), *one who grasps* or *clings* (to existence): Laṅk 357.16 (vs) upādāna-upādātror vibhāgaskandhayos tathā, lakṣaṇaṃ yadi jānāti . . . See **nir-upādātṛka.**

upādāna, nt. (cf. **upādāya, °diyati**; = Pali id., in all senses except 4; in Skt. hardly used in these mgs.), and in Bhvr cpds. (various mgs.) sopādāna (sa-up°) adj., *having, characterized by up°*, and neg. an-up°, nir-up°, *without up°*: (**1**) *fuel* (app. as the *substratum* or *material cause*) of fire: Mv ii.270.14 analo upādānaṃ (sc. bhasmīkaroti); Gv 502.10–11 agnir yāvad upādānaṃ labhate; Śikṣ 226.1 yathāgnir upādānavaikalyān na jvalati; (**2**) *grasping, clinging, addiction*: Śikṣ 104.14 parṣad-anupādānatayā, (by) *having no addiction to company* (Bendall and Rouse); in most passages not clearly distinguishable from (3); Laṅk 23.7 (vs) te bhonti nirupādānā ihāmutra nirañjanāḥ; Mvy 2144 upādānam, foll. by granthaḥ, nīvaraṇam; 7066 upādāna-hetuḥ; LV 180.12 sarvopādānaparigrahair anarthiko (of the Bodhisattva); 244.(2–)3 (nāpi saṃskṛtānāṃ sāśravānāṃ) sopādānānāṃ dhyānasamādhisamāpattīnāṃ doṣo datto bhavet; 358.20 (vs) yāsyanti nirupādānāḥ phalaprāptivaraṃ śubhaṃ; 392.13 anādāno 'nupādāno 'vijñapto ... (of Buddha's dharma); Av ii.188.10 abhinandanāyopādānāya adhyavasānāya (em.) saṃvartate (of a heretical opinion); Dbh 48.9 (saṃskārair avaropitaṃ cittabījaṃ) sāsravaṃ sopādānam ... bhavati; (**3**) *clinging to existence*, specifically (undoubtedly this is meant in some passages cited under 2); esp. as one of the links in the chain of the **pratītyasamutpāda**; it is produced by tṛṣṇā, and produces bhava (as in Pali, taṇhāpaccayā upādānaṃ, upādānapaccayā bhavo): Mv ii.285.10–11 tṛṣṇāpratyayam upādānaṃ, upādānapratyayo bhavo; Mvy 2250; Dharmas 42; modulations of the same formula LV 346.12, 15; RP 48.6; Dbh 48.16; a peculiar one LV 420.4–5 (vs) tṛṣṇāta sarva upajāyati duḥkhaskandhaḥ, (5) upādānato (read upa° m.c.) bhavati sarva bhavapravṛttiḥ, where obviously duḥkhaskandha = upādāna, see below, 4; also pañcopādāna-skandhāḥ (= Pali pañc' upādānakkhandhā), *the five skandha which are the basis of clinging to existence* (otherwise called simply the 5 skandha, q.v.) Mvy 1831; Av ii.168.1; pañcasu upādānaskandheṣu Mv iii.53.3; Divy 294.4; (listed as rūpa, vedanā, saṃjñā, saṃskāra, pl., vijñāna, Mvy 1832–6; Mv iii.53.4–7; Divy 294.5–7;) skandhā sopādānā jñānena mayā parijñātā LV 371.20 (vs); in the first of the 4 noble truths, saṃkṣepeṇa (LV °pāt, Mv saṃkṣiptena) pañcopādānaskandhā (Mvy °dha-) duḥkham (Mv duḥkhā) Mvy 2240; Mv iii.332.4; LV 417.7; (**4**) in SP 75.2 *sorrow, misery* (cf. LV 420.4–5, cited under 3 above), prītiprāmodyajāto nir-upādāno (*free from sorrow*) vigata-nivaraṇo (see s.v. **nivaraṇa**), said of the man whose sons have been brought out of a burning house. Burnouf cites Tib. as rendering upādāna here by mya ṅan, which regularly renders Skt. śoka, *grief*; and no other interpretation seems possible. It is an outgrowth of (3) as used in religious language.

upādāya, ger., postp. (= Pali id.; cf. **upādāna, upādiyati**; also **samupādāya**; note **an-upādāya,** used in a sense not corresponding to any known Pali or BHS mg. of upādāya; formally ger. of Skt. upa-ā-dā-, in BHS and Pali used in special senses), fundamentally (and in Skt.) *taking to oneself, assuming, making use of*, etc.; BHS meanings (probably all paralleled in Pali, see Childers, whose article on this word is far better than that of PTSD): (**1**) *on the basis of*, with preceding acc.: (**a**) *in view of, in consideration of, on the ground of, because of*: LV 395.18 dharmasya cātigambhīrodāratām upādāya, *and in view* (because) *of the very profound nobility of the Law*; Mv iii.61.3–4 pratītyasamutpannāṃ dharmāṃ (acc. pl.) ... śāstā upādāya pratiniḥsargaṃ vijñapeti, *on the ground of states-of-being as originating in dependence, the Teacher teaches abandonment* (of them); Śikṣ 151.6 (sa ... sattvānaṃ ...) praṇamati, dharmagrāhyatām upādāya, (*he salutes creatures,*) *in view (because) of the fact that they must be made to grasp the Law*; (**b**) *making use of, employing*: parikalpam upādāya Śikṣ 87.15, 16; 166.11, *making use of a hypothetical assumption, 'to put an imaginary case'* (Bendall and Rouse); anukampām upādāya (extremely common; also in Pali, °paṃ up°), *employing (manifesting, showing) compassion*, commonly preceded by a gen., or in comp., *as a merciful favor to* ... SP 166.1, 2 (asmākam ...); LV 6.2 (lokasyānu°), 21 (lokānu°); 64.19; 382.13, 21; 413.7; Mv i.255.1; 307.9; iii.171.12–13; Divy 36.27; 52.11–12; Av i.42.4; 290.13; etc. etc.; (**c**) *with reference to*: Bbh 224.2, 3 (katamā ... viśuddhā arthacaryā? sā) daśavidhā draṣṭavyā; bahiḥśuddhim upādāya pañcavidhā, antaḥśuddhim upādāya pañcavidhā; (**d**) *for the purpose of*: Gv 242.4 (sudhanasya ...)-paripākam upādāya; -vaśam upādāya = -vaśena or -vaśāt (see s.v. **vaśa**), the ger. up° being as it were the equivalent of the (causal) instr. or abl. ending, as is neatly shown by SP 320.4 tathāgato 'parinirvāyann eva parinirvāṇam ārocayati, sattvānāṃ vaineyavaśam upādāya, *the T., not entering nirvāṇa at all, lets his nirvāṇa appear, for the sake of conversion of creatures* (see s.vv. **vaineya** and **vaśa**), to which a close parallel in SP 319.1 reads vaineyavaśena, or (v.l.) °vaśāt, omitting upādāya; in a very similar passage Gv 206.5 (na ... tathāgataḥ parinirvṛto na parinirvāti na parinirvāsyati) ... atyantaparinirvāṇenānyatra vainayikasattvavaśam upādāya, ... *except, for the sake of those who are to be converted by his* (apparent or reputed) *absolute complete nirvāṇa*; (**2**) *beginning from* (orig. *taking as basis*), with prec. acc. (usually) or abl., once ā plus acc., once loc.; often followed by a complementary phrase, yāvat *as far as* (with following acc. or nom., once loc., in one doubtful case, Mv i.17.10, possibly abl.); when such phrases with yāvat occur in the examples below, they are quoted; equivalent to prabhṛti with prec. abl. or in comp., and exchanges with it in Av i.255.10 yad upādāya ... tataḥ-prabhṛti, *from what time ... beginning from that time*; (**a**) in expressions of time or temporal sequence: SP 18.6 pūrvakaṃ tathāgatam upādāya yāvat paścimakas tathāgataḥ, so 'pi ... abhūd, *from the first T. to the last T., even he was* ...; LV 160.18 asaṃkhyeyān kalpān up°; Mv i.128.2 prathamāyāṃ bhūmau up° (the only case of loc. noted!), *beginning with* (in) *the first* (bodhisattva-) *stage*, but in i.128.6 below, prathamāṃ (mss. °mā) bhūmim up°; Mv i.170.3 and 246.11–12 dīpaṃkaram up°, *from* (the time of) *D. on*; Mv iii.393.7 adya (mss. asya) saptarātraṃ up°, *from a week ago today*; Bhīk 9b.2 imaṃ divasam up°; Divy 25.29 tam eva divasam up°; 413.19–20 garbhādānam (so text, read °dhānam?) up°; the acc. preceded by ā, Mvy 9215 ā saptamaṃ yugam up°, *beginning from the seventh* (previous) *generation* (so Chin.); Mv iii.44.3 yad upādāya rājā vipravāsito, tad up°, *ever since when* ..., *ever since then* ...; instead of yad ... tad, yataḥ ... tataḥ, Mv ii.211.18 yata up° ṛṣikumāro vijñaprāpto tata up°; and **tata** up° alone = tataḥ-prabhṛti, RP 39.8; Gv 176.5; Sukh 56.17, cf. Av i.255.10, above; (**b**) in expressions of place or local sequence: LV 61.16 ito brahmalokam (note mixture of abl. with acc.! Brahmā Sahāpati is speaking) up° yāvat trayatiṃśad- (so text! see s.v.)-bhavanam; 64.12 adha-āpaskandham up° ... yāvad brahmalokam; 273.16 nadīṃ ca nairañjanām up° yāvad bodhimaṇḍo; Mv i.6.4 pārṣṇi up° yāvad (? adhi-)kṛkāṭikā; i.17.10 pārṣṇi up° yāvat kṛkāṭikāto (abl.! but v.l. °ṭikā, nom., which should perhaps be read); ii.302.3 bhūmitalam up° yāvad bhavāgraṃ; Samādh 8.10 bhaumān devān up° yāvad brahmalokam; Mv ii.2.8 cāturmahārājikān up°; ii.349.20 bhūmyā devā (acc. pl.; v.l. °myāṃ devāṃ) up°; Divy 162.16 akaniṣṭhabhavanam up°; 359.11–12 bodhimūlam up°; Suv 122.4 pṛthivītalam up°; Bbh 122.17–18 vṛddhāntam up° yāvan navakāntam; Mv ii.378.21 heṣṭā (adv.) upādāya bhavāgra-pūraṃ (instead of yāvad bhavāgraṃ, as in ii.302.3 above); the abl. is less common, Mv iii.148.3 mūrdhāto upādāya yāvat pādeṣu (loc.; only case of this recorded); iii.288.6 mūlato up° yāvat puṣpam; (**c**) in serial expressions, neither temporal nor spatial: Bbh 100.3 sarve caite apekṣā-hetum upādāya pratiniyama-hetvantā hetavaḥ, *and all these* (are) *causes, beginning with* *apekṣā-cause and ending with pratiniyama-cause*; a few instances included under (b) above might perhaps be placed here.

upādāya-rūpa, nt. (= Pali id., Childers s.v. rūpaṃ, or upādā-rūpa, PTSD s.v. rūpa), acc. to the Pali Dictt. a group of 24 *'accidental'* or *'derivative' forms* of matter, listed from Vism. in both ll.cc.; contrasting with **bhautika-** (Pali bhūta-)rūpa: Mvy 1846 °pam.

upādi, perhaps = **upādāna**, *clinging to existence*; cf. Pali (an-)upādi-sesa: Mv i.243.16 na rūpaṃ na upādiṃ (mss. upādi or udapādi) gaccheham upādehaṃ (so Senart em., mss. upādehi) ca. The passage is obscure; see Senart's long note.

upādiyati, **°dīyati** (= Pali upādiyati; see **ādiyati**), *takes, assumes* (a burden): Mv i.89.17 (prāpyaṃ ca bhāraṃ) na upādiyanti, aprāpyaṃ ca bhāraṃ upādiyitvā ... (by em.; see s.v. **prāpya**); *takes* (someone as wife, both acc.), Mv i.233.7 yadi mama (acc.) bhāryām upādīyasi (Senart °diyasi), and forms with upādi- 233.11, 17; 234.8; *gets* (evil states of existence, bhava), Mv i.293.1 na te bhavāṃ aṣṭa upādiyanti; *takes to, clings to, assumes* (any kind of worldly existence; opp. to parinirvāyati), Mv iii.447.6 prajānanto kiṃcil loke na upādīyati, anupādīyanto pratyātmam eva parinirvāyati; (the saṃskāras) ib. 17 yo imāṃ ca saṃskārān nikṣipati anyāṃ ca upādīyati (anyatra, Senart adds from 448.6); similarly 448.5. In a number of these passages the mss. are seriously corrupt, but in all there seems to be no doubt that this verb (with long ī or short i) is intended. Cf. **upādāna**, **°dāya**, **anupādāya**.

upādu, see s.v. **utpāta**.

[**upādhāna**, Karmav 22.5, misprint for **upadhāna**, q.v.]

[**upādhu**, stem °dha, LV 241.14, read upārdhu or °dha; see **upārdha**.]

Upādhyāyarājan, n. of a former Buddha: Mv i.141.10.

upādhyāyikā (Skt. = gurubhāryā, Schmidt, Nachtr.; not recorded in Pali), *female teacher*: Bhīk 10b.1 ff.

upānantarīya, nt., *secondary deadly sin* (upa plus **ān°**, or, without upa, **ānantarya**, q.v.): pañcopānantarīyāṇi Mvy 2329, title of Chap. 123; Mironov, instead, pañcānantarya-sahagatāni, but Tib. contains ñe ba, usually = upa. Five such are listed 2330–4: mātur arhatyā dūṣaṇam, niyatabhūmisthitasya bodhisattvasya māraṇam, śaiksasya māraṇam, saṃghāyadvāraharanam (see **āyadvāra**, 2), stūpabhedanam.

(**upānaha**, nt. or m., **°hā**, and **°haka**, Bhvr. [= Skt. upānah, f.; nt. ŚGS, see BR; upānaha- stem in prior part of cpd. Mbh 13.2960; AMg. uvāṇaha, said to be m., Ratnach.], *sandal*: Divy 6.23 °hāni; MSV iv.205.7 °haḥ; anupānahakaḥ ib. 5; upānahābhiḥ ib. 207.15. Cf. **-upāhanaka.**)

? **upānāmayati** = **upā°**, q.v.: LV 118.11 (prose); prob. a corruption, possibly even misprint, tho not corrected.

upānta, adj. (recorded only as n., *vicinity*), *near* (or if subst., *neighbor*), with instr.: LV 90.9 (prose) upāntās te tathāgatena, *they are close to* (*neighbors, associates of*) *the T.*

upānvāharati, *prepares* (food, for the table): MSV iii.22:10 nāpy āhāram °hṛtam; 12 (nāpy āhāra) °hriyate; ib. 97.18–19 upānvāhāraṃ pratyavekṣyopānvāhṛtaṃ cec charaṇapṛṣṭham abhiruhya gaṇḍir dātavyā, *having inspected the food-preparation, if it is prepared, he must mount on top of the house and ring the gong.* Cf. next.

upānvāhāra (m.; to prec.), *food-preparation* (Tib. kha zas kyis gyos): MSV iii.97.18, see prec.

upāya, m. (= Skt.), *means*: three, Dharmas 111, sarvasattvāvabodhakaḥ, sattvārthābhāvakaḥ, kṣiprasukhābhisaṃbodhiḥ; six, of a Bodhisattva, for sattvārthasyābhiniṣpattaye, Bbh 264.7–9: ānulomiko vibandhasthāyī visabhāgāśayaḥ avaṣṭambhajaḥ kṛtapratikṛtikaḥ viśuddhaś ca ṣaṣṭha upāyaḥ. (They are explained in great detail.)

upāya-kuśala, adj. (= Pali °kusala), *skillful in expedients* (see next): Mv i.133.14 °lāś ca bhavanti.

upāya-kauśalya, nt. (= Pali °kosalla), (**1**) *skill in expedients, 'able management, diplomacy'* (Kern, SBE 21.30 note 1); cf. prec., which however is very rare, whereas this is extremely common everywhere, esp. of the Buddha's skill in devising means to impress and convert people: SP 33.8 (also n. of SP Chap. 2) etc.; Gv 248.11 (mahop°), et passim. In Bbh 261.6 text prints °kauśalam, but v.l. °lyam should doubtless be adopted. Mvy 795; and as (**2**) n. of a Buddhist work 1345; in the latter sense °lya-sūtra Śikṣ 66.9; 165.5; 167.3; 168.4, 12.

[**upāyana yebhī** Śikṣ 333.2, read upāya-nayebhī.]

[**Upāyapramathana**, error for **Apāya°**.]

upāyāsa, m. (= Pali id.), *irritation, mental disturbance* or *perturbation*: esp. as last element in the **pratītyasamutpāda**, q.v., immediately preceded (in comp. or as separate words) by jāti and (standardly in cpd.) jarā, maraṇa, śoka, parideva, duḥkha, daurmanasya, Mvy 2258; Dharmas 42; Mv ii.285.12; iii.448.15; SP 179.8; Sāl 81.4 (cited Śikṣ 222.10); Dbh 49.5; Av ii.106.4; Suv 193.13; KP 61.6; parts or variations of this occur in other connections, thus śokaparideva° °upāyāsāḥ Mv iii.337.11–12; same cpd. beginning (jāti-)jarā-vyādhi-maraṇa-śoka- etc. LV 104.16; Divy 210.8; Av i.177.12; Gv 229.17; Laṅk 174.2; 180.9; cpd. or associated with other quasi-synonyms, SP 77.6 sarvopadravopāyāsopasarga- (etc.); Suv 92.12 sarvopadravopasargopāyāsebhyaḥ; KP 93.3 sopadravaḥ sopakleśa(ḥ) sopāyāso, and 4 nir-upa° (same cpds. in neg. form); used alone, Bbh 194.22 (kāyikāḥ klamāḥ, caitasikāḥ apy) upāyāsāḥ, *bodily toils and mental irritations*; Mv ii.161.13 upāyāsehi arttīyanto upāyāsa-samatikramaṇaṃ; Mv iii.401.11 (vs) upāyāsā ca te sarve vidhvastā viralīkṛtā(ḥ) (so read, cf. Senart's note which seems to me not quite correct); neg. Bhvr. cpd. (beside nir-upā°, KP 93.4 above) an-upāyāsa (= Pali id.), *free from irritation*, Suv 77.2; Śikṣ 176.5.

-upāyikā (= Skt. upāya), *means*: in sādhanopāyikā, *means of performance*: Sādh 415.5; 449.17; 468.12; 486.3 (all colophons).

upārabhyate (cf. next; in mg. = Pali upārambhati, Skt. upālabhate), *censures, abuses*: AsP 84.9 yo 'py upārabhyeta (v.l. °labhyeta; trans.!) tam api na samanupaśyati.

upārambha, m. (cf. prec.; = Pali id.), *blame, reproach, fault-finding*: LV 422.17 sarvaprapañcopārambhavigatatvāt; Bbh 42.7 paropārambha-vivāda-; 104.13 nopārambhābhiprāyeṇa, 24 an-upārambha-prekṣī; AsP 78.1 upārambhābhiprāyāḥ; 84.8 sa upārambhān api ... na samanupaśyati. The Skt. is upālambha; note Mvy 5356 upālambhābhiprāyaḥ.

Upāriṣṭa (once printed Upa°, prob. by error, despite the Pali equivalent Upariṭṭha; Chin. on Karmav *sans mal*, see Lévi's note), n. of a pratyekabuddha: Mmk 40.23 (prose; dvau pratyekabuddhau gandhamādanaḥ) upāriṣṭaś ceti; 64.12 (prose) ... upariṣṭa ... (so printed here, in a list of pr. b.); 111.10 (prose, in list of 8 pr. b.) candanaḥ gandhamādanaḥ ketuḥ suketu sitaketu ṛṣṭa upāriṣṭa nemiś ceti; Karmav 67.1, where Lévi prints Upariṣṭha in text, but apparently without ms. authority; in his note he says, read Upāriṣṭa with one ms. (the other is corrupt but begins apā-, indicating ā in second syllable).

[? **upārodha**, *injury*, Bbh 118.7 (prose) prāṇinām upārodhāya; read prob. uparodhāya; doubtless misprint.]

upārdha, adj. and subst. nt. or m. (in Mv mss. written uparddha, semi-MIndic; = Pali upaḍḍha; cf. Ind. Stud. 15.160, last line, for an apparent Skt. occurrence), *half, the half*; adj. upārdhaṃ mārgaṃ Divy 144.11, 12, *half the way*; upārdhena dhanena Av i.23.11; in cpds., upārdha-rājyam Divy 514.15, 16; uparddha-kāśiṃ (mss. °śi) Mv iii.376.1, *half a thousand*, see **kāśi**, and cf. **Upar-**

ddhakāśikā; subst., usually with gen., rajanyā upārdhaṃ (n. sg.) LV 198.8, *half of the night*; ratnānāṃ ... upārdhaṃ dātavyam Av i.23.15; upārdhaṃ ... brahmacaryasya Av i.211.8; 240.2 ff.; upārdhaṃ (sc. āhārasya; MSV °dho) bhikṣūṇāṃ pātre pataty upārdhaṃ (MSV ardho) bhūmāv iti Divy 86.15 (and ff.) = MSV i.85.20; with abl., upārdhu (read so, or upārdha; Lefm. upādhu with some mss.; acc. sg.) sarvarājyād LV 241.14 (vs); in Mv i.49.12 uparddhasya is obscure (adverb? Senart *par moitié*) but is prob. to be taken somehow with the following numeral caturaśīti (otherwise Senart).

upārdhakālaka, adj. with pudgala, see **sarvakālaka**: MSV iii.75.11.

[**Upārdhakāśikā**, see **Uparddha**°.]

Upāli or °**lin** (= Pali id.), n. of one of Buddha's leading disciples, a barber by caste and profession; story of his ordination, Mv iii.179.6 ff. Forms implying stem Upāli in Mvy 1062 °liḥ, nom.; Av ii.112.5 °lir, 112.9; 113.7 °leḥ, gen.; 113.7 °liṃ, acc.; 113.2 °li-kalpako (ms.; Speyer em. °liḥ k°); Śikṣ 148.16 °lir; 164.9 ff. °le, voc.; stem Upālin, Divy 21.21; 197.18 °lī, nom.; 197.21, 24 °lin, voc.; Upāli Sūtra, Hoernle MR 29 passim °lī, nom.; non-Skt. form, Divy 21.24 °li, voc.; in Mv the forms are mixed, as often in BHS: nom. °lir, °liḥ, °lis, iii.179.6; 180.10; 197.1; °li 179.10 (v.l. °lī), 11, 14, 18 (twice); 180.18 (v.l. °lī); 181.10, 16 (v.l. °lim, before vowel), 19; acc. °liṃ i.75.1; °li iii.180.12 (? or stem in comp.?); 181.18 (mss.; Senart em. °liṃ); voc. °li iii.180.5, 13; gen. °lino i.178.2; °lisya iii.179.10, 17; 180.2, 4, 7, 16; 181.11, 13, 15; 182.1, 4, 6, 7. See next items. Written **Udālin** in MSV i.248.11, 14; ii.91.10 (here Tib. cited ñe bar ḥkhor = Upāli); 108.8; 113.14, etc.

Upāli-gaṅgapālānāṃ jātakaṃ, n. (in colophon) of a Jātaka story (= Pali Gaṅgamāla-Jāt., 421): Mv iii.197.3. See the two names.

Upālipariprcchā, n. of a work: °cchā Śikṣ 164.8; 168.15; 178.9; 290.3. Fragments, including two of the Śikṣ citations, also cited from another ms. in IHQ 7.259 ff.

Upālisūtra, n. of a work: Hoernle, MR 27 ff. Is this the same as the prec.? Probably not; it has a Pali correspondent: MN. i.371 ff.

(**upāvartayati**, *provides*, seems not essentially different from Skt. tho recorded in Index to Divy 449.2 puṣkariṇī khātā ... kṣudramṛgarudhiram upāvartayitum ārabdham; 532.12 (bhūrjena prayojanam ... tūlena; sa kathayati, devi śobhanam,) upāvartayāmīti. tena prabhūtam upāvartya praveśitam ...)

upāsaka, m., °**sikā**, once °**sikī**, f., *lay-disciple* (of the Buddha), passim: m. Mvy 8724; Divy 618.13, 17; Av i.338.4 ff., and often; in Mv iii.268.13, description of Rāhula's ordination, acceptance of the first five śikṣāpada makes him an upāsaka, and the further requirements for making him a monk are then stated; f. °sikā Mvy 8725; Divy 618.13; Bhīk 9a.2; °sikī Divy 618.18 (no v.l.).

-upāhanaka, ifc. Bhvr. (cf. Pali sa-upāhana, id., to Pali upāhanā, by metathesis = Skt. upānah; and BHS **upānaha**), in sopāhanaka, adj., *with* (wearing) *sandals*: Prāt 536.16.

upāhiṇḍate (cf. [**anvā**]**hiṇḍ**°), *strolls upon* or *over*: Divy 264.19 (rathyāvīthīcatvaraśṛṅgāṭake) upāhiṇḍamānā(ḥ).

upīḍa, m., *crowding*: Samādh 19.17 (vs) no ca upīḍo. I take this as = *uppīḍa, Skt. utpīḍa, § 2.84. According to Régamey 78, note 116, it represents an unknown *avapīḍa, *opīḍa, with u for o m.c. Cf. 19.22 utpādo. text, where meter requires upādo.

(**upekṣate** (= Skt.), in Mv i.107.10–11 kevarūpāṃ ca janatāṃ upekṣanta iti (subject, bodhisattva cakravartin), *and what sort of people do they suffer?*, i. e. *tolerate, put up with, let do as they like*; the answer is given in lines 16 ff.; Senart's note fails to understand.)

upekṣā (Skt. id., used in much the same sense, but in BHS like Pali upekkhā, upekhā, technical religious term, while also used in general untechnical sense), *indifference* (Tib. btaṅ sñoms), *putting up with whatever happens, patience, long-suffering*: non-religious, LV 304.11 (vs) śreyo upekṣa ma raṇe paribhāvu gacchet, (a son of Māra advises him not to fight the Bodhisattva) *better is patience* (to put up with what can't be helped), *lest one arrive at humiliation in battle*; religious, as the 7th **bodhyaṅga** and as one of the 4 **apramāṇa**, qq.v.; LV 129.10 (prose) aduḥkhāsukham upekṣāsmṛtipariśuddhaṃ caturthaṃ dhyānam; 224.2 (vs) mudito upekṣa-dhyāyī brāhme pathi vidhijñaḥ; 275.18 (yasyā ... brāhmaḥ patho jñāyate) maitrī vā karuṇā upekṣa muditā (see s.v. **apramāṇa**); in 442.5 acquisition of upekṣā leads *to getting rid of love and hatred*, anunayapratighotsargāya; its six **aṅga**, see this.

Upendra, n. of a nāga king: Mvy 3265; Māy 246.15.

upodbala, nt. (cf. Skt. °balana, to °balayati), *strengthening, increase of strength*: Mvy 7677 = Tib. stobs skyed pa.

upoṣaṇīya, adj. (gdve. to next), in °ya-prabha, ep. of Amitābha: Sukh 29.14; Müller SBE 49.2, p. 29, (possessed of) *pleasant* (light), the basis of which is obscure to me; either gdve. of next or of Skt. upa-vas as in BR s.v. (5), *to which one should devote oneself*, or (less likely) *to be honored with observances like those of the upoṣatha* (°dha).

upoṣati (cf. Skt. upavasati, which alone is recorded in Pali too), *keeps* (the sabbath), *observes* (**upoṣadha**, which may well have influenced the form): Mv ii.177.20 upoṣadhaṃ upoṣati (no v.l.).

Upoṣatha, n. of a nāga king: MPS 34.132.

upoṣadha, (**1**) nt. (but see under **poṣadha, posatha**; = Pali (u)posatha, m.; Jain Skt. pauṣadha, m.; AMg. posaha, m. and nt.; except a single case of posatha, q.v., BHS seems to have only forms ending in -dha, whereas Pali has only -tha; see prec. and foll. items), *the Buddhist 'sabbath'*, four times a month, on which good laymen observed 8 śīla (see **aṣṭāṅga**), confessed, etc.: Mvy 7137 °dham, n. sg.; Mv i.255.13 °dhe; ii.177.20 (see **upoṣati**); iii.97.20 and 98.2 (vss), mss. poṣadhaṃ (acc.), Senart em. upo° m.c.; Divy 116.22 upoṣadhoṣitaḥ, but 116.21 poṣadhe and 118.27 poṣadhoṣitaḥ (all prose); (**2**) m., n. of a (cakravartin) king of old, grandson of Kalyāṇa, father of Māndhātar (= Pali Uposatha): Mvy 3556; Mv i.348.8; Divy 210.13 ff.; MSV i.66.7 ff.; 92.16; (**3**) m., n. of a devaputra who visited Buddha: Av i.336.1 ff.

upoṣadhika, f. °ikā (= Pali (u)posathika; cf. **poṣadhika**, °**dhin**), *observing* (*one who observes*) *the 'sabbath'*: masc., Mmk 49.5; 75.12; 304.15; 318.7; fem. °ikāyāṃ, loc., Mv i.205.7 = ii.8.20.

Uppalaka = **Utpalaka** (1), q.v.; cf. also **Upala** (for Uppala = Utpala).

uppharitvā or **upphāritvā**, see **utpharati.**

ubhayaṃ, in cobhayaṃ (= Pali cūbhayaṃ, PTSD s.v. ubhaya), *both*, after two coordinates: krīḍanti ramanti cobhayaṃ MPS 12.9, *they sport and take delight both.*

ubhayato-bhāga-vimukta, adj. (= Pali ubhatobhāga-vimutta), *emancipated from both parts*: Mvy 1028 (misprinted °bhaga°; corr. Index); Divy 404.24 (read: ubhau hi tau ubhayatobhāgavimuktau); Bhīk 27b.1; cf. AbhidhK. LaV-P. ii.205; vi.275–7. Often edd. (Pali and BHS) print ubha(ya)to as separate word, wrongly; it modifies bhāga- directly, as part of the cpd. Tib. on Mvy gñis kaḥi cha las ... *from both parts*; Pali MN comm. iii.188.7 = DN comm. ii.514.3 dvīhi bhāgehi vimutto, arūpasamāpattiyā rūpakāyato vimutto, maggena nāmakāyato (i. e. from the skhandha other than rūpa) vimutto. The AbhidhK. vi.276 has a different interpretation acc. to LaV-P., *delivered from the obstacle of the passions* (impurities, kleśāvaraṇa), *and from the obstacle to* (the 8) vimokṣa (which is stated to be akarmaṇyatā, *l'impuissance corporelle* *et mentale*). This seems to be a later reinterpretation; the Pali comms. make it simpler, referring to the *physical* and *mental* constituents. Which was meant in our texts is not clear from the contexts.

ubhayavyañjana, adj., f. °nā (= Pali ubhatobyañjanaka), *having the marks of both* (*sexes*), *hermaphrodite*: °naḥ Mvy 8775; °nā Bhīk 11a.4; 16a.5 (in questioning a candidate for ordination).

umaka-, in comp. with -puṣpa, nt. (from Skt. umā), *flower of the flax plant* (blue): Mvy 1522 rūpāṇi . . . nīlāni . . . tad yathā umakapuṣpaṃ. Tib. zar ma, usually *sesame*, but also (Das) = kṣauma, *linen*.

Umeśvara, n. of a future Buddha; as such it is prophesied that the goddess Umā will be reborn: Kv 90.20.

uyate, pass. to Skt. vā, *weave* (cf. ūyate, B.S. in Wh. Roots), *is woven*, in uyamāna-(pres. pple.)-vardhanam Mvy 8410 (so Mironov and v.l. Kyoto ed. for text upamāna-), *magnification of* (a robe that is) *being woven* (for oneself), a sin for a monk; Tib. ḥthag pa (*weave*) (b)skyed pa (*make increase*). The short u is supported by Skt. uta (beside ūta), ppp.

[**ura(s),** *womb*? So acc. to Senart on Mv i.199.10 = ii.3.8 (vs), ed. divasāni sapta māsā ca daśa tasyā uram otaret. The meter is bad even so; mss. in i.199.10 read udare-m-, which suggests a form of udara, the word we should expect; I find no record of ura(s) in the required mg. Perhaps the orig. had something like . . . daśa tasyodar' (for tasyā udaram or udare) otaret.]

uraga-garbha, m. or nt. (= Skt. nāga-garbha, Garbe, Ind. Min. 44, *vermilion* as *originating from lead*, nāga; cf. Schmidt, Nachtr. s.v. nāgagarbha), *vermilion*: Mv ii.311.1 (prose) °bha-maṇiratanehi samalaṃkṛtaṃ (mss. uragarbha-, em. Senart).

uragasāra-candana, nt. (not recorded for Pali), a kind of sandalwood: SP 406.8–9; 408.2–3; 411.7; LV 63.18; 64.3; 125.17; 204.11; 215.1; 294.2; Mvy 6255; Gv 123.20; 153.16; 164.18, etc.; Sukh 38.17.

[**uratrika,** in Kv 42.9 noratrikeṣu, read naurabhri°; see **aura°**.]

urabhra, m. (in Skt. only *sheep*, and so MIndic equivalents), said to mean *goat* in Mvy 4824 acc. to Tib. (ra).

urasa, adj. (= AMg. id.; Skt. aurasa, Pali orasa), *own* (*son*): Mv iii.278.20 urasā lokanāthasya te khu bheṣyanti harṣitā. Both mss. urasā; same line ii.354.16 orasā (for aur°, MIndic; read 2d half as in iii.278.20, cf. reading of ms. C). The AMg. form prob. justifies Senart in keeping ur°.

Urumuṇḍa, m. (also occurs as **Rurumuṇḍa,** q.v.), n. of a mountain: Divy 349.19; 350.22 ff.; 385.10, 18, 27; MSV i.3.17.

uruvilvaka, adj., *of Uruvilvā*: Mv ii.207.19; 208.1 °vake vanaṣaṇḍe, or (208.1 and v.l. of 207.19) °khaṇḍe.

Uruvilvā (= Pali Uruvelā), n. of a village where the Bodhisattva sought enlightenment for a time: called a senāpati-grāma(ka), LV 248.7; 267.13; Mv iii.415.11; 425.17; other occurrences LV 261.3; 269.9; Mv ii.123.16; 200.9 ff.; 207.1, etc.; Divy 202.7.

Uruvilvākalpa, m. (nt.? = Pali Uruvelākappa), n. of a town: LV 406.20 °kalpam, acc.

Uruvilvā-kāśyapa (in MSV Uruvilvă°; = Pali Uruvelă-kassapa), n. of one of Buddha's disciples: Av i.148.10 (ms. Uparivilvā°, ed. em. Uruvilvā° wrongly); Karmav 157.3; originally a jaṭila ascetic; story of his conversion, Mv iii.424.6 ff.; usually mentioned with his brothers **Nadī-kāśyapa** and **Gayā-k°**, qq.v., Mv iii.102.12, 20; 430.12, 18; 432.7; SP 2.1; 207.3; LV 1.10; MSV i.196.5; Mvy 1049 (Nadī-k° 1050, Gayā-k° later, 1064): Sukh 2.4.

ulana, nt., a high number; app. error for **tulana,** q.v., tho it occurs three times in Gv 133.7.

Uluka, v.l. for **Huluka,** q.v.

Uluvillikā, n. of a village chief's daughter: LV 265.5.

ulūka-pakṣika- (in comp.; = Pali ulūka-pakkhika, AN i.241.1, 296.1), (a dress or decoration) *made of owl's feathers*, worn by certain ascetics: Mv iii.412.8 °ka-bhaginī (n. pr. acc. to Senart p. xxxvii) śramaṇā. Cf. LV 249.1 gṛddholūkapakṣadhāraṇaiś ca (ātāpanaparitāpanaiḥ).

Ulkādhārin, n. of a Bodhisattva: Gv 442.25.

ulkāmukha, (**1**) (nt., = Pali ukkāmukha) *a* (goldsmith's) *smelting-pot* or *furnace*: LV 405.14 -niṣka ulkāmukhaprakṛṣṭo; Sukh 3.5 (-niṣko . . .) ulkāmukhe (so v.l., better than °khena text) saṃpraveśya supariniṣṭhitaḥ; Śikṣ 182.3 °khaṃ vā hriyamāṇasya (as a form of torture); (**2**) nt., in Mvy 6900, following dīpaḥ, ulkā, followed by pradīpaḥ, = Tib. skar mda-ḥi gdoṅ ṅam snaṅ (read prob. sna with Das), which acc. to Das = *one having either his face or his nose* (sna; snaṅ = light) *glowing as a meteor*; *a demon* (so Skt.); *a meteor-mouthed arrow*; *a kind of fire-arm*; (**3**) m. (= Pali Okkāmukha), n. of a son of King Sujāta Ikṣvāku: Mv i.348.12; 352.9; and of a later descendant, 352.12.

Ulkāmukhī, n. of a rākṣasī: Māy 243.24. Cf. Skt. Ulkāmukhaḥ, a kind of ghost (preta); n. of a rakṣas (BR); and see prec. (2), Tib. (Das).

ulkin (Skt. ulkā plus -in), perhaps *a portent containing a meteor*, or some personified power *characterized by, carrying, wielding a meteor*(?); the passages are obscure and in part clearly corrupt; in verses: Mmk 198.15 °nāṃ (gen. pl.?), 25 °naḥ (gen. sg., see **prapata**); 200.15 ulkino (nom. pl.) bahudhākārā dṛśyante vividhāśrayā; 204.5 °nāṃ (gen. pl.); 223.2 nirghāta ulkināṃ (gen. pl.).

ulla, adj. (= AMg. id., for Skt. ārdra), *wet*; of sorrow, *fresh, new* (so Skt. ārdra, BR): Mv iii.116.8, read ullenaiva śokena, substantially with mss.; Senart em. wrongly.

ullaṅghikā, *act of jumping, springing, leaping*: Mvy 8547 nollaṅghikayā. (So Tib. mchoṅ, and Chin.)

ullapati, or **ullāpayati** (see s.v. **ullāpana**; in Skt. ullapati recorded only in mg. *wheedle, flatter, coax*; in Pali app. only *boast, brag* (falsely); noun derivs. show mgs. pointing to *deceive*, but no verb forms with this mg. have been noted), *shouts* or *yells derisively at* (acc.); associated with **uccagghati,** q.v.: SP 382.12 (prose) ye te taṃ bodhisattvaṃ . . . ullāpitavanta (but most mss. ullap°) ucca(g)ghitavantaḥ; 482.6 sūtrāntalekhakānāṃ uccagghanaṃ kariṣyanty ullapiṣyanti; AsP 385.13 and 388.19 ullāpayiṣyati (see **uccagghati**).

[**ullāṭṭayati,** error for **ullāḍayati,** q.v.]

ullāḍayati? perhaps *stirs* (food, in cooking): Divy 285.25 ārabdhaḥ . . . khādyakāny ullāḍayitum; cf. AMg. ullāliya, ppp., *struck, beaten, tossed* or *flung up* (Ratnach.); note to Divy suggests em. ulloḍayitum (cf. Skt. loḍayati, Pali ullola, *commotion*); but khādyakāny ullāḍayata MSV i.264.1; iii.138.7 (text here ullāṭṭayata).

ullāpana (to **ullapati,** q.v.; see also next two), (**1**) nt., *shouting* or *yelling derisively, abusive derision* (this may possibly be the mg. of Skt. ullāpa in khalollāpāḥ Ind. Spr. 2047, for which Boehtl. *harte Worte von schlechten Menschen*): Mvy 5227 °nam (follows **uccagghanam**) = Tib. (b)stiṅ pa, *abuse*, also rñiṅ pa (? for rñi, *snare, trap*? then belonging to mg. 2 below?); Chin. *disdain*, Jap. *talking in a loud voice, abusing*; Śikṣ 271.6 nāsty uccagghanollāpana-dānam, see **uccagghana**; acc. to note, Tib. here brid, which means *deceit*(ful), (not *wheedling, coaxing*, with Bendall,) but it seems clear from uccagghana that this is an error; (**2**) adj., *deceitful, deceptive*: LV 176.4 (vs) (saṃskāra . . .) bāla-ullāpana **riktamuṣṭivat** (so read, see this); 212.14 (kāmāḥ . . .) ullāpanā riktamuṣṭivat (q.v.); Śikṣ 77.3 bāllollāpanāḥ, *deceiving fools*, said of lusts; 261.8 °nam; RP 39.13 bāllollāpanaṃ, of worldly life, esp. royal pleasures; read so in Dbh 43.6 for bālālāpanaṃ.

ullāpanaka, adj. or subst. (see prec., next, and **ullapati**), *deceiving, deceiver*; or perhaps *deception*: LV 371.19

(vs) iha te ciraṃ samāyata ullāpanakā (n. pl.) vināśaparyantāḥ, *here these* (my) *deceivers* (? *deceptions*; refers to ignorance, error, and the like) *have at long last ended in destruction.*

ullāpayati, see **ullapati.**

ullāpin, adj. (see s.v. **ullāpana,** 2), *deceiving*; fem. °inī: Laṅk 77.7 mṛgatṛṣṇikā mṛgollāpinī, *a mirage that deceives deer.*

ullipta, ppp. (= Pali ullitta, chiefly in cpd. ullittāvalitta, e.g. Vin. ii.117.23; of kūṭāgārāni, AN i.101.10; comm. ii.168.5 on the latter, anto ca bahi ca littāni, and similarly comm. on Vin.), in Mv ii.115.11 kūṭāgārāṇi kārayet ulliptāvaliptāni (mss. ulliptā ca liptāni); if Pali comms. may be trusted the cpd. means *smeared inside and out.* (PTSD *smeared up and down*, evidently an etymological rendering.)

Ulluka, v.l. for **Huluka,** q.v.

ullumpati (= Pali id.; Skt. *herausgreifen*, °*fischen*, BR.), *saves, rescues*: Bhīk 19a.3 ullumpatu māṃ bhadantā ubhayasaṃghaḥ (by ordination; said by the candidate); Mvy 8704 °patu māṃ (same situation; so also in Pali). [Cf. **ullopana.**]

ullokanaka (for **olok°**, q.v.; § 3.54), *window*: gavākṣa-ullokanakehi (cpd., instr. pl.) SP 85.1 (vs); same form in Nep. mss. SP 114.3 (vs), where Kashgar rec. aulok°, and ed. with Foucaux olok°; WT gavākṣa olokanake 'pi (citing their ms. K' as °olokanakeṣu).

ullokanīya, adj. (gdve. to **ullokayati,** q.v.), *to be looked up to, worthy of admiration, of reverence*: of persons, Mv i.103.5, see s.v. **avalokanīya**; ii.378.8 (vs) °nīyo sada puṇyavanto; 391.17 °nīyo bhavati mahānubhāvo; 393.3 °nīyo bahujanapūjito; (in Śikṣ 302.10, parallel to Mv 378.8, replaced by udvīkṣaṇīya, in 308.4, parallel to 393.3, by vilokanīya;) LV 85.7 ullokanīyo bhaviṣyāmi sarvasattvānām (said by the Bodhisattva); ullokanīyaṃ, adverb, of sounds, Mv i.206.17 = ii.10.10 = iii.341.8 (of sounds of auspicious earthquakes), *in a way worthy of admiration*, substantially = *agreeably, enjoyably*, **nirvarṇanīyaṃ** (see this; iii.341.8 instead **nirvāpanīyaṃ**, q.v.) ca ullokanīyaṃ ca āsecanakaṃ ca.

ullokayati, °te (see prec. and **an-ullokita**; = Pali ulloketi), *looks up to* (in admiration or reverence): SP 54.14 ullokayan pādapam eva tatra (at the tree of enlightenment); 100.6 (bhagavantam) abhimukham ullokayamānā(ḥ); 215.10 bhagavantam ullokayamāne (dual); Mv i.204.17 = ii.8.12 ullokayanti tuṣiteṣu jinam; ppp. ullokita, seems to mean *looking up, upturned*, of eyes or face, Gv 46.21 ullokita-vadanair devendrair (in reverence or supplication); in Mvy 6635 ullokitaḥ, perhaps also thus used (or perhaps passive, *looked up to*? lack of context leaves doubt); Tib. gyen du (or, yar; both *upward*) blta ba (*look*).

(-ullocaka,) f. **-ullocikā,** ifc. Bhvr. (= Skt. Lex. and AMg. ulloca, AMg. also ulloya, *canopy*), *canopy*: svastikollocikā(ḥ) lājā(ḥ) Megh 308.14, *canopied by a svastika* (in a painting). See also **mukhollocakaṃ.**

ulloḍayati? see **ullāḍayati.**

[**ullopana,** nt. (ul-lup- not recorded in this mg.; contrast **ullumpati**), *deceit*, in bālollopanam Mvy 7312 = Tib. byis pa ḥbrid pa, *deceit of children* or *fools*. But read **ullāpanam** with Mironov, tho against most mss.]

uvyadha, m. (so also Mironov, as separate item, after utphikā), n. of some disease: Mvy 9543; acc. to Tib. mgo glog, perh. *head-ulcer* (see s.v. **utphikā**); Chin. *dizziness in the head.*

uśī (? cf. Skt. Lex. uśī, *wish*?), perhaps *joy*, or *energy*: in uśī-bahula, Dbh 12.10, followed by utsāhabahula, but preceded by udagrībahula and synonyms of this, see **udagrī.**

Uśīra-giri, m., n. of a mountain: Mvy 4126; or Usīra-giri, Divy 22.2 (to the north); cf. Pali Usīraddhaja, a northern mountain range, and Skt. Uśīra-bīja (or Uṣ°), n. of a mountain.

uśvasati, false Skt. for ucchvasati, apparently *breathes in* (see s.v. **āśvāsa-praśvāsa**): Mv ii.208.4, 8, 9 (paired with praśvasati); correlated with noun āśvāsa.

uṣita (seemingly only Lex. in Skt.), ppp. to uṣ, *burnt*: jvālūṣitā SP 85.9 (vs), for jvāla-uṣ°, *burnt with flames*; so WT (Kashgar rec. jalūṣ°, i. e. for jvala-uṣ°; KN saṃlūṣitā); see § 4.31.

uṣitavant, adj. (perf. act. pple. of vas; = Pali vusitavant(a), ep. of arhats), *having lived the* (proper, right) *life*, ep. of arhats: Sukh 1.14 arhadbhiḥ . . . uṣitavadbhiḥ.

Uṣidatta, see **Ṛṣi°.**

uṣṭradhūmaka (m.?), lit. *camel-smoke*, a kind of worm, cause of calamities: KP 93.2 yasmiṃ . . . deśe °ka kṛṣṇaśira uttānaśāyī bhavati, sa deśa sopadravaḥ . . . Tib. srin bu rṅa mo dud ka zhes bya ba, *the worm called camel-smoke.* See Das s.v. rṅa mo ṅud (mistake for dud) ka, where full confirmation of the KP passage is found.

Uṣṭrapāda, n. of a yakṣa: Māy 82.

(uṣṭrikā, *camel-shaped vessel*, occurs in Skt., Kauṭ. Arth. Sham. 411.14; 416.4; see Meyer, 650 n. 1: Karmav 45.14 yatroṣṭrikāmātrāṇi phalāni; large, rich fruits are compared to it because of its size and bulging shape; see Lévi's note.)

uṣṇi (m. or nt.), app. = **uṣṇīṣa** in sense 1, q.v.; twice in vss of RP, supported by meter: 46.13 giritatam iva (ms. iha) haima śobhate cāsya coṣṇi (end of line); 50.11 girirājatulya tava coṣṇir iha.

uṣṇiṣa (m.c. for uṣṇīṣa), *excrescence on the head*: °ṣodgato (= °ṣa udgataḥ) RP 6.18 (vs).

uṣṇībhavati (to Skt. uṣṇa), *becomes hot*: Divy 68.2 °bhūtvā, ger.

uṣṇīṣa, (1) nt. (in Skt. also m.; = Pali uṇhīsa), in Skt. only *turban*; in cpd. uṣṇīṣa-śīrṣa(n) or -śiras(ka), 32d of the 32 **lakṣaṇa,** q.v. (Pali uṇhīsa-sīsa), acc. to Pali DN comm. ii.452.1 ff. *having a head the size and shape of which makes it seem turbanned.* But in BHS (and Pali) interpreted as *having a head surmounted by an excrescence*, whether a top-knot of hair, or a growth in the skull. So Tib. regularly (uṣṇīṣa = gtsug tor), e. g. on Mvy 236 uṣṇīṣa-śiraska-tā. Confirmed by Gv 401.26 ff. mūrdhni cāsyoṣṇīṣam abhinirvṛttam abhūt, sujātaṃ samantaparimaṇḍalaṃ madhyābhinyastakeśālaṃkāraṃ koṭīśatasahasrapattraratnapadmasaṃdarśitaṃ samantāt samabhāgapratiṣṭhitam aparimitamahārghyatāpradhānamadhyam. Cf. also **uṣṇi,** apparently = uṣṇīṣa in this sense, and **uṣṇiṣa.** In comp. as one of the lakṣaṇa, LV 105.11; 432.13; Dharmas 83; Mv i.227.3; ii.30.6; 307.4; Bbh 376.7; **(2)** m., one of ten **Krodha**: Dharmas 11; **(3)** in Mmk 41.7 aṣṭau uṣṇīṣarājānaḥ are mentioned as to be depicted in a rite; their names, given 41.10–11, are Cakravartin, Uṣṇīṣa, Abhyudgatoṣṇīṣa, Sitātapatra, Jayoṣṇīṣa, Kamaloṣṇīṣa, Tejorāśi, Unnatoṣṇīṣa. They seem not to be related to the Krodha of Dharmas 11, tho the first two names also occur in that list. Nothing significant is said of them.

Uṣṇīṣakośasarvadharmaprabhāmaṇḍalamegha, n. of a Tathāgata: Gv 311.16.

Uṣṇīṣavijayā, n. of a goddess: Sādh 180.7 etc.

[**uṣṇīṣa-śobhana,** erroneous v.l. for **tūṣṇīka-śo°**, q.v., at Mv i.301.14.]

Uṣṇīṣaśrī, n. of a Bodhisattva: Gv 442.9.

uṣmagata, or **ūṣma°**, adj., *become warm*; applied to the first stage of **nirvedha-bhāgīya,** q.v., or to things (cittāni, kuśalamūlāni, etc.) pertaining to it: Mvy 1212; Divy 80.1 (erroneously uṣṇa-gatāni); 166.15; 240.20; 271.12 (ūṣma-gatāni); 469.12; Sūtrāl. xiv.26 comm.; AbhidhK. LaV-P. vi.163 f.; (ūṣmagatam) MSV i.224.10.

Usīragiri = **Uśīra°**, q.v.

uhoḍima, ed. with v.l. once **aho°**, n. pl. °mā(ḥ), probably *deformed*: Laṅk 27.4; 33.15; see s.v. **avakoṭimaka.**

U

***ūjñā, *ūñā,** or ***ūṇā** (Skt. avajñā), see s.v. **ujña-ka.**

ūti, f., *effort* (cf. BR s.v. 7: cited once from BhagP.; no other mg. seems possible in Divy): Divy 654.27; 655.2 utsāhany ūtir aprativāṇiḥ ... yogaḥ karaṇīyaḥ.

ūddhata, in Ud xii.2 °taṃ raja(ḥ), *raised,* for uddhataṃ; note suggests that ū is due to confusion with Pali ūhata; a later var. is uddhṛtam; it may be noted that PTSD associates Pali uddhata with Skt. uddhṛta, from ud-dhṛ.

ūna-māna, m., *pride of* (thinking something) *too little* (i. e. unworthy of oneself): Mvy 1951. So Tib.: chuṅ zad sñam paḥi ṅa rgyal, *pride of thinking small.*

ūna-vāda, m. (corresp. to Pali omasa-vāda, Vin. iv.6.5; see Childers; not in PTSD), *depreciative language, speaking of defects* (of others): Mvy 8421 = Tib. skyon (nas) smra ba.

-ūruṇikā, ifc. Bhvr., fem. (to ūru, thigh; on formation see § 22.45), *having ... thighs*: LV 322.21 (vs) gajabhujasaṃnibha-ūruṇikāṃ, *having thighs like an elephant's trunk.*

Ūrṇatejas (v.l. Ūrṇī°; read Ūrṇā°? Tib. mdzod spu = ūrṇā), n. of a former Buddha: LV 5.8 (prose).

ūrṇapāśa, see **ūrṇākośa.**

Ūrṇaśiriprabhāsamati, n. of a former Buddha: Gv 258.10 (vs); ă here may be m.c.

ūrṇā (= Pali uṇṇā; very rare in Skt. in this sense, see pw; essentially Buddhist term; cf. **ūrṇā-kośa,** which seems unknown in Skt.), *the circle of hair between the eyebrows* of a Buddha (or other mahāpuruṣa): LV 316.9; chiefly in the 31st of the 32 **lakṣaṇa,** q.v. (elsewhere ūrṇākośa is generally used); *white color* is prevailingly mentioned.

ūrṇā-kośa, m., = **ūrṇā,** q.v.; usually as place from which a Buddha emits rays of brilliant light (raśmi, prabhā): bhagavāṃs ... ūrṇākośād raśmiṃ prāmuñcat SP 243.3; similarly LV 393.17; Mmk 169.4; Laṅk 13.4; ūrṇa-(m.c.)-kośā LV 116.7 (vs); bhrūvivarāntarād ūrṇākośād SP 20.8 (ekā raśmir niścaritā); LV 300.7; rarely in lists of 32 lakṣaṇa, Mvy 239, where erroneously °keśa for °kośa (so also Mironov; Burnouf, Lotus 563, records the same error once); Tib., as regularly for both ūrṇā and ūrṇākośa, mdzod (= kośa) spu (= *hair*). In LV 357.9 (vs) na tapati abhibhūtā bhānuvatyorṇapāśā (v.l. °ṇakośā), *does not shine, being surpassed by the* (Buddha's) *resplendent hair-curl,* I understand bhānuvatyā ūrṇa-(m.c. for ūrṇā-)-pāśā (or -kośā), instr. sg. (pāśa, *tie, knot, mass*; but in view of the fem. adj. perhaps an otherwise unknown fem. pāśā must be assumed).

ūrdha- (semi-MIndic, or possibly orthographic error) for ūrdhva of Skt., cf. Weller 23, Senart note on Mv i.116.3 (where ūrddha is said to be the reading of mss., tho the Crit. App. omits r; Lefm. regularly ūrdha, usually without note of variant); LV 85.6; 129.19; 208.11; 249.10–11; 258.13 (twice); 306.19; 307.8, 12, 16; 408.10; 413.9.

? **ūrdhva,** adj. (in fig. sense), *exalted, lofty, great,* of power: Mv i.116.3 adhivāsanaṃ viditvā rājāsya durjayordhva- (mss. °yorddha-, or °yoddha-, see prec.) bala (mss. balam) eva. Senart's note suggests em. durjayarddhi-bala. For this mg. of ūrdhva may be compared Pali uddhehi vatthehi Jāt. iv.154.15, *in rich, lofty clothes* (PTSD, doubtfully); but Dutoit's transl. understands *with uplifted garments* (presumably to wipe his eyes; the person is weeping).

ūrdhvaga, ūrdhvaṃga, see **ūrdhvāgra.**

Ūrdhvajaṭā (printed Ūrddhva°), n. of a rākṣasī: Māy 243.27.

ūrdhvabhāgīya, adj. (Pali uddhaṃbhāgiya), (*binding*) *to higher states* (viz. rūpa-, arūpa-dhātu), only said of the second group of five **saṃyojana** (q.v.), cf. **avarabhāgīya**: Mvy 2155 (without mention of saṃyojana); this in Pugg. 22.14–15 called *external* (bahiddhā).

ūrdhva-lokanā, *consent* (so Tib., gnaṅ bar): °nā dātavyā MSV iv.98.11.

ūrdhva-virecana (nt.; = Pali uddha-vi°), *'purging upward', emetic treatment* (for disease): MSV ii.45.12 °nena.

? **Ūrdhvasaṃdhi,** see **Oddhasaṃdhi.**

ūrdhva-srota(s), **°śrotas** (= Pali uddhaṃ-sota), *going upward in the stream* (of transmigration, i.e. to better existences; so comm. on Dhp. 218): Mvy 1019 °śrotāḥ; Ud ii.9 (= Dhp. 218) °sroto; both nom. sg.

ūrdhvāgra- (ūrdhvāṅga-, ūrdhvaṃga-, ūrdhvaga-; also written ūrdhā° without v, see **ūrdha-**; for other variants see below) **-roma(n),** adj. (= Pali uddhaggaloma), *having* (*body-*)*hair standing up,* lit. *with upright tips,* one of the 32 **lakṣaṇa,** q.v. The form ūrdh(v)āgra-, supported by Pali, is prob. orig. (so Burnouf, Lotus, 571); it is found in Dharmas 83; Mv i.226.18 (mss. kṛtvāgra); ii.305.15 (mss. ūrddhāgraromarājino or uddhā°); but in ii.30.2 mss. ūrddhaṃga, urddhaṃ ca (Senart ūrdhvāgra). Mvy 257 has ūrdhva-ga-romaḥ, but Mironov ūrdhvaṃga° (both *going upward*; cf. mss. in Mv ii.30.2); and Bbh 375.17; 381.24 also ūrdhvaṃga-(romā, adj.; romatā, subst.). In Bbh 379.10 the ms. has the further change to ūrdhvāṅga-(romatāṃ; ed. em. ūrdhvaṃga), as if ūrdhvaaṅga-roma-; so Gv 402.9–10 ūrdhvāṅgaromā (Bhvr.); LV 429.15 ūrdhvāṅga-(dakṣiṇāvarta-)-romakūpa(ḥ). Finally in LV 105.21 there is great confusion; Lefm. (only with B mss.) ūrdhāgrā(bhipradakṣiṇāvarta)-romāḥ (read °mā, Bhvr.); other mss. u(d)dhāṃgā°, uccāśā° (ucca-āśā); Tib. obscure, yan lag gi spu gyas phyogs nas gyen du ḥkhyil ba, lit. *hair of member(s), from (after) right direction* (generally = diś or āśā), *upward twist* (generally = āvarta). As Burnouf points out, Foucaux's transl. is inaccurate. The expression (abhi-pra-)dakṣiṇāvarta is inserted here in the epithet only in LV (both passages); it is attached to the lakṣaṇa ekaikaroma(n) in Mvy 256 and Dharmas 83, and in the commentarial expansion of the latter Gv 402.9; but Pali commentarial expansions of uddhaggaloma have a corresponding term, Burnouf, Lotus, 571.

ūrmi, m. or f. (in this sense AMg. ummi, see Ratnach., but not Skt. ūrmi, Pali ūmi, ummi), *crowd, throng* (of creatures): Mv i.222.14 = ii.24.22 samantormijātā, *forming a crowd all around* (here of gods); LV 173.13 (vs) naṭaraṅgasamā jagi-r-ūrmi-cuti, *like an actor's stage-set is the passing of the crowd* (of people) *in the world*; so if Lefm.'s text is right, but v.l. janmi for r-ūrmi, which (or rather janma) seems supported by Tib. skye.

ūṣmagata = **uṣma°,** q.v.

ūhata, ppp. (both mgs. = Pali id.; cf. § 3.2 and **samūhata**; in Skt. uddhṛta has both mgs.; uddhata, to root han, is somewhat dubiously assigned to mg. 2, still more dubiously to mg. 1; but BHS has **ūhanati,** q.v. in mg. 1), (**1**) *removed, put away, destroyed*: Mv i.247.17 rāgadveṣā ca ūhatā (mss. °tam); 354.4 tiṣṭhaṃ yathā kāṣṭhagataṃ an-ūhataṃ (the context resembles Dhp. 338); Ud x.13 tāla-mastur (see **mastu**) iv' ūhataḥ, *like the top of a palmtree destroyed*; (**2**) *arisen*: Mv ii.58.12 (vs) aruṇasmiṃ (read °smim or °smi, m.c.) ūhate; 415.14 ūhate ca aruṇe; so with mss. both times; Senart em. udgate, but cf. Pali Jāt. v.403.30 aruṇasmiṃ (mss.; ed. em. °smi, m.c.) ūhate (comm. gloss uggate).

ūhate (Vedic ohate, to root ūh- or oh-, see Neisser,

Z. Wbch.d.RV., s.v.; not in this sense Skt.), *heeds, pays attention to*: Mv i.163.(3–)4 parehi ukto paruṣaṃ punaḥ-punaḥ, prabhuḥ samāno kṣamate na ūhate (v.l. ūhyate, uhy°), ... *he endures it, pays no attention.*

ūhanati (= Pali id.; cf. § 3.2; Skt. uddhanti in this sense at most Ved. and BhāgP., hardly Class. Skt.), *removes, puts away, destroys, gets rid of*: Mv ii.404.14 (adya sarvabhavamūlam aśeṣaṃ) ūhanāmi. Cf. **ūhata,** the ppp. to this (? or = Skt. uddhṛta).

ūhasati (= Pali id.; whether it represents Skt. ud-, ava-, or upa-has- is a moot question), *laughs* (in joy): Mv i.218.18 = ii.20.20 (vs), all mss. mahāhāsaṃ ca ūhati, kept by Senart (see his note); I think we must read ūhasi (or °se), 3 sg. aor.; ii.268.13 ff. mahā-ūhasitaṃ ūhase (repeated several times), *laughed a loud laugh*; i.221.20 = ii.24.7 (vs) ūhasāsi (seems guaranteed by meter and sense; mss. in ii.24.7 ūhāsasi, ūhasari; in i.221.20 more remote; the laugh is one of joy over the following thought:) ayaṃ dānim eko bhavo paścimo (t)ti.

ūhasita, nt. (orig. ppp. of prec.; cf. Pkt. ūhasiya, used Deśīn. 1.140 as gloss on Deśī ūhaṭṭha), *a laugh*: Mv ii.268.13 ff., see **ūhasati.**

Ṛ

ṛkta-, hyper-Skt. for rikta-, in tucchata ṛktato 'sārato Śāl 88.14, cited Śikṣ 227.6; ṛkta- LV 212.14 (prose); 214.8; and see **riktamuṣṭi.**

ṛgava, nt., a high number, corruption for **mṛgava,** q.v. (but occurs 3 times): Gv 133.3.

ṛg-iti (also **rig-iti**) = **ṛṭ-iti,** q.v., *instantly*: Mvy 8223 (also in Mironov). Cf. Skt. jhag-iti for the more usual jhaṭ-iti.

ṛjī-kṛta-vant, adj. (perf. act. pple.), *having made straight*: LV 10.11 (prose) adhimuktim ṛjīkṛtavataḥ (gen. sg.). Regular Skt. would be ṛjū°; the only v.l. cited is ms. A ṛjvī°; even Calc. ṛjī°; Tib. also draṅ por byas pa, *having made straight.* Presumably ī is due to analog. influence of stem-form in ī from stems in a, ā, i, ī before kṛ-.

ṛjuka, adj. (also **ujjuka**; = Pali ujuka, ujjuka; Skt. ṛju plus ka), *straight, right*: SP 324.2 (but see s.v. **ujjuka**); KP 8.1 (prose) ṛjukasya bodhisattvasya ṛjukalakṣaṇāni; Śikṣ 285.9 (prose) (āśayo ...) ṛjukaḥ akuṭilatvāt; MSV i.47.4; adv. °**kena,** *straight out, straightforwardly, honestly* (before a **daśavarga** of monks), Śikṣ 169.1 (prose) āpattir daśavarge ṛjukena deśayitavyā; adv. **ṛjukam,** id., Bbh 6.17 (prose) arthikeṣu ca sattveṣu ṛjukaṃ pratipadyate, na māyāśāṭhyenainān vilobhayati; abstr. °**ka-tā,** Gv 186.8 (prose) mārgakuṭilatāṃ mārgarjukatām anuvilokya (here literally, *straightness*).

ṛjubhāva, m. (= Pali uju°), *uprightness*: Mv ii.97.10 °vena.

ṛjju, adj. (also **ujju**; for ṛju, § 2.82; Pali ujju beside uju; AMg. app. only ujju), *straight, right, honest*: Mv ii.63.15, read asaṭh' (or asaḍh' ? mss. asadh') ṛjjubhūto (with one ms.); in ii.80.13 mss. ṛjubhūtaḥ or ṛjū°, meter demands ṛjju°.

ṛṭ-iti (also **ṛg-, rig-iti,** qq.v.), *instantly*: Mvy 8224 (also in Mironov); Dbh.g. 51(77).27, repeated 52(78).2, 18; the same line repeated with sapadi instead of ṛṭ-iti 52(78).6, 10, 14. But for the repeated occurrence one might suspect a merely graphic corruption for Skt. jhaṭ-iti (var. jhag-iti).

ṛṇa-dhara or °**hara,** °**hāraka,** adj., in cliché said after birth of a son, jāto 'smākam ṛṇaharo (254.11 °dharo; 87.17 °hārako) dhanaharo (om. 498.21; 87.18 °hārakaś ca) Divy 87.17–18; 254.11; 301.10; 498.20–21; MSV i.87.5. After saying this, the father announces his intention of going on a business trip to make money. The situation suggests ṛṇadhara, *debt-establisher,* and dhanahara, *remover of wealth*; i. e. a financial liability; cf. AMg. aṇa-dhāraga, rendered *debtor* (Ratnach., Sheth). But (a) ṛṇahara rather than ṛṇadhara, (or else ṛṇahāraka,) is read every time but once (h MIndic for dh?); and (b) in Divy 5.12 mahāsamudram avatīrṇo dhanahārakaḥ, the latter means *to get wealth* (see **hāraka**; Index *with money,* not accurately); similarly, mahāsamudram avatareyaṃ dhanahārikaḥ (read °rakaḥ? but cf. s.v. **-hārika**) Divy 100.28. Not clear.

ṛtīyati, °te, = **ar(t)tiyati,** q.v. Usually written ritī°; only in Bbh; °yate 168.23; °yamāna 166.11; 171.9; °yante 282.23 (perhaps also 282.8 °yeran).

ṛtuka, adj. (ifc.) and subst. nt. (Pali -utuka, in sabbotuka), (**1**) *of, belonging to, a season*: Divy 167.8 kālartukaiś (*of the time and season*) copakaranair anuvidhīyate; Mmk 27.21 yathartukena (text yathā°) vā sugandhapuṣpeṇa; (**2**) *fruit of the season*: Divy 531.5 (navaśasyāni navaphalāni) navartukāni; so MSV i.7.6; Divy 531.8 navaiḥ phalaiḥ navaiḥ śasyakair navartukaiḥ.

ṛtu-pariṇāma and **ṛtu-vipariṇāma**: cf. Pali utu-pariṇāma, *change of season,* as a source of disease, e. g. AN ii.87.30–31 (vedayitāni ...) utupariṇāma-jāni (comm. iii.114.19 = utupariṇāmato atisīta-atiuṇha-ututo jātāni); ṛtupariṇāmāye, Mv ii.15.6 (Senart wrongly), or ṛtuvipari° ii.424.(3–)4, perh. adj. *subject to change of season*; or, prob. reading °nāma-tāye, *because of change of season*?; in vipācanīye grahaṇīye samanvāgatā nāpy atiśītāye nāpy atiuṣṇāye (424.3 na cāti° both times) ṛtu- (424.4 ṛtu-vi-) pariṇāmāye. A like passage Mv i.211.7 reads, instead of ṛtu(vi)pari°, in the mss. samāye cintamatāye (v.l. vinta°), which is obscure; Senart em. sammāpariṇāmāye, but this seems violent; samāye seems sound, as it occurs just before. Senart understands this as *causing good digestion,* and infers that ṛtu-pari° means the same. He does not mention ii.424.3–4, which reads vipariṇāma; this, unlike pariṇāma, seems never to be used in Skt., Pali or Pkt. in the sense of *digestion*; and the established Pali cpd. utu-pariṇāma certainly goes against Senart's view. The only question is, can ṛtupariṇāmāye, fem., be an adj. going with grahaṇīye, or should we take it as a noun? In the latter case an em. to °matāye seems probable.

ṛtupariṇāmika, adj. (to prec. plus -ika), *due to change of season* (disease): MSV ii.45.9 (ābādha).

ṛddhati = Skt. ṛdhyati, *is successful* (§ 28.19): Divy 102.9 ṛddhiṣyati te praṇidhir iti.

ṛddhi, f. (= Skt. id., Pali iddhi), *supernatural* or *magic power,* hardly significantly different from its Skt. use; ṛddhi-vaśitā Mvy 779, one of the 10 vaśitā of a Bodhisattva; knowledge of ṛ° is the fifth **abhijñā,** q.v.; ṛddhi-prātihārya, see **prāti°**; ṛddhi-balatā and -vaśitā, Mv iii.67.2; aiśvarya-ṛ° Mv ii.166.8 simply *the magic power of aiśvarya,* as in Skt. (otherwise Senart); see **ṛddhi-pāda** separately.

-ṛddhika, ifc. Bhvr., in **maharddhika,** q.v.; in Karmav 35.8 Lévi reads nāgena ghoreṇa ṛddhikena, but by em.; ms. marddhikena; read maharddhikena, which gives correct meter and sense. There seems to be no Skt. ṛddhika nor Pali iddhika, uncpd.

[**Ṛddhidatta,** error of mss. at Av ii.9.7 for **Ṛṣidatta,** q.v.]

ṛddhi-pāda, m. (= Pali iddhi°), usually pl., *the* (four) *elements* or *bases of supernatural power,* viz. (Mvy

966–970; Dharmas 46) 1 chanda- (2 citta-, 3 vīrya-, 4 mīmāṃsā-)-samādhi-prahāṇa- (Dharmas prahāṇāya; see s.v. **prahāṇa** 1)-saṃskāra-samanvāgata ṛddhipādaḥ; with number four, Mv ii.324.4; Divy 95.14; 201.9; 208.8; Av i.16.11; KP 95.8; without number, LV 8.5; 183.5; Mv i.74.4; iii.120.12; Divy 264.29; Av i.327.6, 8 (ṛddhipāda-yānayāyin); RP 5.17.

Ṛddhipāda-nipāta (m. or nt.), n. of a section of the canon: Karmav 161.10; cf. Pali Iddhipāda-vagga (part of AN), and four Iddhipāda-suttas (see DPPN), but it is not clear that any of these contains the passage cited.

ṛddhi-prātihārya, see **prātihārya.**

Ṛddhilamātar, n. of a female lay-disciple: Divy 160.6.

Ṛddhivikrīḍita, n. of a samādhi: SP 424.5.

? **ṛdhyati,** perhaps in transitive sense (so Vedic, not Class. Skt.), *makes perfect, makes successful*: LV 178.10 (vs) (svargāmṛtadvāra muñcahī) ṛddhyahi (so Lefm., em.; mss. ṛddhyabhi-, ṛddho bhi-, ṛddhyehi, ṛddhyebhiḥ; Calc. ṛddhi hi, Foucaux ṛddhihi as impv.) śīlavato cintitaṃ. Tib. is confused in order but if I understand correctly it reads for this phrase: tshul khrims ldan paḥi bsam pa ḥgrub ḥgyur gyis, which seems to support an impv.: *make to become accomplished the thought of* (the) *one endowed with morality.*

ṛlla, m. (cf. next), something like *prize-fighter*: naṭanartaka-ṛlla-malla- etc. Mv i.231.12, and in similar cpds. Mv i.259.5; ii.100.10; 150.4; 153.17; 156.9; iii.57.9; 113.3; 141.17; 161.3; 255.11; 266.5; 442.9. Senart on i.231.12, note, was inclined to think the word a graphic error for jhalla, as was Burnouf (see next); but he kept the mss. reading, which seems too common to emend.

ṛllaka, m., = preceding: SP 480.9 (prose) na ṛllakā, all mss. that contain the word (ed. narllakā); in SP 280.6 Burnouf (fol. 150 b) says all his 3 mss. read ṛllakebhir, which KN report for only one ms. (their text jhall°).

? **ṛvraṭā-**(-śabda), onomat., used by Buddha in expelling a snake: bhagavatā °bdena prabodhyābhihitaḥ, gaccha ... MSV ii.126.5.

Ṛṣabha, n. of a former Buddha: Mv i.137.2.

Ṛṣabhagāmin, n. of a former Buddha: Mv i.137.2.

Ṛṣabhanetra, n. of a former Buddha: Mv i.137.6.

Ṛṣabhendrarāja, n. of a Bodhisattva: Gv 4.7.

Ṛṣi, pl., n. of a brahmanical (Yajurvedic) school (!): Divy 633.6, 8 ṛṣayaḥ.

Ṛṣikuśa, n. of a brother of Kuśa: Mv ii.433.16.

Ṛṣigupta, n. of a former Buddha: Mv i.137.11: LV 5.7 (confirmed Tib.).

ṛṣi-tapas-taptā, sc. lipi, a kind of script: LV 126.10; Tib. *ṛṣi-penance-performed* (spyad pa). A v.l. in Lefm. points to prāptā or saṃprāptā for taptā.

Ṛṣidatta, (**1**) n. of a sthapati of Śrāvastī, otherwise called (semi-MInd.) **Iṣi°** and **Riṣi-datta,** qq.v.: Av ii.9.7, by Speyer's em. for mss. Ṛddhidatta- (-purāṇābhyāṃ); Tib. (draṅ sroṅ = ṛṣi) supports the em., as well as the parallel texts; MSV i.75.15 text Uṣidatta (same text as Divy 466.23 Iṣi°); (**2**) n. of a monk, associate of **Ṛṣila**: MSV ii.108.20.

Ṛṣideva, (**1**) n. of a legendary king: Mv i.92.5; (**2**) n. of a former Buddha: LV 5.5 (confirmed Tib.); Mv i.137.12.

Ṛṣipatana (in mss. also °**paṭana,** °**paṭṭana,** °**pattana,** °**bhavana**), or **Ṛṣivadana,** nt. or (LV) m., n. of the deer-park at Benares where Buddha preached his first sermon. On the forms of the name, see Senart, Mv i.631; Lévi, JA 1912 (vol. 20), 499 f.; Pali Isipatana; this form supported by widely-known etym., Mv i.359.17 ṛṣayo 'tra patitā ṛṣipatanaṃ, similarly LV 19.3, and in Pali; -vadana acc. to Senart and Lévi Prakritic. Both forms Mvy 4130 °patanam, Tib. lhuṅ ba, *fall*, and 4131 °vadanam, Tib. smra ba, *speak* (Mironov °pattanam for the latter, but he records v.l. °padanam; Tib. supports °vad°). In Mv, mss. usually vary between -vadana and -pattana, Senart always (in these cases) adopting the former: i.43.15 (one ms. °bhavana); 161.4; 174.2; 307.5; 313.16, 19; 323.14, 16 (in 16 -pahana instead of -pattana); 330.4; 331.3; 337.11; iii.330.3, 17. But in i.243.3 Senarts reads -bhavanasmiṃ with mss. (v.l. °nesmiṃ), and (besides i.359.17 above) in ii.138.2; iii.323.3; 328.20 -patana (only v.l. -pattana in all three); in i.366.8 mss. °paṭṭane, Senart pattano. Divy has only -vadana, 393.21; 464.16; Av only -patana, i.42.9 etc., passim (in i.237.13 the former Buddha Kāśyapa stays there). SP has -patana, once, 69.12; and LV app. only -patana, 18.20; 19.3; 264.22; 402.3; 404.17; 407.16; 413.1; 421.16 (v.l. -paṭana 18.20; 19.3); in 407.16 nom. sg. °no (the only form in LV unambiguous as to gender).

Ṛṣirakṣitikā, n. of a piśācī: Māy 239.23.

Ṛṣila (ms. Riṣila), n. of a monk, associate of **Ṛṣidatta** (2): MSV ii.108.6, 20.

Ṛṣivadana = **Ṛṣipatana,** q.v.

Ṛṣiśṛṅga, n. of a maharṣi (doubtless false form for Ṛśyaśṛṅga): Māy 256.31. Cf. **Ekaśṛṅga.**

Ṛṣīka, n. of a nāga: Māy 221.29.

? **Ṛṣṭa,** n. of a pratyekabuddha: Mmk 111.10; in a list, followed by **Upāriṣṭa**; this suggests that Ṛṣṭa may be a corruption for Ariṣṭa = Pali Ariṭṭha, preceding Upariṭṭha in a list of paccekabuddhas MN iii.69.29.

E

Ekakakṣa, see **Erakakṣa.**

Eka-kānta-rājan, n. of a Bodhisattva: Mvy 730; var. Ekāntarājan, adopted by Mironov with v.l. in Index, his text Ekakānta°, which is confirmed by Tib. gcig tu mdzes pa (om. rājan).

eka-ghana, adj. (= Pali id.), *in one mass, entire,* said of a Tathāgata's body that is not divided into separate relics: SP 240.11 (here Kern *condensed,* inaccurately); 259.15 (na ca śarīraṃ dhātubhedena bhetsyate,) ekaghanaṃ cāsya śarīraṃ bhaviṣyati saptaratnastūpaṃ praviṣṭam.

eka-cīraka, see **cīraka.**

Ekachattra, n. of a Tathāgata: ŚsP 47.16.

Ekajaṭā, (**1**) n. of a goddess, form of Tārā (= **Ekajaṭī**): Sādh 254.1 etc.; (**2**) n. of a mahāpiśācī (the same?): Māy 242.29.

Ekajaṭī = **Ekajaṭā** (1): Mvy 4277 (cf. Tārā 4280).

eka-janmika (cf. **-janmika**), adj., *in, subject to, a single birth*: Divy 422.7 mā tāvat tavaikajanmikasya maraṇabhayāt ... harṣo notpannaḥ, *can it be that you, from fear of death, in a single birth ... have not conceived joy ...*; similarly 422.18 (vs) mā tāvad ekajanmikasya ...

ekajātipratibaddha, adj., *limited to* (or *by,* only) *one* (more) *birth*: LV 10.15 °dhasya (bodhisattvasya); Gv 514.7 °dhānām (bodhisattvānām).

ekatya, pronom. adj. (= Pali ekacca, Aśokan ekatiya, cf. Senart's note Mv i.388 f.; nom. pl. once ekatye, KP 128.2, = Pali ekacce, but otherwise only nominal inflection), (**1**) sing. *some one, anyone,* in general and often hypothetical statements: Mv iii.213.2 yadaikatyo ... pravraje(t), and id. 8, 12 yad ihaikatyo ...; Śikṣ 76.7

iha ... ekatyo brahmacāriṇam ātmānaṃ pratijānīte; Karmav 44.1 ihaikatyaḥ paripṛcchakajātīyo bhavati; KP 122.2 ihekatya (read ihaikatyaḥ) śramaṇa(ḥ)...; Bbh 46.22–23 varam ihaikatyasya pudgaladṛṣṭir na tv evaikatyasya durgṛhītā śūnyateti; 297.11 (tad yathā,) ekatyaḥ anuttarāyāṃ samyaksaṃbodhau cittaṃ utpādayati, and so 12, 14; Mvy 6733 ekatyaḥ = Tib. khaṅ (read kha?) cig, or la la, defined *some, several, a few*; 7096 apy ekatyaḥ, see below; (**2**) *a certain, an* (unnamed) *one*: Karmav 26.19 (vs) dṛṣṭvaiva ekatyam iha pudgalam (his name has actually been given in the prose story); (**3**) *any* (one), *any at all*, substantially = *each and every* (similarly under pl., below): in a cliché, pañcāveṇikā (98.22 and 440.16 °ṇīyā) dharmā ekatye (98.22 ihaikatye) paṇḍitajātīye mātṛgrāme, *there are five peculiar characteristics in any* (= *every*) *intelligent woman*, Divy 2.3; 98.22; 440.16–17; Av i.14.7 etc.; ekatye niṣadya MSV ii.196.2, *sitting in any place at all*; (**4**) pl. ekatyā(ḥ), once ekatye, *some*: Mvy 2289 manuṣyā ekatyāś ca devāḥ (Tib. cig, or kha gcig); KP 128.2 ihekatye (read ihai°; nom. pl.; cited Śikṣ 196.12 ihaike) śramaṇabrāhmaṇo (read °ṇā with Śikṣ) bahūn dharmān paryāpnuvanti...; Divy 327.16, 18 (correlative with eke, kāścit, ... apare); Bbh 46.8, 63.8, 10; (**5**) *some* (only), *some few*: Mv iii.131.17 ekatyeṣu manuṣyeṣu caite (keep, with mss.; Senart em. naite) guṇā sulabharūpā ye imasya gajapotasya, *and in* (only) *some few men are these virtues easily got, which*...; (**6**) *any*, substantially = *each and every, any and all* (as in sg., above): SP 71.11 and 133.2 upamayaikatyā vijñapuruṣā bhāṣitasyārtham ājānanti, *by a comparison* (parable) *in this world any intelligent men come to know the meaning of what is said*; Mv iii.453.13 (vs) upamāye ihaikatyā arthaṃ jānanti paṇḍitā; (7) apy ekatyā(ḥ) ... apy ekatyā(ḥ) (= Pali app-ekacca, mostly pl.), *some ... others*: Mv i.23.9–11; iii.223.8–10; 443.18 ff.; Divy 618.28 ff.; sg. only in isolated citation Mvy 7096 apy ekatyaḥ = Tib. ḥon kyaṅ (= api) kha cig (*some, several*) ni; (**8**) tad-ekatyāḥ, pl. *some*: Bbh 98.9 °tyānāṃ śramaṇabrāhmaṇānām; 151.21; like apy ek°, correl. with another tad-ekatyāḥ, *some ... others*, Bbh 125.17, 19; 296.22 ff.; 403.21 f. (ekāntena samyak pratipadyate sarvam eva, iyam ekā parṣat; ekāntena mithyā pratipadyate sarvam eva, iyaṃ dvitīyā parṣat;) tṛtīyā punaḥ parṣad yasyāṃ tadekatyāḥ samyak pratipadyante, tadekatyā mithyā pratipadyante; (**9**) see next.

ekatya-śāśvatika, m. (= Pali ekacca-sassatika, PTSD s.v. sassatika), *one who holds that some things are eternal*: Bbh 67.(22–)24 śāśvatadṛṣṭikānāṃ śāśvatadṛṣṭiṃ (qq.v.) nāśayati, tad yathā, pūrvāntakalpakānāṃ (see **pūrvānta**) śāśvatavādinām (q.v.) ekatya-śāśvatikānāṃ. Cf. LaV-P. AbhidhK. v.14 (*partiellement éternalistes*).

? **eka-dukāye**, inst. sg. f. adv. to stem eka-*dukā (= *dvi°), *in one or two times*: Mv iii.15.12 °ye sarvaṃ khāditaṃ, *in one or two eatings* (Senart *bouchées*) *he ate all*. Or if v.l. eka-du-kārye is right (du = dvi), *in one or two performances, operations*(?).

ekadeśakālaka, adj. with pudgala, see **sarvakālaka**: MSV iii.75.21; 78.13.

Ekadhāraka, m., n. of a mountain: Divy 450.10, 12; 455.29; 456.1.

ekadhyam, ekadhye, adv. (= Pali ekajjhaṃ, Skt. aikadhyam), *together, in one place*: °dhyam Mvy 6745; Mv i.304.15 (mss.; Senart em. ekā°); Bbh 98.5 (ed., ms. °dhyām); 208.7; 225.18; 377.5; (the Skt. aikadhyam occurs Bbh 186.19; 185.3 is ambiguous;) °dhye Divy 35.24; 40.17, 20, 22; 346.3; MSV i.211.6.

[**ekanāma(nāma)tā**, erroneous reading Mv iii.201.1 for **ekārāma°**, q.v.]

ekapadikā (cf. Pali °dika-magga, id., Jāt. i.315.8), *small footpath*, on which only one person can walk at a time: Mv ii.214.15 etāye ekapadikāye (inst.); 215.6.

ekapiṇḍayati, denom. to *eka-piṇḍa (not recorded), *makes into a single mass, brings together*: SP 73.2 sarvāṇīmāni kumārakāny (so read, or °kāṇy, see KN Crit. note) ekapiṇḍayitvā, *collecting all these boys into one bunch*.

eka-puṭa, adj. (cf. AMg. puḍa, perh. used in this sense of *fold*; Skt. puṭa hardly so used), *in a single fold*, contrasted with **dvipuṭa**: MSV ii.90.6 (of a blanket).

Ekapuṇḍarīka (= Pali id.), n. of King Prasenajit's elephant: Av ii.114.10.

ekaprasūtā, *who has borne once*: Mv iii.282.14. Cf. **dvi-pra°**.

ekamante, adv. (= Pali id., Skt. ekānte; m 'hiatus-bridger'), *at one side*: (all prose) Mv i.35.9; 323.5 (in 3, just above, ekānte); ii.216.2; 257.11 ekamante asthāsi, resumed in next line by ekānta-saṃsthitasya.

ekameka, āmreḍita cpd. (= Pali id., Skt. ekaika; m 'hiatus-bridger'), *one by one*: SP 146.3 (vs) °ke, nom. pl. m. (vṛkṣa); LV 172.21 (vs) ekameka (nom. sg. f.) buddhapūj' acintiyā (so interpret text); 237.3 (vs) ekameka (nom. sg. m.) ... suro; 310.2 (vs) bhujaikamekena (= bhujā, nom. pl., ek°, adv.), *the* (100) *arms, one by one*; Mv ii.49.12 ekameko; *each one* (of a group), *each separate one*, Mv ii.178.14 °ko samartho ...; °kasmiṃ Mv ii.191.21; 273.11, 12; 485.11; 490.12; in Mv iii.358.5 (prose) ekamekāye hastāye, seems to be intensive āmreḍita, *for just one* (single) *hand*, since line 7 refers back to this with hasto chinno, and the second hand is specifically dealt with in line 9; yet in so loosely written a text as Mv it is perhaps possible that the phrase in line 5 means *for each hand in turn*.

eka-yāna, see **yāna**.

ekarakṣa, m. (= **ekārakṣa**, q.v.), *having a single protector*, ep. of Buddhas (in the plural): Divy 95.13; 124.12; 264.27. Perhaps error of tradition for **ekā°**.

ekavacanodāhāra, see **udāhāra**.

ekavīcika, m. (corruption of Pali ekabīji(n) plus ka), *one who has only one more rebirth before him*: Dharmas 103; Mvy 1013 = Tib. bar chad gcig pa, *one hindrance, obstruction, interruption*. One of the stages of a śrāvaka; context same as that of AN i.233.17 ekabījī hoti, ekaṃ yeva mānussakaṃ bhavaṃ nibbattetvā dukkhassa antaṃ karoti. Cf. **kulaṃkula**.

Ekavyūha, m., n. of a samādhi: Mvy 592; ŚsP 1423.3.

Ekaśīrṣā, n. of a nāga maid: Kv 4.3.

Ekaśṛṅga, °ṅgaka, n. of the hero of what the colophon Mv iii.152.19 calls Nalinīye rājakumārīye jātakam; later iii.272.17 it is referred to as Ekaśṛṅgajātakaṃ (punaḥ kartavyaṃ); °śṛṅga iii.144.17 ff.; °śṛṅgaka (prose) 144.18; 145.7 ff. He corresponds to Skt. Ṛśyaśṛṅga, Pali Isisiṅga (in the Naḷinikā-jātaka, 526), and doubtless is meant by the maharṣi **Ṛṣiśṛṅga**, q.v.; both occur Māy 256.31.

ekāṃśa, adj. and subst. (m.? cf. the following items; = Pali ekaṃsa, in PTSD defined only as subst., but in every passage cited could be adj., and in some surely is so; not in these mgs. in Skt.), (**1**) *absolute, complete; concentrated*: Mv ii.50.3 ekāṃśam (*absolute*) vindate sukhaṃ; iii.23.7 (vs) priya-m-(so with mss., 'hiatus-bridging' m) anumataikāṃśo (so with v.l., ed. °so; mss. °mataṃ ek°; *concentrated in being*...) kṛtvā añjaliṃ (read °li m.c.) tiṣṭhati; (**2**) *absolute affirmation, absolute assurance*: Mvy 1658 ekāṃśa-vyākaraṇa (see **vyākaraṇa**), *elucidation* (response to a question) *by absolute affirmation*, cf. Pali ekaṃsa-vyākaraṇīyaṃ pañhaṃ AN i.197.20, explained comm. ii.308.24 cakkhuṃ aniccaṃ ti puṭṭhena, āma aniccaṃ ti ekaṃsen' eva vyākātabbaṃ; Mv iii.374.6 karohi ekāṃśam anugrahāye (mss. anubodhanāye, but) 9 karomi ek° anugrahāye (mss.); in both Senart em. okāśam for ek°, in accord with the Pali corresp. Jāt. v.150.6, 12 okāsam anuggahāya, but *make absolute assurance* (of a state of grace attained) is exactly what the context seems to require; the sense is much better than with the Pali okāsam, and I suspect that the latter is a distortion of an original which agreed with Mv. (As noted by Francis and Dutoit, karomi must be read for karohi in Jāt. v.150.12.)

ekāṃśika, adj. (= Pali ekaṃsika; to prec.), *entire, absolute, whole-hearted*: RP 45.8 (vs) bodhyarthiko hi vicarāmi 'ha sattvahetoḥ ekāṃśiko.

ekāṃśīkṛta, see **ekāṃsīkṛta**.

ekāṃśena, adj. (= Pali ekaṃsena; instr. of **ekāṃśa**), *wholly, exclusively, absolutely*: Mv i.102.7 °na śubhaṃ karma; ii.33.6 °na vyākaritvā; iii.378.8 °na vyākṛto.

ekāṃsam (= Pali ekaṃsaṃ), adv., only in phrase °sam uttarāsaṅgam (°gāni, mss. SP 100.4) karoti (usually in ger. kṛtvā), *put(ting) the upper robe over one shoulder*: SP 100.4; Mv i.98.1; et passim. Cf. next.

ekāṃsīkṛta, adj. (ppp. of *°sī-karoti = °sam uttarāsaṅgaṃ karoti, as a mark of respect, cf. Childers s.v. ekaṃsaṃ), *with* (his upper robe) *put over one shoulder* (in token of respect), always followed by **prāñjalīkṛta**, and said of some one paying respects to a Buddha: Mv i.239.18 (mss. ekāśī°; see Senart's note; in fact ś is always written for s in the mss. of Mv in this word); ii.257.11; iii.300.11; 302.13. I have not found this form recorded in Pali; cf. prec.

Ekākāra, m., n. of a samādhi: Mvy 594; ŚsP 1423.8.

Ekāgramati, n. of a son of Māra (favorable to the Bodhisattva): LV 311.13.

ekātmanībhūtvā, ger. (to *°nībhavati; ek-ātmanī- based on °na, a-extension of ekātman; regular Skt. would be ekātmī-), *becoming of one spirit, concordant*: Av i.378.1 (prose) (sarvair ekasamūhībhūtaiḥ prasannacittakaiḥ prītijātair) ekātmanībhūtais.

Ekādaśā (by em.), (**1**) n. of a devakumārikā in the west: LV 390.6; mss. Ekāhaṃśa-, Ekāndaśā, °dasā; in parallel Mv iii.308.9 mss. Ekānavā (v.l. °naṃ-vā); Tib. not quoted by Foucaux; (**2**) a kind of musical instrument, = next: Mv iii.442.11 (prose; mss. ekāśā, em. Senart); read ekādaśāṃ (acc. sg.) also, with one ms. (v.l. °śa), in Mv iii.82.4 (Senart em. °daśīṃ!).

ekādaśikā, = °**daśā** (2): Mv iii.70.15; 407.20.

[**ekādaśī**, Senart's unnecessary em. for °**śā** Mv iii.82.4.]

? **Ekānavā**, see **Ekādaśā**.

ekāntaka, adj. (= Skt. ekānta), *entire, complete*: in prior member of cpd. Mv i.6.4 (prose) ekāntaka-duḥkhavedanā. The form ekantaka is apparently used in Pali as alternative title for the Sedaka and Janapada Suttas; SN v.168 and 169.

Ekāntarājan, see **Ekakāntarājan**.

Ekānta-raurava (most mss. Ekanta-, MIndic), n. of a hell (cf. **Raurava**): Mv i.5.13.

ekāntīkaroti (to Skt. ekānta), *makes all right, makes perfect, completes*: Divy 572.1 putra jñānakovidāḥ praṣṭavyās te etad ekāntīkariṣyanti; MSV i.55.20.

(**ekāyana**, adj. with mārga (also in Skt. in literal sense; = Pali ekāyano maggo), *narrow* (path), *traversible only by one at a time*: Divy 158.22 (teṣām, sc. ṛṣīṇām, āgacchatāṃ Bhagavatā) ekāyano mārgo 'dhiṣṭhitaḥ; here app. in the literal, physical sense. In Pali it is also applied to the religious 'Path', prob. in the sense of *traversible only by One* (the Buddha); but several other interpretations are offered in the comms., e. g. MN comm. i.229.)

ekārakṣa, m. (= Pali ekārakkha), *having a single guardian or protector*, ep. of a Tathāgata: Mvy 428; in Divy **ekarakṣa** (by error of tradition?), q.v. The 'single guardian' is smṛti, Pali sati: DN iii.269.27 f. ... ekārakkho hoti ... satārakkhena cetasā samannāgato ...; comm. 1051.15 f. sati-ārakkha-kiccaṃ sādheti.

(**ekārāma**, adj. [= Skt. and Pali id.] *delighting in solitude*: in Mv iii.201.1 read eko ekārāmo ekārāmanāmatām anuyukto [ed. partly with mss., which have n for r, eko nāma ekanāmanāmatām; my reading is proved by a Pali parallel DN ii.223.20], ... *the state of having* [deserving] *the name of one who delights in solitude*; Śikṣ 191.10 ekārāmatā, abstr., *delight in solitude* [Bendall and Rouse *keeping to one monastery*!].)

Ekārthadarśin, n. of a Bodhisattva: Gv 441.26.

ekālāpaka, read °**lopaka**, see **ālopaka**.

ekāvacāraka, m., perhaps *having a unitary or single explanation*: Mvy 7615 = Tib. gcig nas rtog(s) pa, *explanation* (or the like) *from one*; so Chin. may intend. Das defines gcig nas rtogs pa by ekavicāraka, apparently a corruption; his English, *one who deliberates with undivided attention*, is evidently based on -vicāra(ka), and does not seem to fit the surroundings of Mvy 7615.

ekāvalikā (= Skt. °li, °lī), *an ornament consisting of a single string of pearls*: Mv ii.492.6, 8 ff. (prose).

ekāsanika, adj. (= Pali id.; BHS also **aikā°**), *observing the rule of using the same seat* (for eating his meal), one of the 12 **dhūtaguṇa**: Dharmas 63; AsP 387.5; MSV iii.122.5; aikā° Mvy 1132. See Pali Vism. i.69 for explanation.

ekāhatya, adj. (= AMg. egāhacca), *to be struck down in a single blow*: Mv ii.74.15 (devadattena) so hastināgo ... ekāhatyaṃ kṛtvā tatraiva ... nihato.

ekāhika, adj. m. (= Pali id., Skt. aik°), *recurring daily, quotidian* (of fever): Mvy 9531; SP 401.6 (prose); Bhīk 17a.2; Māy 220.19.

ekībhūta, ppp. (cf. ekībhāva, *solitude*; in Skt. ekībhavati recorded only in mg. *becomes united*, and so all derivs.), *isolated, lonely*: LV 227.5 (prose) ekībhūtābhiḥ kurarībhir iva.

ekoti-(°tī-)bhāva, m. (= Pali ekodi°, app. not recorded with ī, which is commoner in BHS tho both are written; etym. and lit. mg. much disputed, see refs. in Lévi Sūtrāl. xiv.14n., Renou JA 1939 p. 393 note 1, referring esp. to ŚB 12.2.2.4 prāṇā nānā santa ekotayaḥ samānam (so, not °nām!) ūtim anusaṃcaranti; here ūti surely means *web*, and it is hard to believe with Eggeling's transl. (note) that the second part of the cpd. ekoti could mean anything else; cf. the next two items), *the becoming concentrated, concentration* (of mind, cetasaḥ; seems to mean about the same as Skt. ekāgratā manasaḥ); chiefly in formulaic statement of process leading out of the first dhyāna into the second, found (with slight variants) Mvy 1479; LV 129.3; 343.17; Mv i.228.5; ii.131.18; 283.8; iii.213.9 (here, by a strange confusion of formulas, applies to entrance into first dhyāna); Dbh 34.2: sa vitarkavicārāṇāṃ (var., taking sa as associative prefix, savitarkāṇāṃ savicārāṇām, or the like) vyupaśamād adhyātmasaṃprasādāc cetasa ekotibhāvād (once °vā; ekotī° Mvy; Mv i.228.5; iii.213.9; Dbh; and vv.ll. LV 343.17; Mv ii.131.18) avitarkam avicāraṃ samādhijaṃ prītisukhaṃ dvitīyaṃ (Mv iii.213.9 prathamaṃ) dhyānam upasaṃpadya viharati (or other form of this verb); this passage is prose and the var. in quantity cannot be m.c.; other occurrences, Mvy 1656 ekotībhāvaḥ; Gv 490.15 (prose) sa ekotībhāvagataḥ sarvabuddhadharmeṣu; Gv 305.7 (prose) ekotībhāvagataṃ dharmadhātum avatarāmi.

ekoti-(°tī-)bhūta, adj. (ppp.; = Pali ekodi°; see prec.), *concentrated* (without dependent modifier, but doubtless implying a form of cetas, *in mind*): Mv iii.212.16 (vs; ekoti-, i could be but prob. is not m.c.); 213.10 (prose: Senart ekotī° but mss. °ti°, °ni°).

ekotīkaroti (= Pali ekodi°; see prec. two), *concentrates*: Bbh 109.17 (cittaṃ ...) ekotīkaroti samādhatte.

ekotī-bhāva, -bhūta, see **ekoti°**.

Ekottara, n. of a Bodhisattva: Gv 442.18.

Ekottarika, nt. (Karmav 153.12 °ke, loc.), or °**kā**, f. (Divy 329.1 ff.; 333.13; Karmav 167.2 °kā-sūtram, *a sūtra of the Ek°*), a section of the canon, corresponding to Pali Aṅguttara-nikāya; forms ambiguous in gender (°ka or °kā), Karmav 157.9; Ekottarikāgama, m., Mvy 1421.

?**ekotsava**, adj. or subst., n. or epithet of mus. instruments, in a list of such: SP 51.14 (vs) ekotsavā(ḥ), n. pl.; so 3 mss.; v.l. ekonnaḍā; Kashgar rec. ekāvacārā (for ekotsavā vā). Burnouf, *qui ne servent que pour une fête*; Kern, who in his Transl. knows only the reading ekonnaḍā, leaves it untranslated.

ekodāhāra, m., *united, unified, single utterance*, see s.v. **udāhāra.**

eḍaka-mūka, adj. = **eḍa-mūka**, q.v.: Śikṣ 188.8 idaṃ mayā naiva vaktavyaṃ, jaḍasamena eḍakamūkasamena mayā kalahavivādeṣu bhavitavyaṃ (so punctuate). Here perhaps the literal idea, *speechless*, is dominant, tho the parallel jaḍa-samena suggests that overtones of *dull, stupid* must also be present.

eḍaka-rajas (= **avi-rajas**, q.v.), lit. *sheep-speck*, a small unit of matter; like avi-rajas Mvy 8195, it occurs LV 149.6 and Divy 645.11 in tabular lists of very small weights or measures; in all three, seven **śaśa-rajāṃsi** (q.v.) make one eḍaka-(avi-)r° and seven of these make one **go-rajas** (q.v.). Acc. to St. Julien, cited by Weber ISt. 8.436 note, the mg. is said by Hiuen Ts'ang and a Chin. transl. of LV to be *a grain of dust on the hide of a hare* (*sheep, beeve*). But Tib. on both Mvy and LV says simply *hare-* (*sheep-, cow-*) *speck* (rdul); to be sure, Das s.v. rdul declares that glaṅ rdul means *a mote in the dung of an ox, a small particle of cowdung.* But this, as well as the different guess from Chin., can hardly be anything but implausible guesswork. Why should a speck on the skin, or in the dung, of an animal vary with the size of the animal? The Tib. itself gives no such indication. It seems safe to assume that *hare-speck, sheep-speck*, and *cow-speck* mean only three different sizes of small particles.

eḍamūka, adj. (cf. **eḍaka-mūka**; = Pali eḷamūga), *stupid* (lit. *dumb*) *as a sheep* (this, not *deaf and dumb*, seems to be the regular mg. in Pali and BHS, see CPD s.v. an-elamūga, an-eḷa°, and e. g. Miln. 251.1–2 duppaññā jaḷā eḷamūgā mūḷhā dandhagatikā janā): Mvy 7684 = Tib. lug ltar (*sheep-like*) lkug pa (*dumb*, also *stupid*); Chin. also *dumb, dumb like sheep*, but Jap. *deaf and dumb*; it must be admitted the Jap. editor's view gets some support from the next word in Mvy, hastasaṃvācakaḥ (see **saṃvācaka**); AsP 113.2 eḍamūkajātīyā(ḥ) prajñāparihīṇāḥ; °ka-saṃgha MSV iii.116.18, 21; Śikṣ 51.6 dhanva-(= **dhandha-**, q.v.)-gatiṃ jaḍaiḍamūka-gatiṃ; 284.1 dha- (erasure, read nva for ndha)-jaḍa-eḍamūka-jātīyāḥ. Skt. lexicons seem to have abstracted from this cpd. an adj. eḍa, *deaf*, assuming that the cpd. means *deaf and dumb*; and in some late texts (see Schmidt, Nachtr.), perhaps by direct borrowing from lexx., this usage is actually found in literature. Did Mvy also know this interpretation? Sheep are proverbially stupid in other countries than India.

[**Eḍameḍa**, see **Ela-mela.**]

eḍākṣi-puṣpa, nt. (presumably = Skt. eḍikākṣī, see pw), n. of a certain flower: Mvy 6177 (Tib. renders lit., *sheep's-eye-flower*).

eṇi(jaṅgha), see **eṇī°** and **eṇeya°**.

Eṇī (= Pali id.), n. of a river: Karmav 34.14, 15.

eṇī-, eṇi- (these appear to belong primarily in prior member of cpds. only; see below eṇī-mṛga and -jaṅgha), and **eṇeya**, m. (= Pali eṇi-miga, also eṇimmiga Jāt. v.416.23; eṇi-jaṅgha, also eṇī° MN ii.136.14, but v.l. eṇi°; and eṇeyya, m.; = Skt. eṇa, m., eṇī, f., and aiṇeya, regularly adj. but rarely recorded as subst. = eṇa), a kind of deer, *the black antelope*: (**1**) eṇi, abbreviation meant to suggest °jaṅgha, as one of the 32 lakṣaṇa: Mv i.226.17 (here mss. vaṇi); ii.30.1; (**2**) eṇījaṅghā ca te āsi Mv ii.305.3, *and thou hadst antelope-legs* (one of the lakṣaṇa); this lakṣaṇa = Pali eṇijaṅgha (above); (**3**) eṇīmṛga, m. (= Pali eṇi°, eṇim°, above). = Skt. eṇa, *the black antelope*: Mv ii.221.19 (vs) °gāṇa yūthāni; (**4**) eṇeya, subst., Mv iii.70.13 (in list of flesh of various animals, all nouns, prior parts of cpds., ending) kapiñjala-mānsāni eṇeya-mānsāni; Gv 400.7 eṇeyasyeva mṛgarājño (tasya jaṅghe), in expl. of aiṇeyajaṅgha-tā (as lakṣaṇa); (**5**) eṇeya-jaṅgha, *having legs like the black antelope* (this is the usual form of the lakṣaṇa in BHS; but see also **aiṇeya-j°**): LV 105.22 (here °ya-mṛgarāja-j°); 429.17 (all mss. so, both times); Bbh 375.15; RP 51.3.

Etadagra, n. of a work, or section of one, which = or contains the Dakṣiṇāvibhaṅga sūtra: Karmav 156.12 Bhagavataitadagre Dakṣiṇāvibhaṅge sūtra uktam. It is not the Etadagga-vagga AN i.23 ff. (cf. **Agratā-sūtra**); nor does Lévi's identification with AN Book 4, No. 15 (ii.17) seem certain, since the precise quotation does not occur there.

etarahi (= Pali id.) and **etarahiṃ**, *at this time*, Skt. etarhi; see the next two. Only in Mv, but both very common, and that too in prose; mss. often vary in same passage. All the foll. are prose; in few are mss. unanimous; often etarhi or etarhiṃ (or even **etarahesi**) occurs in same vicinity or in v.l. of same passage: Mv i.39.4, 13; 50.2, 5; 54.12; 56.6; 60.5 ff.; 128.14; 238.16, 19, 20; 239.2 (in 13 etarhi, no v.l.); 262.2; 286.19, 20; 313.2; 330.7, 8; 331.6, 8; 332.9, 10, 11; 335.16 ff.; ii.130.9; iii.67.11; 200.8, 13; 201.2, 7, 10, 14; 202.1; 272.15 etc.

etarahesi, *at this time*, = prec. and next: Mv i.38.13; 39.1, 3. Speculations on the strange form in Senart's note, i.404.

etarhiṃ = **etarahi(ṃ)**, Skt. etarhi; not infrequent in variants of mss.; esp. Mv i.34.16; 239.15; 331.7.

etādṛśaka, adj. (= Skt. °śa), *such*: SP 15.13; 87.11 (both vss, -ka may be m.c.).

eti, = Skt. aiti, *comes*: kuta eti (WT enti) ime śūrā(ḥ) SP 307.2 (vs).

etta, adv. (in mg. = Skt. atra; = Pali etta, at least once for usual ettha, Pv i.5.6, repeated comm., to be sure with v.l. ettha, but the gloss 28.33 has etta without v.l.; cf. **ettha**), *here, hither*: Mv i.35.5 etta, etta, *here, here*! (so app. all mss., at least as far as tt, not tth, is concerned); for SP 16.5 (vs) WT read with their ms. K' kāraṇam etta (= atra), for KN kāraṇeva (unmetr.) allegedly with all Nep. mss. (Kashgar rec. quoted as kāraṇam eta).

ettaka, f. °**akā**, °**ikā**, adj. (= Pali id.; origin of formation disputed; one theory Geiger 27.7; cf. next), *so great, so much*; pl. *so many*: (sg.) SP 208.8 (vs) triguṇaṃ tato ettakam eva kālam; Śikṣ 174.15 (prose) ettakā (f.) guṇānuśaṃsā; ettakena kṣaṇavītihāreṇa, *in just so large* (here = *no larger, so small*) *an instant-passage* (of time), Mv i.56.9; iii.425.16, 22; 450.16; (same phrase i.55.14, Senart ettakena but mss. ekena which is quite sound, as parallels cited s.v. **vītihāra, vyatihāra** prove; note also i.55.2 ekakṣaṇena padavītihāreṇa;) ettako 'yam . . . dharmo, (is) *this all of* . . .(?) Mv ii.118.14, 16; ettakasya janakāyasya, *of such a great crowd*, ii.157.17; ettakaṃ prāṇavadhaṃ ii.99.2; °kaṃ hiraṇyasuvarṇaṃ ii.169.6; ettaka-mātram arhāmi, *do I deserve only so much*? ii.64.10; pl. *so many*, Mv i.18.2 f. (five times); 126.6; ii.98.17; 347.13; 380.22 (ettikā, f., with mss.); iii.131.16; Suv 11.8; 12.3 (both vss); in Mv i.77.14 mss. ettakā kalpā or ettakaṃ kalpānāṃ, *in so-and-so-many kalpas*. On Mv iii.277.13 (one ms. ettikā, f. pl.) see s.v. **ettiya.**

ettāvat-, in cpd. (= Skt. etāvat, cf. prec.; Pali adv. ettāvatā), *to this extent*, noted only in Mv ii.130.8, 11, where mss. are corrupt but Senart's text and interpretation are certainly wrong; read probably, ettāvatpāram ito imaṃ pi kecit nābhisaṃbhuṇanti. or possibly nāpi saṃ° (they experience pains) *to so great an extent as this, and after this* (ito; cf. Pali parallel, MN i.246.22, 25 etāvaparamaṃ na-y-ito bhiyyo; also parallel LV 263.8 etāvatparamaṃ te duhkham anubhavanti) *some do not attain* *even this* (degree of success; said of ascetics who practise self-torture). At any rate, divide ettāvatpāram from ito (Senart °pāramite).

ettiya, adj. (= AMg. ettiya, ettia), = **ettaka,** *so many*: Mv ii.353.10 (vs) ettiyā (f. pl.; no v.l.) sattvakoṭiyo; in same vs iii.277.13 Senart also ettiyā, but one ms. ettikā (f. of **ettaka**), the other etti, with accidental omission of final syllable.

etto, adv. (= Pali id.; abl.), in yāva(d) etto, *up to this point* (yāvat with abl., as in both Skt. and Pali): Mv i.327.20; 329.5; in both read, as clearly indicated by the mss. despite some corruption, yāvad etto pi ativiśvasto, *even to such an extent very intimate* (wrongly Senart).

ettha, adv. (= Pali id.; see **etta** and next), *here*: Mv i.28.11 (three times) ettha vayaṃ (khādiṣyāmaḥ etc.); ii.178.6 ettha (v.l. etthaṃ) caturmahāpathe; 248.2 ettha samudrapāre (no v.l.).

etthaṃ, adv. (= **ettha**; not recorded elsewhere; only in prose, hence not m.c.; Senart em. first two passages to ettha, but keeps etthaṃ iii.316.11; 317.4; 417.6; see below), *here*: Mv i.24.2; ii.99.3 yattakā ete prāṇā etthaṃ yajñe haniṣyanti; repeatedly etthaṃ etaṃ śrūyati, *here the following is recorded,* Mv iii.316.11; 317.4; 417.6, and one ms. in 416.8 where Senart reads itthaṃ with v.l. and with 418.7, where both mss. itthaṃ. The mg. seems to be *here*, not *thus*; but perhaps the form is blended with itthaṃ.

edānīm, adv. (§ 3.59; Pkt. eyāṇim, acc. to Sheth, from the drama Rambhāmañjarī, dialect unspecified; = Skt. idānīm), *now*: Mmk 55.19 (prose) (aham apy) edānīṃ bhāṣiṣye; apy edānīm... MSV i.67.2; 226.14; ii.178.3, 8; 180.11.

edṛśa, f. **°śā, °śī,** adj. (= Pali edisa, Skt. īd°; Pischel 121 has a highly implausible explanation of e-; Geiger 11 a less implausible one), *such*; very common in Mv but rare elsewhere: SP 70.7 (vs; īdṛśa in same position 70.4); 336.7 (vs); Mv i.225.8 and (°śī, f., by em.) 9, 258.21 and 261.14 (°śāye, inst. f.); 284.9; 289.1; 308.16 (°śāye); 364.8; ii.35.3; 58.10 (°śī); 76.16; 110.1; 144.17; 146.13; 147.15 (°śī); 180.1; 208.16; 215.14, 15; 274.9; 307.18; 433.2; 447.3; iii.130.15; 264.6 f., etc.

edṛśaka (= Pali edisaka), = **edṛśa,** *such*: Mv ii.7.7 (vs; v.l. edṛśaṃ; meter is bad either way); ii.35.2 (vs; here -ka may be m.c.).

em, adv. (= AMg. id., chiefly before eva; MIndic for Skt. evam), *thus, so*; only in vss: chiefly before eva, SP 89.11 (most mss.); 99.2; 127.9; 197.9; 213.7; 313.11; rare in LV and Mv and app. never in their mss., but required by meter LV 371.7 and Mv i.119.18 (see Senart's note); 234.1; 298.5; common in KP, em eva 30.7; 31.6; 34.6; 36.7; 49.7 etc.; em eṣa, required by meter LV 420.9, 15 (text evam eṣa); once em seems required by meter before a consonant, Dbh.g. 9(345).1 em (text evaṃ) śruṇitva.

[**eminā**(pi), Mv iii.403.12, 14, see s.v. **acchindati** 1.]

eyaṃ, m.c. for iyaṃ (§ 3.60), *this* (f.): SP 306.7 (vs); so also emāṃ, m.c. for imāṃ, SP 355.4 (vs). Both edd., all mss., read so.

eraka, m. (Divy.) or nt. (Mvy.), (= Pali eraka, see PTSD, or eragu, see below), a kind of grass, prob. = Skt. erakā, used in making coverlets, or a coverlet made of it; in a list of four such materials, Mvy 9180 erakam (= Tib. mal stan, *bed-cover*, var. bal stan, *woolen cover*; Chin. *mattress*); 9181 merakam (= śiṅ śun gyi stan, *coverlet of tree-bark*; Chin. *mattress of leaves*, or *of bark*); 9182 syandarakaḥ (Mironov v.l. syandu°; = Tib. srin bal gyi stan, *coverlet of cotton* or *silk*, and so Chin.); 9183 mandurakam (= Tib. ras bal gyi stan, *coverlet of cotton cloth*); same passage Divy 19.22 evaṃrūpam āstaraṇaṃ pratyāstaraṇaṃ, tad yathā, erako merako jandurako mandurakaḥ; and in Pali, Vin.i.196.6 eragu moragu majjhāru (v.l. majjāru) jantu; see the other words; eraka occurs also Mv i.19.10, where prob. read eraka (°kā?) vārṣikā as separate words, *grass-coverlets for the rainy season*, see s.v. **vārṣikā.**

Erakakṣa (= Pali Erakaccha, see DPPN), n. of a locality: Māy 51, 69. So all Lévi's mss. in 51 (v.l. Bharukaccha in 69); he em. Ekakakṣa with Chin. versions, not knowing the Pali form. The Chin. doubtless have a rationalization.

Eravaṇa, m. (= Pali, Pkt. Erā°, Skt. Airā°), n. of Indra's elephant: Mv ii.275.7, 8 (prose). The short a may be only an error, tho it is repeated; it is otherwise unknown; v.l. both times ai°; e for ai, § 3.67.

erita, ppp. (= Pali id., to ereti; Skt. īrita, to īrayati, which takes the preverb ā only in the Veda, and no erita, ppp., seems recorded even there), *stirred, moved* (by wind), or (of musical instruments) *struck*: LV 194.10 (vs) vṛkṣā māruta-eritā (cf. Skt. vāyv-īrita, Mbh., BR); so Lefm., most mss. -īr°; Mv iii.367.12, 17 (vs) (gandho . . .) upavāyati erito mārutena; Divy 251.3 an-eritāni vāditrabhāṇḍāni madhuraśabdān niścārayanti.

ela, (**1**) m. or nt., a high number: Mvy 7759 (m.) = Tib. yal ḥdas, ya lad; 7872 (nt.) = Tib. thal thal, cited from Gv, which has elam 133.14; (**2**) m., n. of a nāga king: Mvy 3263; Māy 247.28; also dual dvandva Elamelau, two nāga kings, Māy 247.33.

?**elaka** (= Pali eḷaka), *threshold*, perhaps to be read in Mv i.195.15; see s.v. **eluka** (1).

elatā, a high number, = next: Gv 106.5.

elada, m. or nt., a high number: Mvy 7746 (m.), 7875 (nt.), both = Tib. thal yas; the latter cited from Gv, the text of which has instead **elatā** or **eluda,** qq.v.

elapatra, m., (**1**) one of four 'great treasures' (mahānidhi; cf. a similar group of four treasures in Pali, DN comm. i.284.8, saṅkha, ela, uppala, puṇḍarīka), each presided over by a nāga-king of (presumably) the same name (so definitely stated for Elapatra): Mv iii.383.18–384.1 catvāro mahānidhayo saṃkho vārāṇasyāṃ mithilāyāṃ (19) padumo kaliṃgeṣu piṃgalo takṣaśilāyāṃ elapatro; vārāṇasyāṃ saṃkhasya māsiko (20) samājo vartati; tahiṃ nidhānādhipatayo nāgarājāno nimantritakā āgatā; (384.1) tatra ca elapatreṇa nāgarājñā praśnā sthāpitā (see below for Pali equivalent); (**2**) Elapatra, in Mv iii.384.1, above, n. of a nāga-king presiding over the 'treasure' of the same name; presumably the same as the nāga (or nāga-king) named (without reference to the 'treasure') Mvy 3271 (Kyoto ed. Elāpattra, by error; Mironov Ela° with no v.l.); Suv 162.9; Mmk 452.20; Kv 2.9; Māy 222.3; 247.2; certainly the same as the Elapatra (mss.; ed. wrongly em. Elā°) of Divy 61.4, tho here he is not called a nāga but one of the four 'kings' presiding over the four treasures (cf. Mv iii.383.18 ff. above), (Divy 61.1) atha catvāro mahārājāś caturmahānidhisthāḥ, (3–4, vs) Piṅgalaś ca Kaliṅgeṣu Mithilāyāṃ ca Pāṇḍukaḥ, Elapatraś ca Gāndhāre Śaṅkho Vārāṇasīpure. Besides the Pali parallel, DN comm. above, cf. the 9 treasures of Kubera which include Śaṅkha and Padma (with presiding personages of the same names), and among the Jains the 9 treasures of a cakravartin, which in their AMg. forms include piṃgala, paṇḍua (= pāṇḍuka), and saṃkha; the Skt. forms of these are recorded at least lexically. Note also in Pali the nāga-king Erakapatta, of Dhp. comm. iii.231 ff., who however does not seem to be brought into relation to the 'treasure' called in Pali ela (above); but the vss attributed to him, and the replies to them, in Dhp. comm. are reproduced in Mv iii.384, see above.

Elabhadra, n. of a nāga: Hoernle, MR 27.3 (Āṭānāṭiya Sūtra).

[**Ela-mela,** Mironov **Eḍa-meḍa,** n. of a nāga king: Mvy 3291. But a var. in both edd., supported by **Tib.,** makes Ela-Mela a dvandva cpd.; see **Ela** and **Mela.**]

Elavarṇa, n. of a nāga king: Mvy 3267; Māy 247.28.

elā, a high number: Gv 106.9; corresp. to **elu**.

[**Elāpattra**, see **Elapatra**.]

elu, m. or f., a high number: Mvy 7888 (eluḥ, = Tib. yal, or ya lad), cited from Gv which reads **elā** or **delu** (nt.) qq.v.

eluka (m. or nt.), (**1**) (= AMg. eluya, *threshold of a door*; cf. Pali eḷaka, id., wrongly queried in PTSD; DN comm. ii.355.5, on DN i.166.5, = ummāra; possibly supported by Mv i.195.15), *threshold*: (teṣāṃ ...) dvārāṇāṃ ... elukā (pl.; Senart elūkā with v.l. iii.228.11; in i.195.15 both mss. valakā, perhaps to be read elakā in agreement with Pali, above) abhūṣi (i.195.15 abhunsuḥ) Mv i.195.15; iii.228.11; (**2**) (= Skt. eḍūka, m., and Lex. eḍuka), *monument for containing the ashes of a dead person* (occurs as eḍūkān, acc. pl., and eḍūka-, in cpd., Mbh. Cr. ed. 3.188.64, 66, of heretical relic-shrines; prob. Buddhist word): Mv ii.486.5 (prose; refers to the 'bones' of ordinary laymen, not religious persons) asthini sāhareyetvā (so mss., Senart asthīni saṃharayitvā) tato me elūkāṃ (so text, but v.l. elukāṃ; acc. pl.) kārāpayesi. tatra ca elukadvāre (so both mss.; Senart em. elūkā°)...; iii.20.9, 10 (same situation, story told in vss) ekamante dahāpetvā elukaṃ (mss., Senart em. elūkaṃ) mama kāraye, elukaṃ (mss., Senart em. elūkaṃ) me karitvāna ... Since Skt. Lexx. record eḍuka, and eḍūka is read only in one ms. in one passage, it seems best to read eluka in both.

eluda, nt., a high number: Gv 133.15; cited Mvy as **elada**, q.v.

?**elūka**, see **eluka**.

1 **eva** (as in Pali kocid-eva, see PTSD s.v. ka, 2) after kaścid, has extreme indefinitizing force, *some ... or other* (not only unnamed and unknown, but usually imaginary, as in a parable): kaścid eva puruṣaḥ, *some man or other* (any one at all), after tad yathāpi nāma, SP 101.11; 320.6 (vaidya-puruṣo); Śikṣ 166.6 (all prose); taṃ kaścid eva puruṣa upasaṃkramya Śikṣ 166.7, *to him some* (different) *man or other approaching* ...; kenacid eva karaṇīyena MSV i.62.3.

2 **eva** in the sense of evam, occurs in the cpd. **evarūpa**, q.v.; also (in vss, m.c.) as separate word, LV 55.21; 76.2; 216.8. In LV 238.18 (prose) Lefm. reads: te 'bruvan, eva hy etat paśyāmaḥ; Calc. evaṃ for eva (not noted by Lefm.); Weller ignores the passage; the only v.l. is naiva for eva; either this, or evaṃ, must surely be read. Possibly (since the Calc. v.l. evaṃ is not noted) eva is a mere misprint (but it is not corrected).

evaṃvidhi, adj. (= Skt. °vidha), *of such a sort, such*: °dhiḥ prābhṛto (q.v.) Divy 36.21.

evaṃkara, adj. (= Pali id., Jāt. v.148.21), *acting thus* (correl. to **kathaṃkara**): Mv iii.373.5 (vs, = Jāt. above) °ro prajñāvāṃ bhoti manye (mss. manyo, read martyo, cf. Pali macco?), 13.

[**evata**, acc. to Bendall, Śikṣ 343.3 and 7 (vss), taken as a single word, 'connected with evaṃ' and translated *even so*. On the contrary, it represents two words, eva = evam in 7 but eṣa (with mss.) in 3, followed by (a)ta = ataḥ; eṣ' ata, *this* (ray) *therefore* (in 3), ev' ata, *so therefore* (in 7). See §§ 4.21 ff., esp. 4.29.]

evaṃdarśana, adj. Bhvr., = next, *holding such a view*: Mv ii.119.3 evaṃdarśanaṃ ca samānaṃ samānārthatāye sthāpayet, *and* (me) *being a holder of such an opinion* (agreeing with his own, Ārāḍa Kālāma's) ... See also **tathādarśana**.

evaṃdṛṣṭi, adj. Bhvr. (= Pali evaṃdiṭṭhi), = prec. and **tathādarśana**, *holding such a view* or *opinion*: Av ii.188.5 ff. eka evaṃdṛṣṭir bhavaty evaṃvādī, sarvaṃ me kṣamata iti (etc., similar phrases).

evarūpa, adj. (= Pali id.; Skt. evaṃrūpa), *of such a sort* or *form*: very common in vss, SP 83.14; 86.14; 93.4; 94.1; 95.4, 12; 96.8; 97.6; LV 55.9; Dbh.g. 12(348).16; Sukh 50.12; but also in prose, esp. of Mv, e.g. i.39.8; 329.7, 21; 330.11; ii.257.12; iii.317.7; 444.6, etc.; also in prose of LV, 13.22 and 307.13 (so all Lefm.'s mss. and Weller's ms., certainly not misprint as suggested by Weller 16), as well as 441.12, eṣām evarūpāṇāṃ dharmāṇāṃ (no v.l. except Calc. evaṃrū°, cited by Lefm., so that evarū° is not a misprint; not noted by Weller). Pali also uses evarūpa in prose as well as verse. (PTSD cites this cpd. under eva; of course it should be under evaṃ.) Cf. **keva-rūpa**.

evala, adj. (= Ap. evaḍa = iyat, Hem. 4.408; cf. Jacobi, Bhav. Gloss., evaḍḍa, id.), *so many*: Mmk 507.14 (vs) evalā mudravarety āhu = mudrā varā(ḥ) ity āhur(?).

eṣaka, adj. (= Pali esaka, Dhp. comm. iii.417.10; not in PTSD; to eṣati), *seeking, striving*: Bbh 204.4 eṣakaṃ vīryaṃ bodhisattvasya, sarvavidyāsthānaparyeṣaṇatayā.

eṣati, °te (= Pali esati; very rare in Skt., BhāgP. in pw, which associates this with iṣyati; in mg. it belongs with icchati; cf. **adhy°**, **anv°**, **pary-eṣati**), *seeks*: SP 54.10 (vs) na buddham eṣanti; LV 242.10 (vs) na ca so tṛpti labheta bhūyu eṣan; 354.2 (vs) bodhi vara eṣatā (inst. pr. pple.); 364.9 (vs) eṣati; 379.11 (vs) agādhe gādham eṣatha (so read with v.l.); RP 5.14 (vs) eṣamāṇa varabodhim uttamām; 15.14 (vs) na ca punar eṣati kasyacit sa doṣam.

[**eṣikā** ? See **aiṣikā**.]

[**eṣiriṣū**, Gv 254.26, 1st ed.; read osiri; see s.v. **avaśirati**, 3.]

? **eha** = iha (§ 3.59), *here*, in app-eha (read rather apy-eha?): MSV iv.220.4, 5.

ehipaśyika, adj. (= Pali ehipassika; based on ehi paśya, *come see!*; also **aihi°**, q.v.), *that invites* (every man) *to come and see*, ep. of the Buddha's dharma (and, in Mv, vinaya; in Pali, of dhamma): Mv iii.200.10 (svākhyāto ... tathāgatasya ...) dharmavinayaḥ sāṃdṛṣṭika akāliko ehipaśyikaḥ aupanayikaḥ etc. (essentially same formula in Pali and in passages cited s.v. **aihipaśyika**).

ehibhikṣukā, *the act or formula of ordination as monk by pronouncing the words beginning ehi bhikṣu* (bhikṣo; Pali ehi bhikkhu; or pl. bhikṣavo); one of the four forms of **upasaṃpad**(ā), q.v.: ehibhikṣukāya (inst.) upasaṃpadā Mv i.2.15; often followed by the words of the formula, in Mv regularly ehibhikṣukāye (or °ya, inst.) ābhāṣe (3 sg. aor; rarely abhibhāṣe, iii.379.13), or ābhāṣṭo, °ṭā (ppp., subject the initiates): ehi bhikṣu (sometimes followed by the name, as Upāli iii.180.12; or pl. etha bhikṣavo) cara (caratha) tathāgate brahmacaryaṃ Mv ii.234.2 (read etha for Senart's em. ehatha); iii.65.2; 92.7; 180.12; 181.3; 379.13; 413.10; in Divy 48.18; 281.22; 341.27; 558.18 ehibhikṣukayā ābhāṣitaḥ (or °tāḥ; 341.27 mss. ābhāṣya, ger.) ehi bhikṣo cara (eta bhikṣavaś carata) brahmacaryaṃ (omitting tathāgate); also used without quotation of the formula, the instr. °kāye or °kāya (in Mv; °kayā Divy and Av) being followed by ppp. pravrājito (°taḥ, or °tā = °tāḥ; Mv adds upasaṃpādito or °tā = °tāḥ) Mv iii. 376.14; 401.16; 430.14; Divy 463.25; Av ii.113.5; (ayaṃ ca me) caramo bhaviṣyati sākṣāc-chrāvakāṇām ehibhikṣukayā pravrajitānām (non-caus.), ... *of disciples who have become monks through* (my saying) *the ehibhikṣukā formula*, Av i.230.16.

ehibhikṣuṇī-vāda (m.; cf. Pali ehi bhikkhuni, fem. to ehi bhikkhu), = (the fem. equivalent of) prec., *the ordination of a nun by the formula ehi bhikṣuṇi*: Divy 616.19 mātaṅgadārikām ehi°vādena pravrājayitvā.

ehisvāgatavādin, adj., and °**vādi-tā** (Pali ehisāgatavādi, or °svāgata°), (the state or actions of) *one who* (habitually) *says 'come, welcome'!* (ehi svāgata): Bbh 254.20 (sattvānāṃ) pūrvābhilāpī ca bhavati ehisvāgatavādī; Bbh 146.6 saṃmodayati °di-tayā; 217.11 °di-tayā ... sattvān pratisaṃmodayati.

AI

aikāsanika, Mvy 1132, = **ekās°,** q.v.

aiṇeya-jaṅgha(-tā), (state of) *having legs like a black antelope* (= the more usual **eṇeya°,** q.v. under **eṇī-**): Mvy 267; Dharmas 83 (text aineya°); Gv 400.6 °gha-tā, glossed in 7 eṇeyasyeva mṛgarājño (indicating that aiṇ° is adj., eṇ° noun).

aindramārga (m.), lit. *path of Indra = the open air*: °ge Mv ii.157.7. See s.v. **ajina-khipa.**

Airāvata, m., n. of a mountain (= next; occurs as n. of several mountains in Brahmanical and Jain Skt., see Kirfel, Kosm., Index s.v.): Divy 450.11.

Airāvataka, m. = prec., Divy 455.29.

Airāvatī, n. of a yoginī: Sādh 427.5.

airyāpatha, m., = **īryāpatha,** q.v., in mg. 3, *proper deportment*; the form with vṛddhi of first syllable is not recorded elsewhere but seems guaranteed by LV 127.9, in the Bodhisattva's spelling lesson, where the letter ai stands for airyāpathaḥ (so prob. read, Lefm. °patha- with ms. A, other mss. airapathaḥ) śreyān; LV 191.16, text with most mss. prāsādikenairyāpathena (one ms. °kena iryyā°) saṃpannaṃ (bhikṣum); ŚsP 96.7 sarvasattvān airyāpatha-sahagate puṇyakriyāvastuni pratiṣṭhāpayitukāmena (bodhisattvena).

aiṣikā (= Pali esikā; proverbially 'stable, firm', see refs. in PTSD), *pillar* (as that which makes firm, steadfast): Śikṣ 3.7 (vs) niśraya (separate!) kleśa-adharṣikatāyai aiṣika (m.c. for °kā; possibly read eṣika?) śraddha svayaṃbhuguṇānām, *faith is a support, so as not to be subject to attack by the depravities, a pillar for the excellent qualities of the Self-existent.* (Bendall and Rouse wrongly derive from eṣaka, to eṣati.)

aihipaśyika, adj., = **ehipaśyika,** q.v.; ep. of dharma: Mvy 1296; Śikṣ 323.6.

O

o-: see also **ava-** for words with this initial. When the form with ava- is normal Skt., the form with o- is sometimes omitted here; cf. § 3.76.

Oka, n. of a rich merchant, father of Yaśoda: Mv iii.404.13.

okaṭṭati, once **avak°** (see s.v. **kaṭṭati**), (**1**) *draws down* (= Pali ava-, o-kaḍḍhati); Mv iii.29.13 to 30.10, always of a water-ogre who draws down into the water creatures who come to drink (Senart always em. °kaḍḍh°): °ati 29.13, 15 (here Senart with ms. ā-k°, but o-k° must be read), 16; °iyā (opt.; Senart em. °eyā) 30.8; °itāni, ppp. 29.17; °iyanti, and pres. pple. °iyanto (pass.), 30.3 and 4; °itum, inf. 30.10; avakaṭṭitum 30.6; (**2**) *draws out* or *forth* (in this sense = Pali apakaḍḍhati, but in Pali ava- and even o- occur, at least in the mss., in this mg. also): Mv iii.34.8 dāruskandhaṃ nadīye ... oruhyantam okaṭṭitum (inf.); 34.10 okaṭṭitaṃ (mss. °tuṃ by error; ppp.).

okara (mss.), see **avakāra** (2).

okasta, taken by Senart i note p. 556 as ppp. of ava with root kas (see BR), *gone down, descended.* I cannot improve on this suggestion, altho no form of this cpd. has been recorded elsewhere. Usually with acc. or loc. of that to (sometimes into) which the subject has *gone down,* the pple. °to or °tā being a periphrasis for a past tense: to the sea, in order to embark, Mv i.245.4; to a river, ii.212.15 (to draw water); iii.313.8; to a pool, ii.450.2 (by a staircase, sopānena), 15; iii.24.19; 29.16; from the Himalayan region into another country Mv i.232.3 (text uncertain), 12; to the bazaar-street iii.35.17; 37.3; from a wagon iii.39.16; a nāga enters into the Buddha's alms-bowl, iii.429.3. Not found outside of Mv.

okāra, see **avakāra.**

okkarika, m. (= **aukarika,** q.v.; acc. to Feer, Transl. of Av, = Tib. yul tsoṅ [read tshoṅ] pa, see below), some kind of tradesman; Feer, 'country merchant'; but yul, which indeed often means janapada (opp. to *town*), in comp. with tshoṅ pa, *merchant,* could possibly mean *dealer in agricultural products,* something like *truck-farmer*; possibly cf. ogara, oggara, cited by Sheth from Prākṛtapiṅgala as meaning *a kind of grain* or *rice.* Certainly not a keeper of a shop in the country, for the story shows that it means a member of an urban tradesman's guild, parallel with perfumers: Av i.198.7 pitā te okkarika āsīd; 10 tenaukkarikāpaṇo vyavasthāpitaḥ; 12 tenaukkarika-tvaṃ tyaktvā. The story is the same as that in which Divy uses **aukarika.** I see no reason to associate with either of these words the n. pr. **Utkarika** or **Otk°,** qq.v.

okramaṇa, see **avakramaṇa.**

o-kṣapayati (for ava-kṣ°, caus. to Skt. apa-kṣi), *causes to be done away with, orders put away,* with 'inner accusative' vadham, *to death,* i. e. *orders executed*: Mv i.96.7 (prose), read with 5 of 6 mss. (aparādhaṃ ca ananuyujyā, read °jya, q.v.) vadham okṣapayanti (one ms. ākṣap°; Senart em. ākṣep°).

ogamana, nt. (= Pali id.; Skt. ava-ga° not in this sense), *going down, setting* (of heavenly bodies): Mv ii.163.8 (prose; candrasūryāṇāṃ ...) ogamanāni.

ogrāhaka, m., *one who grasps* (intellectually), *acquires* (knowledge): Mv iii.373.3 (vs) ogrāhako ca paripṛcchamāno (... evaṃkaro prajñāvāṃ bhoti). Prob. false Sktization of Pali uggāhako (vā paripucchako siyā, same line as above, Jāt. v.148.19). Alternatively, might be false Sktization of a Pali *ogāhaka to ogāhati, °heti (= Skt. ava-gāh-), *penetrates* (used once with object lokanāthassa sāsanaṃ, Pv. comm. 287.12).

ogha, m. (= Pali id.), *flood* (of evils, passions, or depravities, 'crossing' of which, tar- or ut-tar-, is necessary for salvation); usually *four* in number, presumably as in Pali = the 4 **āsrava** or **yoga,** qq.v. (cf. Mvy 2141 āśravaḥ, 2142 oghaḥ): catur-ogha-pāra-gāmitābhiprāyasya (bodhisattvasya) LV 8.16 (read so with Tib. pha rol tu ḥgro baḥi bsam pa can, *intending to go to the further shore* ...; best ms. A °pāramitābhi°, Lefm. with others °pāragāminābhi°); LV 195.18 (vs) ogha catvāri tīrtvā; caturoghottīrṇānāṃ (Buddhānāṃ) Divy 95.15; Av i.16.11; sattvānāṃ caturoghottaraṇatāyai Gv 492.1; five or six ogha, Mv iii.283.18 (vs) pañcoghatīrṇo taratīha ṣaṣṭhaṃ (text ṣaṣṭaṃ; = Pali SN i.126.22; cf. Windisch, Māra und Buddha, 122 note 1; it is not clear what these are; for one not very plausible conjecture see PTSD s.v.).

Oghaja, n. of two former Buddhas, in the same list: Mv iii.231.5; 237.1 (v.l. both times Oghaṃjana or Oghajana).

Ojaḥpratyāhāriṇī, n. of a goddess: Mvy 4285.

? **ojas,** nt., a high number: Sukh 31.2 (by plausible em.; follows **srotas,** precedes **aprameya**). Cf. **bala** (4).

-ojaska = ojas, *strength,* in Bhvr. cpds.: SP 105.10

(prose) alpaujaskau; Jm 200.20 (vs) anojasko (mss. anau°); 234.2 (vs) svabhāva-saujaska-.

ojā (= Pali id.; derived by Childers and Senart from Skt. ūrj, by PTSD from ojas, which seems more plausible), *food*: Mv i.210.19 = ii.14.20 (prose) (lābhinī bhavati divyānāṃ gandhānāṃ ... mālyānāṃ ... vilepanānāṃ) divyānāṃ ojānām; ii.131.3 (and 6) (prose) (vayaṃ te romakūpa- [mss. °pe] vivarāntareṣu) divyām ojām adhyohariṣyāmaḥ; see s.v. **adhyoharati** (used in Pali, like its noun ajjhohāra, of food). It seems clear that in BHS, at least, ojā means simply *food*, not *essence* or the like.

Ojopati (for Ojaḥpati), n. of one of 4 (masc.) devatās of the Bodhivṛkṣa: LV 278.10 (so all mss.; Lefm. em. Ojāpati). Cf. next.

Ojobalā, n. of one of 8 (fem.) devatās of the Bodhivṛkṣa: LV 331.21. Cf. prec.; but there is otherwise no resemblance between the two lists.

ojovanta-tara, adj. compv. (cf. Pali ojavant(a), Vedic ojasvant; in Skt. only ojasvin), *strong-er*: Suv 164.8 (vs) ojovantatarā bhonti lakṣmīvīryabalānvitāḥ.

ojohāra, adj. and subst. (f. °rī), lit. *strength-robber*; ep. of rākṣasas: Divy 295.6 rākṣasa eva ojohāra ihāgacchati; of yakṣas, Jm 41.14 ojohārāḥ pañca yakṣāḥ; subst. m. and f., in a list of evil supernatural beings, ojohāro vaujohārī vā Laṅk 261.11; 262.13. Cf. next two. See also s.v. 2 **-hāra**; in both Divy and Jm the mg. *to rob the strength* (of people) would be possible.

ojo-hāraka, adj. or subst. m. (cf. prec., but see also s.v. 2 **-hāra, hāraka**), *strength-robbing, -robber*; or, as expression of purpose, *to rob the strength* (of people): Mv i.253.3, said of the 1000 sons of a yakṣiṇī: te 'pi vaiśālim ojohārakā preṣitā, vaiśālim gatvā manuṣyāṇām ojaṃ haranti (so that they all became sick).

Ojohāriṇī (cf. prec. two), n. of a piśācī: Māy 239.6.

oḍigalla? (see s.v. **uḍigalla**).

Oḍiyāna, see **Oḍḍi°**.

Oḍḍiyāna, also **Oḍi°** (and **uḍḍiyāna(ka)**, q.v.), n. of a locality; see GOS 41 p. xxxvii; Lévi, Māy p. 105 ff.: Sādh 80.18 etc.; Oḍiyāna, Sādh 286.11 etc.; Oḍḍiyāna- (or Oḍiyāna, Sādh 283.10 etc.)-Mārīcī, a form of Mārīcī, Sādh 283.10 etc.; 287.10–11.

oḍḍeti (in mg. 2 = Pali id.; in mg. 1 seemingly = Pali uḍḍeti, very rare, only 1 reasonably clear case, Vin. ii.131.16–17 bhikkhu sikkāya pattaṃ uḍḍitvā, text uṭṭitvā, see PTSD), (**1**) *ties, fastens* (on): Mv ii.75.21 (see Crit. App. on 74.8) saptānāṃ tālānāṃ purato bherī oḍḍitā, *in front of* (each of) *the 7 tāl-trees a drum was fastened*; (**2**) specialization of 1, *fastens, sets* (a snare or trap, esp. for birds); with object (or subject of ppp.) pāśa, or kālapāśa (mss. also bāla°): Mv ii.235.1 pāśā oḍḍitā, 6 pāśo oḍḍito; other forms of ppp. 251.1, 8; 253.11; kālapāśāni ca oḍḍeti 252.16; kālapāśe oḍḍitvā 252.17; tasya kālapāśāni ca oḍḍentasya 253.9.

oḍrapuṣpa (nt.; = Skt. Lex., and in late, artificial literature, Schmidt, Nachtr.), n. of a flower, *'the china-rose flower'*: Mmk 213.15 -samākāraṃ, adj., *having a form like* ... (of a heavenly portent).

1 **otarati, otāreti**, see **ava-t°**.

2 **otarati** = Skt. uttarati (§ 3.73), *conquers, overcomes*: pass. otarīyati SP 358.12 (vs), without v.l.; WT with their ms. K' ostarīyati, *is overwhelmed* (virtual synonym, but prob. rationalizing lect. fac.; KN note calls otarīyati 'a mistake for otthar°'). Tib. chod pa med, *not cut off*; Chin. *not destroyed*.

Otalā, n. of a town: MSV i.17.13 ff.

Otalāyana, n. of a rich brahman in Otalā: MSV i.17.14.

Otalīya, adj., *of Otalā*: MSV i.17.14.

Otkarika, n. of the merchant also called **Utkarika** (unless there is a corruption, see s.v.): Divy 228.5, 14 yo 'sāv Otkariko baṇig ...

ottareṇa, acc. to text Dīpaṃkarasya ott° Mv i.250.5 (vs) postposition = uttareṇa; the latter form may have been intended, see s.v. **uttari**, but cf. **pratyottareṇa.**

ottānaka, adj. (= utt°; cf. Pkt. ottāṇa for utt°, Sheth): Mv ii.16.11 (= i.213.7 **uttānako**, q.v.).

otrapa, otrapya (nt.?; cf. **an-otrapa, apatrāpya**, Pali ottappa; the short vowel in the penult is doubtless of MIndic character, and the single p, when it occurs, doubtless m.c., as in **an-otrapa**), *modesty, shame, decency*: Mv ii.357.14, mss. hirī-otrasya (v.l. -otasya)-sampanno; Senart °ottappa°, but read rather °otrapya°; LV 329.13 lajji (read as separate word) hirotrapāt tu, Lefm., but most and best mss. end in -patta for -pāt tu, and this may be the orig. form (abl., see § 8.56).

-odaka (as in Pali, e.g. anodaka) = Skt. udaka, *water*, at end of cpds.; see **an-, nir-od°**.

odadhati, see **ava-da°**, and cf. s.v. **odahana.**

odanakulmāṣopacaya, adj. (= Pali °kummāsūpacaya, MN ii.17.6; wrong ref. in PTSD; in same formula as Mv), *built up* or *grown by porridge and gruel*, ep. of the body (kāya), in a formulaic list of such: Mv ii.269.15; 277.18.

odahana, in Pali, *attention, application*, from odahati = **avadadhati**, q.v.; not noted in BHS, but see **anvodahana, samod°**.

odumbara, adj. (= Skt. aud°), *of the udumbara*: °ram iva kusumaṃ Mv i.270.3.

? **Oddha-saṃdhi**, n. of a former Buddha: Mv i.137.11. So mss.; Senart em. Ūrdhva°; should we understand Oddha- as for MIndic Uddha- (= Ūrdhva-), or emend with Senart?

odhṛta- (looks as if = avadhṛta; but ava-dhṛ is not so used, and it is no doubt really a false Sktization of a MIndic equivalent of Skt. uddhṛta), *removed, laid down* (of a burden): Mv ii.95.4 (rājā Subāhuḥ) rājakṛtyato odhṛtabhāro, *having laid down the burden of* (lit. from) *royal duties*. Perh. cf. AMg. ohariya, ppp., *taken down, placed down* (Ratnach.), supposedly for avadhṛta.

onamanā, see **avanamana, °nā.**

onādeti, see **avanādayati.**

opa-, see **aupa-** (also s.v. **upavusta**, where mss. opa-).

[**opadhika**, assumed by Weller on LV 32.1, but see s.v. **upadhika.**]

opalambhika = **aupa°**, q.v. (prob. with MIndic o for au, or possibly with o m.c. for u, i. e. **upalambhika**, without vṛddhi; the first passage might be for ca-u°, and in the others meter requires a long), *subject to the* **upalambha** *heresy*: ye c'opalambhikāḥ SP 335.1; opalambhikā(ḥ) SP 384.5, 9.

opalipyate, m.c. for upa°, *is stained*: no ca loki kva ci opalipyase LV 53.22 (vs).

Opāsimbha (! nothing like it found recorded), n. of a mountain: Māy 254.9.

(**opunati,**) caus. **opunāpayati** (Pali opunāti, opunāpeti; cf. Skt. nakhāvapūta, MS only, pw 7.351), (*winnows;*) caus., *causes to be winnowed*: Mv iii.178.5 (prose) (dhānyajātāni ...) khaladhāneṣu (mss. °**hāneṣu**, q.v.) saṃhārāpayitavyāni opunāpayitavyāni (gdve.).

Opura (for Avapura), n. of a son of King Sujāta Ikṣvāku: Mv i.348.11; 352.9, 11.

Obhāsa- (in cpds.), = **Avabhāsa-**, q.v.

omāraka, m., n. of a demoniac being (for *ava-mā°?): SP 401.5 stabdho vomārako vostārako, in a list of such creatures (vom° = vā om°, see s.v. **ostārako**).

omuddhaka, adj. (MIndic for **avamūrdhaka**, q.v.; cf. also next, and AMg. omuddhaga), *with head hanging down*: Mv ii.283.1 omuddhakā prapatetsuḥ, of the discomfited party of Māra; cf. Mv ii.412.16, under next.

omūrdhaka, f. °ikā, adj. (= **ava-m°**), = prec.: Mv ii.412.16 °dhakā prapatetsuḥ (of the discomfited host of Māra, cf. under prec.); Mv ii.172.13–14 omūrdhikām lambāviya (so mss.), *having hung her head downwards*; LV 213.12 (vs) omūrdhakāś, of ascetics.

ora (= Pali id., Skt. avara), *hither, nearer,* or *lower*; in ora-pāra (Pali id.), *the nearer and the farther* (state of existence), substantially *the present life and any future life*: Ud xviii.21 so bhikṣu jahāti orapāraṃ = Pali Sn i.(1–)5 so bhikkhu etc.

oravati (ava plus Skt. ravati; not recorded elsewhere), *murmurs, complains*: Mv ii.100.17 (prose) (rājñā...) śabdāpito putro (so with mss.): jānapadā oravanti, ... *the people of the country are complaining.*

orasa, adj., subst. (= Pali id., Skt. aur°), *own, self-begotten* (son): SP 88.3; 192.9; Mv ii.354.16.

orāṭikā (cf. Skt. raṭ-; o- for ava-), *howling, loud crying*: MSV iv.64.12.

[**orāpayi,** SP 331.11, doubtless misprint, read oropayi with WT (for ava-ropayati).]

? **oruṇḍa,** adj., perhaps for ava-ruṇḍa = ruṇḍa, *mutilated* (cf. **ava-kubja, ava-koṭimaka**): LV 333.16 (vs) chinna-kara-caraṇa ivoruṇḍaḥ, *mutilated, as if having hands and feet cut off.* But possibly understand ivo (m.c. for iva, § 3.82) ruṇḍaḥ; in a verse, the meter of which is MIndic and obscure to me.

o-rupta, o-rūp, o-rop-, see **ava-r°.**

olaṅka, m. (Skt. Gr. udaṅka, Pali uḷuṅka), *ladle*: Mv ii.244.10 śobhano mama ayaṃ adya kacchapo olaṅko bhaviṣyati.

Olambā (for Avalambā), n. of a piśācī: Māy 238.19 (prose).

o-līyati, see **ava-l°.**

olokanaka, nt. (= Pali id.; BHS also **avalokanaka, ullok°,** qq.v.), *window*: Mv iii.266.15 (read) olokanakāni dhāvanti, (girls) *run to the windows* (to look at Rāhula as he passes); SP 114.3, see **ullokanaka.**

ovaṭṭikā (Pali °ka, nt., id.), *girdle*: Mv i.321.2 māṇavaṃ ovaṭṭikāyāṃ (mss.; Senart em. kṛkāṭikāyāṃ) gṛhya; in Mv ii.311.11 perhaps read ovaṭṭikāhi (or °kehi, nt. as in Pali?) for mss. ovātakehi (Senart āvāpakehi) ratanadāmakehi paṭṭadāmakehi ... samalaṃkṛtaṃ bodhivṛkṣaṃ saṃjānetsuḥ.

o-vadati, o-vāda-, see **ava-v°.**

ovācu, m.c. for uvāca, *said*: Gv 212.16 (vs); § 3.71; ending of 3 pl. (cf. § 25.30).

o-vāyati (cf. RV ava-vāti, twice; otherwise no ava-vā *blows* is recorded), *blows* (intrans.): Mv ii.275.9–10 (prose; no v.l.) mṛdukā ca vātā ovāyanti.

ovidhyana-khā (so recorded; n. pl.? wrongly divided in Kyoto ed. ovidhya-nakhā; ovidhyana is n. act. from Pali ovijjhati *shoots down,* to Skt. ava-vyadh), *parapet, battlement,* lit. *holes for shooting* (arrows) *down*: Mvy 5524 = Tib. mdaḥ yab, or, ba gam, both having substantially this mg., but the first seems to mean lit. *arrow-shelter.*

ovṛṣṭa, ppp. (to Vedic ava-varṣ-; cf. Pali an-ovassa, °ssaka), *rained upon*: Ud iii.9, old and best ms. ovṛṣṭā (later ms. avavṛṣṭā, with poorer meter) bīraṇā (Skt. vīr°) yathā.

ośaṭuka, nt. (var. ośaḍuka), prob. some kind of *plaster*: Mvy 9364 = Tib. ḥdag rdzas, a kind of clay (Das *dry or wet*); Chin. *a substance for smearing,* or *sticky stuff.*

ośākha-, see **avaśākha-.**

ośirati, see **ava-ś°.**

oṣadha (= Skt. auṣ°), *medicine*: LV 197.11 (vs).

oṣadhi (= Pali osadhi), n. or epithet of a particular star: n. sg. °dhi or °dhī, Mv ii.56.20 and 58.13 (vs) tāravarā va oṣadhī, by Senart's em., which is proved by the Pali parallel Jāt. v.398.30. In Pali more often called osadhi-tārakā, *star of medicine.*

Oṣadhirāja, n. of a Bodhisattva: Gv 442.21.

oṣarati, see s.v. **avaśirati** (oṣaret SP 449.3).

? **oṣita,** in RP 19.10 (vs) apy oṣitā āmiṣapātracīvare (so apparently divide), *set upon, intent upon worldly things* (like) *bowl and robe* (see **āmiṣa**). Cf. Pali an-osita, *not occupied* (of houses; CPD). If correct, oṣita seems = Skt. avasita; used with loc. But api at the beginning is suspicious, and s does not normally become ṣ after MIndic o for ava. I suspect corruption.

osa, see **avaśya.**

osakkati, see **ava-sa°.**

osanna, adj. (= Skt. avasanna; in this sense, of flowers, not recorded), *wilted,* of flowers: Mv ii.394.5 (vs) osanna-puṣpaṃ jinacetiyeṣu (equivalent to jīrṇaṃ puṣpaṃ 394.2, puṣpaṃ purimaṃ milānaṃ 393.9, and others in the vicinity).

osaraṇa, nt. (to next; = Pali id.), *entrance, approach*: Mv ii.37.9 osaraṇe (mss. osakaṇe) ca bharitā addaśi pramadā, *at the entrance* (to the king's palace) ... (otherwise Senart); ii.108.8 kasya eṣa osaraṇaśabdaḥ (? mss. te saraṇa°, or te śaraśa°), *whose noise of approach is this?* In Mv iii.401.1 osaraṇāni, in a line otherwise hopelessly corrupt, corresponds to the same word in the same vs of Pali Sn 538, the rest of which seems also corrupt (so ed.); the comm. says it means *heretical views* (ogahanāni titthāni, diṭṭhiyo). Senart's em. and interpretation of the line are unconvincing; but the Pali is also dubious, and its comm. questionable. I cannot solve the problem.

1 **osarati** (= Pali id. or avasarati; cf. prec.; see **avasarati** 1, and for 2 osarati see s.v. **avaśirati**), **(1)** *enters, approaches, arrives*: Mv ii.108.7 kumāro siṃhasya va (? mss. ca) osarantasya śabdaṃ śṛṇvati; iii.453.3 (vs) na te koṣṭhesmiṃ (so read with 1 ms.) osaranti (the Pali version, Jāt. v.252.20, has upenti); **(2)** caus. osārayati = Pali osāreti, *restores* (a monk to good standing in the order): osārayantu māṃ āyuṣmantaḥ MSV ii.115.2, 14; 116.7, 20; 192.15; osāryate 179.12 f. (prose). See also **utsārayati, vosārayati.**

osāraṇā, also °ṇa (= Pali id.; cf. **avasāraṇa**; to prec., 2, plus -aṇā), *restitution* (to good standing, of a monk or nun that has been disciplined): °ṇāṃ yācantam Bhīk 28b.5; 29a.4; °nāṃ yācasva 29a.1; °ṇā yācitavyā MSV ii.192.6; °ṇaṃ 193.2, 6–7, etc. See also **utsāraṇa.**

osāraṇīya, adj., with karman (cf. prec.), (rite) *of restitution*: MSV ii.193.17 ff.

osirati, see **avaśirati.**

osupta (= Skt. avasupta, see s.v. **avasvāpayati**), ppp. to **osopati,** q.v.

osopati (= Skt. *ava-svapiti; see s.v. **avasvāpayati**; cf. **sopita,** and next), *sleeps, is asleep* (ppp. osupta): Mv ii.31.21 (āgamehi muhūrtaṃ, kumāro saṃprati) osupto. ṛṣi āha: mahārāja na kumāro osopati; ii.159.4 (bodhisattvo) pratibuddho paśyati antaḥpuram osuptam.

osopana, nt. (to prec.; cf. AMg. osovaṇī, *profound sleep* acc. to Ratnach.), *sleep,* or *putting to sleep*: Mv ii.160.6 devehi sarvasya janasya ... osopanaṃ kṛtaṃ. Cf. also **osvāpana, apasvāpana.**

ostarati, pass. ostarīyati, see s.v. 2 **otarati.**

ostāraka, m., and f. °**kī,** n. of demoniac beings (for *ava-st°?): omārako vostārako (v.l. vā ost°) SP 401.5; masc. Māy 219.10 etc.; fem. °kī Sādh 502.11; m. and f. Laṅk 261.9 and 262.11 ostārako vaustārakī vā; Māy 226.11.

osvāpana, nt. (presumably for **ava-sv°,** to **avasvāpayati** with -ana; cf. **apa-sv°**), *going to sleep*; *sleeping*; or perhaps *putting to sleep*: LV 236.8 (vs; avasvāpanaṃ would be metrically better!) devatābhi osvāpanaṃ kṛtam (in the corresponding prose version 217.7 apasvāpanaṃ); Mv iii.296.16 (prose) sarvasya rājakulasya °naṃ kṛtam. Non-causative mg. would be possible in both cases, the causative mg. would seem more natural; but see under **apasvāpana**; see also **osopati, °pana.**

osvāpita, see **ava-sv°.**

ohana, nt. (cf. Skt. ūhati, ūha, *change, derangement*, etc.? or Pali ūhanati *disturbs*?), acc. to Tib. *the making deluded* or *disturbed*: Mvy 4371 °nam = Tib. ḥkhrul byed, or ḥkhrug byed.

ohāra (m.; perh. cf. AMg. oharai, *establish, settle*, 'sthāpan karnā, pratiṣṭhit karnā'; derived by Ratnach. from upa-har-), *domicile, abode*: Mv iii.36.19 te . . . svakam ohāraṃ gatā; 37.3 tato ohārāto (mss. °rito) nirgamya; 40.1. ohāraṃ prasthito.

ohita-bhāra, adj. (= Pali id.; but see **apahṛta-bhāra**, which is prob. the true orig. of the Pali; Mv simply keeps the MIndic form), *who has laid aside his burdens*: Mv iii.262.13, 14 (of Buddha); -tā, *state of* (such a one), Mv ii.260.17 °tām anuprāpnuvanti (Bodhisattvas).

AU

aukarika, m., some sort of tradesman, the same as that designated by the Av form of the same story as **okkarika**, q.v. for discussion: Divy 590.2 (vs) putrakaukarikatvena (so mss.) pitā te mām apūpuṣat; 5 (prose) aukarikāpaṇaṃ prasasāra; 12 cirantanā aukarikās.

autkara (m. or nt.), ? some subject that was part of the education of a brahman: in a list of such, Divy 485.7 (. . . upanyastaḥ . . . samudācāre bhasmagrahe) autkare bhoskāre (mss. bhotk°) ṛgvede . . .; same passage MSV iv 15.19 reads ḍoṅkāre (for aut°) bhoṅkāre.

auttarāpathika, adj. (Skt. uttarāpatha plus -ika), *of the north country*: MSV i.239.1.

autpātika, nt. (v.l. autpatika, which is Mironov's reading but can hardly be right; to utpāta plus -ika, cf. Skt. autpātika, adj., in different mg.), apparently *a sudden, offhand invitation* (to eat), or *food thus offered* (follows nimantranakam): Mvy 5764 = Tib. ḥphral ba bos pa, *sudden invitation*.

autsuka, adj. (= Skt. utsuka; AMg. osuya, osua), *eager*: Mmk 61.5 (vs) °ko sarvamantreṣu nityaṃ grahaṇadhāraṇe.

[**audatya** MSV iii.16.2, read **auddhatya**, q.v.]

[**audarika**, adj., '2. *dem Bauche zusagend*', pw, is to be deleted; in the places there cited, LV (Lefm.) 264.15; 270.15, read **audārika**, *material, substantial* (of food), with all mss.; Calc. auda°. In LV 407.22 (not cited in pw) both edd. audarika without v.l., but certainly read audār°. So also in Mv ii.131.1 and 8, read with mss. audārikam āhāram (Senart em. audar°); the Pali parallel MN i.247.8 ff. has oḷārika; so Mv ii.241.1, 3 (in 3 mss. app. °dar°); and in Mv ii.277.18 read with mss. kāyo audāriko (Senart em. audar°), of the Buddha's body.]

audarīyaka, nt. (cf. Pali udariya, some abdominal organ, said to be the *stomach*), a presumably abdominal organ, only noted in lists of parts of the body: Mvy 4028 = Tib. sgaṅ pa (? perhaps *back*?) or lgaṅ pa, *bladder*; so Chin.; Bcṭ 295.6 (text audanīyakam); and cf. next.

audaryaka, nt., presumably = prec., in a list of parts of the body: Śikṣ 209.9; Bendall assumes *bladder*, but states that Tib. gives leṅ ga = Skt. liṅga; perhaps error for loṅ ga = *intestines, entrails, guts* (Jä.).

audāra, adj. (cf. Pali oḷāra, once, Pv. comm. 110.2 in gloss on atulaṃ, = appamāṇaṃ oḷāraṃ paṇītaṃ, but PTSD would read uḷāraṃ with v.l.; = Skt. udāra, or BHS **audārika**), (**1**) *large, vast*, of radiance, avabhāsa: Divy 207.6 audāre avabhāsanimitte prāviṣkṛte; cf. 63.17 ff. udārāvabhāsaḥ, and 201.22 audārike avabhāsanimitte prāviṣkriyamāṇe; the usual mg. of audārika might suggest *material, corporeal*, i. e. *physically actualized*, but the parallels are against this; cf. Mv i.41.3 aprameyasya udārasya ca mahato avabhāsasya . . ., and similarly in parallels (collected s.v. lokāntarikā); (**2**) *gross, unrefined* (= **audārika**): Gv 534.20 audārādhimuktikānāṃ viśuddhaye; this cannot = udāra- (tho this is compounded elsewhere with **adhimuktika**, q.v.) since that is a complimentary term, and this is not (cf. the parallel 534.23 saṃkliṣṭānāṃ sattvānāṃ viśuddhaye, and similarly 534.26).

audārika, adj. (see also °**ka-tā**; from Skt. udāra plus ika; **udāra, audāra**, qq.v., also occur rarely, but **audarika**, q.v., is a false reading for this; = Pali oḷārika), *gross*; Mvy 2691 in a list of 'synonyms for bṛhat', defined in Tib. by a number of terms including rags pa (text la! corr. in Tib. Index), *gross, corporeal, substantial*; che ba, *great*; sbom pa, *stout, gross, coarse*; also che loṅ, loṅ, and raṅ po, the precise lit. mgs. of which are not clear to me; in Mvy the word is nt. and is preceded by udāraḥ, viśālam, vipulam, and followed by pṛthuḥ. Practically all BHS occurrences may be subsumed under the mg. (**1**) *gross*, as opposed to sūkṣma, *fine, subtle* (so in Pali contrasted with sukhuma), -sūkṣmaudārika- Dbh 15.14; audārikaṃ vā sūkṣmaṃ vā Av ii.169.10 (rūpam); Mv iii.336.15 (id.) and 18 (vijñānam); so of the body, *gross, substantial, material*, LV 122.10 devatā sā audārikam ātmabhāvam abhisaṃdarśya; 219.19 (vs) Puṣyaś ca nakṣatra . . . °kaṃ nirmiṇi ātmabhāvaṃ, P. *created by magic a corporeal body*; Gv 218.20 mahādevo . . . audārikenātmabhāvena sattvānāṃ dharmaṃ deśayati; Dbh 23.11 audārikakāya-viheṭhanayā, *by injuring the actual, physical body* (of creatures); Bbh 61.7 kāyena vā audārikeṇa cāturmahābhūtikena; Av ii.191.4 ayaṃ . . . kāyo rūpī audārikaś cāturmahābhūtika(ḥ); Mv ii.277.18 (Māra says:) mātāpitṛsambhavo śramaṇagautamasya kāyo audāriko (so mss.) . . . mama punar manomayo kāyo; SP 277.7 (a Bodhisattva in speaking to women) nāntaśo dantāvalīm apy upadarśayati, kaḥ punar vāda audārikamukhavikāram, . . . *not to speak of* (showing) *any* (emotional) *alteration* (due to internal feelings) *in his corporeal* (gross, external) *face*; of other things, esp. *food*, āhāra (also in Pali, where oḷārika āhāra, *material* or *substantial* food or sustenance, is contrasted with immaterial kinds of sustenance, see Childers): Sukh 41.(2–)3 ff. (na . . . sukhāvatyāṃ) . . . sattvā audārika-yūṣa-phāṇikārāhāram (so ed. em.; mss. corrupt but beginning audāri-) āharanti, api tu . . . yathārūpam evāhāram ākāṅkṣanti, tathārūpaṃ āhṛtam eva saṃjānanti, prīṇitakāyāś ca bhavanti; in this sense audārika āhāra is always to be understood (not *abundant food*), LV 264.2, 6 etc.; 271.1 (others, see s.v. **audarika**); *material, corporeal* (forms of worship), Dbh 72.7 (a Bodhisattva in the 8th bhūmi) audārikaṃ buddhadarśanapūjopasthānaṃ notsṛjati; others, misc., Bbh. 9.24 bodhisattvasyaudārikāṇy . . . gotraliṅgāni; (**2**) in a few cases possibly *great, large*: Divy 104.24 audārikāś cāsyāśvāsapraśvāsā gurugurukāḥ pravartante yathā meghasya garjato.........śabdaḥ, *enormous breathings*; but since a rākṣasa is being described, perhaps *gross, coarse* would better correspond to the mg., cf. in Pali Vism. i.274.26 assāsapassāsā pi oḷārikā honti, balavatarā hutvā pavattanti etc. (Pe Maung Tin transl. ii.315 *the breathings too are gross* etc.); as to Divy 201.22 audārike avabhāsanimitte, see **audāra**.

audārika-tā, abstr. to prec., *coarseness* (Tib. **rags pa**): Mvy 1651 sthūlabhittikatā audārikatā.

Audumbarā, n. of a gandharva maid: Kv 4.24.

auddhatya, nt. (in Skt. only *haughtiness*; = Pali uddhacca), *frivolity*, in the double sense of *amusement*, *idle sport*, and *mental indolence, lack of seriousness of mind* ('the property antithetical to attention', Aung and Rhys Davids, Compendium of Philos. 18; *frivolité*, AbhidhK. LaV-P. vii.20): Mvy 1979 = Tib. rgod pa, *laughter* (acc. to Jä. and Das also *languor, indolence*, which the Dict. of the Fr. Cath. Miss. questions); here it stands between asaṃprajanyam aud kaukṛtyam, styānam; Bbh 169.5 (see s.v. **drava**; here seems clearly related to *amusement*); see **drava** also for MSV iii.16.2 where read auddhatyaṃ for audatyaṃ (Tib. mig zur gyis lta bar byed, *making glances with the corners of the eyes*); Jm 184.6 (said of women) tyakta-vibhrama-vilāsauddhatyā(ḥ); as one of the 6 **āvaraṇa** (q.v.) to samādhi, Dharmas 118; usually assoc. with such qualities as **styāna, middha,** and esp. **kaukṛtya,** qq.v., in formulaic lists which hardly give much help, Bbh 173.1; 223.13; 243.21; Sādh 365.12; Dharmas 30; auddhatya-kaukṛtya, together, constitute one of the 5 **nīvaraṇa,** q.v.

audbilya, audvilya, nt. (also **udbilya, udvilya,** q.v.; these sometimes occur as vv.ll. for aud°; = Pali ubbilla; acc. to Geiger 15.1 to ud plus vell-; other theories, see PTSD), *joy, pleasurable excitement*: °bilya-prāpta, often with adbhuta-p°, SP 6.5; 60.3; 100.3; Mmk 105.24; °ya-jāta SP 61.6; °ya-kārī (n. sg. °kārin) Mvy 2939; atīvaudbilyam utpannaṃ Divy 82.30; cittasya prāmodyaṃ kāyasyaudbilyam (n. sg.) Śikṣ 183.6; cittaudvilyaprītikaraṇyodārayā prabhayā (cf. under **udbilya**) Gv 203.18; cittaudvilyakaraṇī (prabhā) Sukh 30.2.

aupakramika, adj. (also **upa°**, q.v.; = Pali opakkamika, not well defined in PTSD; cf. AN ii.87.31 opakkamikāni, defined AN comm. iii.114.23 vadhabandhādi-upakkamena nibbattāni), *caused by violence*: Bbh 63.5 dhātu-vaiṣamikāṃś (see **vaiṣamika**) ca aupakramikān amanuṣyābhisṛṣṭāṃś copasargaṃ vyupaśamayati; 246.23 pañcavidhaṃ duḥkhaṃ: (the first of the five is) aupakramikam; so also in 293.10 aupakramika-duḥkha- is one of the same five kinds of duḥkha; 247.12–13 svayaṃkṛtaupakramikaṃ duḥkhaṃ, *pain caused by self-inflicted violence.*

Aupagama (text Opa°), n. of a Bodhisattva: Gv 442.16.

aupacayika, or (Mvy) **aupacāyika,** adj. (Skt. upacaya plus ika), *based on accumulation*: Bbh 247.17 °cayikaṃ duḥkhaṃ (not explained); cf. AbhidhK. LaV-P. i.69 *d'accumulation*, ii.290 *d'accroissement* (venant de la nourriture, etc.); Mvy 7089 °cāyikaḥ = Tib. rgyas pa las ḥbyuṅ ba, *originating from increase* (application not clear).

aupadhika (**1**) adj. (once also **upadhika,** q.v.; Pali opadhika, acc. to PTSD always with puñña = puṇya); in Pali opa° = *relating to the substratum* or *basis of rebirth*, i. e. *leading to rebirth*, so e. g. Vv. comm. 154.23 ff.; in BHS the word acquires a new meaning based on **upadhi** (2), q.v., *material, consisting of* or *relating to material things*; chiefly as ep. of **puṇyakriyāvastu,** q.v., as also **upadhika,** q.v.: Mvy 1703 °kaṃ puṇyakriyāvastu; Śikṣ 138.7 °kānāṃ °vastūnāṃ; similarly MadhK 487.1 (vs) puṇyam aupadhikaṃ; MSV ii.86.5; (**2**) subst., *what relates to material things*: with forms of sthā- (see Lévi, Sūtrāl. xvii.3, note, °dhika-sthiti, refus ... d'accepter un *don matériel*), bhagavān °dhike 'sthāt abhinirhṛtapiṇḍapātaḥ (Divy sthitaḥ, om. abhi°), *the Lord remained* (without partaking of) *the material gift* (a meal which his monks received) MSV ii.128.3; 180.5 (Tib. bsgrubs pa na bzhugs nas, *remained when* [the meal] *was supplied*)· Divy 542.17; both texts (Divy in 18, after another sentence) continue, pañcabhiḥ kāraṇair buddhā bhagavantaḥ aupadhike tiṣṭhanty (MSV adds abhinirhṛta-piṇḍapātāḥ, Divy varies, see **abhinirharati** 1); the five reasons (special things which need attention) are listed in MSV ii.128.5 ff.

aupanayika, adj. (= Pali opa°; ep. of Buddha's dhamma; from Skt. upanaya plus -ika; cf. next), *conducive* (to the desired religious end), ep. of dharmavinaya: Mv iii.200.10 (see s.v. **ehipaśyika**).

aupanāyika, adj., = prec. (in same formula): Mvy 1295. (So also Mironov.)

? **aupapatti-,** in Gv 243.14 nānaupapatti-nirmāṇakāyameghān niścaritvā (read before this -samāpannān, as proved by 243.25; also in 244.9 read sarvasattvasamāpannān nānāvarṇa-); the parallel 244.10, see s.v. **-upapattika,** indicates that either nānopapatti(-ka?)- or nānaupapattika(nir°) should be read; *various clouds of magic bodies spontaneously produced*; or perhaps ... *of various origins* (nānopapatti).

aupapattyaṃśika (= **upa°**; see s.v. **-aṃśika**), *relating to* (the part of) *birth*, opp. to māraṇāntika, Śikṣ 226.7 ff. (cited from Śāl 87.10 ff.); 253.3, 5.

aupapattyaṅgika, app. equivalent to preceding, *participating in birth*, of citta, Laṅk 277.6. See s.v. **-aṃśika.**

aupapāduka (°**dika**?), or **upapāduka,** adj. (the two forms identical in mg. and both included below; list of occurrences of **upapāduka** s.v.; aupapādika only SP 408.12, where 2 mss. °duka; corresp. to Pali opapātika, Jain Skt. aupa°, AMg. uvavāia, °iya; der. from **upapāda**, q.v.; with Leumann, Aup.S.1; Weber I.St. 16.377, I believe BHS shows the etymologically historical form, from upa-pad, contrary to Childers, s.v., and Lévi JA.1912 Pt. 2 p. 503; the counter-argument that upa-pad means *to be born* in the usual [rather, in any] way is inconclusive, since the passages cited below show that in BHS these words are definitely associated with upa-pad, see esp. SP 260.11–12; 408.12; Divy 300.17), *born by spontaneous generation*: often the fourth of 4 kinds of beings classified as to manner of birth, aṇḍajā(ḥ vā) jārāyujā(ḥ vā) saṃsvedajā(ḥ vā)aupapādukā(ḥ vā), SP 346.8; Mv i.211.16 = ii.15.15–16; ii.163.21; Sādh 26.7; or °upapādukā(ḥ vā) Mvy (2279–) 2282; Mv i.212.7 (v.l. aupa°); Dharmas 90 (n. sg. forms); also in cpd. -aṇḍaja-jarāyuja-saṃsvedajaupapāduka- Dbh 15.8; jarāyujāṇḍajasaṃsvedaja-upapāduka-sattva- Mmk 16.14; with omission of one member, aṇḍaja, saṃsvedaja, upapāduka, Gv 264.24; jarāyuja-saṃsvedajaupapādukānāṃ Divy 627.17; sometimes with addition of other terms, as rūpiṇo vārūpiṇo vā saṃjñino vāsaṃjñino vā etc. SP 346.8; Sādh 26.7, and similar additions in some others of the above; other occurrences: Divy 300.17 aupapādukāḥ sattvā ghaṭīyantraprayogena cyavamānā upapadyamānāś ca (*falling and being reborn in the manner of a bucket-machine*, sc. for raising water from a well) kartayvāḥ (as part of the **pañcagaṇḍakaṃ,** q.v., cakram); usually, as here, of human beings, esp. Buddhas, Bodhisattvas, and cakravartins; they often appear sitting on lotuses, which may themselves be *spontaneously generated*, as in SP 260.11–12 yasmiṃś ca buddhakṣetra upapatsyate tasminn aupapāduke saptaratnamaye padma upapatsyate; SP 455.4 (vs; in 3 'there is no sexual intercourse') upapāduka te jinorasāḥ padmagarbheṣu niṣaṇṇa nirmalāḥ; Śikṣ 175.8 te (bodhisattvāḥ) tatra nānāraṅgeṣu padmeṣūpapādukāḥ prādurbhavanti; contrasted with birth in the womb, Sukh 65.16 (anye garbhāvāsaṃ) prativasanti, anye (sc. bodhisattvāḥ) punar aupapādukāḥ padmeṣu paryaṅkaiḥ prādurbhavanti (also 66.6), *some dwell in the dwelling of the womb* (Müller SBE 49, 2, p. 62 *calyx*!), *others, spontaneously generated, appear sitting cross-legged on lotuses*; similarly Mv i.145.4 (na khalu ...) bodhisattvā mātāpitṛnirvṛttā bhavanti, atha khalu svaguṇanirvṛttyā (so with mss., *by the creative power of their own virtues*) upapādukā (v.l. aup°) bhavanti; in Mv i.153.6 ff. it is explained that Bodhisattvas, after rebirth in the Tuṣita heaven, do not engage in sex relations, and hence Siddhārtha was not Rāhula's father; Rāhula nevertheless entered (in some way not explained) the womb of Yaśodharā; but R. was not aupapāduka as cakravartins are, 153.16–154.3 (rājānaś cakravartinaḥ) aupapādukā babhūvu ... cakravartigaṇāḥ aupapādukā āsan, na tathā Rāhulabhadra iti; that cakravartins are aupa° (upa°) is also shown by Gv 254.12 (vs, of a cakravartin, having the 32 lakṣaṇa) upapāduko padumagarbhe; 268.26 cakravartī caturdvīpeśvaraḥ aupapādukaḥ padmagarbhe ...; elsewhere however it is clear that one born from the womb may nevertheless be aup°, Gv 339.4 yayā (sc. Māyayā) sa upapādukaḥ kumāra (sc. the bodhisattva Śākyamuni) utsaṅge pratigṛhītaḥ; SP 408.12 (of a bodhisattva; rājño Vimaladattasya) gṛha upapanna aupapādika (2 mss. °duka) utsaṅge paryaṅkeṇa prādurbhūto 'bhūt; other statements about aup° (up°) are that anything they wish is instantly fulfilled, Av ii.95.11 (see s.v. **upapāduka**) yenopapādukaḥ saṃvṛttaḥ sa(ha)cittotpādāc cāsya yac cintayati yat prārthayate tat sarvaṃ samṛdhyatīti; they have the 32 lakṣaṇa, and otherwise marvelous bodies, SP 205.14 (vs) upapādukāḥ sarvi (sc. sattvāḥ) suvarṇavarṇā dvātriṃśatīlakṣaṇarūpadhāriṇaḥ; SP 202.5 te sattvā aupapādukā bhaviṣyanti ... manomayair ātmabhāvaiḥ svayaṃprabhā(ḥ) ...; such birth results from high moral attainments in the past, Divy 533.25 (striyo yāḥ pañcānām avarabhāgīyānāṃ) saṃyojanānāṃ (q.v.) prahāṇād upapādukāḥ; this word is suggested by the letter au in the young Bodhisattva's spelling lesson, LV 127.10 aukāre aupapāduka-śabdaḥ.

aupabhogika, adj. (Skt. upabhoga plus -ika), *connected with* or *due to enjoyments*: Kv 80.5 kleśā aupabhogikāḥ.

aupamya, nt., a high number: Gv 134.5, cf. **upamya**.

aupalambhika (also recorded **opa°**, q.v.), *characterized by the heresy of* **upalambha** (q.v.), = upalambha-dṛṣṭika: °kānāṃ bodhisattvānāṃ (an inferior type) Śikṣ 315.8; AsP 158.14.

[**aupavana**, in LV 9.8 (prose) caturīryāpatha-vinayanaupavana-suvardhitataror; read -vinayanopavaṇa- with Calc., i. e vinayana-upavana-; Tib. seems to have read -tanor for -taror; it also had a longer text, suggesting haplographic corruption in the BHS; a photostat in my possession reads, spyod lam bzhi (catur-īryāpatha) daṅ ḥdul ba (vinaya, or °yana) ri (*mountain*) nags tshal (*forest*) daṅ nags ḥdab na (*in forest*) skyes paḥi (*made*) lus (*body*) daṅ ldan pa (*having*).]

aupaśamika, adj. (= Pali opasamika; in Skt. only as technical term of Jainas; from Skt. upaśama plus -ika; cf. **an-aupa°**, and **upa°**), *tending to tranquillity*; usually, as in Pali, ep. of dharma: Mv ii.33.3 dharmaṃ ... aupasamikaṃ (so mss. and ed.); 41.9 dharmaṃ tu opasamikaṃ (v.l. aupas°); Av ii.107.7 dharmaś ca ... aupaśamikaḥ; Bbh 24.13 (hitānvayaḥ svaparārtho bodhisattvasya) ... aupaśamikaś ca.

? **aurabhraka**, m., see next.

aurabhrika, m. (= Pali orabbhika; not in this mg. in Skt.; from urabhra plus -ika), *mutton-butcher* (sometimes perhaps *butcher* in general): Mvy 3758 = Tib. (b)śan pa, *butcher*: SP 280.2; 480.9; Laṅk 246.7; 253.5 (here text °bhraka but v.l. °bhrika, which prob. read); Divy 10.2; 15.22; Bbh 302.9; Kv 42.9 (text noratri°, read naurabhri° = na-aur°); 94.22.

aurṇaka, adj. (= Skt. Gr. id.; Skt. aurṇa), *woolen*: °ka-vāsaḥ Mvy 9159.

auśīrika, m., or °**kā**, f. (cf. Skt. uśīra; Sheth cites Pkt. osīra once), pl. °kāḥ, Mvy 9414 = Tib. myu gu, or zha lu, both (the latter acc. to Dict. Fr. Cath. Miss.; acc. to Jä. *cup, bowl*) *shoots* or *reeds*; Chin. *green shoots*.

Auṣadhi(n), or °**dhi(n)**, n. of a Tathāgata: Mv iii.236.10, 11. Senart reads °dhim, acc., and °dhī, nom.; but v.l. °dham (read °dhim) and °dhī resp., which are surely to be read.

auṣarya (nt.; Skt. ūṣara plus -ya; unrecorded), *salty ground*: Mmk 113.11 auṣarye sikatāstīrṇe tathaiva ca.

K

kaṃsa-kūṭa, see **kāṃsa**.

kaṃsa-doha, adj. Bhvr. (= Skt. kāṃsya-doha, also °syopadoha and °syopadohana; kaṃsa, *brass*, MIndic for kāṃsya, recorded in Skt. only Lex. and once in Lāṭy., pw; the pre-classical Skt. kaṃsa means *metal dish*; cf. Pali kaṃsūpadhāra DN ii.192.1, °raṇa AN iv.393.26, kaṃsupadhāraṇā Jāt. vi.503.17, inaccurately reported PTSD, all same mg.), *provided with brass milk-pails*, ep. of cows (like the Skt. and Pali equivalents): Gv 164.15 gosahasrāṇi ... kaṃsadohāni. See also next two.

kaṃsa-pātrī (see prec.), *brass bowl*: Mv ii.282.11; 412.8 (parallels to LV 318.22 **kāṃsa**-pātri, see **kāṃsa**). There are no doubt yet other cpds. of kaṃsa-.

kaṃsopadohinī, f. adj. Bhvr. (perhaps read °dohanī?), = prec. but one: Mv iii 458.11, read with one ms. ṣaṣṭiṃ dhenusahasrāṇi sarve kaṃsopadohinī (or °hanī? f. pl. of either °hin = °ha, or °hana, see under prec. but one); Senart em. wrongly.

Kakucchanda, Kakutsanda, °sunda, see s.v. **Krakucchanda.**

Kakuda Kātyāyana (= Pali Kakuda, Kakudha, or Pakudha, Kaccāyana or Kātiyāna; DPPN s.v. Pakudha), n. of one of the six famous heretical teachers of Buddha's day (see s.v. **Pūraṇa Kāśyapa**), named with the others: Mvy 3549; Mv i.253.13; 256.20; iii.383.16 (v.l. Kakuṭa); Divy 143.12; Av i.231.4.

Kakubha, n. of a deity (devaputra; living in a kakubha tree): Mv iii.313.10 ff.

kakkhaṭa, adj. (also **khakkhaṭa**, q.v.; both Skt. Lex., *hard*; = Pali kakkhaḷa, *hard, harsh, rough, cruel*), *cruel*, if reading of LaVallée-Poussin, JRAS 1911.1074, krūrāḥ kakkhaṭās (sattvāḥ), be adopted for SP 267.4 śaṭhakāḥ (sattvās). See next.

kakkhaṭa-tva, nt. (see prec. and **khakkhaṭatva**), *hardness*: Mvy 1842 v.l. for khak°; Śikṣ 245.2 (associated with pṛthivīdhātu; Bcṭ. 327.12 em. khakkha° in parallel); Mv i.339.16 (?) teṣāṃ kāye gurutvaṃ ca kharatvaṃ ca kakkhaṭatvaṃ (em.; mss. **kalkaṭa°**, q.v., or kaṭk°) ca upanipate.

kakkhaṭī (Skt. Lex., Trik., *chalk*), prob. *chalk*: Mvy 5940 (Tib. transliterates Skt.; follows sudhā, *plaster, mortar*).

kakhorda: Gv 214.6, m.c. for **kākhorda**, q.v.

kaṅkaṇikā = Skt. kiṅkiṇikā, *bell*: MPS 34.72,79, 85.

kaṅkara (once °**la**, once **kiṃkara**), m. or nt., a high number, acc. to LV 100 niyuta, but sometimes 100 **bimbara**, q.v.: m. (°raḥ) Mvy 7830 (cited from Gv); 8004; nt. (°ram) Mvy 7704; 7957 (cited from LV); Tib. in all gtams; LV 147.21; Gv 133.1 (kiṃkaram); Sukh 30.15 kaṃkarāṇi; gender undetermined SP 409.6; LV 151.3 Gv 105.19 (kaṅkala); 206.17.

Kaṅkālī (cf. Skt. Kaṅkālin, n. of a yakṣa; °linī, a form of Durgā), n. of a yoginī: Sādh 584.12; 589.15.

kaca, m., Mvy 5870, acc. to Tib. srin bal = *cotton* or *raw silk* (Chin. app. *cotton thread*); occurs in a list of textile materials.

Kacaṅgalā (= Pali Kajaṅgalā, °la), (**1**) n. of a town: Jm 113.22 °lāyāṃ, loc.; Av ii.41.5 f., id.; (**2**) n. of an old woman who lived in this town, who had been the mother of the Bodhisattva in former births and whom the Buddha initiated as a nun: Av ii.41.6 ff. (this is an embroidered form of the Pali story of the nun Kajaṅgalā, AN v.54 ff.); MSV i.20.4 ff.

kaccati (nt.? cited in this form, without ending; Mironov v.l. kacchati), *corslet* acc. to Tib., synonym of **kavacikā** (q.v.) which follows it in text: Mvy 6077.

kaccha (Skt. kakṣa, kakṣā, MIndic and Skt. Lex. kaccha, kacchā, at least in mgs. 1, 2), (**1**) *arm-pit*: Mv ii.124.3 kacchehi svedā muktā; (**2**) *hem of* (lower) *garment*: Mv iii.13.3 kaccham bandhitvā (Pali id.), *girding himself* (for action, by tying the undergarment at the waist); (**3**) in nikkaṭa-kacchā Mv ii.87.17 (see **nikkaṭa**), possibly *edge* (of a needle)? One expects the mg. *point*, but I find no evidence for it. The allegation that Pali kaccha means *arrow* (PTSD) seems unfounded.

Kacchapā, n. of a river: Māy 253.3. In list of rivers, placed between Narmadā and Payoṣṇī.

kacchāṭikā (Skt. Lex. id.; cf. Pkt. [called Deśī; Rambhāmañjarī] kacchaṭṭī, id.; deriv. of Skt. kakṣa *girdle*; *end of lower garment tucked in at the waist*), in Mvy 5851 = Tib. ske rags, ska rags, defined as *girdle*, prob. also *end of lower garment tucked in at the waist*. Next item is baddha-kakṣyaḥ 5852.

kacchāhāra (m. or nt.; cited in stem form, also in Mironov; v.l. in both edd. kacāhara), acc. to Tib. an *ornamental girdle*: Mvy 5854 = Tib. ska rags phu (Das pho) gu can (acc. to Das = Skt. kakṣa-hāra).

kacchula, adj. (cf. Skt. Lex. kacchura; AMg. kacchulla, printed kacchūlla in Ratnach.), *afflicted with itching* (kacchū), *with a skin-disease*: Mv ii.150.9; 152.3; 153.19; 156.12.

? **kajāva**, m. or nt., a high number: Gv 106.15 (°vasya, gen.); seems to correspond to **kaṣaca** or **kaṣava**, q.v.; cf. also **kalāpa**.

kañcu, perhaps to be read for **kāñcu**, q.v.

kañcuka, m., or °**kā**, f. (doubtless = Skt. kañcuka, also fem. °kī, *bodice*; *coat of armor*; *covering, sheath*; *skin of a snake*), *covering, downy coat* (of flowers): Mv i.236.9–10 = 241.3–4 (vss, but defective in meter) tāni ca karapramuktā surabhīṇi pañcavarṇo (? °ṛṇe? sc. flowers, strewn over Dīpaṃkara), saṃsthihati puṣpakañcuko bhagavato lokanāthasya; Av ii.68.6 (dārako jāto . . .) divyasumanaḥkañcukayā (so read for °kañcikayā) prāvṛtaḥ; 70.3 divyayā ca sumanasāṃ (mss. °syāṃ) kañcukayā prāvṛto; for kañcukā Speyer cites Tib. ral chuṅ, *fine hair*; Feer, *couvert d'un duvet de sumanā* (jasmine) *divin*.

kañcukīya, m. (defined in Skt. as *attendant in the harem*; see s.v. **kāñcukīya**), *eunuch* (?): Mv ii.432.17 varṣavarā kañcukīyā ca rājño nivedayanti; 433.3 varṣavarā kañcukīyā āha.

kaṭa, m. (also, in mg. 2, **kaṭā**?), (**1**) (in specialized application of Skt. kaṭa, *matting*, possibly paralleled in Skt. itself), *matting-screen* or *partition* (cf. late Skt. kaṭa = bhitti, Schmidt, Nachträge, s.v.): SP 72.6 (niveśanaṃ . . .) saṃśīrṇa-kuḍya-kaṭa-lepanam, *the* (ruined) *house had its walls, matting-screens* (or *partitions*), *and plaster destroyed*; 83.1 (vs) viśīrṇa kuḍyaṃ kaṭa lepanaṃ ca (of the same house); Laṅk 169.(10–)11 (list of things which, by intervening, frustrate knowledge of an object) kuḍya-kaṭa-vapra-prākāra- (etc.) -vyavahita- (Suzuki wrongly renders kaṭa *mountain*); (**2**) (= Skt. kaṭaka), some ornament, prob. *bracelet*: Divy 317.13 harṣa-kaṭa-keyūrāhārārdhahārādīn (all ornaments); 540.26 hastāt kaṭān (so text em., mss. kaṭām, implying acc. sg. of a fem. kaṭā) avatārya.

kaṭaka (nt.? cf. **-kāṭaka**, for which Mvy Index suggests reading kaṭaka), a kind of fetter or bond, presumably in form of a *ring*: Gv 353.12 (sattvān nānā-haḍi-)-nigaḍa-kaṭaka-kuṇḍala- (q.v.)-śṛṅkhalā-khalīna-bandhana-baddhān.

Kaṭaṅkaṭa, n. of a yakṣa: Māy 68.

kaṭaccha, and **kaṭacchaka** (m. or nt.), = **kaṭacchu(ka)**, q.v.: °ccha, Divy 165.18; °cchaka, Mmk 322.25.

kaṭacchu, m. or f., °**chuka** (once nt.) and °**chukā** (?), also °**cha** and °**chaka** (app. = Pali kaṭacchu, *spoon, ladle*; cf. Deśīn. 2.7 kaḍacchū, comm. ayodarvī), in most occurrences could be either *spoon* or *bowl*; it seems that Tib. and Chin. sources support mg. *bowl, vessel*; so Mvy 9013 kaṭacchuḥ, Tib. nal ze, which I do not find in Dictt., but nal may be connected with na li, *bowl, basin* (of iron or china, Jä.), while Chin. gives (1) *pillow* (often made of porcelain), or (2) *bowl, basin*; on Suv 86.3 and Mmk 65.2 Tib. is cited as snod, *vessel* (Mmk ap. Lalou, Iconographic, p. 84, line 11, who nevertheless translates *cuiller*, pp. 37, 44); in favor of mg. *spoon* may be cited (besides the Pali and Deśī words) Megh 310.10 sapta-dhūpa-kaṭacchukām utkṣiped ākāśe (hardly *bowlful*! if text is right acc. sg. f., but perhaps this represents °kān, acc. pl. m.); most commonly in cpds. preceded by dhūpa-, *incense-spoon* (? *-bowl*), generally as held in the hand by a painted image, dhūpa-kaṭacchuka-vyagra-hasta Mmk 65.2; 69.12, etc.; 322.25 (here °kaṭacchaka°); eka-dhūpa-kaṭacchu-hasta-parigṛhītān Suv 86.3; dhūpa-kaṭacchukam ādāya Divy 398.28–29; (dakṣiṇahaste) dhūpa-kaṭacchukaṃ (n. sg. nt.!) kartavyaṃ Kv 74.20; dhūpa-°ke dhūpaś copasthāpayitavyaḥ MSV iii.97.16; in Divy 165.18 acc. to Index *vessel*, but this seems less than certain, (Pūraṇaṃ, q.v., dharmaśāṭapraticchannaṃ) kaṭaccha-vrata-bhojanam (might mean *eating according to a vow of spoonfuls*, i. e. of limiting his food to a definite number of them, rather than *eating by a vow of the begging-bowl*). In Divy 475.21 kāṇḍa-kaṭacchu-pūra-kūrca-bhaiṣajya-sthavikāś is obscure to me at more than one point; the cpd. evidently lists articles pertaining to children, and either *spoon* or *bowl* is conceivable.

kaṭasī (= Pali id., °siṃ vaḍḍheti), *cemetery, place where unburied corpses are left*: Mvy 7105 = Tib. dur khrod (id.); 7419 °sī vardhitā; SP 48.4 (vs) kaṭasī ca vardhenti punaḥ-punas te (i. e. they die again and again; Pali also uses the word only with forms of this verb).

kaṭā, see **kaṭa**.

kaṭāhaka, m. or nt. (= AMg. kaḍāhaya; Skt. kaṭāha), *pot, caldron*: kaṭāhakā upasthāpitā(ḥ), nom. pl., Divy 404.28; °kam, nt., in śleṣma-k° Mvy 9019, and kheṭa-k° 9440, *spittoon* (both = Tib. mchil maḥi snod, *vessel for spittle*); śīrṣa-k° (= Pali sīsa-kaṭāha), lit. *head-caldron*, i. e. *skull*, LV 306.17. 18, °kān (acc. pl.); śroṇi-k°, see s.v. **śroṇi-kaṭāha(ka)**.

kaṭi, nt. (?), perh. *straw*, = **kuṭi** (q.v.), for which it is prob. a false reading: Divy 511.19.

[**kaṭīkṛta**, see **saṃkaṭī°**.]

kaṭikā, *chip, piece of wood* (as record): MSV i.4.9 ff. (= Tib. thur ma, = śalākā, Dutt).

kaṭuka (so Index, for text **kuṭaka**), m. or nt., *pool, pond*: Śikṣ 249.14 udapānaṃ vā kaṭukaṃ vā kūpaṃ vā puṣkariṇīṃ vā khānayet; Tib. renders ka° and puṣkar° both by rdziṅ, *pond*.

kaṭuka-taila, nt., acc. to Tib. = yuṅs (d)mar, *oil of mustard*: Mvy 5786; 9346. (Cf. Skt. kaṭuka, *pungent*, and n. of various plants.)

kaṭuṅka, var. for **khaṭ°**, q.v.

kaṭkāra, m. (so also Mironov; vv.ll. in the two edd. kadgara, kaṭkara, kaṅkara), some kind of bird: Mvy 4894, acc. to Tib. (one rendering) and Chin. = the prec. item, krakara, 4893, which in Skt. means a kind of *partridge*; cf. also Pali kakkara, said to mean *jungle-cock*; Tib. also bya baṅ, which acc. to Jä. means *night-hawk, goatsucker*; or *bat*.

kaṭṭati (corresponds to Pali kaḍḍhati, Skt. kṛṣ-; sometimes associated with forms of kṛṣ in BHS, see below; occurs also with cpds., ā-, ut-, o- (ava-), niṣ-, sam-; Senart reads always kaḍḍh-, but his mss. invariably kaṭṭ-

(except once or twice kaṭṭh-, doubtless a graphic variant); ākaṭṭati occurs also once in Megh; -kaḍḍh-, on the other hand, is recorded in SP, see s.vv. **ākaḍḍhana, vikaḍḍhate**), *draws, pulls; takes away, removes*: Mv i.217.7 (devīye nāvāyānena) kaṭṭīyantiye *while the queen was being drawn along by a boat*; ii.75.3 dvārato sapta padāṃ (acc. pl.) kaṭṭito, cf. line 5 sapta padāni apakarṣitvā; line 11 sapta padāni kaṭṭito; 241.18 tataḥ paṃjarehi (abl.) kaṭṭiyanti (birds); 429.15 (rājagṛhāto) kaṭṭiyamānī (see s.v. **ākaṭṭati**). Note that all these forms are passive.

? **kaṭṭāṃkriyati** (contains a form derived from **kaṭṭ-ati**, q.v., compounded with kriyati = °te; possibly read kaṭṭīkriyati with Senart's text), *is dragged, hauled away*: Mv ii.429.12, see **ākaṭṭati**.

kaṭhala, kaṭhalya, kaṭhalla, kaḍhalya, m. (in Pali only kaṭhala; not in Skt. or Pkt.), *gravel*, regularly assoc. with śarkara, *sand* or *pabbles*; kaṭhala noted only Divy 45.10 and Av i.64.3 (v.l. °lla); kaḍhalya only LV 39.22 (with all mss.), also v.l. LV 276.21; kaṭhaṇṇa erroneously printed for kaṭhalla Mmk 37.5; 525.20; kaṭhalya SP 144.9; Divy 155.24; LV 301.10; Mv iii.69.11; Av i.139.12; Karmav 79.4; kaṭhalla in the rest below; masc. wherever used as noun with generically distinctive forms, Mvy 5304 °llaḥ = Tib. gyo mo, *gravel*; Mv i.308.2 aśuci-pāṣāṇa-śarkara-kaṭhallā bhūmiṃ praviśanti; Mmk 525.20 kaṭhallaḥ (text °ṇṇaḥ) śarkarāṅgāraḥ; other substantival occurrences, Laṅk 268.3 tṛṇa-kāṣṭha-kaṭhalleṣu yathā māyā virājate (Suzuki transl. *bricks*, which is another mg. of Tib. gyo mo but surely inappropriate here); Mv i.15.10 macchā kaṭhalla-gatā (mss. kabhalla°) yathā, *like fish on gravel*; Karmav 79.4 (pṛthivyāṃ) śarkara-kaṭhalyādīni ... prādurbhavanti; usually in adj. cpds., especially apagata-pāṣāṇa-śarkara- (or °sark°) -kaṭh° Mv iii.79.18; 141.16; 255.9; Divy 45.10; 155.23–24; 441.12–13; 460.16; Av i.64,3; 76.2; 97.3–4; 107.10; 139.11–12; 144.11; SP 144.9; apagata-śarkara- (°sark°)-kaṭh° Mv iii.69.11; 266.9; LV 276.21; apagata-pāṣāṇa-kaṭh° (printed kaṭhaṇṇa)-bhasmāṅgāra- (etc.) Mmk 37.5; utsanna-śarkarākaṭh° Gv 328.25; ākīrṇa-śarkara- (°sark°) -kaṭh° LV 301.10; Gv 166.18–19; -śarkara-kaṭhallākīrṇāyāṃ (... dharaṇyāṃ) Gv 226.6.

kaṭhina, nt., (**1**) (= Pali id.), the rough cloth from which monks' robes were made: Mvy 8687; 9035; 9104; 9406 (= Tib. sra brkyaṅ); Prāt 490.10 uddhṛte (see **uddharati**) kaṭhine; cpds., kaṭhina-cīvara (= Pali id.), *a robe made of k. cloth*, Av ii.13.6; 18.1; kaṭhināstaraṇa, nt., Mvy 8685; °stāra, m. (so Mironov) or °stāraṇa, nt. (not in Mironov), Mvy 9407; °stara, MSV ii.152.9; all = Pali kaṭhinattharaṇa or °tthāra, *the ceremony of 'spreading out' or dedicating the kaṭhina*; kaṭhināstāraka, m., (*the monk*) *who superintends this ceremony*, Mvy 8686 (with Index); MSV ii.154.10 ff.; on the ceremony cf. SBE 17.148 ff. with notes; MSV ii.151 ff. (long description); (**2**) *hut* (of a caṇḍāla): Av ii.114.9 anyataracaṇḍāla-kaṭhinaṃ piṇḍāya praviṣṭaḥ; 114.13; 115.3 piṇḍapātam ādāya caṇḍālakaṭhinān nirgataḥ.

kaḍaṅgara, (**1**) nt. (= Skt. Lex. and late lit., Schmidt, Nachtr., defined as *straw*; AMg. id., *a kind of grass*, Ratnach.; Pali kaliṅgara, kaḷi°, defined in comms. as *stick of wood*), *stick of wood* (? the mg. *straw* would also be appropriate; something thrown away as worthless): Ud i.35 (kāyo 'yaṃ pṛthivīm adhiśeṣyati) ... nirastaṃ vā kaḍaṅgaram (same vs in Pali, Dhp. 41, kaliṅgaraṃ); (**2**) (= Pali Kāliṅga, Kal°) n. of an upāsaka in Nādikā: MPS 9.13.

kaḍatra (nt.; Skt. Lex., = **kalatra**, in its BHS sense, see s.v.), *family*: Bbh 18.12 sarvasattvāṃś ca kaḍatra-bhāvena parigṛhṇāti, *he cherishes* (or *adopts*) ... *as his own family*; °tra-bhāvena parigṛhītāḥ 192.1; (mātā-pitṛ-)putra-dārādi-kaḍatra- 310.15; sarva-gṛha-kaḍatra-bhogān (*house and family enjoyments*) utsṛjya ... pravrajya 331.23; kaḍatra-parṣatparigraham 349.4.

Kaḍambā (or °bakā? see ed. note), n. of a yakṣiṇī: Mahāsamāj 187.1 (Waldschmidt, Kl. Skt. Texte 4); corresp. to Pali Karumhā (Chin. Ka-da-m-ra).

kaḍiṃtala, m. (cf. Skt. Lex. kaḍitula), Mvy 6093, = Tib. ral gri dgu po, *crooked sword, scimitar*. Same form in Mironov; Kyoto ed. Index cites (as variants?) also kaḍitula, kaḍiṃtula, but neither ed. records them as variants in text.

kaḍevara, nt. (Divy 234.8; 383.18, the only cases where gender is clear; = Skt. kalevara), *cadaver, corpse*: Divy 39.11; 234.8; 383.18; Av ii.26.1; Śikṣ 208.12; Gv 157.13; Jm 45.18; 211.3 (here the ed. strangely emends to kale°!). Mvy 3933 reads kalevaram without v.l., but Mironov kaḍe°.

kaḍhalya, see **kaṭhala.**

kaṇa, m. (= Pali id.; app. not in this sense in Skt., where mg. is *kernel* etc.), *the red coating between the kernel and the husk of rice*: Mv i.343.19 tasya śālisya kaṇo ca tuṣo ca prādurbhavati. See also **akaṇa(ka), niṣkaṇa.**

kaṇaya or **kanaya** (m. or nt.; = Pali id.; on Skt. see below), some kind of weapon, said to be a kind of *spear* or *lance*; occurs only in long cpds. consisting of lists of weapons of all kinds: -kaṇaya- LV 305.9 (no v.l.); 306.14 (-kan°, v.l. -kanapa-); 317.15 (several good mss. -kanaya-); -kanaya- LV 218.12 (no v.l.). The form kaṇaya is recorded as v.l. for kaṇapa in some Skt. passages, BR 2.30, and twice without record of v.l. in late Skt., see Schmidt, Nachtr. The form kaṇapa is not very common in Skt. itself, see BR l.c. and pw; it is found Mbh.Cr. ed. 1.218.24 (Calc. 1.8257) and 3.83* (after 3.21.32 ab; Calc. 3.810 kaṇapa, Bomb. kanapa); no Mbh. ms. is recorded with ya for pa in either place. Yet it seems probable that the variation between y and p is purely graphic; Pali and BHS clearly support y, which even Skt. sometimes shows as v.l. for p and which may be the original (relatively very few occurrences are noted).

Kaṇima, or **Kanima**, n. pl., n. of a brahmanical school, of the Yajurveda (mentioned between the Kaṭhas and Vājasaneyins, and all called adhvaryavaḥ): Divy 633.5 Kaṇimā(ḥ), 6 Kanimā(ḥ) acc. to mss.

kaṇeruka (cf. Pali and Skt. Lex. kaṇeru, Skt. kareṇu), a kind of elephant: MPS 31.21.

kaṇṭaka, (**1**) see **pṛṣṭha-** (**°ṭhi-, °ṭhī-)kaṇṭaka**; (**2**) (nt.? = **kāṭaka**, q.v.), *ring* on which the alms-bowl is hung: Divy 227.29 (mudgāś) catvāraḥ pātre patitā ekaḥ kaṇṭakam āhatya bhūmau patitaḥ; 228.10 mudgaḥ pātra-kaṇṭakam āhatya bhūmau patitas; (**3**) in prākāra-k° Divy 578.18, perhaps *point, projection* (of a wall), i. e. a jutting *battlement* occupied by a guard: sā anyatamena puruṣeṇa prākārakaṇṭake sthitena ... gacchantī dṛṣṭā. (So Index.) See **kaṇṭhakāpāśraya.**

kaṇṭhaka, m. (**1**) as in Pali, alternative spelling for kaṇṭaka, *thorn*: SP 420.4; Mv i.91.16; Divy 350.8 °kān uddharati; see also next, and **pṛṣṭhi-kaṇṭhaka**; (**2**) n. of the Bodhisattva's horse (here as in Pali also Kanthaka, but rarely): Kaṇṭh° Mv i.154.6 ff.; ii.114.14; 159.13 ff.; 189.2 ff.; iii.120.4; 262.5; dies mourning for the B.'s departure, ii.190.9, and is reborn as a god of the same name, 11; LV 94.14; 95.11; 217.11; 221.8; 225.8 ff.; 228.17 ff.; spelling Kanthaka noted only Mvy 4772.

kaṇṭhakāpāśraya (= Pali kaṇṭakāpassaya; **kaṇṭhaka**, q.v., for kaṇṭaka), m. pl., (ascetics) *who lie on beds of thorns*: Divy 350.5, 7 (Index 'corrects' to kaṇṭa°).

kaṇṭha-guṇa, see **kaṇṭhe°.**

kaṇṭha-nāḍyā, see **-nāḍyā**; cf. next.

kaṇṭhanālikā (= Skt. °nālī, also °nāla; cf. prec.), *throat, gullet*: Mvy 3961.

kaṇṭhamaṇi (m. or f.; = Skt. Lex. id. only Trik.), *Adam's apple*: °ṇiḥ Mvy 3962.

kaṇṭhikā, *embrace*: Mv iii.258.10–11 Rāhulo dāni mātṛkaruṇakaṇṭhikāya (inst., *with a pathetic embrace of* *his mother*, i. e. putting his arms around her neck) yācati. In Skt. only *necklace*; AMg. kaṇṭhiyā (1) *necklace*, (2) *a part of a neck*, (3) *a cover of a book* (Ratnach.).

kaṇṭheguṇa, m., nt.; in MSV i.215.10 kaṇṭha° (= AMg. kaṇṭhe°, *a gold necklace*, Ratnach.), *an ornament for the neck*, made of a string of flowers: udārapuṣpāir āsakta- (mss. °puṣpāvāsakta-)-kaṇṭheguṇā(ḥ) Av i.163.8; esp. one made of karavīra flowers, placed (as in Pali) around the neck of a condemned criminal, karavīramālābaddha- (ii.182.6 °lāsakta-) kaṇṭheguṇo (°guṇaḥ; in i.102.8 mss. °kaṇṭhena, em. Speyer) Av i.102.8; ii.182.6 (said of a criminal); kaṇṭheguṇāni Mv ii.463.3 ff., repeatedly, so mss. always, Senart em. kaṇṭha°; kaṇṭheguṇena (mss.) Mv ii.168.9.

? **kaṇḍa**, m. or nt. (either false reading, as Senart assumes, or MIndic, = Pali id., for Skt. kāṇḍa), *arrow*: Mv ii.82.14, 15, mss. kaṇṭho, once kantho; 18 v.l. kaṇḍāto; Senart reads kāṇḍ- always, with both mss. ii.82.17; 83.8, and one in 82.18.

[**kaṇḍaka** SP 94.13, see **kuṇṭhaka**.]

[**kaṇḍarika**, v.l. for **kāṇḍ°**, q.v.]

kaṇḍita, ppp. (= AMg. kaṇḍiya, *pounded*; kaṇḍanta, pres. pple.; cf. Skt. kaṇḍīkaroti, *pounds*, Caraka; ultimately perhaps related to Skt. khaṇḍayati?), *pounded, crushed*: RP 44.10 (vs) dhik kaṇḍitasya tribhave nṛpa kāmarāgaḥ.

kaṇḍuka, kaṇḍu-kāra, see **kanduka**.

kaṇḍūsika, m. (so one var. in Mvy, others gaṇḍūśika, °mika; so also Mironov, v.l. °śika; note dental s!; MSV gaṇḍūṣa; cf. Pali kaṇḍusa, Vin. i.254.31; °saka 290.16, *a small piece of cloth sewn on as a mark or as a patch*), *patch* (on a monk's robe): Mvy 9193 = Tib. lhan pa klon pa (or gon pa), *a patch or patched garment*; MSV ii.159.4 gaṇḍūṣaṃ, nt.; 8 °ṣa-cīvareṇa.

[**kata-** in kata-puṇyo Mv i.198.17 is prob. only a misprint for kṛta-, since it is not mentioned in Senart's notes nor listed in his Index. If correct it would be MIndic for kṛta-; cf. Pali katapuñña.]

katamatra, loc. adv., used instead of loc. sg. fem. of katama, *which*?: Mv ii.72.17–18 °tra kanyāye kumārasya cakṣu (n. pl.) nipatanti, *on which girl . . .*?

katamad-vidha, adj. (katamad- as grammatical stem seems to be unrecorded), *of what kinds*?: LV 383.5 (prose) °dhaiḥ pātraiḥ . . . pratigṛhītam.

katara, pron. adj. (see also **katira**; cf. **anyatara**; used in this way sometimes in Pali and apparently even in Skt., where however the cases are rare and not always certain), *which* (of more than two)?: Divy 102.17; 308.8; 371.23 kataraḥ (of several) kumāro . . . rājā bhaviṣyati; Śikṣ 75.4; KP 97.4 kataraṃ (cited Śikṣ 233.15 as katarat) cittaṃ; MSV iii.136.10 (read kataraṃ tat), 12. In LV 239.15 (Ārāḍasya dharmo . . .) na niryāti tat-katarasya samyagduḥkhakṣayāya, and Mv ii.119.5 (nāyaṃ) Ārāḍasya dharmo niryāti tat-katarasya (so mss.) samyagduḥkhakṣayāye, could at best (but implausibly) be taken to mean *A.'s religion does not result in the complete destruction of the misery of anyone*. But Senart emended to tat-karasya, *of (for) the one who performs it* (sc. Ā.'s religion), which is confirmed by Tib. on LV de byed pa, *one who has done that*. It is indeed strange to find the same corruption in both texts; but the em. seems quite certain; it is confirmed by Pali takkarassa DN i.235.17; MN i.68.12, in a quite similar phrase; and in a close parallel Mv ii.120.16 one ms. reads tatkarasya (the other corruptly taktenasya).

katima, adj. (= Pali id., M. kaima; not derived from kati (PTSD), but = Skt. katama modified to -ima, see § 22.16), *which* (of more than two)?: Kv 80.5, read: katimāḥ ṣaṭ kleśā(ḥ), *which are the six impurities*? (text kati māṣāḥ kleśā). See next.

katira, adj. (= **katara**, q.v., but like it used in ense of katama; in form based on atima, q.v. by analogy of tara: tama forms), *which* (of many)?: Suv 60.4 (vs; read with mss., after 3 paśyāhi . . . eta dharmān), katiro 'tra sattvas tatha pudgalo vā, *which among these* (dharmas) *is the creature, or the person too*? Nobel em. katir atra; kati is, however, not used as sg., and all mss. read -ro.

katīya, adj. (from kati, with suffix īya, cf. dvitīya, tṛtīya, and tadīya etc.), *amounting to how much*?: Karmav 70.10 °yaṃ mahārāja gṛhapater dravyaṃ gṛhītam. (There is a v.l. kevatī; cf. **kevatika**).

katuṅka, v.l. for **khaṭ°**, q.v.

kathaṃkathā (= Pali id.), *doubt*: °thā mahya na bhūya kācit SP 61.7 (vs); °thām āpannāḥ SP 71.3; vicikitsā-k° SP 33.12; Divy 84.9; Mmk 495.17; nirvicikitsās tīrṇa-k° Sukh 59.16; avitīrṇa- (so Senart em., mss. °cīrṇa-)-k°, *not having got rid of doubt*, Mv iii.445.21; krodho mṛṣāvāda ka° ca Mv iii.214.8 (vs); vigata-ka°, *freed from doubt*, SP 70.11–12; Mv iii.61.7; 62.12; 201.12; Divy 617.14; chinna-ka° Gv 30.16. See next.

kathaṃkathin, adj. (= Pali id.; to prec.), *having doubts*: ŚsP 1453.2 na °thī bhaviṣyati; SP 35.4 (vs) °thī (n. pl.; v.l. °thā) vicintentā; MSV i.274.3.

kathaṃkara, adj. (= Pali id.; cf. **evaṃkara**), *acting how*?: Mv i.284.17; iii.212.12 (mss. corrupt); 372.21 kathaṃkaro prajñāvāṃ bhoti . . .

kathatva (nt.; to katham, with -tva; cf. Skt. kathaṃtā, rare), *how-ness, manner*: Gv 526.23 (prose) dharmadhātu - prakṛti - kathatvāyatana - m - ucitatvān na kṣaṇyante sarvaviṣayeṣu (bodhisattvāḥ); -ucitatvān can only be construed as part of preceding cpd. (m 'Hiatus-bridger'); the text seems rather suspicious.

? **katha**, m. = Skt. kathā, *talk*: SP 283.13 (vs) upasaṃharec citrakathān bahūṃś ca, so all Nep. mss.; Kashgar rec. °kathāṃ bahuṃvidhāṃ, which perhaps read; both edd. em. °kathā bahūś ca.

kathāpuruṣa, m., *narrator, teller of the story* (of the dharma or the like): Gv 528.(9–)10 (daśadik)sarvalokadhātuṣu kathāpuruṣo Mañjuśrīḥ; -tva, *state of being a ka°*: Gv 417.(23–)24 (sa tasya bhagavato dharmacakraṃ pratīcchitavān saṃdhāritavān kathāpuruṣatvaṃ ca kārayām āsa.

kathāvastu, nt. (= Pali °vatthu), *theme* or *essence of the story, argument*: Mvy 7674 = Tib. gtam gyi gzhi, *basis of the story*.

kathika (m., = Skt. Lex. id.; Pali id. only at end of cpds., chiefly in dhammakathika = BHS **dharmakathika**, q.v.), *speaker, expounder*: RP 28.7 (vs) bahuśrutaḥ kathika-śreṣṭhaḥ.

-kathin, adj. ifc. (Skt. kathā plus -in; = Pali id., ifc.), *speaking, declaring*: LV 363.11 (vs) satyāsatyakathī, n .sg.

kathina, adj. (= Skt. kaṭhina), *hard*: -śilavat °nāntarātmā LV 158.5, so all mss. acc. to Lefm.; Calc. kaṭh°.

kathyāyitta, m. (v.l. kathya°; so Mironov, same v.l.), Mvy 3814, acc. to Chin. *messenger*; Tib. pho ña (*messenger*) raṅ rta (? see s.v. **kāṣṭhikavitta**). The preceding word is dūta.

kadarya, adj. (Skt. *stingy*, and so Pali kadariya), perh. *evil, wicked* (of persons): °ya-tapanā ghorā Mv iii.454.15 = (so read also) i.9.16; see P. Mus, La Lumière des six voies, 95 f. The mg. assumed by Mus is attributed by Wilson to Skt. kadarya.

? **kadākhya** (so Skt. Lex., nt., a name for the kuṣṭha plant), a name of some plant: Mv ii.86.11 (vs) yato yavā kadākhyā (Senart's em., mss. kadāyā, kaṭhāyā) ca kovidārā ca phullitā. Very uncertain.

kadācikāt, adv. (= kadācit, formed on the model of noun-adj. formations in suffix ka; see Edgerton, JAOS 31.113, § 37), *now and then*: Mmk 340.12 (vs) bhavet kadācikāt siddhiḥ. Is there quasi-diminutive force here, *barely now and then, less than frequently*? Or possibly the extra syllable only m. c.?

kadgara, var. for **kaṭkāra**, q.v.

kanaka, m. (in Skt. *gold*, only nt.), (**1**) *gold*: LV 165.9 dhana-maṇi-kanakāḥ, acc. pl., all mss. and Calc. (Lefm. em. °kā); (**2**) = **Kanakamuni**, q.v.; (**3**) n. of a nāga king: Māy 247.1.

Kanakajālakāyavibhūṣita, n. of a Bodhisattva: Gv 442.9.

kanaka-tāla (m. or nt.; cf. Skt. kāṃsya-tāla, a kind of cymbal), a kind of cymbal, *gold-cymbal*: Mv i.172.12 (vs) jinavācā kanakatāla-patra-(ravā, Senart's em., mss. vadārā or vaddārā).

Kanakanāgarājateja(s), (v.l. om. rāja) n. of a former Buddha: Mv i.140.9 °jaḥ, nom.

Kanakaparvata, n. of a former Buddha: Mv i.114.6.

Kanakaprabha (?), n. of a prince (form uncertain, see Nobel's note): Suv 52.8 (vs).

Kanakabimbābha, n. of a Buddha: Mv i.123.15.

Kanakabhujendra, n. of a prince: Suv 52.8 (vs).

Kanakamaniparvataghoṣa, n. of a Tathāgata: Gv 311.16.

Kanakamaṇiparvatatejobhadra, n. of a Tathāgata: Gv 311.11–12.

Kanakamuni, (Tib. gser thub, *gold muni*), also **Kanaka** (Mmk 130.4, prose, Kanakādyais tathāgatair; Laṅk 365.5, with **Krakucchanda** and **Kāśyapa**), Kanakāhvaya (*the one named Kanaka*, LV 281.14; 283.17, with the same two others), in Mmk 68.27 text corruptly Kabakagrani; in Mv Kanakamuni i.294.20; 318.13 (in the former with the prefix **Bhāna-** or **Bhāma-**, q.v., acc. to text), but otherwise in Mv only **Konākamuni** (or **Koṇ°**; Senart usually gives n, but see his Introd. to i p. xiv f.; also Konāka-nāmo, nom. sg., ii.300.4; 336.8, and Konākasāhvayo ii.401.7); this form occasionally in other texts, Mmk 426.9 in a confused list also containing the other form (Kanakamuni, Kāśyapa, Krakutsanda, Śikhin, Viśvabhu, Konākamuni!), also Laṅk 29.1 = 142.14; Māy 227.17 (but Kanakamuni Laṅk 141.9; Māy 250.10, and Kanaka Laṅk 365.5); Konāgamuni Karmav 97.1, 5 (but Kanakamuni 71.21; and so v.l. 97.1, 5; same vs in Pali Therīg. 518, Koṇāgamana) = Pali Koṇāgamana or Konā° (even in late Pali, Buddhavaṃsa comm. 213.14, acc. to DPPN, the form Kaṇakāgamana is used in a popular etymology of the name; doubtless Koṇāka or Koṇāga- was original), Aśokan Konākamana, n. of a former Buddha, next but one before Śākyamuni, preceding **Kāśyapa** and following **Krakucchanda**, qq.v.; often mentioned with these two, see list of passages s.v. **Krakucchanda**; mentioned alone, besides some passages cited above, Av ii.34.11.

Kanakameghapradīpadhvajā, n. of a lokadhātu: Gv 8.20.

Kanakarāśi, n. of a former Buddha: Mv i.140.11.

Kanakavatī, n. of a lokadhātu: Gv 82.8.

Kanakavarṇa, n. of a king, previous birth of the Buddha: Divy 291.5 ff.; °varṇāvadāna, nt., n. of Divy chap. xx, Divy 298.23.

Kanakavimalaprabha: Gv 297.15, or **°vimalaprabhāvyūha**: Gv 296.7 (both prose): n. of a lokadhātu.

Kanakākṣa, n. of a former Buddha: Mv i.138.6.

Kanakāvatī, n. of the capital city of Kanakavarṇa: Divy 291.11; 294.28.

Kanakāhvaya = **Kanakamuni**, q.v.

kanaya, see **kaṇaya**.

Kanima, see **Kaṇima**.

(**Kaniṣka**, n. of the celebrated emperor; predicted as future incarnation of a boy seen making stūpas: MSV i.2.3.)

kantārika, m., Mvy 9036 = Tib. gzar thag, or bzar thag, *peg-cord* (cord fastened to pegs on a wall, to hang clothes on, Das); Chin. *cord for hanging clothes*.

Kanthaka, see **Kaṇṭhaka** (2).

kanthā, (**1**) (= Skt. Lex. id.) *wall*: MSV iv.74.2; (**2**) n. of a town: MSV i.xvii.11.

kandaraka (m. or nt.; = Skt. °ra; -ka prob. m.c.), *cave*: Samādh 19.28 (vs) ye vanakandarake 'bhiramanti.

kandalī-chinna, adj. (m.), ? Mvy 8797; **°nna-ka**, id., MSV iv.68.14; Chin. *one who is in debt*; Tib. gtaḥ (=*pledge, pawn*) gam(s) pa (? perhaps to ḥgam pa, one mg. of which acc. to Jä. is *to threaten, menace*). A kind of person who should not be initiated into the order; seems possibly to correspond to Pali kaṇḍara-chinna, Vin. i.91.10, interpreted as *one the tendons of whose feet are cut*.

kanduka, and **kandu-kāra(ka)**, or (vv.11.) kaṇḍu°, m. (presumably from Skt. kandu, AMg. id. or kaṇḍu, *iron pan*), an artisan of some sort, presumably *maker (seller) of iron pans*; only in nom. pl. in long lists of persons of various occupations: Mv iii.113.9 kaṇḍukā(ḥ), v.l. kandrukā; 442.14 mss. kandukā(ḥ), Senart em. kaṇḍ°; 443.2 kandu-kārakā(ḥ), v.l. kaṇḍukāro (intending °rā).

Kandha, n. of a yakṣa: Mv iii.328.2 (lives in Gandhapura, which suggests the possible emendation Gandha, or vice versa; but no v.l. in mss.).

kanyakubjaka, adj., *of* (the city) *Kanyakubja*: Mv ii.460.12 (prose) Mahendrakasya kanyakubjakasya Madrakarājño dhītā.

[**kapaḍa-**, error for **kavaḍa-**(chedaka), q.v.]

Kapardin, n. of a nāga: Mmk 454.15.

kapāṭa, in LV 376.13 (vs), to be read approximately: nīvaraṇa-kapāṭāś ca pañca mayehā pradāritā sarve, perh. *all the five doors* (gates, as obstacles) *of the hindrances have been cleft by me here*. Note however that AMg. kavāḍa = kapāṭa is a homonym of kavāḍa = kapāla; I suspect that the latter is really meant here (falsely Sktized), in some such sense as *hard shells*.

? **kapāpikā** (var. kaṣāyikā, which is read by Mironov with vv.ll. kapāyikā, °vikā), *felt*: Mvy 5863 (= **namata**, q.v., Tib. ḥphyiṅ ba).

kapāla-koṭanī (cf. **koṭayati, ā-ko°**), with vidyā, the art of *knocking on the skull* of a dead person and predicting his future fate (in Pali chava-sīsa-manta, DPPN): MSV ii.80.8.

kapāla-mocanī (once **kapālī°**) vidyā, a prized aspect of surgical art: MSV ii.26.6 (here kapālī°), 7, 9; 30.17 ff.; it involves opening a man's skull and extracting an insect (prāṇaka), which caused a disease (kapāla-vyādhi, 30.18), see 31.6 ff., also 33.12 (a centipede is thus removed).

Kapālinī, n. of a goddess: Sādh 502.6.

kapi-citta, adj. (= Pali id.), *'monkey-minded', fickle*: in LV 178.20 (vs) read, kapicittā 'ryapathe sthapeṣya haṃ, *I shall establish the fickle ones in the noble path*. Not only Tib. but a BHS ms. reported by Foucaux (Notes p. 139 l. 2) supports kapi-, and the Pali form confirms it.

kapittha, m. (Skt. id., *the wood-apple tree*, and nt. its fruit), in Mvy 5041 in a list of (colors and) articles used in painting, dyeing, etc.; perhaps the fruit, or some other product of the tree, used in some such way. Tib. transliterates.

Kapitthaka, m. or nt., n. of an āśrama on the Godāvarī river where Śarabhaṅga took residence: Mv iii.363.2. In Pali Sarabhaṅga lived in Kapiṭṭhavana on the Godāvarī.

? **Kapinahya** (nt.; v.l. °naptaṃ or °najyaṃ, read °nāṭyaṃ? cf. Pali Kapinaccanā, DPPN), n. of a caitya in or near Vaiśālī: Mv i.300.10.

Kapila, n. of a yakṣa (in Skt. of a nāga, inter alia): Suv 161.13 (vs; Piṅgala-Kapilas, text, supported by Tib. acc. to Nobel, but most mss. Piṅgala alone, without K., and the one which has K. reads Piṇḍola-Kapilas; one name or two?); Māy 15, 30, 53; 235.12.

Kapilapura, nt.: = next: LV 243.2 (vs).

Kapilavastu (or °vāstu), nt. (= Pali Kapilavattnu); see also prec., and **Kapilasāhvaya, Kapilāhvaya**; n. of the city in which Śākyamuni Buddha was born: its foundation, with explanation of the name (the Śākya princes founded it on the site of the hermitage of the ṛṣi Kapila with his permission), Mv i.351.19 ff.; spelling °vāstu (rare and dubious) Mvy 4118 (but Mironov °vastu); Divy 67.3 (text, but not repeated thus in Index; °vastu 90.30; 390.26); best ms. of Av °vāstu ii.98.5 ff., several times, and 111.7 (here acc. sg. in ms. °vāstum, Speyer em. °vastu; foll. by vowel, m hiatus-bridger? prose), but usually °vastu in Av, as i.345.6, 12, etc.; °vastu otherwise, SP 311.2; LV 26.13 etc., very common here and in Mv (see Indexes), also in Gv, e. g. 222.26 ff., and elsewhere.

Kapilavāstavya, adj., *of Kapilavastu*: Mv iii.101.17 sarve °vyāḥ Śākyā; 113.12 sarve ca °vyā śilpāyatanā.

Kapilasāhvaya, = **Kapilāhvaya**, q.v. (Kapilavastu): LV 54.12 (vs) °yaṃ puraṃ (perh. m.c.).

Kapilā, (1) n. of a kiṃnara maid: Kv 6.5; (2) n. of a rākṣasī: Māy 240.7; 243.8.

Kapilāṅga = Kapila, the 'Sāṃkhya' philosopher: Laṅk 334.13 °go 'pi durmatiḥ (Suzuki 'the school of Kapila', but I know of no such use of aṅga; the word is clearly an epithet of the man himself, *'tawny-bodied'* = 'Tawny').

Kapilāhvaya, usually as adj. with pura or nagara, (the city) *named Kapila*(-vastu), cf. **Kapilasāhvaya**; °ye pure LV 28.3; °ye mahāpuravare LV 48.22; 59.18 (both prose), etc.; without noun accompaniment, e.g. LV 47.19 (vs), read °ya taṃ (text °yataṃ); common also elsewhere, as Mv (see Index); also SP 312.15 (vs), and other texts.

Kapiṣṭhalāyana (mss. Kapiṣṭhil°), m. pl., n. of a brahmanical gotra (= Skt. Kapiṣṭhala): Divy 635.22.

? **kapīdaka**, see **kamībala**.

kapoṭa-mālā (v.l. °malā; Mironov kapota-malā, but most of his mss. ° mālā, no report of kapoṭa-; cf. however AMg. kavoḍa = kapota, *pigeon*), Mvy 9345 = Tib. stegs bu, *stand, board, table*, but also *'a turret where sparrows make their nest'*, Das; Chin. *platform-foundation*; Jap. *place where droppings of doves* (qy: reading -malā?) *accumulate*, also, *where doves perch in rows; upper part of a pagoda*.

Kapphiṇa or °na or other vv.ll., see below (see also **Mahā-ka°**; = Pali Kappina or Mahā-ka°, the only forms noted DPPN), n. of one of Buddha's disciples: MSV i.266.5 ff. (Brāhmaṇa-K°); Kapphiṇa SP 207.4 (vv.ll. °na, Kaphiṇa, Kasphiṇa); Av ii.102.1 ff. (no v.l.); Kapphina, text, SP 2.4 (vv.ll. Kaphina, Kaṃphina, Kaphilla, Kaphiṇḍa); Kaphila LV 1.14 (no v.l. in Lefm., but Tib. Ka-pi-na); Kaphiṇa Mmk 64.11.

kapyāri, m. or f., °riḥ Mvy 3841, following **kalpikāra**, q.v., and similarly defined in Tib.; Chin *male or female slave*. Appears to be Sktization of MIndic form representing **kalpikāra** or °**rin** (something like *kappiyāri).

kaphalikā (prob. = **kabhalli-**, q.v.), Mvy 9012, *pot* (? in the shape of a skull); Chin. *cooking-pot*; Tib. = slaṅ, sla ṅa, defined as *a large iron pan for roasting grain*.

Kaphiṇa, see **Kapphiṇa**.

kaphin (= Skt. Lex. id.), *characterized by phlegm, foam* (one of the bodily humors): Mmk 146.22; 147.1, 7 etc. °ne, dat.

Kaphina, Kaphila, Kaphilla, see **Kapphiṇa**.

kabhalli- (? last akṣara uncertain; cf. **kaphalikā**, and AMg. kabhalla, *skull*, which Pischel 208 connects via *kaphāla with Skt. kapāla), in ka°-tāpa, a form of torture in hell: Śikṣ 80.11 (vs) °tāpān atha dhūmagārān (... pādasya cārcchanti hi kāmadāsā iti); Bendall and Rouse *boiling tortures of the skull*; perhaps rather, *boiling in pots* (so named from their resemblance to a skull in shape). The AMg. suggests em. to kabhalla-.

kama (m.c. for MIndic kamma, Skt. karma-n), *action, rite*: read veda-kamāpanītam (= vedakarma-apa°) Dbh.g. 29(55).2, with Rahder (see note), for text °karmā° (unmetr.).

Kamaṇḍaluka, n. of a nāga king: Mv iii.327.20; lived at **Lohitavastuka**; entertained Buddha.

amara (nt.? gen. °rasya), a high number: Gv 106.14 (follows **kamala**. q.v.); in position corresponds to **agava**, q.v.

kamaraka, m., *purse*: MSV i.252.19 (in place of **nakulaka** 2 of Divy 133.23, same passage, and MSV i.241.8).

kamala, (1) nt., a high number: Mvy 7775; 7904 (the latter cited from Gv); Gv 106.14 (see **kamara**); 133.24; (2) m., n. of a mleccha king: Mmk 621.25.

Kamaladalavimalanakṣatrarājasaṃkusumitābhijña, n. of a Buddha in a distant lokadhātu: SP 423.5 ff.

Kamaladhara, n. of a former Buddha: Mv i.141.4.

Kamalākara, name of a certain laudation (stava) of 'all the Buddhas': Suv 45.1, 5 (ch. IV, entitled Kamalākaraparivarta); 51.9 (but here text corrupt); 54.14.

Kamalākṣa, n. of a former Buddha: Mv i.137.7.

Kamaloṣṇīṣa, n. of one of the 8 Uṣṇīṣa-rājānaḥ (see **uṣṇīṣa** 3): Mmk 41.11.

? **kamībala**, m. or nt., a kind of tree: MSV i.286.10 (so text; but Tib. cited as ka-pi-da-ka; cf. Skt. kapītaka, pw).

? **Kampila**, n. of a disciple of Buddha: Sukh 2.8; so 1 ms. only; one Karmira; two omit the name; possibly = Pali Kimbila?

Kampilla, nt. (= Pali id.; MIndic for Skt. kāmpilya), n. of a city of the Pañcālas: Mv i.283.11 ff.; iii.26.20; 34.3, 5 etc.; 158.6; 160.8 etc.; 361.16 ff. Cf. s.v. **Kāmpillaka** (v.l. Kam°).

kambuka, m. or nt. (= Skt. and Pali kambu), *a shell-bracelet*, forbidden monks to wear: MSV ii.95.7, 15; orig. was prob. kañcuka (as Skt.) with Pali Vin. i.306.27.

Kambugrīvā, n. of a piśācī: May 238.20.

kamboja (cf. **Kāmbojī**), m. or f. pl., designation of a class of malevolent supernatural beings: Mmk 17.4 (prose) (vetāḍā) mahāvetāḍā kambojā mahākambojā bhaginyo mahābhaginyo etc.

kambojaka, adj., *of* (the land) *Kamboja*: Mv ii.185. 12, 17 (vs) °kā aśvavarā sudāntā.

kambhākṛta, see **skambhā°**.

-kara (m. or nt.; apparently related to Skt. and Pali kaṭaka; also **karaka**; see next), *ring* on which the alms-bowl is fastened; only in pātra-kara-vyagra-hasta: Divy 48.21; 159.9; 281.24; Av i.347.10.

karaka, (1) = prec., in same cpd.: Divy 37.1–2; 341.29; Av i.3.5; Speyer, Index, takes kara(ka) in this cpd. as = Skt. and Pali karaka, *water-pot*, but see s.v. **kāṭaka**, which may be related (in cpd. pātra-k°), and even if not related, seems to disprove Speyer; (2) (= AMg. karaga; in Skt. kāraka, not karaka, is used in this sense, as also in Pali) *doer, one who does*: LV 340.4 (vs) karaka-vedaka-vītivṛttāḥ (most mss. kāraka, unmetr.); Dbh.g. 27(53).11 karak'apeta, *without a doer*; in view of Dbh 49.6 (prose) kāraka-vedaka-virahita, the short *a* is prob. m.c. despite the following, all from prose, where to be sure the word is adjectival, *making, producing*: bodhi-karakair dharmaiḥ Av i.69.12; 75.4 etc.; bodhisattva-karakair dharmaiḥ Av i.86.15.

Karakaṇḍa, °**ḍaka**, (= Pali id., also Karaṇḍu, Karakaṇḍu, etc., DN i.92.18, comm. i.258.21), n. of a son of King Sujāta Ikṣvāku: Mv i.348.11 (°ḍaka, v.l. °ḍuka); 352.9 (here Senart Karaṇḍaka, with one ms., a form known in Pali mss.; v.l. Kacakaṇḍaka); also of a later descendant, i.352.11, both °ḍa and °ḍaka.

karakandikara, m., ? ep. of Buddha: Mv iii.269.4 (vs) śrāvakayugaṃ daśabalo āmantraye karakandikaro. Senart can do nothing with it; neither can I; I have thought of divaṃkara-karo, corrupted and metathetized, *sun-rayed*, cf. Pali divaṃkara = divākara, but it does not yield the meter required.

Karakarṇin (cf. Karakarṇa, BR s.v.?), n. of a man: Mvy 3663.

karakiṇī (cf. Skt. and Pali karaka, *water-pot*), *some* *kind of vessel* or *bottle*, app. for carrying water: Mvy 9386 (said to be synonym of kuṇḍikā, 9387) = Tib. ril ba spyi (phyi) blugs, *gourd-shaped bottle* (Das); Chin. *bottle for* (water for) *washing clean hands.*

karaṅka, nt. (in Skt. *skull*; in JM. *skeleton, heap of bones*, also *bone* in general), *skeleton* or *heap of bones*: Mv iii.297.1 sarvaṃ khāditaṃ, asthikaraṅkāni avaśeṣīkṛtāni; 14 hasti-karaṅkāni cāśvakaraṅkāni ca; 16 karaṅkāny evāvaśeṣitāni; 298.1, 2; LV 174.4 (vś; text doubtful, cf. citation Śikṣ 204.14, and Lefm.'s Crit. App.), read probably: yatha śvāna karaṅka (n. pl.) śavair amukhā (?); LV 207.7 (prose) (iha te bālā) adhyavaśitāḥ (read °sitāḥ) kukkurā ivāsthikaraṅkamadhye.

karañjaka? (Mv ii.470.8, mss.), see s.v. **kalandaka.**

karaṇā (cf. **karaṇī**; both = Skt. karaṇa, nt.), *means, cause*: LV 434.2, repeated 3–4, sarva-sāṃkleśikāntarāyika-dharmāntarāya-karaṇā-nirvāṇasye 'ti (both times one ms., a different one each time, with Calc. °karaṇa-).

karaṇī (cf. **karaṇā**, q.v., and **kāraṇī**), *means, cause*: LV 432.2–3 (twice in one long cpd.) -muditā-prāmodya-karaṇī- (only Calc. °karaṇa-; one ms. °karī-)-snigdha-madhura-ślakṣṇa-hṛdayaṃgamā-sarvendriya-prahlāda-karaṇī-(so all mss., only Calc. °ṇa-)-samyagvākya-samyak-prayogatvād.

karaṇīya (nt.; = Pali id.; rare in Skt., but cf. pw 2.297), *affair, business, duty* (*thing to be done*, fundamentally gdve.): deva-karaṇīyeṣu Mv i.32.12 (gods occupied) *in affairs, matters of business, of the gods*; see **sa-karaṇīya**; prob. here also cakṣu-karaṇīyā Mv iii.331.8, 10, 15, jñāna-kar° 11 (of the madhyamā pratipadā), *having insight* (knowledge) *as its business*, i. e. *cause of insight* (knowledge); in Pali parallels cakkhu-karaṇī, ñāna-karaṇī.

karaṇḍaka, nt., in cīvara-k° Mvy 9379, would naturally be taken as *box* (for monk's robe), as in normal Skt. and Pali. So one Tib. version (sprog, or dprog). But another Tib. version is sgrog, *cord*, and Das cites the cpd. chos gos kyi sgrog ma, *strings or bands for fastening a religious robe*, giving the Skt. as cīvara-karaṇḍaka. Corruption in Tib.? See Jäschke's Grammar 8: pr = Skt. ṭ, gr = Skt. ḍ. The Chin. rendering of Mvy gives *cord*, with the second Tib. (Note: on Karaṇḍaka-nivāpa see s.v. **Kalandaka-n°**.)

karati, see Chap. 43, s.v. kṛ.

[? **karada**, m., *small bit*: mss. at Divy 290.23 apaścimaḥ karadaś carama ālopaḥ; ed. em. kavaḍaś, doubtless rightly, as in same phrase 298.5 where mss. kavaḍaś. Pali (tiṇa-)karala (°ḷa), perhaps *wisp* or *bundle* (of grass), is not likely to be concerned here.]

karanta? (Mv ii.470.9, mss.), see s.v. **kalandaka.**

Karandaka-nivāpa (m.), = **Kalandaka-ni°**, q.v.: Av i.107.5 (no v.l.); ed. Divy 143.1, but with only 1 ms., 3 mss. kal°; for other cases of v.l. Karandaka-, and even Karaṇḍaka-, see s.v. **Kala°**.

karapattrikā (= Skt. °pattra and Lex. °pattraka), *saw*: Divy 31.4 °pattrikayā catasraḥ khaṇḍikāḥ kṛtāḥ.

karaphu, m. or f. (nom. °phur), a high number: LV 148.5, cited Mvy 7967 (from LV); = Tib. lag sbyin, *hand-giving*; acc. to ed. note in Mvy, Chin. points to **karabha**, q.v.; most LV mss. kalahu.

karabha, m., a high number: Mvy 8020 = Tib. ḥod mdzes, *beautiful light.*

karama, nt. (= **kalama**, q.v.), *reed* (*-pen*, for writing): Kv 69.16 (bhūrjaṃ na saṃvidyate na masiṃ na) karamaṃ; 69.17.

karaviṅka, m. (in mg. = Pali karavī, °vīka; in form blend of this with **kalaviṅka**, q.v., which in Skt. = *sparrow*), *the Indian cuckoo*, proverbial for its sweet voice; LV 323.19 °ka-rutena svareṇa; 338.3 (vs) °ka-ruta-svareṇā: Mv ii.415.3 (vs) °ka-kokilā; KP 84.1 °ka-potaka(ḥ, n. sg.).

(**karavīra** = Skt. id., *oleander-flower*; for its use in making garlands for criminals, as in Pali, see s.v. **kaṇṭheguṇa.** Cf. next.)

karavīrikā = prec.: Mmk 720.20 (prose) °kāṃ.

karāḍa (cf. karāla?), a kind of elephant: °ḍa-hastin MPS 31.21.

karāpayati, see § 38.53.

Karāla, n. of a yakṣa: Māy 97.

Karāladantī, n. of a rākṣasī: Māy 243.33.

Karālikā, n. of a yoginī, = **Karālī**: Sādh 589.15 (vs; prob. m.c. -kā).

Karālī, n. of a yoginī (cf. prec.): Sādh 584.12; name of a piśācī: Māy 238.20; n. of a rākṣasī: Māy 243.15.

? **karikāra** (-dharma), ? Mv ii.384.14 (vs) dharmaṃ karitvā karikāradharmaṃ ārogyaprāpto care sarvalokaṃ (mss., ed. em. °ke); said of one who is thus rewarded for having decorated a caitya. I am as unable to interpret or emend the form as Senart was.

-kariṇa, adj. or subst. ifc., *doing* or *one who does*: Mmk 57.2 pañcānantarya-kariṇasyāpi, *even of a doer of the five deadly crimes* (see **ānantarya**). (JM. kariṇa = Skt. karin, *elephant*; MIndic for Skt. karin, which is recorded in this sense only once from Kāś. in pw, and nowhere else in any dialect).

kariya (nt.), MIndic for Skt. kārya, *deed*: iti-pramukhā kariyā (n.-acc. pl.) LV 168.1, 10; 169.4 (vss). The shortening of ā to a is regular enough, § 3.103, but this form seems, as far as I can find, not to be recorded in the MIndic Dictt.; and it may be only m.c. in this phrase.

Karuṇatejas (m.c. for Karuṇā° ?), n. of a Buddha: Gv 257.22 (vs) °tejā(ḥ), n. sg.

? **Karuṇā**, n. of a yakṣiṇī: Mahāsamāj 187.1 (Waldschmidt, Kl. Skt. Texte 4). But Pali Aruṇā, which may be right (reading Kaḍambakā before it for **Kaḍambā**, q.v., and see ed. note).

Karuṇābhidhāna, n. of an author: Sādh 391.6, 10; 590.11.

Karuṇāvicintin, used in vs, Samādh 8.26 for **Mahākaruṇācintin**, q.v.

Karuṇāvṛkṣa, n. of a Bodhisattva: Gv 442.26.

karoṭa (m. or nt.; cf. next; = Skt. and Pali karoṭi, *cup, basin*, also *skull*), lit. *cup, basin* (so in **karoṭa-pāṇi**, q.v.); in LV (at least 305.22) fig. *skull*: LV 258.6 (vs) na ca kumbhamukha-karoṭān (abl.) na dhārakuśalāntarāc ca gṛhṇanti; 305.22 (in description of monsters in Māra's host) kumbhodarāḥ karoṭapādā(ḥ) (Tib. *with feet resembling skulls*, rkaṅ pa mgoḥi thod pa ltar ḥdug pa).

karoṭaka (m. or nt.; = prec.), *cup, vessel*: Sādh 47.21 nānāsugandhikusumaparipūrṇaśukla-karoṭakaṃ (Bhvr.); loha-ka° MPS 26.16.

karoṭa-pāṇi, m. (in Pali karoṭi, same mg., Jāt. i.204.3), n. of a class of yakṣas who act as guards for the gods, esp. the Trayastriṃśa gods: Divy 218.8 (devānāṃ trayastriṃśānāṃ pañcarakṣāḥ) sthāpitāḥ, ... karoṭapāṇayo devā(ḥ) ... (mālādhārāḥ, sadāmattāḥ); 319.24 karoṭa-pāṇibhir yakṣaiś; Mvy 3150 = Tib. lag na gzhoṅ thogs, (Cath. Miss. Dict.) *qui tient un bassin à la main, un certain génie*; Mmk 19.13 sadāmattā mālādhārā karoṭapāṇayaḥ vīṇātṛtīyakāḥ; 43.19 (sadāmattāḥ mālādhāriṇo) karoṭapāṇayaḥ vīṇādvitīyakā lekhyāḥ; 232.10 (vs) karoṭapāṇayo devā sadāmattāś ca vīṇakāḥ; Mv i.30.7 °pāṇayo nāma yakṣā (foll. by mālādhārāḥ, sadāmattāḥ); all three also MSV i.95.6.

karoti, *makes*: (idiomatic uses) Mv ii.247.4 (prose) sā dāni śuśumārī glānakaṃ kṛtvā āsati, *the she-crocodile now sat pretending to be sick* (Senart compares *faire le malade*). Or is glānakaṃ a MIndic acc. sg. f. for glānakāṃ? Or even a corruption therefor? See further s.v. **a-, an-**, neg. prefix. For other *forms* from this root see Chap. 43.

karkaṭaka (m. or nt.; cf. karkaṭa, actually °ṭakāṅghri, *a moulding, a kind of joinery resembling the crab's leg*, Acharya Dict. Hindu Arch. 115), (**1**) a kind of moulding on a toraṇa (°ṇā): Mv iii.178.16 tasya nirdhāvantasya toraṇāye karkaṭakasmiṃ makuṭaṃ lagnaṃ, and 20 (uttamāṅgato makuṭaṃ toraṇāgrāto) karkaṭakena **utkṣiptaṃ**; (**2**) in Divy 274.23 (and 281.2) °kena, defined Index as *hook*, but rather *tongs*, a mg. found in Skt.; (**3**) °**ṭikā, f.**, *heart of a flower*: Mvy 6239 = Tib. sñiṅ po, which also renders karṇikā 6238; also in indranīla-kark° 6244; of a lotus, Gv 434.14 mahāratnarājapadma-karkaṭikāyām; ifc. Bhvr. 434.13 (paṅktivairocana)maṇirāja-karkaṭikaṃ; (**4**) °ṭaka (= Pali Kakkaṭa), n. of an upāsaka in Nādikā: MPS 9.12.

Karkarabhadra, n. of a locality of the Śākyas: Mv i.355.12.

karkarava, m., Mvy 6204, and **mahā-k°**, m., 6205 (cf. Pali kakkaru, a kind of creeper, and see **karkārava**), a (heavenly) flower; = Tib. mdog dkar, *white color*.

karkarī (? mss. kakarī both times; Skt. karkarī, AMg. kakkarī, *pot*), lit. *pot*, applied to some protuberance on the head of a crocodile (cf. kumbha, applied to a frontal protuberance on an elephant's head): Mv ii.249.2 (śuśumāro āha, ahaṃ te neṣyāmi, mama) iha grīvāyām āruhya upaśehi, ubhayehi ca hastehi karkarīya lagnehi; 249.5 °rīya lagno.

karkārava, nt. (or m.), and **mahā-k°**, id. (cf. Skt. karkāru, a kind of gourd; Pali kakkāru, id., also a heavenly flower; see also **karkarava**), a kind of heavenly flower: karkāravehi mahākarkāravehi Mv i.266.18 (prose); °vāṇi mahā°vāṇi ii.160.12; 286.16 (both prose); karkāravāṃ ca (acc. pl.) 413.17 (vs); karkāravāṇi iii.94.24, mahā°vāṇi 95.2 (vss).

-karṇaka, m. or nt. (cf. Pali cīvara-kaṇṇa), *edge, border* (of a garment): cīvara-k° Av ii.184.12 and MSV ii.50.6 (prose; °kam, acc. sg.); RP 29.1 (vs, °kā, acc. pl.); Karmav 161.1 (vs, but hypermetric; °kaṃ, acc. sg.); Mmk 68.25 (prose; misprinted -kargakāvasaktā); vastra-karṇake Mmk 721.3 (prose; loc sg.). See also **karṇika**.

karṇadhāraka, m. (Skt. Lex. id., = Skt. °dhāra, so Mironov), *helmsman*: Mvy 3853; see s.v. **pauruṣeya** 2.

Karṇadhārā, n. of an apsaras: Kv 3.10.

karṇika, (**1**) m. or nt., only in cīvara-k°, *edge, border*, (of robe), = **-karṇaka**, q.v.: m. °ko Divy 90.25; 239.27; 577.8; nt. °kāny Divy 350.2; ambiguous as to gender, Divy 90.17, 22; 239.25; 341.3, 4; 345.16; Śikṣ 249.2; (**2**) nt. (= Skt. karṇikā, AMg. kaṇṇiyā), *ear-ornament*: Mvy 6022 = Tib. rna cha.

? **karṇikāyā**, in °yā-keyūrāṇi (in a list of various ornaments, all noms.) LV 121.7 (prose; printed as cpd. by Lefm.). One ms. (A) omits karṇikāyā; another reads °kāyāṃ (loc. of °kā); Calc. karṇikāḥ; Weller 25 states that his ms. reads karṇābharaṇāni muṇḍikābharaṇāni (for karṇikāyā-keyūrāṇi? or for the two preceding words? his statement is not clear). Some form or equivalent of karṇikā, *ear-ornament*, is doubtless meant. Tib. *ear-ornaments* (rna rgyan) *and shoulder-ornaments* (the latter represents keyūrāṇi).

Karṇesumana(s), n. of an elder (sthavira): °manasya, gen., Karmav 99.14; 101.3 (see Lévi's note 4 for Chin. correspondents); °manaḥprabhṛtīnāṃ 154.11. All prose.

kartati (= Skt. kṛṇatti, AMg. kattai; see Chap. 43, s.v. kṛt), *twists, twines*; *spins* (cord): tat karpāsaṃ kartituṃ Divy 213.2; kartiṣyanti 5; taṃ picuṃ kartāpayet (caus.), tat sūtraṃ su-kartitaṃ . . . Mmk 57.7. Cf. next.

-kartin, adj., f. °**inī**, *spinning*: Divy 643.1 (yathā . . .) striyā nātidīrghahrasvakartinyāḥ sūtrodyāmaḥ. Cf. prec.

kartṛma (nt.; either false Sktization of a MIndic kattima, which occurs in JM. [cf. Pali kittima], = Skt. kṛtrima, or = Skt. *kārtrima, vṛddhi deriv. of kṛtrima, with semi-MIndic a for ā and hyper-Skt. ṛ for ri), *trick*: Mv i.129.13 vacana-kartṛme, *verbal trick, trickery in words*. (A v.l. °tume is recorded.)

? **karthika**, cited as 'BSkt.' without reference in PTSD s.v. kattikā (= Skt. kṛttikā; see s.v. **kīrtika**).

karpaṭaka, nt. (or m.?), *a* (small, mean) *village* (= **karvaṭaka**, q.v.): Divy 87.13; 191.27; 498.17; 505.4, 5 (in the last °kam, nom. sg. nt.; other forms ambiguous in gender).

karparaka, m. (= Skt °ra plus -ka), (chamber-)*pot*: MSV iv.54.15 ff.

karpāsa-picu (m.; = Pali kappāsa-picu; cpd. not noted in Skt., where picu is masc.), *cotton* (in some form), used as symbol of lightness: Divy 210.15; 388.15, along with **tūlapicu**, q.v.; both together in Pali in the same way SN v.284.1; there evidently was some difference between the two, but what?

karpāsika, (**1**) adj. (= Pali kappā°, Skt. kārpā°), *made of cotton*: Mv ii.375.19 °kānām atha kambalānāṃ; iii.50.15 °kaṃ paṭapilotikaṃ; 53.14; (**2**) m. (= **kārpāsika**, q.v.), *dealer in cotton goods*: Mv iii.113.8 (in list quite like that in which kārp° occurs).

karmakāraka, m., or °**ikā**, f., *the presiding officer* at an assembly of monks or nuns before which a **jñapti**, q.v., is presented; he or she presents the jñapti, and the following **karmavācanā**, q.v. (if any): °rakaḥ Mvy 8729 (after ācārya and before **raho'nuśāsaka**, q.v.); °rakasya bhikṣoḥ Bhīk 19a.1, °rakena bhikṣuṇā 4; °rikayā bhikṣuṇyā Bhīk 15b.1 ff.

karma-kāraṇa, nt., or °**ṇā**, f. (= Pali kammakāraṇa, °karaṇa, see PTSD s.v. kamma, II.3.A.b), *punishment*: Mv i.22.14 yehi iha atrāṇā anabhisaraṇā karmakāraṇā (so mss., Senart om. kāraṇā) kārāpitā bhavanti, *by whom the helpless and defenceless have been made to undergo punishment*.

karmaṇiya (= Pali kammaniya, cf. next; Skt. °ṇya), *effective, useful, clever*: °yāni (ābharaṇāni) Mv ii.470.14 (prose; mss. karmāṇ°).

karmaṇīya, adj. (= Pali kammanīya, often epithet of citta), *dexterous, capable of work*: mṛducitto °yacitto Mv iii.61.8; 62.12; -mṛdū-karmaṇīya-cittāḥ Dbh.g. 6(342). 12. In Pali mudu is similarly used, parallel with kammanīya. Cf. next.

karmaṇye-sthita, adj. (= Pali kammaniye-ṭhita; read as cpd., ep. of citta, with mudu-bhūta etc., e. g. DN i.76.14; MN i.22.10; °niya = °nīya, see prec.), *abiding in a diligent* (dexterous, working) *condition*, ep. of citta; preceded by mṛdu, cf. corresp. Pali phrase above: LV 345.2, read (citte . . .) mṛduni karmaṇyesthite (Lefm. wrongly °ṇyupasthite with minority of mss.); 345.19 (cittena . . .) mṛdunā karmaṇyesthitena.

karmapatha, m. (nt. noted only Kv 46.1–2 daśa kuśalāni karmapathāny; = Pali kammapatha; seems to be a fundamentally Buddhist term, tho recorded once by BR in Mbh. Calc. 13.583, which is followed by a list of the ten items substantially as in Buddhism, belief in the law of fruition of actions taking the place of No. 10, abstention from heresy), *course of action*; almost always, as in Pali, of a set of ten good (kuśala) actions consisting in avoidance of ten bad (akuśala) actions, three of body (taking life, theft, fornication or adultery), four of speech (lying, harsh speech, spiteful speech, idle or silly, disconnected speech), and three of mind (covetousness, malevolence, heresy); these are listed without use of the term karmapatha, as daśākuśalāni and or daśa kuśalāni, in Dharmas 56 and Mvy 1681–4, 1685–1698; but the same list is given in texts as the ten (a)kuśala karmapatha, so Mv i.107.13–15; Divy 301.22–25; 302.7–10; Śikṣ 69.13 ff. and Dbh 23.6 ff., in both of which each item is treated at some length, esp. in Śikṣ which describes the torments suffered in hell by those guilty of each of the 10 sins; in Mv ii.99.5–12 the ten karmapatha are slightly different; a fourth sin of the body (use of liquor) is added, and the number ten is kept by omitting one of the 4 sins of speech (harshness), also avidyā, *ignorance*, replaces abhidhyā, *covetousness* (this seems likely to be a mere corruption of tradition); in Mv i.26.12 akuśala karmapatha is used more loosely, of sinful acts in general, specifically exemplified by the five **ānantarya,** q.v.; in Mv i.282.14 the term ten kuśala karmapatha (in prose) is immediately followed (in verses) by a list of ten vaśitā, apparently implying that they are the same (not the usual 10 karmapatha); in Suv 6.11 the expression is daśakuśalamūlakarmapatha; often a form of the verb sam-ā-dā-, *adopt, take to, adhere to,* governs the noun, as in Mv ii.77.11 daśa kuśalakarmapathāṃ (acc. pl.) samādāya; Suv 6.11 ... °thaṃ samādāpayet; in Mv ii.425.10 read with mss. daśa-kuśalakarmapatha-samādānaṃ vartitvā (= vartayitvā, *having practised the taking-upon-oneself, the vow, of* ...); cf. **samādiyati, °dāpayati, °dāna**; other references to the 10 kuśala, or akuśala, karmapatha, without listing, are found Mv i.3.1; 46.10; 101.18; 193.15; iii.357.14; Divy 318.22; Karmav 31.13, 14; Gv 521.4.

Karmavajrī, n. of a goddess: Sādh 160.7.

karma-vācanā (= Pali kamma-vācā; PTSD definition does not fit very well Vin. i.317.30 ff., where this Pali word is used exactly like the BHS), *the stating of the matter* that has been moved in the assembly of monks or nuns, see s.v. **jñapti**; it takes the form of a demand that they consent by silence, or oppose by speaking; in the case of jñapti-caturtha the question is triple, prathamā, dvitīyā and tṛtīyā karma°: Mvy 8663–6; Bhīk 18b.4, MSV iii.13.6 f.

Karmavibhaṅga, m. (Pali Kamma°), 'classification of acts', n. of a work (edited by Lévi; our Karmav): Mvy 1372; Karmav 29.31; 105.13 (colophon); 154.10; 163.3; also called **Mahā-karmav°,** q.v.

Karmavibhaṅga-sūtra, n. of a work, not the same as prec.: Karmav 46.11 (see Lévi's note; corresp. to Pali Mahākammavibhaṅga Sutta, MN iii.207–215).

karmasvaka, adj. (= Pali kammassaka), *having* (one's own) *action as one's property,* i.e. subject to the inevitable results of one's own action (and not involved in any other person's): Śikṣ 46.18 (vs) (bhikṣūṇāṃ bhinnavṛttānāṃ parivādaṃ niśamya ca,) karmasvakā bhaviṣyāmo ... (substantially = *we will mind our own business*).

Karmāvaraṇapratiprasrabdhi, n. of a work: Mvy 1383 °dhiḥ.

Karmāvaraṇaviśuddhi-sūtra, n. of a work: Śikṣ 90.6; 172.10.

karmika, adj. or subst. m. (= Pali kammika; Skt. Gr. id., and Skt. karmin), *working, a worker*: RP 31.3 na ca karmiko hy ahaṃ vihāre ātmana-hetur eṣa hi kṛto me. For -karmika at end of cpds. see **ādi-, tatprathama-, sarva-.**

? **Karmira,** v.l. for **Kampila,** q.v.

karvaṭaka, m. or nt. (= Skt. karvaṭa, nt., and Lex. m.; AMg. kabbaḍa and kavvaḍa, m. and nt.), *a* (mean, poor) *village*; acc. to Tib. on Mvy 9356 (°kaḥ, m.) *a mountain hamlet* (so Das for ri ḥor ba; not *Bergabhang* as stated in BR); cf. also **karpaṭaka**: nt. Divy 374.13 (°kam, nom.); masc. Divy 448.7; 451.20 (°kaḥ); ambiguous in gender, Divy 311.24; 541.11; 577.11; 584.22, 27.

karvaṭa-pradeśa, m., Mvy 5283 (var. karvaḍa°), acc. to Tib. ri brag(s), *mountain crag,* or ri boḥi (ri bor gyi) phyogs, *mountain region.* Cf. s.v. **karvaṭaka.**

karṣika, m. (cf. Skt. kārṣaka, and tila-kārṣika; perh. semi-MIndic in having a for ā; or Skt. karṣin plus -ka), *plowman, farmer*: Mv iii.108.20 (vs) punar-punar lābhaṃ labhanti karṣikā.

? **karha-cid,** adv. (cf. Skt. karhi-cid; = Pali karahaci, only after kadā-ci, and in same mg. acc. to DN comm. i.110.3), *ever, at any time*: in one old ms. of SP inserted after kadācid SP 257.1 (prose), Baruch, Beiträge zum Saddharmapuṇḍarīkasūtra, 23 and 28; omitted in all other mss. The coincidence with Pali usage is so extraordinary that I am inclined with Baruch to regard it as old.

kala, perh. = Skt. kara, *hand,* in LV 12.11 (vs) kena sa kalagata (Lefm. prints sakalagata) ti bodhi (so read with ms. A m.c., for bodhī); so Foucaux and Tib. (khyod ni byaṅ chub phyag mthil bzhag daṅ ḥdra, *enlightment is the same as put in thy hand-palm*; kena is difficult; Foucaux seems to have read tena with ms. H; Tib. has no evident correspondent; does sa go with bodhi?).

[**kalaṇḍaka,** see **kalandaka.**]

Kalaṇḍaka-nivāpa, see **Kalandaka°.**

kalatra (nt.; in Skt. only *wife* except once in Harṣac. acc. to Thomas, *retinue,* see Schmidt, Nachtr.; see **kaḍatra**), (**1**) *family* (in the usual Eng. sense): Bbh 362.7 (bodhisattvena sarvaḥ sattvadhātuḥ) kalatrabhāvena parigṛhītaḥ, *cherished like* or *adopted as* (one's own) *family* (oftener **kaḍatra,** q.v.); (**2**) *servants* (familia), esp. perhaps *male servants*: LV 139.12 (vs) dāsī-kalatra-jani (loc.) yādṛśam ātmaprema (in a description of the qualities of a wife, so that kalatra cannot possibly mean *wife*); Foucaux, because of preceding dāsī, understands kalatra as referring to males alone, which is possible but hardly necessary.

kalandaka (or °ntaka? karanta? variants in mss. also karañjaka, kalaṇḍaka; = Pali kaḷandaka, Jāt. vi.224.6 mudukābhisiyā mudu-citta-kaḷandake, comm. sukhasamphassacittattharake), *spread, cover* for a seat: Mv i.306.9 (vs) kāśikapratyāstaraṇaṃ (? em.; mss. °tyottaraṇaṃ) suvicitra-kalandakaṃ (so 1 ms., the other °ṇḍakaṃ; Senart em. wrongly) maṇivicitraṃ; ii.38.3 (vs) read essentially with mss.: atha kanaka-m-aṣṭapādā suvicitra-kalandakā (or, with mss., °ntakā-ḥ?) maṇivicitrā (? mss. °tro or °tra); ii.470.8, for Senart's em. kilaṃjakā (pi kriyanti) mss. seem to intend karaṃjakā; context fits our word as to mg.; note, however, that in the next line (9) mss. have karantā (Senart em. karaṇḍā) pi kriyanti, which might be meant for kalanta(ka), or be another form of the word here concerned.

Kalandaka-nivāpa, m. (= Pali id., *squirrel food-offering*), also written in mss. **Karandaka°,** q.v., and Kalaṇḍaka°, Karaṇḍaka°, see below; n. of a place near Rājagṛha where Buddha often dwelt: Mv i.255.4 (v.l. kar°); iii.47.12 (v.l. kalaṇḍaka°); 60.2 (mss. kalaṇḍaka° or kar°); 91.14 (no v.l.); Mvy 4138 kalandaka-nivāsa, but Index with v.l. and Mironov °nivāpa; Divy 143.1 (ed. Kar° but 3 of 4 mss. Kal°); 262.8; 298.24 (here 3 mss. Kalandani°); 364.19 (printed Kalindaka°); 506.7; 544.22; Av i.1.8 etc. (list, Speyer, Index 213); Burnouf, Introd. 456 cites Karaṇḍaka° from Av but the passage (ii.186.5) in Speyer reads Kalandaka° without v.l.

kalapālī (cf. **kallavāla**), acc. to Tib. (cited as chaṅ ḥtshoṅ ma), *a woman liquor-seller*: MSV i.117.11 (°lyāpaṇam), 12; 120.4.

Kalabha (in Pali Kalābu), n. of a wicked king of Benares, character in a Jātaka (Pali Khantivādi Jāt., No. 313; Jm Kṣānti-Jāt., 181 ff.; unnamed in Mv, no colophon): Mv iii.357.4; 359.16; 361.3; 368.15; 369.16. (Not named in Jm.)

(**kalama,** m., = Skt. Lex. and late lit., Schmidt, Nachtr.; cf. **karama,** and **kalamā**; *reed (-pen,* for writing): Mvy 5900 = lekhanī; Mironov kalāmaṃ.)

kalamā = prec.: Divy 532.11 masinā (= maṣ°) kalamayā tūlena; 535.10 bhūrjāṃ (mss.) kalamā (so divide) tailaṃ tūlam asir (read masir or maṣir?).

(**kalambukā** [rare in Skt., and only Jain?; once in Pali; perh. = Skt. kalamba, °baka, °bikā, *convolvulus repens*?], n. of a creeper, to which a vana-latā is compared in a complimentary way: Mv i.341.6; 345.11.)

kalayati (cf. Skt. kālayām āsa Mbh 3.229.5, *counted, reckoned up,* for which 4 Kashmirian and 3 D mss. read kal°; Pkt id., Sheth), *counts, computes*: Divy 27.5 tāta kalyatām asmadīyaṃ paṇyam iti. tena kalitam (mss. quoted as kalpitam, intending prob. kalyitam), ekaikasya suvarṇalakṣāḥ saṃvṛttāḥ ... (8) mamāpi kalyatām ... (10)

kalyate... kalyatām... (11) kalitaṃ... (12) lakṣā saṃvṛttā (mss. °ttāḥ).

kalaviṅka (m.; = **karaviṅka**, q.v.), *the Indian cuckoo*: LV 353.6 (vs) °ka-rutāya vācā; 355.3 °ka-mañjughoṣaḥ (Bhvr., of the Buddha); 355.17 °ka-rutasvareṇa; Kv 73.24, corrupt, read kalaviṅka-rutena svareṇa; 89.5 °ka-rutasvarābhinirghoṣeṇa.

kalaviṅkaka, m., = prec. (-ka prob. m.c.): SP 358.7 (vs) °kā (n. pl.) kokilabarhiṇaś ca.

Kalaśoda, n. of a nāga king: Mmk 18.10.

Kalaśodara, n. of a yakṣa: Māy 37.

Kalaśodarī, (**1**) n. of a river: Kv 71.15; (**2**) n. of a piśācī: Māy 238.20; (**3**) n. of a rākṣasī: Māy 241.15; see next.

Kalasī (= prec. 3), n. of a rākṣasī: Māy 243.10.

Kalahapriya, n. of a yakṣa: Māy 36.

kalahayati, **°hāyati**, denom. (Skt. kalahati and kalahāyate; Pkt. has equivalents of both these; not recorded in Pali), *quarrels*: °hayati Mvy 5228; °hāyati AsP 420.4 (prose).

kalācikā (so Mironov without v.l.; BR cites °ka, m., which Kyoto ed. cites as v.l.), *spoon, ladle*: Mvy 8958 = Tib. kha gzar.

kalācī (Skt. Lex. id., and kalāci in late lit., Schmidt, Nachtr.; not in Pali; cf. Pkt. kalāiā = Skt. Lex. °cikā, Sheth), *fore-arm*: Śikṣ 228.14 -hasta-kalācī-bāhv-aṃśa- (in a long cpd. listing parts of the body).

kalāpa, m., a high number: Mvy 7780 = Tib. cha tshogs (same as **kaṣaca** or **kaṣava**, q.v.; cf. **kajāva**).

kalāpaka, adj. or adv. (as noun, *bundle*; *string of pearls*, in Skt. and Pali), perhaps *in folds* ('bundles, bunches'?), applied to a monk's robe: Prāt 528.7 na °kaṃ cīvaraṃ nivāsayiṣyāmaḥ; Chin. ... *des plis fins*.

kalāva, m. (= AMg. id., Skt. and Pali kalāya), *a kind of pulse*: Mvy 5652 (text kulatthaḥ, var. kulāvaḥ, but Index also kalāvaḥ, and so Mironov 228.6); Kv 48.5 (kola-mudga-)māṣā-kalāba-(so printed)-masura- etc.; Divy 499.25, read with mss., tena tasya kalāvānām (ed. em. kalāyānāṃ) añjalipūro dattaḥ.

kali, m. (in this sense = Pali id., but not in Skt.), *sin, depravity*: Mvy 621, 622, see s.vv. **Kāyakali-**, **Vākkali-** (Tib. skyon, normally = doṣa); Divy 623.21 (vs, tho printed as prose) pāpakaṃ karma kilviṣaṃ kalir eva ca; Jm 103.24 kali-paddhatiṃ (surām; kali-bala, *the power of evil* (text °vala), Dbh.g. 52(78).8 °parihāropāya-vidyarddhimantaḥ, and 16 vijita-kalivalaughās; kali-mala-paripūrṇa- Kv 90.16; sattva-kali-kaluṣair Śikṣ 279.7; rāga-doṣa-moha-kali-kaluṣa-vinodanī LV 286.12; kali-pāsu (read °sa? for °śu or °śa, so v.l.) LV 371.17 (vs); kali-puruṣa, *man of depravity*, said of Devadatta, Mv i.128.14 (mss. kāli°); kali-nṛpa, *evil king*, LV 165.22; kali-rāja(n), id., Divy 574.10; RP 21.18; MSV i.29.2; (see also s.v. **Kaliṅga-rājan**;) in Ud viii.4 word-play on the other mg. of kali, *bad luck at dice* (Chakravarti ignores this), alpamātro hy ayaṃ kalir ya ihākṣeṇa dhanaṃ parājayet, ayam atra mahattaraḥ kalir yaḥ sugateṣu manaḥ pradūṣayet (same vs Pali Sn 659); see also Ud viii.3; often regarded as characteristic of Māra the Evil One, and so cpd. with Māra-: SP 481.8 nirjeṣyaty ayaṃ... Māra-kali-cakraṃ (*Māra's wheel of depravity*) pravartayiṣyaty ayaṃ dharma-cakraṃ; LV 180.9 Māra-kali-pāśāṃś (cf. LV 371.17, above) ca saṃchinatti sma; Māra-kali-vikiraṇa-vinarditam avatārāmi Gv 206.25; Māra-kali-kleśa-sūdana(ḥ) Gv 483.9 (vs), so read with the citation Śikṣ 104.1 (Gv text corruptly sudama).

kalikā (perhaps lit. *a bud*, i. e. a trifle, nothing of value?) Divy 499.24 kim ayaṃ kalikāyā (abl.? gen.?) dīyate, mūlyam anuprayaccha, *why should it be given for nothing? give me a price.* In LV 276.16 (vs) prāsādāś ca gavākṣa-harmya-kalikā(ḥ), without v.l., kalikā seems uninterpretable; Tib. maṅ ldan pa, *having many*..., which suggests -kalitā(ḥ), *provided with*...

[**Kaliṅga-rājan**, Vaj 31.10, is undoubtedly an error of tradition for kali-rājan; see s.v. **kali**, and cf. SBE 49, Part 2, p. 127, n. 1. The Kashgar version reported in Hoernle MR 184.11 unfortunately has a lacuna where the word occurs, but Chin. and general sense support the em.]

Kaliṅgavana, nt., n. of a city in the **Śroṇāparānta** country: Gv 192.15.

kalina, m., = Skt. kali, *the present world age*: Laṅk 364.5 (vs) kṛtayugaś ca tretā ca dvāparaṃ kalinas tathā. Meter makes another form out of the question; the word has followed the pattern of in-stems, extended by -a, see § 10.3.

[**Kalindaka-nivāpa**, error (misprint?) for **Kalandaka°**: Divy 364.19.]

? **kalī** = Skt. kalā, *part*: LV 341.5 (vs). Doubtful; see **saṭhaḥ**.

kalopī (= Pali kaḷopī), some sort of container, *vessel* or *basket*: Mv iii.453.3 (read) na te koṣṭhesmiṃ osaranti na kumbhe na kalopiyaṃ (loc.); Senart for last word kulopakaṃ, mss. kulopiyaṃ; in same line Jāt. v.252.20 Pali has kaḷopiyā (loc. sg.).

? **kalkaṭa-tva**, nt. (cf. Skt. karkara, Pali kakkhaḷa, AMg. kakkhaḍa, *hard*?), perhaps *hardness*: Mv i.339.16 atha teṣāṃ kāye gurutvaṃ ca kharatvaṃ ca ka°tvaṃ ca upanipate. So acc. to Crit. App. one ms.; v.l. kalkatvaṃ (*impurity*? cf. Skt. kalka); but Senart's note cites mss. as katka° instead of kalka°; he em. kakkhaṭatvaṃ.

kalpa, m., also nt. (**1**) (cf. Skt. id. *style, manner, fashion*, chiefly in Bhvr. cpds., BR s.v. 2b), in tatpuruṣa cpds., esp. gṛhi-kalpa, tīrthika-k°, ṛṣi-k°, *appearance, aspect* (of), *resemblance* (to), sometimes replaced by ākalpa (as in Skt., *ornament* or *attire*), and parallel with **gupti** (gupta), liṅga, dhvaja (see s.v. **gupti** for citations); (**2**) ifc., said to mean *indifferent, alike in regard to*..., in **vāsīcandanakalpa**, q.v.; (**3**) (not recognized in Skt. or Pali Dictt., tho Childers gives *thought* as one mg. of kappa), (false) *fancy*, (vain) *imagining*, often with **vikalpa** and **parikalpa**, qq.v.: LV 34.11 (prose) sarva-kalpa-vikalpa-parikalpa-prahāṇāya; others s.v. **parikalpa**; 250.16 (prose) akalpaṃ tad dhyānam avikalpam aniñjanam...; 419.17 (vs) saṃkalpa-(q.v.; instr.?)-kalpajanitena ayonisena bhavate avidya...; 420.11 (vs) yasmin na kalpa na vikalpa (so most mss.); 422.20 akalpāvikalpa-dharmanayavistīraṇa-cakraṃ; Laṅk 57.3 (vividha-) kalpa-vikalpitam, *discriminated by various false imaginings*; et alibi in Laṅk; Divy 629.18 (vs, printed as prose) (a list of sins attributed to brahmans, ... śāṭhyaṃ) ca dhaurtyaṃ ca tathaiva kalpam (nom. sg.!); (**4**) as in Skt. (and Pali kappa), *world-age*; various kinds, largely but not entirely parallel to Pali usage (best statement of this in Childers): Dharmas 87 lists **antara-**, **mahā-**, **śūnya-**, **sāra-k°** (all m.), qq.v.; Mvy has the first two, also **bhadra-k°**, q.v., 8292; **saṃvarta-** and **vivarta-k°**, qq.v., 8279–80; see **asaṃkhyeya**, adj., which does not seem to be used in BHS, or at least in the texts included in this Dict., as it is stated to be in Pali, as n. of a particular kind of kalpa; (**5**) n. of a king: Av ii.102.6 ff. See **kalpa-kaṣāya** and following cpds.; also **kalpam**, adv.; in **kalpa-dūṣya** or **°duṣya**, and **°puṣpa**, qq.v., kalpa = kalpa-vṛkṣa, as in Skt. Lex.

(**kalpaka**, m., in BR, pw, recorded only as Lex., but cf. pw 2.297; occurs however in Kauṭ. Arth. i.21, Shama Sastri 1st ed. 44.4; = Pali kappaka, *barber*: Mv ii.489.8; iii.70.5; 92.5; 180.10; 191.9, 15; Av ii.112.5.)

kalpa-kaṣāya, m. (see also s.v. **kaṣāya**), *degradation* (degraded state) *of a world-age*: SP 65.13 sa tathāgato (Padmaprabha) na kalpakaṣāya utpatsyate, api tu praṇidhānavaśena dharmaṃ deśayiṣyati (but see s.v. **kaṣāya**, esp. Mmk 5.23; SP 56.8); Gv 307.19–20 anantara-kalpa-kaṣāye pratyupasthite (after disappearance of a Buddha's teaching).

kalpakāra, m., *attendant* (on monks): MSV i.248.10 (allowed to take money for travel-expenses of monks).

kalpa-duṣya, or **°dūṣya**, nt. (see **duṣya, dūṣya**; Senart always prints duṣya in Mv text but cites dūṣya in Index), (fine) *cloth made from the kalpa-vṛkṣa* (for which kalpa is cited Skt. Lex.): Mvy 5883 °duṣyam (so also Mironov) = Tib. dpag bsam śiṅ las byuṅ paḥi gos; Mv i.216.7 = ii.19.4 (vs); ii.337.6; kalpadūṣyavṛkṣāḥ, *trees that bear such materials*, Divy 215.28 ff.; 221.18.

Kalpaduṣyagupta, n. of a former Buddha: Mv i.138.3 (text °duṣya°; Index °dūṣya°).

kalpapuṣpa, nt., *flower of the kalpa-vṛkṣa*: Mv ii.33.20 °puṣpāṇi.

(**kalpana**, Skt. nt. once *das Bilden in der Phantasie, Erfinden*, pw, = **kalpa** (3), (false) *fancy, imagining*: Laṅk 9.5 (vs) mohitā viśvakalpanaiḥ, or °tā hi svakalpanaiḥ, see note.)

Kalpanāmaṇḍitikā, n. of a work, of which Central Asiatic fragments ed. Lüders 1926, = Kleinere Skt. Texte II; p. 38 'Die Sprache... ist durchweg das korrekte Sanskrit der Grammatiker.' But a few items of vocabulary, listed pp. 42–45, have been incorporated here so far as they seemed to me pertinent.

kalpam, adv. (from **kalpa**, q.v.; = Pali kappaṃ), lit. and orig. *for a kalpa, = for a long time*: SP 227.5 (prose) (yaḥ... tathāgatasya) saṃmukhaṃ kalpam avarṇaṃ bhāṣet, *who should for a long time speak ill before* (= towards) *a T.* (The translators misunderstand.) The verse account has (229.7) yaś caiva... jinasya saṃmukhaṃ śrāved avarṇaṃ paripūrṇakalpam, ... *for a full kalpa*, which may therefore be the mg. of 227.5; but the Pali adv. is well established.

kalpayati, with śayyām (= Pali seyyaṃ kappeti), *lies down*: Mv i.210.(13–)14 (prose) (sukhaṃ gacchati) tiṣṭhati pi niṣīdati pi śayyām api kalpayati; nearly same phrase ii.14.(12–)13. See also **kalpāpayati**.

kalpa-vṛnda (nt.), *the whole mass of* (brahmanical) *ritual regulations*: °daṃ prahāya, *abandoning* (these), said of 'ṛṣis' (pre-Buddhistic ascetics): Divy 210.11.

kalpa-sthiti, adj. Bhvr. (cf. also next), *abiding for a world-age*: LV 200.2 kalpasthitīya (nom. pl.) ṛṣayo.

kalpa-sthitika (= Pali kappaṭṭhitika; see **sthitika**), = prec.: °kenāyuṣpramāṇena LV 442.20; Dbh.g. 56(82).8 (both prose!); cf. also kalpakoṭī... (etc.)-sahasrasthitikenāpy āyuṣpramāṇena Sukh 62.2.

kalpāpayati (caus. to Pali kappeti, as in MN ii.155.6 kesamassuṃ kappetvā), *causes to be trimmed* (hair and beard): Mv ii.489.8 keśaśmaśrūṇi kalpāpayitvā. Skt. kḷpta, ppp. of simplex kalpati, is used in mg. *trimmed* (of hair).

kalpāvaśeṣam, adv. (= Pali kappāvasesaṃ), *more than a kalpa*, in the phrase (kalpaṃ) vā... vā (nirdiśet, *he might expound*) LV 436.6; (tiṣṭhet, *would last*) Divy 201.9; 207.1. So Foucaux, apparently supported by Pali DN comm. 554.32 (on DN ii.103.4) appaṃ vā bhiyyo ti, vutta-vassa-satato (= kappaṃ = āyukappaṃ) atirekaṃ vā, *a little more*, or *in excess of the stated 100 years* (the extreme life of a man, which Pali exegesis takes as the mg. of kappaṃ here). So also Tib. on MPS 15.10 = Divy 201.9. But CPD and PTSD (*for*) *the rest of a kalpa*.

kalpika, adj. (= Pali kappiya; see also **akalpika, kalpiya**), *suitable, proper*: Mvy 9196; of a monk's (nun's) robe, cīvara, LV 267.10; Prāt 494.6; Bhīk 15a.1; of food, °kaṃ niravadyaṃ ca māṃsaṃ Laṅk 258.15, cited Śikṣ 133.15; meat, when kalpika, when not, MSV i.236.17 ff.; of gifts, dāna, Bbh 123.7; of monkish paraphernalia in general, LV 2.22; even more generally, of all sorts of useful and ornamental objects, Gv 164.14 (bracketed with anavadya). See also next.

kalpika-śālā, also **°ka-sthāna**, corresp. to Pali kappiya-kuṭī (also -bhūmi), which is variously rendered (in SBE 13.304, on Vin. i.139.36, *kitchen*), in MSV i.235.2, 4 (°śālā), 8 ff. (°sthāna), introduced as a place where broth for a sick monk could be heated, and seems to mean lit. either *hall* (*place*) *for allowable* (*proper*) *perquisites* (see prec.), or possibly *hall* (*place*) *for preparation* of such perquisites (?); five are listed (cf. the somewhat diff. list of four in Pali Vin. i.240.1 ff.), ārabhyamāṇāntikā (sc. śālā; *whose boundaries*, anta, *are being proposed*), ucchrīyamāṇāntikā, **goniṣādikā, udbhūtavastukā, saṃmatikā**; all are 'explained' in 6 ff., but the glosses are not all very clear. In i.234.4 kalpika-sthāna refers to a proper place for preparing (perhaps also storing? see **pratijāgarti**) food, and ten akalpikāni (sthānāni) are listed 5 ff.

kalpikāra, m. (cf. **kapyāri**; possibly connected with Pali kappiyakāraka, Vin i.206.12, but the traditional interpretation is different; see also next), Mvy 3840; ? acc. to confused definitions in Tib., Chin., and Jap., would seem to mean some kind of *servant* of monks in a temple or monastery.

kalpikāraka, m., = prec.: Divy 343.15 (parallel cited with varr. Śikṣ 59.2) te Kāśyapasya samyaksaṃbuddhasya °kā āsan (Śikṣ inserts bhikṣūṇām upasthāpakāḥ), te bhikṣūṇāṃ bhaiṣajyāni kvāthayamānāḥ sthālikāṃ bhañjante (mss.; Śikṣ varies but same general sense).

kalpita, nt. (= **kalpa** 3, **kalpana**; also substantially = **vikalpita** 2), (false) *fancy*, (vain) *imagining*: LV 374.6 (vs) (parikṣīṇā) kalpita-vikalpitāni (dvandva cpd.) ca (certainly noun!); LV 178.1 (vs) viparīta-abhūta-kalpitaiḥ, *by perverted and false imaginings*, parallel with rāgadoṣaiḥ (paridahyate jagat); so better than with Foucaux as adj. modifier of rāgadoṣaiḥ; as ppp., = vikalpita, SP 281.12 (vs), read (cf. WT) anutthitāś cāpi ajāta-dharmā jātā tha bhūtā viparīta-kalpitāḥ, *and the states of being that have never originated or been produced are falsely conceived as produced and real*; kalpito, *imagined*, ŚsP 1534.7.

kalpiya, kalpya, m.c. **kalpīya** (= Pali kappiya; not recorded in this sense in Skt.), *suitable, proper*: Mv iii.305.5 (vs) kalpiyaṃ (tarpaṇam, food and drink; v.l. kalpitaṃ); Laṅk 250.3 kalpyaṃ (bhojanam; prose); kalpīyāni (garments) ca saṃnivāsya (q.v.) LV 271.18 (vs). Cf. **kalpika, akalpya**.

kalpīkaroti, *prepares, makes ready*: °kṛtya MSV i.vii.3.

kalmāṣaka, adj. (= Skt. °ṣa; perhaps m.c.), *spotted*: SP 94.7 (vs) varṇena te kālaka tatra bhonti, kalmāṣakā...

Kalmāṣadamya (= Pali Kammāsadamma), n. of a town in the Kuru country, home of **Mākandika** (as of Māgandiya in Pali): Divy 515.13 ff.

Kalmāṣapāda, n. of a yakṣa: Māy 9. (Cf. the same as n. of a prince changed into a rākṣasa, in Skt. and in Jm 209.9).

kalyato (°**tas**), adv. (cf. next; in Skt. kalyam, kalye, kālyam, kālye), *early in the morning*: Mv iii.177.13 (prose) °to evotthitena.

kalyasya, or **kāl°**, adv., = prec., q.v.; only in phrase °syaiva nivāsayitvā Mv i.34.14 (Senart kāl° with 3 mss., but 3 mss. incl. the two best kal°; most mss. lp for ly); iii.60.3 (Senart kal° with 1 ms., v.l. kāl°); 142.10 (both mss. kāl°); 414.5 (mss. kāl°, Senart strangely em. kal°!).

Kalyāṇa (= Pali id.), n. of a mythical early king: Mvy 3554; Mv i.348.8. In Mvy son of **Roca** and grandson of **Mahāsaṃmata**; in Mv son of the latter; in Pali son of Vararoja, the son of Roja = **Roca**.

kalyāṇa-kāma, adj. (= Pali id.); -tā, *state of being desirous of pleasant things* (a sin in a monk): Prāt 497.1, 7 etc.

Kalyāṇagarbha, n. of an author: Sādh 471.18.

Kalyāṇabhadra, n. of a householder of Benares: MSV iii.132.15; called **Kalyāṇabhadrika** 132.19; 133.1.

kalyāṇa-mitra, nt., f. °ā (= Pali °mitta; there often tho not always ep. of Buddha), *good friend*, regularly said of one (not as a rule a Buddha) who helps in conversion or religious progress: Mv i.243.12 °mitrāṇy āgamya; 313.5 asmākaṃ Mālinī °mitrā (f.; she was the cause of their conversion); Mvy 2380 °tra-parigṛhīta; Divy 347.17 °tram āgamya; Av i.240.8 id.; °tra-tā, *state of*... Av i.240.2. Very common.

kalla, adj. (cf. Skt. kalla-tā acc. to Galanos, and Dhātup. kall-), *stammering*: Mvy 7156 = Tib. dig pa, ldibs pa; AsP 427.1.

kallavāla, m. (cf. **kalapālī**; Skt. kalyapāla, pw 2.38, 297; AMg. kallāla), *liquor-dealer*: Mvy 3779.

kavacikā (Skt. kavaca; in AMg. kavaciyā defined by Ratnach. as *a kind of vessel*, pātra), Mvy 6078 = Tib. ḥthab ber, *war-coat*, i. e. *corslet, battle-garment*.

kavacita, denom. pple. (from Skt. kavaca; = Skt. Lex. id., and cf. kavacayati, once, pw 5.251), *armored*, often in fig. (religious) sense: Mvy 5203; saṃnaddha-k° Mv i.313.16, 18; saṃnaddhavarmā kavacitavarmā ii.320.1; (susaṃnaddha-)dṛḍhavarma-k° LV 82.2; saṃnaddha-dṛḍhavarmita-k° 209.19; dṛḍhasaṃnaddha-varmita-k° 218.12; *armored* with the (32) lakṣaṇa, said of Buddha, LV 110.8, 21; 240.13; Mv ii.299.13; 371.14; miscellaneous, LV 181.5; 311.21; 361.5; Mv ii.316.8.

kavaḍa, m. (Skt. id. in sense of *mouth-rinsing water*; Skt. kavala in both senses), *morsel, mouthful* (of food): AsP 234.5; Divy 290.23 etc. See next.

[**kavaḍaka** (m. or nt.) = prec. (in comp., -kavaḍakāhāra-) Gv 145.19 (prose). But 2d ed. kavaḍīkāhāra; read °kārāhāra, see **kavalīkārāhāra.**]

kavaḍa-chedakam, adv., (in the manner of) *dividing morsels* (of food): na ka° Mvy 8585; the complete phrase in LaVallée Poussin JRAS 1913.845, Stein ms. fragm. 1.2.11, na ka° (ms. kapaḍa°) piṇḍapātaṃ paribhokṣyāma iti. The Pali is kabaḷāvacchedakam, Vin. iv.196.1.

kavalikāra (-bhojana), see next.

kavalīkārāhāra, m. (cf. Skt. kavalīkāra, pw 4.297; = Pali kabaliṃkārā° or °līkārā°), so Mvy (Kyoto) and Dharmas (text), or **kavaḍī°** (Bbh; so read in Gv 145.19, see **kavaḍaka**; also AbhidhK, see LaVallée Poussin's Index) or **kavaḍiṃk°** (Mvy v.l., and Mironov text), *food making a lump* or *morsel*, i. e. real, material food: Bbh 99.18; the first of four 'foods' (with **sparśāhāra, manaḥ-saṃcetanāh°, vijñānāh°**, qq.v.; Pali has same list); Mvy 2284; in Dharmas 70 five kinds, see s.vv. **pratyāhāra** and **dhyānāhāra**; Mmk 103.25 (vs) seems to contain this word, tho the metrical structure is monstrous and some words besides this are corrupt, audārika-m-ākāra-kavaḍīkā(rā, not in text!)-hāraś ca kīrtitāḥ, (26) sūkṣmāhārikasattvā vai ity uvāca tathāgataḥ; in Mmk 104.3 (vs) read kavalikāra-bhojanāḥ (= °kārāhārāḥ) for corrupt and unmetr. kavalikāhārabhojanāḥ.

kavita, denom. pple. from Skt. kavi, *fanciful, thought up, invented*: RP 28.15; AdP, Konow MASI 69.17.23 kavitāḥ kāveyāś (q.v.) caitāḥ (sc. pāramitās), *they are fanciful, the product of poetic invention* (preceded by naitā bhoṇ pāramitās tathāgatair... bhāṣitāḥ, *they were not spoken by the T's*).

kaśambaka-jāta (also written kaṣ°, kas°; = Pali kasambu-jāta, with var. kasambuka-j°), acc. to Tib. on Mvy, *rotten*; this is consistent with the lit. mg. in Pali, applied to a tree the inside of which is rotten, see s.v. **avasruta**; the orig. mg. was forgotten in Pali at an early time, as the vague and inconsistent Pali comms. show; e. g. Vin. ii.236.26, comm. 1287.5 = ākiṇṇadosataya saṃkiliṭṭhajātaṃ; Pugg.p. 27.10, comm. 207.25 either kasambu = kacavara, *rubbish*, or = tinta-kuṇapa-gataṃ kasaṭa-udakaṃ (evidently guessing): Mvy 9139 kaṣ° (but Mironov kaś°) = Tib. śiṅ rul ba (*rotten*) lta bur gyur pa; follows antarpūty avasrutaḥ (all part of a longer cliché found repeatedly in Pali, e. g. in Vin. and Pugg.p., ll.cc.); MSV i.50.7 kaṣ°; Śikṣ 67.20 kaśambakajāto aśramaṇaḥ etc. (as in Mvy 9143–4); AsP 181.20 kas°. Could this word be related to kasavva Deśīn. 2.53, said to have four mgs., (1) stokam, (2) ārdram, *wet*, (3) pracuram, (4) bāṣpaḥ? By the 'law of morae' kasamba could be related to Deśī kasavva.

kaśāhata, adj. (= Pali kasā°, Vin. i.75.29), (marked by being) *beaten with a whip* (as punishment): MSV iv.68.6.

kaśmala, m. pl., apparently n. of a class of evil supernatural beings: Mmk 538.26 (et alibi) sarve ḍākinyaḥ sarve bhūtagrahāḥ sarve ca kaśmalāḥ vaśā bhavanti.

Kaśyapīya, see s.v. **Kāśyapīya.**

kaṣaca, or (with v.l., and Mironov without v.l.) kaṣava, nt., a high number: Mvy 7908 (cited from Gv) = Tib. cha tshogs; cf. **kajāva, kalāpa.**

kaṣaṭa (m. or nt.; cf. **kaṣaṭṭa**, and Pali kasaṭa, which PTSD takes to mean *dregs* in Vv.comm. 288.21, but both form and mg. are doubtful), prob. *dregs*, in fig. sense, i. e. *lowest part*: parṣat-kaṣaṭu (WT's ms. K' °ṭa) tāñ jñātvā SP 44.11 (vs), *knowing them* (to be) *the dregs of the assembly* (WT em. kaṣāya-tām, but this is unnecessary).

kaṣaṭṭa, m. (= AMg. kasaṭṭa, *refuse, dross*, and cf. **kaṣaṭa**), *dregs, sediment, impurity*: °ṭaḥ (Mironov °ṭāḥ, m. pl.) Mvy 7638 = Tib. sñigs ma, or tshigs ma, *sediment, impurity.*

kaṣambaka-jāta, see **kaśam°.**

kaṣava, see **kaṣaca.**

kaṣāya, m. (= Skt. id., BR s.v. 2c; Pali kasāya), *sediment*, and so *impurity, degradation*, etc.: five such, āyuḥ-, dṛṣṭi-, kleśa-, sattva-, kalpa-k° Mvy 2335-40; (order varies) Dharmas 91; SP 43.4–5; Bbh 252.17–19; pañcakaṣāya-kāle SP 58.11; LV 248.13; pañcasu kaṣāya-kāle LV 257.21 (vs); pañcakaṣāye loke Śikṣ 60.14; pañcakaṣāye kāle buddho... śākyamunir utpannaḥ Mmk 5.23; kaṣāyakālaḥ Bbh 15.3; ahaṃ (sc. the Buddha)... utpanna sattvāna kaṣāyamadhye SP 56.8 (vs); see also s.v. **kalpa-kaṣāya**; in vs m.c. for **kāṣāya**, q.v., KP 117.5 (twice, once in text, the other time required by meter for text kāṣāya); five k° in a different sense, *astringent substances* (as Skt.), products of five plants, MSV i.iv.5.

kaṣāyikā, var. for **kapāpikā**, q.v. Seems most likely secondary (influenced by the familiar word kaṣāya).

kaṣmīlita, acc. to Tib. *distorted*, in °litākṣa, adj.: Mvy 8926 = Tib. mig sle ḥo, (having) *distorted eyes.*

kasambaka-jāta, see **kaśam°.**

? **kasina** (Pali kasiṇa) for Skt. kṛtsna; śubha-k° seems to be the intention of the corrupt mss. at Mv ii.319.5 for **śubha-kṛtsna**, q.v., which Senart adopts by em.; see §§ 3.90, 111.

kasulā, v.l. °**rā**, adj. fem. (Senart's text prints kasūlā, but he cites all mss. with u), sc. lipi, some kind of script: Mv i.135.7. Etym. and mg. unknown.

kastūrikāṇḍa, nt. (or **kastur°**, Mironov; cpd. of Skt. °ikā and aṇḍa; Wilson recorded °ikāṇḍaja in same mg., BR), *musk*: Mvy 5832 = Tib. gla rtsi.

[**Kasphila**, a disciple of Buddha; so both edd. LV 1.16, no v.l. It could be understood as intended for Kapphiṇa or °la, who however occurs shortly before in the same list as Kaphila, or acc. to Tib. °na. And Tib. here reads ḥug pa, = **Kauśika**, which I believe is the true reading; and which see.]

kahāpaṇa (= Pali id., for Skt. kārṣāpaṇa, a coin), only in °ṇa-māṃsika, nt., or °kā, f., or °kaṃ, adv. (so read for Senart's text °māsikaṃ, see esp. the ms. reading at iii.260.14), *cutting from the body pieces of flesh the size of a small coin*, a form of torture, called in Pali kahāpaṇaka: Mv iii.258.18 (kāmaṃ) khalu me śākyā kāyaṃ tīkṣṇena śastreṇa kahāpaṇa-māṃsikaṃ (°kāṃ?) pi chindetsuḥ; in Pali lists of tortures, e. g. MN i.87.16, kahāpaṇakaṃ is regularly preceded by balisa-maṃsikaṃ (baḷ°), see s.v. **biliśa-**; in Mv iii.260.14, verse version of the same passage, Senart reads kahāpaṇa-, but the single ms. obviously read **kārṣāpaṇa-māṃsikaṃ** (°kāṃ?), i. e. the Sktized form; see this, and **kārṣāpaṇa-chedikam,** another expression for the same.

kahi, kahiṃ (cit), as loc. of ka-, see § 21.22; sometimes varies in mss. with karhi.

kāṃsa- (false Skt., instead of kāṃsya, for MIndic **kaṃsa-**, q.v.), *brass; brazen*: LV 318.22 kāṃsa-pātrī (in Mv **kaṃsa-pātrī**, q.v.); Bbh 28.25 kāṃsa-kūṭa (v.l. kaṃsa°), = Pali kaṃsa-kūṭa-, *one who cheats by* (substituting) *brass* (for gold; followed by -tulā-kūṭādibhiḥ, see **tulākūṭa**).

kāṃsika, adj. (from **kāṃsa** or **kaṃsa**, qq.v., plus -ika), *made of brass*: SP 50.15 kāṃsikā ... (sugatāna bimbā).

kāṃsikā (AMg. kaṃsiā, also kaṃsia; see Sheth), prob. *a musical instrument* (so AMg.; so pw 7.331; Divy Index *vessel*) *made of brass*: Divy 529.23 tadā tvaṃ sopānake °kāṃ pātayiṣyasīti; 24 °kā pātitā.

kāka-cañcuka, nt., *a knife shaped like a crow's beak*: Mvy 8976; so Tib. gri bya rog gi mchu lta bu.

[**kākaciñcika,** see **kācilindika.**]

Kāka-jātaka, nt., *Crow-Jātaka*: Mv iii.129.17, colophon to story beginning 125.10, = Pali Supatta-Jāt., No. 292.

kākaṇi (nt.?), f. °ṇī (Pali °ṇa, nt., and °ṇikā; Skt. kākiṇi, °ṇī, °ṇikā, and acc. to Galanos kākaṇī), a small weight (of a valuable substance): ekaratnakākaṇiḥ pratipāditā Gv 205.9; *a small coin*: Mvy 9375, in both edd. printed °ṇi without ending (nt.?); Divy 396.6 °ṇiḥ, 8 °ṇī (nom. sg.).

Kākavarṇin, n. of an ancestor of Aśoka: Divy 369.10 f.

kāka-vāṇī, lit. *crow's speech*, n. of a kind of magic: Divy 636.28 °ṇī ca mantraṃ ca indrajālaṃ ca bhañjanī. (Qy: *ventriloquism*, as sounding non-human?).

kāka-śaṅkin, adj., lit. *afraid of crows*, i. e. *easily frightened* or *suspicious*: °kino hi rājānaḥ MSV ii.5.2; 72.6.

kāka-śira(s), adj. (Pali kākasīsa, ep. of the horse Valāha(ka), Jāt ii.129.9), *crow-headed*, ep. of the horse **Valāha**: Mv iii.85.11 °śiro, nom. sg.

kākāsyaka, adj., *in full bloom* (of a flower): Mvy 6231 = Tib. me tog (*flower*) kha phye ba, or kha bye ba, both = phullita, vikasita; ed. implausibly suggests em. prākāsyaka; Minayev is cited in ed. note as having explained 'become open like a crow's mouth' (kāka-āsya).

? **Kākī,** n. of a piśācī: Māy 238.20.

kākhorda, m. (Iranian loanword, Burrow, BSOS 7.781), a kind of evil spirit, often associated with vetālas (vetāḍas): Mvy 4375 = Tib. byad, *an evil demon*: Suv 3.2 (vs) °da-dāruṇa-grahe; 157.8 (vs) °da-graha-dāruṇā; 104.4 and 107.8 sarva-kākhorda-vetāḍāḥ (107.8 °ḍān); Śikṣ 192.8 (daṇḍanītiśāstrāṇi) kākhorda-śāstrāṇi vādavidyā-śā° (transl. *charms for procuring death*, but better *devil-lore*); Gv 214.6 (vs) vetālamantra tha kakhorda (m.c. ka-) sadā prayuktā; 450.25 kākhorda-vetāḍa-pratighāteṣu; Sādh 309.11; 406.10; Māy 220.18 etc.

kāṅkṣati (= Pali kaṅkhati; cf. **kāṅkṣā**, and ff.; in Skt. only *desires*; see also **ākāṅkṣati**), *doubts*: Mv i.85.12 buddhe dharme ca saṃghe ca na kāṅkṣanti ...; *worries*, Mv ii.55.21, read bhumjāhi mā (so v.l.) kāṅkṣiṣu (see § 30.16) bhojam (read bhojyam? Senart bhogam) uttamaṃ; cf. corresponding Pali vs Jāt. v.397.5 mā vicārayi = mā kāṅkṣiṣu, *don't worry*; Sukh 99.6, read prob. mā kāṅkṣayatha, *don't doubt*, see s.v. **ākāṅkṣati**; dvayoḥ kāṅkṣati MSV i.274.2, *he was troubled regarding two* (which he didn't find).

kāṅkṣā (also °ṣa-, m. or nt.? = Pali kaṅkhā; in Skt. only mg. *desire*; cf. prec. and next; this word and relatives are also used as in Skt., tho much less commonly, cf. dharmakāṅkṣā, *desire for dh°*, SP 258.6; kāṅkṣiṇo, *desirous*, LV 399.8), *doubt*: °ṣāṃ tatha saṃśayaṃ ca SP 49.1 (vs); very common, e. g. SP 61.8 (°ṣāṃ ca śokam ca jahāti); 125.12; 223.1; 337.2; LV 87.13; 370.16; Mvy 2129 (foll. by vimati; so also Divy 297.28; 328.1; RP 57.19; Gv 4.26; 32.25; Sukh 37.12 etc.; so often Pali kaṅkhā with vimati); Mv i.162.7 (here v.l. kāṅkhā); ii.308.19; 374.11; 390.23; iii.55.11; 394.16 (misprinted ka°); Divy 573.5; RP 12.10; Bhad 54; niḥkāṅkṣa (niṣk°), *free from doubt*, Mvy 364; SP 63.8; 70.11; 71.5; tīrṇakāṅkṣa, id., Mv iii.61.7; 62.12; Divy 617.14; Av i.233.5; apparently a-stem, m. or nt. (if not misprint or error of tradition), RP 8.10 (prose!) kāṅkṣa-prahāṇaṃ, *riddance of doubt*.

kāṅkṣāyita-tā, f., and **-tva,** nt. (= Pali kaṅkhāyitatta, nt.; abstract from denom. pple. derived from **kāṅkṣā**, Pali kaṅkhā; cf. prec. two and next), *state of doubt*: -tā, AsP 454.10; -tva, Av i.228.6 ff.; AsP 454.9.

kāṅkṣita, adj. (= Pali kaṅkhita; ppp. to **kāṅkṣati**), *affected by doubt*: Divy 69.18 (śrotṝṇāṃ ...) °tānām (.. vyapanaya saṃśayam).

Kāṅgī, n. of a rākṣasī: Māy 243.18.

kāca (1) m. or nt. (Pali, and Skt. Lex., id.; acc. to BR strictly the *cord* used on a carrying-pole for suspending burdens), *carrying-pole, pingo* (for carrying burdens at each end): Jm 137.4 (vs) svasthāvabaddhāv adhiropya kācam; 8 (prose) tau ... kācenādāya; **(2)** see s.v. **Kācī.**

kācaka, m. (acc. to Wilson, *glass; stone*; Skt., Pali kāca), Mvy 5971, acc. to one Tib. definition = ḥchiṅ bu, *spurious, glass jewel.*

Kācaṅgalīya, adj., *of* (the town) **Kacaṅgalā**: Av ii.41.5 °ye vanaṣaṇḍe.

kācamaṇika, m. (= Skt. °ṇi; pejorative -ka), (cheap) *crystal*, (worthless) *quartz-gem*: Gv 500.5, see § 22.37; KP 85.2 (prose; vaiḍūryaṃ ...) °ṇikān abhibhavati; 91.1, 2 (prose). In verses, 85.6; 91.7, kācamaṇi.

Kācarā, n. of a rākṣasī: Māy 240.23.

kācalindika = **kācilindika,** q.v.

kācākṣa, adj., Mvy 8836, lit. *glass-eyed*; Tib. śel mig, *glass-eye*, acc. to Das used for *spectacles*. Does it orig. mean *having a glass eye*, literally? Or *glassy-eyed*, perh. = *staring-eyed* (so Chin.)? Occurs in a list of monstrous or deformed characteristics; followed by **skandhākṣa,** q.v.

kācilindika, nt. (also **kāca**°, Mvy 5879, both edd.; Mv i.152.16; ii.29.13; 262.4 (mss.); and v.l. i.226.10; the readings kākaciñcika, kāciñ°, cited by BR from LV, are worthless corruptions found once each in Calc. but in no mss.), n. of some kind of very soft textile stuff: Mvy 5879 °kam (Tib. transliterates, adding gos, general word for *cloth, clothing*); mṛdu(ka)-kācalindika-praveṇi- Mv i.152.16 = 226.10 (kāci°, v.l. kāca°) = ii.29.13; Mv i.235.19 (text troublesome, but has kācilindika without v.l., clearly applied to clothes); °dika-mṛdu-sama-cittatāṃ Mv ii.261.2; 262.4 (so with mss., except that in 261.2 they read pama for sama); mṛdukā keśā kācilindika-sādṛśā (m.c. for sadṛśā) Mv ii.307.2 (vs); °dika-mṛdu-sparśopama-cittā Mv iii.225.5; °dika-prāvaraṇa- Śikṣ 208.11; very often in cpd. kācilindika-sukha-saṃsparśa (Bhvr.) LV 17.12; 27.4; 64.8; 65.15; 82.21; 163.3; 276.22; 286.6; Gv 194.10; Sukh 43.11; ŚsP 11.16.

? **Kācī,** pl., adopted by Lévi Māy 68 (Kācīṣu, loc.) as n. of a people or region, but apparently by his own em.; if I understand him, all his mss. and Chin. and Tib. transl. vary (**Kāca,** Kāśī, Kāñcī, etc.). Since this form seems unrecorded, it would seem better to have adopted some form supported by at least one authority.

kāñcana, m. **(1)** *gold* (in Skt. only nt.): LV 122.16 (vs) nā bhāsī itaraḥ sa kāñcana (read °naḥ, m.c.) prabhasirirahitaḥ; **(2)** n. of a kind of tree (in Skt. Lexx. applied to several trees; Pkt. kaṃcana, m., acc. to Sheth a kind of tree): Māy 258.10 (mahāvṛkṣa); MSV i.286.10; MPS 49.25.

kāñcana-cakra, nt., *gold-orb*, under the earth (see LaVallée-Poussin, AbhidhK iii.138 ff., esp. kāñcanamayī bhūmi 140): Divy 197.8 (yāvatī bhūmir ākrāntā adho 'ṣītiyojanasahasrāṇi) yāvat kāñcana-cakram...; same passage, with a few slight variants, cited Śikṣ 148.(14–)15, from some unnamed work of the Sarvāstivāda school, doubtless MSV, tho not found there in i–iii; cf. Winternitz, Hist. Ind. Lit., 2 (1933).284–5. The same is called **Kāñcanamayī bhūmi**, q.v., in Kv.

Kāñcanaparvata, n. of a Buddha: Gv 259.1.

Kāñcanamayī bhūmi = **Kāñcana-cakra**, q.v., where AbhidhK. is cited: Kv 24.22 f. sā Kāñcanamayī nāma bhūmir asti yad uttarasyāṃ Kāñcanamayyāṃ bhūmyāṃ gatvā Avalokiteśvaro ... 'dhomukhānāṃ sattvānāṃ dharmaṃ deśayati sma.

Kāñcanamālā, (1) n. of the wife of Kunāla: Divy 406.19; 413.3, 22; (2) n. of an apsaras: Kv 3.14.

Kāñcanavarṇa, n. of a king, previous incarnation of the Buddha: RP 24.2. (Not the same as **Kanakavarṇa**, q.v.)

? **kāñcu** (cf. Pkt., acc. to Sheth, kaṃcu as well as kaṃcua = Skt. kañcuka, *woman's bodice*; perhaps read kañcu, but not kāñci, *girdle*, with Senart's em.), *woman's bodice*: Mv ii.59.15 (vs) (kā dṛṣṭāsi...) sīhāṅgadā (v.l. **siṃh°**, q.v.) kāñcu (so mss.) pramṛṣṭa (or prasṛṣṭa with v.l.?) dhāraṇī (prob. divide so).

kāñcukīya, m. (occurs in Skt., see pw, which calls it a false reading for **kañc°**, q.v.; acc. to Tib. on LV, e. g. 186.2, = ñuṅ rum, more specifically *eunuch*), *eunuch* (? Skt. kañc°, usually defined less specifically as *attendant in a harem*): LV 42.17; 135.3; 186.2; 198.7, 8; Mv ii.422.4 kubja-vāmana-kirāta-varṣavara-kāñcukīyehi; 426.9, 10; 427.13–14 rājā varṣavarāṃ kāñcukīyāṃś ca pṛcchati; 427.15.

-kāṭaka, nt., in pātra-kāṭakam Mvy 8952, *ring* on which the almsbowl is fastened, = Tib. lhuṅ gzed (bzed gzhag paḥi gdu bu, *ring for putting almsbowl*. BR cite the passage with kaṭaka (as in Skt. and Pali), but Mironov also kā°; no v.l. in either ed. (but Index to Kyoto ed. cites both forms). However a form found with the same mg. in Divy and Av is **-karaka** or **-kara**, qq.v. On the other hand, Divy likewise has a form **kaṇṭaka**, q.v., clearly meaning the same thing, which raises doubts as to the etym. Cf. **kaṭaka**.

kāḍa, adj. (= Pali kāḷa, Skt. kāla), *black*: Prāt 496.6. See next.

kāḍiśāma, read prob. **kāḍa°**, adj. (= Pali kāḷasāma; cf. prec.; Skt. kāla plus śyāma), some kind of dark color, acc. to Chin. version of Prāt reported as *black*; acc. to PTSD on the Pali, *dark gray*: Prāt 517.7 (a monk must make the color of a new robe either) nīlaṃ vā kardamo vā kā°mo vā; same passage in Pali, Vin iv.120.22 nīlaṃ vā kaddamaṃ vā kāḷasāmaṃ vā; old comm. glosses yaṃ kiṃci kāḷasāmakaṃ (!).

Kāṇa, n. of a nāga king: Māy 247.24.

kāṇaka, adj. (= Skt. kāṇa; pejorative ka, or m.c.?), *one-eyed*: SP 113.11 (vs) vaṅkāś ca ye kāṇaka kuṇṭhakāś ca; in SP 94.13 (vs) KN bībhatsakāḥ kāṇaku (nom. pl.!) kaṇḍakāś ca, but read with WT for the last kuṇṭhakāś ca, and possibly before it kāṇa ku-(kuṇṭh°), see **kuṇṭhaka**.

-kāṇḍaka (= AMg. kaṇḍaka, kaṇḍaya; Skt. kāṇḍa, perh. with dim. ka?), *small piece*, in trikāṇḍakaḥ Mvy 6716 (lit. rendering in Tib.; real mg. unknown).

kāṇḍa-kāṇḍi or **°ḍī**, in °ḍiṃ kṛtvā, perh. *making an accumulation of injuries* (lit. *darts*, Skt. kāṇḍa in mg. *arrow*): MSV ii.6.11; Tib. mdaḥ daṅ mdaḥ dag hdres par byas nas, *making darts with darts in mixture*, i. e. adding one injury to another.

kāṇḍarika, m. (v.l. kaṇḍ°, but no v.l. in Mironov), Mvy 8783, defined by Tib. smad ḥchal, which is reported to mean *prostitution, dissoluteness* (and Jap. *one who frequents prostitutes*); MSV iv.68.11. But Chin. *one who is defective in the lower parts*; and the surrounding terms in Mvy and MSV (khañja, khela, kāṇa, etc.) are all adjectives referring to physical deformities, thus supporting the Chin. The Tib. word smad means *lower*, and may be used of the lower limbs; ḥchol (ḥchal) ba may mean *to be confused, deranged*.

Kāṇḍyāyana, n. of a maharṣi: Māy 256.33.

Kātyāyana (= Pali Kaccāyana, Kaccāna; occurs Mv iii.382.13 and Divy 635.15 as n. of a brahmanical gotra, as in Skt.; perhaps the same is that mentioned Laṅk 361.1 as the gotra of the Buddha **Viraja** 2, q.v.), n. of an important disciple of the Buddha (Śākyamuni): Mv i.76.5 ff. (here he is made to deliver a discourse on the ten bhūmi); SP 152.3; Divy 11.29; 550.2; identical with **Mahākātyāyana**, which is commoner; in Divy 573.8 he appears to have the epithet (Ārya-) **Kāśyapa**, q.v. (or are they different persons?); Kātyāyanāvavāda MPS 29.15 (see Waldschmidt, p. 284 n. 6).

kāntāra, m. or nt. (see Gray, ZDMG 60.360, citing this word from Vāsavadattā, expl. in comm. by durbhikṣā; Pali kantāra, cpd. with prec. dubhikkha-; said by PTSD to mean *hardship, trouble* in general): *famine*: Av ii.83.8 tena khalu samayena durbhikṣam abhūt kṛcchram, kāntāra-durlambhaḥ piṇḍako yācanakena; Kv 47.15 nādyaiva māṃsabhakṣaṇaṃ viṃśati-varṣāṇi paripūrṇāni kāntārasya ca pratipannasya ca nātra kiṃcid annapānaṃ saṃvidyate; 47.20; MSV i.237.15; in SP 81.11 perhaps in more general sense of *troubles, difficulty, disaster*: parimuktāḥ sarvabhayopadrava-kāntārebhyo nirvṛtisukhaprāptāḥ.

Kāpiñjaleya, m. pl., n. of a brahmanical school (of the Chandogas): Divy 637.27. (Cf. Kāpiñjalāda, pw.)

Kāpilavastava, adj. (= Pali °vatthava), *of Kapilavastu*: Mahāsamāj., Waldschmidt, Kl. Skt. Texte 4.167.14 vanaṃ °vam; 169.2 id.

kāpileya (cf. Skt. kapila), adj.? *drawn by tawny oxen*? or subst., *tawny cattle*?: Mv iii.50.14 (in description of luxurious state abandoned by Kāśyapa on taking up religious life), ekūnaṃ ca halasahasraṃ bhadrāṃ kāpileyāṃ (could be acc. pl. m. or sg. f.) suvarṇasirikāṃ (so Senart em., cf. **hala-sīra**; but mss. suvarṇasamikā or (?) °saṃvikā) avahāya.

Kāpiśī, n. of a locality: Māy 83; 94; cf. Lévi p. 102; the name occurs in Pāṇ. 4.2.99, which Lévi fails to note.

kāpuruṣa, m. (= Pali kāpurisa; in Skt. apparently used only in sense of *coward, contemptible person*), *evil, wicked man*: Mv i.131.7 prāpyo (mss. °ya) khalv ayaṃ mama kāpuruṣo bhasmīkartum (said by a nāga-king of a snake-charmer who was at his mercy).

kāpotaka, m., acc. to Tib. (phug ron) = Skt. kapota(ka), *pigeon*: LV 248.20 (prose) sārasikāpotaka-saṃdaṃśikotsṛṣṭasamprakṣālakaiḥ (of a certain type of ascetics, or their practices, in a list of such types). The ā is strange, and I am not sure that we should not divide sārasikā-potaka, *the young of female cranes*; but Tib. is very clear. (AMg. kāvoya, a type of ascetics, and kāvoyā, *'taking food with great care, like pigeons,'* Ratnach., seem not to be relevant here.) Foucaux: *qui mangent, après l'avoir lavé, ce qui, mordu par les grues et les pigeons, en a été rejeté*; so Tib

kāma, nt. (so cited Skt. Lex. *object of desire*, BR; acc. to PTSD nt. as well as m. in Pali), (*object of*) *desire*: LV 215.7 (vs) bhukta kāmāni (so Lefm. with only ms. A, the best; the others kāmān imāṃ which is bad in meter and sense and seems an attempt to 'correct' the form) rūpāś ca śabdāś ca ... nānāvidhā.

kāmakārika-tā, *condition* (or *power*) *of making at will*: Mv iii.335.14 (repeated 16, 18, etc.) (idam rūpaṃ ce, v.l. ced, bhikṣavaḥ ātmā abhaviṣyat,) na ca (so read with mss., Senart va) rūpaṃ ābādhāya duḥkhāya saṃvarteta, ṛdhyāc ca rūpe kāmakārikatā, evaṃ me rūpaṃ bhavatu evaṃ mā bhavatu (etc.), ... *one could make what he pleased in regard to his form* ... See in Pali Vin. i.13.19 ff., essentially the same passage (but without this word).

kāma-guṇa, m. pl. (= Pali id., defined as *the objects of the five senses*, e. g. AN iii.411.4 ff.), *qualities of desire*, regularly five in number, in some passages clearly understood as the objects of the five senses as in Pali; so Mv iii.417.2 pañca kāmaguṇe (n. pl.; read °ṇā?) loke manaḥ-ṣaṣṭhā praveditā (so read with mss.), tatra me vigato chando ...; SP 79.8 (mā ... 'bhiramadhvaṃ hīneṣu) rūpa-śabda-gandha-rasa-sparśeṣu; atra hi yūyaṃ traidhātuke 'bhiratāḥ pañca-kāmaguṇa-sahagatayā tṛṣṇayā dahyatha; yet in Mv ii.116.17 pañca kāmaguṇāṃ (acc. pl.), specifically listed as nāṭyaṃ gītaṃ vāditaṃ tūryaṃ striyo; the fact seems to be that the phrase became a stock formula or cliché, often used without definite association with any list; so Mvy 5378, 7373 mentions the 5 kāmaguṇa, but never lists them (in 871 even the number 5 is lacking). The old tradition that they are the objects of the 5 senses never died out, however; see LaVallée-Poussin, AbhidhK. iii.86 note 2. With the number 5 they are mentioned SP 78.12; 111.6; 213.6; LV 186.19; 215.3; Mv i.31.5; ii.170.13, etc.; without the number e. g. LV 45.4; 173.19 and 22 (cited Śikṣ 204.7 and 10); Mv ii.142.5, 12.

kāmaṃgama, adj. or subst. m. and f. °mā (= Pali id., Childers, without reference; cf. Skt. kāmaga and Lex. kāmagāmin, kāmaṃgāmin; all these in mg. 1), (**1**) *going at will, freely, where one lists*: Śikṣ 32.15 (sarvasattvā) kāmaṃgamā bhavantu sarvatragāminībuddhabhūmipratílabdhāḥ; (**2**) *going according to the desire* (of someone else, sc. a master); *a servant*: Divy 302.26 yeṣām ahaṃ dāsaḥ preṣyo nirdeśyo bhujiṣyo nayena kāmaṃgamas teṣāṃ pūjyaś ca bhaviṣyāmi; Gv 412.7 (ahaṃ te ...) yathecchāparibhogyā yena kāmaṃgamā sarvatrātyantānugāminī ... sarvakāryotsukā.

kāmacchanda, m. (= Pali id.), *desire for lusts*, one of the 5 **nīvaraṇa**, q.v. (as in Pali): Mvy 2218.

Kāmada, m. or nt., n. of a locality: Māy 93.

Kāmadeva, n. of a former Buddha: Mv i.140.14.

kāma-dhātu, m. (= Pali id.), *the world* (*region, sphere*) *of desire*, including all states of existence up to and including that of the paranirmitavaśavartin gods; the gods who live in this region are called **kāmāvacara** (see **deva**): very common, e. g. Mv ii.314.12; LV 45.15; 48.17; 299.20; Jm 192.11; esp. contrasting with **rūpa-dhātu** and **ārūpya-(dhātu)**, qq.v., LV 428.19; Mvy 3072; KP 94.4.

kāmadhātuka, adj., *of the kāma-dhātu*, q.v.: Gv 203.8 (sarva-) kāmadhātuka-deva-manuṣyātikrānta-.

kāmaṃdada, adj. (cf. **-dada**), *desire-giving*; with vṛkṣa, = Skt. kalpavṛkṣa: Gv 495.3 °dada-vṛkṣa-bhūtaṃ (bodhicittam). See also kāma-dada, s.v. **-dada**.

Kāmarūpin, n. of a mountain: °pī Divy 450.10; 455.29.

Kāmarūpiṇī, n. of a kind of magic: Divy 636.27.

kāma-vitarka, m. (= Pali °vitakka), (sinful) *thinking on lusts*: Mv i.145.16 = 202.13 = ii.6.10.

Kāmaśreṣṭha (cf. Pali Kāmaseṭṭha, n. of a yakṣa), (**1**) n. of a yakṣa: Māy 236.27; (**2**) n. of a gandharva: Suv 162.4.

Kāmāpavādakasūtra, nt., n. of a work: Śikṣ 76.16.

kāmāvacara, m. (rarely f., see below; = Pali id.; cf. **-avacara**), *dwelling in the kāma-dhātu* or *the realm of desire*, ep. of a group (regularly six; ṣaṭ-kāmāvacarā devāḥ Dharmas 127; LV 290.2) of classes of gods (for list see s.v. **deva**): LV 30.5; 59.17 (they are kāmadhātu-stha 59.11); 83.6 (read °cara-deve°); 99.8; 273.16; 290.2; 300.3; 302.5 (here a list of some of their 'overlords'); 369.12; 413.5; Divy 140.18; 203.11; 327.29; Mv i.159.6; 209.6 = ii.11.13; i.265.18; ii.2.8; iii.223.8; Mvy 6895; Suv 10.3; Mmk 69.8; Gv 121.22; Bbh 295.23; Karmav 30.13; °vacarā apsaraso LV 353.9; seemingly used in a broader sense (as also in Pali) to refer to any beings 'subject to desires' Mvy 2154.

kāminikā (= Skt. kāminī), *a loving woman* (endearing dim., § 22.34); applied to daughters of Māra: LV 322.20 (vs) prekṣasu nātha (perhaps read prekṣa sunātha, § 30.16) su-kāminikāṃ; 323.14 (vs) na hi bhuñjasi kāminikāṃ.

Kāminī, n. of a goddess: Sādh 502.8.

Kāmpillaka (v.l. **Kam°**), adj., of **Kampilla** (Kāmpilya): Mv iii.156.12 °ko ca rājā Brahmadatto.

Kāmbojaka, adj., f. °**ikā** (Skt. Gr. id.), *of Kamboja*: °ikānāṃ kanyānām MSV iii.136.20.

Kāmbojī, n. of a rākṣasī: Māy 240.23; cf. **kamboja**

kāya, normally m. (= Skt., but sometimes nt., LV 289.20, vs, naivāsanāt kāyam ataś caliṣyate, *my body shall by no means move from this seat*; Mv i.44.4 hāyiṣyati asura-kāyaṃ, n. sg.; ii.124.2–3 idam eva kāyaṃ, acc. sg., twice; SP 52.8, vs, avanāmitaṃ kāyu, n. sg.; but WT with ms. K′ °taḥ): (**1**) sometimes, as in Pali, *body* used instead of Skt. tvac as term for the organ of touch: Mvy 2036 kāyāyatanam; 2053 kāya-dhātuḥ; its object is **spraṣṭavya,** q.v.; (**2**) as in Pali (Skt. Lex.), *body* in the sense of *group, collection, mass, crowd, totality*: usually at the end of cpds., as jana-k°, mahato janakāyasyārthāya, *for the welfare of a great crowd* (? the vast mass or totality) *of people*, SP 41.1; 81.2; 162.10; mahatā janakāyena parivṛtaṃ, *by a large retinue* ... SP 103.6; taṃ ca mahāntaṃ janakāyaṃ ... adhyabhāṣat LV 124.13; mahājana-kāya = *the body of the populace* (contrasting with kings and great men), Mv i.37.1; 198.15; ii.2.17; and probably LV 131.22; sarva eva Jambudvīpanivāsī janakāya Divy 59.22; bala-kāya, *body of troops, army*, vārāṇasī (so read) caturaṅgena balakāyena veṣṭitā (so with v.l.) Mv ii.82.11; caturaṅgeṇa balakāyena LV 14.22; caturaṅga-bala-kāyaṃ (mss. vara for bala) saṃnahitvā hastikāyaṃ aśvak° rathak° pattik° saṃnahitvā Mv i.30.6; caturaṅgabalakāyo ii.111.7; (hastyaśvaratha)padāti-balakāya-samanvitaḥ LV 22.15; mahāntaṃ hastikāyaṃ ... pattikāyam avahāya Mv ii.161.5 f.; pattikāya-parivṛtaḥ Divy 618.24; sattvakāye, *in the* (whole) *mass of creatures*, Mv i.158.10; 159.5; rājño Māndhātasya putrapautra-kāye napta-pranapti-kāye (so read) bahūni rājasahasrāṇi Mv i.348.9, *in the body* (mass) *of King M.'s sons, grandsons, and remoter descendants there were many thousands of kings* (misunderstood by Senart; fem. forms impossible); tailavyāmiśro gandhakāyo (*a collection of perfume*, i. e. of sweet-scented substances) dattaḥ (at a stūpa) Av i.362.1; sa paśyati mahāprajño dharmakāyam aśeṣataḥ SP 143.3 (vs), ... *the whole mass of conditions of existence* (cf. sarva-dharmān 143.1); in the same sense, māyāsvapnasvabhāvasya dharmakāyasya kaḥ stavaḥ Laṅk 22.12 (vs); (visaṃvādakaṃ sarvam eva) dharmakāyaṃ Mv ii.147.18, *disappointing* (is) *the whole mass of conditions of existence*; probably also, dharmakāyajñānaśarīratvān ... LV 428.21–22, *because his body contains* (or *consists of*) *knowledge of the whole mass of states of existence* (he is called a Great Tree); otherwise Foucaux; prob. also, na rājan kṛpaṇo loke dharmakāyena saṃspṛśet Divy 560.2 (vs), ... *with the mass of material conditions* (surely not 'spiritual body' with Index); acc. to LaV-P. AbhidhK. vii.81, n. 1, 'souvent dharmakāya = le corps des écritures = le deuxième ratna'; I have not found this usage; he refers to Bodhicaryāv. i.1, where I see no such mg. in the word; to Divy 396 (? line 28, śarīraṃ ... dharmamayaṃ); and to Przyluski, Açoka, 359, where it does not have that meaning but contrasts with **rūpakāya**, q.v.; **sparśa-kāya,** see this; nāma-kāyaḥ, *collection of 'names'* = *words* Mvy 1996, vyañjana-k° 1997, *c. of 'letters', sounds, or syllables* (= akṣara), and pada-k° 1998, *c. of phrases, expressions, sentences* (these terms explained in LaVallée Poussin, AbhidhK. ii.238–40; Tib. renders kāva bv tshogs, *mass,* *quantity*, and **pada**, q.v. by tshig, which means both *word* and *speech, utterance*); sometimes, but more rarely, used out of comp. with modifying adj. or appositional noun, as, tuṣite kāye Mv i.199.7 = ii.3.5; (parihāsyante...) asurāḥ kāyāḥ, divyāḥ kāyāḥ paripūriṃ gamiṣyanti LV 401.6; hāyetsu(ḥ) āsurā kāyā, divyā kāyā abhivardhetsu Mv i.330.9 (cf. on the other hand, hāyiṣyati asura-kāyaṃ, nara-maru-saṃgho vivardhanti Mv i.44.4). On the three 'bodies' (kāya) of a Buddha, **dharma-, saṃbhoga-, nirmāṇa-k°**, see these words; Régamey, Samādh. p. 23, with refs. They hardly occur in the texts included in this work. A little better known is the two-fold contrast of **dharma-** with **rūpa-k°**, qq.v.

Kāyakalisaṃpramathana, m., n. of a samādhi: Mvy 621; ŚsP 1426.5.

kāya-bandhana, nt. (= Pali id.), *girdle*: Mvy 5855; 8993; Mv i.19.4 cīvarāṇi vā °nāni vā; Bhīk 29a.1, 5 pātreṇa cīvareṇa śikyena (= Skt.; *loop*, for carrying bowl) saritena (see **sarita** 3; in 29a.1 śar°) kāyabandhanena.

kāya-saṃsarga, m. (= Pali °sagga), *bodily contact* (with a woman, in a libidinous way), one of the saṃghāvaśeṣa sins: Mvy 8370; Prāt 479.8; probably *sexual intercourse* in Mvy 9467 (the preceding word is vivāhaḥ).

kāya-sākṣin (= Pali °sakkhi, Jāt. v.424.12), *personal, bodily, physical witness; one who has seen* (the circumstance) *in the flesh*: Śikṣ 109.9 (vs) (paribhāṣyate cāpi sa paṇḍitebhiḥ,) ye ka-cid (read ke cid) astī pṛtha (read **pṛthu,** q.v.?) kāyasākṣī (n. pl.).

-kāyika, ifc. adj. (from **kāya** 2 plus -ika), *belonging to the company of*...; noted only modifying (as separate word or in comp.) the words deva and devaputra, of various classes of 'gods': tuṣitakāyika LV 183.17; 363.21; Gv 527.15; tuṣitabhavanakāyiko devaputro Mv i.174.1; trāyatriṃśakāyikair devair LV 365.8; gandharvakāyikeṣu deveṣu Mv ii.49.2; mārakāyikā devaputrās LV 300.4; svaviṣayakāyika-devaputrā(s) Mv ii.278.16 (Māra speaking); °yikā dev° 287.11.

? **kāyitāntya**, acc. °tyaṃ (read prob. kāya-; second member uncertain; to tānta with -ya?), acc. to Tib. (lus kyis sñog par byed) *making lust with the body* (towards women): MSV iii.16.3; see s.v. **drava.**

kāyuśa, Mvy 5830, or **kāyūṣa**, 5937, nt. (varr. with a for ā, p for y, s for ś or ṣ; Mironov adopts kayuṣa in 5937 but records numerous varr.), acc. to Tib. *green vitriol, green* or *black sulphate of iron*, Skt. (puṣpa-) kāsīsa, which is rendered by the same Tib. (nag tshur) at Mvy 5829, 5938.

Kāyeśa (kāya-īśa), a name for **Vairocana** (3) as one of the 5 'transcendant' Buddhas, replacing V. in a list of these at Sādh 164.9.

kāyoddharṣaṇa, nt., Mvy 9001, acc. to Chin. *fine-meshed cloth*; Tib. rnag gzan, lit. *pus-eater* (var. gnag gzan, prob. intending the same); possibly *gauze-like cloth for binding suppurated sores*? The apparent composition, kāya-uddharṣaṇa, should mean something like *enlivener of the body*!

1 **kāra**, m. sg. or (oftener) pl. (= Pali id.; pw 7.331 identifies with Vedic kāra, *hymn of praise*, but BHS always makes it object of a form of karoti), *homage, act of worship*: sg. kāraḥ kṛto Divy 133.17; (blend-form in mss.) kārāḥ kṛto (!) 134.1, 6, 10; otherwise only pl., kārāḥ kṛtā(ḥ) Divy 133.12, 22 (mss.); 192.19; 539.10; Av i.349.13; te kārāḥ kṛtās (note masc. pronoun) ii.108.1; kārā (for °rāḥ) kṛtā a- Divy 289.6; 583.29; kārā na kṛtā yena Divy 82.15; 88.18; kārāḥ kartavyā iti Av i.308.7; kārān, acc. pl. Divy 166.26; 329.16 (kurvan); 329.20 (akariṣyat); 539.8; Av i.154.2 (kartum); MSV i.61.19; ii.138.13, 14; acc. often written kārāṃ, which is only an orthographic variant of kārān but has led to the erroneous view that the stem is or may be fem. (kārā); so Divy 47.21, 24; 135.18; 245.1, 3, 9; 251.14; 289.15; 366.18; 420.16; 423.11; 531.8; 579.6; Śikṣ 150.2; Bbh 233.12; 234.16. The very rare sg. occurrences may be corruptions; standardly the word is m. pl.

2 **kāra** = Skt. kāla, *time* (cf. **-kārika** and vikāra for **vikāla**, q.v.): LV 79.18 (vs) kāru (only one inferior ms. kālu) deva pratīkṣa, *await the* (proper) *time, sire*!

-kāraka, see **puruṣa-k°**.

-kārakam, adv., quasi-gerund, ifc., *making*...; see §§ 22.5; 35.5: ālopa-kārakam, *making a morsel of it*, Mv i.339.16; 344.14 etc. (prose); na cuccu-k°, *not making the noise cuccu*, Mvy 8577 (similar onomatopoetic forms 8578–8580); na sikthapṛthak-kārakam 8582; nāvarṇakārakam, *not making dispraise, not complaining(ly)*, 8583. So also in Pali, e. g. capucapu-kār° Vin. ii.221.35.

kāraṇa, *cause* (as in Skt.; a few special uses): (**1**) Laṅk 9.18 f. sarva-kāraṇa-tīrthya-vyapeta-buddheḥ (Laṅkādhipateḥ), prob. *having his intellect turned away from the heretics* (who are characterized by the view that) *all things are caused* (Suzuki's version is impossible); (**2**) acc. adv., *for the sake* (of, gen.): SP 74.8 (prose) āgacchata (read prob. °tha with most mss.) śīghraṃ teṣāṃ kāraṇaṃ nirdhāvata (°tha), *come, run forth quickly for the sake of* (getting) *these* (toys)!; (**3**) loc., quasi-adv., used in a way resembling Skt. sthāne, *with good reason*: Jm 223.20 (vs) jagad idam avakīrṇam kāraṇe tvadyaśobhiḥ.

kāraṇā (= Pali id.; essentially Buddhist word, tho cited in Skt. Lexx. and once from Daśak., BR s.v.), *torture, torment*, esp. applied to torments of hell: with kārayati, *causes to undergo, inflicts*, °ṇāṃ kārayanti Divy 376.12; °ṇāḥ (so with mss.) sattvānām ārabdhāḥ kārayitum id. 16; kāraṇāviśeṣāḥ (in hell) pratiprasrabhyante, *are allayed, quieted*, Divy 68.3; 138.10; 265.23 (°srabdhāḥ); 568.15; Av i.4.10–11; 10.10–11, etc.; kāraṇābhiḥ kārito, *tortured with torments* (in hell and elsewhere) Śikṣ 186.11; of earthly torments, kāraṇāś ca kārenti LV 259.19 (vs), *they make him* (the Bodhisattva, practising austerities) *undergo* (physical) *torments*; ātmanaḥ kāraṇāṃ kārayasi Śikṣ 39.3; *you inflict torture on yourself*.

-kāraṇika, adj. or subst. m. (not recorded in this mg.; from Skt. kāraṇa plus -ika), *one who holds... to be the cause* (of existence, etc.): Jm 149.24 īśvara-k°, *one who holds God to be the Cause*.

? **kāraṇī**, adj. f. or subst. assimilated in gender to f. subject, *cause, thing that gives rise to* (gen.): Laṅk 109.4 yadi... māyāprakhyā bhrāntis tenānyasyā bhrānteḥ (read bhrāntiḥ with all mss. except one bhrāntyāḥ) kāraṇī bhaviṣyati. But kāraṇībhaviṣyati (one word) may be intended; not however stem *kāraṇin with Suzuki, Index. Cf. **karaṇī.**

kāraṇḍava, m. (in Pali *chaff, rubbish*; cf. next), *a kind of grain*: Mvy 5669 = Tib. sre da, *a kind of corn*; confirmed by context (list of cereals).

kāraṇḍavaka, m. (cf. prec.; Pali °va, *chaff, rubbish*), *chaff* as symbol of worthlessness, fig. bodhisattva-k°, *a worthless B.*: AsP 394.17 °ko veditavyaś cauraḥ śramaṇaveṣeṇa.

Kāraṇḍavyūha, n. of a work: Kv 13.20; 23.6 °hamahāyāna-sūtra-ratna-rāja-, etc.; Sādh 30.21.

kārayati, with object **kāraṇām** or **°ṇāḥ**, *causes to undergo* (torments), *inflicts*; hence once with instr. vividhābhiś ca kāraṇābhiḥ kārito Śikṣ 186.11 (prose), *inflicted with various tortures* (see s.v. **kāraṇā**). Cf. **kāritaka, kāritakāraṇa.**

kāravālika, m. (Skt. karavāla plus -ika), (royal) *sword-bearer*: Mvy 3729 (in list of royal officers).

kārasūtra, see **kāla°**.

kārākāra, m., n. of a samādhi, see **kāryakara.**

Kārā-dvīpa (m. or nt.), n. of a dvīpa: Jm 34.16.

kārānusāri(n) = **kālānu°**, q.v. (with r for l in kāla, *black*; cf. **kārasūtra**, and **kāra** = kāla, *time*), a kind of sandalwood: -ri- (in comp.) LV 274.7 (all mss., both edd.); Mv iii.261.4 (so mss., Senart em. kāl°).

kārāpaka, m. (cf. Pali id.; to kārāpayati, with -aka), *he who causes to act,* used in a formulaic list of terms applied to the (heretically alleged) ātman, and as such rejected: Mvy 4678 (follows kāraka); Mv iii.447.11, 16 (kārako vā) °pako vā utthāpako vā...; ŚsP 120.18 °pakaḥ °paka iti vyavahriyate sa ca yathābhūtaṃ parigaveṣyamāṇo nopalabhyate.

kārāpaṇa, nt. (= Pali id.; to next, with suffix -ana), *the causing to be built:* Karmav 39.10 caityastūpa-kārāpaṇam.

kārāpayati, and °**peti** (Pali id.), see Chap. 43, s.v. kṛ (4).

kārāhva (Skt. kārā-āhvā), *what is called a prison:* Mv iii.105.9 (vs), read with mss. bandhasya kathaṃ mukto vacanena kārāhvam abhikrameya, *how, having been freed from a bond by a word, would one enter into what is called a prison* (viz. sensual life)? Meter is to be sure bad, but the sense is perfect; Senart em. wrongly.

-kārika, adj. (= Skt. kālika; cf. 2 **kāra**), ifc., *belonging to a... time:* LV 40.11 (prose) nānāpuṣpaphalavṛkṣā nānartukārikās (only one inferior ms. °kālikās),... *trees belonging to the time of various seasons,* or *to various seasons and times.*

Kāriṇī, n. of a goddess: Sādh 502.9.

kāritaka, adj. (kārita, ppp. of kārayati in sense of karoti, § 38.6, plus -ka, perhaps specifying, § 22.39, or perhaps m.c.), *(the one that had been) constructed:* Mmk 640.7 (vs) paśyate... caityaṃ kāritakaṃ hi taiḥ, *saw the caitya that had been constructed by them.*

kārita-kāraṇa, adj. (on kārita, ppp. of kārayati = karoti, cf. prec.), *having performed his duties, done what he had to do,* said of a Buddha (or a disciple, iii.60.7, or Pratyekabuddha, i.301.7) compared to an elephant: nāgo viya (iii.64.6 yathā) kāritakāraṇo Mv i.237.10; 301.7; iii.60.7; 64.6. Senart, i note p. 560, aptly compares SP 1.7 (arhadbhiḥ...) mahānāgaiḥ kṛtakṛtyaiḥ kṛtakaraṇīyair.

kāritra, nt. (apparently based on Skt. cāritra, blended with forms of kar-, kār-), *action, operation:* Mvy 6698; 7250 (Tib. byed pa, *action*); Bcṭ 261.4; 372.5, 10; repeatedly in AbhidhK, see LaVallée Poussin's Index; repeatedly in Abhisamayālaṃkārāloka (GOS 62), e. g. 276.18 kāritraduṣkaratā; 362.4 (vs) paścimaṃ gatikāritram idaṃ kāritralakṣaṇam.

[**kārīṣi**? form and mg. doubtful, in refrain pāda: kārīṣi (so the mss. seem clearly to indicate; sometimes they read °ṣu, and other vv.ll.) dattvā jinacetiyeṣu Mv ii.384.17, repeated 21, 385.3, 7, 11, 19, 23. A parallel vs occurring in the midst of these, 385.15, has (na) tailavinduṃ jinastūpe dattvā; and in a following vs 386.1 tailasya vinduṃ jinacetiyeṣu occurs. This suggests that possibly tālīśa (°śu, for °śaṃ?) should be read, = Pali tālīsa, tālissa, *a 'powder or ointment'* (PTSD) made from the plant named in Skt. tālīśa; **tālīśa** occurs, perhaps in this mg. (associated with tailam), in Mvy 5787, see s.v. It seems at any rate appropriate; some oily substance used in decorating a caitya is indicated.]

kāruṇa (nowhere recorded), (**1**) adj. (= Skt. kāruṇika), *compassionate:* Mv i.179.6 (vs, metr. indifferent) tato lokānukampārthaṃ kāruṇo (mss. °ṇā) mahadviśāradaḥ; (**2**) subst. nt. (= Skt. kāruṇya), *compassion:* Mv i.51.2–3 ... samyaksaṃbuddhasya mahatā kāruṇena (no v.l.) samanvāgatasya sattveṣu mahākāruṇaṃ (no v.l.) okrami.

Kāruṇika, n. of a former Buddha: Sukh 6.15.

kāruṇyatā (= Pali kāruññatā; Skt. °ṇya plus tā, § 22.43), *compassion:* Divy 194.16.

kārpāsaka, nt. (= Skt. °sa), *cotton cloth:* Mvy 9164 °kam.

kārpāsika, m. (= AMg. kappāsia; one doubtful Skt. occurrence, pw 6.300), *dealer in cotton goods:* Mv iii.442.14 °kā, n. pl., in a list of merchants and artisans. Cf. **karpāsika,** used in very similar list.

Kāryakara, m., n. of a samādhi: Mvy 558. In same list ŚsP 1419.14 kārākāra; read kārakāra? or kārya° as in Mvy? Explained by yatra samādhau sthitvā sarvasamādhīnāṃ kārāgatāṃ kriyāṃ karoti.

Kāryatāvicāra, n. of a former Buddha: Mv i.141.6.

kārvaṭika, m. (Skt. karvaṭa plus -ika; cf. **karvaṭaka**), *chief of a village* (mountain hamlet?): Divy 445.23; 446.5, 20; 531.11; in MSV i.102.13 read -nyatamaḥ kārvaṭiko vyutthitaḥ (text has nt. forms), cf. 17 taṃ kārvaṭikaṃ nirjitya.

kārṣa, m. (Skt. Gr.), *plowman:* Divy 463.8 (prose) (pañca) kārṣa-śatāny, prob. error; in the sequel, 463.11 ff., repeatedly replaced by kārṣaka (Skt.); same passage MSV i.71.3 ff. kārṣika (Skt., KSS.) thruout.

kārṣāpaṇa-chedikam, adv. (or acc. sg. of °ka or °kā?), in °kaṃ vā chidyamānasya Śikṣ 182.5, *or being cut up into small pieces the size of a coin,* a form of torture; = next, and see **kahāpaṇa**(-māṃsika).

kārṣāpaṇa-māṃsika, see **kahāpaṇa** (-mā°).

kārṣikā (or °**ka**; cf. Skt. karṣa), a small weight, app. = karṣa: Laṅk 31.9 (vs) karṣo hi dharaṇāḥ kyantaḥ, palaṃ vai kati kārṣikā (one ms. °kam; must be n. pl.), *how many dharaṇas make a karṣa, how many kārṣikās* (°*kas*?) *a pala*? (Tib. however is reported to render kārṣikā by zho, which is one-tenth of a sraṅ, the word used for karṣa in the same line.)

-kārṣī, see **gomaya-k°.**

1 **kāla** (adj., *black,* as in Skt.), (**1**) (m.? = **kālaka** 3, which is more usual in this sense and which see), *blackhead, pimple:* Mvy 309 vyapagata-tilaka-kāla-gātra, one of the anuvyañjana; so Kyōtō ed., but Mironov °kālaka°; (**2**) n. of some plant: sayyathāpi nāma kālaparvāṇi vā (v.l. adds aśitaparvāṇi vā) evam eva me aṅgāni abhūnsuḥ Mv ii.125.12, and similarly 126.17; 128.5; 129.7; see discussion s.v. **āśītakī**; in parallel LV 254.8 kālāparvāṇi (but most mss. omit), which agrees with the corresp. Pali text kālāpabbāni MN i.80.12; 245.27, but the comm. on the former reads kāḷa-pabbāni (as in Mv!) and repeats the same form in its gloss (kāḷavalliyā vā saṃdhiṭṭhānesu); it may mean the same plant designated as kālā in Skt. (and Pali); (**3**) (= Pali Kāḷa, Mahākāḷa; cf. **Kālaka** 4 and **Kālika**) n. of a nāga king, who came in contact with the Bodhisattva shortly before he reached the bodhitree: Mv ii.265.7 ff.; 302.14; 304.5; 308.4; 397.9 ff.; 400.10 ff.; after the enlightenment he saluted the Buddha and invited him to his home, where B. spent the fourth week after the enlightenment, Mv iii.300.10 ff.; mentioned Mvy 3251; Māy 221.29; (**4**) n. of a yakṣa: Māy 7; 236.10; (**5**) apparently n. of Asita, or epithet given him (synonym in literal mg.), see **Asita** (2): Mv ii.37.13; (**6**) n. of a disciple of Buddha (doubtless intends one of the several disciples named Kāḷa in Pali): SP 207.3; (**7**) n. of a minister of Māra: Mv ii.409.19; (**8**) n. of a brother of King Prasenajit (cf. **Gaṇḍaka** 3): Divy 153.21 ff.; 160.5; (**9**) n. of a mountain, perhaps = **Kāla-parvata** (?), q.v.: Kv 91.13 Kāla-mahākālau parvatarājānau.

2 **kāla,** m. (as in Skt. *time, death,* etc.) (**1**) *day,* opp. to night, see s.v. **akāla**; cf. Pali kāla, PTSD s.v. 2(a), kāle juṇhe, *by day and by night;* (**2**) kālena kālaṃ, adverbial phrase, (**a**) *from time to time* (so Pali, see Childers s.v. kālo): SP 225.5 (or under b?); 276.7, 10; Mv iii.154.14 (or under b?); Av i.241.9; Divy 10.27 (or under b?); Suv 94.3 (or under b?); (**b**) *day in and day out, continuously:* LV 100.13; Divy 62.10; 71.5; 298.25; Kv 28.14; Bbh 239.21, 23; 362.16, 19, 23; and perhaps in some cases noted under a, above; (**3**) *time for functioning:* Mv iii.222.12 āryo khalv asmākaṃ govindo bhartā bhartṛ-kāle (? mss. bharte°, bhartta°) sakhā sakhi-kāle (? mss. sakha°, sakhī°), *to us, you see, G.* (our husband) *is a husband at the time for* (functioning as) *a husband, a friend at the time for a friend* (said by his wives in proposing to follow him into

the ascetic life); see also Mv ii.131.11 cited s.v. **nāganadī**; (**4**) yaṃ kālaṃ, adverbial phrase, quasi-conj., *what time, when* (relative): Mv ii.210.14; iii.144.13, 15; 145.7; 272.9 (v.l. yat k°); yatra kālaṃ, id., Mv iii.295.13, 15, 16; (**5**) phrase, yasya kālaṃ manyasi, or manyatha (= Pali yassa kālaṃ maññasi), *as you think fit*, in assenting to a proposal: Mv iii.210.9 (yasya ca k°, with mss.); 222.15 (yasya dāni k°); yasyedānīṃ kālaṃ manyase, id., Mmk 2.17–8; 73.19.

kālaka, (**1**) adj. (= Pali kāḷaka; Skt. very rarely for kāla, see BR s.v.), *black*: Mvy 8397 śuddhaka-kālakānām (Kyōtō text °nam; Mironov °nām), sc. eḍakalomnām (same passage in Pali suddha-kāḷakānaṃ, Vin. iii.225.28); varṇena te kālaka tatra bhonti SP 94.7 (vs; here ka could be pejorative, or m.c.); kālako vata bhoḥ śramaṇo gautamaḥ LV 255.4; 256.7 (prose; could be pejorative ka); (**2**) *black spot* on a garment, and also *moral defilement* (= Pali kāḷaka, id.), see s.vv. **apagata-kālaka** and **sarvakālaka**; (**3**) (m.?) *blackhead, pimple* on skin (= Skt. Lex., perh. once lit., id.; Pali kāḷaka; = BHS 1 **kāla 1**, q.v., rare): vyapagata-tila-kālaka-gātra, one of the anuvyañjana, Mironov's Mvy for Kyōtō °kāla° 309, and similarly LV 107.5; Mv ii.43.13; (**4**) (cf. 1 **Kāla** 3 and **Kālika**) n. of a nāga: Mvy 3327 (here definitely distinguished as a 'commoner' of the nāgas from Kāla, who is a 'nāga-king'); Māy 221.24; 247.3; however, in Māy 247.13 dvau Kālakau nāgarājānau. See next.

kālaka-pṛṣṭha (ms. thrice kālakā-p°), adj., acc. to Tib. (quite literally) *having a black back* (rgyab nag po), applied to a man suffering for past misdeeds: MSV ii.89.7, 8, 12; in 89.13, 90.1 ff. text kālaka° without note.

kālakarṇin, adj. or subst. m. (Skt. Lex., allegedly °ṇī f.; in Pali and BHS clearly °ṇin, cf. Jāt. ii.153.23, prose, kālakaṇṇi-sakuṇena), *omen of bad luck*; *'Jonah'*: Mv i.257.6 (prose) (tatra), sarve īti- (mss. iti) -kali-kālakarṇi (Senart em. °ṇī; n. pl.) praśāmyanti; Divy 40.16, 17, 19, asau (...) kālakarṇi-prakhyaḥ, said of a man, Pūrṇaka; 19 śrīr vā bhavatu kālakarṇī (surely n. sg. m.) vāgacchaikadhye prativasāmah. The lit. mg. is doubtless *black-eared*.

kāla-kriyā (= Pali °kiriyā; cf. Skt. kāla-karman, once in Rām., BR), *death*: SP 102.11 (prose) mā haiva mama °yā bhavet; 112.2; 347.7 (prose) abhyāśībhūtāś caite kālakriyāyāḥ; Mv ii.32.10 (prose) nacireṇa kālena °yāṃ kariṣyāmi.

(**kālajña,** see **sarva-kā°**.)

kāla-(v.l. kāra-)**pattrika,** m. pl., some sort of artisan or trader, in a list of such: Mv iii.113.16; 443.3; follows vardhakirūpakārakā(ḥ), *carpenters and carvers* (sculptors), and followed by **śelālakā(ḥ)** or **pela°**, q.v. (*masons*?). Senart em. to **kālapātrika,** q.v., but this obviously does not fit here.

Kāla-parvata (= Pali Kāḷa-pabbata; cf. also 1 **Kāla** 9 and **Mahākāla**), n. of a mountain range, always m. pl. when not in comp.; cf. Burnouf, Lotus, 842 ff.: SP 244.10 (in comp.); m. pl. Mv ii.300.19; Śikṣ 246.4; LV 277.9 (prose) na ca kālaparvatā(ḥ).

kāla-pātrika, adj. or subst. m., (a monk) *with black* (alms-) *bowl*: Mvy 8749; rendered lit. in Tib. and Chin.; the Kyōtō ed. suggests that it means *a bad, unworthy monk*, noting that it is followed by **saṃjñā-bhikṣu** and **pratijñā-(bh°)**, qq.v.; this is confirmed MSV iv.67.2, 3 (term of abuse). See **kālapattrika.**

Kālarātrī, n. of a rākṣasī: Māy 243.25.

? **kāla-valla-**: Mv ii.288.13 evaṃrūpāḥ sattvāḥ (sc., like the Bodhisattva) kālavalla-saṃpannāḥ, *perfect in*...(?); in a series of like formulas, preceded by varṇa-saṃpannāḥ, followed by adhyāśaya-saṃpannāḥ. Senart em. kāra-varṇa-saṃ°, which inspires no confidence; but I have found no light on the word. There is a v.l. kālavallabha, which seems no better.

kālavastu, nt., *abode of death* (i. e. place of desolation; so Senart): Mv iii.360.1 (vs) uddahyatu imaṃ nagaraṃ kālavastuṃ (n. sg.) karīyatu. But possibly, as suggested by PTSD s.v. tāla-vatthu, a corruption for tāla-vastu (or tālāvastu); the Pali word means *destroyed utterly*.

[? **kāla-veṣin,** n. sg. °veṣī, said of the Bodhisattva: LV 160.22 and 161.11 (prose), parallel and evidently equivalent to kālākālajña or kālajña, respectively. One ms. in 160.22 (H, generally a poor one) and three (H and B) in 161.11 read kāla-gaveṣī, and this seems the only possible reading: *seeking the right occasions*. So Tib., dus la lta zhiṅ, *considering* (having regard for, caring for) *time(s)*.]

kālasūtra, m.; Pali kāḷasutta, m.; occurs in Skt. but there regularly nt.; n. of a hell: Dharmas 121 (a hot hell); Mvy 4921; etc.; Mv i.5.7 °treṇa sūtritāṅgā (? em.), here taken by Senart as an 'instrument' of torture, better 'an accessory', *blackened cord* (for marking bodies to be cut), see P. Mus, La Lumière des six voies 79, referring to F.W.K. Müller, Ethnologisches Notizblatt I.3 (1896), p. 23 ff.; in Kv 35.10 text kāra°, cf. **kārānusāri(n)**; common in BHS. Cf. **sūtrayati.**

kālākāle, loc. quasi-adv. (kāla plus akāla), *in and out of season*: Śikṣ 167.1: °le punar anenopekṣā karaṇīyeti.

[**kālākṣuṇṇadharmavedhī** LV 181.7, read vālākṣaṇa-dh°; see **vālavedhin** and **akṣaṇavedhin.**]

kālāñjanikā (cf. Skt. Lex. °janī), n. of some plant: Mmk 317.28 (prose) °kā-kusumānām aṣṭasahasraṃ juhuyāt.

kālānukālam, adv. (= Pali id., Dhp. comm. i.323.4; see s.v. 1 **anu**), *from time to time*: Kv 24.19 tadā kālān° mayā tasya ... sakāśāt guṇodbhāvanāvalokiteśvarasya... śrutā; MSV ii.100.16.

kālānusāri (°rin?), or °**ra** (once), also **kārānu°**, q.v. (= Pali id., or kāḷ°, some kind of sandal; in Skt. said to mean another fragrant substance, *gum benzoin*, but Skt. Lexx. define relatives, viz. °sāraka, °sārya, as kinds of fragrant wood or specifically sandal), some kind of *sandalwood*: Mvy 6256 °ri-candanam, Tib. dus kyi rjes su ḥbraṅ baḥi tsan dan (so also in rendering LV; a woodenly lit. version, ... *which follows after time*!; acc. to Das the Tib. phrase means *yellow sandal*, which however appears to be based on Das's interpretation of the Skt. equivalent); SP 406.8 (prose) °ri-candana-meghaḥ kṛta uragasāra-candana-varṣam abhipravṛṣṭam; LV 204.11 pūjākarmaṇe kālānusāri-megham abhinirmāyoragasāra-candana-cūrṇa-varṣam abhivarṣayiṣyāmaḥ; 294.1 pūjākarmaṇe °sārya-guru-megham abhinirmāya (etc.) ... [3] kālānusāri-megha-maṇḍala-mātrād iyaṃ gāthā niścarati sma; Mv ii.116.4 (anulepanam ...) aguru-candanaṃ kālānusāriṃ (acc. sg.) tamālapattraṃ; Mv iii.70.7 gātrāṇi ... lohita-candaṇa-kālānusārehi (only occurrence noted of stem °ra!) viliptāni (in both Mv passages v.l. kārān°); Śikṣ 65.14 ... agaruṃ vā tagaraṃ (ms. °ruṃ) vā kālānusāri (n. sg.) vā dhūpayitavyaṃ (Bendall and Rouse misunderstand); °ri-candana- Gv 64.17; 101.3; 119.12, etc.; °ri-gandharāja-Gv 153.16; -agaru-kālānusāri-tagaroragasāra-candana-Sukh 38.17; kālānusāri-mahā-megha-sadṛśā dharmābhigar-janatayā Sukh 60.6, *because they thunder out the law, they are like a great cloud of kālānusāri* (i. e. of color like that? certainly not *at the rainy season* as rendered SBE 49 part 2 p. 57).

Kālāpa, var. for **Kālāma,** q.v.

kālāpadeśa, m. (see **apadeśa**), acc. to Tib. cited by Wogihara *'black doctrine'*, nag-po bstan pa; but this can hardly be right; perhaps *'timely expression'*; something which a Bodhisattva must know, along with **mahāpadeśa** (of which the precise mg. is also unknown; Tib. renders literally): Bbh 108.10–11 °śa-mahāpadeśāṃś ca yathābhūtaṃ prajānāti; 257.2 °śaṃ ca mahāpadeśaṃ ca yathā° praj°; 108.25 °śa-mahāpadeśa-kuśalo bodhisattvaḥ.

Kālāma (= Pali id.), surname of **Ārāḍa** or **Ar°**, qq.v.; var. Kālāpa.

Kālāma-sūtra (to be read for Kāma-sūtra of text), n. of a work: Bbh 389.10 (the Tib. cited in note = Kālāma or °pa, see Mvy 3515). Perhaps means the equivalent of Pali AN iii.165 (PTS ed. i.188 ff.), preached to the Kālāma tribe.

kāli, f. (ka plus āli), *ka-series*, name for a series of syllables beginning with ka (consonants plus a or ā), used as a magic formula in Sādh and defined there 478.13 ff. Cf. **āli** (2).

Kālika (cf. 1 **Kāla** 3, **Kālaka** 4), n. of a nāga-king: Mvy 3258 (here seems to be distinguished from both Kāla and Kālaka); but in LV 281.10 ff.; 284.11; Divy 392.14 ff. he plays the same rôle attributed to the nāga-king 1 **Kāla** 3, q.v., before the Bodhisattva's enlightenment; see also Māy 247.22.

Kālika-sūtra, n. of a work: Karmav 33.9 (passage cited corresp. to Pali AN iv.247.8 ff.).

Kālikā, n. of a rākṣasī: Māy 241.13; Av ii.66.4.

kālikā-vāta, m. (cf. AMg. kāliā, *hurricane*; Skt. kālikā, defined pw as a dark mass of clouds, Rām.), *tempestuous gale, hurricane*: °vātena rākṣasīdvīpe kṣiptaḥ SP 439.5; °vāta-bhayam Divy 41.11, 13 (mahā-kāl°); 229.24; °vātaḥ ... pratinivṛttaḥ Divy 42.10; vahanam °vātena spṛśyate 12; °vātena tad vahanam... paribhrāmyate Av ii.62.1; °vāta-vitrāsitāni ii.139.4.

Kāliṅga-pravaraṇa (nt.? cf. AMg. kaliṅga, *a cloth made in the Kaliṅga country*, Ratnach.), *Kaliṅga-coverlet*, doubtless = a coverlet made of a textile material characteristic of Kaliṅga: Sukh 67.7 (paryaṅkaḥ...) °raṇa-pratyāstaraṇa-sottarapada-chada(ḥ); **Kāliṅga-prāvāra**, *an outer-garment* of this material, which was soft and pleasant to touch, MSV i.36.20 °ga-prāvāra-mṛdu-saṃsparśāni.

Kāliyaka (= Skt. Kāliya; cf. also **Kālika**), n. of a nāga king: Samādh p. 42 line 31.

(**Kālī**, prob. the name of the well-known Hindu goddess, used as (**1**) n. of a yoginī: Sādh 584.12; 589.15; (**2**) n. of a piśācī: Māy 238.20; (**3**) n. of a rākṣasī: Māy 243.13.)

kāluṣa-, either = Skt. kāluṣya, *turbidity*, or perhaps error for kaluṣa, *turbid*: Gv 327.13 īrṣyā-mātsarya-māyā-śāṭhya-kāluṣāśayaḥ.

Kālodāyin (= Pali Kāḷudāyin; also called **Udāyin**, and possibly Udayin, see the former (1); spelling Kālodayin also occurs, see below), a son of Śuddhodana's purohita, playfellow of the Bodhisattva in his youth, who was sent (with Chandaka) as a messenger from Śuddhodana to the Buddha after his enlightenment: Mv ii.233.11 ff.; iii.91.14; 93.9; sent by Buddha as messenger to Śuddhodana, Mv iii.103.7 ff.; he was given the title *first of those who conciliate the family* (of the Buddha), kulaprasādakānāṃ... agro, which must be read in Mv iii.104.7 (cf. Pali AN i.25.5 kulappasādakānaṃ, sc. aggo, as his standing epithet); also mentioned SP 207.3; Jm 116.2; spelled Kālodāyin, Sukh 92.8; Karmav 78.16.

[**kālpam** LV 407.13, error or misprint for kālyam, *early in the morning*.]

kālyasya, see **kal°**.

Kāviśa, n. of a country (only loc. °śe), evidently in the north; in vss: Mmk 88.4 Kaśmīre Cīnadeśe ca Nepāle Kāviśe tathā; 325.10 Kāviśe Vakhale caiva Udiyāne samantataḥ (in next line, Kaśmīre); 333.4 (in same line Kaśmīre) Kāviśe ca janālaye.

kāveya, *produced by poetic invention*: AdP Konow MASI 69.17.23, see s.v. **kavita**. Cf. Pali kāveyya, *poetic composition*, a reprobated occupation among Buddhists. (From Skt. kavi.)

kāśi (see also **kāśi-sūkṣma**), in mg. 1 also kāśī (f.? in mg. 1 = **kāśika** or °**kā** 1; in mg. 2 = Pali kāsi, Buddhaghosa on Vin. i.281.18, 20, cited SBE 17.195 n. 3, where transl. departs from comm.; this interpretation is confirmed by our word, which can have no other mg. than some large number), (**1**) some valuable textile product of Benares, *fine cotton cloth* (?): Divy 388.17 (vs) tūlopamāḥ kāśi-samopamāś ca; Śikṣ 208.3 (prose) kāśi-kauśeya-dūkūla-; kāśī-, Divy 579.8 kāśī-maha, *festival of kāśī-cloth*; (**2**) *a thousand* (pieces of money): Mv iii.375.18 (gaṇikā) sarvāṃ kāśibhūmiṃ kṣamati, *was worth* (as a fee) *the whole sum of a thousand*; 376.1 uparddha- (mss., for **upārdha-**, q.v.) kāśiṃ kṣamati, *was worth half a thousand*. Cf. **Kāśikā**, **Uparddha-kāśikā**, as proper names (the women were so called because of these rates). The same mg. is given to Pali kāsi by comm. on Vin., above, and in Vin. i.281. 24 occurs upaḍḍha-kāsinaṃ khamamāno, confirming this mg.; see s.v. **kṣamati**.

kāśika, adj., and subst. m. or nt. (see s.v. **kāśi**; as adj. Skt. Gr.; in Pali recorded only as adj., chiefly with vattha, also uttama), adj. *of Benares*: once kāśika-candanaṃ Mv i.286.5; otherwise only of a kind of cloth, or garments made of it, kāśikair vastraiḥ Divy 391.26; °ka-vastra- Divy 29.4–5 ff.; Av i.107.1; 109.12; Kv 39.5; 72.5; 78.23; 86.17; Mv iii.119.8; °ka-śuci-vastra- Mv iii.412. 12; °ka-pratyāstaraṇam Mv i.306.9; °kāṃśu- (see aṃśu) Divy 316.27; °kottama-dhāriṇaḥ (mss. °vāriṇaḥ; see s.v. **uttama** 2) Mv i.296.4; as subst., a *garment of this cloth*, nt., lubdhakasya kāśikāni dattvā Mv ii.189.11; or m., kāśikau (dual) gṛhṇitvā (gṛhītvā) Mv ii.195.8 and 9; hitvā... kauṭumba-kāśikān (dvandva) Divy 559.10 (foll. by dhārayan pāṃśukūlāni; vs); the cpd. kāśika-sūkṣma occurs as adj., °māṇi prāvṛtāni Mv ii.159.11, °māṇi vastrāṇi Mv iii.264.6, but also as subst. nt., Mvy 9176 °mam (Tib. *fine cloth of Kāśi*), and Mv ii.116.7 (vividhāni vastrāṇi... sayyathīdaṃ) kāśikasūkṣmāṇi kambalasūkṣmāṇi; cf. also **kāśi-sūkṣma**, s.v.; as subst. f. **kāśikā**, see next. The word is variously interpreted, sometimes (e. g. Divy Index) as *silk*, but the preponderance of opinion favors a *fine cotton* or *muslin*.

kāśikā (see prec.), (**1**) *a piece* or *garment of Benares cloth*: Divy 576.29–30 putra vātāyanena kāśikāṃ niṣkāsayeti. tena vātāyanena kāśikā niṣkāsitā; 579.7 kāśikā dattā; (**2**) n. of a courtesan in Benares: Mv iii.375.16 ff.; the story told here (see 375.18) is that she got her name not from the city, but because she was worth a fee of a thousand (see **kāśi** 2, **bhūmi** 2, and **kṣamati**); her sister was called **Uparddhakāśikā**, q.v.

Kāśi-kośala, and °**laka**, n. of a (single) people, or part of a people (the Kośalas): Mv i.350.5 and 12 °lena rājñā; 7 °lakā manuṣyā(ḥ); 10 °la-rājño. Contrasted with the Kośalas of Śāketa, Śāketā api Kośalā(ḥ) i.350.19. On the relation between the Kośalas and Kāśi see DPPN s.v. Kāsi.

Kāśivardhana, n. of a city: Mv i.184.19 °ne. Senart, Introduction xxxix, assumes that Benares is meant.

Kāśisundara, n. of a prince (the Bodhisattva): Av ii.27.14 ff.

Kāśisundarī, n. of a princess of Benares: Av ii.31.13 ff.

kāśi-sūkṣma, nt., = **kāśika-sūkṣma**, nt. (see s.v. **kāśika**): Bhīk 22b.4 kṛmivarṇā (q.v.) vā kāśiṣūkṣmaṃ vā.

kāśī = **kāśi** (1), q.v.

Kāśmīra-pura, *the city* (capital) *of Kashmir*: °pure Divy 399.11. Cf. next.

Kāśmīrā, *the capital city of Kashmir*: Karmav 32.12 °rāyāṃ mahānagaryāṃ; 61.12; 62.1; 72.3. Cf. prec. Lévi translates the last three as if they referred to the country.

Kāśyapa (= Pali Kassapa; Tib. ḥod sruṅs, *light-guard*, e. g. on Mvy 93), (**1**) n. of a former Buddha, the one immediately preceding Śākyamuni: often mentioned as having predicted the latter, and esp. as one of a group of three, the others being **Krakucchanda** and **Kanakamuni**, or equivalents; see the former for list of such references; also alone (it being not always certain that this particular Buddha is meant, cf. Mv i.58.8, ref. to 90,000 Buddhas of this name), Mv i.307.4 ff.; 312.2; 318.7 ff.;

iii.249.8; Divy 22.4 ff.; 54.12, 25; 76.26 ff.; 192.25 ff.; 233.21 ff.; 336.21; 337.17; 344.4 ff.; 347.1 ff.; 465.25 ff.; 504.26; Av i.237.11; 247.15, et alibi; Karmav 159.7; LV 172.9; 260.10; Mmk 104.17 ff.; (2) n. of one of Buddha's leading disciples, also called **Mahā-k°** (= Pali Kassapa or Mahā-k°), q.v.; there is no doubt that the same person is, as a rule at least, meant by the two forms, notably Kā° in Mvy 1031; Mv iii.48.2; SP 116.4; 121.3 ff.; 144.2 ff.; 206.8 ff.; Divy 83.10 ff.; 396.1; K. is given the title dhutaguṇāgrapāraga Mv i.64.14 (ff.), where he is involved as an interlocutor at the First Council, perhaps its presiding officer (as in Pali, DPPN); he then and there causes Kātyāyana to discourse on the 10 bhūmi; similarly Divy 61.28 calls him dhūtaguṇa-vādināṃ agro, and cf. Pali AN i.23.19 where Mahākassapa is dhutavādānaṃ (v.l. dhūtaṅgadharānaṃ) agga; mentioned in Candropama Sūtra, Hoernle MR 40 ff., = Pali SN ii.197 ff. where (Mahā) Kassapa corresponds; among mahāśrāvakas, Divy 182.22; 268.6; in Divy 573.8 it appears, strangely, that āryakāśyapasya is an epithet of (the next word) Kātyāyanasya (pañcaśataparivārasya; in the story which follows only Mahākātyāyana appears!); it is not clear whether the same person is meant by āyuṣmān daśabalaḥ Kāśyapaḥ Divy 275.5, and 7 daśabala-Kāś°;* no monk of this title is recorded in Pali; in Vv. comm. 148.24 Kassapassa dasabalassa kāle refers to the Buddha Kāś°, tho I find no evidence to support PTSD and DPPN in stating that dasabala was 'especially' an epithet of his, 'to distinguish him from other Kassapas' as DPPN says; dasabala (BHS daśa°) of course usually refers to a Buddha, and in Pali generally to the B. Gotama; there are at least four other disciples of his having this name, see **Uruvilvā-k°**, **Kumāra-k°**, **Gayā-k°**, **Nadī-k°**; (3) n. of an ascetic (ṛṣi) who once lived in the Himālaya: Mv ii.106.16, a previous birth of **Mahākāśyapa**, q.v., 114.12; (4) n. of another (?) ascetic (ṛṣi) who lived in the hermitage **sāhaṃjanī** (q.v.; this is not mentioned in connection with the prec. Kā°, and the stories told of them are different): Mv iii.143.13 ff. (in story of Ekaśṛṅga and Nalinī; = Pali Kassapa 9 in DPPN); prob. the same (at least also living in Sāhaṃjanī) Mv iii.362.14; 363.19. See also **Pūraṇa Kāśyapa**; **Jaṅghā-k°**; **Vṛddha-k°**. — *Correction in proof: MPS 49.16 names four mahāsthavirāḥ in the world (pṛthivyāṃ) at the time of Buddha's death; two of them were Daśabala-Kāśyapa (one word) and Mahā-Kāśyapa. This settles the above question; D.K. is a separate person.

Kāśyapa-parivarta, n. of a work (our KP); see Stael-Holstein, Intr., XIV note 4; generally called **Ratnakūṭa** or **Mahā-r°**, in itself, and in Śikṣ. (The text, even in its prose parts, contains an exceptional number of MIndic forms.)

Kāśyapa Pūraṇa, see **Pūraṇa Kāśyapa**.

Kāśyapīya, m. pl., (1) *followers or disciples of the Buddha Kāśyapa*: Divy 336.2 (here text Kaś°); 337.5; 338.5; MSV i.57.8; (2) n. of a (Buddhist) sect: Mvy 9079 (v.l. Kaś°).

kāṣāya (= Skt. kaṣāya; cf. Skt. kāṣāya, Pali kāsāya, which = Skt. kaṣāya in other mgs.), (1) nt., *decoction*: Mv iii.70.11 . . . kaṭukāgrāṇi kāṣāyāṇi; (2) *impurity*, in sakāṣāyasya ca kāṣāya-dhāraṇaṃ KP 117.1–2 (prose), *the wearing of the yellow* (robe; Skt. kāṣāya and Pali kāsāya are used in *this* sense!) *on the part of one characterized by impurity*; Tib. *of impure thoughts*, which also translates sakaṣāyacittasya (kāṣāya-dhāraṇaṃ) 117.5 (vs), where note short a in -kaṣāya, m.c.; read also kaṣāya-dhāraṇaṃ, m.c.

Kāṣāya-grahaṇa, nt., n. of a caitya on the spot of the Bodhisattva's first assumption of monk's garb: LV 226.12.

Kāṣāyadhvajā, n. of a lokadhātu: Gv 81.7.

kāṣṭha-puṣpa, nt. (pl.), some kind of flowers; perhaps *flowers of woody plants* or *trees*: Kv 8.4–6 tatra vividhāni °pāṇy utpadyante, tad yathā: campakāśokakaravīra-pāṭalānirmuktaka-sumanā-gandhavārṣikāṇi, etāni manoramāṇi kāṣṭhapuṣpāṇi . . .; Kv 79.2 vividhāni kāṣṭhapuṣpāṇi (text °puṇyāṇi), campaka-karavīra- etc. (similar list).

kāṣṭha-bhāraka, m. (= Skt. °ra plus -ka svārthe), *load of wood*: MSV ii.32.13, 15 (prose).

kāṣṭha-hāraka, m. (= Pali kaṭṭha-hā°; see **hāraka**), *wood-gatherer*: Mvy 3776; Divy 500.3 ff.; Av ii.101.5; Śikṣ 9.5–6.

kāṣṭhikavitta, m. (var. °kācinta; Mironov id., vv.ll. kaṣṭhikavitta, kāṣṭhikacitta), Mvy 3815, acc. to Chin. *messenger*; follows **kathyāyitta**, q.v.; Tib. raṅ rta, which is not in Tib. Dictt. (raṅ = *self*, rta = *horse*).

kāsana, and °**naka**, adj. (cf. AMg. kāsaṇa, nt., *act of coughing*), *afflicted with coughing*: Mv iii.3.15 (vs) kāsano mūrchito cāhaṃ; ii.428.1 (prose) ahaṃ jīrṇo vṛddho kāsanako ca.

kāsi, etc., aor. of kṛ, q.v. in Chap. 43.

-kāsī, see s.v. **gomaya-kārṣī**.

kāhala, adj. (in this mg. only Pkt. acc. to Hem. i.214, 254), *downcast, fainthearted* (= kātara, Hem.): mā °lo bhava MSV ii.20.11; so Tib., mi dgyes par ma mdzad cig.

kāhiti, etc., fut. of kṛ, q.v. in Chap. 43.

[**kiṃkanīkṛta-**, see s.v. **kiṇīkṛta**.]

[**kiṃkara**, (prob. corruption) for **kaṃkara**, q.v.: Gv 133.1.]

Kiṃkara, n. of a yakṣa: Māy 90.

kiṃkaraṇī-, prob. error or misprint for next, q.v.: Gv 463.25 (prose) kiṃkaraṇī-pradakṣiṇa-grāha-tayā (see **pradakṣiṇagrāha-tā**).

kiṃkaraṇīya, also °**ya-ka** (m. or nt.), and °**ya-tā** (all = Pali kiṃkaraṇīya; cf. Skt. kiṃkartavyatā), *job to be done*: Mv i.211.3 (prose) kiṃkaraṇīyaka-pratisaṃyuktehi (not 'abstract-forming suffix ka' with Senart; same mg. as °ṇīya); Śikṣ 21.23 ayam eva mayā kāyaḥ sarvasattvānāṃ kiṃkaraṇīyeṣu kṣapayitavyaḥ; 143.9 sarvasattva-kiṃkaraṇīya-prāpaṇatayā; °yeṣu MSV i.50.2; °ṇīya-tā, Mvy 6448 (sarvasattvānāṃ); Śikṣ 230.2 (sarvasattvānāṃ . . .) °tāyai utsuko bhavati. Cf. also prec.

kiṃkiṇīkā (Skt. °ṇika, m., and °ṇikā; Pali °ṇika, m., nt., see also next), *bell*: Mv iii.227.15, 16; (with v.l. °ṇikā) 229.1.

kiṃkiṇīyā (so Senart, m.c.; mss. °ya-), = prec. (or Skt. kiṃkiṇī), *bell*: Mv i.235.4 (vs) tapanīya-kiṃkiṇīyārucirā.

kiṃcana (= Pali id.), prob. *attachment, defilement* (see Childers and PTSD): RP 35.12 kleśābhibhūtāḥ sakhilāḥ sa-kiṃcanāḥ (Bhvr.). Undoubtedly sa-ki° and the noun kiṃcana (in Pali) were abstracted from a-kiṃcana, adj., orig. *having nothing*, then *disinterested, unattached, without attachment* or *defilement*, whence finally (sa-)kiṃcana, as above. In late Skt. (Schmidt, Nachtr.) sa-kiṃcana occurs, glossed sa-dhana. In RP it could possibly mean *propertied, interested in wealth*, but Pali usage is prob. to be followed.

Kiṃcanaka, n. of a nāga-king: Mvy 3259; Māy 247.23.

Kiṃcanin, n. of a nāga-king: Māy 247.23, °nī, n. sg.

kiṃcitka (= Pali kiñcikkha) to which it may be a hyper-Skt. back formation; kiṃcit plus ka), *a tiny bit*, noted only in āmiṣa-k°: āmiṣakiṃcitkahetoḥ (= Pali āmisakiñcikkhahetu), *for the sake of a trifle of worldly things*, Mvy 2475; Bbh 166.4; āmiṣakiṃcitkābhilāṣī (n. sg. to °ṣin) AsP 246.21.

kiṃcit-prāṇa, adj. (recorded by Monier Williams as Skt., without reference, but not found otherwise), *barely alive*: LV 227.17 (prose) dharaṇītale vinipatitāḥ kiṃcitprāṇāḥ; 253.6 (vs) ko me dady' (= dadyā, dadyāt) ekaputrasya kiṃcitprāṇasya jīvitam, *who would give life to my only son that is almost dead?*

Kiṭāgiri (= Pali id.), n. of town (region?) among the Kāśī, home of **Aśvaka** and **Punarvasu**: MSV iii.17.7, 8 etc.

Kiṭāgirīyaka, adj., *belonging to* the prec.: MSV iii.15.21; 17.14.

kiṭāla-piṇḍa(ka), m., *lump of iron-rust* (? cf. Skt. kiṭṭa and Lex. kiṭṭāla), supposed to have medicinal value: MSV ii.28.14 ff.; used in a poultice, 29.10; Tib. phrum tshud, which I cannot interpret. See **koṭaka.**

Kiṭi, n. of an attendant on the four direction-rulers: Mahāsamāj. 173.9 (Waldschmidt, Kl. Skt. Texte 4).

? **kiṭika**, m. or nt.: Divy 374.7 (prose) pañcastrīśatāni kiṭikaiḥ saṃveṣṭya dagdhāni. (Burnouf, Intr. 365 note 1, conjectures kāṣṭ[h]akaiḥ, implausibly.) Perhaps same word as Pali kiṭaka, in Pv. i.9.2 and 4, something (acc. to comm. [hot] *copper plates*) into which the *clothing* of the petas is changed; thus it fits the Divy passage. There is also a Pali kiṭika, Vin. ii.152.26 and 153.5, perhaps also some sort of *covering*, but very obscure; comm. repeats it without glossing.

[**kiṭibhaka**, m., corruption for **Kirīṭaka**, q.v.]

? **kiṭṭaka**, see **koṭaka**, *iron-rust.*

kiṇikiṇāyamānā, fem. pres. mid. pple., onomat.? (cf. Pali kiṇi; Pkt. kiṇikiṇinta), applied to sandals: MSV iv.206.11.

kiṇīkṛta, ppp. (Skt. kiṇa plus kṛ-), *made callous, hardened*, in fig. sense, of mentality (as in Eng. *hard* or *callous*): SP 319.8 (prose), for KN kilīkṛta-saṃjñā(ḥ), read with WT and their K' kiṇī°, *their fancy made callous*; Laṅk 253.7, read kiṇīkṛta-rūkṣa-cetasāṃ (rākṣasānām iva), *having minds calloused and harsh*: one ms. kiṇī°, another kiṃnī°; text kiṃkanīkṛta-rukṣa°. Suzuki implausibly em. (a-)kiṃkarīkṛta°.

kiṃtikara, adj. (Pali id.), *doing what?* Mv iii.212.12, acc. to Senart's em. following Pali Jāt. iv.339.25; v.148.14; the mss. are hopelessly corrupt.

Kiṃnara, n. of a yakṣa: Māy 40.

kiṃnara-lipi, a kind of script: LV 126.3.

(śrī-)Kiṃnarī-jātaka, nt., n. of a jātaka-tale: (colophon) Mv ii.115.5.

[**kipala**, error for **kimpala**, q.v.]

kimarthiya, adj. (= Pali kimatthiya; Skt. *kimarthya, from kimartha), *having what as its purpose?*: Mv iii.373.22 (vs), read with mss. kimarthiyaṃ āgamanam abhūṣi.

kimi (m.; § 2.6; = Pali id., *glow-worm*, as well as *worm* in general; in this specialized sense Skt. kṛmi, krimi is not recorded), *glow-worm*: Mv i.73.20 (vs) udgate dinakare yathā kimi niṣprabho bhavati.

kimpaka (also **mahā-ki°**), m. pl., a class of malevolent superhuman beings: Mmk 17.6.

kimpala (once **kimphala**), m. (or nt.), a kind of musical instrument; pw suggests loan from Gk. κύμβαλον: LV 163.6 (here ed. kipala, without v.l.; Calc. lacks the word; doubtless misprint, or error); 206.14; 212.4 (all prose, in cpd. lists of instruments of music); Mv ii.322.14 (vs) nakulaka-kimphalāṃ ca (with false etym. adaptation to phala?).

kimpila (m. or nt.?), acc. to Tib. *owl*, in kimpilākṣaḥ Mvy 8910 = Tib. ḥug mig po, *owl-eyed.*

[**kiṃpuruṣa**, Mv i.23.2, or °**ṣaka**, i.20.6; Senart reads °ṣakānāṃ (all mss. dental n!) in 20.6, °ṣāṇāṃ (but mss. again end in -kānāṃ!) in 23.2, assuming mg. *monkey*; but only by violent em. of mss., which, combining the two passages, point rather to something like tampuruka or tamb°; in any case, *monkey* is implausible in mg., since reference seems to be made to animals living in holes; see s.v. **gutti.** I cannot solve this word.]

kiṃpratyaya, adj. Bhvr. (Childers records adv. kiṃpaccayā in Pali), *having what as cause?*: LV 346.6 (so also 8, etc.) kiṃpratyayaṃ (Lefm. prints as two words) ca punar jarāmaraṇam, *and what further is the cause of old age and death?*

kiṃprāptin, adj. (Skt. kiṃ plus prāpta plus -in; = Pali kiṃpattin, Sn 513, 518, etc.), *having obtained what?*: Mv iii.395.6 (here text kiṃprāptam, to be em.); 396.10; 397.12 (kiṃprāptinam āhu vedako ti, the others similarly), in vss corresp. to Sn (in the Sabhiya Sutta; see **Sabhika**).

kimphala, see **kimpala.**

kiṃbhūta, adj., lit. *become what?* = *destroyed, obliterated*: Mv iii.347.2, read with mss. apāyā tatra kiṃbhūtā (v.l. ki-bh°) svayambhū tava tejasā, *evils there are obliterated, Self-existent, by thy glory.* (In this sense not recorded; misunderstood and emended by Senart.)

kiyat- in comp., in interrogative-exclamatory function (in Skt. only with pejorative connotation, = *very little*), with complimentary, or at least (when prefixed to a word in itself uncomplimentary) augmentative force, = *exceedingly, in high degree*: LV 158.2 (vs) kiyad-vibhūṣito bālaḥ pāpacārī na śobhate, (even) *highly adorned, a foolish evil-doer does not shine*; foll. by api, Śikṣ 130.1 kiyatpraṇītam api bhojanam, *even very fine* (? *however fine*) *food*; 130.11 kiyal-lūhenāpi bhojanena, *even with very poor food*; 151.5 kiyad-dhīnānām api sattvānām, *even of extremely low creatures.* Foucaux takes the LV passage as having indefinite kiyat-; even when the cpd. beginning with kiyat- is followed by api, as in the Śikṣ passages, it can hardly be taken as the indefinitizing api. PTSD interprets Pali kīvat as indefinite in Sn 959, but this is an error; it is interrogative (-exclamatory). Cf. next.

kiyattama, adj. (superl. of kiyat), *very few*: °mair divasair āgata eva MSV ii.23.20.

kiraṇa, m., a kind of evil spirit (associated with kākhorda, vetāla or °ḍa): Mvy 4374; Māy 220.18. Tib. on Mvy gyeṅs byed, which acc. to Das = Skt. kiṭi, 'fig. *a pig*'. For Skt. kiṭi, *wild hog*, Lexx. give also kira, kiri. But our word certainly means a demon (possibly supposed to resemble a swine?).

kirāta-lipi, a kind of script: LV 125.21. Tib. transliterates ki-ra-ṭa, with domal ṭ; Pali has Kirāṭa beside °ta for Skt. °ta. No ms. of LV is reported with °ṭa, but some have °ri, instead. See **kuta-lipi.**

Kirīṭaka, n. of a nāga: MSV i.145.5 = 153.1. The Divy (450.17; 456.6) version of this story has corruptly kiṭibhakaś ca; the rest of the line is also corrupt; read as in MSV.

Kirīṭavatsa (Pali Tirīṭavaccha or Tirīṭi°), n. of the father of Unmādayantī: Jm 83.12.

kirttiya (semi-Sktized from MIndic kittiyā = Skt. kṛttikā; see **kīrtika**), n. of a nakṣatra: Thomas ap. Hoernle MR 122.7.

[? **kilañjaka**, *mat* (note Skt. kilañja, BR 5.1297, beside kiliñja), read by Senart Mv ii.38.3; 470.8; but see s.v. **kalandaka.**]

kilamati (MIndic for Skt. klam-), ppp. kilānta, kilanta, etc., *is wearied*, see § 3.109 and Chap. 43, s.v. klam. Cf. **klāmati.**

kilamatha, see **klamatha.**

kilāsa, m., Mvy 6650 = Tib. sñoms las, *indolence* (Jä. and Das; but sñoms (pa), *weariness*). This noun is probably a back-formation from the adj. **kilāsin.**

kilāsitā, *indolence* (see next): SP 128.12; 129.4; 284.3 (cited Śikṣ 353.5).

kilāsin, *weary, indolent, faint-hearted.* Certainly = Pali kilāsu, which Geiger 39.1 derives with Trenckner from Skt. glāsnu; perhaps rightly; change of g to k may be due to confusion with forms of klam- (Pali kilam-), or even with Skt. kilāsin, *leprous*; in this sense in Mv ii.383.16–17 na jātu gilāno (note this form of glā!) bhave pāṇḍurāgo, na cāpi kuṣṭhī nāpi ca kilāsī (clearly *leprous*). Defined ālasyopeta, vīryarahita, in Abhisamayālaṃkārāloka (GOS 62) 320.15: °sī, n. sg. m., Śikṣ 49.16; AsP 243.10. See also **kilāsitā, akilāsin, °sitā**; and **kilāsa.**

kilikila, nt., and **°lā,** f. (cf. Skt. kilakilā, and kilakilāyate, °layati, also Pali kilikilāyati), *a loud noise* (onomatopoetic): nt. Mv ii.410.7 °la- (acc. to text in comp.; but read °lā with mss.; perh. fem.), of noises made by the army of Māra, in attacking the Bodhisattva; °lāni Mv iii.312.13, of applause; fem. Mvy 2800; Divy 459.16, of astonishment; Samādh 19.8 of joy, applause; AsP 203.12 (read kilikilā with most mss. for text kila°), of joy, applause. Usually associated or cpd. with **hāhākāra** and prakṣveḍita. See next.

kilikīlate, *makes a loud noise* (of Māra's army): pres. pple. °lamānā(ḥ), n. pl., seems the probable reading at Mv ii.339.6 (vs), as suggested by mss. (which have hyper-Skt. krīḍ- for kīl-) and meter; Senart reads kilikilāyamānā, which gives the meaning required (see s.v. **kilikila**), but is hypermetric by one short syllable.

kiliṣṭa = Skt. kliṣṭa, see **kliśyati.**

[**kilīkṛta-** in SP 319.8 would mean *joyous* if the text were right; but read **kiṇīkṛta,** q.v.]

kileśa, see **kleśa.**

kilviṣa (nt.; in Skt., and Pali kibbisa, apparently only of moral evils), (physical) *filth* (cf. bībhatsa, given by Ratnach. as one rendering of AMg. kibbisa): LV 208.15 (vs) vastī-pūya-vasā-samastaka-rasaiḥ pūrṇaṃ tathā kilviṣaiḥ, nityaprasravitaṃ . . . (said of the body).

kiśala, m. or nt. (= Skt. kiśalaya, kis°; Skt. Lex. kisala, so also Pkt., Hem. 1.269), *leaf-bud, young sprout* (of a tree): LV 166.21 (vs) suvidita sugaṇita yatha tahi (sc. tarau) kiśalā (n. pl.).

kisara, (**1**) adj. and subst. (= Pali kasira, Skt. kṛcchra), *difficulty,* only in **akisara-lābhin** and **alpakisareṇa,** qq.v. The use of the former, beside **akṛcchra-l°,** proves that the two forms were not felt as identical. In Pali also (Geiger 59.2) kicchena kasirena are used together, and evidently taken as 'different words'. Pkt. only kiccha; our kisara (perhaps influenced by Pali-Pkt. kisa = kṛśa) has no recorded parallel in MIndic; (**2**) m. or nt., 'eine Art wohlriechender Stoff': Kalpanāmaṇḍitikā, Lüders, Kl. Skt. Texte 2.43.

kīṭa (m. or nt.; = Skt. Lex. id., BR 5.1298), *excrement:* Śikṣ 81.5 (vs) kīṭakumbho (*chamber-pot*) yathā . . . pūrṇo mūtrapurīṣeṇa. So with Tib.; Bendall and Rouse very implausibly *pot of worms.*

kīrtana (nt.?), some kind of building; Speyer, *temple*; pw 7, App., *Denkmal, Monument*: Jm 219.14 śrīmanti kīrtanaśatāni niveśitāni, sattrājirāśramapadāni sabhāḥ prapāś ca.

Kīrtanīya (mss. Kīrti°), n. of a former Buddha: Mv i.137.14.

Kīrti, m., (**1**) n. of a maharṣi: Māy 256.24; (**2**) n. of one of the oxen of Trapuṣa and Bhallika: LV 381.7, 17.

kīrtika (m. or nt.; hyper-Skt. for AMg. kittiā = Skt. kṛttikā; Pali only kattikā, °ka), n. of a nakṣatra (Skt. kṛttikā): Mv iii.303.7 eko sujātāye nakṣatre jātako, aparo kīrtike. Cf. **kirttiya, karthika.**

Kīrtimant, n. of a disciple of the Buddha: Mv i.182.18.

kīlayate, °ti (denom. to kīla; Skt. has ppp. kīlita only), *fastens, binds, fixes*: Mmk 476.1 (vs) punaḥ kīlayate mudrāṃ bandhanorundhanādibhiḥ kriyaiḥ; Sādh 171.4 (kaṇṭakena) tu tasyā mukhaṃ kīlayet, prativādimukhaṃ kīlitaṃ bhavati.

[**kīvant,** see **keva.**]

kuṃsana, m. or nt. (also written kunsana; by 'Morengesetz', § 3.4, for *kussana = Skt. kutsana; so Tib., smod pa; Pali and Pkt. record only kucch- for Skt. kuts-, but cf. e. g. Pali ussava = utsava), *blame, abuse*: KP 8.6 (prose) ākrośa-paribhāṣaṇa-kuṃsana-paṃsana-(etc.); 8.16 (vs) ākrośanā-kunsana-paṃsanāsu; 23.6 (prose) pareṣāṃ jñānākunsanatā (jñāna-ak°) niradhimānatayā. Cf. **kucchati.**

kukuṭa-saṃpāta-mātra (read kukkuṭa°?), adj. (cf. Pali kukkuṭa-saṃpāta, °pātika, °pāda, Vin. iv.63.28, see comm. 806.2 ff.; DN iii.75.9, comm. iii.855.27; AN i.159.30, comm. ii.256 infra; wrong interpretation Morris JPTS 1885, 38, adopted PTSD s.v. kukkuṭa), lit. *cock's-alighting* (or *flight*)*-measured,* i. e. so close together that a cock could fly from one to another: Divy 316.11 (saumyā janapadā) babhūvuṣ °mātrāś ca grāma-nigama-rāṣṭra-rājadhānyo babhūvuḥ (in a kind of golden age in the past; the population was so large that inhabited places were close together).

Kukustā (Pali Kukuṭṭhā, Ka°, Kakutthā), n. of a river: MPS 27.12 (Tib. Ka-kus-sta; Chin. both Ka- and Ku-).

kukūla, nt. (in Skt. *chaff*; *a fire made of chaff*), n. of a hell (acc. to Tib. heading, a cold hell): Mvy 4937; v.l. **kukkula,** q.v.; Tib. me ma mur, apparently *coals in a pit* or the like.

kukkuṭa-pakṣaka, nt., *a knife shaped like a cock's wing*: Mvy 8977; so Tib., except that there is some question of the specific bird meant by bya gag = kukkuṭa (acc. to Jä. a kind of duck); in Mvy 4904 kukkuṭa is rendered khyim bya.

Kukkuṭāgāra (m. or nt.) = **Kurkuṭārāma,** q.v.: Av ii.203.1 °raṃ, acc. sg.

Kukkuṭārāma (m.) = **Kurku°,** q.v.: Svay 19.8.

kukkura-vratika, adj. (= Pali °vatika), applied to certain non-Buddhist ascetics *who took a vow to live like dogs* (cf. Pali MN i.387.18 chamā-nikkhittaṃ bhuñjati, and comm. iii.100.25; DN comm. iii.819.17 sunakho viya ghāyitvā khādati, uddhana-vāre nipajjati, aññaṃ pi sunakhakiriyam eva karoti): Karmav 44.19 **govratika-**(q.v.)-kukkuravratika-prabhṛtīnāṃ; Śikṣ 332.3 kukkura-govratika; cf. LV 248.21 govrata-mṛga-śva-varāha-vānara-hasti-vrataiś ca; AbhidhK. LaV-P. iii.86 n. 3.

Kukkuri(n), n. of an author: Sādh 468.13 (°ripādānām, in colophon).

kukkula (nt. or m.; = **kukūla,** q.v.; = Pali kukkuḷa), n. of a hell: Mv i.6.16; i.11.1, 5 = iii.455.13, 17; iii.185.16; 369.4. In Pali the word is recorded as meaning also *hot ashes, embers.*

kukṣi (and **kukṣimatī**; in Skt. only m., except acc. to one Lex. f., and mg. only *belly* or *womb*; so also Pali, Pkt. kucchi), as fem., LV 75.6 (vs) kukṣiye (loc. sg.) pratiṣṭhitaṃ; (like garbha) with mg. *embryo* (and hence **kukṣimatī,** *pregnant*): Mv ii.432.11 devīye kukṣiḥ pratilabdhā (*the queen conceived*); evaṃ dāni pañca devīśatāni kukṣimantāni (so Senart; mss. °matinī, °matīnāṃ; read °matīni?) saṃvṛttāni; Divy 264.10 kukṣimaty eṣā nūnam asyāḥ prasavakāla iti.

ku-gaṇin, m., *bad teacher* (inaccurately BR): °ṇi-pratāpakaḥ LV 4.3 (vs); °ṇi-pramathi RP 51.11 (vs); °ṇi-gaṇa- LV 273.2 (prose); Mv i.117.11 (vs; so all mss., Senart °gaṇī°). See **gaṇin.**

ku-celaka, adj. (= Skt. ku-cela), *having bad clothes*: SP 113.12 (vs) °kā, n. pl. m. (so read with most mss., ed. ku-cai° with 1 ms.).

kucchati (MIndic, § 2.18, for kutsati, or more regularly kutsayati; cf. Pali ppp. kucchita; AMg. kucchai), *contemns*: Mv i.106.9 kucchanti. Cf. **kuṃsana.**

Kuñjaragati, n. of a former Buddha: Mv i.137.1.

[**kuṭaka,** acc. to Index read **kaṭuka,** q.v.]

kuṭakuñcaka = **kuṭu°,** q.v.

kuṭi or **kuṭī,** f. (m. or nt. modifiers, in -aṃ, acc. sg., Prāt 480.8–9; or MIndic for -āṃ?), (**1**) as in Skt., *hut, cell,* esp. of a monk: Divy 338.22 (tasya) kuṭiḥ śūnyāvatiṣṭhati; Av ii.136.8; of leaves, *a temporary shelter,* parṇikāṃ kuṭim abhinirmāya Divy 574.6; parṇa-kuṭiṃ kṛtvā Av i.262.14;

in Mvy 5678 kuṭi- (v.l. kuṭī°, also v.l. in Mironov)-mahaḥ, *cell-festival* or acc. to Tib. vihāra-(*monastery-*) *festival* (gtsug lag khaṅ gi dus ston; var. gtsug log gi etc.); similarly Chin., *sūtra-hall feast*; acc. to Jap., *a feast or ceremony celebrating completion of a new temple-building*; tasya dharmabhāṇakasya caṅkramakuṭīm upasaṃkramiṣyāmi SP 475.1–2, *I will go to that preacher's hall of promenade* (?); (**2**) in maśaka-kuṭī, Mvy 9002, acc. to Tib. sbraṅ skyabs, *insect-protection* (BR conjecture, *a whisk to brush off flies*; but Chin. *mosquito-netting*); (**3**) *straw* or the like, as fodder for a horse (see Turner, Nep. Dict. s.v. kuṭuro): Divy 510.18 tuṣān kuṭiṃ cānuprayacchati (to a horse); 511.19 tuṣāś ca **kaṭi** (q.v.) sakaṇṭaṃ bhakṣitavyam.

kuṭikā (= Pali id.; see **kuṭi**), *hut*, usually as habitation of a monk, whether Buddhist or brahmanical: kuṭikāya (loc.) SP 115.1 (vs); °kāye (loc.) Mv i.328.1; parṇakuṭikā Mvy 5556; Divy 631.10, 13; °kā-dvāre Av ii.156.5; others Divy 338.22; 442.22; 538.20 ff. (of a pratyekabuddha); yaḥ punar bhiksuḥ sāṃghike vihāre uparivihāyasi kuṭikāyām . . . niṣīded . . . Prāt 506.5–6; in Mvy 8374, MSV iii.87.19, abbreviated designation of one of the saṃghāvaśeṣa sins, consisting in a monk's building a hut for himself in an improper place or manner, in violation of Prāt 480.8 ff.

Kuṭigrāmaka, Gv 525.16, MPS 8.4 (here = Pali Koṭigāma, but not in Gv), or **Kūṭagrāmaka**, Gv 527.9, n, of two villages.

kuṭira (m. or nt.; Skt. Lex.; Skt. kuṭīra), *hut*: Kv 60.9 (prose) parṇa-kuṭira-, cf. (parṇa-)**kuṭi**, **-kuṭikā**.

Kuṭilā, n. of a kiṃnara maid: Kv 6.4.

kuṭī, see **kuṭi**.

kuṭukuñcaka, kuṭa°, var. kuṭku°, adj., f. °ikā (cf. Pali kaṭukañcuka-tā, kaṭa°, kaṭakuñca°), *niggardly*: Mvy 2491 (var. kurukuci; acc. to Tib. *hypocrite*, ṅan gyo ḥam tshul ḥchos pa, but this seems clearly an error); Divy 8.3 (with matsarin); Śikṣ 149.13 (so read, see p. 279, n. 3); in a cliché with matsarin and āgṛhītapariṣkāra, see **āgṛhīta**, Divy 302.3; Av i.257.4; 289.9; ii.158.3; fem. °ikā, same cliché, Av i.248.2; 262.3; MSV iii.20.17 (kuṭa°); Bbh 124.16 (kuṭa°).

kuṭṭana (m. or nt.), in ayo-kuṭṭanehi kuṭṭīyantā Mv i.6.5 (prose), *being pounded with iron hammers*. Cf. Pali ayo-kūṭa, and Skt. kūṭa, *iron hammer* (once, Mbh.); the word kuṭṭana is found in Skt. as noun of action, *pounding* (cf. kuṭṭ-ayati); our form looks like an etymological blending, with influence of the 'Morengesetz' (§ 3.4a).

kuṭṭ(ayati), as in Skt. *pounds, crushes*: Mv i.6.5 kuṭṭīyantā, pres. pple. pass., *being pounded*; also *reviles* (Dhātup.), see prec., **anukuṭṭaka, parikuṭṭaka**, and **kuṭṭī**.

kuṭṭā and **kuṭṭāvitā**, two large numbers or ways of calculation (gaṇanā), Mvy 7983 and 7984 (cited from LV), for Lefmann's **kuruṭu** and **kuruṭāvi**, qq.v.; Tib. gcod rtogs (Das = kuṭṭa-cinta) and gcod rtogs ldan, which should render °vatī, as suggested in note to Mvy 7984 (for °vitā).

kuṭṭitika, see **ikṣu-kuṭṭitikam.**

kuṭṭī, *reviling*? (see s.v. **kuṭṭ-ayati**): SP 274.2 (vs) bahukuṭṭī bahūvidhā, with Nep. mss.; but Kashgar rec. upakrośā for bahuk° (confirmed La Vallée-Poussin, JRAS 1911, 1076); WT read bandha- (citing Tib. as bciṅ, *binding*) -kuṭṭī, *imprisonment and reviling*.

kuṭmalībhūta, adj., *budded* (of flowers): LV 76.11 (prose). Skt. kuṭmala occurs beside the more usual kuḍmala.

kuṭhārī (= Pali and Skt. Lex. id.; in Skt. lit. only °ra, m., whereas Pali records only the f.), *axe, hatchet*: Mv i.16.14 vāsīhi paraśūhi kuṭhārīhi; ii.35.13 (vs) kuṭhārihastā (short i m.c.); Ud viii.2 kuṭhāri (v.l. °rī; metr. indifferent) jāyate mukhe (same vs, with kuṭhārī, in Pali, Sn 657 et al.).

kuḍḍa (Pali id., = Skt. kuḍya), *wall*: Mv i.25.14 ff.

kuḍmalaka(-jātam), (= Skt. kuḍmala), *bud*: Mvy 6229.

kuḍya-mūla (nt.; = Pali kuḍḍa-mūla, Vin. iii.15.38, wrongly defined PTSD), *base of a wall*: AsP 498.(2–)3, cited Śikṣ 38.(15–)16 dakṣiṇaṃ coru (Śikṣ coruṃ) viddhvā nirmāṃsaṃ (Śikṣ adds ca) kṛtvāsthi bhettuṃ ku°lam upasaṃkrāmati (sma, Śikṣ om.); kuḍyamūlaṃ niśritya paribhuktam Divy 82.25.

kuḍyā (or kuḍya, m.? in Skt. nt., except f. Gr. and once BhāgP., see BR; acc. to Sheth m. or nt. in Pkt.), *wall*: SP 83.5 (vs) kuḍyāś (WT em. °yā) ca bhittīś ca (influence of the gender of bhitti?); n. pl.

kuṇapa, nt. (cited pw 7, App., as m. in Mvy; but Mironov as well as Kyōtō ed. nt.), n. of a hell, acc. to Mv i.7.3 a narakotsada (see **utsada** 2) or *supplementary hell*, acc. to Tib. on Mvy *a cold hell*: Mvy 4938; Mv i.7.1, 3; 11.5, 9 = iii.455.17, 21.

kuṇāla, or **kunāla**; see also **koṇāla**; m., (**1**) (= Pali kuṇāla; not in Pkt. or Skt. in this sense), a kind of bird, in Pali apparently *the Indian cuckoo*, Skt. kokila: kuṇ° Mvy 4880; LV 40.5; 286.13; 301.14; Av ii.201.2, 4; RP 26.15; Śikṣ 329.6; Gv 100.26; 194.12; kun° LV 162.19–20 (most mss. kuṇ°) and in a passage found only in ms. H but confirmed by Tib. (ku na la; ms. H kunāra), see Crit. App. on LV 11.3; RP 41.9; Divy 406.6 ff.; (**2**) (in this sense not recorded in Pali or Skt., but AMg. Kuṇāla), n. of a son of King Aśoka, so named because his eyes were like those of the bird acc. to Av ii.201.4 ff. (Kuṇ°) and Divy 406.14 ff.; other occurrences Divy 403.8 ff.; 405.14 (in Divy always Kun°); Kunālāvadāna, colophon to Divy chap. 27, Divy 419.13.

kuṇṭha, adj. (in Skt. only *blunt, dull*; in Pali also (a) *mutilated* (person), Jāt. ii.117.18, also koṇṭha in same context; cf. Skt. Dhātup. kuṇṭ-, vikalīkaraṇe; and cf. the following items), probably *mutilated, maimed* (or possibly *deformed*): AsP 426.18 (prose) na kāṇo bhavati na kuṇṭho bhavati na kubjo . . .

kuṇṭhaka, adj., = prec., q.v.; see also **kuṇḍa(ka)**: SP 94.13 (vs), for KN kāṇaku kaṇḍakāś ca, read with WT (and their ms. K′) kā° kuṇṭhakāś ca, or perhaps kāṇa ku-kuṇṭhakāś ca (see s.v. **kāṇaka**); SP 113.11 (vs) ye kāṇaka kuṇṭhakāś ca.

Kuṇṭhā (to **kuṇṭha**, q.v.), n. of a rākṣasī: Māy 240.6.

kuṇḍa, adj., (**1**) in the sense of Skt. (and Pali) kuṇṭha, *dull, blunt*: LV 252.2 (prose) kuṇḍayā śaktyā śiraḥkapālam upahanyād; Tib. rtul pos, *dull, blunt*; despite this, and on no apparent ground, Foucaux translates both the Skt. and even the Tib. (!) by *aiguë*!; no v.l. reported by Lefm.; (**2**) in Mvy 7363 and 8875 acc. to Tib. lag rdum, *maimed in the hand*; so also Chin. and Jap.; same mg. perh. in Pali, Pv. comm. 181.9 catūhi aṅgehi kuṇḍa (*bent*, PTSD); pw 7.332 *krüppelicht, lahm*; cf. Dhātup. kuṇḍ-, vaikalye, and the use of **kuṇṭha** (Skt. *blunt*, a mg. which BHS kuṇḍa has) in BHS and Pali in the additional sense of *mutilated, maimed*. See also next.

kuṇḍaka, adj., presumably = **kuṇḍa** 2, *maimed* (in the hand?): SP 95.5 (vs) te kuṇḍakā (Kashgar rec. khuḍḍakā) **laṅgaka** (q.v.) bhonti tatra; WT keep kuṇḍakā, altho their ms. K′ reads kuṇṭhakā (see s.v.), because Kumārajīva's Chinese, they say, this time is different and suggests kuṇḍa of Mvy.

kuṇḍana (to the root of **kuṇḍa**, q.v.; but the Skt. Dhātup. assigns to this root the mg. *burn* as well as *mutilate*), prob. *mutilation* (barely possibly, *burning*), in a list of tortures in hell: ŚsP 1461.9 tatra (sc. nirayeṣu) chedana-bhedana-kuṇḍana-**snedana-** (! see s.v.) -pacanāny anubhaveyam.

kuṇḍala (**1**) (nt.) *coil* (of rope): Jm 23.11 anyatra rajju-kuṇḍalād dātrāc caikasmāt; see next (1); (**2**) in LV 276.22 nīla-mṛdu-kuṇḍala-jāta-pradakṣiṇa-nandyāvarta-kācilindika-sukhasaṃsparśaiś ca tṛṇair, the word kuṇḍala (vv.ll. kuntala, kuṇṭaka) is obscure; it is omitted from the cpd. in Foucaux's Tib.; a late Skt. Lex. records the meaning *thick* for kuṇṭaka; this mg. would fit here but there is no other support for a word kuṇṭaka. On the other hand, perhaps kuṇḍala-jāta- means simply *curling* (of blades of grass, tṛṇa); cf. **kuṇḍalaka** (2) -jāta, of hair; Foucaux's Note p. 167, bottom, actually cites this form of the cpd. as the reading of one ms., but adds that Tib. indicates a reading kuśa-jāta (of this his Tib. text and its transl. contain no trace); *curling* seems to me a curious epithet to be applied to grass; (3) (cf. Skt. Lex. id. = pāśa), *a ring* as a kind of fetter: Gv 353.12, see s.v. **kaṭaka**; (4) m., n. of a form of a mendicant, created magically by Māra to obstruct Buddha: Mv i.270.13.

kuṇḍalaka, nt., (1) (= prec.; Pali id., Vv. comm. 212.13 rajju-kuṇḍalaka-), *coil* (of rope): Jm 23.14–15 tad rajju-kuṇḍalakaṃ . . .; 24.4 id.; (2) (perhaps adj.?) *curl*, or *curling* (of hair), in °ka-jātaṃ (roma; said of a mahāpuruṣa): Bbh 375.18 (ekaikam asya) roma kāye jātaṃ nīlaṃ kuṇḍalaka-jātaṃ . . .; (3) (cf. **kuṇḍalikā**) in Mvy 9007 °kam, acc. to Tib. zaṅs bum, *copper vessel*; Chin. *cooking vessel*; Mvy 9443 °kaṃ, acc. to Tib. bkru bśal gyi snod, *wash-basin*, so also Chin.

kuṇḍala-vardhana, nt., Mv iii.263.16 and 18, a name for some brahmanical saṃskāra or similar rite performed for a boy (here Rāhula); bracketed with jātikarma (or in 15 jāta°) and cūḍākaraṇa (or in 16 jaṭākaraṇakarma). Could vardhana here mean *cutting* (as in nābhi-var°), and kuṇḍala *curls* (of hair, cf. **kuṇḍalaka**, 2)? Then *cutting of the* (infant's) *locks of hair*?

Kuṇḍalā, n. of a yakṣiṇī: Mv i.253.1.

kuṇḍalikā (cf. °**laka**, 3), *water-jar*: Av ii.87.5 udakapūrṇā °kā dattā; so mss., to be kept; confirmed by °**laka** (3) and Tib. spyi blugs, *vase* (Das); Speyer em. unnecessarily to kuṇḍikā.

[**Kuṇḍaśriyārciścandra**(sya), n. of a Bodhisattva, Gv 442.26, 1st ed.; read with 2d ed. Kuṇḍaśriyo 'rciśc°, two names.]

Kuṇḍaśrī, n. of a Bodhisattva: Gv 442.26 (see prec.).

kuṇḍika (m. or nt.; cf. AMg. kuṇḍiya, *water-pot*, acc. to Ratnach. m.; Skt. kuṇḍaka, kuṇḍikā), *water-pot*: LV 249.9 (prose; no v.l.) (aṅgāradhātu-kaṣāya-tridaṇḍamuṇḍika)-kuṇḍika-kapāla-khaṭvāṅga-dhāraṇaiś ca (all ascetics' paraphernalia).

? **kuṇḍīraka** (m. or nt.), some article used to cover a lamp and keep its light unseen: tayā pradīpaṃ prajvālya °rakeṇa pracchādya sthāpitaḥ MSV i.102.9. (Related to Skt. kuṇḍī, *pot*?).

Kuṇḍopadhānīyaka, lit. app. *using a water-jar for a pillow* (so BR), ep. of **Pūrṇa** (4), q.v.: Divy 44.8; 45.1, where he is declared by the Buddha to be the first of receivers of food-tickets (**śalākā**, 3, q.v.) among his disciples. This identifies him with Pali Kuṇḍa-dhāna (see DPPN s.v.), a name also applied in DPPN to 1 Puṇṇa; Kuṇ° seems to be his regular name, but it is said to have been originally Dhāna, and the prefixation of Kuṇḍa- is explained in a way which would not fit the BHS epithet.

? **Kutarārkaka**, n. of a yakṣa in Kurukṣetra: Māy 57; dual dvandva, Tarārkakutarārkakau; division between the two names uncertain, but Tarārkaku-tarārkakau seems implausible. Lévi, p. 97, refers to Tarantukārantukayor (loc. du.) Mbh. 3.81.178 (Calc. 3.7078), which he calls the name of two yakṣas; but it is obviously the name of two *localities* (acc. to BR, tīrthas) in Kurukṣetra.

kuta-lipi (or, with v.l., **kutana-lipi**), some kind of script: Mv i.135.6. Senart thinks of reading kuṭa, referring to Kuṭaka as n. of a people, but this is recorded only once from the BhāgP., and seems implausible here. The word seems to correspond to **kirāta-lipi** of LV 125.21.

kutupa, m., nt. (Skt. Gr.-Lex. and AMg. id., m.), *oil-flask*: °pam, nt., Mvy 9016; taila-°pāḥ, m. pl. (ms. °kutapāḥ) MSV ii.141.16.

kutūhala-śālā (= Pali °sālā; expl. DN comm. 369.6 ff. etc.), *hall of discussion*, in which various opinions are expressed and questions disputed; ordinarily used of gatherings of non-Buddhists: Divy 143.13; MSV i.221.7.

-kuttaṃ, see **-kṛtvā** for Skt. kṛtvas.

-kutsaka, ifc. (to Skt. kutsayati), adj. or subst., *blaming, contemning*; *one who contemns*: apamārgaka-(q.v.)-kutsakā(ḥ) Mv i.176.8 (prose).

kutsanīya, adj. (cf. prec., and AMg. kucchaṇijja), *offensive*: LV 189.17 (vs) mūtre purīṣi svaki tiṣṭhati kutsanīye.

ku-daṇḍa, m. (= Pali ku-daṇḍaka, Jāt. iii.204.16 °ka-baddhā, *bound by an unmerited punishment*; misinterpreted in translations and PTSD), *unjust punishment*: Mvy 5355 °ḍaḥ; LV 43.7 (vs) na tathā kudaṇḍā notpīḍanā . . .; Gv 213.24 (vs) haḍi-daṇḍa-bandha-nigaḍāś ca tathā kudaṇḍā(ḥ).

kunāla, see **kuṇāla.**

Kunikaṇṭha (cf. Pali Kinnughaṇḍu, n. of a yakṣa?), n. of a yakṣa: Māy 236.27.

kunta (1) m. (Skt. Lex.; see **kunta-pipīlikā**), *a small insect* (ant?): Mvy 4851 °taḥ = Tib. srin bu phre-ḥu, *small insect*; followed by 4852 pipīlikā; (2) nt., *tax, tribute*: Mvy 7301 °tam = Tib. dpya.

Kuntadaṃṣṭrā (text °dāṃṣṭrā), n. of a rākṣasī: Māy 241.14.

kunta-palaka, m., *spear-point*: Mvy 9350 = Tib. mduṅ rtse.

kunta-pipīlika, also °**laka**, m., *a small insect*, presumably *a kind of ant* (see also s.v. **kunta**, m.): Bhīk 25b.1 antataḥ °ko 'pi prāṇī jīvitān na vyaparopitavyaḥ; corresp. to Pali kuntha-kipillaka (°ika, °ikā?), acc. to note in Bhīk. also kunda-kimiṇṇaka (! cited without reference from Kammavākya; not in Dictt.); °likasya Divy 51.4; Gv 160.4; °liko 'pi Divy 161.24; °likā api (n. pl.) Divy 77.15; °likādayo Divy 466.12; °lako 'pi (mss.) Av ii.130.4; °lakam MSV ii.43.12.

kuntala, nt. (in Skt. and Pkt. only m.), *hair* (of the head): LV 49.20 (vs) kuntalānī (-ī m.c.).

Kuntī, or °**ti** (cf. Pali Kuntī, n. of a kiṃnarī?), (1) n. of a rākṣasī: °tī SP 400.6; °ti, voc., 403.6; °ti-, stem in comp., 402.12 (all prose); (2) n. of a yakṣiṇī: Suv 163.2; MSV i.xviii.18 ff.

Kuntīnagara, n. of a city: MSV i.xviii.18 ff.

Kundapuṣpagandha, n. of two former Buddhas: Mv i.141.5, 9 (in the same list).

kundasaka, m., acc. to Dutt = Tib. pho loṅ, *'a kind of jasmine'*: MSV iv.76.6.

kupina, nt., and °**nī**, f. (= Skt. Lex. °nī; Pali kumina, nt.), *fish-net*: Śikṣ 77.4 (matsyānāṃ) bandhanāya kupinam (Tib. dol, *fish-net*); Ud iii.3 baddhā matsyā vā (read va) kupinīmukhe (Pali parallel vs Ud vii.4 kumināmukhe, with ā m.c.).

kupyaka, m. or nt., n. of some unknown tree: Mv ii.203.6 °ka-vana-śākhā; iii.80.5 °ka-vārṣika-mallika- etc. (names of plants).

kupsara, nt., some unknown part of a chariot: Mv ii.62.8 (vs) heṣṭā manesī uparim ca kupsaraṃ, suvarnacandrā ca rathe upāgatā. Mg. of this word and **manesī** both unknown. The vs should correspond to Jāt. v.408.32–409.2, but shows no resemblance to it; there is, however, some resemblance to 407.22 navamhi kocchamhi yadā upāvisī(ti), and kupsara might correspond to koccha, *seat* (comm. kañcanapīṭhasaṃkhāte kocche), the etym. of which is unknown.

Kubera, as one of the four **mahārāja(n)**, see this.

Kubela = Skt. Kubera, n. of a god: LV 130.13 (vs; but several mss. °ra).

Kubjottarā (= Pali Khujjuttarā), n. of a servant of **Śyāmāvatī** (1): Divy 533.5; 538.10; 539.16; 541.4; Jm 115.24 (identified with a slave-girl in a Jātaka, as also in the same Jāt. in Pali).

Kumāra-kāśyapa (= Pali °kassapa), n. of a disciple of the Buddha: Sukh 2.6; Karmav 80.4.

Kumāradarśana, n. of a gandharva-king: Kv 2.20.

kumāra-bhūta, adj., *while still a youth; remaining a youth*; a stock epithet of **Mañjuśrī**, q.v., who is perennially young: SP 7.8–9; 260.16; 275.1 ff.; Mvy 650; but also of others, esp. Bodhisattvas, Mvy 693–5, 698–9, and cf. 883 te ca bodhisattvā . . .bhūyastvena sarve kumārabhūtāḥ; also of Buddhas, with reference to the period before their enlightenment, SP 19.2; 160.9; 311.2 (here of Śākyamuni); and even of an ordinary human being, Jīvaka, Divy 270.12, 20; 506.8 ff.; but this is probably based on a misunderstanding and consequent re-formation of next, q.v.

Kumāra-bhṛta (Pali Komārabhacca), ep. of **Jīvaka**; interpreted here, as in Pali, as meaning *raised by the prince* (**Abhaya** 5); cf. under prec.: MSV ii.25.5 ff.

Kumāravardhana, nt., n. of a city: MSV i.66.2, 6 ff.

Kumārākaragupta, n. of an author: Sādh 574.9.

Kumārikā, see s.v. **Kumārī** (2).

Kumārī, (**1**), n. of four female deities (mahāyakṣiṇyaḥ Mmk 575.10), also called **Bhaginī**, q.v., and noted only in Mmk; they have a brother called Kumāra (but apparently not = Kārttikeya), 45.17; 518.14; but his real name seems to have been **Tumburu** (otherwise known in Skt. as a gandharva), 537.7; 538.1, et alibi; 575.10; in 538.1; 542.9 he is called sārthavāha; otherwise they may be simply bhrātṛ-pañcamāḥ, 44.25; they are to be portrayed standing on ships and living in the ocean, 44.25; 45.17; 575.11; they are called Kumārī 45.17; 518.14; 575.10, but Bhaginī 17.4; 44.25; 519.8 ff. The last begins a long passage dealing with them, extending to p. 546, in which repeatedly their names appear as Jayā, Vijayā, Ajitā, and Aparājitā (523.6 ff.; 528.2, 9 ff.; 537.7 ff.; 539.7, 25; 540.5; 543.3 ff.); (**2**) n. of one specific yakṣiṇī (hardly one of the above-mentioned four): Mmk 567.11; 569.5; also called (yakṣa-) Kumārikā Mmk 569.4.

Kumudagandha, n. of a former Buddha: Mv i.140.12.

Kumudapuṣpā, n. of a gandharva maid: Kv 5.5.

Kumudākaramati, n. of an author: Sādh 14.10.

kumbhaka, m., *the base of a pillar* or *column*: Mvy 5574 = Tib. ka rten. Not recorded in any Dict., but in Acharya, Dict. Hindu Architecture s.v., from inscriptions at Mathurā (Sanskrit?).

kumbhakāraka, m. (not recorded in any Dict. except by Wilson; fem. °rikā occurs in Kathās.), *potter* (= °kāra): LV 207.16 (prose) °ka-cakram (ms. A °kāra-ca°).

Kumbhakārī, (**1**) n. of the daughter of a village chief (grāmika): LV 265.5; (**2**) in Divy 348.20 taken by ed. as n. pr., of a caṇḍālī cowherdess: Apalāla-nāgaṃ vinīya Kumbhakārīṃ caṇḍālīṃ gopālīṃ ca teṣāṃ Mathurām anuprāptaḥ. But in 385.(3–)4 text has (Apalālaṃ nāgaṃ damayitvā) kumbhakālaṃ (!) caṇḍālī-gopālīṃ ca nāgaṃ ca Mathurām anuprāptas . . . Burnouf, Intr. 377, understands Gopālī as the n. pr., and takes Kumbh° as meaning *potter's wife*.

kumbhatūṇa, m. or nt. (Pali °thūṇa; see the derivs. following; sometimes spelled with n for ṇ, but never with th for t, which should always be kept, as Senart belatedly recognized, iii.472; cf. also **tūṇa(ka)**, and **tuṇa**), some *musical instrument*, in Pali acc. to Dictt. *a kind of drum* (Skt. tūṇava said to be a *flute*): Mv ii.52.15 (the corrupt mss. clearly indicate °tūṇaṃ, acc. sg., as the true reading); followed by mṛdaṅga-.

kumbhatūṇin, m. (= next; cf. under prec.), *a player on the* **kumbhatūṇa**: Mv ii.150.4–5 (prose) °ṇī, acc. pl.

kumbhatūṇika, m., = prec.: Mv ii.100.10; 153.17; 156.9; iii.57.10; 113.3; 141.18; 255.11; 442.9 (regularly prose).

(**kumbhadāsī**, once in Harṣac., pw; = Pali id., misdefined PTSD; *harlot*: Mv ii.58.3, read °dāsiye, = Jāt. v.403.6 °dāsiyā; °dāsīye Mv iii.264.10 [text °vāsīye, but see note]; 270.1.)

kumbhāṇḍa, °**aṇḍa**, m. (= Pali kumbhaṇḍa, which is recorded in BHS Gv 46.18; 102.25; 119.23, all prose, tho the Sktized ā is printed later in Gv, see below: = Skt. kuṣmāṇḍa, kūṣ°; in all verse passages where meter determines the quantity of the first syllable, it is short, except only in Gv 214.11; note that in Mv ii.203.16 it is necessary to read with mss. kumbhāṇḍa-su-(mss. śu)-bhairava-rutān, Senart erroneously em. by omitting su, the syllable kum° being short metrically), a kind of *evil spirit*, commonly mentioned with yakṣas, piśācas, bhūtas, etc., and esp. rākṣasas; **Virūḍhaka** is standardly their lord: LV 217.21; 389.2; SP 399.6; cf. Mvy 3436–7; but in LV 130.9 Rudra is called their overlord (adhipati); in LV 302.3 mentioned among Māra's followers, along with yakṣas, rākṣasas, and gandharvas; occurrences in verses where first syllable is short, LV 50.6; 54.13; 307.18; 341.16; Mv ii.203.16 (see above); Bhad 18; Śikṣ 333.9; in verses where meter is indecisive or in prose, SP 86.11; 401.5; LV 249.17; Mv i.257.5; 350.9; ii.106.13; 212.10; 296.10; 351.17; 410.5; iii.71.20; Mvy 3225; 4755; Divy 105.28; 119.9; Av i.67.10; 108.9; Kv 76.10 (in Kv 11.20 the Skt. form kuṣmāṇḍa is printed, prob. by misprint or graphic corruption); Gv (cf. above) 120.2; 169.10; 190.23; Laṅk 261.8; Sādh 411.2; Bhīk 26a.5. Cf. next two.

kumbhāṇḍaka, m. (ka may be m.c.), = prec.: SP 84.7; 85.9; 86.1 (all vss; quantity of first syllable indifferent).

kumbhāṇḍī (= Pali °bhaṇḍī), (**1**) a female kumbhāṇḍa: Laṅk 261.8; (**2**) n. of a rākṣasī: Māy 241.14; 243.17.

Kumbhīra, (**1**) (= Pali id.) n. of a yakṣa: Suv 161.13; Māy 101; Mahāsamāj. 169.9 (Waldschmidt, Kl. Skt. Texte 4); (**2**) n. of a nāga: Māy 221.28 (misprinted °ira).

Kumbhodara, n. of a yakṣa: Māy 98.

kuranṭa (m.; = Skt. Lex.; cf. Skt. and Pali kuraṇḍaka), a kind of tree: Mv iii.80.2, so read with 1 ms., v.l. kulamba, Senart em. kulattha.

Kuru, m. = **Uttara-kuru**; see s.v. **dvīpa**.

kuru, nt. (= Skt. Lex. id.), *boiled rice*: Mv i.28.10 (prose) asti kuru (v.l. kuruṃ; n. sg.) asti yvāgū. Senart em. to kūraṃ, which is Skt.; in i.29.3 he reads kūro ti loke pretasmiṃ paśya yāva sudurlabhaṃ (note nt. adj.!), but mss. all kuro (except one karo); perh. read kurū, kuruṃ, or even kuro with mss. (o for final u, favored by meter).

kurukuci, var. for **kuṭukuñcaka**, q.v.

Kurukulla(-parvata), n. of a mountain: Sādh 343.11 etc.

Kurukullakā (in a vs, Sādh 354.13, prob. m.c.), or **Kurukullā**, Sādh 343.3 etc., n. of a goddess.

kuruṭu, nt., and **kuruṭāvi** (vv.ll. °ṭuvi, °tāvi, °ṭāpi), nt., two large numbers or ways of calculation (gaṇanā): LV 148.16 (in Calc. only kurutā; only A, Lefm.'s best ms., has both; most mss. om. kuruṭu). In the list cited from this LV passage in Mvy the two forms are **kuṭṭā** and **kuṭṭavitā**, qq.v.

kuruvinda, m. (Pali °vindaka, a powder for the bath, made from a 'stone', -pāsāṇa-, acc. to Vin. Comm. 1200.1), a sort of *bath-powder*, acc. to Tib. made of ground lead (zha ñe brdar): Mvy 9291. In Mvy 5981 the same word (m.) certainly means *ruby* as in Skt.; it follows words for *gold* and *silver*. Tib. transliterates, or alternatively renders by zha ñe, *lead* (base metals are named in the sequel); Chin. *tin*.

Kurkuṭārāma (m.; also **Kukku°**, **Kukkuṭāgāra**, qq.v.; = Pali Kukku°), n. of a grove and monastery at

Pāṭaliputra: Divy 375.7; 381.12; 384.28; 406.20; 423.11; 430.14 ff. (here one ms., D, has Kukku° several times); 434.5 (here text is found only in D, which writes Kukku°).

kurvati, see Chap. 43, s.v. kṛ.

kulaṃkula, m. (= Pali kolaṃkola), *one destined to be reborn in several families before liberation*: Mvy 1011 = Tib. rigs nas rigs su skye ba; Dharmas 103 deva-k° manuṣya-k°. One of the stages of a śrāvaka; cf. **ekavīcika.** In corresp. Pali passage AN i.233.15 kolaṃkolo hoti dve vā tīṇi vā kulāni saṃdhāvitvā saṃsāritvā dukkhassa antaṃ karoti. See also **kulākula.**

[**kulaccha**, is surely only a graphic corruption for kulattha, not a genuine variant for it as Senart assumes on Mv ii.131.9 (-yūṣaṃ, cf. Pali kulatthayūsaṃ MN i.245.19) and 204.19.]

kulajyeṣṭhāpacāyaka, see **apacāyaka.**

kula-dūṣaka, m. (= Pali °saka), in MSV iii.88.4 written **°ṣika**, *injurer or spoiler of families* (this is a saṃghāvaśeṣa sin): Mvy 8380; Prāt 485.1; MSV iii.15.22. Corresp. to Pali Vin. iii.184.9 ff.; acc. to 185.1 ff. the 'injury' or 'spoiling' consists in the erring monk's imposing on lay families improper services.

Kulanandana, n. of a former Buddha: Mv i.138.7.

kula-puruṣakeṇa, adv., *at the rate of one man per family*: Mv iii.176.10 (°keṇa tatra śalākāni cārīyanti), 11, 12 (in the first occurrence, only, v.l. °ṣeṇa).

? **kula-baddha**, *consort, wife* (?): (Māyā . . .) Śuddhodanasya °ddha-kalpena (*as Ś.'s wife*?) Siddhārthaṃ bodhisattvaṃ janitravatī (q.v.) Gv 439.1.

kulala, m. (n. pl. °lā; = Pali id.), some bird of prey, associated with gṛdhra and kāka (as in Pali with gijjha and kāka): Mv i.7.4 °lā ca gṛdhrā ca kākolūkā ca; 11.11. One might identify it with Skt. and Pali kurara, *osprey*; but the latter is not used in Pali in close association with gijjha and kāka. In AMg. defined as a *vulture*, or (another) *kind of bird.*

kulavaka, m. = Skt. kuravaka, a kind of tree: Mv iii.80.1 (vs), with only 1 ms. (the other omits the word).

kula-śulka, nt.: acc. to pw and Jap., *betrothal-price*, paid for a bride to her father: Mvy 6797; no Chin. given; Tib. gñod, *strength* (! but also, in Dict. Cath. Miss., gñod ka, *prix, valeur*).

kula-sāmpreya, adj., substantially = **sāmpreya,** q.v., *appropriate to* (your?, or, a good?) *family*, or *wholesome in* (for) *a* (good) *family*; of food: Av i.255.2 °yena bhojanena (sc. me prayojanam; said by a pratyekabuddha). Speyer (Index) would em. to kila sāṃ°, very implausibly.

kulākula, nt., *the state of a* **kulaṃkula**, q.v.: SP 27.8 (vs) kulākulaṃ ca pratipannam (WT °na with ms. K′) āsīt, *and he had attained the stage of one destined to be reborn in several families* (before enlightenment). (ā = aṃ, § 3.3.)

ku-lābha, m., *slight acquisition* (so Tib.): MSV ii.97. 14 ff.

kulāyaka, adj., m., *confined to worldly existence*: Divy 562.9 (vs) etac ca dṛṣṭveha parivrajanti, kulāyakās te na bhavanti santaḥ; te sarvasaṅgān abhisaṃprahāya, na garbhaśayyāṃ punar āvasanti. Prob. from kulāya, *cage*, and lit. *caged, confined*; less likely cpd. of kula plus āyaka (Skt. gr.) or *ayaka (cf. Skt. aya).

kulika, adj. (not in Pali, except in aggakulika; see **agra°**), *of good family*: Divy 366.6 eko 'grakulikaputro dvitīyaḥ kulikaputraś ca.

[**kulina**, misprint or corruption for Skt. kulīna, adj.: Gv 526.16 (prose) (sarvajāter adoṣaḥ . . .) prajāyāṃ kulino (read °īno) bhavati.]

Kuliśika, n. of a nāga king: Mmk 18.11 (prose).

Kuliśeśvarī, n. of a goddess: Sādh 598.17.

kulopaka, see **upaka** (1).

kulopagata, m., = **kulopaka** (cf. **upaga** = **upaka,** with etymologizing adaptation to root upa-gam-, further adapted here to ppp. -gata), *family associate*, see **-upaka** 1: Av ii.67.9 tasmiṃś ca gṛhe sthaviro 'niruddhaḥ kulopagataḥ.

[**kulopi(yaṃ)**, Mv iii.453.3, mss., see **kalopī.**]

Kuvalayā, n. of a daughter of a dancing-teacher: Av ii.24.8 ff.

Kuvera, as one of the four **mahārāja(n)**, see this.

Kuśa, (1) n. of a king, previous incarnation of the Buddha (in the 7th bhūmi): Mv i.128.13 ff.; (2) = Pali Kusa (hero of Kusa Jātaka); his story is told in Mv twice at great length, Mv ii.433.19 ff. and iii.8.3 ff.; (kuśajātakaṃ samāptam iii.27.21;) also MSV i.100.11 ff.; probably referred to (rather than 1 above) in Mvy 3566, in list of cakravartin kings.

kuśaṇḍikā (see BR 5.1313; BHS goes against Aufrecht's em. reported pw 6.300, kuśa-kaṇḍikā), something used for a seat, prob. some kind of reed or grass, or a seat made thereof: Sādh 11.18 pallavopaviṣṭaḥ kuśaṇḍikopaviṣṭo vā.

Kuśadruma, n. of a brother of **Kuśa** (2), q.v.: Mv ii.446.12 ff.; 460.18; iii.10.10; 15.4.

Kuśanagara, nt., = **Kuśinagarī**, q.v.

Kuśamālin, m. (= Pali Kusamāli), n. of a mythical sea: Jm 91.24 °lī samudro 'yam.

kuśala, nt. (= Pali kusala, synonym of puñña; in Skt. Lex. only, also syn. of puṇya), *good in a moral sense* (not so in Skt. literature), *merit, righteous action*; there are 10 kuśala (= Pali 10 kusala or sīla), Mvy 1685, listed 1686–98, = (kuśala) **karmapatha,** q.v. for list. See the next items.

kuśala-pakṣa (m., = Pali kusala-pakkha), *the side of virtue, good morals*: °kṣaṃ pratijāgṛhīti Av ii.145.2; °kṣaṃ pratijāgṛtheti MSV i.237.8; in Śikṣ 128.1 (prose) atisaṃlikhito hi kuśalapakṣa-parāṅmukho bhavati, *too severely restricted* (in food), *he becomes averse to the virtuous life* (wrongly Bendall and Rouse). See **saṃlikhita.**

kuśalapuṇya, *meritorious deed of virtue*, in Mv i.81.1–2 contrasted with kuśalamūla, but whether the former marks a higher, more developed stage of religious advancement than the latter (as Senart seems to believe), is not clear to me: (ye punar . . .) bodhisattvā avaivartikatāyai pariṇāmenti, kin tu khalu teṣām upacita-kuśalapuṇyānāṃ prathamā praṇidhir utpadyati, āho svid upacita-kuśalamūlānām iti. The reply, in vss, first says that worship of Buddhas etc. does not suffice. Then (81.16) te yadā vipula-puṇya-saṃcayā, bhonti bhāvita-śarīramānasāḥ; te . . . bodhaye upajanenti mānasaṃ; yaṃ mayā kuśalamūlam arjitaṃ, tena me bhavatu sarvadarśitā; . . . (82.3) yaś ca me kuśalamūla-saṃcayo, so mahā bhavatu sarvaprāṇibhiḥ . . . Is puṇya of 81.16 something else than kuśala-puṇya of 81.1–2? Both it and kuśala-mūla seem, as far as I can tell, to have the same effect in the verses; no clear answer to the question in the prose has been discovered by me.

kuśala-mūla, nt., usually pl. (= Pali kus°), *root(s) of merit*; Pali has three, alobha, adosa, amoha; the same, with adveṣa = Pali adosa, in Mvy 1936–8; Dharmas 138; two other kinds named separately Mvy 1208–9, abhisamayāntikaṃ ku°, and kṣayajñānalābhikaṃ ku°; a different list of three in Dharmas 15, bodhicittotpāda, āśayaviśuddhi, ahaṃkāra-mamakāra-parityāga; Mvy 7417 avaropitakuśalamūla, *one who has planted* (see **avaropayati**) *roots of merit*; very many other occurrences, e. g. LV 429.14; Mv (see **kuśala-puṇya**) i.134.3; 142.11; Divy 23.18; 65.10; 95.25; Av i.4.2, et passim; often referred to in **praṇidhāna** as basis for making the 'earnest wish'.

kuśala-varta, m., prob. *auspicious procedure* or *functioning*: Mvy 2738, introductory to Chap. 138 kuśalādayaḥ; no Tib., Chin., or Jap. translation; cf. s.v. **varta,** and Pali vatta. Here kuśala has its normal Skt. mg., not that peculiar to Buddh. language.

-kuśalin, in daśa-kuśalī, n. sg. m.: LV 169.11 (vs), *possessing the ten kuśala* (q.v.), i. e. *living a moral life.*

Kuśākṣī, n. of a rākṣasī: Māy 240.23.

Kuśāvatī, (1) name given to Kuśa's city: MSV i.106.18: (2) (= Pali Kusā°) former name of Kuśinagarī: MPS 34.1 ff.

Kuśi-grāmaka (? text with 1 ms.; vv.ll. Kuśilagrā°, Kuśala°), nt., = **Kuṣṭha-grāmaka,** q.v.: Divy 208.14. (Not = next.)

Kuśinagarī (also **Kuśanagaram,** Mvy 4125; Kuśīnagarī, Karmav 36.11), = Pali Kusinārā, n. of a town of the Mallas, where the Buddha entered nirvāṇa: Divy 394.6; Av i.227.5; ii.197.5; MPS 30.4 and 32.4 (which together guarantee the form).

kuśīda, see **kusīda.**

Kuśīnagarī = **Kuśi°,** q.v.

Kuṣṭha-grāmaka, m., n. of a Vṛji village near Vaiśālī: MPS 20.2; 21.6. Not in Pali; Tib. first ku-sti, later ru-rta ('a spicy root', Jä., = kuṣṭha); on Divy equivalent see **Kuśi-grāmaka** (*not* = **Kuśinagarī!**).

kuṣṭhila, adj. (cf. Skt. kuṣṭha, kuṣṭhin; on the suffix § 22.17), *leprous*: RP 30.7 (vs) kuṣṭhilāś, n. pl.

kusīda, kuś°, (1) adj. (cf. kusīda, TS 7.3.11.1, rendered *inert,* Keith; = Pali kusīta; cf. **akuśīda-, kausīdya),** *slothful.* The mg. of this essentially Pali-BHS word is made clear by collocations like Mv iii.436.6 kuśīdo hīnavīryavān; Bbh 182.26 na kusīdo . . . na hīnavīryo; Gv 220.7 kusīda-nyasta-prayogān sattvān; and see s.v. **kausīdya.** The spelling with ś seems to be always found in Mv (i.79.11; ii.93.5, 16; 220.16), and occurs also LV 35.4; Av ii.107.3 (mss., Speyer em. to s); RP 18.7; 34.8; Śikṣ 52.6; so also most mss. Sukh 74.3 (ed. s); otherwise with s, SP 27.7; 203.11 hīnādhimuktāś ca kusīdarūpā; Av i.15.15 ff.; 216.1; Śikṣ 50.17; 275.4; Mmk 73.12; (2) noun, m. or nt., *sloth* (not so recorded in Pali; = **kausīdya**), clearly in RP 35.13 (vs) lābhābhibhūtasya kusīda (n. sg.) vardhate, kusīdabhūtasya praṇaṣṭa śraddhā; perhaps also in Gv 220.7, above.

kusuma, (1) lit. *flower,* used in comp. Laṅk 43.15, -kusuma-dharma-paryāya, lit. *flower (of a) dharma-p°,* i. e. *supreme, beautiful, noble* one? Tib. renders literally; Suzuki *most subtle doctrine* (does 'most subtle' represent kusuma?); (2) n. of two future Buddhas: dvau buddhau kusumanāmau (°nāmānau) Mv ii.355.8 = iii.279.13; n. of a future Buddha, Gv 441.25; followed by **Kusumaśrī,** the two corresponding to Mv's two Kusumas (on the passage see s.v. **Maitreya**); (3) n. of a king, former incarnation of Śākyamuni: RP 24.10.

Kusumakuśa, n. of a brother of Kuśa (2): Mv ii.433.17.

Kusumaketu, n. of a Bodhisattva: Gv 3.19.

Kusumaketumaṇḍalin, n. of a kiṃnara: Mvy 3416.

Kusumagarbha, n. of a Buddha: Gv 256.8.

Kusumagupta, n. of a former Buddha: Mv i.136.17.

Kusumacūḍa, n. of a cakravartin: Mv i.153.16.

Kusumadhvaja, n. of a Bodhisattva: Gv 2.18.

Kusumaprabha, n. of a former Buddha: Sukh 6.7.

Kusumarāśi, n. of a Buddha: Gv 258.26.

Kusumavṛṣṭyabhiprakīrṇa, n. of a former Buddha: Sukh 6.7.

Kusumaśayana, n. of a former Buddha: Mv i.140.8.

Kusumaśrī, n. of a future Buddha: Gv 441.25 (see **Kusuma**); one of 'the 35 Buddhas', Śikṣ 169.12.

Kusumaśrīgarbha, n. of a Bodhisattva: Dbh 2.10.

Kusumasaṃbhava, n. of a former Buddha: Sukh 6.5.

? **Kusumahestha** (so Senart; 6 mss. vary greatly; a better guess might be °hemastha, with one good ms.), n. of a former Buddha: Mv i.138.11.

Kusumā, n. of a legendary queen, instructed and saved by Buddha (wife of **Kusumbha**): Mv i.177.14; 180.14, 17; 181.7 ff.

Kusumābhijña, n. of a former Buddha: Sukh 6.12.

Kusumārcisāgarapradīpa, n. of a Buddha: Gv 256.18.

Kusumāvatī, n. of a lokadhātu, presided over by Saṃkusumitarāja (°rājendra): Mmk 2.5; 5.11; 79.27.

Kusumottama, n. of a Buddha: Mmk 426.7.

Kusumottarajñānin, n. of a Bodhisattva: Gv 2.14.

Kusumottarīya, n. of a former Buddha: Mv i.141.7.

Kusumotpala (mss. °para), n. of a former Buddha: Mv i.140.3.

Kusumbha, n. of a king, husband of **Kusumā**: devī Kusumbharājasya Mv i.180.14, 15.

kusulaka, nt. (also **kusūlaka,** q.v.), *a woman's breast-covering*: Mvy 9000. So apparently Tib.: śiṅ ṅa (d)puṅ chad, cf. Jä. dpuṅ pa bcad, *the part of a woman's dress covering the chest.*

? **kusuvā,** sc. lipi, a kind of writing: Mv i.135.8 (but v.l. kumuvā).

? **ku-sūtra,** in Mv i.144.5 (prose), mss. kusūtre; Senart em. kusūtraṃ, rendering *a very fine thread* (hardly plausible, since ku- is regularly pejorative). The passage is extremely corrupt and its mg. obscure; Senart makes sweeping emendations.

kusūlaka, (1) nt., = **kusulaka,** q.v.: Bhīk 15a.2 evam uttarāsaṅgam antarvāsaḥ kusūlakaṃ saṃkakṣikā adhiṣṭhātavyā; (2) m., a man's garment: Rāhulasya °kaḥ MSV ii.48.15.

kuha, adv. (so Pkt. id., Saptaśatakam, ed. Weber, 507; more usual Pkt. kahaṃ, kaha), *how?*: Mv iii.264.14 (prose) taṃ kuha (mss.; Senart em. kuhaṃ!) nāma saṃbhuṇiṣyasi (mss. °ti, em. Senart), *how will you get that?* (or perhaps with °ti of mss., *how will that be got?*).

kuhaka, adj. or subst. m. (= Pali id.; see next), *hypocritical,* or *a hypocrite* (in the sense explained s.v. **kuhana**): Śikṣ 20.16 kuhako vatāyaṃ, lapako vatāyaṃ, naṣṭadharmo . . .

kuhana, nt., or °**nā** (Skt. both Lex.; Pali °nā, in same technical sense as BHS), lit. *trickery*; as one of the 5 **mithyājīva,** q.v., for a monk, see Wogihara, Lex. 21 ff., *hypocrisy,* specifically *display of behavior designed to stimulate laymen to give gifts*: Mvy 2493 °nā; na lapanā na kuhanā kartavyā Śikṣ 131.3; citta-kuhanā, 131.6; 268.3; kāya-, vāk-kuhanā 268.1; °nāṃ lapanāṃ naimittikatāṃ naiṣpeṣikatāṃ lābhena lābhaṃ (read lābha-) niścikīrṣutāṃ (the 5 mithyājīva) Bbh 168.21–22; a-kuhanatā a-naiṣpeṣikatā (so read), in a list of virtues, Śikṣ 183.15; na ca pareṣāṃ kuhanārthaṃ dānaṃ dadāti Bbh 122.1 (of a Bodhisattva); kuhanārthaṃ, also Bbh 234.20; kuhana-lapana-, in lists of vices, Jm 110.20; LV 372.17; Śikṣ 268.6; kuhana-lapana-tayā KP 123.4; RP 17.5 (so read for text °lepana°; prose); kuhana-lapana- (text °lepana)-niṣpeṣaṇaparivarjitasya RP 15.10. Cf. further LaVallée Poussin, AbhidhK. iv.165, n. 4; and Pali and Chin. parallels, with general discussion, Wogihara l.c.

1 **kuhā** (or kuha, with ā m.c.? Skt. and Pali kuha, only adj. or nom. ag., *deceitful, deceiver*; cf. **kuhana**), *deceit*: RP 13.9 (vs) māyā-kuhā-varjitāḥ.

[2 **Kuhā,** n. of a river: Māy 252.35; prob. error for Skt. Kuhū.]

? **Kūjaka,** n. of a mountain: MSV i.152.12. But Divy here **Kūlaka,** q.v., and earlier **Utkūlaka,** q.v. (for the latter MSV i.144.16 is said to read Kulako in ms., ed. em. Kūjako); and since the ms. has a lacuna covering i.152 (see i.149, note 1), I presume Kūjaka must be based on Tib. (sgra can? see i.144, n. 2).

Kūṭagrāmaka, see **Kuṭigrāmaka.**

Kūṭadaṃṣṭra, n. of a yakṣa: Māy 27.

Kūṭadantī, (1) n. of a rākṣasī: SP 400.4; (2) n. of a yakṣiṇī: Suv 163.2.

kūṭanā (ana-formation to kūṭa, § 22.7), *trickery*: SP

286.12 (vs) śāṭhyaṃ ca mānaṃ tatha kūṭanāṃ ca... ujjhiya.

Kūṭāgāra, nt., n. of a city (in the south): Gv 185.24 etc.

Kūṭāgāra-śālā (= Pali °sālā), n. of a hall or house near Vaiśālī where the Buddha often stayed: Divy 136.7; 200.21 (Bhagavān...Vaiśālyāṃ) viharati... °śālāyāṃ; similarly Av i.8.5; 279.5; MSV i.224.14; Mv i.299.20 idaṃ mahāvanaṃ kūṭāgāraśālaṃ or °lāṃ, mss.; Senart em. sa-kūṭāgāraśālaṃ. See **Markaṭahrada-tīra** (same place?).

[**kūra**, m.? see s.v. **kuru.**]

kūrparaka, nt. (= Skt. °ra, m.), *elbow*: Mvy 3973.

Kūlaka, m., n. of a mountain (= **Utkūlaka**, q.v.): Divy 455.28 (= **Kūjaka** MSV i.152.12).

(a-)kūhaka, adj., (*not*) *deceiving*: Dbh.g. 16(352).18 sumanāś ca akūhakaś ca; prob. m.c. for Skt. kuhaka. Cf. next.

kūhanā (so Skt. Lex. once; but prob. m.c. for Skt. kuhanā), *trickery*: Samādh p. 49 line 22 (vs). Cf. prec.

Kṛkin (= Pali Kiki(n); chiefly Skt. in-stem forms have been noted outside of Mv), n. of a legendary king of Benares in the time of the Buddha Kāśyapa (Mv and Av), father of Mālinī: Mv i.303.5, 7 kṛkisya, gen.; kṛkī, n., Mv i.313.3; 323.14, 17; 325.13, etc.; kṛkīṃ, v.l. kṛkī (Senart em. kṛkiṃ), acc. sg., Mv i.324.3; tried to seduce Padmāvatī (1) after she became a wandering nun, Mv iii.168.18 (gen. kṛkisya); other references, Mvy 3651; Divy 22.10 ff.; Av i.338.1 ff.; ii.39.5 f.; 76.14; 80.6; 124.14; MSV i.200.16 (vs; kṛker, gen.); ii.77.12 (kṛkir).

-kṛta, (**1**) in **dṛṣṭi-kṛta**, q.v., lit. perh. (*what has*) *become*..., or (subst.) *matter of*...; seems = (**dṛṣṭi-**)**gata**; (**2**) acc. to Senart = **kṛtya** (q.v. 2) as equivalent of adj. formation or gen. case-form, in Mv ii.274.4 udyānakṛtā āsanā, allegedly *les sièges du jardin*. But does it not mean quite literally and simply *seats made in the park*? In Mv ii.245.5 read with mss. karaṇḍe mālakṛto, *in the garland-maker's basket* (stem māla-kṛt).

-kṛtaṃ, see **-kṛtvā** for Skt. -kṛtvas.

kṛtaka, adj. (perhaps essentially identical with Skt. kṛtaka, but with peculiar tinge of mg. as opp. of **akṛtaka**, q.v.): *created* (person or thing), *fashioned, material* or *tangible* (person or thing): Laṅk 60.14; 61.1, 9, etc.; 176.11; 187.9. Mistranslated 'creator' (!) by Suzuki e. g. at 61.9.

Kṛtajña, n. of a previous incarnation of Śākyamuni, hero of Avadāna-kalpalatā ch 45, and, acc. to Finot, of Kalpadrumāvadānamālā ch. 34; referred to RP 25.5–6; cf. Finot p. viii.

kṛtaśas, postposition with prec. gen. (used like Skt. kṛtena, kṛte, but this form is nowhere recorded), *for the sake* (of): Mvy 5461 = Tib. phyir; sarvasattvānāṃ k° Śikṣ 282.12; 350.9; evaṃrūpāṇāṃ dharmāṇāṃ k° Śikṣ 37.19; (vratasamādānasya) k° 98.13; -karmakaraṇāṃ k° Suv 190.4; pāramitānāṃ k° AsP 229.12; saddharma-parigrahasya k° AsP 339.7, et alibi (sometimes printed with s for ś).

Kṛtāgada, n. of a Buddhakṣetra in the east: Mv i.123.8.

kṛtādhikāra, see **adhi°**.

kṛtāvin, adj. (§ 22.51; = Pali katāvin, acc. to PTSD applied to arhats; so only in the first BHS citation), *skilled, skillful*: °vi-bhūmi, n. of the 7th and last of the śrāvaka-bhūmi, i. e. that of the arhat, Mvy 1147; ŚsP 1473.14 et alibi, see **bhūmi** 4; but otherwise regularly of worldly skills, and with loc. of the subject of the skill: pañcasu (Divy 442.9 pañca-)sthāneṣu kṛtāvī saṃvṛttaḥ Mvy 4996; Divy 58.28; 100.13; 442.9 (see **vidyā-sthāna**); dāruparīkṣāyāṃ k° Divy 31.1; gaṇitre 263.9; lipy-akṣareṣu 301.17; śabde 496.6; in comp., kauśala-kṛtāvinaḥ (gen. sg.) Bbh 75.2; absolute, kṛtāvī (n. pl.; of tuṣita gods) Dbh.g. 22(358).24.

(**kṛti**, f., *structure, work*, as in Skt., where commonly a *literary work*; applied to relic-stūpas Divy 381.19 tābhyas saptabhyas pūrvikābhyaḥ kṛtibhyo dhātuṃ tasya ṛṣeḥ sa hy upādāya Mauryaḥ; acc. to Index specifically *house for relics* (but in Note *spell* is suggested) here and in 560.13, an obscure passage where the mg. is probably also *work*, and surely not *house for relics*: putrād vepiṇīyām (? v.l. °līyām) āhur bhāryayā kṛtir ucyate.)

kṛtin, adj., acc. to Suzuki *belonging to the kṛta age*: Laṅk 365.6 ahaṃ ca virajo 'nye vai sarve te kṛtino jināḥ; the interpretation is supported by Tib. byaṅ dus, *perfect time*, and by 364.6 ahaṃ cānye kṛtayuge...

-kṛto, see **-kṛtvā** for Skt. kṛtvas.

? **kṛttas, kṛtto**, also written **kṛntas, kṛnto**, n. pl., *how many*? Laṅk 31.2 (vs) kṣetre kṣetre rajāḥ kṛtto, dhanvo (read °ve) dhanve bhavet kati; Suzuki, Index, says 'kṛtta for kyanta', but the same appears 32.3 (vs) in virtually all mss. (ed. kyanto), and in 31.5, 7, 9 (vss) all mss. kṛntaḥ, kṛnto (ed. em. kyaṃtaḥ, kyanto). We seem to be dealing with a hyper-Skt. substitute for a MIndic form related to Pali kittaka, *how many*? (minus -ka, which is metr. impossible).

kṛttima, adj. (semi-MIndic for Skt. kṛtrima), *artificial, unreal*: °ma-bhūṣaṇa- LV 123.6 (vs).

kṛtya, (**1**) m., a kind of demon (cf. Skt. kṛtyā, of which this may be a masc. correspondent created for the nonce, in this passage which is a list of masc. evil spirits): SP 401.5–6 kṛtyo vā vetāḍo vā... (6) yakṣakṛtyo vāmanuṣyakṛtyo vā manuṣyakṛtyo vā; (**2**) nt., or at end of adj. cpds., *business* etc., in some cases apparently transcending normal Skt. usage; bhakta-kṛtya (= Pali bhatta-kicca), lit. *business of food*, so *a meal*: Divy 185.22 °tyaṃ kartum ārabdhaḥ; āhāra-kṛtya, id., Divy 82.26 nānenāhāreṇāhāra-kṛtyaṃ kariṣyati, *he will not make his meal(s) on this food*, i. e. live on this alone; Divy 236.6, text āhāraṃ (read °ra-?) kṛtyaṃ kuru, *get your sustenance*; acc. to Senart, note on Mv i.349.18 (p. 622), used like the Pkt. quasi-suffix -kera(ka) as substantial equivalent of gen. case-ending (Pkt. -kera is to be derived from Skt. kārya with Pischel 176; see **-keraka**); Senart's Index further interprets -kṛtye ii.97.13 as 'periphrasis for instrumental', but this is certainly wrong, since there gītakṛtye pramattā jaladardarake ca clearly means *careless in their occupation with singing and the* (musical instrument) *jaladardaraka*; the cases where -kṛtya is alleged to be a 'periphrasis for the gen.' are also, in some cases, doubtful; in Mv i.349.18 and 350.1 Senart rāja-kṛtyā kośāto, supposedly = *from the king's treasury*, but the mss. read rāja-kṛto or (v.l. in 349.18) °kṛtāto, and the latter, at least, could be interpreted (*the treasury made by the king*); ii.95.4 rājakṛtyato (abl.; v.l. °tāṃ) odhṛtabhāro, *having laid down the burden of* (lit. *from, away from*) *royal duty*; in ii.446.14 rājakṛtye siṃhāsane rājeti kṛtva (°tvā?) upaviśāpito, *he* (who was actually not the king) *was caused to sit upon the throne which was appropriate* (really belonged) *to the king*; ii.478.10 rājakṛtye (v.l. °kṛte) mahānase, and 12 rājakṛtyehi sūpehi, as in prec.; Senart's interpretation may however be substantially correct in the last three, and in ii.113.9 rājakṛtyaṃ udyānaṃ, *the park that belonged to the king*. Since Skt. kṛtya is in fact a synonym of kārya in some of its uses, the comparison with Pkt. -kera(ka), from Skt. kārya, is apposite. But the two alleged parallels from LV cited by Senart in his note, above, are not sound; one rests on a false reading of the Calcutta ed., and the other is to be interpreted otherwise. (**3**) -kṛtya, -kṛtyaṃ, = **-kṛtvā** for Skt. -kṛtvas, q.v.

kṛtyaka = Skt. kṛtya, *affair, business*, at end of Bhvr. cpd., in a vs, perhaps m.c.: Śikṣ 46.8 alpārtha alpakṛtyakāḥ.

-kṛtyā = **-kṛtvā** for Skt. -kṛtvas, q.v.

kṛtyākṛtya (= Pali kiccākicca; § 23.12), *all kinds of duties*: Mv i.279.18; 280.18.

kṛtyānuṣṭhāna-jñāna, nt., *knowledge of the carrying out of duty,* one of the 5 **jñāna** (q.v.) of a Tathāgata: Mvy 114; Dharmas 94.

-kṛtyo = **-kṛtvā** for Skt. -kṛtvas, q.v.

kṛtrimaka, adj. (= Skt. kṛtrima, prob. with dim. or pejorative connotation), *imitation-, false-, toy-,* perhaps with added sense of *little*: Bbh 281.13 (prose) (tasya dahrasyaiva ...) kṛtrimakā mṛgarathakā ... upasaṃhṛtā bhaveyuḥ; in 16 below, teṣv eva kṛtrimeṣu mṛgeṣu.

1 **-kṛtvā** (also -kṛtva, -kṛtvaṃ), for Skt. -kṛtvas, adv., ... *time(s),* after numerals in comp.; kṛtvā is the only non-Skt. form noted outside of Mv, viz. in Suv 115.4; 116.7 (only v.l. triḥ° for triṣ-kṛtvā); Divy 95.24 and 124.20 ṣaṭkṛtvā (mss., ed. em. °tvo); Śikṣ 290.10, 12 triṣkṛtvā. In the mss. of Mv this form is found, along with many others (partial list Senart, note on i.212.5); Senart's text is highly arbitrary and inconsistent, paying often little attention to the mss., but also not attempting to standardize. In the following list the readings of the mss. as given by Senart are cited. Forms showing u in the penult of course are related to AMg. khutto, M. huttaṃ (Pischel 451); those with final nasal, to the latter and to Pali khattuṃ; the vowel u seems not to occur in the final syllable except when preceded by a single t, in which case -tu- is apparently only a misreading or miswriting for -tta- (Senart, l.c.). Forms in -tya, -tyā, -tyo, -tyaṃ seem to be unparalleled in other dialects but are quite common in Mv, which shows (in mss.) the following: -kṛtvā, -kṛtva, -kṛtvaṃ, and very rarely -kṛto, -kṛtaṃ; -kṛtya, -kṛtyā, -kṛtyo, -kṛtyaṃ; -khuttaṃ (cf. the Pkt. forms above), -khutta, -kṣuttaṃ (hyper-Skt.), -kṣunto; -khattaṃ (cf. Pali, above), -kṣattaṃ, -kṣatto, -kuttaṃ, and a few other readings too obviously corrupt to be worth listing (but noted below): Mv (S = Senart's text) i.212.5 S trikhuttaṃ, mss. triṣutum, triṣkṛtvā; 212.13 S triṣkhuttaṃ, mss. °khutaṃ, °kṛtya; 213.5 S triṣkṛtvo, mss. °tvā, °tya; 231.1 S triṣkṛtyo, mss. °tya, °tvā; 246.5 S trikhutto, mss. trikṣunto, trikhattaṃ; 246.8 S trikhutto, mss. trikṣunto, °kṣuttaṃ; 256.15 S triṣkhuttaṃ, mss. triṣkṛtya, triṣṭūbhyaṃ (?); ii.16.1 triṣkṛtyo, v.l. °tya; 16.8 triṣkṛtyo without v.l., so also 268.3 and iii.302.19 (mss.); ii.131.14 and 313.13 triṣkṛtyo, v.l. °tya; 177.19 S triṣkṛtvo, mss. triṣkṛtya, triskṛtvā (dental s); 258.2 triṣkṛtyo, v.l. °tya (passage repeated 259.1 where mss. °kṛtya, Senart em. °tyo); 282.6 S triṣkṛtvo, mss. °tvā, °tyā; ii.45.2 śatakhutto, no v.l.; 412.5, twice, first triṣkṛto in mss. (S em. °tyo), then °tyo, v.l. °to; 424.20 S trikṣutto, mss. trikṣatto, triṣkṛtya; 425.3 trikṣuttaṃ, v.l. triṣkṛtyaṃ; 425.15 S triṣkṣuttaṃ, mss. triṣkṣattaṃ, triṣkṛtyaṃ; 426.7 S triṣkṣuttaṃ, mss. triṣkuttaṃ, triṣkṛtyaṃ; iii.76.2 triṣkṛtyaṃ, no v.l.; 111.8 trikhuttaṃ, v.l. triṣkṛtyaṃ; 76.11 S triṣkṛtvo, mss. °tvā, °ttyā; 139.4 S trikhuttaṃ, mss. triṣkṛtyaṃ, trittaṃ; 139.9 trikṣuttaṃ, v.l. triṣkṛtyaṃ; 255.6 S triṣkṛtvaṃ, mss. °tva, °taṃ; 298.16 and 311.12 triṣkuttaṃ, 301.2 saptakuttaṃ (twice with v.l. °kṛtyaṃ); 410.16 S trikhuttaṃ, mss. trikṣustaṃ, triṣkṛtyaṃ; 446.6 S trikhuttaṃ, mss. tṛkṣuttaṃ, triṣkṛtyaṃ.

2 **kṛtvā,** ger., loosely used without logical subject, *making, treating as, taking as*: LV 421.7 (vs) kauṇḍinyaṃ prathamaṃ kṛtvā pañcakāś caiva bhikṣavaḥ, ṣaṣṭīnāṃ devakoṭīnāṃ dharmacakṣur viśodhitaṃ, *taking K. as the first and the five monks, the dharma-eye of 60 crores of gods was purified.*

kṛtsna, nt., and **kṛtsnāyatana,** nt., *basis of total (fixation of the mind),* as leading to concentration; = Pali kasiṇa and °ṇāyatana, see Childers, which is far superior to PTSD; ten such in Pali, and in Mvy 1528–38, viz. nīla, pīta, lohita, avadāta, pṛthivī, ap, tejas, vāyu, ākāśa, vijñāna (-kṛtsnāyatanam; Vism. slightly different, see PTSD); five-fold manner of practice upon each kṛtsna, only the first eight listed, Mvy 1539–40 (as in Pali, PTSD); see also AbhidhK. LaV-P. viii.213 ff.; Sūtrāl. vii.9; xx–xxi.44; Gv 523.11 kṛtsnāyatanasamāpatti-vihārī bhikṣur; Divy 180.17 f. nīlakṛtsnam (see Mvy 1529); and see **Apkṛtsna.**

Kṛtsnākarā, n. of an apsaras: Kv 3.16.

Kṛtsnāgata, m., n. of a mountain: Kv 91.15.

kṛtsnāyatana, see **kṛtsna.**

? **kṛntas, kṛnto,** see s.v. **kṛttas.**

kṛpaṭa, °ṭaka (nt.), = (Skt.) kṛkāṭaka, *'neck'* (of a column): °ṭa(ka)-śīrṣakaṃ MPS 34.58; Tib. ka zhu (see Mvy 5575).

[**kṛpālava,** if correct, a-extension of Skt. kṛpālu, *compassionate*: Laṅk 245.18 °lavā (n. pl.) bhavanti. Prob. read °lavo by em.]

kṛmi (in sense of *glow-worm,* see **kimi**); Kṛmi, n. of a nāga-king: Mvy 3248; Māy 246.33.

kṛmilika, m., *a kind of cloth*: Mvy 9173; acc. to Tib. and Chin. *a red cloth made of calf's hair.*

kṛmivarṇā, *a kind of red cloth*: Mvy 9174; Bhīk 22b.4; acc. to Chin. on Mvy something like *red gauze.*

Kṛmiśa or **Kṛmiṣa,** n. of a yakṣa: Divy 434.18 ff.

kṛśalaka, kṛśālaka, kṛśāluka, kṛṣ°, adj. (in mg. = Skt. kṛśa; cf. Whitney, Gr. 1227 a and b), *lean*: kṛśālaka Mvy 8812 = Tib. skem po (but Index also cites, app. as vv.ll., kṛśaraka, kṛśāluka, and Mironov reads kṛśalaka without v.l.); kṛśālaka also mss. at Divy 334.1; kṛśāluka Divy 334.3 (mss. kṛṣ°); 571.11, 18, 20, 21; kṛṣāluka MSV i.i.11 ff. In a corresponding phrase in Pali, kiso lūkho (two words) is read, and PTSD, s.v. uppaṇḍuppaṇḍukajāta, assumes that kṛśāluka is a false Sktization of this Pali version.

kṛṣāṇa (m.; cf. pw 2.95 and 7.387), *farmer, peasant*: °ṇa-grāma, *a peasant village,* LV 133.13, 14; 135.6 (all vss).

kṛṣi-grāma, *an agricultural village* (cf. prec.): LV 128.16; Mv ii.45.5.

kṛṣimant, adj. or subst., *devoted to agriculture, an agriculturist*: Divy 646.17 (punarvasau jātaḥ) kṛṣimān bhavati gorakṣaś ca.

kṛṣṇa, adj. and m. n. pr. (mgs. 1–3 = Pali kaṇha), (**1**) *evil, wicked* (in this moral sense app. only Lex. and Gr. in Skt.): Ud xvi.14 kṛṣṇāṃ dharmāṃ (acc. pl.) viprahāya (= Pali Dhp. 87 kaṇhaṃ dhammaṃ vippahāya); ? kṛṣṇā Divy 562.23, see **visāriṇī**; (ekānta-)kṛṣṇānāṃ karmaṇāṃ ekānta-kṛṣṇo vipākaḥ (similarly Pali) MSV i.48.3 etc.; (**2**) as n. or epithet of Māra, *the evil one*: Mv ii.320.5; 407.16; more commonly Māra is called kṛṣṇabandhu (app. not recorded in Pali), Mvy 7385; LV 262.20; 301.3; 303.2; 341.10; 342.6; Mv ii.238.16; 294.15; 327.1; 335.23; (**3**) n. of a king, previous incarnation of Śākyamuni, and hero of a Jātaka (Pali Jāt. 440, Kaṇha-J.): LV 170.16 (vs), where all mss. kṛṣṇabandhu, contrary to meter and sense; Tib. nag po = kṛṣṇa, with no equivalent for bandhu; so read; (**4**) n. of a nāga-king: Kṛṣṇa-gautamakau nāgarājau Divy 50.17, 29; °gautamau 50.22; °gautamakayor nāgarājayor 51.5. App. a secondary interpretation of **Kṛṣṇa-gotamaka** (or °gaut°), q.v., = Pali Kaṇhāgotamaka (°kaṃ ahirājakulaṃ AN ii.72.23; °kehi Jāt. ii.145.20), n. of a (single) nāga family. But see also s.v. **kṛṣṇaka,** 2.

kṛṣṇaka, (**1**) adj. (= Skt. kṛṣṇa plus ka), fem. °ikā, *black, blackish*: Divy 352.20 kṛṣṇikāṃ paṭṭikāṃ; 23, 24, 26 kṛṣṇikānāṃ (sc. paṭṭikānāṃ; all these prose); on the basis of these we must surely read in Divy 352.19 (prose) kṛṣṇikā paṭṭikā (ed. kṛṣṇika-p°) dattā pāṇḍurikā ca; in these there is certainly no dim. force; there is prob. dim. (pejorative) force in SP 113.12 (vs) kucelakā (so read) kṛṣṇaka hīnasattvāḥ (repulsively *black* in complexion); na ca (cā?) chavī kṛṣṇika (m.c. for °kā) tasya bhoti SP 293.2 (vs); (**2**) n. of two nāga kings: Māy 248.1 (see s.v. **kṛṣṇa,** 4).

Kṛṣṇagotamaka, pl. (= Pali Kaṇhāgotamaka, pl.; see s.v. **kṛṣṇa** 4), n. of a nāga family: Māy 221.15. Cf. also next.

Kṛṣṇagautama, n. of a nāga-king: Māy 247.24. Cf. under prec.

kṛṣṇa-pakṣa, see s.v. **śukla-pakṣa.**

Kṛṣṇapakṣika, n. of a nāga-king: Laṅk 179.7; cf. prec. and **-pakṣika.**

Kṛṣṇapāda, n. of an author: Sādh 378.18; or is the name Kṛṣṇa, -pāda being the honorific affix? kṛtir iyam ācārya-śrī-kṛṣṇapādānām.

kṛṣṇa-bandhu, see s.v. **kṛṣṇa,** 2.

kṛṣṇamukha, a member of some heretical sect: Mvy 3536.

Kṛṣṇayamāritantra, n. of a work by Kṛṣṇarāja: Sādh 328.5; 339.19.

Kṛṣṇarāja, n. of the author of prec.: Sādh 328.5.

Kṛṣṇavātamaṇḍalī, n. of a deity or magic potency, fem. if text is correct (pronoun sā): Mmk 106.11. Also called **Mahākṛṣṇameghavātamaṇḍalī**, q.v.

? **Kṛṣṇā**, possibly n. pr. (of a devakumārikā), see s.v. **Draupadī**: LV 390.6; Mv iii.308.9; also short form for next, q.v.

Kṛṣṇājinā (= Pali Kaṇhājinā), n. of the daughter of **Viśvaṃtara**: Jm 59.22 ff.; in 63.14 short form Kṛṣṇā, as in Pali (Kaṇhā).

Kṛṣṇila, n. of a serpent king: Mmk 241.19.

? **Kṛṣṇukta** (! cannot be correct), pl., n. of a class of gods: Mahāsamāj., Waldschmidt, Kl. Skt. Texte 4, 189.2. The Pali parallel has Kaṭṭhaka, v.l. Kaṭhaka (see DPPN). Acc. to Waldschmidt, p. 204 (para. 22), Tib. may represent Kṛṣṇopta.

Ketaka, pl., n. of a people or region: Māy 96.

Ketu, (**1**) n. of a former Buddha: Mv iii.237.7; Gv 104.16; (**2**) n. of a future Buddha: Gv 441.25; Mv ii.354.21 = iii.279.5 (in all these follows **Siṃha** who follows **Maitreya**, or **Pradyota** who follows Siṃha); (**3**) n. of a Pratyekabuddha (cf. Pali Ketumā?): Mmk 111.10.

ketukā, sc. lipi, a kind of writing: Mv i.135.8.

Ketudhvaja, n. of a former Buddha: Mv iii.230.7 f.

Ketuprabhā, n. of a female lay-disciple: Gv 51.16.

Ketumatī, n. of the capital of the future Buddha Maitreya: Mv iii.240.12; cf. Pali Ketumatī, given as a future name for Benares and the birthplace of Metteyya.

Ketumant, n. of a mountain: Dbh 96.4.

Ketuśrī, n. of a Bodhisattva: Gv 4.4.

Ketūttama, n. of a former Buddha: Mv iii.237.7 f.

kettaka, adj. (cf. s.v. **ettaka**; cf. Pali kittaka, Pkt. kettia), *how much*?: kettakasya . . .kālasya Mv i.50.14; 51.11; kettakaṃ (one ms. **kevattakaṃ**, q.v.) puṇyaṃ 80.5. (All prose).

kedṛśa, adj. (= Skt. kīdṛśa; cf. AMg. kerisa), *of what sort*?: Mv ii.99.1 (?); 422.10; 443.6; 463.11.

? **kedhuka**, app. n. of some plant (perhaps error for kecuka or kevuka?): Mmk 81.25 chattrikāṃ kedhuka-pattrāvanaddhāṃ.

Keyūradharā, n. of an apsaras: Kv 3.17.

Keyūrabala, n. of a devaputra, one of the 16 guardians of the bodhimaṇḍa: LV 277.13.

-keraka, ifc. adj., in para-k° (= Pkt. id.; Pischel 176, from Skt. kārya; cf. **kṛtya** 2), *belonging to* (another): LV 175.20 (vs) parakeraka-yācitopamāḥ (sc. saṃskārāḥ).

kela, m., Mvy 7765; **kelā**, Gv 106.10; **kelu**, m. or f., Gv 133.21; Mvy 7894 (cited from Gv), a high number.

kelāyati (or, once, **kelay°**; = Pali keḷāyati, not well defined PTSD; prob. not connected with Skt. keli, but origin obscure), (**1**) *cleans up, puts in order*: so perhaps gdve. kelāyitavyam Mvy 2591 (Jap. *to be cleaned*; this seems to be the mg. of one Tib. rendering, bstsal ba; occurs in list of words headed nisṛjā-paryāyāḥ, *synonyms for* nisṛjā, q.v.); note that Pkt. kelāiya is said to mean *cleaned* (Sheth); also Mmk 52.14 su-parāmṛṣṭaṃ su-kelāyitaṃ su-śobhitaṃ pṛthivīpradeśaṃ kṛtvā gomayena leptavyaḥ; (**2**) *tends, keeps up, looks after* (fields): Divy 631.5 anye sattvā(ḥ) śālikṣetrāṇi kelāyanti gopāyanti vāpayanti vā; (**3**) *tends, cares for* (persons): AsP 253.13 (te putrās tāṃ mātaraṃ . . .) su-kelāyitāṃ kelāyeyuḥ; LV 100.9 (kā . . . samarthā) bodhisattvaṃ gopāyituṃ kelayituṃ (only occurrence of kela-; no v.l.) mamāyituṃ; Mv iii. 154.13 (mānuṣikāye) ca naṃ kelāyanāya kelāyantī, so Senart, taking kel° as 'passive in sense', (the girl) *being tended* (by the ṛṣi) *with human care*; but mss. kelāyanti, possibly for kelāyan ti (= iti), *since he* (the ṛṣi) *was caring for her* etc. (?); the mss. are corrupt in what follows, and the precise sense of the passage is doubtful; (**4**) *cares for, cultivates, devotes oneself to* (states of existence): Dbh 39.22 kelāyitāni mamāyitāni dhanāyitāni niketasthānāni (see s.v. **niketa**), tāni sarvāṇi vigatāni bhavanti sma; (**5**) *attends to, prepares* (by cooking): Mmk 81.26 mṛdvagninā pacet, su-kelāyitāṃ sukhoṣṇaṃ saindhava-cūrṇa-pūtāṃ kṛtvā . . .; (?) Mmk 708.28 śastram aṣṭaśatajaptaṃ kṛtvā chinditaḥ kailapayitvā (! read kelāpayitvā? ger. of caus., *having caused to be cooked*? object pāyasaṃ, line 26) hanet.

kelāyanā (n. act. to prec.), *care*: Mv iii.154.13, see prec. (3).

Kelin, n. of a yakṣa: Keli-mahākelinau, dual, Sādh 567.2.

Kelimālin, n. of a yakṣa: Sādh 560.15; 561.7, etc.; **Kelimālinī**, his fem. counterpart, 563.9.

kelu, see s.v. **kela.**

keva (in AMg. and other Pkt. in cpds. only; see **keva-cira, keva-rūpa**; and cf. **kevaka, kevatika, kevattaka**), *how many*? KP 147.7 (prose) keva yuṣmākaṃ sabrahmacāriṇa(ḥ), *how many are living the religious life with you*? A theory of the origin of the word in Pischel 149; but more likely keva was formed as rime-word to eva- (= Skt. evam); note particularly **keva-rūpa**: eva(ṃ)rūpa. — In MPS 34.53 read (ke)vaṃ for ed. (kī)van (ms. vaṃ, after lacuna), *how great*? (prāsādaṃ).

kevaka, adj., *how many*? (cf. prec.): 5 of 6 mss. at Mv i.111.2 (prose) kevakā (Senart kevattā; one ms. kevantā) śrāvaka-sannipātā. Followed by **kevatika** (mss.), q.v.

keva-cira (= AMg. id.; see s.v. **keva**), *how long*?: kevacirotpannaḥ, v.l. of Kashgar rec. for kiyaccirot°, *how long since produced*? SP 156.5 (prose); adv. kevaciram Mv iii.242.7, 8; °cireṇa yūyaṃ parinirvāsyatha(ḥ) KP 147.2 (prose), *in how long a time* . . .?

kevaṭṭa, m. (= Pali id., Skt. kaivarta), *fisherman*: Mv iii.166.11 (after kaivartakehi 10) te dāni kevaṭṭā (v.l. kaivartakā) . . .teṣāṃ kevaṭṭānāṃ (v.l. kaivarttānāṃ) . . .

kevatika, adj. (cf. **keva**; AMg. kevatiya, kevaiya), *how many*? in Mv i.111.2, after phrase quoted s.v. **kevaka**, 5 of 6 mss. kevatikā prabhā, kevatikaṃ āyuḥpramāṇaṃ (with slight variants, but only one t; one ms. °ttikā, °ttikaṃ, followed by Senart. See **kevattaka**; and note v.l. **kevatī** for **katīya**, q.v.

kevatta, adj., read by Senart for **kevaka**, q.v.

kevattaka, adj. (cf. s.v. **keva**, and prec.), *how many*?: Mv i.101.2 (prose) kevattakāni (mss. °vartt°) karmāṇi; Senart also reads forms of this adj. in i.83.12; 97.3; 351.15 (and see s.v. **kevatika**), but in all of these the mss. are very confused and do not really establish the reading.

keva-rūpa, adj. (see s.v. **keva**; clearly formed as rime-word to **eva-rūpa** = Skt. evaṃ-rūpa), *of what sort*?: Mv i.97.2 °peṇa sukhena; 104.9 °peṇa ovādena; 107.9, 10; 108.4 °paiḥ karmabhiḥ; 127.15; 128.2 ff.; 326.12; iii.60.16 °pā . . . ovādānuśāsanī; 157.15; 159.21 °po . . . ṛṣikumāro; 311.16 (all prose).

kevalaka, (**1**) adj. (= Skt. kevala), *alone*: Mv ii.254.9 (vs) nāyaṃ kevalako (-ka perhaps m.c.) vṛkṣo; (**2**) n. of a region in Magadha: Gv 451.9, 16 (prose).

kevala-kalpa, adj. (= Pali and AMg. kevala-kappa; misdefined PTSD; correctly Childers), *complete, entire*: kevalakalpaṃ jambudvīpaṃ, *all India*, Mv ii.213.17: 217.16; in the latter one ms. kevalaṃ kalpaṃ, which is the reading of both mss. in all the following (but can only be a corruption; all are prose), Mv ii.257.9 °paṃ gṛdhrakūṭaṃ; iii.302.11; 315.9; 316.14; 317.12.

Keśakambala (or °**lin**), see **Ajita.**

keśa-cīvara, nt. (cf. Pali kesa-kambala), *a robe of hair*: MSV ii.91.16; 92.6.

keśa-pratigrahaṇa, nt., *hair-receptacle*: Mvy 8940; one of 13 utensils of a monk. Tib. and Chin. translate literally.

keśara, m. or nt., or oftener keśara-cūrṇa, nt. (cf. AMg. kesara, *pollen*), *a fragrant powder*: keśara, bought of perfumers, Mv i.38.4, 6, 9; presumably prepared from pollen (rather than from the flowers called kesara or keś°, with Senart); otherwise always keśara- (mss. sometimes °la)-cūrṇāni, mentioned with candana-, tamāla(pattra)-, and aguru-cūrṇāni, Mv i.211.20; 212.8, 12; 230.17; 267.2; ii.15.20; 160.16 (mss. °la); 162.6 (mss. °la); 286.15 (here Senart keśala, but v.l. °ra!).

Keśaranandin, n. of a Bodhisattva: Gv 442.8.

Keśarin, (**1**) in LV 170.16, or Kesari-rāja, RP 22.16, n. of a king, former incarnation of Śākyamuni, alluded to in these vss.; his story is unknown to me; (**2**) kesarin, n. of a battle-array (saṃgrāma; so also in Pali, n. of a saṃgāma): Av i.56.4; (**3**) Keśarin, n. of a former Buddha: Sukh 6.13.

[**keśa-lucana,** nt., read °**luñcana** (Skt.) with 93.18, *plucking out of hair*: MSV ii.91.16.]

Keśava, n. of a former incarnation of Śākyamuni: RP 24.6 (vs; he was a vaidyarāja).

? **keśas,** nt. s-stem, for Skt. keśa, masc., *hair*: LV 307.7 (prose) keśāṃsi dhunvantaḥ, see § 8.105. Cf. Mvy 9331 na golomakaṃ keśaś (both edd.; see s.v. **golomakam**) chedayet, which if the text is right supports stem keśas.

Keśasthālin, m., n. of a place where Trapuṣa and Bhallika built a stūpa for the Buddha's hair-relic: Mv iii.310.14 (tehi dāni yatra) keśasthālī nāma adhisthāno tahiṃ keśastūpaṃ kārāpitaṃ.

Keśin, n. of the supernatural horse (the Bodhisattva) who saves shipwrecked persons from the island of ogresses (story of Jāt. 196, Valāhassa-J.): Mv iii.72.18; 75.11, 17 f.; 77.1. This name occurs only in Mv and only in the prose version; in the verse he is called **Valāha** or **Vālāha,** qq.v., as in other BHS and Pali versions.

Keśinī, n. of a rākṣasī: SP 400.5; Māy 240.23; (presumably the same) n. of a Buddhist goddess or yakṣiṇī (associated with **Upakeśinī,** q.v.) Sādh 113.18; 118.15; 120.2; 121.19; 131.18.

keśoṇḍaka, nt., v.l. for °**ḍuka,** q.v.

keśoṇḍu, m. (or f.), = next, only in Laṅk 327.6 (vs; dropping of -ka m.c.? § 22.24) yathā hi darpaṇe bimbaṃ keśoṇḍus . . .

keśoṇḍuka, m. and nt. (recorded once, erroneously, as °ṇḍraka, in Skt., pw, defined as *ringförmige Lichterscheinungen vor geschlossenen Augen*), also °**ḍu,** and v.l. °**ḍaka,** apparently primarily *hair-net* or the like; this lit. mg. apparently in Bcṭ 245.3 °ka-maṇḍitam; standardly used as a symbol of unreality, prob. with mg. as cited from pw above: °ḍukaḥ (so also Mironov; v.l. in both °ḍakaṃ) Mvy 2836, among synonyms for māyā; frequent in Laṅk, e. g. 168.5 (cited MadhK 262.2) keśoṇḍukaṃ yathā mithyā gṛhyate taimirair (MadhK °rikair, unmetr.) janaiḥ (vs); 96.5 skandhāḥ keśoṇḍukākārāḥ; 17.6 °kasvabhāvāvasthitānām; 72.6 and 82.1 °ka-prakhyā(ḥ), etc. Suzuki regularly renders *hair-net*, but this in its literal sense does not fit.

kesarin, Kesari-rāja, see s.v. **Keśarin.**

kaiñjalka, adj. (Skt. kiñjalka plus -a), *derived from filaments* (of flowers): Jm 102.10 °kasya . . . madhunaḥ.

kaiṭabha, (once in LV) **kaiṭubha,** m. (= Pali keṭubha), *ritual science* (of the Veda; = Skt. kalpa, as a Vedāṅga; so Buddhaghosa on the Pali, see PTSD): for the corrupt text of LV 156.18 (in list of sciences) ajalakṣaṇe miśṛlakṣaṇe kauṭubheśvaralakṣaṇe nirghaṇṭe, read, with each word confirmed by Tib. and supported by good mss. (except mss. śvara for śva), but order correct only in Tib., all Skt. mss. kaiṭ° before śva°: ajalakṣaṇe miṇḍhalakṣaṇe śvalakṣaṇe kaiṭubhe nirghaṇṭe; Mvy 5052 kaiṭabhaḥ, following 5051 nighaṇṭuḥ; otherwise only in Bhvr. cpd. sa-nighaṇṭa- (or nirghaṇṭa-)-kaiṭabha, epithet of veda, *along with etymology and ritual science*: (vedānāṃ . . .) sa° °bhānāṃ Mv i.231.18; ii.77.9; 89.17; iii.450.7; Av ii.19.7; (vedān . . .) sa° °bhān Divy 619.22.

Kaineya (= Pali Keniya), n. of a jaṭila ascetic, converted by Buddha, living at **Udumā**: MSV i.255.14 ff.; 262.10 ff. Cf. **Koṭu.**

kaivarta, m., some member (officer?) of a ship's crew; in Av i.200.5 and ii.61.9 named with **āhāra,** nāvika, and karṇadhāra, in ii.61.9 constituting five sorts of members of the crew (the fifth, not named in text, may be **raṇadhara** of Mvy 3854); essentially the same list is found in Mvy 3850–55, kaivarta being named in 3855; here Jap. and alternatively Tib. and Chin. interpret by *fisherman* (as in Skt.), but the first Tib. rendering is rgyal chen, normally = mahārāja; prob. a ship's officer.

Kokadatta, n. of an author: Sādh 426.15.

Kokanada, m., (**1**) (= Pali id. or °nuda), n. of a parivrājaka: Pischel, SBBA 1904, p. 813, fol. 158a; (**2**) n. of a palace belonging to King Kṛkin: Mv i.325.1 ff. (In Pali n. of a palace belonging to a wholly different prince called Bodhi; see DPPN).

Kokanāda, n. of a mountain: Māy 254.11.

Kokālika (= Pali id.), n. of a monk, a partisan of Devadatta: Karmav 49.4 yathā Devadatta-Kokālikādayaḥ; MSV iv.239.5 ff.

kocava, m. (cf. Pali kojava, PTSD *rug* or *cover with long hair*, Childers *a goat's-hair coverlet . . .*), *a woolen blanket* (so Tib.): Mvy 5861 = Tib. bal la ba; so read, in general with mss., at Divy 40.11; 550.16; 553.2, 9; nt., °vaṃ, as material unsuitable for making monks' robes, MSV ii.52.10. Cf. next.

kocavaka, nt., = prec.: Mvy 8982 = Tib. la ba.

[**kocca**: SP 89.6, KN by em. koccair baka-, but read with WT and their ms. K′ **koṭambaka-,** q.v.; see also **kocava,** for which text Divy 553.2 reads kocca.]

[**koccaka,** w.r. for **kocava,** q.v.]

koṭaka, m., Mvy 9423, acc. to Tib. and Chin. *iron-rust*. Ed. suggests em. kiṭṭakam, = Skt. (lauha)kiṭṭa and Lex. kiṭṭaka, nt., *iron-rust*; cf. **kiṭāla-.**

koṭanaka, nt. (to **koṭayati**), *striker, clapper* (of a gong): gaṇḍī-ko° Mvy 9156.

koṭanī, see **kapāla-k°.**

koṭambaka, nt., *a kind of fine cloth*: Mvy 9163 (transliterated in Tib., Chin., and Jap.); SP 89.6 (vs), read with WT and some mss. pratyāstṛtāḥ koṭisahasramūlyair varaiś ca koṭambaka- (KN by em. koccair baka-)haṃsalakṣaṇaiḥ (see **haṃsalakṣaṇa**); Chin on SP indicates a fine *woolen cloth*; °ka-sūkṣma, nt., a fine garment of this cloth, Bhīk 22b.5.

koṭayati (cf. **ākoṭayati**; simplex app. not otherwise recorded, cf. **koṭanaka**), (**1**) *strikes*: Divy 114.22 nagaradvāraṃ triḥ (text tri-, here and in all the following) koṭayitavyam; tri(ḥ) koṭite dvāre Divy 115.27; 117.4, 13; (dvāramūlaṃ . . .) tri(ḥ) koṭayati Divy 115.27 (note 117.26 dvāraṃ trir ākoṭayati); (**2**) ppp. *covered* (with gold, silver, and jewels; perh. orig. *studded*, from *struck*), so Tib., gyogs pa: LV 236.9 (vs) svarṇarūpya-maṇi-koṭitā mahī kaṇṭhakasya caraṇai parāhatā, *the earth, covered* *with gold, silver, and gems, was struck by the feet of Kaṇṭhaka.* (Or could it mean *the earth, as it was struck by the feet of K., was hit with gold, silver, and gems,* with which the gods had magically shod the horse's feet? Tib. favors the other.)

koṭara-yava, m., should be a depreciative epithet of barley (intended for horses, but eaten by Buddha), *wretched* or *coarse barley* (lit. barley gathered from *tree-hollows*?): MSV i.38.9, 13; 42.9; 44.13; 216.14 ff. Pali allusion to this incident Ap i.301.1 says only yava.

koṭi (f.), in Pali often = anta (q.v. in CPD), *end, limit,* esp. in time; this use is illustrated by **aparānta-** and **pūrva-koṭi,** qq.v., and by koṭi alone in LV 242.13 (vs) na vidyati koṭi (so divide; Lefm. as cpd.) saṃskṛtasya, *there is no end* (sc. in either direction of time) *of composite substance* (i. e. of material existence). See also s.v. **bhūta-koṭi**; and (with a different mg. of koṭi) **tri-koṭi.** For akoṭi or °ṭī see s.v. **bhūtakoṭi.**

koṭitama, f. °mī, ord. num., *the ten-millionth:* Vaj 35.8 °mīm api (sc. kalām).

(**Koṭivarṣa,** m. or nt., n. of a locality: Māy 62. Occurs in Skt. Lex., see Lévi, p. 97 f., but also in Varāh. Bṛh.S., see BR 5.1329, a fact not mentioned by Lévi; and see Kirfel, Kosmographie 226, Koṭīvarṣa, capital of the Lāṭa people.)

Koṭīkarṇa, see **Śroṇa Ko°.**

Koṭīviṃśa (= **Śroṇa-ko°,** q.v.), n. of a Buddhist elder, called ārabdhavīryāṇām agryo: MSV i.181.12 ff., 15.

Koṭu (or Koṭṭa? corresp. to Pali Keniya or Keṇiya, see **Kaineya,** a jaṭila), n. of an ascetic (maharṣi): Karmav 155.16 Koṭusya, text with ms., but Lévi suggests em. Koṭṭasya; see his note.

koṭṭamalla, Av ii.116.15, MSV i.85.12, 16; or **koṭṭa-mallaka,** m., Av ii.116.9 ff., MSV i.84.19; 85.10; = **kroḍamalla(ka),** q.v., *beggar.*

koṭṭa-rājan or **°rāja,** lit. *fort-ruler*; precise mg. not clear; sometimes clearly an independent potentate (tho perhaps a minor one, cf. Mvy 3677 °rājā = Tib. khams kyi rgyal po, *king of a realm, region,* or rgyal phran, *petty ruler*); so, °rāja iva mantrigaṇaparivṛtaḥ Divy 126.4; 148.15; 182.9; Av i.108.7; sarvakoṭṭarājānāṃ cāturdvīpakānāṃ ca sattvānāṃ Dbh 81.17; mānitāś ca bhaviṣyāmo 'navadyāś ca sarvakoṭṭarājabhiḥ (so read with several mss. for Lefm. °koṭa°), *and we shall be honored and not contemned by all k°* (surely foreign princes) LV 137.3; viṃśati ca sahasra paryantakāḥ koṭṭarājās tathā... LV 94.16 (vs), here they approach Śuddhodana submissively, possibly they may be vassals of his, but it seems more likely that they are foreign princes; but in other cases they seem clearly to be part of the king's own retinue or at least direct dependents, apparently officers; so in LV 118.10 (Śuddhodana gives orders to the people of his city) saṃnipātyantāṃ sarvakoṭṭarājānaḥ, ekībhavantu śreṣṭhi-gṛhapaty-amātya-dauvārika-pāriṣadyāḥ; Mv i.231.15 rājā aśītihi koṭṭarājasahasrehi sārdhaṃ anyāye ca janatāye; 234.16 rājñā ca arcimena aśītihi ca koṭṭarājāna-sahasrehi (one cpd. word!); Divy 61.16 Śaṅkho 'pi rājā aśītikoṭṭarājasahasraparivāro; KP 84.8 (kumāraṃ) sarvaśreṣṭhinaigamajānapatayaḥ (read °padāḥ) koṭṭarājānaś ca namasyanti; Sukh 68.1 (amātyān stryāgārāñ śreṣṭhino) gṛhapatīn koṭṭarājāṃś ca paryeṣayed. It is, however, perhaps possible to take the word in all these latter cases as meaning *vassal prince.* The context gives no clue to the mg. in SP 433.4; Suv 153.9.

koḍa, MIndic for kroḍa, *breast*: koḍa-sakkino SP 95.3 (vs), so both edd. and most mss. (v.l. kroḍa°). See also s.v. **kola** (2).

Koḍya, Kroḍya, Krauḍya, m. pl. (= Pali and BHS **Koliya**), n. of a people, neighbors of the Śākyas: LV 225.6, Koḍyān (Calc.; Lefm. Kro°, semi-Sktized, no v.l.) atikramya; in MPS 51.13 fully Sktized as **Krauḍya,** living at **Rāmagrāmaka,** q.v.

[**koḍhaka,** read **khoṭaka,** q.v., or **khoḍaka.**]

Koṇākamuni = **Kanakamuni,** q.v.

koṇāla, some kind of bird. RP 43.3 (vs), in a list of birds, kokilāś ca koṇāla (n. pl.); prob. = **kuṇāla,** with o for u m.c. (this is suggested by the preceding kokilāś); cf. however Skt. konālaka, acc. to BR some sort of water-bird.

(? **kotha,** Finot's em. for ms. kutha, m.c., RP 14.6 (vs; meter requires length of first syllable) tṛṇa-kāṣṭha-kotha- (mss. kutha)-sama paśyati sattvarūpaṃ; perhaps = Skt. kotha, *rottenness* or *a foul abscess*: *he regards the form of beings as like* (worthless, vile) *grass, wood, or rottenness* (?).)

kodravaka (m. or nt.; = Skt. °va), *a cheap kind of grain*: Mv ii.210.9 (prose) °kaṃ vā śyāmākaṃ vā (acc. sg.; no special reason for suffix -ka perceptible).

Konāka(-nāma), Konākamuni, Konāka-sāhvaya, Konāgamuni, = **Kanakamuni,** q.v.

kopīna (= Pali id., Skt. kau°), lit. *the immodest bodily parts*; fig. *shame*: Mv i.134.2 parakopīnachādaneṣu aparikhinnāś ca bhavanti, *and they are unwearied in covering the shame of others,* i. e. concealing their disgraceful actions (Senart).

kopya, adj., gdve. (= Pali kuppa; also a-k°), *challengeable, open to valid objection*: °ya-tvāt karmaṇaḥ MSV iii.64.2; others, see s.v. **sthāpana.**

koraṇḍaka (m. or nt.; = Pali id., cf. Skt. kuraṇṭaka, Lex. kuraṇḍaka, and see BR 5.1330 koraṇḍaka, n. pr., and °ṭaka-grāma), n. of a certain shrub and its flower: Mmk 711.6 (prose) raktaśālituṣāgirikarṇikā-koraṇḍaka-bījaṃ.

Koravya, see **Kaur°.**

korpara, kaurpara, m. (= AMg. koppara, Skt. kūrpara; Skt. kaurpara only adj.; not recorded in Pali, where the equivalent word is kappara), *elbow*: kaurparau, dual, Mmk 157.4; in cpds. kaurpara Mmk 69.12; kor° 76.12; 305.10; 436.3.

kola (m.), (**1**) (= Skt. Lex. id.; see also **kaula**; cf. Pali kulla), *boat, raft*: kolopamaṃ dharmaparyāyaṃ Vaj 23.16 *like a* (rescuing) *raft*; kolaṃ hi janāḥ prabandhitā uttīrṇā... Divy 56.9 (vs); same vs begins in same way in oldest (fragmentary) ms. Ud xvii.7 (same vs in Pali, Ud viii.6, kullaṃ); kolaṃ badhnanti śrāvakāḥ Divy 56.11 (same vs Ud xvii.8 contains kolaṃ); Samādh p. 6 line 12; (**2**) (Skt. Lex. and M. kola = utsaṅga; see s.v. **koḍa**), *breast,* or *lap*: Mmk 371.13 (vs) kṛtvā nābhideśe vai kolasthaṃ nimnam udbhavam; (**3**) n. of a rājarṣi: Mv i.353.9; 355.13 (see **Koliya**).

kolaka (**1**) (nt.? = Skt. kola; possibly dim. -ka; but same phrase repeated next line with kolam), *jujube berry*: Mv ii.125.9 (prose) ekaṃ kolakam advitīyam āhāram āhareyam; (**2**) m., n. of a nāga: Māy 222.2.

kolāhala-, acc. to Tib. = ras ma, *rag* (esp. of cotton), in °la-sthavika, m. (see **sthavika**), Mvy 9004, app. *rag bag,* or *bag made of rags*? Jap. *bag for miscellaneous things*; one Chin. rendering is *cloth bag.*

(? **kolika,** perh. = Skt. kaulika, and kolika, Schmidt, Nachträge, *weaver*: Divy 165.3 (vs) āhiṇḍase kolika-gardabho yathā, *like a weaver's ass*? Index understands it as an ethnic name. It is certainly contemptuous; cf. in line 1 rathakāra-meṣa iva nikṛttaśṛṅgaḥ.)

Kolika, n. pr., see **Kolita.**

Kolita (or **Kolika**; = Pali, both; in Mv i.27.4 and 28.4 most mss. Kolika, Senart always °ta), the given name of **Maudgalyāyana**: Mv i.5.2; 27.4; 28.4; 30.3; 62.10, 12; story of his conversion, iii.56.16 ff.; in Mvy 1048 Kolita is named in a list of śrāvakas, not juxtaposed with Maudgalyāyana, who is named earlier in the same list. Cf. next.

Kolita-grāmaka, nt., (Pali °gāma) name of the village (half a yojana from Rājagṛha) where Maudgalyāyana was born: Mv iii.56.13. Cf. prec.

Koliya (= Pali id.; cf. **Koḍya**), n. of a tribe, neighbors of the Śākyas: Mv i.355.13 (story of their origin 352.15–355.13; they were descendants of a Śākya girl and the ṛṣi **Kola**, q.v.; Pali has a similar story, but the father is a king of Benares, there is no personage named Kola, and the mother is not a Śākya); Mv ii.76.7; iii.93.20 (koliyā śākiyā ca). Cf. **Vyāghrapadya.**

Kolisovā (v.l. Koliśovā), n. of a sister of Māyā: Mv i.355.17.

kovidāra, m. (in Skt. n. of a tree, and also, in Hariv., of a heavenly tree, equated by BR with pārijāta; same two mgs. belong to Pali koviḷāra), in Mv i.32.4 and ii.452.1, at least, n. of one of the groves of the Trāyastriṃśa gods; elsewhere it is regularly equated or associated with pārijāta(ka), which seems as a rule to have its Skt. mg., or **pāriyātra(ka)**, q.v.; cf. DPPN 'The pāricchattaka (= pārijātaka, °yātraka; called a tree, but 100 leagues in circumference) is generally described as a koviḷāra'; it is certainly sometimes a (heavenly) tree, e. g. Gv 193.9 -pārijātaka-kovidāra-sadṛśān (vṛkṣān), but at other times it is hard to be sure whether it is conceived as a tree or a grove; e. g. Mvy 4199 (after pāriyātraḥ 4198, which is preceded by names of groves, but with 4200 ff. come words for individual trees); Divy 219.20 pāriyātrako (mss.) nāma kovidāro, 27 pārijātako kovidāro; SP 360.13–14 pārijātakasya kovidārasya, and same Av ii.89.6 (°jātasya); Gv 501.11 (here pāriyātrakasya). Perhaps the explanation is that, like the Pali pāricchattaka, it was a single tree of such size as to be equivalent to a grove.

kośagatavastiguhya, kośavastiguhya, see **kośopagatavastiguhya.**

kośamba (m. or nt.; semi-MIndic for Skt. kośāmra), n. of a plant: °ba-kaṣāya (one of five ka°): MSV i.iv.6. (Or is the Skt. form popular etymology, as if for kośa-āmra? Cf. AMg. kosamba.)

? **kośāvika**, m. (pl.), some sort of tradesman or artisan, possibly a corruption of some form or deriv. of Skt. kauśikāra, see BR, *sheath-maker* or *box-maker*: Mv iii.113.7 (here mss. koṇāvikā or nāvikā); 442.13; both prose; in both °kā stands between gandhikā and tailikā.

kośikāra (m. or nt.; = AMg. kosiyāra; cf. Skt. kauśika, *silken, silk cloth*), *silk cloth*: (read) dukūlapaṭṭorṇa-kośikārehi Mv i.149.5 = 216.1 = ii.18.16 (vs).

kośopagatavastiguhya(-tā), or **kośagata°** (= Pali kosohitavatthaguyha), No. 10 of the 32 **lakṣaṇa**: kośopa° Mvy 258 = Tib. ḥdoms kyi sba ba sbubs su nub pa, *having the privities of the pubic region sunk in a hole* (better, *in a sheath*); LV 105.21; 429.20; kośagata° Bbh 375.16; kośagata° °tā Dharmas 83 (koṣa°); Gv 400.11 (with gloss, making mg. clear, *with privities concealed*); Bbh 379.4 (koṣa°); cf. Mv ii.305.10 kośavastiguhya-.

koṣṭuka (semi-MIndic for kro°; Pali koṭṭhuka), *jackal*: LV 117.2 (vs; v.l. kro°).

koṣṭha(ka), see **caraṇa-, dvāra-k°.**

Koṣṭhaka, m. or nt., n. of a town: Divy 434.15.

koṣṭhikā (to Skt. koṣṭha; cf. Pkt. koṭṭhiyā), *storehouse*, in dhāraṇa-k°, *a place for storing and keeping* (sacred books): MSV ii.143.6.

Koṣṭhila, also **Mahā-k°** and **(Mahā-)Kauṣṭhila**, qq.v. (= Pali Koṭṭhita or °ika or Mahā-k°, who was declared 'first of the paṭisaṃbhidappatta' among Buddha's disciples, cf. below), a disciple of Buddha: in Av ii.195.4 declared first of the pratisaṃvitprāpta; here and in 195.7, 196.9 (also called Mahā-k° 195.5) he is evidently identified with **Dīrghanakha**, q.v.; this identification not recorded in Pali but confirmed MSV iv.15.14 ff.; it should be noted that in Pali (Mahā-)Koṭṭhita is intimately associated with Sāriputta, who in Av, MSV is a nephew of Dīrghanakha, and who was present on the occasion of the Dīghanakha-sutta even in Pali (MN i.497 ff.).

kaukṛtika, adj. (cf. next), *(over-)scrupulous, worried in one's conscience*: MSV ii.107.19.

kaukṛtya, nt. (Skt. Lex.; cf. prec.; = Pali kukkucca, of which or of a MIndic antecedent this is surely a Sktization), usually *regret, remorse, worry, mental disturbance, 'difficulties of conscience'* (SBE 13.51 for Pali kukkucca). This is the usual mg. in Pali; but sometimes the etymological mg., seemingly *wickedness, evil deeds*, must apparently be assumed (as in Jāt. i.119.29 hattha-kukkuccaṃ vā pāda-kukkuccaṃ vā). Cf. LaVallée Poussin, trnsl. of AbhidhK. ii.166: 'le regret (kaukṛtya) . . . au propre . . . est la nature de ce qui est méfait (kukṛtabhāva); mais on entend par kaukṛtya un mental qui a pour objet (ālambana) le kaukṛtya au sens propre, à savoir le regret (vipratisāra) relatif au méfait . . . Le kaukṛtya au sens propre est le point d'appui, la raison d'être du regret; donc le regret est nommé kaukṛtya'. In BHS this is the only certain mg. of the word: Mvy 1358; 1980; 5237 = Tib. ḥgyod pa, *regret, remorse*, in 5237 = vipratisāra; similarly Chin.; Prāt 504.9 bhikṣūṇāṃ kaukṛtyāya vilekhāya . . .; 518.3 bhikṣoḥ saṃcintya kaukṛtyam upasaṃharet, *shall consciously cause disturbance of conscience* (but see below) *to a monk*; Mvy 8487 kaukṛtyopasaṃhāraḥ, *the causing of disturbance of conscience*; KP 3.6 (vs) pareṣu kaukṛty' (= °tyam) upasaṃharanti; SP 285.9, 11 kaukṛtyam upasaṃharati; 287.2 kaukṛtyasthānaṃ (here Tib. the tshom gnas, *position of doubt*, but better *occasion for mental disturbance* in another) ca na jātu kuryān, na lapsyase jñānam anuttara(ṃ) tvam; Mv iii.48.14 °tyam utpādetsuḥ; 173.9 cauro ahan ti tasya kaukṛtyam utpannaṃ; 173.19 mā kaukṛtyaṃ janehīti; Kv 80.5 (mā tvaṃ . . .) kaukṛtyam utpādayasi; Śikṣ 138.1 lajjābhiḥ kaukṛtyasaṃpannaiḥ paralokāvadyabhayadarśibhir; LV 32.19 anupanāho . . . akaukṛtyāya saṃvartate, . . . *leads to freedom from remorse*; SP 71.4 bhikṣūṇāṃ kaukṛtyavinodanārthaṃ, yathā . . . niṣkāṅkṣā nirvicikitsā bhaveyuḥ (see below); Śikṣ 135.16 tena niṣkaukṛtyena bhūtvā nirvicikitsakena . . .; Bbh 83.14 kaukṛtyaprativinodana-paricaryā; 137.24 niṣkaukṛtyo bhavati; 250.20 sva-kaukṛtye samutpanne . . . yā lajjā; one of a list of upakleśa, Dharmas 69, and elsewhere associated with such things as vyāpāda, styāna-middha, auddhatya, vicikitsā, Bbh 173.1; auddhatya-kau°, one of the 5 **nīvaraṇa**, q.v.; **paryavasthāna** (q.v.) or *possession by, fixation in*, these 'depravities' leads to misery and must be avoided, Bbh 145.10 f.; 223.14; 243.22; kaukṛtya-**paryutthānam** (= paryavasthānam) Śikṣ 178.14; similarly, dṛṣṭi kaukṛtya-pratiṣṭhitasya KP 96.4, where Tib. renders as usual by ḥgyod, *regret, remorse*, which tends against interpretation of the word in this connection (as an upakleśa) etymologically, as *state of wickedness*; Śikṣ 191.7 a-kaukṛtya-tā, immediately followed by a-paryutthāna-tā (cf. Śikṣ 178.14 above); Śikṣ 171.4 āpatti-kaukṛtya-sthānaṃ viśodhayituṃ, perhaps *to wipe away any occasion for remorse due to sin* (but Bendall and Rouse *state of sin and wickedness*, taking kaukṛtya etymologically; the Tib. is not cited); Laṅk 139.(13–)14, 15 (yasya kasyacid anyasyānantaryakāriṇaḥ) kaukṛtyaṃ, tasya kaukṛtya-dṛṣṭivinivartanārthaṃ nikṣiptadhurasya kaukṛtyadṛṣṭyabhāvārtham (Suzuki *wickedness*; but *remorse, troubles of mind* or *conscience* would seem preferable); Sādh 17.11 kaukṛtyam ājīvamalaṃ ratiṃ saṃgaṇikāsu ca (here *wickedness* seems more likely than in any other passage, but even here the word may mean only something like *mental perturbation*; note association with vicikitsā, kāṅkṣā, above; Chinese translations sometimes are said to render kau° by *doubt*, e. g. acc. to Finot on Prāt 518.3; so perhaps understand SP 71.4, above).

kaukkuṭika, m. (kukkuṭa plus -ika), *dealer in poultry*: Mvy 3763 (Tib. *poultry seller*, bya gag ḥtshoṅ ba); Bbh

302.10 (aurabhrikasaukarika-)-kaukkuṭika-prabhṛtayaḥ; elsewhere also associated with aura° and sauka°, SP 276.5; 480.9; Kv 42.10.

Kauñcarā (?), n. of a rākṣasī: Māy 243.14.

Kauñcī (? Krauñcī?), n. of a rākṣasī: Māy 243.14.

[**kauṭubha,** see **kaiṭabha** (kaiṭubha).]

kauṭumba- (m. or nt.; cf. Pali koṭumbara; the only BHS occurrence is in vs!), *a kind of fine cloth* (in Pali derived from the name of the country of its origin, Koṭumbara): Divy 559.10 (vs) °ba-kāśikān; see s.v. **kāśika.**

Kauṇḍinya, (**1**) original name of **Ājñāta-k°**, q.v. (so also Pali Koṇḍañña): SP 206.10; 207.7 (Kauṇḍinya-gotra); Divy 480.12; Karmav 161.17; LV 419.4; 421.7; he was the first who *knew* or *understood* the Buddha's Law, hence his name Ājñāta-k°, cf. LV 421.1–2 dharmacakraṃ pravartitaṃ, Kauṇḍinyena ca ājñātaṃ; (**2**) n. of a brahman, seemingly not the same as prec. tho the latter was a brahman in origin: Suv 12.6 ff.; 108.3; 110.1; (**3**) the family name of **Śarabhaṅga,** q.v.: Mv iii.370.12; (**4**) n. of a group of 2000 Buddhas: Mv i.58.10; (**5**) °nya-gotra, *having the family name K.*, said of (Ājñāta-)K. in SP above, and of 300 former Buddhas, each of whom predicted the next following one, except the last who predicted the Buddha Candana: Mv iii.233.8–9, 13 ff.; 234.5.

kautuka, m. (Skt. only nt.), *curiosity*: MSV iii.129.20 (prose) kautukaś ca me mahān.

Kautsya, m. pl. (= Skt. Kautsa), n. of a brahmanical gotra: Divy 635.8 (but perhaps read Kautsāḥ as in 637.24).

Kaudhuma, m. pl. (semi-MIndic, or perh. error, for Skt. Kauthuma), n. of a brahmanical school and gotra: Divy 632.23; and mss. 635.10 (here ed. em. Kauth°).

Kauntīnāgara, adj., *of Kuntīnagara*: MSV i.xviii.20 ff.

Kauberī (Skt. Lex.), n. of a goddess: Sādh 502.8; called a mātar, the Śakti of Kubera, Māy 242.18.

kaumudika, nt. (cf. Skt. kaumudī), *full-moon festival*: Mv iii.188.2 (prose) ramaṇīyaṃ kaumudikaṃ bhaviṣyati, *there will be an enjoyable k°.* Cf. 188.10 ramaṇī kaumudī (mss. °dī na!; Senart °dīyaṃ) bhaviṣyati; ramaṇī here clearly adjective.

kaumodī (= Skt. kaumudī), *festival of the full-moon day*: LV 72.19 (prose), °dyām iva cāturmāsyām; all mss. °mod°, perhaps by analogy of relatives of root mud (moda, etc.); or cf. Skt. kaumodakī (?). The phrase kaumudī cāturmāsī occurs twice in Mv, but no form of this word with medial o for u is otherwise recorded.

Kauravya (= Pali Koravya, which is read in best ms. of Av also), n. of a king of Sthūlakoṣṭhaka: Av ii.118.6.

kaurukullaka, n. of a Buddhistic school (from **Kurukullā,** or **°llakā,** q.v.): Mvy 9086.

kaurpara, see **korpara.**

kaula, m. (var. **kola,** q.v.), *boat, raft*: Mvy 6514 = Tib. gziṅs. Mironov also kaulaḥ, without v.l.

kauśalyaka (nt.; = Skt. kauśalya; -ka perh. m.c.), *welfare*: Mv ii.176.6 (vs) kathaṃ sā . . . mama kauśalyakaṃ bhaṇe.

Kauśāmbaka (written Ko°; Pali Kosambaka), adj., *of Kauśāmbī*: MSV ii.173.7; 186.11 etc.

Kauśika, (**1**) (presumably = Skt. id. as gotra-name), n. of a brahmanical gotra: Mv ii.48.16 ff., and of an ascetic belonging to it, ii.49.3 ff.; in ii.63.18 he is called **Nārada** by personal name, which is due to a confusion in the story, the true form of which is told in Pali, Jāt. 535, where the ascetic is called (Macchari-)Kosiya (Kosika), and Nārada (= Skt. id.) appears as a quite different character; many vss of the Jāt. are paralleled in Mv, including one giving (in Mv, not in the Jāt.) the name Nārada, apparently, to the ascetic (Mv ii.55.3 = Jāt. v.395.12); (**2**) n. of a disciple of Śākyamuni, to be read in LV 1.16 instead of **Kasphila,** q.v., as proved by Tib. ḥug pa = *owl*; he may be the same as Pali 3 Kosiya in DPPN; (**3**) n. of a locality: Māy 81; see Lévi, p. 101, identifying this with Skt. Kuśika; cf. also Kirfel, Kosmographie 90, Kauśika, n. of a people.

kauśīdya = **kaus°** q.v.

Kauśīnāgara, adj. (cf. Pali Kosinārakа), *of* (*inhabiting*) *Kuśīnagarī*, with Malla, pl.: Av i.228.4 (ms. Kośī°, here Speyer Kauśi°); 234.9; 237.2 (all prose).

Kauṣṭhila = **Koṣṭhila,** q.v. (also **Mahā-k°**): so read with best mss. at LV 1.14 for Lefm. Kauṇḍinya (other mss. Kauṇḍilya, so also Calc., and Kauṇḍila); Tib. gsus po che, *great belly*, = **Mahā-kauṣṭhila,** q.v.

kausīdya, kauś°, once **°tya,** nt. (abstract n. from **kusīda**; = Pali kosajja, contrasting with kusīta), *sloth*; note Bbh 73.4–5 vīrya-vipakṣaṃ kau°; almost always written with s; with ś RP 18.2, and v.l. Mv ii.364.14 (prob. to be adopted here since Mv writes kuśīda); v.l., two mss., in Dharmas 30 kausītyam, cf. the Pali kusīta; a-kausīdya, *zeal*, Jm 2.4; other cases of kaus° SP 22.11; 28.1; LV 88.2, 5; Mvy 1974; Dharmas 69; Divy 464.19; Jm 110.20; Av i.18.7; Śikṣ 298.4; Mmk 73.14; 495.18; Gv 91.24; Bbh 15.1; 232.22.

kyant (once in TB., see BR 5.1336; cf. § 3.106), = Skt. kiyant, *how many*?: Laṅk 31.9 (vs) kyanto, n. pl., apparently m.c.; see s.v. **kārṣikā.**

Kraku(c)chanda, (**1**) (= Pali Kakusaṃdha,) also written Krakutsanda (Mv i.2.6; v.l. ii.302.22; v.l. iii.246.9; iii.330.6; Gv 297.26; 441.15; Mmk 68.27; 426.9); Kakucchanda, v.l. Kakutsanda, Karmav 65.7 and 76.14; in Mvy 90 Krakucchanda, 91 also Kakutsunda (but Mironov only the former, with v.l. °tsanda, reporting that 1 ms. adds and then deletes Krakutsunda); the Tib. translation is regularly ḥkhor ba ḥjig, *destroyer of the saṃsāra*, which is given in Mvy 91, while 90 strangely gives log pa daṅ sel (which I have found nowhere else and cannot interpret) for Krakucchanda: n. of a former Buddha, almost invariably the third before Śākyamuni in the standard series (but in Mv iii.231.3 a much earlier Buddha in a long list which later contains at 240.8 the same name in his regular position); as such most commonly named with **Kanakamuni** (or equivalent form, see this) and **Kāśyapa,** the two Buddhas intervening between Kra° and Śākyamuni; in Mv i.2.6 Kanakamuni is omitted, prob. by accident of tradition; sporadically the order is varied; the three together named (often with others in list) in Mvy 90-93; Dharmas 6; Mv i.294.19–20; 318.13, 18; ii.265.9, 11, 14; 266.3; 300.2, 4, 6; 302.22; 304.12, 13; 336.4, 8, 12; 400.12, 14, 17; 401.7, 8; iii.240.8, 9 f.; 241.17; 243.16; 244.6, 7; 246.9; 247.11; 300.12–13, 18–19; 330.6–7; LV 5.16; 281.14, 15; 283.17 (here meter requires krā°; all mss. °chanda, n. sg., Lefm. em. °chandu for no apparent reason); Divy 333.5–6; Mmk 68.27; 397.12, 13; 426.8, 9; Gv 206.11–12; 297.26–298.4; 441.15–16; Laṅk 29.1 = 142.14; 141.9–10; 365.5; Karmav 71.20–21; without Kanaka° and Kāśyapa, Divy 254.3; 418.23 ff.; Av i.285.17; ii.29.7; 100.10; Kv 93.14; Karmav 38.12; 65.7; 76.14; Gv 300.21; 358.19; (**2**) n. of a yakṣa: Māy 1.

Krakucchandaka, = prec. (1) if reading is correct: LV 260.11 (vs) °dakasya; but Tib. (not included in Foucaux's ed.) seems to have had a different reading, without this name, see Foucaux's transl., and his Notes p. 162.

? **krakūnikā,** Mmk 395.26, in a description of a hand-position: saṃkocita-krakūnikā-granthānya-prayogāvasthita- (what follows is corrupt). Meaning? Probably corrupt.

krandanā (or °na, m.), a kind of malevolent supernatural being, in a list of such: krandanā mahākrandanāḥ Mmk 17.8. The immediately surrounding terms in the list are fem., but masc. ones occur not far away.

krandita, nt. (= Skt. Lex.; Pali kandita), *crying, lamentation*: LV 372.21 (vs) iha rudita-kranditānāṃ . . . paryantaṃ.

(**krayika,** m., once in Mbh., BR, *dealer, buyer, pur-*

chaser: Mv ii.242.4 śakuntakānāṃ krayiko, 6 śakunta-krayiko; Divy 505.6 māṃsasya krayiko.)

krāyaka, m. (Skt. Lex. id.), *purchaser*: Śikṣ 38.3 °kaṃ na labhate; 8, 12; AsP 497.17 °ko labdho. Cf. prec. and next.

krāyika, m. = **krayika, krāyaka**: Divy 505.8 yatra krāyiko 'sti (cf. krayika in 6 above).

kriṇati, kriṇeti = Skt. krīṇāti; see § 28.5.

Krimila, (**1**) n. of a mountain: Māy 253.32; (**2**) n. of a maharṣi: Māy 257.5.

kriyā (not in this sense in Skt., nor so far as I have found in Pali; the definition *promise, vow*, given PTSD s.v. kiriyā 1(b), is not supported by a careful study of the few passages cited), *decision, determination*: Mv i.310.6 (cf. line 8 and Senart's note p. 602) eṣa brāhmaṇapariṣāya kriyā anuparivartitavyā, *this decision of the brahman-assembly must be followed* (observed, concurred in); SP 186.6–7 etāṃ kriyāṃ śroṣyanti, *they will hear this decision* (determination, viz. what is then stated, that there is only one nirvāṇa). Cf. **kriyākāra, kriyābandha**, in which kriyā- seems to have this same mg.; neither of them has been recorded elsewhere. In MSV ii.109.8, 16, kriyāhṛta (kriyā-āhṛta), with lābha, kriyā is short for **kriyākāra**, *agreement*; note kriyākāraṃ kṛtvā, 17.

kriyā-kāra, m. (cf. **kriyā**, and next), lit. *the making of a decision, determination*; so, *resolution, agreement*; = pratijñā, Mv iii.329.9, below; commonly as object of a form of kṛ (or subject of a passive thereof), of *making a resolution or agreement*; also with anu-rakṣ, *keep an agreement*, and bhid-, ud-ghāṭay-, or ud-ghātay-, *break* it: LV 407.18 kriyābandham (see next) akārṣuḥ (pañcakā bhadravargīyāḥ), *made an agreement* (to the effect stated in the following quotation), followed 408.17 by kriyākāraṃ (v.l. kriyāṃ) bhittvā, *breaking their agreement*; in account of this same incident Mv iii.329.3 kriyākāraṃ (mss. °kālaṃ) karonti (bhadravargīyāḥ), but below 329.9 bhagnā . . . pratijñā, *the agreement* (promise) *has been broken*; Divy 6.8 °raṃ tāvat kurmaḥ; 32.10; 33.8 ff.; 128.6, 9, 28; 129.9; 130.5 f.; 136.8; 203.20; 338.13 f.; Av i.83.10; 88.8; 90.13 udghāṭyatāṃ kriyākāraḥ; ii.53.10; 136.5; 154.3; Kv 56.24 (misprinted kriyākaraṃ); 58.1, 3, 14; Bbh 162.5 °kāram anurakṣataḥ (gen. sg. pres. pple.); 176.8 °kāram anurakṣitukāmasya, et alibi; MSV iv.133.1, 3 (wrongly Dutt p. xvi).

kriyā-bandha, m., = **kriyā-kāra**, q.v.: LV 407.18 (cited in prec.).

(**kriyā-lakṣaṇa-vinivṛttaṃ**, ep. of the Buddha, Laṅk 12.5, acc. to Suzuki *who keeps himself away from work and form*; better, *who is freed or turned away from* (even) *the appearance* (or characteristic mark) *of activity*.)

krīḍaka, adj. or subst. m. (= Skt. Lex. id.), *playing*, (one) *who plays*: SP 89.10 (vs) vrajanti krīḍakāḥ, *they go* (in all directions) *playing* (with the toy-carts); or, perh. better, *to play* (§ 22.3).

krīḍanikā, rarely °**nakā**, with or without dhātrī (cf. AMg. kīlaṇa-dhāī, and also **krīḍāpanikā**, s.v. °**naka**), *a nurse who amuses* (plays with) an infant, regularly as one of four kinds of nurses: with dhātrī, Mvy 9481; in a cliché, Divy 99.26; 271.20; 441.23; Av i.15.12 (very often); MSV i.132.21 and (°nakā) iii.134.8; without dhātrī, in same cliché, Divy 3.13; 58.13; Av i.219.10; 346.5; 360.1, and in some other places (but less often). See s.v. **kṣīra-dhātrī**.

krīḍāpana, nt. (= °**panaka**, q.v.), *plaything*: SP 86.5 (vs) putrān krīḍāpanaiḥ krīḍana-sakta-buddhīn. So KN without v.l.; but WT with their ms. K′ krīḍāpanaka-krīḍana°, which is also possible metrically.

krīḍāpanaka, (**1**) nt. (= Pali kīḷāpanaka. Sk only krīḍanaka), *toy, plaything*: Kashgar rec. and 1 Nep. ms. at SP 74.1 (prose; ed. krīḍanaka); Mv ii.434.1–4; 475.7; (**2**) m., of animals and men, *plaything, animal* or *person to be used for amusement*: SP 94.6 (vs) sudurbalāḥ śvānaśṛgāla-bhūtāḥ pareṣa (or °ṣu) krīḍāpanakā bhavanti; Mv ii.479.16 antaḥpurikānāṃ krīḍāpanako bhavatu (subject, Kuśa disguised as a cook), 18; 488.21; iii.16.3 antaḥpuraṃ praveśiyati krīḍāpanako bhaviṣyati; (**3**) fem. °panikā, foll. by dhātrī, = **krīḍanikā**, q.v.; Divy 475.13, 17. (Cf. AMg. kīlāvaṇa-dhāī, beside kīlaṇa-dhāī.)

krīḍāpanika, nt., = °**panaka** (1), *toy*: Divy 475.18 °kāni bhavanti, tad yathā, akāyikā etc. (these are toys, not games as stated in Index). For °nikā, fem., see s.v. °**naka.**

krīḍyaka (m. or nt.), *game, sport*: Mv ii.172.3 (prose) puṣkariṇīm otīrṇodaka-(so mss., Senart em. otīrṇā udaka-) -krīḍyakehi (v.l. -krīḍantehi) krīḍitum.

kruñcati = **kroñcati, krauñcayati**; see s.v. 2 **krauñca.**

krudhyana, see **akrudhyana-tā.**

[**kruhi**, Mv i.280.14 and ii.405.15, so Senart with mss.; but read brūmi in both. Note that mss. at ii.405.15 point to (a)ham as subject. In a number of other places the Mv mss. read kruhi or krumi (ii.50.2, 12; 51.2, 12; 52.2; 181.16; 193.10; 256.15; 294.13; 482.12; iii.17.18; 214.4), but Senart always em. brūhi or brūmi; also in i.307.1 mss. krutha, Senart em. brutha, intending brūtha. Sometimes a corresponding Pali passage proves the emendation right, e. g. Mv iii.214.4 = DN ii.242.16 brūhi; Mv ii.50.2 = Jāt. v.387.21 vadāmi (Mv brūmi). In my opinion Senart should have made a clean sweep of these erroneous forms and adopted brūmi in i.280.14 and ii.405.15.]

kroñca (= Skt. krauñca), *curlew*: LV 193.17; 220.7; 315.15.

Kroñcakumārikā, f. pl., n. of certain ogresses on Ratnadvīpa: Divy 230.10; 503.8.

Kroñcakuśa, n. of a brother of Kuśa: Mv ii.433.18.

kroñcati (denom., to Sktized form of Pali koñca, koñca-nāda, *the trumpeting of an elephant*), *trumpets*: Divy 251.2 hastinaḥ kroñcanti. See **krauñca(-nāda)**. Also **kruñcati, krauñcayati**, qq.v.

kroḍa-malla (m.; = next, q.v., 2) *beggar*: °mallānāṃ madhye praviṣṭaḥ Divy 171.16.

kroḍa-mallaka, m. (cpd. of kroḍa, perh. in mg. *hollow*? plus **mallaka**, q.v.), [(**1**) *a hollow* (?) *vessel*, or at least some kind of *begging bowl*: Divy 89.21 tayā kroḍa-mallakena bhikṣāṃ aṭantyā, but read khaṇḍamallakena with same passage MSV i.89.13; cf. Divy 90.2 = MSV i.90.2 (tayā) khaṇḍamallake (MSV °kena) tailasya stokaṃ yācayitvā (MSV yācitvā);] (**2**) Bhvr., lit. *one who has* (carries) *a hollow* (?) *vessel*, i. e. *a beggar* (also **koṭṭa-malla**, °**laka**, and see prec.): Divy 85.20; 86.4 ff.; 172.4; 175.29; 191.8; 192.4.

Kroḍya, see **Koḍya.**

Krodha, m. (Skt. krodha, personified, *wrath*), Mmk 25.26, or **Krodha-rāja(n)**, Mmk 22.8 et passim; 547.6 (°rājā), ep. of Yamāntaka; in Dharmas 11 are listed ten personified Krodha, the first of which is Yamāntaka. Cf. **mahākrodha(-rājan).**

Krodhanā (mss. Ko°), n. of a rākṣasī: Māy 243.31.

Krodharājan, see **Krodha.**

krośika, adj. (Skt. krośa plus -ika), *a krośa* (kos) *in length or distance*: Mv i.41.12 °kāni, and 42.1 dvikrośikāni, *two krośas long*, trikrośikāni, *three* . . .; same forms i.230.8 f.; 240.17 f.; ii.162.17 f.

1 **Krauñca** (cf. Kirfel, Kosm. 108), m. pl., n. of a people, mentioned with Śākyas: MSV ii.16.18. One is tempted to emend to **Koliyāḥ**; but Tib. is cited as kruṅ kruṅ (q.v. in Das) ba rnams daṅ, which seems to support text.

2 **krauñca, krauñca-nāda** (m.; Sktized for Pali koñca-nāda, see s.v. **kroñcati**; perhaps read kroñca-nāda), the *trumpeting of an elephant*: MSV iii.16.11 hasti-krauñcam api kruñcataḥ (dual); Mv iii.256.1 hastinaḥ krauñcanādaṃ muñcanti (but v.l. kroñcaśabdaṃ nādanti).

krauñcayati = **kroñcati**, q.v.: hastināgena °yatā (pres. pple.) MSV i.66.11.

Krauñcāna, nt., n. of a city: MSV i.66.2, 10.

Krauḍya, see **Koḍya**.

? **krauṣita(-śabda)**, (sound of) *shrieking*: Gv 522.16 (prose) °daṃ ca nārakāṇāṃ śṛṇyāt. Evidently a false hyper-Skt. form, based on some MIndic derivative of root kruś; no recorded form suggests itself as the precise source. Textual corruption, beyond the obvious ṣ for ś, is probably concerned.

klamatha, kilamatha, m. (= Skt. Lex. kla°, Pali kilamatha; § 22.44), *weariness, fatigue*: Mvy 7336 klamathaḥ; SP 21.4; 258.8 (vs); LV 392.18; 416.20; Śikṣ 252.10; Bbh 81.1; 185.6; 187.11; kilamatha, Mv ii.483.11 (vs), by plausible em., naitaṃ (so with v.l., text na etaṃ, unmetr.) kilamathaṃ mahyaṃ (the forms are n. sg., as if nt.; otherwise the word is always m.); iii.331.6 (prose) ātmakilamathānuyogo; Gv 488.16 (vs) kilamatho (meter correct).

klāmati (1) = Skt. klāmyati, *gets weary*: klāmed MSV ii.85.1; (**2**) (as in Pali kilamati), *goes short of* (instr.): mā . . . piṇḍakena k . . . tha (lacuna; ed. klāmatha) MPS 13.9; klāntāḥ piṇḍakena MSV iv.137.9.

kliśyati, also **kili°** (= Pali kilissati, ppp. kiliṭṭha, neg. a-ki°; Skt. not in this mg.), *becomes soiled* (see also **saṃkliśyati**): Divy 193.20 akliṣṭāni (em., confirmed by the foll.) vāsāṃsi kliśyanti (mss. kliṣ°); 57.19 akliṣṭāni vāsāṃsi; cf. Pali akiliṭṭha-vasana; ppp. kiliṣṭa, *afflicted*, LV 131.17; Mv iii.446.1.

kleśa (also semi-MIndic **kileśa**), m. (= Pali kilesa), *impurity, depravity*; on relation to **anuśaya**, q.v., see esp. LaVallée Poussin, AbhidhK. v.1 note 4; Dharmas 67 six kleśa: rāga, pratigha, māna, avidyā, kudṛṣṭi, vicikitsā; AbhidhK. v.2, six anuśaya, same list (for the last two, the synonyms dṛṣṭi, vimati); Kv 80.5, read, katimāḥ ṣaṭ kleśāḥ (no list given); the word is extremely common, but usually vague and undefined; Mvy 862; LV 8.18; 11.5; 12.12, etc. etc.; kileśa, Mv i.299.16 (vs; mss. kilena, em. Senart), and others, § 3.109. A discussion in Burnouf, Lotus, 443 ff.

kleśa-jñeya, nt. dvandva, see Suzuki, Studies, Glossary and p. 177, = kleśāvaraṇa and jñeyāvaraṇa, *the* (hindrances constituted by) *depravities and objects of* (false, finite) *knowledge*: Laṅk 23.2 kleśajñeyaṃ ca te sadā viśuddham.

Kleśa-māra, m. (= Pali Kilesa°), one of the four Māras; see **Māra**.

klomaka, m. (= Pali kilomaka; to Skt. kloman plus -ka), *lung*, or *pleura* (seemingly the latter in Pali, cf. Buddhaghosa as quoted by Childers): Mvy 4018 °kaḥ = Tib. glo ba, *lung*; Śikṣ 70.1; 209.9 °kaḥ (in list of bodily parts).

kvātha (m.; in this mg. Skt. Lex.), *misery, sorrow*: asmābhir anena kvātha-kāyena prāptavyaṃ prāptaṃ (so punctuate) MSV i.5.17, *by this body of misery we have got all we could get*.

kṣaṇa, m. (= Pali khaṇa), *birth under favorable conditions*. There are 8 **akṣaṇa** (q.v.) but only 1 kṣaṇa, viz., birth as a man in the 'middle region', where a Buddha is to be expected, at a time when he is born, and with the mental capacity to assimilate his doctrine (Pali AN iv.227.8 ff.): Mv ii.363.4 kṣaṇaṃ (acc.) ekaṃ buddhotpādaṃ suśobhanam; Suv 41.(13–)14(–15) (bhavantu aṣṭākṣaṇavītivṛttāḥ, so read) āsādayantu kṣaṇarājam (*the supreme favorable birth*) uttamaṃ, (labhantu buddhehi samāgamaṃ sadā); Śikṣ 2.4; 114.15 kṣaṇasampad, *the good luck of* (this) *favorable birth*; 282.1 kṣaṇa-gati-pratilabdhena *having obtained the lot of* . . .; Kv 18.19 sarvakṣaṇopapannāḥ sattvā(ḥ), *all creatures born under* (the described) *favorable conditions*, cf. Sūtrāl. xiii.10 kṣaṇopapatti. (In Mv ii.378.1 Senart kṣaṇāṃś ca, but keep kṣaṇāc ca with mss., *and instantly*.) Once, however, kṣaṇa in this sense seems to be pluralized: Mv ii.392.5–6 so akṣaṇāni parivarjayitvā, kṣaṇā ca tasya bhavanti viśiṣṭā (but mss. bhavati viśiṣṭo, taking kṣaṇā as n. sg., § 8.24); the same vs Śikṣ 306.1 even makes 8 kṣaṇa, obviously as mechanical pendant to the 8 akṣaṇa: so akṣaṇaṃ vai vijahāti sarvaṃ, aṣṭakṣaṇāś cāsya viśiṣṭa bhonti. This is a secondary distortion. In LV 327.12 dullabho 'dya labhitaḥ kṣaṇavaro amṛto, *today has been obtained the immortal* (nectar-like?) *excellent favorable birth that is hard to obtain*, followed by 13 . . . varjitā (a)kṣaṇaduḥkhā asurasurapure, *avoided the pains of unfavorable births in the cities of asuras and gods*; evidently both kṣaṇa and akṣaṇa (the latter includes birth as a god!) are used in their standard meanings; but here the use of kṣaṇa is not strictly logical, since the Bodhisattva himself is speaking! [In Divy 76.25; 465.23 read **kṣūṇa**, q.v.]

[**kṣaṇā**, f., acc. to Divy 643.2, = Skt. kṣaṇa, of a definite unit of time; but in line 3 the word is nt., kṣaṇāny; and in the parallel 644.11 it seems to have been recorded first as m., kṣaṇaḥ (mss. however are corrupt), then nt., as in 643.3. See the passages, s.v. **tatkṣaṇa**. Prob. the fem. kṣaṇā is a mere corruption.]

kṣaṇika, adj., *empty* (of the hands): read in Mv ii.252.14 kṣaṇikena (Senart °tena with 1 ms., v.l. kṣamikena) hasteṇa gṛhaṃ gacchati, hato bhavati, *went home empty-handed and was depressed* (of a fowler who caught no birds); iii.171.6, read svakaṃ ca hastaṃ kṣaṇikaṃ (so 1 ms., v.l. kṣeṇikaṃ; Senart em. implausibly) paśyati (having given away a beautiful lotus, and now regretting the gift); repeated 171.9. Is this an extension of the mg. of JM. khaṇika, *idle, unemployed, out of work* (which is itself derived from Skt. kṣaṇin, *at leisure*)? In any case the two Mv passages confirm each other; kṣaṇika is certainly the true form in both, and the mg. is certain.

kṣaṇe-kṣaṇā, adv. (? perh. for °ṇāc = °ṇāt, before c-) *moment by moment, from moment to moment*: LV 321.5 (prose) kāścid (daughters of Māra) avaguṇṭhikayā (? see this) vadanāni chādayanti sma, kṣaṇe-kṣaṇā copadarśayanti sma. So Lefm. with best mss., supported by Weller's ms. 1; Calc. with some mss. kṣaṇena.

-kṣattaṃ, -kṣatto = **-kṛtvā** for Skt. -kṛtvas, q.v.

kṣatra (nt.) = kṣetra, *field*. Cf. Pali DN 3.93.13 khettānaṃ patī ti . . . khattiyo (in an etymology), which shows that a popular association of kṣatriya with kṣetra (or of their MIndic equivalents) existed. Doubtless as a result of this, the secondary etymological blend-form kṣatra occurs often in LV, as in 208.13; 283.8; 352.18; 354.14, 22; 355.16; 357.4; 366.8; in all these all mss. and Lefm. kṣa°; in LV 290.8, 15; 353.1 Lefm. kṣe° but most mss. kṣa°. The mss. of Mv also—sometimes nearly all of them—read kṣa°, as in v.l. for kṣe° at i.121.9, 11, 12; 122.1, 2. In all these cases there is no doubt of the mg. *field*; it seems to me that Lefm. was right in recognizing the existence in BHS of kṣatra in this sense, because of its frequent occurrence, which the etym. in DN supports.

kṣatriyāṇī (= Skt. Lex. and Gr. only; § 22.10; Pali Lex. khattiyānī, only cited by Childers from Abhidhānappadīpikā 236; AMg. khattiyāṇī), *kṣatriya-woman*: Mv iii.21.1 (vs). In literary Skt. only kṣatriyā; Lex. also kṣatriyī = literary Pali khattiyī (also °yā and khattī).

kṣapaṇa, m., *a member of some heretical* (not Buddhist as BR state) *sect*: Mvy 3530. Perh. a Jaina; AMg. has khavaṇa, seemingly applied to Jains; the word is not recorded in Pali.

kṣamam, nt. impersonal adj. (or adv.), *it is fitting*, construed with gdve. (cf. Speyer, VSS §§ 221, 222): LV 315.14 (vs) vāyasa-gardabha-ruditaṃ nivartitavyaṃ kṣamaṃ śīghraṃ, . . . *it is fitting that one turn back quickly*; 315.20 (vs) nivartitavyaṃ kṣamam prājñaiḥ.

kṣamaṇa (nt.; = Pali khamana, with dental n; not in Skt., tho normal formation from kṣam with -ana), *tolerance, patience*: Bbh 171.7 paraṃ kṣamaṇam anāghātaśīlaṃ ca saṃbhāvayet; a-kṣa°, *intolerance*, 171.14 akṣamaṇa-śīlatayā; in Laṅk 237.17 seems = **kṣānti**, q.v., prob. in sense of *intellectual receptivity*, vikalpasyā-pravṛtti-kṣamaṇa-tā grāhyagrāhakaparijñayā sā kṣānti-pāramitā.

kṣamaṇīya, adj. or subst. nt. (= Pali khamanīya, Vin. i.59.10, also with yāpanīya), *tolerable, endurable* (condition): SP 429.4, see s.v. **yāpanīya**. Both this form and **kṣemaṇīya(-tara**, q.v.) are used in what is clearly the same locution, bracketed with yāpanīya; kṣam° is supported by Pali khamanīya, but **kṣemaṇīya-pṛccha**, q.v., supports kṣem°. Etymologically both forms can be justified in a way, but kṣemaṇīya looks strange as a derivative of kṣema (premaṇīya is not a perfect parallel) and may be a blend of kṣamaṇīya with kṣema. Or is it a direct imitation of **premaṇīya**, a near-synonym?

kṣamati, oftener **°te** (in mgs. 2, 3 = Pali khamati), (**1**) *is worthy*: LV 383.17 (vs) (sa bhājanaṃ...) pratigrahītuṃ kṣamate, na cānyaḥ; (**2**) *is worth*, with acc. mūlyaṃ *price*, or another word naming the price or value; so in Pali, Vin. i.281.24 upaḍḍha-kāsinaṃ khamamāno, *being worth half a thousand*: Mv iii.375.18 sarvāṃ kāśi-bhūmiṃ kṣamati, and 376.1 upārdha-kāśiṃ kṣamati, see s.v. **kāśi**, 2; mūlyaṃ kṣamate LV 63.19; SP 264.15; 406.10 (all prose); in the last, text imāṃ sahālokadhātuṃ mūlyena kṣamati, but read with most mss. mūlyaṃ kṣamate, *is worth this whole sahā-world as a price*; the other passages similarly; (**3**) impersonally, *seems good, pleases*: yathā te kṣamate, *as seems good to you, as you think best*, Divy 70.18; AsP 16.7; MSV ii.74.11; sarvaṃ me bho Gautama na kṣamata iti Av ii.187.10 (and ff.); yam (= yad) vā vo kṣamati taṃ karotha Mv i.311.10–11.

kṣamāpayati (in mg. 1 = Skt. id., tho semi-MIndic in form; in both mgs. = Pali khamāpeti), (**1**) *asks pardon*, with acc.: °payanti LV 379.6; °penti Mv iii.359.10; °payed Sādh 108.7; °payām āsa Mmk 640.19; (**2**) *takes leave of, says farewell to*, with acc.: °payitvā LV 38.14; Divy 556.25.

kṣamuda, m., a high number: Mvy 7745 = Tib. bzod yas (cf. **kṣepu**).

Kṣamottara, n. of a former Buddha: Mv iii.233.1.

kṣampana, nt., Mvy 8965, some article of a monk's equipment; acc. to Tib. ḥur rdo, lit. *noise-stone*, but as a cpd. *sling* (for throwing stones; so also Jap. and one Chin. rendering, the other *cannon*, perh. orig. *catapult*?). But what would a monk use a *sling* for? In a wholly different direction leads AMg. khampaṇaya, *winding-sheet* (Ratnach.); if our word is related to this it might mean *sheet* or *large piece of cloth* of some kind. Uncertain.

kṣaya, m. (as in Skt., and Pali khaya), *exhaustion, perishing, decay*; (special uses, **1**) āyuḥ-kṣayāya Mv i.52.6, āyuḥkṣayāya ca karmakṣayāya ca i.338.17, (beings fall from heaven to earth) *in order to 'exhaust'* (work out, finish) *their* (destined) *life* (and the force of their past deeds); so, I agree with Senart, the text seems to mean; but in the Pali form of the same passage DN i.17.27 we find ablatives, āyukkhayā vā puññakkhayā vā, *because of the exhaustion of their lives* (in heaven) *or of their merits* (entitling them to live there, they fall to earth); (**2**) kṣaya-jñāna (= Pali khayañāṇa), *knowledge of* (the fact of) *decay, perishability*, in °na-lābhikaṃ kuśalamūlam Mvy 1209; a-śuddha-kṣayajñāna-viṣayiṇāṃ Laṅk 17.6–7, *that do not belong to the sphere of pure knowledge of perishability*(?) [(**3**) in Gv 106.5 and 18 read **akṣaya**, q.v., for kṣaya, a high number.]

Kṣayāpagata, m., n. of a samādhi: Mvy 550; ŚsP 1418.20.

kṣara (m.? = Pali khara, said by Jāt. comm. to mean *a saw*, twice in Jāt. vss.; used for cutting ivory or an elephant's tusk), *a sharp cutting tool*, perhaps *a saw*: Divy 417.10 (vs) kṣareṇa jihvām atha kartayāmi (cf., in prec. line, chinnāmi(!) nāsām krakacena vāsyāḥ; krakaca, *saw*, in its Pali form kakaca, is the Jāt. comm.'s def. of khara).

kṣānti, f. (= Pali khanti, used in this sense but not properly defined in Dictt., see AbhidhK. La V–P. vi.165, n. 2, et alibi, see Index; good statement Lévi, Sūtrāl. Transl. p. 123, cf. text xi.52 and comm.; Suzuki, Studies in Laṅk., 125–7 et alibi), *intellectual receptivity*; *the being ready in advance to accept knowledge*; a preliminary stage leading to jñāna but distinguished from jñāna by the fact that it is still characterized by doubt, AbhidhK. vii.1–2; the 8 kṣānti there referred to are paired with 8 corresponding jñāna to make up the 16 citta-kṣaṇāḥ Mvy 1217 ff., = caturāryasatyeṣu ṣoḍaśa kṣānti-jñāna-lakṣaṇāḥ Dharmas 96; in this list are 8 pairs of jñāna-kṣānt' and jñāna, e. g., first, duḥkhe dharma-jñāna-kṣāntı, *receptivity to knowledge of the truth in respect to misery*, then duḥkhe dharmajñāna, du° 'nvayajñāna-kṣānti, du° 'nvayajñāna; and so with samudaye, nirodhe, and mārge instead of duḥkhe. So **anutpattika-dharma-kṣānti**, q.v., *receptivity to the fact that states-of-being have no origination*; dharmanidhyāna-kṣānti, *receptivity to reflection on the states of being*, Sutrāl. xiv.26 comm., see transl. n. 3; similarly, sarvadharmasvabhāvanidhyāna-kṣāntiḥ Gv 248.4; dharmanidhyānādhimukti-kṣāntiḥ Bbh 195.10; samyaksaṃtīraṇā-kṣāntiḥ Bbh 81.22; avaivartika-kṣānti-pratilabdhāś ca bhaviṣyanti SP 259.13, *and will become possessed of the intellectual receptivity of non-returners* (see **avaivartika**); ānulomikī kṣāntiḥ Mvy 6571; Dbh 53.24; ānulomika-dharma-kṣānti-dharmālokamukham LV 35.20; nāhaṃ ... teṣāṃ ... ānulomikām api kṣāntiṃ vadāmi, kutaḥ punar buddhajñānam RP 34.13–14, *I do not attribute to them even the intellectual receptivity that conforms* (to continued religious development), *still less Buddha-knowledge*!; ghoṣānugā kṣānti, see **ghoṣānuga**; this with ānulomikī (or equivalent) and anutpattika-dharma- (or equivalent) form a triad of kṣānti, Samādh p. 22 l. 4 ff.; Sukh 55.13 (see Régamey, cited s.v. ghoṣānuga); **anutpāda-** (and °de) kṣāntiḥ, q.v., and anupa-lambhadharma-kṣ° RP 12.2, both = anutpattika-dharma-kṣ°; a different triad of kṣānti, Dharmas 107 (dharmanidhyāna-, duḥkhādhivāsanā-, paropakāradha(r)ma-); kṣānti is the 3d of the **nirvedha-bhaga**, q.v., Mvy 1214 (Sūtrāl. xiv.26, comm.).

-kṣāntika, ifc. Bhvr. (= **kṣānti**, q.v.; cf. Pali -khantika), *characterized by intellectual receptivity*: gambhīra-kṣ° Śikṣ 67.9; apratilabdha-kṣ° 270.6; mṛdu-kṣānti-kenāpi jñānena Bbh 236.13; pratilambha-kṣ° Sukh 56.13 (pratilambha, *acceptance*, sc. of truth; not *patience under censure*, SBE 49 pt. 2, 52).

Kṣāntipradīpaś(i)ri, n. of a former Buddha: Gv 285.18 (vs).

Kṣāntipriyā, n. of a gandharva maid: Kv 5.7

Kṣāntimaṇḍalapradīpa, n. of a former Buddha: Gv 257.23.

Kṣāntivādin, or (once) **°vāda** (= Pali Khantivādin), n. or epithet of an ascetic, previous incarnation of Śākyamuni; in Pali (Jāt. 313) his original name was Kuṇḍaka, but he is commonly referred to as Khantivādin; in Jm 182.1 ff. Kṣā° is an epithet, his name not being given; no other name for him is recorded in BHS; the story is told in Jm, and in Mv, where he is called Kṣāntivāda iii.357.9, °vādin 20 ff. and 369.15; referred to Kv 24.18; Vaj 31.17; and presumably Māy 256.23 (a maharṣi).

kṣāmodara, Mvy 304, or **kṣāma-kukṣi(-tā)**, Dharmas 84, *slender-bellied*, one of the **anuvyañjana**, q.v. (No. 36); LV instead **cāpodara**, q.v.; Mv ii.44.3 mss. corruptly chādoradā, chāto°, Senart em. cāpodarā, but chā- may represent a MIndic form of kṣāma-. Tib. renders Mvy 304 by phyal phyaṅ ṅe ba, *slender-belly*.

kṣāraka- (= khāraya, nt., = mukula, Deśīn. 2.73;

chāraya, nt., id., ib. 3.34, and Pkt. Lex. acc. to Sheth), *bud*, in °ka-jāta, *budded, in bud*: LV 76.13 (prose) (puṣpaphalavṛkṣā . . .)kṣārakajātā na phalanti sma (Tib. kha ḥbus nas rgyas par, cf. Das kha ḥbu ba, *the opening of buds of flowers*); Mvy 6227 °ka-jātam = Tib. sbal mig (= *bud*, Jä.) bye-ba (*open*), or che-ba (*great*).

Kṣitigarbha, n. of a well-known Bodhisattva: Mvy 652; Dbh 2.7; Sādh 49.12; Mmk 406.1; 425.19; one of a list of eight, Dharmas 12; Mmk 62.13; one of sixteen, Mmk 40.13. Cf. next.

Kṣitigarbha-sūtra, n. of a work: Śikṣ 13.7 et alibi. Cf. prec.

kṣitiśa (m.c. for Skt. kṣitīśa), *king*: RP 45.7 (vs).

? **kṣīyati** (= Pali khīyati), *is vexed*; so Senart at Mv ii.480.2, 4; text in 2 (sā . . .) tāsām antaḥpurikānāṃ ruṣyati kṣīyati (but v.l. kṣipati) paribhāṣati, in 4 kiṃ tuvaṃ asmākaṃ ruṣyasi kṣīyasi (but both mss. kṣipasi or °pesi) paribhāṣasi (mss. °ṣesi). Since one ms. in 2, and both in 4, have forms of kṣip, which in normal Skt. means *scold, revile*, it seems at least likely that we should read kṣipati, °si. See, however, s.vv. **vivācayati, dhriyati.**

kṣīraka, in form nt., = **kṣīrikā** (1), q.v., *a kind of* (probably) *date-tree*: Mv ii.248.4 °kāni ca, in a list of trees, all nt. in form and even introduced by the formally nt. vṛkṣāṇi; hence, doubtless, our form. In line 16 below the list is repeated in inst. forms, and here the mss. read kṣīrikāhi, which should doubtless be kept, since kṣīrikā is recorded.

kṣīra-dhātrī, *wet-nurse* (in Divy 475.13, 16 replaced by **stana-dh°**, q.v.), one of four kinds of nurses regularly provided for princes and rich men's sons: Mvy 9479; the others are standardly **aṅka-dh°** (**aṃsa-dh°**), **mala-dh°**, and **krīḍanikā** (dh°), qq.v. As a rule two of each sort, or eight in all, are provided, in a cliché common in Divy and Av: kṣīra° Divy 3.14; 58.12; 99.25; 271.19; 441.22; Av i.15.11 etc. But in Divy 475.12 only four, one of each kind, are provided; their functions are precisely defined 475.13 ff.

kṣīrapaka, adj. (= Pali khī°, only with vaccha; Skt. kṣīrapa is recorded only of humans; °paka not in Skt.), *suckling*, only with vatsa, *calf*: Mv iii.259.9 vatso iva kṣīrapako; Ud iii.3 and xviii.4 vatsaḥ kṣīrapaka iva (these vss correspond to Pali Ud vii.4 and Dhp. 284 respectively, which have khī°).

Kṣīrapūrṇāmbha(s), n. of a former Buddha: Mv i.140.9 °bhaḥ, n. sg.

kṣīrikā, °ka (nt.), °kā recorded as n. of a tree Skt. Lex., and once in Var.Bṛh.S., BR 5.1350; the one occurrence cited from Mbh. in BR, pw, is shown by Crit. ed. 3.155.42d to be a false reading for kṣīriṇas, acc. pl.; cf. Skt. kṣīrin, n. of one or more trees, and kṣīriṇī, n. of various plants; AMg. khīriṇī, n. of a creeper; cf. s.v. **kṣīraka,** (**1**) °kā, n. of a tree, perhaps *date*, but context gives no clue in LV 381.12 (prose) kṣīrikā-vana-nivāsinī-devatā-; Tib. śiṅ ḥo ma can, *milky tree*; in Mv ii.248.16 read prob. °kāhi with mss., see s.v. **kṣīraka**; (**2**) °kā, n. of a kind of grass or herb: Mv ii.137.1, 19 kṣīrikā (v.l. both times sthinikā) nāma tṛṇajāti; medicinal, brought by Śakra from Mt. Gandhamādana, Av i.31.16 kṣīrikām oṣadhīm; (**3**) nt. kṣīrikāni (so; no v.l.), *fruits*, apparently *of the date*: Mv ii.475.16, in a list of names of fruits, all nt. pl.

Kṣīroda, n. of a nāga king: Mmk 18.12.

kṣuḍḍīka, v.l. for **khudrāka,** q.v.

kṣuṇa (so mss.), adj., *failing, unsuccessful* or *mistaken, in error*: Divy 213.28 kṣuṇā (ed. em. kṣuṇṇā) bhavanto, *you have made a mistake* or *you have failed* or *you are wrong*; kṣuṇo (ed. em. haṃ bho, wrongly) bhikṣavo rājā . . . MSV ii.73.18, *the king made a mistake*. Cf. **kṣūṇa** (perh. to be read for this?).

kṣuṇaka, see **ati-kṣ°.**

kṣuṇṇa, adj. (ppp. of Skt. kṣud-, in peculiar use), *injured* (in spirit), *insulted, crushed* (fig.), or *angry*: (Vaiśālako gaṇaḥ) kṣuṇṇo dvāre tiṣṭhati MSV i.229.20.

-kṣuttaṃ, -kṣutto = **-kṛtvā** for Skt. -kṛtvas, q.v.

kṣudra (= **kṣaudra,** q.v.; cf. Pali Lex. khudda, *honey*, Abhidh., see Childers), (**1**) ep. of madhu, = kṣaudra(ṃ) madhu, (a kind of) *honey*: kṣudramadhusadṛśāni phalāni Mv ii.107.4; 108.4, 13; kṣudra-madhu (°dhv, °dhum) aneḍakaṃ (once °ko; or anel°) Mv i.339.8; 340.13; 341.7 (vv.ll. kṣaudra-, kṣudro, kṣudraṃ; at least 1 ms. each time kṣudra-); (**2**) adj., *honey-like, honeyed, honey-, sweet*: with **yvāgu,** *gruel*, Mv ii.84.9–10 (prose) kṣudrāye ca yvāgūye ghaṭikā haste; 13, 16 yvāgu (°gū) kṣudrā (n. sg.); kṣudra-kṣudrāṇi phalāni Mv iii.145.2, see s.v. **kṣudra-pāka,** in which kṣudra- seems to = Skt. svādu-.

kṣudrakānukṣudraka = **kṣudrānukṣudra,** q.v.: °kaiḥ śikṣāpadair Prāt 504.8; Chin. quoted as 'les préceptes mineurs'.

kṣudra-pāka, adj., *very ripe*, of fruits in the last month of summer: Mv iii.143.(14–)15 (grīṣmāṇāṃ) paścime māse kṣudrapākāni phalāni bhuktāni, whereupon he was thirsty, drank much cold water, and got indigestion; substantially the same, 144.5; 153.10; the mg. seems guaranteed by 154.6 where pakva-supakvāni replaces kṣudrapākāni, in what is otherwise virtually the same phrase. Cf. Skt. svādupāka, defined BR as *was sich süss angenehm kocht*, d. h. *verdaut*; **kṣudra** here means *honey-like* = *sweet* (see s.v.). In Mv iii.154.14 the ṛṣi who had the above adventure squeezes such fruits (so that the juice falls) into the mouth of the infant born to the doe who drank his seed: ṛṣi kṣudrapākāni phalāni mukhe pīḍeti. The interpretation is further confirmed by Mv iii.145.2 kṣudra-kṣudrāṇi phalāni (on which see **kṣudra**), of the fruits fed by the ṛṣi to the young Ekaśṛṅga(ka). It seems that the ṛṣi's indigestion was caused by the excessive amount of cold water he drank, not by the fruits.

kṣudraputrā, *poor wretch* (f.): Divy 525.24 °putrāham; 26 °putreyaṃ tapasvanī (read °svinī). Cannot mean literally *daughter of a mean person*, since the speaker in 24 claims to be a king's daughter.

kṣudrānukṣudra (Pali khuddānukhuddaka, recorded only with sikkhāpada; cf. **kṣudrakānukṣudraka**): °drāṇi śikṣāpadāni, perhaps *very minor* (usually rendered *small and minor*): MSV i.59.13; Divy 465.4; °drā . . . oṣadhīyo SP 129.7, acc. to Kern *of different size*, but perhaps *very minute* (?); followed successively by kṣudrīka, madhyā, mahatī, *small, middling, large ones*. See under 1 **anu.**

kṣudrikā, SP 129.10, and **kṣudrīka,** 129.7, *small*; both vss, quantities metrically required; both f., with oṣadhi; in both Kashgar rec. cited as khuḍḍīka, which would be unmetrical in 10. Related to Skt. kṣudra(ka); see s.v. **khudrāka.** For kṣudrīka Burnouf cites his mss. as reading khuḍḍāka or khuḍḍīka.

-kṣunto = **-kṛtvā** for Skt. kṛtvas, q.v.

kṣuraka, m. (cf. Skt. kṣura, kṣurikā, Pali khura, churikā, *knife*), *knife*, applied in pl. to certain 'winds' in the body, in a list of them: Śikṣ 248.13 (kukṣigamāḥ śastrakāḥ) kṣurakāḥ sūcakāḥ . .

kṣurapra-vārin, *wearing a guard against arrows, having defensive armor* (kṣurapra and khurapra both found in Skt.; see s.v. **khurapra-vāra**): Mv ii.339.14 (vs) kṣurapravārī (so read; n. pl.; Senart °cārī; v.l. kṣurasaṃpravārī) . . . mārasya sainyā sthita bodhimūle.

kṣūṇa, adj. (also **kṣuṇa,** perh. by error; see references s.v. in Schmidt, Nachtr.; JM. khūṇa, said to be only a noun, = doṣa; blend of Skt. kṣīṇa and kṣuṇṇa?), *at fault, in error, wrong*: kṣūṇa (Tib. ñes) Ānanda eṣa brāhmaṇaḥ MSV i.74.9; in same text Divy reads kṣaṇa, erroneously, at 76.25 (one ms. kṣūṇa) and 465.23; in Śikṣ

126.6 read with mss. (na ... bodhisattvasya vāk) kṣūṇa-vyākaraṇā, *having faulty grammar*; see **akṣūṇa**(-vyākaraṇa).

kṣeṭa, nt. (hyper-Skt. for kheṭa), *phlegm*: MSV iv.120.10.

kṣetra (*field*, always nt. in Skt., and so khetta in Pali acc. to PTSD), rather often has masc. endings and modifiers: SP 9.4 (end of vs) kṣetrāḥ; 24.3 (vs) kṣetra (n. pl.) tathātra kecid ... tathaiva kecit; Laṅk 12.17–13.1 (prose) te ca kṣetrāḥ sanāyakāḥ; LV 280.9 (vs) sphuṭāḥ kṣetrā hy acintiyāḥ; 280.12 (vs) sarve te ... kṣetrāḥ (most mss. kṣa°, see s.v. **kṣatra**); this substitute kṣatra with masc. endings LV 354.22; 357.4. See **buddha-kṣetra.**

kṣepaṇa (nt.; not recorded in this sense, but cf. Skt. kṣepa, and kṣipati, in corresp. mgs.), *abuse, reviling*: Prāt 504.12 (see s.v. **avadhyāna**).

kṣepayati, (**1**) *spends, passes* (time, with acc. kālam or some expression of time), is found in Skt. (BR 5.1349), and the simple kṣipati is commoner in that sense (ibidem). It is strange that Senart, Mv i. n. 492, PTSD on khepeti (s.v. khipati), and others have overlooked that fact, regarded the usage as specifically Pali-BHS, and assumed confusion with kṣi, *destroy*. I have, to be sure, found no record of kṣepayati used absolutely in this sense in Skt., as it is in LV 276.11 (vs) brahmaśakrabhavane nityaṃ sukhaṃ kṣepituṃ, *to spend* (time) *happily forever in the home of B. and Ś.* (**2**) *exhausts, brings to an end, obliterates*; here influence of kṣi, *destroy*, might more reasonably be suspected, yet Skt. kṣip is sometimes used in nearly or quite the same sense, BR s.v. kṣip 7 (2.549; but as BR suspected, Mbh. Calc. 3.1094 should be read kṣīyeran, not kṣiperan, see Crit. ed. 3.30.30); it prob. is an extension of the meaning *spend* (time). So Divy 367.8 (narakavedanīyāni karmāṇi) kṣepayitvā, *having spent* (*exhausted*) *their deeds that had to be suffered-for in hells*, which may illustrate the transition from *spend* (time) to *exhaust*; the change is complete in LV 237.13 (vs) saptarātra bhaṇamānu ... sā viyūha na pi śakya kṣepituṃ, *tho described for a week, this splendor could not be exhausted* (*'spent'*). But it is doubtful whether any of these uses are strictly non-Skt.

kṣepu, m. or f. (nom. kṣepuḥ; but Mironov kṣepu, as if nt.), a high number: Mvy 7874 = Tib. bzod yas (cf. **kṣamuda**); cited from Gv, which however reads **kṣemu,** q.v.

kṣema, (**1,** as in Skt., adj. *causing peace and comfort*, or n. *comfort*: Mv i.302.1 kiṃ kṣemaṃ, *what* (can we do that) *will cause you peace and comfort*? In the verse form 303.21 replaced by kiṃ karoma. Response to a cry of distress; foll. by kiṃ avidhāvidhaṃ ti krandasi. Senart fails to understand.) (**2**) n. of a king of old (= Pali Khema, oftener Khemaṃkara, q.v. DPPN): Divy 242.5 (his capital was **Kṣemāvatī,** q.v.); (**3**) n. of a Buddha: Mmk 365.17 (vs, but submetrical; one syllable short).

Kṣemaka, m. pl. (corresp. to Pali Khemiya), a class of gods: Waldschmidt, Kl. Skt. Texte 4, Mahāsamāj. 189.1.

Kṣemaṃkara, (**1**) n. of a former Buddha: Divy 242.1 ff.; he lived in **Kṣemāvatī**; in the same story in Pali Khemaṃkara is the n. of the king of the city, who in Divy (242.5) is **Kṣema** (in Pali also alternatively Khema); in Pali the Buddha Kakusaṃdha is born under this king (in Divy Krakucchanda appears in a sequel to the story, 254.3); (**2**) n. of an apparently different former Buddha: Av i.110.10 ff.; (**3**) n. of a son of King Brahmadatta of Benares: Av ii.46.6; 49.8; (**4**) n. of a Bodhisattva: Gv 442.16; (**5**) n. of a nāga: Mvy 3336.

kṣemaṃgama, adj. (formed on the pattern of the commonplace kṣemaṃkara), *attaining comfort* (*peace, weal*); ep. of a Buddha: Mmk 131.11; of a mudra, °gamo mudraḥ 476.9; mahā-kṣemaṃgamaṃ (mudram) 475.11.

kṣemaṇīya-tara, adj. (§ 22.20), *more healthy*: Divy 110.2 (tato Maghasya ...) °taraṃ cābhūd yāpanīyataraṃ ca. Cf. next; and see **kṣamaṇīya** on the etymology.

kṣemaṇīya-pṛccha, adj. (cf. prec.), *asking after the welfare* (with gen. of person): Mv iii.347.19 tasya ... kṣemaṇīyapṛcchā āgatā, *they came inquiring about his health.*

Kṣemā, (**1**) (= Pali Khemā) n. of Śākyamuni's chief female disciple: Mv i.251.21 (agrā ... śrāvikā); (**2**) n. of a daughter of King Prasenajit, who also became a nun in the Buddha's order: Av ii.46.7 ff.; in 50.9 she is, in fact, declared by Buddha to be agrā me ... bhikṣuṇīnāṃ mama śrāvikāṇāṃ, so that she is actually identified with (1); her story, however (Av no. 79) is wholly different from the story of Khemā in Pali. (Mv gives no story about Kṣemā 1.).

Kṣemāvatī (= Pali Khemāvatī), n. of an ancient city, where dwelt King **Kṣema** and the Buddha **Kṣemaṃkara,** qq.v.: Divy 242.4 ff.

kṣemu, m. or f. (nom. °muḥ), a high number: Gv 133.15 (represented in Mvy by **kṣepu,** q.v.).

kṣoḍaka (= the commoner **khoṭaka, khoḍaka,** q.v.), prob. *wall-coping* or *enclosure on a wall*, at any rate some part of a wall: Gv 161.24 (sarve ca vajraratnamahāprākārā(ḥ) ...) jāmbūnada-kanaka-kṣoḍaka-rucira-dantamālā-racitā(ḥ).

kṣomaka, (adj. or) nt. (= **kṣaumaka,** q.v.), (garment of) *linen*: Divy 316.27, in a long cpd. listing various garments or textiles, -prāvarakā-kāśikāṃśu-kṣomakādyāḥ; Bhīk 22b.4, in a series of materials usable for robes, ... kāśisūkṣmaṃ vā kṣomaka-sūkṣmaṃ (*fine linen garment*) vā dukūlakasūkṣmaṃ vā.

(**kṣaudra** = Skt. *honey*, or *a kind of honey*; here possibly adj., *of* or *made by bees*? cf. s.v. **kṣudra**: kṣaudraṃ madhu Mvy 5728; Av i.187.7; 243.1; kṣaudramadhu Karmav 45.14; in all cases immediately foll. by **aneḍakam.** Also occurs, as in Skt., as subst. without madhu, e. g. Dbh 6.8; 8.11; Divy 221.11; 551.27.)

kṣaumaka, (adj. or) nt. (= Skt. kṣauma; Pkt. khomaga beside khoma), *linen garment*: Mvy 9161 = Tib. zar maḥi ras, acc. to Dict. of French Cath. Miss. *cloth made of fibre from nettles* (!); Das *muslin.* See **kṣomaka.**

KH

khakkhaṭa, adj. (= **kakkhaṭa,** q.v.; cited by Thomas JRAS 1899.494 from Harṣac.; see next), *hard*: Śikṣ 342.3 (so ms.); MSV iv.75.8; *harsh* (of sounds), Divy 518.2 (vs) (dviṣṭo naro bhavati hi) khakkhaṭā-svaraḥ (ā m.c.? MIndic pron. -saraḥ).

khakkhaṭatva, nt., also spelled **khakhaṭa°** (to prec.), *hardness*: Mvy 1842 (v.l. kakkh°; opp. to dravatvam) = Tib. sra ba ñid; (= **kakkha°** Śikṣ 245.2;) Bcṭ 328.6 (and with var. 327.12); spelled khakhaṭatvam Mmk 265.20 (gātre).

khakkhara, nt. (= **khakhara-ka, khaṅkhara-ka,** qq.v.), *monk's staff*: Mvy 8955 = Tib. ḥkhar bsil (or gsil), id.

khakkhala, adj. (doubtless onomat.), *stammering* (so Tib., dig pa): Mvy 8887.

khakhaṭatva, see **khakkhaṭatva.**

khakhara, nt. (m.? f. °rā?) = **khakkhara, khaṅkhara(ka)**, and next: Mmk 356.18 (vs) kumbhaḥ... khakharam (n. sg.) text, but meter requires khakkharam or khaṅkh°!; 368.15 kuryāt khakharākāram (meter demands °rakākāraṃ), 16 etan mudram samākhyātaṃ khakharety (f.?) arisūdanā, 17 tad eva khakhara (masc.?) īṣad...; 386.6 khakharaṃ, n. sg. (all vss; meter indifferent as to quantity of first syllable in all these except 356.18).

khakharaka (where gender is clear only m. noted; = prec. and **khakkhara**), *monk's staff*: Mmk 42.26 (prose) °ka-kamaṇḍalum, cf. daṇḍa-kamaṇḍalum 43.8; 91.15 (prose), in a list of monk's belongings, -cīvara-khakharaka-śūcī (read sūcī)-; khakharaka-mudrā 418.11 and 422.4 (both prose); in 471.16 text tadaṅantare khakhavarakaḥ, read khakharakaḥ (hypermetric even then!); 472.8 (vs) khakharakaś ca mahāmudraḥ; in both the last khakharaḥ (or khakkharaḥ) would be metr. better.

Khagarbha, n. of a Bodhisattva: Sādh 49.14; one of 'the eight Bodhisattvas' (cf. **Kṣitigarbha, Maitreya**, etc.), Dharmas 12.

Khagānanā, n. of a yoginī: Sādh 427.6.

khaṅkhaṭa- (in cpd.), acc. to Tib. (re śig) *a little*: -svaro MSV ii.80.10, *a little sound*. (MW quotes from Wilson khaṅkhaṇā, *a tinkling sound*.) **khakkhaṭa** would not be a likely reading here since the omen is favorable, indicating rebirth as a god.

khaṅkhaṭika, nt., some kind of dye-stuff: MSV ii.142.10 (with gairikaṃ).

khaṅkhara, m. (or nt.; Skt. Lex. m., *lock of hair*), = next: Mmk 392.4 (iyam ca) bhagavato buddhasya khaṅkharamudrā.

khaṅkharaka, m., also °**kā**, f.? (= prec.): °ko MSV iv.67.16; Mmk 392.5 eṣa... buddhānāṃ khaṅkharaka-mudrāmantraḥ...; (tāḥ) °kāḥ kṛtvā in MSV ii.142.3 (and 8) certainly means *monk's staff* (= **khakkhara, khakharaka**; Tib. khar sil, cf. Tib. on Mvy 8955); in view of this, prob. this is the mg. (rather than *lock of hair*) in Mmk, here and in prec.; parallel are sarvatathāgatoṣṇīṣāṇāṃ mahāmudrā 391.18, and sarvatathāgatānāṃ pātra-mudrā 392.9–10.

khacana (nt.; to root khac, cf. Skt. khacita), *studding, inlay*: LV 430.13 (prose) suvarṇa-khacana-suvarṇa-puṣpa-suvarṇacūrṇābhikiraṇa-...

(**khaja**, as in Skt., *churning-stick, stirring stick*; Skt. Lex. also *spoon, ladle*: Laṅk 340.8 (vs), repeating 203.15: khaja- (203.15 kheja, mere corruption)-mṛd-daṇḍa- (203.15 bhāṇḍa)-cakrādi bījabhūtādi (i. e. all material things) bāhiram (sc. constituent of the **saṃkalā** or **śaṃ**°, q.v.). Ed. note on 203.15 seems to indicate support in northern translations for mantha = khaja. No need to em. to dhvaja as suggested in ed. on 340.8 and Suzuki's Index.)

khajja (nt.; = Pali id., MIndic for **khādya**), *hard food* (as in Pali, hardly in Skt., contrasting with **bhojya**, or also **bhakta**, q.v., *soft food*): Mv iii.39.4 bhakta-khajjam upaviṣṭo, *sat down to soft and hard food*; 405.1 -khajja-bhojya-gandha-mālya-vilepanaṃ viśrāṇīyati; ii.462.10, read with mss. khajja-rūpaṃ, *thing of the nature of hard food*.

khajjaka, nt. (= Pali id., MIndic for khādyaka), = **khādyaka**, q.v.: Mv ii.190.6 nānāprakārāṇi khajjakāni (v.l. khādya°) allīyanti; 461.21 khajjakasya pūraṃ gopiṭakam (q.v.)... alindaṃ (q.v.) odanasya; similarly 462.3, 7, 9, 11; iii.15.9, 12 (in all these a *basket*, gopitakam, of khajjaka is contrasted with an **alindaṃ** or °**dā**, q.v., of soft food); iii.127.5 khajjakaṃ vā.

khajjati (= Pali id.; MIndic from Skt. khādyate, pass. of khād), *is eaten*: khajjāmi Mv ii.450.6, 8; 452.8, 11; khajje, opt., iii.252.15; fut. khajjiṣyasi Mv ii.78.4; °ṣyatha iii.290.17; note khajjanti Mv i.360.1, repeated as khādyanti 3.

khañjāhva, m., some sort of bird; acc. to pw 7, App., *the water-wagtail* (assuming identity of mg. with Skt. khañjana): Mvy 4911. But Tib. ba mo byi ḥu; acc. to Das, this—or rather ba moḥi byi ḥu—means the Skt. cātaka, *Cuculus melanoleucus*.

khaṭa (m. or nt.; Skt. Lex. m.; cf. Deśīn. 2.72 khaḍaia = saṃkucita), *fisticuff, blow with the fist* (cf. next): Śikṣ 56.17 khaṭa-capeṭa-caṇḍa-prahārāṇāṃ; Karmav 37.5, 6 khaṭa- (by em., ms. śata; Tib. confirms em.) -capeṭa-pradāna; Laṅk 119.14 khaṭa-capeṭa-.

khaṭaka, m. (Skt. Lex.) = prec.: Mvy 3984 (foll. by capeṭa).

khaṭakā = prec.: Divy 372.18 °kā mūrdhni pātitā; 19 °kāṃ nipātayati.

khaṭayati, acc. to Tib. (skyoṅs śig) *guards, protects* (cattle): MSV ii.5.17 (go-mahiṣīḥ...) °yata.

khaṭu (**1**) = **khaṭa**: Divy 173.10 khaṭu-capeṭādibhis; (**2**) khaṭv-ākārān (sattvān) Divy 338.8 (here Dutt, MSV iv.38.17 note, cites Tib. as gtun, *pestle*); 342.11 (here Dutt, ib. 44.19, cites Tib. as phar [read phor] pa, said to mean saraka, *a drinking vessel*); but 342.26, 343.5 replaces this by what is meant for taṭṭv-āk°, see s.v. **taṭṭu**; so read each time.

khaṭuka, oftener **khaṭuṅka** (also abstr. °**ka-tā**), in KP **khaḍuṅka**, adj. or subst. m. (Pali and AMg. khaluṅka; cf. Skt. Lex. kaṭuṅka-tā, and see Schmidt, Nachtr. s.v. khaṭuṅka), *unruly, unmanageable*, in BHS and Pali only of horses (in AMg. said to be used of bullocks too) and figuratively of men: Mvy 2450 (in a list of evil qualities) khaṭuṅkaḥ, v.l. kaṭ° (cf. Skt. Lex. above), Mironov khaṭuka; in Śikṣ always of sattva, *creatures*, and always khaṭuṅka, Śikṣ 149.13 (see note on 279.5); sattvair evaṃ khaṭuṅkair evaṃ durdāntair 283.14; ṛjutā kuṭileṣu, spaṣṭatā khaṭuṅkeṣu (sc. sattveṣu) 285.16; khaṭuṅka-tā Śikṣ 279.5 (see note; Tib. shows the word was in text); 283.13; Jm 5.20; (aśvaḥ...) khaḍuṅka-kriyā vā karoti KP 108.2 (see s.v. **utkumbhati**); kuhakāḥ khaṭukāḥ kuśīlāḥ (sattvāḥ) Mmk 666.13; (sa āghātacittaḥ syāt...) khaṭuṅka-jātīyaḥ Bbh 177.7; mūḍha-śaṭha-khaṭuṅkeṣu sattveṣu Bbh 365.15; (subst.) bodhisattva-khaḍuṅkāḥ, *unruly horses of Bodhisattvas* (i. e. untrained, unruly ones; contrasted with ājāneya in KP 10, as Pali khaluṅka with ājānīya, PTSD), KP 9.1, 7, and khaḍuṅka alone (referring to Bodhisattvas) 16, 18; similarly, bodhisattva-khaṭukāḥ RP 58.6. See also **khāduka-tā.**

khaṭṭika, m. (= Skt. Lex. id. = māṃsa-vikrayin; not in Pali; AMg. khaṭṭia, °iya), *butcher*: Mvy 3759 = Tib. bśan pa. Ultimately, of course, based on a theoretical Skt. *kṣattṛ-ka.

khaḍuṅka, see **khaṭuka.**

khaḍga, (**1**) nt., a high number (cf. **khaḍgin**): Mmk 262.15 adhikā daśa tare (?) tasya (sc. vivāhasya, cf. line 14) khaḍgam ity āhu vāṇijāḥ; 343.14 daśārbudā nirbudaḥ uktaḥ taddaśaṃ khaḍgam iṣyate; (**2**) m., n. of a mountain: Māy 254.6.

Khaḍgajvalanā, n. of a kiṃnara maid: Kv 6.18.

khaḍga-viṣāṇa, *rhinoceros*; **-kalpa**, adj. (= Pali khagga-visāṇa-kappa), *like a rhinoceros*, i. e. *living a lonely life*; esp. (as in Pali) ep. of a Pratyekabuddha: Mvy 1006; Divy 582.8; ekacarā °kalpā Mv i.301.4, and in a vs 357.15, otherwise eko care °kalpo 21 ff., or ekaś caret °kalpaḥ Divy 294.15, refrain of the stanzas of Pali Sn i.3 (vss 35–75: eko care khagga-visāṇakappo), a number of which are reproduced in Mv i.357.12–359.15, and one in Divy l.c.; they are designated khaḍgaviṣāṇa-gāthāḥ Mv i.359.16. Since Skt. khaḍga and Pali khagga mean *rhinoceros*, the Pali comm. on Sn paraphrases kh°-visāṇa by *rhinoceros-horn*. But actually the cpd. means *rhinoceros*, = Skt. khaḍgin, originally *having a sword*(-like) *horn*. The comparison is to the animal, not to its horn. Cf. Samādh 19.29 khaḍga-samā; RP 13.7 khaḍga-vimalāḥ (cited Śikṣ 196.4 as khaḍga-sadṛśāḥ); RP 16.7 (vs) eka viharati yathaiva khaḍgo. In all these khaḍga is the precise equivalent of khaḍgaviṣāṇa (and khaḍgin), *rhinoceros.*

khaḍgika, m., a royal officer of some kind, acc. to Tib. *sword-bearer* (from Skt. khaḍga): Mvy 3730 = Tib. ral gri pa. Cf. however Deśīn. 2.69 khaggia = grāmeśa.

khaḍgin, (1) m., or **khaḍgina**, nt. (cf. khaḍga), a high number: Mmk 262.16 (vs) nikhaḍgaṃ (q.v.) tad vidur mantrī nikhaḍgaṃ cāpi khaḍginam (follows line 15 cited s.v. **khaḍga**, and seems to mean that khaḍga, nikhaḍga, and khaḍgin(a) are interchangeable terms); (2) m., a Pratyekabuddha (because he is often compared to a *rhinoceros*, Skt. khaḍgin; see s.v. **khaḍgaviṣāṇa**): Mmk 67.9, 14; 122.7; 156.7; 238.5; also **pratyeka-khaḍgin**, 108.23; 112.20; 114.21; 169.26.

khaṇapita, read khaṇāpita, ppp. of MIndic caus. to Pali khaṇati = Skt. khanati, *caused to be dug* (for cultivation): Divy 71.5 (vījaṃ ca) navasāraṃ su-khaṇapitaṃ (so mss.; ed. em. sukhāropitaṃ, very violently), kālena ca kālaṃ devo vṛṣyate . . .

khaṇḍa, (1) m., seems to be used not at the end of cpds. in the sense of *quantity, mass, large number* (as in Skt.), but in apposition to the noun, as separate word, if we may trust the reading: ye cānye parvatāḥ khaṇḍāḥ (2 mss. cited as puṣṭāḥ, ghuṣṇāḥ) SP 355.6, *and whatever other mountains there are, quantities of them* (?); (2) n. of the chief minister of a king of Videha: MSV ii.3.17 ff.

khaṇḍaka, (1) adj. or subst. m., *evil, false*: Mmk 73.13 (sattvā bhaviṣyanti kusīdā . . .) aśraddhāḥ khaṇḍakā (?) akalyāṇamitraparigṛhītāḥ . . .; Lalou, Iconographie 51, renders *divisés*; 94 she cites Tib. as mi sruṅ pa, which perhaps could mean *careless, disobedient, not on guard*, but is more likely a misprint for mi srun pa, *evil* (= Skt. khala, *evil, mischievous*; perhaps therefore, em. to khalakā); Gv 116.22 (mārakāyiko vā kalyāṇamitrapratirūpako vā) bodhisattvakhaṇḍako vā, *a rascal of a Bodhisattva*, or *a false, fake B.*; (2) n. of a yakṣa: Māy 41.

khaṇḍa-kāraka, m. (Skt. °kāra, id., plus -ka), *maker of candied sugar*: °kā(ḥ) Mv iii.113.8; 442.14, in closely parallel lists of occupations; in both foll. by modakakārakā(ḥ).

khaṇḍa-khaṇḍam, adv. (Pali khaṇḍākhaṇḍaṃ, id.), *broken to bits*: Mv ii.173.14 (prose) tad ahaṃ kha° chindiṣyaṃ, *then I shall be cut up into little pieces.* Cf. next.

khaṇḍakhaṇḍīkṛta (see under prec.), ppp. of °ḍīkaroti, *smashed to bits*: Mv ii.82.16 (tasya rājño . . . pādaphalakaṃ) khaṇḍakhaṇḍīkṛtaṃ.

khaṇḍa-mallaka (cf. **koṭṭa-, kroḍa-m**°), *broken pot, fragment of a pot, potsherd*: °kena MSV i.89.13; i.90.2; in same passage Divy 90.2 °mallake, but 89.21 kroḍamallakena, see this; Tib. on MSV rdzaḥi chag dum, *fragment of a pot*, and so Tib. on Divy 89.21 (letter from Mr. D. R. S. Bailey).

khaṇḍara (cf. Skt. Gr. and Lex. id. and khaṇḍala = khaṇḍa; in other mgs. literary Skt. has khaṇḍara, pw, and khaṇḍalaka, Schmidt, Nachträge, as equivalents of khaṇḍa), = khaṇḍa, *part, portion*, in vana-khaṇḍara-(v.l. khaṇḍa-, metr. bad)-gatā, *who were present in the grove*: Mv i.236.5 (vs).

Khaṇḍarohā, n. of a yoginī or similar demoness: Sādh 425.13; 427.7; 439.10.

khaṇḍikā (= Pali id.; in Skt. khaṇḍaka is, but °ḍikā apparently is not, used in this precise sense), *piece, fragment*: Divy 31.5 catasraḥ khaṇḍikāḥ kṛtāḥ.

-khattaṃ = **-kṛtvaḥ** for Skt. -kṛtvas, q.v.

-khadā, *pit*; see **agnikhadā**; also aṅgārakhadā, *pit of coals*, Av i.221.8 eṣāṅgārakhadā mahābhayakarī. See Wogihara, Lex. 26, where however it is said that the Buddhists use khadā *only* in agnikhadā (ignoring the above).

Khadiraka, m. (seems to correspond to Pali Karavīka), n. of one of the seven mountains surrounding **Sumeru** (Kirfel, Kosm. 186): Mvy 4143; Dharmas 125; Mv ii.300.18 (mss. corrupt); Māy 253.27; Divy 217.10, 12; n. of what seems to be a different mythical mountain, at any rate one of an otherwise different list of names of mountains, Divy 450.12; 455.29; 456.1.

Khadirakovida, n. of a yakṣa: Māy 236.29.

Khadiravaṇī-tārā, n. of a form of Tārā: Sādh 176.8.

Khadiravanika (cf. Pali Khadiravaniya, there another name for **Revata**, q.v., who in both LV and Sukh is mentioned as a distinct personage immediately before Kha° in the same list), n. of a disciple of the Buddha: LV 2.1 (v.l. °vadika, but Tib. confirms text); Sukh 2.9; Mvy 1066. Is it significant that Mvy does not mention Revata?

[**khadukatā**, misprint or error for **khād**°, q.v.]

khadyotaka, m. (= Skt. khadyota plus -ka; in BHS recorded only in vss, could be m.c., could also be diminutive; cf. AMg. khajjoyaga and Pali khajjopanaka), *firefly*: LV 120.11, 13; 304.20; 334.4 (all vss).

khandhāvāra (= Pali id., MIndic for Skt. skandh°), *army-encampment*: Mv ii.485.14 khandhāvārehi (so read for Senart khandha°; mss. khandhyā°, khandya°) kanyakubjaṃ nagaraṃ samantena veṭhiyāna sthitāḥ.

(**khanya**, *mineral*, cited once from late Skt. in khanya-vāda-vid = BHS °vādin, below, see Schmidt, Nachträge; cf. Skt. khani, *mine*: khanya-vādin, *mineralogist*, Mvy 3753; khanya-dhātu-kriyā, *the working of minerals*, Mmk 346.9.)

khambhīra-pati, Mvy 3702, or **khambhara-pati**, 3703 (evidently a v.l.; not in Mironov, who cites a v.l. khambhāra-pati; for 3703 Tib. miṅ dan, which I do not understand but presume means *idem*), some sort of royal officer, acc. to Tib. either mṅan bdag, *master of imprecations* (i. e. *royal sorcerer*?), or ṅan bdag, *lord of salaries* (i. e. *controller, bursar*?). The prior element is quite unknown.

Khara, nt., n. of a hamlet: Divy 577.11.

Kharakarṇa, n. of yakṣa, associated with **Sūciroma**: Samādh p. 43 line 19; cf. Pali Khara, associate of the yakṣa Sūciloma.

khara-gṛha, nt. (Skt. Lex.; see Schmidt, Nachträge), *tent*: Mvy 5542 = Tib. gur.

Kharapostā, n. sg., n. of a yakṣa: Māy 33. See Lévi 74, who thinks -postā preserves a relative of Skt. pustaka, which acc. to Gauthiot, MSL 19 (1915).130, was borrowed from Iranian pōst, *skin*; *ass-skin* is what at least one Chin. transl. renders; but there is some suggestion of a reading -lomā (Skt. loman) instead of -postā.

Kharaskandha, n. of an asura: SP 5.3; Suv 162.13. Tib. on SP reads phrag rtsub, *rough shoulder*, proving this reading as against Burnouf's (and v.l. of KN) Sura-sk°.

kharukharā-, °**khur-**, see **khurakhurāyate, khurukhura-** (°**rā-**).

Kharuṣṭa, n. of a ṛṣi: Thomas ap. Hoernle MR 123.11. (Cf. Lévi BEFEO. iv. 543–79, esp. 565.)

kharoṣṭī, kharostrī (AMg. kharoṭṭhī; doubtless Skt. but not in dictt.), n. of an alphabet: LV 125.19 °ṣṭī (Tib. kha ro stī); Mv i.135.5 °strī (mss., Senart em. °stī).

kharjuraka, nt. (Skt. Lex. kharjura; otherwise recorded only with ū), *fruit of the date*: °kāni Mv ii.475.16, so read; in a list of various fruits; so 1 ms., v.l. kharjuralatikā (prob. corruption); Senart kharjaralatikā (ja for ju misprint?).

Kharjūrikā, n. of a town: MSV i.1.20 f.

kharta, ? in Mmk 157.4 (vs) ūrū cāsya vartulakau, kaurparau kharta-varjitau, *and the elbows free from . . .*? Prob. corrupt, but I can think of no plausible em.; kharva- would be paleographically close, if only it made reasonable sense.

kharpara, nt. (= Pkt. khappara, see Sheth; Skt. Lex. kharpara and karpara; in Skt. lit. karpara, *bowl*, and once in late Skt. kharpara, said to mean *shell of a tortoise*, Schmidt, Nachträge; cf. next), (*skull*,) *head*: Divy 324.11 kharparam (so read with v.l., ed. kharpam) idaṃ gṛhāṇa (referring to uttamāṅgam in prec. line).

kharparikā (cf. under prec.; Skt. id. said by Galanos to mean *umbrella*), *bowl* or *bowl-shaped object*: ghaṭa-khar°, n. of a mudrā: Mmk 505.13 (vs) °kā jñeyā anāmikāgrasunāmitau (hypermetr.).

Kharvarī, n. of a yoginī: Sādh 427.4.

khalaka, (**1**) m. or nt. (= Skt. khala), *threshing-floor* or *granary*: Kv 28.18 (prose) mahā-khalake mahāntaṃ rāśiṃ kuryāt; (**2**) m. (= Skt. khala; AMg. khalaya, app. in this sense, Ratnach.), *rogue*, or adj. *roguish, evil, bad*: perhaps read khalakā(ḥ) for text khaṇḍakā(ḥ) Mmk 73.13; see s.v. **khaṇḍaka**.

(**khalakhalāyati** = Skt. °te, see pw, onomat., *rattles*; see s.v. **vikhala**.)

khalati (= Pali id., MIndic for Skt. skhalati, cf. 2 **khalita**), *stumbles, wavers*: khali, aor. 2 sg., LV 362.11 (vs).

khala-hāna (nt.; MIndic for Skt. khala-dhāna, see Schmidt, Nachträge), *granary*: °hāneṣu Mv iii.178.5, mss., Senart em. °dhāneṣu; see s.v. **saṃhārāpayitavya**.

khalābhidhāna (nt.; = prec.), *granary*: °dhāne Divy 577.12, 13, 14–15 °dhāne dhānyaṃ vardhitum ārabdham, 17, 18, 20, and 26 °dhāne dhānyaṃ vardhate (or °ta iti), *the grain in the granary increased*. Ed. takes the word as a n. pr., which is clearly impossible.

(**khali** = Skt. id., m., see Schmidt, Nachträge, also Pali id., (*paste made of*) *oil-cake*: Divy 343.9, 12, read khaleḥ (mss. khale) stokaṃ, or with Śikṣ 58.7, 9, citation of this Divy passage, khali-stokaṃ, *a little bit of oil-cake paste*. Divy ed. khala-.)

1 khalita, adj. (= Pali id., Skt. khalati, but note Skt. khālitya, *baldness*), *bald* (?): Mv ii.367.15 (vs) na so kubjo ca khaṃjo vā khalito vā vicakramo (so mss., Senart em. vicaṃkramo). However, it is possible (and this would come closer to the mg. of the surrounding terms) that it belongs to Skt. skhalita (see next) and means *stumbling, unsteady in gait*.

2 khalita, nt. (= Pali id.; MIndic for Skt. skhalita, cf. **khalati**), *error, false step*: Mv i.160.14 (nāsti) khalitaṃ (one of the 18 āveṇika buddhadharma); Bhvr. cpd. a-khalita (= Pali id., *free from false steps*, CPD), *unwavering*: RP 47.6 (vs) svarāṅgā akhalita-m-anavadyā sarva-arthānubodhā. See also 1 **khalita**, which may belong here.

khalu-paścād-bhaktika, adj. or subst. m. (= Pali khalupacchābhattika; see Childers s.v. pacchābhattiko, where the word is fully explained with Buddhaghosa's gloss), *not* (khalu, as in Pali) *eating after* (the time when one should cease): Mvy 1133 (Tib. zas phyis mi len pa, *not taking food after*) and Dharmas 63 (as one of the 12 **dhūtaguṇa**); Śikṣ 135.15 yadi punaḥ khalupaścādbhaktiko (one word) bodhisattvo vā glāno bhavati; AsP 387.5 sacet khalu° bhaviṣyati; MSV iii.122.6.

khalu-bhakta, adj., = prec. (doubtless due to metrical convenience): Laṅk 373.9 (vs) utthitaḥ khalubhaktaś ca . . . śuddhaṃ bhaktaṃ samācaret, *and arising without eating* (beyond the proper point) . . . *he shall carry on his eating pure* . . . (Misunderstood by Suzuki.)

khallaka, nt., Mvy 9021, acc. to Tib. chu tshags gru gsum, lit. *triangular water-filter*; to the lit. mg. of the Tib. Das adds '*(a leather water-bag)*'. Cf. Skt. khalla, acc. to Apte, *leather*, also *a leather bag* (so Skt. Lex., BR); acc. to BR *Düte, cucullus*. In Pali khalla- (and khallaka-)-baddha, only ep. of sandals (upāhanā), perhaps *bound with leather* (?). In Mvy prec. by **parisrāvaṇam**, q.v., and foll. by kuṇḍikā, *water-pot*; all monkish utensils.

Khallāṭaka, n. of a minister of Bindusāra: Divy 372.17.

[? **khalli(n)**, obscure and corrupt: SP 351.5 (vs) so dṛṣṭva teṣāṃ ca jarām upasthitāṃ, valī ca khallī (so KN em., mss. khalī, unmetr.; WT khaṇḍaṃ with their ms. K') ca śiraś ca pāṇḍaram, *seeing* . . . *their wrinkles* . . . *and gray head(s)*. Tib. seems to have no equivalent of the crucial word: mgo 'la skra dkar gñer ma kun byuṅ ste, (*them*) *having become all with white hair on the head and wrinkles*. A noun seems to be required for this word; if khaṇḍaṃ is the true reading, perhaps it could mean something like *decrepitude*.]

[**khallu**, corruption for **khāṇu**, q.v., Gv 482.7.]

Khalvavāhana, m. pl., n. of a brahmanical gotra: Divy 635.21.

? **Khaṣa**, m. pl., cf. **Khāṣya-**, prob. = Skt. Khasa, or Khaśa (cf. **Svaśa**), n. of a barbarian people in the north: MSV ii.31.17 (ff.) Puṣkarasāriṇo rājñaḥ Pāṇḍavā nāma Khaṣā viruddhāḥ; acc. to N. Dutt's note, khaṣa = **pratyantika**; Tib. cited as mthaḥ ḥkhob = *barbarian border country*, often applied to Tibet itself, and fitting Skt. Khasa. I assume that the Pāṇḍavāḥ are meant for the well-known people of the Skt. epic.

Khasarpaṇa, (**1**) n. of a Buddha: namaḥ Khasarpaṇāya (or śrī-Kha°) Sādh 36.9; 38.1; 42.8; (**2**) n. of a village: Sādh 42.11.

[**khāḍa**, error for **khoḍa**, q.v.: Mv ii.150.9, and (ed., without ms. authority) 152.3.]

khāṇu, m. (= Pali id., associated with kaṇṭaka, *thorn*; Skt. sthāṇu; a theoretical *skhāṇu is implied), *stump* (as a worthless and impeding element): Mvy 6970 °ṇuḥ; LV 39.22 (prose) vyapagata-tṛṇa-khāṇu-kaṇṭaka-. . .; Mv ii.350.18 (vs) khāṇū ca kaṇṭa- . . . (corrupt); Gv 482.7 (vs), cited Śikṣ 102.1, rāga-doṣa-tṛṇa-khāṇu- (Gv 1 ed. corruptly khallu-, 2d ed. and Śikṣ khāṇu-)-kaṇṭakaṃ. Furthermore read khāṇu for **khāṇḍa**, q.v., reported as mss. reading Mv i.215.14 = ii.18.10.

[**khāṇḍa**, read **khāṇu**, q.v.; cf. Senart Mv i p. xii: Mv i.215.14 = ii.18.10 (vs), read, apagata-tṛṇa-khāṇu (mss. reported khāṇḍa; in i.215.14 Senart em. khaṇḍa)-pattra-saṃkāraṃ (see s.v. **saṃkāra**). For Skt. khaṇḍa a corruption khāṇḍa is scarcely likely.]

khāta-rūpa-kāra, m., *carver, sculptor* (lit. *maker of carved or engraved forms*): Mvy 3799 = Tib. rko mkhan, or, tshud mo mkhan, both *digger* or *engraver*; Jap. *carver, sculptor*. (BR *potter*, perhaps because the next word is kumbhakāra.)

khādati (= Pali id., e. g. dantakaṭṭhaṃ khāditvā Jāt. i.80.14–15), *uses* (lit. *chews on*), a toothpick: Śikṣ 125.5 na purato dantakāṣṭhaṃ khāditavyam.

khādanikā (cf. Skt. and Pali °na), *eating, feast*: guḍa-khā° MSV i.221.17; 222.1.

khādanīya, nt. (= Pali id.), = **khādya**, *hard food*, regularly paired with **bhojanīya**, *soft food*: cpd. °ya-bhojanīya Mv ii.98.18; iii.272.1; Divy 85.19; 262.22; also triple cpd. with **āsvādanīya** or **svādanīya**, qq.v., as the third member: LV 58.5; 123.17; Mv i.38.7; Śikṣ 208.2; °ya and bhojanīya as separate, juxtaposed words, Mv iii.255.8; Divy 50.14; 85.25; Av i.64.9, etc.

khāditaka (Skt. khādita plus specifying ka, § 22.39), in ardha-khāditako, (a corpse) *that has been half eaten*: Mv ii.78.11 (prose) udakahrade ardhakhāditako plavanto . . . dṛṣṭo, *was seen, floating, a half-eaten thing* (corpse), *in the pool of water*; 11–12 tena . . . ārocitaṃ, Dharmapālo udakarākṣasena khāyito ti, *he reported, Dh. has been eaten* (khāyito, no -ka! simple fact) *by a water-ogre*; but again 13–14 paśyati ca taṃ . . . udakarākṣasena ardhakhāditakaṃ plavantaṃ, *he saw him floating, in the state of having been half-eaten by the water-ogre*. One ms. in this last passage has khāyitaṃ instead of ardhakhāditakaṃ; then simply *eaten*.

? **khāduka-tā** (cf. Skt. Lex. khāduka, *bissig, boshaft*), seemingly *snappiness, inclination to bite, bad temper* (of a horse): Gv 464.1–2 ājāneyāśvasamacittena sarva-khādukatā-(1st ed. °khad°; corr. 2d ed.)-vivarjanatayā; 494.17 ājāneyāśvabhūtaṃ sarva-khādukatā-vigatatayā. But despite the single Skt. Lex. citation, khād- means *eat*, not *bite*; it is not a synonym of daś-. Our word contrasts with **ājāneya**, like **khaṭu(ṅ)ka, khaḍuṅka**, and I believe it is only a rationalizing replacement of some form of that word, q.v. The reading khadukatā, once in 1st ed., may preserve the original short a of the first syllable.

khādya, nt. (also **khajja**; = Pali khajja; in Skt. seems to mean *food* in general), *hard food* (as in Pali); regularly associated with **bhojya**, *soft food*: °ya-bhojyaṃ Mv i.352.21; ii.171.10; 189.17, 18; 462.1; khādya-bhojyasvādanīya (see this last), LV 96.21. Cf. **khādanīya.**

khādyaka, (usually) nt. (m. Divy 404.16 f.; see also **khajjaka**, MIndic for this), some sort of *cake* or *delicacy, confection*; associated with modaka; (apparently never used like khādya or khajja, *hard food*, in association with bhojya, *soft food*;) as v.l. for **khajjaka**, q.v., Mv ii.190.6; Divy 130.21, see **akāla-khādyaka**; 285.25, see s.v. **ullāḍayati**; 404.16 f. khādyakā(ḥ), n. pl., with modakā(ḥ) 17; °kāny MSV i.238.6; Mmk 48.7 aśoka-vartti-khaṇḍakhādyakādyāṃ; and see next.

khādyaka-cāraka, m. (see prec.), *dispenser of cakes* (?), a certain kind of monastery official or servant: Mvy 9059 (prec. by yavāgū-cāraka, and foll. by phala-cāraka).

khānta-samācāra, adj. m., *of vile conduct*; synonym of, or variant for, **śaṅkhasvara-samācāra**, q.v.: Mvy 9141 (not in Mironov).

khāyati (Pali khāyita, ppp., only, Vin. iii.213.8; = Skt. khādati, khādita; § 2.32), *eats*: aor. 3 sg. Mv iii.299.11 na sānaṃ khāyi rākṣasī; otherwise only ppp. khāyita; Mv ii.78.12 udakarākṣasena khāyito; in 14 khāyitaṃ is v.l. for ardhakhāditakaṃ; khāyitā(ḥ) iii.72.13 (and 12 where Senart ākhāyitā with one ms., read either khāditā with v.l. or khāyitā; ā-khād- is Vedic only); iii.84.17, 19; 166.7.

khāraka (m. or nt.; perh. related to Skt. khāra, khārī, a measure of capacity), apparently a (large) number: Gv 396.20 lokadhātu-khārakeṣu, *in* (large numbers of) *world-systems*. Occurs in a long series of terms, 396.17 ff., all cpd. with lokadhātu and app. denoting large numbers.

Khāranādi (Skt. Gr. id. and Kharanādin, also cf. Skt. Kharanāda), n. of a ṛṣi: Mvy 3460 °diḥ.

Khāṣya-(lipi), (from **Khaṣa**, q.v., Skt. Khaśa or Khasa, n. of a people), a kind of script, *writing of the Khaṣa* or *Khasa people*: LV 126.1 (all mss. reported with ṣ; Calc. Khāsya; Tib. kha śa).

khikkhira, nt., presumably *staff* (cf. next and Deśīn. 2.73 khikkhirī = ḍumbādīnāṃ sparśaparihārārthaṃ cihnayaṣṭiḥ): Divy 570.7 Rudrāyaṇasya pātracīvaraṃ khikkhiraṃ (mss. corrupt, pointing rather to khikkhirikaṃ, see next) cādāya . . .; 16 idaṃ pātracīvaraṃ khikkhiraṃ ceti.

khikkhirika, see prec.; **khikkhilikā, °likā**, with various corrupt vv. ll., = prec.: Svay 101.8; 210.1; 219.11.

khijjati, °te (cf. AMg. khijjamāṇa, etc.; in Pali cited by Childers only from Clough, not in PTSD; MIndic for Skt. khidyate), *is tormented, wearied*, or the like: khijjitvā Mv ii.252.14, a-khijjantaṃ (pres. pple.) 15; khijjantasya 253.9, 13; khijjante (3 pl. pres.) 457.13.

khila, nt. (rarely m.; = Pali id.), *hardness* or *harshness of mind*, produced by the passions [rāga, dosa, moha], or the five hindrances [pañca nīvaraṇāni, = pañca cetokhilā], CPD s.v. a-khila), *harshness, hardness of heart, unkind* or *unfriendly attitude*; in Tib. regularly rendered tha ba, defined by Jä. as *bad*, by Das as (1) *rigid, hard, compact, firm*, (2) *bad*, (3) *anger*. Usually in lists of vices of all sorts; context often does not suggest precise mg., but note esp. Bbh 8.2 na ca khilaṃ dhārayati, na cirakālikaṃ vairāśayāṃ vahati; AbhidhK. LaV-P. iv.20 cetaḥkhila-mrakṣa-vastu, *la cause des endurcissements de la pensée et de l'hypocrisie* (cf. Pali cetokhila, above); RP 48.9 citta-khilena, Bhvr., *by a person having hardness of heart* (citta = cetas); Śikṣ 14.3 (vs) vyāpāda-khila-cittaṃ, *a mind* (full) *of malice and harshness*; 16.17 na khila-doṣacittam utpādayati, *does not produce a mind* (thought) *characterized by harshness and hatred* (**doṣa** = dveṣa); SP 94.2 (vs) bhikṣūṣu vā teṣu khilāni kṛtvā, *or having shown a harsh* (unfriendly) *attitude to these monks*; LV 56.20 (vs) na ca mama khila-doṣo (= dveṣa) naiva roṣo; 162.5 (vs) krodhāviṣṭā khila-mala-bahulā; RP 15.14 (vs) na khila mala na cāpi roṣacittaṃ; Dbh 25.3 krodhopanāhakhila-mala- (see **upanāha**); in more miscellaneous lists of vices, LV 35.2 vyāpāda-khila-doṣa-(= dveṣa)-māna-madadarpa-prahāṇāya; 42.5 (vs) vyāpāda-doṣa-khila-mohamada-; in LV 138.19 Lefm. khilo (m.), with ms. A (other mss. and Calc. khilā, less plausible); 279.8 (prose) Lefm. khilo (m.) but most mss. khilaṃ (nom. nt.) and in corresponding vs 280.5 all mss. khilaṃ; 325.15 khilaṃ (nom.); 357.6 khila-mada-doṣā; 365.17 trimala-khila-prahīṇa; Mv ii.295.9 khila- (Senart as separate word!) -doṣa-mohaṃ; RP 10.11 khilaṃ (nom.); Gv 54.7 (vs) māyā-śāṭhiyakhilaiḥ khilīkṛtāḥ, *devastated* or *made powerless by trickery, deceit, and hardheartedness*; Dbh.g. 42(68).13 khila-malavigatā.

khu, indecl. (also **kho, hu**, which are much less common; Pali only kho, except khv before vowels; AMg. khu and hu; all by the side of khalu = Skt. khalu), *of course, obviously, as everyone knows; clearly, certainly, you may be sure*; rarely in prose, Mv i.348.16; ii.165.15; sometimes khu is written in vss when a long syllable is required, e. g. Mv ii.199.19; 200.4 (Senart em. kho); but in e. g. Mv i.69.15 (vs) khalu is written, Senart em. khu, m.c.; other cases of khu in vss, consistent with meter, are SP 113.8; 229.13; 295.2; LV 91.17; 342.4; 366.2; Sukh 22.4, 15; Mv i.11.3 (em.); 126.13; 142.15; 150.3 = 218.4; 204.18; ii.6.10; 141.7–10 (em.); 143.2; 194.14; 201.4; 316.6; iii.77.14 (v.l. kho); 82.12; 134.20; 186.4; 259.17; 386.12; 452.14, et alibi. Cf. **khu-ssa.**

khuṭkhuṭā-(śabda), onomat., imitation of a sound (apparently of something being cooked or heated, cf. Mmk 318.24–319.5, in the latter yāvaj jvalati): Mmk 319.(6–)7 (manaḥśilāṃ haritālam añjanaṃ) vā śrīparṇīsamudgake prakṣipya tāvaj japed yāvat khuṭkhuṭāśabdaṃ karoti.

khuḍḍaka, adj., *small* (see s.v. **khudrāka**): SP 460.4 (prose; twice); v.l. Kashgar rec. for SP 95.5 (vs), text **kuṇḍaka**, q.v.

khuḍḍāka, adj., *small* (see s.v. **khudrāka**): Mv i.302.13 na cāti- (mss. cāpi) khuḍḍākaṃ na cātimahantaṃ.

khuḍḍīka, cited as v.l. for **kṣudrikā, kṣudrīka**, q.v.

[**khuḍḍulaka**, adj., Kashgar rec. v.l. on SP 94.7, see s.v. vrāṇika; may contain a corruption of some form of khuḍḍa-(la?), see **khuḍḍaka.**]

-khuttaṃ, -khutto = **-kṛtvā** for Skt. -kṛtvas, see **-kṛtvā.**

khuddalaka, f. **°ikā**, adj., = next: MSV iv.74.8.

khudrāka, adj. (= Skt. kṣudra-ka; BR 7.1736 and pw record khuḍḍāka, f. khuḍḍīkā, and khuḍḍaka from Caraka; cf. AMg. khuḍḍa-ga, -ya, and khuḍḍāa, khuḍḍāga, khuḍḍiya, but no penultimate long ī), *small*: SP 127.3 (with druma; Kashgar rec. kṣuḍḍika). See **khuḍḍaka, khuḍḍāka, khuḍḍīka, kṣudrīka, °ikā**, and prec.

khura (m.; = Pali and Skt. Lex. id.; MIndic for Skt. kṣura), *razor*: Mv iii.179.15; 270.11.

khurakhura- or **khurukh°** or **°rā-**, or **kharukh°**, **kharukhar°**, onomat. (Skt. has khurukhurāyate, *makes a rattling noise in the throat*; see next; cf. also Skt. ghurughurā-, Pali ghurughuru-, and ghurughurāyati *snores*; the next is evidently a var. of this), imitation of a hoarse or rattling sound made in the throat, characteristic of an old man: Mvy 4092 kharukharāvasaktakaṇṭhaḥ (so Mironov; v.l. in Kyoto ed. khurukharā°), = Tib. ṅar ṅar po, *hoarse, husky*; the same cpd., in same context, LV 188.2, all mss. but A khurukhurāv°; A kharukhurov°; Calc. khurakhurāv°; (Lefm. kharakharāv°;) Tib. as for Mvy. Is the form beginning khar° influenced by reminiscence of khara, *harsh*?

khurakhurāyate (onomat. denom., to prec., q.v.), pres. pple. °yamānāḥ, *snoring*: LV 206.12 (so nearly all mss., v.l. kharukharāy°; Calc. khurukhurāy°, as once in Skt., Caraka).

khurapra-vāra, commonly written -vāla in mss. (see also **kṣurapra-vārin**), *a guard against arrows, defensive armor* (cf. Skt. bāṇa-vāra); only noted in sa-khura°, Bhvr., *provided with*..., said of chariots (yāna or ratha), Mv i.261.12 (mss. sa-khurapra-vāśehi or -māṇehi, with rathehi, read -vārehi; Senart em. wrongly); ii.154.4 (°vāla); 156.16 (mss. °vāra); 420.13 (°vāla, v.l. °vāra); 456.11 (id.); 461.5 (°vāla); of elephants, Mv ii.420.10 (°vāla); 453.17 (mss. °bāla); 461.2 (text °vāla, v.l. °vāra).

Khuramālin (= Pali id.), n. of a mythical sea: °lī, n. sg., Jm 90.20.

khurukhura-, see **khura°.**

khurdati (prob. = Skt. kūrdati, for which Dhātup. records also kurdati, khūrdati, khurdati; and gūrdati, gurdati are surely variants of the same), *leaps, dances*, or the like: in a mantra addressed to a Buddha, Mmk 28.15 khurda khurda avalokaya avalokaya (impvs.).

khusta, and **khustaka,** f. **°ikā,** adj. (? cf. khuṭṭa = truṭita, Deśīn. 2.74; khuṭṭa(a), Ap., Jacobi, Bhav. 42.13; 76.4), ? in Divy 426.28 app. *bald* (of the head), (tasya tena vyādhinā spṛṣṭasya) śiraḥ khustam abhavat, yadā ca vyādhir vigatas tasya virūḍhāni śirasi romāni (so, °ni); in Divy 173.3 of a garment, app. *old, worn*, (tena tau kārṣāpaṇau) khusta-vastrānte baddhvā; khustikā, Divy 329.1, 6, of a religious text, in deprecatory sense, app. *poor, unsatisfactory*, perh. lit. *old, worn-out, stale, out-of-date* (fem. °ikā): ayaṃ tāvat khustikayā ekottarikayā dharmaṃ deśayati, amī bhikṣavaḥ tripiṭā dharmakathikā yuktamuktapratibhānāḥ, kasmān naitān adhyeṣayasi (read °ti?); similarly in 6; pw 7.336, mediating between these three occurrences, conjectures *abgeschabt* for the mg.; Tib. acc. to Dutt, MSV iv.27.1, note, rjub (rdzub?) pa '= *imperfect*'.

khu-ssa, cpd. particle, acc. to Senart = Skt. khalu svid: Mv ii.184.8 (vs) mā khu-ssa me nāga kṛtaṃ na jāne, *do not, O nāga, fail to recognize* (gratefully) *what I have done* (for you). In Pali -ssu, -su, -si occur for svid (Geiger 22; 111.1); PTSD s.v. su[3] states that sa and assa occur, allegedly for Skt. sma, but no such forms are cited in their alphabetic positions in PTSD, nor have I found any other record of them. Cf. **sva** (?).

[**kheja,** Laṅk 203.15, corruption for **khaja,** q.v.]

(**kheṭa-,** or) **kheḍa-**(piṇḍa) (Skt. kheṭa, *phlegm*, Caraka, see pw; = Pali kheḷa, AMg. khela), (a lump, mass of) *phlegm*: Śikṣ 130.18 (pretā...) ye varṣaśatena kheṭapiṇḍam apy āhāraṃ na pratilabhante; generally as symbol of worthlessness, LV 242.4 (vs) jahita mayā yatha pakva-kheṭa-piṇḍaṃ (see s.v. **pakva**); kheḍa-piṇḍam iva (mss.) anapekṣo jahitvā Mv ii.398.22 (vs); Śikṣ 193.11, cited from Samādh p. 17 line 15 (vs) prahāya rājyaṃ (Samādh text rājā) yatha kheṭapiṇḍaṃ; kheṭa alone similarly used, Av ii.113.1 alaṃkāraṃ kheṭavad utsṛjya.

kheda-tā (= kheda, see § 22.43; but possibly read **khedanā,** see next), *lassitude*: LV 237.1 (vs) ma janehi khedatāṃ.

khedanā (Skt. °na, nt.), *lassitude*: ŚsP 1462.10 (prose) na ca kadācit khedanopapadyate.

khelata, m. or nt., a high number: Gv 106.13. Cf. next, and **kheluda, °du.**

khelu, m. or f., a high number: Gv 133.21; cited Mvy 7891 as **śvelu** (n. °uḥ), q.v.; note that the variant **svela,** m., occurs with the same Tib. rendering, and that khelu would be an easy graphic corruption for *svelu (which could also easily be corrupted to śvelu). But cf. also prec., and **rolā.**

kheluka, m. (cf. AMg. khela, *acrobat, tightrope-walker*; Skt. khelati, khelana, °naka), prob. *acrobat, tightrope-walker*, in a list of entertainers of many kinds: Mv iii.255.12. Some such word may be represented by the corrupt mss. reading cited as kelukaṃ- at Mv iii.442.9, in a similar list.

kheluda, m., a high number (= next): Mvy 7771 = Tib. rdzi phyod phyod.

keludu, m. (or f.), a high number (= prec.): Mvy 7900 = Tib. rdzi phyod khyod, or rji phyod phyod; cited from Gv 133.23 °duḥ.

kho = **khu** (Skt. khalu), q.v.; this, which is the Pali form, is rare in BHS: in vss, where meter requires a long syllable, Samādh 8.25; Mv ii.57.22; but in Mv iii.79.12 prob. read khu with v.l., and keep kadācit with mss.; in prose, Mv i.144.10, 12; Thomas ap. Hoernle MR 133 for SP 327.3 (ed. khalu).

khoṭaka (see also **kṣoḍaka**), **khoḍaka,** (**kholaka**?), m. (or nt.; perh. cf. AMg. khoḍa, *log of wood*? JM. khoḍī, *box*? or Deśī khoḍa(ga), *peg, nail*?), some part or appendage of a wall or rampart; acc. to pw 7.336 *coping* of a wall, a mg. said to be that of Skt. Lex. khoḍaka-śīrṣaka; in Mvy 5529 text erroneously koḍhakaḥ, but vv.ll. khoṭ°, khoḍ°, one of which must be read; Mironov khoṭakaḥ, v.l. khoḍh°; Tib. lcog, *turret*, or śiṅ thags skabs daṅ sbyar; the last three words seem to mean *fit for, adapted to* (Das, s.v. skabs), and siṅ thags = *wooden enclosure*; this cpd. is used for khoṭaka LV 193.6 in Tib.; khoṭaka occurs: LV 193.6 (vs) parikhā-khoṭaka-toraṇāś ca mahatā prākāra ucchrāpitā; Mv ii.193.14, read, aṭṭāla-khoṭaka-racite dṛḍha-prākāra-toraṇe (see Senart's note on iii.19.17, p. 468); Gv 162.20 (mahānagaraṃ ... aneka-)-ratna-khoṭaka-pratimaṇḍitaṃ, 21 sarve ca te ratnakhoṭakā...; 167.17 ratna-khoṭakāni; 202.26 sarva-ratna-khoṭaka-racita-prākāraṃ; khoḍaka, in Mv ii.484.16 = iii.19.17 (vs) ete udviddha- (ii.484.16 mss. oviddha)-prākārā aṭṭāṭṭālaka-khoḍakā (in iii.19.17 Senart °kholakā with 1 ms., the other quoted as °ṣodakā, doubtless misprint for °ṣoḍakā = °kho°); Divy 220.21, read (teṣu prākāreṣu caturvidhāḥ) khoḍakā (mss. ṣo°) māpitāḥ; AsP 486.1 (teṣāṃ ... prākārāṇāṃ) ... suvarṇasya khoḍaka-śīrṣāṇi (cf. the Skt. Lex. cpd. cited above) pramāṇavanty upodgatāni. For another case see **kṣoḍaka.**

khoṭana, nt., see s.v. **utkoṭana**; true form doubtful, and etym. and mg. both obscure.

(**khoḍa,** adj., = Skt. Lex. and late lit., Schmidt, Nachträge; Class. Skt. khora, Lex. also khola; *lame*, in a list of adj. for bodily deformities, noms. or accs.: Mv ii.150.9; 152.3; 153.19; 156.11 (in 150.9 ed. with mss. khāḍo, mere corruption; in 152.3 ed. also khāḍo, but the only ms. khoḍo); in all preceded by kāṇo (or kāṇaṃ) vā, then khoḍo (°ḍaṃ) vā dadrulo (°lam, or other variant, see this) vā ...)

khoḍaka, see **knoṭaka.**

? **khodaka,** m. (so text; cited pw 7.336 as khoṭaka, without annotation; cf. next), acc. to Divy, Index, and pw, *pot*: tena śarkarā-°ko labdhaḥ Divy 29.14. This may be right; but if reading of text is correct, the word could be related to AMg. khoda (in khododaga), khoya, *sugar-cane*; or even to Skt. kṣoda, *piece* (pw s.v. 5); any of these mgs. would make possible sense. Uncertain.

khora (m. or nt.; cf. prec. and next), *alms-bowl* (so Tib., sloṅ phor): MSV iv.52.15.

khorakā (cf. AMg. khoraya, nt., *a kind of round shaped pot*, Ratnach.; cf. prec. two, and JM. khoḍī, *wooden box*; Skt. Lex. kholaka = pāka, *cooking-pot?*), *pot*: °kāṃ pūrayitvā (with guḍa, *candy* or *sweets*, solid or liquid) MSV i.222.14.

[**kholaka**? so Senart, Mv iii.19.17; but prob. read khoḍ°, see s.v. **khoṭaka**.]

? **kholā** (Skt. khola, m. or nt.), some sort of head-covering, *hat* or *cap*, or perhaps *helmet* (Tib. zhva, any kind of headcovering): Mvy 8612 na kholā-śirase (but Mironov khola°) dharmaṃ deśayiṣyāmi.

khosayati (cf. AMg. khosiya = jīrṇa?), perh. *wears away, wears off*: marditvā mama lāṅgūlaṃ khosayitvā ca vāladhim MSV iv.228.4; spoken by a wolf; Tib. yaṅ phyis (to ḥphyi ba, *wipe, blot out*?) nas.

khyāti-vijñāna, nt. (Skt. khyāti, *appearance, becoming known*), *pure perception, reflection* 'as the mirror reflects all forms before it' but *with no differentiation even of subject and object* (see Suzuki, Studies, 189 f.); function of the **ālaya**; opp. to **vastuprativikalpavijñāna**: Laṅk 37.15 ff.

G

Gagaṇa-, see also **Gagana-** (as in Skt. there is much variation, but °na seems commoner).

Gagaṇagāmin, n. of a former Buddha: Mv i.138.6.

gagaṇaprekṣiṇī-lipi, a kind of script: LV 126.10. Tib. nam mkhā blta ba, *sky-seeing*.

Gaganakāntarāja, n. of a Tathāgata: Gv 360.13.

Gaganakośānāvaraṇajñānagarbha, n. of a Bodhisattva: Dbh 2.17.

Gaganagañja (or Gagaṇa°, so in LV 295.10; Mvy 1336, but °na 700; °ṇa Kv 38.13 ff., 49.17 ff., but °na 39.8), (**1**) n. of a Bodhisattva: one of eight B's, Dharmas 12; Mmk 62.13; one of sixteen, Mmk 40.13; otherwise named Mvy 700; LV 295.10; Śikṣ 127.1 (from Dharmasaṃgītisūtra); Mmk 68.21; 406.3; Sādh 49.16; Kv, see above; (**2**) m., n. of a work: Mvy 1336 Gagaṇagañjaḥ, prob. = °ja-paripṛcchā, see note ad loc. and note on Śikṣ 33.11, or °**ja-sūtra**, q.v.; (**3**) n. of a samādhi (one of four listed): Dharmas 136 (°ṇa° or °na°).

Gaganagañja-sūtra, n. of a work: Śikṣ 33.11 etc. (perh. same as °ja-paripṛcchā, see prec.).

Gaganagarbha, (**1**) n. of a Bodhisattva: Gv 2.24; (**2**) n. of a dhāraṇī: Gv 66.19.

Gaganaghoṣa, n. of two Buddhas: Gv 258.9 and 285.5.

Gaganacitta, n. of a Buddha: Gv 259.14.

Gagananirghoṣasvara, n. of a Bodhisattva: Gv 4.10.

Gagananetra, n. of a Bodhisattva: Gv 3.3.

Gaganaprajña, n. of a Buddha: Gv 256.7.

Gaganapradīpa-abhirāmaś(i)rī (wrongly printed as two words), n. of a Buddha: Gv 285.7 (vs).

Gaganabuddhi, (**1**) n. of a Bodhisattva: Gv 4.12; (**2**) n. of a Buddha: Gv 257.2.

Gaganameghaś(i)rī, n. of a Buddha: Gv 284.23.

Gaganaśrī, n. of a Bodhisattva: Gv 4.4.

Gaganālaya, n. of a Buddha: Gv 284.11.

Gaṅga, n. of a merchant: Av ii.53.3 ff.

Gaṅgadevī bhaginī, AsP 352.1 (in title of chapter), or Gaṅgadevā bhaginī, 366.8, 13; 367.2 (v.l. in each of the three last Gaṅgādevā); 368.7 and 9 (here in both inst. Gaṅgadevayā, v.l. Gaṅgā°, bhaginyā), n. of a woman for whom Buddhahood was predicted.

Gaṅgapāla (= Pali Gaṅgamāla, in Jāt. 421, but there not an incarnation of Upāli; rather, he becomes a Pratyekabuddha), n. of a barber, previous incarnation of Upāli: Mv iii.191.8 ff. (prose). Cf. next.

Gaṅgapālaka = prec.: Mv iii.191.10 (prose).

Gaṅgarasthā, n. given to **Virūpā**, q.v., after her marriage to Gaṅga (see Speyer's note): Av ii.53.6 ff.

Gaṅgādevā, v.l. for Gaṅga°, see s.v. **Gaṅgadevī**.

Gaṅgā-nāgarājan, n. of a nāga-king: Mvy 3304; Māy 247.8.

Gaṅgika, n. of a householder's son of Benares: Av ii.181.6.

gaṅgeyaka, adj. (cf. Pali gaṅgeyya, Skt. gāṅgeya), *of the Ganges*: Mv iii.423.10 evaṃ āyuṣmato gaṅgeyakasya nāvikasya pravrajyā upasaṃpadā bhikṣubhāvo, ... *of the Ganges-boatman* (who took the Buddha in his boat across the Ganges). Or is this meant to be the boatman's name?

gacchati, seems to be used in the sense of Skt. tiṣṭhati, vartate, *exists, carries on*, or substantially this, in Mv i.22.11 (gharakehi) oruddhā chinna-īryāpathā (mss. oruddha chinna-ir°) gacchanti, (sinners in hell) *shut up in huts, get along with their freedom of action cut off*. So Senart's note. PTSD s.v. 5 gives a similar definition, but the passages it cites obviously do not support it. Here perhaps gacchanti Mv i.17.11, 12.

gacchantaka = Skt. gacchant(-a), *walking*: Mv iii.330.2 (prose) (kiṃ nu khalu purimakāḥ samyaksaṃbuddhāḥ) gacchantakā dharmacakraṃ pravartenti (the only ms. °tanti) tiṣṭhanto vā niṣaṇṇā vā śayantakā vā. No apparent reason for -ka. Cf. next.

gacchamānaka, = °māna = prec.: LV 235.8 (vs; here -ka may be m.c.).

gaja-karṇa, 'elephant's ear', as symbol of impermanence (for some reason which is obscure to me as it was to Feer and Speyer): Av i.144.9 (ime bhogā) jalacandrasvabhāvā gajakarṇa-sadṛśā anityā(ḥ) ...

Gajadeva, n. of a former Buddha: Mv i.137.1.

gajapati, m. or nt., n. of some unknown gem: Mv ii.311.2 anye gajapatīhi maṇiratanehi samalamkrtam (sc. bodhivṛkṣaṃ saṃjānanti).

Gajaprameha, n. of a rain-deity: Śikṣ 247.7.

Gajaśīrṣa, n. of a nāga: Mvy 3325.

gaja-śvasana (= AMg. gaya-sasaṇa), *elephant's trunk* (misunderstood by Senart): Mv i.216.14 = ii.19.11 (vs) °na-sannikāśā śāradamegha khapathe virocanti (so read, combining evidence of mss. and meter).

gajāśva, m., perh. '*elephant-stallion*' = *male elephant*? MSV iii.125.18. I do not know this use of -aśva; later in the story the animal is called simply hastin (126.7 etc.).

? **Gajomānikula**, m. or nt. (doubtless corrupt, tho metrically correct), n. of a country: Mmk 325.18 (vs) °kule cāpi siddhis (sc. mantrāṇāṃ) tatra pradṛśyate.

(**gañja**, m., occurs in late Skt., Kathās., Rājat.; Persian loanword, BR; also in the NW Niya Pkt., Burrow, Kharoṣṭhī Documents, vii; not recorded in Pali or Pkt.; *treasury, jewel-room*, and fig. *treasure-store* (esp. of dharma): dharma-gañju (nom. sg.) LV 73.16 (vs); dūṣyagañjāś ca vividharatnagañjāś ca 77.14; saddharmagañjaḥ Gv 163.15; sarvajina-gañja-rakṣakāḥ Gv 481.17; dharmagañja-paripālana-karāya (sc. Avalokiteśvarāya) Kv 35.7.)

gaḍā (= Skt. gadā), *club*: LV 305.9 (all mss.); 311.17 and 317.15 (in both v.l. gadā).

gaḍita (= Skt. galita, § 2.46; in Pali gaḷita), *fallen in*: SP 83.1 (vs) gavākṣa-harmyā gaḍitaikadeśā (mss. °śāṃ), *its windows and upper apartments* (so Tib.; but prob. rather, *its windowed upper-story-apartments*) *were fallen in in places*. (Tib. bral, *parted, lost, perished*; not to be connected with Dhātup. root gaḍ, āvaraṇe).

gaṇa-guṇa, adj. (cf. **caturguṇam**), *in many folds*: °ṇāṃ saṃghāṭiṃ śirasi pratiṣṭhāpya (as a pillow, Chin.) MPS 27.9.

gaṇanāgati, f., a high number: LV 148.7, cited thence Mvy 7970–1.

gaṇanāvarta-lipi, a kind of script: LV 126.7. See **āvarta**. Does it mean something like *mathematical writing*? Cf. also **śāstrāvarta**.

(**gaṇanā-samatikrānta**, f. °tā, *surpassing calculation*: SP 66.4 (prose); so read with all mss.; KN em. gaṇanāṃ sam°, which WT keep without note.)

gaṇa-bhojana, nt. (= Pali id.), *eating in a group*; forbidden to monks except for special reasons which are stated in Prāt: Mvy 8458; Prāt 510.3.

gaṇa-vācaka, m., *teacher of a group* (of pupils), *school-teacher*: °ko brāhmaṇaḥ ... gaṇaṃ brāhmaṇakān mantrān pāṭhayati MSV i.46.14.

gaṇika = **gaṇin**, *teacher*: Mv iii.392.7 (prose) -tīrthika-gaṇikā (v.l. °gaṇi), n. pl., *heretical teachers*.

gaṇitra (nt.?), Divy 263.9, acc. to Index *astrologer's instrument, abacus*; perhaps quite as likely, (astrological) *calculation*: Bhūriko gaṇitre kṛtāvī śvetavarṇām (q.v.) gṛhītvā gaṇayitum ārabdhaḥ, *Bh., who was clever at g., took śv.* (pw *chalk*) *and began to reckon*.

gaṇin (= Pali id., and more commonly AMg. id.; see also **kugaṇin, gaṇika**), *teacher*: SP 313.1 (vs) mahāgaṇī (n. pl.); 298.5 and 387.4 (prose) gaṇin- mahāgaṇin-gaṇācārya-; Mv i.74.3 (vs) para-gaṇī (n. pl.), *hostile teachers* (niṣprabhā para°); LV 243.19 saṃghe (v.l. saṃgha-) gaṇinaṃ gaṇācāryaṃ, and 20 saṃghe (v.l. saṃgha-) gaṇī gaṇācāryaḥ; read saṃghinaṃ and saṃghī (see **saṃghin**) for saṃghe; the corresp. Pali phrase (PTSD) is saṃghī (ca) gaṇī (ca) gaṇācariyo (ca), and Tib. has three coordinate epithets, tshogs daṅ ldan pa (= saṃghin), tshogs can, tshogs kyi slob dpon.

Gaṇendra, n. of a Tathāgata: LV 295.9.

Gaṇendrarāja, n. of a Bodhisattva: Gv 4.6.

Gaṇeśvara, n. of a former Buddha: Samādh p. 57 line 13.

gaṇḍa, m. (nt.? cf. also **gaṇḍikā** and **gaṇḍaka**), (**1**) *stalk* of a plant (in this sense, somewhat doubtfully, in Pali, see PTSD): ikṣu-gaṇḍā, acc. pl., Mv i.21.9; nāḍāṅkura-gaṇḍa- Laṅk 18.4; aṅkura-gaṇḍa-pattra- Bbh 99.24; esp. as possessing medicinal properties, gaṇḍa-bhaiṣajyam Mvy 5839; mūla-bhaiṣajyaṃ gaṇḍa-bhai° Bhīk 23b.1; mūla-gaṇḍa-pattra-puṣpa-phala-bhaiṣajya Divy 100.16; 109.25; 347.6; 486.16 (om. puṣpa); Av ii.133.12; bhaiṣajya-vṛkṣasya mūlato vā ... gaṇḍataḥ śākhātaḥ tvaktaḥ ... Śikṣ 21.17; (**2**) *piece, part, portion* (cf. gaṇḍa Kathās. 94.66 'fehlerhaft für khaṇḍa', pw, but?): madhyamako gaṇḍaḥ MSV ii.104.19; gaṇḍa-gaṇḍam, adv., *in pieces*, Divy 155.13 (see s.v. **gaṇḍaka**, 3); kati-gaṇḍā, *of how many parts*? (sāvitrī) Divy 638.2, sāvitrī tri-gaṇḍā 3; pañca-gaṇḍa-gati-cakra, Gv 484.9 (vs), *the wheel of the five-partite* (five-fold) *states of existence*, = saṃsāra-cakra, see s.v. (pañca-) **gaṇḍaka** 1; (**3**) *rhinoceros* (so Skt. Lex.; also **gaṇḍaka** 2, q.v.): Mvy 4793 = Tib. bse.

gaṇḍaka (m.? = **gaṇḍa**, q.v.), (**1**) *part*, in pañca-gaṇḍaka, adj., *five-partite, five-fold* (also gaṇḍa, 2), ep. of the (saṃsāra-) cakra or *wheel of rebirth* (not the dharma-cakra as absurdly stated in Divy, Index) referring, as is clear from Divy 300.8–12, to the five states of being in which one may be reborn (see s.v. **gati**), hell-inhabitants, animals, ghosts (preta), gods, and men: Divy 48.25; 180.22; 281.29; 300.8, 9; 301.18; 551.15; 567.10; Av i.50.13–14; 96.5; 104.5 etc. (and in Gv 484.9 pañca-gaṇḍa-gati-cakra); MSV ii.130.18; (**2**) *rhinoceros* (= gaṇḍa 3, q.v.; Skt. Lex. and Pali Lex. id., see Childers; Pkt. Lex. and Deśīn. 7.57 gaṇḍaya): Mv iii.303.10 (prose) gaṇḍaka-bhayaṃ vā (with other dangerous animals); (**3**) n. pr., given to Kāla, brother of King Prasenajit: Divy 155.13 (yatrāsya) śarīraṃ gaṇḍa-gaṇḍaṃ (see s.v. **gaṇḍa** 2; cf. Divy 153.28 ff. for the point) kṛtaṃ, tasya Gaṇḍaka ārāmika iti saṃjñā saṃvṛttā; 157.25.

Gaṇḍa-grāmaka, m., n. of a Vṛji village: MPS 21.6. Corresp. to Pali Bhaṇḍa-gāma; Tib. (dum, *a piece*) and Chin. support g-.

Gaṇḍavyūha, m. (in Śikṣ 2.3 °ha-sūtra), n. of a work, our Gv: in colophon, Gv 548.10, 11; Mvy 1341; Mmk 38.12; Sādh 10.11; various citations from it in Śikṣ, 2.3 ff. (Gv 116.16 ff.); 34.18 ff. (Gv p. 462.5 ff.); 101.13 ff. (Gv 482.3 ff.); 310.1 ff. (Gv 31.9 ff.); these quotations are all abbreviated; Gv contains in 543.9 ff. the entire text of Bhad.

gaṇḍi, only Divy 335.13 °ḍir, n. sg., usually **gaṇḍī**, q.v., *gong*.

gaṇḍikā, (**1**) *stalk* (= **gaṇḍa**, 1; = Pali gaṇḍikā, gaṇṭhikā): ikṣu-g° (= Pali ucchu-g°) Mv i.17.11, 12; (**2**) *piece* (cf. **gaṇḍa**, 2) or *block* of wood (also Pali id., more often spelled gaṇṭhikā): gośīrṣacandanasya tisro gaṇḍikā vastreṇa pidhāya Divy 31.27; (tisro) gaṇḍikā darśitāḥ 32.2; (**3**) = **gaṇḍī, gaṇḍi**, *gong*: Kv 13.8, read, dharma-gaṇḍikām ākoṭayanti (see **ākoṭayati**).

gaṇḍī (= Pali id.; cf. **gaṇḍi**, °**ḍikā**), *gong*; very often with a form of **ākoṭayati**, q.v.: Mvy 9155; gaṇḍy ākoṭitā Divy 336.11; 337.9 (cf. gaṇḍir āk° 335.13); Av i.258.9; 272.1, etc.; in ii.87.2 read with ms. gaṇḍī-m-ākoṭyatām, cf. Kv 36.17 na ca tvayā dharma-gaṇḍī-m-ākoṭyamānā śrutā (fig., *the gong of the dharma*); esp. as a sign of meal-time, gaṇḍī-kāle Av i.264.8; gaṇḍī-deśanā-kāle Av ii.95.1, app. *at the time of the manifestation of the gong*, i. e. at dinner-time, see Speyer's note; in Av i.258.1 and ii.10.8 is printed instead of this gaṇḍī-deśa-kāle, but Speyer on ii.95.1 would emend deśa to deśanā, prob. rightly.

gaṇḍīraka, m. (= Skt. °ra), a kind of pot-herb, growing in water: candana-°kaḥ MSV ii.64.11 (cf. **candana** 1).

gaṇḍūśika, °**mika**, °**ṣa**, see **kaṇḍūsika**.

gata, adj., ppp., (**1**) *understood, grasped* (hardly a Skt. usage; cf. however BR s.v. gam, ppp. gata, 1, l): gatam etad Divy 301.27, *I have understood this* (which you have said); etad api gatam 302.1, 5, 12; (**2**) extensions of the quasi-suffixal use of gata noted for Skt. by Whitney, Gr. 1273c; very close to the Skt. is perhaps Divy 29.21 ekasya gṛhagataṃ kṣetragataṃ ca, ekasyā-vārīgataṃ deśāntaragataṃ ca, *to one went* (in a division of property) *what was in the house and in the field* (? or possibly *the house(s) and field(s)*? as in dṛṣṭigata, rūpagata, see below), etc.; Śikṣ 246.16 (tatra katamo 'bdhātuḥ?) yad idam asmin kāye 'dhyātmaṃ pratyātmam āpaḥ, abgataṃ; aptvaṃ snehaḥ (abgataṃ perhaps *what is water*), snehagataṃ snehatvaṃ ...; on **dṛṣṭi-gata** and **rūpagata**, which seem hardly distinguishable in mg. from dṛṣṭi and rūpa, see s.vv. (the former is found in Pali, the latter in AMg.).

gataka, adj. (gata plus specifying -ka), *the one who has gone*: Mv ii.216.18 udakahārī gatako.

gata-pratyāgatikā, Bbh 122.18–19, or °**tika-tā** (v.l. gati-pratyāgatikā) 121.20 (cf. Skt. gata-pratyāgata, *gone and come back*), *the coming back again after having gone*: instr., (na ca bodhisattvo yācanakaṃ) punaḥ-punar-yācanatayā gata° °tayā (or, gati° °kayā) ... parikliśya dānaṃ dadāti.

gati, f., (**1**) (= Pali id.) *state of existence* into which rebirth is possible; *destiny*, (future) *state*. As in Pali, there are normally five: hell (naraka, niraya; nairayika), animals (tiryak, tiryagyoni, tiryaggata), ghosts (preta, yamaloka, °kika), gods, men; or six, with addition of asuras. The first three are evil, durgati (tisṛṇāṃ durgatīnāṃ SP 260.8, listed 9), or **apāya**, q.v. A brief summary of the 5 or 6 gati in LaVallée Poussin, AbhidhK. iii.11. Lists of 5,

Samādh 19.17; Divy 300.10–11; 301.20; of 6, Dharmas 57; SP 244.12–14; without listing, aniṣṭa-gati-(= durgati)-traya-, and abhimata-gati-dvaya- (= gods and men), Av i.244.14; pañca-gati- SP 131.16; LV 173.16; ṣaḍgati-, v.l. pañcagati-, SP 135.14, ṣaṭsu gatiṣu, or (vss) ṣaṭsū gatīṣū, gatīṣu ṣaṭsū, SP 6.9; 9.6; 48.3; 54.11; ṣaṭsu gatīhi (loc.!) Mv i.42.17 (vs); ṣaṭsu gatiṣu 337.5 (prose); six also Mv ii.368.12 (text uncertain); existence even in the relatively favorable states is still evil, cf. SP 48.3 ṣaṭsū gatīṣū parikhidyamānāḥ; in Śikṣ 147.14 a totally different list of four (evil) gati is given, viz. (1) akṣaṇa-gati (see s.v. **akṣaṇa**), (2) going to a Buddha-field which contains no Buddha, (3) birth in a heretical family, (4) sarvadurgatigati; (**2**) a high number: Mvy 7800; 7930 (cited from Gv); 8026; Gv 106.20; 134.5; (**3**) in **gatiṃ-gata**, q.v., perhaps to be taken in the sense of *understanding, comprehension, knowledge*; Tib. in this cpd. renders rtogs pa, *understanding*, and uses the same translation when gati is associated with such words as smṛti, mati, as in LV 8.2 smṛti-mati-gati-dhṛty-uttapta-; see s.v. **gatima(nt)**. See next two.

gatika, (1) m., *a recourse, refuge*: Kv 53.21 (prose) agatikānāṃ gatiko bhava, advīpānāṃ dvīpo bhava, *be a refuge for* (us, women) *who have no refuge*; (**2**) at end of Bhvr. cpds., = gati in various senses; *recourse, refuge*, agatikānāṃ Kv 53.21, above; *state of* (future) *existence, destiny* (see **gati**), saṃsārasya pañca-gatikasya Kv 69.10 (prose), *of the saṃsāra which is characterized by the five states of existence*, cf. (pañca-)**gaṇḍaka**; agatikā hi te tathāgatāḥ sarvalokagati-niruddhatvāt Gv 238.6, *for Buddhas are not subject to* (rebirth in) *the states of existence* ...; ṣaḍgatikāt (v.l. pañca-ga°) traidhātukāt SP 137.6 (prose); śūnyatā-gatikā ... sarvadharmās AsP 298.5; *passing away, vanishing, perishing*, vicinanti saṃskṛta-gatīkam an-āgatīkam (ī twice m.c.) Dbh.g. 11(347).2, cf. Dbh 31.5–6, and s.v. **an-āgatika**; sarvā dharmā ajātā anirjātāḥ anāgatikā agatikā nātra kaścid dharma utpanno ... nāpi ... niruddho ... AsP 162.2 (prose). Cf. next.

gatikā = **gati** (1), *state of existence, destiny*, in Tatpuruṣa (not Bhvr.) cpd.: RP 34.16 (prose) nīcakulopapattir durvarṇatāndhatva-gatikāḥ pāpamitrasamavadhānaṃ etc., (evil) *states of existence such as* ...

gatigata, adj. = next (unless misprint or corruption?): Mv ii.434.14 (prose) sarvatra niścitā gatigatāḥ (no v.l.).

gatiṃgata, adj. (cf. **gati** 3, prec. and next; nowhere recorded in this sense), *skilled, experienced, adept*; perh. lit. *gone to understanding*, so Tib. regularly, rtogs par khoṅ du chud pa, *entered within understanding*; some editors print gatiṃ gata- as two words, certainly wrongly; with loc. of the field of skill, or in comp.: loc., SP 26.5 (vs) gatiṃgato jñāni (most mss. jñāna; certainly loc.) anāśravesmiṃ (mss.); SP 131.3 (vs) sarvatra traidhātuki ye g°; 313.2 (vs) prajñabale; Mv ii.73.9; 76.14 sarvatra; iii.184.8 (series of locs.) ... iṣvastrajñāneṣu sarvatra; 386.10 nakṣatreṣu; 393.9 sarvaśāstreṣu; 419.2 parivrājakaśāstreṣu; RP 5.18 sarvasattvacarite; 10.16 śūnyatāsu; Suv 175.6 sarvaśāstreṣu; in cpds., Mvy 356 anāvaraṇa-; SP 3.2 prajñāpāramitā-; Laṅk 2.2.; LV 2.8, read with v.l. sarvabodhisattvapratisaṃvid-gatiṃgataiḥ; 179.15 upāya-kauśalya-; Gv 25.11 bodhicaryā-; 31.11, etc.; Sukh 59.4–5; alone, no dependent, Mvy 866; 2888; Sādh 15.17.

gatiṃgatvā, ger., to prec., q.v., *having thoroughly comprehended*, at end of cpd. in Laṅk 72.13 (prose) -pañcadharmasvabhāvanairātmyalakṣaṇadvaya-gatiṃgatvā, cf. 2.2 pañcadharmasvabhāvavijñānanairātmyādvaya-gatiṃgataiḥ; with acc. object, Sukh 36.12 aprameyāsaṃkhyeyāṃl lokadhātūn gatiṃgatvā (here perhaps in physical sense, *having penetrated, permeated*?) sattvebhyo dharmaṃ deśayanti.

Gaticandranetranayana, n. of a Buddha: Gv 284.20.

Gatipravara, n. of a kalpa: Gv 398.21.

gatima(nt), adj., *possessing gati* (perhaps in the sense of *knowledge, intelligence*, see s.v. **gati**, 3): Mv i.229.9 (prose) gatimena smṛtimena dhṛtimena matimena (of the Bodhisattva); cf. Pali MN i.82.37 adhimatta-satimanto, °tta-gatimanto, °tta-dhitimanto.

-gatīka, m.c. for **gatika**, q.v.

Gadgadasvara, n. of a Bodhisattva: SP 423.10 ff.

[**gantra**, said to mean *cart*, in Śikṣ 28.1, ms. ṣaḍgantopetān (hasty-ājāneyān), ed. em. °gantrop°; but Tib. clearly had ṣaḍdantopetān, see Bendall and Rouse, Transl. 30 n. 4, and this should be adopted.]

gandha-kuṭī (= Pali id.), name given to a special private cell of the Buddha (and a similar one of earlier Buddhas, so in Pali, and in Divy 333.4–5); esp. one at the Jetavana at Śrāvastī: Mvy 9151; Av i.96.4; ii.40.1; 153.11; Divy 46.5 and 13 (in both text with mss. °kūṭī); 333.4 (one ms. °kūṭī) and 6. (Divy., Index, wrongly °kūṭī). MSV ii.142.10 seems to imply that any monastery might be provided with one; in iii.133.6 ff. directions for its location (in general, in the center of a vihāra).

gandhatailaka, Mv iii.442.15, or °lika, Mv iii.113.10 (from Skt. gandhataila plus ka or ika), *dealer in perfumed oil*.

Gandhapura n. of a town: Mv iii.328.2. See s.v. **Kandha.**

Gandhapradīpa, n. of a Tathāgata: Gv 81.13.

Gandhapradīpameghaśiri (= °śrī), n. of a Buddhakṣetra: Gv 258.2 (vs).

Gandhaprabha, n. of a Buddha: Gv 284.21.

Gandhaprabhāsa, n. of a Buddha in the zenith: Sukh 98.16.

? **Gandhamadana**, n. of a mountain, = Gandhamādana: Māy 253.26. Occurs in Skt (pw), allegedly only m.c.; prose in Māy! Perh. corruption for °mādana.

Gandhamādana, (1) n. of a park in the city **Ratanakholaka**: Mv i.186.18; (**2**) n. of a pratyekabuddha: Mmk 40.22; 64.12 (here, acc. to Lalou Iconographie 35 n. 7, taken by Tib. and Chin. as two names; she follows them, but the interpretation is impossible in the other passages and must certainly be rejected); 111.10; Av i.156.20 (here a future pr. b.); (**3** = Skt. and Pali id., n. of a mountain, which in Pali is persistently associated with paccekabuddhas, cf. 2 above: Mvy 4151; Mv ii.53.17; 55.4; Divy 157.27 etc.)

Gandhameghavyūhadhvajā, n. of a lokadhātu: Gv 12.14(13).

gandharva, m. (cf. Pali gandhabbā, f., and Skt. gāndharva, nt., id.), *music*: Mvy 4954 (so also Mironov; short a may be MIndic, but note gender!) = Tib. rol mo.

gandharva-kanyā, *a gandharva-maid* (distinguished from Apsaras!): Kv 4.13 ff.; 62.5, 6. Cf. Gv 88.13 (gandharvendrān) asaṃkhyeya-gandharvendra-kanyā-śatasahasra-parivārān.

Gandharva-kāyika, adj., a class of devaputras: SP 4.15 °kāyikair (mss. °kaiḥ; ed. °ka-) devaputraiḥ sārdhaṃ.

Gandharvakāyu-prabharāja, n. of a Buddha: Gv 284.21 (vs). Read °kāya°? In a list of Buddhas. Or possibly, with different division of words, read Maṇisumeruśirī-gandharvakāyu (one cpd. word, n. sg.), followed by Prabharāja?

Gandharvagīta, n. of a former Buddha: Mv i.141.2.

Gandharvamādana, n. of a mountain: RP 43.4 (vs; meter correct). Does it refer to the well-known **Gandhamādana**, q.v.?

Gandharvarāja, n. of a Buddha: Gv 257.10.

gandharva-lipi (= AMg. gandhavva-livi), a kind of script: LV 126.2 (confirmed Tib., dri za).

gandharvika (= Skt. gā°; ă MIndic?), *musician*: Mv iii.111.20 (here Senart em. gā°); 113.2; 442.8 (all prose).

Gandhavatī, (1) n. of a goddess: Mvy 4324; (**2**) n. of a city: AsP 485.13; (**3**) n. of a lokadhātu: Gv 82.6.

Gandhasugandhā, n. of a lokadhātu: Laṅk 105.9.

? **gandha-hasta**, in sa-gandhahastaṃ LV 415.12, in a list of epithets of the dharmacakra; Tib. spos kyi lag ris daṅ bcas pa, *having perfumed lines-on-the-hand.* I do not understand the term. There is no v.l.

Gandhahastin, n. of a Bodhisattva: Mvy 704; AsP 474.2; Sukh 92.11; Samādh p. 36, line 1. The word occurs in Skt. and AMg. (°hatthī) in the sense of *an elephant in the climax of must*, i. e. in the fourth stage of must, described in Mātaṅgalīlā ix.15; this mg. is also found Mvy 8209, where °hasti-balam is contrasted with 8208 prākṛta-hasti-balam, *strength of an ordinary elephant.*

Gandhā, n. of a yoginī: Sādh 157.13 etc.; 324.6.

gandhāra, m. (**1**) (= Skt. Lex. id.; MIndic for Skt. gāndhāra), the third note of the gamut: Mvy 5030 (v.l. gān°, but Mironov gan°); (**2**) n. of a nāga-king: Mvy 3298; Māy 247.37.

Gandhārī, n. of a rākṣasī: Māy 243.17.

Gandhārciḥprabhāsvarā, n. of a lokadhātu: Gv 81.13.

Gandhārcimeghaśrīrāja, n. of a Tathāgata: Gv 311.15 (prose).

Gandhārciravabhāsarāja, n. of a Tathāgata: Gv 310.16 (prose).

Gandhālaṃkāraruciraśubhagarbhā, n. of a lokadhātu: Gv 81.19.

gandhika, (**1**) at end of Bhvr. cpds. (= Skt. gandhin; in Skt. only Lex., except pejoratively = *having only the smell* [semblance] of . . .), *having the odor of* . . .: Mv i.168.16 mukhaṃ cotpalagandhikaṃ, *and his mouth is lotus-scented*: Divy 120.2 (bhūmipradeśam . . .) niṣpūtigandhikam; in LV 293.5–6 (vs) prob. pejorative, as in Skt. (above), yasya guṇaiḥ satataṃ guṇagandhikā bhonti surāsurayakṣamahoragāḥ, *by reason of whose virtues the gods* . . . (etc.) *are* (or perhaps, with v.l. bhānti, *appear*) *possessed of a mere semblance of virtue* (in comparison); (**2**) m. (= Pali id., Skt. gāndhika), *a perfumer, dealer in perfumes*: Mv i.38.1; 44.5; iii.113.7; 442.13; in Divy mss. vary with gāndhika (see note on 348.23): ga° 351.2, 5; 647.3; 649.19.

-gandhinikā, adj. fem. (to gandhin-ī, § 22.34), *perfumed*, in LV 322.9 (vs) surabhīvaragandhinikā, said by the daughters of Māra of themselves, speaking to the Bodhisattva.

Gandhottama, n. of a Buddha in the zenith: Sukh 98.15.

gabhira, adj. (m.c. for gabhīra, gambhīra), *deep, profound*: Sukh 7.18 (vs).

gamantra, nt., a high number: Mvy 7882, cited from Gv 133.17; = Tib. gzhal ḥkhor, which seems to support **ga-mātra**, q.v.; prob. = **saṃgamantrā** Gv 106.7.

gamātra, m., = prec.: Mvy 7753 = Tib. gzhal (= mātra) ḥkhor (*go around*).

gamika, m. (= Pali id.; opp. **āgamika**, q.v., or āgantuka = Skt. id.) (a monk) *setting out on a trip*: Mvy 8747; Divy 50.27 āgantukasya gamikasya glānasya etc., Av i.87.3 (asti te . . . vijite) kaścid vihāro yatrāgantukā gamikāś ca bhikṣavo vāsaṃ kalpayiṣyantīti; id. 4; MSV ii.84.9.

Gambhīraghoṣasvaranādita, n. of a Bodhisattva: Mvy 686.

Gambhīradharmaguṇarājaś(i)rī, n. of a Buddha: Gv 285.3 (vs).

Gambhīradharmaśrīsamudraprabha, n. of a Tathāgata: Gv 282.9.

Gambhīranirghoṣa, n. of a nāga: Mvy 3338.

Gambhīrapakṣa, n. of a king: Mmk 621.2 (so read for text °yakṣa). Cited from Wassiliew by BR 5.1369.

Gambhīrabuddhi, n. of a former Buddha: Mv i.138.4.

Gambhīreśvara, n. of a Bodhisattva: Gv 442.18.

gamya, adj., *belonging to, property of* (with gen.): Divy 42.28 (yasya nāmnā vahanaṃ) saṃsiddhayānapātram āgacchati tat tasya gamyaṃ bhavati; 232.26 (after almost the same first clause) tasyaiva tāni ratnāni gamyāni; 243.19 (etat suvarṇam) asmākaṃ gamyam.

gamyate (pass. of gam, cf. BR s.v. gam 5; but I find no record of the pass. in this use), *it is possible, there is opportunity* (with infin.): Mv ii.248.(17–)18 yadi tava abhiprāyo, āgaccha; nānāprakārāṇi phalāni paribhoktuṃ tahiṃ gamyate.

Gayā-kāśyapa (= Pali Gayā-kassapa), n. of one of Buddha's disciples, mentioned with his brothers **Uruvilvā-kāśyapa** and **Nadī-k°**, qq.v.: Mv iii.102.13; 103.2; 430.13, 18; 432.8; SP 2.2; 207.3; LV 1.11; Mvy 1064 (Uru° and Nadī° 1049, 1050); Sukh 2.5.

Gayāśīrṣa, m. (= Pali Gayāsīsa, Skt. Gayāśiras, Gaya°), n. of a mountain near Gayā: Mvy 4116; LV 246.8; 248.7; Mv ii.121.1; 200.9.

gara-dattaka, adj. (specifying ka, § 22.39), *one that has been poisoned, given poison*: Mmk 53.26 (prose) °kaṃ (sc. ālikhet) ekākṣareṇaiva mantreṇaiva udakaṃ saptābhimantritaṃ kṛtvā tatraiva maṇḍalamadhye pātayitavyaḥ, mucyate. On the construction (*poison-given* = *poisoned*) cf. pw s.v. dā 10, garaṃ or viṣaṃ dā with acc. (as well as gen.); this is the passive equivalent of that syntax. Cf. also -garādi-pradattaṃ Mmk 82.13.

garahati (= Pali id., Skt. garhati), *censures*: Mv ii.376.4 (vs; metr. required).

Garuḍa, n. of a yakṣa on (Mt.) Vipula: Māy 5. Occurs as n. of a yakṣa also in AMg. (Ratnach.)

garuḍa-lipi, a kind of script: LV 126.3 (confirmed Tib., nam mkhaḥ ldiṅ).

gargarī (in Skt. *churn*; = Pali gaggarī, regularly kammāra-ga°), usually karmāra-ga°, *blacksmith's bellows*: LV 251.17 tad yathāpi nāma karmāragargaryāṃ (pw with only Calc. °rāyāṃ, rendered *churn*) mathyamānāyām uccaśabdo . . . niścarati; same figure Mv ii.124.12 karmāragargarī dhamyamānā; 232.2 gambhīraṃ sya (mss. °rasya) tad āśvāsaṃ karmārāṇāṃ va (mss. ca) gargarī.

Gargā (corresp. to Pali Gaggarā), n. of a pool at Campā where Buddha stayed: MSV ii.202.12; 203.1.

Garjanī, n. of a rākṣasī: Māy 243.23.

Gardabha(ka) (cf. Pali Gadrabha, a yakkha), n. of a yakṣa: °bha MSV i.15.4 ff.; °bhaka i.16.15; Māy 37; Samādh p. 43, line 20.

Gardabhakātyāyanī, n. of the gotra of the nakṣatra Pūrvāṣāḍha: Divy 640.20.

gardula, gardūra, gardūla (m. or nt.; = Pali gaddula, °ūla, *thong*), (**1**) *thong, bond*: LV 207.17 (prose) iha te bālā viparivartante kurkurā iva gardūla-(so read with some mss., v.l. gandūla, gadūla, etc.; Lefm. em. śardūla-)-baddhāḥ, . . . *like dogs tied to a thong*; MadhK 218.6 (sattvānāṃ . . .) tṛṣṇā-gardūra-baddhānāṃ (so mss., ed. em. wrongly °gaṇḍura; cf. Pali taṇhā-gaddūla-); (**2**) some kind of forest plant (perhaps one used in making thongs?): as fuel for fire, parallel with araṇī, Śikṣ 248.6–7, text garbhala- (corrected in ms. to gardūla, which read) -sahagatebhyo vā; eaten by ascetics, LV 213.12 (vs) śāka-syāmāka-gardūla-bhakṣāś ca; 258.10 (vs) syāmākasāka-bhakṣā mṛṇāla-gardula-kaṇā-bhakṣāḥ (here short u could be m.c., but it occurs also in Pali gaddula).

Garbha, n. of an author: Sādh 295.18.

Garbhahāriṇī, n. of a rākṣasī: Māy 243.19.

? **garbholika**, in upari-garbholikaṃ (to be read as one word; sc. āsanam) AsP 488.20, *having* (some sort of) *cover on top*; parallel to goṇikāstīrṇam, kāsikavastrapratyāstaraṇam (read kāśi°), etc. The word is otherwise unknown, obscure in etymology, and perhaps corrupt. Possibly read for the cpd. a word containing ubhayato-lohita-(upadhānaṃ, or the like), cf. Sukh 67.8; Mv ii.115.16–17; iii.70.2 (all similar passages).

galita, of Buddha's voice, perhaps *fluent*: Mv i.315.3

°tam (so or °tam mss.; Senart em. gaditaṃ, but his note retracts the em.) āviṣṭaṃ bhāṣati, metr. dubious; i.171.11 galita-pada-saṃcayavatī, of Buddha's voice. It would perhaps be rash to read agalita, which is used in Pali in the sense of (*not dropping,*) *fluent, distinct, agreeable* (CPD). Relation of the two forms obscure.

galli (v.l. gallikā; unrecorded; cf. **ardha-galli**), some sort of vehicle: Mv ii.434.8 (prose). Doubtless = AMg. (etc.) gaḍḍī, *cart.*

gava, m. (Skt. only in cpds., = go), *bull, ox*: SP 363.10 (vs) mahiṣā gavā ye.

Gavayaśīrṣa, n. of a nāga-king: Māy 246.28.

Gavā, n. of a **nagarāvalambikā** (q.v.) at Senāpatigrāma who gave a rag garment to the Bodhisattva: Mv iii.311.18; 312.12.

? **Gavādevagupta** (so all mss.; Senart em. Sarvadeva°), n. of a former Buddha: Mv i.140.8.

Gavāṃpati (= Pali Gavampati), (**1**) n. of a disciple of Buddha: Mvy 1051; SP 2.4; LV 1.10 (see s.v. **Yaśodeva**); Mmk 111.12; Sukh 92.8; Karmav 62.3; (**2**) n. of a nāga-king: Kv 2.10 (cf. 2 Gavampati, in DPPN, who had once been born to a nāga girl).

-gaveṣaka, adj. (= Pali -gavesaka), *seeking*: Sukh 8.13 (vs) śiva-vara-bodhi-gaveṣako.

gaveṣaṇā (= AMg. gavesaṇā; Skt. Lex. id., and Skt. °ṇa, nt.), *search, inquiring, inquiry*: LV 182.21 (vs; final metr. indifferent) paripṛcchatā kiṃ kuśalaṃ gaveṣaṇā.

gavya-dṛḍha, m. (Skt. Lex. = gorocanā), *a yellow dye made from the bile of cattle*: Mvy 5929, in a list of dye-stuffs (Tib. spyin, defined in Dictt. only as *paste, glue*).

gaha, nt., possibly MIndic for Skt. gṛha, *house*, but acc. to Chin. *a shrine, pagoda,* or the lower part of one; see § 3.90: Bbh 231.11, 26; 232.7. Cf., however, **gahastha.**

gahana (nt., or adj.), is sometimes, apparently, involved in word-plays with **grahaṇa**, q.v. (on the basis of MIndic pronunciation of the latter). In Śikṣ 286.1 (aśaṭhatā śaṭheṣu,) amāyāvitā gahanacariteṣu (this is the clear intention of the ms., see ed. note, and must be read), kṛtajñatā akṛtajñeṣu, etc., the Tib. is said to render *guilelessness among the guileful*, which is supported by the parallel phrases surrounding this. The transl. of Bendall and Rouse renders gahana-carita *overreaching*; it seems more likely to mean *of obscure, hidden* (or perhaps *tangled*) *conduct*, and so *tricky*. See next (apparently a quite unrelated confusion).

gahanatā (app. = Pali gahaṇa, below; cf. prec.), designates some sort of heresy: Śikṣ 172.3 (prose) idam agraṃ mithyādṛṣṭīnāṃ, yad uta gahanatā-dṛṣṭiḥ. Ed. note refers to Dhp. comm. iii.494.1 (on Dhp. 318 micchādiṭṭhi-samādānā) gahaṇa-saṃkhātāya micchādiṭṭhiyā samādinnattā, *from being taken by the heresy called gahaṇa*; the domal ṇ suggests connexion with Skt. and BHS **grahaṇa**, which Bendall says is also shown by the Tib. rendering, which he quotes as gziṅs pa (connecting it with ḥdzin pa). The Dhp. context suggests that it consists in taking what is sinful for no sin, and vice versa; perh. then lit. *holding* (perverse views on morals)? Unfortunately I find no other evidence for the heresy referred to, in either Pali or BHS. Bendall and Rouse: *the chiefest of all false doctrine, that is, the heresy of clinging to the world* (would this be called a *false doctrine*, dṛṣṭi?).

gahastha (cf. **gaha**; = Pali gahaṭṭha, Skt. gṛhastha), *householder*: SP 291.11 (vs), contrasting with pravrajita.

gāḍha (m.? = Skt. and Pali gādha; see also **gāha**), *firm ground, solid basis*: in alabdha-gāḍha (Senart °ḍhā, mss. °ḍhaṃ, which could stand as adv., °ḍhe, or once °gāho) Mv iii.284.2, 11 paribāhiro (q.v.) bhavati alabdha-g°, ... *not finding any basis* (support). Cf. Skt. agādhe gādham icchatām Mbh. (Calc.) 7.91; gādha in Pali often with esati, vindati, labhati. In Mv iii.285.13 mss. agāhe gāham eṣatha, which may be kept, see **gāha**; Senart em. agāḍhe gāḍham, which is read by some mss. in the same vs LV 379.11 (Lefm. with v.l. agādhe gādham, also eṣata). Cf. also next.

gāḍham, adv. (to Skt. gāḍha, adj., *firm*), *certainly, assuredly*; in this sense modelled on bāḍham, which is used in the same way in Skt.: LV 121.4 (prose) bāḍhaṃ gāḍhaṃ kriyatām, *certainly, decidedly let it be done.*

gādha (m.; in mg. *ford, solid ground, firm basis,* in Skt. and Pali, see s.vv. **gāḍha, gāha**), *basis*, in the sense of *occasion, opportunity*, (to do something, dat., quasi-infinitive): AsP 472.3 (avatāraṃ na labhate grahaṇāya) gādhaṃ na labhate.

Gāndharva, n. of a cakravartin: Mv i.153.16.

Gāndhāra, n. of a maharṣi: Māy 256.31.

gābhīra-tā, *deepness, depth*: Mv ii.148.3 (prose) (kleśaśatānāṃ) gābhīratā. Skt. Gr. records gāmbhīra, adj. acc. to BR, pw 7.338; but gābhīra-, if not a corruption, is most likely a replacement of gambhīra by the 'Morengesetz' (§ 3.3).

(**-gāmika** as in Skt. = -gāmin: in LV 397.16, vs, read with all mss. and Mv iii.316.20 pratisrotagāmiko mārgo, which Lefm. wrongly em.)

-gāminikā (to gāminī, f. of gāmin, § 22.34), *going*: °kāṃ LV 323.3 (vs), of a daughter of Māra.

gāyanaka, m. (= Skt. gāyana), *singer*: in lists of entertainers of all kinds, Mv iii.113.4 (here mss. śāya°); 255.12; 442.10.

gāyita (nt.), *song*: LV 194.4 (vs) no nṛtte na ca gāyite (Calc. gāyane, most mss. gāyate, ms. A text) na ramite.

gārava, nt. (= Pali id., for Skt. gaurava; vṛddhi to MIndic garu, Geiger 34), *reverence, respect*: Mv ii.230.7; 373.3; iii.345.18; 372.5; 430.11 (in the last three v.l. gaur°).

gārdha, nt. (so Mironov without v.l.) or gārdhā, f., *desire*: Mvy 2227 = Tib. zhen pa. In pw 7.338 this is called an error for gārdhya; but the latter is recorded only once in Skt. (BR 7.1738), and a vṛddhi formation in suffixal -a is as natural as one in -ya.

gārhapatika, adj. (to gṛhapati plus -ika; cf. Pali gahapatika), *of a householder*: MSV ii.161.6.

gāvī (Pali and Skt. Gr. id.), *cow*: Mv ii.125.4 (prose) gāvīye, gen. sg.; Sādh 182.4 and 187.17 (prose) raktavarṇa-gāvī-(text em. go-)-ghṛtena.

gāha (m.; MIndic for **gādha**, q.v.), = **gāḍha** and (Skt., Pali) gādha: Mv iii.285.13, mss. agāhe gāham eṣatha.

girā (= Pali, Skt. Lex. id.; Skt. gir, f.), *voice, speech*: SP 152.2 girām, acc. sg.; Mv i.163.16 -girāhi, inst. pl.; ii.143.23 girāṃ acc. sg.; LV 360.15 girā, n. sg. (all vss). See also next, **-giri-.**

Giri, n. of a nāga-king (cf. next): Māy 246.32. In LV 393.3 (vs) I am doubtful of -giri-, which seems to stand for a form of gir(ā), *speech, words*, and suggest em. to -gira-, m.c. for -girā, see prec. Text apagata-giri-vākpatho hy alipto, said of the Buddha: *unstained, because beyond the range of speech in words*; in Skt. (atīta-)vākpatha (not well defined in BR) means (*beyond*) *the range of words, inexpressible, indescribable*; some such meaning must be involved here. Mss. vākyatho, but Tib., otherwise not clear, confirms a form of -path(a): tshig bral dag gi lam (= *way*) gyis (inst.; does this point to a reading -pathā?) mi gos pa, which seems to mean *not stained by the way of those deprived of speech.* But Calc. and Foucaux understand apagatagiri as a separate word (loc. absolute), which may be right.

Girika, (**1**) n. of a jackal, in the Vṛṣabha-jātaka: Mv iii.28.8 ff. Cf. Pali Giriya, n. of a jackal, Jāt. iii.322.1; but the story is not the same; (**2**) n. of a nāga-king (cf. **Giri**): Mvy 3253; Māy 246.33; (**3**) n. of a weaver's son: Divy 374.14 (also **Caṇḍa-girika**, q.v.).

Girikūṭa, n. of a yakṣa: Māy 24.

Giripradīpa, n. of a Buddha: Gv 259.18.

Girimaṇḍa, n. of a yakṣa: Māy 38.

Giriyagra-samāja (v.l. Giri-m-agra°; MIndic for

Giryagra°; = Pali Giragga-samajja), nt., *mountain-top festival*, n. of a festival held at Rājagṛha (see Hardy, Album Kern, 61 ff.): Mv iii.57.6 Rājagṛhe ... Gir°samājaṃ nāma parvaṃ; also 12. Also called **Girivalgusamāgama**, q.v. Cf. **samajya**.

Girirāja, n. of a Buddha: Gv 258.17.

Girirājaghoṣa, n. of a former Buddha: Sukh 5.12.

Girirājaghoṣeśvara, n. of a former Buddha (in same list as prec.): Sukh 6.7.

Girivalgu-samāgama, m. (doubtless corruption for Giriyagra-) = **Giriyagra-samāja**, q.v.: Av ii.24.6 Rājagṛhe ... Giri°gamo nāma parva (mss. °vata[ṃ]).

girisāra-candana (cf. Skt. Lex. girisāra, n. of Mount Malaya, noted as home of sandalwood), *sandalwood from Mt. Malaya*: Mv ii.310.4.

Giryagra-samāja, see **Giriyagra°**.

gilāna, °naka (= Pali, both; Skt. glāna, BHS **glāna** and **glānaka**), *weak, exhausted, sick*: °na LV 189.19; Mv i.117.7; ii.153.19 (prose); °na-bhaiṣajya SP 13.12; 119.10; 284.8; Mv ii.221.5· °naka-tva, see **glānaka**.

gillapeṭṭa, adj., *pot-bellied*: Mvy 8889 = Tib. gsus ḥphyaṅ, lit. *with belly hanging down*, same as lambodara 8890; spelled **gillapeṭha** MSV iv.194.8 (here as term of abuse).

Gītā, *Song*, personified as one of eight deities or (324.6) yoginīs: Sādh 157.12 and 324.6 Lāsyā-Mālyā (324.6 Mālā)-Gītā-Nṛtyā-Puṣpā-Dhūpā-Dīpā-Gandhāś ca (324.6 °Gandhādy-aṣṭayoginībhir ...); et alibi.

Gīrghoṣākṣaravimukta, m., n. of a samādhi: ŚsP 1423.19. This form, which also occurs in other lists of samādhis in ŚsP, is corrupted in Mvy to Nirghoṣā°, q.v.

guḍa, nt. (in Skt. m.), *ball*: LV 339.11 (vs) kecit sumerusadṛśān (note m. form!) ayasā (v.l. °so) guḍāni ... nikṣipanti.

guḍāguñjika-bhūta, adj., Mvy 5391; so also Mironov; but guñjika seems impossible; see s.v. **guṇāvaguṇṭhita-bhūta**; the mg. of these two cpds. is substantially identical and both go back to one original.

guḍāyati (cf. s.v. **guḍuguḍāyate**), *thunders, roars* (of the noise of a thunder-storm): LV 308.4 (vs) deva guḍāyati (v.l. gud°).

guḍikā (cf. Skt. guḍa), in mālā-guḍikā (nānāpuṣpāṇāṃ) Mv i.302.16, *cluster* (of garlands); cf. (mālā-)**guṇa** (2), and Pali mālā-guḷa, -guṇa, id.

guḍuguḍāyate (onomat., cf. **guḍāyati**, and **gulugula** and following; also Skt. guḍuguḍāyana, *noise of rumbling in the belly*), *makes a kind of noise*, said of serpents: Megh 288.15 °ḍāyamānā(ḥ).

guṇa, (**1**) m. (Skt. and Pali id., not recorded in this use), *advantage*: Mv i.155.7 (vs) kaṃ vā guṇaṃ karoti, *or what good does it do? what use is it?*; (**2**) m. (= Pali guṇa), *cluster, bouquet, garland*: LV 214.19 (vs) sugandhamālāṃ guṇapuṣpasaṃcayāṃ (acc. pl.), *bunches of flowers in clusters, of garlanded flowers*; **kaṇṭhe-guṇa**, see this; mālā-guṇa-parikṣiptaḥ Mvy 9463. See also **antraguṇa** (in which guṇa may perhaps mean lit. *garland, chain*, i. e. of the intestines).

guṇaka, m. (= Skt. guṇa, in vallakī-guṇa, BR; perhaps -ka m.c.), *string* (of a musical instrument): Mv iii.82.4 (vs) ekādaśīṃ ca vīṇāṃ vādenti vallaki-(so Senart em., mss. vallihi, vallakīhi)-guṇakāṃ ca.

Guṇakusumasāgara, n. of a Tathāgata: Gv 310.4.

Guṇaketu, n. of a former Buddha: Mv i.137.10; LV 5.4 (confirmed Tib.).

Guṇakesarīśvara, n. of a Buddha: Gv 284.8.

guṇa-gaṇa, m., also nt., *reckoning, counting, calculation of virtues*; avoidance of this is a merit: (na) kaścid °ṇo 'dhigataḥ Divy 347.5, 9 (anenāhaṃ kuśalamūlena ..., in a **praṇidhāna**), 15 (kiṃcit ... °ṇam adhigatam), 19 (id.).

Guṇagupta, n. of a former Buddha: Mv i.137.11.

Guṇacakravāḍaś(i)rirāja, n. of a Buddha: Gv 284.25 (vs).

Guṇacakravāḍaśiru- [= śiro]**-megha**, n. of a Buddha: Gv 285.17 (vs).

Guṇacandra, n. of a Bodhisattva: Gv 442.19.

Guṇatejas, n. of a Bodhisattva: Gv 442.12.

Guṇapadmaśrīgarbha, n. of a Tathāgata: Gv 310.15.

Guṇaparvatateja, n. of a Tathāgata: Gv 311.6 (prose).

Guṇapradīpa, n. of a Buddha: Gv 256.6.

Guṇaprabha, n. of a teacher: Mvy 3486.

Guṇaprabhānodgata, n. of a Bodhisattva: Gv 3.26.

Guṇamaṇḍala, n. of a Buddha: Gv 258.16.

Guṇamati, (**1**) n. of a Bodhisattva: LV 292.20; (**2**) n. of a teacher: Mvy 3488.

Guṇaraśmidhvaja, n. of a Tathāgata: Gv 421.24.

Guṇarāja, n. of a Buddha: Gv 258.18.

Guṇarājaprabhāsa, n. of a Tathāgata: LV 292.19.

Guṇarāśi, n. of a former Buddha: LV 5.13.

guṇavarta, Mv iii.442.10, designation of some kind of professional man, seemingly a musician (cf. guṇa, *string* of a mus. instrument): **gāyanakā** (q.v.) guṇavartā **tāṇḍavikā** (q.v.). No equivalent in the parallel passages (see Senart, note on iii.113.2).

Guṇaviśuddhigarbha, n. of a Bodhisattva: Gv 2.25.

Guṇaśrīgarbha, n. of a Bodhisattva: Dbh 2.12.

Guṇasaṃcaya, n. of a Bodhisattva: Gv 442.19.

Guṇasamudra, n. of a Buddha: Gv 256.26.

Guṇasamudraś(i)rī, n. of a Buddha: Gv 284.19 (vs).

Guṇasamudrāvabhāsamaṇḍalaśrī, n. of a Buddha: Gv 282.17.

Guṇasāgara, n. of a Buddha: Gv 259.18.

Guṇasumeru, n. of a Buddha: Gv 257.11.

Guṇasumeruprabhateja (n. sg. °tejo), n. of a Buddha: Gv 297.2 (prose).

Guṇasumeruś(i)rī, n. of a Buddha: Gv 284.9 (vs).

Guṇākara, was prob. n. of a former Buddha in orig. text of LV 5.5, after Mahākara (lost by haplography), as indicated by Tib. yon tan (= guṇa) ḥbyuṅ gnas (= ākara). Is the same personage referred to in LV 73.22 (vs) udāgato Guṇākarasya padma ojavinduko?

Guṇākaragupta, n. of a teacher and author: Sādh 541.14.

Guṇākarā, n. of a lokadhātu in the southeast: LV 292.19.

Guṇāgradhārin, n. of a former Buddha: LV 172.9.

guṇā-bhūta, adj. (for Skt. guṇa°, with ā m.c.), *dependent*: Mv i.182.4 (vs) tasya sarvaṃ guṇābhūtaṃ atītānāgatasthitaṃ.

guṇāvaguṇṭhita-bhūta, adj. (see below for Pali), LV 205.11, *entangled in* (or *like; a maze or tangle of*) *cords* (*threads*). Corresp. to Mvy 5391 **guḍā-guñjika-bhūta**, q.v., = Tib. dru gu (*ball* or *skein of thread*) ḥdziṅs pa (*implicatus, embrouillé*, Dict. Fr. Cath. Miss.) lta bu, *become as it were mixed up in a skein of thread*. Parts of this old cliché in Mvy 5390–93 and in LV l.c., and repeatedly in Pali, see PTSD s.v. guḷā, which misinterprets; an approximation to the Tib. transl. of this word (with jāta for bhuta) is given in Pali comms., e. g. DN comm. ii.495.24 ff. LV: aho vatāhaṃ ... lokasya tantrākulajātasya (q.v.; so mss.) guṇāvaguṇṭhitabhūtasyā- (here Mvy adds **muñja-balbajajāta**, q.v., with Pali) -javaṃjavasamāpannasyāsmāt etc. (for the rest see s.v. **ājavaṃjava**; Pali lacks this part, at least in most occurrences). The tradition, both Pali and BHS, is confused on the form of this word, but there seems no doubt of the essential meaning, as stated above. Instead of guṇa, *thread*, Mvy has guḍā, *ball* (sc. *of thread*; both Tib. dru gu and Pali comms. prove this mg., against PTSD). In Pali the mss. in different occurrences show guḷā, guḷi, guṇa, kulā, kula, etc.; I suspect the orig. may have been guḍā (Pali guḷā), as in Mvy, but note the Pali v.l. guṇa as in LV; the mg. of the two is practically identical here. The second member appears in Pali as gunṭhita, gunṭhika, gunḍika, guṇika, ganṭhita, gandhika, etc.; in LV ava-gunṭhita, in Mvy guñjika which seems to be unparalleled and uninterpretable. The orig. was most likely gunṭhita; but possibly gunṭhika (Pali, prob. based on a MIndic gunṭhiya, really = gunṭhita), or gunḍita (AMg. gunḍia, °ya).

Guṇāsaha (? m.c. for Guṇasaha), apparently n. of a nāga: Mahāsamāj. Waldschmidt, Kl. Skt. Texte 4, 177.4 (vs); text printed guṇā saha; Chin. transliteration Yü-nang-so-ho = gu-na-sa-ha, acc. to W.

? **gunṭha**, m. or nt., *covering*?, in LV 284.15 (prose) (divya-mānuṣyaka-mālya-vilepana-)gunṭha-parigṛhītābhiḥ (nāgakanyābhiḥ). Tib. lacks vilepana, and for gunṭha (most mss. and Calc. guṇa) has brgyus pa, acc. to Das = grathita, *make a string of, stitch together.* If correct, the cpd. would seem to mean *enveloped in a covering of*...

guṇya, adj. (cf. AMg. guṇṇa; adj. from guṇa), apparently *relating to virtues* (guṇa, in some sense, not precisely clear owing to lack of context), the fifth sort of **puṇyakriyāvastu,** q.v.: Mvy 1704 guṇyam (without puṇyakriyāvastu, which is added to the first four sorts; possibly then as substantive?) = Tib. yon tan (regularly = guṇa).

gutti (MIndic for gupti, which is recorded in Skt. Lex. in this sense, and similarly AMg. gutta), *hole* or *cave*, used as lair by animals: Mv i.20.6 and 23.1 randhreṣu (? mss. corrupt) vā guttīṣu vā kārāsu vā bandheṣu vā sāhikānāṃ vā kiṃpuruṣ(ak)āṇāṃ (? see s.v.) vā undu-rūṇāṃ vā biḍālānāṃ vā ajagarāṇāṃ vā bile(ṣu)... However, the whole passage is doubtful; mss. very corrupt.

Gupta, n. of a perfumer: Divy 348.23; 351.5 ff.; 385.6; MSV i.4.2. On gupta see also s.v. **gupti.**

Guptakāma, n. of a disciple of Buddha: Mv i.182.20.

Guptā, n. of a yakṣiṇī: Sādh 561.2; 562.4.

gupti, f., in Mv nt. in form (n. sg. °tiṃ), in Mv sometimes written **gupta,** nt., seems to be false Sktization of the word which appears in Pali as kutti, apparently = Skt. kḷpti, *form, formation, fashion*: note esp. svara-gupti = Pali sara-kutti (Jāt. vi.293.19; Vin. ii.108.18, comm. 1202.6 = sara-kiriyā), *form* (timbre? so Lévi, JAs. 1915, I, 404 n.) *of voice*, Bbh 61.(18–)20 (yādṛśī teṣāṃ varṇa-puṣkalatā bhavati, tādṛśī tasya; yādṛśa āroha-pariṇāhaḥ, tādṛśas tasya bhavati;) yādṛśī svara-guptis teṣāṃ, tādṛśī tasya bhavati (Chin. acc. to Wogihara *sound*, i. e. perhaps *timbre, of words*); very similarly Divy 222.21 (Indra made Mūrdhāta like himself; there was no difference between them, na... nānākaraṇaṃ vā yad utāroha-)pariṇāho (so read with mss., as in Bbh; ed. em. °hau) varṇapuṣkalatā svara-guptyā svaragupter nānyatra...; see also s.v. **guptikā;** in Mv a dozen times in a cliché where gupti (sometimes written gupta) is parallel and synonymous with liṅga, dhvaja, and kalpa (sometimes ākalpa; cf. Jāt. vi.293.19 ākappaṃ sara-kuttiṃ vā na raññо sadisam ācare); with minor variants the cliché reads yaṃ (yat) kiṃci(d) gṛhi- (or ṛṣi-, parivrājaka-, tīrthika-)-liṅgaṃ gṛhi-(etc.)-guptiṃ (mss. sometimes guptaṃ, very rarely guptiḥ; Senart sometimes em. gupti) gṛhi-(etc.)-dhvajaṃ gṛhi-(etc.)-kalpaṃ (mss. sometimes ākalpaṃ) sarvaṃ (sam-)antar(a)hitaṃ (antarahāye), describing sudden and miraculous changes in heretics upon their conversion — they suddenly appear like Buddhist monks: Mv ii.234.(3–)4; iii.65.(3–)4; 92.(8–)9; 180.14; 181.5; 329.11; 379.14; 413.(11–)12; 423.8; 430.16; 432.2; here prob. belongs also ācāra-gupti-kuhaka(ḥ) śramaṇaḥ KP 121.3; 123.1, 8; ācāraguptiḥ kuhako 126.12; here Tib. renders literally, (hypocritical) *while guarding* (propriety of conduct); as KP 123 makes clear in detail, it refers to a monk who goes thru all the external proper forms of behavior but for interested, selfish motives (hence kuhaka); 2d and 3d Chin. translations render ācāra-gupti by (*having*) *dignity of demeanor*, and prob. gupti really meant *external form*, as very clearly in Mv. See next but one, and cf. **gutti** (for Skt. gupti, in a different sense).

Guptika, n. of a householder's son of Saupāraka: Av ii.167.5 ff.

guptikā = **gupti,** q.v., *form, fashion* (of voice): Divy 20.23, text parāntikayā (read prob. aparān°, see **aparāntaka**) guptikayā; certainly refers to the voice in which verses were recited. (Index *depth of voice*, certainly wrongly.) Same passage MSV iv.188.8 svara-guptikayā.

gumugumunti, 3 pl. (cf. Skt. gumagumāyita; AMg. gumagumanta, etc.), onomat., *they make a* (pleasant) *noise* (subject, lutes): Mv iii.267.3 vallaki-parivādinīyo (so Senart em., mss. °vādanīyo, °vānīyo) madhuraṃ gu° koṇa-parighaṭitā.

Guru, n. of a maharṣi: Māy 256.24.

guruka, adj. (**1**) (= Skt. guru), *serious, weighty*: praṇidhānaṃ gurukaṃ SP 242.4 (prose); *important* (of persons), *influential* (?), rājño kumāresmiṃ guruko preṣya(ḥ), tena bhūyo-bhūyaḥ pṛcch(y)amānena ācikṣitaṃ Mv ii.73.13 (prose; so read, with mss. except for parenthetized letters), *there was an important servant of the king in the prince's presence; he, on being asked* (by the prince) *repeatedly, said*... (Senart em. violently and needlessly); esp. at the end of Bhvr. cpds., LV 20.4, 5 (prose) yadā brāhmaṇa-guruko (and kṣatriya-gu°) loko bhavati, *when brahmans* (kṣatriyas) *are dominant in the world*; (**2**) (= Pali garuka) *bent, intent on; eagerly desirous, covetous of*, with gen. or in comp.; regularly of desires that are disapproved: lābha-guruko 'bhūt satkāra-guruko jñātra- (q.v.; so read with v.l. for jñāta-)-guruko SP 22.4 (prose); lābha-g°, satkāra-g° Mv i.89.12–13; jñātra-g° RP 34.4 (cf. SP 22.4 above); gurukaḥ Mvy 6773 = Tib. gduṅ ba, gdu ba, *longing, lustful* (esp. in bad sense); lābha-satkāra-śloka-g° RP 58.5; āmiṣa-g° RP 35.2; lokāmiṣa-g° Śikṣ 20.17; yācanaka-g° 145.2, *eager for alms*; upasthāna-g° 199.17 *covetous of service*; middha-guruko... kāyaguruko... sa tena middhagurukatvena ... kāyaklamathena samanvāgato na śrotukāmo bhaviṣyati AsP 245.9, similarly 13; also of desires which are approved, satya-g° Śikṣ 12.8; dharma-g° Śikṣ 323.1; dharmasamādāna-g°, saṃparāya-g° Bbh 7.1; samādhisaṃbhāra-g° Bbh 395.2; also **pratisaṃlayana**-(q.v.)-guruko.

Gurujanapūjita, n. of a former Buddha: Mv i.141.1.

Gurudeva, n. of a former Buddha: Mv i.141.12.

gurudharma, m. (= Pali garudhamma), *important rule of conduct*: Bhīk 4b.2; 6a.3. There are eight such for nuns, listed Bhīk 4b.5–6a.2; they correspond approximately, but with some variation and in a different order, to the Pali list Vin. ii.255.5 ff.

Gurupādaka, m., n. of a mountain: Divy 61.20, 22 (prose).

guruputraka, some kind of heretical ascetic or sectarian, in a cpd. containing a list of them: Mv iii.412.7 tre-(Senart trai-, em.) daṇḍika-m-ānandika-gu°-gautama-dharmacintikavṛddhaśrāvaka-(tṛtīyā ulūkapakṣika-bhaginī śramaṇā).

Gururatna, n. of a former Buddha: Mv i.140.14.

[**gurula,** in Śikṣ 271.13 anubadha(q.v.)-gurulādya-vavicārād, read anubandha-guru-(should be gaurava!)-lāghava-vicārād; transl. *after full consideration of advantage and disadvantage.*]

gurviṇikā (= Skt. gurviṇī; -ka prob. m.c.), (a) *pregnant* (woman): SP 363.11 (vs) striyaś ca yā gurviṇikā bhavanti.

Gulā, n. of a rākṣasī: Māy 243.14.

gulugula, onomat. (cf. s.v. **guḍuguḍāyate,** and see

the foll. items; cf. AMg. gulagula, gulagulāiya, *a sound made by elephants*; Skt. gulugulita, id., Skt. gulagulāyate, °lā-śabda, Schmidt, Nachträge, of the thunder of clouds), a sound made by serpents: °lena Megh 304.8; °la-śabda 308.18.

gulugulāyati (see under prec.), *thunders, roars* (of clouds): Mmk 294.12 meghā °yanti.

guluguluyati (see s.v. **gulugula**), *makes a kind of noise,* of serpents: °luyanto, pres. pple. Megh 304.19.

(**gulma,** a kind of fee, perhaps *transit fee, fee for pass,* or *customs fee*; occurs in Skt., Kauṭ. Shama Sastri 1st ed. 99.2; 143.4 śulka-vartanyātivāhika-gulma-tara-deya-, see Meyer's transl. 149 n. 1: Divy (Index wrongly *wharf-dues*) 92.27 na gulma-tarapaṇyātiyātrā-bhayam; 291.25 aśulkān agulmān muñceyaṃ, and ff.; aśulkenāgulmenātarapaṇyena Divy 34.13; 501.23; Av i.199.12.)

gulmaka, (**1**) (cf. Pali maccha-gumba, *a lot of fish*; AMg. gumma = samūha, Ratnach.), *bunch*: LV 72.6 (prose) māyā devī tṛṇa-gulmakam api dharaṇitalād utkṣipya. In the vs equivalent 75.1 tṛṇasya tūli; (**2**) (= Skt. gulma) *division of an army*: MSV i.95.20.

gulmalā, sc. lipi, a kind of writing: Mv i.135.7.

Guhagupta, (**1**) n. of a Bodhisattva: Kv 1.9; Mvy 716 (so also Mironov) = Tib. phug sbas; (**2**) so doubtless read in SP 3.11 for Guhyagupta of both edd., Tib. printed phug spas (both Burnouf's and Kern's transl. Guhagupta), here as one of 'sixteen virtuous men' (**satpuruṣa,** q.v.).

guhati? prob. error for **gūhati,** q.v.

guhā, *cave* as a residence for Buddhas (or monks): Mv i.54.5 (prose) sapta-ratanamayānāṃ guhānāṃ aśīti sahasrāṇi Arko rājā adāsi Parvata-nāmasya (sc. Buddhasya).

Guhāvāsinī, n. of a yakṣiṇī: Mmk 567.11, 21 (here Guhya°); 568.2 (here Guha°; the last two are prose and should certainly be read Guhā°).

guhmita, ppp. (falsely Sktized. form based on Pkt. gumhadi, Śaur., see Sheth, = Skt. gumphayati), *strung together*: RP 47.3 °tā dharmamālā.

guhya = guhyaka, see next.

Guhyakādhipati (and see **Āguhyakā°**), **Guhyakendra,** also twice **Guhyādhipati** (otherwise guhya for Skt. guhyaka seems unrecorded; the cpds. in Skt. refer to Kubera), epithets of **Vajrapāṇi,** q.v.: LV 66.5 . . . mahāyakṣasenāpatayo Guhyakādhipatiś ca nāma yakṣakulaṃ yato Vajrapāṇer utpattis, te . . .; plainly stated as ep. of Vajrapāṇi, Guhyakādhi° Mmk 36.2 etc.; Guhyādhi° Mmk 36.6, 21 (both prose; in 21 misprinted Guhyădhi°); Guhyakendra Mmk 548.7. Note that Vajrapāṇi is also called Yakṣendra (Mmk 25.12) and the like.

Guhyagupta, see **Guhagupta.**

Guhyasamājatantra, n. of a work publ. as GOS 53 (1931), ed. Bhattacharya; with alternative title Tathāgataguhyaka; but clearly not the work cited in Śikṣ as **Tathāgataguhya-sūtra,** q.v.; see Winternitz, Hist. Ind. Lit. 2.635.

Guhyādhipati, see **Guhyakādhi°.**

gūtha, nt. (Skt. Lex. m., nt., once in late and prob. artificial use, Schmidt, Nachträge, and in karṇa-g°, m.; see also **gūthaka, gūthoḍigalla**), *excrement*: Mvy 4064 and Mv ii.326.3 gūtham, n. sg.; Śikṣ 57.7 gūtha-; Mmk 60.3 gūtha-prasrāvam utsṛjet, so em. Lalou, Iconographie, 27 n. 5, with Tib. for text kuṭi°; ŚsP 1431.12–13, passage cited Śikṣ 210.14, akṣi-gūthaṃ karṇa-gūthaṃ, n. sg., *excretions from the eyes and ears,* in ŚsP both times °gūthakaṃ.

-gūthaka, nt. (Skt. m., only karṇa-g°) in akṣi-, karṇa-g°, see s.v. **gūtha.**

gūthoḍigalla (m. or nt.; gūtha plus **uḍi°**. q.v. or oḍi°?), *cesspool*: SP 144.10 (prose; cited s.v. **syandanikā**); 148.12 apagatagūthoḍigallaṃ (of a Buddhakṣetra), *free of cesspools*; here ed. says mss. all read gūthoḍillaṃ or gūthoḍyaṃ, but Kern, note to Transl., SBE 21.146, quotes the mss. as gūthoḍigalla or °gilla; in SP 425.10 (prose) all mss. are said to read gūthoḍilla (except one °ila)-paripūrṇā. A form of the same word is surely intended by MSV iv.230.8 gūthoḍīraṃ (n. sg. nt.; so ms.; ed. em. gūthādhāraṃ).

gūhati, gūhayati (perhaps connected with Skt. Gr. gumpha(ya)ti, Pali ogumpheti; see **avagūhayati**), *winds* (garlands): Mv ii.426.19 mālāṃ gūhayati; 427.4 (prose) mālāṃ guhāhi (impv.; short u!); iii.4.1. mālāṃ . . . gūhasi (impv. in mg.), v.l. guhasi (unmetrical; cf. preceding citation; the short u is prob. erroneous).

gṛddha (AMg. giddha; semi-MIndic for Skt. gṛdhra; in Pali aberrantly gijjha), *vulture*: LV 77.15 (prose), text gṛdha, prob. intending gṛddha, the reading of Weller's ms. 1; 249.1 (prose, no v.l.); Mv iii.456.1 (no v.l.); also in the mountain name Gṛddha-kūṭa (by the side of Gṛdhra-, also recorded Mv, see Index), Mv i.193.8; ii.257.6; iii.197.12, 15; 224.1.

gṛddhi, f. (= Pali giddhi), *greed, eager desire*: Mvy 2226; Śikṣ 39.15 (not 'for gṛdhyam' as Bendall's note suggests); 137.4; Bbh 129.19; AsP 92.2; Jm 136.9.

gṛdhriṇī (for Skt. gṛdhrī; formed to gṛdhra as yakṣiṇī to yakṣa), *female vulture*: MSV ii.35.7 (prose).

gṛhatara, nt. (compv. to Skt. gṛha; cf. Renou, Gr. scte. 237), *superior house,* the comp. suffix prob. complimentary; or possibly *something like a house* (like aśvatara, *mule*): LV 59.19 śuddhodanena manuṣyātikrāntaṃ divyāsaṃprāptaṃ (*surpassing human but not equalling divine workmanship*) gṛhataraṃ pratisaṃskāritam abhūt (for Māyā).

gṛhapati (= Pali gahapati), lit. *householder,* in °ti-ratna, as one of the 7 'jewels' of a cakravartin: LV 14.5; Mv i.49.4; 193.17, etc., see the lists s.v. **ratna** (3). The function of the gṛhapati-ratna is to discern the location of hidden treasures by means of the divya-cakṣus which he possesses, and bring those of them which are ownerless (asvāmika) into the possession of the king: LV 17.17–22; substantially the same statement in Pali, DN ii.176.7 ff. For this reason, no doubt, PTSD s.v. ratna translates gahapati by *treasurer*; but there is no clear evidence that he had precisely the functions which we should associate with that title. In Pali a gahapati (see PTSD s.v.) is, to be sure, often associated with seṭṭhi = śreṣṭhin; the Pali word is often rendered *treasurer*, but perhaps *capitalist* would be better (orig. *guild-leader*).

gṛhapatika (= °pati, plus -ka; = Pali gaha°), *householder,* in cpd. brāhmaṇa-gṛ° (= Pali brāhmaṇa-ga°), *brahmans and* . . .: Mv iii.317.6, 10; 318.13; 441.21; Śikṣ 38.2.

gṛhāvāsa, m. (= Pali gharāvāsa; cf. Skt. gṛha-vāsa), *living at home, in the householder's state,* contrasted with ascetic life: RP 12.16 (prose), where Finot em. gṛha°; Jm 181.21 (mss.; Kern em. gṛha°); Mv iii.50.12, text gṛhā°, to be sure with v.l. gṛha°. Pali seems to support gṛhā° adequately, tho elsewhere (e. g. Mv ii.69.1; 117.19) the regular Skt. gṛha° occurs.

[**gṛhīṇa,** RP 29.11 (vs), taken by Finot, p. X, line 5, as n. sg. = Skt. gṛhī; I think we should emend to gṛhī na. Read: gṛddho gṛhī na tathā kāmair yādṛśe pravrajitva te gṛddhāḥ, *a householder is not so eager for pleasures as they are eager, after becoming monks* (said of wicked and degenerate monks).]

gṛhītaka (Skt. gṛhīta plus specifying ka, § 22.39), *the one that has been caught, taken*: Mv ii.179.9; Mmk 82.25–26.

gṛhṇana (nt.; nom. act. to gṛhṇati with suffix ana), *act of taking, grasping*: Mmk 118.17 śodhana-vedhana-gṛhṇana-virecanādīni karmāṇi.

geya, nt. (= Pali geyya), the second in the traditional Pali-BHS list of nine (in Mvy twelve) types of Buddhist sacred literature, classified by form and content; *mingled prose and verse*: (sūtraṃ) geyaṃ (Mvy gey(y)aṃ, but Mironov only geyaṃ) (vyākaraṇaṃ...) Mvy 1268; Dharmas 62; (sūtrāṇi... gāthā itivṛttakaṃ jātakam adbhutaṃ ca,) nidāna... geyaṃ ca bhāṣāmi tathopadeśān SP 45.(7–)8 (vss). Tib. on Mvy dbyaṅs kyis bsñad pa, app. *narration with verses*.

Geya-rājan, n. or title of a cakravartin: Mvy 3593; first element confirmed by Tib. glu dbyaṅs, *song*. The adjoining parallel names, all ending in -rājan, suggest that Geya- was a locality; perh. cf. Geyamālava or -marthaka (?), Kirfel, Kosm. 74 (from Purāṇas).

gela, m., a high number: Mvy 7762 = Tib. phyag phyig (= next).

gelu, m. (or f.), a high number: geluḥ Mvy 7890, cited from Gv 133.20; = Tib. phyag phyig (= prec.).

gailānya, nt. (or m.? = Pali gelañña; § 3.70; cf. **glānya**), *sickness*: Mv iii.165.1 (prose, em., but certain; mss. glaināṇyaṃ); KP 65.6 (prose, text gelānyaṃ); 118.3 (prose) dvau... gailānyo (read °nyau, dual; as if masc.!; in 1 above glānyau, in 7 below dve... glānye, nt. dual!); 119.1 (prose) dvau... gailānyau (in 2–3 dvau... glānyo, read °yau); Samādh p. 52 line 25 (vs) gailānyu (for °yaṃ); acc. to Kern, Preface vii, viii, SP Kashgar rec. has (manda-) gailānya for (manda-)glān(y)a of Nep.

go-kaṇṭaka (Skt. Lex., of ground, roads; cf. Pali gokaṇṭaka-hata, of ground, bhūmi; alleged in Skt. Lex. also to mean *the hoofs of cattle*), lit. apparently *having cattle as 'thorns' = enemies, afflictions; trampled by cattle*, of grain: Divy 19.19 kharā bhūmī, gokaṇṭakā dhānā (so mss., ed. em. dhānāḥ). The Pali cpd. could be rendered consistently with this: *afflicted because of being trampled by cattle*. This seems to be substantially what is meant by AN comm. ii.225.11–15.

Gokarṇa, n. of a mountain: Māy 254.5.

goghātaka (= Pali id.), *beef-butcher*: Mvy 3761; °ko vā goghātakāntevāsī vā Mv ii.125.3–4; Śikṣ 210.4.

gocara, m., (**1**) as in Skt., *scope, range*: Laṅk 1.11 svacitta-dṛśya-gocara-parijñāna-, *knowledge of what has as its scope things perceptible to their own minds* (Suzuki, ... *the objective world as the manifestation of their own Mind*, which is not what the words say); pratyātma-gatigocaram, *what has as its scope the course of the individual self*, Laṅk 4.16; 5.5; 7.8, 11; atra gambhīre buddhagocare Śikṣ 174.9, *in regard to this profound sphere* (range, scope) *of the Buddha(s)*; similarly tathāgatagocarābhirataḥ LV 180.13; dhyāna-gocarāṇāṃ... laukikasamādhīnāṃ LV 244.4; etc., common, but hardly transcending Skt. limits; (**2**) (also quite close to Skt. usage, but closer to Pali locutions), *association, the range of persons with whom one associates*; in comp. or parallel with ācāra, *right conduct*; so also in Pali, ācāra-gocara-(dvandva! as all comms. agree; PTSD wrongly)-sampanna, *perfect in conduct and personal associations*, fully explained Vism. 17 f., where proper gocara is defined as avoiding the company of immoral persons, kings and courtiers, heretics, and impious families; so in SP 275.6 a Bodhisattva must be ācāragocara-pratiṣṭhita, *fixed in* (right) *conduct and associations*, which, as the following makes clear, means (besides good conduct, ācāra) avoidance of kings and courtiers, heretics, worldlings, or even followers of the Hīnayāna (276.1–11, in response to 275.11 katamaś ca... bodhisattvasya... gocaraḥ); in this sense, saṃtoṣaṇīyā me sabrahmacāriṇo, yad uta tena tenācāra-gocara-samudācāreṇeti nihatamāno bhavati (does samudācāra, as third member of the cpd., mean *address, manner of speaking to people*?) Śikṣ 150.21; prob. also saṃgaṇikayāpi vivekagocaraḥ Śikṣ 202.20, *even with company, he is in association with solitude*, i. e. he is not contaminated or distracted by crowds; (**3**) (= Pali id.) *sustenance, provisions, food*; particularly used (as in Pali) of food for monks: supriyā śrāvastīm abhisamprasthitā gocaravyavalokanārthaṃ Av ii.9.1; (pātracīvaram ādāya) śrāvastīṃ gocarāya prasthitaḥ 114.9; gocara-grāma (= Pali °gāma), *sustenance-village*, a village where food is supplied to monks, Mv ii.123.19; 127.14; 129.1; 130.4; 131.4; LV 248.9 (read °grāmaṃ with ms. A for ed. °grāmāṃ); 255.3; 267.12; Av ii.145.3; 164.6. Cf. also **gocarika** (1).

Gocarapariśuddha, nt., n. of a work: Mvy 1376. Cf. next.

Gocarapariśuddhi-sūtra, n. of a work (same as prec.?): Śikṣ 350.21.

—**gocarika**, adj., (**1**) *providing sustenance* (see s.v. **gocara**, 3) *for*... (monks): (tatraiko) baṇig bhikṣugocarikaḥ Divy 307.21; (**2**) (= Pali gocariya, see below), ? an epithet of wool, some of which is to be used in making coverlets for monks, Prāt 496.10, 12; they are to be made of two parts 'pure black' (śuddha-kāḍānāṃ) wool, one part white (avadātānāṃ), and the fourth part gocarikānāṃ (gen. pl.), which acc. to Finot is rendered in Chin. by (wool) *of inferior quality*. In the close Pali parallel Vin. iii.226.25 ff. (ignored in PTSD; Childers records it from Minayeff's Prātimokṣa S.) the corresponding epithet, gocariya, is said by the comm. 684.21 to mean *tawny* (kapilavaṇṇānaṃ); this is adopted by Childers; also transl. SBE 13.25 'of the colour of oxen (reddish brown)', or (below) 'tawny'; it seems like a dubious guess.

gocarin, adj., *having as one's scope* or *sphere*; *devoted to*: rājyakāryu no karoti dharmam eva gocarī LV 76.4 (vs), *does not perform the business of kingship, being devoted only to religion* (or dharmam eva may depend on implied karoti).

gocarī (°ri?), f. (not in Skt. or Pali, but cf. AMg. gocarī, JM.goyarī, both defined as *begging*, cf. s.v. **gocara** 3), = gocara, *course, sphere, range*: teṣu (sc. Buddhānāṃ, gen. pl.) ca gocarim (no v.l.) otari nityaṃ Bhad 33 (= Gv 545.22, vs), *and may I enter permanently into the range of them* (viz. of all Buddhas).

goṇa, m. (= Pali id., also Pkt., Hem. 2.174), *ox, bull*: (gorathakān...) goṇair yojitān SP 75.8 (prose); in vss SP 89.1, 7; 358.1; goṇa-mukhāś ca SP 84.13 (vs), *ox-faced* (of demons).

goṇasaka, m. (= Skt. gonasa, AMg. goṇ°; -ka possibly m.c.; all mss. goṇa°, ed. em. gona°), *a kind of snake*: śatāpadī °kāś ca vyāḍāḥ SP 84.2 (vs).

goṇasika, nt. (v.l. gonasīta, with dental n; Mironov as text, v.l. °sīkaṃ), some sort of ornament: Mvy 6037 = Tib. gser gyi mon lhas, which Das renders *suvarṇadāma, a gold braided head-ornament, also a necklace*.

goṇi, n. sg. goṇiḥ, or goṇī (f.?), Mvy 9564 = Tib. do gal gal: Jä. and Das define do gal as *important, importance*, Das adding as Skt. equivalent gauṇī (but Skt. gauṇa = *unimportant, of secondary importance*!). Chin. also *important*. Mironov goṇī, v.l. goṇiḥ.

goṇikā (also spelled gonikā, Sukh 67.6; cf. Pali goṇaka, also gonaka, *woolen cover with long fleece* PTSD; Skt. goṇī = carmamayam āchādanam, Schmidt, Nachtr.; Gaṇapati Sastri uses śayyāstaraṇa-goṇikādiḥ as a gloss on parivāpaḥ Kauṭ. Arth. i, 12th prakaraṇa, line 3), *coverlet, blanket*: SP 75.7 (gorathakān...) tūlikā-goṇikāstaraṇān; Mv ii.115.16 (paryaṅkā, read °kāṃ, °kān, or °kāni, mss. °kaṃ...) ṣoḍaśa-goṇikāstṛtāṃ; iii.70.1 paryaṅkāni... ṣoḍaśagoṇikāstaraṇāni (Senart em. lomaśa- for ṣoḍaśa, which is confirmed by prec.; mss. °śoṇikā°); AsP 488.20 (āsanaṃ...) goṇikāstīrṇaṃ; Karmav 22.5 goṇikāstṛte paryaṅke niṣaṇṇam; Sukh 67.6 paryaṅkaḥ... anekagonikāstīrṇas; Śikṣ 208.11 -goṇikāstaraṇa-.

Gotama, MIndic spelling for **Gautama**, q.v.: Śikṣ 331.11 (here apparently = **Gautama** 3).

Gotamī, MIndic spelling for **Gautamī**, q.v.: LV 201.10 (no v.l. recorded, but Calc. Gau°; perhaps misprint).

gotaraṇi, n. sg. °ṇiḥ, a kind of flower: Mvy 6208

(Tib. transliterates go-ta-ra-ṇi); also in ms. H of LV, see Crit. App. on LV 11.3, cited as govaraṇi, but read gota°, as shown by Tib. which here has ko-ta-ra-ni (dental n).

gotra, m. and nt. (in Skt. only nt., and not in these mgs.; Pali Dictt. also fail to record these mgs. except in cpd. **gotrabhū**, q.v.; but Pali gotta seems clearly used in mg. 1, below, in Vism. i.138.4–5, in definition of gotrabhū: taṃ parittagottābhibhavanato mahaggatagottabhāvanato ca gotrabhū ti pi vuccati; note how Pali here associates the Sktized gotra-bhū with the MIndic gotta! contrast Lévi's note on Sūtrāl. iii.1), (**1**) lit. *family*, but in special technical sense of *religious group* or *communion*: pañca-gotrāḥ Mvy 1260, listed 1261–5 śrāvaka-yānābhisamaya-gotraḥ, pratyekabuddha-yānā°, tathāgata-yānā°, aniyata-gotraḥ, a-gotraḥ; same five, with -gotraṃ, nt., Laṅk 63.2–5 (pañcābhisamaya-gotrāṇi); for the fourth, aniyata-taikatara-gotram, 63.4; in the sequel Laṅk explains at length the first three; aniyata-, *le gotra qui n'est pas définitif*, Lévi, Sūtrāl. iii.1, note, is briefly treated in Laṅk 65.2 f., aniyata-gotrakaḥ punar ... triṣv apy eteṣu deśyamāneṣu yatrānunīyate tatrānuyojyaḥ syāt; apparently this is the class of people who may be drawn to whichever of the three yānas happens to be presented. The a-gotra is not explained but evidently means people outside of any Buddhist communion; in this sense understand gotrāgotraṃ kathaṃ Laṅk 25.2, (religious) *family and lack of it* (dvandva cpd.). Only the first three gotras are listed AbhidhK. LaV-P. vi.175; similarly Bbh 223.5–6 contrasts śrāvaka-pratyekabuddha-gotrāṃ (acc. pl.) with tathāgata-gotrān. In KP 102.9; 103.1, 8 āryāṇāṃ gotraṃ is described as a state in which all normal conditions and activities are at an end, and in 104.1–2 (continuation of the same) it is said, anulomaṃ tad gotraṃ nirvāṇasya. The relation of this to the three or five gotras is not quite clear. In the question, kena pravartitā gotrāḥ suvarṇa-maṇimuktajāḥ Laṅk 26.3, gotra is prob. used in this same sense, but the adj., *sprung from gold, gems, and pearls*, is obscure in application; one is tempted to see an allusion (metaphorically) to the next mg., cf. especially suvarṇa-gotra-vat Sūtrāl. iii.9 and suratna-gotra-vat 10, with Lévi's note; but *producing gold* etc., which one would expect, seems philologically impossible; (**2**) *mine*, of gems or ores: Sūtrāl. iii.9, 10, above; sarvaratnasaṃbhavotpatti-gotrākaramūlyajñāneṣu Gv 451.2; dhātu-gotrāṇi, *mines of ores* (metals), °ṇi yaṃ paktvā suvarṇa-rūpya-vaiḍūryāṇy (°vaid°) abhinivartante Divy 111.20, and (°ūrya-sphaṭi-kāny°) 111.28–29, 112.12–13; catvāro dhātu-gotrāḥ pradarśitāḥ MSV i.106.16; (**3**) like Skt. ākara, also *origin*: nikāyagati-gotrā ye Laṅk 292.16, paraphrasing nikāyagati saṃbhavāt (labhyante) 292.13; *basis, source, cause, seed* Bbh 2.25 punar etad gotram ādhāra ity ucyate, upastambho hetur niśraya upaniṣat pūrvaṃgamo nilaya ity ucyate ... (3.1 gotraṃ dvividhaṃ, prakṛtisthaṃ samudānītaṃ ca, *natural and acquired* ...); 3.6 f. tat punar gotraṃ bījam ity apy ucyate, dhātuḥ prakṛtir ity api (cf. gotra = bīja, hetu, AbhidhK. LaV–P. vii.49); (**4**) prob. as special development of prec., *kind, class, category* (like Skt. **jāti**, of similar origin and lit. mg.): nānāratna-gotra-puṣpaprati-maṇḍite Laṅk 1.7, *adorned with flowers* (made of) *various kinds of jewels*; so prob. vijñapti-gotra-saṃchannam Laṅk 269.12, *covered by* (various) *classes of relative* (worldly, practical) *knowledge* (see **vijñapti**).

-gotraka, m., *belonging to, a member of a gotra* (q.v., 1): aniyata-gotrakaḥ Laṅk 65.2; śrāvakayānābhisamaya-gotrakasya 64.2; similarly 64.4, 10, 17; 65.1.

Gotrakṣānti, n. of a kiṃnara maid: Kv 6.22.

gotrabhū, f. (cf. Pali id., *a member of the religious communion*, see s.v. **gotra**, 1), in Laṅk 266.2 āśritā sarva-bhūteṣu gotrabhūs tarkavarjitā, nivartate kriyāmuktā jñānajñeyavivarjitā, apparently a fem. collective or abstract, *the 'communion of saints'*, corresponding to the Pali masc. which refers to an individual person. Suzuki, *the original source*, which is certainly impossible; the word must have some relation to the Pali word, on which see especially Childers, and Lévi, Sūtrāl. iii.1, note.

gotra-bhūmi, f. (see s.vv. **bhūmi** 4 and **gotra**, the latter in mg. 1? or 3?), (**1**) the first of seven bodhisattva-bhūmi: Bbh 367.3; (**2**) the second of seven śrāvaka-bhūmi: Mvy 1142; ŚsP 1473.11 etc.

gotrāntarīya, adj. (see **-antarīya**, **°yaka**), *belonging to a different* (religious) *'family'* or *sectarian school*: Karmav 60.9; 167.12.

Godānīya = **Apara-go°**, q.v.: LV 149.19 (but Tib. nub kyi points to Apara-!); reported also from AbhidhK., iii.145 of LaVallée-Poussin's Transl.; and with short a, Godanīya MPS 31.46.

godoha (m.; Skt. godohana is used in the same way, BR), (the time required for) *milking a cow*, expression for a short time: antato godoha-mātram api Bbh 156.19; (antaśa) ekarātriṃ dinam apy eka-godoha-mātram api Sukh 72.6.

godha, *greed, attachment* (cf. Pali gedha, and BHS **paligodha**, q.v.); must apparently be read for bodha in KP 111.6 (vs) ākāśa-bodhe imi dve pratiṣṭhite, tau bodhisattvena vivarjanīyau; prose above, line 1, ākāśa-paligodhau, Tib. (nam mkhaḥ la = ākāśa) yoṅs su (= pari) chags pa (= *greed*), while in 6 Tib. (nam mkhaḥ la ni) chags pa. It seems that ākāśa-godhe is intended. But see s.v. 2 **bodha**. Lin Li-Kouang, Aide-Mémoire 169 n. 6, cites wrongly pali-bodhe.

Godhā-jātaka, nt. (= Pali, commonly cited as Godha-j°, tho the word for *lizard* is godhā as in Skt.), n. of a jātaka story (= Pali Jāt. 333): Mv ii.67.14 (colophon).

gonaṅgula (m., = Pali id., Therag. 113 = 601; Skt. golāṅgula, id., see **golāṅgula-parivartana**), lit. *cow-tailed*, a certain kind of (black-faced) *monkey*: Mv iii.438.8, read with mss. (one slightly corrupt) gonaṅgula-niṣevitā (parvatāṃ, acc. pl.); Senart em. golāṅgula°.

gonasaka, see **goṇa°**.

gonikā = **goṇikā**, q.v.

go-niṣādikā (= Pali gonisādikā, Vin. i.240.2; in same context as MSV), *cow-resting-place*; *cow-barn* (?), or merely *place where cattle rest*: MSV i.135.5, glossed in 13 yatra dvārāntas tad goniṣādiketi.

Gopa, n. of a son of Khaṇḍa (2): MSV ii.4.3 ff.

Gopaka, n. of a disciple of Buddha: Karmav 65.7. Perhaps the same as Pali āyasmā Gopako, Vin. i.300.5.

gopakṣma(n), or °ma-netra, adj. (= Pali gopakhuma), *having* (eyes with) *eyelashes like a cow's*, the 30th of the 32 **lakṣaṇa**; in Mvy 240 fused with abhinīla-netra into one term, abhinīla-netra-gopakṣmā; gopakṣmā Bbh 376.7; gopakṣmo (read °mā or °maḥ) sa ... Gv 401.22 (prose); gopakṣma (perhaps sc. -netra; -a m.c.) Mv i.227.2; ii.30.5 (both vss.; in the latter mss. °kṣma, Senart em. °kṣa!); gopakṣma-netra LV 105.15; 432.7 (here text gopekṣa°, v.l. gopakṣa°, read °kṣma°); Dharmas 83 (text gopakṣa-netra-tā, v.l. gopakṣma-bhrū-tā).

Gopagiri, n. of a mountain: Māy 254.10.

Gopā (also **Gopī** and **Gopikā**, qq.v.; in Pali a Sākiya girl named Gopī or Gopikā is known, but not identified with the Bodhisattva's wife), n. of a Śākya girl, who in LV and Suv becomes the wife of the Bodhisattva (in most other texts he marries **Yaśodharā**, q.v.): LV 142.8 ff. (daughter of **Daṇḍapāṇi**); 157.4 ff.; 194.7 ff.; 230.3 ff.; 237.19; Suv 200.8; in Mvy 1071 Gopī or Gopā, named next to Yaśodharā, but there is no reason to assume their identification (Mironov reads Gopā without v.l.); in Gv 385.6 ff. Gopā occurs as a Śākya-kanyā, who in 420.19 is the daughter of **Daṇḍapāṇi** (like the Gopā of LV), but there is here no suggestion that she married the Bodhisattva, tho she mentions him 419.20 (as well as **Vairocana**, 396.23).

gopānasī (once, in mss., °sa; rare in Skt., see BR 5, Addenda, and pw; = Pali id., essentially Buddhist word; cf. Skt. gopāna, °naka, Acharya, Dict. Hind. Arch. s.v.), *framework of a roof, rafters*: Mvy 5580; gopānasī vigaḍita tatra sarvā SP 83.5 (vs; of a ruined house); (-sālāyāṃ ... vivṛtāyāṃ) gopānasy-āntarikāś ca virājante LV 254.11, *the interstices of the roof-frame*; similarly 256.1 and °sīye antarāṇi, or °sī-antarāṇi, vivaṭāni Mv ii.125.14; 127.1; 128.7; 129.9; because of curvature, used as type of the bent-over posture of old men (so Pali °sī-vaṅka), kubjo °sī-vakro vibhagno LV 188.1; Kv 48.12 (text °ṇasī°, and wrongly divided in ed.); in parallel passage, bhagno °sī-vakro Mv ii.150.19; kubja-gopānasī-vaṅkā Mv iii.283.11; kubja-gopānasī- (ms. °sa, em. Speyer)-vakrā Av ii.25.8.

Gopāla (= Pali id.), n. of a yakṣa: Māy 103; 237.1.

Gopālaka, n. of a śreṣṭhin: Gv 525.17.

Gopālī, n. pr.? see s.v. **Kumbhakārī** (2).

Gopikā = **Gopā** (and **Gopī**), wife of the Bodhisattva: °kāya (gen.) LV 235.21 (vs); °ke (voc.) 237.13 (vs); MSV iv.233.17 (but in 234.14 Yaśodharā).

go-piṭaka, nt., lit. *cow-basket*; perh. orig. a receptacle for fodder for cattle; but in Mv always used for human (hard or dry) food or cakes (khajja, khajjaka), while soft food (odana, once **bhakta**, q.v.) is in the same passages placed in the **alinda** or **°dā**, q.v.: Mv ii.461.21; 462.2, 7, 9, 11; iii.15.9, 12; mentioned merely in reference to its size, °ka-mātram, Divy 70.28.

gopitaka, adj. (= Skt. °ta), *hidden, concealed*: (so ca naṃ māṣo) tatraiva gaṅgākūle °ko abhūṣi Mv iii.184.18.

Gopī = **Gopā**, q.v.: Mvy 1071 v.l. for Gopā (but Mironov only Gopā, no v.l.); as the Bodhisattva's wife, Gopi (voc.) LV 235.22; 237.11 (both vss).

[**gopekṣanetra**, LV 432.7, corruption for **gopakṣma°**, q.v.]

? **gomaya**, m., *offal, refuse*, if this word is intended in Mv ii.65.7 gómayo ti (so Senart for mss. gometi) kṛtvā na siddhā, *thinking it was offal, I did not prepare it as food*; foll. by, kumāro āha, na eṣā godhā abhakṣyā, bhakṣyā eṣā manuṣyāṇāṃ. As Senart remarks, this seems a strange use of gomaya, and I share his suspicion of the reading, but can suggest no good emendation.

gomaya-kārṣī (or **-kāsī**), (possibly cf. kasso = paṅkaḥ Deśīn. 2.2?) perhaps *a coating of cowdung*, possibly mixed with something else, seemingly applied as purification: (gṛhaṃ sammārjitaṃ) sukumārī °kārṣī dattā Divy 306.23; MSV ii.100.13; 129.16; in Divy 338.24 text (sā kuṭikā siktā sammṛṣṭā sammārjitā) sukumārī (note same adj.!) gomayakāsiñcānupradattā, but mss. °kāsīñ cānu°, read °kāsī cānu° or °kārṣī cānu°; (gomayena miśrayitvā) yatra caṅkrame tathāgataḥ caṅkramyate tatra gomayakārṣīṃ prayacchati Divy 369.5, and, tatra gomayakārṣī dattā 7. If -kāṣī may be accepted as the true reading, perh. connected with root kaṣ and meaning something like *a rubbing with cowdung*.

Gomardana, n. of a locality: Māy 49.

Gomimukhya, n. of a king: Mmk 619.26; seems to be the same as the next, but the passage is not clear to me.

Gomiṣaṇḍa, n. of a king: Mmk 620.10; see under prec.

gomukhī (= AMg. gomuhī, Skt. gomukha), a kind of wind-instrument: parivādinī gomukhīṃ atha pi veṇuṃ Mv iii.82.5 (vs).

Goyoga, n. of a locality: Māy 64; cf. possibly Pali Goyoga-pilakkha.

go-rajas, lit. *cow-speck*, a small unit of matter, = seven *sheep-specks* (see **eḍaka-rajas**, where the mg. is discussed): Mvy 8196; LV 149.6; Divy 645.11.

gola, m. (in this sense Skt. Lex. nt. and golā, f.), *bottle*: Mvy 9415 = Tib. bum pa; Chin. *large bottle*. Cf. next.

golaka (m. or nt.; cf. prec.; Skt. Lex. *bottle*), *a bottle-shaped* (or ball-shaped?) *ornament on a building* (this is a mg. of Tib. bum pa, see under prec.): (nagaraṃ ...) aṭṭāla-(mss aṭṭala-)-golaka-(v.l. goraka)-toraṇaṃ Mv iii.160.13 (prose).

golāṅgula-parivartana (nt.?), lit. (place of) *turning, moving about, of* (the) *monkeys* (called golāṅgula, see s.v. **gonaṅgula**), n. of a mountain near Rājagṛha: °ne parvate LV 18.14. Tib. (omitting go!) mjug ma (= *tail*) sgyur ba (= *turn*).

golika, also **gaulika**, m. (cf. AMg. goliya-sālā, *a shop for selling treacle*, Ratnach.; from Skt. guḍa with -ika), *dealer in sugar* or *molasses*: golikā, n. pl., Mv iii.442. 13; gaulikā iii.113.8.

golomakam, adv., seemingly *in the manner of a cow's hair*: Mvy 9331 na go° keśaś (so also Mironov; Kyoto ed. v.l. keśāc; read keśāṃś, keśaṃ? or assume acc. form of s-stem **keśas**, q.v.?) chedayet; Tib. skra chan pas mi breg (dreg), *not cut hair with scissors* (!); Chin. simply *hair not cut off*; Jap. ... *like a cow's hair*; corresp. to Pali Vin. ii.134.11 (massuṃ ...) na golomikaṃ kārāpetabbaṃ; comm. 1211.3 hanukamhi dīghaṃ katvā ṭhapitaṃ eḷakamassukaṃ (!) vuccati; SBE 20.138 transl. *nor ... like a goat's beard*; but how can *go-* mean (*sheep* or) *goat*? The Tib. and Chin. renderings, with the Pali gloss, suggest that the real mg. was forgotten in both traditions.

Govardhana, n. of a city in the south: Mv iii.363.6.

Govinda (= Pali id., DN ii.230.23 ff.), n. of the brahman-purohita of King Diśāṃpati: Mv iii.204.9 ff. Cf. the next items.

Govindasūtra (nt.), n. of a sūtra, prob. = next but one (but see Lévi's note): Karmav 157.13.

Govindiya (or **Gau°**, also written **°dīya**), adj., *belonging to* **Govinda**, q.v.: paurohitye govindiye Mv iii.205.8; 206.5, 6 (Senart with one ms. Gauvindīye in 5, Govindīye in 6; v.l. in both Govindiye).

Govindīyaṃ sūtraṃ (to **Govinda**; cf. prec.), n. of a sūtra which corresp. to Pali DN 19: Mv iii.224.9 (mss. somewhat corrupt); also **Mahāgovindīyaṃ s°**, q.v.

govratika, adj. (= Pali govatika; Skt. govratin, see below), applied to certain non-Buddhist ascetics *who adopt a vow to live like cows* (eating grass, etc.; see the Pali and other references, esp. MN and its comm., cited s.v. **kukkuravratika**): Śikṣ 332.3; Karmav 44.19; cf. also Mvy 3535 govratī, and LV 248.21 govrata- (s.v. **kukkuravratika**). The word govratin occurs Mbh. (Cr. ed.) 5.97.13, defined 14 thus: yatra-tatra-śayo nityaṃ yena-kenacid-āśitaḥ, yena-kenacid ācchannaḥ sa govrata (S apparently govratir, which as an irregular form from govratin may be the original!) ihocyate.

Gośālīputra, Gośāli(n), °li(kā)putra, °līputra, see **Maskarin**.

Gośīrṣa, n. of a nāga-king: Kv 2.12.

gośṛṅgavratin, a member of some heretical sect: Mvy 3542. Possibly cf. **govratika**?

Gośṛṅgī, n. of a pious woman who entertained the Buddha: Mv i.261.15; 263.3, 6; 271.13.

goṣṭhika (once written **gau°**; not in this sense in Skt., but only as adj., *relating to a guild*; not in Pali; but = AMg. goṭṭhiya, °iga), m., usually pl., (boon-)*companion, member of a friendly group*: Mv iii.375.13 triṃśa(d) goṣṭhikā udyānabhūmiṃ nirgatā; id. 15 and 376.1–2 tehi goṣṭhikehi; 376.5, 7, 8; Av i.93.6; sambahulāś ca goṣṭhikā ... 163.7; °kānāṃ śataṃ nirgataṃ 377.14; ii.53.9 ff. (in 55.9 ms. gauṣṭhika, see Speyer's note); 100.13 ff.; MSV ii.78.2. Obscure is Mv iii.121.9 (vs), in which Śuddhodana addresses the Buddha: purā tuvaṃ goṣṭhika-tūlikāsu ...; Senart suggests doubtfully *coussins, divans où on est assis de compagnie* (tūlikā, *mattress*, Skt.).

gosāraka (so Mironov also, with v.l. gośālaka), m., an architectural term, acc. to Tib. bcam (gduṅ; cf. Das gduṅ pa, gduṅ ma): Mvy 5577. The surrounding terms seem to refer to parts of a pillar; does this mean a *cross-beam*, connecting pillars?

Gosālikā-putra, see s.v. **Maskarin.**

[**gauḍakamṛga**, see **ghoṭakamṛga.**]

Gauṇāyana, m. pl., n. of a brahmanical gotra: Divy 635.13.

Gautama (also written **Gotama**, q.v.), (**1**) (= Pali Gotama), gotra-name of Śākyamuni, often applied to him especially by those who are not his followers: Mvy 78; Mv i.251.19; 294.21; ii.118.8 ff.; 119.16 ff.; 126.10; 200.1; 241.2; 277.2 ff.; 287.9; 330.11, etc. etc.; LV 238.21; 239.8 f.; 255.4 ff.; 256.8 f.; 306.5; 358.5; 369.2; 378.21; 380.13; 405.7 ff.; 406.4, 8; (**2**) gotra-name of another (former) Buddha: Mv i.113.11; (**3**) (= Pali Gotamaka) n. of a non-Buddhist sect: Mv iii.412.7; Śikṣ 331.11; LV 380.12 (here named with Nirgranthas, Ājīvikas, et al.); (**4**) n. of a ṛṣi and ascetic: Mv ii.210.2 (lived at **Sāhaṃjanī**, q.v.); prob. same as the ṛṣi killed by the wicked King Arjuna, Mv iii.361.7, 10, who occurs as Gotama in Pali also; he was an Āṅgirasa, iii.369.8, as in Pali, see DPPN s.v. 7 Aṅgirasa; (**5**) n. of a brahmanical teacher: Araṇemī (n. sg.) Gautamo Divy 651.7, or °ṇemiś ca Gau° 653.12 (in 632.12 corruptly Araṇemī-gautamau as if a dual dvandva); (**6**) n. of a nāga-king (also **Gautamaka**, q.v.): Divy 50.22; Māy 247.20; (cf. s.v. **kṛṣṇa**, 4;) (**7**) Gautama-nyagrodha (= Pali Gotama-nigrodha, DN ii.116.31), n. of a locality at Vaiśālī, doubtless the caitya called **Gautamaka**, q.v.: Divy 201.5, 14.

Gautamaka, (**1**) n. of a nāga-king (also **Gautama**, 6; cf. s.v. **kṛṣṇa**, 4): Divy 50.17, 29; 51.6; (**2**) n. of a caitya (cetiya) at Vaiśālī: Mv i.300.9 (see Gautama-nyagrodha, s.v. **Gautama**, 7).

Gautamī (= Pali Gotamī; once **Got°**, q.v.), family-name of **Mahāprajāpatī**, to which Gau° is regularly added, see citations s.v. Mahāp°; rarely used alone, Mv iii.137.13 (vs); Karmav 158.19 (voc., in address by the Buddha).

Gaura, n. of a former Buddha: Mv i.140.11.

gaura-khara, m. (AMg. gora-khara, *white ass*, Ratnach., *a kind of ass*, Sheth; once in Late Skt., see Schmidt, Nachträge, gaura-khura [sic] is cited as meaning *a kind of ass*), a kind of *ass*, acc. to BR *wild ass*: Mvy 4797 = Tib. rgyaṅ, which Tib. Dictt. do not record as an animal name; Jap. *a kind of wild horse found in Central Asia*; Chin. *reddish-brown horse*, or (2) *wild mule* (*ass*?).

gaurava-tā = Skt. gaurava, *the condition of regarding* (something) *as important*: tāye dharma-gauravatāye Mv ii.256.8. Cf. § 22.43. But possibly the true analysis is dharma-gaurava, Bhvr., *being in a state of regarding righteousness as important*, plus -tā.

Gaurī, (**1**) n. of a yoginī: Sādh 443.15; (**2**) n. of a rākṣasī: Māy 243.17.

gaulika = **golika**, q.v.

gaulmika, m. (in Skt. *member* or *commander of a troop of soldiers*; AMg. gummi(y)a, defined as *a guard of a fort*; *a watchman*), acc. to Tib. la gcan pa = *a collector of duties on a mountain pass* (Das): Mvy 3803. Follows śaulkika; Jap. *customs officer*; perh. originally *guard at an outpost*, later *one who collected duties* there.

Gauvindīya, adj. = **Govindiya**, q.v.

gauṣṭhika, once written for **goṣṭhika**, q.v.

grathita, ppp. (= Pali gathita, often foll. by mucchita; in this sense not Skt.), *enslaved* (by desire or worldly things): Divy 534.19 (raktaḥ sakto gṛdhro) grathito mūrchito 'dhyavasito... Cf. Pali DN i.245.24 gathitā mucchitā; comm. ii.403.25 gathitā ti gedhena abhibhūtā hutvā; mucchitā ti mucchākārappattāya adhimattataṇhāya abhibhūtā. Cf. next items, esp. **granthita**, used Mvy 2194 in same context as Divy (prec. by raktaḥ, saktaḥ, gṛddhaḥ, foll. by mūrchitaḥ, adhyavasitaḥ, etc.).

grantha, m. (= Pali gantha; Skt. uses granthi, but not grantha, in much the same way; cf. prec. and next), *bond, fetter* (to worldly life): Mvy 2145 = Tib. mdud pa, *knot*; context indicates fig. (religious) application.

grantha-dhāraṇī, see **dhāraṇī.**

granthita, ppp. (Skt. Lex. id., for grathita; Pali ganthita; ppp. either to *granthati = Pali ganthati, Skt. grathnāti, or denom. ppp. to **grantha**, q.v., or Skt. granthi), *enslaved*: Mvy 2194, see s.v. **grathita**; LV 372.3 (vs) iha sā vitarkamālā saṃjñāsūtreṣu granthitā **nipathī** (read with v.l. 'narthī?), vinivartitā aśeṣā bodhyaṅga-vicitramālābhiḥ.

granthi-mocaka, m. (cited by Monier-Williams from Wilson's Dict.), *cutpurse*: Mvy 5362; (pāripanthikā...) janapadaghātakā yāvad gra°kā iti kṛtvā Śikṣ 77.9.

Grasatī, n. of a nāga maid: Kv 4.4.

Grasana (cf. next), n. of a piśāca: Mmk 18.6.

Grasanī, (**1**) (cf. prec.) n. of a piśācī: Māy 239.6; (**2**) n. of a rākṣasī: 243.15.

Grahakośa, n. of a former Buddha: Mv i.141.14.

grahaṇa, nt., confused with **gahana**, *thicket, entanglement* (?): in Mv i.34.7 (prose) -durga-saṃsāra-kāntāra-grahaṇa-dāruṇāto mahā-prapātāto uddharitvā, Senart thinks that grahaṇa is a copyist's hyper-Skt. alteration of gahana, which is a near-synonym of kāntāra (esp. in Pali, where diṭṭhi-kantāra and diṭṭhi-gahana are often closely associated); in spite of this, I think grahaṇa may be sound and orig.: *rescuing from a great abyss that is dreadful because of the grip of the forest of the saṃsāra etc.* In Mv i.91.14–17 occur four lines of verse in which the mss. repeatedly vary between gahana and grahaṇa; the text is both very corrupt and fragmentary; Senart's note is a very earnest effort to disentangle it, but I find it hardly convincing, tho I am inclined to agree that puns are here contained, involving gahana, *entanglement, obstruction, difficulty*, as well as *thicket*, and grahaṇa, *seizure, imprisonment* (perhaps also *eclipse*, as by Rāhu, so Skt.); the text, with the most important vv.ll., reads: 14 vanagahanaṃ (mss. °grahanaṃ or °ṇaṃ) balagahanaṃ (3 mss. °grah°) girigahanāni (em.; 5 mss. °gahanaṃ, one °grahaṇaṃ) tyāgagrahaṇāni (3 mss. °gahanāni), 15 viṣamāprati- (mss. viṣamapati-)-saṃniṣaṇṇavanāni tu manuṣyagahanāni (5 mss. °graha°), 16 tṛṇagulmakaṇṭakalatākulāni vṛkṣagrahaṇā- (mss. °grahaṇya- or °nya-) gahanāni (3 mss. grahaṇāni), 17 śaṭhanikṛtipaiśunyāni tu manuṣyagahanāni (5 mss. °grahaṇāni or °ṇāni). Tho Senart's interpretation seems very dubious, I cannot suggest with confidence any improvements. The meter is meant for āryā. See also **gahana, gahana-tā.**

grahaṇī (Skt. only as n. of an imaginary abdominal organ; Pali gahaṇī app. more loosely used, cf. saṃsuddhagahaṇika, *of pure womb* or *origin*; DN comm. i.281.10 -mātu-gahaṇī kucchīti attho), (*belly, womb*;) *interior* (like Skt. garbha): in SP 239.3 (prose) read pañcabhiḥ puṣpa-grahaṇī-(so with Kashgar rec. and 3 Nep. mss., ed. °ṇīya)-vedikā-sahasraiḥ svabhyalaṃkṛto (stūpaḥ), *adorned with 5000 balconies filled with* (*containing*; Tib. bkram pa, *besprinkled with*) *flowers.*

[**grahaṇīya**, see prec.]

grahāya (= Pali gahāya), irregular ger. to root grah (see § 35.19), used virtually as postposition, lit. *taking*; *with, along with*: SP 211.6 etc. (l.c.).

grahika, adj.,? Mvy 2449, in a list of evil qualities; pw 7.339 guesses 'etwa bissig'; Tib. dus (*time*) po che (*great*), which I cannot interpret (is it connected with sdud pa, which might render grah, *collect, bring together*, perhaps in a corrupt form?); one Chin. rendering *vain, futile, time-wasting* (does Tib. mean [*consuming*] *much time*?), *useless*. Etymologically one might guess *grasping, avaricious*, or the like.

Grāmaghoṣa, n. of a locality: Māy 104.

grāmaṇika, presumably = next: Mv iii.160.19 (prose)

(rājā) brahmadatto amātyapāriṣadyān āmantrayasi: ho bhaṇe grāmaṇikā kṣipraṃ purohitam ānetha.

grāmaṇīya (presumably = Skt. grāmaṇī, Pali gāmaṇī; see prec.), *a military officer of some sort*: ārūḍhā °yehi khaḍgatomarapāṇibhiḥ Mv ii.487.14 = iii.22.5 (vs), and variants ii.487.18; 488.2 = iii.22.9, 13.

grāmaluka, see **grāmeluka**.

(**grāmika**, m., prob. only *village headman*, as in Skt., and as Pali gāmika; °kā, f. *a woman belonging to a village headman's family*. Senart [repeatedly in his Introd., on the passages below] understands simply *villager*: grāmika, m., Mv i.301.8 ff.; 303.12 ff. (his daughter was attended by serving-women, 302.16); **Sujātā**, q.v., was a grāmika-duhitā LV 265.11 or °dhītā Mv ii.263.15–16; 299.9, or grāmikasya dhītā ii.200.17; she is called simply a grāmikā Mv ii.131.10, but this doubtless has the mg. suggested above. Cf. also grāmika-gharaṃ āgami (in search of food) Mv ii.200.16.)

grāmeluka, adj. or subst. m. (= Mg. gāmelua, see Sheth, and Pischel 595, end), *living in a village*, or, *a villager*; *rustic*: grāmelukenāpi (so mss.) dāni puruṣeṇa Mv ii.275.17 (prose); in 19 mss. grāmaluko puruṣo; Senart em. grāmāl° in both.

grāmya, adj. (in Skt. app. only used of speech; Pali gamma used more generally, esp. associated with synonymous hīna), *vulgar, low*: in passage = Pali Vin. i.10.12, hīno grāmyaḥ (sc. antaḥ) LV 416.17 and (om. hīno) Mv iii.331.3; grāmyaṃ nopajīvitaṃ LV 262.10, see s.v. **upajīvita**; grāmyāṃ tṛṣṇāṃ Ud iii.9, 10 = Pali jammī taṇhā Dhp. 335–6.

-grāha, ifc., m. (= Pali gāha), (heretical, erroneous) *belief (in), holding (to)*...: asantagrāhātu (*from false belief*) vimukta bhonti SP 92.9 (vs); esp. ātma-grāha (= Pali atta-gāha), *clinging to the* (false view that there is a) *self*: Śikṣ 198.20 (bhayāni...) tāny ātmagrāhata utpadyante; 21 ahaṃ... ātmagrāhaṃ parityajeyaṃ; Laṅk 177.14 ātmagrāhapatitayā saṃtatyā; Vaj 23.11–12 and 25.16 ātmagrāho bhavet sattvagrāho jīvagrāhaḥ pudgalagrāho bhavet; similarly Vaj 42.12; and 42.13 ātmagrāha iti subhūte agrāha eṣa tathāgatena bhāṣitaḥ; 45.4 sa eva piṇḍagrāho 'bhaviṣyat... (5) agrāhaḥ sa tathāgatena bhāṣitaḥ; LV 205.8 (lokasya...) ātmanīyagrāhānugamānasasya, *having minds that follow after the false belief that there is anything peculiar* (belonging) *to the self*.

grīveya (nt.? = Pali gīveyya, °yyaka; Skt. graiveya, °yaka, usually of a chain put on an elephant's neck), *necklace* or *chain about the neck*: (suvarṇaniṣkāṃ yatha osiritvā) grīveya taptā (perh. read °taṃ? or plural? dharaye ca loke Mv ii.(334.22–) 335.1 (so mss.; Senart em. badly), *as one might put off gold neck-ornaments and wear heated* (i. e. red-hot) *chain(s)-on-the-neck in the world*.

[**grīṣmāṇa-māse**, printed as cpd. in Mv i.294.3 (vs), but read grīṣmāṇa (gen. pl.) māse prathame, *in the first month of the summer*; so also Pali gimhāna māse (so printed), Sn 233. There seems no reason for taking either Pali gimhāna or BHS grīṣmāṇa as a 'stem-form'.]

grīṣmika, adj. (= Pali gimhika; Skt. graiṣmika), *of, for summer*: grīṣmika-vārṣika-haimantikeṣu prāsādeṣv LV 227.3; trayo prāsādā kārayat (so Senart divides) hemantikaṃ grīṣmikaṃ vārṣikaṃ Mv ii.115.9; similarly iii.405.13; trayaś ca (sc. māsāḥ) grīṣmikās Suv 178.4.

gredha (= Pali gedha, m.; cf. **parigredha**; analogically based on Pali giddha etc. = Skt. gṛddha etc.; § 3.68; the nearest Skt. equivalent in mg. is gṛdhyā), *greed*: sukhāpi gredhāśritā Mvy 7553 (= Tib. zhen pa); saṃkalpair gredha-niśritaiḥ Ud xxxi.29; -rasa-gredhāt MPS 31.63.

(**graiṣmika**, m., see s.v. **sāmayika**.)

glāna (also **gilāna**, q.v.; = Pali gilāna; acc. to BR Skt. glāna is not used in this specific sense), *sick, ill*; in glāna-pratyaya-bhaiṣajya, one of the four **pariṣkāra**, q.v. for occurrences, *medicine to cure the sick*.

glānaka, gilā°, adj. (= Pali gilā°) = **glāna**, (one that is) *sick*: MSV i.149.8; glānakaṃ kṛtvā Mv ii.247.4, see s.v. **karoti**; taṃ... glānako ti kṛtvā, *thinking with regard to him, He is a sick one* (specifying ka), Mv ii.242.8; 243.2, 4; ka may be m.c. in Mv ii.221.3 (with mss.; vs) °kā (n. pl.), and in SP 293.1 (vs) gilānaka-tvam, *illness*.

glānya, nt., once m. (Sktized form of **gailānya**, q.v., or directly formed from Skt. glāna plus -ya; but not recorded in Skt.), *weakness, debility*: SP 107.9; Divy 25.8; Av ii.85.18; 133.12; Śikṣ 37.4; 135.16; KP 65.4 tasmād glānyā(t); 118.1 dvāv imau... dīrgha-glānyau (dual m.) katamau dvau; but 118.7 (vs) dve... glānye ukte (nt.); Mmk 147.26 (vs); all but the last two prose; bahuglānyatā Dbh 26.19.

GH

ghaṭaka, m., or adj., *who* or *which reveals* or *expounds*: Divy 442.1; 523.25 (in cliché cited s.v. **udghaṭaka**, for which this is substituted); ekānta-ghaṭake śāsane (loc. abs.) MSV i.237.8.

ghaṭa-bhedanaka, nt.,? Mvy 9051; Tib. rdza (*clay*, or *clay-pot*) gzoṅ (*chisel, graving-tool*); cf. however rdza gzhoṅ, *earthen basin* (Jä.), and rdza gsoṅ, rendered in Das by ghaṭa-bhedanaka, kaṭānaka, *frying-vessel*! Chin. *instrument(s) used in building houses*. The next word in Mvy is karparaḥ, *pot, bowl*; but various implements and tools are listed in the vicinity. BR render (etymologically) *ein bei der Verfertigung von Töpfen gebrauchtes Instrument*.

ghaṭā (Skt. ghaṭa, m.; ghaṭī, ghaṭikā; Weller 24 suggests lengthening of stem-final a in the seam of cpds., but a fem. ghaṭā exists in Skt. tho in other mgs.), *pot, jar*: pañcāpsaraḥsahasrāṇi divyagandhodakaparipūrṇa-ghaṭāparigṛhītāni LV 96.9. Cf. next.

ghaṭā-śiras, adj. (cf. prec.; perh. lit. *pot-headed*?), in Mvy 8807 (not in Mironov), acc. to Chin. and Jap. *having a knotty, uneven head*; this is prob. also the meaning of Tib. mgo (*head*) ḥbar ḥbur can; cf. Jä. ḥbar ḥbar, *uneven, rough*; *pock-marked*; Jä. and Das ḥbur po, *having protuberances, uneven, rough*; ḥbur, *boil, pustule* (as pot-shaped?).

ghaṭī (f.? cf. Pali ghaṭikā, *small stick*), *stick, piece of wood*: samudramadhye patitā kecid ghaṭīm (v.l. vṛttim) ādāya kecit phalakaṃ kecid alābuśreṇiyaṃ Mv iii.68.5 (prose).

ghaṭikā (Pali id., *small stick*; cf. prec.), *stick*; in **vaṃśa-gh°**, q.v.

Ghaṭikāra, MSV **Ghaṭī°** (= Pali Ghaṭīkāra), n. of a potter who was a disciple of the Buddha Kāśyapa, Mv i.319.9 ff.; 326.10 ff., and later became one of the Śuddhāvāsa gods, in which capacity he with others of that class of gods fashioned magically the Four Sights for the Bodhisattva Śākyamuni to see, Mv ii.150.16; 152.10 ff.; MSV i.217.12 (called **Nandīpāla**). He lived at **Veruḍiṅga** or **Vebha°**, **Vaibhiḍiṅgī**, the later **Mārakaraṇḍa**, qq.v. Several parts of his legend (not, apparently, his part in creating the Four Sights) recur in Pali, see DPPN.

ghaṭṭa- (or **ghaṭṭaya,** MIndic for ghaṭṭaka), prob. *polishing-stone*: in Mv iii.81.12 (vs) (bhavanāni rākṣasīnām...) ghaṭṭaya-vimaṣṭaka (? mss. ghaṭṭapa-vi°; Senart em. ghaṭṭa-parimṛṣṭaka), prob. (*the palaces of the ogresses were...*) *polished with polishing-stones* (cf. AMg. ghaṭṭaga, *stone for polishing*; Pkt., acc. to Ratnach. Deśī, ghaṭṭanaka, id.); or possibly (cf. JM. ghaṭṭa, = gāḍha, nibiḍa), *polished hard, vigorously*.

ghaṭṭita, ppp. (= Skt. ghaṭita; cf. udghaṭṭayati), *closed*: kāśikavastrāvarī ghaṭṭitā phuṭṭakavastrāvarī udghaṭitā (mss. in 12 udghaṭṭitā) Divy 29.7, 12.

? **Ghaṇṭa** (in Skt. n. of a Dānava), n. of a rākṣasa king: Mmk 18.1; but see **Yama** (3).

ghaṇṭāka (m. or nt.; Skt. Lex. as n. of a tree with bell-shaped flowers; Skt. ghaṇṭā, *bell*), *bell*: pāśa-ghaṇṭāka-dvāraka-dhanur-nārāca-mudgara- Mmk 46.8 (prose). But this word and dvāraka may be corrupt; some sort of weapons would seem suggested by the other terms.

ghaṇṭikā (Skt. Gr. id.; AMg. ghaṇṭiā), (little, decorative) *bell*: MSV ii.16.8.

Ghanavyūha, m., n. of a work: Mvy 1343.

? **ghana-saṃdhi,** n. sg. °iḥ, LV 106.13, one of the **anuvyañjana,** replacing (it seems) **nirgranthi-śira,** q.v.: acc. to Burnouf, *having solid joints*; but Tib. tshigs (*joint*) mi mṅon pa (*not visible*; also renders gūḍha in the two preceding items, suggesting that the Tib. LV text had gūḍha-saṃdhi).

ghara, nt. (and m.? = Pali nt., and acc. to Childers m.; AMg. m. and nt.; Skt. gṛha), *house*: gharo, mss. (n. pl.; Senart em. gharā) Mv i.24.13; ghara-vāsa-rakṣito 285.22; gharaṃ, acc. sg. iii.289.8 (em.); gharam, n. sg. Mvy 5518.

gharaka (dim. of prec.? so Senart), (small) *house, hut*: nairayikā... gharakehi oruddhā (mss. °ddha) chinna-īryāpathā (mss. -iryā°) Mv i.22.10 (prose).

? **gharaṇī,** see **ghariṇī.**

gharati (Skt. Dhātup., and Ved. jigharti etc.; see **pragharati, parighareti**), *drips, flows* (intrans.): Mv iii.408.1 kāsāṃcil lālā (mss. lolā) gharati (or with v.l. gharanti; in accord with this read in Mv i.227.17–18 kāsāṃcil (ed. with mss. kācil) lālā gharanti (kācil would require transitive mg. for gharanti, lālā being then acc.; but the verb and its cpds. seem to be only intrans.).

gharā, a high number: Mmk 343.25 (= 10 **pragharā,** q.v.; see **aśeṣa**).

ghariṇī (v.l. once °aṇī; Pali gharaṇī; AMg. both °aṇī and °iṇī; cf. **ghara** and Skt. gṛhiṇī), *housewife*: Divy 46.27 °ṇī-śatāni (one ms. gharaṇī°); 47.25 ghariṇī-stūpa. Divy Index *widow*, for reasons not evident to me.

Ghasmarī, n. of a yoginī: Sādh 446.2.

-ghātaka = -ghātaka, in **vadhya-gh°,** q.v.; cf. **ghātin,** and § 2.41.

(? **ghāṭikā,** *pot, jar*, recorded a few times in Kosegarten's Pañcatantra, see BR, who suggest that it is an error for ghaṭikā; in Mv iii.255.10 (prose) Senart prints gandha-ghāṭikā-vidhūpitaṃ, but one of his two mss. °ghaṭikā°. Note however that BR also record **ghāṭa,** 'viell. nur fehlerhaft', as meaning *pot*, = ghaṭa, once in Hariv.)

ghātin, adj. (= ghātin, cf. § 2.41), *destroying*: jagakleśa-ghāṭī Dbh.g. 41(67).14 (no v.l.).

Ghātanī, n. of a rākṣasī: Māy 243.28.

ghātikā (cf. Pali dubbala-ghātikā Jāt. i.176.27; 177.4, *killing of the weak*), *destruction, violation*, in visrambha-gh°, ... *of confidence*: bodhisattvo ... na °tikayā na dhūrtatayā lābham upārjayati Śikṣ 269.2.

-ghātyā, see **nala-gh°.**

ghuṇaghuṇāyate (cf. Deśīn. 2.110 ghuṇaghuṇiā = karṇopakarṇikā; JM. ghuṇāhuṇī = *Gerücht*, Jacobi, Erz.), *buzzes* (of a bee): pres. p. °yamānaṃ (printed °ṇaṃ) Kv 46.21. The Skt. ghuṇa, *a wood-boring insect*, seems probably not connected with this obviously onomatopoetic word.

ghṛta-kuṇḍika, m., in a list of trades and crafts, seems to mean lit. *ghee-potter*: °kā, n. pl., Mv iii.113.8; 442.13 (both times without v.l.). Does it mean *maker of pots intended for holding ghee*? Or *dealer in pots of ghee*? No similar word has been discovered elsewhere.

ghoṭaka-mṛga, m. (cited by BR from Minayev as gauḍaka°; Mironov as text), *wild horse*: Mvy 4798 = Tib. rta rgod.

Ghora, (**1**) n. of a rākṣasa king: Mmk 18.1; (**2**) n. of a piśāca: Mmk 18.6.

Ghoracaṇḍī, n. of a goddess: Sādh 488.7.

Ghorarūpī, read perhaps °pin, n. of a piśāca: Ghorarūpīś (read °pī?) ca (in list of piśācas) Mmk 18.6.

ghorī (Pali ghora or ghorā, n. of a kind of magic, Jāt. iv.496.10; 498.33; also Skt. ghora, nt., see BR), n. of a kind of magic: ghorī vidyā vaśaṃkarī Divy 636.28 (vs, printed as prose).

ghoṣa, m. (Skt. *sound, noise, roar*; in this sense nt. in Mv i.229.16 = 240.5 = 333.7 ghoṣam, n. sg.), *proclamation*: ghoṣam **anuśrāvayati** (q.v.) SP 123.1; LV 266.1; Samādh 8.10; Śikṣ 38.1; or udīrayati LV 401.2; Mv i.40.11.

Ghoṣadatta, n. of a Tathāgata: Śikṣ 8.20 (from Bhadrakalpikasūtra); Samādh p. 16 line 6 ff.

Ghoṣamati, n. of one of the sons of the Buddha Candrasūryapradīpa: SP 19.4.

Ghoṣaśrī, n. of a Bodhisattva: Gv 442.18.

Ghoṣānana, n. of a former Buddha: Samādh p. 57 line 17.

ghoṣānuga, f. **-ā,** a kind of **kṣānti,** q.v.: *receptivity* (kṣānti) *to the oral teaching* (of the Buddha): Samādh 19.37 (see Régamey's note 143, p. 82 f.); Sukh 55.13.

Ghoṣila (corresp. to Pali Ghosaka or Ghosita), n. of a gṛhapati (so Divy 541.19 ff., 575.30 ff.), one of the ministers of King Udayana: Divy 529.6; 531.19; 541.19 ff.; 575.30 ff. The same person is doubtless meant by the gṛhapati Ghoṣila mentioned Mv ii.2.13; Karmav 157.7.

Ghoṣilārāma, m. (Pali Ghositārāma), n. of a residence built for Buddha by the prec. at Kauśāmbī: MSV ii.173.6; iii.28.7.

Ghoṣeśvara, n. of a former Buddha: Samādh p. 57 line 15.

C

(**ca,** as in normal Skt. (BR; Speyer, Skt. Synt. § 441 b, VSS § 282), is used (**1**) in sentences where a contrast seems implied, = tu, *but*: te caivaṃ vācaṃ bhāṣeran, tac ca bhaiṣajyaṃ upanāmitaṃ na pibeyuḥ SP 321.10–11, *on the one hand* (ca) *they would speak thus, and yet* (ca; *on the other hand*) *they would not drink the proffered remedy*; (**2**) in the protasis of conditions, = yadi (acc. to Speyer, VSS l.c., 'in Vedic and older Skt.,' but this is too limited): deśayeyaṃ cāhaṃ dharmaṃ na vā deśayeyam LV 400.7, *whether I preach the dharma or not* — (the same result, as regards some people, will ensue); śakraś ca (mss., Senart em. ce) me varaṃ dadyāt Mv iii.6.15, *if Śakra should give me a boon* —. (**3**) Acc. to Senart, MV i notes pp. 370, 501, 561, ca may introduce a following word, as 'proclitic', no longer enclitic; he says the same is authorized for Pali by the Mukhamattadīpanī, a comm. on Kaccāyana. Alleged cases are cited in Mv i.3.11; 57.10; 83.17 (? read 16?); 158.1; 241.13. In some of these (e. g. 158.1) ca seems to me quite normal; in others the position may be peculiar, as sometimes it is in Pali, see Childers s.v., but I do not believe it ever introduces a following word or phrase; some of the passages cited are violently emended by Senart in other respects. The Pali Dictt. do not recognize the usage alleged by Senart, and I am not convinced that it occurs in BHS.)

cakaṭi, in °ṭy-odana, *some inferior kind of porridge*: Divy 496.9, 11, 12, 26; 497.2; and °ṭi-taṇḍulāḥ, *grains intended for such a porridge*, perhaps *grains of cakaṭi* (some sort of cereal?), Divy 496.21.

cakoraka, nt. (cf. JM. caora, *a kind of dish*, Samarāiccakahā), acc. to Tib. and Chin. apparently *a covered cup* or *vessel used as a lamp*: Mvy 8953 = Tib. skoṅ po (or skoṅ bu, or sgron bu; the first two *cup* or *vessel*, the third *lamp*) kha sbyar (*mouth closed*); Chin. *covered lamp vessel*.

cakra, nt., *circle*; (= Pali cakka) one of the four *circles* or *states of* (desirable, happy) *existence* (in which gods and men may find themselves): catvāri devamanuṣyāṇāṃ cakrāṇi Mvy 1603 (similarly Pali AN ii.32.1), listed 1604–7, pratirūpadeśavāsaḥ, satpuruṣāpāśrayam, ātmanaḥ samyakpraṇidhānam, pūrve ca kṛtapuṇyatā (= Pali ibid. 5 paṭirūpadesavāso sappurisūpassayo attasammāpaṇidhi pubbe ca katapuññatā); see further **cakra-bheda, vidyuc-cakra.**

cakraka (= cakra plus -ka, m.c.?), *circle*: anādibhava-cakrake Mmk 434.21 (vs).

cakra-peyāla, m. or nt. (see **peyāla**), *successive round* (of listed items): MSV ii.206.11; anayā vartanyā °laḥ 208.13; but °laṃ, nt., 209.20.

cakrabheda (m.; = Pali cakka°, parallel with saṃghabheda), *breaking of the 'circle'* (of unity), *sowing discord*: °da-vastu Mvy 9114 = Tib. ḥkhor lo mi mthun pa, *circle non-harmony*.

Cakravartidatta, n. of a former Buddha: Mv i.139.11.

Cakravartin, (1) n. of one of the Uṣṇīṣa-rājānaḥ (see **uṣṇīṣa** 3): Mmk 41.10; **(2)** n. of one of the **krodha,** q.v.: Dharmas 11.

Cakravartinī, n. of a yoginī: Sādh 427.8.

Cakravarti-sūtra, n. of a work: Karmav 59.21; designated as part of the Abhidharma, 94.7; 102.1; 103.6.

Cakravarmiṇī, n. of a yoginī: Sādh 427.7.

cakravāḍa, regularly m. (nt. forms rare; = Skt. °vāla, Pali cakkavāḷa), n. of a mountain or rather mountain-range, supposed to surround the earth: sometimes sg., Mvy 4149 °ḍaḥ; SP 363.5; Dbh 96.4; Mv ii.332.2 śailo . . . °ḍo; more often pl.; often followed by **mahācakravāḍa,** esp. in cpd. (dual dvandva Kv 91.11–12; Dharmas 124), oftener pl., or in longer cpds. where both have stem form, or both sg. (Mvy 4149, 4150), LV 150.1; 277.9; Mv i.6.1; ii.300.17; SP 244.11; Śikṣ 246.2; Suv 86.7; Sukh 36.14–15; 63.3; without mahācak°, SP 355.5 (pl.); LV 316.13 (pl.); Mv ii.341.10 (stem in cpd.); Samādh 19.19 (vs, text cakravāḍa, meter requires cakravāḍo or °ḍā); in fig. use, (puṇya-)cakravāḍaṃ loke parisaṃsthāpayiṣyati Gv 112.22.

Cakravālagupta, n. of a former Buddha: Mv i.139.9 (vv.ll. cakravāḍa°, °vāra°; read prob. °vāḍa°).

Cakravicitra, n. of a lokadhātu: Gv 150.3.

cakravimala, nt., a kind of flower: Mvy 6187.

Cakravegā, n. of a yoginī: Sādh 427.7.

Cakravyūha, n. of a kiṃnara-king: Kv 3.2.

cakraśatapattra, nt., a kind of flower: Mvy 6188.

Cakrākṣaraparivartavyūha, n. of a (perhaps imaginary) Buddhist work (dharmaparyāya): Gv 72.26; 75.12.

Cakrāntara, n. of a future Pratyekabuddha: Av i.133.10.

cakrika, adj., or subst. m., **(1)** some sort of prefessional *entertainer*, perh. *a juggler who does tricks with wheels or discs* (cf. BR s.v. cakrin, 7; a Skt. Lex. possibly gives this mg., but it is uncertain): Mv iii.113.2 (mss. here corrupt); 442.8; **(2)** (*a*) *tricky, crafty* (*person*): °kaḥ Mvy 7326; this seems to be the mg. indicated by Tib. (five renderings), Chin., and Jap., and supported by the adjoining words (jihma, kuṭila, Mvy 7324–5); cf. Skt. (Rājat.) cakrikā, *Ränke* (BR); **(3)** see s.v. **cākrika.**

cakrikā, acc. to Tib. *double door-bar*: Mvy 9344 = Tib. sgo gtan zuṅ can. Chin. contains the words *double* and *bar*. I do not know just what is meant.

-cakṣuka, ifc. for **cakṣus,** q.v.

Cakṣuṣmatī, n. of a goddess: Mvy 4326.

cakṣus, in pañca-c° (= Pali pañca-cakkhu), *the five superior qualities of vision* (partly physical, partly mental or spiritual) possessed by a Buddha (cf. pañcacakṣuḥ-samanvāgata LV 3.5; 403.2, of Buddha): listed, in agreement except for order, Dharmas 66; Sūtrāl. xviii.54, comm.; and Mv i.158.1 ff., where each is explained in some detail, viz. māṃsa-c° 158.8–159.5; divya-c° 159.5–7; prajñā-c° 159.8–9; dharma-c° 159.9–160.7 (= daśānāṃ balānāṃ manovibhutā, 159.10; then follows a statement on the 10 bala, 159.12–160.5, in verse); and buddha-c° 160.7–16 (this = the 18 āveṇikā buddhadharmāḥ, which are then listed). In Pali (see Childers and PTSD) the list contains maṃsa-, dibba-, paññā-, and buddha-cakkhu, but for dharma- substitutes samanta-c° (before or after buddha-c°). A difficult and corrupt line, Mv i.42.15 = 53.12 = 337.4 (in the last printed by Senart as prose), contains some form of bhava-cakṣuka, which Senart regards as containing a *bhava-cakṣu(s) = māṃsa-c°, quite wrongly; his transl. (note on 42.15) misunderstands māṃsa-c° which is a complimentary and superior power, not one to be derogated. Possibly rather *eye of existence* and agreeing with prajñā-skandha (337.4 prajñā-cakṣu[r])? The preponderant evidence of the mss. points to bhava-cakṣuke (or °ko or °kaiḥ) apāye prajñāskandho (or °dhe, °dhā; 337.4 see above) niveśeyaṃ (? °yaḥ, or other vv.ll.). All too obscure to be useful.

-cagghati, see **uc-, saṃ-cagghati.**

caṅkrama, m. and (less regularly) nt. (= Pali caṅkama; to **caṅkramati**), **(1)** *act of walking*, in purely physical sense: vivṛtaḥ śobhate ārya āsana-sthāna-caṅkrame LV 157.15 (vs), *when uncovered* (unveiled), *a noble person shines* (is distinguished) *in sitting, standing, and walking*; these are three of the (usually four) modes of physical behavior (the fourth being lying down), see s.v. **īryāpatha** 4; AsP 520.13; RP 45.18; cognate acc. °maṃ caṅkramyate or °mati, see (4) below; **(2)** *walking, wandering*, as an occupation or mode of life: in Karmav 104.14 one of the daśa guṇāḥ paiṇḍapātikatve, *ten advantages in the mendicant's life*, is, caṅkramo 'sya upārjito bhavati, *he has acquired* (a life of) *walking, wandering about*; **(3)** *place of walking, promenade* (in the sense of *ground where walking is done*): of walks in groves or parks (secular), ekaikaṃ caṅkrama-varaṃ . . . kalpayatha Mv ii.18.16 (vs), Śuddhodana says, *adorn* (or with mss. kalpayama, *let us adorn*) *every excellent promenade* (in the Lumbinī grove, in preparation for Māyā's visit); gṛha-dhana-dhānya-śayana-vasanaṃ caṅkramodyānāni cānekaśo yācanakebhyo nisṛṣṭāni LV 318.5 (prose), . . . *promenades and parks were bestowed on beggars many times*; **(4)** especially, *promenade, terrace, place for walking* (often rendered *cloister*), for monks or Buddhas or other ascetics; sometimes associated with places for 'standing, sitting, lying down', the other **īryāpatha,** see mg. (1) above; samyaksaṃbuddhānāṃ adhiṣṭhitāni caṅkramā niṣadyāni śayyāni Mv ii.163.18; teṣāṃ bhikṣūṇāṃ sthānāni caṅkramāṇi niṣadyāni śayyāni Mv iii.420.15; teṣu ca caṅkrameṣu niṣadyāsv āsaneṣu ca Gv 518.7 (places); oftener associated with a vihāra (from which it seems that one *climbed* or *mounted* to the caṅkrama, cf. Pali Therag. 271 ... vihārā upanikkhamiṃ, caṅkamam abhirūhanto; so frequently abhi-ruh- occurs in BHS with this word): araṇyavāsi (loc.; v.l. °se) tiṣṭhanto caṅkrame (WT °mam with K') abhiruhya ca SP 335.5 (vs); ārāmāś caṅkramā dattāḥ (to Buddha and his monks) 341.13 (vs); ye keci bhikṣū sugatasya śāsane, abhiyuktarūpā sthita caṅkrameṣu 365.5 (vs); (yasmiṃś ca ... grāme vā nagare vā ...) janapadapradeśe vā caṅkrame vā vihāre vā ayaṃ Lalitavistaro ... pracariṣyati LV 442.11; bhikṣūṇāṃ saptaratnacitān vihārān kārayām āsa maṇi-caṅkramān (prob. Karmadh., not Bhvr.) ... RP 56.13; in Mv i.318.10 text, bhagavato Kāśyapasya caṅkrama-ṣaṣṭiḥ, for which Senart's note suggests caṅkrama-bhūmiḥ (violent em.!), but mss. kraṃkrame (or kraṃkame) ṣa°; possibly read caṅkrame yaṣṭiḥ, *stick (pole, flagstaff?) in K's promenade*; (vihārān...) ārāmān ramaṇīyāṃś ca caṅkrama-sthāna-śobhitān SP 334.9 (vs; ca°-sthāna, *place of promenade*, substantially = caṅkrama?); (vihārāḥ ... bhikṣusahasrāvāsā ārāmapuṣpopaśobhitāś) caṅkramavanopetāḥ SP 339.3, ... *provided with promenades and groves*; of a brahmanical ascetic, atha Brahmaprabho māṇavako 'nyatarasmin pradeśe kuṭīṃ kārayitvā caṅkramaṃ (*a walking-ground*, in the wilds) pratiṣṭhāpya sattvānām arthāya tapas taptavān Divy 477.17–19; (Bhagavataś) caṅkrame dattaḥ (sc. pradīpaḥ) Divy 90.3, *a lamp was given to the Lord on his promenade* (i. e. *the place of exercise*? or *on his walk*, to mg. 1?); loc. or acc., followed by form of the cognate verb, bhagavāṃś cāsya nātidūre caṅkrame caṅkramyate Av i.183.1; ānando bahir vihārasyābhyavakāśe caṅkrame caṅkramyate 228.9; (Buddha speaks) yan nūnāhaṃ pauruṣamātraṃ vaihāyasam antarīkṣe dīrghaṃ caṅkramaṃ caṅkrameyaṃ Mv iii.114.12–13, which he does in 15, dī° ca° caṅkramati aspṛśanto pādatalehi bhūmiyaṃ; in a dream the Bodhisattva sees himself, tathāgato ... saṃbodhim anabhisaṃbuddho mahato mīḍhaparvatasya uparim anupalipyamāno caṅkramaṃ caṅkrame (aor.) Mv ii.137.11–12 and 139.7–8; *the long*(-continued) *promenade* (cf. Mv iii.114.12–13 above) seems to have been a special spiritual exercise, to which exceptional importance is attached, and the cognate accus. in the following may be partly a noun of action, tho it seems rarely if ever completely separate from the place-designation; the Buddha, in the 2d or 3d week after enlightenment, (dvitīye) saptāhe tathāgato dīrghacaṅkramaṃ caṅkramyate sma LV 377.4, (tṛtīyaṃ) saptāhaṃ prītisukhena dīrghaṃ caṅkramaṃ caṅkrame (aor.) Mv iii.281.12; (Buddha, vihārāto nirgamya ... smitaṃ prāduṣkaritvā) dīrghaṃ caṅkramaṃ caṅkrame (aor.) Mv i.317.(7–)9; without use of the word dīrgha, the like is presented in SP, with emphasis on spiritual results: (the Bodhisattva Sarvasattvapriyadarśana) dvādaśa varṣasahasrāṇi caṅkramābhirūḍho (Tib. ḥchag pa la zhugs śiṅ, *having begun, undertaken, a walk*) 'bhūn mahāvīryārambheṇa yogābhiyukto 'bhūt SP 405.13, followed by reference to this in 408.14 (vs), spoken by the Bodhisattva S., ayaṃ mamā caṅkrama rāja śreṣṭha yasmin mayā sthitva samādhi labdhaḥ; similarly, yadā ca sa dharmabhāṇako 'smin dharmaparyāye cintāyogam anuyuktaś caṅkramābhirūḍho bhaviṣyati, tadāhaṃ ... tasya dharmabhāṇakasya caṅkrama-kuṭīm (Tib. ḥchag paḥi, = caṅkrama, gnas, = *place*, esp. *abode, habitation*; cf. kuṭīṃ and caṅkramaṃ together in Divy 477.17–19 above) upasaṃkramiṣyāmi (*I will go to his promenade-hut* which perhaps might be in a vihāra, but in any case must be the place where he rested during his caṅkrama with its long-continued attendant spiritual exercises) ... asya dharmaparyāyasyārakṣāya SP 474.11–475.2; ye ... ekaviṃśatidivasāni caṅkramābhirūḍhā abhiyuktā bhaviṣyanti, teṣām ahaṃ ... ekaviṃśatime divase teṣāṃ dharmabhāṇakānāṃ caṅkramam āgamiṣyāmy ... SP 476.3–5 (note here the evident reference to caṅkrama as a definite *place*!); in Kv **caṅkramaṇa,** q.v., is used in the same local sense, but twice followed by caṅkrama in this same sense: tato vimānān niṣkramya svaka-svakāni caṅkramaṇāni pratyudgatāḥ (sc. Bodhisattvāḥ), caṅkramecaṅkrame ... (follows description of their physical beauties and decorations) Kv 65.1–2; (pious kiṃnaras) ṣaṭpāramitāsāṃkathya(ṃ) kṛtvā svaka-svakāni caṅkramaṇāni caṅkramanti (cf. cognate verb with caṅkrama, above); kecit suvarṇamayāś caṅkramā(s) teṣu caṅkrameṣu sāmantakeṣu kalpavṛkṣāḥ, etc. Kv 66.6–7.

caṅkramaṇa, nt. (= Pali caṅkamana; in sense of caṅkrama 4; in Skt. °ṇa only n. act., *walking, strolling*), *place of promenade* (for a monk): (tavārthāya divyāni sauvarṇamayāni) °ṇāni kariṣyāmaḥ Kv 42.21; svakasvakāni caṅkramaṇāni 65.1; 66.6; in both of these followed by forms of **caṅkrama,** q.v., in the same sense, referring to places of promenade.

caṅkramati (= Pali caṅkamati; Skt. caṅkramyate, rarely °mate, °mati; § 39.1), *wanders, strolls, roams*: opt. °mi SP 344.1; °med LV 369.1; aor. °mī LV 368.16; etc., see Chap. 43, s.v. kram (5).

? **caṅkramya-yuktāḥ** SP 13.2 (vs), so both edd., as cpd.; perh. Tib. understood it so, ḥchag pa byed ciṅ, *making wandering* (no other rendering for yuktāḥ in Tib.); if so, we must assume an otherwise unknown noun caṅkramya = caṅkrama(ṇa), *wandering* (based on the normal Skt. pres. caṅkramya-te = BHS **caṅkramati**?). Burnouf clearly understood caṅkramya as separate word, ger. to **caṅkramati**; Kern *actively engaged in walking*, which is ambiguous but suggests rather a cpd.

caccara (m. or nt.; = Pali id., Skt. catvara), *square, four-crossroads*: so it seems that the mss. must read, or intend, at SP 88.1 (vs), where KN sthitu catvarasmin (kept by WT without note), but with note over the final letter: 'O. care the others caresmin'. This very imperfect annotation seems to mean that the Nep. mss. have caccaresmin (*cacaresmin or *caresmin would be unparallelled, morphologically and semantically incomprehensible, and metrically impossible); caccare, seemingly the reading of 'O' = Kashgar rec., would be metrically defective, lacking the necessary last syllable.

cañca, m., acc. to Chin. *box*, but acc. to Tib. gab tse, defined in all Tib. Dictt. as *a tablet used in divination*; BR *Korb* (accepting Chin.?): Mvy 5911; preceded by ṭaṅka, *chisel*, and followed by piṭharī, *pot* (in a list of implements and utensils). Cf. **cañcu.**

Cañcā (Pali Ciñcā), n. of a brahman girl who falsely accused Buddha: Laṅk 240.12; MSV i.161.1 ff.; 212.10.

cañcitāśraya (cañcita, ppp. of Skt. cañc, plus **āśraya,** q.v.), *with shaking* (quivering, trembling) *body*: Av i.243.7, repeated 247.5; 268.10. Speyer, Corr. ii.209, adopts from Kern an em. carvitāśraya, which seems to me singularly implausible; text is quite sound.

cañcu, nt., in Divy 131.21, 22, 24, and same passage MSV i.250.9 ff., said to mean lit. *box* (cf. **cañca**), and to be applied to a type of *famine*: trividhaṃ durbhikṣaṃ bhaviṣyati, cañcu śvetāsthi śalākāvṛtti (Divy mss. °ttiṃ; MSV ms. śilakā°) ca. tatra cañcu ucyate samudgake, tasmin manuṣyā vījāni prakṣipyānāgate (MSV °ta-) sattvāpekṣayā sthāpayanti mṛtānām (MSV asmākam) anena te vījakāyaṃ (MSV anena bījena manuṣyāḥ kāryaṃ) kariṣyantīti. idaṃ samudgakaṃ baddhvā cañcu ucyate.

caṭita, ppp. as adj. and subst. (to caṭ, in this sense only in cpds. in Skt., except caṭita, *zerbrochen*, once acc. to pw; BR s.v. caṭ erroneously *abfallen* for Pañcat. Koseg. 131.1; not recorded in MIndic), *broken down*, or *cracked*: caṭita-sphuṭitān (adj.) vihārān Kv 13.9; stūpa-bimbāni caṭita-sphuṭitāni viśīrṇa-bhūtāni 13.11; tenāsau dṛṣṭaḥ stūpaḥ; caṭita-sphuṭitakaḥ prādurbhūtaḥ Divy 22.27, *he saw that stūpa; it appeared cracked and broken* (ruined);

(subst.) *break, crack, fissure,* or *broken place*: tenāsmin stūpe caṭita-sphuṭitakāni prādurbhūtāni Divy 23.6, here seemingly dvandva cpd., *fissures and breaks appeared in the stūpa.* See next.

caṭitaka, nt. (= prec., as subst.), *break, fissure*: tasmin stūpe caṭitakāni prādurbhūtāni Divy 22.24, *in that stūpa breaks appeared.*

Caṇḍaka, n. of a yakṣa: Māy 77.

Caṇḍa-giri, Mv iii.130.4 (prose), or **Canda-parvata,** 133.12 (vs), n. of a mountain.

Caṇḍa-girika, *the fierce Girika* (q.v.): Divy 374.17 ff.

Caṇḍa-parvata, see **Caṇḍa-giri.**

Caṇḍamahāroṣaṇa, acc. to Bhattacharya, GOS 26 p. viii, n. of a Bodhisattva, 'the principal figure in the Tantra of that name': Sādh 171.15, 172.2 etc. Is he not another name for, or form of, Mañjuśrī? His sādhanas follow those of the latter in Sādh; both have the name or epithet **Pañcavīra** (read °**cīra**)-**kumāra,** q.v. He is in any case an angry personage.

caṇḍamṛga, *a fierce beast of prey* (so Tib. on Mvy): MSV ii.14.2; fig. of a man: Mvy 2958.

Caṇḍa-vajrapāṇi, *the fierce V.,* a form of **Vajrapāṇi,** with epithet mahāyakṣasenāpati: ŚsP 2.2.

Caṇḍā (in Skt., like **Caṇḍikā** and (Lex.) **Caṇḍālikā,** names of deities identified with Durgā), n. of a yakṣiṇī: Suv 163.1 (with Caṇḍikā and Caṇḍālikā); n. of a rākṣasī, Māy 243.30, 34.

Caṇḍākṣī, n. of a yoginī: Sādh 427.3.

caṇḍālaka (= Skt. °la), *an outcaste, caṇḍāla*: (listed among enemies of birds) Mv ii.251.5 (prose; Senart em. cāṇḍ°).

Caṇḍālikā (cf. s.v. **Caṇḍā**), n. of a yakṣiṇī: Suv 163.1.

Caṇḍālinī, n. of a yoginī: Sādh 446.20 (vs).

Caṇḍālī, n. of a yoginī: Sādh 443.16, et alibi; n. of a rākṣasī, Māy 243.34.

Caṇḍikā (cf. s.v. **Caṇḍā**), n. of a yakṣiṇī: Suv 163.1.

catuḥkarṇa, adj. (Pali catu(k)kaṇṇa), *four-cornered, square* or *rectangular*: (of hells) Mv iii.454.11 (= Pali catukkaṇṇā Jāt. v.266.19); in same vs i.9.12 catuḥkalā, prob. corruption, but acc. to P. Mus, La Lumière des six voies 94 ff., supported by a Tib. correspondent and to be adopted in Mv (with same mg., *carrés*).

? **catuḥkala,** see prec.

catutha (m.c. for MIndic catuttha, Skt. caturtha), *fourth*: Dbh.g. 16(352).8 (vs; no v.l.; this form not recorded in MIndic).

[**catur-aṅga,** m. (otherwise ep. of an army, *having the four parts*), *having a fourfold* (*army*), ep. of a cakravartin: LV 101.13; 136.16 (both prose); but in the same cliché Mv has **cātu(r)dvīpa,** q.v., and Pali cāturanta, DN i.88.33; our word is a malformation; Tib. mthaḥ bzhi las (rnam par rgyal ba) suggests cāturanta-(-vijitavant), cpd., as the true reading; or possibly **cāturantam** (see this) vijit°. See **vijitavant.**]

Caturaṅgabala, n. of an ancient king: Mv i.117.3.

caturaśrita (denom. ppp. to Skt. caturaśra), *squared, made square*: maṇḍalapramāṇam ity uktaḥ samantāc caturaśritam, caturdvāram . . . Mmk 526.13 (vs).

caturasraka, nt. (cf. Skt. caturaśrikā, Kauṭ, see Schmidt, Nachträge, and J. J. Meyer, Index; acc. to Meyer *a square shawl* [or *a blanket*] used as protection against cold), prob. *a square blanket* or *shawl*, one of the appointments of monks' quarters: vṛṣi-**kocava** (so read, see s.v.)-bimbopadhāna-caturasraka-śatāni (things furnished to monks) Divy 40.11; 550.16; 553.3, 10; caturasrakam Mvy 8992, rendered in Tib., Chin., Jap. literally, *square*; **bimbopadhāna** and **vṛsikā** (or vṛṣ°, = Divy vṛṣi) occur in the same vicinity, and **kocavaka** not far away (8982).

Caturasravadana (mss. °dara), n. of a former Buddha: Mv i.138.2.

caturahika, adj. (to Skt. °aha), *pertaining to four days*: °kaṃ pañcāhikaṃ śālim Mv i.343.16, 17. Mss. caturāhika (or caturo°); perh. read so.

caturāśīti (= Pali °sīti, AMg. caurāsīiṃ, Pischel 446; see § 19.35), *eighty-four*: in prose, Mv iii.450.13 (v.l. °aśīti); Gv 389.16 (note in 22 below °aśīti); in vss (could be m.c.) Mv i.119.5; 216.10; cf. also (vs) catvāri āśīti, *eighty-four*, Dbh.g. 44(70).25.

caturguṇam, adv. (= Pali catu[g]g°), (so as to be) *folded in four* (thicknesses), of the outer robe: Divy 77.3 (MW *tied with 4 strings*); MPS 30.5, 7 (in 7 ed. em. °guṇa uttarāsaṅgaḥ, but ms. °ṇam, adv.). Cf. **gaṇa-guṇa.**

(**caturdikka,** acc. pl. °kān Śikṣ 26.16, called by Bendall a 'new form'; but it is recorded in Kathās., BR 3.637 s.v. 2 diś, and [°kam, adv.] 5.1407.)

caturdvīpaka-cakravartin, *a universal monarch of the highest rank, who rules over the 'four continents'*: SP 6.4; 20.6. See s.vv. **balacakravartin, maṇḍalin**; cf. next, and **cātur°.**

caturdvīpeśvara (cf. **cāturdvīpeśvara**), with cakravartin, = prec.: °śvarāś cakravartinaḥ Śikṣ 175.10 (prose); sa cakravartī caturdvīpa-īśvaro (so Lefm. em., m.c., for °peśvaro of all mss.) LV 211.6 (vs).

Caturdharmaka-sūtra, n. of a work: Śikṣ 41.7; 160.4.

caturmahāpatha (m.; = Pali catu-ma°; cf. Skt. catuṣpatha and mahāpatha), *crossing of four main roads*: catuḥmahāpathe (v.l. caturma°) sthitvā Mv i.301.19 (in vs form of the same catuṣpathe, 303.18); caturmahāpathe ii.177.20; 178.1; °thāto, abl., 178.2.

caturmahārājakāyika, adj. with deva or devaputra, = next and (the more usual) **cātur°**, *belonging to the group of the four 'World-Guardians'* (a class of gods, see **cāturmahārājika**): Mv i.212.15 = ii.16.3; iii.223.9; 319.13; LV 366.11; 441.15; read so with best mss., supported by Tib., in LV 367.4 for text mahārājakāyika. Some of these prose.

caturmahārājika, adj. (in Pali also sometimes ca°, oftener cā°, acc. to PTSD), = prec. and (much oftener) **cāturmahārājika,** q.v.: Mv i.30.16, 17; 40.15; ii.348.16; Divy 568.24; all these are prose.

? **caturya,** m. (= Skt. cāturya, nt.), *cleverness, strategem, trick*: in Mv iii.74.2 (prose) read with v.l. eṣo caturyo (Senart ca tujyo, see **tujyo**) kāryo. (Or read cāturyo? Pali only cāturiya; in Vv.41.2 read with PTSD ca turiyagaṇā, supported by comm.)

Catuḥśaila, n. of a mountain: Māy 254.2.

catuṣka-nipāta (= Pali catukka-ni°), n. of a section of the Ekottarikāgama: MSV i.45.19.

catuṣkumbhikā (cf. Pali catu-kuṇḍika, adj., *going on all fours*; explained Pv. comm. 181.9; this and the BHS form are certainly based on a common orig., one or the other, or both, being modified by some analogical or blending influence), *way of crawling on all fours*: °kayā sarpati Mvy 9311; so Tib. rkaṅ lag bzhis phye ba (with varr.), *crawling by the four feet-and-hands.*

catuṣkoṭikā (see also **cātuṣkoṭika,** °**kā**; Skt. koṭi, *alternative*), *a set of four alternative propositions* (see Suzuki, Studies in Laṅk., 116 n. 2), viz. that something is, is not, both is and is not, neither is nor is not: Laṅk 122.4–8, defined 5–8 ekatvānyatvobhayanobhayāstināstinityānityarahitām °kām iti vadāmi, etayā °kayā . . . rahitāḥ sarvadharmā ity ucyate.

catuṣpadaka, f. °**ikā,** adj. (= Skt. °pada plus -ka; see also °**pādaka,** and **cātuṣpada,** °**pāda,** °**padaka**), *consisting of four pādas or metrical units*, ep. of gāthā: Mvy 6350; Divy 505.3 (both prose).

Catuṣparṣadasūtra, n. of a work: Karmav 161.20. Seems to correspond to Pali AN ii.8 (Book 4, section 7); cf. Lévi's notes.

catuṣpādaka, f. °**ikā,** adj. (= Pali catu(p)pādikā

gāthā), = **catuṣpadaka,** q.v.: with gāthā, Suv 125.12; 129.2; Śikṣ 37.8; Kv (misprinted catuṣyā°) 40.5, 13, 20; Vaj 28.7, 11; 30.1; 42.5 (all prose; Kashgar rec. of Vaj **cātuṣpādā, °padikā, °padī,** qq.v.).

catuṣpādika, adj. (Skt. °pād or °pāda plus -ika; cf. prec.), *four-footed* (creature, sattva): °kāni sattvāni Kv 25.3 (prose).

catvāra (m. or nt.; = Skt. catvara; only in prose of Gv; ā perhaps influenced by remembrance of catvāraḥ etc.), *crossroads, square* (as meeting of roads): °reṇa °raṃ rathyayā rathyāṃ Gv 179.18; sarvarathyāsu sarvacatvāreṣu sarvaśṛṅgāṭakeṣu 181.9–10; rathyā-catvāra-śṛṅgāṭakebhyaḥ 192.25; sarva-śṛṅgāṭaka-rathyā-catvāreṣu 327.26.

candana, (1) adj. (cf. BR s.v. 2; acc. to Skt. Gr. used at end of a cpd. meaning *best of its kind*), *superior, excellent*: (of the Buddha)... śāntaḥ śāntaparivāraś candanaś candanapari° mukto muktapari°... Divy 96.16; is this the mg. of candana in °na-**gaṇḍīraka** (q.v.)?; (2) n. of a former Buddha: Mv iii.234.5 f.; LV 171.12; Av i.74.9 ff.; Sukh 5.10 (perhaps not all intended for the same person); (3) n. of a devaputra (prob. same as DPPN Ca° 1, described as a yakkha): LV 4.12; 6.12; 7.5; 438.16 (only in lists of names of gods); (4) n. of a gandharva: Suv 162.4 (not likely to be the same as 3); (5) n. of a Pratyekabuddha: Av i.119.8 ff.; (a different one?) Mmk 64.12; 111.10 (in lists of Pr.); (6) n. of a noble elephant, born at the same time with Śākyamuni: Mv ii.25.13.

Candanagandha, n. of two former Buddhas: Sukh 5.9; 6.9 (in the same list!).

candana-godhā, *sandalwood-lizard*, a kind of godhā: MSV ii.40.10; 41.14.

Candanapīṭha, n. of a 'Tathāgata-caitya': Gv 205.16; 206.6.

candanaprabha, m. or nt., a kind of gem: Mv ii.311.1. (Read **candraprabha,** q.v. 8?)

Candanamāla, (1) n. of a mountain: Māy 254.10; (2), see s.v. **māla** (2).

Candanamegha, n. of a Bodhisattva: Gv 442.7.

Candanavatī, n. of a lokadhātu: Gv 82.6.

Candanaśrī, n. of a Buddha: Śikṣ 169.11.

Candanaśrīgarbha, n. of a Bodhisattva: Dbh 2.9.

Candanaśrīcandra, n. of a Buddha: Gv 310.12.

Candābhibhū, n. of a former Buddha: Sukh 5.14. So text without v.l.! Read Candrā°? Caṇḍā°?

? **candīsaka** (m. or nt.; v.l. **śabdīsaka**), some musical instrument: Mv ii.159.5. Nothing like either form has been found anywhere. In a list of mus. instr.; prob. corrupt.

candra, (1) nt. (in Skt. only m. in this sense), *moon*: yathaiva candra... tārakai parivṛtaṃ (no v.l.; read parī° m.c.) LV 75.7 (vs); (2) (= Skt. Lex. id.; Skt. candraka, Pali and AMg. candaka), *spot* or *'eye' on a peacock's tail*: moracandrasamaiś candrair Laṅk 365.12 (vs), *with* (moon-shaped) *spots like the eyes on a peacock's tail*; (3) n. of a former Buddha: Av i.81.1 ff.; (4) n. of a young brahman who died and was reborn as a god: Av i.295.11; (5) n. of a prince: Mv iii.172.9 ff.

candraka, nt., *a* (half-)*moon-shaped ornament*: Mvy 6023 = Tib. zla gam can, or, rgya zla gam.

Candrakāntā, n. of a yakṣiṇī: Sādh 562.5. See s.v. **Citrakāli** (v.l. **Candrakānti**!), and next.

Candrakāli (or **°lī**; dat. °lyai), n. of a yakṣiṇī: Sādh 561.10 (replacing **Citrakāli,** q.v.).

Candragarbha, n. of a Bodhisattva: ŚsP 6.21.

Candrateja(s), n. of a former Buddha: Mv i.137.5 °jaḥ, n. sg.

Candradhvajaketu, n. of a samādhi: Mvy 510; ŚsP 1415.10.

Candradhvajaśrīketu, n. of a Tathāgata: Gv 280.12; called **Indradhvajaketu** 281.7.

Candradhvajā, n. of a lokadhātu: Gv 222.13.

Candrapadma, n. of a former Buddha: Mv i.137.4.

Candrapradīpa, n. of a samādhi: SP 424.4. Refers to subject of our Samādh; see next; Burnouf reads Candraprabha (n. of the Bodhisattva who is prominent in Samādh) in SP.

Candrapradīpasamādhi = next: Mmk 38.12; 109.27.

Candrapradīpasūtra, another name for Samādh (-irājāsūtra), always used for it in Śikṣ, 16.19 etc.

Candraprabha, (1) n. of a former incarnation of Śākyamuni: Divy 315.27 ff., 328.20 (hero of Divy Chap. 22); RP 23.4 (certainly the same); prob. also intended by LV 171.1; (2) n. of another incarnation of Śākyamuni, a śreṣṭhin's son: Divy 475.10 ff.; 480.3–5; (3) n. of a Bodhisattva, chief interlocutor of Buddha in Samādh: 8.1; 19.1 ff., 37; 22.1, 7; (?) perh. the same, Mvy 689; Sādh 96.1 (in these two followed by **Sūryaprabha,** q.v.); 114.2; Mmk 40.15; 62.11; 312.5; (v.l. for **Candrapradīpa,** q.v., as n. of a samādhi, referring to this Bodhisattva;) (4) n. of a yakṣa: Divy 113.22; 114.4, 6; (5) n. of a nāga-king: Māy 246.24; (6) n. of a former Buddha: Sukh 6.6; (7) n. of a mountain: Māy 253.35 (a mountain of this name appears in Skt., Kirfel, Kosm. 59; perh. the same?); (8) m. (or nt.), a kind of gem: Mv ii.317.11. Cf. **candanaprabha.**

Candraprabhā, n. of the queen of Rudrāyaṇa: Divy 545.4; 553.14 ff.

Candraprabhāsā, n. of a female lay-disciple (upāsikā): Gv 51.16.

Candraprabhāsvararāja, see **Candrasvararāja.**

Candrabimbaprabhā, n. of a 'gandharva maid': Kv 5.16.

Candrabuddhi, n. of a Tathāgata: Gv 82.11.

Candrabhānu, n. of a former Buddha (or of two such): Mv i.136.17; Sukh 6.6.

Candravimala, m., n. of a samādhi: Mvy 551; ŚsP 1419.7.

Candravimalasūryaprabhāsaśrī, see **Candrasūryavimala°.**

Candraśubha, n. of a former Buddha: Mv i.139.11.

Candraśrī, n. of a Bodhisattva: Gv 4.3.

Candrasūryajihmīkaraṇa, n. of a former Buddha: Sukh 5.19.

Candrasūryajihmīkaraprabha (v.l. °karaṇaprabha), n. of a Tathāgata: LV 292.7.

Candrasūryapradīpa, (1) n. of a former Buddha: SP 17.9; there were 20,000 former Buddhas of this same name, 18.4; in the verse account 25.1 called **Candrārkadīpa;** (2) n. of a Buddha in the southern quarter: Sukh 97.7.

Candrasūryavimalaprabhāsaśrī, n. of a former Buddha: SP 404.11 ff., (v.l. **Candravimalasūryaprabhāsaśrī;** so both Burnouf and Kern, Transl.).

Candraskandhārcitabrahman, n. of a Bodhisattva: Gv 443.7.

Candrasvararāja, n. of a series of 20 hundred crores of former Buddhas: SP 380.6 (so both edd., no v.l.; Burnouf's and Kern's translations Candraprabhāsvararāja).

candrāṃśujālamaṇḍalagarbha(-maṇirāja), some kind of jewel: lohitamuktāmayeṣu kṣetreṣu °maṇirājavarṇāṃ prabhāṃ pramuñcamānāni, °maṇirāja-śarīreṣu kṣetreṣu lohitamuktāvarṇāṃ... Gv 90.6–8.

Candrānana, n. of a former Buddha: Samādh p. 57 line 19.

Candrābha, n. of a former Buddha: Mv i.137.5.

Candrārkadīpa, SP 25.1 = **Candrasūryapradīpa,** q.v.

candrāvabhāsa, see **candrobhāsa.**

Candrima (cf. Pali candimā = Skt. candramās,

moon), n. of two former Buddhas, in the same list: Mv iii.233.4; 236.17 f.

Candrottarajñānin, n. of a Bodhisattva: Gv 2.15.

Candrottarā, n. of a girl, and °rā-dārikā-paripṛcchā, n. of a work in which she appears: (both) Śikṣ 78.19.

Candrodgata, n. of a Bodhisattva: Gv 442.20.

candrobhāsa (for candrāvabhāsa), m. or nt., a kind of gem: Mv ii.310.16.

candropaniṣad, pl., a class of gods, lit. *based on the moon*: °do devāś candram eva puraskṛtya (sc. āgatāḥ) Mahāsamāj., Waldschmidt Kl. Skt. Texte 4, 183.15 (vs); Tib., ibid. 204.1, zla la gnas pa, *dwelling in the moon*; = Pali DN ii.259.23 candassūpanisā devā candam āgu purakkhatvā; comm. ii.690.12 = canda-nissitakā devā. Or possibly *like the moon*? cf. **upaniṣad.** Similarly **sūryopaniṣad.**

Candrolkādhārin, n. of a Bodhisattva: Gv 441.26.

(**capalam**, adv., rare in Skt., see BR 5.1411; not recorded in Pali, but AMg. capalaṃ, cavalaṃ; *quickly*: chandakā capalu mā vilamba he LV 210.4 (vs), so read for Lefm. vilambahe (§ 30.8), *quickly, Chandaka! don't delay, I say!*; dadāhi capalaṃ LV 220.16 (vs), *give it quickly!*; saṃpūryate capalam eva Mv ii.136.8 (vs).)

camara, m., a high number: Mvy 7787 = Tib. rgod-yas (mg.?).

camasa, m., Mvy 4050, acc. to one Tib. version rna śal, *tip* or *lobe of ear*; v.l. sna śal (not recorded; sna = *nose* but Dictt. do not record śal except in rna śal). Perhaps named from fancied resemblance to the (flat) shape of the utensil called camasa.

camu, camū, (**1**) as in Skt., *host, army*, but with masc. ending (otherwise only fem.): mārasya jetuṃ camūn LV 276.6 (end of stanza; no v.l.); (**2**) f., *coffin* (rare in Skt., only early, see BR s.v. camū 2, and Kauś 48.4): (so mṛtako puruṣo ...) camusmiṃ prakṣipitvā subaddhaṃ kṛtvā ... Mv ii.173.6; etāṃ camuṃ 173.12; camuṃ 173.13, 14; 174.4, 9.

Campaka (same as Pali Campeyya), n. of a nāga-king: Mv ii.177.13 ff.; colophon 188.22 iti śrīcampaka-nāgarājasya jātakaṃ (= Pali Campeyya-Jāt., 506) samāptaṃ.

Campakavarṇā, n. of a lokadhātu, in the west: LV 291.17.

Campakavimalaprabha, n. of a Bodhisattva: Gv 442.24.

caraka, m. (not noted in Pali; rare in Skt., see pw s.v. 1 c; but recorded in AMg. as caraga-, cpd. with parivvāyaga, just as in BHS), one of a heretical sect of ascetics; regularly followed in comp. by parivrājaka, the two possibly (as allegedly in AMg., above, see Ratnach.) denoting a single sect or class of persons, rather than two: usually preceded, immediately or otherwise, by anyatīrthika (LV 2.21; Mv iii.412.7) or anyatīrthya (SP 276.2); caraka-parivrājaka- LV 2.21; 380.12; SP 276.2; Mv iii.412.7; Śikṣ 331.11. The proper Tib. translation seems to be spyod pa pa; so both LV passages (Foucaux reads dpyod pa pa for 2.21, but my photostat of the Lib. of Congr. ed. spyod ...) and SP; spyod = car-. But Jäschke defines this by Mīmāṃsaka, the correct term for which is dpyod pa pa (both terms are given for Mīmāṃsaka in Mvy 3517; Mvy seems to omit caraka); dpyod = *examine* (mīmāṃs-); Tib. tradition has confused the two.

Carakā, n. of a goddess: Mahāsamāj., Waldschmidt, Kl. Skt. Texte 4, 185.17.

caraṇa, nt., (**1**) a high number: Mvy 7914 (cited from Gv; Tib. gdab yas); Gv 106.16; 133.26; (**2**) *residence* (of a king): rājñaś caraṇa-koṣṭhe MSV ii.61.12, *on the top part of the king's residence*; so Tib., rgyal poḥi (*king's*) khap (read khab, *residence*, of a king) kyi (gen. suffix) khaṅ (*house*) tog tu (*on top*); for this mg. of koṣṭha cf. **dvāra-koṣṭha(ka)**.

carama, nt., a high number: Mvy 7915 (cited from Gv; Tib. mthaḥ ḥbyam); Gv 106.16 (follows **caraṇa**; but omitted in Gv 133.26).

carama-bhavika, adj. (Pali carimabhava plus ika), *living in one's last existence, destined to be reborn no more*: said of Bodhisattvas, LV 22.4; 85.11 etc.; Kv 68.23; 75.5; Mmk 324.7; Gv 438.23; (bodhisattvasyaikajātipratibaddhasya, *bound to only one further rebirth*) caramabhavikasya vā Bbh 229.1; without noun, Mvy 7003; of the barber-disciple Upāli, Mv iii.179.8; said of Rāhula before ordination, Mv iii.263.11 (note in 13, said of the same, etehi eva skandhehi parinirvāpayitavyaṃ); said of śrāvaka-pratyekabuddha-yānika, Gv 141.5; of *creatures* (sattva) in general, not specifically classified, Divy 1.17; 174.1; 177.20; 264.2, 6; 331.5; 423.14; Av ii.135.8.

carama-śayana, *'last couch', funeral bier* (wrongly Bendall and Rouse): (-vastraviśeṣair) āchāditasya caramaśayanāvasthitasya ... kālakriyā bhaviṣyati Śikṣ 208.4.

cari, or **carī** (ī chiefly or wholly m.c.), f. (not recorded in MIndic; = Skt. **caryā**, Pali **cariyā**, both also in BHS, see s.vv.; cf. § 3.115), *course of conduct, regular system of action* (esp. *religious*); particularly with reference to the *programmatic course* of a Bodhisattva, leading to enlightenment; (on its four aspects or stages see s.v. **caryā**;) these forms chiefly, but not exclusively, in verse; see also **cāri, cārikā**; in prose the usual expression is (Bodhisattva-)caryā, e. g. SP 7.1; 65.5; LV 90.10; Gv 58.9; but even in prose note (bo)dhisattva-cari-niṣpanda- LV 5.1 (all mss., only Calc. °carita°), and cf. Bhadracari-vidhipūrvakaṃ Śikṣ 139.13 (prose; the bhadra-cari is the bodhisattva-cari; the work of this name is elsewhere called Bhadra-caryā in the prose of Śikṣ, 290.8; 291.9; 297.1); in Bhad itself the form is Bhadracari wherever meter does not require ī, as in the cpd. °cari-praṇidhāna 2, 49, 54, 61, where in the seam of the cpd. the consonant cluster makes the preceding syllable long; cf. also the acc. sg. °cariṃ (not °carīṃ) 17, 22, 26, 51, 62; Watanabe wrongly regards the title as primarily °carī. (All remaining citations in this article are from verses.) caryā may be used even in vss, where meter is indifferent (so SP 67.13) or requires long first syllable (SP 68.6), tho in the latter case **cāri** (°ī) and **cārikā**, qq.v., are also found; nearly all the cases here cited refer to the *religious course* leading to enlightenment, to Buddhahood or Bodhisattvahood, but occasionally the term is applied to any or all human courses of action, including such as are disapproved; iya bāla-carī, *this foolish* (or *childish*) *course* LV 174.9, 11 (vs); jāniya te cariṃ ca SP 45.3, *knowing them* (all the creatures of the world) *and their* (various) *course*(s) *of action*; cariṃ-cariṃ jāniya nityakālaṃ vadāmi sattvāna tathā-tathāhaṃ SP 326.11, *knowing the various modes of conduct* (of beings) *always, I speak to creatures in this or that way* (Kashgar rec., Thomas ap. Hoernle MR 133.1, cari acari, metrically impossible, and uninterpretable; Thomas *the moving and not-moving* [of living beings], which seems unacceptable); jagataḥ prajānase yā carir yatha ca karmasaṃbhavaḥ RP 6.1; otherwise, referring to the *course* of Bodhisattvas, also called the *true* (bhūta), *subtle* (sūkṣma), *pure* (viśuddha), *supreme* (uttama) *course, the course of* (leading to) *enlightenment* (bodhi-), *of morality* (śīla-), or other similar epithets; also duṣkara-, referring to Śākyamuni's temporary experiment with severe austerities; often *former, ancient* (pūrva, **purima**) with allusion to the length of it thru many past births; frequently a form of the cognate verb car (also ā-car) is used with it: sūkṣmāṃ cariṃ SP 12.7; te (sc. of the Buddha) ātmana yādṛśī carī 63.13; bhūtāṃ cariṃ 64.2 (but in adjoining prose, 64.13, 65.5, caryā); 127.10; 193.6; yathā carī mahya sutena cīrṇa 203.4; smara cari purimāṃ LV 161.21; yām evā varacari (acc.) caritas tvaṃ tām evā cari vibhaja jagasya 164.16; purimāṃ praṇidhāna-carīṃ 175.14; tāṃ pūrvacarīm anusmarā 178.5; pūrvacariṃ carantaḥ 219.13; ṣaḍvarṣāṇi caritva duṣkaracariṃ 276.1; bodhicari sarva (n. sg.) 341.2; svacarī viśuddhacari pāragatā 360.3; nigadottamāṃ cariṃ RP 9.6; uttamacariṃ prakāśaya 9.14; cari buddhasutānāṃ Śikṣ 2.16; cariṣyāmy amitāṃ cariṃ 13.19; cari (acc.) samanta-bhadrāṃ Gv 57.17–18; purimacariṃ pariśuddha ācaritvā Sukh 23.14; śīlacariṃ Bhad 17; bodhicariṃ 22, 26, 28.

carita (nt.), (mathematical) *operation, calculation, problem* (in mathematics): (śākyakumāraśatāny ...) apūrvacaritaṃ samuddiśanti sma, bodhisattvaś cāsaṃmūḍho nikṣipati sma LV 147.1, ... *proposed an unheard-of* (mathematical) *problem* ... Tib. rtsis, *calculation.* See also **dharma-carita.**

caritavant = **caritāvin,** q.v.: bodhisattvacaryāṃ ca caritavatāṃ protsāhanārthaṃ Laṅk 241.3, *and to instigate those who have pursued the course of the Bodhisattvas.*

caritāvin, adj. and quasi-pple. (§ 22.51; cf. **caritavant**), *having followed the* (true religious) *course* (sc., normally, of Bodhisattvas; see s.v. **cari**): bodhisattvacaryā-caritāvinaḥ (n. pl.) Laṅk 120.16; dārako 'smin dharmaparyāye caritāvī (only two mss.; most mss. caritavān) SP 464.1 (prose), *pursued the religious course in* (studying) *this dh°*; bahubuddhaśatasahasra-caritāvino (n. pl.) SP 180.9 *having pursued the course of* (under?) *many hundreds of thousands of Buddhas*; text not certain in Mv ii.218.14, Senart, vayaṃ pi ugratapacīrṇa-(v.l. °tīrṇaṃ) -caritāvino (mss. °tāvīna), *we have followed the right religious course in that we have pursued* (? cīrṇa) *severe austerities* (a forest ascetic speaks); in absolute use, without dependent noun, caritāvino hi te bhikṣavaḥ LV 404.19, *for these monks have pursued the* (true religious) *course.*

carima, adj. (§ 22.16; = Pali id., Skt. carama), *last, final*: SP 222.2; 229.6 °masmi kāle, cf. below; Mv i.4.3; ii.8.10 (in parallel i.204.15 carama); 438.14; carimakāle, *at the last hour* (of death), Mv ii.174.5; RP 31.13; 32.4, 5.

carimaka, f. **°ikā,** adj. (= Pali id.) = prec., *last*: °mikāyāṃ Vaj. in Hoernle MR 187.8 (omitted in ed. of Vaj 35.4).

cariyā = Pali id., Skt. caryā, BHS usually **cari,** q.v.: paśyāma sattvācariyā yathā jage LV 367.12 (vs), *we see the course of conduct of creatures as it is in the world*; so read, as cpd. (Lefm. sattvā cariyā), with Tib. ḥgro baḥi spyod; cariyāṃ jinasutasya Gv 1.23 (vs); cariyāya (loc.) sthihitvā Bhad 45.

carī, see **cari.**

[**care,** acc. to Senart ii note 537 interjection ('*Va!*') in Mv ii.214.10 (prose) taṃ care ekaṃ satyaṃ pratiśruṇāmi, addressed by the penitent king to Śyāma(ka) whom he has accidentally shot; evidently understanding 2 sg. opt. (or impv.) of car-. But the division ca re, rejected by Senart, or c' are, is surely to be adopted; in Pali even re seems sometimes used without derogatory implication, and are is so used even in Skt.].

Carendra, n. of a yakṣa: Sādh 560.15; 561.9.

? **carcara,** adj. (cf. Skt. Lex. carcarī, *curly hair,* which BR take to be an error for varvarī or barb°), *curly* (of hair): ardha-carcara-keśāṃ Sādh 310.12 (vs), *with half-curly* (partly curly) *hair*; ardha-carcara-bhṛṅgāṅga-śrīmat (? text śrīsat)-keśair alaṃkṛtāṃ 332.7 (vs). In the latter passage, to be sure, there is a v.l. °varvara°, supporting BR's suggestion; in the first the only v.l. is candana in a single ms.

carci (-gātra), adj. (unrecorded; cf. root carc, *injure,* Dhātup.), (having) *injured* or *defective* (limbs): na ca andha-kāra-vadhirā na pi carci-gātrā, na ca raudra khañjā atha **cāṭaka** (q.v.) prekṣaṇīyā Gv 214.22(-23; vs).

carpaṭa (m. or nt.; Skt. Lex. id.), *flat of the hand*: so read with WT, supported by Tib. thal mo, for KN vāpy-atha (-maṇḍakā) SP 52.1 (cited Śikṣ 93.12), read carpaṭa-maṇḍukā; see the passage, s.v. **maṇḍuka.**

carpaṭaka, nt. (possibly cf. AMg. cappaḍaga, acc. to Sheth = kāṣṭha-yantra-viśeṣa?), *peg* (or *rack*? so the Chin. is interpreted; Tib. and Jap. *wooden peg*) *for hanging clothes*: Mvy 9037 = Tib. gdaṅ bu.

carpaṭikā (Skt. Lex., Trik., °ṭī), *a flat cake*: ye ... gandhā avaśiṣyante °kāṃ kṛtvā pratidivasaṃ śoṣayati MSV ii.60.4 (Tib. re lur byas nas; I cannot find re lur). Cf. Turner, Nep. Dict. s.v. capāti (?).

carma-caṭaka, m. (Skt. Lexx. have corresp. fem. forms, °kā etc.), *bat* (the animal): Mvy 4914 (so Tib., pha lbaṅ). (Lit. 'leather-sparrow'.)

caryā (Skt.) = **cari,** q.v., used like that form (regularly in prose, but also in verses) esp. of the *course of conduct* of Bodhisattvas, which has four aspects or stages: catvārīmāni bodhisattvānāṃ bodhisattvacaryāṇi Mv i.1.2, listed in 3 as prakṛti-caryā, praṇidhāna-c°, **anuloma-c°,** anivartana-c° (cf. Senart i p. xxi); same list, called catasraḥ ... bodhisattvacaryāḥ i.46.6; they are discussed in the following 46.8 ff. (prakṛti-c° 46.8–47.11; praṇidhi-c° 47.12–63.10; anuloma- and avivarta-c°, very briefly, 63.11–14); they seem to be aspects, or possibly successive stages, of the Bodhisattva's long course of development; prakṛti- refers to his original, basic andowment; praṇidhāna- (°dhi-) to his vows to attain enlightenment; anuloma- (also ānulomikī, see s.v. ānulomika) alludes to his progressive approach to the goal, and anivartana- (avivarta-) refers to the point at which it becomes impossible for him to backslide. We also find bodhicaryā(ṇi, with nt. ending, as above) Mv i.252.4, °ryāṃ ii.341.1 (both of these vss), and duṣkara-caryāṃ ii.241.4 (prose), parallel to bodhi-cari and duṣkara-cari. See further **artha-caryā, dharma-caryā.**

Caryākārā, n. of a kṣatriyā: Av ii.9.7 (ms.; Speyer em. Varṣākārā, with Kalpadrumāv.; neither seems known elsewhere, and ms. reading makes good sense).

Caryāgata, n. of a Bodhisattva: Gv 443.4.

caryāpratipatti-bhūmi, third of six bodhisattva-bhūmi: Bbh 84.25, or fourth of seven, 367.4.

cal-, in various derivatives substituted for regular car-, esp. in Laṅk; see **anucālin, antaścālin, vicālana.**

Calakalpaka (corresp. to Pali Allakappaka), adj., *of* next: °kā Bulakāś Calakalpāyāṃ ... MPS 51.11.

Calakalpā (Pali Allakappa, m. or nt.), n. of a city; see prec.

calatthā (f.? Kyoto ed. °tthāḥ, n. pl.? but Mironov °tthā; v.l. in both saṃcal°), *manger*: Mvy 5607; so Tib. bres, and Chin.

calana (m. or nt.; only Mmk 63.2), **calanika,** m. (so also Mironov; only Mvy 5853), **calanikā,** f. (cf. Skt. calanaka, once calanī, pw, and AMg. calaṇiā, defined *a waist-cloth used by a nun,* Ratnach.), *short trousers* (so Tib. on Mvy, dor thuṅ): Mvy 5853 °nikaḥ; otherwise only in Mmk; nīla-(om. 63.2, 8)-paṭṭa-calanikā-(63.2 calana-)-nivasta (75.15 nivasita), *clothed in short trousers of* (*blue*) *cloth,* Mmk 63.2, 8; 75.15, 21, 23; 305.4, 7 (all prose); said of Bodhisattvas, all male; Lalou, Iconographie 33 et alibi, renders the word in all these passages by *vêtement(s) flottant(s),* which misses the true meaning.

Calamakuṭa, n. of a former Buddha: Mv i.137.3.

calu-śiras, see **vattu-ś°.**

cavati (= Pali id., Skt. and BHS. cyavati, § 2.8), *falls* (to a lower existence): cavitvā Mv iii.42.18; 43.10, 14; so Senart, v.l. each time cya°. Cf. **cuti.**

cākrika, m. (= AMg. cakkia, °iya), *disc-bearer,* a royal officer: Mvy 3733 (so also Mironov without v.l.; BR cite **cakrika,** which Kyoto ed. Index gives as a var.).

cākṣuṣya, adj. (= Skt. cakṣ°, cf. cākṣuṣa; Pali cakkhussa), *good for the eyes*: MSV iv.210.5.

? **cāṭaka,** read prob. **cāṭuka** (= Skt. cāṭu, and once cāṭuka, which in the passage cited in BR may be an adj.; in Rājat. 1.213, cited in pw s.v. cāṭu, for cāṭusīt- read with Stein caṭasī-), *agreeable, pleasant,* approximate synonym of prekṣaṇīya: Gv 214.23, see s.v. **carci** (-gātra).

Cāṇḍikā (cf. Skt. Caṇḍikā), n. of a yoginī: Dharmas 13 (misprint or error?).

cātudvīpa, see **cāturdvīpa.**

Cāturakṣa (all mss. °akṣo; Senart em. Cāturanta), n. of a disciple of Buddha: Mv i.182.18.

cāturanta (cf. also prec.), nt. (?), *the whole world* (bounded by the four oceans): °taṃ vijitavān Mvy 6542. In Pali used as adj. f. with words for *earth;* also m. as applied to a king (so also in Skt., Kauṭ. Arth. Sham.[1] 11.10 °to 'pi rājā), *ruler of the whole earth,* Sn 552 etc.; unrecorded in this gender and mg.; cf. Skt. caturantā, adj. or subst., said of the *earth;* see next, and s.v. **caturaṅga.**

cāturarṇavānta-, presumably nt. (= prec., q.v.), *(the world) bounded by the four oceans:* cakravartī °vāntavijetā Divy 140.21 (prose).

cāturāryasatya, *the Four Noble Truths:* MSV i.54.3; 58.13; etc., replaces the usual catur°, see **saṃprativedhaka.**

cāturthya, either *period of four days,* or *the fourth day:* ekāhorātra-cāturthya-pañca-ṣaṭka-kālāntarāś ca LV 248.22, *and* (eating once) *at intervals consisting of a day and a night, or four, five, or six* (days; as a form of austerities).

cāturdaśika, nt., *food given on the festival of the 14th* (lunar day): Mvy 5759; Bhīk 23a.3 (see s.v. **āṣṭamika**).

cāturdiśa, adj. (= Pali cātuddisa; catur-diś plus -a), *pertaining to the 'four directions'* i. e. *the whole world; universal;* ep. of the bhikṣu-saṃgha (as in Pali of the bhikkhu-saṃgha): °diśāryabhikṣusaṃghāya Divy 274.13; °diśāya bhikṣusaṃghāya Av ii.109.7; MSV ii.70.10; °diśasāṃghikena (sc. dravyeṇa? cf. Śikṣ 170.3), adj. *belonging to the universal monk-brotherhood,* Śikṣ 56.5.

Cāturdeva (v.l. Cātudeva), n. of a former Buddha: Mv i.140.11.

cāturdvīpa, also semi-MIndic **cātudvīpa,** (**1**) adj. (= Pali cātuddīpa; from catur-dvīpa plus -a), (ruler) *of the earth consisting of four continents,* ep. of a cakravartin: Mv i.49.2; 52.8; 108.7; 114.13; 193.14; 220.2 = ii.22.3; ii.158.14; iii.102.15; ep. of rājya, *rulership:* Mv i.95.2, 4; (**2**) adj. and subst., *consisting of the four continents,* ep. of the earth: °pāṃ mahīṃ Mv i.208.4 (corrupt in mss.) = ii.12.13; as subst., gender uncertain (f. would be expected, recorded forms ambiguous): daśacātudvīpanayutānāṃ... madhyama cātudvīpa, *the midmost world of ten nayutas of worlds,* Gv 254.6–7 (vss; final short a perhaps m.c. for ā?); cāturdvīpeśvaro, lord of the whole world, Dbh.g. 53(79).2 (as subst., without other noun; cf. **caturdvī°**).

cāturdvīpaka, adj., f. °**ikā** or (rarely) °**akā,** also as subst. m. (nt.?) and f. (cf. Pali cātuddī°, adj., and prec., next, and **caturdvī°**), as adj., *of, containing, consisting of four continents; of the world;* as subst., m. (nt.?) or f., *the world,* as containing four continents: °aka, masc. adj. with lokadhātu, Gv 107.2; 325.3; Śikṣ 282.3, 9; LV 149.21 f.; Mvy 3046; adj. with sattva, °pakānāṃ ca sattvānām, *and of creatures of the world,* Dbh 81.17; adj. f. °ikā, with lokadhātu, Gv 233.23; subst. m. (nt.?), madhye cāturdvīpakasya, *in the middle of the world,* Gv 352.10; subst. f., usually °ikā, once at least °akā, *world-of-four-continents,* but usually regarded as only a part of a lokadhātu, which contains a plurality of cāturdvīpikā: trisāhasramahāsāhasrāyāṃ lokadhātau sarvacāturdvīpakāsu Gv 380.1, but in 380.3 same phrase with °dvīpikāsu; (tasmin ... lokadhātau) madhyamā cāturdvīpikā Gv 232.8, *the middle earth in this world-system;* similarly Gv 268.6; 380.26; in Gv 373.17 the cāturdvipikā named **Bhāgavatī,** q.v., is part of a trisāhasramahāsāhasrā lokadhātu, and itself in turn contains a Jambudvīpa.

cāturdvīpika, adj. and subst. (cf. prec.), (**1**) *containing four continents,* masc. adj. with lokadhātu: °pikalokadhātuṃ Gv 275.23 (or is this, as prior member of cpd., to be interpreted as = 2, subst.?); (**2**) m. or nt., *the whole earth:* °kaṃ vyavalokayituṃ pravṛttaḥ Av i.258.3.

cāturdvīpeśvara, see s.v. **cāturdvīpa.**

cāturmahādvīpaka, adj. m., with lokadhātu, = **cāturdvīpaka,** q.v.: Śikṣ 282.3 (in same line cāturdvīpakalokadhātv-).

cāturmahābhūtika, adj. (= Pali cātu(m)mahā°, and cf. next), *consisting of the four gross elements:* Av ii.191.4 and Bbh 61.7, see s.v. **audārika;** Divy 652.13 (ayaṃ ...) Brahmaṇā ... °tika-mahāpuruṣaḥ prajñaptaḥ.

cāturmahābhautika, adj. (cf. Skt. cāturbhautika), = prec.: °tike ātmabhāve Śikṣ 21.21; °tikaṃ (rūpaṃ) Laṅk 125.3; °tikaṃ ... samucchrayaṃ Bbh 253.20.

cāturmahārājakāyika, adj., = **catur°** and next, q.v.: SP 160.2; 239.6; LV 50.20; 60.7; 396.14; Mv i.333.5; Mvy 3078; Dharmas 127; Divy 195.1; 199.8; 367.9; Bbh 61.27.

cāturmahārājika, rarely and doubtfully °**jaka,** once **cāturmāhā°,** adj., almost always with deva or devaputra (the noun rarely omitted), = prec., and **catur°** (= Pali cātu(m)mah°), *belonging to the group of gods of the four 'World-Guardians',* a class of kāmāvacara gods, see **deva,** and **mahāraja(n):** °jaka (but v.l. °jika), without noun deva, Mv i.263.15; in the rest, °jika, LV 46.19; 150.2; 266.4 f.; 401.8 f.; Mv i.31.10; 240.4 (v.l. °ja-kāyika); ii.2.8; 163.10; Divy 68.12; 83.6; 127.20; 219.8; 367.9; 554.4; Av i.5.1; 10.16, etc.; Mmk 19.12; common. This is the most usual form. Once, at least, cāturmāhārājika, Mv ii.314.5 (prose, no v.l.). Also **mahārājika,** q.v.

cātuṣkoṭika, °**kā** (from **catuṣkoṭikā,** q.v.), (**1**) adj., *relating to, concerned with, involving* or *based on the 'four alternatives':* °kaḥ Mvy 6887; °ka-naya-viśuddhim Laṅk 124.1; skandhāḥ ... °ka-rahitāḥ, *deprived of anything that relates to ...,* Laṅk 125.7; (**2**) °kā, subst. f. = catuṣ°: °kayā Laṅk 152.14; 296.14 (muktaṃ bhavaṃ); 324.14 (yukto).

cātuṣpada, f. °**padī** (Skt. catuṣp°), = **catuṣpadaka,** q.v.; f. with gāthā, Vaj in Pargiter ap. Hoernle MR 192.1 (for Vaj 42.5 catuṣpādikā, see °**daka**).

cātuṣpadaka, f. °**ikā,** = prec.: Vaj in Pargiter op. cit. 183.1 °ikā, with gāthā (for Vaj 30.1 catuṣpādikā).

cātuṣpāda, f. °**dā,** = prec. two; with gāthā, Vaj in Pargiter op. cit. 181.11, 14 (for Vaj 28.7, 11 **catuṣpādikā**).

canāḥ, n. pl. (? cf. Hindi canā, with dental n, = Skt. caṇaka?), *parched grain:* Mvy 5738, so Tib. yos (so read with Tib. Index, misprinted gos), and so one Chin. rendering. Cf. **vahuri.**

Cāpāla, nt. (= Pali id., near Vesāli), n. of a caitya near Vaiśālī: Mv i.299.22 (cf. 297.16); pūrvasmin vai (Mv purimasmiṃ) diśo-bhāge cāpālaṃ (Senart em. cāpalaṃ, but mss. of Mv text) nāma (Mv va nāma) cetiyaṃ LV 388.12 = Mv iii.306.14 (vs); Cāpāla-caityaṃ Divy 201.1 (at Vaiśālī); Vaiśālī Vṛjibhūmiś Cāpāla- (13 °lam)-caityaṃ 4 and 13; °lam caityaṃ Divy 207.11.

? **cāpālya** (nt., for Skt. cāpalya), *instability:* lakṣmī-°ya- Divy 432.13 (prose); prob. read cāpalya.

cāpodara, *having a belly* (slender) *like a bow,* one of the **anuvyañjana,** replacing **kṣāmodara** (No. 36) in LV 107.4, and by Senart's em. in Mv ii.44.3 (see kṣāmodara). Tib. renders LV rked pa gzhu-ḥi ḥchaṅ bzuṅ ltar phra ba, which, if I understand it correctly, seems to mean *with waist slender like the handle* (?) *of a bow;* at least the words gzhu, *bow,* and phra, *slender,* seem clear, and suggest that Tib. rendered both cāpa and kṣāma; in another context Mvy 5207 has cāpodarī, fem., rendered rked pa gzhu-ḥi chaṅ gzuṅs, *waist* (like) *handle* (?) *of bow,* or bzuṅ ltar phra ba, *slender like handle* (?); Chin. *waist like handle of bow.*

Cāmara, n. of a country or division of the world: Mvy 3052. Cf. **Aparacāmara.** See Kirfel, Kosmographie, 90 (var. Ḍāmara).

cāmarā (AMg. and Skt. Lex. id., f.; cf. Pali and Skt. Lex. cāmarī; regularly nt. °ra in Skt., Pali, and Pkt.), *chowrie*: vara-cāmarāye (instr.) Mv i.235.8 (vs).

cāmarika, m. (Skt. cāmara plus -ika), *chowrie-bearer*, a royal attendant: Mvy 3728.

Cāmīkaragaura, n. of a former Buddha: Mv i.139.5.

Cāmpeya and **°yaka, °yika** (= Pali Campeyya, -ka), (**1**) n. of a nāga-king: °ya Mvy 3274; Mmk 18.11; °yaka Māy 247.19; (**2**) **°yikā**, *woman of Campā* (**Viśākhā**): MSV ii.59.1 f.; °yikāḥ (monks) *of C.* MSV ii.120.2. All prose.

cāra (m.; Ap. and Deśīn. id., also Skt. Lex.; = Skt. cāraka, in Kauṭ. Arth. as well as Daśak., BR), *prison*: cāra-pālānām ājñā dattā ... (etān ... cārake baddhvā sthāpayata) Divy 565.19 f. (prose) *to the prison-guards a command was given* (cf. cāraka-pālavad Śikṣ 231.5).

-cāraka, m. (to **cārayati**, q.v., 2), *dispenser, one who deals out* (Tib. ḥgrim pa, or ḥdrim pa, both for more usual ḥbrim pa), in yavāgū- Mvy 9058, khādyaka- 9059, phala- 9060, yatkiṃcic- 9061; all referring to officials or servants in a monastery.

cārakā = **cārikā** 3, q.v., *course, stream* (of a river).

cāraṇa (nt.; = Pali id., see below; = Skt. caraṇa), (**1**) *conduct, practice*; in Pali, Sn 162, comm. takes ā as m.c., which it could be in Mv i.177.2, but elsewhere in prose: Mv i.177.2 (vs) anupakruṣṭa-cāraṇā; Gv 333.2 dharmāṇāṃ grahaṇa-cāraṇa-pratibodhiṣu (dvandva); (**2**) *trained, skilled behavior; practice of an acquired art* (Tib. cited as bslab pa, regularly = śikṣā): MSV i.34.11 (hasti-damako ...) hastiratnam ekāhnā sarva-cāraṇebhir upasaṃkrāmati, and in sequel; likewise with aśvaratnam (both of a cakravartin) i.35.11 ff.; both prose; (**3**) (rare in Skt.: *pasturing, tending* of animals: MSV iv.227.18.)

cārayati, cāreti (caus. to car-), (**1**) *distributes, casts* (lots, **śalākā**, q.v.); so Pali cāreti, read at Jāt. i.239.27–28 te kālakaṇṇi-salākaṃ cāresuṃ, for text °vāresuṃ: śalākā cāryate, *a lot is cast*, Mvy 9204, so read, text caryate; Mironov śalaka-caryā te, v.l. -caryate; Tib. ḥdrim (pa), *distribute*; the process consisted in distributing small pieces of wood (śalākā) to serve as lottery-tickets; śalākāṃ cāraya, yo yuṣmākam utsahate ... Divy 184.15, and śalākāṃ cārayitum ārabdhaḥ 18; śalākāni cāretha (mss. dhār°) Mv iii.176.9, śalākāni cārīyanti (v.l. vār°) 10; (**2**) *hands out, distributes* (cf. s.v. **cāraka**): bhikṣūṇāṃ cāraya, sa bhikṣūṇāṃ cāratum ārabdhaḥ Divy 180.13, *distribute* (flowers) *to the monks! and he began to distribute them to the monks*; cāraya ... peyām Divy 462.4, *distribute the gruel*; °yati (here sc. garments, to monks) MSV ii.106.2.

? **cārayin**, adj.? (to cārayati, caus. of car-; if adj. form, contains suffix -in), *propagating, spreading* (heretical views): vakṣyanty avarṇam asmākaṃ tīrthyavādaṃ ca cārayī (v.l. °yi) SP 273.3 (vs); Kashgar rec. tīrthikā vāca cārayī, which seems better in eliminating the superfluous and disturbing ca; but the form cārayī could not only be n. pl. of an in-stem adj., but also ger. (note v.l. °yi, also ambiguous). WT kārayī with ms. K′.

Cārāyaṇa = **Dīrgha Cār°**, q.v.: Av ii.114.14, 16.

cāri (m.c. for **cari**, q.v.), *conduct*, in Bhvr. cpds.: sugatasya putrān ... śāntapraśāntacārīn SP 12.14 (vs), ... *of calm, peaceful conduct*; paripūrṇacārī (n. pl. m.) ca bhavanti tatra śīlena te prasthita agrabodhim SP 13.4 (vs), *having fulfilled the* (religious) *course of action* (that leads to enlightenment).

-cārika, adj. or subst. m. (= Skt. and Pali -cārin, ifc.; see also **piṇḍa-cārika**), *moving; practising*: pattra-cārikā ṛddhyā harita-cārikā bhājana-cārikāś cāgatāḥ Divy 45.17; similarly 45.20; it seems clear that the reference is to persons who magically *ride* or *move* thru the air on *leaves*, some sort of *plants* or *trees* (harita, cf. Skt. haritaka), and *jars* (bhājana), cf. 45.27–30. Acc. to Burnouf, Introd. 261 note 2, Tib. renders -cārikā(ḥ) by ḥdri ma, which the Dictt. of Tib. do not interpret satisfactorily; I suggest dri bo, *magician*. Tib. renders harita by śiṅ tshe, apparently some tree or shrub. There is a v.l. -vārika, which pw 7.365 adopts for bhājana-cārika, identifying it with °vārika in Mvy 9069, which however means something like *superintendent of vessels* and cannot be intended in the Divy passage. In Śikṣ 332.4 cārika seems to mean *practiser, follower* (cf. Skt. and Pali cārin), sc. of a heretical religion.

cārikā (in mg. 2 = Pali id.), (**1**) = **cari**, q.v., *course of conduct*, esp. *a religious course leading to enlightenment*, pursued by Bodhisattvas; repeatedly used in prose, hence not exclusively m.c.; usually with a form of the cognate verb carati: caranti ete varabodhi-cārikāṃ SP 131.12 (vs); puruṣottama-cārikām acari, so bodhisattva-caryāṃ (note use together of the synonymous forms cārikā and caryā!) ... saṃsarati Mv i.3.9 (prose); duṣkara-cār° (cf. duṣkara-cariṃ LV 276.1) Mv ii.130.12 (°kāye, instr., prose); 237.17 (°kāṃ carantaṃ, prose); bodhisattva-cārikāṃ caranto ii.356.19 (prose); caranto bodhicārikāṃ ii.362.20 (vs); jinacārikā(ye) ii.375.12 (vs); carann uttamabodhicārikāṃ RP 50.2 (vs); cariṣye varabodhicārikāṃ Sādh 29.7 (vs); otari cārika- (a m.c.)-kalpa-samudrāṃ Bhad 29; bodhisattvacārikā Śikṣ 316.18 (prose) and °kaṃ (prob. misprint for °kāṃ) carantaṃ Gv 423.22 (prose); praṇidhisi cārīkām (ī m.c. for i) asamām (referring to the *course* of Bodhisattvas) Gv 57.15 (vs); saṃsāra-cārikaiṣā, naiṣā bodhisattvacārikā AsP 329.15 (prose); eka-cārikā Laṅk 291.13 (vs), *the solitary religious course* (of Pratyekabuddhas); (**2**) *journey, wandering* (also = Skt. caryā, which varies with this in the same passages; Pali cārikā id.), commonly as object of carati or another verb of *going*; the place of the journey is either in the loc. or preceding in comp.: magadheṣu cārikāṃ prakrāmat LV 246.2 (prose), cf. magadheṣu caryāṃ (best ms. cārikāṃ) caran 246.6; caryāṃ caran kāśiṣu janapadeṣu cārikāṃ (v.l. caryāṃ) prakrāmat 405.2–3; janapadeṣu cārikāṃ prakramet(su) Mv i.231.3 (prose), *set out on a journey over the countryside*; cārikāṃ caramāṇo 6; gacchantam ... cārikāṃ 234.14 (vs); janapadacārikāṃ caramāṇo 244.12 (prose); kāśiṣu cārikāṃ prakrāmi 323.10 (prose); magadheṣu °kāṃ caramāṇo iii.47.10 (prose); °kāṃ pratipannasya, *embarked on a journey*, 94.3 (vs); janapada-cārikā Mvy 9355; Kauśaleṣu janapadeṣu °kāṃ caran Divy 80.11; °kāṃ cariṣyati 92.8; Buddha-cārikā, *the journey of a Buddha*, 92.25; 93.2; śmaśānacārikāṃ gantu(ṃ) 267.8, 9, *to go on a trip to a cemetery*; dakṣiṇāgiriṣu janapade °kāṃ caritvā Av i.3.3; janapadacārikāṃ caran RP 5.2 (prose); (Pāñcāleṣu janapadeṣu) janapadacārikāṃ caramāṇo Suv 202.3 (prose); also used of journeys to other worlds or states of existence, inferior or superior: niraya-cārikāṃ gacchati Mv i.4.15 (prose) *went on a trip to (the) hell(s)*; caranto narakacārikāṃ 5.2; so also tiracchāna-cārikāṃ gacchati 27.2, and caranto tir° °kāṃ 4, *a trip among the animal-existences*; pretacārikāṃ 28.3, 5; asura-c° 30.1, 3; deveṣu °kāṃ gacchati 30.16; 31.16; and with acc. instead of loc., devāṃ (= °ān) cār° ga° 33.4, *went on a trip to the gods*; deveṣu cārikāṃ caramāṇena Mv ii.190.17; naraka-cārikāṃ carataḥ Av i.241.9, preta-c° c° 10; (**3**) cārikā or cārakā, *stream, course* (of a river): nadīcārikām avatīrṇaḥ, *went down into a river-stream*, Av ii.86.3; nadīcārakāyāḥ (ms., Speyer em. °cārik°) pāre vṛkṣaḥ 4; nadīcārikām uttīrṇaḥ, *crossed a river-stream*, ii.116.13; nadyāṃ cārakāyāṃ (so Speyer; ms. naṃdyā cārakāyā; read nadyāś, or, semi-MIndic, nadyā, gen.?) patitas, *fell into the stream of a river*, or if nadyāṃ is correct, *into a river, into its stream*, ii.181.17.

cāritra (nt.), in °tram āpadyate (with loc.; = Pali cārittaṃ āpajjati, with loc.), *has dealings with, visits, cultivates*, esp. said of a monk who takes food at the house of laymen: (bhikṣuḥ...) kuleṣu cāritram āpadyeta Prāt 522.4. The Pali phrase is rendered *goes on his* (begging) *rounds* in SBE 13.42.

Cāritramati, n. of a Bodhisattva: ŚsP 34.15.

Cāritravatī, n. of a samādhi: Mvy 579; ŚsP 1421.17.

cāritravant, adj. (= **caritavant**, °**tāvin**), *that has pursued the* (true, religious) *course*: māṃsaṃ sarvam abhakṣyaṃ cāritravato bodhisattvasya Laṅk 246.5 (prose).

cārīkā, m. c. for **cārikā**, q.v., Gv 57.15.

Cāru, n. of a cakravartin king: Mvy 3559. Seems to correspond to Pali Cara, or Caraka Mahāv. ii.2. Cf. **Upacāru.**

Cārugandha, n. of a former Buddha: Mv i.139.7.

? **Cārucaraṇa**, n. of a former Buddha: Mv i.138.14; mss. Cārucaraṇādasiddharaṅgaḥ; Senart em. Cārucaraṇaḥ Prasiddharaṅgaḥ.

Cāruchada (v.l. °chattra), n. of a former Buddha: Mv i.137.8.

Cārudanta, n. of a former Buddha: Mv i.141.3.

Cārunetra, n. of a Buddha: Mv i.123.19.

Cārubhānu, n. of a former Buddha: Mv i.139.4.

Cārumant(a), nom. °taḥ, n. of a cakravartin king: Mvy 3561.

Cāruvarṇa, n. of a disciple of Buddha: Mv i.182.17.

-cāla, see **pṛthivī-cāla.**

cikitsikā (= Skt. °tsā, plus -ka svārthe), *medical treatment*: MSV ii.140.9 °tsikāṃ kurmaḥ (in 10 °tsāṃ kuryāma; both prose).

cikka, m., or **cikkā** (n. pl. °ās; cf. Skt. cikkaṇa, esp. s.v. 5 in pw), *sticky matter*, as secreted from the eyes: cikkās tathākṣṇoḥ krimivac ca jantoḥ Śikṣ 231.11 (vs).

ciṅkhala (adj., or less likely subst. m. or nt.; cf. Skt. Lex. cikhalla, Pali and AMg. cikkhalla, AMg. also cikkhila, all nouns), *muddy* (or *mud, mire*): °le bhūpradeśe MSV ii.79.18; Tib. rdzab can gyi phyogs, *muddy place.*

cicca, or **ciccha**, m., a kind of malevolent supernatural being: Mvy 4377 ciccha, in Index var. cicca; Mironov cicca, v.l. ciccha; follows **kākhorda** and vetāla, followed by **preṣaka**; = Tib. sems (b)sgyur ba (?); in similar lists of evil spirits, cicca Māy 220.18; 245.16.

Cicchaka, var. for **Śīrṣaka**, n. of a nāga-king, q.v.: Mvy 3283; Mironov Cicchaka, v.l. Śīrṣaka.

ciṭiciṭāyati, °te, once **ciṭa**°, once **ciṭiciṭī**° (= Pali ciṭiciṭāyati), onomat., *sputters*, used of the noise made by hot things, especially (at least in Pali) in contact with water: cakraṃ (a hot metal disk, 604.15) ciṭiciṭāyamānadahanakaṇacayodgāraraudraṃ Divy 606.1; with subject sarṣapāḥ, ciṭiciṭāyanti Mmk 298.2; 719.1; °ṭīyanti Mmk 295.6; with subject an ayomaya cakra, or triśūla, ciṭaciṭāyati Mmk 687.9. In these BHS passages it is not clear whether contact with water or other liquids is implied.

cita (orig. ppp. of Skt. ci-), orig. *piled up, heaped up*; so, *thick, dense* (of hair), *stout, large* (of fingers), *full, stout* (of the space between the shoulders), in cpds. (**1**) cita-keśa, *having thick, dense hair*, one of the **anuvyañjana** of the Buddha: Mvy 343 = Tib. stug pa, *dense, thick*; Mv ii.44.10, so read with one ms., the other vivitra° (Senart em. citra°); instead Dharmas 84 has citra-keśa, which I believe is certainly a corruption; lacking in the LV list; (**2**) citāṅguli, *with stout, large fingers*, another **anuvyañjana**: Mvy 274 (here Tib. rgyas = *large*); confirmed by Pali acc. to Burnouf, Lotus, 585; this time the corruption citrā° (above) is more widespread, being printed in Mv ii.43.9 (only one ms., lacuna in the other); Dharmas 84 (but one ms. ciṃtā°); and LV 106.12–13 (Lefm. anupūrvacitrāṅguliś ca, combining this with anupūrvāṅguli; most mss. have the reverse order, as does Tib., which also renders by rgyas pa = *large*, proving that it had citā° and not citrā°); (**3**) citāntarāṃsa (or °śa) (= Pali citantaraṃsa, e. g. DN ii.18.10; comm. ii.449.6 antaraṃsaṃ vuccati dvinnaṃ koṭṭhāsānaṃ antaraṃ; taṃ citaṃ paripuṇṇaṃ assā ti), *with full, well filled-in, space between the shoulders*, one of the 32 **lakṣaṇa**: Mvy 251, Tib. thal goṅ rgyas pa = *large shoulders*; so also Tib. on LV 105.18; all lists of the **lakṣaṇa** (q.v.) intend the same form, only varying between °āṃsa and °āṃśa. In Gv 69.26 read citta with 2d ed. for cita; see s.v. **avabhā.** See also next.

cita-vistara, m., some kind of *ornament*: Mvy 6044 = Tib. tshoṅ-tshoṅ (said to be *a kind of ornament*; as adj. or adv. apparently *even*[*ly*]) bśibs (or gśibs) pa, perhaps literally *arranged evenly*? Chin. *hair-net.* Does the BHS form mean lit. *of full extent*? Cf. **cita.**

citāṅguli, citāntarāṃsa, see s.v. **cita.**

1 **citta** (= Pali id., also citra, = AMg. citta, = Skt. caitra), n. of the first month of spring (as usually reckoned, but here called 'the first month of summer', evidently implying a division of the year into only three seasons, spring-summer constituting one season of four months; see Senart's note): grīṣmāṇa māse prathame cittasmiṃ (so, or cittesmiṃ, mss.; Senart em. caitrasmiṃ) Mv i.294.3 (vs).

2 **citta**, m. (in Skt. only nt.), *thought*: used with masc. adj. and pron. forms in Bhad 19 abhiyukto ... cittu ..., ye ... āvaraṇīyās (sc. cittāḥ).

-cittaka = Skt. citta, *thought*, in Bhvr. cpd.: ekacittakāḥ, *single-minded*, Av i.378.4 (prose).

citta-kṣaṇa, m. (**1**) *a moment of thought*: Gv 222.22, see s.v. **anujava**; adv. praticittakṣaṇam, *in each moment of thought*: Gv 242.21; 252.13; cf. AbhidhK. LaV-P. ii.153; (**2**) in Mvy 1216 ṣoḍaśa-c°, *the 16 ...*, listed in 1217 ff., name for what in Dharmas 96 are called caturāryasatyeṣu ṣoḍaśa kṣāntijñānalakṣaṇāḥ; they are summarized s.v. **kṣānti**, q.v. It is not clear to me what (citta-)kṣaṇa could mean as applied to these categories, and the use in Dharmas of (jñāṇa-)lakṣaṇa instead suggests that kṣaṇa might be a corruption for lakṣaṇa; but Tib. on Mvy has skad cig ma = kṣaṇa.

citta-grāha, m. (or nt.), *fancy of the mind, desire*: devasya °haṃ kariṣyāmi MSV iii.138.2.

citta-dhārā, *stream of thought*: (teṣām, sc. sattvānām, ahaṃ) nānābhāvāṃ cittadhārāṃ prajānāmi Vaj 39.11. Cf. next.

Cittadhārābuddhisaṃkusumitābhyudgata, n. of a former Buddha: Sukh 5.19. Cf. prec.

citta-paryāya = **cetaḥ-p**°, q.v. (see also **abhijñā**).

Cittaratha, MIndic for **Citra**°, q.v.

cittavistarā (Senart suggests that this is Pkt. for citra-vi°), n. of 5th (bodhisattva-) **bhūmi**: Mv i.76.15.

Cittaśāśvata, n. of a Tathāgata: Sādh 445.11, 13.

Cittasthita, m., n. of a samādhi: Mvy 561; or **Cittasthiti** (in same list), ŚsP 1419.21.

[**cittikāra**, false reading for **citri**° or **citrī**°, q.v.: LV 196.3; by em. 270.6.]

cittotpāda, m. (= Pali cittuppāda), *production of intention, resolution*; cf. the phrase cittam utpādayati, common in BHS, see s.v. **utpādayati**: antaśa ekacittotpādenāpy anumoditam idaṃ sūtram SP 224.6, *by even so much as a single* ('*production of intent*', i. e.) *deliberate mental act this sūtra has been approved*; śobhanas te cittotpādaḥ, *that is an excellent resolution of yours, a fine idea!*, Divy 389.10; (anena) kuśalamūlena cittotpādena, *by this resolution which constituted a root of merit*, Av i.4.2; 10.1 etc.; ii.96.9; iha bodhisattvasya prathamaś cittotpādaḥ sarvabodhisattvasamyakpraṇidhānam ādyam Bbh 12.1; yenāsyaikacittotpādo 'pi kṣīyeta Śikṣ 49.10, *even a single resolution* (as in SP 224.6 above); sarvajñatācittotpādaratne Śikṣ 184.10, *in the 'jewel' of a determination to obtain omniscience*; sahacittotpādāt, *as soon as the thought arose*, Divy 212.18, 27; 221.21, 23 etc.; Av i.32.1; ii.95.1–2, 11;

Sukh 16.8–9; sahacittotpādena, id., Mv iii.329.18; 330.2 (read as cpd.; Senart saha cittot°, but the commoner abl. form disproves the implication that saha is a separate word). See next.

-cittotpādika, adj. ifc. (to prec. with -ika; not recorded in Pali), *(one that is) characterized by production of intent, that has formed a resolution* (used only of religious resolves): bodhi-cittot° Śikṣ 101.11, 13, *that has formed the purpose of winning enlightenment*; (eṣāṃ parvatānāṃ...) pārśve kecid ekacittotpādikā bodhisattvāḥ prativasanti Kv 64.17 (so read), here apparently *that have formed a single* (? the One? the first? as in the following) *resolution*; often in prathama-cittot°, always epithet of Bodhisattvas, *that have formed the initial resolution* (to enter on the course of a B.), Śikṣ 153.11; KP 29.4; Bbh 18.16; Gv 500.3; Kv 85.20; 86.4.

Citra, (**1**) (= Pali Citta gahapati) n. of a lay disciple of the Buddha, with the epithet gṛhapati: MSV iii.21.9 ff.; Jm 115.25; (**2**) n. of a nāga king: Mvy 3268, v.l. **Vicitra**, which Mironov reads with v.l. Citta; Tib. ris bkra (each word alone elsewhere renders Skt. citra); Māy 246.30.

[**citraka**, see **cintaka.**]

[**citrakāraḥ** LV 119.9, read citrikāra(ṃ).]

? **Citrakāli** (stem-form, in a cpd. listing yakṣiṇīs), n. of a yakṣiṇī: Sādh 561.1. But v.l. Candrakānti, which may well be right; replaced below in 561.10 (based on the same list) by **Candrakāli**, whereas in 562.5 (a different piece) occurs **Candrakāntā** as n. of a yakṣiṇī.

Citraketu, n. of a king of Vidyādharas: Mmk 655.10.

[**citra-keśa**, error for **cita-**, see s.v. **cita.**]

? **Citrachattra** (so 2 mss.; v.l. °cheḍa; Senart em. °chada), n. of a former Buddha: Mv i.137.7.

citraṇā (to Skt. citrayati with -anā), (the act of) *painting*: antarīkṣa iva raṅgacitraṇā Dbh 6.23 (vs).

Citradhvaja, n. of a man (monk or layman?) mentioned as interlocutor of the Bodhisattva **Akṣayamati**: SP 447.2, 5 (vss).

citrapāṭala, nt., a kind of flower: Mvy 6200.

Citrapiśācikā, n. of a piśācī: Māy 239.23.

Citrabhānu, n. of a former Buddha: Mv i.139.4.

Citramakuṭa, n. of a former Buddha: Mv i.137.3.

Citramalla (mss.; Senart em. Citravarṇa), n. of a former Buddha: Mv i.138.12.

Citramāla, n. of a former Buddha (or of two such): Mv i.137.11; 141.14.

Citramālya, n. of a former Buddha: Mv i.141.11.

Citraratha (once Citta°; = Pali Cittaratha; see also **Caitra°**), n. of one of the groves of the Trāyastriṃśa gods: Mv i.32.5; 149.14; 217.2; ii.19.16 (Citta°); 181.7; 451.20.

[**Citravarṇa**, see **Citramalla.**]

Citraśayana, n. of a former Buddha: Mv i.140.8.

Citrasena, n. of a yakṣa: Māy 99.

Citrasenā, n. of a goddess: Sādh 502.2.

citrastavana, *worthy of all manner of praise* (Senart): Mv i.147.2 (vs), of Māyā's womb.

Citrahemajāla, n. of a former Buddha: Mv i.141.15.

Citrā, (**1**) (Skt. Lex. id.) n. of a river: Divy 451.1 ff.; 456.19 ff.; (**2**) n. of an ogress: Māy 244.1.

Citrākṣa, n. of a nāga king: Mvy 3244.

citrāṅga, adj., *of scarred body* (so Tib. on Mvy, lus rma mtshan can): Mvy 8778; MSV iv.68.7.

[**citrāṅguli**, error for **citā°**, see s.v. **cita.**]

citrānta, *of manifold, miscellaneous* (with pejorative implication) *conditions*: citrānta-cittān sattvān dhyāneṣu pratiṣṭhāpayāmi Gv 318.12.

Citrārtha, n. of a Buddha: Gv 284.15 (vs). But perhaps read Citrārtha-indraśiri as one compound name, and in next line separate **Avabhāsarāja** from **Prabhaketuśirī**, as two names.

citrika, nt., apparently *wonder, marvel, thrilling and pleasing thing or experience*: nāsti loke citrikaṃ yaṃ me na parityaktaṃ tasya arthasya āharaṇatāye Mv ii.279.16, said by the Bodhisattva as a basis for his *noble pride* (ārya-māna); in a series of like formulas, the preceding containing ramaṇīyatā in place of citrikaṃ, and the next aiśvaryaṃ.

citrikāra, see **citrīkāra.**

citritaka, adj. (Skt. °ta with endearing dim. -ka, § 22.34), *made bright, adorned*: (tava rūpa surūpa suśobhanake) vasavarti sulakṣaṇa citritake LV 321.(21–)22 (vs); said by the daughters of Māra to the Bodhisattva; the e-forms seem scarcely construable with suvasantake in line 19 (nor does Tib. take them so; Calc. reads suśobhanako and citritako, but all mss. °ke in both); accordingly it seems that, if the mss. are right, we must understand them either as n. sg. nt. in e, with rūpa (§ 8.37), or as voc. sg. m., addressed to the Bodhisattva (§ 8.28).

citrīkaraṇa (nt.; to next), *paying reverence, respect*: -saṃbuddha-śāsana-gaurava-citrīkaraṇatayā Dbh 13.19–20.

citrī-karoti (= Pali citti°, perhaps also cittī°, see next; derived by Childers and PTSD from Skt. citta-; Senart, Mv i.444, accepts this and regards BHS citrī° as false Sktization; later, he emends the forms occurring in Mv ii and iii to cittī°; whatever the history of the word may be, the BHS form is only citrī° or citri°); (**1**) ppp. *respected, honored*: (vayaṃ hi...) loke 'tīva citrīkṛtāḥ SP 215.6 (prose, no v.l.); (**2**) *pays heed*: na °kariṣyati MSV i.8.1, 10, *he will pay no heed*; caus., *causes to pay heed, gets the attention of* (acc.): (Māra tried to distract the Bodhisattva,) na ca taṃ bodhisattvaṃ citrīkāresi (aor.; so mss., Senart em. cittī°) Mv ii.268.11; with noncaus. mg., and °kar° with short a in mss. except in the first passage, Mv iii.282.6, 12; 283.2, 7, prob. read in all approximately: na ca sānaṃ bhagavāṃ citrīkāraye (or °karaye), *and the Lord paid no heed to them* (the daughters of Māra who were seeking to distract him); the mss. are variously corrupt; Senart em. cittīkāraye; (**3**) citrīkṛta in a quite different sense: hastau saṃpuṭākārau kṛtvā anyonyāv āveṣṭya citrīkṛtau ātmorasi sthāpayet (in a certain mudrā) Mmk 400.28; similarly, hastāv udveṣṭya citrīkṛtāv abhayāvasthitau 401.20; hastāv ubhayāṅguṣṭhavinyastau citrīkṛtau lalāṭe darśayed 401.25; punaḥ citrīkṛtau karau, svastikaṃ ... bandhitavyam 407.21. It is clear that citrīkṛtau here applies always to the two hands in various mudrā-positions, but the mg. is not evident to me; possibly *made elaborate*, by intertwining the fingers (which is apparently characteristic of these mudrās)?

citrīkāra, citri°, once **citrīkara** (?), m. (to prec., q.v.; Pali usually cittikāra, but also cittī° acc. to CPD s.v. acittikāra; the usual BHS form is citrī°, but citri° also occurs, in prose; cittī° or citti° is not authenticated; Lefm. cittikāraṃ LV 196.3, but practically all mss. citr°), (**1**) *respect, reverence*: citrikārānuyuktaḥ LV 56.9 (vs); read citrikāra(ṃ) for text citrakāraḥ 119.9 (vs) and for text cittikāraṃ 196.3 (above); citrikāra-bahumāna- 270.6–7 (prose; so all mss.; Lefm. em. citti°); citrīkāra- (various forms) LV 278.8 (prose; 2 mss. citri°); 429.16 (prose; no v.l.); Mvy 1759 (°raḥ; Tib. gces par byed pa, *making esteemed*); Suv 172.16; 173.6; Śikṣ 41.17; 151.17; 183.14; Dbh 46.8; 62.15; Megh 288.16 (read mahatā gurugauravacitrīkāreṇa; misunderstood by Bendall); AsP 494.15; Gv 467.17; citrikāra- Mv i.89.15 (prose; 1 ms. citrī°); pūrvarāja-citrīkareṇa (mss.; read °kāreṇa, probably) Mv ii.439.18 (prose). Often associated with gaurava, sometimes with prīti, prasāda, and the like. (**2**) citrīkāraḥ in Mvy 7563 (cf. Skt. citrīkṛta, *made into a picture*) = Tib. mtshan mar ḥdzin pa daṅ ḥdom na bkra bar ḥdzin pa, which perhaps means *the taking for a sign or the taking for variegated* (?). Follows **apasphoṭanam**, rūpaṇāt, and rūpyate.

citropacitra, see **upacitra.**

cintaka, m. *inspector, overseer*: rājño Mūrdhātasyāmātyāś cintakās tulakā upaparīkṣakāś cintayitvā tulayitvā... Divy 212.9; karvaṭakaḥ saṃnāmito nipakā gṛhītāś cintakaḥ (*an overseer, manager*) sthāpitaḥ. Divy 451.20; for this last, MSV i.147.2 reads **citrakaḥ**, doubtless by corruption; Tib. sna bo, *leader, commander*.

cintārāja- (m.) (**1**) (cf. Skt. cintāmaṇi?) *a kind of gem* with magic powers, conferring wealth: Gv 498.25; 499.7; 500.18; (**2**) n. of a Bodhisattva: Gv 81.3.

cinnaka, m. (presumably = Skt. cīna, cīnaka, and Lex. cinna, *Panicum miliaceum*; cf. also AMg. ciṇṇa, *Chinese*), *a kind of grain* or *legume*: kodravo vā śyāmako vā cinnako vā priyaṃgur vā... Mv ii.211.14.

-cippitika, in **naḍa-cippitikam**, q.v., seems to be an extension of ppp. of next (implying an active cipyati, cippati? or a caus. MIndic cippeti?).

cipyate, pass. (cf. Pali cippiyamāna, Miln. 261.28, 30; and see prec.), *is crushed*: naḍa-cippitikaṃ (q.v.) vā cipyamānasya Śikṣ 182.2 *or of one being crushed*...

[**ciya** = iva, *like*, acc. to mss. at Mv ii.158.7 (prose) karṣakā ciya, *like peasants*; Senart em. viya, prob. rightly. No ciya or cia is authenticated for iva; Sheth s.v. cia = iva is based on an erroneous statement in Woolner's Introduction to Prakrit, Vocabulary, where cia should be equated with eva, not iva.]

ciraṃ with gen., *it is long since*...; ciraṃ me devanikāyaṃ śuddhāvāsaṃ (or śuddhā° deva°) upasaṃkrāntasya Mv i.56.7, and by plausible em. i.35.1, *it is long since I visited the Śu. class of gods.*

ciratarakena, adv. (to compv. cira-tara plus -ka), *in* or *after a longer time*: yuṣmākaṃ evaṃ cira° vāro bhaviṣyati imehi duvehi potakehi jātehi Mv i.362.3, *the lot* (of death) *will fall on you after a longer time, if these two fawns are born.* But mss. ciratanakena (em. Senart); possibly a deriv. of Skt. cirantana is intended.

cira-sthitika, adj. (= Pali ciraṭṭhitika; Skt. cira plus **sthitika**), *long-enduring, lasting*: gaṇavaro, *the excellent assembly* (of monks), Mv i.301.1 (vs); kulavaṃśa, *family line*, Divy 2.14; 99.6; Av i.14.15 etc.; 277.1; Karmav 59.15; brahmacarya, Mvy 8356; Divy 207.28; (sa āyuṣmān... evaṃdīrghāyur evaṃ-)cirasthitikaḥ Bbh 254.1, ... *lasting for such a long time*; dharmavinaya, Bhīk 4a.3; saddharma, Mvy 6354; °ka-tā, *state of being*..., Bbh 28.20; saddharma-°ka-tā, Bbh 210.11; 229.10; a-cirasthitika-tā, *transitoriness* (sarvasaṃskāragatasya), Dbh 31.4. See also s.v. **sthitaka** (4).

cilimilika, nt., or **ciliminikā** (var.; so Mironov and BR), Mvy 8984, some kind of cloth, or article made of cloth (BR *Halschmuck*, clearly wrong); cf. Pali cilimikā, cimilikā; AMg. ciliminī, *curtain, cloth used as curtain*, also cilimiligā, °miliyā, °milī. Tib. bar thaṅ (? not in Dictt.); Chin. seems to mean *mattress of coarse hair* (or *wool*).

cilla, m. (Skt. Lex.), *a kind of falcon*: Mvy 4905 = Tib. ḥol bu (Jä. and Das ḥol pa, Das *a kind of kite*, Jä. *vulture*?).

ciṣṭā or **ciṣṭhā** (conjectural), see **viṣṭhā**.

cihna-dhara, m., *emblem-bearer*, a kind of royal officer or attendant: Mvy 3727. Tib. translates literally. On cihna cf. Meyer, Kauṭ. Arth. 833, 854.

cīraka, m. or nt. (in mg. 1 = Pali id., Skt. cīra), (**1**) *strip*, primarily of cloth, bark, or the like: °ka-vadhrāṇi, here of strips of flesh, Mv i.19.9 (prose); of either cloth or bark garments, i.19.11 (prose), see **vārṣikā**; (**2**) in Mmk, *lock* or *braid of hair*, artificially arranged (compared to a *strip*) = Tib. (skra, *hair*) zur phud (*hair-knot*), Lalou, Iconographie 66 f. (but I do not think, with Lalou, that this or any cpd. ever refers to a *diadem*); Mañjuśrī's head is adorned with five such, but some passages suggest that in this he was like an ordinary youth in festive garb, sarvabālālaṃkārabhūṣitaḥ (ed. °ta-) pañcacīrakopaśobhitaḥ Mmk 41.24; pañcacīrakopaśobbhita-(text °taṃ) śiraṃ bāladārakālaṃkārālaṃkṛtaṃ 305.6; (kumārākāracihnitaḥ) pañcacīrakamūrdhāno 436.3; note especially pañcacīrakopaśobhitaṃ ekacīrakopaśobhitaṃ śikhopaśobhita-śiraskaṃ (so read for text °bhitaṃ aśiraskaṃ!) vā rājaputraṃ mūrdhābhiṣiktaṃ kṣatriyaputraṃ vā... 49.13 (the youth symbolizes Mañjuśrī, cf. 49.16 f.); Mañjuśrī is pañcacīrakopaśobhitaḥ 41.24; with more specific reference to his head, pañcacīrakaśiraskaḥ 62.8; similarly 68.16; 75.14; (**3**) also in Mmk, cīraka-mudrā is a position of the two hands, interlocked, in which one index finger is made to project (muktvā) between the two thumbs, so that it resembles a *hair-braid*: (anyonyasaktāṅgulimuṣṭayoḥ pradeśinīṃ muktvā aṅguṣṭhayugalaṃ [prob. read °la-]madhyataḥ, eṣā sā Mañjuśrīḥ) tvadīyā aparā cīraka-mudrā 382.(15–)17; prob. this is alluded to by ekacīrakam (sc. mudram; see s.v. **mudra**) 355.27, also sacred to Mañjuśrī; its description in 382.15 ff. occurs in a list of mudrās the names of which refer (presumably because of their shape) to various parts of Mañjuśrī's body, e. g. tvadīyā vaktramudrā 382.11, etc. (note esp. 383.1 ff. śravaṇo grīvā bhujau etc., without specific descriptions).

? **cīra-cīra-cīvaraka**, adj., *tumbledown* (?), of a house: MSV i.82.11 = **avacīra-vicīraka.**

cīvaraka, nt. (= cīvara, the only form otherwise recorded in Skt., Pali, or Pkt.; no dim. or other perceptible force in suffix -ka), *monk's robe*: °kāṇi Divy 125.16; 181.23; 267.9; °ka-śatāni, -sahasrāṇi Bbh 165.10; bhikṣubhir gṛhapati-°kāṇi... dhārayitavyāni MSV ii.48.19. All prose.

cīvara-gopaka, *guardian of the* (monks') *robes*: Mvy 9065; MSV ii.144.15.

cīvarika, acc. to Tib. (gos kyi rin du bcas pa) *the price of a robe*: pātracīvaraṃ sa-cīvara-cīvarikam MSV ii.145.6, 8; 146.1.

cukra, nt., in Mvy 5712 = Tib. tshva, which is said to mean only *salt*; no such mg. otherwise recorded for cukra; the preceding word is amlaḥ, which goes much better with the regular Skt. mg. of cukra; lavaṇam occurs 5709. Cf. **śulukaḥ**, defined in the same way.

cuccu-kārakam, adv., *making the sound cuccu* (smacking the lips? sc. while eating): Mvy 8577 na cu°; completed by piṇḍapātaṃ paribhokṣyāma iti, La Vallée Poussin, JRAS 1913.845, Stein ms. fragm. 1.2.12. May correspond to Pali capucapu-kārakaṃ, Vin. iv. 197.13. Chin. onomat., indicating that one has eaten something sour.

cuti (MIndic for Skt. cyuti; see **cavati**), *fall* (to a lower existence): jagi-r-ūrmi-cuti LV 173.13 (vs); but citation Śikṣ 204.1 jagi janmacyutiḥ, which must be adopted at least as to janma; and most of Lefm.'s mss. read cyuti; of course, meter proves that the pronunciation was cu°, not cyu°, in any event; cuti- Gv 230.25 (vs).

[**Cunanda**, LV 1.15, false reading for **Cunda**, q.v.; Tib. skul byed, *exhortation-maker*, as if from root cud-; so Tib. skul bye = Cunda in Mvy 1045.]

Cunda, (**1**) (= Pali id.; also **Mahā-c°**), n. of one or more disciples of the Buddha: SP 207.4; LV 1.15 (so read for **Cunanda**); Mvy 1045; Divy 153.5 (called a śrāmaṇeraka of Śāriputra); 160.6 (a **śramaṇoddeśa**; this title samaṇuddesa is given to 2 Cunda in Pali, DPPN); (karmāraputra) MPS 26.14 etc.; even in Pali the (apparently) several Cundas are hard to distinguish, and still harder in BHS; (**2**) n. of a yakṣa: Mv iii.327.18 (see next).

Cunda-dvīla (v.l. -vīra), nt., or **-dvīlā** (v.l. -vīrā), f., n. of a locality (adhiṣṭhāna) between Aparagayā and Benares, home of the yakṣa **Cunda** (2): Mv iii.325.11 (nt.); 327.18 (fem.). Seems to be the same as Pali Cundatthiya, °ṭṭhila, °tthika, Pv iii.1.2 and comm. pp. 168–170 (cited DPPN as Cundaṭṭhīla, v.l. Cundavīla, but neither form is recorded in texts or Crit. App.).

Cundā, n. of a goddess: Sādh 270.8 etc. (cf. next).

Cundā-dhāraṇī, n. of a sacred formula: Śikṣ 173.4 (cf. preceding).

culuculāyati (? cf. Hem. 4.127 culuculai = spandate), onomat. verb, perhaps *quivers*: manaḥśilāṃ tri-(text tṛ-)-lohapariveṣṭitāṃ kṛtvā mukhe prakṣipya tāvaj japed yāvac culuculāyati Mmk 319.11, similarly 15; 324.1.

culla, in cullākṣa, see **cūlla.**

Culla-pantha, = **Cūḍapanthaka,** q.v.; so read in Sukh 2.11 for Culla-patka, a monstrous form for which, amazingly, there is no ms. authority, whereas one ms. (reading -patthena) obviously intends -panthena (instr.) as the note points out (two mss. omit the word; the fourth -pacchena, surely for -patthena = panthena).

cūḍa, adj. (= Pali cūḷa; cf. culla, cūlla), *small, petty, insignificant*; always followed by paramacūḍa, and followed or preceded by dhanva (for **dhandha,** q.v.) and paramadhanva: Divy 488.26; 489.19; 490.7, 19; 492.21; 504.18.

Cūḍakā, n. of an apsaras: Kv 3.12.

Cūḍa-panthaka (Cūla°, Cūḍā°; also **Culla-pantha, Śuddhi-panthaka,** qq. v.; = Pali Cūla°), n. of a disciple of the Buddha: Cūḍa° Mvy 1054 (v.l. Cūla°; Mironov Cūḍa° only); MSV i.206.4 ff.; Divy 493.12 (in other places in Divy called simply **Panthaka,** q.v.); Cūḍā° Karmav 43.1 (doubtless by error; v.l. Vṛddha-p°; not in Tib.). The first element has nothing to do with cūḍā but means *lesser, minor*; he is contrasted with **Mahā-panthaka** Divy 493.11, 12.

cūḍā (cf. JM.cūlā, seemingly used in the general sense of *ornament*, see Sheth s.v.), *ornament* (for the head): yat te dṛṣṭā bhūṣaṇā uhyamānā, cūḍā vastrā mahya mañce 'dṛśāsi LV 195.19 (vs). Prob. = the usual Skt. cūḍāmaṇi; Tib. cod pan, *diadem, tiara* (usually = mukuṭa).

Cūḍāpanthaka, see **Cūḍap°.**

cūḍā-pratigrahaṇa, nt., *'reception of the hair-knot'*, n. of the caitya commemorating the Bodhisattva's cutting off of his hair-knot and its reception by the gods: LV 225.19.

Cūḍāmaṇidhara, n. of a nāga: Mvy 3362.

cūḍāmaha, m. or nt., *festival of the* (Bodhisattva's) *hair-knot* (in honor of his cutting it off): (trāyatriṃśatsu) deveṣu °ho vartate LV 225.18; (trāyastriṃśadbhavane . . .) °haṃ ca vartati Mv ii.166.1.

cūḍika, m., or °**kā,** f., applied to a lokadhātu, see s.v. **sāhasracūḍika.**

cūḍikābaddha, adj. (= Pali cuḷi°, read with PTSD cūḷi°, SN ii.182.16), *filled full, crammed* (lit. *to the top*): (sacet . . .) jambūdvīpaḥ paripūrṇaś cūḍikābaddhas tathāgataśarīrāṇāṃ . . . AsP 94.3, etc.; (a silk cloth, kāśikā . . .) pūrṇā cūḍikābaddhā (with dust, in a rain of dust) Divy 577.2. Cf. next.

cūḍikāvabaddha = prec.: Mvy 6356 = Tib. byur bur (read byur with Jä. and Das?) gyur ba, *become heaped up.*

Cūḍeśvara, n. of a suparṇin, previous birth of Vaiśravaṇa (**mahārājan**): MSV i.260.19 ff.

cūrṇa, adj.? in Mv ii.87.12 (kiṃ) karmārāṇāṃ sarvacūrṇa-karmaṃ? sūcīyo, *what is the most delicate* (so Senart; or, *profound, significant, important*?) *work of smiths? Needles.* Perh. cf. JM. cuṇṇa, n., defined by Sheth padaviśeṣa, gambhīrārthaka pada, mahārthaka śabda. Sheth derives from a Skt. caurṇa, of which I can find no trace; if a secondary derivative of cūrṇa, it might mean lit. *polished with powder, rubbed down,* or the like, and so *refined* or *subtle.* Cf. Skt. cūrṇi, cūrṇī, and s.v. **cūrṇika** below (?).

cūrṇa-kuṭṭa, prob. *grinder of powder* (for perfumes): Mv iii.113.10; 442.15; in both foll. by gandhatailika or °laka.

cūrṇika- (perh. for °kā, m.c.; cf. Skt. cūrṇi, cūrṇī), *commentary*: ākhyāyiketihāsādyair gadya-cūrṇika-vārttikaiḥ Laṅk 363.7 (vs).

cūlaka, m., in udaka-c°, *mouthful* or *handful, small draught,* of water: °kāḥ, n. pl., Mmk 690.23; 704.20 (both prose). In place of Skt. culuka (which occurs 714.19) or cūlaka (719.14); the latter is recorded in late Skt. in pw and Schmidt, Nachtr. Is the form with ū a mere corruption?

Cūlapanthaka, see **Cūḍa°.**

Cūlīyā, n. of a sister of Māyā: Mv i.355.17.

cūlla- (= Pali culla, cūḷa), in cūllākṣa, adj., *small-eyed*: Mvy 8834 = Tib. mig chuṅ ba. The Index records also cullākṣa; Mironov only the latter.

cūṣaka, m., *'sucker'*, a class of malevolent superhuman beings: Mmk 17.5. Also **mahācūṣaka,** ibidem.

cetaḥparyāya, m., *way of thought, manner of mind*; less often citta-pa°; commonly preceded by para- or parasya, *of others*; knowledge of *other's mental make-up* is one of the **abhijñā,** q.v.; so also in Pali, where Buddha is parassa (para-) ceto-(citta-)-pariyāya-kusala (-kovida), as one of the abhiññā. In Bhīk 27a.5 cetaḥparyāyasya is not preceded by para- or equivalent, but the meaning is certainly the same, since other abhijñā precede and follow it (divyasya śrotrasya, pūrvanivāsasya). In Mv iii.321.13 Buddhas are called cetaḥparyāyasaṃpannāḥ, probably also with implication of para-, tho here most of the other abhijñā are not listed; but the next following epithet is ṛddhiprātihāryasaṃpannā(ḥ), which recalls one of them.

cetanaka, or (v.l. of Mvy with Mironov) **cait°,** nt. (to next but one, q.v.), *price*: Mvy 8392 °kāni = Tib. rin thaṅ, *price*; Prāt 492.12, 13 (bhikṣuṃ punar uddiśya ajñātinā gṛhapatinā . . .) cīvara-cetanakāny upaskṛtāni syur etair ahaṃ cīvaracetanakair evaṃrūpaṃ cīvaraṃ cetayitvā evaṃnāmānaṃ bhikṣum āchādayiṣyāmi; similarly 493.1, 3, 7 etc., always cet°. The corresponding Pali (see next but one) has (cīvara-)cetāpana, from the caus. of the verb, which alone is recorded in Pali; its mg. can only be substantially the same, *price* (of an article ordered to be bought).

1 **cetayati** (Skt. caus. of cit, not in this mg.; = Pali ceteti), *longs for* (dat.): saṃghasya ca alābhāya apadāya °yati MSV iii.8.14.

2 **cetayati** (the verb on which is based Pali caus. cetāpeti, below), *buys*: cetayitvā, ger., Prāt 492.13; 493.2, 4, 9 etc., see **cetanaka.** In Lang. 22.98 it was stated that the subject of Pali cetāpeti, *causes to be bought, has bought,* 'is always a monk or nun, who instigates (a layman) to buy (something for himself or herself).' This is true only in Vin. iv.250.14–15; in Vin. iii.216.13 and 237.10 the subject is a layman, tho the mg. is certainly *causes to be bought, has bought* (for the benefit of a monk). Vin. iii.216.13 is the same passage as Prāt 492.13 (see **cetanaka**) where cetayitvā, *having bought,* replaces Pali cetāpetvā, *having had* (ordered) *bought* (for a monk). The non-caus. form of Prāt proves the meaning of the caus. Pali form, which Pali interpreters have not understood. The former is not recorded in Pali, nor the latter in BHS. The etymology is unknown but the mg. is clear from the contexts.

? **cetayika** (v.l. ve°), Mv iii.442.10, some sort of entertainer. Form and mg. alike obscure; no correspondent in parallel passages iii.113.4 (see Senart's note here) etc. If the reading ve- were accepted, one might think of reading vetālika or °ḍika (Skt. vaitālika), were it not for the fact that this word seems likely to have been read in 442.8 in the same list (Senart here tālika, but mss. vetaddika, vetarddi°), and in 113.2 Senart em. vaitālika for mss. tetalika, tetarika.

cetasika, adj. (MIndic for cait°), = **caitasika,** q.v.: Mv ii.260.7; iii.66.7, 14 (see **vedayita,** which Senart reads); KP 103.5; Divy 352.15 ff.; Av i.31.14. All cited under **cait°.**

ceti = **cetika, cetiya, caitya,** qq.v. (see § 3.115): ceti bhu (mss. bhū, Lefm. em. m.c., printing cetibhu as one word) trisahasraḥ kiṃ punas tubhya kāyaḥ LV 368.18 (vs), *the 3000-fold world has become* (= abhūt) *an* *object of reverence* (a shrine) . . . So Tib.: stoṅ gsum (= 3,000) mchod rten (= caitya) gyur na (*become*) . . .

cetika, nt. (prob. hyper-Skt. for MIndic cetiya, but cf. **caityaka**) = **ceti, cetiya, caitya**; only in vss: LV 389.10 cetikaṃ (v.l. ceṭikāṃ), parallel to 388.12 cetiyaṃ (v.l. ceṭikā, °ko); dattvā patākāṃ bhagavata cetikeṣū Śikṣ 302.3, parallel to Mv ii.375.9 cetiyeṣu (mss. corruptly jātīyeṣu); so in Śikṣ 303.4, 7; 304.4, 8, etc., cetika regularly where Mv parallels (ii.379.7 etc.) have cetiya.

cetiya, nt. or (when applied to a person) m. (= Pali id., Skt. caitya), *sanctuary, temple*; but also, *object* (of any kind) or *person worthy of veneration*; this form common in even the prose of Mv, only in vss of other texts; cf. also **ceti, cetika.** In sense of a *shrine* (building) cāpālaṃ nāma cetiyaṃ LV 388.12 = Mv iii.306.14 (vs); cāpālaṃ cetiyaṃ Mv i.299.22 (prose), and ff.; cetiyeṣu Mv i.223.11 = ii.26.8 (vs); other forms, ii.354.11; 364.11, 13; 365.20 ff.; iii.50.19; 303.1, etc.; cetiya- (mss. mostly cetiyaṃ-, perhaps read so; one ms. once cetika-)-pūjakaṃ (taṃ kulaṃ) Mv i.198.2 = ii.1.12 (prose), *shrine-revering*, of the family in which a Bodhisattva is born the last time (LV 24.9 caitya-pūjakaṃ in same passage); of the Buddha himself, sarvalokasya cetiyo Mv ii.349.6; 359.8; iii.273.5, the *Revered One of the whole world*; lokasya cetiya (voc.) Mv ii.294.14; cetiyaṃ narāṇāṃ ii.296.13; lokacetiyaḥ LV 97.10 (vs), of the Bodhisattva; utpanno iha loki cetiyo divi bhuvi mahitaḥ LV 363.2 (vs), of the same; of the miraculously produced four bowls, dhāret' ime cetiya saṃmataite (so read with v.l., text °matīte) LV 383.12, *preserve them; they* (shall be) *honored as revered objects*; cetiyārthe (so with mss.) Mv ii.263.12 (prose), *for the purpose of* (making it, viz. the spot where Buddha became enlightened) *an object of veneration* (universal emperors will never master, adhiṣṭhihanti with v.l., that spot except for this purpose).

cetovimukta, adj. (cf. next), *emancipated in mind*: rāgavirāgāya °ktaḥ MSV iii.53.13.

cetovimukti, *emancipation of mind* = Pali cetovimutti, acc. to PTSD always with paññāvimutti: LV 418.18 °tiḥ prajñāvimuktiś ca; both also Mv ii.139.6; iii.333.16; but in iii.333.13 prajñāvi° is lacking. In all four described by the adj. **akopya, q.v.**

ceto-samādhi, f. (= Pali id., also citta-s°), *concentration of mind*, here as leading to the magic power of becoming invisible: tathārūpāṃ °dhiṃ samāpadye yathā . . . mātāpitarau nādṛśetsuḥ Mv iii.409.12 (prose).

? **cedācitta,** instr. cedācittena LV 431.12 (prose; so only one ms.; v.l., two mss., °cintena; all other mss. and Calc. have a haplographic omission here), is uninterpretable to me; I must assume a corruption, perhaps a misprint. Not noted by Weller. Foucaux's Tib. omits the passage. (The particle ced can, it seems, hardly be involved.)

celaka, cellaka, see **cailaka.**

Celā, n. of a daughter of **Siṃha** (8): MSV ii.8.8 ff.

caitanaka, nt., var. for **cet°**, q.v.: Mvy 8392.

caitasika, fem. **°kī,** adj., rarely quasi-subst. with ellipsis of dharma, sometimes written **cetasika,** q.v. (= Pali cetasika); in the following cait° is written except in the passages listed s.v. **cet°**; *mental, of the mind*: often contrasted with kāyika, sometimes also with vācika; sarvakāyika-caitasika-prapīḍitāny Gv 96.4; kāyika-caitasikaṃ . . . sukhaṃ 169.10; kāyikaṃ caitasikaṃ (sc. sukham) Bbh 26.2; cetasikena (parallel to kāyikena and vācikena) sthāmena Mv ii.260.7; kāyikaṃ ca me duḥkhaṃ cetasikaṃ ca Av i.31.14; kāyikāḥ klamāḥ caitasikāḥ (so!) apy upāyāsāḥ Bbh 194.21; without such contrasting words, °kī (sc. vedanā) Mvy 7551; caitasikenābhyāsena Śikṣ 33.16; cittāni caitasika-saṃjñi (acc. pl. of -saṃjñā) vitarkitāni LV 151.13; esp. with dharma, regularly pl., *mental states* or *conditions of existence*, °kā dharmāḥ Mvy 1922; read cetasikā in Mv iii.66.7, 14 (ye . . . dharmā pratītya utpadyante, so substantially with mss., . . .) te . . . cetasikā (Senart vedayitā; mss. in 14 cetasitā or °yitā, one ms. in 7 veṭayitā); na cittaṃ na cetasikā dharmāḥ KP 103.5, *there is no mind, no mental states of existence*; cittacaitasikānām eva dharmāṇām Bbh 99.4, and °kā dharmāḥ 5, apparently *the mind's mental states, states that are mental as belonging to the mind* (?), cf. Pali citta-cetasikā dhammā, Dhammasaṅgaṇi 1022 ff. But in other occurrences of both together, in Pali and BHS, cittam and caitasikā dharmāḥ (cetasikā dhammā), or caitasika (usually masc. pl.) with dh° understood, constitute a duality, *the mind and mental states-of-being.* (For Pali see e. g. Vism. i.84.25 cittacetasikānaṃ samaṃ sammā ca ādhānaṃ; *mind and mental properties*, Maung Tin.) Cf. KP 103.5, above, and: kuśalānāṃ ca citta-caitasikānām (so read) anusmṛtir Śikṣ 33.13, *remembrance of meritorious mind and mental states.* In Divy 352.15 kīdṛśās te cittacetasikāḥ (certainly sc. dharmāḥ) pravartante, kliṣṭā vākliṣṭā vā, and similarly in the sequel, the cpd. may perhaps be a Tatp., *mental states of the mind*, rather than a dvandva. On the other hand cf. Sūtrāl. xi.30, comm., marīcikopamau dvau dharmau, cittaṃ caitasikāś ca; here the duality is obvious, and dharmāḥ is certainly to be supplied with cait°. In AbhidhK. the usual equivalent is **caitta,** q.v.; note that the word dharma regularly has to be supplied, or at least is not expressed, but note LaV-P. viii.159 avasthāviśeṣo 'pi hi nāma cetasaś caitasiko bhavati (is dharmaḥ here also to be supplied with the masc. quasi-subst. caitasiko?). As in Sūtrāl. above, they are false, delusive, illusory.

Caitika (= Pali Cetiya, DPPN 2, = Apacara), n. of a lying king (former birth of Devadatta): MSV iv.245.6 ff.

caitta, adj. from citta in origin but regularly substantivized as masc.; fundamentally a Buddhist word, equivalent to **caitasika,** q.v.; common in AbhidhK., see LaV-P. Index; *mental state* or *condition of being*, regularly cpd. or associated with citta, as a duality: Laṅk 150.14 citta-caitta-kalāpo, *mind and the whole mass of mental things* (et alibi in Laṅk); MadhK 11.9 citta-caittānāṃ; 274.7 -citta-caitta-, *la pensée et ses dérivés*, ed. note. See esp. AbhidhK. ii.149 citta-caittāḥ (note masc.!) sahāvaśyam; LaV-P., note, says citta = manas = vijñāna; caitta = caitasa = caitasika = cittasaṃprayukta (cf. also ii.150).

caitya, nt., like its MIndic substitutes **ceti, cetika, cetiya** (also **caityaka**), seems to be used more broadly than in Skt., as any *object of veneration*: lokasya caityam Śikṣ 56.11 (said of any ornament of a stūpa); 136.2 (of the monkish robes); caitya-bhūtaḥ Vaj 34.12, *of the nature of an object of veneration* (said of any place where 'this sūtra' shall be proclaimed). See **mahācaitya.**

caityaka (nt.; Skt. caitya plus -ka; may possibly be the direct ancestor of **cetika,** q.v., or a further hyper-Sktization of that form if, as I think likely, **cetika** is itself a semi-Sanskritized substitute for MIndic cetiya), *temple, shrine*: °keṣu Śikṣ 301.1 (= Mv ii.373.17 cetiyeṣu).

caitradaṇḍika, see **vetra°.**

Caitraratha(-vana), doubtless to be identified with Skt. id. (n. of a grove constructed by the gandharva Citraratha for Kubera), = **Citraratha,** q.v., as n. of a grove of the Trāyastriṃśa gods: Mvy 4197; Divy 194.2.

cailaka, (**1**) m. (from Skt. cela or caila, *cloth*), *a monk* (cf. Burnouf, Intr., 57; Lotus, 392; Kern, SBE 21.186 note 1), said to mean, specifically, *one who wears no more than a (loin-)cloth*: te cailaka-bhūta SP 192.9 (vs), *turned into monks*; but most mss. read celaka, ceḍaka, or cellaka, or the like; (**2**) nt. (= Skt. cela, caila, also celaka, see Schmidt, Nachträge; AMg. celaa), *cloth*: °kaṃ, acc. sg., Mv iii.163.9 (prose).

cailoṇḍūka (or °ḍuka? m. or nt.; cf. Skt. caila, cela, and uṇḍuka; = Pali celaṇḍuka, or °ḍaka, which in MN i.150.17 clearly means *turban*, with comm. ii.158.28 ff., not *loincloth* with PTSD; celoṇḍukaḥ, *turban* (śiroveṣṭe), also

Skt. Lex., Trik. 2.6.35, Bombay ed. of 1889; BR cites coloṇḍuka from old ed., clearly an error), *turban*: (sacet tvam... dharmodgataṃ bodhisattvaṃ...) cailoṇḍūkam (v.l. cailamaṇḍukam) iva śirasā parikarṣeḥ AsP 493.17, *if you should carry around... on your head like a turban*.

co (m.c. = ca, see JAOS 66.203), *and*: SP 13.15 etc., § 3.82.

coṭa, °ṭaka (m. or nt.; cf. next, and Skt. Lex coṭī, coṭikā), some kind of garment, or textile goods: coṭa-kambalena, Kashgar rec. SP 106.10; coṭakam, Kashgar rec. 112.4.

coḍa, m. or nt. (Skt. cola, defined as *jacket* or *blouse*, Lex. = kañcuka, prāvaraṇa; BHS seems to use coḍa in a wider sense; see next), *garment(s), clothing*; regularly associated with bhakta or bhojana, together = *food and raiment*: paryeṣate bhakta tathāpi coḍaṃ SP 112.4; bhaktaṃ ca coḍaṃ ca gaveṣamāṇo 8; kim adya coḍena ca (so read with most mss. for text tha) bhojanena vā 113.8; (ananyacitto) bhakte ca coḍe ca bhavaty abhīkṣṇaṃ Śikṣ 113.8, *and he always has his heart set on nothing but food and clothing*. (All verses.)

coḍaka, m. or nt. (= prec.; Skt. colaka Lex. and rarely lit., Schmidt, Nachträge), *garment(s), clothing*: with bhakta (like coḍa) bhakta-coḍaka-paramo vatāyam Śikṣ 20.17 (prose); otherwise, coḍaka-dhovakasya, *washerman (of clothes)*, and coḍakāni dhovīyanti Mv ii.466.4, others in sequel; ujjhita-coḍakā (*discarded garments*) sāhartavyā Mv iii.264.11; coḍaka- Divy 415.6.

codaka, adj. (= Pali id.), with bhikṣu, *accusing (monk)*: MSV iii.18.20 f.

codanā (to next, q.v.; = Pali id.), *accusation, reproof*: bhūtāṃ codana saṃśrutya Śikṣ 47.4, *hearing the true accusation*, and °nāṃ bhūtataḥ śrutvā 47.6 (both vss); mamaivārthaṃ codanā kriyate Divy 4.4 (prose); -acodanatā, *state of not accusing* (reference lost).

codayati (= Pali codeti), *accuses* (a person, acc., of an offense, instr.): Śikṣ 98.2 pudgalaṃ... āpattyā codayiṣyāmo (so Pali āpattiyā codeti, *accuses of sin*); SP 326.6 taṃ vaidyu vijño na mṛṣeṇa codayet, *a wise man would not accuse that physician of lying*; in MSV very common with smārayati, e. g. ced... codayeyaṃ smārayeyaṃ MSV ii.177.15, *if I should accuse and warn...*; a necessary preliminary to suspension, ib. 202.9. See **saṃcodayati**.

Caurikā, n. of a yoginī: Sādh 446.1.

caurya (nt.; not recorded in this sense), *stealth*, in the sense of *secrecy*: (ya imaṃ dharmaparyāyaṃ...) rahasi cauryeṇāpi kasyacid... saṃprakāśayed SP 227.3 (prose), *who should declare this dharma-paryāya even by stealth in secret to anyone*...

cyavati, *falls* (to a lower existence); in Skt. and, so far as I have found, in Pali (cavati) construed with abl. of the existence departed from; here sometimes with loc. instead, *dies, passes away in*...: SP 94.3 ff. cyutvā manuṣyeṣu avīci teṣāṃ pratiṣṭha bhotī paripūrṇakalpān, (4)... cyutāś ca tatra prapatanti (Kashgar rec. and WT with ms. K′ cyutāś-cyutās tatra patanti) bālāḥ, (5) yadā ca narakeṣu (Kashgar rec. °kebhya) cyutā bhavanti..., *having fallen* (from existence, i. e. having died) *among men, Avīci becomes their abode for full kalpas... and having fallen* (died) *there, the fools fall* (lower); *and when they come to fall* (die) *in* (Kashgar, *from*) *the hells*...

cyutopapāda (= Pali cutūpapāta), *fall* (from one existence) *and rebirth* (in another), see s.v. **upapāda**.

[**cyūḍika**, read **cūḍ°**; see **sāhasra-cūḍika**.]

CH

chaka (nt.; = Pali id., Childers and Geiger 40.1a; only chakana reported in Pali literature; = Skt. śakṛt), *dung*: in Mv ii.71.14 (vs) read chaka-mūtram eva sṛjaṃ (= sṛjan, pres. pple.) for Senart charda-gūtham... mss. chada-mūrtam, or chanda-mūrtem); my reading is proved by the corresponding prose 70.9 uccāra-prasrāvaṃ muñcamāno.

Chagalapāda, n. of a gandharva: Suv 162.1.

? **chaṭa-**, perhaps to be understood instead of **śaṭa-**, q.v., in Mmk 112.24. Cf. next.

chaṭa-chaṭā, chaṭā-chaṭā (Skt. chaṭā, AMg. chaḍā; āmreḍita), *mass*; instr. adv., *in a mass*, French *en masse*: taṃ tālaskandhaṃ pṛthivīye chaṭāchaṭāye (*in one great mass*; Senart, *lourdement*) upari patitaṃ Mv i.317.1; tāni bandhanāni hastena chaṭachaṭāya (*in one single mass, en masse*; = *all with one stroke*) chindati Mv ii.458.2. Both prose.

chaḍḍeti (= Pali id.) *abandons*: °ti Mv ii.170.18; iii.291.14; mss. corrupt in both, but context makes Senart's em. seem certain; in iii.291.14 the only ms. choḍḍeti (lacuna in other ms.).

chaṇḍikā, acc. to Tib. sgo ḥu chuṅ, app. *small door*, or ske ḥu (? ske = *neck*), in °kā-vārika Mvy 9075, some servant or official in a monastery; Chin. and Jap. *watcher at a small gate or door*, app. agreeing with the first Tib. gloss.

chattraka, nt., and °**ikā**, f. (both Skt. Lex.; cf. Pali ahi-chattaka, nt., *mushroom*), *mushroom*: tad yathā chattrakaṃ (mss.; Senart em. chā°) evaṃ varṇapratibhāso pi abhūṣi Mv i.345.7; same phrase i.340.12 has in mss. vāḍakam, Senart em. chātrakaṃ; chattrikāṃ Mmk 81.25.

Chattramukhā, n. of a nāga maid: Kv 4.8.

Chattrākāra, n. of a locality: °re Māy 50.

[**chaddhva-ṃ**, corrupt reading in KN for SP 352.9; read cipiṭam, *flat* (agreeing with nāsa in next line), with WT, supported by Tib. sna leb, *flat nose*. The mss. cited by KN vary greatly and at random. Burnouf and Kern both translate as if they read cipiṭaṃ.]

-chana for -channa (Skt.), *covered*, in (text) ducchanaṃ and succhanaṃ, yathā hy agāraṃ du° Ud xxxi.11–16 and... su° 17–22; meter favors, indeed almost demands, -channaṃ, which is read in the same vss in Pali, Dhp. 13, 14, and must, it seems, be adopted here, tho the manifold repetition of this obvious error is strange.

chanda, (**1**) m. (rarely nt., LV 262.8), = Skt. and Pali id., used in both bad and good sense; more often in bad, *desire, whim, caprice, passion*, see e. g. **acchanda-gāmin**; in good sense, *zeal*, a characteristic of a Bodhisattva or a Buddha; often associated with vīrya: asti me (sc. Bodhisattvasya) chando 'sti vīryaṃ LV 239.1, same passage as: mahyaṃ pi khalu asti chando... Mv ii.118.10; asti chandaṃ (n. sg.! one ms. °as) tathā vīryaṃ LV 262.8 = asti chando ca vīryaṃ ca Mv ii.239.9 (vs; note chandaś ca LV 262.5, just above); nāsti chandasya hāniḥ Mv i.160.12 (one of the 18 āveṇika Buddha-dharma); (āryasmitaṃ, of the Bodhisattva) chandopastabdhaṃ Mv ii.280.16, *based on zeal*; janemi chandaṃ Sukh 9.6; (**2**) (m.; this mg. in Pali, see PTSD s.v. 2), *approval, consent*, as object of dā-, *give*: dadāti... tathāgataś chandam... SP 248.8, *the Tathāgata* (who sends this message; not Śākyamuni; neither Burnouf nor Kern understands the passage) *gives his consent* (to the opening of this stūpa); chandārhibhyaś

(= Pali chandāraha, see esp. Vin. i.318.11, *one who has the right to a valid vote*) ca chandenānītā bhavanti (*are agreed in consenting*) MSV ii.210.3; (**3**) n. of Buddha's charioteer, oftener called **Chandaka** (4), q.v.: LV 133.6; Divy 391.24; both times in vss, the -ka possibly dropped m.c., cf. § 22.24 (note that Chandaka is the form used in prose two lines before in Divy); but in MSV iii.28.8 ff. (prose) also Chanda, = Pali Channa, assumed in DPPN to be this same person; here as in Vin. ii.21.7 ff. subjected to **utkṣepaṇīya**; MPS 29.15; the corresponding name in Pali is Channa; (**4**) n. of one of the ṣaḍvārgika monks: Mvy 9474.

chandaka, (**1**) nt. (= Pali id.; from chanda plus -ka; see also **chanda-yācaka**), *'free-will offering', general collection of alms* for the community of monks, made by going the rounds of the town and inviting subscriptions from all citizens (Av ii.39.4 ff. describes this); chandakāni Av i.269.9; otherwise only **chandaka-bhikṣaṇa** (nt.) in same mg., MSV i.61.19; ii.77.15; Av i.257.8, 11; 313.9; 314.2, 4; 317.16; ii.39.4 ff.; in i.264.2 (see Speyer's Index) read chandaka-(ed. chandana)-bhikṣaṇa (ms. and ed. bhikṣa; but the missing -ṇa is read in line 7 below); (**2**) in Av ii.55.3 . . . indriyair avikalatvasya kuśaladharma-chandakasya āścaryādbhuto loke prādurbhāvaḥ, Speyer, Index, renders -chandaka by *gathering* (of merit); but cf. Pali dhamma-chanda, *desire for the Law*, opp. to kāma-chanda, *desire for lusts*; this is certainly the word involved; either chandaka = chanda (ka svārthe), or, perhaps better, read -chandatvasya, which matches the preceding series of nouns in -tva-sya, *the appearance in the world of a state of desiring meritorious* (or, *felicitous*) *dharma* (Law, or states of being?) *is a prodigious marvel*; (**3**) in Mvy 2225 text tīvreṇa chandakaḥ, presumably adj., *desiring* (*vehemently*); but v.l. chandena, and so Mironov without v.l. (also Index of Kyoto ed. lists this reference under chanda, not under chandaka); this is prob. the true reading: *with vehement desire* (**chanda**); (**4**) n. of the Bodhisattva's charioteer (in Pali Channa; here rarely **Chanda,** q.v.); sometimes even when the meter seems to demand Chanda, Chandaka is written, as in Mv i.154.9; this is the regular form in prose and vs; Mv i.154.5 (prose), 6, 9; 155.14; ii.25.12 (prose); 114.5 (prose); 159.12 ff.; 189.1 ff.; iii.91.7; 262.8; LV 94.13; 95.10; 123.8; 210.3 ff.; 228.17 ff.; 237.18; Divy 391.22; sent with Kālodāyin by Śuddhodana as messenger to Buddha after his enlightenment, Mv ii.233. 11 ff.

Chandaka-nivartana, nt. (see prec.), n. of a caitya built on the spot where Chandaka left the Bodhisattva as he gave up wordly life: LV 225.13.

chanda-yācaka, adj. with bhikṣu, *monk begging for the* **chandaka** (-bhikṣaṇa), q.v.: MSV i.62.1, 2, 4 °kā (bhikṣavaḥ).

chandasvinī (from Skt. chandas plus -vin; sc. vidyā?), *metrics, versification*: LV 156.19 °vinyāṃ (prose; so nearly all mss., v.l. chandasi nyāya-; . . . bodhisattva eva viśiṣyate sma); Tib. tshig (*word*) sdeb pa (*combining*; also *to make poetry, to compose verses*, Jä.).

chandārhin, m. (= Pali chandāraha), see s.v. **chanda** (2).

chandika (from chanda plus -ika; = Pali id., not well defined PTSD, cf. CPD a-cchandika), *desirous*, with instr., inf., at end of cpds., or without complement: parasmai cārthikāya chandikāya kulaputrāya . . . yācamānāya AsP 102.19; chandiko bhaviṣyati . . . lekhayitum Śikṣ 49.15; (buddhaguṇebhiḥ) Śikṣ 342.20 (vs); bhūyaś-chandika, *desiring more, greedy*, Mvy 2211; °**ka-tā**, abstr., in tīvra-cch° KP 155.6, kuśala- 8.

channa-daśa, adj., (garment) *with hidden fringe* or *border*, forbidden to monks: MSV ii.95.7, 13; prob. corruption for Pali acchinnadasa, in corresp. passage Vin. i.306.25; see **-daśaka.**

chambati (= Pali chambhati, perhaps to be read here; derivs. of this root are spelled with b, not bh, in this text; see also **sa-cchambita**; cf. the next entries, and (**ac**)**chambhin,** (**ac**)**chambhita**(**tva**)), *is frightened*: bibhety api chambaty apy uttrasaty api, Dhvajāgrasūtra, Waldschmidt, Kl. Skt. Texte 4, p. 49, line 23. The MIndic chambhati is clearly based on Skt. skambh-; BHS (rarely) uses the equivalent stambh- in the same sense, see **a-stambhin.**

chambita-tva, nt. (= **chambh°**, see prec.), *state of being frightened*: Dhvajāgrasūtra (as prec.), 47.6, 16, 24.

chambin, adj. (= chambhin, see prec.), *frightened*: Dhvajāgrasūtra, Waldschmidt, Kl. Skt. Texte 4, p. 49, line 22.

chambhita, adj. (ppp., cf. prec. entries and next, also **acchambhita**; Pali id., for Skt. *skambhita = BHS stambh-, § 2.18, cf. **a-stambhin**), *frightened*: °to Mv ii.357.8.

chambhitatva, nt. (= Pali °tatta; cf. prec. entries), *consternation*: SP 63.5; Gv 159.24; 166.5; Dbh 12.23; Dbh.g. 2(338).11, 13.

chambhin, see **chambin** and **acchambhin,** and cf. **astambhin.**

[**chayika,** read **chāyika,** q.v.]

[**challa,** text in Mv ii.125.8 kola-challaṃ pi āhāram āharanti; so one ms., but v.l. kolaṃ curṇṇa, which clearly points to kola-cūrṇaṃ = Pali kola-cuṇṇaṃ, MN i.80.3 in a closely parallel passage; so read; *powder of jujube-berries*. Senart assumes a m. or nt. equivalent of challi, *bark* (Pali, late and lex. Skt., see Schmidt, Nachträge.)]

chava, adj. (also **śava,** q.v.; Pali chava, homonymous with chava = Skt. śava, *corpse*, and perhaps ultimately the same word, cf. Senart, Mv i.583), *base, vile, wretched*: śūrāṃ sāhasikāṃ chavāṃ (acc. pl.) Mv i.278.10; pattrāhāro chavāvāsī Mv iii.435.22, *having a wretched dwelling*.

chavi (= Skt., Pali id., *skin*), *bark* (of a tree): kovidārasya chavigandhaḥ Gv 501.11 (prose). Acc. to the English of Ratnach., chavi may have this mg. in AMg.; this is a translation of Hindi chāl, which seems to mean both *skin* and *bark*; whether the AMg. word also means *bark* I do not know.

chāgalaka, adj. (to Skt. °la), *of a goat*: °ka dṛti, *goatskin bag*, MPS 7.5.

(**chāta,** adj., *thin*; occurs, tho rarely, in Skt., as well as Pkt. chāa, cf. Deśīn. 3.33, with comm.; Pischel 328; Schmidt, Nachträge; acc. to Pischel, Pali chāta, Pkt. chāa, *hungry*, is an unrelated word, from *psāta, while our chāta is from *kṣāta; this theory seems speculative. In Mv i.147.2 = 203.17 = ii.7.13 (vs) Senart em. cāpodare, but read chātodare with all mss. in first and third citations (in second nābhodare); cf. chātodarī in comm. to Deśīn., above; also Jm 3.8 kṣudhā chātatarodarīm.)

[**chāttraka,** nt., see **chattraka.**]

-chāda, ifc. (cf. Skt. chādana etc.; this stem seems not recorded anywhere), *cover, protection*: tad rājyaṃ dharma-chādaṃ (*with dharma as its protection*) prādāt Gv 416.19 (prose).

(**chādayati,** Skt., (**1**) *covers*: in Mv iii.55.4, text, kuñjaraṃ pi so . . . ṣaṣṭihāyanaṃ balaśaktikāye chāditavyaṃ manyeya, yo me . . . ṣaḍ vābhijñā balaṃ (so mss.) vaśībhāvaṃ chādayitavyaṃ manyeyā (the last part, from yo . . ., repeated 6–7, 8, 9–10). For the first chāditavyaṃ, Senart thinks a form of **chaḍḍeti** must be read; but the Pali parallel SN ii.222.10 reads tālapattikāya chādetabbaṃ, (an elephant) *to be covered with a palm-leaf*, which proves chāditavyaṃ correct. Perhaps read before it (with the Pali) tāla-pattrikāye; possibly, however, tala-śaktikāye (closer to our mss.), *with an upheld arm* or *hand*, see s.v. **talaśaktikā.** (**2**) *protects, helps, saves* (cf. pw s.v. 6, *schützen*): in LV 168.8 (vs) read, kṛpakaruṇā janiyā atiraudre chāditu so bho (so best ms. A; all other mss. and Calc. śobhe, which is uninterpretable), (by you) *taking pity and compassion on your very cruel* (foe), *he, lo! was protected* (helped). So Tib. seems clearly to read; it ends, de ni (*that very one*) khyod kyis (*by you*) bskyabs (*protect, help*).

chāya, m., and **chāyā** (see also **duśchāya**, °**yā**, **mahāchāyā**), a kind of evil supernatural being, acc. to Tib. on Mvy 4763 chāyā = grib gnon, *harpy, a demon that defiles and poisons food*; fem. also Mmk 17.8; Māy 219.10, etc.; masc., na chāyaḥ chāyasamatīye sthānaṃ Māy 226.24.

chāyika, nt., or °**kā**, f. (cf. Pali chārikā; AMg. chāria, °ya, nt., and °yā; no form with y for r recorded), *ashes*: chāyikam (so Index; text, also Mironov, chayikam; short a seems clearly an error) api na prajñāyate Mvy 5255 (Tib. thal ba, *dust, ashes*; follows **maśir**, or maśir, q.v., api . . .); (na maṣir) na chāyikā prajñāyate Śikṣ 246.10; in Mv ii.325.9 (vs) read, substantially with mss., na . . . maṣī (mss. add va; read vā? or na?) chāyikā (mss. chā-ikā, or chāyi; Senart em. chārikāṃ) vā (the first part of the line is corrupt but Senart's em. cannot be right; the negative was clearly present); one of four **vikṛta**-bhojana, MSV i.286.8, 9 chāyikā. See also **jambū-chāyaka**.

-chiṭi (acc. sg. °ṭim), in kāñjikacchiṭim, *an inferior kind of sour gruel* (kāñjika): Divy 496.9, 11, 12. Replaced by simple kāñjikam in lines 15, 21, 26.

? **Chitvāsuta** (Oldenburg suggests reading Chibbāsuta; I find no trace of anything like either), n. of a nāga; Māy 221.22.

chidrāchidra (nt.; § 23.12), *all manner of holes*: (na svapet) chidrāchidreṣu sattvānāṃ yac ca sthānaṃ mahadbhayam (Śikṣ mahābh°) Laṅk 257.1, cited Śikṣ 132.7 (one should not sleep) *in all manner of holes of creatures* (animals), *and* (not in) *whatever is a place of great danger*. Both translations are incorrect.

chidrīkaraṇa (nt.; to next), in a-cchid°, *the* (not) *making defective*: °raṇāvipādanatayā (i. e. -avipād°) Bbh 187.14.

chidrīkaroti (cf. prec. and next; to Skt. chidra with kṛ-), *makes defective*: -samādānaṃ na chidrīkaroti (bodhisattvaḥ) Bbh 183.24.

chidrīkāra (m.; to prec.) = °**karaṇa**; in cpd., Bbh 162.19.

chinna, adj. (ppp.; not recorded in this sense), *wearied*; in strī-, bhāra-, mārga-chinna, Mvy 8793–5; MSV iv.68.13–14; Tib. dub pa.

chinna-bhakta, adj. (Bhvr.; = Pali °bhatta), or °**taka**, *with food cut off, fasting, not having eaten*: brāhmaṇaś chinnabhakto (*having had no breakfast*) halaṃ vāhayati Divy 461.13; (same phrase, °ktako) MSV i.68.20. See also **bhakta-chinnaka**.

chinna-vārṣika, *one who has fallen away from observance of the rainy season*: Mvy 9425 (Tib. dbyar gnas pa las ñams pa); also **varṣā-chinnaka** (spelled varṣācchi°) MSV ii.154.12; 157.13.

chuṭī, see next.

chuṭṭa, adj. or subst. nt. (also **chuṭī**; cf. Skt. root chuṭ-; perh. read chuṭṭha? cf. Ap. chuṭṭha, Jacobi, Bhav., Glossar, said to = kṣipta, to chuhai, which prob. = Skt. kṣubh-), seems to mean (*what has been*) *injured*: -stūpeṣu ca khaṇḍa-chuṭṭaṃ (Tib. ral ba daṅ ḥdrams pa, *what is damaged and injured*, cf. ḥgrams pa, *to hurt*, Jä.) pratisaṃskartavyam MSV ii.143.12; khaṇḍa-chuṭyā pratisaṃskaraṇārtham MSV iv.136.10. In parallels **sphuṭa** (q.v., 2); read so?

cheka, adj. (Jain Skt. and Pali, *clever*; also Pali *good*, Jāt. v.366.27, comm. sundara, opp. pāpaka, of odors), *good, proper, seemly*: na chekaṃ na pratirūpaṃ MSV iii.96.15.

cheda (= **chedya**, q.v.), *a martial art*: chede vā bhede vā Mv ii.74.1.

chedaka, m. (only pl. in list of misc. artisans), perh. *cutter* (of wood? quite uncertain): Mv iii.113.17 nāpitā (v.l. nāvikā) kalpikā chedakā (v.l. chedakārakā) lepakā sthapati-; Senart by em. also in iii.443.4 (nāpitā, v.l. nāvikā) kalpikā (mss. °akā) che° (but mss. chādakā) lepakā sthapati-. On adv. **kavaḍa-chedakam**, see s.v.

chedya, nt. (also **cheda**; in this sense not recorded; Pali has chejja-bhejja-, Jāt. v.444.22, and chejjā, fem., alone, Vin. iii.47.7, only as forms of punishment; PTSD inaccurate), always associated with **bhedya**; both in lists of military arts, usually as mastered by the young Bodhisattva or another young prince; precise mg. is never made clear; Tib. on Mvy and on LV renders chedya by bcad pa, *cutting*, and bhedya by dral ba, *splitting, tearing asunder*: chedyam Mvy 4988, bhedyam 4989; otherwise only in loc., usually listed with other martial arts, chedye and bhedye, LV 156.12 and Mv ii.74.1–2 (here Mv chede, bhede, and so v.l. elsewhere in Mv; the young Bodhisattva challenges other Śākya youths to test their skill in such arts); Mv i.129.5; ii.423.17; 434.13; Divy 100.11; 442.7.

choḍayati, see **chor°**.

choraṇa (to next), (**1**) *discharge, expulsion*, of impurities: kheṭa-cchoraṇe (of phlegm) Mmk 113.7; pūti- ib. 14; (**2**) *abandonment*: (yatra na kasyacid dharmasya) choraṇam asti ŚsP 1409.16.

chorayati, rarely (Mv iii.20.2) **choḍ°** (cf. prec.; not in Pali; AMg. and JM. ppp. choḍi(y)a, *discharged, released*; Hindi choṛnā, *let go, release, abandon*, etc., see Turner, Nep. Dict. s.v. choṛnu), (**1**) *clears away, removes*: (withered flowers from caityas) choretva jālaṃ (see **jāla**) jinacetiyeṣu Mv ii.391.22; 392.4, 8, 12, 16, 20 (vss); same passages Śikṣ 306.2, 4 choritva, but 6, 8, 10 apanīya (ms.; wrongly em. to upa° in ed.); Tib. cited by Bendall as bsal ba, which can only mean *remove, clear away*; immediately following verses deal unambiguously with meritorious clearing away of withered flowers, and in Mv ii.394.6, 10 choretva is again used, with objects osannapuṣpaṃ and nirmālyaṃ; Senart and Bendall misunderstand; pātrādhiṣṭhānaṃ chorayitavyam MSV iii.98.3–4, *he must put away the* (*food-*) *bowl-stand*; (**2**) *throws away* (refuse, food-leavings, dirty water, etc.): chorayiṣyāmaḥ Mvy 8595 = Prāt 534.13 (water with which the food bowl has been washed); Mvy 8596 (leavings of food); ekānte chorayitvā (id.; text sthor°) Mmk 107.27; chorito (food regarded as unclean) Divy 86.23; annapānaṃ choryate Divy 84.21; ucchiṣṭodakaṃ choritaṃ 185.28; tad (foul stuff) ekānte chorayitvā Av i.255.7; chorayitvā (a dead body) Divy 166.1; sapta parvatā utpāṭitā, utpāṭayitvā laghunīvānyapradeśe chorayitvā Kv 31.24, *having plucked up and thrown away*; with gen., tasya pātraśeṣaṃ °yanti MSV i.5.14, *threw to that* (ape) *what* (food) *was left in their bowls*; (**3**) *discharges* (bodily discharges): chorayiṣyāmaḥ (°mi; not in an improper place) Mvy 8627–28; *emits* (a sigh), ucchvāsaṃ choritam Kv 57.15, 16; (**4**) *casts off, puts aside, lays down* (garments, ornaments): vastrāṇy ābharaṇāni ca pṛthivyāṃ chorayanti sma LV 321.2; mukuṭaṃ . . . chorayitvā LV 135.11 (vs), (Śuddhodana) *laying off his diadem* (etc., in saluting the Bodhisattva); (**5**) *abandons, leaves* (a place): choritva kṣetrāṇi svaka-svakāni SP 251.5 (vs), *leaving their several* (Buddha-) *fields* (they have come here; misunderstood by Burnouf and Kern); kva tvaṃ gato 'si mama śayi chorayitvā LV 230.18 (vs; Gopā apostrophizes the Bodhisattva), *abandoning my bed*; (**6**) *abandons, gives up*: rājyaṃ ca rāṣṭraṃ ca chorayitvā Mv ii.483.3 = iii.18.6 (vs); choritā (? precise mg. uncertain from lack of context) Mvy 2553; *gives away* (in largess), paṭakāś choritāḥ MSV ii.107.2; (**7**) *abandons, deserts* (a person): taṃ (sc. rājānaṃ) choḍitvā (v.l. choḍayitvā) Mv iii.20.2 (prose); choritaḥ (a man) Divy 6.6; 334.22; chorayantu (a woman, in a cemetery, after cutting off her hands, feet, ears, and nose) Divy 353.23; sa tam ekānte prakramya (read prakrāmya?

caus.) chorayitvā prakrāntaḥ (Speyer em. violently) Av i.245.4, *making him go off to one side and deserting him, he departed*; (**8**) *gets rid of, relieves oneself of* (periods of life in the world): iyataḥ Subhūte kalpān bodhisattvo . . . chorayati viprṣṭhīkaroti saṃsārād vyantīkaroti AsP 343.18–19, *so many aeons the B. gets rid of, abandons, puts an end to, from the round of existence* (i. e. he shortens his necessary stay in the saṃsāra).

J

jakṛt (semi-MIndic for Skt. yakṛt; cf. AMg. jagaya), *liver*: LV 208.18 (vs; v.l. ya°).

Jagatīṃdhara, n. of a Bodhisattva: Mvy 728; RP 2.1.

Jaga(t)pradīpaś(i)ri, n. of a Buddha: Gv 285.19 (vs).

Jagadindrarāja, n. of a Bodhisattva: Gv 4.5.

jagadrocana(-maṇiratna), a kind of jewel: Gv 124.5.

jagadvyūhagarbha, nt., n. of a kind of magic gem: °bhaṃ nāma mahāmaṇiratnaṃ Gv 499.9.

Jaga(n)mantrasāgaranirghoṣamati, n. of a Buddha: Gv 285.21 (vs).

Jaganmitra, n. of a Bodhisattva: Gv 442.25.

Jaṅgamā, n. of a rākṣasī: Māy 243.24.

jaṅgala, m. (Skt. Lex. and Pali id., acc. to PTSD nt., which its citations do not prove; jaṅgalāni Jāt. iv.71.1 is an adj.), *wild place, jungle*: khānayet kūpa jaṅgale SP 235.11 (vs); ujjaṅgalo ca jaṅgalo Mv ii.207.5, 8 (treated as n. pr. by Senart, Index).

Jaṅghā, n. of a (tantalizing) state of preta-existence: Śikṣ 57.6.

Jaṅghā-kāśyapa, n. of a monk: MSV i.204.18 ff.; Karmav. 76.3. Neither the name, nor the story told of him, seems to be associated with any of the Pali Kassapas.

jaṅghā-preṣaṇa, nt. (cf. Pali °pesanika, °ṇika, *running errands on foot*), *'foot-errand', the sending* (someone) *on foot on an errand*: nāsti taj jaṅghāpreṣaṇaṃ yan notsahate Śikṣ 37.1.

jaṅghā-vihāra (m.; = Pali id., 'usually in phrase °raṃ anucaṅkamati anuvicarati', PTSD), *walk, stroll* (on foot): °ram anucaṅkramyamāṇo LV 248.7; °ram anukrāmati Divy 471.8.

jaṭā-karaṇa-karman, nt., *the ceremony of clipping a young boy's hair except for the top-knot*: (Rāhulasya) °karma Mv iii.263.16; = Skt. cūḍākaraṇa, which replaces this as exact synonym in line 18 below.

Jaṭāpura, n. of a town: Māy 77.

Jaṭiṃdhara, n. of a śreṣṭhin and medical authority: Suv 175.1 ff.; 199.10 ff.

Jaṭilikā, n. of a village chief's daughter: LV 265.6.

Jaṭhara, n. of a local ruler (pradeśarājan), previous incarnation of Devadatta: Mv i.128.14.

jaḍa = Skt. jala, *water*: LV 372.15 (all mss., both edd.).

jaḍuvāra (var. **°pāra**), some sort of herb: Mvy 5814 = Tib. zur ba (not recorded in Dictt.).

jatu-yantra, loc. °tre, lit. *lac-machine*, n. of some art, in a list of those in which the Bodhisattva excelled; so read in LV 156.22, for Lefm. jala-yantre; mss. vary, A (the best) cited as janu- (read jatu-)y°; Calc. jatu°, confirmed by Tib. rgya skyegs kyi ḥkhrul ḥkhor, *machine of lac*. The precise mg. is obscure to me; in corresponding lists of arts I have found nothing similar, unless jantunā Mv i.129.9 (in a corrupt and obscure line, included in a passage of similar tenor) conceals jatunā, instr. of jatu.

? **jatya,** perh. by error for a-jatya, itself either error, or with MIndic a for ā, for Skt. a-jātya (= Pali a-jacca); or else (perhaps more likely) error for **a-janya,** q.v.; *ignoble* (person): (na mlecchesu na pāpakuleṣu naurabhrikeṣu [text noratrikeṣu]) na kaukkuṭikeṣu na jatyeṣu pratyājāyante Kv 42.10.

(**jana,** (**1**) or **janā** (*birth*, Skt. Gr., BR s.v.; also cf. ajana, evidently *unborn*, BR 7.1689), kṛta tvayi hitakara bahuguṇa janato (abl., *from birth*) LV 165.1 (vs), so text; but Tib. ḥgro la, evidently based on jagato, *to* (for) *the world*, dependent on hitakara; (**2**) *strange, foreign*, subst. *stranger*, Saundarānanda xv.31, and cf. janī-bhavati, *becomes a stranger*, Buddhacarita vi.9; acc. to Johnston on Saund., jana in this sense is 'common in Buddhist Skt.', but I have not noted it. Cf. however jana, m., *fremdes Volk*, . . . *Land*, pw 7.342.)

jana-kāya, see s.v. **kāya.**

Janakṣetriya (mss., Senart em. °kṣatriya), n. of a former Buddha: Mv i.138.7.

jananī (otherwise only *mother*), *woman* (Johnston's note compares **mātṛgrāma,** q.v.): na saṃrarañje viṣamaṃ jananyām, Buddhacarita ii.34, *loved no woman wrongly.*

-jananīya, adj. ifc. (cf. § 22.20; to Skt. janana, f. jananī), *productive of . . ., producing*: saṃvega-jananīyā kathā Gv 307.24 (prose); cf. Pali saṃvega-jananī (desanā) Pv. comm. p. 1 verse 6.

janapada-kalyāṇī (= Pali id.; Mironov and pw 7.342 with var. °ṇam, disproved by Tib. and Pali), *beauty* (beautiful) woman) *of the country*: Mvy 7630 = Tib. yul gyi bzaṅ mo (fem. suffix mo!); °ṇyā striyā sārdhaṃ paricaret Śikṣ 252.3; °ṇīṃ MSV i.136.4 (= Divy 444.10, text °ṇāṃ).

janapadi, m. (to janapada; representing stem °padin?), *countryman, man of the country*: manuṣyā mahāmanuṣyā janapadayo mahājanapadayaḥ Mmk 17.14 (prose), in long list of beings of all sorts.

janayati (like **upajanayati,** q.v.) is used in BHS in the mg. *conceive* (lit. *produce*) a feeling or notion, in oneself; this seems to Senart, n. on Mv i.47.1, different enough from Skt. usage to record: Mv i.47.1 naiva tāva janayanti mānasaṃ agrapudgalagataṃ; SP 12.6 (vs) harṣaṃ janitvā (metr. bad).

janayitrī (Skt. Lex. and once cited from Rājat.; = **janetrī, janetukā,** qq.v., and Pali janettī; the regular Skt. is janitrī), *generatrix, mother*: mātṛbhūtāni kalyāṇamitrāṇi buddhakuleṣu janayitrī Gv 463.11 (prose), *good friends are like mothers as causing birth in Buddha-families* (°trī for °trīḥ = °trayaḥ, n. pl.? or n. sg., ad sensum, *since each one causes* . . .? followed by daṇḍa, which is followed by p-); janayitrībhūtaṃ sarvasattvānāṃ Gv 494.11 (prose); yena svamātā janayitrī (but most mss. janetrī; *the mother that bore them*) . . . añjaliṃ pragṛhya janayitrīm etad avocatām SP 458.7 (prose); also in SP 462.2 (prose) svamātaraṃ janayitrīṃ, but several mss. janetrīṃ; etc.

Janārdana, n. of a nāga king: Māy 246.30.

janitā (or °ta?), sg. or pl., = Skt. janatā, *people*: daśakuśalī janitā (Calc. °tāḥ) thapitā te brahmapatheṣu LV 169.11 (vs); tvayi purimā janitā (here Calc. janatā) ima dṛṣṭvā dṛṣṭivipannā 169.17 (vs); in both Tib. skye bo = *man, men, people.* The mg. seems clearly that of janatā, but no ms. seems to read so. No record of such a form elsewhere; cf. Skt. jani, *birth, life.*

janitravatī (unrecorded; seems superficially based on Skt. janitra, Pali janitta, plus -vant, -vatī; but corresponds in usage to janita-vatī, periphrastic perf. act. pple. to janayati; perhaps read so?), periphrastic verb-substitute,

(I) *have given birth to*: (ihaiva tāvad ahaṃ . . .) siddhārthaṃ bodhisattvaṃ jan° Gv 439.2 (prose); Māyā speaks, *right here I gave birth to* . . .

Janīsuta, n. of a (virtuous) son of Māra: Mv ii.337.2; 408.10 (prose; here mss. jana°, janaṃ°); 410.2 (vs).

janetukā (semi-MIndic for *janayitṛkā = **janetrī, janayitrī**; § 3.92), *generatrix, mother*; associated with mātar, as are janayitrī, janetrī: mā eṣa mātur hi janetukāya (or °ye; v.l. also °yaṃ; Nobel em. °yāḥ) Suv 238.1 (vs).

janetrī (= prec. and **janayitrī**, q.v.; Pali janettī), *mother*: janetrī-saṃpannāś ca bhavanti samyaksaṃbuddhā Mv i.142.7; jina-janetrī i.149.13 = 217.1 = ii.19.15 (vs); pūrva-janetrī, *mother in a former birth*, ii.205.3 (vs); jātiśatāni janetrī abhūṣi 205.9 (vs); purimabhavajanetriye bhavanighātī 206.15 (vs, so read with mss.); Gv 37.15; 355.5; 381.5 (Vairocanasya janetry evam . . .); LV 82.22; 98.8 (atītānām . . . bodhisattvānām . . .) janetryaḥ; tasya mātā janetrī Gv 354.23, *the mother that bore him* (similarly s.v. **janayitrī**); etc. All these prose except as marked vs.

janta (nt.; also written **jantra,** as well as **yanta**; Pkt. or semi-Pkt. for Skt. yantra), *machine*: Mv ii.475.6 ff., 476.1, 5, in cpds. janta-kāra and janta-**māṣṭa(ka)**, see the latter. The mss. read prevailingly janta or jantra; Senart usually j-, but sometimes y- even against both mss.

? **jantāka** (m. or nt.) is read once or twice in Av (i.286.9, 10, see Speyer's note on i.286.8) for jentāka, see s.v. **jenta**; and jaṃdāka(-snātra) is written in one of the Niya documents, see Rapson and Noble, Kharoṣṭhī Inscriptions (Stein collection), vol. 3, p. 321, where it is suggested that jantāka be adopted in Av; but Av i.286.8 has je-, supporting Mvy and Karmav.

jantita (cf. **janta**), Pkt. = Skt. **yantrita**, q.v.: LV 372.15.

jantu-, in Divy 418.1 jantu-gṛhaṃ praveśayitvā dagdhā (Tiṣyarakṣitā); note conjectures jatu-, *lac*. But cf. Pali jantu, Vin. i.196.6, a kind of grass used for making coverlets (corresponds to Divy 19.22 **janduraka**; see s.v. **eraka**); *a house made of jantu-grass* would make possible sense.

Jantukarṇa, m. pl., n. of a brahmanical school: Divy 635.18. Perhaps read **Jātu°**, q.v.

jantra, see **janta.**

? **jandāka,** see **jantāka.**

janduraka, m., a kind of coverlet: Divy 19.22; corresponds to **syandaraka** (v.l. Mironov syandu°) Mvy 9182, and apparently to Pali jantu, thus supporting j- rather than sy-; see s.v. **eraka.**

Janmacitra, Divy 436.29 ff.; MSV i.124.5; or °**traka,** Divy 435.11; 436.19 ff., n. of a serpent-demon (nāga; not 'elephant' with N. Dutt, Introd. to MSV i p. 16).

janman (for closest approach to this mg. which I have found, see BR s.v. 11), *circumstance, condition, case*; iha janmani, *in this case, under these circumstances*: Mmk 56.18 meha janmani avandhyā me mantrasiddhiḥ; 56.29 iha janmani (Tib. skabs der = *en ce cas*, Lalou, Iconographie, 21) saṃhartavyaḥ (see **saṃharati**). See also **bodhisattva-janman.**

janmanideśa, n. of the eighth (Bodhisattva) bhūmi, in the (isolated) formulation of Mv i.76.17.

janmabhūmika, adj. (to Skt. janmabhūmi plus -ka, or -ika), *belonging to one's native land*: °kānāṃ manuṣyāṇāṃ anugrahāya Gv 456.20; °kaiś ca babubhir jñātisaṃbandhibhir 479.19; °kānāṃ (text °makānāṃ, certainly corruption for °mi°) ca manuṣyāṇāṃ 525.17. All prose.

janmika, ifc. (janman plus -ika), in varṣa-janmika, *born in the rainy season*? or, more likely, taking this as irregular cpd. (§ 23.9) with prec. yāvat-triṇi, *up-to-three-years old*? in Mmk 49.(12–)13 (yāvat triṇi) °mikaṃ pañcacīrakopaśobhitaṃ . . . rājaputraṃ . . . kṣatriyaputraṃ vā . . . praveśayet. See also **eka-janmika, paurva-j°.**

jampatī, dual (= Skt. Gr. and Lex. id.; not in Pali or Pkt.), *husband and wife*: Mvy 3905; = Skt. dampatī, which follows it in Mvy.

jambu-kāñcana, jambū°, prob. to be read, with two mss. in first passage, for jāmbu° in LV 122.15 ekā kākini jāmbu-kāñcane bhavati upahatā, and 17 jāmbūkāñcanasaṃnibhā punar bhavet sakara iya mahī (both vss); the mg. seems evidently *gold from the Jambu river*, and it is hard to believe that ā in the first syllable is anything but a corruption (if an adjectival form, it should be jāmbava; the ā of jāmbunada, jāmbū°, is justified because that is derived from °nadī with suffix -a).

jambuḍa, m. or nt. (Deśīn. 3.41 jambuḍam = madyabhājanam; see next, and **jāmbuḍī**), *a liquor-vessel*: dhyātvā jambuḍa-māṃsa-pañcapiśitair madyaṃ sapañcāmṛtaṃ . . . dadyād balim Sādh 588.17 (vs).

jambuḍikā = prec., q.v.: māṃsa-jambuḍikā-madya-puṣpa-dhūpa-vilepanam . . . sṛjed balim Sādh 583.12 (vs).

jambudvīpaka, in Av ii.91.1 **jambū°**, adj., pl., (people) *of Jambudvīpa*: °kā akarā abhūvan Divy 316.9, with ellipsis of manuṣyāḥ, which in the rest is always found expressed; Divy 317.1 ff.; 335.21; Av ii.91.1 (jambū°); Karmav 36.5; Gv 352.22; 504.6. Also **jāmbu°**, **jāmbū°**, qq.v.

Jambudhvaja, m. (**1**) = Jambudvīpa, n. for India; only in vss: LV 12.7; 13.3; 29.9; 94.7; Gv 336.10 et alibi; (**2**) n. of a group of former Buddhas: Mv i.58.13; 62.3; (**3**) n. of a nāga: Mvy 3359.

jambūkāñcana, see **jambu°.**

jambū-chāyaka or °**ika,** f. °**ikā,** adj., *having the color of the rose-apple* (?), ep. of poles (yaṣṭi): MSV ii.142.2.

jambūdvīpaka, see **jambu°.**

Jambūdvīpaśīrṣa, nt., 'tip of India', = **Milaspharaṇa,** q.v.: Gv 83.20 (here printed Jāmbū°); 84.16.

jambūnada (nt.; = Pali jambu°, Skt. jāmbū°; § 3.32), *gold*: jambūnadārcisadṛśaṃ (all mss.) LV 134.11 (vs).

Jambūnadaprabhāsavatī, n. of a lokadhātu: Gv 80.25.

jambūlikā, presumably = Skt. jambūla, Pandanus odoratissimus: (raṇḍāṃ) māṣa-jambūlikā-homena (. . . vaśyāṃ karoti) Mmk 287.22; raṇḍāvaśīkaraṇe māṣa-jambūlikāṃ juhuyāt 707.18. Both prose.

Jambhaka, n. of a yakṣa: Māy 74. Perhaps to be identified with one of the demoniac beings so named in Skt. (BR); and cf. next.

Jambhala (cf. prec. and next), n. of a supernatural being, a yakṣa acc. to Mmk 549.23; 607.1; 648.6 (yakṣarāṭ); cf. Sādh 421.7 °la-rūpam ātmānaṃ dhyātvā; in Mvy 4331 rendered by Tib. rmugs ḥdzin, which Das renders by jalendra (cf. next), *'the chief of waters,' the sea* . . .

Jambhala-jalendra (see Mvy 4331 under prec.), °dra-nāmā yakṣarūpī bodhisattvo Mmk 45.20; doubtless the same as Jambhala.

jambhi, m. or f., *palate*: °iḥ Mvy 3954; so acc. to Tib. thag ḥgram, see Das, who gives Skt. as jimbha (a different word; see Sheth s.v., and BR s.v. jimbha-jihvatā); occurs in a list of bodily parts, after hanu, śaṅkha, and before danta, tālu, oṣṭha; pw 7.343 suggests reading jambha.

[**jambhīra,** var. for jambīra, nt., Mvy 5808; but Mironov jambīra, m., without v.l.; = Skt. jambīra and Lex. jambhīra, *citron* (m. the tree, nt. the fruit).]

jaya, (**1**) nt. (otherwise recorded only as m.), *victory*: yadi no jayaṃ syāt LV 304.14 (vs); no v.l.; (**2**) m., n. of a youth, previous incarnation of Aśoka: Divy 366.7, 9.

Jayaṃgama, m., n. of a kalpa: Gv 447.5.

Jayadatta, n. of a Bodhisattva: Mvy 724; ŚsP 37.8.

Jayanta (see also **Jenta**), n. of a former Buddha: Mv iii.238.9 f.

Jayantadeva, n. of a former Buddha: Mv i.141.1.

Jayantī (see also **Jentī**), n. of a devakumārikā in the eastern quarter: LV 388.9; and so Senart in Mv iii.306.8, but his defective mss. lack it.

jaya-patākā, *trophy for the winner in a contest*, in fig. use: (Gopā nāma Śākyakanyā) °kā sthāpitābhūt LV 144.8.

Jayaprabha, n. of a king: Gv 352.24. A previous incarnation of **Satyaka**, q.v., the 'great debater': 358.26.

Jayamati, n. of a Bodhisattva, perhaps of several different ones: Mvy 682; RP 2.1; in Śikṣ 6.16, one who was punished for disbelief in śūnyatā.

Jayamitra, n. of a future Buddha: Mv iii.330.10.

Jayaśrī, n. of a nāga maid: Kv 3.22.

Jayā, n. of one of the four **Kumārī**, q.v., or **Bhaginī**: Mmk 537.7; 539.7, et alibi; prob. the same, a yakṣiṇī, Mmk 573.14; 574.4.

Jayottama, n. of a merchant (śreṣṭhin): Gv 189.1 ff.

Jayoṣṇīṣa, n. of one of the 8 Uṣṇīṣa-rājānaḥ (see **uṣṇīṣa** 3): Mmk 41.11.

Jayoṣmāyatana, n. of a brahman: Gv 115.1; 116.4 ff.; 158.2. Cf. next.

(ārya-)**Jayoṣmāyatanavimokṣa**, n. of a section of Gv (viz. 115 ff.): Śikṣ 2.3. Cf. prec.

[**jara**, m., *old age*, instead of jarā, f., according to text LV 175.4 (vs) tatha ojaharo ahu vyādhi jaro; so all mss. acc. to Lefm.; but citation Śikṣ 206.2 has jage for jaro, and is supported by Tib. ḥgro baḥi (in transl. of LV); jage is surely right; jaro is carried over from 174.16–175.2 where jarā occurs repeatedly. Tib. on LV also supports Śikṣ ayu instead of LV text ahu, reading ḥdi.]

jarāprajñāyate, see **prajñāyate.**

jarodapāna, m. or nt. (= Pali jarūdapāna, SN ii.198.3), *an old* (ruined) *well*, as a danger to walkers: tad yathā cakṣuṣmāṃ puruṣo °naṃ vā nadīdurgaṃ vā ... avakṛṣya kāyam avakṛṣya cittaṃ vyavalokayed ..., Candropama Sūtra, Hoernle, MR 42.5–6 ... (43.2–3 ...); cf. note p. 44.

Jalagarbha, n. of a son of **Jalavāhana**: Suv 183.10; 188.10; 200.11.

jala-dardaraka, nt. (cf. **dardaraka**, and Skt. jaladardura), a musical instrument playable in the water: °rake, loc., Mv ii.97.13–14; °rakāni (so) ii.109.9.

jaladhara (in Skt. *cloud*, and Lex. *ocean*; in Pali *ocean*, Milp. 117.31), *ocean*, appears in Pkt. form, and with ā m.c. for a, as jalāhara, in LV 175.11 (vs; cited Śikṣ 206.9) maraṇo (Śikṣ °ṇaṃ) grasate bahuprāṇiśataṃ (Śikṣ °tān) makareva jalāhari bhūtagaṇaṃ (Śikṣ °ro va jalākari bhūtagaṇān); the meaning *ocean*, which alone fits the context, is confirmed by Tib. rgya mtshoḥi. The form is loc. sg., for jala-dhare.

Jaladharagarjitaghoṣasusvaranakṣatrarājasaṃkusumitābhijña, n. of a former Buddha: SP 457.3 ff.

Jalapatha, m., n. of a mountain: Divy 450.10; 455.28.

Jalabindu, n. of a nāga maid: Kv 4.2.

[**jala-yantra**, read **jatu°**, q.v. But in MSV iii.16.10 occurs **jala-yantraka**, lit. *water-machine*, something used in water-play with women; Tib. chu (*water*) la spal paḥi skad ḥbyin (?).]

Jalavāhana, n. of a son of the śreṣṭhin Jaṭiṃdhara: Suv 175.4 ff.; 182.14 ff. (= the Bodhisattva, 200.3–5).

jalahara, *ocean*, see **jaladhara.**

Jalā, n. of a princess: Mv i.348.13.

Jalāgamā, n. of a river: Suv 187.1; 188.11.

Jalāmbara, n. of a son of Jalavāhana: Suv 183.9; 188.9; 190.6 ff.; 200.10.

Jalāmbugarbhā, n. of the wife of Jalavāhana: Suv 183.7 f.; 200.7.

jalāhara, m.c. for jalahara, which is Prakritic for **jaladhara**, q.v.: LV 175.11.

Jalī, n. of a princess: Mv i.348.13.

jalūka, m. (= °kā, f., Skt. Lex., and AMg. jalūgā), *leech*: Mvy 4855 (so also Mironov).

Jalūkā-vana-ṣaṇḍa, n. of a grove at **Pāpā** where Buddha once stayed: MSV i.282.2, 7.

jalūṣita, read °tā with Kashgar rec. SP 85.9 (vs) for ed. saṃlūṣitā (most Nep. mss. saṃtūṣitā), *burnt with flames* (for jvaloṣitā, prob. for jvāl°); confirmed by Tib. tshig par ḥgyur. WT em. jvālūṣitā; but cf. § 4.31.

Jaleniprabha (!), n. of a Buddha in the north: Sukh 98.1.

jalpa, m., or better **jalpā** (= Pali jappā, *desire*), *desire*: in Mv iii.284.19 (vs) mss. sarvāṃ prahāya bhavalobhajalpaṃ, not to be emended; same vs in Pali SN i.123.8 chetvāna (v.l. hitvāna) sabbaṃ bhavalobhajappaṃ. It is tempting to interpret in the same way such passages as Laṅk 186.8, 9 (vss) jalpaprapañcābhiratā hi bālās ... jalpo hi traidhātukaduḥkhayonis, *fools delight in jalpa and idle fancies* (? see **prapañca**) ... *for jalpa is the source of the misery of the universe.* This seems more naturally to mean *desire* than (idle) *talk*; but acc. to Suzuki's Index Tib. (smra ba) supports the latter; this might however only mean that Tib. knew the regular Skt. jalpa and had lost the tradition of the old word represented by Pali jappā.

? **jalla**, nt. (Pali id.), *dirt* or *dirty moisture*; perh. represented by (**rajo-**)**jala** (q.v.; l for ll m.c.?).

? **java**, a high number: Gv 106.13; see **ayava.**

javita (nt., also **jāvita**, q.v.), (**1**) *running* (as an athletic performance), *foot-racing*: laṅghite plavite javite sarvatra bodhisattva eva viśiṣyate LV 151.17; similarly, °te in lists of athletic exercises, LV 156.10; Mv ii.423.16; 434.12; iii.184.8; (**2**) *velocity*; in Bhvr. cpd., śakyo vāyuḥ pāśair baddhuṃ ... gamanajavito nareṇa LV 337.13 (vs), *a man might bind with fetters the wind that possesses impetuosity of motion*, so Tib., ḥgro baḥi śugs can, *having velocity* (śugs, *speed, impetuosity, violent force*, used of the wind, see Das s.v.) *of motion*; prob. in this sense also in KP 154.2, where, after lacuna, -da-java-javitā (in a series of adj. cpds. in fem. gender); Tib. mgyogs paḥi (*swift*, = java) śugs (as above) daṅ ldan pa (*possessing*); (**3**) in LV 337.10 (vs) perhaps ppp., *expelled, uttered* (of cries): **svāmaṃ** (so read) drakṣye duḥkhenārtaṃ bahu-vividha-javita-ravitaṃ ... (perhaps) *I* (Māra) *myself shall see him* (the Bodhisattva) *tormented with pain, and with many and various shrieks uttered* (expelled); Tib. ku co (*clamor*) rnam pa maṅ po (= bahu-vividha) ḥdon (*expel, drive forth*, also *utter* [sounds]) ciṅ.

? **javina**, adj. (if correct, a-extension of Skt. javin; cf. § 10.3; Sheth cites Pkt. javiṇa beside javi), *swift*: so all Nep. mss. in SP 104.1 (prose) for Kashgar rec. and both edd. javanān (puruṣān saṃpreṣayet).

-jaha, adj., f. **-jahā**, ifc. (to jahati, § 28.9, = Skt. jahāti; = Pali id.; cf. Skt. Gr. śardhaṃ-jaha, interesting as a vulgar word evidently borrowed from a MIndic dialect), *abandoning, giving up*: punarukta-doṣa-jahā Mvy 475, said of Buddha's speech: **Rati(ṃ)jaha**, see s.v.; kileśa-jahaṃ LV 46.3 (vs); sarvaṃjahaḥ Ud xxi.1 (v.l. sarvaj°; = Pali sabbaṃjaho, Dhp. 353). In Śikṣ 273.1 text jahā (of śūnyatā), but Tib. bem po = jaḍā, which read (transl. 249 note 3). Cf. next, and see s.v. **raṇa(ṃ)jaha.**

-jahana, f. °**nī**, adj. ifc. (see under prec.; this form not recorded elsewhere), *abolishing, banishing, getting rid of*: **Sarvasattvapāpajahana** (see s.v.) SP 464.2; ariśatrumāra-patha-jahanī KP 154.3, kutīrthya-tīrtha-jahanī 4, (a-)satkāyadṛṣṭiṃ-jahanīṃ 9 (read as cpd.; ed. as separate word).

jahāti, in caus. sense (§ 38.24), *removes, abolishes*: SP 61.8 (vs) sugatāna ghoṣaḥ kāṅkṣāṃ ca śokaṃ ca jahāti prāṇinām. It seems hardly possible to understand it otherwise; so Tib. bsal = *remove, do away* (an evil), *cure* (a disease).

jāgarikā (cf. next; perh. hyper-Skt. to Pali and

AMg. jāgariyā, id.), *wakefulness, staying awake* (as a form of self-discipline): °kā ca saddharma-svādhyāyādinā kartavyā Sādh 11.11; °kāṃ bhajeta Ud xv.6 (in Pali also with bhajati); yukto jāgarikāsu ca Ud vi.6; °kā-yuktaḥ Bbh 139.24; °kānuyukta-tāṃ 206.4 (in Pali often with anuyutta, and cf. the following); esp. common in jāgarikā-yogam anuyukta, *devoted to the discipline of wakefulness*: instr. °ktena Mv i.284.2; ii.48.18; iii.145.14; 152.11; 172.17; 265.12; 362.17; °ktāye, fem., iii.48.17; 49.4; n. sg. °ktaḥ Mmk 146.3; n. pl. Av i.273.7; 297.16; gen. sg. Śikṣ 191.6.

jāgarya (read °yā? which is recorded in Skt. Gr. and Lex., and prob. underlies Pali and AMg. jāgariyā), = prec.: jāgaryam anuyuktasya Ud xv.8, *of one devoted to* (the discipline of) *wakefulness*. There is no metrical reason for shortening ā; °yām would be just as good. I suspect a misprint or error of tradition; prob. jāgaryām should be read.

jāgṛta (nt.; § 34.14), *waking (state)*: MPS 10.12 (ms.; ed. em. jāgarita, Skt., Pali).

jāgraṇa (nt.; = Pali jaggana, °na-tā; from pres. jāgrati, § 28.11, Pali jaggati, plus -ana), *waking, being or staying awake*: suptā idāni yada jāgraṇa-deśakālaḥ Mv i.154.15 (vs), *asleep now when it is the place and time for being awake.*

Jāṅguli, m., n. of a maharṣi: Māy 256.30.

jāṅgulī, f. (Skt. Lex. id.; JM. jaṅguli, AMg. jaṅgolī, id.), (**1**) *the science and art of curing snake-bites*: Śikṣ 142.1 °lyāṃ vidyāyāṃ udāhṛtāyāṃ, *a snake-charm having been recited*; but Transl., p. 139, note 3, reads jāṅgulyā, allegedly 'with Tib.' (which is not cited), and renders *when the snake charmer recites this spell against poison*; there is a stem jāṅguli, m., *snake-charmer*, Skt. Lex., but this form being fem. would have to be taken as meaning *by a female snake-charmer*; (**2**) n. of a goddess: Sādh 177.14 etc.; in 249.5 a personified charm (vidyā) against poison (uttamā viṣanāśanī).

-jāta (= Pali id.; in Skt. rarely found, if at all, in just this use; cf. BR s.v. 1d, end, where it is not cited after an abstract noun except from LV), after an abstract noun, *become characterized by, full of*, equivalent to prāpta (note audbilyaprāpta SP 20.7 = audbilyajāta 61.6 *full of joy, joyous*), or to an adj. based on the abstract; very common in Pali as in BHS; particularly common in both is prīti-saumanasya- (Pali pīti-somanassa-)jāta, *full of joy and gladness*, SP 60.1; LV 58.5; Mv ii.96.4; 163.20; 237.1; Mvy 2933; Divy 297.15; Suv 9.8, etc.; prīti-prāmodya-j° SP 75.2; LV 395.14; harṣa-j° SP 14.1; praharṣa-j° SP 229.13; prasāda-j° Divy 75.20; kutūhala-j°, *interested, curious*, Divy 77.25; 466.21; saṃśaya-j°, *doubtful*, Divy 191.5; vega-j°, *excited*, LV 232.9, 14; *full of haste*, nearly = *speedily*, Mv ii.299.13; vegajātu adade (mss. adaye) tṛṇamuṣṭiṃ Mv ii.399.5 (vs); gaurava-j°, *filled with respect*, LV 410.1; vipratisāra-j°, *remorseful*, Av i.90.10; saṃtāpa-j°, *afflicted*, LV 381.1; antaḥśalya-paridāgha-j°, *tormented with inner anguish*, Mv i.42.3; krodha-j°, *angry*, Karmav 45.6; sometimes, when prec. part of the cpd. is a concrete noun, may be rendered *like* (as in Pali): samaṃ pāṇitalajātaṃ (buddhakṣetraṃ) SP 202.2 (prose), *level, like the palm of the hand*. Cf. Aśokan jāta, nt. (Hultzsch 96 n. 5).

jātaka, nt., rarely m., (**1**) m. pl., *experiences in past births*, particularly of Bodhisattvas: Bbh 67.17 (sa tena pūrve-)nivāsānusmṛtijñānena jātakān pūrvāṃ bodhisattvacaryā-paramādbhutacaryāṃ sattvānāṃ buddhe ... prasādajananārthaṃ ... prakāśayati, *by this knowledge consisting of remembrance of former births he reveals to creatures, in order to make them well-disposed to the Buddha, his experiences in past births* etc.; 397.13 (pūrvenivāsānusmṛtijñānabalena tathāgataḥ pūrvānte itivṛttakāṃś) ca jātakāṃś ca smṛtvā ... vineyānāṃ deśayati; this usage, which is prob. only a late and secondary extension of the next mg., seems not recorded in Pali; (**2**) nt., = Pali id., *a story of a previous birth* of the Buddha, common esp. in colophons to many such stories in Mv, e. g. i.282.13; also as n. of a work or type of literature, sometimes, at least, referring to a specific collection of such stories like the Pali Jāt.: as one of the nine (Mvy twelve) pravacana, *gospel texts* (Mvy dharma-pra°), Dharmas 62; Mvy 1275; in a similar list, SP 45.7; Jātake Śyāmākajātakaprabhṛtiṣu Karmav 50.6, *in the Jātaka* (collection), *in the Śyāmāka* (individual) *Jātaka and others like it*, combining both these mgs. in one phrase; (**3**) in Mv i.104.13; 105.5, 7; 192.19 taken by Senart in sense 2 above, but I think wrongly; I believe it means *nativity* in the sense of (astrologically determinable) *personality and destiny*, as in Skt.; or possibly *future birth*. This seems to me indicated by adjoining parallel terms, esp. **paramata**, q.v., which Senart misunderstands: (bodhisattvacaritaṃ ...) jātakāparamateṣu kovidā (deśayanti ... īśvarā) Mv i.104.13 (vs; -kā for -ka, m.c.), *the Lords* (Buddhas), *being skilled in nativities* (indicating personality and destiny; or, future births) *and in the thoughts of others, proclaim the* (future!) *course of Bodhisattvas* ...; (yānīmāni) ... jātakāni jinabhāṣitāni imāni kutaḥprabhṛtikāni vijñeyāni (? em.; mss. ciṃhneyāni) 105.5, answered by: yānīmāni ... jātakāni jinabhāṣitāni imāṃ aṣṭamīṃ bhūmiṃ (so some mss.) prapadyanti (v.l. prayanti) 105.7; the mg., as Senart suggests, seems (from -prabhṛtikāni) to be that they *begin* with the 8th bhūmi; but as this passage occurs in a description of the 4th bhūmi, it is *future* births or destines that are meant. In i.192.19 (vs), after saṃbuddhāḥ sarvaparamataṃ viduḥ 18, *Buddhas know all the thoughts of others*, we read: adhyāśayaṃ parīkṣanti jātakā sarvaprāṇināṃ, *they perceive the disposition and the destinies* (future births) *of all living beings.*

jāta-maha, m. (or nt.), = **jāti-maha, jātī-mahī**: Divy 515.18.

[**jātaya**, Śikṣ 4.10, 11 (vss), read jātiya = Skt. jātya, prob. *noble*: jātiya-buddhakule anujātāḥ, *they are* (born as) *worthy sons* (like their parents) *in a noble Buddha-family*. Bendall and Rouse propose a less plausible em.]

? **jātarūpya**, if correct = jātarūpa, *gold*: utsada ... rajata-jātarūpyaṃ (most mss., but A °paṃ) LV 276.21 (prose); cited s.v. **utsada** 3.

jāti, (**1**) as in Skt., *kind, sort*, but with forms of nt. gender: tāni sarvāṇi prāṇaka-jātīni Mv ii.95.10 (prose), *all those kinds of living beings*; (prāṇakajātīyo 14, but then, in same sentence) tāni sthalacarāṇi prāṇakajātīni (v.l. °tāni) 15; cf., in ii.132.17, ekaṃ (so mss.) pi jātiṃ duve pi jātiṃ (mss.) trayo pi jātiṃ (mss.), etc.; (**2**) f., *age* (cf. **-jātīya**): daharo 'ham asmi ... jātyā SP 318.2 (prose), *I am young in age* (lit., perhaps, *by birth*); (**3**) (as in Pali, e. g. jāti-vīṇā Jāt. ii.249.24, *noble lute*; and like Skt. kula-) at beginning of cpd., *characterized by nobility; noble, excellent*: jāty-utpalātimuktaiś ca SP 342.8 (vs), *with excellent water-lilies and atimukta-flowers* (Burnouf and Kern transl. have different readings for the last word).

-jātika, adj. ifc. (= Pali id.; = **-jātīya**; often the same cpds. occur with both), ... *by nature or character, of ... sort*: paṇḍita-j° (= -jātīya) Mv i.274.10; ii.241.16, 18; 251.3; prajñā-j°, or sa-pra° (uncertain whether sa- is separate word or not; Senart em. °jña-) iii.71.3; samudra-j° sārthavāho iii.286.17, *a merchant of the sea(-going) class*; duṣprajña-j° Mv iii.289.7; aparokṣa-j°, see **aparokṣa-**; in SP 282.12 Kashgar rec. upārambha-j° for edd. upālambha-jātīya.

jātijarāmaraṇīya, adj. (from dvandva cpd. °maraṇa), *leading to birth, old age, and death*: āyatyāṃ °yā (āśravā vighātā paridāghā) Mv iii.338.3 ff.; 340.2, 7; āyatyāṃ °yaiḥ (pāpakair akuśalair dharmaiḥ) Av ii.107.4.

jātiprajñāyate, see **prajñāyate.**

jāti-maha, m., *birthday festival*: Mvy 5673. Cf. **(jātī-)mahī.**

jātiya, adj. (= Pali id., Childers, for Skt. jātya), prob. *noble*; to be read for text **jātaya,** q.v.

[**jātilinī** Gv 399.25, read with 2d ed. jālinī, see **jālin.**]

jāti-vāda, m. (= Pali id.), *account* or *record of* (a person's) *birth*: padmodbhaveyaṃ na hi jātivādaḥ saṃdūṣaṇām arhati nirmalatvād Gv 414.1 (vs).

jātī-mahī, see **mahī.**

-jātīya, ifc. adj., (**1**) (in this sense unrecorded; cf. **jāti** 2) *of* (such and such) *an age*: bāla-j°, *young in age*, Mvy 7099; (kumārakāś...) SP 73.4 (in this and the next two bāla may also connote *foolish*); bālāḥ (*fools*) kṣaṇyante madhudigdhābhir iva kṣuradhārābhir bālajātīyāḥ (primarily *like children*) LV 208.1; ābhir bālā (as above) badhyante dhūrtakair iva bālajātīyāḥ (as above) 4; yadā... māṇavako 'ṣṭavarṣajātīyaḥ saṃvṛttas Divy 476.27, *eight years old*; (**2**) (not in Pali; but in Skt., see BR s.v., used in substantially the same way, tho much less commonly; here extremely common, and apparently characteristic of this language; = **-jātika,** which is much rarer here but characteristic of Pali), *of* (such and such) *a nature*, cpd. with prec. adj. or noun, concrete or abstract: paṇḍita-j° *of intelligent nature*, SP 80.4; Mvy 2895; °ye mātṛgrāme, *in a woman that is intelligent by nature*, Divy 2.3; 98.22; 440.17; Av i.14.7 etc.; Bodhisattvajātīyo bhikṣuḥ Divy 261.9, *a monk who had the nature of a Bodhisattva*; bāla-j° (v.l. °jātiko) SP 211.5 (prose), *foolish by nature* (cf. 1 above); duṣprajña-j° Gv 508.26; momuha-j°, *confused, deluded by nature*, Bbh 9.20 (a-mo°); 157.2; **aparokṣa-** (q.v.)-j° Mv iii.322.11, 14 (= °jātika iii.415.10); **alparajaska-** (q.v.)-j° Mv iii.322.16; vaṅka-(most mss. vañcaka) -j° SP 268.5, *deceitful*; upālambha-j° (v.l. jātika) SP 282.12, *censorious*; lolupa-j° Mv i.339.10, *greedy*; mānābhimāna-j° i.340.11; alasa-j° Divy 485.18; aroga-j° Av i.168.10; evaṃ-j° Śikṣ 135.2, *of such a sort* (Skt., BR); paripṛcchana-j°, *of an inquiring disposition*, Laṅk 14.10; Śikṣ 50.7; and prob. read so with v.l. Karmav 44.1 (text paripṛcchaka-); adhivāsana(q.v.)-j° Sukh 25.15.

Jātukarṇa, m. pl. (cf. **Jantukarṇa**), n. of a brahmanical (Yajurvedic) school: Divy 633.5, 7; also °**ṇā,** f., n. of the gotra of the nakṣatra Pūrva-Bhadrapadā: °ṇāgotreṇa Divy 641.6.

-jātya, ifc. Bhvr. (= **-jātīya** 2, **-jātika**; cf. **-jātiya**); *of* (such and such) *a nature*: lolupa-j° LV 386.9, *greedy*; sthāvarādhivāsana-j° Śikṣ 23.9, *firmly patient*. Both prose.

jāty-antarīyaka, adj. (see **-antarīya-ka**), *belonging to another birth*: Jm 194.19.

jāna, adj. or subst. m. (occurs, tho rarely, in Pali, e. g. Jāt. iii.24.2; orig. prob. = jānant-, pres. pple., cf. §§ 18.52 ff.; see next), *knowing, wise* (person): drakṣyanti jānu (all mss.; acc. sg.) imu saptapadāṃ kramantaṃ LV 48.1 (vs); puruṣadhīreṇa puruṣajānena (nearly all mss.) LV 350.11 (prose), *by a wise one among men*.

jānaka, adj. (Pali Gr. id., Childers; AMg. jāṇaga; = prec., but prob. formed on the pres. jānati plus -aka), *knowing, wise*: jānako jānakavihārehi Mv i.34.12 (prose); jānakāḥ pṛcchakā Buddhā bhagavantaḥ Divy 184.26; 299.15; MSV i.i.12 (prose), *Buddhas*, (tho) *knowing* (the answers), *are* (in the habit of) *asking* (questions; otherwise Divy Index); a-j°, *foolish, ignorant*: SP 10.1 (so read with Kashgar rec. and WT for ajñā°, unmetr.); 37.5; 47.14; 93.12; LV 323.12 (all vss). With objective gen., *acquainted with*: jānako duḥkhasya Av ii.119.11; 120.3, 11.

[**jānatā** LV 264.1 (prose), na me paścimā °tānukampitā syāt, read janatā, *people*, with v.l.; Tib. skye bo; cf. in the verse account 270.22 no... anukampitā hi janatā... paścimā.]

jānana, nt., *birth, origination*: Mvy 1848 = Tib. bskyed pa. Cf. Skt. janaṇa, perh. to be read here; but Mironov jā°.

jānanaka, adj. (= Pali id.; to Pali jānana, *knowledge*, from jānati plus -ana, with adj. suffix -ka; in BHS only a-j° which could be considered Bhvr., a- plus jānana plus -ka, Bhvr.), *knowing*; a-j°, *not knowing*, with acc.: rāgam ajānanako LV 323.13 (vs); in prec. line ajānaku.

[**jānapati,** in KP 84.8 (prose) sarva-śreṣṭhi-naigama-jānapatayaḥ, read °jānapadāḥ, *people of the country*. Tib. and Chin. lack this sentence.]

jānapada (= janapada; otherwise, in Skt., Pali, and Pkt. jāṇavaya, only in mg. *inhabitant of the country*), *country*: yaṃ velaṃ dharmalabdho kṣemena vārāṇasyāṃ jānapado (so mss., Senart em. °daṃ, read rather °de, loc.) prāptaḥ Mv iii.291.8 (prose); nagarehi ca nigamehi ca jānapadehi ca 13 (prose, no v.l.). Perhaps read jana° both times.

jānayati (= janayati; § 38.15), *produces*: kāyabalasthāmaṃ jānayitvā Mv ii.131.10 (prose), cf. LV 272.9 kāyabalasthāma saṃjanayya; jānayi sarvi vikurvitu teṣāṃ Bhad 45, *may I produce all the miracles of those* (Buddhas); (sa... tathāgato) jānitaḥ Gv 381.17.

[**jānikaḥ,** text Laṅk 26.4 (vs) abhilāpo jānikaḥ, Suzuki *of whom is speech born*? But read 'jāni, or better, m.c., ajāni (aor. pass.) kaḥ.]

Jānutrasta, n. of a former Buddha: Mv i.140.7.

jānu-maṇḍala, nt. (= Pali id.; nowhere else), *knee-cap; knee*; °lābhyāṃ (abl.) niścaritvā Gv 85.13; in list of **anuvyañjana,** q.v., our no. 25, acc. to Mv ii.44.5; LV 106.20, but the lists in Dharmas 84 and Mvy 293 have a different reading which omits jānu; mostly used in a cliché, dakṣiṇaṃ (dakṣiṇa- LV 397.8; Suv 64.4; Sukh 2.16; ubhau Av i.2.11) jānumaṇḍalaṃ (°le Av i.2.11) pṛthivyāṃ pratiṣṭhāpya Mvy 6277; Av i.2.11 etc.; Suv 64.4; Kv 8.14; 17.2; 38.14; Sukh 2.16; SP 100.5; LV 397.8; 398.13-14.

[**jāneya,** in puruṣa-j°, v.l. -jāna, Mv ii.133.8 (prose), read puruṣājāneya; see s.v. **ājanya.**]

jānya, adj. (= Pali jañña), *noble*: durlabhaḥ puruṣo jānyo Ud xxx.27.

jāpanā (Pkt. for Skt. yāp°, cf. next; = AMg. jāvaṇa, nt., and JM. °ṇā, Sheth), *sustenance, maintenance*: kāyajāpanārthaṃ Śikṣ 131.8; (mahābhūtānāṃ) sthitaye jāpanāyai 137.9.

jāpayati (Pkt. for **yāp°**, q.v., cf. prec. and § 2.34; = AMg. jāvei), *lives, sustains life*: kiyal-lūhenāpi bhojanena jāpayanti Śikṣ 130.11 (prose; ed. jñāp°, corrected Transl. p. 129, note 1).

jāmātika, °**tuka** (MIndic for Skt. jāmātṛ-ka, yām°, rare for jāmātṛ; neither in Pali; AMg. jāmāuya), *son-in-law*: °tukasya Mv iii.24.18; °tiko 146.5, 9, 12; all prose.

Jāmbāla (*muddy*, from Skt. jambāla plus -a), n. of a man, hero of Av chap. 50: Av i.279.1; 280.6 etc.

jāmbu-kāñcana, jāmbū°, see **jambu°.**

jāmbuḍī (= **jambuḍa,** °**ḍikā,** qq.v.), *a liquor-vessel*: jāmbuḍī-sīdhum eva ca... baliṃ dadet Sādh 411.5 (vs).

Jāmbudvīpaka, Jāmbū°, adj. (= **jambu°**, q.v.), *of Jambudvīpa*: °budvīpakāni ratnāni Divy 116.6; usually of the people (manuṣya, sattva) of J., jāmbu° Divy 292.9; Kv 13.2, 3; 46.11; 57.17; 87.7; jāmbū° Av ii.94.2 ff.; RP 37.8; Śikṣ 84.1. All prose.

Jāmbunada or **Jāmbū°,** n. of three former Buddhas, all in the same list: Mv iii.233.6 (°bu°); 236.12 (°bū°); 237.9 (°bū°, v.l. °bu°). In all v.l. °nanda; all prose.

Jāmbūdvīpaka, Jāmbūnada, see **Jāmbu°.**

Jāmbūnadatejorāja, n. of a Tathāgata: Gv 421.15 (prose).

Jāmbūnadaprabhāsa, SP 151.6 (prose), or Jāmbūnadābhāsa, 152.9 (vs), n. of a future Buddha, to be an incarnation of Mahākātyāyana.

jāyate = Skt. jayate, °ti (§ 28.33), *conquers*: nāśūro

jāyate senāṃ . . . śūras tu jāyate senām LV 262.12 and 13 (vs, but in the fourth syllable of anuṣṭubh pādas ā can hardly be m.c.). The mg. is certain; no v.l. recorded.

jāyapatika, m. pl. (see also **jāyā°**, **jāyaṃ°**; Pali jāyampatika, jayaṃ°, jāyāpatī, all m. pl.; Vedic jāyāpatī, rare), *wife and husband, a married couple*: duve jāyapatikā (v.l. °kās; pl. for dual) Mv iii.26.20 (prose).

Jāyā, n. of a lokadhātu: ŚsP 37.5.

jāyāpatika, m. dual (= **jāya°**, q.v.; and see next), *wife and husband, a married couple*: dvau °tikau Divy 22.6 (prose).

jāyāṃpatika, nt. sg. (cf. prec. and under **jāya-p°**), *a married couple*: (vikhyāpayamānau) °tikam iti Divy 259.7 (cf. 3, above, jāyāpatīti vikhyātadharmāṇaḥ); °tikam iti khyātau 259.17.

Jāyendra, n. of a Tathāgata (living in **Jāyā**): ŚsP 37.5.

jāla, jālaka, nt., prob. *bouquet of flowers* (here withered ones, to be removed from caityas); so jālaka is used in Skt.; the only plausible alternative would be *spider-web*, which jāla also means in Skt. (cf. Schmidt, Nachträge) and Pali. In any case it means something the *removal* of which from caityas is a work of merit: yo jālakāni apanaye (so read with v.l. for Senart upanaye) cetiyeṣu Mv ii.391.3; choretva jālaṃ jinacetiyeṣu 391.22, repeated in the sequel; parallel Śikṣ 306.2, 4 choritva jālaṃ; 6, 8, 10 apanīya (ed. em. upa°) jālaṃ. On the passage, misunderstood by Senart and Bendall, see s.v. **chorayati**. In the immediately following verses, Mv ii.392.21 ff., Śikṣ 306.11 ff., the meritorious removal of withered flowers is unambiguously mentioned.

jālayati (MIndic for jvāl°, § 2.8; = Pali jāleti), *kindles*: dharmadīpam ayu (so read for unmetr. °dīpamaitrayu; 2d ed. °dīpam atrayu, still unmetr.) jālayiṣyati Gv 482.24 (vs).

jālā (fem.!), *net* = jāla (nt.): jālā-vitānāvanaddhena (pāṇinā) LV 318.14 (prose), *with his hand bound by a web-canopy* (between the fingers). The only v.l. is jālo- for jālā-, which is senseless. Both edd. jālā-.

Jālāntara, n. of a former Buddha: Mv i.140.14.

jālikā (cf. Skt. jālaka, nt., BhāgP.8.20.17, s.v. in BR, same mg.), *a network* (of jewels, used as an ornament): chinnāṃ jālikam (m.c. for °ām) a(d)dṛśāti supine ratanāmikāṃ śobhanāṃ LV 194.20 (vs), *she saw in her dream her beautiful network, made of jewels, cut* (so Tib., rin po che las byas paḥi dra ba . . . *net made of jewels* etc.); here the fem. adjectives prove that °kam is m.c. for °kām; the same must be assumed also in the next: muktā-maṇī-jālika-chāditāś ca SP 89.2 (vs), *and covered with networks of pearls and gems* (°ka m.c. for °kā).

jālin, (1) adj. (= Pali id., Vv.81.16 and comm. 315.30, not in PTSD; from jāla, *web*), *webbed*, of hands and feet, i. e. having the fingers and toes connected by a web (one of the 32 **lakṣaṇa**): hastapādatale jālinī (dual; so read for text jātilinī) abhūtām Gv 399.25; jālinā hastaratnena . . . pāṇinā Mv ii.282.4–6; (2) n. of Viśvantara's son (= Pali Jāli), Jm 59.21 ff. See also next.

jālinī (f. to **jālin**, q.v., but in sense of *ensnaring* or the like: = Pali id., ep. of taṇhā, with or without that word; the comms. have various explanations, three being offered on Dhp. 180 alone), perhaps *ensnaring*, or subst. *enchantress*, as ep. of tṛṣṇā, *thirst, longing*: tasiṇāṃ ca jālinīṃ Mv i.166.20 (vs); jālinīṃ tṛṣṇāṃ ii.307.12; tṛṣṇāṃ chittvāna jālinīṃ 357.15; jālinī . . . tṛṣṇā iii.92.1 = Pali Dhp. 180 jālinī . . . taṇhā; without the word tṛṣṇā, Dharmasamuccaya (unpublished BHS work) 8.44, 47, acc. to Renou, JA Jul.–Sept. 1939 p. 336 note 1; in a personal letter of May 16, 1945, Renou kindly informs me that here jālinī 'a ni plus ni moins le sens de tṛṣṇā, hors de toute ambiance métaphorique; de même pour **viśālā**' (q.v.). We should, then, doubtless recognize the same mg. in: sarvakileśabandhanalatāṃ . . . jālinīṃ (Tib. dra ba, *net*) LV 276.12 (vs), and: iha jālinī . . . ṣaṭtriṃśaticāriṇī LV 373.7 (vs), *thirst which acts in 32 ways* (as does taṇhā in Pali, PTSD s.v.); Foucaux *le filet d'illusion*. Most mss. and Calc. read indrajālinī for iha j° (hence Foucaux's rendering); but this is metr. impossible, and the epithet proves that tṛṣṇā is referred to.

Jālinīprabha, n. of a Bodhisattva: Mvy 705. Tib. renders jālinī by dra ba, *net*, or dra ba can, *having a net*. Perhaps *having seductive* (alluring) *splendor*? See s.v. **jālinī**, which otherwise = tṛṣṇā.

Jālinīmukha, n. of a mountain: Kv 91.15.

jāva, m. (to java, but nowhere recorded), *speed, swiftness*: °vaḥ Mvy 2003 = Tib. mgyogs pa. So also Mironov; no v.l. Follows yogaḥ and precedes anukramaḥ, kālaḥ.

jāvita, nt. (= **javita**, 1; perhaps so read, but Mironov also jā°), *running, foot-racing*: Mvy 4999 °tam = Tib. baṅ, *foot-race*.

[? **jāhu**, in RP 58.18 (vs), printed: dūre jāhu bhujagavad etān (sc. evil companions). Since it is scarcely possible that the Vedic verb aj-, *drive* (away), is concerned ('jā = aja, hu = khalu, *drive them away like serpents*!'), I believe that some form of hā, *abandon* (less likely of han, *smite*) must be involved; the ā might well be m.c. (meter requires two long syllables), but I cannot explain the final u (ū?). Perhaps read jāhā = jaha, 2 sg. impv., *abandon*! (?)]

jighatsita, adj. (ppp. of jighatsati, desid. to ghas-; Skt. jighatsu, BR 5.1444; = Pali jighacchita), *hungry*: Mvy 6306 (see s.v. **pūrṇagātra**); 7328 (v.l. and Mironov **jighaṃsita**, see next; precedes pipāsitaḥ); °tā bhojana mārgamānā(ḥ) SP 84.12 (vs); °tānāṃ ca sattvānām agraṃ varabhojanaṃ dadāti Śikṣ 274.7 (prose). See next.

? **jighāṃsita** (should be ppp. of desid. of han-! but in mg. = **jighatsita**!), clearly means *hungry* in Karmav 46.9 °ta-pipāsitasya kruddhasya kālakriyā; so Tib. bkres śiṅ skom pa, *hungry and thirsty*; and so Lévi translates, without any note, tho a note is surely needed! So v.l. for Mvy 7328, see prec. It seems likely that the true reading is jighatsita; or dare we assume that MIndic (Pali) jighacchita was falsely Sktized as jighāṃsita?

jijñāsanā (cf. Skt. °na, nt., and jijñāsā, f.; perh. a blend of these two), *test, trial*: yūyaṃ kanyakā (Māra speaks to his daughters) . . . bodhisattvasya jijñāsanāṃ (no v.l.) kuruta LV 320.2 (prose).

jitam, apparently interj. or particle, chiefly in phrase: api hi jitaṃ Mv ii.126.9; iii.181.14; 206.10, 12; 209.12; this seems to be an expression of *astonishment*, something like *Who'd have thought it*? *That beats all*! Once, in Mv iii.286.1, jitaṃ (v.l. jidaṃ) occurs by itself; the daughters of Māra, reporting to Māra, say: (any other man than the Bodhisattva, seeing us,) so jitaṃ mūrchitvā prapatiṣyad vā . . . cittakṣayaṃ vā prāpuṇe (but the B. was unmoved); here too *astonishment* might be the connotation of the particle; *he, good heavens! would have fallen down fainting . . ., or lost his wits*. No etymology is apparent for the word.

Jitaśatru, n. of a former Buddha: LV 5.15 (confirmed Tib.); follows **Lokābhilāṣita**, precedes **Saṃpūjita**; Mv i.136.16, follows Lokābhilāṣita, precedes **Supūjita**.

(**jina**, *conqueror*, standard epithet of a Buddha, so used in Skt.: Mvy 12 = Tib. rgyal ba, *victorious*; et passim. The word appears to be used of any head, or at least founder, of a religious sect; see s.v. **jina-śrāvaka**.)

Jinakāntāra, n. of a former Buddha: Mv i.140.10.

Jinacakra, n. of a former Buddha: so read in LV 5.7 for Jinavaktra of both edd.; best ms. Jinacakra, confirmed by Tib. dmag tshogs (*army*) las rgyal.

jinaputra, (spiritual) *son of a Buddha*, common epithet of Bodhisattvas: Mvy 629 et passim. Any synonymous word or phrase is apt to be similarly used; see e. g. **jinaurasa.** Not listed in this work: sugatasya putrā(ḥ) SP 10.5; 12.4; jinendraputrān 12.9; buddhaputro 48.12; sugatātmajānāṃ 57.10; jinātmajānāṃ 116.10, etc.

Jinabhāskara, n. of a Buddha: Gv 284.10 (vs).

Jinarṣabha (corresponds to Pali Janesabha, Janavasabha; but the temptation to emend to Janarṣabha should prob. be resisted; Chin. versions on Māy 85 support Jina-), in Māy 237.1, n. of a yakṣa; in Māy 85 n. of a prince, son of Vaiśravaṇa (Kubera), who dwelt in Tukhāra, *'attended by (a) crore(s) of yakṣas'.*

[**Jinavaktra** LV 5.7, read **Jinacakra.**]

Jinavaruttama, n. of a former Buddha: Mv iii.236.14, 15. (Would be °varot° in Skt.)

? **Jinavrata,** n. of a Pratyekabuddha, predicted as future incarnation of **Sujātā**: Mv ii.206.18 (vs), text °vrato ti, by em., mss. unmetrically and uninterpretably Jinavarttāyī.

jina-śrāvaka, *pupil of a jina,* applied in Mv ii.118.2, 3 to the pupils of Ārāḍa Kālāma, and in ii.119.9, 10 to those of Udraka Rāmaputra. Senart assumes that this means that these teachers were Jains. But in default of any other evidence this seems unlikely; jina is of course also a title of a Buddha, and we may infer from this that it could be applied to the founder of any religious sect.

Jinasūrya, n. of a Buddha: Gv 259.18.

jināti, jinati, *conquers,* see Chap. 43, s.v. ji, 2.

Jinendra, n. of a former Buddha: Mv iii.233.5; n. of 300 successive former Buddhas, 237.12 f.; the last of them predicted the Buddha **Sarvārthadarśin(a),** 238.5.

Jinendraghoṣā, n. of Susaṃbhava's capital city: Suv 147.1.

jinaurasa = **jinaputra,** ep. of Bodhisattvas: Mvy 641 et passim.

Jihnuna, n. of a mleccha king: udayaḥ jihnuno hy ante mlecchānāṃ vividhās tathā Mmk 622.1 (vs), at the end of a list of mleccha kings.

jihma, adj. (in these senses recorded nowhere else; Skt., Pali jimha, and Pkt. jimha, jimma, regularly *crooked* or fig. *dishonest*), (**1**) *bereft of light, obscured, not shining, dull;* regularly said of entities regarded as brightly shining in themselves, but having their light eclipsed or obscured by a greater radiance, esp. that emitted or caused by the Buddha; so at the bodhi-tree Buddha causes a radiance which makes the divine abodes of the gods jihma Mv ii.316.18 or jihmavarṇa Mv ii.313.17; 316.16 and by Senart's em. (for mss. jihmabala) 295.1; 296.9; 304.1; 308.16 (in all these jihma-bala might stand, *of obscured, dulled power*); similarly, jihma vipaśyatha (so divide) divya ātmabhāvāṃ LV 49.12 (vs; Apsarases speak, looking at Māyā's superior beauty), *see how* (our) *divine bodies are eclipsed* (in splendor); jihma sarvatuṣitālayo bhuto (m.c. for bhūto) 54.3 (vs), *the whole abode of the Tuṣita became splendorless;* sarvāṇi mārabhavanāni karonti jihmā 296.16 (vs); jihma (so divide; acc. sg.) kurvati jagat sadevakam RP 6.15 (vs); also fig. of the intelligence and senses; -vijñāna, in Mv ii.355.14 (vs) ye gṛddhā lābhasatkāre jihma-vijñāna-(*dull intelligence*)-niśritā; and Karmav 31.12 (apāyeṣūpapanno) durgandho bhavati jihmendriyo bhavaty avyaktendriyaḥ, . . . *of dull and obscure* (see **avyakta**) *senses;* (**2**) (cf. jihmīkṛtaḥ Mvy 5200, below s.v. **jihmīkaroti,** with Tib.) *disappointed, depressed, saddened, despondent:* in LV 193.19 (vs) read (with v.l.) jihmā-jihma (n. pl., āmreḍita) sudurmanā, *very depressed and downcast;* confirmed by Tib. dman zhiṅ dman; prob. so, a-jihma in Sukh 25.16 (prose) aśaṅko 'jihmo, *free from doubt and despondency* (in a description of a Bodhisattva); to be sure the next words are 'śaṭho 'māyāvī, which suggest the Skt. meaning, *not deceitful,* but these lists of characteristics are apt to go in pairs, and aśaṅka suggests this BHS meaning of (a-)jihma, which is otherwise known and easily develops from mg (1). See the following items, which support both mgs.

jihmīkara, adj. (= next), *obscuring:* in **Candrasūrya-jihmīkara-prabha,** q.v. (*having a splendor that obscures the moon and sun*): LV 292.8 (prose). But v.l. °karaṇa, which, being much commoner (I have noted no other case of °kara), is very likely the true reading.

jihmīkaraṇa, adj. (from next, with -ana), (**1**) *obscuring, making* (what is normally bright seem) *dark* or *dull:* candrasūryajihmīkaraṇayā prabhayā LV 41.5; -indusūrya-jihmīkaraṇa-prabho Sukh 29.16; see also prec.; **-tā,** (jāmbūnada-suvarṇālaṃkāra-bhūtaṃ) saṃskṛtāvacara-kuśalamūlopacaya-jihmīkaraṇa-tayā Gv 496.6, (*it is like an ornament of finest gold*) *because it obscures* (*overshadows, makes seem dull*) *things in the realm* (see **avacara**) *of the conditioned thru the acquisition of roots of merit;* (**2**) *disappointing* (lit. *darkening,* so *making despondent* or the like), in a-ji°, *not disappointing* (beggars): (upasaṃkrāntānāṃ, sc. yācanakānāṃ, cāvi)mānanājihmīkaraṇāvikṣepaṃ (adv.) LV 431.10, *while not showing disrespect to* (beggars) *who come to him, not disappointing them, and not turning them away;* yācanaka-maitrīkāruṇyapūrvaṃgamasaṃprekṣaṇājihmīkaraṇa- LV 432.5, *looking upon beggars with love and compassion and not disappointing them.*

jihmīkaroti (to **jihma,** q.v., in both its BHS senses), (**1**) *obscures, makes* (esp. something normally bright to appear) *dark* or *dull:* bhagavantaṃ... sūryasahasrātirekayā prabhayā sarvaparṣanmaṇḍalaṃ °kurvantam... dṛṣṭvā RP 2.16; (sarvamāramaṇḍalāni) °kurvamāṇān (to pres. kurvate) Gv 87.5; sarvamārabhavanāni jihmīkṛtya (text jihvī°) Mmk 7.20, and (°bhavanaṃ) 78.16; ppp. °kṛta (various forms), with mārabhavanāni LV 300.9 (cf. 296.16, s.v. **jihma**); of Māra's host, 316.10; ābharaṇāni 122.3; jihmīkṛta (so mss., Lefm. em. jihmi°) candrasūryā 354.18 (vs); (candrasūryau . . .) tayā prabhayā te 'pi jihmīkṛtau nāvabhāsyante niṣprabhāṇi ca bhavanti Mmk 78.17; fig. *eclipsed, overshadowed,* jihmīkṛta (so mss., Lefm. em. jihmi°) śakrabrahmā (by the Bodhisattva) LV 354.2 (vs); (**2**) *disappoints* (lit. *darkens, makes dull;* cf. **jihmīkaraṇa,** 2); ppp. °kṛta, *disappointed, despondent, overcome:* °kṛtaḥ Mvy 5200 = Tib. (among various renderings) spa skoṅs pa, *despondent,* or zil gyis non pa, *overcome.* Cf. prec. and next.

jihmībhavati (to **jihma,** q.v.; cf. prec.), *becomes obscured:* °vanti RP 51.2, see s.v. **pāla (jagato).**

jihrīyati (to root hrī, q.v. in Chap. 43), *is ashamed;* so best ms. Karmav 47.26 for text jihreti; and so ed. 49.2, 10, 16.

jihvā-nirlekhanika, m. (= Skt. °khana; not otherwise recorded), *tongue-scraper:* Mvy 8974.

[**jīraṅka,** m., *cummin-seed;* v.l. for jīrakam, nt., Mvy 5801, but prob. only error of tradition. Mironov jīrakaḥ, m., no v.l.; Skt. °ka, m. or nt.]

jīrṇaka, f. **°ikā,** adj. (= Skt. Gr. id., Pali jiṇṇaka; Skt. jīrṇa plus -ka; twice in vss, may be m.c.; once in prose, may be pitying or contemptuous dim.), *old:* LV 109.15 (vs); Mv i.184.21 (vs); tā māradhītaro jīrṇikā vṛddhikā sthavirikā palitikā . . . bhavitvā daṇḍam avaṣṭabhya . . . Mv iii.283.13 (prose). Above, lines 10–11, the other three appear with -ikā, but jīrṇā without the suffix.

Jīvaka (= Pali id.), n. of a physician and follower of Buddha (called in Pali Komārabhacca, in BHS **Kumārabhṛta, °bhūta,** qq.v.): Divy 270.12 ff.; 506.2 ff.; MSV ii.25.5 ff.; has epithet Vaidyarāja(n) KP 96.2, 3; Śikṣ 159.8, 12 (here, amazingly, Bendall and Rouse translate vaidyarāja as n. pr. and jīvaka as adj., *when alive!*). See also **Jīvika.**

jīvakajīvaka, m. (= Skt. jīvajīvaka), a kind of pheasant: °vakā(ḥ), n. pl., SP 358.8 (vs); may be m.c.

jīvati (for Skt. jīyate, pass. to jayati), *is conquered, is lost:* yasya jitaṃ nātha jīvati Mv iii.91.19 (vs) = Pali

Dhp. 179 yassa jitaṃ nāvajīyati, which proves the mg. (and suggests nāva- for nātha = na atha?); if not a mere corruption, change of y to v, § 2.31.

jīvantaka, f. **°tikā** (pres. pple. of Skt. jīvati with a-extension plus ka svārthe), *living*: (prāṇaka) Mv i.24.3, 16, *living creatures*; °tikā evaṃ vivarjitā Mv i.353.19, *abandoned alive*: all prose.

jīvaśūlaka, or **°ika**(?), f. **°ikā**, adj. (to Pali jīvasūla, lit. *live-stake*, plus -ka), lit. *provided with* (= impaled on) *a stake alive*: yehi iha °śūlikā kāritā bhavanti eḍakāyo Mv i.25.10, *who in this world roast she-goats on spits alive*; naṃ ... °lakaṃ karotha ii.168.8, *make him to be impaled alive*; °likam (read °lakam?) api kriyamāṇasya Śikṣ 182.6, *of him even being impaled alive*.

Jīvika, (**1**) = **Jīvaka**, the physician: Av ii.134.6 ff.; [(**2**) in LV 430.20 text jīvika-pariskāra, but most mss. jīvita- or javika-; read jīvita-, *equipment* or *utensils for living*.]

jīvitaka, ifc. Bhvr. (= jīvita plus -ka, Bhvr., perhaps m.c.), *life*: jarjarakāṣṭha va soṣita-jīvitako (for śoṣ°) LV 322.8 (vs), *with life dried-up, withered*.

jīvita-saṃskāra, m., see **saṃskāra** (2).

jugutsu, adj. (unhistorical hyper-Skt., § 2.19, for MIndic *jugucchu = Skt. jugupsu, cf. Pali jigucchā etc., JM. juucchiya, etc.), *abhorring*, with loc.: kāmeṣu jugutsuno Mv iii.438.2 (no v.l.; gen. sg.). Cf. next, Mv iii.407.16.

jugupsanā, **°na** (?nt.), **°na-tā** (Skt. Lex. °na, nt.; Pali jigucchana, nt.), *loathing, condition of abhorrence*, with loc. or in comp.: kāmeṣu ... °nā utpannā Mv iii.407.16, v.l. jogustanā, intending jugutsanā, cf. s.v. **jugutsu**; °na-tā LV 32.4; 34.9; -parigraha-°natayā (instr.) Gv 456.25; °na or °nā, in Bhvr. cpd., alpabhoga-°nāḥ Mmk 46.28. All prose.

juhana (nt., = Pali id., to juhati, § 28.18, = Skt. juhoti, plus -ana), *pouring, offering* (oblation): agnihotraṃ juhanāya (dat., infin.) Mv iii.161.9 (prose).

jṛmbhīkṛta, ppp. (to Skt. jṛmbha plus karoti), *made to appear, caused to stand out*: saptadvārāṇi (so read for text sarva-dv°) °kṛtāni Kv 31.11 (not *opened*! since the gates were heavily locked and barricaded, as the sequel explicitly states).

Jeta-vana, (normally) nt., rarely m. (= Pali id.), n. of the grove at Śrāvastī where Buddha often dwelt and preached: Mv i.4.13; 27.11; 29.13; 30.11; 31.9; 32.14; 33.8; 73.3; iii.224.11; Mvy 4112, °nam; LV 1.5; 4.14 (here masc., sarvāvantaṃ °vanaṃ, acc.); Divy 1.2 etc.; 80.12; Av i.13.5 etc.; also, in vs, the two parts separated, Jetasāhvayaṃ vanaṃ LV 7.4 (vs), *the grove called Jeta*.

Jetavanīya, m. pl., n. of a school: Mvy 9097.

[**jen-**, quasi-root, prob. error: upajenitvā, text LV 36.20, see s.v. **upajanayati**.]

1 **jenta**, nt. (Mironov jontaka, m.), v.l. for jentāka, m., at Mvy 9289, *a hot* (steam) *bathroom*. The true reading is doubtless jentāka, which is Skt. (Caraka 1.14, BR 7, App.) and also occurs Av i.286.8 ff.; ii.205.1; Karmav 38.13; but see also **jantāka**. Regularly cpd. with **-snātra** or -snāna.

2 **Jenta** (cf. **Jayanta**), n. of a bastard son of King Sujāta Ikṣvāku: Mv i.348.13 ff.

Jentī (cf. **Jayantī**), n. of the mother of 2 **Jenta**: Mv i.348.13.

jeṣṭha, semi-MIndic for Skt. jyeṣṭha (§ 2.8), n. of a month: Mvy 8264 (but Mironov jye°); LV 133.2 (vs).

jehrīyate (nowhere else recorded; intens. to hrī-), *is much ashamed*: °yate Mvy 1829; °yante Divy 39.7; °yamāṇam SP 108.6.

joḍa, *chin*: Mvy 8849–8857; = Tib. sko, (s)ko-(s)ko; in cpds., hasti-, aśva-, etc., a-.

-jota, semi-MIndic for -jyota (§ 2.8) = Skt. -dyota (as kha-dy°), *light*: su-jota-caraṇo Mv i.156.13 (vs); so all mss., Senart em. °dyota.

jotiṣ(a), semi-MIndic for jyo°, *light*, in sa-jotiṣa LV 340.18 (vs).

?**jontaka**, m., see 1 **jenta**.

?**jomā**, *a kind of broth* or *liquid food* (drunk; pāsyasi, pītā), with adj. **hilimā**, Divy 497.19 ff. Perhaps error for josā, cf. **yosa**; hardly for *jemā (cf. Skt. jemana; AMg. jemaṇa, *delicacies in food*).

jñapti, for (always in Mvy, but nowhere else) **jñāpti**, f. (= Pali ñatti), *proposal, motion*, made before the assembly of monks or nuns; in the BHS literary passages recorded, usually concerning initiation (upasaṃpadā): jñaptiṃ kṛtvā MSV ii.101.15; Bhīk 17b.3, *having made the motion*: eṣā jñaptiḥ 5, *this is the proposal*; (duḥśīlena bhikṣuṇā ... na ca) jñaptir dātavyā Kv 96.14 (... prāg eva jñapticaturthaṃ 15, see below); jñāpti-karma(n), id., Mvy 8660 (= Pali ñatti-kamma); jñapti° MSV ii.101.16; there are three forms in which the motion may be made (see SBE 13.169, note 2), (**1**) *isolated, simple* (**muktikā**, q.v.) *motion*, not followed by a separate question as to whether the monks (or nuns) present approve, Mvy 8659; Bhīk 15b.3; (**2**) *accompanied* (followed) *by a single such formal question*, called jñapti- (Mvy jñāpti-) dvitīyam (sc. karma; = Pali ñatti-dutiya-kamma), Mvy 8661; MSV ii.178.12; (**3**) accompanied by three such questions, called jñapti- (Mvy jñāpti-)caturtham (karma; = Pali ñatti-catuttha-kamma), Mvy 8662; 8754 °tha-karmaṇopasaṃpanno bhikṣuḥ; Bhīk 31b.1 jñapticaturthena karmaṇā; Divy 356.16 °thaṃ ca karma vyavasitaṃ; Kv 96.15, see above; MSV ii.178.12. The putting of the questions (one or three) to the congregation, after the jñapti, is called **karma-vācanā**, q.v.

[**jñāta**, wrong reading for **jñātra**, q.v.]

Jñātaputra, see s.v. **Nirgrantha**.

jñātika, m., and f. **°kā** (Skt. jñāti, Pali ñāti and ñātaka, for which sometimes v.l. °tika), *kinsman, relative*: mitra-jñātikā(ḥ) Mv i.244.10; jñātikā(ḥ), pl., Mv i.354.11; °ko ii.49.2; 379.10 (v.l. °tṛko); iii.258.6 (mostly prose); -suhṛda-jñātika-bāndhavehi Gv 214.14 (vs); a-jñātikāṃ bhikṣuṇīṃ Prāt 497.13 (prose), *a nun who is not a relative*. [**-jñātika** Mv ii.292.12, 14, read °nika, see s.v. **pañcajñānika**.]

Jñātiputra, see s.v. **Nirgrantha**.

jñātra, nt. (rarely Vedic id., VS 18.7, comm. jñātur bhāvo, vijñānasāmarthyam; PB 5.7, see BR; prob. here too *reputation for skill*; = Pali ñatta, Dhp. 72, badly defined PTSD; it means *public reputation for skill*, which only fools seek, to their ruin, as the Dhp. verse says and the comm.'s story illustrates), *public reputation for skill* or *intellectual accomplishments*, regularly mentioned as something which a good monk or Bodhisattva should not covet: lābhaṃ ca jñātraṃ (so with Kashgar rec., text jñātaṃ) ca gaveṣamāṇaḥ SP 27.7 (vs), *coveting profit and reputation for skill*; in corresponding prose 22.4–5 lābha-guruko 'bhūt satkāraguruko jñātraguruko (so v.l., text jñāta°) yaśaskāmas; aniśrita sarva-jñātra-lābhe RP 16.3 (vs); tyakta ... jñātram aśeṣam 21.6 (vs), of good Bodhisattvas; tyaktva ca jñātra-lābha-yaśa-kīrti 33.2 (vs); jñātra-gurukāḥ 34.4 (prose), of evil Bodhisattvas; jñātra-lābha-mātrakena (so!) 34.12 (prose); jñātra-pratilambhaḥ Bbh 289.10, 16.

jñāna, nt. (= Skt.; Pali ñāṇa), *knowledge*; for distinction from **vijñāna** see the latter; five j° (of a Tathāgata) Mvy 109, listed 110–114 and Dharmas 94, dharma-dhātuviśuddhiḥ (Dh. suviśuddhadharmadhātu-jñānam, No. 5), ādarśa-jñānam (Dh. ādarśana-j°, No. 1), samatā-j° (Dh. No. 2), pratyavekṣaṇā-j° (Dh. No. 3), kṛtyānusthāna-j° (Dh. ° ṣṭhāna°, No. 4); ten j° Dharmas 93 and Mvy 1233–43, eleven ŚsP 1440.10 ff.: duḥkha-j° (Mvy No. 5), samudaya-(Mvy 6), nirodha-(Mvy 7), mārga-(Mvy 8), dharma-(ŚsP 7, Mvy 1), anvaya-(ŚsP 8, misprinted annaya-; Mvy 3), saṃvṛti- (ŚsP 9 erroneously saṃvṛtti; Mvy 4), paracitta- (Mvy 2; ŚsP 10, paricaya-! = Pali paricce DN iii.277.6, expl. ŚsP 1441.20 as pratipakṣa-j° confirming paracitta-), kṣaya (ŚsP 5; Mvy 9, akṣaya), anutpāda- (ŚsP 6, Mvy 10); No. 11 in ŚsP is given as yathāruta-j° 1440.13, but yathākata-j° 1441:21, explained tathāgatasya sarvākārajñatā-j°(perhaps read yathābhūta-j°?); AbhidhK. LaV-P. vii.11 has the ten as in Dharmas and Mvy, in slightly different order, reading kṣaya-j° for No. 9; three jñāna Dharmas 114: avikalpakam, vikalpasamabhāvabodhakam, satyārthopāyaparokṣam. Cf. also **pañcajñānika.**

Jñānaketu, (**1**) n. of one or more former Buddhas: Mv i.137.10; LV 171.18; Gv 423.2; (**2**) n. of a Bodhisattva: Gv 3.18; (**3**) n. of a samādhi: Mvy 559; ŚsP 1419.16.

Jñānaketudhvaja, n. of a deity (devaputra): LV 23.2.

Jñāna-kauṇḍinya, for **Ājñāta-k°**, q.v.: LV 1.6 (so also Calc.; v.l. Lefm. Jñāta°).

Jñānagarbha, (**1**) n. of a Bodhisattva: Mvy 670; (**2**) n. of a teacher: Mvy 3491.

jñāna-tā = jñāna, *knowledge* (§ 22.41): jñānatāparipūrtyai LV 32.18 (prose), not at the end of a cpd.; at end of cpds., in which immediate constituents may be (. . .)jñāna plus -tā: LV 33.18, 21.

Jñānadatta, n. of a teacher: Mvy 3504.

Jñānadarśana, n. of a Bodhisattva: Kv 1.7.

Jñānadhvaja, (**1**) n. of a Buddha: Mv i.123.13; (**2**) ep. of Bodhisattvas (Tatp. or Bhvr.? not recorded in Pali), *banner of knowledge*, or *having knowledge as banner*: °tva, abl. °tvāt, *because they are . . .*, Mv i.153.11.

Jñānaparvatadharmadhātudikpratapanatejorāja, n. of a Buddha: Gv 324.8.

Jñānaprabha, n. of a Bodhisattva: Mvy 691.

Jñānaprasthāna, nt., n. of a work: Mvy 1419.

Jñānabalaparvatateja (nom. °jo), n. of a Buddha: Gv 297.13.

Jñānabuddhi, n. of a Bodhisattva: Gv 4.12.

Jñānabhāskarateja (nom. °jo): Gv 421.25.

Jñānamaṇḍalaprabhāsa, n. of a Buddha: Gv 256.9.

Jñānamati, n. of a Buddha: Gv 284.15.

Jñānamatibuddha, n. of a Buddha: Gv 259.2.

jñānamudrā, (**1**) n. of a samādhi: SP 424.3; (**2**) in Mvy 4298–4313 is a list of cpds. all ending -jñānamudrā, described in 4297 as dhāraṇī-mudrā; they are not listed individually here.

Jñānameru, n. of a former Buddha: LV 172.2.

Jñānaraśmimeghaprabha, n. of a Buddha: Gv 422.2.

[**jñānalotu**? evidently corrupt, in RP 8.18 (vs, rathoddhatā) °tu bhavate kṣayaḥ katham; in laudation of the Buddha, addressed to him. Possibly read jñānaketu, voc., *O Banner of Knowledge*!]

Jñānavajratejas, n. of a Bodhisattva: Gv 2.21.

Jñānavatī, (**1**) n. of a princess, previous incarnation of Śākyamuni: RP 24.18; acc. to Finot viii, her story occurs in Samādh chap. 31; (**2**) n. of a Bodhisattva-dhāraṇī: Mvy 748.

Jñānavatī-parivarta, n. of a (section of a) work: Śikṣ 134.7. Acc. to Wogihara ap. Bendall p. 405, note, = Chap. 34 of Samādh.

Jñānavibhūtigarbha, n. of a Bodhisattva: Mvy 734.

Jñānavaipulya-sūtra, n. of a work: Śikṣ 192.6.

Jñānavairocana, n. of a śrāvaka of old: Gv 150.6.

Jñānavairocanagarbha, n. of a Bodhisattva: Dbh 2.8.

Jñānaśikharārcimegha, n. of a Buddha: Gv 310.6.

Jñānaśrī, (**1**) n. of a Bodhisattva: Gv 4.4; (**2**) (-śirī) n. of a Buddha: Gv 284.16 (vs).

Jñānaśrīpuṇyaprabhā, n. of a 'night-goddess' (rātri-devatā): Gv 296.20.

Jñānasaṃbhārodgata, n. of a Bodhisattva: Gv 4.1.

Jñānasiṃhaketudhvajarāja, n. of a Buddha: Gv 309.20.

Jñānasūryatejas, n. of a Bodhisattva: Gv 150.7.

Jñānākara, n. of a son of the former Buddha Mahābhijñājñānābhibhū: SP 160.9.

Jñānākaracūḍa, n. of a Buddha: Gv 309.11.

Jñānārcijvalitaśarīra, n. of a Bodhisattva: Gv 442.16 (prose).

Jñānārcitejaśiri (for °rcis-tejaḥ-śrī), n. of a Buddha: Gv 258.8 (vs).

Jñānārciḥśrīsāgara, n. of a Buddha: Gv 309.17 (prose).

Jñānārcisāgaraśiri (for °rciḥsāgara-śrī), n. of a Buddha: Gv 285.20 (vs).

Jñānāvabhāsatejas, n. of a Bodhisattva: Gv 2.22 (prose).

Jñāneśvara, n. of a former Buddha: Samādh p. 57, line 1.

Jñānottarajñānin, n. of a Bodhisattva: Gv 2.13.

Jñānodgata, n. of a Bodhisattva: Gv 3.25.

Jñānolka, m., n. of a Bodhisattva-samādhi: Mvy 744; °**lkā,** f., n. of a samādhi: SP 424.6 (prose).

Jñānolkāvabhāsarāja, n. of a Buddha: Gv 297.6.

jñāpti, f., (**1**) *bidding, order*: Mvy 7536 (= Tib. bsgo ba), para-jñāpti-saṃcetanīyatā; (**2**) *proposal, motion*, Mvy 8659–8662, 8754 (= Tib. gsol ba) = **jñapti,** q.v.

[**jñāmaka,** see **vyāmaka.**]

jyeṣṭhataraka, f. °**ikā** (°tara plus -ka svārthe), *elder*: ṣaḍ dārikāyo °tarikāyo Mv i.356.13, and °tarikā ṣaḍ dārikāyo 15.

[**jyeṣṭha-bhavikā,** Divy 28.22; 30.11–12, read **-bharikā,** q.v.]

Jyoti-, often for Jyotir-, Jyotiḥ- (sometimes in vss m.c.); see under the longer (regular Skt.) forms.

jyotika, (**1**) at end of Bhvr. cpd. = Skt. jyotis, *light*; ajyotika in garbhagṛhe °ke Mv ii.444.9 (prose), *without light*; (**2**) ? questionable reading in Mv ii.318.15 (vs), text jyotikāṃ ca (mss. °kaṃ vā, or jyotiṃ ca vā) maṇiratanāṃ grahetvā; some name of a jewel is concealed here, but jyotika does not seem right; the meter is bad with either ms. reading. Perhaps jyotiṣkaraṃ maṇi°, which improves the meter; Finot, Lap. ind. 138, notes jyotiṣkara as n. of a jewel. Or else read jyotīrasaṃ (or °sāṃ = °sān); this is known as n. of a jewel in Skt., and in Pali as jotirasa, AMg. joirasa.

Jyotigupta, n. of a former Buddha: Mv i.140.7.

Jyotiṃdhara, v.l. **Jyotidhara,** n. of a future Buddha: Mv ii.355.4. In repetition of same vs **Jyotīvara** (or v.l. °cara), q.v.

Jyotipāla (both 1 and 2 = Pali Jotipāla), also spelled Jyotiḥ°, Jyotiṣ°, (**1**) n. of a previous incarnation of Śākyamuni under the Buddha Kāśyapa: Mv i.319.11 ff.; also mentioned i.2.8, 9 where (as also e. g. i.319.18–19) Senart adopts Jyotiṣ° in text; (**2**) n. of a son of Govinda, later purohita under Reṇu son of King Diśāṃpati and then called Mahāgovinda (= Pali Jotipāla, DN ii.230.25 ff.): Mv iii.204.12 ff. (iii.224.5 says that he was a previous incarnation of Śākyamuni).

Jyotiprabha, see **Jyotiṣprabha.**

jyotiprabhāsa, m. or nt., a kind of gem: Mv ii.310.16. Cf. **jyotiṣprabhā.**

Jyotiraśmirājendra, n. of a Tathāgata: Mmk 7.13.

Jyotirjvalanārciśrīgarbha, n. of a Bodhisattva: Mvy 712; (°ārciḥśrī°) Dbh 2.16.

jyotirdhvaja, (**1**) a kind of jewel: °ja-maṇiratna- Gv 53.2, 3; (**2**) (Jyoti-dhvaja) n. of a Buddha: Gv 256.17 (vs); (**3**) n. of a Bodhisattva: Gv 2.17 (prose).

Jyotirnāma, m. pl. (= Pali Jotināma): n. of a class of gods: Mahāsamāj., Waldschmidt, Kl. Skt. Texte 4.191.2.

Jyotiṣakūṭa, n. of a dhāraṇī: Gv 66.20.

Jyotiṣka (= Pali Jotika, Jotiya), n. of a rich householder (who in a previous birth was **Anaṅgana**): Mv ii.271.1 ff.; Divy 271.6 ff.; MSV i.197.12 ff.; **Jyotiṣkāvadāna**, n. of Divy Chap. 19: Divy 289.26.

jyotiṣkara, m., a kind of flower: Mvy 6196. Cf. **jyotis**.

Jyotiṣpāla, see **Jyotipāla**.

jyotiṣprabha, m., (**1**) a kind of flower: Mvy 6195; (**2**) n. of a Brahmā: SP 4.9; (**3**) n. of a former Buddha: Sukh 5.13; (**4**) n. of a contemporary or future Buddha: Sukh 70.4; (**5**) n. of a Bodhisattva: Mvy 729; Gv 3.16; (**6**) n. of a king: Gv 335.21 (vs, here Jyoti-p°, but not m.c.); 336.19 (vs); 339.2 (prose).

jyotiṣprabhā(-ratna), n. of a jewel: Mvy 5963. Cf. **jyotiprabhāsa**.

Jyotiṣmati, n. of a Bodhisattva: Mvy 698 (with epithet kumārabhūta).

jyotis, (**1**) a kind of flower (qy: *Trigonella foenum graecum*? so Skt. Lex.): jyotir-mālikā- LV 11.3 (prose); Tib. proves that jyotis was understood as a separate name of a flower: me tog (*flower*) snaṅ ḥod (*bright light*) daṅ ma li ka daṅ, etc.; (**2**) n. of a (brahman-)youth: Jyotirmāṇavakaṃ (acc.) Śikṣ 167.3, cited from Upāyakauśalyasūtra.

Jyoti-sūrya-gandha-obhāsa-śrī (see next), n. of a Tathāgata: Thomas ap. Hoernle MR 101 (prob. error for next).

Jyoti-somya-gandha-obhāsa-śrī, Thomas ap. Hoernle MR 102 (twice; from Mahāsaṃnipāta Sūtra; cf. prec., which refers to the same); or (Sanskritized) Jyotissaumya-gandhāvabhāsa-śrī, Mmk 7.9, n. of a Tathāgata.

Jyotīrasa, n. of a nāga: Mvy 3364.

Jyotīvara, or (v.l.) °**cara**, n. of a future Buddha: Mv iii.279.9 (in previous occurrence of same vs **Jyotiṃdhara**, q.v.).

Jvalatkukūla, n. (or epithet) of a hell: °le narake Jm 196.1.

Jvalanaśirīśa (read °ṣa?) n. of a Buddha: Gv 256.18.

Jvalanādhipati, n. of a contemporary or future Buddha: Sukh 71.3.

Jvalanāntaratejorāja, n. of a god (devaputra): Suv 168.1; 170.1; 171.3 etc.

Jvalanārciḥparvataśrīvyūha, n. of a Buddha: Gv 282.3.

Jvalanī, n. of a rākṣasī: Māy 243.10.

Jvalanolka, m., Mvy 599, or **Jvalanolkā**, ŚsP 1423.21, n. of a samādhi.

Jvalantaśikharā, n. of a 'gandharva maid': Kv 5.11.

Jvalitatejas, n. of a Bodhisattva: Gv 442.3.

Jvalitayaśas, n. of a former Buddha: Mv i.141.16.

Jvālāmukhī, a name or epithet of Vajravārāhi: Sādh 436.4.

JH

Jhalujhalu, n. of a nāga: Mmk 454.15.

jhallaka, m. (= Skt. jhalla), prob. *a kind of prize-fighter, fighter with a cudgel* (listed among entertainers; cpd. with malla): naṭair °ka-mallebhir Śikṣ 48.12 (vs; cited from SP 280.6 where text naṭebhir jhalla-ma°); jhallaka-mallāḥ Śikṣ 330.15 (vs); here Tib. cited as rol mo mkhan = *musician* (so Burnouf, reading **ṛllaka**, q.v., and Kern on SP); but Bendall and Rouse Transl. *fencers* or *musicians*. I am swayed by Skt. jhalla and the composition with malla.

jhāṣayati (cf. Skt. Lex. jhaṣ-, jaṣ-, Pali Lex. jhas-, Childers; Vedic jasate, jāsayati), *pulverizes, destroys utterly* (so Tib. cited on Śikṣ 59.12, thal bar rlog): °ti Śikṣ 59.12 (pūrvāvaropitāni kuśalamūlāni), similarly 61.2, and °nti 60.12; (svakleśāṃś ca parakleśāṃś ca) °ti 89.3.

Ṭ

Ṭakkirāja, n. of a Buddhist deity (one of the krodha): Sādh 137.10 et al. Also **Acalaṭak**°, **Acaraṭarkirāja**, qq.v.

ṭaṅgaṇa-kṣāra, m. (= Skt. ṭaṅkaṇa-kṣāra and Lex. ṭaṅgaṇa), *borax*: Mvy 5903.

ṭiṭibha, m. (cf. **ṭiṭila, ṭiṭilambha**), a high number: Mvy 8016. Tib. mthaḥ (= Skt. anta) snaṅ (*light, brightness*; thinking of Skt. bhā?).

ṭiṭila, nt., a high number: °lam Mvy 7964, cited from LV 148.3 where **ṭiṭilambha**, q.v. Tib. as on LV, confirming -lambha as last part of the word.

ṭippiṭaka, m. (unrecorded; cf. Skt. ṭippaṇī etc.?), acc. to Tib. mdor bśad pa, *condensed explanation*, or, sa bcad (gcad) pa, *synopsis*: Mvy 1448.

ṭivyaka, m., Mvy 9416, Chin. *snapping the fingers in water*, and fig. *a moment, jiffy*; Tib. has a long phrase the first part of which means *snapping the fingers in water*; the rest is obscure to me: chu la ḥdzub (mdzub) mos se gol rdob rkus ḥdzugs pa ḥgal gzugs ḥkhri las ḥdzugs pa.

ṭerākṣa, adj. (= Skt. Lex. ṭeraka; v.l. torakṣa, Mironov ṭorakṣa), *squint-eyed*: Mvy 8882 = Tib. mig noṅ ba (*faulty eye*); Chin. *having eyes with deep sockets*.

ṬH

ṭhapanīya-praśna(-śabda), in the alphabet list in the school scene, to furnish a word with initial ṭh, LV 127.17, *a question that is to be rejected, left unanswered*; ṭhapanīya = Pali id. = Skt. (BHS) sthāpanīya; see **sthāpanīya-vyākaraṇa**.

ṭhapeti (= Pali id.; see **sthapayati**, § 38.52), *places, sets, establishes*: ṭhapetu Gv 34.24 (vs).

ṭhambhana or °**nā** (= Skt. stambhana; from this root Pali records only forms with th-, as thambhanā, and so Pkt. except Gr. and Lex. ṭh-, see Sheth), *restraint, constraint*, (hostile) *immobilization*: avamānanā, tathā vimāna ca ṭhambhanāś ca (. . . mama nāmadheyu smaramāṇa labhanti mokṣam) Gv 213.25 (vs).

Ḍ

ḍambhā, Mvy 6102 = Tib. ḫphaṅ-mduṅ (thuṅ), *a sling-hook* or *spear head to which a string is tied and...* (which) *is flung at a fish or bird* (Das, who gives Skt. śakti as equivalent).

-ḍaha for Pali daha, Skt. hrada (Lex. draha), see s.v. **Deva-ḍaha.**

ḍāmara (**1**) (m. or nt.; = Skt. Lex. id., Skt. ḍamara), *riot, tumult*: kali-kalaha-kaluṣa-ḍimba-ḍāmara-duḥsvapna-vināyaka-pīḍāḥ Suv 104.3 (prose, no v.l.); (**2**) (cf. Skt. id., n. of an attendant of Śiva; perhaps the same), n. of a supernatural being, prob. = **Bhūta-ḍāmara**: Sādh 515.1.

(**ḍāmarika**, once in late Skt. = caura, Schmidt, Nachträge; AMg. °ria; *man of violence, ruffian*: °kānāṃ manuṣyaghātakānāṃ Gv 157.3 (prose).)

ḍimphika (also **mahā-ḍi°**), m. pl., a class of malevolent superhuman beings: Mmk 17.5. (Cf. **ḍimba**?).

ḍimba, m. and nt. (Skt. Lex. id., in lit. rare except in cpd. ḍimbāhava, but see Schmidt, Nachträge; AMg. id.), *disturbance, riot, tumult*: yadi Mālinīṃ na parityajiṣyāmi, ḍimbaṃ bhaviṣyati Mv i.310.9; regularly cpd. with ḍamara, Mv iii.349.13; Divy 98.15; 131.18; 282.27; Av i.120.4 etc.; with **ḍāmara**, q.v., Suv 104.3; ḍamarātha ḍimbās SP 96.3 (vs).

ḍimbara, or (v.l.) **ḍimbala**, some kind of entertainer (at a festival): Mv iii.57.10. Perhaps cf. **dvistvala** (in like contexts).

ḍūma, var. for **hūma**, q.v.

ḍoṅkāra, see s.v. **autkara.**

Ḍombinī, Sādh 445.22, or **Ḍombī**, 443.16 etc., n. of a yoginī.

Ḍombīheruka(-pāda), n. of an author: Sādh 443.9.

ḌH

ḍhalita, ppp. (Pkt. ḍhalai, *dangles, hangs down*; ḍhaliya, *bent, lowered*; Hindi ḍhalnā, etc., see Turner, Nep. Dict. s.v. ḍhalnu, and next), *dangling*: kalipāsu (v.l. °śa) durānugā (m.c. for dūr°? so Foucaux) ḍhalitamūlā (*with dangling roots*) ... chinnā me jñānaśastreṇa LV 371.17 (vs).

ḍhālayati (caus. to prec.; Pkt. ḍhālae, ppp. ḍhālia; Hindi ḍhālnā, Nep. ḍhālnu, etc.), *makes hang down, dangles* (trans.): śakaṭakam ... bhadraghaṭam iva ḍhālayantam (pres. pple.) Sādh 569.19; bhadraghaṭam iva ḍhālayantam 575.7.

ḍholla (m. or nt.: Pkt. and late Skt. id., Schmidt, Nachträge; Skt. Lex. ḍhola), a kind of *drum*: ḍhollāviddhaśrutiṃ Sādh 571.1, *with ears unpierced* (aviddha, cf. 577.9 below) *like drums*; ḍhollakarṇaṃ 574.17; aviddha-ḍholla-karṇadvayam 577.9. All epithets of Jambhala.

T

taka, m., and **taka-karṇin**, m. (Pali taka, and cf. taka-paṇṇi, in corresp. list), n. of two resinous substances (jatu) used medicinally: MSV i.iii.17, and i.iv.1 tako lākṣās, takakarṇī sikthaṃ.

Takṣaśilaka, adj. (from Skt. °śilā plus -ka), *of Takṣaśilā*: °lakā naṭā Mv ii.175.3; °lakānāṃ paurāṇāṃ Divy 409.30. Both prose.

takṣāṇa (for Skt. takṣan; §§ 17.39, 41; cf. Pāṇ. 6.4.9 and Kāś.; Pkt. takkhāṇa, Hem. 3.56), *wood-worker, carpenter*: °ṇo MSV i.117.5; °ṇasya 119.20; °ṇaṃ, °ṇaḥ 120.2 (all prose).

Tagaraśikhi(n), (Pali °sikhi, a Paccekabuddha), (**1**) n. of a former Buddha: °khiṃ, acc., and °khir, n., Mv iii.233.7 (prose); read Tagāra° with best ms. (ā m.c.) LV 172.12 (vs); (**2**) n. of a pratyekabuddha: °khī Karmav 57.18; 58.1; 68.9; 70.2. Is (1) really the same as (2)? Hardly in Mv, where he is predicted by an earlier Buddha and predicts the next one.

taṅgati (only Skt. Dhātup.), *stumbles*; in etym. fantasy, to explain the caste-name mātaṅga: mā taṅga Divy 632.1, *don't stumble!*

tacchaka (= Pali id.; § 2.18; Skt. takṣaka), *carpenter, woodworker*: Ud xvii.10 (same in same vs Pali Dhp. 80 etc.). Cf. next.

tacchita, ppp. (to Pali tacchati, taccheti, see under prec.), *cut* (as with axes): Mv i.16.14.

Taṭiskandha, m. or nt., n. of a locality: Māy 47.

taṭṭa, taṭṭu, taṭṭuka (m. or nt.; = Pali taṭṭaka, *a flattish bowl*; otherwise unrecorded), some kind of *bowl* or *dish*: taṭṭukaṃ (acc.) Śikṣ 58.1; taṭṭa-kāra, *bowl-maker*, Mv ii.468.14, 18; iii.442.17 (here mss. tadva°, Senart wrongly em. taddhu°); taṭṭu-kāraka, id., Mv iii.113.13 (so read for taddhu°); taṭṭv-ākāra, *bowl-shaped*, to be read in Divy 342.26; 343.5, for text tapv-āk°; this passage cited Śikṣ 58.1 taṭṭākāra (taṭṭa-āk°), but 58.5 taṭṭukākāra (taṭṭuka-āk°); miswritten khaṭvākāra, see **khaṭu** (2).

Taḍāgapālinī, n. of a rākṣasī: Māy 243.21.

?**Tataṃjacala** (one ms. out of six Taṭaṃ°), n. of a former Buddha: Mv i.139.7 (Senart em. Pataṃgacara).

tatonidānaṃ, adv., *for that reason*, see **nidāna.**

tatomukha, adj. (unrecorded), *facing that way*: Mv ii.303.9; 351.14, 16, 18, 20; 352.1, 5; 353.13 (this passage repeated iii.275.14 ff.).

[**tat-katara**, false reading for tatkara, in LV 239.15 and mss. of Mv ii.119.5; see s.v. **katara** and next.]

tatkara, adj. or subst. (= Pali takkara), *one who does that*: Mv ii.120.16, and read so ii.119.5; LV 239.15, see s.v. **katara**, end; MPS 2.35.

tatkṣaṇa, m. (see BR s.v. 2, where citation from Julien's 'Hiouen-Thsang' is obviously identical in language with our Divy), the smallest unit of time, of which 120 = one kṣaṇa: Divy 643.1–2 = 644.9–10 (tad yathā...) striyā nātidīrghahrasvakartinyāḥ sūtrodyāmaḥ (see **udyāma**), evaṃdīrghas tatkṣaṇaḥ; viṃśatyadhikaṃ tatkṣaṇaśatam ekā kṣaṇā (read ekaḥ kṣaṇaḥ, or ekaṃ kṣaṇam; 644.10, corruptly, viṃśatyuttarakṣaṇaśataṃ tatkṣaṇasyaikakṣaḥ, mss., ed. °aikakṣaṇaḥ); ṣaṣṭi-kṣaṇāny eko lavaḥ...

tatkṣaṇikā, acc. to Jap. *temporary wife*: Mvy 9454;

9464; = Tib. thaṅ ḥgaḥ ḥphrad pa, *meeting for a few moments*; so Chin. in essence; pw 7.344 *prostitute.*

tattaka, f. **°ikā,** adj. (also, rarely, written **tātaka, tāttaka, tātuka,** and in mss. sometimes with nt for tt; = Pali tattaka, Geiger 111.6; perh. analog. to Pali kittaka, BHS **kettaka,** and Pali, BHS **ettaka,** if Geiger is right in deriving these from kiyat-, iyat-; cf. **yattaka**), sg. *so great, so much,* pl. *so many*; in most texts only in vss, but in Mv common in prose, and KP has tāttaka, q.v., in prose: na ca vīrya sya tattakaṃ SP 254.3 (vs; Kashgar rec., La Vallée-Poussin, JRAS 1911.1073.1, tātakam); gaṇanā yeṣa tattikā (Kashgar rec. tātikāḥ) SP 304.9 (vs), f. pl., *so many*; gaṇanāya tattakāḥ (v.l. tāta°) 330.11 (vs), m. pl.; tattakaṃ, *so great, so much,* Mv i.364.1; ii.90.15; 276.2, 7 (these and most of our Mv citations are prose); tattaka (m. acc. pl.) Dbh.g. 41(67).16, 17; rarely in mg. (only) *so much = so little,* tattakaṃ āhāraṃ (...yathā) Mv ii.242.2, 3; in correlation with **yattaka,** mostly pl., *as many ... so many,* Mv i.266.1; 267.8; 314.1; ii.99.3–4; tattaka before yattaka Mv i.359.22 (both pl.); adverbs, yattakaṃ ... tattakaṃ, *as often, as many times as ... every time,* Mv i.246.5–6.

Tattvārthaikadeśānupraveśa, m., one of the adhimukticaryābhūmi: Mvy 900.

tatprathamakarmika, adj. (cf. next), (a Bodhisattva) *engaging in the* (appropriate) *action for the first time*; regularly associated with **ādikarmika,** q.v.: ādikarmika-tatpra°ka-vīryeṇa Bbh 205.2; on Bbh 395.2 see next; Bbh 394.24.

tatprathamatas, adv. (cf. AMg. tappaḍhamayā, *priority*; if such a cpd. occurs in Pali I have not found it in PTSD or Childers), *for the first time*: °taḥ śalākāṃ gṛhṇatāṃ Divy 44.28; °to Buddhadarśanam 47.6; tadā mama gṛhe tatp° piṇḍapātaḥ paribhoktavya iti 188.24; ādikarmikaṃ tatprathamakarmikam (see prec.) tatprathamata evaṃ avavadati Bbh 395.2. In several of these, notably the last, tat could certainly not be interpreted as an independent word.

tatsvabhāvaiṣīya, m., sc. vinaya, or nt., with karma, (procedure of discipline) *which investigates the special nature of that* (accused monk), a particular type of procedure for settling disputes, one of the 7 **adhikaraṇa-śamatha,** q.v.: MSV ii.207.12 (nt.); m., Mvy 8635 = Tib. deḥi (*of that*) ṅo bo ñid (= svabhāva, *reality, entity*) tshol du (*seeking,* -eṣa) gzhug par (*for entering*?) ḥos pa (*suitable*). The Pali equivalent is tassa-pāpiyyasikā, with which kiriyā is assumed to be supplied; PTSD offers no etym.; Childers, tasya-pāpīyas-ikā; MN ii.249.1 ff. has a description, its comm. iv.49.22 f. glosses tassa puggalassa pāpussannatā, *that individual's abundance of sin*; can the Pali be an unhistorical distortion of the orig. of the BHS form? Or is the latter a secondary rationalization? Childers s.v. gives a description of the performance acc. to Pali tradition (the case is decided on the accused person's general bad behavior).

tathatā, f., and **tathatva,** nt., once **tathatvatā** (= Pali tathatā, tathatta; note that Pali has actually an adj. and subst. tatha = sacca, Skt. satya, *true, truth*; it has not been noted in BHS; it was prob. a Pali backformation from these nouns, and/or from such Bhvr. cpds. as vi-tatha; BHS also has the more Sktized **tathātā, °tva,** qq.v., but they are rare), *true essence, actuality, truth*: (the SP is) asaṃbhinna-tathatā SP 473.8 (prose), *unmixed truth* (Kern); tathatā bhavet katividhā Laṅk 25.17 (vs); tathatāparivarto nāma AsP 306.1 (title of chapter); anujātas tathatāṃ subhūtiḥ sthaviras tathāgatasya 307.1 (prose), *the Elder S. is created after the manner of the truth* (true nature) *of the T.*; and often in the sequel; tathatā tathateti ... śūnyatāyā etad adhivacanaṃ Śikṣ 263.1 (prose), *'truth, truth'— this is a designation for nullity*; sāsau paramā (so prob. read for ed. sā sauparamā) tathatā ... Bbh 38.26 (prose), *this is that supreme truth*; tathatāyāṃ tathatvataḥ (... dharmavideśo) LV 437.1 (vs; v.l. tathātvataḥ), *in truth, according to reality*; both stems together also in tathata-sama tathatvād (dharmatā) Dbh.g. 26(52).2, *alike in true nature according to truth*; tathatvāya (i.319.6 °āye) dhārayiṣyanti Mv i.319.6; ii.257.15; iii.337.15 (prose), *will hold it fast for truth, make certain that it is true*; tathatvāya pratipadyate (Gv °yante) Dbh 19.13; Gv 181.14 (prose); ekā ca tasya (read tasyo; sc. dharmasya) samatā tathatvam SP 128.6 (vs), *it has one sameness and true nature*; tathatvatāyāṃ (! loc. sg.) pratipanno KP 125.4 (prose), *resorted to the truth*; tathatāyāṃ, *in truth,* AsP 320.15; 321.2 (see **pravibhāvayati**).

Tathatāprabha, n. of a Buddha: Gv 285.9.

Tathatāsthitaniścitta, m., n. of a samādhi: Mvy 620 (ed. Tathātā°, but Mironov Tathatā°; var. °niścita, but Tib. sems med pa = niścitta); ŚsP 1426.2.

tathatva, °tvatā, see **tathatā.**

tatha-r-iva (= tathaiva), *just so, also*; see § 4.61.

tathāgata (= Pali id.) = Buddha: Mvy 3 = Tib. de bzhin gśegs pa, *thus gone* or *come* (could = gata or āgata; both theories are held; acc. to Jä. and Das, in Tibet today the commonly accepted interpretation is *who goes,* or *has gone, in the same way,* sc. as earlier Buddhas); seven listed Dharmas 6 (Vipaśyin, Śikhin, Viśvabhū, Krakucchanda, Kanakamuni, Kāśyapa, Śākyamuni); Vipaśyin is the first 'of 7 Tathāgatas, of whom I (Śākyamuni) am the 7th' SP 201.4; same list, with variant forms, Mmk 397.11; Divy 333.3; and with other Buddhas, LV 5.15; 20 listed Mvy 82–101, the above seven, with variants, in 87–94; passim in all texts; as adj., f. °gatī, only m.c. for tāthāgatī, *of* (a) *Buddha*(s), in list of bhūmi: dharmameghā tathāgatī Laṅk 318.12 (vs; tāth° metr. impossible; sc. bhūmiḥ; see s.v. **tāthāgata**).

Tathāgatakulagotrodgata, n. of a Bodhisattva: Gv 4.1.

Tathāgatakośaparipālitā, n. of a kiṃnara maid: Kv 6.12.

Tathāgatakoṣa (i. e. °kośa)-sūtra, n. of a work: Śikṣ 171.13 (see Bendall 407, note).

tathāgata-garbha, m., (**1**) in Laṅk acc. to Suzuki (see Studies 405 with references), *the womb where the T. is conceived and nourished and matured = the Ālayavijñāna fully purified of its ... vāsanā and ... dausthulya*: Laṅk 77.14 ff., etc.; (**2**) n. of a Bodhisattva: Mvy 669.

Tathāgataguhya-sūtra, n. of a work: Śikṣ 7.20; 126.5; 158.16; 242.7; 274.3; 316.5; 357.1. Not identical with **Guhyasamājatantra,** q.v.; whether same as **Tathāgatācintyaguhyanirdeśa,** q.v., is not known to me.

Tathāgatajñānamudrāsamādhi, m. (or f.?), n. of a work: Mvy 1387.

Tathāgatabimba-parivarta, n. of a (? part of a) work: Śikṣ 173.8.

Tathāgatamahākaruṇānirdeśa, m., n. of a work: Mvy 1351.

Tathāgataśrīgarbha, n. of a Bodhisattva: Dbh 2.21.

tathāgata-hṛdaya, nt., *heart of the T.,* n. of a magic spell: Śikṣ 139.3 (it is quoted in lines 4–7).

Tathāgatācintyaguhyanirdeśa, n. of a work: Mvy 1355. See s.v. **Tathāgataguhya-sūtra.**

Tathāgatotpattisaṃbhavanirdeśa, m., n. of a work: Mvy 1378.

tathātā = **tathatā,** q.v.: Mvy 1709; 1716; 1721; Vaj 37.3. In Mvy 620 Kyoto ed. also tathātā-, but the true reading is **Tathatā(-sthitaniścitta,** q.v.).

tathātva = prec. and **tathatva,** q.v.: v.l. in LV 437.1 (vs) tathātvataḥ for tatha° of the text.

tathādarśana, adj. Bhvr. (evidently = **evaṃdarśana, °dṛṣṭi**), *holding such a view*: Mv ii.120.17 (sa) cāhaṃ bhikṣavo tathādarśanato evaṃ va (one ms. omits va) samāno yena gayānagaraṃ tad avasāri, *and, O monks* (realizing the worthlessness of the doctrine of Rāma, taught by his son), *from the holder of such a doctrine* (viz. from Udraka Rāmaputra), *being just as I was, I went off to Gayā-city*; in ii.119.6 we should expect a close parallel, in which the Bodhisattva leaves Ārāḍa Kālāma, but the text seems corrupt: sa khalv ahaṃ bhikṣavo tathādarśanāya (so, or °nāyai, mss.; Senart em. °nāyaiva; required is rather °nato, prob. followed by evaṃ va) samāno, etc. (he goes to Rājagṛha). (Otherwise Senart; ignoring the Bhvr. nature of the cpd. which seems guaranteed by evaṃdarśana, °dṛṣṭi.) Also Mv ii.123.16 (prose) sa khalv ahaṃ . . . tathādarśanasamāno, *I being of this opinion* (as just stated in prec.).

tad-anuvartaka, adj. or subst. m., (the **saṃghāvaśeṣa** offense of persistently, and in spite of remonstrance) *following that one* (sc. a monk who persists in causing **saṃghabheda,** q.v.): Mvy 8379; corresp. to Prāt 483.9 ff.; Pali Vin. iii.175.14 ff.

tadaho-poṣadhe, adv. phrase, see **poṣadha.**

tadāgata, m., a kind of (medicinal) resinous substance (jatu): MSV i.iii.17 and i.iv.2 (here Tib. cited as drod sman, *stimulating* or *heating drug*).

tadāni (= Pali Lex. id., Childers; Skt. °nīm), *then*: Mv i.253.6 (prose).

[**tadāhiṃ** is apparently understood by Senart as meaning *then* in Mv ii.69.5 (prose), yadā bhagavāṃ pravṛtadharmacakro tadāhiṃ etaṃ bhikṣubhi śrutaṃ. But mss. tadā hi or tadā hi-m-(i. e., I suppose, 'hiatus-bridging' m before following vowel); I think the particle hi must be assumed, after tadā. Perhaps Senart assumed a blend of tadā with (e)tar(a)hi(ṃ).]

tad-ekatya, see **ekatya** (8).

[**taddhu-,** read by Senart with mss. in Mv iii.113.13 (v.l. taddhura)-kāraka, and by em. for mss. tadva-(kāra) in iii.442.17; read respectively **taṭṭu-** and **taṭṭa-,** qq.v.]

tad-yathā, tad-yathāpi (nāma), **tad-yathedaṃ**; see s.vv. **yathāpi (nāma), sayyathīdaṃ.** The simple tad-yathā occurs in Skt. (pw and Monier Williams s.v. tad) as well as in BHS: Mv i.55.13; 56.8 (prose), *just as if . . .*

tanu, pl. (in this sense apparently not recorded; Sheth cites taṇu = alpa, thoṛā, from Deśīn. 3.51, a wrong reference; I have failed to find it in Deśīn. elsewhere), *few* (in number): ima ucyante (ms. ucyate) tanubhyas tanutarāḥ Av ii.188.4 (prose), *these are said to be fewer than few* (= *extremely few*). [In LV 243.3, vs, read with v.l. tatu = tatas for text tanu; confirmed by Tib. der.] See also s.v. **Taru.**

tanukībhūta, ppp. (from Skt. and Pali tanuka = tanu with bhavati), *become slight*: apāyā °tā Mv i.175.11 (vs).

tanu-(also **tanū-**)**bhūmi,** f., the 5th of the seven śrāvaka-bhūmi: Mvy 1145; ŚsP 1473.13 et alibi, see **bhūmi** 4.

tanuruha (recorded only in mg. *hair*, or rarely *wing, feathers*, Schmidt, Nachträge), *member, limb of the body*: chini tava tanuruha kalinṛpu ruṣito LV 165.22 (vs), *an evil king in anger cut off thy bodily member(s)*; the mg. is certain and is confirmed by Tib. yan lag.

tanū-bhūmi, see **tanu°.**

tantrajāla-jāta, adj. (see next, which is the older form), *become* (confused) *like a* (tangled) *net of string*: Mvy 5390 (Mironov wrongly jala for jāla) = Tib. thags ḥkhrugs pa lta bu, *like a disordered web* or *texture*, the latter representing tantra; ḥkhrugs pa, *disordered*, prob. indicates that the BHS original had ākula rather than jāla.

tantrākulajāta, adj. (= Pali tantākulakajāta; see under prec.), *become confused like an* (entangled) *web* (or *warp*): LV 205.11 (so mss., wrongly em. in ed.). The Tib. transl. under prec. fits this, which is proved by Pali to be the orig. form, rather than tantra-jāla-. For the rest of the passage (same in LV and Mvy) see s.v. **guṇāvaguṇṭhita-bhūta.**

Tantrī, n. of a daughter of Māra acc. to Mv iii.281.15; 283.15; 284.3; 286.6. The Mv is clearly secondary here; thruout most of the passage it mentions only two daughters of Māra, Tantrī and Arati, but in 286.6 three, the third being Rati. Originally (LV 378.4 ff.; Pali, see Childers s.v. Ragā) there were three, Tṛṣṇā, Arati, and Rati (or, in Pali, Ragā, SN i.124.15 ff.). It is clear that Mv replaces Tṛṣṇā by Tantrī. Could it be a corruption of MIndic *Taṇhī = BHS **tṛṣṇī,** q.v.? Or is the corruption based on some form of the numeral for *three* (which is lost in Mv except in the final verse), cf. tās tisro . . . LV 378.4?

tanmukhikayā, instr. (adv.?) of °kā (see **-mukhaka, °ikā**), *for this reason* or *by that means*: (anāpattayas) tanm° nirgatā bhavanti Divy 330.2, acc. to p. 708 rendered in Tib. *through this consideration they go forth innocent.*

tanvībhavati (for Skt. tanū-bh°, ppp. °bhūta, Pali tanubhūta; -ī due to influence of forms in -ī before bhavati derived from a-stems), *becomes slight, diminishes*: (akuśalāś ca te dharmā . . .) te tanvībhaviṣyanti Divy 236.17 (prose).

tapana, (1) m. or nt., and **°nā,** *box* or *basket*, in which infants are enclosed and thrown into a river: (tāhi dāni) antaḥpurikāhi te dārakā tapanasmiṃ cailakaṃ upastaritvā tatra prakṣiptāḥ, taṃ tapanaṃ sv-apihitaṃ subaddhaṃ kṛtvā rājakyena tāpanīyena tāpayitvā mudrayitvā nadīye gaṅgāye prakṣiptā Mv iii.163.9, *by the harem-women those infants in a tapana, putting a cloth on, were laid in there, and making that tapana carefully closed and tied, soldering it with the royal solder* (? *gold*) *and* (so) *sealing it, they were thrown into the River Ganges*; referring to the same incident, (te) cāsmābhiḥ tapanāye (loc. f.) prakṣipitvā etc. 166.6; the same receptacle is called mañjūṣā, *basket*, in 166.10 ff., which makes the mg. clear. Senart's note compares **tapu,** in Divy, q.v., but this is a false reading. It seems unlikely that Skt. tapanī, *Kochtopf*, Schmidt, Nachträge, or Deśīn. 2.59 comm. tavaṇī, *frying-pan*, are directly connected; **(2)** m., less often nt. (= Pali id.), n. of a hot hell (see also **Tāpana**): Dharmas 121 (°naḥ); Mv i.6.3; 9.9 (m.); 14.15; ii.350.8 = iii.274.10; ii.369.14; iii.454.8 (nt.); Divy 67.22; 138.6; 366.29; Av i.4.8 etc.; Samādh 19.20; Kv 18.13; Mmk 114.26; Mironov tapanaḥ for Mvy 4925 tāp°.

Tapanī, (1) n. of a river (= **Tapantī**): Divy 451.1; 456.19; **(2)** n. of a rākṣasī: Māy 243.22.

Tapantī, n. of a river (= **Tapanī**): Divy 451.4, 8; 456.22, 26.

tapara, nt., a high number: Gv 133.2; cited in Mvy as **tavara,** q.v.

[**tapasvanī,** Divy 525.27, *poor wretch* (f.); read tapasvinī.]

Tapā, n. of one of the 8 deities of the Bodhi-tree: LV 331.21.

[**tapu**: Divy 342.26; 343.5; read taṭṭu; see s.v. **taṭṭa.**]

Tapoda, m. or nt., °**dā** (= Pali Tapodā, n. of a lake and its outlet river at Rājagaha), n. of one or more bodies of water (lake, spring[s], river?) at Rājagṛha: tapoda-dvāreṇa Rājagṛhaṃ . . . prāvikṣat LV 240.1 (prose), *entered R. by the gate of that-which-has-warm-water*, so Tib., chu dron can gyi (*of that which has warm water*) sgo nas (*by gate*); the gate was named for warm springs or for the river outlet from them; (rājagṛhe samasamaṃ giriyagra-[v.l. giri-m-agra-]-samājaṃ) nāma parvaṃ vartati pañcānāṃ tapoda-śatānāṃ (so read for ed. tapo-śa°; mss. tapa-śa°, capośata-śa°). tatra dāni pañcahi tapoda-(so read, ed. tapo-, mss. tapa-, tapota-)-śatehi pañca udyānaśatāni Mv iii.57.7, *at R. at the same time there took place the festival called Mountain-top-gathering, of 500 Warm Springs. Now at these 500 Warm Springs there were 500 pleasure-parks*; Tapodā, as in Pali n. of a river at Rājagṛha,

Pischel, SBBA 1904 p. 813 fol. 158a; n. of a river Māy 253.7 (doubtless the same).

tabdha, ppp. (cf. Pali thaddha; semi-MIndic for Skt. stabdha), *haughty, puffed up*: (devadattaḥ...) mānī ca balavān eva tabdhaḥ śākyamānena ca tabdho... LV 152.15 (prose). So all mss.; only Calc. sta°.

Tamasāvana, n. of a grove: Divy 399.11 (vs; m.c. for tamasa- or tāmasa-? or cf. the river-name Tamasā?).

tamasīkaraṇa, adj. (to *tamasī-karoti; perhaps m.c. for tāmas°), *darkening, making dark*: smṛtiśokakarās tamasīkaraṇāḥ bhayahetukarā... (kāmaguṇāḥ) LV 173.21 (vs).

Tama(ḥ)sundarī (text lacks ḥ), n. of a yakṣiṇī: Mmk 564.26 (here text corrupt); 566.15. Cf. **Andhārasundarī** (same personage).

Tamālapattracandanagandha, n. of a future Buddha (= Mahāmaudgalyāyana, by prediction): SP 153.8; 154.14.

Tamālapattracandanagandhābhijña, n. of a Buddha in a northwestern lokadhātu: SP 184.14 (no v.l. in edd.; Burnouf omits -abhijña, reading as prec.).

tamisrāyita-tva, nt. (abstr. from denom. pple. to tamisrā), *begloomedness*: Mv i.41.5; 229.20; 240.10; ii.162.10; iii.334.8; 341.12; in all of which I believe we should read tamisrāyitatvā (or possibly ti°, cf. Pali timissā) for the corrupt mss.; Senart tamisrārpitā, but the mss. have no -r-. See under **andhakārāpita-tva.**

-tamisrita, ppp. denom., see **andhakāra-tamisrita.**

[?**tam-enaṃ**, Mv i.11.7, 11 (vss), assumed by Senart to be adverbial phrase, *thereupon, straightway*, and identified with Pali taṃ enaṃ, Vin. i.127.32, which is so interpreted PTSD s.v. ta-, II.4(b); neither Senart's nor PTSD's explanation seems plausible. It seems to me that acc. sg. m. pronouns may quite well be intended; if Senart is right in his em. of the rest of the text, i.11.7 would read: tam enaṃ kṛṣṇaprāṇakā agnitīkṣṇamukhā kharā, chaviṃ bhittvāna khādanti..., *him... they eat, cutting his skin*; and similarly line 11 where tam enaṃ may depend on khādanti in line 12. In the Pali passage, also, I believe pronouns are to be assumed, anticipating taṃ bhikkhuṃ of the next line, altho the construction is indeed exceptionally loose.]

Tamodghātana, n. of a Bodhisattva: Mmk 42.5.

? **tampuruka** or **tambu°**, see s.v. **kiṃpuruṣa.**

? **taṃbhū** (for Skt. *tad-bhū), *being that*, as just described; perhaps in Mv i.349.5 rājā ca Sujāto apративacano satyavādī yathāvādī tathākārī taṃbhuvo (so mss.) rājño varaṃ yācāhi, ... *from the king, being that* (as just described), *ask a boon!* Senart em. taṃ tuvaṃ, which seems implausible; taṃ would have to go with varaṃ, which would be separated from it by tuvaṃ.

tayyathāpi nāma, ms. var. for **tadyath°**, **sayyath°**, see s.v. **yathāpi 2.**

Taraṅgavatī, n. of a locality: Māy 42.

(**taraṅgāyate**, denom., Skt., Schmidt, Nachträge, *is wavy, acts like a wave*: (vikalpavijñānam...) mṛgatṛṣṇikāvat taraṅgāyate Laṅk 94.14.)

taraṇa, nt. (Skt. id., *fording* (a river), so also Tib. rgal ba, below; AMg. id., defined Ratnach. *swimming, crossing*), perhaps *boating, rowing*, or *swimming*, in lists of arts and sports: javite plavite taraṇe LV 156.10; °ṇam, after javitam, plavitam, Mvy 5001 = Tib. rgal ba. Foucaux's Tib. rgyal in LV, prob. error for rgal; he renders *la natation.*

taraṇi, °ṇī, f. (Skt. Lex., used of various plants and flowers), a kind of flower: °ṇiḥ Mvy 6207; LV 11.3, reading of ms. H in Crit. App. °ṇī; Tib. in both places transliterates ta ra ṇi or °ni.

tara-paṇya, nt. or m. (= Skt. tara-deya, in Kauṭ. Arth., cited s.v. **gulma**, q.v.), *ferry-money*: Mv iii.328.7 (nāviko dāni āha, dehi) tarapaṇyaṃ; LV 407.4 (same incident) prayaccha... tarap°; aśulkenātarapaṇyena Divy 4.12; similarly Divy 34.13; 501.23; Av i.199.12, see s.v. **gulma**; Divy 92.27, see ibid. See also **tārapaṇyika.**

taraputa, m., Mvy 9371 = Tib. gru btsums (gru = *boat*; btsums = ?) or gru tshugs, *ferry* or *ghat* (Das); next word is pratisrotaḥ; perhaps *ferry-landing*?

?**Tarārka**, n. of a yakṣa: Māy 57. See **Kutarārkaka.**

?**Taru**, n. of a legendary king: Mv i.188.12; 189.7; 191.12; one ms. in the first passage, three in the third, and all in the second, read Tanu; both occur as names of men in Skt., but very rarely.

taruṇaka, adj. or subst. (-ka svārthe, or dim.; AMg. °ṇaa), *young; child*: dārakāṇāṃ dahukānāṃ (so mss., see **dahuka**) °ṇakānāṃ krīḍāpanikāni Divy 475.(17–)18 (prose).

Taruṇārkabhānu, n. of a former Buddha: Mv i.140.3.

tarka, m. (in Skt. *reasoning, philosophizing*), as with Pali takka, in BHS seems normally to have pejorative connotation, *sophistry, vain speculation*; typical are Sutrāl. i.12 with comm., see Lévi's Transl. (*dialectique*), and Laṅk 24.2 kathaṃ hi śudhyate tarkaḥ kasmāt tarkaḥ pravartate, kathaṃ hi dṛśyate bhrāntiḥ..., *how is tarka purified* (got rid of)? *From what does it arise*?

tarjanīya, adj. with karman (= Pali tajjaniyakamma), *act of rebuke* or *threat*, a formal censure against dissident monks: Mvy 8642; MSV iii.5.14 ff. (described, as in Pali Vin. ii.2.20 ff.).

tarpaṇa, nt. (in Skt. *food, sustenance*, in general), a particular kind of food, *dough, paste, meal*(?): Mvy 5753 = Tib. skyo ma, *pap, paste, dough*; bhaktāni vā tarpaṇāni vā (ya)vāgūpānāni vā... Bhīk 23a.2 (in list similar to that of Mvy).

tala, m. or nt. (= AMg. id. = Skt. bhūtala), *surface of the ground*: yehi iha kīṭakamardanāni vā kārāpitāni bhavanti talamardanāni vā... Mv i.21.12; tala-m° acc. to Senart *stamping on the ground*; but perhaps *breaking up the surface of the ground*, as in digging; reprobated as injurious to living creatures.

talaka (tala plus -ka svārthe), *upper surface, top, roof*: °kopari Mvy 9351 = Tib. khaṅ steṅ, (on) *the top of a house.*

talavarga, m. (cf. Skt. talārakṣa, pw 5.255; and AMg. talavara, talāra, some sort of *guard* or *police officer*), some sort of royal officer, acc. to Tib. sku bsruṅs, *body-guard*: Mvy 3724, in a list of royal functionaries.

tala-śaktikā (= Pali talasattikā, also a raising of the hand, but there seems to denote a *threatening gesture*), lit. *palm-spear*, a raising of the hand in a *gesture of salutation*: añjalis (so with WT)... paripūrṇa ekā talaśaktikā vā SP 52.7 (vs), (by whom is made) *either a complete añjali or a mere raising of one hand* (in salutation). On Mv iii.55.4, where this word might be conjectured, see s.v. **chādayati** (1).

talikā, sc. lipi, a kind of writing: Mv i.135.8 (prose).

tallakṣaṇa, nt., a high number: LV 148.11, cited Mvy 7977; Tib. renders literally deḥi mtshan ñid, *mark of that.*

tavara, m., Mvy 7709, or nt., Mvy 7835, a high number; in 7835 cited from Gv which reads **taparam**, q.v.

tasarikā (from Skt. tasara, *shuttle*), in Divy 83.24 (prose), acc. to Index *weaving*, as *operation of the shuttle*; this force of the suffix would seem peculiar, but the context gives little help: (Śacy api...) tasarikāṃ kartum ārabdhā. In the preceding sentence Śakra, in disguise, vastraṃ vāyitum ārabdhaḥ. Perhaps tasarikāṃ kartum, *to make the* (little) *shuttle*, means only *to operate the shuttle.*

tasiṇā (= Pali id.; MIndic for Skt. tṛṣṇā), *thirst*: Mv i.166.20 (vs; may be m.c.; mss. ka°, va°, but em. certain), see s.v. **jālinī.**

tahi, tahiṃ, loc. of pron. stem ta-, also as adv., *there*; see § 21.22.

tāḍa, (**1**) m. or nt. (Skt. tāla, Pali tāḷa, *cymbal* or some percussion instrument; also *clap of the hand* etc.), *a musical instrument, cymbal*: vīṇāś ca tāḍā paṇavāś ca SP 51.13 (vs); saṃgīti-tāḍa-samaye ca viniścayajñāḥ RP 42.17 (vs), but here and in the next tāḍa could mean not the instrument, but the sound made by striking it; vādya-tāḍa-ninādа-nirghoṣa-śabdair SP 338.11 (prose); others, see s.v. **śamya**; see also **tāḍāvacara**; (**2**) m. (= Pali tāḷa, m.; see next), *key* (in Skt. tāla, *lock*, cf. **tālaka**; see Johnston, note on Buddhac.): saddharma-tāḍena Buddhac. 1.74; tāḍam ādāya gṛham asya gatvā Av ii.56.2; tāḍam apahṛtya gṛhaṃ gatvā 3 (ms. tāḍan both times).

tāḍaka, m. (cf. s.v. **tāḍa,** 2), *key*, or some kind of key: °kaṃ kuñcikāṃ ca tāvad dhāraya Divy 577.21, 27; °kaḥ kuñcikā ca 578.11; tāḍaka-kuñcikāṃ (acc.; so read for ed. tāḍhaka°) MSV iii.23.14. Cf. also **tālaka.**

tāḍanā, f. (Skt. °na, nt.), *a beating*: kaści kuryān na tāḍanāṃ . . . SP 285.1 (vs); tāḍanās, acc. pl., to be read LV 214.3 (vs) with practically all mss. for °nā; all the series of nouns in this line are f.

tāḍāvacara, also (doubtless wrongly) spelled **tāḍopacāra,** m. and nt. (= Pali tāḷā°, wrongly defined in PTSD; it means *a musical instrument*, as stated by comm. (596.15) on DN ii.159.16 which glosses turiyabhaṇḍaṃ; Skt. tālāv° seems to mean a person, see BR, and Rām. 7.91.15, BR 5.1469), *a musical instrument* in general or *a particular class* of them, prob. of the *cymbal* type, cf. **tāḍa**; almost always preceded by tūrya: sarvagīta-vādyanṛtya-tūrya-tāḍāvacara-saṃgīti-saṃpravāditaiḥ pūjā karaṇīyā SP 232.3 (prose); nearly this same cpd. LV 82.5; tūryatāḍāvacaraiḥ satkriyate sma LV 96.20; vādyantāṃ sumanojñatūryatāḍāvacarāṇi 118.9; sarvavāditehi sarvatūryatāḍāvacarehi bhagavantaṃ satkṛtya Mv iii. 138.7; sarvatūryatāḍ°rehi 179.2; °raḥ Mvy 5023 = Tib. pheg rdob pa, variously defined as *a small brass plate for music* (a cymbal), or a kind of *drum*; tūrya-tāḍ° Laṅk 3.4–5; 16.1,7; Dbh 85.31; Mmk 79.5; tūrya-tāḍ°ra-nirghoṣeṣu Gv 174.24; sarvatūryāṇi sarvatāḍāvacarān 219.22; spelled (almost certainly by error, yet cf. **upacāra** with **avacara**) tāḍopacāra twice in Gv, -divya-tūrya-tāḍopacāra-saṃgīti- 119.4 and 147.7; in Samādh p. 20 line 2 printed °canaiḥ, read °raiḥ.

(**tāṇḍavika,** m., Skt., Schmidt, Nachträge, = nartaka, *dancer*: twice in lists of entertainers, Mv iii.113.4 (here Senart with mss. bhāṇḍ°); 442.10 (mss. tāṇḍ° or taṇḍ°, MIndic); the passages are closely parallel and tā° must be read in both.)

tātaka, tātuka, tāttaka, all = **tattaka** (§ 3.2), *so much, so great*, pl. *so many*; no such forms are recorded elsewhere; tātaka, only as v.l. of Kashgar rec. of SP for **tattaka,** q.v.; tāttaka, m. pl., Samādh 19.16 (vs); KP 158.3 (prose; twice); 159.5 ff. (prose); tātuka, correl. with **yātuka,** q.v., Śikṣ 346.16 (vs); Gv 487.17 (here the correl. in 1st ed. is spelled **yātaka,** in 2d. ed. yātuka) and 18 (vss).

tāthāgata, adj., f. °ī (from tathāgata plus -a), *of* or *belonging, pertaining to the* (or *a*) *Buddha*: °taḥ (vihāraḥ) Bbh 318.5; 367.13; °taṃ caturthaṃ dhyānam Laṅk 97.7; °tasya padasya Bbh 10.4; °tī (bhūmi) Laṅk 244.11; 318.12 (vs, here m.c. tathāgatī); bodhisattva- °tī bhūmiḥ Bbh 367.3; °tī (vidyā) Mmk 561.20; (pūjā) 600.25; (mudrā) 502.13; tāthāgatī-mantrāḥ Mmk 35.3; 392.17 (here °gatī seems to represent °gatī-mudrā, cf. 392.13 tathāgata-pātra-mudrā-mantra anena saṃyuktaḥ); tatrottarāpathe sarvatra tāthāgatī-vidyā-rājñaḥ (cf. line 4 vidyā-rājñāṃ; here tāthāgatī, which read in composition with vidyā, takes its gender from that word, see Mmk 561.20, above) siddhiṃ gacchanti saṃkṣepataḥ Mmk 325.5–6 (one might expect rājñī instead of rājan after vidyā, but this text tolerates such things).

[**tādin,** Pali id., = **tāyin,** q.v., has not been found in BHS, tho Ud once has a gen. tādṛno = Pali tādino, see next. In Mv iii.397.2 Senart reads tādi, n. sg., but mss. bhāvayi, and the true reading is certainly tāyi, see s.v. **tāyin** 1.]

tādṛ(n), (hyper-Skt. for Pali tādin = BHS **tāyin,** q.v.), *holy* (person): devāpi tasya spṛhayanti tādṛnaḥ (dental n) Ud xix.3, *even the gods envy that holy man*; corresp. to Pali Dhp. 94 which reads tādino.

tādṛśa = **tāyin,** q.v.: Ud xix.1 (oldest ms. tādṛśāḥ, later ms. tāyī).

tādṛśaka, (**1**) adj. (= Pali tādisaka), *such*, = Skt. tādṛśa: Mv iii.287.10 (prose; correl. with **yādṛśaka,** q.v.); (**2**) = BHS **tādṛśa,** and **tāyin,** q.v.; applied to a Bodhisattva or a Buddha; *holy*: (kausīdyaprāptas tada yo babhūva . . .) tvam eva so tādṛśako babhūva SP 28.2 (vs), addressed to the Bodhisattva Maitreya, (*he who was indolent at that time* . . .) *has become none other than thou, the holy one* (misunderstood by Burnouf and Kern); tvam eva so tādṛśako bhaviṣyasi anābhibhūto dvipadānam uttamaḥ SP 69.4 (vs), predicting Buddhahood in the future, *thou thyself shalt become a Holy One* (*a Buddha*), *unconquered, best of bipeds.*

?**tānika,** see **tālika.**

tāpa- = tapas, *ascetic practice* (a mg. unrecorded for tāpa or its MIndic equivalents); in Mvy 1608, chapter-title, tāpa-saṃvāra-paryāyāḥ, *words for ascetic practices and restraints*; **saṃvāra** is also unparallelled in the sense of **saṃvara**; Tib. dkaḥ thub, which regularly = tapas, and sdom pa, which regularly = saṃvara. Perhaps read tapaḥ-saṃvara-; but Mironov (p. vi) cites both words as in Kyoto ed.

Tāpana, (**1**) m. (acc. to DPPN Pali id. = Tapana; but no reference is given; this v.l. recorded in some mss. for Tapana), n. of a hot hell, = **Tapana**: Mvy 4925 (but Index lists Ta° as well as Tā°, and Mironov Tapanaḥ without v.l.); (**2**) n. of a mountain: Māy 254.6.

tāpanīya, m. or nt., acc. to Senart *solder* or some substance melted and used for sealing containers: Mv iii.163.10, see s.v. **tapana** (1), and next. But possibly *gold* (in Skt. adj. *golden*).

tāpayati, *solders*: °yitvā Mv iii.163.10, see under prec.

Tāpasasūtra, n. of a work: Karmav 157.13 (Lévi's note says no such title is otherwise known).

tāpya, nt., *regret, grief*: (mā vaḥ paścāj) jambudvīpagatānāṃ tāpyaṃ bhaviṣyati Divy 230.10 (prose).

Tāmarā, n. of a river: Māy 253.6 (prose). Cf. Epic Skt. Tāmrā, a river(?). In list between Amarā and Pañcālā.

Tāmradvīpa (was prob. known in Skt. tho not so recorded BR or pw; cf. dvīpaṃ tāmrāhvayaṃ Mbh. Cr. ed. 2.28.46), an earlier name for Ceylon, later replaced by (Skt.) Siṃhaladvīpa (cf. Divy 528.12): Divy 525.10, 21, 28; so also in the version of Kv reported by Burnouf, Introd. 223 f.

Tāmradvīpaka, adj., *belonging to, of* **Tāmradvīpa**: Divy 525.3.

tāmra-loha, m. or nt. (= Pali tambaloha), *copper*: °haṃ ca sānaṃ (hell-inhabitants) vilīnakaṃ pāyayanti (mss. pāyanti) Mv i.8.5.

tāmraśāṭīya, m. pl., n. of a school: Mvy 9083.

Tāmrākṣa, n. of a serpent: Divy 106.1, 8, 11.

Tāmrāṭavī, n. of a forest: Divy 102.29; 105.29 f.; 106.12. (So ed.; but perhaps merely a descriptive epithet, *a copper-colored forest*, or *a forest of tāmra trees*, any of several trees given this name in Hindu Lexx.)

tāyaṇa, °na (nt.; MIndic, = **trāyaṇa,** q.v.), (act of) *saving*: jaga-tāyanaṃ smarati Dbh.g. 2(338).7; jaga-tāyaṇārthaṃ (v.l. °trāy°) 16(352).12.

tāyin, m. (= AMg. tāi, defined as *attaining salvation*, i. e. *holy, religious*; also *who protects himself and others*, i. e. a Jina; Pali tādi, see below), originally Prakritic for Pali tādi(n) = Skt. tādṛś; see **tādṛ(n), tādṛśa(ka).** The identity of the two words can hardly be questioned. The mg. of Pali tādi(n) is also quite clear, *such* (= tādṛś); doubt remains only as to whether this meant originally *such as the Buddha,* of the same quality as He, or *such as a religious man ought to be,* thus *holy, following the path of true religion.* On the Pali see esp. Childers s.v., also Senart on Mv ii.256.9, where BHS uses evaṃrūpa in nearly the same sense; Senart points out that tathārūpa glosses tādi in Dhp. comm. Acc. to Childers tādi is usually applied to *holy men,* only rarely to Buddha. In BHS tāyin most often applies to Buddhas, but also fairly often to Bodhisattvas, and occasionally to other holy men. Once, at least, **tādṛśaka,** q.v., is clearly applied to a Buddha, like tāyin. These facts all together make it seem clear to me that the etym. and original mg. are as stated above. It is true that Tib. (see on Mvy below) interprets tāyin as if for trāyin, rendering *protector* or the like; some modern scholars (Burnouf, Lotus 16, on vs 73 of Chap. 1; pw 7.345 'wohl nur fehlerhaft für trāyin') assume that this was the etym. and primary mg. of tāyin. But against this stands not only Pali but BHS **tādṛśa(ka), tādṛ(n)-.** Tib. doubtless has a secondary popular etymology. The forms are typical of in-stems: tāyī n. sg. (SP 45.13; Mvy 15, 1746), tāyinaḥ gen. sg. (SP 69.2; 208.7, etc.), °nām gen. pl. (SP 176.8 etc.), tāyibhiḥ (LV 388.13), etc. Occasionally the mss. write corruptly tāpin (so Mv ii.349.12 text, prob. mere misprint; Mmk 98.8; 499.19; 599.20; 600.17). (**1**) Used of others than Bodhisattvas and Buddhas, *holy*: anigho tāyi tam āhu śrotriyaṃ ti Mv iii.400.2; ariyo (mss., Senart āryo) tāyi pravuccati tathatvā 400.6; in iii.397.2 read, śramaṇo tāyi (mss. bhāvayi, Senart tādi, cf. 400.6) pravuccati tathatvā, *he is called in truth a monk, a holy man* (or, *one such as the Buddha,* or, *such as he should be*); tāyī sa sarvāṃ (read °vaṃ) prajahāti duḥkham Ud xix.1, in later version of line which in oldest ms. reads prahāsate (= °syate) sarvabhavāni tādṛśāḥ, *the holy man (men) gets (will get) rid of all misery (states of being)*: (**2**) used of Bodhisattvas (other than Śākyamuni in his last existence, when in laudations he is often given epithets of a Buddha, even before his enlightenment): SP 304.5 (vs; buddhaputrasya tāyinaḥ), 12; 306.1; Mv ii.370.1 (vs, buddhaputrāṇa tāyināṃ); Sādh 93.10 (of Mañjuvajra = Mañjuśrī); Dbh 29(55).14(? reference not clear); (**3**) but most commonly of the Buddha (Śākyamuni) or of any or all Buddhas: Mvy 15 (text trāyī, tāyī, but Mironov tāyī without v.l.; Tib. skyob pa, *protector*); 1746 (tāyī; Tib. skyob ston, *protector-teacher*); SP 25.1; 45.13; 69.2; 116.9 (tāyinaḥ, *for the Buddha*; wrongly Kern); 176.8; 208.7; 303.13; 331.8; LV 122.20 (tāyino with v.l. for kāyi no); 388.13; 421.5; Mv ii.349.12 = iii.273.11; ii.351.8, 14; 352.15; 353.17; iii.109.20; 124.20; 445.17; Av ii.199.4; Suv 17.11; Śikṣ 260.11; Mmk 98.8; 125.15; 320.14; 375.10, 15; 442.9; 499.19; 599.20; 600.17; nikṣiptaḥ sādhu tāyinā Divy 712.7. All these passages (except Mvy where the word is cited alone) are verses; they are not exhaustive, but it is doubtful whether tāyin occurs anywhere in prose.

tāraka, m. (°kā, f.; Skt. and Pali; °ka, said by Ratnach. to be nt., AMg.), *pupil of the eye*: °kaḥ Mvy 3945 = Tib. mig gi ḥbras bu, lit. *fruit* (cf. Eng. *apple*) *of the eye.*

Tārakākṣa (cf. **Tārākṣa**), n. of a mountain: Divy 102.29 (Nīlodas Tār° ca parvatau).

Tārakopama, n. of a kalpa: ŚsP 309.9; AsP 366.12; 458.7.

tārapaṇyika, m. (**tarapaṇya** plus -ika; cited BR as tara°, but Mironov also tāra° with no v.l.), *ferryman*: Mvy 3804.

Tārā, n. of a Buddhistic goddess: Mvy 4280; Dharmas 4; Sādh 18.16 etc.; Mmk 10.16, at the head of a list of vidyārājñī; 40.10; 65.9, called 'compassion of Avalokiteśvara', Āryāvalokiteśvara-karuṇā; 69.16; 312.6; 576.11 etc.; 647.12 ff.

Tārākṣa (cf. **Tārakākṣa**), n. of a rākṣasa: Divy 105.2, 6 (called a daka-rākṣasa), and by em. text 104.21, where mss. Raktākṣa, Raktāka (described as raktanetraḥ); he lives Nīlode mahāsamudre.

tārāyaṇa- (m. or nt.), once °ṇī, n. or epithet of the bodhi-tree, only noted in LV; Tib. śiṅ sgrol rgyu, *cause-of-salvation-tree* (deriving from tārayati): °ṇa-mūle LV 381.3; 392.7; -samīpe 381.11; -mūlam 385.11; 396.17; 398.11; these both prose and vs; °ṇī-mūlam 387.4 (vs, meter requires long stem-final).

? **tārā-vana,** m., n. of a muhūrta, in list of them: °no (3 of 4 mss. °to) nāma muhūrtaḥ Divy 643.22; (all mss. tārāḥ vacanaḥ) 644.16.

tārāvarta, m. or nt., some kind of flower: °ta-puṣpaṃ juhuyāt Mmk 684.25 (prose).

Tāriṇī = **Tārā**: Sādh 208.2 (prose), etc.

Tāreśvararāja, n. of a Tathāgata: Gv 80.26.

tāla, nt. (in Skt. only m., and so BHS usually), *palm-tree*: (sarvasmāc ca tālād ratnasūtrād, so read with Calc. for Lefm. °trā) dvitīye tālam avasaktam abhūt LV 273.22 (prose), *and from a jewel-thread* (extending) *from each palm-tree,* (each) *palm-tree was attached to the next.* As a measure of length or esp. height, **tāla,** *palm-tree,* occurs also in Skt. (BR), and much oftener in BHS, where previous translators often erroneously render *span,* esp. in the cpd. sapta-tāla; but this (= Pali satta-tāla) means, as in Pali, *seven palm-trees,* and so tāla regularly (confirmed by Tib., regularly śiṅ ta la, *tāla-tree*). Acc. to Mv ii.313.3 ff. a tāla is one-eighth of a krośa, and eight times a **pauruṣeya** 3, q.v. In LV 14.11 the cakra-ratna of the cakravartin is saptatālam uccaiḥ; in LV 154.5 a metal figure of a boar (ayasmayī varāhapratimā) measures 7 tālas (read saptatālā as one word); in LV 273.19 a vedikā is saptatālān uccaistvena; in Av ii.104.4, 14 a throne is saptatālodgataṃ; in SP 428.10 kūṭāgāram abhiruhya vaihāyase saptatālamātreṇa, *having mounted a tower-house seven tālas high in the air.* Most commonly used as a measure of height to which someone, esp. Buddha, magically rises in the air; one tāla only, tālamātraṃ (vaihāyasam . . .) Mv i.239.18; iii.107.12, 13; 108.5; 411.13, 15; oftener sapta-tāla-mātraṃ vaihāyasam abhyudgamya, or variations on this, SP 459.11; 465.7; LV 18.16 (here a Pratyekabuddha, rising 7 tālas, passes thru the 'fire-element', tejodhātu, and disappears); 350.20–21; Laṅk 16.6; Divy 252.16.

tālaka, (**1**) nt. (= Skt. Lex. id. and Skt. tāla), *lock*: Mvy 5905 = Tib. sgo lcags, *door-lock*; cf. **pratitālaka**; (**2**) nt., a kind of ornament, acc. to Tib. shaped like a palm-leaf: Mvy 6029 = Tib. rgyan ta la ḥdab.

Tāladhvaja, nt., n. of a city (in the south): Gv 154.20; 155.10. (In Skt. m. as n. of a mountain, and °jā, f., cited Lex. as n. of a city.)

tāla-mukta (Mvy) or °**ta-ka** (MSV), adj., designates a kind of person not to be accepted as a monk: Mvy 8796; MSV iv.68.14. Acc. to Chin. on Mvy, *one who mixes liquor* (from the palm tree) *with his food.* Tib. obscure, perhaps similar to Chin.

tālavaṇṭaka, nt. (= Pali °vaṇṭa, Skt. °vṛnta), (palm-leaf) *fan*: °kāni Mv ii.475.8; 477.5. See also **tālavṛndaka.**

[**tālavastu**? see **kālavastu.**]

tālavṛndaka (nt., = °**vaṇṭaka,** Skt. Lex. °vṛntaka; no form with d otherwise known), *fan*: na °kam (adv.) Mvy 8529, (the monk's robe is to be worn) *not fan-wise.*

? **tālika,** or **tānika,** Mv ii.311.6, n. or epithet of gems: tālikehi (v.l. tāni°) maṇīhi. Senart has no note. (In Mv iii.442.8 read, instead of tālika, vetāḍika, or vai°, or °lika; Skt. vaitālika; cf. iii.113.2.)

tālīśa, m., prob. an unctuous substance made from the (Skt.) tālīśa plant (= Pali tālīsa, tālissa): Mvy 5787 (see s.v. **kārīṣi**).

tālukā (AMg. tāluyā; Skt. tālu, nt. tāluka, and acc.

to Wilson °kā), *palate*: °kā cābhiraktikā Mmk 156.24 (vs).

[**tālūka**, nt, °kaṃ MSV i.239.16, read śālūka (Skt.), *edible lotus-root*.]

tāva-kālika (perhaps only m.c.), **tāvat-kā°**, adj. (= Pali tāvakā°), *temporary*: (saṃskāra . . .) pāṃśunagaropama tāvakālikāḥ LV 175.20 (vs; may be m.c. for -tk-); °tkālika-vihāra- Bbh 27.1; °ka-yogena 63.4; °ka-MadhK 263.3 (these three prose).

tāvattakaṃ, °ntakaṃ, °ttikaṃ, adv. (from Skt. tāvat; cf. Pali tāvataka, AMg. tāvantia; for the greater variety of forms based on the correl. yāvat-, see s.v. **yāvataka**), *so far* (= tāvat): Mv iii.115.10 (mss. °ttakaṃ, °ntakaṃ); 437.17 (mss. °ttakaṃ, °ttikaṃ); see the passages s.v. **yāvataka**, and next.

tāvantaraṃ, or (text in Dbh.g.) **tāvattaraṃ**, adv. (tāva = tāvat plus antara, MIndic cpd.), *for so long* (a time): Mv iii.252.7; Dbh.g. 12(348).18; see s.v. **yāvantara**.

[**tāhi** in LV 232.3 (vs), read (mā) bhāhi, *fear* (*not*), with v.l. and Tib. ḥjigs.]

1 **ti** (= Pali, Pkt. id.), = Skt. iti; see §§ 4.5, 14, 18, 19.

2 **ti-** = Skt. tri-, *three*, initially in cpds.: (read) vicara ti-gatiṣū LV 165.2 (vs); (read) tṛṣṇānadī ti-vegā 372.16 (vs, so most and best mss., referring to 'thirst' for kāma, bhava, vibhava).

[**Tikṣṇa**, Lefm., **Tikṣu**, Foucaux with v.l., wrong readings for **Tiṣya**, q.v. (Tib. ḥod ldan) at LV 172.3. Calc. reads Vikṣu.]

tiṭilambha, nt., a high number: °bhaṃ (= 100 nāgabala) LV 148.3; cited Mvy 7964 as **ṭiṭilam**, but Tib. in both places ṅogs (! regularly = Skt. tīra) ḥthob (= Skt. labh-, lambh-), confirming -lambha as the last part. Cf. also **ṭiṭibha**.

titila, m., *bat* (the animal): Mvy 4913; so acc. to Tib. pha baṅ (lbaṅ).

tipyaka, nt., acc. to Tib. as cited in note sgo bcad, *locked door*, but context suggests rather *bucket* or *container* attached to a rope, with which water is drawn from a well: MSV i.24.14 (a brahman, thinking the Buddha will damage his well, tato rajjuṃ) tipyakaṃ ca gopāyitvā sthitaḥ; 25.1 (inviting Buddha to use the well) iyaṃ rajjur idaṃ tipyakam, gṛhṇātu pānīyaṃ.

(**timiṅgala**, also Skt., Ind. St. 14.106, and Pali id., more usually Skt. °gila, m., *a kind of sea-monster*: Divy 229.22 (so mss., ed. em. °gila); elsewhere, as 232.4, mss. °gila; in 502.19 mss. mostly °gira, cf. next, and **timitimiṅgila**.)

Timiṅgira (cf. prec.), n. of a nāga king: Kv 2.10.

(**timitimiṅgila**, m., cf. prec. two, once in Skt., BR; Pali °gala; *a kind of sea-monster*: Mv i.245.2, 15, 17, etc.; iii.454.3, where if I understand Senart his mss. read timitimi° and he em. to timiṅ° for metrical reasons, an insufficient ground in this instance, meter being bad in any case; Divy 231.16; 239.29; 502.19, here associated with timiṅgila.)

timira, m. (cf. Skt. °ra, nt., *darkness*; *obscuration of vision, an eye-disease*), *veiling illusion*: °ro mṛgatṛṣṇā vā svapno vandhyāprasūyatam Laṅk 9.2 (vs); in prec. line māyā etc.

Timirāpagata, m., n. of a samādhi: Mvy 578; ŚsP 1421.14.

timirīkṛta, ppp. of *timirī- (to Skt. timira)-karoti, *blinded*: °ta-netro Divy 103.14.

Timisikā, n. of a yakṣiṇī: MSV i.17.9. Perh. cf. **timīsaka**.

? **timisrā** (for Skt. tamisrā; cf. Pali timissā, Jāt. iii.433.10), *darkness, gloom*; perh. to be read in Mv i.229.20; 240.10; iii.334.7, instead of tamisrā; cf. next, and s.v. **lokāntarikā**.

? **timisrāyita-tva**, see **tamisr°**; the corrupt mss. on the whole favor tam°, but sometimes (as at Mv iii.334.8) tim°. Cf. prec.

timīsaka, adj. (§ 3.2; cf. AMg. timissa-, °ssā, Skt. tamisra; Pali timisa), *dark*: yathā ca bhavanaṃ mahyaṃ andhakāra-timīsakaṃ (*dark as night*) Mv ii.398.5 = 401.17 (vs); so mss. at 398.5; in 401.17 timāsakaṃ; Senart em. tamisrakaṃ both times.

-tiraka (= Skt. tilaka), *speck, spot*: lipiphalakam ādāya divyārṣa-suvarṇa-tirakaṃ LV 125.17–18 (prose), so Lefm.; the mss. vary, and none has exactly divyārṣa-, but all but one have -tirakaṃ (that one -tilakaṃ); *taking a writing-board with . . . golden* (decorative) *spots* (Foucaux *paillettes, spangles*).

tiraccha, or (?) **tirakṣa** (hyper-Skt.?), adj.-subst. (= Pali id., in °bhūta, *gone astray, going wrong*; cf. next, and **tiriccha**, **°cchāna**, **tirya**; Skt. tiraśc-a, Wackernagel 3.230; § 2.12) *animal* (sub-human): °ccheṣūpapadyante Mv i.31.8 (prose); in 12 below tiriccha; Mv ii.195.2 (vs), read, paśya tirakṣa-(or, as intended by v.l., tiraccha-)-bhūtena karmaṃ upacitaṃ śubhaṃ (Kern, IF. 31.195).

tiracchāna (m.; = Pali id.; cf. Skt. tiraścīna; ā for ī due to some analogy, somehow related to the stem-final of **tiraccha**, q.v. for other forms), *animal* (sub-human): °na-cārikām Mv i.27.2, 4, *journey to the animals* (cf. tiryagyoniṣu 4); °na-yonīyaṃ iii.274.16, see s.v. **tiricchāna**; °na-gata (= Pali id.), *existing in the state of an animal*: °gatām Mv i.17.5 (acc. pl.); °gatāye (v.l. **tiricchāna**- q.v.) iii.153.19.

tiras-, tiraskṛta- (cf. Pali tiro, *outside*, esp. as prior member of cpds.), in comp. with -prātiveśya, taken by Divy Index (and pw) as meaning *near* (neighbor), but rather *outside* (neighbor), (neighbor) *living outside* (one's own house): tiraḥprātiveśya-suhṛt-svajanādibhyo Divy 234.24; tena tiraḥprātiveśyāḥ pṛṣṭāḥ 272.4; tiraskṛta-prātiveśya-sajana-(read -svajana-?)-yuvatyaś 235.19. See also s.v. **tiryak**, where it is suggested that even Skt. tiras may have this mg. in Mārk. Pur. 17.3 (BR s.v. 2a).

tiriccha m. (= AMg. id., *oblique, slanting*, and °cchiya, *animal*; the penultimate i by 'saṃprasāraṇa' from **tirya(k)**, cf. § 3.115; see next, and s.v. **tiraccha**), *animal* (sub-human): naraka-tiriccha-pretāsureṣu kāyeṣu Mv i.31.12 (cf. **tiraccha**, line 8 above); similarly 32.17; eṣo hi mārgo narake tiricche ii.324.10; narakān tiricchāṃ 344.17; nāyaṃ (na te) tiriccho (°cchā) . . . vayaṃ tiricchā Mv i.365.8–9; ii.236.11–12, said in recognition of greater virtue shown by an animal than by human beings.

tiricchāna (m.; nowhere recorded, but cf. prec. and **tiracchāna**), *animal* (sub-human): °na-yonīyaṃ (loc.) Mv ii.350.14 (vs) = iii.274.16 which reads tiracchāna-; kuto imasyā (mss. °sya) tiricchāna-gatāye mṛgīye mānuṣo apatyo Mv iii.144.3 (prose); in similar phrase 153.19 Senart tiracchāna-gatāye mṛgīye, with one ms., v.l. tiricchāna°.

tirīṭī, °ṭi (cf. Skt. tirīṭa, *Symplocos racemosa*; Pali °ṭa, °ṭaka, this tree, also *a garment* made of its bark), *a garment of bark* (of the above tree): °ṭīṃ dhārayitum, tirīṭi iti valkalaḥ MSV ii.94.13; °ṭim ib. 91.17.

tirya, adj. and subst. (= Skt. tiryañc, tiryak, § 15.3, cf. Pali tiriyaṃ, adv., and AMg. tiri, tiriya, adj. and subst. *animal*; spelling tiriya not recorded in BHS but metrically demanded in Mmk 107.27, 28), (**1**) adj. *oblique, transverse*: ākāśagamanaṃ cāpi tiryaṃ cāpi nabhastale Mmk 148.20 (vs; perhaps adv., or adj. with -gamanam understood); (**2**) subst., *animal* (sub-human): tiryāṇa (gen. pl.; separate word) yonīṣu ca so sadā ramī SP 97.2 (vs); tiryāṇa yonīṣu 358.13 (vs); tiryā, n. pl., LV 336.3 (vs); meter seems to demand tiriya, contrary to text, in tiryebhyo dadau vratī Mmk 107.27 and °bhyo tu dattvā vai 28 (vss). Also for the Skt. cpds. tiryag-gata and °gati, tirya- occurs m.c., Samādh 19.17; Suv 48.1; RP 27.10 (text here tīr°); 32.8. The stem tirya has been recorded only in verses.

The AMg. form tiri, with 'saṃprasāraṇa', suggests the origin of the penultimate i of **tiriccha**, °**cchāna**.

tiryak, adv. (used in the sense of Pali tiro, BHS **tiras**, **tiraskṛta**, q.v.; the converse use of Skt. tiras in the sense of tiryak, *crosswise*, is recorded by BR s.v. 2a from lexicons, and once in Mārk. Pur.; but in this one passage it seems to me that tiras may have its Pali mg. of *outside, away, afar*), *outside, away, afar*, in contrast with iha; neha na tiryak nobhayam antarā Śikṣ 252.15, *not here, not afar, not between the two*. (Bendall and Rouse, Transl. 234 line 2, *across*; but this seems manifest nonsense in the context.)

tiryakkāma(-sevin), (one addicted to) *bestiality, sexual love of animals*: °vī Śikṣ 75.17 (punishment for this sin in future lives is described).

tiryagyonika, adj. (also **tairyag**°; cf. Pali tiracchānayonika), *belonging to the animal state of existence*: °kānām (sc. sattvānām) anyonyabhakṣaṇādiduḥkham LV 86.12.

Tiryag-lokadhātu, m. or f., n. of a fabulous lokadhātu where people walk on all fours: Mvy 3070; Tib. thad ka = tiryak (Das).

tilakocavaka, nt., a kind of *arrowhead*: Mvy 6099 (in a list of weapons); acc. to Tib. (mde ḥu zur bzhi pa) and Jap., *an arrowhead with four edges* or *blades*; Chin. *arrowhead with four layers* (?). I see no etymology for the word; Skt. tila plus BHS **kocavaka**, q.v., seems to make no sense.

tiṣṭhatu (3 sg. impv. of sthā; = Pali tiṭṭhatu; so far as I know, not so used in Skt.), *be it so! all right!* as formula of assent: tiṣṭhatu tāva LV 287.19 (vs), in Svastika's response to the Bodhisattva's request for grass; rendered by Tib. freely, khyod bzhes śig, *do you take it!* (qy: did Tib. possibly take tāva as = tava, and understand literally *let it remain yours*?).

tiṣṭhantika, adj. (= pres. pple. tiṣṭhant-; we should expect °ta-ka, but there is no v.l.; -ika is abnormal here; gender is m.), *remaining* (in the world, of Buddhas, contrasting with nirvṛta, *entered into nirvāṇa*): dattā apratimeṣu maitramanasā tiṣṭhantike (so read, both edd. °ti ke) nirvṛte LV 291.14 (vs), *were given with loving heart to the Matchless Ones* (Buddhas), *to* (one) *that was remaining in the world*, (and) *to* (another) *who had entered nirvāṇa*. Cf. Senart, Mv i.568, who reads this word correctly, equating it with tiṣṭhamāno (mahāvīro) i.252.12, but wrongly understands 'nirvṛte; Tib., at least, supports my interpretation: byams paḥi yid kyis do zla med par bzhugs (*remaining*) daṅ (*and*) mya ṅan ḥdas la (= nirvṛta) phul.

tiṣṭha-vākya, adj. (cf. Pali tiṭṭha-bhadantika, *one who says to a guest, 'wait, sir!'*), *one who says* (to a guest) *wait!*: na ca yatra svānu (= Skt. śvā) bhavatī na cāhitaṃ tena (te na?) tiṣṭhavākyasya LV 258,7 (vs). Acc. to Foucaux's Note, p. 161, Tib. (omitted in F.'s ed.) indicates a reading tiṣṭha vā gaccha.

Tiṣya, (**1**) (= Pali Tissa), n. of a former Buddha: Mv iii.240.5; 241.15; 243.12; 244.3; 245.14 f.; 247.8; 248.17; LV 5.10; 172.3 (so read for Lefm. Tikṣṇa, confirmed by Tib. ḥod ldan, as in Mvy 1046 = Tiṣya; divide Tiṣya lohamuṣṭinā); Sukh 6.3; Gv 206.12; (**2**) n. of a future Buddha: Gv 441.25, in a list of them; cf. Pali Tissa, 2 in DPPN, also in such a list, but the lists do not otherwise correspond; (**3**) (= Pali Tissa, in same vs, DN ii.261.13, cf. DPPN Tissa 6) n. of a Mahābrahmā: Mahāsamāj. Waldschmidt Kl. Skt. Texte 4, 191.11; (**4**) (= Pali Tissa, 5 of DPPN) n. of one of the leading disciples (agraśrāvaka) of the Buddha Kāśyapa: Mv i.307.4, 17; (**5**) in a list of cakravarti-rājānaḥ, Mvy 3605 (Tib. rgyal), but the adjoining names are mostly only those of Śākya nobles, contemporaries of the Buddha, incl. even Siddhārtha (!); stands between Nanda and Bhadrika; (**6**) as n. for Śāriputra (otherwise **Upatiṣya**): SP 91.7 (vs); (**7**) n. of a brother of Śāriputra: Mv iii.56.11; (**8**) n. of Śāriputra's father: Av ii.186.6; (**9**) in a list of 'disciples' (śrāvaka): Mvy 1046 (Tib. ḥod ldan); followed immediately by Upatiṣya; Śāriputra is named, 1032, in the same list; various monks of the name Tissa are mentioned in Pali, see DPPN; (**10**) n. of a householder (associated with **Puṣya** 4) of Rauruka; converted by Kātyāyana and attained enlightenment: Divy 551.6 ff.; 571.3, 5; apparently not the same as Pali Tissa, 13 in DPPN, a rājā of Roruva (= Rauruka).

Tiṣyarakṣitā (cf. Pali Tissarakkhā, here Asoka's second wife), n. of the chief queen of Aśoka: out of jealousy she plotted to destroy the bodhi-tree (as in Pali): Divy 397.21 ff.; made advances to Kunāla, and being rebuffed plotted his ruin, 407.5 ff.

tisra-loka, see § 19.8.

Tīkṣṇa, n. of a nāga: Mvy 3314.

[**tīkṣṇaṃ**, in SP 149.2 (sa ca bhagavān . . .) sthitvā tīkṣṇaṃ dharmaṃ deśayiṣyati, read (a)bhīkṣṇaṃ with WT and their ms. K'; so Tib. rtag tu, *constantly*.]

Tīkṣṇagandha, m. pl., n. of a tribe of serpents living in the Saptāśīviṣa rivers: Divy 107.22.

tīkṣṇendriya, adj. (tīkṣṇa-indriya; = Pali tikkhindriya), *of keen senses* or *faculties*: AsP 387.3 (cited s.v. **ātīkṣṇendriya**).

tīmayati (cf. Dhātup. tīm- = Skt. tim-; M. tīmia, ppp.), *makes wet, sprinkles*: sugandhatailena ca vastrāṇi tīmayitvā Divy 285.25.

tīra (m. or nt.), *side* (of a mountain): (parvatasya vaihāyavarasya) uttare ca (so mss., Senart uttarasmi) tīre varapārśve Mv i.70.17 (vs).

tīraṇa (= Pali id.) = **saṃtīraṇa**, q.v.: AbhidhK. LaV-P. i.81.

-tīrīyaka, adj. or subst. (§ 22.20; cf. Pali -tīriya, Vin. ii.287.4), *dwelling* (one who dwells) *on the bank*: samudra-t° Mvy 7149 (Tib. ṅogs na gnas pa, *dwelling on the bank*).

tīrthaka (°ika), see **sama-tīrthika**.

tīrtha-kara (see the foll. items; = Pali titthakara; cf. Skt. tīrthaṃkara, used by Jains of their own sect-founders; in BHS as in Pali always pejorative, of heretics; see however s.v. **tīrthika**), *heretical sectarian, heresiarch, founder of a heresy*: śramaṇa-brāhmaṇa-tīrthakarehi Mv i.234.17; °karā nigṛhītāḥ Av ii.187.3; °karāṇām Laṅk 11.12. All prose.

tīrthika (also **para-t**°; see prec. and next items; prob. Sktized from MIndic (Pali) titthiya, see **tīrthya**; both are very common in prose as well as vss), (**1**) *heretic*; like its relatives, pejoratively used; there is one seeming exception, tīrthikā vā bhavanti bhavasūdanāḥ Mv i.106.8 (vs), where if the text is correct it seems to be said of Bodhisattvas in the 8th bhūmi that they *become religious prophets* (or the like), *destroying* (the states of normal) *existence*. I suspect a corruption, and cannot explain the text as it stands any more than Senart (his doubtful suggestion based on LV Calc. 313.19 falls now with the reading of that text, which in Lefm. 250.1 is replaced by . . . tīrthyāḥ, *heretics*, kurvante). However, it is barely possible that this one Mv passage preserves the original neutral mg., *adherent* (or *founder*) *of* (any) *religion*. A trace of this may also remain in the not infrequent prefixation of anya- to t°, *other* (than Buddhist) *sectarian*, LV 268.12; Mv iii.49.12 (anyatīrthikapūrvo, *formerly a member of another sect*); 412.7; or **para-t**°, q.v.; cf. kutīrthikā(ḥ) LV 12.10, *members of base* (heretical) *sects*. Otherwise, and very often, tīrthika alone means *heretic* simply: SP 272.10; LV 250.21; 258.1; 260.9; Mv i.45.10; 69.17; ii.135.12; iii.392.7 (śramaṇa-brāhmaṇa-tīrthika-gaṇikā, apparently implying that brahmans were not included among tīrthikas; this cpd. appears in some of the other passages listed); Mvy 3514; Divy 146.19; 152.5; 275.9; Av i.2.6; 16.3 etc., common; Bhad 52; Bbh 173.11 etc.;

yat kiṃcit tīrthikaliṅgaṃ . . . LV 409.17; Mv iii.329.11, *whatever* (external) *mark* (dress etc.) *of heretics* (was borne by converts, all magically disappeared and they wore the aspect of Buddhist monks); tīrthikāvakrāntaka, see **avakrāntaka**; (**2**) n. of a nāga: Mvy 3320; (**3**) see s.v. **sama-tīrthika.**

tīrthikara, *heresiarch, founder of a heretical sect*: Śikṣ 317.17 (prose). Prob. a mere error for **tīrthakara**; but cf. **tīrthyakara,** which tīrthi° might represent by 'saṃprasāraṇa'.

tīrthya (= **tīrthika,** q.v.; Pali titthiya), *heretic*: LV 248.14; 250.1; Divy 81.7, 9; 126.18; 127.25 ff.; 143.13 ff., etc.; Av i.112.7, etc.; Dbh 47.3; Laṅk 2.7; 7.16; common in prose as well as vss, tho in most texts less common than tīrthika; para-t° RP 3.16; tīrthyāyatana, see **āyatana** (2). See next.

tīrthyaka, m., = prec.: MSV i.79.17 f.; ii.204.10 (prose).

tīrthya-kara, *founder of a heretical sect*: Mvy 3513; = **tīrthakara,** which one is tempted to read here, but Mironov also °ya; no v.l.; cf. **tīrthikara** which perhaps supports this.

tīvra, adj. (like Pali tibba, hardly Skt., used of religiously and morally good activity), adv. tīvraṃ, *zealously*: mātāpitṝṣu vīro upasthapetvā tīvraṃ paricarati Mv ii.220.18 (vs), *zealously waited upon* (his parents).

tu, *but*, recorded at the beginning of a sentence: tu tava vijite catvāraḥ prāṇinaḥ . . . MSV iii.130.1. Unless some word has been lost or transposed, no other interpretation seems possible.

tucchaka, adj. (Skt. Lex. and Pali id., acc. to PTSD 'always with rittaka' = BHS riktaka; = Skt. tuccha, with -ka, prob. pejorative), *empty, vain*, only with **riktaka** and **asāraka,** see under the latter; Mv ii.145.19; AsP 346.10.

[**tujyo** Mv iii.74.2, presumably taken by Senart as 2 pers. pron., tho his Notes and Index ignore the form; read (ca-)turyo, see s.v. **caturya.**]

tuṇa (m. or nt.; cf. **tūṇa, tuṇava**; AMg. tuṇā [tuṇa?], an unidentified mus. instrument), some musical instrument: in lists, tuṇa-paṇava-mṛdaṅgāṃ LV 80.5; tuṇaveṇu-(text vaiṇu-)-ravaiḥ 173.9; tuṇa-vīṇā-sughoṣakādibhiḥ 177.14. Tib. confused; it may intend this word by rgyud gcig (pa) in the first two (see under **tuṇava**), but if so the order varies from our text; on 177.14 this Tib. word does not occur, and tuṇa may be gliṅ bu (otherwise = veṇu or vaṃśa), altho the order suggests sgra sñan, but this elsewhere = sughoṣaka. In spite of Tib., which suggests a stringed (or in 177.14 a wind?) instrument, perhaps really a kind of *drum*.

tuṇatuṇāyati (cf. prec.?), onomat., used of the sound made by the kokila: kokilā °yanti Mv iii.256.2 (v.l. bhuṇabhuṇā°).

tuṇava, m. (? cf. Skt. tūṇava, acc. to BR a wooden wind instrument, perhaps *flute*; Pali tiṇava, AN ii.117.6, acc. to comm. iii.121.15 = deṇḍimo or diṇḍ°, a kind of drum; see **tuṇa, tūṇa**), some musical instrument, possibly a kind of *drum*; but acc. to regular Tib. renderings a one-stringed instrument of the vīṇā type: °vaḥ Mvy 5015 = Tib. pi waṅ (= vīṇā) rgyud gcig pa (*one-stringed*); on LV and SP Tib. regularly rgyud gcig (pa); in lists, -paṇava-tuṇava-vīṇā- LV 163.6 (here om. in Tib.); tuṇava-paṇava-vīṇā-veṇu- 212.3; -paṭaha-tuṇava-(so mss., except one tuna-paṇava-; Lefm. tūṇava-)-vīṇā- 301.15; in SP 51.13 read tuṇavā(ḥ) with Kashgar rec., WT, and Tib. rgyud gcig, for KN praṇadā.

tuṇḍa (m. or nt.; in Skt. *beak, snout*, of birds and animals, only contemptuously of men; so Pali tuṇḍa and °ḍaka; cf. next), (**1**) *face* (?), of men, as a part shaven: śiras-tuṇḍa-muṇḍa Śikṣ 59.17 and 68.2 (Transl. once *cheek*, once *chin*), of monks, *shaven of head and face*; śiras-tuṇḍa-muṇḍana Bbh 194.5; (**2**) in **Vajra-tuṇḍī,** Bhvr. cpd., q.v., Hoernle assumes tuṇḍa, *navel* (cf. Skt. Lex. tuṇḍi, tuṇḍikā, tunda, late Skt. tundikā, Schmidt, Nachträge); (**3**) in tuṇḍa-bandham Mmk 110.9, uncertain, possibly (*binding of the*) *belly*? (Skt. tunda, *pot-belly*; AMg. tunda, *belly*); but possibly *face*, as in (1), or *mouth*; (**4**) *trunk* of an elephant: na hasti-tuṇḍāvalambitam Mvy 8528.

tuṇḍaka (m. or nt.; = Pali id., Skt. tuṇḍa; see under prec.), (**1**) *muzzle*, of a dog: mukha-tu° Karmav 28.23; (**2**) *face* or *mouth*, of a man, not contemptuously: (pādayor) nipatito (400.18 patito) mukha-tuṇḍakena ca pādāv anuparimārjya Divy 387.7; 400.18, said of King Aśoka, paying his respects to holy men.

Tuṇḍaturika, n. of a mountain (where **Pūrṇa** 1 stayed): °kāto parvatāto Mv i.245.11 (prose, no v.l.).

tuṇḍi-cela, nt. (with this mg. of tuṇḍi, *excellent*, related to **tuṇḍa,** q.v., cf. Skt. mukha in same mg.; Pkt. tuṇḍa = agra-bhāga, Sheth), *a fine garment*: Mvy 5884 = Chin. *beautiful garment*; Tib. bzhag (gzhag) gos, which I cannot interpret thus, but the Chin. is confirmed by the surrounding words (5883 kalpaduṣyam) and by Divy 221.19 (kalpadūṣyavṛkṣaiś caturvidhāni) tuṇḍicelāni (this om. in mss.) tais tuṇḍicelaiś caturvidhāni kalpadūṣyāṇi.

tudana- or °**nā-** (n. act. to tudati plus -ana), *piercing*: śalyavat tudanātmakaḥ (kāyaḥ) Śikṣ 231.2.

tumbaka (m. or nt.; in Skt. *a gourd*), acc. to Tib. *lamp-oil vessel* (among monks' belongings): MSV iv.107.12.

Tumburu (in Skt. n. of a gandharva), n. of a yakṣa, brother of the four **Kumārī,** q.v., or **Bhaginī**: Mmk 523.11 (read Tumburoḥ); 534.1; 575.10; called a sārthavāha and karṇadhāra, 537.2; 538.1; et alibi in Mmk.

turiya (nt. or m.; = Pali id., MIndic for Skt. tūrya), *musical instrument*; common in vss of LV, e.g. 54.6 (v.l. tūry°); 161.17 (v.l. tūry°); 164.20; 169.22; sometimes turiya and tūrya in the same sentence, LV 175.15 and 16 (no v.l.). But in Mv iii.122.16 (vs) turiya is Senart's em., mss. tūrya (which is metrically inferior).

[**tula,** see **atula.**]

tulaka, m., apparently *counsellor* (of a king), or the like: Divy 212.9 rājño . . . amātyāś cintakās tulakā upaparīkṣakāś . . .; 212.11; cf. **tulanā.**

Tulakuci, m., n. of an ancestor of Aśoka: °cī, n. sg., and °ceḥ, gen., Divy 369.11 (prose).

tulana, nt., a high number: Mvy 7725; 7851 (cited from Gv); Gv 105.24. In Gv 133.7 **ulana,** q.v.

tulanā (= Pali id.; in this mg. Skt. only tulana, nt.), *weighing* (mentally), *consideration*: Mvy 6472; Bbh 193.26 (foll. in comp. by **upaparīkṣaṇā**); ŚsP 615.11 (foll. in comp. by **vyupaparīkṣaṇatā**).

tulākūṭa, (m. or nt.; = Pali id.), *cheating in weights*: Śikṣ 269.2 na °ṭena; as Bhvr., *one who cheats in weights*, Bbh 29.1 (**kāṃsakūṭa-,** q.v.)-tulākūṭādibhiḥ; SP 402.10 (vs) yā gatis tulakūṭānāṃ (ă m.c.)

tulya, adj., used in a peculiar sense in SP, and as I think misunderstood by Burnouf and Kern: *equal* in the sense of *equally available, open to choice* (said of different forms of dharma, *religion*, and specifically thinking of the three yānas): tulye (so with Kashgar rec., text tulya-) nāma dharmadhātupraveśe SP 60.8 (prose), *when entrance into the sphere of religion is, after all* (nāma), *alike* (all the same, open to free choice); the sequel complains that the speaker has been given only the hīna yāna by the Buddha; tulyeṣu dharmeṣu SP 61.12; 62.2 (both vss). Chinese versions confirm this interpretation.

Tuṣita (= Pali Tusita; see **deva**), n. of a class of **kāmāvacara** gods: Mvy 3081; Dharmas 127; sg. Divy 140.14; tuṣitakāyiko devaputro Mv iii.345.16; same, sg. or pl., LV 124.12; 183.17; 363.21; tuṣitabhavanakāyiko devaputro Mv i.174.1; tuṣitavarabhavana- LV 4.18–19; 7.21; tuṣitālaya LV 411.20; °te devanikāye Divy 83.2;

Bbh 271.2 f.; usually pl. with, or sc., pl. of deva, often in lists of classes of gods, Mv i.212.15; 229.15; ii.16.4; LV 46.20; 150.3; 219.8; 396.15; 401.10; Divy 68.13; 140.13; 195.22; 367.10; Av i.5.1 etc.; Suv 86.10; Mmk 19.12; et passim, common everywhere. Their chief is **Saṃtuṣita,** q.v.; in Divy 140.14, by exception (just like **Yāma,** q.v.), Tuṣita (n. of the class in the sg.) is their chief.

tūṇa, and **tūṇaka** (m. or nt.; cf. **tuṇa,** and AMg. tūṇaya), a musical instrument, perhaps *a kind of drum* (= **tuṇa**?): tūṇa- (Senart em. tūṇava-)-paṇava-vīṇā- (so read; Senart veṇu-) Mv iii.113.5; kācit (of the harem-women) tūṇakaṃ Mv ii.159.5; in same scene iii.407.18 kāci tūṇaṃ; in these passages little evidence as to the nature of the instrument; cf. **kumbhatūṇa,** apparently also a kind of *drum.*

[**tūrṇa,** (m. or) nt., a high number: Gv 105.26, read **vitūrṇa,** q.v., with 133.9.]

Tūryaghoṣa, n. of a former Buddha: Sukh 5.14.

tūla, (**1**) m. or nt. (cf. Skt. tūlikā, and Lex. tūli, tuli, f., *paintbrush*), *an instrument for writing* (Index *pencil*): (rātrau pradīpena Buddhavacanaṃ paṭhanti, atra bhūrjena prayojanaṃ) tailena masinā kalamayā tūlena (mss. bhū°) Divy 532.11; (**2**) some musical instrument, prob. = tūra (late and Lex. Skt., Schmidt, Nachträge; also AMg.; cf. Skt. tūrya), which should perhaps be read: vallaki-tūlāṃ Mv iii.82.5 (vs, in list of mus. instruments; prob. acc. pl., rather than acc. sg. f.).

tūla-picu (m.; same cpd. Pali and Skt. Lex.), *cotton* (in some form; symbol of lightness): AsP 286.5 (sa punar evotkṣipyate 'vasīdati tasya) calācalā buddhir bhavati, tūlapicūpamaś ca sa bhavati; Divy 210.14 and 388.14 mṛduḥ sumṛdus tad yathā tūlapicur vā **karpāsapicur** (q.v.) vā.

tūli or **tūlī** (cf. Skt. and Pali tūla; Skt. Lex. tūli, tūlī, *paintbrush*), *tuft* (of grass): tṛṇasya tūli (acc. sg.; m.c.) LV 75.1 (vs).

tūṣṇī, tūṣṇīm, indeclinable (Skt. tūṣṇīm only, even in comp., except once Lex. tūṣṇī-śīla; but Pali tuṇhī, lacking nasal, as separate word, and in tuṇhī-bhāva, -bhūta), as adv., *in silence, silently*: °ṇīṃ ca so āsi SP 191.4 (vs); °ṇī pavane vaseyaṃ LV 393.2 (vs); °ṇī vyavasthitaḥ Divy 7.17 f.; 8.16 f.; adhivāsya bhagavāṃs tūṣṇī . . . vyavasthitaḥ Laṅk 6.15 (vs); in Divy and Av often in lieu of tūṣṇīṃbabhūva, *fell silent,* no verb form being expressed; esp. in the formula . . . kathayā saṃdarśya samādāpya samuttejya saṃpraharṣya tūṣṇīm Divy 80.20; 89.11; 91.18; 189.8; 283.13; 310.6; 506.15, et alibi; Av i.63.9; 290.9; ii.89.11; also, āyusmān Ānandas tūṣṇīm Divy 201.12, 20–21; evam ukte Rāṣṭrapālo gṛhapatiputras tūṣṇīm Av ii.119.13; tūṣṇībhāva (= Pali tuṇhī°), *silence,* SP 167.9; LV 6.2, 3, 20; 392.19; 394.20 (vs, °ṣṇi° m.c.); 416.13; Mv iii.255.4; 257.2, 3 (in 3 °ṇīṃ° but v.l. °ṇī°); 271.17; Divy 20.1; tūṣṇībhūto (= Pali tuṇhī°) Mv iii.314.7; °bhutāḥ (m.c.) LV 421.17 (vs).

tūṣṇīka-śobhana, adj., *having the glory of a silent ascetic* (Skt. tūṣṇīka, *silent*; AMg. tuṇhikka, *one engaging in a vow of silence*), epithet of pratyekabuddhas: Mv i.301.3 (misprinted tuṣ°), 14 (here v.l. uṣṇīṣa-śo°, but context indicates that the *silence* of the pratyekabuddha is the significant thing); iii.414.3.

tūṣṇī-bhāva, -bhūta, tūṣṇīm, see **tūṣṇī.**

tṛṃhaṇa(-tā), (Skt. Gr., n. act. from the Vedic and Gr. root tṛh), *crushing*: vātamaṇḍalībhūtaṃ sarvāvaraṇa-nivaraṇa-tṛṃhaṇa-tayā Gv 495.22–23, *it is like a whirlwind, because it crushes all obstructions and hindrances.* But Śikṣ 6.6, citing this passage, reads °tṛṇa-vikiraṇatayā, *scattering like grass,* for °tṛṃh°.

tṛṇa-kuñcaka, nt., a kind of gem: Mvy 5972 = Tib. sbur len (or loṅ), acc. to Jä. = *amber,* but given in Mvy 5970 as translation of puṣparāga, *topaz.*

tṛṇa-prastāraka, m., sc. vinaya, or in MSV nt. with karman (= Pali tiṇavatthāraka, see Childers and PTSD s.v.), (procedure) *which covers over* (as if) *with grass,* one of the 7 **adhikaraṇa-śamatha**: Mvy 8636 = Tib. rtsva bkram pa (*strewn grass*) lta bur (*like*) ḥos pa (*suitable, fit*); MSV ii.207.13.

tṛtiya, adj. (= Pali tatiya, Skt. tṛtīya), *third*; rare and only m.c. in BHS: SP 92.7; LV 111.11; by em. (mss. tṛtī°), m.c., SP 46.11; Mv i.174.16; in Gv 256.7 text tṛtī°, should be tṛti° m.c. All vss. Cf. s.v. **dvitiya.**

tṛtīyakam, adv. (= Pali tatiyakaṃ, Skt. tṛtīyam; see also **traitīyakam**), *for the third time*: SP 315.4, 9, 11; Mv i.347.2 ff.; iii.49.2, 7, 9; 189.8; AsP 182.13. All prose.

tṛdhā (hyper-Skt. for tridhā, which occurs SP 55.10), so all Nep. mss., or tṛvidham, Kashgar rec., *in three ways*: SP 56.1 (vs).

Tṛptavasantagandha, n. of a former Buddha: Mv i.137.13.

tṛptitā (= Skt. tṛpti), *satiation*: na strīkāmaguṇebhi tṛptitāṃ LV 324.1 (vs).

tṛbhava, hyper-Skt. for **tri-bhava,** q.v.: Gv 483.16.

[**tṛmuṇḍīkṛtā,** read **tripuṇḍī**°: Mmk 40.9.]

tṛvidha, for Skt. trividha, see **tṛdhā.**

tṛṣ- = **triṣ-(kṛtvas).**

Tṛṣṇā (= Pali Taṇhā), (**1**) n. of a daughter of Māra: LV 378.4; cf. **Tantrī**; (**2**) = Skt., *craving*; as with Pali taṇhā, three in Buddhism, kāma-, bhava-, **vibhava-** (2): AbhidhK. LaV-P. v. 29.

tṛṣṇī (unrecorded) = tṛṣṇā, *thirst, longing*: tṛṣṇī-latā vichinnā LV 376.14 (vs); so Lefm. with best ms.; vv.ll. tṛṣṇā and dṛṣṭī (the latter clearly a rationalizing 'correction' of tṛṣṇī); tṛṣṇīyāḥ kāraṇābhiniveśaś ca Laṅk 179.3 (prose; no v.l.; Suzuki Transl. and Index em. tṛṣṇā). Cf. also **Tantrī,** perhaps pointing to an original Tṛṣṇī.

Tejagupta, n. of a former Buddha: Mv i.139.13 (prose).

Tejaguptarājan, n. of a former Buddha: Mv i.141.16 (prose).

Tejavativegaprabha, n. of a Buddha: Gv 285.18 (vs).

Tejaśiri (m.c. for Tejaḥśrī), n. of a Buddha: Gv 257.12 (vs).

tejita, ppp. (could formally belong to tejayati, caus. of tij-, but prob. really denom. to tejas, with which it seems to be usually associated), *illumined*: śatapuṇyatejas-tejitaṃ LV 101.7–8 (prose); puṇyatejastejitasya LV 9.13 (prose); puṇyatejitaḥ LV 211.5 (vs); puṇyatejena tejito Mv ii.367.11 (vs).

Tejeśvara, n. of a former Buddha: Samādh p. 57 line 3.

tejo-dhātu, *the element* (see **dhātu** 1) *fire*: as purifier of bodily impurities, Mv i.357.16 f. and LV 18.22 ff., Pratyekabuddhas in gaining nirvāṇa *attain the element fire* (tejodhātuṃ samāpadyitvā, LV samāpadya), and by this (svakāye tejodhātūye, Mv) their 'flesh and blood' (Mv) or these and other bodily substances, incl. pitta, śleṣman, asthi, snāyu (LV), are burnt up, whereupon their purified bodies fall to earth; as source of supernatural power in a religious person possessing it, Mv i.232.(5–)6 (meghasya) māṇavakasya tejodhātubhāvena, *by reason of the state of fire*(-element) *possessed by the Brahman youth Megha* (no reason to suspect corruption with Senart); Svāgata was declared preëminent among those *attaining the fire-element,* tejodhātuṃ samāpadyamānānāṃ Divy 186.20–21 (cf. above).

Tejo'dhipati, n. of a prince: Gv 399.18 etc.; 428.5.

Tejorāśi, n. of one of the 8 Uṣṇīṣa-rājānaḥ (see **uṣṇīṣa** 3): Mmk 41.11.

Tejovatī, (**1**) n. of a samādhi: Mvy 549; ŚsP 1418.17; (**2**) n. of a dhāraṇī: Gv 66.16.

tena, *there*; see **yena.**

tela, m., a high number: Mvy 7761 = Tib. ñar ñer,

which also renders **bhelu**; cf. next, which occurs, however, in the same context with bhelā.

telā, a high number: Gv 106.9. Cf. prec., and **bhelā**, which occurs in the same context with this. There are three sets of numbers in -el- preceded by various consonants; in one set the stem-vowel a is added, in another ā, in another u. The t- and bh-forms of Mvy seem duplications of each other, but both appear in one Gv version (106.9 and 11), viz. the one ending in ā.

? **teṣā**, acc. to Susa semi-MIndic for tṛṣṇā, *thirst*: Dbh.g. 28(54).3, 11, teṣu in text, v.l. tṛṣṇā in 3, teṣa in 11. Cf. AMg. tisā, from Skt. tṛṣā (equivalent to, but not identical with, tṛṣṇā); teṣa (better than teṣu) might possibly be a curious substitute for that AMg. form, with a for ā and e for i m.c., cf. § 3.60.

tairthika, adj. (from tīrtha-, in **tīrtha-kara**, etc.), *heretical*: °ka-dṛṣṭi- Kv 29.21.

tairyagyonika, adj. (Skt. °yona) = **tiryag°**, q.v.: °ka-yāmalaukikād duḥkhaskandhād Śikṣ 29.12; °kaṃ pretalaukikaṃ Bbh 245.2; °kaḥ yāmalaukikaḥ 295.23; °kāni duḥkhāni Gv 376.4.

taila-kuṇḍikā (v.l. tela°), some kind of bird (in a list of birds): Mv ii.475.13 (prose). Seems to mean lit. *little oil-jar* (from its shape?); no record found elsewhere.

taila-pācikam, adv., in °kaṃ vā kriyamāṇasya Śikṣ 182.1, in a list of tortures, looks etymologically as if it might mean (*or of one being made to be*) *boiled in oil*, but acc. to note in ed., Chin. *making mincemeat of one* (perhaps °ka is the name of some dish, of chopped meat fried in oil?). Cf. next.

taila-pradyotikam, adv., °kaṃ vā dīpyamānasya, Śikṣ 182.2, in the same list of tortures as prec. (*of one being set on fire*) *with oil lamps* (?*like an oil lamp*?).

toṭaka, m. or nt., n. of a meter: °ka-vṛttena Laṅk 4.5, referring to the preceding three vss, the pāda scheme of which seems to be — — ⏑ — ⏑ ⏑ ⏑ — ⏑ ⏑ ×, which is inconsistent with Piṅgala's scheme of the toṭaka, ISt. 8.378 f., ⏑ ⏑ — ⏑ ⏑ — ⏑ ⏑ — ⏑ ⏑ —.

Toṇehāra, or **°hāraka**, see s.v. **Ujjhebhaka**.

Todeya, v.l. for **Tau°**, q.v.

Tomara (mss. sometimes Tomala), n. of a Licchavi leader: Mv i.254.13 ff.; 288.6. Probably a family or gotra name, since the person uses the pl. Tomarāṇām (of whom he is one) in 256.3.

tomara-graha, m., *the art of wielding a lance*: °haḥ Mvy 4984; °he, in lists of martial arts: Divy 58.25; 100.11.

Toyikā (from Skt. toya?), n. of a town: Divy 76.11 f.; 465.11 f. = MSV i.73.17 f.; °kā-mahaḥ, established by King Prasenajit, MSV ii.143.16 ff.

Toragrīva, n. of a cakravartin: Mv i.154.1.

toraṇā, f. (= Skt. toraṇa), *portal, arched gateway*: °ṇāye (gen.) karkaṭakasmiṃ Mv iii.178.16 (see **karkaṭaka**).

toṣaṇā (only nt. Skt. °ṇa, Pali tosana), *gratification*: āvarjana-toṣaṇā-vismāpanā Bbh 140.27.

toṣaṇīya, adj., *satisfying, pleasing*: LV 411.8 (śabdāḥ, *words, sounds*); adv. °yaṃ, (mahāpṛthivī . . .) °yaṃ ca kampayati Mv iii.341.7. Both prose.

Tosala, nt., n. of a city in the country of **Amitatosala**, q.v.: Gv 179.3. Cf. Tosala as n. of a people, Kirfel 76, and AVPariś. 56.1.4.

Taudeya (v.l. To°) = Pali Todeyya, n. of the father of Śuka (Pali Subha): Karmav 21.15 etc.; see Lévi's note ad loc. and DPPN s.v. Subha.

Tyāgagatā, n. of a nāga maid: Kv 4.6.

Tyāgavant, n. of a cakravartin: Mv i.154.2.

Trapu-karṇin, nickname of a brother of Pūrṇa, lit. *tin-ear* (because he wore a tin ear-ornament): Divy 26.29; 45.17 etc. Similarly **Dāru-k°**, **Stava-k°**.

Trapuṣa (var. °sa; = Pali Tapussa, Tapassu), and **Bhallika**, q.v., names of two merchants (in Pali brothers) who visited Buddha soon after his enlightenment: LV 381.4 ff.; Mv iii.303.4 ff. (here regularly written °sa, but °ṣa 304.2); Divy 393.19.

tramidā (v.l. °rā), sc. lipi, *Dravidian writing*: Mv i.135.7. In LV parallel **drāviḍa-lipi**, q.v., v.l. drāmida (dental d).

traya-tiṃśad (-bhavanaṃ), in LV 61.16 (prose), = next; only v.l. cited is trāya°; it seems questionable whether the MIndicism ti- for tri- was orig. found here in prose, perhaps read °triṃś° with Calc.

trayastriṃśa (cf. prec.) = **trāy°**, q.v., in lists of Buddhist classes of gods: Mv iii.223.9 (prose, no v.l.); Divy 68.12 (prose); 138.19; 367.10; 568.24; Av 1.5.1 (prose); Suv 86.9 (prose).

trasa-cchidra (m. or nt.), *drain*: MSV iv.234.8 (Tib. stor khuṅ = **udaka-bhrama**). Is trasa corrupt?

trāyaṇa (nt.; to trāyati plus suffix -ana; also **tāyaṇa, °na**, q.v.), (act of) *saving*: saṃbhūta sarva-jaga-trāyaṇa-saṃgrahāya Gv 212.24 (vs).

trāya-triṃśa (alone, or with -kāyika; semi-MIndic, cf. Pali tāvatiṃsa), = more usual **trāyas-tri°**, q.v., a class of gods; this form seems to occur only in LV (cf. also **traya-tiṃśad**), but is fairly common there in ed. and mss. (with vv.ll. trāyas-t°): LV 150.2; 225.17; 366.9; 396.14; 401.9; °śa-kāyika, 365.8 (v.l. traya-); of these, stem-final t only in 225.17, where most mss. trāyas°.

trāyastriṃśa (cf. Pali tāvatiṃsa, prec., and **trayas-tri°**), adj. with **deva** (q.v.) or subst., n. of a class of Buddhist gods: Mv i.31.16 ff.; 40.15; 212.15 = ii.16.4; i.229.15; 262.1; 333.5; ii.163.11; 314.5; °śa- (v.l. °śe) bhavane Mv iii.302.8; °śe devanikāye iii,302.15; °śāḥ Mvy 3079; Dharmas 127. In other texts than LV, Mv, the form trayas° seems more usual, while in LV **trāya-t°** seems regular.

trāyastriṃśaka, adj., belonging to the class of the **trāyastriṃsa**, q.v.: nāmatidevo (q.v.) nāma °śako bodhisattvo bhūto Mv i.98.1 (prose).

[**trāyin**, reported once at end of cpd. in Skt., pw 3.263, *protector*; given as var. for **tāyin**, q.v., in Mvy 15, but Mironov tāyī without v.l.]

Trikaṇṭhaka, Māy 273.3, or **°kin**, Mahāsamāj. Waldschmidt, Kl. Skt. Texte 4,175.3, n. of a yakṣa or gandharva.

Trikātyāyanī, n. of the gotra of the nakṣatra Śravaṇa: Divy 640.26.

tri-koṭi (f.), *the three 'alternatives'* (as in Skt., BR s.v. koṭi, 3) or *classes* (so Tib., rnam, Śikṣ 135 n. 2) or *ways* in which animals may have been killed, so that their flesh may be lawfully eaten (acc. to some): Laṅk 257.12–13 (cited Śikṣ 132.14–15) trikoṭi-śuddha- (v.l. °dhaṃ; Śikṣ kṣuddhaṃ!) māṃsaṃ vai akalpitam (*not intended*) ayācitam (*not asked for*), acoditaṃ (*not instigated*) ca naivāsti tasmān māṃsaṃ na bhakṣayet; acc. to gloss cited Śikṣ 135 note 2, the three (supposedly) unlawful kinds of killing are tad uddiśya hatam (*killed specifically for this meal*), svahatam, and hanyamānaṃ dṛṣṭam (*seen by the prospective eater as it was being killed*); Śikṣ 135.2 trikoṭi-pariśuddha-bhakṣaṇe, *in the eating of what is pure in respect to the three points*; Laṅk 255.2 (cited Śikṣ 135.6) trikoṭiṃ baddhvā, *restraining, suppressing* (ruling out) *the three points*.

tri-kṣutto, -khattuṃ, -khuttaṃ, etc., = Skt. -kṛtvas; see the second elements, listed s.v. **-kṛtvā**. Cf. also **triṣ-kṛtvas**.

Trigupta, n. of a yakṣa: Māy 34.

tri-cīvara, nt. (= Pali ti°), *the three garments* of a Buddhist monk: °raṃ Mv i.168.17 (vs); see s.v. **saṃghāṭī**.

Trijaṭā, n. of a nāga maid: Kv 3.23.

[**trita-** in LV 96.4 (prose), is an impossible em. by Lefm. The mss. vary greatly and the true reading is uncertain; probably tri-viṣyandāmbukūpāḥ.]

tri-daṇḍaka, nt., ? MSV ii.120.6 and (°ke bhāṣyamāṇe) 7 (after the death of a monk); the latter seems to suggest the figurative use of tridaṇḍa in Manu 12.11, meaning *triple self-control*, in word, thought, and act; MSV iv.80.5.

Trinayana, m., n. of a region (janapada; in the south): Gv 126.26.

tri-nidāna (this category not found recorded elsewhere), *the three motives* (see **nidāna** 2) of worldly creatures, viz. rāga, dveṣa, moha: rāgadveṣamohatriṇidānānugatā (so, with ṇ, text!) vateme sattvā(ḥ) Dbh 28.4; trinidānasattva Dbh.g. 7(343).17.

tri-parivarta, see **parivarta** 1.

tri-piṭa, (**1**) m., °ṭā, f. (in Pali tipeṭaka, °kin, tepiṭaka), (a monk or nun) *who knows the three piṭakas*: m. Divy 261.10, 22; 329.2, 6; 505.2; Av i.334.19 f.; f. Divy 4.938; (**2**) given as name to a son of King Prasenajit who was thus gifted miraculously at birth: Av ii.78.1; 79.4 ff.

tri-piṭaka, (**1**) nt. (= Pali id.), *the 'three baskets'*, the Buddhist canon: Mvy 1411; (**2**) m., = **tripiṭa** (**1**): Divy 54.15.

-tri-puṇḍarī-kṛta, Mmk 44.13, or -tri-puṇḍī-kṛta, 40.9, ppp. (to Skt. tri-puṇḍra, JM. tipuṇḍa, with karoti; both semi-MIndic forms), *having the triple puṇḍra-mark* (made with ashes; both cpd. with bhasma-); text in 40.9 printed tṛ-muṇḍī°.

Tripura, n. of a locality: Māy 88 (app. not the same as Skt. Tripurī which occurs Māy 50).

tri-puṣkara, m. or nt., app. *a kind of drum* (*'having a triple drum-skin'*): paṭaha-°ra-nināda-saṃgītiṃ Mv ii.201.20 (vs); (-ghoṣā) tri°ra-sphoṭika-sāryamāṇāḥ (? mss. °āryamāṇāḥ, āryanāmā) Mv iii.58.4 (vs), (if the em. is right, perh. *sounds*) *being emitted with rattle* (? **sphoṭika**) *of drums*; or is **sphoṭika** (unrecorded) another musical instrument?

tri-pradakṣiṇīkṛtya, ger. (tri- plus Skt. prad°; oftener triḥ prad°, which is normal Skt.), *having passed around thrice keeping on the right*: Mvy 6275 (v.l. triḥ, so Mironov without v.l.); Av i.321.3 (mss., ed. em. triḥ); LV 68.1 and 69.14 (all mss.); also °ṇī-kṛtvā LV 253.21 (prose).

? **triphala** (m. or nt.), in °la-vāhakā dārakāḥ LV 132.18 (prose), form uncertain (vv.ll. triphara, trisphara, tisthara; Calc. tila); acc. to Tib. khriḥu, *a small stool or chair, seat*; Foucaux's Note 126 suggests reading tri(s)paᴚa (Skt. tripadikā is recorded as *tripod* in a lexical citation, BR, and tripāda allegedly in Kauś. but not in 26.41 as BR state).

Triphalin, n. of a yakṣa or gandharva: Māy 237.3; Mahāsamāj. Waldschmidt, Kl. Skt. Texte 4,175.3.

tri-bhava (= Pali tibhava, nt., see Childers), *the triple states of existence* (kāma, rūpa, and arūpa): yadi sarvabhayaṃ tribhave na bhavet Mv ii.149.17 (vs); sarvasattvān . . . tribhave vilagnān SP 128.1 (vs); tribhaveśvaraḥ (= the Buddha) Laṅk 6.9 (vs); (see s.v. **vartmiya**) Mmk 26.22. See also **tṛbhava**.

Trimaṅgala, n. of a former Buddha: Mv i.138.14.

tri-maṇḍala (nt.; not noted in Pali in these senses), lit. *the three circles* or *spheres*: (**1**) of giving, viz. the giver, recipient, and act of giving; all must be 'pure', i. e. unselfish: (dānasya) dāyakasya pratigrāhakasya trimaṇḍalapariśuddhyā dānapāramitā paripūritā bhavati ŚsP 92.15; °la-pariśuddham Mvy 2537 = Tib. ḥkhor gsum (see Das s.v.) yoṅs su dag pa; trimaṇḍala-pariśodhanadāna-parityāgī LV 181.8 (said of Buddha); dadato dattvā ca trimaṇḍala-pariśodhitaṃ dānaprāmodyam Śikṣ 183.11; (**2**) tri-maṇḍalaṃ kṛtvā pūrvaṃ śāstuḥ praṇāmaṃ kārayitvā . . . śaraṇagamana-śikṣāpadāni dadāti Bhīk 9a.4, here prob. *threefold sacred plot of ground* (for the rite), see **maṇḍala** (1), **maṇḍalaka** (3). In Laṅk 35.5 trimaṇḍala-padam a-trimaṇḍalapadaṃ, formulaic, no context; precise mg. obscure.

triyadhva-, only in vss for **tryadhva(n)**, *of present, past, and future* (cf. **adhvan**): °dhva-cittaṃ jānituṃ Mv ii.368.8 (vs), *to know all thoughts, present, past, and future*; °dhva-jinānām Gv 230.15 (Buddhas); dharmaśarīru mamādhiviśuddhaṃ (read mamāti° with 2d ed.) sarvatriyadhva-samanta-sthitābham Gv 231.9 (vs); others, LV 151.12; Bhad 1, 29, 31, 41, 56, etc. In triyadhuvā Dbh.g. 51(77).8 the epenthetic u (§ 3.114) actually spoils the meter! See next two.

Triyadhvapratibhāsaprabha, n. of a Buddha: Gv 285.12 (vs).

Triyadhvaprabhaghoṣa, n. of a Buddha: Gv 256.11 (vs).

triy-antara, f. °**rā**, *one among three* (? so Senart doubtfully): tasya dāni śreṣṭhisya triyantarā (*with two others*?) dārikā jātā Mv iii.389.17 (prose).

tri-yāna, nt., *the triple vehicle*: °nam ekayānaṃ ca Laṅk 155.14 (see **yāna**).

tri-ratna, nt. (= **ratna-traya**, q.v., and see **ratna** 1), *the 'three jewels'*: °nāt AsP 179.20 et alibi.

tri-śakunīya, nt., adj.-subst., (jātaka) *relating to three birds*: °yaṃ nāma jātakaṃ Mv i.282.13 (colophon to the story).

Triśaṅku, (**1**) m., n. of a mountain: Divy 106.17, 18, 20, 24; MSV i.30.12; °**kuka**, id., MSV i.40.8; (**2**) f., n. of a river associated with 1: Divy 103.1; 106.20, and °**kukā** 24; (**3**) m. pl., n. of thorns (kaṇṭakās) growing on 1: Divy 106.18, 20; (**4**) m., n. of a mātaṅga chief: Divy 619.19 ff.; MSV i.109.13 ff. (different story).

Triśaṅkuka, °**kā**, see **Triśaṅku** 1, 2.

Triśatikāprajñāpāramitā, n. of a work: Mvy 1374.

Triśīrṣa, n. of a nāga king: Megh 308.7; = next.

Triśīrṣaka, = prec.: Megh 302.11.

tri-śukla(-bhojin), (eating) *the three pure substances*? or *what is triply pure*?: . . . japet triśuklabhojī, kṣīrāhāro vā Mmk 106.4. I have found no clue to the seemingly technical mg. There seems to be no reason to connect the word with Skt. triśukra (pw).

Triśūla, n. of a rākṣasa king: Mmk 18.2.

Triśūlapāṇi, n. of a yakṣa: Māy 88. Cf. **Triśūlin.**

Triśūlapāṇī, n. of a rākṣasī: Māy 243.32.

Triśūlin, n. of a yakṣa (or gandharva?): Māy 237.4. Cf. prec. but one.

triṣkarma, (nt.) *triple activity*, i. e., presumably, acts of body, speech, and mind: °ma-pariśuddha- (. . . vaiśāradyam, sc. of Bodhisattvas) Mvy 783.

triṣkāla, (**1**) m. (= Skt. trikāla, BHS tryadhvan), *the three times*, past, present, future: °laḥ Mvy 8322 (= tryadhvan 8321); (**2**) adj.? or subst. m.? (Skt. trikāla), (at) *the three times* of day, morning, noon, and night; °lam, and m.c. °la, adv., *at* (these) *three times*: divase-divase °laṃ darśanāya Divy 274.4 (prose); °la vṛkṣehi pravarṣayantu Suv 41.6 (vs; cited with var. Śikṣ 218.15), *let them cause* (flowers etc., objects listed in prec. lines) *to rain from trees* (so Tib.; see Nobel's note) *thrice daily*.

triṣ-kṛtvas (Skt. tri-k°, once, pw; triṣk°, also Vedic, blend of this with tris, *thrice*; in Class. Skt. -kṛtvas is ordinarily not used with dvi-, tri-), *thrice*: Laṅk 3.4; Śikṣ 98.11 (prose); tṛṣkṛtva, m.c., Śikṣ 99.4 (vs). For triṣ- before other representatives of Skt. -kṛtvas, see s.v. **-kṛtvā.**

Trisamayarāja, m. or nt., n. of a work: Śikṣ 138.15; 172.13; 290.13.

tri-sahasra, f. °**rā** or (once, cf. **trisāhasrī**) °**rī**, adj., *consisting of 3,000* (worlds), sc. a world-system of that extent; the word lokadhātu seems to be always lacking; only in vss, and °sah° seems to be m.c. for the regular °sāh° (despite Pali sahassi; °sāh° seems unknown in Pali): ceti bhu (= abhūt; so divide) trisahasraḥ LV 368.18 (vs, see s.v. **ceti**); °srāyāṃ Suv 63.5 (vs); trisahasri (acc. sg., for °rīṃ; the only ī-stem form) Dbh.g. 40(66).4, and °ra (acc. sg., for °rāṃ or °raṃ) 10. See also s.v. **triḥsahasra** (°**rā**).

tri-sāhasra-mahāsāhasra, adj. m. or (°rā) f., or in comp., with lokadhātu (which in BHS is both m. and f., in Pali app. only f.; cf. Pali sahassī, see BHS **tri-sāhasrī**, also ti-, mahā-, which acc. to Childers are synonyms in Pali; no numeral mahāsahasra seems recorded in BHS and it is not clear what precise mg., if any, attaches to mahāsāhasra; in Mvy 7999 ff. and Mmk 343.16 ff. mahā-cpd. with other numbers means ten times the number), (world system) *consisting of a 'triple thousand great thousand'* (worlds): °ra-lokadhātu, cpd., LV 319.3; 377.4; Suv 8.6, 9; 86.4; masc. forms, °ro, °raṃ (acc.), etc., Mvy 226; 3044; LV 276.19; 393.18; 405.2; 410.12, 22; Mv i.40.6; ii.300.16 (mss.); 301.2, 8 (mss.); 349.3 (mss.; prec. by fem. adj.); Divy 68.23; 139.3; 158.6; 266.14; 367.21; Av i.5.10; 11.8 etc.; Samādh 8.9; 19.6; RP 2.11; fem. forms, Mv i.214.12 = ii.17.11 °rāyāṃ °dhātūyāṃ (loc.); ii.281.16; 301.12; 314.10; Suv 87.6 °rāyāṃ °dhātau; Śikṣ 138.10 id.; see also **trisahasra**, and items here adjoining.

trisāhasramahāsāhasrika, adj., with mahābrahmā, (ruler) *of a lokadhātu consisting of 3 thousand great thousand* (worlds): °ko mahābrahmā imaṃ trisāhasramahāsāhasraṃ lokadhātuṃ ... samam adhyatiṣṭhat LV 276.19.

tri-sāhasrā (sc. lokadhātu), = °**srī**: °srāṃ bahuratnadharāṃ ... Mv i.80.9 (prose); imāṃ °rāṃ i.236.15 (vs); °srāya yāvatā (see this) ii.302.20. No noun expressed.

tri-sāhasrika, f. °**kā**, adj. with lokadhātu (cf. adjoining items), *consisting of three thousand* (worlds): sarva-°ka-lokadhātau Suv 149.13 (vs); °kāyāṃ mahāsāhasrikāyāṃ lokadhātau Suv 100.9 (vs; analysis of **trisāhasra-mahāsāhasra**).

tri-sāhasrī, f. (sc. lokadhātu; cf. °**srā**), *the three-thousandfold* (world-system): yaś ca imāṃ trisāhasrīṃ (so most mss., two °rāṃ) ... kampayet SP 253.7. Only here and in Dbh.g. 40(66).4 trisahasri have I noted the fem. (tri-, or mahā-)-sāhasrī(-sah°), corresp. to Pali sahassī, which app. is the regular Pali form, see Childers s.v. Otherwise the BHS fem. stem is °srā, see preceding items.

Triskandha-, perhaps = next, but prob. rather in the sense of **skandha** (3), q.v., in °dha-patha-deśika (Mironov °daiśika), a title of Buddha: Mvy 74.

Triskandhaka, nt. (cf. prec.), n. of a work: °kam Mvy 1384; °ka-dharmaparyāya-pravartanena Śikṣ 171.5; °ka-pravartanam 290.1.

triḥsahasrā (only f.) = **trisahasrā**, see °**ra**; like the latter only in vss, and °sah° presumably m.c. for °sāh°; printed in LV 368.7 (°rā), 11 (°rā) and 21 (°rāṃ, here with medinī = °nīṃ); all mss. in 7 and 21, and all but one (A, the best) in 11, read tri-sah°, unmetr., Lefm. em. m.c.; trī° would be equally satisfactory but A triḥ° in 11; triḥs- can be interpreted as doubling of the sibilant m.c., but doubtless influence of tris, *thrice*, is involved. No noun accompanies the (substantivized) adj. in 7, 11.

trīhika, adj. (§ 3.115; cf. Pali dvīha-tīhaṃ, adv., and **trehika**), (sufficient) *for three days* (to Skt. tri plus aha-n), with śāli, *rice* (as food): °kaṃ Mv i.343.11, 12, 14, so Senart (em. °ko in 14); mss. mostly trehika, once trī° once tri°.

(**truṭi** (f.), Skt., so read with v.l. for Lefm. **truti**, *a small particle*: LV 149.4; as a unit of measure, here = 7 aṇu, one-seventh of a **vātāyana-rajas**, q.v., which in LV is one-seventh of a **śaśarajas**; Tib. rdul chuṅ ṅu = *small speck*. Not in corresp. Mvy list, 8190 ff.; possibly cf. Tib. chu rdul = **ab-rajas** 8193, *water-speck*, between loharajas and śaśarajas, not in LV; can a corruption have occurred based on Tib. chuṅ, *small*, and chu, *water*?)

tre- for **trai-** in vṛddhi formations, see the following items.

tredaṇḍika, m. (Pali te°, late Skt. trai°, Schmidt, Nachträge; Skt. tridaṇḍin), *triple-staff-carrier*, a sort of brahmanical (Schmidt, Śaiva) ascetic: °ka-m-ānandika-guruputraka-, etc., Mv iii.412.7 (prose); mss. tre° or te°, Senart em. trai°.

tremāsika, adj. (= Skt. trai°; cf. **traimāsa** and **dvemāsika**), (suitable) *for three months*: °kaṃ (v.l. trai°) vā bhaktaṃ Mv ii.462.6.

trembuka = **tryambuka**, q.v.: Māy 252.2 (prose), in long cpd., before **trailāṭaka**.

treviṃśat (= Pali tevīsa, for Skt. trayoviṃśat), *twenty-three*: °śad-varṣa-sahasrāni Mv iii.234.3 (vs; v.l. trayastriṃśad°, unmetr.).

trehika, adj. (= AMg. tehia), so mss. mostly for **trīhika** (Senart), q.v.

traikuntaka, nt., Mvy 6045 = Tib. rgyan rtse-gsum pa, *a three-pronged ornament*.

traicīvarika, adj. or subst. m. (= Pali tecī°), *one who wears the three* (monk's) *robes*, one of the 12 dhūtaguṇa: Mvy 1129; Dharmas 63; RP 57.10; AsP 387.6; MSV iii.122.5.

traitīyaka, (1) adj. m., *recurring every third day* (of fever): Mvy 9533; SP 401.7 (prose); Bhīk 17a.2; Māy 220.20 (2) °kam, adv., *for the third time*: SP 37.6; 38.8 (Kashgar rec. trir), 9; 484.8; 486.4 (all prose); also v.l. in some mss. for **tṛtīyakam** SP 315.9, 11.

[**traidaṇḍika**, see **tre**°].

traidhātuka, nt. (= Pali tedh°), *the triple universe* (of kāma-, rūpa-, and arūpa- existence): asmād ... °kān nirdhāvitā nirvāṇasaṃjñino ... SP 101.3; eṣo hi trīhi kramehi °kaṃ laṅghiya (mss., Senart em. °yā m.c.) anavaśeṣaṃ Mv ii.40.21 (vs); °ka-asaktaḥ Mvy 865; °ka-vītarāgaḥ Divy 40.13; 282.1; 488.6; Av i.207.11 etc.; °kam anityatāgninā pradīptaṃ paśyanti Divy 422.16; punar eva °ke virohati KP 39.3; cittamātram idaṃ yad idaṃ °kam Dbh 49.9; others, Mv ii.148.1; Samādh 8.4; Dbh 29.8; Bbh 246.25; Gv 288.16, etc.

traimāsa, m., nt., and °**sī** (sc. varṣā, which is normally pl. in Skt. but sometimes sg., so also in BHS, notably Divy, 401.7, 509.19), f. (= Pali temāsa, which seems, in all passages cited in Childers and PTSD, to mean specifically *the rainy season*, tho not so defined in Dictt.), *the rainy season* (of three months); generally either °sa-in comp., or °saṃ, °sīṃ, acc. sg. adv., *for the period of the rains*; but also °saṃ, n. sg., and °sān, acc. pl.: in comp., adhivāsehi me bhagavan °sa-bhaktena sārdhaṃ bhikṣusaṃghena Mv ii.272.2, similarly 6; adv. °saṃ Mv ii.272.13 °saṃ bhaktaṃ; (ekapiṇḍapātreṇāham ...) °saṃ niṣīdiṣyaṃ iii.225.11; °sīṃ, sa °sīṃ śrāmaṇero dhāritaḥ Divy 18.8; adhivāsayatu me bhagavān °sīṃ ... sārdhaṃ saṃghena 89.13; °sīṃ sarvopakaraṇaiḥ pravārito 283.5, ... pravārayeyam 6; noun forms, yāvat °saṃ (so read with v.l. for Senart °sikaṃ) samāptaṃ Mv ii.273.7, *until the rains were ended*; ṣaṣṭhiṃ traimāsān (*for 60 rainy seasons*) sārdhaṃ bhikṣusaṃghena sarvopakaraṇair upasthitaḥ Divy 242.8.

[**traimāsika**, see **tre**°; in Mv ii.273.7 error for traimāsaṃ, see prec.]

traiyadhvika, adj. (tr(i)yadhva(n) plus -ika), *of the present, past, and future*: namas °kānāṃ tathāgatānāṃ Sādh 2.12 etc.; Śikṣ 139.4 and 140.13 (text erroneous, see note p. 405); °kā pratima buddhakulābhijātā Gv 372.16 (vs; refers to Buddhas; read °kāpratimabu°, i.e. °ka-apratima-bu°).

trailāṭaka, m.(?) = next: Māy 252.2, in long cpd., following **trembuka**.

trailāṭā (so text, also Mironov with v.l. °ṭāka; Kyōtō ed. Index with BR °ṭa; cf. prec.), a kind of *fly*: Mvy 4861; °ṭāḥ, pl., MSV iv.74.22.

Trailokyavajra, n. of an author: Sādh 524 16.

Trailokyavaśaṃkara (-lokeśvara), n. of a deity: Sādh 79.13 etc.

Trailokyavikrāmin, n. of a Bodhisattva: SP 3 7.

Trailokyavijaya, n. of a deity: Sādh 511.6.

traividya, adj., and °**ya-tā,** noun (= Pali tevijja, °ja-tā), (state of) *possessing the three knowledges.* In Pali (see Childers s.v. vijjā and Lévi, Sutrāl. vii.9, note), these are either (1) knowledge that all is anicca, dukkha, anatta, or (2) knowledge of former births (pubbenivāsa), of the (future) rebirths of beings (cutūpapāta), and of the destruction of the depravities (āsava-khaya); of these the first and the third are two of the **abhijñā** (Pali abhiññā), q.v., and the second results from another abhijñā, viz. divyacakṣus (see s.v. **upapāda**), so that these three abhijñā are identified in BHS as the three vidyā, AbhidhK. LaV-P. vii.108. So far as I have found, this second of the two Pali sets is the only one recognized in BHS, where the category is in any case of very restricted occurrence; I have failed to record it except in SP and LV. In SP only the adj. occurs, always associated with ṣaḍabhijña, *having the six* **abhijñā,** as in: te traividyāḥ ṣaḍabhijñā(ḥ)... SP 179.17 (prose), and in verses (always separate ṣaḍabhijña from traividya! text makes them cpd.) 90.7; 129.10; 150.2; 155.2; no such association in LV, where context never helps in interpretation; adj., traividya (voc.) LV 363.16 (vs); noun, traividyatādhigatā 350.14 (so read with best mss. for text traividyādh°); °dyatā daśabalena... prāptā 352.17; °tām anuprāptaṃ 353.13 (prose); the last suggests that in 426.13 (prose) it is necessary to em. to traividyatānuprāpta (text °dyānu°, no v.l.) ity ucyate (said of Buddha).

traivaidika, adj. (Skt. only °vedika), *of the 3 Vedas:* °ke pravacane Divy 620.27.

tryadhva(n), also (in vss, m.c.), **triyadhva(n),** in comp., *of the three times* (**adhvan**), i. e. *present, past, and future;* see next two; nt., *the three times:* Mvy 8321.

Tryadhvalakṣaṇapratibhāsateja (n. sg. °jo), n. of a Buddha: Gv 312.5 (prose).

Tryadhvāvabhāsabuddhi, n. of a Bodhisattva: Gv 4.14 (prose).

tryambuka, m. (= **trembuka,** prob. the true original form), a kind of *fly:* Mvy 4862 = Tib. sbraṅ (misprinted sbruṅ) bu (*fly*) tryam bu ka; prob. by popular etym., as if tri-ambu(ka); MSV iv.74.22.

tvaṃ-sādṛśaka, adj. (see § 20.2 and **tvam-īdṛśa**), *like thee;* °kehi paṇḍitaiḥ SP 31.11 (vs).

tvagbhāra (m.), part of a tree, some part of the bark or a kind of bark: °ra-taś ca Divy 628.1, see s.v. **phalgu** 1. One is tempted to em. to tvaksāra- (Pali tacasāra); the fact that sārataḥ follows is no objection, since it means *as to the pith;* but unless the mss. actually read tvak-, the misreading implied is not easy to assume.

(**tvaca,** nt., *cinnamon:* tvacam Suv 104.7, in list of medicinal herbs; tvak, tvacaḥ (n. pl.?) Mvy 5806 = Tib. śiṅ tsha, *cinnamon;* see BR and pw s.vv. tvac, tvaca.)

tvam-īdṛśa, adj., = **tvaṃ-sādṛśaka,** q.v.: pūrṇaṃ sarvajagat tvamīdṛśair yad iha syāt LV 325.13 (vs).

TH

thaṇḍila (= Pali id., MIndic for Skt. stha°), see **sthaṇḍila-śāyikā.**

Thapakarṇi(n), and °**ṇika** (semi-MIndic for Stha°), see s.v. **Sthapakarṇi(ka).**

thapayati, thapeti (Pali only ṭhap°), see s.v. **sthapayati.**

tharatharāyate, onomat., pres. p. °yamāna (AMg. tharatharai, °ranta, ppp. tharahariya; Pkt. °tharāamāṇa, Sheth), *trembling:* atha balir asurendro 'dhomukhaṃ prapatitaḥ, smṛtibhraṣṭa-tharatharāyamānaḥ sthitaḥ Kv 33.24; bhītās trastāḥ °āyamānāḥ Mmk 182.17; °āyamānāḥ pīḍyamānāś ca vepathu-r-upajātaśaṅkā Mmk 520.17. (n, not ṇ, always written.)

tharu (= Pali id.; § 2.9), *hilt of a sword; sword:* (dhanusmiṃ vā) tharusmiṃ vā Mv ii.74.3; in Mv iii.366.2 (vs) read tharu-khaḍga-pāṇi, for text tara°, with Pali Jāt. v.136.24 tharu-khagga-baddhā.

thala (nt., = Pali id., MIndic for Skt. sthala), *dry land:* Mv iii.32.2,11 (v.l. sthala in both: prose).

thavana, nt., a high number: Mvy 7855 (cited from Gv); Gv 133.8.

thāma (= Pali id., see **sthāma-n**), *fortitude:* LV 127.19 thakāre thāma... śabdaḥ, in the spelling-lesson.

thīna, nt. (= Pali id.), MIndic for **styāna** (§§ 2.12; 3.115; also **stīna**): °naṃ (n. sg.) Mv iii.284.5

thutthu(-kārakam, adv.), (making) *the sound thutthu* (in eating): na... Mvy 8579 = Tib. hu hu (*the sound of one's mouth in eating*) mi bya. Cf. Skt. Lex. thū-thū, said to be imitative of spitting; Skt. thūtkāra, and the like. Chin. onomat., indicating that one has eaten something hot.

thera, m. (= Pali id. cf. **sthera;** MIndic for Skt. sthavira, which has this mg.), *old man* (decrepit; not in religious sense): Mv iii.4.17 (vs).

D

Daṃṣṭrasena, n. of a teacher: Mvy 3507.

Daṃṣṭrānivāsin, n. of a yakṣa: Divy 434.15, 22.

daka (nt.; = Pali id., for Skt. udaka; rare in Skt. except dakodara, *dropsy,* Suśr., but see Schmidt, Nachträge), *water:* khaṇḍaghaṭakaṃ dakasya (v.l. uda°) Mv ii.429.17 (prose); daka-rākṣasa, *water-ogre,* = **udaka°,** q.v., Mv iii.11.19 (v.l. ud°); 29.14, 15; Divy 105.3 ff.; daka-candra, *moon in water,* = **udaka-c°,** q.v., māyāmarīcī-dakacandrakalpā Suv 250.2 (vs; read so, or with v.l. °maricy-ūd°, m.c.; Nobel unmetr.); marīci-dakacandra-samāḥ RP 51.16 (vs); dakacandra also ŚsP 542.12 (prose) and Śikṣ 204.15 (vs, cited from LV which reads **udacandra,** q.v.); in Divy 231.1 (prose) read, uparimaṃ dakaskandham ādāya (see s.v. **skandha** 1); other cpds., Mv ii.152.13; 171.5 (these are prose); Gv 27.21 (vs, could be m.c.).

dakodarika, adj. (from Skt. dakodara), *dropsical:* Mv ii.152.13 (prose).

dakodarin, adj., = prec.: LV 305.21 (prose).

dakṣiṇaka, adj. (= Skt. °ṇa plus -ka), adv. °kena, *on the right:* Divy 111.18, 27; 112.10 (all prose).

Dakṣiṇā-giri, or °**ṇa-giri** (= Pali Dakkhiṇā-giri or °ṇa°), n. of a district: °ṇāgiriṣu janapade Av i.2.1; so also ed. i.3.1, where best ms. °ṇa-giriṣu.

dakṣiṇādeśanā (once °na; = dakṣiṇā-ādeś°), *assignment* (to someone other than the donor or performer) *of the profit from gifts or works of merit* (see s.v. **ādiśati**): Divy 239.2–3 °nam (made by the recipient of alms-food) api bhayagṛhīto 'śrutvā; Divy 179.20 bhagavān dakṣiṇādeśanāṃ kṛtvā prakrāntaḥ; 190.9, similarly, °nāṃ kṛtvā prakrāntaḥ; when the subject is not the Buddha or other recipient of the gift, but the donor or performer of the virtuous action, the ger. of the caus. kārayitvā is used (as ādeśayati tends, tho not invariably, to replace ādiśati with dakṣiṇām in this case): Av i.257.9 asmākaṃ nāmnā dakṣiṇādeśanāṃ kārayitvā; 264.11 pretyā nāmnā dakṣ°-nāṃ kārayām āsa, *caused the profit to be assigned in the name* of . . .

dakṣiṇāvarta, m. (in Skt. as ep. of a conch-shell, śaṅkha, and so Pali, dakkhiṇāvaṭṭa-saṅkha-ratanaṃ Jāt. v.380.5, but seemingly not used in Skt. or Pali as subst., independently of śaṅkha; AMg. uses dāhiṇāvatta thus, defined Ratnach. *the right conch; a particular conch*), *a conch-shell with spirals turning to the right*, valued as a gem (cf. °varta-śaṅkha- Divy 138.3): in lists of gems, . . . lohitakā °vartā etāni ca te ratnāni . . . Divy 115.4; similarly 229.7; 502.7; 543.29; Av i.205.3; Bbh 234.2.

Dakṣiṇāvibhaṅga Sūtra (= Pali Dakkhiṇā°), n. of a sūtra found in Pali MN no. 142, iii.253 ff.: Karmav 61.5; 156.13 (here apparently included in the **Etadagra**, q.v.; prob. the same text but the quotation seems to have no close correspondent in Pali).

Dakṣiṇā-sūtra, n. of a sūtra presumed by Lévi to = prec.: Karmav 163.1.

? **dakṣiṇāhi**, adv. (Skt. Gr. only), *on the right*: so acc. to Lefm., in LV 354.15 (vs) eṣa (all mss.; Lefm. eṣu) vara-dakṣiṇīyo utpātu dakṣiṇāhi, *he* (Buddha) *is the best recipient of homage, a portent appearing on the right*; but I am very doubtful of this. Text is metrically and otherwise dubious (also in next line). Tib. omitted by Foucaux.

dakṣiṇīya, adj. (also °**ṇeya**, q.v.; = Pali dakkhiṇeyya), *worthy of veneration, to be revered*; orig. no doubt *worthy of receiving a sacrificial* or *reverential* (guru's) *gift*, a mg. which seems still alive in LV 358.21 (vs) °yāś ca te loke āhutīnām pratigrahāḥ, na teṣu dakṣiṇā (noun, *present*) nyūnā . . .; but ordinarily simply *venerable*; very common in prose and vss: LV 57.21; 84.20; 89.19, 20; 97.20; 223.9; 407.6; 429.5; Mv i.78.12; 89.15; 291.18; 301.16; ii.195.1; 214.4; 368.5; iii.155.6; 414.4; Mvy 6829; 9218 (here erroneously dakṣaṇ° in text) = Tib. sbyin gnas, *worthy of gifts*; Divy 82.15; 229.10; Av i.173.9; Suv 139.7; Bbh 5.1; often emphasized by prefixing such words as mahā- LV 425.6; Mv ii.300.4 (vs, maha- m.c.); Divy 192.10; vara- LV 354.15; Mv ii.336.13; eka- Divy 132.22; 538.18; sadbhūta- Divy 133.12; 192.13; parama- Divy 404.12; atulya- Sukh 22.6; °ya-tā, abstr., Jm 71.14.

dakṣiṇeya, adj. (= °**ṇīya**; also **dākṣ**°; closer to Pali dakkhiṇeyya, but in BHS noted only in Mv and rare there), *worthy of veneration*: Mv ii.295.13; 300.8; 308.17; 328.15; iii.194.4; 414.3; °ya-tā, abstr., ii.260.13. (Some of these have v.l. °ṇīya.)

dakṣya (nt.; from Skt. dakṣa plus -ya; = Skt. dākṣya, perh. read so), *skill*: dakṣya-dākṣiṇya-cāturya-(text cātūrya-)-mādhuryopetam Divy 109.28 (prose).

dagodara- (= Skt. dako°; AMg. regularly daga for (u)daka; cf. Skt. dagārgala, VarBṛS., BR), *'water-belly', dropsy*: in LV 189.11 (prose) read dagodarābhibhūtaṃ for Lefm. dagdhod°; proved by Tib. dmu rdziṅ can = dakodara Mvy 9558, and Das, Dict.

[**dagdhodarābhibhūta**, see prec.]

Daṇḍaka(-vana), n. of a forest (cf. Pali Daṇḍakārañña? but in LV associated with an evil person named Brahmadatta): LV 316.2. Tib. transliterates, dan ta ka.

daṇḍa-kamaṇḍalu, m. and nt., a sort of *water-jar* (conjectured to mean one with a *handle*): Divy 14.26 (°luḥ), 16.27 (id.), 246.18 (°lu, n. sg.), 473.5 (°lum, acc. sg.). In the first two and last cpd. with sauvarṇa-; in 246.18 sauvarṇakaṃ daṇḍakamaṇḍalu.

Daṇḍaki(n), n. of a wicked king (of Govardhana): Mv iii.363.6, 16; 364.20; 365.16; 368.14; 369.2. His story is comparable to that of Pali Daṇḍakī (DPPN), tho quite different in details; see s.v. **Vatsa** (1).

daṇḍa-parāyaṇa, adj. (= Pali id.), *dependent on a staff* (for walking), said of old people: jīrṇā °yaṇā Mv i.180.16 (vs).

Daṇḍapāṇi, n. of a Śākya, father of **Gopā**, q.v.: LV 140.9 ff.; 153.20 ff.; 157.3; Suv 199.8; Gv 420.19.

Daṇḍapāda, pl., n. of a group of nāgas: Māy 221.17.

daṇḍa-poṇa, see **poṇa**.

daṇḍa-bhāsa, m., a celestial portent: Mvy 4403 = Tib. braṅ ṅer snaṅ ba, *light in upright position*; so, presumably, lit. *staff-light*, or freely, *vertical flash*.

Daṇḍa-lagna, pl., n. of a brahmanical gotra: Divy 635.14 (follows **Lagna**).

daṇḍa-vāsika, m. (= Pkt. °vāsiga, °vāsiya, Sheth, by the side of °pāsi; to be derived from Skt. dāṇḍapāśika, comm. on Deśīn. 2.99; § 2.30), *policeman, local guard* (not *Türsteher*, BR): Mvy 3741 = Tib. yul sruṅs, *place-guard*.

daṇḍāpayati (cf. Pkt. ppp. daṇḍāvia, Sheth), caus. to Skt. daṇḍayati, *causes to fine* or *punish*: °payantı Śikṣ 63.13; °payed 67.10.

Daṇḍin, n. of a brahman: MSV i.116.4 ff. (corresp. to Pali Gāmaṇi Caṇḍa, see DPPN).

Datṛma-, see **Dattrima-**.

Datta, n. of a rich householder at Śrāvastī, father of **Sudatta** = **Anāthapiṇḍada**: MSV iii.133.13 ff.

dattaka, (1) nt., *thing given* (specifying -ka): (vismarāmi satyaṃ yat tava) kiṃcid °kam iti Divy 504.4; see also **gara-d**°; (2) f. °ikā, *given* (in marriage): MSV i.105.1.

Dattā, n. of a yakṣiṇī: Sādh 561.1, 11.

?**Dattrima-daṇḍika-putra**, patron. of **Rājaka**: LV 238.10; Lefm. with most mss. Datṛma°; Calc. Trima°, with v.l. Dattrima°; form and mg. of first element obscure. Tib. gdul baḥi be con can gyi bu, *son of one who has a stick for discipline*.

-dada, adj. (= Pali id., only in comp.; cf. also next; to pres. dadati), *giving*, only at end of cpds.; esp. when prior member is an a-stem, it appears that it regularly has acc. form, -aṃ, except in vss where meter requires short syllable: kāma-d° Śikṣ 331.4 (vs), see also s.v. **kāmaṃ**°; cakṣur° LV 361.7 (vs); 365.16 (vs); 422.6 (vs); cakṣu° (m.c.) LV 359.22 (vs); in Mv i.316.14 (vs) mss. cakṣur°, Senart em. cakṣu° m.c.; abhayaṃ°, dharmaṃ° Kv 11.9 (prose); priyaṃ° Kv 11.7 (prose); sarvaṃ° (see also s.v., as n. pr.) Mv i.287.10 (prose; v.l. sarva°); iii.250.14 (vs); Divy 316.14; 319.2–3, et alibi (prose); Mmk 324.15 (prose); sukhaṃ° Mv ii.297.3 (prose); Gv 481.14 (vs); sukha° LV 363.3 (vs, m.c.); saukhya° LV 45.18 (vs, m.c.); various proper names, see **Dānaṃdadā**, **Dharmaṃ**°, **Pṛthivīṃ**°, **Priyaṃ**°, **Phalaṃ**°.

-dadana, adj. (not recorded elsewhere; = **-dada**), *giving*, at end of cpd.: sarvajagasya saukhyadadanaḥ LV 221.22 (vs; presumably m.c. for saukhyaṃ°, see s.v. **-dada**).

dadantaka, f. °**ikā** (pres. pple. dadant-a plus -ka), *giving*: (apsarā . . . bodhisattvaguṇa bhāṣamānikāḥ) kaṇṭhakasya balu te dadantikāḥ LV 236.22 (vs).

dadrula, dardura (**dardara**), **dardula, dradula**, adj. (all these spellings recorded in the mss.; cf. Skt. dadruṇa, adj., Schmidt, Nachträge; from the noun Skt. dadru, Pali and AMg. daddu, a skin disease variously alleged to be *leprosy* or *ringworm*), *afflicted with* a skin-disease, *leprosy* or *ringworm*(?), in a list of adj. describing physical deformities, see quotations s.v. **khoḍa**, *lame*. Senart's readings vary and are not always related to the wildly varying readings of the mss., which I quote: Mv ii.150.9 darduro, dardaro; 152.3 dradulo (only one ms.); 153.19 dadrulaṃ, dradulaṃ; 156.12 dadrulaṃ, (da)rdulaṃ.

dadhi-pradyotika, adv. °kaṃ (vā dīpyamānasya), Śikṣ 182.3, in a list of tortures, after **taila-pradyotikaṃ**, q.v., and **sarpiḥ-pra°**; Bendall and Rouse render this (*burnt with blazing*...) *ghee*, on what ground I do not know; dadhi seems always to mean *sour milk* or *curds* in Skt., Pali, and (dahi) Pkt. literature. Some inflammable material must be meant; acc. to Skt. Lexicons, dadhi also may mean *turpentine* or *resin* (BR), here perhaps the latter.

Dadhimālin (= Pali °li), n. of a mythical sea: Jm 91.4.

Dadhimukha (= Pali id.), text actually **Dadhī°**, n. of a yakṣa: Hoernle MR 26.13 (Āṭānāṭiya Sūtra, in Hoernle's terminology; see **Āṭānāṭika**).

[**dadhyika**, supposedly *dealer in sour milk*, Senart with mss. Mv iii.113.8; but read **dhānyika**, q.v.]

danta-kāraka (= Skt., Pali, AMg. °kāra), *worker in ivory*: Mv iii.113.7 (prose), in list of artisans and tradesmen.

Dantapura, nt. (= Pali id.), n. of the capital of Kaliṅga (only in Buddh. works): Kaliṅgeṣu °raṃ nāma nagaraṃ Mv iii.361.12; 364.3; in Mv iii.208.16 (vs) read Dantapuraṃ for ataḥ puraṃ, mss. antaḥpuraṃ, and transfer to line 17 before Kaliṅgānāṃ; see the same vs in Pali DN ii.235.19.

Dantaśayana, n. of a former Buddha: Mv i.140.8.

Dantā, n. of a rākṣasī: Māy 243.34.

-dantinikā, f. (= Skt. dantin-ī, plus -ka, endearing dim., see § 22.34), *having... teeth*: -śukla-su-dantinikā(ḥ) LV 322.15 (vs), of the daughters of Māra.

Danturā, n. of a rākṣasī: Māy 243.20.

damatha, m. (= Pali, Skt. Lex., id.), *restraint, control*: duṣṭanāgā °tham āgacchanti Divy 185.24; esp. *self-control*, ātma-damatha Mv i.127.17; iii.52.18; tri- (Divy 95.14 trividha-)-damatha-vastu-kuśala Divy 95.14; 124.13; 264.28; Av i.16.11 (presumably control of body, speech, and mind); damathaḥ (context not clear) Mvy 6727.

damadamā(-śabda-; see Hemacandra, Gr. 3.138, with note in Pischel's Transl.), onomat., perh. as noun, *a kind of drum*: (anta)bhramac-cakra-maṇḍalāloka-pramukta-damadamā-śabdā (!read °da-? °dād?) gambhīra-bhairavam āyasaṃ nagaraṃ Divy 603.18.

? **dayati**, pres. to root dā-, q.v. in Chap. 43.

Darada-lipi, or (in Mv) without lipi, a kind of script: LV 126.1; Mv i.135.6 (here mss. -varada-, em. Senart). In Mv i.171.14 (vs), in a list of dasyu peoples, mss. -dareṣu, Senart em. -daradeṣu in accord with meter. That the (Skt.) Darada people is meant in LV is indicated by Tib. bru śa.

daridraka, adj. (= Skt. °dra), *poor*: °kā preṣaṇakārakāś ca SP 95.9 (vs). (-ka svārthe? m.c.? or dim.?)

dardara, variant for **dadrula**, q.v.

? **dardaraka**, m. or nt. (cf. Skt. Lex. dardara, said to be a kind of *drum*; Skt. dardura, said to be a *flute*; AMg. daddara, some musical instrument; and BHS **jala-dardaraka**), some musical instrument: in Mv ii.159.7 Senart em. jharjharakaṃ, but mss. dardarakaṃ, dardulakaṃ.

[**dardarā**, see **dardurā**.]

dardura, variant for **dadrula**, q.v.

? **dardurā** (most mss. dardarā), sc. lipi, a kind of script: Mv i.135.7. Senart's note mentions this as one of the forms in the list which 'ne laissent guère d'incertitude'; to me it is by no means clear. Did Senart mean to associate it with the Skt. name of the mountain range, often associated with Malaya? As a mountain name. Dardara (rare and doubtful in Skt., but in Pali Daddara) would merit consideration, as supported by most mss. But one would not expect a mountain-name here.

dardula, variant for **dadrula**, q.v.

dardulaka, variant for **dardaraka**, q.v.

Darbhakātyāyana, pl.. n. of a brahmanical gotra: Divy 635.15. So read for Durbha° of text; one ms. Darbhakāyana.

darvikā (= Skt. Lex. id.; Skt. darvī), *spoon, ladle*: Mvy 9047; āyasa-d° Mvy 9347.

darśana, nt., once m. (Skt. nt., not in these senses; cf. °nā), (**1**) nt., = **dṛṣṭi**, *false, heretical view*: tasyedaṃ darśanaṃ abhūt, śubhāśubhānāṃ karmāṇāṃ phalaṃ nāstīti niścayaḥ Mv i.178.11 (vs); (**2**) once m. (= Pali dassana, nt., in sippa-d°), *exhibition* (of skill in arts or exercises): kumāro ... darśanaṃ dāsyati Mv ii.73.18; 74.4, 7; kumāreṇa ... darśano dinnaḥ 75.18; darśana-śatāni vartanti iii.57.9, *hundreds of exhibitions* (as entertainments at a festival).

Darśanakṣama (v.l. °kṣema, so read?), n. of a former Buddha: Mv i.139.12.

-darśana-tā, *state of seeing*: LV 32.17 (prose); in amogha-d°, perhaps to be analyzed as amogha-darśana plus -tā, *state of having unfailing vision*.

darśana-bhūmi, f., the 4th of the 7 śrāvaka-bhūmi: Mvy 1144; ŚsP 1473.12 et alibi, see **bhūmi** 4.

darśanā (nowhere recorded) = Skt. °na, nt., *sight*: (yāye) prabhāye samanvāgataṃ yāye śūkṣma-darśanāye samanvāgataṃ yāye tattva-darśanāye samanvāgataṃ ... Mv i.158.9 (prose); perhaps nonce-form, attracted to gender of prec. prabhāye (the suffix -anā, f., is not rare in other forms beside -ana, nt.).

darśaniya, adj. (§ 3.42), *beautiful*: SP 313.13; LV 240.11 (em., mss. °nīya, unmetr.).

darśayati, in mg. of deśayati, *teaches, instructs* (falsely, in wrong ways), influenced no doubt by **dṛṣṭi**, q.v.: ye ca te darśayiṣyanti (seemingly passive, so Senart) teṣām api ca sā gati (sc. narakaḥ) Mv i.179.15 (vs), *and those who will be taught* (by you) *will suffer the same fate*; the next line is, anyān hi vihato hanti, naṣṭo nāśayate parāṃ (so Senart).

? **darśayin**, possibly adj. (pres. stem darsaya plus -in), *showing*: bhūtāṃ cariṃ darśayi lokanāthaḥ SP 64.2 (vs). But no such stem is recorded, and more likely the form is a verb (aor.), *the World-lord has shown*...

darśāvin, adj. (= Pali dassāvin; § 22.51), *seeing, perceiving*, also intellectually, *realizing*: pūrvabuddha-darśāvīni (or with most mss. °vinaḥ, construction 'ad sensum') SP 36.6–7 (prose); darśāvī pūrvabuddhānāṃ Mv iii.104.15 (vs); anantavarṇa- Gv 30.1; bhaya- Mv iii.52.1; abhaye, bhayadarśāvī Ud xvi.4 (oldest ms.; later ms. °darśino, and so Pali equivalent °dassino Dhp. 317); ādīnava-darśāvī Mv i.283.18 (prose; kāmeṣu); iii.52.5 (prose); anantajñāna-d° Mv i.357.5 (vs); sarva-d° Mv i.254.4 (prose); ii.13.3 and 22.5 (vss); iii.51.7 and 10 (prose); asarva-d° iii.51.6 (prose).

-darśin (from Skt. darśa, *aspect*, plus -in), *having the aspect of, resembling, like*: tathāgatadarśī ca veditavyo SP 226.8 (prose), *and he is to be regarded as like a T*. (because he has similar qualities and behavior; cf. lines 1–2 above, sa hi ... tathāgato veditavyaḥ; so Kern, clearly rightly; Burnouf, wrongly, *as having seen the T.*).

-darśimant (= Pali dassima(nt), see § 22.48), in **artha-, bhūta-d°**, qq.v.

daś(ay)-, m.c. for Skt. darś(ay)- (MIndic dass-, daṃs-), *show*; see § 2.87.

-daśaka, ifc. Bhvr. (Skt. daśā with -ka; = Pali -dasaka, in a-d°), *fringe*: achinnāgra-daśake paṭe Mmk 322.20 (prose); achinna-daśakaiḥ saha Laṅk 365.11 (vs; wrongly Suzuki). See **channa-daśa**.

Daśadharma-sūtra, Śikṣ 5.7, or **Daśadharmaka-s°**, 8.8; 116.16, n. of a work (cf. the ten dharma-caryā, Mvy 902 ff.).

daśabala, adj. (= Pali dasa°), *possessing the ten bala*, ep. and synonym of (any) Buddha, often used in the same way as tathāgata, jina, etc.: Mvy 25; (yo dadyā jambudvīpaṃ saptaratnasaṃcayaṃ) daśabalānāṃ Mv i.80.7, *who gives ... to the Buddhas*: similarly 8; 116.2, etc.; in Divy 275.5, 7 daśabala Kāśyapa (as either two words or one) refers to a monk in Śākyamuni's entourage (not to the former Buddha Kāśyapa, who acc. to PTSD and DPPN was 'especially' called daśabala, a statement for which I have found no evidence; in BHS, at any rate, daśabala applies equally to any and every Buddha); see s.v. **Kāśyapa** (2).

Daśabala-sūtra, n. of a work: Bbh 384.24. Printed (practically) completely by Waldschmidt, Kl. Skt. Texte 4.209 ff. Text is brief, prose, normal Skt. in forms, and has little BHS vocabulary except technical religious terms.

Daśabhūmaka, or °**mika**, m. or nt., also °**ka-sūtra**, n. of a work, = our Dbh; see Rahder p. iii ff. on relations to other texts, esp. Mv, which cites a text certainly different from Dbh, tho resembling it; Śikṣ (ms.) seems always to read °aka; Mvy 1350 °mikam, nt.; Mmk 109.28 °makaḥ, m.; Mv and Bbh record both °aka and °ika: Mv i.63.15 (°ko, m.) and 16 Senart °mika, but 5 of 6 mss. °maka; i.193.8, 9, 10 mss. all °mika(ṃ, nt.); Śikṣ (°maka) 227.11; 291.11; °makasūtra 10.15; 11.10; 126.9; 287.14 (ed. °mika° in 10.15 and 11.10 but ms. °maka°); some, at least, of Śikṣ citations are from Rahder's Dbh, e. g. 227. 11 ff. from Dbh 50.26 ff.; Bbh names several of the ten **bhūmi**, °mika 332.20 f. (naming Pramudita, read °tā); 334.24 (Vimalā); 343.16 (Sudurjayā); °maka 338.17 (Prabhākarā); 341.2 (Arciṣmatī).

daśavarga, adj. or subst. (= Pali dasavagga), *consisting of a group of ten; a quorum of ten* (monks); required acc. to Pali Vin. i.319.33 (cf. 31) normally, 'in the middle regions,' for ordination: MSV ii.205.11 ff., cf. 203.16 ff.; Mv i.2.15 daśavargena gaṇena upasaṃpadā (q.v.); Bhīk 18b.5 bhikṣūṇāṃ daśavarge maṇḍalake (see s.v. **dvādaśavarga**); certain sins to be confessed before such a group, Śikṣ 169.1 āpattir daśavarge ṛjukena deśayitavyā.

Daśaśiras, n. of a Pratyekabuddha: Av i.134.1 ff.

daśikā (Skt. daśā plus -(i)kā; cf. Pali dassikā-sutta, °tta-matta), *hem, fringe* (of cloth): °kāṃ dattvā tantravāyabhūtena Śikṣ 9.3.

daśottarapadasaṃdhi-lipi, see **yāvad-daśot°**.

daṣṭaka (ppp. daṣṭa plus specifying -ka, § 22.39), *one that has been bitten* (by a snake; in magic practices to cure snake-bite): °kaṃ mahāhrade nāgāyatane vā (sc. ālikhet) Mmk 53.22; daṣṭakottiṣṭhati (i. e. °ka ut°) 462.19, °ko nirviṣo bhavati 25; sarpa- (text sarva-) -viṣa-daṣṭakāni cotthāpayati 711.28; daṣṭakopari sthāpayitvā 721.4. All prose.

dahati (= Pali id.; for Skt. dadhāti; cf. also **ni-da°**), *sets, places*: dhvajaṃ dahitvā Mv ii.377.6; dahitva dīpaṃ ... cetiyeṣu 379.7 (both vss).

dahara, (1) adj. (= Pali id.; Skt. not in this sense; cf. next, and **dahra**, which is far less common), *young*; common in prose and vss alike, in Ud xvi.7, 8 even where meter demands dahra! (in corresp. Pali vs, Dhp. 382, daharo metrically correct, with other different readings): ahaṃ ca vṛddhas tvaṃ ca daharo SP 106.14 (prose); (śākyaiḥ) vṛddha-dahara-madhyamaiḥ LV 82.4 (prose); daharā (mss. °ro) ca madhyā ca mahallakā ca Mv i.262.18 (vs; dahrā would be as good metr.); dahara-manohara(ḥ) Sukh 25.14 (prose), *youthfully charming*; as v.l. along with dahra Mvy 4081; 8734 (Mironov dahra); others, SP 293.4; 311.11; 318.2; LV 241.17; Mv ii.41.2; 63.7; 78.18, 19; 79.4 ff.; iii.48.16; 294.20; 457.9; Divy 116.16; Av ii.71.6; Gv 127.19; 129.3; 136.24 etc.; (2) Dahara-Sūtra (= Pali D° Sutta, viz. SN i.68 ff.), n. of a sūtra by which Buddha converted King Prasenajit, as in Pali King Pasenadi: Av i.36.7; also called Daharopama Sūtra, MSV iv.62.3.

daharaka, adj. (-ka svārthe) = prec.: °ka-vayasy (mss. corrupt as to °sy-) avasthitena Av i.178.1 (prose).

? **dahuka**, so mss. of Divy 475.17 (ed. em. dakṣaka), ep. of children, see **taruṇaka**. Prob. read dahara(ka), or dahraka, = next.

dahra, adj. (not in this sense in Skt.; cf. **dahara**, which is much commoner), *young*: LV 100.12; yuvān ... navo dahras ... 212.6; in Mvy 4081; 8734, both times (in Mironov only in 8734) with v.l. dahara; Bbh 75.1; 281.12. All prose.

dākṣiṇeya, adj. (= **dakṣ°**; cf. Skt. id., not in this sense, pw 6.302), *venerable*: Karmav 156.10 (saṃbuddho °yānām agryaḥ); 161.18.

dākṣiṇya-lipi, a kind of script: LV 125.22 (Tib. *of the southern region*).

dāgha, m. (recorded only for Pkt. in Hem. 1.264, but cf. Skt. nidāgha), *burning, conflagration*: (geha-)dāghā vā kṛtā bhavanti vana-dāghā ... Mv i.23.1 (prose); dāgho ca utpanno ... nirvāpitaḥ ii.181.2; (śīlena pariśuddhena kāyo bhoti prabhāsvaro,) na cāsya jāyate dāgho (but v.l. doṣo, perhaps better) maraṇe pratyupasthite Mv ii.358.14 (vs); agnidāghaṃ (pari-)nirvāpayituṃ ii.457.9, 13, also hasti-dāghaṃ 12, *conflagration* (burning) *of elephants*.

-dāṭha, ifc. Bhvr. for *dāṭhā (= Pali id., Skt. daṃṣṭrā; cf. next), (large) *tooth*; in several anuvyañjana, buddhā ... vaṭṭitadāṭhā (m. n. pl.) ca, tīkṣṇadāṭhā ca, abhagnadāṭhā ca, achinnadāṭhā ca, aviṣamadāṭhā ca Mv ii.44.5–6. The mss. vary, usually reading °dāṭā or °dantā; both these occur in the corresponding Pali; but in the other BHS lists (see s.v. **anuvyañjana**) the form is °daṃṣṭra.

dāṭhin, adj. (= Pali id., Skt. daṃṣṭrin; see prec.), *having large teeth* or *fangs*: dāṭhī Mv iii.103.20; 261.10; 410.16 (all prose; always of a lion).

dāṇḍājinika-tā (to Skt. Gr. and Lex. °jinika; cf. late Skt. °jinaka, Schmidt, Nachträge), *state of being a hypocritical ascetic* (characterized by external marks, *staff and skin*, only): Jm 188.3.

(**dāna**, nt., Skt., *gift*; as one of the four **saṃgraha-vastu**, q.v.)

Dānaṃdadā (cf. **-dada**), (1) n. of an apsaras: Kv 3.17; (2) n. of a 'gandharva maid': Kv 5.6.

Dānapraguru, n. of a former Buddha: Mv i.137.15.

Dānavakula, n. of a former Buddha: Mv i.138.4.

Dānavagupta, n. of a former Buddha: Mv i.140.1.

Dānaśūra, n. of a Bodhisattva, previous incarnation of Śākyamuni: Kv 15.16; 93.17 (here printed °sūra).

dāni, dāniṃ, dānim (before vowel), (= Pali dāni, before vowel dānim, Childers; for Skt. idānīm) *now*; dāni SP 113.3; 170.3 (vss); in prose in Mv, i.17.10; 18.10; 21.4, 5; i.226.14 = ii.29.17; i.227.4; 232.2, 7; ii.26.5, etc., very common; also App. to Jm (= Mv) 240.5; in vss of Mv, dāni i.142.15; 143.1; 155.1, 5; i.204.19 = ii.8.14; in i.154.12 (vs) Senart kiṃ dāni ā°, but read dānim with 2 mss., the others dānīm, unmetr.; i.221.21 = ii.24.8 (vs) dānim, before vowel; in ii.11.12 (vs) dāniṃ, before cons., m.c.; in ii.6.18 (vs, = i.203.1, where Senart prints dāni) and i.209.3 (vs) Senart em. dāniṃ, m.c., for mss. dāni. It appears that dāni-m was used only (optionally) before vowels, and dāniṃ only in verses m.c. In Laṅk 336.11 (vs) text yathāpi dāniṃ naivāsti; rather, yathāp' idānīṃ ...

-dāntaka (dānta plus -ka, svārthe?), *tamed, controlled*: sarvadānta-sudāntaka (voc.) Mmk 4.29 (vs), perhaps m.c.; or perhaps specifying -ka, *you who are the one that is well controlled among all controlled ones!* In a formulaic passage in which most lines end in vocs. in -ka.

dāma(n), (only Vedic, and even there rare, in this sense, except, possibly, in the cpd. sudāman, Class. Skt.), *gift*: dāma-carī (*course of almsgiving*) yādṛśā ti pure LV 11.13 (vs). So acc. to Lefm. all mss.; Calc. dāna-; mg. confirmed by Tib. sbyin.

? **dāmaka**, possibly adj. (from Skt. dāman), *garlanded, formed into garlands* (of flowers), in paryaṅkaṃ dāmaka-puṣpa-saṃnibhaṃ Mv ii.183.16 (vs); so Senart reads, but assumes inverted order of parts of cpd., = puṣpa-dāmaka-, *like a garland of flowers*; if the reading is right, perhaps *like flowers that form a garland*. But the text is an em. and quite uncertain; mss. damakaṃ or °ko. In the following line bhāryāṃ ca sadṛśī devīm, understand sadṛśī = °śīṃ, as separate word, *corresponding, suitable*.

Dāmodara, n. of a former Buddha: Mv i.138.1.

dāyika, adj. and subst. m. (= Pali id. ifc., Skt. dāyin, dāyaka), *giving, a giver*: bījam . . . phala-dāyikam MSV i.70.12 (vs); same vs in same story Divy 462.23 -dāyakam; -saṃghasya dāyikaiḥ prajñaptaḥ MSV ii.113.5.

? **dārika** (= Skt. dāraka), and acc. to text °kā- (in comp.), *boy*: dvātriṃśad-dārikā-sahasrāṇi LV 128.11 (prose), all mss. acc. to Lefm.; dārikebhiḥ LV 133.6 (vs), two mss. with Calc. dāra°. There can hardly be a reference to girls (cf. Weller 26), and at least the final -ā of dārikā must, it seems, be a corruption for -a. Perhaps read dāraka both times. Note the same cpd. with dāraka 128.9; the word seems to occur only once in this passage in Tib.

dāru, m. (always nt., acc. to Dictt., in Skt., Pali, and Pkt., except for one Skt. acc. sg. dārum), *tree*: dāruḥ LV 188.14 (vs), end of line, all mss. acc. to Lefm. (Calc. dāru).

Dāruka, n. of a yakṣa, and °**ka-pura**, n. of the town where he lived: Māy 30.

Dāru-karṇin, nickname of a brother of Pūrṇa, lit. *wood-ear* (see s.v. **Trapukarṇin**): Divy 26.28; 45.16 etc.

[**dārvāyasmaya**, prob. misprint for dārv-ayasmaya, *made of wood or iron*, in SP 440.4 (prose), altho uncorrected in Errata and repeated without note in WT: °mayair haḍi-nigaḍa-bandhanair. But the true reading is prob. dārumayair vā ayasmayair vā, with Kashgar rec. Cf. verse version, dārumayair ayomayair 450.1 (vs).]

dālana (nt.; Skt. in diff. mg.; = AMg. °ṇa), *splitting, piercing*; in literal sense, of a military art mastered by the Bodhisattva: (bhedye) dālane sphālane . . . LV 156.13 (Tib. dbug pa); fig., object heresies: sarva-dṛṣṭigata-jāla-dālanāya prayuktaḥ Gv 117.3; adj. (perh. Bhvr.?) *destroying* (heresies): (mahāyogināṃ . . .) akuśala-dṛṣṭidālanānāṃ Laṅk 10.13.

dālāvana (if not corruption), some sort of tree: (panasa-)dālāvana-tinduka- etc. Divy 627.23 (in long cpd. containing list of trees).

Dāsaka, n. of a servant of Śroṇa Koṭīkarṇa: Divy 3.11; 4.22; 5.17 ff.; 6.2, 4; cf. 2 Dāsaka Thera in DPPN, possibly the same personage but presented in a quite different way; and cf. **Pālaka** 1.

? **-dāsitā**, in caṇḍavaco-dā° Mvy 2109 (v.l. in Mironov °dāśitā); acc. to Tib. (tshig brlaṅ(s) pos, = caṇḍavaco, zher ḥdebs pa) and Chin. *reviling with harsh words*. The etym. of dāsitā (app. containing suffix -tā) is obscure.

dāsinikā (to dāsī; see § 22.45), *maid-servant, slave*; tava °kāṃ LV 323.2 (vs).

dāha (m.; in this sense seems unrecorded in Skt., Pali, or Pkt.), fig. *pain, sorrow*: sarva-dāha-vināśanī Mv i.314.13 (vs), said of Buddha's voice.

? **dāhani**, must mean *burning*, as adj. or n. act.; so both edd., no v.l.: tuṣādy-aṅgāra-dāhani-kumbha-sādhana-pakvaśilāpacanāgnijalapraveśana- LV 249.11 (prose). Possibly understand dāhanin (dāhana plus -in)? Or mere corruption for °na?

[**dikṣiṣu**, LV 364.11 (vs), read udikṣ°, see **udikṣati**.]

Dignāga, see **Diṅnāga**.

Digvilokita, m., n. of a samādhi: Mvy 524; ŚsP 1416.18.

Digvairocanamakuṭa, n. of a Bodhisattva: Gv 3.5.

Diṅnāga, n. of a teacher: Mvy 3481 (v.l. Dignāga; so Mironov with no v.l.).

didṛkṣuka, adj. (= Skt. °kṣu with -ka svārthe), *anxious to see*: pretī-didṛkṣukāṇy anekāni prāṇiśatasahasrāṇi saṃnipatitāni Av i.264.9 (prose).

dinna, ppp., = Skt. datta; see § 34.16 and cf. **a-dinna**.

Divasacarā, n. of a rākṣasī: Māy 243.30.

divasa-nirīkṣaka, pl., should mean *observers of the day* or *of days* (astrologers?): in Kv 81.7 referred to as people who are initiated into certain heretical sects (but who cannot attain mokṣa).

divasam, adv.? (if so, = **daivasikam**), *daily, every day*: evaṃ tuvaṃ āryaṃ taṃ divasam āhāreṇa upasthihisi (? so Senart em., mss. °sa, °sā; true reading probably °hasi, 2 sg. pres.) Mv i.302.6, and: sā dāni taṃ . . . divasam āhāreṇa upasthihati 8 (both prose). But possibly, with Senart, understand divasa-m-āhāra, for divasāh°, with 'hiatus-bridging' m.

divasānudivasam, see s.v. 1 **anu**.

divāvihāra (m.; = Pali id.), *relaxation (rest) during the day*: (ārāma, acc. pl. . . .) °hārārtha dadanti . . . puruṣarṣabhāṇām SP 13.18 (vs); °raṃ parigamya 62.5 (vs); (went to a caitya) °hārāya Mv i.300.2, 5 ff.; (nadyāṃ . . .) °hāraṃ kalpayitvā ii.264.1; (vṛkṣamūlaṃ niśritya) niṣaṇṇo °hārāya Divy 201.3; 202.2; Av i.252.9; vṛkṣamūle niṣaṇṇo °hārāya 246.6; bhagavān °hāropagato 319.12; bhikṣavo °hāraṃ (v.l. °hārāya) gatāḥ Karmav 74.10. Regularly of the Buddha or his monks.

diviṃ, prob. m.c. for divi, loc. of div: Mmk 618.26; 625.7; 627.14; 629.16. Otherwise H. Smith (see § 1.38 fn. 15), pp. 4–5 [3.2j; Smith's em. of Mmk 629.16 (see my § 2.74) introduces not only metrical irregularity but a stem *diviya which I have not noted in BHS and do not find in MIndic except once in Aśoka's 4th Rock Edict, Dhauli-Jaugada version.

Divaukasa, n. of a yakṣa, attendant on Māndhātar: Divy 211.5 ff.; MSV i.68.13; 94.11.

Divyānnada, n. of a future Buddha: Av i.116.13.

Divyāvadāna (nt.), n. of a work: Divy 24.8 etc., in colophons.

[**diśa**; m.-nt. forms occur from stem diś(ā), as from other f. ā-stems, § 9.4; ex. daśa-diśebhir LV 416.2.]

diśatā (= Pali disatā; Skt. diś, diśā; PTSD refers to a 'Skt. diśatā' which does not exist), *direction, region, point of the compass*; only in vss except (rarely) in prose of Mv, e. g. ii.295.4; others, vss: SP 27.10; 205.6; LV 162.8 and 167.11 (diśato, acc. pl., § 9.97); 295.21; 421.17 (read daśa-diśata, § 9.68); Mv i.204.6 = ii.8.1; i.305.20; ii.135.12; 140.12; 299.2; 315.19; 409.17; iii.381.7; 438.15; Suv 233.1; RP 55.3, 14; Bhad 21 (text wrongly diśa tāsu); Gv 316.22; Dbh.g. 39(65).25.

diśati, (1) *says, speaks* (so in Ap. disai, Bhav. 232.7): pradakṣiṇāṃ dakṣiṇa (so divide) lokanāthaḥ teṣāṃ diśaiṣa 'pratimo vināyakaḥ LV 391.21 (vs), where we must understand (a)diśa(t) as the verb of the sentence (Tib. gsuṅs, *said*), *the Lord of the World, the Matchless Guide, declared their donation* (dakṣiṇā) *auspicious* (*virtuous*, pradakṣiṇa); direct quotation of his words follows; tatra gatā sukha me diśanti kṣipram Sukh 9.4 (vs), *quickly declare my happiness*; kṣetrārṇavān . . . cintāvyatītāṃś ca diśāmi dikṣu Gv 428.14 (vs), *I proclaim, tell of*; diśe (aor., by em. for diśāṃ which would make construction difficult) sovatthikaṃ divyaṃ Mv iii.305.10 (vs); (2) *teaches* (= **deśayati**, q.v.): dharmaṃ dideśa yakṣāya Laṅk 8.12, and dideśa nikhilaṃ sūtraṃ 13 (both vss); (3) *confesses* (also = **deśayati**): (kṛtaṃ yat) pāpaṃ jinānāṃ purato diśāmi Sādh 56.12 (vs); sarvāṇi pāpāni diśāmi bhītaḥ 90.4 (vs).

Diśadeśa-āmukhajaga(t; so read, as cpd.), n. of a Buddha: Gv 285.23 (vs). In this and the next two diśa-may be regarded as for diśā- m.c.

Diśabhedajñānaprabhaketumati, n. of a Buddha: Gv 285.6 (vs). See under prec.

Diśasaṃbhava, n. of a Buddha: Gv 284.11 (vs). See under prec. but one.

Diśāṃpati (= Pali Disampati, DN ii.230.22 ff.), n. of a mythical king, father of **Reṇu**: Mvy 3579 (here called a cakravartin); Mv iii.197.9; 204.8 ff.; in LV 171.1 (vs) apparently used as n. or epithet of **Reṇu**, q.v., himself (Reṇu bhū Diśāṃpati).

diśi (= AMg. disi, for Skt. diś, diśā; not in Pali), *direction*. Noted only in Mmk, but not rare there; usually acc. sg. diśim; sometimes (notably 205.26, where it seems clearly to be taken so, § 4.59, end) this could be interpreted as loc. diśi plus 'hiatus-bridging' m; among the cases which are certainly acc. are: dakṣiṇāṃ diśim āśritāḥ Mmk 326.18, and ... āśritya 626.26; prāciṃ (°cīṃ) diśim upādāya 620.1 (these all vss). The great corruption of the text of Mmk might tempt to emendation (diśam would be easy), but AMg. seems to confirm the form.

diśodāha, m. (= Skt. digdāha, Pali disāḍāha), *'burning in the sky'* (as omen): Divy 203.9; 206.4; Av ii.198.2; MPS 16.14. In MPS 17.21 ms. **diśodāgha** (ed. em.).

(**dīkṣate**, cf. Skt. id., *undergoes consecration* or *monastic initiation*: Kv 81.6 ff.)

Dīpa, (**1**) n. of the king of Dīpāvatī: Divy 246.9 ff.; (**2**) n. of a serpent king: Mmk 18.24; (**3**) m.c. for **Dīpaṃkara**: buddha Dīpa-nāmā LV 393.12 (vs).

Dīpakāra, m.c. for **Dīpaṃkara**: LV 172.14 (vs).

Dīpaṃkara (= Pali id.; in Pali the first of the 24 Buddhas; here sometimes, e. g. Sukh 5.6, first of a much longer list of Buddhas, but often named without any such preëminence), n. of one of the most celebrated of former Buddhas: his story told at length in the 'Dīpaṃkaravastu' Mv i.193.13 ff.; incomplete list of references, SP 22.3; 27.4; LV 5.4; 172.19; 185.15; 253.16; 415.19; Mv i.1.13; 2.1; 3.3; 57.13; 61.11; 170.3; 227.6 (his name is given to him); iii.239.10 ff.; 241.13; 242.19; 243.20; 244.13; 247.3; 248.3; Mvy 95; Divy 246.5 ff.; Gv 104.13; 222.2; Vaj 26.18; Sukh 5.6; 76.10; Karmav 102.15; 155.9; AsP 48.10. Also, in vss m.c., **Dīpa, Dīpakāra, Dīpasaha.**

Dīpavatī (also **Dīpā°**, q.v.), n. of the capital city of (Arcimant and) Dīpaṃkara: Mv i.194.1, 3; 231.7, 9; iii.239.11 ff.; AsP 48.10.

Dīpaśrī, n. of a Bodhisattva: Gv 442.2.

Dīpasaha, = **Dīpaṃkara**, m.c.: Dīpasahena ti LV 11.11 (vs), so read as suggested by Lefm. in Crit. App. for text °sahenāsti.

Dīpā, n. of a goddess or yoginī: Sādh 157.12 etc.; 324.6.

Dīpāvatī = **Dīpa°**, q.v.: Divy 246.9.

Dīptateja(s), n. of a former Buddha: Mv i.136.17 (°jaḥ, n. sg.).

Dīptabhānu, n. of a former Buddha: Mv i.139.4.

Dīptavīrya, n. of a previous incarnation of Śākyamuni: LV 170.19.

dīrita, ppp. (§ 34.10), *rent, destroyed*: mantradīritā(ḥ) Mmk 143.24 (vs).

Dīrgha (= Pali Dīgha), n. of a yakṣa: Māy 235.11; 237.2.

dīrghaka, (**1**) adj. (Skt. dīrgha plus -ka, ? m.c.), *long*: nātidīrghakaḥ Mmk 154.24 (vs); (**2**) m. (= Pali dīgha), *snake*: tehi halehi °ko ca maṇḍūko (mss. maṇḍ°) ca utkṣiptā Mv ii.45.6; so 'pi °ko kumāreṇa kṣipto 7 (both prose).

Dīrghakātyāyanī, n. of the gotra of the nakṣatra Jyeṣṭhā: °nī-gotreṇa Divy 640.16.

Dīrgha Cārāyaṇa (Pali Dīgha Kārāyaṇa; also called simply **Cārāyaṇa**, q.v.), n. of the charioteer of King Prasenajit: Dīrgheṇa Cārāyaṇena Av ii.114.10; in 13 mss. Dīgha-Cār°, as cpd. word, MIndic in form.

Dīrghanakha (= Pali Dīgha°), n. of a mendicant to whom Buddha preached the Dīrghanakhasya parivrājakasya sūtram: Mv iii.67.7 (*to be put in*, kartavyam, but not quoted here); in Pali it is MN i.497 ff., and a version occurs in Av 99; acc. to DPPN, D. was a nephew of Sāriputta (but no citation is furnished for this; the MN sutta does not say so); in Av ii.186.9 ff. and MSV iv.22.1 he is the uncle (mother's brother) of Śāriputra; in this story his given name was (**Mahā-**)-**Koṣṭhila**, q.v.; he had the surname **Agnivaiśyāyana**, q.v.

Dīrghabāhur-garvita (so, with -r-, no v.l., both edd.), n. of a son of Māra, unfavorable to the Bodhisattva: LV 310.20. See § 12.4.

dīrgharātra-, very commonly adv. °tram (= Pali dīgharattam), *for a long time*: prose, SP 37.10; 320.3; LV 108.7; Śikṣ 37.17; Dbh 7.14; Divy 616.21; Av i.177.7; vss, SP 38.4 (su-); 97.11; 213.8; LV 42.11; 158.11; 219.3; in comp., °trānugata- Divy 84.9; Av i.42.3; °tra-kṛtaparicaya- Divy 264.30.

dīrgha-vārṣika, m. sg. Mvy 9286, pl. Bhīk 22a.3 (°kāḥ), *long rains*; see s.v. **sāmayika.**

Dīrghaśakti, n. of a yakṣa (or gandharva?): Māy 237.4.

Dīrghāgama, m., n. of a section of the canon (= Pali DN): Mvy 1423; Divy 333.12.

Dīrghāyu (= Pali Dīghāvu), n. of a prince, son of **Ariṃdama**: Mv iii.457.8 ff.

dīrghāyuka, app. name of a class of gods, *the long-lived ones*: so dīrghāyukehi devehi upapanno Mv i.51.14, *he is born among the D. gods.*

Dīrghika, MSV ii.173.3, or **Dīrghila**, 182.7 (corresp. to Pali Dīghīti), n. of a king of Kosala, conquered by Brahmadatta of Benares; reference to his story in the Dīrghila-sūtra of the Madhyamāgama (Samādhisaṃyuktaka), 182.8.

dīrghya, gdve. (to Skt. denom. dīrghayati, pw 7.348), °yam, impersonal, (it is) *to be delayed*: tvayā kiṃ punar eva dīrghyam Divy 600.15 (vs).

du- (= Pali id.) for Skt. dvi-, stem for numeral *two*, § 3.117, esp. in cpds.: see **duguṇa, dupadendra, durūpa, ekadukāye.**

duḥ-k-, see **duṣ-k-**.

duḥkhaka (nt.; duḥkha plus -ka, prob. m.c.), *misery*: vedentā bahu duḥkhakaṃ Mv i.11.4 (vs).

duḥkhatā (Skt.), (state of) *misery*; three, listed Mvy 2228-31, and cited SP 108.17 f. (prose) tisṛbhir duḥkhatābhiḥ saṃpīḍitā(ḥ)... yad uta duḥkha-duḥkhatayā saṃskāra-du° vipariṇāma-du°; on this group see AbhidhK LaV-P. vi.125 ff., *state of misery qua misery* (what is grievous by its very nature, from the start, always painful), *state of misery due to conditioning* (saṃskāra; acc. to Vism. 499.20 f. this means particularly experience in itself not painful or pleasurable, but, because impermanent and so undependable, still a cause of misery), and *state of misery due to alteration* (of what was pleasurable to begin with, but cannot last); in Mvy 2232-40 eight duḥkhatā, each consisting of one of the list of evils enumerated in the first of the four noble truths.

duḥkhati (= Pali dukkhati; denom.), *is painful, hurts*: aṅgapratyaṅgāni duḥkhanti SP 100.12 (prose); jihvā pi tasya (read tasyo with v.l.) na kadāci duḥkhati SP 352.7 (vs). See also **duḥkhāpayati.**

duḥkhana, adj. ifc. (duḥkha-ti with suffix -ana), *hurting, causing pain to*: mayā ... jana-duṣkhanena (so spelled) Śikṣ 156.5. But note cites Bodhicaryāv. as reading °duḥkhadena (same mg.).

Duḥkhamukta, n. of a former Buddha: Mv i.137.8.

duḥkhāpayati (= Pali dukkhāpeti; caus. to **duḥkhati**), *causes pain to, hurts, grieves*: sukhitān (mss. °tāny, may be kept) api sattvā tvaṃ duḥkhāpayasi durmate Mv i.179.19 (vs).

duḥkhitaka, m. (ppp. °ta plus -ka, prob. pitying dim., § 22.36), *poor wretch*: °ko 'yam iti kṛtvā Divy 84.1 (prose); santy anye 'py asmadvidhā duḥkhitakā(ḥ) 86.22.

duḥkhila-tā (from duḥkha plus -ila; § 22.17), *state*

of being miserable: Mvy 1652 = Tib. tha ba ṅan pa ltar.

duḥ-p-, see **duṣ-p-**.

? **-duka, -dukā**, for dvi°, see **ekadukāye**.

Dukura, n. of a nāga king: Mmk 18.11.

dukūlaka (nt.?; Skt. °la plus -ka svārthe), *a certain fine textile fabric*: °kānāṃ tatha varakauśakānāṃ Śikṣ 302.6 (vs, may be m.c.); paṭe caiva °ke Mmk 131.21 (vs, may be m.c.); °**laka-sūkṣma**, subst. nt., *a fine garment made of dukūla(ka)*: °maṃ vā Bhīk 22b.4 (prose), in a list of various textile fabrics. See also **daukūlaka**.

dukha (as in Pali, see Childers), **dukhin**, and **dukhita**, m.c. in verses for duḥkha, °khin, °khita, *misery*; *miserable*. The mss. and edd. are quite inconsistent, but write dukha very often, at least, where meter requires it; so SP 54.10; 162.2 (in 92.6 ed. dukha-, acc. to note with only one ms.); LV 173.11 (no v.l.); 220.22 (dukhī, v.l. duḥ°); in LV 252.10 Lefm. properly em. dukhitaṃ against all mss., but in 188.12 he allows the equally unmetr. suduḥkhito to stand; Senart on Mv i.9.17 keeps duḥkhā of mss., noting that meter implies a short penult; so also i.14.16, 15.13, and often, usually not em. by Senart; dukha is rather common in vss of Samādh, e. g. 19.20; also in Gv, dukha 301.22; 488.9; dukhitām 474.23; dukha (v.l. duḥ°) Bhad 21; etc. In my opinion dukh° should always be read where meter indicates short first syllable.

dukhya (nt.; cf. **dukha**; semi-MIndic for *duḥkhya, *dauḥkhya, cf. Pali sokhya = Skt. saukhya, with which dukhya is compounded and to which it was perhaps formed as a pendant), *unhappiness, misery*: lābha atha alābhe saukhya-dukhye (so, as cpd.) RP 47.15 (vs).

du-guṇa (= Skt. dviguṇa), *two-fold, double*: duguṇa-palāśā ca pādapāḥ Mv ii.86.7 (vs); so mss., Senart em. dviguṇa°.

ducchana, read prob. °channa (see s.v. **-chana**); MIndic for Skt. duśchanna, § 2.12.

[**dutiyās** is read by Senart Mv ii.134.7 (vs), but mss. dvitīyās or °yaṃ; meter requires two short first syllables, but **dvitiya** is as good as dutiya. I have found no writing of du- for dvi- in the ordinal numeral.]

Dundubhi (**1**) f., n. of a 'gandharva maid': Kv 4.21; (**2**) m., n. of a nāga king: Māy 247.16.

-dundubhikā, see **mukha-du°**,

Dundubhisvara, (**1**) n. of a former Buddha: LV 171.11; (**2**) (the same? cf. also next, and °svara-rāja), n. of a Buddha in the north: Suv 2.5; 8.2; 120.7; (**3**) n. of a gandharva king: Kv 2.17; (**4**) n. of a Śākyan youth: Av i..371.1 ff.

Dundubhisvaranirghoṣa, n. of a Buddha in the north (cf. prec., 2): Sukh 97.22.

Dundubhisvararāja, n. of a series of former Buddhas (cf. **Dundubhisvara** 1 and 2): SP 380.9.

dupadendra (MIndic for Skt. dvi°; cf. **du-**; dupada not recorded in Pali; AMg. dupaya acc. to Sheth), (**1**) *king*: in Gv 259.20 (vs) read, yada sa niṣkramī dupadendrā (or °dro), *when that king retired from the world*; (**2**) n. of a former Buddha: in Gv 258.8 (vs) read with 2d ed., saptamu teṣa āsi Dupadendraḥ.

dumela (var. dumaila; Mironov dumela), nt., a high number: Mvy 7873 (cited from Gv) = Tib. yal yal; Gv 133.11 f.

duyamana (m.c. for Skt. dūyamāna, pres. pass. pple), *being distressed*: LV 166.8 (vs).

dura, nt. (etym.?), seems to mean something like *worldly existence*: māyopamaṃ hi duram etat, svapnasamaṃ ca samskṛtam avīkṣyam RP 33.3 (vs; meter, Finot's No. 18, p. xiv). The only possible connection I have discovered is duraṃ-daraṃ, Deśīn. 5.46, glossed duḥkhottīrṇam.

duradhimoca, °**cya**, *hard to strive zealously towards* (see **adhimukti** and its congeners): SP 185.9 duradhimocaṃ (tathāgatajñānaṃ; Kashgar rec. °mucyanīyaṃ, cf. **adhimucyanā**, °**natā**); said apropos of the fact that disciples of the Buddha in many past existences are still in the same stage of discipleheod; AsP 185.2, 5, et passim, duradhimocā (prajñāpāramitā); read with 2d ed. duradhimocaṃ Gv 321.19 for text durabhimocaṃ (etat sthānaṃ, sc. anuttarā samyaksaṃbodhi).

dur-anubodha (= Pali id.; cf. **anubodha**), *hard to comprehend*: Mvy 2917 (as synonym of gambhīra); LV 422.12 °aṃ (cakraṃ); Mv iii.314.1 (dharmaḥ).

dur-abhimoca, prob. error for **dur-adhimoca**, q.v.

dur-abhisaṃbodha, see **abhi°**.

dur-abhisaṃbhava, adj. (= Pali id.; to Skt. and Pali abhisaṃbhavati; see **abhisaṃbhāvayati**, and cf. next), *hard to attain*: Mvy 7210; Bbh 10.3; Gv 267.10; 321.19; Jm 78.12; 122.17.

dur-abhisaṃbhuṇa, adj. (= prec.; see **abhisaṃbhuṇati**), *hard to attain*: Mv ii.237.21; 238.13; iii.264.5; 387.4. The last = Pali Sn 701, which has durabhisaṃbhavaṃ (cf. prec.).

durākāra, see **ākāra**.

dur-ākhyāta, adj. (= Pali durakkhāta), *ill-proclaimed, ill-stated, incorrect*: Laṅk 244.12 durākhyāta-dharmair api . . . anyatīrthikair (Suzuki *who hold erroneous doctrines*).

dur-āgata, (**1**) adj. (= Pali id.), *unwelcome, unpleasant, offensive*; associated with durukta, and applied to words, **vacana-patha** (same collocation in Pali, AN ii.117.34; 143.29): sarva-durukta-durāgata-vacanapatha-LV 181.11; durukta-durāgatān vacanapathān sahate Śikṣ 185.2; duruktān durāgatān . . . vacanapathān 188.9; Bbh 238.9, cited s.v. **avaspaṇḍana**; (**2**) name given to **Svāgata** because of his bad luck: Divy 171.14; 172.12; 173.9; 177.7 ff.

dur-ājñeya, see **ājñeya**.

durānuga, m.c. for dūr°? see s.v. **ḍhalita**.

Durāroha, n. of a cakravartin: Mv i.154.2; and **Durārohā**, a name for the first bodhisattva-bhūmi: Mv i.76.13; 90.13. Cf. **Dūrāroha-buddhi**. I think it probable that Dūrāroha (dūra, *far*, plus **āroha**, q.v., *height* or *length*) is the true reading in all these cases.

durāvagāha, adj. (for durava°), *hard to fathom*: samudrakalpa . . . gambhīra-durāvagāhatvāt LV 424.11 (prose). See § 3.10. This is ignored by Weller 39, tho he refers to two other cases of apparent vowel-lengthening in the following lines (see l.c.). The -ā- here may have been carried over from some passage in vs where it was metrically required.

du-rūpa, adj. or subst. (cf. **du-**; for Skt. dvirūpa), (*of*) *two kinds*: (karmā kalyāṇa-pāpakā) Mv i.12.13 = iii.456.19 (mss. du° both times; Senart em. dvi° first time, not the second), see s.v. **paryāya** (4).

dur-opagama, adj. (m.c. for dur-upa°), *hard of access*: LV 46.15 (vs).

durga, (**1**) nt. (Skt. id.), *evil state*; five such, perhaps = the five **kaṣāya**, q.v. (not **durgati**, of which there are only three or at most four): durgāni (so text) pañca, ṣaṣṭi mohānī, triṃśatiṃ ca malināni (. . . chinnā) LV 372.5 (vs); (**2**) m. or nt. (loc. durge), n. of a region (janapada) in the south: Gv 201.10, 25.

durgati, f. (= Pali duggati), *evil destiny* or *state of being*, see s.v. **gati**: SP 260.8; also called **apāya**, q.v.

? **durgandha**, acc to Bendall and Rouse, Transl. 179 (cf. note 3, implying support of Tib.) *danger of a bad destiny*: sarva-durgandham (to be understood as °gandham-, with 'hiatus-bridging' m?) atikramāśvāsanam Śikṣ 183.12 (prose), *giving confidence in passing beyond* . . . If this is the meaning, surely the text must be corrupt.

durgandhita, denom. ppp. to Skt. durgandha, *made ill-smelling*: MSV ii.90.13 (prose).

Durgottāriṇī, n. of a form of **Tārā**: cpd. with -Tārā, Sādh 237.10; or alone, 237.21; 238.4.

Durjaya, (**1**) n. of a former Buddha: LV 172.12; (**2**) n. of an ancient king: Mv i.115.15.

Durjayacandra, n. of an author: Sādh 489.14.

Durjayā, (**1**) n. of a goddess: Sādh 502.6; (**2**) n. of the 7th bodhisattva-bhūmi: Mv i.76.16; of the 5th **bhūmi** (= **Sudurjayā**, the regular name in the standard list), Sūtrāl. xx.35.

durdatta, adj.-ppp., *wrongly imposed* (cf. **su-d°**), of an ecclesiastical penalty: MSV iii.64.1 ff.

durdina, adj. (Skt. id., Pali duddina, and Pkt. duddiṇa recorded only of weather), *gloomy*, fig. of men's faces or eyes: sāśrudurdinavadana- Divy 4.28; 323.24; Kv 29.15; Av i.170.10; 199.15; savāṣpadurdinamukha- Divy 426.24; śokāśrudurdinamukha- Jm 109.22–23; aśrudurdinanayana- Suv 221.2.

Durdharṣa, n. of a Bodhisattva: Mvy 699 (with ep. kumārabhūta).

durbalaka, adj. (Pali dubbalaka, AMg. dubbalaya; once in Skt., Schmidt, Nachträge; Skt. °la plus -ka, svārthe, or pejorative dim.?), *feeble*: kṛśāluko durbalako mlānako (or mlāno) Divy 334.1, 3; 571.11, 18, 22.

durbuda, m. or nt., a high number: Gv 106.4; corresponds in position to **drabuddha**, q.v.

Durbhakātyāyana, see **Darbha°**.

durbhakṣa Māy 220.18 = **durbhukta**, q.v. (in identical list).

(**durbhara-tā**, cf. Skt. durbhara, *hard to satisfy*, pw, and Pali du(b)bharatā, *insatiableness*, of a monk as regards alms-food: Mvy 2473. Cf. **subhara**, **°tā**, and **duṣpoṣatā**.)

durbhukta, nt. (Pali dubbhutta cited PTSD without reference), *indigestion*, or *indigestible food* (Tib. bzaḥ ñes), app. regarded as due to malevolent magic or superhuman powers, in a list including vetāla etc.: Mvy 4380; Māy 245.18; 259.12 (in same list 220.18 **durbhakṣa**).

dur-maṅku, adj. (= Pali dummaṅku; cf. s.v. **maṅku**), *not showing regret* or *remorse at sins committed*: Mvy 2503; 8350; in both Tib. gnoṅ mi bskur (8350 bkur, so Das) ba, which acc. to Das means *not confessing faults*. The mg. assigned is supported by some Pali comms., while others say less specifically dussīla, *immoral*; see esp. Hardy, AN vol. 5, Introd. pp. v-vi, note. Perhaps orig. *ill* (= *not properly*) *disturbed in mind* (?). On Mvy 8350 var. °maṅgu, °madgu (as for **maṅku**).

Durmati, (**1**) n. of a king: Mv ii.485.8; (**2**) n. of a son of Māra, unfavorable to the Bodhisattva: LV 309.3; (**3**) f., n. of a queen: Av i.178.9 ff.

durmanasvin, f. **°nī** (cf. Skt. amanasvin, in same mg., pw 2.291), *melancholy, dejected*: duḥkhitā °vinī Gv 411.6.

Durmukha, n. of a (brahmanical) sage (ṛṣi): Divy 211.24; 217.19; MSV i.93.15.

Duryodhana, n. of a yakṣa: Māy 23.

Duryodhanavīryavegarāja, n. of a Bodhisattva: Gv 9.10; 25.9.

durlaṅghita, nt., some form of hostile magic or its result (see s.v. **durbhukta**): Mvy 4381; Māy 220.19; 245.18 (here dull°). Acc. to Tib. on Mvy, bgo ñe(s), app. *bad clothes*; or sgyuṅ (which I cannot find) ñes. On the basis of Skt., laṅghita could mean *violation, hostile attack*; or *fasting, hunger, starving*.

durlambha, adj. (for usual durlabha; Skt. Gr. ati-durl°; Pkt. M. dullambha), *hard to get*: (kāntāra-)durlambhaḥ piṇḍako yācanakena Av ii.83.9; °bhaḥ . . . Avalokiteśvaro Kv 66.22.

durlikhita, nt., *written hostile magic*: Mvy 4382 = Tib. bri(s) ñes, *bad writing*; Māy 220.19 and 245.18 (in both dulli°). See s.v. **durbhukta**.

durvarṇī-karaṇa (nt.; Pali dubbaṇṇa-k°, Vin. iv.120.21, to durvarṇa plus kar-), *the making to be of an ugly color* (referring to a monk's robe; a new robe must be so treated): Prāt 517.6, 7, 8; also °ṇī-kṛtya, ger., treating (robes) thus, MSV ii.48.19.

dull-, see **durl-**.

dullabha, adj. (= Pali id.; MIndic for Skt. durl°), *hard to get*: LV 113.17; 322.4; 429.1 (this last prose; two mss. and Calc. durll°); Mv i.233.19; 248.2; ii.55.8; 359.14.

duvāra (rare in Pali, see Childers; = Skt. dvāra), *door, gate*: bhavana-duvāraṃ (acc.) Mv ii.37.8 (vs).

duvārika, m. (AMg. °riya, derived by Hem. 1.160 and Ratnach. from Skt. dauvārika; cf. also Skt. rāja-dvārika, Ind. Spr.[2] 5631), *doorkeeper*: karotha °kaṃ LV 337.9 (vs), *make* (him my) *doorkeeper*. Could be m.c. for Skt. dau°, Pali do°.

duve, see **dve**.

duścaraka, adj. (= Skt. duścara plus -ka, perh. m.c.), *hard to carry out, to live thru*: °kaṃ śrāmaṇyaṃ Mv iii.269.18 (vs).

Duścintita-cintin, n. of a son of Māra, unfavorable to the Bodhisattva: LV 314.11 °cinty āha. Tib. ñes par bsam pa sems pa, *thinking bad thoughts*, which clearly supports the text, contrary to Foucaux's statement, which Lefm. quotes, that it indicates Upacitta°; ñes par = dus-.

duśchardita, nt., (*evil*) *vomit* (possibly as food of devils, or perhaps as result of their influence): °tam Mvy 4379; Māy 220.18 etc.

duśchāya, **°yā** (cf. **chāya**, **°yā**), an evil supernatural being, presumably (like **chāya**, **°yā**) *a defiler of food*: °yaḥ Mvy 4384 = Tib. gnod ḥgrib, *injurious defiler*; °yā Māy 220.19; 245.18.

duḥ-śraddadha, adj. (to pres. śraddadhati = Skt. °dhāti), *hard to believe*: SP 57.7; 313.10 (both vss).

duḥ-śraddadheya, adj. (dus- plus gdve. based on pres. śraddadhati, as prec.), = prec.: SP 70.2 (vs).

duṣkara, nt. (= Pali dukkara; Skt. as adj.), *difficult task*, said of the feats of religious performance accomplished by a Bodhisattva: °rāṇi Mv i.83.12; 95.15; °raṃ 104.21; °ra-kārakā bodhisattvāḥ AsP 293.9; Gv 74.10; °ra-kāriṇo bodhisattvasya Suv 203.9; °ra-caryā Mvy 6679; LV 36.2; 250.10 ff., or -cārikā Mv ii.130.12, *course of* (such) *difficult tasks* (engaged in by Bodhisattvas).

duṣkaraka, (**1**) nt. = prec.: °kaṃ hi kartum SP 119.6 (vs; -ka may be m.c.); (**2**) adj. (Skt. duṣkara, also used in this sense, plus -ka svārthe), *difficult* (to get), *extraordinary, rare* (with complimentary implication): durlabha-saṃjñā duṣkaraka-saṃjñā Gv 332.7 (prose).

duṣkuhaka, adj. (possibly cf. dukkuha Deśīn. 5.44, defined asahana, in comm. also arocakin), lit. *hard to deceive, not credulous* (cf. Wogihara, Lex. 24): duṣkuhakā Jāmbudvīpakā (or Jambu°) manuṣyā(ḥ), nābhiśraddadhāsyasi (°yati, °yanti) Divy 7.29; 8.26; 9.30; 10.23; 11.18; 12.8; 13.4; 14.23; 335.20; 336.18; 337.14; (avalokiteśvaraṃ . . .) duḥkuhakaṃ lokam upadeśayantam Sādh 77.14.

duṣkṛta, nt. (Skt. id., Pali dukkaṭa), also, rarely, **°tā**, f., *misdeed, sin*: (amūlikayā, samūlikayā . . .) duṣkṛtayā (sc. vipattyā or āpattyā) MSV iii.109.21 (here text with ms. duṣṭatayā, but Tib. ñes byas = duṣkṛta-); 110.2. (Note duṣṭatayā in parallel 111.1, 3, where Tib. ñes bcas; I am not sure which word this represents.)

duṣkha, regularly in ed. and acc. to note on 1.1 'always' in the ms. of Śikṣ for duḥkha, *misery*.

Duṣṭa, n. of a Prajāpati: Māy 257.20, in a list of twelve P.

duṣṭhula, adj. (also spelled **°ṣṭū°**; = Pali duṭṭhulla, adj. and n.; cf. **dauṣṭhulya**; on etym. see below), *wicked, grievously evil*: °lām āpattim Prāt 504.1 (Chin. *une faute grave*); MSV iii.79.5 (see **atisārin**), duṣṭūlāpattiḥ, a-duṣṭu° Hoernle, MR 12.5 (in a Vinaya fragment), rendered *grave offense, not* . . .; in Mvy 8424 °lārocana, 8473 °la-praticchādana, Mironov °lāprati°, *telling* and (*not*) *concealing what is wicked* (no neg. in Tib. and Chin.), the word could (but need not) be considered equal to dauṣṭhulya; °la-samudācārāḥ, *of wicked behavior*, MSV ii.200.17 (of the **ṣaḍvargika** monks). In Prāt 479.12 duṣṭhulayā vācā (cf. Pali Vin. iii.128.22) could be rendered *with lewd words* (making sexual advances to a woman), which acc. to Childers and PTSD is a special (tho not the exclusive) mg. of Pali duṭṭhulla; since no other BHS occurrence of this word or dauṣṭhulya suggests this mg., it seems more probable that the standard meaning, *gravely evil*, prevails here too. Derivation from Skt. Gr. duṣṭhu (pendant to Skt. suṣṭhu) has been plausibly suggested by Lévi, Sūtrāl. vi.2 note 3, and others. Prob. Pali -ulla shows the older form of the ending; on the Pkt. suffix -ulla cf. Pischel 595. Probably dauṣṭhulya was first constructed as a hyper-Skt. form from duṭṭhulla; it was restricted to substantive use, and duṣṭhula (which seems to have been much rarer) was a back-formation from it, as adj. Leumann, cited by Wogihara, Lex. 27 f., came fairly close to this suggestion as an alternative (his first proposal seems to me implausible).

duṣpoṣata (= Pali duposata-), opp. of **su-p°**, q.v., *the being hard to feed* (to satisfy with alms-food): Mvy 2472, with **durbharatā** 2473.

duṣprativedha, see **prativedha.**

Duṣpradharṣa, n. of a Tathāgata: Śikṣ 9.5; of a Tathāgata in the northern quarter: Sukh 98.1.

[**duṣprasaṃstara** ŚsP 112.15, read duṣya-saṃ°.]

Duṣprasaha, n. of a Buddha in a remote Buddha-kṣetra and different universe, but contemporary with Śākyamuni; he stopped preaching when the latter 'turned the wheel of the law': Mv iii.342.3 ff.; the same personage may be meant (tho this incident is lacking) by Buddhas of seemingly exceptional renown so named at Sukh 70.1, and (spelled Duḥprasaha) Mmk 64.1; 130.3.

duṣprekṣita, Māy 220.19, or **duḥpr°**, Mvy 4383, nt., *evil eye.* See s.v. **durbhukta.**

1 **duṣya,** adj., *evil,* = Skt. dūṣya, which Senart's note would read by em.: ye 'duṣyadharmasampannāḥ Mv iii.320.12, *who are not endowed with evil characteristics.*

2 **duṣya, dūṣya,** nt. (= Pali dussa; see also **kalpa-d°**), a kind of cloth, apparently of cotton but of fine quality; see valuable note of Thomas ap. Hoernle MR 138 n.12 (on Kashgar fragment of SP 329.3), with examples of uses to which it is put in Pali and BHS (dress of laymen and -women, not monks; wrapping of corpses; spreads on chairs, and floors; curtains). Spellings with u and ū seem both to occur in mss., but editions are exceptionally confusing. Even the usually so reliable Senart always prints (kalpa-)duṣya, but in his Index reads (kalpa-)dūṣya, without explanation and without citing any v.l. in the Crit. App. In SP usually and in LV only dūṣya is printed; Lefm.'s mss. of LV often read duṣya, or corruptly puṣpa or the like. Recorded duṣya(m) Mvy 5876 (so also Mironov; BR dū°) = Tib. ras bcos bu, said to mean *calico*; duṣyāṇi Mv i.251.14; duṣya (various forms) Mv i.216.13 = ii.19.10; i.227.14; 236.4; Divy 614.17 (mss.); RP 41.2 f. and 56.15 (ms., Finot em. dū°); Suv 126.18 (no ms. has dū°); SP 89.4; Śikṣ 76.12; duṣya-yuga, see below, Mv i.61.1; 331.12; on the other hand, dūṣya SP 75.7 (**-paṭa,** q.v.); 243.6 (-paṭṭa); 283.10; 331.6; LV 77.14, 187.13; 284.13; 368.5 (misprinted dūṣpa), Suv 7.8 (but so only 1 ms., the rest du°); Divy 297.23; Gv 22.3: dūṣya-yuga, see Thomas loc. cit., *a double piece of d°* (two lengths), SP 119.9; LV 159.12; or, dūṣya-yugma, id., SP 329.3; in Kv 78.22 and 81.7 reap duṣya (or dūṣya) for **dhyuṣita,** q.v.

duṣyati, °te (see **dūṣyate, dūṣaṇa,** and **doṣa** = Skt. dveṣa; = Pali dussati, clearly with this mg., e. g. Jāt. vi.9.5 (rajanīye) arajjantā dussanīye adussantā nāma n'atthi, ... *not loathing the loathsome* ...; some forms of Skt. duṣyati, at least its ppp. duṣṭa in Rām. Gorr. 2.92.16, BR, are so used, and the 'caus.' dūṣayati = Pali dūseti also comes close in some uses), *hates* (intrans.), *becomes hateful* or *malicious*, parallel with rajyati (°te) and muhyati (°te), cf. the standard trio rāga, dveṣa (or BHS **doṣa**), moha: kataraṃ cittaṃ rajyati vā duṣyati (Tib. zhe sdaṅ bar ḥgyur ba, *becomes malicious*) vā muhyati vā KP 97.4; yo rajyeta ... yo duṣyeta ... yo muhyeta MadhK 143.1.

[**duhatṛ-** for duhitṛ-, which doubtless read, *daughter*: cakravarti-duhatābhūt Gv 269.14, and °duhatur 17; -duhitā, regularly, 275.11 etc.]

duhitṛkā (= Skt. duhitṛ plus -ka, here ifc. Bhvr.; cf. Schmidt, Nachträge, s.v.), *daughter*: apagata-putra-duhitṛkā (Māyā) LV 26.16 (prose).

duhitrī (§ 13.15) = duhitṛ, *daughter*: °tryoḥ, gen. dual (or, with v.l., °tryāḥ, gen. sg.), Divy 392.10 (prose); °tryā, instr. sg., 402.1 (prose); °trīr (v.l. °trī), acc. pl., LV 301.21 (prose); °tryāḥ, gen., MSV i.104.5.

[? **dūkūla** = Skt. dukūla, a textile fabric: Śikṣ 208.3. Prob. error or misprint.]

dūtī, substantially = **mahādūtī,** q.v.: Mmk 12.(18–)19, read, (mahādūtyaḥ aneka-)dūtī-gaṇa-parivāritā(ḥ).

Dūraṃgamā, n. of the 7th Bodhisattva-bhūmi: Mvy 892 (erroneously °maḥ; Mironov °mā); Dharmas 64; Dbh 5.9 etc.; Bbh 350.9; Laṅk 125.17 et alibi.

dūravedha, m., *the art of shooting at a target from a distance*: Mvy 4991; Divy 100.12; 442.8.

Dūrāroha-buddhi, n. of a former Buddha: Mv i.140.13. So mss., which I would follow; Senart em. Durā°, but see s.v. **Durāroha.**

dūṣaṇa, nt. (to **dūṣyate,** q.v.; = BHS doṣa = Skt. dveṣa), *hatred, malice*, with doṣa in expl. of dveṣa, parallel with rāga, moha: (rāgasya dveṣasya mohasya; tatra rañjanaṃ rāgo raktir adhyavasānaṃ; rajyate vānena) cittam iti rāgaḥ. dūṣaṇaṃ doṣaḥ, āghātaḥ ... dūṣyate vānena (5) cittam iti doṣaḥ MadhK 457.(3–)4.

dūṣika, *eunuch*: °ka, voc., Divy 165.8. Cf. Pkt. (M., Ratnach.) dūsia, 'a kind of eunuch', Sheth and Ratnach. (derived by them from Skt. dūṣita); cited from a ms.

dūṣya, see 2 **duṣya.**

dūṣyate (= **duṣyati, °te,** q.v.), *becomes hateful, malicious*: MadhK 457.4, see s.v. **dūṣaṇa.**

Dṛḍhadeva, n. of a former Buddha: Mv i.137.7.

Dṛḍhadhana (? cf. next), n. of a previous incarnation of Śākyamuni: LV 170.17 (vs); Lefm. with best ms. °dhanu, Calc. with other mss. °dhano; Tib. nor brtan, *firm wealth*, supporting stem -dhana; metr. indifferent; °dhanu could be regarded as identical with next.

Dṛḍhadhanu, (**1**) (cf. prec.) n. of a cakravartin, previous incarnation of Śākyamuni: Mv i.60.14 (°nunā, instr.); n. of an ancient king, perhaps the same: Mv ii.146.19 (°nuḥ, n. sg.); (**2**) n. of a yakṣa: Māy 56.

Dṛḍhanāman, n. of a yakṣa: Māy 19.

dṛḍha-niṣkramaṇa, adj. (Pali daḷhanikkama), *of firm prowess*, said of the family into which the Bodhisattva is born in his last existence: °ṇaṃ Mv i.198.2, mss., Senart em. °vikramaṇaṃ; Pali supports mss., tho the parallels Mv ii.1.12 and LV 24.7 have vikramaṃ (LV v.l. °maṇaṃ).

Dṛḍhaprabha, n. of a Bodhisattva: Gv 442.23.

Dṛḍhapralamba, n. of a prince: Samādh p. 64 line 20 (reading uncertain, for avatī read avacī?).

dṛḍhapraharaṇatarakā, adj. (cf. next), lit. *of stouter blows*; *more martial* (in some specific way?): (tāḥ ... ātavīkān-tāre bahutarakāś ca śūratarakāś) ca dṛ°tarakāś ca ... AsP 373.4.

dṛḍhaprahāri-tā, or **-tva,** n. of some kind of military art or technique, *dealing vigorous blows* (?); in a cliché list of military arts: °tā Mvy 4995; °tāyāṃ, loc., Divy 58.27; 100.13; 442.8; °tve LV 156.13. Tib. on Mvy and LV tshabs (Mvy tshab) che ba, which ace to Jä. and

Das is an adj., *very great, very serious* (esp. said of diseases or dangers, disasters); its application here is not clear. Cf. prec.

Dṛḍhabala, n. of a king: Samādh p. 16 line 14; probably read so also Samādh p. 66, line 27, where text Dṛḍhavaro, of another king, father of a previous incarnation of Śākyamuni. The first part of p. 60 line 30 corruptly refers to the same person; read dṛḍhabalo (or m.c. dṛḍhābalo) nāma pitāsya bhūṣi?

Dṛḍhabāhu, (1) n. of a Buddha in the nadir: Mv i.124.8; (2) n. of a disciple of Śākyamuni: Mv i.182.17.

Dṛḍhamati, (1) m., n. of a man (in Śūraṃgamasamādhisūtra): Śikṣ 91.8 ff.; (2) f., n. of a girl attendant on **Subhadrā** (1): Gv 52.2.

Dṛḍhamūla, n. of a former Buddha: Mv i.139.9.

Dṛḍhavikrama, n. of a Tathāgata: Śikṣ 9.4. See **dṛḍha-niṣkramaṇa**.

Dṛḍhavīrya, (1) n. of a former Buddha: Mv i.139.8; (2) n. of a kiṃnara king: Kv 3.4.

(**dṛḍhavīryatā**, intended as Bhvr. adj., *characterized by firm heroism*, with Mūlā; not n. of a nakṣatra: LV 389.17 (vs) Anurādhā ca Jyeṣṭhā ca Mūlā ca dṛḍhavīryatā (the Mv parallel iii.308.2 reads Mūlaś ca dṛḍhavīryavān), (18) dvāv Āṣāḍhe Abhijic ca Śravaṇo bhavati saptamaḥ; the count is correct taking Āṣāḍhe as two.)

Dṛḍhaśakti, n. of a former Buddha: Mv i.137.14.

Dṛḍhasaṃdhi, n. of a former Buddha: Mv i.137.11.

Dṛḍhahanu, n. of a former Buddha: Mv i.137.10.

Dṛḍhā, n. of an (or, the) earth-goddess (pṛthivīdevatā): Suv 1.8; 3.12; 85.1; 91.15; 121.1 ff. (here begins Chap. 10, entitled Dṛḍhā-parivarta).

dṛśyati (app. based on Skt. °te, passive; cf. **saṃdṛśyati**), *sees* (active!): °yanti Laṅk 268.14 (vs), foll. by accusatives (see s.v. **spariśa**) which must be objects of this.

dṛṣṭa-, (1) short for **dṛṣṭadharma** or °**dhārmika**, in a cpd.: (sarvadharmāṇām) . . . dṛṣṭasukhasaṃsthānām abhilāpya-(read with Tib. an-abhi°) -gati-viśeṣāḥ Laṅk 18.7 (prose), *innumerable different courses of all states-of-existence which are based on* (saṃstha) *the pleasures of the visible* (world). Suzuki fails utterly to understand the passage. For the phrase dṛṣṭa dharma, see next; (2) perhaps = **dṛṣṭi**, *false view*: āya-vyaya-dṛṣṭābhiniveśena Laṅk 174.12 (see s.vv. **āya** and **abhiniveśa**); the alternative would be to emend to °dṛṣṭy-abhi°.

dṛṣṭa-dharma, m., also as two words (= Pali diṭṭhadhamma, also as two words), *the visible world, the present life*, often contrasted with **saṃparāya** (**sāṃ**°): dṛṣṭadharmaḥ Mvy 2974; °ma-sukha- Jm 3.3; °ma-saṃparāyasukhāya Bbh 198.9; °ma-hitāya Divy 207.25; °ma-duḥkhaś LV 416.20; yogināṃ nilayo hy eṣa dṛṣṭadharmavihāriṇām Laṅk 6.13 (vs), *for this* (mountain, giri, from prec. line) *is the abode of disciplined men that are dwelling in the visible* (present) *world* (badly misunderstood by Suzuki); dṛṣṭe dharme, *in the present life*, SP 279.7; Bbh 25.16; Mv iii. 211.15 = 212.2 (dṛṣṭa-); dṛṣṭa eva dharme Divy 302.20; Av ii.195.1; in LV 409.12 (prose) read dṛṣṭa (with mss.) eva dharma (as loc., or possibly em. to °me with Weller 38); dṛṣṭe ca dharme . . . sāṃparāye ca Ud v.25.

dṛṣṭadharmika (only Mvy 8354), or (commonly) °**dhārmika**, adj. (rarely subst. nt., and °kam, adv.; = Pali diṭṭhadhammika; from prec. plus -ika), *relating to the present world, to this life*; often in contrast with **saṃparāyika** or **sāṃ**°, qq.v.: adv. SP 77.14; subst. nt. SP 482.3 (see sāṃparāyika); adj. SP 420.11; Mv iii.212.5, 7; Suv 80.5; 83.4; 136.5; Mmk 426.16 (cpd. °ka-sāṃparāyikāḥ); Bbh 17.19; 170.17; °mika eko 'rthas tathānyaḥ saṃparāyikaḥ (so Lévi; see s.v.) Ud iv.26.

Dṛṣṭaśakti, n. of a former Buddha: Mv i.137.7.

dṛṣṭā, n. sg., for draṣṭā, to stem draṣṭṛ, *seer*: in same line dṛṣṭavya, for dra°, gdve.: na dṛṣṭā na ca dṛṣṭavyaṃ Laṅk 9.6 (vs), *there is no seer nor object of sight*. Possibly both are errors or misprints.

dṛṣṭānta, m., a high number: Mvy 7870 (cited from Gv); Gv 133.13 (text corruptly dṛṣṭvānta).

dṛṣṭāntaka (m.; = Skt. °ta plus -ka svārthe, perhaps m.c.), *parable, comparison*: °kaiḥ kāraṇahetubhiś ca SP 49.6 (vs).

dṛṣṭi, f. (= Pali diṭṭhi), *view, opinion*; rarely in a good sense, (tena, sc. by Buddha, dṛṣṭam acalaṃ paraṃ sukhaṃ, mss. sukha) dṛṣṭibhiḥ paramasādhudṛṣṭibhiḥ Mv i.73.17 (vs), *he has seen immovable supreme bliss by views characterized by supremely good insight*; but, as in Pali, almost always *wrong opinion, heresy*: SP 71.2; (sattveṣu . . . nānā-)-dṛṣṭi-praskanneṣu LV 248.15, *attacked by various heresies*; Mv i.179.2, 3; prahīna-d° Mv iii.61.7; 62.12, *having abandoned heresy*; dṛṣṭiṃ kurvāmi ujjukām SP 125.14 (vs), *I make a heretical view straight (correct it)*; five dṛṣṭi listed Dharmas 68 and Mvy 1955–59, **satkāya-d°**, **antagrāha-d°**, **mithyā-d°**, **dṛṣṭi-parāmarśa**, **śīlavrataparāmarśa**, qq.v.; these same five under other designations AbhidhK. LaV-P. v.15, as explained in the sequel; there are also, as in Pali, 62 dṛṣṭi, see s.v. **dṛṣṭikṛta**; see the following items, and **upalambha**(-dṛṣṭi).

-dṛṣṭika, ifc. (= Pali -diṭṭhika), *having a (usually false) belief in* . . . ; or, in Bhvr., = **dṛṣṭi**, *(false) belief*, (usually) *heresy*; always said of persons: vigatapāpadṛṣṭikaś ca LV 26.9 (prose), *rid of evil heresies*; pudgala-d° Bbh 46.24, *believing in the person*; ātma-dṛṣṭikaiḥ, sattva-, jīva-, pudgala-, Vaj 34.5–6; in good sense, samāna-°ṭikānām MSV iii.101.8 = samānadṛṣṭibhir 100.9.

dṛṣṭi-kṛta (also **dṛṣṭī**°), nt., app. equivalent to **dṛṣṭigata**, q.v.; *matter, item of heresy, instance of heresy*: Mvy 4650 °tam = Tib. lta bar ḥgyur ba (perhaps *changed into* or *become heresy*), or lta bar byas pa (*made heresy*, a lit. rendering); in 4651 dṛṣṭi-gatam is defined lta baḥi rnam pa (*class, species of heresy*), or lta bar gyur ba (= ḥgyur ba, above); important are KP 18.3 (prose) dṛṣṭīkṛtānām, resumed 18.8 by dṛṣṭi (read m.c. dṛṣṭī)-gatan (m.c. for -gatān = -gatāny), both being rendered by Tib. lta bar gyur pa (cf. above), and so KP 109.2 (prose) dṛṣṭigatānām (Tib. lta bar gyur pa), resumed 109.7 (vs) by dṛṣṭīkṛtānām (Tib. lta gyur); in KP 112.1–2 (prose) and 5 (vs) both times dṛṣṭikṛta (or dṛṣṭī°), Tib. lta bar gyur pa (prose) and lta gyur (vs); SP 62.15 vimucya tā dṛṣṭikṛtāni sarvaśaḥ; Śikṣ 190.1 dṛṣṭikṛtāni vinodayanti; Gv 463.9 vinivartayitāraḥ sarva-dṛṣṭikṛtānām; MadhK 374.7 °kṛtāni (fn.: 'expression assez rare; cf. dṛṣṭigata'); 447.10 (tasyaivaṃ vikalpayataḥ) syād dṛṣṭikṛtam, *if he fancies thus, it would be a case of heresy*. There are 62 heresies: dvāṣaṣṭidṛṣṭīkṛta niścayitvā (read **niśrayitvā**, q.v.) SP 48.6 (vs); see Burnouf's note on this; Childers s.v. diṭṭhi; LaVallée-Poussin, AbhidhK. ix.265, note.

dṛṣṭi-gata (also **dṛṣṭī**°, sometimes even in prose; = Pali diṭṭhigata), nt., rarely masc., lit. *what relates to heresy*, substantially = **dṛṣṭi**, *heresy*; cf. in Pali MN comm. i.71.20 diṭṭhi yeva diṭṭhigataṃ, gūthagataṃ (text gutha°) viya; cf. also **dṛṣṭi-kṛta**, which is not recorded in Pali or elsewhere; and see s.v. **gata**: Mvy 4651; KP 18.8; 109.2, see **dṛṣṭi-kṛta** (Tib. renderings noted there); pāpakāni akuśalāni dṛṣṭigatāny utpannāni LV 398.3 = Mv iii.317.7; dṛṣṭigatāni LV 398.10; Jm 146.7; Bbh 228.1; °gatam Śikṣ 61.19; other, misc. forms Mv iii.67.9; 353.15 (°gateṣu, mss., Senart °gatiṣu); Śikṣ 18.4; KP 154.9; Gv 117.3; 508.15; dṛṣṭī-gatāni Mv iii.318.14 (prose: v.l. dṛṣṭi°); °gatam Suv 61.13 (vs, ī may be m.c.); other dṛṣṭīgata, in prose, KP 94.3; 95.4; masc. dṛṣṭigatān Divy 164.19, 22; dṛṣṭīgatan (m.c. for °tān; °tāny) KP 18.8 (vs).

dṛṣṭi-parāmarśa, m. (= Pali diṭṭhi-parāmāsa), lit. *clinging, attachment* (see **parāmṛśati**) *to heresy*, as one of the five dṛṣṭi: Dharmas 68; Mvy 1958; paraphrased

AbhidhK. LaV-P. v.15, 18 as hīnocca-d°, *regarding as high what is low* (evil).

dṛṣṭiviṣa (subst.; in Skt. as adj. with nouns for *snake*, so also here, LV 317.8, prose), *having poison in the glance, a snake* (perh. a particular kind of snake?): na siṃhavṛndaṃ ... dṛṣṭīviṣāṇāṃ (°ṭī° m.c.) api nāsti vṛndaṃ LV 314.1 (vs); āśīviṣā bhujaga dṛṣṭiviṣāś ca ghorāḥ 339.2 (vs; is this a noun, distinct from āśīviṣā and bhujaga? so the ca seems to suggest).

dṛṣṭī-(in cpds.), see **dṛṣṭi-**.

***-dekkhiya,** MIndic, *worthy to be seen*, implied by **a-dekṣiya,** q.v.

deyadharma, m. (= Pali deyyadhamma, primarily adj. and may have nt. gender, AN i.166.12 deyyadhammaṃ, n. sg., see comm. ii.265.32, 266.3), *meritorious gift*, lit. *having the quality of something that should be given*: °ma-parityāgāt Mv ii.276.10, *as a result of having given meritorious gifts*; °ma-parityāgena Av ii.117.4; °maṃ, acc., Mv iii.426.6; (ayam) asya °mo yat tathāgatasya pāṃśvañjaliḥ pātre prakṣiptaḥ Divy 369.3; bhagavacchāsane sarvadeyadharmāḥ samucchinnāḥ Av i.308.6.

delu, nt., a high number: Gv 133.20; = **elu,** m. or f., q.v.

deva (Skt.), often also **devaputra** (rare in Skt., common in Pali devaputta), *god*. More or less complete and corresponding lists of the classes of Buddhist gods are given in Pali in MN iii.100 ff.; Kvu 207, 208; Abhidh-s. (here called Abh) 21; Childers (Ch) 467 has a list nearly agreeing with the last; in BHS, in Mvy 3075 ff.; Dharmas 127 ff.; Mv (1) ii.314.4 ff.; (2) 348.16 ff.; LV 150.2 ff.; Av i.5.1 ff. (et alibi); Divy (1) 68.12 ff.; (2) 138.19 ff.; (3) 367.9 ff.; (4) 568.24 ff.; Bbh 61.27 ff.; Gv 249.10 ff. (the last in reverse order). There are other lists, mostly fragmentary, and often so confused as to be hardly usable. The gods fall into three grand divisions: **kāmāvacara,** living in the **kāmadhātu** (cf. Mvy 3071–4), usually six in number; **rūpāvacara,** in the **rūpadhātu**; **ārūpyāvacara,** in the **ārūpyadhātu.** Cf. also the 9 **sattvāvāsa,** Mvy 2288 ff. (Pali DN 3.263). — **Kāmāvacara** (deva). The standard list is: **cāturmahārājika** (BHS sometimes cat°); often °**rājakāyika,** so in Mvy, Dharmas, Divy 2, Bbh; **trāyastriṃśa** (Av, Divy, Bbh, **trayas**°); **yāma** (Bbh yama); **tuṣita** (in Dharmas before yāma); **nirmāṇarati** (see also **nirmita**); **paranirmitavaśavartin.** The Gv list omits 1 and 2. Before 1, Mvy inserts **bhauma** and **āntarikṣavāsin,** making 8 instead of 6. So Mv 2 prefixes bhūmyāṃ (see s.v. **bhūmi**) va carā (devāḥ; so read with mss.; va = eva) and **antarīkṣecarā**(ḥ). While no other of the above lists has these two items, **bhauma** and **antarīkṣa** (or **antarikṣa**; adjective) devas are associated with shorter lists (generally of kāmāvacara, or some of them, alone) in LV 266.1; 367.7 and 368.3; 396.14; 401.1; and correspondingly **bhūmya** and **antarīkṣecara** (deva) in Mv i.40.14; 229.14, 15; 240.3, 4; ii.138.12 and elsewhere. — **Rūpāvacara** (deva) dwell in the rūpadhātu (Mvy 3073), divided into the four **dhyāna-**bhūmi (Mvy 3084 ff., see **dhyāna**), the last of which includes, as its final and highest group, the **śuddhāvāsakāyika** gods, in five sub-groups. These being counted separately, the standard list of rūpāvacara contains usually 18 items in BHS, 16 in Pali, as follows. First dhyāna-bhūmi, usually 4 items, in Pali 3: **brahmakāyika** (not in Pali lists, but the word occurs, acc. to Childers as an inclusive term for the classes of the first dhyāna-bhūmi; perhaps rather for all the rūpāvacara, or for them plus the arūpāvacara, since they all inhabit brahmalokas, Childers s.v.; in Gv also omitted; in Mv put second, **brahmā** (devā) being first in Mv 1, and **mahābrahmā** in Mv 2); **brahmapāriṣadya** (Dharmas, LV, Divy 4 °**pārṣadya,** Gv °**pārṣada**; om. Mv 1, Divy 1–3, Av, Bbh; after brahmapurohita in Dharmas, LV, Mv 2, Divy 4; our order is that of Mvy, Gv, Pali); **brahmapurohita** (Gv omits brahma by haplography), **mahābrahman** (or °hma; as no. 1 in Mv 2). Second dhyāna-bhūmi, regularly 3 items in BHS and Pali; but Mv 1 and 2 and Pali MN iii.102.25 prefix another, **ābhā(ḥ)** (misprinted abhā in MN) devā(ḥ): **parīttābha** (Divy 1–3 mss. **parītā**°; Mv 1 omits); **apramāṇābha** (Mv 1 omits); **ābhāsvara** (Divy 3 **apramāṇābhāsvara**). Third dhyāna-bhūmi, regularly 3 items in BHS and Pali; Mv and Pali MN iii.102.30 add another, **śubhā** devāḥ (Pali subhā devā): **parīttaśubha** (Mv 2 omits); **apramāṇaśubha** (Dharmas omits), **śubhakṛtsna.** Fourth dhyāna-bhūmi, usually three items in BHS, one in Pali, plus (sometimes app. included in the 4th dhy. bh. but sometimes not, cf. Childers s.v. jhānaṃ) the five śuddhāvāsa(kāyika), who are usually not given this separate group-designation in the lists (but are so designated e. g. in Mvy 3101 and Abh): **anabhraka** (Pali and Mv omit); **puṇyaprasava** (Pali and Mv omit); **vṛhatphala** (so only Mvy and Mv 2 in BHS, others **bṛh**°, but Pali vehapphala); only in Dharmas, LV, and Abh of Pali there follows **asaṃjñisattva,** Pali (Abh) asaññasatta, a term which occurs as the 5th sattāvāsa in the Pali list of these DN iii.263.9 ff. (preceding the arūpadhātu), while in the corresponding list of 9 sattvāvāsa in Mvy (2297) it is made the 9th and highest, above the arūpadhātu (an obvious error of Mvy); this item is also given in Childers's list and is needed to make up the traditional Pali number of 16 rūpa-brahmaloka. Then all lists have the five **śuddhāvāsakāyika: avṛha** (Av, Divy 1–3, Bbh **abṛha,** Gv **abṛhat**); **atapa** (Gv atapo, as s-stem); **sudṛśa** (Mv 1 omits); **sudarśana** (Mv 2 omits; Divy 1 **sudarśa**); **akaniṣṭha** (for the Pali forms see these words). Here Mvy alone adds as additional stages of śuddhāvāsakāyika, **aghaniṣṭha** and **mahāmaheśvarāyatanam** (see these words). — The **ārūpyāvacara** gods dwell in the four **ārūpyadhātu** bhūmi listed (only in Mvy and Dharmas, and in Pali MN, Abh. and Childers) as **ākāśānantyāyatana, vijñānānantyāyatana, ākiṃcanyāyatana,** and **naivasaṃjñānāsaṃjñāyatana**; the gods dwelling in them are described in Dharmas as °**āyatanopagāḥ** (see s.v. **upaga**; similarly Pali °āyatanūpagā). In Suv 86.11 ff., curiously, the first three 'stages', ending °āyatana, are personified as gods (°āyatanānāṃ koṭiśataṃ), while only with the last °āyatanopagatānāṃ (for °nopagānāṃ) is used. The first of the four is found in the Pali Kvu list also. For the Pali forms of the names see s.vv.

devakulika, see **daiva**°.

Devakuśa, n. of a brother of Kuśa: Mv ii.433.16.

Devagarbha, n. of a former Buddha: Mv i.139.1.

Devagupta, n. of two former Buddhas: Mv i.137.9; 140.12.

Devaguru, n. of a former Buddha: Mv i.141.11.

Devacūḍa, n. of a former Buddha: Mv i.139.7.

Devaḍaha, m. (= Pali Deva-daha; Pali, AMg. daha for Skt. Lex. draha = Skt. hrada; domal ḍ seems not to be recorded anywhere else), n. of a Śākyan village (nigama): °ho Mv i.355.15; °hāto 357.1; in 356.5, 7 mss. corruptly deva-ubha (em. Senart).

devata, m., nt., *divinity*; interpreted by Weller 36 as = Skt. daivata; that may have something to do with it, but see § 9.4; in part it seems also a matter of use of m. and nt. endings (and modifiers) with f. noun (devatā): kasmān name devate (acc. pl.) LV 120.12 (vs), *why should he bow to the gods*?; devataiḥ 221.5 and 10 (vss; only v.l. devaiḥ, unmetr.); -devataiḥ, °tair also 281.5, 8 (vs, no v.l.); kiṃcid giridevataṃ vā nadīdevataṃ vā (n. sg.) 382.6 (prose; Calc. daiv°); ete catvāro bodhivṛkṣadevatās (m. n. pl.) 401.22 (prose), and tān devatān (acc. pl.) 402.2; anye ... -devatāḥ 421.9 (vs), and in next line teṣāṃ, referring to these devatāḥ; in Divy 209.5 (prose) anekābhir Vaiśālīvananivāsinībhir devatair (despite fem. adjs.!).

?**devataṭika** (-pravrajitā, f.), prob. a corruption concealing the name of some kind of (female) ascetics: devanirmālyahomena devat°jitā ca vaśyā bhavanti Mmk 714.11 (prose; in prec. line, by another means, kulastriyo vaśyā bhavanti).

Devatā-sūtra, n. of a work: Karmav 89.6; 94.6. See Lévi on the latter. The corresp. Pali sutta is the Kiṃdada s., but it is part of the Devatā-saṃyutta, the first division of SN.

devatī = **devatā** (the form °tī is cited by Ratnach. from a manuscript work as = Devakī, the mother of Kṛṣṇa!), *divinity*: only noted in Sādh, but fairly common there, by the side of devatā; devatyaḥ, °tyo Sādh 140.11; 180.10; 185.19; -tyor, loc. dual, 191.22; daśadevatīparivṛtaṃ 195.6; sarvāsāṃ °tīnāṃ 199.4, etc.

Devadatta (**1**) (= Pali id.), n. of a Śākyan, relative of the Buddha and inimical to him: son of Śuklodana, brother of Ananda and Upadhāna, Mv iii.176.15; after the Bodhisattva's retirement asks Yaśodharā to marry him, Mv ii.69.2; kills an elephant at the city gate but cannot remove it, Mv ii.74.13 ff.; various previous incarnations identified, Mv i.128.14; ii.72.10; Divy 328.11; instigated Ajātaśatru to parricide, Divy 280.18; Av i.83.6; 308.5; other refs., Mvy 3610; LV 144.10 ff.; 152.14 ff.; 154.1 ff.; enters the order of monks, Av ii.112.4; hostility to Buddha, Av i.88.6; 177.6 ff.; Karmav 45.3; as a typically, proverbially evil person, Karmav 49.4; RP 36.3; Devadattodrakasamācāro Śikṣ 105.17, *characterized by conduct like D. and U.*; (**2**) n. of an evidently virtuous monk, follower of Buddha, to whom in a previous birth he had taught a holy text, and for whom the Buddha now predicts future Buddhahood: SP 259.2 ff. (only in prose; no verse account of this incident; prob. a late intrusion).

devadundubhi, m. or f. (= Pali id.), pl., *drums of the gods* (thunder): Divy 203.10; MPS 17.19, 21.

devaputra, see **deva**.

Devaputra-māra (= Pali Devaputta°), one of the four Māras, see s.v. **Māra**.

Devapurā (v.l. °ra, nt.), n. of the capital of the former Buddha Sudarśana: Mv iii.235.18; 236.8.

Devaprabha, n. of a Bodhisattva: Gv 3.17.

Devamakuṭa, (**1**) n. of a Bodhisattva: Gv 3.4; (**2**) n. of a Buddha: Gv 258.7.

Devamati, (**1**) n. of a past cakravartin, whose wife was later reborn as the goddess Pramuditanayanajagadvirocanā: Gv 255.10; (**2**) n. of a Buddha: Gv 284.15.

Devamatiprabha, n. of a kiṃnara: Mvy 3415.

Devamitrā, n. of a rākṣasī: Māy 241.14.

Devarāja, n. of a future Buddha, who, it is predicted, will be a future incarnation of **Devadatta** (2): SP 259.7 ff.

Devarājagupta, n. of a former Buddha: Mv i.138.1.

Devarājaprabha, n. of a former Buddha: Mv i.141.6.

?**devala**, a high number: Gv 106.2. Cf. **hevara**; perhaps read so, or hevala, here; but Gv 133.9 **hetura**.

deva-lipi, a kind of script: LV 126.2; so also Tib. lha-, *god*.

Devalokābhilaṣita (so most mss.; Senart with one ms. °lāṣita), n. of a former Buddha: Mv i.138.1.

Devavacanā, n. of a 'gandharva maid': Kv 5.7.

Devavālāha, see **Vālāha**.

Devaśarman, n. of a yakṣa: Māy 76.

Devaśiri-, see **Devaśrī-**.

Devaśuddha, n. of a Bodhisattva: Gv 442.23.

Devaśrī, (**1**) n. of a (Buddhist) monk: Gv 47.10; (**2**) (°śiri, m.c.) n. of a kalpa: Gv 256.15 (vs).

Devaśrīgarbha, (**1**) n. of a Bodhisattva: Dbh 2.10; (**2-3**) n. of two Buddhas (in form °śiri°, m.c.): Gv 256.18 and 259.8 (vss).

Devasattva, n. of a former Buddha: Mv i.139.2.

devasika, MIndic for **daiv°**, q.v.

Devasiddhayātra (v.l. °pātra), n. of a former Buddha: Mv i.137.2.

devasumanas, m., a kind of flower: °nāḥ Mvy 6206 = Tib. lha yid dgaḥ, *god-mind-pleasing* (literal); the insertion of ms. H cited by Lefm. on LV 11.3 contains the word in a cpd. devasumanotpala-, confirmed by Tib. lhaḥi sna maḥi me tog, *flower of nutmeg of the gods* (sna ma, reported to mean *nutmeg flower*, Jā. and Das).

Devasopānā, n. of the lokadhātu of the future Buddha **Devarāja**: SP 259.9.

Devābharaṇa, n. of a former Buddha: Mv i.138.3.

Devābhika, n. of a former Buddha: Mv i.141.2.

Devālaṃkṛta, n. of a former Buddha: Mv i.139.6.

Devāvataraṇa, nt., n. of a place: Karmav 78.16. It seems safe to assume that it means **Devāvatāra**; cf. (Sāṃkāśye nagare) devatāvataraṇaṃ vidarśitaṃ bhavati Divy 150.23.

Devāvatāra, m., n. of a place, = **Sāṃkāśya**, q.v.: °raḥ Mvy 4103; °re Māy 105 (the Chin. comms. cited by Lévi 115 make the identification); °re mahācaitye Saṃkaśye mahāprātihārike Mmk 88.14 (vs). Cf. prec.

Devāvatāra-sūtra, n. of a work: Karmav 159.18 (see Lévi's note).

Devī, n. of a yakṣiṇī: Sādh 561.2 (but possibly only an epithet of one of the names which adjoin this word in a long cpd. listing names of yakṣiṇī).

Devendragarbha, n. of a Tathāgata: Gv 360.9.

Devendracūḍa, n. of two presumably different Tathāgatas: Gv 259.1; 361.5.

Devendrabuddhi, n. of a teacher: Mvy 3490.

Devendrarāja, n. of a Bodhisattva: Gv 4.6.

Devendra-samaya, nt., n. of a 'royal science' (rājaśāstra) taught in Suv Chap. 12: Suv 69.18; 131.9; 132.6 ff. It deals with kingship, and seems to have been originally an independent work; Nobel, Introd. XLI.

deśa, nt. (otherwise m.), *part* (here, of the body; not common in Skt., but see śarīradeśebhyaḥ BṛhU 4.4.3; common in AMg., see Ratnach. s.v. desa 5): na ca te 'ntarā kāyu kadāci cālito, na hasta-pādaṃ no pi cānya deśam SP 161.9 (vs; mss., except Kashgar rec. grīva for deśa; KN em. cānyad-aṅgam, kept by WT without note), *and your body never moved, not your hands or feet, nor any other part.*

-deśaka, f. **°ikā**, adj. ifc. (to Skt. deśayati plus -aka), *showing, exhibiting*: pañcadaśa-(and, ṣoḍaśa-)-varṣa-deśikā Mv iii.282.8–9, (girls created by magic) *showing* (an apparent age of) 15 or 16 *years*. See also **dharma-deśaka.**

deśana, nt. (= °nā 2, q.v.), *confession*; see **atyaya-d°**.

deśanatā = **deśanā**, (**1**) *preaching*, ln dharma-d° Bbh 82.18; (**2**) *confession*: Bhad 12.

deśanā (= Pali des°; to Skt. or BHS deśayati plus -anā), (**1**) *preaching*, in this sense Skt., hardly specifically Buddh., but see **°nā-pāṭha, dharma-d°**, (°nā-)**matsarin**; also, deśanā dharmasya Mv i.42.10; 53.5; °nā naranāgānāṃ (= Buddhānāṃ) Mv i.168.4; deśanā-naya, *the way of verbal instruction*, in Laṅk 148.10 ff., 172.6, distinct from and inferior to siddhānta-(pratyavasthāna-)naya, *the finally approved way*, which is that of immediate personal realization, see Suzuki, Studies, 409 (where other citations of this depreciative use of deśanā in Laṅk); LaVallée Poussin, HJAS 3.137 ff.; (**2**) *confession* (so Pali, e.g. Jāt. v.379.22 desanaṃ paṭigaṇhanto; not in PTSD, Childers): °nā-parivarta Suv 20.1, *Confession*, title of Chap. 3; °nāgāthāḥ 21.8; pāpa-d° Dharmas 14; °nādyaṃ tu pāpāder Sādh 72.13, et alibi; see also **atyaya-d°**; (**3**) see s.v. **gaṇḍī**(-deśanā).

deśanā-pāṭha (m.), *sermon-reading, verbal instruction* or *text*; acc. to Suzuki, always depreciative in Laṅk; so (thinks S.) °ṭha-kathāṃ Laṅk 12.17 contrasting with tathāgatapratyātmagocarakathāṃ 16; I am not sure that I understand this passage, but deśanāpāṭhābhiratānāṃ sattvānāṃ 14.2 is certainly depreciative; as to deśanāpāṭhe 16.12, I am again uncertain; yāni deśanāpāṭhe (Suzuki, *canonical texts*) 'nusaṃvarṇitāny ānantaryāṇi 139.9, these are among the *'external'* (bāhyāni, 139.6) *acts-of-immediate-fruition*; in 222.19 etad eva... mayā Śrīmālāṃ devīm adhikṛtya deśanāpāṭhe..., there seems nothing depreciative, even in Suzuki's rendering, *this... was told by me in the canonical text relating to Queen Śrīmālā* (viz., the **Śrīmālāsiṃhanāda-sūtra**?).

deśayati or °**śeti** (= Pali deseti; see also **diśati,** 2, 3), (**1**) *communicates, teaches*: Mvy 2770; almost always with dharma, *the Doctrine,* as object, and very common everywhere: SP 63.10 (ppp. deśitu, dharma), 12; 92.14; 199.7; 264.6; 317.10; LV 409.10; 416.22; Mv i.52.11; 60.6; 73.10 (deśitā daśabalena, subject skandhā); iii.51.12; 201.9; 357.11; dharma in different sense, (nāhaṃ... ye) dharmā anityās te nityato deśayāmi Mv i.173.2, *I do not teach that states-of-being which are impermanent are permanent*; deśanām Suv 28.11 and 29.1; deśayāmo Bhīk 6b.1, *communicate, make known*; text ppp. deśayito, yo imu Bhadracarī-praṇidhānaṃ dhārayi vācayi deśayito vā Bhad 54, but read opt., deśay' ito vā, *or teaches from it*; (**2**) *confesses*: see s.v. **atyaya,** where SP 210.1; 212.7; LV 409.22 are cited; tat (pāpakaṃ karma) ṣarvaṃ deśayiṣyāmi Suv 25.4; similarly 27.8, 10 etc.; (karma kṛtaṃ...) deśayati Karmav 47.26; see also **deśya**; (**3**) *displays, exhibits,* in the sense of darśayati: deśenti Mv i.170.2, cited s.v. **upadeśeti,** q.v. for reasons against em. to darś°.

?**deśayin,** *teaching* (the Doctrine); perhaps so interpret SP 272.5 (vs) raseṣu gṛddha saktāś ca gṛhīṇāṃ dharma deśayī, satkṛtāś ca bhaviṣyanti..., (will, in later ages, be) *teaching the Doctrine to householders,* n. pl. m.(?); but perhaps better as 3 pl. (in form sg.) opt., like deśayuḥ line 10, from deśayati (altho verb forms in this passage are mostly fut.).

deśya, gdve. to **deśayati** (2), *to be confessed*: (āpattayo hy etā...) āryasyākāśagarbhasya... deśyāḥ Śikṣ 67.14.

dehaka (Pali id.) = Skt. deha, *body*: vikopenti (see this) na dehakaṃ Mv i.168.18 (vs; -ka perh. m.c.).

dehalā (or °rā?; Skt. and M. °lī; not in Pali), *threshold*: dehalāya, °ye, gen. sg., Mv ii.437.14, 15, 17 (prose; in the first two mss. °rāya).

dainya-tā (= Skt. dainya), *discouragement*: Mv i.83.17 (vs).

daivakulika (Mironov deva°), m., *temple guard*: Mvy 3748 = Tib. lha khaṅ bsruṅ ba. (M. devakuliya, defined pūjārī, *worshiper*.)

daivasika (also written dev°) adj., and °kam adv. (= Pali dev°, adj. and adv.; Skt. divasa plus -ika), *daily, relating to* or *consisting of a day*; adv., *each day*: Māy 220.20 (of fever, *quotidian*); adv. °kaṃ... pūjeti Mv i.302.14; 309.9 (bhuṃjanti), 10; 360.4 (ekaṃ mṛgaṃ... dāsyāmaḥ); 361.7; iii.255.3 (in i.309.9, 10 mss. dev°, em. Senart; in iii.255.3 Senart dev°, v.l. daiv°); at end of cpds. with numerals, dvi-d°: kiṃ dvidaivasikāṃ bhṛtiṃ dadāsi Divy 305.6, *why do you give two days' wages* (for a single day)?; evaṃrūpai rātriṃdivaiḥ pañcadaśa-daivasikena pakṣeṇa triṃśad-daivasikena māsena... Śikṣ 283.5–6, *with a half-month made up of* 15 *days of that sort, a month made up of* 30...

doṣa, m. (once app. nt., na ca doṣam asti LV 138.19, vs, but perh. doṣa-m-, 'hiatus-bridging' m; = Pali dosa; see **duṣyati, dūṣaṇa**), *hatred, malice, aversion,* for Skt. dveṣa, which also occurs, sometimes in variants of the same passage; usually distinguishable from the homonym doṣa (Skt. id.), esp. by association with rāga and synonyms (also moha), or contrast with *love* (kāma, preman, sneha): premā ca doṣaś ca na me kahiṃ cit SP 128.9 (vs), *I have no love or hatred for any*; nirjita-kāma-doṣāḥ Divy 399.3–4; na ca snehu nāpi doṣas LV 355.10; associated, often compounded, with rāga, and generally also with moha, LV 291.1; 313.3; 403.5 (but also rāga-dveṣa-moha LV 374.19); Mv ii.41.18; Suv 23.10; Gv 54.5; 195.19; Śikṣ 164.6 (cited from Suv 33.9 where text with all mss. dveṣa); Dbh 35.16; MadhK 457.4, in explanation of dveṣa, see s.v. **dūṣaṇa;** dveṣa Śikṣ 232.12, resumed by doṣa 13; maitrīm utpādayitvā doṣaṃ vivarjayiṣyāmi Śikṣ 200.15; among misc. vices, LV 357.6; 372.17.

doṣā, adv. (Skt. chiefly Vedic; cf. Skt. doṣām, Pali dosaṃ), *last evening*: Mv ii.258.5 (prose).

dohalaka, m. (= Skt. dohala, °da; cf. Skt. dohadaka, pw), *pregnancy-longing*: tasyā (mss. tasya) kākīye rājabhojanena dohalako Mv iii.125.16 (prose).

daukūlaka, nt. (Skt. °la plus -ka svārthe), *a garment made of the fine fabric dukūla*: °kam Mvy 9162 (text misprinted °kul°, Index °kūl°).

daumya, adj. (cf. AMg. dūmiya, *white*; dūmaṇa, also dumaṇa, nt., *making white*; not in Skt. or Pali), *white*: site daumye tathā śukle (sc. paṭe) Mmk 131.20 (vs).

daurgandha, nt. (Skt. durgandha plus -a; Skt. daurgandhya; this is a quite possible Skt. formation, cf. Speyer on Av i.280.1), *bad odor*: Divy 57.20 (°dhaṃ mukhān niścarati); 193.21; Av i.280.1; ii.167.2.

daurmanasya-tā (= Skt. °sya), *dejection*: Mv ii.355.17 (vs; not cpd.).

daurmanasyita, denom. ppp. from Skt. daurmanasya, used as subst., *dejection*: Samādh p. 29 line 21. Or is this an error or misprint for °sya-tā, prec.?

daurvacasya, nt. (= Pali dovacassa, which, with dubbaca, is wrongly defined PTSD, see SBE 13.12 n. 1), *the quality of being hard to talk to,* i. e. *not receptive to good advice,* a saṃghāvaśeṣa sin: Mvy 8381 = Tib. bkaḥ blo mi bde pa, *not putting one's mind on advice*; MSV iii.88.5; cf. Prāt 486.6 ff.; Pali Vin. iii.178.3 ff.

daurvarṇika, °**ṇiya** (only Mv ii.392.13), written also **dauv°,** nt. (Skt. durvarṇa plus -ika, -(i)ya; cf. AMg. duvaṇṇa; form without r may be genuine analogical creation to sauv°, suv°, frequent antonym), *ugliness, ill-favoredness*: 18 kinds, cited from gloss on Aśokāvadāna by Speyer, note on Av ii.52.11; the number 18 also Av ii.175.6; Divy 411.14; dau-v° SP 293.1 (vs), all mss. lack -r- acc. to KN, yet WT daurv° without note; Av ii.52.11, ms., Speyer em. daurv°; Mv ii.392.13 (vs), mss. dauvarṇa(m) yaṃ, Senart em. daurvarṇiyaṃ; mss. daurvaṇika Divy 411.14 (em. °varṇ°); daurvarṇika attributed to ms. only Av ii.175.6.

dauṣṭhulya, spelled in Mvy 2102 (also Mironov) °**ṣṭulya,** in Das, Tib. Dict. s.v. gnas ṅan lan (for which Mvy, and Lévi, Sūtrāl. vi.2 note 3, read len, Lévi adds pa) **dauṣṭhūlya,** nt. (Pali duṭṭhulla; see s.v. **duṣṭhula**), *gross wickedness, depravity*; AbhidhK.LaV-P. v.2, *mauvais état*; apparently very general word, applied to any wickedness; e. g. kāya-dau° Śikṣ 116.17 is illustrated by hastavikṣepaḥ etc.; kāya-d° utpādayet, vāg-d°... mano-d°... ŚsP 281.16 ff.; anādikāla-prapañca-d°-vāsanā Laṅk 38.7, etc.; Bbh 9.1; 14.26; 20.6, etc., common in these texts.

dauṣprajña, adj. (in mg. = Skt. duṣprajña, Pali duppañña; app. formally from Skt. duṣ-prajñā plus -a; cf. next), *unwise*: °jñāḥ Mvy 7070; (na) ca bodhisattvo dauṣprajña-dānaṃ (*a gift to the unwise*) dadāti, dadat prājña-dānam eva dadāti Bbh 123.16.

dauṣprajñiya (nt.; from Skt. duṣprajña, or BHS dauṣ°, plus -(i)ya), *unwisdom*: °yaṃ ca vijahati Mv ii.392.14 (vs).

dyutiṃdhara, (**1**) adj. (= Pali jutim°), *brilliant, glorious*: pārthivendrair °dharair Divy 398.21 (vs); (**2**) n. of a nāga-king: Māy 247.11; (**3**) n. of a mountain: Māy 253.28.

[**draṅga,** v.l. for **avadraṅga,** q.v.]

dradula, see **dadrula.**

drabuddha, m., a high number: Mvy 7742; v.l. in

Mironov drabudaḥ; corresponds in position to **durbuda,** q.v. No corresp. in Gv 133.13–14.

[**Drama,** Kv 3.6, read **Druma,** q.v.]

Dramiḍa, n. of a nāga king: Mvy 3299; Māy 247.37.

drava (m., = Skt. Lex., and late lit., id., see Schmidt, Nachtr. s.v.; Pali dava), *sport, play*: Bbh 169.5 saṃkiḷikilāyate auddhatyaṃ dravaṃ prāviṣkaroti pareṣāṃ hāsayitukāmo; MSV iii.16.2 (mātṛgrāmeṇa . . .) saṃkilikilāyete, audatyaṃ (read **auddhatyaṃ**) dravaṃ (Tib. ḥphyar bar byed, *assuming a seductive attitude*) kāyitāntyaṃ(?)kurutaḥ; Jm 225.11 -drava-hāsa-nādaṃ; (?) SP 189.1 mā khalv ima ekam eva buddhajñānaṃ śrutvā draveṇaiva (*in mere sport, lightly, not taking it seriously*? but Burnouf *bien vite*, Kern *suddenly*) pratinivartayeyur . . .

dravīkaroti (Skt. Lex. id.; to drava), *makes liquid*: °kṛtya MSV i.249.13 ff.

-dravyaka, ifc. Bhvr. (= Skt. dravya), *substance*: aṣṭadravyakam etan nu Laṅk 270.6 (vs), *consisting of eight substances* (possibly m. c.).

dravyāmbara, adj., *lacking in wealth, poor*: LV 42.21 (vs) °rāś (acc. pl.) ca puruṣān dhaninaḥ kuruṣva, *and make poor men rich*; confirmed by Tib. nor gyis brel pa *poor in, destitute of, wealth*; Calc. divyāmbarāṃś, without ms. support. *Having* (only) *their clothes as wealth* would seem to require ambaradravya; I do not understand the formation.

drākṣā-latikā (would be expected to mean *grape-vine-creeper*, but actually means) *grape* (the fruit): . . . mātuluṅgāni ca vīrasenakāni ca °tikā ca āmrāṇi ca . . . Mv ii.475.14 (prose; in a list of fruits).

Drāmiḍa, adj. (precisely this form seems to be unrecorded; cf. AMg. Dāmila), *Dravidian*: (avyaktāḥ śabdā yeṣām artho na vijñāyate; tad yathā) °ḍānāṃ mantrāṇāṃ . . . Bbh 69.3.

?**drāva,** nt. (vv.ll. drāṣa, naṣa), some part of the body, in a passage (vss, tho printed as prose) identifying various bodily parts with features of the outside world: (sāgaraś cāpy amedhyaṃ vai) drāvaṃ Brahmā Prajāpatiḥ Divy 628.29. I have no idea what is intended; but sarvaṃ, conjectured in note, seems implausible.

drāviḍa-lipi (v.l. drāmiḍa-, with d; cf. **tramiḍā**), *Dravidian writing*: LV 125.21 = Tib. ḥgro ldiṅ ba (standard word for Dravidian), rendered etymologically by Foucaux.

druma, (1) nt. (otherwise recorded only as m.), *tree*: drumāṇi Mv i.7.3 (prose, no v.l.); (2) m., n. of the king of the Kiṃnaras (in Skt. n. of the king of the Kiṃpuruṣas; not noted in Pali or Pkt.): SP 4.13; Mv ii.97.5; 108.5; Divy 443.2; 451.12; 457.3; Mvy 3414; MSV i.134.11; Śikṣ 261.15; Kv 3.6 (printed Drama); Mmk 19.4; 655.9; Gv 250.4.

Drumakiṃnaraprabha, n. of a gandharva: Mvy 3382.

Drumakiṃnararāja-paripṛcchā, n. of a work: Mvy 1352.

Drumakuśa, n. of a brother of Kuśa: Mv ii.433.17.

Drumachāyā, n. of a yoginī: Sādh 427.4.

Drumadhvaja, nt., n. of a Buddhakṣetra: Mv i.123.16.

Drumaparvata, n. of a Buddha: Gv 284.26.

Drumaparvatateja, n. of a Buddha: Gv 310.20 (prose).

Drumameruśrī, n. of a capital city: Gv 398.23.

Drumaratnaśākhāprabha, n. of a kiṃnara: Mvy 3419.

Drumāvatī, n. of a city: Gv 427.13 (vs; ā may be m.c.).

droṇa-, *valley* (so Skt. droṇī), implied in **droṇamukha,** q.v.; BR state that v.l. droṇī° occurs for droṇa° in Mvy (5285), but Mironov droṇa° with no v.l.

droṇa-kāka, m. (Skt. Lex. id., also droṇa, m., id.), *crow* or *raven*: Mvy 4897 = Tib. bya rog.

Droṇa-grāmaka, m., n. of a Vṛji village: MPS 21.6: here lived **Dhūmrasagotra,** q.v., MPS 51.2.

(**droṇamukha,** nt. [see also next; in BR, pw, only recorded Lex., but Schmidt, Nachtr., shows that it occurs in late Skt.; not in Pali; = AMg. doṇamuha, *a city near a port* . . ., Ratnach.], *a town* [of some sort]; recorded only of **Utkaṭa** or °**ṭā**: Mvy 5285 = Tib. [2d gloss] luṅ paḥi mdaḥ, *outlet of a valley*, said of Utkaṭa; Divy 620.12, 21; 621.11.)

droṇamukhya, nt., Divy 620.28, or °**khyā,** f., 620.26, = prec.; said of **Utkaṭa** or °**ṭā.**

Droṇavastuka, nt., n. of a village in Kośala, home of Pūrṇa Maitrāyaṇīputra; cf. Pali Doṇavatthu, home of Puṇṇa Mantāṇīputta: Mv iii.377.8.

droṇī (= Pali doṇī), *the wooden body of a lute* (from its 'tub'-like shape): AsP 515.19 (cited s.v. **upadhānī**).

Droṇodana, n. of a brother of Śuddhodana; app. corresponds to **Dhautodana,** q.v.: Mvy 3601 = Tib. bre bo (= droṇa) zas; Av ii.111.7, with **Amṛtodana** as a leading Śākya.

drohiṇya, nt. (seemingly Skt. drohin plus -ya; no such formation recorded; = **drauhiṇya,** q.v.), *injurious malice*: Gv 459.15 (prose) sattva-drohiṇyāni soḍhavyāni.

? **Draupadī,** n. of a devakumārikā (or of two? see below) in the Western Quarter: Mv iii.308.9; LV 390.6. Mss. of both confused, and readings doubtful; Senart reads kṛṣṇā śukrā ca dr°, *the dark and light Dr.*; LV may go back to some such reading; some of its mss. and Lefm.'s. text contain kṛṣṇā. It hardly needs to be recalled that Kṛṣṇā was the name of the epic heroine known as Draupadī.

drauhiṇya (nt.), so read for ed. drauhilya, = **drohiṇya,** q.v., *injurious malice*: Śikṣ 279.5 sattva-drauhiṇya-doṣaiḥ (Tib. cited as ḫkhru baḥi ṅaṅ tshul can).

dvaya (nt.), (sexual) *coupling, copulation*: sa nehaiva mātṛgrāmeṇa sārdhaṃ dvayaṃ samāpadyate Śikṣ 76.8, *he does not by any means enter into copulation with a woman*; dvaya-dvaya-samāpattiḥ Mvy 9469, *copulation*, lit. *attaining* (entering into, sc. a state of) *couple by couple*.

dvaya-mati, *doubt* (lit. *double thought*): °ti-vimocaka LV 360.2 (vs), *O freer from doubt!*

dvātriṃśata = °śat, *thirty-two*; see § 19.34.

dvādaśavarga, *consisting of a group of twelve* (nuns), necessary for ordination of a nun (whereas ten monks have this power, see **daśavarga**): Bhīk 19a.1 bhikṣuṇīnāṃ dvādaśavarge maṇḍalake.

dvādaśavargika, fem. °**kā,** with or without bhikṣuṇī, pl., prob. not = next but to prec. plus -ika, *members of the* °**varga**: MSV ii.144.1, 16.

dvādaśavargīya, f. °**yā,** pl., *belonging to a group of twelve* (nuns; clearly not *heretics* as stated in Index): °yābhiḥ śrutam Divy 493.12; °yābhir 495.23. No such group has been discovered in Pali; the context in Divy is my only source of knowledge of the meaning. It can hardly mean *members of the dvādaśavarga*, q.v., in the sense of *quorum for ordination*. Apparently these nuns were given to cavilling and trouble-making; they object to functions assigned to (Cūḍa-)Panthaka.

dvāra-kośa (m.; = Pali °kosa, Vin. iv.47.23), app. *door-frame*: in the corrupt and fragmentary passage Prāt 506.10 ff., mahallakaṃ bhikṣuṇā vihāraṃ kārayatā yāvad dvārakośārgaḍasthā[pa]na ālokasaṃta (read **āloka-saṃdhi,** q.v.?) bhūmi . . . (lacuna). In the same passage in Pali (Vin., above), yāva dvārakosā aggaḷaṭṭhapanāya ālokasaṃdhiparikammāya.

dvāra-koṣṭha (m.), = next: (jetavanavihāre . . . sopānāni . . .) °koṣṭhe ca muktāpaṭakalāpapralambitāni Kv 7.23 (prose). Here seems to mean the upper part, top story, over the entrance(s) to the vihāra.

dvāra-koṣṭhaka, m. (= Pali °koṭṭhaka; cf. **caraṇa-koṣṭha**), lit. *gate-room*; a room, or (often) roofed but open space, over a gate or entrance (to a private house, religious edifice, or city); such spaces, guarded by railings and covered but open in front, are seen in the 'cave-temples' of Ajanta etc. Also, perhaps by extension, seems to be used in the sense of *gate, entrance*; and sometimes it is hard to say which is meant: °ke sthitvā Divy 17.12, *at the gate* (entrance, to a house); bhagavāṃs tasya (sc. of a private person, at his house) dvārakoṣṭhakam anuprāptaḥ; dauvārikapuruṣeṇāsya niveditam, bhagavān dvāre (note! = °koṣṭhake) tiṣṭhatīti Av i.31.10, *is standing at the gate*; Divy 535.11 ff., here app. a city-gate; bahirdvārakoṣṭhaka (= Pali bahidvārakoṭṭhaka), *the space outside the gate*: °kasyaikānte Bhīk 3b.2 (here prob. of the vihāra-gate); jetavanam gataḥ... dvāra°ke sthitvāgarum dhūpitavān Av i.24.2; in the last it is hard to say whether the gateway, or the space over it, is meant; app. of the space over the entrance to a vihāra, °ke pañcagaṇḍakam cakram kārayitavyam Divy 300.8, 9, 25; (stūpasya...) catvāro °kā māpitāḥ Divy 244.17; (dvitīyamaṇḍale) °ke Mmk 47.26; others, Jm 19.17; 20.1; MSV i.168.12 etc.

dvārapālinī (cf. Skt. °pālikā; f. to °pāla), *female doorkeeper*: Sādh 502.13.

Dvārapālī, n. of a town: °liyām, loc., Māy 13 (see Lévi p. 62).

Dvāravatī, n. of a city, said to be in the south, and residence of the god Mahādeva: Gv 218.6 ff.

dvāra-śākhī, acc. to Chin. *door-frame*: Mvy 5569 (so also Mironov; BR °khā) = Tib. sgo (*door*) skyobs (or, skyes; mg. of both obscure to me). BR cite Skt. Lex. dvāra-śākhā, *Thürflügel*.

Dvārasvaraprabhūtakośa, n. of a Tathāgata: Gv 312.3.

dvi, m.c. for **dve**, q.v.

Dvijātirājan (Senart nom. sg. °rājaḥ, most mss. °rājāḥ, pointing to stem °rājan), n. of a former Buddha: Mv i.140.12.

dvijihvika, adj. (Skt. °hva), *double-tongued, falsely speaking*: °kā (m. n. pl.) bhavanti, anyathā nidarśayanti Śikṣ 61.21.

dvitiya, adj. (cf. Pali dutiya, for Skt. dvitīya; § 3.41), *second*; rare and only m.c. in BHS (so also **tṛtiya**, q.v.); in many of the following cases some or all of the mss. read ī, tho meter justifies em. to i: SP 46.11, 14; 91.7; 158.1; LV 94.8; 175.10; Mv ii.134.7 (see s.v. **dvitīyā**; Senart dutiya, but I have not found du- written for dvi- in this word); in Gv 257.10, 20 text dvitīyu, meter requires °iyu. All vss.

dvitīyakam, adv. (= Pali dutiyakam, Skt. dvitīyam; see also **dvaitīyakam**), *for the second time*: SP 315.2, 7; Mv i.346.20; iii.49.2, 7; 189.8; AsP 182.13. All prose.

dvitīyā (Skt. Lex. id.; Pali [purāṇa-]dutiyikā), *wife*, in purāṇa-dv°, *former wife*: Mvy 9262; read dvitiyā m.c. in Mv ii.134.7 (vs) dvitiyās (mss. °tīy°; Senart em. duti°) tathaiva caturo (so mss.) svajanam ca sphītam (vijahitva, from line 6); perhaps also dvitīya- (short a! mss. °ye in 405.18, later only °ya-) -kulika Mv iii.405.18 ff., 407.14; acc. to Senart *wife's kinsman*; but I am doubtful of this; we should expect °yā-; the passage is wholly prose; in 406.1 dvitīya- is omitted, kuliko alone being read; perhaps rather, *a second* (= another) *kinsman*, or a *fellow* (second) *kinsman*.

dvi-daṇḍin, a member of some heretical sect (*carrying two staffs*): Mvy 3541.

dvi-daivasika, see **daiv°**.

dvipadaka, f. °**ikā** (= Skt. dvipada; Bhvr.), (a verse) *consisting of two metrical units*: (na tena) kasyacid dvipadikā gāthā śrāvitā Divy 396.6 (prose).

?**dvipari**(-vartanāveṇī), LV 256.1. If we accept dvipari- with all mss. and both edd. we should have to understand it as part of the foll. cpd.; in that case apparently parivartanā = vartanā, and with preceding dvi- the whole might mean *string of double beads* (lit. *spheres*?), i. e., possibly, extra-large ones? See the whole passage cited s.v. **vartanā(veṇī)**. Note however that the close parallel LV 254.13 lacks dvipari; and Tib. on 256.1 has nothing corresponding. Note also that the preceding comparison, ending pārśve (and cited l.c.), lacks any statement of the tertium comparationis between the Bodhisattva's sides (pārśve) and the 'ribs' of a crab or the roof-frame of a (ruined) stable; 254.10–11 shows the point, viz. that they were 'open', so that light shone thru. Is it possible that dvipari goes with the preceding and contains a corruption of some form of vi-var- (cf. vivṛtāyām 254.10)? Something like opt. vivare(t), vivari? The passage is prose, and MIndic forms are not normal in prose of LV; but no one knows how MIndic its original form may have been.

dvipādaka, adj. (= Skt. dvipāda; cf. Pali dipādaka, said of the human body, Sn 205), *'two-legged', human*, only with puṇyakṣetra, a *human* (personified) *field of merit* (virtue): of a Buddha, Divy 48.6; 63.24, 28; of other pious persons, Mv i.329.11 (not quite rightly Senart).

dvi-puṭa, adj. (cf. **eka-puṭa**), *folded double* (of a cloth): Mvy 9187; MSV ii.90.7.

dviprasūtā, *who has borne twice*: Mv iii.282.14. Cf. **eka-pra°**.

dviruttarapadasaṃdhi-lipi, a kind of writing: LV 126.8; Tib. tshig lan lan gñis su gdab paḥi tshig gi mtshams kyi (yi ge), which Foucaux renders, (*écriture*) *du saṃdhi* (*liaison*) *d'un mot répété deux fois*, which does not make much sense to me, nor can I see how it renders the Tib. (which however I find obscure). The text continues: yāvad-daśottarapadasaṃdhi-lipim; this time Tib. is rather different, tshig gi mtshams bcur brgyud paḥi bar gyi (yi ge), which Foucaux renders as before (with *ten* for *two*); it seems to mean *writing up to a series of ten* (forming) *a combination of words*, or *writing of combinations of words in which up to ten words follow one another*. Possibly dviruttara° means no more than *writing of two words in combination*.

dviṣa, m. (= Pali disa; in Skt. as adj. ifc.; a-extension of Skt. dviṣ), *enemy*: MSV ii.17.1 dviṣo (so ms., ed. em. dviḍ) bhaviṣyāmi.

dvisāhasra (in Skt. as adj., *consisting of* 2000; cf. Pali dvisahassī majjhimikā lokadhātu AN i.228.5), designation of a medium-sized lokadhātu, *consisting of* 2000 (worlds): as subst., sc. lokadhātu, Dbh 81.31 dvisāhasrādhipatir (mahābrahmā); °sro madhyamo lokadhātuḥ Mvy 3043; AsP 95.18; °sre lokadhātau ŚsP 26.10; °sre madhyame lokadhātau AsP 66.3; 67.3; contrasted with **sāhasra**(-cūḍika) on the one hand, and **trisāhasramahāsāhasra**, qq.v., on the other. Cf. next.

dvisāhasrika, adj. (cf. prec. and cf. **sāhasrika**), *consisting of* 2000 (worlds), of a lokadhātu, or *ruling over* such a system, of a Mahābrahmā: dvisāhasriko mahābrahmā sarvasmin dvisāhasrike lokadhātau... Dbh 81.23–24.

?**dvistvala**, m., or (iii.161.4) **dvistvalaka**, m., dubious form assumed by Senart (the mss. in most of the passages vary considerably), some unknown kind of entertainer, in lists of various sorts of entertainers (cf. e. g. kheluka, gāyanaka, kumbhatūṇika, pañcavaṭuka, etc.): Mv iii.113.3; 141.18; 161.4; 255.12; 442.9. Cf. **ḍimbara**.

dvīpa (Pali dīpa, see below; as in Skt. usually m. but sometimes nt., e. g. Divy 214.25; Mv iii.378.2; the gender of the names follows that of the word dvīpa in the context; normally they are m.), one of the 4 continents, which to Buddhists are Jambudvīpa, **Pūrvavideha** (**Prāgvideha** LaVallée Poussin, AbhidhK. iii.145), **Aparagodānīya** (°**ni**, °**dānī**- in comp., °**nika**; rarely **Avara°**, **Godānīya**, qq.v.), and **Uttarakuru** (Kuru alone, AbhidhK l. c.); see the second and third s.vv. Listed LV 19.15 f.; 149.19 f.; the three outer ones cpd. with -lipi LV 126.4 f.; Mv i.6.2; ii.68.6; 158.18; iii.378.2; cf. AbhidhK. l. c.;

Mvy 3045, 3047, 3050, 3054, 3057; Dharmas 120; Divy 214.7, 10, 24; 215.15, 20; MSV i.94.4 f. The Pali forms are Jambudīpa, Pubbavideha, Aparagoyāna (! or v.l. °godhāna), and Uttarakuru.

dvīpaka (m.; dvīpa plus -ka svārthe), *continent*: ... catvāro dvīpā abhūvan; ekaikasmiṃś ca dvīpake... Gv 325.4. Prose; no possible difference of mg. from **dvīpa** appears.

1 **dvīpika,** m., a certain insect: °kaḥ Mvy 4918 = Tib. sril (*silkworm*) or mug pa (*moth*, acc. to Jä. also *worm*). Seems likely to be related to Deśīn. 5.53 dīviā, glossed upadehikā (Skt. Lex., said to be = Skt. upadīkā, a kind of ant).

2 **-dvīpika,** ifc. adj., in pratyantadvīpikānāṃ (brāhmaṇānāṃ) Suv 14.4 (prose), *belonging to the (outlying) continents.*

dvīhika, dvehika, dvyahika, adj. (so the mss. and Senart variously read; § 3.115; cf. Pali dvīhika), (sufficient) *for two days*, with śāli, *rice* (as food): °kaṃ Mv i.343.11, 12, 14; Senart dvyahika in 11 (with one ms.), dvīhika in 12, 14; mss. have v.l. dvehi(ka) in 11; both read dvihika (so!) in 12 and both dve° in 14. Most likely dvehika is to be read; cf. **trīhika, tre°**.

dve, duve, m.c. **dvi,** MIndic for Skt. dvau etc., *two*: see §§ 19.3, 4.

dve-caturaśīti, prob. *twice 84*, expressive of a large number (for Skt. dvi- or dvai-?): Mv i.259.8; 261.15; 271.15 (all prose; in the last duve°).

dvemāsika, adj. (cf. **tremāsika,** and Skt. dvaimāsya), (suitable) *for two months*: °kaṃ (bhaktaṃ) Mv ii.462.6; iii.15.11.

Dveṣaparimuktā, n. of a 'gandharva maid': Kv 5.13.

dvehika, so prob. read for **dvīhika,** q.v.

dvaitīyaka, (1) adj. m., *recurring every second day* (of fever): Mvy 9532; SP 401.6 (prose); Bhīk 17a.2; Māy 220.19; **(2)** °kam, adv., *for the second time*: SP 36.4, 11; 484.8; 486.3 (in first two Kashgar rec. dvir; all prose); also in some mss. as v.l. for **dvitīyakam** SP 315.2, 7.

dvyaṅgula-prajñā, adj. f. (= Pali d(u)vaṅgulapaññā), *having* (only) *two-fingers-intelligence*, said of women in derogation: °jñāye strīmātrāye tvaṃ nigṛhīto ti Mv iii.391.19. Acc. to comm. on Therīg. (67.1–5) the word refers to a feminine habit of taking grains of rice between two fingers to see if the rice is cooked enough.

dvyahika, see **dvīhika.**

DH

?**dhaṭika,** m. (perh. cf. Skt. Lex. dhaṭī, *rag; loincloth*?), acc. to Tib. and Chin. (*a cloth*) *with hemmed edges*: Mvy 9189 = Tib. cha ga btab (or ltab) pa. But the reading is uncertain; vv.ll. vaṭika (so Mironov, who cites no dhaṭika even as v.l.), dhajika, dhaṇika.

Dhaṇapālaka, see **Dhana°.**

dhana, (1) nt., (spiritual) *treasure* (= Pali ariyadhana, the same seven, see s.v. in CPD): Mvy 1565–72, seven such: śraddhā, śīla, hrī, apatrāpya, śruta, tyāga, prajñā; **(2)** n. of a king (= **Mahādhana**): Divy 437.19; 439.26; 441.20; MSV i.123.20 ff.

Dhanagupta, n. of a son of Gupta the perfumer: Divy 351.22.

Dhanaṃjaya-sūtra, n. of a work: Karmav 55.19.

Dhanapati, n. of a king: Gv 399.12.

Dhanapatigupta, n. of a former Buddha: Mv i.140.3.

Dhanapāla (= Pali id.), n. of an elephant let loose by Devadatta, or by Ajātaśatru at his instigation, to kill the Buddha: Karmav 49.21; see also next. In Pali oftener called Nālāgiri.

Dhanapālaka (= Pali id.), = prec.: Av i.177.6 (here ed. with best ms. Dhaṇa°, but v.l. Dhana° as in Pali).

Dhanaśrī, n. of a Tathāgata: Śikṣ 169.13.

Dhanasaṃmata, n. of an ancient king: Divy 62.11 ff. (previous birth of Maitreya, 66.22).

dhanahara, °hāraka, °hārika, see s.v. **ṛṇadhara.**

Dhanāpaha, n. of a yakṣa: Māy 47.

Dhanika, n. of a rich householder of Vaiśālī: MSV i.225.4 ff.

dhanuḥ- in cpds., see **dhanuṣ-.**

Dhanudharā, n. of a rākṣasī: Māy 241.32.

Dhanunāśa, n. of a former Buddha: Mv i.137.9.

dhanuṣ-kalāpa (m., see next; dvandva cpd.; = Pali dhanu-ka°), lit. *bow and quiver*, actually in effect *archery, the art of handling bow and arrows* (so Tib. mdaḥ gzhuḥi thabs, *method of arrow and bow*): °pe LV 156.11, in list of arts mastered by the young Bodhisattva.

dhanuṣ-kalāpaka, m., = prec.: °kaḥ (so also Mironov) Mvy 5005; here Tib. simply mdaḥ gzhu, *arrow* (and) *bow*.

dhanuṣkārika or **°kā,** a kind of flowering tree: (puṣpavṛkṣāṇāṃ...) sumanā-vārṣikā-dhanuṣkārikādīnāṃ Divy 628.15 (prose). Obviously = the commoner **dhānuṣkārin** or **°rika, °rikā** (**°rīka**), q.v. But in Pali recorded only with dhan°: dhanukārika (in a cpd.) Jāt. v.420.7, which (tho prose) is glossed in the comm. 422.28, which replaces this word with dhanukārī(ti), glossing it with dhanupāṭali (otherwise unknown).

dhanuṣkārin, once as v.l. for **dhān°,** q.v., and cf. prec.

dhanuṣketakī (so also Mironov, and so pw 7, App.; cited in BR as dhanu-ke°), n. of some flower: Mvy 6175; Tib. dha nu ke ta ki.

Dhanuṣketu, n. of a king: Mmk 625.21 (text dhanuḥ ketus, n. sg.).

Dhaneśvara, n. of two yakṣas: Māy 26 and 89.

dhandha (= Pali dandha; see also **adhandha**), *slow, weak, dull*: cf. Wogihara, Bbh. Lex. 28; opp. to kṣipra, Pali khippa. In Śikṣ (see note p. 395) and Divy always recorded as dhanva; as to AsP, see next two: dhandhābhijña Mvy 1245, 1246; Bbh 322.26; dhandham, adv., *slowly* Bbh 175.12 f.; other forms and cpds. Bbh 176.6, 19 f.; 193.5; 218.9; 322.26; Śikṣ 7.9; 51.6; Divy 488.27; 489.20; 490.7 f., 20; 492.21; 504.17.

dhandhaka = **dhandha,** *slow; difficult, hardly to be expected*: AsP 238.13 dhandhako (text corruptly dvandhako) hy anyeṣu (sc. hīnayāna-) sūtränteṣu bodhisattvasamudāgamaḥ (Wogihara Bbh. Lex. 28 *unerfahren*, not happily).

dhandhāyati, °te, denom. from **dhandha,** *is slow, is dull* (of wit); in AsP always recorded as dhanvā° (as in Śikṣ, Divy): a-dhandhāyamāna Bbh 284.7, *not going slow*; dhanvāyati AsP 284.4; 326.4; °yiṣyati 176.9; dhanvāyita-tva, *state of being dull of comprehension* AsP 31.16; 454.9; °yita-tā 454.11 (associated with **kāṅkṣāyita-tva,** q.v.); dhanvāyita-tvaṃ Gv 451.7.

dhandhīkriyate (text dhanvī°), *is made dull*, from **dhandha**: Śikṣ 7.11.

Dhanyabhānu, n. of a former Buddha: Mv i.139.13.

Dhanyākara, nt., n. of a city: Gv 2.1; 50.17 ff.; 491.6.

dhanva, dhanvāyati, etc., common miswriting for **dhandha,** etc., q.v.

dham, syllable used in learning to write, see s.v. **si.**

dhamana, nt., a high number: Mvy 7917 (cited from Gv) = Tib. ḥdzin yas; Gv 106.17; 133.26. Cf. next. Mironov has the same reading in Mvy.

dhamara, m., a high number: Mvy 7788 = Tib. ḥdzin yas. Cf. prec. Mironov has the same reading, but it seems likely (in view of Gv's confirmation of °nam) that °ra is an error for °na.

dharaṇa, (1) nt. (in Skt. a certain weight), a high number: Mvy 7726 = Tib. gzhal (*weight*) dpag; cf. **varaṇa;** (2) m., n. of a yakṣa: Māy 13; 235.30.

Dharaṇitejas (perhaps m.c. for Dharaṇī°; yet Skt. has dharaṇi = dharaṇī), n. of a Buddha: Gv 257.2 (vs).

Dharaṇi-teja-śirī, m. (m.c. for °tejaḥ-śrī, possibly also m.c. for Dharaṇī°, but see under prec.), n. of a Buddha: Gv 285.2 (vs).

Dharaṇiṃdhara = Dharaṇīṃdhara, q.v.

dharaṇī, (1) acc. to Tib. on Mvy 5578 = phyam, defined by Jä. *support* (of rafters), *the resting point of a beam*; by Das, *'the resting beam of a staircase or ladder. Also: prop, bracket, mortice'*: dharaṇīyo (v.l. °ya), n. pl., Mv iii.228.5 (prose), as parts of a city gate; (2) a small weight (cf. Skt. dharaṇa, a considerably larger weight): in eka-suvarṇa-dharaṇī LV 63.19 (prose, no v.l.), acc. to Tib. = phye ma zho gcig, *one grain* (a very small weight, which is clearly intended in the context of LV; Jä. defines zho as *dram, a small weight = 1/10 ounce) of dust.* There is no word for *gold* in Tib.; it may be noted that suvarṇa is also used in Skt. as n. of a rather small weight (a karṣa) of gold, but acc. to BR, pw, not of other substances; did suvarṇa-dharaṇī mean *a gold-grain* in some such sense as *a small weight commonly used in weighing gold*? (3) n. of a rākṣasī: Māy 243.12.

Dharaṇītalaśrī, m., n. of a kiṃnara: Mvy 3423.

?**Dharaṇītejas,** °teja(ḥ)ś(i)rī, see **Dharaṇi°.**

Dharaṇīnirghoṣasvara, n. of a Bodhisattva: Gv 4.8.

Dharaṇīnirnādaghoṣa, n. of a Bodhisattva: Gv 3.21.

Dharaṇīṃdhara, or °ṇiṃdhára, (1) n. of one or more Bodhisattvas: SP 3.8 °ṇīṃ°, v.l. °ṇiṃ°; 456.1 °ṇiṃ° (no v.l.); RP 2.1 °ṇīṃ°; Mv i.112.1 °ṇīṃ° (here a cakravartin); (2) n. of a **satpuruṣa,** q.v.: SP 4.1 °ṇīṃ°, v.l. °ṇiṃ°; (3) n. of a nāga king: Māy 247.10 °ṇīṃ°.

dharaṇīprekṣaṇī-lipi, a kind of writing: LV 126.10. Followed by gagaṇaprekṣaṇī°, indicating that dharaṇī-means *earth*; so Tib., sa blta ba, *earth-seeing.*

Dharaṇīśubhakāya, n. of a yakṣa: Mvy 3376.

Dharaṇīśrīparvatateja, n. of a Buddha: °jo, n. sg., Gv 360.10 (prose).

Dharaṇīśvararāja, n. of a Bodhisattva: LV 2.11.

Dharaṇīsurendrāyudha, n. of a yakṣa: Mvy 3369.

Dharananda, n. of a yakṣa leader: Māy 235.30.

1 Dharma, as n. pr., (1) n. of a brother of Śāriputra: Mv iii.56.11; (2) n. of a Pratyekabuddha: Divy 200.12; (3) n. of a Buddha in the nadir: Sukh 98.8; (4) n. of a pupil of **Mati** 4 = **Mahāmati** 5, qq.v.: Laṅk 365.3.

2 dharma, normally m. as in Skt.; occasionally (as in Pali, see Childers s.v. dhammo) nt.: SP 70.2 (vs) acc. to Kashgar rec. duḥśrāddheyam idaṃ dharmaṃ deśitam adya śāstṛṇām (ms.), but Tib. seems to support Nep. mss. which lack dharma; idam ... dharmaṃ śrutvā SP 71.3 (prose; KN em. to imaṃ, which WT keep without note); aśrutvaiva ... idam ... dharmaṃ SP 60.4 (here kept with all mss. in both edd.); mā ... a-dharmaṃ utpadyate LV 15.10 (prose), *may no wickedness arise*; idaṃ dharmaṃ LV 396.1 (prose; acc. sg.); paramaṃ dharmaṃ Mv ii.99.5 (n. sg.; in next sentence dharmo). — (1) *characteristic, quality,* substantially as in Skt. (BR s.v. 2), but used in BHS, as in Pali dhamma, very commonly and in a way which seems specially pointed and deserving of special mention: asti-dharma, see s.v. 1 **asti;** vināśa-dharmeṇa (*subject to destruction, perishable*) mānsena Mv i.94.12; divyāś ca kāyāḥ parihāṇa- (v.l. °ṇi-) dharmāḥ SP 162.3 (vs), *and divine bodies were characterized by diminution,* i. e. became few (meaning proved by parallel 170.2; wrongly Burnouf and Kern); māreṇa ... īrṣyādharmaparītena LV 267.2 (prose), *full of the quality of jealousy*; catvāra ime ... duḥkhavipākā dharmāḥ RP 19.16 (prose), *qualities that result in misery,* i. e. vices; in Mv iii.200.5 are mentioned eight āścaryādbhuta dharma, *marvelous qualities,* of the Buddha, seven of which (the eighth apparently being omitted by mistake) are listed 200.6–202.2; they correspond imperfectly to the eight yathābhucca vaṇṇa of Pali DN ii.222.7, listed 222.13–224.14 (DN nos. 2, 4, 5, 6, and 8 = Mv nos. 2, 7, 3, 4, 6); śuddhāvāsā ca devā aṣṭādaśa āmodanīyāṃ dharmān (*the eighteen 'qualities of rejoicing',* here *conditions of, elements* or *matters for rejoicing*) pratilabhanti Mv ii.259.10 (they are listed in the sequel); (2) like Pali dhamma, dharma (or dharmāyatana) is the object of manas (as rūpa of cakṣus, etc.); sometimes rendered *idea*; it seems likely that, at least in origin, it meant *quality, characteristic* (= 1), as that element in the outside world which the indriya manas (as distinguished from the five external organs of perception) concerned itself with; see AbhidhK. LaV-P. i.45, where it is explained that 'tho all the āyatanas are dharmas' (*qualities*), 'because it includes many and the chief (agra) dharma, one āyatana is specifically so called;' in any case this exclusively Buddhist use occurs: dharmāyatanam Mvy 2039; Dharmas 24; dharmadhātuḥ Mvy 2057 (after manodhātuḥ, as dharmāyatanam 2039 follows mana-āy°); manendriyaṃ dharmavicāraṇeṣu Suv 56.12; similarly 57.8, etc.; see also dharmāyatanika, s.v. **āyatanika;** (3) in Laṅk used in a peculiar sense; pañcadharmāḥ Laṅk 229.6; °rma- id. 2.2; the list of them is given id. 228.5 pañcadharmo (v.l. °mā, which seems surely correct), nimittaṃ nāma vikalpas tathatā samyagjñānaṃ ca, which are then defined in the sequel, but I confess I find the definitions hard to understand; Suzuki, Studies 155 ff., discusses the passage and renders dharma by *category*; it seems likely that it started out as a specilized application of mg. (1), *quality*; (4) very commonly, as with Pali dhamma, *state of existence, condition of being*; crystallized in the phrase or cpd. dṛṣṭa dharma, *the present state, the present life,* see **dṛṣṭa-dharma;** (nāhaṃ ... ye) dharmā anityās te nityato deśayāmi, nāpi ye dharmā nityā te anityato deśayāmi Mv i.173.2, *I do not teach that impermanent states are permanent, nor permanent ones impermanent*; mostly restricted to states of empiric, hence transitory, worthless, existence: nairātmyaṃ ... dharmāṇāṃ Laṅk 1.4; nairātmy' aśubhāś (so divide, as Foucaux implies) ca dharm' ime LV 176.19 (vs); māyasamāṃs tatha svapnasamāṃś ca ... samudīkṣati dharmāṃ; LV 308.9 (vs), but note in 10 that the word is used in two radically different senses, īdṛśa dharma-nayaṃ vimṛṣanto (*considering as such the rule, nature, condition, of the states of existence*) ... dhyāyati saṃsthitu dharme, *he meditated ... steadfast in the Doctrine*; dharma pratītya-samutthita buddhvā LV 308.13 (vs, just after prec.), *realizing that the states of being have originated by dependent-causation*; śāntāḥ kila (read with WT °lā or with K' °laḥ) sarv' imi dharm' anāsravā ... (4) na cātra kaścid bhavatīha dharmo SP 117.3–4 (vs; Burnouf and Kern take dharma in 3 as *law*), *all the conditions of being* (in the saint) *are calmed, free of the impurities* (so that) *there is not* (any longer) *in them under these conditions any state of* (conditioned, empiric) *existence*; by extension, however, even nirvāṇa is called a dharma, *state of being*: (śreṣṭho ...) dharmāṇa nirvāṇaṃ iva Mv i.166.18 (vs), (Buddha is the best of creatures) *as nirvāṇa of states of being*; nirvṛtau ... dharma (loc. sg.) RP 6.9 (vs), *in the state* (of) *nirvāṇa.* See also the following cpds., esp. **dharma-**

kāya. For Dharma as n. pr. see prec.; for dharma as adj. see next. I have not listed dharma *law, doctrine* (second of the 3 ratna, Dharmas 1 etc.), since it is both extremely common and hardly un-Skt. It may refer particularly to the collections of sūtras which set forth the Doctrine; see e. g. **dharma-caryā**. — dharma is also one of the four **pratisaṃvid**, q.v.; on the mg. here see esp. AbhidhK. LaV-P. vii.89 ff., with references (note Dbh 77.3 ff.); it seems likely to belong to mg. (4) but definitions are confusingly variant and obscure.

3 dharma, f. **-ā** or (rarely) **-ī**, adj. (= Skt. dharmya, dhārma; BHS also **dhārmya**, and as element in comp. **dharmī-**, **dhārmī-**, **dhārmi-**, **dharmi-**, **dharmā-**, qq.v.; Pali dhammī, as fem. adj. or as element in comp., as such also dhammi-, only with kathā), *religious*, only with kathā except for the last citations; on the forms cf. Senart i n. 574 (the regular Skt. dharmya also occurs); most commonly instr. sg.: dharmayā kathayā LV 38.13 (prose, all mss.; Lefm. and Calc. °myayā); Mv i.261.18 (prose, no v.l.); 297.16 (ib.); 309.2 (v.l. dhammā-); 329.14 (v.l.; text with 1 ms. °myayā); 333.19 (v.l. °māyā); 334.5 (v.l. °myā); 334.10, 16; iii.272.11 (v.l. dharmā-); dharmyā (v.l. dhārya-, intending dhārmya-?) kathayā iii.142.4; dharmā- (Senart em. °myā) kathayā iii.143.6; dhārmyayā kathayā Mv i.322.6; dhārmi-kathayā Mv i.282.3 (vs); less often acc. sg., dharmi-kathāṃ Mahāsamāj., Waldschmidt, Kl. Skt. Texte 4, 157.8; dharmī-kathāṃ Mv i.319.3 (v.l. dharmayā kathāṃ!); Divy 241.26 (3 of 4 mss. dhārmī- or dhārmi-), 28 (no v.l.); dhārmyāṃ kathāṃ Mv iii.446.9; dhārmyaṃ dharmacakraṃ Divy 393.23. In MPS 34.30 ff. dharma, f. °mā, occurs many times as adj. with other words than kathā (prāsāda, puṣkariṇī, tālavana); ed. always em. to dhārma, f. °mī.

dharma-kathika, m. (also **dhārma**°; = Pali dhamma°; cf. 3 **dharma**, with kathā), *preacher*: SP 200.3; Mvy 2763; Karmav 162.1; Divy 329.2, 7 (by em.). (BR's alternative dharmakathaka is evidently a false reading for Mvy 2763; Mironov only °ika.)

Dharmakāṅkṣiṇī, n. of a gandharva maid: Kv 4.23.

Dharmakāma, (**1**) n. of a son of Māra, favorable to the Bodhisattva: LV 312.8; (**2**) n. of one of the four devatās of the bodhi-tree (so Lefm. with Tib. chos ḥdod; all mss. and Calc. Dharmakāya): LV 401.21.

dharma-kāya, m. (in Pali recorded only as Bhvr. adj. in quite different sense, *having a body that is, or is characterized by, the Doctrine*, DN iii.84.24, said of the Buddha; see below for similar use in BHS); (**1**) *the mass of conditions of existence*, see s.v. **kāya** (2); (**2**) perhaps to be rendered *spiritual body* (?), contrasted with **rūpa-kāya**, q.v.: (dṛṣṭo mayopādhyāyānubhāvena) sa bhagavān dharmakāyena (*in his spiritual form*, or the like; he had not seen him physically) no tu rūpakāyena (*but not in his physical form*) Divy 19.11; similarly 360.19 (. . . na dṛṣṭo rūpakāyo me 20–21); na rūpakāyatas tathāgataḥ prajñātavyaḥ . . . dharmakāyaprabhāvitāś ca buddhā bhagavanto na rūpakāya-prabhāvitāḥ Samādh 22.7 (Régamey, *Absolute Body, Material Body*; R. does not understand prabhāvita quite rightly; it means *recognized*, see BR s.v. bhū with pra, caus., 3); similarly 22.9 and esp. 34, with the explanation, dharmeṇa kāyu nirjito, (His) *body is born* (? see **nirjita**) *by dharma*; see Régamey p. 23; elsewhere, with the same contrast, the word dharma-k° is used as a Bhvr. adj. (cf. the Pali usage above, with which this usage may be directly connected), na hi tathāgato rūpakāyato draṣṭavyaḥ, dharmakāyās tathāgatāḥ AsP 513.15; instead of rūpakāya, simply kāya may be used in contrast, dharmakāyā buddhā bhagavantaḥ, mā khalu punar imaṃ bhikṣavaḥ satkāyaṃ kāyaṃ manyadhvaṃ, dharmakāya-pariniṣpattito māṃ bhikṣavo drakṣyanty AsP 94.11–13; (**3**) perhaps to be rendered in the same way as (2), but considered the highest of three *bodies* of a Buddha, the others being **saṃbhoga-** and **nirmāṇa-k**°; this is a late formula (Régamey, l. c. above) and I have noted the triad only in Mvy 116–118 among texts included in this work (see under the others); (**4**) without specific contrast with other kāyas but most likely belonging to (2) rather than (3): sa dharmakāya-prabhāvito (see Samādh 22.7 above) darśanenāpi sattvānām arthaṃ karoti Śikṣ. 159.7; manomaya-dharmakāyasya tathāgatasya Laṅk 192.1 (AbhidhK. knows a manomaya-kāya, app. not identified with dharma-k°, see LaV-P. Index; acc. to ii.209 it pertains to the rūpa-dhātu); prob., na rājan kṛpaṇo loke dharmakāyena saṃspṛśet Divy 560.2 (vs). [In LV 401.21 all mss. and Calc. read Dharmakāya as n. of one of the four devatās of the bodhi-tree; Lefm. **Dharmakāma**, with Tib. chos ḥdod; the em. seems plausible.]

Dharmakīrti (cf. Pali Dhammakitti), n. of a teacher: Mvy 3483.

Dharmakusumaketudhvajamegha, n. of a Tathāgata: Gv 309.8.

Dharmaketu, (**1**) n. of a former Buddha (or of several such?): LV 5.4; 172.14; Sukh 6.14; Mmk 365.17 (here acc. sg. °ketunaṃ, in a vs); (**2**) n. of a Bodhisattva: Gv 3.18; (**3**) n. of a devaputra, one of the 16 guardians of the bodhimaṇḍa: LV 277.14.

Dharmagaganakāntasiṃhaprabha, n. of a Tathāgata: Gv 311.23.

Dharmagaganābhyudgatarāja (cf. next), n. of a Tathāgata: SP 218.9. (Burnouf's and Kern's translations °gahanā° for °gaganā°, but Tib. confirms the latter with nam mkhaḥ, *sky*.)

Dharmagaganābhyudgataśrīrājan (cf. prec.), n. of a Tathāgata: Gv 360.7.

Dharmagupta, (**1**) n. of a former Buddha: Mv i.138.8 (and by Senart's em. for °**gupti**, q.v.); (**2**) pl. (= Pali Dhammagutta), n. of a Buddhist school: Mvy 9081.

Dharmagupti, n. of a former Buddha: Mv i.137.9 (so mss., Senart em. °gupta; in same list with °gupta above).

Dharmagrāma, n. of a locality in the south: Gv 454.8.

dharmacakra, nt. (Skt. id., but in BHS as in Pali dhammacakka used in a specialized sense, hardly exactly paralleled in Skt.), *the wheel of the law*, which was 'set in motion' (pra-vartayati; pravartana, n.) by the Buddha when he first preached his doctrine: passim; triparivarta-(see **parivarta**)-dvādaśākāra-dharmacakra-pravartanam Mvy 1309; °kra-pravartana- LV 36.3; °kraṃ pravartitaṃ SP 69.13; Divy 393.23; °kraṃ pravartesi SP 69.15 (vs), etc.

Dharmacakracandrodgataśrī, n. of a Tathāgata: Gv 310.26.

Dharmacakrajvalanateja, n. of a Tathāgata: Gv 311.17 (prose).

Dharmacakranirghoṣagaganameghapradīparāja, n. of a Tathāgata: Gv 352.6 (here om. megha), 15, 20; 355.15, 21 (in 21 1st ed. om. gaganamegha); 356.6, 12, 16; 357.8; 359.10; 360.6. All these prose; in vs 362.25 the same personage is called **Saddharmaghoṣāmbaradīparāja.**

Dharmacakranirmāṇaprabhā, n. of a nun: Gv 308.4.

Dharmacakranirmāṇasamantapratibhāsanirghoṣa, n. of a Tathāgata: Gv 360.17.

Dharmacakraprabhanirghoṣa, n. of a Tathāgata: Gv 310.25.

Dharmacakraprabhanirghoṣarāja, n. of a Tathāgata: Gv 360.11.

dharma-cakṣus (= Pali dhamma-cakkhu, nt., defined DN comm. i.237.23 by dhammesu vā cakkhuṃ dhammamayaṃ vā cakkhuṃ), *'eye of the Doctrine'*, *religious insight*: ṣaṣṭīnāṃ devakoṭīnāṃ dharmacakṣur viśodhitaṃ

LV 421.8 (vs); lokottamā dharmacakṣurdadāḥ 422.6 (vs). Others, where this appears as one of the five **cakṣus**, see under this word. In Pali not used as a member of this category.

Dharmacandraprabhurāja, n. of a Buddha: Gv 256.9 (vs). (Qy: °prabha-rāja?).

Dharmacandrasamantajñānāvabhāsarāja, n. of a Tathāgata: Gv 13.4.

dharmacarita = (the 10) **dharmacaryā**, q.v.: Sūtrāl. xx.41, comm.

dharma-caryā (cf. Pali dhamma-cariyā, but the Pali Dictt. do not record any list of ten), (one of the ten) *action(s) with reference to the Doctrine*: Mvy 902; listed 903–912 as lekhanā, pūjanā, dānam, śravaṇam, vācanam, udgrahaṇam, prakāśanā, svādhyāyanam, cintanā, bhāvanā. Mentioned as (ten) **dharma-carita** in Sūtrāl. xx.41 (comm.), without listing; Lévi cites from Chin. a list similar to that of Mvy but containing only nine items. Here dharma = the *teachings*, sūtras.

Dharmacārin, (**1**) n. of a devaputra: LV 204.5; 205.17; 209.2, 8; (**2**) n. of one of the 4 devatās of the Bodhivṛkṣa: LV 401.22.

dharmacintika, apparently some kind of heretical ascetic or sectarian, in a cpd. listing several such: Mv iii.412.7, see s.v. **guruputraka.**

Dharmacinti(n), *'thinking on the Doctrine'*, perhaps n. of a previous incarnation of Śākyamuni (otherwise unrecorded): LV 170.17 (vs). Tib. chos sems confirms the meaning; but it lacks the connective daṅ, which occurs after each of the other three names in the line; accordingly it seems to have understood this word as an epithet of the following Arcimān.

Dharmajālavibuddhaśrīcandra, n. of a Tathāgata: Gv 309.24.

Dharmajñānasaṃbhavasamantapratibhāsagarbha, n. of a Tathāgata: Gv 309.10.

Dharmajvalanārciḥsāgaraghoṣa, n. of a Tathāgata: Gv 312.4.

dharmatā (= Pali dhammatā), *natural and normal custom, habit, natural condition, what is to be expected, normal state, rule, standard custom, ordinary thing*; (as in Pali) often in n. sg., frequently at the beginning of a sentence and often followed by khalu (sometimes hi), (*you are to know that*) *it is the regular thing*, often then gen. of person, as e. g. buddhānāṃ, rarely loc., and a clause stating what the 'regular thing' is; but sometimes also referring to what precedes: dharmatā (usually foll. by khalu or hi) ... Mv i.338.19 (... (i)yaṃ teṣāṃ sattvānāṃ ...); iii.255.17 (... buddhānāṃ ...); Divy 3.2; 18.8; 67.16, etc.; Av i.4.6; 10.6, etc.; Jm 88.3; 98.16; iyam atra dharmatā LV 219.5; RP 10.9; dharmatā hy eṣā dharmāṇāṃ Laṅk 9.4 (vs), *for this is the normal condition of states-of-existence*; lokahitāna dharmatā SP 392.2 (vs); buddhānāṃ eṣā (read with v.l. eṣa, m.c.) dharmatā Mv iii.327.12 (vs); loc., eṣa buddheṣu dharmatā Ud xxi.12 (same vs with gen. in Pali AN ii.21.22); dharmatā-pratilambha eṣa caramabhāvikānāṃ bodhisattvānāṃ ... LV 161.12 (here I fail to see that -pratilambha adds anything in particular; the cpd. seems to mean about the same as dharmatā alone, *it is the established, normal procedure* ...); (bodhisattvasya ...) abhijñādharmatā LV 85.10, *normal state of* (having the) *abhijñā*; dharmatā-prāpta Mv i.301.8, *arrived at the normal* (correct, to-be-expected) *state*, said of the mind of a Pratyekabuddha; pratyātma-dharmatā-śuddhaṃ (nayaṃ) Laṅk 8.1 (vs); śruṇuya yo ti dharmatāṃ LV 54.2 (vs), *who ever hears your true nature* (regular procedure; contrasted with one who just sees or listens, i. e. to a few words); lokānuvartanakriyā-dharmatāṃ anuvartya LV 179.18; jarādharmatāyām anatītāḥ Mv ii.151.7, *not free from* (subjection to) *the normal condition of old age*; jātidharmatāyāḥ (abl.) Av i.211.15, *from the normal condition of birth*; instr., *by the method* (means) *of* ..., *by way of* .... (śatana-patana-vikiraṇa-) vidhvaṃsana-dharmatayā Divy 180.24; 281.31; atyantakṣīṇakṣaya-dharmatayā (so, as cpd.) niruddhāḥ LV 419.16 (vs), Tib. śin tu zad ciṅ byaṅ baḥi chos-ñid-kyis (dharmatayā) ni ḥgags; paramagatigato 'si dharmatāye Mv iii.381.8, *you have gone to the highest goal according to your natural, normal procedure*; dharmatāṃ vā pratisaraty Bbh 255.13, see **pratisarati.** In Bhad 3 Leumann interprets dharmata-dhātuṃ as m.c. for dharmatā-dh° which he assumes = dharma-dh°; but dharmata is rather for °taḥ, abl. of dharma, as a separate word.

dharmatā-buddha, in Laṅk a kind of Buddha: Laṅk 56.10; 57.8; 241.7, etc. See Suzuki, Studies, 142 ff., 208 f., where this is related to the **dharma-kāya** as (later) contrasted with the **saṃbhoga-** and **nirmāṇa-kāya.**

Dharmatrāta, n. of a teacher: Mvy 3508.

Dharmadinnā (= Pali Dhammadinnā), n. of a nun, disciple of Śākyamuni: Mvy 1073 (v.l. and Mironov °naḥ, m.); Karmav 97.3.

Dharmadeva (corresp. to Pali Dhammasena), n. of a leading disciple of Buddha Maṅgala: Mv i.248.17; 252.7.

dharma-deśaka, m. (in Skt. rare and somewhat doubtful, see BR s.v. deśaka; = Pali dhammadesaka, Childers, s.v. desaka, also app. rare), *preacher of the law*; = the much commoner **dharma-bhāṇaka**; in BHS, too, not common, despite the frequency of **dharma-deśanā**: nirāmiṣa-dh° LV 436.2 (prose), of the Tathāgata.

dharma-deśanā (= Pali dhammadesanā; also in Skt., KSS, BR 5.1509; but seems characteristically Buddh.; very common in BHS), *sermon*: SP 39.7; 64.1; 100.11, etc.; Mv ii.99.15, 17; 291.1; Bbh 80.7; 82.15 (= deśanā alone, 82.12); Divy 48.13, Av i.64.13; Suv 18.9; Mvy 2759; 8426.

Dharmadrumaparvatateja(s), n. of a Tathāgata: Gv 296.19 °jo, n. sg.; 296.21, text °jas, read °jasas, gen. sg.; both prose.

Dharmadhanaśikharābhaskandha, n. of a Tathāgata: Gv 310.5.

dharma-dhara, (**1**) adj. or subst. (= Pali dhammadhara), *one who has a good hold on the Doctrine*, i. e. who knows the sūtras well: °ra-saṃgaṇanā Mv i.70.11 (vs); vaistārikān °rān kuruṣva Divy 379.28 (vs); (**2**) n. of a Buddha: Gv 285.17; of a (presumably different) Buddha in the nadir, Sukh 98.8; (**3**) n. of a Bodhisattva: Kv 1.18; (**4**) n. of a king of the kiṃnaras: SP 4.14; (**5**) n. of a samādhi: Kv 51.14; 83.12.

dharma-dhātu, (**1**) m. (cf. Pali dhamma-dhātu), *sphere of religion*; regularly rendered by Tib. chos kyi (*of religion*) dbyiṅs (whereas khams is the usual Tib. for **dhātu**, q.v.); acc. to Das, dbyiṅs = *space, expanse; sphere* ... also *that which is massed in indefinite compass*: tulye (so read with WT) nāma dharmadhātu-praveśe SP 60.8, see s.v. **tulya**; dharmadhātu-gagana-gocarāṇāṃ tathāgatamahājñāna-sūryacandramasāṃ Gv 500.8 (*the sun and moon of the great knowledge of the Tathāgata have the heaven of the sphere of religion as their scope, gocara*); °tum eva vicārayamāṇo RP 4.10 (*meditating on* ...); sarva-dharmadhātu-prasṛtaṃ tathāgatajñānam RP 4.12; dharmadhātuviśuddhiḥ Mvy 110, as one of the five **jñāna**, q.v. (where note variant of Dharmas 94); śive virajase 'mṛte dharmadhātau pratiṣṭhāpayiṣyati LV 227.1, *he will establish* (creatures) *in the auspicious, pure, immortal sphere-of-religion*; (parijñāto) dharmadhātur vyavasthāpitaḥ sattvadhātuḥ LV 351.9, *he* (Buddha) *has completely understood the sphere of religion and established the 'sphere'* (*community, mass*; see s.v. **dhātu** 6) *of creatures* (presumably sc. in religion); dharmadhātu-paramāṇy ākāśadhātuparyavasānāni sarvabuddhakṣetrāṇy LV 290.7–8 (... *which make the sphere of religion their supreme interest* ... ? but Tib. chos kyi dbyiṅs kyis klas pa, prob. *which are beyond the* *dharmadhātu*, otherwise Foucaux); dharmadhātv-asaṃbheda-cakraṃ LV 423.1, *wheel that causes no confusion in the sphere of religion*; ananta-madhya-dharmadhātv-avikopana-cakraṃ 3; dharmadhātu-samavasaraṇa-cakraṃ 7, *wheel of attainment* (see **samavasaraṇa**) *of the sphere of religion.* The cpd. dharma-dhātu seems to be used differently in AbhidhK, see LaV-P's Index. On the other hand, the use of it described by Lévi, Sūtrāl. p. *24, can be reconciled with that which I have described, and which is the only use I have noted in my texts. (**2**) n. of a former Buddha: Mv i.137.10.

Dharmadhātukusuma, n. of a Buddha: Gv 284.13.

Dharmadhātugaganapūrṇaratnaśikharaśrīpradīpa, n. of a Buddha: Gv 283.1.

Dharmadhātugaganaśrīvairocana, n. of a Buddha: Gv 11.4.

Dharmadhātujñānapradīpa, n. of a Buddha: Gv 10.3.

Dharmadhātutalabhedajñānābhijñārāja, n. of a Bodhisattva: Gv 32.3 (= Dharmadhātupraṇidhitalanirbheda).

Dharmadhātunagarābhajñānapradīparāja, n. of a Tathāgata: Gv 312.12 (prose; in vs 314.9, called Dharmameghanagarābhapradīparāja).

Dharmadhātunayajñānagati, n. of a Buddha: Gv 285.16.

Dharmadhātunayāvabhāsabuddhi, n. of a Bodhisattva: Gv 4.15.

Dharmadhātuniyata, m., n. of a samādhi: Mvy 514; ŚsP 1415.16.

Dharmadhātupad(u)ma, n. of a Buddha: Gv 284.17 (vs).

Dharmadhātuparirakṣiṇī, n. of a kiṃnara maid: Kv 6.13.

Dharmadhātupraṇidhitalanirbheda, n. of a Bodhisattva: Gv 15.19 (in 32.3 called Dharmadhātutalabhedajñānābhijñārāja).

Dharmadhātupraṇidhisunirmitacandrarāja, Gv 27.23, = °**dhātusunirmitapraṇidhicandra.**

Dharmadhātupratibhāsa, n. of a Buddha: Gv 257.21.

Dharmadhātupratibhāsaprabha, n. of a palace in Kapilavastu (see **saṃgīti**): Gv 385.18.

Dharmadhātupratibhāsamaṇimakuṭa, n. of a Bodhisattva: Gv 3.4.

Dharmadhātupratibhāsaśiri (n. sg. °riḥ), n. of a Buddha: Gv 285.5 (vs).

Dharmadhātuvāgīśvara, n. of a form of Mañjuśrī: Sādh 127.20. Cf. **Vāgīśvara.**

Dharmadhātuvidyotitaraśmi, n. of a Tathāgata: Gv 81.22.

Dharmadhātuvibhaktipraveśa, n. of a samādhi: Dbh 82.11.

Dharmadhātuviṣayamaticandra, n. of a Buddha: Gv 422.5.

Dharmadhātusiṃhaprabha, n. of a Tathāgata: Gv 312.6.

Dharmadhātusunirmitapraṇidhicandra, n. of a Bodhisattva: Gv 11.24 (23); = **Dharmadhātupraṇidhisunirmitacandrarāja.**

Dharmadhātusvaraketu, n. of a Buddha: Gv 257.1.

Dharmadhātusvaraghoṣa, n. of a Buddha: Gv 259.16. The foll. word is app. an epithet of this, not another name.

Dharmadhātvarcivairocanasaṃbhavamati, n. of a Bodhisattva: Gv 81.23.

Dharma-dhāraṇī, see **dhāraṇī.**

Dharmadhvaja, n. of several different former Buddhas: Gv 257.2; 259.2; 284.8; 427.2; LV 171.17 (no v.l., but Tib. ḥod zer rgyal mtshan, which points to **Raśmidhvaja**); n. of a Buddha in the nadir, Sukh 98.9.

(**-dharman**, = **dharma** at end of cpds., as in Skt., BR; note pratyakṣadharman pw 5.260; *nature, character, characteristic*: yathā bālapṛthagjanā na (WT with K′ om. na) paśyanti pratyakṣadharmā (but mss. °mān!) tathāgataḥ . . . asaṃpramoṣadharmā (mss. °māḥ) SP 318.11–12 (prose; the acc. could be construed, with an implied paśyati, but the last word is clearly meant as n. sg.); jātidharmāṇaḥ sattvān LV 226.19; pratyakṣadharmā bhagavāṃ Mv i.9.7; vipariṇāmadharmāṇo (n. pl.) 31.13; pāpadharmā (n. sg.) 36.13; cyavanadharmā (n. sg.) Divy 193.22 f., *ready to fall* (from heaven to a lower existence); kāladharmaṇā (saṃ)yukta- Divy 210.28; 258.23, *dead*; jātidharmāṇaḥ sattvā(ḥ) Av i.240.8, *creatures subject to birth*: see also **avinipāta-dh°**; common.)

Dharmanagaraprabhaśrī, n. of a Tathāgata: Gv 310.19.

Dharmanayagambhīraśrīcandra, n. of a Tathāgata: Gv 309.9.

Dharmanārāyaṇaketu, n. of a Tathāgata: Gv 423.1.

Dharmaṃdadā, n. of a 'gandharva maid': Kv 4.23.

dharmapada, nt. (once m.; = Pali dhamma°), (**1**) *religious saying*: catvāri dharmapadāni Dharmas 55 (they are: anityāḥ sarvasaṃskārāḥ; duḥkhāḥ sarv°; nirātmānaḥ sarv°; śāntaṃ nirvāṇaṃ ca); (**2**) as n. of a Buddhist work (Pali Dhammapada), sg. or pl.: °pade Mv ii.212.18, followed by vs = iii.156.16–17 = Pali Vin. v.149.22–23; imāṃ dharmapadāṃ bhāṣati Mv iii.91.18, foll. by two vss = Pali Dhp. 179, 180; °padeṣu Mv iii.156.15 (cf. above); 434.12, foll. by verses = Pali Dhp. 100 ff.

Dharmapadmapraphullitaśrīmegha, n. of a Tathāgata: Gv 309.25.

Dharmapadmaphullagātra, n. of a Tathāgata: Gv 310.3.

Dharmapadmavairocanavibuddhaketu, n. of a Tathāgata: Gv 311.1.

Dharmapadmaśrīkuśalā, n. of a deity: Gv 432.1.

dharma-paryāya, m. (Pali dhammapariyāya, not well defined PTSD), lit. *device, means of* (teaching) *the doctrine*, and so, secondarily, *religious discourse.* Cf. Pali (kathā) sapariyāyā and nippariyāyā (e. g. Vism. 473.16–17), *discourse involving indirect devices* (not to be taken absolutely literally), *and discourse to be taken literally, without 'devices'*; cf. AbhidhK. LaV-P. ix.247, note. This fits the regular BHS mg. of **paryāya**, q.v. 2. Tib. renders chos kyi (dharma-) rnam graṅs, *specification, enumeration* (Das); only in this cpd. the Tib. Dictt. allege also the mg. *treatise, dissertation* for rnam graṅs, but obviously that is made to fit this word alone; the Tib. rendering was intended to render Skt. paryāya, *repetition, series*, etc.(only in the Veda does it mean *a piece of text*, and then chiefly if not exclusively one that is *repeated, a refrain*, etc.; this special use cannot be related to the BHS and Pali word, tho PTSD would have it so). Originally, the mg. was close to that of **upāyakauśalya**, indeed it was a verbal manifestation of that quality as clearly in: tathāgatasyaiṣa kulaputrā dharmaparyāyo (so WT with most mss., supported by Tib. chos kyi rnam graṅs te; KN deśanā-paryāyo, which would be substantially equivalent) yad evaṃ vyāharati, nāsty atra tathāgatasya mṛṣāvādaḥ SP 320.5, *this is the Tathāgata's way of* (teaching the) *doctrine* . . . (sc. by giving out statements not literally true); *in so doing the T. does not lie*; cf. dharmāṇāṃ paryāya-jñānam Bbh 214.10 (with dharmāṇāṃ lakṣaṇa-jñānam id.11); ayaṃ mañjuśrīḥ dharmaparyāyaḥ, asmiṃ sthāne pracariṣyati Mmk 657.3, *this, M., is a way of* (teaching) *the doctrine* (does this refer to the following discourse?); (ātmanaḥ parinirvāṇaṃ vyāharati tathā tathā ca sattvān paritoṣayati) nānāvidhair dharmaparyāyaiḥ SP 318.1, here perhaps merely *by various ways of* (teaching) *the doctrine* (but possibly *religious disquisitions*); more commonly the word comes to be used of a specific *religious discourse*: asmin khalu dharmaparyāye bhāṣyamāṇe Divy 340.8; Av i.50.12; 233.4; ii.108.3; ito °ryāyād SP 225.3; ayaṃ °ryāyo Mv ii.297.12; frequently named, buddhānusmṛtir nāma °ryāyo Mv i.163.11; applied to the work in which it occurs, Lalitavistaro nāma °ryāyaḥ LV 4.17; Karmavibhaṅgaṃ ... °ryāyaṃ deśayiṣyāmi (misprinted °yami) Karmav 29.31; other occurrences, °ryāyaḥ Mvy 6263; kiṃ (so! prob. kiṃ-nāmā, cpd.) nāmāyaṃ ... °ryāyaḥ RP 59.20 (similarly in Pali, DN i.46.20–21, Ānanda asks, and is told, what is the name of this dhammapariyāya, viz. the first sutta of DN); imaṃ °ryāyaṃ śrutvā Śikṣ 137.18; °ryāye KP 52.1. Once in SP 28.6 (vs), the simple **paryāya**, q.v., is used for dharma-p° in this sense.

Dharmapāla (**1**) (= Pali Dhammapāla 2 of DPPN), n. of the son of the purohita Brahmāyu (previous incarnation of Rāhula): Mv ii.77.12 ff.; (**2**) (= Pali Dhammapāla 8 of DPPN), n. of a teacher: Mvy 3482; (**3**) n. of a prince (previous incarnation of the Buddha): Av i.178.9 ff.; his story is clearly a modified form of that of the prince-hero in the Pali Culla-Dhammapāla Jātaka, No. 358, where he has the name Dhammapāla (4 of DPPN); (**4**) n. of a gandharva: Suv 162.2; (**5**) n. of a yakṣa: Māy 84.

Dharmapālasya jātakam, colophon of a story (of prec., 1): Mv ii.82.3; = Pali Mahā-Dhammapāla Jāt., No. 447.

Dharmapīṭhā, n. of a nāga-maid: Kv 4.9.

Dharmapradīpavikramajñānasiṃha (1st ed. misprinted Dharmapradāpa°; corr. 2d. ed.), n. of a Tathāgata: Gv 297.11.

Dharmapradīpaśirimeru, n. of a Buddha: Gv 259.8 (vs).

Dharmaprabha, (**1**) n. of a Bodhisattva: Gv 3.16; (**2**) n. of a Buddha: Gv 284.20.

Dharmaprabhāsa, n. of a future Buddha (= Pūrṇa Maitrāyaṇīputra, by prediction): SP 201.12.

Dharmapriya, n. of a gandharva king: Kv 2.21.

Dharmabalaprabha, n. of a Buddha: Gv 257.2.

Dharmabalaśrīkūṭa, n. of a Tathāgata: Gv 311.14.

Dharmabuddhi, n. of an ancient king (= the Bodhisattva): Av i.91.16.

dharma-bhāṇaka, sometimes written °**naka**, as LV 179.10; 432.11 (= Pali dhamma-bh°, Childers, s.v. bhāṇako; not in PTSD), *a preacher of the doctrine, religious preacher*: SP 19.9; 227.5; 343.9; 402.5, 7, 9, 11; Mvy 2764; LV 179.10; 432.11, 18, 19–20; Suv 66.12; 112.8; RP 15.11; Kv 13.12; 27.17; 78.1; Bbh 175.15; Dbh 46.12; °ka-tvam, *state* or *condition of* ..., Dbh 76.24; Gv 417.25.

-dharmabhāṇin, adj. (*dharma-bhāṇa, *exposition of the doctrine*, plus -in; cf. prec.), in aprāpta-dharmabhāṇin (actually to be analyzed as a Bhvr. aprāpta-dharmabhāṇa plus -in), *not having received an exposition of the doctrine*: dhārmaśravaṇikasyāprāptadharmabhāṇinaḥ AsP 244.20.

Dharmabhāskaraśrīmegha, n. of a Tathāgata: Gv 309.5.

Dharmamaṇḍalapaṭalamegha, n. of a Tathāgata: Gv 311.9.

Dharmamaṇḍalaprabhāsa, n. of a Buddha: Gv 257.23.

Dharmamaṇḍalavibuddhaśrīcandra, n. of a Tathāgata: Gv 311.11.

Dharmamaṇḍalaśrīśikharābhaprabha, n. of a Tathāgata: Gv 312.5.

Dharmamati, m. (**1**) n. of one of the sons of the Buddha Candrasūryapradīpa: SP 19.4; (**2**) n. of one of the four deities of the bodhi-tree: LV 401.22; (**3**) n. of a former Buddha: Sukh 6.16; of a Buddha, Gv 285.14.

Dharmamaticandrā, n. of a queen: Gv 232.12.

Dharmamativinanditarāja, n. of a former Buddha: Sukh 6.3.

dharma-mukha, nt., *entrance* or *introduction to the doctrine* or *to religion, way of entering* it; so correctly Burnouf on SP 53.5, *introductions à la loi*, confirmed by Tib. on LV 161.14 chos kyi sgo rnam, *doors* or *entrances to the doctrine* or *to religion*. They are usually said to be very numerous: dharmāmukhā (°mā° m.c.) koṭisahasr' aneke prakāśayiṣyanti anāgate 'dhve SP 53.5 (vs); asaṃkhyeyāni dharmamukha-śatasahasrāṇi niścaranti sma LV 128.8 (as the alphabet is recited, religious dicta come forth); a formulaic list, beginning (akṣayavimokṣa)-saṃbhedaṃ nāma dharmamukha(ṃ) Gv 195.24; sarvadharmaśubhavyūhaṃ nāma dharmam° 196.3, and others in 196.5–6, 8, 11, 14, 17, 20, etc. (the names are pompous but unilluminating); (sarvaromamukhebhyo) vividhāni dharmamukhāni niścaramāṇāny aśrauṣīt Gv 515.5, foll. by: yad uta, bodhisattvaguṇavarṇa-mukhāni dānapāramitā-mukhāni etc. (the cpds. become longer and more embracing as they proceed); precisely *four* are listed in LV 182.5 ff., (bodhisattvaḥ ...) catvāri dharmamukhāny āmukhīkaroti sma... (6) yad idaṃ ... catuḥsaṃgrahavastu-prayoga-nirhāraviśuddhiṃ ca nāma dharmamukhaṃ ... (and three other even more complicated ones, showing no clear relation to the Gv lists; it seems clear that there was no standard or accepted list); (bodhisattvāḥ ...) dharmamukhaiḥ saṃcoditavyā bhavanti LV 161.14, *are to be instigated* (to withdraw from the world) *by* (the utterance of) *introductions to religion* (such as those which then follow in verses).

dharmamukhikā (to prec.; pejorative -ka?), *an (unworthy, deceptive?) introduction to religious teaching*: (Upanandena tan mahalladvayaṃ) °khikayā vyaṃsitam (q.v.) MSV ii.102.12.

dharma-mudrā, *'seal' of the doctrine*: iya ... °drā SP 92.13 (vs); also dharma-svabhāva-mudrā, *'seal' of the true nature of the doctrine*: bhāṣiṣyate °drām SP 28.8 (vs); deśem' imām °drām 47.8 (vs). Tib. renders literally, phyag rgya, and so Burnouf, *le sceau*; Kern, *closing word of my law, fixed nature of the law, (unmistakable) stamp of the nature of the law*; probably the last rendering comes close to what is meant.

Dharmameghadhvajapradīpa, n. of a Tathāgata: Gv 310.10.

Dharmameghanagarābhapradīparāja, n. of a Tathāgata: Gv 314.9 (vs); = **Dharmadhātunagarābhajñānapradīparāja** (in prose), q.v.

Dharmameghanirghoṣarāja, n. of a Tathāgata: Gv 297.4.

Dharmameghavighuṣṭakīrtirāja, n. of a Tathāgata: Gv 311.8.

dharmameghā, n. of the tenth Bodhisattva-bhūmi (in the usual list; cf. **abhiṣeka**, °**ka-vatī**): Mvy 895; Dharmas 64; Bbh 354.26; Laṅk 15.5; Dbh 5.10, etc.

Dharmayaśas, n. of the father of Bakula: Karmav 76.10.

dharma-yoga (m.; in PTSD dhammayoga is recorded, s.v. yoga, only from AN iii.355.6, where it is a Bhvr. adj., °gā bhikkhū), *application to a religious doctrine*, in īdṛśa-dharma-yoge LV 420.20 (here a heretical doctrine); see s.v. **pravādī**.

Dharmarati, n. of a son of Māra (favorable to the Bodhisattva): LV 313.9.

Dharmaratnakusumaśrīmegha, n. of a Tathāgata: Gv 309.14.

dharmarāja(n), (mgs. 1 and 2 = Pali dhammarāja), (**1**) *king of the doctrine* or *religious, righteous king*, ep. of Buddha: LV 214.13; 395.9; 426.19; 437.18; °ja-putra (= jina-putra etc., of disciples or Bodhisattvas) Mvy 1090; (**2**) *lawful* (or *righteous*) *king*, as standing epithet of a cakravartin (cf. Pali DN comm. i.249.29, glossed dhammena rajjaṃ labhitvā rājā jāto ti): Mvy 3618; LV 14.3; 101.13; (**3**) n. of a former Buddha: Mv i.138.2 (°jaḥ).

dharmarājikā, once **dhārm**° (from **dharmarājan** 1),

lit. (edifice) *which belongs to* (serves for relics of) *the king of the doctrine* (= Buddha); *a stūpa*. So correctly BR; Burnouf Intr. 370 n. 1 and 631 is uncertain; Divy Index wrongly *royal edict on the law*. The mg. seems clear from (caturaśīti-)dharmarājikā-sahasraṃ pratiṣṭhāpayeyam Divy 381.14, °sraṃ pratiṣṭhāpitam 18, 23, while in the same passage, describing the same performance, in verse, we read: cakre stūpānāṃ ... sāśīti ... sahasram 21. To my mind this settles the matter. Other occurrences, always with forms of pratiṣṭhāpayati, *establishes, founds*: Divy 379.22; 381.5; 402.19; 405.15, 16; 419.15; 429.13; 433.27; 434.1; also dhārmarājikā 368.28.

dharmarājya, nt. (°rāja, mg. 1, plus -ya), *Buddhahood*: (bodhisattvānāṃ ...) aprāpte °jye Mv i.148.1, *while they have not yet become Buddhas*.

Dharmaruci, (**1**) (= Pali Dhammaruci) n. of a disciple of Śākyamuni: Mv i.246.3, 6, 12 (later incarnation of **Meghadatta**, q.v.); Divy 236.2 ff. (here a number of the same stories are told of him as in Pali); Divy chap. 18 is called Dharmarucy-avadāna, Divy 262.6; (**2**) n. of one of the four deities of the bodhi-tree: LV 401.21.

Dharmalabdha, n. of a merchant (previous incarnation of Śākyamuni): Mv iii.286.16 ff.; °dhasya sārthavāhasya jātakaṃ, colophon, iii.300.9.

Dharmavikurvitavegadhvajaśrī, n. of a Tathāgata: Gv 297.8.

Dharmavimānanirghoṣarāja, n. of a Tathāgata: Gv 422.21.

Dharmavivardhana, n. originally given to Aśoka's son, later called **Kunāla**, acc. to Divy 405.24, 26. Known to Chinese sources: Przyluski, Aśoka, 106 etc. (see Index).

dharma-veṣṭi, see **veṣṭi**.

Dharmaśarīra(-sūtra), n. of a short work: Stönner, SBBA 1904 pp. 1282, 1283 (line 5 of text). Here printed entire; a list of Buddhist religious categories.

Dharmaśikharadhvajamegha, n. of a Tathāgata: Gv 311.6.

Dharmaśūra, n. of a former Buddha: Mv i.141.9.

dharma-śravaṇa, nt. (= Pali dhammasavana), *listening to the doctrine, attending sermons and religions recitations*: Jm 162.8 etc. Forms the basis of the next.

dharmaśravaṇika, also **dhārma-śrav°** and **°śrāv°**, adj. or subst. (from prec. form plus -ika; not recorded in Pali), *listening (one who listens) to religious discourses*: dharmaśrav° SP 283.2, all Nep. mss., ed. with Kashgar rec. dhārmaśrāv°; Śikṣ 49.16; 355.10; Suv 104.2; 107.5; 128.16; dhārmaśrav° SP 20.13; Śikṣ 49.17 and 18 (thrice); 56.2; 197.16; 201.5; AsP 243.9; 244.20; dhārmaśrāv° SP 286.8 (and see above under 283.2).

Dharmaśrī, (**1**) n. of a Bodhisattva: Gv 4.3; (**2**) n. of a Buddha: Gv 258.7 (vs; °śiriś ca, n. sg., m.c.).

Dharmasaṃgīti, f., n. of a work: Mvy 1346; Śikṣ 12.8 (-sūtra); 145.16; 263.1, etc. See **saṃgīti** 2.

Dharmasamudra, n. of two Buddhas: Gv 257.12; (°maḥsamudra, so read, as cpd., § 8.12) Gv 285.16.

Dharmasamudragarjana, n. of a Buddha: Gv 257.1 (vs).

Dharmasamudragarbha, n. of a Bodhisattva: Gv 2.25.

Dharmaḥ- (m. c. for Dharma-; cf. § 8.12) **samudraprabhagarjitaghoṣarāja**, Gv 314.14, and °garjitarājya, Gv 314.7, both in vss, = **Sarvadharmasāgaranirghoṣaprabharāja**, n. of a Tathāgata, q.v.

Dharmasamudravegaśirirāja (for °śrīrāja), n. of a Buddha: Gv 258.6 (vs).

Dharmasamudrasaṃbhavaruta, n. of a Buddha: Gv 259.17 (vs).

Dharmasāgaranigarjitaghoṣa, n. of a Tathāgata: Gv 422.10.

Dharmasāgaranirghoṣamati, n. of a Buddha: Gv 285.3 (vs).

Dharmasāgaranirdeśaghoṣa, n. of a Tathāgata: Gv 309.6.

Dharmasāgaranirnādanirghoṣa, n. of a Tathāgata: Gv 310.21.

Dharmasāgarapadma, n. of a Tathāgata: Gv 423.2.

Dharmasūryatejas, n. of a Bodhisattva: Gv 2.21.

Dharmasūryameghapradīpa, n. of a Tathāgata: Gv 311.7.

dharmaskandha, m. (= Pali dhammakkhandha, on which see Childers, and cf. Kern's note in Transl. of SP, SBE 21, p. 241), *article* or *item of the doctrine*, of which there are said (also in Pali) to be 84,000: Mvy 1417 (°dhaḥ); dharmaskandhasahasrāṇi caturaśīti dhārayet SP 254.11 (vs; so read with most mss. and WT, as required by meter, contrary to note in KN, whose text is unmetrical).

dharmasvabhāvamudrā, see **dharma-mudrā**.

Dharmaḥsamudra(-), see **Dharma-sa°**.

dharmā-(kathā), see s.v. 3 **dharma**.

Dharmākara, n. of a monk (of old): Sukh 7.3 ff.; he became the Buddha **Amitābha**, 28.10.

Dharmākaramati, n. of an author: Sādh 200.9; 417.7 (here called **Madhyamaka-ruci**).

Dharmādityajñānamaṇḍalapradīpa, n. of a Tathāgata: Gv 309.7.

dharmānudharma-, see s.v. **anudharma**.

dharmānvaya (m.; = Pali dhammanvaya), *consecutive* or *constant exposition of the Doctrine*: (yadā devo 'ntaḥpuraṃ) praviśati tadā mamāntike °yam upasthāpayed Divy 531.2; °yaṃ prasādayati (q.v.) 4.

Dharmābhimukhā, n. of an apsaras: Kv 3.15.

dharmāyatana, see 2 **dharma** (2).

Dharmārci(s), n. of a Buddha: °rci (n. sg.) Gv 284.12 (vs).

Dharmārciḥparvataketurāja, n. of a Tathāgata: Gv 309.8.

Dharmārcinagaramegha, m., or **°ghā**, f., n. of a lokadhātu: °gho, n. sg., Gv 307.2; °ghāyāṃ, loc. sg., 307.10. For this the next item, q.v., occurs in vs.

Dharmārcimeghanagaraḥ (or °raḥ-śiri; n. sg.) = prec., in vs, Gv 314.3.

Dharmārcimeru, n. of a Buddha: Gv 257.3 (vs).

Dharmārciḥsaṃtejorāja, or (2d ed.) **Dharmārciṣmattejorāja**, n. of a Bodhisattva: Gv 12.14. In 28.19 replaced in 1st ed. by next; 2d ed. as before.

[**Dharmārthamatitejorāja**, see prec.]

dharmāloka, m., *light of (?on) the doctrine*; acc. to Sūtrāl. xiv.26 comm., āloka iti dharmanidhyānakṣānter etad adhivacanam, *āloka is a synonym for 'readiness to meditate on the doctrine'* (but generally the word seems to be an appositional karmadh.): (avidyāmohāndhakārasya) mahāntam °kaṃ kuryāṃ LV 205.3, *may I make the great light of the doctrine against the darkness of ignorance and delusion*; dharmālokasyādarotpādanārthaṃ LV 395.16, *to produce respect for the light of the doctrine*; (?) bodhisattvānāṃ ... mahanto dharmāloko (but mss. dharma-loko) kṛto bhaviṣyati āśvāso ca datto bhavati Mv ii.294.5 (as a result of a requested statement by the Buddha on how he attained enlightenment); (-Kāraṇḍavyūhaṃ nāma) dharmālokaṃ nāma deśayitvā Kv 38.3; °ka-praveśa, (*means of*) *ingress into the light of the doctrine* (= **°ka-mukha**, see next) Dbh 38.1, where ten such are listed, viz. sattva-dhātuvicāraṇālokapraveśair, and (substituting for sattva in the same cpd.) loka-, dharma-, ākāśa-, vijñāna-, kāma-, rūpa-, ārūpya-, udārāśayādhimukti-, and māhātmyāśayādhimukti-. See under next.

dharmāloka-mukha, nt. (see under prec., and cf. **dharma-mukha**), *entrance, means of ingress, into the light of the doctrine*: Mvy 6973 = Tib. chos snaṅ baḥi sgo, *'door'* (or *entrance*) *to the light of dharma*; in LV 31.2 ff. a list of 108 dharmālokamukhāni; cf. the ten dharmālokapraveśa, s.v. **dharmāloka**; evamrūpasarvasattvasaṃjñāpanaṃ dharmālokamukhaṃ Gv 304.26; dharmālokamukhenāntaḥpuraṃ pratyavekṣamāṇo LV 207.1, *looking upon the harem by the door of the light of the doctrine* (i. e. by entering into that light? perhaps substantially *by way, by the path* or *means, of* that *light*; but the alleged use of mukha in the sense of *means* is certainly very rare in both Skt. and Pali and prob. not to be admitted, unless as a deliberate and intentional figure).

Dharmāvabhāsasvara, n. of a Bodhisattva: Gv 4.10.

Dharmāśoka, epithet of the emperor Aśoka: Divy 381.24; Mmk 608.4.

dharmāsana (nt.; = Pali dhammāsana), *preacher's seat* (used by him in preaching): Śikṣ 355.8.

dharmāsanaka, m. (dharmāsana plus -ka), *occupant of the preacher's seat*: Śikṣ 355.8.

dharmi-(kathā; Pali dhammi-), see s.v. 3 **dharma.**

dharmika, adj. (very rare in Skt. and regarded by BR as error for dhārmika; in BHS doubtless Sktization of MIndic, Pali dhammika), *righteous, pious*: Mvy 3618; Divy 381.24; both times followed by **dharmarājā** (of a king).

[**-dharmita,** Śikṣ 103.8 (vs) karuṇa-maitra-dharmitāḥ, could be taken as a denom. pple. to dharma, *characterized* (by . . .). But the passage is cited from Gv 483.3, which reads īdṛśaḥ karuṇā-(read with Śikṣ °ṇa, m.c.)-maitra-varmitaḥ, *armored with compassion and love*, which is undoubtedly the true reading.]

dharmī-(kathā; Pali dhammī-), see s.v. 3 **dharma.**

Dharmendrarāja, (**1**) n. of a Bodhisattva: Gv 4.5; (**2**) n. of a Buddha: Gv 258.18 (vs).

Dharmendrarājaguṇaghoṣa, n. of a Buddha: Gv 258.7 (vs).

Dharmeśvara, (**1**) n. of a devaputra, one of the 16 guardians of the bodhimaṇḍa: LV 277.14; (**2**) n. of one or two Buddhas: LV 171.14 (vs); Gv 285.21 (vs).

Dharmeśvararāja, n. of an ancient king: Gv 150.8.

Dharmoccaya, m., n. of a palace in the Tuṣita heaven: LV 13.10; 27.17.

Dharmottara, n. of a teacher: Mvy 3502. Cf. Pali Dhammuttara (DPPN).

Dharmodgata, (**1**) n. of a Bodhisattva: AsP 487.14 etc.; Śikṣ 37.16 etc. (cited from AsP); (the same or not?) Suv 120.5; Gv 3.25; (**2**) n. of a Buddha: Gv 285.11 (vs); (**3**) n. of a samādhi: Mvy 568; ŚsP 1420.16.

Dharmodgatakīrti, n. of a Tathāgata: Gv 361.6.

Dharmodgatanabheśvara, n. of a Tathāgata: Gv 422.25.

dharmolkā (= Pali dhammokkā), *the torch of the Doctrine*: Mv i.42.8 = 53.9 = 337.2 (see **vicalayati**); i.250.6 (see **abhidhārayati**).

Dharmolkājvalanaśrīcandra, n. of a Tathāgata: Gv 310.8.

Dharmolkāratnavitānaghoṣa, n. of a Tathāgata: Gv 311.22.

-dharṣika, see **adharṣikatā.**

dhavara, nt., a high number: Mvy 7916 = Tib. laṅ liṅ (not elsewhere in Mvy); cited from Gv; corresponds to **parava** of that text 106.17 (not in the other Gv list, 133.26).

dhātu, m. or f. (nt. forms occur rarely; in Skt. recorded only as m.; in Pali app. usually, acc. to PTSD only, f., but acc. to Childers m. and f.); in BHS most commonly m.; f. examples, ākāśadhātuṃ yaḥ sarvām SP 253.13, pṛthivīdhātuṃ ca yaḥ sarvāṃ 254.1; yattikā pṛthivīdhātu Mv i.126.12; svakāye tejodhātūye (instr.) 357.16–17; see also **lokadhātu,** often f. as well as m.; nt., tāni dhātūni Mv ii.93.20 (vs); in Mv iii.65.10 ff. adj. forms of all three genders, catvāro (dhātavaḥ), repeatedly, 10–12; catvāri, 11; tiṣṭhamānāvo (f. n. pl.) and bhajyamānīyo, 11; (= Pali id. in all mgs. except 6; in some included here, viz. 1 and 2, more or less similarly in Skt.; some Pali mgs. etymologically explained in Vism. 485.2 ff.;) the most fundamental meaning is perhaps *element*, cf. Lévi, Sūtrāl. i.18 note 1, 'l'idée centrale reste toujours celle de *élément primordial, original, principe*'; Tib. regularly renders khams, except in cpd. dharma-dh° where it renders dbyiṅs; once (below, 6) it uses rluṅ; conscious recognition of several different mgs. in a four-pāda vs: sattvadhātu paripācayiṣyase, lokadhātu pariśodhayiṣyasi, jñānadhātum utthāpayiṣyase (meter!), āśayasya tava dhātu tādṛśaḥ Gv 484.15–16, *you will completely mature the* (or, *a*) *mass of creatures, you will completely purify the world-system(s), you will raise up on high the sphere* (*state of mind*? see below) *of knowledge; such is the natural character of your disposition*; (**1**) *physical element, constituent* of the material world, of which, like Pali, BHS normally recognizes (**a**) *four*, earth, water, fire, and air or wind, pṛthivī, ap, tejas, vāyu; listed Mvy 1838–41 pṛthivī-dhātuḥ etc. but given the caption catvāri mahābhūtāni 1837; and cf. Śikṣ 250.14 under (b) below; in a cliché, na . . . karmāṇi kṛtāny upacitāni vāhye pṛthivīdhātau vipacyante nābdhātau na tejodhātau na vāyudhātāv api tūpātteṣv (em., but probable), eva skandhadhātvāyataneṣu vipacyante Divy 54.5 ff.; 131.9 ff.; 141.9 ff.; (with slight alterations 191.16;) 311.18 ff.; 504.19 ff.; 581.29 ff.; 584.16 ff.; Av i.74.4 ff., (*the effects of*) *deeds done do not mature in the four external physical elements, but in the skandha, dhātu* (sense 4, q.v.), *and āyatana* (q.v.); iha dhātu-bhūta (so divide) caturo . . . viśoṣitā me bhavasamudrā LV 373.13(–14; vs), *here I have dried up the four 'oceans' of existence* (there are four oceans in normal Hindu geography, surrounding the earth) *which consist of* (-bhūta) *the* (four) *elements*; catvāro . . . dhātavaḥ Mv iii.65.10; caturo dhātava LV 284.5 (vs; Foucaux renders *directions*, claiming support of Tib., but Tib. khams, the regular rendering of dhātu); abdhātuṃ pratyāpibanti SP 122.5 (pratically simply *water*); **tejodhātu,** see this separately; pṛthivīdhātu Mv i.126.12; SP 254.1; but also (**b**) again as in Pali, not *five* as in Skt. but *six*, the above four plus ākāśa (as in Skt.; note ākāśadhātu alone SP 253.13; 342.11) and also vijñāna (Pali viññāṇa), listed Dharmas 58 as ṣaḍ dhātavaḥ; important is Śikṣ 244.11 ff. (similarly Bcṭ 326.24 ff.): ṣaḍdhātur ayaṃ . . . puruṣaḥ . . . katame ṣaṭ? tad yathā: pṛthivīdhātur abdh° tejodh° vāyudh° ākāśadh° vijñānadh° ca . . . ṣaḍ imāni . . . sparśāyatanāni (see **āyatana** 5) . . . cakṣuḥ sparśāyatanaṃ rūpāṇāṃ darśanāya, (and so) śrotraṃ . . . ghrāṇaṃ . . . jihvā . . . kāya(ḥ) sparśāyatanaṃ spraṣṭavyāṇāṃ sparśanāya, manaḥ spa° dharmāṇāṃ vijñānāya . . . (245.1 ff.) adhyātmikaḥ pṛthivīdhātuḥ, which is whatever is *hard* in the body, as hair, nails, teeth, etc.; (245.4) bāhyaḥ pṛthivīdhātuḥ is whatever is *hard* in the outside world. Similarly with abdhātu 246.16 ff.; tejodhātu 248.2 ff.; vāyudhātu 248.11–249.3; ākāśadhātu 249.3 ff., in the body of man, is such things as the mouth, throat, etc. (*empty space*, we would say); in the outside world, what is hollow and empty (as a hole in the ground); vijñānadhātu 250.5 ff., (line 7) ṣaḍindriyādhipateyā (see **ādhipateya**) ṣaḍviṣayārambaṇā (read °baṇa-, in accord with line 5 cakṣurindriyādhipateyā rūpārambaṇaprativijñaptiḥ; see **ārambaṇa** 3) viṣayavijñaptir ayam ucyate vijñānadhātuḥ (this is only adhyātmika; there is no external vijñāna); in 250.14 ff. it is made clear that the sparśāyatanāni, i. e. the sensory organs or powers (244.15 ff.), are constituted by *equilibrium* or *tranquillity* (**prasāda** 2, q.v.) of the four physical elements (a, above, here called mahābhūtāni, as in Mvy 1837): katamac cakṣurāyatanam? yac caturṇāṃ mahābhūtānāṃ prasādaḥ, tad yathā, pṛthivīdhātor abdhātos tejodhātor vāyudhātor yāvat, etc.; these four only make up the several senses; ākāśa, *emptiness*, cannot be involved, and vijñāna (six-fold) is what results from the operation of each sense on its appropriate objects; (**2**) *element* in the body exclusively and specifically (aside from 1 above which applies to the body but also to all the external world), pretty much as in Skt. (BR s.v. dhātu 3), but I have found no numerical listing of them in BHS (in Skt. various numbers occur, rarely 3 = the 3 doṣa, *wind, gall, phlegm*; but regularly 7, sometimes 5 or 10), *main constituent* of the body: in Suv 179.5 six (ṣaḍdhātu-kauśalya, see below, end, note*); abhiṣyaṇṇā vātātapā saṃvṛttā Mv iii.143.16, cf. abhiṣyaṇṇehi dhātūhi 144.6; 153.11; 154.8, see s.vv. **abhiṣyaṇṇa** and **vātātapa,** *excessive* or *over-exuberant bodily humors* (a cause of disease; Pali uses abhi(s)-sanna of the dosa, Skt. doṣa, [three] bodily humors); dhātu-vaiṣamyāc ca glānaḥ Divy 191.28, *sick from an upset condition of the humors*; tvaṃ vaidya (n. sg.; so divide) dhātu-kuśalas LV 184.21 (vs), *thou, a physician skilled in the humors* or *bodily elements*; kaccid dhātavaḥ pratikurvanti SP 429.4, *I hope your bodily humors* (or *elements*) *are acting properly*?; (**3**) the 18 dhātu, *psycho-physical constituent elements* of the personality in relation to the outside world (Pali id.), are the 12 **āyatana** (i. e. the 6 senses plus 6 sense-objects, see s.v. 5) plus the 6 corresponding sensory perceptions, **vijñāna**; listed Mvy 2040–58, cakṣur-dhātuḥ, rūpa-dhātuḥ, cakṣur-vijñāna-dhātuḥ, and so with śrotra (śabda), ghrāṇa (gandha), jihvā (rasa), kāya (spraṣṭavya), mano (dharma); same in abbreviated form (with sparśa for spraṣṭavya) Dharmas 25; aṣṭādaśa dhātavaś LV 372.7; see also **varṇa-dhātu**; (**4**) *constituent element* of the mind, 'heart', or character, and so by extension (psychic) *character, nature, natural disposition*; as *element* of the citta, Av ii.140.13 ff., śamatha-vipaśyanā-paribhāvitam . . . (14) āryaśrāvakasya cittaṃ dhātuśo (cf. Pali dhātuso in quite similar sense, SN ii.154.19 ff., referring to dhātu 153.23 ff.; note avijjā-dhātu 153.29) vimucyate. tatra sthavira katame dhātavaḥ? yaś ca . . . (141.1) prahāṇa-dhātur yaś ca virāga-dhātur yaś ca nirodha-dhātuḥ, kasya nu . . . prahāṇāt (2) prahāṇadhātur ity ucyate? . . . (3) sarvasaṃskārāṇāṃ . . . prahāṇāt prahāṇadhātur ity ucyate, and so identically with virāga and nirodha; in this sense I understand nānādhātu-jñāna-balam Mvy 123 (one of the 10 balāni of a Buddha), and (also one of the 10 balāni) nānādhātukaṃ (-ka Bhvr.; = °dhātuṃ) lokaṃ vidanti Mv i.159.14; nānādhātum imaṃ lokam anuvartanti paṇḍitāḥ (= Tathāgatāḥ) Mv i.90.17; Pali similarly has anekadhātu and nānādhātu as eps. of loka, and knowledge of them as one of the 10 balāni, e. g. MN i.70.9–10, where comm. ii.29.20 ff. is uncertain, cakkhudhātu-ādīhi (see 3 above) kāmadhātu-ādīhi (see 5 below) vā dhātūhi bahudhātuṃ . . . lokaṃ ti khandhāyatanadhātu-lokaṃ (see below); but DN ii.282.25 ff. seems to prove that the mg. is different, anekadhātu nānādhātu kho . . . loko . . ., yaṃ yad eva sattā dhātuṃ abhinivisanti, taṃ tad eva thāmasā . . . abhinivissa voharanti: idam eva saccaṃ moghaṃ aññaṃ ti; tasmā na sabbe . . . ekantavādā ekantasīlā ekantachandā ekanta-ajjhosānā ti (here, dhātu is surely something like *nature, disposition*, as comm. says, ajjhāsaya, iii.737.18); similarly, nānādhimuktānāṃ sattvānāṃ nānādhātv-āśayānām āśayaṃ viditvā SP 41.3; 71.8, *knowing the disposition of creatures who vary in interests and who vary in character and disposition*; CPD s.v. anekadhātu (as ep. of loka) is not quite clear, saying *with many elements, or natural conditions* (*or dispositions*); confirmation of this interpretation may be found in a cliché, (bhagavāṃs teṣāṃ, or the like) . . . āśayānuśayaṃ (see **anuśaya**) dhātuṃ prakṛtiṃ ca jñātvā (evidently *disposition, character*, or *state of mind*) Divy 46.23; 47.9–10; 48.12–13; 49.11–12; (in 209.12 cpd. āśayānuśayadhātuprakṛtiṃ ca, in view of ca prob. to be read °dhātuṃ;) 462.9–10; 463.18–19, etc.; Av i.64.12–13; also āśayasya tava dhātu tādṛśaḥ Gv 484.16, above, and possibly jñāna-dhātu in the same line, but here *sphere* (5, below) may be meant; here also, it seems, must be included dhātu, *state of mind, psychic characteristic*, when used parallel (or in composition) with skandha and āyatana (where, if sense 3 were intended, āyatana would be included in dhātu so that tautology would result), as: te skandhā tāni dhātūni tāni āyatanāni ca, ātmānaṃ ca adhikṛtya bhagavān tam (mss. etam; Senart's em. leaves the meter still bad) arthaṃ vyākare (v.l. °ret) Mv ii.93.20–21 (vss); na skandha-āyatana-dhātu (read as one dvandva cpd., as suggested by Tib. phuṅ po skye mched khams rnams, the last syllable being the plural suffix, put after the third noun only, saṅs rgyas yin mi smra) vademi Buddhaṃ LV 420.17 (vs), *I do not say that the skandha, sense-organs and their objects, and states of mind are Buddha*; skandhadhātvāyataneṣu Divy 54.5 ff. etc. (see 1a, above), roughly, *in the mental* (not gross-physical) *constitution*; in LV 177.5 (vs) read, skandhāyatanāni dhātavaḥ, with citation of the line Śikṣ 240.5, as required by meter and supported by Tib. (Lefm. skandhadhātvāyatanāni dhātavaḥ); (**5**) *sphere, region, world, state of existence* (Pali id.); so in **lokadhātu,** q.v.; sometimes dhātu alone appears to be short for loka-dhātu, *world*(*-region*): ratnāvatī nāma dhātv aika (read ekā?) yatrāsau bhagavān vaset Mmk 139.1 (vs, bad meter); evam aśeṣata dharmata dhātuṃ sarv' adhimucyami pūrṇa jinebhiḥ Bhad 3, *thus completely according to what is right I devote myself to the world*(*-region*) *that is all full of Buddhas* (wrongly Leumann); three *states of existence*, **kāma-dh°**, **rūpa-dh°** (qq.v.), and **ārūpya-** (q.v.)dh° (all in Pali); nirvāṇa-dhātu (Pali nibbāna°, usually with adj. anupādisesa), the *sphere* or *state, condition, of nirvāṇa*, usually with adj. **anupadhiśeṣa,** SP 21.9; 411.5; Kv 18.19 (text arūpaviśeṣe, read anupadhiśeṣe, nirvāṇadhātau), or **nirupadhiśeṣa,** Divy 22.9; 242.16; 394.8; asadṛśa nirvāṇa-dhātu-saukhyam Sukh 9.1 (vs); see also **dharma-dhātu,** *sphere of religion*; jñānadhātum utthāpayiṣyase Gv 484.16 (above), *you will raise up on high the sphere* (?possibly *state of mind*, mg. 4) *of knowledge*; (**6**) from this last, *world, sphere*, develops the meaning *mass, abundance, large quantity* (not recorded in Pali nor recognized by Lévi, Sūtrāl. i.18 note 1), chiefly in comp. with sattva: tvayā Mañjuśrīḥ kiyān sattvadhātur vinītaḥ SP 261.8, *how large a quantity of creatures have you, M., trained* (*religiously*)? (so both Burnouf and Kern; no other interpretation seems possible); dūrapraṇaṣṭaṃ sattvadhātuṃ viditvā SP 187.1 (Burnouf, *la réunion des êtres*; Kern *creatures*, adopting a v.l. sattvān which is not recorded in either ed.); (yathābhinimantritasya) sattvadhātoḥ paripākakālam LV 180.4 (Tib. khams = dhātoḥ); vyavasthāpitaḥ sattvadhātuḥ LV 351.9 (see s.v. **dharmadhātu**; note that Tib. renders dhātu by dbyiṅs after dharma-, but by khams after sattva-); na tv eva śakyaṃ gaṇayituṃ sarvasattvadhātū (v.l. °tuṃ) daśasu diśāsu . . . Mv ii.295.11; yāvanti buddhakṣetrasmiṃ sattvadhātu (so mss., evidently pl.; Senart °tū) acintiyā 352.12; sattvadhātavaḥ parimokṣitāḥ Kv 13.24; sattva-dhātu- (in comp.) 15.5; °tu paripācayiṣyase Gv 484.15 (vs, above); na ca sattvadhātuṃ parityajanti Gv 471.23; rarely with any other word than sattva, śiśire hi yathā himadhātu mahān (*a great mass of snow*) tṛṇagulmavanauṣadhi-ojaharo (one cpd. word) LV 175.3 (vs), cited Śikṣ 206.1; here Foucaux translates *wind*, claiming support of Tib. rluṅ, which does indeed primarily mean *wind*, but is also used of the bodily *humors*, which is one of the mgs. of dhātu (2, above); Foucaux's mg. could only be right if we em. to vāyu (or vāta), but Śikṣ confirms dhātu, which cannot possibly mean *wind* in the ordinary natural sense; it seems that Tib. misunderstood the passage and used a word which is a synonym of khams (= dhātu) in one of its senses, but does not fit here; (**7**) (orig. *elemental bodily substance*, 2 above; hence) *relics, bodily remains* (after death; = Pali id.), sg. or pl.: (buddhānāṃ) dhātustūpāḥ SP 7.3; 340.12, *relic-stūpas*; dhātu SP 99.1 (sg.); 324.1 (pl.); jina-dhātuṣu 341.2; (yaś ca parinirvṛtasya, v.l. adds tathāgatasya,) sarṣapaphalamātram api dhātum (so read) satkareyā Mv ii.362.15; lokanāthasya dhātuṣu Mv ii.367.3; dhātu-vibhāgaṃ kṛtvā Divy 90.9, *division, distribution of the relics*; śarīra-dhātūn Divy 368.27, °tuṃ 380.19; dhātu-pratyaṃśaṃ dattvā 380.20; dhātavaḥ 381.2; dhātu, sg., Suv 13.6 ff.; dhātu- (in comp.) RP 6.9; dhātūnām 57.3; see also **dhātu-vigraha** and (dhātv-)**avaropaṇa.** — [Note*: on the medical use of dhātu, see Nobel, JAOS Supplement 11 to Vol. 71 No. 3, 1951; on Suv 179.5 (above; **2**) esp. p. 8.]

-dhātuka (-ka ifc. Bhvr.) = **dhātu** 4, q.v.: Mv i.159.14.

Dhātu-kāya, m., n. of a work: Mvy 1418 = Tib. khams kyi tshogs, *collection* (see **kāya**) *of 'elements'* (in which sense of **dhātu**?).

(**dhātukī,** once in Skt., acc. to pw error for dhātakī, n. of a plant: MSV i.iii.13.)

dhātugarbha (cf. **dhātu,** 7; = Pali °gabbha, Childers; not in PTSD), *'containing relics'* i. e. *relic-shrine, dagoba*: mad-dhātugarbha-parimaṇḍita-jambukhaṇḍam Divy 369.1.

dhātu-tantra, nt., *'science of dhātu'* (in which sense? possibly 2, *the bodily elements, physiology*?), one of the subjects studied in school: LV 124.16 (vs); prec. by saṃkhyā, lipi, gaṇanā; no clue to precise mg. in context, nor in Tib. which renders mechanically khams kyi rgyud.

Dhātupriyā, n. of a kiṃnara maid: Kv 6.2.

?**dhātu-rāṣṭra,** in °ṭropaśobhitāḥ Sukh 39.3, epithet of the rivers of Sukhāvatī; Müller, SBE 49.2, p. 39, *adorned with fields, full of metals.* One mg. of Skt. dhātu is *metal* or *mineral*; if that is the mg. here, the cpd. might be rendered *adorned with kingdoms characterized by minerals.* I am very doubtful of this interpretation, but have no guess which seems to me plausible as to what **dhātu,** q.v., means here.

dhātu-vigraha (m.; not recorded in Pali), *'relic-body', relics* (substantially = **dhātu** 7): (vayam api...) Prabhūtaratnasya Tathāgatasya... °haṃ paśyema SP 430.6; (bhagavān darśayatu...) °ham 7.

dhātṛ = **dhātrī,** *nurse*: mātṛbhir dhātṛbhiś (both edd., no v.l.) ca rudantībhiḥ parivṛtāḥ SP 160.14 (prose), *surrounded by their weeping mothers and nurses.* The form has phonetic aspects (§ 3.95) but may and doubtless should be regarded as in part, and perhaps primarily, a riming adaptation to the preceding mātṛbhiḥ.

-dhāna, nt., ifc. (see BR s.v. 2 dhāna, 1, which is fairly common in Vedic, hardly used in Cl. Skt. except in some proper names of doubtful interpretation), *place,* or perhaps *receptacle,* in **varca-dhāna, saṃkāra-**dhāna.

dhānuṣkārikā or °**kā** (in cpds.), = next, q.v.: °ka- Mmk 61.19 (prec. by vāpika, read vārṣika); 111.18 (text dhātuḥ°); °kā- Mmk 63.12 (prec. by vārṣikā).

dhānuṣkārin (= **dhanuṣ°,** q.v. on mg. and Pali equivalent; see also prec. and next), n. of a certain flowering tree; also written °skārin, and corruptly dhātu°; usually in cpds. listing flowering trees, and apt to be preceded by (sumanā-)vārṣika (with variants)-: (sumanāvārṣika-)-dhānuskāri- (mss. dhātu°; Tib. dha-nu-°) LV 366.13; sumanāvārṣikī-dhānuskāri- (v.l. dhātu°, also °ṣkāri-) 431.16; in LV 11.3 Tib. confirms insertion in ms. H and has da nu ska ri (= BHS dhānuskāri or °ṣkāri) for the corrupt dhātusphanite of H; °kāri- to be read (after vārṣikā-, once text vārṣikāṃ but v.l. °ka-, once varṣaka-, in cpds.) in Mv i.249.13 (for vātuṣkāra-, no v.l.); ii.116.10 (for Senart's vātuṣkārī, mss. cited as vānuṣ°, cārukkārī); iii.80.4 (here Senart varṣaka-dhātuḥ kārī; mss. °kāri); °ṣkārī, n. sg., Mvy 6160 (v.l. dhanuṣ°, but Mironov dhān° without v.l.); Mmk 445.24 (vs, metr. indifferent); °ṣkārī, apparently n. pl. (end of cpd.), to be read for dhātu° of ed. and mss. Divy 244.25 (prose).

dhānuṣkārīka- (perhaps read °**rika,** q.v.), = prec., q.v.: stem in comp., Mmk 69.18 (prec. by varṣika-).

Dhānyakaṭaka, n. of a caitya, in the south: śrī-dhānyakaṭake caitye jinadhātudhare bhuvi Mmk 88.10 (vs); in prec. line dakṣiṇāpathasaṃjñike; °ke mahācaitye JRAS Oct. 1875 (N.S. VIII Pt. 1), p. 27, line 1.

Dhānyadrāhyāyaṇa (so read for ed. °drāyāyaṇa; see the readings of the corrupt mss., some of which support this, the obviously correct reading), pl., n. of a brahmanical gotra: Divy 635.19. This passage is omitted in two Chin. translations, my colleague Prof. Rahder informs me. Cf. **Dhyāna-drāhyāyaṇī,** where Chin. seems more favorable to initial Dhā- rather than Dhyā-. It seems that one or the other of these two must be an error, and perhaps Dhānya- should be read in both.

Dhānyaparigraha, n. of a work(?): °he Bbh 100.10.

Dhānyapura, n. of a city: MSV i.xvii.12.

dhānyika (Skt. dhānya plus -ika), *grain-dealer*; in list of tradesmen and artisans; so read with mss. Mv iii.442.14, and also iii.113.8 where mss. **dadhyika** (which Senart reads both times).

dhāraka, adj., subst. (= Pali id.; in Skt. only ifc. and hardly in this sense), *one who retains in his mind* or *memory,* with gen. of a sacred work: sūtrāntānāṃ dhārakā(ḥ) SP 44.1; (sc. sūtrasya) 228.7; (sūtrarājasya) Kv 13.12; dharmaparyāyasya 27.17.

?**dhārakuśalāntara,** in na °rāc ca gṛhṇanti LV 258.6 (vs, see s.v. **karoṭa**), *and do not take* (food) *from*...? Foucaux renders, *from the crack* (fente) *of a door*; I do not understand this rendering, even assuming dvāra for dhāra (for which there seems to be no ms. authority). Tib. omitted in Foucaux.

dhāraṇa (nt.), °**ṇā,** in a list of sciences studied by young men, app. some branch of mathematics (*memory* is an established mg. of the word, but seems hardly possible here); seems to correspond to **uddhāra,** q.v., in Divy (cf. Senart iii n. 520); gaṇanāyāṃ pi mudrāyāṃ pi dhāraṇāyāṃ (loc.) pi Mv ii.423.15; otherwise always °ṇa, -gaṇanāṃ dhāraṇa-mudrāṃ (dvandva cpd.?) Mv iii.184.7; gaṇanāṃ dhāraṇaṃ (mss. vār°) nikṣepaṇaṃ iii.394.9; nikṣepaṇaṃ (mss. add taṃ) dhāraṇaṃ iii.405.12.

[**dhāraṇita,** read dhāraṇ' ita(h), Dbh.g. 20(356).11; see s.v. **udyāna** 3.]

dhāraṇī (recorded nowhere except in BHS), *magic formula*: often consisting of meaningless combinations of syllables (which this Dict. does not record), as e. g. Suv 105.6–8; 106.8, 11, 15 ff.; 108.11 ff.; in Tib. regularly gzuṅs, lit. *hold, support,* or (Mvy 4239) gzuṅs sṅags (= *mantra, incantation*); names of 12 Bodhisattva-dhāraṇī, Mvy 746–758; names of 10 dhāraṇī-maṇḍala Gv 305.18 ff. (not listed in Dict.); a list of dhāraṇī-names (not listed here) Mmk 12.20 ff.; four kinds, ātma-, grantha-, dharma-, mantra-dh° Dharmas 52; another list of four, Bbh 272.13 ff., all defined, dharma-dh° (by which a Bodhisattva is able to remember a book on merely hearing it, without study), artha-dh° (same, except *'its meaning'* is remembered), mantra-dh° (by which he acquires charms to allay all plagues, īti), bodhisattvakṣāntilābhāya dh°; °ṇī-pratilabdha, *having obtained* (being in possession of) *a dh°* SP 263.4; 270.8; Dbh 46.12; sarvabodhisattvadhāraṇīpratibhānapratilabdhaiḥ LV 2.6; °ṇī-pratilambha, *acquisition of dh°,* SP 327.5; koṭīnayutaśatasahasraparivartāyā dhāraṇyāḥ pratilambho 8, *acquisition of the dh. which makes* (very many) *revolutions* (an amulet-wheel?); °ṇī-mantrapadāni SP 396.3, *talismanic charm-words,* or *words of dhāraṇīs and mantras*; mantra-dhāraṇī-padāni 397.2–3; dhāraṇī-padāni 397.6 ff.; °ṇī-mudrā Mvy 4297; sarvadharma-dhāraṇy-asampramoṣitaḥ LV 275.6; others, Mvy 782; 4239; Divy 616.14; Kv 84.9; Suv 30.5; 103.1.

Dhāraṇīgarbha, n. of a Bodhisattva: Gv 2.23.

Dhāraṇīmati, f., n. of a samādhi: Mvy 604; ŚsP 1424.14 (°tir, with adj. katamā).

Dhāraṇīmukhasarvajagatpraṇidhisaṃdhāraṇagarbha, n. of a Bodhisattva: Dbh 2.18.

Dhāraṇīśvararāja, n. of a Bodhisattva: RP 2.1.

dhārayati, (**1**) with infin., *holds out = is able, endures* (to do something): na dhārayiṣyati eṣo bhūyo imaṃ alindam odanasya (so read, see **alinda**) khāditum Mv ii.462.11, (after eating a large basket of hard food he will be full;) *he won't last out* (*be able*) *further to eat this dish of porridge*; (**2**) *makes fast, locks* (a door, gate, against someone, gen.): vaidyānāṃ dvāraṃ dhārayitvā svayam eva cikitsā kṛtā MSV ii.66.10. Or read dvār°? Cf. **avadvārāpayati.**

dhārmakathika, m. (= **dharma°**, q.v.), *preacher*: Divy 493.8; Śikṣ 56.1; Kalpanāmaṇḍitikā, Lüders, Kl. Skt. Texte 2 p. 43; Bbh 162.2; 175.7; -tva, abstr.: Bbh 239.8; MSV iii.122.4.

dhārmarājikā = **dharmarājikā**, q.v.: Divy 368.28.

dhārmaśravaṇika and **°śrāv°** = **dharmaśravaṇika**, q.v.

dhārmi-(kathā), see s.v. 3 **dharma.**

?**dhārmikīkṣita**, acc. sg. °tam (v.l. °kṣitim, but Mironov only °kṣitam), anupradāsyāmaḥ (Mironov °ma) Mvy 7307 = Tib. chos bzhin du (*according to dharma*) dpyaḥ (?dpya, *tribute*?), or kha(?), or cha ḥbul ba (*give portion*); Chin. versions also seem to mean *offer* or *hand over according to law*. I can only conjecture a hyper-Skt. substitute for some MIndic form, Skt. dhārmika, adj., plus possibly icchita, MIndic ppp. to icchati, *what is required by dharma*(?).

dhārmī-(kathā), see s.v. 3 **dharma.**

dhārmya, adj., *religious, holy*; see s.v. 3 **dharma.**

dhāvana, nt., *causing to wash, having washed* (a monk's robe, by a nun unrelated to him; cf. Pali Vin. iii.206.20–22): Mvy 8388; cf. also Prāt 491.8 and Mvy 9258 dhāvayet (caus. of dhāv-, *wash*; recorded in BR, tho the mg. assigned is that of the non-caus.).

dhāvita (nt.? not otherwise recorded as noun), *running*, as an athletic exercise or art, in lists of arts learned by a young man: °te (423.16 adds laṅghite) javite plavite Mv ii.423.16; 434.12; °tesmiṃ (so mss., Senart °tasmiṃ) laṅghite javite iii.184.8. All locs.

dhi, interj. (= Pali id., Skt. dhik), *fie! out upon it!*: hā hā dhi muṣyanti hi (v.l. °ti mi, i.e. °ti ime) sarvasattvā SP 351.6 *alas, alas, fie! for all creatures* (or, *all these creatures*) *are deceived* (or, *lost*). WT read śuṣyanti; both edd. take dhi as the preverb adhi with the verb, but it is surely the interj.

dhigama = **adhigama**, q.v., Laṅk 144.10 = 324.5; see § 4.7.

dhītar-, dhītara- (**°rā-**), **dhītā-, dhītrā-** (= Pali dhītar-, dhītā; Skt. duhitar-), *daughter*: (**1**) forms based on normal Skt. r-stem forms: n. sg. dhītā Mv i.36.10; 44.10 ff.; 302.6, 13; 304.8; 305.6; 349.2; 352.15; ii.97.6; 172.10; 441.8, etc.; dhita, m.c., LV 271.5 (vs); acc. sg. dhītaram Mv i.180.17; ii.88.16; 110.18 (v.l. °tāraṃ); 441.18; 442.1; 485.18; iii.9.1; 20.1; 23.14; gen. (abl.) sg. dhītur, °uḥ Mv i.36.14; 302.10; 306.8; 307.3; ii.444.11; dhītu (v.l. °uḥ; prose, before vowel) ii.458.18; n. pl. dhītaro Mv i.348.12; 355.16; 356.8; ii.490.9; iii.282.7, 13; 283.3, 8, 13; 285.15; 300.4; dhītaro used as acc. pl. Mv ii.490.11; iii.16.4; 285.11; (**2**) forms based on fem. ā-stem, starting from n. sg. dhītā: voc. sg. °te Mv ii.172.16; acc. sg. °tām Mv i.356.12; ii.65.6; 73.5; 337.18 (mss.); 442.3; 490.12; iii.146.8; oblique sg. °tāye Mv ii.66.1; 88.15; 263.16 (note duhituḥ 17); 444.9; 486.10; iii.39.7, 19; n. pl. dhīta, m.c. for °tā(ḥ) LV 170.13; (**3**) stem dhītrā, § 13.15: (read) kuladhītṛāya, inst., Thomas ap. Hoernle, MR 94.2; (**4**) forms based on stem dhītara-, abstracted from acc. sg. °ram, with masc. endings: n. sg. dhītaro Mv iii.88.18, 20; 89.12 (here Senart em. dhītā), 14; inst. °reṇa Mv iii.39.17; loc. (? § 13.37) dhītare Mv ii.65.17; acc. pl. °rāṃ Mv i.356.17 (in 18 °ro); °rāṃś caiva ii.367.21; (**5**) forms based on stem dhītarā-, fem.: acc. sg. °rām Mv iii.146.4; 284.3 (v.l. °raṃ), and read so with 1 ms. 284.17; oblique sg. °rāya Mv ii.58.2 (loc.; mss., cf. Pali Jāt. 5.403.4–5), °rāye ii.111.14 (inst.); n. pl. °rāḥ LV 53.1 (vs); acc. pl. °rā (for °rāḥ) Suv 63.3 (vs); gen. pl. dhītarāṇaṃ Mv i.356.6 (prose).

dhuta, adj. and subst. (= Pali id.; as adj. rarely in Skt., in comp. dhuta-pāpa, *having purified his sin*, BR), *purified, got rid of* (evil, as in Skt.); arahāṃ dhutakleśo Mv i.247.12; *pure*, of persons: buddhaṃ dhuta-janārcitaṃ Mv i.186.13; oftener (as also in Pali tho not clearly indicated in PTSD; cf. dhutadhara, Childers dhutavata, and AN i.23.19 dhuta-vādānaṃ aggaṃ) = **dhuta-guṇa** (**dhū°**), **-dharma** (cf. **dhuta-dhara**): āraṇya-dhutābhiyuktāḥ SP 310.3 (vs; cf. Pali araññakaṅga, ār°); śikṣa dhutāṃś ca RP 30.15 (vs), *the instructions and qualities of the purified man* (Finot p. X strangely *les exhortations*!); dhuta-yāna (ms. dhuna°) deśita jinebhiḥ RP 27.17, *the way of the dhuta(-guṇa), taught by the Jinas*; tatra dhute satataṃ ca prayukto id. 18, *in that dhuta(-guṇa)*... (In SP 83.2 (vs) KN jīrṇapravṛddhaṃ dhutavedikaṃ ca, reporting Kashgar rec. as jīrṇapravṛddhoddhṛtavedikaṃ ca; WT with ms. K′ jīrṇu pravṛddhoddhṛta°; certainly uddhṛta, not dhuta, must be intended.)

dhuta-guṇa, m. (= **dhūta-guṇa**, q.v.; tho not recognized in PTSD, this occurs in Pali, Dhp. comm. iv.30.13, besides dhūta°, q.v., for more regular dhutaṅga; cf. **dhuta**, which is also used alone in this sense, and **dhuta-dharma**), (one of the 12) *qualities of the purified man*: Dbh 98.2; dhutaṃguṇa (nasalization m.c.) Śikṣ 328.2 (vs, from Ratnolkādhāraṇī); dhutaguṇāgrapārago (of Kāśyapa, see s.vv. **dhutadharma, dhūtaguṇa**) Mv i.64.14 (vs).

dhuta-guṇin, *one who possesses the dhutaguṇa*: Śikṣ 98.20 (prose). The word **dhūtaguṇa** is used without suffix, as Bhvr., in this mg.

dhutaṃ-guṇa, m.c. for **dhuta-guṇa**, q.v.

dhuta-dhara, m. (= Pali id.), *maintainer of the dhuta*(-guṇa): Mv i.71.12 (vs) °rā, voc., to Kāśyapa; see s.vv. **dhutaguṇa, dhū°, dhutadharma.**

dhuta-dharma, m. pl. (= **dhuta, °guṇa, dhūtaguṇa**: cf. Pali dhammaṃ dhutaṃ Sn 385, but the sequel shows that this is not used in the technical sense of Pali dhutaṅga; it is very vague and general; Childers cites a dhūta-dhamma but his references fail to show it), *the qualities of the purified man*: °māḥ RP 33.1 (vs); the disciple Kāśyapa is regularly called dhutadharma-dhara, *maintainer of the*..., Mv i.85.11 ff.; 105.12, 13, or the like, as °rma-dhārin Mv i.66.16; °rma-samaṅgin (see **samaṅgin**) i.71.16; in i.69.13 (vs) Senart reads evam ukte dhutadharmaviśuddho (Kāśyapo...), mss. °rma-su-viśuddhaṃ; the syllable su is hypermetric, but the acc. °dhaṃ (tho certainly referring to K.) could perhaps stand as goal of ukte, *it having been thus spoken to the one-that-was-purified-in-the-dhutadharma, K.* (replied); Kāśyapa has similar epithets involving dhutaguṇa (dhū°), a fact which establishes their equivalence of mg. with dhutadharma; and see also **dhuta-dhara.** Similarly in Pali, Mahā-Kassapa in AN i.23.19 is called dhuta-vādānaṃ (v.l. dhutaṅga-dharāṇaṃ) agga.

dhuttūraka (= Skt. dhattūraka, Schmidt, Nachträge; cf. M. dhuttīraya, *flower of the thorn-apple*), °kapuṣpāṇi, *flowers of the thorn-apple*: Mmk 314.18; 316.11.

dhunana, (nt.; = Pali id., Childers, without ref., and °na-ka, ifc. Bhvr., PTSD; AMg. dhuṇana; Skt. dhūnana; to dhunati = Skt. dhunoti plus -ana), *shaking, agitation*: °na-kampana- Sādh 80.12; 82.10, 13, 15.

?**dhunī** (perh. = Pkt. Lex. dhuṇi, Sheth, cf. AMg. jhuṇi, for Skt. dhvani?), *sound* (?), in -mahatī gāthā-dhunī Divy 328.26 (prose).

dhura, subst. and adj. (= Pali id.; Skt. dhur, both mgs., and dhura, at least mg. 1, in less technical sense), (**1**) *burden*, esp. *religious obligation* or *duty* (in Pali, e. g., gantha, *study of texts*, vipassanā, *reflection*, saddhā, sīla, paññā): dhura-(so mss., to be kept; Senart em.

dhuta-)-buddhinām (sc. of Bodhisattvas) Mv i.86.2, *having their minds occupied with their religious obligations*; dhuradhīrāḥ i.90.13, *firm in their religious obligations* (also Bodhisattvas); pravrājayāmi, śāsane dhuram unnāmayatīti Divy 487.28; (**2**) ifc., *best, most excellent* (cf. BR s.v. dhur 3, end): pramadavaradhurā(ḥ) LV 326.2 (vs), so read with best ms. for Lefm. °vara madhurā, which is unmetr. and disproved by Tib. bu moḥi naṅ na gces mchog, *the most excellent and best among girls*.

dhurā-tuṇḍa, °**ḍaka,** m. (= Skt. dhūs-tuṇḍa), *the tip of the wagon-pole*: MSV ii.71.7 (°ḍo), 10 (°ḍakena).

Dhurānikṣepaṇa (ed. °na), nt., n. of a caitya in the general region of Vaiśālī: Divy 201.5, 14.

?**dhurdhūraka,** n. of some plant: °kasya tu mūlāni Mmk 556.24; °ka-mūlaṃ juhuyād ekaṃ 557.14; each phrase should constitute the first half of an anuṣṭubh line, the meter being bad both times.

dhūta-guṇa, m., usually pl. (also **dhuta**°, q.v.; corresp. to Pali dhūtaṅga, dhu°; Pali also has dhūtaguṇa, Dhp. comm. iii.399.18; and dhu°, q.v.; cf. also **dhuta-dharma**), *the qualities* or *virtues of the purified man* (Tib. sbyaṅs pa, *pure*), viz. of an ascetic who lives an unworldly life (see **dhuta,** which is also used alone in the sense of °guṇa); also as Bhvr., *one who possesses these qualities*: °ṇa-samanvāgato SP 135.9; °ṇa-sākṣātkṛtā(ḥ) Divy 62.3; °ṇa-vādinām agro Divy 61.28; 395.23; said of Kāśyapa, see s.v. **dhuta**°; there are 12 °ṇāḥ (Bhvr., m., persons so characterized) in BHS, Mvy 7011 and 1127, listed 1128–1139 as **pāṃśukūlika, traicīvarika, nāma(n)tika, paiṇḍapātika, aikāsanika, khalu-paścād-bhaktika, āraṇyaka, vṛkṣamūlika, ābhyavakāśika, śmāśānika, naiṣadika, yāthāsaṃstarika,** qq.v.; same in diff. order and with minor variants (recorded s.vv.) Dharmas 63, and (without the name dh°) AsP 387.3—8; in Pali there are 13 dhutaṅga, see Childers, and esp. Vism. i.59.15 ff. where they are listed and defined; they include Pali equivalents of all the above except the third, and in addition two others, sāpadānacārika, and pattapiṇḍika.

Dhūtarajas, n. of a Bodhisattva: Gv 442.15.

dhūpanetra, m. (cited as nt. in pw from Caraka, defined *Rauchpfeife*), *incense-burner*: °trāṃ gṛhetvāna or grahe° (v.l. gṛhī°) Mv ii.351.2 = iii.275.4; ii.352.18 = iii.277.1; said of gods paying homage to the Bodhisattva.

Dhūpā, '*Incense*', n. of a goddess or yoginī: Sādh 50.3 etc.; 324.6.

dhūmakālika (Pali id., see below; from Pali °kāla, *death, destruction*, Jāt. iii.422.14, plus -ika), *subject to destruction*; *destroyed, lost*: (17–18 tīrthikā . . . krāyur, so mss. for Senart kreyur, apratimaśāsana-doṣaṃ) dhūmakālikam iti śramaṇasya, etad eva ca tu rakṣaṇīyatā (so with most mss.) Mv i.69.19–20 (vs), *the heretics may do harm* (or, *cause enmity*) *to the matchless doctrine of the Monk* (*Buddha*), *saying that* (iti) *it is perishable* (*is now going to be destroyed*); *but this very thing is a state that we must guard against* (Senart quite differently, ignoring iti); saṃgātavyam imaṃ vācyaṃ mā haiva (text °vaṃ) dhūmakālikaṃ Mmk 600.10 (vs), *this text must be recited in unison, lest it be destroyed* (*lost*); °ka-tā, abstr., (mā haiva pravacanaṃ kṛtsnaṃ . . .) dhūmakālikatāṃ vrajet Mmk 596.25 (vs), *lest the whole Gospel become destroyed* (*lost*). This, I believe, is the mg. of the Pali word too; both the Pali comm. and modern interpreters misunderstand it. In Vin. ii.288.20 (bhavissanti vattāro:) dhūmakālikaṃ samaṇena Gotamena sāvakānaṃ sikkhāpadaṃ paññattaṃ, (if we do not preserve the Gospel, *people will say*:) *a perishable set of religious teachings was taught by the monk G. to his disciples*, or in other words, these teachings are perishing, or will perish. In Vin. ii.172.15, the only other passage recorded, dhūmakālikaṃ pi pariyositaṃ vihāraṃ navakammaṃ denti, *or they give as new work* (the reparation of) *a completed monastery that has proved perishable*, that has fallen into ruin, or begun to. The adj. dhūmakālika cannot mean, as is supposed, *lasting to* (the monk's) *funeral*, for then it would be synonymous with yāvajīvikaṃ, just before it, in line 15; the time expressions vīsativassikaṃ, tiṃsavassikaṃ, yāvajīvikaṃ, lines 14–15, all forbidden, contrast with lines 26–29 where jobs lasting from 5 or 6 to 10 or 12 years are permitted, but only upon an akataṃ or a vippakataṃ vihāraṃ; it is these latter expressions, in line 25, which contrast with the (forbidden) work on a dhūmakālikaṃ pariyositaṃ vihāraṃ. It seems that this derivative of (Pali) dhūmakāla came to be used figuratively in a way fairly remote from its original and literal mg., like English *to go up in smoke* = *to be destroyed, completely lost*.

dhūma-gāra, m. (acc. pl. °rān; so text with corr. for first hand ms. dhūpa-rāgān), some kind of torture in hell: Śikṣ 80.11 (vs), see s.v. **kabhalli-**; Bendall and Rouse *suffocation*; Tib. cited as du bas bdug, *fumigation by smoke*. Possibly *swallowing smoke*? (but I find no noun gāra with this mg.); or *houses of smoke*? (gāra is used in AMg. for agāra, *house*; and here dhūmag° might be m.c. for dhūmāg°).

Dhūma-netra (cf. dhūpanetra), m., n. of a mountain: Divy 103.2 (here reading is doubtful, °tram udakaṃ); 107.6, 8, 13, 19.

Dhūmrasagotra, n. of a brahman livivg at **Droṇa-grāmaka**: MPS 51.1 ff.; plays the rôle of Pali Doṇa (DPPN 1; = droṇa).

Dhṛtamatiteja, n. of a Bodhisattva: Gv 442.26.

dhṛtarājya, apparently a kind of bird (haṃsa?) with a pleasant voice (cf. Skt. dhārtarāṣṭra, BHS **Dhṛtarāṣṭra** 2, and BR s.v. dhṛtarāṣṭra 3): LV 43.21 (vs) parivārayātha dhṛtarājya- (Calc. °rāṣṭra)-manojñaghoṣaṃ devyābhayārtha . . . (Tib. understood a bird of the haṃsa type, ṅaṅ skya, rendered by Foucaux *cygne*). The syntax is not clear; the cpd. °ghoṣaṃ ought seemingly to be acc. sg. fem., agreeing with Māyā understood (°ṣaṃ, fem., MIndic for °ṣāṃ?). But Tib. seems to make it agree with the retinue prescribed by the impv. parivārayātha.

Dhṛtarāṣṭra (in mgs. 1 and 2 = Pali Dhataraṭṭha), (**1**) n. of one of the four 'world-guardians', see **mahārāja(n)**; guardian of the east and lord of gandharvas; (**2**) (see s.v. **dhṛtarājya**) n. of a haṃsa-king (previous birth of the Bodhisattva): Gv 399.26; Jm 127.24; also n. of the haṃsa-king in the story which = the Pali Nacca Jātaka (32), MSV ii.92.17 ff.; (**3**) n. of a former Buddha, or (probably) of two such: Mv i.138.1; iii.235.1; (**4**) n. of one of Śuddhodana's palaces: LV 49.1; Mv ii.5.5 ff.

Dhṛtarāṣṭragati, n. of a former Buddha: Mv i.136.16. See under prec. 2.

dhṛti-pada (nt. or m.), *word of weighing*, i. e. *of measurement* (cf. dhar-, BR s.v. 7, *weigh*): RP 59.16 . . . upaniṣām api dhṛtipadam api nopaiti, *does not permit even any comparison, any word of weighing* (see s.v. **upaniṣad** 2).

Dhṛtiparipūrṇa, n. of a Bodhisattva: SP 67.1 ff., predicted to become the Buddha **Padmavṛṣabhavikrāmin.**

Dhṛtimant, n. of a king, former birth of the Buddha: RP 23.12.

-dheya (only ifc.; = Pali -dheyya), *realm, sway, control* (normally subst. in Pali, despite PTSD, and in BHS): anāgataṃ mṛtyudheyaṃ Ud ii.8, . . . *the realm of death* (so Pali maccudheyya); parispandati vai cittaṃ māradheyaṃ (Pali also has māradheyya) prahātavai Ud xxxi.2; **bhrūṇa-dheya,** q.v.

?**dhopati** (this spelling occurs also in Pali mss., app. always with v.l. dhov°) = **dhovati,** *washes*, q.v.: acc. to text dhopāmi Śikṣ 154.18.

dhova (m., or nt.; to **dhovati**; = Pali id., subst., kilesamala-dhove vijjante Bu.v. ii.15), (*the*) *washing, cleansing*: danta-dhovaṃ ca sevanti Mv i.168.16 (vs).

dhovaka, m. (to **dhovati** plus -aka; M. dhoaga; not recorded in Pali or AMg.), *washerman*: Mv ii.466.4, 8; 467.10; iii.113.15.

dhovati (= Pali id.; to Skt. 2 dhāvati, ppp. dhauta which yielded MIndic dhota, as in Pali; from such forms the o became generalized, Geiger 34; less plausibly Pischel 482), *washes*; except for one case of the noun dhovana, and one of saṃdhovita, this verb and its derivs. are found only in Mv, the Appendix to Jm, and the Bhikṣuprakīrṇaka as cited in Śikṣ (the two latter contain prose of the same type as Mv): dhovati Mv ii.466.7; Śikṣ 155.1; °vāmi Mv ii.244.15; Śikṣ 154.18 (text dhop°, see s.v. **dhopati**); Jm (App.) 241.1; °vanti Mv i.168.12; impv. °vāhi Mv ii.430.3; °va Śikṣ 154.20; °vatu Śikṣ 154.19; ppp. (su-) dhovita- Mv ii.466.9; ger. °vitvā Mv ii.244.13; iii.313.7; inf. °vitu-kāma- Mv iii.312.15; pass. °vīyanti Mv ii.466.4, 5.

dhovana (nt., = Pali id.; to **dhovati**), (act of) *washing*: read (cīvara-)dhovana-śoṣaṇa-sīvana- (etc.) Sukh 19.12 (prose), with most (three) mss.; ed. dhāvana with 1 ms. (Sktization).

dhovanaka, m. (from prec. plus -ka, perhaps by blending with **dhovaka**), *washerman*: coḍa-dhovanako Mv ii.467.1 (prose).

dhovāpanika (nt.; to unrecorded MIndic *dhovāpeti, caus. to **dhovati**, plus -ana, plus -ika), *fee for having clothes washed, washerman's fee*: Mv ii.466.17; 467.4, 5, 7; in all °kaṃ, acc. sg. Cf. **rañjāpanika**, which occurs a little later in the same text, and on which this form may possibly be modelled.

Dhautodana (= Pali Dhot°), n. of a brother of Śuddhodana: Mv i.352.13; 355.20; app. corresponds to **Droṇodana** (which read for Dhonodana as cited from Rockhill by DPPN s.v. Dhot°).

Dhaumrāyaṇa, m. pl. (Skt. Gr.), n. of a brahmanical gotra: Divy 635.20.

?**dhaura** = (or error for?) Skt. dhaureya, in (puruṣa-siṃhena puruṣarṣabheṇa) puruṣa-dhaureṇa (puruṣajāneyena, see **-jāneya**) Mv ii.133.8 (prose); in essentially the same passage in which other texts read puruṣa-dhaureyeṇa, but in Mv with v.l. °dhaureṇa, LV 350.12; Mv i.229.8; ii.284.18. The word dhaureya, = Pali dhoreyya and (purisa-)dhorayha, occurs occasionally in Skt., and seems to mean primarily *stout animal, capable of bearing burdens*, but then secondarily *best of his kind* (= mukhya, Schmidt, Nachträge). In the cliché passage just mentioned, it refers to superior men, esp. Buddhas (used in reference to Śākyamuni at the moment of enlightenment). In ... dhīrā dhaureyā dhṛtimanto ..., in the midst of a long description of the inhabitants of Sukhāvatī, Sukh 61.6 (prose); in Mv ii.364.16 (vs), of a man who worships at stūpas, dṛḍhavīryo dṛḍhasthāmo dhaureyo (replaced by vīraś ca in citation Śikṣ 299.3) dṛḍhavikramo. In all these it is not entirely clear how definite the lit. mg., *stout animal*, remained. In any case (puruṣa-)dhaureya seems pretty well established as standard Skt.; and I suspect that -dhaura is a mere error.

dhmātaka, ms. at Śikṣ 211.1, for **vyādhmātaka**, q.v., which Bendall reads by em., and which indeed is read in ŚsP 1431.19, the source of Śikṣ 211.1. Cf. however next.

[**dhyātaka**(-saṃjñā), corruption for **dhmātaka** (see preceding) = **vyādhmātaka**, q.v.: ŚsP 59.2.]

dhyāna, nt. (Skt. id.; in technical sense = Pali jhāna), lit. *meditation* or *contemplation*; *mystic 'trance'*; Lévi (Sūtrāl.) *extase*. Normally *four*, as in Pali, described in some detail in a long ancient passage (the Pali form, virtually identical, cited in Childers), found with hardly a true variant LV 129.1–11; 343.14–344.4; Mv i.228.3–10; ii.131.16–132.5; Mvy 1478–1481; an abbreviated form, giving the central points, as follows: savitarkaṃ savicāraṃ vivekajaṃ prītisukham iti prathamadhyānaṃ, adhyātmapramodanāt prītisukham iti dvitīyaṃ, upekṣāsmṛtisamprajanyaṃ sukham iti tṛtīyaṃ, upekṣāsmṛtipariśuddhir aduḥkhāsukhā vedaneti caturthaṃ dhyānam iti Dharmas 72; they are the first four of the nine **anupūrvavihāra-(-samāpatti)**, qq.v.; these are related to the four dhyāna-bhūmi constituted or occupied by the various classes of **rūpāvacara** gods (see **deva**), as explained by Childers, in that attainment in worldly life of (various stages of adeptness in) each of the four dhyāna leads to rebirth in successively higher stages among these gods; catu-dhyāna-(meter proves single initial consonant pronounced for written dhy-)-dhyāyino (as before) SP 131.5 (vs); *three* dhyāna, listed as sadoṣāpakarṣa-, sukhavaihārika-, and aśeṣavaibhūṣita- (read °**vaibhūtika-**? see this word), Dharmas 109; I have found no other trace of this list; the names sound vaguely as if the first might apply to the first of the 4 dhyāna, the second to the 2d and 3d combined, and the third to the 4th; in Laṅk 10.11 na ṣaḍdhyānādidhyāyinā (tvayā bhavitavyam), *you should not meditate on such things as the six dhyāna*; apparently some reprehended practices are meant, but I have no more idea of the specific meaning than had Suzuki (Studies, 414).

dhyānagocara, a class of gods: LV 219.11 (vs); 250.7 (prose, no v.l.). They are included among, or associated with, the **rūpāvacara** gods (who occupy four dhyāna-bhūmi, see **deva**), in both these passages; in the second, °rāṇāṃ ca rūpāvacarāṇāṃ ca devānāṃ.

Dhyāna-drāhyāyaṇī, n. of the gotra of the nakṣatra Uttarapadā: Divy 641.9. Chin. (Taisho Chin. canon text 1300, p. 405a, line 6 from left) begins with a character which usually represents dha (dhā), tho allegedly sometimes dhyā. See **Dhānya-drāhyāyaṇa**; perhaps read Dhānya- for Dhyāna- here.

dhyāna-bhūmi (four), see s.v. **deva** (rūpāvacara).

dhyānāṅga (nt.; = Pali jhānaṅga, nt., misdefined PTSD), *factor in dhyāna*: °ga-vibhajanārthaṃ LV 251.2 (cf. **vibhajana**). No specification here; in Pali, Vism. i.190.2, refers to vitakko (vitarka), vicāro, pīti (prīti), sukhaṃ, ekaggatā (ekāgratā).

dhyānāhāra, one of five kinds of 'food' (**āhāra**), Dharmas 70. Seems to correspond to **vijñānāhāra** of Mvy 2287, but cannot have the mg. attributed to the Pali corresp. of that term, q.v. Prob. a corruption; orig. there are only four 'foods', see s.v. **kavalīkārāhāra.**

[**dhyāni-**(buddha, -bodhisattva), *produced by meditation* (*trance*): Burnouf, Introd. 117 and Lotus 400; Müller on Dharmas 3, where five such Buddhas are listed. I have failed to note any actual occurrence in my texts. P. Mus calls them 'transcendent' Buddhas in his searching study cited s.v. **Buddha**, end.]

dhyāpayati or °**peti**, see **dhyāyati.**

dhyāma, adj. (Skt. Lex. and late lit., Schmidt, Nachtr.; also Skt. dhyāmala; acc. to Senart Mv i note 407, hyper-Skt. for Pali jhāma = Skt. kṣāma, *burnt*; the mg. does not fit very well, but cf. AMg. jhāma-vaṇṇa, *black color*), *dark, darkened, eclipsed, lacking luster*: dhyāmāni ca abhunsuḥ (abhūnsuḥ) mārabhavanāni Mv i.41.12; 230.7; 240.16 (in all these mss. dhyānāni); ii.162.16 (here mss. vyāmāni); māraḥ ... svakaṃ balaṃ dhyāma-balaṃ (mss. dhyāna°) saṃjānati Mv ii.314.14; °tā, abstr., (kramau mune, *the Buddha's feet*) dhyāmatām (mss. mostly dhyāyatāṃ; em. certain) upagatau, *become less resplendent*, Mv i.68.2 (vs). Cf. the next two.

dhyāmīkaraṇa, adj. and subst. nt. (to next), *making dark, eclipsing*: (f. adj. °ṇī) sarvagrahanakṣatra-dhyāmīkaraṇi (voc. sg.) Sādh 416.23; °ṇam, presumably subst. nt., Mvy 6624 = Tib. mog mog par bya ba (byas pa), *making (made) very dark.*

dhyāmīkaroti (to **dhyāma**, q.v.), *darkens, eclipses*: ger. °kṛtya (sarvamārabhavanāni) Dbh 8.17; 84.6; ppp. °krta Mvy 6625; LV 260.9 (vs; °ta tīrthikā).

***dhyāyati** or ***dhyāyeti,** *burns* (trans.), *cremates*; caus. ***dhyāpayati** or **°peti,** id., hyper-Skt. to Pali jhāyati (intrans.), jhāpeti (caus.); § 2.14. Cf. **abhidhyāyati,** which is intrans.; otherwise BHS seems to have only caus., or at least trans., forms; emendation of y to p in four occurrences would make them all caus. in form. Used of *cremating* dead bodies: dhyāpiyantānāṃ (em. Senart, mss. dhyāniy°), pres. pple. pass. gen. pl., *of* (Buddhas) *being cremated*, Mv i.126.2; (-buddhaṃ) dhyāyetvā Mv i.302.12; 304.12 (mss.); dhyāyito Mv ii.78.15; 174.11; dhyāpita- (same mg.) Mv i.357.17; RP 57.2.

[**dhyāyi,** LV 325.6 (vs), read either dhyāna (= °ne, before ut-) with best ms., or dhyāni; in any case a loc. of dhyāna, parallel with śīle; so Tib.]

dhyāyikā (to Skt. dhyāyati, cf. dhyāyin), *intent contemplation*: śīrṣavyavalokanenānuvilokayati sma (Tib. mgo byol nas bltas kyaṅ), unmeṣa-dhyāyikayā vā (*or with open-eyed intentness,* sc. anuvilokayati; for this phrase Tib. has no correspondent in Foucaux's text), na ca śaknoti sma draṣṭuṃ (Tib. mthoṅ bar mi nus so) LV 62.6. All mss. agree on the cpd.; only Calc. unmeṣādhyāyikayā, which is plainly nonsense.

?**dhyuṣita,** adj., ep. of garments or cloth, acc. to pw *blendend weiss*: cīvarāni (so) °tāni Kv 78.22; °ta-paṭam 81.7, see s.v. **indra-paṭa.** There is a very dubious record of a Skt. n. pr. Dhyuṣitāśva, BR, but this is prob. incorrect. The word paṭa is often preceded in comp. by duṣya- or dūṣya-, designating *a very fine cloth,* and I am inclined to read this; the text of Kv is so corrupt that it seems not implausible.

dhriyati, *holds back, resists* (cf. pw s.v. dhar- 3, d, *Widerstand leisten*): avadhyāyanti dhriyanti vivācayanti Divy 492.17. But see s.v. **vivācayati**; Divy perhaps corrupt for kṣīyanti (cf. **kṣīyati**) or kṣipanti (Mvy).

Dhruva, (1) n. of a śreṣṭhin, instructed and saved by Buddha: legend referred to Mv i.177.14, told 184.19 ff.; (2) n. of a king: Mmk 625.16; (3) n. of a yakṣa: Māy 72.

Dhvajaketu, n. of a former Buddha: Mv iii.230.7.

Dhvajadhvaja, n. of two former Buddhas in the same list: Mv iii.230.8 f.; 237.6 f.

dhvaja-baddhaka, f. **°ikā,** adj. (= Pali dhaja-baddha, Vin. i.74.30 °dhaṃ coraṃ; comm. 997.14 dhajaṃ bandhitvā viya caratīti dhajabandho [so also several mss. in text!], Mūladevādayo viya loke pākaṭo ti vuttaṃ hoti, i. e. *notorious,* as if *having raised a banner of thievery*; SBE 13.196 *who wears the emblems* [*of his deeds*]; it is not clear where PTSD, which renders *captured,* gets authority for the allegation that āhaṭa is meant, since this is not in the comm. on the above Vin. passage, the only one quoted in PTSD s.v.), prob. *notorious* (as a robber): cauro dhvaja-baddhakaḥ Mvy 8799 = Tib. chom rkun por (*as a robber-thief*) grags pa (*famous*; but, curiously, this word may also mean *bound,* acc. to Jä. and Das!); mā caurī, mā dhvaja-baddhikā Bhīk 16b.2, *you aren't a* (female) *thief? a notorious one?* (in examination of a candidate for initiation, who must make negative answers). But note that mā is found before *both* caurī *and* dhva°, as if each were a noun; this arouses some uneasiness.

Dhvajamaparājita (i. e. dhvaja-m-apar°, m 'hiatus-bridging'), n. of a former Buddha: Mv iii.230.9 f.

Dhvajarucira, n. of a former Buddha: Mv iii.230.6.

Dhvajavatī, n. of one of the four goddesses protecting the Bodhisattva in his mother's womb: LV 66.8. Tib. rgyal mtshan ldan pa supports this form, not the v.l. Dhvajapatī, contrary to Foucaux's assertion.

dhvajāgra, nt. (= Pali dhajagga), *top of a banner* or *standard*: °grāṇy api (240.19 adds asya, v.l. cāsya) prapatetsu(ḥ; mss.) Mv i.230.10 = 240.19.

Dhvajāgrakeyūra, (1) m., n. of a samādhi: SP 424.1; Mvy 530 (not in ŚsP); (2) n. of a work: Mvy 1410 (cf. **Dhvajāgrasūtra**).

Dhvajāgrakeyūrā, n. of a goddess: Sādh 403.1 etc.

dhvajāgra-niśrāvaṇī, a high number or means of computation (gaṇanā): Mvy 7980 (Tib. ṅes par, often = ni-, nis-, sgrogs pa, *proclamation,* for niśr°); cited from LV 148.14 where Lefm. niśāmaṇī; best ms. niśrā°; no ms. °vaṇī; note domal ṇ; Tib. as for Mvy 7980, except sgrog pa, which is the form given by Jä.

dhvajāgra-maṇi, a high number or means of computation (occurs just before prec.): °ṇir, n. sg., Mvy 7979; cited from LV 148.13 where Lefm. -vatī for -maṇir, but best ms. -maṇī; Tib. on both LV and Mvy nor bu = maṇi.

Dhvajāgravatī, n. of a capital city (rājadhānī): Gv 444.7.

Dhvajāgrasūtra, n. of a work, fragments publ. in Waldschmidt, Kl. Skt. Texte 4, pp. 7–8 (excerpted in this book). Cf. Pali Dhajagga(-sutta), SN i.218–220; and (?) **Dhvajāgrakeyūra.**

Dhvajottama, n. of three former Buddhas in the same list: Mv iii.230.4 f.; 237.5 f.; 238.7.

N

1 na, pronoun (Pali id.) = ena, see § 21.48.

2 na- acc. to Senart i n. 381 used in comp. for a-; see **ana-,** which may well be intended here: Mv i.14.10. See however **na-yācanaka,** where ana- cannot be assumed without emending.

naṃ, see **nam.**

nakula, (1) (m.; cf. next; = AMg. ṇaula), a kind of musical instrument: LV 163.6; 206.14; 212.4; Mv ii.159.4; iii.407.19; all prose; Tib. transliterates; (2) n. of a gandharva: Suv 162.4.

nakulaka, m., (1) = prec. (1), some musical instrument: Mv ii.322.14; iii.70.15; 82.5 (°kāṃ, acc. pl.); 270.5 (iii.70.15 prose, the others vss); (2) *money-bag* or *purse*: °ko (°kaḥ) kaṭyāṃ (133.23 adds upari) baddhas Divy 124.2; 128.29; 133.23; MSV i.241.8. See under (3). Hertel, ZDMG 67.125, states that nakula is used in this sense in Jain Skt. (3) °kaḥ Mvy 6024, acc. to Jap. *a purse* (cf. 2) *made out of a mongoose's skin* (adding that in India purses are so made). However, Tib. glosses rgyan (*ornament*) ne-ḥu le (*mongoose*) can (*having, with*), the whole cpd. interpreted by Das as *ornament made in the shape of a weasel's head.* Not only Tib. rgyan, which seems to mean only *ornament,* or at least not *purse,* but also the context supports this general sense; it occurs in the midst of a long list of what are certainly ornaments.

nakṣatra, m. (= Skt. nt., once m. in RV), *star, constellation* (recorded only as nt. nakkhatta, ṇa°, in Pali and AMg., Ratnach., but acc. to Sheth also m. in Pkt.): ete sapta nakṣatrā (best ms. °trāḥ) lokapālā ... (n. pl.) LV 388.1 (vs), repeated 21, 389.19.

Nakṣatragupta, n. of a former Buddha: Mv i.138.5.

Nakṣatrarāja, (1) n. of three former Buddhas: Mv i.137.14; iii.231.9 f.; Śikṣ 9.1; n. of a Buddha in the zenith: Sukh 98.14; (2) n. of a Bodhisattva: SP 3.9.

Nakṣatrarājaprabhāvabhāsagarbha, n. of Bodhisattva: Dbh 2.16.

Nakṣatrarājavikrīḍita, n. of a samādhi: SP 424.3.

Nakṣatrarājasaṃkusumitābhijña, n. of a Bodhisattva: SP 404.2 ff.; 425.4.

Nakṣatrarājāditya, m., n. of a samādhi: SP 458.2; v.l. tārā for rājā, which acc. to note agrees with Kumārajīva's version; Burnouf °tārārājāditya; WT as in KN without note.

Nakhaka, n. of a nāga king: Mvy 3290.

nakharikā (= °**rī,** q.v.), *nail, claw*: (pāda-)nakharikābhir avalikhitamadhyaṃ Karmav 28.23 (prose; of a dog).

nakharī (cf. prec.; Senart with v.l. °lī, both times; = Skt. °ra, m. or nt., f. in Lex.), *nail, claw*: nakharīhi pānīyārthaṃ (75.4 tr. pān° nakh°) bhūmiṃ khananti Mv iii.71.17; 75.4 (prose). The mg. is certified by the vs account of the same incident, bhūmiṃ nakhehi vilikhanti iii.83.14.

Nagarabindu (cf. Pali Nagaravinda), n. of a city in Kośala: MSV i.66.5.

nagarāvalambaka, m., and °**ikā,** f., seemingly *city-washerman* and *-woman*: m. only Śikṣ 9.4 tṛṇapradīpaṃ dattvā nagarāvalambaka-bhūtena (Bendall and Rouse, ignoring the fem. counterpart, *inhabitant of the outskirts of the town*, without evident justification); f. °ikā Mv iii.311.8, 18; 312.12 (no v.l.), apparently a woman whose job it was to hang out clothes (to dry?), cf. 311.11 pāṃsukūlaṃ (which she has just presented to the Bodhisattva) vṛkṣaśākhāye olambitvā; the gerund seems to suggest her occupation. Senart Introd. p. xxix, *étendeuse de linge* (which is surely far better than his suggestion, note p. 505, that velambikā be read by em.; this is clearly impossible, see s.v. **velambaka**); Divy 82.11, 28; 84.24; 89.20, 26 = MSV i.80.16 ff. (in these passages no light seems to be thrown on the meaning by the context).

nagna, m. (cf. on the etym. and exact mg. the commoner **mahā-nagna,** of which this is essentially a synonym), *great man, mighty man, champion*: sarvi bala-upeta nagnāḥ samā duṣpradharṣāḥ paraiḥ LV 94.11 (vs); -nagnabalānupradāna- 429.22 (prose), *the granting of the might of champions*; (ekasmin dvāre eko) nagnaḥ sthāpitaḥ, dvitīye dvitīyaḥ, tṛtīye Rādhaguptaḥ (an agrāmātyaḥ), pūrvadvāre svayam eva rājāśoko 'vasthitaḥ Divy 373.13.

nagnacaryā (= Pali naggacariyā, Dhp. 141, same vs as Divy), (ascetic) *practice of going naked*: Divy 339.23 (vs).

nagna-śravaṇa, pl. (= Skt. °śramaṇa; § 2.30), *naked monks*, a sect of ascetics (Digambara Jains?): Kv 81.8; see s.v. **Vailmavegarudra.**

Naṅgā, n. of a river: MSV i.146.3 ff.; 153.13 ff.; so read with mss. Divy 456.19 ff., and for mss. **Raṅgā** 451.1 ff.

naṅgula (= Pali id., for Skt. lāṅgula), see **go-na°.**

na ca (as in Skt., see pw s.v. 3 vara, 2, e; Speyer Skt. Synt. § 250; but here used in a rather peculiar way which has misled Burnouf, Kern, and Lüders ap. Hoernle MR 154), *than*, after comp.: (śīghrataraṃ) samyaksaṃbodhim abhisaṃbudhyeyaṃ na cāsya maṇeḥ pratigrāhakaḥ syāt SP 265.3 (prose), *may I attain perfect enlightenment more quickly than there could be a receiver of* (i. e. than one could accept) *this jewel.*

Naṭa, n. of a śreṣṭhin: Divy 349.11; MSV i.3.17.

Naṭabhaṭikā, °**ka** (m.), n. of a monastery (vihāra; also called araṇyāyatana) founded by Naṭa and his brother Bhaṭa: Divy 349.13 ff.; 356.15; 385.11 ff.; MSV i.3.18 (°ka iti).

naṭa-raṅga, m., lit. *actor-stage*, as symbol of *deceptive* or *illusory* character: °gaḥ Mvy 2837, in chapter headed māyādayaḥ, *such things as māyā*; na naṭaraṅga-vacanaḥ (sc. bhavati) Śikṣ 126.3, *his speech is not deceitful* (Bendall and Rouse, *fictitious*).

[**Naṭā,** see **Naṭṭā.**]

Naṭikā = next, n. of a yakṣiṇī: Mmk 565.1 (prose).

Naṭī = prec.: Mmk 564.25 (vs).

Naṭṭā, n. of a yakṣiṇī: Mmk 565.18 (Naṭṭāyā(ḥ), gen.; prose); in 564.25 (vs) the same name is printed Naṭa, read Naṭṭā (no metr. reason for short a). Or should Naṭā be adopted in both places?

Naḍa, n. of a nāga: Mvy 3311.

naḍaka (m. or nt.; Skt., *hollow of a bone*; = Skt. naḍa), *reed*: Mv i.359.23 (prose).

naḍa-cippitikam, adv., *by being crushed like a reed*, as a form of torture: Śikṣ 182.2, see **cipyate.**

naḍinī (= Skt. nalinī; § 2.46), *lotus-pond*: LV 328.16 (vs; °ni, m.c.); Gv 374.9 (°nīṣu, prose); 531.9 (prose).

Naḍera (= Pali Naḷeru), acc. to Pali comm. n. of a yakṣa; see **picumanda.**

Nadin, n. of a brahman: nadī nāma Mv iii.325.2. The same personage is referred to, but not named, in Pali, Vin. i.2.32.

nadī-kāla(-samaya), *time for the river*, i. e. perhaps time for bathing in it (?): nadīkāla- (v.l. °kāle) samaye nadīye nairaṃjanāye snāyitvā Mv i.4.5. Senart has no note. See s.v. **nāga-nadī,** Mv ii.131.11.

Nadī-kāśyapa (= Pali Nadī-kassapa), n. of one of Buddha's disciples, mentioned with his brothers **Uruvilvā-kāśyapa** and **Gayā-k°,** qq.v.: Mv iii.102.12; 103.2; 430.12, 18; 432.8; SP 2.1; 207.3; LV 1.11; Mvy 1050 (misprinted Nadi°); Sukh 2.5.

Nadīdatta, n. of a Bodhisattva: Mvy 722; = Tib. chu bos byin, *given by a river.*

Nanda, (**1**) (= Pali id., DPPN Nanda Thera 1; also called **Sundarananda,** q.v.) n. of a monk, disciple of the Buddha, and his half-brother: Mv iii.132.20 (mama, sc. Buddha's, pitriyaputro); prob. also meant by Mvy 1041; 3604; LV 2.2; Sukh 2.11; 92.7; is he also the Nanda of Mvy 9471? (one of the ṣaḍvārgika monks, cf. **Upananda** (1) and **Nandopananda**); cf. also **Nandana** (1); (**2**) n. of a nāga-king, always associated and almost always compounded (regularly as dvandva, Nandopanandau or °nandakau) with **Upananda(-ka),** q.v.: SP 4.11 (here not a cpd.); LV 83.21; 204.10; Mvy 3278; Divy 162.9; 395.11; Suv 162.9; Kv 2.13; Mmk 62.2; 437.2; Gv 119.11; Karmav 72.18; Māy 221.18; 246.17; 247.33; (**3**) n. of a monk in a Jātaka story: Mv i.36.6 ff.; (**4**) n. of a devaputra: Mv ii.257.7, 12 etc.; LV 4.12; 6.12; 7.5; same (?) LV 438.16; (cf. DPPN Nanda 8 ?); (**5**) n. of a teacher: Mvy 3501; (**6**) n. of a Śākya youth (same as 1 above?): LV 152.12, and perhaps Av i.148.9; (**7**) n. of a king, said to be grandfather of Aśoka: Divy 369.12; (**8**) n. of a son of a śreṣṭhin of Śrāvastī, called 'the lazy': Av i.15.10; (**9**) n. of a yakṣa: Māy 17; 235.19; (**10**) n. of a cowherd, converted by Buddha: MSV i.51.1 ff.

Nandaka (= Pali id., 1 or 2 in DPPN), n. of one (or more?) disciple(s) of the Buddha: Mvy 1042 = Tib. dgaḥ byed, *making joyous*, whereas Nanda in 1041 is dgaḥ bo, *joyous*, and Nandika in 1043 is dgaḥ yod, *being joyous*; Av i.267.6 ff.; Karmav 161.5 (= Sundara-nanda? so Lévi).

Nandadatta, n. of a Bodhisattva: ŚsP 52.22.

Nandana, (**1**) n. of a Śākyan, son of Śukrodana (cf. **Nanda** 1), who retired from the world: Mv iii.177.1; (**2**) n. of a yakṣa: Māy 236.26; (**3**) n. of a nāga-king: Māy 246.25, 29; (**4**) nt., n. of a mythical city: Divy 602.2; Av i.201.12.

Nandabalā, n. of the girl who fed the Bodhisattva after his fast, associated with **Nandā,** q.v.: Divy 392.9 (prose); in Buddhacarita xii.109 Nandabalā alone does this deed; here she is a cowherd girl. More often the girl is **Sujātā,** q.v.

Nandaśrī, n. of a Tathāgata: ŚsP 52.19.

Nandā, (**1**) n. of the daughter of a village chief who gave food to the Bodhisattva when he broke his fast after his long austerities; otherwise known as **Sujātā**, q.v.: Divy 392.12 (vs); in 392.9 (prose) associated in this act with **Nandabalā** (they seem to be regarded as sisters, dual grāmikaduhitryoḥ), q.v.; (**2**) n. of a lokadhātu: ŚsP 52.18; (**3**) n. of a rākṣasī: Māy 240.7; 241.13.

Nandika, (**1**) (prob. = Pali Nandiya, particularly 1 of DPPN) n. of a disciple of Śākyamuni (or of more than one?): MSV i.187.5 ff.; in lists of mahāśrāvakas Gv 17.23; Sukh 2.8; of śrāvakas Mvy 1043 (on Tib. see s.v. **Nandaka**); of bhikṣus LV 1.16 (Tib. here dgaḥ byed, which in Mvy 1042 = **Nandaka**); prob. a different person is Nandika (v.l. °aka) the son of Śukrodana and brother of **Nandana** (1), mentioned as having retired from worldly life Mv iii.177.1; (**2**) n. of a village chief at Uruvilvā, father of **Sujātā**, q.v.: LV 267.13, 18; (**3**) n. of a yakṣa (? or, acc. to some versions, n. of a locality): Māy 44. (3 Nandaka in DPPN is n. of a yakkha.)

Nandika-sūtra, n. of a work: Karmav 33.14; 42.5 (see Lévi's note here); 44.6.

nandikāvarta (perh. hyper-Skt. for Pali nandiyāvatta), n. of a mystic diagram, = Skt. nandyāvarta, which is also recorded in LV: sa-n°, Bhvr., LV 415.13 (prose, no v.l.)

Nandigupta, n. of a former Buddha: Mv i.139.8.

(**nandi-ghoṣa** [also **nandī**°, q.v.], some sort of *bell* or other sound-making instrument, normally referred to as attached to chariots; the word occurs in Skt. but is not rightly defined in BR, pw; not recorded in Pali; acc. to Ratnach., AMg. ṇandighosa = *a sound produced by playing upon twelve kinds of instruments at once*: this could scarcely fit nandīghoṣa Śikṣ 29.1 in ep. of umbrellas; and AMg. ṇandighosā is *the bell of* (a certain deity) acc. to Ratnach.; sa-n°, ep. of chariots: Mv ii.339.17, 19; 420.13; 456.11; iii.22.7 (°ṣālaṃkṛta); 178.13; 267.5; 449.20; read nandighoṣa-m-alaṃkṛtā Mv ii.487.16, of chariots.)

nandi-janana, m., = Skt. nandi-kara, *son*: Śākya-°ne Tathāgate Mv i.64.9 (vs).

nandidhvaja, some kind of gem: °ja-maṇiratnopama Gv 295.5.

Nandin, n. of two yakṣas: Māy 35; 104.

Nandinagara, n. of a town: Māy 104.

Nandinī, n. of a devakumārikā in the eastern quarter: LV 388.10 = Mv iii.306.7.

Nandirakṣitā, n. of a devakumārikā in the eastern quarter: Mv iii.306.7 (= **Nandivardhanī** of LV).

Nandivardhana, (m. or) nt., n. of a locality: Māy 35 (see Lévi p. 78); MSV i.xviii.3 f.

Nandivardhanī = **Nandirakṣitā** (of Mv): LV 388.10.

Nandisenā, n. of a devakumārikā of the eastern quarter: LV 388.10 = Mv iii.306.7.

Nandihāra, nt., n. of a city: Gv 189.1 etc.

nandī (= Skt. nandi, f.; both in Pali), *joy*: yo rāgo yā nandī yā tṛṣṇā Samy Ag 1.2; nandī-rāga, m., app. not dvandva (as taken by PTSD), but *passion for joys* (cf. Pali MN i.145.3, 4, in sing. and not compounded with another word): °gaḥ Mvy 2217 = Tib. dgaḥ baḥi ḥdod chags, *passion for joy(s)*, so also Tib. on LV below; °gasya MSV i.49.16; °rāgāndhāś ca Śikṣ 288.1; (tṛṣṇā . . .) nandīrāgasahagatā (as in Pali with taṇhā) LV 417.8, 10 (in 10 v.l. nandi°); Mv iii.332.6, 7 (no v.l.). All these are prose.

nandīghoṣa, (**1**) = **nandi**°, q.v., but here in °ṣa-manojña-śabdopacārāṇi, Śikṣ 29.1, Bhvr., ep. of chattrāṇi; (**2**) n. of Indra's chariot: Av ii.104.3,13.

Nandīdhvaja, n. of a śreṣṭhin: Gv 427.19 (vs).

Nandīpāla, a name given to **Ghaṭīkāra** in MSV i.217.11; cf. **Jyotipāla** 1, who was a friend of Gh.; °la-sūtra, an account of this story, in the Madhyamāgama, ibid. 12.

nandī-mukhā, °**khī**, adj. (cf. AMg. nandi, *the sound of a particular drum*, Ratnach.), with rajanī or rātrī (= Pali nandimukhī), (the time at the end of night) *just before the beating of the* (morning) *drum*, i. e., substantially, *dawn*; so Tib. on LV, rṅa brduṅ baḥi (*of beating the drum*) nam tshod tsam na (*at the point of time of the night*), for °khyāṃ rātrau; in phrase, rātryāṃ paścime yāme aruṇodghāṭanakālasamaye °khyāṃ rātrau LV 345.20; 350.9; nearly the same, but °mukhāyāṃ rajanyāṃ, Mv i.229.6; ii.133.7; 284.16; 415.18; in Pali, . . . pacchime yāme uddhate aruṇe nandimukhiyā rattiyā Vin. i.288.12; ii.236.15 (comm. has an absurd etymological attempt to explain nandimukhī, 1287.1–2).

nandī-rāga, see **nandī**.

Nandottarā, n. of a devakumārikā in the eastern quarter: LV 388.10 = Mv iii.306.7.

[**Nandopananda**, Divy 307.1; 329.9, 14, acc. to ed. name of one individual monk, a member or associate of the ṣaḍvargīya or ṣaḍvargika group, which acc. to Mvy 9471–2 contained two monks named Nanda and Upananda. This is, I believe, also the intention of Divy. In 307.1 understand Nandopananda- as cpd. with the following bhṛtaka-puruṣaḥ sa, *he* (the householder just mentioned) *is a serving-man of Nanda and Upananda*. In 329.9 and 14 understand two vocs., Nanda-Upananda. However, in MSV i.95.4 Nandopananda, sg., is presented in the text as n. of one nāga king; cf. s.v. **Nanda** 2.]

napta = Skt. naptṛ (§ 13.4), (*nearer*) *descendant*: napta-pranapti-kāye (mss.) Mv i.348.9, *in the crowd of his near and remoter descendants*; cf. **pranapti**.

nam (naṃ = Pali naṃ, Pkt. ṇaṃ; variously regarded as from Skt. nanu or nūnam), asseverative particle, *assuredly, certainly, of course*; recognized by Senart only at Mv i.314.11 (see his note), where it is not wholly certain. Clearer cases: āgatvā ca bhuvaṃ śreṣṭhi(m) naṃ (so several mss.) dhruvaṃ pratipatsyase, . . . yaṃ śraddhā taṃ samācara (misunderstood and wrongly em. by Senart) Mv i.187.5(–6), *and having come, śreṣṭhin, to the spot* (where Buddha is), *you will assuredly attain security*; . . . (now) *do what seems best to you*; na ca śaknoti ārādhayituṃ, tāye (mss. yāye) ca naṃ godhā hṛdayaṃ gatā ii.66.11, *and he could not pacify her*, (because) *of course the* (incident of the) *lizard had gone to her heart* (turned her against him); tāta mā naṃ antarāyaṃ karohi ii.408.10, *father, do not, assuredly, make any obstacle* (for the Bodhisattva); Mv i.168.18 (vs), see s.v. **vairambha**.

namata (cf. Pali namataka), m. Mvy 5862, or nt. Mvy 8981, MSV ii.52.2 ff., *felt*; Tib. (ḥ)phyiṅ ba; as material for monks' garments. Cf. **nāmatika**.

namati, in LV 259.21 (vs) said by Foucaux to mean *arise, get up*, and vinamate, *sit down*. But I think the mgs. of both are close to or identical with those of normal Skt. Line 20 reads, na ca iñjate bhramati vā dhyāyaty āsphānakaṃ dhyānaṃ, *and he does not stir nor swerve, he practises the āsph° dhyāna*; then 21, na ca namati no vinamate na kāyaparirakṣaṇā spṛśati, *and he does not bend* (to one side?) *nor stoop down* . . . On the other hand, namati is used as in Pali (apparently not in Skt. so far as recorded) with object cittaṃ, *bends, inclines the mind, thought*, with loc. (dat.), *towards* . . .; see **nāmayati**, also used similarly: pravrajyāyai (so Senart, but °ye, which might be loc., is just as plausible; mss. °āryeś, °āyaiś) cittaṃ name (aor.) Mv i.322.20; ppp., pāṃśukūle cittaṃ nataṃ LV 266.3.

namantra, nt., a high number: Gv 133.18; Mvy 7883 (cited from Gv) = Tib. gzhal med (cf. **namātra**).

namaskara, nt., = °kāra (masc.), *homage-paying*: nidāna-namaskarāṇi samāptāni Mv i.2.12 (colophon).

namātra, m., a high number: Mvy 7754 = Tib. gzhal med (cf. **namantra**). The Tib. fits this form (gzhal, *measure*).

Namuci (= Pali id.), a name for Māra, used chiefly in vss (but also in prose, Dbh 28.17; 90.5); LV 261.6; 302.21 ff.; 311.15; 328.3; 357.14; Mv i.264.9; ii.238.6; 413.2;

iii.254.6; 381.10; Divy 393.11; Mmk 171.18; Samādh 19.36; RP 58.15; Namucibalanudaṃ, not n. pr. but ep. of the Bodhisattva, Mv i.208.12 = ii.10.20; in same cpd. with Māra, nihata-namuci-mārā(ḥ) Dbh.g. 52(78).4, Bhvr.; pl., perh. used of Māra and his hosts, or like the pl. of **Māra**, q.v.: tāṃ namucināṃ (but v.l. °cino, gen. sg.) mahatīm avasthām LV 356.9.

na-yācanaka, adj. or subst. (see **yācanaka**, 2; = yācana plus -ka), hastapralehakair °kair LV 248.17 (prose), (ascetic practices) *consisting of not begging* (qy: perhaps sitting and waiting for food to be brought unsolicited?); mss. vary but Tib. mi sloṅ ba confirms the text and mg. In a list of ascetic practices of various sorts.

nayuta, m., nt. (not in Pali, which has nahutaṃ, nt.; AMg. ṇaua, ṇauya, defined as 84 lacs of niyutāṅgas), seems to occur in BHS as replacement of Skt. niyuta, with which it frequently varies in mss.; a moderately large number, generally 100,000,000,000 (niyuta in BHS usually the same), and rendered in Tib. (like niyuta) khrag-khrig, which is given the same value by Jä.: nayutam, nt., Mvy 7956, cited from LV 147.21 where Lefm. niyuto, m., allegedly with all mss.; but nayutaḥ Mvy 8000, and niyutaṃ, nt., 7702, 7828, 8056 (in the last, however, the value is only 1,000,000, as shown by the position in the list and Tib. sa ya). Common everywhere: ambiguous as to gender, SP 316.6; LV 36.10; 52.17; Mv iii.443.12; Divy 318.10 (mss.); KP 155.2; Gv 255.20 (etc., but niyuta 267.26, 268.14, etc., prob. equally common); Mmk 25.16; Dbh 19.27, 29; masc. (besides the above) LV 12.2, 21; both this and niyuta common in LV, side by side in 151.2–3 (vss), koṭīśataṃ ca ayutā nayutās tathaiva, niyutānu kaṅkaragatī tatha bimbarāś ca; Mv i.119.8 (°tāṃ, acc. pl.); 247.1 (°tā, n. pl.); RP 5.13 (°tān, acc. pl.); nt. forms, °tāni, Mv i.72.12; 171.12; 209.5 = ii.11.12; Sukh 30.15 (but niy° seems commoner in Sukh); in Suv I have noticed only niy°. Cf. **mahā-nay°**.

naraka-kumbha, n. of a (minor) hell: Mv i.7.8. Senart compares Skt. naraka-kuṇḍa.

narada, nt. (Skt. Gr.), a medicinal plant or a product of it, presumably = nalada, which Nobel reads with support of Tib.: Suv 105.3 (mss.)

Naradatta, (**1**) n. of a nephew and pupil of the ṛṣi Asita: LV 101.2 ff.; in Mv as in Pali named **Nālaka**; (**2**) n. of a Bodhisattva: ŚsP 6.8; (**3**) n. of a virtuous man (**satpuruṣa** q.v.): SP 3.11 (Kashgar rec. Nāla°; Burnouf Ratnadatta, noting that all mss. but one read Nara°; Tib. mes byin, which should render Pitāmahadatta, doubtless understanding Nara as the Primeval Spirit, also sometimes called Pitāmaha).

naradamyasārathi = **puruṣa-damya**°, q.v.: SP 359.7 (vs); LV 235.10 (vs); Mv i.234.3 (vs); Divy 72.14 (vs). Apparently used only m.c. for puruṣa°.

Naradeva, n. of a former Buddha: Mv i.141.12.

Naraṃpravāha (half the mss. Nara-pra°), n. of a former Buddha: Mv i.137.7.

Nara-rāja, n. of a yakṣa: Māy 237.1. Read probably Nala°; corresponds to Pali Naḷo rājā (cited Waldschmidt, Kl. Skt. Texte 4, 175 n.3).

Naravāhana, n. of a former Buddha: Mv i.141.13.

Naravīrā, n. of a yakṣiṇī: Mmk 567.11; 568.22.

Narasiṃha, n. of a nāga king: Māy 246.29.

Narendra, n. of a former Buddha: Sukh 6.15.

Narendraghoṣa, n. of a former Buddha: Samādh p. 58, line 23 ff.

Narendrarāja, n. of a contemporary or future Buddha: Sukh 70.16.

Nareśvara, n. of a former Buddha: Mv i.112.7.

narottama (= Pali naruttama), *highest of men*, standard ep. of a Buddha: Mvy 40 = Tib. mi mchog, *best man*; et passim.

Nardana, n. of a nāga king: Mvy 3243; Māy 246.25.

Nala (see also Nara-rāja), n. of a nāga king: Māy 246.18.

Nalakūvara, n. of a yakṣa: Māy 94.

nala-ghātyā, *reed-slaying* (so Tib., literally, ḥdam bu bcom bzhin): hanmy eṣāṃ (gen. for acc.) nalaghātyayā MSV i.177.13; °tyayā haniṣyanti 17. Just what form of killing is meant I do not know. The second member (not in Skt.) = Pali -ghaccā.

Nalamālin (= Pali Naḷamāli), n. of a mythical sea: Jm 92.9 (vs; °māly eṣa sāgaraḥ).

Nalinī (= Pali Naḷ°, oftener Naḷinikā), n. of the heroine of the Nalinī Jātaka (colophon °nīye rājakumārīye jātakaṃ Mv iii.152.19), a daughter of a king of Benares, who seduced Ekaśṛṅga: Mv iii.146.4 ff.

nava, oftener **navaka**, m. (= Pali, both), *newcomer to the Buddhist order, junior, recently ordained monk*; see also **nav(ak)ānta**: nava, Māy 219.29; navakaḥ Mvy 8742; navakair ādikarmikair acirapravrajitair RP 5.1 (prose); °kair acirapravrajitair (text °varjitair) Gv 47.8 (prose); daharo jātyā °kas tu pravrajyayā 129.3 (prose); sthaviramadhya-navakeṣu bhikṣuṣu Śikṣ 199.16 (prose).

navakarmika (= Pali °kammika, said to mean *repairer of buildings*, but see below): Mvy 8735 °kaḥ = Tib. lag gi bla, which Das defines as *one who does general menial service to the congregation of lamas in a monastery*; MSV i.235.6, 9; ii.145.13; he was as a rule himself a monk, but inferior in position and function, as shown by Jm 113.22 (vs) āvāsikaḥ so 'stu mahāvihāre kacaṅgalāyāṃ navakarmikaś ca (as a punishment). That the navakammika in Pali, too, was low in station among monks is shown by the story of Sudhamma, Vin. ii.15.30 ff. (āvāsiko ... navakammiko dhuvabhattiko), and navakamme in Jāt. iv.378.29 seems to mean *manual labor* (certainly not *repairing*, since a new structure was being built). I have found no Pali comm.'s interpretation, but the Pali word seems to need reexamination. Perhaps lit. (*one who performs*) *new-initiate's work* (see **nava**).

navakānta (m.) = **navānta**, q.v.: Divy 404.14; Bbh 122.18.

nava-dānta, adj. or subst. m., *newly broken in* (to work), *a new hand*: tvaṃ °taḥ, sthānam etad vidyate yad asmākaṃ pṛṣṭhato gamiṣyasi Divy 304.25.

Navamikā, n. of a devakumārikā in the West: LV 390.6 (Calc. with v.l. navanāmikā, which is hypermetric).

nava-yāna-saṃprasthita, adj. (also **acira-yāna**°, q.v.), *newly entered upon the Vehicle*, (a- Bodhisattva) *that is in the early stages of the* (*mahā-*)*yāna*: SP 32.5; 218.5; yaḥ kaścid ... bodhisattvo 'sya dharmaparyāyasyottraset saṃtraset ... navayānasaṃprasthitaḥ sa ... bodhisattvo mahāsattvo veditavyaḥ. sacet punaḥ śrāvakayānīyo 'sya (etc., as before) adhimānikaḥ sa ... śrāvakayānikaḥ pudgalo veditavyaḥ SP 233.13 ff. This last passage is decisive. Kern correctly renders the 2d and 3d passages but mistranslates the first; Burnouf misunderstands all three. Similarly SP 312.8; ŚsP 910.11; AsP 139.12 et alibi.

navara, m., a high number: Mvy 7783.

Navaśīrṣaka, n. of a nāga king: Megh 302.16. App. = **Meghasaṃcodana**, q.v., with epithet navaśīrṣa.

navāṅga, adj. (= Pali navaṅga), with śāsana, (the) *nine-fold* (Buddhist sacred texts): °gam etan mama śāsanaṃ ca SP 46.1 (vs); see Kern, SBE 21.45 note 4.

navānta, m. (= Pali navanta, CPD s.v. anta), *the juniors' end* or *place*, in an assembly of monks; opp. to **vṛddhānta**: Mvy 8744 °taḥ; Divy 349.26. Also **navakānta.**

[**navutpattika**, Mv iii.179.7, ed. °ko āryadharmāṇāṃ, if the text were right, would seem to mean *freshly productive, given to ever-new production* (of noble qualities). But this seems forced, and the true reading is doubtless na utpathika, nearly with one ms.; see **utpathika**.]

? **navodaka** (nt.?), some kind of food: °kaṃ ca

tailalavaṇakvathanaṃ Mv i.329.13. Senart has no suggestion. Read perhaps navodanaṃ (navaud°), or some other cpd. of odana?

nasta-karaṇa, -karman, nt. (perh. for Skt. nastaḥ-k°; but cf. nasta, BR 4.82, 5.1539), *'nose-operation'*, *sternutatory treatment* (of disease): °karaṇam Mvy 9034; °karmaṇā MSV ii.45.13.

naharū, or **°ru**, f. (Pali nahāru, nhāru; AMg. etc. ṇhāru; no form with short penultimate a recorded; cf. Skt. snāyu), *sinew*: °rūḥ Mvy 3989 (but Index cites stem °ru, and Mironov °ruḥ) = Tib. chu ba, *a large sinew*; note snāyuḥ Mvy 3990 = rgyus pa, small, finer *fibers*.

nahimantra, nt., a high number: °tram Gv 133.18, and (cited from Gv) Mvy 7884 = Tib. gar gzhal, which also renders **hemātraḥ** Mvy 7755; gar = *strong*, gzhal = *measure* (mātra). But in Gv 106.8 occurs **himantrā**, f.

? **Nahīnagarbha**, n. of a former Buddha: Mv i.138.10. All six mss. virtually agree on this form (two with unimportant variations), but it seems implausible.

Nāgakulottama, n. of a former Buddha: Mv iii.232.20.

Nāgakulodbhavameghavirājita, n. of a Tathāgata: Megh 296.16.

Nāgadatta, n. of a former Buddha: LV 172.2.

nāga-nadī, *'river of nāgas (serpent-demons)'*, epithet of the Nairañjanā, given to it because nāgas lived in it (LV 270.2 ff.), as in the Pali (see 1 Nerañjarā, DPPN): (bodhisattvas...) nāganadīṃ (10) pūrvāhna- (v.l. °hne) kālasamaye nadī- (so mss., Lefm. nadīṃ) nairañjanāṃ upasaṃkramya... (11) nadīṃ (so Lefm., but most and best mss. nadī-, again) nairañjanāṃ avatarati sma LV 269.9 ff.; this word is confirmed by Tib. which also connects it syntactically with nadī-nair° of line 10, kluḥi (*of nāgas*) kluṅ (*river*) chu bo (*water, river*) nai ra ñja naḥi (*of the N.*) ṅogs su (*to the bank*) soṅ ste (*being gone*); similarly twice in Mv, ... nāganadī- (so mss., Senart wrongly °nandī)-kālasamaye (does this mean *betimes, at the appropriate hour*? cf. **nadī-kālasamaya**; perhaps *at the proper time for* [bathing in] *the nāga-river*?) yena (? this word may not have been in the text) nadī-nairañjanā (v.l. °nān) tenopasaṃkramitvā ... Mv ii.131.11; and similarly ii.264.3, except that here one ms. is reported to read -nandī- (instead of nadī-)kālasamaye with Senart's text (and both have nāma- for nāga-), but the LV parallel (and reading of the other ms. here and both in 131.11) proves this wrong.

Nāgapālaka, n. of a yakṣa king: MSV i.xviii.3.

nāgabala, (1) nt., a high number: °laṃ LV 148.2 and (cited from LV) Mvy 7963; (2) m., n. of a former Buddha: Mv iii.239.7.

Nāgabāhu, n. of a former Buddha: Mv i.137.15.

Nāgabhuja, n. of a mythical king: Mv i.95.1. (Read with mss., rājā nāgabhujo nāma tadā so.)

Nāgabhogabāhu, n. of a former Buddha: Mv i.141.4.

nāgamaṇi, also **°ṇi-varma**, a kind of gem: nāgāmaṇiṃ (-gā- m.c.; Senart em. °ṇīṃ; acc. pl.) ca śubhavarṇanīyāṃ ... Mv ii.318.19 (vs), here brought by guhyas to decorate the bodhi-tree; °varma-mahāmaṇiratnaṃ Gv 498.18 (worn by fishermen and others who go into water, it protects them from injury by any serpent); in line 21 misprinted -dharma for -varma.

nāga-maṇḍalika, m., *snake-charmer*: Mvy 3765 = Tib. sbrul tshogs can, lit. *having a collection of snakes*; MSV i.288.16 ff.

Nāgamuni, n. of a former Buddha: Mv iii.230.13 f.

? **Nāgayana**, n. of a gandharva: Suv 162.5 (no v.l. but Tib. and Chin. help to make the reading doubtful; see Nobel's note).

Nāgara, n. of a locality: Māy 64.

Nāgarabindava, m. pl., (people) of **Nagarabindu**: MSV i.220.12 ff.

nāga-lipi, a kind of script: LV 126.2 (confirmed by Tib. klu-).

Nāgādhipati, n. of a kumbhāṇḍa: Mvy 3438.

Nāgābhibhū, n. of one or two former Buddhas: LV 172.7; Sukh 5.12; of a contemporary or future Buddha: Sukh 70.9.

nāgāmaṇi, m.c. for **nāgamaṇi**.

Nāgārjuna, n. of a teacher: Mvy 3474; Sādh 194.17; 267.4.

Nāgāhvaya, n. of a teacher (= Nāgārjuna?): Laṅk 286.13; Mvy 3475.

Nāgendracūḍa, n. of a Bodhisattva: Gv 3.9.

Nāgeśvararāja, n. of a Buddha (or of two): Śikṣ 169.8; Gv 12.14 (13).

Nāgottama, n. of two former Buddhas in the same list: Mv iii.233.2; 239.6.

nāgnya, nt. (to Skt. nagna plus -ya; = Pali naggiya, AMg. nagga), *nakedness*: MSV ii.92.8 ff.

nāḍa (Skt. Lex.; = Skt. nāla, § 2.46), *stalk*: SP 122.4; 127.5.

Nāḍakanthā, n. of a town: Av i.78.6 ff.

Nāḍakantheya, adj., *of Nāḍakanthā*; pl., *the people of N.*: Av i.78.8 ff.

Nāḍikā, n. of a rākṣasī: Māy 243.10.

nāḍīkerī (cf. **nālīkera** and Skt. nālikerī), n. of a tree, presumably the cocoa-palm: Gv 501.26.

-nāḍyā (perh. hyper-Sktism based on a MIndic form like AMg. nāliyā, from Skt. nālikā, with ḍ for l, § 2.46), *hollow tube*: in kaṇṭhaṃ vā kaṇṭhanāḍyā vā Śikṣ 249.6 (prose), *throat* or *gullet* (Bendall and Rouse). Cf. Skt. kaṇṭha-nāla, *throat*.

nāda, acc. to mss. for nāḍa = nāla, *stalk* (of a flower): -padumehi... nīla-vaiḍūrya-nādehi Mv ii.302.1 (prose), so mss.; Senart em. °nāḍīhi.

nādana (nt.), *roaring*: (mahāsiṃha-)nāda-nādanārthaṃ LV 275.12 (prose).

Nādikā (= Pali id., also Ñātikā), n. of a village: MPS 9.2 ff.

[**nāna**, misprint for nagna: nānāś ca kṛṣṇāś ca... pretāḥ SP 84.11 (vs); so, without v.l., both edd.; but ms. K′ (photostat) nagnā; Burnouf and Kern both transl. *naked*, without note; so Tib. gcer bu; read nagnā(ś).]

nānākaraṇa, nt. (= Pali id.), *difference, distinction*: Divy 222.20, see s.v. **abhiprāya**; piśācasya ca etasya ca nāsti kiṃcit nānākaraṇam Mv ii.459.4, *between the piśāca and him there is no difference*; kiṃ nāsti nānā° Karmav 58.12; kiṃ nānā° Mvy 6892; AsP 346.15; **nir-nānā°**, adj. Bhvr., *without difference*: Thomas ap. Hoernle MR 95.13 (Mahāparinirvāṇa Sūtra); tulyāṃ ... nirnānākaraṇāṃ Bbh 164.22.

nānā-bhāva, (1) adj., *different, various*: (teṣām ahaṃ) nānābhāvāṃ cittadhārāṃ (see this) prajānāmi Vaj 39.11; (2) m., *the becoming separate(d)*; sarvehi priyehi manāpehi nānābhāvo vinābhāvo Mv ii.215.2, *from all loved and charming things separation* (? or, possibly, *alteration, becoming different*; but the instr. is then hard to construe) *and deprivation occurs*; similarly MPS 31.70.

Nānāratnavyūha, m., n. of the Bodhisattva's palace in Kapilavastu: LV 100.7.

nānā-vāsa, nt. (°saṃ, n. sg.), *dwelling separate* (from the generality of monks in a monastery); imposed on monks who wish to conduct a ceremony of ordination, as also on those guilty of immorality: Kv 96.8, 9, 10, 11, 14. Cf. next.

nānā-saṃvāsika, m., and f. **°kā** (Pali °saka), *one who lives apart* (from the generality of monks or nuns), under restrictions which bar him or her from certain rights of association (such as participation in the uposatha along with the rest, Vin. i.134.2 ff.); see prec.: °kaḥ Mvy 8757; °kā Bhīk 16b.2; masc. MSV ii.178.14 ff.; ii.204.10; opp. **samāna-saṃvāsika**. The transl. of Vin. in SBE 13.293f. is not correct.

nāpinī, *woman of the barber caste*: Divy 370.1, 3.

One might be tempted to assume a misreading for Skt. nāpitī. But note Pali nahāminī, Pv iii.1.13, repeated in comm. 176.1 with gloss kappaka-jātikā. Our word looks like confirmation of Kern's conjecture, cited PTSD s.v. nahāmin, that the Pali form stands for °pin(ī).

Nābhigarbha, n. of a Bodhisattva: Gv 2.26.

1 nāma = **avanāma**, q.v., *depression* (of spirits), only in Śikṣ 108.12, see s.v. **unnāma**. In this verse avanāma or onāma would be unmetrical; but it is barely possible that the text unnāmanāmāni should be taken for unnāma-(o)nāmāni, with MIndic elision in saṃdhi of initial o (for ava) after final a in comp.

2 nāma, adv., particle, *pretendedly, quasi-*: hitakāma iva nāma Jm 20.9, *as if pretendedly desiring his welfare*; dharmātmako nāma bhūtvā Jm 143.21, *assuming a righteous character, forsooth*; so also in Aśvaghoṣa's language: Buddhac. iv. 29 (see Johnston's note), Saundaran. iv.15, 17.

nāmaka (nt.; AMg. ṇāmaya; nāma-n plus -ka svārthe), *name* (in Skt. only ifc. Bhvr.): (rājā Kuśo, ātmano) nāmakena ālikhati Mv ii.463.9 *marks with his own name*; Kuśasya nāmakaṃ 13.

nāmatika, adj. (to **namata** plus ika), *wearing garments of felt*, one of the **dhūtaguṇa**: Mvy 1130; Dharmas 63; in both v.l. **nāmantika**, q.v. (so text AsP 387.8, but can hardly be right); Mironov cites v.l. nāmāntika; nāmatikaḥ MSV iii.122.5. Not in Pali.

Nāmatideva (?so, no v.l.; meaning?), n. of a divine Bodhisattva, one of the trāyastriṃśaka gods: Mv i.98.1 (prose).

nāman, nt., usually as in Skt. *name, noun*; but in contrast with **pada**, q.v., *sentence*, and **vyañjana**, *sound*, seems to mean (any) *word*: Mvy 1996 nāma-kāyaḥ (see **kāya** 2); defined AbhidhK. LaV-P. ii.238 by saṃjñākaraṇa, *ce qui fait naître une idée*; the examples given are in fact nouns, but other parts of speech, if they are not included under this term, are completely ignored here.

nāmana (cf. Pkt. ṇāmana, *bending, lowering*), see **a-nāmana-tā**.

Nāmaniyatapraveśa, m., n. of a samādhi: Mvy 576.

nāmantika, adj., = **nāmatika**, q.v.: AsP 387.8. Can hardly be anything but an error of tradition, despite its widespread occurrence, and should doubtless be emended. (Here too in list of **dhūtaguṇa**.)

nāmayati (cf. also nāmita; caus. of namati, which alone seems to be recorded in Pali in these senses, tho nāmeti occurs in the literal sense, *bend*, trans.; see **namati**, which in BHS is much rarer in these senses), (**1**) *inclines*, with object cittaṃ, and remoter object (*to, towards*) dat. or loc. or infin.: āhāram āhartuṃ cittaṃ nāmayati sma LV 264.12–13, *inclined* (made up) *his mind to take food*; bodhāya cittaṃ nāmetvā Mv ii.362.17; 364.11; cittaṃ bodhāya nāmaye 367.13; nāmetva cittaṃ sahalokanāthe 385.24, *directing* (centering) *his thought towards* (upon) *the Buddha*; cittaṃ bodhāya nāmayet Śikṣ 5.18; (**2**) with other objects than cittaṃ, *directs, applies*, something (acc.) to (dat. or loc.): (citrācāryo . . .) citrārthe nāmayed raṅgān Laṅk 48.9 (vs), *would put colors to use for a picture*; yac ca śubhaṃ mayi saṃcitu kiṃcid bodhayi (dat.) nāmayamī (= °yāmi, m.c.) ahu sarvaṃ Bhad 12; sabhāgacarīye (dat.) nāmayamī kuśalaṃ imu sarvaṃ 42; nāmayamī kuśalaṃ imu sarvaṃ 55 (construe with next), . . . kuśalaṃ imu sarvaṃ nāmayamī vara-Bhadracarīye 56; sarva kuśalamūlaṃ bodhaye nāmayāmaḥ LV 369.4 (vs), *let us apply all roots of merit unto enlightenment*; seems used almost in the sense of **upanāmayati**, q.v., *presents*, in: gṛhītva Brahma ojavindu bodhisattva (loc. in sense? § 8.11) nāmayī LV 74.2 (vs), *Brahma, taking the drop-of-might (elixir), applied* (presented?) *it to the B.*

nāmāvaśeṣa, adj. (cf. Skt. nāmaśeṣa, same mg.), *of which* (only) *the name is left*, i. e. *destroyed, dead*: Divy 185.28 (°ṣam enaṃ karomi); 187.4; 334.6 (always with forms of kṛ-).

nāmita (ppp. of **nāmayati**; seems unrecorded in this sense; nearest approach is Pali pitthiṃ nāmetvā Jāt. vi.349.24), *bent*, of limbs; *distorted, deformed*: na khañjakubjo nāpi ca nāmitāṅgaḥ Śikṣ 304.11.

?**nāmnas**, adv. (abl. of nāman, cf. Skt. nāmatas, adv.), *by name*; so all Nep. mss. in SP 68.2 (vs), virajā ca nāmnas tada lokadhātuḥ; Kashgar rec. nāmā (m.c. for nāma, *by name*); ed. em. nāmnā.

nāyaka, *guide*, very common ep. of Buddha, as in Pali: Mvy 20 = Tib. ḥdren pa, *guide*; LV 4.4, et passim.

nāyin = **nāyaka**, but applied to a Bodhisattva (Mañjuśrī): bhāṣitā bodhisattvena Mañjughoṣeṇa nāyinā Mmk 32.18 (vs).

nārakīya, adj. (Skt. Lex.; cf. next), *of hell*: °yā (printed nārakī yā) vedanā Kv 36.11; °yaṃ karma Karmav 49.9, 15, *deed that results in* (rebirth in) *hell*.

nārakeya, adj. (subst.; cf. prec.), *inhabitant of hell*: Śikṣ 69.15; 70.6; 72.2.

Nārada, (**1**) occurs as the n. of the well-known sage, as in Skt., e. g. Mv iii.401.9; (**2**) in Mv ii.55.3; 63.18 given as n. of the ascetic **Kauśika** (1), q.v., owing to a confusion of tradition (in Pali, which has the original form of the story, he is the same as Skt. Nārada and not = Kosika, Kosiya); (**3**) in Mv ii.42.19 and 43.2 (here v.l. nālada) the name seems to replace **Nālaka**, q.v., perhaps by corruption of tradition (but cf. the form Nālada in Av, also v.l. at Mv ii.43.2).

Nārāyaṇa, (**1**) (also **Mahā-n°**, q.v.; presumably the name of the Hindu god, but used in BHS as a proverbially powerful personage; so also in Pali, see DPPN s.v. Nārāyana-saṃghāṭa-bala, *'name given to a certain measure of physical strength . . . [it] was the strength of the Buddha'*; but in MPS 31.21 Buddha has the power of many hundreds of Nārāyaṇas): Nārāyaṇa-balam Mvy 8214 = Tib. sred med buḥi (*of Nārāyaṇa*, so Das; lit. seems to mean *of son of the desireless one*) stobs (*strength*); °ṇa-sthāmavān LV 109.11; 110.8; 291.15 (all vss), *having the might of N.* (Tib. on the last, sred med bu yi mthu ldan pa); °ṇa-saṃhananakāyaḥ SP 428.9–10, said of a Bodhisattva; °ṇa-saṃhananaḥ MSV i.271.10; vajradṛdha abhedya nārāyaṇo ātmabhāvo guru LV 202.17 (vs) = Tib. sku (*body*) ni sred med bu yi stobs ldan (*having the strength of N.*), which seems to imply that Tib. took nārāyaṇo as an adj., *Nārāyaṇa-like* (in strength); it could perhaps be understood as for °ṇa-, in comp. with -ātmabhāva (§ 8.12), *having the body of a N.* (i. e. like N.); sarvaparvasu caikasmin (read caikaikasmin?) parvaṇi Nārāyaṇa-bala-saṃniviṣṭatā (. . . *a state of being invested with the power of N.*) Bbh 74.27; see the similar cases s.vv. **Ardhanārāyaṇa**, **Mahānārāyaṇa**; (**2**) n. of a Buddha: Śikṣ 169.12; (**3**) n. of a yakṣa: Suv 161.6; (**4**) n. of a nāga-king: Māy 247.4.

Nārāyaṇaparipṛcchā, n. of a work: Śikṣ 21.1; 147.1; 189.7.

Nārāyaṇavīrya, n. of a Tathāgata: Gv 421.20.

Nārāyaṇavratasumeruś(i)rī, n. of a Buddha: Gv 284.25 (vs).

Nārāyaṇaśrīgarbha, n. of a Bodhisattva: Dbh 2.12.

[?**nārāśībhāva-ḥ**, n. sg., Mvy 2588 (so Mironov, no v.l.), but prob. read with v.l. in Kyōtō ed. na rāśi°, which accords with Tib. spuṅs paḥi dṅos pa med pa, *not becoming a heap*; this also fits the context, a chapter entitled **nisṛjā**-paryāyāḥ.]

Nārīkela, see **Nālikera**.

[**nāryadhanahīna** LV 178.5, preceded by anusmarā; read āryadhana°, with Tib., which has no negative. The n- belongs with the preceding word, which should be read either anusmaran(n), or with some mss. anusmaram, intending the same form, a n. sg. m. pres. pple.]

Nāla = next: Mv iii.387.4 (vs; doubtless m.c.).

Nālaka (= Pali id.), n. of a nephew and pupil of the ṛṣi Asita (also **Nāla,** and perhaps **Nālada,** q.v.; in LV called **Naradatta**; see also **Nārada** 3): Mv ii.30.14; 33.14; iii.382.14 ff. (his story told at length); belonged to the Kātyāyana gotra, 382.13; 386.8; colophon, Nālaka-praśnā (mss., Senart em. °naṃ) 389.12.

Nālada, (1) v.l. in Mv ii.43.2 for Nārada (3), q.v., referring to **Nālaka**; prob. the same person is meant by the sthavira Nālada Av i.274.6 ff.; **(2)** = **Nālanda,** birthplace of Śāriputra (Tiṣya): °da-grāmake Tiṣyo... (here father of Śāriputra) Av ii.186.6 (so text, no v.l.).

Nālanda, nt. (Pali Nālandā, also Nāla, Nālaka, Nālika), or °**dā,** n. of a village near (one-half yojana acc. to Mv) Rājagṛha, birthplace and family home of Śāriputra; also called **Nālada** acc. to Av ii.186.6: rājagṛhasya ardha-yojane nālanda-grāmakaṃ (v.l. nālandaṃ) nāma grāmaṃ Mv iii.56.6; śrī-nālandā Mvy 4120.

Nālayu, m. or f., n. of a province (janapada; in the south): °yur nāma Gv 110.11; 111.6.

?**nāli,** m. or f. (°liḥ, n. sg.), Mvy 7521, from the context should mean something connected with weaving; Tib. son pa, *arrived*(!) and so also Chin.!; Jap. *pipe*, or *vein*, which fits Skt. nāḍī (and Lex. nālī), but not the context in Mvy.

nālikā, (1) (= Pali nāḷikā), *a tubular vessel* or *receptacle*: pucchaṃ sauvarṇāyāṃ °kāyāṃ prakṣiptam Divy 514.6; bhaiṣajyāñjana-nālikā Mvy 9014; **(2)** (= Pkt. ṇāliā, AMg. ṇālī), *a metal plate on which the hour is struck*: Jm 83.24.

Nālikera (= Pali Nāḷikera, °kīra), n. of a wicked king of Dantapura in Kaliṅga: Mv iii.361.12 (text Nārīkela, v.l. nālikela); 368.14 (v.l. °la); 369.12 (v.l. °la).

Nālī, n. of a yakṣiṇī: MSV i.xviii.17.

nālīkera, nt. (cf. **nāḍīkerī,** and Skt. nālikera, nārīkela), *cocoanut, the fruit of the cocoa-palm*: Mv ii.475.15 °rāṇi (v.l. °lāni).

(**nāvika** = Skt. id., *sailor*; see **pauruṣeya** 2.)

nāśita-saṃgraha, m. (nāśita, ppp. of Skt. nāśayati, Pali nāseti; cf. Pali nāsita, Vin. iv.139.5 ff., where the situation contemplated is described), *social relations with* (a monk who has been) *banished*: Mvy 8481.

nāsti-bhāva, *condition of not-being*, see s.v. 1 **asti** (3).

niḥk(h)-, see in general **niṣk(h)-.**

[**niḥkṣepa,** see **nikṣepa.**]

niḥkṣobhya (nt.; imitation of **akṣobhya,** which occurs in the same line), a high number: akṣobhyaṃ pare vindyān niḥkṣobhyaṃ ca tataḥ pare Mmk 262.13 (vs).

niḥp-, see **niṣp-.**

Nikaṭa (= Pali id.), n. of an upāsaka in Nādikā: MPS 9.13.

Nikaṇṭha, n. of a gandharva: Suv 161.17.

Nikaṇṭhaka (cf. Pali Nighaṇḍu?), n. of a yakṣa: Māy 236.27.

nikaruṇa, adj. (m.c. for Skt. niṣk°, Pali nikk°), *pitiless*: LV 235.8 (vs).

nikāya, (1) (as in Skt., but nt., in Skt. m.) *collection, group*: yena... deva-nikāyaṃ tenopasaṃkrameyaṃ Mv i.54.13; Buddha is saptabhiś ca nikāyaiḥ saṃpuraskṛto Divy 159.15; **(2)** (= Pali id.) *'collection'* of sūtras in the Buddhist canon, or more loosely, *the canon* collectively: nikāya-gati-saṃbhavāt Laṅk 292.13, *from* (having their) *origin in the course of the canon*, and °gati-gotrā(ḥ) 16, said of the abhijñā (*psychic powers*, Suzuki) as acquired by orthodox canonical lore; Suzuki misunderstands the mg., which is made clear by **naikāyika,** q.v., shortly after; **(3)** *school* (of religious opinion), in **nikāyāntarīya,** q.v. (orig. and lit., no doubt, *canon* as under 2). The four Nikāyas of the Pali canon are usually called Āgamas in BHS.

nikāyāntarīya, adj. or subst. m., *belonging to* (adherent of) *another school* (nikāya): Mvy 5149; MadhK 312.1 (and see ib. 10 n. 5, 145 n. 1).

Nikuṇṭhā, n. of a rākṣasī: Māy 240.7.

nikubja, adj. (= Pali nikujja, nikk°; cf. next), *prone, lying face down*: kāścin nikubjāḥ LV 206.11 (prose; v.l. nikujj-, as in Pali; most mss. nikukṣ-).

nikubjana, nt. (to **nikubjayati,** see Addendum p. 627), *upsetting, making to be prone*: pātra-°nam Mvy 9252.

nikūla, adj., *low, descending*; see s.v. **utkūla.**

nikṛnta (also nikṛntana? prob. only by error) adj. (= Pali nikanta, MN i.364.17), *cut off*; common in Divy and Av in mūla-ni°, *cut off at the roots*; mss. regularly read so; in Divy 539.5 they read °nikṛntana, which ed. em. °nikṛntita; otherwise edd. of both texts always em. to nikṛtta, but the Pali word supports the reading of the mss. It is doubtless derived in some way from kṛntati, but the precise process is obscure to me: Divy 192.9; 313.15; 362.17; 387.6; 400.17; 425.5; 539.5 (see above); 583.15 (in 537.14 occurs nikṛntita-mūlaṃ); Av i.3.16 (one ms. here nikṛta, v.l. nikṛnta); 9.12; 24.11; 37.12; 51.2, etc.

niketa (m. or nt.), *state of existence, life*: paścime bhave paścime nikete paścime samucchraye paścima ātmabhāvapratilambhe Divy 70.2; 73.16; niketa-sthānāni, *bases for* (further) *lives*, Dbh 39.23, quoted s.vv. **unmiñjita, kelāyati** (4).

nikkaṭa, adj. (= Deśī ṇikkaḍa, *hard*), in nikkaṭa-kacchā Mv ii.87.17, ep. of a needle (so one ms.; Senart wrongly em. nikkaṭṭa-), *with hard* **kaccha** or **kacchā** (?perhaps *edge*? see s.v.).

nikranda- (in comp.), *loud pronouncement* (Bendall and Rouse *boasting*): nāsti nikranda-dānaṃ Śikṣ 271.5, *there is* (to be) *no giving with*...

nikṣipaṇa (nt.; = Pali nikkhipana, Childers, pada-ni°; Skt. nikṣepaṇa; to nikṣipati plus -ana), *putting, setting down* (of the feet): vimalapadma-krama-nikṣipaṇa-gatiḥ (mahāpuruṣāṇām) LV 272.19.

nikṣipati, (1) *figures, calculates, works out* (a mathematical problem): LV 146.12, 15, 16, 20, 22; 147.2; see s.v. **uddiśati; (2)** *lets down* in sense of *permits to descend*: LV 186.13 f. (see s.v. **utkṣipati,** 1); Tib. ḥbebs, *cause to descend*.

nikṣepa (m.; cf. next; presumably n. act. to prec., 1, q.v.), *working out mathematical problems*(?), in stock lists of arts, (gaṇanāyāṃ mudrāyāṃ uddhāre nyāse) nikṣepe Divy 3.19; 26.12; 58.17; 100.2; 441.28; same spelled niḥkṣepe MSV iii.20.1; (lipiśāstra-mudrā-saṃkhyā)-gaṇanā-nikṣepādīni Dbh 45.22. See also **nyāsa, nyasana**; cf. also **nikṣepa-lipi** (here in diff. sense).

nikṣepaṇa (nt.? presumably = prec., q.v.), *working out mathematical problems*(?), in a list of arts: lipiṃ... gaṇanāṃ dhāraṇaṃ (mss. vār°) nikṣepaṇaṃ Mv iii.394.9; lipiṃ... nikṣepaṇaṃ dhāraṇaṃ vyavahāraṃ ca iii.405.12. (In Mv ii.287.9 na... paśyāmi śramaṇasya gautamasya kaṃcid devamanuṣyeṣu nikṣepaṇaṃ, the word means *subjugation*, as in normal Skt., or at best *conqueror*, as nom. ag.; not *égalité* with Senart.)

nikṣepa-lipi, LV 126.5, and **nikṣepāvarta-lipi,** 7, n. of two kinds of script; see s.v. **utkṣepa-lipi.**

nikhaḍga, nt., a high number: Mmk 262.16 (cited s.v. **khaḍgin,** q.v.); 343.15 (vs) daśa-khaḍga-(text as cpd., but read as separate word?) nikhaḍgaṃ tu daśanikhaḥ (?hypermetric; I should expect daśa nikhaḍgā-ni) kharvam iṣyate (follows l. 14, cited s.v. **khaḍga**).

nigama, nt., a high number: Gv 134.1; Mvy 7919, cited from Gv; = Tib. dpag bral. Equivalent to **vigama,** q.v.

nigarjati, °**te** (this and its derivs., see next two, have been noted only in Gv), *roars, cries forth*, often with obj. a sacred text or doctrine, then fig. *proclaims loudly*: °jamāna, pres. pple., Gv 43.10 (vs; ruṭāni bauddhāni);

92.10, 23; 532.4 (all prose, object -meghān in fig. sense, e. g. prajñāpāramitā-m° 92.10); similarly -meghān (fig.) nigarjayamānā(ḥ) 272.26 (prose; is this a true caus., *causing to roar forth*? or = °jamānāḥ? most likely the latter); -ghoṣu . . . nigarjita 241.7 (vs), . . . *was cried forth*; sūtraṃ nigarjasu (certainly intends 3 sg. aor.; read °si? § 32.62) narendraḥ 259.23 (vs).

nigarjana (nt., to **nigarjati, °te,** plus -ana), *roar*: (sarvadharmadhātv)a-saṅga-nigarjana-spharaṇa-candra, n. of a samādhi: Gv 37.3 (seems strange, perhaps corrupt); (-meghonnata-)nigarjanaṃ (acc.) 68.10; -dharma-nigarjanena 247.21, et alibi (in Gv only).

nigarjita (nt.) = °rjana: -megha-nigarjita- Gv 86.22; -nirghoṣa-nigarjitān (Bhvr. adj.) 88.3; -sāgara-nigarjitaghoṣaṃ 94.21.

nigarhaṇīya (to Skt. ni-garh-), adj. with karman (corresp. to Pali nissaya-kamma, Vin. ii.8.1, '*act of subordination*' SBE 17.344), *action of* (severe) *condemnation* (more serious than **tarjanīya**): MSV iii.12.2 ff. (description); Mvy 8643.

(**nigala**, m. or nt., = Skt. Lex. and late lit. id., see Schmidt, Nachträge; Skt. nigaḍa, Pali °ḷa; *fetter*: °lehi Mv ii.484.2, mss., Senart em. °ḍehi.)

niguṇa, adj. (m.c. for Skt. nirguṇa, Pali nigguṇa), *virtue-less*: LV 206.20 (vs; most mss. corrupt, haplog.).

Nigrantha, var. for **Nirgr°** (Jñātiputra), q.v. Cf. next.

nigrantha and **°thaka** (cf. prec.), *a Jain monk*: Kalpanāmaṇḍitikā, Lüders, Kl. Skt. Texte 2 p. 43, where evidence is cited to show that ni-gr° was, at least sometimes, not an error but a deliberate and malicious alteration of nirgr°.

nigha, m. (also **nīgha**, q.v., and cf. **anigha**), *evil, sin*: Mvy 7308 = Tib. sdig pa, *sin*. In Pali only anigha, anīgha seem to be in real use; nigha and nīgha are given in comms. and said to mean dukkha; they have the look of abstractions from anigha (anīgha); alternatively the comms. analyze an-īgha. Real etym. of anigha uncertain. But BHS seems clearly to have used nigha, and probably nīgha, independently (tho perhaps by secondary backformation from an°).

(**nighaṇṭa, nirghaṇṭa**, rare in Skt. for usual nighaṇṭu, *word-study, lexicology*, esp. as a Vedāṅga; AMg. has nighaṇṭu, nigghaṇṭu, acc. to Sheth also nigghaṇṭa: LV 156.18 nirghaṇṭe; in cpd. sa-nighaṇṭa-kaiṭabha (with veda), see s.v. **kaiṭabha**: Mv i.231.18; ii.77.9; 89.17; iii.450.7; Av ii.19.7; Divy 619.22; in Mv mss. vary between nigh° and nirgh° in i.231.18 and ii.89.17, both nirgh° ii.77.9; iii.450.7; also with ṭh for ṭ.).

[**nighoṣa**, m., prob. error of tradition for nirghoṣa, *sound*: Suv 231.5 (vs), but meter seems bad in any case; best ms. -nirghoṣaḥ, which gives better approach to good meter.]

nicūta, a kind of tree: Māy 258.14.

nicchavi-(v.l. °vī-)**-kṛtvā**, ger. (MIndic form of nis, neg., plus Skt. chavi, plus karoti), *having skinned, removed the skin of*: sā . . . godhā tena . . . nicchavi- (v.l. °vī; Senart prints nirchavi-)kṛtvā pakvā Mv ii.65.9. (For standard Skt. ***niśchavī°**.)

[**nijinitu** (only v.l. °nita) LV 165.2 (vs), foll. by jinaguṇa; certainly corrupt; Tib. gñug mar (= nija, with 'terminative' ending) byas (*made*, = kṛta), *made* (your) *own*; read prob. nija-kṛta, or niji- (m.c. for nijī-)kṛta.]

nitīraṇa, nt. (looks like deriv. of *nitīrati, MIndic pass. of *ni-tarati; cf. next; note that in Pali nitiṇṇa occurs in mss. as v.l. for nittiṇṇa = Skt. nistīrṇa), *complete and conclusive investigation*: Mvy 7471 = Tib. ṅes par (or, phye ste) rtog pa; sarvadharmajñāna-nitīraṇam Dbh 57.13; satya-nitīraṇaṃ Dbh.g. 20(356).25.

nitīrayati (prob. corruption for **nistīr°**, q.v.; but cf. prec.), *accomplishes, solves* (problems, questions): gambhīra-gambhīrān praśnān svaprajñayā °yati MSV i.114.13; °rayitvā (a legal question) id. 116.13.

[**nitya**, acc. to Senart used as synonym for nirvāṇa, Mv ii.140.16 (vs), see his note, comparing ii.144.4. But this seems hardly sufficient evidence, and I have been unable to find elsewhere in Pali or BHS or Skt. any such use of nitya. Text: nityāntareṇa manasā kṛtamokṣabuddhiḥ, mārgaṃ (?mss. āryaṃ) va (mss. ca) tāva mama putra cara prasīda, jīvāmi yāvac ca ahaṃ (so mss.) . . ., (Śuddhodana pleads with the Bodhisattva to wait for his own death before renouncing the world; text in part uncertain;) *with constantly internal mind fixing your will on salvation* (i. e. keeping it to yourself, not doing anything about it yet) . . . *as long as I live* . . . The word nitya, at any rate, seems to have its Skt. meaning.]

nityaka, nt., *constant provision, regular food*: yan tu brāhmaṇānāṃ rājakule nityakaṃ . . . taṃ pi na vartati Mv i.309.18; na śakyaṃ brāhmaṇehi rājño nityakaṃ pratīcchituṃ 310.4; pl., either subst. or perh. adj., contrasting with **nimittika**, q.v.: bhaktais tarpaṇair yavāgūpānair nityakair nimittikair (*regular food* and *food for special occasions*; but both words may be understood as adjectives with the adjoining nouns) dīpamālābhiḥ kaṭhina-cīvarair dānapradānāni dattvā Av ii.13.5.

nitya-jvara, m., *permanent* (uninterrupted) *fever*: °raḥ Mvy 9535; = **satata-jvara**, q.v.

Nityaparinirvṛta (v.l. °parivṛta; so Burnouf), n. of a Buddha in a southern lokadhātu: SP 184.10.

Nityaprayukta (so Mironov on Mvy, and ŚsP), or **Nityaprabha** (so Mironov v.l.), or **Nityayukta**, n. of a Bodhisattva: Mvy 715; Tib. rtag tu (= nitya) sbyor ba (misprinted spyor ba; = prayukta or yukta), or ḥod (= prabhā); ŚsP 6.19.

Nityotkṣiptahasta, n. of a Bodhisattva: ŚsP 7.6.

Nityodyukta, n. of a Bodhisattva: SP 3.4; LV 2.14; Mvy 696; Sukh 92.11.

nidarśana, (nt.) *exhibition* (of skill or powers); cf. **darśana** (2) in same sense: paścime nidarśane bāṇā vidhyanti Mv ii.75.20.

nidarśayitar, *one who sets forth, expounds*: °tāro niryāṇamukhānām Gv 463.7 (prose).

[**nidaśa**, read with 2d ed. **nirdeśa**, q.v., Gv 106.18.]

nidahati (= Pali id., for Skt. nidadhāti; cf. **dahati**), *puts down*: nidahiya (ger.; Senart em. nidahya, which is not an improvement metrically or otherwise) jānu bhūmyāṃ Mv ii.320.16 (vs).

nidāna, nt. (Skt. id. in mg. 1, but even here BHS develops the word differently from Skt.; most, perhaps all, mgs. found in Pali id.), (1) *cause, underlying and determining factor*; may be associated with virtual synonyms hetu, pratyaya, nimitta: paribhoga-nimittaṃ ca kāmahetu-nidānaṃ ca . . . dṛṣṭadhārmikaṃ ca paryeṣṭi-nidānaṃ parigraha-nidānaṃ ca SP 77.14–15; sa-hetu sa-pratyayaṃ ca sa-nidānaṃ LV 376.21; jātī-nidāna jaravyādhiduḥkhāni bhonti LV 420.7 (vs), in the pratītya-samutpāda, where the regular term is pratyaya; Tib. here gzhi, *underlying cause*; dāne nidāne ca sukhodayānāṃ Jm 24.25 (vs), *and since giving is the cause of happiness and advancement* (word-play on dāna); (bodhisattvāḥ . . .) mahantānāṃ utpādānāṃ nidānam anuprāpnuvanti, bhūtānāṃ (*true*) utpādānāṃ nidānam anuprā° Mv ii.260.16, 17; sākāraṃ soddeśaṃ sa-nidānaṃ pūrvanivāsam anusmarati sma Mvy 229, *he recalled his former births with their forms, locations, and underlying causes* (i. e. what made them what they were; Tib. gzhi ci las ḥgyur ba daṅ bcas pa, *together with from-what-cause-origination*); the acc. sg. nidānaṃ is used adverbially, *because of* . . ., sometimes with dependent gen. preceding, mama nidānaṃ Mv ii.111.1, *on my account*; asmākam eva ni° Mv iii.221.9, tava . . . ni° 13; or in comp. with preceding pronominal stem, tan-nidānaṃ, *for that reason*, Bbh 29.2, 7; 72.18, etc.; Laṅk 251.2; (kasya hetoḥ, so read with v.l.) kiṃnidānaṃ vā baddhaṃ SP 211.4, *for what reason or cause was it tied on?*; yan-nidānaṃ, *inasmuch as*, MSV ii.191.1 (= yad, 190.14), 11, and ff.; esp. commonly preceded by tato, yato, less often ato, ito, it being open to question whether these latter forms are compounded with nidānaṃ (like tan-, kiṃ-, yan-, above), or are dependent ablatives (like the gens. mama, etc., above); editors vary in printing them as one word or two (and so in Pali, tato-, yato-nidānaṃ): tato-nidānaṃ SP 347.12; Mv i.351.12; iii.66.5, 11; Śikṣ 84.6; Vaj 24.15; Bbh 46.25; ato-ni° Divy 448.4; MSV i.51.4; yato-ni° Śikṣ 100.12; Bbh 163.12; Ud ii.20 (duḥkhaṃ hi yo veda yatonidānaṃ, *who knows misery, whence it is caused*, = Pali id. in SN i.117.3; same line in Divy 224.18 reads yaḥ prekṣati duḥkham ito nidānaṃ, *as caused from this*); (**2**) (*cause of action*, so) *motive, motivation*, in **tri-nidāna**, q.v.; also prob. in Av i.169.14, teṣāṃ sattvānāṃ nidānam āśayānuśayaṃ copalakṣya svayam ārabdhaś cikitsāṃ ... kartum, *noting the motives, the disposition and inclination* (see **anuśaya**) *of these creatures* (who were afflicted with a pestilence; i. e. finding them worthy), *himself undertook to give them medical treatment*; otherwise Feer, who understands *cause* (of the disease) *of these creatures*; it is true that Pali nidāna means *cause (aetiology) of disease* in Miln. 272.13, but it seems to me forcing the Av passage to read that mg. into it, esp. since the coordinated āśayānuśaya can hardly be applied to disease (tho Feer makes the attempt); (**3**) *beginning, introduction* (cf. Pali Nidānakathā, the introduction to Jāt.): nidāna-parivartaḥ prathamaḥ Suv 5.6, colophon to Chap. 1, *the first, Introductory Chapter*; nidāna-namaskarāṇi samāptāni Mv i.2.12, colophon, *the introductory salutations*; iti śrīmahāvastu-nidāna-gāthā samāptā Mv i.4.11, colophon, *the first gāthā of the Mv* (lines 9–10, which Senart prints as prose but which obviously were a verse, and the first one in Mv); (**4**) *theme, content, subject-matter*: vaipulyasūtraṃ hi mahānidānam LV 7.9 (vs), ... *having an exalted theme*, Tib. gleṅ gzhi (*subject of discourse*) chen po (*great*); yathā Śrāvastyāṃ tatra vinaye tantravāyasya) nidānaṃ varṇayanti Karmav 71.(10–)11, *as here in the Vinaya they describe the theme* (*matter, account*) *of the weaver at Śrāvastī*; Śrāvastyāṃ nidānaṃ Divy 123.16; 198.1: MSV i.v.4, at the beginning of a story, *the theme* (subject-matter) *is* (laid) *in Ś.* (so also Pali, e. g. SN v.12.9); yad-yat tvayābhihitaṃ nidāne Divy 626.29 (vs), ... *on* (this) *theme, subject*; uktaṃ nu te saumya guṇe nidānaṃ 627.1, ... *the subject-matter* (theme, account) *on* (the subject of) *quality*; ... vadāmi dharmaṃ, bodhiṃ nidānaṃ kariyāna nityam SP 128.7 (vs), *I declare the doctrine, making enlightenment my constant theme*; sanidānaṃ ahaṃ ... śrāvakāṇāṃ dharmaṃ deśayāmi na anidānaṃ Mv iii.51.12–13, *I preach to my disciples the doctrine including its content, not devoid of content*; vistareṇa nidānaṃ kṛtvā, a phrase indicating abbreviation of a cliché, *making the content* (theme, subject-matter) *in full*, Mv i.4.13–14 (here Senart em. kṛtyaṃ, all 6 mss. kṛtvā, which he keeps in the rest); ii.115.7; iii.224.12; 377.1, 8; 382.9; 389.14; 401.20; in all these reference is to the cliché given in full e. g. Mv i.34.1 ff.; (**5**) as title of a class or type of work or subdivision of the Buddhist canon, acc. to Tib. on Mvy = gleṅ gzhiḥi (ed. bzhiḥi) sde, *statement of subject-matter, table of contents, summary* (of a work): Mvy 1272, in list of dvādaśaka-dharma-pravacanam (omitted in Dharmas 62, navāṅga-pravacanāni, see Müller's note); in more informal lists of the same kind SP 45.8; Kv 81.21; (**6**) *theme, subject*, hence virtually *occasion*, parallel with prakaraṇa and velā, once also **utpatti,** vastu: etasmiṃ nidāne etasmiṃ prakaraṇe tāye velāye (Divy tasyāṃ, misprinted tasyaṃ, velāyāṃ) Mv iii.91.17–18; Divy 654.21, *on this occasion, in this connexion, at this time*; (asyām utpattau) asmin nidāne (asmin prakaraṇe asmin vastuni) Mvy (9209,) 9210, (9211–12).

nideśita, m.c. for nirdeśita, *expounded*, ppp. of *nirdeśayati (either unrecorded 'caus.' to Skt. nirdiśati, in same mg. as this, or denom. to Skt. nirdeśa): tatra nideśitu (so all mss., Calc. nird° unmetr.; Lefm. em. ti de°) dharma udāro LV 364.3 (vs).

nidrākṣa, adj., f. **°ī,** *sleepy-eyed* (nidrākṣan): in Mv ii.203.1 (vs) read, nānā-udyānagamana-śrāntā pramadā viya nidrākṣyā (n. pl. f.). So the mss.; Senart em. violently. The meter is almost perfect; we must understand pronunciation nidā° for nidrā°.

nidhūpita, or **nirdhūpita,** q.v. (ppp. of an unrecorded *ni(r)-dhūpayati), *perfumed*: LV 187.15 (one ms. and Calc. nir°); 203.18 (only Calc. nir°); Mv iii.266.9 (ni-dh° mss., Senart em. vi-dh°); Mvy 6133 (no v.l.; but Mironov nir-dh°, no v.l.). All prose.

nidhyapta, adj., quasi-ppp. (=, and prob. hyper-Skt. back-formation from, Pali nijjhatta; contrary to PTSD, note Vv. comm. 265.24 where nijjhatto is glossed nijjhāpito, saññāya paññattigato; I believe other Pali occurrences may be similarly interpreted; cf. next and the following items), *made to understand, comprehending*: nidhyapta-cittena Śikṣ 130.13, *with comprehending mind.*

nidhyapti, f. (=, and prob. hyper-Skt. back-formation from, Pali nijjhatti, on the mg. of which see s.v. **nidhyāpayati,** also cf. **nidhyāna** and **nidhyapta**), *profound meditation*, (leading to) *comprehension*: °tiḥ, prob. so read with Mironov for nidhyāptiḥ Mvy 7460 = Tib. ṅes par sems pa, *deep thought* (the usual Tib. rendering); gambhīra-ni° Samādh 19.37; dharma-ni° Śikṣ 131.8; 190.18; Gv 163.20; (buddha-)dharma-ni° Samādh 19.14, 15; sarva-dharmasvabhāva-ni° Gv 72.23; citta-ni°, *meditation on*, or *comprehension of, the mind, thoughts*, Śikṣ 152.2; KP 107.4; 118.2, 5 (in 5, vs, °ti cittasya); Gv 110.20; svacitta-ni° Dbh 33.28; samādhi-nidhyapti-jñāna- Dbh 70.10; anāgatānāṃ kuśalamūlānāṃ nidhyapti-bodher Śikṣ 33.15, *illumination of comprehension of future roots of merit.*

nidhyāta (ppp. of Skt. ni-dhyā; not in Pali), *comprehended, realized mentally*: Vaj 32.14 (with dharma).

nidhyāna, nt. (= Skt. Lex. id., Pali nijjhāna; PTSD def. requires revision, see s.v. **nidhyāpayati**; °naṃ khamati acc. to PTSD *to be pleased with*, but MN comm. ii.106.32, on MN 1.133.28, defines it by upaṭṭhahanti, āpāthaṃ āgacchanti, i. e. *become known*, lit. *submit to comprehension*), *profound reflection*, (leading to) *comprehension*: dharma-nidhyānato 'pi kṣamate Bbh 196.26, *also thru reflection on* (or, *comprehension of*) *the states-of-being he is receptive*; cf. dharma-nidhyānādhimuktikṣāntiḥ Bbh 195.10, and sarvadharmasvabhāva-nidhyāna-kṣāntiḥ Gv 248.4, both cited s.v. kṣānti; sattvārtha-nidhyāna-virahitaḥ Bbh 23.11; see s.v. **saṃlakṣaṇā** for Bbh 83.6.

nidhyāpaka, adj., *causing comprehension*: ārakṣāsmṛti nidhyāpaka- (so mss., Senart em. °pana-)-smṛtiḥ (Bhvr.) Mv iii.52.4, *with mental-intentness on guard and causing comprehension.*

? **nidhyāpayati** (= Pali nijjhāpeti, *give to understand*, Childers; certainly means this in MN i.321.7, = saññāpenti, comm. jānāpenti; in same line nijjhatti, see **nidhyapti,** defined by comm. ii.393.32 as synonym of saññatti; PTSD defs. of this group of words need revision), *causes meditation* or *comprehension*; noted only in a probably spurious sentence, atha śuddhāvāsakāyikā devā nidhyāpayanti sma, bodhisattvam āharitum LV 187.19 (bracketed by Lefm., om. most mss., Calc., and Tib.); would seem to mean, *then the Ś. gods instigated earnest thought, to draw the Bodhisattva out.* (In lines 21 ff. they cause the first of the Four Sights to appear to him.)

nidhyāpti, Mvy 7460, prob. error for **nidhyapti,** q.v.

ninandati (unrecorded elsewhere), *rejoices, applauds*: °dimsuḥ (or v.l. °ditsuḥ), 3 pl. aor., Mv iii.267.8 (vs, but metr. poor).

nindiya, adj. (= Pali id., Skt. nindya), *blameworthy*:

(with antonym **praśaṃsiya**) Ud viii.3 (same vs in Pali, Sn 658 etc.)

nipaka, (1) m., *chief* (cf. Jain Skt. nipa, doubtless semi-Skt. for AMg. ṇiva = Skt. nṛpa, Ind. Stud. 14.386): Divy 447.27; 451.20; **(2)** adj., = Pali id., in Pali tradition app. always interpreted as *wise, prudent*, and so nepakka, *wisdom, prudence*; occurs in Ud several times, mostly in vss which also occur in Pali with the same word, viz. vi.8; xii.18; xiv.13, 14; xv.6 (here text nṛpaka, not corrected in ed.; if genuine, could only be hyper-Sktism; the Pali vs, It. 47.3, has nipako); in all these occurrences *zealous* (see 3 below) would make quite as good sense; **(3)** in phrase nipakasyāṅgasaṃbhāraiḥ Mvy 7023 and Bbh 145.23, *with the collection of parts of the nipaka* (man)? Acc. to Tib. on Mvy, ḥgru skyaṅ, *zealously attending* (?), *zealous*, and so Chin. on Mvy appears to take nipaka; Wogihara's Index to Bbh renders it by two Chin. characters which may mean *constantly self-possessed* (possibly associating the word with Pali niya, niyaka, = Skt. nija, *own* ?). It would be possible to identify this occurrence of the word with mg. 2; it might mean *prudent, wise*, here; or contrariwise the occurrences under 2 might mean *zealous*. Further complication is caused by **niyaka**, which Tib. seems to interpret as the same as nipaka, suggesting graphic confusion; this is proposed in the Index to Mvy and in pw 7.352, where niyaka is assumed to stand for nipaka and the mg. *wise* is given for both Mvy passages, but doubtfully for the one here under discussion.

nipacchita (related to **nepatthita**, q.v.), seems to be denom. ppp., *clothed*: Kalpanāmaṇḍitikā, Lüders, Kl. Skt. Texte 2, p. 44, q.v. Since cch and tth are often confused, possibly nipatthita (or even ne°) should be read. However, acc. to Pischel 280 AMg. has nevaccha and nevacchiya, by the side of ṇevattha and ṇevatthiya, Ratnach.; and Pischel believes that cch is the only 'correct' spelling.

[**nipathī**, LV 372.3 (vs), seems uninterpretable and has very little ms. support; v.l. (a)narthī, which is metrically and semantically good (see citation s.v. **granthita**), *disadvantageous*, and seems implied by Foucaux's transl.; Tib. omitted in Foucaux but the mg. attributed to Tib. in his Note (193) to transl. of the BHS LV accords well with anarthī.]

nipanna, adj. (= Pali id., ppp. of Pali nipajjati, Vedic nipadyate; not recorded even in Vedic Skt.), *lying down*: Mvy 8602.

nipāta (m.; = Pali id.), *section* (of a literary work), in titles like **Brāhmaṇa-n°**, **Ṛddhipāda-n°**, qq.v.

nipātayati (caus. of Skt. nipatati), *applies* (a word, to ..., gen.): katamasyāyaṃ ... arhacchabdo nipātyate (pass.) Laṅk 120.12, *to which is this word arhat applied*?

nipātin, adj. (= Pali id.; not in this mg. in Skt.), *lying down* (to sleep), *going to bed*: (kalyotthāyī) sāyaṃ nipātī Bbh 8.7.

nipuṇa, °na, adj. (as in Pali, ep. of dhamma), *subtle*: (gambhīraḥ ... dharmo) ... sūkṣmo nipuno (duranubodhaḥ) LV 395.20; 397.13 (both prose; in the second some inferior mss. °ṇa). Acc. to pw 7.352, *fein, zart, zärtlich* also in Jm 20.25 yuktā ... daivateṣu parānukampānipuṇā pravṛttiḥ; but here the usual Skt. mg. *skillful* would seem possible (so Speyer).

Nipura, n. of a son of King Sujāta Ikṣvāku: Mv i.348.11, 352.9; and of a son of his son Opura, 352.11. Corresp. to Pali Sinipura (also written Sīn°, °sura, and Nipura), see refs. in DPPN.

nibaddha, ppp. of ni-bandh, in aṣṭāpada-ni°, *adorned, laid out, marked out with* (or, *in*) *a checkerboard*: Mvy 6062 = Tib. mig maṅs (*checkerboard*) ris su bris pa (*drawn or painted in the form of*); SP 65.10 and 145.1 suvarṇasūtrāṣṭāpadanibaddhaṃ (*with gold threads ...*). This seems to have been a fairly standard expression; **vinibaddha** (q.v., 2) was also used; the use of **vinaddha** (q.v.) in the same cpd. seems to be a mere corruption.

nibhanakti (cited in BR only once from the artificial Bhaṭṭ.; cf. AMg. ṇibhaṅga), *breaks*; pass. pple. nibhajyamāna, to be read in Śikṣ 230.13, see s.v. **nibhunakti**.

nibhā (= Pali id.), *appearance, sheen*: LV 255.6; 256.5, 10 (all prose). In Skt. recorded only as -nibha in Bhvr. adjectives; but the existence of the noun in Pali makes Weller's note, 30 f., quite valueless.

[**nibhunakti**, pres. pass. pple., acc. to text kadalīvan nibhujyamānāsārakaḥ Śikṣ 230.13. But Transl. of Bendall and Rouse assumes nibhajy°, *broken*, citing Tib. bśig na, 217 note 3; this is surely right, since it accords with the usual fig. use of the comparison.]

nimantraṇaka, nt. (Skt. °ṇa plus -ka), *a meal to which monks or nuns are invited*: Mvy 5763; Bhīk 23a.3 (in list of kinds of food); Av ii.150.3, 5; 154.12 (all prose).

nimantraṇā (= AMg. ṇimantaṇā; in Skt. and Pali only °ṇa, nt.), *invitation*: na °ṇāṃ svīkaroti Bbh 162.11.

nimantritaka (°ta, ppp., plus specifying -ka, § 22.39), *one that has been invited, an invited guest*: Mv iii.383.20; Divy 486.14.

Nimi, (1) (= Pali id., also **Nemi**, q.v.) n. of a king, former incarnation of Śākyamuni; the hero of the Pali Nimi Jāt. (541): LV 170.16 (Tib. mu khyud, *rim*, suggesting Nemi); MSV i.112.18 ff.; **(2)** n. of a former Buddha: Sukh 6.9.

nimiñjita, nt., or adj. (see s.v. **miñj-**, and cf. especially **unmiñjita**, opposite of this and regularly associated), *closing* (as of the mouth): Mvy 2669, 6303 = Tib. btsum(s) pa; *ending, finishing* (of an act etc.), AsP 268.19 ff., see unmiñjita; adj. (ppp.) *closed* = *concluded, finished*, Dbh 39.22, see ibid.

[**nimiṇati, °ṇāti**, see **nimināti**.]

nimitta, nt. (masc., nimittā ime LV 109.8, 193.16, vss; besides the Skt. mgs., the following seem worthy of distinct listings; all seem to be also in Pali, for which Childers must be consulted to correct and supplement PTSD), **(1)** (*sign, mark*, and so) *external aspect* or *feature, appearance* (but not only visual; cf. AbhidhK. La V-P. i.28 saṃjñā nimittodgrahaṇātmikā, *la notion consiste dans la préhension des caractères*; comm. nimitta = vastuno 'vasthāviśeṣa, *les diverses conditions ou manières d'être de la chose*; quite similarly Laṅk), defined, yat saṃsthānākṛtiviśeṣākārarūpādilakṣaṇaṃ dṛśyate, tan nimittam Laṅk 228.6–7; each of the 5 objects of sense-perception has or consists of a nimitta, cf. Suzuki, Studies, 156, end: na jātu rūpa-nimittam udgṛhītavān na śabda-ni° na gandha-ni° na rasa-ni° na sparśa-ni° RP 42.3–4; na nimitta-saṃjñāyām api pratitiṣṭhet Vaj 21.10, 19; cf. 8–9 above, na rūpapratiṣṭhitena ..., na śabda-(etc.); duḥśraddadhaṃ etu ... nimittasaṃjñīn' (gen. pl., for °īnām) iha bālabuddhinām SP 57.7 (vs) ... *for fools who form notions based on appearances*; nimittacārīṇa (gen. pl.) bravīti dharmam SP 120.3 (vs) ... *to men who follow appearances*; anitya-saṃjñānimitta-kāmehi Mv i.54.6, *desires for what is impermanent*, (mere) *name and appearance* (wrongly Senart's note); (for the Bodhisattva about to attain enlightenment) śūnyā nimittā Mv ii.341.12; 344.9, *appearances* (esp. prob. as objects of the senses) *are void* (wrongly Senart); so (Buddha) cakṣuṣā rūpaṃ dṛṣṭvā na ca nimittagrāhī bhaviṣyan na cānuvyañjanagrāhī Mv iii.52.6, and with the other senses, incl. manasā dharmāṃ vijñāya, na ca etc. (10–)11, *when he perceives the objects of sense he is not one who grasps appearances or minor marks* (Pali also associates nimittaggāhin and anuvyañjanaggāhin in the same way); similarly Śikṣ 357.2, of Bodhisattvas; saced ... bodhisattvo ... rūpe (and below with vedanāyāṃ, saṃjñāyāṃ, saṃskāreṣu, vijñāne, the 5 skandhas) carati, nimitte carati (*he operates in, on superficial appearance*) ŚsP 683.4 ff., also ... rūpaṃ nityam iti carati, nimitte carati 8, etc.; (**2**) *personal, physical mark* or *trait* or *characteristic*, esp. of the body, but also of dress or ornament: mūrdhāto upādāya yāvat pādeṣu nimittaṃ paśyati Mv iii.148.3 (the following details include muñja-mekhalaṃ!); nimittāni 19; as basis for prognostication by soothsayers (cf. **nimittika, nai°**), te tasya nimittam udgṛhītum ārabdhā(ḥ) Divy 579.20; (**3**) (*sign*, in sense of) *hint, suggestion of something wanted*; sometimes with **avabhāsa**, q.v., as in Pali, see Childers s.v. obhāsa, 298; avabhāsa-nimittaṃ Śikṣ 131.6 (designed by a monk to extract donations); na bodhisattvo dānapatiṃ vā dṛṣṭvā nimittaṃ karoti Śikṣ 268.6; so prob. MSV ii.36.12 sā kāmarāgādhyavasitā nimittam upadarśayati, *showed an intimation* (of her desire). Cf. **naimittika(-tā, -tva)**.

nimittaka, adj. or subst. (cf. °ttika 2), *sign-reading, -reader*: °kānāṃ brāhmaṇānāṃ Mv ii.155.18 (prose, no v.l.).

Nimittaprajña, n. of a Bodhisattva: Gv 443.6.

nimittika, (**1**) subst. or adj., (*food*?) *for special occasions*: Av ii.13.5, see s.v. **nityaka** (cf. Skt. naimittika, Pkt. ṇemittia); (**2**) *sign-reader, soothsayer* (not in Skt. or Pali, but AMg. nimittia; = **naimittika**): Divy 131.20 (prose, no v.l.; ed. em. nai°).

[**nimināti**, °nati, *exchanges, barters*; so Pali; in Mv ii.176.12, 14 *nirmiṇati is implied in this sense; see s.v. **nirminoti** 3.]

Nimiṃdhara, (**1**) n. of a king, previous incarnation of Śākyamuni: LV 170.16 (Tib. mu khyud ḥdzin, *rim-holding*, as if Nemi°); (**2**) m. sg., once pl., n. of one of the mountains (or mountain-ranges), regularly seven (with the central **Sumeru** sometimes counted as eighth, e. g. Dharmas 125 where **Nemiṃ°**; see Kirfel, Kosm. 186), surrounding the earth (= Pali id., also Nemiṃ°, q.v.): Mvy 4140 (Tib. as above); Mv ii.300.18; Divy 217.1, 3; Dbh 96.4; Māy 253.29; pl., Śikṣ 246.4; (**3**) n. of a nāga-king: Māy 247.11.

Nimi-sūtra, n. of a sūtra of the **Rājasaṃyuktakanipāta**: MSV i.112.19.

nimūlayati, m.c. for Skt. nirm°, *uproots*: RP 45.1 (vs) nimūlayitum.

nimna, adj. (= Pali ninna; cf. **abhi-nimna**; in this sense once in Skt., pw 7 App.), *inclined to, bent upon, headed for*; often parallel with pravaṇa and **prāgbhāra**, as final in cpds.: LV 180.16 viveka-ni°, -pravaṇa, -prāgbhāra; Mv iii.62.13 nirvāṇa-ni°, pra°, prāg°; iii.61.8, same without °nimna; Mvy 808 (read sarvajñatā-ni°); 5163 (separate word, but associated with the other two); Divy 50.12 buddha-ni° dharma-pravaṇā saṃgha-prāgbhārā; same 80.4; Av i.65.3–4 etc. (cliché); apāya-ni°, -prav°, -prāg° *headed for* ..., Divy 95.28; Av i.16.17; dharma-nimnatā °pravaṇatā °prāgbhāratā Śikṣ 191.8.

nimbarajas, nt., a high number: °jaḥ Mvy 8028.

niyaka, adj., in Mvy 1795, acc. to Tib. rtag tu ḥgrus che ba, (having) *constantly great zeal*; Chin. perhaps *constantly respectful* (?). Tib. seems to indicate (graphic) confusion between this word and **nipaka** (2 and 3), q.v., which itself is problematic.

niyatacaryāpratipatti-bhūmi, fifth of six bodhisattva-bhūmi: Bbh 85.2; in 367.5 called **niyatacaryā-bhūmi**, as 6th of seven b° bh°.

Niyatadhvajaketu, m., n. of a samādhi: Mvy 515; ŚsP 1415.18.

? **niyatana**, perh. *determination, fixation* (an irregular formation, as if with suffix -ana, based on niyata, *fixed*; § 22.7; cf. Pali accanta-niyata, -niyāmatā, (*possessing*) *final assurance*, CPD): ye te gambhīrapratītyasamutpādavyupaparīkṣaṇavihāriṇaś ca na cātyanta-niyatanavihāriṇaḥ Gv 472.11–12; may refer to fatalistic beliefs, in contrast with belief in the **pratītya-samutpāda.**

niyata-bhūmi, fourth of six bodhisattva-bhūmi: Bbh 85.1; in id. 367.5 called niyatā bhūmiḥ, as fifth of seven bo° bhū°.

Niyatāniyatāvatāramudrā-sūtra, n. of a work: Śikṣ 7.1; 87.14.

niyati, *absorption, addiction* (sc. to worldly things): Śikṣ 19.18 (na ... parigraho ...) nādhyavasānaṃ, na niyatiḥ, na tṛṣṇānuśayaḥ kartavyaḥ. Not so recorded in Skt. or Pali; but Skt. niyata is used similarly (BR s.v. yam plus ni, 3: *sich beschränkend* ... *ganz bei einer Sache seiend*). Elsewhere **niyanti**, q.v., an irregular formation, is used in the same sense.

niyanti, nom. °tiḥ, *addiction to, absorption in*, so read with v.l. Mvy 5383 for (kāma-)niyantrī, text; Mironov -niyanti (so!); = **niyati**, q.v.; the Jap. definition (for kāma-niyantrī) means *one who pursues pleasure*; Bhīk 24a.3 kāmaniyantiḥ, without v.l., confirming the form and mg.; occurs in a list of synonyms, kāma-snehaḥ, -premaḥ, kāmālayaḥ, kāmaniyantiḥ, kāmādhyavasānam. The Tib. on Mvy 5383 is confused and contains, after ḥdod pa la, *for lusts* (kāma-), either ḥtsuṅs pa or ḥchums pa; the latter is prob. correct and means *wishing, longing for* (see Jä. and Das, the latter s.v. ḥchum pa).

niyāma, also **nyāma**, q.v., m. (= Pali and Skt. Gr. niyāma; Skt. niyama), *fixed regulation*; *certainty, unchangeableness*: °maḥ Mvy 6501 = Tib. ṅes par ḥgyur ba, *what is certain to come to be*; dharma-niyāma-tā Mvy 1714 = Tib. chos mi ḥgyur ba ñid, *the doctrine's being unchangeably the same*; SP 53.9 (vs); Laṅk 143.13; cittanagaraniyāma-vidhijñena Gv 431.8 (*fixed, established rules*; text °vidha°, but cf. -vidhijñena line 9); bodhisattvaniyāma Dbh 11.27 (°maṃ jāto, *born into the fixed way of Bodhisattvas*); Dbh.g. 54(80).11; sattvān niyāmam avakrāmayitum Dbh 63.14 (see Śikṣ, below, and cf. Pali (niyāma)-avakkanti, CPD), *to make creatures enter into the fixed course*, or *unchangeable condition*; yaiś ca ... bhikṣubhir anavakrānta-niyāmair etad bhojanaṃ bhuktaṃ teṣām evāvakrāntaniyāmānāṃ pariṇaṃsyati Śikṣ 270.4–5. See on this and nyāma Wogihara, Lex. 28 ff. There is no doubt that these two words are the same, tho Tib. and Chin. have a different (and fantastic) explanation of nyāma; indeed, acc. to Wogihara, still other interpretations occur in northern Buddhist (Chin.) texts. They are certainly negligible. Most of the above passages are prose.

niyuktaka (= Pali niyuttaka; Skt. °ta plus specifying -ka? § 22.39), (*one that has been*) *appointed in command*: Mvy 3713 = Tib. snar bskos pa.

(**niyuta**, nt., Skt. id., a large number, in Skt. variously defined; = **nayuta**, q.v.; like the latter usually defined in Tib. by khrag khrig, 100,000,000,000; so Mvy 7702; 7828; LV 147.21, which is cited in Mvy 7956 as nayutaṃ; but in 8056 ni° is defined as only 1,000,000, Tib. sa ya.)

niyojayitar, *one who unites, provides with* (instr.): °tāro bodhisattvasamādānena Gv 462.26.

Niraṅkuśa, n. of a former Buddha: Mv i.141.9.

niraṅgaṇa (= Pali id., CPD s.v. aṅgaṇa) = **an-aṅgaṇa**, *spotless, free from evil* (also spelled with °na): LV 7.1; 179.4 (ed. with ms. A nirañjanaṃ, perhaps rightly); 345.2; Śikṣ 121.2; KP 136.7.

Nirañjanā = **Nair°**, n. of a river: noted only in tīru nirañjanā (gen. sg.) LV 243.12 (vs); i m.c. for ai (MIndic e)? The modern vernacular name is given by BR as Niladjan, by DPPN as Nīlājanā.

Nirati, n. of the city of the king of the Kiṃnaras: °tiṃ, acc. sg., Mv ii.101.9; 102.9; 108.6, 16; 109.2.

niradhimāna-tā, *absence of arrogance* (**adhimāna**): °tayā KP 23.6.

Niradhiṣṭhāna, m., n. of a samādhi: Mvy 591; ŚsP 1423.1.

-nir-abhinandin (cf. Skt. abhinanda, Skt. and Pali abhinandin), *not desiring* (end of cpd.): Mvy 607.

nir-abhiramya (cf. **abhi°, an-abhi°**), *unpleasant*; Mv i.41.12; 230.7; 240.17 (here mss. niramyāni); ii.162.17;

iii.420.16; (nir-ābhi°, m.c.) Gv 334.4; Suv 60.1 (mss. all nirā°, Nobel em. nira°, unmetr.).

nirabhilāpya, adj., neg. gdve. (= **an-abhi°**), *inexpressible, that cannot be put in words*; °pya-svabhāvatā Bbh 41.16; 43.24; °pye vastuni Bbh 266.5; °pyo Samādh 22.33 (kāyo me).

nirayika, adj. (= **nair°**, q.v.), *of hell*: °kaṃ duḥkhaṃ ŚsP 1264.17 (prose).

nirargaḍa, (**1**) adj. (= Skt. °la, Pali niraggaḷa), *unimpeded*, used as ep. of sacrifices in Skt. (among other ways), and so here apparently: yajñā nirargaḍa LV 341.5 (vs); °ḍa-sarva-yajña- 432.17 (prose); °ḍa-yajñāḥ Mvy 2867 (but here could have mg. 2); (**2**) subst. m., n. of a specific brahmanical sacrifice (also Pali, e. g. Sn 303; defined in comm. i.322.4 ff. as a specially elaborate and *'unrestrained'* form of the aśvamedha; Pali Dictt. need correction on this), in lists of brahmanical sacrifices (as also in Pali Sn 303); (mahāyajñāni ca yajāhi aśvamedhaṃ puruṣamedhaṃ) **śamyāprāsaṃ** (q.v., so read for text somaprāsaṃ) nirargaḍaṃ padumaṃ puṇḍarīkaṃ ca Mv ii.237.20 (prose); aśvamedhaṃ puruṣamedhaṃ puṇḍarīkaṃ nirargaḍaṃ 405.11 (vs); (aśvamedhaṃ) puruṣamedhaṃ śamyāprāsaṃ (so read) nirargaḍaṃ Divy 634.7, similarly 11, 18 (°ḍo, n. sg.), 21; not in a list, but app. in this same mg., yajño mayeṣṭas ... nirargaḍaḥ pūrvabhave 'navadyaḥ LV 318.8 (vs), *I sacrificed a perfect nir° sacrifice in a previous birth*. Above, in prose, the word **nirgaḍa** (2), q.v., is used instead.

nirarthaka, adj. (read perh. °thika? cf. **arthika, anarthika**), *not desirous* (of, instr.): aśucībhi (sc. strībhiḥ) °thako 'haṃ RP 43.18 (vs).

Nirarbuda, m. (= Pali Nirabbuda), n. of a cold hell: Mvy 4930 °daḥ; Dharmas 122; Divy 67.23; 138.7; Av i.4.9 etc.; Ud viii.5.

[**niravadya**, nt., a high number: LV 148.7, 8 (prose); the only v.l. is nīra°; but Tib. sgrib pa = nīvaraṇam, as read in Mvy 7971, which is cited from this LV passage; we may assume nīvaraṇam as the true reading.]

niravaśeṣa, adj. (= Pali an-avasesa, defined Vin. v.153.25), (a sin) *that is absolute, complete* (*'without remainder'*; acc. to Vin., *that can never under any conditions be atoned*; CPD, contrariwise, *of which nothing is left, all done away*); opp. **sāvaśeṣa**: MSV iii.111.10 f., 15 f. kṛtena °ṣeṇa etc.; iv. 125.4.

niravaśeṣya, ger. (to a denom. verb based on Skt. niravaśeṣa), *making complete*: AsP 146.17 (tāni sarvāṇy ekato 'bhisaṃkṣipya piṇḍayitvā ... °ṣya niravaśeṣam anumoditavyāni) et alibi (only in this text).

?**niraṣṭa**, so Lefm. with ms. A in LV 210.21 (vs), perh. read nirasta, *cast* (*down*), with several mss.: jarāmaraṇa-pañjara-nirasta-sattva-parimocanasya samayo, *time to free creatures cast into the cage of old age and death*; cf. however nyaṣit, § 2.60.

nir-ānurakta, adj. (m.c. for nir-anu°), prob. Bhvr., *having no one devoted to them, not* (fit) *object of devotion*: sarve priyā ripusamā hi nirānuraktā RP 43.15 (vs).

nir-āparādha, adj. Bhvr. (m.c. for nir-a°), *inoffensive*: °dheṣv aparādhyate (so read) yaḥ LV 342.16 (vs).

nir-ābhiramya, m.c. for **nir-a°**, q.v.

nir-āmagandha, adj. (neg. Bhvr. from **āmagandha**, q.v.; = Pali id., wrongly analyzed and defined in PTSD s.v. nirāma, a 'word' which does not exist), lit. *free from foul odors*; so defined in Tib. on Mvy 6784; otherwise recorded only in fig. sense of (*free from vice*, hence) *saintly, virtuous*, applied to holy men: Mv iii.212.17 (= Pali DN ii.241.14) °gandho; 214.1; 388.16 (= Pali Sn 717), in a description of the typical bhikṣu; Divy 578.22 Mahākātyāyanasya nirāmagandhasya; Sukh 61.4; Samādh p. 59 line 4 (text ināma°); applied to actions, Gv 65.10 °dhakarma-.

?**nirāmika**, adj. (from an unrecorded noun ni-rāma, to ni-ram-, plus -ika?), *calm*: sāgaro ca nirāmiko (so 1 ms., v.l. niromiko; Senart em. nirāmito) kṣubhye (aor.) Mv ii.162.5, *en plein calme l'océan se prit à s'agiter* (Senart).

nir-āmiṣa, adj. (= Skt., Manu 6.49; much commoner in Pali and Pkt. °sa), (**1**) *free from worldliness* (see **āmiṣa**): contrasted with sāmiṣa, Mvy 6752; °ṣa-dharmadeśakaḥ Mvy 842; LV 179.12; 436.2; °ṣāṃ ... prītiṃ Mv iii.125.3; 250.6; -nirāmiṣa- in cpd., prob. modifies prīti, Śikṣ 7.15; °ṣeṇa ... premṇā Bbh 225.12; °ṣa-citta RP 57.11; Bbh 83.10; °ṣeṇa cittena KP 2.4; SP 199.3; (**2**) *spiritual, non-physical*: nirāmiṣāhāra, *living on spiritual sustenance*, Śikṣ 31.4; guruśuśrūṣaṇā ... nirāmiṣasevanatayā (anugantavyā) RP 14.14, *by spiritual service, not aiming at worldly rewards*; in Mmk 286 of the bodies of Buddhas, (yathā hi buddhānāṃ śarīrā pravṛttā dhātavo jane, line 2, sc. as relics) sāmiṣā (their *physical* remains) lokapūjās te, nirāmiṣāḥ tu (text ṣu) viśeṣataḥ 3, saddharmadhātavaḥ proktā nirāmiṣā lokahetavaḥ 4 (their *'spiritual'* relics), sāmiṣā kalevare proktā, jinendrāṇāṃ maharddhikā(ḥ) 5, ... sāmiṣā nirāmiṣāś caiva prasṛtā lokahetavaḥ 7, etc.

nirārambha, in Śikṣ 263.3 °bho bodhisattvaḥ, taken by Bendall and Rouse, Transl., as n. pr. of a Bodhisattva, subject of āha following. Perhaps better: (*a Bodhisattva is*) *free from undertakings*; or with same passage as cited Bcṭ 377.19 nirālambo, *without* (*sensory*) *hold* or *attachment*.

nir-ālambya, adj. (see **ālambya**), *without anything to be supported*: Laṅk 190.2 (yac ca na) kāryaṃ na kāraṇaṃ tan nirālambyaṃ yan nirālambyaṃ tat sarvaprapañcātītaṃ.

nir-ālaya, adj., *free from attachment* (**ālaya**, mg. 2): jñāne ... ratis teṣām (sc. Buddhas) ... nirālaye Gv 30.20 (vs).

nirikta (so Mironov; Kyōtō ed. °ti), *what is left* (of food), *leavings*: akṛta-nirikta-khādanam Mvy 8456, °kti-(Mironov kṛta-nirikta-)-pravāraṇam 8457; (same situation) akṛta-nirikte khādanīya-bhojanīye Prāt 509.10. Cf. Pali Vin.iv.82.21 and 84.14, where an-atiritta occurs.

nirikṣate (= Skt. nir-īkṣ°), *views*: ger. nirikṣya LV 56.11 (vs).

?**nir-iṅgita**, adj. Bhvr., *motionless*; written niliṅgita in all occurrences in mss., except that in iii.276.5 one ms. seems corruptly to have both ri and li: yena bodhi niriṅgitā Mv ii.352.11, 13; iii.276.5, 9, 11, 13, 15; yathā vṛkṣā niriṅgitā (while the wind blows) Mv ii.402.2.

nirīkṣaka, f. °**ikā**, *intending to inspect* (§ 22.3), = **prekṣaka**: Mv iii.12.13, 16 (in 16 Senart °akā with v.l.).

nirīkṣyate = Skt. nirīkṣate (kṣy for kṣ? cf. **parīkṣyate, upaparī°**), *views*: °kṣyamāṇaḥ Divy 408.8.

nir-īhaka, adj. (= Pali id.; Skt. nirīha), *indifferent*; often associated with śūnya: SP 14.5 (vs); LV 176.14; 437.4 (vss); Mv ii.147.17 (prose); AsP 465.19 (prose); °ka-tva, abstr., Śikṣ 262.3 (vs); °ka-tā, AsP 465.20 (prose). See next.

nirīhika, adj., = prec. (perhaps corruption for °aka?): kathaṃ loko nirīhikaḥ Laṅk 25.9 (vs, no v.l.).

(**nirukta** = Skt., *explained*, in: likhāpayen naraḥ kaścit su-niruktaṃ ca pustake SP 342.5 (vs), *a man shall cause* (this sūtra) *to be written and well explained* (commented upon) *in a book*; Burnouf and Kern strangely *renferme, have it well put together*.)

nirukti, f. = Skt. id., Pali nirutti, *explanation*, not necessarily etymological, of the meaning of a word or text; one of the four **pratisaṃvid(ā)**, q.v.; other cases: nānābhinirhāra-nirdeśa-vividha-hetu-kāraṇa-nidarśanārambaṇa-nirukty-upāyakauśalyair SP 41.2, 12; 71.7; nānā-nirukti-nirdeśābhilāpanirdeśanair 39.11; nānāniruktīhi ca kāraṇehi 45.5 (vs), *by various explanations and reasons*; nirukti dharmāṇa bahū prajānati 238.1 (vs), *he knows many explanations of the dharmas*; nirukti-rutebhir Gv 231.3 (vs).

Niruktiniyatapraveśa, m., n. of a samādhi: Mvy 522; ŚsP 1416.13.

[**niruttamaka**(-saṃjñā), ŚsP 1258.6, is a strange corruption for **vipaḍumaka**, or a related form; see this.]

nir-uttrāsam (or, once, **nir-uttrastam**; see **uttrāsa**), adv., *in a manner that causes no terror*: Mv i.207.1 = iii.341.9 (mahāpṛthivī... kampe...) °saṃ (in same cliché ii.10.12 niruttrastaṃ).

nirupaka, see **upaka**.

Nirupaghāta (most mss. nirūpa°), n. of a former Buddha: Mv i.140.7.

nir-upadhi-śeṣa (= Pali nirupādisesa, cf. under **upadhi**, and **nirupādhi**°), *free from upadhi = skandha*, ep. of nirvāṇa(-dhātu), i. e. *absolute, complete*; opp. to **sopadhi**°, q.v.; also **an-upa**°, q.v.; see LaVallée-Poussin, AbhidhK. ii.109; vi.211, 279, and Childers, s.v. nibbāna: °śeṣa-nirvāṇam Mvy 1727; °śeṣe nirvāṇadhātau Divy 22.9; 202.24; °śeṣaṃ °dhātuṃ Divy 583.21.

Nirupamā, a 12th Bodhisattva-bhūmi (one of three added to the usual 10): Dharmas 65.

nir-upalepa, adj. Bhvr. (once in late Skt., Schmidt, Nachträge), *unstained*: Mvy 6672; Mvy 623 = ŚsP 1426.12; AsP 170.8.

nir-upavadya, adj. (gdve. to **upavadati**, q.v., with nis-; cf. **Anupavadya**), *not to be blamed, faultless, irreproachable*: Mv i.117.6 (vs) śayyāsanaṃ ca vipulaṃ kārayate pārthivo nirupavadyaṃ (mss. nirūpa°, which seems unmetr.; Pali has anūpa° beside anupa°).

nir-upahatya, see **upa**°.

nir-upādātṛka, adj. (Bhvr. cpd., nis plus **upādātar**, q.v., plus -ka), *without one who grasps or clings* (to existence): MadhK 286.3 (upādānam api) nirupādātṛkaṃ nāsti.

nir-upādāna, see **upādāna**.

[**nirupādhiśeṣa**, error for **nirupadhi**°, of nirvāṇadhātu: MSV ii.77.11; 87.13.]

nir-upāyāsa, see **upāyāsa**.

nir-upāyena, adv., *inescapably, absolutely, unconditionally*: °na sarvaṃ (sc. māṃsabhojanaṃ) pratiṣiddham Laṅk 255.4.

nirūḍha, ppp. (to ni-ruh-, in sense otherwise unrecorded), *climbed down* (in active mg.): °ḍhaḥ Divy 527.9.

?**nirūha-mārga**, probably a corruption; I cannot offer an interpretation, any more than Senart: (yatrāpi) nirūhamārgaṃ pratipadyati Mv iii.223.18 (contrasted with *whenever he dwells near a town or village*; not however a *wild* or *desert place*, since the following shows that people were present).

nir-odaka, adj. (see s.v. **odaka**), *waterless*: Mv ii.178.10 etāni ca puṣkariṇīni (mss. °ṇīna) nirodakāni.

nirodha, m. (= Skt. and Pali id.), *suppression*; in statements of the 3d Noble Truth, see **ārya-satya**; **ni°-samāpatti**, see this; mg. obscure in (sukhito pramuditaḥ pratikrośaṃ) pratilabhati (sc. in the decadence of religion) purima-nirodha-dṛṣṭaṃ Mv ii.371.(10–)11 (vs); Senart's note has what seems to me an unacceptable suggestion. Could it mean (*revilings*) *seen in earlier repressions* (of religion)? [See s.v. **Rodha** for a wrong reading which would make Nirodha the n. of a former Buddha, LV 171.17.]

Nirodhanimna, n. of a Bodhisattva: Gv 442.15.

nirodha-samāpatti (= Pali id., see Childers s.v. nirodho; helpful but not entirely accurate), an abbreviated equivalent of **saṃjñā-vedayita-**(°**vedita-**)-**nirodha-sam**°, see esp. AbhidhK. LaV-P. ii.213; called the chief (pradhāna) of all samāpatti: Bbh 291.21; others, Dharmas 82; Mvy 1500; in this sense understand Laṅk 24.10 (vs) ārūpyā ca samāpattir nirodhaś (sc. °dha-samāpattiś) ca kathaṃ bhavet.

nir-opadhi (only m.c. for nir-upadhi; see **upadhi**; sometimes recorded as nir-aupadhi, e.g. Ud vi.10, an error or possibly hyper-Sktism), *free from the upadhi, things which attach to rebirth*: Mv ii.239.13 (of the Bodhisattva); 294.8 (here nirupadhi, unmetrically, read nirop°); iii.456.22 (of dharma); Ud vi.10, 12; vii.5; xxx.51; SP 307.1.

nir-gaḍa, adj. (neg. cpd. of Skt. Lex. gaḍa, *obstruction*, presumably orig. *bar*, = **argaḍa**, Skt. argala), (**1**) *without bars*, of doors, in a-nir°, *not unbarred*: dvārā pithetha sarvā suyantritānirgaḍāṃ dṛḍhakapāṭāṃ LV 201.17 (vs); (**2**) *unrestrained*, as n. of a specific sacrifice = **nirargaḍa** (2), q.v.: rājñāpi... yathā Sudhanunā kumāreṇa saṃdṛṣṭaṃ (so with mss.) tathā nirgaḍaṃ yajñaṃ avadyaṃ (sc. kṛtam, or iṣṭam) Mv ii.100.3 (prose); tvayā tāvat pāpīyann ekena nirgaḍena yajñena kāmeśvaratvaṃ prāptaṃ; mayā tv anekāni yajñakoṭīniyutaśatasahasrāṇi nirgaḍāni yaṣṭāni LV 318.2–4 (prose); in vs below, 8, nirargaḍaḥ in same sense.

?**nirgarati**, perhaps rather nirgalati, *spits out*: LV 306.21 (prose) nirgaranto; but best mss. nirgalanto; object ayoguḍāni, *spitting forth*. Cf. BR s.v. gal plus nis, nirgalitāmbugarbhaṃ śaradghanam Ragh. 5.17, which could very well mean *an autumn cloud that has ejected its water-content*. On the other hand, nirgīrṇa is recorded in BR once from Rām. Neither nir-gṝ nor nir-gal seems recorded otherwise, in Skt. or MIndic. Since galati is the regular present to gal, it seems more likely that the best mss. of LV have the true form, nirgalanto.

nirgūḍha, ppp. (= Skt. nigūḍha, Pali nigūḷha; cf. Pkt. ṇiggūḍha = sthira rūp se sthāpit, Sheth), *hidden, concealed*: °ḍhenopacārakrameṇa Divy 256.10.

nirgṛhīta, ppp. (= Skt. nigṛ°; cf. Pali niggahīta, and § 2.7), *checked, humbled*: Divy 401.18 (vs, could be m.c.).

(**nirgrantha**, cf. next; Skt. id., Pali nigg°, *a heretical monk*, commonly assumed to mean a Jain; so clearly, nirgrantha-tīrthakara-Ṛṣabhaḥ nirgrantharūpī Mmk 45.27, text both times ndha for ntha; others, SP 276.3 (to be avoided by a Bodhisattva); LV 380.12; Mvy 3529; Bbh 244.6; Divy 154.4; 155.20; 262.9; 264.17; 270.7 ff.; often mentioned together with **Ājīvika**, and in Divy 427.2 f. apparently means the same as this, as indicated by line 7.)

Nirgrantha Jñātiputra (cf. prec.), also written **Nigrantha**, and in Av Jñataputra (= Pali Nigaṇṭha Nātaputta or Nātha°), one of the six famous heretical teachers of Buddha's day (see s.v. **Pūraṇa Kāśyapa**): named with the others, Mvy 3550; Mv i.253.17 (v.l. Nigr°); 257.1; iii.383.17 (v.l. Nigr°); Divy 143.12 (mss. Nigr°); Av i.231.5 (Jñātap°; best ms. Nigr°). His followers are supposed to be the Jains.

nir-granthi-, *free from knots*, in °thi-śira (n. sg. m. °raḥ), one of the **anuvyañjana**, *having veins* (Tib. rtsa) *free from knots*: Mvy 276. The corresp. list Mv ii.43.9 has in mss. vinigrantha-śirā, which Senart em. to **nirgranthi-**. App. not in the Pali (Burnouf, Lotus, App. VIII, 2); in LV seems perhaps replaced by **ghana-saṃdhi**(?).

(**nirghaṇṭa**, see **nighaṇṭa**.)

-nirghātin, adj.-subst. (cf. Skt. nirghāta, plus -in), *destroying*, in bhava-nirghātiṃ (acc. sg. m.) Mv i.113.4 (vs; Senart is wrong in supposing that a stem in °ti must be assumed; cf. § 10.43).

nirghoṣa (m.? = Pali nigghosa), *blame, censure*: BHS Sūtranipāta, fragment corresp. to Pali Sn 818 (nigghosaṃ, acc. sg.), Hoernle, JRAS 1916, 711.

Nirghoṣākṣaravimukta, m., n. of a samādhi: Mvy 598; Tib. sgra dbyaṅs kyi yi ge daṅ bral ba; the Mvy form is a corruption for **Gīrghoṣā**° q.v.

nirjava (to next), *impetuousity, eager movement*: samanta-nirjavena samādhy-anugamena Gv 434.7 (prose).

nir-javati (Chap. 43, s.v. ju), *rushes forth*: nirjavāmi Gv 434.4 (prose).

nirjavana (from prec. plus -ana), presumably nom. act., *impetuosity, eager rushing forth*, but only noted ifc.

Bhvr.: sarvabuddhaparṣanmaṇḍaleṣu sabhāga-nirjavanāni (strīṇāṃ... sahasrāṇi) Gv 140.26; samanta-mukha-nirjavana, n. of a 'bodhisattva-vimokṣa', Gv 216.23.

nirjāta, ppp. adj. (cf. AMg. nijjāya, *gone or come forth or out*, and **niryāta**, which is app. blended or confused with this in BHS, and which the AMg. word could represent historically), (**1**) *produced, originating, born* (understood as ppp. of nir-jan-; Tib. on LV yas skyes pa, *born from*): anekaśatasahasra-nirjāto 'yaṃ (of a courtesan's son) MSV ii.21.16; prītiprāmodyena tathāgatagauravamanasikāra-nirjātena LV 370.1–2; śraddhāgaurava-nirjātena ca kāyaprāṇāmena Gv 96.20; puṇyanirjāta, *produced by merit* (thru former good deeds) Divy 463.4; Karmav 67.18; (svapuṇyātiśaya-nir°) Jm 22.1; Tathāgatakāyaḥ śatapuṇya-nirjātayā buddhyā ekārthanirdeśo dharma-nirjāto (...dharmakāyaḥ) Samādh 22.9, *the Buddha's body, born of dharma, is to be defined as synonymous with enlightenment born of hundreds of* (deeds of) *merit* (...*the dharma-body*); mahābhijñāparikarma-nirjāta SP 66.9 (for SP 312.2 see **niryāta**); Samādh 22.12 (in SP of Bodhisattvas, in Samādh of the body of the Tathāgata), *born of* (produced by; Tib. on SP las skyes pa) *the* (preparatory) *performance of the great abhijñās*; ato nirj°, *born from this*, Vaj 25.4, 5–6; paśyako dṛśyanirjāto dṛśyaṃ kiṃhetusaṃbhavam Laṅk 360.16 (vs), *the seer is produced from the thing to be seen; what does the thing to be seen have as its causal origin*?; (**2**) app. occasionally = **niryāta**, *adept, perfected, perfectly skilled*: sarvabodhisattvapāramitā-nirjātaiḥ (of Bodhisattvas) LV 2.5 (no v.l.); Tib. ṅes par skyes pa, *made fine, right*, cf. ṅes par ḥbyuṅ pa for **niryāta**, q.v.; acc. to Lefm., sarvabodhisattvacaryā-sunirjātaḥ LV 274.20–21 (Lefm. divides °caryāsu nir°), but several mss. °niryātaḥ, and Tib. tshar phyin pa, which is a regular rendering of niryāta; prob. read so.

nirjita, seemingly *born* (Régamey suggests a blend of nirjāta with nirmita): dharmeṇa kāyu nirjito Samādh 22.34 (vs), see s.v. **dharmakāya** (2). So Tib., skyes pa, and acc. to Régamey Chin.; the meaning seems almost necessary; forced and improbable would be *the* (sc. material) *body is conquered* (suppressed) *by dharma* (in the state of the dharmakāya): cf. dharmanirjāto ... dharmakāyaḥ 22.9 (prose).

nirjināti (see Chap. 43, s.v. ji 2), *conquers*: rājyaṃ nirjināti SP 289.3 (prose).

nir-jvara, adj. Bhvr., *free from disease, healthy, sound*: Mvy 1293.

nirṇayana (Skt. Lex. id.), *settling, deciding*: saṃśayanirṇayanārthaṃ Divy 234.30.

nirṇāmayati, also nirnām°, and (once) nirnam° (= Pali ninnāmeti, only in mg. 2, of the tongue), (**1**) *bends, inclines*, = **abhinirn°**, q.v. (object cittam, and with dat. of remoter object, *to*...): nirnāmesi, aor. Mv i.228.12, parallel to LV 344.8 which has abhinirn°; (**2**) *sticks out, extends*: Mv ii.282.4 (-bāhāṃ, *his arm*) nirnāmayitvā; otherwise only of the tongue: jihvāṃ nirnāmayya Divy 7.6, nirnamayya (or, acc. to Index, nirṇam°) 71.14; nirṇāmya Bbh 376.4; jihvendriyaṃ nirṇāmayataḥ SP 387.9; °yaṃ nirnāmayām āsa Mvy 6446.

nirdāraṇa (cf. AMg. ṇiddāriya, ppp.) *plucking out, destroying*: sarvābhiniveśa-nir° Gv 189.21; dṛḍhātmasaṃjñāśaila-nir° 220.17. Cf. next.

nirdārayitar (cf. prec.), *one who rends, destroys*: (kalyāṇamitrāṇi...) °tāro dṛṣṭibandhanānāṃ Gv 462.22.

nirdeśa, (**1**) (m.) *elucidation*, particularly of religious or philosophical questions; in this sense only slight specialization (as in Pali niddesa) of Skt. id.: lokadhātu-paripṛcchā-nirdeśeṣu Dbh 72.14; (**2**) m., once nt., a high number: °śaḥ Mvy 7792; 7921 = Tib. ṅes bstan; in 7921 cited from Gv 134.2, where °śaṃ, nt.; read -nirdeśasya Gv 106.18 (1st ed. nidaśasya, or perh. nird°?); -nirdeśaḥ Gv 324.11, and ff.

nirdeśana (nt.) or °**nā**, f., *explanation, exhibition, revealing, making clear*: nānā-nirukti-nirdeśābhilāpa-nirdeśanair (four-member dvandva? so Burnouf and Kern) SP 39.11; sarvabodhisattvavyavasthāna-nirdeśana-tayā Gv 496.2, *because of the fact of making clear*...; °nā, (buddhānāṃ ... mahāyāna-samudayāvatāra-)-nirdeśanām avatarati Dbh 56.15.

***nirdeśayati**, see **nideśita**.

nirdeśya, adj. or subst. m. (cf. Skt. nirdeśa, *command*), *one subject to command, attendant, servant*: Divy 302.26 (see s.v. **kāmaṃgama** 2).

nirdhānta, adj., ppp. (cf. next; non-Skt. ppp. to nir-dham-, § 34.11, = Pali and AMg. niddhanta, which is used in Pali of *gold*, jātarupa, and in comp. with mala, both as in BHS), *purged, purified by fire*; of metals: dvi-(read dvir-?)-nirdhāntaṃ suvarṇaṃ (so read for °ṇa-) kuśalena karmakāreṇa supariniṣṭhitam LV 63.12 (prose); in comp. with -mala, *with impurities purged* (as if by fire), nirdhāntamalā Ud xvi.3 (= Pali Dhp. 238 niddhanta°); recorded nirdhā[nta]malo as 'Skt.' gloss for Toch. lyalyitku, Sieg and Siegling, Toch. Sprachreste 359.9 (Toch. Gram. 466.2); in Mv ii.470.13 read su-nirdhānta-mala-kaṣāyāṇi for °nirvānta° (mss. add -vanta!), said of gold ornaments made by a skillful goldsmith.

? **nirdhāyate** or °**ti** (pass. corresponding to the preceding ppp.; possibly based on a MIndic form corresp. to Skt. dhmāyate? cf. § 37.38), pres. pple. su-nirdhāyantāni, *being purged* or *purified by fire*: so read Mv ii.470.13 for Senart su-nirvāy° (v.l. °vāp°), same context as under **nirdhānta.**

[**1 nirdhāvana** (nt.; Skt. nir-dhāv-, *run out, escape*, plus -ana), *running out, escape*: nirdhāvanārthāya (sc. traidhātukāt) SP 90.6 (vs). But most mss. nirvāpanārthaya.]

2 nirdhāvana (nt.; nir- with Skt. dhāv-, *wash*, plus -ana), *washing away*: vāribhūtaṃ sarvakleśamala-nirdhāvana-tayā Gv 494.3 (prose), *it is like water, because it washes away*...

nirdhūpita, or **nidhūpita**, q.v., *perfumed*: LV 30.9; 162.17; 277.20; Sukh 41.7; so also Mironov for nidh° Mvy 6133. All prose, no v.l. except in Mvy.

Nirdhautālaya, n. of a Bodhisattva: Gv 442.21.

nirnamayati, see **nirṇāmayati.**

nirnāda, m. (= Pali ninnāda; cf. also **saṃnirnāda**; Skt. only ninādа; all cases of this and related words, see the following, either occur in prose, or in vss in positions where quantity of the first syllable is indifferent; in many places associated with nirghoṣa, whence possibly nir- for ni- is derived by blending), *sound, cry, shout*: LV 226.17; (? 266.9, see saṃnirnāda;) 401.18; 435.13–14; Mv ii.215.14; 282.2 (so prob. read with 1 ms., v.l. nidāna, Senart em. ninādа); Gv 251.24 ff.

-nirnādana, only ifc. Bhvr., f. °**nī**, = prec.: mahādharma-nirnādanaṃ Dbh 90.4, *shouting out, proclamation*; nāga-nirnādanī (sc. vāc) LV 286.17 (prose; v.l. -nirnāda-, cpd. with next word).

nirnādayati (cf. prec. two and next; perh. denom.), *sounds*, or *makes resound*: (mahāmbudaḥ) °yanta(ḥ, n. sg. pres. pple.; no expressed object, but perh. sc. vasuṃdharām, line 2) SP 126.4 (vs).

nirnādita, ppp. of prec. (see **nirnāda**; perh. denom.), *caused to resound*: °tā dundubhayaś ca SP 51.12; others, LV 11.7; Divy 315.12; 318.2; 320.15; Kv 64.20 (cf. next).

Nirnāditasūrya (misprinted °bhūrya), n. of a gandharva-king: Kv 2.19. Cf. nirnāditaṃ sūryaṃ dhārayanti Kv 64.20 (subject gandharvas).

nir-nānākaraṇa, see **nānākaraṇa.**

nirnāma (m.?; not recorded in this sense), *turn* or *extension*; *course* (of time): kālanirnāmasampanno cāsi Mv ii.158.6, *and you* (the Bodhisattva) *are come at* (or *to*) *the right time* (to retire from the world); lit. *perfect in the turn* or *course of time*. (Mss. kālaṃ nir°, which seems scarcely interpretable.)

nirnāmayati, see **nirṇām°**

nirbuda, m. (presumably = nyarbuda, Ved. and BhāgP.), a high number, = 10 arbudas: Mmk 343.14 daśārbudā nirbudaḥ uktaḥ.

nirbhacchita, ppp. (semi-MIndic, to Pali nibbhaccheti, Skt. nirbhartsayati; cf. the following), *reviled*: RP 32.14 (vs).

nirbhatsanā (to next plus -anā; cf. also prec.), *reviling*: °nām Śikṣ 82.18 (so mss., ed. em. °rtsanām).

nirbhatsayati, also written °bhāt° (doubtless an imperfect Sktization of MIndic nibbhaccheti, as in Pali; see Chap. 43, s.v. bharts), *reviles*: nirbhatsya, ger. LV 319.10 (prose, both edd., no v.l.); nirbhātsitaḥ or °bhat°, ppp., Mvy 7183, text °bhāts°, v.l. nirbhansitaḥ; in Index recorded as °bhats°, °bhāts°, and °bhārts°; Mironov nirbhārtsitam, v.l. nirbhāsitam. See prec. two.

nirbhidyati (to Skt. nir-bhid-, 4th class pres. or pass. with act. ending and mg.), *destroys*: nirbhidyet tribhavaṃ ko 'sau Laṅk 24.14, *who is he that could destroy the triple state-of-existence?*

nirbhukta, ppp. (to nir- plus Skt. bhuj, *use*), *used up; that has served its purpose*: LV 222.17 (vs) nirbhukta mālyam iva paryuṣitaṃ.

nirbhedana (nt.; once in late Skt., Schmidt, Nachträge; M. ṇibbheyaṇa), *splitting, destroying*: sarvāraṇaparvata-nirbhedana- Gv 244.15; -dṛṣṭiparvata-nirbhedanaṃ 245.14; (nivaraṇa)kavāṭa-nirbhedana-tāyai 491.23.

nirbheda-bhāgīya, adj., = **nirvedha-bh°**, for which this is clearly a corruption or malformation: °yaiḥ kuśalamūlaiḥ Av ii.181.10.

-nirmatha, adj. (to Skt. nir-math-, used of *churning* the ocean), *churning*, i. e. *doing violence to* (a figurative ocean): sarvasattvābhiniveśasāgara-nirmathānāṃ (bodhisattvānāṃ) Gv 188.23.

nirmadana, only in **mada-nir°**, q.v.

nirmadhya, adj. or subst., apparently (the part) *off the middle*: nāṅgāre na bhasmanirmadhye bandhed mudrāṃ kadācana Mmk 365.25 (vs, first half hypermetric).

nirmardayati, *rubs* (hands, in reflection): hastau °dayan MSV iv.236.8.

Nirmala, (**1**) n. of a future Pratyekabuddha: Av i.162.5; (**2**) n. of a Buddha: Śikṣ 169.9.

nirmāṇa, nt. (cf. Pali nimmāna, in cpd. issara-ni° -hetu, *supernatural creation*), *a magical creation*, usually concrete, and used as symbol of unreality: (samāsato nirvastukaṃ) nirmāṇaṃ Bbh 63.24 (definition of the word), *in brief, a magic-creation is what has no material basis*; (sarvadharma-māyā-svapna-)pratibhāsa-pratiśrutkodakacandra-pratibimba-nirmāṇa-samatayā Dbh 47.14; sarvatathāgata-nirmāṇāny Gv 469.1; dharmasya nirmāṇam ivopaviṣṭam Buddhacarita x.19, (the Bodhisattva) *sitting like a magic-image of dharma*, i. e. *a 'picture'* of Dh. (otherwise Johnston, ... *magically projected by Dh.*; Weller, *wie eine übernatürliche Schöpfung des Gesetzes*; Tib. chos kyi (gen.) sprul pa, which seems to support my interpretation).

nirmāṇa-kāya, m., *body of magic transformation*: Mvy 118; Dbh.g. 6(342).22. In Mvy contrasts with **dharma-k°** (3) and **saṃbhoga-k°**; see s.v. **kāya**, end. In Sūtrāl. ix.60, 63 nairmāṇikaḥ k°; Lévi *métamorphique*. See also Mus, Barabudur (II) 643 ff. (*corps d'artifice*). In Laṅk 241.7 nirmāṇa-kāyair may be an early occurrence of this; see Suzuki's transl., and Studies p. 145; cf. also Laṅk 314.2. Cf. nairmāṇikaṃ (q.v.) kāyaṃ Laṅk 73.9 (vs), but the same vs 276.10 reads nairvāṇikaṃ.

nir-māṇa-tā (domal ṇ; so all mss.; Skt. nir-māna, *prideless*), *pridelessness*: LV 182.20.

nirmāṇa-buddha, *Buddha of magical craeation*, a kind of Buddha in Laṅk, contrasted with **dharmatā-** and **niṣyanda-b°** and acc. to Suzuki, Studies, 142 ff., 208 f., related to the later **nirmāṇa-kāya**, q.v.: nirmita-nirmāṇa-b° Laṅk 57.10; niṣyanda-dharma-nirmāṇā jinā nairmāṇikāś ca ye 283.6 (vs). Cf. **nirmāṇika, nair°**.

nirmāṇarati (= Pali nimmānarati), lit. *enjoying magical creations* (of their own), n. of a class of kāmāvacara gods, see s.v. **deva** (also called **nirmita**, q.v., chiefly in vss); commonly in lists along with other classes of gods: LV 46.21; 51.1; 150.3; 266.6; 396.15; 401.10; in Mv, even prose, n.-acc. pl. may be °ratino i. 240.4 (v.l. °rati); ii.16.4; °ratī ii.348.17 (v.l. °tiś); °rati i.212.15; °ratayaḥ i.40.15; 229.15; 333.6; gen. pl. °ratīnāṃ ii.163.12, etc.; Mvy 3082; Dharmas 127; Divy 68.13; 367.10; Suv 86.10; Śikṣ 257.9; Av i.5.1, etc. Their chief is **Sunirmita** (once **Sunirmāṇarati**).

Nirmāṇāṅgulimālaka, (?) n. of a work, see s.v. **Aṅgulimālika.**

nirmāṇika = **nair°**, *magically created*; with buddha, = **nirmāṇa-b°**: kena nirmāṇikā buddhāḥ Laṅk 28.5 (cf. 34.2, nairm° buddh°).

nir-mādayati (nowhere in this sense; cf. **mada-nirmadana**?), *washes*: notthitāḥ pātraṃ nirmādayiṣyāmaḥ Mvy 8598 (Tib. bkru, *wash*); (pātraṃ) °yati Divy 53.18; (hastau) nirmādya (em., mss. °pya) 185.21; vārakaṃ °yati 343.1; ādarśo °yitavyaḥ MSV ii.57.18; 68.6.

nirmāya, adj. Bhvr., *without guile* (māyā): Śikṣ 285.9.

nirmālyaka (nt., = Skt. °lya; -ka may be m.c.), *left-over garland, remains of a garland*: °kaṃ yo 'panayeta caitye Śikṣ 307.10; same line Mv ii.393.20, read with mss. nirmālya so apanaye cetiyeṣu.

nirmiṇoti, see **nirminoti** (recorded more prevailingly, while from **abhi-nir-m°** I have, perhaps by accident, more forms with domal ṇ; the orthographic variation probably means little).

nirmita (= Pali nimmita), (**1**) ppp. of **nirminoti**, q.v.; (**2**) nt., *a magic creation*: bhagavān °taṃ visarjayati Divy 138.13; Av i.4.12; nirmitopamaṃ māyopamaṃ SP 137.10, *like a magic creation, an illusory thing* (mirage); (**3**) as n. of a class of gods, = **nirmāṇarati**; so very clearly in Mv ii.349.13 (vs) °tā (devāḥ), the verse equivalent of nirmāṇaratī 348.17 (prose); elsewhere, SP 235.1–2 (prose, see s.v. **samāvartayati**); 237.2, 6; LV 45.11; 50.5 (read nirmitāś for nim°); 213.15; 215.13; 219.8; sg., one of the class, 241.2; (**4**) n. of a former Buddha: Mv iii.237.11; (**5**) n. of a Bodhisattva: Gv 442.3.

nirmitaka, f. °ikā, subst. (nirmita plus specifying -ka, § 22.39), *one that has been created by magic*: °kāv KP 142.4; 143.4 ff., *the two that ...*; samyaksaṃbuddhena yo nirmitako nirmito AsP 442.15, *a magically-created individual that has been magically-created by a Buddha*; sa nirmitako yasya kṛtyasya kṛtaso (= °śo) nirmitas, tat kṛtyaṃ karoti AsP 443.1, *that magically-created form does the act for the sake of which he was magically-created*; same mg. MadhK 47.6; 330.2, 10; 338.7; nirmitikā Bhīk 16a.4, *a woman created by magic* (not to be admitted to the order), so if text is right, mā (sc. asi) °kā; but this may correspond to Pali animittā, Vin. ii.271.17, 23, *lacking the (female) characteristics*; in which case the orig. reading would be mānimittikā instead of mā nirmitikā.

nirmita-nirmāṇa- (sc. tathāgata), not dvandva with Suzuki but (Buddhas) *of magically-formed magic-creation*: nirmita-nirmāṇa-bhāṣitam idaṃ bhagavan dharmadvayam, na maulais (so for text maunais) tathāgatair bhāṣitam Laṅk 16.13. See s.v. **maula.**

nirminoti, °nati (also with domal ṇ), and nirmimīte (see also **abhi-nirm°**, which has perhaps even more variations of inflexion; = Pali nimmināti, °nati; Skt. only nirmimīte or °mimāti, used without the implication of 'magic' which is almost always present in Pali and BHS), (**1**) rarely *creates, builds*, without implication of 'magic', as in Skt. nirmimīte: Divy 59.15 maṇḍalavāṭaṃ nirminu (impv.), and 18 °vāṭo nirmito; (**2**) regularly, as in Pali, *creates by magic*: (**A**) forms implying presents in nirmin-

(cf. nirminu, above): nirmiṇati Mv i.179.7 (mss. °miśati, Senart em., certainly rightly, cf. nirmito 10); opt. nirminuyām Divy 50.3; aor. nirmiṇi LV 219.19; nirmiṇe Mv i.189.6; ger. nirmiṇitvā Mv iii.282.15; nirmiṇiya (mss. °ye) Mv i.366.10; (**B**) forms of the pres. nirmimīte, and others from Skt. root mā: nirmimīte SP 245.11; LV 290.20; (perf. nirmamire, Buddhacarita iii.26;) ger. nirmāya Laṅk 8.2; (**C**) ppp. nirmita (see also s.v.), *magically created*, SP 242.8, 9, 11; 247.12; 248.10 (svān nirmitān . . . viditvā, *seeing his own magically created persons*, sc. tathāgatān?); 307.4 (ye te tathāgatā . . .) śākyamunes tathāgatasya nirmitā(ḥ), *the Tathāgatas magically created by Śākyamuni*; note gen.!); LV 45.11 nirmitapure; 237.7 kaṇṭhaka . . . trāyatriṃśabhavane sunirmito (? mss. corruptly °mitāpsaraiḥ, but the word apsaraiḥ belongs to the next line), *being magically created* (i. e. brought into existence) *in the heaven of the Tr.*; 350.19 nirmitām (acc. pl. m.) abhinirmiṇvanti *they create-by-magic magic personages*, cf. SP 248.10 above; Mv i.270.13; 365.17; Divy 50.4; 128.17; (**3**) in Mv ii.176.12, 14 nirmiṇeyā, opt. (in 14 by em.) used in sense of *exchange* (one thing, acc., for another, instr.); this = Pali nimināti, used in the same verse in Pali, Jāt. iii.63.9, 10. Meter guarantees, and perh. is the reason for, nirmi° in Mv. See **nirmitaka.**

nirmṛṣa, read prob. °**śa,** nt., only in semi-etym. explanation of āmiṣa; doubtless understood as *enjoyable contact* or the like (root mṛś, not cpd. with nis in Skt. or Pali); so Tib. ñug pa, *touch, caress*: (tatrāmiṣaṃ . . . katamad? yad utāmiṣam) āmṛśam ākarṣaṇam nirmṛṣaṃ parāmṛṣṭiḥ svādo . . . Laṅk 180.7.

nirmocana, see **saṃdhi-nir°.**

nirmocayitar, *one who frees*: °tāro mārapāśebhyaḥ Gv 462.23.

niryāṇa, nt. (Pali niyyāna, in mg. 3; Pali and Skt. also *going out*, literally, and so BHS bhavaty aparyādattaḥ sarvapradīpaniryāṇaiḥ Gv 502.15, said of a light from which many other flames have been lighted, *it does not become exhausted by the going forth from it of all the lights*; in Skt. also in mg. of a military art, *marching forth*, as in Mvy 4986 = Tib. mdun du bsnur (rnur, rgyu) ba, *going forth*; and niryāṇe LV 156.12, in list of arts mastered by the Boddhisattva as prince; Divy 442.6), (**1**) as in Skt., *departure*: (bheruṇḍakā . . . manuṣyakuṇapāni vi-[WT ca] bhakṣayantaḥ,) teṣāṃ (sc. bheruṇḍakānāṃ) ca niryāṇu pratīkṣamāṇāḥ śvānāḥ śṛgālāś ca vasanty aneke SP 83.12 (vs), *and waiting for them to leave . . .*; Burnouf and Kern, *matter, issue* (of the putrescent corpses); (**2**) *expertness, surpassing knowledge, skill*, as n. act. (abstract) to **niryāta** 2, q.v.: bahulipi-niryāṇataḥ LV 146.1–2, *as regards expertness in many scripts*; in niryāṇam iva sarvakuśalamūlasya (Bodhisattvasya) LV 10.4 something seems wrong with the reading; mss. vary greatly; Tib. dge baḥi rtsa ba (=kuśalamūla) ṅes par byas pa, *with rightly made* or *accomplished roots of merit*, as if niryāta-kuśalamūlasya (perhaps rather **nirjāta-**?); it is often hard to distinguish this mg. from 3, below; the foll. cases seem to me more likely to belong here: parārthapratipatti-niryāṇa- Śikṣ 7.16–17, *expertness* (not *dying*, Bendall and Rouse) *in accomplishing the interests of others*; so prob. when praṇidhi (°dhāna) depends on this, *expertness, skill in accomplishing* (the Bodhisattva's vow), -bodhisattvapraṇidhicaryā-niryāṇa- Gv 98.8; -praṇidhāna-niryāṇa-mukhāni Gv 490.2; (mahāpraṇidhānabalaṃ vā saṃvarṇayituṃ) (sc. praṇidhāna-?) niryāṇa-mukhaṃ vāvabhāsayituṃ Gv 99.8; less certain, perhaps to (3) *deliverance*, bodhisattva-niryāṇa-viśuddhiparimārgaṇaṃ Gv 59.26; sarvajña-jñāna-niryāṇa-mārgavidhiṃ pradarśayamānān Gv 86.5; mahāyāna-niryāṇam abhidyotayamānān Gv 92.18; surely here, because associated with niryāta, and rendered in Tib. ṅes par ḥbyuṅ ba, Mvy 2543 (tho found in a chapter headed pariśuddhaparyāyāḥ, which might suggest *deliverance*); **-aniryāṇa,** q.v., Tib. mi ḥgyur ba, *not arriving at*, in -anyayānāniryāṇa- Mv 785; (**3**) (= Pali niyyāna) *deliverance, salvation* (cf. **niryāṇika, nair°**), often hard to distinguish from 2 above: na cātyanta-niryāṇa-vihāriṇaḥ Gv 472.13 (this is a distinction of Bodhisattvas in the Mahāyāna); yaḥ punar dharmaṃ pratikṣipati śrāvaka-niryāṇa-bhāṣitaṃ vā pratyekabuddha-nir°-bhā° vā mahāyāna-nir°-bhā° vā pratikṣipati Śikṣ 59.15–16, seems most likely to mean *deliverance, 'Scheme of Deliverance'* (Bendall and Rouse); if so, the same must follow with parapudgalānāṃ ca yānatraya-niryāṇāya Bbh 87.20; śrāvakayāna-niryāṇādhimuktinānātvam avatarati Dbh 56.11; less certain, perhaps to 2 above, nidarśayitāro niryāṇa-mukhānām Gv 463.7; bodhisattvasyāvibhrānta-niryāṇam abhidyotitaṃ bhavati Bbh 258.2; -paramayāna-niryāṇa- Mvy 795 = Tib. ḥbyuṅ ba, *arriving at . . .*; (**4**) *deliverance from, curing of* (a disease): MSV i.x.15.

niryāṇika, adj. (to prec., 3; = Pali niyyā°, nīyā°; also **nairyā°**, q.v.), *conducive to deliverance, emancipation*: nāyaṃ mārgo niryāṇiko Mv ii.200.8; in LV 239.14 Lefm. ayaṃ khalv Ārāḍasya dharmo na nairyāṇiko, with ms. A only, other mss. and Calc. niry°; Tib. ṅes bar ḥbyuṅ ba ma yin te (see **niryāti** and **niryāta** 2). Cf. also **nirvāṇika.**

niryāta, ppp., adj. (for AMg. nijjāya see under **nirjāta,** with which this seems blended or confused in BHS; Pali once niyyātaṃ, in MN i.360.9 [puttānaṃ dāyajjaṃ], *property* or *inheritance bestowed upon his sons*; comm. niyyātitaṃ, cf. **niryātayati**; perh. corruption for that word; or possibly lit. *went out to*?); (**1**) in sense of **nirjāta** (1) hardly used, but seems clearly to mean *come from, produced from*: sarvaratana-niryāta-siṃhāsanaṃ (mss.) Mv ii.312.7, *throne made of all jewels*; in mahābhijñāparikarma-niryātā(ḥ) SP 312.2 perhaps to be read -nirjātā (q.v. for the same cpd., occurring twice); this cpd. is not in Tib. nor acc. to WT in their ms. K′, but may have been omitted by haplography, since the next word is mahābhijñākṛtaparikarmāṇaḥ; (**2**) = **nirjāta** (2), which is very little used in this sense and should perhaps be em. to niryāta, *adept, perfected, perfectly skilled*, in (loc. or comp.): Mvy 864 = Tib. ṅes par ḥbyuṅ ba, *become perfect* or the like; 2544 = Tib. same, or, tshar phyin pa, *completely arrived* or the like; these two regularly used in Tib. for this word: dharmeṣu niryātāḥ syāma SP 60.12; na tāvan niryāto (Kashgar rec. pariniṣpanno; Tib. ṅes par ḥbyuṅ pa) 'nuttarāyāṃ samyaksaṃbodhau SP 241.1; kṣānti-niryātaḥ LV 179.14 (here Tib. acc. to Foucaux ṅes par byuṅ ba); (mayāpy eṣa . . .) dharmo 'dhigato yatra tvaṃ niryātaḥ LV 245.9, . . . *in which you are adept*; pūrvaśubhakarma-niryāta LV 46.22, *adept* (perfected) *thru previous good deeds*; abhisaṃjāta-kuśalamūla-niryātā Mv ii.312.6; mahāyāna-niryātaś ca bhavati Bbh 413.16–17; samantabhadracaryā-niryātānāṃ Sukh 15.14; sa niryātaḥ sarvaśikṣāsu Gv 489.26. See s.v. **niryāṇa.**

niryātanā (to next), *gift, offering*: Sādh 64.7.

niryātayati, °**teti** (also °**dayati**; rare in Skt. except in mg. *returns, repays, gives back*; in general sense common in BHS and Pali, where usually niyyādeti, more rarely °teti), *gives, presents*; act., with acc. of thing, dat. or gen. of person; pass., with instr., rarely gen., of giver, also, rarely, recipient in nom., both giver and gift instr.: sarvam asmai . . . °tayāmi SP 108.11; °tayāmi Mv iii.457.17; RP 56.9; °temi Mv i.63.9; °tayati Mv i.118.11; °teti 119.13; ātmānaṃ °tayet Sādh 3.17; °tayanti Kv 49.1; LV 367.10; 368.5; °tema, opt., Mv i.299.20; °tayanto, pres. pple., SP 13.16; °tayiṣyāmy SP 115.4; °tayi, 1 sg. (pres. mid., for °ye, or aor.? either is possible) SP 115.9 (vs); °tesi, aor., Mv i.49.16; °tayī, aor., Suv 152.10 (vs); °tayām āsa (āsuḥ) SP 165.13; 429.1; Jm 127.15; °titvā, ger., Mv i.117.8; °tetvā i.243.5; °tayitvā iii.204.17; °tya LV 367.11; Av i.70.1; 96.4; °tita, ppp., various forms,

SP 60.9 (vayaṃ bhagavatā hīnena yānena niryātitāḥ, exactly as in English, *we have been presented by the Lord with the Lesser Vehicle*; but this is a very rare construction); SP 211.3 (niryātitaṃ te ... mamaitan maṇiratnaṃ, *to thee by me this jewel was given*); 339.6 (te ca, sc. vihārāḥ, which Kashgar rec. inserts, mama saṃmukhaṃ śrāvaka-saṃghasya niryātitās, *and they have been presented in my presence to the assembly of disciples*); generally the gift is nom., the giver instr., and the recipient gen. (dat.), or loc., with niryātita, Mv i.295.15; iii.57.2; Divy 23.4; 155.12; 274.13; Av i.87.7; 198.11; Suv 146.2; Kv 36.17; etc. Very common in most texts.

niryāti (= Pali niyyāti; in this special sense not noted in Skt.), *goes forth, issues* (unto deliverance); (after clause cited under **niryāṇika,** q.v.) na niryāti tat-katarasya duḥkhakṣayāya LV 239.15 (Tib. translates just like the prec., niryāṇiko or nair°); Mvy 2545 (follows niryātaḥ; Tib. includes the same two translations as for that, one of which agrees with LV).

niryātitaka, adj. (niryātita, ppp. of **niryātayati,** plus specifying -ka, § 22.39), (the one) *that has been* (previously) *presented* (with kalaśa): Mmk 51.9, 15, (pūrva-) 25.

niryādayati (the usual Pali form, °deti, for **niryātayati,** q.v.): niryādayinsuś, 3 pl. aor., v.l. of Kashgar rec., SP 191.2 (vs).

niryāmaka, m. (Skt. niy° or niry°, see Schmidt, Nachträge, s.v. niy° with references; Lex. niyāma, °maka, niryāma; Pali niyyāmaka), *pilot, helmsman* (of a ship): read niryāmaka āha Mv i.245.5 (mss. niryāmukha; Senart em. niryātamukha, which does not seem to me to make sense).

niryūha, *abandonment, withdrawal,* opp. of āyūha, with which it is compounded in Laṅk 80.7; 115.15, see **āyūha**; also in neg. **a-nir°**, q.v. (As an architectural term, *turret* or other excrescence on a building, e. g. LV 10.20; 302.15; Gv 124.4, the word is familiar in Skt.; see BR, pw, and Acharya's Dict. Hind. Arch. s.v.)

niryūhati (Pkt. ṇijjūhai; see also **nirvyūhati**), (**1**) *abandons, withdraws from* (Sheth, ṇijjūhai: parityāg karnā), Laṅk 115.13–14, cited s.v. **āyūhati**; (**2**) at least in Gv used as a near-synonym of **āyūhati,** meaning presumably *effects, accomplishes* (cf. Sheth's second mg. for ṇijjūhai: racnā, nirmāṇ karnā; and so noun derivs.; cf. niryūha as architectural term): Gv 69.23–24 bodhisattvavimokṣam āyūhatā niryūhatā anusaratā etc.; so, parallel forms of ā-yūh- and nir-yūh-, in what must be nearly identical mgs., with objects tathāgatavimokṣam Gv 80.24, 25; 83.12; jñānālokamukham Gv 199.24. This may well be the mg. of nirvyūhati, q.v., in MadhK; discussion s.v. **āvyūhati.**

nir-lapaka, adj. or subst. m. (Bhvr., nis plus **lapa,** q.v., with -ka Bhvr.; Pali nillapa); read so, or nirlapana, for (akuhako) nilapako (Müller 'ni°), *not boasting, free from* (religious) *boasting* or *humbug*: Sukh 26.2. See **lapa(ka)**, °**na.**

nirlikhita, ppp. (to Skt. nir-likh-, rare, in not very different mg., pw), *erased, blotted out, done away with*: °tam Mvy 2595 = Tib. śin tu phyis pa (*wiped out*), bsrabs pa (*vanished*, see Das), bzhar ba (*scraped off*), bsubs (*blotted out, erased*).

nirlopa (m.? = Pali nillopa; not in Skt.), *plunder*: °paṃ harati Mvy 5366; °pāpahāraka, or °pāhāraka (so Mironov), or °pa-hāraka, °pa-haraka, *a carrier-off of plunder*, robber: Mvy 5363.

nir-lomaka, adj. Bhvr. (= Skt. nirloma; perhaps m.c.), *hairless*: SP 94.8 (vs).

nirvaṇa, adj. (= Pali nibbana), *free from desire*: Ud xviii.3 (see s.v. **vana**).

? **nir-vamhaṇa,** f. °**ṇī** (cf. Pali vamha, vambhanā, vamheti, etc., etym. unknown; Deśī bambhaṇī, °ṇiā, *poison*, seems hardly pertinent), *free from contempt* or *ill-will*: of Buddha's speech (girā), nirvamhaṇī Mv i.314.13 (vs), so Senart by em.; cf. **parivambhita.**

nirvarṇanīya, adj. (gdve.), lit. app. *praiseworthy* (so Tib. on LV), and so *agreeable, enjoyable,* of sounds: (śabdāḥ) prahlādanīyā nirvarṇanīyā (411.9 adds **aprativarṇanīyā,** q.v.) asecanīyā LV 52.7; 411.9; adv. °yaṃ, *agreeably,* of the sound of earthquakes at the Bodhisattva's conception, Mv i.206.17 = ii.10.10, see s.v. **ullokanīya.**

nir-vastuka, adj. Bhvr. (to vastu; -vastuka ifc. in Skt.), *without material basis*: Bbh 63.23, as definition of **nirmāṇa,** q.v.

Nirvāṇapriyā, n. of a 'gandharva maid': Kv 5.8.

Nirvāṇāṅgulimālika (loc. °ke), n. of one or (more likely, with Suzuki and Bendall and Rouse) two works: Laṅk 258.4 (v.l. Nirmāṇ°, one ms. Nirvāṇe 'ṅgu°), cited Śikṣ 133.4 (mss. °aka). The first work, Nirvāṇa(-sūtra), presumably means the (Mahā-)parinirvāṇa-sūtra; for the second see **Aṅgulimālika,** °**līya.**

nirvāṇika, f. °**kī**, adj. = **nairv°**, q.v.: Mv ii.33.3 (of dharma); Kv 25.6 (of dharmaparyāya); °kīṃ bhūmim (cf. under nairv°) Kv 24.2. Cf. also **niryāṇika.**

[**nirvānta,** see **nirdhānta.**]

nirvāpanīya, adv. °yaṃ (app. from Skt. nirvāpayati), *refreshing*: Mv iii.341.8 (? no v.l.), of the sound of earthquakes after Buddha's first sermon; but parallels suggest **nirvarṇanīya,** q.v.

[**nirvāyate,** °**ti,** see **nirdhāy°**.]

nirvāha, see **a-nir°**.

? **nirvikalpayati** (if correct, denom. to °lpa = Pali nibbikappa, Vism. 193.7), *makes free from uncertainty* (or *false discrimination*) = *distinguishes, considers carefully*: nirvikalpayanti ca virāgam ayīha (read apīha) teṣāṃ Gv 473.19 (vs); but very likely read nirvikalpa (= °paṃ) yanti ..., *go to virāga that is free from vikalpa.*

nirvighaṭṭa (°am, adv.), *without obstruction* or *disturbance*: utkṣiptaśaṅkāṅkuśanirvighaṭṭaṃ Jm 87.9.

nirvidā (= Pali nibbidā, Skt. nirvid), *world-disgust, aversion from worldly things*: °dāye Mv iii.331.4 (prose; in LV 416.18 parallel nirvide); °dāya KP 126.10, 15 (vss).

nirviśiṣṭa, adj. (nir- in neg. sense! = Skt. nirviśeṣa, Pali nibbisesa; only M. ṇivvisiṭṭha in this sense), *without distinction* or *difference, alike*: Laṅk 141.16; 142.4, 8; 197.18; 231.15; 348.6; 350.10.

nirviṣī (Skt. Lex. id.; Pkt. nibbisī, Sheth), a grass used as antidote for poison, acc. to Tib. a kind of *wolfsbane*: Mvy 5820 = Tib. boṅ ṅa nag po.

nirviṣīkaraṇa (nt.; n. act. to Skt. °ṣī-karoti), *the making free from poison*: Gv 495.21.

nirvṛta (ppp. to Skt. nir-var-, but even in Skt. used in ways which suggest secondary association with nir-vā-; so in Skt. *extinguished,* of fire, also BHS, Mv i.66.1; Divy 157.12; Av i.48.8; and esp. often *happy, blissful,* in worldly sense, also BHS, SP 106.13; Mv i.131.14), (**1**) like Pali nibbuta functioning as ppp. to nirvāṇa and its relatives, *released, entered into nirvāṇa* (oftener **pari-nir°**; see also **nirvṛtaka** and **nirvṛti**): SP 392.9; 393.2, etc.; (**2**) in Mv iii.214.6, 13 (vs) = Pali DN ii.242.18, 243.6, nirvṛta-(Senart with mss. unmetr. °tā; Pali nīvuta-, text with Cambodian sources, others nivuta-, ni- being unmetr.)-brahmalokaṃ (adv.; Pali °lokā, n. sg. f. adj.); (*in such a way that the brahma-world is*) *cut off*; *shut out, excluded* (*from the br. world*). So DN comm. ii.665.19 ff., nivuto pihito (and later paṭicchanno) brahmaloko assā ti. This implies Skt. nivṛta; the Pali nīvuta, adopted by ed., must have ī m.c.; Mv nirvṛta also, directly or indirectly, m.c., perhaps directly derived from a misunderstood MIndic nīvuta with false Sktization.

nirvṛtaka, adj. (= nirvṛta, plus -ka, prob. m.c.), *entered into nirvāṇa*: SP 250.15; 393.6 (vss).

nirvṛti, f. (parallel to **nirvṛta,** q.v.; already in Skt. *extinction,* of fire, so e. g. Mv i.66.9; also *bliss, happiness,* in worldly sense, so e. g. Mv i.293.8), (1) like Pali nibbuti (see Childers) = nirvāṇa (Pali nibbāna); so even in Skt. of Jains, Ind. St. 14.385: Mv iii.418.11; LV 38.1 (vs); 46.17 (vs); 245.11 (prose); 355.22 (vs); (2) also like Pali nibbuti (see esp. Childers), *destruction, annihilation*; but in Pali cited only of *destruction of evils*, whereas app. in Mv i.134.2–3 used of good things: phala-nirvṛty-aparikāṅkṣiṇaḥ (of Bodhisattvas), *not desiring extinction of the Fruits*; v.l. °apratikāṅkṣ°.

nirvṛtta, in a-nir°, prob. error for (a-)**nirvṛta**, (not) *happy* (see BR s.v. vart plus nis, 6): Mv ii.215.17, 18.

nirveṭhana (= Pali nibbeṭhana; to next), *exposition* (verbal): Sukh 97.5, 11 etc., °naṃ kurvanti.

nirveṭhayati (= Pali nibbeṭheti, which also means *explains*; on this mg. the prec. item is based), *denies, rejects*: abhūtaṃ cābhūtato nirveṭhayitavyam Bhīk 16a.2, *and the false is to be rejected as false* (follows bhūtaṃ ca bhūtato vaktavyaṃ, *the true is to be declared as true*).

nirveditvā (?), ger., *becoming disgusted*: Mv ii.198.1. See Chap. 43, s.v. 2 vid (4).

nirvedha (= Pali nibbedha; related to Skt. nir-vyadh-; cf. the foll. items and **nairvedhika**), (intellectual) *penetration, insight*: °dha-bhagakramaḥ Mvy 1210, cf. °**dha-bhāgīya** (Tib. ṅes par ḥbyed pa); °dha-vīrya-vajra-prākāreṇa Gv 161.21; cf. AbhidhK. La V-P. vi.169, '*nirvedha* signifie *niścita vedha*, c'est donc le Noble Chemin... il est donc *niścita*, et les vérités sont distinguées (*vibhājana, vedha*).'

nirvedhana (nt.?; cf. **nirvedha**, and Skt. nir-vyadh-), (physical) *piercing*: bāṇabhūtaṃ duḥkhalakṣa-nirvedhanatayā Gv 495.6, *like an arrow, because it pierces the target of misery*; perhaps by double entente both this and intellectual *penetration* (like nirvedha), vajrabhūtaṃ sarvadharma-nirvedhana-tayā Gv 494.19–20, *like a vajra because it penetrates* (physically, and intellectually?) *all dharmas* (states of existence, and religious doctrines?).

nirvedha-bhāgīya, adj. (subst.; = Pali nibbedhabh°), *belonging* or *conducing to the* (four states of) *penetration, insight*, which are **uṣmagata-** (avasthā), **mūrdhan** (mūrdhānaḥ, mūrdhāvasthā), **kṣānti**, and **laukikāgr(y)a-dharma** (the last = ānantaryasamādhi, Sūtrāl. comm.): Mvy 1211; °gīyāni (kuśalamūlāni) Divy 50.8; cf. Sūtrāl. xiv.26, comm., and AbhidhK., see s.v. **nirvedha.** For this Av once reads **nirbheda-bh°**, q.v.

nirvedhika, adj. (to **nirvedha**; = **nairve°**, q.v.; Pali only f. nibbedhikā, with paññā = prajñā), (intellectually) *penetrating*: sarvadharma-nirvedhika-(all mss.)-jñānatvāt LV 424.14, *because he has penetrating knowledge of all dharmas*.

nirvyādadāti (cf. Skt. vyādadāti), *opens wide*: mukhaṃ nirvyādehi Jm 236.22.

nirvyādhita, ppp. (denom. ppp. from Skt. nirvyādhi; cf. Pkt. ṇivāhia, id., analyzed by Sheth as = Skt. *nirvyādhika), *free from disease*: °taḥ sa ca kṛto me RP 24.8 (vs).

nirvyūhati = **niryūhati**, q.v. (cf. also **a-nirvyūha**), MadhK 298.14; 517.20. It is uncertain which of the two meanings of niryūhati applies here; see s.v. **āvyūhati.**

nirharati (cf. **abhinirharati**; cf. Pali nīharati, in Pali Dictt. said to mean only *takes away* or the like; but it certainly sometimes has the mg. recorded below, e. g. bhūmiṃ nīharati Miln. 219.4, *provides, makes available, land* (which was formerly jungle); also piṇḍapāta-nīhāraka SN v.12.11–12 et alibi clearly means *one who brings food*, not one who takes it away, with PTSD; acc. to pw s.v. har with nis 10, Kern cited from SP this verb in the mg. *bekommen, erhalten, theilhaftig werden*, in a passage which I cannot trace), *produces, makes effective, carries out*: tān (= tām, sc. pūjām; in prec. line abhinirhṛta pūjā) ahu nirhari Bhad 6[a]; yair iyaṃ cari (= caryā) . . . praṇidhībhir nirhṛtā Gv 488.6 (vs).

nirhāra (m.; = Pali nīhāra, which certainly sometimes has this mg., e. g. in nīhāra-bhatto Vin. i.13.3; see s.v. **nirharati**; this entire group of words in Pali needs serious study), Tib. (b)sgrub pa, *production, accomplishment, bringing to pass*: Mvy 6865, see **āṇī-pratyāṇī-**; samādhi-vikrīḍita-śatasahasra-nirhāra-kuśalaḥ Mvy 863; (catuḥ-)saṃgrahavastu-prayoga-nirhāra-viśuddhiṃ ca nāma dharmamukham LV 182.7; samādher . . . guṇānuśaṃsanirhārapadāni śrutvā Samādh 19.1; citta-carita-caryānupraveśa-nirhāra-ceṣṭitaṃ jñātuṃ Mmk 6.2; tathāgata-nirhāra- 6.3; tena raśmi-dhātu-maṇḍalī-samuddyotita-nirhāreṇa 7.8.

nirhāraka, (1) m., some member of a ship's crew (see s.v. **pauruṣeya** 2), after **āhāraka**, q.v., Mvy 3852 = Tib. sel ba, *remover*; acc. to Chin. *one who looks after boats* (possibly *unloader* of freight?); (2) adj. (see s.v. **nirharati**), *bringing, producing*: Bbh 209.22 (durbhikṣeṣu . . .) vṛṣṭi-nirhārakaṃ dhyānaṃ, *bringing* or *producing rain* (to relieve famine; an activity of Bodhisattvas). In Pali nīhāraka only recorded in piṇḍapāta-nī°, *one who brings food* (esp. to Buddha; = **abhinir°**; see s.v. **nirharati**); the same, °ta-nirhārakaḥ piṇḍapātam ādāya bhagavatsakāśam upasaṃkrāntaḥ MSV ii.130.2; °ta-nirhārakaṃ bhikṣum 180.15, 17.

[**nilapaka**, see **nirla°**.]

nilamba, nt., a high number: Gv 133.11; in Mvy, cited from Gv, replaced by **nivala**, q.v.

-nilambha, only in **a-ni°**, q.v.

nilihati (once in Skt. nilīḍha in fig. sense, pw 5.264), *licks*: jihvayā nileḍhum ārabdhaḥ Divy 137.8.

nilīyati (ni with Skt. ḍī), *flies down*: °yathā (mss., Senart em. °tha) Mv i.219.3 (= ii.21.5, where abhi-lī° is read, see **abhilīyati**).

nivaraṇa, see **nīvaraṇa.**

nivartaka, f. °**ikā**, adj. (to caus. of next, q.v.), *creative, productive*: (tṛṣṇāyāḥ . . .) janikāyā nivartikāyā(ḥ) LV 417.11 (prose; no v.l.), *which is creative and productive* (Tib. sgrub pa for niv°); occurs in the 3d ārya-satya, in the Dharmacakrapravartanasūtra, but unparalleled in other versions; sarvakāma-nivartakam SP 211.2 (prose), *effecting all desires*.

nivartati, °te, ppp. nivṛtta, caus. nivarteti (cf. vart plus ni, caus., BR 7 and 8, *verschaffen, vollführen*, and s.vv. **nivartaka, nivuṭṭati**), (1) nivṛttā ratanā trayaḥ LV 421.2 (both edd. nirvṛ°, but all mss. niv°; metr. indifferent), *the three Jewels were produced, realized* (Tib. mṅon du grub, *accomplished so as to be manifest*); divyāni ca saṃgīti nivartetsuḥ (so mss., Senart em. nirvartensuḥ) Mv ii.160.19 (prose), *were manifested, occurred, took place*; (2) caus., *puts down* (under water); tāṃ Śyāmāṃ kaṇṭhe samāliṅgaṃ kṛtvā nivarteti Mv ii.172.4; just below occur nivuṭṭiya and nivuṭṭāpiya, for nivart-, see s.v. nivuṭṭati.

nivala, nt., a high number: Mvy 7864 = Tib. stobs yas *without strength* (as if nirbala!); cited from Gv, which however reads in the corresponding list **nilamba**, q.v. (metathesis of syllables has taken place in one direction or the other). Cf. **nevala.**

nivasta, ppp. (= Pali nivattha, for Skt. nivasita), *clothed*: LV 157.21; ajinena nivasto ca prāvṛto ca Mv ii.211.12; kṛṣṇājinena ni° iii.157.1; often varies in mss. with **nivastra**, q.v., in cpds. where either could be interpreted, *clothed in* . . . (Karmadh.), or *having* . . . *as clothing* (Bhvr.); where mss. are unanimous they should be followed in such cases; where they vary, either may be accepted; in such cpds. -nivasta Mv ii.322.10; iii.210.13; 267.9 (but in 11 mss. °vastrā); Mmk 63.2; 68.25; sunivastā, v.l. °strā, Mv ii.430.2.

nivastra, nt. (see prec.; Senart, ii note 515, regards the form as false Sktization for Pali nivattha, but cf. Skt. vastra): kāścit sunivastrāṇy (so some mss., others °vastāny, Lefm. em. °vastā) api durnivastrāṃ (so best mss., v.l. °vastām; Lefm. em. °vastāḥ) kurvanti sma LV

320.18–19, *some* (daughters of Māra) *made even fair garments appear poor garments*; āhata-vastra-nivastro Mv ii.95.19, *having freshly washed garments as clothing*; in cpds. Mv iii.6.2 (sunivastrā); 167.17; 267.11, mss. all °stra, as Bhvr., and so sometimes as v.l. for °**sta**, where either can be interpreted.

nivāta, adj. (= Pali nivāta, given in Dictt. only as noun, but clearly adj. in MN i.125.6 nivātā Vedehikā gahapatānī, *gentle*, parallel with soratā and upasantā), *gentle, mild*: as ep. of princes, parallel with **maheśākhya, sukhasaṃsparśa**, qq.v., Mv i.350.6; ii.64.15; with akarkaśa, sukhasaṃvāsa, in similar description, Mv ii.423.19; in Mv i.171.4 (vs) Senart em. -nivātā (mss. nivānāṃ or nirvāṇāṃ) in pralalita-(so mss.)-kalahaṃsa-barhiṇa-nivātā, of the Buddha's voice, *gentle as the sweet* (voice) of *kalahaṃsa or peacock* (?). I have some doubt of the em., partly because nivāta seems not otherwise used of the voice, partly because I doubt whether the peacock's voice would be referred to in this complimentary way.

nivāpaka(-bhojana, nt.; = Pali nivāpa-bhojana; -ka svārthe), *rations, food* (provided for animals intended to be slaughtered for human consumption): Mv i.17.1; 25.2.

nivāraṇa, nt., see s.v. **nīvaraṇa.**

nivāsa, m. (= Pali id.), (former) *state of existence*; usually in cpds. **pūrva-(pūrve-) ni°**, qq.v.; with separation of the cpd., pūrve (so all mss., Senart em. °vaṃ) ca nivāsa-vāraṃ (*time, turn*) Mv i.4.8; rarely otherwise, nivāsānuttarya-saṃpanna Mv iii.320.5 (see **anuttarya**), *perfect in the supreme excellence of* (former) *births*. See also s.v. **pūrve-vāsa.**

nivāsana, nt. (= Pali id.; to next), *wearing*, or (concretely) *a garment*, esp. *an undergarment*: (-carma)-nivāsanair LV 249.2, so read with Tib. gyon pa, *to wear*, for Lefm. -niveśanair (mss. mostly nives°), *by the wearing of ... as garments*; parimaṇḍala-nivāsanam Mvy 8525, prob. n. act., *putting on* (one's undergarment) *'in a circle'* (not hanging down before or behind, cf. Vin. iv.185.4, 18); concretely, Mvy 8938 = Tib. śam thabs, *petticoat*: Bhīk 11a.4, see s.v. **nivāsayati.**

nivāsayati, generally as in Skt. *puts on* (a garment, regularly undergarment). So also Pali nivāseti, wrongly defined in PTSD *to dress oneself ... to get clothed or dressed*. It is true that in the common cliché (kālyam eva, or the like) nivāsayitvā, LV 240.11 (vs); Mv i.34.14; 54.10; 307.14; iii.60.3; 255.15; 272.5; 414.5; or nivāsya, LV 407.13; Divy 20.2; Av i.290.16, etc.; no object is expressed. It is unnecessary to say what the monk puts on before starting his round of begging; the gerund however means strictly *having put on* (sc. the undergarment; cf. Prāt 527.8 cīvaraṃ nivāsayiṣyāmaḥ, with Chin. transl.; contrast prāvariṣyāmaḥ 529.1 ff., of the upper garment; same contrast in Pali, Vin. iv.185.18, 27). Once the verb is used in the causal sense of *cause* (someone else) *to put on* (an undergarment): Bhīk 11a.4 nivāsanaṃ nivāsayitavyā, (the nun) *is to be caused* (by the instructress) *to put on the undergarment*.

nivāsikā, adj. f. (prob. to °saka, m., Skt. Gr., to ni-vas-, *dwell*; cf. Pali nivāsiko, m., Jāt. ii.435.14, vs, in comm. repeated with v.l. °ako), *dwelling*: Lumbinīvane devatā °kā Mv ii.145.6.

nivuṭṭati (MIndic for **nivartati**, in mg. 2, q.v.), *sinks down* (in water): nivuṭṭiya, ger., Mv ii.172.6 (cf. nivarteti, in line 4, caus., *puts down* under water); caus., ger. nivuṭṭāpiya 7, *putting down* (under water).

nivṛta, ppp. (related to **nivaraṇa, n** , and rendered by related words in Tib.; = Pali nivuta, which may mean *obscured*, as in avijjāya nivutassa SN ii.24.30, cf. avijjā-nīvaraṇassa in 5 above; nivutānaṃ tamo hoti SN iv.127.26), *obscure* (of intellectual questions), *subject to obstruction*: nivṛtāvyākṛtāḥ Mvy 6889, *obscure and not explained*, and a-ni° 6890; Tib. bsgribs pa, or bsgrib ba, for nivṛta.

niveśaka, f. °**ikā** (to Skt. niveśayati with -aka), *introducing, bringing in*: (prajñāpāramitā na kasyacid dharmasya ...) °ikā AsP 203.10.

[**niveśana**, read **nivāsana**, q.v., in LV 249.2.]

niveśayitar (to Skt. niveśayati), *one who causes to enter into* or *settle in*: °tāraḥ sarvabuddhadharmeṣu Gv 463.10.

nivyāpara, adj. Bhvr. (pronounced ni-vāpara, or the like; m.c. for nir-vyāpāra), *without activity*: kāyaś ca niśceṣṭa nivyāparaś ca Suv 57.13 (vs; Tib. byed pa med, *not acting*).

Niśācarā, n. of a rākṣasī: May 243.30.

? **niśāṭhaka** or **niśāthaka**, in: kalaha-raṇa-°kā(ḥ) Mv i.176. 6–7, ep. of Buddhas; clearly corrupt; Senart em. -niśātakā, rendering (*sharp* =) *redoubtable in* (spiritual) *fights and battles*. But niśāta is not recorded in this use, and moreover I question such a complimentary fig. use of kalaha-raṇa. It seems more likely that some deriv. of niśāmyati, *is pacified*, is involved; a caus. to this would mean *quieters* (of strife and evil). Possibly niśāmakā(ḥ)?

niśādā-putra, m. (cf. next, and Pali nisada-pota; see s.v. **śilā-putra**; = Skt. dṛṣat-putra, *upper and smaller millstone*), *upper millstone*, or *pestle*: Mvy 7516 = Tib. mchig gu.

niśādā-śilā (cf. prec., **niṣidā**, and Pali nisadā, also °da), *lower millstone*, or *mortar*: Mvy 7515 = Tib. mchig, *grindstone, mortar*, or gtun gyi gzhi, *what is below a pestle*.

Niśāntāyu, n. of an ancient king: Mv ii.146.19.

niśṛṇoti (not in Skt. or Pali, but = AMg. nisuṇai, ṇi°), *hears*: gopi niśṛṇohi LV 235.22; niśṛṇotha 296.2 (both vss).

niśṛtya, see **niśritya.**

[**niścayitvā**, SP 48.6 (vs), would mean *having determined, made sure of* (heresies, dṛṣṭi). But Kashgar rec. āśrayitvā, and WT with their ms. K′ niśrayitvā, both *relying on*, supported by Tib. brten nas su; prob. the latter is to be read, mg. same as **niśritya** or **niśrāya.**]

niścara, adj. (to Skt. niścarati), *coming forth, issuing* (of sounds): ime ślokāś ca niścarāḥ Suv 22.2.

-niścārakam, in jihvā-ni°, adv. (= Pali jivhā-nicchārakaṃ, Vin. iv.197.6), *putting out the tongue*: na jihvā° piṇḍapātaṃ (pari-)bhokṣyāmaḥ Mvy 8581; Prāt 533.9; La Vallée Poussin JRAS 1913 (Stein fragments) 846.3.

niścāraṇa (nt.; to next), *utterance*: °ruta-pratiruta-niścāraṇa- LV 435.11; vāgniścāraṇena Divy 116.26; 119.4.

niścārayati (caus. to Skt. niścarati; = Pali nicchāreti), (**1**) *utters* (words, sounds): avarṇaṃ (sc word) niśc° SP 282.13; vācaṃ LV 264.15; Divy 116.26; Av ii.161.10; 162.5; 163.4; vacanaṃ, °nāni, Divy 119.4; Śikṣ 268.3; -śabdaṃ LV 352.9; (**2**) *emits, sends forth*: rays of light LV 274.11; poison LV 306.13.

niścikīrṣā, Mvy 2456; La Vallée Poussin, AbhidhK. iv.189, note 3; or °ṣu-tā, Bbh 168.22 (= Pali nijigiṃsanatā, or °gīs°), in lābhena lābha-(Bbh ed. lābhaṃ) niś° (also **-niṣpādanā**, q.v.), *extraction of a profitable gift* (from a layman, by a monk) *by* (referring to) *a gift received* (from others); one of the 5 **mithyājīva** for a monk; see references s.v. **kuhana.** Wogihara, Lex. 26, believes the original form was nirjigīṣā or °ṣutā, relying on the Pali; I believe the contrary.

Niścitārtha, n. of a former Buddha: Mv i.136.17.

Niścitta, m., n. of a samādhi: Mvy 539; ŚsP 1417.18. Cf. **Sthitaniścitta**; **Tathatāsthitaniścitta.** Tib., all three times, sems med pa, *without thought*.

***niśchavī-kṛtvā**, see **nicchavi°.**

niśraya, m. (= Pali nissaya, not completely or perfectly described in the Dictt.), fundamentally, *support, basis* (Tib. gnas, *place, abode, place of settlement*; or rten, *support*): niśraya-bhūtaṃ sarvabodhisattvacaraṇa-tayā Gv 494.10, *it* (bodhicitta) *acts as a support, because it con-*

stitutes legs for all Bodhisattvas; niśraya . . . śraddha Śikṣ 3.7 (vs), *faith is a support* (see s.v. **aiṣikā**); niśraya-sampanna Mv ii.259.14; 280.1 (here text wrongly niḥśraya°), *perfect in the* (five) *supports* or *aids*, for getting rid of evil and cultivating good; so in Pali nissayasampanna AN iv.353.18; they are there listed in 21 ff. as saddhā, hiri, ottappa, viriya, paññā; by relying on (nissāya) them one akusalaṃ pajahati kusalaṃ bhāveti; in Mvy 820 Bodhisattvas are described as sarvapraṇidhāna-niśraya-vigata, *for whom all basis for* (further) *praṇidhānas is removed* (because they are already *perfect in praṇidhānas*, as stated in Mv ii.280.1 and substantially in 259.14, along with niśrayasampanna); app. *support* (of life; Tib. rten) Mvy 1849; in Mvy 8669 °yaḥ (Tib. gnas), of the four technical '*requisites*' or *supports, supplies*, which a Buddhist monk needs and is allowed, listed 8670–3 as vṛkṣamūlam (for sleeping), **piṇḍapātaḥ** (for food), **pāṃsukūlaṃ** (for garments), **pūtimukta**-(q.v.) -bhaiṣajyam (for medicine); the same four in Pali (nissaya); in this sense niśraya-dāyaka, m., *a giver of* . . ., Mvy 8731; in Bbh 193.2 also four, the list in 3–5 is (1) cīvara-, (2) piṇḍapāta-, (3) śayanāsanam, and (4) glānapratyayabhaiṣajyapariṣkārāś ca; for nuns there are only three of these niśraya, since living in the woods, 'at the foot of a tree', is forbidden to them (Vin. ii.278.14); hence trayo niśrayā(ḥ) Bhīk 22a.5–22b.1; na ca skandhaāyatana-dhātau (one cpd. word) niśrayu tubhya vidyati kadācit Gv 253.10 (vs), *reliance* (dependence) *on* (the external world), *the being based on* (it); in Mvy 5623 (Tib. gnas or rten) the context suggests *residence, fixed abode* (between āspadam and niketaḥ); in KP 103.1 tatra na śikṣā na niśrayo nāniśrayaḥ, the exact mg. is not too clear, and Tib. as printed in ed. omits this phrase; perhaps as in niśraya-sampanna, above, *there is no instruction, no support and no non-support* (for moral development)(?); Chin. *no keeping nor not keeping of the moral code*; niśrayāhṛta (lābha), *received thru support*, MSV ii.109.8, explained 112.15 ff.

niśrayitvā, so WT for SP 48.6 **niścayitvā**, q.v.; so Tib. brten nas su; niśray° seems to be the true reading, as a sort of cross between **niśritya** and **niśrāya**, as if based on pres. niśrayati but ger. of MIndic type; this form should also be read in SP 335.11 (vs) where both edd. niṣevitvā (but all Nep. mss. niśrayitvā) imām kriyām, *relying on* . . .

niśrāya, postposition w. acc. (= Pali nissāya, partly Sktized; a further Sktization produced **niśritya**, q.v., which is commoner and has the same mgs.; § 35.20): (**1**) *relying on, based on*: balacakraṃ hi niśrāya dharmacakraṃ pravartate Mv i.277.3; (**2**) *near, by, at, on, in*: Upatiṣyaṃ ni° Mv iii.271.7 *near, with U.*; vṛkṣamūlaṃ ni° tiṣṭhe Mv iii.53.13, *at the root of a tree*; mahāpṛthivīṃ ni° (. . . sarvabījāni virohanti) Mvy 6368, *on the whole earth*; vanaṣaṇḍa ni° (bodhisattvāḥ) SP 12.15 (vs), *living in* . . .; mātur yoniṃ ni° tiṣṭhanti Mv i.144.3, *in the mother's womb* (and others in what follows); bodhisattvā pṛthivīpradeśaṃ niśrāya gacchanti vā tiṣṭhanti niṣīdanti Mv ii.260.9, *go to or stay or sit in* . . ., also 261.10; cīvarakarṇakaṃ cen niśrāya ākramanti pade-pade, aparādhena tiṣṭhanti na te buddhasya sāntike Karmav 161.1(–2), vs, seems to mean *if they step on the fringe of the* (monk's) *robe at every step* (i. e. who violate or disgrace the monkish garb they wear), *they abide in offense; they are not near to the Buddha.* (Otherwise Lévi, who understands ni° as *because of*.)

niśrita, ppp. (Pali nissita; cf. prec. and next items, and see **a-ni**°), *depending, relying, based on* (normally with acc., or at end of cpds.); sometimes (placed) *on, in* (of physical location): bhūmir na cātra paratīrthikaniśritānāṃ LV 420.19 (vs; so read for Lefm. nissṛt°; some mss. niśṛt°; Tib. gnas); māṃ caiva ye niśrita bhonti SP 90.7 (vs), *and those who are relying on me alone*; viveka-niśritam, virāga-, nirodha- Mvy 972–4 (= Tib. gnas pa); lokanāthānāṃ, kṣetraṃ tattvārthaniśritaṃ Mv i.121.8, *based on* . . .; pravāda-niśritāni Mv iii.400.20, *based on talk, casuistry*; saṃjñākṣara-saṃjñā-niśritāni 21 (on this passage cf. **osaraṇa**); (na ca bodhisattvaḥ kīrtiśabda-) śloka-niśritaṃ dānaṃ dadāti, na ca parataḥ pratīkāra-ni° Bbh 121.23 f., cf. niśritya Bbh 135.5; rūpa-niśritāni AsP 269.1, *things based on form*; dvayaniśrito 'yaṃ . . . loko, yad utāstitvaniśritaś ca nāstitvaniśritaś ca Laṅk 145.4–5; pṛthivī-niśritaṃ Mv ii.435.16, *placed on the ground* (lit. and physically), in 18 reinterpreted with an extension of mg., (a king will enjoy) *what exists on earth* (still physically).

niśritya (sometimes recorded as ni-śṛ°, ni-sṛ°, niḥ°; formally ger. to Vedic ni-śri), postposition with acc. = **niśrāya**, used in same senses; doubtless Sktization of MIndic nissāya: (**1**) *relying on, taking one's base on*: dṛṣṭiṃ ni° Ud viii.7 (same vs Pali Dhp. 164 diṭṭhiṃ nissāya); na pṛthivīṃ (etc.) ni° dhyāyati Bbh 49.16 ff.; (-parijñānaṃ) ni° 55.11; alobhaṃ ni° 125.7; yān (sc. trīn niśrayān, see **niśraya**) ni° Bhīk 22b.2; dāna-vipratibandha-pratipakṣaṃ ni° Bbh 130.2 (ni-śṛ°); *aiming at*, (na . . . kīrtiśabdaghoṣaślokaṃ) ni° dānaṃ dadāti Bbh 135.5; (**2**) *near, by, at*: ye māṃ ni° kuśalamūlāny avaropayanti LV 90.17; vṛkṣamūlaṃ ni° Divy 201.2, 26; 516.6–7; kuḍyamūlaṃ ni° paribhuktaṃ Divy 82.25; dakṣiṇaṃ (vāmaṃ) pārśvaṃ ni° niṣaṇṇāḥ Divy 162.7, 9 (in 9 text with mss. nisṛtya); *in* (the womb), dakṣiṇaṃ (vāmaṃ) kukṣiṃ (sc. *part of the womb*) ni° tiṣṭhati Divy 2.7, 8; 98.26 f.

niḥśaraṇa, see **niḥsar**°.

niḥśrayaṇikā (cf. Skt. °ṇī), *ladder*; in alābu-°, *gourd-ladder*, serving as a *raft* on a river: MPS 7.5.

[**niḥśritya**, see **niśritya**.]

niḥśreṇībhūta, adj., see s.v. **viśreṇīkṛtvā**.

niḥśreya(s), adj. (Skt. niḥśreyasa and MIndic derivs. only in opposite sense, *having no superior, supreme bliss*, etc.), *deprived of happiness* or *weal*: (gṛhaṃ) niḥśreyaṃ saṃvṛttaṃ, sarvā lakṣmī antarahitā Mv ii.101.8.

niṣaṇṇa, nt. (not recorded as subst.), *sitting down*: gamanaṃ (mss. gataṃ, unmetr.) sthitaṃ niṣaṇṇaṃ śayitaṃ lokottaraṃ munino (= Buddhasya) Mv i.167.18, *supra-worldly is the going, standing, sitting, lying of a Buddha* (a Lokottaravādin doctrine); note that Skt. (tho rarely) uses sthita as a noun (like gamana); perhaps this otherwise unknown use of niṣaṇṇa and **śayita** is influenced by that.

niṣaṇṇaka, f. °ikā, adj. (Pali nisinnaka; = Skt. niṣaṇṇa with -ka svārthe, in some cases perh. m.c.), *seated*: na . . . mātā bodhisattvaṃ janeti śayānā niṣaṇṇikā vā yathānyāḥ striyo Mv ii.20.9 (prose); (yadi . . .) svake āsane niṣaṇṇako pratisaṃmodayiṣyāmi Mv iii.114.8 (prose); in vss, may be m.c., (buddhāṃ) niṣaṇṇaku (acc. pl.) Bhad 28; niṣaṇṇakā(ḥ), of Buddhas, Gv 34.17 (in same context with **saṃniṣaṇṇaka**, q.v.)

niṣadana, nt. (in Skt. rare, chiefly Ved., and not in this concrete sense; = **niṣīdana**, q.v.) *a seat*, sometimes a *mat* or *article for sitting on*: Mvy 8514 = Tib. gtiṅ (read gdiṅ with Tib. Index) ba; 8942 = Tib. gdiṅ ba, v.l. pratyāstaraṇa (cf. the Pali cpd. nisīdana-paccuttharaṇa); bodhimaṇḍa-niṣadana, *the seat on the Bodhimaṇḍa*, Bbh 94.5–6; Mmk 131.5; *a king's seat, throne*, ekachattra-mahāpṛthivy-anuśāsana-niṣadanābhiṣiktāni Śikṣ 28.13.

[**niṣadā**, see **niṣidā**.]

niṣadyā (Skt. Lex. id., Pali nisajjā), rarely °ya (with nt. forms, see below), (**1**) *act of sitting*: (mātṛgrāmeṇa sārdhaṃ . . .) rahasi praticchanne āsane (*seat*) niṣadyāṃ kalpayet (*should perform the act of sitting*) Prāt 488.10; (same) rahasi niṣadyā (with a woman) Mvy 8449; as an **īryāpatha**, q.v. (4), Bbh 193.17; antaśo niṣadyā-cittam (so read with ms.) api Śikṣ 17.18, *even so much as a thought of sitting down*; sthānena caṅkrameṇa niṣadyayā RP 45.18; (?)-niṣadya-sthānān Dbh.g. 22(358).9, prob. *places for* *sitting* (short a may be m.c.); cf. also °dyā Mvy 8465, n. act.; as a formal religious practice (yoga), MSV iv.72.16 ff.; (2) concretely, *a seat*; fem. °yā forms Mv i.318.12; ii.398.20; 403.1 (? mss. °dya); Divy 259.10 (read °yāyāṃ with mss.); Śikṣ 28.14; 215.7; Dbh 87.12; Gv 518.7; caṅkramā (iii.420.15 °māṇi) niṣadyāni śayyāni Mv ii.163.18 and iii.420.15 (prose; note the nt. ending śayyāni, stem normally śayyā); acc. to text, niṣadya-saṃpadaṃ ca śayyā-saṃpadaṃ ca Mv ii.262.6 (prose), here °dya- with short a, but śayyā. See also **Sīhaniṣadya** (for °yā?), **naiṣadyika.**

niṣāda, m., in Skt. as n. of a hunting tribe; here = **naiṣāda,** q.v.; in Pali nisāda said to mean *robber*, comm. (366.27 f.) on Jāt. iv.364.14; (*bird-*)*hunter, fowler*: Jm 134.24.

niṣādikā, see **go-ni°.**

niṣidā (cf. Skt. dṛṣad; also **niśādā-**; = Pali nisadā; Senart reads niṣadā by em. except in iii.7.19 where he keeps niṣi°; mss. (except one at 433.3) always niṣi° or niṣī°; perh. popular etym., as if to niṣīdati?), (lower) *mill-stone*: °dāyāṃ, °dāye, °dāya Mv ii.432.7 ff.; 433.3, 4; iii.7.19.

niṣīdana (= Pali nisī°; = **niṣadana**; to niṣīdati, § 22.7), (1) *act of sitting*: °nārthaṃ SP 251.7 (vs); °na-saṃstara Prāt 497.3 ff., *rug for sitting on*; (2) concretely, *seat*, acc. to Chin. specifically *rug* or *mat* for sitting on (so also Pali): Prāt 524.6.

niṣedyati (a sort of hyper-Skt. denom. to Pkt. ṇisejjā, AMg. ṇisijjā, ni°, also nisajjā, = Pali nisajjā, BHS **niṣadyā,** q.v.; the y shows that the verb is based on this noun, and the e can only be Pktic.), *sits (down)*: tvayā pratigupte sthāne niṣettavyam (gdve.); sāhaṃ pratigupta eva niṣedyāmi (so ms., ed. em. niṣīdāmi) MSV ii.68.16, 17; fut. niṣetsyāmi iv.195.6.

niṣkaṭṭati (see s.v. **kaṭṭati**), *draws out, removes*: Mv ii.242.12 (śakuntakāṃ . . . pañjarāto) niṣkaṭṭiya (ger.). So surely read; Senart niṣkuṭṭiya with mss. (except that they read tiṣ- or ti- for niṣ-).

niṣkaṇa, adj. Bhvr., *free from* **kaṇa,** = **akaṇa**: Śikṣ 158.15.

niṣkarṣaṇa, nt. (in Skt. not in this exact sense; in mg. = Pali nikkaḍḍhanā), *expulsion, ejection* (of a person from a place): °ṇam Mvy 8436.

niṣkāṅkṣa, adj. Bhvr. (see **kāṅkṣā**), *free from doubt* or *uncertainty*: °kṣo Divy 619.25; °kṣa-prāptā puruṣarṣa-bhatve SP 130.2 (vs), *become* (see s.v. **prāpta**) *free from doubt in regard to becoming Lords of Men* (Buddhas).

niṣkāruṇika, adj. (cf. Skt. kāruṇika and niṣkaruṇa; Pali has nikkaruṇa adj., but also nikkaruṇā, subst., *lack of compassion*, Pv. comm. 55.23; our form might be based on that), *pitiless*: raudracitto °ṇiko Divy 323.3; °ṇiko MSV i.94.1.

niṣkāsati (unrecorded; seems to be kind of back formation to the 'caus.' Skt. niṣkāsayati, *drives out*), *goes out*: mṛgavyaṃ niṣkāsati Mv i.361.3, *goes a-hunting*.

niṣkāsayitar (to Skt. niṣkāsayati), *one who drives out*: °tāraḥ saṃsārapurāt Śikṣ 35.4.

niṣkuṭa, nt. (AMg. nikkhuḍa, acc. to Ratnach. *balcony, entrance*), *small room* (so Tib., khaṅ phran), *cell* (Kern), *chambre* (Burnouf): SP 83.4 (vs) bahūni cā (so read) niṣkuṭa (separate word, n. pl.) saṃkaṭāni uccāra-pūrṇāni jugupsitāni, *and there were many small rooms* (closets), *narrow, full of excrement, revolting*.

[**niṣkuṭṭati,** *draws out, removes*: read **niṣkaṭṭati,** q.v.]

-niṣkramaṇa, see **dṛḍha-niṣ°.**

niṣkramya (m. or nt.; cf. next; = **naiṣkramya**), *departure from the world, renunciation of worldly life*: Mv i.88.10 (°myābhiratāḥ, see Senart's note); °myasyāyaṃ kālaḥ LV 161.5 (prose, all mss.); °mye LV 184.2 (cf. naiṣkramya 12, 18); Mv iii.407.17.

niṣkramyati (on the surface looks like ya-present from niṣ-kram; actually prob. denom. from **niṣkra-mya**), *retires from the world, renounces worldly life*: 2 sg. impv. °myāhī LV 161.22; 162.10; °myā 163.20; 164.11 (all vss.).

niṣkrāmayitar (from caus. of niṣ-kram, cf. prec. items), *one who causes to retire, depart*: °tāraḥ saṃsārād Gv 462.22.

[**niṣṭhapada** in Laṅk 214.3, error or misprint for **niṣṭhāpada,** q.v.; Chin. and Tib. as for niṣṭhā°.]

niṣṭhapeti (caus. of ni, or nis, plus sthā; = AMg. niṭṭhav-iṃsu, aor.), *makes stop*: antaḥpurikāṃ °peti Mv iii.165.15, *makes the harem-women stop* (their songs etc.).

Niṣṭhāgata, app. n. of a devaputra (sing. in all mss., pl. in Calc., but possibly referring to a class of gods? not otherwise noted): LV 44.13 (prose).

niṣṭhāgamana-bhūmi, the sixth of six bodhisattva-bhūmi, Bbh 85.3, or 7th of 7 such, 367.5.

niṣṭhātva, nt. (cf. Skt. niṣṭhā, used in same mg.), *assurance, certitude*: °tvaṃ tatra gacchethā(ḥ) LV 90.6 (prose), *be assured on this point*. In akopyaṃ tac cakram atyantaniṣṭhatvāt LV 422.17 (prose), the last word must be interpreted as atyanta-niṣṭha, Bhvr., *having infinite certitude* (or the like; Skt. niṣṭhā) plus -tva.

niṣṭhāna (nt.? in Skt. Lex. said to mean *sauce, condiment*; cited once by BR from Rām., in passage where the mg. given below would fit very well; = AMg. ṇiṭṭhāna, ni°, defined as *wholesome food; eatables*, Ratnach.), *food*, seemingly of any kind (served to monks): sapta-saptehi niṣṭhānehi Mv i.325.11, (seven servants served each monk) *with seven dishes of food each*.

niṣṭhā-pada, Laṅk 123.7, and (doubtless by error written) niṣṭhāpāda 160.16, or niṣṭhapada 214.3, *fundamental term* (Suzuki *inexhaustible vow*), cf. **aniṣṭhāpada,** which seems used as a synonym. They are ten, and furnish the basis for the ten mahāpraṇidhānas: see Dbh 17.1 ff. where they are listed; cf. Suzuki, Studies, 231 note 1 and Glossary, which gives the list s.v. daśa-ni°. Dbh 17.1 tāni ca mahāpraṇidhānāni daśabhir niṣṭhāpadair abhinir-harati, *he effects the 10 vows by ten fundamental terms*; the list here is sattva-(dhātu-niṣṭhā), loka-, ākāśa-, dharma-, nirvāṇa-, buddhotpāda-, tathāgatajñāna-, cittālambana-, buddhaviṣayajñānapraveśa-, and lokavartanīdharmavar-tanījñānavartanī-(dhātuniṣṭhā). Suzuki's list is identical except for omission of praveśa in 9.

niṣṭhāpana, nt., *conclusion* (? Pali niṭṭhāna), one of the 8 reasons for kaṭhinoddhāra: MSV ii.161.15, 17; 162.5; 164.2.

(**niṣṭhita** [= the regular Skt. niṣṭhita, Pali niṭṭhita; regarded as obscure by Divy, Index], *ready, fixed, properly arranged* or *done*; esp. °ta-cīvara, *having his* (three monkish) *robes all fixed, provided*: Prāt 490.10 ff. (so Chin., *au complet*); RP 5.1; Divy 18.20; 565.25; also [tasmiṃś ca stūpe sarvajātakṛta-]niṣṭhite Divy 245.8.)

niṣṭhīva, m. (= Skt. Lex. id.; M. ṇiṭṭhīva), *spittle*: Kalpanāmaṇḍitikā, Lüders, Kl. Skt. Texte 2.44.

niṣpad (root-noun to niṣ-pad-; in mg. = Skt. niṣpatti; cf. next; Pali, see below), *accomplishment, attainment*: yāvad arthasya niṣpadaḥ (abl.) Ud xvi.2, *until attainment of the goal*; Chakravarti with only ms. reported niṣpātaḥ, metr. impossible (end of anuṣṭubh line); same vs in Pali SN i.225.33 yāva atthassa nippadā (abl.; to read nip-phādā, as nom. of a stem *nipphādar, with PTSD, is impossible on both metrical and formal grounds).

niṣpadi (m.c. for °dī? = **niṣpad,** and Skt. niṣpatti; Sheth cites a Pkt. ṇippaddi [! possibly read ṇippadi?] by the side of ṇippatti and ṇipphatti), *production, attainment, accomplishment*: tasya mi niṣpadi bheṣyati adya LV 287.8, 10 = Tib. de ni de riṅ ṅa la ḥgrub par ḥgyur, *that today for me at accomplishment arrives*. It seems that niṣpadi must be a nom. sg.; this seems confirmed by 287.6 where Lefm. prints the same reading, but Tib. has thob par, *obtaining, getting*, = prāpti, instead of ḥgrub par = niṣpadi, thus confirming the v.l. of the best mss. prāpti bhaviṣyati instead of niṣpadi bheṣyati; it would be very forced, in view of n. sg. prāpti (and for other reasons), to see anything but a n. sg. in niṣpadi.

[**niṣpanda**, for **niṣyanda**, q.v., at LV 5.1 (prose).]

niṣparidāha, adj. Bhvr. (see **paridāha**), *free from feverish longing*: Mvy 465 (Tib. renders pari° by yoṅs su gduṅ ba, *great desire*, also *distress*); śītalo niṣparidāhaḥ Samādh 22.12 (parallel śītalo, *cool*, shows that lit. mg. is still felt in the word, tho both are certainly used in this fig. sense); LV 279.4; Sukh 19.16; Śikṣ 121.9.

[**niṣparuṣa**, error for **niṣpuruṣa**, q.v.]

niṣpalāpa, see s.v. **palāva**.

niṣpalāyati, °**te** (in Śikṣ written niḥpalāyate; seems unrecorded anywhere), *runs away*: Divy 151.21, 23; 164.3, 18, 26; 170.7, 9; 186.23; 527.10; Śikṣ 72.16; 74.14; caus. niṣpālāyita, f. °tā, ppp. (see § 38.14), *banished, forced to flee*: paraviṣayaṃ °yitā Bhīk 28b.1; niṣpalānaḥ (ppp.) MSV i.288.10.

niṣpalāva, see **palāva**.

[**niṣpāta**, see **niṣpad**.]

niṣpādanā = **niścikīrṣā**, °**ṣutā**, q.v.: in lābhena lābha-niṣ° Mvy 2497.

niṣpādita, *prepared, made ready*: °ta-pāṇi-pātraḥ MSV i.222.7, *having prepared his hands and bowl* (for eating, sc. by washing them).

niṣpālāyitā, see **niṣpalāyati**.

niṣpīḍayati (Skt., and Pali nippīḷeti, in other mgs.), *torments* (the body, by asceticism): LV 251.5, 7 (kāyaṃ; parallel with nigṛhṇīte).

niṣpīḍin, in su-niṣpīḍi-hanuḥ Gv 401.2–3, (having a jaw) *that produces a tight, contracted pronunciation in speech*; on the meaning of niṣ-pīḍ in phonetics see BR s.v. pīḍ with nis, end. The mg. is confirmed by **apa-vivāraḥ**, q.v., in the same passage.

niṣpīṣati (see § 28.4 and Chap. 43, s.v. pīṣ-ayati), *crushes*: °ṣanto MSV ii.76.7 (see **abhiniṣpeṣayati**).

niṣpudgala (also written niḥp°), adj. Bhvr. (see **pudgala**), *without personality*: °lāḥ sarvadharmāḥ Mvy 158; Vaj 38.5; -tva, nt., *state of being ...*, °tvena samā sānuttarā samyaksaṃbodhiḥ Vaj 41.18; °leṣu dharmeṣu KP 97.2.

niṣpuruṣa, adj. Bhvr. (occurs in Skt.; but special uses noted here are not recorded there; = Pali nippurisa, e. g. °sehi turiyehi DN ii.21.10, comm. ii.455.4 purisavirahitehi, explaining further that all participants in the performance, not only the instrument-players, were women), *without men, performed by women only*: °ṣeṇa tūryeṇa krīḍati (°te) Av i.321.7, see Speyer's Index (Tib. cited by Feer as bud med ḥba zhig, which means (*with*) *women only*); same phrase erroneously written niṣparuṣeṇa ... Divy 3.24 (here v.l. niṣpur°); 442.13; 460.4; niṣpuruṣeṇa (mss. mostly niḥp°) nāṭakena Mv iii.165.6; 177.5; niṣpuruṣeṇa (nāṭakena must be intended, as the next sentence, 148.1, shows, and was prob. actually in the text; mss. corruptly kena, na-kena) Mv ii.147.19.

? **niṣpula**, nt. (Mironov niṣphalam, v.l. niṣpulam, nippulam; Kyoto ed. has the same vv.ll.), acc. to one Tib. gloss, sñigs ma med pa, *without impurity* (sediment) Mvy 7635; so one Chin. interpretation; precedes apagataphalguḥ (see **phalgu**), of similar mg.; AMg. pula is cited Ratnach. v.73 as meaning *tumour*, but whether it is connected with our word does not appear; another Tib. gloss is śin tu (or, te) med pa, which would seem to mean *completely non-existent* (unless we should em. śin tu or te to śiṅ tog, *fruit*, in which case the cpd. would mean *without fruit*, niṣphala). Very obscure.

niṣpeṣaṇa (nt.) = **naiṣpeṣikatā**, q.v.: RP 15.10, see s.v. **kuhana**.

niṣ-poṣa, see **poṣa**.

niṣ-pratibhāna, see **pratibhāna**: miswritten niṣpratibhāta in MSV ii.101.14.

niṣpratimāna, adj. Bhvr. (to Skt. pratimāna), *matchless*: °na-dhvajā(ḥ) Mv i.176.6, *having a matchless standard* (viz. the dharmadhvaja, just mentioned), said of Buddhas.

niṣprapañca, see **prapañca**.

niṣprabhaṃkara, adj. (cf. **prabhaṃkara**, and Skt. niṣprabha, *splendorless*), *making bereft of splendor*: °karasya LV 9.11 (written niḥpr°).

niṣprabhīkṛta, adj. (ppp., to *°bhī-karoti, to Skt. niṣprabha, see prec.), *made without splendor*: prabhā niṣprabhīkṛtā Divy 474.19; 476.25.

niṣprāṇa(ka), see **prāṇa(ka)**.

niṣprītika, adj. (= Pali nippītika), *free from* (disturbing) *joys*; here and in Pali as ep. of the third dhyāna: LV 129.8; 344.1; Mv i.228.8; Mvy 1480 (all substantially the same prose passage).

niṣyanda, m. (see also **nisyanda** and **syanda**; = Pali nissanda), *issue, outcome, natural result*; Tib. regularly rgyu mthun pa = *cause-correspondence*, i. e. what follows naturally from an antecedent cause: (sarvabodhisattva)-cari-niṣyanda-(so read for text niṣpanda, without v.l.; Tib. as above) -niṣpatti-phalādhigama-parikīrtano LV 5.1 (prose), *description of the attainment of fruit in* (by) *achievement of the natural result of all* (his previous) *course as a Bodhisattva*; svapuṇya-vipāka-niṣyanda-parimaṇḍite siṃhāsane LV 30.7; LV 126.11, see **sarvauṣadhi-ni°**; acintvaḥ puṇyavipāka-niṣyanda iti LV 278.9; buddhānāṃ śubhaniṣyandānāṃ Mv i.169.3 (vs), *characterized by excellent results* (of their actions); ii.230.7 mātāpitugāravasya ni°; 270.15 (here by em., text uncertain); 359.7 (śīlasya); °daḥ sa Tathāgataḥ puṇyānāṃ Mvy 373, *the T. is the result of meritorious deeds*; karmaniṣyando jātiḥ Dbh 48.31, *birth is the natural result of action* (in pratītyasamutpāda); niṣyandato Bbh 13.12, *in regard to the outcome* (of cittotpāda); prajñāpāramitā-niṣyandena AsP 74.11, *as a result of ...*; tathāgatadharmadeśanā-niṣyandena Gv 319.1; bodhisattva-saṃbhāra-bala-niṣyandā(ḥ) Gv 524.5, *the outcome, results of ...*; °da-phala, one of the five **phala** (q.v.), Mvy 2272, acc. to Sūtrāl. xvii.31 of karuṇā; comm. there explains, svabhāvadatvena ... viśiṣṭakaruṇāphaladānāt; Bbh 102.17, explained in 22 f., kuśalābhyāsāt kuśalārāmatā kuśalabahulatā pūrvakarmasādṛśyena vā paścātphalānuvartanatā.

niṣyanda-buddha, *issuance*-(or *natural-result*)-*Buddha*, a kind of Buddha in Laṅk 56.8, 14; 57.8; 283.6; contrasting with dharmatā- and nirmāṇa-b°, and acc. to Suzuki, Studies, 142 ff., 208 f., an early form of the later **saṃbhoga-kāya**, q.v.

niṣyandāyate (denom. to **niṣyanda**), *results naturally from* (abl., or gen.): (tathāgatadharmadeśanāyā eva ...) eṣa °yate AsP 4.13.

nisaṃśayam, adv. (m.c. for Skt. niḥs°, niss°), *without doubt*: LV 316.10 (vs).

nisattva, adj. (m.c. for Skt. niḥ-s°), *without essence*: śūnya nisattva Śikṣ 336.4 (vs).

nisṛjā, *giving up, renunciation*: °jā-paryāyāḥ Mvy 2546 = Tib. spaṅs pa. Cf. **niḥsarga**.

[**nisṛtya**, see **niśritya**.]

[**nistara**, see **nistāra**.]

nistāḍana (nt.; to next), *the striking down, overcoming, subduing*: Gv 495.6 (prose), see s.v. **satkāya**.

nistāḍeti (for °ḍayati; cf. prec., and Pali nitāḷeti Jāt. iv.347.27, comm. paharitvā gaṇhati; neither nistāḍ- nor ni-tāḍ- has been noted otherwise), *strikes down*: °ḍeti, °ḍitvā, °ḍetvā, ppp. °ḍita, Mv ii.76.1–3, 12. Only nis- recorded here, never ni-.

nistāra, m. (so Mironov with v.l. nistara, which Kyoto ed. reads with v.l. nistāra; only the latter recorded in Skt., Pali nitthāra, also ne°, AMg. ṇitthāra), *finishing, termination*: Mvy 7209 = Tib. zin pa, or mthar phyin pa, or ṅes par brgal ba, all substantially same mg.

nistīraṇa, (to next, plus -ana), *accomplishment*: LV 429.18; Dbh 3.22 (pratisaṃvid-bhūmi-°ṇāya); 4.7; 42.21; Gv 201.25; 344.19 (-samārambha-nis°); all prose.

nistīrati or **°rayati,** ppp. °rita (see § 38.10; cf. Skt. nistarati, AMg. ṇittharaṇa, *a successful performance*; Pkt. tīrei, *accomplishes*, Sheth; see also prec.), *accomplishes*: su-nistīrita-kauśalya- Dbh 3.20, *well accomplished*. See also **nitīrayati.**

nisyanda, m. (= **niṣyanda,** q.v.), *outcome, result*: sādhuḥ puṇyasya °daḥ LV 280.22 (vs).

nisrāva, m. (Skt. not in this sense), *issue* (of the body) = *offspring*: mamaiṣo aṅga-nisrāvo (mss. niśr°) Mv iii.144.8, *fruit of my body*.

nisvara (cf. niḥsvarate), *sound*: °rāt Divy 447.16 (same passage MSV i.140.15 nisvanāt).

niḥsara- (evidently from Skt. niḥ-sṛ-), acc. to Tib. phu chu, *mountain torrent*: -dhārāḥ Mvy 4186.

niḥsaraṇa (cf. also **a-niḥ°, niḥsṛti**; often written niḥśar°; = Pali nissaraṇa), nt. (in Mvy 1201 m. in Kyoto ed., but nt. in Mironov), *escape* (from the world), *salvation*; in this sense only lex. in Skt., where the word is however standardly used as (means of) *riddance* (from anything). It has this mg. also in BHS; esp. *getting rid* of evil or misfortune, as Bhīk 28b.5, MSV iii.7.15 *escape* from religious punishment; or *riddance* from sins, Mvy 1597 ff.; Śikṣ 64.14; 191.7 āpattiṣu niḥśaraṇajñānam (Translation wrong); jara-niḥs° *from old age* LV 174.18; more generally loka-niḥs° *from the world* Gv 191.25; bhavaniḥsaraṇe (so read with v.l. and citation Śikṣ 203.16 [ś for s] for Lefm. bhavani saraṇe, unmetr.) LV 173.12, *from existence*. The last two mean virtually *salvation*, mokṣa, and show how hard it is to draw a clear line between the standard Skt. and the specialized Pali-BHS mg. Substantially *salvation* is the mg. in LV 346.2 asya ... duḥkhaskandhasya niḥśaraṇam, *salvation from this* (world which is a) ... *mass of misery*; Mv i.73.6 so hi niḥsaraṇam (all mss. s, Senart ś) uttamaṃ prabhuḥ, *he, the Lord, is the supreme salvation*; i.180.5 niḥśaraṇajñaś ca (here all mss. ś, Senart em. s!; he also em. wrongly °jñasya); ii.418.8; Mvy 853 anantakalpakoṭī-niḥsaraṇa-kuśalaḥ, *skilled in* (attaining) *salvation after endless crores of kalpas* (said of a Bodhisattva); Divy 616.23; Śikṣ 236.7; KP 64.8; sa-niḥsaraṇam Bbh 219.4, 8, of dharma, *containing* (bringing) *salvation*; niḥsaraṇaprajña (= Pali nissaraṇa-pañña; -prajña can be defended as Bhvr., *having knowledge of salvation*, but may also be a MIndicism, cf. -prājña below) *knowing salvation* Mvy 1105 (of śrāvakas); Mv iii.201.6; niḥśaraṇa-prājña (so with 1 ms.; Tatpuruṣa), id., Mv iii.52.5; others, see **a-niḥsaraṇa.**

niḥsaraṇīya, adj. (to Skt. niḥsaraṇa, *riddance*, plus -īya), *relating* (conducing) *to riddance* (of evil qualities in man): ṣaḍ-niḥsaraṇīya-dhātavaḥ Mvy 1596, *the six elements that lead to* ..., listed 1597–1602, e. g. vihiṃsā-niḥsaraṇam karuṇā 1598.

niḥsarita, nt., Gv 351.19; see s.v. **āsarita.**

niḥsarga (m.; not in Pali, except paṭi-nissagga, see **pratiniḥs°**), *abandonment* (= prati-niḥs°): sarvopadhi-ni° (Bhvr.) LV 392.11 (Tib. bor ba, *forsaking*); 395.21 (both prose), *abandoning all upadhi*, ep. of dharma. Cf. **nisṛjā.**

niḥsargika, adj. (also **naiḥs°**; = Pali nissaggiya, there as a group among the pācittiya offenses), *involving forfeiture* (of a monk's right to share in garments belonging to the order, SBE 13.18, note 1); °kāḥ **pātayantikā** (q.v.) dharmāḥ Prāt 490.8; °kā pātayantikā (subst., without dharma) 11 ff.

niḥsṛti (f.) = **niḥsaraṇa,** *deliverance, salvation*: hīnayāna-°tiṃ cārabhya mahāyāna-°tiṃ vā ~~Bbh~~ 223.2.

niḥsvarate, *emits sounds, cries*: °rante Mv i.14.16 (so 5 mss., the sixth °svasante; Senart em. °svanante, but this seems to me no better than the mss. reading; Senart assumes the correct mg.). See **nisvara.**

[**Nihatatejas,** read **Anihata°** q.v.]

Nihatadhīra, n. of a Bodhisattva: Gv 442.23. Here to read Anihata° one must em. preceding final -sya to -syā; and the cpd. seems possible as it stands: *one who has struck down the stout*, i. e. *heroic*.

nihitaka, f. **°ikā** (Skt. nihita plus specifying ka, § 22.39), *the one that had been deposited*: Mv i.353.13.

Nihitaguṇodita, n. of a Bodhisattva: Gv 442.11.

nihīnataraka, adj. (compv. of nihīna plus ka), *rather low* or *mean*: Bbh 16.2, 9 (the latter quoted s.v. **utkṛṣṭataraka,** q.v.; in the former the contrasting word is utkṛṣṭatarebhyaḥ, without ka.).

ni-huhuṃka, adj. (= Pali id., in same vs as Mv, Vin. i.3.5), *one who is not characterized by using the interjection* **huhuṃ,** q.v.; i. e., one who is not haughty or irritable: Mv iii.325.7 (so Senart; mss. slightly corrupt).

nīgha, m. (see **nigha, anigha**), *evil*: Mv ii.374.23, by Senart's plausible em., na tasya nīgho (mss. nīyo) bhavati janasya, *to that man no evil comes*; the Pali dukkha, given by Pali comms. for nīgha, fits here very well.

nīcataraka, adj. (cf. Pali nīcatara, Dhp. comm. i.111.12; Skt. nīcaistara), *lower*: Mvy 8603 (see s.v. **uccataraka**).

? **nīḍaka,** seems to represent corruptly a form of **aneḍaka,** q.v.: madhv iva nīḍakāt sravat MSV i.270.19 (vs); surely corrupt; Tib. cited as sbraṅ rtsi ma bskol (= aneḍaka, see Mvy 5729) ro (*taste*, = rasa) lta bu (*like*); the last suggests rasa-vat, which would be unmetr. (end of śloka line).

nītārtha, adj. (cf. BR s.v. nī, 12, *establish, determine*; = Pali nītattha), *of clear, definite, well-established meaning*; opp. a-nītārtha or **neyārtha,** *having a meaning that is not* (clearly) *established, that has to be determined* (by inference or the like); see LaVallée-Poussin, AbhidhK. ix.246–8 for very complete and illuminating discussion of these terms in Pali and BHS. (In Pali neither is ipso facto preferred to the other; one errs only in interpreting one as if it were the other, nītattha as neyyattha, or vice versa; see esp. AN i.60.13–15, and comm. ii.118.7–27; Dīpav. 5.34, Oldenberg p. 36, and LaV-P. l.c.) In BHS a nītārtha text, *de sens explicite* (La V-P.), is recommended as a guide in preference to one that is neyārtha, Mvy 1549; Bbh 257.10 ff. Equivalent to neyārtha is a-nītārtha, for which see LaV-P. l.c. 248.

nīti, f. (seems not used in quite this sense elsewhere), *management, control*, and so *object of management, thing under control*: sarvā eṣā bodhisattvānāṃ nīti Mv i.135.4; sarvāṇy etāni bo° nītiḥ 9 (prose).

Nīlaka, n. of a hunter (in the story of the deer **Śiriprabha**): Mv ii.234.19.

Nīla-kāyika, n. of a class of gods, noted only in LV 383.9 °kair devaputrair, and 11 **Vairocano** (q.v., 7) nāma Nīlakāyiko devaputraḥ. I have been unable to find anything more about this term. Tib. renders sṅon po (*blue*) ris (*form, figure*; also *party*, like BHS **kāya**). This suggests that Tib. understood *belonging to the group of Nīla* (*blue*) *ones*, rather than *blue-bodied*. In LV they, and their spokesman Vairocana, seem to be superior to the four **mahārāja** gods.

nīla-kṛtsna, nt., see **kṛtsna.** (Divy Index wrongly *kind of lotus*.)

Nīlakeśa, n. of a disciple of Buddha: Mv i.182.19.

Nīlagiryanilavega (text °anīla°), n. of the horse-jewel of a cakravartin: Gv 418.8.

Nīlagrīva, n. of a rākṣasa: Divy 102.29; 105.9, 24.

Nīladaṇḍa, n. of one of the ten **krodha**: Dharmas 11; Sādh 137.11 etc.

Nīlabhūti, n. of a learned brahman: MSV i.8.3 ff.

nīlamuktā, *blue pearl*, a kind of gem: -hāra, Sukh 54.11. Follows **lohitamuktā**(-hāra), a form otherwise known; perhaps invented to match the latter (blended with Skt. nīla-maṇi?).

Nīlavāsas, perh. n. or ep. of Kubera as lord of yakṣas: pañcabhir Nīlavāsaso yakṣaśatair Divy 238.23.

Nīlā, n. of a rākṣasī: Māy 244.1.

Nīlāda, n. of a yakṣa: Divy 113.11; 122.23.

Nīlāmbuda, n. of a nāga king: Mmk 18.12.

Nīlotpalā, n. of an apsaras: Kv 3.15.

Nīloda, n. of a sea (so Skt. Gr.) and of a mountain: Divy 102.28; 104.20, 21; 105.8, 10, 20, 24.

nīvaraṇa, nt. (also written nīvā° in text with one ms. Mv ii.143.16, but v.l. nīva°, metr. indifferent; niva° SP 75.2, but Kashgar rec. nīva°; niva° v.l. for nivā° Mvy 6511; niva° also Divy 567.19; Śikṣ 280.13; Bbh 9.1; 218.19, 20; Gv 491.22; Laṅk 49.7; nivā° Mvy 6511, with v.l. niva°, also acc. to Mironov nivā° for nīva° Mvy 2146), (**1**) (= Pali nīvaraṇa), *disturbance, trouble, interference*: in ordinary worldly sense, prītiprāmodyajāto nirupādāno vigata-nivaraṇo 'bhayaprāpto SP 75.2; in beginning a story (vs), nīvaraṇāni vijahitva ekāgreṇa manasā mama śṛṇotha Mv ii.33.7, *getting rid of hindrances* (to attention) *listen to me with intent minds*, and similarly nīvaraṇaṃ vijahitvā . . . iii.133.6 (vs); usually, as in Pali, *hindrance* or *obstruction to a religious life*, '*besetting sin*' (Childers); Tib. regularly sgrib pa = *darkness*, also *sin*; there are five such, listed AbhidhK. LaV-P. v.98 (in accord with Pali, see Childers, PTSD) as kāmacchanda, vyāpāda, styāna-middha, auddhatya-kaukṛtya, and vicikitsā: Mvy 651; 2146; 6511 (here, for nivāraṇa, Tib. chod pa, *covering over*, is alternative to the usual sgrib pa); nīvaraṇa-kaṭhina-granthi (read °thī, metr. required) LV 371.18 (vs), *having the hindrances as its hard bulb* (of avidyā, compared to a plant); °ṇa-vananī (so with v.l. for °rī) dagdhā me kuśala-mūlatejena LV 372.1; °ṇa-kapāṭāni ca pañca mayeha pradāritā sarvaṃ (text °va; or °ve, v.l.) LV 376.13; nivaraṇa-kavāṭa-nirbhedana-tāyai Gv 491.22; vigata-nīvaraṇa (adj. Bhvr.) SP 123.11; apagata-nī° Dbh 56.26; mandani° Bbh 9.1; pañca nīvaraṇāni Mv i.147.15; °ṇā pañca ceta-sāvaraṇā (mss. °ṇāṃ; = cetas', for cetasaḥ, āv°) i.248.1; °raṇāpagataṃ cittaṃ ii.143.16; nāsti °ṇāni ca iii.401.12, said of Buddha; (Sukhāvatyāṃ . . .) sarvaśo °ṇa-śabdo nāsti Sukh 40.8; °ṇānāṃ viṣkambhanatā Śikṣ 191.7; mukto . . . śalyair nivaraṇais tathā Divy 567.19; -middha--nivaraṇa-vigatena Laṅk 49.7; avidyā-nivaraṇāvṛtāḥ Śikṣ 280.12–13; °ṇa-prahāṇāya Bbh 218.19; also 20; see also **vi-nīvaraṇa**; (**2**) a high number: Mvy 7971 = Tib. sgrib pa, as for mg. 1; in LV corruptly **niravadya**, q.v.

nīharati (= Pali id.; Skt. nir-h°), *carries out*: Mv iii.429.14 pātreṇa nīharitvā (object, a dangerous snake); Śikṣ 155.3 (from Bhikṣuprakīrṇaka) bahirdhā nīharitvā (so with ms.; ed. em. haritvā) snāpayet (a sick monk; see s.v. **anuparigṛhṇīte**).

nu, in kiṃ nu, acc. to mss. and ed. Av i.191.2; 209.5, for Skt. kiṃ tu, *however*. Not noted in Pali or Pkt.

nudantaka (ka svārthe with a-extension of nudant-, pres. pple), *rejecting, repulsing*: °takaṃ Mv i.321.11 (prose).

Nūpurottamā, n. of a kiṃnara maid: Kv 6.15.

Nṛtyā, (*dramatic*) *Dance* or *Drama*, n. of a goddess or yoginī: Sādh 157.12 etc.; 324.6.

? **nṛpakaṃ**, text Ud xv.6; Chakravarti's note says read nṛpakaḥ; but the true reading is surely **nipakaḥ**, q.v., as in the Pali equivalent Itiv. 47.3, unless nṛ° is a hyper-Sktism.

[? **neti**, f.: (smṛtiṃ) pratilabhate netiye Mv ii.264.2; Senart suggests nītiye, *la conduite à tenir*; more likely read netriye, or MIndic nettiye, gen. sg. of **netrī**, q.v.]

netra, m. (otherwise nt.), *eye*: netrā . . . tvacanaddhāḥ (n. pl.) LV 324.11 (vs; no v.l.).

Netraśrī, n. of a bodhimaṇḍa-deity: Gv 444.10.

netrika, nt. (= Skt. netra; cf. Pali nettika, *tube, pipe*), *clyster-tube*: °kam Mvy 9033 = Tib. sman gce ḥu, *medicine-tube*.

netrikā, as ep. of tṛṣṇā, = **bhavanetrī**, q.v.: tṛṣṇā nāsya (mss. nāsti, which may be kept) kahiṃ pi (mss. vi, cin) netrikā Mv iii.92.1 (vs), *he has no craving that takes him towards* (any bhava, *state of being*). Metrical considerations are no doubt concerned in the form.

netrita, denom. ppp. (based on Skt. netra), *guided*: kalyāṇamitra-ne° Gv 461.12 (prose).

netrī (= Pali netti), (**1**) adj., in **bhava-netrī**, q.v. (and cf. **netrikā**), *leading, conducive* (to . . .); (**2**) subst., *way, method, rule, usage*; Tib. (on Mvy 6325) tshul (ed. tshal, but Tib. Index tshul), or lugs: usually in cpds. dharma- (Pali dhamma-netti) and buddha-n°, *the way* (or the like) *of the Law, of Buddha*; rarely alone, so prob. in Mv ii.264.2 where I would read (smṛtiṃ . . .) netriye, *recollection* or *contemplation of the Way*, see s.v. **neti**; mama netrī Laṅk 201.3 (vs; Buddha is speaking); dharma-netrī SP 10.4; 25.13; 53.7; 251.6; LV 439.1; Mv ii.373.5 (śāstu varadharmanetrī); iii.234.12, 17; Suv 69.3; KP 20.18, etc.; Dbh 14.17; Bbh 56.16; 297.4; in RP 9.6 (vs), text dharmanetri rayina pramuhyata, read °netrir iya (= iyaṃ, m.c.) na pramuhyata (or °te), *this rule of the Law has not become confused*; buddha-n° Mvy 6325 (Tib., see above); SP 92.1 (Kashgar rec. dharma-n°); 93.13; 94.12; 96.6; 154.16; Śikṣ 147.3; Laṅk 70.14.

nepattha (= Skt. nepathya), *costume, clothing*: karma-nepatthaiḥ Mmk 100.7 (vs), *with costumes* (fig. for external things) *consisting of deeds*.

nepatthita, or (?) **nepathyita** (denom. ppp. to Skt. nepathya), *clothed, garbed*: some such form (possibly with Prakritic v for p) must be read in Divy 48.24; 49.16; 159.12; 342.2; 463.26; 558.22; Av i.284.11; 347.9; MSV i.71.19; in all these the mss. (followed by edd.) are corrupt, showing such readings as neva (naiva) sthita, nopasthita, (once, Av i.347.9) nepathyasthita, in Divy 436.26 te panthitā; cf. also **nipacchita**, representing the same form.

nema, nt., a high number: Mvy 7712; 7838 (cited from Gv); Gv 105.21; 133.3.

Nemi (cf. also **Nemin**), (**1**) (prob. = **Nimi**, Pali Nimi, Nemi), n. of a cakravartin: Mvy 3583; (**2**) (= Pali id.) n. of a pratyekabuddha: Mmk 64.13; 111.10.

-nemika, ifc. Bhvr. (= Skt. nemi; Pali sa-nemika, PTSD s.v. sanābhika), in sa-ne°, *provided with a rim*: (cakrāṇi . . .) °kāni Gv 399.23 (prose), prec. by sanābhīni.

Nemin (possibly n. pr., = **Nemi** 1 ?), or **Nemina**, ep. of the Buddha: °naṃ, acc. sg., in a formulaic list of such epithets: Laṅk 192.15.

Nemiṃdhara, m. sg. (= Pali id., also **Nimiṃ**°, q.v.), n. of one of the 'eight mountains' (including **Sumeru**): Dharmas 125.

neyartha, adj. (= Pali neyyattha), *of meaning which has to be determined* (by inference or the like), *which is not clear on the surface*: Mvy 1549; Bbh 257.12; opp. **nītārtha**, q.v. with references.

nela (**1**) adj. (= Pali id.), *pure*, of speech, see **aneḍa**; (**2**) m., a high number: Mvy 7764 = Tib. gtaṅ yas; cf. next two.

nelā, a high number: Gv 106.11. Cf. prec. (2) and next.

nelu, m. or f., a high number: neluḥ Mvy 7892 = Tib. btaṅ yas; cited from Gv 133.21. Cf. prec. two.

nevatthita, or the like, see **nepatthita**.

nevala, m., a high number: Mvy 7736 = Tib. stobs yas; cf. **nivala**.

naikāyika, adj. or subst. m. (cf. Pali nek°), (**1**) *follower, devotee of the nikāya*, q.v., i. e. of the literal canon: naikāyikāś ca tīrthyāś ca dṛṣṭim ekāṃśam āśritāḥ Laṅk 294.3 (vs); clearly reprobated and associated with heretics, in accordance with the general position of Laṅk, which is hostile to literalism and even to acceptance of any verbally expressed doctrines; (**2**) sapta-naikāyikaṃ (prā-timokṣa-saṃvara-samādānaṃ) Bbh 138.24, *pertaining to the seven groups* (of Buddhist adherents, listed 25 f. as bhikṣu-bhikṣuṇī-śikṣamāṇā-(! so text)-śrāmaṇera-śrāmaṇery-upāsakopāsikā).

naikhanya, in tripauruṣa-naikhanyāni (iṣikāni, or iṣī°) Mv i.196.2; iii.228.13, (having) *a part sunk in the earth* (measuring three man-lengths). Mss. naikhadya or nakhanya; Senart on i.196.2 reads naikhānya, but in his note adopts °kha° from the parallel; however, naikhānya may be right, for the word is clearly the same as that cited by BR from Ṣaḍv. Br. 4.4 yūpasya yan naikhānyam.

naigama (= Pali ne°; from Skt. nigama, *town,* plus -a), *townsman*; pl. *townspeople*: SP 115 5; Mv i.313.4; 364.5; (? ii.64.16 naigama-sthānāṃ sarvasya, read nigama° ?;) iii.38.2; LV 117.17; Divy 87.1 and 89.2, read sa-naigamam, cf. note p. 706; Divy 404.14; janapadeṣu naigamāḥ LV 391.13 (vs); often (as in Pali) cpd. or associated with jānapada, *countryman, countryfolk*: SP 108.8; Mv ii.100.14; 424.2; Mvy 3746 (foll. by jānapadaḥ); Divy 143.17; Jm 86.24; Av i.87.9; 184.7; RP 41.15; Bbh 122.2; with janapada, prob. only an error for jāna°, Mv ii.439.7; 440.1 (but here v.l. jāna°, so read); Divy 211.13.

Naigameśa, n. of a yakṣa: Māy 55.

Naitarī, n. of a town: MSV i.xvii.12.

naityaka, nt. (cf. Pali nicca-bhatta, and Skt. naityaka, adj.), *food regularly and permanently provided by laymen for monks and nuns*: °kam Mvy 5762 = Tib. rtag re (stag res) ḥkhor, *constantly recurring*; tayā °ka-samucchedaḥ (*suspension of regular provision*) kṛtaḥ Av i.269.12; in Bhīk 23a.2, in a list of kinds of provisions included in **atireka**(lābha), q.v. (beyond regular piṇḍapāta); context of Mvy 5762 was surely the same.

naibhṛtya (nt.; seems not recorded in this sense; Skt. nibhṛta plus -ya), *stillness, quietude*: °tya-nirmukta-samagra-toyaḥ Jm 89.12, *all of whose water was deprived of stillness,* of the ocean in a storm.

naimitta, m. (= Skt. Lex. id., Pali ne°), *soothsayer* (much rarer than **naimittika,** q.v.): Divy 168.23; Mv iii.59.3 (?).

naimittaka, m. (= Pali ne°) = prec.: Divy 168.19; 234.30.

naimittika, m. (= Pali ne°, both mgs.; from nimitta plus -ika), (**1**) *one who hints at a desire for a gift* (from a lay patron): RP 58.7 °kāḥ; cf. Wogihara, Lex. 21, 24 f., and next; (**2**) (commonly) *sign-reader, soothsayer, fortune-teller* (also **nimittika, naimitta,** °**ttaka**; but these are much rarer than **naimittika,** contrary to Wogihara's statement, above, that the latter is found in Buddhist sources only in the LV and Mvy passages; to disprove this statement, I cite a few of many occurrences, altho the word is also recorded in Skt.): LV 186.15; Mvy 3793; Mv ii.32.6; iii.178.17; Divy 132.8; 168.17; 319.14 ff.; 410.18 f.; 474.26; Av i.13.11 etc.; Gv 53.6.

naimittika-tā (from prec., mg. 1; = Pali nemit°), Bbh 168.21, or °**tva,** nt., Mvy 2496: *hinting* at desires, to get particular gifts; one of the 5 mithyājīva of a monk; see references s.v. **kuhana.** Tib. renders Mvy gzhog sloṅ, *indirect begging.* See also s.v. **nimitta.**

naimittikī, *hermaphrodite*: Mvy 8930 = Tib. mtshan tsam yod pa, *of doubtful sexual characteristics* (?); Chin. clearly means one with both male and female characteristics; Bhīk 16b.1, in list of persons who must not be initiated as a nun.

Nairañjanavāsinī, n. of a goddess: Suv 3.11.

Nairañjanā, once Nir° (q.v.; = Pali Nerañjarā), n. of a river in Magadha: LV 248.8; 252.15; 261.3 ff.; 272.8 ff.; 380.12; Mv (incomplete, for others see Index) ii.123.20; 131.12; 207.19; 237.17; 263.16 ff.; 300.14; 302.6 f.; iii.301.8; 425.18; Mvy 4191; Divy 202.7; Mmk 581.12; Buddhacarita xii.90, 108 (in the latter ms. Nir°, see s.v. **Nir°**).

nairayika, once **nir°,** q.v., adj., also subst. m., and rarely nt. (= Skt. Lex. id., Pali ner°, which is used in very similar phrases), *of hell*: adj. with sattva, *creature reborn in hell* (said of the damned, not of fiendish tormentors of them with Senart on Mv i.6.14), LV 86.11; Mv i.6.14, etc.; ii.301.6; as subst. without sattva, *inhabitant of hell,* Mv i.17.6; iii.43.5 (°kāni); *one destined for hell,* Divy 165.19 (°ko, of a man); adj. with duḥkha, *pains of hell,* Mv i.5.1; ii.350.6; iii.274.8; Gv 522.20; with kāraṇa, *torment,* Śikṣ 181.14; °ka-mārga-, Śikṣ 215.1, *the path to hell*; °ka-kāya Dbh 68.7, *body* (existing) *in hell*; with āyuḥ, *span of life in* (an existence in) *hell,* Karmav 30.17.

[**nairātma,** prob. only error for °tmya: śamatha-dhanu gṛhītvā śūnyanairātma-bāṇaiḥ LV 156.5 (vs), but best ms. °ātmya-; nairātmā sārthavan nityaṃ cittena saha vartate Laṅk 372.12 (vs), corrupt in the beginning, read doubtless nairātmyā- (the following word can hardly be right but no plausible em. occurs to me).]

nairātmya, nt. (cf. prec.; to Skt. nirātman plus -ya), *the not having a self*; *the doctrine that there is no self*: LV 9.10 etc.; 436.21 (see s.v. **ātmya**); Mv ii.145.10; 363.9; Mvy 783 °myādhigamāt; KP 97.2; Dbh.g. 20(356).14; Laṅk 1.4, etc.; two kinds, pudgala-n° and dharma-n°, Dharmas 116; Bbh 280.19–20 (see the next lines); dharma-n° Bbh 41.16. Cf. next.

Nairātmya-yoginī, also **Nairātmyā,** n. of a yoginī: °myā Sādh 443.8, etc.; in 502.15 (the same personage?) named as one of four 'doorkeepers'; °mya-yoginī 445.4 etc., in vss and usually where short a might be m.c., but this could hardly be said of 448.4.

Nairṛta, or °**ti** (?), m. (Skt. Lex. id.), n. of the guardian (lokapāla) of the southwest; cf. Skt. °tī (diś): °taḥ Dharmas 8; °tiḥ Mvy 3156 (read °taḥ? Mironov, however, °tiḥ, printed Nairṭiḥ).

[**nairnitya,** LV 325.10 (vs), false em.; read, substantially with best mss., no vai 'nityaśubhā-anātmabhir vasi sārdhaṃ (i. e. anitya-aśubha-anātmabhir etc.). No ms. has nai-.]

nairmāṇika, f. °**kā** or °**kī,** adj. (= nirm°; from nirmāṇa plus -ika), *related to magic creation*; usually, *created by magic*: °kenāgninā Divy 186.26; °kaṃ kāyam Laṅk 73.9 (see **nirmāṇa-kāya**; but in same vs 276.10 **nairvāṇikam,** q.v.); of a class of Buddhas, contrasted with **vipāka-**stha, Laṅk 34.2 or **vaipākika** 283.4, 11, *magically created* as against *naturally developed*; as ep. of ṛddhi, f. °kā Bbh 55.21, or °kī 58.20; 63.23 ff., that kind of magic (ṛddhi) *which creates something out of nothing* (nirvastukam 63.23), as opposed to **pāriṇāmika,** °**kī,** *that which is based on or involves alteration, transformation* of things which have a 'real', natural existence. See next.

nairmita-nairmāṇika (-vyapetaṃ, sc. Tathāgatam), (cf. prec., and s.v. **nirmita**), (*who transcends*) *the* (forms) *connected with the magically transformed and with magic transformation*: Laṅk 11.17 (prose). Such seems to be the lit. mg., but I do not understand what distinction may have been felt between the two, and Suzuki gives no real help.

nairyāṇika, f. °**kī,** °**kā,** adj. (= **niry°,** q.v.), *conducive to deliverance*: LV 239.14 (see s.v. niry°); °ka-pratipad LV 428.17; Mvy 134 (in the 4th **vaiśāradya,** q.v.; for this Dharmas 77 **nairvāṇika**); °kīṃ pratipadaṃ LV 434.5 and 7; Bbh 80.26; 219.11–12; nāyaṃ mārgo nairyāṇiko Mv ii.198.2; adj. with dharma Mv ii.259.15; iii.59.14; (dharma-vinaya) Mvy 1299; śīla Bbh 187.12; artha (the Bodhisattva's goal) Mv ii.279.7; atyanta-nairyāṇika-tā Bbh 298.12; of cittotpāda (of a Bodhisattva), nairyāṇikaś cānairyāṇikaś ca. tatra nairyāṇiko ya utpanno 'tyantam anuvartate na punar vyāvartate; a-nairy° ... nātyantam anuvartate punar eva vyāvartate Bbh 13.14–17; and so, nairyāṇikānairyāṇika-tā Dbh 69.32; dṛṣṭir āryā °ṇikā MPS 2.35.

nairvāṇa, adj. (= Skt. nirvāṇa, as ppp.; note AMg. nevvāṇa = nirvāṇa as noun), *extinguished,* lit., of lamps:

dīpā nairvāṇāḥ Divy 90.11 (same passage MSV i.90.13 parinirvāṇāḥ).

nairvāṇika, f. °**kī**, adj. (= **nirv°**; neither seems recorded anywhere), *relating* or *conducive to nirvāṇa*: Dharmas 77 (same passage in Mvy 134 **nairyāṇika**, q.v.); °kaṃ kāyaṃ ... labhante Laṅk 276.10 (but same vs Laṅk 73.9 nairmāṇikaṃ, which is prob. the correct reading); °kīṃ bhūmiṃ, *the basis of nirvāṇa*, Kv 65.9; 66.19; 67.6.

nairvedhika, adj. (to **nirvedha**; = **nirvedhika**; cf. next), *penetrating*, in lit. and fig. sense: °ka-prajñā (= Pali nibbedhika-paññā), Bhvr., °jñaḥ Mvy 1106 = Tib. ṅes par ḥbyed pa (= nirvedha); ākāśasadṛśāḥ sarvadharma-nairvedhika-tayā Sukh 60.4, *like ether, because they penetrate* (intellectually, as ether does physically) *all dharma(s)* (religious doctrines, or conditions of existence); dṛṣṭir ... °kā MPS 2.35.

Nairvedhika-sarva-bhava-talopagata, m., n. of a samādhi: Mvy 596. This seems the correct reading; Mironov °tamopagata; ŚsP 1423.13 °talavigata, but this is certainly an error; Tib. khoṅs-su chud pa for the end of the cpd. = *entering within*.

nairhetuka, adj. (from nir-hetu(ka), vṛddhi deriv.; cf. **āhetuka**), *arising from no cause*: fem. °kī AsP 516.8.

naivakiṃcanya, m. pl., a class of gods: Mmk 19.11. Nonce-formation, pendant to **ākiṃcanya**, q.v., perhaps influenced by **naivasaṃjñānāsaṃjñāyatana**.

[**naiva-jīva**, assumed by Senart's em. to be adj., *not at all alive*: yathā naivajīvāni evaṃ tiṣṭhanti Mv i.18.8. But the mss. are quite different; em. very uncertain, and even if correct might be taken as separate words, naiva jīvāni.]

naivaśaikṣanāśaikṣa, *one who is neither a śaikṣa nor an aś°* (qq.v.): Mvy 1735.

naivasaṃjñānāsaṃjñāyatana (= Pali nevasaññānāsaññāy°), (**1**) nt., *stage of neither consciousness nor unconsciousness*: as 4th of the stages of arūpāvacara gods, Mvy 3113; Dbh 34.15; as 4th of the ārūpya samāpatti, Mvy 1495; Karmav 47.22; naivasaṃjñānāsaṃjñāyatanasamāpatter mārgaḥ LV 244.13 and 245.3; as condition of the 7th vimokṣa, Mvy 1517; as 8th of the sattvāvāsa, Mvy 2296; in Bbh 49.17–18 ākāśavijñānākiṃcanyanaivasaṃjñānāsaṃjñāyatanam, the four 'stages' are telescoped in one cpd. (āyatana being understood with all four); Rudraka (Mv Udraka) Rāmaputra taught as the goal association with this stage, °tana-sahavratāyai dharmam deśayati LV 243.17 and 403.10 = Mv ii.119.9 and iii.322.12; (**2**) m. pl., °yatanā devāḥ Mmk 45.7 = next.

naivasaṃjñānāsaṃjñāyatanopaga, °**paka**, m. pl., *the gods who are in the stage* named in the prec.: Dharmas 129; Bbh 229.21; Suv 86.12 (here Nobel with 1 ms. °opagatānāṃ, read with the other mss. °opagānāṃ). For the variant form in °opaka see s.v. **upaka**.

naivākāśānantya, m. pl., a class of gods: Mmk 19.11. Nonce-formation, pendant to **ākāśānantya**, q.v., perhaps influenced by **naivasaṃjñānāsaṃjñāyatana**.

Naivāla (read Naipāla or Ne°?), *Nepal*: MSV iv.209.4.

naivāsika, (**1**) adj. (cf. Skt. Gr. id.; = Pali ne°), *resident*: Divy 390.4 (vs) °kā yā ihāśokavṛkṣe ... devakanyā; MSV ii.176.3; (of a monk, *dwelling in* a monastery) Mvy 8745; Av i.286.4; 287.1 (perhaps *servant*; = **āvāsika**, q.v.); (**2**) m., some sort of monster, *python* or the like: Mv iii.33.4 (Māro tena kālena ... ajagaro) naivāsiko abhūṣi; Candropama Sūtra, Hoernle MR 41.3 vyāḍo vā yakṣo vā amanuṣyo vā naivāsiko vā ...; Bbh 19.26 (vyāḍā vā yakṣā vā) [ed. manuṣyā vā, omit with v.l. and Tib.] amanuṣyā vā naivāsikā vā viheṭhāṃ kartum.

naiṣadika, m., = next: Mvy 1138 (both edd., no v.l.); MSV iii.122.6.

naiṣadyika, m. (see also prec.; to **niṣadyā** plus -ika; = Pali nesajjika), *one who sleeps in a sitting posture*, one of the 12 **dhūtaguṇa**, q.v.: Dharmas 63; AsP 387.7; RP 57.10. All prose.

naiṣāda, m. (= **niṣāda**, Pali nesāda; Skt. naiṣāda referring to the tribe Niṣāda), *(bird-)hunter, fowler*: Jm 134.23 ff.

naiṣkramya, nt. (= Pali nekkhamma; cf. **niṣkramya**), *departure from the world, renunciation of worldly things*: °myāśrita Mv i.173.13 (opp. to gṛhāśrita); Mvy 6755; 7554; °myābhiprāyo Mv i.283.19; °mya-cittasya Śikṣ 69.8 (Tatp., *the thought of* ...); °mya-cārin Dbh 19.17; others, LV 136.8; 164.6; 170.10; 184.12, 18; 196.14; 439.10; Mv i.107.3; iii.321.12; 357.13; 422.10; Jm 3.2; Bbh 8.26; 26.10 (°mya-sukhaṃ); 246.20; Ud xv.19; Laṅk 307.2; kāmeṣu °myam Mvy 6444, *renunciation as regards desires* (lusts).

naiṣkramyin, adj. (to prec. plus -in), *characterized by withdrawal from the world*: °miṇo (by em.) Gautamaśāsanesmiṃ (mss.) Mv i.293.6 (vs) = Pali Sn 228 nikkāmino (one ms. nikkh°), interpreted by Khp. comm. i.184.22 kata-nikkhamana.

naiṣpeṣika-tā (= Pali nippesikatā), *extraction of gifts* (from laymen, by monks) *by means of threats*, one of the 5 mithyājīva, see references s.v. **kuhana**: Bbh 168.22; a-naiṣpeṣikatā, so read, Śikṣ 183.15. Cf. **niṣpeṣaṇa** and next.

naiṣpeṣika-tva (text °peś°), nt., = prec.: Mvy 2495 = Tib. thob kyis ḥjal ba, app. something like *extortion of property* (cf. Das s.v. thob pa II); one Chin. rendering, *desire to get something by annoyance*.

naiṣyandika (to **niṣyanda** plus -ika), *of the outcome* or *result*: °kaṃ vīryaṃ Bbh 203.14 (defined by: pūrvahetubalādhānatayā).

naisargika, see **naiḥsargika**.

naistārika, adj. (cf. Pali netthāraṃ vattati, the first word representing a Skt. *naistāra; wrongly PTSD), *involving termination* (of), *riddance* (from, some penalty or evil): °kaṃ phalasaṃbhavam Mmk 352.22.

naiḥsargika, adj. (= **niḥsargika**, q.v.; also written **naisar°**), *involving forfeiture*: °kāpattiḥ Mvy 9309 (text nai-sa°, Index naiḥs°, so Mironov with v.l. nai-sa°); °kāḥ pāyattikāḥ (see this; in Pali the corresponding pācittiya offenses include the nissaggiya) Mvy 8383; in both Tib. spaṅ ba, *giving up, renouncing*, or the like; applied to robes (cīvarāṇi), *subject to forfeiture*: Divy 19.26 (here mss. nai-sa°); 21.21.

naiḥsvabhāvya, naiḥsvā°, nt. (to Skt. niḥsvabhāva plus -ya), *state of having no essence*; only in vss, but quantity of 2d syllable indifferent: °sva° Laṅk 274.3; 295.10; 311.6; 336.2; °svā° 266.12; 280.15.

no hīdaṃ (= Pali no hi idaṃ, PTSD s.v. no), *not so!*: SP 323.1 (prose).

nau-krama, m., Divy 55.17, 19, or **nau-saṃkrama**, m., Divy 55.24 ff.; 386.10; Av i.64.1, 5; 66.3; acc. to Divy Index and Speyer's Index to Av, *bridge of boats* (joined together): e. g. naukramo māpitaḥ Divy 55.17, 19. But this interpretation is difficult in Divy 386.(9–)10, (nauyānenāgamiṣyatīti yāvac ca Mathurāṃ) yāvac ca Pāṭaliputram antarān nausaṃkramo 'vasthāpitaḥ, *thinking, 'he will come by boat,' established a boat-course from Mathurā as far as Pāṭaliputra*. Not only is this a long distance for a 'bridge of boats', but in line 12, as a result of this arrangement, Upagupta *mounts on a ship* (nāvam abhiruhya) and proceeds to Pāṭaliputra. Here, at least, the mg. seems then to be *course for boats, water-way, navigable passage for ships*; and this is possible in all the other passages.

Nyagrodha, m. (**1**) (= Pali Nigrodha, or °dha-miga), n. of a deer-king: Mv i.359.19 ff. (in the story called in Pali Nigrodhamiga Jātaka); (**2**) n. of a deity, formerly a goatherd who had planted a nyagrodha tree under which Buddha spent the 6th week after enlightenment: Mv iii.302.3; this tree was the **Ajapāla-nyagrodha**;

(3) n. of the deity inhabiting a nyagrodha tree at Benares: Mv iii.403.10.

Nyagrodharāja, n. of a former Buddha: Mv iii.238.8.

Nyagrodhārāma, m. (= Pali Nigro°), n. of a park at Kapilavastu where Buddha often stayed: Mv iii.101.14 ff.; 107.11; 114.6; 138.1, 5; 141.17; 179.3; Av i.345.6 etc. (see Speyer's Index).

Nyagrodhikā, n. of a village near Kapilavastu: Divy 67.1 ff.

Nyaṅku, n. of a cakravartin king: Mvy 3575.

Nyaṅkuṭā (Mironov Nyaṭkuṭā; vv.ll. both edd. Nyaṭkā, Nyakuṭa), n. of some hellish creature: °ṭā nāma prāṇī Mvy 4948; Tib. ḥbu mchu rnon, *worm with sharp beak.*

ny-asati (cf. **nyāsa** 2, and next; = **nikṣipati**; for Skt. -asyati, Epic -asati), *calculates, reckons* (in mathematics); so Tib., rtsi: huṃkāreṇa nyaseya (3 sg. opt.) ekinaiṣo LV 151.8 (vs), *he could reckon in a single instant (saying 'hum!').*

nyasana (nt., or m.; cf. prec.), one of the arts, presumably = **nyāsa**, and perhaps also **nikṣepa**, qq.v.; at least seems clearly mathematical; perhaps *solving mathematical problems* (? acc. to Wogihara Lex. 31, rendered *measuring* by Hiuen-thsang): lipi-gaṇana-nyasana-saṃkhyā-mudrā- Bbh 7.4; 103.3; 210.13.

nyāma, m., certainly = **niyāma**, q.v.; § 3.106; this is demonstrated by parallelism of phraseology accompanying the two words: nyāmaḥ Mvy 6502, following niyāmaḥ, but expl. by Tib. skyon med pa, *lack of defect* (as if ni plus āma!), and so Chin.; nyāmāvakrānta (cf. us(of niyāma with ava-kram in BHS and Pali) Mvy 6503, acc. to Tib. *entered* (zhugs pa) *into lack of defect*; nyāmāvakrānti-vihāraḥ Bbh 358.2, samyaktva-nyāmāvakrānti-prayogavihāraḥ id. 1; bodhisattva-nyāmam avakramya Gv 320.22; °mam avakrāmanty ŚsP 272.8, °mam ... avakramitukāmena 67.11; °nyāmāvakrāntas (printed °nyāmava°) AsP 331.10; read nyāmāvakrāntau 322.5; for Lefm. nyāyākramaṇatāyai LV 31.20 and 34.10, read with Wogihara, Lex. 29 nyāmāvakram° (so most mss. in 34.10, and traces of the same in mss. 31.20). All passages are prose.

nyāsa, m. (**1**) *threshold, door-sill*: Mvy 5571 = Tib. them pa; (**2**) one of the arts, presumably = **nyasana**, and perhaps **nikṣepa**, qq.v., hence *working out mathematical problems*(?): Divy 3.18; 26.12; 58.17; 100.2; 441.28 (in a cliché quoted s.v. **nikṣepa**); MSV iii.20.1.

P

paṃsaka, m. (see next two), *one who disparages, vilifies* (others): parapaṃsakaḥ Mvy 2445; KP 1.7; pareṣāṃ paṃsako AsP 184.10.

paṃsana, nt., and °**nā** (cf. Skt. -pāṃsana, ifc., *besmirching, disgracing*, e. g. kula-p°; once pāṃsanā, see Schmidt, Nachträge; Skt. Gr. paṃs-, paṃś-; not in Pali; see prec. and next), *speaking ill of, disparaging, degrading* (by speech); almost always cpd. with para-, the cpd. often coupled with ātmotkarṣa or the like, *exaltation of oneself, bragging*: °na, nt., Mvy 2631 (syn. of nindana, °nā); KP 1.16; 8.6; Śikṣ 10.14 (margin, note 4); 67.8; °nā, f., KP 8.16; 135.7; Bbh 158.5.

paṃsayati, °te (Skt. Gr.; AMg. paṃsei, rendered *defiles*; not in Pali; see prec. two and **vipaṃsayati, pratipa°**), *speaks ill of, disparages, reviles* (others): °yati, °yanti, Bbh 107.10; 174.21; Śikṣ 62.3; 63.6; 90.14, 16; 158.3; opt. °yema, °yeyur, Śikṣ 98.17; 186.6; °yate KP 107.24; °yiṣyati AsP 385.14; 388.20; ppp. paṃsita KP 107.2, 4; paṃsitavanto Śikṣ 68.16.

[**pakti-** is printed for paṅkti-, *row, line*, in LV 43.18, without correction; and occurs several times in mss. of Mv, e. g. i.194.4, both mss., and i.249.14, one ms.; Senart reads paṅkti-, doubtless rightly.]

pakva, adj. (cf. BR s.v. 8, pw s.v. 1, i; more clearly and commonly in this sense Pali pakka), *decayed, near destruction, rotten, foul*: pakva-gātrā Divy 82.11 (= Pali pakkagatta); pakva-kheṭa-piṇḍaṃ LV 242.4, *a rotten lump of phlegm.*

pakva-taila (cf. Pali telaṃ pakkaṃ, Dhp. comm. i.12.8, *oil has been prepared*, lit. *cooked*, sc. to be used as ointment), *prepared oil* (ointment?): te dāni °lena bhagavantaṃ nimantrayetsuḥ Mv iii.329.14. The corresp. Pali cpd. seems to be pāka-tela; e. g. Dhp. comm. iii.311.8–9 sata-pāka-telena, *with oil a hundred times refined* (Burlingame, HOS 30.105). Is -āk- here for -akk- by the Morengesetz? The form to be expected is Pali pakka = pakva.

pakvamāna (quasi pres. mid. pple. to pac-, see § 34.1), *being baked*: °mānānāṃ bhāṇḍānāṃ Divy 510.8.

(**pakṣa**, m. = Skt., *party*; see **kuśala-p°, śukla-p°** and **apakṣya**.)

pakṣagupta, m. (doubtless = **pattragupta**, q.v.), a kind of bird: Mvy 4907 = Tib. ḥdab skyoṅs (or, skyob), both = *wing-guarded.*

[**pakṣati**: °nti in LV 88.15, if correct could only be a denom. from pakṣa, *party*; cf. Dhātup. pakṣa(ya)ti = parigrahe; with object pratipakṣaṃ, *adhere to the opposite party*. But several mss. vakṣanti, which could intend vakṣyanti, as read by Calc., and this seems supported by Tib. brjod pa, *speak*; prob. therefore read so.]

-pakṣika, adj. (= Skt. pākṣika, -pakṣin, Pali -pakkhika, in brāhmaṇa-p°, Childers), ifc., *belonging to the party* (of ...): Māra-p° Mv ii.353.15; Śikṣ 314.8; see also **Kṛṣṇa-pakṣika**, and cf. **śukla-pākṣika.**

Pakṣin, pl., n. of a brahmanical gotra: Divy 635.16.

Pakṣu, n. of a nāga king: °ur Mvy 3307. Cf. **Vakṣu.** Tib. Pag-śu. But it seems to be a river-name; the three preceding names are Gaṅgā-, Sindhur, and Sītā-nāgarājā; similarly in MSV i.164.1. (Nāgas are often thought of as living in rivers, as is well known; cf. Mvy 3304–6.) Since Vakṣu occurs as n. of a river in Skt., it is probably the correct form.

pacanikā (cf. Skt. pacana; AMg. payaṇaga), *a cooking vessel* of some sort (-ikā diminutive?): Mvy 9011 = Tib. dog le, *an iron pan with a handle* (Jä.).

paccate, MIndic for pacyate: paccamāna- Mv iii.45.14.

pacchā (em.; Pali id.) or better **pacche** (with mss.), MIndic for Skt. paścā(t), *behind*: te dāni kusumāni pa° dṛṣṭvā anugacchanti Mv ii.106.2, *they now seeing the flowers* (which she had left) *behind* (her), *follow after*. The mss. reading may stand, possibly as a blend of pacchā = paścāt with its synonym pṛṣṭhe, *in the rear, behind*; in any case it is supported by the statement of Hem. 1.79 that in AMg. (ārṣe) pacche-(kammaṃ) may be used for paścāt-, and by the stem **paśca**, q.v., even in BHS, in loc. paści m.c. for paśce, and in comp.

pacchimaka = **paścimaka**, q.v.

pacyate (pass. of Skt. pac-, in Skt., as usually in Pali and BHS, used lit., *is roasted* in torments of hell), *is tormented* in general (so also Pali paccati): manasi ... pacyamānasya Divy 422.19.

pañcaka, adj. (as in Skt. and Pali in this mg.), *consisting of five, forming a group of five*; regularly of the **bhadravargīya** (or the like, q.v.) monks; pañcakā bhadra° LV 245.16; 246.2; 404.7, etc.; Mv ii.241.2; iii.322.20; 415.7, et alibi; without the word bhadra° but certainly or probably referring to them, as bhikṣavaḥ Jm 51.19; Suv 239.10; SP 56.10; pañcakehi (by em.) saha tehi munīhi (same group) Mv i.72.10.

pañca-gaṇḍa(ka), adj., see s.vv. **gaṇḍa, gaṇḍaka.**

pañcagatika, adj., = **pāñca°**, q.v.: mss. at MadhK 269.9 (ed. em. pāñca°).

pañca-cakṣus, see **cakṣus.**

Pañcacīra (cf. also **Pañcavīra**), an epithet of Mañjuśrī: Trikāṇḍaśeṣa 1.1.22 (BR); Lalou, Iconographie, 67 with note 4; see s.v. **cīraka** (Pañca-c°). Lalou thinks this epithet ultimately related to the gandharva **Pañcaśikha,** q.v. for some evidence tending to support the theory. See **pañcacīrā.**

pañca-cīraka, see **cīraka.**

pañca-cīrā, in °rāsu vinyastaḥ Mmk 334.4; lacuna precedes these words, so that application is not clear; perhaps *on five strips of cloth* (? the fem. cīrā occurs in Skt. tho very seldom, see BR s.v. cīra).

Pañcacūḍa, n. of a nāga king: Māy 247.20.

pañca-jñānika, adj. (= Pali -ñāṇika, ep. of samādhi, DN iii.278 infra, where the five kinds of knowledge are set forth), *based on five kinds of knowledge*, ep. of samādhi: °ka-samādhi-saṃpannā (of Buddhas) Mv. iii.321.16; ārya-mahā-°nika- (mss. pañcājñātikasya)-samyaksamādhiprāptā 322.1; with the mss. reading in the last cf. Mv ii.292.12, 14 ārya-(14 adds mahā-)pañcajñātika-(read °jñānika; sc. samādhi)-saṃpannā(ḥ), of Bodhisattvas. Mvy 109 pañca-jñānāni, see s.v. **jñāna**; but these have no relation to pañcajñānika-samādhi, at least acc. to the Pali DN.

[**Pañcabhūryābhimukhā**, see **Pañcasūryā°**.]

pañcavaṭuka, m.? some kind of entertainer, in lists of various kinds (cf. **kumbhatūṇika, kheluka, gāyanaka, dvistvala,** °**laka**, etc.); very likely corrupt: Mv iii.113.4; 255.12 (here mss. pañcabahuka); 442.10.

pañcavarga (= Pali °vagga, Vin. i.319.30), *consisting of a group of five*; *a quorum of five* (monks), sufficient to perform ordination 'in border countries' in Pali, Vin. i.197.31, cf. i.319.31: pañca-vargena (so, n!) gaṇena upasaṃpadā (q.v.) Mv i.2.16; a quorum for performing pravāraṇā, MSV ii.203.15–16, cf. 204.18 ff.

pañcavarṣika (so Divy 403.16, 27; 405.11; and Kalpanām., below), or (in all others) °vārṣika, adj. and subst. nt., *of five years*, or as subst., *the festival-gathering of the Buddhist order every five years*; as adj., °ka-mahaḥ Mvy 5676 = Tib. lo lṅahi (*of 5 years*) dus ston; °kaṃ satkāraṃ Divy 398.24, *the 5-yearly entertainment* (of the order, on this festal occasion); but usually nt. subst., °ke vartamāne, Kalpanāmaṇḍitikā, Kl. Skt. Texte 2, 44 (Lüders, *das grosse, alle fünf Jahre gefeierte Ordensfest*); ghuṣyatāṃ °kaṃ Divy 403.7, 16, 27; others, Divy 242.11; 405.11; 419.15; 429.15; Av i.88.1 (title of Chap. 16, with story of origin of the festival); 89.14; 90.1; 92.2, 4; ii.39.5, 6. (Divy Index wrongly *entertainment for five months of the rainy season*, with Burnouf, Introd. 394, but B. in his note shows awareness of the possibility of the other, true interpretation.)

Pañcaviṃśatisāhasrikā, n. of a work: Mvy 1327. (Understand: -prajñāpāramitā.)

? **Pañcavīra-kumāra**, n. or epithet of Mañjuśrī: Sādh 111.18; of **Caṇḍamahāroṣaṇa** (q.v.), 174.8. Read prob. **Pañcacīra**, q.v.

Pañcaśikha (**1**) m. (= Pali °sikha), n. of a celebrated gandharva: Mv iii.197.15 ff.; 215.5 ff.; Av i.95.8–9 ff.; 113.5; Samādh 19.11 ff., 37; king of gandharvas, Mmk 46.1; as in Pali (DPPN) sometimes regarded (like Śakra) as an office rather than an individual, so that a person may be reborn as the gandharva P., Mv ii.49.3; (**2**) f., or adj., °khā **mahāmudrā** (q.v.), a mudrā belonging to Mañjuśrī (cf. Lalou's theory cited s.v. **Pañcacīra**), Mmk 26.15; printed °kha-mahāmudrā Mmk 37.8, but in 37.26–27 and 58.24 mahāmudrā(ṃ) pañcaśikhāṃ baddhvā, and so regularly (fem.).

Pañcaśīrṣaka, n. of a nāga king (in the south): Megh 302.13. In 308.8 evidently the same individual is named Prasphoṭana, with the epithet pañcaśīrṣa, *five-headed.*

Pañcasūryābhimukhā (misprinted Pañcabhūr°, cf. **Nirnāditasūrya**), n. of an Apsaras: Kv 3.13.

pañcāṅga, see s.v. **aṅga**, and cf. next.

pañcāṅgika, adj. (in general sense Skt.), (**1**) ep. of tūrya (as in Pali pañcaṅgika-turiya), (instrumental music) *of five kinds* (listed in PTSD s.v. for Pali): °kasya tūryasya Mv i.194.13; iii.229.4; °kaṃ tūryaṃ Karmav 87.16; °ka-tūrya-śabdo 88.2; in view of this last, °ka-tulya-ravā Mv i.171.4 (vs), ep. of the Buddha's voice, is doubtless to be em. to °ka-tūrya-ravā; (**2**) ep. of samādhi (as in Pali pañcaṅgika is ep. of jhāna; the five elements listed PTSD s.v. from Dhs 83; a partly different list s.v. **samādhi**): ārya-pa°-samādhi-saṃpannāḥ Mv iii.321.15, and ārya-mahā-pa°-samyaksamādhi-saṃpannā(ḥ) 16 (the difference, if any, is not made clear); (**3**) as ep. of gods, °kānāṃ ca devakoṭīnāṃ Mv iii.339.2, mg. not clear; perhaps *possessing the five 'gentlemanly qualities'* (Pali pañcaṅga, see s.v. **aṅga**); or *of five groups?*

pañcāṅgula, nt. (= Pali pañca°, also °laka, °lika), (magic) *five-finger-mark* (see Vogel, Versl. en Med. d. K. Akad. v. Wet. Amsterdam, Afd. Letterk., v.4.218 ff., and PTSD s.v.): °lāni (to be made on stūpas) Mv i.269.14; Kalpanāmaṇḍitikā, Lüders Kl. Skt. Texte 2, 44.

pañcātapika, m. (from Skt. °tapā plus -ika), *an ascetic observing the five-fires penance*: Kalpanāmaṇḍitikā, Lüders Kl. Skt. Texte 2, 44.

Pañcāla, n. of a nāga king: Mvy 3257. Cf. **Pāñcāla.**

Pañcāla-gaṇḍa, n. of a yakṣa: Māy 89; 236.2; 237.2. Corresp. to Pali Pañcāla-caṇḍa, which acc. to Lévi is suggested by some Chin. renderings of Māy 89, but others, and perhaps the Tib. which Lévi cites(?), point rather to °gaṇḍa.

Pañcālā, n. of a river: Māy 253.7; in list between Tāmarā and Suvāsu.

pañcāśati (analogical alteration of pañcāśat, like rare Skt. triṃśati; recorded by BR once from Rājat.), *fifty*: °tīnāṃ sama yojanānām SP 95.1 (vs). Burnouf and Kern wrongly *500*.

pañcāśima, ord. num., *fiftieth*: SP 351.1 (vs). See §§ 19.36; 22.14.

pañcāhika, adj. (to Skt. pañcāha), *pertaining to five days*: Mv i.343.16, 17 (see **caturahika**).

Pañcika, n. of a yakṣa: Mmk 44.2. Note that Pañcaka is a well-supported v.l. for Paṇḍaka as n. of yakkha in Pali, Mahāv. 12.21.

pañjala, m. or nt. (= Skt. pañjara), *cage*: LV 420.8 (all mss. l); repeatedly in mss. of Mv, where Senart always em. °ra, ii.241.14, 17 (one ms. °ra), 18; 242.5, 6, 7 (one ms. °ra), etc.; in these contexts both mss. sometimes °ra.

paṭa, m. (rarely nt.), (**1**) *cloth*, as in Skt., seemingly in very general sense: in Mvy 5864, 9168 Tib. snam bu, which is said to mean *woolen cloth* (contrast paṭaka Mvy 9169); in SP 75.7 (prose) both Burnouf (who reads paṭṭa, see his note p. 369–370) and Kern translate *silk*; the word is cpd. with prec. **duṣya-** or **dūṣya-**, q.v.; B. and K. regard the cpd. as a dvandva, but it is surely a karmadh., meaning some kind of *fine cloth* (see **duṣya**); in Kv 81.6 f. (likewise in Mv ii.157.7) it also means *cloth* in general, as used to garb persons initiated in various religious orders, see s.v. **indra-paṭa**; (**2**) in Mv iii.31.11 apparently *piece, fragment* (of a stone; cf. Skt. paṭati, *splits*), if the text is right: (upalānāṃ) paṭaṃ (so mss., Senart paṭāṃ) chittvā, *splitting off a piece of the stones*; (**3**) in LV 315.15 (vs) assumed to be a kind of bird, but reading uncertain; Lefm.

vīkṣasva bodhimaṇḍe paṭukroñcāhaṃsakokilamayūrāḥ, with v.l. paṭa for paṭu; Calc. paṭa-; Tib. pa ta kun ta (presumably understanding it as n. of a single bird) for paṭa(or paṭu-)krośca (the rest of the cpd. is correctly rendered in Tib.); neither paṭa nor paṭu seems to be known as a bird-name; if paṭu is right, could it not be taken as adv. with vīkṣasva? *look keenly, sharply, at the*...; [(**4**) on LV 127.17 for paṭopachedana read vaṭṭopa°, supported by best ms. and Pali; see s.v. **vaṭṭa.**]

paṭaka, m. (cf. Skt. paṭa, AMg. paḍaga), *cloth*, acc. to Tib. on Mvy 9169 *a large piece of cotton cloth* (ras yug chen); Divy 308.12 f.; 547.16; Av ii.112.8.

? **paṭapaṃsin,** n. pl. °sī (written °śī), a doubtful and prob. corrupt word, applying to ascetics, and prob. in derogatory sense; possibly *vilifying* (? *besmirching, degrading*) *the* (monk's) *cloth* (garment): śailāraṇyaguhānivāsino bhavateha tatrasthāś ca ma (m.c. for mā) ātma manyathā paṭapaṃśī RP 59.7 (vs); cf. **paṃsayati** and its group.

paṭa-bhedaka, m. or nt., substantially = Skt. and Pali puṭabhedana (for which a var. paṭa° is cited in BR from Amara acc. to Loiseleur), *city, metropolis*, or perhaps *castle, citadel* (so Bendall and Rouse on Śikṣ, citing Tib. mkhar which has that mg. and also *house*): rājyaṃ vā parityajan paṭabhedakaṃ vā nagararājadhānīṃ... Śikṣ 27.5. Perhaps read puṭa° (and °na for °ka?).

paṭahikā, (to Skt. paṭaha, with -ikā, perh. dim.; cf. M. paḍahiyā, defined as *a small drum*), *a* (small?) *drum*: bherī-śaṅkha-mṛdaṅga-paṭahikā Mv iii.113.4 (prose).

paṭākā (= Skt. Lex. id., Skt. patākā; Pali records paṭāka, nt., PTSD, beside patākā; AMg. paḍāgā; ṭ doubtless due to blending influence of Skt. paṭa), *banner*: LV 273.20; 295.15; 359.4; 365.9; 367.9; 413.4; 424.1; 430.10, 13 (in all these Lefm. paṭ°, sometimes with all mss., but often v.l. pat°).

? **paṭijāgareti**(°**jāgarti**) = **pratijāgarati,** q.v., read by Senart by em. for (agnihotraṃ) paṭipākaroti (so, or prati°, pati°, mss.) Mv iii.148.20; 156.8, *attends to, cares for*; and amātyehi yathāṇattaṃ sarvaṃ paṭiyākṛtaṃ (mss., Senart paṭijāgṛtaṃ) iii.161.7 (here Senart is supported by the closely similar ii.180.5–6 amātyehi pratijāgṛtaṃ). On the whole Senart seems likely to be right, but cf. next.

[**paṭipākaroti,** so mss. for **paṭijāgareti,** q.v.; or in Mv iii.161.7 mss. paṭiyākṛtaṃ (y could be graphic error for p). While Senart's em. seems probably right, we must note Pali paṭipākatika, also simply pākatika, *set right, fixed up*, or the like; esp. *restored to normal* or *desirable condition*; formally, the mss. forms of Mv could be related to the Pali paṭi-pā°, retaining partially MIndic phonology; Skt. would require prati-prākaroti, or °pra°.]

paṭipāṭi (§ 2.47; = Pali id., Skt. paripāṭi), or °**ṭikā,** *order*; only adv. paṭipāṭiyā (Pali id., Skt. paripāṭyā), *in order, in due course*, Mv i.3.3 (em., but surely right); °ṭikāye, *in order* (of age, or rank) Mv i.354.16 (v.l. pari°); iii.181.11, 12, 13 (in 11 and 13 v.l. prati°).

paṭimoka, or **paṭi**°, m. (= Skt. pratimoka, defined pw 5.260 *das Umlegen, Umhängen*, but may rather be concrete, *an ornament fastened on*; certainly this is the mg. in BHS), *an ornament fastened on*: caturṇāṃ varṇānāṃ paṭimokā (so mss., Senart em. °modakā) abhunsuḥ suvarṇasya ca rūpyasya... Mv i.195.14, of a city gate; so also iii.228.7, where mss. and text pratimodakā, v.l. pati°; twice in Bhvr. cpds., of elephants (hasti-sahasrāṇi), dantapatimokāni śuṇḍā-patimokāni (so Senart, essentially with mss.) Mv ii.453.17, *with ornaments* (garlands?) *on their tusks and trunks.*

paṭisaṃdheti, see **pratisaṃdadhāti.**

paṭisubhati (cf. **subhati**; Pali ppp. paṭisumbhita, also parisumbhati), *strikes*: anyam-anyaṃ... °bhanti Mv i.20.3.

[**paṭu** is sometimes written by error for Skt. paṭṭa, esp. in the sense of (honorary) *fillet* or *turban*; or even seemingly for Skt. paṭa, see s.v. **paṭa** 3, and Kv below. In LV 275.4 most mss. point to °paṭv-ābaddha, but it seems we must read with Lefm. vimukti-paṭṭābaddho, *bound* (decorated) *with the honorary-turban of emancipation* (Tib. confusedly rnam par grol paḥi, = vimukti, thabs thob pa, acc. to Foucaux *il a trouvé le moyen de*..., but thabs might well indicate paṭu as the BHS reading); in LV 367.9; 430.10 and 13 both edd. paṭṭa, some mss. in all, all mss. in 430.10 paṭu; in Kv 84.20 text muktāpaṭu-dāma-kalāpa-pralambitāni, but read paṭṭa or else paṭa as in 87.5 muktāhāra-paṭa-dāma-kalāpa-pralambitāni.]

paṭumaka, see **paḍumaka.**

paṭṭa (once in Skt., pw, and not found elsewhere; error for Skt. paṭṭana?), *city*: Kāśī-paṭṭam, -paṭṭe MSV i.280.8, 9.

paṭṭikā, once °**ka,** m. (fundamentally *strip*, as in Skt., where it is primarily a *strip of cloth*), (**1**) *strip of land* around a building, in pradakṣiṇa-p° Mvy 4361, = Tib. ḥkhor sa (khor ba); abhyantara-, bahiṣ-p°, *inside* (*outside*) *strip of land, path*, around a structure, Mvy 4362–3 = Tib. naṅ rim, phyi rim; (**2**) °kā-saṃnāha, m., *coat of mail*: Mvy 6075 (Mironov paṭṭika°) = Tib. khrab; (in Mvy 8994 and MSV ii.89.11 paṭṭikā, *belt*, as in Skt., Tib. śur bu;) in Mvy 9191 ānanda-paṭṭikaḥ, acc. to Tib. mthaḥ skor, lit. *border-circle*, perh. *edge of a garment*(?).

paṭhita (nt.; not recorded as noun, only as ppp.), *reading*, in a list of arts: °te LV 156.15 = Tib. yi ge bklags paḥi mig ḥor, a curiously awkward paraphrase, which seems to mean *fixing the eyes for reading letters*(?); at least bklags = *reading.*

paḍumaka, or **paṭumaka,** *worm*; implied in **vi-pa**°, q.v. Related to Pali puḷava(ka) or puḷu°, *worm.*

paṇana, nt., *traffic*, in dharma-p°, *selling religion*: Mvy 9430 = Tib. chos ḥtshoṅ ba.

paṇayati, see **paṇeti.**

paṇitaka (m. or nt.; = Pali id., read paṇitako, or °kaṃ, in Jāt. vi.192.22 for text paṇītako; Skt. paṇita, nt.), *wager, stake* (in gambling): °kaṃ badhnanti Mvy 9417.

paṇidhi (MIndic spelling) = **praṇidhi,** *solemn vow* (to win enlightenment): LV 163.16 (vs). Only 1 ms. pra°.

Paṇḍara (= Pali id.), n. of a nāga king: Mvy 3281.

Paṇḍaravāsinī, see **Pā**°.

paṇḍitaka, adj. (Skt. id.; here endearing dim., § 22.34), (*sweetly*) *learned*, of the daughters of Māra: divyaratīṣu su-°kāṃ LV 323.6.

Paṇḍulaka, MIndic (if not misprint) for **Pāṇḍ**°, n. of a nāga king: Māy 247.3.

Pataṃga, n. of a nāga king: Māy 247.26.

[**Pataṃgacara,** em. for **Tataṃjacala,** q.v.]

Pataṃgā, n. of a river: Divy 451.1 ff.; 456.19 ff.

Pataṃgī, n. of a rākṣasī: Māy 243.16.

patapyanti (MIndic for pratapyante), *are tormented*: Mv i.10.4 (vs); repetition iii.454.20 pratapyanti.

patika (in Skt. and Pali only ifc. Bhvr.), = Skt. pati, *husband*: (asmākam) apatikānāṃ (Bhvr.) patikā bhaviṣyatha Mv iii.68.16 (prose); is the -ka endearing dim.? or influenced by the prec. Bhvr. cpd. apatikānāṃ?

Patidhara(!), n. of a Bodhisattva: Mmk 40.16.

patimoka, see **paṭi**°.

patīyati = **pattīy**°, q.v., *believes*: fut. patīṣyanti Mmk 73.15, parallel with śraddhāsyanti.

pateka, var. for **padeka,** q.v.

[**Patka,** text Sukh 2.10, read **Pantha,** q.v.]

pattikā, or °**ka,** cpd. with -āstaraṇa, as ep. of paryaṅkā, *couches*, in pattikāstaraṇāṃ (acc. pl.) Mv ii.115.16, *having coverlets* (āstaraṇa) *of*...? Either error or corruption for paṭṭikā, *strips of cloth*, or possibly MIndic for pattrikā, = Skt. pattra, pattraka, *leaf* (in lit. or transferred sense)?

pattīyati, and caus. **pattīyāpayati**; also (rarely) **patīyati,** and (oftener) **pratīyati,** qq.v. (see Chap. 43 for etym. and forms; closest is AMg. pattiyai; in Pali pattiyāyati, prob. denom. to Pali adj. -pattiya, *trusting*), *believes, trusts*; often parallel with forms of śrad-dhā (e. g. in SP 44.3; 286.8; KP 16.8, cf. 16.2): °yati Mv ii.110.9; 208.6; iii.189.14; KP 16.8; °yasi Śikṣ 174.7, 18; °yanti Śikṣ 174.15; °yata SP 44.3; °yiṣyanti SP 286.8; 312.9; °yitam Mv ii.249.14; caus. °yāpayiṣyāmy (Kashgar rec. °yāpayāmi) SP 288.5.

pattragupta (m., doubtless = **pakṣagupta,** q.v.), a kind of bird: LV 11.3, acc. to ms. H, see Crit. app., confirmed by Tib. bya (*bird*) ḥdab sbed (*wing-guarded*); 162.19; 320.17 (Tib. as on 11.3).

pattracārika, see s.v. **-cārika.**

pattrachedaka (so Index and Mironov, text °ika), m., Mvy 3792, acc. to Tib. glegs (*board*, esp. *panel of a door*, Mvy 5567) ḥbra (? this word I have not found) mkhan (*one who is concerned with*); so, perhaps, *board* or *door-panel cutter*; but AMg. patta-chejja is said to mean *art of shooting leaves* (with an arrow), and cf. patta-chejjaka, *activity of one who shoots down leaves from a tree*(!). Cf. Jacobi, Ausgew. Erz. 19.37 (here piercing leaves with pebbles). In any case, designation of some trade or occupation. Chin. is obscure; Jap. *paper-maker* (note pattra also of leaves used for writing!).

pattra-mukha, nt., *border* (? on a robe; so, acc. to N. Dutt, Tib. snam bu rnams kha): MSV ii.50.16 ekena pārśvena °khāni pātayanti, 51.2 ubhayapārśvayoḥ °khāni dattāni.

pattrayāna, nt., *a vehicle moving on wings*: Mv ii.434.8 (associated with ākāśayāna).

Patnīya, n. of a locality: Māy 100, loc. sg. Patnīye; could also be from a stem Patnī, f.

patha, nt. (in Skt. m.), *way*: marutpathāni LV 117.9 (vs). See also **Laṅkā-patha.**

pathājīva, adj. m., *one who makes his living on roads*(?): MSV i.52.7 (gopālakā) aśvapālakās tṛṇahārakāḥ kāṣṭhahārakāḥ pathājīvā utpathājīvāś ca manuṣyāḥ; ii.146.12.

(**pathy-adana,** nt., *journey-provisions*, tho not in pw, is good Skt., see Schmidt, Nachträge; commoner is pathyodana. In Mvy 7182 °adana with v.l. °odana, which Mironov reads without v.l.; in Divy 60.1 read sva-pathyadanam as one word; in Dbh 21.6 pathyodana, but below 21.19 pathyadana.)

pada (= Pali id.), *sentence, complete utterance*, in contrast with **nāman,** *word*, and **vyañjana,** *sound* (same triad in Pali, PTSD s.v. pada, 4): Mvy 1998 (-kāyaḥ), see s.v. **kāya** (2); defined AbhidhK. LaV-P. ii.238 as = vākya, *a complete statement which makes sense*; this may perhaps be the mg. in **agra-pada**; where the context contains no contrasting word for *word*, that common Skt. meaning of pada may ordinarily be assumed; see s.v. **vyañjana** for one or two such passages where pada is thus ambiguous (*word* or *sentence*).

padaka, adj. or subst. m. (in Skt. Gr., *versed in the padapāṭha*; Pali id., interpreted by PTSD in this latter sense, but by Pali comms. generally more broadly, *learned*, esp. in brahmanical learning), *learned*, in brahmanical learning (possibly more narrowly, in the padapāṭha): °ko vaiyākaraṇo Divy 619.24; 620.19; Speyer on Av ii.19.8 would em. Divy. to padaśo with text of Av, but this seems hardly necessary.

Padakrama, n. of a mleccha king: Mmk 621.25.

pada-parama, adj. (= Pali id.), *who makes the word* (not the meaning) *the main thing, literalist*: LV 400.2 and Mv iii.318.4 (in both after **vipañcitajña,** q.v.; virtually same passage); Mvy 2477 = Tib. tshigs la ḥchol ba.

pada-bandha, m. (= **pāda-b°,** q.v.), a particular technique of *holding* or *wielding* (the bow), viz. apparently by using *the foot* in some way; Tib. on LV renders gom stabs, *step-manner* (making a step?); in a list of arts to be mastered by a prince, and associated with **muṣṭibandha,** q.v.: LV 156.12; Divy 100.12; 442.7. On the Tib. see s.v. **pāda-b°.**

(**pada-śas,** occurs in Skt. in mgs. *step by step, gradually*, and *letter by letter*; the latter mg., or *piece by piece, part by part*, is to be assumed in LV 337.12 (vs), which read thus: śakyākāśe lekhyaṃ citraṃ bahu vividha vikṛta padaśaḥ (Lefm. fails to divide correctly) prakartu pṛthak-pṛthak.)

padasā (= Pali id.; instr. sg. of pada, § 8.41), *on foot*: Mv ii.199.8; iii.115.11.

(**padāta,** *footsoldier*; also in Skt., stigmatized by Boehtlingk as erroneous for padāti; but padātā, n. pl., Mv ii.282.17, prose, tends to confirm its correctness.)

padāvihāra, see **vihāra** (3).

Padāśva, n. of a prince: Karmav 80.4; corresp. to Pali Pāyāsi, see Lévi's note.

paduma, MIndic for Skt. and BHS **padma,** q.v. (and in cpds. thereof), *lotus*; very common; examples § 3.114.

Padumuttara, Padumot°, see **Padmottara.**

padeka, m. (so Mironov; var. pateka), *sparrow-hawk, falcon*: Mvy 4901 = Tib. khra.

padma (paduma), m. or nt., (**1**) n. of a kind of brahmanical sacrifice: Mv ii.237.20 (prose) padumaṃ puṇḍarīkaṃ (this occurs in Skt. in this sense) ca, in a list of sacrifices, see **nirargaḍa**; (**2**) m. (paduma), n. of one of the 4 'great treasures' (cf. Pali puṇḍarīka; see s.v. **elapatra**): Mv iii.383.19 (known in Skt. as n. of a nāga); (**3**) n. of a former Buddha (Paduma): Mv iii.233.7 f.; (**4**) n. of the world-age (paduma kalpa) in which 62 Buddhas named Śikhin succeeded each other: Mv iii.235.6; (**5**) nt., also m., n. of a hell (= Pali Paduma; cf. **Mahāpadma**): Divy 67.23; 138.8; Av i.4.9 etc.; it is cold acc. to Mvy 4935; Dharmas 122, but hot (at least sufferers are boiled there) in Śikṣ 75.8, where (and in 10) the spelling is Padumo, n. sg., tho in prose!; (**6**) nt., n. of a cetika (caitya) in the south: LV 389.10; in the parallel Mv iii.307.17 **Abhipaśya**; Pali has Paduma as n. of a cetiya (DPPN s.v. 8), but it is not clear whether it is the same.

Padmaka, n. of a king (the Bodhisattva): Av i.169.6 ff.

padmakā, n. of a (medicinal) plant (prob. = padmā, Suśr., BR): MSV i.iii.8.

padma-kūṭāgāra, *lotus-apartment*, n. applied to the place (magically produced from a lotus, Mv i.227.18 ff.) in which Dīpaṃkara attained enlightenment and then received the adoration of the gods: °re Mv i.230.12.

Padmagarbha, (**1**) n. of one (or two?) former Buddha(s): LV 171.21; Gv 104.18; (**2**) n. of a Bodhisattva: Mvy 673; Gv 2.24; Dbh 2.5.

Pad(u)magarbhaś(i)rī, n. of a Buddha: Gv 284.20 (vs).

Padmaḍākinī, n. of a yoginī: Sādh 460.4 etc.

Padmadhṛk-, stem in comp. for °**dhṛt** (in Skt. -dhṛk is said to be used only as n. sg. for -dhṛt at end of cpds.), n. of a Tathāgata: °dhṛk-pramukhaiḥ sarvatathāgataiḥ Sādh 362.18.

Padmanarteśvara, n. of a deity: Sādh 75.6 et alibi.

Padmanetra, (**1**) n. of a Tathāgata: Mvy 96; (**2**) n. of a Bodhisattva: Mvy 676.

Padmaprabha, (**1**) n. of (a future birth of Śāriputra as) a Buddha-to-be, predicted: SP 65.5 ff.; (**2**) n. of a devaputra, one of the 16 guardians of the bodhimaṇḍa: LV 277.15.

Padmaprabhā, (**1**) n. of a mythical city: Gv 232.8; (**2**) n. of a queen: Gv 335.21.

Padmabimbyupaśobhita, n. of a former Buddha: Sukh 6.8.

Padmabhadrābhirāmanetraśrī, n. of a princess,

daughter of a cakravartin: Gv 269.14. For other forms see s.v. **Samantajñānaratnārciḥpadma°**.

Padmamāla, n. of a former Buddha: Mv i.140.11.

Padmayoni, n. of a former Buddha: LV 171.19.

Padmarajavarṇa, n. of a former Buddha: Mv i.138.12.

Padmavajrī, n. of a goddess: Sādh 160.6.

Padmavana, n. of a grove where Dīpaṃkara was born: Mv i.215.11.

Padmavara, n. of a Bodhisattva: Mmk 576.15.

Padmavardhana, n. of an author: Sādh 317.4.

Padmavāsinī, n. of a goddess: Sādh 75.16.

Padmavṛṣabhavikrāmin (v.l. °vikrama), n. of a future Buddha (= Dhṛtiparipūrṇa Bodhisattva): SP 67.4, 6.

Padmavyūhā, n. of a 'Bodhisattva-dhāraṇī': Mvy 753; padmavyūha-(m. or nt.?)-dhāraṇī-: Gv 66.17.

Padmaśrī, (**1**) m., n. of a Bodhisattva: SP 3.8; 431.3 ff.; 470.3; (**2**) m., n. of a Tathāgata: ŚsP 50.7; (**3**) f., n. of a lokadhātu: Gv 536.22.

Padmaśrīgarbha, n. of a Bodhisattva: Gv 2.26; Dbh 2.6.

Padmaśrīgarbhasaṃbhavā, n. of a queen: Gv 399.16.

Padmahasta, n. of a Bodhisattva: ŚsP 42.14.

Padmā, (**1**) n. of a brahman woman who entertained the Bodhisattva: LV 238.7; (**2**) n. of a lokadhātu: ŚsP 50.6; (**3**) (Padumā) n. of a rākṣasī: Māy 243.9 (prose).

Padmākaramati, n. of an author: Sādh 42.7.

Padmākṣa, n. of a Śākyan youth: Av i.367.12 ff.

Padmāṅka-mudrā, n. of a certain mudrā: Kv 74.8.

Padmāntaka, m., one of the 10 krodhas: Dharmas 11; Sādh 137.9.

Padmābha, n. of a former Buddha: Mv i.136.17. (In Mmk 452.12 prob. adj., *colored like a lotus*, as in Skt. [Schmidt, Nachträge], agreeing with Mahāpadmo ['tha nāgendraḥ padmābhaś . . .], rather than n. of another nāga-prince; cf. 452.14 where padmābhau, dual, is certainly an adj., referring to Vāsuki and Takṣaka of line 13.)

Padmālaṃkārā, n. of a 'gandharva maid': Kv 5.2.

Pad(u)māvatī, (**1**) n. of a girl of miraculous birth who became the wife of King Brahmadatta of Kāmpilya; heroine of the 'Pad(u)māvatī parikalpa' (colophon Mv iii.170.10): Mv iii.155.7 ff. (mss. vary between Padumā° and Padmā°, Senart prints the former); (**2**) n. of a devakumārikā in the northern quarter: Mv iii.309.8 (Padumā°) = LV 391.3 (Padmā°, meter rectified by a 'patch-word'), vs; (**3**) n. of a wife of King Aśoka, mother of Kunāla: Divy 405.17.

Padmoccā, n. of a yakṣiṇī: Mmk 573.14, 16.

Padmottama, (**1**) n. of a future Buddha: Av i.40.13; (**2**) n. of a past Buddha: Samādh p. 66 line 16; (another?) Kv 70.5 ff.; 74.1, etc.; also (**3**) m., n. of the lokadhātu where the last-named lived: Kv 70.4; 76.16 (here misprinted).

Padmottara, in Mv spelled also **Padumot°**, **Padumuttara**, (**1**) (= Pali Padumuttara), n. of a former Buddha, one of the standard list of 24 in Pali, in most BHS cases doubtless the same individual: Mv iii.240.2; 241.14; 243.3, 4, 22; 244.18; 247.5; 248.8; LV 5.4; 172.13; Gv 206.13; Mmk 499.22; a group of 500 Buddhas of this name (Padmot°) are recorded Mv i.58.1, 7; 61.16; (**2**) n. of a future Pratyekabuddha: Av i.128.6; (**3**) n. of one or two Bodhisattvas: Gv 442.1; ŚsP 50.10.

Padmottaraśrī, n. of a Tathāgata: ŚsP 42.11.

Padmodgata, n. of a Buddha: Gv 284.13.

Padmoṣṇīṣa, n. of a former Buddha: Mv i.138.2.

padya (m. or nt.; Skt. only padyā f. in this mg., Lex. and rarely lit., Schmidt, Nachträge; = Pali pajja), *way, path*: padyena kṛtena ātmanā Mv iii.395.11 (vs) = Pali Sn 514 pajjena katena attanā.

? **pana**, indecl. (= Pali pana, Skt. punar), *but*: acc. to Senart's em. in Mv i.188.10 (vs), for mss. pannā; but the whole line is corrupt and dubious. (Senart has no note and omits the word in his Index.)

paneti, read **paṇeti** (= Skt. paṇayati), *evaluates, rates*, in LV 330.13 (vs) kāyā sarva paneti, *he rates all bodies* (at their true worthlessness); Tib. rtogs, *perceive, know*. The alternative, which seems unattractive, would be to assume a strangely distorted MIndic form of Skt. pra-jñā- (cf. AMg. paṇṇāyati etc.).

pantha (m.; = Pali id.; Skt. panthan with altered stem-final), (**1**) *way*: acc. pantham, Mv i.363.16 (prose, v.l. pathaṃ); vss, ii.199.1, 3; iii.82.17; abl. panthāto iii.74.17 (prose); 82.12 (vs); instr. panthena iii.74.19 (prose); (**2**) n. of a disciple of Buddha, = Pali (Mahā-) Panthaka: so read for text Patka (!) in Sukh 2.10, where the only mss. read Paccha or Pattha, both based on Pantha, as the note observes; see also **Culla-P°**, and (**Cūḍa-**)**Panthaka**.

Panthaka = **Cūḍa-p°**, q.v. (younger brother of **Mahā-p°**): Divy 485.28 ff.

panthalika, m. or nt., and **°kā**, f. (obviously based somehow on panthan, but formation obscure; unrecorded elsewhere), *path, way*: taṃ °kaṃ, acc. sg., Mv iii.82.14, 16; °kāṃ gṛhītvā Kv 54.13, 21; 55.5; Divy 335.1; °kāyāṃ, loc., Divy 485.19, 26, 27.

[**panthitā(ḥ)**, Divy 463.26, error: see s.v. **nepatthita**.]

pamatta-bandhu (= Pali id.; with MIndic phonology, both mss., Senart em. pra°), *friend of the indolent*, ep. of Māra: °dhuno, gen., Mv ii.319.13 (vs). See also **pramādabandhu**.

payyaka, m. (= Pali id.; Skt. *prāryaka), *great-grandfather*: Mv ii.426.16. Cf. **ayyaka, aryaka**.

para, adv. **pareṇa**, see this.

? **parakṣa**, adj. (MIndic for parokṣa), perhaps *when* (the owner) *is absent*, ep. of dhana, *wealth*: Gv 407.2; see **aparakṣa**.

Paragaṇamathana, n. of a Bodhisattva: Gv 443.3 (read with 2d ed. °mathanasyānila°).

paratantra, *dependent on something else*, as one of the three **svabhāva**, q.v., in Laṅk: explained Laṅk 67.15; mentioned 130.9; Suzuki, *relative knowledge or relativity*; the same triad called **lakṣaṇa**, q.v., in Mvy and Sūtrāl.; paratantra-l° Mvy 1664; °trasya lakṣaṇaṃ Sūtrāl. xi.40 (Lévi, *indice du relatif*).

paratara, adv. °raṃ and °reṇa, chiefly following **pareṇa**, q.v.; also alone, postpos. with prec. gen., *beyond* (in space): saptānāṃ prākārāṇāṃ paratareṇa kṣipto Mv ii.75.14, *hurled beyond seven walls*.

(**paratas**, *afterwards*, as in Skt., and Pali paṛato; in specific sense, *after this life* = *in a future existence*, perhaps not specifically so used in Skt. or Pali, but hardly deserving Senart's note which ascribes it to 'confusion' with Skt. paratra: imasmiṃ loke parataś ca Mv i.164.6 (vs), *in this world and* (in the) *hereafter*.)

para-tīrthika, adj. or subst. m. (= **tīrthika**; not recorded in Pali, but cf. añña-titthiya, see anya-tīrthika s.v. **tīrthika**; occurs in Jain Skt., see ISt. 10.257), *adhering to* (*adherent of*) *a heretical sect*: °ka-niśritānāṃ LV 420.19 (vs; so read, see Crit. App.); 436.10; in Mv i.87.5 (vs) read with (most) mss. paratīrthikamataṃ teṣāṃ (Senart em. apara° and om. teṣāṃ, which does not improve the sense). Also para-tīrthya, see **tīrthya**.

paratraṃ (m.c. for °tra), *in the world beyond*: Ud vii.6 (see § 2.74, end).

Paranirmita, m., (**1**) sg., = **Vaśavartin**, chief of the **paranirmitavaśavartin** gods: °to RP 52.18 (vs), see s.v. **Suyāma**; (**2**) pl., that class of gods: paranirmitā ye devā Mv ii.349.14 (vs), resuming prose, paranirmitavaśavartī ca devā 348.18; brahmātha Śakra paranirmita sākaniṣṭhāḥ LV 342.18 (vs; or is this sg., to 1 ?); °tā, pl., Mmk 19.12 (prose), cited s.v. **sunirmita**, pl.

paranirmitavaśavartin (= Pali paranimmitavasavatti-n), n. of the highest class of kāmāvacara gods, see **deva**; lit. *controlling* (enjoyments) *magically created by others*; they rank higher than the **nirmāṇarati**, who create their own magical enjoyments: LV 46.21; 51.1; 150.4; 266.7; 396.15; 401.10; Mv i.33.3; 212.15; 229.16; 240.5; 263.17; 333.6; ii.16.4; 163.12; 348.18; 360.6; iii.223.11; Mvy 3083; Dharmas 127; Divy 68.13; 367.10; Av i.5.1; Suv 86.10; Sukh 41.2, etc.; sg., of the chief of this class (parallel with **Sunirmita** etc.), LV 44.10; 59.9; 361.13 (later he is referred to as Vaśavarti-, q.v., in 362.15); he is more regularly known as **Vaśavartin**, also (in vss) as simply **Paranirmita**, q.v. The interpretation of the name is correctly given by Childers, and supported by the paraphrase **paranirmitodyukta.**

paranirmitodyukta = prec., in a vs, doubtless a paraphrase to fit the meter: LV 219.8; interesting because the mg., *devoted to* (*zealous for*) *the* (enjoyments) *magically created by others*, confirms the interpretation of **paranirmitavaśavartin.**

para-praṇeya, *needing to be guided by others* (on account of blindness): Mv ii.212.4 (prose) and 214.4 (prose), Senart both times °prāṇeya (with both mss. 212.4 and one 214.4, also v.l. 221.2), interpreted as *whose life* (prāṇa) *depends on others*; 221.2 (vs) °praṇeyeṣu (Senart em. °yyeṣu), here short a in °praṇ° is required by meter; that Senart's theory is incorrect seems to me proved by 218.3 where the persons in question say that, being blind, they cannot go anywhere vinā praṇetareṇa, *without a guide.*

-parapratyaya, see **a-para°**.

para-pravāda, m. (= Pali parappavāda), *rival* (false, heretical) *doctrine*: nihatāḥ °dā(ḥ) LV 260.9 (vs); in LV 7.12 (vs) read parapravādān for paraṃ pra° (Tib. phas kyi rgol, see next); Laṅk 10.12.

parapravādin (prec. plus -in; not recorded in Pali), *false teacher, one who promulgates false doctrine*: Mvy 2730 = Tib. phas kyi rgol ba, which seems the usual term; Mvy 831 °dy-anabhibhūta, said of Bodhisattvas, Tib. here pha rol gyi rgol ba; LV 5.19; 273.2; 275.13; 375.1; 377.15; 439.5; 440.8; Divy 202.12; Dbh 53.15; Sukh 60.11 (sarvaparapravādy-akampanatayā); Gv 195.8; 221.6, etc. See also **para-vādin.**

[**para-prāṇeya,** read **para-praṇeya.**]

param, indecl. (nowhere recorded; Skt. paramam is so used), particle of assent, esp. to a command, *assuredly, certainly*: Divy 288.13; 292.24; 293.8; 390.1; 407.29; 460.3; in LV 102.9 (prose) Lefm. parameti, with all his mss., read surely param iti with Calc., supported in sense by Tib.; a verb eti is not construable, and paramaṃ ti (for iti), or paramam iti, would be much less probable emendations.

parama, m. or nt., a high number: °masya Gv 105.20. Corresponds to **mapara,** nt., **mavara,** also **savara** (2), qq.v.

para-mata (nt.), *thought(s) of others*, known to a Buddha by his supernatural knowledge: jātakā-paramateṣu kovidā (sc. Buddhas) Mv i.104.13; sarvaparamataṃ viduḥ i.192.18; see full discussion of both passages s.v. **jātaka** (3); Senart misunderstands.

paramatā, *supreme quality* of the paramā bodhi, supreme enlightenment of a Buddha; there are seven such, Bbh 89.10 ff. (they are in no way related to the **pāramitā**), viz., āśraya-, pratipatti-, saṃpatti-, jñāna-, prabhāva-, prahāṇa-, and vihāra-p°, defined in the following.

paramantra, nt., or °**trā,** f., a high number: Mvy 7886 = Tib. gzhal thag; cited from Gv 133.19; in Gv 106.8 °mantrāyā(ḥ), gen. sg. fem.; corresponds to **paramātra,** q.v.; °mantraśaḥ Mv i.13.8 (vs), by Senart's em. which is prob. right (mss. mostly °mantiṇo, one good ms. °mantriśo).

paramāṇurajaḥpraveśa, m., Mvy 7987 (cited from LV), or °praveśānugatā, LV 148.20 (in both foll. by nāma gaṇanā), lit. (*following*) *the entrance* (*penetration*) *into ultimate atom-dust*, n. of a high number or method of computation (gaṇanā). Tib. on both rdul phra rab la ḥjug pa (in LV adding rjes su soṅ ba = anugata).

paramātra, m., = **paramantra**: Mvy 7757, also = Tib. gzhal thag, which suggests that Tib. read °mātra rather than °mantra (gzhal, *measure*).

Paramārthadharmavijaya, m., n. of a Buddhist work: Mvy 1380.

Paramārthavikrāmin, n. of a Bodhisattva: Gv 442.17.

Paramārthasaṃvṛtisatyanirdeśa (see s.v. **saṃvṛti** 2), n. of a Buddhist work: Mvy 1368.

Paramārthasattva, n. of a former Buddha: Mv i.141.8.

Paramāśva, n. of a deity: Sādh 510.7 etc.

paraṃparabhojana, nt. (= Pali id.), *eating* (almsfood, on the part of monks) *in* (chosen) *sequence, by* (chosen) *turns*: Prāt 508.11 (a sin, unless the monk is sick, or robes are to be given at one house; cf. SBE 13.38 note 4).

parava, m. or nt., a high number: Gv 106.17. Corresponds to **dhavara,** q.v.

Paravāḍa, n. of a nāga-king: Mvy 3284. Cf. **Maravāla.**

paravādin (= Pali id.) = **parapravādin,** q.v.: mathiya (most mss. pathiya, but cf. Pali Miln. 348.5 paravādivādamathanaṃ) °di (acc. pl.) Mv i.72.16 (vs); °dibhir Bbh 251.8 (prose).

parasparā-saṃsakti(n), adj. Bhvr. (cf. Pali andhaveṇi paraṃparāsaṃsattā DN i.239.25; Skt. saṃsakta, ppp., with parasparaṃ, adv., BR s.v. sañj with sam, 4), *connected with one another, succeeding one another*, of kings: te ca °tinaḥ ... mahārājānaḥ Mmk 47.8 (prose); if not corrupt, parasparā may be a blend of the adv. °ram with the noun paraṃparā, both Skt.

parākarṣayati (Skt. only ger. °kṛṣya and ppp. °kṛṣṭa, once each in BR; not noted elsewhere), *draws away*: Mvy 6747 = Tib. phar ḥdren.

Parākramavikrama, n. of a Bodhisattva: Gv 442.17.

parājinati = parājayati, Chap. 43, s.v. ji, 2.

parādha, aphetic form of aparādha, *offence* (§ 4.22): deśikaś ca parādhāparāddhaḥ Mv i.132.10 (prose; no v.l.).

[? **parāntaka,** f. °**ikā,** doubtful reading in several Divy passages, listed s.v. **aparāntaka.**]

parāpata, m. (vv.ll. pārāp°, pārāvata, both Skt., see on the first Schmidt, Nachträge; Mironov parāpata with no v.l.), *pigeon*: Mvy 4902 = Tib. phug ron.

parāparajñatā, *condition of knowing successive states*: pudgala-(mss. puṅgala-)parāparajñatā-kuśalo Mv i.4.2; (?) indriya-°tā SP 317.14, so KN without report of v.l.; but WT very differently, omitting this word, acc. to the note with their ms. K′ and Tib.

parāpṛṣṭhīkaraṇa, nt. (n. act. to next), *the putting to flight*: sarvamārabala-abhibhavana-°naṃ (so read, cpd.) Mmk 55.11, *conquest and putting to flight of all Māra's host.*

parāpṛṣṭhīkṛta (ppp. to °karoti, noted only in this and °**karaṇa,** preceding; cf. next), *put to flight, routed*: jitā bhagnāḥ parājitāḥ °kṛtā(ḥ) Divy 223.16; in virtually identical list, °kṛta(ḥ) Av i.55.3.

parāpṛṣṭhībhavati (cf. prec.; cpd. of parā with **pṛṣṭhībhavati,** q.v.), *turns one's back*; in simple, literal sense, nirgacchantaṃ °bhūtvā Divy 259.24, *as he was going away* (from the house) *turning his back* (to it); *turns away* (in disgust) *from* (someone deemed unworthy), °bhūtaḥ Śikṣ 283.14, of a Bodhisattva, from greedy people; resumed in -vimukhyasya (so mss., ed. em. vai°) 15–16.

parāmarśa, m. (to next; = Pali parāmāsa), *clinging to*; see **dṛṣṭi-p°** and **śīlavrata-p°**.

parāmṛśati (= Pali °masati; in Skt. seems not used in same mgs.), *cleaves* or *adheres to, takes up* or *is attached to* (in an unworthy, disapproved way): Laṅk 119.2 śilaṃ ... na parāmṛśati srotaāpannaḥ, *does not adhere to moral rules* (in an unenlightened way, as the sequel explains; see **śīlavrataparāmarśa**); AsP 292.15, 17; 293.4 mā ... samyaksaṃbodhiṃ rūpataḥ (etc.) parāmṛkṣaḥ, *do not attach yourself* (cleave) *to enlightenment as form* (etc.); followed 292.18; 293.5 by **aparāmṛṣṭā** (q.v.) hi ... sarvajñatā, *for omniscience is unattached* (not unworthily affected, untarnished). See also **parāmṛṣṭa**.

parāmṛṣṭa (ppp. of prec.; = Pali °maṭṭha; cf. **a-parā°**), (*unworthily*) *adhered to*: Ud xi.4 (= Pali Dhp. 311) śrāmaṇyaṃ duṣparāmṛṣṭam *evilly adhered to*; the next vs 5 is a secondary imitation of this, and only as such has śrāmaṇyaṃ suparā°, *well* or *properly adhered to* (su-parā° is really a contradiction in terms, as if one said 'a righteous infatuation'); Mvy 7031. [In Ud xiv.7 = MSV ii.183.4 parāmṛṣṭa = *considered, deliberate*, a Skt. mg. of the verb; so Tib. indicates; MSV ms. paramṛṣṭa, ed. wrongly em. parimuṣṭa, cf. Pali. The whole vs is substantially right in text of Ud, wrong in MSV.]

parāmṛṣṭi, f. (= **parāmarśa**: to **parāmṛśati**, q.v.), (unworthy, disapproved) *adherence, clinging to*: Laṅk 119.3; 179.2; 180.7.

-parāyaṇīya, adj. (or subst., nt.; Skt. parāyaṇa plus -īya), *that which has ... as its goal*; *what tends towards ... as its goal* or *refuge*: likhāpanīyaṃ bodhi-parāyaṇīyaṃ (delete daṇḍa or transpose it to here); bodhiparāyaṇaṃ niyataṃ Mmk 38.21, *what tends to the goal* (or refuge) *of enlightenment is to be depicted*; (then) *the goal* (refuge) *of enlightenment is certain.*

Parārthasavihāraś(i)rī, n. of a Buddha: Gv 285.24 (vs).

parāvṛtta, ppp., and **parāvṛtti**, n. act. (both Skt.), *reversed*, and *reversion, revulsion*, of the basic mentality (esp. called **āśraya**, q.v., in Suzuki, Studies, 390 with refs.); technically of the fundamental change in mental attitude which is taught as necessary to knowledge of the true doctrine: parāvṛttāśraya (text °vṛtā°) Laṅk 9.11; cf. 10.14; parāvṛtty-āśraya, *having the basis* (of consciousness) *characterized by* (this) *revulsion* 93.3 (or read °vṛttāśra°?); parāvṛtta, e. g. 284.11; °tti 10.14; for others see Suzuki's Index and Glossary; also in AbhidhK, see LaV-P's Index; Sūtrāl. ix.12–17 (Lévi *20, *24).

parāhaṇana, nt. (to next; here domal ṇ), *beating* (of a drum, here the 'drum of the law'): mahādharmabherī-°naṃ SP 16.12 (prose).

parāhanati (also °ṇati), °**hanti** (not recorded in MIndic; in Skt. not in this mg.; cf. **parāhaṇana**), *strikes*; esp. a drum (bherī, dundubhi, either lit., or fig. dharma-bh°, -du°, *the drum of the law*): °hananti SP 12.12 (read °tī m.c.); 69.11; °haṇe, 1 sg. opt., Mv i.42.8; °hanasva (Kashgar rec. °hanāhi) SP 178.10; °haniṣyati SP 421.8; °haniṣyasi Suv 90.9; °ghnanto, pple., Sukh 61.2; °hanantaṃ Suv 20.8; °hanyamānair, pass. pres. pple., LV 274.12; °hatā Suv 62.3; a gong (gaṇḍī), °hatya, ger., Av i.272.1; vāditrabhāṇḍāni parāhatāni Divy 203.14; (piṇḍapātaṃ) parāhatya Av ii.156.2; the earth (mahī, pṛthivī, dharaṇī) °hanti LV 266.14; °hanati Mv ii.282.8; °hatya Gv 221.23; °hanitvā LV 12.19 (vs).

parikaṭṭaka, m. (mss.; Senart °ḍḍhaka; to next, plus -aka), *leader, manager, ruler*: Mv ii.254.15 (of a flock of birds); 256.20 (of deer). Cf. **parikarṣaka**.

parikaṭṭati (mss.; Senart °kaḍḍhati; see Chap. 43 s.v. kaṭṭ-ati; in mg. = Skt. pari-kṛṣ), *leads, governs, manages*, said of the leader of a flock of deer: °ti Mv ii.255.17, 18.

parikathā (= Pali id., both senses; Skt. Lex. only), (1) *roundabout talk*; *indirect allusion* (see s.v. **avabhāsa**): Divy 92.18 ff.; (2) more generally, *talk*, perhaps *lengthy speech*: LV 242.22 (vs) parikatha bhikṣu yadī na bhārasaṃjñā, *if a* (long) *tale does not seem to you a burden*; but Foucaux takes parikatha as 2 sg. impv. to °kathayati; Tib. dge sloṅ (= bhikṣu) khur gyi ḥdu śes (*notion of burden*) med (*not*) na (= yadi) gsuṅs (*speak*; verb or noun?); more especially of a *religious talk, sermon* or *dialogue*, Divy 225.26; 235.25 (bhikṣavo ...) °thāṃ kurvanti.

parikaraṇa (nt.; to next, plus -ana), *help, assistance, service*: paraduḥkheṣu parikaraṇakuśalāś ca (of Bodhisattvas) Mv i.133.18.

parikarati (= Pali id.; possibly denom. to Skt. parikara; cited °karoti PTSD, but all its citations fit the stem in -a-), *aids, serves, waits upon*: (mātaraṃ pitaraṃ ...) parikared Divy 51.23 (prose).

(**parikarma-kathā**, Divy 210.9, acc. to Index, *prayer* (?); but rather *speech of preparation* (Skt. parikarma), sc. for religious life: (mayā ..., Buddha speaking of his past existences) evaṃvidhā parikarmakathā kṛtā yad ... prāṇiśatasahasrāṇi gṛhāśramam apahāya ṛṣayaḥ pravrajitvā etc.)

parikarmaṇa, nt., n. sg. °ṇaṃ, = **parikarma** (§ 17.28), or n. act. to Skt. parikarmayati with -ana, *working over, preparation* (of Bodhisattvas, compared to jewels): buddhorasānāṃ parikarmaṇaṃ tathā KP 92.8 (vs; cf. vaiḍūryaratne parikarma nīyaṃte, read nīyate, line 6).

parikarmī-karoti (Skt. parikarma-n plus kar-; = Skt. parikarmayati), *works up, makes ready*: °kuru MSV i.31.2.

parikarṣaka, m. (to Skt. parikarṣati; cf. **parikaṭṭaka**), *one who controls, manages*: (dvāv agrāmātyau ...) rāja-parikarṣakau rājaparipālakau Divy 318.19–20.

parikarṣaṇa, nt. (not noted in these mgs.), (1) *carrying about in the mind, thinking on, planning*: idam agraṃ vyāpādānāṃ yad utānantarya-parikarṣaṇam Śikṣ 172.2. Acc. to Bendall 408, a parallel text has ānantaryopakramaṇam; Tib. cited as byed par śom pa, *preparing to commit*; (2) (cf. Pali parikaḍḍhati, in this sense) *attracting, drawing to oneself*: svapakṣa-parikarṣaṇākāraṃ Śikṣ 190.18, *having the form of attracting* (*drawing to oneself*) *one's own allies* (presumably 'good friends' who help one in the right path); parikarṣaṇārthaṃ bālānāṃ Laṅk 135.5 = 321.7 (vs), *for the sake of drawing the simple-minded to myself.*

parikarṣayati, °te (1) (= Skt. parikarṣati, *carries around*; in Skt. karṣayati is used in the sense of karṣati) *carries around* (a child, said of a nurse): Divy 475.14, see s.v. **aṅkadhātrī**; (2) perhaps *attracts, draws to oneself* (see s.v. **parikarṣaṇa**, 2): (buddhavaṃśam anudhārayiṣyasi dharmavaṃśa pariśodhayiṣyasi) saṃghavaṃśa parikarṣayiṣyase Gv 484.12 (vs). Or can the word here mean *you will support, nurse, carry around the Order* (as a nurse carries a child; above)?

parikalpa, m. (not in Skt., except rarely Jain Skt., see Schmidt, Nachträge, where it is rendered *Täuschung*; Pali parikappa, acc. to PTSD *assumption, supposition, surmise*; once, Therag. 940, said to mean *preparation, intention, strategem*, but at least as possible would be *vain, false imaginings* for parikappehi there), fundamentally (1) *surmise, assumption, hypothesis, figment of imagination*, regularly with implication of falsity or unreliability (cf. **parikalpayati**); sometimes of an innocent *hypothesis* or frankly *imaginary assumption*: parikalpam upādāya Śikṣ 87.15, 16; 166.11, *assuming a hypothetical case, to take an imaginary hypothesis*; but chiefly with derogatory implication, *vain fancy*, as something to be got rid of; often with **kalpa** and **vikalpa**, qq.v.; sarva-kalpa-vikalpa-parikalpa-prahāṇāya LV 34.11; na kalpo na vikalpo na parikalpaḥ Śikṣ 272.7; kalpavikalpa-parikalpa- KP 94.3

(prose; Tib. omits the equivalent of parik°, doubtless by haplography); parikalpa-saṃjña-vigatā(ḥ) Gv 478.8 (vs); (avikalpe bodhisattvajñānamaṇḍale) sarva-kalpa-parikalpā na saṃvidyate (= °yante; read so?) Gv 350.6; sukham atra (sc. gṛhāvāse) kutaḥ kathaṃ kadā vā parikalpa-praṇayaṃ na ced upaiti Jm 108.6, *whence, how, and when could there be happiness in this* (householder's life), *if* (as has been shown in the prec. vs) *it does not come to one who is devoted to vain imaginings?* (otherwise Speyer); abhūta-(q.v.)-parikalpa- Laṅk 38.4; abhūta-parikalpa-samutthitaś ca Suv 58.1 (said of the body), *arisen from unreal imaginings*; -parikalpa-samutthita- Gv 466.21; parikalpa-samucchrita LV 174.8 (vs), *produced by vain imaginings*, said of kāmaguṇāḥ, which are called māyā-marīci-samā(ḥ) and the like in the same vs; parikalpa-samucchritaḥ (Mironov -samutthitaḥ) Mvy 7423; Tib. here yoṅs su rtogs pa, and regularly so or with rtog (pa) for rtogs (pa), as in Suv 58.1 and LV 34.11 (but in LV 174.8 rtogs); this is a woodenly literal rendering; yoṅs su = pari, while kalpa is rendered rtog(s pa), defined *consider, reflect, discern, perceive, understand* (the distinction between rtog and rtogs which Jä. sets up is clearly not maintained in the texts); the derogatory connotation is recognized s.v. rtog pa by Jä. and Das, yet Das erroneously renders the cpd. yoṅs su rtogs pa las byuṅ ba, '*having arisen from quite reliable information* (parikalpa-samucchriti)'; vikalpa is rendered rnam par rtog(s) pa; (**2**) nt. or m., *prose version of a jātaka* or *legend*; four times in colophons of Mv, always at the end of prose accounts; in the first three followed by verse accounts of the same story: parikalpa-padaṃ Mv ii.181.3; samāptaṃ śyāmakajātakasya parikalpaṃ 219.17; samāptaṃ hastinikājātakasya parikalpaṃ iii.133.5; padumāvatīye parikalpo samāpto (v.l. °paṃ samāptaṃ) 170.10 (here not followed by any version in verse).

parikalpayati (cf. prec.), *imagines* or *distinguishes falsely*: °payan, pres. pple., Laṅk 57.6; °pita, ppp., Laṅk 19.1; °pita as one of the three **svabhāva**, q.v., *wrongly imagined*, 51.1, 2; 130.9; explained 67.3 ff.; with **lakṣaṇa,** 3, q.v., instead of svabhāva, °pita-lakṣaṇam Mvy 1663; Sūtrāl. xi.38, 39 (Lévi: *indice imaginaire*).

-parikāṅkṣin, adj., in a-pari°, (*not*) *desiring*: Mv i.134.3, see s.v. **nirvṛti** 2. (There is a v.l. a-pratikāṅkṣ°.)

parikātara, adj. (pari-, intensive), *very cowardly*: Jm 223.12.

Parikāla, n. of a nāga king: Māy 247.35.

Parikīṭa, n. of a nāga king: Māy 247.35.

parikīleti (pari plus denom. from kīla, *stake*, cf. Skt. kīlita), *puts stakes around* (a tree, for protection): (so dāni taṃ) nyagrodhapotaṃ . . . parikhaneti parikīleti parikuddāleti (? see this) Mv iii.301.16.

parikuṭṭaka, *abusing, reviling*: °kāḥ, v.l. of Kashgar rec. and La Vallée-Poussin JRAS 1911.1076 for SP 272.8 parivādakāḥ and 12 **anukuṭṭakāḥ.**

? **parikuḍyeti,** perhaps to be read in Mv iii.301.16 (see **parikuddāleti**), *walls about* (?).

? **parikuddāleti,** so Senart's note for his text parikuḍḍāleti; he assumes pari plus denom. from Skt. kuddāla, *hoes or spades around* (a tree): Mv iii.301.16, see **parikīleti.** But the mss. read °kudeti or °kūḍyeti, which looks more like a denom. from kuḍya (Lex. also kūḍya), *wall*; perhaps *walls about?*

Parikūṭa, n. of a nāga king: Mvy 3295.

? **pari-krūḍyate,** read prob. **pari-kūḍyate,** (pass. of pari with kūḍ-, kūl-, qq.v. in pw), *is roasted*: (iha te) bālāḥ parikrūḍyante (all mss. -kr-, but read °kūḍ°) sūnā-kāṣṭheṣv (most mss. śūnā°; read śūlā°) ivorabhrāḥ LV 207.10 (prose), *in this* (life) *fools are roasted all around* (turned over fires) *like rams on spits* (lit. *spit-sticks*).

-parikha, ifc. Bhvr. (= Skt. parigha, Pali usually paligha, once palikha, Geiger 39.2, where kh is explained as dialectic for gh; another possible explanation would be confusion with Skt. and Pali parikhā, *ditch, trench*), *obstacle*; chiefly in cpd. utkṣipta-p°, *with obstacles removed*: LV 428.16 (prose), Lefm. em. °parikheda, but mss. clearly tho corruptly point to °parikha, confirmed by Mv iii.225.6; Samādh p. 28 line 13; also udīrṇa-p° Samādh p. 28, line 14.

parikhaṇḍa, see **pariṣaṇḍa.**

parikhanati (= Pali pali°; Skt. only ger. parikhāya, once in AGS, see BR), *digs up, roots out*: (mūlaṃ) parikhanya Mv iii.284.18 (em., but confirmed by same line in Pali with palikhāya, SN i.123.6; one ms. palikhan-, perhaps read so).

-pariga (Skt. Gr. only), *going about*: -gaganaparigā nadanti mahatsvarāḥ Mv i.100.8 (vs).

parigaṇa, m., *house*: Mvy 7511 = Tib. khaṅ khyim; MSV ii.128.11. Orig. doubtless *attendants, household,* like Skt. parijana.

parigardha (m.), *greediness*: upasthānaparicaryā-parigardham adhipatiṃ kṛtvā Bbh 171.23.

parigaveṣaṇa (to °gaveṣate plus -ana), *act of searching for*: °ṣaṇāvipravasitenāśayena (so read, 2d ed., see **vipravasati**) Gv 533.1.

parigaveṣatā, read prob. °ṣaṇa-tā, or possibly °ṣaṇā, f.; = prec.: citta-parigaveṣa-tāye (loc.; so text) KP 97.3, see next.

parigaveṣate, rarely °**ti** (this cpd. of Skt. gaveṣate is recorded only in BHS; cf. prec. two), *searches all round for, looks intently for* (acc.): kumāraṃ °ṣamāṇaḥ LV 132.1; gṛhapatiṃ parimārgati °veṣati Gv 142.23; arthān parimārgate °veṣate Dbh 19.9; -devatāṃ °veṣamāṇo Gv 365.19; °ṣamāṇa- Gv 532.24; cittaṃ °veṣate KP 97.4, *looks hard for, tries to find* (Bendall and Rouse *inquires into*, but the sequel shows that the point is that the citta cannot be found however hard one searches for it); this is cited Śikṣ 233.15; ātmanaḥ parigaveṣyamāṇānupalambhāt KP 104.7 (pres. passive pple.).

parigṛddha, adj., *greedy, grasping*: Divy 351.10; RP 29.14; Gv 387.5; a-parigṛddha-cetasaḥ Gv 323.18; see **paliguddha,** and **parigredha.**

parigṛhīta, ppp. (in mg. *comprehended*, °taṃ bodhisattvaiḥ LV 423.14, may be regarded as standard Skt., where at least close relatives of this word are so used), *ungenerous, close-fisted, stingy*, in neg. a-pari°: amātsaryo 'haṃ (Buddha speaks) kulaputrā aparigṛhītacitto . . . buddhajñānasya dātā SP 485.1, *I am, gentlemen, one who gives out the Buddha-knowledge without selfishness, with heart not niggardly* (restricted); Tib. ḥdzin pa (= parigṛhīta; note that zin pa, a form of the same Tib. verb, renders **parigṛddha,** q.v.) sems (= citta) med do (*I am not*). The word of course is not connected with **parigṛddha;** Skt. parigṛhīta has mgs. like *limited, restricted*, of which this is a specialization.

parigodha, m., see **pali°.**

? **parigohya,** in Mv i.196.2 tripauruṣa-parigohyāni, is or represents a word meaning *circumference* (epithet of iṣikāni, so ed., see **iṣika**); mss. corrupt, see Senart's note. The same word, whatever it was, should surely be read as final member of the word read by Senart tripauruṣoccāni iii.228.13 (see s.v. **udvedha**).

parigraha, nt. (Skt. only masc.), *property*: SP 85.4 (vs), here predicate noun to subj. gṛham, neut.; perhaps by assimilation of gender; (may be m. or nt.,) (saddharma-puṇḍarīkaṃ nāma) dharmaparyāyaṃ . . . sarvabuddha-parigrahaṃ . . . saṃprakāśayām āsa SP 181.6, perhaps *which is the property of all the Buddhas* (one Chin. transl. *protected, guarded,* or *preserved by the Buddhas*); vaipulya-sūtrāṇa parigrahe SP 98.3 (vs), *in the acquisition of the . . .* (substantially so used in Skt.).

-parigrāhaka, adj. or subst. m., *completely grasping, comprehending* (not recorded in this mg.): °kaḥ, mahāyāna-p° Mvy 6351; saddharma-p° 6352; pravacana-p° Divy 379.9.

parigredha, m. (= Pali paligedha; see **paligodha, parigṛddha**, and esp. s.v. **gredha**), *greed*: Mvy 2200 = Tib. yoṅs su zhen pa, *extreme desire*.

parighareti (caus. to pari plus ghar-, Skt. ghārayati; see s.v. **gharati**), *moistens round about*: Mv iii.301.17 (Senart em. °ghār°), after pariṣyandeti (and acc. to Senart paryārdreti; mss. corrupt).

paricaraṇā (cf. next three), (*sexual*) *commerce*: kutaḥ punar anayā sārdhaṃ °ṇā Śikṣ 252.9.

paricaryā, lit. *service* (of the body), with special reference to (*sexual*) *enjoyment*: Prāt 480.2 (kāya-pa°); °ryā-saṃvarṇana Mvy 8372 *commending of 'service'* (Tib. bsñyen bkur), i. e. *of sexual pleasure* (in speaking to a woman; one of the saṃghāvaśeṣa sins); paricaryā (alone, in this sense) MSV iii.87.18. The Pali term is attakāma-pāricariyā, Vin. iii.133.13, *ministration to one's lusts* (CPD). See also **pāricaryā**.

paricāraṇa, nt., or °**ṇā**, f. (= Pali °ṇā; n. act. to next, mg. 1; in Skt. recorded only in mg. *attendance*; cf. AMg. pariyāraṇā, *sexual pleasure*), *amusement* (not necessarily sexual); only in °raṇārthaṃ, and only after krīḍārthaṃ ratyarthaṃ (cf. the grouping of the corresponding verbs, s.v. **paricārayati**; see also **pravicāra**, °**cāraṇa** or °**ṇā**): Mv ii.115.9; 116.2, 5, 7, 10, 15, 18, 21.

paricārayati, °**reti** (= Pali °reti, AMg. pariyārei; Skt. °rayate, only BṛhU. 6.1.1 Mādhy., 6.2.1 Kāṇva, and KaṭhaU. 1.25, defined BR *sich bedienen . . ., aufwarten lassen*, but rather *amuses oneself*; cf. Charpentier IA 57(1928), note 96, on KaṭhaU. 1.25, where it means . . . *with women*), (**1**) *amuses oneself*: very often preceded by krīḍati ramati (°te), the latter sometimes omitted, as in Mv ii.97.8; of any kind of amusement, as krīḍanakaiḥ krīḍanti ramanti paricārayanti SP 72.13, and so (not of sexual pleasures) SP 78.2; 80.1; 361.4; Mv i.194.17 (with liquor; read with mss. paricāretsu, proved by corresp. passage in Pali DN ii.172.5 paricāresuṃ); but esp. of sexual enjoyment with women, krīḍāhi ramāhi paricārehi Mv ii.103.6; similarly 443.8, 11; 444.10; 452.10; iii.36.6; 37.14; Divy 1.6; 24.14 and often; Av i.13.8 etc.; RP 42.7; same trio of verbs but not clearly or exclusively of sexual pleasures Mvy 7349 (cf. 7347–8); Suv 183.2; LV 157.7; Mv i.32.6; 194.17 (mss.); Divy 3.25; Sukh 42.9; used alone, without krīḍ- and ram-, in the specific sense of *has sexual intercourse* (with, instr. with sārdhaṃ), Bhavena . . . tayā sārdhaṃ paricāritaṃ Divy 25.28; tāḥ parapuruṣaiḥ sārdhaṃ paricārayanti 496.5; anayā parapuruṣeṇa sārdhaṃ paricāritaṃ 538.1, and similarly 2; °yati MSV ii.36.3; °yāvaḥ, dual, MSV i.213.16; (**2**) *attends, waits upon* (a person; so simplex paricarati in Skt.): teṇa dāni pratyekabuddhena ye paricāritā (v.l. °vāritā) pratyekabuddhā(ḥ) Mv iii.347.18; sarve pi devasaṃghā devīṃ (ii.20.7 Māyāṃ) paricārayitva ākāśe Mv i.218.8 = ii.20.7 (vs), so Senart in ii.20.7, in i.218.8 he reads °vārayitva (the mss. vary between these two both times); note that acc. to PTSD, Pali parivāreti is 'often erroneously' used for paricāreti; similarly, paricaritā (so read m.c. for Lefm. paricārita, v.l. °vārita) purime nara ye te sarvasukhenā LV 168.13 (vs), *those men who formerly were attended* (Tib. rim gro byas, *made homage* or *offerings*) *by you with every joy*; *attends* (a corpse, said of the funeral procession), paricārayitva LV 190.16 (vs; no v.l.); ppp. *attended, accompanied* (of the mind), guṇagaṇa-paricārita-matī Mv iii.104.16, *his mind attended by flocks of good qualities*; *frequented, occupied* (of a place), nairayikehi sattvehi śūlopetehi tāni parvatāni paricāritāni Mv i.6.14, *these mountains are frequented by hell-inhabitants impaled on stakes* (wrongly Senart's note); (**3**) possibly to be read for paritārayanti Dbh.g. 44(70).11 in the mg. *they get full knowledge of* (cf. pw 4.39 s.v. paritāraṇīya, where it is suggested that paricār° be read, to be sure not in this mg.); this is the regular Skt. mg. of **pravicārayati**, q.v., which occurs in this mg. in the preceding line 10, and which in BHS is also used in the mg. of paricārayati (1), hence perhaps the latter may have come to be used also in the regular mg. of the former; but I have no parallel case; (**4**) *summons* (monks to a meeting): bhikṣūn paricārayitum ārabdhaḥ MSV ii.175.9, so ms., ed. em. pracār°; Tib. bsgrags pa, *call*.

-paricārika, see **bodhi-pari°**.

paricita, ppp. (essentially = Skt. and Pali id.), *familiarized, well practised* (in): °taḥ (supply vacasā, as in 2411, see **paricetar**) Mvy 2412 = Tib. (yoṅs su, legs su, legs par, = pari) byaṅ ba, acc. to Das *skilled*; Pali vacasā paricita, in similar context, AN ii.185.4; Vin. ii.95.36. Mironov parijitaḥ; cf. **parijaya**.

paricūrṇayati (cf. Skt. cūrṇayati; the cpd. unrecorded), *pulverizes completely*: cakravāḍāḥ kacci sthiro (voc., = sthira in prec. line) me (used for acc. sg.) paricūrṇayeyuḥ Gv 412.16 (vs).

paricetar (cf. **paricita**), *one who practises, is versed in* (with instr.): vacasā °tā Mvy 2411 (v.l. °jitā; Mironov °jetā; cf. s.v. **parijaya**) = Tib. byaṅ ba, as for **paricita, parijaya**.

parichinatti, *reaps* (grain); pass. (śasyāni) . . . °chidyante Kv 71.7.

Parichedakara, m., n. of a samādhi: Mvy 589; ŚsP 1422.18.

parijapati (Skt. id., in good sense, *recites sacred formulae over*; Pali id., *recites magic spells*, object vijjaṃ), *recites magic charms over* (with acc.), esp. of hostile or 'black' magic: mantraiḥ parijapto Divy 397.26, *bewitched*; arkapuṣpaṃ parijapya 612.15; parijapya (object supplied) Mmk 61.18.

parijaya, m. (see next; = Skt. paricaya, § 2.28, cf. s.vv. **paricita, paricetar**), *intensive cultivation, thorough acquaintance, familiarity, careful consideration* (with loc.): Mvy 6532; Bbh 11.16 a-parijayād; AsP 293.1 prajñāyāṃ parijayaṃ karoṣi; 322.3; 332.9 dhyāna-parijayaṃ ca karoti; 356.14 ānimitte ca parijayaṃ karoti; 370.3 śūnyatāyāṃ; 370.16, 17. Prakritic j for c: Leumann cited by Wogihara in Bbh. Lex. 32. According to Wogihara, in AsP 332.9 the word would mean *conquest, mastery*, from root ji, and also in a ms. citation from Yaśomitra, AbhidhK. (cf. LaV-P. vi.150) yogācāras trividhaḥ, ādikarmikaḥ, kṛtaparijayaḥ (*un maître*, LaV-P.), atikrāntamanasikāraś ca. I see no reason to separate these passages from the others. It is clear to me that BHS has only one word parijaya, and I think Leumann's interpretation is the true one. Tib. on Mvy yoṅs su (= pari) byaṅ bar (sometimes *purification*, but also acc. to Das *skilled*; also used for **paricita**, °**cetar**, qq.v.; note that Mironov reads parijita, °jetar for these) byas pa (*made, the making*), or ḥdris par (*acquaintance*) bya ba (*making, being made*). Chin. and Jap. seem to follow Tib.

parijayati, prob. not *masters*, but the verb corresponding to **parijaya**, q.v., for Skt. paricaya: *cultivates, considers carefully, gets well acquainted with*: (bodhisattvavimokṣaṃ) bhāvayann avataran . . . parijayan paricintayan Gv 385.17.

parijāgarati, °**grati** (= the more usual **prati-jā°**), *tends, cares for*: sthānāni . . . parijāgriṣu (3 pl. aor.) Mv i.76.4 (vs); (bodhisattvamātaraṃ devakanyā . . . ucchādana-) parimardanehi (or °mardana-, ii.14.16) pariṣekehi (so read, nearly with mss., see Crit. App.) pratijāgaranti Mv i.210.17 = ii.14.16 (prose).

[**parijāta**, in °tāni puṣpāṇi Mv iii.99.19, = Skt. pāri°, *a* (heavenly) *flower*; not in Senart's Index, hence no doubt merely an uncorrected misprint for Skt. pāri°.]

parijita, var. for **paricita**, q.v., and cf. **parijaya**.

parijūna, adj. (= Skt. paridyūna; Pali parijunna, Ud. ii.7; cf. **paridyāna**; not *parijūrṇa, *old*, as assumed by Childers, PTSD, and evidently Senart), *wretched*, *miserable, poor*; also **parijūnya** (nt., abstr. from prec.; once written in one ms. °juñña, in MIndic fashion), *weakness, debility, poverty* (Pali has the noun pārijuñña, nt.; the same four kinds as in Mv are listed in MN ii.66.9 ff.; the Pkt. adj. parijuṇṇa, °junna, is defined by Sheth *weak, poor*, durbala, daridra, nirdhana, and doubtless belongs with this word): read in Mv ii.161.14–15 na ... bodhisattvo jarāparijūnyena parijūno ... abhiniṣkramati; in 17 ... vyādhiparijūnyena (one ms. here °juññena) pari°...; in 19 ... bhogapari° pari°...; in 162.3 ... jñātipari° pari°...; the mss. are corrupt in all these, but in 17 and 19 one of them is nearly right, reading °parijūtena parijūto or °parijūnena parijūno.

parijūnya (nt.), *weakness, poverty*; see under prec. Should we read pārijūnya, with Pali pārijuñña?

parijetar, var. for **paricetar**, q.v., and cf. **parijaya.**

parijñā (= Pali pariññā), *(thorough) knowledge*; here not used in any special or technical way: Mvy 6910 = Tib. yoṅs su śes pa; LV 33.5 (nāmarūpa-pa°); Mv iii.400.13 (vs, parijñācārī, read °jña° m.c. as in the same vs in Pali, Sn 537, pariññacārī); Gv 38.4; 70.1; Bbh 294.10 (yathābhūta-parijñāyai); Laṅk 184.13.

parijñāta, ppp., *distinguished, renowned*: Mv i.197.15, ep. of the family into which the Bodhisattva is born in his last existence; must mean about the same as abhijñāta, which it follows; but omitted in the other versions of the same passage, Mv ii.1 and LV 23.11 ff. Cf. next two.

parijñāta-bhojana, adj. Bhvr. (= Pali pariññāta-bh°), *having true knowledge about food*: pratyekabuddho pari° sarvāśuciparikṣiṇo mahābhāgo Mv i.302.9; ye °janā(ḥ) Ud xxix.35 = Pali Dhp. 92 ye pariññātabhojanā, expl. in comm. ii.172.1 ff. as *having the three pariññā*, viz. ñāta-pa°, knowing what the food is that he is eating; tīraṇa-pa°, keeping in mind while eating that food is repulsive; and pahāna-pa°, keeping in mind the rejection of pleasure in eating. I have found no evidence in BHS for this or any specific understanding of the term.

parijñātāvin, adj. (= Pali pariññā°; cf. Skt. parijñāta and § 22.51), *knowing thoroughly*: (cyutyupapatti-) parijñātāvinaś ca Gv 472.2.

-parijñāna-tā = Skt. parijñāna, *(state of) knowing*; but perhaps rather analyze duḥkhaparijñāna plus -tā(yai): LV 33.8, *unto a state of having thorough knowledge of misery.*

pariṇamana, nt., or °**nā**, f., also °**ṇa-tā** (once Skt. °na in mg. *transformation, changing into...*; so also M.; not in Pali; cf. **pariṇāmana, °nā**, and Skt. pariṇamati), (**1**) *change* of state or occupation, in the sense of giving up one for another: pṛthivīsamacittena sarvabhāravahanāpariṇamana-tayā Gv 463.21, *with mind like the earth, in that it does not change* (a-pari°) *from bearing all burdens*; cited Śikṣ 35.6, where ed. as in Gv text, but ms. **aparitasyana-tayā** (see this), *in that it does not become wearied with...*, which fits quite as well, tho presumably a secondary change; (**2**) *ripening, maturing* (in religious contexts): kuśalamūlānāṃ °nād Bbh 30.10; (bodhisattvasya) °nā Bbh 307.8; 309.15 (the process consists in this, that ... bodhisattvo ... kuśalamūlaṃ ... prasādena pariṇāmayati 309.15–19); °nā, the last of the seven anuttara-pūjā, *supreme forms of worship*, Dharmas 14 (following bodhicittotpādaḥ; probably understand bodhicittasya, or bodheḥ, with pari°); sarvabodhisattvapariṇamanā-jñāna- Gv 466.3; (sc. of Bodhisattvas) °nā Gv 469.4; kuśalamūla-°nā 499.5.

pariṇāma, nt. (= Skt. id., m.; also Pali; and cf. next), *development, ripening, maturing*: (sc. bodhisattva-) bhūmīnāṃ pariṇāmāni Mv i.77.3 (vs).

pariṇāmana, nt., or °**nā**, f. (cf. **pariṇamana, °nā**; Skt. pariṇamati, *changes*, intrans.; also *ripens*; Pali °na, only noted in mg. 4; AMg. °maṇā, °maṇayā for °manatā, *transformation, change of form*), (**1**) *change, alteration*: priyavastu-pariṇāmana-tayā (*because of the fact that there are alterations of the desired object*) śokabhājano lābhasatkāraḥ Śikṣ 105.13; *change* of one physical element into another, mahābhūteṣv anyonya-pariṇāmanānyathābhāvakriyā Bbh 60.13; (**2**) *ripening*, lit., of a seed; (ṛtur api) bījasya pariṇāmanā-kṛtyaṃ karoti Śāl 74.17 (Tib. bsgyur baḥi bya, see below), *the act of causing the seed to ripen* (or *grow*); (**3**) fig. *development, causing to grow, ripening, maturation*, usually of religiously desirable conditions; Tib. somewhat confused, sometimes yoṅs su (b)sṅo ba (so on Mvy 794 and Suv 44.5), said to mean regularly *bless* (certainly not the mg. of pariṇāmana); other mgs. cited are *devote, design, intend*; elsewhere (e. g. Mvy 1675; Śāl 74.17) Tib. bsgyur ba, *change, transform*, but app. also *multiply, increase, make grow*; Chin. on Mvy *turn, change* (in direction): sarvā bodhisattvacaryāpagata-kleśakalmāṣā bodhipariṇāmanādhipatyena pratyetavyā(ḥ) Dbh 58.18–19, *all depravities and impurities foreign to the Bodhisattva-course are to be recognized, thru mastering the development* (ripening) *of enlightenment*; bodhi-pariṇāmanā Śikṣ 33.14; 158.6; (prob. understand bodhi- also in) pariṇāmanakuśalena Śikṣ 282.2; prathamāyām eva pariṇāmanāyām Śikṣ 29.10, sc. of kuśalamūlāni; cf. 29.13–14, 21; also pariṇāmanā 31.2; bodhisattva-°nā- 31.18–19; imāya pariṇāmana-varṇitāya Suv 44.5 (vs), *with this* (sc. deśanā) *which is praised as a cause of ripening*; imaṃ °ṇa-rājaṃ Bhad 48, *this King of Ripeners* (the Bhad itself); yā pariṇāmana varṇita agrā Bhad 56; parahita-pariṇāmanāt Jm 41.11-12, *thru developing (increasing, furthering) the welfare of others*; pariṇāmanaṃ Bbh 307.2, uncertain reading, replaced by **pariṇamanā** in line 8; iṣṭārthe pariṇāmanām Sādh 34.15; said of the *development* of an evil trait, (read) evam apsarasaḥ prārthanayābrahmacaryapariṇāmanān mahāpadumo nāma naraka uktaḥ Śikṣ 75.10, *thus, as a result of the development (stimulation, ripening) of unchastity thru desiring an apsaras* (wrongly Bendall and Rouse); (**4**) (= Pali °nam, Vin. iv.157.12) *diversion* (of something to the use of someone for whom it was not intended): °nam Mvy 8415.

pariṇāmayati, °meti, (**1**) (in Skt. and Pali recorded only as caus. to pariṇamati; acc. to Senart Mv i note 439, these BHS forms are denom. to **pariṇāma**; identical forms are also used, as in Skt. and Pali, in caus. sense, e. g. Bbh 309.19; Śikṣ 29.13 ff.; Senart's theory may be right; but cf. § 38.23), = Skt. pariṇamati, *ripens, matures, develops* (intrans.): bodhisattvā avaivartikatāyai (or °ye) pariṇāmenti Mv i.81.1 (prose), *develop* (themselves) *towards...*; pariṇāmayanto iha agrabodhau vayaṃ ... SP 10.14 (vs); pariṇāmayanti (with loc. of goal) Laṅk 119.7; (**2**) (= Pali °ṇāmeti; caus. to Skt. pariṇamati, *is changed into*) *changes into*: yo vārṣikaḥ (sc. lābhaḥ) sa haimantikaḥ pariṇāmitaḥ, yas tu haimantikaḥ sa vārṣikaḥ °mitaḥ Śikṣ 59.5; see s.v. **saṃparivartayati**; pariṇāmyamānaṃ Laṅk 159.8, *being changed*, see s.v. **svasti.**

pariṇāyaka, m. (very rare in Skt., BR, only in mg. 1; commoner in Pali, in both mgs.), (**1**) *leader*: °ka-saṃpannā Mv ii.255.17, said of a herd of deer, *perfect in their leader* (who was Surūpa, a former birth of the Bodhisattva); as ep. of a Buddha, °kaḥ Mvy 21; mārga-°kaḥ 439; andhe loke anāyake apariṇāyake Buddho... tārayitā etc., in a cliché, Av i.4.2; 10.2; 210.13, etc.; ep. of Bodhisattvas, (loka-)°kānāṃ Mv ii.297.17; (sattvānāṃ...) pariṇāyakabhūtaḥ Gv 219.7; (**2**) specifically, the 7th of the 7 **ratna** (q.v. 3) of a cakravartin: Mvy 3628 = Tib. blon po, *officer, minister of state*, app. with both civil and military functions of the highest rank under the king, so also Chin., while Jap. seems to make him more specifically military; same Tib. regularly elsewhere, e. g. on LV 14.5; for his functions, see LV 18.3, paṇḍito vyakto medhāvī rājñaś ... cintitamātreṇa udyojayitavyaṃ (read surely °vyāṃ, as Tib. appears to take it, bsko bar bya baḥi dpuṅ rnams) senām udyojayati sma, *he activates as quick as thought an* *army that is to be activated for the king* (here only military functions); Divy 217.20–21 suggests military functions; but contrariwise Mv i.109.14–15 mārgagato pranaṣṭānāṃ hatahatanayanānāṃ (read °nāna, m.c.) deśayati (so mss.) mārgaṃ, tena pariṇāyakavaraṃ labhati ratanaṃ (read °nam, m.c.; one ms. ratnam) uttamanāyakaṃ; for Pali cf. DN comm. i.250.12 pariṇāyakaratanena vijitaṃ anurakkhati; DN ii.177.5 paṭibalo rājānaṃ . . . upayāpetabbaṃ upayāpetuṃ apayāpetabbaṃ apayāpetuṃ ṭhapetabbaṃ ṭhapetuṃ, *he is competent to bring to the king what needs to be brought, to remove what needs to be removed, to hold* (make stay) *what should be kept*; comm. ii.628.3, on this passage, says that he is the eldest son of the king, rañño jeṭṭhaputto va; a sort of *viceroy* or *chief assistant* to the king seems to be meant; very often in lists of the 7 ratna, without specific statement of his functions, e. g. LV 14.5; 101.16; 136.18; Mv i.49.4; 193.17; ii.323.5; iii.377.21; Divy 60.18; 140.25; 211.18; 548.27; Kv 17.20; 49.4; Gv 418.12.

pariṇiṣpanna, see **pariniṣ°**.

paritamana, see **apari°**.

paritarṣaṇa (nt.) or **°ṇā**, f. (cf. **a-paritarṣaṇā**, and Pali paritassanā), *desire, longing*: Bbh 271.16 °ṇārthaṃ; °ṇārthena tṛṣṇā Śāl 81.8; Bca.ṭ. 259.6; ŚsP 1456.17 °ṇacittaṃ parivarjayitavyam; 1465.20; 1463.20 °ṇā-cittam (with reference to a bhikṣuṇī; *sexual desire*). See also next, and **paritṛṣita.**

paritasana, nt. (prob. MIndic for °tṛṣ° to Pali paritasati, and esp. °tasita, ppp., see **paritṛṣita**), *great longing*, = utkaṇṭhā: tāṃs tathāgatān apaśyan (pres. pple.) mahatīm utkaṇṭhāṃ paritasanaṃ cāpannaḥ AsP 494.8 (prose), sc. to see the vision which had disappeared. Cf. also prec. The neg. **a-paritasana,** q.v., has been noted only as a noun from the different verb **parit(r)as(y)ati**; in Pali the two seem to be confused, at least if the Pali Dictt. are to be trusted. It must be noted, however, that the meaning *discouragement, mental trouble* (as in **a-paritasyana** etc., cf. **paritasyati, °tras°**) would be possible in the above AsP passage, and could also be the meaning of **utkaṇṭhā,** as in Pali ukkaṇṭhā and BHS **utkaṇṭhati**; the disappearance of the vision could lead to *depression* of mind, as well as to *eager desire* to see it again.

paritasyati (= **paritrasyati, °sati**; Pali paritassati, °tasati, which seems to be blended with derivs. of Skt. tṛṣ-; cf. MN i.136.16 (na) paritassati; comm. ii.111.11 ff. glosses, bhaya-paritassanāya taṇhā-paritasanāya vā na paritassati, *is not disturbed either by fear*(?) *of danger or desire*(?) *for cravings*, distinguishing the two nouns paritassanā and °tasanā but associating both with the verb paritassati; the forms with -tras- may indicate the true origin, or may be hyper-Skt., association with root tras being then secondary; cf. Dhātup. tas = upakṣaye, but with var. upakṣepe), *is wearied, exhausted, troubled, disturbed*; cf. AbhidhK. LaV-P. vi.145 note 5 paritasyati, upakṣīyata ity arthaḥ (see s.v. **paritāsa**): na °syati Mvy 6813 (ed. adds, as variant?, paritrasyati; Mironov °tas° without v.l.; follows parikhedaḥ; forms related to this word occur with other forms mentioned in this article) = Tib. yoṅs su (= pari) mi (= na) (ḥ)chad = *decay, cease*; so Chin. and Jap.; notkaṇṭhyate (see **utkaṇṭhati**) na °syati Bbh 193.6; a-paritasyamānaḥ Bbh 218.9. Cf. **a-paritasyana(tā)**, and Wogihara, Lex. 32 ff.; Leumann's theory there cited seems hardly conclusive.

paritasyana(-tā), see **a-pari°**.

paritāpana (nt.; = Pali id.), *(self-)torture* (in ascetic practices), esp. in cpd. ātāpana-pari°, see s.v. **ātāpana**; also LV 258.4 kāyaparitāpanārthaṃ.

paritāyati, °te, gdve. °tāyitavya (MIndic, to Skt. °trāyate), *saves, rescues*: paritāyitavya maya sattva duḥkhārditāni (read dukhā°) Dbh.g. 3(339).19.

paritārayati, see **paricārayati** (4): °yanti Dbh.g. 44(70).11.

paritāsa, m. (nom. act. to **paritasyati**), *troubled mental state, discouragement*: AbhidhK. LaV-P. vi.145 note 5 paritāso daurmanasyam, tena hi paritasyate, upakṣīyata ity arthaḥ.

pari-tikta, adj., *very bitter*: Jm 29.10.

paritulana (nt.; except in LV 431.2 could also be understood as °nā, f.; n. act. to next; not recorded), also **°na-tā**, *weighing* (mentally), *consideration*: -doṣa-paritulanākāraṃ (sc. of śruta) Śikṣ 191.1; śrutārtha-°na-tā 191.6; °nābhimānatā Bbh 289.2; °nāsaṃmoha-(-asaṃmoha-) LV 430.16; °na- 431.2.

paritulayati, °te (= Pali °tuleti; cf. prec.), *weighs* (mentally), *considers*: °yati Bbh 254.12 (ātmānaṃ); °yataḥ, gen. sg. pres. pple., Bbh 9.2 (svārthaṃ); °yamānena, pres. pple. mid., AsP 483.6; °yitvā LV 208.7 (antaḥpuraṃ).

paritṛṣita, adj. (ppp. of next, q.v.; = Pali °tasita, presumably subst., *extreme craving*, in DN i.40.2 taṇhāgatānaṃ paritasita-vipphanditam eva; see **paritasana,** and **°tarṣaṇa, °ṇā**; Skt. has no form of pari plus tṛṣ-, but the ppp. of tṛṣyati is Skt. tṛṣita; in Pali there seems to be great confusion between forms of this root in -s-, based chiefly on tṛṣita, leading even to a present tasati, and in -ss-, based partly on tṛṣyati, partly on Skt. full-grade forms in tarṣ-; in DN i.40.2, above, the v.l. °tassita is recorded in text and comm.; both these are moreover confused in Pali with the homonyms related to BHS **paritasyati, °tras(y)ati**), *eagerly desirous, longing*, with dat. or instr. or preceding stem in comp.: °tāḥ smo bhagavato darśanāya (ii.90.11 °nena) Av i.325.8; ii.90.11; darśana-pari° Gv 223.17; 530.18; dharma-pari° Kv 80.13; (absolute use) Dbh 5.23.

paritṛṣyate (see prec.; Pali paritassati beside °tasati), *longs eagerly for*, with gen.: sa tasyāḥ (sc. sukhāyā vedanāyāḥ) punaḥ-punaḥ saṃyogārthaṃ °te MadhK 555.5 (prose).

paritta, adj. (= Pali id., = **parītta**, q.v.), *small*: LV 20.16 (so Lefm. with all mss.); KP 78.5, 7 (read parittaṃ for text pariktaṃ or, with dittography, pariktaktaṃ; separate from the preceding word, see **abhyantarita**; Tib. chuṅ ba, *little*).

parityakta, ppp. (Pali pariccatta; cf. BR s.v. tyaj with pari, 5; cited only Gr.), (*food that is*) *left over*: yadi (or, sacet) te (bhagini) °ktam ākīryatām (or, dīyatām) asmin pātre Divy 67.12; 82.19; 88.22 (in a modest request).

parityajana (nt.; = Pali pariccajana), *giving up, giving away*: -lokadhātoḥ °naṃ ŚsP 1469.22 (syntax not clear; there seems to be no verb in the sentence as printed).

paritrasyati, °sati (looks like cpd. of pari plus Skt. trasyati, trasati, cf. Skt. ppp. paritrasta; but equivalent to **paritasyati,** q.v.; Pali usually paritassati, °tasati, but occasionally paritt°, as in parittase Sn 924, cf. parittāsin SN i.201.28), = **paritasyati,** and used in similar contexts: na paritrasyati Gv 351.15 (in same line na parikhidyate, cf. Mvy 6812 parikhedaḥ, and see s.v. paritasyati Mvy 6813; in next line nāvasīdati); (na parikhidyante na saṃsīdanti . . . na) paritrasyanti Gv 366.9; na paritrasanti Gv 526.22 (parallel na parikhidyante, line 20).

[**paritrasyana** or **°nā, °natā**, false em. for °tasya°; see **a-paritasyana.**]

paritrāyaka, m. (= Pali parittāyaka; to Skt. °trāyate plus -aka), *rescuer*: °kā mama kalyāṇamitrāḥ Gv 171.11 (prose).

paritrāyaṇa (nt.; n. act. to Skt. °trāyate plus -ana; cf. Skt. paritrāṇa, Pali parittāṇa), *rescuing, saving*: sattva-°ṇārthaṃ LV 223.16 (vs); jagat-°ṇārthāḥ Dbh.g. 1(337).6; sarvasattvadhātu-°ṇena Gv 440.13 (prose).

paridamana (= Pali id.), *control*: AsP 54.11 °nāya (bodhisattvānām).

pari-daśa, adj., *full ten*: Jm 170.15 °śā(ḥ) . . . striyaś ca.

paridahana, adj., fem. °nī, *tormenting*: Dbh 24.10 (vāg . . .) hṛdaya-paridahanī.

paridahyati, °te (pass. to Skt. paridahati, which seems recorded only in lit. sense, *burns*; Pali pariḍayhati, subject cittaṃ, Therag. 1224), *is tormented* (with passion or desire; cf. **paridāha** etc.): rāgeṇa °hyāmi Divy 420.6; āhāratṛṣṇā-°hyamānāḥ SP 84.14.

paridāgha, m. (nowhere recorded; cf. next; Pali pariḷāha in all mgs.), (**1**) *hot weather*: °gha-samayaḥ Prāt 517.12 (not noted in this sense in PTSD, but found in Vin. iv.117.30 pariḷāha-samaye); (**2**) *ardent desire* (Pali kāma-pariḷāho MN i.241.5), kāma-paridāghā, Bhvr., *having an ardent desire for lusts*, Mv ii.121.4; read °ghaḥ in Karmav 37.19 with ms. for text pradāśaḥ; vimuktaḥ paridāghaiḥ Mvy 401, said of a Tathāgata, perhaps rather to mg. 3; Tib. yoṅs su gduṅ ba, which is equally ambiguous, having the same two mgs.; (**3**) *torment, anguish*: antaḥśalya-paridāgha-jāta, see s.v. **antaḥśalya**; śokaśalya-paridāghaṃ (acc.) Mv ii.224.4; rūpa-(or, in 8, vijñāna-)-pratyayā ... paridāghā Mv iii.338.2, 8; jvara-°ghaḥ Dbh 48.19; dvau...°ghau (text °gho) KP 117.1, 3 (Tib. as on Mvy 401 above; parallels vraṇa in 116.1 and glānya 118.1 indicate this mg. rather than 2).

paridāha, m. (Skt. only lit. *burning*, and fig. *mental anguish*; = Pali pariḷāha; cf. **paridahyati, paridāgha,** and **nişparidāha**), (**1**) *fever* (disease): Mvy 9485, in list of diseases, Tib. tsha ba, *heat*; (**2**) *feverish longing, ardent desire*, substantially = tṛṣṇā, as a vice: kāmeṣu °haḥ LV 246.13; in lists of vices, LV 52.14; Śikṣ 198.8; Dbh 25.4.

paridīpana (? nt.), **°na-tā, °nā,** f. (= Pali °na, °nā; n. act. to next; clear cases of °na, nt., not recorded, prob. by accident), *explanation, clarification, expounding, setting forth*: (sattva-) °nā kṛtā AsP 47.8; sarvasaṃsāranityatva-paridīpanatāyai Gv 527.17; °panān, ifc. Bhvr., Gv 278.13; °panākāraṃ, Bhvr., Bbh 96.21 ff.

paridīpayati, °te (= Pali °peti; cf. prec.), *makes clear, explains, expounds, sets forth*: °yanti SP 53.14 (ekaṃ ... yānaṃ); °yāmi Gv 152.19; °yati Bbh 50.8 (arthaṃ); °yan (pres. pple.) Sukh 49.2; °yamāna Bhad 26 (bodhicariṃ); Gv 88.15 (bodhicittaṃ); 243.20; °yituṃ, inf., LV 377.14 (jñānaṃ); Gv 135.15; °dīpita, ppp., Śikṣ 124.6; anāmakāḥ sarve dharmāḥ nāmnā tu paridīpitāḥ Śikṣ 241.14 (vs), ... *but they are distinguished (conventionally) by name(s)*.

[**paridyāna, °nāḥ** Ud v.10, acc. to Chakravarti from Dhātup. dyai-, nyakkaraṇe; but v.l. paridyūnā, which is confirmed by Pali parijunnā in the same vs Ud ii.7; see **parijūna.**]

paridrava (m.? = Pali pariddava, to which it is prob. a hyper-Sktism; etym. of the Pali word obscure, see PTSD for Trenckner's not very attractive theory), *lamentation*: saha-śoka-paridravaṃ ca Dbh.g. 11(347).3, so all Susa's mss.; text em. °pardevanaṃ (!), as if for parid°; this is not only formally monstrous but metrically impossible.

paridhāvana, nt. (not in Pali, and not in this sense in Skt.; to pari-dhāv with suffix ana), *running around*: Śikṣ 268.13, see s.v. **ādhāvana.**

paridhauta, ppp. (cf. Skt. dhauta; = Pali °dhota, to paridhovati, Chap. 43, s.v. dhovati), *washed, cleaned*; as periphrasis for verb, *was cleaned*: garbhamalaṃ °taṃ Mv iii.144.11.

[**parinikāsa,** LV 371.11 (vs), kāmakrodhā mohaprabhavā jagatparinikāsāḥ, both edd., no v.l.; but read jagaty arinikāśāḥ, *having the aspect of enemies in the world*.]

parinikşipta, adj. (cf. next; ppp. of unrecorded pari-ni-kṣip), app. *formed, fashioned*; su-parinikṣipta-lalāṭo SP 350.12, *he has a well-formed forehead* (so ~~Kern; Bu~~rnouf *very high*); Tib. dpral baḥi (*forehead*) dbyes che ba (said to mean *of great size*, used for vistīrṇa, and app. for pṛthu); cf. the 71st **anuvyañjana** in Mvy 339 suparīṇata-(*well-developed*?)-lalāṭaḥ, Tib. dpral ba legs par dbyes pa; cf. Burnouf, Lotus, 604 (other texts speak of a *broad*, pṛthu, forehead).

parinikşepa (m.; see prec.), *form* (?): paramapuruṣās te p' ime imasya mānuṣasya (so mss.) parinikṣepaṃ pi na jānanti Mv ii.278.4 (one of the sad reflections of Māra about the Bodhisattva), *these Supreme Persons do not know even the form of this human* (species), i. e. they are completely superhuman (?); otherwise but implausibly Senart, who was not aware of **parinikşipta** SP 350.12.

parinirvāṇa, nt. (= Pali °nibbāna), *complete nirvāṇa*: Mvy 186; 1370 (mahā-p°); 4106; SP 319.5; LV 428.15; Mv ii.157.5; Av ii.197.6 ff. (with description); etc., passim. Note Bbh 55.17–18 prapañca-nirodho bodhisattvasya mahāyāna-parinirvāṇam iti veditavyam (a reinterpretation of the old term); see **prapañca.**

Parinirvāṇa(-sūtra) = **Mahā-pari°**: Karmav 156.15.

parinirvāti, °vāyati, caus. **°vāpayati** (= Pali id., caus. regularly °vāpeti; cf. **prati-nir°**), (**1**) *enters* (caus. *brings to*) *complete nirvāṇa*: °vānti Divy 150.18; °vātu Divy 202.4; °vāsyanti LV 401.7; °vāsyati Divy 90.10; °vāyanti Mv i.63.3; 301.4; a-°vāyan, pres. pple., SP 320.4 (Kashgar rec. °vāyamāṇaś); °vāyamāṇa(ḥ) SP 319.4; aor. °vāyet Mv i.267.18 (v.l. °ye); °vāye Mv iii.97.7; caus. (see **parinirvṛta**) °vāpayati (mss. °yanti), °vāpayiṣyanti Mv i.126.6, 7; °vāpayanti Mv iii.414.4; °vāpayitavya Mv iii.178.8; 263.13; seemingly in mg. of simplex, yathāyaṃ bhagavān ... °vāsyati evam aham api... °vāpayeyam Divy 90.10, ... *so may I also enter complete nirvāṇa*; (**2**) in literal sense: dīpāḥ parinirvāṇāḥ (ppp., *went out*) MSV i.90.13; caus. °vāpayituṃ, inf., *to put out completely* (a fire), Mv ii.457.10, 12.

parinirvāyin, adj. (= Pali °nibbāyin), *attaining complete nirvāṇa*: Mvy 1015–1018; fem. °yinī Divy 533.25.

parinirvṛta, adj.-ppp. (= Pali °nibbuta; used as ppp. to parinirvā(ya)ti, cf. Skt. and BHS **nirvṛta,** similarly used), *completely emancipated or entered into nirvāṇa*: Divy 22.9; 242.16; in collocation with forms of caus. parinirvāpayati (*being emancipated ... emancipates others*), °to (°taḥ) parinirvāpayeyaṃ Mv i.39.5; 50.6; 335.20; °vāpaya Divy 39.15; °vāpayiṣyasi Mv i.239.13.

pariniḥśvasati, *sighs deeply*: °santo, pres. pple., Mv i.154.8.

parinişṭhura, adj., *very harsh*: Jm 55.14.

parinişpatti, f. (n. act. to next), *perfect development, perfection; the bringing to that state*: bodhisattvānāṃ pariniṣpattihetoḥ SP 219.1, similarly 233.13 (in both Kashgar rec. pariniṣpādana-h°), *in order to bring Bodhisattvas to perfect development*; (bodhisattvasya) rūpakāya-°ttiṃ dṛṣṭvā LV 48.18, *beautiful body-development*; Mvy 758, see **Buddhakāyavarṇa-pari°**; rūpakāyapariniṣpattyā (of the Buddha) Samādh 22.39; Vaj 40.7 (and ff.), (*full*) *development* (or *perfection*) *of* **rūpakāya,** here *physical, material form*; Dbh 52.15 and Śikṣ 214.5, see s.v. **parinişpanna**; caryāpariniṣpattito Dbh 7.27, *because of development from the* (Bodhisattva) *course*; cittakarma-°ttiḥ Śikṣ 121.10; others, Gv 53.17; 461.5; Bbh 273.24 (apari°); 298.11.

parinişpadyati, °te (in Pali only ppp., see prec. and following items), (**1**) *becomes perfected*: °padyeyuḥ SP 228.2 (samyaksaṃbodhau); vipulībhavati pariniṣpadyate Gv 296.2; °padyante Dbh 58.9; °padyemahi AsP 509.11; (**2**) *is turned into* (orig. doubtless *develops into*, cf. **parinişpatti**): bhasmamuṣṭim upakṣiptam api amṛtaṃ pariniṣpadyate Kv 29.20.

parinişpanna, sometimes spelled °ṇiṣ°, ppp. of prec. (rare in Skt. and as parinipphanna in Pali, perhaps not in the same mgs., but see a-parinipphanna in CPD), (**1**) *completely perfected* (Tib. yoṅs su grub pa): °naḥ sa ... anuttarāyāṃ samyaksaṃbodhau veditavyas SP 226.6–7; pariniṣpannaṃ cātmānaṃ jāne Śikṣ 38.11; °nnabhūmir ity ucyate apunaḥkāryatvāt Dbh 71.14; (mahābhijñā-)vipāka-parinişpannaś (bodhisattvaḥ) 71.24; (mahāratnarājapadmam...) māyāsvabhāvagocara-parinişpannam 82.25; aparinişpannānāṃ bodhyaṅgānāṃ parinişpattaye 52.14–15; aparinişpannānāṃ sarvapāramitānāṃ parinişpattaye Śikṣ 214.5; mg. obscure in Bbh 279.25; *perfected* in the sense of *arrived at the supreme goal*, cf. SP 226.6–7 above: bodhisattvā ito buddhakṣetrāt °nnā(ḥ) (here spelled pariṇi°) ... sukhāvatyāṃ ... utpatsyante Sukh 69.11; parinişpannānām avaivartikānām 14–15 (here instead of nirvāṇa, permanent life in Sukhāvatī is their reward); (**2**) °nna-svabhāvaḥ (text °ṇṇa-) Laṅk 67.15, *nature* (based on knowledge of) *absolute* (truth), see **svabhāva**, contrasting with **parikalpita, paratantra,** qq.v.; as one of this same triad, but with substitution of **lakṣaṇa**, q.v., for svabhāva, °nna-lakṣaṇam Mvy 1665; Sūtrāl. xi.41 (Lévi, *indice absolu*).

parinişpādana (nt.), once **°na-tā,** *the making perfect*: sarvasattvānāṃ °danāya Śikṣ 282.14; bhūmyaṅga-°danāya Dbh 20.23; sarvaloka-°danārthaṃ Gv 371.17; twice as v.l. for **parinişpatti,** q.v., in SP; buddhakṣetra-°dana-tā ŚsP 1469.21.

parinişpādita (ppp. to caus. of °**padyati**, q.v.), *completely developed* or *accomplished*: bodhisattvacaryā (so divide)°ditā SP 319.2; asmābhiḥ sarvabuddhadharmāḥ °ditāḥ AsP 510.18; °ditāḥ sarvasamādhayaḥ Gv 489.22–3; na ca mayaikasattvasyārthe ātmabhāvaḥ parinişpāditaḥ (misprinted) Kv 39.(21–)22, *and I have not developed* (formed; pw *zur Erscheinung bringen, offenbaren*, not quite accurately) *a* (material) *body for the sake of a single creature* (Avalokiteśvara speaks).

parindanā (also **parī°**; to **parindāmi**), *the giving over, presenting*: °nārthaṃ SP 391.1; °nayā LV 443.9; Dbh.g. 56(82).5 (prose, not vs); see s.v. **parīndanā** on Vaj 20.5, 11.

parindāmi (also **parī°, anu-par°**, qq.v.; peculiar to BHS; formation unexplained, see below), *I present, hand over*: °āmi SP 410.10; 484.5; LV 443.9 (Lefm. paridāmy, read with v.l. parind°); ppp. parindita, see **Parinditārtha,** and Pargiter ap. Hoernle MR p. 179, where parindita is read for parī° Vaj 20.4, 10. Could nasalized vowel -in-(-iṃ) be a substitute by the 'law of Morae' for parī-dāmi (cf. ppp. parītta), and the forms with parind° be blends? Not satisfactory. But parī- occurs for pari-. Dr. Paul Tedesco would derive by the Morengesetz from *pariddāmi for paridadāmi with loss of -a-; as a parallel he cites Skt. ujjhāmi etc., which he also derives directly from uj-jahāmi with loss of -a-. That ujjh- is somehow derived from ud plus root hā, few will doubt; but I am not sure that this is the precise way (for a different one see Uhlenbeck s.v.); and I should like other examples of such loss of -a-.

parindāyin (see prec.), *one who presents*: Dbh.g. 56(82).5 (prose, not vs) °dāyī.

Parinditārtha (cf. prec. items), n. of a former Buddha: Mv i.141.13.

(**paripakva,** = Pali °pakka; cf. **paripācayati** etc.; used in virtually the same sense in Skt.; *fully developed*, intellectually and religiously: a-paripakvānāṃ ca sattvānāṃ ... paripakvānāṃ ca ... Bbh 221.9–10, etc.)

[**paripaṇḍita,** in LV 404.20 (prose) suparipaṇḍita-śukla-dharmāṇo, Lefm., but v.l. °paripiṇḍita°, supported by Tib. bsdus pa, *accumulated*, and proved by the same cpd. Dbh 11.10–11; see **paripiṇḍayati.**]

paripantha (m. or nt.; in Skt. only adv. °tham in Pāṇ.; = Pali id.), *obstacle, blockage, obstruction*: catvāro ime ... bodhisattvānāṃ bodhiparipantha-kārakā dharmāḥ RP 18.1 ff. (listed); aṣṭau bodheḥ paripantha-karān dharmān vadāmi RP 34.15 (also listed; list entirely different from prec.); adv. °thaṃ tiṣṭhati (cf. Pāṇ. 4.4.36; in Pali °the is so used) Mvy 5351, *in a manner obstructive of a road* (as a robber); Tib. lam (*road*) gcod, or chod (*cutting off*).

paripācaka, f. **°ikā,** adj. (to °pācayati plus -aka), *bringing to maturity* (in religious sense): °kāḥ pudgalāḥ Bbh 84.21; (kalyāṇamitrāṇi...) samyaksaṃbodhau ... °cakāni SP 466.7; jñāna-°kair dharmaiḥ Dbh 38.8; bodhi-°cikā ... devata (= °tā) LV 185.11 (vs).

paripācana, nt., **°nā** (?), **°na-tā** (to next), *ripening, bringing to maturity*, in religious sense: sattva-°na(m) Dbh 42.6; 56.2; Kv 24.21; Gv 178.21; -sattvendriya-paripācanābhimukha- Gv 265.7; antaḥpurasya °canārthaṃ LV 182.13; bodhicitta-°na- Śikṣ 51.16; in Śikṣ 328.16 (vs) paripācanulomā seems to stand by haplology for paripācan(a)-anulomā; the alternative would be to assume a stem *paripāca, instead of (Skt. and BHS) paripāka; sattvānāṃ paripācanā Bbh 221.9 (but v.l. °nāya, dat. of °na); sattva-°canatāyai LV 34.21; 35.1; °tayā Gv 460.14 (all prose).

paripācayati (= Pali °pāceti), (**1**) *causes* (food) *to be cooked* (for someone else): bhikṣuṇī-paripācita, (*food*) *which a nun has instigated* (*a layman*) *to have cooked* (for a monk; he must not accept it) Prāt 508.9; Mvy 8451 (= Pali Vin. iv.67.1, 19); (**2**) *ripens* (grain etc.): (nānāsasyaphaloṣadhīḥ) °cayati Suv 166.10; (**3**) fig., *ripens, brings to maturity* (in religious sense): object sattvān, expressed or understood, °cayati Kv 14.8; 21.21; °cya, ger., Samādh 8.18; sattvān paripācayamānān Gv 249.9 (mid., *maturing themselves*, or as pass., perh. to be read °pācyamānan, *being matured*); (bodhisattvas) °cayati Kv 63.14; (tvaṃ, addressed to a bodhisattva) ... samyaksaṃbodhau paripācitaḥ AsP 493.12; (kuśalamūlāni) paripācayeyam Divy 125.1.

paripāṭana (nt.; n. act. to next), *cutting open* (of a sore): vraṇo yadā °ṭanāya niṣṭhāgato bhavaty anantaraṃ pāṭanārhaḥ, sa paripakva (*ripe*) ity ucyate Bbh 78.11.

paripāṭayati (cf. prec.; JM. paripāḍia, ppp., rendered vidārita, *torn*; no relation to Pali paripāteti, with which PTSD connects it on the strength of a single corrupt v.l. °ṭeti in Sn comm., ii.1, p. 353, note 9; the Pali word belongs to root pat, caus., the BHS clearly to root paṭ), *cuts* or *tears all around*: utpāṭya netre paripāṭayāmi gātraṃ kim asyā nakharaiḥ... Divy 417.6 (vs; note the cognate utpāṭya; not *destroy* with Divy Index).

[? **paripāṭhayati,** in ŚsP 381.21 sattvān paripāṭhayan buddhān ... satkurvan, said of a Bodhisattva, should mean *causing creatures to be enumerated* or *named, and honoring Buddhas*, which seems improbable; I suspect a corruption for paripālayan, *protecting*.]

Paripātrikā (= **Pāri°**), n. of a river near Benares: Mv ii.244.5 (prose; v.l. °yātrikā); in corresp. text Jm (App.) 240.4 corruptly Pāripāḍīkā, confirming Pāri°, however. See **Pāri°**.

paripārayati (= °pālayati, § 2.49), *protects*: sarvasattvavaṃśāḥ paripārayitavyāḥ Gv 410.18. The only other interpretation would be to connect it with pārayati, *saves*, which seems otherwise not to be compounded with pari.

paripiṇḍa(-**tva**), cf. next two, (*state of being*) *accumulated*: °tvāt kuśalasya bodhisattvā kāmāṃ (acc. pl.) na pratisevanti Mv i.153.9.

paripiṇḍayati (only noted in gdve. and ppp.; denom., cf. prec. and next; Skt. ppp. °ḍita, acc. to pw *zusammengeballt*; AMg. ppp. °ḍiya, *accumulated*, Ratnach.), (**1**) *makes into the shape of a ball* or *lump*: suptoragarājabhoga-paripiṇḍitaṃ (*like a sleeping snake-king's coils*...) paryaṅkaṃ baddhvā Divy 567.6; (**2**) *accumulates* (so Skt. piṇḍita): buddhadharmāḥ °ḍayitavyāḥ Gv 69.5 (2d ed. absurdly paripīḍay°); °ḍita-kuśalamūlāḥ Mv i.142.2; suparipiṇḍita-śukladharmāṇāṃ Dbh 11.10, and so read in LV 404.20 for text °**paripaṇḍita°**, q.v.

paripiṇḍī-kṛta (ppp. of °ḍī-karoti, see **paripiṇḍa**), *made into the shape of a ball* or *lump*; = paripiṇḍita, see °**ḍayati**, in the identical word and phrase there cited from Divy 567.6: Divy 516.7; 582.25.

paripūrayati, °**te;** once °**pūrati,** once °**pūryati**? (= Pali paripūreti, used similarly to mg. 1; not, seemingly, in these mgs. in Skt.), (**1**) *accomplishes fully, completes, perfects, fulfils* (cf. next): daśamāṃ bhūmiṃ °rayitvā Mv i.142.3; Bhadracariṃ (17) or bodhicariṃ (22) paripūrayamāṇaḥ Bhad 17, 22; sarvākāraṃ (*every form*, of Tathāgatas) °rayiṣyāmaḥ Sukh 10.1; ṣaṭpāramitāḥ °rayati Kv 68.19; 82.9; -pāramitā °rayitavyā Kv 50.17, 19; sarvatyāgādhimuktiṃ paripūrye (tyāga-) Śikṣ 34.1 (prose), read some 3 sg. opt. form, °ryet? °rayet? °ret (cf. under 2)?; (**2**) peculiarly used in Mv iii.356.6 (vs), so bhinnayānapātro (*his ship being wrecked*) paripūrati (v.l. °rayati, but meter seems to support °rati) sāgaraṃ (so mss.) narapravaro (so Senart em. for unmetr. ms. naravaro), which seems to mean *the noble man 'filled the sea'*, i. e. gave his life up to it (for the benefit of his companions); this is what the story certainly attributes to him. I have no exact parallel to this usage but can conceive no other interpretation; Senart's is very unsatisfactory (and involves the most implausible em. sāgare).

paripūri, °**rī,** f. (see also **pūri, pūrī**; this word serves as n. act to prec.; in Skt. paripūrti, also BHS, e. g. LV 32.18; also **pāripūri,** q.v.; both in Pali, but pāri° seems to be commoner, so that PTSD and pw 7.356 consider pāri° the 'correct' form; this is disproved by BHS, where pari° is commoner, and °ri commoner than °rī; pari° could, of course, not be explained by Senart's theory, Mv i.373, which involves the vṛddhi of secondary derivation), lit. *filling up*: divyāḥ kāyāḥ °riṃ gamiṣyanti LV 401.6; usually fig., *fulfilment, accomplishment*: pāramitānāṃ °pūryā(i, dat.) SP 256.11 (prose); (pratijñā-)paripūri- LV 275.14 (prose); praṇidhi-paripūriye (so read with mss.) Mv ii.205.16 (vs), *by fulfilment of my previous vow* (instr.); praṇidhāna-paripūryai (dat., so with mss., Lefm. wrongly em. °rtyai) LV 31.22; manorathāśā-paripūrī Mvy 6334; śūnyatāyāḥ °rir Śikṣ 117.9 (prose); icchā-°riḥ Bbh 123.25 (prose); other forms, °riḥ Dbh 56.28 (prose); °rim id. 59.26 (prose); Sādh 34.15 (vs, metr. indiff.); °raye Gv 73.10, 26 (prose); °ryāṃ Śikṣ 30.6; 119.14 (prose). See also **pratipūri.**

paripūrika, adj. (= rare Skt. °rin, pw; cf. °ri), *fulfilling*: sarvābhiprāya-°rika-darśanaḥ Gv 402.21 (prose).

Paripūrṇacandravimalaprabha, m., n. of a samādhi: Mvy 611; = **Paripūrṇacandrābhavimala,** ŚsP 1425.7.

Paripūrṇamanoratha, n. of a Bodhisattva: Gv 442.6.

Paripūrṇaśubha, n. of a Bodhisattva: Gv 442.17.

Paripūryābhayaprada, n. of a future Buddha: Av i.62.3.

paripṛccha-tā (cf. Pali paripucchakatā, see PTSD), *questioning*: (gurūṇāṃ) °tā LV 182.21 (vs); read, utthitā lokapālehi brahmendra-°tā Suv 133.6 (vs), so best ms., Nobel with other mss. °cchayā, which I cannot construe; *there arose (began, took place) a questioning of . . . by . . .*; paripṛcchatotsukaḥ Suv 221.1 (prose), *eager to question.*

paripṛcchana (nt.) or °**na-tā** (Ap. paripucchaṇa, Jacobi, Bhav., Index; AMg. paripucchaṇayā; n. act. to Skt. paripṛcchati), *questioning* (esp. of a teacher or authority), *investigation, inquiry* (into a subject): °na-jātīya, *given to . . .*, Laṅk 14.10; Śikṣ 50.7; (tathāgatasya . . .) °nāya Sukh 71.7; °nārthika Śikṣ 103.12; °na-, in cpds., LV 430.15, 16; Gv 44.21; Bbh 240.5 (all prose); iha śāsane cariṣyanty āparipṛcchanaśīlāḥ RP 34.9 (prose), so text; I cannot understand the ā-(pari°) and suppose it to be a misprint or corruption, perhaps for a-, *not interested in (religious) inquiry* (the epithet is uncomplimentary, describing false Bodhisattvas; people are expected to be °na-jātīya, above); sarvapraśna-°natā RP 8.12, *capacity for investigating all questions*; °na-tā Gv 163.21 (end of a cpd.).

paripṛcchanikā (cf. prec.), Divy 489.14, or °**cchinikā,** 489.23 ff. (cf. **svādhyāyanikā,** °**yinikā**), *subject for investigation* or *inquiry.* The form in -inikā seems suspicious, but occurs repeatedly in the mss., as also in **svādhyāy°.**

paripṛcchā (= Pali paripucchā, paṭipucchā), *question(ing), interrogation*: Mvy 1352, 1357, 1361 etc.; Samādh 19.2; Dbh 62.19; 72.14; Bbh 217.10, 11; title **Rāṣṭrapālapari°,** q.v.; paripṛcchā-vyākaraṇa, nt., *elucidation* (response to a question) *by questioning* (the questioner), Mvy 1660 (see **vyākaraṇa** 1); cf. Pali paṭi-(not pari!)-pucchā-vyākaraṇīyaṃ pañhaṃ AN i.197.21–22, explained comm. ii.308.30 ff. yathā cakkhuṃ tathā sotaṃ . . . ti putthena, ken' aṭṭhena pucchasīti paṭipucchitvā, dassanaṭṭhena pucchāmīti vutte, na hīti vyākātabbaṃ, aniccaṭṭhena pucchāmīti vutte, āmā ti vyākātabbaṃ. The precise equivalent of the Pali, *pratipṛcchā, *asking in reply*, has not been noted. See also **pṛcchaparipṛcchikā.**

pariprakāśa, adj., *very clear*: Jm 79.6 (em.).

paripraśnati, °**te,** °**nayati** (denom. to Skt. paripraśna; cf. **praśnati,** Pali paripañhati, AN v.16.2, following paripucchati, and Skt. praśnayati), *questions*, usually after or before paripṛcchati; so, °nayati LV 70.22; Śikṣ 88.6; 152.10; °nayanti AsP 199.3; otherwise, °nayataḥ (acc. pl. pres. pple.) Gv 518.11; °nase Mmk 218.17; °nitavyam (gdve.) Mmk 229.16. All prose.

paripraśnīkaraṇa (n. act. to next; see also prec.), *questioning, interrogation*: Sukh 48.17 (of Amitābha); (paripṛcchanāya) °karaṇāya 71.8.

paripraśnī-karoti (to Skt. paripraśna plus kar-; cf. prec. two), *questions, interrogates*: pass. °kriyate AsP 31.1; paripṛṣṭāḥ °kṛtāś ca (ppp.) 208.12. See **saṃparip°.**

pariprāpayati (Skt. only noun derivs., as pariprāpti; no record of the verb), (**1**) *gets, acquires* (prāpayati, sometimes = prāpnoti in Skt., BR): (śalākāṃ, *small pieces of wood*) °payituṃ Mv ii.274.7, 8; (**2**) oftener, *gets = gets done, successfully finishes, brings to a conclusion*: of mathematical problems, (**nikṣipati,** q.v., sma) na ca °payati LV 146.13, similarly 15, 17, 20, and Mvy 6658 (after **uddiśati** sma); of kāryaṃ, karaṇīyaṃ, *gets* (a job, task) *done*, kāryam āśu pariprāpyam Divy 410.6; tat (karaṇīyaṃ) °payiṣyāmi 545.27; °payāmi 583.19, *I'll get it done*; Śikṣ 278.7 f.; svakāryaṃ vā °payeyuḥ 282.6; sarvaṃ kṛtvā pariprāpya MSV iii.143.22; pariprāptaṃ ca taiḥ sarvakāryam LV 89.15 (prose), formally ppp. to non-causative *pariprāpnoti, which has not been found, in mg. belonging to caus. °payati.

pariprīṇayati (unrecorded; Skt. pari-prī- only in ppp. °prīta), *delights* (trans.): (abhiṣyandayati pariṣyandayati) °ṇayati (parispharayati) Mvy 1648 (DN i.73.26–27 has this list in Pali forms but with paripūreti for °prīṇayati); saṃpramodayāmi °nayāmi Gv 138.8; pariprīṇitendriyaḥ Gv 489.3.

pari-prokṣate (unrecorded), *sprinkles thoroughly*: (kṣīreṇa) °kṣasva Av i.375.15.

paribāhira, adj. (= Pali id.), *external, outside, alien*: Mv iii.284.2 and 11 paribāhiro (so with mss.) bhavati; same vs in Pali, SN i.126.24, paribāhirā, n. pl.

paribāhya (written °vāhya; gdve. to pari plus **bāhayati, bāheti,** q.v.), *to be excluded*: saṃghāt °hyā bhaviṣyanti AsP 179.19; sarvatriratnāt °hya-bhāvo bhaviṣyati 20; triratnāt °hya-bhāvo bhavati 183.19.

paribudhyati (unrecorded; Skt. has gdve. °bodhanīya and n. act. °bodhana in mg. *admonition, exhortation*), *understands*: na °yāmi kim atra antaraṃ Mv ii.66.15; etaṃ tatra antaraṃ na °yāmi ii.444.16; etat kāraṇaṃ na °yāmi 21; fut., katham ete buddhajñānaṃ paribhotsyante SP 78.15; ger., kāyam imaṃ . . . marīcidharmaṃ paribudhya caiva Ud xviii.18 (also 19, 20), in later mss., oldest ms. abhisaṃbudhāna(ḥ), supported by Pali Dhp. 46, for pari° caiva (see § 34.4); caus. *enlightens, makes to understand*: tān (sc. pṛthagjanān) . . . āryās . . . paribodhayanti MadhK

58.3; ppp. (avatāritāḥ) paribodhitāḥ SP 309.7 (said of bodhisattvas).

(**paribubhukṣita**, desid. ppp., once in Mbh., pw 4.301, *very hungry*, prob. really cpd. of pari, intens., and bubhukṣita: °tā(ḥ) Mv i.8.2, prose, but mss. paribhukṣitā, em. Senart.)

paribhāvita, ppp. (= Pali id., to paribhāveti), *made to be completely pervaded, saturated*: °tā śūnyata dīrgharātram SP 117.7 (vs), *we have long been thoroughly imbued with* (the notion of) *void*; śubhākāra-°ta-cetāḥ LV 181.17 (prose); -tva, abstr., kuśala-°ta-tvāt Mv i.153.12, *because* (Bodhisattvas are) *completely saturated with merit* (otherwise Senart).

paribhāṣaka, adj. or subst. m. (= Pali °saka; cf. next two), *reviling, one who reviles*: SP 273.8 (vs); with **roṣaka**, Divy 38.10; Bbh 120.19.

paribhāṣaṇa (nt.), °**ṇā** (to next; Skt. °ṇa, defined BR *Zurechtweisung, admonitio*), *blame, rebuke, reviling*: °ṇa-, in comp., after ākrośa, LV 181.12; Gv 244.2; °ṇābhiḥ, °ṇām, Śikṣ 19.9; 177.5 (in 19.9 with svacittam paribhāṣitavyam); ātmaparibhāṣaṇayā SP 60.14, *with self-reproach*; but Kashgar rec. °bhāṣāya.

paribhāṣati, °**te**, °**ṣayati** (cf. prec. two: = Pali °sati, °seti Jāt. iv.285.8; Skt. °ṣati, defined BR *Jmd zusprechen, zureden, admonere*; it is at least questionable whether anything close to the Pali-BHS mg. appears with the Skt. verb; yet the noun paribhāṣā seems clearly so used, pw), *rebukes, reviles* (often with forms of ākrośati, sometimes also of roṣayati, as also in Pali, e. g. SP 375.3; 378.10; Bhīk 5b.3): °ṣati Mv ii.480.2; 485.19; 487.2; iii.20.1; 23.14; °ṣasi Mv ii.480.4; °ṣante SP 378.10; ātmānam °ṣathā RP 59.8 (vs); °ṣi, aor., Mv ii.93.1; °ṣiṣyanti, fut., SP 375.3; °ṣyamāṇāḥ, pres. pass. pple., Mv i.18.7; (paribhāṣaṇābhiḥ svacittam) °ṣitavyam, gdve., Śikṣ 19.9; °ṣayitavyaḥ, gdve., and °ṣayitum, inf., Bhīk 5b.3; °ṣayitvā, ger. SP 213.4 (vs).

(**paribhukta**, ppp., SP 339.6, *enjoyed, utilized*, as in Skt.: te [sc. vihārāḥ; follows phrase cited s.v. **niryātayati**; Kern misunderstands the reference of the pronoun] ca mayā °tā veditavyāḥ, *and these* [monasteries] *are to be regarded as having been utilized by me*; cf. mayā sa bhuktaḥ pṛthivīpradeśo 344.5.)

paribhuktaka, adj. (= Skt. °kta), *utilized*; specifically, *worn, used* (of a garment): Divy 277.21 ff. (vastram).

paribhukṣita (cf. **bhukṣita**), *very hungry*: Mv i.8.2 (prose, mss.; Senart em. paribubhu°).

paribhūtaka (= Skt. °ta, -ka pejorative?), *despised*: RP 31.17 (vs).

? **paribheda** (m. or nt.), a high number: Gv 106.2. Corresp. to **haribha**, nt., q.v.

paribhoga, m. (commonly, as in Skt. and Pali, *enjoyment, usufruct, use*, also *article of enjoyment*; e. g. bodhisattvasya paribhogārtham LV 95.15, °gāya 16), *property to be enjoyed*, in LV 60.18 ff. . . . ratnavyūham bodhisattvaparibhogam draṣṭum yo mātuḥ kukṣigatasya bodhisattvasya paribhogo 'bhūt, refers to a physical (tho of course magical) structure, described in detail 63.1 ff., which houses the Bodhisattva in his mother's womb; it had three turrets or apartments, kūṭāgāra, one within the other, and within the third a couch or litter, paryaṅka; it was hard 'like vajra' yet soft to the touch (64.7–8); all the bhavana-vyūha of the kāmāvacara gods appeared in it (64.9); it always develops or appears in the right side of a Bodhisattva's mother in his last earthly existence (65.20, here called **ratnavyūhaḥ**, q.v., kūṭāgāro); in 73.3 referred to again, drakṣasi (so text and app. all mss.) tvam Ānanda ratnavyūham bodhisattvaparibhogam yatra bodhisattvo mātuḥ kukṣigato vyāhārṣīt. Tib. on LV 60.18 renders literally, *complete enjoyment*, yoṅs su spyad pa, cf. Mvy 7369 paribhogaḥ = Tib. yoṅs su spyod. SP 337.13, kūṭāgāraparibhogeṣu cātra bodhisattvān nivasato drakṣyati, does not refer to this magical structure in the womb, but to structures occupied by bodhisattvas while attending on the Buddha Śākyamuni.

paribhogīya, adj. (cf. next two), *usable, fit for use*: sati °gīye (vv.ll. °gike, pāribhogīye) pātre ūnapañcabandhane Prāt 498.12. But pari° seems to be lacking in Chin., acc. to Finot, and is lacking in the Pali, Vin. iii.246.10.

paribhogya (cf. prec. and next), (**1**) adj., *usable, fit for use, suitable, salutary*: pānīyam °gyam LV 408.2; (**2**) subst. (nt.), *use*: puṣkariṇyo jala-paribhogya-sthās LV 40.13; bhaiṣajya-śarāva-°gyena paribhoktavyāni Divy 275.24.

paribhojya, adj. or subst. nt., *useful (object*, sc. for monks): sarvam °jyam Mv i.115.3.

[**parima**, adj., read **pārima**, q.v. (not Pali parima = Skt. parama, *supreme, highest*), *further* (with tīra, *bank*): KP 154.9 (prose) °ma-tīra-gāminī.]

Parimaṇḍanārtha, n. of a former Buddha: Mv i.139.1.

parimardana, see s.v. **ucchādana**.

parimāṇa-vant, adj. (corresp. to Pali parimāṇa, as adj., Vin. ii.62.7 etc.), f. °vatī (āpatti), (sin) *of* (definite) *extent* (?): MSV iii.69.8, 12, etc.; opp. a-parimāṇavatī 70.11; 72.7 ff. (= Pali aparimāṇa). The real mg. is not clear, nor is it clear which category is more serious. Pali is equally uncertain, see SBE 17.421, n. 1. It does not mean 'if the period is known' (N. Dutt, Introd. xiv), for the period (rātriparyanta) may be known or unknown in the case of an aparimāṇavatī, 72.7 ff.

parimārgaṇa, adj., and °**ṇā**, subst. (Skt. only °ṇa, nt., subst. = BHS °ṇā), (**1**) adj., *searching*: °ṇaḥ paripṛcchan Gv 491.5; (**2**) subst., *(act of) searching*: (kalyāṇamitra-) °ṇāsu Gv 460.22.

-parimārjaka (= Pali °majjaka), *touching, attaining to*: candrama-sūrya-°jako maharddhiko . . .ṛṣi Mv ii.49.1, *who* (by magic) *can travel to the moon and sun*; so Pali canda-suriya-parimajjaka Miln. 343.16.

parimīmāṃsate (= Pali parivīmaṃsati), *considers thoroughly*: °se, 1 sg., SP 22.15 (prose).

parimīmāṃsā (to prec.; = Pali parivīmaṃsā), *investigation, careful consideration*: Mv ii.297.11; AsP 62.15 etc.

parimocaka, adj. or subst. (to °**cayati**), *saving, one who saves*: saṃsāraduḥkha-pa° Gv 416.13.

parimocana, nt. (to next; cited by Childers without reference; AMg. °moyaṇa acc. to Sheth), *saving, salvation, freeing*, either from the saṃsāra etc. (religiously), or in ordinary worldly application: SP 77.11; LV 210.21; Kv 11.17; Dbh 44.15; Śikṣ 280.16; 281.2, 8; Karmav 33.19; Laṅk 160.9; kleśavyādhi-°na-tayā Gv 463.16, *because he saves from* . . .

parimocayati, °**te** (= Pali °moceti; in Skt. only non-caus. °muñcati), *saves, rescues* (usually but not invariably in religious sense, cf. °**mocana**): °caya Mv i.180.9; °cayeyam i.337.5, 7; °cayasva SP 321.2; active finite forms, Divy 39.11; 95.28; Suv 91.2; Gv 354.15; LV 226.19; ger. °cya LV 226.21; °cayitvā Kv 8.20 (prose); gdve. °cayitavya SP 78.7; Śikṣ 280.9; inf. °cayitu-kāma Suv 95.2; ppp. °cita RP 24.6; Suv 82.3; Vaj 42.9 ff.

parimocayitar (to prec.), *one who frees*: °tāro 'jñānagahanāt (so read with 2d ed. for 1st ed. jñāna°) Gv 462.24.

parimrakṣaṇa (nt.; n. act. to *pari plus mrakṣ-), *smearing, rubbing on*: -pāṃśu-paṅka-°ṇaiś ca LV 249.7 (prose).

pariyanta, m. (= Pali id., Skt. paryanta), *end, limit*: parvatacakravāḍa-pariyantāḥ (so text, acc. pl. m.; . . . āvasati sarvān) Gv 254.18 (vs).

pariyeṣate, see **paryeṣati.**

[**pariruddha**(text adds -dha) SP 54.11, see **paligud-dha.**]

parilābha (m.; to the very rare Skt. pari-labh-), *acquisition*: sudurlabha-buddharatna-parilābha- Gv 416.11 (prose).

parivandita, adj. or ppp. (perhaps really cpd. of pari, intensive, and vandita; Skt. has pari-vand only once in RV.; but cf. AMg. parivandijjamāṇa, pres. pass. pple., and n. act. parivandaṇa), *highly praised*: naramaru-°ditaṃ sugataṃ Mv i.152.17 (vs).

parivambhita, ppp. (cf. Pali vambheti), acc. to KN Preface VIII, v.l. of Kashgar rec. of SP for Nep. parivañcita. Cf. **nirvamhaṇa.**

parivarjanatā and **°nā** (= Pali id., both; Skt. only °na, nt.), *avoidance*: caturvāgdoṣa-°natāyai LV 31.16; mātsarya-°natā ŚsP 1464.1; pāpamitra-°nā Śikṣ 52.4 (all prose).

parivarjayati, in yo (mss. ye) evarūpaṃ (mss. °pena) naradamyasārathi (Senart em. °thiṃ) dṛṣṭvā maharṣiṃ parivarjayeyaṃ (Senart em. °ya), hastehi pādehi ca so mahāśiriṃ praṇāmaye ... Mv iii.327.(14–)15 (vs) acc. to Senart *satisfaire, rendre favorable* (= ā-varj-); but I find it hard to believe that it could mean anything else than *avoid*. Should we read something like parivārayeya (or paricār°), *would wait upon*? This would at least make good sense.

parivarṇayati (= Pali °vaṇṇayati; Skt. ppp. °varṇita, *described*), *extols, describes with laudation*: yaṃ buddhaśreṣṭho °ṇaye (aor., or opt.?) śuciṃ Mv i.291.10 (vs) = Pali Khud.p. 6.5 yaṃ buddhaseṭṭho parivaṇṇayī (comm. 181.7 pasaṃsi pakāsayi, aor.) suciṃ.

parivarta, m. (in mg. 2 rarely nt.; in mg. 1 = Pali parivaṭṭa), (**1**) *turn, revolution* (so in Skt.): ekasmi citta-parivarti LV 151.15 (vs), *in a single turn of thought* (= *in one instant*); substantially = *method, process*, ime punaḥ pañca dharmāḥ (= bodhisattvaliṅgāni, line 4, cf. 306.1 pañca bodhisattvaliṅgāni pañcaparivartena veditavyāni) pañcaparivartena veditavyāḥ Bbh 301.8; esp. applied to one of the three *'turns'* of the 'wheel of the law' or stages in development of knowledge of the four noble truths; they are most clearly stated in Mvy beginning 1310 āryasatyānāṃ prathamaparivarto darśanamārgaḥ, *the first turn ... is the way of seeing*, sc. what the 4 truths are; these are stated 1311–14; 1315 ... dvitīyaparivarto bhāvanāmārgaḥ, ... *the way of putting them into effect*, viz. as stated in 1316–19, duḥkham āryasatyaṃ parijñeyam, duḥkhasamudayaḥ prahātavyaḥ, duḥkhanirodhaḥ sākṣātkartavyaḥ, duḥkhanirodhagāminī pratipad bhāvayitavyā; 1320 āryasatyānāṃ tṛtīyaḥ parivarto 'śaikṣamārgaḥ (so Tib. mi slob paḥi lam), the stage in which the efforts of the 2d stage have succeeded, 1321–4 duḥkhaṃ parijñātam, samudayaḥ prahīnaḥ, nirodhaḥ sākṣātkṛtaḥ, duḥkhanirodhagāminī pratipad bhāvitā. Similarly LV 417.15 ff. Similar (but somewhat less clear) detailed statements in Mv iii.332.13 ff., 333.3 ff. (here the last two parts of the 2d parivarta and the first two of the 3d are omitted, by accident or compression), and in Pali Vin. i.11.1–18 (here all is stated, but the three parivarta as relating to each of the four noble truths are each compressed into a single statement). The whole is referred to in LV 418.14 as triparivartaṃ dvādaśākāraṃ (because each parivarta refers to each of the four truths) jñānadarśanam, and similarly Mv iii.333.11 (omitting jñānadarśanaṃ; trip° and dvād° seemingly adverbs, the noun is āryasatyāni); Pali Vin. i.11.25 tiparivaṭṭaṃ dvādasākāraṃ ... ñāṇadassanaṃ. With reference to this, the dharmacakra is called triparivarta (usually also dvādaśākāra) SP 179.1; LV 422.2 (vs); Divy 205.21; 393.23; (**2**) m. or (rarely) nt., (orig. *turn*,) *section, part, chapter* of a literary work; °taṃ (acc.) Samādh 8.20; asmin ... dharmālokamukhaparivarte LV 36.6, here *section*, not one of the formal chapters of the work, and so 150.19; parivartān Gv 66.12 ff., *chapters*; °taḥ Mvy 1467 = Tib. le ḥu, *section, chapter*; regularly in the colophons of various works, m. in SP, LV, Suv, Samādh, Dbh 99.33 parīndanā-parivarto (read as one word), cf. 98.12 ff. dharmamukhaparivarto, in body of text; nt. °taṃ Mv i.27.1 (colophon); I have failed to note the word elsewhere in colophons of Mv; idaṃ saddharmapuṇḍarīkasūtra-parivartaṃ (so with WT) śroṣyati SP 260.7 (prose; acc.); (**3**) m. or nt., math., *square* (of a number): (after asaṃkhyeyam Mvy 7802) asaṃkhyeya-parivartaḥ Mvy 7803 (Tib. bsgres pa, *multiply*, Jä.); and so in 7805 etc., and in the similar table of large numbers 7933 ff. (cited from Gv); Gv 106.20 ff.; 134.8 ff. (which last makes the mg. unmistakable; e. g. aparimāṇam aparimāṇānām aparimāṇaparivartam).

parivartaka, m. or nt. (= **°ta**, 2), *chapter, section* (of a work): prathame °take Mv iii.411.18 (referring to what?).

parivartati (= Pali °vattati; in Skt. without complement, *changes*), (**1**) *changes into* (with nom.): Mv i.29.8–9 = Pali Pv iii.6.5, which proves Senart's text wrong; read, nadīm upemi (so one ms.; most mss. upeti, Senart upenti) tṛṣitā, riktikā (mss. °kāṃ) parivartati (*it is changed so as to be empty*); chāyām upemi (mss. °ti) saṃtaptā, ātapo parivartati (*it changes to sunshine*); (**2**) like Skt. pariṇamati, (*changes*, then) *develops, ripens, matures*: ye caivaṃ parivartantā (most mss. °tentā, perh. read so, but not in caus. mg.) na vivartanti paṇḍitāḥ Mv i.90.12 (vs), *who are thus maturing* ... (otherwise Senart).

parivartana (nt.? to Skt. parivartati; not recorded precisely in this sense), *turning-place, place of habitual movement*, in **golāṅgula-p°**, q.v.

parivartikā, v.l. °vartatā, in cakṣuḥ-pari°, *rolling* (*of the eyes*): instr. °ayā, LV 227.10.

? **parivalliya**, see **°velliya.**

parivahin, adj. (to Skt. and Pali °vahati), *carrying around*: hayanavarehi °vahī (mātāpitaraṃ ... rājā) Mv i.109.1 (vs).

parivādaka, adj. or subst. m. (cf. Skt. °vāda), *reviling, one who reviles*: asmākaṃ °kāḥ SP 272.8 (vs).

parivādanī (so, or parivānī, mss.; = Skt. °vādinī, so Senart em., perhaps rightly; °vādinī, no real v.l., Mv iii.82.5), *a seven-stringed lute*: °nīyo, n. pl., Mv iii.267.3.

parivāra, nt. (= Pali °ra, m., title of the Appendix to Vin., v.226.3, colophon), *accessory* (text), *appendix, addendum*: avalokitaṃ nāma sūtraṃ mahāvastusya parivāraṃ Mv ii.397.7, colophon to second version of the Avalokita sūtra.

parivārayati, °reti (Skt. has ppp. °vārita; Pali °vāreti, regarded by PTSD as error for °cāreti, but may easily be denom. from Skt. parivāra, *retinue*), *attends, waits upon* (with gen.?): tasyā (mss. tasya) ... parivāresi (aor.; but mss. °retvā) Mv i.303.4; note on Divy 1.6 says mss. of Divy 'sometimes' read parivārayati for paricār°.

parivāsa, m. (Skt., *period of residence*; = Pali id. in technical sense), *period of probation* to which certain monks were subjected, as a disciplinary measure, for concealment of a **saṃghāvaśeṣa** offense: °saḥ Mvy 8649; mūla-pari° 8650; mūlāpakarṣa-pari° 8651 (on these see s.v. **mūla**); same three MSV ii.207.15; iii.32.21 ff.; Tib. spo ba, *change*, esp. *of residence*. Its extent was equal to the period of concealment. See next, and 1 **paryuṣita-** (parivāsa). In MSV passim; origin and prescription of the three varieties, as in Mvy, MSV iii.94.12 ff. (in the **pārivāsika-**vastu).

1 parivāsita, in paryuṣita-pari°, seems equivalent to **parivāsa**, q.v.: paryuṣita-parivāsitena bhikṣuṇā Prāt 487.10–11, *by a monk who has completed his period of probation*; the Pali is parivuttha-(or °ṭṭha-)-parivāsa, see 1 **paryuṣita.**

2 parivāsita (= Pali id., Jāt. i.51.27; cf. Skt. parivāsa, 2, BR 5.1587), *perfumed*: sugandhi-(v.l.°dha-)-taila-pari° LV 76.15; divyagandha-pari° LV 96.5; Sukh 43.4;

in Mvy 6595 assoc. with **vāsanā**, q.v., prob. means something like *conditioned, habituated*, and if connected with our word, used only in fig. sense (so Jap. understands it, but not Tib. or Chin.; I do not understand the Tib. renderings, yoṅs su bskos pa or bgos pa, the latter *clothed*, suggesting association with root vas, *dress*).

parivāhya, see **paribāhya**.

parivijñapanin, adj. or subst. m. (no cpd. of pari-vijñā recorded), *making (one who makes) completely known*: trisahasra ājña-parivijñapanī (n. or voc. sg.; short a may be m.c., cf. Pali viññāpana; v.l. °jñāpana, unmetr. in antepenult and ultima) jagasya, kṣipraṃ pramuñca bhagavan mahabuddhaghoṣaṃ LV 116.19 (-20; vs).

parivitarka, m., rarely nt. (= Pali °takka), *reflection, consideration, thought*: tasyāsi °ko Mv iii.355.9 (vs), *he reflected*; almost always, as in Pali, preceded by cetaḥ- (always in comp. with pari°, tho sometimes printed separately in edd.), or gen. cetasaḥ; eva(ṃ)rūpaś (°po) cetaso parivitarka udapādi (also °pāsi, utpadye, aor.) Mv i.51.9; 329.21; 330.19; ii.257.12–13; iii.314.15; 416.11; same but with cetasi cetaḥparivitarka (Divy °kam) udapādi Divy 291.24; Av i.211.8; 240.2; evaṃrūpaś cetasaḥ (v.l. cetasaiva cetaḥ-) °tarka utpannaḥ Suv 195.1; of someone, regularly Buddha, 'recognizing' the mental processes of others by his own mind, cetasaiva cetaḥparivitarkam ājñāya (very common, e. g.) SP 8.4; 33.13; 206.7; 218.8; 250.8; 269.7; 303.1; LV 69.9–10; 264.4–5 (read with best ms. A, text tr. cetaś cetasaiva pari°); Mv i.330.11; cetaso parivitarkam ājñāya iii.53.15; 315.2; 424.15; 444.6; Gv 6.11; with pl. subject, cetobhir (for cetasā) . . . LV 285.21; with aor. ājñāsīt (for ājñāya) LV 393.21; evaṃrūpeṇa (adv.; sc. cetasā? but this adj. does not otherwise occur in this phrase and is prob. introduced by confusion with the phrase cited previously) cetaḥpari° ājñāya LV 396.5; ākāra-pari° (= Pali ākāra-parivitakka), *careful consideration of appearances* (or *conditions*), MSV i.236.21.

parividita, adj. or ppp. (prob. not ppp. to Vedic pari-vid, but noun cpd. of pari, intens., with Skt. vidita), *well known*: Jm 190.10.

pariviśiṣṭa (= AMg. parivisiṭṭha), *especial, particular*: pariviśiṣṭān āveṇikān (sc. dharmān) Bbh 377.9. Prob. n. cpd. of pari, intens., plus viśiṣṭa.

pariviśuddha, adj. or ppp. (prob. n. cpd. of pari plus ppp. viśuddha), *completely purified*: triguṇa-pari° Dbh.g. 52(78).21.

pariviṣati, also written °sati in mss. (= Pali °visati; Epic Skt. °veṣati and AMg. °vesai), *serves* with food: °ṣati Mv ii.211.17 (to be read for mss. parivasati or prativas°, Senart em. praticarati); 276.9; iii.145.10; opt. °viṣeyaṃ ii.276.6; ger. °viṣitvā iii.145.12 (mss. °śitvā, Senart em. °sitvā); iii.130.12 (mss. °śitvā, here Senart °ṣitvā); fut. °viṣiṣyāmaḥ ii.275.12; pass. °viṣīyati ii.276.4.

pariveṭheti (Pali so cited by Childers without reference; ppp. °ṭhita in PTSD; MIndic for Skt. °veṣṭayati), *wraps up*: °ṭhitvā Mv ii.82.14 (taṃ bhūrjaṃ kāṇḍe, mss. kaṇṭho, kaṃtho); 253.17; °ṭhitaṃ Mv i.302.17 (mss. °veṭ°, °veṣṭ°).

[? **pariveṇa** (= Pali id.), *cell, apartment* (of a monk or nun); only by Senart's em., sā parivrājikā upadarśitā svake °ṇe . . . svādhyāyaṃ karontī Mv iii.391.8. Both mss. purimante, or (omitting svake) °tena, for pariveṇe; prob. a form of **purima**, q.v., is contained here; perhaps purimaṃ, adv., *in front, before him*, foll. by tena (with foll. svareṇa).]

parivellayati (cf. Pkt. parivellira, defined kampana śīla; to Skt. root vell), *makes wavering*: °yiṣyanti AsP 215.13 (cittāni). Cf. next (?).

parivelliya, ger.? (or °valliya?), in Mv i.203.2 = ii.6.19 kusumalatā va drumavaraṃ śayanaṃ parivelliyā (mss. °ya, i.203.2 °valliya; Senart °yā, required by meter) śayitā, perh. *embracing*: *she lay hugging the couch as a flowering creeper* (embraces) *an excellent tree*. It is uncertain whether the root vell or (chiefly Dhātup.) vall should be recognized. Senart prints as if cpd. with śayitā and interprets otherwise.

parivyakta, adj. (= Pali °vyatta; pari, intensive, plus vyakta), *very clear, distinct*: °tenākṣarapadavyañjanena AsP 461.21.

parivyaya, m. (= Pali paribbaya), *allowance for* (daily) *expenses*: Divy 28.10 (divasa-pari°) and ff.; Śikṣ 146.17; Jm 24.13; fig. bāṣpa-parivyayena Jm 120.17, *with spending* (lavish pouring forth) *of tears*. Cf. **pārivyayika**. (In Mvy 5708 = Tib. spod, *spice*, as in Skt., Manu 7.127.)

parivyākula, adj. (pari, intensive, plus vyā°), *completely confused, disordered*: Jm 158.11; °lī-kṛta, *made* . . ., Jm 111.18.

pariśakti, *capacity*, in yathā-°ti-tas, adv., *according to capacity*: Mmk 110.2.

pariśaṅkā (= Pali °saṅkā; to Skt. pari-śaṅk-), *suspicion*: Jm 144.2; dṛṣṭena śrutena °kayā vā Bhīk 5a.4.

? **pariśara**, app. nearly = śara, *dart, arrow*: śoka-pariśara-viddha-(mss. °ddho) hṛdayo Mv ii.274.5 (prose). Should we read by transposition śoka-śara-parividdha-?

pariśithila, adj. (pari, intensive, plus śi°), *very loose* or *lax*: Jm 54.5; °la-śirāsthicarmagātra Divy 512.15.

Pariśuddhakarma, n. of a former Buddha: Mv i.140.14.

Pariśuddhasuviśālābha, n. of a Bodhisattva: Gv 442.4.

(**pariśuddhi**, f., seems to me used in no different mg. from *purification, purity*, = Skt. id., Pali °suddhi; so even in maṇḍala-pariśuddhiṃ kathaṃ saṃjānīte Kv 74.10, where pw renders *richtige Beschaffenheit, Correctheit*. A few other passages: LV 87.15; 440.2, 3; Dbh 26.8.)

pariśodhaka, adj. (to Skt. BHS °śodhayati, Pali °sodheti, *purifies*), *purifying*: °kaḥ Mvy 1113; bodhicaryā-°kā dharmāḥ RP 15.9 (here misprinted pāri°), 12; bhūmi-°kān dharmān Dbh 20.11 (cf. **pariśodhika**).

pariśodhika, adj. (= °**dhaka**; perhaps wrong reading for that), *purifying*: bhūmi-°kāni Dbh 60.5.

Pariśobhitakāyā, (**1**) n. of an apsaras: Kv 3.11; (**2**) n. of a 'gandharva maid': Kv 5.3.

[**pariśraddhāḥ**, em. in LV 184.5, where mss. unmetrically gṛha-dhana-(Lefm. em. m.c. gṛhe dhane)-putra-bhārya-pariśuddhaḥ or °dhaṃ; Tib. for the last member chags, *devoted, attached, fond*; no pari-śrad-dhā is recorded, and the em. seems implausible, but the mss. reading can hardly be right. The best em. that has occurred to me is pariṣaktāḥ, to Skt. pari-sajjate; see **pariṣakta** for another possible occurrence.]

pariśraya, nt. (= Pali parissaya), (*obstacle*?) *difficulty, danger*: abhibhūya sarvāṇi pariśrayāṇi Ud xiv.13 (= Pali Dhp. 328 parissayāni). See **parisrava**.

pariśrāvaṇa, see **parisr°**.

pariṣakta, *attached, enmeshed, involved*, prob. to be read for pariṣikta(m idaṃ kalipāśa jagat) LV 173.18, cited Śikṣ 204.6 (Bendall and Rouse *entangled*; Tib. thogs, *hindered*, which elsewhere translates derivs. of root sañj). See s.v. **pariśraddhāḥ**.

pariṣaṇḍa (once written °khaṇḍa), (**1**) m., or °**ḍā**, f., acc. to Tib. (baṅ rim) *terraced approach, flight of steps* (leading to a mountain, usually Sumeru, or to a building, acc. to Jä. a chorten, i. e. stūpa): °ḍaḥ Mvy 6760; dvāra-koṣṭhake °ḍāyāṃ caṅkrameṣu MSV ii.90.19; most often Sumeru- (pariṣaṇḍaḥ) Mvy 4159; MSV i.94.3; Divy 212.8 (°khaṇḍaṃ, acc.); °pariṣaṇḍāyāṃ, loc. f., Divy 217.17; 344.12; Av ii.127.8, 9; pariṣaṇḍo tadā Mero(r) Mmk 203.4 (vs); pariṣaṇḍa-vārika, m. (see **vārika**), Mvy 9072, (monk) *in charge of the flight of steps* (to a building, no doubt a stūpa); (**2**) m., MSV ii.159.5 °ḍaḥ, 9 °ḍa-cīvareṇa, perh. corruption for Pali paribhaṇḍa, which SBE 17.154

renders *binding along the back* (of a robe); Tib. zegs pa (? zegs ma = *dirt*, Jä., *water-spray*, Das).

? **parişadā**, see **parşadā**.

parişadya, m. (Skt. Lex.) = **pāri°**, q.v.: amātya-pari° (mss., Senart em. -pāri°) Mv ii.442.19 (prose).

parişā (also **parşā** and rarely **parşadā**, qq.v.; § 15.4; = Pali parisā, Skt. parişad and parşad), *assembly*: in prose of SP acc. to LaV-P. JRAS 1911.1074 °şāyaḥ (abl.-gen.), instead of parşadi (loc.) of KN 267.10; °şāya (gen.) SP 98.7 (vs); °şāṃ LV 361.10 (māra-); 363.13 (naramaru-; both vss); in Mv prose, i.133.16; 158.3; 310.6; 354.21; ii.419.1; 446.16, 17; iii.10.15, 16; catuhi parişāhi (of a Buddha, viz. monks, nuns, male and female upāsakas, as in Pali) 53.1; vss, i.75.3 (meter bad, °şāyāṃ, but Senart's suggestion parşadi requires further change to correct it); 171.12, 14, 16.

[**parişikta**, for **parişakta**? q.v.]

parişiñcana (nt.; n. act. to Skt. parişiñcati; = Skt. parişecana), *sprinkling*: -pravrajita-. . . -sugandhataila-mūrdhni-°naṃ (nt. acc. adv., or n. sg. of separate statement?) sarvayācanakebhyaś cūrṇamālya- . . . -pradānatvād LV 432.15.

parişkāra, m. (also **pariskāra**; = Pali parikkhāra), *equipment, utensils, personal belongings*: = Tib. yo byad; Mvy 2856; °ra-vaśitā, one of the 10 vaśitā of a Bodhisattva, Mvy 772; Dharmas 74; °ra-cīvaram Mvy 8945, presumably the robe as part of (a monk's) *standard belongings*; not of a monk but of an ordinary (poor) man, SP 106.13; often in a standard list, (a monk's) cīvara-piṇḍapāta-(or °tra-)-śayanāsana-glānapratyayabhaişajya-parişkāra (or °skāra; same in MIndic form in Pali, counted as four items), Mv i.49.10; 52.13; 295.17; Av i.1.7–8; Divy 143.6, 19; 470.1; Suv 112.9; LV 2.22; Sukh 27.1; Śikş 41.18 (and 215.7 same list without the word parişkāra); Kv 19.9; 20.20; 40.17; 82.13; elsewhere without list, referring to anything which could properly be given to a monk, Av i.271.13, 15; six parişkāra (of a monk) Av ii.81.6, MSV ii.123.6, not listed (it is hard to see how the above list could count up to six; perhaps the 'eight' listed PTSD s.v. parikkhāra are meant, the three robes counting as one item); āgṛhīta-pari°, see **āgṛhīta**; doubtful is LV 181.1 parişkāra-vigata-malāmātsarya-sunigṛhīta-citta, where pw renders implausibly 'etwa *an sich geübte Zucht*'; Foucaux must have read susaṃgṛhīta-puṇya-parişkāraḥ, as part of the preceding word, assuming mg. *parure* (as in Skt.); Tib. omitted in Foucaux's ed.; saptasamādhi-parişkāra- (dāyaka, of Buddhas) Divy 95.20, explained by Pali DN ii.216.31 ff., the seven pari° (comm. ii.645.28 gloss paricārikā, v.l. parivārikā) are the first seven stages of the noble 8-fold path, because they lead progressively to the eighth stage, sammā-(samyak-) samādhi; the word here seems to mean *utensils* in the sense of *means leading towards* (DN l.c. 32 sammāsamādhissa bhāvanāya samādhissa pāripūriyā). In MSV iv.108.1; 109.7 (bheda-)parişkāra (tho rendered in Tib. yo byad!) is false Skt. for Pali (bheda-)purekkhāra.

parişkārika, adj. (to prec. plus -ika; Pali parikkhārika recorded only as *one possessing the p.*), *belonging to the personal belongings* (of a monk): mṛta-°ka MSV ii.120.16, 20 (in 20 quasi-subst., *what belongs* . . .); 145.1, 9 (with **prativastu**).

parişṭhita, ppp., in su-pari°, app. used in sense of Skt. pratişṭhita, Pali patiṭṭhita, with confusion of MIndic paṭi (pati, = prati) and pari, § 2.47, (*well*) *established* (or, acc. to Tib., *properly taught*? gnas par bstan): °tā (spelled °sthitā) sā varabuddhabodhis SP 63.8 (vs); parallel with darśitā in 7.

parişyanda, m. (to °şyandayati; unrecorded in this sense), *moisture*: Mvy 6949 = Tib. rlon pa, brlan pa, gśer ba.

parişyandana (nt.; to next; cf. prec.), *saturation* (fig.): asmimāna-°na-taḥ Dbh 48.11.

parişyandayati, °deti (= Pali parisandeti), = **abhişyandayati**, q.v., which often precedes it, as in Pali; *saturates, irrigates, moistens*: literally (plants) Mv iii.301.17; of the mind (citta), Gv 83.7 kuśalamūlaiḥ svacittam eva parişyandayitavyam; AsP 92.1 manasikāra-parişyanditena cittena; as a yoga-practice, after abhişyand°, Mvy 1647.

parişvedana (nt.; n. act. to caus. of pari plus svid, used in Suśruta, BR), *sweating* (as a form of medical treatment): Gv 152.10 °danam (. . . . prajānāmi), in list of methods of treating diseases.

parisaṃstuta, adj.-ppp. (cf. Skt. pari-sam-stu-, *praise*, once in Mbh., BR), in (bodhisattvāḥ . . .) tathāgata-°tā(ḥ) SP 66.8, either *praised by* . . . (so Tib. and later Chin.), or *intimate with* . . . (cf. **saṃstuta**; so earliest Chin., Dharmarakşa).

parisaṃsthāpana-tā (to next), *establishment*: -sarvajñatā-mahāpura-°pana-tayā Gv 170.8.

parisaṃsthāpayati, and (perhaps only m.c.) °sthapeti (cf. next; caus. of pari-saṃ-sthā-, not recorded Skt. or Pali; cf. Pkt. parisaṃṭhaviṃta, °ṭhaviya), *establishes, fixes, makes firm, arranges in fixed order*: °sthāpayati SP 246.5, 7 (buddhakşetra); SP 247.5 (lokadhātu); °sthāpayāmi Gv 66.21 (parivartān, chapters or sections of a literary work); °sthapemi SP 308.12 (vs, perhaps m.c.; yuşmān, followers of Buddha); °sthāpayişyati Gv 112.22 (puṇya-cakravāḍaṃ loke); °sthāpitāḥ SP 309.7 (bodhisattvas); °sthāpayitavyaṃ Śikş 56.2 (parşanmaṇḍalaṃ).

? **parisaṃsthita** (ppp. of pari-saṃ-sthā, of which no other form seems to be recorded except the caus., see prec., and Pali parisaṃṭhāti, in a very different mg.; °sthita occurs once in Mbh.Crit. ed. 1.114.59 in mg. *standing round about*, of attendant deities; AMg. parisaṃṭhiya, *well-established*, Ratnach.), *established*: (iyaṃ sarvāvatī lokadhātū . . .) apagatanadīmahānadī parisaṃsthitā SP 244.12 (prose; ed. fails to separate from the prec. word). But perhaps the caus. parisaṃsthāpitā (see prec.) should be read with WT; no ms. is reported with it but some mss. have caus. forms, and the parallel 246.7 looks in this direction.

parisakkati (cf. Pali id. in mg. *sets out to, tries*, with dat.; see **-sakkati**), *walks around*: Mv ii.254.3 parisakkantaṃ (acc. sg. m. pres. pple.; but mss. °sakkāntaṃ or parisaṃkrāntaṃ) dṛştvā, *seeing him* (a man covered with branches, imitating a tree) *walking about*.

parisaṅga (cf. Pkt. id., Sheth, one of whose definitions is saṅga), *sticking, cleavage*: in Gv 401.9 (prose), nābhūt saṅgo vā parisaṅgoparuddhaṃgo (read °ddhāṅgo?) vā upakledo vā . . ., said of a mahāpuruşa, as possessor of the lakşaṇa samacatvāriṃśad-danta-tā: *there was no* . . . *obstructed member due to cleavage* (?).

parisaṃtuşṭa (ppp. of unrecorded pari-saṃ-tuş-, or cpd. of pari, intensive, and saṃtuşṭa), *completely satisfied*: Gv 457.26 (prose).

parisamanta (m. or nt.; see also **parisāmanta, °taka**; Pali parisamanta-to, adv., rendered *from all sides*, perh. lit. *from the vicinity*), *neighborhood*; only in quasi-adverbial instr. and loc., with dependent gen., *near* . . ., usually with a form of the verb carati (or a synonym): °ntena Mv ii.253.3 (nivāpasya ca °ntena carati); iii.126.2 (°ntena rājakulasya); iii.144.2, 14; 155.9; °nte Mv ii.251.11 (sānaṃ); iii.144.1 (v.l. °ntena). All prose.

parisaṃbhavati (twice in AV., otherwise unrecorded), *develops completely*: (saṃbhavanti) parisaṃbhavanti parinişpadyante Gv 371.7.

? **parisara**, nt., in a colophon Mv i.193.12, daśabhūmayaḥ mahāvastuparisaraṃ, acc. to Senart *introduction* (from the mg. *environs, vicinity*); he also thinks of possibly emending to **parivartam** (q.v.), *section*.

parisarpikā, *writhing*, or *stumbling*? in LV 227.8, kāścin (women of the harem, on finding the Bodhisattva gone) nānā-kāya-parisarpikayā rudanti sma, *wept with* *various contortions, grovelings,* or *stumblings, of the body;* Tib. rdeb, rendered by Foucaux *se frappent* (le corps), but the meaning *stumble,* and others, is also given for it.

parisarpyaka (gdve. of pari-sṛp- plus -ka), *capable of being run about in* (or, acc. to Bendall and Rouse, *easy to traverse*): (sthānāni...) sukha-parisarpyakāṇi Śikṣ 197.3 (prose; to be cultivated by an ascetic).

parisāmanta (AMg. id., said to be m., *neighborhood;* see next, and **parisamanta**; all seem to be variants of one word, or at least equivalents), m. noun or adj., *neighboring, belonging to the vicinity:* °ntaḥ (so Index, misprinted pārisam° in text; Mironov °samanta, but most mss. °sām°) Mvy 6493 = Tib. khor yug (*round about*) or ñe khor (*'those about us'*); in cpd., bodhimaṇḍa-°ta-gatā(ḥ) AsP 56.7, *those who were in the neighborhood of...;* either adj. or acc. adv., nirdhāvati taṃ vanaṣaṇḍaṃ parisāmantaṃ Mv i.359.21 (so mss., Senart em. °samantaṃ), *went out to that forest-thicket in the vicinity;* otherwise adv. °te or °tena, with gen., = **parisamanta** (°te, °tena): °te Mv ii.211.6 (āśramapadasya); °tena Mv ii.252.7 (kālapāśānāṃ); iii.153.15 (āśramapadasya... carati).

-parisāmantaka (cf. **sāmantaka**), in Bhvr. adj. (= prec.), ardhayojana-parisāmantakaḥ Mvy 5603, *having environs* (surrounding area) *of half a yojana* (= of that circumference?); cited by BR as °samantaka, but Mironov also °sām°, no v.l.; °kena, adv., = °ntena (see prec.), SP 159.11 (bodhimaṇḍasya).

parisṛṣṭa, ppp. (recorded only in one very doubtful Vedic passage, AV. 8.6.20, see Whitney-Lanman), *mingled, set* (with precious stones): jātarūpaṃ vaiḍūrya-parisṛṣṭaṃ Dbh 54.7.

pariskāra (m.; = **pariṣkāra,** q.v.), *equipment, utensils:* LV 429.22 (no v.l.); 430.20 (only v.l. parihāra); also in some citations s.v. **pariṣkāra.**

paristhita, see **pariṣṭhita.**

parisnāti, °**snāyati** (unrecorded), *swims thru* or *across:* bhikṣavo 'tra (sc. arṇave, fig. of the saṃsāra) parisnānti Divy 56.11 = °vaḥ parisnāyanti MPS 7.10.

parispharayati (prob. caus. to Pali parippharati, *suffuses, permeates*), *causes to expand:* Mvy 1649, so also Mironov 85.12; BR cite °sphār°; = Tib. yoṅs su rgyas par byed pa.

parisphuṭa, adj. (see next, and **sphuṭa, pratisphuṭa;** = Pali paripphuṭṭha, or MN iii.94.2 °pphuta, read °ṭa?), *completely filled, full:* Mvy 6295 (ābhayā); 6867; LV 77.12 (ratnajāla-pa°... gṛhaṃ); 231.7; 307.16; SP 175.3; Mv ii.349.21, 22; 350.2, 20; 351.3, 6 (all these in vss, repeated iii.274.1 ff.); ii.359.22; RP 40.18 (puṣpaphalavṛkṣaiḥ); Śikṣ 28.7 (mahākaruṇā-pa°); Gv 8.6 (tathāgatakāya-); 167.21; Sukh 41.11; °ṭaṃ tu paṭaṃ kṛtvā Mmk 60.13; 553.18; 554.1, of a magic cloth, woven and painted so as to be *full* (of figures).

parisphūṭa, adj. (cf. **sphūṭa,** on same page of LV, for **sphuṭa**), = prec.: (prabhayā...) °ṭo 'bhūt LV 86.3 (prose).

parisrava, m. or nt. (Aśokan id.), seems used in the sense of **pariśraya** = Pali parissaya, *difficulty, trouble,* perh. by folk-etym. confusion with Skt. parisrava: pratighānunayā na santi te na ca te santi mune °vāḥ MSV i.11.11 (vs); sarvāṇi parisravāṇi ib. ii.185.3 (vs, = Ud xiv.13 pariśrayāṇi, see this).

parisrāva (m., = next), *filter, water-strainer:* Mvy 9120 = Tib. chu tshags (°va-kalpaḥ); a-parisrāvaṃ... pānīyaṃ Karmav 160.13, *unfiltered water.*

parisrāvaṇa, also written °śrāv°, nt. (= Pali parissāvana; cf. prec. and next), = prec.: Mvy 9020; pātrapariśrāvaṇaṃ (dvandva, *bowl and strainer*) yathāsthāne sthāpya Divy 582.24. (The preceding pātraṃ ca is to be construed with nirmādya.)

(**parisrāvita,** = Pali parissā°, ppp. of Skt. °srāvayati, Pali °ssāveti, *filtered,* of water: LV 249.8.)

-parisrāvin, in **a-pari°**, *not provided with (made like) a filter* or *sieve,* of the webbed hands and feet of a mahāpuruṣa, see s.v. **jālin:** vicitra-suvibhakta-chidrāparisrāviṇī (dual) Gv 399.26, (if text is right) *in a manifold and well-separated way not made like a filter with holes;* but perhaps read °chidra-pari°, *having* (the nature of) *a filter by reason of various well-divided holes.*

parisruta, ppp. (cf. prec. items), *strained* (of fat): (vasā...) akāle °tā MSV i.v.16.

pariharati, °**reti,** (**1**) (= Pali id.; cf. also **parihāra,** °**hārya**), once ger. °hārya as if from 'caus.' °hārayati, *protects, guards, looks after:* (śiṣya-)gaṇaṃ LV 239.11; 245.10; śrāvaka-, bhikṣu-saṃghaṃ Mv i.39.3; 60.6; 238.20; 239.14; 331.6; ii.119.2; a herd (yūtha, of deer, apes, birds, the subject being their leader), Mv i.359.18 (mss. °reti); ii.234.17; 251.3; iii.31.6; parents (subject being their son), janetrīṃ Mv iii.134.9; mātaraṃ... pitaraṃ... pariharet Av i.205.2; pass., mātāpitarau... parihriyete Av i.193.7; the embryo in the womb, subject the mother (so also Pali), parihārya (seemingly to *°hārayati, but reading doubtful) kukṣiṇā Mv iii.109.13; one's own speech, Dbh 24.21, see s.v. **parihārya;** (**2**) (cf. *umschlingen* in BR s.v.) *wraps up,* a purchase (otherwise Senart): (keśaraṃ, q.v.) parihariyāhaṃ bhagavato... adhikāraṃ karomi. pariharetsuḥ (mss.)... te duve gandhikamahattarakā śatasahasrakeśaraṃ Mv i.38.4–5, *having wrapt up* (the perfume being bought), *I shall pay service to the Lord* (with it). (So saying) *the two perfumers wrapt up the perfume worth 100,000;* (**3**) *brings, moves* (trans.; cf. *umherbewegen* in BR s.v.): bhagavāṃ dakṣiṇam eva caraṇaṃ kanakakamalaṃ, pariharati indrakīle (loc. of goal) tatra bhavati adbhuto ghoṣo Mv i.235.11–12 (vss), in account of Dīpaṃkara's entrance into Dīpavatī-city.

(**parihāṭaka,** nt., Mvy 6020, and **parihāraka,** nt., Mvy 6028 [in both = Tib. gdub bu, with addition of tham pa = pari in 6028] or °raka m., Mv ii.352.6 [°kāḥ, n. pl., in vs]; in Mvy 6028 v.l. °harakaṃ, which Mironov reads without v.l.; *bracelet* [or *anklet*], acc. to Tib.; certainly some bodily ornament. The two are surely different forms of one word, which also appears in BHS as **pārihāraka,** q.v. It occurs in Mbh. crit. ed. 1.67.2; 4.15.2 and 18.19, always following a parallel form of kuṇḍala, °hāṭaka in text [with most mss.] but always with v.l. °hāraka. Taken by BR 4.560 as noun, identical with Mvy °hāṭaka, but in 7.1768 as adj., *ganz von Gold* [with kuṇḍala]; the existence of the v.l. °hāraka, and BHS pārihāraka, give support to BR's earlier interpretation, to which I adhere. See § 2.47.)

parihāṇa (nt.; = Pali °hāna; in Skt. rare, only twice in a Brāhmaṇa, BR s.v., in neg. a-pari°), *loss, ruin:* Śikṣ 105.14, 15; abhavyaḥ °ṇāya Ud vi.7 (so with abhabba in Pali).

-parihāṇikā (to Skt. parihāṇi plus -kā), in pada-°ṇikayā, adv., *'by diminution of a step', one step behind* (another monk): caṅkramanti... MSV iii.97.3.

parihāpaṇa (nt.; to Skt. °hāpayati, Pali °hāpeti), *abandonment, quitting:* saṃgha-°ṇāya Karmav 40.2.

parihāpita, ppp. (= JM. °hāviya = Skt. Pali °dhāpita, to °dhāpayati), *clothed:* vastraṃ °to Mv ii.170.12.

parihāra (m.; = Pali id.; to **pariharati,** 1), *watchful care, guard, ward, act* or *process of guarding:* teṣāṃ bhavanto ardhaparihārā (em.) Mv iii.63.8, *of these* (disciples) *you* (two) *have half the guardianship* (Bhvr.; are half-guardians); parihāradharmaṃ na mārgayati Śikṣ 152.6, *he seeks not to follow the law of watchful care* (of religious practices; wrongly Bendall and Rouse); saparihārā śikṣā Śikṣ 178.13, *full of watchful care* (here B. and R. correctly).

parihāraka, nt. or m., = **parihāṭaka,** q.v.

parihārya, adj. (quasi-gdve. to **pariharati** 1, or to **parihāra** plus -ya), *guarded,* of speech, opp. to **saṃbhinnapralāpa:** saṃbhinnapralāpāt prativirataḥ... suparihāryavacanaḥ (Bhvr.) Dbh 24.18; vacanaṃ parihāryaṃ pariharati 21, *keeps his speech guarded.*

parīkṣā, Skt., *investigation, testing,* of valuable things: Divy mentions eight parīkṣā in the cliché cited s.v. **udghaṭaka,** q.v., 3.19 etc., and **ghaṭaka**; single complete lists are rare but by combining the Divy lists preceding occurrences of the cliché it seems that we get vastu-, dāru-, ratna-, hasti-, aśva-, kumāra- (or puruṣa-), kumārī (°rikā-, or strī-), and vastra- (442.1, in a list also containing vastu-) parīkṣā; these all occur, in different order, MSV iii.20.3 ff.

parīkṣyate = Skt. parīkṣate, *examines*: Divy 407.5; cf. **upaparīkṣ°**; **nirīkṣyate**; § 2.23; Chap. 43, s.v. īkṣ (2).

1 parītta, adj. (= **paritta**, q.v.; cf. also **parīttaka, parīttaśubha, parīttābha**), *small, limited, restricted, minor*; very common: Mvy 1918; SP 211.10; LV 402.3, 4; 438.10; Mv i.316.2; ii.49.17; Av i.329.10; Suv 6.5; 9.12; Divy 498.12; 504.12; Śikṣ 54.3; Dbh 26.21; Bbh 125.6; Sukh 25.4; mā parīttamanām (! for °manas) utpādaya Gv 528.19, *don't be faint-hearted* ('small-minded'); a-parītta, *not small,* Mv ii.44.8.

2 parītta (nt.; = Pali 2 paritta, see PTSD, or °ttā), *protection, safeguard, refuge* (from Skt. pari-trā-): suparīttaṃ (v.l. °ītaṃ) bhāvayiṣyati Mv ii.145.8, *he* (the Bodhisattva) *will produce, effect, a good safeguard* (refuge, against the ills of life); otherwise, but very implausibly, Senart. The ī may be due to influence of the very common homonym, 1 **parītta**; but, of course, the i of the preverb pariis otherwise capable of lengthening in Skt.

parīttaka, adj. (= Pali parittaka), = **1 parītta,** q.v.: Mv i.57.5 (prose); iii.244.8 (vs, meter bad).

parīttaśubha (= Pali parittasubha), m. pl., *of limited magnificence,* one (usually the 1st) of the classes of **rūpāvacara** gods in the 3d dhyānabhūmi; usually with **deva,** q.v.: LV 150.7; Mv ii.314.8; 360.19; Mvy 3094; Dharmas 128; Divy 68.15 (mss. mostly parīta°); 367.12; Gv 249.13; Av i.5.3 etc.

parīttābha (= Pali paritt°), m. pl., *of limited radiance,* one (usually the 1st) of the classes of **rūpāvacara** gods of the 2d dhyānabhūmi; usually with **deva,** q.v.: LV 150.6; Mv ii.348.19; Mvy 3090; Dharmas 128; Divy 68.14 and 367.12 (mss. in both parītā°); Mmk 43.21; Gv 249.14; Av i.5.2, etc. Once, in Mv ii.163.17, seems to be used otherwise, as adj., but the expression is very strange, possibly corrupt; at the time of the Bodhisattva's abhiniṣkramaṇa, the habitations of various gods became completely purified; at the end of the list, in 16, śuddhāvāsānāṃ (highest of rūpāvacara gods, and far higher than parīttābha gods) devānāṃ bhavanāni (etc.); then, in 17, evaṃ ca teṣu śuddhāvāseṣu deveṣu parīttābhānāṃ samyaksaṃbuddhānāṃ adhiṣṭhitāni caṅkramā niṣadyāni śayyāni tāni pi atīva pariśuddhāni abhūnsuḥ paryavadātā. I cannot explain the dwelling of Perfectly Enlightened Buddhas 'of limited radiance' among śuddhāvāsa gods.

parīndanā (also **pari°**; to next), *the giving over, presenting*: °nā- Dbh 95.10; 99.33; °nayā Vaj 20.5, 11 (Pargiter ap. Hoernle MR 179 pari°); °nāṃ Sukh 73.11; AsP 462.16.

parīndāmi (= **parin°**, q.v.), *I present, hand over*: °āmi AsP 460.14; 461.12; ppp. °dita AsP 218.18; Vaj 20.4, 10 (Pargiter ap. Hoernle MR 179 parindita).

pareṇa (in Skt. seems to be used in time expressions only in meaning *afterwards, later,* as adv., or prep. with abl. or gen., *after, later than*; acc. to PTSD, Pali para is used also of 'remote past'), (**1**) alone, postpos. with gen., *before* (of remote past time; lit. *beyond*): kalpānāṃ p° Gv 232.5; (**2**) in collocation with following parataraṃ or °reṇa, as postpos. with abl. or gen., of both future and past time; future, *beyond, later than, after*: tataś ca bhūyaḥ pareṇa paratareṇa SP 151.4, 153.6; (tataḥ) pareṇa paratareṇa SP 269.1; tataḥ pareṇa parataraṃ SP 156.9 (prob. temporal, *after that,* but could possibly be local, *beyond that point*); after gen. of noun, *after, later than*: pareṇa parataraṃ SP 206.10–11; Sukh 5.7 (Dīpaṃkarasya) and ff.; of past time, *before, long before,* with prec. gen. of noun, pareṇa paratareṇa Gv 150.3; 222.13; °taraṃ Gv 380.21–22; in a longer phrase, prec. by abl. of pronoun or gen. of noun, tataḥ (or tebhyaḥ, SP 375.10, or gen. of noun, Gv 352.3) pareṇa paratareṇa yad āsīt tena kālena (following an expression for a very long time in the past) SP 156.2; 375.10; Gv 352.3.

paropara, pron. adj. (= Skt. paraspara, AMg. paroppara; not recorded in Pali), *one another*: °raṃ ca yathābhiprāyaṃ samāgacchanti Mv iii.394.1.

parṇaka, (**1**) nt. (= Pali paṇṇaka), *leaf*: śīrṇa-°kāni samudānīya Divy 582.22; *feather,* (paryaṅkaḥ . . .) tūlikāparṇakāstīrṇaḥ Sukh 67.7; (**2**) adj. (or parṇika = parṇin?), fem. °ikā, *leafy, made of leaves*: °kāṃ kuṭim abhinirmāya Divy 574.6.

parṇakula, °**kulaka** (m. or nt.), acc. to Senart a certain kind of rice; more likely, I think, some special preparation (*curry*?) of rice: ekam-ekaṃ ca (sc. bhikṣuṃ) sapta-sapta puruṣā sapta-saptehi niṣṭhānehi parṇakulakena ca śālīnāṃ Mv i.325.11 (so mss.; Senart śālinā by em.!), *seven men served each monk with seven dishes and with . . . (curry?) of rice*; parṇakula-śālisya śata (mss. śaka) vāhāṃ preṣayet Mv i.329.12, *sent . . . carts (loads) of . . .(? curry-) rice,* i. e. of rice prepared in this style.

Parṇaśabarī, Mmk 318.13, or °**śavarī**, Sādh 306.11 et alibi, n. of a goddess.

-parpaṭaka, m. (= Skt. °ṭa, a kind of cake; AMg. pappaḍa, *a thin paper-like dried cake,* Ratnach.; in Pali only recorded in bhūmi-pappaṭaka), noted only in **bhū-, bhūmi-, pṛthivī-p°**, qq.v., all of which (certainly the first two) seem clearly to mean a kind of *edible mushroom* (like Pali bhūmi-p°, above); lit. *earth-(pan)cake* or the like.

[**parmakanaka**, nt., see **varmakānaka.**]

paryaṅkin, adj. (unrecorded), *squatting in the position called* (Skt.) *paryaṅka*: °naṃ Sādh 35.6 et alibi; see also **ardha-paryaṅkin.**

[**paryaṇṭhate**, *roams about*: so Kashgar rec. for paryeṣatī SP 251.2 (vs), see **paryeṣati** (2); so also, in the same passage, LaV-P in JRAS 1911.1071; read prob. paryaṇvate, see next.]

? **paryaṇvati**, *roams about* (cf. **aṇvati**): sā codyānaṃ paryaṇvantī . . . Mv i.99.8 (vs), so Senart by plausible em. for hopelessly corrupt and metr. deficient mss. Cf. prec.

paryadhigacchati, *attains completely*: sujātadarśanatvaṃ ca śreṣṭhī paryadhigacchasi (3 sg. aor.) Mv i.188.3 (vs).

paryanta, (**1**) nt. (in Skt. only m.), *end*: °taṃ (n. sg.), prāptaṃ mayā . . . LV 372.21 (at end of line of vs; in 374.3 paryantaḥ . . . prāpto, in same series of vss; both times no v.l.); (**2**) at end of a cpd., pātra-paryanta, m. Prāt 499.3 (= Pali patta-pariyanta, Vin. iii.246.13; comm. iii.708.33 evaṃ parivattetvā pariyante ṭhitapatto), *the last, worst* (of its kind, here *bowl*), Chin. *le plus laid*; cf. the following; (**3**) adj., in obscure passage LV 147.2 evam aparyantāḥ sarvaśākyakumārā atha paryantaś ca bodhisattvaḥ; essential mg. must be *thus all the Śākya youths were unsuccessful* (didn't get to the solution? sc. in mathematical computation), *and on the other hand the B. was successful.* The Tib. reads as if the two terms pary° and apary° were reversed: de ltar (= evaṃ) sā kya gzhon nu de dag (*youths*) thams cad (*all*) ni phug thug par gyur (*? became arrived at end*? Foucaux, *furent poussés à bout*), byaṅ chub sems dpaḥ la ni thug paḥi mthaḥ med par gyur to (Foucaux, *sans que le B. eût été poussé à bout lui-même*; Tib. is not quite clear to me but certainly contains a negative). If the apparent transposition in Tib. authorized the assumption that the true text was paryantāḥ śākyakumārā athāparyantaś ca bodhisattvaḥ, this and the preceding (2) would authorize setting up an adj.

paryanta, *'at the end'*, *inferior*, and then a-pa°, *not inferior*. But aparyanta also occurs in its Skt. mg. of *limitless*; see e. g. aparyanta-tvāt LV 180.1, *because of the limitlessness*.

paryantaka, adj. (to Skt. paryanta plus -ka), *of the border, frontier*: °kāḥ koṭṭarājās LV 94.16 (vs). Cf. also next.

paryantika (or °taka?; Pali, see below), f. °tikā, ifc. (Bhvr.?), *having . . . as its limit, ending in, limited to*: kāya-°tikāṃ vedanāṃ Av ii.193.3, and jīvita-°tikāṃ ve° 4, = Pali SN ii.83.1 ff. kāya-pariyantikaṃ vedanaṃ and jīvita-par° (acc. sg.); these, like the Av forms, might be fems. to °taka, but in Vism. i.69.17 ff. occur masc. forms (bhojana-)pariyantiko etc.

paryantīkṛta, ppp. (to °tī-karoti, from Skt. °ta plus karoti), *ended*: Divy 97.19; 236.18; Sukh 14.3.

-paryaya (m.; seemingly = **paryāya**, q.v., which perh. read?), *course, regular procedure*: ifc. Bhvr. in aviparīta-paryayo (v.l. °pratyayā) śāstuḥ śāsane Mv iii.254.11 (prose), *having (adopted) an unreverting course in the Teacher's teaching*, said of one who has realized the śrotāpattiphala.

paryavagāhayati or **°heti**, and ppp. **°gāḍha** (= Pali pariyogāhati and °heti, ppp. gāḷha), *examines, investigates, penetrates intellectually*: ger. a-paryavagāhitvā Mv iii.153.2; 167.5; °hetvā 165.11; 170.7 (mss.); ppp. in °gāḍha-dharma(n) = Pali °ogāḷha-dhamma: °mā (n. sg. m.) Av i.233.5; ii.194.9 (em.); MSV ii.46.17; stem °ma-, Waldschmidt, Kl. Skt. Texte 4,111.12 and 143.5.

paryavadāta, ppp. (to pary-ava-dā-, *purify*, recorded only in the foll. and in caus. forms chiefly with -dap- in Pali, except °dāta rarely in Skt., Kād., BR 7.1752, 1768), *completely purified*: exceptionally in the sense of *educated*, nānāpaṇyaparīkṣāsu °dātaḥ sarvaśāstrajñaḥ Divy 100.4; otherwise noted only following pariśuddha, one or the other sometimes preceded by ekānta- in comp.: °ddhaṃ °dātaṃ brahmacaryaṃ LV 3.9; Mv ii.117.17; ii.140.3; iii.50.11; 214.16; Av i.211.12; RP 2.14; Mvy 1289; of citta, Mv ii.132.14; Mvy 829 (su-pary°); misc., LV 405.8 ff.; Mv ii.163.4 ff.; iii.325.15.

paryavadāna (nt.; to prec.), *complete purification*: tat sarvaṃ tejasā °nam agacchat LV 18.18; sarvākuśaladharmaparyavadāna-karaṇa-tayā Gv 494.19.

paryavadāpaka(-tva, nt.; = Pali pariyodāpaka), (*state of*) *completely purifying*: °tvāt Bbh 91.22.

paryavadāpana (nt.; to next; Pali pariyodapana), *complete purification*: °nāya Dbh 3.28; sarvadharmamukha-°nāya Gv 492.20.

paryavadāpayati (Pali pariyodapeti; see prec. items and next), *purifies completely*: °payati Bbh 363.19; (dharmaparyāyaṃ . . .) °payan (pres. pple.) SP 465.5; gdve., dharmamukhāni °dāpayitavyāni Gv 460.10; ppp. °pita, Dbh 98.4; with suffix -tā, su-paryavadāpita-tayā Gv 391.15, *because of being well purified*.

paryavadāpayitar (to prec.), *one who purifies completely*: svasya vādasya °tāro Divy 202.13.

paryavanaddha, ppp. (Skt. Gr. only; cf. next two; = Pali pariyonaddha), *covered, overgrown, concealed, beset*; rarely in a good sense: (bhūmipradeśaṃ) Divy 120.3, *covered* with useful grain; almost always in bad sense (so in Pali, DN i.246.23); Mvy 2140 = Tib. yoṅs su dkris pa (*enwrapped*, esp. *ensnared*, as in sin); -timira-paṭala-paryava° (often °ddha-nayana, or -netra) LV 104.21; Divy 125.2; Av i.17.2; Śikṣ 192.2; KP 84.4; avidyāṇḍakośa-paṭala-pary° Dbh 44.7; Śikṣ 288.8 (°koṣa°); mātsarya-pary° Gv 319.9; Śikṣ 11.2.

paryavanahati (cf. Pali pariyonandhati; Skt. regularly nahyati, Mbh. also nahet, but with pary-ava- only as stated in prec.), *grows over, covers*: śālisya kaṇo ca tuṣo ca paryavanahe (aor.) Mv i.346.2.

paryavanāha, m. (= Pali pariyonāha, or °naha DN i.246.16 = nīvaraṇa; cf. prec. items), *growing over, covering* (only in bad senses): -timira-paṭala-paryav° SP 77.6, 11 (see **paryavanaddha**); in Gv 401.10 (because of the even and well-spaced teeth of the mahāpuruṣa, as he eats food: nābhūt . . .) paryavanāho vā (follows **abhiṣyanda**, q.v.; precedes **abhiṣajjana** or **atisarjana**, qq.v.), app. some pathological condition of the teeth, *growing over, covering* (with remnants of food? with tartar, or decay, caries?). One might think of impacted teeth which fail to grow out, except that the whole list of non-existent defects seems modified by asyāhāraṃ paribhuñjānasya.

paryavarodha, m., *obstruction*: Mvy 7381 = Tib. yoṅs su ḥdzin pa, or ḥgag pa, bgag pa. Neither this nor any form or deriv. of pary-ava-rudh- is recorded elsewhere.

paryavasthāna, nt. (once m., Divy 458.14; seems = Pali pariyuṭṭhāna in mg. 1, but see BHS **paryutthāna**), (**1**) (*state of*) *possession* (by vice or depravity; cf. AbhidhK. LaV-P. v.1, n. 4, where it is shown that some schools equated this with **kleśa** and **anuśaya**): nānā-dṛṣṭy-anuśaya-°na-kleśa-praśamana-kuśalaḥ (of a Bodhisattva) Mvy 862 (= Tib. kun nas dkris pa, *complete wrapping up, ensnaring*); °nam (erroneous var. paryupasth°) Mvy 2139 (Tib. id.), follows **upakleśa**; -anuśaya-parya° Gv 387.4, see s.v. **anuśaya**; kāma-chanda-°na-duḥkhitānāṃ sattvānāṃ Bbh 145.8 f.; a longer list of vices in cpd. ending °na-duḥkhitānāṃ sattvānāṃ 10; -anuśayopakleśa-°nānām Bbh 202.20; kleśa-°nam anuśayo vā Bbh 388.8; raktānāṃ rāga-°naṃ vigacchati Bbh 76.3; tasyā yad rāga-°naṃ tad vigataṃ, dveṣa-°nam utpannam Divy 520.9–10, *possession by passion (desire) disappeared, and possession by loathing arose*; niṣparyavasthāna-jñāna- Śikṣ 24.7, acc. to note in Transl. = Tib. yoṅs su dkrigs pa (*obscuration*, instead of dkris pa, above, *enwrapping*), *knowledge that is free from possession* (by vice, impurity); (**2**) more particularly cpd. with krodha, *possession by anger*: krodha-°na Bbh 158.11 (Tib. as in Mvy above); Divy 186.9; Av ii.128.4–5; °nena paryavasthitaḥ Bbh 149.17 (Tib. as in Mvy above, for both noun and ppp.); cf. krodha-**paryavasthita**, under next; (**3**) hence, more specifically, without expression of krodha, *anger* (cf., with a different implication, Eng. *possessed*, orig. sc. by an evil spirit): tena tīvreṇa °nena kharavākkarma niścāritaṃ Divy 54.20 and, yadāsya °naṃ vigataṃ 23; tīvreṇa ca °nena śirasi mallakena prahāro dattaḥ Divy 177.8; tīvreṇa °nena paryavasthitaḥ Divy 185.29; tīvra-°na-paryavasthito 'yaṃ Śikṣ 58.10; °no vigataḥ (m.!) Divy 458.14, *his anger departed*, tato vigata-°naḥ (Bhvr.) kathayati 15; °nam Divy 521.2. Cf. next.

paryavasthita, ppp. (cf. Pali pariyuṭṭhita, but it is not clear that Pali shows the senses here recorded, corresponding to **paryavasthāna** 2 and 3), orig. *possessed*, but specifically by anger: krodha-pary° Divy 565.19, and see others s.v. **°sthāna** 2; alone, without krodha (see also s.v. **°sthāna** 3), or without even paryavasthāna, *angry, enraged*: Divy 54.22 (cf. °sthāna 54.20, 23); 180.1; 191.29; 520.27; 530.18, 20; 574.1.

paryavāpti (f.; n. act. to next; corresp. to Pali pariyatti = paryāpti, not used in this sense in Skt.), *mastery, comprehension* (of a text): (dharma-paryāyasya...) °āptaye (text wrongly paryāvāptaye) Sukh 72.4; vācanāya paryavāptaye AsP 460.16 (cf. vācayati with **paryavāpnoti**).

paryavāpnoti (used like **paryāpnoti**, q.v., **paryāpuṇati**, which = Pali pariyāpuṇāti; Pali records no pariyavāp°; cf. prec.), *masters, understands* (words, a speech, a text, learning): often follows parallel form of Skt. vācayati, so, vācayed vā °pnuyād vā SP 226.4; vācaya °pnuhi Divy 613.27 (vidyām); vācayiṣyanti °āpsyanti Kv 61.10; Vaj 28.14; 30.17; Sukh 73.2; vācayitavyā . . . paryavāptavyā AsP 461.15; likhiṣyanti yāvat °āpsyanti Śikṣ 49.11; °pnoti (dharmān) Dbh 79.18; following udgṛhya (or in Divy 18.18 gṛhya), paryavāpya Divy 18.12, 18; 207.27; Samādh 8.15; Karmav 28.12 (bhagavatā bhāṣitam, *what the Buddha said*). The n is recorded only as dental, not domal ṇ.

paryādadāti (Pali pariyā°, in ger. °dāya, and acc. to Childers inf. °dātuṃ, also ppp. °dinna, and pass. °di(y)-yati which however is also used in active mg.; see s.v. **ādiyati**; cf. **paryādāna, a-paryātta** etc.), (1) *masters, overcomes*; (2) *exhausts*. Forms: °dadāmi; ger. °dāya; inf. °dātum, also °dattum (°datum? see § 36.12); ppp. paryātta, paryādatta, and °dinna; pass. °dīyate. Mgs.: (**1**) KP 33.2 and 3 abhibhavituṃ paryāda(t)tuṃ vā, *to conquer* (of an army); Mv iii.429.11 paryādinno (gautamasya tejena), 15; Gv 502.6 °dātum, *to overcome* (a magic fluid; said of copper, meaning *to turn it into copper*); 502.8 °dāya, ger.; Gv 66.16 parivartān paryādadāmi, *I master* (intellectually) *chapters* (of a text); SP 200.7 muktvā . . . tathāgataṃ nānyaḥ śaktaḥ pūrṇaṃ . . . arthato vā vyañjanato vā paryādātum, *except the T. no one else can master* (*overcome, surpass*, in learning) *Pūrṇa, either as to the spirit or as to the letter* (of the texts; wrongly Burnouf and Kern); RP 1.10 sarvaguṇavarṇa-paryādattaiḥ (ppp. but in active mg.; said of Bodhisattvas) *who had mastered* . . .; of *mastering, overcoming* the mind on the part of deleterious forces (cf. **a-paryātta** etc., with citta etc.), Av ii.191.7–8 tac cāsya cittaṃ na paryādāya tiṣṭhati, *and that does not continue mastering his mind*; similarly Śikṣ 20.2 na . . . cittaṃ paryādāya sthāsyati; Bbh 9.3 (pāpakāḥ asad-vitarkāḥ) . . . na (sc. cittaṃ) paryādāya tiṣṭhanti; Mv i.128.15 kāmarāgo mānasaṃ paryādinnavān, *love-passion mastered his mind*; for KP 5.2 see below; (**2**) KP 5.2 paryādīyante (kuśalā dharmāḥ), might be understood as *are overcome, repressed*, but Śikṣ 148.9 cites the passage reading parihīyante, suggesting that it means *are exhausted*; Bbh 62.23 (pratibhāne) paryādatte, *exhausted, given out, expired*; AsP 141.3 paryātta-vāṣpa, *whose tears are at an end*.

paryādāna, nt. (= Pali pariyā°; to prec.), (**1**) regularly, *exhaustion, giving out*: esp. common in comb. parikṣayaṃ °dānaṃ plus a form of gacchati, *give out and be completely exhausted*, Divy 4.3; 10.29; 100.24; 169.25; 488.10; 567.30; Av i.48.8; ii.193.7; Karmav 65.6; na kṣīyate na °dānaṃ gacchati Gv 138.9; (without parikṣaya) LV 207.14 °dānaṃ (Calc. paryavadānaṃ, and so pw) gacchanti pātālasaṃdhigatam iva vāri; Mvy 2113; 2579; Av ii.193.6 jīvita-paryādānād *from* (after) *the end of life*; Śikṣ 177.15 sarvākuśaladharma-paryādāna-karaṇatayā; (**2**) in Gv 495.22 -viṣa-paryādāna-tayā, perhaps *because of the condition of mastering* (*overcoming*) *of poison* (but perhaps rather *exhaustion*?).

paryā-dinna, -dīyate, see **paryādadāti.**

paryāpanna, adj. (= Pali pariyā°; prob. pari, intensive, plus Skt. āpanna, in specialized mg., rather than ppp. of unrecorded *pari-ā-pad-), *belonging to, included in, involved in*: °naḥ Mvy 6728 = Tib. gtogs pa, *belonging to*; kāmadhātu-(q.v.)-pary° Mvy 2153; Mv ii.314.12; Laṅk 16.2–3; Śikṣ 281.10; trisāhasra-pary° LV 307.15–16, *belonging to the system of 3000* (*great-thousand worlds*); (trisāhasramahāsāhasra-)-pary° Sukh 13.13; naika-(or other modifier)-lokadhātu-pary° Gv 107.2 ff.; 138.20; pūrvāntā-parānta-pary° Gv 207.13; sarva-paryāpanna-sarva-sattva-Gv 250.13, *all beings comprised in all* (classes of beings, many of which have been listed just above); tarka-paryāpannāyāṃ bhūmau sthitānāṃ Bbh 37.24; (duḥkhaṃ . . .) sugati-paryāpannaṃ Bbh 245.2, (misery) *that is involved* (even) *in 'good' forms of existence* (in addition to hell, etc., preceding); saṃgha-paryāpannaṃ śaikṣakaṃ (q.v.) karma Śikṣ 55.10, . . . *'included in the routine of the Order'* (Bendall and Rouse); pravrajyā-paryāpanno bodhisattvaḥ Śikṣ 144.13, . . . *that is involved in* (included in, a practitioner of) *wandering monkhood*; pātra-°nnaṃ Śikṣ 312.14 (so in Pali patta-pariyā°), (*food*) *that is contained in the* (*monk's*) *bowl*.

paryāpuṇati, °nati (semi-MIndic, = **paryāpnoti**, q.v., and Pali pariyāpuṇāti), *masters* (in Pali, DN comm. i.288.6, rendered by jānāti; may take object dhamma): dharma (read as separate word) paryāpuṇeyā (3 sg. opt.) Samādh p. 30 line 22 (text paryāyaṇeyyā) = Śikṣ 189.5 (vs); kuśalā dharmā paryāpuṇiṣyanti Mv iii.52.18 (prose), *will be mastered* (fut. in pass. mg., representing Skt. mid.); (bhaiṣajyāṃ) paryāpunitvā KP 130.4 (prose), *having mastered* (*controlled*) *remedies*; (bodhi, sā na śakyam . . .) paryāpunituṃ KP 139.9, *it cannot be mastered*.

paryāptaṃ (= Pali pariyattaṃ = alaṃ, *it is enough*), *it is enough*: paryāptaṃ yaṃ bhagavāṃ . . . eko abhiniṣkrānto, tat sādhu bhagavaṃ (mss. °vāṃ) rāhulakumāraṃ anujānāhi yaṃ na pravrajiṣyati Mv iii.263.9 (Śuddhodana to the Buddha); (Mākandikālaṃ, i. e. -ka alaṃ) paryāptam iti Divy 532.14.

paryāpnoti (= **paryāpuṇati**, q.v., but also **paryavāpnoti**, q.v.; in Pali only pariyāpuṇāti, or °ṇati, seems recorded), *masters, understands* (a text): °pnuyād, opt., KP 159.19 (after likhāpayed); 160.4 (object dharma-paryāyam; after udgṛhṇīyād and likhed, cf. paryavāp°).

paryāya, m. (= Pali pariyāya; in these mgs. not in Skt.), (**1**) *arrangement, disposition for doing anything*: °yam akārṣīt . . . iha āgamanāya Mv i.35.7, *has made arrangements to come here* (so Pali, pariyāyaṃ karoti); brāhmaṇai(r) . . . paryāyo hy eṣa cintitaḥ Divy 624.7, *this procedure has been devised* . . .; (**2**) *way, means*, virtually = upāya: ko nu khalv asyāt paryāyo yena . . . Mv iii.439.15, repeated 440.11, *what would be a way* (means) *whereby* . . .; in this sense esp. **dharma-paryāya**, q.v.; cf. dharmāṇāṃ paryāya-jñānam Bbh 214.10, and paryāya alone = **dharma-p°**, in SP 28.6 (vs) tam eva 'yaṃ (so with WT for KN yaṃ) icchati bhāṣaṇāya paryāyam agraṃ tada yo mayā śrutaḥ (so WT with K' for KN yaṃ . . . śrutaṃ); here doubtless also Mv i.104.15 (vs), where mss. bodhisattvaparyāya-(unmetr., but MIndic °pariyāya- gives good meter and sense; Senart em. °pariṣāya)-īśvarā, *lords of the manner* (*method*; of teaching, **dharma-p°**) *of Bodhisattvas*; alternatively, °pariyāya = °yaṃ, acc. with deśayanti in 14, *the Lords teach the way* (*manner, course*, mg. 3) *of bodhisattvas*; (**3**) *way, manner*: loka- (so read with v.l., Senart loke) -paryāya-kovidu Mv ii.405.6, *knowing the ways of the world*; **cetaḥ-(citta-)-paryāya,** q.v., *the ways of thought, of the mind* (esp. of others, as known by Buddhas); anekaparyāyeṇa, *in various ways*, Av i.63.8 etc.; anekaparyāyeṇa aśmin kāye duḥkhāni saṃkramanti Mv ii.146.3; anena paryāyeṇa, *in this way*, SP 107.5; 316.8; Vaj 33.8–9; *in this* (*changed, alternative*) *way* SP 110.8; sometimes esp. anenāpi paryāyeṇa appears to mean *even in that alternative, on that different supposition*, SP 76.14, and prob. 82.9 (parallel to 76.14); hence (**4**) (alternative) *kind, sort*, in **durūpa-**(q.v.; so with mss.)-paryāyā (same vs iii.456.19 durūpam āgamya) karmā kalyāṇapāpakā (iii.456.19 karma °pakaṃ) Mv i.12.13 (vs), *actions are of two alternative kinds, good and bad*.

Paryāyasaṃgrahaṇī, n. of the 4th division of the **Yogācārabhūmi**: Bbh 392.19. See **saṃgrahaṇī.**

[**paryāvāpti**, read **parya°**.]

paryāhiṇḍati (see **hiṇḍati**), *wanders about*: pres. pple. °ḍanto Mv i.353.4; °ḍantiye (gen. sg. f.) iii.155.1.

paryutthāna, nt. (= Pali pariyuṭṭhāna; used substantially like **paryavasthāna**, in mg. 1, q.v.; cf. LaV-P. note on AbhidhK. v.4, 'la distinction entre paryavasthāna et paryutthāna paraît surtout verbale; il y a paryut° lorsque la passion se lève . . . paryava° lorsque la passion enveloppe'; so Tib. kun nas ldaṅ ba, *rising all around*, for paryut°), *rising all about, overwhelming, possession* (always by depravities or vices): sarvāvaraṇa-vivaraṇa-paryutthāna-vigataḥ Mvy 814; °nam 2137 (after **anuśaya,** before **upakleśa** and **paryavasthāna**); °na-viṣkambhaṇamātreṇa (*with merely blocking the uprising*, sc. of depravities) tuṣṭiṃ vindati, na cānuśayasamudghātāya (see Bendall and Rouse 50 note 1) mārgaṃ bhāvayati Śikṣ 50.8; °na-viṣkambhanam Samādh p. 5 line 1; kaukṛtya-pary° Śikṣ 178.14; (after akaukṛtyatā) aparyutthānatā 191.7, *state of having no possession* (by depravities); nivaraṇāvaraṇa-pary° 198.13; niṣpary° KP 8.3 (= a-pary°, Śikṣ 191.7 above); vigatarāga-doṣa-moha-paryutthānāṃ Gv 195.19; paryutthāna-kiśalayā nirdagdhā jñānatejena (referring to anuśaya in prec. line) LV 372.14 (vs), *the 'shoots'* (fig., alluding to literal mg. of paryutthāna) *of the risings-up of (possession by) them* (the anuśaya) *have been burnt out by the fire of knowledge.*

[**paryupasthāna,** erroneous var. for **paryutthāna** Mvy 814; and for **paryavasthāna** Mvy 2139.]

paryupāsana, nt., and **°nā** (= AMg. pajjuvāsaṇa; Skt. in nearly the same mg.; to Skt. paryupāste in similar sense; Pali payirupāsana, °nā, °sati), *respectful, reverent waiting upon, service, worship*: °nam Mvy 1763, 1780; vandanāya °nāya ca (of the Bodhisattva) LV 265.2; °nāya (of Buddha) Mv i.255.5; iii.379.2 (read with mss. upasaṃkramaṇaṃ °nāya, *for purposes of worship*, of Buddhas); °nāya (of Buddha) also Divy 147.9; 149.26; Av i.341.9 (bhagavantaṃ darśanāyopasaṃkramituṃ °nāya); RP 54.7 (vandanāya °nāya; so also Kv 63.20; 78.5); °nena Gv 36.10 (misprinted paryupas°); °sana° in comp. Gv 386.8 (here could be °sanā°); 438.18 (in both these of kalyāṇamitrāṇi); f., bhagavantaṃ darśanāyopasaṃkramiṣyāmi °nāyai Divy 147.1; 149.19.

paryupāsita, ppp. of Skt. paryupāste (cf. prec.; normally in passive sense, *honored, revered, respectfully attended*, e. g. Divy 57.5; Śikṣ 35.2, cited from Gv 462.13; but also) in active sense, *having honored, revered, attended*: °tāḥ sugata (object) Dbh.g.1(337).2; na . . . te . . . eka-buddha-paryupāsitā bhaviṣyanti Vaj 22.19, *they will not have served one Buddha* (only); bahubuddhaśatasahasra-paryupāsitair (Bodhisattvas) SP 2.12; bahubuddha-paryupāsitaḥ (Mañjuśrī) 7.9.

paryupāsitāvin (§ 22.51) = prec., in active sense: bahubuddhakoṭīnayutaśatasahasra-°tāvino (. . . tathāgatāḥ) SP 29.3–4; similarly (buddha . . .) °tāvinas te . . . bhaviṣyanti SP 225.1, *they shall become ones-who-have-worshiped . . . Buddhas*, i. e. shall accomplish such worship.

1 paryuṣita (Skt., ppp. of pari-vas), in °ta-parivāsa (see also **1 parivāsita**; = Pali parivuttha-(or °ṭṭha-)-parivāsa, in technical sense, see **parivāsa**), (**1**) *having undergone probation*: MSV ii.157.16; iii.41.15; °ta-mūla-parivāsaḥ, and mūlāpakarṣa-paryuṣito ib. 16 (see **mūla** 3); mūlaparivāsa-paryuṣitaḥ 42.15; (**2**) *having completed residence* (in heaven; said of gods reborn there after having been lower beings previously; is divine existence regarded as a kind of *probation*? prob. merely *change of residence*, sc. from earth): in a cliché Av i.259.9; 282.3, nāsmākaṃ pratirūpaṃ syād yad vayaṃ paryuṣitaparivāsā bhagavantaṃ darśanāyopasaṃkrāmema, yan nu vayam aparyuṣitaparivāsā eva . . ., *it would not be proper that we should approach the Blessed One to see him after finishing our residence (probation?); let us, while this is still unfinished*, (visit him); similarly MSV i.53.19.

2 paryuṣita (for Pali and BHS **2 parivāsita**; form app. assimilated, by some analogical process, to **1 paryuṣita** = Skt. id.), *perfumed*: candana-karpūrakuṅkuma-°ṣitena Mmk 304.16; -paryuṣite 311.12.

paryeṣa (m.? cf. **paryeṣati** 2, with its ppp. paryeṣita), *circumference, enclosure, circle*, orig. seemingly *a going around*: in Bhvr. cpds., samanta-jvālāvabaddha-(text °buddha)-maṇḍala-paryeṣaḥ (of a figure of Mañjuśrī) Mmk 62.10–11, lit. *having a round-about-flame-bound-circle-circumference* (or *enclosure*); ratnaprabhā-vicchurita-dyoti-paryeṣam (acc. sg.; of a Tathāgata) 63.26, *having a jewel-radiance-covered-light-circumference* (or *enclosure*); Lalou, Iconographie 35, *auréolé du rayonnement fulgurant des joyaux* (similarly 31 for passage above, *entouré . . .*).

paryeṣaka, adj. or subst. m. (to paryeṣati with -aka), *seeking, one who seeks*: asadguṇa-paryeṣakasya RP 35.4; yathābhilāṣiṇo yathāvastuparyeṣakān Gv 332.11.

paryeṣaṇā (Skt. Gr. id., = Pali pariyesanā; Skt. °ṇa, nt.), *seeking, striving after*: °ṇāṃ Divy 56.13; 151.25 (pakṣa-; here ed. em. °ṇaṃ); °ṇā Bbh 22.22 (bhogānāṃ); 194.10; 294.10 ff.; Mvy 7276.

paryeṣati, °te, °ṣyati, °ṣayati, rarely (semi-MIndic). **pariyeṣate** (Skt. °ṣati, rare, cited pw 1.208 once from Mbh.13; Pali pariyesati; only in mg. 1; cf. prec. and following items), (**1**) *seeks, searches for, strives after*: °ṣanti Mv i.89.15 (bodhisattvacaritaṃ); 170.8 (vs; object tīrthe, acc. to Senart *religious teachers*); °ṣate SP 112.4 (bhakta); LV 140.8 (kanyāṃ); 245.20; Suv 186.12; 213.5 (śastraṃ; last four prose); °ṣase Av i.339.8; °ṣante LV 248.16 (kāyaśuddhiṃ); impv. °ṣatha Mv iii.217.6; 220.16; °ṣadhvam Divy 511.1; pple. °ṣamāṇa SP 112.5; LV 239.16; 246.17; 417.6; Mv ii.121.8 (= LV 246.17); m.c. pariyeṣamāṇaḥ Suv 62.18 (vs); and even in prose, parato vā pariyeṣitaiḥ (sc. bhogaiḥ) Bbh 235.1, *or with such as have been sought from others*; paryeṣyanti Suv 227.2 (vs, only one ms., but that the best, has y after ṣ); paryeṣyāmaḥ Mv iii.59.15 (prose, but v.l. °ṣāmaḥ); °ṣayanto, pres. pple., Suv 225.5; fut. °ṣayiṣyāmi Mv i.232.3; ger. °ṣayitvā SP 105.13; ppp. paryeṣita-(Tib. yoṅs su btsal ba, *thoroughly sought*)-sarvakuśalamūlasya LV 10.3; a-paryeṣitam, *unsought*, after a-mārgitam, SP 110.9, and doubtless read so in close parallel 101.8 (both prose) with Kashgar rec. for a-paryeṣṭam (with only 2 Nep. mss.!) in both edd. (cf. however **paryeṣṭi,** which supports paryeṣṭa as a possibility); (**2**) *wanders around*: parinirvṛto pī (so read with v.l. and WT, m.c.) imu sarvalokaṃ paryeṣatī (Kashgar rec. **paryaṇṭhate**) sarvadaśaddiśāsu SP 251.2 (vs), *tho entered into nirvāṇa, He wanders over* (so Tib., yoṅs su rgyu) *this whole world . . .*; hence, ppp. paryeṣita, *gone around, enclosed, encompassed*: samanta-jvālā-māla-(= mālā, perh. read so)-paryeṣitāṃ Mmk 65.14 (prose; of a figure of Tārā), *enclosed by a garland of flames on all sides*; so Lalou, Iconographie, 38; see **paryeṣa.**

paryeṣṭi, f. (= Pali pariyeṭṭhi; to **paryeṣati**), *search, striving for, seeking*; often with worldly things as the object, āhāra-cīvara-paryeṣṭi-hetoḥ SP 102.5; 105.8; 210.8, *seeking for food and raiment*; apariśuddhajñāna-kṣānti-saṃbhoga-paryeṣṭiḥ (. . . duḥkhavipāko dharmaḥ) RP 19.18–19; lābha-paryeṣṭy-arthaṃ 34.4; lokāyata-mantra-paryeṣṭi-tā KP 111.2; or with implication but no expression of such objects, paryeṣṭi-vyasanādīni duḥkhāni Divy 299.4; °ṭi-samudācāra-duḥkhaṃ 422.12; °ṭi-duḥkhānugatāṃ . . . gṛhasthatāṃ Jm 106.1; °ṭi-nidānam SP 77.15 (see **nidāna** 1); but also with expressed or implied neutral, or even religiously commendable, objects (as in Pali pariyeṭṭhi), mantracaryāparyeṣṭiḥ Mmk 23.12; śruta-p° Bbh 336.13; buddhadharma-p° SP 340.1; Dbh 32.19; dharma-p° LV 179.11; °ṭim (for religious enlightenment) āpadyeyaṃ (or °haṃ) Mv ii.120.16, to be restored also in Mv ii.119.5–6 (cf. Senart's note and parallel paryeṣamāṇaḥ LV 239.16).

paryeṣyati, see **paryeṣati.**

parva, see **parvan.**

parvata, (**1**) prob. error (but see s.v. **parvan**!) for parva(n), *joint* of a plant: Laṅk 18.4 -gaṇḍa-parvata-pattra-palāśa-puṣpa-; (**2**) n. of a former Buddha: Mv i.54.5 (cf. Parvataś(i)rī); (**3**) n. of a yakṣa: Māy 64. (Also n. of the well-known brahmanical sage, associate of Nārada: Mv iii.401.9.)

Parvataś(i)rī, n. of a Buddha (cf. **Parvata,** 2): Gv 284.12 (vs).

parvan, nt., also **parva**, nt. and m. (in mss. sometimes written parvata, which is prob. a mere corruption; cf. s.v. parvata 1, where the same is recorded for parva(n) in mg. *joint* of a plant; in mg. *holiday* = AMg. pavva, nt.; cf. Skt. parvan, *day of change of the moon's phases*, which was a holiday; hence this more generalized mg.), *holiday*: Mv i.232.10 kim idaṃ . . . parvaṃ (v.l. parva) vā prayogaṃ vā utsavaṃ vā; ii.109.15 (kiṃ) atra nagare parvo 'yaṃ, *is today a holiday in this town*? and 16 (na adya) kiṃcit parvo na utsavo; iii.57.7 parvaṃ (v.l. parvataṃ), see **Giriyagra-samāja**; Av i.121.10 nagara-parva pratyupasthitam; 302.6 sālabhañjikā nāma parvataṃ (so mss., one perhaps parvanaṃ, dental n; Speyer em. parva; read parvaṇaṃ, n. sg.? so in next) pratyupasthitam; ii.24.6 parva (mss. parvata[ṃ]), see **Girivalgu-samāgama**; 53.9 kasmiṃścit parvaṇy upasthite; 144.14 parva pratyupasthitam; Divy 307.20 parva (mss. parvaḥ!) pratyupasthitam.

parṣacchāradya, see **śāradya**.

-parṣatka (= Skt. parṣad plus -ka, Bhvr.), *assembly*, ifc. Bhvr.: jita-p° Jm 152.22; sa-p° 155.1.

[**parṣadasādya**, error for **parṣacchāradya**.]

parṣadā (= **pariṣ°**, Skt. parṣad; § 15.9), *assembly*: °dānāṃ Mv i.29.13 (prose); °dāyāṃ Suv 21.14 (vs), so Nobel em. m.c., for pariṣ°, some mss., or v.l. parṣadi with different following text but correct meter.

parṣadya, m. (= **pāriṣ°**, **pārṣ°**, **pariṣ°**), *member of an assembly*: amātya-p° Suv 232.1 (vs), but same cpd. with pārṣ° 230.9 (vs).

parṣavant (for parṣā plus vant; short a can hardly be called m.c. since ā would also be possible metrically), *attended by an assembly*, or *by the* (four) *assemblies* (of a Buddha): parṣavantāna tāyinām SP 303.13 (vs).

parṣā (= **pariṣā**, etc.; Skt. parṣad), *assembly*: SP 354.12 (vs); Mv i.310.5 (prose); of the four *assemblies* of a Buddha (see s.v. pariṣā), SP 9.1; 237.13 (both vss); Mv i.27.11 (prose).

-palaka, m. (etym. not clear), app. *point* (of a spear), see **kunta-p°**.

palagaṇḍa, m. (= Pali and Skt. Lex. id.), *mason, plasterer*: Mvy 3772; Av i.339.12; AsP 236.19 f.; 443.7.

palāta, pple. (to Skt. palāyati; = Pali id., cf. next, and § 34.12), *fled*: in Śikṣ 347.4 prob. read palāt' (for text palātv) asurendrāḥ, *the asura-lords fled* (§ 8.84).

palāna, pple. (= JM. palāṇa, Pischel 567, cf. prec., and § 34.19), *fled*, or sometimes seemingly with pass. force, *put to flight*, with instr. of person causing the flight, e. g. bhagavatā te (mss. tena) amanuṣyakā (*demons*) palānā Mv i.270.11–12; so several times Mv i.283.7 ff., regularly with instr.; used absolutely, without instr., *fled*, Mv ii.172.16; 235.2; iii.350.1. Cf. also **palāyaka**, with v.l. palānaka, and **prapalāna**.

palāpa, see **palāva**.

? **palāyaka**, m., *a fugitive*: SP 112.1 (vs), but Kashgar rec. palāyitaḥ, and WT with K' palānakaḥ = palānaḥ, see **palāna** and § 22.4.

palāva (m. or nt.; once in AV.) or **palāpa** (= Pali id.; so Kashgar rec. of SP, both times), *chaff*: niṣpal° SP 39.3; 44.13 (both edd. with Nep. mss. °va), *free from chaff*.

palāśa, see **pallāśa**.

palāśaka, m. (= Skt. °śa; -ka svārthe), *leaves, foliage*: Divy 631.10.

palikuñca, °**cika** (m. or nt.), °**cikā** (to pali = pari plus a form of Skt. kuc-, kuñc-, *bend*, cf. Skt. saṃkuc-, *bring together, close*; AMg. paliuñcai, in diff. mg., *conceals* a fault, *deceives*), (*thatched*) *hut*, in most cases prec. by kaṭa-, *of grass, straw*: kaṭa-palikuñcikāyām, text, loc sg., SP 106.2; 107.7; 108.3 (all prose), but mss. vary greatly one v.l. each time palikuñce; niveśanasyo (so Nep. mss., m.c. for °sya) palikuñcikesmin (read as one word, loc. of °ka) SP 114.2 (vs; Kashgar rec. has very different and certainly secondary reading; WT here °syopari ku°; this division is inconsistent with the above forms where kaṭa- precedes pali°; in these WT read kaṭapali-kuñc°, with printed hyphen! which I cannot interpret at all): **Tib.** khyim gyi druṅ du rtsva yi spyil po na, *in a hut of straw*, or *grass, near the house*.

palikhanati, see **pari°**.

paliguddha, adj. (ppp., MIndic for **parigṛddha**, q.v.; § 3.92; I find only (pari-)giddha recorded in MIndic records; confirmed by the analog. **paligodha**, q.v.), *attached* (*to*), *greedy* (*for*), usually worldly and unworthy objects: bahu-paligodha-paliguddha Śikṣ 105.12; kāmāhāra-pali° 186.10; a-pali°, *not affected*, lit. *not greedily fastened upon* (rūpagatena, see this) 249.8; in SP 54.11 (vs) read prob. gatiṣu ṣaṭsū (so mss.) paliguddha- (text em. pariruddha; mss. mostly pali-, or pari-, śuddha; Tib. zin pa, one mg. of which is *captivated*; WT with K' parigṛddha)-cittāḥ; so too in Śikṣ 146.20 read tad gṛhasukha-paliguddham (text °śuddham) adhikṛtyoktaṃ, *this is said with reference to one eager for household-joys*; but also with worthy objects, dharma-pali° Śikṣ 100.3–4. Cf. Thomas, JRAS 1915.99 ff.

paligodha, m. (= Aśokan [a-]pari-[pali-]godha; analog. back formation to °**guddha**, q.v., on such models as rodha and cpds. to ruddha; § 3.68; similarly Pali gedha, analog. to Pali giddha = Skt. gṛddha, not a phonetic development of the latter as assumed by Geiger 10; corresp. to Pali paligedha, BHS **parigredha**, of similar origin, tho no Pali *paligiddha is recorded), *attachment* (*to*), *greed* (*for*), usually but not always worldly and unworthy objects: °dhaḥ Mvy 6524 = Tib. chags pa, *attachment*, among other (and irrelevant) renderings; ākāśa-(see this)-paligodhau KP 111.1 = Tib. yoṅs su (= pari) chags pa; in 111.6 (vs) ākāśa-bodhe (Tib. chags pa), read prob. °godhe, see **godha** and 2 **bodha**; vaiyāpṛtya-paligodhe (so with ms) Śikṣ 50.15, *attachment* (*devotion*) *to duties* (here no offensive connotation); see **paliguddha** for Śikṣ 105.12; °dha-mantreṣu ratim janitvā 109.1; laukikakṛtya-°dhaḥ 114.4.

palitaka, f. °**ikā**, adj. (palita with -ka, perhaps pitying or contemptuous dim.), *gray* (*-haired*): Mv iii.283.11, 13; see s.v. **jīrṇaka**.

? **palimbha** (m. or nt.), a high number: Gv 106.2. Corresp. to **halibha**, q.v.

[**paliśuddha**, Śikṣ 146.20, read **paliguddha**, q.v.]

? **palīkṛta**, in Av ii.136.10 (vs) ādīptaṃ kānanaṃ sarvaṃ parvatā pi °kṛtā, perh. *even the mountains are made into straws* (pala, Skt. Lex., *straw*). Speyer, *a-glowing*, with little if any support, and evidently thinking the word must have a mg. similar to ādīptaṃ; but this is quite unnecessary; two entirely separate situations are referred to, related only in that they are things hard to conceive as accomplished. Speyer cites Tib. as ser bo, which he identifies with ser po, *yellow*; this, even if justified, does not give the meaning he assumes.

pallatthikā (= Pali id.; MIndic for Skt. paryastikā, the form used Mvy 8544), n. of some posture or attitude regarded as undignified for a monk; the exact mg. is differently given, see refs. in PTSD: Prāt 536, note 2 (app. Finot's only source reads so, he em. paryastikā with Mvy; Chin. acc. to him *les reins aécouverts*); La Vallée-Poussin, JRAS 1913.844, lines 1, 4.

pallānati (cf. next; = JM. pallāṇei, to Skt. paryāṇayati, denom. to paryāṇa, *saddle*), *harnesses*. or the like (*saddles*?): tena . . . kaṇṭhakaṃ (the horse) pallānatena (pres. pple.; so mss., to be kept) Mv ii.160.4.

? **pallāśa**, or **palāśa** (so mss., varying; cf. prec.), refers to some part of the harness on a horse's back: mss. aśvapṛṣṭhapallāśasya pṛṣṭhato bandhyati Mv iii.158.9; mss. aśvapṛṣṭhe pṛṣṭhato pallāśabaddhatena (v.l. palāśe baddhena) baddham abhūṣi 12. Senart em. pallāṇa, said to mean *saddle* (Pkt., Sheth, and rarely in Skt., pw), prob. rightly.

palvara (= Skt. palvala; § 2.49), *pool*: alpamatsye va °re Ud xvii.3 (in Pali Dhp. 155 pallale).

pavana (nt.? = Pali id.), *wood, forest*; so Pali comms. regularly, cf. MN i.117.23 araññe pavane (clearly near-synonym of arañña), comm. ii.85.2 vanasaṇḍe; DN comm. ii.680.14–15 (on DN ii.254.6) pavanaṃ vuccati vanasaṇḍo; use of the word in Pali and BHS clearly refers to life in the wilds, contrasting with life in society; Tib. on SP 13.2 nags tshal, *wood*; etym. of the word not certain, but unlikely to be connected with Skt. pravaṇa (PTSD; others = upavana, see PTSD): pavane vasanti SP 11.13 (Nep. mss. ya vane); 13.2 (Nep. mss. hi vane); ekāntasthāyī pavane (Nep. mss. ha vane) vasāmi 90.1; °ne vaseyaṃ LV 393.2 (v.l. upavane, unmetr.); viharatha pavane udagracittā Mv ii.361.18; pavanaṃ vrajitvā Mv ii.382.14, *going into the forest*. All these vss, but in Pali also in prose.

pavara (= Pali id., MIndic for Skt. pravara), *excellent*: so if text is right, Dbh.g. 12(348).17 yāvattareṇa pavararṣiṇa (v.l. parikarṣiṇa) jñānalābhas.

paśurathagatika, adj., *who rides in an ox-cart*: °ko bodhisattvaḥ (= one who follows the Hīnavāna) Śikṣ 7.1 (parable follows).

paśca, adj., subst. (= AMg. paccha- in comp., M. paccha, separate word; cf. **pacchā, pacche**, and **paścā-kāla**), *later, last* (of time): yaśodharā sarvapaścā (*last of all*) āgatā Mv ii.72.16; paści (m.c. for paśce) kāle Samādh p. 10, line 1 (so read); p. 12, line 28; p. 19, line 20 (kālasmi); as subst., *later time*, id. p. 19 line 22 sa paści nirvṛtaḥ. In SP 45.13 (vs) na tu (read tatu with WT) paśca bhāsate, paśca = paścāt m.c.; in SP 92.13 (vs) paścakāle doubtless also m.c. for paścāt-(or **paścā-**, q.v.)-kāle.

[**paścama**, in sarva-paścamu Gv 314.10 (vs), doubtless misprint for Skt. paścima. No such form noted anywhere.]

paścā, adv. (Vedic, = Skt. paścāt; here semi-MIndic form of paścāt, cf. **paśca, pacchā** or °**che**), *afterwards*: Mv ii.391.2 (vs); in paścā-kāla, *later time*; instead of paścāt-k° of SP ed. 253.11, 16; 254.6; 255.12, La Vallée-Poussin's version, JRAS 1911.1072 f. has paścā-k°; and so Kashgar rec. for the same word SP 278.8.

paścācchirāśayana, adj., acc. to Tib. *dead* (śi ba): MSV ii.102.6. Lit. seems to be (*be*)*hind-head-lying* (or, *-bed*).

paścācchramaṇa, m. (= Pali pacchāsamaṇa) *a* (*junior*) *monk who walks behind another monk*: Mvy 8740; Divy 154.17, 28; 330.12 ff.; 351.6 ff.; 494.3; Av ii.67.11; 68.1; 150.4 f.

paścādbhakta (or **paścābh°**), (**1**) adj., *after eating* (the midday meal): atha khalu bhagavāṃ . . . paścābhaktaḥ (v.l. paścādbh°) purastāt saṃmukho niṣaṇṇo . . . (turned the 'wheel of the law') Mv iii.340.16; (**2**) (nt.?) *the afternoon, period after eating* (so adv. pacchābhattaṃ in Pali, see Childers, *in the afternoon*): tam (a long time) evaikaṃ paścādbhaktaṃ saṃjānante sma SP 300.10, *took* (*felt*) *it as a single afternoon*; (**3**) in cpd. °kta-piṇḍapāta-(also written °tra) -pratikrānta Mv i 56.1 (mss.), i.329.16 (mss.); LV 407.15; Divy 516.5; 566.3; in mss. of Divy and Av, and in ed. of the former, sometimes °pātaḥ° or °pātraḥ°; = Pali pacchābhattaṃ (only recorded in this form, as adv.) piṇḍapātapaṭikkanta, *having returned from* (*collecting*) *alms-food in the afternoon*; (besides above citations, all of which have °pātra°) Divy 155.29; 200.23; 550.9; 552.24; Av i 252.7; 267.7; 274.7.

paścānmukha, adj. or subst., also °**mukhīkṛta**, adj. (Skt. id. in mg. *turned back*, so LV 319.19, or *turned towards the west*, so Sukh 62.7 °mukhībhūtvā), perh. fig. (made) *inferior, surpassed outdone*: bahava śatasahasra paścānmukhā bodhisattvā kṛtāḥ LV 421.22 (vs), sc. by Śākyamuni's 'turning the wheel of the law' (? or simply *turned back, stopped*, without attaining Buddhahood? Foucaux, however, renders *sont, ensuite, devenus muets*, as if reading paścān mukā = mūkā, m.c.; no such reading is recorded in Lefm., nor in Calc., which glosses parāṅmukhā ity arthaḥ; Tib. phyir ni bsñil ba, acc. to Jä. *banished, exiled*); Maitreyo . . . ekena galaparityāgena paścānmukhīkṛtaḥ Divy 481.5, *M. was outdistanced by a single sacrifice of his own throat* (on the part of a previous incarnation of Śākyamuni). In Śikṣ 167.6 paścānmukho nivartya seems to mean *turning backward* (on the religious path), and 167.8 paścānmukham akārṣam, *I made a retrograde movement* (on the same).

paścābhakta = **paścādbhakta**, q.v.

paścima, adj. (= Pali pacchima; Skt. not in this mg.), (*last* =) *lowest, mean, vulgar*: °mā janatā (Pali id., Vin. ii.108.19), *vulgar folk*, AsP 182.15, 18.

paścimaka, pacchi°, f. °**ikā**, adj. (= Pali pacchi°; to Skt. paścima, -ka svārthe), (**1**) *last, latest, later, subsequent*: paścimake samucchraye SP 68.7 (vs), *in his last body* (*incarnation*); paści° SP 27.14 (vs); pacchi°, v.l. paści° Mv iii.232.15 (vs); the rest in prose; paści° Mv i.348.10; ii.273.5, 10; Mmk 51.13; Bbh 283.8; 356.7; paścimikāyāṃ Vaj Hoernle MR 187.8 (ed. Vaj 35.4 °māyāṃ); (tac ca) paścimakaṃ dāridryam Karmav 67.3, *and that was his last poverty* (i.e. he was never poor again); (etāvan me samucchrayasya) °makaṃ parinirvāṇaṃ SP 43.13, perh. *this* (lit. *so far*) *is the final complete nirvāṇa of my body*, or *there is final* etc. (? Tib. ṅaḥi lus ḥdi tham mya ṅan las ḥdaḥ ba ḥo); (**2**) *western*: (mahāpṛthivī . . . purastimaṃ, v.l. °mena) unnamati paścimakaṃ (one ms. °mako, v.l. pacchimako; Senart em.) onamati Mv iii.256.8, *in the west*.

paśyaka, m. (to paśyati plus -aka), *seer, one who sees*: Mvy 4681; ŚsP 121.4; Laṅk 360.16.

paśyana (nt.; to paśyati plus -ana; cf. Pali anupassana etc.), *seeing, sight*: °nāya, inf., Mv ii.450.14; 451.1 etc.; iii.163.19; -paśyana-tayā Gv 61.10, *because of the fact of seeing* . . .

paśyin, adj. (= AMg. passi; to paśyati plus primary -in), *seeing*: samudayāstaṃgamān (em.; one ms. °dayād ast°) paśyī Mv iii.53.3.

pāṃśava, m. (in late Skt. adj. *dusty*, once only), = pāṃśu, pāṃsu, *dust*: tatra masiḥ pāṃśavāś ca varṣanti LV 315.17 (vs); the only v.l. is the impossible pāṃśuvāś.

pāṃśu-kūla (or **pāṃsu°**), nt. (= Pali paṃsu°), *refuse rags* (from a 'dust-heap', used for garments by monks): °śu° LV 265.21 ff.; Mv iii.54.10 ff.; 311.8 ff. (here mss. favor °su°); Divy 153.13; 424.2; 425.12; 559.11; Bhīk 22b.2; in Av i.182.8 Speyer °su° but acc. to his note ms. regularly °śu; ii.69.1; 114.12; °su° Mvy 8672; Divy 56.26; 57.4; Jm 123.9; 125.14; in Jm 18.18 bālyaprajñaiḥ pāṃsudānaṃ sudānam Speyer assumes that pāṃsu = pāṃsukūla, but this is unprecedented and implausible; render, (*even*) *a gift of dust made by people of childlike minds is a good gift*, cf. SP 50.11–12.

pāṃśukūlika, m. (= Pali paṃsu°), *one who wears pāṃśukūla*, q.v., one of the 12 **dhūtaguṇa**, q.v.: Mvy 1128; Dharmas 63; AsP 387.4; MSV iii.122.5.

pāṃśu-kṛta, adj., *dusty*: °tāni gātrāṇi LV 255.1; Mv ii.126.7, 8; 127.12, etc.

pāṃśukrīḍana, m. adj. or subst. (in Skt. cited only as nt. n. act.; cf. next, and **saha-pāṃśu-krīḍanaka**; Bloomfield, Mūladeva, Proc. Am. Philos. Soc. 52.616, n. 3, cites Skt. pāṃsu-krīḍita = Pali paṃsukīḷita from Pariśiṣṭaparvan and Harṣacarita; and saha-pāṃśukrīḍita is Skt.), once v.l. °ḍaka (adopted by Senart in each case, twice against both mss.), lit. *dust-player*, = *boyhood comrade*, with sahāya: Mv iii.451.6 (= Jāt. v.249.8, where paṃsukīḷita), 10, 20.

pāṃśukrīḍanaka, m. = prec., q.v.: Mmk 602.3, 26 (vss).

pāṃśu-piśāca(ka), m. (= Pali paṃsupisācaka), *dust-goblin*, presumably one covered with dust: °cam LV

257.5 (prose), °cakaṃ LV 259.18 (vs), mockingly applied to the Bodhisattva performing austerities.

pāṃśulika, nt., or **°kā** (= AMg. paṃsuliyā; cf. Pali phāsulī, °likā; the aspiration in Pali ph- is unhistorical), *rib*: °likāni °likāntarāṇi Mv ii.125.15; 127.2; 128.8; 129.10; to be read thus, or else pāṃśulikāntarāṇi (omitting °likāni), *(ribs and) interstices between the ribs*; so the mss. clearly indicate tho with various corruptions; confirmed by AMg.; Senart em. pārśuli°. The form is of course related to Skt. parśu(kā), BHS **pārśukā**, q.v., and is hyper-Sktized from the MIndic represented by AMg., which has nasalized vowel for double consonant (or long vowel), by the 'law of morae'.

pāsatti(-ka?), see s.v. **pātayantika.**

pācana, nt., *means of cooking* (referring to *wood*): °naṃ preṣitam Divy 31.11.

pācanīya, adj. (to prec. plus -īya, in specialized mg.), *heating, softening* (a boil): °yāni dravyāni MSV ii.39.1 f.

pañcagatika, adj., *containing five states of existence*, see **gati** (1), ep. of the saṃsāra: Śikṣ 91.9; MadhK 269.9 (here mss. **pañca°**, q.v.); 304.8; 323.5. BR refer to Mvy (chap.) 90, but I have been unable to find the word in either ed., in this or any other place.

pañcadaśika, nt., *food given on the festival of the 15th* (lunar day): Mvy 5760. Cf. s.v. **āṣṭamika**, and next.

pañcamika, nt., *food given on the festival of the 5th* (lunar day): Mvy 5757. See under prec.

Pañcāla, n. of a nāga king: Māy 247.20. Cf. **Pañcāla.**

Pañcālī, n. of a city: Māy 55.

Pañcika (cf. Pañcaka, DPPN, as var. for Paṇḍaka, n. of a yakṣa), (**1**) n. of a yakṣa: Mvy 3379; Māy 78 (see Lévi 101); Samādh p. 43, line 21; a yakṣa-general, (mahā-) senāpati, Divy 163.18 f.; 447.7 ff.; MSV i.24.15; LV 202.9; Māy 236.2; 258.30; (**2**) n. of a gandharva: Suv 162.1.

pāṭapāṭika, m. (adj. or n. ag.? or n. act.?), °kaḥ Mvy 9397, acc. to Tib. lan (g)cig gñis sprad (phrad) pa, and Chin., *meeting once or twice*. Etym. not clear; possibly related to AMg. pāḍaya, *street, lane*?

? **pātala**, nt. (= Skt. paṭala, which is read in one ms. of AsP and should perhaps be adopted), *film on the eye, cataract*: akṣirogo vā pātalaṃ (v.l. pa°) vā bhavet AsP 97.10.

pāṭalaka (nt.; = Skt. °la plus -ka), (**1**) the plant called in Skt. pāṭala, *trumpet-flower*: Divy 619.19; (**2**) n. of a caitya at Pāṭaligrāmaka: MPS 4.2 ff.

pāṭalikā, see **pātalikā.**

Pāṭaligrāmaka, m. (= Pali °gāma), n. of the city of Pāṭaliputra: MPS 4.1 ff.

Pāṭaligrāmīyaka, adj., *of the prec.*: MPS 4.5, 19 etc.

pāṭahika, m. (= M. pāḍahiga, °hiya; Skt. paṭaha plus -ika), *drum-beater*: Mv iii.442.11 (prose).

pāṭiyaka, adj. (= Pali pāṭekka, pāṭiyekka; AMg. pāḍikkaa, pāḍiekka; to Skt. pratyeka), *individual*: Mv ii.242.13 (prose), °kaṃ nivāpaṃ, °kaṃ pānīyaṃ. So mss.; Senart em. pāṭiyekaṃ; but is the em. necessary? An analogical blend form ending in (MIndic) °yaka seems quite conceivable.

pāṭirāja (= Pali paṭi°, Skt. prati°), *rival king*: Mv i.276.6, 8 (in 8 one ms. pāḍhi°; note in 281.1 pratirāja). On the ā see Senart's note, citing parallels in Pali, and § 3.11.

-pāṭha, m. (to paṭh-; cf. Skt. pāṭhaka), *reader* (otherwise only n. act.): vedasupinapāṭhā ye (so divide) LV 57.1 (vs); śāstrapāṭhān 6 (vs).

pāṇa, m. (= AMg. id.), *a cāṇḍāla, 'untouchable'*: Mv ii.487.1 (mss. yā°), 4; iii.21.10. (Orig. = MIndic pāṇa, *creature*? see **prāṇa.**)

pāṇi (or pāṇī? nt.; = AMg. id.; preserved in many modern Indo-Aryan vernaculars; cf. Skt. pānīya), *water*: pāṇi-pratigrāhakā Mv iii.304.7 (prose); amṛtasya pāṇinā Suv 37.12 (all seven mss.; Nobel em. vāriṇā); heṣṭā ca toyasya ananta-pāṇī (v.l. pāni) Mv ii.92.13 (vs), *and under the ocean there is infinite water* (Senart takes pāṇī = prāṇin, surely wrongly).

Pāṇikhātā (°ta, °da or °dā; cf. Skt. °ta, below, and **Pāṇihatā**), n. of a river magically created by Śakra for the Buddha: °tā (mss. °dā) nāma nadī Mv iii.312.16; °ta-nadī- (so text with mss.) 313.7; °tāto, abl. (so Senart; mss. °dāto) nadīto 313.8. Cf. Pāṇikhāte, loc. sg., a sacred bathing place, Mbh. Crit. ed. 3.81.75.

pāṇisvara (m.? in Mv ii.52.15 seemingly nt.; = Pali pāṇissara), prob. *recitation* or *singing to the accompaniment of clapping of the hands*, a form of entertainment; PTSD, a certain *kind of musical instrument*, but there seems to be no evidence for this; on the contrary, pāṇissare (acc. pl.; need not be personal, as PTSD assumes) in Jāt. vi.276.28 is expl. in comm. 277.1 by ... ti pāṇippahārena gāyante; doubtless persons performing the same activity, to (especially) waken in the morning and entertain a high personage, are meant by paṭhanti pāṇisvanikāḥ Mbh. 7.2912 (Nīl. hastena tālasvanaṃ kurvante, prob. *palm-clapping*, not *cymbal-sound*; so pw s.v. tālasvana), also 12.1899 (no comm. in Nīl.): pāṇisvaraṃ kumbhatūṇaṃ (see this) mṛdaṅgānāṃ svarāṇi ca ... pratibodhenti Mv ii.52.15 (= Jāt. v.390.25); pāṇisvarākhyāna- iii.122.17.

pāṇisvaraka, **°ika**, m. (to prec. plus -ka, -ika), *one who performs the pāṇisvara* (cf. also next): °aka Mv iii.57.9; °ika iii.113.3; 442.9; and (with v.l. °aka) iii.141.18; 255.11; 266.5.

pāṇisvarya, m., = prec.: Mv i.231.13; 259.5; ii.100.10; 150.4; 153.17; 156.9; iii.161.3 (all prose).

Pāṇihatā (corresp. to **Pāṇikhātā**, q.v., a river), n. of a lake (puṣkariṇī) magically created for the Buddha by a (here unnamed) god: LV 266.14 (prose).

pāṇī, see **pāṇi.**

Pāṇḍaka, n. of a nāga king: Māy 246.20 (corruption for **Pāṇḍuka**, q.v.?).

Pāṇḍara, see next, and s.v. **Pāṇḍava.**

pāṇḍara-bhikṣu, a member of a certain heretical sect (Śvetāmbara Jain? or = AMg. paṇḍuraṅga, defined as a southern sect who smear their bodies with ashes?): Mvy 3538; AbhidhK. LaV-P. iii.86 n. 3 (vyākhyā).

Pāṇḍaravāsinī, or **Paṇḍ°**, n. of a Buddhist goddess, associated with Tārā (Mvy 4279; Mmk 621.19), with Avalokiteśvara (Mmk 40.7); prob. the same as **Pāṇḍarā** or **Pāṇḍurā**: Mvy 4279; Sādh 75.8; Paṇḍ° Mmk 40.7; 611.1; 621.19.

Pāṇḍarā (in Dharmas 4 text Pāṇḍurā, v.l. °arā which prob. read), n. of a Buddhist goddess, associated with Tārā, and prob. identical with prec.: Sādh 18.15 etc.; Dharmas 4.

pāṇḍala, adj. (= Skt. °ra, Pali paṇḍara; cf. next), *pale, white*: Mv i.207.8 = ii.11.19, both mss. both times °la (v.l. pāṇḍula; Senart em. °ra); in i.207.12 = ii.12.2 Senart also pāṇḍara, with 1 ms. each time, v.l. pāṇḍala, pāṇḍura; in ii.487.6 Senart pāṇḍala with 1 ms., v.l. pāṇḍura.

Pāṇḍalameghā, n. of a nāgą maid: Kv 4.5.

Pāṇḍava, m. (= Pali Paṇḍava), n. of a mountain near Rājagṛha: LV 239.19; 240.10; 241.4, 10; Mv ii.198.14, 17; 199.5 (but here mss. pāṇḍaro or °ulo); in iii.438.12 text with mss. Pāṇḍaro, but Senart cites the passage without comment s.v. Pāṇḍava; it certainly refers to the same mountain. (For °vāḥ, m. pl., MSV ii.31.17, see s.v. **Khaṣa.**)

Pāṇḍu (doubtless = **Pāṇḍuka**, q.v.), n. of a nāga king: Mvy 3246.

pāṇḍuka, (**1**) adj. (= Skt. Lex. id. = Skt. pāṇḍu), *whitish*: Mv ii.152.15, read with mss. (pīto) pāṇḍukavello, *with* (morbidly) *whitish hair*; (**2**) (cf. Skt. Lex. id., as Jain term; AMg. paṇḍua), n. of the guardian of one of the 4 mahānidhis: Divy 61.3 (see s.v. **elapatra**);

certainly the same as the nāga king of the same name, Māy 247.2 (and cf. **Pāṇḍu, Pāṇḍaka**).

Pāṇḍukambalaśilā (= Pali Paṇḍu°silā), *the throne of Indra* (perhaps orig., the stone of which it is made): Divy 194.3, 11; 195.10; Av ii.89.5; °lā-talam Mvy 7127.

pāṇḍuraka, (**1**) adj., f. °ikā (= Skt. pāṇḍura), *white*: °ikā (paṭṭikā) Divy 352.19 (prose; in next line °rāṃ); (**2**) m. (cf. **Paṇḍaraka, Paṇḍulaka, Pāṇḍu**), n. of a nāga king: Mvy 3250.

Pāṇḍurā, see **Pāṇḍarā.**

pāṇḍula, v.l. for **pāṇḍala,** q.v.

Pāṇḍulaka, see **Paṇḍ°.**

Pāṇḍu-lohita, °**taka,** °**tika** (= Pali Paṇḍu[ka]-lohitaka, here named for two members of the chabbaggiya; not mentioned among the **ṣaḍvārgika** in BHS), adj. pl. with bhikṣavaḥ, a group of troublesome monks: °ta MSV iii.5.2 (vs, bad meter); °taka ib. 12.; °tika 1.2; 5.7; 6.6, 14, 20, etc.

Pāṇḍya-māthura, n. of a town, acc. to Lévi 92 the modern Madura: Māy 39.

pāta, m., *attainment, getting, what comes* or *is got*: bhikṣūṇāṃ cīvara-pāto (Tib. rñed pa = lābha) deyaḥ MSV ii.97.6; in this sense also in **piṇḍa-pāta,** q.v.

pātayati (caus. of Skt. pat), (**1**) *puts back into a whole* (what has been divided, to divide it again): °yitvā MSV ii.119.19, and ff.; (**2**) with roma (= Pali lomaṃ pāteti), *lets* (the hair) *hang down*, as sign of humble penitence (see **romapāta** and s.v. **prakaca**): Bhīk 28b.4; MSV iii.7.14.

pātayantika, adj., and °**kā,** subst. (for alternative Pali and BHS forms see below), *causing fall* (to an evil existence, if not repented and expiated); this is clearly the usual Northern interpretation; one of the three main kinds of monkish transgressions, the others being **pārājika** and **saṃghāvaśeṣa,** qq.v.: as adj., °ka with dharma, (trayāṇāṃ dharmāṇāṃ anyatamānyatamena dharmeṇa vadet pārājikena vā saṃghāvaśeṣeṇa vā) pātayantikena vā Prāt 489.(1–)3, and ff.; there are 30 offenses called **niḥsargikāḥ** (q.v.) pātayantikā dharmāḥ 490.8, listed in the following where each is called °gikā °yantikā (subst. fem.), 490.11–12 and ff.; they are followed by 90 pātayantikā dharmāḥ 502.13, each again styled pātayantikā (subst. fem.) 502.15 ff.; °tikā dharmāḥ also Mvy 8417 = Tib. ltuṅ byed, lit. *making fall*, usually rendered *transgression*; the Pali correspondents are 30 nissaggiyā pācittiyā dhammā Vin. iii.195.1, each one styled nissaggiyaṃ pācittiyaṃ (nt., not f.) id. 18, etc., followed by 92 pācittiyā dhammā, Vin. iv.1, each one styled pācittiyaṃ 2.14 ff. On the various forms of Pali and BHS see (besides older treatments, now obsolete) S. Lévi, JA. Nov.–Dec. 1912, 506–8, and esp. Waldschmidt, Kl. Skt. Texte 3.116f., who says inter alia: In den späteren Turfanfragmenten erscheint ganz allgemein als Sanskritform pātayantikā' (so e.g. op. cit. 41.1). He notes that pāteti is used in Pali in explaining pācittiya, Vin. v.148.30, and that pātayati is similarly used in BHS in explaining the mg. of other (substitute) forms, see below. He states that Chin., like Tib. (regularly ltuṅ byed, above), supports this mg. On the other hand he reports a BHS ms. reading pāca(tt)i, which reminds one of the Pali form; and shows that pātayantika, and other alternative forms, are rendered in ways which suggest association (certainly unhistorical) with root pac-; he cites a passage (p. 117) reading pātayantikā, pacati dahati uddahati avyutthitasyāvaraṇakṛtyaṃ karoti, tenāha pātayantikā, and compares Divy 544.10 pāyantiketi (text pāpānti°, as also 543.24; in 544.15 mss. pāyantikāṃ, read thus all three times with Lévi l.c. above) dahati pacati pātayati (so with Lévi for text yāt°). Besides the popular etymology pāpāntikā of the Divy mss., just cited, Das gives pāpātmikā for Tib. ltuṅ byed. The same word is read pāyattikāḥ (sc. dharmāḥ) Mvy 8360; (naiḥsargikāḥ, q.v., = niḥsa°) pāyattikāḥ 8383, and pāpattikā (f.) 9223, but with vv.ll. in one or more of these places (besides pāyattikā in the last) pāyantika (pāyantikām āpattim, acc., MSV ii.174.9), pāpantika, pāṭāyantika, pātavantika, (acc. to Waldschmidt also pādayantika,) and with °kā as subst. f. (pāyantikayā, instr., MSV iii.109.20). There is moreover (besides pācatti cited by Waldschmidt above) prāyaścittikāḥ (sc. dharmāḥ) Mvy 8418 (śuddha-p°, acc. to Tib. *only, merely prāy°*, ḥbaḥ zhig tu ḥgyur ba); (snāna-)prāyaścittikaṃ 8484 (both these = Tib. ltuṅ byed); and prāyaścittikaḥ (sc. dharmaḥ) Mvy 9307 (= Tib. ltuṅ ba, *fall*), which is followed by śuddha- (Tib. ma ḥdres pa, *unmixed*) -pāpattikaḥ (sc. dharmaḥ; Tib. again ltuṅ ba, = prec.) 9308, cf. 8418 above, and s.v. **śuddhaka.** Lévi l.c. points out the phonetic difficulty of deriving Pali pācittiya from BHS prāyaścittika, and proposes an orig. *prākcitta plus -ika, thru *paccittika to pāci°, *la pensée en avant*, = either (des actes commis) *avec précipitation*, or *qui précipitent* (aux enfers). He cites a Tocharian loan pāyti, which he says goes back to pāyantika. It is obvious that the orig. form and mg. of the word can not be confidently reconstructed.

pātalikā, or **pāṭ°,** *receptacle, pouch*: lavaṇa-p° Mvy 9018 = Tib. tshva (*salt*) khug (*pouch*). Text pāt° (and so Mironov); Index pātalikā, but lavaṇa-pāṭalikā (so BR). Etym.?

Pātāla, n. of a locality: Māy 90 (cf. Lévi p. 103, suggesting the port at the mouth of the Indus).

pātra, regularly nt., (**1**) with masc. forms, in Skt. mg. *bowl*: caturi pātrāṃ, acc. pl., LV 185.8 (vs); tenemi pātrāś (acc. pl.) caturaḥ . . . dadanti 385.7 (vs; in prec. line pātrāṇi); (**2**) = Skt. yāna-pātra, *ship* (cf. Eng. *vessel* in same mg.; not recorded elsewhere), in siddha-pātra, *with successful ship* (after a voyage): Mv iii.287.8; 288.15; 298.17; v.l. each time siddha-yānapātra, which is read in text with both mss. iii.286.17.

pātra-kara, -karaka, or **-kāṭaka,** see the latter forms.

pādaka, (m. or nt., in mgs. 1 and 2 = Skt. pāda), (**1**) *foot* of a bed or seat: Mvy 8512 = Tib. ḥkhri ḥi rkaṅ ba (°ka-sampādanam); (**2**) *upright pillar* of a balustrade: Mv i.194.20 (em.); 195.1, 4; iii.227.8, 11 ff. (see **sūcikā**); (**3**) adj., *connected with, relating to* (Tib. sbyor ba) *a word* (Skt. pada = Tib. tshig), in pūrva-pā° Mvy 7616, paścāt-pā° 7617.

pāda-dhāvanikā, *place for washing the feet*: Mvy 9348; so Chin., and Tib. rkaṅ pa pa bkru baḥi sa (BR understand *sand for foot-washing*, but Tib. sa here means *place*).

-pādapaka, ifc. (= Skt. pādapa, with ka prob. endearing dim., § 22.34), *tree*: LV 321.20 (vs).

pāda-phalaka, nt. (cf. Skt. pādaphalikā, Schmidt, Nachträge), *foot-board, foot-rest*, some sort of board, platform, or rest under the feet: °kaṃ Mv ii.82.15 (cf. pādamūle phalake 18); °kāni 465.1; read °phalakāni 475.9 (mss. °phullakāni, Senart em. °phalakā).

pāda-bandha, m., = **pada-b°,** q.v.: Mvy 4980 (after **muṣṭi-b°, śikhā-b°**) = Tib. gom staṅs, *step-posture*, or gom stabs, *step-manner* (the latter used by Tib. on LV for pada-b°). The definitions given by Das for these Tib. cpds. cannot apply to our passages, which clearly relate to archery; see **muṣṭi-b°.**

pādamaya, in danta-°mayā (v.l. -pādakāma) pi kriyanti Mv ii.473.12, some product of the ivory-worker's craft; prob. corrupt.

pādamūlika, m. (= Pali id.), *servant, attendant*: rāja-°kānāṃ LV 2.20 (prose) = Tib. rgyal poḥi zham riṅ (Foucaux) or zhabs ḥbriṅ (var. for the same, Library of Congress text) ba, *king's subordinate followers* or *servants*.

pādalikhita-lipi, a kind of script *written with the foot*: LV 126.8 (so Tib.).

pāda-vanda, adj., f. °ī (cf. AMg. pāya-vandaya acc. to Sheth, °vandaṇa acc. to Ratnach, id.), *saluting (one who salutes) the feet*: °vando Mv ii.108.4, 10; °vandīyo, n. pl. f., iii.265.17.

pāda-veṣṭanikā (so also Mironov; BR °ka), *stocking, sock*: Mvy 8970 = Tib. ḥbog, which Jä. and Das define as a *kind of upper garment*; but Chin. as above.

pādādhiṣṭhāna, nt., *foot-support, footstool*. Mvy 9054 = Tib. rkaṅ (misprinted rkan) rten.

pādāstaraka, m., and °**raṇa**, nt. (cf. Skt. āstaraṇa, and Pali attharaka, *rug*), *foot-rug*: (antaḥpurasya arthāye...) pādāstaraṇāni pi kriyanti Mv ii.470.7, and . . . pādāstarakā pi kriyanti 11. In the same long sentence; what difference there may have been between the two is not clear.

pāpaka, once °**ika**, f. °**ikā**, adj. (Skt. Pali id. only *bad, evil*), (physically) *ugly*: (°ka)rūpeṇa Mv ii.440.8, 15; kāyena pāpakā iii.15.18; without any such qualifying noun, ii.440.10, 11, 12, 18; iii.8.5 ff.; note esp. na me . . . śrutaṃ vā dṛṣṭaṃ vā rājā pāpiko (only case of masc. °ika) ti, nāpi rājā pāpikāye striyāye sārdhaṃ abhiramati ii.440.12–13, *I have never heard of or seen that a king was called ugly*, etc.; always with reference to Kuśa (who was very ugly but not at all wicked) and a possible bride for him.

pāpattika, pāpantika, pāpāntika, see **pātayantika**.

Pāpā (= Pali Pāvā; recorded in Jain texts, Colebrooke, Misc. Essays 2.215, or 2d ed. 193, as Pāpāpurī, Pāvāpurī), n. of a city of the Mallas: MSV i.282.1 ff.

pāpīmant (cf. Pali pāpimant, id.), *(the) Evil (One)*, ep. of Māra, = the more usual (Skt.) pāpīyāṃs (whence the ī by blending, otherwise based on the Pali form): n. sg. °māṃ, before t- °māṃs SP 289.15 Kashgar rec., for text with Nep. °yāṃs; °māṃ Mv i.42.3; 230.10; 240.19; ii.268.9; 404.20; iii.281.12; 416.1; voc. °maṃ Mv ii.238.1; iii.416.6; °māṃ (nom. used as voc., so mss., Senart em. °maṃ) ii.238.16; °maṃ (to MIndic stem in °ma for °mant, § 18.58, q.v. for others), acc. sg. (v.l. °māṃ), Mv iii.416.4; °matā, instr., Mv i.270.12; °mataś, °mato, gen., KP 33.1; Mv ii.264.10 (note māro pāpīyāṃ, v.l. °māṃ, in prec. line).

Pāpīyaka, adj., *of Pāpā*: °kā Mallāḥ MPS 31.2.

Pāpeya, pl., *people of Pāpā*: MSV i.282.4 ff.

? **pāma**, see **yāma** 2, **poma**.

-pāya, adj. (M. id. defined as subst. m., *act of drinking*) in pānīya-p°, with implication of purpose (so in **pāyaka** 1, q.v.), *drinking (in order to drink) water*: (yo) tatrodakahrade otarati pānīyapāyo mṛgo va . . . Mv iii.29.12; similarly 13; 30.1; 31.8.

pāyaka, adj. or subst. m. (Skt. *drinking, drinker*), (**1**) *drinking*, with implication of purpose (see **-pāya**, and § 22.3): pānīyaṃ pāyako Mv iii.29.11, *to drink water*; (**2**) *young* (of an animal), orig. presumably *'drinker'*, *suckling*: yathā āraṇyakaṃ nāgaṃ pṛṣṭhato 'nveti pāyako Mv iii.459.21 (vs); mg. confirmed by same line in Pali, Jāt. v.259.21 . . . poto anveti pacchato (pota = pāyaka).

pāyattika, pāyantika, see **pātayantika**.

pāragata, adj. (= Pali id.; Skt. pāraga; Skt. °gata in lit. mg., of a river, Ind. Spr. 1047, and in Jain Lex. = an arhant or Tīrthaṃkara), *gone to the farther shore* (of existence), ep. of Buddha and arhants or disciples of his: pāragato pāragataparivāro (of Buddha) Mv iii.64.11.

Pāragā, n. of the mother of Śyāmaka in the Ś. Jātaka: Mv ii.210.6 ff.; 218.9; 229.12. In the corresp. Pali Sāma Jāt. she is named Pārikā.

Pāraṃgata, (**1**) n. of a former Buddha: Mv iii.231.7; (**2**) n. of a Bodhisattva: Gv 442.1.

pārajanmika, adj. (para-janman plus -ika), *of a future birth*: Mvy 2979.

pārami-, °**mī** (f.; = Pali id., in Pali used both as in BHS, pāramippatta, °miṃ-gata, Childers, and, usually in the form pāramī, as equivalent of BHS **pāramitā** 2; BHS seems to use it only once in this latter sense; seems clearly deriv. in secondary -a, fem. -ī, from parama), *mastery, supremacy*; usually in vss; in LV 414.19 (vs) read ṣaḍi pārami te, *the six supremacies* (= **pāramitā** 2) *are thine* (see § 19.24); otherwise noted by me only in forms °mi-, °mī-, and (with -gata) most commonly °miṃ-, in comp. with following -gata or -prāpta (edd. often print the cpd. as two words), *arrived at, attained to mastery*, often in comp. with preceding word stating the field of mastery, but also used absolutely, aham atra °mī-prāpto SP 35.6 (vs; so ed. with Kashgar rec.; Nep. mss. pāramitā-, cpd. with foll. nirdiṣṭaḥ); or with gen. or loc. preceding; pāramiṃgata SP 451.5 (vs, ṛddhībala-); 453.2 (vs, svaramaṇḍala-), 5 (vs, sarvaguṇa-); LV 28.6 (vs, iṣvastraśiṣyeṣu ca); 398.19 (vs, āryadharmeṣv iha); Divy 637.5 (vs, printed as prose; mantrāṇāṃ); Mv i.47.4 (vs, vaśi-, q.v.); 74.4 (vs, ṛddhipādabala-); 129.6 (vs, śastre hi, so divide), *for I have attained supremacy in weapons* (even beyond you, see **ati-r-iva**); 164.11 (vs, cittasthititve asi); 166.9 (vs, śreṣṭheṣu dharmeṣu; 3 mss. unmetr. °mi-gato; the other three °miṃ-gato; Senart em. °mī-gato, why?); 169.18 (vs, puṇyeṣu); Gv 488.22 (vs, sarvabuddhaguṇa-); the preceding nouns are only rarely those included in the lists of **pāramitā** (2), but such occur with °miṃgata Mv ii.368.2 (vs, kṣāntiye); RP 5.16 (vs, prajñ' upāya sada); °mi-gata RP 13.11 (vs, dhyāne vīryaguṇe ca); in the last, and in the foll. cases, it seems likely that the short i is m.c.: mi-gata LV 110.7 (vs, vararūpa-, read as cpd.); Mv i.215.4 and ii.18.1 (vs, rūpa-, in 18.1 read anurūpa-); ii.33.16 (vs, devaguṇa-); iii.355.12 (vs, cittacarita-); but before prāpta I have found °mī-prāpta only in the doubtful passage SP 35.6, above; no certain case of °miṃ-prāpta (cf. Mv i.226.9 below); and otherwise only °mi-prāpta, once in prose, Mv i.237.12 (uttamadamaśamatha-); and in vss (note that the syllable °mi- may be metrically either long, as in Pali °mippatta, or short!), LV 437.12 (vineya-); Śikṣ 324.20; Mv i.115.7 (vaiśāradyavara-); 152.11 = 226.5 = ii.29.8 (lakṣaṇa- or °ṇa-guṇa-; mss. always °mi-, but the syllable is long in the last two cases, short in the first); i.152.15 = 226.9 (here mss. °miṃ-prāp°! but °mi in the others; syllable is long) = ii.29.12 (lakṣaṇaguṇa-).

pāramitā (= Pali id., to prec. plus -tā; in Pali synonym of pāramī or °mi in all respects), (**1**) = prec., *mastery, supremacy, perfection*, in general sense, cpd. with preceding attribute indicating the field of mastery: garbhāvakrānti-°tā Mv i.214.12 = ii.17.11, *supremacy (supremeness, perfection) as regards entry into the womb*; sarvakuśaladharma-vaśibhāva-°tāṃ Mv ii.261.7; jina-°tāve 402.22 (*of the Jinas*); uttama-damatha-śamatha-°tā-prāpta Mv iii.64.6 (cf. i.237.12 s.v. **pārami**); sarvacetovaśi-(see **vaśin**)-parama-°tā-prāpta LV 425.22 (prose); in LV 376.18 (vs), read probably daśabalaguṇa-pāramita-(m.c. for °tā, which all mss. read; Lefm. em. °mi-)-prāptaṃ; possibly to be classed with (2) below are mahopāyakauśalyajñāna-(29.10 adds darśana-)-parama-°tā-prāpta SP 29.10; 77.8 (both prose); (**2**) one or more of a technical list of (usually six, sometimes ten, rarely five or seven) *supreme virtues*, of Buddhas, or (to be cultivated by) Bodhisattvas; usually rendered *perfection*; Burnouf, Lotus 544 (App. VII deals with this category) *vertu transcendante*; the lit. mg. was surely *supremacy*: (*five*) SP 334.2 °tāḥ pañca (and pañca is v.l. for ṣaṭ ca SP 142.7); pañcasu °tāsu SP 332.10 (prose), listed in the foll. as dāna, śīla, kṣānti, vīrya, dhyāna; but a sixth, prajñā-p°, is separately mentioned after the list in 333.1; (*six*) listed, as just cited from SP 332.10 ff., Dharmas 17 (cf. 18 cited below); Mv iii.226.2 ff.; Divy 476.2 ff.; Bbh 4.13 ff.; 58.16 f.; Laṅk 237.6; Sūtrāl. xvi.2 and 3, comm.; described in brief statements Śikṣ 187.5–15; in Kv 50.16 ff. with substitution of dhairya for vīrya; without listing, but with number 6, SP 17.15; 142.7 (v.l. pañca, above); 256.10; 259.3; 262.1; 264.10; Divy 95.19; 265.2; 490.16,

18 Av i.7.4; 16.13; Suv 37.13; 42.7; RP 21.7; (*seven*) the above six plus upayakauśalya-(LV mahopā° and adds parama-)-paramitā SP 457.11–12; LV 8.2–3; also LV 34.20 ff. (with upāyakauśalam); (*ten*,) the above seven (with upāya for upāyakauśalya in Mvy, Dharmas [upāyam, nom.!], Gv) plus praṇidhāna (Dharmas praṇidhi), bala, jñāna, Mvy 913–923; Dharmas 18 (immediately after 17 which lists the six); Bbh 371 5 ff.; and in Gv 295.10–25 where, curiously, the same list is given but called **mahā-vitānadharma**, q.v., instead of pāramitā; in Pali, be it noted, the list is (so far as has been recorded) always *ten* in number, but not quite the same as in BHS: dāna, sīla, nekkhamma, paññā, viriya, khanti, sacca, adhiṭṭhāna, mettā (or metti, Childers), upe(k)khā; in Pali they are called pāramī as well as °mitā; note further a list of ten jñāna-pāramitā-vihāra in Gv 537.11 ff., not noted elsewhere, seemingly a nonce-elaboration of the tenth (jñāna) pāramitā; pāramitā without indication of number, LV 274.21 (sarva-°tāsu pāraṃgataḥ); Bhad 19; individual members of the category, dhyāna-p° SP 335.10; dāna-p° Mv i.102.5; esp. frequent is **prajñā-p°**, q.v., Mv iii.67.4; LV 179.14–15; 427.17; and passim in ŚsP, AsP, and other works of this school which makes prajñā-p° its central point; the word is rendered in Tib. pha rol tu phyin pa, *going to the other shore*, a fantastic etymological rendering, as if from pāram plus a form of root i; often forms of (pari-)pūrayati, and noun or adj. derivs., are used governing pāramitā, e.g. SP 256.10 (°tānāṃ paripūryai); Kv 50.16 ff. (each °tā paripūrayitavyā)

pāramī, see **pārami**.

? **pāraloka** (m., = AMg. pāraloga, acc. to Ratnach.; Skt. paraloka), *the other world*: imaṃ lokaṃ °kaṃ (acc.) Mv i.9.2 (vs; v.l. pala°; first part of śloka). Senart quotes Aśokan pālaloka, but the passage he cites (Dhauli Sep. II.6; Jaugada Sep. II.7) is now read pala° (Hultzsch 98, 115); cf. however pālate, °taṃ (acc. to Hultzsch 119 n. 3 to Skt. adv. paratra; rather *para-tva?).

pāraśvadhika, m. (= Skt. Gr. and Lex. id.; to Skt. paraśvadha plus -ika), *battle-axe wielder*: Mvy 3732.

pārājayika, adj., *grave, extremely serious* (sin), = **pārājika**, q.v.; the identity of the two is proved by °jayikādhyāpanna Bbh 159.22 = Pali (pārājikaṃ) ajjhāpanna (q.v. in CPD), see **adhyāpadyate**; similarly Bbh 180.26, see ibid.; bodhisattvasya catvāraḥ °jayika-sthānīyā dharmāḥ Bbh 158.3, 5, etc.; 159.3; they are described in this passage, but bear no resemblance to the four **pārājika** of monks, being evidently a recent invention patterned on that ancient category.

pārājika, f. **°kā**, adj. (= Pali id.; on etym. see Lévi, JA. Nov.-Dec. 1912, 505 f., who assumes Pktic form for *pārācika, from parāc-, parāñc-, plus -ika; as Lévi notes, Pali comms. connect with parā-jayati; so also Northern Buddhists must sometimes have taken it, since Bbh uses **pārājayika**, q.v., which may be only a hyper-Sktism, see Wogihara, Lex. 34; Lévi notes AMg. pārañciya as supporting his view, suggesting derivation from Skt. parāñc-; a mysterious Skt. pārañcika, acc. to Schmidt, Nachträge, *Bruch, Verletzung*, occurs in Kauṭ. Arth., 195.16 in Sham.[1], hastapāda-°kaṃ vā kurvataḥ, *or of one causing injury* (?) *to hands or feet*; neither Meyer, 307.11 and note 4, nor Gaṇapati, who glosses by parāñcikam anyathābhāvaṃ saṃdhivighaṭanam iti yāvad, can offer any real explanation of the word, but it looks startlingly like the AMg. form), *involving expulsion from the order of monks; of the utmost gravity* (of a sin): catvāraḥ °kā dharmāḥ Mvy 8358; the four are listed 8364–7 as unchastity, stealing, taking life, and falsely claiming superhuman powers (uttaramanuṣya-dharma-pralāpa, see s.v. **uttari**); the same four in Pali (for the last, uttarimanussadhammaṃ . . .) Vin. iii.1 ff.; °kā dharmāḥ Prāt 476.7; °Kenā dharmeṇanudhvaṃsayet 481.6, *should accuse falsely of a pār° offense*; f., without noun (sc. vipatti or āpatti), amūlikayā °jikayā MSV iii.109.21; āpat pārājikā Śikṣ 66.16, *a pār° offense*; said of the person guilty of such an offense, *deserving of expulsion*, °ko bhavati Prāt 477.1, 5; 478.5; similarly Śikṣ 143.7; (bhikṣuṇī . . .) °jikā Bhīk 28b.1; in Śikṣ 59.12 read parājitaḥ, with same phrase in 60.12, 61.3, instead of text pārājikaḥ, cf. Bendall and Rouse p. 61 note 3. Cf. also next.

pārājikīya, see **a-p°**, and prec.

pārāyaṇa, n. of a Buddhist work, presumably = the P°-vagga of Pali Sn (976–1149): Divy 20.23; 34.29.

Pārāśara, n. of a yakṣa: Māy 95.

pāri (f.; cf. AMg. pārī, *a particular vessel*, Ratnach.; pārī dohaṇabhaṇḍe, Deśīn. 6.37, and pārī in Gauḍavaha, Sheth), *a kind of* (milking?) *vessel*: suvarṇa-pāri-sahasrāṇi, rūpya-pā°, Mv iii.450.3–4 (prose); ṣaṣṭi pārisahasrāṇi 459.3 (vs, i not m.c.).

pāricaryā, or (MIndic) **°cariyā** (= Pali pāricariyā; see also **paricaryā**), *service*: upasthitā (mss. °to) pāricaryāye (instr. sg.) santo Mv i.286.2 (vs), so mss., Senart em. paricariyāye, which if final e be read short corrects the meter; in Mv ii.225.2 Senart pāricaryāye, but see the readings of the mss.; meter would be better if we read tāṃ guru-su-paricariyāya (all supported by one ms. or the other except that both read °caryāya) but the rest of the line is defective; Senart's reading is bad; pāricaryā Mv iii.348.9 (prose); -pāricariyāye 348.13 (vs), so Senart em. m.c., mss. -pari°.

(**Pārijāta**, n. of a mountain: Māy 254.3. Recorded in Skt, Kirfel 98 f., as n. of a mountain in the west; not in BR, pw in this sense.)

? **pārijūnya**, perhaps to be read (as in Pali pārijuñña) for **parijūnya**, q.v.

pāriṇāmika, f. **°kī** (pariṇāma plus -ika), ep. of ṛddhi, (*magic*) *involving transformation*, see s.v. **nairmāṇika**, with which this is contrasted: ṛddhiḥ . . . °kī Bbh 58.19; °ka-ṛddhi-prakāra-bhedaḥ 22; °kyā ṛddhyāḥ prakārā(ḥ) 63.18.

pāridhvajika, m., *standard-bearer*: Mvy 3725 (so Tib. rgyal mtshan thogs pa).

pārinirvāṇika, adj. (**parinirvāṇa** plus -ika; cf. Pali parinibbānika), *dealing with, leading to, complete nirvāṇa:* dharmaś ca . . . °kaḥ Av ii.107.7.

Pāripātrikā (°trī? = **Pari°**, q.v.), n. of a river near Benares: Jm (App.) 241.5; corresp. to Mv ii.245.1 where text Pāripātri, v.l. °trī; the text is uncertain; in Jm 240.4 text corruptly Pāripāḍikā for Mv ii.244.5 Paripātrikā.

pāripāna, nt., a kind of drink: °nam, n. sg., Divy 221.28.

pāripūraka, f. **°kī** or **°ikā**, adj. (= Skt. pari°; cf. next), *making full* or *complete*: sarvāśā-p° Mmk 2.23; 6.15, 17; 26.25; f. °kī 27.3; f. °ikā 28.1; abhiprāya-°ka 9.22; (sarvabodhisattvacaryā-)°ka 55.11; all prose; et alibi, in Mmk only.

pāripūri, **°rī**, f. (Pali id., = **paripūri**, q.v.; cf. prec.), *fulfilment, accomplishment*: śīlaṃ samādhiḥ prajñā ca °riṃ na gacchati Ud vi.13 = °riṃ Pali Therag. 634; arthasya °rir (v.l. pari°) bhavati Av ii.107.6 (prose); arthapāripūrī (acc., sg. or pl.) . . . dhāraya RP 60.1 (prose); (vratasya) °riṃ LV 197.18 (vs); °riṃ Mmk 22.26; 23.8 (both prose); -kuśaladharma-pāripūryai (so read, dat., for text °ryaiḥ) KP 95.7 (prose).

pāripūrṇa, adj., ppp. (m.c. for pari°), *full*: śubha-°ṇaṃ Mv ii.299.11 (vs). Cf. prec.

pāribhogika, adj. (cf. Pali id., in special slightly different application; = **paribhogya**, **°gīya**, qq.v.), *fit for use*, of articles for personal use, specifically of a nun's robe: cīvaraṃ kalpikaṃ °gikaṃ Bhīk 15a.1.

pāribhogīya, v.l. for **pari°**.

pārima, adj. (= Pali id.; cf. also **a-pā°**; from Skt. pāra plus -ima, § 22.15), *further* (bank or shore, only with tīra or kūla): °maṃ tīraṃ LV 437.14; Mv ii.259.7; 260.1; °me tīre Mv iii.407.9; AsP 434.12; Av i.148.14; Gv 351.3; °me kūle Mv i.261.17. See **parima.**

pāriyātra, °traka, m. (= Skt. pārijāta, °taka, which also occurs here, n. of a heavenly tree; Pali pāricchattaka, also rarely pārijāta, °taka, cf. Childers; see DPPN, and under our **kovidāra,** which is sometimes equated with this; the form °yātra(ka) is supported by Chin., Ware, JAOS 48.160, note, and Tib. below, and should not be emended), n. of a heavenly tree: °traka Mv i.267.1 (v.l. °jātaka); of a heavenly grove (perh. formed by a single enormous tree, cf. s.v. kovidāra), Mv i.32.4, read °yātra with v.l. for Senart °pātra; Divy 194.3, 11 °yātraka; either grove or tree, Mv i.358.6 (read °yātro for mss. and Senart °pātro); Mvy 4198 °yātraḥ, so also Mironov (without v.l.), not to be em., Tib. ḥdus-brtol supports yātrā, *assembly*; Divy 219.20, mss. °yātrako, while in 219.27 they seem to read °jātakaḥ; Gv 501.11 °yātrakasya.

Pārileya (= Pali °leyya), n. of an elephant who ministered to Buddha: Jm 116.1.

pārivāsika, adj. (= Pali id.; **parivāsa** plus -ika), *one on probation*: MSV ii.154.14; 204.3, 11; iii.34.15; also mūla-pāri°, ib., see **parivāsa** and **mūla**; upārdha-pāri°, *half-way thru with probation*, MSV iii.86.14; yadbhūyaḥ-pāri°, *having finished most of a probation*, ib. 18; °ka-vastu, a part of MSV, MSV iii.93.1.

pārivyayika, adj. (to **parivyaya** plus -ika), *relating to ordinary, regular* (daily) *expense*, contrasting with **utsavika,** q.v. (wrongly Senart): vyayakarmeṇa (em.) utsavikena °yikena ca Mv iii.177.17.

pāriśuddhi (f.; = Pali °suddhi, for Skt. pariś°; § 3.10), *purification*: MSV iv.99.7 ff.; kāyakarma-pāri° KP 161.1 (prose).

pāriṣadya, m. (also **pārṣadya**; = Pali pārisajja; pāri° Skt. Lex. and once Rājat., for regular pāriṣada; also Skt. Lex. pārṣadya for regular pārṣada; see also **par(i)ṣadya,** and s.v. **brahmapār(i)ṣadya**), *member of an assembly or group*; pl. *retinue*; esp., and almost always, said of members of the retinue of a king (or god, or Māra, or the like), and often associated or cpd. esp. with amātya (so e.g. LV 26.10; Mv iii.160.19, and many others in the foll.), or with this and other royal retainers such as dauvārika (e. g. LV 118.11); usually pl.: LV 26.10 (prose); 43.15; 50.9; 78.17; 118.11 (prose); 219.19; Mv ii.443.2 (prose, v.l. pari°), 12, 17, 18; iii.160.19; Divy 291.27; Suv 227.11, read °dyāḥ (all mss. contain y, and meter is better so) for Nobel °dāḥ. See also **pārṣada** which is used absolutely, like Skt. gaṇa.

pārihāṇa (nt.; = Skt. and Pali pari°; § 3.10), *loss*: prajñā-°ṇāya (dat.) KP 1.2, 8 (prose). Cf. next.

pārihāṇi, or **°ni,** f. (cf. prec.; = Skt. and Pali pari°; § 3.10), *loss*: °ṇi Mv ii.238.1 (prose); °ṇiṃ (acc.; mss. °ṇi, unmetr.) 391.21 (vs); °niṃ (n. sg.) 395.18 (vs, perhaps m.c. for °ni, which Senart reads by em.; parallel Śikṣ 308.8 seems to have read in ms. parihāṇir, but ed. pāri° m.c. with Mv); °ṇiṃ (acc.) Samādh p. 53 line 1; °ṇir (n. sg.) KP 8.3, 4.

pārihāraka, m. (= **parihāraka, °hāṭaka,** q.v.; cf. § 3.10), *bracelet* (or *anklet*?): °kā (so mss., Senart em. °hāryakā) pi kriyanti Mv ii.470.10 (prose); nūpurā valayā ...°rakā (here kept by Senart) iii.276.8 (vs).

pāruṣaka, (1) nt. (and, in °kā-vana, or pārūṣakā-, seemingly fem.; = Pali phārusaka; cf. **pāruṣyaka**; perh. cf. Skt. parūṣa, °ṣaka, *Grewia asiatica*? cf. next, 2), n. of a flower (cf. also **mahāpāru°**): °kam Mvy 6162; pāruṣakā-vanam (Mironov pārūṣakā-) Mvy 4196 = **pāruṣyaka,** q.v.; (2) adj. = **pāruṣika** (1), q.v.: Gv 159.14.

pāruṣika, (1) adj. (also **°ṣaka** 2, q.v.; to Skt. paruṣa plus -ika), *harsh in speech*: Divy 301.24; Gv 228.14; 352.18; Bbh 168.11; (2) (-pānam), acc. to Dutt, *juice of Grewia asiatica*: MSV i.ii.19 (cf. prec., 1).

pāruṣyaka (nt.; = Pali phārusaka; also pāruṣakā-vana, or pārū°, see s.v. **pāruṣaka**), n. of one of the groves of the trāyastriṃśa gods: °ke (loc.) Mv i.32.4; °ka (voc.) Divy 194.2, 10; 195.9.

pāruṣya-lipi, a kind of script: LV 125.21; Tib. transliterates pa ru śa. Not in the Mv list i.135.5 ff. Could Pārasa- (or °sī) be the original? Or cf. **pāruṣaka, °ṣyaka**?

pārevataka, v.l. for **pāle°.**

? **pārṇa-vāsin,** m. (cf. Skt. pārṇa, *hut of leaves*, acc. to Galanos; Pkt. paṇṇa, *leafy*), perh. *hermit as dwelling in a hut of leaves*: °sī Mvy 7134 = Tib. ṅom(s) pa, *hermit* (Das). But Mironov reads vārṇa-(v.l. raṇa-)-vāśī (vv.ll. -vāsī, -pāsī).

pārthagjanaka, °nika, f. **°nakī, °nikī,** also **prāthujjanika** (influenced by the rare and questionable Skt. prathu? or by some other form of prath-? note u in the Pali), and mss. v.l. **prārtha°,** adj. (to Skt. pṛthagjana, plus -ka, -ika, but partially, at least, a back-formation from MIndic, cf. Pali pothujjanika), *vulgar, common, characteristic of low people*: prāthujjaniko (sc. antaḥ) Mv iii.331.4, and pārthagjaniko LV 416.17 (prose; in LV vv.ll. prārthakjanako, prārthajjanako and °iko); (vāg...) pārthagjanakī Dbh 24.9; (bhūmau...) pārthagjanikyāṃ (loc. f.) Bbh 37.25; pārthagjanikāni karmāṇi MadhK 319.2.

? **pārthika,** *king*: °ka-varaḥ LV 43.15 (vs); = Tib. rgyal po, *king*. Seems prob. a graphic error for pārthiva (which Calc. reads), but acc. to Lefm. in all his mss.

pārśukā (= Skt. Lex. id., Pali phāsukā; cf. **pāṃśulika, °kā,** and Skt. parśu, °śukā, as well as BHS **pārśvakā, pārśvika**), *rib*: LV 254.9 (twice), 11; 255.22 (v.l. in all **pārśvakā,** q.v.); (of a house) *'rib', rafter*, Ud xxxi.7 (spelled pārṣukā); same vs in Pali, Dhp. 154, phāsukā; see s.v. **visaṃskāra**).

pārśva (m., nt.?), *lying* or *leaning on one's side, leaning, slouching*: in comp. with -sukham, (divaṃ nidrāsukhaṃ) pārśvasukhaṃ śayanasukhaṃ ca svīkurvataḥ Bbh 156.18, *of one who is attached to the pleasures of sleeping by day or lying (leaning) on his side or (keeping to) his bed*; (nidrāsukhaṃ śayanasukhaṃ) pārśvasukhaṃ ca Bbh 172.2; as object of verb of giving, (na tv akāle) pārśvam anuprayacchati mañce vā pīṭhe vā tṛṇasaṃstare vā ... Bbh 193.(19–)20, *but he does not lie down* (? *lean, slouch*; lit. *give a side*) *at improper times on a couch or stool or grass-bed*; na jātu pārśvaṃ dattavān, na styāna-middham (q.v.) avakrāmitavān RP 57.10, *he did not at all 'give a side', nor give way to sloth and torpor*; in MSV i.237.7–8, 11 seems to mean *leans, lounges, slouches*: (bhikṣavaḥ) pārśvaṃ dattvā tiṣṭhanti ... kimarthaṃ pārśvaṃ dattvā tiṣṭhatha? ... kṣudhārtā durbalā jātāḥ, ataḥ (11) pārśvaṃ dattvā sthitāḥ; possibly, however, it may mean *stays* (at home) *lying down*.

pārśvakā (see s.vv. **pārśukā, pārśvika**), *rib*: Śikṣ 228.13 (ed. note suggests reading pārśukā); v.l. in some mss. for pārśukā LV 254.9, 11; 255.22.

pārśva-dāha, m. (cf. Skt. pārśvaśūla), a kind of disease, *burning (pain) in the side*: Mvy 9524; Bhīk 17a.2.

pārśva-sūtraka, nt., a kind of ornament, *'string for the sides'* (?): Mvy 6030 = Tib. se ral (mg.?) (ḥ)phreṅ (= sūtraka).

pārśvika, m. (cf. **pārśvakā, pārśukā**; Skt. pārśvaka, m.), *rib*: Mvy 4005 = Tib. rtsib (so read with Index) ma.

(**pārṣada** = Skt. id., a kind of supernatural being, *attendant*, sc. on a god; similar to gaṇa, which immediately follows, and after which pitṛ must be read with Tib. mtshun for text pati, which was a natural error induced by gaṇa-: LV 249.17, prose, in long cpd. listing supernatural beings. Cf. **pāriṣadya, pārṣadya.**)

pārṣadya = **pāriṣ°,** q.v. for other forms; used exactly in the same way: SP 474.8 (prose, māra-p°); LV 2.20 (prose, amātya-p°); 55.17 (prose); 118.2 (prose);

302.19 (prose); 383.18 (prose); Divy 297.16; amātya-p° Mv iii.129.2; Suv 230.9; 236.1.

pāla jagato, *protector of the world,* = lokapāla; so read, as two separate words, in RP 51.2 (vs) brahmendra pāla jagato bhagavan jihmībhavanti tava te prabhayā, *Brahma, Indra, the Protectors of the World, O Lord, these are obscured by thy radiance.*

Pālaka, (1) n. of a servant of Śroṇa Koṭīkarṇa: Divy 3.12; 4.22; 5.17 ff.; 6.3; mentioned with **Dāsaka,** q.v.; (2) n. of a yakṣa: Māy 46.

pālaloka, v.l. for **pāra°.**

pālika, m. (= Skt. pālaka; perhaps to Skt. pālin plus -ka), *protector:* °ka vardhika (q.v.) sarvaguṇānām Śikṣ 2.18 (vs).

Pālita (= Pali id.), n. of an attendant on the Buddha Maṅgala: Mv i.248.20; 252.9.

Pālitaka, n. of a yakṣa: Māy 26.

Pālitakoṭa, n. of a yakṣa king: MSV i.xviii.3.

pālevata, once **°taka,** m. (= Skt. pālīvata, and Lex. and once in Rājat. pāle°, BR 4.693; Schmidt, Nachträge, s.v.; Pali and Skt. Lex.-Gr. pārevata), a kind of tree bearing edible fruits: °ta Mv i.249.11; ii.248.3, 15; iii.80.10; °taka iii.324.2 (prose; v.l. pāre°).

pāśa-graha, m., *the art of casting a noose or lasso,* one of the martial arts studied by a prince: Mvy 4983 = Tib. zhags pa gdab pa, *noose-casting;* LV 156.11; Divy 442.7.

? **pāśā,** f. = Skt. pāśa, *mass:* LV 357.9 (vs); see s.v. **ūrṇākośa.**

pāśālepa, m. (pāśa-ālepa), lit. *snare-smearing,* a method practised by hunters for catching animals, associated with kūṭa: Divy 582.11 (°pāṃś ca, acc. pl.); kūṭāḥ °pāś ca 582.13; 583.1; in 582.29 kūṭān pāśāṃś (alone) ca.

pāṣaṇḍika (= Skt. Lex. id., Skt. °ḍin, Pali pāsaṇḍika), *heretic:* Av i.2.6.

pāṣī, pāṣi (not found elsewhere; perh. cf. **paṃsayati;** AMg. paṃsei is rendered *defiles*), *dung:* pāṣī Mvy 5309 = Tib. lud, *dung;* pāṣiṃ, acc., MSV ii.33.10 = Tib. lci ba, (esp.) *cow-dung.*

-pāsa(ka), f. **-ikā,** ifc. (Pali sūci-pāsa, Vism. 284.14), *eye (of a needle),* in **vaṭṭa-p°,** q.v., Mv ii.87.17; text °yāsikā; same vs in Pali, Jāt. iii.282.13, su-pāsiyaṃ (v.l. °kaṃ), acc. sg. with sūciṃ; comm. sundarena suviddhena pāsena samannāgatattā supāsiyaṃ (suggesting that -iya or -ka, -ikā, accompanies the Bhvr. cpd. only); and, in fact, pāse (loc.) occurs in the prose iii.282.3, 5, with vijjhi(tvā), where the translators render wrongly *dice;* rather, *piercing* (the needle) *at the* (place for the) *eye.* From Skt. pāśa, *loop?* A Deśī word (Deśīn. 6.75) pāsa = akṣi, *eye,* is recorded. Hindi āṅkh, *eye,* is given the meaning *hole of a needle* (sūī kā ched) in Hindī Śabdasāgara (1914), 1 p. 312, s.v. āṅkh, mg. 4; I have found no confirmation of this, or of any use of a word for *eye,* of a *needle's eye,* in any Indian dialect, in any other source. The Hindi usage (evidently limited) could possibly be explained as due to English influence. Professor W. N. Brown informs me that the common Hindi word for *eye of a needle* is nākā. However, Jä. says that Tib. mig, regularly *eye,* also means *eye of a needle,* and *hole for the handle* of a hatchet etc.

pi = Pali id., Skt. and BHS api, § 4.3, 11, 12, also m.c. pī, § 3.14.

piṅga (m.; in one Skt. Lex. said to mean *buffalo*), *young* (male) *elephant,* parallel with kareṇu, as in prec. line kiśora, *male colt,* with vaḍavā: pañca kareṇu-sahasrāṇi pañca piṅga-sahasrāṇi LV 95.11 (prose; vv.ll. kapiṅga-, piśa-); confirmed in Tib., ba laṅ gi phrug gu pho, (usually *bullock* but also) *young male elephant* (for kareṇu Tib. has the same phrase with mo, *female,* instead of pho, *male*).

piṅgala, m. (Skt. Lex. id., as Jain term; AMg. piṃgalaya), n. of one of the four 'great treasures', Mv iii.383.19, or of the 'king' who guards it, Divy 61.3; see s.v. **elapatra;** doubtless this guardian is the same as the nāga so named Mvy 3315; Māy 247.2; as n. of a yakṣa Suv 161.13 (?), see **Kapila.**

Piṅgalavatsājīva, n. of a wandering mendicant: Divy 370.14 ff.

Piṅgalā, n. of a rākṣasī: Māy 241.13; 243.16.

Piṅgalāyanī, n. of the gotra of the nakṣatra Maghā: Divy 639.24.

? **pici-** (perhaps a corruption), seems to designate some impurity, defect, or undesirable quality in a cloth on which images are to be painted: site daumye (see this) . . . pici-varjite (sc. paṭe) Mmk 131.20 (vs). Possibly read picu, *cotton?*

picut-kāra (m.; onomat.), a sound made by Māra's hosts, see s.v. **phuphu-kāra:** LV 306.3 (v.l. picuk-kāra; Tib. pi tshi).

picumanda (m.; Skt. Lex. and Pali id., Pali oftener pucimanda), *the nimba tree:* **Naḍera-**(q.v.)-picumandamūle (viharati) MSV i.25.15, 19 (Pali Naḷeru-pucimanda), at **Vairambhya;** MPS 31.56, at **Vairaṇyā.**

picuvā, n. of a formula and rite in honor of Mārīcī: Sādh 298.15; 299.9, 11. (Origin acrostic?)

piccaṭa, or (Mironov) **°ḍa,** m., Mvy 8883, app. adj., *red-eyed* (owing to a disease), so app. Chin. and Jap.; Tib. tshag po, which is not clear to me.

piccayati (Skt. Dhātup.; ppp. piccita used in Suśruta; cf. AMg. picchiya, *pounded bark*), *presses, squeezes, torments:* śīrṣāṇi piccīyanti (pass.) Mv i.24.3, 5; nakhehi piccitā 21.14; śīrṣāṇi °tāni 24.4.

piñjala = **°ra,** *reddish:* so text with mss. in śirigarbha-°lehi (padumehi) Mv ii.301.4, see **śrīgarbha;** but l perhaps mere corruption for r, since below in 302.3 we must certainly read śirigarbha-piñjarehi (Senart with mss, -pañjarehi), see ib.

piṭa (nt.? or m.; Skt. Lex. id., not in Pali) = **piṭaka,** *basket* in the fig. sense of *collection of literary works,* esp. of the Buddhist canon; only in **tri-piṭa** (Bhvr.), q.v.

piṭaka, nt., m. (= Pali id.), = prec.; of the Buddhist canon, in **tripiṭaka,** q.v.; also in Bodhisattva-piṭaka, *collection of writings on bodhisattvas:* Mmk 22.12 (°kaṃ . . . bhāṣiṣye, referring to Mmk itself or its doctrine), et passim in Mmk (not noted elsewhere, but cf. -piṭakīya); (also, m., as in Skt., *blister, pustule, swelling on the skin:* [krodhāviṣṭasya mahānagnasya] yāval latāṭe piṭakās tiṣṭhanti . . . Gv 504.6.) On **piṭakā** see **piṭṭakā.**

-piṭakīya, adj., *belonging to a collection of literary works* (see prec.): vidyādhara-pi° Sādh 151.15.

piṭṭaka, m. (= Skt. piṭaka, piḍaka, Pali piḷakā), *blister, swelling on the skin:* Divy 210.14.

[**piṭṭakā** or **piṭakā,** mss. Divy 256.24, ed. em. paṭṭikā or paṭikā, *cloth,* prob. rightly.]

[**piṭhaka,** error for **piṭaka,** *basket* (in literal, Skt. sense): Kv 52.23; 71.8. Cf. **pīṭhaka.**]

piṭharikā (= Skt. and Pali °ra and °raka), *(small) pot* (perh. dim. -ikā): Divy 496.14 (so read with most mss. for ed. pipar°); Gv 137.7; 138.1 ff.

? **piṇḍaka-yuddha,** nt. (after aja-yuddha, etc.; before strī-y°, puruṣa-y°), perhaps error for paṇḍaka-y°, *a fight of eunuchs* (?): MSV iii.17.3.

piṇḍakā (= Skt., Pali piṇḍa, piṇḍaka; cf. also **piṇḍikā**), *(alms-)food:* Divy 87.2, 7, 10.

piṇḍa-cārika, adj. (=Pali id.), *(engaged in) going on the round of food-begging,* said of a monk: yo bhikṣuḥ °ko bhavati Śikṣ 55.12; °keṇa bhikṣuṇā 130.12, and ff.

piṇḍapāta, m. (see **pāta**), or **°pātra** (the latter very often, esp. in mss., tho editors often em., cf. Speyer Av i.13 note 1; Index to Divy suggests two different words, 'often confused', but note that even in the cliché list of

pariṣkāra, q.v., piṇḍapāta occurs as always in Pali, beside °pātra, the latter e. g. Suv 112.9; Śikṣ 41.18: Sukh 27.1; LV 2.22; also mss. at Av i.13.4 et alibi, Speyer, note ad loc.; it seems that both forms mean simply *alms-food* (*-attainment*, put into a monk's bowl), as is quite obvious in Pali, see Childers and PTSD, and in some BHS passages; the BHS °pātra was doubtless due to popular etym., association with pātra = Pali patta, *bowl*; tho secondary and unoriginal it occurs so often that it seems probably to have been used in BHS tradition, by the side of °pāta), *food thrown into a monk's almsbowl*; see also (besides s.v. **pariṣkāra**) s.v. **paścādbhakta**: °pāta Mvy 2374; 8571; 8581; 8591; 8671; Divy 188.24; 236.28; 262.23; 553.3, 10; 573.10; Jm 19.25; RP 29.13; Śikṣ 128.2, 8; 215.7; Prāt 500.4 ff. (so regularly in Prāt); Bhīk 23a.1; °pāta-cārika, *living by alms-begging*, RP 57.10 (= °**pātika**), °pātra, besides cases in cpds. cited above, Śikṣ 312.14; v.l. in Mvy 8571, 8581, 8591, above; ekapiṇḍapātreṇa Mv iii.225.10, 13, 21, *with nothing but (a bowl of) almsfood*.—See Rahder, Hobogirin 158.

piṇḍapātika, m. (= Pali id.; to prec.; BHS also **paiṇḍ°**, q.v.), *one who lives on alms-food*, one of the 12 **dhūtaguṇa**, q.v.: AsP 387.4; Divy 141.21; Av i.248.4; °ka-tva, abstr., Karmav 105.5 (note paiṇḍ° in 104.14).

Piṇḍavaṃśa, n. of an ancient king. MSV i.63.4, etc.

piṇḍa-veṇu, m., a kind of bamboo: °ṇuḥ Mvy 4216.

(**piṇḍāraka**, presumably = Skt. °ḍāra; in Skt., Schmidt, Nachträge, s.v.; -ka svārthe; n. of one or more plants: °ka-puṣpāṇām Mmk 712.15, 18, prose.)

piṇḍārtha, m. (= Pali piṇḍattha), *meaning of the sum or whole mass, summary meaning*: (asya tu granthavistarasyāyam) °tho . . . dhārayitavyaḥ Śikṣ 127.9.

piṇḍālu, m. (f.? Skt. Lex. id.; °lū, f., Schmidt, Nachträge; AMg. °lu, m.), an edible root or tuber: °luḥ Mvy 5769 = Tib. do baḥi rdog ma, do baḥi dag pa, cf. Das do baḥi tog ma, *root of Jerusalem artichoke*, also *potato*.

piṇḍikā (see s.v. **piṇḍakā**; recorded in late Skt., see Schmidt, Nachträge, defined *Opferkloss*), *(alms-)food*: Divy 88.8, 11, 19, 23, 27; 89.4 (but in 89.1 note piṇḍakaḥ, m., as in Skt.); MSV i.86.12 ff. (always this, never °akā).

piṇḍita, adj. (= Pali id.; the word is Skt. but is not there recorded of sounds), *full, compact*, of sound: Mv i.171.7 (vs), cited s.v. **aviṣtara**, q.v.

piṇḍī (in Skt. app. not precisely in this sense; also in AMg., whether in this sense is not clear), *large group, collection*: buddhapiṇḍī nirmitā Divy 162.15; buddhapiṇḍyā (gen.) nimittam 163.1.

piṇḍoddāna, nt. (see **uddāna**), apparently *abridged summary* or *statement of contents*: Mvy 1474 = Tib. sdus paḥi (*abridgement*) sdom; MSV ii.3.1, 5; iii.61.1.

piṇḍopadhāna, nt. (cf. Skt. upadhāna, *cover*), *cover for alms food*, i. e. *for the alms-bowl*: °nam Mvy 8960 = Tib. lhuṅ bzed gyi (read kyi?) kha gyogs, *cover for the open (top) of the alms-bowl*; tasmād anujānāmi °naṃ dhārayitavyam iti Divy 84.22 = MSV i.84.2, *therefore I authorize an alms-food (bowl) cover to be maintained* (to prevent undesired things falling into it). Wrongly Dutt Introd. p. 10.

? **Piṇḍola-Kapila**, see s.v. **Kapila**.

Piṇḍola Bharadvāja (Divy, Mmk, MSV) or **Bhārad°** (Karmav), = Pali Pi° Bhāradvāja, n. of one of Buddha's disciples, called 'chief of lion's-roarers (**siṃhanādin**; so in Pali sīhanādin, °dika)': Divy 399.30 ff.; 404.1 (represented as still living in the time of Aśoka, to whom he presents himself); Mmk 111.12; Karmav 62.5; MSV i.183.18 ff.

Pitānandin, n. of a yakṣa: Māy 44.

Pitāputrasamāgama (once Pitṛ-pu°), m., n. of a work: Mvy 1333; Śikṣ 181.12; 244.11 (Pitṛ°) = Bcṭ 326.24.

pitṛjña, *father-honoring*, see under **mātṛjña**, which regularly precedes this.

Pitṛputrasamāgama, see **Pitā°**.

pithati, oftener **pithayati**, or **pitheti** (see also **(a)pidheti**; to Skt. api-dhā-; Geiger 39.5; in Pali only pass. pithīyati, pithiyyati, in some mss. pidhiyyati; cf. AMg. pihei) (**1**) *covers*: etaṃ maṇiṃ pāṇinā pithiyeyāsi (2 sg. opt. of caus. of pass., *you are to cause to be covered*) Mv iii.25.6 (Senart em. pidhi°); (śarāveṇa, sc. pratikṛtiṃ) pithayet Mmk 287.1; pithayet sarvavidiśāṃ 362.15; yaṣya pāpakṛtaṃ karma kuśalena pithīyate Ud xvi.9, 10 (= Pali Dhp. 173, where pithīyati); (**2**) *shuts, closes*, esp. a door, also a window, the mouth: dvārās te pithitā(ḥ) LV 220.20; dvārā pithetha LV 201.17 (vs), *shut the doors*; nagaradvārāṇi pithayata LV 228.2 (prose); in Mmk 560.27 perh. read dvāraṃ (for text **śuddhāraṃ**, q.v.) pithayitvā; sa pithad evaṃ cittam utpādayati Śikṣ 348.10–11 (prose), *he, closing* (the door), *forms this thought*; here pithad stands for pithan, pres. pple. n. sg. m., perh. owing to association with Skt. (a)pidadhat? cf. Bendall's note; pithita-vātayāne Mv iii.122.5 (vs, so read, see **vātayāna**); mukhadvāraṃ . . . pithitaṃ Divy 232.20; (**3**) *blocks, suppresses* (the senses, ascetically): na cendriyāṇi pithayati sma LV 257.2 (prose; Tib. bkag), of the Bodhisattva performing austerities (yet he did not grasp the objects of sense); (**4**) *blocks* (a way), in lit. sense: mārgo . . . pithitaḥ Divy 7.1; (**5**) *closes* (the door to) or *blocks* (the way to), evil states of existence (either dvāra or mārga, or a synonym, may be used, or neither; the figure is clearly derived from 2 and 4 above): (tisṛṇāṃ durgatīnāṃ) dvāraṃ pithitaṃ bhaviṣyati SP 260.9; pithitā apāyapatha LV 117.9 (vs); pithituṃ apāyapatha yeṣa matir vivṛtuṃ ca ṣaḍ-(Calc. ṣaḍ-; read sad-)-gatipathaṃ hy amṛtaṃ LV 46.7 (vs), . . . *to block the ways to evil and open the immortal way to good fates* (Foucaux *la bonne voie*); (sarvā)pāyadurgati-pithita-gatiḥ LV 273.1 (prose); sarvāṇy akṣaṇāni pithitāny abhūvan LV 278.22; pithitāni . . . apāyapathāni Suv 62.10; kumārga sarvaṃ pithita apāyabhūmiḥ Śikṣ 307.3 (vs; Bendall's note misunderstands); (sarvākṣaṇa-dvārakapāṭāni) pithapayiṣyati Gv 112.20 (prose; would seem to be fut. of a caus. analogous to sthapaya-, dapaya-, etc., but prob. read pithayiṣyati); -pīthita, m.c. for pi°, Gv 55.1, see s.v. **pithana**; pithanti (2d ed pibanti, which is absurd) sarvākṣaṇāpāyadurgativinipātadvārāṇi Gv 63.15.

pithana- or **°nā-** (n. act. to prec., suffix -ana, -anā), *the shutting off, blocking*: pithanārthāya apāyabhūminām LV 178.7 (vs; Tib. lam ni bcad pa, *blocking the way*); vitathagrāha-pithanā-su-pīthitam Gv 55.1 (vs; °nā could be m.c., as pīth° certainly is); sarvākṣaṇagati-dvārapithanārthena Gv 98.1 (prose).

? **pithānita** (!), in kṛtarakṣā-pithānitam, Mmk 57.18; 60.18; acc. to Tib. and Chin. the cpd. means *having made the rite of security*. See Lalou, Iconographie, 23 note 1; as there suggested our word seems to be related to, or corrupted from, some form of vi-dhā (perh. vidhāna).

pidhayati, pidhāyati, pidheti (also **apidheti**; to Skt. (a)pi-dhā; and cf. **pitha(ya)ti**), *covers*; also *closes* (a door): (dvāraṃ) pidhāyitvā Mmk 566.18, and pidhayitvā 21 (one of the two seems likely to be a corruption, but see Chap. 43, s.v. dhā); apidheti, *covers, conceals*, Mv ii.493.8; pidheti 17; 496.2; pidhehi 494.7; avidyā-pidhitā (ppp.) bālāḥ Śikṣ 81.1; pidhāpetha, caus. impv., Mv iii.126.18 (prose); pidhīyantu, pass., iii.23.18 (vs).

? **pinya**, m., (mg. unknown) Divy 650.9, pinyādhyāyaḥ, colophon of a section omitted in ed., which only quotes in a note the following: kṛttikāyāṃ jātasya mukhe caturaṅguliḥ (mss. °leḥ) pinyo dakṣiṇato 'syai lomaśaḥ kṛṣṇalohitaḥ.

[**Pipāsā**, Māy 253.1, n. of a river, read (Skt.) Vipāśā.]

? **pipāsin**, adj. (= Pali °si; Skt. °sā plus -in), *thirsty*: read prob. bhukṣa-pipāsino (ed. °sitā, mss. cited as °sito; a n. pl. is needed) madhukarāḥ LV 328.12 (vs).

Pippalāyana, of a brahman (māṇava) living at **Pippalavatī**, who got a share of the fuel used in cremating the Buddha: MPS 51.19 ff. He replaces the

Pipphalivaniyā Moriyā (pl.) of Pali; acc. to DPPN a Pali Pipp(h)ali-māṇava was a previous birth of Mahā-Kāśyapa.

pibana, nt. (Pali pivana; also °nā, f.? but only in dat.-inf. °nāye, which may belong to stem °na, § 36.16; to pibati with -ana), *drinking, drink*: °na-bhājanāni Mv ii.468.16, 17; 469.15, *drinking-vessels*; pānaka-pibanāni (mss. -pibānāni) pītvā Mv iii.147.11, *having drunk draughts of water*; infin. °nāye, Mv ii.432.4, 5; °nāye ... dinnaṃ ii.479.10, *given to drink*.

(**1 piyāla**, m., = Pali id.; MIndic for Skt. priyāla, but occurs also in Skt.; n. of a tree: Mv ii.60.16; 248.16; Jm 167.4.)

2 piyāla = **peyālaṃ**, q.v.: AdP, Konow, MASI 69.34.2 (prose). Corruption?

pilakṣa (m.; = Pali pilakkha; semi-MIndic for Skt. plakṣa), n. of a tree: read pilakṣa-śākhāṃ in Mv i.149.15 = ii.19.17 (vs), as suggested (but in i.149.15 not adopted) by Senart, confirmed by LV 83.3 ff.

Pilindavatsa (= Pali °vaccha), n. of one of Buddha's disciples: SP 2.5; Mmk 111.12; MSV i.x.12.

pilipalipāyeti, onomat., *rattles*? (the razor; said of Upāli the barber in) Mv iii.179.16 °pāyeti, 3 sg., and °pāyehi, impv.

pilotika (m. or nt., in mg. **2** perhaps °kā f.; = Pali °kā, once °ka m. or nt., Jāt. iv.365.19; MIndic for **plotika, ploti**, qq.v. for discussion), (**1**) *piece of cloth, rag*: karpāsikaṃ paṭa-pilotikam ādāya (in becoming a monk) Mv iii.50.15; paṭa-pilotika-saṃghāṭī(ṃ) Mv iii.53.14, 16; 54.1 ff.; (**2**) (gender uncertain), when modified by chinna, perh. *connecting cord* or *thread, binding cord, bond* (presumably of karman, see s.v. ploti-ka): chinnā (mss. °ne) pilotikā Mv iii.63.10, *cut are the cords* (of dharmavinaya, by the Buddha); (Bhvr.) daṇḍachinna-pilotiko (said of dharmavinayo) Mv iii.412.11, *whose cords are cut* (as) *with a stick* (? no other use of daṇḍa in this connexion has been noted; note that chinna-pilotika in Pali is an ep. of dhamma, and chinna-**plotika**, see the latter, in BHS of dharma; here also of dharmavinaya). See also **pailottaka** (?), **°ttika**.

piśācinī (= Pali pis°; Skt. only piśācī; formation like Skt. yakṣiṇī, f. to yakṣa), also written °canī (doubtless by error), *female piśāca, ogress*: Mv iii.163.18 (prose, no v.l.; in prec. line piśācī); 164.3, 8; 295.17 (v.l. °canī); °canīyā, n. pl. (Senart em. °yo) iii.292.1 (both mss.).

piṣṭaka, nt. (Skt. Lex id.), *cake*: °kāni rasarasāgropetāni Kv 48.2.

piṣṭa-pācanika, acc. adv. °kam (cf. Skt. piṣṭa-pacana, Wilson also °pācaka, *meal-baking-pan*), *in (by the use of) a baking pan (for meal)*: °kaṃ vā pācyamānasya Śikṣ 182.5 (a form of torture).

[**pīṭhaka**, error for **piṭaka**, *basket* (in lit. sense as in Skt.): Kv 28.17. Cf. next, and **piṭhaka**.]

pīṭhikā, (**1**) *base, pedestal* (of a divine figure; cf. Skt. pīṭha): pṛthivī tasya pī° Kv 15.9 (misprinted pīthikā); this is the definition of pw, but perhaps *footstool* is at least equally probable; (**2**) in Kv 32.18 perh. error for piṭakā or piṭikā = Skt. piṭaka, *basket*, in lit. sense (cf. **pīṭhaka**): pīṭhikām upagṛhya, said of Rāma (Viṣṇu) masquerading as a brahman dwarf in mendicant's garb; pīṭhikā surely means something which an ascetic might carry (hardly *footstool*!).

pītaka, (**1**) adj. and subst., ifc. *one that has drunk*, in viṣa-pītaka (= Skt. °pīta), *one that has drunk poison* (specifying -ka?): Mmk 462.26; subst. (= Skt. pīta), *drink*: Av i.179.6 f.; (**2**) n. of two nāga kings (? from the other Skt. pīta, *yellow*): Māy 247.14 dvau Pītakau nāgarājānau.

Pītaṅgalya, pl., n. of a people or region: Māy 42. See Lévi 93 (= Petirgala of Ptolemy, prob. modern Pitalkhora, near Chalisgaon, Khandesh).

pīthita, m.c. for pithita, see **pitha(ya)ti**, end.

pīthī = Skt. vīthī (by hyper-Sktism? § 2.30), *street, bazaar, public market-place*: pīthīṃ gato Divy 172.10; nagarasya pīthī (n. pl.) Divy 221.3 (so mss.; ed. em. vīthyaḥ; Tib. *market-place* acc. to Schiefner, cited Divy Index).

Pīlu, n. of a piśāca: Mmk 18.5; piśāco pīlu-nāmataḥ Mmk 611.19 (vs).

-pīṣaka, f. °ikā (to next; cf. Skt. peṣaka), *one who pounds, crushes*, or *grinds*: varṇaka-pīṣikā Mv ii.427.5 (prose; so Senart em., plausibly, for mss. °pīdhikā, °mīdhikā), *woman who grinds* (materials for) *paint*; note Mv ii.427.9 under next.

pīṣati, pīṣayati, pīṣeti (very rare in Skt., see § 28.4 and Chap. 43; AMg. pīsei; for Skt. pinaṣṭi, Pali piṃsati), *pounds, grinds, crushes*: pīṣayanti Mv ii.273.15 (prose); opt. pīṣayet Suv 105.4 (vs); Mmk 82.15; impv. pīṣehi Mv ii.427.9 (varṇakaṃ, *paint*; cf. prec.); so, pīṣahi iii.3.17; ger. pīṣayitvā Divy 409.18; Mmk 81.29; 82.5, etc.

Pukkasī, n. of a yoginī: Sādh 445.21.

puṃgala, see **pudgala**.

pucchati (= Pali id.; MIndic for Skt. pṛcchati), *asks*: ger. pucchitva (vv.ll. buddhitva, vṛddhitva) Dbh.g. 4(340).10.

puja (m.c. for Skt. pūjā), *homage*: puja karoti (so read, as two words) Gv 215.3 (vs).

puñchati or °**te** (= Pali °ti, with object upāhanā; cf. poñchate), *wipes off, cleans* (upānahān): inf. puñchitum Divy 491.7 (so mss., ed. em. po°); forms of **poñchate** follow, perhaps justifying the em.

puṭa, see **puṣpa-puṭa, eka-, dvi-puṭa**; also s.v. **paṭa-bhedaka**.

puṭāpuṭī, some sort of (comfortable) *foot-gear*: MSV iv.208.2.

puḍinī, *pool*: puḍinī-puṣkariṇīṣu LV 193.20 (vs), *in pools and lakes*, Tib. rdziṅ (*pool*) daṅ rdziṅ chen (*large pool*, = puṣkariṇī); ke cāgatāḥ ... puḍinī (acc. pl.) gṛhītvā LV 298.3 (vs), *and some* (Bodhisattvas) *came* (to honor the Buddha) *bringing* (magically) *pools*; so Foucaux; the whole scene is full of magic marvels, of which this is not less natural than some others. Etym. obscure; cf. Pkt. (Deśī) puḍaiṇī = puṭakinī, *lotus* (?), or Skt. pulina?

puṇḍa, puṇḍara, implied as MIndic forms of Skt. puṇḍra, see **tri-puṇḍarī-kṛta, tri-puṇḍī-kṛta**.

Puṇḍakakṣa, n. of a mountain (but acc. to Tib., Bailey, JRAS 1950.173, a grove): Divy 21.25; presumably semi-MIndic for Puṇḍra°, which is not recorded; cf. **Puṇḍavardhana**.

puṇḍara, see **puṇḍa**.

Puṇḍarīka, (**1**) n. of a locality: Māy 91; (**2**) v.l. for **Pauṇḍarīka**, 2, q.v., n. of a former Buddha.

Puṇḍarīkanetra, n. of a former Buddha: Mv i.137.4.

Puṇḍarīkarājan, n. of a former Buddha: Mv i.141.7.

Puṇḍarīkā, n. of a devakumārikā in the Western Quarter: LV 390.5.

Puṇḍarīkākṣa, n. of a former Buddha: Mv i.140.6.

Puṇḍavardhana, nt., n. of a city: Divy 21.24; 402.2, 4, 8; 427.2. Semi-MIndic for Skt. Puṇḍra-va°, which is the form cited Mvy 4113 and by Burnouf, Introd. 399, 423, in translating Divy (last four occurrences).

Puṇyakusumaprabha, n. of a park in Aḍakavatī: Suv 116.1.

Puṇyaketu, n. of a Bodhisattva: Gv 3.18.

puṇyakriyāvastu, nt. (= Pali puññakiriyavatthu, or, acc. to Childers, °kriyāvatthu), *object* or *item of meritorious action*; in Pali 3 kinds are listed, dānamaya, sīlamaya, and bhāvanāmaya: in Mvy 1699–1704 five kinds, dānamayaṃ 1700, śīlamayaṃ 1701, bhāvanāmayaṃ 1702, aupadhikaṃ (q.v.) 1703, and guṇyaṃ (q.v.) 1704; upadhika-pu° (= aupa°) LV 32.1; (aupadhikānāṃ) °vastūnāṃ Śikṣ 138.8; see AbhidhK. LaV-P. iv.15, 94, 231 f., 237.

Puṇyadatta, n. of a former Buddha: Mv i.137.6.

Puṇyaparitrātar, see s.v. **Lokaparitrātar.**

Puṇyaparvatatejas, n. of a Bodhisattva: Gv 2.21.

Puṇyapradīpadhvaja, n. of a Tathāgata: Gv 422.1.

Puṇyapradīpasaṃpatketuprabhā, n. of a goddess: Gv 296.14.

Puṇyaprabha, (1) n. of a monk, disciple of Śākyamuni: Gv 47.9; (2) n. of a lay-disciple: Gv 51.10.

Puṇyaprabhāsaś(i)ri, n. of a Buddha: Gv 285.8.

puṇyaprasava, m. pl., *having increase* or *abundance of merit*, the 2d (but om. in Mv and Pali) of the classes of rūpāvacara gods in the 4th dhyānabhūmi; with or sc. **deva**, q.v.: LV 150.8; Mvy 3099; Dharmas 128; Divy 68.16; 138.23; 367.13; Mmk 43.22; Gv 249.11; Bbh 62.5; Av i.5.3 etc.

puṇya-maheśākhya, see the latter.

Puṇyaraśmi, n. of a previous incarnation of Śākyamuni: LV 170.19; RP 23.18; 37.5 ff. (his story at length).

Puṇyarāśi, n. of a former Buddha: Mv i.140.1.

Puṇyavant(a), n. of a prince (the Bodhisattva), son of a king of Benares: Mv iii.33.15 ff.; the Puṇyavanta Jātaka ends 41.11.

Puṇyaśrīgarbha, n. of a Bodhisattva: Dbh 2.11.

Puṇyasama, n. of a former incarnation of Buddha: RP 23.6.

Puṇyasumeru, n. of a Buddha: Gv 258.18.

Puṇyasumerudgata, n. of a Bodhisattva: Gv 3.26.

Puṇyābha, (1) n. of a Buddha: Mmk 305.13; 426.7 (both times following Amitābha in lists); (2) n. of a god or class of gods: Mmk 19.10 (a nonce-form, invented here? cf. **śuddhābha**).

Puṇyālaṃkāra (v.l. °lamkṛta), n. of a son of Māra (favorable to the Bodhisattva): LV 311.19.

Putkasa (Pali Pukkusa), n. of a Malla official: MPS 28.24, 46 ff.

putrapautrikā, *line of descendants, family line*; °kayā, adv.: Av ii.19.13 (soma-nāmāni kriyante).

putramoṭikāputra, *bastard* (as term of abuse): °trair ājīvikair MSV ii.83.19 = Tib. ḥtsho ba pa (= ājīvika) nal phrug (*bastard child*); yena na kaścit °putro 'lpaśruta utsahate bhikṣuṇīr avavadetum Divy 493.20–21. No doubt moṭikā means *basket* or the like (cf. **moṭa-ka, muṭa**), and the lit. mg. is *child-basket child*, i. e. *foundling*. Cf. **vāta-putra.**

putrimant (= Pali putti°), *having* (*one who has*) *sons*: Mv iii.417.15 (vs, = Pali Sn 33). See § 22.48.

Putrīvaṭa, n. of a locality: Māy 94.

pudgala, m., often written **puṃgala** (so regularly in LV, ŚsP, e. g. 4.1, and mss. of Mv, also Mmk 108.23; 112.19 etc.; RP 19.2; this writing also occurs in Skt., see BR, and Tedesco, JAOS 67.172 ff., who rightly observes that the word is essentially Buddh. and Jain, and offers an etym. which does not convince me; another reading found in Mv mss. is puṅgava, a Skt. word which may have influenced the form with nasal, puṃgala; = Pali puggala; see also **aprati-pu°, niṣ-pu°**), = Skt. puruṣa, *person, man, creature, soul* (often in the latter sense = ātman, esp. in **niṣ-pu°**): SP 120.7; LV 103.14; 420.10; 423.13; 439.2; Mv i.4.2 (Senart always prints pudgala, contrary to most or all his mss. puṃg°); 47.2, 8; 80.13; 119.14; 142.4; 163.18; Bbh 46.22; Śikṣ 236.15 (puruṣo vā pudgalo vā); Ud xiii.14; Mvy 4674; 7028; ŚsP 4.1 etc.; Mmk 108.23; 112.19 etc.; catvāra ime . . . pudgalā bodhisattvena na sevitavyāḥ RP 18.17 (wicked persons, listed in sequel; here text repeatedly pudgala but in 19.2 puṃgala); puṃgalādhyāśaya (Senart em. pudga°) Mv i.85.10; 88.12; 14, acc. to Senart, Introd. xxviii note, (*inclinations*) *tournées vers la grande personnalité* (i. e. the Buddha), which seems to me doubtful; rather = Skt. ātma-, *with self-determined* (*-directed, -controlled?*) *dispositions*; catvāraḥ pudgalāḥ Mvy 2968–72 (as in Pali, Puggala-paññatti 51 f. same terms in Pali form), tamas (separate word) tamaḥparāyaṇaḥ, tamo jyotiṣparā°, jyotis tamaḥpara°, jyotir jyotiṣparā°, i. e. one who is in a low state of existence and does evil (tending to still lower states), ditto but does good, who is in a good state but does evil, ditto and does good; eight pudgala Mv i.291.16 = Pali Khp. 6.6, on which comm. 182.11 f. says, te hi cattāro ca paṭipannā (viz. the four just listed above) cattāro ca phale ṭhitā (i. e. as reaping the fruits of their good or evil courses) ti aṭṭha honti.

punarbhavika, f. **°kī**, adj., = **paunar°**, q.v.. (tṛṣṇāyāḥ) °kyā(ḥ, gen. sg.) LV 417.10 (prose); (paridāghāḥ . . .) °kā(ḥ, m. nom. pl.) Mv iii.338.3.

Punarvasu (= Pali Punabbasu), n. of one of the ṣaḍvārgika monks: Mvy 9473; also called **Punarvasuka,** MSV i.xviii.5 (later incarnate as a nāga); iii.15.21 ff. (see **Aśvaka** 2).

[**punaḥśramaṇa**, error for **puraḥ°**, q.v.]

punā, for punar, *again*, or rather *but, yet*, prob. m.c. for MIndic puna: Gv 476.9 (vs: before ca). So also Pali Jāt. iii.437.26 punā atthi (vs, m.c.). The form occurs in Pkt., as uṇā or puṇā- (in comp.), where it seems not to be m.c. and is regarded by Pischel 342 end, 343 end, as abl. to the 'stem' (p)uṇa-; cf. under **puni**; or in the case of puṇā- perhaps due to lengthening in the seam of cpds., Pischel 70.

puni, in LV 151.8 (vs) seemingly m.c. for *pune, certainly represents punar, *but*; both edd. read so, no v.l. No *pune seems to be recorded, even in a MIndic equivalent (as *puṇe, *uṇe). Possibly it may be assumed as loc. to the 'stem' puna- (Pkt. puṇa-, uṇa-) recorded by Pischel (see under **punā**). Less likely, in my opinion, *pune as 'Māgadhism' for MIndic puno.

? **pubba** (m., = Pali id., for Skt. pūya, Geiger 46.1), *pus*: Mv i.28.9 (prose). So Senart; but several mss. cited as pucca, clearly intending **puvva**, which must underlie the Pali pubba and may well be the true reading here.

pura, (1) *city*, as masc. (Skt. nt.): LV 300.22 (vs) pūrṇām . . . purām (acc. pl., for pūrṇān . . . purān); (2) in cpds. with numerals, tri-pura etc., an element in the architecture of a vihāra, acc. to Tib. (b)rtseg, *upper chamber*: MSV iii.133.9 ff., monks' vihāras have five, nuns' three; a **gandhakuṭi**, and a **bālāgrapūtikā**, of monks have seven each, of nuns five.

Puraṃjaya, n. of a yakṣa: Māy 56.

Puraṃdara, n. of a former Buddha: Mv i.137.6 (v.l. °dhara).

puram, adv. = Skt. purā, *before* (in time), *formerly* (or to be analyzed pura-m plus vowel?): Mv i.133.4 (vs) yathā puram (iti, quoting the vs), *as before*. In AMg. puraṃ is used for Skt. puras, but I find no record of this use.

pura(ya)ti (for Skt. pūr°), *fills*: pureya Suv 37.13 (vs, only two mss. pūr°; may be m.c., in the first syllable of a pāda; the other pādas in this vs have short initial syllables; but surrounding vss show longs in the same place). Dialectic forms with pur- for pūr-(aya-) are recorded for Ap. in Sheth s.v. pur = pūr (puraha), and in modern vernaculars, Turner, Nep. Dict., s.vv. purnu, purāunu.

puraḥśramaṇa (= Pali puresamaṇa), *leading monk, one who walks before another monk*; opp. **paścācchramaṇa,** q.v.: Divy 494.7 f. (ed. with mss. punaḥ°, clearly error).

purasta, adv. (= Skt. purastāt, m.c.; cf. Pali puratthaṃ), *in front*: kāmaṃ prabhāṣanti purasta (so divide) nāyake Sukh 50.11 (vs), *they declare their wish to the Ledder before* (*him*). Cf. next.

purastataḥ, adv. (from Skt. purastāt, cf. prec., or Pali puratthaṃ, plus.-tah: = Pali puratthato, misdefined in PTSD), *to the east, on the eastern side*: Pāṇḍavasmiṃ purastataḥ Mv ii.198.17 (vs) = Pali Sn 416 Paṇḍavassa puratthato. Render Mv *on* (Mt.) *Pāṇḍava, on its eastern part*. Confirmed by Jāt. i.66.14 puratthābhimukho.

purastima, adj., with case-forms used as adv. and

quasi-prep. (= Pali, AMg. puratthima; § 22.15), orig. no doubt *in front*, a mg. which is possible in one or two passages, but as a rule, and prob. always, used in the sense of *eastern, in the east, easterly*: °time diśo bhāge Mv i.123.6, 8, 10, 12, 14; ii.34.19; iii.306.6 (in same vs LV 388.8 pūrvasmin vai for °time, with 'patchword' vai indicating secondary correction to pūrvasmin); °māyāṃ (diśāyāṃ) Mv ii.139.8; iii.116.1, 3; 410.12, 13; °maś ca anto iii.334.2, 3; other cases of adj., Mv i.26.1; 40.7, 8 (°mā diśā); ii.95.20 (also with diśā); 136.17; adverbs, °maṃ Mv iii.256.7, 8, *in the east*; °meṇa Mv i.194.2; 249.3; ii.31.6; iii.226.7; Suv 120.5 (prose); °me, Mahāsamāj., Waldschmidt, Kl. Skt. Texte 4, pp. 5, 171 (ms. 127 V 1); as prep., °time nagarasya Mv iii.186.16, *to the east* (possibly *in front*) *of the city*. Cf. **purima**, which however rarely means *eastern* or *in front* (of space), but regularly *former, first* (of time).

purākṛta, ppp. (for Pali purakkhata, Skt. puraskṛta, § 3.2), *put in front*: devaiḥ ... °tās te LV 297.14 (vs).

Purāṇa (= Pali id.), n. of a sthapati of Prasenajit, associate of **Iṣidatta**, Divy 77.27; 466.23, or **Ṛṣidatta**, spelled **Riṣidatta** in Av i.224.3, and **Ṛddhidatta** in mss. Av ii.9.7. He, and perhaps his associate, were doubtless referred to in MSV ii.70.4, which must contain a lacuna as well as more than one corruption. See also next.

Purāṣa (so ed. with mss.), n. of a former Buddha: Mv i.137.13. Senart's note rightly expresses doubt of the reading, which he says could at best represent Vedic Purāṣāḍ (once in RV). I suggest that Purāṇa is apt to be the true reading.

puri, m.c. for **pure**, q.v.

purima, adj. (also °maka, q.v.; = Pali id., also usually *former*; PTSD gives only this mg., but Jāt. v.398.29 proves that it can also mean *eastern*; in mgs. 1 and 2 based on Skt. puras or MIndic equivalent, in mg. 3 on Skt. purā, in both with -ima, § 22.15; cf. **purastima**; there is no 'Skt. purima' as alleged by PTSD), (1) rarely, *eastern*, = **purastima**: SP 9.3 (vs, purimā-diśāya); Mv ii.56.19 (vs, °māṃ diśaṃ; same vs in Pali Jāt. v.398.29 °maṃ disaṃ); ii.163.3 (°mā diśā); iii.305.19 (°māṃ diśāṃ; in same vs LV 387.18 pūrvikāṃ); (2) *front*, esp. in °maṃ kāyaṃ, *front (part of the) body*: Mv ii.126.5–6 (= kukṣi of LV 254.20, udara-chavi of Pali MN i.246.3); ii.131.15; 232.15; read prob. purimaṃ, adv., *in front*, Mv i.217.3 and 227.13 (mss. corrupt, Senart em. violently); (3) regularly, *former, preceding* (in time), *ancient, first*: SP 48.1; 49.3; 55.9; 93.3; 115.11; 351.12 (here *previously mentioned*; all these vss); LV (also only vss) 123.3; 161.21; 163.20, etc.; 363.5; 393.6; Mv (often in prose as well as vss) i.108.10; 142.11; ii.52.18; 200.12, 14; 206.15 (with mss. purimabhavajanetriye, *of his mother in former births*); 361.5; Suv 225.8 (vs); RP (vss) 39.3; 52.7; 59.8; Sukh 23.14 and 24.3 (vss); purime yāme, *in the first watch of the night*, Mv i.4.6; 228.12; ii.283.14 (in parallel LV 344.7 prathame); purimā koṭi Mv ii.148.3, *the prior end* (i. e. *beginning*, of the drama of the saṃsāra); adv. purime, = **pure** and **pūrve**, qq.v., *of old, in former time*: LV (vss) 167.13; 168.13; 169.9; 393.9; Śikṣ 177.7 (vs); purime bhaveṣu Mv ii.341.4 (vs, favored by meter, lit. *formerly in incarnations*; cf. purima-bhava Mv ii.361.5 et alibi; text bhavesu with 1 ms., v.l. bhavetsu, both hard to interpret); °meṇa, adv., *formerly*, RP 55.10 (vs).

purimaka, adj. (= **purima** 3), *former*: LV (vss) 165.3; 234.9; 366.5; Mv (mostly prose) ii.148.7; 170.18; 257.13; 302.13; 313.13; iii.179.7; 300.12; Gv 301.10 (vs); prob. with specifying -ka (§ 22.39), *the former one*, yathā so °ko śreṣṭhiputro Mv ii.170.18 (= prathamaka, id. 15).

purima-kāraka, m., °kā(ḥ) n. pl., some sort of artisan or tradesman, in a list of occupations: Mv iii.113.14; 443.1 (so without v.l. both times, except one ms. in 443.1 °kārā). What *makers of purima* means is not clear, but this word can hardly be identified with the adj. **purima**. It is prob. connected with AMg. purima as cited by Sheth (as a Deśī word) from Ohaṇijjutti 265 (I have not found it in Ratnach.) cha ppurimā nava khoḍā; the word khoḍa = *cleansing* a part of a garment (see Ratnach. s.v.), and Sheth says purima, like khoḍa, is a part of the Jain cleansing ceremony, (prasphoṭana or) pratilekhana. If *cleaning* is the mg., our cpd. would perhaps mean *professional cleaners* (of clothes). I have no access to the Ohaṇijjutti.

-puruṣaka, see **kula-puruṣakeṇa**.

puruṣakāra- (= Skt.), in °ra-phalam, one of the 5 **phala** (q.v.): Mvy 2274; sc. of karuṇā acc. to Sūtrāl. xvii.31, comm., *fruit consisting of heroic deed, because it brings happiness to others and penance* (austerity, tapas) *to oneself*, reading in text and comm. tāpaka instead of tāyaka, with Lévi's note in transl., but Lévi's transl. (*qui éclaire le Moi*) seems clearly wrong; it brings pain to oneself, pleasure only to others; tapas surely cannot mean *illumination*; it is this quality which makes it *heroic*; in more general sense Bbh 102.17, expl. 103.1–5, puruṣakāreṇa yadi vā kṛṣyā ... sasyādikaṃ lābhādikaṃ ca phalam abhinirvartayati ...

puruṣakāraka, nt. (! = °kāra, normally m.), *manly performance*: na °kaṃ bhavati asmākaṃ Mv iii.126.9, (if I do not do the bidding of the crow-king) *I* (shall) *have no manly performance* (fail in my duty; wrongly Senart's note).

puruṣa-damya-sārathi (= Pali purisa-damma-sā°; expl. Vism. 207.22 ff. essentially as here interpreted), *charioteer* (*driver, tamer, controller*) *of human ones-that-need-to-be-tamed* (= *trained* religiously; as Vism. indicates, dam = vi-nī, *discipline*); the figure clearly refers to taming animals, particularly horses, and indeed is no doubt directly based on Pali assa-damma-sārathi, q.v. in CPD; cf. such expressions as puruṣājāneya (see s.v. **ājāneya**), *noble steed of a man*. Ep. of a Buddha, or a Bodhisattva just before his attainment of Buddhahood. Often misunderstood; further evidence supporting the interpretation here given will be found below. Tib. (on Mvy 10, LV 3.4 etc.) skyes bu ḥdul baḥi (*of human [to-be-] tamed ones*, more lit. *of [to-be-] tamed men*) kha lo (b)sgyur ba (*helm-governor* = *charioteer*). In Tocharian yātāṣlyes yāpy ā(śa)nt, *leader of one to be tamed* (omitting puruṣa; yāpy is uncertain, possibly *helm* as in Tib.). Regularly in cliché listing characteristics of a Buddha: SP 17.11; 65.6; 144.6; 156.4; LV 3.4; Mvy 10; Mv i.38.12; 238.15; 330.2; 331.1; 332.4; 335.16; Divy 54.13 etc.; Av i.65.12 etc.; Suv 168.10; in Mv i.4.9 (read with mss., and print the sentence as an āryā vs, not prose as in Senart) puruṣasiṃhasārathinā (Senart em. puruṣadamya°), *controller of lions of men*, evidently meant as a much stronger variant of the usual term, but incidentally confirms our interpretation of the latter; so also does the epithet puruṣadamyasārathinā in another formulaic series of epithets applied to the Bodhisattva just before his enlightenment, in which several preceding epithets compare him to animals, such as puruṣarṣabheṇa, puruṣasiṃhena: LV 350.12; Mv i.229.9; ii.133.9; 284.19; 415.21; in less formulaic passages LV 428.5; abstr. °sārathi-tā, *state of being ...*, meaning the state of Buddhahood which Bodhisattvas are to attain: Mv ii.260.11; 261.12.

pure, and m.c. **puri**, adv. (= Pali, AMg. pure, Skt. puras), in BHS only of time (but see **purebhāga**), *formerly, before*: quasi-adj., pure bhave LV 385.6 (vs) *in a former existence*, and (m.c.) puri bhavi LV 165.9 (vs), id.; tatpure Mv i.192.13 (vs), *before that*; as simple adv., pure LV 11.13; 282.21; Mv ii.34.17; 169.2 (see Senart's note), in a vs virtually repeated iii.148.11 and 185.9 (in the last Senart strangely em. to purā, tho mss. read pure, which he keeps in the other places, or v.l. puro); iii.445.13; RP 27.18; puri, only in vss m.c., LV 165.13; 169.1; 230.13; 352.19.

purebhāga (m.; cf. **pure** = Skt. puras; = Skt. purobhāga), *forwardness, insistent pressing forward, Zudringlichkeit* (BR), *obtrusiveness*: read sa-purebhāgo (Bhvr.; so 1 ms., v.l. so pure bhāge; Senart em. so puregāmī) Mv i.232.13, *with obtrusive insistence* (he questioned . . .).

purojava (in mg. 2 = Pali purejava), (**1**) m., *attendant, follower*: (tasya . . . yakṣaḥ) °vaḥ Divy 211.6; 214.5; MSV i.68.13; (me) nāgāḥ °vā bhavantu; tatas te nāgā . . . (15) 'nuyāyino jātāḥ Divy 218.14(–15); purojava= anuyāyin; (**2**) ifc. Bhvr., (orig. *having . . . as attendant*) *characterized, marked by . . .*: saptaratna-purojavaḥ Divy 214.19; 215.8, 23; sattveṣu kāruṇya-purojaveṣu Divy 379.26; dharmacakraratanaṃ-purojavā Gv 54.16 (vs), voc., addressed to Mañjuśrī; one cpd. word, not two as printed; *O thou characterized by the jewel of the wheel of the Law!*

purobhakta (nt.; = Pali purebhatta; cf. next), *morning meal, breakfast*: as expression of time, eka-°ktena Sukh 57.4, *during* (or, *at the time of*) *a single breakfast* (they go to other world systems and wait on countless Buddhas); ekena °ktena koṭiśatasahasraṃ buddhānāṃ vandanti Sukh 94.12, same mg.

purobhaktakā (see prec.), *breakfast*: °kāṃ kurmaḥ Divy 307.2, . . . kuruta 4, . . . kṛtvā 7; °kā kṛtā 5.

purobhakṣikā = prec. (cf. **pūrva-bhakṣikā**): Divy 175.8.

purohitya (nt.; = Skt. pauro°, Pali porohicca, also written °hacca; to Skt. purohita plus -ya), *purohitaship*: °tyaṃ labhate Mmk 319.27 (prose). Childers cites a Pali purohicca from Turnour's Mahāv. (11.26), but the PTS ed. (of Geiger) reads poro°, to be sure with v.l. puro°.

pula, nt., or **pulā**, f. (dual pule), designates something given by Mahākātyāyana to a devatā as relic or keepsake, with the thought that these two articles were *not to be worn* or *kept* (na dhārayitavye) in Madhyadeśa, by Buddha's instructions: Divy 581.7. May it be related to Skt. pulaka, AMg. pulaga, pulaa (all said to be masc.!), *a kind of gem*? Not mentioned in Divy Index; no further clue to mg.

Pulindā, n. of a nāga maid: Kv 4.7.

Pullīramalaya, n. of a place or region: Sādh 376.7.

? **puvva**, see **pubba**.

Puṣkara, n. of a former Buddha: LV 5.8 = Tib. śin· tu rgyas, *very extensive*.

puṣkaraṇī (cf. Skt. puṣkariṇī, the only form recorded in lit., Lex. also pauṣkariṇī; BHS also **puṣkiriṇī**, °**ṇikā**, and °**ṇīya**, nt., qq.v.; and Pali pokkharaṇī, the only form recorded), *lotus-pool*: °ṇīye Mv i.227.18 (v.l. °kiriṇīye).

puṣkaratā (= **puṣkalatā**, q.v.; despite the Pali there cited, the orig. surely = Skt. puṣkala plus -tā), *excellence*: parama-puṣkaratayā samanvāgatā Mv i.352.16; paramayā śubhavarṇa-puṣkaratayā samanvāgatā(ṃ) SP 263.7; LV 140.11 (in Pali only cpd. vaṇṇa-pokkharatā is recorded).

Puṣkarasārin, (**1**) n. of a brahman, ruler of the droṇamukha **Utkaṭa**, q.v.: Divy 620.11 ff. As suggested in DPPN, prob. identical with Pali Pokkhara-sāti or °sādi, dwelling in Ukkaṭṭhā; but the Divy story about him seems not paralleled in Pali. See also s.v. **Pūraśāyin**; (**2**) n. of a king of Taxila, app. = Pali Pukkusāti: MSV ii.26.12 ff.; 31.15 ff.

puṣkarasārī (in mss. of Mv °śārī; cf. AMg. pukkharasāriyā, *'one of the 18 kinds of script'*, Ratnach.), n. of a kind of script: Mv i.135.5 (°sārī, Senart); LV 125.19 (°sāriṃ, acc. sg.; Tib. pad maḥi sñiṅ po, *heart of lotus*).

puṣkarāstika, adj. nt. (false Skt. for Pali pokkharaṭṭha), (thing) *produced from lotus-clumps* (so Pali Vin. and comm. cited s.v. **vanāstika**, q.v.), such as **tālūka** (q.v., read śālūka), lotus fibers and seeds: °kāni MSV i.239.13, 16 (all edible)

puṣkariṇī, n. of one of the groves (udyāna) of the Trāyastriṃśa gods: Mv i.32.4. (As common noun = Skt. id., *lotus-pool*, by the side of **puṣkaraṇī**, **puṣkiriṇī**, °**ṇikā**, and °**ṇīya**, qq.v.)

puṣkalatā (also **puṣkaratā**; = Pali pokkharatā, in vaṇṇa-p°, cf. below; PTSD gives wrong etym.), *excellence*, in comp. with varṇa-: varṇa-p° Bbh 61.18 and Divy 222.21, see s.v. **gupti**; in Av ii.202.13 parallel with varṇa: kumārasya rūpaṃ śobhāṃ varṇaṃ puṣkalatāṃ ca . . . (dṛṣṭvā); or should we em. to varṇa-puṣ°?

Puṣkalāṅga, n. of a former Buddha: Mv i.140.12.

Puṣkalāvata, nt., n. of a city: Divy 479.19.

puṣkiriṇī (see also puṣkaraṇī and next two), a very common spelling instead of Skt. puṣkariṇī, *lotus-pool*; not noted elsewhere; editors often em., and mss. sometimes vary; so for °karaṇī of text Mv i.227.18 there is a v.l. °kiriṇī, while Senart prints °kiriṇī Mv iii.329.16, with v.l. °kariṇī; in Divy mss. seem regularly to write °kiriṇī, so 114.10; 116.6 (in these two, but not later, ed. em. °kariṇī); 118.5 (here ed. em. °karaṇī); 165.9; 194.2; 221.6 ff.; 244.20; 248.23, 25, etc.; in Av regularly °kiriṇī, acc. to Speyer on i.75.11, who does not em.; in RP likewise in ms., but Finot em. °kariṇī, 40.14 ff.; 56.14; others, Kv 54.1; Gv 193.17; 519.2.

puṣkiriṇīkā (mss.; v.l. puṣkar°, see prec.; Senart em. °ṇikā), = prec.: °kāto Mv ii.438.5. See also next.

puṣkiriṇīya, nt. (! see prec. two), *lotus-pool*: °yāni (printed °yāṇi) Kv 45.20.

puṣṇāti (Skt.), used in Laṅk in a curious way which I find it hard to interpret; Suzuki omits the word in his transl.: (people who fail to abandon false distinctions) vikalpayanti (*discriminate*, sc. falsely) puṣṇanti (? *develop*, i. e. expand, in worldly activity; the opposite of praśama) na praśamaṃ pratilabhante (*do not attain tranquillity*) Laṅk 21.2. Perhaps cetanāṃ, or a synonym, is to be supplied as object; cf. MSV ii.79.9–10 cetanāṃ puṣṇāti, *develops* or *cherishes* (the following) *thought*.

puṣpa, m., (**1**) as common noun, *flower* (regularly nt.): puṣpāṃ = °pān, acc. pl., LV 92.16; (**2**) n. of a plurality of former Buddhas, puṣpa-nāmaka or the like, numbering 300: Mv i.46.3, but 3 crores, 58.4; 61.13; n. of an individual former Buddha, iii.239.7–8, 432.12; occurs also as v.l. for **Puṣya** (1), q.v., in mss. and some edd.; (**3**) n. of a future Buddha (cf. **Puṣya** 2): Mv ii.355.12 = iii.279.17; (**4**) n. of a king: Puṣpa-nāmo Mmk 625.22 (possibly means *with a name containing the element puṣpa*, and may even refer to more than one king).

Puṣpakūṭadhāraṇī, n. of a work: Śikṣ 173.13.

Puṣpakṛta, n. of a former Buddha: Mv iii.239.10 (read Puṣpakūṭa?).

Puṣpaketu, (**1**) n. of a former Buddha: Mv i.137.10: LV 5.7 (confirmed Tib.); (**2**) n. of a yakṣa: Māy 29.

[**Puṣpadatta**, mss. for Puṣpadanta, Mv i.115.9.]

Puṣpadanta, (**1**) n. of a former Buddha: Mv i.115.9 (here mss. °datta), 16; 116.1; in 116.11 referred to as Puṣpa-sāhvaya; (**2**) n. of a palace belonging to King Udayana: Divy 529.1 f.; 535.9, 19; (**3**) n. of a yakṣa: Māy 63.

Puṣpadantī, n. of an ogress (rākṣasī): SP 400.5.

Puṣpadrumakusumitamukuṭa, n. of a gandharva: Mvy 3384.

Puṣpadhvaja, n. of a contemporary or future Buddha: Sukh 70.19.

Puṣpanivāsinī, (?) n. of a goddess (or epithet of Umā?): Mahāsamāj. Waldschmidt, Kl. Skt. Texte 4, 185.16.

puṣpa-puṭa, nt., °**pūṭa**, m., °**pūṭī**, f., *flower-sheath, calyx*: so Tib. me tog gi phur ma (acc. to Das) on Mvy 6112 °puṭam, n. sg., in list of 'articles of worship' (pūjā-pariṣkārāḥ), between cūrṇa and gandha; Sukh shows how they were used, viz., thrown upon a Buddha, or up in the air where they remain magically fixed and form umbrellas; in Sukh the forms are puṣpa-pūṭī 49.5 and 50.9, or gandha-pūṭī, *fragrant calyx* (of a flower), 50.1, but puṣpa-pūṭa, masc., in 50.13 (all these are in vss) and, in prose, 57.11 ff., repeatedly, always with ū; Müller renders the second member *handfull*, BR *Düte*, but the use in Sukh confirms Tib. on Mvy. It is, to be sure, doubtless connected with Skt. puṭa, puṭī, *pocket, cavity, container*, etc.

Puṣpabherotsa, n. of a village in Gāndhāra (not of a man, BR with Burnouf, Introd. 433): Av ii.201.10, 15.

Puṣpamañjarimaṇḍita, n. of a former Buddha: Mv i.140.4.

Puṣpamaṇḍitā, n. of the 3d Bodhisattva Bhūmi: Mv i.76.14.

puṣpa-lipi, n. of a kind of script: Mv i.135.5; LV 126.2 (both without v.l., but Tib. on LV rgyal gyi = puṣya°).

(**puṣpaloha,** once in Skt., 'a kind of precious stone', Schmidt, Nachträge (from Thomas): °ha-mayīṃ muṇḍiṃ Mmk 691.25, see s.v. **muṇḍi.**)

Puṣpaśrīgarbha, n. of a Bodhisattva: Dbh 2.9.

Puṣpā, n. of a goddess or yoginī: Sādh 157.12 etc.; 324.6.

Puṣpākara, (**1**) n. of a former Buddha: Sukh 6.1; (**2**) n. of a kalpa: ŚsP 323.2.

Puṣpāvakīrṇa, n. of a kiṃnara king: Kv 3.3.

Puṣpāvatī, n. of the capital of the former Buddha **Śirasāhvaya**: Mv iii.231.13 ff.

Puṣpāvatīvanarājasaṃkusumitābhijña, n. of a former Buddha: Sukh 5.20. Cf. next.

Puṣpāvalivanarājikusumitābhijña, n. of a Tathāgata: LV 291.17 (v.l. Puṣpāvanti°; °saṃkusumitā°); cf. prec.

Puṣpika, n. of the present **Bhadrakalpa** (q.v.): Mv iii.330.5.

Puṣpita, n. of a former Buddha: LV 5.8; 171.22; in both Tib. me tog (= puṣpa) rgyas pa (= vipula or the like, also phullita, vikasita).

puṣpitaka (= Skt. puṣpita; -ka svārthe), *flowering, in bloom*: padmāni ca °kāni Mv ii.448.16 (prose).

Puṣputtara (semi-MIndic for Puṣpo°), n. of a former Buddha: Mv iii.239.8.

Puṣpendra, n. of a Buddha: Mmk 130.4.

Puṣya, (**1**) (= Pali Phussa) n. of a former Buddha, following **Tiṣya** (1) in the list well-known in Pali: LV 5.10, Tib. skar (= nakṣatra) rgyal, cf. Mvy 3192 where Tib. rgyal = (Skt.) Puṣya, n. of an asterism; prob. the same person LV 172.7 (so Lefm. with no v.l., confirmed by Tib. rgyal; Calc. and Foucaux Puṣpa); prob. also the same Av ii.175.14 ff. (inferior v.l. Puṣpa); certainly the same Gv 206.12; also in Mv iii.240.6 ff. clearly the same, tho mss. call him **Puṣpa** (q.v.) 240.6; 243.13; 247.8; these Senart emends to Puṣya, in accord with mss. at 241.16; 244.3; 245.16 f. (here with etym. allusion to the month Puṣya [Pauṣya] ! proving the true form); 248.19; (**2**) n. of a future Buddha: Gv 441.25 (cf. **Puṣpa** 3); (**3**) n. of a śreṣṭhin of Śrāvastī: Av ii.36.6; (**4**) n. of a householder of Rauraka who, with **Tiṣya** (10), was converted by Kātyāyana and entered nirvāṇa: Divy 551.6 ff., 571.3, 5.

Puṣyagupti (Senart em. °ta), n. of a former Buddha: Mv i.138.6.

Puṣyadharman, n. of a king, descendant or successor of Aśoka: Divy 433.23 f. He was succeeded by **Puṣyamitra.**

(**Puṣyamitra,** n. of a king, son or successor of **Puṣyadharman,** and ultimately successor of Aśoka: Divy 433.24 ff.; known in Brahmanical sources as founder of the Śuṅga dynasty.)

? **puṣyala,** (*Buddhist*) *monk*? In Skt. Lex. °laka, id., see BR s.v. puṣkalaka; there puṣyalaka is called a wrong reading. Mv i.137.13 has a n. pr. of a former Buddha: Ajitapuṣyalaḥ (v.l. °puṣyaḥ, °puṣyāḥ), which Senart suggests may contain this. But it does not seem very appropriate in comp. with Ajita-; I have assumed that -pusvaḥ is the true reading.

pusta-, acc. to Tib. *letter* (of the alphabet); perh. more generally (painted) *figure* (for decoration; in Skt. said to mean *modelled figure*): LV 95.12 (prose) tāni (elephants, perh. also other animals born at the same time with the Bodhisattva) sarvāṇi rājñā Śuddhodanena pusta-varopetāni (Tib. sna graṅs yi ger bris te, which Foucaux 97 renders *marqués d'un grand nombre de peintures diverses*) kumārasya krīḍārthaṃ dattāny abhūvan; Foucaux renders the Skt. *marqués* (*à la trompe*) *de belles lettres peintes.* (In Skt. *manuscript, book*, = the more usual pustaka.)

pūjanā (= Pali id.; in Skt. only °na, nt., recorded), *worship, reverence*: SP 144.3; 148.6 (both prose); LV 282.8 (vs).

pūjayati (= Pali id., see Childers; not in PTSD, but occurs e. g. Mahāvaṃsa, PTS ed., 36.125 pūjayitvā maṇiṃ; not in this sense in Skt.), *presents respectfully*, with acc. of thing and gen. of person: lokadhātuyo (acc. pl.) . . . lokanāthāna pūjayet Mv i.80.11 (prose); Senart's note correctly.

Pūjita, Divy 509.16; 514.21; or °**taka,** 511.7, 10, n. of a place (adhiṣṭhāna).

pūṭa, m., and **pūṭī,** *sheath, calyx* (of a flower); see s.v. **puṣpa-puṭa**; only in comp. with puṣpa-, except once with gandha-.

pūta (Skt. Lex., n. of various plants), n. of some plant: Mmk 85.11.

pūti-mukta, m. or nt. (Mvy 9435 app. either °taḥ or °tam; = Pali pūtimutta, interpreted even by Pali comms. as containing mutta = Skt. mūtra, *urine*; this is prob. a late and secondary interpretation, suggested by pūti-; it seems unlikely in MN i.316.24 pūtimuttaṃ nānābhesajjehi saṃsaṭṭhaṃ; BHS prob. has the true form), *a medicinal decoction*, of herbs acc. to the apparent mg. of Tib., Chin., and Jap. on Mvy; one of the four **niśraya,** q.v., or *requisites* of the Buddhist monk: Mvy 8673; 9435 (misdefined in BR); Bhīk 23a.4.

pūpika (= Pali pūvika; Skt. pūpa plus -ika), *cakemaker*: Mv iii.113.8 (in a list of trades).

pūra, adj., *full*, and subst. m. (= Pali id.), mss. often pura, in vss meter proves pūra, *full measure, full extent, full contents* (Skt. also nearly in this sense, but usually of water, *flood*, acc. to BR only fig. of other things); it is doubtful to which mg. some instances belong; (**1**) adj., udupānā pūrā (or °naṃ pūraṃ) Mv i.220.20 = ii.23.5 (vs); pūraṃ ca te bhaviṣyati sahasraṃ putrāṇāṃ, *and you shall have a full thousand sons*, Mv ii.158.17, and similarly Mv iii.107.6; 124.3, 8 (vs, putrāṇa te, or me, pūrasahasraṃ, *a full thousand of sons*); 377.21; yadi pi lokadhātu pūrā bhave . . . sarṣapehi Mv ii.295.10, *if the universe were full of mustardseeds*; (kṣetrā . . .) pūrā bhavetsuḥ yadi sarṣapāṇāṃ 379.13; kṣetrā sahasrā bahuvastra-pūrā 380.9; in Mv ii.461.21; 462.2, 3, as in some others of our citations, mss. puraṃ (**gopiṭakaṃ,** q.v.), but Senart seems surely right in his em. pūraṃ, *full* (*cow-basket*); contrasted with ūnakaṃ, *empty*, yaṃ ūnakaṃ (mss. corrupt, but cf. next line) taṃ svanati (?) yaṃ pūraṃ śāntam eva taṃ Mv iii.389.6; pūrārgheṇa, *with full value*, Śikṣ 143.6, see s.v. **prātimokṣa;** (**2**) subst. m.: (dvau trīn vā) pātra-pūrāṃ (acc. pl.) Prāt 509.4, *bowls-full*; dva-tri-pātra-pūrātiriktagrahaṇam Mvy 8455; pātrapūra Divy 51.16, 18; °ro dattaḥ 262.22; **kaṭacchu-**(q.v.)-pūra- Divy 475.21; añjalipūro dattaḥ Karmav 67.16; saptāhapūra, *the full extent of a week, a full week*, °raṃ ekaparyaṅkenātināmesi Mv ii.348.15, *he spent a full week* . . .: °ram, adv., *for a full week*, Mv ii.343.3; 349.2, 3, 5; bhavāgra(q.v.)-pūra, *the* *full extent of the top of the universe* (or adj.?), heṣṭā upādāya (*beginning from the bottom*) bhavāgrapūraṃ jāmbūnadasya imaṃ (unmetr.) buddhakṣetraṃ Mv ii.378.21 (in same vs Śikṣ 303.1 vi-, for which read pi, bhavāgru yāvat); 380.2, etc.

Pūraṇakarṇa, n. of a nāga: Māy 222.1.

Pūraṇa Kāśyapa, or (in Mv always) Kāśyapa Pūraṇa (= Pali Pūraṇa, v.l. Purāṇa, Kassapa), n. of a celebrated heretical teacher of Buddha's time one (usually the first in listing) of a group of six (śāstāraḥ, tīrthyāḥ): in Divy 154.4 nirgranthāḥ; P. himself called a nirgrantha, Divy 165.14; the others are Maskarin Gośālīputra, Saṃjayin Vairaṭīputra, Ajita Keśakambala, Kakuda Kātyāyana, and Nirgrantha Jñātiputra (with variants), qq.v.; P.K. named with the rest, Mvy 3545; Divy 143.10; Av i.231.3; in the order K.P., Mv i.253.o and (as cpd., Kāśyapa-pūr°) 9; 256.20; iii.383.15; P.K. without the others, Av i.281.1; K.P. without the others, Mv ii.200.10; 207.2; Pūraṇa alone (without Kāśyapa, and without the names of the others, but often as one of the 'six teachers' or the like) Divy 143.9, 13; 154.4 ff.; 164.17, 26; 165.14 ff.: Av i.16.3; 47.7; 48.6; ii.24.11; 134.10.

? **Pūraśāyin** (so mss.; perh. the person called in Pali Pokkharasāti or °sādi; Lévi suggests reading **Puṣkarasārin**, q.v.), n. of a brahman convert to Buddhism: Karmav 157.5.

pūri, pūrī, f. (not recorded; cf. paripūri, °rī), *the fulfilling; full measure*: bodhi-saṃbhāra-pūrye (for °yai, dat.) Dbh.g. 52(78).11; daśapāramitā-pūryai 55(81).13; bodhisattva-caryā-praṇidhi-pūrim adhigamiṣyante Gv 493.9 (prose); *full measure* . . .

pūrṇa, adj. and n. pr. (adj. as in Skt., *full*, with numerals; wrong division in edd., notably that of SP, often makes the construction seem strange, when it is really quite normal Skt., e. g. [read] aṣṭādaśa kṣetrasahasra pūrṇāḥ [ed. as one word!] SP 9.3 and 24.1; aśīti so antarakalpa pūrṇāṃ [with aśīti, acc.] 26.12; aśīti pūrṇāḥ 62.3 [ed. as one word]; dvātriṃśatī [so mss., acc.] antarakalpa [so divide] pūrṇāṃ 68.11; cf. next vs, dvātriṃśatī antarakalpa sthāsyatī 69.1; note the same use of paripūrṇa, in: °ṇa so antarakalpa [so divide] ṣaṣṭim 25.8, *for full 60 intermediate kalpas*; sahasr' aśītiḥ paripūrṇa ye sthitāḥ 35.12; all these are vss), (**1**) also **Pūrṇaka** (1), **Saṃpūrṇa**, qq.v. (= Pali Puṇṇa, -ka, No. 1 in DPPN), n. of a sthavira, a well-known disciple of Buddha; his story is told Av i.2.8 ff. (here always called Pūrṇa except twice **Saṃpūrṇa**, q.v.); and more fully Divy 26.8 ff. (here regularly Pūrṇa, occasionally **Pūrṇaka** without difference of mg.); a fragment of the story in Mv, with name **Pūrṇako** i.245.10; referred to as Pūrṇa Jm 115.23; Karmav 63.3; (**2**) Pūrṇa Maitrāyaṇīputra (= Pali Puṇṇa Mantānīputta), n. of another disciple of Buddha: as two separate words Mv iii.377.13 (here Maitrāyaṇīye . . . putro); 379.3, 12, 17; 382.7; SP 199.1; 200.1, etc.; as one cpd. word, Pūrṇa-Maitrāyaṇīputra, SP 2.7; EV 1.15; Mvy 1036; Gv 17.23; and so Sukh 2.4, where he seems to be confused with Pūrṇa (3), see s.v. **Yaśodeva**; (**3**) n. of another disciple of Buddha, corresp. to Pali Puṇṇaji, which should = Pūrṇajit: LV 1.9 and Sukh 2.4, above (see **Yaśodeva**); (**4**) n. of another disciple of Buddha (the same as 1?) called **Kuṇḍopadhānīyaka**, q.v. (once also **Pūrṇaka**): Divy 44.8; 45.1; (**5**) n. of a former Buddha: Av i.117.10 ff.; see **Saṃpūrṇa** 2: (**6**) (= Pali Puṇṇaka; also BHS **Pūrṇaka** 3), n. of a yakṣa: Sādh 562.20 (prose).

Pūrṇaka, (**1**) = **Pūrṇa** (1): Mv i.245.10; Divy 29.22, 26; 30.5, 10, 14, 16; 31.22; 40.18; 44.15; only the last is in a vs, the rest are prose, often occurring close to the form Pūrṇa which is much commoner, and without any discernible difference of mg.; (**2**) = **Pūrṇa** (4): only in a vs, Divy 44.15; (**3**) = **Pūrṇa** (6): Māy 40; 54; 235.12; 236.29; (**4**) adj. pūrṇaka (= Skt. pūrṇa; nowhere recorded in this mg.), *full*: pañcāśa varṣāṇi su-pūrṇakāni SP 115.7 (vs), *full 50 years*; here perhaps -ka m.c.; but prose in MSV i.252.20 (same passage Divy 133.24 pūrṇa).

pūrṇa-gātra, adj. Bhvr., *full-bodied* in the sense of *satiated* with food: jighatsitāḥ pūrṇagātrā bhavanti Mvy 6306, *the hungry become filled*; Tib. ḥdraṅs pa, *satiated*. or lus rgyas pa, *full-bodied*.

Pūrṇacandra, (**1**) n. of a Buddha: Mv i.124.6; (**2**) n. of a Bodhisattva: SP 3.6.

Pūrṇabhadra, n. of a future Buddha which it is predicted that **Pūrṇa** (1) will become: Av i.7.4.

Pūrṇabhadrikā, n. of a piśācī: Māy 239.23.

pūrṇamā (= Skt. Lex. id., Pali puṇṇamā; Skt. pūrṇimā), *day* (or *night*) *of the full moon*: loc. °māyāṃ, all mss. but one, and Calc., LV 55.1; Lefm. with ms. A pūrṇamāsyāṃ (to °māsī, rare in Skt., cf. paurṇamāsī); several mss. add paurṇamāsyāṃ (gloss?).

Pūrṇamukha, (**1**) n. of a yakṣa: Māy 97; (**2**) n. of a jackal: MSV ii.103.9 ff. (in story = Pali Jāt. 400); in 105.4 his mother calls him Pūrṇika and Supūrṇika, affectionate hypocoristics.

Pūrṇa-maitrāyaṇīputra, see **Pūrṇa** (2), and **Maitrāyaṇī.**

Pūrṇika = **Pūrṇamukha** (2), q.v.

(**pūrvakārin**, adj., *that has previously done a favor*: °kārisya, gen., Mv ii.184.12, vs, so mss., Senart em. °karisya, m.c.; Skt., pw 7.359, and Pali pubba-kārin.)

pūrva-koṭi, f. (= Pali pubba-koṭi; see **koṭi**, and cf. **aparānta-koṭi**), *the 'first end'* (in time), *the very beginning*: Mvy 8306. (In Pali used of the saṃsāra, see PTSD.)

pūrvaṃgama, adj. (= Pali pubbaṃgama), *foremost, first*: °maḥ Mvy 6270; sarvatra °maḥ Divy 333.17, 26; °maṃ (-saṃprasthānaṃ) Gv 504.17; used much like Skt. -ādi, *et cetera*, Mahāmati-bodhisattva-pūrv° Laṅk 1.10 (= *including the bodhisattva M.*); similarly Gv 149.20; pūrvapraśna-pūrvaṃgama- Mmk 6.10, *preceded by* . . .; abhivilokanā-(q.v.)-pūrvaṃgamehi dharmehi Mv ii.259.8; 260.1, *preceded (and conditioned) by intimate examination*; **°ma-tā**, abstract: bodhicitta-°ma-tayā Śikṣ 53.18, *by keeping . . . in the foreground*; **°mī-karoti**, *makes (puts, keeps) in the foreground*: Śikṣ 216.2.

pūrvaṃgamana, = prec., q.v.: Gv 494.18, see s.v **pratilayana.**

pūrva-carama, m., (a distribution of goods to monks beginning with) *the first and the last* (monk): °maḥ Mvy 9271; written pūrvācaramaṃ (kṛtvā) MSV ii.121.1 (the process explained in ff.); Tib. thog ma (in Mvy daṅ po) daṅ tha ma, *first and last*.

Pūrvajanmāvadāna, see s.v. **Pūrvāvadāna.**

pūrvajanmika, see **paurva°.**

pūrva-nimitta, nt. (= Pali pubba°), *advance-sign*, prognosticating something that is to happen in the future: °tāni LV 76.9 and 77.21, of the 32 signs which precede and forecast the birth of the Bodhisattva (so also in Pali); they are listed in detail between these two points in LV; in Gv 373.20 ff. only ten pūrvanimittāni are listed as preceding the Bodhisattva's birth; in Divy 193.20 of the five signs that a god is about to 'fall' (so also in Pali); used (as also in Pali) of dreams that foretell events, so LV 186.5 of Śuddhodana's dream presaging the Bodhisattva's retirement from the world; in Gv 375.2 ff., ten pūrva-ni° occurred in the Lumbinī-grove when Māyā came out of Kapilavastu; in Gv 531.4, ten precede the revealing of the Bodhisattva Samantabhadra (these are all esoteric, dealing with occurrences in Buddhakṣetras).

pūrva-nivāsa, m., = **pūrve-ni°**, usually with forms or derivs. of anusmarati (as in Pali with anussarati): Mv i.160.3 (°saṃ vetti, one of 10 bala); 228.16; 229.5; 319.3; ii.132.15; 284.7, 8; iii.67.6; 321.9; Mvy 229 (see **nidāna** 1); Divy 619.8 ff.; Bhīk 27a.5; °sānusmṛti, one of the **abhijñā**, q.v.

Pūrvapraṇidhānasaṃcodanasvara, n. of a Bodhisattva: Gv 4.11.

Pūrvapraṇidhinirmāṇacandra, n. of a Tathāgata: Gv 422.24.

pūrva-preta, m. (= Pali pubbapeta, wrongly defined PTSD as = peta; it means *spirit of an ancestor*, or at least *of a deceased member of one's family*; this is clear from DN comm. i.90.28, on i.8.2, atīte ñāti-kathā, as gloss on pubbapetakathā; and Pv comm. 17.26–27 pubbe keci pitaro, gloss on i.4.1 pubbe pete), *spirit of an ancestor* or *deceased membe. of the family*; as object of worship: pūrvapeta-pūjakaṃ tat kulaṃ (in which the Bodhisattva is to be reborn in his last existence) LV 24.10 (replaced in same passage Mv i.198.2 by pūrvapitṛpūjakaṃ, in Mv ii.1.13 by pūrvamitrapūjakaṃ; the latter may be an error, mitra for pitṛ); in a list of venerable persons and benefactors, a cliché in which all are contrasted unfavorably with the Buddha, Divy 47.13; 97.16; Av i.149.3 etc.

Pūrvabuddhānusmṛty-asaṅgājñānā-(read °asaṅga-jñāna, as in Mvy 186, cf. Tib. below)**-lokālaṃkāra**, nt.: °raṃ, n. sg., nāma raśmiś, LV 3.13, n. of a ray emitted from the crown of the Buddha's head; in 4.6 repeated as abl. fem., °**jñānālokāyā** raśmyā(ḥ), omitting pūrva and alaṃkāra; Tib. both times sṅon gyi saṅs rgyas rjes su dran par bya ba la chags pa med paḥi ye śes snaṅ ba, *light of unattached knowledge for making to remember past Buddhas*, omitting alaṃkāra both times; Tib. ye śes = jñāna, not ājñāna, confirming ms. A in 3.13, °asaṅga-jñāna°.

pūrva-bhakṣikā = **puro-bha°**, *breakfast*: Divy 30.18, 20.

pūrva-yoga, m. (in Mv also nt.; = Pali pubbayoga), lit. *former connexion*, i. e. *deeds, adventures, lives in former incarnations*: pratibhātu te vāgīśa tathāgatasya °go Mv i.267.10–11, *let a previous life of the T. recur to your mind* (there follows a story of a former life of the T. and of Vāgīśa together; but Senart is wrong in supposing that this '*réunion antérieure*' is inherent in the mg. of the word); eteṣu pūrvayogā prakīrtitā śāstuno Mv i.338.9, *previous lives* or *adventures* in them; pūrvayoga-saṃpanna, *perfected in (thru) previous lives*, said of the Buddha or Bodhisattva, Mv ii.259.11; 287.13; iii.320.2 (ye te sattvā °saṃpannā bhavanti te āryadharmacakraṃ pravartenti); colophons, Padumāvatīye pūrvayogaṃ Mv iii.172.4, and Rāhulabhadrasya pū° 175.19; etam eva °ga-parivartam Samādh 8.20; °ga-parivarta, title of SP Chap. 7 (not 'ancient devotion' with Kern, nor 'l'ancienne application' with Burnouf, but *a former existence*, of Śākyamuni and others, under an ancient Buddha).

Pūrva-videha, one of the 4 Buddhist continents (see **dvīpa**); -lipi, a kind of script: LV 126.5. (Prāg- for **Pūrva-** is reported in AbhidhK, see s.v. **dvīpa**.)

pūrvaśas, adv., *of old, in former time*: LV 221.6 and 20 (vss).

Pūrva-śaila, m. pl. (= Pali Pubba-seliya, see **Apara-ś°** and CPD s.v. Apara-seliya), n. of a (heretical) school: Mvy 9090.

pūrvasyām (loc. sg. of Skt. purvā, f.), or **pūrvikāyam** (loc. sg. of f. of Skt. pūrvaka; in both sc. jātau or jātyām), *in a former birth*: kiṃ punar Bhagavān ... Śaṅkhakuñjarasyāsmākaṃ pūrvasyāṃ jātaṃ jānīte Karmav 27.15–16, *but does the Lord know what, in relation to me, happened to* (jātaṃ) *Ś.* (we should expect acc., °kuñjaram, *as what in relation to me was Ś. born) in his former birth*?; kiṃ punar Bhagavān ... asmākaṃ Śaṅkhakuñjaraṃ pūrvikāyāṃ jātaṃ saṃjānīte 27.19–20, ... *as what in relation to me Ś. was born in a previous birth*?; saced bhavāñ Chaṅkhakuñjaro 'smākaṃ pūrvikāyāṃ jātaḥ pitābhūt 28.2–3, *if you, Ś., were born as my father in a previous birth* (Ś. in his present birth was a dog).

pūrvānta, m. (= Pali pubbanta; sometimes in contrast with **aparānta**, q.v.), *the past*: °nte, *in past time* LV 164.3, 7; Divy 427.20; Bbh 67.3; °ntata eva LV 180.11, *from past times already* (wrongly pw *in advance*); in LV 422.16 read with many mss. and Calc., supported by Tib., pūrvāntāsaṃbhavatvāt (Lefm. °ntasaṃbh°), *because it has no origin in the past*; Mvy 8305 °ntaḥ, n. sg.; Mv i.176.6 °nta-naya-saṃpannā, *perfected thru past behavior* (wrongly Senart); Gv 49.25, read pūrvāntāparānta; Dbh 17.15; 31.4; Śāl 88.16, cited Śikṣ 227.7; pūrvāntakalpakānāṃ Bbh 67.23 (see s.v. **ekatya-śāśvatika**), *qui se forgent des systèmes sur le passé* (LaV-P., AbhidhK. v. 14).

pūrvāntika, fem. °**kī** (from prec. plus -ika), *of the past*: Śikṣ 228.1; quot. from Dbh 51.2 where **paurvāntiky** is read.

Pūrvāparāntaka Sūtra, *Sūtra of the Past and Future*, n. of a work: Karmav 39.13 (see Lévi's note); 67.3.

pūrvābhilāpin, adj. (unrecorded; cf. pūrvālāpin), *speaking (greeting) first, a mark of graciousness or respect*: °pī. n. sg., Mvy 848 (of Bodhisattvas); 1787; Bbh 6.16 and 123.12, read °lāpī for text °bhāpī; 254.20, text °lāpī, em. for ms. °lāṣī; °pinyaḥ (n. pl. f.) smitamukhāś ca RP 41.18; abstr. °**pi-tā** Śikṣ 183.15.

? **pūrvābhūtvā** (v.l. omits pūrvā; should we read pūrvībhūtvā?), *having existed in a previous time*: Laṅk 251.5.

Pūrvārāma (m., = Pali Pubbārāma), *Eastern Park*, n. of a locality at Śrāvastī, where **Viśākhā** built the **Mṛgāramātuḥ prāsāda**: MSV ii.70.11; 82.8.

pūrvālāpin, adj. (cf. AMg. puvvālavaṇa, n. act.), = **pūrvābhilāpin**, q.v.: Av i.243.2 etc. (of Buddhas); Mv ii.64.16 (of a prince); 367.23; 423.19.

Pūrvāvadāna, m. or nt., n. of a work or section in an unnamed work: Śikṣ 10.12. Doubtless = Pūrvajanmāvadāna, 13.16, named as part of the **Mañjuśrībuddhakṣetraguṇavyūhālaṃkāra-sūtra.**

pūrvāhṇikā, app. *morning meal*: MSV ii.144.6 ff.

pūrvi, m.c. for **pūrve**, q.v.

pūrvika, adj., or subst. (unrecorded; Skt. -pūrvika in Mbh 5.7553 is an error for -pūrvaka, as BR saw, and as is proved by Crit. ed. 5.193.62), *former, of old; (one) of olden time*: °kāḥ, n. pl., Mvy 6549; °kāni stūpabimbāni Kv 13.10.

pūrvikāyām, loc. sg., sc. jātau (jātyām), *in a former birth*: Karmav 27.20; 28.3; see s.v. **pūrvasyām**.

pūrvīkaroti, ger. °kṛtya, *bringing to the front*, and so *raising* (his tail, of a peacock): kalāpaṃ °tya (Tib. bsgreṅ nas, *raising*) MSV ii.93.2.

pūrve, and m.c. **pūrvi**, adv. (= Pali pubbe; in Skt. pūrvam), *of old, in former time; first, beforehand*: in prose of Mv, otherwise hardly found except in vss, but note pūrve SP 158.13 (prose, only Kashgar rec. and one Nep. ms.); pūrve adattvā Mv ii.56.4, *not having first given*; Mv i.26.7; ii.98.14 (pūrve vā saṃnivāsena, *either by dwelling together in a former birth* ...); 121.1 (pūrve aśrutā caiva aśrutapūrvā ca, cf. parallels LV 246.9 aśrutapūrvā(ḥ), only, and Pali MN i.240.30 pubbe assutapubbā); 130.14; 192.19, 21; 337.13; 356.19; 469.10 (so with mss.); iii.332.13, 15, 18, and 333.2 (in some v.l. pūrvaṃ, once followed by Senart), etc.; the rest are only vss: RP 21.14; 23.8; Gv 230.13; LV 163.16; 164.1; 196.5; 215.15; 231.11; 331.6; 340.15; 376.6; 386.14; **pūrvi**, m.c., LV 170.11; 365.13; cf. also the foll. cpds., and see **pūrvasyām, pūrvikāyām.**

pūrve-jāti (f.), substantially = **pūrve-nivāsa**, and noted only in a line of vs also containing that word; pūrvenivāsaṃ bhagavān pūrvejātim anusmaran Mv i.282.4 = ii.93.18 = 188.9 = 237.5 = iii.26.6 = 89.21.

pūrve-nivāsa, m. (= Pali pubbe-ni°; also **pūrva-ni°** and rarely **pūrve-vāsa**, qq.v.; cf. s.v. **nivāsa**), *former birth* or *state of being*; usually with forms or derivs. of anusmarati (as in Pali with anussarati): LV 375.15; Mv i.282.4; ii.93.18; 133.5; 188.9; 237.5; 300.12; 415.13; iii.26.6; 89.21; Gv 104.12; Bbh 58.14; 389.15.

pūrve-vāsa = prec.: pūrve-vāsa-nivāsena Mv iii.148.8 = 185.6, *because of birth in a previous state of existence.*

pūla, m. pl. (pūlān), MSV iv.107.12, or **pūlā**, n. sg. f., Mvy 8967, *buskin(s)*; so Tib., both times, lham sgro(g) gu can; Chin. *laced boots.* Cf. **maṇḍa-pūla.**

pṛṅga, m. (n. sg. °gaḥ, v.l. bṛ°; Mironov pṛṅgaḥ, vv. ll. pridgu, priṅgā, vradgāḥ), *figured silk* (so Tib., dar ri mo can): Mvy 5866. Reported but not defined in Schmidt, Nachträge, from comm. to Harṣac.

-pṛccha (= Skt. pṛcchaka), ifc., see **kṣemaṇīya-pṛccha.**

pṛcchati, (1) *requests, asks* something to be done by another: bhagavato vandanaṃ °ti Mv i.307.7, *she asks* (us to make) *a salutation of the Lord*; (2) in mg. of Skt. āpṛcchati, *says goodby*: mātāpitṝṇāṃ mama vacanena pṛcche (2 sg. opt.) LV 231.17 (vs), *say goodby to my parents in my name.*

pṛcchā-paripṛcchikā (or °**akā**; cf. Skt. pṛcchā, BHS **paripṛcchā**), *repeated questioning*: °chikāya or °chakāye (instr. sg.; so mss.) Mv iii.391.5 (prose).

pṛcchika, = Skt. pṛcchaka, *one who asks*, see s.v. **sukharātrī.**

-pṛthakkārakam, adv., in siktha-pṛ°, *separating the lumps of rice*: na ... (we will eat) Mvy 8582; corresp. to Pali sitthāvakārakaṃ, see CPD s.v. avakārakaṃ (*'scattering about'*). This is supported in sense by Prāt 534.1 which is printed śista-vikiraṃ, with note: 'Corr. śiṣṭa'; Chin. *sans jeter des morceaux*; it seems clear that either the MIndic (Pali) sittha, or a Sktized (perh. hyper-Skt.) form of it, was intended; Chin. suggests this rather than śiṣṭa, *what is left.*

pṛthagudāhāra, m., *separate utterance*: ŚsP 567.6; 615.7 (here text °haro), see s.v. **udāhāra.**

pṛthagjana-kalyāṇaka, m. (= Pali putthujjana-), *a good kind of ordinary man*, one striving for religious improvement: śaikṣāṇāṃ °kānāṃ ca Divy 419.17; 429.17; saṃvṛti-saṃghaḥ katamaḥ? sarve °kāḥ MSV iii.117.1.

pṛthagjanatā (= Pali puthujjanatā), *quality of common folk*: sāmante °tāye (gen.) Mv i.102.13 (prose), *near (in association with) vulgarity.*

pṛthagbhavati (cf. ppp. M. puhabbhūya; noun, Skt. pṛthagbhāva; the finite verb not recorded), *is peculiar to* (gen.): in phrase (mahāntaṃ pṛthivīmaṇḍalam abhinirjityādhyāvasatāṃ, or in 58.23 °dhyāsatāṃ, prob. by error, but Skt. adhy-ās and adhy-ā-vas are both used in the sense required) °vanti śilpasthānakarmasthānāni (MSV rājakṛtyāni) Divy 58.23; 100.9; 442.5; MSV ii.74.9.

pṛthita-pṛthita, adj. (prob. hyper-Skt. for AMg. pahiya = Skt. prathita, ppp., partly under influence of Skt. pṛthu etc.), *scattered, spread out* (drops, spots, sc. of water): °tāni (sc. udakāni) Śikṣ 247.16.

Pṛthivī, or **Pṛthvī**, n. of a devakumārikā in the northern quarter: Pṛthivī Padumāvatī Mv iii.309.8 (vs) = Pṛthvī Padmāvatī tathā LV 391.3; note how LV Sanskritizes and then patches the meter! Both without v.l.

pṛthivī-cāla, m. (cf. Skt. bhūmi-cala, and Pali mahā-bhūmicālo, Mahāvaṃsa 17.55), *earthquake*: SP 164.2; Mv ii.30.15; mahāntaḥ °lo abhūṣi Mv ii.300.15. All prose.

Pṛthivīṃdadā, n. of a 'gandharva maid': Kv 5.4.

pṛthivī-parpaṭaka, m. (so read with Index; text °parvaṭaka; Mironov °paryaṭaka, vv.ll. °parv°, °parp°), prob. = **bhūmi-, bhū-p°**, a kind of *edible mushroom*: Mvy 5287 = Tib. sa zhag, lit. *earth-fat (-grease)*, acc. to Das *bitumen* (or *rock-oil, petroleum*); follows pṛthivī-rasa and precedes vanalatā and pṛthivī-maṇḍa.

Pṛthivīpaśyin, Pṛthivīpāla, names of future Buddhas: Mv iii.330.10, 9 respectively.

Pṛthivīvaralocana, n. of a Bodhisattva: Kv 2.1.

Pṛthivīvijaya, n. of a future Buddha: Mv iii.330.10.

Pṛthivyupasaṃkramaṇā, n. of a kiṃnara maid: Kv 6.19.

pṛthu (like Pali puthu = Skt. pṛthak- in pṛthag-jana), *common, ordinary*: pṛthu pratyekarājāno Mv ii.270.10 (prose), contrasted with rājā cakravartī. But pṛthukāyāḥ (one or two words) Mv i.350.10 prob. means *numerous* (so Skt. pṛthu) *classes* (of beings); and so pṛthu(-)tīrthyā(ḥ) Śikṣ 332.9 (vs), *numerous* (rather than *worldly*, Bendall and Rouse 295) *heretics*; in Śikṣ 109.9 (vs) pṛtha (for pṛthak? or read pṛthu, in sense of *numerous*?) kāyasākṣī (see °**kṣin**). In pṛthu-**vaiśāradya** (see this) Mv ii.261.6; 262.7 mg. uncertain; perh. *manifold, inclusive, general confidence*? Contrasts with kāya-, vācā-, and citta-vai°.

pṛthuka, adj. (not recorded in this sense; = Skt. pṛthu, -ka svārthe), *broad*: (paṭe ... trihasta-, text tṛhasta-)-pṛthuke Mmk 311.12 (prose).

Pṛthurāṣṭra, nt., n. of a country (in the south): Gv 182.10.

Pṛthvī, see **Pṛthivī.**

pṛśati (semi-MIndic for spṛś-, based on MIndic phus-, phas-; cf. Weller, Prosa des LV, 25; cf. also Whitney, Roots, s.v. pṛś), *touches*: pṛsiṣyati (for pṛś°, fut.) LV 153.18 (vs); mā ... prākṣur (aor.) LV 379.18, 21; 380.2; mā prākṣīr Divy 443.21 (vs, = MSV i.135.7 sprākṣīr); praṣṭum, inf., Mv ii.427.7; iii.158.5; Divy 519.18; ppp. pṛṣṭāni LV 122.7 (prose; all mss.); pṛṣṭho, read pṛṣṭo, Divy 190.11; vyādhina pṛṣṭā Śikṣ 330.6 (vs), *touched by disease*; gdve., see s.v. **praṣṭavya.**

pṛṣṭa-vācikā (cf. Pali vācikā, *speech*), °kayā (instr.) bhikṣūn samanuyujya MSV ii.145.3, *questioning the monks by words involving the matter asked about*; same 153.7; 156.8.

pṛṣṭha-kaṇṭ(h)aka, see **pṛṣṭhi-k°.**

pṛṣṭhato-mukha, adj., f. °**khī**, *with face turned backwards*: °kha(ḥ) Divy 333.15; °khī Mv ii.102.3.

pṛṣṭhi, °**ī**, f. (or m.? cf. late Skt. pṛṣṭi, pw; BHS mss., in fact, mostly ṭ, not ṭh; = Pali piṭṭhī; for Skt. pṛṣṭha), *back*: °ī MPS 30.5; loc. sg. pṛṣṭhīyam Mv ii.232.13; -pṛṣṭhismin iii.73.3; adv. pṛṣṭhito (= Pali piṭṭhito), *in back*, Mv i.31.3; pṛṣṭhi-vaṃśo LV 260.2 (vs), *backbone*, and see next.

pṛṣṭhi-(pṛṣṭha-, pṛṣṭhī-; mss. sometimes pṛṣṭi-) **-kaṇṭaka**, often spelled °**kaṇṭhaka** (see this) in mss. of Mv, m. or nt. (= Pali piṭṭhi-kaṇṭaka; also piṭṭhī-?), *backbone*: LV 254.13 evaṃ me pṛṣṭhīkaṇṭako 'bhūd; 20 pṛṣṭhikaṇṭakam evāsprākṣam; 256.1 pṛṣṭhīkaṇṭakaḥ; Mv ii.125.16 pṛṣṭhakaṇṭakāni; 127.5 pṛṣṭhikaṇṭakāsthikāni; 128.10 pṛṣṭhikaṇṭakāni; 129.12 evam eva me pṛṣṭhakaṇṭakaṃ (mss., Senart em. °kā) abhūnsuḥ (all passages are prose); pṛṣṭhikaṇṭakam Mv ii.127.10; 128.15; 129.17, see prec. and next.

pṛṣṭhima, once (Mv ii.126.6, prose) °**maka**, adj. (to **pṛṣṭhi** or Skt. pṛṣṭha, § 22.13), *of the back, back-, rear*: °makaṃ (sc. kāyaṃ) Mv ii.126.6, *back* (part of the body), contrasted with purimaṃ kāyaṃ; the LV (similarly Pali MN) parallels (see s.v. **purima** 2) have pṛṣṭhi-kaṇṭakaṃ (or Pali equivalent), and so also (or spelled °ṭhakam) in repetitions Mv ii.127.10; 128.15; 129.17; but pṛṣṭhimaṃ, sc. kāyaṃ, Mv ii.232.15 (vs, same incident); adverbs, °mena (āhatā) Mv ii.455.18, *in the back, behind*; °mena °maṃ samanubaddho Mv ii.255.2, 4; iii.28.2; 53.11, *pursuing ever behind*; °mena °maṃ anugacchati iii.291.7; pṛṣṭhena pṛṣṭhimaṃ samanubaddhā iii.296.9; pṛṣṭhimaṃ (but mss. pṛṣṭiṃ me, or se) āruhitvā Mv ii.479.19, *mounting on* (a person's) *back.*

pṛṣṭhī-kaṇṭaka, see **pṛṣṭhi-k°.**

pṛṣṭhībhavati (cf. parā-, vi-p°, and **avapṛṣṭhīkṛta**; Pali vipiṭṭhi-katvā(na) clearly means *turning one's back on* worldly things, evils, Sn 67, 362, substantially *abandoning*; and Pali piṭṭhito karoti is used in the lit. sense, *turns one's back on*, Jāt. i.71.23), (**1**) in Divy 326.9 pṛṣṭhībhūtaḥ, and in 11 avapṛṣṭhīkṛtaḥ, both seem to have the mg. suggested by Pali vipiṭṭhikatvā(na), above: (*made*) *averse, turned away* (from worldly things); see the passage cited s.v. **Maitrīya.** In Mvy 2590, also, pṛṣṭhībhavati may have this mg., *becomes averse* (followed by **kelāyita,** q.v., in a chapter headed '*synonyms* of **nisṛjā**'); but the two Tib. renderings are not clear; pw 7.359 understands this as belonging to (2); of course pw's assumption that the 'correct reading' is piṣṭī° is wrong; (**2**) *becomes depressed* (= **vipṛṣṭhībhavati,** q.v.), orig. doubtless *turns one's back* as a sign of unhappiness: cittaṃ nāvalīyate na saṃlīyate na pṛṣṭhībhavati AsP 320.17 (prose).

pṛhā (semi-MIndic = Skt. spṛhā), *longing*: Śikṣ 195.8 (vs, from Samādh).

pe (= Pali id.), abbreviation for **peyālam,** q.v.: Śikṣ 53.15; 55.18, etc.

peja, m. (sg. or pl.; MIndic for Skt. peya, Mvy 5701; cf. Pkt. pejja, and see **peyya**), *broth*: pejaḥ Mvy 5702 (Mironov pejāḥ, n. pl., peja in Index; BR cites pejā) = Tib. thug pa, as for peya 5701.

(**peyā,** in the **uddāna** MSV i.66.4, is not the n. of a city like most other words in it, but refers to the peyā of i.68.21 ff.)

peyāla, prob. orig. m., see **cakra-peyāla**; also seemingly nt.; regularly °**laṃ,** prob. acc. adverb, rarely °lena, instr. (see also 2 **piyāla** and **pe**; = Pali peyyālaṃ; presumably MIndic for Skt. paryāya, adverbial acc.), *et cetera*, indicating abbreviation, usually but not always of a passage previously cited in the text, and often but not always with implication that the full text is supposed to be recited: SP 174.6 (only in 2 mss.); LV 247.13 (iti sarvaṃ °laṃ); 349.4; 418.7, 8, 9; Mvy 5435; Mv iii.219.10; 220.2; Śikṣ 6.2; 15.16; Bbh 19.8; 146.13; AsP 87.11; Mmk 94.13; °laṃ vistareṇa kartavyaṃ Mmk 61.16; 107.10; °laṃ yāvat Mv iii.202.11; 203.6; LV 150.15; 161.7; 248.4; 255.16; 397.14; pūrvavad eva peyālaṃ yāvad LV 417.22; 418.1 (but here and in lines 7, 8 read prob. peyālaḥ with best mss.); (note in the same mg., without peyālam, sarvaṃ pūrvavad yāvad LV 417.21; pūrvavad yāvad LV 403.19; 418.4, 5; sarvaṃ pūrvavat LV 409.3; yāvad, alone, LV 403.20; sarvaṃ yāvad 418.3;) instr. peyālena, noted only in evaṃ °lena kartavyam AsP 109.11; 159.9; used where the passage has not occurred before in the text in question, but where presumably its sense is regarded as well-known or obvious, like Eng. *et cetera*, SP 424.8, perhaps with connotation *in short, in a word*; so in LV 295.21 (vs), the opening words of a series of stanzas, peyālam eṣa, *this is the story in brief*; similarly LV 314.21 (prose), beginning a résumé of a prec. series of stanzas, peyālam, evaṃ, *in brief, thus* . . .; in Divy 103.1–2 (prose) read with mss. Triśaṅku-peyālaṃ, that is, *Triśaṅku etc.* (the name that is understood with T. is not found in Divy until 106.24 ff.).

peyya (m.? cf. Pali id., Skt. peya, and **peja**), *beverage*, or *broth* (the latter, Tib. thug pa, given for peyaḥ Mvy 5701): Av i.3.11 (in cpd.).

(**pela,** m., *testicle*: Mvy 4002; so in Skt., Schmidt, Nachträge.)

? **pelalaka,** see **śelālaka.**

? **pelavaka,** m. (mss. pelacaka, palavaka), in Mv ii.161.2, see passage quoted s.v. **anuśrotaṃ.** Senart assumes P. as proper name of a horse; it might as well be a common noun, *horse* (cf. pelin, *horse* acc. to Wilson); but the whole passage, esp. this word, is doubtful and likely to be corrupt.

pelā (**1**) (= Pali pelā, *basket*, also *chest, box*, see **phelā**; = Skt. peḍā, *basket*), *basket*: pelāyāṃ, loc., Mv i.92.4 (vs); pelāya, loc., ii.245.2 (vs), here for carrying flowers; (**2**) a high number (= **pelu, phela,** qq.v.): Gv 106.11.

? **pelāṅka,** m., in akṣi-pe°, acc. to Tib. (mig gi ḥbras bu) *pupil of the eye*: MSV ii.37.2 (corrupt?).

Peliyakṣa (= Pali Piliyakkha), n. of a king of Benares, in the **Śyāmaka** Jātaka: Mv ii.212.15 ff. In 226.1 (vs) Senart reads Peliyaśo; the mss. are clearly corrupt; perh. read Pĕlīyakho, or Pil° (cf. Pali), an adaptation m.c. of a MIndic form of the name.

pelu, m. or f., a high number: peluḥ Mvy 7896, cited from Gv 133.22, same; but in Gv 106.11 **pelā,** q.v., and in Mvy 7767 **phelaḥ,** m.; Tib. phyol yas in both passages of Mvy. Occurs in a long list of stems which rhyme, in one list fems. in ā, in one mascs. in a, in one m. or f. in u.

Paiṅgika (cf. Pali Piṅgiyānī, Piṅgiya), n. of a brahman (māṇava) of Vaiśālī: MPS 11.12.

paiṇḍapātika, m., = **piṇḍa°,** q.v.: Mvy 1131; Dharmas 63; Sādh 541.14; °ka-tva, abstr., Karmav 32.2; 104.14 (note piṇḍa° in 105.5). Cf. also next.

? **paiṇḍilika,** m., read prob. **paiṇḍinyika,** *mendicant, monk*, like prec. and **piṇḍapātika** a complimentary term: °ko 'smi saṃvṛtaḥ Śikṣ 150.18. I derive °nyika from Skt. Lex. (Trik., which has many Buddhist words) paiṇḍinya, nt., *mendicant monk's life*, which BR derive from piṇḍin (cited with appropriate mg. only from Wilson). Pali and AMg. have a word piṇḍola(-ka, -ga), *mendicant monk*, but this cannot be used to interpret the Śikṣ text form, unless by em.

? **paitṛkya,** adj. (cf. Skt. paitṛka), *paternal*: °kyehi (but v.l. °kehi) Mv ii.424.12 (prose).

pailottaka, or (var. in Index) °ttika (so Mironov), nt., Mvy 9445, acc. to Tib. rdol ba, *leak*; Chin. *leak-instrument*; Jap. identifies with Pali pilotikā, see **pilotika** (despite double tt). Follows varatram, app. = more usual Skt. varatrā, *strap*. Could it possibly mean *stopper against leaks*, made of *rags*? Improbable. Cf. next.

pailottika, adj. (see also prec.), *thin* (of a blanket): MSV ii.90.7 °kena vā dviputena, in contrast with ghanena vā ekapuṭena; Tib. seṅ bzhig na, *thin*; *made of thin cloth* (of a robe), or *pieced out by adding such a cloth*, ib. 160.15; 161.2; here Tib. gso maḥi seṅ ras (same for **plotikā,** q.v.).

paiśunika, adj. (= Pali pesunika, not °ṇika with PTSD; to piśuna plus -ika), *slanderous*: after **mṛṣāvādika** or °vādin, Divy 301.23; Gv 159.14; 352.18 (all prose). Cf. next.

paiśunya, adj. (Skt. id. and Pali pesuniya, °ṇiya, pesuñña, only as nt. abstr.), = prec.: mṛṣāvādinām °nyānāṃ Gv 228.14 (prose).

poñchate (= **puñchati,** q.v.; semi-MIndic from Skt. proñch-, see BR s.v. uñch), *wipes off, cleans*: °chasva Divy 491.7, °chitum (inf.) 7, °chate 12.

poṭṭalikā (= AMg. °liā; Skt. °laka, and Lex. °la, °lī), *package, bundle*: Mv ii.90.12 (°kā; Senart em. poṭalikā); Sādh 366.2 (°kāṃ kṛtvā).

-poṇa, nt. (for Skt. -pavana, in danta-p°; = Pali -poṇa, in danta-p°, *tooth-cleanser, toothpick*, = dantakaṭṭha, cf. Miln. 15.7 with 9 and 10), in daṇḍa-poṇam, *filter with a stick* (i. e. handle): Mvy 9026 = Tib. sbyaṅs tshags, *cleaning-filter*; Chin. *filter*; Jap. translates daṇḍa, *handle*.

-poṇika, m. (perh. cf Deśīn. 6.28 poṇia = pūrṇa, 6.61 poṇiā = sūtrabhṛt tarkuḥ?), *receptacle, container* (Tib. snod), in Mvy 8950 pātra-poṇikaḥ, *bowl-carrier*. Under Tib. snod Das cites Skt. yonikā! corr. for poṇika? But MSV iv.67.15 reads pātra-yoṇikā (fem., but ṇ, not n); Tib. snod bzhag. Same mg. is given for Mvy 8951 pātra-sthapikaḥ (Index °sthavikaḥ); see **sthavika.**

Potana, nt. (= Pali id.), n. of a city, capital of the Aśmakas or (in Mv) Asmakas: read Potanaṃ (ms. cited as yo°) Mv iii.208.17.

potalaka, m., (**1**) also °**ikā,** f. (cf. Skt. pota, potaka, and go-potālikā in BR 7.1740; also AMg. poāla, poyāla), *young* (of an animal): nāga-°ka(ḥ) Av ii.127.9, 10; also kumbhāṇḍa-potalako vā °likā vā, Āṭānāṭika Sūtra, Hoffmann, Kl. Skt. Texte 5, 65.5–6; (2) n. of a mountain (also **Pautalaka,** q.v.): Mvy 4154; Avalokiteśvara dwells on it, Gv 208.8; (3) n. of a maharṣi: Māy 256.25.

potāra, m. or nt., *boat*: loc. °re Gv 499.26; 500.3 (here misprinted °ro). Cf. Skt. pota, id.; see § 22.11.

pontī, so with pw 7.359, rather than text potrī (= Pali pontī, or °ti, see PTSD, which wrongly questions the form; Pali and BHS confirm each other), *cloth*: Divy 256.26 (ātmīyām) evopariprāvaraṇa-pontīm (mss. cited as yontīm, yontim, yāntīm, ed. em. potrīm) alabhamānas... (below, line 28, the same article is referred to as tam evātmīyaṃ prāvaraṇaṃ); the context indicates that it was a *headcloth* (*turban*?) in this case; in Pali it is a garment worn by a Buddhist nun.

popphala, nt. (= M. id., Hem.; Skt. pūgaphala), *betel-nut*: Mvy 5804 (v.l. **pohala,** q.v.); the next entry is pūgaphalam, 5805.

poma, nt., a high number: Mvy 7837 = Tib. zam zim; cited from Gv 133.2 which reads **yāma**; in Gv 105.21 **anaupamya.** Also = **hūma,** q.v.

poṣa, m. (= Pali posa, which is said by PTSD and Geiger 30.3 to be used only in vss; doubtless somehow derived from Skt. puruṣa, but Geiger's theory is not compelling), *person, individuality, soul, spirit*; occurs often in prose of various texts, regularly associated with near-synonyms like jīva, jantu, pudgala (puṃgala), and even with puruṣa itself, which clearly had come to be felt as a different word (if it was derived from the same original): in Mvy 4672 defined by Tib. gso ba, *nourishment*, as if from root puṣ-, tho the context proves it means the same as puruṣa, which is the next word; puruṣa also adjoins it (along with other words of like mg.) in Śikṣ 236.15; Laṅk 63.15, et alibi; ŚsP 120.12 (puruṣa in parallel phrase 13), et alibi; otherwise with similar words, Śikṣ 199.8; KP 125.6; 142.8 (in these two miswritten pauṣa); Dbh 39.21; MSV ii.76.15; **niṣpoṣa,** *without personality*, along with nirjīva, niṣpudgala, etc., KP 97.2; Dbh 43.13; Vaj 38.5.

poṣadha, m. (on gender and forms see **upoṣadha**; cf. the following items) = upoṣadha, 'sabbath': Mvy 8676 °dhaḥ; 9101 °dha-vastu; 9287 °dha-sthāpanam; 9403 chanda-poṣadham, acc., *p. of profound desire* or *faith* (so Tib., Chin., Jap.); poṣadha-sthāpana-vastu, title of a section of MSV, MSV iii.107.1; poṣadha-parigṛhītāyā mātuḥ LV 25.21; 55.2; gṛhṇāmi... aṣṭāṅga-poṣadham LV 41.18, see **aṣṭāṅga** (1); also aṣṭāṅga-poṣadhe Gv 521.5; aṣṭāṅga-samanvāgataṃ (so Pali, aṭṭhaṅgasamannāgata) poṣadhaṃ gṛhṇāmaḥ Karmav 52.7; tantuvāyasya poṣadhaṃ dattvā Mmk 58.11; on Divy 116.21 and 118.27, see upoṣadha; Jm 15.5; 28.14; 52.18 etc.; poṣadhāmukha, nt., with or sc. vāstu, (a site) *fitting for the poṣadha*, MSV iv.81.8 ff.; mss. at Mv iii.97.20 and 98.2, see upoṣadha; tadaho-poṣadhe Mv i.255.5 (= Pali tad-ah-uposathe; Pali also tadahe and tadahū, *on that day*), adv. phrase, *on that day* (*which was*) *a 'sabbath'*; see **poṣadheya.** (Senart prints as two separate words, perh. rightly.)

poṣadhika, f. °ikā (= **upoṣ°, poṣadhin,** qq.v.), *keeping* (*one who keeps*) *the 'sabbath'*: Mvy 8726 °kaḥ; Mmk 76.26 °kena vā apoṣadhikena vā; 322.20; f. poṣadhikāye Mv i.207.9 (mss. °kāyāṃ) = ii.11.20 (mss. upoṣa°, unmetr.; vs).

poṣadhin (cf. Pali uposathin, and prec.), *keeping the 'sabbath'*: LV 76.3 °dhī, nom. sg.

poṣadheya, adj. (from **poṣadha**), *of the 'sabbath'*: only in adv. phrases, tad-aho poṣadheyaṃ Mv iii.210.12, *on that day, a 'sabbath' day*; tad eva (sc. aho) poṣadheyaṃ, id., LV 14.8. Cf. tadaho-poṣadhe, adv., s.v. poṣadha; perhaps °dheyaṃ was based on that form.

posatha, m. or nt. (= Pali id., BHS **poṣadha, upoṣadha**), *'sabbath'*: Ud xvi.15 śuddhasya posathaṃ (so oldest ms., later ms. posathaḥ; nom. sg.) sadā.

pohala, nt., var. (also in Mironov) for **popphala,** q.v.: Mvy 5804. Cited from a Pkt. Lex. by Sheth s.v.

pauṇḍarīka, (1) (Skt. as adj.; AMg. poṇḍarīya, id., = pu°), *white lotus*: Gv 136.8 (at end of a Bhvr. cpd.); (2) n. of a former Buddha: Mv iii.236.16 f. (v.l. Puṇḍ°).

Pauṇḍra, n. of a serpent (nāga) king: Megh 306.3.

Pautalaka = **Po°,** n. of a mountain: Māy 253.27 (prose).

paudgalika, adj. (Pali puggalika; to pudgala plus -ika; in different sense recorded pw 4.302), *individual, personal*, always contrasted with **sāṃghika,** sometimes also **staupika**: sāṃghikāḥ puṣpavṛkṣāḥ...°ka-paribhogena bhuktāḥ Divy 342.19, ... *were put to individual, personal* (not *selfish* with Index) *use*; staupikaṃ sāṃghikaṃ... vittaṃ °kaṃ ca RP 29.8; similarly Śikṣ 63.14; Bbh 166.26; MSV ii.123.19.

paunarbhavika, f. **°kā** or **°kī,** adj. (also **punar°,** q.v.; = Pali ponobbhavika; to Skt. punar-bhava plus -ika), *pertaining to rebirth*: of tṛṣṇā, °kā Mv iii.332.6; °kī LV 417.8; Laṅk 138.11–12; 162.15; of masc. nouns, (... paridāghā...) °kā(ḥ) Mv iii.338.4, 9 (in both v.l. punar°), 11; (akuśalair dharmaiḥ)...°kaiḥ Av ii.107.3; Bbh 182.27.

paura, only f. °rī, with or sc. vāc(ā) (cf. Skt. paura, subst.; = Pali porī, with vācā; PTSD wrongly gives stem as porin), *urbane, courteous, elegant* (speech): pauriye vācāye (instr.) Mv iii.322.2; (vāg...) na paurī Śikṣ 127.5 (wrongly transl. Bendall and Rouse); with vāc, Dbh 24.13; Bbh 65.11; sc. vāc, in cpd. paurī-sāṃkathyam Mvy 2808.

paurāṇaka, adj. (= Pali por°; Skt. only °ṇa and °ṇika), *previous, former, ancient, of olden time*: °ṇakaṃ LV 379.5 (Lefm. with all mss.; Calc. °ṇikaṃ); Mv ii.492.10; iii.25.5 (here Senart with v.l. °ṇika).

pauruṣa (= Pali porisa; cf. next three), *servant, henchman, attendant*: yama-°ṣāḥ Mv i.12.5 (vs); pau- could be m.c. for pu-.

pauruṣaka = prec.: nṛpa-pauruṣakebhyo Divy 447.24 (vs, could be m.c.).

pauruṣeya (not recorded in these senses; cf. prec. and next), (1) m., *servant, laborer*: Divy 86.13; 153.28; 168.28; 274.15, etc.; Av i.189.8; 315.9, etc.; Mvy 3833; often in cpd. dāsī-dāsa-karmakara-pauruṣeya (the other words precede Mvy 3833), either alone as dvandva subst., or in Bhvr. preceded by prabhūta-, bahu-, or the like: SP 102.2; LV 24.20; Mv i.36.5; 198.8; ii.2.4; 168.13; 420.18; iii.56.9; 177.16; 377.11; Divy 229.9; Kv 35.24; Dbh 18.28; Bbh 119.11; putra-dāra-dāsī-dāsa-pauruṣeya Bbh 119.22; (2) m., specially, pañca pauruṣeyān (acc. pl.), *the five* (*kinds of*) *members of a ship's crew*: Av i.200.5; ii.61.9; but in both places only four are named, viz. **āhāra, nāvika, kaivarta,** karṇadhāra; in Mvy 3850–55 six are named, **nāvika, āhāraka, nirhāraka, karṇadhāraka, raṇadhara, kaivarta**; (3) adj., or subst. (nt.?) ifc. Bhvr. (cf. Pali porisiya, AMg. porisīya, Ratnach. 5.74, adj. ifc., *as high as a man*), in sapta-, ṣaṭ-, etc., -pauruṣeyaṃ, *of seven* (*six*, etc.) *times the height of a man*: Mv ii.313.6 ff.; follows tālamātraṃ, in descending order, implying that one **tāla,** q.v., = 8 pauruṣeya (if this is to be understood as a noun; the noun might be pauruṣa, so used in Skt.; see **pauruṣya**; in the Mv passage, 313.8–9, a single man's height is expressed by puruṣa-mātram).

pauruṣya (1) (nt.; Pali porisa is used in this sense; cf. **pauruṣa**), *service, position* or *activity of a servant*: -rāja-pauruṣyādi Bbh 195.3, *the position of a king's henchman*; (2) ifc., perh. adj. (= Pali porisiya), or subst. in Bhvr. cpd. (na) sādhika-pauruṣyaṃ (vṛkṣam adhirokṣyāmaḥ) Mvy 8629, (a tree) *above a man's height*; but Mironov °pauruṣam, and so Prāt 537.18, implying the noun pauruṣa, *man's height*, so used in Skt. Instead of na sādh° (Mvy prints nasādh° as one word) Mironov nāsādh°, erroneously; cf. Pali MN i.74.12 sādhika-porisā, *of more than a man's height*; this is confirmed by Tib. mi gaṅ tsam las mthor, *to the height of an average man.* For na sādhika Prāt (l.c.) has a lacuna, which Finot fills by the erroneous nāsādhikaṃ from Minayeff's Mvy. Cf. prec. (3).

(**paurvaka**, adj., f. °**ikā**, once in Rām., BR 7.1773, defined *von den Vorgängern stammend, ererbt*, but scarcely to be differentiated from this; *of former times*, = the more usual Skt. pūrva and paurvika, f. °kī: °kaṃ caryāpraṇidhānaṃ SP 64.13; °vikayā daridracintayā 108.6; °akaiḥ ... jinendraiḥ LV 285.12 (vs); Divy 245.28; °kaḥ puṇyaskandhaḥ Vaj 35.7; all except LV prose.)

paurvajanmika, adj. (Skt. pūrva-janman plus -ika), *of former births*: °kāny aśubhāni karmāṇi Vaj 34.17, 18; but Kashgar rec., Pargiter ap. Hoernle MR 187.1, 2 pūrvajanmikāny. Neither form has been noted elsewhere.

paurvāntika, fem. °**kī** (= **pūrv**°, q.v.), *of the past*: Dbh 51.2 (cited as pūrv° Śikṣ 228.1).

Pauṣpaka, nt. adj. (?) or subst. in apposition (= Skt. Puṣpaka, or adj. from this), with vimāna or yāna, n. of Rāvaṇa's car: Laṅk 3.2; 4.12 (in 6.16 Puṣpaka but v.l. Pau°).

prakaca, adj., *with dishevelled hair* (so Chin.): Mvy 9198 (follows **utkaca**, q.v.); Bhīk 28b.4 tam (bhikṣum) utkacaprakacaṃ saṃghe roma pātayantaṃ ... evaṃ vaden mā tvam ārya utkacaprakacaḥ saṃghe roma pātaya ... ; modulation of MSV iii.7.14 ff., et alibi, where penalized monks, asking release from **tarjanīya**, utkacaprakacāḥ saṃghe roma pātayanti (cf. **romapāta**; all this indicates humble penitence) ... osāraṇāṃ yācante.

Prakaraṇapāda, m., n. of a work: Mvy 1420.

prakaraṇikā (? partly conjectured; to Skt. °ṇa), *subject of study* (Tib. bstud par bya): °kayā MPS 41.4.

(**prakarṣin**, adj., *distinguished, excellent*: Jm 100.12; once in late Skt., Schmidt, Nachträge.)

prakānta, ppp. (semi-MIndic for Skt. prakrānta), *set forth, departed*: LV 58.2; so nearly all mss.; vs, but metr. indifferent.

prakāra? in SP 146.5 (vs) puṣpaiḥ (so all mss., KN em. puṣpa-, kept by WT without note) prakāraiḥ samalaṃkṛtaṃ ca; acc. to Tib. *adorned with many flowers* (me tog maṅ pos). On the face of the reading of the mss. and the Tib. rendering, prakāra should be an adj., *many*; it is otherwise known only as a noun, *kind, sort.* KN's em. hardly helps; *with kinds of flowers* could not, so far as I know, serve as a substitute for *with many kinds ...*; for this we should expect bahu-, nānā-, or the like, modifying prakāra. I have thought of reading pravāraiḥ, taking it as = pravaraiḥ, *excellent*, with ā for a m.c.; but Tib. does not support this.

prakāśa, nt. for regular m., *light*: yad andhakāraṃ tat prakāśam iti saṃjānīṣe, yac ca prakāśaṃ tad andhakāram iti saṃjānīṣe SP 135.4 f. (prose). Perh. attracted to gender of andhakāra.

Prakāśadharma, n. of a former Buddha: Mv i.141.6.

prakāśanā (Skt. °na, nt.), *illumination, explanation*: (dharmasya) Mv i.42.10 = 53.5 = 337.1 (vs; in the last text corrupt, printed as prose by Senart); as one of the ten dharma-caryā, Mvy 909.

Prakāśavarṇa, n. of a former Buddha: Mv i.137.14.

prakīrṇa-lapi-tā (to *prakīrṇa-lapin, cf. AMg. pakiṇṇa-vāi = °vādin), *incoherent talking*: Bbh 42.8.

prakusumita, adj. (pra, intensive, plus Skt. kusumita), *in full flower*: Mv ii.203.2, 6.

-prakṛta, adj.-ppp. ifc. (= Pali -pakata), ... *by nature*, in īrṣyā-prakṛta, *jealous* (= Pali issā-pakata): °tena Mv i.36.12; 44.13; °taiḥ Av i.199.4. For another mg. of prakṛta (= Skt.) see s.v. 2 **Prakṛti**.

1 prakṛti, f., once in Mv nt. in form (= Pali id., Pv ii.8.9 saṃghe ārocayi pakatiṃ, *told the occurrence to the assembly of monks*; comm. 110.5 pakati-pavuttiṃ, doubtless *the above-mentioned occurrence*, the one here treated; not in this mg. in Skt., but doubtless connected with the use of Skt. prakṛta mentioned s.v. 2 **Prakṛti**), (*above-mentioned*) *matter, occurrence, circumstance, story*; usually object of a form of ārocayati: kumārasyaināṃ prakṛtim ārocayanti sma LV 137.11, *told the prince this circumstance*; bodhisattvāya tāṃ prakṛtim ārocayati sma 143.18; similarly 200.16; 386.6; 407.8; teṣāṃ bhagavāṃ bhikṣūṇāṃ etāṃ prakṛtiṃ vistareṇārocayati Mv i.246.11; tasya imāṃ prakṛtiṃ ārocehi 287.10; also with other verbs, etāṃ prakṛtiṃ śrutvā LV 157.13, *having heard this circumstance*; (tāṃ) prakṛtim ācikṣati (the verb is an em., supported by the next) Mv i.244.6; as if nt., tehi taṃ prakṛtiṃ (n. sg.) sarvam (Senart em. -aṃ) ācikṣitaṃ Mv i.355.2. See also s.v. **caryā** for prakṛti-caryā (here prakṛti in another, normal Skt. mg.). [Senart reads, in part with mss. of Mv, prakṛtyaiva for pratikṛ°, see **pratikṛtya**.]

2 Prakṛti, n. of an outcaste girl (mātaṅga-dārikā): Mvy 3665; Divy 611.6 ff.; also of a previous incarnation of the same person, when she was a brahman's daughter, Divy 620.22 ff. Acc. to Senart, i.xliv infra, also n. of another girl, who plays a role in the story of **Megha**; but I believe this is an error. The girl is introduced but not named Mv i.232.13; she is then referred to as prakṛti (for °tī) māṇavikā 232.16, and, in oblique forms, °tiye °vikāye 233.14; 238.3; there is no indication that these passages state her name, and I believe they contain the Skt. adj. (ppp.) prakṛta, *above-mentioned* (BR 2.95), in fem. form (°tī, § 11.3).

prakṛtisthaka, m. (Skt. °stha plus -ka), *one who is in normal condition*, esp. (a monk) *in good standing*, opp. to utkṣiptaka, *one suspended*: MSV ii.113.16 ff.; opp. to faulty monks, iii.93.9.

Prakṛtīśarīraśiribhadra, n. of a Buddha: Gv 285.24 (vs); m.c. for Prakṛti ... śrī ...

prakrāmaṇī, n. of a kind of magic: Divy 636.27.

prakṣeḍā, °**ḍita** (semi-MIndic for Skt. prakṣveḍ°), *shout*: °ḍā (in °ḍoccair-) Av i.48.9 (ms., Speyer em. °kṣve°; in 49.6 he reads °kṣve° without report of variant); °ḍita LV 151.9; 153.4; 155.7, 21; 226.17; 306.3 (Weller 27 would read °kṣve° everywhere); cf. § 2.17.

prakṣepa-lipi, a kind of script: LV 126.6; see s.v. utkṣepa-lipi.

prakṣveḍana, nt. (to next), *shout*: Mvy 2784 = Tib. bśuṅ ba (also spyugs pa, which I do not understand in this situation; the context clearly proves that some sort of noise is meant). Cf. **prakṣeḍā**, °**ḍita**.

prakṣveḍayati (cf. prec.), *shouts*: mahāśabda(m) °yantaḥ MPS 31.8.

prakharati, pres. pple. °rantaḥ (semi-MIndic for Skt. pra-kṣarati), *flows forth*; perh. to be read for both edd. **prākh**°, q.v.: SP 126.8 (vs).

prakhalati (semi-MIndic for Skt. praskhalati, cf. Pali pakkhalati), *staggers*: °lamānair gātraiḥ Mv ii.151.3, and read so (avaṣṭabhya pra° gā°) above in 1, where corrupt mss. are not emended in text.

prakhyālana (nt.); semi-MIndic or false hyper-Skt. (based on derivative of Pali pakkhāleti) = Skt. prakṣālana, *washing*: āsanapādaprakhyālanakarma Śikṣ 153.21.

pragalbhāyate, see **apraga**°.

praguṇa, adj. (seems not used in Skt. in this mg.; = Pali paguṇa), *skilled, familiar, versed*: nirayāgnicittapraguṇāḥ (so!) bhavanti Śikṣ 184.7 (prose; so read for °guṇṇāḥ, see note 1 in ed. for Tib., supporting this).

pragṛhīta, (ppp.) adj. (= Pali paggahīta, °hita, see Childers), *high, lofty*, synonym of ucca, which is usually bracketed with it: (gorathakān ...) uccān °tān SP 75.6; -caityam ... uccaṃ °taṃ 231.9; of vihārāḥ 339.1 (without ucca); prāsādāṃ (acc. pl.) ... uccāṃ mahantāṃ pragṛhītāṃ Mv ii.117.13; in Divy (always with parallel ucca)

7.13 (nagaram); of mountains, (mahā-)parvata, 102.26; 107.27; 113.8.

pragṛhṇāti (not in this mg. in Skt.; = Pali paggaṇhāti, used with cittaṃ as object), *exercises, activates* (the mind): cittaṃ °ṇāti Mvy 964 (follows vīryam ārabhate); pragrahakāle (see **pragraha**) cittaṃ °ṇāti Bbh 205.16.

praggharati, see **pragharati**.

pragraha (m.? = Pali paggaha), *exertion, energetic activity*: Bbh 205.16 (see **pragṛhṇāti**; contrasted with śamatha-kāle, prec. line).

pragrahaṇa (nt.?), *seizure, convulsion*, as caused by famine: °ṇe Divy 471.4 (see s.v. **apatāna**).

pragharati (praggh°? below; see **gharati**; Pali paggharati, which because of the double ggh is customarily associated with Skt. kṣar-, Geiger 56.2; even Skt., and still more BHS, has forms which at least look as if they came from a root ghṛ-, ghar-, see Wh. Roots and BR; cf. also **parighareti**), *flows forth*: °ti Mvy 6967 (here v.l. praggharati, and so Mironov; the only trace in BHS tradition of the double ggh); Divy 57.21; 409.1; Śikṣ 249.7; Av i.202.13; Karmav 66.4. See also **prākharati** (**pra°**?). It may be, perhaps, that the BHS forms of ghar- (not in Pali) originated as simplex back-formations from MIndic paggharati, and that pragharati (instead of praggh°) was influenced by gharati. How are the Skt. forms to be interpreted? Uhlenbeck connects them with ghṛta, *ghee*.

pragharā, a high number: Mmk 343.24, 25 (= 10 mahāsāgara; see **gharā**).

praghātana (to next), dat. °tanāya, quasi-infin., Divy 531.10 (after praghātyate 531.9, see next): sā ca tasyāḥ °tanāya . . . avasthitā, *she set about to kill her* (or, *to have her killed*).

praghātayati (caus. to Skt. prahanti, but seems nowhere recorded), *causes to be killed* (by another), so clearly pass. praghātyate Mv i.181.3; possibly also in Divy 10.2 praghātya (ger.), 9 °tayasi, 14 °tita, ppp. (of a butcher or meat-dealer, perhaps *having killed*, but perhaps *killing*, etc.); in Divy 376.21 praghātita, *killed*, seemingly not caus., and prob. so praghātayitvā 530.13; praghātyate 531.9 (but this last perh. caus., *is caused to be killed*); MSV i.5.2 °tayati. Cf. prec.

Pracaṇḍā (cf. Skt. id., *eine Form oder Śakti der Durgā*, BR), n. of a yoginī: Sādh 427.3.

pracala (m.?), *setting out*; in °la-parivarta, title of LV Chap. 5: LV 54.17 (colophon), *chapter of departure* (sc. of the Bodhisattva from the Tuṣita heaven to earth).

pracalāyati, °te (= Pali pacalāyati; in Skt. only ppp. °yita and n. act. °yana recorded), *nods* (the head, while sleeping sitting up): °yataḥ Jm 233.8, and °yamānayā Gv 405.9, both pres. pples.

(**pracāra** [m.; cf. Skt. id.], in uncertain mg., Laṅk 13.15 [bhagavān . . . rāvaṇasyaiva yoga-]-gati-pracāram anuvicintayamānaḥ, *meditating on Rāvaṇa's own conduct in the way of discipline* [? or, *on the appearance of the way of discipline to R.*?]. Otherwise Suzuki.)

pracāraṇā, *going about, behavior* (with unfavorable implication): Av ii.136.7 °ṇāyāṃ vartamānāyāṃ, *while his* (worldly) *behavior* (just alluded to) *continued* (he was rebuked by his monk-superior). Feer, *au moment de l'exercice*; which seems in every way improbable.

pracārika, m. or nt., **°kā**, f., in pāda-pra°, *journey on foot*: Mmk 694.3–4, ūṣmāyamāne pādapracārikaṃ pañcayojanaśatāni gacchati, sarve cāsya pādapracārikā vaśyā bhavanti, *if it steams*, (it augurs that) *he is going a journey of* 500 *yojanas on foot, and all foot-journeys come under his control*; but the mg. in the next two is obscure to me: ūṣmāyamāne (as above!) pādapracārikāṃ (so!) pañcavarṣasahasrāyur bhavati Mmk 713.17, and: pādapracārike (! loc. sg.?) saptavarṣasahasrāṇi jīvati 718.8–9; in both of these it seems that omens of very long life are inferred, in the first depending on *steaming* of the offering; the word pādapra° is obscure in application; perhaps read °rikāyāṃ for °rikāṃ in 713.17, and render both words *in case of* (his making) *a foot-journey*?

pracārita (nt.; orig. ppp., cf. Pali pacāreti, *goes about in, frequents*; so, *parts frequented, dwelt in*?), *town*, or perhaps *region* (about a town): aham api tatra (sc. **Rauruka-**) pracārite gamiṣyāmi Divy 563.28; ahaṃ pracāritaṃ Raurukaṃ gamiṣyāmi 564.5. (One ms. out of four pravārita, both times.)

-pracālaka, (**1**) °kam, adv. (= Pali -ppacālakam, with kāya-, bāhu-, sīsa-, Vin. ii.213.22 f.; iv.188.4, 17, 28), *with shaking* (motion) *of* (body, arms, head): na kāya-, bāhu-, śīrṣa-p° Mvy 8550–2; (**2**) adj., *shaking, moving* (various parts of the body); in passage corresponding to Pali and Mvy above: Prāt 531.7 ff. na bāhupracālakā antargṛhaṃ pravekṣyāmaḥ (°gṛhe niṣatsyāmaḥ), and so with aṃsa-, śīrṣa-, kāya-, for bāhu-; this form is intended by the Stein ms. fragments publ. La Vallée Poussin, JRAS 1913, 844.14 ff., where text na bāhupracālakāntargṛhaṃ etc. (like Prāt, also with aṃsa-, śīrṣa-, kāya-).

? **pracoḍaka**, see **praccopaka**.

praccaya (semi-MIndic for **pratyaya**, q.v., = Pali paccaya), in bhojana-gilānapraccayam ṛṣiyogyaṃ Mv i.117.7 (vs); g(i)lānapratyaya (bhaiṣajya) is the fourth **pariṣkāra** (q.v.) for a monk. It should be noted that the meter proves that paccaya was pronounced.

? **praccopaka**, m. pl., v.l. **pracoḍaka**, Mv iii.442.17, see **pradhvopaka**.

-pracchandika-tā, *desirous-ness, eager-ness*, in tīvrapracchandikatayā bodhisattvamārgaṃ paryeṣante Gv 492.26, *with ardent eagerness* . . .; cf. Pali tibba-chanda. No *pracchanda, *eager desire*, seems to be recorded anywhere, but it seems implied as an intensive to Skt. chanda, underlying this adjective.

pracchanna-bhartṛ (cf. AMg., acc. to Sheth, pacchaṇṇa-pai, id.), *'secret husband'* = (a woman's) *paramour*: °tā Karmav 73.10.

pracchāyā (= Pali pa°), *shady place*: MPS 5.3.

prachoḍayati, *rears aloft* (its body, śarīraṃ), said of the horse **Vālāha**: °ḍayitvā, ger., Kv 55.16; 56.19; °ḍayati 58.7, 8; °ḍayāmi 58.12. The corresp. expression is atyunnamayati in Divy (120.5), unnāmeti in Mv (iii.75.17); the Pali Jāt. (196) seems to lack a correspondent.

[**prajanīyām**, 1 sg. opt., in Śikṣ 283.10 (sarvasattvānām . . .) svacittacaritāni pra°; read instead prajānīyām, *of all creatures may I learn to know the own thoughts and conduct*; cf. line 9 (ekaikasyāpi) sattvasya cittacaritaṃ jānīyām. Bendall and Rouse, 259, interpret as if from pra-jana(ya)ti, *produce*; this is most implausible on formal (linguistic) as well as philological grounds; it assumes an unbelievable opt. of a thematic verb which does not exist in Skt. (only pass. prajāyate, °ti) or Pali.]

prajahana (nt.; n. act. to prajahati = Skt. °hāti with -ana), *riddance, the getting rid*: sarvasattvakleśaprajahanena Gv 356.3.

Prajāgu, n. of a nāga: °guś ca Mahāsamāj., Waldschmidt, Kl. Skt. Texte 4, 177.4. The Pali version has Pāyāgā, n. pl.

-prajāna-tā (from prajāna = Skt. prajānant, *knowing*, pres. pple., §§ 18.52 ff., plus -tā), in dharma-°tāyai, (for) *state of knowing* (the dharma): LV 34.3–4 (prose; no v.l.; both edd.).

prajānāti, °nīte (app. not recorded in Skt. or MIndic in this mg.), *claims, makes profession*: with predicate nom., anācāryo bhagavāṃ Gautamo prajānāsi Mv iii.326.9–10, *you profess to be untaught*?, and similarly 13–14, 17–18; in the corresp. passage LV 405.22 and 406.4 pratijānīṣe (in 405.22 v.l. pra-jā°), which is more normal Skt.; also with acc. (? gen.) of the thing claimed, mātṛgrāmo 'saṃvidyamānaguṇo 'pi guṇān (so prob. read with v.l. for Lefm. with best mss. guṇānām) ātmani prajānīte LV

141.9, *womenfolk, even when no virtues are found, profess* (claim) *virtues in themselves*; the meaning is certain (wrongly Foucaux); some (inferior) mss. prati-jā°; Calc. guṇān.

Prajāpati, m. (**1**) n. of one of the 16 devaputra who guard the bodhimaṇḍa: LV 277.12; (**2**) n. of a brahman, father of the Buddha Viraja: Laṅk 364.13; (**3**) n. of a yakṣa: Māy 236.26. (For **prajāpati**, f., see °**tī**.)

Prajāpatinivāsinī, n. of a 'gandharva maid': Kv 5.10.

prajāpatī, °**ti**, °**vatī**, f. (= Pali pajāpatī; believed to be hyper-Skt. for prajāvatī, which occurs once in Divy), *consort, wife*: (of a king, as Kuśa), °pati, voc., Mv ii.484.7, 10; iii.17.8 (so with one ms., v.l. °tiḥ, Senart em.; his note is wrong); 19.21; °tiṃ, acc. (Senart em. °tīṃ) iii.9.2; °tyāḥ Divy 2.2 (of a gṛhapati); 98.21; Av i.14.7 etc.; 277.9; °tī, nom., Av i.138.2; prajāvatīṃ, acc., Divy 620.10; °pati-putra-duhitṛ-(cpd.) AsP 241.9.

prajñapayati, °**te**, or °**peti** (in all mgs. = **prajñāpayati**, q.v., but commoner than it in BHS, tho not recorded in Pali; see the following items), (**1**) *makes known, declares, teaches*: kiṃ bhagavāṃ (mss.) prajñapento prajñapeti Mv iii.65.8, *what does the Lord expound* (*teach*) *when he is expounding*?, answered in 10, catvāro ... dhātavaḥ prajñapento prajñapemi (or, v.l., °ti; Buddha is speaking; Senart misunderstands and em.); in iii.447.14 Senart em. prajñapeti (I am not sure that prajñapti of mss. may not be kept, as noun, n. sg.: *there is a declaration, it is declared*, viz., as follows); (yān, sc. dharmān ... agraprajñaptiṣu ca) prajñapayanti Bbh 291.13; gurudharmān prajñapayāmi Bhīk 4b.2; yāvān kaścit sattvadhātuḥ (text °tur) prajñapyamānaḥ prajñapyate (pass.) Vaj 20.19, ... *being made known, is made known*; *defines*, (taṇḍulāhāratāye, or other instr.) śuddhiṃ prajñapenti (or °payanti) Mv ii.126.14; 128.1; 129.5, *they define purity as* (instr.) ...; (**2**) *arranges, provides* (a seat): °payasva SP 410.8 (prose; mañcaṃ); °payet Mv i.325.8 (āsanāni; Senart em. prajñā°); °pīyanti, pass., ii.274.4 (āsanā); °petha iii.63.15 (āsanāni); °paya Divy 20.8 (mañcaṃ), and so, prajñapya, ger. 10, and prajñapto (mañco) 11; °pitvā SP 194.3 (vs; āsana); °pya Suv 203.2; (**3**) *arranges, spreads out* (a cloth or garment, to sit on): ger. °petvā Mv i.238.12 (ajinaṃ); 318.15 (-saṃghāṭiṃ); °payitvā i.241.1 (ajinaṃ); tṛṇasaṃstaraṃ ii.131.14 (for himself; LV parallel, 289.13, saṃstīrya); 268.3; prajñapya (uttarāsaṅgaṃ) Divy 77.4; 465.30. See next.

prajñapta, ppp. of prec. (= Pali paññatta), (**1**) *arranged, provided* (of seats, see prec. 2): esp. with āsana, often prajñapta evāsane, *in the seat expressly provided*, SP 183.2; LV 6.8; Mv i.318.16; ii.258.5; Divy 49.29 and often; others with āsana, SP 283.7; LV 67.14; 408.21; Mv i.306.10; Suv 203.2, 4; RP 41.1; Divy 222.8, 10; siṃhāsana, SP 159.9; 245.4–5; 246.10; LV 288.21, and padmāsana 22; mañca Divy 20.11; (**2**) *arranged* in the sense of *covered, strewn* (with cloths or garments, see prec. 3): praveṇīpraṇīta-prajñaptā(ḥ) SP 341.12 (vs), *elegantly spread with cover-cloths*; paryaṅkāni ... ratnadūṣyapaṭaiḥ prajñaptāni Suv 7.8, ... *spread with* ...; (**3**) in a cliché occurring Divy 2.19; 99.10, and often in Av, i.15.3 etc., vaidyaprajñaptair āhārair, perh. *with food provided* (*arranged*) *by physicians* (in description of the care bestowed on a pregnant woman; Divy Index *ordered*, but this does not seem to be a mg. of this or related words).

prajñaptaka, adj. (prec. in mg. 1 plus specifying -ka, § 22.39), (the seats) *that have been provided*: yāny etāny āsanāni prajñaptakāny ... Divy 222.13–14 (cf. prajñapta with āsana above, lines 8, 10); (Panthakena siṃhāsanaṃ) dṛṣṭaṃ prajñaptakaṃ (*the one that had been provided*), dṛṣṭvā saṃlakṣayati, kiṃ tāvat prasādajātābhiḥ prajñaptaṃ (*was it provided* ...?) Divy 494.14.

? **prajñaptāpayati**, ppp. °**pita**, caus. to denom. from **prajñapta**, *causes* (a seat) *to be arranged* (for himself): Mv iii.93.3 and 4, see s.v. **prajñāpayati** (2) and § 38.56.

prajñapti, f. (in Skt. recorded once, Bhāg.P., in mg. 1, BR; in general used much like Pali paññatti, cf. **prajñapayati** and relatives; see also **prajñāpti**), (**1**) *making known, declaration*: agra-°tiṣu Bbh 291.12, see prajñapayati 1; (**2**) śabda-pra°, *manifestation in words* (cf. Pali sadda-paññatti, Compendium of Philosophy 4), *verbal expression*: Samādh 8.11 yāvatī ca tatra lokadhātau śabdaprajñaptiḥ, *every ... in this world* (took on the same sound, when the Buddha became enlightened); (**3**) *statement, manifesto*: icchāmi ekāṃ prajñaptiṃ (*I wish*, sc. *to make, a statement*) brāhmaṇapariṣā yadi pramāṇaṃ ti Mv i.311.5; the brahmans reply, jalpa yā te vijñapti, *say what your statement* (? *request*?) *is*; (**4**) *désignation* acc. to LaV-P. AbhidhK. ii.214, where °ti-dharma is contrasted with dravya-dharma, *chose en soi*; *notation*, Lévi on Sūtrāl. xix.43 (Tib. brtags, *signe, symbole*; Chin. kia, *faux, simulé*); 'le mot désigne la notion comme purement verbale, comme moyen de se faire entendre;' lokānuvartanāṃ buddhā anuvartanti laukikīṃ, prajñaptim anuvartanti yathā lokottarām api Mv i.168.8–9 (vss), ... *Buddhas imitate* (or *follow*) *the conventions* (*which pass current in the world*; i. e. they *seem* to carry on worldly activities) *as if* (all this were) *super-worldly* (esoterically real); bahubhir abhilāpaiḥ prajñaptaya upacārāḥ (*access*) kriyante Bbh 44.14, and repeatedly in sequel, esp. in cpd. °ti-vāda; (rūpādisaṃjñake) vastuni yā rūpam ity evam-ādyāḥ prajñaptayaḥ tāḥ saṃvṛtaya (see **saṃvṛti**) ity ucyante Bbh 49.4; nāma-saṃketa-°tiḥ 50.10; (nāmadheyamātraṃ saṃketamātraṃ saṃvṛtimātraṃ) prajñaptimātraṃ Śikṣ 257.8 (said of the 5 saṃskāra; note saṃvṛti again, virtually = prajñapti); wrong actions are of two sorts, some like adultery *wrong by nature* (prakṛti-duṣṭa-tvād), others like remaining in the householder's life *blameworthy by convention* (prajñapti-sāvadya-tvād) Śikṣ 192.13; Buddhas are prajñapti-samatikrāntā(ḥ) Mv i.176.18, *passed beyond convention* (*exoteric things*); in Laṅk 153.10 (vs) an ātman exists prajñapti-satyato, *by* (*exoteric*) *verbal convention*, it is not dravya-sat, *real in itself* (cf. AbhidhK, above), and so in line 11, skandhānāṃ skandhatā tadvat prajñaptyā na tu dravyataḥ, ... *by conventional designation, not in reality*; (**5**) *arrangement, provision* (of a seat; n. act. to prajñapayati 2, prajñapta 1): śatasāhasrikā āsana-prajñaptī kriyati Mv ii.273.12, *a seat-provision worth 100,000 was made*, i. e. a seat worth that was provided; similarly, āsanaprajñaptī ca me na tādṛśī bhaviṣyati 274.9.

prajñā (Skt., and Pali paññā), *knowledge*: three kinds, śrutamayī, cintāmayī, bhāvanāmayī (so in Pali cintāmayā, sutamayā, and bhāvanāmayā paññā, Childers): Mvy 1550–3; Dharmas 110.

Prajñākūṭa, n. of a Bodhisattva: SP 260.14 ff.

Prajñāntaka, n. of one of the ten krodha: Dharmas 11; Sādh 137.8.

prajñāpayati (caus. of Skt. pra-jñā, = Pali paññāpeti, but in BHS, in all mgs., less common than **prajñap**°, q.v., which does not exist in Pali unless in paññatta, °tti, see **prajñapta**, °**pti**; both practically unknown in Skt., acc. to BR prajñap° once in ŚB. in mg. 1, prajñāpita in one questionable v.l. in Śak., also in mg. 1), (**1**) *makes known, declares, teaches*: prajñāpayanti ca saṃmūḍhāḥ LV 248.16 (prose), *and foolish* (teachers) *make public announcement* (or, *teach*; Tib. ston pa; sc. their doctrines, just listed; but no object is expressed); (**2**) *arranges, provides* (seats; so also Pali): LV 439.15 (dharmāsanaṃ prajñāpayiṣyati, no v.l.); Divy 198.14 (āsanaṃ prajñāpayatā); Suv 203.1 (āsanaṃ prajñāpaya, but in next line, āsanaṃ prajñaptaṃ, prajñapya ca ...); (siṃhāsanaṃ) prajñāpayanti Mvy 6282, and prajñāptam 5602 (Tib. bśams pa, see Tib. Dictt. s.v. śom pa); ger. prajñāpya, SP 182.6 (siṃhāsanaṃ); LV 102.14 and 268.7 (āsanaṃ; but in both most mss. prajñapya); Av i.227.9 (mañcaṃ); a strange caus., of doubtful form, prob. to a denom., mss. prajñāpāyitaṃ or prajñaptāpitaṃ (prob. read the latter, see § 38.56), Senart em. prajñāpayitaṃ, with āsanaṃ, Mv iii.93.3 and 4, (by Buddha) *a seat was caused to be arranged* (for himself); (**3**) *arranges, spreads out* (cloths, garments, etc., for sitting on; so also Pali); Mv iii.53.13 prajñāpayeyaṃ (-saṃghāṭīṃ).

Prajñāpāramitā (see **pāramitā** 2), as n. of a work or class of works, extant in several versions, of which I have excerpted for this study two, **Aṣṭasāhasrikāp°** (AsP) and **Śatasāhasrikā-p°** (ŚsP), qq.v.; there are other references under the name of Prajñāp° alone: so Mvy 505 refers to, and 506–623 cites, a list of samādhis as Prajñāpāramitodbhavita-(the list occurs ŚsP 1412.8 ff.); so, (Ārya-) Prajñāp° Śikṣ 49.5; 120.11; 313.18, 349.6; 351.9; called Mahatī Praj° Śikṣ 275.14; °tā-parivarta Gv 124.26; °tā-mukha-parivarta 125.1 ff.; see also 149.1 ff. et alibi; °tā-pustaka Sādh 127.5, et alibi; personified and depicted in Mmk, Ārya-pra° 109.27; 318.9; Bhagavatī Pra° 38.11; 40.11; 312.7, 17, 24–25.

Prajñāpāramitāpañcaśatikā, n. of a work: Mvy 1373 (cf. prec.).

prajñāpti, f., noted only in Mvy as substitute for the usual **prajñapti**, q.v., cf. **vāhana-pra°** where in citing LV the Mvy substitutes ā for a in the word. Besides this cpd., the word occurs Mvy 1415, 6496, 9213; and see **anu-pra°**. Tib. on the first two gdags pa (also used for prajñā), *making known*, but in 9213 bcas pa (and so for anu-pra°), which is ambiguous (context suggests perhaps mg. of prajñapti 2 or 3), and on 6496 alternatively bcaḥ ba, probably intending the same; Jap. *deciding, settling, fixing*. (Acc. to LaV-P., Index, also occurs in AbhidhK, = prajñapti.)

Prajñāptivādin, m. pl. (cf. prec., and prajñapti 4, in the sense of which prajñāpti is here used), n. of a school: Mvy 9094.

Prajñāptiśāstra, nt., n. of a work: Mvy 1415 (see **prajñāpti**).

Prajñāpradīpa, m., n. of a samādhi: Mvy 555 (not in ŚsP).

Prajñāpradīpaprabhaketuś(i)ri, n. of a Buddha: Gv 285.15 (vs); printed as two words.

-prajñāyate, denom. from -prajñā, in jāti-prajñāyate jarā-pr° vyādhi-pr° maraṇa-pr° LV 19.12 (prose), *there is knowledge of birth, old age, disease, death*; based on cpd. jāti-prajñā, etc. Weller 18 wrongly assumes that jāti etc. are separate nouns, n. sg., and prajñāyate pass.; this is the construction in Mv i.52.10 jarā vyādhi maraṇaṃ (so mss.; Senart as one dvandva cpd., em. °maraṇā) ca prajñāyanti, *old age, disease, and death become known*. In prose of LV it is hardly conceivable that jāti, vyādhi, and maraṇa would occur in one sentence as n. sg.; while in prose of Mv vyādhi is not at all surprising as n. sg.

Prajñāvant(a), n. of a companion of **Puṇyavant(a)**, q.v.: Mv iii.33.20 ff.

Prajñāvabhāsaśrī, n. of a merchant's daughter: Gv 233.20..

prajñāvimukta, adj. (= Pali paññāvimutta), *emancipated as to intelligence* (acc. to Pali Pugg. i.31, p. 14, thru destruction of the āsava = āśrava): Mvy 1027. Cf. next.

prajñāvimukti, f. (= Pali paññāvimutti), *emancipation of intelligence* (cf. prec.); with **cetovimukti**, q.v. (so also Pali): LV 418.18; Mv ii.139.6; iii.333.16.

prajñopaka, see **upaka**.

prajvara, m., acc. to Tib. on Mvy 9530 *a virulent contagious disease* (rims drag po); also Bhīk 20b.2, in a list of diseases. Doubtless a fever.

[**praḍīna, praḍīyati**, see **pralī°**.]

praṇata, ppp. (to Skt. pra-namati, in mg. *depart*, implied by Pali caus. paṇāmeti, *sends away, dismisses*; cf. AMg. paṇaya, acc. to Sheth = prāpta), *departed, set out towards*: yena himavāṃ parvatarājā tena praṇatā Mv ii.101.16; yena himavantaparvatarājā tena praṇato 103.17; (yena rājakulaṃ) tena praṇato iii.39.1; yena veṇuvanaṃ tena praṇatā 63.11. In Mvy 426 praṇata-pratyekasatya (see the latter), ep. of a Tathāgata, must mean *from whom individual* (heretical) *doctrines are departed*, if the reading is right; it corresponds to Pali panunna- (or panuṇṇa-)-paccekasacca, DN iii.270.5 etc.; should we boldly em. to praṇunna-? Tib. bstsal ba, or btsal ba, possibly (= bsal ba, to sel ba, see Jä. s.v. stsol ba, 3) = *removed* (of impurities).

[**praṇada**, SP 51.13, read **tuṇava**, q.v.]

praṇamati (?), **praṇamayati** (cf. Skt. id.), (**1**) ger. praṇamayya, *saluting* (in non-caus. mg.): Bhagavantaṃ Divy 463.22; but MSV i.71.16, same passage, añjaliṃ praṇamya; (**2**) añjaliṃ praṇamya, *making an añjali*: SP 60.2 (prose; so all mss., ed. em. praṇāmya); and so all Nep. mss. and WT, SP 100.5 (prose), KN with Kashgar rec. praṇāmayitvā; añjaliṃ praṇamayya Av i.347.4; ii.3.9. Is praṇamya ger. of praṇamati, or of praṇamayati? See **praṇāmayati**, which like Pali paṇāmeti is so used with añjaliṃ; is the literal mg. *bends*, or rather *extends, holds out*?

Praṇāda (= Pali Panāda, both mgs.), (**1**) n. of a king (acc. to Mvy a cakravartin): Mvy 3576; Divy 57.9 ff.; (**2**) n. of a yakṣa: Māy 236.28.

praṇāmayati, °**meti** (in mgs. 1 and 2 = Pali paṇāmeti; cf. also **abhi-praṇam°**), (**1**) with object añjali, *makes* (a gesture of reverence); so also praṇamya and praṇamayya, see s.v. **praṇamati**; was the lit. mg. *bends*, or *extends, holds out*, as in (2)?: añjaliṃ praṇāmetvā Mv i.255.12; °liṃ praṇāmayitvā SP 100.5 (prose; so KN with Kashgar rec., Nep. mss. and WT praṇamya); Mv iii.97.9; praṇāmehi añjaliṃ Mv iii.358.2; (**2**) *holds out, holds forth, extends*, e. g. a hand or arm: hasto praṇāmito Mv ii.450.3, *the hand was extended* (to pluck flowers); (ekaśṛṅgasya hastaṃ) praṇāmi (aor.) Mv iii.147.19, *held out her hand to E.*; (bāhā) praṇāmitā iii.313.13; also a bowl, pātraṃ . . . praṇāmaye (aor.) Mv i.303.14, *held out his bowl* (for inspection); so in Pali, pattaṃ paṇāmetvā Vin. ii.216.11 means *holding out his bowl* (with his right hand; wrongly PTSD and SBE 20.88, 290–1); (**3**) *gives, furnishes, provides* (in this sense app. not in Pali, but AMg. and other Pkt. paṇāmai, °mei, *offers*, Hindi arpaṇ karnā, Ratnach. 3.440 and Sheth 652), doubtless as specialization of *holds out towards*: so app. dhārmyāṃ kathāṃ praṇāmaye (aor.) Mv iii.446.9, *presented, gave a sermon*; possibly daṇḍo praṇāmayitavyo Mv ii.457.3, *punishment must be given* (i. e. administered, meted out), but here v.l. pradāpayitavyā (for °vyo), *must be caused to be given*. (In LV 172.2 (vs) kāyu praṇāmi (prob. verb, aor., not noun with Senart Mv i note 427; Tib. lus btud) *bowed your body*, the mg. is substantially Skt.)

Praṇālin, n. of a gandharva: Suv 162.2.

praṇitar (m.c. for Skt. praṇetar), *leader, guide*: °tāro Mmk 167.17 (vs; delete jagati before this word).

praṇidadhāti, praṇidheti (= Pali paṇidahati, paṇidheti, Childers), orig. *fixes firmly* the mind (cittam, manas), but often with ellipsis of such an object, used absolutely, *makes an earnest wish, cherishes an ardent desire* (**praṇidhāna, praṇidhi**, qq.v.) for something (usually dat., sometimes loc., rarely acc.), *vows, assumes a vow*; sometimes (like the related nouns; and cf. **apraṇihita**) applied to worldly desires, so praṇidadhāti Dbh 24.26, used absolutely, synonym of abhidhyām utpādayati, and lobhacittam utpādayati, in the context; usually some sort of religious purpose is involved, so: praṇidhehi tuvaṃ tatra śreṣṭhikule cittaṃ upapattīye (prob. loc., cf. kule in 14 below) Mv iii.404.11, *concentrate your mind on being born there in a merchant's family* (with the understanding that he should become a monk), and cf. śreṣṭhisya kule cittaṃ praṇihitaṃ 14; the wish may be for the enlightenment (bodhi, or the like) of others: evaṃ ca (sc. Sujātā) praṇidadhāti sma ('after eating my food, may the Bodhisattva attain enlightenment!') LV 265.14; bodhāya cittam atulaṃ praṇidhāya sattvāṃ (gen. pl.) LV 356.11 (vs), *fixing our minds in an unequalled degree on the enlightenment of creatures* (Bodhisattvas speaking); varāgrasattve praṇidhenti bodhaye LV 183.12 (vs), (women) *earnestly wished for enlightenment for* (loc., lit. *in the case of*) *the Supreme Being* (the Bodhisattva); but commonly the object is enlightenment or Buddhahood for the maker of the vow, which is very often taken under the inspiration of an earlier Buddha: (bodhāya cittaṃ) praṇidadhad Bbh 12.5, *fixing the mind on enlightenment*; bodhāye (or °ya) praṇidhento, pres. pple., Mv i.80.7, 9, 10, 12, 14 (mss. often praṇidhyanto); °dheti Mv i.83.8 (narasiṃhatāye, *for Buddhahood*); °dhesi (aor.; used absolutely) Mv i.42.6 = 53.3 = 336.19; i.49.16; purā praṇidhitvā (ger.; absolute) Mv i.96.10; °dhenti i.120.5 (bodhāye); mss. °dhenti, °dhyanti, Senart em. °dhento i.120.12 (bodhāya); °dhintāna (gen. pl. pres. pple.; Senart °dhentāna) bodhāya i.124.18 (vs); °dhenti i.127.1 (samyaksaṃbodhāye); 193.9 (buddhatvāya); °dhento i.127.4 (bodhāya); yebhir manaḥ praṇihitaṃ varabuddhabodhau LV 343.10 (vs); yaṃ mayā bodhāya praṇihitaṃ Mv i.46.1 *that* (or, *since*) *I have made a vow for enlightenment*; bodhāye praṇihitaṃ i.47.16; with cognate noun, asaṃkhyeya-praṇihitā praṇidhi Mv iii.281. 8–9 (sc. for bodhi); with goal in acc., praṇidhisi (m.c. for °dhesi, 2 sg.) cārīkām asamām Gv 57.15 (vs), *thou vowest the matchless course* (of a Bodhisattva), and similarly praṇidhisi 57.20 (samantabhadrām . . . cārika, acc.).

praṇidhāna, nt. (m. modifiers Bhad 58; = Pali paṇidhāna; like **praṇidhi**, n. act. to **praṇidadhāti**, **praṇidheti**), *fixation* of mind (ceto-pra° Mv i.239.5; iii.138.19; Pali ceto-paṇidhi), and so *ardent desire, earnest wish, vow*; sometimes (but rarely) of purely worldly desires, which are reprobated, praṇidhāna-vivarjitam SP 142.8 (vs); usually religious at least in basis, fulfilment being expected on the ground of acts of merit, which are often mentioned in a solemn declaration of wish; the thing desired may nevertheless be worldly (wealth, or special marks of grace), tho often the intention is stated to use it for religious purposes: Mv i.302.19 (magic possession of garlands); iii.414.12 (fortunate rebirths); Divy 23.17; 65.10 (to become a cakravartin); or it may be truly religious, yet not Buddhahood or Bodhisattvahood, SP 242.4 (here made by a past Buddha, to do services to Buddhas to come); most commonly to win enlightenment, i. e. to become a Buddha, SP 43.12; LV 31.22 (°na-paripūryai, so with mss.; cf. **praṇidhi**-paripūriye); 180.1; 415.15; Mv i.39.8; 104.3; 239.5; iii.138.19; Divy 66.22; 90.3; Av i.8.12; praṇidhāna-caryā, *a whole course of praṇidhānas*, Mv i.1.3, see s.v. **caryā**; when made by a Bodhisattva it may mean rather the vow to follow the Bodhisattva-course, and may then be called specifically caryā-pra° SP 64.13, 14, or bhadracarī-pra° Bhad 2, etc.; praṇidhāna is one of the ten bala of a Bodhisattva, Mvy 764, and one of his vaśitā, Mvy 778; anuloma-pra° Mv i.1.11, *continued successive pra°*, seems to mean a pra° repeated by the same individual (Śākyamuni in previous incarnations as cakravartin), in similar terms, as described later in i.48.17 ff.; there are ten mahāpraṇidhāna of a Bodhisattva, Dbh 14.15 ff., described at length (ten such are referred to in Sūtrāl. iv. 12, but the list quoted from another source by Lévi, note to Transl., is quite different from the Dbh list); four pūrva-praṇidhāna-padāni LV 204.16, each described in the sequel in an entire paragraph; three kinds of pra° Dharmas 112, viz. susthāna-prābandhikam (see **prābandhika**), sattvārtha-prābandhikam, buddhakṣetra-pariśodhakam. Rarely **prārthanā**, q.v., appears to be used of the *'earnest wish'* for enlightenment.

Praṇidhānasāgaraprabhāsaś(i)rī, n. of a Buddha: Gv 285.13 (vs).

praṇidhi, m., sometimes f., even nt. (= Pali, and once BHS, **paṇidhi**, q.v., f. acc. to PTSD, m. acc. to Childers; both are right) = **praṇidhāna**, q.v. for development of mgs.; gender f., (praṇidhim . . .) yā ti (= te) abhūṣi LV 167.15 (vs); yā praṇidhi 175.13 (vs); saiṣā te . . . praṇidhī 283.2 (vs); °dhī . . . paripūrṇā 364.10 (vs); °dhī iyam evarūpā (mss. °pāḥ) 415.21 (vs); prathamā praṇidhi (v.l. °mo °dhiḥ) Mv i.48.16; caturthī tadā praṇidhiḥ āsīt 54.6; pañcamā °dhiḥ 54.7; prathamā °dhir 81.2 (these in Mv all prose); neut., taṃ yuṣmākaṃ mūlapraṇidhiṃ Mv i.45.8 (complete sentence!); dvitīyapraṇidhiṃ tadāsi 54.3, *then was the 2d pra°* (Senart em. °yo praṇidhi); of worldly desires, nāstīha me praṇidhi saṃskṛtasarvakāmaiḥ RP 45.7 (vs), and so in **a-praṇidhi**, q.v.; religious in basis, for desired fate in rebirths on basis of past merit, Av i.171.1; of religious desires, but other than Buddhahood or Bodhisattvahood, Mv ii.276.10; LV 386.14, 16 (Trapuṣa and Bhallika had made a praṇidhi in a former birth that the Buddha might 'turn the wheel of the law' after eating their food; this was fulfilled); a Bodhisattva is called praṇidhī-sāgaru SP 447.4, *an ocean of pious vows*; mūla-pra°, *the original* or *primary vow* leading to ultimate enlightenment, Mv i.45.8; commonly of the vow to gain enlightenment, LV 161.19; 167.13; Mv i.237.18; ii.259.14; Jm 204.1; Av i.4.1; Gv 255.17; praṇidhi-paripūriye Mv ii.205.16 (so mss., instr., see s.v. **praṇidhāna**-paripūryai); paripūritavya praṇidhī Gv 58.4 (vs); to this, the common, sense also belong the citations of pra° with f. and nt. gender, above.

praṇidheti, see **praṇidadhāti**.

? **praṇidhyeti** (if correct, cpd. of Skt. dhyāyati), *meditates on*: °dhyenti te prathamajanmasthitāḥ Gv 371.24 (vs); object may be in prec. line 23, sarvaṃ jināna aparāntaviyūhameghān, but this could be object of paśyanti in line 22, in which case °dhyenti could be an error for °dhenti, *make a solemn vow*, to **praṇidheti**, °**dadhāti**, q.v. for similar corruptions recorded in mss. of Mv.

praṇīta, adj. (= Pali paṇīta, esp. of food, but also of dhamma, sattā, *creatures*, etc.), *superior, excellent, distinguished, first-class*; esp. of food (and drink) and sometimes used, without noun, of fine food: °ta-vijñāpanam Mvy 8462, *asking for fine food*, = Tib. zas (*food*) bsod pa (*good*) sloṅ ba (*begging*), something forbidden to monks by Prāt 511.2 (°ta-bhojanāni . . .); elsewhere, of food (sometimes drink), LV 387.5; Mv i.113.6; 211.9 = ii.15.8; ii.274.9; iii.39.5; 142.2, 15, etc.; Divy 13.7; 50.14, etc. (common); Jm 19.25; Av i.64.9; 264.11, etc. (common); LV 214.21 (rasām praṇītām, acc. pl.); of living creatures (sattva), esp. bracketed with hīna, *low*, sometimes also with madhya(ma), *middling*, SP 9.8; 370.2; LV 151.14; 344.11; 399.22; Mv ii.132.8; Bbh 391.2, 3; of dharma, LV 393.16; Mv i.173.11 f. (opp. hīna); Divy 385.20; Bbh 33.16; of divine existences, Divy 98.21 (devanikāya); Av i.259.4 and 292.1 (trayastriṃśa); misc., Mvy 1200, 2527 (unspecified; = Tib. gya nom pa); SP 341.12 (see **prajñapta**); 214.2 (jñānaṃ); 350.11 (praṇīta-mukhamaṇḍalaḥ, *having an excellent round mouth*, or *face*); LV 47.7 (dhyānasukhaṃ); 196.5 (dāna); 196.7 (bodhimārga); 242.9 (kāma, *desires* = *desirable things*); Mv i.290.20 and 291.2 (ratanaṃ); ii.279.4 (artha, the *goal* of the Bodhisattva); Bbh 120.9 (vastu).

praṇetara or °**tāra** (MIndic extension in -a of Skt. praṇetar), *leader, guide*: vinā praṇetareṇa (v.l. °tāreṇa) Mv ii.218.3 (prose).

pratata, adj. (ppp. of Skt. pra-tanoti; in this mg. seems not recorded), *extensive, great*: paritrāyate tasmād vicitrāt pratatād ugrād bhayāt Bbh 5.6; (kusīdo nodagra-) pratata-vīrya-samanvāgataḥ 11.12.

pratara (m. or nt.), perhaps = Pali patara (Jāt.

iv.32.21; Geiger 39.4; = Skt. pradara, § 2.29), *hole, crevice*: pratarādiṣu mahārogaspṛṣṭāsu (! but the interpretation is far from certain) Mmk 54.4.

pratarkya, adj. (gdve. to pra-tark-; cf. BR 5.1617, a-pra°), *discoverable*: mā jñātīnāṃ °kyo bhaviṣyati Divy 174.29.

pratāna (Skt., *creeper, tendril*), lit. *creeper, tendril*, used fig. of lightning, cf. the common vidyul-latā: vidyut-pratāna-jvalitaṃ (so with all mss. but one for Lefm. °taḥ) LV 216.19.

Pratāpa, m., (**1**) n. of a large number of former Buddhas: Mv i.58.9; (**2**) = next, prob. only by corruption: Mv i.6.13 (no v.l.); some mss. read so in i.15.7 (vs), but unmetrically.

pratāpana, m., n. of a hot hell: Mvy 4926, so with v.l., Tib. rab tu tsha ba, and Mironov without v.l., for text mahātāpanaḥ; Dharmas 121; in these and most other places occurs in lists of various hells (cf. **Pratāpa** 2); Mv i.9.9; 15.7, 12; ii.350.8; 369.14; iii.274.10; Divy 67.22; 138.6; 366.29; Av i.4.8, etc.; Samādh 19.20; Kv 18.13 (text pretāyane!); 66.16 (text pretāpane! some copyist thought of preta); Mmk 114.26.

Pratāpavant(a), n. of two former Buddhas: Mv iii.237.4 (°ntaṃ, acc., °ntas, nom.); Ṣukh 5.7 °vān, n. sg.

pratikaṇṭhukayā, adv., read with v.l. °ṭhakayā, or with pw 7.360 °ṭhikayā (= Skt. pratikaṇṭham), *singly, severally, one by one*: Divy 244.8.

pratikaraṇa (nt.; n. act. to Skt. pratikaroti), *expiation*; in yathādharma-°ṇa-tā, *state* or *condition of making expiation according to what is right*: vyatikrāntena ca °ṇatayā pratyāpattiḥ karaṇīyā Bbh 180.21–22; (skhalitasya) ca °ṇatāyai vīryam 204.10.

pratikaroti, (**1**) (= Pali paṭi°, Jāt. ii.406.19) *imitates* (with dat. of person): ko nāma śaktaḥ pratikartu tubhyam SP 119.4 (vs); naiva kadācit pratikartu śakyam 11 (vs); (**2**) *works in accordance with what is expected, acts normally*: kaccid dhātavaḥ pratikurvanti SP 429.4, see s.v. **yāpanīya** (Burnouf, *sont-ils en parfaite harmonie?*).

pratikāṅkṣaṇa (nt.), °**ṇā** (unrecorded; cf. next items), (**1**) *desire*: akāla-°ṇa-tā mārakarma Śikṣ 51.14, *state of having untimely desires*; (**2**) *expectation*: vipāka-°ṇā-viśuddhaṃ (dānaṃ) Śikṣ 270.11, *free of expectation of reward*; (dānaṃ) vipākāpratikāṅkṣaṇa-tā KP 16.4 (°ka-aprati°); sarvadāneṣu vipākāpratikāṅkṣaṇa-cittaṃ Gv 319.14.

pratikāṅkṣati (in Skt., and Pali paṭikaṅkhati, seems recorded only in mg. *desires, longs for*; cf. however Pali bhaya-paṭikaṅkhin MN i.21.4, *expecting dangers*), *waits for, expects*; noted only in ppp. °kṣita, once, and otherwise gdve. °kṣitavya; na paraḥ °kṣitavyaḥ Śikṣ 282.16, *I must not wait for another* (to do my duty as a Bodhisattva); bhikṣubhyaḥ sakāśād ānanda mātṛgrāmeṇa pravrajyopasampad bhikṣuṇībhāvaḥ °kṣitavyaḥ Bhīk 4b.5; °kṣitavyaḥ Mvy 6382 (context suggests *to be expected*); °tavya, various forms, Divy 618.1 (vṛddhi); Bbh 155.15 (id.); Śikṣ 84.6 (trīṇi bhayāni); Sukh 54.18 (śrotrarogo na...); Vaj 35.17 (vipākaḥ); Śikṣ 138.10 (puṇyakriyāvipākaḥ); °kṣitaḥ, ppp., RP 57.12 (a return for a favor done, not *expected*).

pratikāṅkṣā (cf. prec.), *expectation, hope*: read °āṃ with Corr. for text pratijñāṃ LV 184.14 (meter demands the correction); see s.v. **uttārayati**. Cf. also **a-pratikāṅkṣa-tā**.

-pratikāṅkṣin, see s.v. **-parikāṅkṣin**.

pratikubjita, adj. (denom. ppp.; = Pali paṭikujjita), *covered, enclosed*: Mvy 6947, one Tib. version is bskor ba, *surrounded*; ayaḥprākāraparikṣiptā ayasā pratikubjitāḥ Mv i.9.14 (of hell-inhabitants); ayasā prati° iii.454.13 (of the same).

? **pratikūla**, nt., would seem to be a part of a city gate: (teṣāṃ dvārāṇāṃ dvinnāṃ) varṇānāṃ pratikūlaṃ abhūṣi, suvarṇasya ca rūpyasya ca Mv iii.228.8. The parallel passage i.195.10 ff. seems, as far as I see, to have no correspondent, unless far-reaching corruption has concealed relationship. Could this be for *prati-kūṭa, as if *counter-pinnacle*?

-pratikṛtika, in kṛta-prati°, adj. (to Skt. pratikṛti, app. not recorded in this sense of *requital, repayment*, but Skt. pratikaroti and Pali paṭikara are so used), one of the six upāya of a Bodhisattva, *containing, consisting of* or *concerning requital* (*repayment*) *for* (favors previously) *done* (by the Bodhisattva; he declines any recompense, other than virtuous life by his debtor): Bbh 264.9; described 270.9 ff.

pratikṛtya, ger. used as adv. (= Pali paṭigacca, with Pkt. g for k, Geiger 38.1; usually followed by eva, i. e. °gacc' eva), *in advance*, always foll. by eva: mss. sometimes pratikṛtyaivaṃ (so LV 182.1); in Mv ii.449.8; 451.14, 16; 454.2, 4; 455.9; 456.14, 18 prakṛ° for pratikṛ°; and Mv mss. often °tyeva (or °tveva; °tyevaṃ iii.12.9) for °tyaiva; Senart reads always prakṛtyaiva, rendering *simplement, sans aucun appareil qui fasse connaître ton rang* (ii.570), tho his mss. read pratikṛ° in ii.448.16; 449.10; iii.11.18 and 12.9; moreover the mg. he assumes for his reading prakṛtyaiva can hardly be correct, since in 449.10 and 451.16 the word is preceded by prākṛtakena veṣeṇa, *in common garb*, which would be duplicated by the assumed prakṛtyaiva: pratikṛtyaiva (text with mss. °vaṃ) dharmavihāry... LV 182.1, *even in advance* (of enlightenment, while still dwelling in worldly life, in the harem), *he* (the Bodhisattva) *was dwelling according to what was right*; Mv ii.448.16; 449.8, 10; 451.14, 16; 454.2, 4; 455.9; 456.14, 18; iii.11.18; 12.9.

pratikṛṣṭa, ppp., adj. (= Skt. Lex. id., Pali paṭikiṭṭha; see s.v. **pratikruṣṭa**, where it is suggested that both Pali forms may derive from pratikṛṣṭa historically, °**kruṣṭa** being hyper-Skt.; but possibly the two are independent, tho virtual synonyms): *bad, evil*: ayaṃ bodhisattvasya pratikṛṣṭo mṛṣāvāda iti Śikṣ 12.12.

pratikopayati (= Pali paṭikopayati, *breaks, violates*, uposathaṃ; in Skt. only the noun pratikopa is recorded, from a spurious vs of Mbh., 4.970*), *attacks*, or *rebels against*: °yanti AsP 460.6 (prajñāpāramitāṃ; parallel with **pratikrośanti**).

pratikramati, *abstains* (from sin, abl.): mss. in Mv i.145.10 (vs) paruṣavacanāc ca naravara pratikramāmi tathaivaṃ paiśunyaṃ (read °yāt, or with Senart °yā, abl.); Senart em. to prativiramāmi, which to be sure seems to be intended by prativiremi of mss. in parallel i.202.7; but there is no need to em. i.145.10; the ppp. pratikrāntaḥ is evidently meant in a closely similar way in Mvy 2563, in a list of 'synonyms for **nisṛjā**', *abstained, withdrawn* (from evil).

pratikrānta, (**1**) nt., *recession*; only in association with **abhikrānta** 3, q.v.; (**2**) ppp. as adj., see **pratikramati**.

pratikruṣṭa, adj. (felt as ppp. of Skt. prati-kruś- which is not used in an appropriate mg.; = Pali paṭikuṭṭha, which is a synonym of paṭikiṭṭha and may represent historically another form of **pratikṛṣṭa**, q.v.; to this our word may be a hyper-Sktism; § 3.96; yet cf. next): *poor, bad, inferior*: of land, Mvy 5300; °ṭam etad vairāṇāṃ yad uta strīvairam MSV ii.18.8; similarly 65.6; compv. °**ṭa-tara**, of an occupation, *low, despicable*: pratikruṣṭataraṃ bāṇijyānāṃ yad uta kāṣṭhabāṇijyam Divy 500.21, also 26; 501.2.

pratikrośa (m.? to next; cf. Pali paṭikkosana), *rejection, scorn, disregard*: °śena AsP 179.6 (prose; refers to action of 179.4, see next); *rejection of, opposition to*, action in the saṃgha, MSV ii.210.5, 9 ff. In Mv ii.371.10 (vs) Senart reads sukhito pramuditaḥ pratikrośaṃ pratilabhati purimanirodhadṛṣṭaṃ, and interprets prati° as referring to the contempt and ill-treatment which pious men will accept with joy in the time of decadence of religion; but this does not seem a natural interpretation, and the mss. read, one, prītiḥ krośaṃ, the other prati-kośaṃ; combining parts of each we would get prīti-kośaṃ, *a treasure-store of joy*, which makes good sense and which I would read. The meter is very puzzling to me in this whole passage, so that I cannot rely on it.

pratikrośati (= Pali paṭikkosati; cf. prec. and °**kruṣṭa**; if the latter is hyper-Skt., then °krośati would seem to be based on °kruṣṭa), *rejects, scorns, treats with contempt*: (yaḥ śāsanaṃ hy arhatāṃ ...) °śati Ud viii.7 (= Pali paṭikkosati Dhp. 164); (imāṃ prajñāpāramitāṃ...) pratikrokṣyanti (fut.) AsP 179.4; so also °śanti 460.6; in Mv iii.7.16 (vs) read, yā mamāṇā(ṃ) pratikrośe (aor.), *who has scorned* (*disobeyed*) *my command*; *rejects, opposes* action in the saṃgha: prativahanti °śanti MSV ii.210.4 (and ff.).

pratikṣaya (m.?), *loss, ruin, disappearance*: sad-dharma-pratikṣayāntakāle SP 287.11 (prose); KN suggest a Pkt. *paḍikkhaya for parikkhaya = Skt. parikṣaya, cf. § 2.47.

pratikṣepaka, m. (to Skt. °kṣipati), *one who rejects, contemns*: saddharma-pra° RP 19.1; Mmk 73.16.

pratigarvita, adj., *showing hostile pride*: °tān ari-gaṇān Divy 431.14 (vs).

pratigṛhṇāti, °**ṇīte**, with atyayaṃ (= Pali accayaṃ paṭigaṇhāti), *accepts* (confession of) *a sin, forgives*: atyayaṃ no sugato °ṇātu LV 379.7; yuṣmākaṃ dārikā atyayaṃ °ṇāmi 12 (both prose); atyayam atyayataḥ pratigṛhṇīṣva MSV i.43.4; others, see **atyaya.**

pratigopaka, m., *'concealer', one who acts secretly, on the sly*: MSV iv.195.9 (Tib. sbad pa).

pratigraha, m. (lit. *receiver*; in a similar sense in Skt., Car., see BR 7.1774; Pali paṭiggaha, *receiver for scraps and refuse*, Vin. ii.115.16, 19), *bed-pan* (acc. to Tib., chol zaṅs): Mvy 8964 (among utensils of monks).

pratigrahetar, m. (= Pali paṭiggahetā, DN i.89.10, cited as °hītā PTSD; Skt. °hītar; cf. graheti, Chap. 43, s.v. grah 3), *one who receives*: dharmāṇāṃ °tāraṃ (Ānan-daṃ) Mv iii.49.13, 18; 50.3; pāṃśukūlānāṃ °tāro 54.16.

pratigrāhaka, m., *one who took* or *has taken*: Mv iii.304.7, see § 22.4.

pratigrāhita, ppp. (of 'caus.', AMg. paḍiggāhia, *received*, to °ggāhei), *received*, in a-pratigrāhita-bhuktiḥ, *eating what has not been received* (as a gift): Mvy 8461.

pratigha, generally m., in LV 329.22 nt. (Pali paṭigha, acc. to PTSD m. and nt.; Skt. pratigha, m., *resistance*; [Lex. and a few doubtful literary occurrences] *anger*), *aversion, repugnance, loathing, hostility* (hardly *anger*, at least I find no clear proof for this mg.; but in Mvy 1945, where it follows and seems to contrast with rāgaḥ, Tib. renders khon khro ba, *anger*). It is often bracketed and contrasted with **anunaya**, q.v. for citations; both (= rāga and dveṣa) are evil and must be shunned. Etymolog. gloss Śikṣ 149.5 *it is called pratigha because it destroys*, pratihanti, *roots of merit*. One of six kleśa, Dharmas 67 (follows rāgaḥ). Other occurrences (without anunaya): LV 11.5; Dbh 25.4; Bbh 7.16; 161.13; Śikṣ 6.17; 52.9; 251.15; 271.12. See also next.

pratighāta, m. (= Pali paṭi°; substantially = prec., but not standardly associated with anunaya; see however Gv 351.24, under **anunaya**), *malice, hatred*; seems to be contrasted with maitrī: LV 430.11 aprati-ghāta-maitrī- (a dvandva), *non-malice and kindliness*; Śikṣ 101.4 pratighātaṃ na janayet, maitracittaḥ sadā bhavet; 128.9; KP 27.7.

praticāra (m.; = Pali paṭicāra; Skt. not in this mg.), *dealing with, having relations with*: kalyāṇamitro-pāya-saṃdhi-(q.v.)-lokānuvartana-praticāreṣu Gv 461.1–2. See also **prāticāraka** (read **prati**°?).

praticārin, adj. (to prec.), *practising, dealing, behaving*: anudharma-°rī Mvy 1123, acc. to Tib. *behaving according to the dharma* (but perh. practising the **anu-dharma**, q.v.?); apratihatamatigati-(acc. to Lalou, Iconographie 18 n. 8, read gatimati- with Tib. and Chin.)-praticāriṇām Mmk 55.23.

praticālayati (= Pali paṭicāleti, Jāt. v.434.4, cited as °caleti PTSD), *causes to budge* or *stir, move*: śakyo nāhaṃ... drumāt praticālitum LV 337.15 (vs).

? **praticinoti**, *investigates, studies carefully*: pari-vartān vibhāvayāmi °nomi Gv 66.15 (prose); perh. error for pravicinomi.

praticodayati (= Pali paṭicodeti, in this mg. rather than *blame, reprove*, as given in PTSD; even Skt. may have this mg. in Rām. 4.61.48, BR s.v.), *countermands, forbids*: gdve., a-praticodya-(so to be read, as cpd. with next)-pratijñā-vaiśāradya-prāpta(-tvāt) LV 434.6, 8, *not to be countermanded* or *interfered with.*

praticchati (= Pali paṭi°, Skt. pratī°), *receives* etc.: ppp. praticchita, see § 3.38; Chap. 43, s.v. iṣ.

pratichadana, once for °**chādana**, q.v.

pratichāda (= Pali paṭi°), *covering*, in probably Bhvr. cpd. (but possibly adj.): svaka-mukha-pratichādā tasya jihvā prabhūtā RP 46.18.

pratichādana, nt., °**na-tā**, °**nā**? (in mg. 1, *concealment*, once in Skt., Schmidt, Nachträge), (**1**) *covering*, for protection: citta-nagara-prati° Śikṣ 123.6; *concealment*, gambhīrārtha-dharma-°na-tā Bbh 82.17; esp. *concealment* of one's own faults, duṣṭhula-°nam Mvy 8473; svadoṣa-(text °dauṣa-)-°na-tā KP 116.2; kukṛta-°na-tā (v.l. °nā) Bbh 403.24; (**2**) (= Pali kaṇḍu-paṭicchādī, f., Vin. iv. 172.11, 15, glossed paṭicchādanatthāya) a cloth *covering* or *bandage*, in kaṇḍu-°nam, *itch-covering*, allowed to monks afflicted with a skin disease: Prāt 524.3; Mvy 8516; spelled kaṇḍū-pratichadanam Mvy 8943 (Index °chād°, but Mironov °chad°).

pratijaneti (m.c. for °jāneti, see Chap. 43, s.v. jñā 2, = Skt. °jānāti), *approves*: yādṛśīṃ (what noun is understood?) pratijaneti sūrata eva (= evam) yūyam anu-śikṣatho sadā Gv 481.22 (vs), *whatever the Gracious One approves, thus do ye imitate it always.*

pratijāgarti, °**jāgarati**, °**jāgrati** (also **paṭi**°; forms, see Chap. 43; the verb seems to be Vedic only, but a few Skt. noun derivs. are recorded; Pali paṭijaggati, defined in PTSD *nourish, tend, feed, look after* etc., hardly covering the Pali range of mg.), (**1**) *watches = stays awake* (opp. sleeps): devī... pratijāgaritvā Mv i.154.16 (vs); (**2**) *watches = guards*: yāmaṃ °jāgreta Ud v.15 (= Pali paṭijaggeyya, Dhp. 157; the real meaning of yāma is obscure in both, but prob. lit. *night-watch*, with thought of mg. 1 preceding; acc. to Dhp. comm. the three *ages* of man), not to be em. with ed. (°jāgṛyāt unmetrical!); kṛtyaṃ °jāgareta Ud xvi.1 (one's own acts); here, perhaps, **kuśalapakṣaṃ** (q.v.) °jāgṛhi Av ii.145.2, etc.; (**3**) *attends to, looks after*: °jāgaranti Mv i.147.11 (apsarases... the toilet operations of the Bodhisattva's mother); (amātyehi) °jāgṛtaṃ ii.180.6, *the ministers attended to, carried out* (sc. what the king had commanded); yadā ekamātraṃ °jāgarti, tadā saptamātrāḥ saṃpadyante Divy 124.9 (preceded by: sā yadaikaṃ vastu rakṣati tat saptaguṇaṃ syāt: perhaps rather with mg. 2, *guards*; but it may well be *attends* to a job); (**4**) *prepares* (food): °jāgaritvā Mv i.307.13; 324.8 (with mss. °jāgarayetvā, to caus., or °jāgaritvā); °jāgrāhi (impv., to °jāgrati) ii.274.12 (bhaktaṃ); iii.141.15; 255.8; 272.1 f.; Divy 306.12 (food and entertainment); Av i.257.14 (bhojanaṃ); MSV i.233.17 ff.; (**5**) *fixes up, decorates, adorns* (orig. prepares, for a festive event), a place: yathājñaptāni sthānāni yathoktaṃ pratijāgriṣu Mv i.76.4 (vs), so read with v.l. for text pari-jā°, unless MIndic paṭi-jā° was the orig. reading, cf. § 2.47 (this might account for pari°

of some mss.); MSV i.264.2; esp. of a *road, way* (usually mārga) over which a distinguished person is to pass, pratijāgratha (impv.), *prepare, adorn, decorate*, Mv ii.150.2; °jāgaretha (opt.) 153.14; °jāgariṣyāmaḥ iii.323.10; ppp. °jāgṛta- Mv i.258.16 (amātyehi ca sarvaṃ °jāgṛtaṃ yathā āṇattaṃ; could belong to 3 above, like Mv ii.180.6, but the king's command was to *adorn* the road); ii.111.8 (amātyehi ... sarvaṃ °jāgṛtaṃ mahatā samṛddhīye pratyudgamanaṃ kṛtaṃ; situation like prec.); devehi mārgo °jāgṛto iii.324.10; °jāgritaṃ Mv i.270.13; ii.150.8; mārgaṃ °jāgraṃsu (v.l. °jāgṛsuḥ; § 32.76) Mv i.259.3; in Mv i.231.11 some form of this verb seems to be intended, (daśakrośamārgaṃ) pratijāgṛhansuḥ (Senart, almost as one ms. which has °jagṛhansuḥ; v.l. pratigrahetsuḥ); Senart suggests contamination with prati-grah-, but this hardly makes sense; what was done is shown by the following (they made the road level, clean, adorned, etc., for the Buddha Dīpaṃkara to pass over).

pratijāgraka, adj. (to prec. plus -aka), *attending to, in charge of*: prahāṇa-°ko bhikṣuḥ MSV iv.77.11.

[**pratijṛmbhitā**, see **pravijṛ°**.]

pratijñā (= Pali paṭiññā, ifc. Bhvr. -paṭiñña, in samaṇa-pa°... brahmacāri-pa° Vin. ii.236.25, same phrase as below), *claim, profession* (to be something, with implication of falseness and presumption; cf. Skt. jñā with prati in BR, mg. 4), only noted in comp., pratijñā-bhikṣu Mvy 8751, *a monk by* (his own) *claim* (only), Tib. here and below khas ḥche ba, *promise with the mouth*; otherwise only at end of cpds., esp. in cliché (as in Pali above) aśramaṇaḥ śramaṇapratijñaḥ, abrahmacārī brahmacāripratijñaḥ Mvy 9143 and 9144 (text °cārī-prati°, both edd.; Mironov °pratijñāḥ both times, as if pl.!); Śikṣ 67.20; MSV i.50.8; plural thruout, same phrase, Śikṣ 64.4–5; ṣaṭ śāstṛpratijñāḥ, *the six false, self-alleged teachers*, **Pūraṇa** (q.v.) etc., Av ii.134.10; ṣaṭ śāstāra-pratijñā(ḥ) (id.) Mv iii.383.15; gen. ṣaṇṇāṃ śāstārapratijñānāṃ 17.

pratijñā-kāraka, m., sc. vinaya, or in MSV nt. with karman (= Pali paṭiññāta-karaṇaṃ, MN ii.248.21 ff., with description, cf. Childers s.v. paṭiññāto), (procedure) *which effects confession* (of the erring one), one of the 7 **adhikaraṇa-śamatha**: Mvy 8637; MSV ii.207.12.

pratijñottaraka, adj. (pratijñā-ut°?), Mvy 1796, perh. *surpassing one's promise; exceeding expectations*; context indicates something like *zealous, energetic*. Tib. kha ḥog tu lus ḥkhrus pa, *bathing the body with face downward* (!); but Chin. *bathing the body with lower part covered, that is, observing propriety even when alone* (a famous Confucian precept).

pratitāḍayati, *beats in return*: tāḍito na °ḍayati KP 107.2; Śikṣ 185.5; tāḍitaḥ °ḍayati Bbh 170.20; tāḍitena (Bhīk °tayā) na °ḍitavyam Mvy 8712; Bhīk 31a.4.

pratitālaka, nt., *key*: Mvy 5906 = Tib. lde mig. Cf. **tālaka**.

pratitiṣṭhati (virtually = Skt. id.), *bases oneself on, relies on* (loc.; pw 7.211; *believes in*, acc. to Müller, SBE 49.2 p. 114, n. 1, = *depends on*, or *accepts as real*): Vaj 21.7–11, 20 (see **nimitta** 1); cf. SP 63.10 upāyakauśalya (uninflected stem form?) pratiṣṭhihitvā (?).

pratidakṣiṇa, adj. (= the usual pradakṣiṇa), with karoti, (*makes so as to be*) *on the right hand*: praṇamya pādau pratidakṣiṇaṃ ca kṛtvaiva māṃ tasthur ihāgrato me LV 7.7 (vs). (No v.l. for prati°.)

pratidiśati (= **pratideśayati**, q.v.), *confesses*: sarvaṃ pratidiśāmy agham Sādh 29.1 = 106.13 (vs; m.c.?).

pratideśa, m., *message*, or *direction, instruction*: rājñā °śo dattaḥ, nirviśaṅkā tiṣṭha MSV ii.24.3.

pratideśanā (to **pratideśayati** with -anā), *confession*: Sūtrāl. xi.62, comm.

pratideśanikā (adj., sc. vipatti or āpatti), = next: MSV iii.109.20 °nikayā.

pratideśanīya, gdve. (to next; = Pali pāṭidesanīya), *requiring confession*, as adj. with dharma: (four) °nīyā dharmāḥ Prāt 525.1; (sc. dharmāḥ) Mvy 8361; as nt. subst., referring to the same set of four offenses, °nīyāni Mvy 8518 (listed in the sequel).

pratideśayati, (**1**) (= Pali paṭideseti; cf. **pratidiśati**), *confesses* (a sin): taṃ (sc. pāpaṃ) pratideśayamī ahu sarvaṃ Bhad 8; also with obj. pāpam Suv 34.4; Kv 31.5; Mmk 146.4; (pāpakaṃ karma ...) °yāmi Sādh 55.14 (prose), etc.; with āpattiṃ Śikṣ 65.6; misc. LV 379.13 (see s.v. **atyaya**); Bbh 263.21; gdve. impersonal, °śayitavyaṃ Prāt 525.5, *he must confess*; (**2**) *renounces, rejects*; only noted in AsP 328.6 bodhicittaṃ (so read) °śaya pratiniḥsṛja (q.v.; the two are synonyms here), and 14 yad etat tvayā pūrvaṃ śrutaṃ tat pratideśaya, yat tvayā pūrvaṃ parigṛhītaṃ tat pratiniḥsṛja (thus Māra tempts Bodhisattvas).

pratidvandvayati (denom. to Skt. pratidvandva, *rival*), *rivals, acts as a rival*: ko 'yam asmābhiḥ sārdhaṃ °yaty alokajñaḥ Divy 403.18.

pratidvāra (= AMg. paḍiduvāra), *small gate, wicket-gate*: svakasya niveśanasya °dvāre asthāsi, bhagavantaṃ ... pratipālayamāno Mv i.324.18.

pratinaya (m.? cf. pratināyaka, acc. to pw 7.389 *Ebenbild, Gegenstück*), *imitation, matching, copying* (but I have not found prati-nī, or MIndic equivalent, recorded in this mg.): (seeking the company and advice of good friends, kalyāṇamitra) tad-guṇa-pratinayeṣu prayujyamāno (*and applying yourself to the imitation of their virtues*) na parikhidyase ... Gv 386.8.

[**pratināva** or **°vā**, acc. **°vaṃ**, see **pratinau.**]

? **pratinirvāti**, may be error, = **parinir°**: °vāsyāmi MSV i.259.12; in the context parinir° occurs. Cf. however § 2.47.

pratinivārayate (cf. noun pratinivāraṇa, once in late Skt., BR), *wards off, keeps away*: (vihiṃsācittān, Bhvr.) °yamānān Gv 87.7, *keeping away those minded to injuriousness*.

pratinivāsana, nt. (= Pali paṭi°, wrongly transl. in PTSD; see SBE 13.155), (monk's) *undergarment*: Mvy 8939 = Tib. śam thabs kyi gzan; Chin. *underpiece for a monk's garment* (lining?); Kalpanāmaṇḍitikā, Lüders, Kl. Skt. Texte 2, p. 44.

pratiniviśati, ger. °viśya (recorded only in ppp. °viṣṭa, BR, *ganz mit Etwas beschäftigt, nur für Eines Sinn habend*), perh. *taking a keen interest*: tatra (sc. nagare) praviśya (*having entered there*) pratiniviśya nagaraṃ nagarakriyāsukham anubhavet Laṅk 143.16.

pratiniṣaṇṇa, *severally seated*: vaiḍūryāsaneṣu (mss. °sane; Tib. plur.) °ṇṇān Suv 20.5 (prose).

-pratiniṣevaṇa(-tā), ifc., *cultivation* (of), *adherence* (to), *severally, in each case* (prati): (karmaṇaḥ ...) °vaṇena (by em.; Tib. cited as so sor bsten cin, read ciṅ) samudānayanam Bbh 107.27; pañcāṅgāpramāda-°ṇa-tayā 187.5.

pratiniṣkrānta, ppp. (=AMg. paḍinikkhanta), *returned*: MSV iii.17.17; 18.1.

pratinisarga, pratinisṛjati, see **pratiniḥs°**.

pratinistarati, *accomplishes, fulfils* (*in a way corresponding to promise*, prati): pratijñāṃ °reta Divy 102.14.

pratiniḥsaraṇa (nt.; cf. Pali paṭinissarati, *escapes*; see next), *escape*, in duḥ-prati° (Bhvr.), *hard to escape from*: duḥ°ṇam copādānaṃ (see **upādāna** 3) RP 48.6.

[**pratiniḥsarati**? mss. reading at Mv i.192.1; Senart em. pratiniḥsṛja, see s.v. **pratiniḥsṛjati.**]

pratiniḥsarga, m., also written °**nisarga** (to next; = Pali paṭinissagga), *abandonment, renunciation*: in LV 31.21 text °sargāyai, as if f., but best ms. °sarga-tāyai, so read, in cpd., sarvopadhipratiniḥsarga, m. (except here, in LV 31.21; note synonym parivarjana-tāyai LV 31.16); Mv ii.285.20; iii.314.4–5 (em.; but certain); Mvy 2549 (°nisargaḥ); of dṛṣṭi, or wrong opinions, Av ii.188.1; 190.2 (both °nisargo); Prāt 516.2; of tṛṣṇā, Mv iii.332.9; Samy.

Āg. 1.3; of dharmas, esp. as being pratītyasamutpanna, Mv iii.61.4; Av ii.194.3; kāmānāṃ Bhīk 24a.3; of misc. or unspecified evils, LV 431.3; Gv 189.21; Mvy 7666 (°nisargaḥ).

pratiniḥsṛjati, often written °**nisṛjati** (= Pali paṭinissajjati; cf. prec.), *renounces, abandons* (usually a wrong opinion, or something evil): °nisṛjya Mvy 2547; °nisṛjati 2556; °nisrakṣyati 5232 (v.l. and Mironov °kṣati); °nisṛjati... dāruṇaṃ manaṃ (=manaḥ) Mv i.184.11 (Senart em. °niḥsṛ°); tāṃ dṛṣṭiṃ pratiniḥsṛja 192.1, Senart's em., mss. °niḥsara; tāṃ dṛṣṭiṃ °niḥsṛjya (mss. mostly °jā) 192.2, confirming the em.; °niḥsarati would seem to require an abl., *depart* or *escape from*; Pali has paṭinissarati, Nett. 113.1, 9, 11, used absolutely, without dependent noun, *escape, be freed* (comm. acc. to PTSD niyyāti, vimuccati; the extracts from the comm. in PTS ed. do not contain this or any gloss); kleśagaṇaṃ... pratiniḥsṛṣṭaṃ Divy 44.17; (°nisṛṣṭaṃ) 275.8; dṛṣṭiṃ pratiniḥsṛjaty Av ii.190.2 (mss. °jyaty; Speyer em. °nisṛ°!); pratiniḥsṛja AsP 328.6, 15, see s.v. **pratideśayati** (2); pratiniḥsṛje(d) Prāt 514.14, 15 (a wrong opinion); caus. pratinisṛjāpayiṣyanti MSV iv.140.7.

pratinau (cf. AMg. paḍiṇāviyā, *boat coming to meet another boat*), *meeting-boat, landing-boat* (to bring persons ashore from a sea-going ship): so dāni tataḥ yānapātrāto pratināvaṃ (acc.) āruhiṣyatīti Mv ii.90.11; same form 13.

pratipaṃsayati (see **paṃs**°), *disparages, reviles, in return*: (paṃsito na) pratip° KP 107.3.

pratipakṣa, nt.? (in Skt. only m., *rival, enemy*; acc. to PTSD, Pali paṭipakkha also adj., *opposed, opposite*; perh. *obstacle* in Vv. comm. 20.24 [puññakiriyā...] paṭipakkha-chedana-samatthā), *obstacle* (? so Index): (vatsa yadi kevalaṃ) cittaṃ parijñātuṃ na śakyasi, pratipakṣaṃ mocayitum Divy 352.18, *there is an obstacle to setting you free* (? *it interferes with*...).

pratipakṣika, adj. (= Pali paṭipakkhika), = **prāti**°, q.v.

pratipaṇya, *merchandise in exchange*: °yaṃ, acc., Divy 173.5; 271.27; 564.2. (Schmidt, Nachträge, records Skt. pratipaṇyatā, once.)

pratipattavya, gdve. of prati-pad-, nt. as quasi-postpos. with gen., *on account of*: devasya °tavyam MSV ii.20.10, (it is) *on account of your Majesty*; so Tib., lhaḥi slad du ḥo.

pratipatti, f. (not far in mg. from Skt. id., BR s.v. 5; but closer to Pali paṭipatti), *behavior, practice, performance*, esp. *good behavior*, religiously; opp. to **vipratipatti,** q.v.; here are included some passages previously misinterpreted (esp. those from SP): pratipatti (acc.) darśeti bahuprakāraṃ (v.l. °rāṃ) SP 120.5 (vs), (the Buddha) *shows* (to men of various sorts) *good behavior in many ways*, or *the various sorts of good behavior*; pratipattyā ca saṃpādayet 395.12 (prose), *and* (who) *shall put into effect* (this sūtra) *by his behavior* (*conduct, in practice*); ye tubhya dharma śrutvā pratipattim eṣyatī hi LV 355.12 (vs), *who, having heard the dharma from you, will arrive at proper behavior* (i.e. will put it into practice); °ttīya saṃpanno Mv ii.357.20, *perfect in behavior*; ārādhyate satpratipattimadbhir dharmo Jm 106.19, *by those having virtuous behavior*; °tti-guṇasauṣṭhavāc ca 142.17, °tti-śobhayā 20; vācayā yatha vadanti te budhās tatra caiva pratipattiyā (*in actual practice*) sthitāḥ RP 11.1 (vs); śrutvā ca tasmin pratipattiye sthito 36.12 (vs), *and having heard it he remains steadfast in it by his behavior*; °ttiś ca mayāpi bhāṣitā iha sūtre 59.10 (vs); pratipattitu Śikṣ 4.16, *thru their holy behavior*; sarvabodhisattvaśikṣā-pratipattayaḥ Gv 461.9 (Bhvr., *characterized by practice of*...); °ttiṣu vyādhinirghātanasaṃjñā Gv 464.10, misquoted śatrunirghātana° Śikṣ 36.4, *to good behavior* (*should be applied*) *the name of destroyer of diseases*; bhūtapratipattiḥ śramaṇaḥ KP 125.1, *a monk of true* (*correct*) *behavior*; Bbh 3.22; 4.2 (see s.v. **pratipanna**); 213.18; pratipatti-kāmo Dbh.g. 16(352).17; Dbh 25.13 ff.; note esp. line 15, ... anavakāśo yad ātmā vipratipattisthitaḥ parān samyak-pratipattau sthāpayet..., *it is inconceivable that myself remaining in evil behavior should establish others in good behavior*; pratipatti-vipratipattisthitānā(ṃ) sattvānām anutsargaḥ (*not dismissing*) ekāṃśavacanatā (*speaking to them in the same way*) KP 25.7; (eteṣu...) dharmeṣu pratipattir na vipratipattiḥ Samādh p. 14 line 2, *good, not bad, behavior*; sarvatragāminī-pratipattijñāna-balam Dharmas 76, see s.v. **pratipad,** which is here and often interchangeable with pratipatti. In MSV ii.86.10 read with ms. amuko bhikṣuḥ sa bhagavatā pratipa(t)tyeva vyākṛtaḥ (ed. °tāḥ, doubtless misprint); pratipattyā iva, *as it seems by his intellectual realization* (so Skt. pratipatti), or *with confidence due to experience* (so AMg. paḍivatti); the ed. em. to pratipadyeva, stating in note that Tib. reads sṅa nas, which means *formerly* and which I cannot relate to either reading. Is there a corruption?

pratipad, f., also °**dā** (= Pali paṭipadā), *course of conduct, practice, behavior*, esp. *good, approved behavior*, = **pratipatti,** q.v.; acc. to Childers and PTSD, so also primarily Pali paṭipadā; this mg. is recognized by Speyer on Av ii.130.2, which he reads by em. araṇya-°daṃ samādāya (better, I think araṇāṃ pra°, see s.v. **araṇya**; in that case render *passionless way of behavior*); he also accepts this mg. in puṇyāṃ pratipadam udbhāvayan dānadamasaṃyamādibhiḥ Jm 100.10, *displaying meritorious behavior by*...; vākpragraheṇa pratipanmayena Jm 105.2, *by* (the kind of) *acceptance of his words which consists of behavior*, i.e. by not only assenting verbally but putting them into practice; (anayāpi... caryayānayāpi) pratipadā LV 263.11 (pratipad = caryā), and similarly 264.18; often rendered *way, path*, and called 'a quasi-synonym of magga' in PTSD; this is due to the fact that the *middle course of conduct*, madhyamā pratipad(ā), is (in BHS as in Pali) identified with the eight-fold way (mārga) stated in the fourth Noble Truth, but the terms are quite differently defined, ma° pra° being the course of *behavior* which steers between the two extremes (anta) of violent asceticism and worldliness; the lack of real synonymity between Pali magga and paṭipadā is shown, e.g., by DN ii.154.25–26 (kaṅkhā vā vimati vā) Buddhe vā dhamme vā saṃghe vā magge vā paṭipadāya vā (obviously different things must be meant); madhyamayaiva pratipadā LV 416.21 (contrasted with amadhyamā pratipad = violent asceticism, 416.19); here as elsewhere such a statement introduces the Four Noble Truths, the fourth of which is duḥkhanirodhagāminī pratipad (with or without āryasatyam, in LV 417.3, 12 without it, in 12 = eṣa evāryāṣṭāṅgamārgaḥ); so Mvy 1314, 1319, 1324; Mv ii.138.5 (with āryasatyam) and 10 (without it); 285.4 (without it); SP 179.3 (with it); more metaphysical interpretations of the term madhyamā pratipad in Bbh 39.26; KP 52.6 and repeatedly in following sections; one of the ten bala of a Tathāgata is sarvatragāmanī-pratipaj-jñānam Mvy 125, cf. sarvatragāminī-(the more usual form)-pratipatti-jñāna-balam Dharmas 76 (note obvious equivalence of pratipad and pratipatti!), *power of knowledge of courses of conduct which may lead to any result*; in same context sarvatragāminīṃ ca pratipadaṃ (v.l. °dāṃ) vetti Mv i.159.13 (vs), and, for another, see s.v. **pratipadā**; parānukampā-pratipad Jm 28.7, *conducting oneself with compassion for others*; nairyāṇika- (and °kī) pratipad, see s.v. **nairyāṇika**; śaikṣa-pratipady uttarikaraṇīyam (see this) Sukh 2.13, *in the course* (*practice*; here we could also, no doubt, translate *path*) of the **śaikṣa** (q.v.); there are four *courses of conduct* (Tib. lam, *way, path*, but also *manner of conduct*) Mvy 1244–1248, viz duḥkhā pra° dhandhābhijñā, sukhā pra° dhandhābhijñā, duḥkhā pra° kṣiprābhijñā, sukhā pra° kṣiprā° (for the corresponding Pali list, and interpretation, see Childers s.v. paṭipadā). See also next.

pratipadā = prec. (as in Pali paṭipadā), but very much rarer; hence, where saṃdhi is ambiguous, I have assigned the doubtful forms to **pratipad**: dharmadeśanā-pratipadā-saṃpannaṃ ... śāstāraṃ Mv iii.201.9, *perfected in the practice of preaching the law*; ye sarvatragāminīpratipadāṃ tatratatragāminīpratipadāṃ ... prajānanti 320.14, in list of the ten **bala** of a Tathāgata, see pratipad, towards the end; nirvāṇagāminī °dā 201.15, 18; madhyamā °dā 331.8, 10, between the two extremes, introducing Four Noble Truths; in 12 the word mārga is omitted, text reading yad idam āryāṣṭāṅgikā, sayyathīdaṃ samyagdṛṣṭiḥ etc.; but one ms. reads āryāṣṭāṅgikaḥ, implying mārgaḥ as in all known parallels, and the adaptation to the fem. gender of pratipad in one ms. (followed by Senart) is prob. an error, resulting from the accidental omission of the noun mārgaḥ; below the usual formulas are found, duḥkhanirodhagāminī pratipad-āryasatyaṃ 331.18; tatra katamā (mss. °mo!) duḥkhanirodhagāminī pratipad āryasatyā (! so mss. and Senart), eṣaiva āryāṣṭāṅgo mārgo, etc., 332.9–10.

pratipadyati (Pali paṭipajjati seems so used, but hardly Skt.; cf. **pratipatti, °pad, °panna**), *behaves*, with instr. of manner: yan nv aham alpāhāratayā pratipadyeyam LV 254.2 (prose), *suppose now I behave with (practise according to the method of) taking scant food*. This seems the most probable interpretation; otherwise Tib., which renders the instr. -tayā by la, as if dative, and then has nan tan bya ḥo, *I shall make earnest effort to eat scant food*; I can hardly believe this is what the text means.

pratipadyana-tā (to prec., with -ana plus -tā), in bodhisattvamārga-°tāyai Gv 367.14 (prose), *unto state of practice of the bodhisattva-way*.

pratipanna, ppp. (to **°padyati**; Pali paṭipanna similarly used), *practised* (sc. in religiously proper behavior): impersonally (passive), (sārthavāhenāpi) kiṃcit pūrvaṃ pratipannaṃ Mv iii.354.4, *the merchant, for his part, had to some extent engaged in previous practice* (of a religious course); so Senart in 19 (vāṇijakehi) pūrvaṃ (read pūrveṇa, mss. pūrvāṇa) pratipannaṃ, but mss. pratipannās, n. pl., as if with active mg., *having practised*; cf. Pali Vv.34 vs 23 cattāro ca paṭipannā (comm. 154.31 paṭipajjamānā, maggaṭṭhā ti attho) cattāro ca phale ṭhitā; also, as in Pali, *behaving, acting* (for the purpose of, dat.), ātmahitāya pratipanno ... parahitāya etc. Bbh 4.3.

pratipannaka, (adj. or) subst. (Pali paṭipannaka; = Skt. °nna, with specifying ka, § 22.39), *one that has resorted to ...*, in adhva-pra° (= Pali magga-paṭi°, Dhp. comm. i.233.16 ff.), *one that has taken to the road, gone traveling*: MSV i.249.7.

(**pratipādaka**, nt. (= Pali paṭi°), *leg* (support) *of a bed*: Mvy 9044 = Tib. khri ḥu rkaṅ rten, supported by Pali; there seems to be a Tib. var. skra ḥi, *of hair*, for khri ḥu, *of a bed*; hence BR *eine Schale für Haare*, and Chin. *cut-hair receptacle* (or *instrument*). The adjoining words in Mvy seem to me to support the other interpretation. And in fact Skt. has the word in this mg.; see Schmidt, Nachträge.)

pratipādanaka (nt.; = Skt. °na), *bestowal*: yācanaka-saṃgha-pratipādanakārthaṃ (adv.) Gv 403.17 (prose).

pratipādayati, *gives, presents* (so Skt., with acc. of thing and loc., dat., or gen. of person; used thus regularly in BHS; note passive pratipādīyati, Divy 226.21, prose, mss., ed. em. pratipradīyate), used occasionally with acc. of person and instr. of thing presented, as in Eng. *presents with*: pass., eka-kola-tila-taṇḍula-pradānena ca pratipādito 'bhūt (sc. Bodhisattvaḥ) LV 265.3, *was presented with ...*; ebhir (sc. kārṣāpaṇair) amba śramaṇa-brāhmaṇa-kṛpaṇa-vanīpakān pratipādayasveti Av i.198.11, *present monks ... with these*; same, with anena for ebhir, i.262.2–3, et alibi.

pratipāditaka, adj. (°dita, ppp. of °dayati, plus specifying -ka), (*the one*) *that has been* (previously) *presented*: °kam pūrṇakalaśaṃ Mmk 51.4.

(**pratipālaka**, once in late Skt., Schmidt, Nachträge, not in Pali, *protector*: LV 277.15, prose.)

pratipibate, *drinks back* (the subject's own poison): viṣaṃ pratipibasva Mmk 462.22 (prose; addressed to a snake, in a magic practice).

pratipīḍā (cf. Skt. °pīḍana, Pali °pīḷana), *affliction*: Mv ii.145.13, 15, 18.

pratipudgala, °puṃgala (see **pudgala**), (**1**) = Pali paṭipuggala, and cf. a-prati°, *match, equal, counterpart*: nāsti me pratipuṃgalaḥ LV 406.3 (vs); (**2**) pl., *several, distinct personalities*, if text is right: tathāṣṭau pratipudgalāḥ Dharmas 103; but text is badly corrupted here; the foll. list contains more than 8 items confusedly drawn from list found in Mvy 1008–28 and in Pali, Pug. p. 3.

pratipudgalika, adj. (to prec., mg. 2; = Pali paṭipuggalika, pāṭi°, misdefined in PTSD), *particular, individual, belonging to a specific person*: etad agraṃ ... °kānāṃ dakṣiṇānām Karmav 156.13. Also **prātipaudgalika**.

pratipuṣṭa (ppp. of otherwise unknown prati-puṣ-), *nourished on, fed with*: (nṛṇāṃ, *of ordinary men* ...) tīrthakara-dṛṣṭi-prativikalpa-(q. v.)-vāsanā-(q. v.)-°ṭānāṃ Laṅk 150.13.

pratipūra, adj. (to Skt. pratipūrayati; cf. **pūra** and Pali paripūra, *full, complete*), *full, complete, replete*: sarvākāra-°raṃ (dharmaṃ, as preached by Buddha) Mv i.60.5; ii.259.16; °raṃ arthaṃ prārthayamāno (*seeking a complete, full, aim, goal*) bodhisattvo ... Mv ii.279.3 (v.l. °pūrṇam); yathā gaganaṃ pratipūraṃ (read °ra) tārakehi ii.371.15.

pratipūraka, adj. (to Skt. pratipūrayati with -aka; see prec.), *filling*: apāya-pratipūrakā bhavetsu(ḥ) Mv i.61.4–5 (mss.), *they were filling* (i. e. crowding, occupying in great numbers) *the evil states of existence*.

pratipūri, f. (= **paripūri**, q.v.), *fulfilment*, (perfect) *accomplishment*: traividyavidyā-pratipūryā LV 441.7 (prose; so, or °ryai, mss.; not to be em. to °pūrtyā with Weller 39); kāya-°riṃ Śikṣ 30.14 (prose), *perfect development of body*.

pratipūrti, f. (to Skt. pratipūrayati), *fulfilment*: °tyai LV 35.13, 22 (no v.l.); in 32.18 and 33.16 Lefm. paripūrtyai for Calc. prati°, in the former with most mss., in the latter with the best (but most others prati°).

pratiprakhyā (cf. Skt. prakhyā), *resemblance*, implied in Bhvr. cpd. -khya: dharmakośaṃ cintāmaṇi-pratiprakhyaṃ Mmk 301.5 (prose), *having a resemblance to* ...

prati-pratidivasam, adv., *every single day*: LV 256.11 (prose). The double prati seems not to be represented in Tib., and may be dittography, but is found in most mss. incl. the best.

pratipraśrabdha, ppp. (or °srabdha; = Pali paṭippassaddha; ppp. to **pratipraśrambha(ya)ti**; cf. **a-prati°** and **praśr°**), *quieted, allayed, finished, ended*: Mvy 845 karmāvaraṇa-prati°, of Bodhisattvas; LV 428.11 sarvasaṃskāra-pratipraśrabdha-tvād, *because all his saṃs° are quieted*; kāraṇāviśeṣāḥ pratiprasrabdhā(ḥ), *all torments are allayed*, Divy 68.9; 138.16; 265.23; 367.3, 6 (here mss. °śra°); ṛddhyabhisaṃskārāḥ prati° Divy 340.11; yan mayā (253.5 yāvat) prayogo na °srabdhaḥ MSV i.252.15; 253.5, *until my use for them is finished*.

pratipraśrabdhi, f. (or °srabdhi; = Pali paṭippassaddhi; to **pratipraśrambha(ya)ti**; cf. **a-prati°** and **praśra°**), *allaying, quieting, putting an end to*: LV 33.12 and 34.14, read °śrabdhyai for Lefm. with all mss. °śraddhyai, unless semi-MIndic assimilation be assumed (Tib. rgyun chad; cpd. with sarvavedita-, sarveṣaṇa-, respectively); Mvy 1383 karmāvaraṇa-prati° (n. of a work); Śikṣ 29.12 narakāpāya-pra°; Gv 165.21 °dhaye, *unto becoming peaceful*; 217.22, see a-prati°; Dbh 66.19 sarvasattvakārya-prati°, *relaxation, abandonment of the interests of all beings* (would ensue if Bodhisattvas entered nirvāṇa); Bbh 63.3 °dhi-sukham, apparently sc. of obstacles, nivaraṇa; cf. the next sentence; or possibly as in Gv 165.21 above, *becoming peaceful*?

pratipraśrambhaṇa, nt. (or °srambh°; to next; = Pali paṭippassambhanā, f., BHS °**śrabdhi**), *allaying*: Dbh 83.15 sarvāpāya-pra°; Bbh 210.16 -duḥkha-pratiprasrambhaṇa-tāyai; *ceasing*: Laṅk 212.16 sarvakārya-pra°. See **a-prati°.**

pratipraśrambha(ya)ti, (or °sram°; see **praśrabhyate;** = Pali paṭippassambheti; PTSD records also °mbhati as pass. or intrans., but only °śrabhyate or °srabhyate, °ti, is so used in BHS), *quiets, allays, puts an end to*, regularly said of evils, but rarely also, apparently, of good things: °mbhayati, °yanti, duḥkhāni Bbh 63.10; Megh 296.13; Dbh 83.26; opt. °śrambheyuḥ, for °bhayeyuḥ, Megh 292.19 (duḥkhāni); inf. °śrambhayitum Mv i.254.2 (vyādhim); ger. °śrabhya or °srabhya, duḥkhāni Mmk 182.3; Dbh 8.17; ṛddhyabhisaṃskārān (once written °rām, 163.3) Divy 161.11; 163.3; 190.22; 494.22; sarvakarmāntān Divy 549.10; in Gv 53.23 (Mañjuśrīḥ) sattvānāṃ dharmadeśanādhiṣṭhānaṃ pratipraśrabhya prakrāntaḥ, *having brought to an end* (by fulfilment), *completed* (?); pass. °srabhyati, subject disease (vyādhi), Mv i.253.9(?), 10 ff.; °bhyate or °bhyante, kāraṇā-viśeṣāḥ Divy 68.3; 138.10; 367.1; 568.15; Av i.4.11; 10.11, etc.; duḥkhāni Mmk 183.6.

[**pratiprahītavyam** LV 408.2, misprint for **pratigrah°.**]

[**pratiprākaroti,** see **paṭipā°.**]

pratiprākāra, m., Mvy 5541 = Tib. phyi ra, *outer* (or *rear*) *wall.*

pratipriya, adj. or subst. nt. (in Skt. *return favor*), *a matching, corresponding kindness*: °yaṃ duṣkarakaṃ hi kartum SP 119.6 (vs), *for it were a hard task to perform a kindness corresponding* (to those done by the Buddha); wrongly Kern, *resistance*; better Burnouf, *rivaliser.*

pratibibharti, see **pratibharati.**

pratibimbya, adj. (Skt. °mba plus -ya), *acting as reflection*: -pratibimbya-rūpāṇi (Bhvr.) Gv 96.6.

pratibodhi (cf. Skt. pratibodha), *realization, comprehension*: Gv 333.2 (prose) dharmāṇāṃ grahaṇa-cāraṇa-pratibodhiṣu (dvandva).

pratibhajati, °te, (**1**) (once recorded from Mbh 12 in pw but considered error for pravibhajati; however, Pali paṭibhajitvā MN iii.91.5, and BHS, suggest that Skt. prati° may be genuine) *divides, gives a share in*: amṛtaṃ pratibhajamānaṃ Mv ii.42.8, (the Buddha) *when he is sharing out amṛta* (to the people); (dharmadeśanāṃ . . .) matyā pratibhajāmi Gv 207.5, but in repetitions of the same phrase lines 11, 26, pravibhajāmi; (**2**) (cf. Pali paṭibh°, *divides*) *distinguishes, makes distinctions in*: Bbh 401.12 pratipadaṃ . . . °ti, iyaṃ pratipat saṃkleśāyeyaṃ vyavadānāya . . .; ppp. pratibhakta, *several, separate,* nakṣatreṣu °kteṣu Divy 642.17. See also **pratibhāgeti.**

pratibhaṇati, see s.v. **pratibhāṇita.**

pratibhaṇḍayati (Pali paṭibhaṇḍati), *abuses, quarrels, in return*: bhaṇḍitaḥ °yati Bbh 170.20; bhaṇḍito na °yati KP 107.3; bhaṇḍitena (Bhīk °tayā) na °bhaṇḍitavyam Mvy 8711; Bhīk 31a.4.

pratibharati, pratibibharti, *supports in return*: bhṛtaḥ pratibibhṛyād (Divy 99.5; 440.27 pratibhared), said of a son, in a cliché, Divy 2.13; 99.5; 440.27; Av i.14.15 etc.; MSV i.131.12.

? **pratibhāga,** m. (perh. read pravibhāga, which has this mg. in Skt.; but note Pali paṭibhāga, *opposite, counterpart,* MN i.304.8 ff.), *difference, distinction*: (mṛtpiṇḍa-paramāṇvoḥ) °go na syāt Laṅk 38.13, *there would be no difference between the lump of clay and the atoms* (composing it).

pratibhāgeti (denom. to Skt. pratibhāga; cf. **pratibhajati**; pw regards pravibhāga as the 'correct' form of the noun), *shares, gives a share in*: striyāye pratibhāgehi Mv ii.426.8, *give me a share in* (i. e. the use of) *a woman.* So by Senart's em., which seems probable; mss. °bhānehi or °bhāṇehi.

[**pratibhāṇa** is read by the mss., and sometimes in Nobel's text, of Suv, for **pratibhāna,** q.v.; it seems to be a mere corruption. Cf. next.]

[**pratibhāṇika,** see °**nika.**]

pratibhāṇita, ppp., m.c. for °bhaṇita (to pratibhaṇ-, recorded in Skt. only in a single artificial passage; not in Pali; AMg. paḍibhaṇai), *answered, responded to*: °to Mv ii.37.17 (vs: v.l. °bhaṇito; meter requires ā).

(**pratibhāti,** as in Skt. [BR s.v.4], in pratibhāti no bhagavan SP 101.9, means *it is perfectly clear to us, we are completely reassured, Lord.* Kern's transl. is correct; his note suggests needless uncertainty; Burnouf is wrong.)

pratibhāna, nt., also written °**ṇa** in mss. and some edd. (= Pali paṭi°; usually considered a Buddhist word, see e. g. Senart Mv i.511, Lévi Sūtrāl. on i.12, and PTSD s.v., where 'late Skt.' prati° is derived from Pali; yet Epic and Class. Skt. use at least the adj. pratibhānavant repeatedly, and see Ind. Spr. 6451 pratibhānavattvam, *Geistesgegenwart*; the difference is surely not great, but perhaps association with *readiness in speech* is more marked in Pali and BHS), *presence of mind, self-confidence* or *brilliance*, esp. as manifested in speech; *quickwittedness, inspiration*; Tib. spobs pa, *courage, confidence*; one of the four **pratisaṃvid,** q.v.; equivalent to commoner Skt. pratibhā, *wit, presence of mind,* whence **niṣpratibhāna** (Mvy, Av) is replaced in Divy by niṣpratibha, in a cliché cited s.v. **maṅku,** q.v., where the mg. seems to be *without presence of mind, abashed, out of countenance*: SP 393.11 (vs; the 3 other pratisaṃvid in 12, same vs); sarvabodhisattvadhāraṇī-pratibhāna-pratilabdhaiḥ LV 2 6; **utkṛṣṭa-pra°** 439.10; jñānaparamā asaṃkliṣṭapratibhānāś ca Mv i.134.7; miscellaneous, Mv i.166.8; 282.17 (one of ten vaśitā of bodhisattvas); ii.290.18 (°na-saṃpannāḥ, of bodhisattvas); anāchedya-pra° Mvy 851 (of bodhisattvas); Suv 13.2 (tasya °nam utpannam, *he became inspired to speak his thoughts*); 102.17 (spelled °ṇam, as often in mss. of Suv, here kept in ed.); Mvy 389 (anantaḥ °nena, of Tathāgatas); Samādh 19.30; RP 14.15; Bhad 6[2]; Kv 14.9 (here the quality by which Avalokiteśvara 'matures', paripācayati, creatures); Sukh 4.4. See also **pratibhānatā, -vant; asaṅga-prati°.**

Pratibhānakūṭa, n. of a Bodhisattva: Mvy 703.

pratibhānatā = **pratibhāna**: Karmav 82.5 (here by em. but quite certain), 9.

pratibhānavant (= Pali paṭi°; occurs in Skt.), *possessing* **pratibhāna,** q.v.: LV 299.7; Mv i.133.11 (°vantāś, mss. °vāṃś, n. pl.); Suv 80.10; RP 15.2 (vs; °vān, as n. pl.; § 18.88).

pratibhānika, adj. (from °**bhāna** plus -ika): (nāpi ca) svayaṃpratibhāṇiko (grantho) Mv ii.231.4 (vs; so with one ms.), *of one's own invention or native wit*; read °niko for °ṇiko (Senart em. wrongly).

[**pratibhāṣyate,** error for °syate, fut. of Skt. pratibhāti, *seems good*: (na . . . rasatṛṣṇāvyavasitānām idaṃ praṇītaṃ) bhojanaṃ pratibhāsyate Laṅk 250.6, *this excellent food will not seem pleasing to* . . .]

pratibhāsa, m. (in this sense unrecorded elsewhere; also used as in Skt. in mgs. *appearance*, Dbh 16.4, *presentation to the mind*, LV 397.15), *reflected image*: (śakrasya . . . devānāṃ ca) °saḥ saṃdṛśyate sma LV 69.6 (so Tib., gzugs brñan; possibly however only actual, literal *appearance*, as in Skt.); commonly as (mere) *semblance*, with emphasis on *unreality*, (kāmaguṇāḥ) . . . pratibhāsasamā naṭaraṅgasamāḥ. LV 174.6; māyā-marīci-svapnodakacandra-pratiśrutkā-pratibhāsa- LV 181.21; 428.14; in similar lists Mvy 854; Dbh 47.14; Dbh.g. 29(55).3; (parallel with chāyā, svapna, pratiśrutkā) Gv 468.21; with things of no value, tṛṇa-kāṣṭha-kuḍya-(Dbh adds vartma-)-pratibhāsopama Dbh 18.14; Śikṣ 201.9 (here said of the body, as also in) Śikṣ 272.10 and (ātma-pratibhāsavat, *like an illusion, illusory image, of self*) Śikṣ 199.6; saṃsārasāgari anantān darśayase gatīyu (gen. sg.) °sān Gv 253.13 (vs), *in the ocean of saṃsāra thou displayest endless semblances of* (human) *fate(s)*; in Bbh 282.7 of toys, imitations of real things; in Dbh.g. 40(66).13 of the reflection of sun and moon in water.

pratibhinnaka, adj. (from ppp. of Skt. prati-bhid-, *show up, reveal*, plus -ka, perh. pejorative), *shown up, betrayed, revealed*: sa °kaḥ saṃlakṣayate Divy 280.16 (Index *undecided?*).

pratibhuka, m. (= Skt. pratibhū; M. paḍihua), *surety, guarantor*: pratibhuko Mv ii.141.4, 5 (prose); 143.8, 10, 13 (vss); elsewhere in the context pratibhū, e. g. 142.20 °bhūr.

pratibhūṣyaṃ, 1 sg. fut., cf. Skt. pratibhū, *I will warrant*: Mv ii.142.17 (vs); no v.l.; meter correct; a nonce-form based on the noun; § 31.15.

[**pratima**, in Gv 372.16, read apratima-; see s.v. **traiyadhvika.**]

pratimaṇḍana (nt.; to next plus -ana), *ornamentation*: LV 432.22 (prose); -sarvavyūha-pratimaṇḍana- Gv 343.25 (prose), and in Gv 320.10 (prose) read -vyūha-pratimaṇḍana- for text °ḍala-.

pratimaṇḍayati (in Pali only ppp. paṭimaṇḍita), *adorns*: perf. °ḍayām āsa Gv 415.6; inf. °ḍayitum LV 187.18; ppp. °ḍita (various forms) SP 68.3; 227.7; 239.4; LV 211.17; 277.6; 402.6; Laṅk 1.7; Mv ii.360.10; iii.246.15; Divy 315.9 (°ḍikā, ed. em. °ḍitā); Av i.87.6; Suv 202.4; RP 6.13; 40.11; Gv 8.5; 100.20. Cf. prec.

pratimānayati (in this sense not in Skt.; whether so used in Pali I am not sure; I have been unable to find the majority of references for paṭimāneti in PTSD), *provides, presents with* (instr., usually *food*): āhāreṇa pratimānetvā Mv i.302.5; °netha iii.304.2; °nito, ppp., iii.414.11; (scilicet) a woman, Mv iii.2.15 (vs), mss. corrupt, perh. read: stryāgārārthiko iha gacche me pratimānaya, *I came here wanting a woman; provide me* (with one); daivatāni bhūtāni vṛṣṭyā °yanti Jm 69.3 (vs), *the deities present creatures with rain.* See also **saṃpratimān°**.

pratimudrā, lit. *'counter-seal', seal impression*: mudrāt pratimudra (a m.c.) dṛśyate LV 176.15 (vs). Cited by BR also from Mvy, but not in Index to Kyoto ed. or Mironov.

pratimuhyati (otherwise known only in caus. pratimohaya- in AV), *becomes confused*: na °hyema Laṅk 211.5.

pratimoka, see **paṭimoka.**

pratimokṣa = **prātimokṣa**, q.v. (the literary work): na ca pratimokṣa-vinaye vā RP 30.11 (vs; perhaps pra- for prā- m.c., but meter is obscure to me); pratimokṣa-saṃvara-saṃvṛtā(ḥ) Kv 98.23 (prose).

pratimokṣita, ppp. (either to Skt. mokṣayati, denom., with prati, cf. Skt. pratimokṣaṇa; or ppp. to denom. from pratimokṣa, Pali paṭimokkha), *ransomed, redeemed*: (evaṃ Bhagavatā) sārthaś caurasahasrāt pratimokṣitaḥ Divy 94.18.

[**pratimodaka**, false reading for **paṭimoka** (or prati°), q.v.]

pratiyatta, ppp. (to Skt. prati-yat-, not in this sense; Pali paṭiyatta), *prepared, made*: yehi iha advārakā gharā pratiyattā (mss. gharo pratipattā) bhavanti Mv i.24.13, *by whom in this life doorless houses are prepared.*

pratiyācate, *begs, requests*: sattvā āgatyābhayaṃ °cante sma LV 90.11 (prose, no v.l.).

pratiruta (nt.? in Skt. as ppp. only, not recorded otherwise; = Skt. pratirava), *echo*: (sarva-)ruta-pratiruta-niścāraṇa-kauśalya-prāptatvād LV 435.11 (prose, no v.l.).

pratirodana, nt. (= Pali paṭi°, Jāt. iii.80.25, in closely similar vs), *crying back*, rejecting the 'cry' of one who asks for something: yācanāṃ rodanam āhu adānam pratirodanaṃ Mv iii.419.13 (vs).

pratiroṣayati (Pali paṭirosati), *is angry in return*: roṣitaḥ °ṣayati Bbh 170.19; roṣito na °ṣayati Śikṣ 185.5; KP 107.3; roṣitena (Bhīk °tayā) na °roṣitavyam Mvy 8710; Bhīk 31a.4.

pratilakṣaṇa, *perfect observance* (of the Law): saddharma-°ṇa-tayā LV 440.20, *by reason of the fact that he perfectly observes the Good Law*; so Tib., dam paḥi chos yoṅs su sruṅ bas. No v.l., but em. to °rakṣaṇa (so Foucaux, Notes p. 209)? Or l for r, § 2.49? Prose; not in Weller.

-pratilambhika, adj. (also **prāti°**, q.v.; to Skt. pratilambha plus -ika; cf. pratilābhika), *suited (fit, ready) for attainment* (*of*...; ifc.): (kāmāvacarāṇāṃ) devānām upapatti-pratilambhikam (see s.v. prāti°) api tāvad divyaṃ cakṣuḥ Bbh 390.16, ... *suited to the birth* (*existence*) *of kāmāvacara gods* (cf. **upapatti**); śamaikāyana-mārga-°kasya (sc. arhataḥ) Laṅk 120.13, 15, (one) *who is fit for getting* . . .

pratilayana, (app. to Skt. prati-lī-, Pali paṭilīyati, *withdraws, turns back*, and derivs.), should mean *withdrawal* (from), *non-adherence* (to): only in Gv 494.18, said of bodhicittam, (sārathibhūtaṃ) mahāyāna-pratilayana-pūrvaṃgamana-tayā; it seems probable that the true text was mahāyānāprati°, with neg., *it acts like a charioteer because of the fact that it is accompanied (conditioned,* see **pūrvaṃgamana**) *by not withdrawing (holding back) from the Great Vehicle.*

pratilābhika, adj. (to Skt. pratilābha plus -ika; cf. **pratilambhika**), *(what is) conducive to getting*: dharmatā-°kam Mvy 6982 (Tib. rñed pa).

pratilābhin, adj. (to Skt. °lābha plus -in), *getting, winning*: tridaśādhipatyaṃ °bhino bhaviṣyanti Suv 14.6; abstr. °**bhi-tva**, nt.: nirābhāsa-gocara-°bhi-tvāt Laṅk 226.13.

pratilīna, adj. (ppp. to Skt. prati-lī-; not noted in this mg.), *veiled*: (read) navavadhūkā hi nāma pratilīnā tiṣṭhatīyaṃ punar vivṛtaiva sarvadā LV 157.12 (wrong punctuation in Lefm., corrupt text in Calc. with apratilīnā, so recorded pw 3.252).

(**pratilekha**, m., *letter in reply*: MSV ii.11.10; Skt., see Schmidt.)

prativarṇika (var. °ṇaka), m., or °**ṇikā** (in mg. = Skt. pratirūpaka, which is also BHS; both = Tib. ltar bcos pa, Mvy 6687–9), *counterfeit*, (false) *imitation* (of something, which usually precedes in comp.): prajñāpāramitā-°ṇikaḥ Mvy 6687 (Mironov °ṇakaḥ); the gender of the first element makes °ṇikā seem preferable, and this is used in the same cpd. AsP 112.16 ff.; tasyāḥ (sc. prajnāpāramitāyāḥ) °ṇikām 113.3 (in the foll. passage it is said to consist in the doctrine that impermanence, anityatā, of the skandhas means destruction, vināśa, of them); na (sc. prajñāpāramitā-)-prativarṇikāpi 181.5, *not even the counterfeit* (of it); bodhisattva-prativarṇikaḥ 394.16, *a counterfeit bodhisattva.* In several of these passages there are parallels with pratirūpa(ka). (See Schmidt, Nachträge, for a different mg. in Skt.)

prativarṇita (ppp. of prati with denom. Skt. varṇayati), *correspondingly* (or, *in return?*) *described* or *praised*: buddhā deśenti vai yogaṃ mayā ca °tāḥ Laṅk 343.5 (vs), *the Buddhas teach yoga, and are described (praised) by me accordingly* (or, *in return?*).

prati-vaśa, adj., *obedient* (to), *subject to the will* (of), with gen.: mama °śāś ca syuḥ Ud xiii.4, in a vs = Pali Dhp. 74 mam' evātivasā assu. The Pali ativasa is isolated, strange, and difficult (see CPD), and BHS prativaśa seems a more natural and comprehensible form, tho also unparalleled as far as I know.

prativastu, nt., in Skt. (*thing that is*) *equivalent* (to something else): so Tib. (nor daṅ ḥdra ba) on Mvy 9405; but in MSV ii.127.19 and 145.1 ff. Tib. (dṅos paḥi) skyin pa, (*personal*) *loan*; here it seems to mean *property left in trust*, for safe-keeping, with another person. Cf. next.

prativastuka, m. (to prec.), *recipient of a fiduciary deposit*: MSV ii.145.11 f.

prativahati, *opposes*, *rejects* (advice; a person), *disobeys* (a command, instruction); once 'caus.' **prativāhayati** in same mg.: ājñāṃ prativāhayāmi Gv 122.8 (prose); (ājñāṃ) prativahati Divy 562.26; na mayā... bhagavataḥ...ājñā pratyūḍha-pūrveti (= °vā iti) Divy 178.11; vāṇīm a-prativahan (pres. pple.) Gv 216.17; (ye caināṃ prajñāpāramitāṃ) na pratikrośanti na prativahanti AsP 460.6; (bodhisattva-piṭaka-)-prativahatānām aśrāddhānāṃ sattvānāṃ Bbh 157.6, *of those disobeying* (gen. pl. pres. pple.)...; prativahaty (so with mss., wrongly em.) eṣo 'smākam Divy 329.9, *he opposes* (or *rejects, repulses*) *us*; evaṃ ca vyavacārayati na ca prativahati AsP 433.2; te prativoḍhum ārabdhāḥ MSV ii.109.5. See next.

prativahana, nt. (n. act. to prec.), *opposition, rejection, disobedience*: °nam Mvy 6607 = Tib. slar bzlog pa, *turning back*; (arthabhūtam) anartha-prativahana-tayā Gv 496.8, *it is of the nature of advantage, because it goes counter to disadvantages*; dharmarājājñāprativahanatayā (i. e. °ājñā-aprati°) Gv 464.8, *because of not disobeying the commands of*...

prativāṇi, °ṇī, f. (and °ṇi, nt.?; cf. **a-prati°**, which see for Pali correspondents), *opposition, repulsion, aversion* to spoken words, especially to preaching or teaching; apparently a cpd. of prati and vāṇī: °ṇī, n. sg., AsP 244.20, and °ṇiḥ, id., 484.7, both in reference to preaching or teaching; prativāṇi (? Mironov °ni without v.l., and Kyoto ed. suggests that their mss. read °ni, and that their °ṇi in text is an em.; cf. however aprativāṇi, where both edd. have °ṇi) Mvy 5239 = Tib. mi ḥphrod pa, *unsuitable, disagreeable* or the like; prob. of attitude towards teaching (the preceding entry is śaikṣābhir nikūjitaṃ). Form dubious; ending seems confirmed by aprativāṇi; n. sg. nt.? Or possibly adverb? In pw 7.360 °vāṇi by em., rendered *Opposition*, which I think is about right.

prativāhayati = **prativahati**, q.v.

prativikalpa, m., *separate* (and false) *discrimination, making distinctions where fundamentally none exist*; in Laṅk seems interchangeable with **parikalpa**, etc., see Suzuki, Studies, Glossary s.v. (where pratikalpa is also cited, but this is not in Suzuki's Index, and I have not noted it) and Index to Laṅk: bālaprativikalpam upādāya Laṅk 17.12, etc. Cf. next.

prativikalpana (nt.) = prec.: vāg-akṣara-prativikalpanaṃ ca vinihatya Laṅk 160.14; (anādikāla-prapañca-) -dauṣṭhulya-sva-prativikalpanā 171.11, Bhvr., with bālapṛthagjanā(ḥ).

prativikalpayati (denom. to °**kalpa**, q.v.), *makes a (false) discrimination, discriminates (falsely)*: (na) lakṣaṇataḥ °payitavyāḥ Laṅk 18.18, *they are not to be (falsely) distinguished according to their* (external) *marks*; dharmādharmaṃ °payanti 21.1; et alibi in Laṅk.

prativigacchati (= Pali paṭi°, so e. g. AN iii.243.5; see also **saṃpratívig°**), *is dispersed, becomes scattered, vanishes*: sā (dṛṣṭiḥ, *wrong opinion*) °vigatā Divy 573.4; °gataḥ Av i.163.12 (madya-madaḥ? uncertain); ii.28.8 (rūpa-madaḥ); 105.1 (aiśvarya-madaḥ), 11 (bala-madaḥ); 129.4 (sattveṣv āghātaḥ); abhūtvā bhavati bhūtvā ca prativigacchati Śikṣ 248.10; (yo dohadaḥ sa) °gataḥ MSV ii.15.6, 9.

prativijñapayati (caus. to Skt. prati-vi-jñā-), *recognizes (severally, specifically)*: ger. °pya Śikṣ 250.9. Cf. next.

prativijñapti, f. (to prec.), (separate, specific) *recognition*: Śikṣ 222.2, in definition of vijñāna as vastu-prativijñaptir; 226.1 (? reading uncertain); 250.5, 6 (but in 7 replaced by vijñaptiḥ; see s.vv. **ādhipateya, ārambaṇa** 3).

prativídhyati, °te (= Pali paṭivijjhati), *penetrates*; physically, aṅgāni °yanti (passive!) Mv i.7.13 (prose), *are penetrated*; = *reaches, attains* (a place): °yate padaṃ śāntaṃ Ud iv.31, *reaches the peaceful place* (same vs in Pali Dhp. 368 adhigacche); usually fig., *penetrates* intellectually, *understands*: °yati Śikṣ 317.10 (dharmān); Bbh 129.24 (prajñayā); 273.21 (arthaṃ); 347.4 (tathāgataviṣayaṃ); Gv 252.20 (parallel with **vyavacārayati**, q.v., and other synonyms); °yate Bbh 273.22 (arthaṃ); na kiṃcin na °yati ŚsP 1423.15, *does not fail to comprehend anything*; °yan (pres. pple.) Gv 160.23; °ya (ger.) Bbh 130.2; 273.20 (arthaṃ); °viddha, ppp., dharmasvabhāva-°ddha-cittāḥ (Bhvr.) Gv 323.16; su-pratividdha, Śikṣ 286.9 (dharmo... bodhisattvena...); Bbh 48.6 (śūnyatā samyakprajñayā); Gv 286.8. See next.

prativídhyana (nt.; to prec. plus -ana; Pali a-ppaṭivijjhana), *comprehension*: aśarīrasarvadharmanaya-°natayā Gv 431.17 (instr. of -tā).

prativinaya, m. (= Pali paṭi°; cf. **prativinīta**), *removal, suppression*: Mv iii.200.11 pipāsā-°vinayo (same phrase in Pali AN ii.34.24 has pipāsa-vinayo).

prativinisṛjati, *abandons*: Mvy 2557; so also Mironov; acc. to pw 7.381, error for prativiniḥsṛjati, and = **pratiniḥ°**, q.v. (pratinisṛjati precedes this in Mvy).

prativinīta (ppp. of °nayati = Pali paṭivineti, °nīta; cf. **a-prati°**, **prativinaya**), *removed*: °tā Mv ii.122.15, of kāmādhyavasānā and the like.

prativinudati (rare), usually °**nodayati** (= Pali paṭivinodeti), *dispels, removes, gets rid of*: simplex only in prativinudanti (rajaḥ) in vs Divy 491.21 = 25 = 492.1 (perh. m.c.?); otherwise only °nodayati, as in Pali: mārgaśramaṃ °nodya (ger.) Divy 27 4; 34.21; 451.17; Av i.23.13; 73.8; ii.104.11; °dayeyaṃ (daurmanasyaṃ) Mv iii.439.16; 440.12; °dayati Bbh 145.9 (duḥkhaṃ); 177.19 (ālasyakausīdyān); °dayituṃ Av i.228.7 (**kāṅkṣāyitatvaṃ**, q.v.); object, (the effects of) sin: °nodituṃ (kaukṛtyaṃ) Mv iii.174.19; °dayāmi, etc. (vadhaṃ) Divy 571.15 f.; °dayitu-kāmaḥ (āghātaṃ) Bbh 169.10. See next.

prativinodana, nt. (to °**nodayati**, see prec., plus -ana; = Pali paṭivi°), *removal, dispelling, getting rid of*: Mv iii.175.2 (kaukṛtyasya, i. e. *of the effects of sin*); Śikṣ 120.15 (nidrāklama-); Bbh 56.15 (saṃśayānāṃ); 83.14 (śoka-kaukṛtya-); 168.25 (tad-, sc. āpatti-).

prativipaśyati, *perceives distinctly*: evaṃ vidarśanayā prativipaśyataḥ (gen. sg. pres. pple.) Laṅk 19.2; °śyati 123.14, 17; °śyan 15.

prativibudhyate, *wakes up* (perh. orig. *re-awakens*; no record of the cpd. elsewhere): °yate Divy 175.13, 17 f.; ger. °dhya Suv 218.1; ppp. °buddha, *having awakened*, or as periphrasis for pret., *woke up*: (various forms) LV 186.2; Mv iii.357.16; Divy 15.7; 318.29; Jm 185.19; Suv 21.1; 196.2; Kv 55.19; Gv 405.10.

prativibhāvayati, °te, *considers thoroughly* or *individually*: svakāyaṃ °yan (pres. pple.) LV 208.8; °yanti Laṅk 171.14; °yamānā(ḥ) 42.13.

prati-vibhinna, adj., *altered to the reverse*: MSV iv.235.11.

prativimānanā, *dishonoring*: kalyāṇadharma-°nā KP 11.5 (prose). No cpd. prati-vi-man- seems to be recorded.

prativirata, ppp., adj. (to °**ramati**; = Pali paṭi°, also a-ppaṭi°), *abstained, ceased*, usually with abl., or preceding stem in comp., of sin *abstained from*: Divy 302.7 (prāṇātipātāt); 585.18; Suv 6.10 (prāṇātipāta-prati°); LV 86.5, read as one cpd. sarvākuśalakriyāprativiratā(ḥ), and delete punctuation before and after; Mv i.326.14 ff. (prāṇātipātāto, etc.); Śikṣ 78.7; Dbh 23.7; a-prati° Mvy 7299.

prativirati, f. (= Pali paṭi°; cf. prec. and next), *abstention* (from sin): Mvy 1691–1698, in cpds., precisely parallel to virati 1687–89; Divy 303.9 (prāṇātipātāt); Bbh 220.9 f.; 223.18 ff.; Bhīk 9a.3.

prativiramaṇa (nt.; to next plus -ana), = prec.: Śikṣ 104.13; Bbh 194.15 ff. Cf. also **prativairamaṇa**.

prativiramati (= Pali paṭi°, cf. prec. three items), *abstains* (from sin): °ramāmi Mv i.202.7 (vs; akhilavacanāt; mss. °viremi, em. Senart); Divy 10.8; 11.23; Bhīk 9b.3; °ramanti Bbh 151.20; fut. °ramiṣyaṃ (1 sg.) Mv iii.268.11 ff. (prāṇātipātāt, etc.); °raṃsyanti Av i.249.13; 274.14.

prativirahita, ppp. to unrecorded prati-vi-rah- (cf. Skt. virahita), *let go, given up, abandoned*: su-°hitāḥ Gv 328.1 (sarvopakaraṇakośā . . . vividhopakaraṇavidhayaḥ).

prativiruddha, ppp. (= Pali paṭi°; see next), *hostile, at odds* (with, instr. with saha): uttarapañcālarājo dakṣiṇapañcālarājena saha °ddho babhūva Av i.41.6; tāv anyonyaṃ °ddhau babhūvatuḥ 47.6; (tasya rājño vijite 'nyatamaḥ kārvaṭikaḥ) °ddhaḥ Divy 445.24 (wrongly rendered *rebellious* in Index and pw 7.371).

prativirodha (m.; = Pali paṭi°; like prec. to Pali paṭivirujjhati, which would be BHS prativirudhyate, °ti, but has not been recorded), *hostility*: Bbh 394.8 °dha- (in comp.).

prativilomayati (cpd. of **vilomayati,** q.v.), *opposes, goes against*: bhāṣitaṃ °mayanti KP 141.3.

prativiśiṣṭataraka, adj. or subst. (to compv. of Skt. °śiṣṭa; specifying -ka? § 22.39), (one that is) *more (especially) distinguished*: bodhisattvaḥ vṛddhatarakaṃ guṇa-prati°kaṃ dṛṣṭvā samyak saṃbhāṣayaty . . . Bbh 254.6.

prativiśodhayati, *purifies*: °śodhya, ger., Laṅk 51.3.

prativiṣa, nt. (cf. id. cited pw 4.145 as adj. from Rājat., *ein Gegengift enthaltend*, and °ṣā, ibid., a kind of aconite, in medical texts), *antidote for poison*: acc. to Tib. (boṅ ṅa dmar po; there is an alternative gloss, ḥab śan tse ḥu, which I cannot interpret) on Mvy 5822, *red wolfsbane (aconite)*; prativiṣa-bhūtaṃ (sc. bodhicittaṃ) karma (2d ed. kāma-)-rativiṣanirviṣīkaraṇatayā Gv 495.21.

prativeṭhāpeti (caus. of prati with **veṭhayati,** not recorded in Pali or Pkt., while Skt. prati-veṣṭ- is not recorded in this mg.), *causes to be enveloped*: puṣkariṇīṃ pratisīrāhi (q.v.) °ṭhāpehi (em., but sound; cf. line 15 pratisīrāhi veṭhāpitā) Mv ii.171.12.

[**prativedin,** error for **pratisaṃvedin,** q.v., LV 345.14.]

prativedha, m. (= Pali paṭi°; to Skt. prati-vyadh-, cf. Skt. vedha), (intellectual) *penetration* (only in this fig. mg.): LV 128.2 (dharma-pra°); 428.9 (-satyanaya-pra°); Mv i.86.13 (prativedha-parākramāḥ, mss. °vikramāḥ, unmetr., *possessing heroism of penetration*); Śikṣ 214.15 (buddhadharma-pra°); Gv 229.19 (atyantājarāmaraṇadhātu-pra°); 251.5 (dharmadhātu-prativedha-jñāna-); Dbh 97.23; Bbh 131.8; 202.10; duṣ-pra° *hard to penetrate* (= Pali duppaṭi°), RP 48.4 (of saṃskāra); Laṅk 222.14 (of yogins).

prativeśaka, f. **°ikā** (= Skt. °veśa), *neighbor*: avidhāvidhaṃ prativeśikā(ḥ) Mv iii.15.15 (vs; so read with 1 ms.; Senart em.), *O neighbors* (fem.)!

prativaikārika, adj. or subst. m. (cf. Skt. vaikārika, from vikāra), °kāḥ, '*counter-disturbing(-elements)*', people who cause dissension and trouble: MSV iii.100.3, in uddāna vs, referring, it seems, to 102.6 ff., quarrelsome monks.

prativairamaṇa, nt. (= **prativiramaṇa** and **vairamaṇa**; blend of these two?), *abstention*: prāṇātipāta-pra° Suv 6.8 (prose).

? **prativrata,** f. **°ā,** adj., *true to vows* (of chastity): °tānāṃ Mv iii.151.5, 7, applied to female ascetics (tāpasīnāṃ 5); v.l. both times pati°, which could not apply here in its normal mg. *true to one's husband* (so also Pali patibbatā); AMg. paivvayā is glossed prativratā, and rendered thus in both Guj. and Hindi, yet the Skt. gloss is patiṃ vratayati (Ratnach.); for Skt. prati AMg. usually has paḍi, rarely pai. For Mvy 7261 pativratā a v.l. prati° is recorded; but there is no such v.l. in Mironov, and Tib. says clearly *not unfaithful to her husband.* Possibly MIndic forms of Skt. pativratā came to mean simply *chaste*, and then became applicable even to female ascetics; the form prati° might then be an unhistorical hyper-Sktism.

pratiśamayati = **pratiśām°,** q.v.

pratiśaya (treated as nt.; for Skt. pratiśraya, m.; semi-MIndic), *lodging*: so . . . anyasmiṃ grāme vāsopagato, anyatarāye vṛddhāye pratiśayaṃ dinnaṃ Mv iii.15.7.

pratiśaraṇa, often written for **pratisaraṇa,** q.v.; no distinction of mg. between the spellings.

pratiśāmaka, m. (to next), *one who stores up, collects* (creatures, gen., as if treasures; said of a bodhisattva): (sarveṣām eva . . . sattvānām . . .) samyak-pratiśāmakaś ca Bbh 254.20–21.

pratiśāmayati, also **°śam°** and erroneously **°śrām°, °sam°** (= Pali paṭisāmeti, *puts away, stores*; wrongly PTSD), (**1**) *stores away* (property): hiraṇya (so read) . . . (etc.) °śāmayet (so Nep. mss., KN with Kashgar rec. °yīt) SP 114.13 (vs); bhāṇḍaṃ °śāmitaṃ (mss. °śrām°) Divy 6.9; bhāṇḍaṃ °śāmayanti Divy 341.7 (subject merchants); bhāṇḍaṃ °śāmya MSV ii.68.20 (subject a housewife); (**2**) *puts away* (a monk's bowl and robe, after his begging-round): pātracīvaraṃ °śāmayitvā Mv i.56.2; °śrāmya, ed. with mss., read °śāmya, Divy 156.1; °śāmya 516.6; Vaj 19.9; (a monk's bed, or bed and seat, preparatory to setting out on a journey, on which he takes bowl and robe with him), (paribhuktaṃ) śayanaṃ pratiśāmya Divy 550.10; yathāparibhuktaṃ śayanāsanaṃ pratiśamayya Divy 552.25; 566.4; written °samayya, pātracīvaraṃ pra° Divy 20.4; 199.27; 201.1; 493.28; yathāparibhukta-śayanāsanaṃ pra° Divy 39.20; (**3**) *harbors* (a person), *entertains (privately)*: (surakṣitaḥ kartavya iti. sa) tena pratiśāmitaḥ MSV ii.99.15; (ye āgantukā bhikṣavo . . .) tān asau pratiśāmya ib. 199.7; others, 200.17 etc. See also **pratisamarpayati.**

? **-pratiśiṣyakā,** in śiṣya-pra°, perhaps *(pupil's) pupilhood*: (yasya tāvad) vayaṃ śiṣya-pratiśiṣyakayāpi na tulyāḥ Divy 153.14, *of whom* (viz. the Buddha), *you see, we are not equal to the pupil's pupilhood* (having been shown to be inferior to Cunda, the novice-attendant of Śāriputra, the disciple of Buddha). Cf. Pali sissānusissa, *pupil and pupil's pupil.*

(**pratiśṛṇoti,** *hears*, tho rare in this sense in Skt., occurs Mbh. Crit. ed. 3.261.16 pratiśrutya; so, also pratiśrutya, LV 58.4; Av i.2.10; 315.12.)

pratiśoka (m.?), *grief*: sarve saduḥkhā janā atyantapratiśoka-śalya-vihatāḥ Divy 321.15.

pratiśodhayati (caus. of unrecorded prati-śudh-), *purifies*: bodhisattvacittaṃ °dhayitavyaṃ Gv 457.4 (prose; perhaps error for pariśodhayitavya, which occurs in prec. line; or false Sktization for MIndic pari-, confused with paṭi-, paḍi-, § 2.47).

pratiśrama, m. (= Skt. pariśrama; perh. for MIndic *paḍissama, cf. paḍissanti, Sheth, and § 2.47), *toil, trouble*: saphalo me °maḥ syād Divy 108.26.

[**pratiśrāmayati,** false reading for **pratiśām°,** q.v.]

pratiśrukā (semi-MIndic for **°śrutkā,** q.v.; may be m.c.), *echo*: read dakacandra-°śrukāḥ with best mss. (dvandva cpd.) in LV 436.15 (vs, end of anuṣṭubh; Lefm. °śrutkā, unmetr.).

pratiśrutakā or **°ka** (= next), *echo*: -pratiśrutakopamāṃ LV 177.12 (vs), cited Śikṣ 240.12 with varr.; but uncertain, see § 3.101.

(**pratiśrutkā,** occurs in older Skt., VS., Kauṣ., Up., *echo*; here always as symbol of what is *transitory, ephemeral*, or *unreal*: SP 137.11; 142.14; LV 181.21; 428.14, where read °kā with most mss. for text °ka; Mvy 854; 2823; Dbh 47.14; in Laṅk 20.17 text °kāni, note suggests °kāpi. Cf. prec. two.)

pratiṣevate, see **pratisevati.**

? **pratiṣkūla** (= Skt. pratikūla), in a-prati°, *not offensive*: Mv iii.341.8 (prose), acc. to Senart, °laṃ. If correct, could be taken as false Sktization of Pali paṭikkūla (explained JAOS 41.462 ff.). But v.l. apratikulaṃ (so!), and parallels i.207.1; ii.10.11; iii.343.1 all pratikūla without v.l.

pratiṣṭhapayati, °**peti** (cf. M. paḍiṭṭhavia, ppp.; Pali only patiṭṭhāpeti, with ā), *establishes*: °pemi SP 47.2 (vs; so with Kashgar rec.); °peyaṃ 47.4 (vs); ger. °ṣṭhapiya Mv i.108.15 (vs).

(-**pratiṣṭhāna**, *basis*: in Laṅk 42.4 read deha-bhoga-pratiṣṭhānam for ed. °sam, Suzuki, Studies, Gloss., which see for other occurrences in Laṅk; Suzuki transl. *body, property*, and *abode*, as a triple dvandva; it seems rather to mean *the basis of bodily enjoyments*, i. e., approximately, the visible, empiric world.)

pratiṣṭhāpaka, f. °ikā (AMg. paiṭṭhāvaa), *one who* or *that which establishes*: m., LV 351.13; Gv 416.13; f. °ikā (buddhiḥ) Laṅk 122.2.

pratiṣṭhāpana (nt.) = Skt. °ṣṭhāna, *stool* (for the feet), in pāda-pra° LV 408.19 (prose), corresp. to pāda-pratiṣṭhāna 408.3; both times without v.l.

Pratiṣṭhitacāritra, v.l. for **Su-prati°**, q.v.

[**pratiṣṭheti**, acc. to Lefm. LV 317.5 (prose) with all mss., but read praviṣṭeti = °ṭā iti with Calc.: mama camū bodhisattvasya vadanaṃ praviṣṭeti manyamānaḥ prapalānaḥ..., confirmed by Tib. (which Foucaux fails to understand) bdag gi dpuṅ byaṅ chub sems dpaḥi khaḥi naṅ du zhugs so sñam du sems śiṅ bdud bros par gyur pa daṅ, *thinking in his mind, My army has entered the mouth of the Bodhisattva!* (cf. Bh.G. 11.27), *the demon* (Māra), *while taking flight...*]

pratisaṃyukta, adj. (ppp., once in pw from Mbh 12, Bombay only, Calc. different; = Pali paṭisaṃyutta), *connected with, related* or *suitable to, concerning*: SP 18.1 (ṣaṭpāramitā-pra°, of dharma); Mv i.211.4 = ii.15.2 (kiṃkaraṇīyaka-pra°); Mvy 2147–9 (kāma-, rūpa-, ārūpya-); Divy 339.21 (brāhmaṇa-); 631.25, 26 (vivekakāla-, artha-); Av i.68.8 (anityatā-°ktāṃ dharmadeśanāṃ); Samādh 19.15 (śabdo... dharmatā-°ktaḥ); Śikṣ 50.10, 13; 202.9; Gv 16.1; AsP 460.20; Bbh 17.14; 46.8 f.; 317.17; Mahāsamāj. Waldschmidt, Kl. Skt. Texte 4,157.8 (nirvāṇa-°ktāṃ dharmikathāṃ); hrīvarṇa-°kteṣu lokādhipateyeṣu (see **ādhipateya**) ceti (sc. upaneyam) Jm 80.13–14.

[**pratisaṃlapana**, error for °layana, q.v.: SP 277.10 (corrected in WT); AsP 236.4.]

pratisaṃlayati (cf. the foll. items; = °**līyate**; Pali only paṭisallīyati, °liyati), *withdraws, goes into seclusion* (for meditation): °yiṣyāmi aham atrāgniśaraṇe Mv iii.428.15 (prose; cf. pratisaṃlayanāya 429.1); pratisaṃlātu-kāma (§ 36.11) MSV ii.128.5.

pratisaṃlayana (see also **atisaṃlayana**), nt. (m. acc. to Mvy 1488; to prec.; = Pali paṭisallāna), = **pratisaṃlāna**: °naḥ Mvy 1488, as a type of dhyāna; °nam Mvy 1642, as a yogāṅga; vihāraṃ praviṣṭaḥ °layanāya SP 182.2–3; Divy 156.2; 494.1; °layanād vyutthāya, *coming out from* (meditative) *seclusion*, Mv i.231.3; 317.7; iii.225.15; Divy 197.1; Av i.187.6; 242.11, etc.; °layana-guruka SP 340.2 (on SP 277.9–10 see next); (ayaṃ kālo dharmadeśanāyā) ayaṃ kālaḥ °layanasya LV 161.10; niṣīde (aor.) °layanāya Mv iii.429.1; °layana-**sārūpya**, also °**pyaka** and °**sāropya**, qq.v., *suitable for private meditation* (Pali paṭisallāna-sāruppa), said of āśrama-pada, śayyāsana (śayanāsana), and the like: Mv ii.123.18, read °layana- (so v.l.) -sārūpyāṇi with Senart's Index (wrongly ii.519 note); iii.143.13 and 200.17 (°sāropya); Bbh 8.25 (°sārūpyaka); in similar passage LV 248.11 bhūmipradeśo ... pratisaṃlayanānurūpaḥ; °layanam (text printed °lapanam) appears to be associated with the lower methods of śrāvakas and pratyekabuddhas in AsP 236.4.

pratisaṃlāna (nt.; = °layana, Pali paṭisallāna), *retirement, withdrawal into privacy* (for the purpose of meditation): °lāna-utthito Mv iii.305.8 (vs; v.l. °sīna, intending °līna-, which is an unhappy 'correction'); °lāne punar eva yogam āpadyeta AsP 345.17; °lānaṃ sevate, reading of WT's ms. K′ at SP 277.10 (prose), where KN wrongly °lapanaṃ, WT °layanaṃ; in SP 343.2 both edd. °lāna-gocaraḥ by em., read with mss. °līna-; in SP 277.9 read prob. °lāna-guruko, see next.

[**pratisaṃlāpa**(-guruko), wrong reading in SP 277.9 for °lāna- (K′ cited in WT as °līna-) or °layana- (so WT ed.).]

pratisaṃlīna, adj. (ppp. of next and of °**layati**; = Pali paṭisallīna; cf. also °**layana**, °**lāna**), *retired, withdrawn*, (**1**) usually for the purpose of meditation; often with rahogata (and other synonyms): LV 392.8; 395.18; Mv i.51.9; 329.21; 330.19; iii.416.11; Divy 291.23; Av i.211.8; 240.1; for the period of the rains, Mv iii.210.5; °līna-gocaraḥ (all mss., ed. em. °lāna-) SP 343.2; others, SP 182.3, 6; Divy 196.19; Av i.238.3; RP 39.11; Śikṣ 67.12; (**2**) to sleep: Divy 90.13, see next.

pratisaṃlīyate (cf. prec. items; Pali paṭisallīyati, °liyati, only in mg. of BHS **pratisaṃlayati**), *retires* in the sense of *goes to bed*: (dharmatā khalu Buddhānāṃ ... na tāvad) upasthāyakāḥ °līyante na yāvad Buddhā ... °līnāḥ Divy 90.13, ... *attendants of Buddhas do not go to bed until Buddhas have gone to bed* (and put out lights; context demonstrates this mg.).

[**pratisaṃvartanīya**, error for pratilābha-**saṃvartanīya**, as read in surrounding parallels: Divy 482.9.]

Pratisaṃvitprāpta, n. of a Bodhisattva: LV 2.13.

pratisaṃvid, f. (also °**vidā** and app. °**vida**; see following items; = Pali paṭisaṃbhidā, which is often, but questionably, assumed to be the orig. form), *special knowledge*, of which there are four (the same in Pali), dharma, artha (or in reverse order), nirukti, pratibhāna; on their mgs. see LaV-P. AbhidhK. vii.89 ff.; Lévi, Sūtrāl. xviii.34; Burnouf, Lotus, App. XVII; and for Pali, Childers, and Kvu. transl. 377–382; lists of the four: Mvy 196–200; Dharmas 51; SP 393.11–12 (here without the term pratisaṃvid); listed with more or less detailed definitions of each, Dbh 77.3 ff.; Bbh 214.11 ff.; 258.4 ff.; °vid-avatāra, LV 8.13; 35.16; °vid-gatiṃgata, SP 202.10; LV 2.8 (so read with v.l., confirmed by Tib., for text pratisamyag-gati°); °vidāṃ lābhy (lābhī) SP 200.11; °vit-prāpta Divy 97.26; 180.27; 240.25; Av i.96.8 etc.; anāvaraṇa-°vit-prāpta LV 426.5; others, LV 343.4; Bbh 207.22; Gv 4.21.

pratisaṃvidā, f. (cf. Pali paṭisaṃbhidā), and app. °**da**, nt., = prec.; the four listed, artha-°vida-prāptā dharma-°vida-prāptā nirukti° pratibhāna° (each time vida) Mv iii.321.14–15 (prose); also, with dharma° first, and n. sg. °vidā each time, Bbh 89.25; catvāri ca (mss. confused) pratisaṃvidāni (no v.l.) sākṣīkare Mv iii.67.2–3, and again 4; in LV 287.10 (vs) mss. confused, read prob. sa-pratisaṃvida-(a could be m.c.)-satyabalaṃ ca; °vidānāṃ... lābhī SP 204.11 (vs); °vidāsū ca gatiṃgatānām 205.12 (vs); °vidāto, abl., Śikṣ 109.6 (vs).

pratisaṃvidita, adj.-ppp. (Pali, in neg. a-ppaṭi°, in mg. 1), (**1**) *experienced, known*: °ditānāṃ vedanānāṃ saṃjñānāṃ tarkānāṃ utpādaḥ sthānaṃ nirodhaś ca Bbh 75.20; mahājana-prati° MSV ii.99.14, *known to a lot of people*; in this sense app. back-formation from **pratisaṃvedayati**, as if from its non-caus. present, cf. CPD s.v. appaṭisaṃvidita; (**2**) *possessed of* (full) *special knowledge* (in this sense doubtless based directly on the noun **pratisaṃvid-ā,-a**): (ye janā) aśrāddhā mandaprasādās te dāni pratisaṃviditā bhavanti Mv iii.256.5 (on Buddha's entrance to a city; along with other miracles); (**3**) see **a-prati°**.

Pratisaṃvin-niścayāvatārā, n. of a Bodhisattva-dhāraṇī: Mvy 755.

pratisaṃveda, see **a-prati°**.

pratisaṃvedaka, adj. (to °**vedayati**), (**1**) *experiencing* (pleasure or pain): sukhaduḥkhāprati°kāny (sapta vijñānāni, other than ālayavijñāna) Laṅk 221.5, *they do not experience*... (so Tib. mi myoṅ ba, as cited in Suzuki's Index; he translates *they do not give exact information regarding*...); (**2**) in Mvy 9413 kula-prati°kaḥ = Tib. khyim so sor bsgo ba, *speaking* (or, *giving orders*) *to families individually*, and so Chin.; in default of context or known Pali parallel the exact mg. is not clear; app. °vedaka in caus. sense to °**vedayati** (2).

pratisaṃvedanā (Skt. °na, nt., reported rarely in Skt., pw, as also **pratisaṃvedin**, tho other related forms, noun or verb, are not recorded for Skt.), *experience* (of the fruition of past deeds): (vipākasya) °nā Śikṣ 253.6, 14 (in the latter prob. read prajñāyate, for ed. prajāyate, with line 6 and the ms. of Śikṣ). Cf. **a-prati°**.

pratisaṃvedayati, °te (not in Skt., but see °**vedanā**; = Pali paṭisaṃvedeti, at least in mg. 1), (**1**) *experiences* (joy, sorrow, the effect of past deeds): sukhaṃ (ca) kāyena °dayati (or °te; in the third dhyāna) LV 129.7; 343.19; Mv i.228.7; ii.132.2 (°dayāmi); Mvy 1480; out of context, Mvy 7283; prītiṃ °dayan Jm 210.4; vimuktisukhaṃ °dayataḥ (gen. sg. pres. pple.) Av i.234.5; pipāsāduḥkhaṃ °dayamāno Divy 235.28; asya karmaṇo vipākaṃ °dayeyaṃ Av i.287.7; nātra kaścid ātmā...yaḥ karoti °dayate Śikṣ 172.6; (**2**) *perceives, recognizes*: (te tena jñānadarśanena) yathābhūtaṃ evaṃ °dayanti Bbh 155.9; aham anena pitrā °ditaḥ (*recognized, known*) Divy 258.18; (dārako na) kenacit pāpakaṃ karma kurvāṇo 'bhiśaṅkito vā °dito vā, 24, ... *was not suspected or recognized* (*known*) *as doing an evil deed*; (sa iha...) °dayiṣyati, eṣāsya dārakasya māteti (misprinted ma°) 259.16, *he will know* (*recognize*) *that she is this boy's mother.*

pratisaṃvedin (to prec.; = Pali paṭi°; recorded from Skt., rarely, in pw, see °**vedanā**), (**1**) *experiencing; having experience* (usually of something which precedes in comp.): sukha-°dī LV 369.11; sukhaduḥkha-°dībhir (masc.!) Gv 377.12, 19; evaṃsukhaduḥkha-°dī (same cpd. in Pali, PTSD) Mvy 230; Mv i.229.4; ii.133.3–4; 284.13; Bbh 253.27; and read so in LV 345.14 for °pratìvedī, both edd., no v.l.; sarvakāya-pratisaṃvedy āśvasan (so read with Mironov; same cpd. in Pali, e.g. MN i.425.13; Vism. i.267.4 ff.) Mvy 1177, and modulations of this 1178, 1181–4, 1187–8; vimuktiprītisukha-°dī Divy 181.1; 567.18; (aparimāṇaduḥkha-)°dī Dbh 29.14; neg. a-prati°, svamativikalpasukhaduḥkhāpratisaṃvedināṃ Laṅk 221.8; (**2**) *perceiving, recognizing, knowing*: pūrvaṃ cāham alpaprajño 'lpapratisaṃvedy andhabhūto 'smy āsīt SP 135.12, see § 41.1.

pratisaṃśikṣati, only in Mv, otherwise °te, (corresp. to Pali paṭisaṃcikkhati, as noted by Speyer on Av ii.189.8 below; under this PTSD cites Mv ii.314.15 as pratisaṃcikṣati!), (*learns exactly*,) *realizes perfectly, becomes well aware that*..., always foll. by direct quotation of the subject's thoughts: imaṃ (v.l. idaṃ) °ti Mv ii.314.15; °te, prec. usually by idaṃ, Av ii.189.8 (parallel in Pali, as above, MN i.499.10, 25); Bbh 190.11; 191.3, 18, 25 (in last three printed prati śikṣ°); or by evaṃ, Śikṣ 232.8; Dbh 26.14, or itaḥ, Śikṣ 167.15; Laṅk 123.13 (the thought here quoted is tat satyaṃ... asaṃbhavo; what then follows depends on **prativipaśyati**, q.v., which seems to be a synonym of this, peculiar to Laṅk); idaṃ °kṣitavyam Av ii.107.9.

[**pratisaṃskaraṇa**, prob. error, see next.]

pratisaṃskāra, m. (to Pali paṭisaṃkharoti, and Skt. pratisaṃskaroti is used in substantially the same way; the noun seems not recorded, but Pali has adj. °khārika, °khāriya), *repair, restoration* (of ruined or damaged buildings): (stūpe khaṇḍasphuṭa-) °kāra-karaṇāya Divy 22.19 and 23.1; read so in 22.11 and 23.3 for text °pratisaṃskaraṇāya (haplogr.); similarly in Karmav 34.5, text with inferior ms. (stūpacaityavihārāṇāṃ śīrṇānāṃ) pratisaṃskaraṇam, read with better ms. pratisaṃskāra-karaṇam; (khaṇḍasphuṭa-) °kāraṃ kuruta Divy 23.8, and (°sphuṭita-)°kāraḥ kṛtaḥ 23.11; jīrṇagṛhavat °kāra-dhāryaḥ Śikṣ 231.3, *to be held up* (only) *by repair*; °kāraṃ karoti, with acc. of things to be repaired, (te satpuruṣāḥ ye caṭitasphuṭitān vihārān) °kāraṃ kurvanti Kv 13.10, similarly 11.

pratisaṃskāraṇa (nt.), = prec.: caitya-viśīrṇa-°raṇa- (in cpd.) LV 430.5 (prose, no v.l.).

pratisaṃskārayati, ppp. °kārita (prob. denom. to saṃskāra, cpd. with prati; hardly caus. to Skt. pratisaṃskaroti, *repairs*, also perhaps *unites*), *prepares, fixes up* in an elaborate, ornate way for someone: gṛhataraṃ (q.v.) pratisaṃskāritam abhūt LV 59.(19–)20.

pratisaṃstara, nt., *distribution severally* (of gifts): °ram Mvy 2859 = Tib. so sor ḥged (ḥgyed) pa, *separate distribution*; so also Chin.; acc. to pw 7.361 *freundlicher Empfang*, perh. based on the mg. assigned to Pali paṭisaṃthāra, °tharati, which seems not to apply here (surrounding terms refer to aspects of giving alms); MSV i.279.20 (vs) namasyanty... samādhiṃ °ram (Tib. cited ḥgyed pa).

pratisaṃstaraṇa (nt.; cf. prec.), *arranging* (monkish perquisites for distribution): MSV iii.121.3 °ṇa-bhūmim = Tib. gśibs pa, *arranging in line.*

pratisaṃsthāna (nt.; nowhere recorded), *establishment*, in garbha-°nāya, *for the establishment-in-the-womb* (*incarnation*, of the Bodhisattva in his last existence): LV 20.19; 21.11, 17, etc.

pratisaṃharaṇa (nt.), (**1**) *restoration, bringing back* (from exile): Bbh 83.21 pravāsanā punaḥ-pratisaṃharaṇāya, *exile with later restoration in view*, opp. to **apratisaṃhārya**, q.v.; (**2**) *withdrawal, turning back* (to Skt. pratisaṃharati): Bbh 142.5.

pratisaṃharaṇa-tā = °**haraṇa** (2): ŚsP 1469.9 indriyāṇāṃ prati°tā.

pratisaṃharaṇīya, adj. nt., with or sc. karman (corresp. to Pali paṭisāraṇiya; to °**haraṇa** plus -īya), prob. (action of the saṃgha) *leading to withdrawal* (in the stock example, as in Pali Vin. ii.18.9 ff., of contemptuous treatment of a layman on the part of an offending monk): Mvy 8645 = Tib. phyir (ḥ)gyed (or skyed) pa(r) (ze) spaṅ ba or pa (the last = *give up, renounce*), i. e. acc. to N. Dutt, MSV iii Introd. iv, *making up a disunion*; MSV ii.207.13; iii.24.10 ff. (description). Cf. Pali AN comm. ii.165.5 gihīnaṃ akkosakassa... paṭisāraṇīya-(so here!) -kammaṃ. The offender had to apologize to the layman, MSV iii.26.10.

pratisaṃhṛta, adj.-ppp. (perh. cf. **pratisaṃharaṇa** 1; but perh. hyper-Skt. for °hita, ppp. of **pratisaṃdadhāti**; replaces °dhita in same phrase 236.4), *restored* (? or *re-created*): °tāni... kuśalamūlāni MSV iv.238.20.

pratisaṃkakṣikā, some sort of garment: Mvy 8937 = Tib. ṅul gzan gyi gzan, *shirt for undershirt*; Chin. *sweat-garment*; *undershirt.*

pratisaṃkhyā (= Pali paṭisaṃkhā; see **apratisaṃkhyā**), *careful* (*point by point*) *consideration, thorough knowledge*, in °khyā-nirodha, *suppression* (of rebirth) *by*..., one of the 3 asaṃskṛtāni (see **asaṃskṛta**); it is a synonym of nirvāṇa: Mvy 2185; Dharmas 32; see esp. La Vallée Poussin, AbhidhK. i.8–9 (*suppression due à la sapience*). In Mv ii.283.14 Senart reads by em. -jñānadarśana-pratisaṃkhāya (for °khyāya) for mss. °saṃlāpa, or acc. to note °saṃlāya; but the em. is not supported and seems implausible; the parallels Mv i.228.12, ii.132.16 read °pratilābhāya or °ye; LV 344.7 °sākṣātkriyāyai.

(**pratisaṃkhyāna**, nt., *careful consideration*, occurs in Skt., see pw s.v., but Pali paṭisaṃkhāna, and the verb °khāti, are commoner; note Pali cpd. °na-bala: °nabala Bbh 251.19; Jm 186.4; °na-balika, adj., Bbh 9.21; 17.3; °na-mahant Jm 181.17; 190.13; °na-bahula Av ii.24.10.)

pratisaṃkhyāya, ger. (cf. **pratisaṃkhyā, aprati-**

saṃkhyāya, Pali paṭisaṃkhā-ya), *having reflected, considered* (carefully, point by point): SP 73.5 (after quotation) iti prati°, *so reflecting*; KP 124.2 ff. prati° (śīlaṃ rakṣati), *calculatingly* (to gain a reputation for virtue); so in Bbh 129.27 na prati° dāsyāmi; other passages Bbh 8.9; 35.24; 255.13; tad (sc. food) api bhikṣavo mātrayā pratisaṃkhyāya paribhuñjanta iti MSV ii.88.6–7, *monks eat that in moderation, with careful consideration* (cf. Pali MN iii.2.28 bhojane mattaññu hohi paṭisaṅkhā... āhāreyyāsi).

pratisaṃgraha (m.; to Skt. prati-saṃ-grah-), *acceptance*: saddharma-°hāt Śikṣ 45.6 (vs).

pratisaṃtuṣṭa, adj. (ppp. of unrecorded *prati-saṃ-tuṣ-), *contented*: °ṭā LV 26.20 (prose; no v.l.; in description of Māyā).

pratisaṃdadhāti, °saṃdheti, also in Mv **paṭi°** (cf. next; = Pali paṭisaṃdahati; specialized use of Skt. prati-saṃ-dhā; Pali and BHS generally but wrongly understood as if medio-passive), *connects, makes connexion, again* (with a new body), substantially = *takes on a new existence,* so *is reborn*: °dadhāti Mvy 2171; paṭisaṃdheti Mv iii.65.9 and °dhenti 12; pratisaṃdheti 65.14, 19, and (mss. °veti) 66.1 (twice) and 3; ppp. °dhita, *re-created,* °tāni... Devadattena kuśalamūlāni MSV iv.236.4. See next. The Pali verb is recorded in PTSD only from Miln. 32(.12 ff.); it occurs elsewhere, at least in Miln., e.g. 46.5 ff.

pratisaṃdhi, m. (so Divy 234.8; perhaps f. Mv iii.447.19? = Pali paṭisaṃdhi; nom. act. to prec.), (**1**) *rebirth*: Mvy 2164; °dhi-bandhaḥ 7695; °dhi na me bhaveyā LV 200.7 (vs); °dhir gṛhītaḥ Divy 234.8; usually acc. °dhiṃ, obj. of grah-, Divy 14.15; 57.24; 68.10; 138.17; Av i.4.15; 10.15 etc.; bhava-°dhiṃ ca karoti Dbh 49.22; °dhi-balena Gv 105.11, but read with 2d ed. pratisaṃvidbalena; sahetukā saṃskāra-(mss. °rā)-pratisaṃdhir Mv iii.447.19; (**2**) fig., *the forming a connection with* (adoption of) a philosophical view: anyāyāś ca dṛṣṭer a-pratisaṃdhir anupādānam aprādurbhāvaḥ Av ii.188.1, *not taking on, not accepting, non-appearance of* (*any*) *other view.* Could be rendered, perhaps, *no birth... of another view.*

pratisamayati, ger. **°mayya,** for **°śam°**, see **pratiśāmayati.**

pratisamarpayati, ger. °arpya (rationalizing hyper-Sktism, if not error, for pratiśamayya, see **pratiśāmayati**), *having put away* (bowl and robe): pātracīvaraṃ pra° Av i.252.8 (see Speyer's note); 267.7; 274.8.

pratisaṃmodate, °modayati, °te (= Pali paṭisaṃmodeti; cf. **saṃmodate**), *greets, salutes*: sometimes clearly not *in return,* esp. in LV 68.6 and 10 where prec. by pūrvataraṃ, *greet first* (before being greeted); not *in return* also Mv i.256.18; LV 62.20; but sometimes *in return,* Mv ii.443.17; Jm 138.13; Bhīk 26b.4, 5; prob. SP 277.3, 4, and doubtless elsewhere (often there is no evidence on the point); °date LV 68.11 (and in the sequel; prose); Gv 53.14 (prose); °dante Bhīk 26b.4, 5 (prose); °dayati (prose) SP 277.3, 4; Bbh 146.5; °denti Mv iii.180.18; °dayate LV 68.6 (prose); °dayante LV 62.20 (prose); °dayiṣyāmi Mv iii.114.8 (prose); ger. °detvā Mv i.256.18; iii.117.1; 160.4; °ditvā i.273.10 (mss.); ii.443.17; iii.450.20; °dya Divy 117.1; Bbh 124.18; inf. °ditum LV 68.10; Jm 138.13 (both prose); ppp. °dita Divy 439.15; pass. pres. pple. °dyamānaḥ Bbh 161.14.

pratisaṃmodana (nt.), **°nā** (= Pali paṭisaṃmodana, Childers, from Dhp. comm. kata-°no, Bhvr.; nom. act. to prec.), *greeting, salutation*; not necessarily *return greeting,* cf. LV 68.8–9 where read sattvān pratisaṃmodana-(Lefm. °naḥ)-kuśalo with several mss.; Divy 248.7 °naṃ, acc.; 403.1 °nāṃ; MSV iii.141.21 bhagavantam °nayā pratisaṃmodate; but °na- *return greeting* Jm 123.20; 147.24; and perhaps SP 280.8 (vs; °naṃ, acc.).

pratisaraṇa, nt., **°ṇa-tā** (also written °śar° without differentiation of mg.; = Pali paṭi°; see esp. La Vallée Poussin, AbhidhK. ix.246–8, with valuable bibliography; Wogihara, Lex. s.v.; n. act. to next, q.v., but influenced, prob. secondarily, in mg. by Skt. śaraṇa = Pali saraṇa), (1) basically, *reference, point of reference, 'point d'appui'* (LaV-P, better than Lévi's *'ressource-respective'*, Sūtrāl. xviii.31), *going back to* (*something*), and then also *the thing to which the going back occurs*; so, *basis, point of dependence, support,* thus naturally leading to (2) *support* in the sense of Skt. śaraṇa (MIndic saraṇa), *refuge, that on which one relies*; often the two mgs. cannot be clearly distinguished; Tib. (b)rten (pa, or ba), see Jä. (*keep, hold, adhere to... depend, rely on... be given, addicted, depend on, arise* or *issue from... support*), also rton (pa), *to place confidence in, rely on*; but sometimes (e.g. on **apratiśaraṇa,** q.v., LV 189.12) Tib. skyabs, regular equivalent of Skt. śaraṇa, *refuge*; (**1**) *'point d'appui'*, four in number: Mvy 1546 artha-pratisaraṇena bhavitavyaṃ na vyañjana-pra°, *one must refer to, rely on, the real meaning, not the 'letter'*; 1547, dharma-pra°... na pudgala-pra°, *the Law as such... not* (as, or because, taught by) *any person* (Bbh 257.4 f.); 1548 jñāna-... na vijñāna-, see these words; 1549 nītārtha-(sūtra)-... na neyārtha- (sūtra-), see these words; same four listed Dharmas 53 (here written °śaraṇa); discussed in some detail Sūtrāl. xviii.31–33, and more clearly Bbh 256.23–257.22 (see also LaVP, above); artha-pratisaraṇānāṃ (bodhisattvānāṃ) Laṅk 223.8 (Tib. don la, *to meaning,* rten pa); (a sinful bodhisattva) vyañjana-pra° ca bhavati nārtha-pra° Bbh 175.16–17; caturbhiḥ pratisaraṇaiḥ (not listed) Bbh 219.9, ... tasmād eṣāṃ dharmaḥ sapratisaraṇo bhavati 11 (*becomes provided with its points of reference or bases*); prob. in this sense, sarvārtha-°ṇatvād Bbh 91.20; (śrutaṃ...) artha-pratiśaraṇākāraṃ dharma-pratiśaraṇākāraṃ Śikṣ 191.1; (dharmārthikatā para-)mārthārthapratisaraṇa-tayā KP 156.2; (sarvajñatābhimukhānāṃ sarvajñatā-)-pratisaraṇānāṃ Gv 166.24; prob. also sa-pratiśaraṇaḥ (of the Buddha's dharma) Mvy 1301 (Tib. brten ba; cf. Bbh 219.11 above); (bhavamūlakā... dharmā, *states of being,...*) bhavaprabhavā... bhava-pratiśaraṇā Mv iii.337.14 and 339.13, *founded on existence* or *on becoming*; uncertain whether here or with (2), dharmacaraṇaṃ... dharma-pratiśaraṇa-tāyai saṃvartate LV 32.11; (dharmārthikatā, cf. KP 156.2 above) ... arthapratiśaraṇa-tāyai saṃvartate LV 33.2; karma-pratiśaraṇa or (Mvy) °sar°, Bhvr., *one who* or *that which has,* or *recognizes,* (past) *actions as the base* (of what happens to the doer): °ṇam, nt., Mvy 2316 (Tib. brten pa); (sattvān...) karmayonīn karma°ṇān Karmav 30.4; °ṇo bhūtāvāvasthitaḥ Divy 427.22 (a monk saw a murderer about to kill him, but perceiving that it was the result of his own past deeds, he made no attempt to escape, but calmly) *waited, accepting* (past) *deeds as the basis* (of his fate; here clearly not refuge!); Av ii.86.5 (wrongly em. Speyer); more fully, karmavipākapratiś° Śikṣ 316.16; (bodhicittaṃ...) dharaṇi-bhūtaṃ, sarvaloka-pratiśaraṇatayā Gv 494.2, cited Śikṣ 6.1, *like the earth because it is the basis* (*support*) *of all people* (Bendall and Rouse *refuge,* implausibly); similarly (cakravāḍabhūtaṃ) sarvalokapratisaraṇatayā Gv 494.15 (same passage; note variation between ś and s, not significant); (**2**) *refuge,* = Skt. śaraṇa (see above); some of the above cases may belong here; (bodhisattvaḥ... dharmatrāṇo dharmaśaraṇo) dharmapratiśaraṇo... LV 179.14 (but Tib. rten pa, perhaps understood as *support,* for the Law); °ṇabhūtaḥ (of the Tathāgata) 426.6; (bodhisattvānāṃ) sarvajagat-pratisaraṇa-bhūtānāṃ Gv 99.6; (bodhisattvāḥ) pratiśaraṇa-bhūtā lokasya Gv 219.5; pratiśaraṇāvatāro dharmālokamukhaṃ LV 35.17 (? or to 1); (beggars) ye tasya gṛhaṃ (? read gṛha-) pratiśaraṇa-bhūtā Divy 176.26, *who had come to be in a state of having his house as their refuge, reliance,* i. e. his regular pensioners.

pratisarati (cf. prec.; = Pali paṭisarati, which is

a unitary verb and has nothing to do with Skt. pratismarati, despite PTSD; paṭisaranti in DN comm. i.267.24 occurs in a gloss on gotta-paṭisāriṇo which belongs with BHS °sarati), (lit. *returns to;*) *attends to, refers to*: Laṅk 196.8, (as if one should point out something to someone with his finger, and that person) aṅgulyagram eva pratisared vīkṣitum, *should turn his attention only to the fingertip* (instead of the indicated object) *to look at*; Śāl 88.16 na pūrvāntaṃ °ti, *pays no attention to the past* (nor future, 89.3, nor present, 89.6); this passage cited Śikṣ 227.7, 8, 10; (kvacit...) na °ti Śikṣ 229.6, *pays no heed to anything*; śūnyatā (for °tāṃ, acc.)... pratisaratha KP 64.3; °saranti id.5; (paraiś ca...) āhataḥ san... dharmatāṃ vā °raty ātmānam eva vā aparādhikaṃ paśyati Bbh 255.13, *and when attacked by others, he either takes it as a natural thing* (see **dharmatā**), *or regards himself, rather, as to blame*; -nītārthaṃ sūtraṃ °rati na neyārthaṃ Bbh 257.10 (cf. Mvy 1549, s.v. **pratisaraṇa**), *he attends to a sūtra of clearly defined meaning, not one of which the meaning needs definition*; dharmatām eva °rati AsP 329.3 (as in Bbh 255.13 above); MSV iii.108.8, 9.

Pratisarā, n. of a **rakṣā** (q.v.): Dharmas 5; Sādh 397.9 etc. (in this text oftener **Mahā-pra°**).

pratisāra, m. (cf. Pkt. paḍisāra, Sheth, and Hem. 1.206), *turning back, regression*: (lokadhātum...) avagāhya ...°ro na kartavyaḥ Sukh 72.1.

[**pratisārin**, n. sg. °rī, *regretful* (for having given a gift), Karmav 65.4 dattvā ca khalu °rī bhavati. But one ms. is cited as reading ripuṇisārī, which points to vipratisārī as the correct reading; this is confirmed by 66.7 vipratisārī. This word is applied to one who, after giving something, regrets his generosity.]

pratisīrā (Skt. Lex. only), *curtain*: °rāhi, instr. plur., Mv ii.171.12, 15 (a pond is enclosed, enveloped, with curtains for privacy); mss. °śīlehi or °sīharāhi; Senart's em. seems certain.

[**pratisubhati**, see **paṭi°**.]

pratisṛjyati (4th class pres. to prati-sṛj-, which in Skt. is rare and doubtful, and seems recorded nowhere else), *abandons, gives up*; icchema (mss. ikṣema; read īkṣema?) pratisṛjyantau icchema (so most mss., two ikṣema) maraṇam ātmanaḥ Mv i.181.1 (vs), ... *abandoning* (life), *we desire our own death*. (Otherwise but implausibly Senart.) Note several cpds. of sṛj in Mvy 2547–58, including prati-ni-, prati-vi-ni-; and the 4th class pres. **utsṛjyate** (not pass.) 2558.

pratisevati, °te (sometimes written °ṣev°; Pali paṭi°; Skt. °te, *devotes oneself to a person*, once in pw), (**1**) *indulges in* (pleasures, acc.): (active) kāmāṃ (kāmān, kāmā) Mv i.153.6 and ff.; Divy 258.6; maithunaṃ (as in Pali, meth°) Mv i.199.13 (v.l. pari°) = ii.3.11; ii.3.10 (for which same line i.199.12 pari°); (māṃsabhojanam) °vitavyaṃ Laṅk 254.6; *adheres to* (obstructive conditions, **antarāyika**, q.v., dharma) Prāt 514.6, 13 (°vato, gen. sg. pres. pple.); (**2**) *makes use of* (medicine), auṣadhaṃ °vanti Mv i.169.4; (**3**) *undergoes* the fruit of deeds, evil or good: evil, vipākaṃ pratiṣevataḥ Ud ix.11; (middle) vipākaṃ pratiṣevate (evil), and °sevate (good), Ud ix.14–15 = Pali Dhp. 67–68 where paṭisevati.

pratisevin, f. °vinī (to prec.), akṣudrasattvā-(ā m.c.)-pratisevinī (so read as cpd.) Mv ii.57.19, *attaching myself to creatures that are not ignoble* (Śraddhā speaks). There is a v.l. °sattā for °sattvā.

pratisphuṭa, adj. (= the much commoner **parisphuṭa**; cf. § 2.47; here perhaps error, since pari° occurs just below, 40.18), *completely full*: (udyānam)... -ratnavṛkṣa-°ṭam RP 40.13.

pratismṛta, adj. (= Pali paṭissata; orig. ppp. of Skt. prati-smṛ-), *mindful, heedful*: saṃprajāna (separate word) °to Mv ii.359.6 (vs); other cases (all adj., not pple.) Ud xii.18; xv.6; xix.1; MSV ii.185.4.

pratisyandana (nt.; no prati-syand- otherwise known), perh. lit. *moistening, making to flow*, and so *making tender*: cittanagara-pratisyandana-prayuktena te kulaputra bhavitavyaṃ vipulamahākaruṇā-sarvajagadanukampanatayā Gv 430.25.

pratihanyate, °ti (pass. of Skt. prati-han-), (**1**) *is struck against* (to Skt. prati-han-, rarely, BR s.v.1): yatra ... indriyāṇi °yante te viṣayā ity ucyante Śikṣ 251.12, *the things against which the senses are struck* (wrongly Bendall and Rouse) *are called the sense-objects* (cf. pratihanyanā); (**2**) *is echoed*, of sound: (mahārāvaṃ ravantānāṃ ca śabdo...) parvatehi °yante (so mss.) Mv i.6.2; (**3**) *is reflected*, of light: in Senart's text pratyahanyanti Mv i.6.9 ff., repeatedly, with most or all mss.; in i.7.9 pratyāhanyanti, with some mss., others pratya°; but in i.25.14 ff., in similar passage, all mss. repeatedly pratihanyanti, which is probably what the passages all mean; cf. § 32.8.

pratihanyanā (nom. act. to prec., mg. 1), *the being struck against*: °nā teṣāṃ (sc. indriyāṇāṃ) nirdiṣṭā Śikṣ 251.14.

pratihāraka-pakṣa = **prāti°**, q.v.

pratihārayati, °reti (prob. denom. from Skt. pratihāra, *usher*, rather than caus. to prati-har-), *announces*: (speaking to the king's pratihāra) Śuddhodanasya pratihāretha, Asito ṛṣi darśanakāmo; pratihāreṇa rājño niveditaṃ Mv ii.31.12; *has announced, causes to be announced*: rājñaḥ pratihārayām āsa Jm 118.13 (that he wished an audience).

(**pratīcchati**, Skt., *receives, accepts, acquires*;) non-Skt. forms: fut. pratīcchiṣyati Mv ii.435.12; inf. °cchituṃ Mv i.310.4; ppp. °cchita AsP 204.15; Gv 349.7; spelled praticchita (MIndic, cf. Pali paṭicchati) Mv ii.165.19; 189.12; °īcchitavān Gv 417.24; caus. °cchāpaya Mmk 27.24, *cause to accept*; *make* or *consider acceptable*. Cf. next, **saṃpratī°**, and **pratyeṣita**.

pratīcchana (nt.; nom. act. to prec.; cf. Schmidt, Nachträge, s.v., and AMg. paḍicchaṇa), *reception, acceptance, acquisition*: °na-tayā, at end of cpd., Gv 430.13. Cf. **saṃpratī°**.

[**pratīta**, *past, departed*, in Mv iii.330.6 trīṇi pratītāni ahaṃ caturtho, is prob. a misreading, or error of tradition, for atīta (pra and a are easily confused), altho a Hindu Lex., cited BR, gives prasthita as a mg. of pratīta.]

pratītya, ger., also used virtually as postpos. (derived from Skt. prati-i-; = Pali paṭicca), *dependent on, based on*: daśa bhūmayo buddhajñānaṃ pratītya prajñāyante Dbh 95.27; hetuṃ pratītya bhavaśūnya śruṇitva dharmā (or °māṃ) LV 117.1 (vs; so read), *hearing that the states-of-being are based on a cause and void of* (real) *existence*; yatha muñja pratītya valvajaṃ rajju ... vartitā LV 176.7, cited Śikṣ 238.5 (vs; so read), *as, on the basis of muñja or valvaja* (grass), *a rope is produced*; cakṣuś ca pratītya rūpataḥ cakṣuvijñānaṃ LV 176.17, cited Śikṣ 239.5 (vs); yatha tantri pratītya dāru ca ... LV 177.13, cited Śikṣ 241.1 (vs); hetuṃ pratītya imi saṃbhuta (= °bhūtāḥ) sarvadharmā LV 419.9 (vs); skandhā (acc. pl.) pratītya samudeti hi duḥkham evaṃ LV 419.13 (vs); upadhi (mss.) pratītya duḥkhasya saṃbhavo Mv ii.418.10; used absolutely, without object, *in dependence* (on something else): pratītya sarve imi bhāva utthitāḥ SP 191.12 (vs); pratītya dharmaṃ (read °mā?) pravicito (v.l. °tā, so read?) bodhisattvaḥ... Mv ii.346.3 (vs; but construction is not clear); dharmā (n. pl.) pratītya utpadyante (or °ti; so with mss.) Mv iii.66.6, 12; also in comp. with a following or prec. word, as in **pratītya-samutpāda**, q.v., but in this and in some of the following pratītya could be understood as a separate word, as in the prec. cases, *in dependence*: hetu-pratītya-kuśalo LV 125.2 (vs), *wise in regard to* (things that are) *dependent on causes*; anyonya-pratītya-hetutaḥ LV 176.6 (vs); sāmagri-pratītyataś ca sā vāca-mana-buddhi-vaśena niścarī LV 177.9, cited Śikṣ 240.9 (vs), or perhaps understand sāmagri pratītya (a)taś ca°, *depending on the totality, and hence by force of voice, mind, and consciousness, this* (utterance) *has gone forth*; dharma (acc. pl.) pratītya-samutthita buddhvā LV 308.13 (vs); pratītya-jātā (dharmā ime) LV 340.3 (vs); pratītya-samudāgataṃ jagac chūnyaṃ LV 375.11 (vs); pratītya-samutpannāṃ dharmām Mv iii.61.3; pratītyāvatārobhayāntadṛṣṭisamatikramaṇa-cakraṃ LV 423.2, *the wheel that transcends the false view of two alternatives* (see next passage) *by penetration of* (what exists) *by depending* (on other things, Tib. rten ba la ḥjug śiṅ...); ubhayānta means, not the extreme types of behavior, violent asceticism and sensuality (see **pratipad**), but the notion of contrast between oneself and others, as is shown by Gv 469.9 ātmaparasaṃjñā-dṛṣṭi-vigatena pratītyāvatārajñānena; so also pratītyāvatāraviruddhaṃ (so read with 1 ms. for Lefm. °ddha-; Tib.... mi ḥgal ba, and in a new, separate, phrase zhi ba = śāntaṃ) śāntaṃ LV 423.11, *unhindered thru penetration of*... (as above), *and calm.* Cf. next.

pratītya-tā (abstr. from prec.), in sattva-pra° Gv 473.22, *the fact that creatures are dependent* (in origination, on ulterior causes).

pratītya-samutpāda, m. (= Pali paṭicca-samuppāda; commonly taken as cpd. in both languages; see **pratītya**), *origination by dependence* of one thing on another; applied to the celebrated 'chain of causation', the (usually twelve) steps of which are the same as in Pali, from avidyā to (a compound ending in) upāyāsa: elaborate analysis Śāl 76.13 ff. (valuable discussion by LaVallée Poussin), cited Śikṣ 219.10 ff.; more briefly Dbh 48.23 ff.; schematic lists of the terms, Mvy 2241–58; Dharmas 42; SP 179.4 ff.; Mv ii.285.8 ff.; 345.13 ff.; iii.448.12 ff.; Av ii.105.16 ff.; KP 61, 62; Suv 193.9 ff.; an approximate, not quite complete, analysis in reverse order (some of the above lists have this order or both together) in LV 346.1 ff.; the name is found, without listing of the terms, LV 181.19; Mv ii.416.20; 417.5; iii.314.4; KP 94.2; Divy 300.18; 487.24; 547.19; 549.12, 15; Av i.287.14; Gv 89.13, etc. The standard list may be cited from Mvy 2241 ff., where the twelfth item is split up into its elements, not put into a cpd. as often: 1 avidyā, 2 saṃskāra (here sg.), 3 vijñāna, 4 nāmarūpa, 5 ṣaḍāyatana (here sg.), 6 sparśa, 7 vedanā, 8 tṛṣṇā, 9 upādāna, 10 bhava, 11 jāti, 12 jarāmaraṇa, śoka, parideva, duḥkha, daurmanasya, upāyāsa.

pratīyati = **pattīyati**, q.v. (cf. also next), *believes, trusts*: °yasi Kv 54.12, 16; impv. °ya Mv ii.223.20 (mss., Senart em. pattīya); °yatha Sukh 97.5; 99.6; °yiṣyanti SP 36.7; 37.10 (in both Kashgar rec. pattīy°).

pratīyapayitar, read °yāp° (n. ag. to caus. of **pratīyati**, cf. **pattīyati**, caus. °**yāpayati**), *one who causes to believe* or *trust* (in, loc.): °tāro (sc. bodhisattva-) bhūmiṣu Gv 463.3 (2d ed. pratiyāp°, which seems implausible).

-pratīśa, °**sa**, see **a-pra**°, **sa-pra**°, **su-pra**°.

pratodana, nt. (Skt. pra-tud- plus -ana), *thrusting, poking*, in aṅguli-°nam (= Pali aṅguli-patodaka), *poking with the fingers, tickling*: Mvy 8488; Prāt 518.6 (Chin. *chatouille*).

pratyaṃśa, m. (prati plus Skt. aṃśa), (individual) *part, portion, share*: SP 446.8; LV 90.8 (Bhvr., te samaguṇa-°śās te tathāgataguṇa-°śās); Divy 30.5 f.; 132.29 ff.; Śikṣ 129.4.

pratyakṣa, adj. (cf. °**kṣin**; once in nearly the same mg. in Skt., with gen., °kṣāḥ sarvadharmāṇāṃ Mbh. Cr. ed. 3.181.15), *seeing before the eyes, witness to*, with loc.: LV 146.2 (°kṣo bodhisattvasya lipijñāne), 7 (vs; atra °kṣu); 257.14 (Bodhisattvasya guṇeṣu °kṣās); Av ii.139.8 (guṇeṣu); Divy 71.8 f.

Pratyakṣadeva, n. of a former Buddha: Mv i.141.7.

pratyakṣa-dharman (?), see **dharman.**

pratyakṣin = **pratyakṣa**: in comp., tat-pratyakṣiṇām Jm 128.8.

Pratyagrarūpa, n. of a former Buddha: Mv i.138.1.

pratyajati, *abandons*; gdve. pratyaktavya: -sarvāṅgapratyaṅgāni °vyāni Gv 411.2 (prose).

praty-adhiṣṭhāna (nt.; noun cpd. of prati plus adhiṣṭhāna), *separate, several, respective* (prati) *basis*: anyabhavagati-°naṃ ca karoti (subject bhavaḥ, in pratītyasamutpāda) Dbh 50.11, *makes the respective basis for entrance into* (various) *other births.*

pratyanukampate, *is correspondingly compassionate*: (te cāsya sarve... bhrātur iva) kalyāṇair manobhiḥ °pante, evaṃ kalyāṇamanaḥ-°pitasya (ppp.)... Bbh 155.13 f.

pratyanubhavati (= Pali paccanubhoti), (**1**) generally, *experiences, undergoes*, often indistinguishable from (Skt.) anubhavati: °vati Mvy 7280 = Tib. so sor myoṅ bar ḥgyur, *experiences severally* (cf. 7281 vedayati = Tib. myoṅ bar ḥgyur), but it is doubtful whether prati should ever be rendered *severally* in this cpd.; a possible case is sukhaṃ duḥkhaṃ °vati Karmav 56.21 and 57.3, where for 56.21 Lévi says *éprouve respectivement*, but in the close parallel 57.2 anubhūtam is used, without prati; on the other hand, in many cases the word refers definitely to what is experienced as a result af past deeds, so that one is inclined to render prati *in return, as recompense*; so in Karmav above, and in: (paśyantu... aniṣṭaṃ) phalavipākaṃ pratyanubhūyamānam (in hells) Bbh 151.19; karmāṇāṃ (karma-) vipākaṃ °vanti Mv i.16.13; 18.6; (Pūrṇena) karmāṇi kṛtāny upacitāni ko 'nyaḥ °viṣyati, *who else will experience* (*in return*, sc. the effects of) *deeds done and accumulated by*..., a familiar cliché, Divy 54.4; 131.9; 141.9; 191.14; Av i.74.4; 80.10, etc.; puṇyaphalaṃ °bhavataḥ (gen. sg. pres. pple) Divy 213.26, and °bhavanti 222.3; sukhaṃ °vāmi Divy 10.14; 11.30; sukhāni °bhaveyuḥ Suv 113.8; 127.16; duḥkhaṃ °vāmi Av i.339.3; vividhā duḥkhāni °bhavanto (pres. pple.) Mv i.27.3; duḥkhāni °viṣyanti SP 78.1, and °vanti 2; kam arthaṃ °viṣyati, or °vati, *what advantage will* (does) *he experience* (*in recompense*)? Av ii.140.10, 11; 141.10, 11; 142.8, 9; there is, however, no clear evidence of the notion of *recompense* in duḥkhāni °vanti SP 77.14; saṃsāraduḥkhaṃ °bhavataḥ... sattvān dṛṣṭvā Gv 319.10; and in some cases such a notion seems improbable or even impossible, as in: (Māyā) na codaragatāni °vati LV 71.7; mahatīṃ ratiṃ °viṣyatha SP 80.2, *you will enjoy yourselves very much*; ratikrīḍāṃ °vati Divy 531.7, *enjoys lovesport*; praśāsana-ratiḥ (so both edd.; prose, no v.l.; but an acc. is certainly meant, as Foucaux's transl. correctly renders; read °ratiḥ or °ratiṃ?) °vati LV 16.5, (a cakravartin) *enjoys the pleasures of rulership*; (nagaraparva) °vitum Av i.122.3, *to take part in* (*experience, enjoy*) *the city-holiday*; divyamānuṣīṃ śriyaṃ °viṣyati Divy 262.20; 263.7, 20–21 (predicted of an unborn child); idaṃ... duḥkhaṃ na kadācit °vanti... yādṛśaṃ vayaṃ °vāmaḥ Kv 25.13–14; also 27.8, 21, 22; (**2**) with object *magic power* (ṛddhi, etc.), uncertain whether mg. is *experiences, enjoys*, as prec., or *gets, acquires* (so anubhavati in Pali, CPD): anekavidhāṃ ṛddhiṃ (Dbh ṛddhividhiṃ) °vati Mv iii.409.2; Dbh 34.24; anekavidham ṛddhiviṣayaṃ °vati Mvy 215, where Tib. myoṅ bar byed pa, *makes experienced*; but in mentioning one of the specific powers of ṛddhi, in the sequel to the same passage, Dbh 34.26 and Mvy 218 āvirbhāvaṃ (Mvy āvirbhavati) tirobhāvam api °vati, substantially *he is able to appear and disappear* by magic, Tib. on Mvy simply ḥgyur, prec. by 'terminative' (in -r), *attains to* (the power of)...; perhaps so in Dbh 82.19 (sa tān sarvān samādhīn samāpadyate ca... samādhikauśalyānugataś ca yāvat samādhikāryaṃ tat sarvaṃ) °bhavati, ... *until he attains* (? *experiences*? or perhaps *reaches* in the sense of *is adequate to*, see 3 below?) *that whole matter of the samādhis*; (**3**) *suffices for, is sufficient to produce* (= **anubhavati**, q.v., and in passage parallel to those there cited): (sūryācandramasāv . . . ābhayābhāṃ na) pratyanubhavatas Divy 205.25; possibly also in Dbh 82.19, under 2 above.

pratyanubhāva (m.; cf. prec.), in a sense derived from Skt. anubhavati which may mean (*experiences* and so) *attends*, a public gathering (so in Mbh. Cr. ed. 3.51.8 anubhūyatām ayaṃ . . . svayaṃvaraḥ which means *let be attended* . . .): *attendance at, participation in* a meeting (**samajya**, q.v.): Mv iii.393.3.

pratyanubhāṣati (occurs in Skt., Kauṭ. Arth. Sham.[1] 74.2, where interpretations differ, see Meyer 105 note 1, *read again*, or *read aloud* [to the king]; perh., however, *having made an oral reply*, i. e. having composed and recited a reply, pratyanubhāṣya, *he should then write a reply*, pratilekho bhavet kāryo; Pali paccanubhāsati also has a different mg. acc. to PTSD), *speaks in reply*: ppp. °bhāṣṭam (see § 34.11) Mv iii.393.17 (tāye ca . . .) tam uttaraṃ na °ṣṭam.

pratyanuyukta, adj. or subst. m. (cf. next), in Mvy 7664, opp. of anuyukta 7665, Tib. respectively phyir (= *back, in return*) brgal, and brgal ba; this may be derived from rgal ba, *cross(ed) over* (e. g. a river); so Chin. interprets, and also praty-anu° *crossed back*; but Jä. also allows brgal to be connected with rgol ba, *contend with, attack*, and states that phyir rgol ba refers to *defense against attacks*; derivatives of these two are used of *plaintiff* and *defendant* in lawsuits, and of *disputants* in academic arguments. In this latter sense Jap. interprets pratyanuyuktaḥ Mvy 7664, and this seems likely to be right; anuyukta then prob. *examined, questioned* (ppp. of Pali anuyuñjati, b in CPD), and praty-anu° *counter-questioned, cross-examined*.

pratyanuyujyate (pass. to *°yunakti; cf. prec. and next), *is interrogated*; both verb and noun equivalent to Skt. paryanuyunakti, °yoga, which occur in the vicinity (°yuñjīta 84.6, °yogo 84.12) and elsewhere in AsP; the exceptional use of prati for pari denotes prob. *hostility, counter-*, since it is hostile sectarians who are referred to: paraiś ca °jyamānaḥ pratyanuyoga-vyākaraṇasamartho bhaviṣyati AsP 84.20, *and when he is cross-examined by others* (hostile teachers), *he will be able to elucidate the questions asked*.

pratyanuyoga (m.; once in Skt., BR 7.1775, defined *Gegenfrage*; see prec. two), *cross-questioning, (counter-) interrogation*: AsP 84.20.

pratyanuśaṃsate, *expects, looks for*: gdve., pañca tasmin kule 'nuśaṃsāḥ °śaṃsitavyāḥ Karmav 40.22, *to be expected* (not *à célébrer*, Lévi, inconsistently with his rendering of 64.7); mātāpitaraḥ pañca sthānāni (see **sthāna**) °śaṃsamānāḥ putram icchanti 64.7 (here Lévi correctly *ont . . . en vue*).

pratyanta, adj. (= Pali paccanta), *on the border, outside, outer*: MSV ii.188.14 °tāni śayanāsanāni (= **pratyantima**).

praty-antarāpatti, f., *a second repeated offense*, the same as the original one, performed while the culprit was on **mūla-parivāsa** (cf. **antarāpatti**) and concealed: MSV iii.37.15. It leads to **mūlāpakarṣa**.

pratyantika, adj. (not in Pali; cf. next and AMg. paccantiya, °tiga), (*located*) *on the extreme boundary, edge, or frontier*: Mv ii.262.14; Kv 42.8.

pratyantima, adj. (= Pali paccantima; § 22.15), *belonging to the border* or *frontier*, cf. prec.: Divy 21.17; 426.25; °māni śayanāsanāni MSV ii.188.13 (in 14 pratyantāṇi); 190.8, 10, *seats on the border, the outer rim*.

praty-andhakāra- (adj.), in °viṭapam (nyagrodhapādapam) Jm 175.18, (*whose branches were*) *a counterpart of night* (prec. by meghasaṃghātam iva; all acc. sg.).

pratyabhijñāta, ppp. of praty-abhi-jñā- (not recorded in this mg.), *assented to, promised*: (rājñā) °ta evam astv iti MSV ii.24.19, *he was promised* . . .

pratyaya, m. (once **praccaya**, q.v.; in mg. 1 Skt.; in all mgs. = Pali paccaya), (**1**) *cause*; often clearly a synonym of hetu, tho metaphysical writers try to distinguish the two in various ways; see e. g. AbhidhK. LaV-P. ix.241, note 3, vyākhyā: hetur āsannaḥ pratyayaḥ, viprakṛṣṭas tu pratyaya eva; janako hetuḥ, pratyayas tv ālambanamātram ity apare; paryāyāv etāv ity apare, *hetu is the proximate cause* (pratyaya), *the remote one is pratyaya rather*; *others say hetu is what generates (produces), pratyaya only the underlying condition*; *others say the two are synonyms*; where hetu and pratyaya occur together in parallel phrases older interpreters (Burnouf, Kern on SP, Foucaux on LV) often mistakenly render pratyaya by *effect*: ko . . . hetuḥ kaḥ pratyayaḥ SP 8.5; ayaṃ . . . hetur ayaṃ pratyayo LV 120.19; so, the two being clearly synonyms, LV 128.11; Mv i.66.7; 153.7; ii.283.19 (taddhetos tatpratyayāt); Divy 204.7 etc. (ko . . . hetuḥ kaḥ pratyayo, common here); Divy 199.12 (ahetu-pratyayaṃ, mss. °yāṃ, adv.); Mv iii.57.15 (hetu-pratyaya-cārikā, Bhvr.); Av i.82.4 (taddhetu tatpratyayaṃ ca, adverbs); with the further synonym nidāna, sahetu sapratyayaṃ ca sanidānaṃ LV 376.21 (vs), *with* (good) *ground, cause, and reason*; with kāraṇa (Skt.), dvau kāraṇau tasya . . . dvau ca pratyayau Suv 11.9 (vs), *two causes and reasons*; technically there are four pratyaya listed, viz. hetu-pr°, samanantara-pr°, **ālambana**-pr°, **adhipati**-pr° (equivalents among 24 paccaya in Pali, Vism. 532.11), elaborately discussed AbhidhK. LaV-P. ii.299 ff.; listed Mvy 2266–2270; Bbh 98.26 ff. (brief definitions); seemingly in corrupt form ŚsP 80.4 ālambanāmateya-samanantara-hetupratyayatā (see s.v. **adhipati**); in Bbh 13.21 ff. a (totally unrelated) list of 4 pratyaya and 4 (different) hetu of cittotpāda in a Bodhisattva are listed, the pratyaya being *occasions*, conjunctions of events which stimulate cittotpāda; they are external to the Bodhisattva, while the 4 hetu seem more personal and mostly internal (the 4 hetu are gotrasampad, buddha-bodhisattva-kalyāṇamitra-parigrahaḥ, sattveṣu kāruṇyam, and saṃsāraduḥkhād . . . abhīrutā, 15.11 ff.); kadācit pratyayaṃ nārāgayiṣyāmi MSV ii.14.11, *perhaps I shall not get an occasion* (*opportunity*, = avakāśa); in Mv iii.338.2, 8 are listed three pratyaya, viz. āśravā(ḥ), vighātā(ḥ), and paridāghā(ḥ), for each of the five **skandha**, q.v.; -pratyayā (ifc.), for °yāt (= Pali paccayā), abl. as adv., *because of* . . . (what precedes in comp.), kiṃpratyayā, *because of what*? Mv iii.65.13, 15; avidyāpratyayā, etc., various cpds., id. 15 ff.; idaṃpratyayā 66.1; esp. in the **pratītya-samutpāda**, q.v. for lists, the regular formula begins avidyāpratyayāḥ (Bhvr.) saṃskārāḥ yāvaj jātipratyayaṃ jarāmaraṇam iti Śāl 76.14, and similarly as a rule when the formula is cited in full in prose, as Mv ii.285.8 ff., iii.448.12 ff. (but even in prose it may be modulated with avoidance of this stock terminology, as Dbh 48.25 ff.); with rather clear reference to this but not in the standard formula, pratyayasaṃbhava (Bhvr. adj., *dependent in origin*) Suv 57.14; 60.6; 61.2; otherwise used quite as in Skt., *cause*, e. g. dveṣa-pratyayopasaṃhāraḥ Av ii.129.14, see **upasaṃhāra** (1); svapratyayān (*based on themselves*) dharmān prakāśayati SP 29.8, and similarly 131.9 (vs); (**2**) in glāna-pratyaya-bhaiṣajya, *medicine to cure the sick*, the fourth of a monk's 4 **pariṣkāra**, q.v. for lists (in Kv 19.9; 20.20; 40.17 yāna is misprinted for glāna); here the word pratyaya (Tib. on Mvy 5893 misprinted gos, read gso with Tib. Index and 6139) means substantially *cure*, orig. however clearly (*required*) *means* (*of treatment*); note that pratyaya in BHS is *not* used as equivalent of **pariṣkāra** in this sense, as Pali paccaya is alleged to be used by both Childers and PTSD; bhojana-gilānapraccayaṃ (semi-MIndic) Mv i.117.7 (vs); (**3**) pratyayabuddha, one who becomes *a Buddha by* (understanding of) *causes*, = a **pratyeka-buddha**, q.v.: Śikṣ 344.7 (vs), where a marginal gloss has pratyekabuddha (which would be unmetr.); so also pratyaya-jina Dbh.g. 51(77.)2; and pratyaya-yāna = pratyeka-(buddha-)yāna Śikṣ 328.8 (vs; follows śrāvakayāna, and followed by uttama-yāna = mahāyāna; misunderstood by Bendall and Rouse); the same mg. is expressed by pratyayair jinā(ḥ) LV 443.17 (vs; refers to pratyekabuddhas, mentioned two lines before); the application of the term is made clear by a passage in SP ch. 3, p. 80, where first, line 5 f., we read: tatra kecit sattvāḥ paraghoṣaśravānugamanam ākāṅkṣamāṇā ātmaparinirvāṇahetoś caturāryasatyānubodhāya tathāgataśāsane 'bhiyujyante, ta ucyante śrāvakayānam ākāṅkṣamāṇās... (the hīnayāna followers); then, 8 f., anye sattvā anācāryakaṃ jñānaṃ damaśamatham ākāṅkṣamāṇā ātmaparinirvāṇahetor hetu-pratyayānubodhāya tathāgataśāsane 'bhiyujyante, ta ucyante pratyekabuddhayānam ākāṅkṣamāṇās...; and finally, 11 ff., apare punaḥ sattvāḥ sarvajñajñānaṃ... ākāṅkṣamāṇā... sarvasattvaparinirvāṇahetos tathāgatajñānabalavaiśāradyānubodhāya tathāgataśāsane 'bhiyujyante, ta ucyante mahāyānam ākāṅkṣamāṇās...; here it is very clearly characteristic of pratyekabuddhas that they seek *to understand* (anubodhāya) *grounds and reasons*, whereas śrāvakas seek to understand only *the four noble truths*, and mahāyānists seek to understand the whole *knowledge*, etc., *of Tathāgatas*. The śrāvakas are also said to be content with following what they hear said by others (i. e. of the gospel); pratyekabuddhas go deeper, but not so deep as mahāyānists. In Prāt 520.9 pratyaya-pravāraṇāyā (see **pravāraṇā**) is, in a v.l., read pratyeka-prav°, which seems to have been the reading used by Chin. (*secrète*); the Pali parallel, however, Vin. iv.102.38, has cātumāsapaccaya-pavāraṇā, and the old comm., Vin. iv.103.4 ff., understands paccaya = gilāna-paccaya, i. e. our 2 above; it may be that some confusion has occurred in the tradition; did the Prāt redactor, reading pratyaya-, have in mind both the above-mentioned use of pratyaya-buddha for pratyeka-b°, and at the same time the curious use of **pratyeka** described under that word (and did he even substitute pratyaya for it)?

pratyayana (-tā; to Skt. praty-eti, prati-i-), *state of reliance upon* or *confidence in*: (prajñāpāramitāyāḥ...) °yanatā-cittatā ŚsP 615.11 (prose), *state of having a mind characterized by reliance upon*...; tatpratyayanārthaṃ MSV iv.229.17, *to give assurance of this* (so Tib.).

praty-araṇya-(cara), adj., (*dwelling*) *in* (or *near*) *a forest*: (dadṛśuḥ) °caram... gopālakaṃ Jm 42.4.

pratyarthika, m. (in Skt. only ifc. Bhvr. = pratyarthin; = Pali paccatthika), *enemy*: sometimes ifc. Bhvr. as in Skt., Mv ii.77.6; RP 1.8; Gv 325.14; but in the rest an independent word; often foll. by the synonym pratyamitra; Mvy 2731; Mv i.198.8 = ii.2.5; Av i.177.7; KP 100.4; Bbh 98.16; 190.15; Mmk 24.16; *opponent* in a dispute, MSV i.56.4; arthika-praty°, *the two contending parties in a dispute* (Pali attha-paccatthika), MSV ii. 180.20 ff. (ms. sometimes arthi-pra°).

pratyarha, adj., *worthy*: kā ca pratyaraha-(semi-MIndic)-saukhyā Mv i.143.5 (vs), *and who possesses felicity worthy* (to become the Bodhisattva's mother)?; dhūpasya tathāgata-bodhisattva-pūjā-pratyarhasya Sukh 18.5; yathā-pratyarha, adj., *according to deserts* (Skt. yathārha): °rheṣu siṃhāsaneṣu LV 13.16; °rha-dharma-deśanā-kuśalatvād °rha-dharmadeśanā-kuśala ity ucyate LV 435.8-9; adv. yathāpratyarham Mvy 6374.

pratyavakrānta, ppp. (of *praty-ava-kram-, unrecorded), in periphrastic use, representing preterite verb, *withdrew, retreated*: (bhadravargīyā...) °tāḥ Mv ii.241.2; (Māro...) °to (from the Bodhisattva) Mv ii.241.6; iii.28.3.

pratyavagama, m. (to Skt. praty-ava-gam-, BR; cf. °gantavya, *to be known*, Laṅk 188.7, 16), *precise knowledge*: Bbh 74.1 (jñeyavastu-yathārtha-); 282.3 (°mo yathābhūta utpadyeta), 19 (yathābhūtaḥ °ma utpadyate); 388.23 (°maḥ).

pratyavatarati (AMg. paccoyarai, see Sheth), *descends, disembarks*: vahanāt (*from a ship*) °tarasva Divy 229.18.

pratyavabhāṣati, *addresses, calls to* (from a distance, in the places recorded): (sa tair dūrata eva dṛṣṭaḥ.) te taṃ °ṣitum ārabdhāḥ Divy 9.16; (sā taṃ dūrata) eva °ṣitum ārabdhā 12.18.

pratyavasarati, *departs, withdraws, steps back*: ppp. °sṛteṣu bhikṣubhikṣuṇīṣu Divy 235.27, *when... had departed*; ger. °sṛtya Gv 338.15, *having stepped back, withdrawn*.

pratyavasthāna, nt. (cf. AMg. paccavatthāṇa, *'clearing of a doubt'*; M. id., *refutation*), in Mvy 6507 is defined in Tib. and Chin. as (**1**) *rejection*; *getting rid of* (Tib. phyir gzhil ba), or (**2**) *arrangement, establishment* (Tib. so sor, *severally*, gzhag pa, *arranging*). Both mgs. are supported by forms or derivs. of Skt. praty-ava-sthā-, see pw. The word has been noted elsewhere only in Laṅk, where it usually, and I think always, has the second mg., *establishment* (of an intellectual truth or argument): tattva-pra°-kathā 77.7; pramāṇatrayāvayava-pra° 92.18; pra°-gati-svabhāva- 93.11; siddhānta-pra° 172.6; svanaya-pra° 179.12 (°na-kathāṃ cintayan, *thinking on a discourse for establishment of his own philosophic method*; here only, Suzuki assumes mg. 1, *rejection*, but certainly wrongly); also svanaya-pra° 193.12; 230.14, 15; -jñānādhigama-pra° 194.18.

pratyavekṣaṇa-tā = next: yoniśodharma-°tāyai LV 33.3; yathāśrutadharmayoniśaḥ-°tayā Dbh 13.23. Cf. **saṃpratyav°**.

pratyavekṣaṇā (Skt. and BHS °ṇa, nt., and Pali paccavekkhanā, °na; Skt. and BHS also °vekṣā, Pali °vekkhā), *thorough consideration, reflection, intellectual mastery*; pratītyasamutpāda-pra° KP 94.2; °ṇā-jñāna, one of the five **jñāna**, q.v., Mvy 113; Dharmas 94; Gv 251.7. (The verb pratyavekṣati in Skt., also BHS, e. g. °kṣitvā, ger., Mv i.275.19.)

pratyāgacchati (not in this sense in Skt., but = Pali paccā°), *backslides* (in religion): labhyaṃ satpuruṣā °anti (mss. pratyaga°) akuśalena karmaṇā (mss. karmāṇāṃ), vipratisārī bhavanti Mv i.37.4 (wrongly Senart's note), *it is possible that good men may backslide*...

pratyācikṣati (= Pali paccācikkhati; see s.v. **ācikṣati**), *rejects*: ppp. °kṣito Mv iii.196.1, 3.

pratyājaniṣyate, see °**jāyate**.

pratyājāti, f. (to next), *rebirth*: ucceṣu kuleṣu °tiḥ Bbh 28.22.

pratyājāyate, once with active ending (once in Skt., Kauṣ Up. 1.2; = Pali paccāj°), *is reborn*: °yate LV 23.5; Bbh 72.5; °yante Sukh 55.17; Kv 42.9, 10; opt. °yeyaṃ (active ending) Śikṣ 170.7 (prose); °yeran Sukh 12.11; fut. °janiṣyante, *will be reborn*, Sukh 40.16; 55.18; ppp. °jāta SP 225.3; LV 386.12; Sukh 11.12, 15; 40.16; 55.17; Av ii.55.3 (°ta-tva, by em., abstract n.); 125.13; Bbh 16.14; Karmav 33.1; 66.1; Gv 506.22 (read with 2d ed. °jāta for °jātā).

pratyāṇī, see s.v. **āṇī-pratyāṇī-nirhāra-yoga**.

pratyātma-, in comp., and °mam, adv., rare in Skt.; = Pali paccatta(ṃ), like BHS fairly common, and in general parallel to it; (*by*) *one's own* (*separate, individual*) *self*: adv. °mam, Mv iii.317.19 (? by em.); 447.7 (°mam eva parinirvāyati); Śikṣ 246.16 (yad idam asmin kāye 'dhyātmaṃ pratyātmam āpaḥ); AsP 103.14 (yaḥ svayam eva °maṃ pūjayet); °ma-mīmāṃsājñānena Sukh 3.19; °ma-vedanīya (of dharma), *to be personally realized*, Mvy 1297; Śikṣ 323.7; °ma-vedayitavya (of dharma-vinaya) Mv iii.200.10; esp. common in Laṅk, °ma-gati, *the way* (of salvation) *by personal realization*, Laṅk 4.16; 5.5, 14; 6.2, etc.; °ma-dharma 6.11; °ma-dharmatā-śuddhaṃ (nayaṃ) 8.1, (*the doctrine*) *pure with* (*in*) *the true nature of* (*realization by*?) *the inner self*; in Laṅk 2.7 (where Suzuki assumes loss of a negative by corruption) sva-pratyātmāryajñāna - tarkadṛṣṭitīrthya - śrāvaka - pratyeka-buddhāryaviṣaye tadbhāvito dharmo deśitaḥ, perhaps meaning: *in the exalted sphere* (āryaviṣaye) *of* (1) *the exalted knowledge based on one's own inner self* (on the one hand) *and* (2) *of sophistic and false views, of heretics, śrāvakas, and pratyekabuddhas* (on the other), — *the dharma as realized in relation to these* (various doctrines, tad-bhāvito) *has been taught* (by former Tathāgatas on this peak of Malaya).

pratyātmaka, adj. (cf. next; to prec.), *belonging to oneself*: °kaṃ dhanam SP 108.12, *wealth that is my own.*

(**pratyātmika**, f. °kī, adj., found in Skt., *peculiar, pertaining to the individual*; *private, personal*, contrasting with *general, universal*: °kaṃ jñānabalaṃ mamaitat SP 54.6 (vs), *this is my* (Buddha's) *peculiar power of knowledge*; Buddha saves all men by the Buddha-(= mahā-) yāna alone, and *does not preach individual* (*personal, private*) *release for any creature*, i. e. by the śrāvaka or pratyekabuddha ways, na ca kasyacit sattvasya °mikaṃ parinirvāṇaṃ vadati SP 81.14 (prose); similarly, °mikīṃ nirvṛti kalpayāma ... na bhūyaḥ SP 117.1 (vs); in this light interpret SP 93.10 (vs) ete 'pi śraddhāya mamaiva yānti, °mikaṃ jñānu na caiva vidyate, *they too walk in* (*by*?) *faith in me alone, and there is no individual* (*private*) *knowledge at all found in them*, which would lead to their seeking selfish, individual nirvāṇa; Burnouf and Kern see a contrast between the two halves of the line, which seems unjustified.)

praty-ādeśa, m. (cf. Skt. ādeśa), with lābha, *substitute, surrogate* (munificence, to monks): MSV ii.109.9; defined 113.8–10 as one made at all, or only one, of the four **mahācaitya**, q.v.

pratyādeśana (nt.; = Skt. °deśa, for which the definition *Anerbieten*, referring to Jm 84.13, is wrong; the word is used in a Skt. sense), *rejection, refusal*: (buddhaviṣa)yābhilāṣiṇaḥ a-pratyādeśana-parāś ca bhavanti (bodhisattvāḥ) Mv i.134.8 (prose).

pratyāpibati, *drinks in severally*: °nti SP 122.5 (prose).

pratyāya, m. (Skt. Lex.), *tax, tribute*: °yaḥ Mvy 7302; kara-pra°, pl., Divy 22.12 ff.; 59.24; 510.22 ff. (not in Index or Notes); MSV ii.32.5; (printed prāt°) ii.72.4.

pratyālīḍha, nt. (Skt. Lex.; Pkt. paccā°, Sheth), a stance for a bowman, with *left foot forward, right drawn back* (so BR and Tib. on Mvy): Mvy 4267; Sādh 86.14; 123.6, etc.; opp. of ālīḍha, Mvy 4266, which occurs in Skt., BR. (Sheth reverses the mgs.)

pratyālepana, nt., some kind of medical treatment, '*counter-anointing*', paired with ālepana: ālepana-pratyālepanāni vamana-virecanāni ca kriyanti (by physicians, treating kuṣṭha-vyādhi) Mv i.352.18.

Pratyāsannabuddhi, n. of a former Buddha: Mv i.138.8.

pratyāstaraṇa, nt. (= Pali paccattharaṇa), *cover, spread, rug, carpet*: kāśika-°ṇaṃ Mv i.306.9 (em. for mss. pratyottar°, which may point to semi-MIndic °pratyātth° or °pratyatth°); avadāta-°ṇāṃ (v.l. °pratyast°) ii.115.17; avadātapaṭa-°ṇāni iii.70.2; upastaraṇa-°ṇaṃ (by em.) 152.2; °ṇam Mvy 8942 = Tib. gdiṅ ba, v.l. **niṣadanam**, which Mironov reads; °ṇam Divy 19.20 ff.; °ṇa- Sukh 67.7; °ṇena MSV ii.89.2; in ib. 89.10–11 kalpa-pra° mala-pra° seem to mean *cover designed to keep* (a bed or seat) *in good condition*, and *cover* (to prevent) *soiling* (it); for kalpa, Tib. is cited as miṅ cam (read can), lit. *having a name*, so *reputable*.

[**pratyāstāra** = prec., Mvy acc. to BR, cited from Minayev; not in Index to Mironov or Kyoto ed., but for Mvy 8942, see under prec., Mironov cites this as a v.l.; is this the source of Minayev, cited by BR?]

pratyāstīrṇa, ppp., = next, q.v.: dūṣyapaṭa-°ṇān SP 75.7.

pratyāstṛta, ppp. (no Skt. praty-ā-star- recorded; = Pali paccatthata), *spread over, bespread*: Mvy 5178 = Tib. rab tu btiṅ pa; °tā (mss. and WT °tān) duṣyavaraiḥ SP 89.4.

pratyāhāra, m. (also as misreading or var. for **pravyā°**, q.v.), in Dharmas 70 one of five 'foods'; otherwise only four are listed in BHS and Pali, see s.v. **kavalīkārāhāra**; this seems to be an addition and its mg. is not clear; the Dharmas list is otherwise questionable.

pratyuccāra, m. (= M. paccuccāra), *repetition* (of an utterance): Mvy 2798 = Tib. slar gsuṅs pa, *saying again.*

[**pratyuttareṇa**, see **pratyot°**.]

pratyutpanna, ppp. (to Skt. praty-ut-pad-, but used in Skt. only as adj., *present*, like Pali paccuppanna, so also usually BHS; Skt. also, cpd. with -mati, *ready-witted*, and in math., *resulting from multiplication*), = Skt. utpanna, *produced, conceived, engendered*: hṛṣṭo bhavāhi (or °si, mss. bhavasi, i.207.17) naravara yasya tava kulesmin °no ... varagarbho ... mahāsattvo Mv i.207.17 = ii.12.7 (vs).

Pratyutpanna-(Dbh adds **sarva-**)-**buddha-saṃmukhāvasthita**, m., n. of a bodhisattva-samādhi: Mvy 745; Dbh 82.14.

pratyudāvarta, see **a-pra°**.

pratyudāvartate (= Pali paccudāvattati; cf. next, and **a-pratyudāvarta**, **°vartana**, **°vartanīya**, **°vartya**, **a-punaḥ-pratyudāvartya**), *turns back* (intrans.), usually from a religiously proper course: pres. °varte 1 sg. Śikṣ 280.7; °vartante Gv 144.12; 169.17; fut. °vartsyante AsP 248.1; ppp. °vṛttaḥ, *turned back*, Mvy 5106; in Gv 169.21 read °vṛttāni for text °vartāni; AsP 79.2 °vṛttaḥ *repulsed*, said of Māra; gdve. °vartya (see also **a-praty°**) Gv 287.12 avaivartya-pratyudāvartya- (read °tyāpraty° with 2d ed.); 529.9 °vartya-vīryair; in LV 423.6 certainly read apraty°, q.v., for praty°; pratyudāvṛtya, *turning around* (*back*), Gv 48.16 (nāgāvalokitena, see **avalokita**); caus. °vartayati, *turns back* (trans.) Bbh 290.16 (object cittam); pass. of caus. Śikṣ 7.4 °vartyeta, *would be carried back*; 7.10 °vartyate (by a whirlwind).

pratyudāvartana- (nt.) or °nā- (in comp.; = Pali paccudāvattana; to **°vartate** q.v.), *turning back*: in Śikṣ 296.8 text -gaty-apratyudāvartanāvabhāsa-, but Tib. cited in note indicates pratyud° without negative, and so Bendall and Rouse render in Transl.; read -gati-praty°. Cf. **a-praty°**.

pratyudāhāra (m.?; to Skt. praty-ud-ā-har-), *response, reply*: paripṛṣṭaś ca na yuktarūpeṇa vāk-pratyudāhāreṇa pratyupatiṣṭhate Bbh 161.15; pṛṣṭasya ca °hāra-mātre 172.12.

pratyudgamaka, adj. or subst. m. (to Skt. °gacchati), *going* (*one who goes*) *out to meet* (a guest or new arrival): MSV ii.38.3 (prose).

pratyuddeśa, m. (substantially = Skt. uddeśa), *direction, region, place*, sometimes app. with added sense of *specific, particular* (prati): yehi °śehi teṣāṃ ... gamano, tehi uddeśehi ... Mv ii.251.19, similarly tehi tehi °śehi 252.2; anuhimavante (10 °ta-) °deśe iii.29.9, 10; dakṣiṇāpathe sāgaramukho nāma dikpratyuddeśas, tatra ... bhikṣuḥ prativasati Gv 62.13, *a place* or *region*; so also 63.5; 529.4, dik-pra°; (samudrakaccho) nāma digmukha-praty° Gv 456.13 (the same place is called a janapada 466.16); (dakṣiṇāpathe samudravetāḍī) nāma pratyuddeśas tatra ... udyānaṃ Gv 99.11 (the same place is called a pradeśa in 100.9–10).

pratyuddharati (to praty-ud- with Skt. har-, not used in this sense in Skt.; Pali paccuddharati is usually wrongly interpreted; it means *removes* [water, or coloring, with a cloth], Vin. ii.122.37 and 151.26; see also next items; the range of mg. in Pali and BHS, for the whole group, is something like *remove, take away, take back, withhold, restrain*), *holds back, restrains, moderates*: °dhareti or °dharesi, to be read for mss. °dharehi (Senart em. °dhāreti), Mv iii.339.3, see s.v. **samajya.** In MSV ii.156.5 (at the kaṭhina rite) yuṣmābhiḥ svaka-svakāni cīvarāṇi pratyuddhartavyānīti (prob. read so, text pratyudvar°), *you* (monks) *are to receive back your several robes.*

pratyuddhāra, m. (to **praty-ud-dharati**, q.v., but in somewhat different mg.; cf. next), *the act of taking back* (approval, or a gift, once given): chanda-°raḥ Mvy 8477 = Tib. dad pa phyir bsgyur ba (*approving, then later changing*); so Jap., which understands the monkish rules of discipline as the object; Chin. *first showing respect for another* (person, or possibly thing) *then going back on it; changing one's mind*; so interpret pratyuddhāra-tām avabhāsa-tāṃ (q.v.) ca pratilabdhukāmena Śikṣ 140.6, *by one who* (wrongfully) *seeks to take back* (prob. a gift he has promised, see next)...

1 **pratyuddhārya**, adj. (gdve. to °dharati, or adj. to °dhāra), in a-pra°, *that is not to be restored or taken back*: apratyuddhāryam asya (Bhīk asyā) bhavati śrāmaṇyam Mvy 9133; Bhīk 23b.5, *not to be restored is his monkhood* (*her nunhood*), of a person permanently expelled; a-pratyuddhārya-paribhogaḥ Mvy 8493, *use of* (a gift once given or promised) *which ought not to be taken back*; so Tib. phyir ma blaṅs (or slaṅs, a form of which is used in Tib. version of 9133 above) par spyod pa; Chin. *using again after giving trickily.* The form in °-rya- might perhaps be interpreted as a gerund, see next; it is certainly so used in Prāt 519.5; but the corresp. Pali, Vin. iv.121.16, 19, 22, 31; 122.17 ff., has an adj. apaccuddhāraka (and in 122.21 ff. paccuddhāraka), which means *that ought not* (*ought*) *to be taken back*; applied to a monk's robe, as in Prāt; misinterpreted even in CPD. The old Vin. comm., iv.122.19–25, makes my interpretation unmistakably clear; note especially 24 paccuddhārake paccuddhārakasaññī, anāpatti, *there is no offense in the case of a thing that may* (properly) *be resumed, when* (the one who so acts) *knows that it is*; cf. 17–18 which explains the circumstances under which it is apaccuddhāraka (implying that it is paccud° in other cases).

2 **pratyuddhārya**, ger. (to **pratyuddharati**, q.v., or formally to its caus.; influenced by prec.), *having taken back* (something promised as a gift to another): (yaḥ punar bhikṣur bhikṣor ... cīvaram uddiśya) tataḥ paścāt pratyuddhārya paribhuñjita Prāt 519.5 (Chin ... *et la reprend ensuite brusquement pour la porter lui-même*); in the light of this possibly interpret Mvy 8493 as containing a ger., see prec.

pratyudyāna, nt. (to Skt. pratyudyāti, Pali paccuyyāti), *going out against* (the enemy, in warfare): Mvy 3614.

? **pratyudvartavya**, see s.v. **pratyuddharati.**

pratyupatiṣṭhati (not recorded in this sense), *resorts to, takes one's position upon* (a notion, loc.): na dharmasaṃjñāyām api °tiṣṭhet Vaj 45.16.

pratyupasthāna, nt. (Pali paccupaṭṭhāna; cited by pw once in Skt. from Śaṃkara, defined *nahes Bevorstehen*), (**1**) *presence* (of), *adhering* (to), *engaging* (in), usually cpd. with preceding noun; Tib. on Mvy 185, 7233, ñe bar gnas pa, *remaining near* or *adherence to*, see s.v. **viṭhapana** (-praty°): -sarvakleśadāha-°na-tvāt LV 424.15; avidyā dvidhakārya-°nā Dbh 49.18, *has a tendency to* (produce) *results of two kinds*; (sattvānāṃ ...) cittayathāgati-°natāṃ Dbh 74.5, *the fact that the minds* (of creatures) *follow their respective courses*; nānopasthāna-°nānāṃ (Bhvr.) Gv 85.4; (pratyutpannasarvabuddhadharmasamudāgama-) °nena Gv 467.4; (pratyayasya) a-praty° Bbh 34.6, praty° 7; (**2**) (cf. **pratyupasthita**; Pali paccupaṭṭhāna, at least as v.l. gilāna-pacc° for text gilānupaṭṭhāna DN iii.191.3), *waiting on, tending*: mātāpitror a-pratyupasthānam Karmav 40.11; mātāpitroḥ °naṃ 40.17.

pratyupasthita, ppp. (to Skt. praty-upa-sthā-; cf. Sudeṣṇāṃ pratyupasthāsye Mbh. Cr. ed. 4.3.18, *I shall wait on S.*), (**1**) *waiting upon*, often foll. by a form of bhū, *waits upon* (with gen. of person, instr. of thing): buddhakṛtyena sattvānaṃ °to 'bhūt SP 201.2–3, (Pūrṇa) *waited upon creatures with Buddha-service*; buddhakṛtyena ca °taḥ (no person, no form of bhū) SP 204.10 (vs); (rājā ...) samyaksaṃbuddhasya ... sarveṇa °to abhūṣi (52.12 om. abhūṣi) Mv i.49.9; 52.12, *waited upon the Enlightened One with everything* (which he needed); (tasyāṃ) dharmadeśanāyāṃ °tā bhavāmaḥ SP 100.11, *we are in attendance* (on the Buddha) *at this preaching of the Law*; prob. also tvam evaṃrūpayā sattvārthakriyayā °sthitā Gv 232.3, *you wait on* (creatures) *with such activity advantageous to creatures* (but possibly passive, as in next passage); with passive force, pañcasu sthāneṣu °tau (mātāpitarau) Karmav 56.4, *waited upon in five matters* (by their son); (**2**) *concerned in* (a specialization of the meaning *present, on hand*, Skt. and BHS), with loc. and instr.: (na hy ākāśadhātur) gamane vā āgamane vā °taḥ, na strībhāvena na puruṣabhāvena °taḥ Śikṣ 250.1, *for the space-element is not concerned in going or coming, nor in femininity or masculinity* (with instr., perh. lit. *attended by*?).

pratyupāsana (nt.; no cpd. of ās- with praty-upa- is recorded anywhere; one might think of em. to **paryupā°**, q.v., but in Pkt. this appears as AMg. etc. pajjuvāsa-, whereas pratyup° would give *paccuv°; hence such an em. could not easily be based on the Pkt. confusion of paḍi- with pari-, § 2.47), *service, waiting upon*: °na-vaineyānām Gv 348.26.

pratyuptaka, f. °ikā (= Skt. pratyupta, ppp.; the suffix ka may be specifying in Divy 3.7, but apparently not in 2.28), *set* (with jewels), *studded*; see s.v. **āmukta.**

pratyeka-, adj., chiefly as prior member of cpds. (but cf. pratyekāṃ bodhiṃ Divy 294.10; Av i.99.17; °kāyāṃ bodhau Divy 70.6; 209.16; °kā bodhiḥ Av i.136.7), primarily as in Skt., *for a single person, individual, personal*; esp. common in **pratyekabuddha** and other cpds. showing this mg., see the foll. items; in some BHS cpds., in part with equivalents in Pali, this seems to have developed special connotations, possibly owing to the standard contrast between a pratyekabuddha's rating (far inferior) and that of a real (samyak-saṃ-)buddha. So **pratyekaniraya** (Pali pacceka-n°) or °**naraka** seems clearly to be a place of less severe punishment than a (mahā-, or regular) niraya: note Mv i.103.(7–)9 (yadi kecit, sc. bodhisattvāḥ, kathaṃcid ... avīciṃ mahānirayaṃ gacchanti, atha khalu) pratyekanirayaṃ gacchanti (text adds, they are never born as pretas, asuras, etc.); also Mv ii.350.10, 12; pratyekanarakaḥ Mvy 4944 = Tib. ñi tshe baḥi (*ephemeral; single, simple*, Jä.; Das adds, *very small, minute; animals that do not live more than a day*) sems can (*creatures*) dmyal ba (*hell*), app. then *a hell in which creatures live for a short time*; Chin. *individual hell*; no Jap. rendering; iha pratyekanarakeṣūpapannāḥ ... asmābhir itaś cyutair narakeṣūpapattavyaṃ bhaviṣyati (app. for further, more serious punishment) Divy 335.25; bahuśaṅkur nāma pratyekanarakaḥ Śikṣ 57.1; śramaṇavarṇapratirūpakaṃ nāma pra°narakaṃ (n. sg.!) Śikṣ 136.10; °narakān Bbh 151.16; °narakaḥ Karmav 53.13–14; (tasminn eva janmani) pratyekasvargaṃ pra°narakaṃ (n. sg.) cānubhūtam 57.2 (refers to story of which 53.13–14 is part); here *private, personal heaven* and *hell* seem to fit, since the one who experiences both seems to be a single individual (at a given time; a former inhabitant of the pra°naraka is released as the new one arrives); pratyeka-rājan Mv ii.270.10 (see s.v. **pṛthu**), contrasting with cakravartin, either *minor, subordinate*, or *individual* (belonging to a single land?);

pratyeka-brahman (= Pali pacceka°, PTSD *an independent Brahma*), Karmav 34.8, see s.v. **Baka** (Lévi, *devenu un des Brahmas*, which can hardly suffice); in Mv i.103.1, most strangely, the words brāhmaṇa and pratyeka-brā° seem used for (the god) Brahman and pratyeka-brahman: (bodhisattvā avaivartikadharmā... never enter an evil existence,) atha khalu brāhmaṇā bhavanti pratyekabrāhmaṇā vā indrāś ca upendrāś ca yakṣādhipatayaś ca yakṣāś ca... (note parallelism between pratyeka-br°, contrasting with br°, and upendra and yakṣa, contrasting with Indra and yakṣādhipati).

pratyeka-khaḍgin = **pratyeka-buddha**; see **khaḍgin**.

pratyeka-jina = prec.: Mv i.197.5; 357.7 (vss).

pratyeka-naraka (m. or nt.), **-niraya**, see **pratyeka**.

pratyeka-buddha, m. (= Pali pacceka-; also °**kakhaḍgin**, **-jina**, and **pratyaya-bu°**, see **pratyaya** 3), a *Buddha for himself alone*, who has won enlightenment but lives in solitude and does not reveal his knowledge to the world; in Mahāyāna-texts often mentioned with śrāvakas (followers of Hīnayāna) and bodhisattvas (Mahāyānists), between the two: when there is no Buddha in the world, Pra° Buddhas arise, Mv i.301.3; iii.27.1; Divy 132.20 ff.; exceptionally, future Pra° Buddhas are predicted by name, Av i.99.17; 167.1; stories involving them are numerous, e. g. Mv i.301.5 ff. (loosely called saṃbuddha 303.12; 304.5, 11, in vss); Divy 70.3; 73.17; pratyekabuddhayānam Mvy 1251; SP 80.10, or simply pratyeka-yāna SP 10.4; a (corrupt and obscure) list of names of pra° bu°, described Mmk 13.4 ff., listed 13.11 ff. (not included in this Dict.).

pratyeka-bodhi, f. (= Pali pacceka°), *the enlightenment that belongs to the prec.*: Divy 50.11; 69.5; 74.14, etc.; Av i.65.3 etc.; also as two words, pratyekā bodhi, see **pratyeka**.

pratyeka-brahman, **-brāhmaṇa**, see **pratyeka**.

pratyeka-yāna, see **pratyeka-buddha**.

pratyeka-rājan, see **pratyeka**.

pratyeka-satya (nt., = Pali pacceka-sacca), *individual* (alleged) *truth*, applied to doctrines of heretical sects: **praṇata**- (q.v.)-°tyaḥ Mvy 426, ep. of a Tathāgata, *rid of*...

pratyeṣaka, m. (cf. next), *recipient*: (-vyākaraṇa-) °kaś Dbh 71.25; (prajñāpāramitāyāḥ...) AsP 40.16.

pratyeṣita, ppp. (to pratīcchati, cf. **eṣati**), *received*: samyaksaṃbuddhaiḥ °taṃ ... dharmacakram LV 415.17 (prose).

pratyottareṇa, adv., *after* (with prec. gen.; cf. **ottareṇa**, also preceded by Dīpaṃkarasya): (Dīpaṃkarasya tathāgatasya) pratyottareṇa (all mss.; Senart em. tasyott°, but tasya is implausible in this position) Mv i.2.2, *after D.* Em. to *pratyuttareṇa is unnecessary; § 3.73.

[**pratretu-**(kāma), LV 408.10 (prose), seems clearly corrupt; it is parallel, and must be virtually synonymous, with utpatitukāma; both are rendered in Tib. by ḥphur (bar) ḥdod (pa), *desirous of flying up*, said of birds in a cage, under which a fire is lighted. The vv.ll. are pratrentu-, pratetu-, prakrāmatu-, and Calc. prakramitu-, the latter clearly lect. fac. Prob. read praitu-k°, *desirous of going away*.]

[**pratha**, LV 34.12, read (vākya-)patha- with v.l., or (Skt.) vāk-patha, which is read in Calc. and prob. intended by another v.l. cited by Lefm. as vākyatha-.]

prathamaka (specifying -ka, § 22.39, to Skt. prathama), *the former one*: Mv ii.170.15 (= **purimaka** id. 18).

prathamakalpika, adj. (= Skt. prāthama°, Manu 9.166, where v.l. pratha°; cf. **prāthama°**), *first, leading, principal, best*: Gv 270.22; 307.15; 314.8 (vs) pūrvaṃgamaḥ prathamakalpika(ḥ), these two adj. being synonymous.

prathamacittotpādika, see **cittotp°**.

Prathamarājan, n. of a former Buddha: Mv i.141.7.

pradakṣiṇa, adj. (= Pali padakkhiṇa; not in these mgs. in Skt.), (**1**) *skillful, clever*: sarvākāra-pradakṣiṇacittāyāṃ (loc. sg. f.) Mv i.205.8, read prob. with repetition ii.9.4–5 pradakṣiṇa-cittāyāṃ sarvākārasaṃpannāyāṃ; pradakṣiṇa-citto (of Bodhisattva) i.206.4 = ii.9.20; (**2**) *successful*: (bodhisattvasya parārtha-, or sattvārtha-)-kriyā pracurā ... pradakṣiṇā Bbh 32.18, 21, *abundant and successful*.

-pradakṣiṇa-grāha-tā (= °**grāhi-tā**, which should prob. be read for it; Pali has no *padakkhiṇaggāha recorded), *adequate learning* (how to do), *competence* (in): bhṛtya-sama-cittena, kiṃkaraṇī-(q.v.)-pra°ha-tayā Gv 463.25.

pradakṣiṇa-grāhi-tā (= Pali padakkhiṇaggāhitā; to next, and cf. prec.), *state of 'grasping'* (learning) *well, adequate competence* (in): °tānuśāsanīṣu Śikṣ 286.4 (transl. wrong); (no complement expressed but referring to 492.22, see next) °tayā Gv 493.4; (-avavādānuśāsanīṣu) °tayā 529.22.

pradakṣiṇa-grāhin, f. °**iṇī**, adj. (= Pali padakkhiṇaggāhi), *skillfully* or *successfully 'grasping'* = *learning*; *adequately competent*; usually without complement, in lists of virtuous qualities: Mvy 2365 = Tib. mthun par ḥdzin pa, *adequately grasping*; LV 25.10 (f., of Māyā), 27.1 (id.); 91.3; with loc., (-avavādānuśāsanīṣu) °grāhī Gv 492.22; see prec.

pradakṣiṇatas, adv. (= Skt. °ṇam, °ṇena, adverbs), *keeping on the right* (as mark of respect): devim (m.c.) upagatā °ṇato Mv i.218.7 = ii.20.6 (vs; mss., three out of four times, °ṇāto, unmetr.)

Pradakṣiṇārtha (or, with v.l., °thin), n. of a former Buddha: Mv i.138.12.

pradakṣiṇīya, adj., *worthy of veneration* (lit. of circumambulation to the right): vandanīyaḥ °ṇīyaś ca Vaj 34.11.

pradattaka, f. °ikā (Skt. °tta plus -ka, svārthe?), *given* (in marriage): (mama duhitā ...) Kuśasya ... °ttikā MSV i.104.16. In 105.1 dattikā; in 105.9 anupradattikā.

pradadhāti (= Pali padahati, with cittaṃ, DN iii.221.14), *exerts* (the mind, cittaṃ): evaṃ cittaṃ pradadhyās tvaṃ Śikṣ 101.10 (vs, from Samādh). From this verb, as used in Pali, are derived **pradhāna** and **prahāṇa** (1), also **prahita**, qq.v.; and in Mv ii.208.1 (prahāṇaṃ) pradadhāti, *exerts himself in exertion*, should prob. be read (for corrupt mss.) instead of Senart's em. pratidadhāti; cf. both pradhāna and prahāṇa dependent on prahita, q.v. [In pw s.v. dhā with pra cited from LV Calc. as mg. *sich einer Sache* (acc.) *hingeben*, but Lefm. 385.12 (vs) reads with some mss. pradadhyau (to dhyā), which is proved right by meter and Tib. dgoṅs.]

-pradarśanaka, ifc. Bhvr. (= Skt. °na), *containing a revelation of*...: nirmāṇanirmita-°nakam Laṅk 3.15 (vs, perh. m.c.), with dharmanayam of line 13 (as all accs. in 14–16; wrongly Suzuki).

pradarśaniya, by em. m.c. for °nīya of mss., adj. (pra, intensive, plus darśanīya), *very handsome*: °yo Mv iii.259.16 (vs).

pradalita, adj. (once in late Skt., Schmidt, Nachträge; ppp. of pra-dal-; Pali only padālita, padāleti; but AMg. padalia), *dispersed, destroyed*: Mvy 7390; ŚsP 254.7, 9 (karaṇīyāni, kleśāḥ). Cf. **pradālayati**.

[**pradāna** ed. Dharmas 30, line 4; read **pradāsa**.]

Pradānaruci, n. of an ascetic, previous incarnation of Vītaśoka: Divy 428.27.

Pradānaśūra, (**1**) n. of a Bodhisattva: SP 3.6; 397.8; 398.3; 425.4; 436.10; (**2**) n. of a former incarnation of Śākyamuni: LV 171.2 (Lefm. °sūra).

-pradāraṇa, f. °**ṇī** (Pali padār°, ifc.; late Skt. once °ṇa, nt., *destruction*, Schmidt, Nachträge; to Skt. pradārayati), *destroying*... (in adj. cpds.): sarvakleśapradāraṇi (so mss., acc. sg. f., with vāṇim, Buddha's *voice*; end of line of vs; Senart em. °ṇīm) Mv iii.385.4;

mārgaṃ . . . bhavatṛṣṇā-pradāraṇam (so oldest ms.; later ms. °**pradālanam,** see next) Ud xii.1.

-pradālana, v.l. (later ms.) for **-pradāraṇa,** q.v., in Ud xii.1. Cf. next.

pradālayati (= Pali padāleti; cf. prec., **pradalita,** and Skt. pradārayati), *destroys*: ger. °layitvā Ud xii.18; tamaḥskandhaḥ pradālitaḥ MSV iii.27.19. (In Mvy 7390 Kyoto ed. reports var. pradālita for pradalita of both edd.)

pradāsa (°**śa**), m. (= Pali paḷāsa, see Pugg. 19.1–3), *envious rivalry*, the quality of being unwilling to see another get any advantage over oneself; M. Müller on Dharmas 69 *contentiousness*; always associated with mrakṣa and īrṣyā (similarly in Pali, where comms. gloss yugaggāha, see s.v. **mrakṣa**): Dharmas 30, line 4, read °saḥ for pradānaḥ (between īrṣyā and mrakṣa); 69 (text °śaḥ); °saḥ Mvy 1964 = Tib. ḥtshig pa, *burning*, also of violent pain; acc. to Lévi, Karmav 37.19 and 38 note 1 (and Tib. p. 185) Tib. has ḥchig (read ḥtshig?) pa for pradāśaḥ, as he prints it (but his only ms. paridāghaḥ, which corresponds to Tib. ḥtshig pa; it follows mrakṣaḥ, as in some other passages, and is surely to be kept! cf. Śikṣ 198.8 -mrakṣa-paridāha-, and see **mrakṣa**); I do not find ḥchig pa in a suitable mg. in Tib. Dictt.; Chin. on Mvy has, as second gloss, *irritation, anger* (the first gloss is obscure).

pradīkṣate (cf. § 2.28), in LV 185.7 (vs) seems = pratīkṣ°, *gazes* (longingly) *towards*: catvāri lokapālāḥ sasainyakās te tava °kṣante, dāsyāma caturi pātrāṃ . . . Cf. parallel udīkṣate, line 9. The mss. are unanimous (exc. one pravīkṣ°); Calc. interprets by pratīkṣ°, and no other mg. seems possible (pra plus dīkṣ-, *be consecrated*, is implausible).

Pradīpa, (**1**) n. of a former Buddha: Mv iii.230.12; (**2**) n. of a serpent king (cf. next): Mmk 18.25.

Pradīpaśaraṇadhvaja, n. of a serpent king: Mvy 3430 (cf. prec., 2).

pradīrghaka, adj. (= Skt. pradīrgha), *very long, very tall*: °kaḥ Mmk 593.6 (vs, -ka may be m.c.)

pradugdha, ppp. (of *pra-duh-; ppp. occurs in Skt. in passive mg., *milked*), in active mg. as periphrastic expression, *having milked out*: (gāvaḥ) sarpimaṇḍaṃ pradugdhāḥ (or, °gdhā abhūvan) LV 386.5 and 7, *the cows* (*have*) *milked forth butter-cream.*

pradūṣaṇa (nt.; in Skt. cited only as adj.; to next with -ana), *corruption*: in citta-°ṇād Karmav 26.15, *from corruption of the mind = from anger*, cf. next.

pradūṣayati (Skt., *corrupts, injures*; Pali padūseti, also padoseti, used as in BHS with object citta, also manas, manaṃ), (**1**) with obj. citta, lit. *corrupts* (*one's own*) *mind*, = (as in Pali) *becomes ill-disposed, irritated, angry, malicious* towards someone (usually loc., or gen. with antike, sometimes gen. alone): (devānām . . . antike) cittāni pradūṣayitvā Mv i.30.9–10; arhato 'ntike Av i.287.7; dakṣiṇīyeṣu ii.148.2; dagdhasthūṇāyā (prose; gen.? MIndic loc.? or corruption for °yām?) api cittaṃ na °ṣayiṣyāmaḥ prāg eva savijñānake kāye (note loc.!) Divy 197.25; mamāntike cittaṃ pradūṣitam Karmav 26.15, *he got angry at me*; no dependent case-form, Divy 286.5; Av i.248.4; 289.10 etc.; ii.130.4; (**2**) without cittam, but app. in same mg.: mā bhavanto bhagavato kāśyapasyāntike bhikṣusaṃghasya bādhituṃ pradūṣetha Mv i.314.8–9, *do not be malicious towards the Lord K., or* (*his*) *order of monks, to injure them.*

pradeva, *super-god*? So if text is right: devagaṇapuruṣa-pradevaṃ abhivādya nandituṃ narasiṃhaṃ (the Bodhisattva) Mv i.151.11 (vs). Last part much emended, and still not metrical, but no v.l. in first part.

pradeśa, m. (cf. **prādeśika**), acc. to Lévi *une question particulière*: (anyad api tāvad vayaṃ bhagavantaṃ Gautamaṃ pṛcchema kaṃcid) eva pradeśaṃ saced avakāśaṃ kuryāt . . . Karmav 29.23. Perh. cf. use of Pali padesa-, initial in cpds., mg. *of limited extent* or the like; but perh. the word has one of its Skt. mgs., such as *example*, or *reference* (*some example or other*? see 1 **eva**).

pradeśakālaka, adj. with pudgala, see **sarvakālaka**: MSV iii.76.9.

pradeśa-rājan (= Pali padesa°; Vin. comm. 309.5 f. ekadīpassa padesissaro Bimbisāra-Pasenadi-ādayo (text °ādāyo) viya; cf. **prādeśya**), *a local ruler, king of a* (*single*) *country* (not a universal emperor): Mv i.128.14.

pradeśeti (°śayati), *exhibits, displays*: Mv i.170.10 (cited s.v. **upadeśeti,** q.v.).

pradoṣin, adj.-subst. (= Pali padosin; cf. s.v. **pradūṣayati**), *malicious, hostile* (*person*): śatrūṇāṃ nāśayet kṣipraṃ hṛdayāṃsi pradoṣiṇām Mmk 496.5 (vs).

Pradyumna, (**1**) (= Pali Pajjunna, which is commonly derived from Skt. Parjanya, Geiger 23; if so, this would be hyper-Skt.; acc. to Waldschmidt, note ad loc., Fa-t'ien also points to Pradyumna), n. of a god of rain: Mahāsamāj. Waldschmidt, Kl. Skt. Texte 4,185.19; (**2**) n. of a nāga king: Māy 247.21.

Pradyota, (**1**) n. of a large group of former Buddhas: (8,000) Mv i.58.3, (60,000) 61.12; (**2**) n. of a future Buddha: Mv ii.355.2 = iii.279.7; Gv 441.25 (see s.v. **Maitreya**).

pradveṣaka, m., *one who hates*: °kā (n. pl.) śramaṇabrāhmaṇānāṃ Mv ii.53.1 (vs).

-pradharṣaka, see **supra**°.

pradhāna (nt.; also, oftener, **prahāṇa** 1, q.v.; see also **prahita**; = Pali padhāna; n. act. to **pradadhāti**), *exertion*: rūkṣa-pradhānaṃ prahitātmanaḥ LV 255.3 (prose), *of* (*me*) *having exerted myself in harsh exertions*; rūkṣapradhānaprahitātmakatvāt LV 256.6 (prose); the Mv parallels to these passages read lūha-prahāṇa-, see these words; samyakpradhānā caturo me aśvā Mv iii.120.14 (vs), *my horses are the four right exertions*, for which see also (samyak)prahāṇa; cf. Pali sammappadhāna; the four (cited in Childers and PTSD) are, exertion to prevent sinful states (dhamma = dharma) from arising, to get rid of those that exist, to produce good states, and to maintain those already existing; for BHS definitions (agreeing with this) see prahāṇa. In AbhidhK. LaV-P. vi.281, Vyākhyā, four samyakpradhāna; the older Chin. rendering has *effort*, the later *abandonment*, as if (Skt.) prahāṇa; Tib. also the latter.

pradhūpayati (Skt. only ppp. °pita; cf. Pali padhūpita, and aor. padhūpāsi), *perfumes*: pres. pass. pple. °pyamānaiḥ Gv 403.9. (Pali mg. is different.)

? **pradhvopaka,** m. pl., so (implausibly) Senart Mv iii.113.13; in a list of traders or artisans; mss. pradhvopraka, prabdhopaka. Corresponds to iii.442.17 praccopaka (v.l. pracoḍaka). Wholly obscure.

pranapti (MIndic for Skt. Lex. pranaptṛ), *remote descendant*: in Mv i.348.9 read, nearly with mss., rājño māndhātasya putrapautri-kāye napta-pranapti-kāye bahūni rājasahasrāṇi; see s.v. **napta,** and § 13.20.

Pranaṣṭaduḥkha, n. of a former Buddha: Mv i.137.7.

prapañca, m. (cf. Skt. id., Pali papañca, and the foll. items), is a word which in Pali and BHS is very hard to define; a careful and searching study of the Pali is needed, and has not been made. Northern translations are unusually bewildering; Tib. regularly spros (pa), which seems to mean (1) *spreading out, enlargement*, and (2) *activity*. Suzuki's Index to Laṅk cites three Chin. renderings, (1) *frivolous talk* (this is the only Chin. recorded in Index to Bbh, with reference to 51.15), (2) *falsehood*, (3) *the error of false statement*. Das s.v. spros pa (two items) offers a confused variety of interpretations; for the neg. (niṣ-pra°, a-pra°, etc.) he says *the state of an absolute inactivity*. The state of freedom from prapañca is always praised; common is niṣ-(niḥ-)prapañca, *free from . . .*, Mvy 2925 (among synonyms for gambhīra); Mmk 12.4 (form corrupt); 13.21; Gv 471.8; (of the dharmacakra) LV 436.11; of Buddhas and Bodhisattvas Mmk 164.9; Gv 25.19; Dbh.g. 26(52).1; Bbh 42.17; RP 15.15 (vs: aśaṭha akuha niṣprapañca-citto bhavati, which rather suggests *falsehood* for pra°, with some Chin.); aprapañcaṃ tac cakraṃ, sarvaprapañcopārambhavigatatvāt LV 422.16 (see **upārambha**); vigata-prapañcāḥ (bodhisattvāḥ) RP 15.2 (vs); in a number of passages pra° is bracketed or closely associated with vikalpa, and the contexts suggest *vain fancy, false imagining*: viṣayavikalpahetukam anādikāla-prapañca-vāsanāhetukaṃ ca Laṅk 38.1–2, and similarly 42.2; vikalpa-prapañcādhiṣṭhānaṃ vikalpa-prapañcālambanaṃ vastu janayanti rūpādi-saṃjñakaṃ Bbh 51.3–5; vikalpādhiṣṭhānasya prapañcavastunaḥ (dṛṣṭy-asmimānasya...) 15; vikalpa-prapañca-vastv-āśrayā sat-kāyadṛṣṭir... 16–17; tasya savastukasya vikalpasya nirodho yaḥ, sa sarva-prapañca-nirodho veditavyaḥ; evaṃ ca prapañca-nirodho (etc., as cited s.v. **parinirvāṇa**) Bbh 55.15 ff.; saṃjñāvikalpāḥ prapañca-saṅgānugatā(ḥ) 266.5–6; sarva-vikalpa-prapañcātītā(ḥ) (tathāgatāḥ) Laṅk 19.18; jalpa-prapañcābhiratā hi bālās Laṅk 186.8, see **jalpa**, the interpretation of which is doubtful, which increases the uncertainty of prapañca; prapañcārāma-Śikṣ 105.3, *delight in pra°*; °cārāmam adhikṛtyāha 114.13. followed by a series of vss on the subject (prapañca-cārin, *acting with* or *according to*... 114.17, 19); pra° bracketed with vigraha, *strife*, 115.2; its object is possessions, 4–7 (na vo 'sti kṣetraṃ na kṛṣir vaṇijyā syur yasya arthāya prapañca ete 6–7); next a vs devoted to vigraha, as based on family and possessions, 8–11; then again a vs on pra°, ending prapañca varjitva janetha kṣāntim 15; prapañca-cāra, *the course of pra°*, again contrasted with kṣānti, 18–19; parallel with iñjana, manyana, spandana (text syan°), Gv 253.14 (vs), see **prapañcana** and **°cita**, similarly used; important is MadhK 448.1 ff., (prakṛti-) śānte niḥsvabhāve tathāgate sarvaprapañcātīte manda-buddhitayā śāśvatāśāśvatādikayā nityānityāstināstiśūnyā-śūnyasarvajñāsarvajñādikayā (here a kārikā vs:) prapañcayanti (see this) ye buddhaṃ prapañcātītam avyayaṃ, te prapañca-hatāḥ sarve na paśyanti tathāgataṃ. (Comm. continues:) vastu-nibandhanā hi prapañcāḥ syur, avastukaḥ (so!) ca tathāgataḥ, kutaḥ prapañcānāṃ pravṛtti-saṃbhava iti. ataḥ prapañcātītas tathāgataḥ... tam itthaṃvidhaṃ tathāgataṃ svotprekṣitamithyā-parikalpa-mala-malina-mānasa-tayā vividhair abhūtaiḥ parikalpa-viśeṣair ye buddhaṃ bhagavantam prapañcayanti, te svakair eva prapañcair hatāḥ santas...; here *false fancy, vain imagining*, seems not far wrong; note **parikalpa** associated with it; prapañcopaśamaḥ MadhK 538.3 (vs), with sarvopalambhopaśamaḥ.

prapañcana (nt.? = **prapañca**; on the surface, from **prapañcayati** with -ana; prob. really riming adaptation to the parallel nouns in -ana), *idle fancy*: sarveñjana-manyana-(so read with 2d ed.)-spandana-prapañcanāpagata-cittam Gv 128.6 (see s.v. **prapañca**, used with the same series of words Gv 253.14, and **prapañcita**, similarly).

prapañcayati (denom. from **prapañca**; Pali papañceti), *falsely fancies, imagines*: MadhK 448.3, 8 (see prapañca); vikalpo prapañcayaṃ(s), pres. pple., Bbh 51.7 (see 51.3–5 s.v. prapañca); sa eṣa prapañcyate (pass.) kalpe (kalpo?) niḥprapañcās tathāgatā(ḥ) Mmk 164.9. In Mv ii.221.2 na khu me prapañcayitavyaṃ, Senart's em., assumed to mean *I must not delay*; this mg. of this verb is said to occur in Pali; but the Mv mss. read prapadyetavyaṃ; curiously, PTSD proposes to derive papañceti from papajjate = prapadyate, but this is impossible on both formal and semantic grounds. I have no very good suggestion for the Mv passage; perh. *I must certainly not rely on, be a burden to* (my blind old parents).

prapañcita, nt. (orig. ppp. of prec.), *idle fancy, imagination*, = **prapañca(na)**: iñjita-manyita-prapañcitāni SP 372.7 (cf. Gv 128.6; 253.14, prapañca and °cana used with iñjana, manyana); yasya ha prapañcitaṃ hi no sat Ud xxix.61 (51), = Pali Ud. vii.7 yassa papañcā ṭhiti ca n'atthi.

prapata (m.? cf. Skt. prapāta), *fall*: ulkinaḥ (see **ulkin**) prapate (*on the fall of*...) yuddhād (sc. apakramet, see prec. line) Mmk 198.25 (vs); cf. ulkāpāta 200.13. See also **aprapata.**

[**prapati**, assumed by Senart, = durgati, *evil fate*; but prapatiṣu (or °tīṣu) is a 3 pl. aor. to prapatati: kāmanidānaṃ (mss. kāmaṃ-ni°, keep?) prapatiṣu (v.l. °tīṣu) durgatīṣu (...narā) Mv ii.326.10 (vs), *on account of desire, men have fallen into evil states*; durgatiṣu prapatiṣu (mss. °tīṣu) paśukāle (read °kāye? Senart em. pāṃsukūle) 333.15, (*people*) *have fallen into evil states, into the body of a beast.*]

prapatnī, f., *chief consort*: Mahendrako... rājño Kuśasya... dhītāṃ Sudarśanāṃ °nīṃ prayacchati Mv ii.442.3.

praparīkṣate, *examines intently*: °kṣamāṇa (pres. pple.) na patanti vidū praśānti Gv 473.23 (vs).

prapalāna, once perh. °līna (cf. Pischel 567; see **palāna**), *fleeing, in flight*: LV 317.5 (prose; in prec. line prapalāyānaḥ, cf. Whitney 584b, 1043f); LV 319.14 (vs; no v.l., metr. guaranteed); Mv i.71.2 (vs: most mss. °līna, § 34.19); ii.213.6 (prose); 216.1.

prapācayati (cf. Skt. prapacati, *cooks*, and Pali papaccati, pass., *is cooked, ripened*; caus. not recorded), *matures, brings to full development*: ger. prapācayitvā (sc. sattvān) Gv 411.20 (vs).

prapāṭikā (cf. Pali papaṭikā, *splinter, shoot, sprout*), (**1**) *shoot, creeper*: so acc. to Mironov, and pw 7 App. (Minayev), for Kyoto ed. Mvy 433 latikā (so Index, text misprinted laṭikā), Tib. khri śiṅ, *creeper*; (**2**) in ayas-pra° Mvy 7014 (Mironov °ṭikā, v.l. prapaṭika) = Tib. lcags kyi (*of iron*) tsha tsha, prob. lit. *shoot of iron*, acc. to Jap. *sparks cast off from red-hot iron*; Chin. seems to support this.

prapāṇḍara, adj. (Skt. °ḍura id.), *very white*: SP 75.8.

prapāta, m., fig. *fall* from grace, or perhaps *pitfall* or (fig.) *precipice, danger-spot* (for bodhisattvas): catvāra ime...°tāḥ RP 17.3 ff., listed, (1) agauravatā, (2) akṛta-jñatāśāṭhyasevanatā, etc.

prapīḍana, *massaging, rubbing down*: (adhvapari-śrāntānāṃ...) aṅga-prapīḍanena śramaklamaduḥkhaṃ prativinodayati Bbh 145.19. (No such use of any deriv. of pīḍ- has been noted.)

prapuṣpaka, nt. (= Pali papupphaka, only in Dhp. 46, same vs as Ud xviii.18), *flower-tipped* (arrows), of Māra: Ud xviii.18 prapuṣpa- fragmentarily recorded in oldest ms., as in Pali papupphakāni; a later ms. changes to: tu (pu)ṣpa(kā)ni (so!).

prapūra, adj. (see also **saṃ-pra°**), *full*: °ra-vākyaṃ Mv ii.395.4, (*of*) *full* (*rich?*) *voice*; acc. to Senart also ii.331.4, see **saṃprapūra.**

praprīṇayati, *makes delightful*: madhuramadhuraṃ dharmaṃ deśayati kṣaudram iva madhuraṃ °yati Divy 551.27.

praphullana (nt.; n. act. to *pra-phullati, cf. Pkt. pres. pple. papphullanta, and next two items), *blooming* (of trees): sarvavṛkṣa-°na- Gv 313.13.

praphullita, ppp. (= Pkt. papphullia; cf. prec.), *in bloom, burst forth* (of a flower, and fig., of a person): °tas tvaṃ... padmam iva... LV 332.5.

praphullin, adj. (cf. prec. two), *blooming*, fig. of members of the body: °llibhir aṅgapratyaṅgair Suv 102.2.

prabandha, m. (Skt., *continuation, continuity*), in Laṅk 37.10 ff., 38.5 ff., 39.3, seems to be nearly a synonym for pravṛtti (which occurs as var. for it in one ms. 39.3; see **pravṛtti-vijñāna**), *continuous activity* or *existence*, viz. of vijñāna, contrasted with lakṣaṇa, the *external mark* or *manifested aspect* (Suzuki, Studies, 183) of vijñāna; both must be subjected to suppression (nirodha); 38.5 f. prabandha-nirodhaḥ . . . yasmān na (so, with Tib.) pravartate, *as a result of which it no longer operates*; the prabandha of vijñāna is analogous to the relation between atoms of clay and a lump of clay composed of them, 'neither different nor not different', 38.9 ff.

Prabuddhaśīla, n. of a former Buddha: Mv i.138.10.

? **prabudhyati**, or °**te** (so mss.), perh. *is taught* or *proclaimed*: nāmena vaipulyam idaṃ pra° (KN em. pravucyati, kept by WT without note) SP 23.10 (vs); Tib. does not seem to render any verb; Kern *which by name is called* (adopting the em.?); Burnouf *il expliqua* (active verbs, of which Buddha is the subject, precede and follow, but it seems not impossible to take this as passive: *this sūtra of great extent is taught by name as*. . .); na cāpi nirvāṇam (text °ṇām) idaṃ prabudhyati SP 62.16 (vs), so all Nep. mss. reported; WT pravucyati, citing K' as pravuceti.

Prabodhana, n. of a former Buddha: Av i.100.12.

prabha, m., (**1**) = Skt. prabhā, *light* (abstracted from cpd. **prabhaṃkara**?), acc. to all mss. in LV 123.1 (vs) candrasūrya-prabhaś ca jyotiṣā . . . na bhāsate, *the light of the sun and moon, the stars*, (etc.) *do not shine*; not a Bhvr.; we must interpret in this way, or em. to °prabhā; (**2**) n. of a maharṣi: Māy 256.28; (**3**) Prabhanāmā sahasrāṇi . . . (anantā nṛpatayo proktā Yādavānāṃ kulodbhavāḥ) Mmk 625.24, *thousands of kings named Prabha* (literally; prob. meaning, *whose names contained the element -prabha*).

prabhakara, see **prabhaṃkara**.

Prabhaketurājamati, see **Prabhā°**.

Prabhaketuśirī (m.c. for Prabhāketuśrī), perhaps n. of a Buddha (separating this from prec. **Avabhāsarāja**, q.v.): Gv 284.16 (vs).

prabhaṃkara, in vss (m.c.) prabhakara, once prabhāṃkara (cf. Skt. and BHS **prabhākara**, in Skt. said of sun and moon; = Pali pabhaṃkara, often ep. of Buddha; MIndic-aṃ for āṃ), (**1**) *light-making, light-maker*: candrāditya prabhaṃkarā prabhakarā khadyotake no name LV 120.11 (vs), *the moon and sun, makers of light, O maker of light* (Buddha)! *would not bow down to a firefly*; prabhāṃkaro Mv i.296.11, of the moon; fig., (sarve ca te, sc. sattvāḥ, *human beings* . . .) prabhaṃkarā bhontu paraspareṇa Suv 40.11 (vs), *shall give light* (i. e. help, or spiritual illumination) *to one another*; esp. (as in Pali) ep. of Buddhas, SP 301.4; LV 363.9; 424.2; 438.1 (prajñājñāna-°raḥ); Mv i.232.19 (vs; text prabhaṃkaraṃ, v.l. prabhak°, better metr.; of Dīpaṃkara); ii.353.2 = iii.277.5; ii.389.5; RP 5.7; Sukh 74.1; Gv 391.26; as name of a supernatural ray emitted by Bodhisattvas, Śikṣ 334.1; (**2**) n. of two former Buddhas: Mv i.136.17; iii.231.4; (**3**) n. of two yakṣas: Māy 34; 77. Cf. **niṣprabhaṃkara**.

prabhaṅgura, adj., °**ra-tā** (= Pali pabhaṅgura, also °guṇa), (*state of being*) *perishable*: °ram Mvy 2589 = Tib. rab tu ḥjig pa, or, phuṅ por gyur ba, both (*completely*) *ruined* (a neg. supplied from 2588 where read na rāśībhāvaḥ); °raḥ Śikṣ 232.1 (of the body); °raṃ (rūpaṃ) Ud i.34 (= Pali Dhp. 148 °guṇaṃ or °raṃ); °ra-tā (mss. always so or °la-tā; Senart em. °ṇa-tā) Mv iii.338.1, 7; 339.18; 340.5.

prabhañjaka, ifc., *destroying*: aribala-prabhañjakāḥ Māy 248.8.

Prabhañjana, n. of two yakṣas: Māy 32, 92.

Prabhadrikā, n. of a river: Māy 253.7 (in list between Suvāsu and Tapodā); MSV i.266.3.

[**prabhayanti**, read **prabhaṣanti**; see next.]

prabhaṣati, *barks*: for text (by em.) prabhayanti (mss. °vanti, °panti) read °ṣanti in Laṅk 246.14 śvāṇaḥ, (on seeing an outcaste, who eats dog-flesh) prabhaṣanti, bhayena maraṇaprāptāś caike bhavanty, asmān api mārayiṣyantīti.

Prabhākara (cf. **prabhaṃkara**), (**1**) n. of a former Buddha: Sukh 5.8; of a Buddha in the northern quarter, Sukh 98.2; (**2**) n. of a samādhi: Mvy 542; ŚsP 1413.17; 1418.2.

Prabhākarakīrti, n. of an author: Sādh 171.16.

Prabhākarasiddhi, n. of a teacher: Mvy 3505.

Prabhākarī, n. of the third bodhisattva-bhūmi: Mvy 888; Dharmas 64; Dbh 5.8; Bbh 338.17.

Prabhāketu, (**1**) n. of a Bodhisattva: Gv 3.19; (**2**) n. of a Buddha (Prabha°, m.c.): Gv 256.19.

Prabhā-(m.c. Prabha°)-**keturājamati**, n. of a Buddha: Gv 284.15 (vs).

Prabhāketuśrī, see **Prabhaketuśirī**.

[**prabhāga-tā**, in sarva-kalyāṇamitra-°tāṃ pratyalabhata Gv 342.9–10; read **sabhāgatā**, q.v.; cf. bodhisattva-sabhāgatāḥ, line 25 below, and sabhāga-mitra-samavadhāna- Gv 110.19.]

prabhāṃkara, see **prabhaṃkara**.

prabhāta, m. (recorded only as nt. in Skt. and pabhāta in Pali), *dawn, getting light*: rātriprabhāto 'bhūt (all mss.) LV 225.7 (prose).

Prabhāvatī, (**1**) n. of one of the four goddesses who guard the Bodhisattva in his mother's womb: LV 66.9; (**2**) n. of a yoginī: Sādh 427.3.

Prabhāvyūha, apparently n. of one of the **Ābhāsvara** (q.v.) gods: LV 44.12 prabhāvyūhābhāsvaraś ca (so Lefm., mss. vary, one ms. prabhāvyūhaś cābhā° which may be correct); in a list of classes of gods and individual representatives of some of them.

Prabhāśrī, n. of a Bodhisattva: Gv 4.2.

Prabhāsaśrī, n. of a Buddha: Śikṣ 169.11.

prabhāsvara, (**1**) adj., *clear* (of a voice): °rā Mvy 451, of Buddha's voice; (**2**) m., n. of a class of gods: devā (mss. divyā) ca brahmā ca prabhāsvarā ca Mv iii.122.12 (vs); in sg., following **ābhāsvara** (of which it is prob. a variant; perh. read ābhāsvarā in Mv?), Mmk 19.9 (cf. **śuddhābha** and **puṇyābha**, which follow); (**3**) m., n. of a yakṣa: Māy 91; (**4**) °rā, f., n. of a magic plant: Divy 113.27 ff.

? **prabhinna** (m. or nt.), if textually sound, *part, portion*, or some measure of capacity: mudga-prabhinnaṃ vā māṣa-pra° vā taṇḍula-pra° vā pūretvā utkiritvā (mss. utkāritvā) Mv i.327.2–3.

Prabhu, n. of a yakṣa leader: Māy 235.26.

? **Prabhuvidehakarṇa** (v.l. Prabho°), n. of a former Buddha: Mv i.139.14 (Senart em. Prabhūtadehakarṇa).

prabhūtajihva, adj. (= Pali pahūtajivha), *long-tongued*, ep. of Buddha: LV 366.17; as one of the 32 **lakṣaṇa**, q.v., in lists of them.

prabhūtataraka, adj. (= Skt. °tara), *rather abundant*: Bbh 162.24 (= °tara 162.6); 178.26 (all prose).

Prabhūtadhanaskandha, n. of the 'householder-jewel' of a cakravartin: Gv 418.11.

Prabhūtaratna, n. of a former Buddha in a distant world (**Ratnaviśuddhā**): SP 240.13 ff.; 299.15; 300.4; 328.16; 387.7 ff.; 421.13; 430.12 ff.; 487.2.

Prabhūtavarṇa, n. of a former Buddha: Mv i.138.9.

Prabhūtā, n. of a lay-disciple (upāsikā): Gv 135.18; 136.16 ff.

[-**prabhūti**, in °tiṣu Bbh 5.11 (prose), at end of cpd., *and so forth*, = Skt. -prabhṛtiṣu, which should almost certainly be read. It is barely possible that a MIndic form of this word (Pali pabhuti) was orig. intended, in which case read -prabhutiṣu.]

prabheda, m., (**1**) *ten thousand*: Mvy 7993 (mg. proved by position and Tib. khri); (**2**) *analysis, solution* (of questions): praśna-°da-kuśalaś SP 340.2.

prabheda-tā (v.l., best mss.), or °dana-tā (text), *thorough analysis*: mati-nidhānaṃ (sc. pratilapsyate) buddhi-°tayā LV 440.17 (prose).

? **Prabhemi** (so mss., except one Prahemi; Senart em. Praheti), n. of a former Buddha: Mv i.137.9.

pramaṇḍita, *adorned*: kiṅkiṇibhiḥ °tā Sādh 261.3 (vs).

pramattaka (unrecorded; PTSD cites a-ppa° from Pv. comm. 201.16, but the word here found is rather appa-matta-ka, = Skt. alpa-mātra(-ka), as correctly stated CPD); = Skt. pramatta, *heedless, negligent*: RP 37.15 (su-pra°) and 16, both vss; may be m.c. (or pejorative -ka?).

pramatta-bandhu, see **pamat°**.

-pramathaka, adj. (Skt. pra-math- plus -aka), *crushing*: paracakra-°kasya Suv 69.7 (prose).

pramada, nt., (= **pramāda** 2, q.v.), *a high number*: Gv 106.17 (°dasya); 134.1 (°daṃ, n. sg.).

Pramadā (m.c. °da), n. of an ogress: in RP 23.15 (vs) read, bālisa (or °śa) rākṣasī pramada-saṃjñā.

pramantā, gen. sg. °tāyā(ḥ), a high number: Gv 106.6. Error for **pramātra**, q.v.

pramardaka, adj., m. (Skt. pra-mard- plus -aka, but nowhere recorded), *destroying, one who destroys*: sarvāpara-°ka(ḥ) LV 433.2, of Buddha; chiefly in a cliché describing heroic sons, gen. pl. parasainya-°kānāṃ Mv i.49.5; 193.18; ii.158.17; iii.378.1; Divy 548.28; Gv 399.15; LV 18.6–7; in LV 22.7 same cpd., gen. pl., which here seems to have been carelessly repeated from the cliché (tho no v.l. is reported); a n. sg. is required, like the prec. series of epithets of a king.

Pramardana, n. of two yakṣas: Māy 32 and 88.

pramāṇa, *authority, evidence*, rarely (as sometimes in Skt.) agreeing in gender with the subject, but in Skt. fem. °ṇī acc. to BR; in LV 318.19 (vs) iyaṃ (sc. mahī) pramāṇā mama, *she* (the earth) *is my witness*; above in 318.10 iyaṃ . . . pramāṇaṃ (prose; but meter could not be concerned).

pramāṇika, adj., f. °kī (Skt. Lex.; = Pali pamā°), *having a measure, limited, restricted*: °kaṃ kuṭiṃ kārayīta Prāt 480.8, (a monk) *shall make himself a hut of limited extent* (= Pali Vin. iii.149.11; not quite accurately rendered in PTSD and transl.); (if) pramāṇikī me prabhā bhaved Sukh 13.17 (then may I not attain perfect enlightenment! here mg. is very clear); °ka-buddhakṣetra-Gv 458.2.

? **-pramāṇin**, *having . . . as measure, measured by . . .*: lakṣa-°ṇibhiḥ Mmk 139.25 (vs); but see § 8.114.

pramātra, m., Mvy 7751, or nt., 7879 (cited from Gv); Gv 133.16; a high number (corruptly **pramantā**, f., q.v., in Gv 106.6).

Pramāthin, n. of a nāga: Mmk 454.15.

pramāda, m., (**1**) an intoxicating liquor: na pāsyi (fut.) pānaṃ na ca madhu na pramādaṃ (only v.l. °modaṃ) LV 230.19 (vs); (**2**) a high number: Mvy 7789; 7918 (here cited from Gv, which reads **pramada**, nt., q.v.).

pramāda-bandhu (not recorded in Pali, but = **pamatta-b°**, q.v.), *friend of indolence*, ep. of Māra: Mv ii.334.5 (mss. prasāda°); 335.3 (one ms. prasāda°), 11 (no v.l.).

pramilāyita, ppp. (to Skt. pra-mlāyati), *faded, exhausted*: śīrṣaṃ maharṣisya tapena °taṃ Mv ii.232.4 (vs); mss. prapil°.

? **-pramuktaka**, presumably = Skt. °kta, *discharged*: (sarvaratna)-paṅktirucirasūkṣma-kusuma-reṇu-pramuktakān Gv 100.12 (prose); so text, but there is something wrong with it; it occurs in a long series of acc. nt. or m. epithets, mostly ending -aṃ, applied to a park (udyānaṃ, line 11). The following word begins with s-, so the form could only be acc. pl. m., which makes no sense. It would be unsatisfactory to em. to °kaṃ; I have no suggestion.

Pramukhī, (prob.) n. of a goddess or yakṣiṇī: Mahāsamāj., Waldschmidt, Kl. Skt. Texte 4,187.3; in Pali parallel, DN ii.260.23, pāmokkhā, taken as adj. by comm. and modern interpreters; the Skt. adj. pramukha might be assumed in our text (with **Avadātakeśā**), but its fem. seems to be only noted as pramukhā.

-pramuñca, adj. (= Pali pa°), *emitting, sending forth*: -prabhā-vyūha-°cāni Gv 358.8.

-pramuñcaka, adj., = prec.: °kānāṃ Gv 426.5 (prose).

pramuñcati, (**1**) *utters* (words; so in Pali with object vācaṃ), used absolutely: naivam āryāḥ pramuñcanti (no object expressed in stanza, but clearly means *utter words*) Ud viii.9; (**2**) *sheds* (tears): aśrūṇi pramuktāni Kv 70.2, or pramuñca 70.4.

pramuñcana (nt.), or adj. (in comp.; to prec. with -ana), *sending forth* (usually rays of light): clearly subst. in raśmijāla-°ne Suv 166.7, *upon the emission of a mass of light* (from the sun); in cpds. usually hard to tell whether adj. or n. (if n., in Bhvr. cpd.): Gv 3.11; 18.9; 29.24 (jñānaraśmi- °naḥ, ep. of Buddha); 117.6 (raśmi-); 210.13; 269.7 (prabhā-); raśmi-pramocana-, text of KN in SP 17.3 (most mss. pramuñcana) and 7 (here no v.l. in KN; but WT in both places pramuñcana, with their ms. K′). Cf. **saṃpramuñcana**.

Pramuditanayanajagadvirocanā, n. of a goddess of night: Gv 240.12 etc.

Pramuditapralambasunayana, n. of a gandharva: Mvy 3386.

Pramuditā (also **muditā**, q.v., 2), n. of the first bodhisattva-bhūmi: Mvy 886; Dharmas 64; Dbh 5.7 etc.; Laṅk 226.15; Śikṣ 10.17; °tāyāṃ tu paṭhyate Śikṣ 11.3; Daśabhūmike pramudita-(read °tā-)-bhūmi-nirdeśam ārabhya Bbh 332.20–21.

pramūrchita, adj.-ppp. (= Pali pamucchita), *infatuated*: sarve skhalitā āsi sarve (mss. pūrve) āsi °chitā Mv ii.425.7 (prose); similarly 8; Māy 223.12.

Pramokṣaka, m., (**1**) n. of a nāga-king: Mvy 3276; Māy 247.32; (**2**) n. of a mountain: Divy 455.30, called **Pramokṣaṇa** 450.11.

pramokṣaṇa, (**1**) (nt.; in this sense not in Skt.; cf. AMg. pamokkhaṇa, defined as *abandoning, giving up*), *liberation, salvation*: sattva-pramokṣaṇa-maitra-ratiś ca LV 313.11 (vs); teṣāṃ pramokṣaṇa-nimittam RP 44.18 (vs); (**2**) n. of a mountain, = **Pramokṣaka** 2, q.v.

pramocaka (to pra-muc-, caus., plus -aka), (**1**) adj. or subst. m., *freeing, one who frees, savior*: dharmaṃ jātimṛtyu-°kaṃ LV 131.18 (vs); otherwise of the Bodhisattva, or Buddha(s); prādurbhūtaḥ °cakaḥ LV 131.14 (vs); utpanno vaidyarājaḥ °cakaḥ LV 351.12 (prose); sarvaloka-°cakāḥ Gv 31.6 (Buddhas); (**2**) *sending out, emitting* (light): raśmi-°kaṃ dhyānaṃ Bbh 210.17. See next.

[**pramocara**, read] **pramocana** (Skt.), or °**caka** (q.v.), *sending forth, giving out*: nānāsvaramaṇḍala-pramocareṣu (read °neṣu or °keṣu; said of creatures in existence) Gv 330.22.

pramocin, *one who frees, savior*: dukhebhyaḥ pramocī (voc., to the Bodhisattva) LV 285.2 (vs).

Pramodā, n. of a yakṣiṇī: Mmk 573.14 (text here erroneously Samodā); 574.20.

[**pramohayitvā**, read pramodayitvā, *having gratified*: MSV iv.130.1, 3.]

prayāma, m., *extension*, lit. and physical: avakubjaḥ prayāmeṇa (om. in several mss.) prāpatam LV 254.21, *I fell prone at full length* (on the ground); usually of the *extent* of qualities, also of disease, gate prayāmaṃ (text prayāsaṃ, see Crit. App.) . . . vyādhau Jm 21.2, *when a disease has made progress*; śakti-°maḥ Jm 78.2, *extent of power*; dhairya-°maḥ Jm 111.16; 238.11; labdha-prayāma, *having acquired great extent*, Jm 171.15 (karmāṇi;

of the power of karman); 182.3 (kalāsu saṅgaḥ, *interest in the arts*).

prayuktikā (= Skt. °ti, plus -ka, doubtless m.c.), *application*: bhogināṃ viṣanāśaṃ ca mūlamantraprayuktikā (... nirnāśayati) Mmk 363.3 (vs).

prayujyate, °ti (to Skt. pra-yuj-, *apply*, pass.), *applies oneself*, with instr. of means of application: āśayena (mss. āśrayeṇa)... yoniśaḥ prayujyate RP 12.9 (vs); adhyāśayena ca prayujyati... 14.7 (vs; °ti may be m.c.); prayujyantena ghaṭantena vyāyamantena Mv i.246.4 (prose), *by him applying himself, striving, exerting himself*.

prayoga, nt. (Skt. only m.), *presentation* of a dramatic performance: kiṃ idaṃ adya... parvaṃ vā °gaṃ vā utsavaṃ vā Mv i.232.10.

prāraṇati, *resounds*; always of the world, or world-systems, at the time of an earthquake; usually followed by **saṃprāraṇati**, q.v.: prāraṇat LV 318.21 (mahāpṛthivī); 352.4 (lokadhātavo); prāraṇan Dbh 98.31 (lokadhātavaḥ); prāraṇitaḥ Mvy 3014; Samādh 19.6 (lokadhātuḥ); °ṇitā Mmk 514.17 (mahāpṛthivī).

prarucira, adj., *very bright*: Divy 601.14.

prarunda, adj., quasi-ppp. (on etym. see **ruṇḍa**), (**1**) *weeping*: te... praruṇḍā (mss. °ḍo) aśrukaṇṭhā rudanmukhā paridevetsuḥ Mv ii.217.11, *they lamented, weeping, with tears in their voices* (lit. *throats*), *with tearful faces*; (**2**) as periphrasis for past tense, *wept*: rājā °ḍo Mv ii. 216.19, *the king wept*; devī °ḍā 426.16; (parivāro) °ḍo 427.12; Alindā °ḍā 427.17; others iii.263.5 (thrice).

prarodana, nt. (Skt. pra-rud- plus -ana; unrecorded), *weeping*: °nam Mvy 6926 = Tib. ṅu ba.

pralagna, ppp. (of *pra-lag-, unrecorded), *attached* (an ox, to carts etc.): °gno Mv ii.70.7.

pralambana- (recorded only Skt. Lex. as nt. n. act.), *hanging down*: pañca ca kanyāsahasrāṇi nava-vicitra-°namālā-parigṛhītāni LV 98.19 (prose).

Pralambabāhu, (**1**) n. of a disciple of the Buddha: Mv i.75.7 (°huṃ, by em. for °hur, which would make the word an ep. of **Kāśyapa** 2, but cf. lines 11, 15, 18, 76.1, which support the em.); (**2**) n. of several former Buddhas: Mv i.137.12; Gv 174.21 (lived in the Vimalaprabha kalpa); 422.23.

pralambayati (caus. of Skt. pra-lamb-), *hangs down* (trans.), *dangles, swings*: hārā-sahasranayutāni °yantaḥ (pres. pple.) LV 296.4 (vs).

Pralambā, n. of a piśācī: Māy 238.19. See also s.v. **Vilambā**.

Pralambodara, (**1**) n. of a kiṃnara-king: Kv 3.4; (**2**) n. of a mountain: Kv 91.14.

[**pralambha-(bāhu)**, in Divy 99.18, misprint or error for Skt. and BHS pralamba-.]

pra-lalita, adj. (cf. Skt. lalita; Pkt. palaliya, not in this mg.), *very sweet*: °ta-kalahaṃsa-barhiṇa-nivātā (see this last) Mv i.171.4 (vs), of Buddha's voice. Senart em. pralulita, without good reason.

pralīna, (nt.; orig. ppp. to next; = Skt. praḍīna, ppp., and as subst., *flight*), also °**naka**, *flight*, in haṃsa-pralīnaṃ (mss. °prā°; Senart em. °praḍīnaṃ) buddhā bhagavanto gacchanti Mv iii.255.17; also in Mv i.307.16 read some form of haṃsa-pralīnaka (mss. °prahīnakasya; Senart em. °praḍīnakam iva) buddhā bhagavanto nagaraṃ praviśanti; both adverbs, *in the manner of the flight of* (a flock of?) *haṃsas*.

pralīyati (for Skt. pra-ḍī-, only recorded in ppp. and noun praḍīna, see prec.), *flies down*: Mv i.216.11 = ii.19.8 (vs); also ii.19.2 for o-lī° of i.216.5; in all mss. pralīyanti, kept by Senart i.216.11, but em. to praḍī° ii.19.2, 8.

pralugna, ppp. (of **pralujjati**; = Pali palugga), *broken, destroyed, ruined*: Mv ii.429.18 (ābharaṇehi lugna-°nehi); Śikṣ 56.8 (stūpa); Bbh 147.2 (karmānta); Gv 280.14 (tathāgata-vigraha).

pralujja- (to pralujjati; perh. m.c. for *pralujyā), *destruction*, in °jja-kāle jinaśāsanasya Mv ii.388.1 (vs), *at the time of destruction of*... (v.l. pralujya-). The reading is, however, not certain; the same vs in Śikṣ 305.3 reads **pralopa-**(q.v.)-kāle.

pralujjati (semi-MIndic), °**jyati**, °**te** (see **lujjati**), *is broken, destroyed*: Mv ii.356.9 (? v.l. pralujyamānaṃ for text lujy°); 370.22 (mss. °jyanti or °jjati, perh. pres. pple. loc. abs.?); 371.4 and 373.4 (°jjamāne, v.l. °jya°); 412.12 °jje (aor.); in ii.354.13 read pralujjaṃ (= °jan, pres. pple.; one ms. pulujjaṃ) for Senart's puluvaṃ, and perh. so in iii.278.17, same line of vs, unless pralujyanto (same mg.) be adopted, with Senart, as suggested by the corrupt mss. (it would be hypermetric); saddharme °jyamāne Śikṣ 17.3; °jyante AsP 256.8.

praluḍita = **pralulita**, q.v. (cf. also Skt. vipraloḍita, BR s.v. luḍ-), *agitated*, esp. by lusts: (manuṣyās) tāhi rājapatnīhi sārdhaṃ °tā(ḥ) (so 1 ms., Senart em. °ṭhitā) Mv ii.425.8; in list of synonyms, kāmeṣu gṛddhaḥ etc., Māy 223.12.

pralulita, adj., ppp. (despite **praluḍita**, q.v., which may well be an instance of ḍ for l as per § 2.46, prob. a noun cpd. of pra-, intensive, with Skt. lulita), *greatly agitated*: (yāṃ padminīṃ...)- paṅkā-(so mss., Senart em. paṅke)-jala-pralulitāṃ Mv i.130.12 (vs); by lusts, kāma-°tā i.180.18 (vs); in i.171.4 read with mss. **pralalita**, q.v., for Senart's °lul°.

pralepaka, m., Mvy 5998 = Tib. thod le skor gyi phye ma, *chalk-dust*.

pralehaka, in hasta-pra°, n. or adj., ep. of a kind of ascetic practice, in a long series of such: °hakair LV 248.17 (prose); lit. rendered in Tib. lag pa la ldag pa, *hand-licking*.

pralopa (m.? to Skt. pra-lup-), *destruction*: saddharma-°pe Śikṣ 116.2; °pa-kāle Śikṣ 305.3 (vs) = Mv ii.388.1 pralujja-(q.v.)-kāle; otherwise only °pa-dharma(n), *subject to destruction*: saṃskāra pralopadharm' ime LV 175.21 (vs); duḥkhaṃ...°padharmaṃ Dbh.g. 10(346).21; kim...°pa-dharma kim atra loke 'pralopa-dharma, rūpaṃ... pralopa-dharma... (etc.) Av ii.168.10 f.; read pralopadharmaṃ MPS 45.8 for ed. (p)r(a)lo(ka°; only r and lo in ms.); also (em.) 44.13.

pravacana, nt. (Skt. id., in closely corresponding mgs.; Pali only pāvacana), (**1**) °ne, with prec. gen., *under the preaching* (of..., a Buddha or Bodhisattva): mama SP 64.12; tasyaiva Divy 505.2; Kāśyapasya Av ii.97.6; samyaksaṃbuddhasya Sukh 7.3; tathāgatasya Gv 280.12; once instr. °nena in same mg., following the temporal tena kālena, tena samayena, tasya bhagavato... pravacanena Samādh 8.12; (**2**) designation of the groups or types of sacred texts of Buddhism, which are listed as nine Dharmas 62, as twelve (the same with three added after the fifth) Mvy 1266–78.

pra-vajita, ppp. (semi-MIndic for pra-vraj°, see § 2.16), (*having*) *become a wandering monk*: °ta nirapekṣaḥ (so divide) LV 57.19 (vs; most mss. pra-vraj-; meter requires short first syllable).

pravaṇṇa, adj.-ppp. (= AMg. pavaṇṇa; semi-MIndic for Skt. prapanna), *resorted to*: raudrair narair aśubhakarma-m-ati-pravaṇṇaiḥ Mv i.84.3 (vs), *by violent men who resort too much to evil deeds*. So one ms., the rest °pravarṇaiḥ, which makes no sense; Senart em. °vaṇaiḥ, but his note recognizes that the penult is required by meter to be long; he suggests that doubling of ṇ of pravaṇa took place m.c. But the AMg. form fits without change.

pravayati (used in somewhat similar way in Vedic; in Skt. only ppp. prota), *adorns, attaches to... by weaving* or *trimming*, with acc. of thing adorned and instr. of trimmings: vividhavasanaratnaiḥ sarvavṛkṣāṃ pravethā (for pravayata) LV 79.12 (vs), *trim all the trees with various garments and jewels*; so Tib., brgyan par gyis (impv. of bgyid pa), *make adorned*!

pravara, m. Mvy 7706, or nt. id. 7832 (cited from Gv), a high number: Gv 105.20; 133.1 (nt.).

Pravaraśrī, n. of a Bodhisattva: Gv 4.2.

? **Pravarāgramati**, see **Varāgramati**.

Pravarendrarāja, n. of a Bodhisattva: Gv 4.7.

pravarjanā- (possibly hyper-Skt. for M. pavajjaṇa to pavajjai = Skt. prapadyate), *assent, promise* (?): jñānaketava akhinnavacanāḥ pravarjanā-kuśalāś ca bhavanti (bodhisattvāḥ) Mv i.134.8 (prose). Senart suggests emendations which are not attractive.

pravartana-tā (= Skt. °tana), *setting in motion*: dharmacakra-°tanatāyai LV 394.2 (in repetition 7 °tanāya); 397.5; both prose.

pravahaṇaka (nt.? = Skt. °ṇa), *ship* (? at least some kind of vehicle): dārikā bhartari °ṇakena pratipādīyati (so mss., pass. of pratipādayati; ed. em. pratipradīyate) Divy 226.20 (prose).

pravāḍa, m. or nt. (= Skt. °la), *coral*: SP 10.12; 102.2; 111.7; LV 108.19; Mv ii.316.5; 383.6; Mvy 5947; Divy 51.24; 67.19; 115.3; 138.4; 229.6; Av i.201.2 etc.; Suv 171.5; RP 40.8; Gv 164.8; Dbh 18.26.

Pravāḍasāgara, n. of a former Buddha: LV 5.6.

pravādita (nt.; orig. ppp. of Skt. pravādayati), *musical sound*: tūryasahasra-°tair (so, as one cpd.) LV 313.7 (vs).

? **pravādī**, f., n. sg. °**di** m.c., *disputation, argument*: śūnyā pravādi iha īdṛśa-dharma-yoge (so, one word) LV 420.20 (vs), *empty (vain) is discussion regarding this application to such a kind of doctrine* (of heretics, mentioned in prec. line). So Tib. seems clearly to understand: chos sbyor ḥdi ḥdra ḥdi la rab tu rtsod pa stoṅ, which definitely opposes taking pravādi as loc. for °de; this construction would in any case be difficult, since śūnyā could then not agree with this word (as Tib. makes it and as natural interpretation requires); to take śūnyā with bhūmir in prec. line would be forced. No v.l. is recorded for pravādi (Calc. with some mss. reads śūnya-); perhaps it should be em. to °da (n. sg., for °daḥ).

pravāraka, (**1**) nt. (cf. Skt. pravāra), a kind of cloth: °kam Mvy 8983, acc. to Tib. (be ḥu ras) and Chin. *cloth made of calf's hair*; (**2**) ? in Av i.56.1 (tāvat suvarṇam anuprayacchāmi yena devaḥ) punar api yatheṣṭa-pravārakaṃ kariṣyati, acc. to ms.; Speyer em. to °pracāraṇaṃ; but perh. keep ms. in mg. of **pravāraṇa** (1), or read °raṇaṃ, ... *will again make any desired presentation* (i. e. charitable gift).

pravāraṇa, (**1**) nt., also °**ṇā** (= Pali °ṇā; once °ṇam in Mbh. Cr. ed. 5.7.15; to 1 **pravārayati**), *offer, tender* of entertainment or of some gift, *presentation*: samyak-°ṇā Bbh 303.2, one of the Bodhisattva's duties; caturmāsikā bhikṣuṇā °ṇā svīkartavyā Prāt 520.7, and ff. (refers to situation of Mvy 8500, and Pali Vin. iv.102.38 ff., see 1 **pravārayati**); akṛtanirikti- (Mironov kṛtanirikta, see **nirikta**)-°ṇam Mvy 8457; see also **pravāraka** 2; (**2**) nt., also °**ṇā** (= Pali °ṇā; to 2 **pravārayati**, which may be a denom. to this; see also °**rika**, and °**rita**), *the ceremony performed by monks at the end of the rainy season*: °ṇam Mvy 8682 = Tib. dgag dbye (also dgag phye); °ṇa-vastu id. 9103; °ṇa-sūtra, n. of a work (= Pali SN i.190–192, called Pavāraṇā), Hoernle MR 39.25; °ṇā Divy 91.12 (mss. prāvar°), 93.10; Prāt 501.4; Av i.308.7; ii.136.7 (read °ṇāyām with Corrig. 211); MSV iv.119.5 ff. (in the °ṇāvastu).

Pravāraṇa-sūtra, see prec. (2).

1 pravārayati (Pali pavāreti; cf. **saṃprav°**; app. caus. of Skt. pra-var-; once in Rām. ii.77.15, see BR, with loc., bhojyeṣu ... ābharaṇeṣu ca pravārayasi, Bomb. ed. °ti, comm. prakarṣeṇāsmadiṣṭavaraṇaṃ kārayati bhavān; Mbh. 5.6006, also cited BR, is a wrong reading, read with Crit. ed. 5.173.5 praveritā), *offers, tenders, presents*, generally with acc. (also gen.) of recipient, instr. (but sometimes acc.) of thing tendered: aham enaṃ vareṇa pravārayeyaṃ Av i.58.2, and śreṣṭhinaṃ vareṇa pravārayati 3; cīvaraiḥ °rayed Prāt 492.8; te (ed. em. tvāṃ, but see Mv ii.427 etc. below) sarveṇa °rayāmi Av ii.9.4; amanuṣyair ... pravāryate (pass.) 8; lābhena pravāryamāṇo (pass. pple.) Śikṣ 268.4, *being tendered a profitable gift*; ratnaiś ca °rayanti Divy 116.17; ratnaiś ca pravāritaḥ Divy 439.15; °ritaḥ, °ritaṃ Prāt 509.6, 10, *having been tendered* (food); the situation is identical with that of Mvy 8456 and 8457, see **pravāraṇa** 1, and Pali Vin. iv.82.21 ff. and 84.14 ff., where pavārito, °taṃ, as in Prāt; divyair vastrair pravāritaḥ Kv 44.11, not *clothed* (pw) but *offered, presented*; rājena me ... pravāritā (so with mss.), yā te strī ruccati tāṃ gṛhṇāhīti Mv ii.427.16, *she was offered to me* ...; mama strīyāya (stri°? in 3 v.l. striyā; in 13 both mss. strī, Senart em. strīṃ) pravārayitvā Mv ii.428.3, 13; devīṃ vareṇa pravārayati ii.430.11; confused text Mv ii.431.12, ahaṃ varaṃ pravāritā (woman speaking) vareṇa (? orig. with pravāritā; varaṃ later addition? Senart em. varaṃ varehi) bhadre (this voc. may be construed separately from prec., introducing the foll. vs spoken by Śakra to her in granting the boon; cf. iii.6.11 below); priyaṃ ... pravāretvā Mv iii.4.8; yaṃ (= yad) me striyaṃ pravāretvā 5.10, but yo (mss. ye) me strībhiḥ pravāretvā 5.12; (sā dāni) śakreṇa vareṇa pravāritā 6.11, *she was presented with a boon by Śakra* (same context as ii.431.12 above, which see); pravāritaṃ me khalu mahābrahmaṇā praśnavyākaraṇena, kiṃ dāni mahābrahmāṇaṃ pṛccheyaṃ iii.212.4–5, *I have been granted by Mahābrahman the expounding of a question*; pravāritārthātisevā Mvy 8500, *taking excessive advantage of things of value* (artha) *that are tendered* (a monk), referring to the situation of Prāt 520.7 ff., see **pravāraṇā** 1; (na tu) kadācit traimāsīm (q.v.) sarvopakaraṇaiḥ pravārito, yan nv ahaṃ Vipaśyinaṃ ... sarvopakaraṇaiḥ pravārayeyam Divy 283.5–6. On pravāritvā Mv ii.489.10 see **pravarati**.

2 pravārayati (= Pali pavāreti), *celebrates the* **pravāraṇa** 2 (°**ṇā**) *ceremony*, at the end of the rainy season: pravāraṇāṃ pravārayitvā Divy 93.10; varṣoṣitayā ... bhikṣuṇyā ubhayasaṃghas ... pravārayitavyo (here caus. in mg.) Bhīk 5a.3–4, *after the rainy season a nun must have both orders* (monks and nuns) *perform the pravāraṇā* (for her); pravārayitavyam Av ii.136.6, so read with Corrig. 211, *the pravāraṇā ceremony is to be performed*.

pravārika, m., (a monk) *making, or about to make, the pravāraṇa* (q.v., 2) *rite*: Mvy 8683 = Tib. dgag ḥbyed pa, or, dgag dbye byed.

pravārita, nt., = **pravāraṇa** (2), q.v.: Mvy 8684 = Tib. dgag dbye.

pravāsanā (= Skt. °na, nt.), *banishment, exile* (as punishment): Bbh 83.19 ff.; 140.24.

pravāsanīya, nt., with or sc. karman (to prec. plus -īya), *action leading to banishment* (from the monkish community): Mvy 8644; MSV ii.208.16 f.; iii.18.19 ff.; corresp. to Pali pabbājaniya.

(**pravāsayati** = Skt., *banishes*, with acc. of place of banishment: Divy 127.5, 9; badly defined in Index as *make to dwell in*.)

pravikatthate (cf. Pali ppp. pavikatthita, *boasted*; AMg. pavikatthai), *talks grandiloquently*: svābhāvikaṃ jagad iti pravikatthase tvaṃ Jm 148.23 (vs).

pravikampati, *shakes* (active): °pyamānā rudanti LV 227.16 (prose), the women of the Bodhisattva's harem *being shaken* (pass. pple.; fig., by grief) *wept* (but one ms., the best, A, viprakam°); pravikampya (no v.l.) corvīṃ LV 385.10 (vs), *and having caused the earth to shake*.

pravikarṣaṇa (nt.), *dragging along*: svavadhra-cīrapravikarṣaṇāturāḥ Jm 195.24 (vs), *afflicted with dragging along their thongs* (*and*?) *rags*.

pravikalpayati, *chooses alternatively, exercises option upon*: dṛṣṭyanvayaṃ hi pravikalpya (ger.) tat-tad Jm

153.10 (vs), *for choosing this or that* (action) *according to his view.*

pravikṣipta, ppp., (carelessly) *thrown down, scattered about* (Tib. bzhag pa): MSV iv.120.11 (here em.), 17; 121.7.

pravicaya, m. (= Pali pavi°; to Skt. pravicinoti), *discriminating comprehension* (generally rendered *investigation*, PTSD, *Untersuchung*, pw, which seems to me not quite exact); Tib. on Mvy rab tu (= pra) rnam par (= vi) ḥbyed pa (*separate, divide, classify, select*): esp. dharma-pra°, one of the (**saṃ**)**bodhyaṅga** (Pali dhamma-vicaya), Mvy 990; LV 34.4; and dharma° elsewhere, LV 181.16 (°ya-kuśalo); KP 50.2 (°ya-kauśalya); Mvy 846; buddha-dharma-pra° Dbh 71.5; dharmāṇāṃ (here prob. *states of being*) pra° Bbh 212.4; loka-pra°-saṃpannā(ḥ) Mv ii.290.3 and iii.320.12, of Bodhisattvas or Buddhas; (acintyajñāna-māhātmyaṃ ca pravicinvan, dhāraṇīsamādhi-)°cayaṃ ca pariśodhayan Dbh 73.13; pravicaya-(v.l.°ye) buddhyā Laṅk 15.2, *with mind set on discernment* (no dependent noun; could hardly be *investigation*); ā paramāṇu-°cayād Laṅk 52.6; others, Bbh 31.25; Gv 248.23.

pravicāra (m.; cf. next, and AMg. paviyāra, *sexual intercourse*), *amusement*: only in °cārārthaṃ, following mama eva krīḍārthaṃ ratyarthaṃ, Mv ii.115.13, 17; of luxurious apartments; there is nothing to indicate specifically sexual enjoyments.

pravicāraṇa, nt., or °**ṇā**, f., (**1**) = prec. (from next plus suffix -ana; cf. paricāraṇa, °ṇā, used in exactly the same phrase; JM. paviyāraṇā, *sexual intercourse*), *amusement* (not necessarily sexual): only in °cāraṇārthaṃ, in the same formula in which pravicāra and paricāraṇa (°ṇā) occur: Mv ii.117.4, 6, 8, 11, 14; (**2**) (from Skt. pravicārayati; Skt. °cāraṇā defined BR 7.1776 '*Unterscheidung*, so v.a. *Art*'), *investigation, thorough consideration*: (sarva)dharma-pravicāraṇābhinirhāra- Gv 364.26.

pravicārayati, °**reti** (see prec. two; in Skt. *investigates fully, becomes well cognizant of, knows well*, and so in BHS, e. g. Dbh.g. 44(70).10, see s.v. **paricārayati** 3), *amuses oneself*, especially (but not exclusively) sexually with women; in this sense the verb is unrecorded outside of BHS, and almost limited to Mv; but see prec. two items for AMg. and JM. related nouns; as Senart points out, i note 396, this seems to be somehow due to confusion with **paricārayati** (1) with which its use is identical; but it occurs once in LV, and too often in Mv to be emended, esp. in view of the noun relatives in AMg. and JM.; nārīhi pravicāreti Mv iii.8.17; almost always, like paricārayati (1), follows forms of krīḍati and ramati (°te), so (not always of sexual pleasure) LV 72.18; Mv i.31.6 (repeated with paricār° 32.6); 32.8; ii.111.15, 16; 144.10, 13; 146.6; 151.6; 170.14; 171.16; 444.12; iii.37.10, 11; 162.10; caus. in force, suṣṭhu kumāraṃ krīḍāpethạ ramāpetha pravicārayetha (so mss., Senart em. °cārāpetha) Mv ii.151.13, *amuse the prince* . . .; pass. (cf. Pali paricāriyati to paricāreti) *is entertained*: devī Māyā . . . sukhaiḥ pravicāryate Mv i.99.3.

pravijṛmbhitā, ppp. f. (to Skt. pra-vi-jṛmbh-, once in pw in somewhat different mg.), *spreading out* (*her legs*), of a woman in childbirth: (sā, i. e. Māyā, in bearing the Bodhisattva) °tā salīlaṃ (or °lā) Mv i.149.16 (here Senart keeps pratijṛ° with mss.) = 217.17 = ii.19.18 (vs; in the two last Senart pravi°, which is suggested by readings of mss. ii.19.18 and should certainly be read each time); cf. LV 83.5 (prose) vijṛmbhamānā sthitābhūt, which means the same; wrongly Senart's note Mv i.495.

Praviṇa, n. of a rākṣasa king: Mmk 17.27.

pravidarbhayati (= **vidarbh**°, q.v.), ger. °bhya, *intertwining* (writing letters between the letters of a mantra): Sādh 367.7 (prose).

pravidarśayati (= Pali pavidaṃseti), *reveals*: sarvajñabhūmiṃ °yanti Gv 364.16 (vs).

pravidārayati (unrecorded, but cf. Skt. °dāra, subst., and Lex. °dāraṇa), *rends, splits*: °dārayaṃ (for °yan, pres. pple.) Divy 606.3 (śiraḥ); °dārya, ger., Divy 592.12; °dāryamāṇa-(pres. pass. pple.) Divy 592.6 (-hṛdaya); 604.15 (-mūrdhan).

pravidāha- (m.?), *destroying* or *consuming flame*: °ha-jena tīvreṇa duḥkhena Divy 606.6; 607.24. (No pra-vi-dah- recorded.)

pravibhakti (f.; = AMg. pavibhatti; cf. Pali °bhajati, Skt. °bhāga), *division, distribution*: āryalaukika-°ti-tāṃ (prajānāti) Dbh 74.18; daśabhūmivyavasthāna-nirdeśa-°tiṃ avatarati 78.11.

pravibhāvayati (cf. Skt. °bhāva, subst.), *makes to appear*: bodhisattvānāṃ tathatāyāṃ (q.v.) °vyamānānāṃ (*being made to appear*): AsP 320.15; 321.2.

pravibhāsayati, *illumines*: (bodhisattvavimokṣam ..) °sayatā (pres. pple. instr. sg.) Gv 69.25.

pravirājate (AMg. pple. pavirāyamāṇa), *gleams forth*: ābheyaṃ (ābhā iyaṃ) °te surucirā LV 108.18 (vs).

pravirohati (once in late Skt., Schmidt, Nachträge), *grows up* or *out, develops*: pravirokṣyamāṇa-taruṇa-pakṣaḥ Jm 98.8, of a young bird, *whose tender wings were still to grow out*; pakṣau samyak pravirurohatuḥ 98.14; pravirūḍha-vilāsa-śikhāgaru-vṛikṣa-vanaṃ Divy 598.8.

praviloma, adj. (pra-, intens., plus Skt. viloma, unless error for pratiloma), *very contrary, opposed, averse*: saṃsārasrota-°ma-sthitāḥ sumedhāḥ Gv 393.4.

praviveka, m. (= Pali pa°; cf. Skt. pravivikta, *solitary*), *solitude, seclusion*: °ka-jaḥ Mvy 6344 (Tib. rab tu dben pa las . . .); LV 161.6; 180.17; Śikṣ 50.12 (ms. °vekya); 124.18; Bbh 9.2; 26.11; 246.20; Jm 11.21; 107.6; 108.21, etc.

? **praviśāmayati**, perhaps *stills, causes to subside*: smṛtim upasthāpayati (q.v. 2) praviśāmayati Divy 542.22; seems to be opposite (or, perhaps, equivalent?) of upasthāp°, but I do not understand the passage; Index leaves praviś° untranslated; context seems to throw no light on it. Cf. **pratiśāmayati**, which however does not seem to fit in this place.

praviśiṣṭa-tara, adj. comp. (prob. pra- intens. plus viś°; cf. AMg. pavisiṭṭha, printed °siṭha in Ratnach.), *more highly distinguished* (*excellent*): Divy 252.17 (prose).

praviṣajati (cf. Skt. viṣajjati, regarded as pass. to vi-sañj-, of which active is viṣajati), *applies oneself earnestly*: MSV ii.88.2 (and ff.), see s.v. **ātāpayati.**

praviṣṭaka (specifying -ka, to praviṣṭa), *one that had entered in*: Mv ii.169.11 (śreṣṭhisya ekaputrako dvādaśavarṣikena) krayeṇa °ko.

praviṣṭamāna, see § 34.1.

pravisarpin, adj., *spreading out, pushing out* (intrans.): Jm 96.21. No *pra-vi-sarp- seems to be recorded.

pravisārayati (caus. to Skt. *pravisarati in ppp. °sṛta, BR, and adj. °sārin, Schmidt, Nachträge), *causes to go apart*: (stūpasya) dve bhittī °yati sma SP 249.1 (prose); °sāryate, pass., id. 2, so Nep. mss., Kashgar rec. apāvṛṇvanti, KN em. °sāryete because of dual subject, unnecessarily.

pravistaraṇa (nt.), °**ṇa-tā** (cf. Skt. pravistara, °stāra), *expansion, spreading out*: cittanagara-°ṇa-prayuktena Gv 430.22, cited Śikṣ 123.5; °ṇa-tā (in cpd.) Gv 152.24; śāstrāṇāṃ °ṇa-tayā Bbh 264.24.

pravuccati, °**te** (= Pali pavuccati; semi-MIndic for procyate), *is said, declared*: SP 129.14 °ti, and 130.4 °te, both with v.l. °cya°; both vss. Cf. also **saṃpravutta.**

(**pravṛtta**, acc. to Senart nt. noun, *la mode d'action*, but rather ppp. as in Skt., in Mv i.159.5 [tac ca samyaksaṃbuddhānāṃ mānsacakṣuṣaḥ] varṇaṃ pravṛttaṃ, sthānaṃ ca yathānyeṣāṃ sattvānāṃ . . ., *and that color of the fleshy eye of Buddhas is developed, and its position, just as of other creatures*; so line 7, [divyacakṣuḥ,] tat pravṛttaṃ manomayeṣu rūpeṣu [tat = divyacakṣuḥ].)

pravṛttaka, adj. (= Skt. pravṛtta), *who have set out, embarked* (on, comp.): buddhānāṃ . . . lokānugraha-°ttakānāṃ Av i.16.10 (prose; in same cliché, °ttānāṃ i.30.8); *that took place, were engaged in*, °ttakāni chandakāni Av i.269.8 (prose; perh. specifying ka, § 22.39).

pravṛtti-vijñāna, *the vijñāna as characterized by evolution*: contrasted with **ālaya**-vi° Laṅk 2.13; trividhaṃ vijñānaṃ, pravṛtti-lakṣaṇaṃ karma-la° jāti-la° ca Laṅk 37.13; Suzuki, Studies, 182 infra, obviously misrepresents this by making the triad pravṛtti (*evolution*), lakṣaṇa (*'modes of being'*), and karma (*'function'*), whereas lakṣaṇa here means *characterized by* and goes alike with pravṛtti, karma, and jāti; see loc. cit. 186 which recognizes this. See also **prabandha.**

Pravṛddhakāyarāja, n. of a Bodhisattva: Gv 442.14.

pravedha (m.? = Pali pabbedha; in Skt. once, see pw, *shot*, sc. of an arrow), *shot* as a measure of breadth (? or possibly, *breadth*, cf. **udvedha, āvedha**): Divy 56.16–17 yo 'sau yūpa ūrdhvaṃ vyāmasahasraṃ tiryak ṣoḍaśapravedho (cf. Jāt. ii.334.4 tiriyaṃ soḷasapabbedho), . . . *across* (in diameter) *16 shots*, or possibly *across having a breadth of 16* (sc. vyāma?); cf. the vv.ll. cited in the note; virtually same text 59.16.

pravedhati, once °**dhayate** (= Pali pave°; see also **pravyadhati**; regularly follows **vedhati**, q.v.), intenser substitute for **vedhati**: prāvedhat LV 352.2; 411.1; °dhanta Dbh 98.31; read pravedhayamānaḥ LV 188.3 (prose) with most and best mss., intrans., *trembling*, for Lefm. °vep°; °dhita, ppp. Mvy 3008; Divy 250.23; 365.15; Samādh 19.6.

praveśa (m.), in LV 149.18, 21 (prose) anena praveśena, acc. to pw *Art und Weise, Methode*; Foucaux, *entrée* (dans la numération des atomes subtils, mentioned in the preceding part of 18 and supplied with praveśena both times by F.); Tib. renders literally, ḥjug pa, *entrance*; the pw rendering is probably close to the intended mg.; perhaps *procedure, process*; 21 reads: an° pra° imaṃ cāturdvīpakaṃ lokadhātuṃ pramukhaṃ kṛtvā paripūrṇakoṭīśataṃ.

praveśaka, adj. (= AMg. pavesaa), *entering*: katham etāni °kāni bhaviṣyanti Divy 249.4, *how will they enter* (lit. *come to be entering*)?

praveśitā, fem. ppp. (of caus. of Skt. pra-viś-): ahaṃ . . . dārakaṃ praveśitā Divy 541.28, *I am pregnant with a boy* (lit. *caused to be entered*).

praveṣṭuka (app. MIndic for °ṭṛ-ka; § 13.22), *one who enters*: (maṇḍalaṃ) °kānāṃ mukhaṃ veṣṭayitvā Mmk 49.12, *having covered the faces of those that enter the* (magic) *circle*.

praveṣye, iṇ LV 189.6, vs, āvartayāśu mi rathaṃ punar ahaṃ (read puna 'haṃ, m.c.?) pra°, *turn my car about quickly, I'll enter the city again*, if not corruption for pravekṣye, which Calc. reads, must have ṣ for (kh for) kṣ, § 2.26. Tib. ṅa . .ḥgro, *I go*.

pravyathā (to Skt. pra-vyath-, cf. Skt. vyathā), *perturbation*: mā bhadre °thā Suv 219.9 (prose).

pravyadhati, only Divy, = **pravedhati**; citations s.v. **vyadhati**, q.v.; Pali also has pavyadhita.

pravyāharaṇa (nt.; to Skt. pravyāharati, see next), *speech*, esp. *the faculty* or *power of speech*: mūkāḥ °ṇa-samarthā bhavanti Divy 250.27; Av i.109.4; tiryañco vāk-°ṇa-samarthā bhavanti MSV ii.134.7.

pravyāhāra, m., sometimes acc. to texts nt. (in Skt. recorded once, Mbh 12.8088, where mg. is doubtful; °rāya, Nīl. prakṛṣṭoktaye, which BR 5.1630 take to mean *um weiter in der Rede fortzufahren*; otherwise P.C. Roy; to Skt. pravyāharati), *speech, utterance*: corruptly written pratyāhāra in Mmk 4.21 and always in Kv except only 90.14; a-°raḥ, *not speaking, non-utterance*, Mvy 6986; KP 59.4 (neg. proved by Tib.; see s.v. **udāhāra**); pravyāhāraṃ (acc.) vācā Bbh 160.21; °raḥ kartavyaḥ Kv 44.23; mayā (or, me) °raḥ kṛtaḥ (55.20 °raṃ kṛtaṃ), followed by directly quoted words, Kv 54.9, 11; 55.8, 20; 56.11, 14; similarly Kv 55.16; 56.8; 90.14; idam (gender!) . . . vāk-°raṃ śrutvā Divy 324.7; (imebhir) akṣarapadapratyāhārair bhagavantam abhyaṣṭāvīt Mmk 4.21 (read °pravyā°); in Bhvr. cpd., duḥpravyāhāraṃ (etat sthānaṃ) Gv 321.20, *hard to describe in words*.

pravyāhṛtavatī, Av ii.10.9, following uvāca (fem. subject), can, it seems, only be a periphrastic form substituting for the perfect, from Skt. pravyāharati, *speaks*; render, *she spoke and uttered* (the following, which directly quotes her speech). Feer, *s'écria à haute voix*; Speyer, Index, does not translate, but attributes 'inchoative force' to pra (i. e. *began to speak*?); this is not supported by Skt. or BHS usage as far as I know.

Pravrajyāntarāya-sūtra, n. of a work: Śikṣ 69.4.

pravrājayati, used in non-caus. mg., *enters ascetic life*: yan nv ahaṃ bhagavato 'ntike °jayeyam Gv 417.15. Cf. the opposite, sādhu ca (ca om. in 1 ms.; Senart em. tvaṃ, unnecessarily) pravrajāhi (Senart pravrājehi, metr. impossible!) māṃ Mv iii.386.13 (vs), *and please initiate me into ascetic life*! Here, to be sure, meter may be concerned in the short a.

praśaṃsiya, adj. (= Skt. °sya, Pali pasaṃsiya), *praiseworthy*: Ud viii.3 (with **nindiya**, q.v.).

? **praśaṭha**, °**ṭhā**, °**ṭhatā**, uncertain; in KP 154.1 (prose) samyakprahāṇa-(see **prahāṇa**)-prasaṭhā (so divide) ri-(lacuna; Tib. rdzu ḥphrul = ṛddhi-); Tib. renders prasaṭhā by ḥgro ba, here doubtless *entrance into* . . .; the syllable ṭhā seems corrupt but I think of no attractive em. Dubious also is praśaṭhatā Mvy 2101 (both edd., no v.l.), which looks as if it meant *trickery, deceitfulness* (so pw 7.362; cf. AMg. pasaḍha, *rogue, trickster*); but Tib. renders rnal du (*into tranquillity*) (ḥ)bab (*entrance into*) or ḥdug pa (*state of*), which suggests a form of śam (cf. **śamatha**); Chin. acc. to Ting, *elimination of differences among things*, resulting in tranquillity (the last phrase not in Chin. here but cited from a parallel passage).

[**praśabdha**- LV 224.8, read **praśrabdha-**, q.v.]

Praśamagandhasunābha, n. of a Buddha: Gv 422.7.

Praśamarūpagati, n. of a Buddha: Gv 284.22.

Praśamasukhābhijñā, n. of a (Bodhisattva-) samādhi: Gv 122.17.

? **praśasta**, ppp. (to pra plus śas, *cut*; but this cpd. hardly exists), *cut*: so Senart's em., (in hell) kartarikāhi praśastā (mss. °sattā or °śaktā) bhavanti Mv i.24.14 (prose).

? **Praśastaguṇarāśi**, n. of a former Buddha (by em.): Mv i.136.15.

Praśastavarṇa, n. of a former Buddha: Mv i.138.3.

Praśānta, n. of a śuddhāvāsakāyika devaputra: LV 4.13; 6.13; 438.16. Cf. **Praśāntacitta.**

Praśāntacāritramati, n. of a Bodhisattva: LV 2.13.

Praśāntacitta, n. of a devaputra: LV 7.5 (vs); confirmed in Tib.; seems to be a vs correspondent of the prose **Praśānta**, q.v.

Praśāntaprabha, n. of a kalpa: Gv 232.6.

Praśāntamati, n. of a Buddhist monk: Gv 47.10.

Praśāntamatitejas, n. of a kalpa: Gv 257.19.

Praśāntarutasāgaravatī, n. of a goddess of the night: Gv 286.10 ff.; in the final list, Gv 549.14–15, text omits ruta, prob. by accident.

Praśāntaroga, n. of a former Buddha: Mv i.138.12.

Praśāntaviniścayaprātihāryanirdeśa, m., n. of a work: Mvy 1377; (same?) °prātihārya-sūtra (om. nirdeśa), Śikṣ 16.2 (here printed °pratihārya°); 83.20; 86.13; 146.16.

Praśāntavinīteśvara, n. of a devaputra, acc. to LV 4.13; but the true reading is **Vinīteśvara**, q.v., as in repetitions; Tib. indicates this even in 4.13; the prec. name is **Praśānta**, and this has corrupted the tradition in 4.13.

Praśāntasāgaravatī, Gv 549.14–15, = (and prob. error for) **Praśāntarutasāgaravatī.**

Praśāntasvara, n. of a Bodhisattva: Gv 4.8.

praśobhita, ppp. (to *praśobhayati; no form of pra-śubh- recorded exc. pra . . . śobhe, once RV), *adorned*: sarvaratna-°tam LV 415.10 (prose).

praśoṣita, ppp. (to *pra-śuṣ-, caus.; or pra-, intens., plus Skt. śoṣita), *completely dried up*: tṛṣṇānadī . . . °tā LV 372.16 (vs).

praśnati (denom.; Skt. praśnayati; cf. **pari-pra°**), *questions* (two accus.): (tathāgatam) etam artham praśnasi Mmk 666.23 (prose).

praśraddadhāti, *believes*: karmāṇi, yāni loke na praśraddadhati (3 pl.) Karmav 155.11 (prose).

praśrabdha (also prasr°; = Pali passaddha), ppp. (see next two and pratipraś°), *allayed, stilled*: kṣutpipāsā prasrabdhābhūt LV 86.7; duḥkhaṃ . . . prasrabdhaṃ 86.12; ṛddhiḥ (*operation of magic*) prasrabdhā Divy 48.10, *was put an end to*; the quieting of misery and other disturbing influences leads to the body and mind being *calmed, at peace*, prasrabdhakāyaḥ sukhaṃ vedayati Mvy 1588 (see 1587 s.v. **praśrabhyate**); praśrabdha-kāyo Mv iii.284.8; Gv 522.4; kāya-praśrabdha-citto LV 224.8.

praśrabdhi, prasr°, f. (= Pali passaddhi; see prec. and next, also **pratipraś°**), *alleviation, calming*, of pain etc., sarvopadrava-prasrabdhi- Śikṣ 255.14; (after bodily pain has been alleviated, in the prec.,) sa kāyikaṃ prasrabdhi-sukhaṃ labdhvā . . . Av i.32.4; hence, *calm, serenity, lack of any disturbance*, bodily or mental, kāya-prasrabdhiḥ citta-°dhiḥ Bbh 110.6; (kāyika-)caitasika-prasrabdhi-janakaṃ Bbh 207.14; praśrabdhisukha- Gv 165.22; (misprinted °mukha-) 189.12; prasrabdhiḥ (alone) Mvy 1940; as one (5th in the list) of the seven **(saṃ)bodhyaṅga**, q.v., Mvy 993; Dharmas 49; LV 34.7; Dbh 39.8 (so also Pali passaddhi).

praśrabhyate, pass., praśrabhya, ger. (written °sra°; see also **praśrabdha**, ppp.; all to *praśrambhayati, noted in BHS only in **prati-praś°**, q.v.), *is calmed*: prītimanasaḥ kāyaḥ °srabhyate Mvy 1587; ger. °srabhya kāya- (and, citta-)saṃskārān Mvy 1179 f.; 1185 f.

praśreṣṭha, adj. (pra-, intensive, plus śr°; = Pali paseṭṭha, Pv. ii.9.75, wrongly em. PTSD), *very superior*: (kathaṃ) hīna °ṭhena saṃbandhaṃ kartum icchasi Divy 623.11 (vs, printed as prose).

praśvasati, and **praśvāsa**, m., apparently *breathes out*, and *breathing out*; see s.v. **āśvāsa-praśvāsa.**

praṣṭavya = **spraṣṭavya**, q.v. (cf. **pṛśati**), *object of touch*; parallel with rūpa and the other objects of sense: Mv i.31.2; 337.17; ii.341.18 (v.l. sparśa); iii.52.11 °vyāṃ, acc. pl. (on gender see **spraṣ°**); Śikṣ 64.5.

prasadaniya, °nīya, adj., = **prasād°**, q.v.

prasanna, ppp., adj. (= Pali pasanna, used in same way, with loc.; cf. **abhi-pra°**, and **(abhi-) prasāda**; seems not to be recorded in Skt.), *believing in* (loc.): yada puna janatā prasanna brahme LV 393.14 (vs), *but since people have faith in Brahma* (I will turn the wheel of the law only on his request); cittam abhiprasannaṃ, prasanna-cittaś ca . . . Divy 137.1.

Prasannagātra, n. of a Tathāgata: Gv 421.12.

Prasannabuddhi, n. of a former Buddha: Mv i.138.6.

Prasannavadanotpalagandhakūṭa, pl., n. of a group of (predicted) future Buddhas: Suv 172.5.

Prasannavarṇa, n. of a former Buddha: Mv i.140.9.

Prasabha, n. of a yakṣa. Māy 55.

prasameti, *comes forth*: Śikṣ 347.8 (vs, from Ratnolkādhāraṇī) prasamentī (3 pl. pres.).

[**prasaraṇīya**, Senart's text in Mv i.207.1, read prasadanīyaṃ, see **prasād°**.]

1 **prasavate, °ti** (= Pali pasavati; not in Skt. in this sense), *produces, acquires* (merit): kettakam puṇyam °vanta (v.l. °vanti) iti Mv i.80.5; °vati 7 ff. For **prasavitā**, ppp., see next but one.

2 **pra-savati** (semi-MIndic for Skt. °sravati), *flows forth*: śroṇitanadyo ca °vanti Mv i.5.11 (prose; only 1 of 6 mss. °sra°; Pali only passavati).

prasavāyitā (so mss.; could be denom. ppp. to Skt. prasava), *delivered* (of a child): tayā (*by her*, the midwife) sā °tā Divy 484.8 (ed. em. prasavāpitā, ppp. of MIndic caus. to Skt. prasavati, *bears*); the reading of the mss., and my interpretation, seem supported by the close parallel tayā **prasavitā** 485.12, *by her she was delivered*, where the form in °tā can at any rate not be caus., and seems likely to be denom. from prasava (rather than a MIndic ppp. to prasavati, = Skt. prasūtā).

prasātika, °kā, Mv ii.60.22, see **prāsādika** (2).

prasāda, m. (= Pali pasāda, see Childers; cf. **a-pra°** and **prasanna**, also **abhipras°**), (**1**) *faith* (*in*, with loc., so commonly in Pali): Mvy 6822–24 (no locs.); Mv iii. 434.20 Buddhe prasādasya; °da-jātaḥ (after **abhiprasannaḥ**, q.v.) Divy 23.14; 75.20; = śraddhā, AbhidhK. La-VP. viii.158; (**2**) *tranquillity* of the four physical elements (dhātu) in sense-organs, as resulting in the sensitivity of the organs and so in sense-perception: Śikṣ 250.14 ff.; cf. 251.4, which by contrast with kṣobha *agitation* proves what prasāda means. Pali pasāda is so used, see PTSD; for Mrs. Rhys Davids' interpretation see her Dhs. transl. 174.

prasādanatā (cf. Skt. °na; Pali cittassa pasādanam, Pv. comm. 132.15), *the making clear, pure*: prasādo dharmālokamukham āvila-citta-prasādanatāyai saṃvartate LV 31.13.

prasādanīya, also **prasadanīya** and **°niya**, adj., once (by corruption?) prāsādanīya in mss. (= Pali pasādaniya, °nīya, the latter not noted PTSD, but it occurs e. g. Pugg. 50.3; PTSD def. seems not happy, Childers is better, *causing happiness*), *cheering, gracious, pleasing*, cf. **prāsādika**; in the foll. citations the form is prasādanīya except as stated: applied to a past Buddha Mv i.3.4 (Senart em., mss. pramadanīya, prob. read prasad°!); to another person, iii.260.19 (Senart em. °niyaṃ m.c.); to an utterance, °yāṃ . . . kathāṃ i.312.9; to sounds, °yāḥ . . . śabdāḥ LV 411.9; to the sounds made by (auspicious) earthquakes, °yam, adv., Mv ii.10.11; iii.341.8 (prasadanīyaṃ); and read prasadanīyaṃ in the same cliché Mv i.207.1 where Senart prasaraṇīyaṃ but mss. prasaranīyam or prasam°; to lotuses, prasadaniyāni Mv i.238.11 (only v.l. is praśa°); to trees, iii.302.2 (here mss. prāsād°, em. Senart); 401.21 (v.l. prasamadanīyo, intending prasad°).

Prasādapratilabdha, n. of a son of Māra (favorable to the Bodhisattva): LV 311.5.

prasādayati (caus. of Skt. pra-sad-, not recorded in this construction; or possibly denom. from prasāda), *grants the favor of* (acc.): Śyāmāvatyā antike **dharmānvayaṃ** (see this) prasādayati Divy 531.4.

Prasādavatī, n. of a samādhi: SP 424.5.

prasādika, (**1**) adj. = **prāsādika** (1), q.v.: so mss. at Mv i.3.4, applied to a past Buddha; Senart em. prā°; (**2**) v.l. for **prāsādika** (2), q.v.

prasādhi-vārika, see **prāsādi°**.

prasārita (nt.; in Skt. as ppp.-adj. to prasārayati, *extended, stretched out*; so also in BHS), *extension, stretching out*, = Skt. (and BHS) prasāraṇa; esp. of the arms; citations see s.v. **saṃmiñjita**, with which in this mg. it is associated.

prasiddha-karmānta (opp. of Pali paṭicchanna-kammanta, Sn 127; in Pali pasiddha is recorded only from a Lex. in Childers), *of open, frank behavior*: (of bodhisattvas) Mv i.133.18.

? **Prasiddharaṅga**, acc. to Senart's em., n. of a former Buddha: Mv i.138.14; see s.v. **Cārucaraṇa.**

Prasiddhavedana, n. of a former Buddha: Mv i.138.10.

prasuta, m., a high number: Mvy 8002 (perh. for Skt. prayuta, as suggested by the ed.; but same in Mironov, no v.l.).

prasūyat-a, pres. pple., *being born*: Laṅk 9.2; see § 18.41.

? **prasena,** nt. (in Skt., acc. to pw, *eine Art Gaukelei*, which seems certainly not what our word means), acc. to Tib. gsal snaṅ, *bright light*, or *bright clear*: °nam Mvy 4268; Chin. also *clear bright*. Follows pratyālīḍham and precedes siddhiḥ; lack of context leaves mg. very obscure.

(**Prasenajit** [= Pali Pasenadi], n. of a king of Kośala, with capital at Śrāvastī: Divy 77.23; 146.23; 466.19; (the same?) n. of an ancestor of Aśoka, Divy 369.12. Doubtless identifiable with the king of Śrāvastī known by this name in Skt.)

prasotar (= Skt. prasavitar), *one who produces, generates*: (aprameyapuṇya-)°tā bhavati (bodhisattvaḥ) Bbh 128.19.

praskanda, °dha (?), in SP 54.8 (vs) adj., *fallen, sinking*: praskanda (sc. sattvān; acc. pl.) saṃsāri, (*I see creatures*) *fallen into* (*sinking in*) *the saṃsāra*; note in KN says praskanna is to be expected, and WT read so, by em.; Pali pakkhanna is said in PTSD to be often written pakkhanta; AMg. pakkhanda = *moving, walking*, Ratnach.; in LV 104.18 (prose) nānā-kudṛṣṭi-grahaṇa-(read gahana-, below)-praskandhānāṃ (so!, dh) sattvānāṃ, paralleled by Gv 288.13 dṛṣṭi-kṛta-gahana-praskandhānāṃ sattvānāṃ; Tib. on LV ḥthibs pos, *dense, close, a covering*, confirming gahana as in Gv for grahaṇa; khebs pa, *covering*, for praskandha; see below, and note Dhātup. root skandh as v.l. for skand; twice Mvy has what may be the same word, but both times there are variants in the text, and northern translations are confused; Mvy 6815 praskandaḥ, v.l. °dhaḥ (so, °dhaḥ, Mironov); Tib. ḥjug pa, or, ḥgro ba (both something like *enter* or *move*), or skem pa (*dry up*!); Chin. *going in*, or, *going away*; Jap. *enter*(*ing*); Mvy 7172 praskannaḥ, v.l. (with Mironov) praskandhaḥ (Mir. v.l. °ndaḥ, and, above line, skannaḥ); Tib. rab tu zhug pa (*entering*), or byiṅ ba (*sinking*); so Chin., *going inside*, or *sinking*. The mg. *sinking*, as adj., which fits Skt. pra-skand- fairly well, would fit both the SP passage and the LV-Gv parallel passages, *of creatures sinking* (*entered* would also be possible) *in the thicket of heresy*.

Praskandaka, m., n. of a village: Mv ii.207.5, 8 (vss).

praskandin (= Pali pakkhandin, *bold, braggart, a bravo*, PTSD), (*a*) *violent* or *insolent and belligerent* (*person*): °di-balam Mvy 8212 = Tib. rab gnon (gyi stobs); °dinā, applied to a crow, Jm 98.21; °dī MPS 26.24; 31.21.

praskandha, see °**nda.**

[**praskṛta,** in -devagaṇa-°taḥ Gv 405.13 (prose), read with 2d ed. (Skt.) puraskṛta.]

-prastāraka, see **tṛṇa-pr°.**

prastārika, or °**raka,** in Mv iii.113.7 °ikā, v.l. °akā, in a list of guilds or occupations, after maṇikārakā; perhaps *merchant*, if related to Pali (kaṃsa-)pattharikā (pl.) Vin. ii.135.16, acc. to comm. 1211.15 *dealers in brass-ware*; in similar passage Mv iii.442.13 maṇi-prastārakā (omitting kārakā), perh. *jewel-merchants*?

praspanda, adj. (or noun? to Skt. pra-spand-), *quivering* (from grief): (atyantapratiśokaśalyavihatāḥ) praspanda-kaṇṭhānanāḥ Divy 321.16.

prasphulita, adj.-ppp. (= Skt. prasphurita, cf. root sphul-), *quivering, flashing*: °ta-marīcijālavasanāsu . . . dikṣu Jm 30.10.

Prasphoṭa, n. of a nāga king: Megh 306.13. Cf. next, and **Prasphoṭana** 2.

Prasphoṭaka, n. of a nāga: Mvy 3346. Cf. under prec.

prasphoṭana, (**1**) nt. (cf. Skt. id., esp. in Schmidt, Nachträge; AMg. papphoṭana, *winnowing*, Ratnach.; to Skt. prasphoṭayati), °nam Mvy 9422, acc. to Jap. *cleansing* (*of grain*) *by beating*; Tib. sbugs pa, or phyi ba (obscure; the second gloss may intend the above mg.); Chin. (*cleaning by*) *wiping*, or *dusting*; (**2**) m. (cf. **Prasphoṭa,** °**ṭaka**), n. of a nāga king (also called **Pañcaśīrṣaka,** q.v.): Megh 308.8.

prasrabdha, °dhi, prasrabhya(te), see **praśra°.**

prasravaṇī (cf. Skt. °ṇa, nt., *flowing forth, flux*, and acc. to BR *spring, well*; in LV 77.10 sarvanadī ca prasravaṇāni ca na vahanti sma, it seems more likely to mean *stream*), *stream, water-course*: nadīyo ca °ṇīyo ca Mv i.360.20. In Mvy 8928 sadā-prasravaṇī, *a woman who is constantly menstruating* (Tib. rtag tu zla mtshan zag pa), may be interpreted as a fem. Bhvr., *having a constant flux*, to Skt. °ṇa, above.

prasrāva-kuṭī, *hut for urinating*: °ṭī varcaḥkuṭī (q.v.) MSV ii.91.6; °kuṭiḥ ib. 157.3.

prasrāviṇī, subst. f. (cf. **prasravaṇī**; less likely adj. f. to *prasrāvin), *stream, flood* (or, if adj., *flowing*, with dependent gen.): (striyo . . .) prasrāviṇī (n. pl.) rudhiramūtra-śakṛn-malānāṃ RP 43.19 (vs).

? **prahata,** ppp. or adj., app. *practised* or *controlled*: gocaro 'sya prahato bhavati Karmav 104.15, *on a la pratique de sa tournée* (Lévi); acc. to Lévi Tib. *il a la pratique de son domaine*, using goms par ḥgyur ba, which also renders upārjita in the prec. sentence; Chin. *il devient expert en êtres vivants*. Prob. prahata conceals some corruption; read **prahita**?

? **Praharāja** (so text, prob. corrupt), n. of a Bodhisattva: ŚsP 7.8.

praharṣā, f. (Skt. °ṣa, m.), or (v.l.) °ṣa-tā, (*state of*) *joy*: tayā °ṣa(ta)yā Suv 181.11 (prose).

Praharṣitatejas, n. of a Bodhisattva: Gv 442.19.

Prahasita, n. of a kiṃnara-king: Kv 3.2.

Prahasitanetra, n. of a former Buddha: LV 5.13 (Tib. rab tu ḥdzum paḥi spyan, *very smiling eye*); Mvy 97 (Tib. spyan gsal rgyas, *full-bright-eye*).

Prahasitanetranihitarāgarajas, n. of a Bodhisattva: Gv 442.14.

prahāṇa, nt. (besides the mgs. here noted, also as in Skt. id., *getting rid of, abandonment*; only this mg. seems to be recognized by Tib. which regularly renders spoṅ ba; mg. 1 = Pali padhāna, BHS also **pradhāna,** q.v., here in Pktic form, cf. AMg. pahāṇa-vanta, Ratnach. = Hindi saṃyama samādhivālā; rendered *one who concentrates on self-restraint*, better . . . *on strenuous exertion*; mg. 2 = AMg. pahāṇa, Skt. pradhāna), (**1**) *exertion, strenuosity*: four such Mvy 957–961 (as in Pali, see s.v. pradhāna for list); oftener called samyakprahāṇa (also °pradhāna; Pali sammappadhāna); Dharmas 45 (with list); Śikṣ 105.14; KP 95.6; Divy 208.8; in long cpds. containing lists of virtues and religious requirements, LV 8.5; 426.7; prahāṇa less technically, of zealous religious activity, in a series of vss similar, tho not quite identical, in Mv ii.238.3 ff., LV 261.2 ff., and Pali Sn 425 ff.: LV 4 prahāṇāyodyataṃ . . . dṛḍhavikramaṃ (subject), cf. Mv 4 prahāṇaṃ prahitaṃ (q.v.) mayā, Sn 425 maṃ padhānapahitattaṃ; Mv 8 saṃhara mahā-prahāṇaṃ, *restrain your great* (ascetic) *exertion*! (Māra speaks), not in LV or Sn LV 13 kiṃ prahāṇe kariṣyasi, (Sktization of) Mv 12 kiṃ prahāṇena kāhisi, Sn 428 kiṃ padhānena kāhasi; LV 14 duḥkhaṃ mārgaṃ prahāṇasya, Mv 13 text dūraṃ (mss. duraṃ, duraṃgaṃ, read perh. duḥkham?) āśā prahāṇasya, Sn 429 duggo maggo padhānāya; similarly, prahāṇāya gamiṣyāmi Mv ii.199.18 (vs) = Pali Sn 424 padhānāya gamissāmi; in a prose passage not found in LV or Sn, but introducing the above series of vss, Mv has (in words said by Māra to the Bodhisattva) kiṃ prahāṇena kariṣyasi ii.237.18, prahāṇaṃ ca duṣkaram 21; bodhisattvaḥ prahāṇārthī viharati LV 246.8, which supports reading of v.l. at Mv ii.124.1 (alaṃ punaḥ me...) kulaputrasya prahāṇārthikasya prahāṇāye, yan nūnāhaṃ ihaiva (mss. °vaṃ) prahāṇaṃ hareyaṃ (so mss., Senart prahar°; better would perhaps be vihareyaṃ, *dwell in*..., see s.v. **vyapakṛṣṭa**, where cliché is cited with prahitātmā and forms of viharati); the first part of this Mv passage is supported by Pali MN i.167.6–7 alaṃ vat' idaṃ kulaputtassa padhānatthikassa padhānāyā ti; prahāṇaṃ **pradadhāti** (so prob. read for Senart's em. pratidadhāti, mss. corrupt) Mv ii.208.1; -prahāṇa-jñāna- LV 434.9; lūhaprahāṇena Mv ii.126.12 and in sequel (= rūkṣa-**pradhāna**, see the latter); °ṇa-śālā, *hall of religious exercise, concentration*, in a monastery, MSV iv.74.4 ff.; śaithiliko bāhulikaḥ prahāṇa-vibhraṣṭaḥ (*fallen away from religious exertions*) LV 407.19; Mv iii.329.3–4 (here text with mss. vikrānto, prob. intending vibhrānto, for vibhraṣṭaḥ, cf. Pali bāhuliko padhānavibbhanto Vin. i.9.1 and Jāt. i.68.2, in the same incident); **utkuṭuka-pra°**, see **utku°**; in the formula of the four **ṛddhipāda**, q.v., always -samādhi-prahāṇa-saṃskāra-samanvāgata (Pali -samādhi-padhāna-saṃkhāra-samannāgata, e. g. DN ii. 213.7); (**2**) twice I believe prahāṇa (= AMg. pahāṇa) = Skt. pradhāna, *the chief thing*, at end of Bhvr. cpds. = *chiefly consisting of* or *characterized by*: kuhana-lapana-prahāṇaṃ māyā-mātsarya-doṣa-irṣyādyaṃ, (iha te kleśāraṇyaṃ chinnaṃ...) LV 372.17 (vs), *here you have cut down the forest of the impurities, consisting chiefly of* **kuhana** *and* **lapana** (qq.v.), *including deceit, malice, hatred, jealousy*, etc.; tasya tahiṃ āśramapade prativasato kṣama-dama-prahāṇasya Mv ii.221.15 (vs), *while he was dwelling... characterized by...* In both these the Skt. mg. *abandonment* is manifestly impossible (tho Foucaux tries to adopt it in LV, by flagrant violation of the text), and *exertion* in the sense of Pali padhāna seems certainly implausible. The word is very common in AMg. in this mg.; note that BHS has usually this AMg.-like form for Pali padhāna.

prahāṇika, adj. (= Pali padhānika), *characterized by religious strenuosity* (**prahāṇa** 1): °kānāṃ bhikṣūṇāṃ Śikṣ 64.8.

prahārā, f. (= Skt. prahāra, m.; no other record of f. °rā, but cf. next), *blow, stroke*: instr. sg. tala-prahārāya (v.l. °ye) Mv ii.74.15; ekāye tala-°rāye hato 18; ekāya tala-°rāye nihato 75.9.

prahārikā (to prec. plus -ka, in the usual fem. form -ikā; prob. svārthe), *blow*: apy edānīṃ paraspara-°kāṃ apy āgamayanti MSV ii.180.11, *they come to blows with each other*; same with āgamitāḥ 181.2, 8.

prahita (cf. **prāhita**; = Pali pahita; ppp. of **pradadhāti**; Pali comms. regularly identify it with pahita = Skt. prahita, to pra-hi-, *sent*), *exerted*: prahāṇaṃ prahitaṃ maya Mv ii.238.4 (vs), *exertion was engaged in by me*; otherwise noted only in cpd. prahitātman (or °tmaka) = Pali pahitatta, acc. to PTSD the only use of the word in Pali, *having exerted oneself*: rūkṣapradhāna(ṃ) prahitātmanaḥ (°tmaka-tvāt), see s.v. **pradhāna**; prahitātmanāṃ LV 262.2 (vs); repeatedly in cliché cited s.v. **vyapakṛṣṭa**, q.v. (in Divy 618.4 corruptly prahitāni, prob. intending prahitātmanī, fem.). Cf. **prahata**.

praheṇaka, nt. (= Skt. Lex. id., also prahelaka, prob. by error; Pali paheṇaka, also °hiṇ°, see Childers; AMg. paheṇa, Pkt. also °ṇaga, °ṇaya, *sending of estables to the relatives, a present of food*, Ratnach., and so Sheth, bhojopanāyan, khādya vastu kī bhemṭ; in Pali, e. g. AN iii.76.13, usually *a gift of food*; in Jāt. vi.369.9 cūḷāmaṇiṃ paheṇakatthāya pahiṇi, the gift was a jewel, which to be sure was concealed in a vessel containing takka, *dates*? at any rate, food; note the verb pahiṇi, which points to connexion with Skt. pra-hinoti), *a present*, in BHS, at least, only of delicacies to be eaten: Divy 13.26 (mama jñātayaḥ) °ṇakāni preṣayanti, and in ff. lines; maṇḍīlakāḥ praheṇakam anupreṣitam Divy 258.19.

? **Praheti, Prahemi**, see **Prabhemi**.

(? **prahelika**, m., Mvy 7351 [one Tib. rendering, lde ḥu, = *riddle*, Das; so Jap.], but Mironov reads °kā, which in Skt. means *riddle*.)

prahruta, ppp. (to pra- with Skt. hru-, hvṛ-), *gone astray*: °taṃ vatedaṃ kulaputra cittaṃ viṣayeṣu Śikṣ 42.5.

prahlādanīya, adj. (to Skt. °dana plus -īya), *refreshing, comforting, cheering*, of sounds: °yāḥ (śabdāḥ) LV 52.6; 411.9; °yaṃ, adv., of the sounds of an (auspicious) earthquake, Mv i.206.17; iii.341.7; as quasi-gdve. to Skt. pra-hlād-, *to be greeted with joy*, °yāḥ (of Bodhisattvas), following saṃkīrtanīyāḥ, Mv i.103.6.

prākaṭa, adj. (= Pali pākaṭa, °ṭa; semi-MIndic for Skt. prākṛta, cf. next), *vulgar, low, common*: upāsikāś ca varjeta prākaṭā yā avasthitāḥ SP 279.6 (vs); prākaṭendriya (= Pali pākaṭindriya), °yāḥ Samādh p. 53 line 5; capalāṃ prākaṭendriyāṃ (mss. pra°, v.l. prakṛt°) Mv i.305.15.

prākṛtaka, adj. (= Skt. °ta; cf. prec.), *common, vulgar*: °kena veṣeṇa Mv ii.449.10, *in mean garb* (contrasted with royal garb); *ordinary, natural*, as distinguished from supernatural, divine: śrotrendriyaṃ... anāvilaṃ prākṛtakaṃ ca tāvat SP 357.10 (vs), *and yet his power of hearing is still natural* (not 'divya'); similarly 359.12 (vs); in both -ka might be m.c.

? **prākṛti** (f.), sometimes in text of Divy for prakṛti, *nature*, e. g. 310.26 °tiṃ ca jñātvā; elsewhere in the same phrase, e. g. 47.10, the regular prakṛtiṃ is printed. Not recorded in Index; perhaps only misprint.

prākharati, pres. pple. °rantaḥ (semi-MIndic for Skt. prakṣarati), *flows forth*: SP 126.8 (vs; quantity of prā-, pra- metr. indifferent; two mss. pra-, which perhaps read). Cf. also s.v. **pragharati**; both edd. refer to Pali paggharati, taking ā as replacement of the double consonant by the 'law of morae'.

Prāgajita, n. of a former Buddha: Mv i.140.1.

prāg eva (= Pali pageva; cf. Kunst, BSOS 10.983f.; in Skt. = *formerly*, and so sometimes in BHS, e. g. LV 235.18), in sense of Skt. kim u, kim uta, *how much more* (or *less*), *a fortiori, not to speak of*...: SP 141.4 (taṃ śrotuṃ na samartho 'si prāg evānyaṃ vidūrataḥ); Mv iii.251.6; 356.11; 359.15; 360.11; LV 154.16, 20; 313.20; 314.18; 338.18; Laṅk 17.2; 244.14; 251.3; Divy 51.4; 90.25; 102.16; 108.17; 110.21; 185.10; 241.6; Av i.89.3; 248.3; Jm 33.14; 40.19, 23; Suv 7.1; 89.5; RP 56.19; Śikṣ 21.7; Kv 20.15, 22; 52.21 (note wrong paragraph division, showing editorial misunderstanding); Mmk 292.9; Gv 48.25; 160.4; 176.8; Bbh 3.11; Karmav 164.15; very common in most texts; occurs even in some texts the vocabulary of which is otherwise virtually standard Skt., e. g. Buddhacarita iv.10, 81; xi.7.

prāgbhakta, *forenoon* (*time before dinner*): Śikṣ 352.1 (= Tib. sṅa dro).

prāgbhāra (see also **a-prā°**), (**1**) adj. (= Pali pabbhāra), *inclined*, usually but not always at end of cpds.: lit. and physically, (vṛkṣāṇāṃ chāyā) prācīna-pravaṇā prācīna-°rā Divy 579.22, *inclining towards the east*; of an old man's body, *bent over*, with or without preceding purataḥ (*forward*): prāgbhāreṇa kāyena, Mvy 4093, and so LV 188.2 (prose) in Lefm.'s text with ms. A, seemingly supported by Tib. (lus dgu bas, *with bent body*, no word for purataḥ), but all other LV mss. read purataḥ-prāg°, like Mv ii.150.19 (in the same passage) purata-(so mss., Senart em. °to-)prāgbhāro (agreeing with the subject, the old man); oftener fig., *inclined to* or *headed for* some condition or religious entity, assoc. with **nimna** (q.v. for citations) and pravaṇa; (**2**) m., acc. to Tib. = bya skyibs, lit. *bird-shelter, rocky overhanging crag with ledge beneath* (Das): Mvy 5259 °raḥ (follows parvataḥ, precedes darī); 5558 kṛta-°raḥ.

Prāgvideha = **Pūrva-vi°**, q.v., and see **dvīpa.**

[**prājina**, in Gv 414.16 ed. na prājineṣu praṇatā sadaiva, read namrā jineṣu..., *she was always humble and obedient before the Jinas.*]

prājīvika (nt.; looks like formation in -ika with vṛddhi, but I find no record of *prajīva or MIndic equivalents), *livelihood, sustenance*: °kaṃ prājīvikārthikebhyaḥ (LV °rthibhyo) LV 58.10 (sc. dāpayati); ŚsP 276.1 (... upasaṃharanti); 1353.12 (dadāti).

prāñjayati (no *pra-añj- otherwise recorded), *anoints*: gātrāṇi °yitvā (v.l. pāṃcayitvā), ger., Mv iii.70.7.

prāñjalīka, adj. Bhvr. (m.c. for °li-ka), *making a gesture of reverence in front*: LV 81.12 (vs).

prāñjalīkṛta, adj. (ppp.; = Pali pañj°), or sometimes °likṛta, *assuming a position making an añjali in front*: Mv i.239.18; ii.257.11; iii.300.11; 302.13 (in all these follows ekāṃśīkṛta, for **ekāṃsī°**, q.v.)

prāṇa, m. (= Pali pāṇa; cf. next; Skt. only prāṇin), (**1**) usually, *living being, creature*, in very inclusive sense: SP 27.15; LV 394.19 (bahuprāṇakoṭyaḥ, all mss.); Mv i.3.3 (prāṇa-koṭīṣu); 13.14 (pīḍayanti bahu prāṇāṃ); 128.8 (prāṇāṃ jīvitād vyaparopayanti); 145.8; 247.1; ii.6.2 (vs, prāṇeṣu, for prāṇiṣu, same vs, i.202.5); (**2**) rarely, *animal* (excluding human and superhuman beings), see **prāṇaka** 2: ye te sthalacarāḥ prāṇā... sarvāṇi **prāṇaka**-(NB!)-jātīni samānetha... ye kecij jalacarā prāṇāḥ... sarvabhūtehi yajñaṃ yajiṣyāmi Mv ii.95.9–11; note at end of this story, te sarve prāṇaka-jātīyo... osṛṣṭā 99.17; (**3**) once even more specifically of *insects*, = **prāṇaka 3**: niḥprāṇenodakena Mmk 37.19 (prose).

prāṇaka, m. (= Pali pāṇaka; cf. prec.), (**1**) allegedly = **prāṇa** 1, *living being* in general: ko nu so bhavam upetya prāṇako, yo na mṛtyuvaśam āgamiṣyati Mv i.67.5 (vs), so Senart, but mss. (besides sā for so) prāṇanta, unmetr., for the em. prāṇakó; highly questionable; (**2**) = **prāṇa** 2, *animal*: LV 197.1 (vs), see s.v. **śubha** 3, *white*; tatra (sc. in the **kuṇapa** hell) kṛṣṇehi prāṇakehi ayomukhehi khajjanti Mv i.7.2, *there they are devoured by black beasts with iron jaws*; kṛṣṇa-prāṇakā i.11.7, by em.; prāṇaka i.16.14; 24.16, etc., common; ii.95.10 and 99.17, see **prāṇa** 2; Mvy 4827 = Tib. srog chags, *living being*, but in a list of animals; °ka-jātaḥ Mvy 4908, (various) *sort(s) of animals*; (kākair) vā khādyamānāni kurarair vā... anyair vā nānāvidhaiḥ prāṇaka-jātaiḥ Śikṣ 211.5 (also °jāti, Mv ii.95.10, 99.17, above, and see under 3 below); prāṇaku saumya tadā ca yadāsīt RP 26.10 (vs), *a gracious animal* (? Finot, p. viii, takes Saumya as n. pr.; the story referred to is not identified); Mv ii.417.6 (perhaps to 3); (**3**) more specifically, = **prāṇa** 3, *insect*: Mv i.270.13; of an insect called **lohitaka**, q.v., Mv ii.137.4; 138.19; °ka-jātayaḥ (n. pl.) Mmk 37.15, *(any) kinds of insects* (on a designated spot of ground); °kā(ḥ) Kv 47.1, referring to worms and the like; of insects found in water, saprāṇakam etat pānīyam Karmav 160.13; niṣprāṇakenodakena (or niḥ°) Mmk 37.6 (text corrupt); 56.8; 58.18, etc., *with water free from insects*; MSV ii.31.6 ff.

Prāṇahāriṇī, n. of an ogress: Māy 241.32.

prāṇātipātika, adj. or subst. m. (cf. Pali pāṇātipātin), *one who is guilty of taking life*: ete °kā adattādāyikāḥ... Divy 301.22 (prose).

-prāṇika (m.; = Skt. prāṇin, Pali pāṇin, plus -ka; cf. **prāṇaka**), *living being*, particularly *insect* (**prāṇaka** 3): sa-prāṇikopabhogaḥ Mvy 8439, *use of* (water) *that contains insects*; corresp. Pali, Vin. iv.49.3, sappāṇakaṃ (udakaṃ).

prātaṃ, adv. (= Pali pātaṃ, analog. modification of Skt. prātar), *in the morning*: prātaṃ prātar-aśāya (for °āśāya) Mv i.343.5 (prose).

? **prātarāśika** (nt.?) = Skt. °rāśa, *breakfast*: °kam akārṣīt MSV i.35.1 (prose); close parallel 36.1 °śam ak°, which perhaps read.

prātikṣepika, nt. (adj.? from Skt. pratikṣepa plus -ika), *what has to do with negation*, or the like (in a context app. dealing with terms of logic): °kam Mvy 7604.

prāticāraka (m.; perh. misprint or error for prati°; = AMg. paḍiyāraga, but Skt. and Pali paricāraka, § 2.47), *attendant*: °kebhyo baliṃ haste dattvā Mmk 676.9, *putting the offering in the hands of the attendants.*

prātipakṣika, in mss. once **prati°**, adj. (Pali paṭipakkhika only; Skt. pratipakṣa plus -ika), *adverse, opposite*: duḥkha-°kaṃ sukhaṃ Bbh 25.12; vipakṣa-°kaś ca virodhaḥ 98.17; °kaṃ... karma 377.24; in 392.8 mss. tat-(sc. āśrava-)pratipakṣikaṃ (ed. em. prāti°) anāśravaṃ cittaṃ.

prātipathika, m. (or adj.; to Pali paṭipatha, *opposite way*; cf. AMg. paḍipahia, and acc. to Sheth pāḍi°, defined by Sheth like our word, but by Ratnach. as *waylayer*, i. e. *highwayman*), *one met along the way, going in the opposite direction*: sa ca panthānaṃ gacchan °thikān pṛcchati Divy 242.21.

prātipaudgalika = **pratipudgalika**, q.v., *individual*: MSV iv.237.16 (so read; ms. cited as prātimaud°; ed. em. viśeṣā).

-prātibhānika, f. °**kī**, adj., in (bhūmau...) svayaṃ-°kyāṃ, loc. sg., Bbh 37.24, *based on one's own wit.*

prātimokṣa, m. (on etym. and literal mg. cf. Winternitz, H.I.Lit. 2.22; = Pali pātimokkha, pāṭi°), n. of the code of precepts in the Vinaya according to which monks are controlled and corrected (with penances etc.): Mvy 9217 = Tib. so sor thar pa, *individual* (as if = prati) *release* (sc. from sin), which is accomplished by confession and penance. As in Pali, cpd. with **saṃvara**, q.v. for this cpd. Generally seems to refer to the literary text containing this code, one version of which is our Prāt: °kṣa-sūtroddeśam (acc.) Prāt 476.8; Av ii.21.12; °śaḥ MSV iii.107.9; prātimokṣād Śikṣ 125.9 (seems to refer to a literary text); pūrārgheṇa (see s.v. **pūra**) prātimokṣe Śikṣ 143.6–7, *in the* (book of) *expiation according to full value* (of the requirements, i. e. matching the offense). See also **pratimokṣa.**

-prātilambhika, adj. (= prati°, q.v.), *suited for getting*: upapatti-°kaḥ Mvy 6979 = Tib. skye ba (see **upapatti**) (ḥ)thob pa.

prātiveśaka, m. (Skt. °veśika, °veśya), *neighbor*: Divy 264.14.

prātisīma, adj. (see next two; based on Skt. prati-plus sīman, unrecorded anywhere), *neighboring* (king): MSV i.100.13; °maiḥ... rājabbhiḥ Av ii.32.3; Divy 546.13; °mā rājānaḥ Av ii.32.11, 13; 104.10.

prātisīmaka, adj., = prec.: °kehi pratirājānehi Mv ii.485.3 (prose).

prātisīmantika, adj. (cf. Skt. sīmanta) = prec. two: te °tikā (Senart em. °sāmantikā) rājāno Mv ii.490.13 (prose).

prātihāraka-pakṣa, m. (only once, Mmk 79.19, is pakṣa not expressed), more rarely **prati°**, **prātihāra-**, °**hārika-** (= Pali pāṭihārika-pakkha or pāṭihāriya-p°, inaccurately defined PTSD; the mg. is evidently related to that of **prātihārya**, q.v., but *quinzaine du miracle*, Lalou, Iconographie 24, is hardly likely to be the true mg., tho it is the lit. mg. of the Tib. cited, cho phrul gyi...), *extraordinary, exceptional half-month.* The Pali comms. vary greatly in their explanations; see citations in PTSD; note specially AN comm. ii.234.25 ff. on AN i.144.2 (cited PTSD °hārika-, but actually °hāriya-) in contrast with Vv. comm. 71.26 ff. on Vv. 15 vs 6 (same stanza as in AN, wholly discordant glosses in comms.; at least one of them clearly a baseless guess). Evidently the tradition of the true mg. was lost at an early time. In BHS noted only in Mmk, where it is fairly common, but I have found no evidence as to mg., except that pakṣa has its usual mg. *half-lunar-month* (not *holiday* with PTSD); this is proved by prātihāraka-pakṣa-pūrṇamāsyāṃ Mmk 669.19–20, *on the full-moon day of*... Otherwise, usually °raka-pakṣe

Mmk 58.11; 75.10; 289.19; 669.22–23 (°rakapakṣe pūrṇamāsyām); 675.28; 676.28; 715.6, et alibi; śuklapūrṇamāsyāṃ prātihāraka-pratipūrṇāyāṃ 79.19, *on the full-moon day of a bright fortnight, when* (the moon) *is full in a prātihāraka* (sc. pakṣa; the only case noted in which this is omitted); prātihārika-pakṣe 290.1; śuklapakṣe prātihārapakṣe vā 145.21 (prose; is the omission of -ka a mere corruption?), *in a bright fortnight, or in a prāti° one*; pratihāraka-pakṣe 36.25; 675.7 (foll. by śuklatrayodaśyāṃ; evidently the 'extraordinary' fortnight could be either 'light' or 'dark'); pratihāraka-pakṣam ārabhya 675.22 (passages with prati° all prose).

prātihāra-pakṣa = prec., q.v.

prātihārika, (1) -pakṣa, = °**raka**, q.v.; **(2)** in mahāprā°, adj., either *highly exceptional* (place), or (prob. more likely, adj. to **prātihārya**), (place) *of extraordinary things, miracles*: Devāvatāre (q.v.) mahācaitye Saṃkaśye (q.v.) mahāprātihārike Mmk 88.14 (vs).

prātihārya, nt. (cf. **prātihāraka-pakṣa**; = Pali pāṭihāriya, °hārika, °hera, °hīra), *extraordinary occurrence, miracle*: three kinds attributed to Buddhas, ṛddhi-pr° *magic performance* (as by indrajāla), ādeśanā-pr° *mind-reading*, and anuśāsanī-pr° *miracle of admonition* (effecting destruction of someone's vices), see LaVallée-Poussin, AbhidhK. vii.110; in Pali iddhi-, ādesanā-, anusāsanī-pāṭihāriya; listed Mvy 232–4; Dharmas 133; Mv i.238.4–5; iii.137.17–18 (dharmadeśanā- instead of ād°); 321.13; Bbh 210.4–5 (here anuśāsti for anuśāsanī); Gv 537.8, read sarvānuśāsany-ādeśanarddhi-prātihāryāṇi (text corruptly °ādeśena viprāti°); ṛddhi-prā°, without the other two, SP 388.2, 4; 406.12; LV 73.1; 83.8; 85.12; 88.7; Mv i.266.17 (a clear indrajāla, multiplication of Buddha figures so that one sits under each of many parasols); ii.314.18; iii.409.17; 412.9; Divy 144.4 ff.; Av i.3.4; Mmk 182.14; Bbh 82.5; ṛddhi and prātihārya separate and parallel, Sukh 42.16 ṛddhyā vā prātihāryeṇa vā; yamaka-prātihārya (Pali yamakaṃ pāṭihāriyaṃ, Mahāv. 17.44; yamaka-pāṭihīra; see LaVallée-Poussin, l.c.), 'twin miracle', one which manifests itself in a double way, Mv iii.115.19 (illustrations in the sequel); 116.18 (described as examples of ṛddhi-prāt° 116.6, 19); 254.8; yamakāni prāt° 410.5 (examples follow); mahānimittaṃ prāt° SP 7.4, 6; nimitta-prāt° Dbh.g. 50(76).2; mahā-prāt° SP 17.6; Divy 126.16; 147.23 ff.; Suv 88.11; other occurrences SP 392.8; 459.8; LV 88.9 bodhisattva-prāt°; 101.3; 377.16; Mv iii.51.13–14; 242.12; Divy 49.19; 133.9; 313.14; 365.19; Av i.24.5; 83.1 (title of chap. 15) etc.; Suv 157.15; Kv 13.14; Bbh 13.24.

prātihāryaka (nt.; = prec.), *miracle*: vividhaiḥ °yakaiḥ Sādh 32.8 (vs; -ka may be m.c.).

Prātihārya-sūtra, title of Divy xii: Divy 166.28 (colophon); a version of **Mahāprātihārya**, q.v.

[**pratyaya**, error for **pratyaya**, q.v.]

prāthamakalpika, adj. (in Skt. used in sense of BHS **prathamakalpika**, q.v.; so also Gv 281.25; 352.6; 358.10; 381.9; here in the sense of Pali paṭhamakappika, Childers, and Andersen, Reader, 4.10; 10.25), *belonging to the first world-age*: °kānāṃ sattvānām Divy 631.2; also Buddhacarita ii.49.

prāthujjanika = **pārthagj°** (q.v.).

prādakṣiṇa (seemingly nt. = Skt. °ṇya), *circumambulation to the right, respectful behavior*: kurvanti °ṇaṃ LV 283.4 (vs); but perhaps prā- m.c. for Skt. pradakṣiṇaṃ, adv.

prādu(ḥ)karma (nt.; = Pali pātukamma; cf. Skt. prāduṣkaraṇa etc.), *manifestation, making visible*: Mv ii.121.10 (Senart prādur-k°, but mss. prādukarmāye, or prādurkamāya with misplaced r; read prob. prāduka°, semi-MIndic); prāduḥkarmāye 122.5; 123.2 (all datives).

? **prādur-bhāmi** (=°bhavāmi), *I appear*: Gv 70.9 (prose), immediately following antardhāmi, *I disappear*, and may be modelled on it; see Chap. 43, s.v. bhū, 7; but 2d ed. °bhavāmi.

prādeśika, f. °**kī**, adj. (see **pradeśa**; in Skt. usually *local*, so also Mmk 268.5, vs, °ke 'tha durge vā ekadeśe nṛpo bhavet; but also see BR 5.1634, which shows that Skt. usage is not far from BHS), *restricted* (in scope), *limited*: °ka-yāna (= **hīnayāna**, which in Mvy immediately precedes) Mvy 1254; Śikṣ 183.10; na cāyaṃ vidhiḥ °kaḥ Śikṣ 125.8 (i. e. it is universal and absolute); °kī śūnyatā (read °ta, m.c.) tīrthikānām Samādh p. 31 line 16; °ka-citta-tā Dbh 25.22; of jñāna, Bbh 236.13; ŚsP 615.13.

prādeśya, adj. (= Skt. °śika; see **pradeśa-rājan**), *local, of a country*: °yāś ca rājānaḥ Mv i.103.3 (contrasted with cakravartinaḥ).

prānta, adj. (see next two; = Pali panta, said to occur only with senāsana; Skt. as noun only, *border*, etc.), *secluded, solitary, distant, remote*, perh. sometimes with implication of *in the jungle*; orig. *bordering, on the border* (between jungle and settled country?): in Mvy °taḥ, alone, 2990 = Tib. nags mthaḥ, *forest border*; 7224 = Tib. mthaḥ, *border*; but in prānta(ṃ) śayyāsanaṃ 2988 = Tib. bas mthaḥi, *of border country*; vṛkṣamūlāni prāsādikāni . . . prāntāni viviktāni Mv ii.123.17; prānto pravivikto iii.130.6, *lonely and solitary*; prānta-vāṭikā Divy 631.14; (bodhisattvaḥ) saputradāraḥ prānta (mss. prāpta) eva tu Jm 60.6 (paradox; *tho with son and wife, he was quite solitary*); prāntavane . . . abhinivasanti RP 31.14; prānta-śayyāsana (cf. Pali, above) Mv ii.212.9; iii.422.9 (vs); RP 14.14; in Mvy 2988 printed prānta(ṃ) śayyāsanaṃ, Mironov °taṃ śa°, no v.l.; śayyāsanāni . . . prāntāni Mv iii.200.16; °ntāni ca śayyāsanāni 348.4; prānta-śayanāsana-(sevinas) Divy 312.9; prānta-śayanāsana-bhakta(ḥ) Divy 88.14; 132.21 (°śayana-bhaktā); 191.26; 538.17; 582.8; °tāni śayanāsanāni Divy 344.10; Av ii.119.12; °taṃ ca śayanāsanam Ud xxxii.27(32).

prānta-koṭika, adj. (cf. prec.), *extreme* (lit. *having a remote end*): °kaṃ dhyānam Mvy 1482 = Tib. rab kyi mthar phyin pa.

prāntaśayyāsanika, adj. (see s.v. **prānta**), *having bed and seat in a lonely* (forest?) *place*: (tatra ye bhikṣava) āraṇyakāḥ °kās . . . Śikṣ 55.9 (prose).

prāpadyate, *falls to the lot of* (gen.): MSV ii.98.14 °ta iti, parallel to pratipadyate in same line; but no parallel in lābhaḥ kasya prāpadyate ii.110.4, 7, etc.; 113.17 etc.; 119.8. No pra-ā-pad- otherwise recorded.

prāpuṇati, also °**ṇeti** (and with n for ṇ), (= Skt. prāpnoti, Pali pāpuṇati), *attains*: prāpuṇehi Mv iii.270.14 (mss.; Senart em. °āhi); °ṇeti Mv iii.418.11 (taken by Senart as caus., but the mss. are extremely corrupt and the text very doubtful); °ṇitvā Sukh 24.12; °ṇe (3 pl. aor.) Mv ii.302.21; °ṇetsuḥ (mss.; aor., 3 sg. subject) Mv iii.338.20.

-prāpta, ppp. (= Skt. id., Pali -patta), in āścarya-, adbhuta-pr°, generally means *filled with astonishment and wonder* (e. g. SP 188.5). But in SP 183.4–5 āścaryaprāptā . . . adbhutaprāptā ime ṣoḍaśa śrāmaṇerāḥ, rather, something like *arrived at a wonderful thing* or *condition, marvelously successful*. In KP 9.5 and 10.5 dāntājāneya-prāpta (bodhisattva), and KP 9.14; 10.17, 20 ājanya-prāpta (bodhisattva), clearly *arrived at* (*the condition of being* . . .) i. e. *become* (*tamed*) *noble* (*steeds*, see **ājanya, ājāneya**). In most of these, Tib. renders prāpta by thob pa, which acc. to Jä. primarily means *get, attain*, but in expressions like saṅs rgyas thob pa *become* (lit. *get*) *a Buddha*. This latter seems clearly parallel to the use of -prāpta in these KP passages. Ordinarily a cpd. ending in -prāpta has as its prior member an abstract noun. Note however that some such prior members may be either abstract or concrete; thus adbhuta may mean either *surprising* or *surprise*. Possibly the KP usage arose by analogy of such compounds. There are other cpds. of prāpta with a preceding adj.; see s.v. **niṣkāṅkṣa.**

[**prāptayu** (kālu), so Lefm. LV 326.16 (vs); analyze prāpt' ayu, or prāpta 'yu = Skt. prāpto 'yam.]

Prāptasena, n. of a former Buddha: Sukh 6.5.

prāptikā (f. to *°taka, to prāpta), seemingly some kind of *servant* or *slave*, at any rate one not to be accepted as a nun: mā (sc. asi) °kā Bhīk 16a.4; follows **vikrītikā,** precedes **vaktavyikā,** qq.v.

prāpya, adj. (gdve. of pra-āp; not recorded in this sense; cf. Jm 183.17 prāpya-rūpāṇi . . . puṣpāṇi, *which are easy to get*), *easy*: Mv i.89.16 prāpyaṃ ca bhāraṃ na upādiyanti, aprāpyaṃ ca bhāraṃ upādiyitvā viharanti (mss. corrupt; so I would read for text vitaranti), *they do not take up an easy* (*possible*) *burden* (viz. the religious life), *and they live assuming a difficult burden* (viz. the cares of worldly life; so essentially Senart's note); with inf., *easy to* . . . Mv i.131.7 prāpyo. . . 'yaṃ . . . bhasmīkartuṃ *it would be easy to burn him to ashes,* and so 131.10; 132.2; mss. prāpya each time.

prābandhika, f. °kī, adj. (Skt. prabandha plus -ika), *continuous, characterized by continuation*: °kaṃ (cittaṃ) Bbh 263.5 (contrasted with ekakṣaṇika, *momentary*); duḥkhā vedanā °kī Bbh 302.4; susthāna-°kam, and sattvārtha-°kam, two kinds of **praṇidhāna,** Dharmas 112.

prābhāvya, adj. (to Skt. prabhāva plus -ya), *majestic, mighty*: rājābhūt °yaḥ MSV i.114.7; 116.3; 122.11 (all prose), etc.

prābhṛta, m. (Skt. nt.), *present, gift*: (nāsti tathāgatasyaivaṃvidhiḥ) prābhṛto yathā vaineya-°ta iti Divy 36.21.

prāmāṇika, adj. (Skt., not quite in these mgs.), (**1**) *measurable, subject to measurement*: mā ānanda tathāgataṃ (so read, Foucaux, Notes, p. 113) °kaṃ akārṣuḥ . . . aprameyo hy ānanda tathāgato LV 89.9–10, *let them not make* (*consider*) *the T. measurable* . . .; (**2**) °kā(ḥ) sahāyakāḥ Mvy 7607 = Tib. tshad mar ruṅ ba, *fit to be measured*; Chin. either *based on accurate measure*, or *reliable*; (**3**) (puṣkariṇī . . .) °kā MSV i.142.1, perhaps *extensive* (but Divy 448.12, same passage, puruṣa-prāmāṇikā, *of the measure of a man*).

prāmukhya, adj. (Skt. pramukha plus -ya; = Pali pāmokkha, AMg. pāmukkha), *chief, principal*: °yena Bbh 379.22.

prāmudya = **prāmodya** (cf. Pali pāmujja beside pāmojja): AdP Konow MASI 69,35.32 prītiprasādaprāmudyaṃ.

prāmodya (and rarely **prāmudya**), nt. (= Pali pāmojja, pāmujja), *joy*: SP 123.9 (°karaṇīṃ, WT with most mss. °ṇīyāṃ, sc. -kathāṃ); LV 31.14 (as a dharmālokamukha); Mv i.266.12; ii.143.23; Mvy 1585 (misprinted pra°, Index prā°); 2936; Divy 13.12; 82.28; 239.19; 258.16; Gv 155.5; Dbh 12.9; Bbh 72.15; 187.21; °dya-vant Dbh 12.17; often °dya-jāta, SP 12.11; Mv ii.299.5; 317.17; Divy 553.5; Jm 180.9; Gv 75.10; very often prīti-prāmodya, SP 75.2; 199.4; LV 89.12; 162.22; 370.1; 427.9; Mv i.59.14; 233.13; iii.42.8; Jm 36.3; Av i.189.6 (-jāta); 286.6; Suv 19.8; Sukh 30.3, etc.; also with other synonyms, prīti-prasāda-prā° LV 11.6; -sukha-prīti-prasāda-prā° LV 281.11–12; prā°-harṣa SP 170.15.

Prāmodyarāja, n. of a Bodhisattva: RP 2.15; 4.9, 18.

prāyaścittika, see s.v. **pātayantikā.**

? **prāraṇya,** acc. to Foucaux *edge* (*lisière*) *of a forest*, in āraṇya-prāraṇyābhimukhaḥ LV 180.16 (prose; no v.l.); pw would em. to prāvaṇya (from pravaṇa), but no such form is recorded, and it does not seem very plausible in this context. The Tib. version is omitted in Foucaux's ed. and transl.

[**prārthak-**(prārthaj-)**-janaka, °nika,** vv.ll. for **pārthagj°,** q.v.]

prārthanā seems = **praṇidhāna, praṇidhi,** in SP 70.10 (vs) ārāgitaś ca yad (WT with most mss. saṃ-) buddhaḥ °nā bhotu bodhaye, . . . *may there ensue* (*for us*) *an earnest wish for enlightenment.*

? **prārdhate,** acc. to Divy Index *attains*, interpreted as from pra- plus root ṛdh-: Divy 146.11 (see s.v. **śava**). But no present *ardhati or °te, and no cpd. of this root with pra-, is recorded. Prob. read prārthadhve for prārthayadhve, or the latter.

prāvacana (nt.; = Pali pāv°, AMg. pāvayaṇa; in Skt. only as adj. and rare), *words, teaching, gospel* (of the Buddha): ahaṃ . . . pravrajito tava svayaṃbhu prāvacane Mv i.247.11 (vs); mss. pravacane, the regular Skt. form, but meter seems to demand Senart's em.

[**prāvaṇya,** to pravaṇa, em. in pw for **prāraṇya,** q.v.]

prāvarakā (cf. Pkt. pāvaraa, Sheth, beside pāvāraya = Skt. prāvāraka, *cloak*), perh. *cloak*; certainly some kind of garment or textile: Divy 316.27, cited s.v. **kṣomaka**; cf. **prāvāraka.**

prāvarati (= **prāvṛṇoti**; and see **prāvṛta**; not noted in MIndic; § 28.13), *dresses oneself*, more particularly *dons the* (monk's) *outer robe*: prāvaranti SP 11.12 (vs); ger. prāvariya Mv ii.441.14; prāvaritvā 445.4, and other forms, see Chap. 43, s.v. 1 vṛ (2); in Mv ii.489.10 (prose) pravāritvā, read prāvar°?, caus. in mg., *having clothed* (another); prāvarayantyā (caus.) Bhīk 11a.5, by the (nun) *who is dressing* (the novice).

prāvāraka, nt., some kind of material listed as not proper for monks' robes: MSV ii.52.10. In Skt. °ka, m., =prāvāra, *cloak*. Cf. **prāvarakā,** which may be either a material or a garment.

prāvivekya, nt. (to **praviveka,** q.v., plus -ya), *state* or *life of solitude*: Av ii.119.11; 120.4, 11 (duṣkaraṃ prā°); Bbh 8.26 f. (with naiṣkramya); 333.11.

prāviṣkaraṇa (nt.; to next, plus -ana), *manifestation*: Divy 199.14; Mmk 78.25.

prāviṣkaroti (to pra- with Skt. āviṣkaroti; unrecorded elsewhere, but common in BHS, and wrongly questioned in pw 7.362), *manifests, shows*: Divy 67.17; 69.26; 72.16; 138.1; 140.7; 199.11; 201.23, etc.; Av i.4.6; 10.5, etc.; Śikṣ 194.8 (from Samādh p. 31 line 24); Mmk 78.24; Bbh 6.1; 122.15; 146.5.

prāvṛṇoti (Skt. id.; cf. **prāvarati**), sometimes specifically (like Pali pārupati) *puts on the* (monk's) *outer robe*, contrasting with **nivāsayati** (which occurs Prāt 527.8 ff.): prāvariṣyāmaḥ Prāt 529.1 ff., better, perhaps, to **prāvarati**; Whitney, Roots, records no fut. to root vṛ(ṇoti) in Skt. lit.

prāvṛta, nt. (= Skt. Lex. id.), *cloak, outer garment*: (kāśikasūkṣmāṇi) °tāni Mv ii.159.12; (kumārīṃ . . . śucivastra-)prāvṛtena sunivastām kṛtvā Mmk 56.7, *having made her well-clothed by use of an outer garment of fine cloth* (Lalou, Iconographie 19, *recouverte d'un voile d'étoffe pure*).

prāvṛti (cf. prec.), *covering, cover*: (tūlikāyāṃ) māṃsapūrṇāṃ prāvṛtiṃ devyā ātmānam upanaya MSV ii.15.3, *present yourself to the queen as a meat-filled covering in* (or *on*) *a cotton mattress.*

prāśaṃsya (= Pali pāsaṃsa, acc. to PTSD gdve., with prā- for pra-, but could be from Skt. praśaṃsā plus -ya), *praiseworthy* or *resulting in praise*: dṛṣṭe ca dharme prāśaṃsyaḥ Ud v.25; cf. Pali Pv. iv.7.13 diṭṭhe va dhamme pāsaṃso.

[**prāśālika,** v.l. for **prāsādika** (2), q.v.]

[**prāsa,** Lefm.'s em. in prāsasya muṣṭiṃ LV 313.14 (vs), *a handful of straw* (so Tib., phub ma); mss. prasasya, vegasya (so Calc.), dharṣasye; read buṣasya with Foucaux, Notes 178, or better bus°.]

prāsādaka (= Skt. °da), *palace, terrace*: -daśa-°kamaṇi- Gv 100.24 (prose).

prāsādika, (**1**) (see also **a-prā°**), adj., f. °kā, once at least pras° in mss. (= Pali pās°), *gracious, attractive, fair*, usually but not always applied to persons: Mvy

5216 = Tib. mdzes pa, *fair, handsome*; SP 425.13; 441.14; LV 26.10; 63.4; 107.1; 191.16; 240.2, 3; 278.13; 424.7 (samanta-prā°, of the Buddha); 432.21; Mv i.3.4 (mss. pra°); ii.212.8; 447.3; iii.27.3 (common in Mv); Divy 74.23; 99.18; Samādh 8.12 etc.; Kv 42.5; 45.11; Suv 39.17; 80.15; 175.5, etc.; RP 37.5; Gv 203.6; °kā, f., Mv i.196.20; 199.1; 232.14; ii.9.1; Av i.8.9; like **prasādanīya,** q.v., with which it may be closely associated, of trees, Mv ii.123.17; iii.302.1; 401.21; also like the same, in kāya-prā° citta-prā° (or in inverse order) Divy 82.13–14; 132.27; of actions (karma), °ka-saṃvartanīyaṃ Karmav 30.8; adv. °kaṃ, of the sounds of an (auspicious) earthquake (like **prasādanīya**), Mv i.207.1; iii.341.8; °ka-taro Mv ii.446.9, with superlative force (§ 22.40), *fairest*; °ka-tva, abstract, Bbh 28.21; (**2**) m. (cf. Skt. prasātikā and Lex. °dhikā, *a kind of rice*; Pali pasādiyā, Jāt. vi.530.14, comm. = the kind of rice called saṃsādiyā *when it has fallen on the ground,* misunderstood PTSD; Skt. prāśātika, ApŚ 4.3.8, *legume* acc. to pw), some edible plant, vegetable or grain, in lists of such: Mv ii.210.10 (v.l. prāśālika); °ko (v.l. prādiko) 211.14; °ka- (v.l. prasā°) iii.362.13; in Mv ii.60.22 (vs) text prasātikā (n. pl., perh. = Skt., above), v.l. prasādita (intending °kā = prās°?).

prāsādi-vārika, m., so Mironov for Mvy 9071 prasādhi° (v.l. prāsādi-vāraka), some official in a monastery; Tib. mdzes (cf. mdzes pa = **prāsādika** 1) (ḥ)chos, perh. *maker of fine things*; Chin. believed corrupt, em. in Kyoto ed. would mean *maker of metal objects*; Jap. *person in charge of ornamental utensils.*

prāsika, adj. or subst. m. (Skt. Lex.; to Skt. prāsa plus -ika), *armed with a spear; spear-man*: °kaḥ Mvy 3731.

prāhavanīya, adj. (= Pali pā°, cf. Vism. i.220.17; more usually Pali pahuneyya, or °huṇ°; °havanīya prob. by popular etym., tho found in both Pali and BHS; see **āhavanīya**), *worthy of receiving the hospitality due to guests*: Mvy 1773.

prāhāṇika, adj. (to **prahāṇa** 1 plus -ika; cf. Pali padhānika, without vṛddhi), *engaging in* (ascetic) *exertion*: MSV i.56.21; 57.10.

prāhita (if not error or misprint, = **prahita,** q.v.), *intent, concentrated* (here, on evil desires): kathaṃ ca tvaṃ °to mūrchito 'dhyavasito ... Śikṣ 78.2 (prose).

prāhṛta (app. ppp. to prā- [for pra-] hṛ-, but prahṛta is not normal Skt. in this mg.; perh. semi-MIndic for Skt. prābhṛta, *present,* cf. AMg. pāhuḍa), (what has been) *extorted, stolen* (so Transl.); or, perh., *present*: (śramaṇair apahṛtya) teṣāṃ prāhṛtaṃ pradāpyante Śikṣ 63.15 (prose), *they are caused to give to them...*

Priya, n. of a Śākyan youth: Av i.363.11 ff.

Priyaṃkara, (**1**) n. of a Bodhisattva: Śikṣ 168.4 f. (quoted from Upāyakauśalya-sūtra); (**2**) n. of a king: Śikṣ 255.11 (quoted from Pitṛputrasamāgama); (**3**) = Pali Piyaṃkara (see DPPN), n. of a yakṣa-child: Mmk 44.1 (here associated with, and apparently regarded as the son of, Hārītī).

Priyadarśana, (**1**) n. of a cakravartin: Mv i.114.12; (**2**) n. of a kalpa: SP 431.9; 457.6; (**3**) n. of a Bodhisattva: Śikṣ 124.5 (quoted from Dharmasaṃgīti-sūtra); (**4**) n. of two yakṣas: Māy 48, 100.

Priyadarśanā, n. of a female doorkeeper: Sādh 502.15.

Priyaṃdadā, n. of a 'gandharva maid': Kv 4.14.

priyamāṇa, adj. (quasi-pres. pple. pass. or 4th class mid., = Skt. prīyamāṇa; doubtless influenced in form by priya), mutually *affectionate, fond* (of each other), always of two persons; in first and third passages follows **sammodika**: Mv i.231.19; ii.246.15; iii.57.4; all prose.

Priyamukhā, n. of a 'gandharva maid': Kv 4.14.

priya-vacana, nt. LV 182.6; Dharmas 19; **-vadya,** nt. (both these two occur in Skt., not in the Bu. technical sense) Mv i.3.12 (most mss.); ii.395.8; LV 38.17; Dbh 20.6; °**vadya-tā** LV 429.12; **-vākya,** nt. LV 160.6; °**vādi-tā** Mvy 926; Bbh 217.2, 6 ff.; 302.26; [**-vādya,** nt., Senart with 1 ms., Mv i.3.12] (in Pali peyyavajja), one of the four **saṃgraha-vastu,** q.v., *speaking in a kind, loving manner.*

Priyasena, n. of a merchant: Divy 98.17.

priyākhyāyin, adj. (Skt. °khya), (a messenger) *who brings good news*: Divy 386.17; 529.8 f.

(**priyānna,** adj. Bhvr., cf. Skt. °nna-tva, pw, *characterized by expensive food*: °no kālo, *a time of high prices for food,* Mv i.301.10 (mss. pray°), 12 (mss. priyānno, priyono); in both Senart em. prāyonna-.)

(**priyāyati,** °**te,** denom.; in Skt. rare, either absolute, *is friendly, is pleased,* AV, Mbh. Cr. ed. 2.56.5, or with instr., once RV.; *is friendly to, makes friends with* (acc.): so °yitavyaḥ (mss. priyāt°, priyot°) Mv ii.479.1, *he must be made friends with*; anyam-anyaṃ °yanti iii.453.7; vicitrāṃ (sc. dharmadeśanāṃ) na °yate Śikṣ 197.13, *takes kindly to.*)

-prītika, see **niṣ-pr°.**

prītibhakṣa, adj. (= Pali pītibhakkha, ep. of ābhassara gods), *feeding on joy,* ep. of gods: of śuddhāvāsa, Mv i.33.6; as in Pali, °kṣā bhaviṣyāmo devā hy ābhasvarā yathā Ud xxx.49 = Pali Dhp. 200.

prīti-saumanasya-jāta, see **-jāta.**

Prītyāhāravyūha, n. of a samādhi: LV 370.7.

prīyaṇā (n. act. from Skt. prīyate plus -anā), *amiability*: Sūtrāl. xi.62.

prekṣaka, f. °ikā, *intending to view* (§ 22.3): devī ... āmravanaṃ °ikā nirgatā Mv iii.12.9 (prose).

? **prekṣaṇa** (perh. hyper-Skt., see § 2.26, or error, for Skt. preṣaṇa), *sending forth,* in dautya-prekṣaṇe LV 432.18–19, so all mss., Calc. °ṇa-.

prekṣikā (Skt. prekṣā plus -ka svārthe), *look, gaze*: yugamātra-, saviśvasta-, and anābhoga-prekṣikayā Śikṣ 267.15–268.1, *with look extending only a yoke's length* etc.; fig., sukha-prekṣikayā Śikṣ 323.5, *with regard to pleasure.* See also **prekṣaka.**

prekṣya, adj. (= Pali -pekkha; to Skt. prekṣā plus -ya; seems not used in Skt. in this mg.), *intending...*: hāsya-prekṣyam (adv.) api Prāt 518.11; 519.1, *even intending a jest.* (Pali correspondent, Vin. iv.123.14, hāsāpekkho, containing -apekkha.)

(? **pretaka,** once in late Skt., Schmidt, Nachträge, = Skt. preta, *dead person, ghost*: manuṣya-°ko Sukh 42.12; but acc. to note in ed., Chin. indicates -paṇḍako instead, which as note says seems better.)

preta-maharddhika, f. °**kā,** see s.v. **maharddhika.**

Pretasaṃtarpita-lokeśvara, n. of a deity: Sādh 89.6.

Pretī, n. of a piśācī: Māy 239.6.

premaṇī, adj. f. (to *premaṇ-a? might be error for **premaṇīyā,** see next, but occurs twice), *lovely, charming* (of speech, vāc): LV 286.11; Śikṣ 126.11 (both prose).

premaṇīya, and (§ 3.42) °ṇiya, adj. (= Pali pemanīya; cf. prec. and § 22.20), *lovely, charming*: esp. of the voice (usually of the Buddha), or other sounds, SP 367.2; 368.11; LV 52.6; 242.1 (°ṇiyā, m.c.); 411.9; Mv i.172.16 (mss.); ii.306.12; iii.343.1 (Buddha's voice); RP 47.7 (id.); Dbh 24.13 (Bodhisattvas' voice); °yaṃ, adv., of sounds made by (auspicious) earthquakes, Mv i.206.17; iii.341.7; of a man, Mv ii.388.19, cited Śikṣ 305.12; of a (buddha-) kṣetra SP 146.2; of bowls (pātra; °ṇiyā, m.c.) LV 385.6; of cakṣuḥ (? divyaṃ) Mv ii.374.15; of splendor, °ya-prabhaḥ (Bhvr.), said of Amitābha, Sukh 29.13.

premna (see § 17.28), and **premnaka,** nt. (= Skt. preman, Pali pema and pemaka), *love, affection*: tasya (must be f.; read tasyā?) ... tehi goṣṭhikehi putrasya premnakena putrapremnaṃ Mv iii.375.15, *because of love for her son, she had a love as for a son for those companions.*

preṣaka, m., a kind of malevolent supernatural

being: Mvy 4378 (follows **cicca** or **ciccha,** q.v.); Mmk 17.9 (followed by **mahā-pre°**); Māy 220.18; 245.16.

preṣayati, preṣeti (cf. Skt. id., Pali peseti, *sends*), with cittaṃ, *directs* the thought (with dat., or loc., towards, see **sampreṣayati**): cittu preṣeti varāgrabodhaye LV 179.6 (vs). Acc. to Senart, Mv i note 535, preṣayati would have this same mg. with ellipsis of cittaṃ in Mv i.202.14 = ii.6.11 (vs); and, I would add, surely the same form (preṣaya) should be read in the same line i.145.17, where all mss. omit the verb altogether but Senart by em. inserts prekṣasva, instead of preṣaya of the other passages. Senart's interpretation of preṣaya seems hardly necessary; it may mean *order, direct, command*; cf. Pali Vin. ii.177.19 (ārāmikā) a-pesiyamānā (pass. pple.), *not being directed, commanded*; and SP 116.5.

proṇa, adj. (semi-MIndic for Skt. pravaṇa; Pali poṇa), *directed* towards (in comp.): tatproṇu (Pali tappoṇa) KP 10.16 (vs; = tatpravaṇaḥ 10.6, prose).

protsṛjati, *throws away* or *down* (impetuously): arthān ... °sasarja pradānaiḥ Divy 587.7; śailataṭād ... śarīraṃ °sṛjataś (gen. sg. pres. pple.) RP 22.3.

prodyāyate or **°ti** (pra-ud-yā-, cf. Skt. prod-i-), *sets out, goes forth*: prodyayāmāna, pple., m.c. for °yāyamāna, Dbh.g. 51(77).25.

pronmathyate, pass. (cf. Skt. pronmāthin, rare), *is disturbed*: keśariṇo balena mahatā °yamānā (read °naṃ) gajam Divy 599.2.

pronmūlita, ppp. (to pra- plus Skt. unmūlayati), *uprooted, cast out*: yūyaṃ ... °tā bhūmayaḥ Divy 603.9.

prollīḍha, ppp. (to pra- plus Skt. ul-leḍhi), *licked voraciously, much used for food*: madavārilolamadhuliṭprollīḍha-gandhasthalam (gajam) Divy 599.1 (vs). It seems that gaṇḍasthalam should be read for gandha°.

proṣṭa, ppp. (of pra- plus uṣ, *burn*, this cpd. unrecorded), *burnt*: must be read for ploṣṭa-, which is senseless (pluṣṭa- would be possible) and is recorded from only one ms., while one has the correct proṣṭa- (the others vary; WT keep ploṣṭa- without note): kumbhāṇḍakāḥ proṣṭamukhā bhramanti SP 85.9 (vs); confirmed in Tib., gdoṅ tshig, *burnt face*.

Proṣṭhapada, pl., n. of a brahmanical (Yajurvedic) school: Divy 633.6 f.

plavita, nt., *swimming* (as exercise, sport, or art); so Tib. rkyal on Mvy and LV 151.17: Mvy 5000 (°tam); °te, loc., LV 151.17; 156.10; Mv ii.423.16; 434.12.

plāvīkṛta, ppp. (to Skt. plāva plus kar-), *made to overflow*: udapānaṃ °tam MSV i.24.15.

plīha, m. (= Skt. plīhan), *spleen*: °haḥ Mvy 4021 = Tib. mchin pa, acc. to Jä. *liver*; Chin. also *liver*.

plīhaka, m. (cf. Pali pihaka), = prec.: °kaḥ Śikṣ 209.9 (prose).

Plīhakānanda, n. of a Buddhist monk: MSV ii.96.10 (Tib. cited as mchin nad can, *having liver-disease*); see **plīha.**

ploti, f., see also next, and **-plotika,** ifc. Bhvr. (= **pilotika,** q.v.; Skt. ploti, *piece of cloth*, so read with Gaṇapati Sastri for plauti of Shama Sastri, Kauṭ. Arth., Shama S.[1] 80.9, in ii.11; also Skt. plota; both for *proti, *prota, from Skt. pra-vayati; note the denom. ger. protayitvā, implying protayati, thrice in KātyŚrS, see BR; this seems to mean *having fastened, tied on* or *in*, which implies a meaning like that here suggested for the underlying noun *proti or *prota), seems to mean *cord*, as *connecting link* or *bond*: chiefly in karma-ploti, e. g. pūrvikā °tir vyākṛtā bhavati Divy 150.24, *the previous action-(binding-)cord has been explained*; so, regularly with forms of vyākaroti, Divy 87.8; 89.5; 241.25–26; Av i.242.9; 244.1; 246.11 et alibi; Mārāś ca Mārakarmāṇi ca karmaplotayaś ca Laṅk 240.11 (as matters of which an explanation is asked); -plotika alone in chinna-°kaḥ, ep. of dharma, Mvy 1306; Av ii.106.11; Tib. on Mvy rgyun ma (? rgyun = srotas, *stream, continuity*; error for rgyu, *cause*? cf. Chin.) bcad pa (*cut*); Chin. *having cut off causes*; Jap. *cut off ties* or *bonds of karman*. Also (chinna-)**pilotika,** q.v. Both Mvy and Av use this cpd. in a cliché occurring in Pali, e. g. MN i.141.21; here the comm. ii.119.19 ff. explains chinna-pilotiko (of dhammo) as *having its rags cut off*, like a fresh garment (cf. **pilotika,** 1), but he offers two different, and equally fantastic, explanations of the specific application of the term, and gives the impression that he is merely guessing.

plotikā (= prec., in Skt. mg.), *piece of cloth* attached to a monk's robe in mending it: °kā-cīvareṇa MSV ii.159.9; in the uddāna above, line 5, represented by upadhiḥ; is this used in the mg. *addition* (*Hinzufügung*, pw 1.240)? The ed. note cites avadhi from Pali Vin. i.254, 297, where I have not found it; Tib. renders plotikā as it does **pailottika,** q.v.

[**ploṣṭa** SP 85.9, read **proṣṭa,** q.v.]

PH

phakka, adj. or subst. m., *lame, crippled, maimed*: °kaḥ Mvy 8876 = Tib. grum po.

[**phaṭika-,** see **phalikha.**]

phaṇika, m. (= Skt. phaṇin), *snake*: Mv ii.305.19; iii.380.8 (both vs, in both v.l. phali°).

[**phana,** allegedly = Skt. phena, *foam*; cited as phaṇa once from TB. in BR; Lefm. phanapiṇḍeva LV 176.2 (vs), *like a heap of foam*, symbol of transitoriness; but all mss. phena°, so also citation of the line Śikṣ 237.11 phenapiṇḍāvad, where note says 'scan phena-'; see § 3.65.]

phara, nt. (once in Skt. acc. to pw; = id. Deśīn. 1.76; AMg. pharaya; Skt. phalaka), *shield*: °ram Mvy 6079 = Tib. phub; Mmk 356.6; 362.24.

pharaṇa (nt.; Pali id.; to **pharati**; = **spharaṇa,** q.v.), *suffusion, penetration, pervasion*; noted only in Bhvr. cpd., = *pervading* ...: dharmadhātu-pharaṇaṃ (241.2 °ṇāḥ) pratikṣaṇam (240.20 misprinted pratilakṣaṇam) Gv 240.20; 241.2 (vss).

pharati (= Pali id.; see also **phalati, spharati, sphurati**), *pervades, fills*, esp. with radiance, or with love or the like: (in Mv iii.124.15 mss. phalitvā, Senart em. phar-;) in Mv iii.374.11, 16 Senart rightly em. pharetha (16 pharema) for mss. har° kāyaṃ vipulāya prītaye (16 prītiyā); Pali uses pharati with kāyaṃ or synonym as object; *thrill the body with great joy*; pharitva (v.l. sphalitva; Lefm. em. sphar°) LV 116.15 (vs; amṛtodakena); in Gv 230.14 (vs) read kāya (text 'pāya, at beginning of a line!) pharitva; pharanti Gv 236.6; pharitvā 236.8; °tva 240.24; phari (aor.) 240.25, et alibi, in vss of Gv.

pharapharāyate, onomat., *crashes* (?): Mmk 674.4 (prose; subject app. kumbhīra-dhāraṇam, *a crocodile-holder* [?], from prec. sentence); cf. Ap. pharaharantu, pres. pple., Bhav. (Jacobi) 155.11.

? **pharasaka,** see **phalasaka.**

phala, nt. (**1**) (= Skt. and Pali phalaka) *bark, bast* (used for garments): phala-muñjāsana-valkala ... LV 249.1 (prose); (**2**) (= Skt. and Pali id.) *religious fruition* or *attainment*, passim; prathama phala Mv i.174.12, 14;

192.7, 8, = the first stage of religious advancement, cf. śrotāpattiphale i.175.1; five phalāni, sc. of karuṇā, *compassion*, acc. to Sūtrāl. xvii.31 with comm., which explains all five, in different order: Mvy 2271–7, **niṣyanda-, adhipati-, puruṣakāra-, vipāka-, visaṃyoga**-phalam (see the various prior members). However, nothing is said of karuṇā in Mvy, and it probably intends them as different kinds of *results* of anything; so Bbh 102.16 ff. and AbhidhK. LaV-P. ii.287 ff., iv.185 ff. treat the same terms.

phalaka, (**1**) m., °kaḥ Mvy 9192 = Tib. sgrog guḥi rten ma, *holder for a strap*; perhaps a *fastener*, something like a *button*, to be affixed to a monk's robe, and to which a *strap* is fastened; I believe phalaka has this mg. in Pali gaṇṭhika-pha° pāsaka-pha° Vin. ii.136.38; 137.1, 3 (not a kind of cloth, perhaps made of leaves, as assumed SBE 17.246); so Chin. on Mvy, *leather bag* or *pocket with button(s)*; (**2**) nt., in ŚsP 1430.9, cited approximately in Śikṣ 210.5 as: gāṃ hatvā tīkṣṇena śastreṇa catvāri phalakāni kṛtvā, acc. to Bendall and Rouse *four quarters* (of the animal), which seems implausible; possibly four *leather bags* (of the hide)? cf. Chin. cited above; or *belts*? (this mg. given for AMg. phalaga in Ratnach.); (**3**) nt., *grain* (of sand): vālikā-phalakāni Gv 134.20 f.; (**4**) see s.v. **Halaka**; (**5**) see also **phalaha**. (In Divy 316.26 phalaka may mean *bark*, as in Skt., used as material for garments.)

phalakinī, acc. to Index *plank*: kim etat kāṣṭham syād athāsthiśakalātha °nī syāt Divy 240.3.

phalakha, see **phalaha.**

phalati = **pharati**, q.v.: phalī (3 pl. aor.) Mv ii.349.17 (vs), see s.v. **akṣamātra**; tam enaṃ (read ena, m.c.) jñānena phalitva (mss. °tvā; Senart em. pharitva) iii.124.15 (vs).

Phaladharā, n. of a rākṣasī: Māy 241.33.

Phalaṃdadā, n. of a 'gandharva maid': Kv 5.2.

phalasaka (m. or nt.), a kind of tree, in a list of them: Divy 628.10; mss. phara°; ed. em., presumably on the basis of Skt. Lex. phalasa, said to mean *breadfruit tree.*

phalaha-, also written °**kha**, °**ka**, in comp. with -stāra (cf. AMg. phalaha, defined as *a big plank*, Ratnach., and identified with Skt. phalaka), some part of a gate or door: Mv i.195.13; iii.228.10 (prose; same passage; following the sentence containing **phalikha**-(q.v.)-phalakāni; in i.195.13 mss. phalaha-stārā(ḥ), Senart em. phalaka-; in iii.228.10 he reads phalaka° without v.l., but acc. to his note i p. 530, on the other passage, one ms. at least reads phalakha-stārā(ḥ); it seems reasonably clear that the AMg. form, conceivably with °kha for °ha, was read in Mv. (Cf. **phalikāstaraṇa**? but I cannot mediate between these two forms, both enigmatic.)

phalāphala, nt. sg. or pl. (= Pali id.; § 23.12), *all manner of fruits*: Mv ii.475.13; iii.45.3; 159.13; Sādh 411.12.

[**phalika**, see **phalikha.**]

phalikāstaraṇa, adj., perh. *having couch-covers* (cf. AMg. phalaga, one mg. of which is said to be *cot*, Hindi palang): ep. of a palanquin (paryaṅka), Mv ii.115.16, parallel with citrāstaraṇa, ubhayato bimbopadhāna, etc. (all indicative of luxury).

phalikha, (m.? = Skt. parigha, AMg. phaliha, see § 2.29 and Pischel 208), *bar* (as to a door or gate): in Mv ii.379.5 (vs) read phalikha-(mss. °khaṃ)-bhujo achambhī, as proved by same line Śikṣ 303.3 parigha-bhujo . . .; accordingly, read doubtless phalikha-(so mss. in iii.228.9; in i.195.12 mss. phaṭikāya-, sphaṭikāya-)-phalakāni (so, or with v.l. °khāni, mss. in i.195.12; mss. very corrupt in iii.228.9) Mv i.195.12; iii.228.9 (same passage, prose); Senart reads phaṭika- the first time, phalika- the second; in a description of parts of gates or doors. In both of these last passages the next sentence contains another part of the gate, printed by Senart phalaka-stārā (pl.); see s.v. **phalaha.**

phaleṣin, adj. (Skt. phala plus -eṣin; = Pali °sin, in same vs as Mv, Therag. 527 = Jāt. i.87.2), *seeking* (to bring forth) *fruit*, ep. of trees, acc. to Pali: (read) °ṣiṇo Mv iii.93.11. The Mv is very corrupt and has omitted the word for *tree* (drumāḥ, Pali dumā), but there is no doubt that the text was substantially the same; Senart with mss. s for ṣ, but one ms. has ṇ for (Senart's) n!

phalgu (gender not known, only in cpds.; in Skt. adj., *worthless*; Pali pheggu in mg. 1, phaggu in mg. 2), (**1**) '*accessory wood . . . next to the pith, but inferior and worthless*' (PTSD): Mvy 433 apagata-śākhā-pattra-palāśā-laṭikā-(read latikā with Index, Tib. khri śiṅ, *creeper*; or with Mironov **prapāṭikā**)-tvak-phalguḥ, Bhvr. (here Tib. skyon, *fault, defect*, not parallel with prec. words but having them as dependents); apagata-phalgu, adj., = Pali °phegguka, *free from weak wood* (PTSD), Mvy 7636 (°guḥ; here Tib. sñiṅ po ma yin pa, *what is not the pith*); SP 39.4 (°guḥ); (parṣad) phalgu-vyapagatā (so with WT, cpd.) SP 44.14; tvagbhārataś ca phalgutaś ca sārataś ca (of trees) Divy 628.1, similarly 12; fig., of **dauṣṭhulya** in men, tvaggataṃ phalgugataṃ sāragataṃ Bbh 356.25; (**2**) nt., a certain religious observance (defined for Pali, MN comm. i.179.1 ff.): śuddhasya hi sadā phalgu Ud xvi.15 = Pali MN i.39.19.

phāṇī(-kṛta), (cf. Skt. phāṇita and Lex. phāṇi, f.), (*mixed with*) *syrup* or *treacle*: °kṛtaṃ mudgayūṣaṃ hareṇukayūṣaṃ . . . LV 264.16 (prose). Senart by em. puts phāṇikṛtam into Mv ii.204.19, relying on the LV passage; but a comparison of the corrupt Mv mss. with Pali MN i.245.19–20 seems to make it clear that Mv should be read: mudgakulattha-hareṇuka-kalāya-kṛta-yūṣam upabhuñje.

phāṣa, adv. phāṣam (see **a-phāṣa** and s.v. **sparśa-vihāra-tā**; also the following items), *comfortably*: KP 141.8 (prose) sukhaṃ phāṣaṃ vihariṣyāmaḥ.

phāṣaka, adj. = **phāṣa** (as adj.): Prāt 513.6 na me . . . phāṣakaṃ, *it is not agreeable to me.*

phāsa, adj. (= **phāṣa, phāsu**; see **sparśa-vihāra-tā**), *agreeable, comfortable*: noted only in v.l. of Kashgar rec. -sukha-phāsa-vihārārthaṃ for SP 211.2 (prose); text omits phāsa with Nep. mss.

phāsu, adj. (= Pali id.; see **phāṣa, phāsa**, and esp. **sparśa-vihāra-tā**), *comfortable, agreeable*: Mv iii.48.12 phāsu-vihārāye (mss. cchāsu-, em. Senart); adv., sukhaṃ phāsuṃ viharantu Śikṣ 129.8; yathāsukhaṃ yathāphāsu Mv iii.169.9.

phuṭa, adj. (= Pali id.; MIndic, = **sphuṭa**), *full*: prīti-phuṭā Śikṣ 334.17.

phuṭṭaka, adj. (cf. Skt. phuṭṭikā, BR 5.1640), description of some kind of cloth of small value (contrasting with kāśika-): phuṭṭaka-vastra-, phuṭṭakair vastrair, phuṭṭakāni (vastrāṇi) Divy 29.7–9, 12.

phutphu(-kārakam, adj.), *making the sound phutphu* (in eating), regarded as offensive: Mvy 8580 (so also Mironov; cited in BR, pw as phupphu°). Cf. **phuphu-(kāra)**. Chin. onomat., indicating that one has eaten something cold.

phupphusa, (**1**) m. (recorded only in mg. *lungs*), app. some sort of instrument, used by monks: °saḥ Mvy 9446 = Tib. snod rñeṅ (sñeṅ) khyer ba (obscure to me; possibly *an instrument for stretching some abdominal organ*, as the bladder? snod, *vessel*, is used in cpds. of abdominal organs, Jä. s.v. 2); Chin. also obscure; lit. *love instrument* (!); (**2**) nt. MSV ii.159.5 °sam, 160.1 °sa-cīvareṇa, applied to a monk's robe; Tib. deṅs pas, *old, stale, worn* (Das).

phuphu-kāra (onomat.; cf. **phutphukārakam**), one of the noises made by Māra's host, described as horrible and harsh: (kecid bhinna-vikṛta-bhairava-)rūkṣa-svarāḥ phuphukāra-(v.l. huṃhuṃkāra, and so Calc.; Tib. similarly hu hu; Lefm. em. phutphutkāra-)-picutkāra-(q.v.)-phuluphulu-(q.v.; most mss. °la; Calc. and Tib. huluhulu-)-prakseḍitāni kurvanti sma LV 306.(2–)3.

phuluphulu (or °**la**, or **huluhulu**), onomat., a sound made by Māra's hosts: LV 306.3. See prec.

phulla, adj. (like Skt. id. from Skt. phalati, *bursts*; but not in this sense in Skt.; = Pali id.), *broken*: khaṇḍaphu° (= Pali id.) Mvy 9427; replaced by (khaṇḍa-)sphuṭa (see **sphuṭa** 2) in Divy 22.11, 18; 23.1, 3, 8, or sphuṭita, 10.

phullita, adj. (= Pali id.; denom. pple. to Skt. phulla, cf. rare Skt. phullati), *in full bloom*: Mvy 6233 (°tam); Mv ii.449.2, 3 (of lotuses); °ta-pādapake LV 321.20 (vs).

phullitaka, adj., = prec.: Mv ii.449.4, 16 (of lotuses; prose).

phuṣphasa, Mv ii.326.2; 331.18, 22 (in 22 v.l. phaphasa); **phuṣphuṣa,** ŚsP 1431.10, **phusphuṣa** 1430.21 (Skt. and Pkt. phupphusa, cf. Pali papphāsa), *lungs*.

phela, m., a high number: Mvy 7767 = Tib. phyol-yas; see s.v. **pelu** (also **pelā** 2).

(**phelā,** *box, chest*; so Skt. bhāṇḍa-phelā, Kauṭ. Arth., Sham.[1] 314.2, 4; cf. **pelā**; Pali peḷā means *chest, box*, as well as *basket*; see also **phelikā**: phelā vā phelikā vā Mv ii.465.14, in list of objects made of wood by carpenters; suvarṇasya phelāṃ pūrayitvā Divy 503.24, *making a chest full of gold*; Index to ed. *dish*, wrongly.)

phelikā (dim. of **phelā**, q.v.), *small chest* or *box*: Mv ii.465.2 (? by em.), 14 (see **phelā**). Possibly cf. (śunaka-) phelakāḥ Kauṭ.Arth. Sham.[1] 418.6, but the mg. of this is doubtful; cf. Meyer's Index s.v.

B

Baka (= Pali Baka-brahman), n. of a pratyekabrahman (q.v.), in **Baka-pratyekabrahma-sūtra,** n. of a work: Karmav 34.8; see Lévi's note.

baka-puṣpa, nt. (Skt. Lex., *Agati grandiflora*, BR), n. of a flower: Mvy 6213 = Tib. spra baḥi me tog, which Das says is *Aeschynomene grandiflora*.

Bakkula, Bakula, Vakkula, Vakula, Vatkula, (**1**) (= Pali Bakkula, Bākula, Vakkula), n. of a disciple of Buddha: Bakkula SP 2.5; 207.4; Bakula (the same person?) Karmav 76.11, called king of Kashmir and son of Dharmayaśas, noted for his health and long life, which in Pali is a characteristic of the thera Ba°; Vakkula LV 2.2 (v.l. Vakula; Tib. Ba ku la); Sukh 92.8; Mvy 1065 (var. Vakula; Tib. Ba ku la, or Bag ku la); Vakula Sukh 2.9; MSV i.192.18 ff.; Vatkula Divy 396.2 f.; (**2**) n. of two vakṣas: Māy 6, 54 (Lévi Vakula).

Baḍi = the asura Bali: Mahāsamaj., Waldschmidt, Kl. Skt. Texte 4,181.1.

Badara, n. of a kiṃnara prince: Divy 118.22.

Badaradvīpa, m., n. of a town: Divy 102.11 ff.; 108.12 ff.; RP 23.14.

? **baddha,** m. or nt., in Divy 40.2 gacchanti baddhaṃ (ed. note qy. bandhaṃ?) mṛgāḥ, perh. = Pali baddha, which = Skt. vadhra, vardhra, vārdhra, *strap, thong* (here of a *snare*).

baddhaka, adj. (= Skt. baddha; AMg. baddhaga; in Skt. cited only from AV, mg. *prisoner*), *bound, fastened*: mekhalībaddhakāś ca devadārakā(ḥ) LV 76.20; dvārāṇi °kāni Mv iii.297.3, 6; f. °kā Divy 226.22; all prose, not dim.

baddhati (§ 28.19), *binds*: baddhitvā Mv iii.7.5. Cf. also **baddhāpayati.**

baddhamālā, *having a garland bound on*, n. of the 2d bodhisattva-bhūmi; so read for ed. °mānā Mv i.76.14. It is inconceivable that such a name as the mss. present should be applied to a bhūmi; and my em. is supported in sense by puṣpamaṇḍitā, n. of the 3d bhūmi immediately following. This word cannot, therefore, be cited (with Renou, Études de gram. scte., 1936, p. 18) as an example of -māna added to a ppp. (§ 34.1).

baddhāpayati, caus. to **baddhati,** q.v.: °payitavyaḥ Mmk 50.16, *to be caused to be bound*.

[**badha,** m., read vadha (Skt.): Mvy 8366; **badhra,** see **vadhra.**]

bandhaka, nt., *container, case* (for holding knives): śastraṃ nāsti, tayā °kaṃ gṛhītam, śastraṃ dattaṃ MSV ii.79.8. Cf. Skt. kṣura-bhāṇḍa, Pali khura-bhaṇḍa, *razor-case*; perh. read bhāndakam in MSV?

Bandhanāntakara, n. of a former Buddha: Mv i.140.10.

bandha-nikṣepa, *bond-pledge, guarantee* (to support an assertion): Av i.47.10.

Bandhuma (MIndic for °**mant,** q.v.), (**1**) = °**mant** (Pali °mā), father of **Vipaśyin**: °mo Mv ii.271.5; °masya 7 (both prose); (**2**) n. of a former Buddha: °maṃ (acc.) Mv iii.230.16; °mas (v.l. °mano), nom., 231.1.

Bandhumatī (= Pali id.), n. of the capital city (rājadhānī) where **Vipaśyin** was born: Mv ii.271.6; Divy 141.19; 227.23, 25; 282.23 ff.; Av i.137.9; 349.5; ii.109.5, etc.

Bandhumatīya, and °**yaka,** adj., *belonging to* **Bandhumatī**: °ye dāve Divy 283.23; °yake dāve Divy 282.24; Av ii.109.5 (all prose).

Bandhumant (= Pali id., nom. °mā; cf. also **Bandhuma**), n. of a king of **Bandhumatī,** father of **Vipaśyin**: Divy 282.25; 283.21 ff.; Av i.349.7 etc.

Bandhumā (presumably = °**matī,** cf. °**ma** = °**mant,** but app. a different city), n. of a capital city where it is prophesied that the Buddha Maitreya will be born: °māyāṃ rājadhānyāṃ Mv i.51.7 (prose).

Babbaḍa, n. of a yakṣa, living in **Babbaḍādhāna** (cf. Skt. Babāḍa, Inscrip., n. of a village, and Pali Babbarā, as well as Lévi 103): Māy 93.

barhaka, nt. (= Skt. barha plus -ka), a peacock's *tail-feather*: °kāṇi MSV ii.93.7, 10 (vs, may be m.c.).

bala, (**1**) m., n. of a yakṣa: Māy 48; (**2**) m. = Skt. (and usual BHS) nt., *force, power*: balāś ca, n. pl., SP 47.2 (vs); abalo balo LV 301.4 (vs), (Māra's)*power* (force, host) *is powerless*; daśa-balāṃ = °lān, acc. pl., *the ten bala* (see 3), LV 343.4 (vs); (**3**) nt., technically, *power*, esp. one of the 10 bala of a Tathāgata: often referred to, e. g. SP 67.14; LV 343.4 (above, 2); Mv iii.64.5; Divy 9516; Av i.7.5; hence **daśabala,** q.v., means a Buddha; so also in Pali, where the ten bala are listed and elaborately explained MN i.69.31 ff.; AN v.33.7 ff.; virtually the same list Mvy 119–129 (all but the tenth are various kinds of jñāna, viz., sthānāsthāna-jñānabalaṃ, karmavipāka-, nānādhimukti-, nānādhātu-, indriyavarāvara- [others °parāpara-, prob. orig.], sarvatragāmanīpratipaj-, sarvadhyānavimoksasamādhi-samāpattisaṃkleśavyavadānavyutthāna-, pūrvanivāsānusmṛti-, cyutyutpatti-, and as No. 10, āśravakṣaya-, but Dharmas and Bbh add jñāna-, balam); Dharmas 76; Bbh 384.18 ff.; Mv i.159.10 ff. (here more variation from the standard; Senart's long note, 502 ff., cites inter alia a list as from Mvy, which differs, notably in the last three items, from our Mvy, which is confirmed by Mironov); see also Burnouf, Lotus, App. XI; no complete list in Sūtrāl., but four of the ten (approximately = Mvy 1, 2, 7, and 5) listed xx–xxi. 51 comm.;

ten wholly different bala of a Bodhisattva are listed Mvy 759–769, and a still different list Dharmas 75; five bala, (*moral*) *powers*, corresponding to the five moral faculties identically named (see **indriya** 1), Mvy 982–7; Divy 208.8; Dharmas 48; four bala leading to a bodhisattva's cittotpāda, Bbh 13.22, listed 17.8–9 as adhyātma-, para-, hetu-, prayoga-b°; a trividhaṃ balam Dharmas 113, listed (no parallel found); (**4**) nt., a high number (cf. **ojas**): Mvy 8032.

balaka, (**1**) (nt., = bala, may be m.c.), *power*: Dbh.g. 41(67).6; (**2**) m., n. of a nāga king: Māy 247.23.

bala-kāya, *army-body*, see **kāya.**

Balaguptā, n. of a village chief's daughter: LV 265.4.

bala-cakravartin, a kind of inferior cakravartin: stands intermediate between (**caturdvīpaka-**)**cakravartin** and (rājan) **maṇḍalin** (q.v.), SP 6.4; 20.6; 362.8; without mention of maṇḍalin, (ordinary) rājānaḥ ... balacakravartino 'pi rājānaś cakravartino 'pi SP 367.15; balacakravarti-rājyam distinguished (as inferior) from cakravarti-rājyam, Divy 139.11 = Av i.5.15; (after nṛpatiḥ, simply,) balacakravarty api ca dvīpapatiḥ RP 52.15 (vs); here it seems probable that dvīpapati is not the same as balacakr° but rather = the supreme (caturdvīpaka-)cakravartin. Acc. to Childers and PTSD (without citation of passages), Pali distinguishes cakkavāḷa-cakkavatti, who 'rules over the four great continents', dīpa-cak°, who rules 'over only one', and padesa-cak°, who rules 'over a portion of one'. The BHS terms seem not recorded elsewhere.

balatā (= Pali id.), *quality of strength*: kīrtir yaśaś ca balatā guṇavatī LV 45.21 (vs); na me 'sti śaktir balata parākramo vā 231.22 (vs).

Baladatta, n. of a former Buddha: Mv iii.239.4 f.

Baladeva, n. of a nāga king: Mvy 3300; Māy 247.4.

bala-dharaṇīya, °**ṇīyā,** or °**ṇī** (§ 10.174; cf. **dharaṇī** 1), a part of a palace, Tib. mdun gduṅ, *front beam:* °ṇīyā māpitā(ḥ), n. pl., MPS 34.60.

Balaprabhāsamati, n. of a Buddha: Gv 285.9.

Balabāhu, n. of a former Buddha: Mv i.137.15.

Balabhadra, n. of a nāga king: Māy 247.12.

Balamitra, n. of a householder of Campā, father of Viśākhā: MSV ii.53.16; 70.5.

Balavant, n. of a Śākyan youth: Av i.359.11.

Balavyūha, m., n. of a samādhi: Mvy 520; ŚsP 1416.9.

Balasena, n. of a householder: Divy 1.3.

Balā, (**1**) n. of a village chief's daughter: LV 265.4; (**2**) n. of a rākṣasī: Māy 243.15.

Balākalpa, (?) n. of a place (so Senart): Mv ii.207.5, 8.

balākṣa, nt., a high number: Mvy 8038.

-balādhāna, nt. (Skt. bala plus Skt. ādhāna, on this use of which see pw s.v. ādhāna 6), *assumption, attainment, of* (usually some particular) *power* (said of Buddhas and Bodhisattvas): Mv i.134.11–12 kṛtaniścaya-balādhānāś ca bhavanti (Bodhisattvas); SP 316.1 śṛṇudhvam idam evaṃrūpaṃ mamādhiṣṭhāna-balādhānam; 414.4 (bodhisattvasya) jñānabalādhānena puṇyabalādhānena ca (as manifested in his 'act of truth', satyādhiṣṭhāna); 420.7 evaṃ jñānabalādhānaprāptaḥ sa ... bodhisattvo bhaviṣyati, *this B. will be thus arrived at attainment of the power of knowledge*; 426.6–7 tathāgatabalādhānena, *by the T.'s acquisition of* (*the*) *power*(*s*) (*appropriate to him*).

Balāntīputra, see **Upasena** (3).

Balābhijña, n. of a contemporary or future Buddha: Sukh 70.18.

Balāhaka, m. = the horse **Valāha,** q.v.: Mvy 4774.

balāhukka? some sort of martial exercise; reading not certain: Mv ii.74.2 jave vā balāhukke (?) vā hastismiṃ vā ... (in list of martial exercises to which the Bodhisattva challenges the Śākya youths). Senart gives it up, and I too have been able to think of nothing attractive; for I should not call plausible an em. to *balāhikke, assuming bala plus āhikka, Pkt. for ādhikya, *superiority of strength.*

Bali, n. of a yakṣa: Māy 104. See also s.v. **vali.**

-balika, (**1**) adj. (only ifc.; = Pali id., Skt. balin), *strong, having strength of ..., in ...*: bāhu-°kaḥ SP 73.1, 2; 79.1 (all prose); others Bbh 9.21; 17.3; 73.12; 322.7; Sukh 61.10 (all prose); (**2**) n. of a nāga king: Mvy 3260; Māy 247.22.

balīyati (= Pali id.), *grows strong*: so read in Mv ii.423.10 (rājakumāro ... yathā utpalaṃ) vā padumaṃ vā ... balī° (Senart bahvīyati without report of v.l., recorded in Index, but certainly error of some sort); *overpowers*, with gen. of object (so also in Pali, e. g. Pv. ii.6.1): pramattasya ... paraśatru (n. sg.) balīyati Mv i.275.10, *his enemy prevails over the indolent.*

Balendraketu, n. of a king: Suv 132.3, 12.

bahidhā, prob. m.c. for (Skt.) bahirdhā or (= Pali) bahiddhā, in the sense (also in Pali) of *outside* of the Buddhist faith: tīrthikā ca bahidhānugatāś ca Mv i.69.17 (vs), *heretics and followers of outside* (teachers); so Senart, plausibly; mss. mostly vahidānu°, one vahir-anu°; the 2d syllable must be short, the 3d long, metrically.

bahirāyāma, m. (text vahir°), some kind of disease: Mvy 9548 = Tib. glo laṅs pa (*cough*?) or glab thams pa (?); Chin. *cholera.*

bahir-dvārakoṣṭhaka, see **dvāra°.**

bahirnagara (nt.; Pali bahinagare, loc.), (*the region*) *outside the city*: °rāto (abl.) Mv ii.74.12.

? **bahirṣu,** if correct, loc. pl. adv. as if to bahir = Skt. bahis (cf. **bāhira,** Pkt. bahira), *outside*: LV 145.12 (vs) kṣiptu bahirṣu purātu (so v.l.; Lefm. bahi ṣupurātu! unmetr.) ayaṃ hi. Perhaps bahirṣu is a misreading for bahirdha, which could be m.c. for bahirdhā, which occurs in the parallel 145.14.

bahuka, adj. (= Pali id.; Skt. bahu plus ka svārthe, perhaps partly m.c.), *much*, pl. *many*: °kāḥ SP 95.10 (vs); as quasi-subst., bahukaṃ dinnaṃ Mv ii.67.16, 17 (prose), *much was given.*

bahukara, adj. or subst. nt. (cf. Pali bahukāra, in same mgs.), *very useful, very helpful*; or, *a great favor*: etad evāsmākaṃ bahukaraṃ SP 109.9 (prose), so both edd. with Kashgar rec., confirmed by Tib. maṅ du (= bahu) bgyis par (= kar-); all Nep. mss. bahutaraṃ; MSV i.287.13.

bahukaraṇīya, adj. (= Pali id.), *busy*, with unfavorable implication, *thinking oneself too busy for duties* (in a list of vices; so sometimes, perhaps regularly, in Pali): Mvy 2467. Cf. next.

bahukṛtya, adj. (= Pali bahukicca), = prec.: Mvy 2466; used however without unfavorable implication, simply *busy*, in Śikṣ 128.10.

bahujana (m.; in Skt. only recorded as Bhvr.), *many people, a multitude*: °na-priyaḥ (adj.) Mvy 2940; (nagaraṃ ...) bahujana-manuṣyaṃ Mv i.36.2 (prose), *whose men constitute a great multitude.* Cf. next.

bahujanya, bāhu°, (usually) adj. (to prec. plus -ya; = Pali bāhujañña and, e. g. SN ii.107.3, v.262.13, bahu°), *pertaining to many people, to a multitude*: brahmacaryaṃ cariṣyanti bāhujanyaṃ pṛthubhūtaṃ Divy 202.15; (brahmacaryaṃ cirasthitikaṃ) syād bahujanyaṃ pṛthubhūtaṃ Divy 208.1, 6, 13; possibly subst. nt. (? no context) °yam Mvy 6449, where Kyoto ed. bāhu° with var. bahu°, Mironov bahu°.

Bahujāta, pl., n. of a brahmanical gotra: Divy 635.13.

bahutaraka (Skt. °tara plus -ka), *more numerous*: AsP 373.3; 430.2. Cf. **alpataraka.**

Bahudevataka, n. of a cetiya (caitya) in which Buddha passed the 7th week after enlightenment: Mv iii.303.1.

Bahupakṣa, n. of a cakravartin: Mv i.154.1.

Bahuputra, nt. (= Pali Bahuputta, °taka-cetiya,

near Vesāli), n. of a caitya (cetiya) near Vaiśālī: Mv i.300.9; MSV i.173.9; recorded as Bahupattraka, doubtless by error for °putraka, in Divy 201.14. Cf. next.

Bahuputraka, (nt.; cf. prec.; = Pali Bahuputta, see below), (**1**) n. of another caitya (cetiya) near Rājagṛha: Mv iii.50.19; in Pali (same story) SN ii.220.6 called Bahuputta cetiya, and located between Rājagaha and Nāḷanda; correct DPPN on this point; (**2**) = prec., so read in Divy 201.14.

Bahuprabha, n. of a former Buddha: Mv i.140.7.

Bahubuddhasūtra, n. of the passage Mv iii.225–250: 250.8 (colophon).

Bahumukha, n. of a nāga: Mmk 454.16.

Bahurājan, n. of a former Buddha: Mv i.140.6.

bahurāśi, f., lit. *having many signs of the zodiac* = *night*: īdṛśa bhīṣaṇikā bahurāśī LV 308.6 (vs), *such a terrible night it was.* So Tib. very plainly: mtshan mo, *night.*

Bahurāṣṭra, n. of a former Buddha: Mv i.137.14.

bahula, nt., a high number, = 100 utsaṅga (Mvy ucchaṅga): LV 148.2, cited Mvy 7962 = Tib. maṅ ḥdzin, *much hold.*

Bahulakeśa, n. of a former Buddha: Mv i.140.4.

[**bahulin,** assumed by Senart Mv iii.283.17 and ff. as an adj., *zealous,* cf. next; but the text should be em. to contain forms of Skt. and Pali bahula, as shown by the identical Pali passage SN i.126.21 ff.]

bahulīkāra (m.; see next; = Pali id., actually printed bahuli° in the only passage cited PTSD, MN iii.25 24 ff.), *repeated going over, conning*: (dharmeṣu yoniśo) manasikārād bahulīkārāj jñānam udapādi LV 348.2; same (utpannam for uda°) 417.16.

bahulīkṛta, ppp. (see prec.; = Pali °kata), *repeatedly conned, studied, gone over, practised*: śamatha(ḥ) ... āsevito bhāvito bahulīkṛtaḥ Av ii.140.10, and similarly ff.; Mvy 2322 °tam, after āsevitam, bhāvitam.

[**bahu-vādyakāra,** see **vād°**.]

Bahuśaṅku, m., n. of a pratyeka-(q.v.)-naraka: Śikṣ 57.1.

Bahuśruta, n. of a Buddhist elder (not in DPPN): MSV i.207.4 ff.

bahuśrutya (nt.; = **bāhu°**, q.v.; = Pali bāhusacca, also bahu°, which PTSD would em. to bāhu°): *great (excessive) learning,* disparagingly: Mv i.96.10 °tyam, all mss., Senart em. bāhu°; in same line bāhu°, most mss., but one good one bahu°.

Bahusena, n. of a former Buddha: Mv i.140.12.

Bahūdaka, n. of a nāga-king: Kv 2.11.

Bahvāśrayā, n. of a kiṃnara maid: Kv 6.23.

[**bahvīyati,** see **balīyati.**]

[**bāḍita,** em., Divy 505.10, see **vāḍita.**]

Bāṇḍyāyana, pl., n. of a brahmanical gotra: Divy 635.20.

bālaka, var. for **valaka,** *finger-ring,* q.v.

Bālakāṇḍa-sūtra, n. of a work, part of Abhidharma: Karmav 155.2.

Bālapaṇḍita, n. of a monk: Divy 375.7.

? **bālayati,** denom., *acts the fool, is foolish*: somabhāṣkarayor bhūtvā ye bālenti na te sutāḥ Laṅk 330.1 (vs). Acc. to note in ed., Tib. points to °rayor bhānuṃ (or, bhāṃ vā) nāśenti; Suzuki's Index, p. 202, s.v. cal, would em. to cālenti.

bālavyañjana, see **vāla°**.

? **bālāgrapūtikā** (cf. BR, pw s.vv. bālāgra, and vālāgrapotikā, AMg. vālaggapoiyā, *an open palace built in a lake,* Ratnach.; Sheth prefers spelling bālaggapoiā, defining first like Ratnach., secondly by valabhī, aṭṭālikā, which fits our word; true form and etym. obscure to me), an upper part of a vihāra, acc. to Tib. sgo khaṅ steṅ gi bsil khaṅ = *cool-room (summer-house) over the entrance-porch*: MSV iii.133.11 sapta-purāḥ (see **pura** 2) °tikāḥ; ib. 12. For other spellings see **vātāgravedikā.**

Bālāha, n. of the horse called **Valāha,** q.v.: Divy 120.4 ff. (story told at length); 524.20.

Bālāhaka = prec.: Av ii.104.2 °ka-sadṛśā aśvā(ḥ); LV 16.11, said of the 'horse-jewel' who belongs to a cakravartin, Bālāhako nāma aśvarājaṃ (so!).

bālikā, see **vāl°**; **Bālikā(chavī),** see **Vāl°**.

Bāṣpa = **Vāṣpa,** q.v.

bāṣpāyati, °te (also written vāṣ°; denom.), *steams, turns into vapor* (intrans.): °yantaḥ (pres. pple.) LV 251.8, 12; °yetsu(ḥ) (mss., vā°, aor.) Mv ii.124.4, 5, 8; vāṣpāyamānaḥ Divy 462.2 (so read for vāpyā°; sa jīrṇakūpo vāṣpāyamānaḥ peyāpūrṇaḥ, *steaming, full of rice gruel*; confirmed by 6, nearly same phrase, and by MSV i.69.14, same passage), 6.

bāhanikā, see **bāhunikā.**

bāhayati, bāheti (commonly written **vāh°**, cf. also **paribāhya,** written °**vāhya**; certainly identical with Pali bāheti, which seems to be a caus.-denom. to bahi = Skt. bahis, rather than caus. to Skt. vah-, cf. Senart, Mv i n. 431), *casts off, expels, puts aside*; ger., puṇyaṃ ca pāpaṃ ca vāhetvā Ud xi.12 = Pali Dhp. 267, bāhetvā; otherwise only ppp. bāhita-(vāh°) in comp. with pāpa, as often in Pali: bāhita-pāpa, of Buddha or his saints (mss. corrupt in some places; vāh° often for bāh°) Mv i.305.22; 306.6; iii.64.12, 13; Mvy 2554; °pāpa-tvāt LV 424.16; °pāpa-karmāṇaṃ LV 353.14; °pāpa-dharma, standard ep. of Buddha, Mv iii.64.14; 325.6; Mvy 420; LV 426.15 (so v.l., Lefm. °pāra-). (Note that bāhitaka, or vāh°, is also written for **bāhiraka,** q.v., as ep. of mārga, but I believe wrongly; °raka must be read.)

bāhā (= Skt. Lex. and, rare and late, lit., Schmidt, Nachträge; Pali and AMg. id.; not 'specific' to Pali, as stated in PTSD) = Skt. bāhu, *arm*: only noted in Mv, i.55.14; 56.8, 9 (in same phrase 55.1 bāhuṃ); 347.9, read with mss. bāhāyāṃ (loc.) bāhāṃ pragṛhya; ii.136.18; 159.9; 192.10; 282.4; iii.313.12; 354.3 ff.; 407.21; 425.15, 16, 22.

[**bāhitaka,** written for **bāhiraka,** q.v.]

bāhira, adj. (= Pali id.), *outside, external,* contrasting with abhyantara, ābhy°: bāhira-vāiśālakā(ḥ) Mv i.263.1, 11, *the people living outside Vaiśālī* (in prec. lines abhyantara-vaiś°); janasya ābhyantarasya bāhirasya Mv ii.160.6; abhyantara-bāhira, cpd., Mv iii.178.5; other cases of the adj., Mv i.264.6 (ye bāhirā); ii.147.17; 189.3; iii.298.1; in special sense with **āyatana,** q.v. (here contrasted with ādhyātmika); adv. °re, *outside,* Mv iii.22.21 (contrasting with abhyantare); abhyantare bāhiri (m.c. for °re) ye (both edd. bāhiriye as one word) vasanti SP 373.5 (vs); as quasi-prep. with abl., bāhire nagarāto ... sthitakena Mv i.310.15, *remaining outside the city*; adv. °reṇa, id., abhyantareṇāpi ca bāhireṇa SP 359.10 (vs); āmreḍita cpd., as quasi-prep. with gen., imasya śakuntayūthasya bāhira-bāhireṇa gacchati Mv ii.254.4, *is moving constantly* (? or *just*) *outside this flock of birds.*

bāhiraka (cf. prec.; = Pali id.), *external,* but in BHS noted only in the special mg. *outside (the Buddhist religion), non-Buddhist, heretical*: brāhmaṇo °rako Mv iii.223.4; with tīrthya, Śikṣ 332.9; in Pali with -pabbajjā and -tittha in this sense; in BHS esp. with mārga, *a non-Buddhist (religious) path,* °keṇa mārgeṇa Mv i.284.1; ii.210.7 (by em.); iii.450.9; and read so in ii.30.11; 48.19; iii.152.11, in which Senart keeps the corruption bāhitakena (or vāh°) mārgeṇa, inconsistently (the phrase is obviously the same and must be read in the same way; Senart, i n. 431 and 587, expresses the belief that the true reading is °taka, but fails to act on it in the first three passages above; Pali bāhiraka helps to prove him wrong). For the general sense cf. bahidhānugatāḥ s.v. **bahidhā.**

bāhirī (cf. **bāhira,** and AMg. bāhiriyā, *quarter* or *group of houses outside a city*), *outbuilding* for animals: hasti-, aśva-bāhirīye (loc. sg.) Mv iii.298.1 and 2 (seen after entering the bāhira-rājakula-dvāra).

bāhujanya, see **bahu°**.

-bāhunikā, or with v.l. and Lefm. -bāhanikā (= bāhu, **bāhā**; cf. **-ūruṇikā** and § 22.45), ifc. cpd. adj., *having ... arms*: valayanirantara-bāhunikāṃ (-bāha°) LV 322.22.

bāhu-balika, adj., see **-balika**. Note Skt. bāhubalin.

bāhulika, adj. (= Pali id. or bāhullika), *luxurious* in manner of life, acc. to Tib. esp. in eating, *gluttonous, gourmandizing*; always with **śaithilika**: (eṣa sa... śramaṇo) Gautama āgacchati sma, śaithiliko bāhulikaḥ LV 407.19; (same situation) Mv ii.241.3 (Senart wrongly em. °kaṃ, mss. °ko); iii.329.4 (here Senart keeps °ko of mss.); śaithilikā bhavanti, bāhulikā bhavanti Śikṣ 64.4.

Bāhuśrutīya, pl., n. of a (Buddhist) school: Mvy 9082.

bāhuśrutya (nt.; also **bahu°**, q.v.; = Pali bāhusacca; once in Skt., Mbh 12.6214, in complimentary sense), *great (excessive) learning*, disparagingly, as something which does not lead to the true goal: SP 218.10; Dbh 79.21 (cited s.v. **udgrahaṇa**); Samādh p. 30 line 24, cited Śikṣ 189.6.

bāhyaka, adj. (Skt. bāhya plus -ka svārthe; cf. **bāhira-ka**, in same mg.), *external*; after ito, *to this* (i. e. Buddhist); *heretical*: ito-bāhyakeṣu tīrthikeṣu Bbh 222.6; ito-°keṣu śramaṇa-brāhmaṇeṣu Bbh 389.7 (both prose); (dhārmikān, i. e. Buddhists) ... no tu bāhyakān MSV iii.123.15.

biḍāla-bhastrā (or **°tra**, or, MIndic, **°ta**, **°tā**; = Pali biḷāra-bhastā), lit. *cat-bag*, acc. to comm. ii.101.29 on Pali MN i.128.21 *catskin-bag* (biḷāracammapasibbako); as in Pali used as symbol of something very soft: so read (mss. somewhat corrupt; Senart °trasta, in ignorance of the Pali parallel) in Mv ii.261.2, °trā- (or °tra, °ta, °tā)-sama-cittatāṃ, and in repetition 262.3, where perhaps some other word (bhoga, *delight, pleasure*?) was inserted after this word in the cpd.

Bindu, n. of a nāga king: Māy 247.21.

Bindusāra, in Divy written **Vindu°**, n. of a Maurya king, son of Candragupta: Mmk 613.6 (text Binduvāra), 12 (text Bimbasāra); 614.2; father of Aśoka, Divy 369.13 ff.

bibhatsa, adj. (m.c. for Skt. bī°), *loathsome*: LV 206.2 (vs).

bibhatsana, see **bī°**.

bimba, nt., a high number: Mvy 7912, cited from Gv; Gv 106.16 (not in the list of Gv 133).

bimbaka (m. or nt.; = Pali id., Skt. bimba; Vv. comm. 168.12, = bimba of Vv. text), in mukha-bi° (text writes vi°), *orb of the face*: Divy 172.10; 174.5; 525.16.

bimbara, m. or nt., also written **viṃvara**, **vimbara** (**viṃb°**), once erroneously vivara in mss., a moderately large number; when defined, either 100 **kaṅkara**, or vice versa, a hundredth of a k° (for the latter's variants see s.v.); regularly = Tib. dkrigs (pa), which is given varying values, see Jä., but seems prevailingly = 100 gtams (= **kaṅkara**, 1000 billion); acc. to Suzuki, Index, on Laṅk 31.6 = Tib. śu rdog: LV 147.22 (all mss. and both edd. vivaraṃ, no v.l., but Tib. dkrigs pa, as for 151.3), cited Mvy 7958 as viṃvaraṃ; LV 151.3 (vs), bimbarāś ca (m. pl.); bimbara, m. or nt., Gv 105.20; 206.17; nt., 132.26; cited from Gv as viṃvaraḥ Mvy 7829; bimbara, nt., Sukh 30.15; m. Mvy 8006; viṃvara, nt., Mvy 7703; m. Laṅk 31.6; ambiguous, m. or nt., vimbara- Mmk 380.7; 383.13 (read vimbara-koṭini); bimbara Śikṣ 157.11; 318.1; 346.16.

Bimbasāra, see **Bimbi°**;**-sūtra**, n. of a work: Waldschmidt, Kl. Skt. Texte 114 ff.; text 121 ff.

bimbahu, a high number: Gv 106.16; = **mirava** (°pha), **mirahu**, qq.v.

bimbi or **bimbī**, app. *gold, gold-color* (see PTSD s.v., with cpd. bimbijāla): so perh. in **Padma-bimby-upaśobhita**, q.v., Sukh 6.8, *adorned with the golden color of lotuses* (?).

Bimbisāra (= Pali id.; mss. sometimes **Bimba°**, Divy 145.24 f.; 146.10; 545.6; Av i.2.7; Waldschmidt, Kl. Skt. Texte 4, 114 n. 1; 121.2 etc.; text Bimbāsāra-suta = Ajātaśatru Mmk 602.23), n. of a king of Magadha in Buddha's time, father of Ajātaśatru: he is oftenest called **Śreṇiya** (or **Śreṇya**, **Śreṇika**) Bi°, see these names, which are always accompanied by Bi° except in Mvy 3652 where Śreṇika occurs alone, Bimbisāra in 3647 (in the same list); but Bimbisāra also occurs often alone, Mv ii.2.9; LV 241.7, 9; 407.8, 10; Divy 253.24; 269.9; 369.8; 392.1; 393.28; 545.6 ff.; Av i.2.7; 107.6 ff.; 290.4 ff.; 307.6 ff.; 319.6 ff.; 326.12 ff.; in the mss. of Mv the name is also written °śāla and °śāra (i.254.15; 256.14, 17; 257.9, etc.); Mmk 602.23 (above).

bimbopadhāna, mss. once **°opahata**, once **°opana**, nt. (related to Pali bimbohana, AMg. bibboaṇa, Ratnach., Pkt. biṃbovaṇaya, bibboa, bibboyaṇa, Sheth, all same mg.; doubtless a loan from a non-Aryan dialect, variously adapted by popular etym.), *pillow, cushion*: Mvy 8988 = Tib. sṅas (*pillow*) naṅ (tshaṅs) can (?); Chin. *thick pillow*; Jap. *pillow*; Divy 40.11 (here text vimbo°); 550.16; 553.9; sumeru parvatarājā °dhānam (v.l. bimbopanam, °mam) abhūṣi (sc. for the Bodhisattva) Mv ii.136.17 and 137.15; ubhayato-°dhāna Mv ii.115.16–17, *having cushions on both sides*, ep. of paryaṅka, *couch, palanquin*; also ep. of paryaṅkāni Mv iii.70.2, where mss. ubhayato-lohita-bimbopahatāni, Senart em. °bimbohanāni (= Pali); in MPS 7.5 °panair, prob. corruption for °padhānair (with Tib.).

biliśa (so once in Skt. for regular baḍiśa, Suparṇ., pw 4.226; and note Pkt. biḍisa, Sheth; Pali only baḷisa, bal°), *fishhook*; some form or cpd. of this word is to be read in Mv iii.259.2, for mss. bilaśa (v.l. billaśa)-tāni-kāyetsuḥ, and 260.16 (vs), same reading, except that both mss. read billa° here; evidently a verb is concealed in the end; Senart reads pāṭensuḥ, and before it bila-śatāni, which is impossible. It is possible that bilaśa-(with one ms.) is the true reading, tho it is not recorded anywhere. The phrase follows, both times, that containing **kahāpaṇa-māṃsikaṃ** (or **kārṣāpaṇa°**), q.v., while in Pali lists of tortures kahāpaṇakaṃ regularly follows balisa-maṃsikaṃ. It is certain that we must understand some torture by means of *fishhooks*; should we read biliśa-tāṃ, *fishhook-condition*, i. e. being torn with fishhooks? The preceding words are much like those quoted as occurring before **kahāpaṇa-māṃsikaṃ**.

bībhatsaka, adj. (= Skt. °tsa; -ka may be m.c.), *loathsome*: SP 94.13 (vs).

bībhatsana (to Skt. bībhatsate plus -ana), *loathsome treatment* or *behavior*: ākrośa-tāḍana-bibhatsana-(short i, m.c.)-tarjanāś ca Gv 213.26 (vs).

bukkati (Skt. Gr. id.; Pkt., Hem. 4.98 = garj; cf. next), *barks* (of a dog): Karmav 22.7; 26.1.

buk-kāra (m.; cf. prec.; Skt. Lex. and Pkt. Lex. *roar*, in Skt. of a lion, but here perh. read cukkara, q.v. in Schmidt, Nachträge), *barking noise* (of a dog): Karmav 22.9.

Buddha, *an 'Enlightened One'*, passim; Mvy 1 (and regularly) = Tib. saṅs rgyas; 35 Buddhas before whom serious offenses are to be confessed by Bodhisattvas, Śikṣ 169.4, see note. Many long lists of B's in most of the texts here included; in general, each name in such lists has been entered in my Dict. But one such list, Mmk 7.24-8.18, has been ignored; the text is very corrupt and obscure; division of the words is often uncertain; few of the names are known elsewhere, Five Buddhas called 'transcendent' by P. Mus, Barabudur, p. 577 ff. (*L'origine des Cinq Jina*; a full discussion here), Dharmas 3 et alibi, see the names **Vairocana**, **Akṣobhya**, **Ratnasaṃbhava**, **Amitābha**, **Amoghasiddhi**.

-buddhaka = **Buddha**, ifc. Bhvr.: sabuddhaka-kalpābuddhaka-kalpa- Dbh 87.20 (prose).

Buddhakapāla, n. of a deity: Sādh 500.10; 503.9, 11.

Buddhakāyavarṇapariniṣpattyabhinirhārā, n. of a Bodhisattva dhāraṇī: Mvy 758.

buddha-kṣetra, nt. (= Pali, late, °khetta), *Buddha-field, region or* (usually) *world* or *world-system* in which a particular Buddha lives and operates; see Teresina Rowell, 'The background and early use of the Buddhakṣetra concept,' The Eastern Buddhist 6.199–430 and 7.131–176, where the term is ably discussed; a few out of many occurrences are here recorded: descriptions of a b°, SP 65.9 ff.; 144.9 ff.; its 'jewels' are Bodhisattvas SP 66.3; in Mv ii.301.16 Bodhisattvas in numberless b° take the form of gods and come to Śākyamuni as he is about to become enlightened; misc., Mvy 3065; Mv ii.319.11; 349.17; iii.139.3; 342.1; in Mv i.123.4 ff. enumeration of some 'present' Buddha-fields and their Buddhas; buddha-kṣetraṃ viśodhenti bodhisattvā(ḥ) Mv i.283.3; atuliya (so mss.) aprameyaṃ °traṃ aparimitaṃ bharitvā (*having filled*) sameti (= śamayati) khila-doṣa-mohaṃ (so read, see s.v. **khila**) Mv ii.295.9; on *'emptying'* of buddha-fields, see s.v. **riñcati**; in Mv i.121.14 ff. the question is asked whether Buddhas are produced in all Buddha-fields, and the answer, 122.2–3, is negative; in many there is no Buddha; Śikṣ 147.15 speaks of going to a buddhaśūnya-buddhakṣetram as an evil fate; so in SP 68.2 (vs; cf. 66.3 ff., prose, same subject) buddhakṣetra is clearly equated with **lokadhātu,** meaning merely *world-system*, presumably as *potential field for a Buddha*, but not necessarily containing one; on this see Rowell, op. cit., 415. See also **upakṣetra.**

Buddhagaganaprabhāsacūḍa, n. of a Tathāgata: Gv 422.11.

Buddhaḍākinī, n. of a yoginī: Sādh 461.10 etc.

buddhati = Skt. and BHS budhyate; see § 28.19 and Chap. 43, s.v. budh.

Buddhadrumarāja, n. of a Buddha: Gv 257.10.

Buddhapālita, n. of a teacher: Mvy 3494.

Buddhaprabhāmaṇḍalaśrīpradīpā, n. of a lokadhātu: Gv 420.2.

Buddhabhūmi, n. of a work: Mvy 1354.

Buddhamati, n. of a buddhakṣetra: Gv 257.7.

buddha-yāna, nt. (also **bodhisattva-y°**), = **mahāyāna,** *the* (great) *Buddha-vehicle*: SP 41.15 etc. (see KN, Index). Also **bauddha**(ṃ . . . yānaṃ), q.v.

Buddharakṣita, n. of a householder: Divy 330.3 ff.

Buddhalocanā, n. of a Buddhist goddess: Mvy 4278 (= **Rocanī, Locanā**).

Buddhavajrasaṃdhāraṇasaṃdhi, n. of a Bodhisattva: Mvy 735.

Buddhavicīrṇā (v.l. °vistīrṇā), n. of a pool near Benares: Mv iii.329.16. In the LV version of the story, 410.2, we find bahuvicitra-puṣkariṇyāṃ; there is no evidence that the first member of the cpd. is meant as a n. pr.

Buddhaśrīgarbha, n. of a Bodhisattva: Dbh 2.21.

Buddhasaṃgīti, f., n. of a work: Mvy 1360.

buddhānusmṛti, quoted Mv i.163.11 (prose) as name of a dharmaparyāya, *'recollection of Buddha(s)'*.

Buddhālaṃkāravyūha, m., n. of a samādhi: LV 3.10 (confirmed Tib.).

Buddhālaṃkārādhiṣṭhitā, n. of a Bodhisattva dhāraṇī: Mvy 756.

Buddhāvataṃsaka, nt., n. of a work: Mvy 1329. Also in mg. a *collection* or *large number of Buddhas*, see **avataṃsaka.**

Buddhika, n. of a nāga-king: Mvy 3289; Māy 247.32. (Also -buddhika, ifc. Bhvr., = buddhi, *intelligence*; so in Skt. n. pr. Sthira-bu°, and in Pali; in BHS, e. g. tikṣṇa-bu° Mv i.232.2; alpa-bu° and others, AsP 249.17.)

-buddhivant, see **subuddhivant.**

buddhyāyate, pple. °yamāna, prob. denom. to buddhi, *being mentally alert* (hardly *thinking him a Buddha*, Note p. 711): Divy 574.8 te buddhyāyamānāḥ parivāryāvasthitāḥ.

budbudaka (= Pali bubbuḷaka, Skt. budbuda), *bubble*: Laṅk 92.12, 14 (prose) jala-, udaka-bud°.

budbudākṣa, adj., Mvy 8838, lit. *bubble-eyed*; Tib. mig chu bur lta bu, *eyes like bubbles*, which acc. to Das means *round eyes* (s.v. mig).

budhyana (nt.; spelled buddhy°; n. act. to budhyate plus -ana; cf. Pali bujjhana), *the becoming enlightened*: no śaktā siya budhyanāya LV 271.4 (vs), dat., quasi-inf.; °na-nayān Gv 340.14 (vs).

budhyāpaka (spelled buddhyā°), *causing to become enlightened*; to *budhyāpayati (Pali bujjhāpeti), MIndic caus. to budhyate; acc. to Kern, SP Preface viii, in Kashgar rec. for Nep. pratibodhaka. This and the next are known to me only from Kern's Preface; I have searched for them in vain in the notes to the KN ed.

budhyāpana (spelled buddhyā°), *the* (act of) *causing to become enlightened*; see under prec.; like it, this is said by Kern, loc. cit., to be used in Kashgar rec. for pratibodhana of Nep.

bubhukṣitaka, adj. (= Skt. °ta plus -ka, perh. pitying dim.), *hungry* (*poor fellow*!?): mā me putro °takaḥ sthāsyati Divy 88.7.

Bulaka, pl., n. of a tribe (in Pali pl. Bulayo): see **Calakalpaka.**

buli (Skt. Lex., said to be f., *vulva*, acc. to Galanos also *buttocks, behind*), in Mvy 4008 buliḥ, defined by Tib. rkub, acc. to Das *buttocks, behind*; acc. to Jä. the same (Skt. pāyu), but also *vulva*.

? **busaplāvī,** acc. sg. °vīm, something disagreeable (hard, or foul, offensive) to eat; parallel with ayoguḍa, svamāṃsa, pūyaśoṇita: Divy 12.25; 13.17; all things which niggards wished a mendicant should eat, and which later they were therefore obliged to eat themselves. The Index renders *beetle* (?); I do not know why. The first member seems to be Skt. busa, *chaff, refuse, rubbish*; perh. the ed. of Divy understood the latter part as *leaping* (*in chaff* of grain; even this need not lead to the mg. *beetle*). Same passage MSV iv.176.7; 177.11; Tib. cited as phub ma, *chaff* (= busa), for the entire word.

bṛṃhayitar, vṛ° (= Pali brūhetā, see below), *one who magnifies, exalts*, in the sense of *devotes himself to, frequents* (solitude, solitary places): vṛṃhayitā śūnyāgārāṇām (see **śūnyāgāra**) Mvy 2437 = Pali brūhetā suññāgārānaṃ MN i.33.11; comm. i.157.13 ff. . . . rattiṃdivaṃ suññāgāraṃ pavisitvā nisīdamāno bhikkhu brū° suññā° ti veditabbo. (From the same Skt. bṛṃhayati the ppp. Skt. bṛṃhita is also used in BHS. In Mv iii.351.17 (vs) I understand manorathāśā balabṛṃhitā me, *my desires and hopes were mightily swollen, augmented*; otherwise Senart.)

bṛṅga, var. for **pṛṅga,** q.v.

bṛsikā (**bṛṣ°**), see **vṛṣikā.**

(**bṛhatikā,** *cloak, outer-garment*: MSV ii.47.18 °kāprāvaraṇam; in BR, pw only cited Gr., but see Schmidt, Nachtr.)

bṛhatphala, m. pl. (written vṛh° only Mv ii.349.1 and Mvy 3100; but = Pali vehapphala, which, if it really represents historically the BHS equivalent, that is if the latter is not a rationalizing hyper-Sktism, would seem to be a MIndic 'vṛddhi' form based on *vihap°; cf. **avṛha** or **abṛha(t)** = Pali aviha; if not this, the origin of the Pali is obscure), *having great fruition*, one (the 3d, but in Mv and Pali 1st) of the classes of rūpāvacara gods in the 4th dhyānabhūmi; with or sc. **deva,** q.v.: LV 150.9; 396.16; Mv ii.314.8; 319.6; 349.1; 360.21; Mvy 3100; Dharmas 128; Divy 68.16; 138.23; 367.13; Bbh 62.5 (misprinted bhṛh°); Gv 249.11; Av i.5.3, etc.

Bṛhat-sāgaranāgarāja-paripṛcchā, n. of a work, see **Sāgara°.**

Bṛhadratha, n. of a yakṣa: Māy 22.

Bṛhaspati, (1) n. of a king, descendant of Aśoka: Divy 433.23 (written Vṛh°); **(2)** n. of a yakṣa: Māy 10.

Bṛhaspatigupta, n. of a former Buddha: Mv i.138.6.

1 **bodha,** m. (? = bodhi, normally f. in BHS as in Pali; but Pali records also bodha, m., and Skt. bodha is used not very differently), **(1)** = **bodhi,** *enlightenment,* in the technical Buddhist sense; so far as noted, seems limited in BHS to the forms bodhāya and (rarely, prob. only in Mv) bodhāye, which are usually interpretable as datives: bodhāye Mv i.47.16; 60.11 (so mss. indicate); ii.130.18 (in prec. line bodhāya, but v.l. °ye, in same phrase); Senart, whose note i.369 on i.3.2 discusses both the forms, calls bodhāye fem., but such datives are recorded from indisputably m.-nt. stems, § 8.45; more tempting to the fem. interpretation is the occasional, tho rare, occurrence of bodhāya (in vss) where dat. syntax seems hard to accept; so gen., te sarvi bodhāya (mss.) abhūṣi lābhinaḥ SP 49.14 (vs), repeated often in the sequel, as 50.2 etc.; in 50.12 and 51.4 bodhāya is confirmed by citations Śikṣ 92.13; 93.5; bodhāya . . . varṇam SP 10.6 (vs) = 12.16; loc., bodhāya sthāpitāḥ SP 306.3 (vs); it is possible that the fem. gender of bodhi (in Pali and BHS) has led to some forms suggesting a stem bodhā (oblique °āya, °āye), but bodhāya is usually dat., and occurs often in prose; KN ed. of SP often keeps it but as often emends to bodhīya, with utter inconsistency; dat. occurrences of bodhāya, SP (in mss.) 14.2; 33.1; 46.10; 47.13; 303.12; 334.11; LV 209.9 (prose); 284.8; Mv i.46.1; 63.2, 11; 97.2; 234.5; ii.130.13, 17; Suv 42.6; Śikṣ 5.18; KP 20.9; Gv 105.15 (prose); Bbh 13.19 (prose), etc.; **(2)** n. of a householder: Divy 167.2 ff.; he lived in Śiśumāragiri; cf. Pali Bodhi (DPPN), a prince whose capital was Suṃsumāragiri; but the two stories seem quite unrelated otherwise.

[2 **bodha,** m. (or nt.), read prob. **godha,** q.v.: KP 111.6. Cf. however Pali palibodha, which is interpreted, with support in Aśokan id., as meaning *fetters,* by Lüders SBAW 1914.841. Cf. also Thomas, JRAS 1915.103 ff.]

bodhi (in mgs. 1–3 = Pali id.), **(1)** (in this sense regularly f., as in Pali, when modifiers determine gender; hardly used at all in Skt. except Jain Skt., rarely Skt. as m., BR 5.1650) *enlightenment,* the quality attained by a Buddha: clearly f. SP 63.8; 70.8; 140.4; 323.8; 335.9 (all vss); so regularly in LV, e. g. 365.1 (vs), Mv, e. g. i.170.9, and most texts; so also **(samyak-)saṃbodhi,** qq.v.; gender undetermined, Vaj 34.3, 19; possibly m. SP 64.7 (vs; imu buddhabodhim, acc. sg.); LV 243.7 (vs; anuprāptu . . . bodhis, n. sg.), but possibly the forms in -u are to be understood as f. (§§ 9.13, 23); **(2)** (in this sense said to be m. in Pali, see Childers; most BHS passages do not reveal the gender) = **bodhi-druma, °yaṣṭi, °vaṭa,** *the tree of enlightenment,* under which the Bodhisattva became enlightened: clearly f. at least once, bodhīya mūle Mv i.3.1; gender undetermined, Mv i.249.2; 252.1; Divy 397.21, 24; 403.3, 7; bodhi-mūla, *the root* (foot) *of the bodhi-tree,* Mv i.158.1; ii.302.18; iii.272.18; **(3)** n. of a wandering mendicant, previous birth of the Bodhisattva (= **Mahābodhi**; in the corresp. Pali story both forms occur, but Bodhi is commoner): Jm 143.18; **(4)** name said to be given to the 'elephant jewel' of a cakravartin: LV 16.1 (prose); not noted elsewhere.

-bodhika, see **abodhika.**

Bodhiketu, n. of a Bodhisattva: Gv 3.19.

bodhicitta, nt., *thought of enlightenment,* the mental attitude which aspires to Buddhahood or Bodhisattvahood; Mvy 2351; LV 8.18; 34.17; and passim; esp. Gv 494.1, where begins a passage glorifying it, cited with abbreviations Śikṣ 5.20 ff.

Bodhicittāsampramoṣa, m. (cf. **asampramoṣa**), n. of a samādhi: Śikṣ 65.11; the word occurs as an adj., in a list of virtues (guṇa), Mvy 2351.

bodhi-druma = **bodhi** (2), also **bodhi-yaṣṭi,** *the tree of enlightenment:* LV 272.6; 275.19; 276.1; 282.4; etc.

bodhipakṣa, m., subst. and adj. (rare, and possibly only a phonetic variant for the commoner °pakṣya, q.v.), *assistant, aid, to enlightenment,* of which there are 37 (see **°pakṣya, °pakṣika, °pākṣika**): seemingly subst., Sūtrāl. xviii (entire chapter entitled °pakṣādhikāra); saptatriṃśad-°kṣa-bhāvanātaḥ xx–xxi.16, comm.; °kṣā bhavet kutaḥ Laṅk 25.12; as adj. with dharma, saptatriṃśad °kṣān dharmān Divy 350.14; saptatriṃśad-°kṣa-dharma- LV 9.5; °kṣa-dharma- LV 8.6; 181.18; 182.11.

Bodhipakṣanirdeśa, m., n. of a work: Mvy 1382.

bodhipakṣika, adj., = next and **°pākṣika,** q.v.: saptatriṃśatsu °keṣu dharmeṣu SP 458.1; °ka-dharma-saṃpannāḥ Mv ii.290.6; (dharmāṇāṃ) °kānāṃ (so, dental n, text) Bbh 227.10.

bodhipakṣya, adj. (cf. **°pakṣa,** also **°pakṣika, °pākṣika,** which see for list; = Pali °pakkhiya and °pakkhika), *assistant, aid, helpful, to enlightenment;* usually with dharma; there are 37 such (the same 37 dhammā in Pali), saptatriṃśad °kṣyā dharmāḥ Dbh 57.17; Av i.340.2; KP 45.3 (text saptātriṃśad bodha-p°); Bbh 259.7 (loc.); without the number, but with dharma, as separate adj. Bbh 236.17, or in comp. °kṣya-dharma- Gv 495.23; Dbh 42.6; also °kṣya-kuśalamūleṣu dharmeṣu Śikṣ 12.17; and, instead of dharma, with mārga, °kṣya-mārga- Śikṣ 52.2; °kṣyāṇāṃ mārgāṅgānāṃ Dbh 42.9, referring app. to the °kṣya-dharma- of 42.6, above.

bodhipaṭa-pattrakā, adj. or subst., applied to a kind of sandal: MSV iv.206.12. (Read **bodhi-vaṭa-**?)

bodhi-paricārika, adj. (cf. **bodhi** 2, and rare Skt. paricārika, commoner in Pali), with devaputra, (deity) *attending on the tree of enlightenment:* LV 333.19; 335.9.

bodhipākṣika, adj. (= Pali °pakkhika; cf. **°pakṣika, °pakṣya, °pakṣa**) = **bodhipakṣya,** q.v.; usually with dharma, *the* (37) *conditions favorable to enlightenment* (same 37 in Pali): listed as 4 **smṛtyupasthāna,** 4 **samyakprahāṇa,** 4 **ṛddhipāda,** 5 **indriya** (q.v., 1), 5 **bala,** 7 **bodhyaṅga,** and the 8-fold noble path (mārga), Dharmas 43; list, without the name, Divy 208.7–9; °ka-dharma- Dbh 53.22; Laṅk 213.7; also AbhidhK. LaV-P. vi.290 (otherwise Index to this text shows only form °pakṣya, vi.282); in LV 424.12 read, with v.l., sarva-bodhipākṣika-(text °kā)-dharma-ratna-pratipūrṇatvāt; not with dharma, but °ka-mahāpuruṣa-lakṣaṇeṣu Śikṣ 283.11.

bodhi-maṇḍa, nt. (= Pali id.), *platform* or *terrace* or *seat of enlightenment,* name given to the spot under the bodhi-tree on which the Buddha sat when he became enlightened; Tib. (on Mvy and elsewhere) byaṅ chub (kyi) sñiṅ po, *essence* (lit. *heart;* = **maṇḍa,** q.v.) *of enlightenment;* Chin. acc. to Burnouf, Introd. 387 n. 2, *platform of the bodhi-tree;* very common: Mvy 4114; SP 16.3; 54.13; 316.3; etc., see Index to KN; LV 36.2 (here BR follows Calc. in reading °maṇḍala, but Lefm. with all mss. °maṇḍa, the only true form; others, see Index to Lefm.); 273.7 ff.; Divy 392.17 etc.; Suv 89.15 etc.; Bbh 94.5; 405.11. For equivalent expressions see s.v. **maṇḍa.**

Bodhimaṇḍacūḍa, n. of a Bodhisattva: Gv 3.10.

Bodhimaṇḍamakuṭa, n. of a Bodhisattva: Gv 3.5.

[**bodhimaṇḍala,** error for **bodhimaṇḍa,** q.v.]

Bodhimaṇḍavibuddhaśrīcandra, n. of a Tathāgata: Gv 310.7.

Bodhimaṇḍālaṃkāravyūha, m., n. of a samādhi: Dbh 82.12.

Bodhimaṇḍālaṃkārasurucirā, n. of a lokadhātu: ŚsP 42.10.

Bodhimūla-sūtra, n. of a work: Karmav 160.8 (see Lévi's note).

bodhi-yaṣṭi, f. (oblique °ṭīye, °ṭiye; unrecorded except here), = **bodhi-druma:** Mv ii.131.13 f.; 264.4 f.; 268.2: 282.1; 404.20.

bodhi-vaṭa, = prec., see **vaṭa**.

bodhisattva (= Pali °satta), *person destined for enlightenment, Buddha-to-be*, passim; Mvy 625, followed by list of standard epithets of such persons incl. **jinaputra**; other epithets meaning *son of Buddha* are frequent; there are many lists of names, such as the 92 beginning Mvy 645; each name in such lists as occur in works here included is, generally speaking, recorded in this Dict., but e. g. the list Mmk 8.21 ff. is omitted because it is very corrupt and obscure, even the word-division being often doubtful; eight special B's listed Dharmas 12, **Maitreya, Gaganagañja, Samantabhadra, Vajrapāṇi, Mañjuśrī, Sarvanivaraṇaviṣkambhin, Kṣitigarbha, Khagarbha**, qq.v.; in SP 64.12–13 (sa tvaṃ) Śāriputra bodhisattva-sammantritena °ttva-rahasyeneha mama pravacana upapannaḥ, sa tvaṃ . . . bodhisattvādhiṣṭhānena . . ., refers to Śāriputra's own **sammantrita** (q.v.) etc. as a Bodhisattva, not (with Burnouf and Kern) to the Buddha's (they use the word Bodhisattva in translating, but understand it as referring to the Buddha, which is contrary to usage).

bodhisattvakṣāntilābhāya dhāraṇī, see **dhāraṇī**.

bodhisattva-janman, *birth of a Bodhisattva*; ten such: daśemāni . . . janmāni yaiḥ samanvāgatā bo°tvā jātā bhavanti Gv 366.5; described in detail 366.14 ff., sarvabuddhopasthānapraṇidhiprayogagarbhaṃ nāma prathamaṃ bodhisattvajanma, etc.; all the names are cpds. ending in -garbhaṃ.

Bodhisattva-piṭaka, nt., n. of a work: Mvy 1330: Śikṣ 190.12; 311.13; **°ka-mātṛkā**, given as alternative name for Bbh, Bbh 409.14; either this, or Bodhisattvasūtra-piṭaka-mātṛkā, mentioned also Bbh 156.8; 157.3–4; 180.16; 332.22–23. See **mātṛkā** (2).

Bodhisattva-prātimokṣa, n. of a work: Śikṣ 11.11 etc., common; in 36.15 printed °pratimokṣa, but °prāti° in Transl. A work called by this name (°kṣa-sūtra) was published by Nalinaksha Dutt in IHQ 7 (1931).259–286; but as the editor states, 260, it 'has very little to do with the B.Pr.S. cited in the works of Śāntideva'.

Bodhisattva-bhūmi. n. of a work: Bbh, colophons, regularly, 11.20 etc.; in text (not colophon) 409.14 f. alternative forms of the title are given as **Bodhisattvapiṭaka-mātṛkā** and **Mahāyāna-saṃgraha**, qq.v. See s.v. **bhūmi** for the mg. of the term.

bodhisattva-yāna, often = **mahāyāna**, *the* (great) *'vehicle' of the Bodhisattvas*: SP 79.6; 416.14, etc.; **°yānika**, adj., *adhering to this °yāna*: SP 183.8 (bhikṣavaḥ . . °nikāḥ); **°yānīya**, adj., id.: SP 224.4; 285.8 (v.l. °yānika); RP 34.1.

bodhisattva-vimokṣa, see **vimokṣa**.

bodhisattva-samādhi, Mvy 736; a list of nine, named ib. 737-745. It means, evidently, *samādhi practised by bodhisattvas*.

Bodhisattvasamuccayā, n. of a goddess: Suv 1.7; 45.2; 167.8; 172.10; 199.5; 247.1; regularly called kuladevatā; acc. to Chin. the deity of the bodhi-tree (Nobel, 247, note 2)

Bodhisattva-sūtra-piṭaka, Bbh 156.8; see **Bodhisattva-piṭaka**.

bodhyaṅga, m. and (oftener) nt., also **saṃbodhyaṅga** (= Pali bojjhaṅga, sambo°, acc. to Childers m.; CPD gives aṅga as nt.), *member of enlightenment*: there are seven (same list in Pali), viz smṛti, dharmapravicaya, vīrya, prīti, praśrabdhi (prasra°), samādhi, upekṣā; listed Mvy 988 (bodhy°) to 995 (each item called saṃbodhy°); just so Dharmas 49; sambo° LV 34.3 ff.; Dbh 39.6 ff.; referred to without number (bodhyaṅga) SP 80.1; as seven, but not listed, bodhyaṅgāni Divy 208.9; KP 95.10; bodhyaṅgān Mv ii.357.16; °ga- Divy 95.20; 265.3; Av i.16.13.

Bodhyaṅgavatī, n. of a samādhi: Mvy 586; ŚsP 1422.9.

Bodhyaṅgāyuṣya (? printed °puṣya), n. of a large group of future Buddhas (predicted): ŚsP 323.1.

bodhyaṅgika (sarva-b°), adj., *of the bodhyaṅgas*: sarva-°kā dharmāḥ Dbh 57.18 (prose).

bollaka, adj., subst. (to Pkt. bollai, *talks*), in bahu-b°, *very loquacious, great talker*: Divy 338.13 (°kāḥ śramaṇāḥ, so read for śrā°, Śākyaputrīyā bhavanti), 19.

bauddha, adj., *of (a) Buddha*: °dhaṃ . . . yānaṃ SP 91.12 (vs), cf. **buddha-yāna** (= **mahāyāna**); °dhasmi (so with WT and their ms. K'; KN baudhasmi) jñānasmi SP 323.9 (vs); °dhā vikurvitaviyūha vidarśayanti Gv 373.3 (vs); °dha-vaineyaka, *to be trained by Buddha*, °kā sattvā Mv i.51.4 (prose; = buddha-vaineya, see s.v. **vaineya**).

brahmakāya, *the company of Brahman*, i. e. gods who attend B.: Mv i.229.16 = 240.5 (prose) yāva(d) brahmakāyaṃ, *as far as* . . . (the sound arose). Cf. next.

brahmakāyika (see prec.), adj. or subst. (= Pali id., but not used in the same technical sense), usually with **deva**, q.v., one (usually the first) of the classes of rūpāvacara gods of the first dhyāna-bhūmi: SP 4.10; 159.10; LV 39.13 (here an individual one named Ugratejas, who is present in the Tuṣita heaven); 47.1; 150.4; 266.7; 359.16 and 360.7 (in these two Subrahma(-devaputra) is their leader); 394.3 (here Mahābrahmā is their leader); 396.15; 401.11; Mvy 2290 (here as example of the 2d **sattvāvāsa**, q.v.); 3085; Dharmas 128; Mv i.33.3; 40.16; 212.16; 263.21; ii.16.4; 163.15; 314.6; 348.18; 360.11; Divy 68.14; 367.11; Av i.5.2, etc.; brahmakāyikā devanikāyā (abl.) Mv i.333.7, *the divine dwelling-place of the br°*.

Brahmakīrti, n. of a former Buddha: Mv i.136.14.

Brahmakuśa, n. of a brother of Kuśa: Mv ii.433.16.

Brahmaketu, (1) n. of a Bodhisattva: Gv 3.19; (2) n. of a former Buddha: Sukh 6.16.

Brahmagupta, n. of a former Buddha: Mv i.137.4.

Brahmaghoṣa, (1) n. of a Bodhisattva: Gv 3.21; (2) n. of two former Buddhas: Sukh 5.14; 6.10 (in same list!); (3) n. of a Buddha in the zenith: Sukh 98.14.

brahmacariya (= Pali id., Skt. °carya), *chastity*: Mv i.202.5 (vs, but °carya is metr. equally good and occurs in same vs ii.6.2).

Brahmajyotirvikrīḍitābhijña, n. of a Tathāgata: Śikṣ 169.12.

Brahmatejas, n. of a former Buddha: LV 5.12.

Brahmadaṇḍa, n. of a mountain: Māy 254.4.

Brahmadatta (= Pali id. in mg. 1), (1) n. of various kings of Benares city and the land of Kāśī, Kāśi (cf. Mv i.271.19 et alibi, nagare Vārāṇasī Kāśijanapade); in many Pali Jātakas formulaic at the beginning of the story, and playing no part in the story itself; DPPN suggests that this was the 'dynastic name' of kings of Benares; somewhat similarly Mv ii.77.5; Divy 73.25; 98.13; 121.7; 538.14 ff.; 540.1; but elsewhere plays a more real rôle in various stories, Mv i.271.19 ff. (in Triśakunīya Jātaka); 359.20 (in Nyagrodhamṛga Jāt.; unnamed in the Pali version); iii.125.10 (in āka Jāt. = Pali Supatta Jāt., where the king has the same name); iii.183.19 ff. (in Upāli-Gaṅgapāla-Jāt.; in the Pali version named Udaya, but addressed as Brahmadatta Jāt. iii.452. 16, 25); Divy 131.15; 132.6; 134.16 f.; 510.19 ff.; Jm 128.25 ff. (called Bahuputtaka in corresp. Pali story); Av i.120.3; 134.11; 174.14, etc.; MSV ii.182.7, 10 (in story of Dīrghila; as in Pali); (2) n. of two kings of Kāmpilla or Kamp°: Mv iii.156.13 ff. (in Padmāvatī Parikalpa); 361.16 ff. (father of Śarabhaṅga); (3) n. of two former Buddhas: Mv iii.239.4 f.; Śikṣ 169.10; (4) n. of a king, previous incarnation of Śākyamuni, perhaps one of those mentioned under 1: LV 170.16; (5) n. of some evil person who mistreated a former incarnation of Śākyamuni: LV 316.1; (6) n. of an unidentified king (perhaps belongs to 1): Mvy 3645; (7) n. of a bhikṣu under Siṃhadhvaja Buddha: Samādh p. 52 l. 20; he later became Dīpaṃkara id. l. 29.

Brahmadattā, n. of a girl attendant on Subhadrā (1): Gv 52.2.

Brahmadeva, n. of a Bodhisattva: Gv 443.8.

Brahmadhvaṃsadeva, n. of a former Buddha: Mv i.139.9.

Brahmadhvaja, n. of a Buddha in a southwestern lokadhātu: SP 184.12.

Brahman, (**1**) n. of two former Buddhas: Av i.69.5 ff.: Śikṣ 169.10; (**2**) n. of a nāga king: Māy 246.14.

Brahmaparipṛcchā, n. of a work: Śikṣ 125.8.

brahma-pāriṣadya, **-pārṣadya**, once **-pārṣada**, m. pl. (= Pali °pārisajja), usually with **deva**, q.v., one (usually the 2d or 3d) of the classes of the rūpāvacara gods of the first dhyānabhūmi: °pāriṣadya Mv ii.348.19; Mvy 3086; °pārṣadya LV 150.5; Mv ii.360.14; Dharmas 128; Divy 568.26; °pārṣada Gv 249.15 (prose).

? **brahmapālikā**, loc. °kāyāṃ, app. some locality (for performing a magic rite): Mmk 54.5 (prose); perhaps corrupt.

brahmapurohita, m. pl. (= Pali id.), usually with **deva**, q.v., one (usually the 3d, or 2d) of the classes of rūpāvacara gods of the first **dhyāna-bhūmi**: LV 150.5; 283.13 (brahmā brahmapurohitāś ca); Mv ii.314.7; 348.18; 360.12; Mvy 3087; Dharmas 128; Divy 68.14; 367.11; 568.26; Gv 249.15; Av i.5.2 etc.

Brahmaprabha, (**1**) n. of a brahman's son, previous incarnation of Śākyamuni: Divy 476.26 ff.; (**2**) n. of a kalpa: Gv 256.23; (**3**) n. of a Buddha: Gv 285.5.

Brahmamati, n. of a son of Māra, unfavorable to the Bodhisattva: LV 313.18.

Brahmavatī, n. of a city: Māy 31. See also **Brahmāvatī** (1).

brahma-vali(-lipi), LV 125.21, or **brahma-vāṇī** (vv.ll. °cārī, °rārī), sc. lipi, Mv i.135.5, n. of a kind of script. Instead of this word, Tib. transl. of LV has two other terms, ya ba na (= yavana-; note that the preceding word in Mv is **yonānī**, q.v.), and bag le pa, which I cannot interpret. Lefm. reports no v.l. in his mss. (Calc. °valli-).

Brahmaviśeṣacintiparipṛcchā, n. of a work: Mvy 1367; Mironov prefixes the honorific Ārya-, and reads citta (v.l. cinti) for cinti.

brahma-vihāra, m. (= Pali id.; cf. **vihāra**), *brahmic (supreme, highest religious) state*; four such: Dharmas 16 maitrī, karuṇā, muditā, upekṣā (as in Pali); °rāś catvāraḥ SP 142.11; catvāri °rān bhāvayitvā Divy 224.28 (prose); °ram (sg.) ācare Mv iii.105.17; same expressed by brāhmo (adj.) vihāraḥ Bbh 90.13 = catvāry apramāṇāni, see **apramāṇa** (in Pali also called appamaññā, fem., see CPD); brāhmya (as separate adj.) vihāra Sūtrāl. vii.3; xvii.17 comm. See AbhidhK. LaV-P. viii.196.

Brahmaśuddha, n. of a former Buddha: Gv 104.19.

Brahmasabha, n. of a pool: Divy 442.28, 443.12, MSV i.134.8.

Brahmasama, pl., n. of a brahmanical school (of the Chandogas): Divy 632.23, 25.

brahma-sthala (m. or nt.), *holy ground* (?): catvare brahmasthale vā ālikhitavyam (in a magic rite for a man or a woman desirous of glory, yaśas) Mmk 54.1. The precise mg. is quite obscure.

Brahmaspasa (! °spṛśa?), n. of a former Buddha: Samādh p. 57 line 25 f.

Brahmasvara, n. of a former Buddha: Mv iii.231.11 f. (v.l. once °śvara; cf. **Brahmeśvara**?).

Brahmasvaranādābhinandita, n. of a former Buddha: Sukh 6.4.

Brahmānana, n. of two former Buddhas: Samādh p. 57 line 11 and line 23 (in the same list!).

Brahmāyu(s), (**1**) °yu, n. of the purohita of Brahmadatta king of Benares, in the Dharmapālasya Jātaka (previous incarnation of the Buddha, and father of **Dharmapāla** 1): Mv ii.77.9 ff.; (**2**) n. of the purohita of King Śaṅkha: Divy 60.23 ff. (showing stem in °yus, as °yuṣe 61.6); (**3**) °yu (= Pali id.), n. of a brahman who became a disciple of the Buddha: Karmav 157.5 (°yu- in cpd.).

Brahmālaya, n. of a mountain: Māy 253.30.

Brahmāvatī, (**1**) (= Pali Brahmavatī) n. of the mother of Maitreya: Divy 60.24 (so mss., ed. em. Brahma°); (**2**) n. of a pond near Benares: Divy 514.11; (**3**) n. of the gotra of the nakṣatra Abhijit: Divy 640.24 (°tī-gotreṇa).

Brahmendracūḍa, n. of a Bodhisattva: Gv 3.9.

Brahmendrarāja, n. of a Bodhisattva: Gv 4.6.

Brahmeśvara, n. of two former Buddhas: Samādh p. 57 lines 7, 8, 9 (cf. **Brahmasvara**).

Brahmottama, (**1**) n. of a former Buddha: Mv iii.235.17; (**2**) n. of a Buddhist monk: Gv 47.10.

Brahmottara, (**1**) n. of a purohita among the gods: LV 44.11; (**2**) (nt.) n. of a mythical city: Divy 602.4; in Av i.202.2 and 203.2 called a 'palace', prāsāda.

brāhmaṇa, (**1**) m., seemingly = (the god) Brahma: pl., Mv i.103.1, see s.v. **pratyeka**; (**2**) nt. (once in Pali, acc. to text °ṇam, Therag. 631, for usual brahmañña = Skt. brāhmaṇya), *brahmanhood, brahmanic condition*: (na) śrāmaṇāya na brāhmaṇāya (no v.l.) na nirvāṇāya saṃvartate LV 245.13 (prose).

brāhmaṇaka, adj. and subst., (**1**) adj., f. °ikā, *of brahmans, brahmanic*: °keṣu deveṣu Mv i.231.18, (orthodox) *brahmanical gods*; °ṇikāyām īryāyāṃ Divy 485.6; °ṇakān mantrān (vācayati, various forms) Divy 60.26; 487.2; 621.19; (**2**) subst., = brāhmaṇa, *brahman*: māgadhakānāṃ °ṇakānāṃ Mv i.261.17 (prose; -ka svārthe); perh. dim., *young brahman*, MSV i.46.15 (see s.v. **gaṇavācaka**), but prob. adj., to (1); at end of Bhvr. cpds., f. °ikā, saśramaṇa-brāhmaṇikāḥ prajāḥ Mvy 6425, and other case-forms of this same cpd. SP 21.8; 64.9; Suv 9.18; Sukh 25.7, etc.

Brāhmaṇanipāta, n. of a section of the Madhyamāgama: Karmav 156.11; MSV i.98.15.

Brāhmaṇa-sūtra, n. of a work: Karmav 155.14. Identified by Lévi with Verañja(-brāhmaṇa)-sutta, AN iv.172 ff. (with citation cf. 176.18).

brāhmaṇya, adj. (in Skt. only brah°, and in Pali only brahmañña; regularly follows śrāmaṇya, the long ā of which seems to have influenced this word in BHS), *devoted to brahmans*; regularly after mātṛjña, pitṛjña, śrāmaṇya; see s.v. **mātṛjña** for references. In some passages of Mv the mss. read brahmaṇya. Cf. **a-brā°**.

brāhmī, (**1**) (sc. lipi; surely Skt. tho not in Skt. Dictt.) n. of an alphabet: Mv i.135.5; LV 125.19; (**2**) n. of a rākṣasī: Māy 243.21.

BH

bhakta, nt. (Skt.) *food*, is occasionally used instead of bhojya of specifically *soft food*, in contrast with khādya or khajja, *hard food*; so in Mv iii.39.4 bhakta-khajjam, see **khajja**; and more clearly iii.15.9 (tasya prabhūtaṃ khādya-bhojyaṃ) dinnaṃ, mahantaṃ gopiṭakaṃ khajjakasya, mahatī ca alindā bhaktasya . . ., which is resumed below, l. 12, by taṃ khajjakasya gopiṭakaṃ ekadukāye sarvam khāditaṃ, sā ca odanasya mahatī alindā . . . Here it is obvious that bhakta is not only contrasted with khajjaka but identified with odana, which is regularly the food put in an **alindā** or **°da,** q.v.

bhaktaka = Skt. bhakta, *food*: yady aham asyaika-bhaktakam (*even a single* [*little*?] *meal*, prob. -ka dim.) api nādhivāsayāmi MSV i.43.18 (prose). He has just refused to accept longer entertainment; and see **chinna-bhakta(ka)**.

bhakta-kṛtya, see s.v. **kṛtya.**

bhakta-chinnaka, adj. or subst. (cf. next and **chinna-bhakta**), *one cut off from food, hungry*: MSV i.249.7.

bhakta-cheda, m. (= Pali bhatta°, °daṃ katvā Jāt. i.156.13), *abstention from food, a fast*: °daṃ kāritaḥ Av i.248.7, *was made to go without food*; tenaiko °daḥ kṛtaḥ ... yāvat ṣaḍ °dāḥ kṛtāḥ Av ii.80.15; 119.8; °dam akarot 155.1 ff.; dvirātraṃ trirātraṃ vā bhaktacheda-(text °cchada-)chinnena Śikṣ 130.17, *cut off* (from food) *by fasting for two or three days*. Cf. **chinna-bhakta(ka)**.

bhaktāgra (m. or nt.; = Pali bhattagga), *refectory*: °gram upaviṣṭo Mv ii.478.14; 479.4; °gre Divy 335.24 f.

-bhakṣikā (in Skt. Gr. ikṣu-bh°, and Lex. uṣṭra-bh°, n. of a plant), *food, meal*, in **puro-, pūrva-bh°**, qq.v.

Bhagavatī, (**1**) app. n. of a celestial city: Mv iii.251. 4 ff. Is Pali Bhagalavatī (DPPN) to be compared? (**2**) n. of a work, a version of the Prajñāpāramitā: Śikṣ 188.5; 202.4; 210.3 (here citation, not quite accurate, of ŚsP 1430.5 ff.); 243.15; 262.12.

bhagavant (= Skt. id.), as in Pali standard designation of the Buddha, passim: Tib., e. g. Mvy 2, bcom ldan ḥdas, *victorious(-ly) passed beyond*.

Bhaginī = **Kumārī** (1), q.v.

bhagnaka, adj. (= AMg. bhaggaya; Skt. bhagna plus -ka, perh. pejorative), (*miserably*) *routed*: devānām asurair °kānāṃ Divy 223.8.

bhagnapṛṣṭhī-karoti (from *bhagna-pṛṣṭha, lit. *broken-backed*, only known in Skt. Lex. and strangely defined there by saṃmukha, plus karoti; cf. next), *makes depressed*, synonym of **vipṛṣṭhīkaroti**; both, with object mānasam, *depresses* (his own) *mind*, = *becomes disturbed, alarmed*: (na vipṛṣṭhīkariṣyati mānasaṃ) na bhagna-pṛṣṭhīkariṣyati (misprinted magna°) nottrasiṣyati ... AsP 139.19.

bhagnapṛṣṭhībhavati (see prec.), *becomes depressed*: nāsya vipṛṣṭhībhavati mānasaṃ na bhagna°vati nottrasyati ... AsP 5.7; 7.22, etc. (cliché in this work).

? **bhaṅgakula,** Mv ii.251.6, in a list of enemies of birds, all gen. pl., after sākuntikānām (śā°), cāṇḍālakānām (mss. ca°), mṛgalubdhakānām, biḍālakroṣṭukānām, and nakulānām, comes (in text) bhaṅgakulānām (but mss. both °kulān; one ms. bhaṅgeṇa — so, ṇ! — for bhaṅga-). Senart thinks of muṅgusa-kulānām (Pali Lex. muṅgusa, *mongoose*, Childers); closer to the mss. would be AMg. maṅgusa, id. As Senart notes, this would seem to duplicate nakulānām, the preceding term. Possibly, however, maṅgusānām may have been the orig. reading, the last part corrupted by confusion with nakula. It might, possibly, have designated a different species of *mongoose* from nakula, which would justify the collocation of the two words.

bhajjati (MIndic for bhajyate), *is broken*, see Chap. 43, s.v. 2 **bhaj** (3).

bhañjanī (f. to Skt. bhañjana, *one who breaks*; so Pkt. °ṇī, Sheth), n. of a kind of magic: Divy 637.1.

Bhaṭa, n. of a śreṣṭhin, brother of **Naṭa**: Divy 349.11; MSV i.3.17.

bhaṭṭā (f., which I do not find recorded, to bhaṭṭa, title of respect), (**1**) *lady* (applied to a queen): bhaṭṭe, voc., Mv ii.445.6; 447.7 (em); bhaṭṭāye, instr., 445.14 (em.); (**2**) n. of a yakṣiṇī (cf. the yogeśvarī named Bhaṭṭā, Rājataraṅgiṇī, ed. Stein, i.331): Mmk 564.25 (read bhaṭṭā for °ṭa); 565.20 (°ṭe, voc.).

Bhaṭṭika (for the usual **Bhadrika** 3, q.v.), n. of a Śākyan, son of Amṛtodana, brother of **Anuruddha** and **Mahānāma(n)**: Mv iii.177.3. This form of the name has not been noted elsewhere.

? **bhaḍḍalikā,** perh. n. of some animal: Pischel SBBA 1904 p. 817, fol. 169 b; Pischel p. 824 suggests dubiously connexion with (ambaka)maddarī of the corresp. Pali passage AN i.188.2. He is probably right, but unfortunately this doesn't help much; the Pali word is very obscure; acc. to the comm. ii.304.14 the cpd. means *a young hen* (khuddaka-kukkuṭikā).

bhaṇe (1 sg. mid. of Skt. bhaṇati; = Pali id.), *I say! look here!*: in Mv i.320.3, 6, 14; 321.1, 11; 322.11, used by Jyotipāla in addressing his friend Ghaṭikāra; otherwise only bho (twice **ho**) bhaṇe, and always used by a person of superior social station, usually a king, in speaking to subjects or inferiors: Mv i.272.15; ii.74.17 (here Sundarananda, to the populace); 151.6, 10; 152.14–15, 19; 154.10, 14; 155.11; 165.14; 426.10; 427.14; 436.7; 478.17; iii.102.10; 111.16; 441.19; ho (for bho) bhaṇe iii.160.19; 166.17.

bhaṇḍa, nt. (related to AMg. bhaṇḍaga, defined gṛha, sthāna, Sheth and Ratnach.), *hut, arbor*: aśoka-bhaṇḍaṃ (so one ms.; Senart with v.l. °bhāṇḍaṃ) kārāpitaṃ Mv ii.48.4; bhaṇḍa-mūle āsatha Mv ii.172.1, *sit near the* (pleasure-)*arbor*, and ... āsanti 2; in both of these Senart em. bhāṇḍa° but mss. bhaṇḍa°.

(**bhaṇḍati** or) **bhaṇḍayati, °te** (Pali bhaṇḍati; Skt. Gr. bhaṇḍ-; cf. next), *quarrels with, abuses*: °ḍayate KP 107.25 (vs; °te may be m.c.); °ḍita, ppp. *abused, quarrelled with*, Mvy 8711; KP 107.3, 5; Bbh 170.20; Bhīk 31a.4.

bhaṇḍana, nt., once written bhāṇḍana (to prec.), *quarrel, strife*; commonly cpd. or associated with kalaha: Mvy 2630; kalaha-bhaṇḍana-(vigraha-) Mv iii.48.13; Śikṣ 281.14; Bbh 7.8; 179.26; kalahajāta, bhaṇḍanajāta Suv 93.11; Prāt 521.4; Divy 164.25 (here bhāṇḍana°, prob. read bha°); akalaha with abhaṇḍana Suv 73.9; 74.5; others, Mv iii.5.3; RP 19.14.

bhaṇḍikā (also **bhāṇḍikā**, q.v.; in mg. 1 = Skt. bhāṇḍaka, Pali bhaṇḍaka; Pali bhaṇḍikā is defined *heap, bundle*), (**1**) *implement*: karmāra-bha° Mvy 9049; ayaskāra-bha° (so mss., ed. em. °bhā°) Divy 521.25; (**2**) in cīvara-bhaṇḍikā Mvy 9378, app. *pocket* or *fold* in a monk's robe, for carrying things; so one Tib. rendering, chos gos kyi (*of a robe*) snod (*receptacle, holder*), and Chin. *receptacle for holding* (apparently *for holding the robe!*?); another Tib. rendering substitutes for snod the word rin, which usually means *price, value*.

Bhaṇḍin, and **Bhaṇḍīsuta,** n. of two nāga kings: Māy 247.6.

bhats(ayati), etc., semi-MIndic (or false Sktization of MIndic forms) for bharts-, q.v., Chap. 43.

bhadanta (= Pali id., see below; used also in Skt. as address to Buddhist monks; AMg. bhayanta, app. in general application), *venerable, reverend person*; in Pali voc. °ta or °te, other forms as from stem °ta, see Childers; sometimes written in Pali bhaddanta, °te, etc.; acc. to PTSD derived from phrase bhadraṃ te (Skt.), a theory app. accepted by Lévi, since he translates (p. 108) Karmav 26.12 bhadanta (to Buddha) by *la paix sur toi*; in BHS often, but by no means always, refers to Buddha; °te, voc., Mv ii.194.11 (not to Buddha); so mss. in i.306.2, 4 (vss), addressed to a plurality, Senart em. °ta, which seems favored by meter (which however is difficult, text being corrupt); °ta, voc., addressed to Buddha, Mv iii.197.17; 198.1; acc. to Kern's SP Preface p. viii, often in Kashgar rec. for bhagavan of Nep.; Karmav 26.12; Bhīk 3a.3 etc.; Av i.2.15 etc.; to others, Divy 15.17 ff. (an elder); Bhīk 3b.4 (Ānanda); Bbh 153.14 (a bodhisattva); other than voc. forms, °taḥ, nom., Mvy 9220; Av i.244.8; °tam, acc., Divy 506.4; Jm 19.21; °tena Jm 106.18; °tasya Av i.263.4.

Bhaddālin (presumably = Pali id.), n. of a disciple of Buddha, who in a previous incarnation was **Aśoka** (5), q.v., uncle of King Mahāpraṇāda. Note that in Pali (see DPPN) King Mahāpanāda was a previous incarnation of Bhaddaji. A confusion of tradtion, with phonetic bearings, seems to have occurred: Divy 56.25; 57.4; 60.11.

Bhadra, (1) short for **Samantabhadra** (2), q.v.: Bhadra-vidusya Bhad 43; (2) n. of a Bodhisattva, seemingly different from Samantabhadra, who is mentioned in the same sentence: Kv 93.19; (3) n. of a yakṣa: Māy 25; (4) n. of a nāga king: Māy 247.11

bhadraka, (1) adj. with kalpa, = **bhadrakalpa**, q.v.; (2) = **Bhadrika** (2), one of the **bhadravargīya** monks: Mv iii.328.20. (As adj. = bhadra, found in Skt.; prob. with endearing diminutive flavor Divy 38.15, 23, 30.)

Bhadrakanyā, n. of the mother of Maudgalyāyana, as she was reborn in the Marīcika world: Divy 52.16, 22 ff.

Bhadrakarṇa, n. of a yakṣa: Māy 47.

bhadrakalpa, also **bhadraka kalpa**, m. (= Pali bhaddakappa, see Childers s.v. kappo, and DPPN), *a kalpa such as the present in which 5 Buddhas are to appear* (four, from Krakucchanda to Śākyamuni, and the fifth, Maitreya); so in Pali, and see Gv 300.21; 358.19 s.v. **bhadrakalpika**, which support this; yet in Mv iii.330.5 Puṣpiko nāmāyaṃ ... bhadrakalpo, bhadrakalpe ca buddhasahasreṇa utpadyitavyaṃ! (text in part emended but 1000 Buddhas in both mss.); Mvy 8292; asminn eva bhadrakalpe Divy 344.4 (vv.ll. bhadrake k°, bhadraka-k°); 464.14; Av i.250.11; asminn eva bhadrake kalpe Divy 346.24; Av i.237.10; etc. See next.

bhadrakalpika, adj. (to prec. plus -ika), *belonging to* (the present) *bhadrakalpa*: °ka-bodhisattva Mvy 726; 884; °ko bodhisattvaḥ Divy 440.15; 447.4; āryamaitreyapūrvaṃgamāḥ sarva-bhadrakalpikā bodhisattvās Gv 548.5; °kās tathāgatāḥ Gv 300.21; 358.19 (in both Krakucchanda is the first, and in 300.21 Śākyamuni is the last to date).

Bhadrakalpika-sūtra, n. of a work: Śikṣ 8.20. Cf. Konow, Saka versions of the Bhadrakalpikā-(sic)-sūtra, Oslo Akad. hist.-fil. kl. 1929, 1.

bhadrakalpīya, adj., = °pika: °yo bodhisattvaḥ MSV i.101.7.

Bhadrakānta, n. of a nāga-king: Māy 246.24.

Bhadragupta, n. of two former Buddhas: Mv i.137.8; 139.11.

Bhadraṃkara, see **Bhadrika** (6).

Bhadracari, m.c. °carī, or more fully °cari-praṇidhāna, n. of a work, our Bhad (part of Gv); in prose (of Śikṣ) generally called Bhadracaryā; see s.v. **cari**: *the (vow to perform the) excellent course (of Bodhisattvas)*.

Bhadrajit, n. of a disciple of Buddha: Sukh 2.3; in form the name = Pali Bhaddaji, but actually it is evident that it is a substitute for **Bhadrika** (2), since it follows the names of the four other **bhadravargīya**; perh. it was altered under the influence of **Aśvajit**, the second of this list.

Bhadrateja(s), n. of a former Buddha: Mv i.139.11 (°jaḥ n. sg.).

Bhadrapada, n. of a nāga king: Māy 247.16.

Bhadrapāla, (1) n. of the first of the 16 'virtuous men' (**satpuruṣa**): SP 3.10 (with list of 16 names); RP 2.2 (characterized as such, but without names of the others); (2) n. of a Bodhisattva: SP 383.1; Mvy 692; (and prob.) Mmk 311.16 (more likely than the 'satpuruṣa'). A Bhadrapāla Sūtra exists in Chin., and a BHS fragment of it is recorded by Thomas ap. Hoernle MR 88 ff.

Bhadrapura, n. of a city: Māy 2; Lévi 59 thinks it = **Bhadraṃkara, Bhadrika** (6), q.v.

Bhadramati, fem., n. of the queen of Viśāṃpati, a previous birth of **Pramuditanayanajagadvirocanā**: Gv 260.23.

bhadramuṣṭika (nt. in ending; app. = Skt. °musta and Lex. °mustaka, °mustā; cf. Pali bhaddamuttaka, AMg. bhaddamutthā), n. of a kind of water-plant: °kāni Mv ii.274.16. See Senart's note; prob. a false Sktization of a MIndic °muṭṭhikā or °mutthikā.

bhadravargīya, m. pl., also written °**vargiya**, and °**vargika**, °**vargīka**; regularly preceded by **pañcaka**, q.v., or rarely (e.g. LV 264.17) pañca, as separate adj. (= Pali pañcavaggiyā, or °ikā, with or without bhikkhū), the five first disciples of Buddha (Tib., e. g. on LV 245.16, lṅa sde bzaṅ po, *five good-class*); no corresp. for bhadra seems ever to occur in this group in Pali, where bhaddavaggiyā applies to a very different group, DPPN: °gīya LV 245.16; 264.17; 265.3; 404.7 etc.; 407.16 etc.; 416.15; Mv ii.241.2; iii.329.2, 6, 9, 14; 331.1; 335.12; 337.13; 353.14; 415.7 (in several of these v.l. °giya, in 331.1 °gīka, in 335.12 °gika); °giya iii.322.20 (v.l. °gīya); 323.4; 328.20; °gika iii.335.8 (so, or °gīka, mss.); 337.7, 16; 339.3; 353.17; 415.13; °gīka iii.337.10 (mss., no v.l.); pañcakānāṃ bhadravargikānāṃ jātakaṃ iii.356.19 (colophon). Their names given e. g. in Mv iii.328.20, and elsewhere, sometimes without the designation bhadrav°, as SP 1.9 f.; LV 1.6–8; Sukh 2.2 f.; the approved forms seem to be **Ājñātakauṇḍinya, Aśvajit, Vāṣpa, Mahānāman** (3), and **Bhadrika** (2), qq.v. for variants and Pali equivalents.

Bhadraśilā, n. of a city in the north: Divy 315.5 ff.; acc. to 328.3–4 = Takṣaśilā (Taxila).

Bhadraśaila, (1) n. of a city or locality: Māy 33 (= prec.?), but the Chin. versions vary, see Lévi's note, p. 74; (2) n. of a mountain: Māy 253.36 (qy: that mentioned in Kirfel, Kosm. 98?).

Bhadraśrī, (1) n. of (one, or more prob.) two Buddhas: Gv 536.22; Śikṣ 169.11; (2) n. of a male lay-disciple: Gv 51.11; (3) n. of a female lay-disciple: Gv 51.16.

Bhadraśrīmeruteja(s), n. of a Tathāgata: Gv 311.12 (prose), °jo, n. sg.

Bhadrasena, n. of a general of Māra: LV 315.1.

Bhadrā, (1) n. of a female lay-disciple: Gv 51.16; (2) n. of a girl attendant on **Subhadrā** (1): Gv 52.1; (3) n. of a yakṣiṇī: Sādh 562.4; (4) n. of a lokadhātu: SP 269.12 (prose); (5) n. of a courtesan: MSV i.213.13 ff.

Bhadrāyudha, n. of a **mahānagna** (q.v.): Divy 373.20.

bhadrika, (1) adj. (= Skt. bhadra-ka, Pali bhaddaka), *felicitous*: °keṇa śākyarājena (refers to Śuddhodana, hence not n. pr.) LV 122.1 (prose, no v.l.; possibly, however, read bhadrakeṇa?); (2) (= Pali Bhaddiya) n. of one of the five **bhadravargīya** monks, q.v. (also **Bhadraka, Bhadrajit**, qq.v.): Mv iii.337.5; 339.1; LV 1.8; SP 1.10; Divy 268.6; (3) (app. not the same as 2, but also = Pali Bhaddiya, 2 in DPPN; BHS also **Bhaṭṭika**, q.v.), n. of a Śākyan youth, usually associated with **Aniruddha** or **Mahānāman** (2) or both; became a disciple of Buddha: LV 229.12; Mvy 3606; Av ii.112.4; 113.6 ff.; as one of 8 **mahāśrāvaka**, q.v., Mmk 64.11; see also **Lavaṇabhadrika**, prob. not the same; (4) n. of a pratyekabuddha: Mv iii.414.4; (5) n. of a yakṣa: Māy 66 (living at **Bhadrikā**); (6) (= Pali Bhaddika, or Bhaddiya), n of a city: °ke nagare Karmav 68.8 (acc. to Lévi's note, a Chin. version points to **Bhadrikā**, q.v., but I do not see how it gives any clue to the quantity of the a-vowel); the same city is called **Bhadraṃkara** Divy 123.16; 125.10 ff.; MSV i.241.1; ii.32.8; the country containing it is given the same name, Bhadraṃkareṣu janapadeṣu Divy 125.16 ff.; cf. also **Bhadrapura**.

Bhadrikā (cf. prec., 6; the same?), n. of a city or locality, where the yakṣa Bhadrika (5) lived: Māy 66 (°kāyāṃ).

Bhadrottamā, n. of a lay-disciple: Gv 451.10 etc.

[**bhaya**, read **Abhaya** (4), q.v.: Mv i.135.7.]

Bhayaṃkara, n. of a son of **Māra**, unfavorable to the Bodhisattva: LV 311.10.

Bharata, (**1**) n. of a cakravartin; perh. the one well-known in Skt., perh. = Bharata 7 of DPPN, or one of the others of that name (5?) in DPPN: Mvy 3581; (**2**) app. n. of the father of Śyāmaka: RP 22.1.

bharati, bharayati (in mg. 1 = AMg. bharai, bharei; denom. to Skt. bhara, cf. Skt. bharita, more rarely bhṛta, *filled, full*; § 38.37 and Chap. 43, s.v. bhṛ 2), (**1**) *fills (up)*: yojanaśatam prabhāye Dīpaṃkaro bharitva (mss. °tvā) asthāsi Mv i.231.5 (vs); buddhakṣetraṃ aparimitam bharitvā ii.295.9; (na ca śaknoti, Senart em. °nonti, tāni karakāni) bharayituṃ iii.427.14 (mss. haray°); (tāni karakāni udakena) bharayetsuḥ (so one ms., v.l. bhavetsuḥ; Senart em. bharensuḥ) 16; (**2**) (cf. Skt. ppp. bhṛta, *hired*; otherwise recorded only in bharasva, v.l. bhajasva, mām Mbh. Crit. ed. 3.64.4; cf. bhajasva mām 4.7.5, no v.l.), *hires*: dviguṇayā divasamudrayā . . . bharayitvā (caus.?) SP 105.11 (prose); *having (caused to be?) hired for a double daily wage*; but Kashgar rec. bharitvā.

Bharadvāja (cf. **Bhāra°**, the only form recorded for Pali in DPPN), (**1**) n. of a disciple of Śākyamuni (in lists of names; not clear which of the several Pali disciples named Bhāra° is meant): SP 2.6; Sukh 92.8, see also **Piṇḍola Bhara°**; (**2**) gotra-name of the Buddha **Candrasūryapradīpa**: SP 18.5; (**3**) n. of a yakṣa: Māy 236.26; (**4**) n. of a monk, former incarnation of Śākyamuni: MSV i.211.3 ff.

bharayati, see **bharati.**

bharikā (hyper-Skt., § 2.33, for MIndic (Pali) bhariyā = Skt. bhāryā), *wife*; in Divy 28.22; 30.11–12 read jyeṣṭha-bharikā, *elder brother's wife*, with some mss. both times, for ed. °bhavikā. Bailey, JRAS 1950.175–6, would read -bhartṛkāyā in 28.22 (Tib. jo mo, *mistress*), and -bhrātṛke in 30.11 (Tib. mnaḥ ma, *daughter-in-law*). I prefer my interpretation.

Bharuka, n. of a yakṣa (lived in Bharukaccha): Māy 17.

Bharukaccha, n. of a nāga: Mvy 3318.

Bharga, m. pl. (= Pali Bhagga; possibly to be identified with Skt. Bharga or Bhārga, Mbh. Cr. ed. 2.27.10; 6.10.49), n. of a people, whose capital was **Śuśumāragiri**, q.v.: Divy 181.22 ff.; 189.1.

bhali, acc. to Tib. bu ma rta, *messenger*: MSV iv.62.14. The Ap. word bhali in a vs, Hem. 4.353, could be interpreted in this sense (*whose messenger is longing for things hard to get, they think naught of distance*), but the comm. glosses abhyāsaḥ.

Bhallika (in Mv var. °iya; = Pali Bhallika, °iya, °uka), n. of a merchant, associated with **Trapuṣa**, often in dvandva cpd.: LV 381.4 ff.; Mv iii.303.5 ff. (°iya, with v.l. °ika, 303.13; 305.6); Divy 393.19.

bhalluka, m. (= Skt. Lex. id.; Skt. bhallūka, Deśīn. bhallu), *a bear*: Mvy 4781.

bhava, (**1**) (threefold) *state(s) of existence*, see **tribhava**; (**2**) n. pr., father of **Pūrṇa** (1): Divy 24.10 ff.

Bhavaketu, n. of a former Buddha: Mv i.140.9.

bhavati (Skt.), *comes to be*; in peculiar use, bodhisattvo mātāpitaraṃ bhaṇāsi mā khu bhave Mv ii.221.7 (vs), *the B. said to his parents, Be it not so! (Perish the thought!)*; next line continues, na khu tāva śocitavyaṃ . . ., *you must not grieve!*

Bhavatrāta, n. of a son of **Bhava**: Di 24.21.

Bhavadeva, n. of a king: MSV i.xviii.4.

Bhavadevagupta, n. of a former Buddha: Mv i.140.7.

Bhavana, n. of a mountain: Kv 91.16.

Bhavanandin, n. of a son of **Bhava**: Divy 24.22.

bhavanetrī, °trikā (= Pali bhavanetti, seems to be a virtual synonym of taṇhā; defined by Childers *desire, lust*), *leading (that which leads) to (continued) existence*; ep. of tṛṣṇā: tṛṣṇāṃ °trīṃ Mv ii.307.12; alone, but clearly implying tṛṣṇā, in Mv i.247.18 (vs) aśeṣā bhavanetrisaritā ucchoṣitā, *all streams of* (thirst) *which lead to further existence are dried up*; dharmā (*states of being*) bhavanetrikā(ḥ) Mv iii.337.13; 339.12. (In Mv ii.206.15 Senart puts this into text by em., but read with mss. purimabhava-janetriye bhavanighātī, which is sound in meter and sense.) See **netrikā**, and next.

-bhavanetrī-ka, adj. Bhvr., = prec.: chinna-prapañca-bhavanetrīkānāṃ (said of Buddhas) AsP 136.1; 141.2–3 (prose). Cf. Pali ucchinna-bhavanettiko DN i.46.9.

bhavant, used (as in Pali, e. g. MN i.241.7 te bhonto samaṇabrāhmaṇā . . . vediyanti) like bhagavant, *venerable, respected*, not necessarily in address (cf. Senart Mv i note 558, on i.235.17): muñcanti yaśasvino bhavato (gen. sg.) Mv i.236.8 (vs); bhavanto śramaṇā vā brāhmaṇā vā . . . vedayanti Mv ii.121.2, 5, etc. (not in address, but simple narration, referring to persons not present); similarly ii.126.13; 127.17; 129.4; 130.7; ya ime bhavantaḥ śramaṇabrāhmaṇā . . . vedayanta iti LV 247.19; voc. bhavanto, *Sirs! gentlemen!*, not as subject of a verb in polite address as in Skt.: Mv ii.442.1, 19; beginning a story, bhūtapūrvaṃ bhavanto . . . rājā . . . abhūṣi Mv iii.204.8, *Once upon a time, Sirs, there was a king . . .*, and in the sequel; bhavanto yūyaṃ na . . . śabdaṃ śruṇiṣyatha iii.297.10, *sirs, you shall not hear . . .*; often in Divy, e. g. 34.23 (bhavanto 'sti kaścid yuṣmābhir dṛṣṭaḥ . . .); 35.3, etc.; and in MSV, e. g. i.64.15.

bhava-saṃskāra, see **saṃskāra.**

Bhavasaṃkrānti, n. of a work: Mvy 1379; °ti-sūtra, id.: Bbh 48.11 (cited).

[**bhavasyu**, Gv 488.5 (vs), read with 2d ed. bhavaḥ su-.]

bhavāgra, m. (nt.? = Pali bhavagga), *the highest point of the universe, of existence; the limit of existence*; often locally, but also figuratively: (read) °nimagna (with prec. cpd.) sthitā (voc. sg.) bhavāgre LV 116.22 (vs), *O thou stationed at the peak of existence!* (misunderstood by Lefm. and Foucaux); divyā bhavāgraparyantāḥ LV 374.7; bhūmitalam upādāya yāvad bhavāgram Mv ii.302.3, *from the earth's surface to the peak of the universe*; yāvad bhavāgraṃ, also, Mv ii.312.6; SP 370.4; (manuṣyopapattim ādiṃ kṛtvā) yā° bhav° Dbh 25.20, *to the limit* (here temporal) *of existence*; bhavāgrā lokadhātūyo Mv ii.350.3, *the extreme summits of the universe*; bhavāgra-pūraṃ Mv ii.378.21 etc., see s.v. **pūra** (2); bhavāgrāc ca gāminī pratipat Bbh 277.14.

Bhavila, n. of a son of **Bhava**: Divy 24.19.

bhavi-vādi-kathā? Mv i.144.13 (prose), so mss.; Senart bhava°: (Bodhisattvas in their mothers' wombs) °kathāṃ kathayanti kuśalamūlata iti; one ms. bhaviṣya° for bhavi°; perhaps, then, bhavin = Skt. bhāvin, *relating to the future*? or, (of) *living beings* (so, tho rarely, Skt. bhavin)? or again, for Skt. bhavya, as bhavi- is used in Ap. (Jacobi, Bhav., Glossar)?

bhavya, (**1**) adj. (= Pali bhabba; not in this sense Skt.; cf. a-bh°), *able, capable*, with inf. or dat., once gen.: inf., LV 247.15 (sākṣātkartum), 19; 248.5; 394.14; Bbh 78.9; dat., Mv ii.123.2 (abhinivartanāye); Bbh 159.20; gen., Śikṣ 197.12 (dharmadeśanāyāḥ); (**2**) n. of a teacher: Mvy 3495.

bhasati (m.c. for bhāṣati), *speaks*: bhasi, 2 sg. aor., LV 235.9 (vs).

bhasmagraha (m. or nt.), some part of the education of a brahman: Divy 485.6 (see s.v. **autkara**).

(**bhasmita**, denom. pple. from bhasman, *reduced to ashes*, occurs in Skt., see Schmidt, Nachträge: °taṃ kuryāt Mvy 6537, with var. bhasmīkuryāt.)

Bhasmeśvara, n. of a future Buddha (which, it is predicted, the god Maheśvara = Śiva will become): Kv 90.6.

Bhākrama, n. of a mleccha king: Mmk 621.25. Cf. **Bhāgupta, Bhāvasu.**

? **bhāgayati** (seemingly denom. to Skt. bhāga), *gives a share to, shares with*: māṃ sudhāye . . . bhāgaya, *give me a share of the nectar*! Mv ii.57.5 (vs), repeated 57.21 (here v.l. bhogaya); 59.1; but same line in Pali, Jāt. v.399.4, 8, bhājaya, which should perhaps be read in Mv.

bhāgavatī, (1) (in Skt., *a [female] follower of Viṣṇu*, or also acc. to Schmidt, Nachtr., of Śiva; perhaps so here), *a female follower of Viṣṇu* (?): Vasumitrā nāma bhāgavatī Gv 201.11; similarly Vasumitrā bhāgavatī 201.26 ff.; (2) n. of a **cāturdvīpikā**, q.v. (world-system of four continents; in 373.17 and 381.4–5 specifically includes a continent Jambudvīpa): Gv 373.17; 379.25; 381.4–5; 438.26.

-bhāgīya, adj., ifc. (= Pali -bhāgiya), *of . . . kind, sort; belonging to, connected with; sharing, headed for*: puṇya-bh°, phala-bh°, vāsanā-bh° (sattva) Mv i.34.4, 5; ii.419.4, 5; esp. *leading, conducive to*: **ūrdhva-, avara-bh°**, qq.v., Mvy 2155–6; mokṣa-bh° (kuśalamūla) Divy 50.7; 363.28–29; **nirvedha-bh°** (**nirbheda-bh°**), qq.v.; hāna-bh°, *conducive to loss* or *degradation* (= Pali hānabhāgiya, in PTSD defined as just the opposite, *conducive to relinquishing of perversity and ignorance*; but see DN iii.273.3, where ayoniso-manasikāro is hāna-bh°, glossed comm. iii.1055.10 apāyagāmī, parihānāya saṃvattanako), hāna-bhāgīyānāṃ (misprinted hāta°) viśeṣabhāgīyānāṃ (the opposite, *conducive to distinction*) dharmāṇāṃ pāraṃ gantukāmena bodhisattvena ŚsP 93.19 ff.; pañca ime bodhisattvasya hānabhāgīyā dharmā veditavyāḥ. katame pañca. agauravatā dharme dharmabhāṇake ca; pramāda-kausīdyaṃ; etc., Bbh 288.24; the opposite (besides viśeṣa-bh°, = Pali visesa-bhāgiya, ŚsP above) is ahāna-bhāgīyā (dhyānārūpyasamāpattiḥ) Bbh 35.28; ṣaḍāyatana-bhāgīyaḥ sparśaḥ Dbh 49.14, *connected with* . . . (not *conducive to* here! in pratītyasamutpāda; rather *based upon*); evaṃbhāgīya, *of such sort(s), kind(s), division(s), part(s)*, Bbh 6.3; 299.16; Mvy 1999; anyathā-bh° Mvy 9402.

-bhāgīyaka, adj. or subst. ifc., = prec., in avaśya-bhā°, (*what is*) *inevitable, certain in nature*: Uttaro nāma māṇavo . . . avaśyabhāgīyakasya bhāvyatāyāṃ buddho vyākṛtas Divy 347.11.

Bhāgīratha, n. of one or two former Buddha(s): Mv iii.239.5; Av i.65.11.

Bhāgupta, n. of a mleccha king: Mmk 621.26. Cf. **Bhākrama, Bhāvasu.**

bhāṅgaka, nt., Mvy 5882, or m., MSV ii.3.2, acc. to Tib. (in both) gso ras, app. *worn-out* or *ragged garment* (of cotton, ras). Perh., then, derived from Skt. bhaṅga (with BR). The surrounding terms designate garments of fine materials, and one is tempted to assume the mg. *linen garment* (Skt. bhaṅgā, adj. bhāṅga, *hemp-en*); and so Chin., clearly; but even if we assume that Tib. gso is an error for gos, *garment*, the word ras is said to mean only *cotton*.

bhāṅgeya, adj. (to Skt. bhaṅgā plus -eya), *hempen*: (cīvaraṃ) MSV ii.91.16; 92.2.

-bhājaka, m. (= Pali id., in cīvara-bh° and other cpds.), *dispenser* (of articles among monks in a monastery): bhāṇḍa-bh° Mvy 9063; cīvara-bh° 9066; MSV ii.124.5 etc.; = Tib. ḥg(y)ed pa.

bhājana, (1) as m. (otherwise nt.), *pot*: bhavanti bhājanās (ed. em. °nā; Kashgar rec. varies) tasya SP 138.6 (vs); dhāret' ime (sc. bhājana; acc. pl.) cetiya saṃmataite (n. pl., ete; Lefm. °tīte, see Crit. App.) LV 383.12 (vs); (2) *inanimate object*, as dist. from sattva, *living being*: °na-loka Sūtrāl. iv.15–20, comm. (Lévi, n. 4); AbhidhK. LaV-P. iii.138; °na-**vivartanī** and **-saṃvartanī** (qq.v.) ibid. iii.181 n. 3, cf. Wogihara, Lex. 38. Prob. so understand sarva-sattva-bhājana- (text °nā-)-loka-vyavacāreṣu Gv 180.8, *in wanderings* (or *searchings*) *through the world(s) of all living beings and inanimate objects*.

bhājanaka, nt. (= Skt. °na plus -ka svārthe), *pot*: °nakāni Mv i.327.1 and 3 (in 2 bhājanāni; all prose).

bhājana-cārika, see **-cārika.**

bhājana-vārika, see s.v. **-vārika.**

bhāṇaka, *reciter* (as a kind of entertainer): Mv iii.113.3; 255.12; 442.9. Cf. Pali bhāṇaka, f. °ikā (only of one who recites religious texts?) and **dharma-bhā°**.

-bhāṇin, adj. ifc. (= Pali id.), *speaking*: -manojña-bhāṇī Bbh 376.6; manda-, mṛdu-, and priya-bhāṇī Śikṣ 268.2; alpa-bhāṇiṃ, acc. sg., m.c. for °bhāṇinaṃ Ud xxix. 55 (45).

Bhāṇḍa, n. of a nāga king: Mvy 3256. (In Mv ii.48.4; 172.1, 2 Senart bhāṇḍa, read **bhaṇḍa**, q.v.)

bhāṇḍana, see **bhaṇḍana.**

bhāṇḍāvārī (°ri), f., *shop for wares*, see **āva...**

bhāṇḍikā (= **bhaṇḍikā**, q.v.), *implement*: parivrā-jaka-bhā° Jm 144.10. (In Divy 521.25 read bhaṇḍikā with mss.)

Bhāṇḍyāyana, n. of a maharṣi: Māy 256.33.

bhāti (= M. bhāi; analog. to trāti, see s.v. **bhāyati**), *fears*: bhāhi, impv., LV 232.3 (with v.l., text tāhi); Mv iii.403.17, and v.l. 408.11.

bhānaka = **bhāṇaka**, see **dharma-bh°**.

Bhāna- (Index), or **Bhāma**-(text)-**kanakamuni**, Mv i.294.20, appears to be another designation of **Kanaka-muni**, q.v., unless the text is corrupt, which is probable.

Bhānuprabhā, n. of a śreṣṭhin's daughter: Gv 427.20.

bhānuvant, adj. (= Skt., Pali bhānumant), *shining*: LV 357.9, see s.v. **ūrṇākośa.**

Bhāmakanakamuni, see **Bhāna°**.

bhāyati, °te (= Pali id., Skt. bhayati, bibheti; on this and **bhāti** see § 28.23), *fears*: °ti Mv ii.236.9; °si i.163.18; Ud ix.3 (later ms. bibheṣi); °se Mv ii.58.19; impv. bhāya ii.134.3; Śikṣ 154.17; bhāyāhi Mv i.363.1; iii.408.11 (v.l. bhāhi); bhāyatha, read °thā both times, SP 26.4; 197.1; °tha Mv i.361.15; iii.303.17; aor. bhāyi Mv ii.308.16.

Bhāradvāja (= Pali id.; see also **Bhara°**), (1) n. of one of the two leading disciples of the Buddha Kāśyapa (= Pali id. 1 in DPPN): Mv i.307.4, 17; (2) n. of a brahman convert to Buddhism, associated with **Vasiṣṭha** 1 (= id. 4 in DPPN): Karmav 157.6. See also **Piṇḍola Bhara°**.

bhārgava, m. (acc. to Nīlak., so in Mbh., see pw 7.365; Pali bhaggava, see PTSD), *potter*: Mv iii.347.19 (twice); 348.2, 9 (= kumbhakāra 347.16, 17); SP 138.8; Speyer, Preface to Av, p. LXII, line 4 (śloka 219), cf. p. CXII.

bhāryaram, bhāryāraṃ, acc. sg. to Skt. bhāryā, *wife*: Mv i.129.2; 233.17; 234.8, etc., see § 9.25.

-bhāryāka, ifc. Bhvr., = Skt. bhāryā, *wife*: sa-bhāryāko Mv i.304.6.

bhāvati (m.c. for **bhavati**), *comes to be*, etc.: śāstā-rasaṃjñā tvayi sada bhāviṣyanti (read °ṣanti, m.c.) LV 232.5 (vs); bhāvāmy ahu Samādh p. 66 line 3 (so read for text bhāvāmbahu; same corruption bhombahu for bhomy ahu pp. 64 line 25, 65 lines 1, 3, etc.) = bhavāmy aham.

? **bhāvana** (= Skt. °**nā**?), in LV 182.21 (vs) anusmṛtī bhāvanu śabda niścarī, *the sounds* **anusmṛti** (q.v.) *and bhāvana* (°nā) *came forth*; nt. for fem.? or u, nom. sg. for fem. ā (§ 9.13)? or, finally, perhaps cpd. °tī-bhāvana, adj. agreeing with śabda, *a sound producing* **anusmṛti** (but this seems less likely; parallel words in the vs are nouns in apposition with śabda).

bhāvana-tā (see § 22.42), in mārgabhāvana-tā (= Pāli maggabhāvanā), *realization of the* (8-fold noble) *Path*: LV 33.10 (prose).

(**bhāvanā**, substantially as in Skt., in Mv i.66.12 (vs) tasya eṣa khalu ṛddhi-bhāvanā, *this is his* (Kāśyapa's) *accomplishment of magic*, or perhaps *this is the effect of his magic*, viz. that the Buddha's body does not burn.)

Bhāvasu, n. of a mleccha king: Mmk 621.24. Cf. **Bhākrama, Bhāgupta.**

Bhāvitātma(n), n. of a former Buddha: Mv iii.236.18.

bhāṣaṇaka, m. (to Skt. °ṇa plus -ka), *a reciter or knower of sacred texts*: (sacet pratibalo bhavati śāstur guṇakīrtanaṃ) . . . kartavyam, noced °kaḥ praṣṭavyaḥ MSV iii.97.18.

bhāṣamānaka, f. °**ikā** (pres. mid. pple. of bhāṣ-, plus -ka), *speaking* (of), *describing*: °nikāḥ (dental n in text) LV 236.21 (cited s.v. **dadantaka**).

bhāṣiṇikā, see **bhās°**.

bhāṣṭa (= Skt. bhāṣita), ppp. of Skt. bhāṣati, *says, speaks* (§ 34.11): Laṅk 283.8 (vs) twice, and 11 (vs).

-bhāsinikā, read with most mss. (sumanmatha-) **bhāṣiṇikā** (dim. to fem. of Skt. -bhāṣin), *speaking affectionately* (see § 22.34): LV 323.4 (vs).

Bhāskaradeva, n. of a Bodhisattva: Gv 442.20.

Bhāskarapradīpa, n. of a Buddha: Gv 256.16.

bhikṣāka-vṛtta, nt. (bhikṣāka is rare in Skt., but bhikkhāa, °khāga frequent in AMg.; not in Pali), *mendicant's mode of life*, of seven aspects (with description): Bbh 194.4, 17. Cf. **bhaikṣāka.**

bhikṣā-da-(-kula), *alms-giving* (family; wrongly Bendall and Rouse): only in mitrakula-bhikṣādakula- Śikṣ 98.8; 104.13; 105.12; in all mentioned as people with whom it is wrong to try to curry favor.

bhikṣuṇikā (= °ṇī, perh. -ka m.c.), *nun*: read °kāna, gen. pl., with Kashgar rec. and v.l. of Nep., for KN °ṇiyāna SP 283.13 (vs); cited Śikṣ 353.4 with bhikṣuṇikās (acc. pl., with change of construction).

bhikṣuṇī (= Pali bhikkhunī), *nun*: common everywhere, e. g. Mvy 8447–8; 8718; LV 89.7; 161.9; Mv iii.49.10 ff.; Divy 160.7; 202.14; 552.8 ff.; Av ii.11.2 ff.; Bhīk 3a.1 etc.

Bhikṣuṇīkarmavācanā, n. of a work (our Bhīk), acc. to BSOS 1 p. 123.

Bhikṣudeva, n. of a former Buddha: Mv i.138.9.

Bhikṣuprakīrṇaka (nt.?), n. of a work, cited: °ke Śikṣ 154.17. The quotation is in prose, but shows many Middle Indic forms, resembling the prose of Mv.

bhiṇḍipāla, m. (cf. Skt. Lex. and AMg. bhiṇḍimāla), = Skt. bhindipāla, a kind of missile weapon: Mvy 6103 = Tib. mtshon rtse gcig pa, *one-pointed dart*.

bhittī-phalaka, m., lit. *wall-board*, a sitting-bench or stool against a wall, for an infant of six months to be placed on: (paryaṅkaḥ . . . tad yathāpi nāma) ṣaṇmāsajātasya dārakasya °kaḥ (no v.l. in mss.) LV 63.7 (prose).

bhit(t)vara, adj., *ruined, broken-down*: (of a house,) read bhitvara (with ms. K′) or °ru (with 3 mss., KN) in SP 85.4 (vs), for durbalam of both edd., which the preceding and parallel sudurbalaṃ makes improbable; Tib. ḥjig (ñe) supports a form of bhid-; read for the next word bhairavaṃ, with all Nep. mss. of KN, also K′, and Tib. ḥjigs, for KN's em. itvara; this word (q.v.) is inappropriate here, yet similar enough in mg. to have helped in the creation of bhit(t)vara, as if bhid- plus tvara, modelled on i-tvara and Skt. ga-tvara; the latter has a mg. virtually identical with that required here. Is this the word intended by vidvarena (vi = bhi repeatedly here) in Dutreuil, C fragm. XIIIvo, for which Pali SN i.131.11 has bhindanena, v.l. °rena? See Barua and Mitra 211, 213.

Bhiru, n. of a minister of Rudrāyaṇa (bracketed with **Hiru**): Divy 545.5.

Bhiruka, (**1**) m., = prec.: Divy 556.8, 13; 562.15; 563.25; 564.10; 570.26; 571.2, etc.; (**2**) nt., n. of a city founded by the prec.: Divy 576.24.

Bhirukaccha, nt., another name for prec. (2): Divy 576.25.

bhiṣaṅka (= Pali bhisakka, for Skt. bhiṣaj- plus -ka, by the 'law of morae', § 3.4; see also next), *physician*: bhiṣaṅkā LV 285.1 (Lefm. with all mss.).

bhiṣaṭka (see under prec.), *physician*: mahā-°kaḥ SP 161.6; 292.11; 294.6 (all vss); for the last two Senart Mv i note 367 cites vv.ll. bhiṣaka (metr. impossible) and bhiśaṃka (for **bhiṣaṅka**, prec.); on ṭ for j see § 2.38.

Bhīma, (**1**) n. of a cakravartin king: Mvy 3584; (**2**) n. of a nāga: Mmk 454.16; Māy 247.6.

Bhīmadarśanā, n. of a goddess: Sādh 502.10.

Bhīmaratha, (**1**) (= Pali id., 1 in DPPN) n. of a king, concerned in the story of **Śarabhaṅga**: Mv iii.364.5; 365.18; 366.7; 373.23; (**2**) n. of a cakravartin king: Mvy 3485.

Bhīmā, n. of a goddess: Sādh 502.6.

Bhīmottara, n. of a kumbhāṇḍa: Mvy 3441.

bhīru (nt.? = Pali id.; in Skt. only adj.), *fear*: ṣaṣṭhī (sc. Mārasya senā) bhīru pravuccati (so Senart, mss. pranandita, (u)panandati) Mv ii.240.5 (vs); in parallel LV 262.16 bhayaṃ (v.l. bhaya) ṣaṣṭhī nirucyate.

Bhīṣaṇa, (**1**) n. of a yakṣa: Mmk 44.3; (**2**) n. of a nāga: Mmk 454.16; (**3**) n. of a locality: Māy 28.

Bhīṣaṇikā, n. pr. (?); in °**kā-vana**, n. of a park (mṛgadāva) in **Śuśumāragiri**: Divy 182.25.

bhīṣaṇīya (cf. § 22.20; to Skt. bhīṣaṇa, rather than quasi-gdve. to bhīṣ-), *terrifying*: parama-°yaṃ . . . pṛthivīpradeśaṃ Kv 39.11; °yā Gv 334.4 (vs).

bhīṣma, (**1**) nt., n. of some (heavenly) flower (cf. **mahābhīṣma**, which regularly follows it; with **mandārava** etc.): Mv i.230.16; 267.1; ii.160.13; 286.17; iii.95.12; 99.11; (**2**) adj. (?) *formidable, mighty*, in SP 119.1 (vs) teno vayaṃ śrāvaka bhīṣma-kalpāḥ, = Tib. (cited by WT) de bas (= tena) bdag cag (vayaṃ) sgrogs pa (śrāvaka) mi bzad (*irresistible*, Jä.) ḥdra (*like*, = kalpa); this mg. seems hardly matched in the use of Skt. bhīṣma; cf. **mahābhīṣma** 2; (**3**) n. of a great seer (maharṣi): Māy 257.1 (possibly referring to Bhīṣma of the Mbh?).

Bhīṣmagarjitanirghoṣasvara, n. of a former Buddha: AsP 481.3; identical with **Bhīṣmagarjitasvararāja** (vv.ll. add nirghoṣa, or ghoṣa, before svara; Burnouf reads ghoṣa), n. of a former Buddha who was succeeded by a long series of Buddhas of the same name: SP 375.10 ff.; under this Buddha (or in SP the first of them) the Bodhisattva **Sadāprarudita** (in SP **Sadāparibhūta**), qq.v., started his career.

Bhīṣmamātaṅga, n. of a great sage (maharṣi): Māy 257.1.

Bhīṣmayaśas, n. of a Bodhisattva: Gv 442.20.

Bhīṣmottaranirghoṣa, n. of a sage (ṛṣi): Gv 110.12 ff.

bhuktāvin (= Pali bhuttāvin; § 22.51), *having eaten*: gen. °visya Mv ii.116.14; otherwise n. or acc. sg., °vī, °viṃ (°vi), and always followed by dhautahasta (or dhautapāṇi; not in i.312.15) apanītapātra (mss. sometimes avan°, e. g. i.325.13), *having washed the hands and laid aside the bowl* (but once, iii.143.4, mss. dhautapātro apanītapāṇi, *having washed the bowl and removed the hands*, sc. from it); the corresp. Pali phrase is bhuttāvi(ṃ) onītapattapāṇi(ṃ), regularly explained by comms. as *having eaten and removed the hands from the bowl*; but comms. (e. g. DN comm. i.277.18) sometimes cite another reading, onitta or oṇ°, *washed*, for onīta. The BHS form seems to make better sense than the Pali but may be a rationalizing lect. fac.: Mv i.38.8; 309.1; 312.15; 325.13; ii.276.9; iii.142.4; 143.4.

bhukṣa, adj. (= AMg. bhukkha, Ratnach.; cf. next two; all from unreduplicated desiderative stem = Skt. bubhukṣ-, lacking first syllable; such forms are well established in Pkt., tho ignored in Pischel and, so far as I am aware, in other Pkt. grammars; they live on in modern vernaculars, cf. Hindi bhūkh, subst., bhūkhā, adj., and Turner, Nepali Dict., s.vv. bhok, bhoko, etc.), *hungry*: bhukṣa-pipāsitā madhukarāḥ kusumam abhigatāḥ LV 328.12 (vs).

bhukṣā (cf. prec. and next; = Pkt. bhukkhā for Skt. bubhukṣā, Sheth, and Jacobi, Ausgew. Erz. 60.26), *hunger*: tṛṣa-bhukṣa-(short a, m.c.)-pīḍitā, fragment of Candragarbha section of Mahāsaṃnipāta Sūtra, Thomas ap. Hoernle MR 105, note 10 (seemingly in a vs).

bhukṣita (= Pkt. bhukkhia for Skt. bubhukṣita, see under prec. two), *hungry*: tṛṣita-bhukṣitasya te Mv ii.202.3 (vs); Śikṣ 341.1 (vs).

bhuja (normally *arm*; said to mean also *hand*, pāṇi, kara, Skt. Gr. and Lex., see BR; once, at least, interpreted thus in an old Pali text, see PTSD), *hand*: keśān addaśi lūna dakṣiṇi bhuje LV 194.12 (vs), *she saw her hair cut off in her right hand.* Tib. is strangely different: lag pa gyon pas skra yaṅ rab tu ḥbal... mthoṅ, *she saw her hair dishevelled by her left* (so!) *hand.*

bhujiṣya, adj. (in Divy 302.26, see s.v. **kāmaṃgama** 2, as in Skt., *dependent, in service*; but Skt. Lex. *free*, and so regularly Pali bhujissa, see notably Vv. comm. 11, last line), *free, independent* (so Tib.; see also next): nt. °yam, presumably sc. śīlam, Mvy 1624, in a list of epithets of moral restraints very similar to Pali Vism. i.221.25, bhujissāni (sīlāni); Vism. i.222.12–13 explains that they are *free* because they cause freedom from the slavery of craving, taṇhādāsavyato mocetvā bhujissabhāvakaraṇena; (śīlāni...)°ṣyāṇy MPS 2.34 (Tib. id.).

bhujiṣya-tā (from prec., q.v.), *freedom*: °tāṃ gato LV 398.18 (vs), *arrived at freedom = salvation*, of the Buddha.

? **Bhuḍhuka,** or better **Bhudhuka,** ed. at Laṅk 366.14 (vs), but apparently by em.; mss. Pudruka, Buddhaka; Tib. Bhu-dhu-ka (dental dh!); I see no reason to assume domal ḍh, but the true form is very incertain. Seems to be the name of an astronomical work: bhudhuka-jyotiṣādyāni bhaviṣyanti kalau (so read) yuge.

bhuta, m.c. for Skt. (and BHS) **bhūta,** *become*, etc.; *true*: (only vss) LV 54.3 (but in 53.8 prob. read tuma); 197.2 (read sakuṇā, or śa°, bhutā, with Tib.); 222.20; Gv 334.20.

Bhudhuka, see **Bhuḍhuka.**

? **bhumī,** LV 155.11 (vs), so Calc. and Lefm., who cites all mss. as bhūmī (unmetr.): na ca utthitu āsani no ca bhumī; Tib. gdan las ma bzheṅs (*from seat not arise*) brtsol ba ma mchis su (*not making any effort*; brtsol = vyāyāma, vyavasāya). Possibly read bhramī, aor. of root bhram? *and did not stir.*

bhuyo, adv. (m.c. for Skt. bhūyas), *more, further*: LV 54.9; bhuyu LV 240.19; 242.14; Dbh.g. 7(343).16; 8(344).7. All vss.

Bhūcarī, n. of a yoginī: Sādh 446.3.

bhūt, aor. of Skt. bhū, seemingly as a kind of particle; Tib. seems to render by graṅ, *perhaps*: LV 193.11 (vs), see § 41.1.

bhūta, (**1**) adj. (cf. also **abhūta**; not unknown in this sense in Skt. but quite rare; in Pali and BHS very common), *true, real, not false* (= satya): satyavādī bhūtavādī Dbh 23.21; similarly SP 39.9; bhūtāṃ vācaṃ SP 315.2; vācaṃ... bhūtāṃ vābhūtāṃ vā SP 227.6, *true or false*; mitrāṇi bhūtavādīni na mṛṣāvādīni LV 91.7 (in 8 read °vādīni with v.l.); bhūtā LV 286.14 (vāc); bhūtasaṃdhāya-vacanaṃ RP 8.11; paśyāmaḥ kiṃ bhūtam abhūtaṃ vā Divy 572.20; (sc. dharmasya) bhūtaṃ... artham SP 32.4, *true meaning*; bhūta-vacano Mv iii.112.11, *whose word is true*, i. e. *true to his word*; pareṣāṃ bhūtān guṇān nodbhāvayati, bhūtaṃ varṇaṃ na bhāṣate Bbh 179.4 f.; (ātmabhāvasya) bhūta-varṇā(ḥ), *true description*, Samādh 22.44; so also bhūtaṃ varṇaṃ Divy 229.3; bhūtena varṇena Mv iii.344.5; bhūtāḥ putrā(ḥ) SP 110.3 and 5, *true, real sons* (bhagavato, or tathāgatasya); bhūtakalyāṇamitra- Gv 122.7, and °trāṇi Śikṣ 2.6, *true 'good friends'* (also bhūta-nayānuśāsanyupasaṃhāraḥ Śikṣ 2.6); (sa bodhisattvaḥ) pratirūpakaś ca bhavati, no tu bhūto bodhisattvaḥ Bbh 159.8, *he is a counterfeit bodhisattva, not a true one*; (ayaṃ) sa bhūto (*true*) bodhisattvānāṃ... vīryārambha iyaṃ sā bhūtā tathāgatapūjā SP 408.1; bhūtaṃ (phalavipākaṃ, acc. sg.) Mv i.207.14 = ii.12.4; bhūtaṃ padaṃ śāntam anāsravaṃ ca... prakāśayanti SP 24.17 (vs), *they make known the true place (state), calm, free from impurities* (i. e. enlightenment, presumably); adverbs, bhūtaṃ *truly, in truth*, śmaśānamadhye vasito 'smi bhūtaṃ LV 206.2 (vs); bhūtataḥ Śikṣ 47.6, *according to truth*; (**2**) (nt., = Pali id.), *vegetable*: bījagrāma-bhūtagrāma-vināśanaṃ Mvy 8431, and °bhūtagrāma-pātanāt Prāt 504.11 (cf. Pali bhūta-gāma, Vin. iv.34.34), *all sorts of vegetables.* See next.

bhūta-koṭi (°ṭī?), f. (cf. **koṭi,** *end, goal*; and Pali koṭi-gata, *having reached the end = perfection, salvation*), *the true goal*: listed Mvy 1708 among 'synonyms for paramārtha, *the supreme truth*' (note 1707 tattvam, 1709 tathātā, etc., all *intellectual* terms; not nirvāṇa!) = Tib. yaṅ dag paḥi mthaḥ, *real end*; Mvy 407 sthito bhūtakoṭyām, of a Tathāgata, *abiding in*... (presumably *absolute truth*); LV 351.8 jñātā dharmatathatā avabuddhā bhūtakoṭiḥ; 423.1 bhūtakoṭy-avikopana-cakraṃ, *the wheel which does not disturb* (move, upset, confuse) *the true end* (perfect knowledge or enlightenment); 428.11 bhūtakoṭy-avikopita-jñāna-viṣayatvād avitathānanyathāvādī; 437.1 bhūtakoṭīm (v.l. °ṭim) akoṭīm (v.l. °ṭim) ca tathatāyāṃ tathatvataḥ... dharmacakraṃ nirucyate, *the wheel of the law is declared to be the true end* (goal, conclusion), *and that which has no end* (or beginning, in time).

bhūta-caram, adv., *in former time*: MSV i.266.20 (prose); = the usual bhūtapūrvam (as in Skt.), which should perhaps be read; Tib. cited as sṅon byaṅ (read surely byuṅ) ba = bhūtapūrvam (Mvy 8302).

Bhūtaḍāmara (see **Ḍāmara**), n. of a deity: śrī-Bh° Sādh 512.15, etc.

bhūta-darśimant (see **darśimant**), *truly wise*: °mān Mv i.184.16, said of Buddha.

Bhūtamukha, n. of a yakṣa: Māy 67.

Bhūtaraśmi, n. of a Bodhisattva: Gv 442.26.

Bhūtārthaketu, n. of a former Buddha: Mv i.139.12.

bhūtārthika, adj. (from Skt. bhūtārtha, subst., plus -ika), *real, genuine*: ime te °kā mṛgarathakā(ḥ) Bbh 282.3.

Bhūti, n. of a brahman, father of **Subhūti** (2): Av ii.127.12.

bhūtika, (**1**) ifc. Bhvr. (= Skt. bhūti), (having... as) *origin, basis*: [kālasūtra-bhūtikaṃ Mv i.17.7, but this is prob. a corruption, see P. Mus, cited s.v. **saṃjīva**;] abhūtikāś ca bhūtāś ca Laṅk 239.9, or °kā ca bhūtāni 368.14, *having no* (real) *origin* or *basis*; (**2**) adj. (to bhūta, in different senses, plus -ika, cf. Skt. and BHS bhautika), *what is derived from the elements* (in this sense AMg. bhūtiya, and cf. Pali cātummahābhūtika): Laṅk 355.2 janma bhūtānāṃ bhūtikasya ca (cf. bhautikam in prec. line); from bhūta in another mg., sarvabhūtikā balir deyā Mmk 39.18 (prose), *an offering to all goblins* (or *creatures*?) *is to be made.*

bhūtvā-śraddha, adj., see **abhūtvā-śraddhā.**

bhū-parpaṭaka, m. (= **bhūmi-p°,** q.v.), a kind of *edible mushroom*: °kāḥ (in list of foods) Śikṣ 291.2 (not 'medicinal herbs' with Bendall and Rouse).

Bhūma, n. of a yakṣa leader: Māy 236.9.

bhūmi, f., (**1**) (as in Skt.) *earth, ground*: bhūmyāṃ va carā(ḥ) = **bhūmya** (q.v.) or **bhaumya** (gods); in LV 187.12 (prose) udyāna-bhūmim upaśobhitaṃ (n. sg.) seems to present bhūmi as nt., but Tib. seems to have read simply udyānam (skyed mos tshal), without bhūmi; udyānabhūmi (Pali uyyāna°) is however common, SP 96.11 etc.; (**2**) *capital, amount* (of money; unrecorded, but seems used in same mg. Mbh. Crit. ed. ii.47.2c, where it contrasts with phala, *interest*): kāśibhūmiṃ kṣamati Mv iii.375.18, see s.v. **kāśi,** 2; (**3**) (= Pali id.) *stage, state,* *condition*: kumāra-bhūmīm (*childhood*) atināmayitvā SP 68.7 (vs); śaikṣa-bhūmau, loc. (Pali sekha-bh°), *the stage of a śaikṣa*, q.v., SP 70.13; nirvāṇa-bhūmi-sthitā(ḥ) sma ity ātmāna (i. e. °naṃ? WT ātmanaḥ) saṃjānatāṃ (gen. pl. pres. pple.) SP 71.2 (prose), *supposing themselves* (erroneously) *to be fixed in the state of nirvāṇa*; apāya-bhūmiḥ, *state of misfortune* (one of three such, see **apāya**) SP 96.11; pithanārthāya apāyabhūmināṃ LV 178.7 (vs), *to block the way* (see **pithana**) *to the states of misfortune*; in LV 178.9 (vs) text baddhvā dvāra nirayāya bhūmināṃ, but read tri-r-apāya-bhū° with Tib. ṅan soṅ gsum poḥi sayi sgo chod de; dānta-bhūmim (*state of being self-controlled*) anuprāptaḥ SP 256.2; more specifically, (**4**) *stage* of progressive religious development; for the **śrāvaka**, seven are listed Mvy 1140–1147: **śuklavidarśanā-bh°**, **gotra-**, **aṣṭamaka-**, **darśana-**, **tanu-** (var. tanū-), **vītarāga-** (var. vigatarāga-), **kṛtāvi-**; the same ŚsP 1562.21 ff.; in ŚsP 1473.11 ff. (where śuklavipaśyanā-bh° for the first) and 1520.20 ff. these (nirdarśana- for 4) are followed by pratyekabuddha-bh°, bodhisattva-bh°, and buddha-bh°, making in all ten **bhūmi** *of a bodhisattva* (!), bodhisattvasya . . . daśa bhūmayaḥ, 1473.17–18; this list noted only in ŚsP; the usual list of ten bodhisattva-bhūmi is that given Mvy 885–895; Dharmas 64; Dbh 5.7 ff.; Sūtrāl. xx–xxi.32 ff., viz. **pramuditā** (Sūtrāl. muditā), **vimalā**, **prabhākarī**, **arciṣmatī**, **sudurjayā** (Sūtrāl. durjayā), **abhimukhī**, **dūraṃgamā** (Mvy Kyoto ed. °maḥ, read °mā with Mironov), **acalā**, **sādhumatī**, **dharmameghā**; the last three are named Laṅk 15.5; in Bbh 332.20 ff. the ten bodhisattva-bhūmayaḥ of Dbh (which is specifically referred to) are called bodhisattva-vihārāḥ; the 10 bodhisattva-bhūmi usually means this group, often referred to, so e. g. in Mmk 15.24 (while in Mmk 13.8 eight bodhisattva-bhūmi, presumably the first eight of the standard ten, are mentioned as attained by Pratyekabuddhas); a different list of ten 'bodhisattvāna bhūmayo' in Mv i.76.11 ff. (vss), viz: durārohā, **baddhamālā** (q.v., text °mānā), puṣpamaṇḍitā, rucirā, cittavistarā, rūpavatī, durjayā (cf. No. 5 of the list above), janmanideśa (-bhūmi?), yauvarājya(-bhūmi?), and **abhiṣeka**(-bhūmi); only the last of these, q.v., is mentioned elsewhere, in Gv; on the other hand, Bbh has an otherwise unknown list of bodhisattva-bhūmi, numbering six, 84.22 ff., or seven, 367.6, listed 367.3 ff. and identical with the other list except for an additional first member, gotra-bhūmi; the (other) six are **adhimukticaryā**-bh°, **śuddhyadhyāśaya-** (or **śuddhādhy°**), **caryāpratipatti-**, **niyata-** (or **niyatā** bhūmi), **niyatacaryā-** (or **°ryā-pratipatti-**), and **niṣṭhāgamana**-bh°.

-bhūmika, ifc. (**bhūmi** 4 plus -ka), *belonging to . . . stage*, of Bodhisattvas, in eka-°kāḥ, dvi-°kāḥ, etc., down to daśa-°kāḥ: Kv 64.10 ff.; (also in other mgs. of bhūmi, e. g.) kuto-bhūmikas tvaṃ MSV iii.143.10, *from what country are you*?

Bhūmideva, n. of a former Buddha: Mv i.140.6.

[**bhūmin**, acc. to text occurs in gen. pl. LV 178.9, but see **bhūmi** 3.]

bhūmi-parpaṭaka, (properly) m. (= Pali °pappaṭaka, m., DN iii.87.1, compared to ahicchattaka, *mushroom*, and eaten, line 3; PTSD fails to define), a kind of *edible mushroom* (see s.v. **parpaṭaka**): °kaṃ (here nt. in form, but the foll. epithets m., and so **bhū-p°**, **pṛthivī-p°**) prādurbhaveya sayyathāpi nāma chātrakaṃ (em.) evaṃ varṇapratibhāso, so . . . Mv i.340.12; also 341.1, 5, 8, 13. The mss. are variously corrupt.

Bhūmibalavaiśāradyadhara, n. of a Bodhisattva: Mvy 731.

Bhūmimati, n. of a Bodhisattva: Gv 442.18.

? **bhūmi-sūcaka**, m., acc. to Burnouf and Kern, *dog* (a mg. given to sūcaka in Hindu Lexx.): khara-sūkarā kroṣṭuka bhūmi-sūcakāḥ pratiṣṭhitasyeha bhavanti nityam SP 96.12 (vs). Tib. seems to intend to render literally. sa ḥdzul (bar) *ground glide*, i. e. (animals) *that glide along the ground* (?); for the preceding animal names Tib. has *ass, hog*, and *fox* (wa; but cf. wa-spyaṅ, *jackal*). Could not the BHS mean: *asses, swine, and jackals mark* (indicate) *the 'ground'* (*state, condition*? see **bhūmi** 3) *of him always as he is established here on earth* (preceding line says he always dwells in an **apāya**-bhūmi)? However, Chin. *dogs* in the later versions; the oldest version seems to lack the word.

bhūmya, adj. (= Pali bhumma, of gods, also creatures, bhūtāni), *of the earth*; common in Mv, not noted elsewhere (= **bhauma**); almost always used of a class of gods, with **deva**, q.v.: Mv i.40.11, 14; 229.11, 14; 239.20; 240.3; 332.15; ii.138.6 ff.; 314.4; 349.20; iii.319.8 (same passage LV 401.1, bhauma); 334.13; on ii.348.16 see s.v. **deva** (read with mss. bhūmyāṃ va carā); also, rarely, (bhūtāni) bhūmyāni Mv i.290.16.

Bhūmyavacāraṇānugama, n. of a dhāraṇī: Gv 66.15.

bhūyaś-chandika (see **chandika**), *greedy* (*for more*): Mvy 2211.

bhūyas-kāma-tā (= Pali bhiyyo-kamyatā; cf. prec.), *desire for more, greed*: Mvy 2208.

bhūyasya, °syā, °so, **bhūyosya**, with (in Mv rarely without) mātrayā (instr. of Skt. mātrā), or once mātrāṃ, = Pali bhiyyoso-mattāya, adv. or adverbial phrase, *in specially high degree*. The common BHS expression is bhūyasyā (instr. fem. of Skt. bhūyas-) mātrayā, e. g. SP 23.1; LV 321.17; Mv ii.345.2 (vs, prob. read with v.l. °sya, m.c.); exceptionally bhūyasya (a m.c.?) mātrāṃ (so mss., Senart em. °aṃ) Mv ii.338.13 (vs); twice, at least, in Mv the noun mātrayā is omitted (by error?), and text presents bhūyasya (so, a! but here prose) alone, i.231.13, or, acc. to Senart with 5 of 6 mss., bhūyosya (cf. Pali) i.3.14 (prose); in SP 71.10 (prose) ed. with Nep. mss. has the usual bhūyasyā mātrayā, but Kashgar rec. bhūyaso (intending Skt. °śo; cf. Pali bhiyyoso) mātrayā. See also s.v. **yadbhūyasā**.

bhūyo-'bhiprāya, m., *desire for more, greed*: Mvy 2213.

bhūyo-rucitā (so Index, and so Mironov except that he reads -rūcitā, with ū which seems surely erroneous; Kyōtō ed. text °rucitaḥ, which ght be a Bhvr. adj. from -rucitā), = prec.: Mvy 2212.

bhūyosya, see **bhūyasya**.

bhūri, f. (= Pali id. or °rī; cf. Renou, JA 1939 p. 384 n. 1), *intelligence*: vidyā udapāsi buddhir ud° bhūrir ud° Mv iii.332.14, 17, 19; (vidyodapādi) bhūrir uda° medhoda° LV 348.3, 18; so with utpannā for uda° 417.17. Cf. next.

bhūrika, adj. or subst. m. (to prec. plus -ka), (an) *intelligent, wise* (man): tasya nātidūre bhūrikas tiṣṭhati, sa saṃlakṣayati Divy 263.1; °kaḥ kathayati 29. Taken as n. pr. in ed., which is obviously impossible; if it were a man's name he would be somehow identified, but he is not.

Bhūriṇī, n. of a goddess: Sādh 75.15.

Bhūrisattva, n. of a former Buddha: Mv i.139.10.

Bhūruṇḍa, n. of a serpent king: Mmk 18.24. Cf. **Bheruṇḍa**, **Maruṇḍa**.

? **bhūṣaṇā**, f. (only nt. in Pali and Pkt.; in Skt. nt. or 'exceptionally' m.), *ornament*: hā istrigārā vigaḍita bhūṣaṇābhiḥ LV 231.6 (vs), *stripped of ornaments*; v.l. °ta-bhūṣaṇāni (could be construed as Bhvr. adj. with istrigārā, or better istrigārā-vigaḍita-bhūṣaṇāni as one word, *alas for the ornaments fallen from the harem-women*!).

Bhūṣaṇendraprabha, n. of a kiṃnara: Mvy 3421.

-bhūṣiṇikā (Skt. -bhūṣiṇ-ī plus endearing -ka, § 22.34), *adorned*: īdṛśarūpa-su-bhūṣiṇikāṃ LV 323.5 (vs), of daughter(s) of Māra.

-bhṛkuṭika, ifc. Bhvr. (Skt. °ṭī plus -ka; cf. Pali bhākuṭika), *frown*: vyapagata-°kā (f.) LV 26.22; °kaḥ 118.17; cf. **-bhrūkuṭika**.

Bhṛkuṭinī (cf. next), n. of an attendant on the four direction-rulers: Mahāsamāj. Waldschmidt, Kl. Skt. Texte 4, 173.10.

Bhṛkuṭī, n. of a goddess (= **Ārya-Bhṛ°**, q.v.), regularly associated with Hayagrīva: Sādh 37.9 etc.

bhṛkuṭīka, adj. (cf. Pali bhākuṭika, adj., and **-bhṛkuṭika**), *frowning*: in RP 31.2 (vs) read āvāsagṛdhra (= °rāḥ) °kās (n. pl. m.).

Bhṛgin, and **Bhṛgīratha**, names of two great seers (ṛṣi): Māy 256.18. The latter perh. hyper-Skt. for Bhagīratha, and the former abstracted from it? But cf. **Bhṛṅgin.**

Bhṛgu, (**1**) n. of a cakravartin: Mvy 3573; (**2**) n. of an attendant on the four direction-rulers: Mahāsamāj. Waldschmidt, Kl. Skt. Texte 4, 173.10.

Bhṛṅgānaṅga = **Alimanmatha**, q.v.: Sādh 146.3.

Bhṛṅgin, n. of a great ṛṣi: Māy 256.17.

bhṛtikā (= Pali bhatikā, Skt. bhṛti), *service for hire, wages*: °kayā karma karomi Divy 303.30, and ff.

bhekṣāka-, see **bhaikṣ°**.

bheda, a martial art, = **bhedya**; associated with **cheda**, q.v.: Mv ii.74.2.

-bhedanaka, see **ghaṭa-bhe°**.

bhedya, nt., a martial art (also **bheda**, q.v.); always associated with **chedya**, q.v. for occurrences.

bheraṇḍa(ka), **bheruṇḍaka**, m. (Pali bheraṇḍaka, *jackal* acc. to Jāt. comm. v.276.9; the form bheruṇḍa, cited by Burnouf, Lotus 371, is read bheruṇḍaka in our SP, and has, doubtless by chance, not been noted elsewhere in BHS), some sort of beast of prey which makes a terrible sound (Mv ii.140.15 °ḍa-bhairava [mss. bhīrava, bhīruva]-ruteṣu; iii.123.9; 264.12) and eats human flesh (SP 83.11; 85.13); Tib. renders variously, on Mvy 4785 spyaṅ (*wolf*) or ce spyaṅ (*jackal*, acc. to Das also *fox*); on SP 83.11 ce spyaṅ, on 85.13 and 86.12 lce spyaṅ (= ce spyaṅ); on LV 306.6 wa (*fox*, but cf. wa spyaṅ, *jackal*); the word śṛgāla, *jackal*, is prob. a different animal, since it is closely associated with our word in LV 306.6; SP 83.11 and 86.12; in LV, where Tib. wa renders our word, śṛgāla is rendered by ce spyaṅ, while in the two SP passages the reverse is the case, wa rendering śṛgāla! Kern on SP renders *hyena*, a plausible guess. Forms: bheraṇḍa Mv ii.140.15; °ḍaka Mv iii.123.9 (both vss); bheruṇḍaka Mvy 4785; Mv iii.264.12 (prose); SP 83.11; 85.13; 86.12 (all vss); LV 306.6 (prose). In Deśīn. 6.108 bheruṇḍa is defined dīvī (= dvīpin; comm. citrakaḥ); the hyena is 'spotted', as well as the leopard.

Bheruṇḍa, n. of a serpent king: Mmk 18.24. Cf. **Bhūruṇḍa, Maruṇḍa.** (Cf. also prec.)

bhelā, a high number: Gv 106.11. Cf. next, and **telā.**

bhelu, m. or f., a high number: Gv 133.21; Mvy 7893, cited from Gv; Tib. ñar ñer, which also renders **tela**, q.v.; cf. prec.

bhaikṣāka (to Skt. and BHS **bhikṣāka** plus -a), as adj., *relating to a mendicant*: Buddhacarita xii.40 °kaṃ liṅgam āśritaḥ, and as n. *mendicancy*, ib. x.23; xiii.10; in BHS bhaikṣāka-kula, nt., *a family that* (regularly) *gives almsfood* (to a monk), is to be read for bhaikṣākulaṃ Divy 263.2 (yad apy asmākam ekaṃ °kulaṃ, tad api śramaṇo Gautamo 'nvāvartayati, said by a non-Buddhist), for bhaikṣyāka-kula MSV iv.226.17, and for bhekṣāka-kula KP 114.2, 5, where a monk is warned not to cultivate such relations. Tib. on KP zas ster (baḥi) khyim.

[**bhaikṣākula**, see prec.]

bhaikṣuka, m. (= Skt., BHS bhikṣu), *monk, mendicant*: Mvy 2999 = Tib. spoṅ ba pa, *monk* (Das); here used of a person living in the fourth āśrama of the Hindu system (but not, as pw 7.365 states, as epithet of that āśrama itself! prec. by vānaprastha, which in Skt. is usually applied to an individual person); puṇyaparikṣīṇa iva bhaikṣukaḥ LV 333.13 (vs), *like a mendicant who has spent his store of merit.*

bhaiṣaja, (**1**) m. (not recorded in this sense), *physician*: vaidya-°jādayaḥ sulabhāḥ Av ii.167.8 (prose); (**2**) nt. (= Skt. Lex. id., AMg. bhesaja; Skt. °jya), *medicine, curing drug*; only noted in vss and in positions where °jya would be metr. impossible; perh. m.c.?: LV 4.3 (sa vaidyarājo 'mṛtabhaiṣajapradaḥ); RP 22.15; 23.5; 26.9.

Bhaiṣajyaguruvaiḍūrya-(also °**dūrya-**)**-prabha**, n. of a Tathāgata: ŚsP 1.10 (°dū°), and (m.!) of a work in which he is prominent, Mvy 1404; the latter called °prabha-sūtra, Śikṣ 13.12; the name adds -rāja after °prabha-, Śikṣ 174.5 (in citation from the work), etc.; Mmk 7.9 (°dū°); the work is called °prabharāja-sūtra Śikṣ 174.1. The same person is prob. meant by **Bhaiṣajyavaidūryarāja**, q.v.

Bhaiṣajyarāja, (**1**) n. of a Bodhisattva: SP 3.5; 224.1 ff.; 267.1; 395.1 ff.; 404.3, 5; 414.7 ff.; 425.3; 470.11; (**2**) n. of a former Buddha: LV 172.8.

Bhaiṣajyarājasamudgata = **Bhaiṣajyasamudgata**, q.v.: SP 425.6.

Bhaiṣajyavaidūryarāja, n. of a Tathāgata: Mmk 64.2; prob. intends the same as **Bhaiṣajyaguruvaiḍūryaprabha(rāja)**, q.v.

Bhaiṣajyasamudgata, n. of a Bodhisattva: SP 3.5; 470.11; in 425.6 called Bhaiṣajyarājasamudgata; associated with **Bhaiṣajyarāja**, q.v.

Bhaiṣajyasena, n. of a Bodhisattva: Kv 1.15.

Bhoganagaraka (nt.; = Pali °gara), n. of a town, apparently of the Mallas: MPS 21.7.

Bhogavant, n. of a nāga: Māy 221.24.

bhoṅkāra, see s.v. **bhoskāra.**

bhojana (cf. the cognate Skt., BHS bhoga, in this mg.; normally bhojana only *food*, in Skt., Pali, Pkt., and BHS), (carnal) *enjoyment, sexual intercourse*; only in phrase (or cpd.) sabhojana kula, *a household in which sexual intercourse is going on or about to be practised*; in such a house a monk is forbidden to 'intrude' (see **anupraskandati**) and sit or stand: Prāt 511.8 (a Chin. version interprets as a house where man and wife engage, sc. habitually or excessively, in sexual intercourse); Mvy 8465 sabhojanakula-niṣadyā, and 8466 °sthānam (Tib. ñal po byed pa[r] śom paḥi khyim na, *in a house where preparations are being made to perform sexual intercourse*); so in Pali Vin. iv.95.7, interpreted in this way by both the old and the later comms.; modern interpreters consistently refuse to admit this mg., but the agreement of northern and southern tradition forbids anything else, and the cognate bhoga has the same mg.

bhojanīya, nt. (= Pali id.), *soft food*; regularly cpd. or associated with **khādanīya**, *hard food*, q.v. for examples. Cf. also **bhojya.**

-bhojika (Skt. -bhojin plus -ka), in nitya-bhojikā (v.l. °bhojanakā), n. pl. masc., Mv i.309.4, *enjoying continuous feeding* (said of brahmans, at a king's house).

bhojya (nt., = Pali bhojja, less common than bhojanīya, in cpd. khajja-bh°), *soft food*, = **bhojanīya**; regularly cpd. or associated with **khādya** or **khajja**, qq.v. for examples.

bhoti = Skt. bhavati (MIndic o for ava, see § 1.29 and Chap. 43, s.v. bhū 2).

bhoskāra (m.?; em.; mss. bhotk°; MSV iv.15.19 bhoṅkāra), some part of the education of a brahman, acc. to Index *rules of address*: Divy 485.7 (see s.v. **autkara**).

bhautika, (adj.?) subst. nt. (cf. Skt. id.; here in specialized mgs.), (**1**) possibly adj., *real* or *material*, in Laṅk 17.5, but the reading is very doubtful and the sense at least equally so, see s.v. **abhauti** and below; (**2**) subst. nt., *object of sense*: in Dharmas 40 = viṣaya or indriyārtha (five are listed: rūpa, śabda, gandha, rasa, and sparśa, corresponding, tho in different order, to the five mahābhūtāni listed in 39 just before). Acc. to Suzuki's Index to Laṅk, the Chin. versions of Laṅk indicate bhautika = *the*

4 viṣaya or *color, odor, flavor, contact* (note omission of *sound*, and the fact that in Laṅk 124.8 ākāśa is added only parenthetically; cf. the 4 dhātu of Pali, paṭhavī-, āpo-, tejo-, vāyo-dhātu, Childers, s.v.); in Laṅk 205.10 (omit bhūta- with 2 mss.) bhautika-svalakṣaṇa-vināśānupalabdhir, evidently *products of the bhūtāni*, presumably as in Dharmas 40. The passage Laṅk 123.11–124.16 must, it seems, somehow be interpreted in the light of these passages, but is obscure to me (cf. also Laṅk 355.1). Suzuki is not very helpful on it; e. g. 124.13 na tu mahābhūtānām certainly cannot mean *which* (primary elements) *are non-existent*, but rather: (the mahābhūtāni are the causes of the bhautikāni), *but not* (the bhautikāni) *of the mahābhūtāni*, i. e. *but not vice versa*. In Mvy 1847 bhautika-rūpam appears to be parallel and complementary to 1846 **upādāya-rūpam**, q.v.; this suggests that bhautikarūpam = Pali bhūta-rūpa (Childers and PTSD s.v. rūpa), which acc. to Vism. = the four mahābhūtāni, earth, water, fire, and air (listed Mvy 1838–1841), contrary to Dharmas and the Chin. as cited by Suzuki, above; for the viṣayas are included among the 24 upādā(ya)-rūpa of Pali. On the basis of Mvy 1846–7 we might conjecture that in Laṅk 17.5 (see **abhauti**) abhautika = upādāya(-rūpam), and bhautika = bhautika(Pali bhūta)-rūpam. But if Dharmas and Chin. are right, bhautika would mean virtually the opposite of Pali bhūta(-rūpa).

bhauma, adj. (Skt., *of the earth*, but not used of gods), a class of gods, = **bhūmya**, q.v., and see **deva**: Mvy 3076; LV 266.1; 368.3; 396.14; 401.1. See also **bhaumya**.

bhaumadeva-lipi, a kind of script: LV 126.4; confirmed Tib. sa blaḥi lhaḥi yi ge.

bhaumya, adj. (presumably = **bhauma, bhūmya**), *of the earth*, ep. of devas: bhaumyā devāś ca yakṣāś ca rākṣasāś ca kāmāvacarāś ca rūpāvacarāś ca devāḥ Mv i.159.5.

bhraṃśanin, adj. (Skt. bhraṃśana plus -in; cf. bhraṃśin), *causing to fall*: (kāmāḥ . . .) dhyānarddhītapasaś (so with mss.; Lefm. °saṃ) ca bhraṃśanī (n. pl.) abudhānāṃ LV 323.22 (vs), *causing to fall the contemplation, supernatural powers, and penance of the ignorant* (so Tib., which for bhraṃśanī has ñams par byed, *damaging*).

bhrama (m.? Skt. Lex. *spring*), *water-course, conduit*, in **udaka-bhrama**, q.v.; and in Divy 538.10, where text Kubjottarānukrameṇa niṣpalāyitā; mss. are cited as reading -bhrameṇa, which must certainly be kept; it is not clear whether the syllable -nu- is in the mss. or not; if it is, we should have to assume an otherwise unknown stem anubhrama; if not, since Kubjottarā is fem., bhrameṇa gives excellent sense. See Lévi, Karmav p. 269.

bhramantra, nt., a high number: Mvy 7881 = Tib. gzhal thim (thil); gzhal = mātra, suggesting **bhramātra**, q.v., as the true reading. However, the form is cited from Gv, and Gv 133.17 has the same form as Mvy. In Gv 106.7 **atramantrā**, q.v., seems to correspond.

bhramarikā (= AMg. bhamarī; Skt. °rikā and Pali bhamarikā = *humming-top*), a kind of musical instrument: Mv iii.407.20.

bhramātra, m., a high number: Mvy 7752b = Tib. gzhal thims (see **bhramantra**).

bhrami (f.? in this sense Skt. bhrama and Pkt. bhami, Sheth, but not Skt. bhrami), *giddiness*: gātrakampaṃ bhramiś cāpi chardi praśravanaṃ bahuḥ Mmk 151.16 (vs).

bhramu (= Pali bhamu, also bhamuka, bhamukha; cf. **bhrumukha**), *eyebrow*: asita-bhramū ca snigdhalomabhramū ca Mv ii.44.8 (prose, in list of the **anuvyañjana**).

Bhraṣṭālā(?), n. of a town: MSV i.xvii.10; corrupt; Tib. yul gñis grogs.

bhrumukha (or perhaps **bhrū°**? cf. Pali under **bhramu**; adaptation to Skt. bhrū, secondarily?), *eyebrow*: prabhāsayantī bhrumukhāntarātu (Nep. mss. °ta; all mss. bhrumukhā° or bhrū°, which is not 'nonsensical' as the note says but the true reading; ed. em. bhramukā°) ūrṇāya kośād iyam ekaraśmiḥ SP 8.11 (vs); lalāṭe va (read ca?) bhrūmukhe (one ms. ru°, for bhru°) ca śobhe yathaiva candramaso Mv ii.297.3 (prose; so read with mss.); mahānilā (? so mss.; Senart em. °nalaṃ) ca bhrūmukhāṃ (so one ms., the other has short u, intending bhru°; one of these must be read) candro vā pūrṇamāsiye Mv ii.306.19 (vs).

-bhrūkuṭika, ifc. Bhvr. (= **-bhṛkuṭika**, so v.l.; cf. Skt. bhrūkuṭī, Schmidt, Nachträge), *frown*, in apagata-°kaḥ: Mvy 2405.

bhrūṇa-dheya (see **-dheya**), in °yam idaṃ cittaṃ niḥsāram anidarśanam Ud xxxi.4. This cpd. of -dheya not recorded in Pali; is it a false Sktization of the troublesome Pali word bhūna-ha- or °hu? This word the Pali comms. seem evidently to misunderstand. Cf. Renou, JA 1939, p. 348 with n. 1, who connects the Pali word with Vedic and Skt. bhrūṇa-han; acc. to his note 1, the Skt. form is to be 'restored' in Dharmasamuccaya 16.8. Renou apparently did not know our BHS form, which seems only to complicate the question further. It is clear, in any case, that it is an uncomplimentary epithet. The Pali comms. interpret the Pali as *destroying prosperity* or *welfare*.

bhrūmukha? see **bhru°**.

bhraiṅgarika, m., some sort of cook (followed by sūpakāra): Mvy 3767 = Tib. phyag tshaṅs (or phyag tshaṅ, = *cook*, Das) skyems (*drink*) mal (*place*?) ba; BR doubtfully suggest derivation from *bhriṅgāra for bhṛṅgāra, *water-pot* (note difference of quantity of the vowel in the second syllable). Chin. seems to mean *preparer of seats and beds*.

M

ma, m.c. for neg. mā, § 3.27.

Makara, n. of a nāga king: Mvy 3236; Māy 247.5.

Makaradhvaja, n. of a yakṣa: Māy 98.

Makaraṃdama, n. of a yakṣa: Māy 50.

Makaraputra, n. of a nāga king: Māy 246.17; 247.5.

makuṭa, nt. or m. (= Pali and Skt. Lex. id.; one doubtful Skt. occurrence, Schmidt, Nachträge; Skt. muk°), *diadem, crown*: Mv i.129.7 (vs, read with mss. śiraṃ . . . sa-makuṭaṃ; Senart's em. impossible in meter and implausible in sense); Mv i.153.1 = ii.29.16 (vs; same vs i.226.13 muk°); ii.316.11 (vs, read with one ms. śīryanto, or °ta, mahyaṃ makuṭo . . .); iii.178.16, 19 (°ṭam, n. sg.); Divy 411.12 (°ṭaṃ dattam, n. sg.); Mmk 63.2 etc.; of flowers, gandha-makuṭā Mv ii.463.3, and °ṭāni 4 (prose), *fragrant crowns* (of flowers).

Makuṭadantī, n. of an ogress: SP 400.5; two mss. cited as Maṭṭa-dantī, °caṇḍī, intending perhaps Maṭuta°; Burnouf Maṭutacandī (so!).

Makuṭabandha (m. or nt.), = next: caitye °dhe tu Mmk 598.23 (vs; metr. correct).

Makuṭabandhana, nt. (= Pali id.; cf. prec.), n. of a caitya of the Mallas: Divy 201.6 (°naṃ, n. sg.); Mmk 595.4 (vs; °ne).

makunda (m.; = AMg. maunda; also **mukuṇḍa**,

mukunda), a kind of drum: Mv ii.159.6 (prose) °daṃ, acc. sg.; so mss., Senart em. mu°; after mṛdaṅgam.

Makkoṭaka(-parvata), m., n. of a mountain of torment in hell: °te Śikṣ 71.2. Acc. to Bendall and Rouse, Tib. gnad ḥjoms pa (*destroying the vitals*), which fits the description of torments there. (AMg. makkoḍaa is defined *ant*; Deśīn. 6.142 makkoḍa, *a pile*, rāśi, *for setting up a machine*.)

makṣita (cf. Pali makkhita), semi-MIndic spelling for Skt. mra°, *smeared*: -bhasmādi-makṣitā nagnāḥ LV 258.3 (vs); some mss. and Calc. mra°.

makṣī (= AMg. macchī; cf. Skt. makṣikā, Ved. makṣ, makṣā; Pali only makkhikā recorded), *fly*, or other winged insect: Mv i.211.5 = ii.15.5 (prose) makṣī pi, *even a fly* (did not fly over the bodhisattva's mother while he was in her womb). So, or °kṣi, the mss. both times, unanimously; Senart em. pakṣī, quite needlessly.

Magadha-lipi, *Magadhan script*, a kind of writing: LV 125.20.

magara, Gv 133.1, in place of **āgāra**, q.v., a high number.

magava, m., Mvy 7776, or nt., id. 7905, a high number, = Tib. brtag(s) yas. (Cf. **mṛgava, mīgava**; but the Tib. rendering and Gv equivalents are different.) Mvy 7905 is cited from Gv, which in its place reads **agava**, q.v.

maguli-, some kind of bird: (tittiri)pakṣaiḥ strīṃ, magulipakṣaiḥ putrāṃ (acc. pl.; sc. dadyāt) Mmk 465.7 (prose).

Magha, n. of a merchant: Divy 108.8 ff.

Maghā, n. of a yakṣiṇī: MSV i.17.7. See **Ālikāvendā**.

maghī, n. of a medicinal herb, antidote for poisons, esp. of snakes: maghī nāmauṣadhī sarvaviṣapraśamanī AsP 52.11 (prose); similarly Gv 497.2 (tayā... sarvāśīviṣāḥ palāyante).

maṅku, maṅgu, madgu, adj., also in comp. with -bhāva, -bhūta (= Pali maṅku; cf. also **durmaṅku**; maṅku once in Vedic, ŚB, app. *staggering*, BR, but perh. not the same word): *mentally disturbed, upset, abashed, out of countenance*; all three forms are clearly variants of each other (cf. pudgala:puṃgala etc., § 3.4), as is shown notably by a cliché, tūṣṇībhūto (once °tvā, Divy 633.24; not in Mvy) madgubhūtaḥ srastaskandhaḥ adhomukho niṣpratibhānaḥ (Divy °pratibhaḥ; in Mvy before adho°) pradhyānaparamaḥ (Mvy °paraḥ) Mvy 7122–26; Divy 633.24, 27 (here accs.); 636.7; Av i.48.10, in which, for madgu- of the other texts, Mvy 7122 reads maṅgu-, or with Mironov maṅku-(v.l. maṅgu-). The form madgu also in Av i.286.5 vyāpadyate madguḥ pratitiṣṭhati kopaṃ saṃjanayati; in MSV ii.86.2 madguvo (n. pl. f.); see also **amadgu**; and in Bbh 123.10 (na ca bodhisattvo) yācanakam avahasati... na madgubhāvam (so ms., ed. em. maṅku°) asyopasaṃharati; but maṅku elsewhere in Bbh, (bhūtaṃ ca) doṣaṃ (of someone else) pratichādayati, na vivṛṇoti, yenāsya syān maṅkubhāvaḥ 254.15, *so that he would be embarrassed*; maṅku-bhā(vam..., lacuna) 150.4, filled by Tib. bag ḥkhums pa, *timidity, 'little-mindedness'*, and elsewhere: maṅkur bhavati, Hoernle, JRAS 1916.711 (= Pali Sn 818 maṅku hoti), *is upset, disturbed* (by the criticism of others); abhīru acchambhina-m (! n. sg. m. required; 'hiatus-bridging' m?) a-maṅku-bhūtaḥ dṛḍhavīryaḥ Mmk 93.24. There seems to be even, once, an apparently related **madgībhūta**, q.v., implying a stem madga, but this is doubtful. See Pischel, SBBA 1904 pp. 816 (fol. 169a), and 823 f., for a discussion which in my opinion leads in a quite wrong direction.

maṅgala, (1) adj., *greeting festively, honoring*, ifc. (so Senart): buddha-dharma-saṃgha-maṅgalo Mv i.36.6; (2) n. of a former Buddha (= Pali id., there third of the 24 Buddhas), the next after Dīpaṃkara acc. to Mv i.248.7 ff., where his story is told; a (perhaps the same) former Buddha, LV 5.9; (3) n. of a nāga-king: Mvy 3308.

Maṅgalasena, n. of an author: Sādh 546.8.

Maṅgalya, (1) n. of a former Buddha: Mv i.137.13; (2) n. of a nāga king: Māy 247.9.

maṅgalya-lipi (v.l. māṅga°), a kind of writing: LV 125.20 (Tib. bkra śes pa = maṅgala).

maṅgu-, see **maṅku**.

maṅgula, see **madgura**.

? **maṅgusa**, see **bhaṅgakula**.

maccha (Pali id.), MIndic for Skt. matsya, *fish*: Mv i.15.10.

macchara (Pali id.), MIndic for Skt. matsara, *envious*: a–m° RP 37.17 (vs). Cf. next.

macchari(-jātaka), so read in colophon Mv ii.64.7 for text **maṃjarī**°; MIndic for Skt. matsarin (cf. prec.), *the selfish man*. The main character in the Pali version, Jāt. 535, is called Macchari-kosiya (once °ika), Jāt. v.383.14 ff. Cf. prec.

majjā-gata, adj., lit. *penetrating to the marrow*, with prema, *intense, heartfelt* (love): Śikṣ 287.9, 10.

mañcakāmañcaka (§ 23.12), *all sorts of couches* or *biers*: mahājanamarako jātaḥ, mṛtajane niskāsyamāne °cake.., Divy 578.24.

[**maṃjarī-jātaka**, read **maccharī**°, q.v.]

mañjiṣṭha, adj. (once in Skt., acc. to BR by error, for Skt. māñj°, from mañjiṣṭhā, *madder*, plus -a; Pali mañjeṭṭha; cf. next), *crimson, bright red*: mañjiṣṭhāśvā etc., repeatedly, Mv i.260.3–7 (no form in mā° noted in mss.); in cpd., or series of words, listing colors, after nīla, pīta, lohita, avadāta, and before sphaṭika, Divy 366.26; Samādh 22.38.

mañjiṣṭhikā (cf. prec.; = Pali mañjeṭṭhikā), lit. *the crimson* (disease), a disease affecting sugar-cane: ikṣukṣetre °kā nāma rogajātir nipatet Bhīk 4b.1 (cf. Pali Vin. ii.256.26).

Mañjughoṣa = **Mañjuśrī**, q.v.; usually in verses: SP 10.7; 14.7; 296.1; Sādh 49.15 etc.; Gv 489.10; Mmk 32.18; 65.22; 69.27 etc. (all these vss).

Mañjudhvaja, (1) n. of a future Buddha, predicted rebirth of **Mañjuśrī**: Mmk 591.26 (vs); (2) n. of a Buddha in the eastern quarter: Sukh 97.3 (prose).

Mañjunātha = **Mañjuśrī**: Sādh 108.2 (vs) etc.

mañjubhāṇin (1) adj. (= Pali id.), *sweetly prattling*: (of children) bālakā °ṇino Mv iii.84.18; (2) n. pr., = **Mañjuśrī**: Mmk 628.1 (vs); and prob. Mmk 434.16, where text seems clearly corrupt, perhaps orig. a verse; text has mañjubhāṇī immediately after bhagavāṃ (= Śākyamuni), possibly then adj., *sweetly speaking*, but more likely refers to Mañjuśrī who has just questioned the Buddha (an acc. sg. form in original?). In Mmk 32.23 (vs) read. prob. Mañjubhāṇī (text °bhāṣiṇī, unmetr.) tato bhāṣe (refers to Mañjuśrī, cf. Mañjughoṣeṇa 18).

Mañjurava = **Mañjuśrī**: Mmk 441.10; 442.10; 448.3; 470.13 (all vss), etc.

Mañjuvajra = **Mañjuśrī**: Sādh 93.10 (vs) etc.

Mañjuvara, = **Mañjuśrī**: Sādh 108.17 (vs) etc.; Mmk 436.2 (vs). Error for **Mañjurava**?

Mañjuśrī or °**śiri**, °**śirī**, in vss (for alternative forms see prec. items, and **Mañjusvara**), n. of a celebrated Bodhisattva, with the stock epithet kumārabhūta: Mvy 650; Dharmas 12; SP 3.3; 7.8 ff.; 260.16 ff.; 275.1 ff.; 386.8; 425.3; Suv 157.18; 239.8; Śikṣ 6.12; 7.7, etc.; Gv 1.11; 46.26; 260.20; 527.22 ff., etc.; Sukh 92.10; Sādh 92.12 etc.; in vss often in semi-MIndic forms, as Mañjuśirī SP 8.10; 11.9; Gv 235.24; Bhad 44; 55; in RP 2.2 listed not among Bodhisattvas but as the first among 60 **anupamacitta**, q.v.; in Mmk often in stem-form Mañjuśriya, see § 10.4; his regular title kumāra-bhūta has led to curious blend with (Kumāra =) Kārttikeya (= Skanda) in Mmk, Kārttikeya-Mañjuśrī Mmk 33.2, 15 (in the latter, Mañjuśriyasya kumārabhūtasya Kārt°-°śrīr nāma Kumāraḥ anucaraḥ, as attending Mañjuśrī!); 45.12 (to be depicted sitting on a peacock, like Skanda Kārttikeya); this blend seems to me secondary; a rather different theory in Lalou, Iconographie, 66 ff., esp. 69.

Mañjuśrībuddhakṣetraguṇavyūha, m., n. of a work: Mvy 1381; °**vyūhālaṃkāra-sūtra** (the same?): Śikṣ 13.16; 53.14; 175.17.

(Ārya)**Mañjuśrīmūlakalpa**, n. of a work, our Mmk; final colophon 721.25.

Mañjuśrīvikrīḍita-sūtra, n. of a work: Śikṣ 149.5.

Mañjuśrīvihāra, m., n. of a work: Mvy 1369.

mañjuṣaka, see **mañjū°**.

Mañjusvara (**1**) = **Mañjuśrī**: (in vss) SP 15.10; 16.8; Mmk 35.10; (**2**) pl., n. of a group or class of future Buddhas: Sukh 76.8 (prose).

mañjūṣaka, nt. (cf. Pali mañjūsaka; m. SP 8.13, °kāṃś, in vs), also **mañju°**, a kind of heavenly flower: SP 5.11; 8.13; 20.1; Mv ii.160.13 (°kāṇi); 286.18 (id.); iii.95.8; mañjuṣakam (n. sg.) Mvy 6164; mañjuṣaka-Kv 79.1.

? **maḍḍuka** (Skt. Lex.), *a kind of drum*, perh. to be read SP 52.1 for maṇḍaka; but see **maṇḍuka**.

Maṇi (in Pali n. of a yakkha), (**1**) n. of a kiṃnara-king: Kv 3.3; (**2**) n. of a yakṣa: Māy 236.28.

maṇika, m. (Skt. maṇi plus -ka, pejorative, see § 22.37), *worthless* (glass-)*gem*: Gv 500.5 (prose).

Maṇikaṇṭha, (**1**) (= Pali id.) n. of a nāga: Mvy 3350; (**2**) n. of a gandharva: Suv 161.17.

Maṇikarṇa, n. of a former Buddha: Mv i.139.6 (so text, v.l. Maṇikuṇḍala; cited in Index as Maṇivarṇa).

Maṇikāṇa, n. of a nāga king: Māy 247.13.

Maṇikānana, n. of a yakṣa: Māy 70.

maṇikāraka (= Skt. and Pali °kāra), *jeweller*: Mv iii.113.7 (prose).

Maṇikuṇḍaladhara, n. of a former Buddha: Mv i.141.3.

Maṇiketu, n. of a Bodhisattva: Gv 3.20.

Maṇigarbha, (**1**) n. of a Buddha: Gv 259.1; (**2**) n. of a park in Bhadraśilā (also **Maṇiratnagarbha**, q.v.): Divy 315.23.

? **Maṇigarbharājaś(i)ritejavatī**, n. of a Buddha: Gv 284.22 (vs). The apparently fem. form can not be right. Should we read °vato, MIndic nom. sg. masc. of -vant-stem? In a list of names; no construction of a fem. adjective seems possible.

Maṇicakra, n. of a former Buddha: Mv i.139.8.

Maṇicakravicitrapratimaṇḍitavyūhā, n. of a loka dhātu: Gv 281.22.

Maṇicūḍa, n. of a nāga: Mvy 3331.

Maṇicūḍā, n. of a kimnara maid: Kv 6.9.

Maṇidharā, n. of a certain mudrā: Kv 74.9 (cf. **Mahāmaṇidhara**).

Maṇidhāriṇī, n. of a kiṃnara maid: Kv 6.9.

? **maṇiprastāraka**, Mv iii.442.13; see s.v. **prastārika**.

? **Maṇiprastha** (so text), n. of an apsaras: °sthanāmāpsarasā Kv 3.12; read °sthā, or perhaps, with pw, Maṇiprabhā.

maṇi-bhūmi, f. (Skt. Lex. and Pkt. id., Sheth), *jewel-inlaid pavement*: (dvāraśālāyāṃ) °mir uparacitā Divy 279.6.

Maṇimakuṭa, n. of a former Buddha: Mv i.138.3.

(**Maṇimanta**, nom. °taḥ, n. of a mountain: Māy 254.4, doubtless = Skt. Maṇimant.)

Maṇimeruvirocanadhvajapradīpā, n. of a loka-dhātu: Gv 10.3.

Maṇiratnagarbha (= **Maṇigarbha** 2), n. of a park: Divy 325.8 ff.

Maṇirāja, n. of a Bodhisattva: Gv 442.22.

Maṇirocanī, n. of a kiṃnara maid: Kv 6.10.

Maṇivatī, n. of a city: MSV i.66.2, 15 ff.

[**Maṇivarṇa**, see s.v. **Maṇikarṇa**.]

Maṇiviraja(s), n. of a cakravartin: °jaḥ, n. sg., Mv i.154.1.

maṇiviṣa, *'having* (head-)*gem poison', serpent*, acc. to Senart on Mv i.276.19 (vs), where mss. māṇiviṣāṇāṃ, gen. pl. (Senart maṇi°; meter demands maṇī°); see s.v. **śataghnī**.

Maṇiviṣāṇa, n. of a cakravartin: Mv i.119.7.

Maṇisuta, n. of a nāga king: Māy 247.17.

Maṇisumeru, n. of a Buddha: Gv 256.17 (vs; before this read anantaraṃ).

Maṇisumeruś(i)rī, n. of a Buddha: Gv 284.21 (vs); see s.v. **Gandharvakāyu-prabharāja**.

Maṇisūryacandravidyotitaprabhā, n. of a loka-dhātu: Gv 280.11

Maṇisūryaprabhāsagarbhā, n. of a lokadhātu: Gv 13.4.

maṇḍa, m. (used as in Pali; these fig. mgs. seemingly not in Skt.), (**1**) (lit. *cream*; fig.) *best part, highest point* (cf. Pali comm. on Jāt. iv.233.17, 234.6, maṇḍo sāro): agrayauvana-maṇḍa-prāptā, *arrived at the flower of her highest youth*, Mv i.147.13; (°prāptāyāṃ, loc.) i.205.7 = ii.9.3; śāsanaṃ guṇamaṇḍam RP 59.6, *the highest of* (in?) *good qualities*; navamaṇḍaprāpte dharmavinaye AsP 225.10, *when the dharma and vinaya have just newly arrived at the peak* (*of development*); (**2**) in **bodhimaṇḍa**, q.v., the lit. mg. of maṇḍa is clearly *the best, supreme point* (Tib. sñiṅ po, *heart, essence*); it is used alone, or with other qualifiers (esp. words for earth, as in Pali, puthaviyā . . . maṇḍo Jāt. iv.233.17) referring to **bodhimaṇḍa**: gacchitva maṇḍaṃ vara-pādapendraṃ Mv ii.378.19, *having gone to the supreme place, the excellent king of trees* (i. e. the bodhi-tree); pṛthivīya (gen.) maṇḍe SP 53.10; mahī- (or mahi-, m.c.)-maṇḍa LV 48.9; 315.18, 20; 316.14, etc.; Mv i.161.12; ii.401.12; dharaṇi-maṇḍa LV 12.18; 156.4 (both vss., °ṇi° m.c.); (**3**) in LV 87.17 and 20 *fluid* (cf. Pkt., Sheth, = rasa), with Tib. (khu): Lefm. in 17 (bodhisattvasya . . .) mātuḥ kukṣigatasyoccāraprasrāva-maṇḍoparimiśrasya (read with vv.ll. °maṇḍe, or °maṇḍa-pari°); Tib. . . . btsog paḥi (*unclean*) khu (*fluid*; = maṇḍa, see **maṇḍānupūrvī**) śugs (*power*) daṅ ḥdres pa (*mixed with*); in line 20, (na) sukṛtakarmaṇāṃ sattvānāṃ uccāraprasrāva-maṇḍe kāyaḥ saṃbhavati; Tib. lus (*body*) mi (*not*) gtsaṅ baḥi (*pure*) khu baḥi (*fluid*) naṅ du (*within*, governing preceding; loc. case) mi ḥbyuṅ ṅo (*does not happen, occur*).

maṇḍaka, (**1**) doubtless error for mandaka = manda, *sluggish, indolent*: LV 143.11 (prose) (kiṃ vayaṃ) maṇḍakasyopasthānaṃ (v.l. maṇḍasyo°) kariṣyāma iti; confirmed in mg. Tib.; and no other mg. seems possible in context; (**2**) for maṇḍaka SP 52.1 read **maṇḍuka** (or less likely **maḍḍuka**).

maṇḍanīya, adj. (gdve.?), *joyous*, or *to be greeted with joy*: vasanto yoṣitāṃ maṇḍanīyo LV 78.12 (vs).

Maṇḍapa, n. of a yakṣa (or possibly of a locality, Lévi p. 69): Māy 24.

maṇḍapa-vāḍa = **maṇḍala-māḍa**, q.v.

maṇḍa-pūla, m. (so Mironov, no v.l.; Kyoto ed. v.l. muṇḍa°; cf. **pūla**), acc. to Chin. *boots, short boots* (definitely not *slippers* but shoes with uppers): °laḥ Mvy 8968 = Tib. lham yu can; Jä. and Das cite a word lham yu chad (acc. to Das = muṇḍa-pulā) as meaning *a sort of slippers to which cotton leggings are attached*. MSV iv.208.7 muṇḍapūlā by em., ms. puṇḍapolāḥ.

maṇḍa-peya, adj. or subst. nt. (= Pali °peyya; cf. **maṇḍa**), *best of its kind*: °yaṃ (idaṃ) pravacanam Av i.1.8, note 3; ii.107.6.

maṇḍamā, a high number: Gv 106.6. Seems to have no correspondent in other lists.

Maṇḍara, v.l. °na, pl., n. of a brahmanical gotra: Divy 635.17.

maṇḍarava, nt. (for **mandārava**, **māndā°**), a heavenly flower: °vāṇi mahāmaṇḍaravāṇi (no v.l.) Mv ii.160.12.

maṇḍala, (**1**) m. or nt. (= **maṇḍalaka** 3), *spot of* *ground marked out and ceremonially prepared*, in **trimaṇḍala** (2, q.v.; note also trimaṇḍala 1, in different technical mg.); (**2**) m. or nt., = **maṇḍalaka** 4, q.v.: praṇipatya pañcamaṇḍala-namaskāreṇa vandiṣyante Sukh 19.8; see also **jānumaṇḍala**; (**3**) m., n. of a yakṣa: Māy 82.

maṇḍalaka, (**1**) m. (adj.?), a kind of *disease which destroys a family*: °ko rogajāto yahiṃ kule nipatati, na kiṃci śeṣeti, sarvaṃ harati Mv i.253.4 (see **adhivāsa, ārddha**); (**2**) nt., acc. to Chin. a *standard* (either connected or not connected with that which stands on it), *base* for something: trapu-°kam Mvy 8954 (both Tib. and Chin. render trapu as *lead*); Tib. zha ñeḥi dbyar (prob. read sbyar), with or without ḥdab (= ḥdabs, *surface*), which could mean (*surface*) *attachment of lead*(?); follows **cakoraka**, q.v.; the Tib. (contrary to Chin.) could apparently mean a *cover*, just as well as a *base*, and our word seems likely to mean that in MSV ii.24.12 maṇḍalakaṃ kṛtvā, *putting a cover on* (a box containing an infant); (**3**) = **maṇḍala** (1) m. (nt.?), a *'circle'* (but in Kv actually square in shape, hence rather), *piece of ground* specially prepared in honor of a Buddha or saint (for him to sit on), or for the performance of a sacred rite: Bhagavato maṇḍalakam āmārjaya Divy 333.18; tayor dve te āsanaprajñaptī kṛtau(!) dvau maṇḍalakāv āmārjitau 345.22; (ye) 'valokiteśvarasya purataś caturasraṃ maṇḍalakaṃ kurvanti, te rājāno bhavanti Kv 49.2; agrato °kaṃ puṣpābhikīrṇaṃ kṛtvā praṇamya bodhicittaṃ utpādya ... Sādh 1.12, and so often in Sādh, as a place for a rite; in this sense AbhidhK. LaV-P. iv.94, 102, and (tri-)maṇḍala Bhīk 9a.4; (**4**) (= **maṇḍala** 2), *one of the parts of the body which touch the ground in a reverential prostration*: pañcamaṇḍalakena vandanaṃ kṛtvā Mvy 9278 = Tib. yan lag lṅas ..., *with five limbs* (Jä. *arms, legs*, and *head*; or more precisely *knees, hands, and forehead*?). [BR's maṇḍalaka-rājan, cited from Mvy, is replaced in both modern edd. by māṇḍalika-, which is Skt.; see s.v. **maṇḍalin**.]

maṇḍala-māḍa, in Mv °**māla** (see also s.v. **-māla**), in Divy °**vāṭa**, so also in MSV but once **maṇḍapa-vāḍa** m. (= Pali °māḷa, °māla, in DN comm. i.43.3–7, on DN i.2.8, several definitions, ending: idha pana nisīdanasālā °māḷo ti veditabbo), *a circular hall* or *space*, acc. to Tib. *courtyard*, ḥkhor gyi (ḥ)khyams (on Mvy), defined by Das *courtyard, an open space near a temple or a ... house where people assemble to witness a spectacle*: °māḍaḥ Mvy 5536; °māḍe viharati Mmk 1.4; °māḍe niṣaṇṇaṃ AsP 381.1; ahaṃ āsanaprajñaptī kariṣyaṃ °mālaṃ taṃ māpayiṣyaṃ ... Mv ii.274.13; °mālaṃ samanvāhara praṇītaṃ ca śayyāsanaṃ 18; °mālo abhinirmiṇitvā ... (line 4) āsanaprajñaptī kṛtā 275.1; °mālaṃ (acc.) 9 (in these Mv passages mss. are sometimes cited as reading °mātraṃ; qy. °māḍaṃ?); similarly for maṇḍalamātraṃ LV 291.10, 22, read °mālaṃ or °māḍaṃ; the same word is written °vāṭa in: divyo °vāṭo divyāsanaprajñaptir divya āhāraḥ samanvāhṛtaḥ Divy 288.15 (note āsanaprajñapti and the like in Mv above, and samanvāhara in Mv ii.274.18); and corruptly maṇḍavāṭa, in: maṇḍavāṭaḥ (read maṇḍala-v°) kāritaḥ, tasmin ... āsanaprajñaptiḥ kāritā Divy 286.15; pratijāgrata maṇḍapa-vāḍam (for entertaining Buddha and monks) MSV i.264.2, but °grata maṇḍala-vāṭam (as in Divy) iii.138.8.

maṇḍalavāṭa = prec. (Divy Index *garden*?).

Maṇḍalāsana, n. of a locality (?see Lévi p. 101 f.): Māy 82.

maṇḍalika, adj. or subst. m. (= next 1; Pali id., cf. Skt. māṇḍalika), *ruler of a* (minor) *region*: (rājābhūt) °kas Gv 399.13. (PTSD defines as *district officer, king's deputy*, which seems inadequate; Vin. comm. 309.7 = ye dīpadese pi ekam-ekaṃ maṇḍalaṃ bhuñjanti.) See also **nāga-maṇḍalika**.

maṇḍalin, adj., or subst. m., (**1**) usually with rājan (= AMg. id., Sheth; cf. prec. and Skt. māṇḍalika; māṇḍalika-rājan Mvy 3674, so also Mironov, cited in BR from Minayev as maṇḍalaka°), *ruler of a* (minor) *region*; as subst. *king*: mṛgamaṇḍalīva Mv ii.405.2 (vs) *like a king of beasts* (= *a lion*); maṇḍalino rājāno praṇata mahyaṃ Mv ii.40.9 (vs), said by Śuddhodana, referring to the time of the Bodhisattva's birth; esp. in contrast with more powerful monarchs, rājānaś ca maṇḍalino balacakravartinaś (see this) caturdvīpakacakravartinaś (see this) ca SP 6.4 and 20.6 (prose); the same three in reverse order, rājñāṃ ... cakravartināṃ balacakravartīn' atha maṇḍalīnāṃ SP 362.8 (vs); rājāno maṇḍalinas ... (rājānaṃ cakravartinaṃ pratyuttiṣṭhanti) LV 15.2; (**2**) m. or nt., in Divy 359.19 (vs, printed as prose) seems to be used of a small body of water, in contrast with the ocean, as a mustard-seed with Mt. Meru, or a firefly with the sun: (kiṃ) sarṣapena (so!) samatāṃ nayasīha Meruṃ, khadyotakena raviṃ (read ravi, m.c.) maṇḍalinā samudram, *why are you here making ... the sea equal to a maṇḍalin*? I cannot explain the word, which is not noted in Index or Notes to ed.

[**maṇḍavāṭa**, Divy 286.15, read **maṇḍalavāṭa** = **maṇḍalamāḍa**.]

Maṇḍavī, n. of a locality (cf. Skt. Māṇḍavya?): Māy 54.

Maṇḍavya, see **Māṇḍavya**.

maṇḍānupūrvī, (medical treatment consisting of a) *series of liquids* (**maṇḍa**, 3; so Tib., khu baḥi rim pa): MSV ii.47.14. There is no clue to the more precise mg.; the treatment is for a cold.

maṇḍitaka, f. °**ikā** (= Skt. °ta plus endearing dim. -ka, § 22.34), *adorned*: -su-°ikāṃ LV 323.1, of a daughter of Māra; °ikā, n. of an ogress, Māy 243.31.

maṇḍīlaka, m. (cf. Deśīn. 6.117 maṇḍillo apūpaḥ), a kind of sweetmeat or cake: Divy 258.9, 12, 14, 19 etc.

maṇḍuka, m. (nt.?), acc. to Skt. Lex. (pw 5.262) *a kind of drum*; prob. read so with Kashgar rec. twice for both edd. maṇḍaka (vv.ll. Nep. mss. madduka, maḍaka, etc.; note in KN says 'probably to read maḍḍukā' which is also cited in Skt. Lex. in same mg.) in SP 52.1 (vs), KN vādāpitā ... yehi (Śikṣ yehī) jala-maṇḍakā vāpy-atha maṇḍakā vā, cited thus (except yehī) in Śikṣ 93.(11–)12; WT **carpaṭa-**, q.v., for vāpy-atha, no other change; Tib. for the pāda, chu la brdabs daṅ thal mo brdabs pa daṅ, apparently *striking on water and striking on the palms of the hands*. That some instrument, presumably of percussion, was meant seems clear from vādāpitā, tho I find no record of such a mg. for Tib. brdabs. These noises were made in honor of relics of Buddhas.

Maṇḍūka, n. of a nāga: Mvy 3330.

Mati, (**1**) n. of a prince, son of the Buddha Candrasūryapradīpa: SP 19.2; (**2**) n. of a brahman youth, previous incarnation of Dharmaruci; corresponds to **Meghadatta** of Mv, Megha of Pali, as associate of the previous incarnation of Śākyamuni (here called **Sumati**) under Dīpaṃkara: Divy 247.2 ff.; (**3**) n. of a prince, previous incarnation of Śākyamuni (is this the same as Sumati of Divy?): Samādh p. 52 lines 21 (here text satī, read mati) and 30; (**4**) n. of a teacher (a Buddha?) in the kṛta yuga: Laṅk 365.3; also called **Mahāmati** (5); in 365.7 apparently a different Mati (a Buddha, nāyakaḥ) is named, a later one, tho still in the kṛta yuga (Suzuki's transl. is wrong on this).

Matijñānaś(i)ri, n. of a Buddha: Gv 285.16 (vs).

mativant (= Skt. matimant, Ap. maivanta, see § 22.49), *intelligent*: LV 299.7.

Mativikrama, n. of a Bodhisattva: Śikṣ 122.4 (from Dharmasaṃgītisūtra).

mati-vijñāna = **mano-vi°**, q.v.: in Laṅk 10.14 read sūkṣma-mativijñāna-(text °mam abhivi°)-parāvṛttikuśalānāṃ, with Suzuki s.v. sūkṣma, Studies, Glossary, and

Index; but Suzuki translates wrongly; render, *able to produce revulsion in their subtle mati-*(= mano-)-*vijñāna*.

Matisāra, n. of an ancient prince, son of **Satyavardhana**: Mv iii.104.16; 105.3 etc.

Matīśvara, n. of a former Buddha: Samādh p. 57 l. 5.

matsarin (Skt. id., Pali maccharin), in deśanā-°riṇaś ca Mv i.90.3, of backsliding would-be Bodhisattvas, prob. *resentful of religious instruction*.

[**mathya,** so Lefm. in LV 264.16 (prose) mathyodanakulmāṣam; so 2 mss.; one pathod°; two maṇḍādana°; the others senseless; Lefm.'s reading seems impossible; possibly pathyodana° is to be read, or maṇḍādana°, maṇḍodana°? Tib. has three members of the cpd., zan (*food, pap*; possibly for maṇḍa?) daṅ ḥbras chan (*boiled rice*) daṅ ḥdren mar (*mixture*)...]

Madana, n. of a maharṣi: Māy 256.25.

Madanā, n. of a piśācī: Māy 239.5.

mada-nirmadana, adj. (or subst. nt.? = Pali madanimmadana), *getting rid of pride* or *intoxication*; ep. of virāga in Pali, AN ii.34.24; expl. Vism. 293.21 as *de-intoxication of intoxication*; PTSD takes nimmadana s.v. from Skt. root mṛd, *crushing*; possibly, in BHS at least, it may mean *washing away*, see **nirmādayati** (but in Pali nimmādeti, sometimes written nimmadeti, means *insults*): Mv iii.200.11 yam idaṃ °danam pipāsā-prativinayo ālayasamudghāto ... virāgo ... (close parallel to Pali, above).

Madanī, n. of an ogress: Māy 243.18.

Madā, n. of a piśācī: Māy 239.5.

Madotkaṭā, n. of a piśācī: Māy 239.5.

madgī-bhūta (implying stem *madga = **madgu,** see **maṅku**), presumably *embarrassed, out of countenance*, in a fragment without context, Hoernle, JRAS 1916 p. 711 (cf. p. 722); later on same page maṅkur.

madgu-, see **maṅku.**

madgura, once (by error?) **madguru, madgula,** also (v.l.) **maṅgula,** in comp. with chavi (= Pali maṅgurachavi; also maṅgula, as separate adj.; cf. perh. AMg. and general Pkt. maṅgula, *evil, homely, inauspicious*; prob. not connected with Skt. madgura, Lex. maṅgura, a certain fish, unless indeed the fish was named for its color), something like *sallow(-complexioned), unhealthy* (in aspect): madgura-chavir vata bhoḥ śramaṇo gautamaḥ LV 255.5 and (with vv.ll. maṅgula°, mañjura°) 256.8; same passage, madgura-(but one ms. once, both mss. the other time, madgula-)-chavi dāni śramaṇo gautamo Mv ii.126.11; 127.15; read (a-)madguru-cchavir MSV i.36.17, of a cakravartin's strīratna.

Madyapura, perhaps n. of the city in which **Maitrakanya(ka)** lived (in Pali, Catudvāra Jāt., and Av he lived in Benares; statements in Karmav are confused, see Lévi, p. 50, note 10): Divy 590.25 (but if the prec. vai be read with this word, the name would be Vaimadyapura).

Madrī (= Pali Maddī), n. of the wife of **Viśvaṃtara** (or **Sudaṃṣṭra**): Jm 56.22 ff.; RP 22.17 (vs; m.c. Madri).

Madhudātar, n. (or epithet) of a monkey who once gave honey to the Buddha (see the story s.v. Pārileyya, DPPN): Jm 116.1. In the corresp. Pali vs, Jāt. iv.314.23, the name is Madhuvā (n. sg. of °vant).

madhumādhava, m. (Skt. °dhavī, f.), a kind of spirituous liquor: °vaḥ kādambarī pāripānam Divy 221.28.

[**Madhu-yakṣī,** see **Vadhu°**.]

madhura, (1) sc. -lipi, a kind of writing (perhaps belonging to the city of Mathurā = Pali Madhurā?): Mv i.135.6; **(2)** n. of a gandharva: SP 5.1.

Madhuranirghoṣa, n. of a son of Māra (favorable to the Bodhisattva): LV 309.8.

Madhuravadana, n. of a former Buddha: Mv i.140.2.

Madhurasvara, n. of a gandharva: SP 5.1.

madhuvāsava (MIndic for Skt. and Pali madhvāsava), a kind of liquor: Mv iii.69.4 (prose).

madhu-śira(s), nt. (cf. Skt. madhu-mastaka, -śīrṣaka), a kind of cake: Mmk 48.8 (see s.v. **śrīveṣṭa**).

Madhusaṃbhava, n. of two future Buddhas which it was predicted that Trapuṣa and Bhallika would become: LV 391.22.

madhusiktha, or (MIndic) °**sittha,** and °**thaka** (= Pali madhusitthaka, Vin. ii.116.6; Skt. siktha, and Lex. sikthaka), *beeswax*: °sitthena (so mss.) Mv iii.23.18 (prose, printed as vs); °sikthakena Mv ii.489.19 (mss. °sithak° or °sikkak°).

Madhuskandha, n. of a brahman friend of **Anāthapiṇḍada**: MSV iii.136.6 ff.

madhya, adj., seems to be used (as rarely in Skt.) in the sense of Skt. madhyama, madhyastha, *neutral, impartial*; here perh. more specifically *umpire*: tatra bhavantehi madhyehi bhavitavyaṃ Mv iii.390.14, *there* (where the speaker is to engage in a debate with another person) *your worships must be umpires* (less likely, *must be present, in the midst*).

Madhyadeśika, adj., (people) *belonging to the 'middle country'* (Madhyadeśa): Mv i.2.13.

madhyantika (nt.? = Pali majjhantika, AMg. °tiya; as if semi-MIndic for Skt. madhyānta plus -ika), *noon*: °ke Mv iii.185.16.

Madhyaṃdina (also **Mādhy°**, q.v.; seems to corresp. to Pali Majjhantika, a word which means *noon, midday*, see prec.; both were missionaries to Kashmir), n. of a Buddhist missionary to Kashmir: Karmav 61.11 (for northern sources see Lévi's note).

Madhyama (m.?) = **Madhyamāgama,** q.v.: Divy 333.11 °mam, acc.

Madhyamaka, presumably = **Mādhyamika,** q.v., in °ka-ruci, *one who favors the M. school*: kṛtir iyaṃ paṇḍita-ma°rucer Dharmākaramateḥ Sādh 417.7 (colophon).

Madhyamakīya, n. of a yakṣa: Māy 73 (but reading is uncertain).

Madhyamāgama, m., n. of a section of the canon (= Pali MN): Mvy 1422; MSV i.93.10; 98.15; 111.20, etc.

madhya-strī, *woman in middle life, fully mature woman*: LV 321.8 °strī-rūpāṇi, in contrast with kumārī, *girl*, and **aprasūti,** q.v.; Mv iii.283.5 °striyāyo, acc. pl. In Pali majjha is used in the sense of *middle-aged*, contrasted with *young* and *old*; I have not found this cpd. elsewhere.

madhyākṣaravistara-lipi, a kind of script: LV 126.1.

[**madhyāhāriṇī-lipi,** see **adhyā°**.]

madhyima, adj. (= Pali majjhima, Skt. madhyama, § 22.16), *middle, middling*: anumadhyāto madhyimaṃ Mv ii.49.20 (vs; = Pali Jāt. v.387.19 reading majjhakaṃ). Cf. **anumajjhima.**

[**madhyena** plus gen., alleged to mean *to*, equivalent of loc. of goal (Hindi meṃ), acc. to Senart Mv iii n. 502, on iii.287.2 ahaṃ rākṣasīdvīpasya madhyena gacchāmi. But this means, not *I am going to the island of ogresses*, but *I am going by way of the island* ... (so madhyena in Skt.), as is proved by 291.4–5; the merchant's goal was a puṇya samudrapattana, where he collected jewels and then returned home.]

mana-, apparently m.c. for māna, *pride*, in Laṅk 358.11 (vs, 2d half of anuṣṭubh) upakleśair manādibhiḥ; see **upakleśa.**

manaāpa, adj. (Skt. Lex., Trik. only), *captivating the mind, charming*; relatively rare, usually **manāpa,** q.v.: Mvy 6827; Gv 228.5 (prose); SP 74.5, 10 (prose, no v.l.); in 74.1 and 76.1 also ed. manaāpa, but most or all mss. manāpa.

mananā, acc. to Foucaux *pride*, but perh. rather *intellection* (Skt. manana): (tejaḥsama ity ucyate) durāsada-sarva-mananā-prahīṇa-sarvakleśadāhapratyupasthānatvāt LV 424.15. (Tib. omitted in Foucaux.)

manayate (= Skt. manyate; see Chap. 43, s.v. man 2), *thinks*: °yase Bbh 226.9.

Manasā, n. of a kiṃnara-maid: Kv 5.22.

manasi-(also **manasī-**, q.v.)**-karoti** (= Pali manasi-k°; very rare in Skt., essentially Buddhist word; cf. **manasi-**, **manasī-**, **manas-kāra**, which seem not to occur in Skt. at all), *concentrates the mind on, reflects* (intently) *on*, with acc. (a rare case of gen. s.v. **manasī-k°**): sādhu ca suṣṭhu ca °kuru Mvy 6315; SP 38.10; 346.6; Sukh 5.1; °karoti LV 378.16; °kurvanti SP 72.15 (KN printed, as sometimes elsewhere, as two words); °karotha Mv i.334.1, 2, etc.; °kurvāṇasya Gv 504.19; °kariṣyanti SP 478.7; °kartavya Av ii.140.8; °kṛta (ppp.) SP 60.14; very common, often (as in some of the above) with parallel synonyms like cintayati; esp. with **yoniśaḥ** (or **ayoniśaḥ**), q.v. for examples.

manasi-kāra, m. (= Pali id.; to prec.; also **manasī-**, **manas-kāra**, qq.v.), *fixing in mind, mental concentration*, (esp. *intense*) *attention, thought, notice*; esp. with **yoniśaḥ** or **ayoniśaḥ**, qq.v. for examples; nāpi nirgamana-°ram utpādayanti SP 72.15, *nor do they put their minds on going out* (lit. *produce putting of the mind on*...); na duḥkha-manasikāra saṃjñām utpādayanti SP 78.5; asmṛtya-°kāra-tāyai LV 34.15, *to the keeping in mind of what is not memorable*; dharma-°kāreṇa LV 179.8; tathāgatagaurava-manasi° LV 370.1; manasikārāmanasikāratvāt LV 422.13, *because it cannot be reflected upon by mental reflection*; uddeśa-yoga-°kārān (°kāra-viśeṣān) (ud)gṛhya Divy 18.12, 17; tato 'sya bhagavatā °kāro dattaḥ Av i.284.12, *then the Lord gave him* (the power of) *mental concentration*, and similarly 348.1; ii.68.10 (not any 'task' as Speyer renders; Feer also wrongly); nānya-°kāraḥ RP 56.17, Bhvr., *having no other thought in mind*; evaṃrūpaiḥ saṃjñā-°kāraiḥ Dbh 56.27; other, miscellaneous cases, SP 103.11; Mv ii.278.7; Mvy 1926; LV 180.21; Divy 180.21; 236.20; 240.1; 407.3; Suv 7.3; Gv 177.3; 241.24.

manasī-karoti = **manasi°**, q.v., but rather rare; ī not always m.c., e. g. °karotha Mv iii.339.7 (prose); in vss, ī required m.c., °karontā (pres. pple.) Mv iii.83.7; and with gen. object, na cāpi teṣāṃ manasīkaronti SP 87.2 (vs), *and they do not even take heed of these things* (that have been said). Cf. next.

manasīkāra (to prec.) = **manasi°**: KP 71.8 (prose), see s.v. **yoniśaḥ**.

manaskāra, m. (= **manasi-**, **manasī-kāra**), *concentration of mind, mental application* or *activity*: SP 320.3 (prose); cittāśaya-°kārair Dbh 30.28 ff.; cintā-°kārā abhūvan LV 26.2 (prose), Bhvr., *came to have concentration on the thought* (which follows), and so, cintā-°kāra-prayuktānām 26.4; asan-°kāra Jm 192.12, *evil mental activity*; others, see s.vv. **yoniśaḥ**, **ayoniśaḥ**.

Manasvin, (**1**) n. of a nāga king: Mvy 3285; SP 4.12; LV 204.9; 219.9; Megh 288.6; 306.11; Māy 221.23; 247.29; (**2**) pl., n. of a people: Māy 19 (cf. Lévi p. 68).

manaḥsaṃcetanāhāra, m. (= Pali mano-s°; °nā plus āhāra), also **saṃcetanikāhāra**, one of the four kinds of *'food'* (see s.v. **kavalīkārāhāra**), viz. *living on hope* (in the belief that food is, or will soon be, available; see LaVallée-Poussin, AbhidhK. iii.124 f.): Mvy 2286; the prior member is (manaḥ)saṃcetanā, AbhidhK. iii.121.

manā (= Pali manaṃ, before vowel man', for Skt. manāk; in the sense here recorded found in Skt. only with neg., e. g. manāg asi mayā na śaptaḥ Mbh. Cr.ed. i.3.164, *you were almost cursed by me*; but in Pali, as here, man' amhi, without neg., *I was almost*...), *almost*: ma-nāsmi... khāditā (°taḥ), *I was almost eaten*..., Mv ii.450.16; 451.1; 453.3, 8.

manāpa, adj. (= Pali id.; contraction of **mana-āpa**, q.v., but far commoner than that in prose as well as vss), *charming, agreeable*: SP 74.1 and 76.1 (so most or all mss.); 347.1; LV 9.14; 27.11; 46.13; 90.2 ff.; 187.10; Mv i.103.6; 109.5; 146.3 = 202.18 = ii.6.15; i.150.5; 207.11 = ii.12.1; i.303.8; ii.111.18; 373.23; 424.2, etc.; Divy 74.9; 403.4; Av i.179.1; Suv 146.3; Bbh 217.3; very common; also a-ma°, *unpleasant*: LV 71.11; 187.9; 246.15; Av i.71.9, etc.

Manu, f. (in Skt. Lex. Manu, f., is recorded as the wife of Manu, m.), n. of the 'mother of mankind': (tadya-thā)ditir devānāṃ mātā Manur mānavānāṃ Surabhiḥ saurabheyānāṃ... Divy 635.3.

manujña, adj. (semi-MIndic for Skt. manojña; § 3.54; cf. Pali manuñña), *charming*: Kashgar rec. of SP 110.13 (vs) °jña-ghoṣa, for ed. with Nep. manojña-.

manuṣyaka, adj. and subst. m. (Pali manussaka, adj., is cited by Childers from 'Kh' = Khuddakapāṭha '14', but I cannot find the occurrence; Pali a-manussaka, CPD), (**1**) adj., *of men, human*: manuṣyakā (so mss., Senart em. mā°) kāmāṃ (acc. pl.) Mv ii.405.8 (vs), *human desires*; [sarvāṇi deva-manuṣyakāṇi (*of gods and men*; but here mss. °ṣyāṇi, em. Senart) chattrasahasrāṇi Mv i.264.3 (prose);] (-vimānāni) divya-manuṣyakāṇi Sukh 63.4 (prose); manuṣyako bhavati narasya rājā Śikṣ 308.7 (vs); (**2**) m., *man*: bhavanto °kā apy... Divy 309.20 (prose).

Manuṣyadatta, n. of a former Buddha: Mv i.138.5.

Manuṣyadeva, n. of a former Buddha: Mv i.138.4.

Manuṣyanāga, n. of a former Buddha: Mv i.138.9.

manuṣya-raha-śayyāka, °**sayyaka**, or °**seyyāka**, adj. (= Pali manussa-rāha-seyyakaṃ, sc. uyyānaṃ, Vin. i.39.6, 12, or °seyyākāni, sc. rukkhamūlāni, MN ii.118.18; ā in rāha unexplained), *providing sleeping-places secluded from men*: (vṛkṣamūlāni...) °sayyakāni Mv ii.123.18 (read approximately so; mss. partly corrupt, wrongly em. Senart); (āśramapadaṃ...) °seyyākaṃ iii.143.13 (read approximately so; mss. have a different corruption, Senart em. wrongly); (śayyāsanāni...) manuṣya-raha-(v.l. °rahe-) seyyākāni (v.l. śayyākāni) iii.200.17 (so with mss.).

manuṣya-vigraha, m. (= Pali manussa-viggaha, PTSD s.v. viggaha), *one that has human form*; somewhat broader than manuṣya (incl. at least the human embryo; see Pali Vin. iii.73.21–23): manuṣyo vā °graho vā Bhīk 25b.1.

manesī? Mv ii.62.8, some unknown part or adjunct of a chariot; see s.v. **kupsara**.

manojana, adj. (seems to = Skt. manojña, with MIndic epenthesis, § 3.101), *charming*: bhāṣanto ca °janaṃ (perh. adv.; mss. °janāṃ) Mv i.77.9 (vs), perh. m.c.

manojalpa, m., *mind-talk, imagination*: Mvy 2116 = (alternatively) Tib. rtogs pa, which in 998 = saṃkalpa.

manojavā, n. of a kind of magic: Divy 636.27.

Manojña, n. of a gandharva: SP 5.1.

Manojñanirṇādasvara, n. of a kiṃnara: Mvy 3418.

Manojñaśabdābhigarjita, m., n. of the kalpa of future Buddha Sāgaravaradharabuddhivikrīḍitābhijña: SP 216.11.

Manojñasvara, n. of a gandharva: SP 5.1; Kv 2.17 (here a gandharva king).

Manojñā, n. of a yakṣiṇī: Mmk 567.12; 570.23.

Manojñārutasiṃhadhvaja (so Mironov; var. Samano°), n. of a gandharva: Mvy 3387.

Manobhirāma, nt., n. of the Buddha-field of the future Buddha Tamālapattracandanagandha: SP 153.10.

Manoragā (! sic), n. of a rākṣasī: Māy 243.33.

Manoratha, n. of a piśāca: Mmk 18.5.

Manorathar akṣita, n. of an author (a bhikṣu): Sādh 334.20.

Manorama, nt., n. of two Buddhakṣetras: Mv i.123.18; 124.5.

Manoramā, n. of a 'gandharva maid': Kv 5.6.

mano-vijñāna (-dhātu), *perception by the thought-organ*, the sixth of the vijñāna(-dhātu), the other five being cakṣur-, śrotra-, ghrāṇa-, jihvā-, and kāya-; its object is dharma(-dhātu): Mvy 2058 (in this sense = Pali mano-viññāna); in Laṅk peculiarly used (see Suzuki, Studies 177 f.), bracketed or cpd. often with citta and manas: citta-mano-manovijñāna-svabhāva-viveka-ratasya Laṅk 9.17; cittamano-manovijñāna-vigatena tvayā 10.6, etc. etc.; ālayaṃ ca kathaṃ kasmāt, manovijñānam eva ca 24.18; Suzuki regularly keeps the word in his Transl. Once also **mati-vijñāna,** q.v.

[? **manovibhu(-tā),** said of the daśa balāni; so Senart em. for various corrupt readings of mss. at Mv i.159.10; 160.6, 7. Implausible; I have no alternative suggestion.]

Manoharā, n. of the daughter of **Druma,** king of the kiṃnaras; her story at length, with her marriage to prince **Sudhanu** (Divy, MSV **Sudhana**): Mv ii.97.5 ff. (in the Kiṃnarī Jātaka); Divy 443.2 ff.; MSV i.134.11 ff.; mentioned as last in a list of kiṃnara maids, Kv 7.1.

mantraja, error for mantrajña ? (as suggested in note, ed.): °jā (n. pl. m.) °jā iti saṃjñā Divy 212.11 f.

mantra-dhāraṇī, see **dhāraṇī.**

mantrā, f. (only recorded as m. or nt.) = Skt. BHS mantra, *formula* etc.: Mmk 27.3 āhvānanamantrā cātra bhavati; (7–)8 (eṣa . . . mañjuśriyaḥ) āhvānanamantrā; 17–18 āhvānanamantrāyāś ca ayam eva mudrā . . . (Regularly m. or nt. in Mmk as elsewhere.)

Mantrānusāriṇī, n. of a **rakṣā** (q.v.): Dharmas 5. Also **Mahā-m°,** q.v.

manthā (nom. sg.; fem., if not masc. to a stem manthan) = Skt. mantha, a mixed beverage: Mvy 5755.

Mandaka, n. of a yakṣa: Māy 69. (See also **maṇḍaka** 1.)

Mandara, n. of a yakṣa: Māy 76.

[**mandavāś** ca LV 38.4 (vs), read with v.l. (sadārjavā-) mārdavāś ca; so Tib. mñen.]

Mandavalāhaka, pl. (= Pali id.), n. of a class of gods: Mahāsamāj. Waldschmidt, Kl. Skt. Texte 4, 185.2 (see note 3); cf. **Varṣavalāhaka, Vātavalā°.**

mandārava, m. and nt. (= Pali id.; cf. Skt. mandāra; = the much commoner BHS **māndārava;** also **māndāra, °raka;** once **maṇḍarava;** there are also parallel forms with **mahā-** compounded with each of these, but only in association with the form without mahā-), applied (in comp. or as adj.) to a heavenly tree, or rather usually to its flowers, which are often 'rained' down on earth as celestial salutation to a Buddha or Bodhisattva: Mvy 6202 (mahā-ma° 6203); °vaiḥ puṣpair Divy 220.26; otherwise mand° with short a noted only in Mv, i.147.13; 200.11; 219.6 = ii.21.8; ii.17.10; 19.3; 33.19; 39.9; 299.5; 303.7; followed by mahā-ma° i.230.15; iii.94.20 (mahā° 22).

Mandāravagandha, n. of a former Buddha: Mv i.139.7.

manduraka (1) m. Divy 19.23, or nt. Mvy 9183, a kind of coverlet; see s.v. **eraka;** (2) n. of a nāga: Māy 221.20.

manyate (= Skt. id., Pali maññati), *thinks good, approves;* as in Pali phrase yassa dāni kālaṃ maññasi (see PTSD s.v. maññati), so yasyedāni (yasya dāni) kālaṃ manyase, *whatever you think appropriate,* in formula of consent; in Mv several times preceded by sukhī bhava(tu), see **sukhin,** the whole meaning *all right, be it as you say:* sukhī bhava . . . manyase Mv i.320.15; 321.12; in 323.22 f. the Buddha Kāśyapa replies to King Kṛkin's invitation by messenger, sukhī bhavatu Kṛkī . . . yasya dāni kālaṃ manyase (2d person!); in 324.6 (without any sukhī bhava) adhivāseti ca bhagavāṃ K° yasyedāni kālaṃ manyase; so also in 324.10, 15 (yasya, 15 adds dāni, bhagavaṃ [mss. °vāṃ] kālaṃ manyase); in 325.7, consenting to dwell in Kṛkin's new palace, the Buddha K. says: sukhī bhava yasyedānīṃ kālaṃ manyase.

manyanā, °na chiefly m.c. (= Pali maññanā; cf. next; to manyate plus -anā), (1) *conceit* in the sense of *vain, illusory imagining,* Tib. ṅor sems, in Suzuki's Index to Laṅk; (2) *conceit* in the sense of *pride,* Tib. rlom(s) sems, so rendered in Mvy, Śikṣ, and KP below. The two mgs. cannot always be distinguished with certainty but (1) is doubtless regularly meant when the word is associated with **iñjana, °nā,** or **iñjita,** qq.v. for passages like Gv 128.6; 253.14; Dbh 64.13; so in LV 259.9 (vs) where read na ceñjanaṃ nāpi manyana-(m.c. for °nā)-pracāraṃ (Lefm. manyena, metr. impossible), and prob. in KP 136.8 (vs) iñjanā-manyana-, tho Tib. here rlom sems, *pride;* prob. in Gv 199.20 sarva-manyanā-samudghātitasya bodhisattva-vimokṣasya; certainly in Laṅk 127.2; 278.1; 300.4; and esp. note the vs 265.9, 10: asārakā ime dharmā manyanāyāḥ samutthitāḥ, sāpy atra manyanā śūnyā yayā śūnyeti manyate; (2) *pride:* in LV 332.14 (vs) read with best mss. (and Tib., rlom sems) sarva-manyanā-(Lefm. manyunā)-prahīnāḥ; in LV 371.13 (vs) read, with vv.ll. and Foucaux, iha me hatā navavidhā mānavidhī (m.c., mss. all °vidhi) manyanāpur' aniketāḥ, *here I have destroyed the nine-fold varieties of conceit, which have pride as their home* (or *body,* pura) *and* (now are left in me) *without any resting-place;* in LV 374.5 (vs) read manyanāś with v.l. for mamiyitā; Mvy 7082 = Tib. rlom(s) sems; Śikṣ 251.8 (Tib. cited as rlom sems); śīla-manyanā KP 135.7 (prose), *pride in* (one's own) *morality,* = Tib. tshul khrims kyis rlom sems; Bbh 207.14; AsP 389.20; avamanyana-manyana (acc. sg.; a m.c.) tyaktvā RP 21.4 (vs). See also **a-manyana-tā.**

manyita, nt. (orig. MIndic ppp. to manyate; = Pali maññita; cf. prec.), *conceit* in the sense of *vain imagining, illusion:* vyapanīta sarvāṇi mi manyitāni SP 63.3 (vs); associated with **iñjita** (q.v. for the foll. passages), SP 336.3; 372.7 (here also **prapañcita**).

mapara, nt., a high number: Gv 133.2. Cited in Mvy 7833 as **savaram** (2, q.v.), but read there **mavaram** with v.l.; cf. also **parama.**

[**mama** and **mamama,** nt., read **amama,** q.v.]

mamāyati, °te (denom. to mama; = Pali °ti; Skt. once °te, Mbh 12.8051, where it means *cherishes* as here, wrongly BR), *cherishes;* esp. with **kelāyati,** q.v. (as with keḷ° in Pali), so in LV 100.9; AsP 254.2 °yeyur; Dbh 39.23 (here mamāyitāni, foll. by dhanāyitāni niketasthānāni), all cited s.v. **kelāyati;** yasya nāsti mamāyitam Ud xxxii.18(17); na mamāyamāno, *not cherishing* (as one's own), Bimbisārasūtra, Waldschmidt, Kl. Skt. Texte 4, 125.10; labdhā (read °dhvā, probably) lābhaṃ na mamāyate na dhanāyate na saṃnidhiṃ karoti Śikṣ 269.6, *does not hoard;* in LV 374.5 (vs) Lefm. mamiyita, understood as ppp. to this verb, but read **manyanāś** with v.l.

Mayūrakuśa, n. of a brother of Kuśa: Mv ii.433.18.

mayūra-(mayūrāṅga-, mora-)-hastaka, also **-hasta** (= Pali mora-hattha, defined in Vv. comm. 147.27 as *a fan made of peacock's tail-feathers*), *a peacock's feather fan:* mora-°kā Mv ii.475.9 (context indicates *fans*); mayūra-°kā-parigṛhītāni LV 98.14 (prose; -kā for -ka in cpd.); mayūrāṅga-°ka-parigṛhītā LV 77.3 (prose); mora-hastehi Mv ii.275.5 (prose); morahastena Mv iii.446.6 (prose).

mayūrāṅkī, a jewel, prob. *turquoise:* Mvy 5969 = Tib. gyu (*turquoise*) phal pa (*common*), or sbur len (which, or sbur loṅ, is defined by Jä. as *amber,* by Das as an unnamed gem; but in Mvy 5970 sbur len, or loṅ, occurs with other expressions for Skt. puṣparāga, *topaz*).

mayūrāṅga-hastaka, see **mayūra-h°.**

maraṇa, as m. (?), and f. **°ṇā,** *death* (otherwise nt.): in LV 175.11 (vs) Lefm. maraṇo with ms. A only, but all others °ṇam (or a few °ṇa), and so citation of the vs Śikṣ 206.9; in Mv i.165.8 (vs) maraṇāya (3 mss. unmetrically °ṇāye) pāraṃ, *to the farther shore of death;* can hardly be taken as dat., or as anything other than gen., which seems to imply stem °ṇā.

maraṇaprajñāyate, see **prajñāyate.**

maraṇāṃśika, see s.v. **-aṃśika**, and cf. **māraṇāntika**.

-maraṇīya, see **jātijarā-ma°**.

Maravāla, n. of a nāga king: Māy 247.29. Cf. **Paravāḍa**.

Marīcika, m., n. of a lokadhātu: °ke °dhātau Divy 52.5; °kaṃ °dhātuṃ 52.15.

Marīcijāla, n. of a former Buddha: Mv i.140.10.

maru, m. (in mgs. 1, 2 = Pali id.; cf. **marut, maruta**), (**1**) in the sense of Skt. Marut, a class of Vedic gods: indro . . . maruhi parivṛto Mv iii.267.16 (vs); in this sense rare; (**2**) very commonly, *god*, = deva, sura; oftenest in vss, but also in prose, e. g. nara-maru-kanyā- LV 82.15; often, as here, bracketed with nara or a synonym: SP 12.13; 30.9; 208.9; LV 12.13; 80.19 (read ca marusahasrair); 129.19; 370.14; Mv i.71.21; 72.11, 15, etc.; 90.18; 100.9; 113.15; 143.16; 268.15; ii.299.5; 328.5, etc.; Av ii.176.12; passim; (**3**) a kind of drum (not recorded anywhere): Mv i.259.11; ii.180.8; 410.7; iii.443.13; (**4**) n. of a future Buddha: Mv ii.355.10, but this is prob. a misprint for **Meru**, in the same passage iii.279.15.

Maruṇḍa, n. of a serpent king: Mmk 18.24. Cf. **Bhūruṇḍa, Bheruṇḍa**.

marut (cf. next) = **maru** (2), *god*: marutaḥ, n. pl., LV 93.10; Mv ii.28.6; nara-marutaś (v.l. °tāṃś), acc. pl., SP 251.5; marut-, stem in comp., Mv iii.82.9; LV 44.3; 124.3 (prose); Av i.67.7 ff. (prose); marud, n. sg., LV 113.16; marud, perh. n. pl., LV 113.19 (§§ 15.16; 23.10); marut'(as) āgata (= °tāḥ) LV 114.20; marutaivam = maruta(ḥ) evam LV 115.3. All these vss except as indicated. This mg. seems essentially Buddh. (in Skt. Lex. and Raghuvaṃśa 12.101).

maruta (a-extension of prec.; not recorded in Pali), *god*: nara-maruta-sahasra (cpd.) LV 95.5 (vs); marutāna (gen. pl.) Samādh 19.21 (vs).

Marudeva, n. of a cakravartin: Mv i.154.2.

Markaṭa, (**1**) n. of a gandharva: Suv 162.2; (**2**) nt., n. of a town (nigama) in Avanti: Mv iii.382.10 (v.l. karttakaṃ); cf. Pali Makkarakaṭa, a locality (once called nagara) in Avanti (DPPN).

markaṭa-jāla, nt. (cf. Pali makkaṭa, Skt. Lex. and late lit., Schmidt, Nachträge, markaṭa, *spider*), *spider-web*: Mvy 6761 = Tib. ba (b)rgya (see Das).

Markaṭa-hrada-tīra, nt., n. or epithet (*monkey-pool-bank*) of a cetiya (caitya) at or near Vaiśālī: Mv i.300.11 ff.; the same (?) place called also **Kūṭāgāraśālā**, q.v. (rather than a caitya), °tīre °śālāyāṃ Divy 136.7; 200.21; Av i.8.5; 279.5; MSV i.224.14; in these passages, however, it could be interpreted as a separate loc., *in the K. on the bank of the Markaṭahrada*; note that Kūṭāg° is mentioned separately in Mv i.299.20.

margati (= Skt. mārgati, Pali maggati; semi-MIndic, cf. § 3.34), *seeks*: KP 125.7; 137.7.

marj(j)a, if to be kept with Senart and mss., is hyper-Skt. for majja(n), *marrow*: asthi-marj(j)aṃ (acc. sg.) Mv i.20.2 (v.l. °rjja; one ms., only, repeats the word with majja; Senart, strangely, has no note).

[**marṭita-** SP 420.4 (prose), misprint for mardita-, *crushed*; so WT; not corrected in KN Corr.]

Mardana, n. of a yakṣa: Māy 14; in Māy 24 perh. n. of a place (or of a yakṣa? Lévi, p. 69).

Mardanī, n. of an ogress: Māy 243.28.

maryādā-bandha (m.; = Pali mariyādā-b°), *the keeping in control*: (śaknumo . . .) Pūrṇakasya ca °dhaṃ kartum Divy 29.26.

marṣa, m. (Skt. Lex. id.), *patience*: manaso marṣa utpanno Divy 232.13.

marṣaṇā (= Skt. °ṇa, nt.), *patience, endurance*: (parāpakārasya) °ṇā sarveṣāṃ ca °ṇā . . . Bbh 189.4 f.

marṣayati (caus. to Skt. mṛṣ-), *asks to be excused from, declines* (politely): marṣehi grāmavaram Mv iii.192.1, *ask* (the king, who had offered a present of a village) *to excuse you from the boon of a village*, i. e. decline it. (This seems a natural development of Skt. mṛṣ-, caus.; Senart finds it troublesome.)

marṣayitar, *one who pardons* (to Skt. marṣayati): ugravacanamarṣayitāraś ca bhavanti (Bodhisattvāḥ) Mv i.133.16.

Malada, n. of a people: Gv 525.16; see s.v. **Mālaṭa**.

mala-dhātrī, *nurse who tends to an infant's uncleannesses*: Mvy 9480; Divy 3.14; 58.12; 99.26; 271.19; 441.23; 475.12, 15 (here defined); Av i.15.12 etc. One of four kinds of nurse; see s.v. **kṣīra-dhātrī**.

malara, m., a high number: Mvy 7784 = Tib. bsñal yas, bskal yas.

Malina, n. of a nāga king: Megh 306.10.

maluda, m., a high number: Mvy 7744 = Tib. gzuṅs sbyin (spyin); also cited (nt.) as var. for **māluda**, q.v., but Tib. differs there.

maluma, m., a high number: Mvy 7747 = Tib. tshad yas.

malla (m.? = Skt. Lex. and JM. id.; also = next, q.v.; cf. **koṭṭa-, kroḍa-malla**), *pot, bowl, vessel*: only in Bhvr. cpd. (riktahastā) rikta-mallāś ca Divy 171.27.

mallaka, m. (= prec.; Skt. Lex. and Pali id., AMg. mallaga, *an earthen bowl*, Ratnach.; cf. **khaṇḍa-, koṭṭa-, kroḍa-mallaka**), *pot, bowl, vessel*: Divy 172.7, 10; 174.26 mallakaś; 176.21; 177.8; in Bhvr. cpds. rikta-, pūrṇa-mallaka (regularly preceded by rikta-, pūrṇa-hasta), *with empty (full) bowl*: Divy 171.18 ff.; 172.1, 3, 6; 176.3 ff.

mavara, m., Mvy 7707, or nt., 7833 (so read with v.l. for text **savara**, q.v., 2), a high number; Tib. ban bun. Cf. also **mapara, parama**.

maśaka-kuṭī, Mvy 9002, acc. to Chin. *mosquito-netting*; Tib. sbraṅ skyabs, *insect-protection*.

maśaka-varaṇa, nt., *fan to drive off mosquitos*: Mvy 8987; follows **vidhamanam**, q.v.

maśī or (Mironov) **maśi**, f. (= Skt. maṣi, see below), prob. *soot*, but acc. to Tib. (du ba) and Chin. on Mvy *smoke*: maśīr (Mir. maśir) api na prajñāyate Mvy 5254, foll. by **chāyikam** (q.v.) api . . .; in same context spelled maṣi (= Skt., and Pali masi); (of the earth, burned by fire) maṣir api na prajñāyate, tad yathāpi nāma sarpiṣo vā tailasya vāgninā dahyamānasya na maṣir na chāyikā prajñāyate . . . Śikṣ 246.9–11; similarly Mv ii.325.9, on which see **chāyikā**. (Both edd. of Mvy cite v.l. maśiram.)

maṣṭa(ka), see **māṣṭa(ka)**.

Masakkasāra (= Pali id.), n. of the abode of the Trāyastriṃśa gods: °sāra-pravarāsmi devatā (so with mss.) Mv ii.58.21 (vs) = Pali Jāt. v.400.28 °sāra-ppabhav' amhi de° (possibly read in Mv °prabhavāsmi). One ms. reads Masatkusāra.

masina, adj. (MIndic, = AMg. masiṇa, for Skt. masṛṇa), *soft*: Mv iii.54.2 (prose). Prob. read °ṇa.

Masurākṣa, n. of an author or 'ṛṣi': Laṅk 367.3 (vs); v.l. Mathasurākṣa (unmetr.); Tib. Ma-la-ya, acc. to Suzuki, Index. Monier Williams, Skt. Dict., cites Masūrākṣa as n. of a poet; I do not find this in BR, pw, or elsewhere.

(**masūrikā**, *cushion, pillow, bolster*: Bhīk 19a.1, see s.v. **viṇḍaka**; once in late Skt., Schmidt, Nachträge; cf. Skt. and Pali masūraka, in Skt. m.)

Maskarin (once **Mās°**) **Gośālīputra** (°liputra, °likāputra, Gośalīp°), also Gośālin (= Pali Makkhali Gosāla, said to be founder of the Ājīvakas), n. of one of the six heretical teachers of Buddha's day (see s.v. **Pūraṇa Kāśyapa**); named with the others: Mvy 3546 (M° Gośalīputra, so also Mironov); Divy 143.11; Av i.231.4 (Māskarī, n. sg., Gośā°); Mv i.253.11 Maskarisya (ms. °ṣya) Gośāliputrasya; 256.20 °rī Gośālī (n. sg.); iii.383.15 °rī Gośālikāputro (mss. °līka°; v.l. Gośā°).

mastaka-luṅga, m., nt. (= next, q.v.; this form, with °ka-, otherwise unknown), *brain*: m., Mvy 3936 =

Tib. klad rgyas; Śikṣ 69.16 (°gān, acc. pl.); nt., Śikṣ 209.10; 210.14 (citing ŚsP 1431.12); 229.3; ŚsP 1431.1 (read °luṅgam for text °gañjām), 12 (read id. for text °śaṅgam).

masta-luṅga, m. or nt. (= Pali mattha°, cf. prec.; Skt. mastu°, and Pkt. matthu° only), *brain*: in Mv ii.326.7 (vs) kapho 'tha pittaṃ anugataṃ masta-luṅgam (so read; meter requires long penult: mss. masta-rugaṃ, v.l. maṣṭa°; Senart em. °rogaṃ).

mastika, m. or nt. (Skt. Lex., nt.; cf. Skt. mastiṣka), *head*: upari-°kaṃ (adv.) bhakṣayantī Divy 11.13. Bailey, JRAS 1950.170, suggests upariṣṭhān mastakaṃ, from the Tib.

mastu, m. (cf. Skt. mastu-luṅga, which perhaps confirms such a stem by the side of masta-ka), *head, top*: Ud x.13 tāla-mastur iv' ūhataḥ (see **ūhata**, 1); a later ms. has tālamastakavad dhatāḥ.

[**masniya**, v.l. maśniya, as n. of an animal: Mv i.349.20 (balivardehi) vā °yehi vā ajehi vā eḍakehi vā . . . Senart recognizes the word as corrupt, and suggests (Pali) meṇḍehi; this may well be approximately right, but the precise form may be **miṇḍha**, q.v., for which Lefm.'s text of LV reads miśṛ-, suggesting something resembling the Mv corruption.]

mahaṃgata, adj. (= **mahadgata**, Pali mahaggata, § 2.76), *great, extensive, lofty*: -vipula-mahaṃgatāpramāṇa- Gv 320.19; contrasted with parītta Gv 518.2, and so °ta-tā with parītta-tā 349.24.

mahat, nt. of Skt. mahant (possibly adv.), *great* (*greatly*?); used in Epic Skt. (BR s.v.) instead of (acc.) masc., allegedly m.c.; so possibly (but not m.c.; end of line of vs) nom., narako dāruṇo mahat Mv i.179.14 (or adv., *greatly*? this usage has not been found recorded); perh. also mahad viśāradaḥ Mv i.179.6, but here mahad- may be stem form in comp., = normal Skt. mahā-; see § 18.3 for other cases of this.

mahatī (Skt. id., of Nārada's 'seven-stringed' lute; AMg. id., a kind of lute), a musical instrument (in long lists of them; °tīm, acc. sg.), presumably a kind of *lute* (vīṇā): Mv ii.159.5; iii.407.19; Divy 108.4.

mahattarakā (AMg. °riyā, ib.), *chief queen*: tenaiva sā °kā mahatā janakāyena sārdhaṃ . . . rājakulaṃ praviṣṭā (so mss.) Mv i.364.4.

Mahattarī-Tārā, n. of a form of Tārā: Sādh 177.5.

mahadgata, adj. (also **mahaṃgata**; = Pali mahaggata), *great, extensive, lofty*: contrasted with **parītta**, Śikṣ 248.15; Gv 370.2; 522.9; dānena °gatena Divy 227.4; 228.1; 245.26; associated with vipula, Gv 522.9; Dbh 15.1; (cittena) vipulena °gatena Mvy 1508; Dbh 34.18; (cetasā . . .) vipulena mahadgatena Mv iii.213.13, so read, mss. madgatena, Senart em. m-udgatena; essentially the same passage in Pali, DN ii.242.10, (cetasā . . .) mahaggatena, besides in Mvy, Dbh above.

mahantaka, or **mahān°**, f. °**tikā** (a-extension of mahant-, mahānt-, plus -ka), *great*: °kā duḥkhaparaṃparātra SP 86.10 (vs); ed. with Kashgar rec. mahan°, kept by WT; all Nep. mss. mahān°; mahantikā MSV iv.74.8.

maharddhika, f. °**kā**, Bhvr. adj. (= Pali mahiddhika, acc. to PTSD 'always' with mahānubhāva, but this is not true, see e. g. Pv i.10.1; Mahāvaṃsa 1.39), *of great supernatural power* (ṛddhi), or more loosely, *of great power, majesty*, or perhaps (as in Skt.) *of great wealth*; with mahānubhāva, of ṛṣis, Mv ii.49.1; 96.1, 3; of a gṛhapati, Divy 277.28 ff.; said of Buddha(s), Mv i.294.22; Av ii.199.13; of deities, Mv i.305.1; iii.302.4; Kv 10.15; Suv 101.9 (lokapālas); of Māra, said by himself, Mv ii.276.19; of miscellaneous persons, Mv ii.92.17; iii.1.3; 63.18; sometimes as final member of a cpd., the prior member denoting the class of being so designated (this usage not recorded in Pali): devamaharddhikā vā devā vā nāga-°kā vā nāgā vā etc. (long series of similar terms) Gv 75.3; esp. preta-°ka, said of a class of pretas whose position as such has been mitigated, though not completely relieved, either by their own actions or by merit transferred to them by others (see **dakṣiṇādeśanā**), Divy 14.19; Av i.264.16 ff.; 273.1; even these pretas may still manifest evil propensities, Av i.265.8 ff.; altho the cpd. *peta-mahiddhika seems not to occur in Pali, the adj. mahiddhikā is used of a petī who, like the pretas so described in BHS, was enjoying partial happiness because of some merit acquired, Pv. 1.10.1.

Maharddhiprāpta, n. of a garuḍa prince: SP 5.5.

mahalla, adj. and subst. (cf. next, where etym.; this form without -ka not recorded in Pali, tho cited from Fausböll Dhp. comm., 315.23, by Childers; however, for this PTS ed. iii.116.12 has mahallik' itthi-; AMg. id. in mg. 1), (**1**) *old; an old man, elder*: Divy 329.1 ff. (Tib. *old man*, Index, citing Feer); 520.11 ff.; Av ii.139.8 (all these prose); Mmk 592.20, 21; 593.5, 10; cf. °llakas 593.25 (Mmk all vss); (**2**) *eunuch* (so Skt. Lex.): Mvy 3822 = Tib. ñug rum pa.

mahallaka, f. °**ikā**, adj. and subst. (= prec.; etym. Pischel 595, wrongly PTSD; = Pali and AMg. id., both mgs.), (**1**) *old; an old person, elder*; oftenest of humans: commonly after jīrṇo vṛddho, in stock phrase, SP 72.2; 102.10; 322.3; LV 102.12; Mv ii.150.18; 425.17; Mvy 4097; 7657; Kv 48.12; Av i.228.3 (prec. by jīrṇa-vṛddho); Suv 176.5 (prec. by vṛddho jīrṇo); jīrṇānāṃ vṛddhānāṃ °llakānāṃ Divy 112.22; mahallaka-mahallikāḥ Śākyā(ḥ) LV 100.11; 118.3, *the male and female Śākya-elders*; daharā ca madhyā ca °llakā ca Mv i.262.18; °llakas Mmk 593.25 (vs; see **mahalla**); °kaḥ Mvy 8722, *a senior monk* (? Tib., rgan zhugs, lit. *having entered when old*; Chin. also seems to mean *one who entered the order after middle life*); of an elephant, °ko hastināgas Divy 370.26, and °ke (without noun) 'bhiruhya 27; grāme °kāḥ Mv i.302.3, *the elders in the village*; not clear in corrupt line Mv ii.63.7 (mss. mahallikāya, or maharddhikāya, perh. referring somehow to Hrī?); at end of cpds., yakṣa-mahallako vā yakṣa-mahallikā vā Mmk 395.1, *a male or female yakṣa-elder*; so in Māy 225.14 ff. deva-mahallaka and °likā, and a long series of other such cpds.; (**2**) *large* (so AMg., and Pali, at least with vihāra, e. g. Vin. ii.166.20; iii.156.15; this use ignored PTSD, tho noted in Childers), noted only as ep. of a vihāra: MSV ii.128.12; Mvy 8375 °kaḥ, sc. vihāraḥ, and °ka- MSV iii.88.1, referring to the saṃghāvaśeṣa sin of Prāt 481.4, where lacuna in BHS text but Chin. (*une*) *grande* (*demeure*), = Pali Vin. iii.156.15 °kaṃ . . . vihāraṃ; also °kaṃ . . . vihāraṃ Prāt 506.10 = id. Pali Vin. iv.47.22.

[**mahā**, read **sahā**, q.v.: lokadhātu mahā (so text) nāma Mv iii.342.8, referring to the earth, in which Śākyamuni is preaching the Law.]

mahākaṅkara, m., a high number: Mvy 8005. Cf. **kaṅkara**.

Mahā-kapphiṇa, Av ii.103.3 ff. (no v.l.); Sukh 92.6 (no v.l.); or -kaphila (vv.ll. -kaphira, -kasphina, -kasphila) Sukh 2.7 (Pali Mahā-kappina); = **Kapphiṇa**, q.v.

Mahākara, n. of a former Buddha: LV 5.5 = Tib. ḥod zer chen po, *great ray*.

mahākarabha, m., a high number: Mvy 8021. Cf. **karabha**.

Mahākaruṇameghaś(i)rī, see **Mahākaruṇā°**.

mahā-karuṇā (cf. Skt. karuṇā; = Pali id.), *great compassion*: LV 181.5; Mv ii.2.7, et alibi; 32 mahāk° of a Tathāgata, Mvy 154, listed 155–186.

Mahākaruṇācandrin, n. of a Bodhisattva: LV 2.15. So all mss.; but Tib. sems dpaḥ = sattva instead of -candrin.

Mahākaruṇāciti, n. of a Bodhisattva: ŚsP 7.6.

Mahākaruṇācintin, n. of a prince: Samādh 8.12 (prose). See **Karuṇāvicintin**.

Mahākaruṇānayameghanigarjitaghoṣa, n. of a Bodhisattva: Gv 3.24.

Mahākaruṇāpuṇḍarīka, n. of a work: Mvy 1348. Cf. **Mahākaruṇāsūtra.**

Mahākaruṇāmeghadhvaja, n. of a Tathāgata: Gv 281.24.

Mahākaruṇā-(m.c. °ṇa-)**-meghaś(i)rī,** n. of a Buddha: Gv 285.8 (vs).

Mahākaruṇāsiṃha, n. of a future Buddha: Gv 358.13.

Mahākaruṇā-sūtra, n. of a work: Śikṣ 94.14; 309.5 (so Index; text °ruṇa-); doubtless = **Mahākaruṇāpuṇḍarīka,** q.v.; acc. to Bendall, Tib. inserts the word puṇḍarīka before sūtra in 309.5.

mahā-karkarava, m., and **°karkārava,** nt., a heavenly flower, see s.v. **karkarava, karkā°.**

Mahākarṇa, n. of a yakṣa: Āṭānāṭiya Sūtra, Hoernle MR 26.11 (Obv. 6).

Mahākarmavibhaṅga = **Karmav°,** q.v.: Karmav 167.8 ff. (Not the same as Pali Mahākammavibhaṅgasutta; but see s.v. **Karmavibhaṅgasūtra.**)

(**mahākalpa,** m. (= Skt. id., Pali mahākappa), *great kalpa*: Mvy 8291; Dharmas 87; see s.v. **kalpa** 4. Acc. to PTSD, 'when kappa stands by itself, a Mahākappa is understood'. In Pali it is said to be the most inclusive (i. e. the longest) kind of kappa. For some Pali schemes of its relation to other kappas see PTSD and Childers; for alleged northern Buddhist schemes see LaVallée Poussin, AbhidhK, references in Index. In works here included I have noted no precise definition.)

Mahākātyāyana (= Pali Mahākaccāna, °kaccāyana), n. of a disciple of the Buddha, also called simply **Kātyāyana,** q.v.: SP 2.3; 100.1; 146.13; 150.8; LV 1.13; Mv i.80.3; 84.11, etc.; Mvy 1034; Divy 10.3; 11.21; 12.12; 13.8 etc.; 15.12, etc.; 17.20, etc.; 550.3 etc.; Mmk 40.25; Sukh 92.6.

Mahākāya, n. of a garuḍa prince: SP 5.5.

Mahākāruṇika, n. of a future Buddha: Gv 358.10.

Mahākāla (cf. Pali Mahākāḷa, n. of a nāga king and of a mountain; see s.vv. **kāla, kālaka**), (**1**) n. of a yakṣa: Māy 12; (**2**) n. of a gandharva: Suv 161.18; (**3**) n. of a deity, doubtless borrowed from Hinduism (Mah° = Śiva): Sādh 583.1 (here Vajra-Mah°), etc.; (**4**) n. of a mountain: Kv 91.13 (see s.v. **Kāla**).

Mahākālikā, n. of a deity or yoginī: Sādh 589.15 (vs, perhaps -kā m.c.); **Mahākālī,** id., 584.13.

Mahākāśamātar, see **ākāśamātar(ā).**

Mahākāśyapa (= Pali Mahākassapa) = **Kāśyapa** (2), q.v., one of the Buddha's leading disciples: Mv i.80.3; ii.114.12; iii.47.14 ff., 48.4 ff. (rebukes Ānanda and tells him the story of his own ordination; corresp. to Pali SN ii.218 ff.); SP 2.1; 100.1; 110.11; 121.1 ff.; 206.8; LV 1.13; 443.6; Divy 81.25 ff.; 395.21; Mmk 586.1; Sukh 2.6; 92.5; Karmav 45.1; as a mahāśrāvaka, LV 444.13; Divy 361.18; Mmk 40.25 etc.

Mahākimpaka, m. pl., see **Kimpaka.**

Mahākuśa, n. of a brother of Kuśa: Mv ii.433.17; n. of a king (the same?): Mvy 3568.

Mahākṛṣṇameghavātamaṇḍalī, f. (?), n. of a deity or magic potency (also called **Kṛṣṇavātamaṇḍalī,** q.v.): Mmk 106.9.

Mahāketu, (**1**) n. of a former Buddha: Sukh 6.14; (**2**) n. of a group of future Buddhas (predicted): ŚsP 309.8.

Mahākelin, n. of a yakṣa: Sādh 567.2 (see **Kelin**).

Mahākośa, n. of a former Buddha: Mv i.140.4.

Mahākośalī, n. of a city: Karmav 53.15.

Mahā-koṣṭhila = **Koṣṭhila,** q.v.: Av ii.195.5; AsP 40.13.

Mahā-kauṣṭhila = prec. (see also **Kauṣṭhila**): Mvy 1063 = Tib. gsus po che; SP 2.5; Sukh 2.7 (so read with v.l. for text °ṭhilya); 92.6.

mahākrandanā (or **°na,** m.), see s.v. **krandanā.**

Mahākrodha(-rājan) = **Krodha(-rājan)**: °krodhaiḥ Mmk 11.25; °krodha-rājan, ep. of Yamāntaka, Mmk 16.7.

mahākṣobhya, m., a high number: Mvy 8009. Cf. **akṣobhya.**

? **Mahāga,** acc. to all mss., n. of a disciple of Buddha: Mv i.182.18 (vs); Senart em. **Mahānāga,** q.v., but this makes the verse hypermetric.

mahāgaṇin (= Pali id.), *a great leader of a group of disciples, great teacher*; see s.v. **gaṇin.**

mahāgati, a high number: Mvy 8027. Cf. **gati** (2).

Mahāgandharājanirbhāsa, n. of a former Buddha: Sukh 5.16.

Mahāgiri, n. of a yakṣa: Māy 20.

Mahāguṇadhara, n. of a former Buddha: Sukh 6.11.

Mahāguṇadharabuddhiprāptābhijña, n. of a former Budha: Sukh 5.18.

Mahāgovinda (= Pali id.), name given to Jyotipāla after he succeeded his father Govinda as purohita of King Diśāṃpati: Mv iii.206.12 ff. See next.

Mahāgovindīya sūtra, n. of a sūtra, = Pali Mahāgovinda s° (DN 19): Mv iii.197.9 (by em.). See also **Govinda-, Govindīya sūtra.**

Mahāgrāsa, n. of a nāga: Suv 161.18.

Mahāghoṣasvararāja, n. of a Bodhisattva: Mvy 684.

Mahāghoṣānugā, n. of a goddess: Mvy 4323.

Mahāghoṣeśvara, n. of a yakṣa: Mvy 3368.

mahācakravāḍa, m. sg. or pl., n. of a mountain (-range), only in composition or association with **cakravāḍa,** q.v. for references.

Mahācandra, n. of a minister (previous birth of Śāriputra): Divy 318.18 ff.

mahācitrapāṭala, nt., a kind of flower: Mvy 6201. Cf. **citrapāṭala.**

Mahācīnakramā, n. or form of Tārā: Sādh 208.18; 209.5.

Mahācunda (= Pali id.; cf. **Cunda,** q.v.), n. of a disciple of the Buddha: Sukh 2.8.

mahācūṣaka, m., Mmk 17.5, see **cūṣaka.**

mahācaitya (nt.), *'great holy place'*, one of four, viz. the sites of Buddha's birth, enlightenment, first sermon, and parinirvāṇa: MSV ii.113.9 f.

mahāchāyā, Mmk 17.8, with **chāyā,** q.v.

Mahājñānagītā, n. of a goddess: Mvy 4322.

mahāṭiṭibha, m., a high number: Mvy 8017. Cf. **ṭiṭibha.**

Mahāḍimphika, m. pl., Mmk 17.6; see **Ḍimphika.**

[**mahātapamanda,** m., cited as mss. reading Divy 443.15 (tayāmoghapāśa-śritayā, read -pāśitayā with MSV i.135.2) hrade °daḥ kṛto; ed. em. mahāhatamandaḥ, acc. to Index *great cry* (obscurum per obscurius); MSV i.135.2, same passage mahān **upamardaḥ,** which prob. read in Divy.]

Mahātamālapattracandanakardama, n. of a former Buddha: Sukh 6.11.

[**Mahātāpana,** n. of a hell (cf. **Tāpana**): Mvy 4926; but read instead Pratāpanaḥ with v.l. and Mironov (no v.l.), supported by Tib. rab tu tsha ba.]

Mahāturuṣka, n. of a king: Mmk 623.14.

Mahātejaḥparākrama, n. of a king: Gv 444.8.

Mahāteja(s), (**1**) n. of an ancient king: Mv ii.146.19 (°jo, n. sg.); (**2**) n. of a garuḍa prince: SP 5.4 (°jasā, inst.); (**3**) n. of a Bodhisattva: Gv 2.20 (°jasā).

Mahātejogarbha, m., n. of a samādhi: SP 458.4.

mahādūtī, or **°ti,** f., *'great envoy'*, a class of superhuman potencies attending on a Buddha or Bodhisattva: Mmk 11.8; 12.3, 18 (between the last two is a long list of names of them, which are not included here). Also **dūtī,** q.v.

Mahādeva, (**1**) n. of a king, of the race of Mahāsammata and corresp. to Pali Makhādeva(!): Mvy 3582; MSV i.111.19 ff.; (**2**) n. of a prince, son of Mahāratha and brother of Mahāsattva: Suv 206.12; 225.13 ff.; (**3**) n. of a god: Gv 218.6 ff.; perhaps understood as the same as Skt. Mahādeva (Śiva); but his residence is **Dvāravatī** (q.v.), and he has four arms (219.1); both things suggest Kṛṣṇa.

Mahādevasūtra, n. of a work, part of the **Rājasaṃyuktakanipāta** of the **Madhyamāgama**: Karmav 161.14; MSV i.111.20.

mahā-dyutika, adj. Bhvr. (= Pali mahā-jutika, PTSD s.v. jutika; Skt. mahā-dyuti plus -ka Bhvr.), *of great splendor*: (puṇyavipāko...) °kaḥ Śikṣ 138.7.

Mahādyotā, n. of a goddess: Mvy 4319.

Mahādhana, n. of a king: Divy 435.5. Later called **Dhana,** q.v.

Mahādharma, n. of a kiṃnara king: SP 4.14.

Mahādhipati, f. (so evidently intended; surrounding forms f.; and so Tib., bdag mo chen mo), n. of a Buddhist deity: Mvy 4318.

Mahādhvaja, n. of a former Buddha: Mv iii.230.3 f.

mahā-nagna, m. (cpd. of mahā and **nagna,** q.v.; seems to correspond to Pali mahānāga, DN i.51.10 °gā, n. pl., in a list of kinds of fighting men which includes uggā rājaputtā ... sūrā cammayodhino etc.; comm. i.157.6 mahānāgā viya mahānāgā; hatthiādisu pi abhimukham āgacchantesu anivattitayodhānaṃ etaṃ adhivacanaṃ, all of which only proves that the comm. did not understand the term; it is omitted in PTSD, altho Childers properly refers to Burnouf, Lotus, 452, n. 4, who in translating the Pali suggests equivalence to BHS mahānagna, which he takes to be the older form; Skt. nagna would give MIndic nagga, for which nāga might be substituted; Burnouf also compares the Skt. n. pr. Nagnajit, perh. *conquering champions*; pw and Speyer, Av Index, render *athlete*, but this is only an attempt to explain the word etymologically; it is implausible in several passages, and opposed by Tib.), *great man, champion* (orig. in warfare); *man of distinction, dignitary, grandee, nobleman*; regularly (in Mvy and LV) rendered by Tib. tshan po (Jä. *dignitary, grandee*) che (*great*): (tasya dvau) °gnau saṃśritau Divy 372.12; tasyāpi °gno Bhadrāyudho nāmnānekasahasraparivāraḥ (can hardly mean *athlete*!), sa bhagavacchāsane pravrajito 'rhan saṃvṛttaḥ 373.20; krodhāviṣṭasya °gnasya Gv 504.5; (vajraṃ mahāpraharaṇaṃ) na śakyaṃ mahānagnenāpi saṃdhārayituṃ 509.4; °gnā(ḥ) Kv 41.21 (printed mahāmagnā); Av ii.102.15; often in comp. with bala (the might of a mahānagna being evidently proverbial): °gnabalam Mvy 8210; °gna-balopetāni LV 200.21 (prose); sarve °gna-balair upetā LV 28.5 (vs); others, cpd. with -bala, MSV i.100.10; Av ii.108.12; 110.3; with -balin, Av i.376.1, 4, 18; without -bala, duṣṭamalla-mahanagna-samā LV 153.8 (vs; maha = mahā, m.c.). Cf. next.

mahānagnin = prec.: MPS 31.21.

Mahānanda (= **Nanda** 1), n. of a disciple of Buddha: SP 2.6; but Kashgar rec., one Nep. ms., and Tib. (dgaḥ bo) omit mahā, reading simply Nanda.

mahānayuta, m., = ten **nayuta**: Mvy 8001.

mahānāga, 'great elephant', ep. of śrāvakas: Mvy 1081; in Pali a thera of this name is known, and Senart assumes this name for **Mahāga,** q.v., of mss., Mv i.182.18.

Mahānāma(n), (**1**) regularly °ma, in Mv the name of Yaśodharā's father, a Śākyan noble: Mv ii.48.7; 73.4 ff. (refuses the first request to give his daughter to the Bodhisattva); identified with characters in stories of the past, ii.114.17; 496.11; iii.26.12; 152.16; (**2**) (= Pali Mahānāma 3 in DPPN, son of Amitodana and brother of Anuruddha), n. of a disciple of the Buddha, seemingly not to be identified with (3): son of **Amṛtodana,** brother of **Anuruddha** and **Bhaṭṭika,** Mv iii.177.2 ff. (stem °ma); mentioned with **Bhadrika** (3) and **Aniruddha** LV 229.12 (stem °man); Mvy 3607 (nom. °maḥ): (**3**) (= Pali °ma 2 in DPPN), n. of one of the five **bhadravargīya** monks; seems not the same as (2), tho in some lists of disciples, e. g. Divy below, his name occurs at the end of a list (partial or complete) of these five, but also just before **Aniruddha** (like 2): stem °ma, Mv iii.329.1; 337.6; 339.1; Mvy 1044 (°maḥ; prob. belongs here; the names of the five monks are not grouped together in this list); stem °man, SP 1.10; LV 1.7; Sukh 2.3; stem °ma- in comp., Divy 182.21; 268.6; Av ii.134.12. In Śikṣ 69.4, cited from Pravrajyāntarāyasūtra, voc. Mahānāman, prob. addressed to (2) or (3) but unidentifiable; (**4**) n. of a Licchavi of Vaiśālī (cf. Pali Mahānāma 4 in DPPN): MSV ii.15.17 ff.

Mahānārāyaṇa (= **Nārāyaṇa**), given as ep. of Buddha, Mahānārāyaṇabalopetatvān Mahānārāyaṇa ity ucyate LV 433.1–2; the first occurrence, in the cpd., may be purely secular (or at least non-Buddhistic; see **Nārāyaṇa**), as also in: (vajraṃ mahāpraharaṇaṃ) na śakyaṃ mahānagnenāpi saṃdhārayitum anyatra Mahānārāyaṇasthāma-bala-vegena Gv 509.4, ... *cannot be withstood, even by a great champion, except by* (one who has) *the impetuosity of the might and power of Great Nārāyaṇa.*

Mahānāśā, n. of a yoginī: Sādh 427.3.

mahānimbarajas, a high number: Mvy 8029. Cf. **nimbarajas.**

Mahānirnādin, n. of a nāga: Mvy 3339.

mahāntaka, see **mahan°**

? **mahāpaka,** adj., perhaps to Skt. -āpa (in dur-, mana-āpa) plus -ka, *attaining great* (results): bodhisattvacaritaṃ °kaṃ Mv i.104.12 (vs). Senart assumes that it represents mahā-pākam, m.c., *grande* (c'est à dire *difficile, longue*) *à murir.*

mahāpadeśa, see s.v. **kālāpadeśa.**

Mahāpadma, m. (cf. **Padma** 5), n. of a cold hell: Mvy 4936; Dharmas 122; Divy 67.23; 138.8; Av i.4.9 etc.; °padumo (n. sg.) Śikṣ 75.10 (prose).

Mahāpadmā, n. of a medicinal or magic herb: Gv 497.24.

Mahāpanthaka (= Pali id.), n. of one of Buddha's disciples: Mvy 1055; story of him and his brother **Panthaka** or **Cūḍa-p°** told at length in Divy 485.3 ff.

mahāparidevita, *great lamentation*, in 16 forms, indulged in by Māra on seeing the Bodhisattva about to win the victory: Mv ii.276.17 ff.

Mahāparinirvāṇa, nt., Mvy 1370; Karmav 159.12; °**ṇa-sūtra,** Karmav 158.2; 159.2; n. of a work (also **Parinirvāṇa-sūtra**; = Pali Mahāparinibbāna-sutta, DN sūtra 16). See Waldschmidt, NGGW, ph.-h. Kl., Fachgr. III, NF II Nr. 3 (1939); AbhGGW, ph.-h. Kl., 3te Folge, Nr. 29, 30 (1944, 1948); Abh. AW Berlin, ph.-h. Kl., 1949, Nr. 1 (1950).

mahāpāṭala, nt., presumably a kind of *trumpet flower*: Mvy 6199. Follows (Skt.) pāṭala.

Mahāpāraṇika, n. of a disciple of Buddha: LV 2.1. Not noted elsewhere in BHS or Pali, but confirmed as to general form by Tib. pha rol tu ḥgro ba chen po, *great thru-goer.*

mahāpāruṣaka, nt. (see **pāru°**), n. of a flower: Mvy 6163.

Mahāpāśa, n. of a nāga: Mvy 3335.

Mahāpura, n of a locality: Māy 91.

Mahāpūrṇa, n. of a garuḍa prince: SP 5.5.

Mahāprajāpatī (= Pali Mahāpaj°), n. of the sister of Māyā, after whose death she took care of the infant Bodhisattva; later made the head of the order of nuns; regularly with addition of her family name **Gautamī** (once, at least, written Go°), q.v.: SP 268.6 ff.; LV 100.14, 16; 118.14, 16; 121.17; 201.9; 228.4; 229.15, 18; Mv ii.165.2; 233.2; iii.116.7 ff.; 142.6; 256.13 ff.; Mvy 1068; Bhīk 3a.2 et alibi; without the word Gautamī, SP 2.9; Mv i.355.17; Divy 391.7; Suv 239.9; Av ii.4.9; 21.6, 13; 33.5; 50.3.

Mahāprajñā, n. of a female lay-disciple: Gv 51.15.

Mahāpraṇāda, (**1**) n. of a (cakravartin) king (= Pali Mahāpanāda): Mvy 3577; Divy 56.17; 58.9 ff.; (**2**) n. of a prince, son of Mahāratha and brother of Mahāsattva: Suv 206.12 ff.; 225.13 ff.

Mahāpraṇālin, n. of a gandharva: Suv 162.4.

Mahāpraṇidhivegaś(i)ri, n. of a Buddha: Gv 285.19 (vs) °śiri, n. sg., end of line!

Mahāpratibhāna, n. of a Bodhisattva: SP 3.7; 240.7 ff.; 267.1.

Mahāpratisarā, n. of a **rakṣā,** q.v.: Sādh 396.4 etc., 401.11 etc. Also **Pratisarā.**

Mahāpratyaṅgirā, n. of a goddess: Sādh 402.14, 18. Perhaps a **rakṣā,** q.v.; the context suggests this.

Mahāpradīpa, n. of a former Buddha: LV 172.13; of (some) Buddha: Suv 120.2.

Mahāprabha, (**1**) n. of a Buddha in the west: Sukh 97.15; (**2**) n. of a Bodhisattva: Gv 3.15; (**3**) n. of a king: Gv 160.15 ff.; (**4**) n. of a kalpa: Gv 281.23; (**5**) (presumably nt.) n. of a city: Gv 99.11.

Mahāprasāda, n. of a former Buddha: Mv iii.231.8.

mahāprasuta, m., a high number, 10 **prasuta,** q.v.: Mvy 8003.

Mahāprājña, n. of a lay-disciple: Gv 51.9; n. of a householder (the same?): Gv 52.1.

mahāprātihārika, see **prātihārika.**

Mahāprātihārya, sc. **sūtra,** n. of a work (cf. **Prātihārya-sūtra**): Karmav 157.1.

Mahāprītiharṣā, n. of a goddess: Mvy 4321.

mahāpreṣaka, m., a kind of evil supernatural being: Mmk 17.9 (follows **preṣaka,** q.v.).

Mahāphaṇaka, n. of a nāga: Mvy 3337.

mahābala, (**1**) nt., a high number: Mvy 8033; cf. **bala** 4; (**2**) m., n. of two former Buddhas, in the same list: Mv iii.231.5; 237.3; (**3**) perh. n. of a disciple of Śākyamuni (or merely adj.?): Mv i.182.18; (**4**) n. of a nāga: Mvy 3343; (**5**) n. of a king: Samādh p. 16 line 15 ff.; (**6**) n. of one of the **krodha,** q.v.: Dharmas 11; Sādh 137.12 etc.

Mahābalavegasthāma, n. of a garuḍa-king: Gv 250.7.

Mahābalasūtra, nt., n. of a work: Mvy 1406.

Mahābalā, n. of a yoginī: Sādh 427.7.

mahābalākṣa, nt., a high number: Mvy 8039. Cf. **balākṣa.**

mahābimbara, m., a high number: Mvy 8007. Cf. **bimbara.**

Mahābodhi (= Pali id.) = **Bodhi** 3, q.v.

Mahābodhyaṅgavatī, n. of a goddess: Mvy 4325.

Mahābrahma(n), (= Pali id., in both senses, see Childers) (**1**) m. sg., *great Brahmā* (the god), guards the Bodhisattva upon his conception and praises him: Mv i.208.14 = ii.11.2; i.209.11 = ii.13.4; (**2**) m. pl., one (usually the 4th) of the classes of rūpāvacara gods of the first dhyānabhūmi, usually with **deva,** q.v.: LV 150.5 (a stem); Mv ii.360.14 (id.); Divy 367.11 (id.), the rest n-stem forms, Mvy 3088; Divy 68.14; 568.26; Dharmas 128; Av i.5.2 (text °maṇaḥ, acc. pl.; ms. °māṇaḥ; prose), etc.

mahābrahmapurohita, in Gv 249.15 (prose), is a haplographic error for **mahābrahma-brahmapurohita;** see these two.

Mahābhāga, (**1**) n. of a gandharva: Suv 162.1; (**2**) acc. to Senart, Index, n. of a Buddha: Mv i.124.10; but see **Arisūdana.**

mahābhāgā, n. of a medicinal plant: Suv 104.7 (? or adj. with **indrahastā,** preceding).

Mahābhijñājñānābhibhū, n. of a former Buddha: SP 156.2; 157.5; 158.11; 160.7 etc. The only form used in prose; see **Abhijñājñānābhibhū.**

mahābhīṣma, (**1**) nt., n. of some (heavenly) flower; regularly follows **bhīṣma,** q.v.: Mv i.230.16; 267.1; ii.160.13; 286.17; iii.95.14; 99.13; (**2**) n. of a nāga (? or adj., *very fierce,* cf. **bhīṣma** 2, with airāvaṇo?): Mahāsamāj., Waldschmidt, Kl. Skt. Texte 4, 177.7 airāvaṇo °mo prāpto nāgo...

Mahābhuja, n. of two yakṣas: Māy 45; 84.

mahābhūtasamatāsādhana, nt., a kind of **samāpatti,** q.v.: Mvy 1501 = Tib. ḥbyuṅ ba chen po ḥthun par sgrub pa, *attainment of state of equality of* (*to*?) *the great-elements;* see AbhidhK. LaV-P ii.213. (Mironov corruptly °pādānam for °sādhanam; LaV-P. °pādanam.)

Mahābhairavā, n. of a yoginī: Sādh 427.5.

mahā-mañjūṣaka, or °**mañju**°, once (in a vs, prob. m.c.) °mañjūṣa-puṣpāṇi Mv iii.95.10; only occurs after mañjūṣaka (°juṣ°): SP 5.11; 20.2; Mv ii.160.13; 286.18; °mañju° Mvy 6165; Kv 79.1.

Mahāmaṇicūḍa, n. of a nāga: Mvy 3353.

Mahāmaṇidhara, n. of a Bodhisattva: Kv 74.14 (cf. **maṇidharā**).

Mahāmaṇiratna, m., n. of a mountain: Kv 91.16.

mahā-maṇḍarava. see **maṇḍarava.**

Mahāmaṇḍalika, n. of a nāga: Mvy 3355.

Mahāmati, (**1**) n. of a Bodhisattva who plays a leading rôle in Laṅk, 1.10 etc.; (the same, or another Bodhisattva?) Mmk 40.16; 63.4; 68.20; (**2**) n. of a yakṣa: Mvy 3370; (**3**) n. of a lay-disciple: Gv 51.11; (**4**) n. of a king: Gv 360.22; (**5**) in Laṅk 365.2 (vs) apparently a different person from (1), a pupil of the Buddha Viraja, called **Mati** (4), q.v., in 365.3 (vs).

Mahāmatī, n. of the mother of a previous incarnation of Śākyamuni: Samādh p. 60, line 30.

Mahāmanasvin, n. of a nāga: Māy 221.23.

Mahāmantrānusāriṇī = **Mantrānu**°, q.v.: Sādh 401.1 etc.

mahā-mandāra = °**mandārava**: mandāramahāmandāra Suv 196.1 (prose; so with best ms., the others lack this form).

mahā-mandārava, only following **mandārava,** q.v.

Mahāmayūrarājan, n. or epithet of a supernatural being (? = Skanda or Kumāra): Mmk 91.1.

Mahāmahā (mss. °ha), n. of the mother of the Maruts: Divy 635.5.

Mahāmaheśvarāyatana, nt. (nowhere else; see **deva**), in Mvy 3108 an additional stage of śuddhāvāsakāyika gods. Cf. **Maheśvara** (1).

mahā-māndāra and °**māndārava,** only following **māndāra(va),** qq.v.

mahāmāya, m., a high number: Mmk 343.19; see s.v. **māya.**

Mahāmāyā, (**1**) = **Māyā** 1: Divy 390.2; Av ii.44.6; (**2**) n. of a sister of prec.: Mv i.355.17; (**3**) n. of a deity: Sādh 434.4 etc., mother of guhyakas, 434.6; cf. next.

Mahāmāyātantra (cf. prec., 3), n. of a work: Sādh 486.3.

Mahāmāyūrī (also **Māyūrī,** q.v.), n. of a work (our Māy) and of the charms it contains: Mmk 109.28; Waldschmidt, Kl. Skt. Texte 4, 152 ff.; Lévi, JA 1915.19 ff.; personified, Mmk 312.6; Sādh 177.11 etc.; 402.4; seemingly regarded as a **rakṣā,** q.v., in Sādh (cf. BR 5.648 s.v. **mahārakṣā**), where this form replaces **Mārīcī** of the list in Dharmas 5 (but BR's reference to 'Vjutp.', i. e. Mvy, is a mystery to me, since I have been unable to find this list in either of the edd. of Mvy accessible to me); in MSV i.286.15 ff. applied to a short charm to cure snakebite.

mahāmucilinda (equivalent to, or associated with, **mucilinda** 1–3, q.v.), (**1**) n. of a tree and flower (follows muci°): LV 11.1; °dam Mvy 6168; (**2**) n. of a mountain (follows **muci**°): SP 244.11; Samādh 19.19; Sukh 63.3; Kv 91.12; (**3**) n. of a nāga king: Māy 246.31.

mahāmudrā, (**1**) acc. to Lalou, Iconographie, 19 n. 6, in Mmk regularly = **pañcaśikhā** (q.v. for citations) mudrā; also Mmk 56.7 et alibi; (**2**) a high number: Mvy 8031 (cf. **mudrā** 3).

Mahāmuni, n. of a former Buddha: Mv iii.230.14.

Mahāmekhalā, n. of a goddess or the like: Mmk 318.9 (with **Prajñāpāramitā**, personified).

Mahāmegha, n. of a work: Laṅk 258.4, cited thence Śikṣ 133.4; a passage cited directly from Mahām° in Śikṣ 184.5.

Mahāmeghaśrīteja(-s), and **Mahāmeghasphoṭaka**, the first two of 'some twenty' names of Tathāgatas all beginning in Mahāmegha-: Megh 306.21, 22. The other names are omitted by the ed.

Mahāmeru, n. of a Buddha in the east: Sukh 97.2.

Mahāmaitrīmahākaruṇāmukho(d)dyotana, n. of a (perh. imaginary?) work (dharma-paryāya): Gv 209.7.

Mahāmaitryudgata, n. of a Bodhisattva: Gv 4.1.

Mahā-maudgalyāyana (Pali Mahā-moggallāna), = **Maudgalyāyana**, q.v.: Mv ii.190.16; SP 2.2; 100.2; 146.13; 152.13; LV 1.12; Divy 50.24 ff.; 160.7 ff.; 298.25 ff.; 299.18; 395.6 ff.; Av i.112.7 ff.; 242.3; ii.89.7 ff.; Sukh 2.7; 92.5 (here with Śāriputra, who never seems to receive the prefix Mahā-); Karmav 72.10, et passim.

Mahāyaśas, (**1**) n. of a past Buddha: Mv i.117.12 (vs), °yaśo, n. sg.; (**2**) n. of a Bodhisattva or future Buddha: Gv 442.22; (**3**) n. of a yakṣa: Māy 73; (**4**) n. of a kalpa, in which lived 300 Buddhas successively, all named Jinendra: Mv iii.237.19 (vs), °yaśasmiṃ, loc. sg.; (**5**) f., n. of a goddess: Sādh 502.12, °śā(ḥ), n. sg.

mahāyaśākhya, adj., = **maheśākhya**, q.v., Śikṣ 303.11 (vs; meter correct). Is this only a hyper-Sktism, or does it give a clue to the real etymology of maheśākhya and Pali mahesakkha? *Having a very glorious name* fits the word at least as well, and is in my opinion at least as plausible etymologically, as the traditional (but rather mechanical) analysis mahā plus īśa plus ākhyā.

Mahāyāgika, pl., n. of a brahmanical school (of the Chandogas): Divy 632.24, 26.

mahāyāna, nt., *the 'Great Vehicle'* (also called **buddha-**, **bodhisattva-yāna**, qq.v., and see **yāna**, **vajrayāna**, **agrayāna**): passim, e. g. Mvy 1250; bhikṣur °naṃ dhārayamāṇaḥ Suv 192.1; kecin °nam abhiśraddhayanti id.8.

Mahāyānaprasādaprabhāvana, nt., n. of a work: Mvy 1365.

Mahāyānasaṃgraha, m., given as alternative name for Bbh: Bbh 409.15.

mahāyānika, *follower of the mahāyāna*, see s.v. **-yānika**.

Mahāyānopadeśa, m., n. of a work: Mvy 1366.

mahāyuta, m., a moderately large number, 10 ayutas: Mvy 7999.

mahārakṣā, see **rakṣā**.

mahāraṅga, m. (= Pali id.; cf. Skt. mahārajana), *safflower* (used as a dye): MSV ii.142.9.

Mahāratnakūṭa = the work otherwise called **Ratnakūṭa** or **Kāśyapa-parivarta**, qq.v.: KP 52.1; 150.2.

Mahāratnaketu, n. of a Buddha in the west: Sukh 97.16.

Mahāratnapratimaṇḍita, m., name of the kalpa of the future Buddha Padmaprabha: SP 66.1 ff.

Mahāratnavarṣā, n. of a goddess: Mvy 4320.

Mahāratha, n. of a king: Suv 206.11; 225.9 ff.

mahārambha, see **ārambha**.

Mahāraśmijālāvabhāsagarbha, n. of Bodhisattva: Dbh 2.13.

mahārāja(n), (= Pali id.), (**1**) *one of the four guardians of the cardinal directions*, corresponding to Skt. lokapāla, and called by this name Dharmas 7, MSV i.255.17, and Mvy 3145 as sometimes in Pali, but usually mahārāja(n) in both Pali and BHS: catvāro (°raś ca) mahārājāno or °rājā LV 202.13; 366.11; Divy 218.9; Av i.67.10; ii.104.2, 12; instr. Mv i.230.12; often, as in some of the above, included in lists of other gods; mahārāja-sthānam SP 264.12, *the position of world-guardian*, as one of five states which a woman cannot attain. Pali and BHS differ from Skt. in the names assigned to the four individuals, except that Kuvera (Kubera), oftener called Vaiśravaṇa (Pali Vessavaṇa), sometimes Dhanada or other synonyms, is the guardian of the north, as usually in Skt. The other three (in Skt. normally Indra, Yama, and Varuṇa) are **Dhṛtarāṣṭra** (east), **Virūḍhaka** (rarely Virūḍha; south), and **Virūpākṣa** (west; Pali Dhataraṭṭha, Virūḷha(ka), and Virūpakkha). These four are named, Dharmas 7 (as lokapāla); Mvy 3146–9 (as prec., lokapālaḥ 3145); SP 4.6–7; LV 217.16, 20; 218.4, 9; Suv 64.2–3; LV 382.19 ff. (names 384.6, 10, 11, 15, 16, 20, 21; 385.3); LV 388.3, 389.1, 21, 390.19 = Mv iii.306.9, 307.13, 308.13, 309.13; Mmk 654.21; the four are mentioned as devādhipatayaḥ among the kāmāvacara gods whom Māra perceives as favoring the Bodhisattva, LV 302.5–6; and elsewhere in lists of other gods, e. g. Mv i.245.8–9 where Vaiśravaṇa is separated in the list of gods from the other three; sometimes not all are named, thus only Virūḍhaka, Dhṛtarāṣṭra, Kubera (with other gods) Mmk 434.27–435.1; only Vaiśravaṇa and Virūḍhaka, both styled mahārājo, SP 398.8, 399.5; only Virūḍhaka Mv iii.72.3 (mahārājo), and 84.1, 6; Indro Virūḍhakādyāś ca (-ādya including the other three?) Laṅk 367.14; in some of the above the fact is mentioned that Vaiśravaṇa is lord of the yakṣas, Dhṛtarāṣṭra of gandharvas, Virūḍhaka of kumbhāṇḍas, and Virūpākṣa of nāgas; these functions, rather than their position as mahārāja (lokapāla), are exclusively noted in Mvy 3367 (Vaiśr°, first of yakṣas), 3381 (Dhṛt°, of gandharvas), 3437 (Virūḍhaka, of kumbhāṇḍas; no similar statement in Mvy about Virūp°); and, in longer lists of gods, also in Divy 126.6–8; 148.18–19; Av i.108.8–9; Gv 249.24–250.2. The forms of the names Dhṛtarāṣṭra and Virūpākṣa never vary; Virūḍha without final -ka (also recorded in Pali) has been noted only Av i.108.9 and Mmk 654.21 (here vs, perhaps m.c.); Vaiśravaṇa (see also °ramaṇa) is the regular form, for which Kuvera or Kub° is found Dharmas 7; LV 218.9; 390.19 = Mv iii.309.13; Mmk 435.1; Dhanada Divy 126.8; 148.19; Av i.108.9; yakṣarāṭ Mmk 654.21 (vs). In MSV i.258.2 ff. Dhṛtarāṣṭra and Virūḍhaka are said to be Aryans (ārya-jātīya), Virūpākṣa and Vaiśravaṇa Dasyus; the Buddha resolves to convert them using āryā vāc and dasyu-vāc respectively; he then preaches to the first two in normal BHS, to the others (259.2, 7) using what appear to be meaningless groups of sounds. (**2**) n. of a former Buddha: °jaḥ Mv i.138.14.

[**mahārājakāyika**, adj., text at LV 367.4, but best mss. **caturmahā°**, q.v.; so read, with support of Tib. (despite Foucaux's translation of Tib. which omits 'four').]

? **mahārājā**, adj. or subst. f., used (if text is right) with fem. entities: LV 391.4 (vs) upasthitā mahārājā (but v.l. mahāvāiā) Āśā Śraddhā Hirī Śirī (four of eight devakumārikā, the other four named in line 3; cf. Mv iii.309.9, which proves this interpretation); these personages belong to the directions (in this case the north); is mahārājā a fem. equivalent of **mahārāja(n)**, q.v., = Skt. lokapāla?

mahārājika, adj. (from **mahārājan**, q.v.), with or sc. deva, *of the group of world-guardian (gods)*: °keṣu deveṣu Karmav 155.6; °ka-devaparṣadi Gv 513.22; °ka-rūpeṇa LV 39.10, *in the form of one of these gods.*

Mahārūpa, n. of the kalpa of the former Buddha Mahābhijñājñānābhibhū: SP 156.5.

mahā-rūpiṇī, a kind of malevolent supernatural being (see **rūpiṇī**): Mmk 17.8 °ṇyaḥ, pl.

mahāroca, m., n. of a flower: Mvy 6184. Cf. **roca**.

mahārocamāna, nt. (cf. prec.), n. of a flower; only occurs after **rocamāna**, q.v.: Mv i.267.1; ii.160.12; 286.17; iii.95.6; 99.5.

Mahāraurava, m., n. of a hot hell, usually named after **Raurava**, q.v.; alone, e. g. Karmav 70.16; Jm 20.9.

Mahārciskandha, n. of three Buddhas in the same

list in Sukh: one in the south, 97.8; one in the north, 97.21; one in the zenith, 98.16.

Mahārciskandhin, n. af a former Buddha: LV 171.16.

Mahārṣacūḍa, v.l. (better?) Mahāharṣacūḍa, n. of a former Buddha: Mv i.139.13.

Mahālakuṭa, n. of a nāga king: Mmk 18.12. Cf. **Lakuṭa**.

Mahāvana, n. of a grove: Divy 399.12. Context indicates location in the north (in prec. line Kāśmīrapure); acc. to Burnouf, Introd. 396 note 1, in the country of Udyāna, q.v. in BR (udyāna 4). This would hardly fit any of the four groves of this name mentioned in DPPN.

Mahāvastu, n. of the work (Mv): Mv i.1.2; colophon i.4.11; glorification of it, iii.250.10 (and ff.).

mahāvādin (Pali id., see PTSD s.v. vādin), *a great disputant* or *debater*: Gv 358.26 (said of **Satyaka**, q.v.).

mahāvārṣikī (cited pw as °kā, but Mironov °kī; Tib. cited as bar śi ka chen po!), n. of a kind of jasmine, cf. **vārṣikī**, **°kā** (2): Mvy 6154.

mahāvāhana, m., a high number: Mvy 8015. Cf. **vāhana**.

Mahāvikrama, n. of a nāga: Mvy 3341.

Mahāvikrāmin, vv.ll. **°kramin**, **°krama**, n. of a Bodhisattva: SP 3.7.

Mahāvijaya, n. of a monk: Dbh 89.15.

mahāvitāna-dharma, *quality* (ten in number) *of high development* or the like, is applied to what are elsewhere called the 10 **pāramitā** (q.v.) of a Bodhisattva: Gv 295.10 (list 14 ff.).

Mahāvidyutprabha, n. of a nāga: Mvy 3317.

mahāvibhūta, m., a high number: Mvy 8037. Cf. **vibhūta**.

Mahāvimāna, n. of a former Buddha: Mv i.141.14.

mahāvivāha, m., a high number: Mvy 8011. Cf. **vivāha**.

Mahavihāravāsin, pl., n. of a school: Mvy 9096.

mahāvīci (°cī), f. or m., n. of a hell (= **avīci**, q.v.): °cī Mv i.9.9 = °ciṃ iii.454.8 (the first nom., the second acc.).

Mahāvīryā, n. of a yoginī: Sādh 427.8.

mahā-vaipulya, nt., *a great* **vaipulya** (q.v.), said of Buddhist works: SP 19.12; said of SP itself, 21.6; 22.15; 65.1; 181.6; LV is called °lya-nicayo LV 4.18; in 438.20 it is called dharmaparyāya-sūtrānto mahāvaipulya-bodhisattva-vikrīḍitaḥ.

mahāvaistāra, adj. (can be interpreted as from *mahā-vistāra, a normal Skt. cpd., *great extent*, plus -a; Whitney 1204e), *of great extent*: (te kārāḥ . . . mahānuśaṃsā mahādyutayo) °stārā(ḥ) Av ii.108.2.

Mahāvyutpatti, f., n. of a work (Mvy): Mvy p. 611 l. 1.

Mahāvyūha, (**1**) n. of two former Buddhas: LV 172.4 (vs; m.c. °viyūha); Sukh 6.10; (**2**) n. of a Bodhisattva: ŚsP 7.7; (**3**) n. of one of the 16 gods who guard the bodhimaṇḍa: LV 277.14; (**4**) n. of the kalpa in which Kāśyapa is predicted to become a Buddha: SP 144.5; (**5**) n. of a samādhi: Mvy 613; ŚsP 1425.10.

Mahāśakuni, n. of a (cakravartin) king: Mvy 3565; cf. **Śakuni**; = **Śakuna**, MSV i.100.14 etc.

Mahāśakti, n. of a yakṣa (or gandharva?): Māy 237.4.

? **mahāśakya**, adj., *mighty*: °kya-mahāśakyā devatā MPS 5.3, 11 (contrasted with madhya, nīca). But Pali DN ii.87.2 mahesakkhā = **maheśākhya**, of which our word is prob. a folk-etym. alteration, tho well supported in the mss., and despite Pali mahābhisakka (Therag. 1111); Tib. mthu che ba mthu che ba; cf. Mvy 6411 maheśākhya-maheśākhya (Tib. dbaṅ [= mthu] che ba).

mahāśālikā, some sort of mechanical device or toy (piece of furniture?): Mv ii.475.9 (uninterpretable to me as to Senart; in a list of artifacts).

mahāśeṣa, nt., a high number: Mmk 344.1 (= 10 **aśeṣa**, q.v.).

mahāśrāvaka (= Pali mahāsāvaka), *important disciple* (of Buddha). In general BHS, like Pali, knows no definite number or list of them (Vism. 98.26 speaks of the number 80); a typical list of 26 names in SP 1.9 ff., but at the end it adds, 'and others'; no number given ~~in~~ SP 33.5; 121.1; LV 6.15; Divy 489.11, etc. Only Mmk makes tentative starts at lists; twice it mentions groups of eight: Mmk 64.9 ff. Śāriputra, Mahāmaudgalyāyana, Mahākāśyapa, Subhūti, Rāhula, Nanda, Bhadrika, Kaphiṇa; but 111.11 ff. varies (1–2 = 2–1 of 64.9 ff.; then Gavāṃpati, Piṇḍola-Bharadvāja, Pilindavatsa, 6 = 5 above, 7 = 3 above, and 8 Ānanda, who in SP 2.8 is a mere śaikṣa, excluded from the mahāśrāvaka group); in Mmk 40.25 Mahākāśyapa and Mahākātyāyana constitute a pair of mahāśr°; in 13.22 ff. is a very long list, including some familiar and many fanciful and textually doubtful ones; the same is true of the list of females, mahāśrāvikā, which follows in 14.19 ff. (beginning with Yaśodharā); the names in both these lists are omitted here as being largely unreliable.

Mahāśvāsa, n. of a nāga, previous birth of **Virūḍhaka**: MSV i.260.18.

mahāsaṃvidhāna, nt., *the Great Arrangement* or *Preparation*, made by a Bodhisattva in the Tuṣita heaven when he is about to descend to earth for his last existence: Mv i.198.12; ii.2.7. It consists in the departure of many devas from heaven to be reborn on earth so as to support the Bodhisattva in his mission.

Mahāsamsṛṣṭa (cf. **Samsrsṭa**), m., n. of a mountain: Kv 91.13.

mahāsaṃjñā, a high number: Mvy 8035. Cf. **saṃjñā** (7).

mahāsattva, m. (**1**) *'great Being'*, standard ep. of Bodhisattvas: Mvy 626 et passim (very often follows **bodhisattva**); (**2**) n. of a prince, hero of Vyāghrīparivarta (ch. 18) of Suv: Suv 206.13 ff. Several times in the verse version, 225.11, 234.13, 238.14, Mahāsattva-varo (°varaḥ) is printed as if a cpd., tho the name otherwise appears as Mahāsattva also in vss, e. g. 226.6 etc.; perhaps better division would be Mahāsattva (m.c. for °vo, °vaḥ) plus (adj.) varaḥ.

Mahāsanārcis, n. of a Bodhisattva: Gv 442.22.

Mahāsaṃnipāta Sūtra, n. of a work, identified by Thomas after Watanabe as source of fragment Hoernle MR 104 ff.

Mahāsama, pl., n. of a brahmanical school (of the Chandogas): Divy 632.23, 26.

mahāsamantagandha, nt., a kind of flower (only following **samantagandha**): Mv i.230.16; 267.1; ii.160.14; 286.18; iii.95.18; 99.17.

Mahāsamājasūtra (corresp. to Pali Mahāsamaya-sutta, DN no. 20), n. of a work; fragments ed. Waldschmidt, Kl. Skt. Texte 4, 149 ff. Cf. next.

Mahāsamājīya = prec.: Karmav 156.15.

mahāsamāpta, m., a high number: Mvy 8025. Cf. **samāpta**.

mahāsamudra, nt. or m., a high number, = ten samudra (Skt.): °draṃ Mmk 343.21, °dras 22.

Mahāsaṃbhava, nt., n. of a city in the south: Gv 142.10, 22.

Mahāsaṃbhavā, n. of the lokadhātu where dwelt the Buddhas named Bhīṣmagarjitasvararāja: SP 376.2 ff.

Mahāsaṃmata (= Pali id.), n. of an ancient mythical king, the first king of men in the present world-age: Mvy 3552; (mahatā janakāyena sammato iti) Mahāsaṃ° (mss. °samanto, em. Senart) Mv i.348.4; in 8 one ms. correctly Mahāsaṃmatasya, Senart with v.l. Saṃmatasya (om. mahā); in ii.146.19 mss. °samanto, em. Senart; MSV i.3.6.

Mahāsahasrapramardana, nt., n. of a work: Mvy 1395. Cf. **Mahāsāhasrapramardanī**.

mahāsāgara, nt., a high number, = 10 **sāgara**, q.v.: Mmk 343.23, 24.

Mahāsāṃghika, n. of a school: Mvy 9089; Mv i.2.13 (see **Lokottaravādin**).

Mahāsāhasapramardanī, n. of a **rakṣā**, q.v.: Sādh 400.13 etc. Cf. also **Sāhasra°**, **Mahāsahasrapramardana.**

mahāsāhasrikā, f., see **trisāhasrika.**

Mahāsiṃhatejas, n. of a former Buddha: LV 5.9.

mahāsiṃhanādika, adj., *characterized by a great 'lion's roar'*: °ke dharmaparyāye MPS 31.75.

Mahāsitavatī, n. of a **rakṣā**, q.v.: Sādh 401.5 etc.; the v.l. °sītavatī occurs 402.9; 408.18; = **Śītavatī**, q.v.

Mahāsudatta, n. of a monk (bhikṣu): Gv 47.8. Possibly the same as Pali Sudatta 11 in DPPN.

Mahāsudarśana, (**1**) (= Pali °dassana; cf. **Sudarśana** 7). n. of a cakravartin: MPS 34.14 ff.; Mvy 3570; MSV i.97.14; (**2**) n. of a nāga king (cf. **Sudarśana** 6): Māy 247.34.

Mahāsena, (**1**) n. of a yakṣa: Māy 62; (**2**) n. of a rich man of Benares: MSV i.xiv.10.

Mahāsenāvyūhaparākrama, n. of a yakṣa: Mvy 3374.

Mahāsthāma, n. of a Bodhisattva: Mmk 576.15; almost certainly short form for next, m.c.; in same line **Samanta**, q.v., for **Samantabhadra.**

Mahāsthāmaprāpta (cf. prec.), n. of a well-known Bodhisattva: Mvy 653; SP 3.4; 375.1 ff.; Kv 1.13; Sukh 56.8; Samādh p. 36 line 1 (text °sthāna°); Sādh 71.4 etc.

mahāsthāla, nt., a kind of flower: Mvy 6186. Cf. **sthāla.**

Mahāsmṛti, n. of a (virtuous) son of Māra: Mv ii.337.2. Text seems confused; verses attributed to him seem to be attributed to **Janīsuta** in 333.21.

Mahāsmṛtyupasthāna, nt., n. of a work: Mvy 1401.

[**mahāhatamanda**, see **mahātapamanda.**]

? **Mahāharṣacūḍa**, see **Mahārṣacūḍa.**

mahāhetu, m., a high number: Mvy 8019. Cf. **hetu.**

mahikā (Skt. mahikā, *cold*, in °kāṃśu: cf. mihikā, *mist*, Schmidt, Nachträge; Pali mahikā, AMg. mahiyā, defined in both mgs.), *mist, fog*: Mvy 1872 = Tib. khug rna; 7158 = Tib. na bun rmugs pa; Dharmas 34.

Mahita, n. of a devaputra: LV 4.12 (= Tib. mchad byas, *honored*); 6.13; 7.5; 438.16.

Mahiṃdhara (so all mss.), n. of a devaputra, one of the 16 guardians of the bodhimaṇḍa: LV 277.13 (prose).

Mahiṣī, n. of a rākṣasī: Māy 243.9.

mahī (= Skt. maha), *festival*, in jātī-mahī saṃvṛttā Divy 515.18; in same line, **jātamahaṃ** kṛtvā; both *birth-festival*; is the otherwise unrecorded -mahī adapted to the gender of jātī-? Cf. **jāti-maha.**

Mahīdhara, n. of a minister: Divy 318.18 ff.; previous birth of Maudgalyāyana, 328.15–16.

[**mahīśākhya**, see **maheś°**].

Mahīśāsaka, pl., n. of a Buddhist school: Mvy 9080; Karmav 60.8 (by plausible em., see Lévi's note).

mahīsthāma (all mss.; Senart em. mahi°, m.c., but the meter requires rather abhūṣi cāturdvipo, with shortened i, mahī°), ep. of the cakravartin Maṇiviṣāṇa, *having earth-power* (acc. to Senart, *having in his hands the powers of all the earth*): Mv i.119.6 (vs).

mahendra, (**1**) m., a high number: Mvy 8023 (cf. **indra** 2); (**2**) n. of a king of Kanyakubja and of the Madras, father of **Sudarśanā** who married **Kuśa**; also **Mahendraka** 1, q.v.; in the Pali Kusa Jāt. he is called Madda (= Madra), king of Sāgala: Mv ii.460.8; iii.27.19 (here °dra-nātha-; both prose); (**3**) n. of a king of Hastināpura (also **Mahendraka** 2, q.v.): Mv iii.432.11; 433.4; the story told here is basically (tho with some confusion) the same that is told of Uruvela-Kassapa and his brothers in Pali (see DPPN 1.433 f.), in which Mahinda (3 in DPPN) is the father of the Buddha Phussa (BHS Puṣya); (**4**) n. of the well-known apostle to Ceylon (= Pali Mahinda 1 in DPPN): Karmav 63.1; (**5**) n. of a nāga king: Māy 246.15.

Mahendraka, (**1**) = **Mahendra** 2: Mv ii.441.7; 442.9 etc. (prose); iii.13.16 (vs); (**2**) = **Mahendra** 3: Mv iii.432.16 ff.

Mahendradeva, n. of a Bodhisattva: Gv 442.10.

mahelikā (Skt. Lex.; cf. late Skt. and Pkt. mahelā, Skt. mahilā), *woman*: strī-mahelikā (n. pl.; so mss., Senart em. °mahallikā) . . . bhagavato pādavandīyo Mv iii.265.17 (prose).

maheśākhya, adj. (cf. **alpeśākhya**; = Pali mahesakkha; by error mahīś° MSV i.95.12; see also **mahāśakya**; once **mahāyaśākhya**, q.v.; hyper-Sktism?), *distinguished, exalted, great*; usually of persons, such as kings, Bodhisattvas (Bbh 31.18), or other high personages: SP 180.12; LV 23.16; 24.15; Mv i.36.3; 189.1; 193.14; 197.17; 198.4, 17; ii.64.15; 420.7; 485.3; iii.125.11; Divy 434.1; Av i.354.10; 363.9; Mmk 100.25 (text °kṣā, read °khyā); 215.4; contrasted with its opposite **alpeśākhya**, q.v., Mvy 6411; Karmav 29.26; puṇya-ma° *one who is a great personage by reason of merit* (acquired by past deeds) Divy 8.5; 42.1; 98.20 (udāra-puṇya-ma°); 219.11; 579.17; vipāka-ma°, same (*distinguished thru the maturing of his karma*) Av ii.67.10; mah° said of gods LV 413.12; Mv i.30.9, 17; iii.318.16; of Māra, by himself Mv ii.277.4; of the sun and moon LV 51.12; 410.15; of a nāga king Mv i.249.18; of noble animals Mv i.287.7; 288.19; maheśākhyataram, compv., of a caitya, Divy 243.8. In some of the above (Mvy 6411; LV 413.12) intensive āmreḍita, maheśākhya-mah°.

maheśākhya-tā, Bbh 29.9; 31.22, or **°tva**, Mv ii.289.15, abstracts from prec.

Maheśvara, (**1**) sg. or pl.; in LV 112.3; 113.1, 11, a devaputra, evidently a leader of the **śuddhāvāsakāyika** gods, with whom he comes to salute the infant Bodhisattva and predict his future Buddhahood; in Mv i.224.3, 5 = ii.27.3, 5 (vss) pl., 8000 gods named Mah° come to cast the horoscope of the infant Bodhisattva; prob. interpret in this sense maheśvara-rūpeṇa (the Bodhisattva, it is suggested, should enter his mother's womb thus) LV 39.12; Mvy 3108 **mahāmaheśvarāyatanam**, q.v., a special stage of **śuddhāvāsakāyika** gods; (**2**) n. of a yakṣa: Divy 41.2 ff.; Suv 161.6; Māy 9; (**3**) n. of one or two Bodhisattva(s): Sādh 71.4 (here between Avalokiteśvara and Mahāsthāmaprāpta); Gv 442.6 (in a long, rigmarole list).

maheśvaradatta, m. or nt., a kind of gem: Mv ii.311.3.

mahotsaṅga, m., a high number: Mvy 8013. Cf. **utsaṅga.**

Mahodadhi, n. of a nāga: Mmk 454.15.

mahoragaka, adj., *of great serpents*: Śikṣ 333.9 (vs).

mahoraga-lipi, a kind of script: LV 126.3 (confirmed Tib., lto ḥphye chen po).

Maholūkhalamekhalā, n. of a yakṣī: Māy 58. So the Chin. versions clearly indicate; text Aholū°, prob. misprint.

Maholkādhārin, n. of a Bodhisattva: Gv 442.1.

(**mahaujaska**, adj., *of great might*: Mvy 727; 6410; occurs in Skt., Schmidt, Nachträge.)

Mahauṣadha, n. of a youth (the Bodhisattva), hero of a jātaka = Pali Sūci-j., No. 387 (unnamed there): Mv ii.83.20 ff. He marries Amarā; both names are used in Pali in the different Mahāummagga-j., No. 546; see s.v. **Amarā** (1) for discussion.

Mahauṣadhi, n. of a nāga maid: Kv 4.2.

-māṃsaka (= Skt. māṃsa, with -ka Bhvr.), in a-matsya-māṃsakair LV 248.17 (prose), *involving no* (eating of) *fish or meat*, said of ascetic practices.

māṃsakīla, m., *wart*: Mvy 4056 = Tib. mdzer pa.

māṃsacakṣu(s), nt. (= Pali maṃsa-cakkhu),

fleshly, bodily eye, one of the five **cakṣus**, q.v.: prākṛtena °ṣā mātāpitṛsaṃbhavena SP 354.7, cf. 9; 355.3; tasya dāni tava viśuddhaṃ °kṣuṃ Mv iii.177.8; buddhyā na (two mss. om. na) °ṣā Laṅk 13.3; others s.v. **cakṣus.**

māṃsaja, *'flesh-born', physically begotten (son)*: pravrājemi katham ahaṃ Rāhulaśiri °jaṃ (spelled mānsajaṃ) jinasya Mv iii.269.8 (vs).

māṃsabala, m. or nt., n. of a (supposed) magic herb: m., MSV ii.134.9; nt., madīya-snānodakaṃ °lam ib. 11–12, 16.

māṃsika, m., (**1**) (= Pali maṃsika), *butcher*, or *meat-dealer*: SP 276.5; (**2**) see s.v. **kahāpaṇa.**

Mākandika (also **Māgandika**, q.v.; = Pali Māgandiya), n. of a parivrājaka who lived at **Kalmāṣadamya**, q.v.: Divy 515.14 ff.; °dikāvadānam, colophon of Divy chap. 36, Divy 544.21.

Mākkoṭaka, *living in* **Makkoṭaka**, q.v.: Śikṣ 71.2 °kaiḥ prāṇijātibhiḥ.

Māgadha, n. of a yakṣa: Māy 63.

māgadhaka, f. °**ikā** (Pali id., Childers; AMg. Māgahaa), *of, belonging to, Magadha*: °kānāṃ (brāhmaṇakānāṃ) Mv i.261.17, 18; with brāhmaṇa-gṛhapati(ka), Mv iii.317.6; 443.12; Divy 393.29; janapada, Divy 92.24; paura, Av i.107.8; sattvāḥ, Kv 48.8; °ikā kaṃsapātrī, some special kind of brass vessel called *Magadhan*, Mv ii.412.8; °ikāye kaṃsapātrīye Mv ii.282.10; so interpret °ikānāṃ (partitive gen.) kāṃsapātrī LV 318.22, *a brass vessel of the Magadhan ones* (not 'of the Magadhan people'!); subst. m., *the people of Magadha*, °akānāṃ Rājagṛhaṃ nagaraṃ LV 239.18.

Māgandika, (**1**) = **Mākandika** (Pali Māgandiya): in the 'Skt. Suttanipāta', Hoernle, JRAS 1916.714–5; (**2**) as common noun, in Mv iii.412.7 (prose), applied to some kind of heretical (brahmanical) ascetics or sectarians, in a cpd., after parivrājakā, traidaṇḍika-mānandika-(so mss., read māga°, or māka°?)-guruputraka-gautama- etc.); cf. Pali AN iii.276.32 f., similar list, paribbājako ... māgaṇḍiko ... tedaṇḍiko ... aviruddhako ... gotamako, etc.; the word māgaṇḍika (note ṇḍ) is not recorded in PTSD or Childers; it seems doubtful whether it is related to the n. pr. Māgandika (1).

Māṭhara, n. of a brahman, father of **Śārī**: Av ii.186.7.

māḍa (cf. **māla** 2; Pali māḷa, māla), m. pl. māḍāḥ Mvy 5548 (v.l. and Mironov māṭāḥ), some sort of building: Tib. rṅa (*drum*) khaṅ (*house, building*), or sṅa (= pūrva) khaṅ; Chin. has two renderings, perh. intended like the two Tib. glosses; could the first Tib. mean *drum-shaped hall*? cf. **maṇḍala-māḍa.** PTSD derives the Pali word from Tamil māḍam, *house.*

Māṇa, n. of a nāga king: Mmk 18.10.

māṇava (also mānava, MSV i.261.20), usually (as in Skt. and Pali) *youth*, esp. *brahman youth*; more commonly (again as in Skt. and Pali) °vaka. Once °va is used of an adult brahman, a king's purohita, and contrasted with his pupils, called °vaka: Divy 60.23 rājño Brahmāyur nāma brāhmaṇaḥ purohito bhaviṣyati ... (25) Brahmāyur māṇavo 'śītimāṇavakaśatāni brāhmaṇakān mantrān vācayiṣyati. This seems to be highly exceptional.

Māṇicara (= Pali id., 'to be invoked in time of need'), n. of a yakṣa: Māy 236.28; Mmk 609.7; pl., sarve Māṇicarā yakṣā sidhyante sarvakālataḥ Mmk 337.24 (vs).

māṇḍaleya, *member of a maṇḍala* or (*mystic*) *circle*: Vajratārāṃ sa-māṇḍaleyāṃ (Bhvr.) Sādh 189.7; māṇḍaleyānāṃ tu saṃbhavaḥ 230.13.

māṇḍalya, nt. (to Skt. maṇḍala plus -ya), *circularity*: dīrghahrasvādimāṇḍalyaṃ parikalpasya saṃgrahāt Laṅk 350.6 (vs).

Māṇḍavya, (**1**) n. of a ṛṣi in the 'Padumāvatīye parikalpa': Mv iii.153.7 ff. So Senart, with one ms. in 153.20; v.l. here, and both mss. in most passages, Maṇḍ° (MIndic), which should prob. be read; (**2**) pl., n. of a brahmanical school (of the Bahvṛcas): Divy 632.18 f., and n. of a gotra, Divy 635.8, 20.

Mātaṅga, (**1**) (= Pali id., DPPN 2) n. of a Pratyekabuddha: LV 18.15; (**2**) (perh. = Pali id., DPPN 3) n. of a maharṣi: Māy 257.2; (**3**) n. of a nāga king: Mvy 3262.

Mātali, n. of a yakṣa: Māy 93; 237.4. In Pali Mātali, Indra's charioteer (as in Skt.), is assumed in DPPN to be identical with a yakkha who is to be called on in time of need. This yakkha, in any case, is presumably the same as our Mātali.

mātāpitṛ, sg. or pl. (not otherwise noted in this sense), *family, relatives, 'home-folks'*: (a king has granted a wish to a courtesan, his concubine; she replies) Mv i.348.16–17 mahārāja yāvatā khu mātāpitaraṃ āpṛcchāmi tato devasya sakāśāto varaṃ yācayiṣyāmi. tāye mātāpitṛṇāṃ ārocitam. (18–349.1) tehi dāni yaṃ mataṃ so taṃ jalpati ... tahiṃ aparā parivrājikā (2) paṇḍitā ... sā āha: Jenti, tvaṃ vailāsikāye dhītā ... It is obvious that a plurality of persons is meant here, and certainly not the 'mother and father' of Jentī. On this basis I think it likely that in LV 279.11 mātāpitṛsaṃjñino means *regarding* (each other) *as members of the same family*: (sarvasattvāś ca tasmin samaye maitracittā hitacittāḥ) parasparaṃ mātā° 'bhūvan. Cf. next.

mātāpitṛka, adj. (cf. prec. and next but one), *inherited, innate, natural*, contrasting with what is due to *training*: (the Bodhisattva had not received martial or athletic training, so that Yaśodharā's father refused him as a son-in-law; but he,) mātāpitṛkena balena Mv ii.75.13, *by natural, innate strength*, threw a dead elephant over seven city walls.

mātāpitṛjña, see **mātṛjña.**

mātāpaitṛka (Pali mātāpettika) = prec. but one: MPS 31.17.

mātula, m. (var. ma°), a high number: Mvy 7772 = Tib. ma gzhal; cf. **māludu.**

mātṛkā (= Pali mātikā), (**1**) a name for the **Abhidharma(piṭaka)**: °kādhītā Divy 18.6; sūtrasya vinayasya °kāyāḥ 18.15; sūtraṃ mātṛkā ca 333.7; MSV iii.122.4 °kā-dharo; Prāt 520.13; (**2**) (see also **Bodhisattva-(sūtra-)-piṭaka-mātṛkā**) *summary, condensed statement of contents*; the **Abhidharma** probably professed originally to be a summary of the main points of certain aspects of the Dharma (see CPD s.v. abhidhamma): Bbh 210.10; 274.21; (prob.) 303.25; aṣṭau mātṛkā-padāni MSV ii.161.14, *eight summary points.*

mātṛgrāma, m. (= Pali mātugāma), *womankind, the female sex*; in BHS (acc. to Childers in Pali too) occasionally used mg. *an (individual) woman*, as in SP 418.9 sacet ... mātṛgrāma imaṃ dharmaparyāyaṃ śrutvodgrahīṣyati ... tasya sa eva paścimaḥ strībhāvo bhaviṣyati; 441.13 putrakāmo mātṛgrāmo ... tasya putraḥ prajāyate; and in a cliché (see s.v. **āveṇika**) ekatye paṇḍitajātīye mātṛgrāme Divy 2.3–4; 98.22; Av i.14.7 etc., *in every intelligent woman*; some of the following may also be interpreted thus, but most of them are abstract or collective: Mvy 3922; 6864 (°ma-bhāva); 8490; SP 202.5; 206.2; 277.1; 405.1; LV 25.14; 141.9; Mv iii.49.20; Divy 257.13 ff.; 493.6; 531.6; Suv 110.5; Bbh 94.7; 167.7; Prāt 479.7, 11 (prob. individual); Karmav 167.3; Bhīk 3a.1.

mātṛjña, adj. (ending app. analog. to Skt. kṛtajña), *mother-honoring*: Mv iii.131.16. Almost always followed by **pitṛjña, śrāmaṇya, brāhmaṇya**, *honoring fathers, monks, brahmans*; corresp. to Pali matteyya (or me°), petteyya, sāmañña, brahmañña; also (in both languages) neg. forms in a-: LV 24.15 = Mv i.198.6 = ii.2.2; Mv i.46.9; ii.423.17; Bbh 267.5; mātāpitṛjña-tā, śrāmaṇya-tā, brāhmaṇya-tā Karmav 40.16.

[**mātryo**, Senart Mv i.351.4, 8; read mātrīyo; see **mātrī.**]

-mātra (for -mātraṃ, adv.; m.c.), in comp. with

preceding gerund, as in Skt. and Pali often with participles: utsṛjya-mātra bhaviyā (ger.) navapuṣpadāmāḥ LV 298.9, *as soon as they had thrown* (their bodies), *having become fresh-flower-garlands*, ... (or is -mātra for -māṭrāḥ, adj., with same mg.?). On *mātra, adj., *maternal*, see **mātrī**.

mātrajña, adj. (= Pali mattaññu; cf. next, and **a-mātrajña**), *moderate* (in eating): Mvy 2393; Śikṣ 143.20; Ud vi.6 (bhojane); xxix.16.

mātrajña-tā (also written °jñā-tā, which it seems must be an error, tho it occurs repeatedly in mss.; once mātraṃj°, § 2.76; abstr. from prec., = Pali mattaññutā), *moderation* (in eating): Mv iii.265.11 (v.l. mātṛjñātā); Śikṣ 144.2; Ud xxxii.27 (32); bhojana-mātraṃjñātā LV 430.3–4 (prose), so Lefm., v.l. -mātrajñ°, but apparently all mss. °jñātā; cf. under **a-mātr°**.

mātrā-bhojin (cf. Pali matta-bhojana Dhp.c. iii.265.8 *moderate eating*, and prec. two), *eating in moderation*: Śikṣ 129.13.

mātrī, adj. f. (to m. *mātra, from Skt. mātṛ plus -a?), *of the mother, maternal*: (svaka-svakā yeva) mātrīyo bhaginīyo parasparasya vivāhitā Mv i.351.4, (the princes) *gave to each other in marriage each their own sisters by the same mother* (thus avoiding the marriage of any with his co-uterine sister). So the Tib. version cited by Senart p. 625; Senart misunderstands the Skt. text; he reads mātṛyo with v.l. (and with both mss. line 8 below), but this can only be a corruption. The Pali adj. mātiya which he cites is not known to PTSD; Childers cites it with no textual reference; even if a genuine Pali word, it can hardly be concerned here.

mātsika (Skt. Gr. id.; cf. Pali macchika), *fisherman*: Mvy 3756 (so Mironov; no v.l.). Looks like hyper-Sktism.

[**Mādana**, see **Gandhamādana** 2.]

Mādhāta, cited as equivalent to **Māndhāta**, q.v.: Divy 210.21.

Mādhyandina, = **Madhyaṃdina**, q.v.: MSV i.xvii.4; i.4.4.

Mādhyamika, m., an adherent of the Buddhist school of this name: Mvy 5144. Cf. **Madhyamaka**(-ruci).

māna-kūṭa (= Pali id.), *cheating in measures*: Śikṣ 269.2 na °ṭena (Bendall and Rouse *false pretensions*! the correct mg. is already found in Childers s.v. kūṭo); as Bhvr., *one who cheats in measures*: SP 402.10 (vs) mānakūṭānāṃ (KN wrongly add ca with only 1 ms.) yā gatiḥ (Tib. bre confirms māna, *measure*, yet WT, who cite Tib., read kānsya by em., with corrupt support from one or two mss.).

mānatva, nt. (also **mānāpya**, q.v.; = Pali mānatta), a kind of penance which is superimposed, after **parivāsa**, on a monk guilty of a saṃghāvaśeṣa offense which he has concealed: Prāt 487.11–12 bhikṣuṇā ... mānatvaṃ (12) caritavyaṃ bhavati, cīrṇa-mānatvo (*after he has undergone the m°*) bhikṣur ...; for **mānāpya**, Mvy 8652–5, v.l. mānatva (so Index; ed. mānātva), but Mironov mānāpya without v.l.; Tib. renders Mvy mgu bar bya ba, *making glad* (Das = ārādhanā); Chin. *respectful behavior*; this accords with the Pali comm. (629.29) on the Vin. passage (iii.186.15 f., bhikkhunā ... bhikkhu-mānattāya paṭipajjitabbaṃ, ciṇṇamānatto bhikkhu ...) corresponding to Prāt 487.11–12 above; the comm. says, bhikkhu-mānattāyā ti bhikkhūnaṃ mānanabhāvāya, ārādhanatthāyā (cf. Das on Tib. above) ti vuttaṃ hoti; it thus appears that, according to both northern and southern tradition, this penance consisted in, or at least involved, some kind of ceremonial homage paid by the culprit to the general community of monks. This can be interpreted as supporting the apparent etym., māna-tva, *condition of* (paying) *respect*.

Mānabhañja, n. of a nāga king: Mmk 18.11.

Mānava, n. of a yakṣa: May 2. (Also written for **māṇava**, q.v.)

mānavaka (sometimes written for Skt. māṇavaka, as LV 101.9 and 108.5, all mss.; f. mānavikānāṃ, perh. rather to Skt. mānava, mānavī, *human being*, Mv ii.432.4, used of king's wives), m. or nt., in Av i.265.7 is, or corruptly represents, a word meaning *peg, post*, or the like, for hanging clothes: yena ... sā **yamalī** (q.v.) krītā, tena mānavake sthāpitā Av i.265.7; Tib. cited by Speyer as gdaṅ, which (or gdaṅ bu, Mvy 9037) = **carpaṭaka**, q.v. The context proves that this is approximately right in mg. But Speyer's suggestion that we em. tenārambhaṇake (should be °mbaṇake, see **ārambaṇaka**) is improbable; that word seems to mean a different kind of *peg*, tho also rendered by Tib. gdaṅ (bu). Could our word be related to AMg. māṇavaya, n. of a divine 'caitya-stambha' (see Ratnach. s.v.)?

mānasaka (nt.; Skt. °sa plus -ka, § 22.34), *mind* (endearing): nivartaya °kaṃ LV 322.4 (vs), *turn back your* (sweet) *mind* (said by the daughters of Māra to the Bodhisattva).

Mānasī, n. of a kiṃnara-maid: Kv 5.22.

Mānastabdha (= Pali Mānatthaddha), n. of a proud brahman converted by Buddha: Av i.148.10.

mānātimāna, m. (= Pali id.; māna plus **atimāna**, q.v.), *pride and conceit*: Mvy 1948 (following māna and **adhimāna**; followed by **asmimāna** and abhimāna); °na-vivarjanatayā Gv 463.26.

[**mānātva**, see **mānatva**.]

mānāpika, adj. (= Pali manāpika, and **manāpa**, q.v.; see also **amanāpika**, and cf. next; no form with ā in first syllable is recorded otherwise), *pleasant, charming*: °kāni Mv ii.150.5, 14; 151.18; 152.8; 153.17; 156.10; iii.68.11.

mānāpya, nt. (cf. prec.; app. popular etym. for **mānatva**, q.v., which is cited in Mvy Kyoto ed., tho not in Mironov, as v.l. for this; the implied etym. is manāpa plus -ya, *state of being*, or *making oneself, agreeable*, sc. to the monastic community by homage), = **mānatva**: °pyam Mvy 8652 (on Tib. and Chin. see **mānatva**); mūla-°pyam 8653 (Tib. gzhi nas for mūla-), mūlāpakarṣa-°pyam 8654 (Tib. yaṅ gzhi nas bslaṅ ste for °karṣa); on these see s.v. **mūla** (3); cīrṇa-°pyam Mvy 8655, *having undergone the m°* (penance; we should expect °pyaḥ, see under **mānatva**); Tib. mgu bar byas; carita-°pya, id., MSV ii.157.16; (gurudharmādhyāpannayā ... bhikṣuṇyā) ubhayasaṃghe anvardhamāsaṃ **mānāpyaṃ** caritavyaṃ Bhīk 5b.5; 7b.4; 30b.5 (in the last, ubhayasaṃghena); cf. Pali Vin. iv.52.26–27, where in close parallel pakkha-mānattam; mānāpya-cāra, *one undergoing this discipline*, MSV ii.154.14, and mūla-mān° 15; °pya-cārika, id., MSV ii.157.16; in ii.207.16 occur the three items of Mvy 8652–8654, but in iii.43.1 ff. only mānāpyam, imposed for six days after completion of the mūlāpakarṣa-(parivāsa) penance; in iii.61.18 imposed for six days as penance for a saṃghāvaśeṣa offense which, if concealed, would entail parivāsa (as in Pali, Vin. ii.38.1 ff.).

Mānuṣa, n. of a nāga king: Māy 247.25.

mānuṣaka, f. °**ikā**, adj. and subst. (= Pali °saka; Skt. adj. daiva-mānuṣaka, once, BR 5 s.v.), *human*; *a human being*: °ṣikāye vācāye Mv iii.131.9; nāpi jñāyate °ṣikā eṣā Mv i.353.4.

māndāra (cf. Skt. mandāra), rare, = **māndārava**, q.v.: LV 6.6, so all mss., but Tib. mandāraba (in Calc. 318.16 also māndāra but Lefm. 253.21 °rava with all mss.); °ra-mahāmāndāra ŚsP 322.3; Kv 8.3; 65.4; māndāra-mahāmāndāravāṇi (! presumably read māndārava-mahā°) Kv 79.1.

māndāraka = °ra(va), always as adj. with puṣpa (so also °**rava** and other forms): only in Divy 158.16; 186.5; 251.9; 327.12.

māndārava, m. or nt. (= **mandārava**, q.v., and other varr., see prec. two; most commonly as adjectival epithet of puṣpa or kusuma, but also sometimes alone): LV 45.8; 253.21; 296.21 (vs, read °vāṃ, acc. pl., with all mss.); Karmav 159.3; Mv i.214.11; 216.6; ii.286.13; 393.19; Divy 554.14; Gv 118.23; Sukh 94.12; Suv 102.3; 150.9; (Kv 79.1, see s.v. **māndāra**;) followed by mahā-mā°, SP 5.11; 20.1; 69.9–10; 240.1–2; LV 10.21; Mv i.266.18; ii.286.15–16; Mmk 111.17; Suv 196.5 (mahā-mā° 7, but here best ms. °**māndāra**).

Māndhāta, °**tṛ** (and other forms, see below; = Pali Mandhātā, n. sg., stem °tu-; there seems to be nothing in Buddhist legend suggesting identity with Skt. Māndhātṛ, except the name), n. of an ancient cakravartin king, sometimes (e. g. in Laṅk, also in Pali) regarded as a previous incarnation of Śākyamuni: °taḥ, °to, n. sg., Mvy 3558; Mv i.348.9; Divy 210.20; 214.20; °tasya Mv i.348.9; Divy 210.21; 213.23; MSV i.67.14 ff.; 93.6 ff.; Mmk 609.1; °tṛ- (stem in comp.) Karmav 37.3; °tā, n. sg., Mv i.154.1; Divy 210.23; 214.21; Karmav 36.11; Laṅk 141.5; Mmk 608.22; °tuḥ, gen. sg., Divy 278.13; 576.10, etc.; Mādhātaḥ, cited as used by 'some', Divy 210.21; **Mūrdhātaḥ** (q.v.), as n. sg. Mvy 3557 (so v.l. of Mironov, who reads Mūrdhagataḥ, Kyoto ed. Mūrdhataḥ), also Divy 210.19, and forms of this stem are much used in this Divy and MSV story, interchangeably with stems Māndhāta and °tṛ; e. g. Mūrdhātasya Divy 212.9, 18; °tena 212.19, 22.

Māndhātṛ-sūtra, cited from the **Rājasaṃyuktaka-nipāta** of the **Madhyamāgama**: MSV i.93.10 (story of prec.).

Māmakī, n. of a Buddhist goddess: Mvy 4275; Dharmas 4; Mmk 41.5; Sādh 18.14 etc.

māya, (**1**) nt. acc. to text, a high number: mahāvivāhas tathā dṛṣṭas, taddaśaṃ māyam ucyate Mmk 343.18 (vs); or understand māya(ḥ)-m-ucyate, with m. gender? In next line: taddaśamāyāṃ(!) **mahāmāyaḥ**; (**2**) apparently nt. for Skt. māyā, *trick, wile*: bahūni māyāni darśayati Mv ii.174.12 (prose; no v.l.).

? **māyatā**, prob. read māyitā (Skt.), *trickiness, deceit*: no ca śāṭhya na khilaṃ na māyatā teṣu vidyati... RP 10.11 (vs).

māyati (= Skt. māti), *is measurable in, is contained in*, with loc. (so Skt. māti): (sa puṇyaskandho...) trisāhasramahāsāhasreṣu lokadhātuṣu na māyet AsP 157.19, *would not be measurable in* i. e. *would be greater than.*

Māyā (Pali id.), often Māyā-devī as cpd., also **Mahāmāyā**, q.v., (**1**) n. of the wife of Śuddhodana and mother of Śākyamuni: Mvy 1069 (Māyādevī); her origin and history, Mv i.355.17 ff. (many other refs. to her, see Senart's Index); LV 26.15; 28.8 ff.; 78.1; 252.13, 15; Suv 239.5 (vs, Māya-devī, m.c.); Gv 375.1; in Gv, where **Vairocana**, q.v., seems blended with Śākyamuni, she is also Vairocana's mother (381.5; 338.25, cf. 339.3) in all his existences (as a result of a praṇidhāna made ages ago, 444.20 ff., that she might always be the mother of a certain cakravartin who became Vairocana, 445.4); in Gv 426.11–12 she is called bodhisattva-janetrī and located bhagavato Vairocanasya pādamūle; in 438.8 she made a praṇidhāna to be the mother of all Bodhisattvas and Buddhas (sarvabodhisattva-jina-janetrī-pra°); in 438.23 ff. she says that she has been the mother of all **caramabhavika** (q.v.) Bodhisattvas in all the lokadhātus of the Lord **Vairocana**, and then (439.1–2) that she gave birth to the Bodhisattva Siddhārtha, 'in this very Bhāgavatī cāturdvīpikā', in Kapilavastu, as Śuddhodana's wife; in 441.6 ff. she says that as she was the Buddha Vairocana's mother, so she was the mother of all past Buddhas, and will be of future Buddhas, Maitreya etc.; (**2**) n. of a deity attendant on the four direction-rulers: Mahāsamāj. Waldschmidt, Kl. Skt. Texte 4, 173.9; = Pali id., DN ii.258.9 (not in DPPN).

māyākāra, m. (= Pali and Skt. Lex. id.), *conjurer, sleight-of-hand-performer*: Mvy 7242.

Māyājālamahāyoga-tantra, n. of a work by Kṛṣṇapāda: Sādh 378.16.

māyūravratin, a member of some heretical sect: Mvy 3537. Cf. **go-(śṛṅga-)vratika, mṛga-śṛṅga-vratin.**

Māyūrī (= **Mahā-māyūrī**), n. of a book of spells called vidyārājñī: Māy 218 lines 3 and 1 from bottom.

Māra, m. (= Pali id.), *the Evil One, the adversary and tempter*; regularly with ep. pāpīyāṃs; often styled **Namuci**, q.v.; sometimes *the great* **yakṣa**, q.v.: in the singular, so usually, as the One who tries to thwart the Bodhisattva or Buddha and his followers, SP 63.6; 64.2; 145.2, 3; LV 260.17 ff.; 267.2; 299.20 ff. (long chapter on his temptations of and attacks on Śākyamuni); Divy 144.14; 145.4; 201.22 ff.; 202.2 ff. (here, as often, tempts Buddha to enter nirvāṇa); Jm 19.20 ff.; an unspecific plurality of Māras, SP 64.3; Śikṣ 49.7 f. mārāḥ pāpīyāṃso bodhisattvasya viheṭhanām (so with ms.) upasaṃharanti; in Gv 444.12 there is a Māra named **Suvarṇaprabha** who tries to interfere with a Bodhisattva named Vimalaprabha in his quest of enlightenment; Māra is converted(!) by Upagupta, Divy 357.1 ff.; there are ten Māra-karmāṇi, *deeds of Satan*, of which an erring Bodhisattva may be guilty, Śikṣ 151.13–152.19 (listed in detail); plurality of Māras, in Pali 3, 4, or 6 (in the latter case including Abhisaṃkhāra-māra, which has not been noted in BHS, cf. **abhisaṃskāra**), whereas in BHS they are standardly four, viz. (the order varies) Kleśa-māra, Skandha-māra, Mṛtyu-māra, and Devaputra-māra (the last means the anthropomorphic Evil One; excellent brief statements on the others, which mean in effect quasi-personifications of kleśa etc., in Childers s.v. Māro); to these corresp. Pali Kilesa-, Khandha-, Maccu-, and Devaputta-māra (but in Pali, even when the Māras number four, it need not be *these* four); only two named SP 290.9 (śrāvakāṃś) ca bodhisattvāṃś ca skandhamāreṇa vā kleśamāreṇa vā sārdhaṃ yudhyamānān..., in next line (10) sarva-māranirghātanaṃ; similarly in Mv iii.273.2 only two, Kleśamāro bhagno; Devaputramāro bhagno; but usually all four are named, so Mv iii.281.7 f.; Dharmas 80; Śikṣ 198.10 f.; Sādh 20.1–2; exigences of meter may cause abbreviations, as in LV 224.18–19 where all mss. and Calc. have all four names in full, but meter requires Devamāra instead of Devaputra°; so LV 354.11–12 (vss) anena jitu Skandhamāras tatha Mṛtyu-Kleśa-mārāḥ (v.l. Mṛtyumāra-Kleśamārāḥ, bad meter), anena jitu Devaputramāras; four Māras referred to but not listed Dbh.g. 55(81).3, 14; Gv 472.15.

-māraka, ifc. Bhvr., = **Māra**: in sa-māraka, *including Māra*, common in phrases like sadevakasya lokasya samārakasya... SP 21.7; loc. of same, Suv 9.17; etc.

Mārakaraṇḍa, m., n. of a village of the Kosalas: Mv i.317.5; 319.3 (mss. °kaṇḍa), 8 (mss. corrupt but indicate -karaṇḍa); site of the former **Veruḍiṅga**, q.v., or Vebhaḍiṅga; n. sg. °ḍo 317.5 and 319.8.

mārakāyika, adj. (= Pali id.), *belonging to the entourage of Māra*, regularly with deva(-putra) or devatā, also as subst. without noun (Māro vā Mārakāyiko vā Mv ii.263.7): SP 421.1; 474.7; LV 46.22; 300.4; Mv i.220.1 = ii.22.2; ii.163.14; Av i.215.7; Bbh 116.20.

māraṇāntika (= Pali °ṇantika, Milp. 48.11), *relating to* (the part of) *death*, contrasted with aupapattyaṃśika, Śikṣ 226.7 ff. (cited from Śāl 87.10 ff.); = **maraṇāṃśika**, q.v., and see s.v. **-aṃśika.**

Māradhvaja, n. of a group of 18,000 former Buddhas: Mv i.58.5; i.61.14.

Mārapramardaka, n. of a son of **Māra** (favorable to the Bodhisattva): LV 316.22.

Mārabalapramardin, n. of a Bodhisattva: ŚsP 7.4.

Māramaṇḍalanirghoṣasvara, n. of a Bodhisattva: Gv 4.11.

māri, f. (Skt. mārī, and Lex. māri; AMg. both), *plague, pestilence*: mārir utsṛṣṭā Divy 578.23.

Mārinī, (**1**) n. of Māra's consort: LV 301.18; (**2**) n. of a goddess (the same?): Sādh 502.9.

Mārīca, n. of a serpent king: Mmk 18.24.

Mārīci, n. of a yakṣa: Māy 83.

Mārīcī, (**1**) n. of a **rakṣā**, q.v.: Dharmas 5; surely to be identified with the personification of a charm Śiks 142.5, 9; and prob. Sādh 215.8 etc.; cf. (**Mahā**)**māyūrī**, which sometimes seems to replace this; (**2**) n. of an ogress: Māy 243.12.

māruta, a high number: Gv 106.12; cf. **māluta**, in same list.

mārga, m. (Skt. id.; special uses, the first and third as in Pali magga), *way*; (**1**) aṣṭāṅga-m° (= Pali aṭṭhaṅga-magga), the (*noble*, ārya) *8-fold path*: Mvy 996 etc.; the 8 steps (as in Pali) listed e. g. Mvy 997–1004, samyag-dṛṣṭi, -saṃkalpa, -vāc, -karmānta, -ājīva, -vyāyāma, -smṛti, -samādhi; (**2**) daśāryagotra-mārgaṃ pratilabhate Laṅk 222.4, acc. to Suzuki *the ten paths of discipline which belong to the noble family* (*of the Tathāgatas*); what does this mean? the ten kuśala-karmapatha? Tib. renders literally, ḥphags paḥi rigs kyi lam; (**3**) four kinds of śramaṇa (as in Pali, Sn 83–89, where this is made clear, and the magga-jina, -desaka or -desin, -jīvin, and -dūsin are defined), Mvy 5127–30, mārga-jina, *conqueror of the way* (of religion), -deśika, *teacher of the way*, -jīvin, *living in the way*, -dūṣin, *defiling the way* (by hypocrisy and wickedness).

mārgaka, adj. or subst. (cf. M. maggaa), *seeking*; *one who seeks*: sūtrāntamārgakā(ḥ) SP 476.1 (prose).

mārgaṇatā (AMg. maggaṇayā), = next: kuśalamūlānāṃ °ṇatāyai Śikṣ 214.7.

mārgaṇā (Skt. Lex. id., Skt. °ṇa, nt.; Pali magganā), *act of searching, seeking*: °ṇā kāritā (mss. mārgeṇā karitā; kar° may be kept) Mv ii.112.14 (prose).

mārgika, adj. (mārga plus -ika), *of, consisting of*, or *marked by a road*: °kam (sc. nimittam, *mark*, as boundary) MSV iv.88.8.

Mārgo(d)dyotayitar, n. of a former Buddha: Mv i.141.3.

Mārjanī, n. of a rākṣasī: Māy 243.29.

mārjara, m. (cf. Pkt. maṃjara; Skt. mārjāra), *cat*: Mvy 4790 (so also Mironov, with v.l. mārjāra).

mārjāla (m.; = Skt. Lex. id.; Skt. mārjāra), *cat*: °lādayaḥ Kv 19.21.

mārdava, adj. (= Pali maddava; in Skt. only as nt. abstract n., the adj. is mṛdu), *mild, gentle*: associated with mṛdu, as Pali maddava with mudu(ka), in SP 324.3 and 325.9 (vss) mṛdu mārdavāś ca (what difference is there in mg. between them?); also with (Skt.) ārjava, Mvy 2364 (follows ārjava); ārjavu °vaś ca SP 287.3 (vs); in LV 38.4 (vs) read with v.l. sadārjavā mārdavāś ca; °vāḥ Mv i.133.9 (prose); SP 66.9; °vā (f.) Gv 404.15 (prose).

mārṣa, only voc. sg. or pl. (hyper-Skt. for Pali mārisa = Skt. māriṣa; the short form seems unquotable in Skt. lit., tho cited Lex.; in BHS mārṣa is usual, māriṣa little used except in Mv, e. g. i.185.20; 229.12, 17), *friend(s)*! *good sir(s)*!: commonly pl., SP 88.2; 104.2 (prose); 171.11; 175.3 (vs, mārṣa, pl., m.c.); 389.5 (prose); LV 18.12; 23.4; 383.9; Mv i.41.1; iii.86.2 (mārṣa, prob. pl., but somewhat obscure); Mvy 6391 mārṣāḥ = Tib. grogs po dag, *friends*! *comrades*!; Gv 490.26; Kv 36.16 mārṣā(ḥ), prose, prob. pl. referring to plurality just spoken of, tho followed by na tvayā . . . (to one individual of the group); quasi-nom., with 3 pers. vb. like bhavantaḥ, Mmk 35.27 śṛṇvantu mārṣāḥ; sg., Divy 57.16; 59.4; 194.8; Jm 21.16; 36.18; 38.8.

māla, (**1** = Skt. mālā, *garland*, as prior member of cpd., so also in Skt., see BR: samantajvālā-māla-paryeṣitām (Tārām) Mmk 65.14;) (**2**) = **māḍa**, *hall, pavilion*, in **maṇḍala-māḍa**, °**māla**, q.v. Perhaps this same word is to be recognized in the Bhvr. cpd. candana-māla, *having halls of sandalwood*, ep. of prāsāda, *palace*, in Divy 43.1, 7; 49.27 ff., and of a vihāra in Karmav 64.1. But Lévi in his note ad loc. identifies (**3**) -māla here with **mālā**, q.v., and supports his theory with the cpd. **mālā-vihāra**, q.v.; he may be right (in that case, *having tops* or *crowning pavilions of sandalwood*); the matter seems to me doubtful.

Mālaka, n. of a hunter in the Kiṃnarī Jātaka (story of **Manoharā**); cf. **Halaka**: Mv ii.102.1; 104.8; 105.18; 114.8, 10.

Mālaṭa, n. of a people, acc. to Gv 527.8; but in Gv 525.16 the text has for the same people Malada, which (as well as Mālada) is recorded in Skt. (Kirfel 74).

mālā, (**1**) (cf. AMg. id., *'upper deck or storey on a ship'*, Ratnach.; see mālikā in Acharya, Dict. Hind. Arch. s.v., and cf. **mālāvihāra**, **-māla** 3), *upper part, top, crown*, of a building; in navachadanā āveśana-mālā (so mss. each time; Senart em. °śālā) Mv i.328.6, 9, 10, 12, 14, 20; 329.1, *the newly-thatched crown* (top) *of a* (potter's) *workshop*. The AMg. mg. could be derived from a mg. *pavilion* (on top), so *cabin* (on the deck of a ship); (**2**) n. of a goddess or yoginī (*Garland* personified): Sādh 324.6 (replacing **Mālyā** of 157.12 etc.).

Mālādharin (so all mss.; Senart em. °dharī, metr. better), n. of a Buddha: Mv i.124.2 °rī, n. sg.

mālādhāra, also °**rin**, q.v., m. (regularly pl.), n. of a class of godlings, in Mv i.30.7 yakṣas, associated with **karoṭapāṇi** and **sadāmatta**, qq.v.: Mv i.30.7 °rā(ḥ); Mvy 3151 °rah (but Mironov °rāḥ); Divy 218.8; Mmk 19.13.

mālādhārin, m. pl., = prec.: Mmk 43.18 (see s.v. **karoṭapāṇi**). See also **Mālādharin**.

Mālādhārī, n. of a rākṣasī: SP 400.6 (no v.l.; so WT; Burnouf °dharī).

mālā-vihāra, m., acc. to Tib. (on Śikṣ) phreṅ baḥi khaṅ, *garland-building*: Mv ii.367.3 (vs, = Śikṣ 300.8) °raṃ kṛtvāna (Śikṣ kṛtvā ca) lokanāthasya dhātuṣu, constructed at a place where relics of Buddha are kept. But Lévi, Karmav 63 n. 2, argues, perhaps rightly, that mālā here means not *garland* but *pavilion* (on top of a building); see **mālā**; he finds the same word in the Bhvr. candana-māla, see **-māla**.

Māli, n. of a nāga king: Māy 247.15 (n. sg. Mālir).

Mālikā, n. of a queen, wife of Prasenajit: Av ii.9.6.

Mālinī, (**1**) n. of a pious princess: Mv i.303.7; 305.4, 12; 306.19 etc.; (**2**) n. of a female arhat: Karmav 100.3, 8.

mālu(-latā; Skt. Lex. mālu, f.; = **mālutā** (2), **māluvā**; Pali māluvā; AMg. māluyā), a kind of creeper, which strangles trees (śāla trees are especially mentioned in Pali) on which it grows: jara śoṣayate naranārigaṇaṃ yatha mālu-latā ghanaśālavanaṃ LV 174.19 (vs).

māluta, a high number (twice in same list with °**tā**, see next; °tā seems better to correspond in position to **māluda**, q.v.): Gv 106.4, 13 (the list seems confused at this point); cf. also **māruta**.

mālutā, (**1**) a high number (cf. prec.): Gv 106.5 (seems to correspond to **māluda**); (**2**) (= **mālu**, q v., with Pali and AMg. correspondents), n. of a creeper, symbol of cause of unhappiness (because it chokes trees on which it grows): (kāmāḥ . . .) mālutā-latevāsukhadā(ḥ) LV 212.17 (prose; v.l. mārutā°, but Tib. ḥkhri śiṅ ma lu ta); mālutā-latā-jālāvabaddheṣu (mss. mārutā°, ed. em.) MadhK 441.5 (prose).

māluda, nt. (var. maluda, but Mironov mā°), a high number: Mvy 7876 (= Tib. thal yas), cited from Gv 133.15; seems to correspond in position to **mālutā** Gv 106.5.

māludu, m. or f., a high number: Mvy 7901 = Tib. ma gzhal; cf. **mātula**; cited from Gv 133.23.

māluvā (= Pali id.; BHS also **mālu,** q.v., and **mālutā** 2), a kind of creeper: sālaṃ vā māluvā yathā Ud xi.10 (= Pali Dhp. 162).

mālya, nt. (in this sense Skt. Lex. and once in late Skt., Schmidt, Nachträge; so also, allegedly, Pali malya, mālya, and mālā), *flower*: Mv i.249.12 (prose) imāni . . . sthalajajalajāni mālyāni . . . (list follows, atimuktaka-campaka- etc.); ii.449.2.

Mālyacitra, n. of a mountain: Māy 254.5.

Mālyadhara, n. of a yakṣa: Māy 18.

Mālyā, n. of a goddess or yoginī (*Garland* personified): Sādh 157.12; 312.3; in 324.6 **Mālā,** q.v.

(**māṣa-rāśi-varṇa,** adj., *having the color of a heap of beans*, i. e. black and gray spotted: Mv ii.432.16, 19, etc., often in description of **Kuśa** (2); regularly preceded by kāla, *black*. So the mss. invariably; they are proved right (against Senart's em. maṣi-rāśi°) by Mbh. Cr. ed. 3.268.34 māṣarāśi-sadṛśair . . . kṣaṇadācaraiḥ; the adj. fits rākṣasas as well as Kuśa.)

māṣṭa and **māṣṭaka,** nt., also in mss. maṣṭa(ka), and with ṭh for ṭ, seems to mean something like *construction, product, contrivance, ingenious device*; usually in comp. with prec. yantra-(yanta-, janta-, jantra-): Mv ii.475.7 ff., many times; in 476.3 māṣṭakāni alone, but v.l. jantra-m°; seems to refer esp. to toys: (antaḥpurasya arthāye) nānāprakārāṇi janta-māṣṭa-(mss. maṣṭa-, °ṭha-)-daṇḍakāni kriyanti, krīḍāpanakāni ca vividhāni ca janta-māṣṭakāni kriyanti, vījanakāni pi jantamāṣṭāni kriyanti 475.7–8; āsandikā pi jantamāṣṭa-pādakā 9, etc.

[**māsopavāsaka,** °**ika,** see **śvāsopa**°.]

Māskarin = **Maskarin**; Av i.231.4 ('probably a clerical error', Speyer).

Māhiṣmatī (= Pali Māhissatī), n. of a city, capital of the Avantis, as in DN ii.235.20; originally so in Mv iii.208.18, where mss. are corrupt; Senart correctly em. to Māhiṣmatī, but leaves a blank for the people-name; mss. ca vartināṃ; read c' Avantīnāṃ with DN. In Sn 1011 Māhissatī is mentioned along with Ujjenī, which confirms its association with Avanti.

? **mijī,** *drop, small bit*: ekā odanamijy avatiṣṭhate Divy 346.1. Prob. corrupt, but I think of no good em. (those suggested in ed. note are clearly worthless).

miñj-(ayati, ppp. -**ita,** etc.), see s.vv. **unmiñja,** °**jita, nimiñjita,** and (for etym. discussion) **saṃmiñjayati** (and congeners). Simplex has not been noted.

miṇḍha (= AMg. id.; Skt. Lex. meṇḍha, Pali meṇḍa), *ram, sheep*: LV 156.18 read miṇḍhalakṣaṇe with ms. A for miśṛ-la°; see s.v. **kaiṭabha.** (Tib. lug, *sheep*.) This form, or something like it, may have been intended by the corrupt **masniya,** q.v. See also next.

miṇḍhaka, m., (**1**) (cf. prec.; extensions in -ka in Pali and Pkt.) *ram*: Divy 450.14; 456.3 (so mss. both times, ed. em. me°); (**2**) n. of a rich householder, = **Meṇḍhaka,** q.v.: Karmav 68.8 (and sometimes Divy mss.).

mita-vārṣika, m. sg. or pl., *'short rains'* (consisting of a night and a day): Mvy 9285; Bhīk 22a.2, 3, where definition is given; see s.v. **sāmayika.** See also **mṛta-v**°.

mitra, (**1**) *friend* (in Skt. nt.), sometimes with m. gender (also in Pali; not by inheritance from Vedic, but a MIndic change of gender, caused by the mg.; in Class. Skt. extremely rare and perhaps only in word-plays): kalyāṇamitrāṃś ca niṣevamāṇāḥ pāpāṃś ca mitrān parivarjayantāḥ SP 98.1 (vs); purāṇamitraḥ 210.10 (prose); mitraṃ ca tasya (read tasyo, WT), with nt. epithets, 212.10 (vs), but Kashgar rec. mitraś and m. epithets; pūrvamitro 213.3 (vs, no v.l.); (**2**) n. of a merchant, father of **Maitrakanya(ka)**: Divy 586.16; 589.12; 593.16; Av i.195.3 ff.

Mitrakālikā, n. of a piśācī: Māy 239.23.

mithyatva = (Skt.) mithyātva, see °**tva-niyata** and s.v. **rāśi.**

-**mithyācārika,** adj.-subst. (to Skt. mithyācāra plus -ika), *sinful*; in kāma-m°, *sexually sinful*: Divy 301.23 (follows **adattādāyika**; followed by **mṛṣāvādika**).

mithyājīva, m. (= Pali micchājīva), *wrong way of getting a living*; for a monk, there are five such: Bbh 168.23, listed 21–22 as kuhanā etc., also listed Mvy 2493–2497, see s.v. **kuhana** (or °**nā**); the others are **lapana** (°**nā**), **naiṣpeṣikatā** (°**tva**), **naimittikatā** (°**tva**), and lābhena lābha-**niścikīrṣā** (°**ṣutā**), or °**niṣpādanā.**

mithyātva-(also written **mithyatva**-)-**niyata,** adj. (= Pali micchatta-niyata), *fixed in falsehood*, ep. of one of the three **rāśi** of creatures; q.v. for references.

mithyā-darśana, nt., = next: Mv i.107.15, as one of the three akuśala **karmapatha** of the mind.

mithyā-dṛṣṭi, f. (cf. prec. and next; = Pali micchādiṭṭhi), *false view, heresy*; fundamentally = **dṛṣṭi** alone: in Dharmas 68 and Mvy 1957 more specifically, one of the five dṛṣṭi, paraphrased AbhidhK. LaV-P. v.15, 18 by nāsti- or apavāda-d°, *negation* ('because tho all heresies are false, this is the worst of them'); also one of the three akuśala **karmapatha** (q.v.) of the mind, Mvy 1698; LV 31.17; Mv ii.99.11; Śikṣ 75.1; Bbh 224.1 (with **abhidhyā** and **vyāpāda**); other, misc. occurrences, Mvy 7027; LV 22.3; Mv i.145.13; ii.99.5; 132.9; 283.18; Jm 155.7; 192.13; Mmk 73.15.

mithyādṛṣṭika, adj. and subst. (= Pali micchādiṭṭhika, to prec.), (*a*) *heretical* (*person*), *heretic*: Mv ii.132.9; 283.18; Divy 293.25; in lists of persons guilty of the akuśala **karmapatha,** Divy 301.24; Gv 353.1.

mithyā-praṇidhāna (nt.; cf. Pali micchāpaṇihita, adj. with citta), *a wrong, improper, earnest wish* (**praṇidhāna,** q.v.): Divy 14.19 °na-vaśāt; MSV ii.14.8, 13.

mithyāpratipanna, adj. (= Pali micchāpaṭi°), *devoted to false* or *wrong ways of life*: Mv i.314.4.

mithyā-māna, m. (not recorded in Pali), *false* (*wrong*) *arrogance*: (na) māno nādhimāno na mithyāmānaḥ SP 481.5 (prose).

middha, nt. (= Pali id.; orig. unhistorically abstracted from **styāna-middha,** q.v.), *drowsiness, sleepiness*; sometimes simply *sleep*, with neutral or at least unobjectionable connotation, as in middham avakrāntaḥ, *went to sleep*, MSV i.281.1; Divy 102.5, 21; 579.20; ma (= mā, m.c.) ca bhavatha middhavihatāḥ pataṃga iva rakṣathā netraiḥ LV 202.2 (vs), *and don't be overcome with drowsiness* . . .; Mvy 1982 middham = Tib. gñid, *sleep* (follows styānam 1981); middhāvastha-locanāparisphuṭo Divy 555.22; perhaps in this sense LV 179.6; but also as something definitely reprehensible, Dharmas 69 (in list of *upakleśa*; styāna occurs earlier, but separately, in same list); saṃgaṇikā-saṃsarga-middha-nivaraṇa- Laṅk 49.7; middha-**guruka** (see this) AsP 245.9, 13; middha-sadābhibhūta RP 28.4 (vs); others, Śikṣ 128.1; 197.6; Bbh 223.13; SP 13.1.

middhin (= Pali id.; to **middha**), *characterized by drowsiness* or *sloth*: Ud xxix.13 middhī ca yo bhavati . . . = Pali Dhp. 325 middhī yadā hoti . . .

mirava, v.l. °**pha** (so Mironov with v.l. °va), m., a high number: Mvy 7913, cited from Gv, which reads **mirahuḥ** 133.26, **bimbahu**(sya, gen.) 106.16; Tib. on Mvy lhun yas = **meruṭu,** q.v.

mirahu, see prec.

Milaspharaṇa, nt., n. of a place (not found elsewhere); called 'tip of India' and located in the south; Cape Comorin?: ihaiva dakṣiṇāpathe °ṇaṃ nāma Jambūdvīpaśīrṣaṃ (text here Jāmbū°) Gv 83.20; °naṃ Jambūdvīpaśīrṣaṃ 84.16.

milāyati (= Pali id., Skt. mlā°), *wilts, withers, becomes faint*: Mv iii.131.4 (prose); haritacchinnamilāyitaṃ Mv ii.232.3 (hypermetric! final half anuṣṭubh line); ppp. milāna Mv ii.393.9; a-milāna (-gandhamālya) ii.102.2 (prose).

millati, milleti (= AMg. and other Pkt. millai;

= **mellati**, q.v.), *abandons, lets go, releases, gives up, leaves, rejects*: millehi (sc. mṛgīm; *let her go!*) Mv i.363.14; (mā . . . etām striyaṃ . . .) millehi (mss.; Senart em. mel°) iii.291.17, *don't abandon (forsake)*. . .

[**miśṛ**(-lakṣaṇa), corruption for **miṇḍha**, q.v.]

miśraka, nt., (**1**) a kind of literary composition, acc. to Tib. spel ma, *a mixture of prose and verse* (cf. Skt. miśra, -ka): Mvy 1456; the surrounding terms denote kinds of commentaries, paddhati and ṭīkā; (**2**) (= Pali missaka, nt.), n. of a pleasure-grove of the gods, presumably = next: °ke, loc. sg., LV 45.5 (vs).

Miśrakāvana, nt. (cf. Skt. °vaṇa, Pāṇ. 8.4.4, and Pali Missakavana, e. g. Vin. comm. i.164.29; in BHS only °kā-vana has been noted; all the following prose except the first; cf. also **Miśraka** 2 and **Miśrāvana**), n. of a pleasure-grove of the gods (of the Trāyastriṃśa, Mv): LV 44.7 (vs); 82.12; Mv i.32.5; ii.451.20; Mvy 4195; Divy 194.3, 10; 195.9; KP 47.1; Gv 194.14.

Miśrakeśī, n. of a devakumārikā in the western quarter: Mv iii.308.8 = LV 390.5.

Miśrāvana, m.c. for **Miśrakāvana**, q.v.: °vane KP 47.6 (vs), replacing °kāvana of 47.1 (prose).

Miśrika, pl., n. of a class of gods, = Pali Missaka (DN ii.260.24, same passage as ours): Mahāsamāj., Waldschmidt, Kl. Skt. Texte 4, 187.6.

mīgava, nt., a high number: Mvy 7714 = Tib. zar zer (= **mṛgava**, q.v.); there is a v.l. mīvagam (prob. influenced by the preceding item avagam), which Mironov presents without v.l.

mīṭa, mīḍa (m.), = next, *dung*: mīṭa-sthāne yathā krimiḥ Śikṣ 81.4; (varāha) iva mīḍa-kuṇape (cf. BR 5.1302 s.v. kuṇapa) KP 101.5; satkāra-mīḍe patanaṃ KP 131.8 (vs; in 3 above, satkāra-uccāra-patanaṃ).

mīḍha, m. (= Pali mīḷha; cf. also prec.), *dung*: Mvy 6966; mahato (mss. mahānto) mīḍha-parvatasya upariṃ Mv ii.137.11; mīḍhaṃgirī LV 197.3, *mountains of dung*; varjeti kāmāṃ yatha mīḍha-kumbhaṃ Mv ii.377.21 (vs), *like a pot of dung*; this is a favorite comparison, esp. with mīḍha-ghaṭa, LV 173.20; 174.3; 213.5; RP 19.9 (vs; text °ghatām, read °ghaṭāṃ, acc. pl.); mīḍha-viṣayā(ḥ) LV 127.18; mīḍhāvaliptaḥ Śikṣ 173.8.

mīmāṃsana (nt., = Pali vīmaṃsana), *investigation* (= Skt. °sā): LV 430.16 (prose).

mīvaga, var. for **mīgava**, q.v.

mukuṇḍa, m. (= **makunda, mukunda**), a kind of drum: tuṇapaṇavamṛdaṅgāṃ vīṇaveṇūmukuṇḍāṃ (all mss. ṇḍ) LV 80.5 (vs); Tib. seems to render by rṅa, see s.v. **mukunda**, qualified by same epithet.

mukunda, m. (= **mak°, mukuṇḍa**), a kind of drum: °daḥ Mvy 5020 = Tib. rṅa (*drum*) mu kun da, or rṅa zlum (*round*); prob. read this word for the corrupt mukkanda of Samādh p. 34 line 9.

Mukulitā, n. of a 'gandharva maid': Kv 4.18.

mukuṣṭa, m. (Skt. makuṣṭha, Lex. makuṣṭa, mukuṣṭha; not in Pali or Pkt.), a kind of bean: Mvy 5651 = Tib. mon sran nag gu, *black bean*.

mukta, adj.-ppp. (in Skt. used of fruit fallen from its stem), *loose, fallen* (from its stalk), of a flower: muktakusuma SP 103.4 (Burnouf and Kern *pearls*, as if muktā); the oldest Chinese transl. (Dharmarakṣa, dated 286 A.D.) renders *loose flowers*; mukta-puṣpa Karmav 31.22; 52.13; 100.11 (Lévi *une simple fleur*, also wrong).

Muktaka, (**1**) n. of a śreṣṭhin (called **Vimuktaka** in the list, Gv 549.3): Gv 76.20; 77.23; 79.8, etc.; (**2**) n. of an author: Sādh 94.19 etc. See also **muktikā**.

Muktakusumapratimaṇḍitaprabha, n. of a former Buddha: Sukh 5.15.

Muktachattra, n. of a former Buddha: Sukh 6.13.

Muktachattrapravātasadṛśa, n. of a former Buddha: Sukh 6.2.

muktaprabha, m. or nt., a kind of gem (*that emitted splendor*; Senart em. muktā°): °bhehi maṇiratnehi samalaṃkṛtaṃ Mv ii.310.18; (read) °bhā maṇiratanāṃ grahetvā 317.15 (vs).

[**muktahastā**, read °**hastatā**, *liberality*: Bbh 303.13.]

Muktā, *Pearl*, n. of a daughter of **Puṣya** (3) of Śrāvastī: Av ii.36.12 ff.

muktāphalaka, nt., a kind of flower: Mvy 6194.

Muktāsāra, n. of a goldsmith: Gv 452.7, 15.

muktikā, (**1**) adj., f. of **muktaka** (which is used at least once in Skt. in this sense, BR s.v.), *isolated, unaccompanied*: with **jñapti**, Bhīk 15b.3, or **jñāpti**, Mvy 8659, qq.v., *isolated motion*, unaccompanied by (one or three) supplementary questions (contrasts in Mvy with jñāpti-dvitīyam and °caturtham, explained s.v. **jñapti**); = Tib. gsol ba gcig pu, *isolated question (demand, proposal)*. Seems not recorded in Pali; (**2**) *pearl* (so Skt. Lex., cf. Skt. muktā, mauktika): Mvy 5952; -maṇi-°kasya (in nt. sg. dvandva) SP 88.11 (vs). Cf. **lohita-m°**.

(**mukha**, nt., seems to me to show no uses essentially different from Skt.; a few which have caused or might cause questions to arise are here listed: (**1**) ifc., (in a given) *direction*, cf. BR s.v. 3: bāhyamukhaṃ kṣiptāni Mv ii.458.1, *thrown outside*; bāhyato-mukhaṃ kṣipati iii.13.4; see also **paścānmukha**; sthānāsanaṃ śayanacaṅkramaṇaṃ na kariṣya (mss. °ṣye, unmetr.) 'haṃ kapilavastumukhaṃ LV 223.5 (vs), *in* (lit. *in the direction of*) *K.*: (**2**) *entrance, ingress* (BR s.v. 5 and 8) = *introduction*, in **dharmamukha, dharmālokamukha**, qq.v.; also samādhi-mukha SP 312.2, where Kern suggests em. °sukha, but Tib. sgo, *entrance*; in Laṅk samādhi-mukha 12.1 and 13.13 is, to be sure, said to be rendered by Tib. bde ba, *happiness*, i. e. sukha, and this cpd. is found in the text 222.2–3, while in 72.19 Tib. and Chin. are stated to omit mukha after samādhi; in LV 181.20 trimokṣasukha- is app. a misprint for °mukha (so Foucaux; no v.l. cited in Lefm. but Calc. mukha); in LV 352.16 (vs) Lefm. dhyānā-mukhaṃ, but v.l. with Calc. °sukhaṃ, so Foucaux (the construction is obscure; no verb in text; perh. the word is governed by the foll. abhimukhaṃ, *in the direction of* . . .); upadeśa-mukhaṃ Mv i.193.8, *introduction to* (religious) *instruction* (said of the long section on the 10 bhūmi which follows); prajñāpāramitāmukha Gv 125.1; 149.3 ff., here a long list of such °mukhāni, all named, beginning śāntigarbhaṃ nāma °khaṃ; another list of such names 448.23 ff., forty-two items, as stated 450.19, which adds that they are however innumerable.)

-mukhaka, f. °**ikā** (Skt. mukha plus -ka, Bhvr.), *having . . . mouth*, in eka-m°: ekamukhike dve sthālyau kartum Divy 496.19 (and f.). See also **tan-mukhikayā**.

mukha-dundubhikā (cf. AMg. dundubhiyā, Skt. dundubhi), some musical instrument: MSV iii.17.1.

mukha-puṣpaka, nt., Mvy 6049; LV 201.19 (vs), and **mukha-phullaka**, nt., Mvy 6048; Mv ii.470.9, some kind of ornament, in lists of ornaments: Tib. on Mvy for both me tog (*flower*) rgyan (*ornament*), for °puṣpaka also spen tog (*ornament, finery*) rgyan; Tib. on LV only me tog, om. mukha. The force of mukha is uncertain: *face-flower* (some ornament for the face or head?), or *prime, first-class flower*? In Mv they are made by goldsmiths; evidently therefore of precious metal, which seems suggested by the context in LV also.

mukha-proñchana, nt. (v.l. with Mironov °pocchana; cf. Pali mukha-puñchanacolaka, Vin. i.297.1), *face-(or mouth-)-wiper, handkerchief* (so Tib., gdoṅ phyis): Mvy 8961.

mukha-phullaka, see **mukha-puṣpaka**.

mukhara, adj. (in Skt. *noisy*, esp. *garrulous*, but also of animals and inanimate objects; Lex. as subst. *a crow*, and acc. to MW as adj. *scurrilous*, a mg. which the word is said to have in Pali), perh. *impudent* (in action, by transfer from *scurrilous, impudent* in speech?): in Mv iii.127.15 said of a crow which kept snatching food from a king's servants, eṣo kākaḥ dhṛṣṭo mukharo pragalbho . . . ; the regular Skt. mg. seems impossible here, since the complaint was not against the crow's noise but his impudent behavior. Cf. **amukhara.**

mukha-vāta (m.; = AMg. muha-vāya, id.), *breath of the mouth*: read in Mv ii.315.6 saced bodhisattvo mukhavātam (so v.l.; Senart °vāṭam, *l'ovale de sa face*) osireyā.

mukhullocakaṃ, adv. (Pali mukhullokaka, adj.; defined DN comm. i.168.28 sāmino tuṭṭha-pahaṭṭhaṃ mukhaṃ ullokayamāno vicaratīti mukhullokako), *cheerfully*: Mv i.27.5 (tiryagyoniṣu sattvāṃ. . .) tṛṇāni mukhullocakaṃ paribhujantāṃ.

Mukhendra, n. of a yakṣa: Sādh 560.15 etc.

muṅga (m.; = Pali mugga, Skt. mudga; § 3.4; modern vernaculars have the nasalized form, Hindi mūṃg, Nep. muṅ, etc.), *bean*: LV 171.17 (vs, no v.l.); 264.16 (prose), ed. mudga-, most mss. muga- or mugaṃ(-yūṣaṃ; intending muṃga-?), best ms. muṃga-.

Muci, n. of an ancient king: Mvy 3562. Seems to correspond to Pali Mucala, DPPN.

Mucila, n. of an asura: Mahāsamāj., Waldschmidt, Kl. Skt. Texte 4, 179, last line; cf. **Mucilinda** 5 (who is associated with **Vemacitrin,** as Mucila is with **Vemacitra**; see Waldschmidt's note, which makes the definite identification).

mucilinda (in mgs. 1–3 also **mahā-muc°**; in mgs. 1–4 = Pali mucalinda, which Geiger 34 assumes was 'more original' than muci°, perh. because of Pali mucala; but I see no convincing ground for preferring either to the other), (**1**) n. of a tree (m.) and its flower (nt.): Mv ii.60.18 (vs; read mucilinda-ketakā, see Pali Jāt v.405.24); °dā (n. pl.) ca ketakā ii.254.7; °da- (in comp.) iii.80.11; LV 11.1; °dam, nt. (the flower), Mvy 6167; (**2**) n. of a mountain (= Pali Muca° 6 in DPPN): SP 244.10–11; Samādh 19.19; Sukh 63.3; Kv 91.12; (**3**) n. of a nāga king (= Pali Muca° 2 in DPPN) who protected the Buddha in a celebrated incident told LV 379.15 ff.; Mv iii.300.16 ff.; referred to as a nāga, or nāga-king, Suv 162.9; Mmk 241.17; 452.17; Megh 288.6; Māy 222.5; 246.31; (**4**) n. of an ancient king (cakravartin), prob. = Pali Muca° 1 or 3 in DPPN: Mvy 3563; cf. also Pali Mucala, DPPN; (**5**) n. of an asura prince: Mv iii.138.2; 254.9; cf. **Mucila.**

Mucilindā, n. of a nāga maid: Kv 3.23.

muñcati, *emits words, speech*; in Skt. and Pali used with object vācaṃ or the like, but here absolutely, no object noun expressed (also **pramuñcati, vimuñcati,** in the same context): kalyāṇikāṃ vimuñceta naiva muñceta pāpikām Ud viii.8 (vācaṃ is clearly understood with the f. adj., but does not occur in the passage); similarly viii.9 muñcamāno.

muñcana, (nt., = Pali id.), *the sending forth, emission*: -prabhāsa-muñcana-vidhijñena Gv 431.12; (in Bhvr. cpd.? or adj., *emitting*?) dvārā . . . krośasvarā-muñcanāḥ LV 193.7 (vs), *sending forth sound as far as a kos.*

Muñjakeśa, n. of a yakṣa: Māy 70.

Muñjana, n. of a mountain: Māy 254.7.

muñja-balbaja-jāta, adj. (= Pali °babbaja-bhūta), *become* (confused) *like muñja and balbaja* (reeds or grasses after they have been woven into ropes): Mvy 5392. This is the mg. given the Pali word by DN comm. ii.496.1 ff., and is clearly right. All the parallel terms, on which see **guṇāvaguṇṭhita-bhūta,** refer to *confusion.*

muṭa, mūṭa, mūḍha, moṭa, moṭaka, and see s.v. **moṭikā** (m.? cf. Vedic mūta, mūtaka; late Skt. mūṭaka, pw; Pkt. mūḍa, mūḍha, *'a large measure of grain'*; and s.v. **mūtoḍī,** which may be related), some sort of *basket, bag,* or *large container*; chiefly in an identical cliché, a list of containers and means of transporting goods: śakaṭair bhārair muṭaiḥ (etc.) piṭakaiḥ (this word is once or twice transposed before m°; in Kv it is spelled piṭhakair, once pī°), so, with muṭaiḥ, Kv 28.17; 71.8; one ms. at Divy 524.16 (and ed. by em. 501.27); mūṭaiḥ Av i.199.14; Kv 52.23; and ed. em. Divy 524.16; mūḍhaiḥ, all mss. Divy 332.5 (kept in ed.); 501.27 (ed. em. muṭaiḥ), and 3 of 4 mss. 524.16 (ed. em. mūṭaiḥ); moṭaiḥ Divy 5.8; kuśa-moṭakaṃ baddhvā MSV i.100.6.

Muṇḍa, (**1**) n. of a king of Magadha, grandson of Ajātaśatru and ancestor of Aśoka: Divy 369.10; prob. the same as Pali id. (DPPN), tho his position in the genealogy is not quite the same; (**2**) adj.(?), in muṇḍa-śayanāsana-vārika Mvy 9074, see s.v. **vārika**; follows śayanāsana-v° 9073; Tib. renders muṇḍa by ḥbogs pa (?perh. *removable*?) or phogs; Chin. seems to intend *curtains* (mosquito-nets for the bed?).

muṇḍaka, adj., (**1**) (= Pali id.; cf. **muṇḍā, muṇḍika**) *shaveling,* pejorative ep. of Buddhist monks (with **śramaṇaka,** q.v. for citations; -ka contemptuous or imprecatory): Divy 13.15; 39.26; 574.2; (**2**) f. °ikā, ep. of **gaṇḍī,** *gong*: Av i.272.1; Feer *funereal, for the dead* (suggested by context; Feer cites Tib. as mjug med pa = *tail-less*; could this mean *without a cord*?).

muṇḍanā (= Skt. and Pali muṇḍana, nt.), *clipping of the hair*: Mvy 9332 = Tib. skra breg(s).

[**muṇḍapūla,** v.l. for **maṇḍa°,** q.v.]

muṇḍā (Skt. Lex. id.), *shaveling woman,* contemptuous ep. of a Buddhist nun (cf. **muṇḍaka, °ika**): Kalpanāmaṇḍitikā, Lüders, Kl. Skt. Texte 2, 44.

muṇḍāpayati (caus. to Skt. muṇḍayati, Pali muṇḍeti; = AMg. muṇḍāvei), *causes to be shaved*: °payitvā Divy 261.15.

muṇḍi, f. (perh. muṇḍī Deśīn 6.133 = Skt. nīraṅgī), *veil*(?): puṣpalokamayīṃ (? see **puṣpaloka**) muṇḍiṃ lakṣaṇopetāṃ kṛtvā, paṭasyāgrataḥ kṛtapuraścaraṇaḥ . . . Mmk 691.25.

muṇḍika (= **muṇḍaka,** q.v.), (**1**) adj., *shaveling,* contemptuous ep. of Buddhist monks: °kehi śramaṇehi Mv i.320.4 (prose, no v.l.); (**2**) subst., *a shaven head*: -muṇḍika-kuṇḍika-kapāla-khaṭvāṅga-dhāraṇaiḥ LV 249.9, said of ascetic practices, *characterized by wearing . . . a shaven head* (i. e. by shaving the head) . . . ; one ms. (A, the best) muṇḍaka.

Mutkhalin, reading of Calc., supported by Tib., for **Sūtkhalin,** q.v.

Muditapuṣpā, n. of a 'gandharva maid': Kv 4.19.

muditā, (**1**) (= Pali id.; acc. to Senart, Mv i.629 and iii.523, also PTSD s.v., an altered form of mudutā, = Skt. mṛdutā, which has a quite diff. mg. in Pali), *joy* (esp. of the spirit); so the unanimous tradition, both of Pali comms., and of northern texts and transl.; if orig. derived from Skt. mṛdu-tā, all practical traces of this origin have certainly been lost; the word is always associated with root mud, as is proved by a number of clear descriptions, cited below; esp. as one (usually the 3d) of the four **apramāṇa** or **brahmavihāra,** qq.v. (with **maitrī** or **maitrā,** karuṇā, and **upekṣā**), LV 8.4; 112.6; 183.3; 275.18; 297.12; 376.1, 2; 426.4; Mv i.357.19; ii.362.5 (here upekṣā omitted); iii.421.14, 22; Mvy 1506; Dbh 34.21; Bbh 209.4; 236.7; 241.16; Sādh 57.13 ff.; AbhidhK. LaV-P. viii.196 (*joie*), citing the vyākhyā, muditā cārateḥ pratipakṣaḥ saumanasyarūpatvāt; with this cf. Mvy 1599, aratiniḥsaraṇaṃ muditā; similar description in Sādh l. c. (57.18 hṛṣṭacittatā); esp. elaborate description Śikṣ 183.4, katamā muditā? . . . prītiḥ prasādaḥ prāmodyaṃ cittasyānavalīnatā . . . cittasya prāmodyaṃ kāyasyaudbilyaṃ buddheḥ saṃpraharṣaṇaṃ manasa utplavaḥ, etc.; Tib. regularly dgaḥ ba, *joy*; (**2**) rarely, and only in vss (prob. m.c.), = **pramuditā** as n. of the first bodhisattva-bhūmi: Laṅk 286.15; Sūtrāl. xx–xxi.32.

mudgara, nt. (in Skt. m.), *hammer*: in SP 271.9 (vs) read with Kashgar rec. daṇḍāni mudgarāṇī ca (supported confusedly by 2 Nep. mss. and the fragment publ. by LaVallée-Poussin JRAS 1911.1076).

mudgalikā, or (Index) **mudgarikā**, var. for **mūrkhalikā**, q.v.

mudra, m. and nt. for Skt. mudrā, f., *position of the hands*: very often in text of Mmk, tho the f. is still commoner; e. g. mudraiḥ 423.7; mudreṇa 422.8; 424.9; mahāmudraḥ 472.8, mudro 9, dharmamudram (n. sg. nt.) 10; with f. in same vicinity quite often, e. g. padmamudreṇa 424.18, padmamudrayā 20; mahāmudraṃ (n. sg. nt.) 475.5, mahāmudrām 9, sarvamudreṣu 13; kṣemaṃgamo mudraḥ 476.9, etc. Once mudrāt in LV 176.15; see § 9.71. See also s.v. **mudrāhastaka.**

mudraka, nt. (Pkt. muddaga, °ya, m. acc. to Sheth; = Skt. mudrikā, mudrā), *signet*, in anguli-°keṇa MSV ii.22.8, etad aṅguli-°kaṃ 9–10, and below; cf. aṅgulimudrā ii.20.16; 21.1.

mudrā (in these mgs. not in Skt.), (**1**) (= Pali muddā, acc. to PTSD *art of calculation*; assoc. with gaṇanā; acc. to DN comm. i.95.19 hattha-muddā-gaṇanā, cf. Tib. below, while gaṇanā is acchiddaka-(q.v. CPD)-gaṇanā), some method of calculation, acc. to Tib. on LV (cf. DN comm. above) lag rtsis, *hand-calculation*, that is, presumably, figuring by using the fingers in some conventional way (Das renders this Tib. *lines or marks in the hands, palmistry*, and so Burnouf on Divy 26.12 *chiromancie*, Introd. 237, but the regular context seems to disprove this); always in a list of arts learned by a young man, and associated with mathematical terms: between saṃkhyā and gaṇanā, LV 4.21; after saṃkhyā and gaṇanā, before **dhāraṇā,** Mv ii.423.15; -gaṇanām (v.l. °nā-)dhāraṇamudrāṃ Mv iii.184.7; after saṃkhyā and gaṇanā, before uddhāra, Divy 3.18; 26.12; 58.17; 100.1; 441.28; 485.5 (here uddhāra is omitted); after gaṇana-nyasana-saṃkhyā- Bbh 7.5; 103.3; 210.13; (**2**) *wages* (perh. cf. Skt. Lex. id., *coin*, and AMg. muddā, *coin?*): divasa-mudrā SP 105.11; 109.3–4, *daily wage* (so Tib., gla ba); (**3**) a high number: Mvy 8030. See also **dharma-mudrā.**

mudrā-bala, nt., a high number: Mvy 7972, cited from LV 148.8. Cf. (**mahā-**)**mudrā,** (**mahā-**)**bala,** as high numbers.

mudrā-lipi, a kind of script: °pī (v.l. °pi), n. sg., Mv i.135.6.

mudrāhastaka (mss. mudra°), some sort of ornament for the bodhi-tree: °takehi (in a list of ornaments) Mv ii.311.11. I see no way of connecting this with Pali muddā-hattha.

? **mudhāma**, see **mūdhāma.**

mudhāya, seems to be a quasi-instr. sg. fem. to Skt. and Pali (adv.) mudhā (= Pkt. muhāi, Sheth s.v. muhā), *in vain*: na mudhāya bhavān samudgato LV 364.22 (vs). Alternatively, ya could perhaps be taken as rel. pron. (= yaḥ), but this seems forced.

munigāthā, pl. (Aśokan id., Bhabra 5), n. of a Buddhist text, doubtless = Pali Munisutta, Sn vss 207–221: Divy 20.24; 35.1.

Munipravara, n. of a former Buddha: Mv iii.230.15.

Munihata, m., n. of King Bandhuma(nt)'s pleasure-park: Mv ii.273.9.

Munīndrā, n. of a kiṃnara maid: Kv 6.21.

murava, m. or nt. (= AMg. id.; cf. Skt., Pali muraja), a kind of drum (in cpds. with dundubhi or paṇava): Mmk 56.19; Kalpanāmaṇḍitikā, Lüders, Kl. Skt. Texte 2, 44.

murucikā, prob. *a small belt* or *sash*: Mvy 8997 = Tib. śor bu phreḥu (acc. to Jä. and Das, śur bu phreḥu has the above mg.).

muluta, a high number (°tasya, gen.): Gv 106.13 (follows **māluta**).

muṣaṇa (nt.; = M. musaṇa; to Epic Skt. and BHS muṣati, § 28.37, for Skt. muṣṇāti plus -ana), *stealing, theft*: sarvakuśalamūla-°ṇa-tayā KP 101.2.

muṣitaka, adj. (ppp. °ta plus -ka, in Divy prob. pejorative), *miserably robbed*: (paśyati) °kaṃ Divy 175.23; in MSV ii.158.6 ff. specifying -ka, *those that have been robbed.*

muṣita-smṛti, f. (cf. Pali muṭṭhassati, adj.; pace PTSD, this may very well be from Skt. muṣṭa = muṣita), also °**ti-tā**, *heedlessness, forgetfulness, inattentiveness*: °tiḥ Dharmas 69, in list of upakleśa, between pramāda and vikṣepa; °tā Mvy 1976, between the same two terms, = Tib. brjed ṅas pa, *forgetfulness*; nāsti °titā Mv i.160.14, Dharmas 79, and Mvy 138 (here v.l. °tiḥ), as one of the 18 **āveṇika** (q.v.) buddhadharma; neg. Bhvr. a-°ti, adj., and -tva, nt., amuṣitasmṛtitvād amuṣitasmṛtir ity ucyate LV 434.15–16.

muṣṭi, f. (used in Skt. of the *handle* or *grasping-point* of a weapon), (**1**) = **muṣṭi-bandha,** q.v., *grip*, a manner of *grasping* (the bow): (bhagavatā, or maye, mayā, spoken by the Buddha) ciraprаṇaṣṭā Śāk(i)ya-muṣṭi jñātā Mv ii.77.2, 3; 82.2, *the long-lost (bow-)grip of the Śākyas was known*; referring to the young Bodhisattva's exploit of wielding the bow of his grandfather Siṃhahanu, which no one else could wield; (**2**) see s.v. **ācārya-muṣṭi**; (**3**) since **rikta-muṣṭi,** q.v., is used in lists of things empty and delusive, the word muṣṭi alone is, acc. to text Śikṣ 261.8, used in the same sense: evaṃ cakṣuś cendriyaṃ ca rikte (app. dual) muṣṭisadṛśam (but read rikta-muṣṭi-sadṛśam?) alīkam asadbhūtaṃ etc.; note that after rikte the epithets are (at least mostly; but see **moṣadharma**) singular, which makes the dual rikte suspicious, depite the double subject; and the standard use of **riktamuṣṭi,** occurring actually in the preceding line of Śikṣ, makes the em. seem called for.

muṣṭika, also **mauṣṭika, moṭṭ(h)ika** (cf. Pali muṭṭhika, app. only *boxer, prize-fighter*, assoc. with malla; from Skt. muṣṭi; AMg. muṭṭhiya, id.; Skt. muṣṭika, n. of a roaming despised caste who guard corpses and eat dog-flesh, acc. to Rām. comm. = ḍomba; Skt. Lex. also *goldsmith*), (**1**) perhaps = Skt. muṣṭika, n. of a gypsy-like low caste: SP 276.5 (prose) na caṇḍālān na mauṣṭikān na saukarikān ... (considerably later in the list, na mallān nānyāni pareṣāṃ ratikrīḍāsthānāni tāni) nopasaṃkrāmati; SP 279.2 (vs), cited Śikṣ 48.2, (kuryāt tehi na saṃstavam) caṇḍālamuṣṭikaiḥ śauṇḍais (so also Śikṣ, but WT cite K' cāpi for śau°, and so Tib., gdol ba daṅ ni zol ba for entire pāda) tīrthikaiś ...; but both these may be otherwise interpreted; Tib. for both zol ba, *trickster*; the Pali mg. *boxer* is also not out of the question (note malla in 276.6, with reference to *entertainers*; does Tib. zol ba mean here *juggler, sleight-of-hand performer* ? see 2); (**2**) (cf. Tib. on SP under 1) mauṣṭikaḥ Mvy 3808, followed by vidūṣakaḥ, *buffoon*; acc. to Tib. zol pa, *trickster* (possibly in the sense of *juggler*); (**3**) possibly (= Pali muṭṭhika) *boxer, fist-fighter*: Mvy 7072 muṣṭikāḥ, v.l. mauṣṭikāḥ (Mironov, and pw 7.368, musuntikā, clearly corrupt) = Tib. khu tshur, *fist* (Skt. muṣṭi); Chin. also *fist*; Jap. *fist*, also *trickster, low-class person* (prob. based on Tib. on 3808); (**4**) (as in Skt. Lex.) *goldsmith*: (after **suvarṇa-dhovakā,** q.v.) mauṣṭikā Mv iii.113.19, or (same passage, list of artisans and craftsmen) moṭṭikā (so mss., Senart moṭṭhikā) iii.443.6; goldsmiths are proverbially tricky, hence perhaps this is derived from mg. 2. The word mauṣṭika occurs, without preserved context, in Kalpanāmaṇḍitikā, see Lüders' discussion, Kl. Skt. Texte 2, 44.

muṣṭi-bandha, -saṃbandha, m., a particular technique of *grasping* (the bow) *with the fist* (see s.v. **muṣṭi**); several times muṣṭi-b° is mentioned in a list of arts to be mastered by a prince: Mvy 4978; LV 156.12; Divy 100.12 and 442.7, along with **pada-bandha** or **pāda°,** and (in all but Divy 100.12) also **śikhā-bandha**; in both Divy passages these words are directly followed by **dūra-vedha,** which occurs not far away in Mvy (4991). That a manner of wielding the bow is meant is suggested by the context in all, and proved by Mv ii.82.17 muṣṭisambandho ca, yatra nāma vārāṇasyāṃ sthitena kāṇḍaṃ kṣiptaṃ. Tib. on Mvy and LV ḥdzin staṅs, *grasping posture*.

Musalaka, m. (or n.), n. of a mountain: Divy 49.2 f.

musāra, musāgalva (often in Mv, nowhere else), **musāragalva** (the regular BHS form), **musāragalvārka, musālagalva**(?), sometimes miswritten **susāra(galva, °galvārka)** in mss. and even in edd. (Divy 67.18, Mmk 120.22), m. (rarely nt.), a kind of precious stone. Recorded once in Skt., musāragalva, said to mean a kind of *coral* (pw); otherwise forms with mu- only noted in BHS; but cf. Skt. masāra and masāragalvarka (rarely written °vārka), said to mean *sapphire* or *emerald*; Pali masāragalla, usually said to mean *cat's eye*, but Burnouf found a Pali Lex. source identifying it with pavāla, *coral* (Lotus 319 f.) and hence adopted this mg. for BHS, followed by Senart Mv i.415, and doubtfully by Kern SBE 21.147 n. 2; AMg. masāra and °ra-galla, said to mean *sapphire*; in recent years most interpreters of BHS have left the exact mg. undetermined; it usually occurs in rigmarole lists of various gems (once, at least, pravāla, *coral*, occurs earlier in the same list, Mv ii.472.1–2); Tib. on Mvy 5956 spug, a gem which Jä. leaves unidentified, while Das gives as Skt. equivalent (kakkatana and) karketana, said to mean *cat's-eye* (cf. Pali above); clearly masc. gender when unambiguous, as a rule, e. g. Mvy 5956; Divy 51.25, etc., but musāraṃ, n. sg., Mmk 120.22; besides this last, stem musāra Mv iii.323.13 in one ms. (v.l. musāgalva; Senart musāragalva); vaiḍūrya-musāra-pratyuptāṃ Laṅk 3.5; musālagalva (rare) Mvy 5956 (but Mironov musāra°, no v.l.); Mv iii.304.12 (so, or musā-g°, mss., Senart em. musāra°); musāgalva in text, no v.l., Mv i.194.9, 10; 196.17; 249.6; iii.227.7; 228.2, 14; 229.13; 323.16; 324.6; read musā-g°, with most mss. or requirements of meter, i.49.11; 63.2; ii.186.13; text musāra° but mss. divided evenly with v.l. musā°, i.49.14; ii.177.17; 180.14; 191.5; 310.8; 316.8; 472.2; iii.226.11; 232.10; musāragalvārka (cf. Skt. above) Divy 67.18 (ed. susā°); 138.3; the regular form in all texts is, however, musāragalva, Divy 51.25; 115.3; 229.7; 297.25; 502.7; Av i.205.3; Gv 52.15; 89.25; 148.13; Dbh 46.19; Bbh 5.10; 234.1; SP 151.2; 153.4; 239.7; 256.12; LV 383.2, etc.

musāragalvaka, adj. (to prec.), *made of* **musāragalva**: Mv ii.301.4 (prose; mss. °la-ga° or musā-g°).

musuṇḍi or **°ḍī** (AMg. musuṇḍhi, Sheth, musaṇḍhi, Ratnach.; Skt. bhuśuṇḍi, °ḍī, bhuṣ°, also in Kauṭ. Arth. Sham.[1] 54.6 musṛṇṭhi or °ṭhi, see Meyer's transl. 73 note 2), a kind of weapon: khaḍga-cakra-°ḍyādīnāṃ Mmk 721.5.

(**muhūrta** = Skt.; names for each of the 30 m° of the day [of 24 hours] are given Divy 643.5 ff. [cf. BR s.v. muhūrta, and Weber ZDMG 15.133, 139 f., wrongly cited in BR]; the names are included in this Dict. only when they are words not otherwise recorded.)

mūṭa, mūḍha, see **muṭa**.

? **mūḍhāma**, see **mūdhāma**.

mūtoḍī (prob. related to **muṭa**, etc., q.v.; = Pali mutoḷī, °ḷi, also with ū for u and ṭ for t), *a* (farmer's) *basket, bag*, or *large container*: karṣakasya mūtoḍī pūrṇā nānādhānyānāṃ Śikṣ 210.8 (cited from ŚsP 1431.2 which has corruptly mṛtotriḥ); mūtoḍīvan nānāśuciparipūrṇaḥ (= nānā-aśuci°, doubtless *manure*?) Śikṣ 231.1.

? **mūdhāma** (m.; so text by em.; read rather mudhāma or mūḍhāma), acc. to context apparently *idle* or *deluded religious longings*, see s.v. 2 **āma**: ŚsP 485.(14–)15 (na ca bodhisattvo mahāsattvo) mūdhāmaṃ patati, text. But this is an em.; all mss. mūrdhānaṃ, and so in same locution 17, where ed. inconsistently reads with mss. Note to 15 suggests reading mudhāmaṃ and interprets by vyartha-dharmābhilāṣaḥ. The ŚsP itself authorizes this interpretation of **āma**. It gives no hint as to how it read or interpreted the prior member; it might be Skt. and Pali mudhā, as ed. suggests, or mūḍha, *deluded*. It seems clear from the context that the mss. reading is corrupt and that the true text had a cpd. ending -āmaṃ (acc. sg.).

[**mūyate** Gv 496.23, 25, read **mṛyate** with 2d ed.]

mūrkhalikā (so Mironov, no v.l.), or (v.l.) **mudgalikā** (or, in Index, °rikā), acc. to Tib. *an arrow-head shaped like a bird's heart*: Mvy 6101 = Tib. mdeḥu byiḥu sñiṅ ma ḥdra.

mūrchita, ppp. (= Pali mucchita; in this sense not Skt.), *infatuated* (by desire or worldly things), after **grathita** or **granthita**, qq.v.: Divy 534.19; Mvy 2195.

mūrchitaka = Skt. °ta (no special force in -ka discernible), *unconscious*: sa dṛṣṭvā °kas tiṣṭhati Divy 508.20; sa °kaḥ pṛthivyāṃ nipatitaḥ 515.2.

-mūrdhaka, ifc. Bhvr., = Skt. mūrdha(n) (cf. AMg. muddhaya), *head*: adho-mūrdhakāḥ LV 193.19 (vs); see also **ava-m°**.

Mūrdhaṭaka, n. of a deity: Mvy 4276; Mmk 28.25 (text Mūrdhūṭaka); 29.2; perh. 617.23 (text Mūrdhnaṭaka).

[**Mūrdhata**, Mvy 3557, see **Mūrdhāta**.]

mūrdhan, mūrdhāna (cf. Skt. mūrdhan), *head* (condition), *summit*, the second of the 'stages of participation in penetration', see **nirvedha-bhāgīya**: mūrdhānam, n. sg., Mvy 1213 (so Mironov; Kyoto ed. v.l. °naḥ) = Tib. rtse mo, *summit(s)*; same is meant by mūrdhāvasthā Sūtrāl. xiv.26 comm.; mūrdhāgatāni Divy 79.28, but in next line, 80.1, and 166.15; 240.20; 271.12; 469.12, mūrdhānaḥ (sometimes mss. mūrdhnānaḥ), n. pl., as also AbhidhK. LaV-P. vi.164, where the mg. of the term is explained.

mūrdha-pidhāna, see **mūrdhāpi°**.

Mūrdhāta = **Māndhāta**, q.v.: Divy 210.19 ff., where (as in MSV below) the identity is explicitly stated; read °ātaḥ for Mūrdhataḥ, n. sg., in Mvy 3557, where Mironov Mūrdhagataḥ, but most of his mss. Mūrdhātaḥ; with etym. explanation (mūrdhni jātaḥ) MSV i.67.10–11; 93.7–8.

mūrdhāpidhāna, nt., Mv ii.470.7, or mūrdha-pi° (v.l. mūrdhni pi°) 472.3 (both prose), *'head-covering'*, an ornament for the head, made of gold or jewels.

Mūrdhnaṭaka, see **Mūrdhaṭaka**.

-mūrdhni or **°na**, ifc. = Skt. mūrdhan, *head*: -uṣṇīṣaśīrṣānavalokita-mūrdhnir (v.l. °na; both edd. em. °dha) ity ucyate LV 432.13.

mūla, (**1**) m. (in Skt. only nt.), *root*: mūlān bhakṣayato dhārayati (edible roots, for a horse) Divy 513.14, 23, *holds roots for* (the horse) *as he eats*; (**2**) nt. (Skt. id.) *root* = *foundation*; peculiar use in Divy 491.6, śakṣyasi tvaṃ . . . bhikṣūṇāṃ upānahān mūlāc ca puñchitum (mss.), *can you clean the monks' sandals thoroughly* (from the ground up)? and 11, sa bhikṣūṇāṃ upānahān mūlaṃ kramataś ca ponchate, *he cleaned the monks' sandals thoroughly* (lit., *going to the very foundation*?); (**3**) nt. (Skt. id.), *root, beginning*; in names of penances for monks, **mūla-parivāsa** (see **parivāsa**), *probation starting over from the beginning* because the original offense was repeated while parivāsa was in force (see **antar-āpatti**): Mvy 8650; MSV ii.207.15; iii.35.6 ff. (explained); **mūla-pārivāsika**, *one undergoing this penance*, MSV iii.37.15 etc.; **mūlāpakarṣa-parivāsa**, *probation starting a second time from the beginning* because the offense was repeated while mūla-parivāsa was in force (see **praty-antarāpatti**), Mvy 8651; MSV ii.207.15; this is abbreviated to **mūlāpakarṣa**, m., MSV iii.38.11 etc., 41.13; in Pali, instead of mūlaparivāsa and mūlāpakarṣa-(parivāsa), there seems to be a single category, samodhāna-parivāsa, often qualified by mūlāya paṭikassantā (Vin. ii.7.20) or the like (N. Dutt, MSV iii Introd. iv f. makes Pali mūlāya paṭikassanā and samodhāna-parivāsa separate penances corresp. to the above two in BHS, but this seems hardly supported by Pali evidence; possibly Vin. ii.62.6–12 may imply it, but it is not very clear). There is also mention of **mūla-mānāpya** and **mūlāpakarṣa-mān°**, which are analogous to **mūla-parivāsa** and **mūlāpakarṣa-p°**, except that acc. to MSV iii.77.2 and 5 the repeated faults are concealed (altho the fault leading to the original mānāpya was, of course, unconcealed, 76.20–21; otherwise parivāsa, not mānāpya, would have been the penalty); in a similar case iii.81.16 ff. the original and repeated faults are all unconcealed, leading to mūla-mānāpya 82.9 and mūlāpakarṣa-m° 83.2; (**4**) nt. (= Skt. Lex. and Pkt. id., Sheth; Skt. and Pali mūlaka), *radish* (Tib. la phug); Mvy 5767 bāla-mūlam, *young radish*, and 5768 mahā-m°, *old radish*; (**5**) m., n. of a former Buddha: Mv iii.236.10. See **mūlaṃ, mūlāto, mūle.**

(**mūlaṃ**, as postpos., in Skt. rather rare, BR s.v. mūla 3, *to* (*the neighborhood of*), with gen.: (kumārasya) mūlaṃ allīno Mv ii.32.1; gantuṃ amukasya sārthavāhasya mūlaṃ ii.90.3–4; rākṣasīnāṃ mūlaṃ preṣito iii.296.17–18. Cf. **mūle, mūlāto.**)

mūlaka, m. (Skt. nt., only Gr. m.), an edible root, perh. *radish*: °kā bhakṣitavyāḥ Divy 511.21.

mūlagrantha, m., *original text* (of words attributed to the Buddha): Mvy 7673.

Mūlaphalguna (evidently same as Pali Moliyaphagguna; like him a friend of the nuns), n. of a Buddhist monk: MSV ii.143.17 ff.

Mūlamānuṣa, n. of a nāga king: Māy 247.25.

mūlasarvāstivāda, pl., n. of a school: Mvy 9078.

mūlāto, abl. of **mūla** used as postpos. with gen., *from*; *away from*; *as a result of*, *because of* (the phrase = the abl. of the dependent noun); cf. **mūlaṃ, mūle**: (teṣāṃ sarva-)kāśikośalakā manuṣyā mūlāto prītā Mv i.350.7, ...*were pleased because of them*; samanantaraprakrānto ca kāśirājā Śyāmakaśirisya mūlāto Mv ii.215.7, ...*from Ś.*; mama mūlāto gatvā 246.17 and 18, *going away from me*; (sa teṣāṃ śakuntakānāṃ, gen. for acc.) parirakṣati sākuntikānāṃ (v.l. śā°) api mūlāto (etc., several similar phrases) 251.5 ff., *he protected those birds from fowlers*, etc.; Kuśasya mūlāto palāyitvā 485.5, *fleeing from K.*, and similarly 20; vayasyakānāṃ mūlāto nirdhāvitvā iii.34.17; nalinīye mūlāto ... putrā jātā, aparāṇāṃ pi devīnāṃ ... putraśataṃ jātaṃ 152.8–9, *from N. were born ... sons, and from the other queens ... 100 sons*; mukto tāye piśācinīye mūlāto Mv iii.163.18, *escaped from that ogress* (Senart punctuates wrongly); icchāmi tava mūlāto putraṃ 403.1, *I desire a son thru you* (*by your grace*; addressing a tree supposed to have supernatural power).

mūlāpakarṣa, see **mūla** (3).

mūlāpatti, f. (see **āpatti**), *radical sin*: Śikṣ 10.14 °śravaṇāt; 168.2; five, of a ruler, listed Śikṣ 59.11 ff. (no relation to the pañcāpatti-nikāyāḥ of Sūtrāl xi.4 comm., on which see Levi's note in Transl.); other mūlāpatti mentioned 60.9; and in 60.10 ff. detailed statement of eight mūlāpatti of beginners in the Mahāyāna.

mūlika, adj., (**1**) (Skt. Lex. id.) *living on roots* (as an ascetic practice): śatabhiṣāyāṃ jāto °ko bhavati Divy 647.1; mūliko brāhmaṇaḥ, sa mūlānām arthe 'nyatamaṃ parvatam abhirūḍhaḥ Av ii.125.6; aneka-mūlika, ep. of ascetic practices, (ātāpanaparitāpanaiḥ ...) aneka-mūlikair LV 248.17, *consisting of living on many roots*; (**2**) ifc. Bhvr., *having ... as cause*, = Skt. -mūlaka, and perh. corruption for this: kiṃmūlikā (n. pl. m.) utpadyanti Mv iii.337.11, *having what source do they arise?*, but the normal Skt. -mūlaka is used in parallels below, 13, 16 ff., and kiṃmūlaka 339.10; prob. read °laka.

mūlikā (cf. Skt. mūla, *capital*), *stock*, *supply*, in kāṣṭha-°kā, *stock*, *supply of wood*: Divy 500.9–10, 15.

mūle (cf. **mūlaṃ, mūlāto**; Pali uses mūle sometimes in ways corresponding to some of these mgs., see Childers, dvāramūle ṭhito, *at the door*), as postpos. with gen., or rarely at end of a cpd., may be used as periphrasis for loc. of governed noun in any sense: (**1**) *under* (here doubtless with persistence of lit. mg. of mūla), in pāda-mūle, *under the foot*: so kāṇḍo (mss. kaṇṭho) tasya rājño pādamūle sthitvā Mv ii.82.15, *the arrow, stopping under that king's foot*; mama pādamūle ... nipatito 18; (**2**) *near* (of location): in comp., dvāramūle AsP 502.4; bhaṇḍa-mūle Mv ii.172.1, 2, *near the arbor*, see **bhaṇḍa**; with gen., tena ... brāhmaṇānāṃ mūle sthitakena Mv i.310.15, *staying near* (*with*) *the brahmans*; varaṃ tava mūle mṛtaṃ na Viśākhamūle jīvitaṃ (in the 2d form, a cpd.) 365.20, *better to die with you* (in your company) *than to live with V.*; ṛṣisya mūle ii.96.19; 210.4, *in the presence of the ṛṣi*; (hastino, mss. °nā) mūle 454.5; (rathānāṃ) mūle (mss.) āsati 456.19; mālākārasya mūle 463.20; (**3**) *towards*, *to* (of motion): mama mūla (Senart em. mūle!) āgatā Mv i.364.22, *she came to me*; devīya mūle na kiṃcid aparityaktaṃ ii.66.8, *there was nothing that was not handed over to the queen*; gato Brahmāyusya mūle 78.16, *went to Brahmāyu(s)*; kumbhakāramahattarasya mūle allīno 464.1, and similarly 19, 470.6; praviṣṭo devīya mūle iii.25.11; (**4**) *towards*, *in reference to* (of respect, disrespect, love, regard): brāhmaṇānāṃ mūle abahumānam Mv i.309.15, *disrespect for the brahmans*; devīya mūla (mss., read mūli? meter requires short syllable; Senart mūle) i.204.16 = māyāya mūli ii.8.11 (vs), (obeisance) *towards ...*; mama mūle premā (mss. °mnā; n. sg.) ii.65.15, *love for me*; rājaputrasya mūle premnaṃ iii.39.2; rākṣasīnāṃ mūle sāpekṣā 76.15–16, *having regard for the ogresses*; parasparasya mūle ... premnaṃ Mv iii.391.13.

mūṣati (= Pkt. mūsai, Sheth, = muṣati, § 28.36, Skt. muṣṇāti; ū blended with mūs, mūṣikā?), *steals*: fut. mūṣiṣyate Divy 281.8; inf. mūṣitu-kāmā 276.24; both prose.

Mūṣikāhairaṇyika, 'Mouse-goldsmith,' n. given to a merchant because of his history: Divy 501.3 ff.; a previous incarnation of Panthaka, 504.11.

mūṣī (= Pali mūsī), *rat* or *mouse*; in mūṣī-utkira, m., *rat-(mouse-)up-throwing*, i. e. earth dug up by rats or mice: Mv i.326.20 (prose) ye te bhavanti mūṣī-utkirā (v.l. °kilā; Senart em. mūṣotkirā) vā vāripraropitā (mss. °ropyā, °ropā) vā vārucchinnā (?em.) vā mṛttikā.

mṛgaka, m. (= Skt. mṛga; -ka may be m.c.), *deer* or *animal*, in comparison with monks: mṛgakā va (so Senart em. for °kāṃ ca) asaṅgacāriṇo praviviktā viharanti bhikṣavaḥ Mv iii.421.6 (vs). See also **mṛgikā.**

mṛgacakra, nt., *the zodiac*: °kraṃ Divy 630.20 (in a list of things studied by brahmans; foll. by nakṣatragaṇo); mṛgacakrāṅkavidyā- Gv 451.3; mṛgacakra-lipi, a kind of writing (the symbols for the signs of the zodiac?), LV 126.3 (Tib. translates literally).

mṛga-carya, adj., applied to some non-Buddhist ascetics *who behave like deer*: Śikṣ 332.3; cf. **mṛga(-vrata)**, also in cpd. LV 248.21, cited s.v. **kukkura-vratika**, and **mṛgaśṛṅgavratin** (= this).

[**mṛgadāya,**] **mṛga-dāva**, m. (cpd. only recorded in BHS and as miga-dāya in Pali, tho both constituents are Skt.), *deer-park*, almost exclusively used of the park **Ṛṣipatana, °vadana**, etc., at Benares, where Buddha is said to have first preached; the form °dāya is never recorded in mss., tho Senart adopts it by em. in Mv i.366.8, where the etym. offered seems naturally to call for it (but cf. LV 19.4 below): mṛgāṇāṃ dāyo dinno mṛgadāve ṛṣipattane (mss.; Senart em. mṛgadāyo ti ṛṣipattano); the foll. all refer to the Benares park, usually in loc., Ṛṣipatane (°vadane, etc.) mṛgadāve: SP 69.12; LV 18.20; 19.4 (abhayadattāś ca) tasmin mṛgāḥ prativasanti iti ... mṛgadāva iti saṃjñodapādi, cf. Mv i.366.8, above; LV 264.22; 402.3; 404.17; 407.16; 412.9; 413.1; Mv i.161.4, 323.14, 17; 330.4; 331.3; ii.138.2; iii.323.3; 330.17; Divy 464.16;

Av i.42.9; Mvy 4129; once, in Divy 182.25, of a quite different *deerpark* called **Bhīṣaṇikāvana,** in **Śuśumāragiri.**

Mṛgadeva, n. of a former Buddha: Mv i.138.11.

Mṛgapatiskandha, n. of a Buddha: Mv i.123.7.

Mṛgapatisvara, n. of an ancient king: Mv i.118.2; he worshipped a Buddha and made a vow.

Mṛgarājaghoṣa, n. of a former Buddha: Mv i.136.15.

Mṛgarājinī, n. of a 'gandharva maid': Kv 5.10.

mṛgava, nt., a high number: Mvy 7840 (cited from Gv) = Tib. zar zer (= **mīgava,** q.v.); Gv 105.21; in Gv 133.3 corrupted to **ṛgava,** q.v.; Mv i.13.12 sattvā mṛgavaśo praveśitā(ḥ); so by Senart's plausible em.; mss. begin mṛgav-; cf. **paramantra**(-śaḥ, in line 8 above).

mṛgavyā (prob. blend of Skt. mṛgayā and mṛgavya, nt.; cf. Pali migavā, which could represent this form), *hunting, the chase*: °vyāṃ aṇvati (Senart em. aṇvanti) Mv ii.101.18; mss. (ed. em. °vyaṃ) ib. i.360.6; 361.3, 15.

mṛgavrata = **mṛgacarya, mṛgaśṛṅgavratin**: AbhidhK. (vyā.) LaV-P. iii.86 n. 3.

Mṛgaśiras (= Pali Migasira), n. of a son of an ascetic and a doe, master of the **kapāla-koṭanī** vidyā, converted by Buddha: MSV ii.80.7 ff.

Mṛgaśirā- (stem in comp.; for Skt. °śiras; so once Skt. Lex., acc. to BR f.), n. of a nakṣatra (perh. n. sg. m. in comp.?): °rā-nakṣatraṃ Divy 639.12.

Mṛgaśīrṣa, n. of a nāga king: Kv 2.12; Māy 246.28.

mṛgaśṛṅgavratin, adj. (= **mṛgacarya,** q.v.), *having adopted the style of life of a deer, and wearing a horn like deer,* said of a sort of ascetics: Mvy 3534 (cf. also LV 248.21).

Mṛgāyaṇī, the gotra of the nakṣatra Mṛgaśiras (°rā): Divy 639.13.

Mṛgāra (= Pali Migāra), n. of a rich man, or acc. to MSV the chief minister, of Śrāvastī: Divy 44.13; MSV ii.52.12. Acc. to MSV, as in Pali sources, father-in-law of Visākhā (our **Viśākhā** 2); she was instrumental in instructing him, and he called her his mother, whence she is called **Mṛgāra-mātar** (Migāra°), cf. MSV ii.69.10 ff.; see next (but acc. to some Pali sources she actually had a son, also named Migāra: DPPN).

Mṛgāra-mātar, ep. of **Viśākhā** (2): Mvy 3668 (here alone); for others see Viśākhā (2); MSV ii.70.11 (alone); 72.17 etc.

Mṛgāramātuḥ prāsāda (m.; = Pali Migāramātupāsāda), n. of a monastery built by **Viśākhā** (2): Karmav 161.11; Laṅk 75.11 (here text śṛgāla-m°); MSV ii.70.11 etc.

mṛgikā (to Skt. mṛgī, f. of mṛga, plus -ka; cf. **mṛgaka**), *doe*: °kā iva saṃtrastāḥ Mv ii.425.5; iii.1.8.

Mṛgila, n. of a nāga: Māy 222.5.

Mṛgī, n. of a Śākyan woman, mother of Ānanda, to whom is attributed the stanza attributed in Pali (Jāt. i.60.30–33) to Kisāgotamī: Mv ii.157.9, 16; iii.176.16.

Mṛṇāla, n. of a libertine, former incarnation of Śākyamuni: MSV i.213.13 ff.

mṛta-gṛha, nt., *'house of the dead', tomb*: Mvy 7104 = Tib. mchad pa (also ḥchad pa, mtshon pa).

mṛta-vārṣika, nt. or m., hyper-Skt. or error for **mita°,** q.v.: (°kam) MSV iii.124.3, 5; also v.l. Mvy 9285 (°kaḥ, m.).

mṛttikama, adj. (seems to be shortened for mṛttikamaya; mṛttika- in Skt. m.c. for °kā, BR; loss of syllable -ya MIndic, § 3.118), *made of clay*: Mmk 139.24 (vs) sauvarṇe bhājane raupye tāmre mṛttikame 'pi vā; the meter certainly favors the form; and the mg. is clear.

Mṛtyu-māra (= Pali Maccu-), a form of **Māra,** q.v.

Mṛditakukṣika, n. of a wood at Rājagṛha: Divy 274.15.

mṛduka, f. **°kī** (cf. also next), adj. (= Pali muduka, Skt. mṛdu; adv. °kam recorded BR once from Lāṭy ŚS.), *soft*: °kāna paṭṭāna (gen. pl.) SP 89.5 (vs); -śayane °ke LV 42.15 (vs); paryaṅke . . .°ke Divy 559.14 (vs); *subtle* (? so Régamey; Tib. phra mo, which may have this mg.), °kī saṃjñā Samādh 22.27; (relatively) *slight, ineffective,* of paripāka, *religious maturation,* and abhyāsa, *practice*: Bbh 87.4, 6 f.; adv. °kaṃ: bodhisattvavimokṣaṃ sūkṣmamṛdukaṃ *(easily and lightly)* pratyalabhata Gv 308.12.

Mṛdukā (cf. prec.), n. of an Apsaras: Kv 3.13.

mṛdugandhaka, Divy 628.19, or **°dhika,** Divy 244.23; Mvy 6149, nt., a kind of water-lily; in all follows saugandhika and other names of similar plants.

mṛyati, °te (hyper-Skt. for mriyate), *dies*: °yanti Mv i.193.2; °yate ii.176.8; Gv 498.17, 18 (prose); so read also 496.23, 25, see **mūyate**; also **mṛyyati, °te** (§ 37.27), Mv ii.79.4 ff.

mṛṣa (m. or nt.; otherwise only adv. mṛṣā, and Pali-Pkt. musā), *falsehood, lying*: mṛṣeṇa codayet SP 326.6 (vs), *should accuse of lying*; mṛṣaṃ bhaṇe Mv i.356.7.

mṛṣāvādika, adj.-subst. (to Skt. °vāda plus -ika or °vādin plus -ka), *lying, a liar*: Divy 301.23; follows (kāma-)-**mithyācārika.**

mṛṣṭa(-yava), ppp. (to Dhātup. mṛṣ = secane?), *poured, sprinkled*: mṛṣṭa-yavān MSV ii.142.11; so Tib., yos blugs; context indicates use in fermentation.

Mekhala, n. of a pupil of 1 **Dharma** (4): Laṅk 365.3 f.

Mekhalā, n. of a yakṣiṇī: Mmk 564.26; 566.9.

mekhalī (= Skt., Pali °lā), *belt, girdle*: °lī-baddhakāś ca LV 76.20 (prose); so all mss.; Calc. °lā-.

Megha, (**1**) n. of a previous incarnation of Śākyamuni under **Dīpaṃkara,** who predicted his enlightenment: Mv i.2.1; 232.1 ff. (corresponds to Divy **Sumati** (4), q.v., and to Pali Sumedha, while Pali Megha corresp. to our **Meghadatta,** q.v.); (**2**) n. of another Bodhisattva, a Dravidian (dramiḍa): Gv 2.7; 72.13 ff.; Śikṣ 36.14 (quotation from Gv 76.26); 95.6 (allusion to events of Gv 73.14 ff.).

Meghakūṭābhigarjitasvara, n. of a Bodhisattva: LV 293.20. So best ms.; most mss. °śvara; v.l. also, with Calc., °jiteśvara, but Tib. dbyaṅs confirms °svara.

Meghadatta, n. of an associate of **Megha** (1), q.v.: Mv i.232.1; he corresponds to Pali Megha, whereas BHS Megha = Pali Sumedha; in both BHS and Pali he was a former incarnation of **Dharmaruci,** Mv i.246.12.

Meghadundubhisvararāja, n. of a former Buddha: SP 431.7 ff.

Meghanirghoṣasvara, n. of a Bodhisattva: Gv 4.9.

Meghamālin, n. of a yakṣa: Māy 41.

Megharāja, n. of a Tathāgata: LV 293.19.

Meghavatī, n. of a lokadhātu in the northwest: LV 293.19.

Meghavilambita, n. of a Buddha: Gv 259.7.

Meghaśrī, (**1**) n. of a monk: Gv 2.7; 58.17; 59.8 ff.; (**2**) (°śiri, m.c.), n. of a Buddha: Gv 257.3 (vs); (**3**) n. of a Bodhisattva: Gv 442.5.

Meghasaṃcodana, n. of a nāga-king: Megh 308.10; with epithet navaśīrṣa; app. = **Navaśīrṣaka,** q.v.

Meghasaṃbhava, n. of a nāga: Mvy 3347.

Meghasūtra (our Megh), n. of a work of which extracts are ed. by Bendall, JRAS, N. S. 12 (1880) 288 ff.

Meghasvara, n. of a former Buddha: Mv i.136.15; LV 5.13; Mvy 99.

Meghasvaradīpa (v.l. Meghasvara, so Burnouf; Kern's transl. Meghasvarapradīpa; the Chinese indicates Megheśvara), n. of a Buddha in a northern lokadhātu: SP 184.16.

Meghasvararāja (v.l. Meghasvara, Megheśvara: Chin. indicates Megheśvararāja), n. of another (cf. prec.) Buddha in a northern lokadhātu: SP 185.1; also (no v.l.) n. of a very long series of former Buddhas, SP 380.11.

meghāgaru, *cloud aloe,* a kind of perfume: Gv 153.17 °ru-gandharāja-.

mecaka, nt. (cf. pw s.v. 2c; no other record found), a kind of precious or semi-precious stone: Mvy 5965 = Tib. gzi, acc. to Das *onyx*.

meḍī, (*court-*)*yard* (so Tib., khyams): MSV iv.120.12 etc.; 122.2.

meṇḍa-viṣāṇikā (cf. Pali meṇḍa), *'ram's horn'*, a kind of sandal: MSV iv.206.12.

Meṇḍhaka (= Pali Meṇḍaka), n. of a rich householder: Divy 123.17 ff.; 131.2 f.; MSV i.241.2 ff. Also **Miṇḍhaka**, q.v. (so sometimes mss. of Divy).

metra (semi-MIndic for **maitrā**, with a m.c., or Skt. maitra), *love*: metra-varmita- LV 53.15 (vs).

methaka, m. (= Pali medhaka, °ga; cf. Skt. methana), *quarrel, strife*: śāmyanti methakā (= °kāḥ) Ud xiv.8 (same vs Pali Therag. 275, MN iii.154.13, Vin. i.349.37, tato sammanti medhagā); MSV ii.183.7 °kāḥ (ed. medhakāḥ, read meth°; ms. meṣakaḥ).

medhāvika, adj. (= Skt. °vin), *wise*: Jm 80.6 (prose).

medhī, acc. to PTSD (s.v. medhi, citing no passage from Pali!) = Skt. methi, *pillar*, as part of a stūpa. But the context suggests rather one of several (here three) concentric *galleries* running around a stūpa (as at Borobudur), or the *story-structures* supporting them: Divy 244.9 f. (stūpasya . . . catvāri sopānāny) ārabdhāni kārayitum, yāvad anupūrveṇa prathamā medhī tato 'nupūrveṇa dvitīyā tatas tṛtīyā medhī yāvad anupūrveṇāṇḍam (see **aṇḍa**). This is confirmed by Tib. ḥkhor sa = medhī, Bailey, JRAS 1950.180; read medhyāṃ for yaṣṭyāṃ Divy 47.23.

meraka, m. (Divy) or nt. (Mvy), (= Pali moragu, and prob. both from Skt. mayūrakaḥ), a kind of grass used for coverlets, or a coverlet made of it: Divy 19.22; Mvy 9181; see s.v. **eraka**.

meraṇḍu = **melanduka**, q.v.

Meru, (**1**) n. of a former Buddha: Mv iii.239.9; (**2**) n. of a future Buddha: Mv ii.355.10 (here text Maru, prob. misprint) = iii.279.15 (vs); (**3**) n. of a cakravartin (= Pali Neru; note that Pali has Sineru for the mountain name Sumeru): Mvy 3574.

Merukalpa, n. of a Buddha in a northwestern lokadhātu: SP 184.15; Chin. points to Sumerudhvaja.

Merukūṭa, (**1**) n. of two former Buddhas, in the same list: Sukh 5.12; 6.6; (**2**) n. of a Buddha in an eastern lokadhātu: SP 184.7 (Chin. indicates Sumerukūṭa); (**3**) n. of a Bodhisattva: ŚsP 7.8.

meruṭu (vv.ll. meruhu, merutū; but Mironov °ṭu, no v.l.), m. or f., a high number: Mvy 7786 = Tib. lhun yas = **mirava** (°pha), q.v.

meruta, m. or nt., a high number: Gv 106.12; corresponds to **merudu**, q.v.

meruda (v.l. **meluda**, so Mironov), m. Mvy 7770, or **merudu**, m. or f. Mvy 7899, a high number; = Tib. rdzi phyod; 7899 cited from Gv 133.23, meruduḥ (= Gv 106.12 **meruta**).

Merudhvaja, (**1**) n. of a Buddha: Gv 285.4; (**2**) n. of a Buddha in the east: Sukh 97.1; (**3**) n. of a Bodhisattva: Gv 2.18.

Merupradīpa, n. of a Buddha in the south: Sukh 97.8.

Merupradīparāja, n. of a Tathāgata: Gv 81.5.

Meruprabhā, n. of a lokadhātu: Gv 426.26.

Meruprabhāsa, n. of a Buddha in the east: Sukh 97.2.

Merubalapramardin, n. of a yakṣa: Mvy 3375.

Meruviśuddhavyūhadhvaja, n. of the capital city of King Ratnārcinetraprabha: Gv 381.1.

Meruśikharadhara, n. of a Bodhisattva: Mvy 693 (with ep. kumārabhūta).

Meruśrī, (m.) n. of a former Buddha: Gv 104.17; (f.) n. of a nāga maid: Kv 4.11.

Meruśrīgarbha, n. of a Bodhisattva: Dbh 2.20.

Merususaṃbhava, n. of a kumbhāṇḍa: Mvy 3443.

Merūdgataśrī, n. of a lokadhātu: Gv 444.2.

mela, m. (**1**) a high number: Mvy 7768 = Tib. (ḥ)phrad yas = **melu**, q.v.; (**2**) n. of a nāga king, in cpd. Ela-melau, dual dvandva: Mvy 3291 (so read with v.l., also v.l. in Mironov and Tib., see s.v. **Ela-mela**); Māy 247.33.

melanduka, m. (also **meraṇḍu**; Skt. Lex. melāndhu), *ink-bottle*: Mvy 8966 = Tib. ram phyis (? cf. rams, *indigo*?); Chin. *ink-bottle*; listed among monks' appurtenances; Kv 28.24 (sumeruḥ parvatarājaḥ . . . sa . . . bhūrjarāśir bhavet, mahāsamudro) melanduka-parimaṇḍalaṃ bhavet; 92.7 sumeruḥ parvatarājo bhūrjarāśir (text bhūryya°) bhavet, mahāsamudro (text °dra) meraṇḍumaṇḍalaṃ bhavet.

melā = next: Gv 106.12.

melu, m. or f., a high number (= prec., and **mela** 1): meluḥ, n. sg., Mvy 7897 (= Tib. ḥphrad yas), cited from Gv 133.22.

meluda, see **meruda**.

mellati, melleti (= Pkt., but not AMg., mellai) = **millati**, q.v. (much commoner in BHS, but both recorded only from Mv): brāhmaṇāṃ mellitvā (*abandoning*) śramaṇānām abhiprasannā Mv i.311.13; mellitvā ii.463.17; 464.13 (v.l. °etvā); 465.15; 466.1; 469.19; 470.2; 471.12, 16; 473.1, 4; 474.16; 475.2; 476.17, 20; with gen. (as acc.) object, mama mellitvā anāthāye iii.132.15; mss. mellitvā, Senart em. mellitā (ppp.; better sense) iii.164.10; melletvā ii.463.15; mellehi ii.448.4; 454.16.

Meṣaka, n. of a yakṣa: Samādh p. 43 line 19.

Maitraka = **Maitreya** (1) (only in vss and prob. m.c.): °ku (n. sg.) Gv 488.25; °kasya 489.7.

Maitrakanya, °nyaka (both forms occur in prose; corresp. to Pali Mittavindaka, and to BHS **Maitrāyajña**, q.v.), n. of a merchant's son, later a Bodhisattva: °nya Divy 589.4 (vs); 593.19; 600.3 (both prose); usually °nyaka, Divy 590.4, 28; 592.1; 593.12, 28 (all prose), etc.; Av i.193.1 (title); 197.13 ff.

Maitranātha = **Maitreya** (1) (in vs, prob. m.c.): °tha (n. sg.) Gv 489.8.

Maitra-nāma(n), 'whose name contains maitra', = **Maitreya** (1) (in vs, prob. m.c.): °ma (acc. sg.) Gv 489.4.

Maitrabala, n. of a king: Jm 41.4 (prose; not to be em. to Maitrībala with Speyer).

Maitraśrī, n. of a Bodhisattva: Gv 442.3.

maitrā (rarely **maitryā**, q.v.; = Pali mettā; the Skt. equivalent maitrī is also extensively used, notably instead of this as one of the **apramāṇa**; Skt. also maitra, maitrya), *love, benevolence*; sometimes as one (the first) of the four **apramāṇa** or **brahmavihāra**, qq.v.: maitrāya, oblique case, Mv i.175.3 (vs; same line maitryāya iii.346.15, see maitryā); maitrāya (instr.; v.l. °tryāya) sphuṭā Mv ii.350.15; (cf. maitryā, stem maitrī, sphāritvā Mv i.313.17, and see maitryā;) maitrā-vihārī Mv iii.421.18; Ud xxxii.20 (22); (cf. mahāmaitra-vihārī LV 426.3, prose, with Skt. maitra;) maitrā-pariśuddho Mv ii.362.5; with the other three apramāṇa, maitrāyāṃ (loc.) LV 164.15 (vs); maitrāya (gen.) 183.3 (vs); other cases, maitrā vijitya . . . mārapakṣaṃ LV 343.6 (vs), *by love* (instr.); maitrām anusarati Kalpanāmaṇḍitikā, Lüders, Kl. Skt. Texte 2, 44; acc. to Kern, Preface viii, used in Kashgar rec. of SP for text maitrī; maitrātmaka Divy 319.20, 26, could contain this or Skt. maitra; see also next.

Maitrāyajña, the personage otherwise called **Maitrakanya(ka)** (q.v.): Karmav 50.16 etc.; 60.12; variants Maitra° and Maitre-yajña are cited by Lévi, p. 50 note 10, who conjectures a MIndic original *Metteyañña.

[? **maitrāyana** (for °ṇa?), n. sg. °naḥ, Dbh.g. 41(67).14, if text is right, would seem to be synonym of **maitrā**, *love*: °naḥ śubhaprabhā jagakleśaghāṭī. But it is prob. a corruption; acc. to Susa's note, Tib., Chin., and Mongol versions point to maitrāśayaḥ]

Maitrāyaṇī, (**1**) (= Pali Mantānī), n. of the mother of **Pūrṇa** (2), who is therefore called Pūrṇa Maitrāyaṇīputra (as in Pali Mantānīputta), either as two words, or as a cpd., see s.v.; (**2**) n. of a king's daughter: Gv 123.1, 18 ff.

maitrāyati, °**te** (= Pali mettāyati; denom. from **maitrā**, or from Skt. maitra), *shows love, benevolence*: °yate Bbh 369.15; °yamāṇena (pple. mid.) AsP 395.12; °yatā (pple. act., instr.) Divy 105.17; 123.7.

maitrāvant, adj. (**maitrā** plus -vant), *possessing maitrā*: maitrāvatas tasya muneḥ LV 310.4 (vs; v.l. and Calc. maitrī-).

maitrāsa-tā (for *maitrāṃśa-tā, below; § 3.3), *loving-kindness, benevolence*, is the stem to be assumed Mv iii.373.11 (vs), where read: maitrāsatāṃ (or °taṃ, MIndic for °tāṃ; mss. cited as °naṃ or °na; Senart em. maitrābhāvanāṃ, metr. impossible and otherwise implausible) bhāvaye apramatto, maitreṇa cittena hitānukampī, etc. The stem maitrāsa = Pali mettāsa, which occurs as v.l. for mettaṃso Itiv. 22.4; in the same vs Jāt. iv.71.25 mettaṃso is glossed 72.5 by metta-koṭṭhāso (for *koṭṭhaṃso!) mettacitto; the word is a noun, not an adj. as stated in PTSD, and means the same as BHS maitrāsa-tā (for *maitrāṃśatā); otherwise BHS records only maitra (adj.) as separate word with **aṃśa** (q.v., 2) in the mg. of the cpd. The use of -āsa for -āṃśa (Pali -aṃsa) is confirmed by Pali koṭṭhāsa.

Maitriya, m.c. for **Maitreya** (1), q.v.

maitrī (used as in Skt. = BHS **maitrā**, see s.v. **apramāṇa**; also) (**1**) n. of a kind of magic (vidyā): Divy 636.26; (**2**) n. of a goddess: Mahāsamāj., Waldschmidt, Kl. Skt. Texte 4, 181.11; foll. by **Varuṇikā**, which W. prints as part of the same name with this.

Maitrīya, in Kv 2.2 the last of a rather short list of Bodhisattvas; we should expect the name of **Maitreya** (1) here, and probably the text has a mere error or misprint for it. More curious however is Divy 326.9–11 eṣa eva devate sa (separate from the next) pṛṣṭhībhūto Maitrīyo yo vyāghryā ātmānaṃ parityajya catvāriṃśatkalpasaṃprasthito Maitreyo bodhisattva ekena śiraḥparityāgenāvapṛṣṭhīkṛtaḥ; here, if the text is correct, Maitrīya would seem to be the name of Maitreya in an earlier birth; but the passage is otherwise puzzling. On the basis of these two passages should we recognize Maitrīya as a real variant (like **Maitraka**, q.v.) for **Maitreya** (1)?

? **Maitrīyaśa(s)**, n. of a future Buddha: °śo, n. sg., Mv iii.330.9, Senart; the only ms. reads Maitreyaśo.

Maitrīvyākaraṇa, nt., n. of a work: Mvy 1403.

Maitreya, (**1**) also **Maitriya** m.c., and **Maitraka**, **Maitra-nātha**, °**nāman**, and perh. **Maitrīya**, qq.v.; = Pali Metteyya), n. of the next Buddha to follow Śākyamuni, predicted by him; has special ep. **Ajita**, q.v.: SP 3.9; 7.4 ff.; 302.11, 16; 307.11; 308.1; 309.1; 310.13; 311.1; 312.13; 315.5; 316.12; 327.2; 329.11; 332.5; 345.1 ff.; 478.11; Mv i.59.2 (etc., see Senart's Index); iii.240.11 ff.; 243.19; 246.16; 247.15; 330.8; LV 2.10 (first of a list of Bodhisattvas); 39.2 ff.; 422.7, 11; 443.7; 444.12; Mvy 646 (= Tib. byams pa, second in a list, after Avalokiteśvara); Divy 60.25 ff. (prediction of his history); 326.10 (in an earlier existence gave his life for a tigress); Av ii.176.3; Suv 117.5 (M°-prabhṛtīnāṃ bodhisattvānāṃ); 157.19; 239.6 (here Maitriyo, m.c.; v.l. Maitrayo); Śikṣ 15.13 etc.; Dharmas 12 (first of 8 Bodhisattvas); Sukh 2.13 (M°-pūrvaṃgamaiś ca saṃbahulair bodhisattvair); Karmav 71.22; Mmk 40.14; 62.16, etc.; Sādh 20.8 etc.; as the first in a long list of future Buddhas Gv 441.23; as the first of a much shorter list, not over ten, Mv ii.354.17 = iii.279.1, most of the names being found at the beginning of the Gv list, which is evidently an enormous expansion of an old traditional list; even the order is nearly the same; Maitreya is succeeded by **Siṃha**, then **Pradyota, Ketu** (these two are interchanged in the Mv order), **Sunetra** (in Mv preceded by **Jyotiṃdhara** or **Jyotīvara**, or the like, which Gv lacks), **Kusuma** and **Kusumaśrī** (in Mv these two are represented by 'two Kusumas'), **Tiṣya** (so Gv, prob. unorig.; T. regularly precedes P. in lists of *past* Buddhas; Mv has instead **Meru** or **Maru**), **Puṣya** (Mv **Puṣpa**); here the Mv list ends. In Mv iii.279.19–20 there follows a reference to the four Buddhas of 'this bhadrakalpa', still put in the future; these two lines seem to be a secondary addition of Mv iii.279, being not found in the parallel ii.355; because of them Senart, iii Introd. XXVI note 1, attributes the whole list to the past, which is scarcely conceivable with a list headed by Maitreya, and is disproved by the Gv parallel; in Gv 456.19 introductory to long chapter on M°, Gv 466.15 ff., special glorification of him; (**2**) n. of a brahmanical gotra (sg. as n. of various persons in Skt.): pl. Divy 635.12.

Maitreyavimokṣa, n. of a work: Śikṣ 9.8; 177.14.

maitryā = **maitrā** (Skt. maitrī, and maitrya, nt.; our stem seems to be a rare blend of more than one of these), *love, benevolence*: maitryāya (instr.) sphāritvā Mv i.314.1 (prose; cf. maitryā sphāritvā 313.17); tasmāt te sadṛśo nāsti maitryāya (obl.; loc., or instr.?) Mv iii.346.15 (vs; same line with maitrāya i.175.3).

maithunābhāṣaṇa, nt., *the* (**saṃghāvaśeṣa** offense of) *speaking* (to a woman) *about sexual intercourse*: Mvy 8371; corresp. to Pali Vin. iii.128.21–23 (duṭṭhullāhi, see s.v. **duṣṭhula**, vācāhi ... methunupasaṃhitāhi ...) and to Prāt 479.11–13, also with maithunopasaṃhitayā (vācā).

Maineya, n. of a people: LV 225.6. Nowhere recorded; Tib. transliterates me ne ya. See **Anuvaineya**.

Mokṣaka, n. of a nāga king: Māy 247.31.

mokṣāyaṇa (nt.; to *mokṣāyati in mg. of Skt. mokṣayati, *saves*, denom. to mokṣa), *saving, rescue*: cakṣūtpāṭana-°ṇe Karmav 102.14–15, *saving from* (*after*? so Lévi) *plucking out of eyes*.

moca(-pāna, nt.; = Pali id.), (juice of) *the plantain* or *banana tree*, acc. to PTSD; Vin. comm. 1102.9–10 = anaṭṭhikehi (see CPD) kadaliphalehi katapānaṃ; acc. to N. Dutt, *gum of the śālmalī tree*: MSV i.ii.18; 262.14.

mocana-paṭṭaka, nt., *'clearing-cloth'*, a kind of *filter* or *strainer*: Mvy 9025 = Tib. brtsal tshags, gsal tshags; Chin. *cloth for straining water*.

mocika, m. (from moca, Deśīn. 6.139, *shoe*; modern vernaculars moci, mocī, see Turner, Nep. Dict. s.v. moci; said to be Iranian loanword), *cobbler, shoemaker*: Mvy 3796 = Tib. ko lpags mkhan, *leather-worker*, or lham mkhan, *shoemaker*.

moṭa, see **muṭa**, and **valo moṭa**.

moṭaka, moṭikā, see **muṭa** and **putra-moṭikā-putra**.

moṭṭika, or (em.) **moṭṭhika**, Mv iii.443.6, see **muṣṭika** 4.

modakakāraka (= Skt. °kāra), *sweetmeat-maker*: Mv iii.113.9; 442.14.

? **modayati**, perh. *augments* or the like (prob. corrupt): (pariśiṣṭaṃ [sc. grits, saktu] ghṛtena) modayati, tatpramāṇā eva bhavanti MSV ii.60.7.

(**modi**, in LV 53.16, vs, text modiprāpta, read modi, m.c. for mode, loc., prāpta, *arrived at joy*.)

momuha, momūha (= Pali momūha; cf. momugha, once in ŚB), *confused, bewildered, deluded*: a-momuha-jātīyaḥ Bbh 9.20; na momuha-jātīyasya 157.2; manda-momūha-tā *state of being dull and deluded*, 372.14.

mora, m. (= Pali, Pkt. id. = Skt. mayūra), *peacock*: (prose) Mv ii.264.17; iii.256.1; (vss) Mv ii.202.15; iii.133.16; Suv 47.8; Laṅk 365.12; written maura, Mv ii.266.19 = 402.14 (in the latter v.l., text mora; vs); also in mora-hasta(ka), see **mayūra-ha**°.

moraṅgī, n. of a plant, presumably = Skt. muraṅgī: Mmk 463.12 (prose).

moramba, n. of some sort of bird: Mv ii.475.12

(prose). The mss. agree; since mayūra occurs shortly before in the same list, it seems unlikely to be a corruption for moraka = mora, as suggested in Senart's note.

mora-hasta(ka) = **mayūra-h°**, q.v.

Morikā (MIndic for Mayūrikā), n. of a rākṣasī: Māy 243.9 (prose).

moṣaka, m. (**1**) (Skt. and [mosaka] Pali Lex., see Childers; = Skt. moṣa), *robbing*; *a robber*: udyāna-°kāḥ puruṣāḥ Divy 175.12, 15; ayaṃ cauro rājakula-°ko Mv ii.167.18 (prose; here perh. specifying -ka), *this is the thief that has been robbing the palace*; (**2**) (= Skt. moṣa) *plunder, stolen goods*: MSV iv.62.2, 5; 63.7 ff.

moṣa-dharma, adj. or subst. (Bhvr. or Karmadh.? = Pali mosa-dhamma, by 'false' Sktism; Pali mosa is quasi-vṛddhi formation to Pali musā = Skt. mṛṣā; § 3.68), (*of*) *deceptive quality*: Śikṣ 261.8 evaṃ cakṣuś cendriyaṃ ca rikte muṣṭisadṛśam (but prob. read rikta-muṣṭi°, see **muṣṭi** 3) ... tucchaṃ mṛṣā-moṣadharme (dual? *two things that have*, or *are*, *false and delusive qualities*? but all other epithets except the very doubtful rikte are sg.!) bālopalāpanaṃ ...; Dbh 43.6 (sarvasaṃskṛtaṃ) riktaṃ tucchaṃ mṛṣā-moṣadharmā-visaṃvādakaṃ (so text; note suggests °dharmaṃ vi°; possibly °dharmā, pl., though subject is sg., *false and deceptive qualities* or *states*?) bālālāpanam (read bālollāp°); note that once in Pali, AN v.84.24–25, musā immediately precedes mosadhammā (kāmā ... tucchā musā mosa°, so printed), and should perhaps be regarded as cpd. with it. See next.

moṣadharmin (to prec. plus -in), *characterized by the quality of deceit*: °miṇaḥ, pl., Mvy 7314 = Tib. slu baḥi chos can. Note that the prec. entry is mṛṣā 7313; perhaps orig. the two were one cpd. word, see under prec.

moha, nt. (Skt. only masc.), *delusion*: LV 258.12 (vs) satyam idaṃ moham anyad iti mūḍhāḥ, *foolishly thinking, 'this is true, all else is delusion'* (is -m 'Hiatustilger'? for moha anyad? but next is unambiguous); LV 372.5 (vs) mohānī (m.c. for °ni).

mohaṃ, adv. (= AMg. id.; Skt. and Pali moghaṃ), *in vain*: Mv iii.431.14, 17; 445.7, 10; also mss. twice Mv ii.50.20 (once sohaṃ), Senart em. moghaṃ. Cf. **amoham.**

Mohadharmeśvara, see **Amoha°**.

Mohaparimuktā, n. of a 'gandharva maid': Kv 5.13.

moha-puruṣa (= Pali mogha-purisa; cf. **mohaṃ**), *stupid, vain fellow*: MSV i.222.16.

Mohā, n. of a rākṣasī: Māy 240.22.

Maudgalyāyana, (**1**) also **Mahā-m°**, = Pali Moggallāna, gotra-name and usual appellation of **Kolita**, often paired with **Śāriputra** as leading disciples of the Buddha: story of his conversion, Mv iii.56.16 ff.; 57.18 etc.; the forms without and with Mahā- often interchange in the same passage and sometimes without significance, but the Buddha himself always speaks of or to him as Maud° (without Mahā-), e. g. in contexts where Mahā- is usually prefixed, Divy 160.13, 17; 299.16 (but in 18 Ānanda calls him Mahā-m°); Av ii.91.15; Aśoka refers to him without Mahā-, but in a vs, Divy 395.20; other cases without Mahā-, Mvy 1033; Divy 50.29 ff.; 182.22; 268.6; 314.15; 486.25; Av i.241.7 etc.; Sukh 31.3; Karmav 161.18; et passim; (**2**) pl., n. of a brahmanical gotra: Divy 635.13; cf. Maudgalyāyanīgotreṇa, of the nakṣatra Uttarāṣāḍha, Divy 640.22.

maudrika, m., Mvy 3810, acc. to pw 7.369 *Verfertiger von mudrā*; Tib. rgya ḥdebs pa, *one who seals*, or, yi ge ba, *letter-writer*.

[**mauna**, read **maula**, q.v., Laṅk 16.14.]

maunīndra, adj. (to Skt. munīndra plus -a), *of the prince(s) of sages*: °draṃ (pra)vacanaṃ Divy 490.14, 16.

mauneya, nt. (once in RV.; = Pali moneyya), *sagehood, state of being a muni*: muni pravyāhara dharmaṃ °yaṃ uttamaṃ padaṃ Mv iii.387.2, *sage-hood*, (which is) *the highest station*; °yaṃ ca pṛcchasi nāla duḥkaraṃ ... 4 (these vss = Pali Sn 700, 701); evaṃ °yaṃ (em., but this word supported by corresp. vs in Pali Sn 716) upeṣyasi 388.14.

maura = **mora**, q.v.

[**Maurin**, n. sg. Maurī, printed in text of Laṅk 362.11 pāṇḍavāḥ kauravā rāma paścān maurī bhaviṣyati. Tho ed. note says that Tib. and Chin. support this reading, the Skt. mss. read saurī, and this or śauriḥ is surely to be read (Skt. Śauriḥ = Kṛṣṇaḥ). The reading with m for s, or ś, is due to anticipation of the name mauryā(ḥ) in the next line; see the following entry.]

(**Maurya**, = Skt. id., family name of the emperor **Aśoka**, q.v.: Divy 381.20, 26; 405.6; pl., n. of the dynasty, Laṅk 362.12 °yā nandāś ca guptāś ca.)

maula, adj. (Skt., not quite in this mg.), *fundamental, essential*: as ep. of dhyāna, Mvy 1486 = Tib. dṅos gzhi, *the thing itself, the real essence* (otherwise used for mūla); of Tathāgatas, (nirmitanairmāṇikānāṃ ... tathāgatānāṃ) ... na maulānāṃ tathāgatānāṃ ... maulo hi ... tathāgataḥ ... Laṅk 242.7, 8; Suzuki *original*, which does not hit the mark; read also maula for text mauna (tathāgata) in Laṅk 16.14, see s.v. **nirmita-nirmāṇa**, where Suzuki (Transl. 16 note 2) gives *original* for the Chin. translation.

mauṣṭika, see **muṣṭika.**

mrakṣa, m. (= Pali makkha, which never means *hypocrisy*, as usually rendered; CPD under (a-)makkha more correctly *disparaging*, sc. good qualities of others; = paraguṇa-makkhana-lakkhaṇo, tesaṃ vināsana-raso, tadavacchādanapaccupaṭṭhāno (see **pratyupasthāna**) MN comm. i.106.26 f., on MN i.15.35; similarly tho less fully comm. on Dhp. 150 and 407; AN comm. ii.162.28, on AN i.95.15; in Pugg. 18.25, 22.29 f. read niṭṭhuriya for niddhuniya; AN and MN comms. l. c. define the associated paḷāsa, our **pradāsa**, q.v., by yugaggāha, *grasping after preëminence for oneself over others*), despite usual rendering *hypocrisy* or the like, never has that mg.; primarily, *concealment of the good qualities of others, jealous disparagement, nasty disposition, ill-will*, finally (like **mrakṣya**, q.v.) virtually = krodha, *anger*: this last development seems clearly complete in Karmav 37.19 text krodhaḥ, upanāhaḥ, mrakṣaḥ, pradāśaḥ, but for the last read with ms. paridāghaḥ, cf. Śikṣ 198.8 below; yet Mvy 1963 and Dharmas 69 mrakṣaḥ after krodha, upanāha, and before pradāsa (°śa); prob. same mg. in LV 262.17 (vs) krodha-mrakṣau; usually in rather misc. lists of vices; between māna and mada (after which comes krodha) LV 52.13; 411.16; after māna and mada Mv ii.229.20; between mātsarya and māna SP 481.4; after māna and mada, (before paridāha) Śikṣ 198.8, (before krodha) KP 7.3; after māna Mv i.166.20; Ud xvi.23 (= Pali Dhp. 150 māno makkho); after śāṭhya, vakratā, kauṭilya, māna SP 107.1; krodherṣyā-śāṭhya-mrakṣādayaś Bbh 20.15; krodha upanāhaḥ śāṭhyam īrṣyā pradāso (ed. °dāno) mrakṣo mātsaryaṃ ... Dharmas 30. Tib., in all passages known to me (Mvy, LV, KP), renders ḥchab pa, *concealment*, which is somewhat etymological (mrakṣ, *smear, anoint*), but not erroneous, only incomplete; it means primarily *concealment of the good qualities of others*, not (as nearly all have assumed) of one's own faults.

Mrakṣaṣaṇḍā, or **°ḍa**, m. (= Pali Macchikāsaṇḍa), n. of a place in the Kāśi land, home of **Citra** (1): °ḍā MSV iii.21.8; 24.5; °ḍa 21.8–9, 10, 13, etc.

mrakṣitaka, adj. (= Skt. mrakṣita, ppp.), *smeared*: madhu-°ka, with mūla(ka), (edible) *roots*: Divy 511.20; 513.14; maṣi-°ka (text masi°, Index maṣi°), m., (a person or animal) *that is smeared with ink* (specifying -ka?), Laṅk 274.5.

mrakṣin (= Pali makkhin; see **mrakṣa**), *ill-natured, churlish*: raktāna duṣṭāna tathaiva mrakṣiṇāṃ SP 364.2 (vs).

mrakṣya (nt.; cf. Pali makkha, Vin. i.25.4, comm. 971.20 kodha, the only possible mg.; see **mrakṣa**), *anger*:

(caṇḍībhūto) 'nāttamanāḥ kopaṃ ca dveṣaṃ ca mrakṣyaṃ ca tatpratyayāt saṃjanayitvā Divy 622.12.

mreḍita, nt. (orig. ppp. of Gr. mreḍ, not used as simplex), *expression, speech*: uvāca madhurāṃ vāṇīṃ karuṇārdramreḍitena tu Mmk 479.14 (śloka line; hypermetric by one syllable).

? **mrotaka**, a kind of tree: °ka (pl.) Mv iii.80.11 (in list of trees, āryā vs; v.l. āmrā, equivalent metrically).

mlānaka, adj. (= Skt. mlāna plus -ka; see s.v. **durbalaka**), *faint*: Divy 334.1, 3 (but in 571.11 etc. mlāna in same phrase).

Y

yaṃ = yat, see **yac ca, yat khalu**; yaṃ velaṃ, see **velā**.

yakṣa (as in Skt.): (**1**) mahāntaṃ yakṣaṃ, applied to Māra: Mv ii.260.10; 261.11. Cf. yakkha, applied to Māra, Sn 449 (seems to be a rare use in Pali); (**2**) n. of a rākṣasa king: Mmk 18.1.

yakṣaṇī = the regular Skt. yakṣiṇī, *a female yakṣa*: Laṅk 7.3 (perh. corruption? repeated in Index).

yakṣa-lipi, a kind of script: LV 126.2 (confirmed Tib., gnod sbyin = yakṣa).

yaṃ khalu, with opt., see under **yat khalu**.

yac ca, yaṃ ca (or **ced**?), (**1**) (= Pali yañ ce) *than*, in comparisons: saṃgrāme maraṇaṃ śreyo yac ca jīvet parājitaḥ LV 262.11 (vs); (śreyo hy ayoguḍā bhuktā...) yaṃ ca (or ced? lacuna in mss. for ca) bhuñjīta duḥśīlo (mss. °jita °śilo)... Ud ix.2 = Pali Dhp. 308; Itiv. 43.9, ... yañ ce bhuñjeyya...; (**2**) used somewhat as in Caraka (pw 5.126, *wenn nämlich; und zwar*): (this spot will be used by two Buddhas,) yac ca (*namely*) Kāśyapena ... yac caitarhi Bhagavateti Divy 77.7 = 466.3 (Index says *both ... and*); similarly LV 186.5, (Śuddhodana speaks) abhiniṣkramiṣyati avaśyaṃ kumāro 'yaṃ yac cemāni (so Lefm. em., but mss. either kumāro yaṃ, or 'yaṃ, or yaś, cemāni; read kumāro yaṃ, or yac, ce°) pūrvanimittāni saṃdṛśyante sma, *the prince is certainly going to leave worldly life, as namely...*; Tib. sṅa ltas su snaṅ ba ni ḥdi dag sñam nas (*from the thought*, app. rendering yac ca or yaṃ ca).

yajña, nt. (otherwise m.), *sacrifice*: mahāyajñāni yajamāno Mv ii.405.10 (vs, but so far from being m.c., the added syllable spoils the meter; first half of anuṣṭubh; no v.l.).

Yajñakoṭigupta, n. of a former Buddha: Mv i.140.14.

Yajñadatta, the name originally given to **Śarabhaṅga**, q.v.: Mv iii.361.17 ff.

yaṃ ca = **yac ca**, q.v.

yato-adhikaraṇaṃ, see **adhikaraṇa** (2).

yat khalu, or **yaṃ khalu**, with a 2d (or polite 3d) person form of jñā (regularly opt.), the whole phrase meaning *please be informed; allow me to inform you* (a courteous introduction to a statement made usually to a king or the like); nivedayati (Mv ii.454.1 āmantrayati; 457.16 niveditaṃ; 488.15 nivedayate, v.l. °ti) putra (457.16 and 488.15 mahārāja) yaṃ khalu (457.16 khu) jānesi (in 451.12 mss. corruptly ānesi, Senart wrongly em. āṇesi, with wrong interpretation in note; in 456.13 mss. jānāsi; 488.15 text jāneyāsi, v.l. jānesi) Mv ii.449.6; 451.12; 454.1; 456.13; 457.16; 488.15; (Asita) mānavakam āmantrayate, yat khalu mānavaka jānīyā(ḥ)... LV 101.9 f.; (the king's porter) Śuddhodanam evam āha, yat khalu deva jānīyā(ḥ) 102.11–12; (Śākyan elders) āhuḥ, yat khalu deva jānīyāḥ 118.4; (the purohita) āha, yat khalu devo jānīyād 121.3; āhuḥ, etc. (as prec.) 136.12; etad avocat, yat khalu ... jānīyās 396.6.

yattaka, f. °**ikā**, adj. (= Pali id.; also written **yātaka, yātuka, yāttaka**; AMg. jatta), *as much, as great*, pl. *as many*; in prose of Mv, otherwise recorded only in vss: puṇyaṃ bhavi yattakaṃ SP 351.2 (vs); yattaku tasya puṇyam 12 (vs); yattaka (pl.) loki virūpa suraudrāḥ LV 307.19 (vs; mss. yantaka or yantraka, cf. the reading **yāntak(a)** Gv 384.4, and similarly under **tattaka**; Lefm.'s em. is certainly right in sense, as Tib. confirms); yattaka, sg. forms Mv ii.273.2; 435.15; iii.266.3; pl. forms Mv i.356.10; ii.95.8; 99.2; iii.23.18; 34.19; 266.5; Suv 53.8 (vs); 54.9 (vs); yattikā, f. pl., Mv i.126.12 (vs); ii.149.21 (prose); in correlation with **tattaka**, see this word.

[**yat tu**, see **yan nu**.]

yatra hi nāma (= Pali id.), *inasmuch as*: evaṃ durlabhā bodhir yatra hi nāma kalpānāṃ śatasahasreṇa Mv i.55.12, *in that case* (evaṃ) *enlightenment is hard to get, inasmuch as* (it is got only) *in 100,000 kalpas*; similarly i.57.2, variant of i.35.12, where **yad idaṃ**, q.v., is used instead of yatra hi nāma; āścaryaṃ yāvad (Kashgar rec. and 2 Nep. mss. om. yāvad) yatra hi nāmāsya ... paribhoktopalabdhaḥ SP 103.14, *O wonderful! inasmuch as* (now) *someone to enjoy this* (wealth) *has been found!* (yāvad is prob. to be omitted; if kept, it goes closely with āścaryaṃ; *what a great wonder!* or, *it's nothing less than a miracle!*).

yatha-r-iva (Pali id., = yathaiva), *just as*, see § 4.61.

yathākāri(-tā, etc.), see **yathāvādi-tathākāri(n)**.

yathājñaka, adj. (Skt. yathā plus ājñā, *command*, plus -ka), *according to directions*: °kāni sthānāni Mv i.76.4 (vs); so mss., Senart em. yathājñaptāni.

yathātmya (nt., = Skt. yāthātmya), *true nature*: Mvy 858 °myāvatārakuśalaḥ (of Bodhisattvas; see s.v. **avatāra** 3).

yathādhauta, adj. (= Pali yathādhota), °tena pātreṇa, *with begging-bowl just as cleaned*, i. e. not having received any almsfood: piṇḍāya caritvā °tena pātreṇa tataḥ grāmāto nirdhāvati Mv i.301.10, and similarly 17; 302.3; Divy 296.3.

yathāpi, (**1**) (in this sense unparalleled so far as I know) alone, or esp. followed by idam (**yathāpīdam**), also by tat, and rarely by nāma, *because of course, because obviously*, in giving a (more or less evident) reason for what has just been said: tat kasya hetoḥ? yathāpīdam bālabhāvatvāt SP 73.11, *and why? because, you see, of the fact that they were* (*foolish*) *children*; in same context, yathāpi bālā(ḥ) SP 86.6 (vs); yathāpi ... (without idam or the like) 90.4 (vs); yathāpi (so Kashgar rec.; Nep. tathāpi; WT em. tathā hi, perh. supported by Tib. ḥdi ltar) buddhena adhiṣṭhitatvāt 238.2 (vs), *since, of course, they are inspired by the Buddha*; yathāpīdaṃ, in this same mg., SP 38.14; 110.10; 210.2; (tat kasya) hetoḥ? yathāpīdaṃ sukhasthānasthitatvāt 283.2; yathāpīdaṃ rūkṣapradhānaṃ prahitātmanaḥ LV 255.3, *of course because* (there was) *harsh exertion*; similarly, yathāpīdaṃ adṛṣṭapūrvaṃ dṛśyate Mv iii.210.18, *of course because a previously unseen thing was seen*; yathāpīdaṃ anuttare upadhisaṃkṣaye samyaksuvimuktacitto Mv iii.282.6, *because, of course, he had his mind...*; repeated 12; 283.2; and, only in 283.8, otherwise same phrase and situation, **sayyathāpīdaṃ**, which is an otherwise unknown use of the form **sayyathāpi**, see under 2 below; in the same mg., more rarely, with nāma for idam: tat kasya hetoḥ? yathāpi nāma vayaṃ tathāgatasya bhūtāḥ putrā(ḥ) SP 110.4; yathāpi nāma ...

Śikṣ 40.12; also with tat for idaṃ (or nāma): yathāpi tac cittavaśavartitvād LV 244.22, *of course because he was in control of his thoughts*; yathāpi tat (mss.; ed. wrongly em. tataḥ) sphuṭo Māreṇa pāpīyasā (referring back to same words in lines 21–22) Divy 201.23, *of course (you see) because* ...; yathāpi tad 230.16; MSV i.51.21; also read in LV 256.6, with v.l. incl. best ms. A, (śubhavarṇatanutā) sāpy antaradhād, yathāpi (Lefm. tad yathāpi, but this tad should surely not be in the text) tad rūkṣapradhāna-prahitātmakatvāt (cf. above, LV 255.3); (**2**) **tad yathāpi nāma,** and (only Mv) **sayyathāpi nāma** (very rarely the word nāma is omitted, Mv ii.124.12, in a clause of comparison ending bhavati); mss. of Mv also **tayyathā°**, **sadyathā°**; **saṃyadhāpi nāma** (! cf. **saṃyathīdaṃ**) balavān puruṣaḥ ... bāhuṃ prasārayet Mmk 3.25 (= Pali seyyathāpi, with or without nāma, very rarely sayathāpi, Therag. 412; = Skt. tad yathā, also in Pali as taṃ yathā; note Mv i.55.13 and 56.8 tad yathā, repeating 54.13 tad yathāpi nāma, balavān puruṣaḥ ..., same clause as in Mmk 3.25 above, a cliché in which Mv elsewhere has sayyathāpi nāma), *just as* (followed by nominal phrase or verbal clause), or *just as if* (followed by hypothetical clause, or series of clauses, or, esp. in SP, by an entire long parable, which may fill most of a chapter): sayyathāpi (so Senart but mss. tayyathā° or tad yathā°) nāma kalambukā (*just like k's*), evaṃ varṇapratibhāsāpi abhū Mv i.341.5; in 7 below Senart with mss. tad yathāpi nāma kṣudraṃ madhum anelakaṃ (or °ḍakaṃ, mss.), evamāsvādā; tad yathāpi nāma ... etāni buddhakṣetrāṇi saṃdṛśyante SP 20.10, *just as these b° appear*; tad yathāpi nāma ... udumbarapuṣpaṃ kadācit karhicit saṃdṛśyate, evaṃ ... SP 39.8, *just as an ud° fruit rarely appears, so* ...; introducing rather long parables, SP 101.11; 121.11, etc.; the range of usage is sufficiently indicated by these quotations; tad yathāpi nāma very often, e. g. LV 246.17; 247.17; 251.9, 17; Mv i.194.13; 341.7; iii.229.3; 425.15, 21 (and in mss. as v.l. for sayyathā°, below); both in one sentence, (imasmiṃ ca pṛthivīyaṃ unmajjana-nimajjanaṃ karoti) sayyathāpi nāma udake pi abhidyamāno (mss. °nā) gacchati, tad yathāpi nāma pṛthivīyaṃ Mv iii.410.2, (*he plunges up and down in this earth,*) *just as if he were going in water unbroken, just as if on land* (awkwardly expressed, but the mg. is certain in my opinion); tad yathāpi nāma, also Sukh 19.16 et al.; Śikṣ 21.17 et al.; Gv 20.1 et al.; Dbh 7.23; RP 40.1; in RP 40.20 and 42.1 read tad (for text syād) yathāpi nāma; **sayyathāpi nāma,** only Mv, often with vv.ll. tad ya° (not here recorded) and others, i.339.8 (twice); 340.12, 13, 15; 345.12; ii.121.7; 124.5; 125.3, 12, 13, 16, etc.; ii.270.3 ff. (repeatedly, with v.l. sadyathā°); 282.10; 313.16, 17; 412.8; iii.103.14, 17, 20; 108.7; 180.16; 181.7; 226.18; 282.8, 14; 283.5; 318.5; 325.16; 329.5, 13 (the last four corresp. to LV 400.3; 405.10; 408.8; 409.19, all reading tad yathā°); 379.16; (**3**) **sayyathāpi,** very rarely (like Pali seyyathāpi, see Childers 468, column 2, lines 10, 13, etc.) = **sayyathīdaṃ,** q.v., *namely, to wit, viz.*: (evaṃrūpehi) śabdehi, sayyathāpi (no v.l.) hastiśabdehi rathaśabdehi (etc.) Mv i.196.12.

yathā-paurāṇa, adj., *as of old, as* (it had been) *before*: (nāgabhavano) ca °ṇa-(Senart em. °ṇaṃ) saṃvṛttaṃ devabhavanasaṃnibhaṃ, tasya ca nāgarājño parivāro °ṇaṃ nāga-bhavanaṃ (so read with 1 ms.) dṛṣṭvā ... Mv ii.179.15; āśramapadaṃ vinaṣṭaṃ °ṇaṃ bhavatu Divy 48.9; °ṇaṃ saṃvṛttaṃ 10; sa bāhur yathāpaurāṇaḥ (ed. as two words) saṃsthito 'bhūd SP 414.3.

yathāvadbhāvikatā (Skt. yathāvad plus bhāvika plus -tā), *true* or *full actualization, state of coming to be truly actualized as the thing is* or *should be*: °tāṃ ca dharmāṇām ārabhya yā bhūtatā, yāvadbhāvikatāṃ cārabhya yā dharmāṇāṃ sarvatā Bbh 37.1–3; (tattvārthe dvividhā, sc. prajñā) yāvadbhāvikatayā yathāvadbhāvikatayā ca tattvārthasya grahaṇāt 215.2; yat sarvadharmāṇāṃ sarvaparyāyeṣu yāvadbhāvikatayā °katayā ca bhāvanāmayaṃ ... jñānam 258.5–7; similarly 9.

yathāvādi-tathākāri(n), adj. and **°ri-tā, °tva,** subst. (also as two separate adj., yathāvādī tathākārī Mvy 2408: so clearly in Pali, the two separated by other words, DN ii.224.3; Itiv. 122.2 ff.; in Sn 357 yathāvādī (v.l. °di-) tathākārī, possibly as single cpd.), *acting as one speaks, according to one's word*: °kāry-avitatha-vāk-karma-samudāhārakasya LV 8.7; yathāvādī-(! prob. read °di-)-tathākāricittaṃ Gv 367.13 (prose); abstract nouns in -tā, -tva, yathāvādi-tathākāri-tāṃ (acc.) LV 440.3; RP 8.11; °ri-tayā (instr.) RP 10.7; Dbh 14.1; °ri-tvena Śikṣ 22.16; yathāvāditā-tathākāritā (read as one word) ŚsP 1460.11; in Mv occur, in the mss., forms ending in °taṃ for both members (kept by Senart for the second member, while he em. the first to °ta-), also with reversed order of the two parts (as in Pali ll.cc. above): yathākāritaṃ tathāvāditam anuprāpnuvanti (one ms. adds, yathāvāditaṃ tathākāritaṃ anuprāp°, so surely read) Mv ii.260.13–14; in 261.15 both mss. invert the order, yathāvāditaṃ tathāk° anu°, yathāk° tathāv° anu°. If the ending °taṃ is textually sound, it can only represent °tāṃ with MIndic shortening of the vowel; perh. it should be em. to °tāṃ or °tvaṃ.

yathāvṛddhikā, *order by age*: °kāyāṃ prajñaptāyām MSV iii.125.8, °kām āgamya 9; esp. adv. instr. (Skt. yathāvṛddham, Pali °vuḍḍhaṃ), *in order of age*: MSV ii.175.11; 192.8; iii.124.18.

yathāsaṃstarika, m. (= Pali yathāsaṃthatika, as if from Skt. -saṃstṛta; Pali uses both saṃthata and saṃthara in mg. *seat, mat,* = Skt. saṃstara; BHS also **yāthā°**, q.v.), *taking any seat (mat) which may be offered,* one of the 12 **dhūtaguṇa,** q.v.: Dharmas 63; MSV iii.122.7.

yathopakam, see **upaka.**

yad, see following items, also **yac ca, yat khalu, yan nu, yan nūna(m).**

yad api (not found recorded in this mg.), *furthermore, also*: (Śaṅkhọ rājā ... Maitreyaṃ ... pravrajitam anupravrajiṣyati,) yad apy asya strīratnaṃ Viśākhā nāma sāpy ... anupravrajiṣyati Divy 61.17.

yad idam, (**1**) (= Pali id.; cf. s.v. **sayyathīdaṃ**), *namely, to wit*: ekakulagotrāṇāṃ yad idaṃ Bharadvājasagotrāṇāṃ SP 18.5, *of the same family and family-name, namely, Bharadvāja-kinsmen*; (katamac ca ... mahākṛtyaṃ ... yena kṛtyena tathāgato ... loka) utpadyate? yad idaṃ tathāgatajñānadarśanasamādāpanahetunimittaṃ ... SP 40.3, *it is, to wit* ... (answering a rhetorical question); (ekam evāhaṃ ... yānam ārabhya ...) yad idaṃ buddhayānam SP 40.14, *namely, the Buddha-vehicle*; devagulmāni ... yad idaṃ karoṭapāṇayo (etc.) Mv i.30.7; paryāyaṃ (see this) akārṣit, yad idaṃ iha āgamanāya 35.7, *has made arrangements, namely for coming here*; (duḥkhasamudānīyā anuttarā saṃyaksambodhiḥ) yad idaṃ kalpānāṃ śatasahasreṇa 35.12 (see under **yatra hi ṇāma**), *obtainable with difficulty is ..., namely in 100,000 kalpas*; (ayam ... udyānānāṃ mahā-udyānaṃ) yad idaṃ mahāvanaṃ kūṭāgāraśālaṃ (or °lāṃ; Senart em. sa-kū°) 299.20; (teṣāṃ ced ahaṃ ...) na puratas tiṣṭheyaṃ yad idaṃ cittāvikṣepatāyai Sukh 14.16, *'if ... I should not stand before them ... that is, so that their thoughts should not be troubled'* (SBE 49.2.15); yathārūpair ākārair ... yad idaṃ suvarṇena vā rajatena vā (etc.) Sukh 16.4; similarly 44.15; (**2**) in LV 99.15 seems perhaps used nearly like **yathāpi** (1), q.v.: na ca mānuṣā apsarasāṃ rūpaṃ dṛṣṭvā pramādam āpadyante sma, yad idaṃ bodhisattvasya tejo'nubhāvena, ... *of course, you see* (? but perhaps, as above, *namely, to wit*), *because of the power of the B's majesty*; cf. under **yad uta** (2).

yad uta (not recorded elsewhere; uta not recorded in Pali), (**1**) = **yad idam** (1), *namely, to wit* (in Tib. on LV 392.11 = ḥdi lta ste, which Das renders by *tad yathā, yad idaṃ, for example, for instance, to wit, such as, viz.*;

all these could be used in rendering yad uta as well as yad idam): SP 109.1 katamābhis tisṛbhir (sc. duḥkhatābhiḥ)? yad uta duḥkhaduḥkhatayā (etc.); Dbh 77.4 katamāś catasro (sc. pratisaṃvidaḥ)? yad uta (they are then listed); LV 25.7 (katamair dvātriṃśatā, sc. guṇākāraiḥ?) yad uta (list follows); SP 18.10; 124.3 (ekaraso yad uta vimuktiraso . . .); LV 269.15 (kusumāni jale kṣipanti sma, yad uta bodhisattvasya pūjākarmaṇe, *namely, to do homage to the B.*); LV 392.11; 416.22; Divy 45.1 (eṣo 'gro . . . yad uta pūrṇaḥ), and similarly 49.18; (dharmatā khalu . . .) yad uta daśāvaśyakaraṇīyāni bhavanti Divy 150.17, *it is the normal condition . . . viz., that . . .*; similarly Jm 88.4; 98.16; dharmadeśanāṃ karoti, yad utedaṃ duḥkham (etc.) Divy 198.5; āyuḥpramāṇaṃ yad utāśītivarṣāṇi Suv 6.6 and 9.12; others, Divy 208.7; 320.26, etc.; Av often e. g. i.211.8; Bbh 6.22 etc.; Bhīk 4a.3; Gv 501.9; Kv 66.4; (**2**) perhaps = **yad idam** (2), q.v., giving a reason, *because, of course* (but perhaps not to be separated from 1): SP 414.3 sa bāhur yathāpaurāṇaḥ (ed. as two words) saṃsthito 'bhūd, yad uta tasyaiva bodhisattvasya . . . jñānabalādhānena, (*namely*?) *because* (*of course*?) *of that same B's attainment of power of knowledge*; (**3**) once or twice yad uta seems, I feel, to be used with a slightly different connotation, *and that too*, with implication of *especially, particularly*: Av ii.142.17, repeated 143.6, (āścaryaṃ bhadanta yāvac chāstuḥ śrāvakāṇāṃ cārthenārthaḥ padena padaṃ vyañjanena) vyañjanaṃ saṃsyandate sameti, yad utāgrapadaiḥ, *it is a marvel, Lord, how the teacher and his disciples agree and are identical, meaning with meaning, word* (or *topic*) *with word, letter with letter, and that too with the highest words* (*most sublime topics*); SP 77.2 (it was no deceit, when three kinds of vehicles had been promised by the man to his sons in the burning house, that) ekayānāni dattāni, yad uta mahāyānāni, *he gave them single vehicles, and* (*especially*) *that too* (Kern, *and those*; but Burnouf *c'est à dire*, = 1 above) *great vehicles*.

yadbhūyasā, adv., also °**yastvena** (°**yatvena**?), vv.ll. **yadbhūyaso** and **yadbhūyena**, in Mv **yobhūyena** (= Pali yebhuyyena, adv.; cf. yebhuyya-, in comp., and bhiyyo, bhiyyoso), *for the most part*: °yasā (the regular form) SP 66.6 (Kashgar rec. bhūyaso); LV 136.13; Divy 50.12; 80.4; 142.3; 419.18; RP 34.1; Bbh 252.21 etc.; yadbhūyastvena SP 60.8 (no v.l.); 378.9 (text °yatvena, Kashgar rec. yadbhūyena, but WT °yastvena with ms. K'); yobhūyena Mv i.61.4 (5 mss. yobhūtena); 313.4; 338.14; 354.11; iii.176.9, 10; 393.14 f.

yadbhūyasikīya, m., sc. vinaya (= Pali yebhuyyasikā, sc. kiriyā, described MN ii.247.19 ff., see Childers and PTSD s.v.), (procedure) *decided by vote of a majority* (of monks), one of the 7 **adhikaraṇa-śamatha**: Mvy 8634. In MSV ii.207.12 yadbhūyaiṣīyaṃ (nt., with karma) = this; it follows **tatsvabhāvaiṣīyaṃ** and imitates it in ending (by secondary corruption?); it is however repeated below, 207.19 etc.

yadbhūyaso, yadbhūya(s)tvena, yadbhūyena, see **yadbhūyasā**.

yadbhūyaskālaka, adj., with pudgala, see **sarvakālaka**: MSV iii.75.1.

yadbhūyaiṣīya, see **yadbhūyasikīya**.

yadbhūyopita, gen. °tasya (printed yadbhūyo 'pi tasya), MSV ii.108.13, 15, seems to represent a single word; perh. read °yo'rpita (°yo-arpita, *generally fixed in location*?)? Tib. gaṅ yun riṅ du gnas pa la ḥo, *to one who has dwelt there a long time*.

yantra-kalā, *the art of mechanics*: MSV iv.247.1; °lācārya, *a master of* this: ib. 246.15 ff.; Divy 532.20 (here °karāc°); 535.13.

yantra-māṣṭa(ka), also spelt **maṣṭa(ka)**, etc., see **māṣṭaka**.

yantrita, in MIndic form **jantita**, ppp. of Skt. yantrayati, *engineered* in the sense of *set in motion*, of a river-stream (so interpreted in Pali Therag. 574 by PTSD s.v. yantita): kāṅkṣāvimati-samudayā dṛṣṭījaḍa-jantitā (no v.l.) . . . tṛṣṇānadī LV 372.15 (vs), *the river of thirst . . . set in motion by the water of heresies*.

yan (yaṃ) nu (cf. next; in Pali represented by yan nūna), conj., *suppose now*, with opt. of 1st person; extremely common in most texts, but I have failed to note it in Mv, which uses **yan nūna(ṃ)** instead: SP 73.2, 14; 322.1; LV 14.16; 95.22; 101.5; 137.17; Divy 95.10; Av i.3.4; Samādh 19.12, 14; etc.; in text of MSV regularly printed yat tu (yat tv aham . . .), possibly by misreading? (e. g. i.90.1).

yan (yaṃ) nūna, (before aham) also **nūnam** but in Mv **nūnāhaṃ**, rarely **nūnaṃ** (= Pali yan nūna, rarely nūnaṃ; cf. prec.), *suppose now*, with 1 sg. opt. or (rarely) indic.; acc. to PTSD, Pali yan nūna is or may be used in the mg. *suppose rather*, suggesting an alternative to some other course: once SP seems clearly to favor this; after yan nu . . . nirgamayeyaṃ SP 73.2–3, *suppose I cause them to come out . . .*, a tentative proposal, there follows: yan nūnam aham etān saṃcodayeyam 73.5, *suppose rather . . .*, with nūnam instead of nu; no other so clear case, but *rather* may, at least possibly, be meant in yaṃ nūna . . . SP 55.10 (vs), *suppose* (instead of entering nirvāṇa) *that I* (reveal the Buddha-bodhi); 196.7 (vs); LV 393.2 (vs); also in yan nūnāhaṃ Mv i.35.1; 37.7; 54.12; 343.6; ii.117.18; but the mg. *suppose rather* seems hardly possible in yan nūnam aham . . . LV 258.21 (vs; verb here samārabhe, could be opt. or 1 sg. ind. mid.); nor in most of the following: yaṃ nūnaṃ Mv i.268.3; yan nūnāhaṃ i.51.7 (prose; verb is tiṣṭhehaṃ, see § 31.21, v.l. °eyaṃ), 14 (verb is sthātum icchāmi, pres. ind.); ii.118.5, 11 (in 11, if Senart's text is right, no verb! only dats. of nouns! since adhigami and sākṣākari in 12 seems clearly aorists, statements of fact, not dependent on yan nūnāhaṃ, which is foll. by etasyaiva dharmasya prāptaye sākṣātkriyāyai; which seems to complete the sentence); 124.9; with pres. indic. verb ii.149.21 (here *rather* is perh. possible for yan nūnāhaṃ). In Pali, besides opt., fut. indic. is recorded: Childers 603, top of 2d column; cf. tiṣṭhehaṃ Mv i.51.7, above.

Yama, (**1**) n. of a nāga: Mvy 3328; (**2**) m. pl., n. of a class of gods, = **Yāma**: Bbh 62.1 (unless misprint for yāmāṃs; in standard list of god-classes, see **deva**); (**3**) n. of a rākṣasa king: Mmk 17.28 and 18.1 (twice in the same list!); but prob. both cpd. with the next following name, which in 17.28 is printed Ghibhīṣaṇa (! read Yamavibhī°), in 18.1 Ghaṇṭa.

yamaka (= Pali id. in sense 1), *pair, paired*; (**1**) adj. with **prātihārya**, *paired miracle* (= Pali ya° pāṭihāriya, °hīra), sc. a miracle in which pairs of opposites, such as e. g. water and fire, are simultaneously produced: °kāni prātihāryāṇi SP 459.12–460.1; read so in Bbh 152.10 for text ayamakāny (api) prāt°; (**2**) designation of a kind of yoga practice, = Tib. zuṅ gzug (Das) or zuṅ ḥjug (Jäschke), 'a technical term of practical mysticism, the forcing the mind into the principal artery in order to prevent distraction of mind' (Jä.) Mvy 798 yamaka-vyatyastāhāra-kuśalāḥ = zuṅ daṅ snrel zhi ḥi rgyud la mkhas pa rnams, *clever in the technique* (rgyud, see s.v. **āhāra**, 2; or, *the bringing in*) *of the pair and the inverted* (yoga practices). How the word *pair* applies to the above definition, given by Jäschke and Das, is not clear to me.

Yamaka-śāla-(or -śālaka-)vana, n. of a grove at or near the town of Kuśinagarī, where the Buddha died; named for a pair of śāl-trees (Av i.227.7) between which his couch lay, and which are mentioned also in the Pali accounts (e. g. DN ii.137.11), tho no such name is there given to the grove. See s.v. **upavartana**, where the passages are cited: Yamakaśālavana Divy 208.25; 209.3; Av i.227.6; ii.197.6; Mmk 598.22; °śālakavana Mmk 580.10, 17.

yamadaṇḍika, m. (to Skt. °daṇḍa), *agent of Yama's power prophet of doom*: MSV ii.118.8.

Yamadūtī, n. of a rākṣasī: Māy 243.25.

Yamamathanī, n. of a goddess: Sādh 497.3.

yamalaka, (**1**) m., *twin* (= Skt. yamala): Mvy 3911; (**2**) m. or nt., some kind of (presumably *double*) receptacle, fastened to a part of a horse's harness, in which food was carried: (modakāni . . .) yamalakaṃ pūretvā aśvapṛṣṭhe. . . Mv iii.158.9, 12; °kāto modakaṃ ukkaṭṭetvā (so with mss.) 13. Each time there is v.l. °raka.

yamalita, denom. ppp. from Skt. yamala (= AMg. jamaliya), *juxtaposed*, lit. *made like a pair of twins*: hastau yamalitākārau . . . Mmk 392.2.

yamalī (to Skt. yamala, adj., of which f. is regularly °lā), *a kind of dress consisting of two garments*: Av i.265.6 f.; Divy 276.11 (°lī vāyitā) ff., cf. 277.6, 21 ff., referring clearly to the two garments which constituted the yamalī.

yamalokika, adj., subst. (cf. **yāma**° and AMg. jamaloiya), *belonging to* or *inhabitant of Yama's world*: °kānāṃ sattvānāṃ . . . -duḥkhaṃ vyupaśāntam abhūt LV 86.13; sarva-niraya-tiryagyoni-yamalokikāḥ sarve devamanuṣyāś ca LV 289.7.

Yamānta = next, app. only in vss, m.c., § 22.24, in Mmk, and as a (mahā-)krodha: Mmk 549.2; 550.5; 552.25; 577.2, etc.

Yamāntaka (= prec.), the usual form in Skt. (as a Hindu figure) and in BHS, e. g. (Ārya-)Ya° Mvy 4333; usually as one of the (mahā-)krodha, regularly the first in a list of them, as in Dharmas 11; frequent in Sādh, e. g. 107.11. See next.

Yamāri = prec.: Sādh 95.19 etc. This suggests that the prec. came to be interpreted as *destroyer of Yama*.

Yambhaka, m. pl. (prob. hyper-Skt. for Jambha-ka, n. of various demons in Skt.; as if with Pkt. j for y), n. of a class of yakṣas, named as attendants on kiṃnaras: Mv ii.112.6.

Yavakacchaka, nt., n. of a village near Mithilā (v.l. Timilā): Mv ii.83.17; 86.5, 9, 12.

(**yavanānī**, see **yonānī** and **yāvanī**.)

Yaśa, see **Yaśas**.

Yaśaḥparvataśrīmegha, n. of a Tathāgata: Gv 310.12.

Yaśaḥpūrṇa, n. of a disciple of the Buddha: Divy 268.7 (in a list).

Yaśaḥprabha, n. of a Buddha in the south: Sukh 97.7.

Yaśaḥprabhāsa, n. of a Buddha in the nadir: Sukh 98.8.

Yaśaketu, n. of a former Buddha: Mv i.137.7 (prose).

Yaśadatta (2 of 6 mss. yaja°), n. of a former Buddha: Mv i.137.15. Cf. **Yaśodatta.**

Yaśaparvata (for Yaśaḥ°), n. of a Buddha: Gv 284.9 (vs).

Yaśaprāptā, n. of a devakumārikā in the south: LV 389.7 (vs).

Yaśamatī LV 389.7 (vs) = **Yaśāmatī** (Senart em. Yaśo°) Mv iii.307.8 (vs), n. of a devakumārikā in the south.

Yaśarāśi (for Yaśo°), n. of a former Buddha: Mv i.136.16.

Yaśavatī, m.c. for **Yaśovatī** = **Yaśodharā**, prob. to be read with Calc. and Tib. for **śayavatī** in LV 221.5 (vs).

Yaśavrata, n. of a former Buddha: Mv i.111.8 (vs).

Yaśaḥśuddhodita, n. of a Bodhisattva: Gv 442.4.

Yaśas, also (even in prose of Divy and Sukh) **Yaśa**, (**1**) n. of a Buddhist elder (sthavira): MSV i.188.8 ff.; in the time of Aśoka, but possibly meant as identical with Pali 1 Yasa Thera of DPPN (see **Yaśoda, Yaśodeva**), disciple of the Buddha (see **Piṇḍola Bharadvāja**, whom Yaśa introduces to Aśoka), sthavira-Yaśasam Divy 381.12, °śasā 16; Yaśo (n. sg.) 385.2; 399.26; 404.11; 406.21; 423.11; is this personage, or Pali Yasa (2) of DPPN, meant by the (Sthavira-)Yaśas of MSV i.196.6 ff.?; (**2**) n. of a minister of Aśoka: Yaśo (v.l. Yaśā) nāma Divy 382.6; Yaśāmātya, *the minister Y.*, 382.11, 16; (**3**) n. of a Tathāgata: Yaśasā Śikṣ 9.2; (**4**) n. of a Tathāgata in the nadir: Yaśo (n. sg.) nāma Sukh 98.7 (prose); (**5**) n. of two Bodhisattvas in the same list: Yaśaso, °saḥ (gen.) Gv 441.26; 442.21.

Yaśaskāma, n. of a Bodhisattva, previous incarnation of Maitreya: SP 22.6 ff.; 27.10 (yaśa-k°, in vs, m.c.).

Yaśāmatī, see **Yaśamatī.**

Yaśottara, (**1**) n. of a former Buddha: Mv iii.240.3; 241.15; 243.7, 8; 244.2; 245.9; 247.7; 248.11; Gv 206.12. All the Mv passages, and prob. also Gv, seem to refer to the same individual, tho somewhat confusedly; (**2**) n. of an upāsaka in Nādikā: MPS 9.13.

Yaśoda (= Pali Yasa Thera, 1 in DPPN), n. of a disciple of Buddha: Mv iii.405.4 ff.; colophons, Yaśodasya śreṣṭhiputrasya vastum 413.16; (after story of his former birth) Yaśoda-jātakaṃ 415.5. Cf. **Yaśas** (1), **Yaśodeva** (1).

Yaśodatta (cf. **Yaśadatta**), n. of a former Buddha: LV 172.1; and acc. to Senart Mv i.137.6 (but here two mss. Daśo- for Yaśo-, one Deśa-; all 6 mss. °dattaraḥ for °dattaḥ; note also that the name Yaśadatta occurs just below, in the same list, Mv i.137.15. Some other form must have been intended in Mv.

Yaśodeva, (**1**) n. of a disciple of Buddha: LV 1.8 (no v.l.). Evidently corresponds to Pali Yasa (Thera, 1 in DPPN; cf. **Yaśas** 1, **Yaśoda**), of Vin. i.15.1 ff., as is shown by the next four names in LV, Vimala, Subāhu, Pūrṇa, and Gavāṃpati, who correspond to the four friends of Yasa named in Vin. i.18.36 f., Vimala, Subāhu, Puṇṇaji, and Gavampati. So also Sukh 2.3, followed by Vimala, Subāhu, and Pūrṇa (Maitrāyaṇīputra). (**2**) n. of an upāsaka or lay-disciple, surely not the same as 1: Gv 51.10.

Yaśodgata (for Skt. *Yaśa-udgata), n. of a Bodhisattva: Gv 3.26 (prose).

Yaśodharā, (**1**) (= Pali Yaso°) n. of the wife of Śākyamuni as Bodhisattva (see also **Yaśovatī, Yaśavatī, Gopā**): Mvy 1070; Mv ii.25.12 (birth); 48.7 (meets the Bodhisattva); 69.2 ff. (rejects Devadatta); 72.18 ff. (coquets with the Bodhisattva); 73.5 ff. (requested in marriage; her father first refuses); 135.13 (her dream); previous incarnations, Mv i.128.13; ii.64.4; 67.11, 16 (other refs. in Mv, see Index); Divy 253.26; enlightenment predicted SP 269.6 ff.; mentioned also SP 2.10; (**2**) n. of a devakumārikā in the south: Mv iii.307.8 = LV 389.7.

Yaśomatī, n. of a daughter-in-law of the general Siṃha (5): Av i.8.9 ff. (mss. seemingly °mati, nom. °matiḥ). See also s.v. **Yaśamatī.**

Yaśomitra, n. of a merchant's son of Śrāvastī: Av ii.83.14 ff.

Yaśovatī, = **Yaśodharā** 1, Śākyamuni's wife: LV 95.9 (prose, no v.l.). Cf. also **Yaśavatī** (m.c.?).

yaṣṭa, ppp. and subst. (= Skt. iṣṭa; AMg. jaṭṭha, Pischel 565, cf. ger. jaṭṭhā = Skt. iṣṭvā, Ratnach.; Pali yiṭṭha, blend of Skt. and MIndic), as ppp., see § 34.13; as subst., *sacrifice*: tasmān na yaṣṭe na hute ramāmi Mv iii.445.5 (vs; same vs in Pali Vin. i.36.28, yiṭṭhe). See also next.—On LV 112.11 -mahāyajña-yaṣṭaḥ see § 13.5.

1 **yaṣṭi**, f. (= Skt. iṣṭi, cf. prec.), *sacrifice*: yaṣṭi-(stem in comp.) Mv iii.145.20 (prose; so both mss. intend, Senart em. iṣṭi-); yaṣṭyā RP 54.18 (vs).

2 **yaṣṭi**, f. (Skt. id.), in Mv used of a marvelous kind of *flagpole* which is said to have adorned the capital cities of five former Buddhas; that of the city of **Dīpavatī** was named **Valguyā**, of the other four **Valayā**, qq.v.; it is described in Mv i.196.15 ff. as citrā darśanīyā, of seven colors (gold, silver, and jewels), 12 yojanas high and four in diameter; so iii.229.12 ff.; 232.9 ff.; the cliché is abbreviated iii.234.11 f.; 238.14.

Yaṣṭīvana (once v.l. Yaṣṭi°; = Pali Laṭṭhivana), n.

of a grove outside of Rājagṛha, on the mountain **Antagiri, Antarāgiri**: Mv iii.60.1; 441.15; 442.4; 443.14.

yāgu (f. = Pali id., Skt. yavāgū; § 3.118; cf. also **yvāgū**), *gruel*: yāgu Mv i.298.10 (end of line of vs; acc. sg.; Senart em. yāguṃ).

yācanaka (Skt. and Pali only m., *beggar*), (**1**) m. *wooer* (of a girl, on behalf of another): Divy 168.1 sārthavāhaputrāś ca bhāryārthaṃ °kān preṣayanti; (**2**) nt., *begging*, in **na-yācanaka**, q.v.; (**3**) nt., *alms*, the result of begging: Mv iii.184.17 (prose) māṣa aparasya puruṣasya sakāśāto yācanakaṃ (mss. vāc°, but em. certain) labdhaṃ; Śikṣ 145.2 °ka-guruko, *eager for alms*.

yācanatā (Pkt. jāyaṇayā, Sheth; = Skt. yācanā), *request*: Bhad 12.

yācita, subst. (from Skt. id., ppp., *borrowed*), *a borrowed article*, as symbol of the undependable and impermanent: yācitopamam aśāśvataṃ RP 38.8 (vs); so in Pali yācitakūpama (yācitaka plus up°).

[**yāt**, Lefm. in LV 62.12 (prose), evidently supposed to mean *since* (Vedic yāt, assumed by Pischel 427 as base for Pkt. jā, which others derive from Skt. yāvat). But no ms. reads yāt; some yā, others omit the word (prob. with orig. text) or have other variants. Such a Pktism, and a dubious one at that, can hardly be assumed in the prose of LV.]

yātaka (?), **yātuka, yāttaka**, f. °**ikā**, and acc. to mss. **yāntaka** (q.v.), = **yattaka**, q.v.; cf. the like equivalents of **tattaka**; yāttika, f. pl., correl. with tāttaka, Samādh 19.16 (vs); read yāttika gaṅgavālikā Samādh p. 24 line 19 (vs; text yānti kagaṅga°); yātuka Śikṣ 328.11, 12; 339.10, 346.16 (vss); in Gv 487.17 (vs) yātakā (pl.) ... tātuko (sg.), but 18 (vs) yātukā ... tātukā (both pl.); but 2d ed. yātukā in 17; I have noted no other case of yātaka, but tātaka is recorded at least in the Kashgar rec. of SP.

yāthāva-tas, adv. (= Pali °to), *exactly*, with expressions of knowing: Dbh.g. 27(53).11 (viditvā); Śikṣ 260.2, 6 (vss; with forms of jñā).

yāthāsaṃstarika, m. = **yathā°**, q.v.: Mvy 1139; AsP 387.6.

yādṛśa, *of what sort!* (exclamatory; cf. similar use of **yāvat** 1): aho yādṛśā ṛṣikumārāḥ prāsādikā(ḥ) ... Mv i.354.17 (prose), *Oh how gracious ... the ṛṣi-youths are!*

yādṛśaka, adj. (= Pali yādisaka; = Skt. yādṛśa plus -ka svārthe; no mg. of suffix perceptible), *of which sort*: SP 30.16 and 125.13 (vss; in these might be m.c.); correl. with **tādṛśaka**, q.v.: °ko eṣo ... puṇyaṃ saṃgṛhṇāti tādṛśakaṃ yūyaṃ pi saṃgṛhṇatha Mv iii.287.9–10.

yāna, nt. (sometimes with m. endings), *vehicle*, as in Skt. and Pali; in Pali also used of the 8-fold Noble Path, as the *vehicle* to salvation; by extension of this use, in BHS applied to the two vehicles (**mahā°, hīna°**), or three, with pratyeka(buddha)-yāna between the two; that is, *religious methods*, within the fold of Buddhism. See SP 75.11, 76.2 ff. (parable of the burning house, the 3 yānas compared to *carts* of different sizes); for mahā-y° synonyms are buddha-y°, bodhisattva-y°, eka-y° (because, SP 40.13 f. says, this is really the *only vehicle*, na kiṃcic ... dvitīyaṃ vā tṛtīyaṃ vā yānaṃ saṃvidyate); eka-y° also Mvy 1255; **agra-yāna**, q.v., id.; triyānam ekayānaṃ ca Laṅk 155.14; the 3 yānas mentioned, but not named, Mv ii.362.8 f., where it is specifically stated that one can attain parinirvāṇa by any of them, and no preference is expressed; in SP 43.7 (in times of corruption, the Tathāgatas) upāyakauśalyena tad evaikaṃ buddhayānaṃ triyānanirdeśena nirdiśanti; synonym of hīna-y° is also **śrāvaka-y°**; see the various terms, also **nava-(acira-)-yāna-saṃprasthita.**

yānapātraka, adj. (cf. next; to Skt. °tra plus -ka), *sea-faring*: °keṇa vaṇijā MSV ii.64.11.

yānapātrika, m. (Skt. °tra, *ship*, plus -ika), *shipper, merchant by sea*: Divy 589.19.

[**yānayātrā**, allegedly *Seereise*, em. of pw 7.370 for saṃsiddhayānapātra āgataḥ Divy 503.18–19; but text is correct; *returned with a successful* (*uninjured*) *ship*.]

-yānāti, -yānati, after na, = Skt. jānāti, *knows*, with Pktic. loss of j after proclitic na, § 2.32 (= AMg. JM. ṇa-yāṇai, Pischel 170): na-yāneyā, 3 sg. opt., Mv ii.449.9 (prose; so mss.; Senart em. jā°).

-yānika, -yānīya, adj. (cf. Pali yānika, yāniya, not in this sense; from **yāna** plus -ika, -īya), *one who adheres to* (*one of the three Buddhist*) *yāna*; the two forms seem quite interchangeable, and both are common; note esp. śrāvakayānīyasya vā mahāyānikasya vā Bbh 180.24; śrāvaka-pratyekabuddha-yānīya (Kashgar rec. °yānika) SP 137.5, śrāvaka-yānīya 6 (no v.l. cited); 234.1 (Kashgar rec. °nika); °nika (no v.l.) 2; śrāvaka-, pratyekabuddha-, and bodhisattva-yānika SP 183.8 and Śikṣ 314.9, but same with yānīya SP 224.3–4; śrāvaka-pratyekabuddha-yānika Gv 141.5; Laṅk 171.18; mahāyānika-pratyekabuddhayānika-śrāvakayānikeṣu SP 132.1; śrāvaka-yānīya Śikṣ 7.8; KP 13.2; pratyekabuddhayānīya KP 13.3; mahāyānika Śikṣ 13.8; 43.2; bodhisattvayānīya SP 312.12; RP 34.1; °yānika LV 5.21; 439.2; Śikṣ 92.5.

-yānin (to **yāna** plus -in), *possessed of* (one of the Buddhist) *yāna*: agrayānī, n. sg., LV 438.8, said of the Buddha, *who knows the* **agrayāna**, q.v.

yānīkṛta, adj. (= Pali yānikata), *travelled, gone over*, in fig. sense = *mastered*: Mvy 2418 = Tib. lam du (or, bgrod par) byas pa, *made travelled*.

-yānīya, see **-yānika.**

[**yāntaka**, f. °**ikā**, prob. error for **yāttaka**, q.v.: yeṣu yāntak' (n. pl. m.) upapanna nāyakā te ... sarvi pūjitāḥ Gv 384.4 (vs); cf. also Samādh p. 24 line 19, s.v. **yāttaka**, where text yāntika, fem.]

yāpanaka (nt.? = Skt. yāpana; -ka svārthe), prob. either *curing* (sc. diseases), or *sustenance*, (furnishing) *livelihood* (to others): °ka-saṃpannāḥ, said of Bodhisattvas, Mv ii.289.9; both these mgs. recorded for Skt. yāpana; Senart *vitalité*.

yāpanīya, adj. or subst. nt. (to Skt. yāpana plus -īya; = Pali id., Vin. i.59.10, with khamanīya), *livable, comfortable*: kaccit te bhagavan kṣamaṇīyaṃ kaccid yāpanīyaṃ kaccid dhātavaḥ pratikurvanti SP 429.4, *I hope, Lord, things are tolerable and comfortable for you, and that your bodily elements are working all right*?; °yatara, compv., Divy 110.2, see s.v. **kṣemaṇīya.**

yāpayati, (**1**) trans., *nourishes, maintains*: ppp. (sa dārako ...) yāpitaḥ pālito vardhitaḥ Divy 499.1, *was maintained, protected, nourished*; (**2**) intrans. (as in Pali yāpeti; orig., no doubt, with ellipsis of kālaṃ, which with yāp° in Skt. = *spends time*), *lives, spends time*: (buddhā bhagavantas) tiṣṭhanti dhriyante yāpayanti SP 6.10; 42.2; 184.5; (same verbs, 3 sg.) Sukh 62.9; (buddhā bhagavanto) jīvanto dhriyanto yāpayanto Divy 93.6; 150.16; 196.18; (tathāgatam etarahi tiṣṭhantaṃ) yāpayantaṃ Mv ii.362.13; with instr., *lives* (*on* ...), (kola-vikṛtīhi, taṇḍula-vi°, tila-vi°) yāpenti Mv ii.125.9; 126.15; 128.2; phalāphalehi yāpayituṃ iii.159.13; pakvabhaikṣeṇa yāpayiṣyāmi Av i.209.2; instr. (not of food but) pāṃśukūlena cīvareṇa yāpayitum Bhīk 22b.3, *to live with a robe consisting of refuse-rags*; abs., (during a famine) na sukaraṃ ... yāpayitum Divy 471.4, *it was not easy to live*. See also **jāpayati.**

yāma, (**1**) m., regularly pl. (= Pali id.), n. of a class of kāmāvacara gods, see s.v. **deva**: Mv i.33.3; 40.15; 212.15; 229.15; 240.4; 333.6; ii.16.4; 163.11; 359.21; iii.319.13; LV 45.9; 46.20; 150.3; 219.8; 327.18; 364.15 (see s.v. **Suyāma**); 396.14; 401.9 f.; Mvy 3080; Dharmas 127; Divy 68.13; 140.12; 367.10; Av i.5.1; Suv 86.9; Mmk 19.12, etc.; as sg., one of this class, presumably =

Suyāma, q.v., yāmeṣu ... yāmasya devasya putro Divy 140.12; (2) nt., a high number: Gv 133.2 f. (cited Mvy as **poma**, q.v.).

[**Yāmagupta**, see **Vāma°**.]

yāmalokika (only Gv 75.23) or °**laukika**, adj. (cf. **yama°**; to Skt. yamaloka plus -ika), *of Yama's world*: with sattva, pl., *creatures of*..., Mv ii.301.7; Gv 75.23; with pretāḥ Śikṣ 130.17; after nārakaḥ tairyagyonikaḥ Bbh 295.23; °kāni duḥkhāni Gv 376.5.

yāmika, adj. (not in this mg. Skt. or Pali; same mg. in Pali yāmakālika), lit. *relating to a night-watch* (yāma); of food or medicine, substantially *to be applied at brief periods*: Mvy 9437; (of medicine) Bhīk 23b.1; MSV i.ii.16 ff. (i.iv.10 = yāme paribhoktavyaṃ).

? **yāmikā** = Tib. zug (mg.? *pain, torment? institution, founding?*), in uddāna verse MSV iii.72.6 yāmikāṃ (Index yamikā!) navikāṃ (*nine*) kṛtvā; uninterpretable to me.

Yāminī, n. of a yoginī: Dharmas 13.

Yāmyā, n. of a mātar (śakti of Yama): Māy 242.18.

yāvat, yāva, (1) (= Pali yāva, Vin. ii.196.5 yāva pāpo ayaṃ Devadatto; see also Childers s.v.), *how* (exclamatory)...! Skt. would use an interrog., not rel.; the origin of the idiom may be seen in such a sentence as: āścaryam adbhutam idaṃ paśyatha yāvat mahard-dhikaḥ śāstā Mv i.206.11 = ii.10.5 (vs), *see this wonder and marvel, the extent to which the Teacher is*...!; aho yāva kalyāṇā ... dhārmikā ca Mv i.350.7; so also i.301.16; 303.8 (acc. to Senart; I am not certain of this); 365.7; ii.10.7; iii.412.10; see **yādṛśa**, once used similarly; (2) *as far as*, indicating omission of part of a quoted or repeated passage, which is to be supplied (this usage seems not recorded): yāva Mv i.52.9; ii.428.14 (v.l. yāvad); yāvad Mv i.339.7, 12; Śikṣ 6.1 etc., very common here. Differs from **peyālaṃ** and equivalents in that yāva(t) is always followed by the concluding word(s) of the passage, while peyālaṃ need not be; (3) **yāvac ca** ... **yāvac ca** (spatially) *from* ... *to* (this usage not noted elsewhere); the nouns are in acc., nom., rarely abl.; after the second, the phrase may (but need not) be concluded by atrāntare, *in the space between* (Mv ii.150.2; MSV ii.74.15; Divy 574.28), atrāntarā (Av i.107.10–11), **antarāt** (q.v., Divy 386.9–10), tasminn antare (LV 273.9–10), etad antaram (Divy 250.7); the ca after the first yāvat is rarely omitted (so in the first ex.): yāvad rājakulaṃ yāvac ca udyānabhūmiṃ atrāntare Mv ii.150.2; so, yāva(c) ca ... yāva(c) ca, with accs., ii.150.7; 151.19; 153.14; 156.6; yāvac ca Mathurāṃ yāvac ca Pāṭaliputram Divy 386.9–10; veṇuvanaṃ ... rājagṛham Av i.107.10–11; with noms., MSV ii.74.15; yāva(c) ca bodhi (or bodhir) yāva(c) ca Vārāṇasī (v.l. °sīṃ, once °sīyo), *from the bodhi-tree to Benares*, Mv iii. 323.10, 14; 324.3; vihāro ... nagaram Divy 250.7; gṛhaṃ ... nadī, *from the house to the river*, Divy 574.28; with abl., yāvac ca nadyā Nairañjanāyā yāvac ca bodhimaṇḍādes (vv.ll. °maṇḍād, °maṇḍas) LV 273.9, *from the river N. to the bodhi-tree*. See also **yāvatā, yāvad etto** (s.v. **etto**), **yāvad eva**.

yāvataka, °**ttaka**, °**ntaka**, °**tika**, °**ttika**, adj., and °**kam**, adv. (based on Skt. yāvat; Pali yāvataka; AMg. jāvanta, jāvantia; the forms in °ntaka could be ka-extensions of an a-extension of Skt. yāvant; AMg. °ntia supports °ntika), *as much*, pl. *as many*; adv. *as long, as far*: yāvantakam (all mss., Senart °ttakam) avakāśam Mv i.158.11 (prose); yāvantakena mūlyena krītāni Mmk 695.10; pl. yāvattakā nāga-rājāno Mv i.208.6 (here v.l. yāvatākā) = ii.10.18 (prose); yāvatakā(ḥ) ii.301.10 and 12 (prose), v.l. both times °ttakā(ḥ); adv. yāvatakaṃ (v.l. °ttakaṃ) ... vasitukāmaḥ iii.255.3 (prose), *as long* (a time) *as you want to stay*; (mss.) yāvattakaṃ (v.l. yāvatakaṃ; in iii.437.17 mss. °tikaṃ, °ttikaṃ) yānasya bhūmi(ḥ) tāvattakaṃ (i.255.9 tāvad; in the others vv.ll. tāvantakam, tāvattikaṃ) yānena gatvā (or, yātvā) Mv i.255.9; iii.115.10; 437.17, *as far as there was room for the wagon, so far going by wagon*. See **tāvattakaṃ**.

yāvatā (= Pali id.; not in this mg. Skt.), *up to, as far as*, with abl.: yāvata (a m.c.) brahmalokāt SP 331.10 (vs); trisāhasrāya (oblique, presumably abl., from **trisāhasrā**) yāvatā Mv ii.302.20.

yāvatṛtīyaka, adj. (= Pali yāvatatiyaka), *requiring punishment only after the third offense*, said of the last four saṃghāvaśeṣa offenses: Prāt 487.8.

yāvattaka, °**ttika**, see **yāvataka**; **yāvattara**, see **yāvantara**.

yāvad-etto, see **etto**.

yāvad-eva, adv. (= Pali id., PTSD s.v. yāva), *merely, just simply*: LV 58.10 (the king gave all sorts of gifts) yāvad eva bodhisattvasya pūjākarmaṇe, *just simply to do honor to the Bodhisattva*; in Śikṣ repeatedly after **anyatra** (1, q.v.) following a negative expression: 127.18 na raktaḥ paribhuṅkte ... anyatra yāvad eva kāyasya sthitaye, *he does not eat greedily ... on the contrary, merely to keep the body alive* (cf. Pali yāvad-eva imassa kāyassa ṭhitiyā MN i.10.10 etc.); 252.9 anyatra yāvad eva sa puruṣo ... syāt, *on the contrary, this man would simply be* ...; 254.6, 19.

yāvaddaśottarapadasaṃdhi-lipi, a kind of writing: LV 126.8. See s.v. **dviruttarapadasaṃdhi-lipi**.

yāvadbhāvikatā, *actualization to the full extent, state of becoming actualized in full*, see s.v. **yathāvad-bhāvikatā**: Bbh 37.2; 215.2; 258.5, 9.

yāvadvidha, adj., *to the extent of which sort*: katamaṃ kevalaṃ evaṃ guṇasamanvāgataṃ bhaved, yāvadvidham anena satpuruṣeṇa nirdiṣṭaṃ LV 26.3.

[**Yāvana** (in Skt. recorded only as adj.) = Skt. yavana, a barbarian people (Greek, or western): śaka-yāvana-cīṇa-ramaṭha- etc. Mv i.171.14 (vs), so Senart, by em. But nearer to mss. would be śaka-yavana-cīṇa-ramaṭhā, which is also better metrically; read so.]

[**Yāvanī**, Senart's em. for yonārī, read instead **yonānī**, q.v.]

yāvantaka, see **yāvataka**.

yāvantara, instr. adv. °reṇa (yāva = yāvat plus antara, MIndic cpd.), (*as long as*) *until*; correl. tāvantaraṃ: yāvantareṇa paramārthavidū (°dur) bhaveyaṃ, tāvantaraṃ yadi avīcigato bhaveyaṃ Mv iii.252.6–7 (vs), *until I become a knower of the highest goal, if for so long I should dwell in Avīci*; similarly, written with tt for nt (as if compv. with intensive force, but prob. error for nt), yāvattareṇa pavararṣiṇa jñānalābhas, tāvattaraṃ dukham avīcikam utsahāmi Dbh.g. 12(348).17–18.

yāvasika (= Skt. yavasa plus -ika; = AMg. jāvasia, *grass-seller* acc. to Ratnach.), *grass-seller*: so Tib. (rtswa ḥtshoṅ) on Mvy 3775; said of **Svastika**, q.v. (usually rendered *grass-mower*): LV 286.4 ff., 287.1; Mv ii.131.12 f.; 264.6.

yuga, nt. (Pali id., I believe, in Sn 834 dhonena yugaṃ samāgamā, *you have come under subjugation by the Pure*, i. e. by Buddha; otherwise PTSD, Chalmers), *yoke*, in fig. sense of *subjugation*: yuga-m-antarasmi (for yugāntare) sthita māru LV 338.11 (vs), *Māra, abiding under* (lit. in the middle of) *the yoke* (being subjugated).

yugaḍa (= Skt. yugala, which is v.l. here), *pair, brace*: LV 337.9.

Yugaṃdhara (once °dhāraḥ?), (1) n. of an ancient king (identical with Skt. id.?): Mv ii.146.19; (2) n. of one of (usually 7 or with **Sumeru** 8) major mountains or mountain-ranges (cf. Skt. id., n. of a mountain; also Pali, and see Kirfel, Kosm. 186): Mv ii.300.18 (seven); Mvy 4145 (°dhāraḥ, but Mironov °dharaḥ, no v.l.); Dharmas 125 (eight); Divy 217.14, 16; Dbh 96.4; pl. Śikṣ 246.4.

yugotpāda, adj. (Bhvr.), *characterized by* (unique) *production in one aeon* (said of a Buddha since only one

B. appears in an aeon; Senart ii.544 fails to understand): °da-saṃpanna (of Buddha) Mv ii.259.12; 291.13; °daṃ (in series with śreṣṭhotpādaṃ ... praṇidhipūrvotpādaṃ, of the Bodhisattva) 264.13; °da-vikrāntaṃ 399.10.

[**Yudhiṣṭhira,** see **Āyudhiṣṭhira.**]

yūkila, adj., possibly *deficient*?: AsP 326.11–12 tasya ... avinivartanīyasya bodhisattvasya ... śarīre cīvaraparibhogo na yūkilo bhavati. Prob. corrupt.

yena, *where* (rare in Skt. Epic.: prādravad yena vai saraḥ Mbh. Cr. ed. 3.137.15; common in Pali, esp. yena ... tena): yena daridravīthī tatrāsmākam ... SP 103.8, *where the street of the poor is, there we* (shall easily get food); gaccha tvaṃ bhoḥ puruṣa yenākāṅkṣasi SP 105.5, *go where you like*; even used of time, so 'yaṃ kṣaṇo ... vadāmi yeneha ca bhūtaniścayam SP 45.14, *and this is the moment at which* (yena) *I shall declare the true nature of things*; esp. common in yena ... tena, *where ... there*, as yena bhagavāṃs tenopasaṃkrāmann LV 4.15; similarly LV 50.17; Mv i.35.1; 54.13; Laṅk 3.3; SP 75.3; Divy 64.16; Av i.8.7; RP 5.2; Bhīk 3b.5; common everywhere; yena yenaiva prakrāmet tena tenaiva ... añjalīkaraṇīyaḥ SP 227.9, *wherever he goes, he is to be revered*; yena bhagavāṃs tenāñjaliṃ praṇamya Mvy 6278; Kv 8.14; similarly Suv 9.8, etc. Without correlative yena: tena tenaiva, *in that same place*, SP 73.10. See also next three.

yena-kāma, adj. (?), and °kāmaṃ, adv. (= Pali, adv.; usually printed as two words in Pali and BHS; cf. prec. and next), *wherever one likes*: vrajāhī ... yenakāmaṃ LV 233.12 (vs); adj. (?), gacchati yenakāmo va Mv ii.406.9 (vs; or yena kāmo, *where desire was*?); adv., °maṃ prakraminsuḥ (°mensuḥ, °tsuḥ, etc.) Mv i.212.5, 13 = ii.16.2, 9; (vahati yena°) iii.120.6; Ud xxxi.5 (with yenecchakaṃ); yenakāmaṃ-gama, *going wherever one wishes*, Mv i.31.4 = 32.3; 344.2; °ma-tā, abstract, i.339.18; °gata, 338.19; 339.1 (v.l. °gama), 7 (by em., mss. °gama).

yen'icchakaṃ (= Pali id.), Mv ii.484.8, or **yenecchakaṃ,** Ud xxxi.5 (with yenakāmaṃ; = Pali Dhp 326, yen'icchakaṃ); KP 36.6, 8, adv., *wherever one likes, at will*. Cf. prec. two.

[**yenaiva ... yenaiva,** acc. to Senart, *either ... or*: Mv i.298.22 f. But the first yenaiva is Senart's own improbable em.; read with one ms. kāyena (instead of yenaiva) vācā ... (standard association of kāya and vāc!); in the next line yenaiva (Senart adds ca, but vā is more likely and better metrically) karmasabhāgatāye, yenaiva = *precisely because of which* (meritorious gifts just mentioned).]

yeva (= Pali id.) = Skt. eva (§ 4.66), only in Mv and not common; usually after vowels, sometimes after anusvāra (prob. by extension; Geiger 66.1); after vowels: dūrato yeva Mv i.35.4 (mss. yena, which might perhaps be kept, mg. *where*); 237.7; svaka-svakā yeva mātrīyo (so read, see **mātrī**) bhaginīyo i.351.3, 8; others, ii.54.6; iii.51.6, 11; 91.7 (sa yeva, prose, no v.l.); 216.12 (kuśalāni, em. for mss. kuśalena, yeva, v.l. evaṃ; not certain); 443.17; after anusvāra, etarahiṃ yeva i.286.20; ii.77.2; gantuṃ yevādhyavasito ii.105.11.

yoga, m. (Pali id., PTSD s.v. 3; not in Skt.), *bond, tie, attachment* (in Pali numbering 4, = the 4 **ogha** or **āśrava**): yogehi vuhyati bālo yogaṃ nudati paṇḍitaḥ, sarvayoga-asaṃyukto yogakṣemīti vuccati Mv iii.384.12–13 (vss); cf. Pali Dhp. comm. 3.233.21–22; similarly, yogaiḥ samuhyate bālo yogāṃ nudati paṇḍitaḥ, ... sarvayogāṃ pranudyeha sarvaduḥkhāt pramucyate Ud xxix.49(39). See foll. items, also **dharma-yoga, pūrva-yoga.**

yogakṣema (m.? so Pali yogakkhema; not in this sense in Skt.), *spiritual success, = enlightenment, peace,* or *salvation*, virtually same as nirvāṇa and may be bracketed with it: anuttare °me nirvāṇe pratiṣṭhāpita (various forms) Divy 98.2; 123.10; 498.13; anuttaraṃ °maṃ nirvāṇam anuprāpnuvato 303.2; saṃprāpnoti amṛtaṃ śāntaṃ °mam anuttaraṃ Mv iii.441.4 (vs); °masya prāptaye LV 261.5, said of the Bodhisattva's striving *for attainment of spiritual success* (*enlightenment, peace*). Cf. next.

yogakṣemin, adj. (= Pali yogakkhemin), *possessing* **yogakṣema,** in the sense stated s.v.: °mī kathaṃ bhoti Mv iii.384.10 (= Pali Dhp. comm. iii.233.19); on ib. 13 see s.v. **yoga**; this passage indicates interpretation of this cpd. as *at peace from the bonds of attachment* (cf., similarly, Dhp. comm. i.231.2 ff.) or the like, which of course cannot be the orig. mg.; neg. a-y°, ime sattvā ayogakṣemiṇo Dbh 28.13.

yogācāra, m., (**1**) (AMg. jogāyāra; rare in Skt., not in Pali, where yogāvacara seems to correspond), *practice of spiritual discipline*: Mvy 1638; Śikṣ 55.17 (°cāra-bhūmy-anukūlāni khādanīya-bhojanīyāni); (**2**) as Bhvr., = °**cārin,** *one who is characterized by* yogācāra (1): °cāro (or read °cārī?) bhikṣur KP 108.4; (**3**) n. of a samādhi: Kv 83.10; (**4**) pl., adherents of the Buddhist school of this name; social relations with them cause or constitute backsliding for Bodhisattvas: Mv i.120.9. Cf. foll. items.

Yogācārabhūmi (see **yogācāra** 1), n. of the work of which Bbh is a part: Wogihara, Preface to Bbh, page i.

yogācārin, (a monk) *who engages in* **yogācāra** (1): Śikṣ 55.13 ff.

Yogānugatā, n. of a kiṃnara maid: Kv 6.22.

yogodvahana, nt., *support, furnishing of livelihood*: aham asya sukhaṃ bhaktena °naṃ kariṣyāmi Divy 87.24, similarly 26; sā tava °naṃ kariṣyati 172.28; tvayā Panthakasya °naṃ kartavyam 486.18, similarly 531.21; others, 312.19; 498.27; MSV i.122.3.

?Yojananābha (mss. °tābha, °tāṃbha; Senart em. Yojanābha), n. of a former Buddha: Mv i.138.2.

Yojanasahasradarśin, n. of a former Buddha: Mv i.138.13.

yojanika, adj. (= Pali id.; in Skt. recorded only in comp. with prec. numeral, so also here, e. g. Śikṣ 247.14 dvi-yoj° etc.), *measuring a yojana*: °kāni (khaṇḍāni) Mv i.42.2 = 230.9 = 240.18 (prose; in the last mss. °naka); °kam (parikṣayaṃ, of water) Śikṣ 247.13.

?-yoṇikā, see **-poṇika.**

Yodhana, n. of a rākṣasa king: Mmk 18.1.

yonānī (= Skt. yavanānī, Pat. on Pāṇ. 4.1.49, Vārt. 3), *Greek writing*, in a list of scripts; § 22.10; so read for mss. yonārī (Senart yāvanī, more remote and less plausible): Mv i.135.5. Followed by **brahma-vāṇī,** for which LV 125.21 has brahmavali-lipi; and before this, Tib. on LV ya ba na-ḥi yi ge, *writing of the Yavanas* (not in Skt. text of LV). Cf. **śakānī.**

yoniśas (see also a-yo°; from Skt. yoni with suffix -śas; = Pali yoniso; often written °sas, °so; and m.c. °śa, °sa, °su), *fundamentally, thoroughly, from the ground up*: (**1**) as independent adv., LV 37.12 (vs) nirīkṣathā yoniso imā dharmā; 188.19 (vs) yoniśa cintayiṣye; 418.13 °so manasikurvato; Mv i.4.7 °śo (? by dubious em.) viśodhetvā; Divy 488.3 °śo bhāvayatā, instr. sg. pres. pple.; RP 12.9 °śaḥ prayujyate; 59.4 (vs) saṃcintya yathābhūta yoniśaḥ; KP 52.2 °śo dharmaprayuktena; Kv 61.11 yoniśaś (so read, text yo'niśañ!) ca manasikariṣyanti; 78.2 °śaś ca manasikurute; Dbh.g. 12(348).21 yonisu (or °śu; text yoniṣu by em.!) cintayāti; Bbh 395.10 °śo manasikurvan; Vaj 34.15 °śaś ca manasikariṣyanti; (**2**) in comp. (tho often printed as a separate word in edd., it sometimes cannot be construed as such, and in all the following is best taken as cpd.; in Pali also often cpd., especially with manasikāra, also with citta) yoniśo-manasikāra, *fundamental mental comprehension* or the like: SP 309.9; LV 348.1; 417.16; Mv iii.332.13, 16, 18; 333.2; 438.3; 440.10; Mvy 1641; 1680; Divy 611.15; Av ii.112.10; °manasīkāra KP 71.8; Sktized °manaskāra LV 161.6 (prose); yoniśodharmapratyavekṣaṇatāyai LV 33.3 (prose); dharmayoniśaḥpratyavekṣaṇatayā Dbh 13.23 (prose). Others, see **ayoniśas.**

yobhūyena = **yadbhūyasā**, q.v.

yosa (= Skt. yūṣa, Pali yūsa, AMg. jūsa), *juice, sap*: sāmagriye (mss. °yā) bhavati rasagandhayoso Mv i.298.1; note s, not ṣ. See **jomā.**

yauvanika, or °**aka** (Skt. Gr. and Lex.), = yauvana, *youth* (abstract), in cpd.: LV 322.3 (vs) paribhuñja suyauvanikaṃ (v.l. °akaṃ), if m., *excellent youth*, if f. (Bhvr.), *a woman in the bloom of youth*; in either case endearing dim., § 22.34.

yauvarājya(-bhūmi), apparently n. of the 9th Bhūmi: navamī yauvarājyāto (so mss., except one °yatā; read the latter? Senart em. °yato) Mv i.76.17.

yvāgū, °**gu**, f. (= BHS and Pali **yāgu**, Skt. yavāgū; see § 3.118; a MIndic form, not the Skt., was pronounced, i. e., always two syllables in vss), *gruel*: yvāgu-pāna LV 171.18 (vs; most mss. point to yv- but A yāgu-); yvāgūpānaṃ Mv i.47.16; 48.15; 335.9; 336.17; yvāgū ti i.28.10; 29.6; yvāgū (mss. pyagu) 111.10; yvāgūye ii.84.10 (gen.), yvāgu 13 and yvāgū 16 (n. sg.), see s.v. **kṣudra** 2.

R

Raktacandanagandha, n. of a former Buddha: Mv i.141.15.

Raktamāli, n. of a nāga king: Māy 247.15.

Raktākṣa, n. of a heretical ascetic: Divy 151.25 ff. (See also s.v. **Tārākṣa.**)

[**raktāṅgī** (Skt. Lex. *coral*), a kind of gem: Mv ii.318.7 (vs), by em., °giyo (acc. pl.; mss. lakkātviyāṃ, raktāsiyāṃ) ca rucakāṃ grahetvā. The em. is not plausible; some acc. pl. m. (or nt.) seems to have been intended.]

rakṣā, a set of magic formulas personified as a tutelary deity; five such: Dharmas 5 Pratisarā, Sāhasrapramardanī, Mārīcī, Mantrānusariṇī, Śītavatī; the same, often preceded by Mahā-, in various places in Sādh, see the names; pañcarakṣā- Sādh 413.6; mahā-pañcarakṣā 402.13; see also, especially, Sādh 401.10 ff.; 405.1 ff. Instead of Śītavatī occurs (**Mahā-**)**sitavatī.** See Lévi, JA 1915.1.19.

rakṣāvaraṇagupti, dvandva cpd., f. sg. (= Pali rakkhāvaraṇagutti), *guard, protection, and defense*: °guptaye (in i.208.6 text °guptīye, v.l. °guptaye) Mv i.208.6 = ii.10.18 (prose).

rakṣika, m. or °**kā** f.?, a small weight, orig. prob. a berry: °kā sarṣapāḥ kati Laṅk 31.7, *how many sarṣapa = 1 rakṣikā* (read °ko?); kati rakṣiko (read °kā, n. pl.?) bhaven māṣo 8. Acc. to Suzuki's Index, = Tib. ḥol si; cf. Jä. ḥol mo se, *an officinal plant*; ḥol ma sa, *a certain small berry*; *a small weight.*

Rakṣita, n. of a ṛṣi (previous incarnation of Śākyamuni): Mv i.283.18 ff.

Rakṣitikā, n. of a piśācī: Māy 239.22.

raghu (= Skt. laghu), (*light*,) *quick*(*ly*): raghuṃ Mv ii.5.9, mss.; Senart em. laghuṃ, with parallel i.201.14.

raṅga-stambhana, nt., Mvy 5928 = Tib. (ḥ)tshur, defined as *pigment, mineral paint* (in a list of coloring substances).

[**Raṅgā**, n. of a river: Divy 451.1 ff.; 456.19 ff. (here mss. **Naṅgā**, which read).]

-raṅgika (to Skt. raṅga), in **pañca-ra°**, adj., *of five colors*: °kena sūtreṇa Mmk 37.23; °kair eva cūrṇaiḥ 53.8.

Racanārciparvatapradīpa, n. of a Buddha: Gv 256.10 (vs).

? **Racitamāla** (em.; mss. Navita°), n. of a former Buddha: Mv i.141.16.

raccha, in Thomas ap. Hoernle MR 106.2 (prose), conjectured to be for Pali racchā = Skt. rathyā, *highway*: in cpd. (sphītāḥ karvaṭa-)raccha-grāma-nigamā(ḥ).

raja, m. (= next), *dyer*: raja-mahattarakasya Mv ii.467.11 (no v.l.); sarve rajā (v.l. rajakā) 15. In Skt., Pali, and Pkt. rajaka is applied to a *washerman*, who combined this trade with dyeing; in Mv seems clearly distinguished from (coḍaka-)dhovaka, *washerman* (of clothes), which occurs in the preceding section, 466.4 ff. Only dyeing, not washing, is mentioned in 467.10 ff.

rajaka, m. (= prec., q.v.; Skt. id., applied to a *washerman*), *dyer*: Mv ii.467.11 and 468.5 (both em. by Senart); 468.13 (no v.l.).

Rajakaratha, n. of a former Buddha: Mv i.139.5.

rajata, nt., some kind of disease, in lists of diseases: Mvy 9540; Bhīk 17a.1 (rajabhaṃ, doubtless corruption for °taṃ); MSV iv.68.17. Acc. to Tib. on Mvy = glog pa, which Jä. equates with lhog pa (which Tib. gives for **lohaliṅga**, q.v.), *a large ulcer, sore*, or *carbuncle*. Chin. a skin disease.

rajana (nt.? = Pali id.), (the process of) *dyeing*: vastram apagatakālakaṃ rajanopagataṃ (*gone to be dyed*) raṅgodake prakṣiptaṃ . . . Divy 617.8.

rajanīya, adj. (= Pali id.; gdve. to raj-? § 22.20), *exciting* (to the senses), *stimulating, charming, seductive*: °yās (ep. of kriyāḥ, *activities*) KP 105.8.

[**rajabha**, nt., see **rajata.**]

rajasvara, adj., prob. intended as equivalent of Skt. rajasvala, connected with rajas, and interpreted as *passionate, subject to passion*: kathaṃ bhoti rajasvaro Mv iii.384.3 (vs), and rājye bhoti rajasvaro id. 6. The vss = Pali Dhp. comm. iii.231.21 and 233.3, which read rajissaro (Bhvr., as if raja-īśvaraḥ, *having passion as his master*; our word may be a mangled form of this).

? **rajojala**, nt., Mv iii.412.17 (vs), perhaps intended as dvandva cpd., *dirt and water*; but perhaps same mg. as rajomalaṃ in same vs (this word occurs in Pali, e. g. Jāt. i.24.23, in different vs) Divy 339.24, *dirt and impurity*; in a list of characteristic practices of ascetics, which are said to be ineffective for purifying a man still subject to desire; the vs occurs in Pali Dhp. 141, where edd. and mss. vary, but Fausböll, 2d ed., rajovajall'; better with Mrs. Rhys Davids (Minor Anthologies, 1931) rajo va jall' (cf. jallaṃ Sn 249), two separate words (va prob. m.c. for vā); note that Pali repeatedly has rajo-jalla (PTSD); it is possible that Mv rajojalaṃ stands for (Pali) rajo-jallaṃ, m.c.; jalla is derived in PTSD from Skt. *jalya, deriv. of jala (questionable!). The line (in which Divy prefixes na, unmetrically, before rajomalaṃ) is completed by votkuṭukaprahāṇaṃ (Mv mss. vo utk°; Divy notk°; Dhp. ukkuṭikappadhānaṃ).

rajopaharaṇa (i. e. rajo'pa°), gender unknown, *sweeper*, either personal, or (= **rajoharaṇa**) *instrument of sweeping, broom*: °ṇa-samacittena, mānātimānavivarjanatayā Gv 463.26; cited Śikṣ 35.8, where ed. rajoharaṇa-, but v.l. rajopa°; note cites Tib. as phyag dar ba, translated *the act of sweeping*, but this interpretation is not clear, and Bendall and Rouse render *like a mere sweeper* (personal); Tib. Dictt. only phyag dar pa (Das, *sweeper, duster*; perh. intending *broom, mop*?).

rajomala, nt., see **rajojala.**

Rajovimalatejaḥśrī, n. of a lokadhātu: Gv 233.15.

(**rajoharaṇa**, in Jain Skt. used of the broom which Jain monks use; see s.v. **rajopaharaṇa.**)

rajyanā, f. (cf. Pali rajjana, nt.; to Skt. rajyati plus -anā), *lustful excitement*: no vā mahya khilaṃ na rajyanā na ca moho LV 325.15 (vs).

rañjāpanika, also °**panīya**, °**paṇīya**, nt. (to Pali rañjāpeti, caus. to rañjati, *dyes*, plus -ana, plus -ika; cf. **dhovāpanika**, shortly before in same passage), *fee for having clothes dyed, dyer's fee*: °nīyaṃ (no v.l.), n. sg., Mv ii.468.2; °nikaṃ (v.l. °ṇīyaṃ) 7; mss. confused, °nī or °nīkā, in 8; °nikaṃ, n. sg. (no v.l.) 10.

raṇa (**1**) m. (rarely nt.; = Pali id.), *passion, sin, depravity*, = **kleśa**, and regularly rendered in the same way (ñon moṅs pa) in Tib.; chiefly in Bhvr., **sa-raṇa**, and esp. the common **a-raṇa**; see next; cf. Renou, JA 1939.369 n. 1: Mvy 7528; jita-raṇaḥ Divy 396.24; raṇachedo Śikṣ 199.12; a so raṇaṃ Śikṣ 263.11, see s.v. **raṇati**; (**2**, in pw only Lex.,.but cited from lit. in Schmidt, Nachträge, *sound*: brāhmasvarādhika-raṇo Divy 401.3–4, Bhvr.; said of the Buddha).

raṇaṃjaha, also **raṇajaha** m.c., (**1**) adj. (cf. **raṇa**; = Pali raṇaṃjaha), primarily *abandoning impurities* (so Tib. usually, ñon moṅs (pa) spoṅ ba, or spaṅs ba), but in some contexts, both in Pali and BHS, apparently understood as *victorious in battle* (Skt. raṇa), so that Trenckner (see PTSD. s.v.) wished to em. to raṇaṃjaya; once, at least, Tib. (on LV 304.19) renders thus, gyul las rgyal; Speyer on Av ii.131 note 3 suggests *pacifier, peacemaker*, but this is clearly inappropriate to the contexts; nor is Seidenstücker's *dem Kampfgewühl entronnen* (see PTSD s.v.) any more plausible; the orig. and primary mg. seems certain in LV 358.2 (vs); 361.20 (vs, here raṇajaha, m.c.); 423.22; context tempts to assuming contamination with raṇa, *battle* (but it is hard for me to guess how, in that case, -jaha was interpreted) in LV 304.19 (vs; on Tib. see above) śūru (nom.) balavāṃś ca raṇaṃjahaś ca; LV 437.21 (vs) śūro mahā-raṇaṃjahaḥ; and possibly LV 116.12 (vs) jātī-jarā-maraṇa-kleśa-raṇaṃjahasya; in all these ep. of Buddha, or the Bodhisattva; (**2**) n. of a former Buddha: Sukh 5.18; (**3**) n. of a samādhi: Mvy 535 (Tib. as usual); ŚsP 1417.10.

raṇati (unrecorded in this mg.), acc. to Bendall and Rouse *makes contact with* (loc.), perhaps rather *delights in* (so Vedic), or better yet *is attached to, is* (wrongly) *involved with, contaminated by* (in the sense of the Pali-BHS noun **raṇa**, q.v.): Śikṣ 263.9–11 cakṣū rūpeṣu na raṇati, śrotraṃ śabdeṣu (so punctuate), yāvan mano dharmeṣu na raṇati ... saṃsargābhāvāt, na hi cakṣū rūpeṇa saṃsṛjyate ... yan na saṃsṛjyate, tan na raṇati; advitīyasya ... dharmasya raṇaṃ nāsti. Note the noun raṇaṃ in the last sentence: ... *for the eye does not come in contact with form ... what does not come in contact is not contaminated; of an isolated state-of-being there is no contamination*.

raṇadhara, m., some member of a ship's crew, acc. to Tib. and Chin. *oarsman*: Mvy 3854 = Tib. ru skya ḥdzin pa. In a list of members of a ship's crew; see s.v. **pauruṣeya** 2. The word prob. occurred in the original form of Av i.200.5; ii.61.9, but has been lost by textual corruption.

raṇḍā, n. of a class of evil supernatural beings: sarve raṇḍāḥ sarve ḍākinyaḥ (also fem.!) ... (see s.v. **kaśmala**) Mmk 538.26; raṇḍā (sc. -vaśīkaraṇe) māṣahomena (sc. juhuyāt) 684.7; raṇḍāṃ 287.21, raṇḍā-vaśīkaraṇe 707.18, see s.v. **jambūlikā**.

ratana, MIndic (in most texts usually m.c.) for ratna, *jewel*, see § 3.99 for examples; also in many cpds., see cpds. with **ratna-**.

ratanāmaka, f. °ikā (hyper-Skt. for **rat(a)nāmaya**, Pkt. rayaṇā°, contaminated with MIndic offshoots in -ya of Skt. forms in -ka; § 2.33; cf. AMg., acc. to Sheth, and JM. rayaṇāmaya, as well as rayaṇamaya), *made of jewels*: jālikam (for °kām) ... ratanāmikāṃ LV 194.20 (vs), rendered by Tib. rin po che las byas paḥi dra ba, *net made from jewels*, exactly rendering Skt. ratna-maya.

Ratanendra, n. of (presumably a Buddha?) an instructor of the Bodhisattva in a former birth: Mv i.54.7.

Rati (= Pali id.), n. of a daughter of Māra: Mv iii.286.6 (Ratī, n. sg.); LV 378.4 (Ratiś ca).

Ratika, n. of a yakṣa: Māy 53.

ratikara, m., (**1**) *lamp* (? possibly a corruption for some other word of that mg.; this mg. is proved by Burnouf, Introd. 223 infra, where in a transl. of a verse recension of Kv it is a *lamp* which gives the merchant Siṃhala(rāja) the information which in the prose Kv he receives from a ratikara; no plausible em. occurs to me): Kv 54.7; 55.7, 9, 12 (warns the merchant that he is in danger of being devoured by an ogress); (**2**) m., n. of a samādhi: Mvy 545; ŚsP 1418.11. Cf. **ratiṃkara.**

Ratikarā, n. of an apsaras: Kv 3.14.

ratiṃkara, (**1**) adj. (= Skt. ratikara; perh. m.c.), *causing joy*: (kāyāṃ ...) °karaṃ devasahasrakoṭīnām Suv 153.5 (vs); (**2**) subst., n. of a supernatural ray of light coming from Bodhisattvas: Śikṣ 335.3 (vs).

Raticaraṇasamantasvara, n. of a gandharva: Mvy 3385.

Ratijaha, m., Mvy 567, or **Ratiṃjaha** (same list) ŚsP 1420.14, n. of a samādhi.

Ratipradhāna, n. of a city (built for Puṇyaraśmi): RP 39.16 (see Corrigenda); 54.2; 56.9.

Ratiprapūrṇa (so both edd. and Burnouf; v.l. and Kern's transl. °pratipūrṇa; v.l. also °paripūrṇa), n. of the kalpa of the future Buddha Tamālapattracandanagandha: SP 153.10.

Ratiprabhā, n. of a goddess: Gv 413.8.

Ratirāgā, n. of a goddess: Mvy 4290.

ratilambhā, n. of a medicinal or magic herb: Gv 497.19.

Ratilola, n. of a son of Māra, unfavorable to the Bodhisattva: LV 313.6.

Rativyūhā, n. of capital city (rājadhānī): Gv 352.10.

ratna (or MIndic **ratana**), nt. (m. forms, see § 6.10), *jewel, gem*, as in Skt.; (**1**) three (Buddha, dharma, saṃgha, as in Pali): Dharmas 1, etc.; see **triratna, ratna-traya**; (**2**) seven precious substances, or their respective colors, suvarṇa, rūpya, muktā, vaiḍūrya, sphaṭika (or sphā°), **musāragalva** (or variants, see s.v.), **lohitikā**: Mv i.49.10–11; 63.1; 194.5, 19; 195.9; 249.6; iii.226.10; 227.6; 323.16; a different list of seven, muktāmaṇi, vaiḍūrya, śaṅkhaśilā, pravāla, sphaṭika, musāragalva, lohitikā, Mv ii.472.1; the usual list in other texts is nearly like Mv i.49.10 etc., but omits muktā, and for Nos. 5–7 (6 and 7 of Mv) has **lohitamukti**, aśmagarbha, **musāragalva**: SP 151.1; 153.3; Divy 297.23 ff.; Gv 52.15; 161.16; in SP 239.7 sphaṭika is omitted, karketana added at the end, and the order is abnormal; in Pali no standard list of 7 ratana seems recorded except in the lex. Abhidh.p., which is cited in Childers and PTSD as suvaṇṇa, rajata, muttā, maṇi, veḷuriya, vajira, pavaḷa (Miln. 267.23 ff., cited by PTSD, is not apposite, since this list far exceeds seven in number); yet seven ratnanāni (unspecified) are several times mentioned in Pali (PTSD); (**3**) fig., the seven '*jewels*' of a cakravartin, viz. cakra, hastin, aśva, maṇi, strī, gṛhapati, **pariṇāyaka** (same list in Pali forms also); see Senart, Légende du Buddha (1st ed.), 20 ff.: LV 14.5 and ff., full descriptions of each ratna; also MSV i.31.16 ff., in great detail; lists, Mvy 3621–8; Dharmas 85 (here, aberrantly, khaḍga instead of gṛhapati); Mv i.49.3; 108.5 ff. (account of how they are acquired, by previous deeds of merit); 193.16; ii.158.16; iii.107.5; Divy 548.24 ff.; (**4**) m., n. of a former Buddha: Mv i.62.16 (prose); later called **Rat(a)navant**, q.v.

Ratnaka, n. of an **ārāmika** (2, q.v.): Divy 157.27; prob. the same as **Rambhaka** (q.v.), one or the other being a corruption.

Ratnakara, n. of a Bodhisattva: ŚsP 6.5.

Ratnakaraṇḍaka, nt., n. of a work: Mvy 1408; °**ka-sūtra,** id., Śikṣ 356.2. See next but one.

Ratnakaraṇḍaketu, n. of a former Buddha: Mv i.140.4.

Ratnakaraṇḍa-sūtra = prec. but one: Śikṣ 6.11.

Ratnakirīṭin, n. of a kiṃnara king: KV 3.1.

Ratnakīrti, n. of a former Buddha: LV 5.11.

Ratnakumāra, n. of a Bodhisattva: Samādh p. 36, line 2.

Ratnakuśa, n. of a brother of Kuśa: Mv ii.433.17.

Ratnakusumaguṇasāgaravaiḍūryakanakagirisuvarṇakāñcanaprabhāsaśrī, n. of a mythical Tathāgata: Suv 113.14; 116.5; 131.10.

Ratnakusumapradīpā, n. of a capital city (rājadhānī): Gv 268.22.

Ratnakusumaprabha, n. of a Buddha: Gv 419.25.

Ratnakusumasaṃpuṣpitagātra, n. of a Buddha in the zenith: Sukh 98.17.

Ratnakūṭa, (**1**) n. of a Bodhisattva: Mvy 659; (**2**) m., n. of a work (includes, sometimes = **Kāśyapaparivarta**; also **Mahā-ratnakūṭa,** qq.v.): Mvy 1364 °ṭaḥ; KP 160.1 °ṭo; Śikṣ 52.12; 53.17; 54.11; 55.3; 148.8; 196.11; 233.15; also °kūṭa-sūtra, Śikṣ 146.4. See Stael-Holstein, KP, p. XV f.

Ratnaketu, (**1**) n. of several Buddhas: Suv 2.4; 8.1; 120.2, 6 (here presides over the south); Sukh 6.14 (here a former Buddha); repeatedly in Mmk, 42.21; 129.9; 130.2 f.; 132.25; 139.2 (lives in **Ratnāvatī,** q.v.); 289.12; 305.14; 426.7; (Ratana°, in a vs) Gv 256.7 (a former Buddha); (**2**) n. of one or more Bodhisattvas: Mvy 654; AsP 449.20; Samādh p. 36 line 1; (**3**) n. of a work: Mvy 1349; the ed. note conjectures relation to a Chin. text the title of which is rendered Mahāsaṃnipāta-ratnaketudhāraṇī; this is possibly confirmed by Mmk 109.28 where there is reference to a **Ratnaketu-dhāraṇī** (misprinted °dhāriṇī).

Ratnaketurāja, n. of 2000 future Buddhas (which 2000 disciples, it is predicted, will become): SP 221.8; the name is analyzed as ratnasya ketu in the verse SP 222.5.

Ratnakeśa, n. of a gandharva: Suv 162.3.

Ratnakoṭi, n. of a samādhi: Mvy 564; ŚsP 1420.7.

Rat(a)nakholaka, n. of a city ('jewel-helmet'): Mv i.186.17.

Ratnagarbha, n. of one or more Bodhisattvas: Mvy 665; Gv 2.24; Dbh. 2.5 (in all these in lists of B.'s, among other names ending in -garbha); LV 294.20 (here one living in the buddhakṣetra of **Samantadarśin** in the nadir).

Rat(a)nagātraś(i)rī, n. of a Buddha: Gv 285.12 (vs).

Ratnacaṅkrama, n. of a former Buddha: Mv i.140.14.

Ratnacandra, (**1**) n. of a Buddha: Śikṣ 169.9; of a former Buddha, Sukh 6.8; (**2**) n. of a Bodhisattva: SP 3.6.

Ratnacandradhvaja, n. of a Tathāgata: Gv 422.17.

Ratnacandrapradīpaprabhā, n. of a world (cāturdvīpikā) in the lokadhātu **Ratnaśrīsaṃbhava**: Gv 232.7.

Ratnacandraprabha, n. of a Buddha: Śikṣ 169.9.

Ratnacūḍa, Ratana°, (**1**) n. of a Buddha: Mv i.118.16 and 119.10 (vss, Ratana-, could be m.c.; but in 119.10 mss. Ratna°, unmetr.); referred to 119.9 as taṃ ratanajinaṃ (vs, but not m.c.); (**2**) n. of one or two previous incarnations of Śākyamuni: Ratna° LV 171.2 (vs); Ratana° RP 23.10 (vs, meter obscure); (**3**) n. of a Bodhisattva: Mvy 658; (**4**) n. of a righteous merchant (dharmaśreṣṭhin): Gv 147.12 ff. (Ratna°, prose); (**5**) = next but one, q.v.

Ratnacūḍa-paripṛcchā, n. of a work: Mvy 1363 (same as next?).

Ratnacūḍa-sūtra, n. of a work: Śikṣ 117.12; 120.7; 232.6; 235.1; 272.9; 317.13; called **Ratnacūḍa,** simply, 229.13; 236.13; cf. prec.

Ratnachattrakūṭasaṃdarśana, n. of a Bodhisattva: LV 291.6.

Ratnachattrābhyudgatāvabhāsa, n. of a Tathāgata: LV 294.9.

Rat(a)najinaṃ Mv i.119.9, refers to **Ratnacūḍa** (1) q.v.

Ratnaḍākinī, n. of a yoginī: Sādh 460.2.

Ratnatejas, (**1**) n. of a former Buddha: LV 5.12, before Brahmatejas, indicated as present originally by Tib. rin chen gzi brjid, altho not in Lefm. nor reported in any Skt. ms.; (**2**) n. of a Bodhisattva: Gv 2.20.

Ratnatejobhyudgatarāja, n. of a Tathāgata: SP 473.1.

ratna-traya (= Pali ratana°; cf. **ratna 1, triratna**), *the 'three jewels'* (Buddha, dharma, saṃgha): namo °yāya Divy 481.25.

Ratnadaṇḍa, n. of a cakravartin: Mv i.153.16.

Ratnadatta, n. of a Bodhisattva: ŚsP 6.7.

Rat(a)nadānaś(i)ri, n. of a Buddha: Gv 285.17 (vs; meter obscure).

Ratnadāma, n. of a former Buddha: Mv i.137.1.

Ratnadhvaja, n. of one, or two, Bodhisattvas: Mvy 662; Gv 2.18.

Rat(a)nadhvajāgramati, n. of a lokadhātu: Gv 258.13 (vs).

Ratnanetra, (**1**) n. of a Buddha: (Ratana°, in vs, may be m.c.) Gv 257.11; (**2**) n. of a Bodhisattva: Gv 3.3.

Ratnanetrā, n. of a 'city-goddess' (nagaradevatā): Gv 430.1 ff., cited in abbreviated form Śikṣ 122.14.

Ratnapadmapraphullitagātra, n. of a Tathāgata: Gv 421.26.

ratnapadmavikrāmin, (**1**) adj., *walking on jewel-lotuses,* i. e., with such lotuses appearing under their every step (so Chin. versions of SP; see Burnouf's note, Lotus, p. 364): SP 66.6 (prose), of Bodhisattvas in a future buddhakṣetra; (**2**) n. of a Buddha: Śikṣ 169.15.

Ratnapadmasupratiṣṭhitaśailendrarāja, n. of a Tathāgata: Śikṣ 169.15.

Ratnapadmābha, n. of a Tathāgata: Gv 82.7.

Ratnapadmāvabhāsagarbha, n. of a Tathāgata: Gv 311.2.

Rat(a)naparvata, n. of a Buddha: Mv i.113.10 (vs, but not m.c.).

Ratnapāṇi, n. of a Bodhisattva: Mvy 655; SP 3.5; Mmk 425.19; Kv 1.12; 17.1, etc. (plays prominent rôle in Kv).

Ratnapīṭhā, n. of a 'gandharva maid': Kv 5.14.

Ratnapuṣpa, n. of a former Buddha: Mv i.141.11.

Ratnaprabha, (**1**) (Ratana°) n. of a Buddha: Gv 284.23 (vs, may be m.c.); (**2**) n. of a Bodhisattva: SP 3.6; Gv 3.15; (**3**) n. of a deity (devaputra): SP 4.4.

Ratnaprabhā, (**1**) n. of a śreṣṭhin's daughter: Gv 332.23; (**2**) n. of a lokadhātu: Gv 352.3.

Ratnaprabhāsa, nt., n. of Arciṣmant's capital city: RP 37.2.

Ratnabuddhi, n. of a Bodhisattva: Gv 4.12.

Ratnamakuṭa, n. of a former Buddha: Mv i.137.2 (cf. °**mukuṭa**).

Ratnamati, (**1**) n. of one of the sons of the Buddha **Candrasūryapradīpa**: SP 19.3; (**2**) n. of a future Buddha (future birth of **Yaśomatī**): Av i.12.18.

Ratnamālā, n. of a 'gandharva maid': Kv 4.19.

Ratnamukuṭa (cf. °**makuṭa**), n. of a Bodhisattva: Mvy 657.

Rat(a)namudra, v.l. Rat(a)nasamudra, n. of a former Buddha: Mv i.138.10.

Ratnamudrā, n. of a samādhi: Mvy 507; ŚsP 483.12; 1267.10; 1412.8; 1415.4.

Ratnamudrāhasta, n. of a Bodhisattva: Mvy 656; ŚsP 7.5.

Ratnamegha, m., n. of a work: Mvy 1337; Śikṣ 7.13 etc. (common); °**gha-sūtra,** nt., Śikṣ 51.21; 135.12.

Rat(a)nameru, n. of a Buddha: Gv 256.26 (vs).

Ratnayaṣṭi, n. of a Tathāgata: LV 293.10.

Ratnayūpa (? Senart's em. for °yūṣa, °yūtha), n. of a former Buddha: Mv i.140.2.

Ratnaraśmipradīpadhvajarāja, n. of a Tathāgata: Gv 296.25.

Rat(a)narājaś(i)ri (nom. °riḥ), n. of a Buddha: Gv 285.4 (vs).

Rat(a)narāśi, n. of a Buddha: Gv 259.1 (vs). See also next.

Ratnarāśi-sūtra (in 128.3 Ratnarāśau, loc., without sūtra), n. of a work: Śikṣ 55.7; 128.3; 136.8; 137.17; 200.12; 312.3. A fragment of this work in Hoernle, MR 116 ff.

Ratnaruciraśrīrāja, n. of a Tathāgata: Gv 311.21.

Ratnarudhiraketu, n. of a former Buddha: Mv i.139.12.

Ratnalakṣaṇavibhūṣitameru, n. of a Tathāgata: Gv 309.22.

Ratnavajrī, n. of a goddess: Sādh 160.5.

Rat(a)navant, n. of a Buddha, also called **Ratna**, q.v., in the same passage: °vato Mv i.62.19; 63.9 (both prose).

Ratnavara, n. of a Bodhisattva: Gv 442.21.

Ratnavastrāvabhāsadhvajā, n. of a lokadhātu: Gv 11.4 (2d ed. line 3).

Ratnaviśuddhā, n. of a lokadhātu: SP 240.13.

ratnavṛkṣa (m.; Skt. Lex. id.), a kind of (heavenly, or supernatural) tree: LV 11.2; Kv 17.14.

Ratnavyūha, (**1**) nt., n. of a city in the south: Gv 201.10; (**2**) m. (? or nt.), n. of a bodhisattva-**paribhoga** (see the latter): LV 60.18; 61.12 etc.; 63.2; 73.3. Tib. renders literally, rin po che bkod pa.

Ratnavyūhā, n. of a lokadhātu in the south: LV 291.5.

ratna-vyomaka, see **vyomaka**.

Ratnaśayana, n. of a former Buddha: Mv i.140.8.

Ratnaśikhara, n. of a Bodhisattva: Mvy 661.

Ratnaśikharārciḥparvatapradīpa, n. of a Tathāgata: Gv 282.13.

Ratnaśikhin, n. of a former Buddha: Mvy 98; LV 171.19; Divy 62.17 ff.; Suv 119.10; 146.8; 152.10; 174.3, 7; 192.2 ff.; Mmk 63.17; 68.26 (n. sg. °khiḥ, prose); 499.20 (vs; °śikhe gurau, app. meant for loc. sg.!; corrupt?).

ratnaśilā, said to mean *mosaic*, acc. to Schiefner (Tib.): Divy 211.4, 6 (tena °lā ānītā).

Rat(a)naśṛṅga, n. of two former Buddhas in the same list (both prose): Mv i.137.5 (Ratana°); 138.11 (Ratna°).

Ratnaśaila, n. of a former Buddha: Av i.91.13 ff.

Ratnaśrī, (**1**) n. of one, or two, Buddhas: Śikṣ 169.8; Sukh 6.15; (**2**) n. of a Bodhisattva: Gv 4.4.

Ratnaśrīpradīpaguṇaketu, n. of a Tathāgata: Gv 259.19 (vs; °śirī°); 261.3 (prose).

Ratnaśrīśikharameghapradīpa, n. of a Tathāgata: Gv 311.3.

Ratnaśrīsaṃbhava, n. of a lokadhātu: Gv 232.6.

Ratnaśrīhaṃsacintā, n. of a lokadhātu: Gv 82.11.

Ratnasamudgata, n. of a Bodhisattva-samādhi: Mvy 737.

Ratnasaṃbhava, (**1**) n. of a Tathāgata (3d in list of five 'transcendent' Buddhas; in Sādh also called Ratneśa in vss): Dharmas 3; Mvy 84; Sādh 16.9 etc.; (**2**) n. of a Bodhisattva, in **Ratnasaṃbhavā**: LV 293.10; (**3**) nt., n. of a buddhakṣetra of the future Buddha Śaśiketu: SP 148.10.

Ratnasaṃbhavā, n. of a lokadhātu in the southwest: LV 293.9. Cf. prec., 2.

ratna-saṃmata, nt. (= Pali ratana°, Vin. iv.161.26; 162.19; 163.13, always ratanaṃ vā ratana-sammataṃ vā; comm. 163.21 f. = yaṃ manussānaṃ upabhogaparibhogaṃ, etaṃ °mataṃ nāma), *something considered to have value*: anirhṛteṣu ratneṣu °mateṣu vā Divy 543.21, glossed in 544.1–2 °matam ucyate sarvaṃ saṃgrāmāvacaraśastraṃ sarvaṃ ca gandharvāvacaraṃ bhāṇḍam.

Ratnasālavyūhameghapradīpa, m., or °**pā**, n. of a capital city (rājadhānī): Gv 325.6, here °po, n. sg. (as if masc.); but in 8 °pāyāṃ (loc. sg. fem.); 326.1 stem in comp., °pradīpa-rājadhānī.

Ratnasiṃhāvabhāsajvalā, n. of a lokadhātu in the nadir: Gv 81.22.

Ratnahasta (v.l. Ratnadeva), n. of a former Buddha: Mv i.141.13.

Ratnākara, (**1**) n. of (prob.) two Buddhas, both in the eastern direction: Sukh 70.3; ŚsP 29.6 ff.; (**2**) n. of a Bodhisattva: Mvy 660; (**3**) n. of a **satpuruṣa**, q.v.: SP 3.11; (**4**) n. of a Bodhisattva-samādhi: Mvy 741; (**5**) n. of a mountain: Māy 253.32.

Ratnākaragupta, n. of an author: Sādh 17.20 etc.

Ratnākaraśānti, n. of an author: Sādh 236.15.

Rat(a)nāgni, n. of a former Buddha: Mv iii.239.9.

Ratnāgraprabhateja, n. of a Tathāgata: °jo, n. sg., Gv 422.19 (prose).

? **Ratnāṅkarā**, n. of a 'gandharva maid': Kv 5.8.

Ratnābha, n. of a Tathāgata: Gv 82.7.

Ratnābhibhāsa, n. of a former Buddha: Sukh 6.9.

rat(a)nāmaya, adj. (Pkt. rayaṇāmaya; = Skt. ratna°; cf. **ratanāmaka**), *made of jewels*: (in prose) Mv i.31.5; 32.3, 5, 10; ii.109.3 (twice), 5; others in vss, see § 8.16.

Ratnārciḥparvata, n. of a Bodhisattva: Gv 442.1.

Ratnārciḥparvataśrīteja, n. of a Tathāgata: °jo, n. sg., Gv 422.15 (prose).

Ratnārci-netraprabha, n. of a king: Gv 381.2 (prose).

Ratnārci-parvataś(i)rī, n. of a Buddha: Gv 284.19 (vs).

Ratnārcis, n. of one or several Tathāgatas: LV 291.6; ŚsP 34.12; Śikṣ 169.7.

Ratnāvatī, n. of two lokadhātus: Mmk 139.1 (the Buddha Ratnaketu dwells here); ŚsP 29.6 (in the east; the Buddha Ratnākara dwells here).

Ratnāvabhāsa, (**1**) n. of the kalpa of the future Buddha Śaśiketu: SP 148.10 (no v.l. in texts; Kern's transl. Ratnaprabhāsa, noting v.l. °āva°); (**2**) n. of the kalpa of the future Buddha Dharmaprabhāsa: SP 205.8 (v.l. Ratnaprabhāsa).

-ratnika (ifc.) = Skt. *ratnin, *having jewels*, in sarvaratnikāḥ, *having all jewels*: LV 280.13 (vs), no v.l. (not fem.; with kṣetrāḥ).

Ratnendra, n. pr., see **Ratanendra**.

Ratneśa = **Ratnasaṃbhava** (1): Sādh 164.9 (vs; in list of 'transcendent' Buddhas, replacing Ratnasaṃ°), et alibi.

Ratnoccaya, n. of a preacher (dharmabhāṇaka): Suv 147.4 ff.; Ratano° (m.c.) Suv 149.11 and elsewhere. He became the Buddha Akṣobhya, 152.15–16.

Ratnottama, (**1**) n. of a future Buddha: Av i.27.18; (**2**) n. of a former Buddha: Kv 69.23; (**3**) n. of a Bodhisattva: ŚsP 47.19.

Ratnottamā, n. of a goddess: Mvy 4293.

Ratnotpalaśrī, n. of a Buddha in the zenith: Sukh 98.18.

Ratnolkā, (**1**) n. of a goddess: Mvy 4287; (**2**) n. of a work: Mvy 1375; in Śikṣ (2.15 etc.) called °kā-dhāraṇī.

Ratyudgata, n. of a nāga king: Māy 247.36.

rathaka, m. and nt. (Skt. ratha, m., plus -ka dim.), *toy cart*: m., Jm 63.10; Bbh 281.13 f., 23; SP 75.5, 9 (prose), but nt. (go-rathakāni, aja-r°, mṛga-r°) SP 74.4 f.; 75.4 (also all prose). Acc. to PTSD, nt. in Pali, but I think the form rathakaṃ in the recorded passages may be understood as acc. m. In Buddhacarita iii.62 mss. rathaṃ, nom. sg., Johnston em. rathaḥ.

[**Rathasyā** Māy 253.10, read Rathasthā, n. of a river (Epic Skt.).]

Rathābhirūḍhā, n. of a nāga maid: Kv 4.6.

Ramaṭha (n. of a people, Skt.; listed among dasyu peoples Mv i.171.14), sc. lipi, the script of the R. people: Mv i.135.7.

Ramaṇa, nt., = next: Divy 599.24 (prose).

Ramaṇaka, nt., n. of a city (= prec.): Divy 599.5; Av i.200.8 (both prose); 203.1, 4 (vs).

ramaṇīyaka, adj. (= **rām°**, q.v., and Skt. ramaṇīya), *lovely, charming*: SP 74.3 (prose), and Kashgar rec. for ed. °ṇīya 75.4 (prose); Divy 375.4 and 376.24 (prose); Ud xxix.28 (18) (= Pali Dhp. 98, rāmaṇeyyaka); subst., *lovely thing*, mahā-°ka-samanvāgatāni SP 79.12.

ramita (nt.? = AMg. ramia; in Skt. and Pali only as ppp. and adj.), *sport, amusement*: ramitasya kālo Mv iii.58.8, *time for*...; no nṛtte na ca gāyite na ramite bhūyo manaḥ kasyacit LV 194.4 (vs); hāsya-lāsya-krīḍita-ramita-sukhilamadhuropacāraṃ 212.5 (prose); kāścit pūrvahasita-ramita-krīḍitā anyonyaṃ smārayanti 321.6 (prose).

[**ramin**, see **sadāramin**.]

Rambhaka (see **Ratnaka**), n. of an **ārāmika**: Divy 160.5.

rava (**1**) nt. (Skt. only m.), *sound*: ravaṃ, n. sg., LV 299.11 (vs); [(**2**) **Rava**, v.l. Rāva, n. of an ancient king, acc. to Mv i.348.8; prob. a corruption for **Vara-(kalyāṇa)**, but also confused with **Roca**, q.v., in one ms.]

? **ravaṇa**, nt. or adj. (JM. id., subst. nt.; Skt. Gr., Lex., and artificial lit., as adj. or n. ag., *crying*), (**1**) *cry*, perh. to be read in Mv i.154.9 (vs), Senart saśoka-ravitāni (... bāṣpāṇi), mss. corruptly (one syllable short) saśokabalāni or -vanāni, read -ravaṇāni?; (**2**) *crying, resonant*, in LV 162.9 (vs) Lefm. (with ms. A only) tūryair ghoṣā jinaruta-ravanā (so, n); but read prob. -ravitā(ḥ) with v.l.; Calc. and v.l. -racitā(ḥ); see **ravita**; (**3**) f. °ravaṇī, at end of a (Bhvr.?) cpd., either adj., *speaking, proclaiming*; or (*having*...) *speech*: LV 286.20–21, see s.v. **rutā**.

ravaṇaka, nt., some kind of *filtering vessel*: °kam Mvy 9024 = Tib. bum tshags gceḥu can, *filter-vessel provided with a pipe*; Chin. *water-filter that has a tongue (spout)*; Jap. *filter made of bamboo*. Prob. = Pali ravaṇaghaṭa, to which the bladder is compared in Vism. 264.37, 362.36, app. because (265.1 ff.) *no way of entrance* (of the urine) *into it is evident, while the way of exit is evident*. This suggests that our words (Pali and BHS) designate a vessel of porous material (bamboo acc. to Jap.) thru which water could be soaked in (and filtered), then to be poured out thru a spout.

Ravigupta, n. of a teacher and author: Mvy 3510; Sādh 153.2.

ravita, nt. (= Pali id., sakuṇa-ruta-ravitaṃ Miln. 178.22, *the sound of birds' cries*, as a science to be studied), *sound*; always subst. in unambigous cases; at end of adj. cpds. which may be interpreted as Bhvr.: nāsti ravitam Mvy 137 (= Tib. ca co med pa), Mv i.160.14, *there is no crying, bawling, clamor*, one of the 18 **āveṇika** (q.v.) Buddha-dharma; (saśoka-ravitāni, Senart, Mv i.154.9, but see **ravaṇa**;) bahuvividha-javita-ravitaṃ LV 337.10 (vs), see **javita** 3; in LV 326.8 (vs) Lefm. kokila-haṃsa-mora-raviśā dvija-gaṇa-kalilaḥ, with some good mss., but raviśa (cf. Whitney 1229) is not otherwise known, and v.l. ravitā may be adopted, prob. in comp. with the following, *full of crowds of birds characterized by* (i. e. *emitting*; so Tib., sgra ḥbyin) *sounds of cuckoos, haṃsas, and peacocks* (or is ravita here adj., ... *noisy birds such as cuckoos* ...?); often preceded by **ruta** (as in Pali, above), or **rutā**, qq.v., brahmasvara-rutā-ravitā Mvy 482, and jīvaṃjīvakasvara-rutā-ravitā 483, ep. of Buddha's voice, *having the sound of the voice of*...; sarva-ruta-ravita-parijñānataḥ Dbh 76.21; ruta ravita (Tib. sgra skad, *voices and cries*) ya asti sarvaloke LV 366.18 (vs); sarvasattva-ruta-ravita- (cpd.) LV 435.15 (prose); on LV 162.9 (vs) see **ravaṇa**; brahmasvara-ruta-ravitena (so ms.; Finot wrongly em. °rāvitena) ... ghoṣeṇa (of the Buddha's voice) RP 2.11 (prose).

[**raviśa**, LV 326.8, Lefm., see prec.]

raśami = next, § 3.101, m.c.: raśami-śata- LV 357.3 (vs); best mss. rasami-, others raśmi-, metr. inferior.

raśmi, f. (in Skt. m. except Ch. U. 8.6.2 etā ... raśmayaḥ, em. Boehtl. ete; but in Pali f. forms, such as rasmiyo n.-acc. pl., are not rare), *ray*: sā hi raśmir SP 24.1 (vs); raśmiś cacāra, sā sarvā ... LV 3.14, and tasyā ... raśmyā(ḥ, abl.) 4.6 (both prose).

Raśmiguṇamakuṭajñānaprajñābha, n. of a Tathāgata: Gv 310.25.

Raśmicandrapratimaṇḍitavidyuttejaghoṣeśvararāja, n. of a Tathāgata: ŚsP 2.5.

Raśmicandrorṇamegha, n. of a Tathāgata: Gv 422.12.

Raśmijvalanacūḍa, n. of a Tathāgata: Gv 421.24.

[**Raśmidhvaja**, Tib. for **Dharmadhvaja**, n. of a former Buddha, q.v.]

Raśminetrapratibhāprabhacandra, 2d. ed. °**pratibhāsa-pra**°, n. of a Tathāgata: Gv 309.16.

Raśmiparvatamegha, n. of a Tathāgata: Gv 311.24.

Raśmiprabhāsa, n. of a future Buddha (incarnation of **Kāśyapa** or **Mahākāśyapa**, disciple of Śākyamuni): SP 144.5; 146.12.

Raśmipramukta, m., n. of a samādhi: Mvy 519; ŚsP 1416.7.

Raśmimaṇḍalaśikhhararāja, n. of a Tathāgata: Gv 311.5.

Raśmimukha, n. of a Bodhisattva: Gv 442.20.

Raśmivimalaprabha, n. of a mountain peak in Laṅkā: Laṅk 15.16.

Raśmiśatasahasraparipūrṇadhvaja, n. of a future Buddha (incarnation of **Yaśodharā**): SP 269.10, 13.

Raśmisaṃkusumitapradīpa, n. of a Tathāgata: Gv 309.19.

rasaka (m. or nt.), some sort of gem: anye (devā) rasakehi samalaṃkṛtaṃ (bodhivṛkṣaṃ saṃjānanti) Mv ii.311.3 (in a list including various jewels etc.).

rasanā n. of an artery, vein, or passage-way (nāḍī) in the body: Sādh 448.11 ff.; nāḍyo lalanā-rasanāvadhūtayaḥ 11; rasanopāyena saṃsthitā 13; rasanā raktapravāhinī 15; cf. **lalanā** and **avadhūtī**.

rasarasāgra(-tā), see **rasāgra**.

Rasasaṃbhava, n. of a Bodhisattva: Samādh p. 36, line 1.

rasa-haraṇī, pl. (= Pali id., *nerves of sensation* acc. to Childers, either these or *'salivary canals of the mouth'* PTSD), *taste-conductors*, supposed organs of taste in the vicinity of the mouth and throat: (tasya yāvatyo grīvasāmantakena) mukhasāmantakena ca °ṇyas tāḥ sarvāḥ samā abhūvan Gv 401.1.

rasāgra (only noted Mv ii.478.18, perhaps hapl. for rasarasāgra), **rasarasāgra**, subst. and adj. Bhvr., also adj. **rasarasāgrin**, and subst. °**sāgratā**, (*state of, possessing*) *excellent taste* or *flavor*, lit. ... *best taste of tastes* (the Pali equiv. is rasagga-saggi, adj., or °ggi-tā, not °ta as stated PTSD; the meaning of the -s- in -saggi is obscure; Skt. sa-?); applied both to food and to persons: of food, āhāro siddho ... na me kadācid edṛśo rasāgro ... svāditapūrvo Mv ii.478.18 (rasāgro could be subst. or Bhvr. adj.), *I have never before tasted* (*food containing*?) *such excellent flavor*; (divya-, or divyai) rasarasāgropeta, adj. with āhāra, or once with piṣṭaka, Kv 30.18 (misprinted rasārasā°); 44.2–3, 11; 48.2; 54.4 (misprinted rasarāsogrope°); 56.3; 60.23 (in all these rasarasāgra must be subst.); adj. Bhvr., said of the Bodhisattva by Gopā, hā mama rasārasāgrā LV 234.21 (vs; mss. rasa°, Lefm. em. m.c.); rasarasāgriṇaḥ, n. pl., said of Buddhas, among the 32 lakṣaṇa, Mv ii.306.4

(by em. but sound); °sāgra-tā, abstr., Mvy 245 etc., 21st of the 32 **lakṣaṇa**, q.v.

rahasy-anuśāsikā = **raho'nuś°**, q.v.: Bhīk 15b.1.

rahāyati (= Pali id., MN ii.119.29, *is hiding, is secretive*; wrongly defined PTSD), *is in hiding, is secret, is* or *remains hidden*: yeṣa na jātu na tiṣṭhati buddhaḥ, teṣa na jātu rahāyati dharmaḥ Śikṣ 4.20 (vs).

raho'nuśāsaka, f. °**ikā** (also **rahasy-anu°**, q.v.), *instructor in private*, a monk or nun chosen to administer a private preparatory examination to a new initiate, acc. to Bhīk in sight, but out of hearing, of the community of nuns: °akaḥ Mvy 8730; °ikā Bhīk 15b.5 etc.

rākṣa (nt.? in mg. = Skt. rakṣā, Pali rakkhā; Skt. rakṣa only adj. and n. ag.), *protection*: rākṣe ca sthitvā jina satkaroti Śikṣ 309.2 (vs), *and he pays homage to the Jina(s), abiding in* (their) *protection*.

Rākṣasa, n. of a nāga king: Māy 247.7.

rākṣasī-dvīpa, m., *island of ogresses*, referring to the story associated in Divy and Kv with Siṃhala(-rāja); there it seems to be identified with Ceylon (cf. **Tāmra-dvīpa**): SP 439.5, 6; Mv iii.68.9 ff.; 287.2.

Rāgaparimuktā, n. of a 'gandharva maid': Kv 5.12.

Rāghava, n. of a nāga king: Mvy 3269; Māy 246.32.

Rājaka (v.l. Rājyaka), n. of a man who entertained the Bodhisattva: LV 238.10; Tib. ḥod ldan, *shining*.

rājakya, adj. (cf. M. rāikka; Pischel 598, end), *royal, of a king*: °kyaṃ udyānaṃ Mv ii.48.5; (on 112.9, 11 see **rājanya**;) °kye udyāne 112.18; °kya-(mss. °kyaṃ)-aśoka-vanikāyāṃ (so read for °vaṇi°) 438.4; sā (so read for sa) rājakyā pariṣā 446.16, *this royal assembly*; sarvā ca rājakyā pariṣā 447.8; others, 447.5; 451.3; 453.14; 457.16; 469.4; iii.39.6; 163.10; 166.6, 11.

Rājakṣetragupta, n. of a former Buddha: Mv i.140.11.

Rājagṛhaka, adj. (Childers cites only °gahika for Pali; not in DPPN or PTSD; cf. next), *of Rājagṛha*: °kā manuṣyā(ḥ) LV 240.5; Mv i.289.11; (brāhmaṇa-gṛhapa-tika) Mv i.288.20; iii.441.20; °ko brāhmaṇo Mv i.289.19; °kam amanuṣyavyādhiṃ i.289.8, *the demoniac epidemic of R.*; °kānāṃ, as subst., i.289.9, *of the people of R.*

Rājagṛheyaka, adj., = prec.: °kāni ca parvatāni Mv iii.438.1 (prose, no v.l.); °kāḥ (sc. bhikṣavaḥ) MSV ii.120.2.

rājanīya, adj. (cf. Skt. rañjanīya; § 3.3; replaces usual ramaṇīya, which is commonly bracketed with **pre-maṇīya**), *causing joy*: °ya-prabhaḥ premaṇīya-prabhaḥ Sukh 29.13.

rājanya, adj. (seems not recorded elsewhere in this sense), *belonging to a king, royal*: of a park, udyāna, Mv ii.112.9, 11; Senart em. **rājakya,** q.v.; but he keeps rājanyaṃ ii.452.1 (of an āmravanaṃ) and °nyāni kaṇṭhe-guṇāni (so mss.) 463.3. In the vicinity of all these passages **rājakya** occurs; possibly it should always be read (with Senart on 112.9, 11).

rājapaṭṭa, nt. (in Skt. said to mean an inferior sort of diamond), a kind of (blue) dye-stuff, in a list of dyes: Mvy 5921 = Tib. (m)thiṅ śiṅ, variously defined as *the indigo plant, indigo* (dye or color), *mountain blue* (the mineral azurite), and (Das) *'monolith of turquoise'*; in MSV ii.142.9 ms. cited rājavadyādayas (Tib. thiṅ śiṅ); ed. em. rājapaṭyād°, but prob. read rājapaṭṭād° (or rājavaṭṭād°?).

(**rājamātra,** m., occurs in Skt. but is misdefined BR and pw; Keith on KBr. 27.6 *vicegerent*, which is approx-imately right; = Pali (rāja-) mahāmatta, listed among 'rājāno', i. e. people who in one way or another exercise royal functions, in Vin. iii.47.2, where comm. 309.13 ff. mahāmattā ti ṭhānantarappattā mahāamaccā, te pi tattha tattha gāme vā nigame vā nisīditvā rājakiccaṃ karonti; *chief minister, vizier*, always preceded by rājan: rājā vā rājamātro vā Śikṣ 12.13; similarly SP 108.8; 113.2; Divy 143.2; 290.5; Chin. on SP 108.8 is said to render *equal of a king*.)

Rājaśrī, n. of a 'gandharva maid': Kv 4.20.

Rājasaṃyuktaka-nipāta, n. of a section of the **Madhyamāgama**: MSV i.93.10; 111.20; 112.19; called **Rājasaṃyukta-nikāya** MSV i.217.13.

Rājahaṃsagāmin, n. of a former Buddha: Mv i.138.2.

Rājāvavādaka, nt., 'giving instruction or admonition to kings', n. of a religious work, or of several such: Mvy 1429; °ka-sūtra, Śikṣ 206.11; see also **Apara-rājāvavā-daka-sūtra,** and cf. Pali Rājovāda Jātaka, Rā° Sutta, DPPN.

Rājopakīrṇaka sūtra, n. of a work: Karmav 70.7; corresponds in subject to Pali Aputtaka sutta, SN i.91.22 ff. See **upakīrṇaka.**

rātriṃvāsa (m.), *night's lodging, staying over night*: jetavane °sam upagato Av i.327.11 (prose); °sāya MPS 4.19.

rātriṃdivasa, nt. (= M. rattiṃdiaha; cf. Skt. rātriṃ-dina, Pali rattiṃdina), *night and day*: tāni sapta °sāni LV 380.4 (prose), adverbial, *during the seven days-of-24-hours*; °sasya Divy 124.20; °sehi Mv i.340.4.

Rādhagupta, n. of a son of Bindusāra's minister, who became Aśoka's minister: Divy 370.24; 373.9 ff., 403.12 ff.; 425.11; it is clearly implied that he was a rein-carnation of **Vijaya** (2), 402.15; 429.22 ff.

[**rādhyate,** wrong reading in LV 342.16 (vs), where for Lefm. nirāparādhyeṣv api rādhyate yaḥ, read with v.l. °yeṣv aparādh°; so Tib., ñes byed pa.]

Rāma (Pali id.), n. of the father and teacher of **Udraka Rāmaputra,** q.v.; his doctrine, called naiva-saṃjñānāsaṃjñāyatanam, was taught by the latter to the Bodhisattva: Mv ii.120.7 ff.

Rāmakakṣā, n. of a locality: Māy 83.

Rāmagrāma (= Pali °gāma), n. of a town (seat of a relic-stūpa): Divy 380.22, 26; also °**maka,** seat of the **Krauḍya** (see **Koḍya**) people, MPS 51.13; **Rāmagrāmī-yaka,** adj., ibidem.

rāmaṇīyaka, adj. (= **ram°**, q.v., and Pali rāma-ṇeyyaka), *lovely, charming*: krīḍanakāni °yakāni SP 160.12 (prose).

Rāmaputra, see **Udraka, Rudraka.**

Rāmavratin, an adherent of some heretical sect: Mvy 3533. Perhaps adherent of **Rāma,** q.v.(?).

Rāmāvarānta, n. of a region in the south: Gv 58.16 (prose; here text wrongly Rāmāvartanta); 59.5 f.

[**Rāva,** v.l. for **Rava,** q.v.]

Rāvaṇa, (**1**) n. of a nāga king: Mvy 3245; Māy 246.32; (**2**) n. of a yakṣa: Māy 99.

Rāvaṇī, n. of a rākṣasī: Māy 243.18.

rāśi, m., *group, collection*; (**1**) (= Pali rāsi) applied to three *groups* or *categories of* (human) *beings*, called mithyātva-(or mithyatva-)-niyata, samyaktva-ni°, and aniyata, respectively (= Pali micchatta-niyata, sam-matta-ni°, ani°); Childers, PTSD, and Senart Mv i.517 (on 175.13–16) all wrongly apply the term to *views* or *behavior* instead of *creatures*. Very clear is LV 400.2: trīn sattvarāśīn, ekaṃ mithyatvaniyatam, ekaṃ samyaktvani-yatam, ekam aniyatam; it is then explained that the first is *fixed in falsity*, permanently unable to know the doc-trine; the second *in truth* (they will learn the doctrine whether a Buddha preaches it to them or not); while the third is *undetermined* (they will learn the doctrine if they hear it preached, not otherwise); substantially the same is said in Mv iii.318.5 (reading mithyātva°); in Mv i.175.13–16 (vss), the *group fixed in falsehood* (mithyātva-niyato rāśiḥ) will fill up the *undetermined group* (aniyataṃ rāśiṃ) on Buddha's appearance, and the aniyato rāśiḥ will fill up the rāśiṃ **samyak** (= samyaktva-niyataṃ rāśiṃ); similarly Mv iii.347.4 ff.; saṃvarṇitaḥ samyaktvaniyato rāśir vivarṇito mithyātva-ni° rāśiḥ parigṛhīto (*embraced, brought into the fold*) 'niyata-rāśir LV 351.9; in Mv i.316.17 read mithyatva-niyato rāśi(ṃ? n. sg.) for corrupt mss. nityatva-;

samyaktva-niyata-rāśiḥ, mithyātva°, aniyata-r° Mvy 1737–39; mithyātva° also Mvy 6830; sattva-rāśīnāṃ samyaktva-niyata-tāṃ ca, mithyātva-niyatatāṃ ca, ubhayatvāniyatatāṃ ca yathābhūtaṃ prajānāti Dbh 76.1; the aniyata and mithyātvaniyata rāśi do not exist in Sukhāvatī, Sukh 44.15 f. (in 14 the people there are called niyatāḥ samyaktve); the 3 rāśi listed (with spelling mithyatva-) Hoernle MR 21.1 (from Saṃgīti Sūtra); (**2**) there are also three rāśi, *groups*, of dharmas which are abhisaṃbuddha by a Tathāgata: Bbh 404.23, defined 24 ff. as arthopasaṃhitā dharmāḥ, anarthopasaṃhitāḥ, and naivārthopasaṃhitā nānarthopasaṃhitāḥ.

Rāśīna, n. of a locality: Māy 100 (°ne, loc.).

rāśya, m.(?), apparently = Skt. rāśi, *sign of the zodiac*: Mmk 179.2, 5; 180.6 (all vss). But the text is dubious and corrupt: rāśya makara-nirdiṣṭā sarvānarthanivārakaḥ 179.2; rāśyaḥ kumbhanirdiṣṭā proktā munibhiḥ purā 179.5; tasmād yuktitaḥ karma na graho nāpi rāśya-jā 180.6.

[**rāṣṭa-** LV 360.22 (vs), read rāṣṭra- with most mss.]

Rāṣṭradeva, n. of a former Buddha: Mv i.137.8.

Rāṣṭrapāla (= Pali Raṭṭhapāla), n. of a disciple of the Buddha: RP 4.20 ff.; Av ii.118.1 ff. (hero of chap. 90); Mv iii.41.1; MSV i.200.10 ff.; Karmav 59.8. Cf. next.

Rāṣṭrapāla-paripṛcchā (cf. prec.), n. of a work (our RP): Mvy 1361; called Rāṣṭrapāla (only), Śikṣ 203.8 (quotation from RP 18.15 f.), or Rā°-sūtra, Śikṣ 54.16 (quotation from RP 20.5–9).

Rāhu (= Skt. and Pali id.), in BHS chiefly noted in formulaic lists of asurendras (Rāhu is an asura also in Skt., BR and pw s.v. asura): so Mv iii.138.1; 254.8; SP 5.3; Gv 250.8; Rāhor āgamanam asurāṇām adhipateḥ (so read, text corrupt) Mmk 218.5. In none of these is there any clear indication of association with eclipse. Cf. next.

-rāhuka = **Rāhu**, ifc., Bhvr.: grahe . . . sarāhuke Mmk 224.22 (vs).

Rāhula, (**1**) (= Pali id.; Aśokan Lāghula with gh, held to be older than h, but quite possibly hyper-Skt.) n. of Śākyamuni's son; also **Rāhulabhadra** (= Pali °bhadda), so in Mv i.154.3; iii.175.16, 19; Gv 51.11; SP 219.12; 220.2; also **Rāhulaśiri** Mv i.128.13 (°śirisya, gen.); iii.271.3 (°śiriṃ); his birth was miraculous but not **aupapāduka**, Mv i.153.8, 14; 154.3; he descended from the Tuṣita heaven into Yaśodharā's womb, Mv ii.159.3; discovers that the Buddha is his father and insists on becoming a monk, Mv iii.257.17 ff.; is ordained by Śāriputra at the Buddha's command, 268.5 ff.; remained 6 years in his mother's womb because of an offense against the Bodhisattva in a former birth, Mv iii.172.5; 175.16, 19; in a list of 8 mahāśrāvaka Mmk 111.12; No. 33 of a list of 34 mahāśrāvaka Sukh 2.11; last of 26 mahāśrāvaka, SP 2.8; in list of śrāvaka Mvy 1039; of bhikṣus, LV 2.3; other references Mv i.170.4; ii.114.7; iii.142.15 et alibi (see Index); SP 215.3; 220.5, 9; Sukh 92.7 (as a mahāśrāvaka); Suv 12.12; 200.9; Yaśodharā is called Rāhulaśirisya mātā Mv i.128.13; Rāhulasya jananī Mv ii.135.14, and cf. next; (**2**) n. of a cakravartin king: Mvy 3611.

Rāhulamātar (= Pali id.), *mother of Rāhula*, applied to Yaśodharā: SP 2.10; see also s.v. **Rāhula** (**1**).

Rāhuvamin, n. of a former Buddha: Mv i.140.1.

riktaka, f. °**ikā**, adj. (= Pali rittaka; once in Skt., Manu 8.404, where perhaps m.c.), *empty* (= Skt. rikta, usually perh. with pejorative -ka): Mv i.29.8 (vs), read with mss. nadīm upeti tṛṣitā riktikā parivartati (= Pali Pv. iii.6.5, with rittakā), . . . *it* (the river) *turns empty*; Mv ii.145.19, and AsP 346.9, see s.v. **asāraka**; hardly pejorative in Divy 123.20 (prose) sa yadi riktakāni koṣa-(read kośa-)-koṣṭhāgārāṇi paśyati, sahadarśanād eva pūryante.

rikta-muṣṭi, m., *an empty fist*, used as symbol of vanity and deceitfulness: Mvy 2831; Śikṣ 261.7 tad yathāpi nāma rikta-muṣṭir alīkaḥ, *deceptive as an empty fist*; °ṭi-vat, adv., LV 176.4 (vs) (saṃskāra . . .) bāla-ullāpana riktamuṣṭivat (text ukta°, see Bendall on Śikṣ 238.2, which cites LV); LV 212.14 (prose) (kāmāḥ . . .) ullāpanā (see this) rikta° (text ṛkta°, some mss. mukta°); in Śikṣ 261.8 read prob. rikta-(text rikte)muṣṭi-, see **muṣṭi** 3.

rikṣa (semi-MIndic for Skt. ṛkṣa), *bear*: MSV i.v.15.

rig-iti, var. (perhaps merely error) for **ṛg-iti**, q.v.: Mvy 8222 (not in Mironov).

ricchaṭā(-śabda), onomat. (cf. **acchaṭā**?), *chattering* (sound made by an ape): MSV i.6.15, 17. Possibly for ṛcchaṭā.

riñcati (Pali id., Skt. riṇakti), *leaves, empties*, in special sense, with object buddhakṣetra; gods address pratyekabuddhas when the Bodhisattva is about to descend to earth for his last incarnation: riñcatha buddhakṣetraṃ Mv i.197.1, 4; 357.4, 6; riñcata mārṣā buddhakṣetraṃ LV 18.12; *empty the buddha-field*, sc. by entering nirvāṇa, so that there will be no Buddha (not even a Pratyeka-b.) in the 'field' when the Bodhisattva enters it. (The mg. *neglects, ignores*, seems supported in Skt. tho perh. commoner in Pali, and in BHS: RP 34.12 [read riñcitvā]; Bbh 396.20; AsP 243.6.)

riñcana (= Pali id.), *abandonment*, see **ariñcana.**

ritīyate, °**ti**, several times in text of Bbh for **ṛtīyate**, q.v.; see **ar(t)tīyati.**

ritu (MIndic = Skt. ṛtu; cf. AMg. riu), *season*: Gv 408.1 (vs; after vowel).

riddhi, possibly intended at Mv ii.322.1 for ṛddhi; see s.v. **iddhi**; in prose of Divy 133.10; 134.15, 17, 20; 144.1; 160.25 f., always after a final vowel; sva-riddhi-Mmk 6.7 (prose).

ridhyate, °ti (= Skt. ṛdh°, Pali ijjhati), *succeeds*: RP 59.4 (vs); Bhad 15 ridhyatu (v.l. ṛdh°); MSV i.97.17 (vs) yatra ridhyanti.

riṣi (semi-MIndic = Skt. ṛṣi), *holy man*; always after vowel, but in prose: Av 1.209.11; Divy 321.5; 338.11; 350.4; 638.6; Gv 96.14.

Riṣidatta, = **Iṣi°** (**Ṛṣi°**), qq.v., Av i.224.3, n. of a sthapati of Śrāvastī.

rukṣa, adj., and **-tva**, abstr. n. (semi-MIndic for Skt. rūkṣa; cf. **ruccha**, and see under **lūkha**); (**1**) adj., *coarse*, of food: Śikṣ 131.4; (**2**) n. °tvaṃ, *harshness, evil*: Mv iii.388.5.

rugma (semi-MIndic for Skt. rukma; no such form recorded elsewhere), *gold*: rugma-varṇa Mmk 214.20.

Rucika, pl., n. of a class of gods: Mahāsamāj., Waldschmidt, Kl. Skt. Texte 4, 187.7.

Rucitabhānu, n. of a former Buddha: Mv i.139.5.

Ruciraketu, n. of a Bodhisattva: Suv 6.2 ff.; 9.6 ff.; 20.2 ff.; 120.3; 132.5 ff.; 168.5; 243.7.

Ruciradhvaja, n. of a Bodhisattva: Gv 2.19.

Ruciraprabhāsasaṃbhava, n. of a serpent king: Mvy 3435.

Rucirabhadrayaśas, n. of a Bodhisattva: Gv 442.17.

Ruciraśrīgarbha, n. of a Bodhisattva: Dbh 2.9.

rucirā, n. of the 4th Bodhisattva bhūmi (q.v.) acc. to Mv i.76.15.

ruccati, see **rucyati.**

ruccha, adj. (MIndic for Skt. rūkṣa, but this form seems not recorded in MIndic, tho AMg. has rukkha and lukkha; see s.v. **lūkha**), (1) *harsh, severe* (of forest ascetic's life); (2) *cruel, savage*: (**1**) ruccha-vṛtti or °vṛttika (= AMg. lūha-vitti, see Ratnach.), *the harsh life* (of a forest ascetic), or as Bhvr. *one who leads that life*: °vṛttikā, pl., Bhvr., Mv iii.182.16; in Mv ii.30.10 ruccha-vṛttiḥ, Bhvr., and 33.13 (Senart) rucchāṃ vṛttiṃ (but corrupt mss. point to cpd. in -a- before vṛtti, possibly Bhvr.; in 30.10 mss. are also corrupt but em. seems sound); (**2**) śastra-ruccha Mv i.73.14, *cruel as a knife* (of desire; separate this from the following cpd., and construe as n. pl.).

rucyati, also **ruccati** (= Pali ruccati, M. ruccai; see Chap. 43), *pleases*, with gen. of person (Skt. rocate): na cāsya rucyanti kadācid anye SP 98.11 (vs); yaṃ te rucyati Mv ii.464.10; (na . . .)ruccati Mv ii.485.6; yā te strī ruccitā (ppp.) Mv ii.427.16.

ruṇḍa, m. or nt. (see also **praruṇḍa**; clearly related to AMg. ruṇṭ-, authorized by Hem. 4.57 as substitute for ru-, and found in various derivs., Ratnach.; prob. related thru MIndic dialectic processes to Skt. rud-, more specifically to the ppp. ruṇṇa-, which in Pali is used as a noun like our word), *weeping*, always in instr. (after kiṃ or na . . .) and foll. by śocitena: kiṃ ruṇḍena śocitena Mv ii.218.13; nāpi ca ruṇḍena śocitenārtho 224.10; similarly 227.12; 228.12; 229.12; in some of these occurs v.l. rund°, and in some (vss) Senart em. m.c. to ruṇḍa-śoc°, but mss. never read so; exact readings hard to determine.

ruṇṇa, adj. (= Pali id., as ppp. of rud, *weep*), ruṇṇanayana, *with weeping eyes*: Mvy 6663; LV 195.2 (vs; so read; Lefm. rūṇṇa). Senart reads ruṇṇa in Mv iii.116.8, but read, virtually with mss., **ulla,** q.v.

ruta, nt. (= Pali id.; in Skt. seems to be used only of cries of animals and esp. birds; see also next), (**1**) *voice, cry, sound*, esp. (perh. exclusively) of any living being, incl. men and notably Buddhas: sattvānāṃ rutāni SP 357.5, of all creatures in the universe; sarva-ruta-kauśalyāvartāṃ (see **āvarta**) ca nāma dhāraṇīṃ 475.9; ruta madhura LV 421.14 (vs), of Buddha's voice; of the voice or speech of various creatures incl. Buddhas, Bhad 4, 18, 30, 31; snigdharutaiḥ LV 173.17 (vs), *by sweet sounds*, here parallel with rūpa, gandha, rasa, and sparśa, hence may be more general, = -śabda, *sound* of any sort; rutāni ca divyāni . . . saṃpravādyetsuḥ Mv ii.160.18; (**2**) in Laṅk, and cf. Sūtrāl. i.7 with Lévi's note, used in derogatory sense (Lévi connects it directly with the Skt. application of ruta to animal cries), (mere) *words*, the *'letter'* as distinguished from the (real, esoteric) *meaning* (artha): yathārutārthābhiniviṣṭānāṃ Laṅk 14.3, *attached to the* (superficial) *meaning according to* (literal) *words*; yathārutārthagrahaṇaṃ na kartavyaṃ bodhisattvena 154.8; definition of ruta, *physiological speech*, 154.14 ff., while in contrast (true, esoteric) artha is defined 154.17 ff.; in substantially the same sense **vyañjana,** q.v., is commoner.

rutā = **ruta,** *voice, speech*: in LV 286.20–21 (prose) read, ekarutā-(Lefm. °tāṃ, misprint?)-sarva-ruta-ravaṇī (Lefm. °racanī, v.l. °ramaṇī; our reading proved by Tib. skad cig gis skad thams cad sgrog pa daṅ, *by one speech proclaiming all speech*), ep. of the Buddha's voice or speech; this form, in prose, confirms rutā in Mvy 482–3, cited s.v. **ravita,** despite the fact that the same passage in Sūtrāl. xii.9, comm. (p. 80, lines 19–20) has ruta.

Rutāvatī (mc. °ti), n. of a 'deity of the sea': Śikṣ 346.3, 5 (vss, from Ratnolkādhāraṇī).

-rutāvin (to ruta, cf. § 22.51), in sarvabhūta-°vinaḥ Mmk 546.8 (vs), *having the voices* or *cries of all creatures*; perh. m.c. for *ruta-vant.

Rudanī, Divy 451.1, 456.19, or **Rudantī,** Divy 451.5, 9; 456.23, 27, n. of a river.

rudan-mukha, adj., f. °**khī,** once °**khā** (= Pali rudammukha), *with weeping face*, always associated with, and ordinarily following, aśrukaṇṭha (Skt.): Mv ii.78.16 aśrukaṇṭho °kho; 110.7 (f. °khā); 117.19; 154.9; 217.11; Av ii.182.11; f. °khī Mv ii.429.12; 486.9; iii.5.19; 20.5.

Rudraka Rāmaputra = **Udraka R°,** q.v., only in LV 243.15 ff.; 403.8 ff. Clearly a corruption for Ud°.

Rudradeva, n. of a former Buddha: Mv i.137.8.

Rudrāyaṇa (see also **Udrāyaṇa**), n. of a king of Roruka or Rauruka: Divy 545.1 ff.; hero of the Rudrāyaṇāvadāna = Divy ch. xxxvii (colophon 586.9).

Rudhirāhāriṇī, n. of a rākṣasī: Māy 243.19.

rundhana (nt., or °**nā**? n. act. to rundhati = Skt. ruṇaddhi; cf. AMg. rumbhaṇa), *confinement* (as punishment): bandhanā rundhanā (nearly all mss. °nās) tāḍanā . . . LV 214.3 (vs).

rupa (m.c. for Skt. rūpa), *form*: read kupita-rupavaṃs (before t-) LV 327.14 (vs), Lefm. °vaṃ.

Rurubha, n. of a mountain: Māy 254.7.

Rurumuṇḍa, m., a variant form (used in the first two occurrences) for **Urumuṇḍa,** q.v., n. of a mountain: Divy 349.8, 12. (Saṃdhi is not concerned; presumably an error of tradition, but neither form has been found elsewhere.)

[**ruṣya,** see **aruṣya.**]

rūkṣaka, f. °**ikā** (= Skt. rūkṣa; cf. **rukṣa, ruccha, lūkha, lūha**), *harsh, disagreeable* (of food): °ikāyā(ḥ) alavaṇikāyā(ḥ) kulmāṣapiṇḍakāyā(ḥ) or °ḍikāyā(ḥ) Divy 87.1; 89.3 = MSV i.86.12; 88.20 (°piṇḍikāyāḥ only).

[**rūḍha-cīvara**: Prāt 492.3 (and 6) (ācchinnacīvaro) vā bhikṣuḥ syān naṣṭacīvaro vā dagdhacīvaro vā rūḍhacīvaro vā (Finot prints vārūḍha°); Chin. 'emporté par l'eau'; Pali Vin. iii.213.8 udakena vā vuḷhaṃ. This seems to prove that the Prāt intended ūḍhacīvaro, altho the repetition in 492.6 has vā rūḍhacīvareṇa. Neither rūḍhanor ārūḍha- seems to make any possible sense. We must either emend to vā ūḍha°, or understand vā-r-ūḍha° with hiatus-bridging r.]

-rūpa used as quasi-suffix, in emphasizing sense prescribed by Pāṇ. 5.3.66 praśaṃsāyāṃ rūpam: ko nāma śaktaḥ pratikartu tubhyam udyuktarūpo bahukalpakoṭyaḥ SP 119.4 (vs), *who pray could imitate you,* (even) *if he exerted himself greatly for many crores of kalpas*?; . . . prītisaumanasyajātaḥ śīghraṃ-śīghraṃ tvaramāṇarūpo rājānaṃ . . . adhyabhāṣata LV 132.5 (prose), *in great haste*; naiva tvayā kupuruṣa śrutapūrvarūpaṃ Mv i.130.9 and 13 (vs), *base man, you have never before heard at all* (= śrutapūrvam, with emphasis; wrongly Senart's note).

rūpa-kāya, m., *'form-body', material body* (of a Buddha); regularly contrasted with **dharmakāya** (2), q.v. for citations; without any contrasting term: etac ca bodhicittaṃ rūpakāyadarśanotpannaṃ Śikṣ 10.12 (i. e. *produced by the mere sight of the Buddha's physical form*). See also s.v. **pariniṣpatti.**

rūpa-gata, nt. (cf. AMg. rūva-gaya = mūrtadravya, rūpavān padārtha, *a corporeal substance*; see s.v. **gata**), substantially = rūpa, *form*: tādṛśaṃ sukarmavipākābhinirvṛttaṃ śubhaṃ rūpagataṃ Mv iii.375.17, and similarly 19; cakṣvindriyaṃ rūpagateṣu dhāvati Suv 56.7; yad . . . rūpagatenāpaliguddhaṃ Śikṣ 249.8, *what is not affected* (lit. *greedily fastened upon*) *by form*; bhūtagrahāviṣṭaḥ puruṣo vividhāni rūpagatāni paśyati Gv 522.26.

[**rūpaṇya,** in āśrayabhūta-rūpaṇyāt Mvy 2084, read °rūpaṇāt with Mironov.]

rūpa-dhātu, m. (= Pali id.), *the world (sphere, region) of form*, in which dwell the **rūpāvacara** gods; regularly in contrast with **kāma-dhātu** and **ārūpya-**(dhātu), qq.v.: Gv 471.19; LV 428.20; Mvy 3073; KP 94.4.

rūpadhātuka, adj., *of the* **rūpadhātu**: LV 421.9 (vs) °ka-devatāḥ.

rūpavatī, n. of the sixth Bodhisattva-**bhūmi** (q.v.) acc. to Mv i.76.16.

Rūpavant(a), n. of a companion of **Puṇyavant**(a), q.v.: Mv iii.33.19 ff.

rūpāvacara, m. (= Pali id.; cf. **avacara**), *dwelling in the* **rūpa-dhātu** or *realm of form*, ep. of a group of (18) classes of gods (for list see s.v. **deva**): LV 30.5; 99.8; 219.11; 250.7; 369.13; 413.5; Mv i.159.6; Mvy 6896; Dharmas 128; Suv 10.4; Mmk 69.8; 103.27; 419.7; Karmav 30.13.

Rūpāvata, see next.

Rūpāvatī, n. of a woman (previous incarnation of Śākyamuni): Divy 471.5 ff.; 479.23; by an act of truth she changed herself into a man, **Rūpāvata,** 474.5 ff.; referred to RP 25.2, where read sā Rūpāvatī for text sārūpyavatī, cf. Finot p. viii; the same story in Avadānakalpalatā, chap. 51, where the name is Rukmavatī.

-rūpiṇikā, in su°kāṃ LV 323.8 (vs), endearing dim., § 22.34, of -rūpiṇī, f. of Skt. -rūpin, *charmingly fair-formed*, of a daughter of Māra.

rūpiṇī, a kind of malevolent superhuman being: Mmk 17.8, pl. °ṇyo (also **mahā-r°**); n. of a yoginī or similar demoness, Sādh 425.13, 439.10; n. of a 'goddess' (the same?) Sādh 502.7.

rūpya, nt., (**1**) (Skt. Lex. id.; otherwise *silver* in general), *silver coin*: suvarṇa-rūpya-(etc., various jewels)-jātarūpa-rajata-samanvāgataś ca SP 102.1 (prose); note occurrence of rajata in same cpd., and collocation with suvarṇa; (**2**) in RP 6.15 (vs) rūpyam (sc. of the Buddha) apy asamakaṃ manoramaṃ, if text is sound must = rūpam, *form*; perh. read this.

Rūpyaketu, Suv 169.2, and **Rūpyaprabha**, Suv 169.7, n. of two sons of **Ruciraketu.**

Rūpyamayī, n. of a region (bhūmi): Kv 25.2 (here by error Rūpa°), 21.

[**Rūpyavatī**, read **Rūpāvatī**, q.v.: RP 25.2.]

Reṇu (**1**) (= Pali id., DN ii.230.24 ff.), n. of the son and successor of King **Diśāṃpati**: Mv iii.204.11 ff. In LV 171.1 he seems to have the epithet Diśāṃpati himself, and further, by a confusion in the story, he is represented as a previous incarnation of Śākyamuni: Reṇu bhū (= abhūḥ) Diśāṃpati. In both the Mv and the Pali versions it is the purohita **Jyotipāla** (**Mahāgovinda**) who was the future Buddha. In Mvy 3580 called **Sureṇu.** (**2**) n. of a former Buddha: LV 171.13.

Revata, (= Pali id.) n. of a disciple of Buddha (only in lists of names): SP 2.4; 207.4; LV 1.17; Av i.213.10; ii.112.4; 135.1; Gv 17.22; Sukh 2.9; 92.7. See also **Raivata.**

Revataka, n. of a stream (raya; Burnouf Intr. 396 with note 2 evidently read ratha, as he renders *char*, but context makes this hardly possible): Divy 399.12.

Revatī, n. of a yakṣiṇī (= Skt. id.? see BR s.v. Revant, 2e): Mmk 564.25; 566.1. Cf. next (?).

revatī-graha, n. of a class of demons (follows rākṣasa; followed by śakuni-graha, which occurs in Skt., see BR): Mvy 4765 = Tib. nam gruḥi gdon, *demon of* (the constellation) *Revatī*. Perhaps to be connected with prec.

Raivata, (**1**) n. of a brahman ascetic who entertained the Bodhisattva: LV 238.9; (**2**) = **Revata**, q.v. (perhaps read so): Divy 182.22; 198.8 (in lists of names of disciples).

roca (Vedic as adj. once; not in Pali; M. roa once in different mg.), (**1**) nt., *light* (or, possibly, adj., *shining*): sarvabuddhānuśāsanīcakrarocaṃ nāma prajñāpāramitāmukhaṃ Gv 449.20; (**2**) m., a kind of flower: Mvy 6183 = Tib. me tog mdog mdzes, *fair-colored flower* or *rose*; (**3**) (= Pali Roja 2 in DPPN) n. of an ancient king, in Pali and Mvy son of **Mahāsaṃmata**; in Mv, acc. to the (corrupt) ms. which contains the word, son of **Kalyāṇa** and grandson of Mahāsaṃmata: Mvy 3553; in Mv i.348.8 the v.l. of one ms. shows that this name was in the list, tho it is confused with **Rava** q.v.; (**4**) (= Pali Roja 1 in DPPN) n. of a minister of the Mallas in **Pāpā**: MSV i.282.2 ff. (uncle of Ānanda, but unbelieving; converted by Buddha).

rocana-piśācakā, v.l. °**piśācanakā** (nom. pl.; Sen. em. °piśācikā), some sort of product of the art of the **śaṅkha-valaya-kāra**; the adjoining words in Mv ii.473.11 suggest that it is a small article made of ivory, perh. for holding unguents or the like (and made in the shape of a piśācī? so Senart suggests).

Rocanī, n. of a Buddhist goddess (= **Buddhalocanā**, **Locanā**): Dharmas 4.

Rocaneya, pl., n. of a brahmanical gotra: Divy 635.17.

[**Rocama**, corruption of a name of a future Tathāgata: Gv 443.16: (yathā ca maitreyasya . . .) evam . . . siṃhasyaivaṃ yāvad rocamasya tathāgatasya jananī bhaviṣyāmi. Maitreya and Siṃha are the first two of the preceding long list of future Buddhas: 441.21–443.10; we should expect in place of the impossible Rocama the last name of the list, which is Abhyuccadeva in the text, intending Atyuccadeva.]

rocamāna, nt. (also **mahā-r°**; cf. **roca** 2, **mahāroca**?), n. of some flower: Mv i.230.16; 266.18; ii.160.12; 286.17; iii.95.4; 99.3.

rocamānā, sc. lipi, a kind of script: LV 126.10. Tib. lha ṅes pa, which is prob. an error for lhaṅ ṅe (pa), *clear, distinct, bright*, etc.

? **rocayati** = **ārocayati**, q.v., *tells, says*: sā . . . putrasya Kuśasya rocayati Mv ii.442.15 (prose); perh. read ārocayati, but no v.l.

rodantaka, adj. (-ka extension of a-extension of pple. of rud-), *weeping*: LV 221.18 (vs) rodantako durmanā.

? **rodita** (nt.), *lamentation*, acc. to Senart's much emended text in Mv i.68.8 (vs); the form roditehi is well supported, but perh. originally stood for roditāhi, adj. with following pramadāhi of mss. (for which Senart em. mathitā hi-, very violently). The orig. form of the passage defies reconstruction.

roditavyaka, adj. (= Skt. gdve. °vya plus -ka, prob. m.c.), *to be wept over*: te na . . . °vyakāḥ LV 237.11 (vs); na sa °vyakaḥ id. 12 (vs).

? **Rodha**, acc. to Lefm.'s text, n. of a former Buddha: LV 171.17; Calc. and Foucaux, by diff. word-division, read Nirodha; Tib. seems to read gsal, usually *distinct, clear, bright, glorious* (= **Roca**? q.v.), which seems inappropriate to either; text perh. corrupt, but no v.l. However, the syllable -ni surely belongs with the prec. word, -pradāni (for °ne), cf. dāni 19, 20, 22.

roma, m. (otherwise only nt.), *hair*: n. pl. romāḥ LV 310.1 (end of line of vs).

romapāta or (Mironov) °**pāda**, m., prob. adj., acc. to Tib. spu(ṅ) sa la lhuṅ ba lta bu, and Chin., *like* (one with) *hair falling to the ground*: °taḥ (Mironov °daḥ) Mvy 9199; see **pātayati**, and s.v. **prakaca**, which precedes this in Mvy.

romavivara, m. and nt., n. of a series of mythical regions which belong to Avalokiteśvara, each one given a name (Suvarṇa, Kṛṣṇa, etc.), and its inhabitants (e. g. gandharvas, ṛṣis, Bodhisattvas, etc.) specified: Kv 59.13 ff.; 60.3 ff.; 62.3 ff.; 64.8 ff., 65.12 ff.; 67.7, colophon (read romavivara-varṇanaṃ for text °vivaraṇa-var°); 84.13 ff.; 87.14–15. The word occurs in Skt. in the mg. *pore of the skin* (= Skt. romakūpa), but this can hardly be concerned here; has roma something to do with Skt. Romā, *Rome*, Romaka, *Roman(s)*, etc.?

Romaharṣaṇīya-sūtra, n. of a work: Karmav 158.11 (= Pali Lomahaṃsanapariyāya, aliter Mahāsīhanāda-s°, no. 12 of MN).

Romā, n. of a goddess: Mahāsamāj. Waldschmidt Kl. Skt. Texte 4, 185.15. Pali parallel has Rojā (supported by one Chin. version which points to reconstructed ro-ya; but another Chin. indicates so-ma).

Roruka (var. **Rauruka**), nt. (= Pali Roruka), (**1**) n. of a town, capital of the Sauvīras (Pali Sov°): Mv iii.208.18; home of Rudrāyaṇa, Divy 544.23 ff.; in 545.26 (mss.), and usually later in the story (550.1–11; 551.6; 552.17 ff.; 556.16 ff.; 559.4; 563.12 ff.), called Rauruka; (**2**) n. of a city in the south (and so apparently not the same as 1, which is in the northwest): Gv 453.18, 25.

rolā, a high number: Gv 106.10; perhaps graphic corruption for *khelā = **khelu**, q.v.; occurs in same context as the latter; 2d. ed. **elā**, which duplicates this word in prec. line.

roṣaka, adj. or subst. m. (= Pali rosaka), (*one who is*) *angry*: Mv i.321.21; ii.52.22 (vs, read roṣaka, n. pl., as separate word); with **paribhāṣaka**, Divy 38.9; Bbh

120.18; roṣitāraṃ (sc. labhate) ca roṣakaḥ Ud xiv.3 = Pali SN i.85.31 rosetāraṃ ca rosako (cf. next).

roṣitar (= Pali rosetar), *one who is angry*: Ud xiv.3 (see under prec.)

roṣin, n. pl. roṣiṇo, Mv iii.113.13, or **roṣyaṇa,** n. pl. °**ṇā,** Mv iii.443.1; in a list of traders or artisans. Obscure; perh. cf. Pkt. (Deśī) rosāṇai, ppp. rosāṇia, *cleans, cleaned*; or Skt. ppp. rūṣita, *bestrewed, covered* (with powder).

Rohaka (v.l. Rāh°), n. of a deer-king, father of Nyagrodha and Viśākha: Mv i.359.18.

rohaṇīya, adj. (Skt. rohaṇa plus -īya), *healing, causing to grow over* (a wound): °yāni dravyāṇi MSV ii.39.3 f.

rohati (in Skt. used esp. with neg., *is fruitless*), *is valid, is effective*: MSV ii.210.5, 10; definition of categories of those whose objections to actions (in the saṃgha) are and are not valid, 11 ff.

Rohiṇa, n. of a rich Śākyan: Av ii.14.6 ff.

Rohiṇī, n. of a rākṣasī: Māy 243.12.

(**Rohitaka,** m. pl., prob. = Skt. id., n. of a country or people: Divy 107.29; nt. sg. their city, id. 107.30 (here mss. Rohitakaṇṭha); 109.10, 12; MSV 1.2.6; m. its king, Divy 108.7 (read °ka- for °kaṃ); 111.7. Also **Rohītaka.**)

Rohitavastu (m.? acc. sg. °vastum), n. of a town: LV 406.19 (= **Lohitavastuka, Lohitaka** (2), qq.v.).

rohitāvarta (m. or nt.), some sort of (loose or reprehensible) behavior (with women): MSV iii.16.9 °tam api (kurutaḥ); Tib. ña tshar (not clear to me; ña, *fish*? cf. rohita as n. of a fish) kyis kyaṅ skor bar byed (*waving* or *moving around*, like -parivarta, so Skt., just before).

Rohitāśva, (**1**) m. pl., n. of a people (or region): Māy 25; (**2**) n. sg., n. of a maharṣi: Māy 257.3; possibly cf. R. the son of Hariścandra, see BR s.v., or Pali Rohitassa 2, see DPPN s.v.

(**Rohītaka,** prob. = Skt. id. and = **Rohitaka,** n. of a city: MSV ii.33.16.)

raukṣa, adj. or subst. (Skt. rūkṣa plus -a, cf. Skt. raukṣya, nt. subst., which may be intended here), *harsh, savage,* or *harshness, savagery,* in raukṣa-cittā, Bhvr. fem.: Divy 471.11, *having a mind that is savage* (or, *characterized by savagery*).

Raudrā, n. of a rākṣasī: Māy 241.31.

Raudrākṣa, n. of a brahman: Divy 320.19 ff.; RP 23.3; demanded the head of **Candraprabha** (1), q.v.

Raurava, m. (= Pali Roruva), n. of a hot hell, very common: often followed by **Mahāraurava,** from which in Mv i.5.13 it seems to be specially distinguished as ekānta-raurava (mahā-r° occurs in 14); the two referred to as dvau ca rauravau Mv i.9.8 = iii.454.7 (vs); foll. by mahā-r°, Mvy 4923; Dharmas 121; Divy 67.22; 138.6; 366.28; Av i.4.8, etc.; without mahā-r°, Mv iii.274.11; Kv 18.12, et alibi.

Rauruka = **Roruka** (1), q.v.

[**rauhiṇī,** read prob. rohiṇī with Mironov, Mvy 5831, n. of some plant; Skt. uses rohiṇī of several plants.]

L

Lakuṭa, n. of a nāga king: Mmk 18.11. Cf. **Mahā-l°.**

lakṣa (Skt.), *mark*: anena ca lakṣa-nikṣepeṇa SP 316.10 (prose), *and by this depositing of the sort just described,* lit. *by this mark-deposit,* or, perhaps better, *by this depositing on the* (designated) *mark* (target, lakṣa). Acc. to Senart, lakṣa is read for **lakṣaṇa** (4) by mss. at Mv i.207.16, where he keeps it, tho in the repetition ii.12.6 he keeps lakṣaṇa with mss. there; in i.62.12 he em. lakṣa for lakṣaṇa, alleging metrical grounds, but the resulting meter is not correct; read rather maha-(m.c. for mahā-)puruṣalakṣaṇavarāṇāṃ; and in i.207.16 we must also read, with ii.12.6, dvātriṃśallakṣaṇadharo (or °śa-lakṣaṇadharo?). There is no evidence that the Buddhist 32 lakṣaṇa were ever called lakṣa, despite Skt. lakṣa for lakṣaṇa, Vikr. car. JR VII.0.2 (HOS 27.233).

lakṣaṇa, nt., *mark* (Skt.); (**1**) in Laṅk 37.10 ff.; 38.5 ff., *external mark, manifested aspect,* of the vijñāna (cf. Suzuki, Studies, 183); contrasted with **prabandha,** q.v.; fuller expression seems to be svajāti-lakṣaṇa, see Laṅk 38.16 ff., esp. 18 f., svajātilakṣaṇe punar nirudhyamāne (mss.) ālayavijñānanirodhaḥ syāt, suggesting that with its suppression, the ālaya-vijñāna itself is suppressed; for the aṣṭalakṣaṇa **vijñāna** see **vij°** 2; (**2**) in Divy 513.15, 24, sauvarṇena lakṣaṇena laḍḍīś (sc. of a state horse) chorayati, *removes the dung with a golden . . .* (? some sort of implement; acc. to Index, *spoon*?), perh. *shovel* or the like; (**3**) = **svabhāva** (2), q.v., *characteristic,* of existing things, there being three such, viz. **parikalpita, paratantra, pariniṣpanna,** qq.v.: Mvy 1662 (to 1665 incl.); Sūtrāl. xi.38–41 (Lévi, *indice*); svabhāva-lakṣaṇa-trayakuśalena bhavitavyam Laṅk 67.2; (**4**) *characteristic mark* of a superior person (a cakravartin or a Buddha), of which there are standardly 32 (anomalously 28 in Gv 353.7, aṣṭaviṃśatibhir mahāpuruṣalakṣaṇair upeto; no list). There are various lists; in Pali (lakkhaṇa), DN ii.17.10 ff. and iii.143.5 ff. (here followed by lengthy treatments of each item); MN ii.136.6 ff.; in BHS, LV 105.11 ff. (here referred to as LVa) and 429.3 ff. (LVb); Mvy 235 ff.; Dharmas (here abbreviated Dh) 83; Gv 399.20 ff., with valuable brief explanations of each term; Bbh 375.9 ff., with a few brief glosses, but followed on 378.3 ff., 381.8 ff., by more extensive treatments of the various items, with a few minor variants which are mostly not recorded here; finally, Mv i.226.16 ff. = ii.29.19 ff. has, in 7 lines of verse, extremely brief one-word designations for the 32 items, in part so corrupt in the text that I have failed to identify a few items (here, Mv without reference refers to this list); again, Mv ii.304.14 ff. has a very loose, inaccurate, and incomplete list, mingled with some **anuvyañjana** and other extraneous materials; this is cited below by page and line when it is important. Finally, a few stray lakṣaṇa are unsystematically mentioned in RP 46.13–47.12, and again 50.11–51.5; they will be referred to by page and line under the appropriate items. In modern literature, correlations of various Pali and BHS lists (but without the Gv, Bbh, and Mv lists) have been recorded by Burnouf, Lotus, 558 ff.; Müller, note on Dharmas 83 (but note that in a number of cases Müller here cites Dharmas itself inconsistently with his own text). In Mvy and LVa (as also in the stray fragmentary lists of RP) the order of all other texts is reversed, so as to begin with the head instead of the feet; in citing numbers I have reversed the numbering of these two lists, to facilitate comparison with the other lists; therefore when I cite 'Mvy 32, LVa 32', I refer to Mvy and LVa 1; 'Mvy 31, LVa 31' means Mvy 2, LVa 2, etc. I believe the following list is substantially correct and original, tho the precise language is not always certain; all important variants are cited. The order of the items in BHS varies greatly, no two lists being alike; but the relative order in the Pali lists is, I believe, always or nearly always supported by some BHS evidence, and I see no serious reason to doubt that it represents the original; it is therefore adopted here.

1. supratiṣṭhitapāda (Pali suppatiṭṭhitapāda), Mvy 3;

LVb, Gv, Bbh 1; LVa 1 inserts sama before pāda; Mv prob. means this by 1 samā; Mv ii.304.14 samā ... caraṇā supratiṣṭhitā; Dh 2 -pāṇipādatala(tā) for -pāda. — **2.** adhastāt pādatalayoś cakre jāte ... (epithets), so Bbh 2, similarly LVa, Gv 2; Pali heṭṭhāpādatalesu cakkāni jātāni ... (epithets); Mv 2 heṣṭā, also heṣṭā ... Mv ii.304.16; LVb 2 compresses the epithets into a long cpd. ending cakrāṅkitapādatala; Mvy 4 cakrāṅkita-hasta-pāda, and so Dh 1 adding -tala and with pāṇi for hasta, which, tho supported by Tib. phyag, is only a false interpretation of adhastāt or semi-MIndic heṣṭā. — **3.** āyatapādapārṣṇi (Pali āyatapaṇhi), so Mvy 2, Bbh 4, Gv 5 (LVa 6 āyata-pārṣṇipāda); or āyatapārṣṇi, LVb 3, Dh 7, with Pali; Mv 4 āyatā. — **4.** dīrghāṅguli (Pali dīgha°), LVb 4, LVa 7, Mvy 5, Dh 6, Gv (2d ed.) 6 dīrghā asyāṅgulayo, Bbh 3; Mv 3 dīrghā; Mv ii.305.1. — **5.** mṛdutaruṇahastapāda (Pali mudutaluṇahatthapāda); LVa 4, LVb 6; Bbh 5 (mss. om. hasta, Tib. phyag, for which ed. pāṇi); Dh 4 and Mvy 7 add -tala; Gv 7 mṛdūni ... hastapādatalāni; Mv 11 mṛdu; cf. RP 47.10. — **6.** jāla-(jālāvanaddha-?)-hastapāda; Pali jālahatthapāda, to which Bbh 6 jāla-pāṇipāda is closest; LVa 3, LVb 7 jālāṅgulihastapāda; Mvy 6 jālāvanaddha-hastapāda, cf. Mv ii.304.14 (combined with No. 1 above) jālāvanaddhā (caraṇā); Dh 3 corrupt, jālābalabaddhāṅgulipāṇipādatala(tā); Gv 4 hasta-pādatale jālinī (2d ed.); Mv 12 jālā. — **7.** ucchaṅkha-(?)-pāda (Pali ussaṅkha°), so Gv 3, and so read (ucchaṅkha) Mv 5 and Mv ii.304.19, also with Mironov Mvy 8; Mvy Kyoto ed. utsaṅga°, so LVa 5, Dh 9, and Bbh 7 (-caraṇa for pāda); LVb 8 ucchaṅga°. — **8.** aiṇeyajaṅgha (Pali eṇi-j°), so Gv 8, Mvy 1, Dh 11; eṇeya° LVb 10, Bbh 8 (and RP 51.3); eṇeyamṛgarājajaṅgha LVa 8; Mv 6 eṇi; Mv ii.305.3 eṇī-j°; RP 47.12 eṇajaṅgha. — **9.** sthitāna-vanata-pralambabāhu Mvy 15, and sthito'vanata° (as Mvy) LVa 15; cf. Pali ṭhitako va anonamanto ubhohi pāṇitalehi jaṇṇukāni parimasati ...; Bbh 9 anavana-takāya; LVb 12, Dh 12, Gv 15 pralambabāhu; cf. Gv 13 anūnagātraḥ, (read) anunnatagātro 'pariṇatagātraḥ; Mv(?); Mv ii.305.8 anonatena kāyena pāṇīhi jānukāṃ spṛśe; cf. RP 47.9 dīrgha-parigha-bāhū. — **10.** kośopagata-vastiguhya (Pali kosohitavatthaguyha; it seems that vattha is a mistake for vatthi, cf. Pali vatthi-kosa), so Mvy 10, LVa 10, LVb 11; or kośagata-vas° Bbh 10, Gv 10, Dh 13; Mv 9 kośa; Mv ii.305.10 kośavastiguhya; RP 47.11 guhyakośo. — **11.** suvarṇavarṇa (Pali suvaṇṇavaṇṇa, with appended kañcanasannibhataca, cf. Bbh), so Dh 14; LVb 15 suvarṇachavi; Gv 29 suvarṇavarṇachavi; Bbh 15 kāñcanasaṃnibhatvac (cf. Pali); Mv 22 suvarṇa; Mv ii.305.7 kāñcana-chaviśobhanā; in LVa 16 and Mvy 16 combined with next, sūkṣmasuvarṇachavi (Lefm. adds varṇa, by em., after suvarṇa); kanakavarṇa RP 47.10; 51.5. — **12.** sūkṣma-chavi (Pali sukhumachavi), so LVb 14 (mṛdutaruṇa-sū°), Gv 28; Dh 15 śuklachavi(-tā); for LVa and Mvy see prec.; Bbh 16 ślakṣṇatvāt (but 379.18 sūkṣma-ślakṣṇa-tvacatā, and 381.11 sūkṣmatvaktā) tvaco rajo ... nāvatiṣṭhate, and ślakṣṇa, instead of sūkṣma, is read also in Mv 16; Mv ii.305.14 and RP 51.5 ślakṣṇachavī. — **13.** ekaikaroma (or °man; Pali ekekaloma), so LVa 12; Gv 30; Mv ii.305.15; Mv 14 ekā; LVb 16 ekaikanicitaromakūpa; Bbh 14 °romā, adding ... pradakṣiṇāvartam; Mvy 12 °roma-pradakṣiṇā-vartaḥ; Dh 16 pradakṣiṇāvartaikaroma(-tā); cf. RP 47.11; see next. — **14.** ūrdhvāgraroma, °man (Pali uddhagga-loma), so Dh 10; Mvy 11 ūrdhvaga-roma; Bbh 13 ūrdhvaṃga°; Gv 31 ūrdhvāṅga°; Mv 15, mss. intend ūrdhvāgra or ūrdhaṃga; LVa 11 ūrdhvāgrābhipradakṣiṇā-vartaromā(ḥ); LVb 9 ūrdhvāṅgadakṣiṇāvartaromakūpa; see prec. — **15.** bṛhad-ṛju-gātra (Pali brahmujjugatta), so Gv 16, Bbh 21; Mv 7 bṛhat; Mv ii.305.18 prahvarjugātra (corruption for brahmarj°?); Dh 8 ṛjugātra(-tā); LVb 5 bahujanatrātā, obvious corruption; not in LVa, Mvy (replaced, perhaps, by suvartitoru, Lefm. suvivart°, 9 in both?). — **16.** saptotsada (Pali sattussada), LVa 18; LVb 17; Mvy 18; Gv 9; Dh 5; Bbh 17 °da-kāya; Mv 20 utsadā; RP 47.9. — **17.** siṃhapūrvārdhakāya (Pali sīha-pubbaddhakāya), LVa 14; LVb 18; Mvy 14; Bbh 18; Gv 11; Dh 18 (°ānta° for °ārdha°); Mv ii.305.6; prob. concealed in Mv 18 or 19, corrupt. — **18.** citāntarāṃsa (or °śa, Dh; Pali citantaraṃsa), LVa, Mvy 17; LVb 19; Bbh, Dh 20; Gv 12; prob. citā to be read in Mv 17. — **19.** nyagrodhaparimaṇḍala (Pali nigrodha°), LVa, LVb, Mvy 13; Dh 22; Bbh 11; Gv 33; Mv 10 nyagrodha. — **20.** susaṃvṛttaskandha (Pali sama-vatta-kkhandha), LVa, Mvy, Bbh, Dh 19; LVb 20; Gv 14 (omits su); Mv 24 samā (cf. Pali); Mv ii.305.17 (omits su); RP 47.9 śānta-saṃvṛtta-skandhaḥ; the erroneous spelling °saṃvṛta° in Dh, Mvy text (but Index and Mironov saṃvṛtta), and Gv (but followed in gloss by vṛttāv asya skandhāv ... pīnau, etc.). — **21.** rasarasāgra(-vant? Pali rasaggasaggi); °gra-(-tā) Mvy 23; Dh 21; °gra-vant LVa 22; LVb 25; °gra-prāptaḥ Bbh 27; rasaṃ Mv 21; °griṇaḥ Mv ii.306.4; in Gv 17 represented by kambugrīva(-tā) (400.25), on which see BR s.v. kambu; it is paraphrased by adīnakaṇṭhaḥ, *with not inferior neck*, but for the real meaning see following passage cited s.v. **rasaharaṇī**, proving connexion with (rasa-)**rasāgra**, q.v.; cf. also RP 47.9 kambu-rucira-grīvā (among lakṣaṇa). — **22.** siṃhahanu (Pali sīha°), LVa 20; LVb 21; Mvy 11; Gv 18; Dh, Bbh 25; Mv 23 sīho (or siṃho); Mv ii.306.4; RP 46.15. — **23.** catvāriṃ-śaddanta (Pali cattālīsadanta), Mvy 27; cf. Mv ii.306.5; catvāriṃśatsamadanta LVb, Bbh 22, Gv 19 (1st ed.); samacatvāriṃśaddanta LVa 26; Gv 19 (2d ed.); not identified in Mv; cf. RP 46.17; 50.17. — **24.** samadanta (Pali id.), Mvy 26; Dh 27; Gv 21; Mv 26 samā; for Bbh, LVa, LVb, see under prec.; they seem to combine the two (but note that Gv has this item separately, while including sama with the prec.); RP 46.17. — **25.** aviraladanta (Pali avivara°, but v.l. aviraḷa°), LVa, Mvy 25; LVb 24; Bbh 23; Dh 29; Gv 20 aviralāviṣamadanta(-tā); cf. RP 50.17. — **26.** suśukla-daṃṣṭra, or °danta (Pali susukkadāṭha): °daṃṣṭra Gv 401.13 (in gloss on No. 24 above); śukra-daṃṣṭrā (v.l. suśukladanta) Mv ii.306.6; °danta LVb 23; Mvy, Bbh 24; śukla-danta LVa 24; śukla-hanu(-tā) Dh 26; śuklā Mv 25; cf. RP 46.17. — **27.** prabhūtajihva (Pali pahūtajivha), LVa 21; LVb 29; Dh 24; Gv 22 (su-pra°); prabhūtatanujihva Mvy 21; Bbh 26; Mv ii.306.7; pra-bhūtā Mv 27; jihvā prabhūtā RP 46.18; 50.15. — **28.** brahmasvara (Pali brahmassara), LVa, Gv 23; LVb 26; Mvy 20; Bbh 28 (with gloss kalaviṅkamanojñabhāṇī; some Pali texts gloss karavīkabhāṇī); Mv 28 brahmā; Mv ii.306.11; not in text of Dh, but one ms. is cited in Müller's note as reading corruptly prastasvara(-tā), which should doubtless be emended and adopted, deleting Dh 28 haṃ-savikrāntagāmi(tā), which is properly an anuvyañjana; cf. RP 47.1 brahmaghoṣā. — **29.** abhinīlanetra (Pali °netta), LVa, LVb 27, Bbh 29, Dh 31; Mv 29 nīla; Mv ii.306.15; Gv 24 (2d ed.); Mvy 28 abhinīlanetra-gopakṣmā, combining this with next. Cf. RP 46.15; 50.13. — **30.** go-pakṣma, or °man (Pali gopakkhuma), Bbh 30 °mā (n. sg.), Gv 25 °maḥ; °ma-netra LVa 28, and intended by corrupt readings LVb 28; Dh 32; Mv 30 °ma (mss.); for Mvy see prec. — **31.** ūrṇā bhruvāntare jātāvadātā mṛdutūlasaṃ-nibhā (? exact language uncertain, but Pali uṇṇā bhamu-kantare jātā odātā mudutūlasannibhā); Pali seems supported by Mv ii.306.17–18, where read bhruvāntare(ṇa) ... ūrṇā hi prakāśāvadātā (mss. cited as °śā ca vātā) mṛduka-(so v.l.)-tūlasādṛśā; LVa 29 ūrṇā ... bhruvor madhye jātā himarajataprakāśā; Dh 17 ūrṇālaṃkṛtamu-khatā; Gv 26 bhruvāntare ... ūrṇā jātābhūn mṛdvī ... śuddhā prabhāsvarā himaguḍikā-tuṣāravarṇā ...; Bbh 32 ūrṇā ... bhruvor madhye jātā śvetā śaṅkhasaṃnibhā pra-dakṣiṇāvartā (cf. LV, Mvy); LVa 31 (cf. LVb below, LVa 29 above, Bbh, and Mvy) ... pradakṣiṇāvartakeśaḥ;

Mvy 29 ūrṇākośaḥ (so read), and 31 pradakṣiṇāvartakeśaḥ; LVb 31 bhrūmadhye-sujātapradakṣiṇāvartottaptaviśuddhavarṇābhāsorṇā(ḥ, n. sg., Bhvr.); Mv 31 ūrṇā. Cf. RP 46.14; 50.12. — **32.** uṣṇīṣaśīrṣa (see s.v. **uṣṇīṣa**; Pali uṇhīsasīsa), LVa 32; Mv 32; Mv ii.307.4; Bbh 31 (°ṣāḥ); °śiraska(-tā) Mvy 32; Dh 23; mūrdhni . . . uṣṇīṣam Gv 27; uṣṇīṣaśīrṣānavalokitamūrdha LVb 30; uṣṇi RP 46.13; 50.11. — A few secondary insertions in individual lists are here ignored. References to the 32 lakṣaṇa, usually as seen on a Buddha, are frequent, e. g. SP 47.10; and see s.v. **lakṣa** for two cases where Senart assumes, wrongly I think, that Mv substitutes that word for lakṣaṇa.

Lakṣaṇapariśodhana, m., n. of a samādhi: Mvy 600; ŚsP 1424.1.

Lakṣaṇaparvatavairocana, n. of a Tathāgata: Gv 310.17.

Lakṣaṇabhūṣitagātra, n. of a Tathāgata: Gv 421.16.

lakṣaṇa-mātreṇa, *by mere definition, merely because of inherent form* or *nature, ipso facto, automatically*: (ity evamādinā) °treṇa, samyaksaṃbuddhānāṃ mānsacakṣuḥ upadiśyate (so mss.) Mv i.159.1.

Lakṣaṇamerumegharutaghoṣa, n. of a Buddha: Gv 258.17.

Lakṣaṇaruciravairocanā, n. of lokadhātu: Gv 81.25.

Lakṣaṇarucirasupuṣpitāṅga, n. of a Tathāgata: Gv 311.26.

Lakṣaṇavibhūṣitadhvajacandra, n. of a Tathāgata: Gv 311.24.

Lakṣaṇaśrīparvata, n. of a Tathāgata: Gv 360.23.

Lakṣaṇasumeru, n. of a Tathāgata: Gv 361.2.

Lakṣaṇa-sūtra (= Pali Lakkhaṇa-sutta, DN 30), n. of a (part of a) work: Bbh 378.3.

Lakṣaṇasūryacakrasamantaprabha, n. of a Tathāgata: Gv 309.26.

lakṣaṇāhata, adj. (= Pali lakkhaṇā°, Vin. i.76.1), *branded*: MSV iv.68.7.

lakṣaṇeya (to **lakṣaṇa**; cf. Skt. lakṣaṇya, *possessing auspicious marks*), either adj., *possessing auspicious marks*, or n. pr. of a disciple of the Buddha: Siṃhanandi(ṃ) viśālākṣaṃ °ṇeyam anuttamaṃ Mv i.183.1 (vs). (Senart's Index lakṣ°, without capital letter, evidently taking it as adj.)

Lakṣaṇottamā, n. of a kiṃnara maid: Kv 6.16.

lakṣaṇya, *interpreter of bodily marks*: brāhmaṇā °yā naimittikā(ḥ) . . . Divy 474.26.

lakṣmitā (Skt. lakṣmī plus -tā, i m.c.), *state of fortune, majesty*: yatha lakṣaṇā yatha ca darśita lakṣmitā ca LV 116.5 (vs; so all mss. but one; both edd. lakṣitā, interpreted in Calc. as = lakṣyatā), *as the* (32) *marks* (of a mahāpuruṣa) *and a state of majesty are displayed* (in the Bodhisattva) . . .

Lakṣmīṃdadā, n. of a kiṃnara maid: Kv 6.1.

Lakṣmīpatī (so mss., Senart em. °matī), n. of a devakumārikā in the southern quarter: Mv iii.307.8.

Lakṣmīputra, n. of a former Buddha: Mv i.141.4.

laggati (= Pali id., BHS **lagnati,** q.v.), *sticks, clings*: Mv ii.429.13 (v.l. lagneti).

lagna (**1**) (nt.? otherwise only ppp., *stuck*), *the being stuck, obstacle, obstruction*: nāsti tayor lagnabhayaṃ LV 381.8 (prose, no v.l., except tayol-lag°), *they two* (oxen) *had no fear of obstacles*, or *of being stuck* (in mud); Tib. thogs; (**2**) m. pl., n. of a brahmanical gotra: Divy 635.14; cf. **Daṇḍa-lagna.**

lagnati, lagneti? (also **laggati,** q.v.; and **anulagnati, vilagnita**; = Pali laggati, Pkt. laggai, acc. to Geiger 136.2 and Pischel 488 from Skt. *lagyati; but see § 28.19), *sticks, clings*: °nati Mv iii.148.2 (twice); impv. °natha Mv iii.354.10; opt. °neyaṃ Mv iii.128.3. In Mv ii.429.13 lagneti is v.l. for **laggati,** q.v., of text.

laghūtthānatā (Skt. laghu plus utthāna; in mg. = Pali lahuṭṭhāna, without -tā), *good physical condition*, always in a cliché inquiring after a person's health and well-being, with **alpābādhatā, alpātaṅkatā,** yātrā, bala, sukha, anavadyatā, **sparśavihāratā** (or, in SP, Mvy, sukha-sparśa° for the last three): SP 429.3; Mvy 6287; Divy 156.13; Av i.325.13; ii.90.14. Pali (above) in very similar cliché, e. g. Ud.15.18.

Laṅkā-patha, nt. and m., *a region in Ceylon* (this use of -patha would seem rather anomalous in Skt.): Sāgaratīraṃ nāma °thaṃ (n. sg.) Gv 67.17, or °thas 68.3.

Laṅkāvatāra (with or sc. sūtram), nt., n. of a work (our Laṅk): Mvy 1338; Laṅk 1.5; °**ra-sūtra,** nt., id.: Laṅk 5.6; 258.5 (cited Śikṣ 133.5); Śikṣ 131.13; 135.5 (here a passage from Laṅk 255.1 is quoted).

Laṅkeśvara, n. of a yakṣa: Māy 83.

Laṅkeśvarī, n. of a yoginī: Sādh 427.4.

laṅgaka, adj. (= Skt. laṅga; may be m.c.), *lame*: SP 95.5 (vs), cited s.v. **kuṇḍaka.**

laṅghaka, m. (= Pali id.), *jumper, acrobat*: Mv iii.113.3.

? **laṅghanaka** (conjecture; mss. all corrupt), Index *means of crossing* (?): °nakopamaḥ Divy 340.22; Tib. (Dutt, MSV iv.42.14 note) gziṅs, *boat, ferry*.

laṅghayati, *transports* (grain): (tatas te śakaṭair) . . . gardabhādibhir laṅghayitvā tasmin khalābhyantare prakṣiperan Kv 71.8.

laṅghita, nt., *jumping* (as exercise or sport): Mvy 4997 = Tib. ḥchoṅs pa, but Tib. on LV 156.9 mchoṅs pa, *jumping* (Jä.); foll. in Mvy 4999, 5000, by jāvitam, plavitam; with dhāvita and javita Mv ii.423.16; iii.184.8; °te plavite javite LV 151.17; °te LV 156.9 (later in list, javite plavite).

lajjitavya (gdve. of lajj; = Pali lajjitabbaka, v.l. °bba, Jāt. vi.395.18, and a-lajjitabba), (*matter*) *which one should be ashamed of*; also neg., a-lajj°: both Ud xvi.4 (alajjitavye lajjanti lajjitavye alajjitā).

lajjin, adj. (= Pali id.; cf. **alajjin**), *ashamed*: MSV iii.62.11.

lañcaka, adj. (Pali id., ifc.), *excellent, fine*: kasyetaṃ (v.l. °yaitaṃ) nimittaṃ, lañcakaṃ (v.l. lambakaṃ) pāpakaṃ vā Mv i.421.8, *what does this predict*? (is it) *good or bad*?; sarvāṇi lañcakāni 467.7, *all fine*; also v.l. for (nara-)lambaka Mv i.191.5 (mss. evenly divided). See s.v. **lambaka.**

[**laṭikā,** app. misprint for latikā (so Index): Mvy 433 = Tib. khri śiṅ, *creeper*; but Mironov **prapāṭikā,** q.v.]

laḍita, adj. and subst. nt. (= Skt. lalita), (**1**) adj., *playful*: °ta-mīnakulam Jm 229.19; (**2**) nt., *playful movement*: °tam Mvy 7136 (v.l. and Mironov lāḍitam). See also **Lalitavyūha** (v.l. Laḍita°, sometimes adopted by Lefm.).

[**laḍḍī,** see **laddī.**]

laṇḍaka, m. or nt. (from Pali and rare Skt. laṇḍa, *dung*; cf. Pali aja-laṇḍikā), *piece of dung*, in vatsa-°kānāṃ Mmk 674.28 (prose).

latā, *creeper*, as in Pali ep. of desire or greed, as entangling: (na) saritāṃ (see **saritā**) latāṃ śoṣayato MSV iii.54.2; 57.16.

latārka, m. (Skt. Lex., *green onion*, BR), *onion* of some sort: Mvy 5732, among other names for onions; = Tib. me mo, or, sgre ḥu (mg.?).

laddī (= Pkt. id., *dung of an elephant* etc., Sheth), (piece of) *dung* (of a horse): laddīś (acc. pl.) chorayati Divy 513.15, 24 (ed. wrongly em. laḍḍīś).

-lapa, (m.?), seems to be implied in mg. of **lapana,** q.v., by **sthita-lapa** and **nir-lapaka**; the same seems implied by Pali nil-lapa (n. pl. °pā, *free from lapa*, Bhvr.) AN ii.26.25, altho in line 23, just before, both kuhā and lapā are adj., n. pl., = **kuhaka, lapaka**; so comm. iii.42.18 lapā ti upalāpakā (v.l. upalapakā).

lapaka, adj. or subst. m. (= Pali id.; see next), *boasting*, or *one who boasts* (in the sense explained s.v. **lapana**): Śikṣ 20.16, see **kuhaka.**

lapana, nt., and °**nā** (= Pali id.), *boasting* (of one's own religious qualities, to extract gifts from patrons; one of the 5 **mithyājīva** of a monk, see references s.v. **kuhana**): Mvy 2494 °nā = Tib. kha gsag, *vain mouth*; twice written lepana (certainly a mere corruption) in RP, see s.v. **kuhana** for these and other occurrences. Cf. prec. and next.

lapayati (= Pali lapeti; wrongly defined PTSD), *boasts* (in the sense explained s.v. **lapana**): Ud xxx.52 na kāmahetor lapayanti santaḥ.

labdhaka, adj. (= Skt. labdha, with -ka svārthe), *obtained*: Av ii.147.12; 148.3, 4; in repetitions of phrase which in 147.11 has labdha; all prose.

labdhapūrvāpara (mss. °vara, °cara), adj., *in possession of continuity* (with kulam): Mv i.198.3; see **ātmapūrvāpara.**

Labdhāmitābhagarbhatantra (em., mss. Labdhāmat°), n. of a work: Sādh 221.14.

labhā (m.c., see below), **labhyaṃ, labhyā,** indecl. (= Pali labbhā), (*it is*) *possible*, usually in the sense of *allowable*; usually with infin., the 'logical subject' of which is instr. and the 'logical object' nom., showing that, as with (Skt.) śakya and BHS **śakyā,** the infin. is (or may be) passive in mg.; it happens often that this 'logical object' (nom.) is fem., which might tempt one to consider labhyā a fem. adj., but in one case at least labhyā ... puruṣo occurs, which, with Pali labbhā and BHS śakyā, helps to prove that all these forms are indecl.; without infin., evaṃ labhyaṃ Mv ii.272.10, *it is possible so*; with finite verb, labhyaṃ satpuruṣā pratyāgacchanti akuśalena karmaṇā vipratisārī bhavanti Mv i.37.4, *it is possible, good men* (may) *backslide, and* (afterwards) *feel remorse for their evil action* (wrongly Senart); labhā, m.c. for (Pali) labbhā or (BHS) labhyā, in Mv ii.144.5 (vs), read with mss. parityajya dhṛtir labhā, *by abandoning* (worldly things), *steadfastness is possible* (obtainable), wrongly Senart; with infin., labhyā strībhiḥ puruṣo (with mss., Senart wrongly em. °ṣaṃ) vāhayituṃ Mv ii.480.3, *can women cause a man to carry them*? (cf. line 6 below, with 1 ms., na śakyo yuṣmābhir eṣo vāhayituṃ); labhyā etena ... agramahiṣī (mss.; Senart em. °ṣīṃ) ... āhanituṃ ii.455.20, *can he* (be allowed to) *strike the chief queen*?; so also 457.3 °mahiṣī (mss., Senart °ṣīṃ); no labhyā yuṣmābhiḥ anyam-anyaṃ (adv.) tyajituṃ iii.151.12, and, na labhyā yuṣmābhiḥ parasparasya (adv.) tyajituṃ 19, *you may not be mutually abandoned* (*by one-another*); na labhyaṃ atra puruṣeṇa praviśituṃ Mv iii.151.7, *a man may not enter here*; MSV i.249.12 (see **āmiṣa**); labhyā mithyādṛṣṭiḥ prahātuṃ Mvy 7027, *heresy can* (*may*) *be abandoned* (Tib. nus pa, *possible*, or ruṅ ba, *proper, right*); labhyam ebhir adharmeṇa karmaṇā kartum MSV iii.117.4, *it is possible* (here not *allowable*) *that they may act by an incorrect rite.*

lampa, nt. (cf. AMg. lambaṇa, *mouthful*), *mouthful*, or *titbit*, or the like: anye madhumrakṣitāni lampāni mukhe allīyanti Mv ii.190.5 (prose), *some put honey-smeared bits into their mouths.* So mss.; Senart em. ālopāni (see **ālopa**).

lampaka, nt., some sort of garment: Mvy 8999 = Tib. stod (s)kor (*waistcoat*, Das) naṅ tshaṅs can (?); Chin. *silk garment for upper part of body.*

lampuṭa (mg. unknown), in Mmk 505.(19–)20 (vss), (eṣā Suparṇine mudrā Suparṇīti pragīyate,) tad eva lampuṭākāraṃ (*lampuṭa-shaped*), viparyastākāraceṣṭitam (hypermetric!); line 21 continues: sā bhaved yamalamudrā tu garutmasyāpi mahātmane (!).

lamba, mss. reading for **lumba,** q.v.

?-**lambaka,** adj., only ifc., (like Skt. vara) *excellent, fine*: = **lañcaka,** with which it varies in mss. of Mv; see Senart's notes i.466 f., ii.545, 572; Senart varies in his procedure; in ii.264.6 he em. mss. -lambako to -lañcakam; -lambaka is found oftener in Mv mss., but in view of Pali -lañcaka should perh. be emended to this always: pārthiva-lambaka, *excellent king*, Mv i.115.5; nara-lambaka, *excellent man, best of men* (usually of the Buddha), i.154.18; 156.6, 18; 191.5 (three mss. -lañcaka); ii.26.15; tṛṇarāśilambako, mss. (except tṛṇakāśi-), ii.264.6 (see above).

Lambadāma, n. of a former Buddha: Mv i.137.1 (see s.v. **Hemavarṇa**).

lambana, nt., *fringe, trimmings* (of a garment): Mvy 5848 (misprinted 5858, also in Index) = Tib. śam bu.

Lambā (**1**) n. of an ogress: SP 400.4; (**2**) n. of a piśācī: Māy 238.19.

lambika, app. *the Indian cuckoo*: lambikarutena svareṇa nirghoṣeṇārocayati Kv 73.24.

Lambikā, n. of an ogress: Māy 241.15.

Lambuka, n. of a nāga king, or of two in the same list in Mvy 3237, 3247; Māy 246.33.

Lambodara, n. of a yakṣa: Māy 45.

-layanaka, f. °**ikā** (to °na plus -ka), Bhvr., *having ... cells*: dvi-°nikā, daśa-, dvādaśa-, MSV iv.74.8, 9.

lardayati (cf. laddaṇa, subst., cited as Deśī word from Samarāiccakahā 537 in Ratnach. 5.823; and Hindi lādnā), *loads*: sthorāṃ (q.v.) lardayantaṃ Divy 5.22, lardayituṃ 23, lardayitvā 26 and 334.19.

lalanā, n. of an artery, vein, or passage-way (nāḍī) in the body: Sādh 448.11 ff.; nāḍyo lalanā-rasanāvadhūtayaḥ 11; lalanā prajñāsvabhāvena 13; akṣobhyāvahā lalanā 15; cf. **rasanā** and **avadhūtī.**

Lalitagupta, n. of an author: Sādh 267.15; 270.7.

Lalitavikrama, n. of a former Buddha: Mv i.116.15.

Lalitavistara, m., n. of a work (our LV): LV 4.17; 6.16; 438.20 ff.; Mvy 1331; Śikṣ 203.14; °**ra-sūtra,** id., Śikṣ 5.12 etc.

Lalitavyūha, (**1**) n. of a (trāyastriṃśa) devaputra: LV 203.14; 217.6 (ms. A in both Laḍita°); (**2**) n. of a Bodhisattva: LV 290.10; (**3**) n. of a samādhi: LV 289.1 ff. (here Lefm. Laḍita° with best mss., v.l. Lal°). Cf. **laḍita.**

lalla, adj. (cf. Skt. lalalla or °lā, BR; AMg. lalla, adj. acc. to Sheth, subst. acc. to Ratnach.), *speaking brokenly* or *indistinctly* (onomat.): na lolo bhavati na lallo bhavati na kallo bhavati AsP 427.1.

Lavaṇabhadrika, n. of a disciple of Śākyamuni: Mvy 1061. Cf. **Bhadrika** (3), prob. not the same.

lavāpayati (= Pali lavāpeti; both MIndic caus. to Pkt. lavai, recorded by Sheth from Mārkaṇḍeya, = Skt. lunāti), *causes to be reaped*: gdve. lavāpayitavyāni (dhānyajātīni) Mv iii.178.4 (prose).

Lavuruka, n. of a nāga: Māy 222.3.

lasa, adj. (otherwise recorded only in neg. a-lasa), *active, quick-moving*: suku (= Skt. śuko) lasu (= laso; only v.l. in mss. rasu) guṇadhara ... LV 167.1 (vs), (when you were once incarnate as) *a virtuous parrot, quick-darting.* No other interpretation seems possible, unless we em. to a deriv. of lap-, cf. AMg. lava, *speaking*, and BHS **-lāpika.** Tib. seems to omit the word.

lahu and **lahuka,** °**ka-tara,** adj. (= Pali id., both; MIndic for Skt. laghu, once laghuka, Schmidt, Nachträge), *light*, etc. (mgs. as in Skt.): lahu (v.l. laghu) Mv iii.159.5; lahuṃ Mv i.222.10 (vs; in parallel ii.24.18 laghu); iii.2.17 (v.l. laghuṃ); best ms. at Suv 38.11 (for Nobel laghu; end of line of vs); lahukataro Mv ii.249.11; lahukā-d-ayam iii.54.4 (prose; v.l. laghu°; d Hiatus-bridger).

lāghava (nt.; cf. Skt. id.; Pali lahu, lahuka, seems to approach a mg. similar to this more closely than Skt. laghu etc., but I have found no precise parallel), *buoyancy, not sinking*, of a fishline, taut because a fish has caught the bait: tena sūtra-lāghavena jānāti, gṛhīto matsya iti Śikṣ 94.18.

Lāṅgala, m. pl., n. of a brahmanical gotra: Divy 635.14; (n. of a brahmanical school, of the Chandogas: Divy 637.27; cf. pw s.v., 2b).

lāṅgula (in this mg. only Skt. Lex.), *penis*: °lachinnaḥ Mvy 8868 = Tib. pho mtshan (chad pa).

Lāḍa, m., also adj., f. **Lāḍī** (cf. Pali Lāḷa, Pkt. Lāḍa, the latter identified by Sheth with Skt. Lāṭa), n. of a country or province, and pl. people, in India: Lāḍodreṣu (read °ḍreṣu?) tathā Sindhau Mmk 233.7; Lāḍī vācā, *the language of L.*, id. 9; Lāḍānāṃ janapade Mmk 624.8; °nām adhipatir 625.2, 17.

lāḍika (cf. Schmidt, Nachträge, s.v., citing Skt. lāḍīka), *boy*: Mvy 4076 = Tib. bus pa.

lāḍita, ppp. (cf. next; = Skt. lālita; Gr. lāḍ°), *cherished*: sa tair jñātibhis tathā lāḍito... Av i.206.12; by em. (? see Corrig. p. 210) i.277.9. [In LV 80.17 (vs) read tāḍitā, *beaten* (subject ghaṇṭa) for Lefm. lāḍitā, vv.ll. lāl°, nāḍ°.]

lāḍyate, pass. (to Skt. lālayati, Pali lāḷeti), *is cherished, fondly tended*: MSV iii.134.22.

lāpana, m. (Pali only nt., n. act.), *speaking, one who speaks* (n. ag.): gāthābhir gītābhir °naḥ Mvy 849, said of a Bodhisattva.

-lāpika, adj. (= Skt. -lāpin plus -ka), *talking*, in manuṣya-lāpiko śuko Mv i.271.13 (prose), *a parrot talking in human speech*; so mss.; Senart °ṣyālāpiko, because of the parallel °ṣyālāpino (Skt. ālāpin) i.274.3, which perhaps justifies the em.; yet Skt. has -lāpin.

lābha-niścikīrṣā, °ṣu-tā, lābha-niṣpādanā, see the second parts of the cpds.

[**lābhā**, in lābhā te mahārājo sulabdhā **Mv** i.226.14 (prose), taken as fem. by Senart, wrongly; it is n. pl. m.; so also in the parallels alleged in Senart's note, incl. Pali Dhp. 204.]

-lābhika (Skt. lābha plus -ika, or -lābhin plus **-ka**; cf. AMg. lābhiya acc. to Sheth, lābh-yukta, lābh-**wālā**), *leading to the acquisition of*...; see s.v. **kṣaya** (2); sarvalābhikam MSV iii.93.4, (the rule) *regarding all profits*; refers to 99.20, (pārivāsikasya) sarvapaścāc ca lābho deyaḥ, *a probationer gets a share last of all.*

lābhin (Skt. rare and recorded only ifc.), *acquiring, getting*, with gen., once loc. (lābhino bhavanti dhāraṇīṣu te sadā... RP 11.6, vs): pratisaṃvidāṃ lābhy abhūt SP 200.11 (prose); vimānānāṃ lābhī 349.12 (prose); bodhisattvavimokṣasya lābhinī Gv 287.8 (prose); lābhinī bhavati divyānāṃ gandhānāṃ (etc.) Mv i.210.18 = ii.14.19 (prose); similarly i.211.9 = ii.15.8; lābhī plus gens. ii.139.10 ff.; iii.200.14; 201.3; alābhy (masc.) eva saṃl (= san, *being one that gets nothing*) lābhy aham asmy anityasaṃjñāyā... Bhīk 26b.5–27a.1.

Lāmā, n. of a yoginī or similar demoness: Sādh 425.13; 439.10.

lālapya (m.? = Pali lālappa), = next, q.v., *lamentation*: so read in Mv i.154.14 (vs) for lālasya(-śoka-, with v.l., or text -soka-, -parideva-).

lālapyana, nt. (to Skt. lālapyate with -ana; = Pali lālappana, also in definition of parideva), *lamentation*: °naṃ paridevaḥ Śikṣ 222.8 (definition).

lālayita, m. (! to Skt. lālayati, caus. of root lal-; formally, MIndic ppp. based on caus. present, for Skt. lālita), perh. *desire* (or, with Foucaux, *jouissance*): iha °yitā sarve martyā divyā bhavāgraparyantāḥ, tyaktā mayā... LV 374.7 (vs).

lālasaka, f. **°ikā**, adj. (= Skt. lālasa, plus endearing -ka; acc. to MW. °saka occurs in Pkt., but it is not recorded in Sheth or Ratnach.), *eager, desirous*: rati-lālasikāṃ LV 322.16; kāma-su-lālasikāṃ 323.9; both in vss, both of daughters of **Māra.**

[**lālasya**, see **lālapya.**]

lālāṭikā (cf. Skt. lālāṭī, id.), *forehead*: °kām anuprayacchataḥ (dual) MSV iii.16.7, *give applause*, = Pali nalāṭikaṃ pi denti Vin. ii.10.30; PTSD *frown*, which is impossible in the context; see SBE 17.349 with note 4.

Lāsyā, n. of a goddess or yoginī (*Dance* personified): Sādh 157.12 etc.; 324.6.

likhitaka, adj. (to likhita, ppp.; seems to have -ka svārthe), *peeled, stripped*, of sugar-cane: (asti) madhutarpaṇaṃ likhitakāś cekṣavaḥ; te madhutarpaṇam ikṣulikhitakāṃś cādāya... LV 382.10 (prose).

liṅgita (nt.; = Skt. āliṅgita, perhaps to be adopted here by em., but forms of liṅg-, without ā-, seem to be reported, tho rarely, from Skt., see BR; Pali, as liṅgiya, Therīg. 398, comm. āliṅgetvā; and Pkt., see Sheth), *embrace*: -capeṭa-liṅgita-cumbita- etc. Laṅk 119.14; all erotic practices; Suzuki, absurdly, *suggesting!*

Licchavi (= Pali id.), or **Litsavi** (Suv), n. of a people, with capital **Vaiśālī**: Mv i.254.15 (v.l. Le°), 17 (in the sequel regularly **Le°**, q.v.); ii.76.8; Divy 55.18 ff.; 136.8; Mmk 621.13; **Litsavi** (confirmed Tib.) Suv 13.1 ff. Cf. Licchivi, Manu 10.22, and see Lassen IA. 1.138 note 1.

lipi, f. (Skt.), *writing*; in LV 125.19 ff. the Bodhisattva lists 64 kinds of script; in Mv i.135.5 ff. a similar but much shorter list; Senart's note compares the two. Non-Skt. items from either list are included here.

lipika (from lipi), *writer, clerk, scribe*: Divy 293.5, 9.

-līḍa, ifc. Bhvr. for līḍā = Skt. līlā (§ 2.46), *grace, attractiveness*: suślakṣṇa-sulīḍa-vastravaradhāriṇī (Māyā) LV 41.9 (prose); salīḍa-rūpāḥ (apsarases) 49.9 (vs); sadṛśaliṅga-līḍāḥ (Bodhisattvas) Gv 378.26 (prose).

līna, adj. (= Pali id.; not in this sense in Skt.; for true definition see CPD s.v. alīna, q.v.; wrongly Childers and PTSD), *dispirited, faint-hearted*: Mvy 7269 = Tib. zhum pa; 850 apagata-līna-citta (of Bodhisattvas); Śikṣ 20.15 līnaṃ cittaṃ bodhisattvānāṃ na saṃvidyate. Cf. 2 **līyati.**

līna-tā, Śikṣ 179.14, and **°tva**, nt., 180.10, abstr. from prec.

līpyase, *thou art stained*: Gv 389.2, prob. misprint for lipyase.

1 **līyati** (= Skt. ḍī-), *flies*, only in cpds.; see **abhi-, ava-, ni-, pra-lī°.**

2 **līyati** (Skt. līyate, hardly in this mg.; cf. **līna**), *is cast down, dispirited*: līyanty alābhair na ca RP 13.8 (vs).

līyanā (= Pali id.; to prec. plus -anā), *faintheartedness*, or *sluggishness*: °nāṃ sarva varjitvā śṛṇuyāt sūtram īdṛśam SP 235.9 (vs). (Burnouf *faiblesse*; Kern *distractedness.*)

līlāyitatva, nt. (cf. Skt. līlāyita), *bodily transformation*: Mvy 9428. So Tib. lus bsgyur ba, and second Chin. gloss; first one seems to mean *swaying of the body*, doubtless thinking of the primary mg. of Skt. līlā.

līlin, adj. (from Skt. līlā with -in), *enjoying sport* or *pastime*: ajarāmaralīlī Mmk 80.3; 83.20–21.

lugna, ppp. (to **lujjati**; = Pali lugga, Skt. rugna), *broken*: lugna-pralugna Mv ii.429.18.

? **luṅga**: in Divy 650.22 iti luṅgādhyāyaḥ, colophon to a chapter which is not given in the text; the word is not mentioned in Index or notes; the following colophons suggest that the chapter may have dealt with signs or omens of some sort. Skt. Lex. luṅga = mātuluṅga, *citron*, (fruit or tree); otherwise not recorded.

[**-lucana**, see **keśa-l°.**]

lujjati (MIndic), **°jyati, °te** (= Pali lujjati; not recorded in Pkt. Sheth or Ratnach.; = Skt. rujyate; see also **pra-lu°, vi-lu°**), *is broken*: °jyamānaṃ Mv ii.356.9 (vs; v.l. pra-lu°) = iii.280.15 (vs; here Senart lujja° with v.l.); lujjanti, v.l. lujyanti (pres. pple. loc.; Senart em. °te) Mv ii.371.3; lujjamānaṃ, v.l. lujy°, ii.371.13, 17, and repeated below; lujje (aor.) ii.412.11; lujyata iti lokaḥ (etymologizing) Mvy 3061; lujyante AsP 256.7. See **lugna.**

luḍati (= Pali luḷati, trans. and intrans.), intrans. *stirs, moves, is agitated*: LV 308.4 (vs) vṛkṣa (n. pl.) luḍanti. Cf. **luḍita.**

luḍita, adj. (pple. of **luḍati**, q.v.; = Pali luḷita; cf.

Skt. lulita, loḍita; see also a-luḍita), *agitated*, sometimes physically: Gv 202.21, of water, *stirred* by perfumed breeze; Sukh 38.1 (nadyaḥ . . .) nānāratna-luḍita-puṣpa-saṃghāta-vāhinyo; oftener intellectually, Laṅk 285.5, with citta; Gv 338.4 °ta-saṃtānaiḥ (see **saṃtāna**, which here = citta); Mvy 6819.

lumba, a kind of tree, acc. to Senart (who em. thus for mss. **lamba**) the *plakṣa*, in lumbodyānaṃ Mv i.99.6 (vs), applied to what is otherwise known as the **Lumbinī** grove; since in line 8 **lumbinī** (q.v., 2) seems to be a tree-name, the em. seems plausible, tho no other record of lumba (or **lamba**) or lumbinī as a tree-name has been noted.

lumbinī, (**1**) (= Pali id.) n. of the grove where Śākyamuni was born: LV 78.19; 79.11, 16; 81.8 (°nīye, loc. sg., attributed to a non-existent adj. lumbinīya in BR); 91.16; all these vss, also, with °ni m.c., 234.19; 252.19; 411.21; °nī Mv iii.112.9; Mvy 4123; Karmav 82.1; often °nī-vana, Mv i.149.3; ii.18.10 ff.; 145.6; Divy 389.16; Gv 365.5, etc.; (**2**) seemingly, n. of a tree, = plakṣa: dadarśa 'tha lumbinīṃ Mv i.99.8 (vs), foll. by tasyāḥ śākhāṃ . . . (the subject is Māyā, in the Lumbinī grove); see also **lumba**; (**3**) n. of a class of deities: Mahāsamāj., Waldschmidt, Kl. Skt. Texte 4, 191.1 lumbinī lumbinī-śreṣṭhā(ḥ); confirmed Tib.

Lumbinīśreṣṭha, n. of a class of deities, see prec. (3).

lūkha, adj. (= Pali id., Skt. rūkṣa; see also **lūha, rukṣa, ruccha, a-lūkha, a-lūha**, and next), *coarse, poor* (of food); *inferior, bad* (of inclinations); once perhaps subst., *evil*: of food, Mv ii.233.7, 8 (note lūha in 5); 234.9; 460.15; iii.120.22; 178.7; lūkhādhimuktikā Mv ii.313.9; seemingly subst., *evil*, Mv iii.364.14 śuddhalūkhā (ṛṣayo) *purified of evil* (does it really refer to their diet? improbable; but they are mūlaphalāhārā in preceding line; possibly, then, *of pure and coarse* [*simple*] *food*?).

lūkha-tā (abstr. from prec.), *harshness* = (ascetic) *severe austerity*: Mv ii.208.2.

lūna-lipi, a kind of script: LV 126.1 (between Cīna- and Hūna-l°). Omitted in one ms., one corrects to dūna-; Tib. phu na; not in the Mv parallel list i.135. Kirfel, Kosm., records, as names of peoples, Lūta (84), and Līna (88).

[**lūnāti**, prob. uncorrected misprint for Skt. lunāti: LV 286.4 (prose). No v.l. in Lefm., yet Calc. reads lu°; not noted in Weller.]

lūha, adj. (= AMg. id., by the side of lukkha, rukkha; see under **lūkha**), (1) *coarse, poor*, of food; (2) *poor, inferior*, of bodily condition; (3) *harsh, severe*, of practices; (4) *inferior, bad*, of inclinations, mental tendencies; (5) *coarse, rough*, of garments; (6) *bad*, of more than one of the above, or in a general, unspecified way; adv. lūhena: (**1**) Mv ii.208.7; 233.5; iii.14.20; Divy 13.27; 425.13; Av ii.114.12; 115.2; in Av i.285.4 lūhenābhiramate, *he takes pleasure in* . . . (no noun expressed), but perhaps referring to appetite for filthy food, or perhaps more general, cf. lūhādhimukta in next line; Śikṣ 128.16; 129.9 f.; 130.5; 131.4 (Bendall and Rouse, Transl. 128 ff. *poor*, tacitly withdrawing Bendall's erroneous interpretation in ed. 128 note 4); KP 123.3; Bbh 120.10 (? contrasted with praṇīta, as often when this word is used of food); (**2**) LV 257.7 lūha-nyūna-durbala-kāya; in LV 263.22 read lūha-durbala-kāya, with Weller 32, supported by Tib. (text with mss. lūhaṃ, which could only be adv., = lūhena, 6 below); (**3**) lūha-vrata LV 259.3; °prahāṇa (q.v.) Mv ii.126.12 etc., repeatedly; °karman Mv iii.14.20 (? text uncertain); (**4**) lūhādhimukta LV 264.4, 10; Mv ii.131.5 (followed by lūhābhiprasanna); Av i.285.5 (see under 1 above); (**5**) cīvara Divy 81.26; 427.14; (**6**) of the 4 **niśraya** (q.v.) collectively, Bbh 193.5; defined by Tib. ṅan pa, *bad, poor* Mvy 2700; this is the ordinary Tib. rendering (acc. to Bendall Śikṣ 128 note 4 Tib. in a couple of Śikṣ passages renders by ñuṅ, *little, scant*); adv. lūhena, *poorly*, LV 271.3.

Lūhasudatta, n. of a householder: Divy 159.20; 160.4.

Lekuñcika, n. of a brahman's son of Śrāvastī: Av ii.153.1 ff.

lekhanā (cf. Skt. and Pali °na, nt.), (act of) *writing*: Mvy 903 (in sense of *copying* sacred works).

lekha-lipi, a kind of writing, Senart *epistolary*, i. e. *cursive writing*: Mv i.135.6; **lekha-pratilekha-lipi** LV 126.6, in passage corresp. to Mv; Tib. literally, *script for sending a letter and return* (*reply*), spriṅ yig daṅ lan gyi yi ge.

lekhahārika (cf. Skt. °hāraka, °hārin), *courier, letter-carrier*: Mvy 3817. Cf. s.v. **lehari**(**ka**).

Lecchavi = **Licchavi**, q.v. (vṛddhi formation, § 3.67? or MIndic e for short i, § 3.59, as Senart assumes on 255.9?): Mv i.254.13 ff., in a long passage, almost always Le° (down to p. 299).

Lecchavika (also °vaka?), pl., = **Licchavi**, cf. prec.: Mv i.283.12 (mss. °vakā, n. pl.; Senart °vikā); 300.4.

leḍu (Pkt. id.; AMg. lelu, leṭṭhu; Pali leḍḍu; Skt. leṣṭu), *clod*: acc. to Kern, SP Preface p. viii, in Kashgar rec. (along with leṣṭu) for Nep. loṣṭa.

lena, leṇa, nt., also m. (= Pali lena, leṇa, often with tāṇa, saraṇa; Skt. layana), *refuge*, esp. with synonyms such as trāṇa, śaraṇa; may be m., as epithet of a Buddha: alene lenasaṃjñino Mv i.7.7 (prose), *thinking a refuge that which is not*; lenaś ca Mv i.186.8; lenaṃ (n. sg.) ca i.242.1; mss. leṇo (v.l. layaṇo) i.257.4 (prose), with trāṇo śaraṇo (Buddha); lenaṃ (n. sg.) ii.328.11 (vs, of Buddha); alena, *no refuge*, Mv i.7.7 (above); Bhvr., *refugeless*, alenā atrāṇā aśaraṇā Mv iii.353.18 (prose); sattva alena atrāṇyāḥ (v.l. °ṇāḥ), śaraṇavihīnā . . . Suv 53.1 (vs).

lepa, m. (Skt. and Pali id.), *lime, sticky matter*, as a snare to catch monkeys: markaṭānāṃ bandhanāya leyaḥ Śikṣ 77.4, text, read certainly lepaḥ, cf. Transl. 82 note 2; Tib. rñoṅ, *snare, trap*; Chin. said to render *dung*.

lepaka (Skt. Lex. id.), *plasterer, layer of mortar*: in lists of craftsmen, Mv iii.113.17; 443.4.

[**lepana**, error for **lapana**, q.v.]

[**leya**, see **lepa**.]

lelohita, nt., some sort of material listed as unsuitable for monks' robes: MSV ii.52.10; acc. to Tib. seṅ ras = **viralikā**.

leśi- (stem in comp.; read leśa- ?) = **laiśika**: MSV iii.88.2.

lehari, m. (so Kyoto ed., text, v.l. lohāri), or (Index) **leharika**, Mironov **lohariḥ**, vv.ll. lehari, **lehāri, lehārika**, *courier, letter-carrier*: Mvy 3816 (precedes **lekhahārika**, q.v.) = Tib. baṅ chen pa. Presumably related to JM. lehāriya, on which see Meyer, Kauṭ. Arth. 679 (derives it from lekhacārika; perh. rather from lekhahārika, MIndic leha°, with haplology? the two forms are synonyms and bracketed in Mvy). Prob. read in Mvy **lehāri** or °**rika**.

laiśika, adj. or subst. nt. (from leśa), lit. *concerning a trifling thing*: Mvy 8377, the saṃghāvaśeṣa sin of accusing a monk of a **pārājika** sin on the basis of some trifling matter but afterwards repenting and confessing; cf. Prāt. 482.1 ff. (2 leśamātraṃ dharmam); Tib. bag tsam pa, *trifle*. Pali leṣa interpreted only as *trick*, PTSD; but cf. Childers. The corresp. Pali is Vin. iii.168.1 ff. (with lesamattaṃ).

[**loka**, see **aloka**.]

Lokakṣetriya (Senart em. °kṣatriya), n. of a former Buddha: Mv i.138.8.

Lokagati, n. of a Bodhisattva (one of 16): Mmk 40.16.

Lokaguru, n. of a Buddha in the east: Mv i.123.11.

Lokaji, MIndic for °**jit**, n. of a rākṣasa king: Mmk 18.1 (prose) °jiḥ, n. sg.

lokajyeṣṭha, *supreme one of the world*, a standard ep. of a Buddha: Mvy 13 = Tib. ḥjig rten gyi gtso bo.

? **Lokadhara**, see s.v. **Lokaparitrātar**; and cf. **Lokaṃdhara.**

lokadharma, m. (= Pali lokadhamma), (the eight) *conditions of the world*, listed Dharmas 61 as lābho 'lābhaḥ sukhaṃ duḥkhaṃ yaśo 'yaśo nindā praśaṃsā (same 8 in Pali forms, not in same order, PTSD): anupalipto °maiḥ, *not defiled by* . . ., Mvy 873; LV 352.10; aṣṭalokadharmānupalipta LV 275.5; Śikṣ 180.2.

lokadhātu, m. and f. (= Pali id., only f. acc. to Childers; see s.v. **dhātu**, 5), *world-region, world-system, world*; extremely common everywhere: three sorts, **sāhasracūḍika, dvisāhasra, trisāhasramahāsāhasra** (qq.v.; under the last, many examples showing both genders for lokadhātu are cited) Mvy 3041–4; other Mvy cases (all m. when unambiguous), 226, 361, 816, 860, 3046, 3060, 3063, 3070; besides the forms with trisāhasramahāsāhasra, both m. and f. forms occur, the mss. frequently varying; in SP 40.16 KN with 3 mss. m., 3 others f., ed. note says f. 'seems preferable, dhātu being usually of fem. gender in SP', but this is hardly borne out by the evidence of this edition; e. g. it is clearly m. in 156.7 (prose, no v.l.); 157.1 (one ms. f.); 306.10; in 41.10 and 42.1 (parallel 40.16 above) ed. with all mss. but one masc.; in 121.11 ff. ed. prints fem. forms, but Kashgar rec. masc., usually with some Nep. mss.

Lokanātha, frequent as ep. of the historic Buddha, as in Pali, e. g. LV 97.16; in Sādh (29.17 etc.) n. or ep. of a Buddha; it is not clear that Śākyamuni is meant, tho he may be.

Lokanāthavyākaraṇa, n. of a work: Śikṣ 241.9.

lokaniṣṭha (cf. **aghaniṣṭha**), n. of a class of gods: Mmk 19.10 (follows akaniṣṭhā sukaniṣṭhā).

Lokaṃdhara, n. of a former Buddha: Mv i.137.3.

lokapati = normal Skt. lokapāla, one of the 4 guardians of the points of the compass: catvāri lokapatino (n. pl.; i.204.12 mss. °nā) Mv i.204.12 = ii.8.7 (vs).

Lokapadma, n. of a former Buddha: Mv i.138.4.

Lokaparitrātar (v.l. two names, Lokadhara and Puṇyaparitrātar), n. of a former Buddha: Mv i.137.8. The v.l. (two mss.) seems likely to have been original, rather than Senart's reading, which looks like a secondary telescoping of the two.

Lokapālarājan, n. of a former Buddha: Mv i.141.5.

Lokapūjita, n. of a former Buddha: LV 172.11.

Lokapradīpa, n. of a contemporary or future Buddha: Sukh 70.7.

Lokapriya, n. of a former Buddha: Mv i.141.13.

lokavijita, nt., (n. or) epithet of the samādhi attained by the Buddha at his enlightenment: °taṃ nāma samādhiṃ (so the only ms. which has the word) samāpadyate Mv ii.418.4. (I fail to find in this word what Senart finds, Introduction p. xxxvii, n. 2.).

lokavid, *world-knowing*, a standard ep. of a Buddha: Mvy 8, etc.

Lokasundara, n. of one or more former Buddhas: Mv i.139.14; LV 5.11 (confirmed Tib.); Sukh 6.16.

Lokākṣa, pl., n. of a brahmanical gotra: Divy 635.16. Cf. **Laukākṣa.**

lokākhyāna-kathā, Divy 304.27, and **lokākhyāyikā**, 26, 29, *story-telling about the world*. Here a workman tells entertaining stories to his fellow workmen. Certainly not *philosophical discussion about* (the creation, etc., of) *the world*, which is the scholastic interpretation of Pali lokakkhāyikā (e. g. DN comm. i.90.32; MN comm. iii.223.15), adopted in PTSD. I am not sure that this is not late commentarial pedantry; in the canonical and other early Pali texts, so far as I can see, the Pali word might have the mg. which it clearly has in Divy.

lokānujñā, see **anujñā.**

lokānuvartanā, see **anuvartanā.**

lokāntarikā, subst. f., usually pl. (= Pali lokantarikā, subst., not adj., 'scil. Niraya', with PTSD), *interstice(s) between the worlds*; they are dark, gloomy places, a kind of purgatories: chiefly in a well-known cliché, recorded SP 163.8; LV 51.10; 410.13 (and the first part, ending andhakārās, as abbreviation, 351.22–352.1); Mv i.41.4; 229.20; 240.9; ii.162.9; iii.334.7; 341.12; Divy 204.22; 205.4, 13, 23; 206.5, 16; Samādh page 7 line 9; ŚsP 102.17 (abbreviated); and in Pali, DN ii.12.10; MN iii.120.9; AN ii.130.24; SN v.454.16. There are minor variants thruout, not all reported here, and in Mv the mss. are mostly quite corrupt and vary widely; Senart em. rashly; I shall quote a blended version which seems at least close to a common Mv text. For convenience the passage is divided into sections, (a) to (g); Divy lacks (b) and (f); ŚsP lacks (a) and (g) ; in Samādh, (b) is lacking, (a) and (c) come after (f); in Mv (all six passages) and in ŚsP, (b) comes after (c): (**a**) om. ŚsP; yā (a)pi tā (Divy adds lokasya; 204.22 lacks api tā, and so also SP; 3 of 6 Mv passages add loke) lokāntarikā (Pali lokant°); (**b**) omitted in Divy, Samādh, and prob. corrupt in all; I believe orig. had aghā aghasaṃvṛtā (Pali aghā asaṃvutā, for which Senart, Mv i.406, brilliantly conjectured aghā aghasaṃvutā; the Pali comms. seem to me fatuous, and I cannot feel attracted by CPD's interpretation of aghā, see s.v. **agha**; Mv supports Senart, and so in a measure do SP, LV and ŚsP); the Mv tradition seems to point to aghā aghasaṃbhūtapūrvā, in which with Senart I regard saṃbhūta as a corruption for saṃvṛta, or MIndic saṃvuta; close in sense, also, is aghā aghasphuṭā (*full of misery*), the reading of LV and ŚsP (in ŚsP after **c**); finally, SP, tho substituting (tāsu ya) akṣaṇāḥ for the first aghā, and omitting the 2d agha-, actually preserves saṃvṛtā(ḥ), alone among BHS texts (note that it has no negative! thus tending to show the corruption of the Pali); (**c**) andhakārā andhakāratamisrā(ḥ) (Pali andhakārā andhakāratimisā); so Samādh; SP ed. omits andhakārā (haplogr.), but v.l. has it; either it or andhakāra- is omitted in ŚsP and both LV versions (haplogr.); Divy andhās tamaso 'ndhakāratamisrā; Mv (very confused) seems orig. to have read, andhakārā andhakārāpitatvā (or °rāyitatvā) tamisrā (or ti°) tamisrāyitatvā (or ti°); (**d**) yatremāu (yatra ime, etc.) candrasūryā(v; or variants) evaṃ maharddhikā(v) (sometimes omitted) evaṃ mahānubhāvā(v); SP, LV, ŚsP, Samādh add other adjectives prec. by evaṃ; Pali yattha p' ime candimasuriyā evaṃ mahiddhikā evaṃ mahānubhāvā; (**e**) ābhayā (or ābhāya, etc., Mv; Pali ābhāya) ābhāṃ (or ābhāsaṃ; om. Pali) nānubhavanti (so prob. orig.; LV om. nānu°; Pali nānubhonti, but SP nānubhavataḥ, Divy na pratyanubhavataḥ, ŚsP and Samādh na bhāsato, omitting ābhayā ābhāṃ before it; Mv clearly intends nābhisaṃbhuṇanti, all 6 times; Pali comm. on DN, ii.433.23, attano pabhāya na-ppahonti, on which the 'old ṭīkā' cited CPD glosses . . . obhāsituṃ an-abhisaṃbhuṇanti, cf. Mv!); (**f**)? not in Pali or Divy, perh. not orig.; SP varṇenāpi varṇaṃ tejasāpi tejo nānubhavataḥ; LV varṇena varṇaṃ tejasā tejo nābhitapato nābhivirocataḥ (best mss. nāti° for nābhi° both times); ŚsP, Samādh, na tapato na virocataḥ; Mv ālokena vā ālokaṃ na spharanti; (**g**) uncertain; not in ŚsP; Pali tattha pi appamāṇo uḷāro obhāso pātubhavati; SP, LV (in LV after insertion) tatrāpi (SP tāsv api) tasmin samaye mahata udārasyāvabhāsasya (SP mahato 'vabhāsasya) prādurbhāvo 'bhūt; Divy tā api tasmin samaye udāreṇāvabhāsena sphuṭā bhavanti; Samādh tā api tasmin samaye tenāvabhāsena sphuṭā abhūvan; Mv te (once tā) pi tena obhāsena sphuṭā abhūnsuḥ, with varr. The entire cliché means approximately: *And even those world-interstitial-spaces*, (which are) *miseries and covered over with miseries, darknesses, glooms of darkness, — in which the moon and sun here, which possess such great supernatural power and dignity* (or *capacity*), *are not capable of* (producing) *light by* (their) *light*, . . . (f varies too much to admit a unified rendering,) *even in them a great, magnificent radiance appeared (at that time)*. — Besides this cliché, lokāntarikā occurs in, na ca vedayanti duḥkhaṃ °rikā vipadyamānā (?em.) Mv ii.34.16; alone, Mvy 3062; lokadhātor °rikā duratikramā Dbh 58.11; sarva-°rikāś ca tasmin samaye mahatāvabhāsena sphuṭā abhūvan LV 86.19 (cf. the cliché, g); (na ca bhūyo) °rikā . . . prajñāyante sma LV 277.9.

Lokābharaṇa, n. of a former Buddha: Mv i.136.14.

Lokābhilāṣita, n. of a former Buddha: Mv i.136.16 (v.l. °laṣita); LV 5.14 (confirmed Tib.; no v.l.). In both followed by **Jitaśatru**, q.v.; cf. next.

Lokābhilāṣin (cf. prec.), n. of a Tathāgata: Mvy 101.

lokāyatana (nt.?), = Skt. lokāyata, the system so named: °ne Divy 635.25; in BR cited from Colebrooke, Essays 1.404 as personal, meaning *a follower of the lokāyata* (the usual Skt. and BHS lokāyatika); it is cited from Rāmatīrtha on Sadānanda; BR suggest that it is an error, and indeed a note to the 2d ed., 1.428, states that lokāyatāḥ is read in 'the printed edition'.

Lokālokanihitamalla, n. of a former Buddha: Mv i.141.9.

lokika, f. **°kī**, adj. (= Pali id., BHS and Skt. **laukika**), *worldly*, opp. to **lokottara**: (creatures in Sukhāvatī) lokikīṣu kathāsv anapekṣā viharanti, lokottarābhiḥ kathābhiḥ sāraṃ pratyayanti Sukh 59.9.

? **Lokinī**, (perhaps) n. of a yakṣiṇī, see **Ālokinī**.

Lokendra, n. of one or two former Buddhas, in the same list: Sukh 6.2; 6.15.

Lokendrakāyapratibhāsaprabha, n. of a Buddha: Gv 285.1 (vs).

Lokendraghoṣa, n. of a Bodhisattva: Gv 3.21.

Lokendrateja(s), n. of a Buddha: Gv 257.13 (vs).

Lokendrapravaraprabhaghoṣa, n. of a Tathāgata: Gv 312.1.

Lokendrarāja, n. of a Tathāgata: Mmk 7.11.

Lokeśvara, n. of a Bodhisattva: Sādh 20.11, 23.3, etc.

Lokeśvararāja, n. of a former Buddha: Sukh 6.18 ff.

lokottara, adj. (cf. Skt. id., Pali lokuttara; cf. **lokika, laukika**), *super-worldly*, esp. (but not invariably) said of a Buddha and all his aspects and activities, acc. to the **Lokottaravādin** school: °rasya Buddhasya Śākyamunino Mv i.48.15; °rā(ḥ), said of Buddhas, i.96.12; (na hi kiṃcit samyaksaṃbuddhānāṃ lokena samaṃ,) atha khalu sarvam eva maharṣiṇāṃ lokottaraṃ i.159.3 (a summary statement of the doctrine of the L. school); various functions of the Buddha specifically called lok° Mv i.167.17, 18 (see s.v. **niṣaṇṇa**); 168.1, 2, 3, 4, 9; in Divy 161.25 no creature can comprehend a Buddha's lokottara-cittaṃ, but any creature can understand his laukikaṃ (q.v.) cittaṃ (line 23); (Bodhisattvas) budhyanty āśayasaṃyuktā loke lokottare tathā Mv i.86.4, *are enlightened in regard to the world and the supramundane*, which I think may mean (in the dogmatic sense) what pertains to the Buddha, tho Senart thinks differently; °raṃ arthaṃ (*supramundane goal*) prārthayamāno Bodhisattvo Mv ii.279.8; °rābhiḥ kathābhiḥ Sukh 59.10, see s.v. **lokika**; in Laṅk 156.15 (cf. 157.9, 11) jñāna, and in 237.2–3 ff. pāramitā, are of three kinds, laukika (of worldly persons and heretics), lokottara (of śrāvakas and pratyekabuddhas), and lokottaratama (of Bodhisattvas); here the word can hardly have its technical dogmatic meaning.

Lokottaraparivarta, m., n. of a work: Mvy 1334; Śikṣ 151.13.

Lokottara-vādin, pl., n. of a school: Mvy 9093; part of Mahāsāṃghika, Mv i.2.13.

locanaka, f. **°ikā**, = °na, *eye*: (Bhvr. with endearing dim. -ka) -sulocanikā(ḥ) LV 322.12 (vs), of the daughters of Māra; (Bhvr.) rakta-locanaka, *red-eyed*, Mmk 64.27, of Yamāntaka.

Locanā, n. of a goddess (= **Buddhalocanā, Rocanī**): Sādh 18.13 etc.

loṭhakā (var. lothakam, but no v.l. in Mironov), allegedly *a kind of girdle*, acc. to Tib. lcag phod (Jä. and Das pod), *a girdle, made of plaited . . . strips* [*like*] *a chain*: Mvy 8995; **loḍhakam**, acc., MSV ii.89.11 = Tib. lcag guḥi gdiṅ ba, here app. a material to cover beds and seats.

loḍayati (Skt. in mg. *stirs, agitates*), *mixes, stirs in*; Skt. āloḍayati has this mg. and is used in LV 269.14 (prose), but in 271.14 (vs), the same incident is told with: (gandhāmbu cūrṇāni ca) oruhyā nadi loḍayanti salilaṃ, *descending into the river, mix perfumed water and powders into the* (river-)*water* (two accus.).

loḍhaka, see **loṭhakā**.

loṇa (nt.; = Pali id., Skt. lavaṇa; Skt. Lex. id. in cpds.), *salt*: so dāni loṇaṃ ca aloṇakaṃ ca . . . paribhuñjāsi (so mss., Senart °asi) Mv iii.120.21 (vs); SP 114.8 (vs).

lothaka, nt., var. for **loṭhakā**.

loṣṭu (Skt. Lex.; blend of loṣṭa and leṣṭu?), *clod of earth*: loṣṭuṃ KP 105.5; loṣṭunā 4; śva-loṣṭv-anujavana- (see anujavana) KP 105.2; 106.8; 107.1, 5; loṣṭu-patane LV 319.16.

[**lohari, lohāri**, see s.v. **lehari**.]

lohaliṅga, m., Mvy 9507 = Tib. lhog pa (also ldog pa), some kind of large carbuncle or ulcer; also Māy 238.6; 245.23; 248.31; 259.22. See also **rajata**.

lohitaka, m. (**1**) some sort of insect: °kā prāṇakā kālaśīrṣakā (bodhisattvasya) pādatalehi yāvaj jānumāṇḍalāni chādayitvā asthānsuḥ Mv ii.137.4; repeated 138.19 with °ka-prāṇakā; (**2**) n. of a town: Mv iii.328.2; also **Lohitavastuka**, 327.20, and **Rohitavastu**, q.v.; see also **Kamaṇḍaluka**; (**3**) n. of two nāga kings: Māy 247.14; cf. Skt. Lohita, BR s.v., 2 k. See also **lohitakopadhāna**.

lohitakā = **°tikā** (cf. Pali lohitaṅka), a kind of gem: musāragalvamuktāhi maṇi-lohitakāhi (mss. °kāni) ca Mv ii.191.5 (vs); °kā-mayānāṃ (chattrāṇāṃ) 302.10; °kā-, in cpd., lists of gems, Divy 67.19; 138.3; °kā, separate word, in list of gems, 502.7.

lohitakopadhāna, adj. (= Pali °kūpadhāna), *having red pillows*, ep. of a couch, paryaṅka: Mv ii.115.17. Cf. lohitopadhāna SP 75.8.

Lohitanyāyatana, m. pl., n. of a brahmanical gotra: Divy 635.16.

lohitamuktā, **°kti**, **°ktikā** (once **°ktika**, prob. by error), a kind of gem, evidently = **lohitikā**; like the latter, °kti is listed among the seven **ratna**, q.v. 2; °muktikasya, text, but read °muktisya with v.l., Mv ii.492.6; °muktikā Mvy 5953 (Tib. mu tig dmar po, *red pearl*); otherwise only °muktā: Gv 53.1; 89.26 (text °mukta°; corr. 2d ed.); 90.1, 6, 7; 148.14; 158.25; Sukh 54.11 (lohitamuktāhāra, *a necklace of l°*), et alibi (frequent in Sukh); in Mv ii.302.12 °ktā-puṣpa-gṛhītā (so mss., Senart em. °parigṛhītā; does this mean *lohitamuktā-colored flowers*?); in list of gems SP 256.12.

Lohitavastuka, see **Lohitaka** (2).

lohitākṣa, *red-eye*, (**1**) (n. of a gem, not in Skt. dictionaries, but occurs in Pūrṇabhadra's Pañc., Hertel, 1, vs 67, and see Finot, Lapidaires indiens 137; also AMg. lohiyakkha: Mv ii.311.2; 318.3;) (**2**) n. of a rākṣasa: Divy 119.21; 122.26 (here called a mahāyakṣa); (**3**) n. of a maharṣi: Māy 256.27.

Lohitākṣī (cf. prec., 2), n. of a rākṣasī: Māy 240.23.

lohitikā, a kind of gem (also **°takā**, q.v.; evidently = **lohitamuktā**, **°kti**; app. not *ruby*): in Mv as one of the standard list of 7 **ratna**, q.v. (2); otherwise, usually in lists of gems, Mv ii.275.3; Divy 51.25; 115.3; 229.7; 231.18 (°kā-rājir, read as cpd.); Av i.205.3; Bbh 234.2.

lohī (in AMg. and other Pkt. said to mean *a shallow metal pan, frying pan*, which hardly fits our word), *kettle*, a large metal receptacle: mañjūṣa lohī ca tathā supūrṇā (so read with WT) SP 364.4 (vs); (nararudhiravasāmūtrapurīṣasaṃkulāyāṃ) mahā-lohyāṃ prakṣiptaḥ (a man is the subject) Divy 378.11; tāṃ lohīṃ paśyati 13; lohy-antarasthaḥ 17 (the same man); lohī-saṃghāṭā, see **saṃghāṭa.**

Laukākṣa, pl. (Skt. Gr.), n. of a brahmanical school (of the Chandogas): Divy 632.23, 25. Cf. **Lokākṣa.**

laukika, adj. (Skt. id.; BHS also like Pali, **lokika**), with citta, (thought) *about the world*; said of the Buddha when he concerns himself with the welfare of some person or persons: °kam (137.16 °ka-) cittam utpāditam, or utpādaya(n)ti (subject, a Buddha or Buddhas) Divy 63.11 ff.; 77.14 ff.; 137.16; 161.23 f.; in the last contrasted with a Buddha's **lokottara** (q.v.) citta; MSV i.255.19.

laukikāgra-(or °**grya-**)-**dharma,** m., sg. or pl., *prime-in-the-world condition(s)*, fourth and highest of the **nirvedha-bhaga** (-**bhāgīya**), qq.v.: Mvy 1215 °grya-, but Mironov °gra-; Sūtral. xiv.26 comm. °gra-; here identified with ānantarya-samādhi; °gra- also AbhidhK. LaV-P. vi.167.

V

va (**1**) (= Pali id.; see also **vā**), MIndic for Skt. iva, most commonly in vss, *as, like*; often written ca in mss. of Mv, and em. by Senart; among the cases where mss. read va (sometimes with v.l. ca) are: dharmaṃ imaṃ pāṇitala va (v.l. ca) darśaye Mv i.297.14 (vs); others, iii.5.5 (vs); 14.13 (vs); 78.11 (vs); 110.11 (vs, v.l. ca); 119.12 (vs, v.l. ca); 123.19 (vs, v.l. ca); 290.12 (prose); 384.19 (vs); padumaṃ va vāriṇā SP 313.3 (vs, no v.l.); gagane va pakṣī Gv 473.15 (vs); others after final -e or -o, SP 26.7; 127.9; 128.13; LV 49.21; 173.6; 188.14; Mv i.75.6; ii.115.4; Samādh 19.26; Bhad 20; abhramukto va Ud xvi.5, 7, oldest ms., changed in later mss. to °mukta iva (unmetr.) or °muktaiva; after -ā, Mv i.203.2 = ii.6.19; after -ā for -ās, drumā va SP 131.4; after -a for -am, kāṣṭha va LV 322.8; bhadraṃ va Ud xix.12, oldest ms., later v.l. bhadram iva (unmetr.); naḍāgāram iva kuñjaraḥ Divy 68.20 = 138.27 (vs), so text, but meter requires °raṃ va (or °reva?); a few cases where va is Senart's em., but quite certainly right, are: Mv ii.241.8 (vs; mss. vā or yā; meter requires va; for iva); in the rest Mv mss. ca, em. Senart va: Mv ii.38.12 (vs); āmapātraṃ va ambunā 240.11 (vs; same line, āmapātram ivāmbunā LV 263.1); 250.2; iii.110.10; 123.20; there are many other cases where Senart reads va for mss. ca, not all certain; (**2**) (see also **vā**) perhaps for Skt. eva, as in Pali, but the cases noted are few, and most could be em. to ca (the reverse of ca for va = iva, just mentioned): kālaṃ (mss. kāla; metr. indifferent) va nātināmenti Mv i.192.14 (vs); (taṃ rājyenābhiṣiñcatha,) so va rājā bhaviṣyati Mv ii.436.14 (prose), possibly *he and no other* (but prob., with ca, *and he*) *will become king*; (amṛtaṃ) mayā bhikṣavaḥ sākṣātkṛto(!) 'mṛtagāmī va (v.l. ya; Weller 38 'Schreibfehler für ca', prob. rightly) mārgaḥ LV 409.8 (prose); darśenti dharmacaryāṃ (meter requires cariyāṃ) va sudharmaniṣṭhāṃ Gv 477.6 (vs: printed vasudhar°, which is impossible; va = eva could be assumed); kukṣigatā va Mv i.144.13 (prose), here clearly = eva, *still in their mothers' wombs*; viśiṣṭarūpaṃ v' iha SP 90.11 (vs), all mss., could be for eva; both edd. em. c' iha; in 91.12 (vs) WT em. va, with Tib. ñid, for mss. ca (plausibly); (**3**) va m.c. for vā (as in Pali), *or*: mañjughoṣu yatha yādṛśo va ham Gv 489.10 (vs), *like Mañjughoṣa, or such as I* (Maitreya) *am*.

vaṃśa, m., (**1**) (cf. Pali vaṃsa, *tradition*, as in Dpvs. 18.3 saddhamma-vaṃsa-kovidā, *knowing the tradition of the true religion*; cf. Miln. 190.24, 27, syn. paveṇi 31, *traditional usage*, orig. *line of descent*), *tradition*: (na ... parinirvāsyāmi) yāvan mayā buddhadharmasaṃgha-vaṃśo loke na pratiṣṭhāpito bhaviṣyati LV 377.17 (prose); Tib. sgra, *voice, sound*, hence Foucaux (for BHS) *renommée*, but I cannot find evidence for this mg. in Skt. or MIndic; (**2**) (= Pali Vaṃsa = Skt. **Vatsa,** q.v., which is also used as Vaccha, personal name, in Pali) n. of a people: idaṃ Vaṃśarājakulaṃ ṛddhaṃ ... LV 21.1 (no v.l.), also 3 (v.l. Vaṃsa); Tib. bad sa (= Vatsa).

vaṃśa-ghaṭikā (see **ghaṭikā**), *bamboo-stick*, as a kind of toy (rather than 'game', as Index and pw Addendum): Divy 475.19. It may have been *used* in a game; cf. Pali vaṃsaṃ DN i.6.13, comm. i.84.26 = veṇuṃ ussāpetvā kīḷanaṃ; indeed, the true translation may be *stick used in (the game of) vaṃśa*, instead of the above.

vaṃśa-dalikā, *a bamboo blade* (? cf. Skt. dala): °kayā nirlikhyodakena prakṣālayitavyaḥ (sc. guḍaḥ, added to monks' food) MSV i.249.15.

(**vaṃśarāga,** *bamboo-colored*, adj. applied to a kind of vaiḍūrya-gem in Kauṭ. Arth., Shama-S.[1] 76.19; so also Jm 92.2 vaṃśarāga-vaiḍūrya-prabhā-vyatikara-harita-salilam; in line 4 (vs) the same is described as marakata-harita-prabhair jalair..., which misled Speyer into taking va° as a synonym of marakata, *emerald*; but it is clear from Kauṭ. that it is another green gem.)

vaṃśarocanā (Skt. Lex. id.; Skt. vaṃśalocana, and Lex. °nā), *tabasheer, sugar of bamboo*: Mvy 5790; in Suv 105.2 (vs) mss. samocakaṃ tu; Nobel em. sarocanā, implausibly; a Chin. version supports vaṃśarocanā, which should prob. be read, despite the 'metrical difficulties' (Nobel) which it causes (omit tu, as a patchword introduced after the corruption?).

(**vaka** = Skt. baka, *trickster*: Mūrdhātā nṛpatir hy eṣo naite Vaiśālikā vakāḥ Divy 217.23.)

Vakula, see **Ba°**.

[(**maṇi-**)**vakkala,** false reading Mv ii.472.3; read maṇi-valayā (with ms. C, quoted as °valapā).]

vakkali, nt., a kind of textile material: °li (both edd., no v.l.) Mvy 5871 = Tib bag le ba(?); Chin. *colored, variegated cotton* (= **kaca,** q.v., the prec. word in Mvy). Surely not connected with Pali, AMg. vakkali(n), *wearer of bark*, from Skt. valkala.

Vakkalin (= Pali id., for Skt. valkalin), n. of a ṛṣi who was converted by Buddha: Divy 49.3 ff. His story as told here is clearly related to some incidents told of him in Pali (see DPPN).

Vakkula, see **Ba°**.

vaktavyikā (f. to *°vyaka, to vaktavya, in mgs. 4 or 3 of BR), some kind of person not to be initiated as a nun; *subject to orders*(?), or *worthy of reproach, blameworthy*(?): mā (sc. asi) °kā Bhīk 16a.4.

[**vaktra,** nt., Mv iii.185.17, repeated 19 (vs) atha gāyasi vaktrāṇi, either corruption or false Sktization for Pali vattāni, same line, Jāt. iii.447.18; Senart assumes that this Pali word = Skt. vṛttāni, *meters*, which is plausible. However, Ratnach. records (without citation from literature) an AMg. vatta = Skt. vyakta, defined *singing while making the syllables and sounds distinct, an excellent mode of singing*. May not the Pali vattāni, and our word, be equivalents of this? Our word might then be a false Sktization, or error, instead of vyaktāni.]

Vakṣu, n. of a nāga king: Māy 247.8. Occurs as n. of a river in Skt., and in Māy 252.34; identified with the

Oxus. The n. of the river is used as the n. of a nāga-king, cf. Mvy 3304–7, and s.v. **Pakṣu.**

Vakhala, n. of a country: Mmk 325.10 (vs), see s.v. **Kāviśa.**

[**vaga,** in Gv 105.22 sattva-vagasya, read sattvāvagasya, and see **avaga.**]

vagura, m. (= Skt. bakula, vak°), name of a plant: puṣpaṃ vaguro (vi)pramuñcati Ud xviii.13.

? **vagūhayati,** perh. for **avagūh°,** q.v.

vaṅka, adj. (= Pali id., Skt. vakra, which exists side by side in BHS, sometimes juxtaposed with vaṅka; § 3.4; cf. **a-vaṅka**), *crooked,* (**1**) literally and physically: SP 113.11 vaṅkāś ca ye kāṇaka kuṇṭhakāś ca; 350.9 vaṅkoṣṭho, and 10 vaṅkamukho (in same context vakradanto 8, vakranāso 9); Mv iii.283.11 kubjagopānasī-vaṅkā; both lit. and fig., RP 58.7 (kāya-)vāk-citta-vaṅkāḥ, *crooked in body, speech, and mind;* (**2**) fig. *crooked, dishonest, deceitful:* SP 48.7 vaṅkāḥ śaṭhā; 268.5 śaṭhā vaṅkajātīyāḥ (with only 1 ms., others vañcaka-j°; but LaVallée Poussin JRAS 1911.1075 vaṅka-jātikāḥ); 272.1 durbuddhinaś ca vaṅkāś ca śaṭhā . . .; Mv i.96.5 akṣa-vaṅkadyūta-krīḍā-; 164.14 vaṅkāvakāśā (so Senart for mss. °kāśaṃ ca, unmetr.) vigato, *free from possibility of deceit*(?); Mvy 7322 (the next word is vakraḥ); Śikṣ 230.3 doṣavaṅka-śāṭhya-kuhanāṃ; (**3**) n. of a mountain (= Pali id.) to which Viśvantara was banished: Jm 55.12 ff.

Vaṅga-(= Skt. id.)**-lipi,** a kind of writing: LV 125.20 (most mss. Māṅga, which Tib. supports, maṅ ga; see also **vandā**).

Vaṅgāla (= Skt. and Pali Vaṅga; Pkt. has this form, cited as Baṅgāla in Sheth), *Bengal:* Mmk 275.14 °lādhipatiḥ.

vacana-patha, m. (= Pali id.), *way of speaking,* virtually = vacana, *speech, utterance, words:* LV 181.11; Śikṣ 185.2; 188.9; Bbh 238.9 (for citations see s.v. **durāgata**).

[**Vacanasaṃpraveśa,** see **Adhivacanapraveśa.**]

vacī (once in Skt. vaci-bhedāt, BR; Pali id., mostly in cpds.; AMg. vai, common), *speech, word:* kāyakarma vacīkarma manokarma . . . Mv i.102.4 (vs; ī could be m.c.).

Vaji (the usual form in mss. of Mv, Senart always Vajji), or **Vajji** (= Pali Vajji) = **Vṛji,** q.v., n. of a people and country; associated with (Skt.) Malla, and with **Licchavi,** who in Pali are one unit in the Vajji confederacy, but the two are also treated as interchangeable: Mv i.34.9 (prose), text vajji-, v.l. vaji-; 264.13 (vs), mss. vajim abhimukho, read vajiṃ a°, m.c.; Senart vajji; 326.2 (prose), mss. vajiṣu or varjiṣu; ii.419.9 (prose), mss. -vaji- or -vajri-; iii.421.5 (vs), vaji- required by meter, mss. vajī-, vajrī-, Senart vajji-.

vajira (= Pali id.), MIndic for Skt. vajra, in mg. *diamond* (or *thunderbolt*?), only in vss m.c.: vajirakāya LV 298.19; vajirasāra- Gv 56.1; 372.8.

Vajji, v.l. for **Vaji,** q.v.

Vajra, (**1**) n. of a samādhi: Mvy 516 (var. **Vajropama,** q.v.): ŚsP 1416.1; (**2**) n. of a future Buddha: Gv 441.26.

vajraka, (**1**) adj. (from vajra; in Skt. only with taila, a medicinal oil), *diamantine, hard,* fig.: adhyāśayair vajrakaiḥ LV 216.4 (vs); (**2**) n. of a guhyaka (cf. Pali Vajira, n. of a yakkha): Mmk 532.16 (vs); (**3**) n. of a mountain: Divy 450.10, 13; 455.29; 456.1; (**4**) m., n. of a muhūrta: Divy 643.13; in 644.15 written varjanakaḥ.

Vajrakukṣi, n. of a cave: Kv 23.3; 24.12.

Vajragarbha, n. of a Bodhisattva: Mvy 663; Dbh 2.4, 26 ff., etc.

Vajragāndhārī, n. of a goddess: Sādh 352.17 etc.

Vajragir, n. of a Bodhisattva: Gv 442.16.

Vajragupta, n. of a former Buddha: Mv i.139.13.

Vajracarcikā, n. of a goddess: Sādh 395.13.

Vajrachedikā, n. of a work (our Vaj): Śikṣ 171.9; 275.11; Vaj 46.11.

Vajrajñānaparvata, n. of a Bodhisattva: Gv 442.9.

Vajrajvālānalārka, n. of a deity: Sādh 512.1.

Vajraḍāka, n. of a supernatural being (cf. next): Sādh 466.1 etc.

Vajraḍākī, or °**ḍākinī,** n. of a yoginī (cf. prec.): °ḍākī Sādh 445.20 (vs; v.l. °ḍākinī, contrary to meter!); °ḍākinī 459.21 (prose); 488.8 (vs), etc., the regular form.

Vajratārā, n. of a form of Tārā: Sādh 178.10 etc.

Vajratīkṣṇa, n. of a form of Mañjuśrī: Sādh 148.17 etc.

Vajratuṇḍa (Skt. Lex. id.), *vajra-beaked,* n. or epithet of Garuḍa: LV 270.9 (prose).

Vajratuṇḍī, ep. of Tārā: Hoernle MR 54.2; said (see n. 14) to mean *vajra-navel;* cf. **Vajranābhi.**

Vajradṛḍhanetra, n. of a yakṣa: Mvy 3372.

Vajradrumakesaradhvaja, n. of a gandharva: Mvy 3389.

Vajradhara (cf. **Vajrapāṇi**?), n. of a Bodhisattva or deity: Mmk 312.6; Sādh 515.4 etc.

Vajradharā, n. of a rākṣasī: Māy 243.22.

Vajradhātvīśvarī, n. of a goddess: Mvy 4291; Sādh 65.1; 280.16.

Vajradhvaja, n. of a number of Tathāgatas: Dbh 99.18.

Vajradhvaja-sūtra, n. of a work: Śikṣ 22.5; 278.14; also called Vajradhvaja-pariṇāmanā, Śikṣ 213.3; 291.10.

Vajranābhi, n. of two former Buddhas: Gv 104.20; 257.20 (here Vajira°, in a vs).

Vajranārāyaṇaketu, n. of a former Buddha: Gv 281.26.

Vajranetra, n. of a Bodhisattva: Gv 3.3.

Vajrapadavikramin, n. of a Bodhisattva: Gv 81.8.

Vajrapadmeśvarī, n. of a goddess: Sādh 76.1.

Vajrapadmottara, n. of a Tathāgata: Dbh 89.14.

Vajrapāṇi (in Skt. ep. of Indra; in Pali Vajirapāṇi is n. of a yakkha, also of Indra, the two being identified, at least sometimes; on his character see DPPN; in BHS sometimes = Indra, as in Mv i.183.10 where his form is assumed by Buddha; prob. also in Gv 250.20, where he parallels, and forms the climax of, a series of devatās; and prob. SP 445.6), n. of a yakṣa, Māy 3 (living at Rājagṛha); cf. **Vajra-rājagṛha;** usually not, as in Māy, a mere local yakṣa, but a much more imposing and even terrifying yakṣa, who e. g. in Bbh 152.1 may be conjured up by a Bodhisattva to frighten evil-doers (cf. also **Caṇḍavajrapāṇi**); often called by epithets like mahāyakṣasenāpati Suv 85.3, **guhyakādhipati** 91.17 (see the word, and cf. LV 66.6), yakṣendra 158.13; similarly Mmk 548.7, and often; elsewhere he is an important Bodhisattva, at or near the head of lists of them, Kv 1.7; Mvy 649; one of eight, Dharmas 12; a special attendant on Buddha Laṅk 240.10; a Bodhisattva in the 8th bhūmi is Vajrapāṇisatatānubaddha, Dbh 71.22; other references to V. the Bodhisattva, Śikṣ 274.3; Sādh 49.13 etc.; Mmk 11.6; 62.28; 68.20, etc.; it is clear, however, that for Mmk, at least, the Bodhisattva and the yakṣa or guhyaka prince are the same person; so Vajrapāṇir bodhisattvo 25.8 is referred to in 12 as (**Ā**)**guhyakādhipatinā** yakṣendreṇa; in addressing Vajrapāṇiṃ guhyakādhipatim, 36.2, he is called **jinaputra** (= bodhisattva) in the next line; he is called a bodhisattva in 145.2 and 13, and addressed as yakṣeśa in 14.

Vajrapāda, m. pl., n. of a brahmanical gotra: Divy 635.11.

Vajrapura, nt., n. of a 'Dravidian town' (Dramiḍapaṭṭana): Gv 72.13.

Vajrapramardanin, n. of a Tathāgata in the north: Gv 81.7.

Vajrapramardin, n. of a Tathāgata: Śikṣ 169.7.

Vajrabhāskarī, n. of a goddess: Sādh 488.7 etc.

Vajrabhṛkuṭī, n. of a goddess: Mvy 4281.

Vajrabhairavī, n. of a goddess: Sādh 488.6 etc.

Vajramaṇḍala, m., n. of a samādhi: Mvy 529; ŚsP 1417.8.

Vajramati, n. of a Bodhisattva, or of two: Kv 1.17; Gv 442.21.

Vajramālā, n. of a 'gandharva maid': Kv 4.16.

Vajramuṣṭi, n. of a kiṃnara maid: Kv 6.4.

Vajrameruśikharakūṭāgāradhāraṇī, n. of a work: Mvy 1388.

vajrayāna, nt., a Tantric form of Mahāyāna: Sādh 225.10.

Vajrayoginī (cf. **Vajrā**), n. of a yoginī: Sādh 452.6 etc.

Vajraratnagiritejas, n. of the 'elephant jewel' of a cakravartin: Gv 418.8.

? **Vajra-rājagṛha**, Karmav 55.19, n. of a city; or is Vajra an epithet of the well-known Rājagṛha? A local yakṣa named **Vajrapāṇi**, q.v., lived there.

Vajraraudrī, n. of a goddess: Sādh 488.8.

vajra-lipi, a kind of script: LV 126.6; confirmed Tib.

Vajravārāhikā, = next: Sādh 442.8 (vs, m.c.).

Vajravārāhī, n. of a yoginī: Dharmas 13; Sādh 424.1; 427.1, etc.

Vajravetālī, n. of a goddess: Sādh 352.10.

Vajraśuddha, n. of a Bodhisattva or future Buddha: Gv 441.26.

Vajraśṛṅkhalā, n. of a goddess: Sādh 413.9, 10 etc.

Vajraśrī, (**1**) n. of a 'gandharva maid': Kv 4.15; (**2**) f., n. of a number of lokadhātus: Dbh 99.17.

Vajrasaṃhata, n. of a former Buddha: LV 5.5 (confirmed Tib.; cf. **Vajrasaṃghāta**).

Vajrasaṃhanana, m. pl., n. of (a range of?) mountains: Laṅk 29.6, 32.8.

Vajrasaṃghāta, n. of a former Buddha: Mv i.137.10 (cf. **Vajrasaṃhata**).

Vajrasarasvatī, n. of a goddess: Sādh 326.1 etc.

Vajrasāgaragarbhā, n. of a lokadhātu: Gv 9.9.

Vajrasāgaradhvajamegha, n. of a Tathāgata: Gv 310.11.

Vajrasāra, n. of a Bodhisattva: Mvy 713.

Vajrasena, (**1**) n. of a merchant, former birth of Śākyamuni; in the story of Śyāmā: Mv ii.166.19 ff.; (**2**) n. of one or two Bodhisattvas: Kv 1.8; Mmk 576.18.

Vajrā, n. of a yoginī: Sādh 445.19 etc.; cf. **Vajrayoginī**.

Vajrākara (? em., but plausible), n. of a mountain: Suv 133.5.

Vajrāṅkuśa, m., n. of a mountain: Kv 72.1, 3.

Vajrāṅkuśī, n. of a goddess: Mvy 4284; Sādh 50.3 etc.

Vajrānaṅga, a name of **Mañjuśrī**: Sādh 124.3 etc.

Vajrābha, n. of a Tathāgata: Gv 82.6.

Vajrāmbujā, n. of a goddess: Mvy 4283.

Vajrāyudha, n. of a yakṣa: Māy 11.

Vajrārciḥśrīvatsālaṃkāragarbha, n. of a Bodhisattva: Dbh 2.15.

Vajrāśayo-giri-śirī, n. of a Buddha: Gv 285.13 (vs; m.c. for Vajrāśayagiriśrī).

Vajrottarajñānin, n. of a Bodhisattva: Gv 2.16.

Vajropama, n. of a samādhi: Mvy 560; ŚsP 1419.18. Also v.l. for **Vajra** (1), another samādhi in the same list, but Tib. confirms Vajra (rdo rje śes bya ba, *called Vajra*).

vañcitaka, adj. (Skt. °ta plus -ka, perh. pitying or contemptuous), *deceived*: suvañcitako 'si LV 323.10 (vs), said by daughters of Māra to the Bodhisattva, in the passage in which they apply to themselves many forms in ka which I have interpreted as endearing in tone, § 22.34.

-vaṭa, usually *banyan*, is sometimes applied to the **bodhi**-tree (see s.v. **bodhi** 2): bodhi-vaṭa LV 308.4; 364.8, etc.; bodhi-su-vaṭa LV 360.18; all vss.

vaṭika, v.l. for **dhaṭika**, q.v.

vaṭṭa (= Pali id., both mgs.; Skt. vṛtta, adj., not used as n. in this sense), (**1**) adj. *round*, see **vaṭṭa-pāsaka**; (**2**) = saṃsāra, *the round of rebirths*: LV 127.17, read vaṭṭopachedana-śabdaḥ (text paṭopa°; ms. A vaṭṭoma°, with m corruptly for p; = Pali vaṭṭūpacheda).

vaṭṭanā(valī, i. e. °nā-āvalī; = Pali °ḷi), (*string of*) *bead(s)*; so to be read for Senart's em. vaṭṭanaveṇī Mv ii.125.16; 127.4; 128.9; 129.12; and (em. veṣṭanaveṇī) 231.17. The mss. are all corrupt but clearly point to (ā)valī, in accordance with Pali, rather than veṇī in which Senart follows the LV parallels, see **vartanā(-veṇī)**; the mg. is the same and is explained under the latter word.

vaṭṭa-pāsaka, f. °**ikā**, *having a round eye* (of a needle): Mv ii.87.17, read °pāsikā, or °pāśikā, sūcī; see under **pāsa(ka)**; mss. **maṭṭa-** or vartta-, Senart em. vaṭṭa-, yāsikā(ṃ).

vaṭṭita (MIndic for vartita = Skt. vṛtta), *rounded, round*: °ta-dāṭhā (n. pl. m.) Mv ii.44.5 (v.l. vartita°), in the list of **anuvyañjana**, q.v., No. 53; other texts vṛtta-(-daṃṣṭra).

? **vaṭhara**, adj. (= Pali Lex. id.; rarely in Skt. *stupid, dull*), *large, gross*: Mv ii.65.3, applied to a lizard, godhā; but the reading is quite doubtful; v.l. jaṭharā; and in 5 both mss. (raudrāṃ) japarāṃ, intending jaṭh° (Senart em. vaṭharāṃ); it seems likely that (Skt.) jaṭhara, *hard* (or *old*?), should be assumed.

vaḍa (m., = AMg. id., Skt. and Pali vaṭa), *banyan*: Kv 8.3, in a list of flowers, -mahāmāndāra-vaḍāudumbara-puṣpa-.

Vaḍi, n. of a yakṣa: Māy 236.28.

Vaḍika, n. of a rich householder's son (hero of Av ch. 6): Av i.28.3, 13 etc.

vaḍḍa, adj. (cf. next; Deśīn. 7.29 = mahān, comm.; Hem. 4.364; AMg. vaḍḍa-kumārī, *old maid*, supporting Senart's derivation, ii n. 541, from Skt. vṛddha; see Edgerton, JAOS 69.229, largely anticipated, as I learned too late, by Lüders, KZ 52.106–9), *large, big, fat*; of birds in captivity, fattened for slaughter and sale as food: vaḍḍa-vaḍḍā(ni) Mv ii.241.15, 17, 20; 242.7; vaḍḍo (so read with mss., if not vaḍḍī-, see next) bhaviṣyati 242.14; of udumbara fruit, vaḍḍa-vaḍḍāni 246.11; in 249.19 (vs) mss. vaḍḍā ca vṛndi, (*your*) *body* (see **vṛndi**) *is big*.

vaḍḍī-bhavati (see prec.), *gets big, fat*, of birds, as under prec.: Mv ii.242.2, 4, and in 11 read vaḍḍībhūto; in 14 perh. vaḍḍī-(mss. vaḍḍo)-bhaviṣyati.

Vaṇālā, see **Vaśālā**.

[**vaṇi(n)**, as in Pali vani (Jāt. vi.232.29), *beggar*; so most mss. at Mv i.87.14 (vs); but prob. the true reading is **vaśi(n)**, q.v., with Senart.]

vaṇika (perh. hyper-Skt. for Pkt. vaṇiya = next; or, a-extension of Skt. vaṇik, n. sg. treated as 'stem', § 15.8, owing to its use as stem in composition; acc. to Senart i.367 MIndic vaṇi (= vaṇij) plus -ka; the parallel *bhiṣaka there cited is a false form; SP 292.11, vs, reads bhiṣaṭka without v.l., and *bhiṣaka would be metr. impossible), *merchant*: vaṇika-śreṣṭhi-bhūtena Mv i.1.8 (prose).

vaṇija (a-extension of Skt. vaṇij, § 15.7, cf. prec.; occurs in Skt. as n. pr. and in other mgs.; Skt. Lex. vaṇijaka in this mg.), *merchant*: vaṇija-gaṇena LV 385.13 (vs), similarly 16 (vs); °jāḥ 208.6 (prose); °jānāṃ 387.10 (prose).

vaṇijya (nt.? seems blend of Skt. °jyā, f., and vāṇijya, nt.), *commerce*: -kṛṣi-°jya-prabhūtaś ca bhavet SP 102.4 (prose).

[**vaṇir-yatha**, must intend Skt. vaṇikpatha, *trade*, or a MIndic equiv.: MPS 5.12, ms. āryā vaṇir-yathā, etad . . .; ed. em. vāṇir yathaitad . . ., but Pali vaṇippatho, and so Tib. tshoṅ pa ya rabs rnams kyi lam.]

vaṇīpaka, (only Mv ii.100.4; 182.4, 9; also text iii.254.18 but without ms. support), otherwise **van°** (Skt. vaṇīpaka and °yaka, one of them certainly a graphic variant for the other; I have no doubt that °paka should always be read; in Vikramac. MR 29.35 all mss. °paka; in BHS °yaka recorded only Divy 83.19; cf. Pali vaṇibbaka, AMg. vaṇīmaga, °maya, supporting °paka), *beggar, mendicant*: sometimes *mendicant monk*, e. g. **Asthisena** vanīpaka Mv iii.419.4; once used in reference to a snake-charmer, in a way which I do not understand (it suggests *snake-charmer* as another mg. of the word, perhaps because they are a sort of wandering beggars?), hastatvam āgacche (subject, a nāga, captured by a snake-charmer) vaṇīpakasya Mv ii.182.4, 9; usually the last of a quartette, śramaṇa, brāhmaṇa, kṛpaṇa, vanīp° (as recipients of alms), often in a cpd., LV 430.19; Mv ii.100.4; iii.41.17; 43.8; 44.19; Jm 15.4; Av i.198.11; same with omission of kṛpaṇa, Mv i.188.14 (here Senart vanīyakaṃ, but all mss. °pakaṃ); iii.254.18; without śramaṇa, brāhmaṇa, but with kṛpaṇa (and usually other near-synonyms) Divy 83.19 (vanīy°); 319.4; Jm 105.14; alone, Divy 414.18 (v.l. °pagaḥ); Jm 7.10.

Vatkula, see **Bakkula.**

? **vattī-bhavati,** see **varttī°.**

[**Vattula,** see **Vartula.**]

vattu-śiras (Mironov vandu°, v.l. in both calu°, perh. for Skt. caru, *kettle, pot*; preceded by **ghaṭā-śiras,** q.v., for which Mironov has vattu-ś° without v.l.), *bighead(ed)*, acc to Tib. klad (glad) po che, also Chin. and Jap.: Mvy 8808. If we could accept the v.l. calu, and assume it = Skt. caru, the word would be comprehensible.

Vatsa (cf. **Vaṃśa** 2): (**1**) a pupil of the ascetic Kāśyapa, thus fellow-pupil of Śarabhaṅga: Mv iii.363.3 ff. In the Pali story (see DPPN), Kisavaccha, or Vaccha Kisa, is a pupil of Sarabhaṅga, and his adventure with King Daṇḍaki is somewhat differently told. In Mv iii.364.16 called Vatsa-gotro, cf. Pali Vacchagotta, and in 17 described as vātehi ābādhehi kṛśo (cf. the Pali Kisa-vaccha?). (**2**) n. of a nāga king: Māy 247.16.

Vatsaka, n. of a mleccha king: Mmk 621.26 (vs).

vatsara, adj. (= Skt. vatsala), *affectionate*: mss. at Mv i.155.2; Senart em. °la.

vatsa-hāra, m. (prob. false Skt. for MIndic, incl. AMg., vaccha = Skt. vakṣas, plus Skt. hāra; cf. Skt. vakṣo-maṇi), *a string of gems worn on the chest*, in lists of ornaments: Sukh 41.16, °hārā(ḥ); 54.10.

vadatha (m.? § 22.44), *speaking, speech*: Mv i.184.3 (vs) vadatha-kovidaḥ, *skilled in speech* (of Buddha).

[**Vadanasatyaṇḍatāra,** mss., as n. of a former Buddha: Mv i.139.10; see **Samīkṣitavadana.**]

Vadālī, n. of a goddess: Sādh 276.18 etc.

? **vadi, vade,** assumed by Senart to be interj. of grief, cf. Skt. vata: aho vadi (v.l. vade ti) aho vadīti Mv i.341.9 (and, by Senart's em., 341.8, 11); aho vade aho vade ti 342.4. Text doubtful; see Senart's note.

vaddhaka, see s.v. **vardha.**

vaddha-paṭikā (MIndic for Skt. vadhra, or vardhra, plus paṭikā, *strip* (of cloth); Senart em. °paṭṭikā, which in 260.12 is unmetr.), *strip of leather, leather strap*: kāyaṃ tīkṣṇena śastreṇa °paṭikāyaṃ (instr.; § 9.51) pāṭayensuḥ Mv iii.258.16 (prose); similarly 260.12 (vs).

vaddhāpayati; see **vardhayati.**

vadya (nt.? = Pali vajja, which is usually derived from Skt. varjya, tho this is not used as a noun in this sense; if so, vadya would be a false Sktization of vajja, as in next), *fault, sin*: (read) aṇumātreṣu vadyeṣu bhayadarśāvī Mv iii.52.1 = Pali aṇumattesu vajjesu bhayadassāvī (see CPD s.v. aṇumatta), *seeing danger in* (even) *very small faults*; a common phrase in Pali; since Pali vajja is common in other locutions, there seems no doubt that we must read vadyeṣu; mss. corrupt, °mātreṣevadyeṣu or °mātreṣvabandheṣu; Senart em. °mātreṣv āvadyeṣu (intending Skt. avadyeṣu? this would seem plausible but for the close Pali parallel).

vadyate (false Skt. for MIndic [Pali] vajjati, cf. prec.), *is rejected, excluded*: sā me va santike api ca vadyase Mv ii.58.8 (here mss. vādyase); 59.10, *it is you, being such as this, who are in my presence, and you are rejected* (by me). Otherwise Senart (*I tell you to your face*).

Vadrākara, n. of a mountain: Māy 253.33.

vadhaka, *intending to kill* (§ 22.3): dhruvaṃ khu mahyaṃ °kā upasthitāḥ SP 113.8 (vs); vadhake 'pi Jm 163.21 (prose), *even towards one who intended to kill* (him).

vadhati (= Pali id.; no pres. in Skt.), *kills*: see § 28.14. Cf. **vahati.**

vadhukā (= Pali id., Skt. vadhū; see also vadhūkā), *young woman, young matron*: na ca dārikāṃ vā kanyāṃ vā vadhukāṃ vā... SP 277.3 (prose); kuleṣu cāpi °kāṃ (WT with v.l. °kāḥ) kumāryaś ca vivarjayet 279.12 (vs); *bride*, mi (= me)... vadhukāṃ vṛṇīṣva LV 139.16 (vs); *daughter-in-law*, °kāye Sudarśanāye (in reference to **Alindā,** her mother-in-law) Mv ii.445.12; 446.19 (both prose); śreṣṭhi-°kā Av i.255.9 (prose).

Vadhu-yakṣī (text corruptly Madhu°; in vs) Mmk 567.12, or **Vadhu-**(also **Vadhū-**)**-yakṣiṇī** 569.25 (prose; both forms), n. of a yakṣiṇī.

vadhūkā (= **vadhukā,** q.v.), *young woman*, esp. *young wife, young matron*: sarvā etā °ūkā navā dahrās... LV 100.12 (volunteer nurses for the infant Bodhisattva); nava-vadhūkā LV 157.12, *a young wife; a young matron* or *woman*, Divy 632.1; 651.15; *daughter-in-law* (as in Mv ii.445.12 **vadhukā**) Mv ii.446.20 (mss.). All prose.

vadhū-kumārī, *a young newly-married bride*: MSV i.118.17; 121.12.

Vadhū-yakṣiṇī, see **Vadhu°.**

vadhya-ghāṭa(ka), -ghāta(ka), m. (written ba° in Mvy, Divy; = Pali vajjha-ghātaka; on ṭ for t see § 2.41), *executioner of criminals*: °ṭaka Mv ii.168.10, and v.l. 169.9; °ṭa, v.l. for °ta 170.9; °taka (seems to be the most usual form) Mvy 3836 (ba°); Divy 421.1, 9 (ba°); Mv ii.169.9; °ta, Divy 421.4 (ba°); Mv ii.169.6; 170.8, 9.

vadhyapāna, *a drink given to a criminal before execution* to stupefy him: Kalpanāmaṇḍitikā, Lüders, Kl. Skt. Texte 2, 45.

(**vadhra,** in Skt. as m., Mbh.Cr.ed. 1.26.19a for Calc. vadhrī as cited in BR; also as nt., BR; vadhrī, f., in Skt. only Lex.; Skt. also vardhra, Lex. °rī, and Pali vaddha; see **vaddha-paṭikā;** *strap, thong*: badhreṣu Mv i.13.8; cīraka-vadhrāṇi 19.9, refers to *strips* of flesh; so also **vadhrī,** acc. pl., with Senart, the mss. being corrupt, 19.7, 8.)

vadhrayati (denom. to Skt. vadhri), *castrates*: puruṣāṃś ca °yanti Mv i.96.8.

vadhrī, see **vadhra.**

vana, (**1**) (m. or nt.; once apparently in Skt. Kenop. 31; seems pretty clear in Pali vana, tho interpretations of some passages vary; CPD recognizes avana, *free from lust*; cf. **vanatā, vanatha, avanatā, nirvaṇa**). *desire*: Ud xviii.3 and 4 = Pali Dhp. 283–4, vanaṃ (punningly *desire* and *grove*; so Pali) chindatha mā vṛkṣaṃ vanato jāyate bhayam, chit(t)vā vanaṃ samūlaṃ ca (Pali vanaṃ ca vanathaṃ ca) nirvaṇā bhavatha bhikṣavaḥ; yāvad vanatā (Pali vanatho) na chidyate (later ms. na chidyate yāvatā vanaṃ), etc. [In Gv 105.25 -vanasya, gen., is a false reading; see under **avana.**] (**2**) n. of a yakṣa: MSV i.17.7.

vanatā (see **vana**), *desire*: in Ud xviii.4 (cited s.v. **vana**) equivalent to Pali vanatho, see **vanatha.** Cf. also **avanatā.**

vanatha (= Pali id., m.; § 22.44; replaced once by **vanatā,** q.v.), *desire*, in prahīna-vanatho, *having got rid of desire*: Mv i.204.3 (here by Senart's em.) = ii.7.18.

vanada, nt. (Skt. Lex. id.), *cloud*: (tad yathāpi) nāma śāradaṃ vanadaṃ pāṇḍu pariśuddhaṃ... Sukh 3.2.

Vanavāsin, m., n. of a region (janapada; in the south): Gv 76.20; 77.22.

Vanaspati, n. of a 'gandharva maid': Kv 4.17.

vanānī (vana plus suffix -ānī, § 22.10), *vast forest*: iha nīvaraṇa-vanānī (so with v.l., text °vanārī; *the vast forest of the hindrances*) dagdhā me kuśalamūlatejena LV 372.1 (vs).

Vanālā, see **Vaśālā.**

vanāstika, adj. (false Sktization of Pali vanaṭṭha, like **puṣkarāstika**; cf. Vin. i.215.18 vanaṭṭhaṃ pokkharaṭṭhaṃ, comm. 1093.13 vane c' eva paduminigacche ca jātaṃ), *growing in the forest*: MSV i.239.2 °kāni phalāni.

vanīpaka, [**vanīyaka,**] = **vaṇīp°**, q.v.

vandaka, adj. (Pali vandikā, f.), in caitya-v°, *venerating caityas*: adyāpi caitya-°kā bhikṣavo vandante Divy 579.8–9; 581.2; *intending to salute*, see § 22.3.

? **vandana,** adj.? (in Skt., Pali, Pkt. noted only as n. act.), *greeting, saluting*, possibly in SP 166.8 (vs) yato vayaṃ vandana āgatā jinam, *whence we have come to the Jina greeting him.* But prob. more likely loc. sg. of n. act., for °ne: *in the matter of greeting* (= *to greet*) *him.*

? **vandā** (sc. lipi), a kind of writing: mss. at Mv i.135.7 (Senart **vaṅgā** by em., with LV 125.20).

? **vandu-śiras,** see **vattu°.**

Vapuṣmant, n. of a Śākyan youth: Av i.355.1 ff.

? **vambh-, vamh-** (Pali vambheti, vamheti), *despise, contemn, show ill-will*; see s.vv. **nirvamhaṇa, parivambhita.**

vayana, nt. (so also Mironov; BR vāyana), a kind of perfume or incense: Mvy 6248 = Tib. rgya spos, *Chinese perfume* or *incense.* [For **vayana** as v.l. for **vāyana,** see this.]

[**vara,** read **avara,** q.v.; Gv 105.20, text sattvavarasya, read sattvā°.]

Varakalyāṇa (= Pali id.), n. of a king, son of **Kalyāṇa,** q.v., and father of **Upoṣadha,** q.v. In Mv i.348.8 text is corrupt; the form **Rava** (v.l. Rāva) prob. represents Vara(-kalyāṇa), but in one ms. seems also confused with **Roca,** q.v., who should have been named earlier in the list.

Varagagaṇā (Lefm. with most mss.), or **Varagaṇā** (v.l., with Tib.), n. of a lokadhātu in the zenith: LV 295.9; Tib. tshogs (= gaṇa) kyi dam par (= vara).

varaṭa (m.? Skt. Lex. °ṭa, °ṭā, *a kind of wasp*; Deśī varaḍā), a noxious insect (*wasp*?): Māy 252.2.

varaṭaka, m. or nt., *border, edge*(?): tasya (sc. nīlotpalasya) varaṭake candrastha-oṃkāraṃ bhāvayet Sādh 139.18; cakrābhyantara-varaṭake dhīḥkāraṃ . . . bhāvayet, bāhya-°ke kāliyogaṃ (see **kāli**) . . . cintayet 156.6–7.

varaṇa, nt., a high number: Mvy 7852 (cited from Gv); prob. = **vivaraṇa,** Gv 105.25; but cf. also Gv 105.26, perh. read sattva-varaṇasya (gen.) for sattva-ṇavaraṇasya; no equivalent seems to occur in the similar list Gv 133 (it should occur about line 10). Tib. on Mvy gzhal dpag, the same as the rendering of **dharaṇa,** q.v.; this suggests that one or the other is a corruption. But Gv supports varaṇa, while the Tib. rendering seems to support dharaṇa, which in Skt. is the name of a weight (Tib. gzhal).

varaṇḍikā, some sort of bag or container (to be hung on a wall-peg): MSV i.xi.1.

varatraka, adj. (Skt. varatrā plus -ka), *made* or *consisting of straps*: sahasaiva tāni dṛḍhāni varatrakāni (so!) bandhanāni chittvā Divy 137.5.

varadhara (m. or nt.! or em. °rā? cf. Skt. vasuṃdharā), *earth*: sāgara-varadhara-vipula-buddheḥ (bodhisattvasya) LV 9.22 (prose); so Tib., blo (buddhi) rgya mtsho (sāgara) daṅ (*and*) sa (*earth*) ltar (*like*) rgya che baḥi (vipula).

Varadharmamudrā, n. of a samādhi: Mvy 565; ŚsP 1420.9.

Varaprabha, (**1**) n. of a Bodhisattva, previous incarnation of Mañjuśrī: SP 21.18 ff., 22.9 ff.; 25.4 ff.; (**2**) n. of a former Buddha: Sukh 5.16.

Varabāhu, n. of a former Buddha: Mv i.137.6.

Varamakuṭa, n. of a former Buddha: Mv i.137.3.

Vararūpa, n. of a former Buddha: LV 5.7 (confirmed in Tib.).

Varalakṣaṇaḥśiri (so, one word), n. of a Buddha (same name as next): Gv 284.24 (vs, m.c.).

Varalakṣaṇaśrī (same name as prec.), n. of a Tathāgata: Gv 310.24 (prose).

?**Varāgramati** (mss. have atra before this; Sen. em. Pravarā°) n. of a former Buddha: Mv i.141.10.

varāṅga, adj. (Skt. vara-aṅga; in Skt. recorded as Bhvr. only in a gloss in Amarakośa; not noted Pali or Pkt., but see below), lit. *having excellent (bodily) members*; so Tib. yan lag mchog, on LV and Mvy: ep. of heroic sons, . . . śūrāṇāṃ vīrāṇāṃ °ga-rūpiṇāṃ parasainyapramardakānāṃ Mv i.49.5; 193.18; ii.158.17 and LV 18.6; of the four divisions of an army, rājā caturaṅgād balakāyād vara-varāṅgān hastino 'śvān rathān manuṣyāṃś ca vahaneṣv āropya Tāmradvīpaṃ saṃprasthitaḥ Divy 527.27, *the king loaded on boats the severally* (i. e. in each department; vara-va°) *best-membered elephants, horses, chariots, and men from his four-membered army, and* . . .; varāṅga-balam Mvy 8211, *strength of a varāṅga.* Acc. to pw 7.372, the mg. would be *elephant* (so Skt. Lex.) in Mvy and Divy (so also Index to Divy). But the word in Divy clearly applies to all four regular divisions of an Indian army, specifically named here; if it meant *elephant* it would duplicate hastino. And in Mvy it is placed between **mahānagna-** and **praskandi-**balam (see these words), and separated from prākṛtahasti and gandhahasti-b° in 8208–9. In MPS 31.21 a varāṅga's power rates very high, just below that of an **ardha-nārāyaṇa,** above that of a **mahānagna** and **praskandin.** PTSD s.v. vīra regards this as 'distorted' from vīraṅga- as in Pali; on the contrary, I believe the Pali cliché DN i.89.5 etc. is compressed from an original closer to Mv i.49.5 etc.; it reads puttā . . . sūrā vīraṅgarūpā parasenappamaddanā (vīraṅga- for BHS vīrā varāṅga-).

Varālikā = next, in vs, m.c.: Sādh 589.16.

Varālī, n. of a yoginī: Sādh 277.2 (prose) etc.; cf. prec.

varāhaka (m. or nt.; = Skt. valā°, balā°), *cloud*: pāṇḍala-(so, or pāṇḍula, mss.)-varāhaka-nibho Mv i.207.8 = ii.11.19 (vs).

Varāhamukhī, n. of a yoginī: Sādh 277.4 etc.

varuṭa, m. (Skt. Lex. id., Skt. AMg. varuḍa), *a canesplitter, mat-maker* (by trade): repeatedly in Mv ii.477.4 ff.; mss. usually ṭ or ḍh, sometimes even t, but apparently never ḍ acc. to Senart; ū often in mss. for u.

Varuṇa, (**1**) n. of a former Buddha: Mv iii.234.13, called **Varuṇottama** line 20; n. of (presumably) another Buddha, Śikṣ 169.10; (**2**) n. of an arhat (**vaśibhūta**), disciple of Śākyamuni: Mv i.75.18; (**3**) n. of a nāga (cf. DPPN Varuṇa 15 and 17): LV 204.9; Megh 288.6; Māy 221.20; (**4**) n. of a yakṣa: Māy 236.25.

Varuṇadatta, n. of a **satpuruṣa** (q.v.): SP 3.11.

Varuṇadeva, (**1**) n. of one or two Buddhas: Śikṣ 169.10; Gv 104.20; (**2**) n. of a Bodhisattva: ŚsP 6.10.

Varuṇamati, n. of a Bodhisattva: Mvy 694 (with ep. kumārabhūta).

?**Varuṇarāja,** or °**rājan** (mss. Valu-, Valuṇa-r°), n. of a former Buddha: Mv i.139.13.

Varuṇavegā, n. of a kiṃnara maid: Kv 5.23.

Varuṇaśrī, n. of a Bodhisattva: Gv 442.11.

Varuṇā, n. of a locality (city); Māy 56, see Lévi, p. 96.

Varuṇikā, and **Varuṇī,** n. of two goddesses: Mahāsamāj., Waldschmidt, Kl. Skt. Texte 4, 181.11 and 9 respectively (cf. s.v. **maitrī,** 2).

Varuṇottama, see s.v. **Varuṇa** (1).

Varendraketu, n. of a king: Suv 132.7, by em.; mss. Valendra°, Velendu°; Tib. mchog gi dbaṅ poḥi tog = the em.

? **varkika**, adj.? or subst.? modifying, or parallel with, kūrcaka, *paint-brush*; mg. unknown: kūrcakair varkikair mukto mṛtakeśasusaṃbhavaiḥ, (abhuñjānas tathālikhya svayaṃ vā citrakareṇa vā) Mmk 553.13(–14). Qy: read varṇikair or vartikair? Cf. Skt. Lex. varṇikā, *a paint-brush*; Skt. vartikā, id.

varga-cārin, *living with a crowd*, one of the two classes of pratyekabuddha, contrasting with the **khaḍga-viṣāṇakalpa**, which is the only type known to Pali: Mvy 1007; AbhidhK. LaV-P. iii.194; vi.177.

vargu, adj. (= Skt. valgu; § 2.49), *charming* (of sound): vargu (separate word; **śabda** nt.) manojñaṃ śravaṇīyaṃ śabdam anuravanto Gv 167.19.

varcaḥkuṭī, varcask° (= Pali vaccakuṭī; cf. next items), *privy for defecation* (cf. prasrāva-k°): MSV ii.91.6; °kuṭiḥ ib. 157.4.

varcaḥkumbhikā, varcask° (cf. next), *chamber-pot, commode*: MSV ii.174.5.

varca-ghaṭa, m. (= Pali vacca-gh°; varca = Skt. varcas plus ghaṭa; cf. prec. and next items), *pot of dung*: Av i.252.1.

varca-dhāna, nt. (= Skt. varcas, for which varca-may be m.c., and Pali vacca, plus -dhāna), = **saṃkāra** (q.v.)-dhāna, *dung-heap*: °nāni Av i.254.5 (vs).

varcask-, see **varcaḥk-**.

varcāhāra, adj. Bhvr., Av i.254.2; 255.11; text var-cohāra but read varcāh° with v.l., 253.2 (Skt. varcas plus āhāra, irregular saṃdhi, or semi-MIndic varca, Pali vacca, and cf. varca-ghaṭa, -dhāna, plus āhāra), *feeding on dung* (of a pretī).

varco-mārga (m., = Pali vaccamagga), *anus*: Mvy 9227.

varjanaka, m., n. of a muhūrta: Divy 644.15; in 643.13 written **vajraka** (4).

varjayati, in phrase ārdravṛkṣe vā (or va) varjayitvā (varjetvā, varjitvā) Mv i.7.5; 11.12; 17.9; 20.12; 24.9 (or °vṛkṣeṣu varjitāḥ 12.15, mss.), object being the wicked in various hells, subject their tormentors; acc. to Senart (note 375) *rejetant, repoussant* (les damnés) *sous un arbre verdoyant* (they tear or devour their flesh, or the like). I venture to guess that it means *impaling* them *on a fresh, green tree* (stump or branch). But I cannot explain this mg. in terms of varj- or ā-varj-; vā (almost always preceding the gerund) is also difficult (Senart assumes it stands for eva); I suspect some corruption.

varṇa-dhātu, f. (= Pali vaṇṇa-dh°, which is said in Pv. comm. 137.2 to be meant by the word rūpa in Pv. ii.9.59, while vaṇṇa in 60 is distinguished from this and glossed saṃṭhāna; I understand **dhātu** in mg. 3, q.v., and varṇa-dh° substantially = rūpa-dh°; Pv. comm. 14.26 glosses vaṇṇa-dh° by chavi-vaṇṇaṃ; the PTSD def. is confused and obscure), (bodily) *element of beauty* (*of external appearance*): kā varṇadhātū (so m.c., mss. °tu) iha strīya vidyati Mv ii.60.3 (vs), so read with mss. (except °tū; Senart misunderstands), *what beauty-element of* (? *in*) *a woman is seen here* (in you)!

varṇanīya, gdve. (to varṇayati, which even in Skt., as in Pali vaṇṇeti, may mean *praise*, as recognized by Apte), *worthy of being praised*: śubha-v°, . . . *for beauty*, Mv ii.318.12, 19 (vss), of gems (muktā, nāgāmaṇi, m.c. for **nāga°**).

Varṇasvara, n. of a group of future Pratyekabuddhas (predicted): Av i.99.17.

varṇita, ppp. of Skt. varṇayati, perh. as in pw s.v. (1), *painted*, or else *displayed, depicted*, or even *regarded* (BR and pw s.v. 3); acc. to Senart ifc., *having the aspect of* . . . (as Skt. varṇin): te tu . . . dṛṣṭvā nirmitā (mss. °to; *magically created*) bhikṣu varṇitā (acc. pl.; mss. °to) Mv i.189.9 (vs); Senart bhikṣuvarṇitā; so also, dhyāyante bhikṣu varṇitā 190.1 (n. pl.; mss. °to).

[**varṇin**, *painter* (so Skt. Lex.), possibly in Mmk 134.12 (vs) ālikhet śāstu varṇibhiḥ, *he shall depict the Teacher by means of painters*? but prob. rather m.c. for varṇebhiḥ = varṇaiḥ, *with the colors of* (appropriate to) *the Teacher*.]

Varṇu (Skt. Gr.), pl., n. of a people or region: Māy 30; see Lévi p. 71.

varta (m. or nt.; = Pali vaṭṭa, usually derived from Skt. vṛtta, which is not known in this sense; if this is true, varta shows false Sktization), *round of existences* (= saṃsāra): varte (so mss., Senart em. vatte, which is not noted in this sense in MIndic) apratima dharmadarśanam . . . Mv i.63.17 (vs), *in the round of existences matchless is the revelation of the Law*.

vartakā (= Pali vaṭṭakā; Skt. Gr. °akā; Skt. °aka, m., °ikā), *quail*: °kā-potaka, *young quail*, Jm 98.7, 15; 99.10 (all prose).

Vartanaka, nt., n. of a city in **Kevalaka** (2), q.v.: Gv 451.9, 16.

vartanatā (= vartana, § 22.42), dat. °tāyai, quasi-inf., *for turning*: Bhad 10.

vartanā(-veṇī; for Pali see below), (*string of*) *bead(s)*. Note that veṇī in Pali, and at least veṇikā in Skt., are used in the fig. sense of *line, string*; Tib. on LV (both times) renders lan bu (or, bur) blas pa, rendered by Foucaux *le tissu d'une tresse*; I cannot find blas pa in Tib. Dictt., but lan bu does indeed seem to mean *braid of hair*, the normal Skt. meaning of veṇī; it may be that Tib. mistranslated. Occurs twice in LV, in the same comparison: 254.13 (tad yathāpi nāma) vartanyā veṇy (read vartanā-veṇy) unnatāvanatā bhavati samaviṣamā, evaṃ me pṛṣṭhīkaṇṭako . . .; and 256.1 (tad yathā karkaṭakapār-śukā) vāhanaśālāyāṃ vā gopānāsī pārśve (cf. 254.9–11) dvipari-(see this!)vartanā veṇīvat (read as one cpd. word) pṛṣṭhīkaṇṭakaḥ. The Mv parallels clearly had **vaṭṭanāvalī**, q.v., in accord with the Pali. The Pali MN i.80.15 (cf. also 81.12; 245.30) has: (seyyathā) pi nāma vaṭṭanāvaḷī evam eva ssu me piṭṭhikaṇṭako unnatāvanato hoti; comm. ii.50.5, yathā rajjuyā āvuṇitvā katā vaṭṭanāvaḷī vaṭṭanā-naṃ antarantarā ninnā hoti, vaṭṭanaṭṭhānesu unnatā . . . See also **vartita** (°tā . . . veṇī).

vartamānī (app. subst. use of pres. mid. pple. fem. of vart-; what fem. noun is understood?), *occurrence, circumstance* (Skt. vṛttānta): (in response to question, *tell us what you have seen or heard*!) sārthavāho teṣāṃ vāṇija-kānāṃ vartamānīṃ (v.l. °nīṃ) sarvām (mss. °vaṃ) ācik-ṣati Mv iii.74.16 (prose), *tells them the whole story*.

varti (= Skt. vartikā, which also means *wick* = Skt. varti), *paintbrush*: sūkṣma-varti-pratigṛhītapāṇir anāyāsa-cittaḥ taṃ paṭam ālikhet Mmk 61.21 (prose).

vartikā, in pāṣāṇa-v°, app. *gravel*: MSV ii.28.13 ff.; in 29.12 replaced by pāṣāṇa-śarkarā.

vartita, ppp. (see s.v. **vartanā-veṇī**), *beaded*, i. e. *made of beads* (cf. Skt. varti, to which this might be denom.; or it may be from Skt. vartayati, *rolls*, hence *rolled, made into balls*); in any case associated with **vartanā-(veṇī)**: udarāc ca pṛṣṭhivaṃśo vidṛśyate vartitā yathā veṇī LV 260.2 (vs), *like a beaded string* (string of beads).

vartitaka (cf. **vartanā-veṇī** and prec.), either adj., *strung*, or *beaded* (*made of beads*, cf. line 8 akṣaphalayukto, 9 akṣāṃ vedhayen), or subst., *a strung rosary*: kuryād vartitakaṃ vratī Mmk 120.14 (vs).

Vartitārtha, n. of a former Buddha: Mv i.139.1.

Vartula (? text Vattula), n. of a yakṣa: Samādh p. 43 line 21. Cf. Vartula Skt. Lex., n. of an attendaı of Śiva.

vartulaka, adj. (= Skt. vartula; -ka may be m.c.), *round*: Mmk 157.4 (vs) ūrū cāsya vartulakau.

vartuli, m. or f. (= late Skt. vartula, AMg. vaṭṭhula), *a kind of bean or pea*: Mvy 5653 = Tib. sran ma (general word for *legume*).

Varttālī, n. of a goddess: Sādh 276.16 etc.

varttī-bhavati (semi-MIndic, from Skt. vārtta, AMg. vatta = ārogya, plus bhavati), or in i.352.17 **vattī°** (pure MIndic), *gets well* (from a disease): vaidyā ghaṭanti sarvakriyā kriyanti na ca °vati (mss. varddhī° or vattī°, perh. read the latter, cf. AMg.) Mv i.352.17, *physicians were active, all treatments were tried, and she did not recover*; yāvad °vāmi ii.173.17, *until I get well*; na °vati 18. Senart em. vārttī° in all, but no ms. ever has ā.

vartmani, or **°nī** (Skt. Lex. °ni; perh. blend of Skt. vartman and vartani; or false Sktization of MIndic (Pali) vattani, °nī), *way*: buddhānāṃ . . . chinnavartmanāṃ chinnavartmanīnāṃ AsP 143.9; 145.10, *who have cut off the way* (of worldly existence; cf. next).

vartmīya, adj. (Skt. vartma-n plus -īya), *what concerns the way*: (applied to a sacred formula) . . . mahāpavitraṃ tribhava-vartmīya-chedaṃ (*cutting off what belongs to the way of the triple states of existence*, cf. prec.) sarvadurgatinivāraṇaṃ . . . Mmk 26.22.

[**vartya-** in Gv 331.3, by wrong word-division in text; see s.v. **anivartya.**]

vardala, nt. (see next; AMg. vaddalaa, °laga, nt., Skt. Lex. vār°, possibly with ā by pop. etym., association with vār, vāri?), *rainy weather*: saptāhikaṃ akāla-vardalaṃ (Senart em. vār°) utpannaṃ Mv iii.301.1.

vardalikā, pl. (= Pali vaddalikā, AMg. °liyā) = prec.: saptāha-°likā jātāḥ Divy 500.20 (prose).

vardha, vardhaka, also **vaddhaka**, nt. (semi-MIndic; JM.vaḍḍhaya, and cf. AMg. vaṭṭa), a (metal) *cup* or *bowl* or *pan*: so loha-vaddhakaṃ tattakaṃ ādāya samudrakūlam āgataḥ (proposing to bale the water out of the sea) Mv ii.90.15 (here v.l. °vardhakaṃ); vaddhakaṃ nikṣipitvā 16; dīrghā brāhme (so ms., Senart em. brahmā) ahorātrā loha-vardhaṃ (no v.l.) ca tattakaṃ (n. sg.) 91.3 (vs).

Vardhana, n. of a yakṣa: Māy 35.

vardhanikā (see next, and cf. Skt. vardhanī, rarely vār°, acc. to BR from vār-dhanī, *water-holder*; AMg. vaddhaṇia, m.), *a* (monk's) *water-pot*: Mvy 8963 = Tib. ril ba (acc. to Das sometimes one used to carry water for mouth-rinsing).

vardhanīya (nt., cf. prec.), *water-pot*: in Divy 500.1 text confused, prob. read: śītalasya pānīyasya vardhanīyaṃ pūrṇaṃ gṛhya (or: °pūrṇaṃ kṛtvā tad gṛhya).

Vardhamānaka, n. of a nāga king: Mvy 3288; Māy 247.31.

Vardhamānamati, (**1**) n. of a Bodhisattva: Mvy 706; RP 1.12; (**2**) n. of a 'virtuous man' (**satpuruṣa**, q.v.): SP 3.12.

vardhayati (Skt., with or without diṣṭyā, pw), **vaddhāpayati** (MIndic for vardh°), 1 **vardhāpayati** (rare in Skt.; Pali vaḍḍhāpeti; but both unrecorded in this sense), always with jayena, *hails, greets with good wishes* (object a king or the like): (rājānaṃ) . . . jayenāyuṣā ca vardhayitvā Divy 324.3; jayena vaddhāpito (sc. rājā) Mv i.287.16; vaddhāpayitvā 289.8 (or, here, °petvā; in these last two Senart em. vardh°); ii.421.11; vardhāpayitvā Mv i.310.2; ii.31.17; 441.16 (v.l. vaddh°); 443.14; °paye (aor.) ii.38.1.

2 **vardhāpayati** (once, late Skt.; to Skt. vardh-, *cut*), *causes to be cut off*: read, hastau vardhāpayata MSV i.119.14 (text hastau ardh°) and 120.5 (text hastāvardh°).

vardhika, m. (cf. Pali -vaḍḍhika; perh. to Skt. vardhin plus -ka), *one who increases*: Śikṣ 2.18 (vs, cited s.v. **pālika**); mama buddhi-vardhikā(ḥ), n. pl. m., Gv 481.5 (vs).

[? **vardhībhavati**, v.l., see **vārttī-bh°**.]

? **varmakānaka**, nt., Mvy 9023 °kam; form uncertain and mg. obscure; vv.ll. parmakanakam (so Mironov with no v.l.), marmakā°; ed. suggests dharmakaṇakam as em.; Tib. ril ba zhabs tshags can, which is obscure to me; Chin. said to mean *filter that has legs* (Tib. zhabs, *foot*). In a list of utensils.

varṣaka, (**1**) m. (Pali only vassika as adj.), *house, hut for the rainy season*, for monks or nuns: °kaḥ Mvy 9154 = Tib. dbyar khaṅ, which means not *summer-house* (BR) but the above; bhikṣuṇī-varṣakaḥ Av i.269.6; varṣake 11; (**2**) prob. for **varṣika-** or **varṣikā**, q.v., a kind of jasmine: varṣaka-dhānuṣkāri- (so read, see s.v. **dhānuṣkārin**) Mv iii.80.4 (vs); cf. next.

varṣakī (cf. prec., **varṣikā, vārṣika**, °**kā** 2, °**kī**), a kind of jasmine: Ud xviii.13 (in the oldest ms.) = Pali Dhp. 377, where vassikā.

Varṣaṇa, n. of a nāga king: Māy 246.26.

Varṣaṇī, n. of a rākṣasī: Māy 243.22.

Varṣadhāra, n. of a nāga: Mvy 3349.

Varṣavalāhaka, pl. (= Pali Vassa-va°), with devaputra, a class of gods: LV 273.10 (written Varṣabal°); Mv iii.324.7; Divy 127.19; MSV i.243.21; cf. s.v. **Mandavalāhaka** (note 3 in Waldschmidt).

varṣa-sthāla (nt.) or °**lī**, also **varṣā-sthālī**, lit. *rain-receptacle* (on a building, specifically a stūpa or caitya), i. e. doubtless *gutter* (so Feer); always as a place which the pious decorate with gems: °sthāle mahāmaṇiratnāni tāny āropitāni Divy 244.13; (tan maṇiratnaṃ . . .) stūpavarṣasthālyām upari nibaddhaṃ Av i.370.4; (maṇiratnaṃ . . .) caitye varṣāsthālyāṃ samāropitaṃ Av i.383.6.

Varṣākāra (= Pali Vassakāra, minister of Ajātasattu; became a monkey in next existence, as in BHS, see Pali MN. comm. iv.73), n. of a brahman, minister of Ajātaśatru: was reborn as a monkey, for reasons told Karmav 44.22 ff. (made fun of a disciple of Buddha, comparing him to a monkey); 72.2; MPS 1.4 ff. (another incident, = Pali DN ii.72 ff.)

Varṣākārā, see **Caryākārā**.

varṣāgra, nt., *the beginning of the year*: MSV iii.123.20 ff. (Pali vassagga in different mg.)

varṣā-chinnaka = **chinna-vārṣika**, q.v.

Varṣādhipati, n. of a gandharva: Suv 161.17.

varṣāvāsa, m. (= Pali vassā°), *residence* (of a monk) *during the rainy season*: . . . me °so bhaviṣyati Mv i.326.2; (adhivāsetu bhagavāṃ vārāṇasīye) nagare °saṃ Mv i.325.17; similarly 329.8.

varṣā-śāṭī (cf. Pali vassika-sāṭikā Vin. i.292.9, and **udaka-śāṭikā**), lit. *rain-garment*, but used as in Pali of a garment worn while bathing: -cīvara MSV ii.84.10; 85.14 ff.

varṣāsthālī, see **varṣa°**.

varṣika or °**kā** (cf. **varṣaka**, °**kī**, and s.v. **vārṣika**, **vārṣikā** 2), a kind of jasmine: kumuda-varṣikopamaṃ LV 236.15 (vs); and see LV 221.17 s.v. **vārṣika** (read perh. var°).

varṣopanāyikā, see **upanāyika**.

[**vala**, so Lefm. with most mss., and Calc. bala, in LV 429.22 (prose)-nagnavalānupradāna-, which certainly must mean *giving clothes to the naked*. Neither bala nor vala nor even vara is recorded in any such mg. as *garment* or *cloth*. Two mss. are reported as reading vaila, which obviously intends caila; so read with Foucaux (Notes 206).]

valaka, (**1**) m., see s.v. **eluka** 1; (**2**) nt., *finger-ring*: Mvy 6027 (so also Mironov; v.l. Kyoto ed. bālakam, perh. read **vālakam**?) = Tib. sor gdub.

Valayā, n. of the (2) **yaṣṭi** (q.v.) of the capital cities of four former Buddhas (cf. **Valguyā**): Mv iii.229.12; 232.8; 234.11; 238.14.

Valāha (= Pali id.; also **Vālāha**, °**haka**, **Balāhaka**, **Bālāha**, °**haka**, qq.v.), n. of the horse (in Mv prose called **Keśin**, q.v.), hero of Pali Valāhassa Jāt. (196), used in verse version of Mv iii.85.8 (along with Vālāha).

vali, f. or m. (perh. cf. Skt. Lex. balikā? see pw), a kind of flower: Mvy 6209 baliḥ; also Tib. ba-li in the passage cited from ms. H by Lefm. on LV 11.3, instead of varṇa as cited.

Valikaśīrṣa, n. of a nāga king: Māy 246.27.

valikā-saṃnāha, m. (so Mironov), some style of armor or military dress: Mvy 6074 (var. vālika°) = Tib. tshem tshem (tshem = *seam*: -pa, *tailor*), which Das equates with **paṭṭikā-saṃnāha**, q.v., but translates *a patched cloth*!

valitaka, m., some sort of ornament: Mvy 6031 = Tib. lcams kris can, lcam khris can; cf. Das lcam dkris, *wrinkled*; *n. of an ornament* (= valitaka).

valo moṭa (so also Mironov; vv.ll. moḍha(ḥ), moḍa; Ratnach. cites AMg. vala, nt., *twisting*, and moḍhari, *a kind of vegetation*), some medicinal herb: Mvy 5824 = Tib. myaṅ rtsi ('n. of an officinal plant', Das) ḥbras (*rice*; var. sbras).

Valkala, pl., n. of a brahmanical school (of the Bahvṛcas): Divy 632.18 f.

Valkalin, pl., n. of a brahmanical gotra: Divy 635.15.

valganā, perhaps *analysis, classification*: Mvy 7559; may be for Skt. vargaṇā, *Eintheilung, Abtheilung* (pw); occurs between (Skt.) vivakṣā, and **apasphoṭana** or **ava°** (q.v.). Tib. ḥber bar byed pa, or ḥber ba, which I cannot interpret; Chin. *opening wide*, which suggests Tib. ḥbye ba or ḥbyed pa, which mean *open(ing)*, also *separate, resolve, analyze* (or as nouns).

Valgu, (**1**) n. of one of the 4 devatās of the bodhi-vṛkṣa: LV 278.10; (**2**) a particular kind of tree (presumably = Skt. valguka): Divy 628.5 -nyagrodha-valgu-ity-evam-ādīnāṃ (vṛkṣāṇām).

?**Valguyā**, n. of the (2) yaṣṭi (q.v.) of the city **Dīpavatī**: Mv i.196.15. In the four parallels (relating to the cities of other former Buddhas) the name is always **Valayā**; is our word (no v.l. reported) a corruption for that?

Valgusvara, pl., n. of a (predicted) group of future Pratyekabuddhas: Av i.167.1.

vallaka, a kind of aquatic animal or monster (error for next?): makara-kacchapa-va°-śiśumārādīnāṃ (mss. śuśu°) Divy 105.27.

vallabhaka = prec.: matsya-kacchapa-va°-śuśumāra-makarādyā matsyajātayo Divy 231.4.

vallarī, once °**ri**, (**1**) (= AMg. id.) a musical instrument, acc. to Tib. *three-stringed lute* (vīṇā): Mvy 5019 = Tib. pi-waṅ (vīṇā) rgyud gsum pa (*three-stringed*); veṇu-vallari-sughoṣakā Divy 221.24 (only case written °ri); always in cpd. lists of instruments, Divy 315.12; 317.23; 320.6; 459.4; (**2**) *a stalk* or *panicle of rice-kernels*: śāli-°ryo MSV ii.61.12, Tib. ḥbras kyi (*of rice*) sñe ma (regularly *ear* of corn); = **śīrṣan**, q.v. (Cf. Childers and PTSD s.v. vallarī, citing a Pali Lex. with mg. *a compound pedicle*.)

valliki, °**kī** (presumably = Skt. valla°), a musical instrument, kind of lute: vīṇā-°kī-mahatī-sughoṣakaiḥ Divy 108.4; in Mv ii.159.6 read(?) vallikiṃ (acc. sg.), v.l. vallakaṃ, Senart em. vallakiṃ.

? **vallita** (if correct, denom. pple. to Skt. valli, *creeper*), *curled, curly* (? like a creeper), of hair: -vallita-pradakṣiṇāvarta-keśaḥ LV 105.13; v.l. varṇita-; only Calc. **vellita-**, q.v., which should nevertheless perhaps be adopted.

Valluka, n. of a nāga king: Māy 247.27.

Valluragṛha, n. of a mountain: Māy 254.10.

Vaviṣa, n. of a mleccha king: Mmk 621.24.

vaśa, m.; app. as an extension of the Skt. use of -vaśena, -vaśāt, *on account of, for the sake of, by reason of* (so very often BHS, e. g. vaineya-vaśena, *for the sake* or *purpose of conversion*, SP 319.1; Mv i.238.8; 307.9; 312.5), we have first a periphrasis of -vaśena by -vaśam upādāya, SP 320.4; Gv 206.5, see s.v. **upādāya** (1d), *adopting the purpose of* . . .; so that vaśa seems to acquire a mg. (for which I have found no exact parallel elsewhere) *basis, motivation, (controlling) motive*, as in: sa imam arthavaśaṃ saṃpaśyan Śikṣ 22.3, *he, perceiving this basis (motivation) of* (his) *aim*, i. e. perceiving that the processes just described have their aim thus based or motivated.

vaśaṃkarī, n. of a kind of magic (vidyā): Divy 636.28.

vaśa-nīta, adj. (cf. Skt. vaśa-gata, and vaśam used as goal with forms of nī-), *brought under control*: Mv i.131.6.

vaśavartana (nt., = Pali vasavattana; in late Skt. ifc. as adj. acc. to Schmidt, Nachträge), *control*: (cittanagara-) °na-vidhijñena te . . . bhavitavyaṃ Gv 431.14, *you must become cognizant of the rules for controlling* . . .

vaśavartin, (**1**) adj. (also written vasa°; = Pali vasavattin; in Skt. only *subject to*, and so sometimes BHS, e. g. brahmā pi tasya (WT tasyo with v.l.) vaśavarti bhoti SP 369.7, vs), also **-tā, -tva**, abstracts; *controlling, having control over*: devā maheśvarā nāma cittavaśavartī Mv i.224.3 = ii.27.3 (vs); svacitta-vaśavarti-tāṃ LV 180.1 (prose), *state of controlling one's own mind*; tac-cittavaśavarti-tvād 244.22; sarvadharma-vaśavartī LV 275.8; 423.18; Laṅk 13.10–11; sarvadharmeṣu vaśavartī Mv ii.144.19; sarvayoga-va° Laṅk 11.16; -vihāra-va° Gv 341.1; (tava rūpa surūpa . . .) vasavarti (so text) LV 321.22 (vs; Māra's daughters say to the Bodhisattva), *thy fair form dominates* (us); iha khalu kāmadhātau Māraḥ . . . adhipatir īśvaro vaśavartī LV 299.20 (prose), *in control*; vaśavartī Mahābrahmā LV 275.16, *the dominant* (all-powerful) *great Br.*; vasa-(so ed.)-vartimanuṣyeṣu, *among dominant* (powerful) *men*, Mv ii.286.7; daśaśata-vaśavarti-prativiśiṣṭānāṃ (Buddhānāṃ) Divy 95.23, *who are the* (most) *eminent among ten hundred dominant* (all-powerful) *persons*; (**2**) m. sg. (= Pali Vasavattin, DN i.219.31), n. of the chief of the **paranirmitavaśavartin** gods: LV 45.11 (vs, °ti-devabhavane); 302.6; vaśavarti-devaputra-pramukhāḥ paranirmitavaśavartino devaputrās 362.15 (the same personage was called Paranirmitavaśavartī, q.v., in 361.13; both prose); 439.18; 441.19; Mv i.208.14; 230.13; ii.11.2; Divy 140.16; Bbh 349.21; Gv 503.3; for some passages in Gv and Dbh.g. in which there is a deceptive appearance of use of this as a name for the whole class of paranirmitavaśavartin gods, see s.v. **Suyāma** (actually it seems never to be so used).

Vaśavartiyajñayaśayaṣṭimati, n. of a Buddha: Gv 285.22 (vs).

Vaśālā (or, v.l., Vaṇālā, Vanālā), n. of a city, where the Buddha preached to the brahman **Nadin**: Mv iii.325.2, 10. In Pali this incident occurred at the **Ajapāla** Nigrodha (**Nyagrodha**), q.v., Vin. i.2.29 ff.

vaśika, adj. (**1**) (= Pali vasika; Skt. vaśin) *subject, under the power* (of, gen.): vaśiko te bhaviṣyati Mv iii.281.19 (vs), *he will be subject to you*; (**2**) (occurs rarely in Skt., pw, Schmidt, Nachträge; vaśin in same mg., rarely, BR), *empty*: kṣaṇikāṃ vaśikāṃ tadādṛśī (tadā ad°, aor.) LV 177.12 (vs); written vas°, kṣaṇikā vasikā imi kāmaguṇāḥ LV 174.7 (vs), cited Śikṣ 205.1.

vaśitar (n. ag. from Skt. vaś-; once in Bhāg.P., BR), *controller*; *one who rules, is mighty*: kāmeśvaro 'smi vasitā (so spelled) iha sarvaloke LV 336.2 (vs; Māra speaks).

vaśitā (from **vaśin** plus -tā; rare in Skt.; once from Bhāg. P. in BR; occurs also, as one of the Eight Mahāsiddhis personified, in Vikramac. MR 21.106, see HOS 27.163; her glance subdues the entire universe), (**1**) in loose sense, = bala, *power, control*: Mahāmaudgalyāyano . . . ṛddhibalatāṃ ṛddhivaśitāṃ ca anuprāpuṇe Mv iii.67.2; and so in 4, Śāriputra got abhijñāvaśitāṃ prajñāpāramitāṃ ca; ṛddhīye vaśitāṃ prāptā Mv iii.289.6, said of rākṣasīs; kulavaśitā-prāptam (of the kulam of the Bodhisattva) LV 24.14 (Mv has vaśi for vaśitā, see s.v. **vaśiprāpta**); maraṇaṃ vaśitām avaśīkurute LV 175.9 (vs), *death makes power powerless*; sarvadharmaiśvarya-vaśitā-prāptyarthaṃ LV 275.14; citte vaśī tvaṃ vaśitāṃ parāṃ gataḥ Mv i.164.13 (vs, but only by Senart's violent and dubious em.); buddhadharmavaśitānuprāpuṇe, so read, Mv ii.415.16 (mss. °tāni prā°; Senart em. wrongly); vinaya-vaśitā cāsmim Mv i.180.11 (vs; so read with 2 mss.), *and there is power of training in him* (Buddha); samādhi-vaśitāprāptasya Bbh 58.2; sarva-ceto-vaśitā-parama-pāramitā-prāptair (of arhant monks) SP 1.8 (see s.vv. **vaśin** and **vaśiprāpta** for similar expressions, esp. LV 425.22); (**2**) in more technical sense, one of ten *masteries, supremacies*, attributed to Bodhisattvas: listed Mvy 770 ff. and Dharmas 74, in virtually identical terms but differing in order, (Dharmas) āyus (āyur-v°), citta, pariṣkāra, dharma, ṛddhi, janma (instead of this Mvy **upapatti-v°**, q.v., or v.l. utpatti°), adhimukti, praṇidhāna, karma, jñāna; the same ten, with definitions, Dbh 70.8–18 (closer to Mvy); in Mv i.282.15–20 (vss) a slightly variant list, text partly corrupt, āyus, pratibhāna (which Senart would identify with jñāna, implausibly; jñāna is the last item in both Mvy and Dharmas; alternatively and more probably, S. suggests a corruption for praṇidhāna), upapatti, karma, citta, dharma, ṛddhi, abhiprāya (acc. to Senart = adhimukti), kāla, deśa (the last two entirely divergent); references to these, without number or names, vaśitāsu Gv 83.10; for Gv 489.24 see s.v. **vaśiprāpta**; Laṅk 1.10; vaśitapāragato LV 45.14 (vs, a m.c.); 94.19 (vs), read vaśita-prāptu with ms. A; sarvabodhisattvabhūmiṣu vaśitāprāptaḥ LV 274.21 (prose; all these said of the Bodhisattva, or of Bodhisattvas).

vaśin, adj.-subst. (as adj. = Skt. in mg. *in control*, sc. *of oneself*, or also of other things), as subst. used, like **vaśībhūta** (**vaśī°**), in the sense of **arhant**; this is esp. clear when there is contrast with pratyekabuddhas and Bodhisattvas or Buddhas: (buddhaśatasahasrān pūjayitvā . . .) pratyayajina (q.v.; = pratyekabuddha; acc. pl.) vaśīṃś ca pūjayitvā . . . Dbh.g. 51(77).2; vaśi (so Senart em., mss. **vaṇi**)-pratyekabuddhānāṃ na spṛhenti kathaṃcana Mv i.87.14 (vs), *they* (Bodhisattvas) *are not envious of arhants and pratyekab°*. Besides **vaśībhūta** (vaśi°), the stem is cpd. with various other elements; in some, such as **vaśiprāpta**, q.v., we should expect an abstract noun, such as **vaśitā**; other similar cases are vaśi-pāramiṃgatā Mv i.47.4 (vs), *arrived at the supreme point of mastery* (*of being in control*), less likely, *of* (being) *an arhant*; sarvadharmavaśi-pāragaṃ jinaṃ RP 7.19; sarvacetovaśiparamapāramitā-prāpta ity ucyate LV 425.22 (cf. vaśiprāpta, preceded by ceto, and SP 1.8, s.v. **vaśitā**).

vaśiprāpta, adj. (= Pali vasippatta, acc. to PTSD only in comp. with ceto-, e. g. AN ii.6.17, glossed in comm. iii.5.5 cittavasībhāvaṃ patto, evarūpo khīṇāsavo hoti; idha pana anāgāmī kathito), *arrived at* (state of being) *master, in control*; elsewhere vaśitā-pr° (see **vaśitā**); see also s.v. **vaśin**: note Mv i.198.4 = ii.2.1 kulavaśiprāpta, *attained to mastery over* (other) *families*, said of the family in which the Bodhisattva is born in his last existence; the LV 24.14 parallel to this has vaśitā for vaśi; cetovaśiprāpta, of a Buddha, Mv i.34.12, cf. Pali, above, and LV 425.22 s.v. **vaśin**; sa (Maitreyaḥ) vaśiprāptaḥ sarvabodhisattvavaśitāsu Gv 489.24; anuttarajñānajñeya-vaśiprāptena (of Buddha) Divy 210.4; anuttarajñānajño vaśiprāpto (of Buddha) Divy 546.29; see also **vaśībhāvaprāpta**.

vaśi-bhāva, -bhūta, see **vaśī°**.

vaśirāja, nt., (n. of) a kind of magic gem: asti °jaṃ nāma maṇiratnaṃ Gv 500.5 (it can display on earth the splendor of solar and lunar palaces).

vaśībhāva, vaśi°, m. (nt.; cf. next; = Pali vasī°, esp. with balesu), (*state of*) *mastery*: ṛddhi-vaśibhāvabalasthā (. . . jinaputrā) Mv i.70.20 (vs), so by em. but seems plausible; short i required metr.; sarvakuśaladharmavaśibhāvapāramitāṃ (no v.l. for vaśi°) Mv ii.261.7 (prose); esp. cpd. with bala-(vaśī°), as in Pali with balesu, *mastery of the* (religious) **bala**: °vaṃ sākṣātkṛtaṃ Mv i.246.4; °vaṃ (mss. °vaḥ, but acc.!) chādayitavyaṃ manyeyā iii.55.5, repeated in sequel; °vaṃ prāpuṇetsuḥ (mss.) 338.20; 340.13; all these prose. Cf. next.

vaśībhāvaprāpta, adj., = **vaśībhūta** (**1**): balavaśībhāvaprāptehi Mv i.52.2, *arrived at the state of being masters of the bala*, said of monks; so . . . balavaśībhāvaprāpto iii.379.19. Both prose. Cf. prec.

vaśībhūta, (**1**) adj., also vaśi° (= Pali vasī°, defined PTSD *mastering*; in Skt. has opposite mg., *subjected, subdued*), *become possessed of control*, in BHS regularly, perh. always, a synonym of **arhant** (doubtless orig. as *controlling himself*, or *controlling his destiny*): Mvy 1077 = Tib. dbaṅ du gyur pa, *attained to power*, in a list of śrāvaka-guṇāḥ; as ep. of monks who are also called arhant, SP 1.6; yāni . . . °ta-śatāni bhagavatā pūrvaṃ śaikṣabhūmau sthāpitāny evam avavaditāny . . . abhūvan SP 70.13, . . . *arhants who, when formerly located in the* **śaikṣa** (q.v.) *stage, were thus instructed* (what follows is Hīnayāna doctrine, appropriate to śrāvakas!), misunderstood by Burnouf and Kern; pañca tāni vaśibhūtaśatāni Mv i.69.2 (vs), Senart p. xxvi *cinq cents arhats*, correctly; the same, vaśibhūtā(ṃ) 69.14; 70.8 (vss); vaśibhūtā 74.21 (prose!), Senart *arhats*, which is proved by 75.7, 11, 15 etc. where individuals are named, in the acc. case, Pralambabāhuṃ vaśibhūtaṃ, Vicitracūtaṃ (? Senart with mss. Vicinta°) vaśi°, Haryakṣaṃ nāma vaśi°, etc., *the arhant* . . .; (Bodhisattvāḥ) . . . asādhāraṇā pratyekabuddhādibhiḥ vaśibhūtagaṇādibhiś ca śaikṣa-pṛthagjanādibhiś ceti Mv i.142.5 (prose), *who are unlike Pratyekabuddhas, companies of arhants, śaikṣas and common people, and their like*; śāstā vaśībhūtapuraskṛtaḥ i.187.15 (vs), *the Teacher attended by arhants*; pañcānāṃ vaśībhūtaśatānāṃ (v.l. vaśi°) samavāye i.193.8 (prose), *in a company of 500 arhants* (on Mt. Gṛdhrakūṭa); also (like arhant, Mvy 4 and often) *a Buddha*: vaśibhūta ity ucyate LV 425.18; pūjayanti (sc. Bodhisattvāḥ) vaśibhūta-koṭiyo (acc. pl.) Mv i.47.3 (vs); vaśībhūtasya (so mss., Senart em. °tāna) yā ceṣṭā, bodhisattvāna tādṛśī Mv i.107.6 (vs), *as the behavior of a Buddha, such is that of Bodhisattvas* (in the eighth bhūmi; cf. 105.13 aṣṭamāṃ bhūmiṃ prabhṛti . . . bodhisattvāḥ samyaksaṃbuddhapūjayā pūjayitavyā iti); (**2**) n. of a Bodhisattva: Vaśī° Gv 442.12.

Vaśībhūtā, n. of a lokadhātu: ŚsP 47.15.

vaśetar (semi-MIndic for Skt. vaśayitar, see Schmidt, Nachträge; n. ag. to Skt. vaśayati, 'caus.', really prob. denom. to vaśa), *one who controls, masters*: vidyādharakanyānāṃ vaśetā bhavati Mmk 83.25 (prose).

vaśyāpaka, nt., in pātra-°kam Mvy 8959, acc. to Tib. (lhuṅ bzed kyi) kha yogs, seemingly *bowl-cover*; Chin. *bowl with cover*. Etym.? All I have thought of is (a)vaśyā-, as if *cooler*; implausible.

vasa-, see **vaśa-**.

vasati (**vasayati**), used like Pali vasati with neg. (mā . . . avasī Jāt. v.66.10), ma (m.c. for mā) vasayathā (not caus., = Skt. vasata) LV 202.5 (vs), *don't stop* (*stay, rest, delay*)! Is this paralleled in Skt.?

vasana, m., *ardent desire, passion, attachment*: °naḥ Mvy 7534 (so also Mironov) = Tib. chags zhen; mg. confirmed Chin. and Jap. Nowhere else recorded. We should naturally think it a MIndic equivalent of Skt. vyasana, cf. AMg. vasaṇa (Pali = Skt.), but this word is otherwise nt.

vasantaka, (**1**) (= Skt. vasanta, with endearing dim. -ka), *spring*: su-vasantake ṛtuvara āgatake LV 321.19 (vs); (**2**) n. of a follower of prince **Sudhanu**: Mv ii.103.16; 105.18.

Vasantagandhi (mss. Vaś°), n. of a former Buddha: LV 5.10 (confirmed Tib.).

vasayati, see **vasati**.

vasika = **vaśika** (2), q.v.

[**vasitā**, LV 336.2, see **vaśitar**.]

Vasiṣṭha (= Pali Vāseṭṭha), (**1**) n. of a brahman convert to Buddhism (= Pali Vās° 4), associated with **Bhāradvāja** 2: Karmav 157.6; (**2**) n. of a ṛṣi living in **Anomiya**, q.v., in the Malla country (cf. Pali Vās° 3 in DPPN): Mv ii.164.18, etc.; 195.12 ff.; (**3**) n. of a brother of **Bharadvāja** 4: MSV i.211.6 ff.

Vasutrāta, n. of a yakṣa: Māy 16.

Vasudatta, n. of a lay-disciple: Gv 51.9.

Vasudhārā, n. of a goddess(?), possibly a form of Tārā; like T. associated with **Sudhana** (3), q.v., in Sādh 46.11; n. of a yakṣiṇī (the same?), consort of **Jambhala**, Sādh 561.1 etc.; cf. next.

Vasudhāriṇī, n. of a yakṣiṇī (= prec.): Sādh 561.10 (prose).

Vasuṃdhara, (**1**) n. of a śreṣṭhin, previous incarnation of the Bodhisattva: Mv i.93.11; (**2**) n. of a former Buddha: Mv i.136.14.

Vasuṃdharā, (**1**) n. of a goddess (not the same as **Vasudhārā**, apparently): Sādh 421.12; (**2**) n. of a rākṣasī: Māy 243.24.

Vasubandhu, n. of a teacher: Mvy 3478.

Vasubhadra, (**1**) n. of a yakṣa: Māy 27; (**2**) n. of a nāga king: Māy 247.12.

Vasubhūti, n. of a yakṣa: Māy 16.

Vasumata (for °mat), nt., n. of a city: Mv i.35.14 ff. (always a-stem); scene of the story of **Abhiya**, q.v.

Vasumati, n. of the mother of the Buddha **Viraja** (2): °tiḥ, n. sg., Laṅk 364.13 (vs).

Vasumatiśrī, n. of a goddess: Sādh 421.13.

Vasumitra, n. of a teacher: Mvy 3487.

Vasumitrā, n. of a **bhāgavatī** (q.v.): Gv 201.11, 26 ff.

Vasumukha, n. of a nāga: Māy 221.21.

Vasumukhī, n. of a goddess: Sādh 421.12.

Vasuśrī, n. of a goddess: Sādh 421.12.

vastu, nt. (semi-MIndic, = Skt. vāstu; Skt. vastu in this sense noted only in vraṇa-v°, *Sitz, Ort einer Wunde*, BR; in Pali vatthu = Skt. vastu and vāstu), *site, place*: etasmiṃ ... pṛthivīpradeśe bhagavato Kāśyapasya āgama-(? v.l. āramana-; Senart's note em. ārāma-)-vastuṃ abhūṣi Mv i.318.7; ... Kāśyapasya kuṭī-vastu (v.l. °vastum) abhūṣi 9, *the site of the hut of K.*; ṛṣiṇā taṃ vastuṃ teṣāṃ ... dinnaṃ i.352.3, *the ṛṣi* (Kapila) *gave them the site* (on which they were to build the city called, for this reason, **Kapila-vastu**, q.v.). Also in i.318.10, parallel to 7 and 9 above, I would read caṅkrama-vastu for text °ṣaṣṭiḥ (rather than °bhūmiḥ with Senart's note). [In LV 106.18 śuci-gātra-vastu-saṃpannaḥ read with v.l. vastra for vastu; so Tib., *perfect in having clean garments* (na bzaḥ) *on his body*.]

vastu-kṛta, adj. (= Pali vatthukata), *practised, actively pursued*: Mvy 2419 (var. vāstu°, but Mironov vastu°, no v.l.) = Tib. dṅos por (= vastu) byas pa, or, rten tu (could = vāstu!) byas pa.

vastu-prativikalpa-vijñāna, nt., *discrimination between individual objects*, and between subject and object; function of the manas; opp. to **khyāti-vijñāna**, q.v. (see Suzuki, Studies, 189 f.): Laṅk 37.15 ff.

vastu-vidyā, read so (or with pw 7.373 vāstu°, but see **vastu**) for vastra-v°, *science of sites*: Divy 630.22 (see s.v. **śivā-vidyā**), not *architecture* (Skt. vāstu-v°, BR); = Pali vatthu-vijjā, the art of determining the qualities of sites proposed for houses or parks, DN comm. i.93.14.

Vastusaṃgrahaṇī, n. of a work, the last division of the Yogācārabhūmi (so Wogihara's note to both passages): Bbh 103.11; 182.15.

[**vastra-vidyā**, see **vastu**°.]

vasyati (false Skt. from Pali vassati = Skt. vāśyate; § 3.34), *cries, shrieks*: (devī avidhāvidhaṃ ti, so read) vasyati (Senart em. vakṣyati) udakarākṣasena khajjāmi Mv ii.450.8, *the queen shrieks, O horror! I am being eaten by a water-ogre!*

vahati (AMg. vahai; Pktic. for **vadhati**): vahiṣyāma (tti), *we will kill*, Mv i.17.2 (essentially with mss.; Senart em. vadhiṣyāmi).

vahuri, acc. to Kyoto ed. n. sg. °riḥ, m. or f., but acc. to Mironov °ri, nt. (? perh. cf. Hindi buhrī, *parched grain*), *parched grain*: Mvy 5737 (same Tib. and Chin. as for **cānāḥ**, q.v.). In a list of vegetable foods.

vaheḍa, m. (= AMg. bahelaga, other Pkt. baheḍaya; Pali vibhītaka, °ṭaka; Skt. vibhīta(ka), vibhīdaka), a certain tree: Mvy 5796.

(**vā**, see also **va**, in the mgs. of iva and eva; also in Skt., see BR, pw; not in Pali, but in AMg.; in BHS used in prose and in metr. indifferent positions in vss; (**1**) = iva, *as, like*: siṃho vā asaṃtrasto Mv i.4.6 (prose); (Lumbinivanaṃ ...) manojñaṃ karotha (mss.) ... devabhuvanaṃ vā 149.4; siṃho vā nadate vane 188.7; jvalito agniskandho vā 252.14; (abhiramantu, mss. °ta, °tā) ... nandanagatā vā maruputrā iii.71.1 (prose); kṣubhitajalanidhir vā śrūyate eva śabdo LV 80.15 (in LV noted only in vss, but sometimes in metr. indiff. positions); gehaṃ praviṣṭa nṛpater amarālayaṃ vā 115.6; adhruva capalagāmi mārutaṃ vā 242.6, *like the wind*; sudurbalā (confirmed in Tib.) bṛṃhaṇa kāṅkṣiṇo vā (Tib. ḥdra, *like*) 399.8; others, LV 79.13; 132.13; 241.6; (**2**) = eva (rather than vai with Senart i note 376), *precisely, just*: na ca vā (= na caiva, *and not at all*) loke kiṃcit pāpaṃ karma karaṇīyaṃ Mv i.8.14; 28.1; 31.14; read with mss., āvṛṃhato chavi-māṃsa-rudhiraṃ vā i.13.2; yathā vedaṃ (= vā, or va, for eva, idaṃ) ... 39.4, *exactly as* (but in repetition 40.1 yathāpi); ettakakalpā vā 77.14, *of just so many kalpas in extent*; the bhūmis of Bodhisattvas can not be measured thus.)

vāka (= Pali id., AMg. vāga; for *vakka = Skt. valka; § 3.2), *bark*: certainly contained in reading of mss. (see Senart i n. 558) Mv i.236.1 cirā-vākodbhava, in what was orig. a vs, but is so corrupt in tradition that it cannot be restored in default of a parallel; if cirā- was orig. read, it stands for cīrā or cīra-, m.c.; ep. of garments worn by Dīpaṃkara; *originating from* (made of) *bast and bark*.

Vākkalividhvaṃsana-gaganakalpa, m., n. of a samādhi: Mvy 622; ŚsP 1426.7 (here °gagaṇa°); Tib. ṅag gi skyon rnam par ḥjig pas nam mkhaḥ ltar gyur pa, *becoming like air* (or *sky*) *by destroying depravities* (see **kali**) *of speech*.

Vākyacheda, n. of a Bodhisattva: Gv 442.24.

Vākyanuda, n. of a Bodhisattva: Gv 442.12.

Vāgīśa (= Pali Vaṅgīsa), n. of a disciple of Buddha: Mv i.163.12 (praises Buddha); 267.10; 269.10 (tells an incident in a past existence of Buddha and himself); Pravāraṇa Sūtra, Hoernle MR 38.1 (with Pali parallel, SN i.191.28 ff.); MSV i.182.19 ff.

Vāgīśvara, a name of **Mañjuśrī**: Sādh 94.7 etc.

[**Vācanopāsikāvimokṣa**, in Śikṣ 36.4, error for **Acalopās**°, see s.v. **Acalā** 3.]

vācikā (= Pali id.), *speech*; see **pṛṣṭa-v**°; also tri-, eka-vācikayā, *with triple* (*single*) *pronouncement*, MSV iv.119.3, 5.

vāṭa-dattikā (v.l. vāta°, so Mironov, with v.l. vāḍa°; cf. s.v. **maṇḍala-māḍa**), *garden-house* or *enclosed arbor* (?): Mvy 5549; = Tib. sab ma (*grass-covered arbor*? in 5546 = Skt. kāyamānam), or, sab mos bskor ba (*surrounded by a* ...), or, rib mas bskor ba (*surrounded by a hedge*; *hedged-in enclosure*).

vāṭāgravedikā (etc.), see **vātāgra**°.

-vāḍa, see s.v. **maṇḍala-māḍa.**

[**vāḍaka**, nt., mss. at Mv i.340.12, should = Skt. vāṭaka (pw) = vāṭa, *enclosure*; but Senart is prob. right in emending (to chātrakaṃ, or perhaps better) to **chattrakaṃ**, q.v.]

? **vāḍita**, ppp. (to Skt. Gr. vālayati, beside Skt. valayati, *causes to roll*), prob. intended in Divy 505.10 (sā) naus taiḥ (sc. sūkaraiḥ) parispandamānair vāḍitā (for vālitā), *was made to roll* (ed. bāḍitā, said by Index to mean *sunk*; mss. voḍitā, voditā, vāditā).

vāḍiśika, m. (= Pali bālisika, Skt. baḍiśa, vaḍ°,

plus -ika), *fisherman*: °kena . . . sāmiṣaṃ vaḍiśaṃ prakṣiptaṃ Śikṣ 94.15.

[**vāḍhavya,** read voḍh°: śakaṭam iva bhārodvahanārthaṃ . . . °vyam Śikṣ 34.16.]

vāṇa-, m., (**1**) *woven textiles* (Dutt): kati vāṇā iti . . . pañca vāṇāḥ, muñja-śāṇa-valvaja-kauśeya-vaṃśajāḥ MSV iv.75.11–12; cf. **vāna,** which perh. read for this; (**2**) n. of some bird: °śatāni Mv ii.400.4 (parallel with haṃsa, krońca, etc.); 402.6 (id.); 403.7. Cf. next.

Vāṇāravaghoṣa (so mss., Senart em. Vīṇā°, but cf. prec.; *whose voice is like the sound of the vāṇa-bird*), n. of a former Buddha: Mv i.141.2.

vāṇitaka, adj. (ka-extension of ppp. of unrecorded verb, possibly denom., related to Deśīn. 7.54 vāṇaa = *bracelet-maker*, valayakāra), something like *wrought* by a jeweler: kathiṇa-śubha-vāṇitaka-raśana-(mss. °ṇa-) Mv ii.147.9 (so one ms., v.l. vāśitaka, Senart em. vās°, which is implausible; *perfumed*?), *having hard, beautiful, wrought* (or, *beautifully wrought*) *girdles* (of precious metals and jewels), said of women of the harem.

vāta, nt. (otherwise m.), *wind*: vātāni Mv i.7.8 (prose).

Vātajava, n. of a son of Māra, unfavorable to the Bodhisattva: LV 313.12.

vāta-pratoda, m., some disease: Mvy 9549 = Tib. gzer (*pain*) thabs (or thegs),?; Chin. *piercing pain*.

vāta-putra, acc. to Skt. Lexx. *rogue*, or *libertine*, or the like: viṭa-°tra-dhūrtakair MSV ii.56.14; Tib. cited as nal phrag (read phrug), *bastard* (perhaps meant as term of abuse like that Eng. word, Skt. dāsīputra, and BHS **putramoṭikāputra**).

vāta-maṇḍalī (= Skt. Lex. id.; Pali °la and °likā; cf. (Skt.) **vāyu-maṇḍala-vat**), *whirlwind, tornado*; there are four whirlwinds, presumably one from each point of the compass: asaṃhāryā . . . catasṛbhir °lībhiḥ Dbh 54.13; anāchedyaprabhā ca bhavati catasṛbhir °lībhiḥ Bbh 345.19; °lībhir asaṃhāryā Dbh 46.26; anābhogavāhano °lī-praṇīto Dbh 67.13, see s.v. **anābhoga** (1); (bodhicittaṃ . . .) °lī-bhūtaṃ (*it is like a whirlwind*) sarvāvaraṇanivaraṇa-tṛṇavikiraṇa-(so read with Śikṣ; Gv text corruptly °tṛṃhaṇa-)-tayā Gv 495.22, cited Śikṣ 6.6; mahatyā °lyā . . . pratyudāvartyeta Śikṣ 7.4; °lī-parivartaḥ, *whirlwind Chapter*, Megh 308.16 (here text °li-pari°); 310.13; others, Gv 251.23; 351.14.

vātayāna, *window*: read in Mv iii.122.5 (vs) kūṭāgāre pithita-vātayāne, with v.l., for text °pāne. The word = Skt. and Pali vātāyana, and might stand for that m.c.; but it could also be an equivalent cpd., vāta-yāna, *way for air* (otherwise unrecorded).

Vātavalāhaka, pl. (= Pali id., DPPN), with devaputra, a class of gods: LV 273.10 (written °balā°); Divy 127.17; MSV i.243.19. Cf. s.v. **Mandavalāhaka** (n. 3 in Waldschmidt).

? **vātāgra-vedikā** (var. vāṭagra-petikā; Mironov vātāgra-peṭikā, v.l. °petikā), Mvy 5550, = **bālāgrapūtikā**; Tib. as for that item, q.v.; spelling -vedikā doubtless by popular etym., but orig. form obscure.

vātāṇḍa, adj. (cited BR from Skt. Lex. as subst.), *having swollen testicles*: Mvy 8869 = Tib. rlig rlugs (see Das).

vātātapa, m. pl. (ordinarily *wind and sunshine* as in Skt., e. g. Mv iii.350.10; but also) *wind and heat* as bodily *humors* (dhātu): Mv iii.143.16 abhiṣyaṇṇā (q.v.) vātātapā, resumed 144.6 by abhiṣyaṇṇehi dhātūhi, which, as well as the general context, appears to prove that ātapa is here one of the bodily *humors* (as well as vāta, which is normal in this sense), viz. = pitta (q.v., BR).

[**vātānuvṛttane,** wrong reading Śikṣ 249.2; read vā tālavṛntena, (*or*) *with a fan*; so Transl.]

vātāyana-rajas, LV 149.5; Divy 645.10; or **vātāyana-chidra-rajas,** Mvy 8197, a small particle, used as a measure; = Tib. (LV and Mvy) ñi zer gyi rdul, *sunbeam-speck*, prob. *a speck of dust seen thru* or *in a* (*hole*, chidra, *in a*) *window*; in LV = 7 truṭi, one-seventh of a śaśarajas; in Divy (text corrupt) the smallest unit, one-seventh of śaśaka-rajas; in Mvy a larger unit, placed between go-rajas and likṣā.

[**vātāsparśārgaḍāni,** Mv ii.115.12, see s.v. **sparśita.**

[**vātuṣkāra** Mv i.249.13, °kārī ii.116.10; errors for **dhānuṣkāri(n),** q.v.]

Vātsīputra (Ved. as n. of a teacher), n. of a nāga king: Kv 2.13; of a nāga, Māy 222.2.

Vātsīputrīya (cf. under prec.), n. of a Buddhist school: Mvy 9088. See refs. in BR.

vāda, m. (= Skt.), *talk*; in phrase kaḥ punar vādaḥ (not noted elsewhere, common in BHS), *not to speak of*; *to say nothing of*; *geschweige denn*: SP 298.7 ff. (prose; after ṣaṣṭi-, line 6) kaḥ punar vādaḥ pañcāśad-, *not to speak of* (i. e. a still larger number with) *fifty* . . ., and so on with *forty*, *thirty*, etc.; (ya imaṃ . . . dharmaparyāyaṃ śrutvāvatared . . .) k° p° v° ya imam . . . śrāvayed vācayed . . . SP 337.4–5, i. e. *how much more* . . .; similarly Vaj 33.11; (kusīdo dārakas . . . cakṣuḥsamprekṣaṇām api na kṛtavān) k° p° v° utthāsyati . . . Av i.16.6, *not to speak of rising* (*much less would he rise*; note future tense, tho referring to failure to act in the past); (srotaāpannasamudācāram api na samudācarati,) k° p° v° laukikān samudācārān samudācariṣyati (fut., as in prec.) Dbh 65.3; (yatrāgatir makara-°śuśumārādīnāṃ . . ., so mss.) k° p° v° manuṣyāṇām Divy 105.28, *where even makaras* (etc.) *cannot go, not to speak of men*; (mahāphalaṃ dharmaśravaṇaṃ . . .) k° p° v° dharmadeśanā . . . Divy 200.14, *how much more* . . .; ka eva vādaḥ in same sense Jm 143.10 (vs), eva for punar perh. m.c.?, (adṛṣṭabhaktiṣv api . . . hitaṃ vivakṣanti . . .) ka eva vādaḥ . . . premaguṇotsuke jane.

vādin, adj. m. (specialized mgs. of Skt. id.), (**1**) *one who proclaims* (the doctrine, or learning); as ep. of a Buddha: Mvy 70 (cf. next and **vādi-siṃha**); n. sg. vādi or vādī, followed by pravādi (°dī), *a declarer, a proclaimer* (of learning), or perh. *an eloquent proclaimer* (acc. to Senart vādi-pravādin, cpd., which seems less likely), (brāhmaṇo vedapārago . . .) vādi pravādi (Senart with v.l. pravādī) Mv iii.390.8 (prose); (adhīyāpito) vādi (v.l. vādī) pravādī 394.10 (prose); (**2**) ifc., *calling oneself* . . . (without justification): ye ete tubhyaṃhi (mss.; instr. pl.) ānītā (em.) aśāstārā (mss., n. pl.) śāstāra-vādino Mv i.254.1 (prose), *who are no teachers but call themselves teachers* (so mss., Senart em. wrongly).

Vādirāj, a name or form of Mañjuśrī: °rāḍ-Mañjuśrīrūpaṃ Sādh 104.5; etc.

? **vādiśa,** m. or nt., some musical instrument: Mv iii.407.19; represents, prob. corruptly, the same orig. as **vevādika** (or °aka), q.v. (both follow **mahatī** in the list).

vādi-siṃha, *lion of proclaimers* (of doctrine; see **vādin** 1), ep. of a Buddha: Mvy 39; trayo koṭiyo °hānāṃ Mv i.61.13 (vs); °ha, voc., LV 50.13 (vs), here addressed to Śākyamuni while still Bodhisattva.

vādya-kāra, or °**kara** (Skt. once vādyakāra = vādyaśilpajña, Schmidt, Nachträge), *a player on a musical instrument*: read bahu °kārā or °karā, n. pl., after a list of players of various instruments, Mv iii.113.5 (mss. °kānāṃ; Senart em. °kā ca); 442.11 (Senart °karā, mss. °karo).

vādya-bhāṇḍa (nt.; Skt. Lex. id.), *musical instrument*: caturvidhā °ḍa-vṛkṣā Divy 221.24 (supernatural trees that bear mus. instr.); acc. to pw also reported by Kern from SP.

vāna, nt. (Skt. Lex., *woven stuff, mat*), acc. to Tib. *fibre made from bark*: Mvy 5878 = Tib. thag ran. Follows sūtram; followed by kācalindikam. Cf. **vāṇa.**

Vānārasī (prob. intends Vāṇā° = the commoner, with Skt., Vārāṇasī), *Benares*: °syāṃ (v.l. Vārāṇ°) Mv i.174.2.

vāntīkaroti (cf. next; from vānta, ppp. of Skt. vam-; so regularly Pali vanta; plus karoti), *rejects, throws out from himself*: pūrvakāṃś cittotpādān vigarhiṣyati °kariṣyati jugupsiṣyati AsP 390.11; °kṛtam Mvy 2548.

vāntībhāva, m. (cf. under prec.), *the being rejected, thrown out*: (asyāś ca dṛṣṭeḥ prahāṇaṃ) bhaviṣyati pratinisargo °bhāvaḥ Av ii.188.1; °bhāvaḥ (so with Index and Mironov, text °bhavaḥ) Mvy 2600.

vāpayati (caus. to Skt. vā-), *causes to weave*: tair... vastrāṇy ārabdhāni vāpayitum Divy 213.8; °yanti 10; °yiṣyante 11.

[**Vāpibhūmi, Vāpila,** see **Vāy°**.]

[**vāpyāyamānaḥ** Divy 462.2, read vāṣpā° (or bāṣpā°) with line 6; see s.v. **bāṣpāyati**.]

vāmaka, (1) (Skt. adj., *left*), °kam, adv., *on the left*: devaputrau pradakṣiṇaṃ vāmaku (= °kaṃ) supratisthitau (no v.l.) LV 219.17 (vs), *stationed to the right and left*; **(2)** (unrecorded in this sense; = Skt. vāma plus -ka svārthe) *charming*: asaṃkhyeyaratna-°ka-viracanālaṃkāram Gv 511.22 (prose); **(3)** n. of a cakravartin king: Mvy 3571; **(4)** (= Pali id.) n. of a great (brahmanical) ṛṣi: Māy 256.13.

Vāmagupta (mss.; Senart em. Yāma°), n. of a former Buddha: Mv i.138.5.

vāmānuka, a kind of elephant: °ka-hastin MPS 31.21.

vāyana, nt. (recorded once in Skt., pw 7.373 °nakriyā, *weaving-activity*), **(1)** (act of) *weaving*: paṭa-vāyana Mmk 57.27, 29; 59.27; **(2)** *causing* (a weaver) *to weave* (a robe for himself; a sin for a monk): Mvy 8409 = Tib. ḥthag tu ḥjug pa, *causing to weave*; refers to the rule of Pali Vin. iii.256.26–27; var. vayanam, which Mironov adopts, but noting v.l. vāyanam; in view of the causative mg., the ā-form seems likely to be right (cf. **vāpayati**, Pali vāyāpeti); vayana is unrecorded except Skt. Gr. (BR). [In Mvy 6248 pw reads vāyana for **vayana**, q.v.]

Vāyavyā, see **Vāyuvyā**.

vāyasa-ruta-lipi, a kind of script, app. the writing used in a 'magic' dealing with sounds made by crows: LV 126.4; mss. all vāyu°, em. Lefm., confirmed by Tib. khva skad śes pa, *knowledge of crows' sounds*, a phrase which in Mvy 5057 renders vāyasa-vidyā.

vāyita (MIndic ppp. to root vā, *weave*; = Pali id.; Chap. 43, s.v. 1 vā 1), *woven*: **yamalī** (q.v.) °tā Divy 276.11 (prose).

Vāyibhūmi, n. of a locality and **Vāyila**, n. of a yakṣa dwelling there: Māy 36 Both forms uncertain; v.l. Vāp° in both, and other vv.ll. for the place-name (Lévi 89).

Vāyu, n. of a yakṣa leader: Māy 236.17.

(**vāyu-maṇḍala-vat**, adv., = Skt., Mbh. 12.6886, *like a whirlwind*: °vad ākāśe paribhramanti Av i.256.9 *rush around in the sky like a whirlwind*; Chin. acc. to Speyer *moving rapidly to the four points of the compass*; from this Speyer infers that vāyumaṇḍala was taken as *the circuit of the compass*; but Chin. evidently rendered ākāśe by that phrase, and vāyumaṇḍalavat, loosely, by *rapidly*. Cf. **vātamaṇḍalī**.)

Vāyuvegā, (1) n. of a kiṃnara maid: Kv 5.23; **(2)** n. of a yoginī: Sādh 427.5.

Vāyuvyā (doubtless to be read **Vāyavyā**), n. of a mātar (śakti of Vāyu): Māy 242.19.

vāyvādhika, read **vāyv-a°** acc. to pw 7.373, adj., *suffering from morbid excess of the wind humor* (acc. to Index, *palsied*; acc. to pw, *gouty*): Divy 540.25; the victim's bowl shook as he ate. But prob. read as next.

vāyv-ābādhika, adj. (cf. **ābādhika**), *due to disease of the wind*: °kaṃ glānyaṃ MSV i.xiii.1; i.30.8. Prob. read so for prec.

1 **vāra** (m.; Skt. Lex. and Jain; Pkt. id. = samūha, yūtha, Sheth), *crowd, multitude*: naitad vibuddhi (opt.) ... taṃ sopitaṃ puravaraṃ hi samṛddha-vāraṃ Mv i.155.19–20 (vss), *for this excellent city with its vast multitudes, being put to sleep ..., would not awake* (even if loud noises were made, 17–18); (saṃbhava-vibhavau mohād eva) vāra-lokena (*by the world of the multitude*. the vulgar herd?) dṛśyete MadhK 419.8.

2 **vāra** (m. or nt.; = Skt. Lex., Pali, AMg. id.; Skt. and Pali vāraka, id.), *pot, vessel*: so 'pareṇa samayena pānaka-vāram uddiṣṭas tad vārakaṃ (v.l. tat pānakaṃ) nirmādayati (q.v.) Divy 343.1.

3 **vāra** (m. or nt.), app. *platform* (so Burnouf, Introd. 401, *estrade*): (rājā ...) bodhivṛkṣasya ca caturdiśaṃ vāraṃ baddhvā svayam eva ca vāram abhiruhya ... bodhi-snapanaṃ kṛtavān Divy 404.2.

vāraṇa (m., = Pali id.; ignored by Senart), a kind of bird, which had a pleasant voice (Jāt. vi.539.16) and beautiful eyes (Mv); only in cpd. °ṇa-cakora-nayana: Mv iii.259.6; 267.15; 269.15; applied to Yaśodharā and Rāhula. In some Pali texts identified with the hatthiliṅga (cf. vāraṇa, *elephant*), which is described as *a sort of vulture with a bill like an elephant's trunk* (Childers, PTSD); but it seems questionable whether such attractive qualities as the above would be attributed to any vulture-like bird.

vāratraka, adj. (to varatrā; Skt. Gr. id.; Pali vārattika), *made of straps, leathern*: chinde (v.l. chinda, with Pali) vāratrakaṃ pāśaṃ Mv ii.235.7, and: dṛḍho °ko pāśo 10 (vss); same vss in Pali (vārattikaṃ, °ko) Jāt. iii.184.20; 185.3.

? **vāra-nibandhana**, see **āvāra-ni°**.

vārayati, vāreti, *shares, hands out in turn* (as gifts), *distributes* (? either 'caus.' to vṛ-ṇāti, like Skt. varayati, or perh. denom. to Skt. vāra, *turn*?): (so) dāni brāhmaṇo modakāni krīṇiya brāhmaṇāṃ śabdāvitvā modakāni vāreti (v.l. vārayati) Mv ii.442.2 (prose). Senart ignores the word, which surely deserves a note, and seems to me puzzling; the Skt. caus. to vṛ, regularly varayati, not vār°, seems to mean only *choose for oneself*. To this prob. MIndic caus. **vārāpayati** (§ 38.57), *causes to distribute*: tāttakā caiva vārāpeya (opt.) KP 158.3 (here text vārāvāpeya); 159.6–7. [In MSV iii.11.13; 15.19; and elsewhere, for (etad) vārayāmi, read dhār°, at the end of a vote in the saṃgha.]

Vāravatī, n. of a city: Mmk 625.22.

Vāravālī, °**lī** (also v.l. °ri, °rī), n. of a city, in the Śiri Jātaka: Mv ii.89.16; 90.11; 94.9, 11.

Vārāṇasīya and °**yaka**, adj. (cf. next), *of Benares*: °yāḥ MSV ii.120.1; °yasya śreṣṭhisya Mv iii.403.16; °sīyako (v.l. °sīko) Kāśirājā Mv iii.168.18.

Vārāṇaseya and °**yaka**, adj. (Skt. Gr. °seya; Pali Bārāṇaseyyaka), = prec.: °seyo rājā Av i.175.16; °seyānāṃ brāhmaṇagṛhapatīnāṃ 179.1; ii.159.8; °seyaḥ śreṣṭhiputraḥ ii.183.11; saṃpannaṃ vā °seyaṃ vastraṃ Mvy 1522–24; °seyakasya vā saṃpannasya vastrasya Bbh 390.26 (prose).

Vārāyaṇīya, pl., n. of a brahmanical school (of the Chandogas): Divy 637.27.

vārika, in Mv iii.113.8 (no correspondent in parallel 442.14) °kā (n. pl.) in a list of tradesmen and artisans, placed between gaulikā and karpāsikā; mg. obscure, prob. corrupt; ifc., in names of monastery officials, *charged with ..., superintendent of ..., one who watches over ...*, in **upadhi-v°**, q.v.; bhājana-v° Mvy 9069; pānīya-v° 9070; **prasādhi-**(Mironov **prāsādi-**, q.v.)-v° 9071; **pariṣaṇḍa-v°** 9072; śayanāsana-v° 9073; muṇḍaśayanāsana-v° 9074; **chaṇḍikā**(q.v.)-v° 9075; in most of these Tib. zhal (l)ta pa, *guard, superintend(ent)*; once ḥchos, *prepare*; once bsruṅ ba, *guard*.

vāritra (nt.? = Pali vāritta; formed in direct imitation of Skt. cāritra, Pali cāritta, with which this is closely associated in Pali and BHS), *restraint, control* (religious): °tra-saṃpannaḥ Mvy 1631, after cāritra-saṃpannaḥ 1630.

Vāriyoginī, n. of a yoginī: Sādh 445.19.

Vāruṇī, n. of a rākṣasī: Māy 243.13.

vārṇa-vāśin, see **pārṇa-vāsin.**

[**vārttībhavati**, Senart's em. for **varttī°**, q.v.]

[**vārdala**, see **vardala**, **°likā.**]

vārṣika (Pali vassika, nt., as well as °kā) = next (2); sometimes may have a for ā m.c., as in LV 214.19 (vs, vārṣika-campakāṃs tathā); 221.17 (vs), read with Foucaux's ms. B (Notes 150) so taṃ vārṣika-varṇa (or varṣ°? Lefm. mss. begin va-) kāñcana-khuraṃ; but also in prose, -vārṣika-mallikā- Mv ii.109.7; at end of cpd. containing list of flowers, -sumanā-gandha-vārṣikāṇi Kv 8.5–6 (prose), ... *fragrant jasmines*; v.l. °vārṣika- also in Mv ii.116.10, see next (2). See also s.v. **sāmayika.**

vārṣikā (**1**) Mv i.19.11, taken by Senart as subst., *garment for the rainy season*; he reads (eraka)vārṣikā vā kārāpitā cīrakavārṣikā kārāpitā vā; but see **eraka**; it seems more likely that eraka and **cīraka** (perhaps read °kā in both) are separate words, substantives, and vārṣikā adj., *grass-coverlets* and *bark-* (or *cloth-*)*strip-garments for the rainy season*; (**2**) (= Pali vassikā; cf. prec., also **varṣaka**, **°kī**, **varṣikā**, and next), a kind of jasmine: Mv i.249.13 (prose, in cpd., list of flowers); ii.116.10 (text °kāṃ, v.l. °ka-).

vārṣikī (Skt. Lex. id.; cf. under prec. (2), and see **mahā-vārṣikī**), a kind of jasmine: Mvy 6153, transliterated in Tib. var śi ki; in LV 27.7 (prose), cf. Weller's note, read as cpd. vārṣikī-suviśuddha-darśanā (it is not certain that sumanā, before vār°, is part of the cpd. as Weller believes).

vālaka, (**1**) nt. (= Skt. Lex. id.) *finger-ring*, perh. to be read Mvy 6027 for **valaka** 2, q.v.; (**2**) m. or nt., *lock, bolt*, or *bar*? see **ṣaḍvālaka** (read **°vāraka**?).

vāla-vedhin, in Pāli *hair-splitter*, an archer (and fig. arguer) who hits a very fine mark; implied in LV 181.7 (prose), where I would read vālākṣaṇadharmavedhī (ed. with no v.l. kālā°); see **akṣaṇa-vedhin.**

vāla-vyañjana (nt., = Skt. °vyajana, Pali °vījanī, AMg. °vīyaṇa, °vīyaṇī; recorded as 'error' for °vyajana, BR, from a Skt. Lex. and from SP, but the SP passage, KN 103.3, has °vyajana without v.l. in both edd.), *yak-tail fan, chowrie*: Mv i.259.15; 260.4, 9, 14; 261.1, 6 (all prose, ifc. Bhvr.); written bāla-vyañjanaṃ (acc.) Divy 147.13.

? **vāla-śollaka**, see **śollaka.**

vālākṣaṇa-(etc.), see s.v. **vālavedhin.**

Vālāha = **Valāha**, q.v.: °ha-kulena, of the family or breed to which this wonder-horse belonged (so Pali Valāhaka), Mv iii.85.11; sg. of the horse himself (so also Pali Jāt. ii.130.9; not in DPPN in this form), Mv iii.89.20 = Ud xxi.15; Mv iii.90.3; Kv 55.13 (here Deva-vālāha, as if the cpd. were the horse's name); 56.16; 58.5, 11; Vālāhāśvarāja- Gv 520.19.

Vālāhaka = prec., the horse Valāha: Kv 58.4; 59.9.

Vāli (supported by Tib.; most mss. Vāri), n. of a gandharva: Suv 162.2.

1 **vālikā**, once written bāl° (Skt. Lex. and Pali id.; = Skt., also Pali and BHS, vālukā), *sand*: mss. often vary between °ikā and °ukā, e. g. SP 253.3 (text with Kashgar rec. °ikā, Nep. mss. °ukā); yatha gaṅga-vālikāḥ SP 10.9; 96.9; yathā gaṅgāya vālikāḥ 255.4; 303.10 (these all vss); gaṅgā yathā vālikāḥ LV 283.20 (vs); 284.1 (vs); 360.19 (vs); tvatsaṃnibhair vālika-gaṅga-tulyaiḥ 310.14 (vs), *by such as you, like the Ganges as to sand* (= very numerous); the sands of the Ganges are proverbially used for vast numbers, very often, e. g. LV 311.8; 314.17; 376.5; Sukh 8.11; Śikṣ 16.3 (prose; in next line, same cpd. with vālukā); ṣaṭtriṃśad-gaṅgānadī-vālikā-samānāṃ Gv 125.1 (prose); other phrases, **vālikā-nagara**, q.v.; suvarṇa-vālikā-saṃstṛto Mv i.217.8, or °kā-saṃstīrṇo Gv 403.12; mahān vālikā-rāśir abhūd Gv 134.19; (the sun scorches above, and) heṣṭā tapati vālikā Mv iii.185.18; taptā vālika yā śarīri nipatī LV 282.3 (vs); taptām ayovālikāṃ pravarṣantaḥ 307.1 (prose); vālikā-varṣa-(= Pali °vassa, *a rain of sand*, as a plague)-Suvarṇi-(see **Suvarṇin**)-bhayāny apanayanti Gv 119.15; in all the above text vālikā, usually with no v.l.; in Divy 165.14 mss. bālikā, ed. em. bālukā; in Vaj., Pargiter ap. Hoernle MR 189.11 f. thrice vālikāḥ for Müller's ed. 39.4 f. vālukāḥ, but in 189.13, 14 vālukāḥ as in Müller.

2 **Vālikā** (text Bāl°), n. of a Licchavi woman; and **Vālikāchavī** (text Bāl°, with 1 ms. Bālika-, v.l. Pārikalecchavī, which suggests that the second member was a form of the tribal name!), n. of a place donated by her to the Buddha and the order (identified by Senart with Pāli Vālikārāma, v.l. Vālukā°; Pali seems to know no Vālikā; the v.l. suggests the word for *sand*): Mv i.300.17, printed, bālikāye bhagavataḥ saśrāvakasaṃghasya bhaktaṃ kṛtvā Bālikāchavī niryātitā. Does the name of the place mean *Vālikā's radiance*, or *having a covering of sand* (the woman's name being secondarily based upon the place name)?

vālikā-nagara (cf. AMg. vālua-ppabhā, °ppahā, JM. vāluā-puḍhavī, n. of a particular hell), *sand-city*; possibly, like the Pkt. words, n. of an infernal locality; but possibly rather a *mirage-city*, seen in the *sands* of a desert: dhig bhavāṃ sarada-abhra-saṃnibhā, vālikānagara-rūpa-saṃnibhā Mv i.74.(8–)9, *fie on the states of existence which resemble an autumn cloud or a 'sand-city'*. A third possibility might be *a city built of* or *on sand*, hence not substantial.

Vālikhila, n. of a maharṣi: Māy 257.4. Cf. Skt. Vālakhilya, acc. to BR often 'miswritten' Vāli°.

Vālukṣa, m. (°kṣo, n. sg.), n. of a city where Trapuṣa and Bhallika built a stūpa for the Buddha's nail-relic: Mv iii.310.14 (sentence found in only 1 ms.).

vālkala, adj. (from Skt. valkala), *made of bast*: Mmk 131.22 (paṭa; see s.v. **ātasya**).

Vālkali (= Pali Vakkali), n. of a monk: Saṃy. Āg. 13v.3 (corresp. to Pali SN iii.119.11).

Vāśiṣṭha, for **Vās°**, q.v.

[**vāśīcandanakalpa**, see **vāsī°**, the only spelling recorded in BHS mss.]

[**vāśyate**, *cries*, see **vasyati.**]

Vāṣpa (written **Bā°** in SP, Av; = Pali Vappa), n. of one of the five **bhadravargīya** monks: Mvy 1052; Mv iii.329.1; 337.6; 339.1; SP 1.10; LV 1.7; Divy 182.21; 268.6; Av ii.134.12; Sukh 2.3.

vāṣpāyate, see **bāṣpāyati.**

vāsa, nt. (this gender questioned for Skt., BR s.v. with App. 7.1803), *dwelling*: asmāku vāsaṃ (n. sg.) gagaṇe dhruvaṃ mune LV 367.12 (vs, no v.l.).

vāsana, nt., much more commonly **°nā** (= Pali °nā, no °na recorded; °nā, but not °na, is used in a closely similar way in Skt.), *impression, result* of past deeds and experience on the personality; Lévi, Sūtrāl. xx–xxi.54 *imprégnation, les appétits en tant que résultant d'actes antérieurs*; commonly (PTSD, LaV-P. on AbhidhK. iv.249, Suzuki, Gloss.) derived from Skt. vāsayati, *perfumes*; Suzuki, l. c., *perfuming impression, memory, habit-energy*; LaV-P. op. cit. vii.72, 77 etc., *traces*; the nt. °nam occurs in AbhidhK. LaV-P. iv.249 and Index, also Laṅk 265.17 (vs) vāsanair; regularly in bad sense, as something to be got rid of, Sūtrāl. l. c., above; rāgadoṣakaluṣā sāvāsanā (for sa°, m.c.) uddhṛtā LV 291.1 (vs), *passion, hatred, and impurity, with the* (evil) *impressions* (of the past; so Tib., bag chags bcas), *are destroyed*; sarvā rāgakileśa bandhanalatā sāvāsanā (as in prec.; so mss., here Lefm. em. so vā°!) chetsyati LV 294.6 (vs), *he will cut off all the creepers of bondage ... together with the impressions* (Tib. as above); °nā Mvy 6594 = Tib. bag chags (so regularly), *habit, inclination, propensity* (Das), Jä. *passion* instead of *habit*; stated to be usually bad tho sometimes good; LV 428.2 (prose); 433.19 (prose); Gv 496.13 (prose); Laṅk 37.19; 38.2 ff.; vāsanā-vāsita, *per-*

meated by impressions, Laṅk 92.16 etc., here regularly in bad sense (cf. below); vāsanābhiniveśa-vāsita Laṅk 80.8–9; sometimes in a good sense, vāsanā-bhāgīyāṃ sattvāṃ vāsanāyām avasthāpayanto (or °yamāno) Mv i.34.5; ii.419.5, (the Buddha) *making creatures that participate in* (good) *impressions* (note preceding parallels puṇya and phala) *firm in* (such an) *impression*; see **vāsita-vāsana**, which is complimentary in LV and Mv; perh. indifferent, incl. both good and bad, yathāgatisaṃbandha-vāsanā-vāsita-tāṃ ca (yathābhūtaṃ prajānāti) Dbh 75.21–22.

Vāsantī, n. of a 'goddess of Night': Gv 223.1 ff.

vāsarin, prob. from Skt. vāsara plus -in, = Skt. Lex. vāsareśa, *planet*, as *'regent of a day* (of the week)': pūjāṃ °riṇāṃ kuryāt Mmk 316.28 (complete sentence; prose; context gives no help).

Vāsava, (**1**) n. of a former Buddha: Mv iii.233.3; (**2**) n. of an ancient king, previous incarnation of Śaṅkha: Divy 62.7 ff.; (**3**) n. of another ancient king, vassal or neighbor of Dīpa: Divy 246.13 ff.; (**4**) n. of a yakṣa: Māy 20.

Vāsava-grāma, Divy 1.3, or (**1**) °**grāmaka**, 4.10; 10.2, 19, etc. (all prose), n. of a village near Śrāvastī; (**2**) °**grāmaka**, m., n. of a village in the Kāśi country, home of **Senāṃjaya**: MSV ii.199.2 ff.; adj. n. pl., *of* (*living in*) this village, ib. 5 ff.

Vāsavagrāmīyaka, adj., *of Vāsavagrāma(ka)* (2): MSV ii.200.3.

Vāsavadattā, n. of a harlot in Mathurā: Divy 352.28 ff.

vāsita-vāsana, adj. Bhvr. (vāsita, ppp. of Skt. vāsayati, plus **vāsanā**, q.v.), *having impressions* from previous births *duly formed*, here in good sense: (upālir ... kṛtakuśalamūlo) purimakehi samyaksaṃbuddhehi vāsitavāsano chinnabandhano ... Mv iii.179.7; (carimabhaviko) ... eṣo sattvo kṛtādhikāro vāsitavāsano 263.12; (kṛtādhikāro ...) vāsit° kṛtapūrvayogo ... 406.11; (bodhisattvasya ... paryeṣitasarvakuśalamūlasya) vāsitavāsanasya ... LV 10.4.

[**vāsitā**, acc. to text Laṅk 250.5 °tā-vāsitānāṃ, would = **vāsanā**, q.v.; so Suzuki, Index, *habit-energy*. The formation is isolated and seems to me inexplicable; prob. error, anticipating the pple. vāsita; read vāsanā-vās°.]

vāsin, adj. (Skt. Lex. id.; Skt. vāsa, *perfume*, plus -in), *fragrant*: (mahānadyo ...)-varagandha-vāsi-vāri-paripūrṇāḥ Sukh 38.18.

Vāsiṣṭha (= Pali Vāseṭṭha, so used e. g. DN ii.158.32; 159.5; iii.209.8, cf. Senart, Mv i note 403; mss. of Mv usually Vāśiṣṭa; the mg. not recognized in Pali Dictt.), voc. in polite address to anyone without regard to ancestry, *sirs! gentlemen! mes amis!* (Senart, l. c.): sg. Mv i.257.9, King Śreṇiya Bimbisāra to Tomara the Licchavi; iii.368.4 (mss. Vāśiṣṭo), to Śarabhaṅga, whose gotra was Kauṇḍinya 370.12, as in Pali Koṇḍañña Jāt. v.140.17; generally pl., -ā or (oftener) -āho; -ā Mv i.283.13 (v.l. -āho), 14; 286.14 (in all three Buddha to Licchavis); -āho Mv i.38.4 (Abhiya to two unnamed perfume-merchants in Vasumata); to Licchavis, the speaker being usually the Buddha, i.257.13, 15, 19; 271.12, 18, 19; 283.9; 286.13, 22; 288.1, 4, 11, 13; 289.12, 14, 16; 290.1, 3, 4; 300.1 ff.; Śuddhodana to Śākyas, iii.108.7; Buddha to men of Vaiśālī, MSV i.225.18; 228.22.

vāsī-candana-kalpa, adj. (= AMg. vāsī-candaṇa-kappa, see below), a stock ep. of an arhat; in effect, *indifferent*; only in a cliché list of such epithets, always following (and in every case but one immediately) samaloṣṭakāñcana and ākāśapāṇitalasamacitta, with other similar terms: Divy 97.26; 180.26 (here v.l. vālī°); 240.25; 282.2; 551.19; MSV ii.131.3; Av i.96.7 (ms.); 104.7; 207.12, etc.; acc. to Ratnach., *indifferent alike to being cut with a hatchet* (Skt. vāśī, also written vāsī) *or anointed with sandalwood paste*; this is clearly the Jain traditional interpretation, misunderstood by Jacobi, SBE 45, p. 99, note 1; in transl. of Kalpa Sūtra 119 Jacobi renders vāsī by *ordure*, and Charpentier on Uttarādh. 19.92 also thinks it means something ill-smelling, in contrast with sandal; they both agree with the Jain tradition in understanding -kalpa as *indifferent to* (pairs of opposites, like Skt. sama); perhaps this is right, but if so I know of no parallel for it; ordinary usage, both Skt. and MIndic, would make it mean *like, resembling*...; in this case, possibly, *resembling a knife or sandalwood* in 'coldness', dispassionate nature?. So in effect Feer, Av transl. p. 14, *il était devenu froid comme le sandal*; but Feer omits vāsī!

Vāsudeva, n. of a Bodhisattva (in a long list of them): Gv 442.14.

vāsodghātikā, see **udghātikā**.

[**vāstu-vidyā**, see **vastu°**.]

[**vāstha**, MSV ii.151.16, 18; 152.2, acc. to note on 151.16 = Skt. vasatha! but read, kutra vā stha varṣā uṣitā iti, *or where have you spent the rains*? So vā sma (for smo) 151.20; 152.2.]

[**vāha**: in Mmk 343.17 (vs) text corruptly (-ni) vāhas, read vivāhas; see **vivāha**.]

vāhana, m., a high number: Mvy 8014 = Tib. deḋ ḥdren; cf. **vāhana-prajñapti**, and **mahā-vāhana**.

[**vāhanakāra**, LV 254.9, read **vāhanāgāra**, q.v.]

vāhana-prajñapti, or °**jñāpti**, f., a high number or method of computation: °jñapti LV 148.15, cited thence as °jñāpti Mvy 7981 (see **prajñāpti**). Cf. also (**mahā-**) **vāhana**.

vāhanāgāra (= Pali id.; °na plus agāra, āg°), *stable for vehicles* or *beasts of burden*: -śālā, *a building serving as a stable for vehicles* or *beasts of burden*: tadyathāpi nāma vāhanāgāra-(text vāhana-kāra-, no v.l.)-śālāyāṃ vā hastiśālāyāṃ (text both times °sālāyāṃ) vā jīrṇāyām ubhayato vivṛtāyāṃ LV 254.9; em. proved by Tib. bzhon paḥi (*of vehicles* or *beasts of burden*) bres (*stable*) khaṅ (*house*) ṅam (*or*) glaṅ poḥi (*of elephants*) bres khaṅ ...; parallel in LV 256.1 only vāhana-śālāyāṃ, perhaps by accidental omission, Tib. as before; the em. also confirmed by corresponding passage in Mv ii.125.14; 127.1; 128.7; 129.9, where always vāhanāgāraśālāyā or °yāṃ, usually with no v.l.

vāhayati, vāheti; see **bāhayati**. (Otherwise = Skt. vāhayati, as in MSV i.57.1 manasikāraṃ vāhayitum *to work at, accomplish*. Does lālā (acc. pl.) vāhayati MSV i.285.16, *froths at the mouth* (from snakebite), belong here or with bāhayati?)

-vāhika (Skt. vāhin plus -ka), *carrying, carrier*, in lekha-v°: dārakas tena lekha-vāhika-manuṣyeṇa sārdhaṃ ... gataḥ Divy 258.13.

vāhikā, (*manner of*) *carrying*: (tā dāni antaḥpurikā tena sārdhaṃ viśvastaṃ krīḍanti keliṃ) kurvanti, pṛṣṭhimaṃ (? see this) āruhitvā nānāvāhikāye vāhenti Mv ii.479.19, *the harem-women ... carried him, when he had mounted on their backs* (in amorous sport), *in various ways-of-carrying*; or possibly, *in the manner of various vehicles*. Acc. to Cappeller, HOS 15, Glossar, vāhikā means *Reihenfolge, das Nacheinander*, Kir. 15.25; nānā- makes it difficult to understand it so here (but perhaps not impossible; *variously taking turns* in the sport?).

[**vāhitaka** (mārga), see **bāhiraka**.]

vi, or (a)vi (AMg. etc. vi, avi) = **pi**, Skt. api; perh. in SP 198.6 (vs) kāvi, all mss., = Skt. kāpi, ed. em. kāci (= kācid).

viṃvara, see **bimbara**.

viṃśativarga, m., *a quorum of twenty* (monks), required for **āvarhaṇa** rite: MSV ii.205.21 ff., cf. 203.16.

Vikaṭa, n. of a yakṣa: Māy 75.

vikaṭaka, adj. (= Skt. °ṭa plus -ka svārthe), *deformed*: Mvy 8813 = Tib. lus ñams pa, (of) *imperfect body*.

Vikaṭaṃkaṭa, pl., n. of a group of yakṣas: Māy 71.

Vikaṭāsya, n. of a yakṣa: Samādh p. 43 line 21.

vikaḍḍhate (see s.v. **kaṭṭati**; cf. Pali kaḍḍhati),

tears, rends: SP 84.1 (vs) yakṣā manuṣyakuṇapāni vikaḍḍhamānāḥ.

vikampana (nt.; noted only in neg. **a-vi°**, q.v., except that Skt. uses it of motion of the sun and as a n. pr.), *wavering*: (ta evaṃ bodhisattvena samādāpyamānāḥ) saced °nena na (ms. omits na) pratipadyante... Bbh 269.8.

vikara, and **°ra-ka** (to Skt. vi-kirati; cf. **vikira**): kusuma-°rakaṃ (so mss., Senart em. -nikarakaṃ)... abhikiranti Mv i.236.6 (vs), *they strew a strewing of flowers on* (the Buddha Dīpaṃkara); kusuma-vikaraṃ (Senart em. °nikaraṃ) muncanti 8 (vs); °kusuma-vikaraṃ ii.18.11, see **vikira.**

vikaraṇa = **vikiraṇa,** q.v.; also in sarvasattva-tamovikaraṇa- (*dispelling the darkness of all creatures*)-dharmāvabhāsa- Gv 234.7; (om. sattva) 235.5.

vikarin, f. -ṇī (in cpd. with mg. of **vikaraṇa, vikiraṇa,** qq.v.), *dispelling*: mohatamas-timira-°ṇī (prajñāpāramitā) AsP 170.16, *dispelling the gloom of the darkness of delusion*; vv.ll. °vikaraṇī, °vikiraṇī.

Vikarāla, n. of a piśāca-prince: Mmk 45.23.

vikartana (nt. or m., = Pali vikattana, vikantana), *knife*, in go-vi° (also Pali), (*cow-*)*butcher-knife*: (sayyathāpi ... goghātako vā) ... tīkṣṇena go-vikartanena gāvīye śīrṣakapālaṃ dāleya Mv ii.125.4 (Pali Vin. iii.89.14 tiṇhena govikattanena; in same simile as Mv, MN i.244.15 °vikantanena).

vikalpa, m. (**1**) (Skt. id., BR s.v. 1 g, at least in very similar mg., but in BHS more technical; whether Pali vikappa occurs in this sense is not clear; cf. **vikalpayati** 1), (*vain*) *imagining*, esp. *false discrimination* between true and false, real and unreal; seems substantially identical with **kalpa** 3 and **parikalpa** 1: compounded or associated with one or both of them, qq.v., LV 34.11; Śikṣ 272.7; KP 94.3; LV 250.16; 420.11; 422.20; Gv 350.5–6; eṣo asaṅgaprājñaḥ kalpair vikalpamukto LV 223.21 (kalpair here = *long periods of time*; in next line kalpair is Lefm.'s insertion, mss. defective); in Dharmas 135 three vikalpāḥ, viz. anusmaraṇa-vi°, saṃtiraṇa-vi° (read **saṃtīraṇa-,** q.v., with v.l.), sahaja-vi° (cf. AbhidhK. LaV-P. i.60); eight vi° Bbh 50.23, listed 25–27, svabhāva-vi°, viśeṣa-, piṇḍagrāha-, aham iti vi°, mameti vi°, priya-, apriya-, tadubhayaviparītaś ca vikalpaḥ (all expl. in the sequel); Laṅk 227.18–19 also says, vikalpo 'ṣṭadhā bhidyate, but I find no evidence as to what the eight kinds are (are they connected with the eight vijñāna, mentioned in 227.10?); vikalpa is a common and important word in Laṅk, one of the five **dharma** (2, q.v. 3); kleśendhanavikalpa-kṣayakaraṃ Laṅk 12.3–4, (Buddha) *who destroys* (*false*) *discrimination, the fuel of the depravities* (wrongly Suzuki); Suzuki's transl. seems also wrong in Laṅk 9.7 ff. (vss) anyatra hi vikalpo 'yaṃ buddhadharmākṛtisthitiḥ, ye paśyanti yathādṛṣṭaṃ na te paśyanti nāyakam, apravṛttivikalpaś ca yadā buddhaṃ na paśyati, apravṛttibhave buddhaḥ saṃbuddho yadi paśyati, *on the contrary* (**anyatra**) *this is a false discrimination, viz. abiding in* (*resting upon*) *the external form of the Buddha and Doctrine. Those who see him as seen* (with worldly sight), *they do not* (truly) *see the Buddha. And when, having no productive-*(*false-*)*-discrimination, one does not see the Buddha* (as an earthly figure), *in non-originative condition, he is a Buddha, a Perfectly Enlightened One, if he sees* (thus; the Wei rendering cited in Suzuki's note seems to me to support this); (**2**) (to **vikalpayati** 2; the noun not recorded in Pali) *gift, provision* (for a monk or saint or Buddha), esp. of garments: vayaṃ bhagavato divyāṃ vikalpāṃ duṣyāṇi (so mss.) dāsyāmaḥ. bhagavāṃ teṣāṃ devatānāṃ vikalpaṃ (Senart em. °pa; mss. kalpaṃ) duṣyapradānāni nādhivāsayati Mv iii.312.10–11, (let not the Lord accept a garment of linen rags;) *we will give the Lord supernatural gifts, fine cloth garments. The Lord did not accept the present of those gods, the gifts of fine garments*; vikalpa-hetoḥ Bbh 128.16, *as a gift* (see the preceding passage s.v. **vikalpayati** 2).

vikalpaka, adj. (**1**) (cf. prec.) *which falsely discriminates, imagines*: °kasya manovijñānasya Laṅk 126.11; (**2**) (to Skt. vikalpa) *optional*: °ka-cīvara-dhāraṇam MSV ii.152.11.

vikalpana (nt.), **°nā** (adumbrated in Skt.; see prec. two and next), *false discrimination*: akalpāvikalpana-taḥ (a-kalpa plus a-vikalpana) Laṅk 231.5 (prose); yā khalv eṣu dharmeṣv avicāraṇā a-vikalpanā (so mss.), ayam ucyate ... bodhisattvasya ... ācāraḥ SP 275.10 (prose), *when there is no doubt or false discrimination about these conditions of being, this is called the B's* (right) *conduct*; no ca vikalpana (m.c. for °naṃ or °nā) vidyati mahyam Gv 231.12, 14 (vss); dharmāṇām evam a-vikalpanā, *no false discrimination of states of being*, Bbh 260.11 (see s.v. **vipaśyanā**).

vikalpayati, (**1**) (cf. **vikalpa** 1 and other adjoining items), *distinguishes falsely*: (na ca dharmādharmayoḥ prahāṇena) caranti, vikalpayanti puṣṇanti, na praśamaṃ pratilabhante Laṅk 21.2; °yiṣyanti Mv i.224.4 = ii.27.4, see § 42.7; (**2**) (= Pali vikappeti; cf. **vikalpa** 2), *hands over, assigns, presents, gives*, regularly a garment to a religious person (so also Pali, cīvaraṃ): (sarvapariṣkārāḥ sarvadeyadharmā ... nisṛṣṭā bhavanti) vikalpitāḥ, tadyathā nāma bhikṣur ācāryāya vā upādhyāya vā svacīvaraṃ vikalpayet, sa evaṃ vikalpa-hetoḥ... Bbh 128.15–16.

vikalpā = **vikalpa** (1): paraspara-vikalpayā Laṅk 287.7 (vs); perhaps m.c. for °pena, which would not fit metr. here.

vikalpita, (**1**) ppp. to **vikalpayati** (1), *falsely distinguished* or *imagined*: viparīta-saṃjñīhi ime (sc. dharmāḥ) vikalpitā asanta-santā hi abhūta-bhūtataḥ SP 281.11 (vs), *by men of inverted notions these* (states of being) *are wrongly discriminated as existent and non-existent, true and false* (respectively; i. e. with inversion of terms); very common in Laṅk (see Index), e. g. bālair vikalpitā hy ete 167.17; (**2**) subst. nt., *vain imagining, false discrimination*: kalpita-°tāni LV 374.6 (vs), see **kalpita.** This use does not seem to occur in Laṅk.

vikāla, °ra (m.; = Pali id.; in Skt. *evening*, so also Pali and BHS), *wrong time*: paradāre prasakto (v.l. °te) tatra kāle vā vikāle vā gacchati (mss. °nti) Mv i.243.18, *in season and out of season*; °la-caryā (cf. Pali °la-cariyā), *walking abroad at night* (so Tib., mtshan mo ḥphyan pa) Mvy 2507 (Pali acc. to Childers, *going on the monk's begging rounds in the afternoon*); one of the six **apāyasthānāni** (bhogānām); **vikāla-bhojana** (nt.; = Pali id.), or with Senart and mss. **vikāra°** (§ 2.49), *eating at the wrong time*, or *eating at night* or *after noon*, °bhojanāt prativirato Mv i.326.18.

Vikālarātrī, n. of a goddess: Sādh 502.11.

Vikiṭi, n. of an attendant on the four directionrulers: Mahāsamāj. 173.9 (Waldschmidt, Kl. Skt. Texte 4).

vikira (see also s.v. **vikara**; m. or nt.; Skt., not precisely in this sense; cf. Skt. vikiraṇa), (*act of*) *strewing, throwing about*: in Bhvr. cpd., (padminivanaṃ, or Lumbinivanaṃ ...) varasurabhikusuma-vikiraṃ (so mss. first time, second time °vikaraṃ; Senart em. °nikaraṃ) Mv i.215.15 = ii.18.11 (vs), *having a strewing of beautiful fragrant flowers*; °ram, acc. sg. as adv., *with throwing about of ...*, Prāt 534.1, where text **śista-vi°**, but see under **śista** and **-pṛthakkārakam.**

vikiraṇa, (**1**) (nt., = Pali id., occasionally Skt. in mg. *strewing about*; also **vikaraṇa,** q.v., which is recorded by Sheth from AMg.), *destruction*: (kāmāḥ ...) vikiraṇa sarvaśubhasya LV 242.6 (vs), *the destruction* (? *destroyers*) *of all that is fair*; Mv ii.269.15 and 278.1, see **ucchādana**; in the cpds. cited s.v. **śatana,** q.v. (instead of vikir°, **vikaraṇa** is read Av i.50.14; 348.3, see note here, et alibi; also in ms., Śikṣ 229.12); cyavana-patana-vikiraṇavidhvaṃsanādīni (duḥkhāni) manuṣyāṇāṃ Divy 299.22; (see s.v. **ucchada**) KP 152.3; in LV 4.19 text tuṣitavara-bhavana-vikiraṇa-, no v.l., but read certainly °bhavanāvataraṇa-, with Tib. ḥbab pa (vikiraṇa is senseless; Foucaux *descente*); (**2**) m., n. of a samādhi: Mvy 569; ŚsP 1420.18.

vikuṭṭanā (cf. AMg. viuṭṭanā, rendered pīḍā, saṃtāpa, Sheth), *censure, criticism* (Skt. Gr. kuṭṭ- = bharts-): na pareṣāṃ °nā kartavyā, ayam īdṛśo 'yam īdṛśa iti Śikṣ 100.2. Tib. cited as ḥphyas, said to mean *censure*.

vikutsayate (cf. Ap. ppp. vikucchia; Skt. vikutsā, and kutsayate, denom.), *reviles*: °yase kim asmān Jm 148.24 (vs); bhavān apy asmān na śobhate °yamānaḥ 150.23 (prose); (bhavān) apy asmān kasmād iti °yate 152.9 (prose).

vikurvaṇa, nt. (= Pali vikubbana; n. act. to **vikurvati**; cf. Skt. vikurvaṇaḥ, Mbh 13.1244, n. of Śiva, doubtless semi-MIndic to **vikurvati** as n.ag., *Miracle-worker*; not with either BR or Nīlak.; see also next items), *miracle*: dharmacakra-pravartana-vikurvaṇasya praveśaṃ (? Tib. phyogs, app. = pradeśaṃ, *region*! but better read prakāśaṃ with most and best mss.) śrotukāmās LV 422.9; samantajñānavikurvaṇa ity ucyate 427.7, *he* (Buddha) *is called one who possesses the miracle of complete knowledge*; esp. of Buddha's miracles, Dbh 8.21 (buddha-vi°); 16.15; Mmk 7.21 (buddha-vi°); or bodhisattva-vi° Mmk 1.8; °ṇa-balam Mvy 767, one of the 10 bodhisattva-bala; printed °nam Samādh p. 5 line 18; of all Tathāgatas (as part of their life pattern) Gv 15.8.

vikurvaṇā (= Pali vikubbanā) = prec. and **vikurvā**: °ṇā-dharmiṇaṃ (acc. sg.) LV 16.1 (prose), *characterized by magic performances*, of the cakravartin's elephant-jewel; (bodhisattvasya . . .)-vikurvaṇāḥ (misprinted °vāṇaḥ) saṃdarśayataḥ Gv 504.20 (prose), *displaying miracles*; prabhāva-°ṇā bodhisattvānāṃ Bbh 332.11 (prose); ṛddhi-vikurvaṇā AsP 508.20 (prose; of a bodhisattva).

vikurvati, **°te**, (**1**) (= Pali vikubbati; specialized form of Skt. vi-karoti, § 28.6), *works a miracle* (this seems to be the regular, nearly universal, mg. of the rather rare verb, and of its much commoner derivs., see prec. and next items, in BHS, and prob. also in Pali; no doubt it started from the Skt. mg. of vikaroti, *change, alter*, but Senart, Mv i note 425 f., seems to me wrong in finding that mg. here): (bhūmayo dáśa jināna śrīmatā; so, or °to, mss.) yair vikurviṣu sadā paṇḍitāḥ Mv i.64.3 (vs, metr. deficient), *there are ten glorious Stages of the Jinas, in which the Wise Ones always wrought miracles*; °vati Śikṣ 347.5 (vs), °vī 6 (vs; aor., or opt.?); °vitu-kāma Samādh p. 6 line 23, *wishing to perform miracles*; vikurva vikurva Mmk 55.26 (prose; impv., in a mantra); vikurvayato (n. pl. m., for vikurvantaḥ; not caus.) cakraṃ pravartya vinayanti jagat Gv 267.3 (vs); saṃdṛśyase loki vikurvamāṇā (n. sg. f.) Gv 302.14 (vs); pres. pple., n. or voc., nṛpati . . . tvaṃ sa vikurvan LV 168.2 (vs), to the Bodhisattva, *O King, such art thou* (*hast thou been*), (being a?) *miracle-working one*! (so Tib., rnam par ḥphrul pa de ñid khyod); (**2**) vikurvate, *contends, acts in* (friendly) *rivalry* (with, instr.), not with the hostile mg. usual in Skt.: Kunālo guṇavān pitrā sārdhaṃ °vate Divy 403.21 (viz. in works of piety; thus is answered the king's angry inquiry in 18, ko 'yam asmābhiḥ sārdhaṃ **pratidvandvayati**).

vikurvā (not in Pali; = °vaṇā), *miracle*: īdṛśyā . . . vikurvayā (v.l. vikrīḍayā) SP 446.10 (prose), of Avalokiteśvara; vikurvā- (but most mss. vikrīḍita-)-nirdeśaṃ 456.5 (prose), of the same; mahatyā bodhisattva-vikurvayā 472.4 (prose), of Samantabhadra; bahu tubhyaṃ vīrya-vikurvā (n. pl.) LV 169.4 (vs); dhyāna-vikurvā id. 8 (vs; the first part of this line is certainly corrupt; most mss. omit the first words, which do not make sense here); jinānāṃ . . . akhilā vikurvā Gv 43.19 (vs); bodhisattva-vikurvābhir 224.11 (prose); others, Śikṣ 327.20 (vs); 328.9 (vs), 15; 333.12; 345.12.

Vikurvāṇarājaparipṛcchā (so also Mironov, one of whose mss. first wrote Vikurvaṇa°; I believe this latter was the true reading, as Tib. suggests, rnam par ḥphrul baḥi rgyal pos zhus pa, *questioning by the king of miracle-working*): n. of a work: Mvy 1409.

vikurvita, nt. (seems commonest of this group in BHS; orig. ppp. of **vikurvati**, but noted only as noun; not so used in Pali), *miracle*: dṛṣṭvā vikurvita mamā LV 119.8 (vs); buddha-vi° Mv i.266.17; ii.33.4 (both prose); nirīkṣituṃ Śākyamuner °tam Divy 269.7 (vs); others, Av i.258.9; Samādh 22.19; Bhad 45 (°vitu, acc. pl.; no v.l.); Kv 13.17; 24.10; Mmk 6.1 (read °taṃ for °tuṃ); Gv (common) 6.5; tathāgata-vi° 18.26, et passim.

Vikurvitaprabha, n. of a Bodhisattva: Gv 3.17.

vikurvī = **vikurvā** (which perh. read, with two mss., but see § 11.3), *miracle*: bahu tubhyaṃ śīlavikurvī LV 168.10 (vs); closely parallel with 169.4, 8, vikurvā; this is against understanding a voc. of *vikurvin, which is not plausible otherwise).

vikūṭaka, some musical instrument: °kaṃ (acc. sg.) Mv iii.407.19, in a list.

vikṛta, (**1**) (nt.? = AMg. vigaya = vikār utpanna karnevālā . . ., *objects that cause a change*, Ratnach.), *alterant, deteriorating substance* (affecting ornaments): Dbh 72.18 (jātarūpaṃ supariniṣṭhitaṃ . . .) asaṃhāryaṃ bhavati . . . ābharaṇavikṛtaiḥ; same 81.18; (**2**) *foul, filthy* (things to eat, prescribed for snakebite): MSV i.286.2 ff.; defined 8 as dung, urine, ashes, earth (so Pali Vin. i.206.8, here mahāvikaṭāni).

vi-kṛtajña, adj., *ungrateful*: RP 25.5, ep. of **Akṛtajña**.

vikopayati, **°peti** (= Pali vikopeti), *disturbs*: Mv i.168.18 vairambhā (q.v.; so read) . . . (some form of vāta, *wind*) vikopenti na dehakaṃ; Divy 350.7 teṣām īryāpathān vikopayitum ārabdhaḥ; Gv 84.1 kalyāṇamitrajñān avikopayan, *not disturbing those who know worthy friends* (? so text, prob. corrupt; perhaps read °mitrajñānam avik°); MSV i.6.2. See also **a-vikopita**, **a-vikopana**; **vyākopayati.**

vikrandati (Skt. only ppp. °dita, nt., as noun, *Wehklagen*; = Pali vikkandati), *wails, laments*: so sattvo bāhāyāṃ bāhāṃ (so mss.) pragṛhya vikrande (aor.) vikrośe Mv i.347.9, similarly 12.

vikrama, (**1**) nt. (for Skt. m.), *valor*: °maṃ, n. sg., Mv i.78.16, as one of 8 **samudācāra** (q.v., 1); (**2**) *foot* (so Skt. Lex.), or *footstep* (cf. the mg. *step, stride* in Skt.): govikrama-saṃsthānaṃ, *shaped like a cow's foot*(*-step*), Divy 640.19, of the Pūrvāṣāḍha-nakṣatra; so gaja-vikrama-saṃsthānaṃ 21, of the Uttarāṣāḍhanakṣatra.

Vikrāntagāmin, n. of a Buddha: Śikṣ 169.14.

Vikrāntadevagati, n. of a Buddha: Gv 284.17 (vs).

vikrāmin (unrecorded elsewhere) (**1**) = Skt. vikramin, *possessing prowess*; chiefly m.c.; °mī, n. sg., Mvy 2400 (Mironov vikramī); Tib. rtsal (po) che (ba), usually = vikrama; in n. pr. **Vijaya-vikrāmin**, q.v. (here Mironov also °krā°); in padmaśrīvikurvitasamanta-vikrāmin, one of a list of bodhisattva-samādhis, Gv 39.19; in voc. mahāprajñājñāna-vikrāmin, addressed to **Sudhana** (2), Gv 385.21; all prose; (**2**) see **ratnapadma-vikrāmin.**

vikrāyati (AMg. vikkāyamāṇa, *being sold*; see § 37.39), *is sold*, for Skt. vikrīyate: vikrāyetsuḥ, opt., *would be sold*, Mv ii.241.20 (Senart em. vikrī°); vikrāyiṣyati 242.14 (? text vikray°, misprint? only v.l. is vikrāmāṣyati), and vikrāsyati 11, fut., §§ 31.2, 3.

vikriṇati (= Pali vikkiṇati; Skt. vikrīṇāti), *sells*; see § 28.5; Chap. 43, s.v. krī (2).

-vikrīḍana(-tā), (cf. Pali vikīḷanika), substantially = **vikrīḍita**; here *easy mastery* seems about right: acintya-bodhisattvavimokṣa-vikrīḍana-tā, one of a long list of svacittādhiṣṭhānāni, Gv 83.3; abhijñā-vikrīḍana-tā ŚsP

1458.1, one of four dharmāḥ which are to be fulfilled (paripūrayitavyāḥ) by a Bodhisattva in the 8th bhūmi.

vikrīḍita, nt. (orig. ppp. of Skt. vi-krīḍ-; as n. rare in Skt.; Pali vikkīḷita), (**1**) lit. *sport*: yenaite sattvāḥ krīḍiṣyanti ramiṣyanti paricārayiṣyanti vikrīḍitāni (ca, only 2 mss.) kariṣyanti SP 78.8; (kiṃnaradārikā...) strīvikrīḍitāny upadarśayati Av ii.28.5; (**2**) oftener, fig., something like *easy mastery*: °tam Mvy 6404 = Tib. rnam par rol pa (and so often in cpd. n. pr. in Mvy), which Jä. renders *to practise sorcery, to cause to appear by magic*; lit., however, it would seem to be like the Skt., *variously* (rnam par = vi) *sporting* (rol pa, or °ba, also used for Skt. lalita); often of Buddhas and Bodhisattvas, bodhisattvavikrīḍiteṣu vā tathāgata-vi° vā SP 101.2, something like *miracles, exhibitions of supernatural power*; tasya sattvapradhānasya (i. e. Buddha) śṛṇu vikrīḍitaṃ śubhaṃ Mv i.178.8 (vs); tathāgata-vi° SP 308.5; 426.7; tad buddhavikrīḍitaṃ Divy 401.15, refers to a mahā-prātihāryam, *great miracle*, just mentioned; so 19 (vs) °taṃ daśabalasya; buddha-vi° LV 160.16 (here referring to the dharmacakrapravartana); vikrīḍitāṃ (acc. pl.) ca sugatasya 356.10 (vs); tasmin kṣaṇe 'prameyāni buddha-°tāny abhūvan, yāni na sukaraṃ kalpenāpi nirdeṣṭuṃ 14 (prose); mama (sc. Bodhisattvasya) siṃhavikrīḍitaṃ (in vanquishing Māra) LV 300.4; mahopāyakauśalya-vi° (of the Bodhisattva) LV 179.16; trivimokṣa-mukha-(Lefm. sukha-, misprint?)-vikrīḍito LV 181.20, Bhvr., (the Bodhisattva) *having perfect mastery of entrance to the three-fold salvation*; similarly, (bodhisattvair ... aneka-)-samādhivaśitā-balābhijñā-vikrīḍitair Laṅk 1.10, *'perfect masters of...'* (Suzuki).

vikrīṇati (for Skt. °ṇāti), *sells*; forms, see Chap. 43, s.v. krī (1).

vikrītikā (f. to *°taka, to vikrīta, ppp.), *one that has been sold* (as a slave): mā (sc. asi) °kā Bhīk 16a.4 (not to be initiated as a nun).

? **vikrīya**, (a dead monk's belongings, bhikṣubhiḥ...) vikrīya bhājitam MSV ii.119.15, and similarly 121.2, 125.6. Should, in Skt., mean *having sold*, but Tib. bsgyur nas, or sgyur te, *having altered, transformed*, as if false Sktization of some Pkt. ger. of vi-karoti (vikariya? cf. pass. Pali vikiriyyati).

vikreti (AMg. vikkei; see § 28.49; Chap. 43, s.v. krī 3), *sells*: vikrenti SP 280.4 (vs).

[**viklambhayati, (siṃha-)viklambhita**, corruption or misprint for **viṣkambh°**, or possibly for MIndic vikkhambh°.]

[**vikṣāntam** (as if ppp. to vi-kṣamati = Skt. kṣamati), *pardoned*: in LV 168.14 (vs) all mss. tac ca vi°, Lefm. em. ti (= te) kṣ°, *and that was forgiven by you*; the em. is surely right, because (1) no vi-kṣam- in this sense is recorded anywhere; (2) in 18 below taṃ ca ti kṣāntaṃ is read in all mss. in a precisely similar phrase; (3) Tib. also supports the em., khyod kyis (*by you*) de dag (*those things*) bzod (*pardoned*).]

vikṣipa, see **saṃkṣipa-vi°**.

vikṣiptaka, nt. (= Pali vikkhittaka), *a dismembered corpse* (the members strewn about); -saṃjñā, *contemplation of the notion of such a corpse*, one of the **aśubha-bhāvanā**, q.v., or -saṃjñā: Mvy 1162; Bhīk 27a.3; ŚsP 59.13; 1258.7; 1431.21.

vikṣiptacittaka (= Skt. °citta plus specifying -ka), *one whose mind is distraught*: MSV ii.67.11 °ka-tvam.

vikṣiptikā, a certain posture (of the hands?): Stein ms. fragm. 1.1.25, 26 (La Vallée-Poussin, JRAS 1913.844) na °tikākṛtāntargṛhaṃ (°he)...

vikṣepa, m., (**1**) *a putting off, excuse* (for not acceding to a request); in American slang, *a brush-off*: Av i.94.4 prasenajitā tasya vikṣepaḥ kṛtaḥ (Speyer *refusal*; but he did not precisely *refuse*, as the sequel shows, only put the other off, temporarily); (**2**) in vikṣepādhipati, m., Mvy 3088, Tib. khyab bdag, or dmag dpon, both *commander, general*; pw 7.374 suggests vikṣepa = *camp, cantonment*; (**3**) vikṣepa-lipi, a kind of script: LV 126.5, see s.v. **utkṣepa-lipi.**

vikṣobha, m. or nt., a high number: °bhaḥ Mvy 7738; °bham Mvy 7866, cited from Gv; °bhasya Gv 106.2; °bham 133.12.

vikṣobhi-tā (to adj. vikṣobhin, in one Skt. cpd., from vikṣobha plus -in), *state or condition of one who shatters or disperses*; virtually *power of dispersing*: sa (sc. Maitreyaḥ) śūraḥ sarva-kleśa-vaṃśa-vikṣobhitāsu Gv 490.6 (prose).

vikhata, nt., a high number: Gv 133.7, cited Mvy 7850 = Tib. grags yas, which also = **vikhyāta**, q.v.; in Gv 105.24 corruptly **vigdhanta.**

vikhala, adj. (prob. = Pkt. vihala, acc. to Pischel 206, 332 always = Skt. vihvala, acc. to Sheth s.v. vihala once = Pkt. viala, Skt. vikala; if Pischel is right, and perhaps even if he is wrong, this would be a hyper-Sktism), *broken, breaking* (of the voice): Mv i.172.3 (vs) na ca vikhala (so read, as separate word, m.c. for °lā) khalakhalāyati ... sugatavācā, *and the Buddha's voice does not break and rattle.*

vikhādati, °te (as vb. nowhere recorded; noun derivs. in Skt. and Pali; cf. next), *gnaws at, devours* (said chiefly of animals), Ger. *frisst*: vikhādyamānā bahuprāṇikoṭibhiḥ SP 95.3 (vs); (animals) kṣudhābhibhūtā deśeṣu deśeṣu vikhādamānāḥ SP 83.13, *very hungry, gnawing (devouring) in all places*; lohaṃ dantair vikhādatha LV 379.10 (vs), *you* (daughters of Māra) *are gnawing metal with your teeth* (attempting the impossible); (yadā mṛtaśarīrāṇi paśyati śmaśāne utsṛṣṭāni) vikhāditāny (*gnawed*; see next) aśucīni Śikṣ 211.8.

vikhāditaka, nt. (to ppp. of prec., q.v.; = Pali vikkhāyitaka), *a corpse devoured* (by animals); -saṃjñā, *contemplation of the notion of such a corpse*, one of the aśubha-bhāvanā (q.v.) or -saṃjñā: Mvy 1161; Bhīk 27a.2 (printed vikhyād°); ŚsP 59.11; 1258.7 (printed corruptly vivādika-saṃjñā); 1431.20.

-vikhinna, *greatly wearied* (prob. noun cpd., vi-, *excessively*, plus -khinna; no verb vi-khid- is proved to exist), in a-vi°, *unwearied*: eṣa sada vīryavanto avikhinna (so divide) kalpakoṭyaḥ LV 223.17 (vs), *not (greatly) wearied thru crores of kalpas.*

vikhyāta, m., a high number: Mvy 7724 = Tib. grags (*fame*) yas; cf. **vikhata.**

vigaḍita, ppp. (= Skt. **vigalita**, q.v. below, Pali vigaḷita; cf. **gaḍita**; § 2.46), *fallen down* or *off*: SP 72.5 (niveśanaṃ...) vigaḍita-prāsādaṃ ca bhavet; 83.5 (vs) gopānasī vigaḍita tatra sarvā; LV 231.6 (vs) hā istrigārā vigaḍitabhūṣaṇābhiḥ, *alas, O harem, with ornaments fallen off!*; 329.4 (vs) vigaḍita-vasanā, *with garments fallen off*; Samādh p. 43 line 23 (vs) vigaḍita-ābharaṇā.

vigata, as adj., either *lost, hopeless* (so perh. vigaya in AMg. and Pkt., Ratnach., Sheth; but their definitions are not clear), or (Skt. Lex. *glanzlos*, BR) *unenlightened, dark*: ākāṅkṣamāṇā vigatā vipaṇḍitā, sattvā na jānanti samanta-udyamāṃ Mv i.165.3 (vss), *the creatures* (before Buddha appeared), *in doubt, lost* (? *dark*), *ignorant, do not know all the exertions* (of the Buddha; next line). Senart fails to see the situation envisaged.

vigata-rāga-bhūmi, see **vīta-rāga°.**

Vigatarājasaṃbhavā, n. of a lokadhātu: ŚsP 45.3.

Vigatareṇu, n. of a former Buddha: Mv i.137.15.

Vigataśatru, n. of a former Buddha: Mv i.137.11.

Vigataśoka, (**1**) n. of a Bodhisattva: Mvy 725; ŚsP 32.4; (**2**) n. of a brother of Aśoka: Divy 370.12.

vigandhaka, f. °ikā (in this sense unrecorded, = Skt. °dha, °dhi; -ka perh. m.c.), *malodorous*: sroṇi (v.l. śr°; read °ṇī or °ṇiḥ, m.c.) prasravate vigandhikā pratikūlā LV 324.19 (vs).

vigama, m. (**1**) a high number: °maḥ Mvy 7790 =

Tib. dpal (read dpag) bral; °masya Gv 106.17; corresponds to **nigama**, q.v.; both cited in Das as = Tib. dpag bral; (**2**) n. of a medicament: vigama-bhaiṣajya-bhūtaṃ Gv 494.23; °mo nāma bhaiṣajyaṃ 497.7.

vigarha, m., and °**hā** (Skt. Gr. °ha; to Skt. vi-garh-), *censure*: °haḥ Mvy 2634; °hā repeatedly in Jm, kā śāstra-dṛṣṭe 'pi naye °hā 152.15 (vs); mithyādṛṣṭi-°hāyām apy upaneyam 155.7 (prose); °hāṃ 166.11 (vs), et al.

vigarhaka, adj. or subst. m. (to Skt. vi-garh-), *speaking ill to, abusing*: priya-°hako bhavati Bbh 150.9.

(**vigalita**, as in Skt., *fallen off* or *down*: Mv i.153.1 = 226.13 = ii.29.16 (vs), read in the last two substantially (with minor variants) mūrdhani vigalita-mukuṭā nipatetsu mahītale hṛṣṭā (in the first, °ṭā dharaṇivaratale praṇipatetsuḥ), of gods worshiping the Bodhisattva, *with diadems fallen down at his head, they fell on the ground, delighted.* Wrongly Senart's note on i.153.1. Cf. **vigaḍita**, and **ā-vigalita**.)

vigava, nt., a high number: Mvy 7716; (cited from Gv) 7842; Gv 133.4; prob. read so also in Gv 105.22 for **vivaga**.

vigāhana (nt.; in diff. mg. Schmidt, Nachträge), *the plunging into, being immersed in*: mahājñānasāra(2d ed. om. sāra)-sāgara-°nāya dharmajñāna-sāgara-°nāya Gv 513.14.

vigopita, ppp. (to Skt. vi-gopayati, pw 5.253, cf. vigopa 6.81), *bared, uncovered*: kāścid (sc. harem-women) °ta-gātryaḥ LV 206.5 (prose), *with limbs bared*; vigopayati, *uncovers*, also MPS 49.15 (see **avikopita**).

[**vigdhanta**, see **vikhata**.]

vigrāhayati (cf. Pali ppp. viggahita, or, in AN ii.157.20–21, °hīta, *seduced*), *seduces, misleads*, esp. by false doctrines: evam anya enaṃ °hayām āsa Jm 146.19 (but °hayām āsuḥ Jm 143.17 = *alienated, caused to be hostile*, as in Skt.); ppp. vigrāhita, tvayā Nirgrantha-°tena Divy 272.20; tīrthyair °taḥ 419.19; also by wicked advice, (Ajātaśatruṇā) Devadatta-°tena pitā . . . jīvitād vyaparopitaḥ (or vyava°) Divy 280.18; Av i.83.6; 308.5 (in the last, ms. °hikeṇa, em. Speyer), *seduced by Devadatta*; (kumāreṇa . . .) duṣṭāmātya-°hitena Divy 557.28; 571.22.

[**vigrāhika**, error of ms. for °hita, see prec.]

vigrāhin, *grasping, laying hold of* (Tib. ḥdzin): svacittārtha-vigrāhiṇaḥ Laṅk 374.6 (vs), app. *seizing* (*apprehending*?) *the objects of one's own mind* (? no subject expressed in the vs; Suzuki supplies *all things*; he renders otherwise and implausibly); °hiṇaḥ may also be gen. sg., *for one who apprehends* . . . Or perh. *seduced by* (cf. **vigrāhayati**)? Tib. ḥdzin, lit. *seize*, also *to be taken in*, . . . *captivated*, as by sin (Jä.). One Chin. rendering (misprinted in Suzuki's Index) means *bind* (as with ropes).

vighaṭṭa, *obstruction, disturbance*, in **nir-vi°**, q.v.

? **vighāṭana** (nt.; cf. Pali id., and next), *opening*: bhramaragaṇo vighāṭanonmiṣitakamala iva kamalākaraḥ Gv 136.8; but 2d ed. bhramaragaṇodvighā°, implying **udvighāṭana**.

vighāṭayati (= AMg. vihāḍei, *opens*, Ratnach. s.v. vi-ghaḍ; cf. Skt. vighaṭayati), *opens* (muṣṭim, the fist or hand, to indicate that one is concealing nothing): sa muṣṭiṃ vighāṭya kathayati, kumāra na jāne kutra (sc. maṇiḥ) gata iti Divy 280.9.

vighāta, m. (= Pali id.; Skt. in other mgs.), *distress, trouble, adversity*: ye . . . utpadyetsuḥ āśravā vighātā paridāghā . . . (in Pali also foll. by pariḷāha) Mv iii.338.2; esp. used of the needs of poor ('needy') people: vighāto me cīvareṇa . . . pātreṇa . . . glānabhaiṣajyena Śikṣ 268.7, (Bendall and Rouse, *I am worried about*, but it really means) *I need a robe*, etc., said by a monk to a wealthy patron; °ta-kṛtaṃ (dānavipratibandhahetuṃ; in 8, duḥkhaṃ) Bbh 130.6, 8; vighātārthika (cf. **vighātin** with arthin), *a petitioner, beggar, in distress*, °ka-yuktaṃ . . . dānaṃ Bbh 114.5, °ka-dānam 14; °kaṃ, prob. error for °ka-, dānaṃ 133.3, resumed by °ka-dānaṃ 10; others, in cpds., see Index.

vighātin, adj. (from prec. plus -in; not recorded in this mg.), *distressed, in trouble, subject to adversity*: °tinām anāthānām apratisaraṇānāṃ sattvānāṃ Bbh 18.20; °tiṣv arthiṣu (cf. vighātārthika, under prec.) bhojanapānaṃ dadāti 133.4.

vighuṭṭha, ppp. (MIndic for Skt. vighuṣṭa, so v.l. here; AMg. id. as subst. nt.), *cried aloud*: Mv i.245.15, see § 2.12.

Vighuṣṭa, n. of King Daṇḍaki(n)'s minister: Mv iii.363.10; 365.3.

Vighuṣṭakīrti, n. of a merchant: Gv 233.20.

Vighuṣṭaśabda, n. of a Bodhisattva: Gv 442.2.

Vighnāntaka, n. of one of the 10 **krodha**: Dharmas 11; Sādh 137.9 etc. See next.

Vighnāri = prec.: Sādh 558.8.

? **vicakrama**, mss., or vicaṃkrama, Senart's em., adj., Mv ii.367.15 (vs), denotes some sort of bodily infirmity; perhaps *limping, halt, not walking well*? (cf. Pali a-caṅkama, *a place not good for walking*, CPD); see the passage, cited s.v. 1 **khalita**.

vicakṣu(s), adj. (= Pali vicakkhu-, with -kamma; in Skt. *blind*, but in the Skt. Lex. Trik. = vimanas, a BHS-Pali usage), *perplexed, confused* (in mind); only in comp. with karaṇa or karman, *the making perplexed*: vicakṣuḥ-karaṇāya, *in order to make confused*, Mvy 6528; yan nv aham (Māra) upasaṃkrāmeyaṃ °ṇāya (sc. the Buddha) AsP 78.7; so also °karmaṇe LV 378.15 (the daughters of Māra); (yaṃ nūnāhaṃ upasaṃkrameyaṃ) °karmāya Mv iii.416.1, 15 (Māra); °karmāsya (sc. dharmabhāṇakasya) karoti dharmaṃ pratikṣipati Śikṣ 96.10, (*he who*) *causes confusion for the preacher, rejects the Doctrine.*

vicaṃkrama, see **vicakrama**.

vi-cañcita, ppp. (Skt. cañc-, otherwise not recorded with vi-), *tremulous*: pakṣmānta-°tāśrur Buddhac. i.61, Johnston. Cowell (i.66) reads virañcita; Leumann's speculations reported in Wogihara, Lex. 37, are now seen to be baseless.

[**vicara(ya)ti**, see **vicalayati**.]

vicarcika, adj. (cf. Skt. °kā, *mange*), *mangy*: (na . . . kaṇḍūlo vā kacchulo vā) °ko vā anyo vā kiṃcid amanāpaṃ . . . tiṣṭheyā Mv ii.150.10; 152.3; (by Senart's em. 156.12;) akṣi-vicarcika (so with var. and Mironov for text °vivarcika), °kaḥ, *mangy in the eyes*, or the like: Mvy 8917 (text and Index misprinted 8817; could be called Bhvr., akṣi plus Skt. °cikā).

vicalayati (caus. to Skt. vi-calati; note that calayati occurs beside cāl°, as caus. of calati), *waves, brandishes* (as, a torch): (read) dharmolkāṃ vicaleyaṃ parāhaṇe dharmabheri sapatākāṃ (or °kaṃ) Mv i.42.8 = 53.9 = 377.3 (vs, in the last printed as prose), *may I swing the torch of the doctrine, may I beat the drum of the doctrine* . . .; for vical° (= vicalayeyaṃ, § 38.27) mss. vihareyā at 42.8, vical° or vicar° at 53.9, vicar° at 337.2, where Senart em. prajvāleyaṃ (not noting the parallel).

vicasta, m., a high number: Mvy 7733 = Tib. bsko (bsdo) yas (cf. **vyatyasta** 3).

vicāra, m., Mvy 7732, or nt., id. 7860 (cited from Gv); Gv 105.26; 133.10, a high number.

-vicāraka, ifc. (neither this nor vicāra seems recorded in quite this sense; cf. car with vi 11 in BR), *use, employment*: (in list of ascetic practices) tad yathā, mantra-°rakair . . . LV 248.16, *such as, those that consist in the use* (*performance*) *of mantras* . . .; Tib. sṅags (= mantra) spyod pa (*accomplish, perform, use*).

vicārayati, *withdraws, draws back*: (the Bodhisattva in his mother's womb) pāṇim utkṣipya saṃcārayati sma, saṃcārya vicārayati sma LV 67.20, *raising his hand, waved it* (as a sign of permission for the attending gods to depart; so Tib. specifically says), *and having waved* *it, withdrew it.* Tib. bskum par byed = *made* (for) *withdrawal.*

vicālana (= AMg. vi(y)ālaṇa; Skt. vicāraṇa), *consideration, mental reflexion*: svabuddhi-°na-kuśalasya Laṅk 9.14 (Tib. mthoṅ ba).

vicikitsaka, adj. or subst. m. (to Skt. °tsati plus -aka), *doubting; a doubter*: °ko bhoti sa dṛṣṭiprāptaḥ Śikṣ 111.7 (vs).

(**vicikitsā**, Skt. id., *doubt*; one of the five **nīvaraṇa**, q.v.)

vicikitsita, (nt.; orig. ppp. of Skt. °tsati), *doubt*: °taṃ ca (WT co) jahathā aśeṣam SP 326.3 (vs); **satkāyadṛṣṭi**-(see this)-°tsitā ca Mv i.292.2 (so mss).

vicittaka, adj. or subst. m. (cf. Skt. 2 vicitta, BR), *witless, unthinking, foolish*: unmattako 'si puruṣa athavāsi vicittako Mv ii.88.5 (vs).

Vicitra, var. for **Citra,** q.v., as n. of a nāga king: Mvy 3268.

Vicitrakuṇḍalin, n. of a yakṣa: Sādh 560.15; 561.8; °linī, n. of a fem. counterpart of this yakṣa (apparently): 563.8.

Vicitragātra, n. of a Bodhisattva: Gv 442.25.

?**Vicitra-cūta** (Senart with mss. as reported Vicinta°; my em. seems almost necessary, tho I have not found the name), n. of one of Buddha's disciples: Mv i.75.11.

Vicitradhvajā, n. of a capital city: Gv 233.23.

Vicitrapratibhāṇālaṃkāragarbha, n. of a Bodhisattva: Dbh 2.13.

Vicitrabhūta, n. of Bodhisattva: Gv 442.5.

Vicitrabhūṣaṇa, n. of a kiṃnara: Mvy 3417.

Vicitramakuṭa, n. of a former Buddha: Mv i.140.1.

vicitrayati (denom. to vicitra; Skt. only ppp. °trita), *makes variegated in color*: moracandrasamaiś candrair uttarīyaṃ °trayet Laṅk 365.12 (vs).

Vicitraraśmijvalanacandra, n. of a Tathāgata: Gv 421.17.

Vicitrasaṃkrama, n. of a Buddha: Śikṣ 169.14.

Vicitrālaṃkārasvara, n. of a serpent king: Mvy 3433.

vicitrika, adj. (Skt. vicitra plus -ika), *various, of all sorts*: sarvaloka-°trikeṣv anabhiratiḥ KP 25.4 (prose), *not taking pleasure in all sorts of worldly things* (here quasi-subst.; Tib. sna tshogs, *of various sorts*); °trikā vṛścika (n. pl. m.) mūṣikāś ca SP 83.8 (vs), *all sorts of scorpions and mice.*

vicintaka, adj. (Skt. vi-cint- plus -aka), *thinking upon*: gṛhacintā(WT °vitta with v.l. and Tib.)-°kāḥ SP 272.7 (vs).

?**Vicintacūta,** see **Vicitra°.**

vicīraka (vi, neg., plus cīra, with -ka Bhvr.?), see **avacīra-vi°.**

vicūṣayati (vi- plus Skt. cūṣ-, caus.), lit. *causes to suck*, i. e. *represents* (in a picture) *as sucking*: °ṣayet Sādh 361.1; 377.10, *he shall represent* (bees) *as sucking* (what is depicted on flower-petals in the magic picture); v.l. in both passages vibhūṣayet, in one also vibhāvayet.

vicetar (Skt. cited once from ŚB, *one who picks over, sifts out*, wood etc. from soma-plants), *sifter, arranger*? or *one who knows thoroughly*?: vicetā sarvaprāṇinām Mv ii.405.5 (vs), said by Māra of himself.

vi(c)chandanā (to next, n. act.; Wogihara gives °na, but without convincing evidence), *dissuasion, determent*: mahāyānaprasthitānāṃ ca sattvānā(ṃ) °nā KP 118.3; vicchandanāyāpi (read °nā yāpi) ca buddhayānaṃ (read °nād, abl.? so Tib., -las) id. 6 (vs), referring to 3 above, must surely mean *and dissuasion from the Buddha-vehicle*; °danayā (so read with v.l. for text °danatayā) ca striyaḥ strībhāvābhiratānāṃ ca strībhāvāt Bbh 29.21; tatparasya °danārthaṃ 173.13; duṣkaracaryādhimuktānāṃ sattvānāṃ vicchandanārthaṃ 271.13 (misprinted).

vi(c)chandayati, for which forms of vi-chind- occur in mss., cf. also **vicchindika** and prec.; see Wogihara, Lex. (mss. vary in Bbh between a and i); in Pali (kāya-)-vicchinda occurs as title of Jāt. 293, surely meaning *aversion from the body*, not *cutting off of*...; in Pv. comm. 129.26 atidānato vicchinditukāmo clearly means *wanting to dissuade from over-generosity*, = BHS vi-chand-; Pali (kāya-)vicchandaniya(-kathā) and (kāya-)vicchandanika-(-sutta) cannot be separated from (kāya-)vicchinda, above; in Divy 590.24 even the v.l. vicchedayām āsuḥ occurs for vicchandayām āsuḥ. It is clear that Pali and BHS both show what must, therefore, be a very old confusion between -chand- and -chi(n)d- here. As Kern (cited PTSD s.v. vicchinda), Wogihara, and some others have seen, the orig. form was surely **vicchandayati**; the forms with -chi(n)d- are due to popular etym. (in some occurrences the word means something close to *cuts off*). The fundamental mg. is *makes undesirous* (denom., vi plus chanda); so Tib. mos pa zlog pa on Mvy, ḥdun pa zlog on KP, both mg. *desire-deterring, desire-dissuading*, but on LV simply zlog par byed pa, *dissuasion-(deterring-)making*: °dayati Mvy 6527, foll. by vicakṣuḥ-karaṇāya; bhūyobhūyaḥ sa māṃ °dayati, bhadramukhāniṣṭo 'sya karmaṇo phalavipākaḥ Divy 10.6, similarly 11.24, *dissuades*; °dayām āsuḥ (v.l. see above) 590.24; (Māraḥ...) bodhisattvaṃ ... evaṃ °dayiṣyati AsP 331.16, *will* (*try to*) *dissuade*; (iha ... bodhisattvasya ... pāpamitraṃ, yaḥ prajñāpāramitāyāṃ) carantaṃ virecayati (q.v.) vichandayati ŚsP 1185.19, modulated in the sequel (the means of dissuasion are given 1186.1 ff.; they consist of attacks on the dogmatic interpretation of Buddhism accepted in this school); (devaputrāḥ ... Māraṃ ...) vicchandayanti LV 333.20 and 335.10 (prose), *dissuade, discourage Māra* (by predicting his defeat); °dayati vikṣipati KP 1.6; when the thing dissuaded from is expressed it is regularly abl., dānād vicchandayan Jm 24.7; (saṃgrahavastubhyo) vicchandya Śikṣ 50.12; adattādānād °dayati Gv 155.15; vichandya (v.l. vichindya) with ablatives Bbh 16.2 ff., so also °dayet 27.12; °dayati (v.l. °chind°) 262.13; but once apparently acc., (yasmāt tvaṃ bhikṣucaraṇapraṇāmam) māṃ °dayitum icchasi Divy 383.6, *since you wish to dissuade me* (against, from) *bowing at the feet of monks* (or is this acc. a Bhvr. adj., *me characterized by bowing* etc.?).

-**vi(c)chidra,** in **chidra-vi°** (= Pali chidda-vichidda, used of leaves shot full of holes), *perforated with holes* (pores? so transl.; or, the nine apertures?): (kāyo hy ayaṃ ...) chidra-vicchidraḥ Śikṣ 77.12, in description of its worhtlessness and disgusting character.

vi(c)chindika, read, or understand a synonym of, vicchandika or °daka (see s.v. **vicchandayati**), *dissuading from*: bodhicitta-°dikānāṃ Gv 228.19.

[**vijaga,** see **vijāga.**]

vijagha, nt., Mvy 7846 (cited from Gv), or vijaṅga, Gv 105.23, or vijaṅgha, nt., Gv 133.5, a (moderately) high number; Tib. on Mvy thab thib; = **vijāga,** m., q.v. (v.l. **vijaga**).

vijaṭāpayati (caus. to Pali vijaṭeti, *combs out* etc., which is denom. to vi-jaṭa, adj., in Skt. *unbraided*, of hair), *causes to untangle, comb, card* (wool): (yaḥ punar bhikṣur ajñātikāṃ bhikṣuṇīm eḍakalomāni) dhāvayed vā ... °payed vā Prāt 498.1.

vijambha, m., a (moderately) high number: Mvy 7719 = Tib. nab nub (see **vibhaja**).

Vijaya, (**1**) n. of a minister who made a praṇidhi under the Buddha Suprabha: Mv i.112.17; (**2**) n. of a youth, who was later reborn as **Rādhagupta,** q.v.: Divy 366.7, 10; (**3**) n. of a future Buddha, predicted as incarnation of a king of Pañcāla: Av i.46.4; (**4**) n. of a yakṣa: Māy 39.

Vijayantī, n. of a devakumārikā in the eastern quarter: LV 388.9. Senart's text gives this (from LV) in the corresp. line Mv iii.306.8, but his defective mss. lack it.

Vijayavikrāmin, n. of a Bodhisattva: Mvy 723; ŚsP 39.20.

Vijayaśrī, n. of a nāga maid: Kv 3.22.

Vijayasenā, n. of a village chief's daughter: LV 265.5.

Vijayā, n. of one of the 4 **Kumārī**, q.v., or **Bhaginī**: Mmk 528.2; 537.8 etc. [In LV 272.10 (prose) Lefm. reads pratasthe (sc. the Bodhisattva, to the Bodhi-tree) vijayayā tayā ca gatyā. But the best mss. read vijayāya, *for victory* (over Māra, Tib.), with v.l. vijayāye, also a possible dat. form of an a-stem. There seems no reason to assume a fem. stem vijayā.]

vijahana-tā (only a-vi°) and **vijahanā** (n. act. to vijahati plus -ana-tā, -anā), *abandonment*: kleśa-vijahanā Bbh 213.20; (vṛkṣamūle ca Bodhisattvasya Tathāgatasya vā niṣaṇṇasya... tasya vṛkṣasya) chāyayā kāyāvijahanatā Bbh 75.17, *there is no leaving his body by the shade of that tree*; adhiṣṭhāna(ṃ) mahākaruṇādig-avijahanatāsu Gv 98.24 (see **adhiṣṭhāna** 3).

***vijahayati**, irreg. caus. to vijahati, *causes to leave*: śravaṇopavicāraṃ vijahayya (ger., Whitney 1051d) Bhīk 15a.5, *having caused* (the initiate) *to leave the range of hearing*, see **upavicāra** 2.

vijāga, m. (so Mironov), a (moderately) high number: Mvy 7720 (v.l. **vijaga**) = Tib. thab thib = **vijagha** (with varr.), q.v.

vijānana (nt.; = Pali id.; to pres. vijānati plus -ana), *knowledge, knowing*; dat. °nāya as inf., § 36.15: te śaknuvanti imi (better with best mss. ima = imaṃ) dharma °nanāya LV 420.22 (vs); most mss. and Calc. °natāya (vijāna = °nant plus -tā), but °nanāya is more normal in BHS.

vi-jāla, adj., *without deceit*: vakṣyāmi te avitathāvacanaṃ vijālaṃ (ṃ not in mss.) Mv ii.135.3 (vs).

vijigupsati (for Skt. viju°, with vocalism of Pali vijigucchati), *is disgusted*: °psatā or °psantā, pres. pple. n. pl., so nearly with mss. at Mv i.343.1, see s.v. **artīyati** 3; in i.358.15 (vs, = Pali Sn 41) read, nearly with v.l., priyāviyogo (ms. priyo°) vijigupsanīyo (closer to Sn piyavippayogaṃ vijigucchamāno than the v.l. adopted by Senart, which is a lect. fac.); in 19 Senart reads vijigupsamāno (but in 23 viju° with mss.).

vijita (in Pali, and presumably BHS, nt.), orig. *conquered* (land), but commonly *realm, country*, regularly however with reference to its ruler(s), *territory under control*: mama (a king's) vijite LV 243.8 (vs); tasmin (sc. Mārasya) vijite 300.2 (prose); svaka(ṃ) °taṃ (of the Licchavis) Mv i.257.10, 11, 17; Lecchavīnāṃ vi° 258.1; tuhyaṃ (a king's) eva °te 326.10; Māgadhasya ii.299.9; nāśetha vijitā mama iii.7.15, *banish from my realm*; others, 437.6; 451.11; Divy 22.16; 32.7; 63.19 f.; 445.23; Av i.42.9; 48.2, etc.; Bbh 269.21 f.; vijita-vāsinaḥ, pl., *the inhabitants of the realm*, Mv i.96.7; ii.95.8; Gv 159.22; rarely used referring to the *land* of others than kings or rulers, (gacchantu bhavantaḥ) svakasvakeṣu vijiteṣu... Divy 121.16.

vijitavant, adj. (in mg. = **vijitāvin**, of which it is a Sktization), *victorious*, in cliché description of a cakravartin: **caturaṅgaś** (q.v.) cakravartī vijitavān dhārmiko... LV 101.13; (cakravartī) caturaṅgo °tavān dhārmiko... 136.16 (both prose).

Vijitā, n. of a princess: Mv i.348.12.

vijitāvin, adj., (**1**) (= Pali id.; § 22.51), *victorious*, ep. of a king, usually cakravartin, and mostly in the cliché found also in Pali, e. g. DN i.88.33–34 cakkavatti dhammiko... cāturanto vijitāvī...: this, with some variants, occurs in Mv, cakravartī cāturdvīpo vijitāvī... dhārmiko... i.49.2; 52.8; 193.15 etc. (see **cāturdvīpa**); ii.158.14; iii.102.15; 377.19; in vss, less like the cliché, i.268.11; iii.8.18; for the LV form see **vijitavant** and **caturaṅga**; (**2**) n. of a king of Mithilā, former incarnation of Śākyamuni: Mv iii.41.15 ff.; colophon, Vijitāvisya Vaideharājño jātakaṃ 47.9; (**3**) n. of a former Buddha: Mv iii.231.2; (**4**) n. of a prince, son of **Jayaprabha**: Gv 353.6.

vijugupsaka, adj. (Skt. °psati, °te, plus -aka), *loathing, shrinking* (*from*): (ye te...) na kāmadhātūpapatti-°sakāḥ Gv 472.7.

vijugupsana-tā (n. act. in -ana plus -tā to Skt. vijugupsati), *shrinking from*: sarvakarmasamādānāvijugupsanatayā (°dāna-avi°) Gv 463.24, *because of not shrinking from taking on oneself all duties*: sarvasaṃsāradoṣa-vijugupsanatāyai pratipannaḥ 491.25.

vijjhati (= Pali id., MIndic for vidhyati), see § 2.14; Chap. 43, s.v. 1 vyadh (1).

vijñapana (nt.; cf. Skt. vijñāpana, Pali viññāpana; to Skt. vijñapayati), *the making known*: (rātridevatāṃ...) sarvasattvakāyasaṃsthānasadṛśasvaśarīra-°na-kāyāṃ Gv 341.17, and, (samantamukhābhimukha-)-°na-kāyāṃ 19; (ekaikasmāt paramāṇurajasaḥ) sarvaratnameghasarvatathāgatapratibhāsa-°panān niścaritvā 531.25.

(**vijñapayati**, in Skt. oftener vijñā° except ppp. vijñapta; in Pali only viññāpeti recorded; *asks, begs* (for alms or a favor), a mg. known also in Skt.: na vijñapeyā pariṣāya kiṃcit SP 284.8 (vs), *he shall not ask anything of the assembly*; rājānaṃ vijñapemaḥ (or °ma, so mss., Senart em. vijñā°) Mv i.364.1 (prose), *let's ask the king*; jānapadā rājaṃ vijñapenti (Senart em. vijñā°) 366.3 (prose); tena yāyinā (em.) puruṣo vijñapto Mv i.232.6, *as he journeyed he asked a man* (for alms); vijñapta also i.362.16; 365.1; ii.100.14.)

vijñapti, f. (in Skt. generally from an inferior to a superior, implying a request; Pali viññatti), (**1**) *proclamation, announcement, making known* (a mg. found also in Skt.): Mvy 1887 = Tib. rnam par rig byed (wrongly pw 7.374); abhāvasamudgata-°ti-śabdo niścarati Samādh 8.11, *the sound of proclaiming* (all things as) *arisen from non-becoming came forth*; svapnopama-°tim Gv 82.19, and many like cpds. in the foll.; (divyaśrotra-)°ti- Gv 251.10, *announcement of* (the gift, or faculty, of) *supernatural power of hearing*; Mv i.311.6, possibly *request*, see s.v. **prajñapti** 3; (**2**) in Laṅk, *relative, exoteric knowledge*, = **vijñāna** in this mg. and **prajñapti** 4, q.v.: e. g. Laṅk 270.1 lokaṃ °ti-mātraṃ; 274.10 °ti-mātraṃ tribhavam; 269.12, see **gotra** (4); see Suzuki, Studies, 440.

-vijñaptika, ifc. Bhvr. (= prec.), in a-vi° (Tib. rnam par rig pa med pa, cf. Mvy 1887 s.v. °ti), *without any making known*, or (cf. **vijñapti** 2) *free from* (*limited, qualified, exoteric*) *knowledge*: (yad... nityānityayor madhyaṃ tad arūpy anidarśanam anābhāsam) °tikam apratiṣṭham aniketam KP 56.3; cittaṃ hi... (very similar list of epithets) KP 98.2 (cited Śikṣ 234.2) with °tikam.

vijñā (cf. AMg. a-viṇṇā; no such noun seems recorded in Skt. or Pali), *discretion, mature intelligence*, in vijñāprāpta or vijña° (with MIndic shortening before cons. cluster? § 9.6), *arrived at years of discretion*, of a child reaching maturity: ṛṣikumāro vijña- Mv ii.211.18 (prose; v.l. vijñā-); iii.145.8 (here mss. both āvijña°); yadā vijñāprāpto 'smi iii.131.12 (no v.l.); sā dārikā vijñaprāptā 156.4 (no v.l.); yatra kāle vivṛddhā vijñaprāptā 184.6 (no v.l.); all prose. Since **prāpta**, q.v., may be preceded in comp. by an adj., we might assume the Skt. adj. vijña as prior member here; but the occurrence of vijñā- makes this doubtful.

vijñāna, nt. (in mgs. 3–5 = Pali viññāna; orig. in Skt., *practical knowledge*, opp. to **jñāna**, *theoretical knowledge*, see Edgerton, Festschrift Winternitz, 217 ff.), (**1**) *practical knowledge, applied knowledge*, as in Skt., still clearly in LV 422.13 durvijñānaṃ (or v.l. °jñeyaṃ) tac cakraṃ jñāna-vijñāna-samatānubaddhatvāt, *this wheel* (of the Doctrine) *is hard to know* (practically), *because it is* *inseparably connected with identify of theoretical and practical knowledge* (i. e. can only be known by one whose theoretical knowledge is at the same time applied in practice); in Laṅk 156.11 ff. a dissertation on the difference between jñāna and vi°, rendered by Suzuki, Studies 272, *transcendental* (i. e. absolute) *and* (merely) *relative knowledge*; I should prefer *abstract* and *applied knowledge*; but it is true that to the author of Laṅk *applied knowledge* (vij°) has only *practical*, and hence in the last analysis no *real*, application; the passage cited makes this very clear. Essentially similar is the contrast in jñāna-pratisaraṇena bhavitavyaṃ, na vijñāna-pratisaraṇena Mvy 1548; more at length Bbh 257.16 ff. bodhisattvaḥ adhigama-jñāne sāradarśī bhavati, na śruta-cintā-dharmārtha-vijñāna-mātrake; sa yad bhāvanāmayena jñānena jñātavyaṃ na tac chakyaṃ śrutacintā-vijñāna-mātrakeṇa vijñātum iti viditvā paramagambhīrān api tathāgatabhāṣitāṃ dharmān śrutvā na pratikṣipati; (**2**) two kinds of vi°, **khyāti-vi°** and **vastuprativikalpa-vi°**, qq.v., Laṅk 37.14 f.; vi° is aṣṭa-lakṣaṇa, ib., the list of 8 being given 235.7 ff., Suzuki, Studies, 189 ('Ālaya, Manas, Manovijñāna, and the five sense-vijñāna', on which see **dhātu** 3; the sixth is mano-vij°); (**3**) the sixth of the six 'elements', see **dhātu** 1b; (**4**) the fifth of the five (**upādāna-**)**skandha,** qq.v.; (**5**) the third link in the **pratītyasamutpāda,** q.v. In the last four categories often rendered *consciousness,* etc.; no single word or brief phrase can, of course, really suffice. In Bbh 49.17–18 (see s.v. **naivasaṃjñānāsaṃjñā°**) short for **vijñānānantyāyatana,** in a cpd.

-vijñānaka = **vijñāna,** ifc. Bhvr., in sa-°ke kāye Divy 534.25, *the body possessing consciousness* (same phrase in Pali, saviññāṇake kāye).

vijñānanā, *comprehension*: Mvy 7564. Not to be read vijān° with pw 7 App.; confirmed by **saṃjñānanā**; see § 22.7.

vijñānavādin, a member of the well-known Buddhist school of this name: Mvy 5145.

vijñānānantyāyatana (= Pali viññāṇānañcāy°), (**1**) nt. *stage of infinity of consciousness*: as 2d of the stages of arūpāvacara gods, Mvy 3111; Dbh 34.13; as 2d of four arūpya samāpatti, Mvy 1493; Karmav 47.21; as condition of the 5th vimokṣa, Mvy 1515; as condition of the 8th abhibhvāyatana, Mvy 1527; as 6th sattvāvāsa, Mvy 2294; abbreviated in a cpd. to **vijñāna,** Bbh 49.17–18, see **naivasaṃjñānāsaṃjñā°**; (**2**) m. pl., = next: Suv 86.11.

vijñānānantyāyatanopaga, m. pl., *the gods dwelling in the* prec.: Dharmas 129.

vijñānāhāra, m. (= Pali viññā°), the fourth kind of *'food'* (see s.v. **kavalīkārāhāra**), acc. to PTSD consisting of vijñāna as the *food* or *material cause* from which rebirth arises: Mvy 2287. Dharmas 70 seems (corruptly) to have **dhyānāhāra** instead. Cf. LaVallée-Poussin, AbhidhK. iii.121, which however does not furnish a clear defiinition.

vijñāpaka, adj. or subst. (= Pali viññāpaka; Skt. vijñāpayati plus -aka), *instructing*; *instructor*: in su-vi° SP 301.1, 10; LV 403.5, 9; 404.8, Bhvr., lit. *having a good instructor*, but in the sense of *making things easy for an instructor*, i. e. *easily instructed* (proved by SP passage, s.v. **viśodhaka,** q.v.).

vijñāpana, f. **°nī,** adj. (= Pali viññāpanī, as in BHS; Skt. °na only as n., *request*, so also in BHS, Mvy 8462 = Tib. sloṅ ba), *enlightening*, *giving instruction*, of the voice or speech, vāc(ā), of the Buddha or Bodhisattva: yāsau vāg ājñāpanī vijñāpanī . . . LV 286.9; (vācāye . . .) arthasya °panīye Mv iii.322.3.

vijñāpanīya, f. **°yā,** = prec.: °yā Mvy 472, in a list of epithets of Buddha's speech. Cf. § 22.20.

vijñin, adj. (**vijña,** q.v., plus -in; = Skt. vijña, and next), *wise*: bodhisattvasya vijñinaḥ SP 303.9 (vs).

vijñu, adj. (Sktized form of Pali viññu, AMg. viṇṇu, = Skt. vijña, and prec.), *wise*, *prudent*: anyatra vijñupuruṣāt Prāt 503.7, *except* (there be) *a wise man* (present); so Chin. acc. to Finot.

viṭapa (m.; in Skt. *branch*, also *foliage*; Skt. °paka and °pin, *tree*; cf. AMg. viḍava, defined vṛkṣa vistāra, *tree-spread*? Ratnach.), *tree*, in bodhi-viṭapa, = °druma etc.: °pāc cāletu kampetu (inf.) vā LV 283.21 (vs); °pe upaviṣṭu (ppp.) guṇodadhiḥ 293.8 (vs).

viṭṭāleti (= Pkt. id., see Sheth, and Jacobi, Ausgew. Erz. 2.6; read viṭṭālitāḥ for viṭvāl° in my Pañc. Rec. II § 130; here a MIndic form is borrowed in Skt.), *makes unclean* or *untouchable*: (atra mahānase kāko aparādhyati) rājabhojanam ucchiṣṭīkaroti °leti vidhvaṃseti Mv iii.126.16.

viṭhapana, nt., and **°nā,** once **viṣṭhapana** (n. act. in -ana to next), *fixation, establishment, creation, making*; esp. with implication of something illusory and fleeting: sarvadharmā viṭhapana-(so with Mironov)-pratyupasthāna-lakṣaṇāḥ Mvy 185, *all states of being are characterized by involvement in* (*illusory*) *creation*; °na-pratyupasthāna-lakṣaṇam Mvy 7233, Tib. rnam par bsgrub pa (this, or with bsgrubs, is the usual Tib. rendering); māyākṛtaṃ sarvasaṃskṛtaṃ °na-pratyupasthāna-lakṣaṇam Śikṣ 180.4 (here māyākṛtaṃ is decisive; Bendall and Rouse cite Tib. as rnam par bsgrabs pas, read bsgrubs); Gv 524.1 corrupt, eṣāṃ dharmāṇāṃ dharmatā, aviṣṭhapana-(read viṣṭh°, for viṭh°)-pratyupasthāna-lakṣaṇāḥ . . . sarvadharma-(read °mā with 2d ed.) bodhisattvajñānādhiṣṭhitāḥ, evaṃ svabhāvāpariniṣpannā māyāsvapnapratibhāsopamāḥ; (sattvānāṃ . . .) citta-māyā-°na-tāṃ Dbh 74.4, *the fact that creatures are created by mental illusion* (cf. māyopamaṃ cittam iyam ucyate cittadharmatā Śikṣ 236.2); but in Śikṣ 236.3 this implication is hardly to be found: yat punaḥ sarvasvaṃ parityajya sarvabuddhakṣetrapariśuddhaye pariṇāmayatītīyam ucyate viṭhapanā (fem.); here, in a formal definition, the mg. seems to be *firm fixation* (Bendall and Rouse *edification*, which I do not find in it); at least no very clear suggestion of unreality seems found in the foll.: abhisaṃbodhivikurvita-°nena bodhisattvasamādhinā Gv 38.17–18; upāyakauśalya-°na-dharmatayā 469.18 (cf. however KP 32.1, 7, s.v. **viṭhapayati**); nt., °na, Gv 449.7, 15; f., °nā, 524.6; buddhakṣetra-°panālaṃkārābhinirhāratayā, or °nirhṛtatayā, or °nirhāraṃ, Dbh 39.14; 45.6; 55.17; same cpd. (°nirhāraṃ) with traidhātuka-instead of buddhakṣetra- 55.10–11, with rūpakāyalakṣaṇānuvyañjana- instead of id., 55.18–19; in this cpd. viṭhapanālaṃkāra is to be taken as a dvandva, *establishment and adornment*, as proved by reverse order in: -vyūhālaṃkāra-viṭhapanā-prāptaś 62.11 (here f. °nā).

viṭhapayati (cf. prec. and **vithāpita**; a MIndic form of caus. of Skt. vi-sthā, but not found recorded except in BHS), *fixes, effects, makes*, usually with implication of something illusory and unreal; perh. always so, the only possible exception being the first: yathā . . . vāyudhātuḥ sarvabuddhakṣetrāṇi °yati, evam eva . . . bodhisattvasyopāyakauśalyaṃ sarvabuddhadharmān °yati KP 32.1 (prose), perh. with implication of magic appearance; in 32.7 (vs) read viṭhapeti or °penti (for °panti) dharmān sugatokta-m-agrān; Tib. rnam par sgrub po; kalpanā-viṭhapitāḥ (text °yitāḥ; *fashioned by fancy*) sarvadharmā ajātā(ḥ) . . . AsP 162.1; anityāḥ . . . citta-viṭhapitāḥ (so read for text °yitāḥ) . . . sarvadharmāḥ Sādh 111.2; kāmadhātuḥ kalpito viṭhapitaḥ (text °yitaḥ, and so below) saṃdarbhitaḥ, anityo 'dhruvo . . . ŚsP 1534.7, repeated below; sarvajñatācittotpādaś . . . sarvadharmadhātuṃ ca viṭhapayati Gv 504.24, *makes up* (as a figment out of itself).

viḍaṅgikā (not found recorded), in na °kayā Mvy 8563; the rule (one of the śaikṣa-dharmāḥ) is completed by adding antargṛhe pravekṣyāmaḥ, and niṣatsyāmaḥ, Prāt 531.17, 18; La Vallée Poussin, JRAS 1913.844, Stein ms. fragm. 1.1.37, 38. Acc. to Tib. mdom (ḥdoms) mi snañ, also Chin. and Jap., on Mvy, *showing the private parts*; but acc. to Finot's report of Chin. on Prāt, *bending over* (*nous courber*).

viḍambaka, m. (= AMg. °ga), *buffoon*, a sort of entertainer; assoc. with naṭa; cf. next: na te naṭā nāpi °kāḥ smaḥ Jm 115.11; see also **velambaka.**

viḍambita (nt.; related to prec., q.v.), *buffoonery*, as an art of entertainment, assoc. with nāṭya: nāṭye °te LV 156.16 (in list of arts).

viṇḍa (prob. only m.c.) and **viṇḍaka** (nt. in Mmk 57.7 kuśa-°kaṃ, n. sg.; prob. MIndic for Skt. piṇḍa, °ka which replaces it in kuśapiṇḍakopaviṣṭa Mmk 47.5; cf. however AMg. viṇṭiā, *bundle*, and Skt. vṛnda, see s.v. **vṛndi**), *grass-cushion*, used as a seat: viṇḍake masūrikā-yāṃ (q.v.) vā niṣadya Bhīk 19a.1; otherwise only in comp., preceded by kuśa (rarely darbha), and only in Mmk: kuśaviṇḍakaṃ Mmk 57.7; °viṇḍakopaviṣṭa, *sitting on* . . ., Mmk 37.28; 39.21; 47.18; 57.4 (°ṣṭikāṃ); 61.20; 74.26, etc., common; °ḍaka-śiropadhāna- 146.2; kuśaviṇḍe pallave caiva . . . upaviṣṭaḥ 488.13 (hypermetric!); darbhaviṇḍopaviṣṭas tu Mmk 137.8 (vs).

[**vitaṃsayati,** °**yanto** by em., SP 84.10; read a form of bha(r)ts-, see s.v. **vibhartsayati.**]

vitaṇḍana, nt. (cf. Skt. vitaṇḍā), *slighting, fault-finding*, or *contemptuous* (verbal) *behavior*: Mvy 8429 = Tib. khyad du gsod pa.

vitanati (MIndic for vitanoti; Pali id.), *extends, draws* (a bow): Mv ii.221.20 (°ne, aor.); *stretches* (cloth); read prob. vitanatā (instr. pres. pple.) MSV ii.156.1, and vitanitaṃ (ppp.) 159.4, for ed. vitar°; the mg. is certain; Pali Vin. i.254.28–29 (cīvara-)vicāraṇa, app. in same mg.

vitapana (nt.; Skt. vi-tap- plus -ana), *heating, warming* (of oneself): yaḥ punar bhikṣur aglāno °na-prekṣī (*desiring to warm himself*) . . . dāhayed Prāt 513.9. (Pali Vin. iv.115.21 has visibbana; see SBE 13.44 note 5, which our word confirms.)

[**vitarati,** assumed by Senart at Mv i.89.15 (mss. viranti) and 17 (mss. all vistaranti acc. to note; correct Crit. App.), in mg. *pass the time, live* (doing so and so); the true reading is, I think, viharanti, which is normal Skt. in this mg. See also **vitanati.**]

vitāna, nt., *woof*: Mvy 7520 = Tib. spun. Contrasted with **ātāna,** q.v.; nowhere recorded in this sense. See also **mahāvitānadharma.**

viturṇa, nt., Mvy 7730; 7858; or **vitūrṇa,** nt., Gv 133.9; a high number. Read vitūrṇa also for **tūrṇa,** Gv 105.26. (Mvy 7858 is cited from Gv; but Mironov like Kyōtō ed. reads viturṇam without v.l.)

vitkoṭikā or °**ka,** n. pl. °**kā(ḥ),** some kind of toy (not 'game', Index): Divy 475.19, in a list of such; doubtless corrupt.

-vitthara-ka, f. °rikā, adj. Bhvr. (from MIndic vitthara, so AMg., = Skt. vistara, plus -ka, endearing dim., § 22.34), (*having* . . .) *great breadth* (sc. of hips): jaghanāṅgana (= °nāṃ) cāru-su-vittharikāṃ LV 322.19 (vs), of a daughter of Māra; Tib. yaṅs śiṅ (mdzes, *fair*, = cāru), *the woman characterized by hips, who is* (i. e. whose hips are) *charmingly broad*.

vitramantrā, a high number: Gv 106.8; corruptly represents **vimantra,** q.v.

vithāpita (semi-MIndic ppp., of same derivation and mg. as viṭhapita, see **viṭhapayati**), *illusorily created* (Tib. rnam par bsgrubs pa, as regularly for viṭhap°): māyāraṅ-gam ivā vithāpitaṃ svamatena LV 324.8 (vs), *like illusory color* (or, *stage-setting*), *created by* (the fancy of) *one's own mind*.

vidagdhaka, nt. (not in this sense in Pali; Vism i.110.29 vicchiddakaṃ seems to take its place vaguely, but of course is quite different in mg.), *a corpse burnt by fire*; -saṃjñā, *contemplation of the notion of such a corpse*, one of the **aśubha-bhāvanā** (q.v.) or -saṃjñā: Mvy 1163; ŚsP 59.17; 1258.8 (here misprinted vidagnaka).

vidarbhaṇa, nt., ? Mvy 4351 = Tib. smos pa, *speaking*, or *naming*; occurs among terms relating to ritual; follows codana, precedes argha, naivedya, bali. Perh. some verbal ritual act, *recitation, invocation*, or *laudation*? (In Mvy 5989 smos pa = saṃmata; in 805 = nāman.)

vidarbhayati (see GOS 41 p. lxxxvii, citing a noun vidarbha, perh. the same which pw 7.374 defines *das Innere*; the verb presumably denom.; see also **pra-vidarbh°**), *intertwines* (letters), i. e. writes them between the letters of a mantra: °bhayet Sādh 532.18; 584.7; °bhya, ger., Sādh 357.17; ppp. °bhita Sādh 125.6 et alibi.

vidarśana, nt., and °**nā** (AMg. vidarisaṇa, and with caus. mg. vidaṃsaṇa; to Skt. vi-darś- plus -ana), (**1**) °nā, *insight, vision*, lit. and fig.; in this mg. app. always fem., and often assoc. with samatha, or śam°, replacing more usual **vipaśyanā**: samatha-(so, or śam°, read with v.l. and Tib.)-vidarśanā-suviśuddha-nayanasya (bodhisattva-sya) LV 9.6 = Tib. zhi gnas (śamatha) daṅ lhag mthoṅ (*wide vision*) etc., *with eye well purified in* (or *by*) *tranquillity and insight* (*vision*); °nā-saṃbhāro dharmālokamukhaṃ 35.15; -samatha-(so with v.l., = śam°)-°nāloka-(°nā plus āloka)-prāpta(ḥ) 426.8; samatha-°nā-paripūrṇa-saṃbhā-ra(ḥ) 427.22; °nā-saṃbhāraṃ paripūrayiṣyati 441.6 (cf. samatha-saṃbh° parip° 5); śukla-°nā-bhūmiḥ (one of the śrāvaka-bh°) Mvy 1141 (Tib. rnam par mthoṅ ba), *clear insight*; °nayā prativipaśyataḥ Laṅk 19.2; (**2**) °na, nt., with caus. mg., *display, making to appear* (by magic): Bbh 58.23; defined 59.20 ff. as magical display, by a Buddha or Bodhisattva, of various edifying visions to an assembly; one kind of dhyāna is (pāpakāriṇām) apāya-bhūmi-vidarśanaṃ dhyānaṃ Bbh 210.7.

vidalikā (to Skt. vidala plus -ikā, dim.), *splinter* (of bamboo): vaṃśa-°kayā nirlikhitaḥ MSV ii.129.14; iii.137.8.

? **vidigdha** (ppp. of unrecorded vi plus dih-? or cpd. of vi plus Skt. digdha?), *smeared, covered all over*: dadrūya kaṇḍūya vidigdha-gātraḥ SP 112.6 (vs), *with body covered over* (disfigured) *with eruptions and scabs*. Not to be em. to vidagdha with Kern; Tib. yog, *covered*. But perh. ca digdha- with WT and K'.

Viditayaśas, n. of a Śākya youth: Av i.385.1 ff.

vidu (**1**) adj. (= Pali id., Skt. vidus-; § 16.49), *wise, skillful*, commonly as ep. of Buddhas and Bodhisattvas; in most texts only in vss: SP 25.4, 5; 26.5; 325.4 (printed viḍū!); LV 45.22; 46.6, 14, 18; 192.10; Mv ii.299.8; 300.7; Suv 42.5; Mmk 132.1; 436.4; Dbh.g. 4(340).5; lokavidu (Buddha) SP 31.7; 47.10 etc.; Samādh 19.22; paramārtha-vidu Mv i.82.10 (vs); iii.252.6 (vs); vara-vidu Mv i.220.12 = ii.22.13; vidu-pravara Sukh 24.10; a-vidu, *unwise, ignorant*, SP 212.7; (**2**) f. Vidu (v.l. Vidū), n. sg. °uḥ, n. of one of the 8 deities of the bodhi-tree: LV 331.21 (prose).

vidu-tā (to prec.), *state of being wise* (= Buddha-hood): (naiva tāva janayanti mānasaṃ) sarvadharma-vidutāya (dat.) paṇḍitā(ḥ) Mv i.47.10 (vs); subject Bodhi-sattvas.

Vidurā, n. of a rākṣasī: Māy 243.16.

viduṣa-ka, adj., = **vidu,** for Skt. vidus (changed to a-stem, § 16.50, plus -ka), *wise, skilled* (in . . ., end of cpd.): sarvasattvasaṃgrahaṇa-°kāś ca Mv i.134.11 (prose; said of Bodhisattvas).

viduṣṭa, ppp. (of Skt. vi-duṣyati, Viṣṇusm. 24.41, *does wrong*, pw), *corrupt, evil*: dīrghānudarśiny a-viduṣṭa-ceṣṭā Gv 410.8.

vidūṣa, m. (= Skt. vidūṣaka), *buffoon, jester*: Mironov (without v.l.) for °ṣaka (without v.l.) Mvy 3809; mano vidūṣasādṛśam Laṅk 224.2 = 319.17 (vs; here could be m.c.).

vidūṣaṇā(-samudācāra), (performance of) *self-denunciation* (of one's own past sins), one of four ways of counteracting past evil deeds, by which a Bodhisattva 'kṛtopacitaṃ pāpam abhibhavati' Śikṣ 160.5; tatra °ṇā-samudācāro 'kuśalaṃ karmādhyācarati (so read) tatraiva ca vipratisārabahulo bhavati 6; a long description of the ways in which this is done follows, ending ukto °ṇā-samudācāraḥ 171.7; the Bodhicaryāvatārapañjikā (Bibl. Ind.) p. 153, line 5, glosses vidūṣaṇā: akuśalaṃ karma kṛtvā vipratisārarūpātma-(misprinted)-vigarhaṇā pāpadeśanā.

vidṛṣṭi, f. (unrecorded; = Skt. kudṛṣṭi, BHS **dṛṣṭi** as ordinarily used), *wrong doctrine, evil heresy*: hanto °ṭi-patitā imi bālabuddhī Dbh.g. 7(343).14; svabhāvatrayagrāheṇa (see **svabhāva** 2 and **grāha**) grāhyagrāhavidṛṣṭayaḥ Laṅk 348.10 (vs), *by* (wrongly) *holding to* (*accepting*) *the three svabhāva,* (there ensue) *the erroneous views of something that is to be held, and holding* (it; or, *of holding something as a thing to be held*); Suzuki wrongly.

[**viddha-,** in (makara-)viddhāśritaḥ Gv 505.12, read °vidyāśritaḥ; and so in 505.14 read -vidyāśrito for -viddhā°]

vidyate (Skt., *is found, occurs, exists, is* . . .), seems to be used practically as a passive auxiliary, with ppp., like Eng. *be,* Ger. *werden,* in: yathaite upacīrṇā (line 2) vidyetsuḥ (Senart em. °nsuḥ), svastinā ca abhinirbhedaṃ gacchanti Mv i.273.1–2 (prose), *that these* (eggs) *may be cared for, and may felicitously come to hatching-out.*

(**Vidyā,** n. of a goddess: Sādh 502.8; so also in Skt., see BR s.v. 3.)

vidyācaraṇasaṃpanna, adj. (= Pali vijjā°, in same situation; discussion Vism. 202.25), *perfected in wisdom and good conduct,* in the standard cliché describing a Buddha: Mvy 6; LV 3.3; SP 65.6; 67.4, etc.; common everywhere.

vidyādhara (= Pali vijjādhara; in Skt. seems to be used only of the supernatural beings so called), *magician, practitioner of magic*: Mmk 56.23 (here used of the master of holy Buddhist magic with the use of paṭas); 58.11.

Vidyādharapiṭaka, n. of a work (collection of spells): Śikṣ 142.12.

Vidyādharā, n. of a rākṣasī: Māy 241.32.

? **vidyānulomāvimiśrita-lipi,** a kind of script: LV 126.9, *conforming to science* (or *magic*?) *and unconfused*? But Calc. (acc. to Lefm. without support in his mss.) vidyānulomalipiṃ vimiśritalipiṃ, with which Tib. agrees: rig pa daṅ mthun paḥi yi ge, *writing agreeing with science,* and rnam par ḥdres paḥi yi ge, *variously mixed writing* (no negative!).

vidyārāja(n), °**jña,** f. °**jñī,** *lord* or *master* (f. *mistress*) *of magic* (*spells*), a sort of superhuman being: °rājñaiḥ Mmk 10.6; abjakule (°kūle? see 40.18 below) vidyārājñaḥ (app. nom. sg. or pl.), tad yathā (there follows a list of names, mostly unknown otherwise, and some uncertain in form and word-division; not included here) 10.7; °rājñībhir lokeśvaramūrtisamādhivisṛtaiḥ (! gender), tad yathā (there follows another list, as above, fem., beginning with Tārā) 10.14–15; pradhāna-vidyārājaḥ (*the chief V.*) vidyārājñī abjakūle rūpakamudrā 40.18 (figures to be depicted); without apparent personification, referring to a particular magic rite, *king of spells,* ayaṃ °rājā, Mañjuśriyo 'pi kumārabhūto 'nena vidyārājñā ākṛṣṭo vaśam ānīto . . . 81.7.

vidyā-sthāna, nt., *'subject of knowledge'*, one of the five *'sciences classiques'* (Lévi): Sūtrāl. xi.60 and comm.; Mvy 1554–9, listed in the latter as śabda-, hetu-, adhyātma-, cikitsā-, śilpa(karma)-sthāna-(vidyā), and essentially so Sūtrāl.; referred to simply as **sthāna** 1, q.v., Mvy 4996 = Divy 58.27; 100.13; 442.9; MSV ii.4.6–7 pañcasu (Divy 442.9 pañca-)sthānesu kṛtāvī (saṃvṛttaḥ), with reference to the education of a prince.

vidyuc-cakra, prob. adj., ep. of aśani, (*a thunderbolt*) *accompanied by a wheel* (*large flash*?) *of lightning,* in comparisons, of something destructive: °krāśani-sadṛśo lābhasatkāraḥ Śikṣ 105.11 (Bendall and Rouse, *like to a wheel of lightning and the thunderbolt*); (saṃpanne śālikṣetre aśanir nipated vidyuccakrā (em., but plausible) yāvad etat saiva śāler utsādāya Bhīk 4a.5.

Vidyujjvāla, n. of a nāga: Mvy 3316.

vidyutā (= Pali vijjutā; in Skt. as n. pr., and in °tākṣa, n. pr.), = Skt. vidyut, *lightning*: °tāṃ (acc. sg.) LV 214.16 (vs); vidyuta-prajña (°ta m.c.) vipaśyana LV 414.11 (vs).

Vidyu(t)pratiṣṭha (written Vidyu-p°), n. of a (virtuous) son of Māra: Mv ii.337.5; 338.3.

Vidyutpradīpa, m., (**1**) n. of a samādhi: Mvy 546; ŚsP 1418.13; (**2**) n. of a Tathāgata: Śikṣ 9.2.

Vidyutprabha, (**1**) n. of a former Buddha: Mv i.136.14; (**2**) n. of a samādhi: Mvy 612 (not in ŚsP); (**3**) n. of a mountain (also in Jain Skt. and Pkt. Vijjuppabha, Kirfel, Kosm. 233, 245): Māy 253.35; (**4**) m. (or nt.), vidyu-pr°, a kind of gem: Mv ii.317.9; cf. next but one.

Vidyutprabhā, n. of a nāga maid: Kv 4.1.

vidyu(t)prabhāsa, m. or nt., a kind of gem: Mv ii.310.17; cf. **vidyu(t)prabha** (4).

Vidyuddatta, n. of an ancient king: Gv 174.22.

Vidyullocanā, n. of a nāga maid: Kv 3.24.

Vidyotana, n. of a nāga king: Māy 246.26.

Vidyotanī, n. of a rākṣasī: Māy 243.23.

vidrāpaṇa, adj., f. °ṇī, or subst. nt. (to next, with -ana), *routing, putting to flight*: sarvamāra-vidrāpanaṃ (read °ṇaṃ) nāma mahāmudrā Mmk 389.12; (eṣā, sc. mudrā . . .) sarvamāra-vidrāpaṇī 402.26; -māra(2d ed. adds maṇḍala)-vidrāpaṇa-(subst.!) . . . vikurvitāny apaśyat Gv 96.9.

vidrāpayati (caus. to Skt. vi-drā-, cf. Skt. vidrāvayati to vi-dru-; cf. prec.; also Ap. vi°dāv° ppp., Jacobi, Bhav. 336.4, ms., wrongly em. to cidd°), *routs, puts to flight*: °yati bhūtāni Mmk 34.2; 138.16 (both vss); nāgāṃ °yati 298.5 (prose).

Vidrāyaṇa (ms.), or **Vidrāvaṇa** (em. Bendall), n. of a serpent (nāga) king: Megh 306.12.

Vidrāvaṇa (see also prec.), n. of a rākṣasa king: Mmk 17.28.

Vidvajjanaparisevitā, n. of a kiṃnara maid: Kv 6.10.

vidvala, vidvasu, see **a-vi°**.

Vidvāṃs (n. sg. °vān, acc. °vāṃsam, weak stem Viduṣ-), n. of a householder (gṛhapati): Gv 142.10 ff.

vidveṣaṇā (= Pali viddesanā; Skt. °ṇa, nt.), *hatred*: mā me °ṇā bhavet Mv iii.419.8 (vs).

vidveṣika, adj. (cf. Skt. °ṣaka, or °ṣin, Pali viddesin, plus -ka), *hating*: (mahāyāna-)°kānāṃ (sattvānāṃ) Gv 228.19 (prose).

vidhama (m.?), *blowing away, removing, dispersal*: sa tamo-'ndhakāra-vidhamaṃ gacchati Gv 499.13 (prose), *he attains to dispersal of the gloom of darkness.*

vidhamana, nt. (cf. next two), *fan*: Mvy 8986; so Tib. bsil gyab (yab); next word is **maśaka-varaṇam.**

vidhamanaka (nt. or m.; cf. prec.), *bellows*: °kena vā (in series of methods of producing wind) Śikṣ 249.2; so acc. to Tib. sbud.

vidhamana-tā (= Pali °na; cf. prec. two), *the blowing away, removal*: sarvajñāna-°natāyai LV 33.1; a-vi° neg., in sarvabuddhadharmāvidhamanatāyai 35.8.

vidhamitar (n. ag. to vi-dham-; cf. prec. items), *one who blows away, disperses, scatters*: °tāro 'vidyāndhakārasya (kalyāṇamitrāṇi) Gv 462.21.

vidhāna (nt.; Skt.), *arrangement* (of a heavenly city), i. e. *pomp,* or the like; *l'appareil, la splendeur* (Senart): Sudarśanasya devanagarasya taṃ vidhānaṃ dṛṣṭvā Mv i.32.10. A Skt. Lex. gives dhana as a mg. of vidhāna.

vidhi, f. (only m. in Skt., and acc. to Childers in Pali; PTSD gives it as f., but I have found no evidence for this; acc. to Ratnach., AMg. vidhi, vihi, only m., but acc. to Sheth, Pkt. vihi also f.; a fem. adj. form with the word is cited), *way,* etc. (as in Skt.): n. pl. (oṣadhi-, better °dhī-)-vidhīyo (rather with mss. -vidhiyo) Mv i.115.1 (vs; this ending usually fem.); bhojanavidhiṃ ca citrāṃ 116.6; etāye vidhiye 209.9 = ii.11.16 (vs); yādṛśāye ca vidhīye ii.208.11 (prose).

? **vidhunayati,** perh. for Skt. vidhūn°, *shakes* (u possibly m.c., or influenced by dhunoti beside dhū°): vidhuneṣyase LV 333.12, *you will be shaken*, for °nayiṣyase; but v.l. °niṣyase, to pres. -dhunati (MIndic for -dhunoti).

[**vidhūtika,** error for **vipūtika** or **vipūyaka,** see the latter.]

vidhūna, adj. (? nt., °nam; cf. Pāṇ. 8.2.44 dhūna, ppp. to dhū-, not in Skt. lit.; AMg. vihūṇa, defined by rahita, hīna, śūnya), in Mvy 6983 = Tib. bcad pa, dgag pa, *cut off, stopped, hindered, averted*, etc.; Chin. *cut off*, or *perished*; similarly Jap.

vidhyati, *shoots* (arrows); pass. °ti (for °te): paścime nidarśane bāṇā vidhyanti Mv ii.75.20, *in the last exhibition* (of skill in military arts) *arrows were shot.*

[**vinaga,** prob. error for **vināga,** see s.v. **vināka.**]

vi-nagna, adj. (unrecorded; vi-, intens.), *quite naked*; also **vinagnī-kṛtya,** *having made quite naked*: tāś ca °kṛtya pratyavekṣante, tā hriyāpayanti Bhīk 11a.4, also 5; (text uncertain in) nagne vinagnatara te vicaranti loke LV 158.22 (vs), so Lefm., mss. confused; Tib. de dag sgren mo bas kyaṅ sgren mor ḥjig rten rgyu, (?) *they go in the world to (in?) nakedness even more than the naked* (perh. read nagnebhi, instr. for abl., nagnatara, *more naked than the naked*?); in LV 206.11 (prose) kāścid (harem-women) vibhagna-gātryaḥ, all mss. and both edd., but Tib. lus sgren mor gyur indicates vinagna-g°; vinagna-vasanā LV 220.12 (vs) *with completely bared* (i. e. *removed*) *garments*, Tib. gos bral (*garments removed*) gcer bur gyur (*became naked*), a double translation; kāścid (daughters of Māra) vinagnān ardhorūn upadarśayanti LV 320.16 (prose); others, MSV i.14.14 f.; ii.41.4.

Vinataka, m. (= Pali id.), n. of one of the seven mountains forming a ring around Sumeru (cf. Divy 216.30–217.1 and Kirfel, Kosm. 186): Mv ii.300.18; Divy 217.3, 5; Mvy 4146; with Sumeru in list of 8 mountains, Dharmas 125.

[**vinaddha** is read for (aṣṭāpada-)nibaddha (or vinibaddha) in SP 244.10 and 337.12 suvarṇasūtrāṣṭāpada-vinaddhā, °dhāṃ; in the latter no v.l., and WT the same (but no reliance can be placed on either ed.); in the former, Nep. mss. reported °pada-bhinaddhā, WT °pada-nibaddhā. The word vinaddha is nowhere recorded except in AV, where it means *unbound*. It should surely be emended to either **nibaddha,** q.v., or **vinibaddha,** q.v.]

(**vinamate,** LV 259.21, said by Foucaux to mean *sits down*, but see s.v. **namati.**)

Vinaya, m. (= Pali id.), (book of) *discipline*, one of the sections of the canon: Mvy 1414 (after sūtram, abhidharmaḥ); sūtra-vinayābhidharmeṇa Laṅk 290.8; Vinaye, *in the (text of the) V.*, Karmav 59.18; 60.9; 71.10; 158.17. In Śikṣ 190.4, kim-ākāraṃ śrutaṃ bodhisattva-vinaye praśastaṃ, Bendall in text and transl. understands bodhisattvavinaya as n. of a work, but I believe it means merely *in the training of Bodhisattvas*; there follows immediately a citation from the **Akṣayamati-sūtra.** See next items.

Vinaya-kṣudraka, nt., n. of a part of the canon (presumably = Pali Cullavagga): Mvy 1427.

vinaya-dhara, m. (= Pali id.), *one who has mastered and knows the Vinaya*: Mvy 5142; pratyantimeṣu janapadeṣu vinayadhara(mss. °raṃ)-pañcamenopasaṃpadaṃ Divy 21.23.

vinayanā (in Skt., Pali, and Pkt. only °na, nt.), *instruction, training*: samādāpanā °nā niveśanā pratiṣṭhāpanā Bbh 221.6 (note all fems.).

Vinayapiṭaka (= Pali id.), = **Vinaya**: ārya-Mahāsāṅghikānāṃ Lokottaravādināṃ Madhyadeśikānāṃ pāṭhena Vi°kasya Mahāvastuye ādi Mv i.2.13.

Vinaya-vastu, n. of a part of the canon: Mvy 1426. Follows next, and precedes **Vinaya-kṣudraka**; does it correspond to Pali Mahāvagga?

Vinaya-vibhaṅga, n. of a part of the canon: Mvy 1425. Cf. DPPN s.v. Vibhaṅga.

vinardita, (**1**) (nt.; ppp. of Skt. vinardati), *shout, cry*: Māra-kali-vikiraṇa-vinarditam avatarāmi Gv 206.25; (**2**) n. of a nāga: Mvy 3340.

Vinarditarāja, n. of a Bodhisattva: Gv 442.24.

vināka, var. **vināga** (see Index; so Mironov), or virāga (**vinaga**?), all nt., a high number: Mvy 7841 = Tib. khrab khrib; cited from Gv, which in 133.4 reads virāgaṃ (nt.); 105.22 seems to have a double corresp., vināha and virāga; in Mvy 7715 the corresp. is **viraga** = Tib. khrab (or khrib) khrib.

vinādayati, *mocks, derides* (not *reviles*, Index): (a woman imitates a bent Pratyekabuddha by bending her own back;) yad anayā pratyekabuddho °ditas tasya karmaṇo vipākena kubjā saṃvṛttā Divy 540.19. In Laṅk 244.7 (yathā ca te kravyādabhojinaḥ sattvā) vinādya rasatṛṣṇāṃ . should mean *abandoning, getting rid of the craving for the taste* (of meat); to render *mocking, deriding*, seems implausible; ed. suggests reading virāgya; perh. rather vināśya.

vinābhāvika, adj. (Skt. °va plus -ika), *connected with deprivation*: iṣṭa-°vikāni ca duḥkhāni SP 78.1 (prose).

vināyaka (= Pali id.), common epithet of a Buddha, either *guide, leader*, or *trainer, discipliner* (cf. Pali Vv. comm. 83.18 veneyyasatte vinetī ti vināyako): Mvy 22 (Tib. rnam par ḥdren pa); LV 437.12, 14; Divy 166.26, et passim.

vināha, a high number: Gv 105.22; see s.v. **vināka.**

vinigata, ppp. (m.c. for Skt. vinirg°, Pali vinigg°), *departed*: °tu, n. sg., LV 232.17 (vs).

vinigrantha-(śirā), (read perhaps vinirgrantha-, or °thi-?) mss. at Mv ii.43.9, for **nirgranthi-,** q.v.

[**vinipāta,** see **vi-vipāta.**]

vinipātayati (perh. denom. to Skt. vinipāta; in Skt., and Pali °pāteti, only caus., *destroys, ruins, causes disaster to*; the BHS form could also be taken as caus. in mg. of simplex, § 38.23), *suffers evil*: (asureṣu cyavitvā) vinipātentā Mv i.30.3, *suffering evil after falling to existence among the asuras*; some mss. °tantā; all have ā in root syllable.

vinibaddha, ppp. (cf. the foll. entries; = Pali id., in first mg. only), (**1**) *bound, fastened, attached*: Dbh.g. 11(347).14 bhavacārake dukhaśatair vinibaddhacittāḥ, *fettered*; Gv 353.12 paraspara-śarīra-vi°, *fettered to each other's bodies*, of criminals; Gv 162.21 ratnajālāś cānyonya-ratnasūtra-vinibaddhāḥ, *fastened to one another*; Śikṣ 211.9–10 asthisaṃkalikāṃ . . . snāyu-vinibaddhāṃ, *fastened together with sinews*; in fig. sense Dbh 31.8 priyāpriya-vinibaddhaṃ (ātmabhāvaṃ) *attached to* (or *bound by*) *pleasant and unpleasant things*; (**2**) in comp., aṣṭāpada-vi°, *adorned, laid out, marked out with* (or, *in*) *a checkerboard* (arrangement of squares): Mv ii.301.4 (prose, no v.l.; said of a lokadhātu); LV 211.20 (said of pools, puṣkariṇyaḥ; here most mss. aṣṭāpadānibaddhā(ḥ), only A, the best, °da-vini°), also, āvalī-vi° (of fields), *marked out with lines*, MSV ii.50.9. In this sense, **-nibaddha** is also used.

vinibadhyate (pass. of vi-ni-bandh, which is not recorded in Pali and only once in Skt., see pw; but cf. the prec. and foll. entries, esp. **vinibandhayati**), *is fixed, fastened* (fig. of the eyes): Jm 211.7 °yamāna-nayanaḥ *with eyes fixed, with fixed gaze.*

vinibandha, m. (= Pali id.), *bondage, attachment*: Mvy 2199; 7232 (both °dhaḥ); Dbh 51.14 utpāda-vinibandha eṣaḥ, and 15 vyaya-vi° eṣaḥ.

vinibandhana (presumably nt.; nowhere recorded, except with a different mg. in Schmidt, Nachtr.), = prec.: Dbh 29.7 priyāpriyavinibandhane (cf. under **vinibaddha**);

51.24 utpāda-vyaya-vinibandhanataś ca; Dbh.g. 28(54).14 vinibandhana-vyaya.

vinibandhayati (cf. the prec. entries, esp. vinibadhyate), *binds, ties* (in literal sense): Jm 103.5 °yed api tarau pitarau.

vinibhāga, see **vinirbh°**.

? **vi-nimiśra**, adj., *unmingled*: yam amaravasana (Senart °nā; could also be °naṃ, or with v.l. and ii.4.10 yaṃ ... °na) praśamana-manoramā (mss. °māḥ) śokaduḥkha-vinimiśraṃ (mss.) Mv i.200.13 (āryā vs); repeated ii.4.10 with -vimiśrā(n), submetrical; the extra syllable is required unless we read vīmiś° or the like. A form nimiśra is doubtful; it is recorded only as n. pr. in Skt. Gr.; Vedic nimiśla, adj.

viniyojana (nt.; = Skt., Pali °yoga), *application*, in a-vi°, neg.: lokasaṃbhinnapralāpa-vinivartana-dvayabhaṇitāviniyojanaṃ satyapratiṣṭhāpanaparyavasānaṃ jānāmi Gv 313.1.

vinirbhāga (m.; corresponds to Pali vinibbhoga; see **avinirbhāga**), *discrimination, differentiation, distinction*: Dbh 53.4 vinirbhāgāvinirbhāga(-śūnyatā), *discrimination and non-d.*; Dbh.g. 40(66).2 vinibhāga- (m.c. for vinirbhāga; v.l. vinibhoga, cf. Pali above).

vinirbheda (m.? to Skt. vi-nir-bhid-), *shattering, destruction*: sarvābhiniveśa-°dāya Śikṣ 180.16; cited from Gv, but I have failed to note it there; cf. next.

vinirbhedana (nt.), = prec.: sarvasattva-kleśaparvata-°dana-mahājñāna-vajra-praharaṇaḥ Gv 319.19.

Vinirbhoga, n. of the kalpa of Buddha **Bhīṣmagarjita(nirghoṣa)svararāja**: SP 376.2.

vinirmucya (ger. of Skt. vi-nir-muc-, not recorded in this use), *except*, as postpos. w. acc.: (na tava ...) sadṛśo vidyate, Tathāgatam ekaṃ vi° SP 420.5 (prose).

vinirmokṣaṇa-tā (cf. Skt. °mokṣa), *state of being freed*: Bbh 29.23 (prose; °ṇatayā, instr.).

vi-nivaraṇa, see **vi-nī°**.

vinivartayitar, m.: *one who causes* (something, gen.) *to turn back* (from, abl.): Gv 462.25 °tāraḥ kumārgāt; 463.9 °tāraḥ sarvadṛṣṭikṛtānāṃ.

vinivarti (f.? in mg. = Skt. vinivṛtti; prob. hyper-Skt. for MIndic represented by AMg. viṇivitti, Pkt. viṇiyatti, °vatti; not recorded in Pali), *turning away, release* (from): śubhaṃ dharmamayaṃ cakraṃ saṃsāra-°taye Divy 393.25 (vs).

viniścaya, m. (also nt. = Pali vinicchaya), *philosophical, doctrinal exegesis* or *disquisition, discussion*; also, *a text containing this*: gambhīram idaṃ śrāvakāṇāṃ viniścayam SP 236.3 (vs), acc. sg., *this profound piece of exegesis for* (the benefit of) *śrāvakas*; °ye vartamāne Av i.47.8 and 334.19, loc. abs., *while ... was going on*; tayā ca saha °yaṃ kurvanti ii.20.7, *and engaged in philosophical conversation with her*; (yā dharmadeśanā sāṃkathya-)°yakriyā Bbh 218.26; dharmaviniścayena Ud xix.1, *by exegesis of the Doctrine* (= Pali Dhp. 144, dhammavinicchayena).

viniśrita, adj.-ppp. (or, with Senart and half his mss., viniḥśr°; but the antonym saṃniśr° in the same line makes this implausible; cf. also **aniśrita**), *detached from, not dependent on*: karmasaṃniśritāḥ santaḥ kautūhala-viniśritāḥ, āpatsu na viṣīdanti (mss. viṣād°) na ca modanti vṛddhiṣu Mv i.102.2(-3, vss).

? **viniṣṭha**, app. *intent on, aiming at, devoted to* (with dat.): ye vā sattvā pratyekabuddhatvāya °ṣṭhās Mv i.103.13; Senart's note suggests °tva-pariniṣṭhās; perhaps rather °tvāya viniviṣṭās (cf. Pali vinivesa). The whole passage is dubious; see Senart, Introd. xxx n. 2.

viniḥsṛti, f. (to Skt. vi-niḥ-sar-), *escape, going out* (from captivity): vihaga pañjaramadhyagatā yathā na hi labhanti kadāci °tiṃ LV 206.21 (vs).

? **vinīta**, in suvinītāṃśā LV 27.7, said of Māyā, (of) *well-proportioned* (shoulders) acc. to Foucaux; Tib. (confirming *shoulders*) reads for su-vinīta, legs par (su) byin gyis ḥtsham pa, which Foucaux renders in the same way; no v.l. is recorded, but this seems not a normal mg. for vinīta.

Vinītadeva, n. of a teacher: Mvy 3500.

Vinīteśvara, n. of a śuddhāvāsakāyika devaputra: LV 6.13; 438.16. In 4.13 **Praśāntavinīteśvara**, q.v.

vinīlaka, nt. (= Pali id.), *a corpse turned blue-black*: -saṃjñā, *contemplation of the notion of such a corpse*, one of the **aśubha-bhāvanā** (q.v.) or -saṃjñā: Mvy 1156; Bhīk 27a.2; ŚsP 59.9; 1258.7 (here corruptly vilīnaka-); 1431.20; Śikṣ 211.1 (cited from ŚsP).

vi-nīvaraṇa, once written **vi-ni°**, adj. Bhvr. (= Pali id., usually with citta), *free from 'hindrances'* (**nīvaraṇa**, in religious sense): °ṇe ca dharme (acc. pl.) abhisameti Mv i.312.9; °ṇaḥ Mvy 422, of Tathāgata; °ṇa-citta, Mv iii.225.3; Divy 616.27; 617.2 (here mss. vi-ni°); Sukh 58.17.

vineya, (**1**) gdve.-adj. (hardly differs materially from Skt. id.; = Pali vineyya; cf. **vaineya** 1), *one that is to be* (religiously) *trained*, or *converted*, used in ways parallel with vaineya: °ya-jana Divy 130.7; °yāpekṣayā Divy 463.15; 543.6; (**2**) subst. (m.?) = **vaineya** 2, *conversion*: mahad °ya-kāryaṃ kartukāmo Divy 269.16.

-vinodana, adj. ifc., f. °nī (= Pali id.), *dispelling*: (vāg ...) rāgadoṣamohakalikaluṣa-°nī LV 286.12 (prose).

Vindu, n. of a mountain: Māy 254.1.

Vindusāra, see **Bi°**.

Vindhaka, n. of a nāga king: Māy 247.24.

vindhati, vindhayati = **vedhati**; see § 28.32; Chap. 43, s.v. 1 vyadh (3).

vinyastaka (**1**) = Skt. °ta, *deposited*: Mmk 63.6 (prose); (**2**) fem. °tikā, a certain posture (of the hands?); cf. **udvyastikā, vyastikā**, and **atyastikā** (this latter adjoins vinyastikā and must therefore have a different meaning): Stein ms. fragm. 1.4a (La Vallée-Poussin, JRAS 1913.844).

vinyāsita, ppp. (= JM. vinnāsia = saṃsthāpita, Sheth; since no caus. to vi-ni-as- is otherwise known, and the mg. is not caus., the form is prob. a denom. ppp. to Skt. vinyāsa), *laid down*: bodhisattvasya pādayor °taśirasaḥ prāhuḥ Divy 600.4, *laying their heads at the B.'s feet, they said*.

? **vipaṃsayati** (see **paṃs°**), *defiles* (a woman, sexually); so I would read in Gv 335.2 (vs): (adharmarāgeṇa narā hi raktāḥ) nāryaḥ kumāryaḥ ... vipaṃsayanti (text viṣaṃ sapanti) sma purā prasajya; the em. is graphically simple, and the text seems senseless; to be sure I have found no other case of vi-paṃs-.

-vipakṣa, adj., in karma deśāntara-vipakṣaṃ, *an act which has its fruition* (*result*) *in a foreign country*: Karmav 30.20; 50.12, 14; 57.4; 64.13. So the mss. always, kept by Lévi in 30.20, otherwise em. to vipākaṃ; but the form is clearly a hyper-Sktism for MIndic (Pali) vipakka = Skt. vipakva, confused with MIndic vipakkha = vipakṣa.

vipakṣika, adj. (= Pali vipakkhika; Skt. °kṣa plus -ika, or °kṣin plus -ka), *hostile*: sarvajñatā-vipakṣikāvidyā-Gv 20.7.

vipañcanaka, m., = next: Divy 548.22 (mss.). Cf. **vaipañcanika**, for which mss. at Mv i.207.13 = ii.12.3 point corruptly to vipañc°, unmetrically.

vipañcika, m., regularly pl. (to Skt. vipañcayati; cf. prec., also **vaipañcaka, °cika, °canika**), *soothsayer*; regularly preceded (like its relatives just listed) by parallel **naimittika**, both usually qualifying a preceding brāhmaṇā(ḥ): brāhmaṇā ye naimittikā °kāś (mss.) Divy 319.14, 16, similarly 391.5; 475.5.

[**vipañcikā**, Senart's em. for **vevādika**, q.v.; cited in one Skt. Lex., BR.]

vipañcita, adj. (ppp. of Jain Skt. vipañcayati, once pw; cf. next), *explicitly declared* or *made known*: yo lābho niyato °taḥ MSV ii.113.1; niyato 'vipañcitaḥ 112.18; yo lābho 'niyato 'vip° 113.6.

vipañcitajña, adj. or subst. m. (= Pali vipañcitaññu; cf. prec. and **prapañcayati**), *understanding* (only by) *a full, detailed explanation*, opp. of **udghaṭitajña**, and noted only in association with that word, q.v. for quotations: Mvy 2385; LV 400.1 = Mv iii.318.3; AsP 243.20; in Bbh 295.15 replaced by **vyañjitajña**, q.v.

vipaṭumaka, °**muka,** nt. = **vipaḍumaka,** q.v.

vipaṭmaka, nt. = **vipaḍumaka,** q.v.

vi-paḍumaka, or **vipaṭumaka,** nt., *a corpse destroyed by worms* (so Tib. on Mvy 1158): Gv 157.16 vipaṭ°; -saṃjñā, *contemplation of the notion of such a corpse*, one of the **aśubha-bhāvanā** (q.v.) or -saṃjñā: Mvy 1158 vipaḍ°; Bhīk 27a.2 vipaṭ°. Also vipaṭumuka, MSV iii.54.11; vipaṭmaka, Śikṣ 211.1; and (corruptly) vipadāka- ŚsP 59.4; niruttamaka- (!) ŚsP 1258.6. See s.v. **paḍuma(ka).** Cf. Pali puḷuvakaṃ, Vism i.110.31 (*worm-foul*, Pe Maung Tin).

vipaṇḍaka(-tva), (Skt. paṇḍaka, *eunuch*; this form unrecorded, and not noted by Senart in Notes or Index), (*state of being*) *a eunuch*: (strītvaṃ na gacchanti) vi°tvaṃ na gacchanti Mv i.103.11.

vi-paṇḍita, *ignorant*: Mv i.165.3, see s.v. **vigata.**

vipatha, m., a fairly high number: Mvy 7727 = Tib. yal yol; corresp. to **vivara** (1).

[**vipadāka(-saṃjñā),** false reading at ŚsP 59.4 for **vipaḍumaka,** q.v.]

viparigata, ppp. (unrecorded, but cf. Skt. viparīta), *failed, given out, perished*: (evaṃ saṃviditvā ṛṣikumāro) °gata-śarīro kālagato Mv ii.215.4.

vipariṇāma, m. (in Skt. neutral word, *change*; here as in Pali) *vicissitude, change for the worse*: **ṛtu-vipariṇāma** Mv ii.424.4, see **ṛtu-pariṇāma**; one of the 3 **duḥkhatā,** q.v., is °ma-du°, Mvy 2231; SP 109.1; Bbh 191.16; 280.15; Mv i.31.9; devā pi ... °ma-dharmāṇo Mv i.31.13; all pleasurable states are °ma-dharma(n), (-dharmin, Mv i.32.16,) Mv i.33.10; iii.373.7; Av ii.169.4; KP 152.2; anityatāṃ viditvā calatāṃ (mss. cara°) prabhaṅguratāṃ (mss.) °ṇāma-virāga-nirodhatāṃ viditvā Mv iii.338.1; a-°ṇāma-dharmā (n. sg. m., to °man) Mvy 7287, *not subject to* ...

vi-parokṣa, adj. (= M. vivarokkha, °rukkha), (*quite*) *out of sight* (vi- intensive? essentially = Skt. parokṣa); also **a-vipar°**, *not out of sight*, and °kṣa-tā: paramāryāṇāṃ viparokṣāṇāṃ api sarvatra sarvasattvā-viparokṣabuddhīnāṃ Bbh 154.23–24, *tho out of sight, yet whose buddhi is always not out of sight of all creatures*; saṃmukhāvasthitaṃ, viparokṣāvasthitaṃ Bbh 290.7; (tathāgatam eva ca teṣu buddhadharmeṣv) a-viparokṣa-tāyāṃ (*in manifest state*) samanupaśya Bbh 174.18.

viparya, m. or nt., a high number: °yaḥ Mvy 7728 = Tib. (ḥ)khrul yas; °yam (nt.) Gv 133.8; = **vivaryam** Mvy 7856 (same Tib.), which is cited from Gv (yet Gv agrees, except for gender, with Mvy 7728 instead; om. in Gv 105).

[? **viparyata,** surely corrupt in Gv 228.10, in a list of epithets of ignorant worldlings, saṃjñācittadṛṣṭi-viparyatānām, read perhaps °viparyastānām, *perverted by* (false) *notions, thoughts, and heresies.*]

viparyāya, m. (Skt. Lex. id., Pali vipariyāya, = Skt. viparyaya), *contrariety, the being opposed* (of signs, omens): nimitta-°yaḥ Mvy 9303.

(**viparyāsa,** see **viprayāsa.**)

[**Vipaścin,** error for **Vipaśyin,** q.v.]

vipaśyaka, adj. (Skt. vi-paśyati plus -aka), *perceiving correctly, having insight into*: (sarvajagadbhūta-)-koṭī-°kānāṃ (bodhisattvānāṃ) Gv 40.14; sarvalokagati-°kānāṃ (ib.) 41.7; mahāprajño vipaśyako Mv ii.166.5 (vs; of Śākyamuni as bodhisattva). (Pali vipassaka; cf. next.)

vipaśyanā (Skt. vi-paśyati plus -anā), *correct insight*: with other virtues LV 415.7 (°na, vs); °na-vāyu-samā LV 414.11 (vs), *like the wind in (penetrating) insight*, so Tib., lhag mthoṅ rluṅ (daṅ) ḥdra; °na-vidyu-mālī RP 45.5 (vs; in all these °na m.c.); °nāyāṃ śikṣec ca Ud vi.9; śama-śīla-°nā-balair Divy 44.24 (vs); but almost always closely associated, often cpd., with a preceding **śamatha**; cf. AbhidhK. LaV-P. vi.301 n. 2, 'la pensée parfumée par le śamatha (*calme*) peut obtenir par la vipaśyanā (*intelligence*; elsewhere *vision, contemplation*) la vimukti'; another def. Bbh 260.11–14 tatra yā bodhisattvasyaiṣā dharmāṇām evam avikalpanā (see **vikalpana**), so 'sya śamatho draṣṭavyaḥ. yac ca tad yathābhūtajñānaṃ pāramārthikaṃ, yac ca tad apramāṇavyavasthānanayajñānaṃ dharmeṣu, iyam asya vipaśyanā draṣṭavyā; in Mvy 1678 vi° (Tib. lhag mthoṅ) follows śamatha 1677, and forms a tetrad with it and yogaḥ, yoniśo-manasikāraḥ; śamatha-°nā-vihārin Divy 95.13; 124.12; 264.27–28; Av i.16.10; 283.2; °nā-vihāra-vihārin Gv 471.21; otherwise cpd. or assoc. with śamatha, LV 128.3; 181.19; 183.7; Mv i.120.10; Av ii.140.10; Śikṣ 260.12; 261.2; KP 154.5; Bbh 83.8; 109.9, etc. (Pali vipassanā; cf. prec. and next.)

vipaśyin (cf. prec. two; miswritten Vipaścin Divy 141.16; Mmk 397.11; = Pali vipassi(n), both mgs.), (**1**) adj., *having insight* (*into*, in comp.): sarvāvaraṇabuddha-samudra-°nā bodhisattvasamādhinā Gv 37.6; sarvāvara-ṇavigatena °nā kauśalyena 60.7; (**2**) n. of a past Buddha, as in Pali the sixth before Śākyamuni, and so often as 'first of seven Buddhas', see s.v. **tathāgata**; otherwise named as a former Buddha: Mv i.2.5; 294.19; iii.240.6; 241.16; 243.14; 244.4; 245.18 ff.; 247.10; 249.1; Gv 206.12; stories of incidents which occurred during his Buddhahood, Mv ii.271.7 ff.; Divy 141.16; 227.21 ff.; 282.19 ff.; Av i.137.7 ff.; 349.3 ff.; ii.70.11; 96.3; 109.3; Kv 14.12.

vipāka, m. (Skt. and Pali id.), *maturation, coming to fruition* (of action): °ka-stha, of Buddhas, = **vaipākika,** q.v.; °ka-**maheśākhya,** see this; °ka-phalam Mvy 2276, one of the 5 **phala,** q.v. (2), expl. by iṣṭahetutvena in Sūtrāl. xvii.31 comm., in Bbh 102.19–20 by akuśalānāṃ dharmāṇāṃ apāyeṣu vipāko vipacyate, kuśala-sāsravāṇāṃ sugatau; -karma-samādāna-hetuso-vipākaso-(for °śo; *according to causes and results*)-jñāna- LV 433.6; dattvā ca vipākāpratikāṅkṣī LV 181.2, *not looking for 'maturation'* i. e. *recompense, reward* (for the gift.)

vipākana, vipācana, adj., f. °**nī,** *digesting*: in phrase, samāye (ii.424.3 adds samyag-) vipācanīye (i.211.6 vipāka°) grahaṇīye samanvāgatā (or °to) Mv i.211.6 = ii.15.6 = 424.3 (prose), *provided with an even (steady), well-digesting grahaṇī*; the corresp. Pali is sama-vepākiniyā gahaṇiyā samannāgato DN ii.177.27 et al. Senart keeps mss. reading in ii.424.3; in the others he em. wrongly.

vipāka-śas, see **vipāka.**

vipākya, adj. (to vipāka plus -ya), *coming to fruition*: dvaidha-vi° MPS 18.8.

vipācana, see **vipākana.**

vipācayati, reading of Mironov for **vivācayati,** q.v.: Mvy 9360.

vipāṭaka, adj., °kaḥ Mvy 8818, in a list describing bodily characteristics, esp. unusual ones or deformities; acc. to Tib. lus glebs pa ḥdra ba, *with body like something flat*; Chin. *body like a flat platter.*

vipāsa (m. or nt.), a high number: °sasya, gen., Gv 105.21; replaces **ārāva,** q.v., of Mvy 7839.

vi-puṇya, adj., *un-virtuous*, in °ya-mānā Mv ii.63.4 (vs), see s.v. **surati.**

vipula, (**1**) adj. (like **udagra,** q.v., a near-synonym in Skt.), appears to be used (at least once) in the mg. *rejoiced, very happy*: prītī (? so both edd.; v.l. °tyā, °tya; perh. read prītyā, instr.?) udagrā vipulā sma jātāḥ SP 214.4 (vs); Tib. bdag cag (*we*) dgaḥ zhiṅ (*being glad*) mgu pa raṅs ba skyes (app. *have become joyous and rejoiced*), which points to this interpretation of vipulā; several mss. read jātā, but against taking prīti as subject of jātā, and udagrā and vipulā as pred. adj., is the form sma (= smas), as well as the Tib.; (**2**) (= Pali id.; also **Vaipulya**) n. of a mountain near Rājagṛha: Māy 5; 101.

Vipulakīrti, n. of a Buddha: Gv 258.6.

Vipulaguṇajyotiḥprabha, n. of a Tathāgata: Gv 422.15.

Vipulatarāṃsa (Senart wrongly em. °śa), n. of a former Buddha: Mv i.139.2.

Vipuladharmādhimuktisaṃbhavateja (n. sg. °jo), n. of a Tathāgata: Gv 423.8; later called Vipulādhimuktisaṃbhavatejas, Gv 424.1 (read °tejasas, gen.), and (in vs) **Adhimuktitejas**, q.v.

Vipulapārśva, n. of a mountain: Mvy 4157.

Vipulabuddhi, n. of two Buddhas: Gv 284.23; 285.15.

Vipulamati, n. of a Bodhisattva: RP 1.12.

Vipulamahājñānaraśmirāja, n. of a Tathāgata: Gv 421.19.

Vipulayaśa (for °śas), n. of a former Buddha: Mv iii.238.8 f.

Vipulā, n. of a river: Māy 253.9. Not in BR, pw; cited Kirfel, Kosm., 68 from Mbh. Calc. 6.321, which however seems to be wrong reading; Crit. ed. 6.10.13 seems right in reading bahulā.

Vipulādhimuktisaṃbhavatejas = **Vipuladharmādhimukti**°, q.v.

Vipuloja, n. of a former Buddha: Mv i.137.3 (for Skt. °laujas).

vipuṣpayati, *smiles*; °pita (cf. also **vaipu**°), ppp., *it was smiled*: (tena) °tam, *he smiled*, Divy 585.10; similarly 26, 28; MSV ii.29.13; vipuṣpya, ger., MSV ii.86.1.

vipūtika, nt. (and °ka-saṃjñā), = **vipūyaka**, q.v.: ŚsP 59.6; 1258.6; 1431.20 (which is cited in Śikṣ 211.1 reading vipūyaka). Note also the corrupt variant vidhūtika, Mvy 1157, which might intend vipūtika; but the true reading seems to be vipūyaka.

vipūyaka, nt. (= Pali vipubbaka), *a corpse destroyed by putrefaction*; -saṃjñā, *contemplation of the notion of such a corpse*, one of the **aśubha-bhāvanā** (q.v.) or -saṃjñā: Mvy 1157 (so Mironov without v.l., and var. of Kyoto ed., which first reads vidhūtika; this might intend **vipūtika**, q.v., the ŚsP version of vipūyaka); Bhīk 27a.2; Śikṣ 211.1 (cited from ŚsP): Gv 157.15.

vipṛṣṭhīkaroti (see next; for Pali vipiṭṭhikatvā(na) see **pṛṣṭhībhavati**), (**1**) *makes depressed, discourages*: na viṣādam āpatsyate na vipṛṣṭhīkariṣyati mānasam AsP 139.18; (**2**) (cf. **pṛṣṭhībhavati** 1) *turns one's back on, abandons*: AsP 343.19, see s.v. **chorayati** (8).

vipṛṣṭhībhavati (cf. prec., and s.v. **pṛṣṭhībhavati**), *becomes depressed, discouraged*, = **pṛṣṭhībhavati** (2): (na viṣādam āpadyate) nāsya vipṛṣṭhībhavati mānasaṃ AsP 5.7; (cittaṃ nāvalīyate na saṃlīyate, 7273) na vipṛṣṭhībhavati asya mānasam Mvy 7274.

vi-prakampya, adj. (vi, neg., plus Skt. pra°; cf. Pali appakampin), *not subject to being disturbed*: sukhaduḥkhavi° Samādh 22.10, . . . *by pleasure or pain*, of the Buddha's body, in a long series of epithets of it; Régamey *not oscillating between bliss and suffering*, claiming support of Chin. for *not oscillating*; at least Chin. seems to support the neg. (= vi).

viprakṛta, ppp. (= Pali vippakata), *interrupted, uncompleted*: MSV iii.111.19 pārājikakathā na °tā bhavati (cf. Pali Vin. ii.243.17–18); 112.1, 2.

viprakramaṇa, nt. (n. act. to next; not recorded), *departure*: tūṣṇīṃ °ṇam Mvy 8503.

viprakramati, °krāmati (= Pali vippakkamati; cf. prec.), *departs, goes away*: asmiṃ (sc. tathāgate) janapadacārikāṃ vā viprakrānte parinirvṛte vā Bbh 93.18, *and when he has gone away on a journey over the countryside, or has entered nirvāṇa* . . .; °kram° MSV i.224.21; °krām° iii.112.12.

vipraghāta (m.), *destruction, slaying*: tau parasparam eva mahājana-°taṃ kurutaḥ Av i.42.3.

vipraghātika, adj. (cf. prec.), *murderous*: niyatam anyonya-°tiko bhaviṣyati MSV ii.18.10; °**tikā**, subst., = prec.: anyonya-°kāṃ kartum MPS 51.6.

vipraṇaṣṭaka, see **vipraṇa**°.

vipraṇāśayati (otherwise unrecorded caus. of Skt. vipraṇaśyati; cf. **vipraṇaṣṭaka**), *causes or allows to be wasted*: mā ca me tvaṃ kiṃcid ato (sc. dravyād) °śayiṣyasi SP 107.13 (prose).

viprakṛṣati or °**karṣati**, *maltreats*: paro 'pi tāvan nanu rakṣaṇīyaḥ, pāpātmabhir viprakṛṣyamāṇaḥ (pass.) Jm 125.4 (vs).

vipratipatti, f. (**1**) (= Pali vippaṭi°; cf. next) *evil behavior, sin*; opp. to **pratipatti**, q.v.: °ti-sthita Dbh 25.15, see s.v. **pratipatti**; KP 25.7 and Samādh p. 14 line 2, see ib.; °ti-duḥkhaṃ (yad dṛṣṭe vā dharme . . . labhate) Bbh 245.3; vicitrā vineya-kṛtā °tiḥ 251.6; teṣv (sc. sattveṣu) iha prājñasyāghāto na yuktarūpaḥ, prāg eva °tir Jm 76.22; mama °tiś ca keyam asminn anāgasi Jm 164.23 (vs), *and how could I sin against this innocent one*?; (**2**) (*something going wrong, amiss,*) *mishap, misfortune*: mā khalu kumārasya kācid °tiḥ LV 104.4–5, *I hope there isn't* (going to be) *some misfortune for the child*?

vipratipadyate (= Pali vippaṭipajjati; cf. prec. and next), *sins*: with loc., *towards, in regard to*, (sattveṣu) Śikṣ 12.10; 146.7; with instr. and sārdhaṃ, *sins sexually with*: Divy 293.20; KP 80.2; (na . . . bodhisattvasya) sarvacaryāsu vipratipattavyaṃ Śikṣ 99.17, *must not commit a sin in reference to* (sc. find fault with) *any actions of a B.* (see s.v. **vimoktavya**).

vipratipanna (ppp. to prec.; = Pali vippaṭipanna), *sinful*: °nāś ca bhavanti Mv i.96.8 (leads to retrogression in Bodhisattvas); ārakṣaṇatā °neṣu Śikṣ 286.3 (prose), prob. *being on guard with reference to the sinful*.

vipratibaddha, ppp. (to unrecorded *vi-prati-bandh-; cf. next, also recorded only in BHS), *obstructed*, in a-vi°, *unobstructed*: bodhisattvānām avipratibaddha-sarvavākpathasvabhāvajñānānāṃ Gv 313.2.

vipratibandha, m., *obstacle, obstruction*, see s.v. **vibandha.**

vipratilambha, (*varied*? vi-) *acquisition*: Gv 70.7 abhāvapratiṣṭhitānabhisaṃskāra-vipratilambhena, *by the* (*varied*) *acquisition of non-accumulation* (of karman) *which is established in non-becoming*; cf. Gv 180.6, s.v. **anabhisaṃskārika** (°kā).

vipratisāra, m., rarely nt. (= Pali vippaṭi°; Skt. Lex., once in lit. BR), *discontent with something done or not done* (usually, but not always, by oneself) *in the past*; *regret*; (especially) *remorse*: Mvy 2115; 5236 °raḥ; Mv iii.171.10 °raṃ (n. sg.) saṃjātaṃ (no v.l.); Kv 33.12 °raṃ (n. sg.); Divy 473.17 mā (so with mss.) bhūc cittasya vipratisāraḥ, *I hope you did not feel regret of mind* (at having given your breasts); 585.6 °ra-cittam, *regretful thought*; Av i.90.10 °ra-jāto, *characterized by regret*; 149.12; 180.10; 287.2; ii.71.2; 100.15; Śikṣ 160.7; Bbh 6.9; 141.27; 163.8. Cf. the next entries, and **a-vipratisāra.**

vipratisāravant, adj. (to prec. with vant), *remorseful*: °vān Jm 21.15.

vipratisārin, adj. (= prec. = Pali vippaṭi°; to °sāra, and cf. **a-vipratisārin**), usually *regretful* of something done or undone in the past by oneself, sometimes an act of generosity, in which case the *regret* is a sin: Karmav 66.7, and read vipratisārī Karmav 65.4, see s.v. **pratisārin**; often an evil deed or error, or at least failure to perform a good action; then *remorseful*: LV 407.6, of the boatman who regrets not having ferried the Buddha; Mv i.37.4 satpuruṣā . . . akuśalena karmaṇā (mss. karmāṇāṃ) vipratisārī (n. pl.) bhavanti, *good men . . . become remorseful for an evil action* (or, with mss., *for the evil of their actions*? Senart misunderstands); Mv iii.165.1; Divy

344.11; 638.10, read sa vipratisārī; Av i.215.3 vipratisārībhūtaḥ *became regretful, remorseful*; ati-vi° Śikṣ 178.14 nātivipratisāriṇā bhavitavyam; sometimes *regretful, saddened* by circumstances beyond one's control, especially of Māra, *saddened* by his failure to interfere with the Bodhisattva or Buddha, LV 260.20; vipratisārī usually in this case preceded by duḥkhī durmanā (or °no in Mv) LV 263.4; 378.2; Mv i.42.3; 230.10; 240.20; ii.163.1; iii.281.13; 416.8; of a devatā, saddened by a king's refusal to heed her warning, duḥkhinī durmanaskā vipratisāriṇī Divy 322.13.

vipratihīna, ppp. (=, or perhaps error for, Skt. viprahīṇa), *deprived of, free from*: pañcāṅga-vi°, ep. of Buddhas (see **aṅga**), Divy 124.15; but same cpd. with viprahīṇa in same context 95.17; 265.1; perhaps read so.

vi-pratyanīka (= Pali vipaccanīka; cf. °nīya(ka), **vipratyayanīya**, and **a-pratyanīya**; cpd. of vi, intensive, and pratyanīka; the forms with -ya(ka) are semi-Pktic, partly no doubt assimilated to suffixal forms in -īya, § 2.32), *antipathetic, opposed, hostile, unwelcome*: Bbh 98.15 °ka-virodha, *hostility between* (creatures that are by nature mutually) *antipathetic* (like snakes and mongooses, cats and mice, as the text explains); 389.7 (parasparaviruddheṣu...) anyonyadṛṣṭiruci-vipratyanīka-vādiṣu; Mv iii. 196.8 °kaṃ khalu devatānāṃ, *contrary* (to the ways of men), see Jāt. iv.108.8 which makes clear the true form and mg. of the verse (not understood by Senart); in BHS commonly in cpd. sarvaloka-vi°, as epithet of dharma-(-paryāya), *antipathetic* (not acceptable, unwelcome) *to the whole* (ignorant) *world*, sometimes accompanied by parallel sarvalokāśraddheya (SP 290.12) or °kāśraddadhanīya (SP 230.7), *not believable by*...; with this usage cf. in Pali Pugg. 20.13 (sahadhammike vuccamāne, *when something in accord with* [the Buddha's] *dhamma is being said*)... vipaccanīka-sātatā, *taking delight in contradicting it*: so SP 230.7; 290.12; LV 89.21; 395.21; Mv iii.314.2, 16 (in both one ms. ends in °ya instead of °ka); Suv 81.7; AsP 305.3.

vipratyanīya = prec. and next; I have noted this form only as v.l. (of Kashgar rec. and two Nep. mss.) for °nīka of text in SP 230.7, and v.l. for the same Mv iii. 314.2, 16.

vipratyanīyaka = °**nīya**, °**nīka**: SP 17.5 (prose) sarvaloka-vi° (of dharmaparyāya, as °nīka is often used).

vipratyayanīya, adj. (cf. Skt. vipratyaya, m.; Skt. pratyeti, Pali pacceti, but no cpd. of vi- with this verb is noted; in fact, this form is doubtless a distortion of **vipratyanīka**, °**nīya**, used in precisely such phrases, blended by folk-etymology with the noun vipratyaya), in sarvaloka-vipratyayanīyo (*which all the world is reluctant to accept*, Müller, SBE 49.2 p. 102) dharmo deśitaḥ Sukh 99.17.

vipranaṣṭaka, adj. (spelled here with n; Skt. °ṣṭa plus -ka), (one) *that has disappeared, been lost*: putro mamāyaṃ cira °kaḥ SP 115.6 (vs, end of line, not metr. determined; specifying ka? or pitying dim.? said by the father about his lost son). Cf. **vipraṇāśayati.**

viprapañca, see **a-vi°**.

vipramādayati (= Skt. pramādayati), *wastes*: (ye ca vaiyāpṛtyakarā vā ārāmikā vā sāṃghikaṃ staupikaṃ vā) dravyaṃ °dayanty anayena Bbh 166.26.

vipramuṣita (ppp. to *vi-pra-muṣ-), *forgotten, lost* (of sacred learning): (taṃ sarvaṃ smarāmy ekapadavyañjanam api) me tato dharmanayān na °tam Gv 283.13.

vipramūḍha, ppp. (of vi-pra-muh-, of which Skt. has caus. °mohayati), *bewildered*: arthe ca dharmeṣu ca vipramūḍhā Mv ii.92.8 (vs).

viprayāsa, m. (a distortion of Skt. viparyāsa, = Pali vipariyāsa, °yesa, vipallāsa), *error, delusion*: caturo °sān prahātukāmena bodhisattvena ŚsP 478.22. On the four viparyāsa see Lévi, Sūtrāl. xviii.44 with note.

vipralambhayati (= Pali vippalambheti; in Skt. only non-caus. vipralabh- in this mg.), *deceives, disappoints*: °bhayitum MSV iii.135.2 (prose).

vipralopa (m.; to Skt. vi-pra-lup-), *ruin, destruction*: saddharma-°pe vartamāne SP 282.10; Śikṣ 104.11; Vaj 22.9 (°pa-kāle), 13; puruṣendriya-vipralopāyopāttānāṃ upanītānāṃ manuṣyāṇāṃ Bbh 29.23; °pa-tā, *destructibility*: (sarvasaṃskāra-gatasya)...°tāṃ ca... pratyavekṣate Dbh 31.3.

vipralopin, adj. (prec. plus -in), *destroying* or *robbing*: parasattvabhoga-°pināṃ Gv 157.1; samabhilaṣitārtha-°nas tān vānarān Jm 177.17.

vipravasati (= Pali vippav°, see Childers; not in this use in Skt.), *is separated* (*from*, instr., or in cpd.): na °sati kuśalamūlapariṇāmaiḥ Śikṣ 279.5; neg. ppp. a-vipravasita, *not separated* or *removed* (from): samantabhadrabodhisattvārambaṇaparigaveṣaṇāvipravasitenāśayena (1st ed. °pravaśi°) Gv 533.1.

vipravāti, *blows* (*wildly*?): vātā ca vipravānti Mv ii.225.16 (vs), an evil omen; meter is bad in any case, but reading °nti would make this pāda correct; below, line 19, vātā pravānti (good meter, the rest of the line different).

vipravādana, nt. (to next plus -ana), *deceit, imposture*: Mvy 9431 = Tib. slu ba; so also Chin.

vipravādayati (cf. prec.; nowhere else in this mg.), *deceives, disappoints*: (anena dānena) vilobhya paścād enaṃ °yiṣyāmīti Bbh 122.8; (na mithyāprayogena) °yati 363.12 (Tib. cited in Index as slu bar byed pa).

vipravāsa, m. (= Pali vippavāsa), *the being parted from* (monkish robes): Mvy 8386; chiefly in neg. a-vi° (Pali a-vi°), *not*... (see CPD), MSV ii.153.12 ff. (cīvarāṇām).

vipravāhayati, *carries about hither and yon*: yathā hi kāṣṭham udadhau taraṅgair vipravāhyate (pass.) Laṅk 135.8 (vs).

vipraveśa (m.; to next?), *disappearance, exhaustion, lack*(?), in anarthayoga-°śaḥ, *characterized by absence of union with undesirable things*(?): LV 393.5 (vs) na ca punar ayu śakya akṣarebhiḥ praviśatu anartha°; Tib. don tshul ḥdi ni yi ge rnams kyis su, śes par mi nus ḥdzaṅs pas rig pa yin; I do not understand this, nor Foucaux's translation; acc. to Jä. ḥdzaṅs pa = *spent, consumed, exhausted*; whether this represents vipraveśa I am, however, far from certain.

vipraveśa(ya)ti (cf. prec.), *disappears, passes away*: vistīrṇo ca jñātivargo na °veśeyā (v.l. °veśayā) Mv ii.146.14 (prose), *and may our extensive throng of kindred not disappear* (*pass away*); the context hardly permits doubt about the mg.

viprasanna, ppp. of next (= Pali vippa°; once in Skt., pw, Caraka, of dhātu in medical sense), *calm, serene, unperturbed*: of the sense-faculties (indriya), LV 405.7; 409.2; Mv iii.61.14, 16; Sukh 2.17; °na-manāḥ Mvy 423 (of a Tathāgata); of a Buddha's mukha-varṇa Mv iii.325.16; in comparison to a pond, hradam iva accho anāvilo viprasanno... Mv i.237.12 (of a Buddha), and similarly Gv 195.13; Ud xvii.11 (yathā hradaḥ sugabhīro °nno hy anāvilaḥ; for the conclusion see next); Mvy 7293.

viprasīdati (= Pali vippa°), *becomes serene, calm*: śrutvā hi saddharmaṃ °danti paṇḍitāḥ Ud xvii.11 (= Pali Dhp. 82, vippasīdanti); see under prec.

vipraharṣa (m.), *gratification*: tasya °ṣa-saṃjananārthaṃ... haṃsarājo gaganatalam abhyudgamya... prātihāryāṇi vidarśayitum ārabdhaḥ Av ii.117.1.

? **vi-baddha**, adj. (app. vi plus baddha; cf. next two), *dis-connected*, and so *showing gaps* (in the framework of a roof, and in the Bodhisattva's ribs): sayyathāpi nāma ubhayato pārśve vibaddhāyāṃ (so 1 ms., v.l. vivṛddhāyāṃ, Senart em. vivṛtāyāṃ) vāhanāgāraśālāyāṃ gopānasīye antarāṇi vivaṭāni vītiloketsuḥ vītikāsetsuḥ, evam eva pāṃśulikāni (q.v.) pāṃśulikāntarāṇi vibaddhāni (kept with mss. by Senart) vītiloketsuḥ vītikāsetsuḥ Mv ii.125.13–15. If vibaddha is kept in the last part of the sentence, it should be kept in the first. It is true that in repetitions of the phrase (listed s.v. **pāṃśulika**) the mss. support **vivaṭa,** not vibaddha. Uncertain; but the next items give some support to vibaddha.

vibaddhana(-tā; n. act. to next), *state of being unbound, freed, released*: (sarvajñapuṇyasāgarākarasaṃjñāṃ) pratyalabhata, sarvaśukladharmasamārjana-°dhanatāyai Gv 342.18, *so as to result in being freed thru acquisition* (see **samārjana**) *of*...

vibaddhayati (app. denom. to **vibaddha,** cf. **baddhati**), *unbinds, releases, makes freed*: kaḥ ... svayam ātmanecchati vibaddhayituṃ LV 45.2 (vs), *who wishes to make himself free by himself*?

vibandha, m., and **vipratibandha,** m. (= Pali vibandha, Pv. comm. 207.16, *obstacle,* not *fetter* with PTSD), *hindrance, obstacle, obstruction* (wrongly defined by Wogihara, Lex. 37; correctly LaV-P. on AbhidhK. vi.300, vibandha = *obstacle*); the two words have been noted (except as just stated) only in Bbh and are used there interchangeably: (129.16) bodhisattvaḥ dāna-vibandham api dāna-vibandha-pratipakṣam api (*what is an obstacle to giving, and what counteracts that obstacle*) yathābhūtaṃ prajānāti. (18) tatra catvāro dāna-vibandhāḥ (v.l. °vipratibandhāḥ; they are described in detail) ... (130.2) dāna-vipratibandha-pratipakṣaṃ niśṛtya (*taking recourse to that which counteracts the obstacle* ...) ... dadāti ... (130.6) vighāta-kṛtaṃ dāna-vipratibandha-hetuṃ ... (131.6) caturvidhasya dāna-vibandhasya caturvidhaṃ dāna-vipratibandha-pratipakṣa-jñānaṃ veditavyaṃ ... (131.23) dāna-vipratibandha-pratipakṣa-jñānam upādāya; again, one of the 6 **upāya** (q.v.) of a bodhisattva is the vibandha-sthāyin (upāya), *that acts as a block* (misunderstood by Wogihara l. c.), Bbh 264.8, discussed 267.3 katamo bodhisattvasya vibandha-sthāyī (v.l. °stha) upāyaḥ? iha bodhisattvaḥ ... (5) sattvānāṃ vipratibandhenāvatiṣṭhate (*is in the position of a block, hindrance,* to the natural, worldly behavior of creatures); the text then explains how the Bodhisattva bribes creatures to abandon their natural immorality and live morally by promising them the worldly enjoyments they crave, on that condition; in this passage vipratibandha is constantly used, 267.5, 14, 19, 24; 268.3, 6; but at the end, 268.11, vibandha-sthāyī (or rather in mss. °stha) upāyaḥ is used again, and in 268.9, just above, evaṃ vibandha-sthitasya bodhisattvasya; once more, Bbh 388.6 (aprāpteṣu caiṣu, sc. dhyānādiṣu, cf. lines 3–4) prāptaye vibandha-saṃkleśaḥ, *the* (sort of) *impurity* (one of two kinds) *that, when they have not been attained, consists in an obstacle to their attainment.*

vibuddha, ppp. (not noted in Pali; Skt. id., in somewhat different mgs.), (**1**) *thoroughly enlightened*: sātivibuddha (= sa ati-vi°, *O thou who art exceedingly well enlightened*!) pravartaya cakravaraṃ LV 415.4 (vs); (**2**) *made noticeable, conspicuous*: prāsāda-harmiyaṃ taṃ (mss. °harmiye) gavākṣa-vara-śaraṇa-pañjara-vibuddhaṃ Mv ii.36.4 (vs).

Vibuddhajñānabodhidhvajateja, n. of a Tathāgata: Gv 311.10 (prose).

vibuddhati (cf. **buddhati**; = Skt. vibudhyate, AMg. vibujjhai), *awakes*: vibuddhi, 3 sg. opt., *would awaken,* Mv i.155.19 (vs); vibuddhitvā iii.191.12 (prose); for vibudhyiya (1 sg. opt.) of text Bhad 41, all Jap. and some Nep. mss. vibuddhiya, which prob. read.

vibuddhana (nt.; n. act. to prec.) = **vibudhyana,** q.v.: tryadhvaika-lakṣaṇa-(so read)-vibuddhana-nirvikalpā Dbh.g. 1(337).9.

Vibuddhi, n. of a Bodhisattva or future Buddha(!): Gv 442.15 (gen. Vibuddher, in a long list of them).

vibudhyana (nt.; see also **vibuddhana**; n. act. to Skt. vibudhyate, see **vibuddhati**), *awareness, realization, becoming conscious* (*of* ..., usually in comp.): sarvabuddha-bodhimaṇḍa-°na-(text vibudhyāna-)-jñānamaṇḍalāvabhāsapratilābhāya Gv 344.12; abhisaṃbodhivyūha-°na-370.26; -bodhi-°na-jñāna- 375.17; teṣu (gen. pl., sc. of future Buddhas) vibudhyana (acc. sg.) Bhad 35, here prob. = *becoming enlightened* (attaining Buddhahood).

vibodhaka, adj. (cf. Pkt. vibohaga, °ya, and BHS **vibodhita**; to Skt. vibodhayati plus -aka), *causing* (a flower) *to 'awaken'* i. e. *to bloom* (cf. Skt. vibuddha, of flowers): in a metaphor, buddha-vibuddha-manuja-kumuda-°kasya (bodhisattvasya) LV 9.16.

vibodhana (cf. Skt. id.), applied to a perfume twice in Gv: vibodhana-gandharājapramukhā(ḥ) Gv 153.15, in a list of perfumes all cpd. with gandharā°; °na-gandhamaṇirāja- Gv 101.9, a jewel supposed to emit a perfume, cf. **anuracitagandhagarbha-,** which precedes this.

vibodhita, ppp. of Skt. vibodhayati (see s.v. **vibodhaka**), *brought to full bloom,* of flowers; fig. of women's faces compared to flowers: makuṭakuṇḍalapattra-°ta-ānanikā LV 322.10 (vs; read as one cpd. word).

vibhakta, nt., or °**ti,** f., a high number: °tam Mvy 7849 (cited from Gv); Gv 133.7; °tiḥ Mvy 7723; °ter, gen. sg., Gv 105.24.

Vibhaktāṅga, n. of a Bodhisattva: Gv 442.13.

[**vibhakṣayati,** *devours,* unrecorded; °yantaḥ SP 83.11 (vs), prob. read either ye (short e) bhakṣayanti with Kashgar rec., or yi (= ye), or ca bhakṣayantaḥ with WT and their ms. K′.]

vibhaṅga, m. (= Pali id.; consult Childers), (**1**) *distribution, classification*: °ga eṣāṃ (categories stated just before) yathāsūtram eva veditavyaḥ Bbh 25.4; see also **Karma-vi°**; (**2**) *explanation, commentary*: Cakravartisūtra-vibhaṅga Karmav 102.1; prob. in this mg. **Vinaya-vi°,** q.v.; Vibhaṅge MSV iii.29.6 prob. = this.

vibhaja, nt., a (moderately) high number: Mvy 7845 = Tib. nab nub (see **vijambha**); cited from Gv 133.5; omitted in Gv 105.23.

vibhajati (= Pali id.), *explains* or *understands in detail*: arthaṃ vibhaktum Divy 494.26; yāvad gāthārthaṃ na vibhajati 495.18; (duḥkhaṃ āryasatyam) ācikṣati deśayati prajñāpayati vivarati vibhajati Mv iii.408.18; (alpaṃ vyapadiśāmi, tat svaśaktyā) °ti MSV ii.27.17.

vibhajana, nt. (= Pali id.), *differentiation, classification*: °nam Mvy 5174; dhyānāṅga-(q.v.)-vibhajanārthaṃ LV 251.2.

vibhajitar (cf. Skt. vibhaktar; new n. ag. based on pres. vibhajati), *one who classifies, differentiates,* or *explains in detail*: °tāraḥ kṣāntīnāṃ Gv 463.4, in a long list of epithets of kalyāṇamitrāṇi.

Vibhajyavādin, pl., n. of a school: Mvy 9084; cf. Pali vibhajja°, ep. of Buddha, as expounder of °vāda = Theravāda, orthodox Southern Buddhism.

vibhajya-vyākaraṇa, nt. (cf. Pali vibhajja below), *elucidation* (response to a question) by *analyzing* or *distinguishing* (different aspects involved beyond what the question itself raised): Mvy 1659; cf. Pali AN i.197.21 vibhajja-vyākaraṇīyaṃ pañhaṃ, explained comm. ii.308.27 aniccaṃ nāma cakkhuṃ puṭṭhena pana, na cakkhum eva, sotaṃ pi aniccaṃ, ghānaṃ pi aniccaṃ ti evaṃ vibhajitvā vyākātabbaṃ. See **vyākaraṇa.**

vibhaṇḍayati (cf. Pkt. vihaṇḍana, *abusive,* of language, Sheth), *distorts* (the facial expression); mukhaṃ vi°, *makes a wry face*: °yati MSV i.285.16; Divy 263.14; °yasi 15; ger. vibhaṇḍya 575.24.

[**vibhartsayati**: LV 335.1 (vs) vibhartsyase, but best mss. vihatsyase; a fut. of vi-han- is to be read, see § 31.24; Tib. *you will be made poor,* phoṅs par ...; for SP 84.10 (vs) vitaṃsayanto, em., WT read vibhartsayanto; a form of bharts- is indicated by Tib. bsdigs pa, *menace, threaten,* but vi is very weakly supported; read rather ca, or tha, bharts°, or bhats°.]

vibhava, (**1**)? adj. Bhvr., *free from existence*: (bahu bodhisattvās tatha śrāvakāś ca . . .) bhavaprahīṇā vibhavāś ca sarve SP 152.11 (vs), *rid of existence and free from it, all of them*; so both edd., no v.l.; but Burnouf *exempts de terreur*, implying vibhayāś, supported by Tib. ḥjigs pa rab spaṅs; prob. this is the true reading (vi-bhava would duplicate bhava-prahīṇa); (**2**) m. (= Pali id.) *annihilation, destruction* (Tib. regularly ḥjig pa): (sarva-)dharmaprakṛti-svabhāvam-(read °va- with Calc.?)-saṃdarśana-vibhava-cakraṃ (of the dharmacakra) LV 422.19; vibhavaḥ Mvy 6469 = Tib. (read) ḥbyer ba or ḥjig pa; often assoc. with its antonym saṃbhava, *coming into existence*, Mvy 6845 loka-vi° (6846 loka-saṃ°); (lokadhātusaṃbhavaṃ ca . . .) lokadhātuvibhavaṃ ca vicārayati Dbh 67.23; (kalpadāhaṃ) saṃdarśayanta vibhavaṃ tatha saṃbhavaṃ ca LV 298.12 (vs); saṃbhavaṃ vibhavaṃ caiva mohāt paśyanti bāliśāḥ, na saṃbhavaṃ na vibhavaṃ prajñāyukto vipaśyati Laṅk 269.2–3 (vs); lokasya saṃbhavaṃ ca vibhavaṃ ca vyavalokayate Dbh 47.24; vibhava ucyate prahāṇaṃ tyāgaḥ (definition) Bbh 50.14; with bhava, instead of saṃbhava, vibhavaṃ ca bhavaṃ ca jñātva loke Mv iii.395.13 (vs); it is heresy to believe in either, bhava-vibhava-dṛṣṭi-vigatenānutpādanirodhajñānena Gv 469.11; ātmadṛṣṭi-(add bhavadṛṣṭi- with WT)-vibhavadṛṣṭi- SP 71.2.

Vibhavagandha, n. of a Bodhisattva: Gv 442.12.

? **vibhāgīya** (app. to Pali vibhāga plus -īya), *one who is an expert in scholastic classification* (cf. Senart, Mv ii note 536): dharmo gatir °yānāṃ Mv ii.212.20 (vs); but the pāda is hypermetric; in a repetition of the same vs iii.156.17 Senart reads the metrically correct dvijātīnāṃ, *of brahmans*, but mss. vibhātīnām (read vibhāgīnāṃ, gen. pl. of vibhāgin = vibhāgīya?); Pali has the same vs, Vin. v.149.22–23, but with a quite different pāda for this: vibhavo gati dhammānaṃ.

Vibhāvanagandha, n. of a Bodhisattva: Gv 442.12.

vibhāvita, ppp. (to Skt. vibhāvayati, Pali vibhāveti; Pali °vita used as in BHS, see PTSD s.v. vibhūta, and cf. BHS 2 **vibhūta**), ifc., *free from, deprived of* . . .: sarvanimitta-°to Samādh 22.9 (prose), in a list of epithets of the tathāgata-kāya (others are animittaḥ sarvanimittāpagato . . . animittasvabhāvaḥ).

Vibhāvitamati, n. of a Bodhisattva: Gv 442.7.

? **vibhāṣati** (cf. Pkt. vibhāsai, Sheth), *expounds variously*: yaṃ nūna haṃ pī (so all mss. and WT, metr. required) ima buddhabodhiṃ tridhā vibhāṣyeha (= vibhāṣya, ger., plus iha) prakāśayeyam SP 55.10 (vs), *having expounded it in three ways* (sc. the 3 yānas), *may I here proclaim* . . . But WT vibhajyeha, citing K′ as vibhajyāha, and Tib. phye, *divide*.

vibhāṣā (cf. AMg. vibhāsā, *'relating some broad meanings out of the innumerable meanings of a sūtra,'* Ratnach.), *extensive commentary*: Mvy 7568 = Tib. bye brag tu bśad pa, or, smra ba, *explanation in detail*; referred to in Chin. Buddhist sources, BR s.v.

Vibhīṣaṇa (doubtless a reminiscence of the brother of Rāvaṇa so named), (**1**) n. of a yakṣa (living at Tāmraparṇī): Māy 14; (**2**) n. of a nāga king: Mvy 3303; Māy 247.7. (In Mmk 17.28 prob. read Yama-vibhīṣaṇa; see **Yama** 3.)

vibhugna, adj. (ppp. of unrecorded vi-bhuj-), *bent* (with age): °naḥ Mvy 4100 = Tib. sgur ba, *crooked* (of a man's back).

Vibhudatta, n. of a Buddhist monk: Gv 47.9.

1 **vibhūta**, m., a high number: Mvy 8036 = Tib. rnam ḥbyuṅ, *variously* or *extensively become*.

2 **vi-bhūta**, adj. (vi- privative; cf. **vibhava** 2), *abolished, put away, abandoned, annihilated*: °tam Mvy 2570 = Tib. bral bar ḥgyur, or, med par ḥgyur, *become lost, become not*; sā ca saṃjñāsya vibhūtā bhavati Bbh 50.13, *and for him that notion becomes lost* (text continues, vibhava, q.v. 2, ucyate . . .).

vibhūtaṃgamā, f., or (v.l.) °**ma**, nt. (n. sg. °maṃ), a high number: LV 148.10; cited in Mvy 7976 as **vibhūtigama**, nt., q.v. Tib. in both places rnam ḥbyuṅ.

Vibhūtapati, and **Vibhūtabhūta**, names of two Bodhisattvas: Gv 442.19.

Vibhūti, n. of a Bodhisattva: Gv 442.8 (°teḥ, gen.).

vibhūtigama, nt., Mvy 7976, citing °**taṃgamā** (or °**gama**, nt.) of LV 148.10, q.v.

Vibhūṣaṇadharā, n. of a nāga maid: Kv 3.21.

Vibhūṣita, (**1**) m., n. of a Bodhisattva: Gv 442.8; (**2**) nt., n. of a Buddhakṣetra: Mv i.123.10.

vibhūṣitā, (**1**) (? to Skt. vibhūṣin plus -tā), *magnificence, splendor, ornate condition*: na śraddadhī mahyam imāṃ vibhūṣitāṃ SP 113.10 (vs), *he has not believed, 'this magnificence is mine'*; no v.l. in KN; WT cite ms. K′ as vibhūṣāṃ (Skt.), which they em. to vibhūtāṃ, implausibly; Tib. ḥbyor ba (read pa), *wealth, treasure*; vibhūṣāṃ of K′ looks like a secondary change, to a familiar Skt. word; all the other three pādas of the stanza are jagatī (supporting °ṣitāṃ); the same form prob. occurs in prose in: tāṃ divyāṃ vibhūṣitāṃ (ms. °tān, mere orthographic var.) dṛṣṭvā Av i.68.4, *having seen this magnificence* (Speyer em. to °ṣikāṃ, which is unrecorded and implausible); (**2**) (ppp. of vi-bhūṣ-) n. of an apsaras: Kv 3.10.

Vibhūṣitāṅga, n. of a Bodhisattva: Gv 442.2.

Vibhūṣitālaṃkārā, (**1**) n. of a 'gandharva maid': Kv 4.22; (**2**) n. of a kiṃnara maid: Kv 6.24.

-vibhedika, lit. *separater*, see **aṅguṣṭha**°. (Not recorded; to Skt. °din plus -ka.)

vibhramati (= Pali vibbhamati), *leaves the order of monks*: vibhrāntaḥ MSV iii.66.4.

vibhrāmaṇa, adj. (Skt. vibhrāmayati plus -ana), *causing distraction*: buddhi-°ṇo lābhasatkāraḥ Śikṣ 105.12 (in a list of epithets of lābhasat°).

vimati, f. (= Pali id.), *doubt*: prāṇināṃ ma bhavatu vimatiḥ LV 288.4 (vs); devaputrān °ti-prāptāñ jñātvā 350.20 (prose); idam avaci °ti-haraṇaṃ 370.14 (vs); °ti-samudghaṭita ity ucyate 425.15; °ti-chedakaṃ jinaṃ RP 5.8; °ti-śamakarī (of Buddha's speech) 47.2; often with **kāṅkṣā**, SP 223.1; Mvy 2130; RP 8.10; Gv 5.1; 32.25; at the end of Jātaka stories often as in Divy 297.28, syāt khalu bhikṣavo yuṣmākaṃ kāṅkṣā vimatir vā . . ., similarly 328.1 etc.; misc., Mv i.98.14; 115.14; Dbh 7.6, etc.; vīmati, m.c., Samādh 19.35. See next items.

Vimati-vikiraṇa, (**1**) n. of a Bodhisattva: Gv 442.4; (**2**) n. of a samādhi: Mvy 590; ŚsP 1422.20.

Vimatisamudghāṭī, n. of one of the sons of the Buddha Candrasūryapradīpa: SP 19.4; see **-samudghāṭin.**

vimada, nt., a high number: Mvy 7878 = Tib. dgaḥ yas; cf. **vimuda**. Cited from Gv 133.16, where **visada** (q.v.) is printed.

vimadhyama, adj. (cf. RV vimadhya, Pali vemajjha, n.; AMg. vimajjha, adj.), *middling*: iti hīna-vimadhyamottamānām Jm 115.1 (vs).

vimantra, nt., a high number: Gv 133.19; (cited from Gv) Mvy 7885 = Tib. gzhal (= mātra) saṅs (= vi-, ve-); cf. **vemātra**, also **vitramantrā.**

vimardanatā, see **a-vi**°.

Vimala, (**1**) n. of one or more former Buddhas: Mv i.140.10 (v.l. Vimala-, cpd. with foll. **Marīcijāla**); Śikṣ 169.9; Gv 104.15; (**2**) n. of a disciple of Śākyamuni (= Pali id.; see s.v. **Yaśodeva**): LV 1.9; Sukh 2.4; (**3**) n. of a devaputra, (a) one of the 16 guardians of the bodhimaṇḍa: LV 277.13; (b) as representative of a class of gods(?), Mmk 69.6; (**4**) n. of a nāga king: Māy 246.27; (**5**) n. of a samādhi: SP 458.2; Dbh 82.10.

Vimalakīrti, n. of a Bodhisattva: Mmk 40.15. In a list of 16 Bodhisattvas; is this the same as the Vimalakīrti so well known in Chinese Buddhism? See s.v. **satpuruṣa.**

Vimalakīrtinirdeśa, n. of a work: Mvy 1340; Śikṣ 6.10 etc.; its verses are in BHS, Śikṣ 324.11–327.4.

Vimalaketu, n. of a Bodhisattva: Mmk 40.15.

Vimalagati, n. of a Bodhisattva: Mmk 40.14.

Vimalagarbha, (**1**) n. of an ancient prince, previous birth of **Bhaiṣajyarāja**: SP 457.9 ff.; cf. 470.11; (**2**) n. of a Bodhisattva (seemingly not = 1): Mvy 711; Dbh 2.13; (**3**) n. of a samādhi: SP 424.7; (**4**) a certain gem: °bha-maṇiratna- Gv 219.16; °bha-maṇirāja- 295.4.

Vimalacakrabhānuprabha, another form of the name **Vimalavaktrabhā°**: Gv 308.5.

Vimalajendra (v.l. Vimalendra), n. of a former Buddha: Mv i.139.7.

Vimalatejaḥprabha, n. of a Bodhisattva: Gv 3.15.

Vimalatejas, n. of a previous birth of Śākyamuni: RP 23.2; (the same?) n. of a Bodhisattva: Gv 2.21, and prob. Śikṣ 189.9 ff. (?).

Vimaladatta, (**1**) n. of an ancient king, as whose son **Sarvasattvapriyadarśana** (2) was reborn: SP 408.11; (**2**) n. of a samādhi: SP 424.2.

Vimaladattā, n. of a queen: SP 457.8 ff. (previous incarnation of **Vairocanaraśmipratimaṇḍitadhvajarāja**, 470.6).

Vimaladharmaparvatajñānaśikharābha, n. of a Tathāgata: Gv 309.3.

Vimaladhvaja, n. of a Bodhisattva: Gv 2.18; 444.11.

vimalanā (to Skt. vimalayati plus -ana), *purification*: Mvy 7543 = Tib. sbyoṅ ba.

Vimalanirbhāsa, n. of a samādhi: SP 458.3.

Vimalanetra, (**1**) n. of a past Buddha: Sukh 6.6; (**2**) n. of a future Buddha (predicted rebirth of the Bodhisattva **Śrīgarbha**): SP 21.13 (prose); called **Vimalāgranetra** in vs 26.6; (**3**) n. of an ancient prince, previous incarnation of **Bhaiṣajyasamudgata**: SP 457.9 ff.; cf. 470.11; (**4**) n. of a Bodhisattva: Mvy 677; Gv 3.1; (**5**) n. of the 'leader-jewel' (see **pariṇāyaka** 2) of a certain cakravartin: Gv 418.11.

Vimalapradīpa, m., n. of a samādhi: Mvy 540; ŚsP 1417.20.

Vimalaprabha, (**1**) n. of a former Buddha: Sukh 5.11; (**2**) n. of a Bodhisattva: Gv 3.15; (**3**) n. of a śuddhāvāsakāyika god: LV 267.9; (**4**) n. of two samādhis, in the same list: Mvy 544 = ŚsP 1418.9, and Mvy 609 = ŚsP 1425.2; also one of (only) four samādhis, Dharmas 136; (**5**) n. of a former kalpa: Gv 174.21; of another, also called **Vimalābha**, q.v., Gv 307.9 (prose).

Vimalaprabhā (text °prabhāsa, with only one ms., but repeated in WT), n. of a samādhi: SP 424.7.

Vimalaprabhāsa, n. of a Tathāgata: LV 290.9.

Vimalaprabhāsaśrītejorājagarbha, n. of a Bodhisattva: Dbh 2.14.

Vimalabāhu, n. of a Tathāgata: Gv 361.3.

Vimalabuddhi, n. of a Bodhisattva: Gv 4.13.

Vimalabhāsa, n. of a samādhi: SP 458.3 (so Burnouf; Kern, Transl., Vimalābhāsa; v.l. in ed. °ābhāṣa, °ābhasvara).

Vimalamakuṭa, n. of a former Buddha: Mv i.137.3.

Vimalavaktrabhānuprabha, n. of a cakravartin: Gv 307.15; later called **Vimalacakrabhā°**, q.v.

Vimalavatsa, n. of a Tathāgata: Gv 360.25.

Vimalavyūha, n. of a park at Kapilavastu: LV 121.16.

Vimalaśikhala (so mss.; Sen. em. °ra, but cf. **śikhala**), n. of a former Buddha: Mv i.140.13.

Vimalaśrīmegha, n. of a Tathāgata: Gv 421.22.

Vimalasaṃbhavaprabhā, n. of a nurse of the Bodhisattva **Īśvaraguṇāparājitadhvaja**: Gv 381.17.

Vimalā, (**1**) n. of a princess: Mv i.348.12; (**2**) n. of a deity of the park **Vimalavyūha**: LV 122.10; (**3**) n. of a rākṣasī: Māy 243.11; (**4**) n. of the second Bodhisattvabhūmi: Dbh 5.8 etc.; Mvy 887; Dharmas 64; Sūtrāl. xx.33; Bbh 334.24; (**5**) n. of one or more lokadhātus: Mmk 292.16; (in the east) LV 290.9; (in the south) SP 265.6, 11; (**6**) n. of a river, listed between Tapodā and Nairañjanā: Māy 253.8; prob. not identifiable with rivers of this name in Kirfel, Kosm., 65, 67, 68.

Vimalāgranetra, see **Vimalanetra**.

Vimalānana, n. of a former Buddha: Sukh 5.11.

Vimalābha, n. of a kalpa (= **Vimalaprabha** 5): Gv 312.10 (prose); 314.4 (vs; both edd. corruptly Vimāl°).

Vimalendra, see **Vimalajendra**.

Vimalottarajñānin, n. of a Bodhisattva: Gv 2.15.

Vimalottarīya, n. of a former Buddha: Mv i.139.8.

vimaṣṭaka (semi-MIndic for Skt. vimṛṣṭa-ka; cf. Pali vimaṭṭha), *polished*: so read with mss. in Mv iii.81.12 (vs), see s.v. **ghaṭṭa-**.

vimātra-tā (implies an adj. *vi-mātra, *diverse*, which has not been noted; see next, also **vaimātra**, °**tra-tā**, °**trya**; all these seem to be used only as nouns, except one case of vaimātra as adj., Mv iii.320.16, acc. to mss.; Pali also has no adj.), *diversity, variety, heterogeneity*: sarvasattvendriyavīrya-°tā-jñāna- LV 433.8; naikabuddhasthānapraṇidhāna-°tāvaraṇāya (see **āvaraṇa**) Gv 107.22; (-praṇidhāna-)-vimātratāvaraṇāya (so read for °vimātrāvara°) 24, and so read -praṇidhāna-vimātratānugamāya (for °vimātrānu°) 109.5; anantabodhisattvādhimukti- (2d ed. anantasattvādhimukti-) °tāṃ sampaśyan, anantasattvavibhakti-°tāṃ sampaśyan 115.26 f.; kvacid bodhicitta-°tāṃ (etc., a long series of cpds. ending -vimātratāṃ) ... aśrauṣīt 516.13 ff.; others Dbh 15.15; 75.4; at end of cpd. used like Skt. viśeṣa (see Sukh 66.12 s.v. **vaimātrya**) at end of cpds. = *various* ...: nānāsattvakula-°tābhyo Gv 145.15, *from various varieties of families of creatures*.

vimātrya (nt.) = prec. and **vaimātrya**: kvacit tathāgatapūjā-vimātryavimātratāṃ (... aśrauṣīt) Gv 516.15; in a list of cpds. all ending -vimātratāṃ (see prec.); here alone this synonym precedes, rather pleonastically; *the variety of the diversity of Tathāgata-worship*.

(**vimāna**, nt. and m., = Skt. id.; on use in Pali, see elaborate article in PTSD; even in Skt., see BR, it is not exclusively used of divine, nor yet of mobile, residences, but may apply to any luxurious dwelling-place, which in India would naturally include the surrounding grounds; see Mrs. Rhys Davids, Minor Anthologies of the Pali Canon Part IV, 1942, p. vi: '... more than houses, including gardens, woods, lakes' etc... '*estates* might have been more literally correct', but she uses *mansions*; several times in Jm the word is applied to something located in woods and used by a king for amusement; Speyer *arbors*, pw 7.375 'etwa *Hain*', but surely buildings seem to be involved: vimāna-deśeṣu Jm 182.22, 183.3; the king takes a siesta śrīmati °na-pradeśe 183.10; the king stays for a time śrīmati pravivikte °na-deśe 192.23; vane manoharodyāna-°na-bhūṣite 208.20. Pali certainly also uses the word, as does Skt. more commonly, of the air-traveling palaces of the gods; and I question whether either Pali or BHS gives it any meaning which could not be matched in Skt. On Divy 399.18, where pw also sees the meaning *Hain*, see **Śairīṣaka**; nothing in the context suggests any reason for departure from the common meaning, *celestial*, and no doubt *mobile, palace*.)

Vimānarājan, n. of a former Buddha: Mv i.139.1.

[**Vimālābha**, see **Vimal°**.]

? **vimiśra**, adj., *unmingled* (vi, neg.?): Mv ii.4.10 instead of **vinimiśra**, q.v.; metr. deficient. The word is known otherwise only with intensive force in vi-, *mixed up* (Skt. and MIndic).

vimiśrita, adj. (Ap. vimīsiya, Jacobi, Bhav. 90.10; denom. ppp. to Skt. vimiśra), *mixed*: °taḥ Mmk 149.13 (vs); -lipi, LV 126.9, see s.v. **vidyānulomāvimiśrita**.

Vimukta, n. of a former Buddha: Mv i.137.2.

Vimuktaka = **Muktaka** (śreṣṭhin), q.v.: Gv 549.3.

Vimuktaghoṣa, n. of a Bodhisattva: Gv 442.24.

vimukti, f. (= Skt. id., Pali vimutti), = **vimokṣa,** q.v.: the three vi°, vimuktayas tathā tisro Laṅk 135.6 = 321.8 (vs).

Vimukticandra, n. of a Bodhisattva: Mvy 674; Dbh 2.21; 5.28, etc.

vimuñcati, *emits, utters words* (no noun object expressed): Ud viii.8, see s.v. **muñcati.**

vimuda, m., a high number: Mvy 7749 = Tib. dgaḥ yas; cf. **vimada.**

vimūrchita, adj.-ppp. (= Pkt. vimucchia, Sheth), *stupefied, in a faint*: °taṃ māṃ Divy 454.30.

vimṛṣṭa (**1**), ppp.-adj., lit. *rubbed off,* so *obliterated, obscured*: api tām evaikottarikāṃ vimṛṣṭarūpāṃ prajvālayāmi Divy 333.13, *I will illumine the Ek°, the form of which has become obscured*; (**2**) a high number: Gv 106.1 (error for **viśiṣṭa,** q.v.).

vimoktavya, gdve. of Skt. vi-muc-, lit. *to be let go, passed over,* so *let pass, accepted, not criticized*: (after passage cited s.v. **vipratipadyate**) sarvāḥ kriyās tasya vimoktavyāḥ Śikṣ 99.17, *all his actions are to be let go* (uncriticized); Tib. (Transl. p. 102 n. 1) bya ba la mos par byas. Text proceeds: *one must think,* nāhaṃ paracittaṃ jāne, etc.

vimokṣa, m. (Skt. id., Pali vimokkha), *release, salvation.* As in Pali, there are three, or eight, vi°; the three are in Pali suññato, animitto, appaṇihito vi°, explained Vism. 658, and in Dharmas 73 śūnyato 'nimitto 'praṇihitaś ca; in Mvy 1541–4, three vi°-mukhāni, *approaches, entrances to . . .,* listed as śūnyatā-, animittaṃ (sc. °mukham), apraṇihitaṃ; references to the three (or threefold) vi° (often foll. by -mukha, or corruptly -sukha), LV 9.6; 181.20; 205.3; 359.22; 374.10; Gv 472.9; in Laṅk 163.4 vimokṣa-traya seems, however, to mean the opposite of the three **saṃgati** (q.v. 2), which seems to mean the three **saṃdhi** (q.v. 6); the eight vi° explained at length Mvy 1510–1518 (corresp. to Pali vimokkha); more briefly, and with accidental omission of the third, Dharmas 59; references to 8 vi°, SP 150.2; 180.1 (prose, read aṣṭavimokṣā(ḥ) with mss., Bhvr., *possessing the 8 vimokṣa,* exactly like ṣaḍabhijñā(ḥ) just before; note in ed. and em. wrong); 202.11; Av ii.69.2; **Bodhisattva-vimokṣa** means a Mahāyāna method of salvation; various fanciful names are given to such mystical (and not specifically described) methods; e. g. in Gv 261.4 a 'night-goddess' claims to have learned the Bodhisattva-vi° called samantabhadraprītivipulavimalavegadhvaja. See also **vimukti.**

Vimokṣakarā, n. of a kiṃnara maid: Kv 6.17.

Vimokṣacandra, n. of a Bodhisattva: Gv 443.7.

Vimokṣā, n. of a dhāraṇī: RP 50.4 (prose).

vimogha, either hyper-Skt. = Skt. vimoha, *delusion,* or cpd. of vi-, intens., and Skt. mogha, adj., *completely vain, empty*: in (rājyasukhaṃ) vimogha-dharmaṃ RP 39.13 (prose).

vimbaka, vimbara, see **bi°.**

vi-mrakṣayati, *stains, defiles*: a-vimrakṣito (by Senart's em.; mss. avimbakṣito) aśucinā bhagavāṃ Mv i.147.3 (vs), *unstained by impurity is the Lord.*

viya (= Pali id., Skt. iva), *like, as*; only in Mv, but frequent there in prose and vs alike: prose, i.237.10; 301.7; 339.7; 344.9; ii.158.7 (mss. ciya); 268.10, 11; iii.48.19; 49.6; 60.7; 182.13; 183.5; 414.15; vss, ii.4.1 and 19.16 (same vss with varr. have iva i.200.4 and 149.14; in ii.19.16 Senart em. wrongly); ii.36.14; 57.9; 181.5; 203.1, 5; 423.13 (here viya in mss., hypermetr.); iii.9.11; 79.9; 87.4; 184.4, 5; 405.11.

viyākaroti (Pali id., Jāt. v. 140.7, 28; not in PTSD) = **vyā°,** q.v., (**1**) *explains*: (praśnāni) °rotu Mv iii.368.2, °rohi 4, °riṣyaṃ 11 (vss); (**2**) *predicts*: viyākṛtu (= °taḥ) LV 222.20 (vs, most mss. vyā°, unmetr.).

viyūbha, hyper-Skt. (§ 2.36) for MIndic **viyūha** = Skt. vyūha, *arrangement*: Vaj., Pargiter ap. Hoernle MR 180.16, see note 9 (corresponds to text of Vaj 27.4; 38.7, 8, where vyūha).

viyūha, m., = **vyūha,** q.v.

viyūhati (MIndic for Skt. vyūhati, but Pali and BHS have evolved a quasi-root yūh-, see **āyūhati, niryūhati,** and Pali saṃyūhati), *arranges*: āyūhantī (q.v.) viyūhantī (pres. pple. f.) Gv 222.15 (prose).

viyūhana, (adj. or) subst. (either to prec., or analogical creation to **vyūha, viyūha** 2, cf. § 22.7), (supernally) *manifesting,* or *manifestation*: dharmadhātugaganaṃ viyūhanam (. . . dharmayānam abhivāhayāhi me) Gv 56.7 (vs).

viyūhā = **vyūhā,** q.v.

viraga, nt., a high number: Mvy 7715; Tib. khrib (khrab) khrib. See s.v. **vināka.**

Viraja (cf. also **Virajas**), (**1**) n. of two former Buddhas in the same list: Mv iii.231.11; 234.6 (prose); (**2**) n. of a former Buddha, of the kṛta age (see 364.6): Laṅk 364.14 (vs; he was of the Kātyāyana gotra); 365.6 (vs); (**3**) nt., °jaṃ, n. of the Buddhakṣetra of the future Buddha **Padmaprabha**: SP 65.8 (prose); in 68.2 (vs) it is called the lokadhātu Virajā (f.), or (v.l.) °jo (m.).

Virajaḥprabha (cf. **Virajaprabha**), n. of a contemporary or future Buddha: Sukh 70.10.

Virajadhvaja, (**1**) n. of a lokadhātu: Suv 169.3, 8 (prose); (**2**) n. of a Bodhisattva: Gv 2.19 (prose).

Virajaprabha (cf. **Virajaḥprabha**), (**1**) n. of a Buddha: Gv 285.2 (vs); (**2**) n. of a Bodhisattva: Gv 3.16.

Virajas, n. of a future Buddha: Gv 441.26. Cf. **Viraja.**

Virajastejaḥsvara, n. of a serpent king: Mvy 3427.

Virajottarajñānin, n. of a Bodhisattva: Gv 2.16.

Virajomaṇḍala, n. of a kalpa: Gv 267.21; 281.21 (in vs, Viraja°, 284.5).

Virajovatī, n. of a lokadhātu: Gv 233.22

[**virañcita,** see **vi-cañcita.**]

viraḍa, adj. (= Skt. virala), *scarce, rare, sparse*: (māra-sena . . .) viraḍīkṛta LV 342.2 (vs).

viralikā (cf. next, and Pkt. virali, *a kind of garment,* Sheth), a sort of thin cloth: Mvy 8985 = Tib. seṅ ras; Chin. (1) *silk,* (2) some other kind of cloth; MSV ii.23.16; 24.10.

viralī = prec.: MSV ii.20.16 f.; 23.15; Tib. seṅ ras.

virahitāt, abl. of ppp. Skt. virahita, used as prep. with gen., *except*: °tād Avalokiteśvarasya Kv 48.14, *except A.*

virāga, nt., var. for **vināka,** q.v.

virāgaṇa, see **a-vi°.**

virāgayati (denom. to virāga; = Pali virāgeti; very rare in Skt.; opp. to, and often used with, **ārāgayati,** q.v.; cf. **a-virāgayati**; Skt. vi-rādh- also approaches this in mg., as Skt. ārādhayati = **ārāg°,** and **saṃrādhayati** resembles **saṃrāg°**), (**1**) *is averse to, offends, displeases* (usually a Buddha, or some worthy entity, acc.): °yati Mvy 2395; opt. °yeyaṃ (with neg.) Divy 23.20; 133.15; 192.16; Av i.287.9 (ms. virāmayeyaṃ); °yema Bbh 271.5; °yi (1 sg. opt.) Bhad 24; ppp. °gita (the object being made into subject nom.) Divy 131.6; 135.20; 233.20; Vaj 35.3 (but Kashgar version, Pargiter ap. Hoernle MR 187.7, virādhitā(ḥ), the 'correct' Skt. equivalent); sā te . . . ārāgayitavyā na virāgayitavyā (gdve.) Bhīk 31b.3; (**2**) *turns away from* = *avoids, gets rid* of (cf. **ārāgayati** in meaning *attains*): tiryagyoniṃ virāgya Av i.291.14; °niṃ virāgayiṣyatha MSV i.58.3; abhidhyāṃ ca virāgayan Av ii.69.9; (**3**) in caus. sense, *makes* (the mind, cittaṃ) *averse* (from, abl.): cittaṃ virāgaya Av i.272.11 (pariṣkārāc); 291.9 (nidhānāc); ppp. without cittaṃ and without dependent, used absolutely, (buddhāḥ) virāgitā(ḥ) RP 59.8 *turned away* (from the world).

viriya (= Pali id.) = Skt. vīrya, *heroism*; only in

vss: viriy' (= vīryam) ārabhante Dbh.g. 13(349).8; °ya 26(52).10.

[**virukta,** LV 426.21, Lefm. with one ms., seems uninterpretable; read vimukti with the other mss. and Calc.: asaṅga-mahājñāna-vimala-vimukti-paṭṭābaddha ity ucyate, *bound with the fillet of salvation*...]

Viruḍhaka, m.c. for **Virūḍhaka,** q.v.

? **viruta,** ppp.-adj., in LV 337.15 (vs) seems to mean *surpassing*; so Tib. ḥdas pa (normally = Skt. ati-kram-): śakyo nāhaṃ tvatsādṛśyair bahubhir api gaṇana-virutair (no v.l.) drumāt praticālituṃ, *I cannot be made to retreat from the Tree* (of enlightenment) *even by many such as you* (Māra), *surpassing count.* The word seems surely corrupt but I have not thought of a good em.; ti-(for ati-) might be read for vi-, but what -ruta represents escapes me; perh. -gata? Foucaux, Notes 182, cites a v.l. viratai.

Virupākṣa, m.c. for **Virūp°,** q.v.

Virūḍha (= Pali Virūḷha) = next: Av i.108.9 (prose); Mmk 654.21 (vs, may be m.c.).

Virūḍhaka, (**1**) (= Pali Virūḷhaka), n. of one of the four 'world-guardians', see s.v. **mahārāja(n)**; guardian of the south, and chief of kumbhāṇḍas; Viru° (m.c.; text °dhaka) Samādh p. 42 line 4; (**2**) n. of a former Buddha: Mv iii.235.9; (**3**) n. of a cakravartin king: Mvy 3597; (**4**) n. of a general (senāpati) of King Prasenajit: Divy 77.27; 466.23; MSV iv.63.7; (**5**) n. of a nāga-king: Māy 247.18, see **Virūpākṣa** (1).

Virūḍhabhūmi, n. of a former Buddha: Mv i.139.2.

virūḍhi, f. (= Pali virūḷhi), *growth, increment*: only in phrase vṛddhiṃ °ḍhiṃ vipulatāṃ, foll. by āpadyate Mvy 7435, by āpāttuṃ Bhīk 23b.5, by gataḥ AsP 129.2.

Virūpa, n. of a householder's son: Av ii.174.3 ff.

Virūpā, n. of a daughter of King Prasenajit: Av ii.52.11 ff. Cf. **Gaṅgarasthā.**

Virūpākṣa (= Pali Virūpakkha), (**1**) n. of one of the 'world-guardians', see s.v. **mahārāja(n)**; Viru° (m.c.) Samādh p. 42 line 4; guardian of the west, and lord of nāgas; doubtless intended by the nāga-king of this name Māy 247.18; (**2**) pl., used (as also in Pali) of nāgas, presumably as followers of Virūpākṣa: Māy 221.15; (**3**) sg., Virūpākṣaḥ (alone!) as final colophon, Sādh 601.4, perhaps meant as name of the author of the last section? (But the usual way in Sādh of indicating authors' names is something like kṛtiḥ plus gen. of the name.)

virecayati (cf. AMg. viregа, *division*; M. vireaṇa, virikka, see Sheth), seemingly *separates* from the religious community, or tries to do so (lit. *purges*, i. e. *gets out, removes*); parallel with **vicchandayati,** q.v.: ŚsP 1185.19 ff.

virocana, (**1**) (= **vairocana** 2; cf. Skt. virocana, Lex. and once in late lit., Schmidt, Nachträge, *fire*; so also AMg. viroyaṇa), a certain gem: kāṃścid °na-maṇiratnāvabhāsān Gv 519.24 (prose); (**2**) n. of a Buddha, perh. the 'transcendent' B. otherwise called **Vairocana** (3): Gv 240.21; 241.10 (vss); (**3**) n. of a former Buddha (prob. not = 2; cf. **Vairocana** 4): LV 171.10 (vs), so Lefm. with ms. A, other mss. and Calc. Vairo° (meter indecisive); (**4**) n. of a yakṣa: Māy 52.

virolayati (Pkt. virolai, ppp. °lia, cf. Skt. vilolita, viloḍayati, Pali viloḷeti), *stirs, agitates*: °layitvā (sc. kṣīraṃ kalaśe) Mmk 711.2 (prose); ppp. °litaḥ Mvy 5339 = Tib. dkrugs pa, bsrubs pa.

vilakṣa, nt., *a million* (= 10 lakṣas, 1/10 koṭi): daśa lakṣā vilakṣaṃ tu vilaksaṃ daśa koṭim Mmk 343.12 (vs, but meter bad at end; also the 2d vilakṣaṃ should be pl.).

vilagnita, ppp. (= Pali vilaggita, Jāt. iv.20.5; to vi plus **lagnati** or **lagneti,** q.v.), *hanging down, pendant*: yathā vṛkṣā °tā Mv ii.266.13 (vs), *as the trees are made pendant* (heavy with fruits), one of the signs of the Bodhisattva's approaching enlightenment.

Vilambā, (**1**) n. of a rākṣasī: SP 400.4 (Burnouf Pralambā, citing a var. Vilambā; two mss. reported in KN as reading first Vilambā, then Pralambā); (**2**) n. of a piśācī: Māy 238.19.

Vilāsendragāminī, n. of a 'gandharva maid': Kv 5.3.

vilīnaka = Skt. vilīna, *melted*: Mv i.8.5 (prose); 12.7 (vs). In ŚsP 1258.7 vilīnaka-(saṃjñā) is a corruption for **vinīlaka-,** q.v.

vilujyati (= Skt. virujyate; cf. s.v. **lujjati**), *is destroyed*: so 'lpapuṇyaḥ vilujyati (so read with Senart's note for viruhyati) Mv ii.423.13 (vs).

[**viluta,** corrupt: citrāntacittā vilutendriyāsi Mv ii.181.13 (vs), addressed to a nāginī; the true reading is indicated by the same vs in Pali, Jāt. iv.459.19, vibbhantacittā kupitindriyāsi; read in Mv vibhrāntacittā kupitendriyāsi.]

vilekha, m. (see **vilekhya**; = Pali vilekha; cf. Skt vilikhati, *wounds*, also fig. *vexes, offends*), *perplexity, mental disturbance, annoyance, perturbation*: Mv iii.140.4 (vs) chindahi saṃśayitāna vilekhaṃ; Śikṣ 98.6 vilekhaṃ vā cittasyotpādayema; Dbh 42.4 dṛṣṭi-kāṅkṣā-vimati-vilekhāpanayana-; Prāt 504.9 bhikṣūṇāṃ kaukṛtyāya vilekhāya vihiṃsanāya (v.l. lekhāya viheṭhāya; is the var. lekhāya to be associated with **ālekhya** or **ālekha,** q.v.?)

vilekhana (nt.?), = prec.: saṃśaya-vimati-°nasamuddharaṇatāyai Gv 491.24 (prose).

vilekhya, m., Mvy 5235 °yaḥ, defined in Tib. and Chin. as *regret* or *impressing on the mind, paying careful heed*; same definition for **ālekhya** (or °**kha**), **vipratisāra,** and **kaukṛtya,** 5234, 5236, 5237. Obviously related to **vilekha,** which is recorded as v.l. in both edd. of Mvy and should perhaps be read for this.

vilepanā (otherwise only °na, nt.), *unguent*: °nāṃ gṛhītvā LV 49.8 and 50.12, both vss, but note that °naṃ is as good metr.; all mss. with text; °nā ca kṣipiṣus LV 282.16 (vs), so Lefm. em., read with ms. A °nāś (other mss. °nāṃś, as if m.).

? **vilepanikā** (corrupt?), acc. to Tib. = stan, *mat, rug, carpet* (for sitting on): (bhikṣuṇā ca sā pāṭayitvā)... °kāyāṃ sīvitā Av i.266.3, *the monk tore it up and sewed it into a rug.*

vilokita, nt., (**1**, as in Skt., *look, gaze*: bhagavāṃ... nāga-°tena vilokayanto Mv iii.281.4; nāga-°tenāvalokya Mvy 6371; see **ālokita-vi°, avalokita, vyavalokita,** and **āryamahāsiṃhavilokita**;) (**2**) fig. (in this mg. = Skt. and Pali vilokana), *consideration, reflection*: (bodhisattvas tuṣitavarabhavanasthitaś catvāri) mahā-°tāni vilokayati sma... kāla-°taṃ dvīpa-°taṃ deśa-°taṃ kula-°taṃ LV 19.7–9, and similarly Mv i.197.10–12; ii.1.1–3 (as to the time, continent, country, and family in which he is to be reborn for the last time).

Vilokitamūrdha, m., n. of a samādhi: Mvy 513; ŚsP 1415.14.

Vilokinī, n. of a goddess: Sādh 75.13.

-vilomana, see **a-vi°.**

vilomayati (= Pali vilometi; cf. **prati-vi°**; in Skt. ppp. vilomita once, BR), *goes contrary to*: MadhK 338.5 bhagavata eva tāvad ete bhāṣitaṃ vilomayanti; Gv 493.3 vilomayanti; Dbh 47.18 a-vilomayan (pres. pple.); Dbh.g. 27(53).3 a-vilomanta (read °mata, m.c.; nom. pl. pres. pple., m.c. for °mayantaḥ; follows anulomayanta); Bcṭ 283.8.

vilohita, nt., (**1**) *blood* (? = Skt. lohita): Śikṣ 81.14 (vs) vṛkkau vilohitaṃ pittaṃ, in a list of parts of the body. The alternative would seem to be to take vi = (a)pi, with Prakritic v. for p; I do not think this likely; (**2**) -saṃjñā = **vilohitaka-,** q.v.: ŚsP 59.8.

vilohitaka, nt. (once **vilohita,** q.v.; = Pali lohitaka), *a bloody corpse*; -saṃjñā, *contemplation of the notion of such a corpse*, one of the **aśubha-bhāvanā,** q.v., or -saṃjñā: Mvy 1160; Bhīk 27a.3; ŚsP 1258.6; 1431.20. Cf. Pali lohita-makkhitaṃ MN i.58.26

vilva, nt., *pool*: Mvy 4172 = Tib. lteṅ ka; placed between taḍāga and utsa.

vivaga, a high number: Gv 105.22; = **vigava**, which prob. read for this.

vivaṭa, adj. (= Pali id., Skt. vivṛta), *open*: gopānasīye antarāṇi °ṭāni Mv ii.125.14; vivaṭāyāṃ vāhanāgāraśālāyāṃ gopānasī-antarāṇi °ṭāni ... pāṃśulikāntarāṇi °ṭāni 127.1 f.; similarly 128.7 ff.; 129.9 ff.; one or both mss. are apt to read vivata, sometimes even vivṛta, in the repetitions of this passage, on which see **gopānasī**; the LV version (254.10) has vivṛta.

vivata, see prec.

vivana, a high number: Gv 105.25; = **vivara** Mvy 7853 (cited from Gv; not in Gv 133).

vivara, (**1**) nt., a fairly high number: Mvy 7853 (= Tib. yal yol), cited from Gv, which in 105.25 has **vivana**, while Gv 133 omits the item; it corresponds to **vipatha** of Mvy 7727; (**2**) m. or nt., a much higher number: °raḥ Mvy 7782, °ram 7911, both = Tib. bsñad yas; the latter cited from Gv but not found in either Gv list (106 or 133); (**3**) by corruption for viṃvara or **bimbara** (q.v.), LV 147.22 (but this is cited from LV in Mvy 7958–9 as viṃvara, and LV itself in 151.3 (vs) has bimbarāś); also SP 409.6 (prose) has in text vivara, intending this same unit as is shown by the preceding **kaṅkara**; vv.ll. of SP quoted as viśvara, visvara, certainly intending viṃvara or bimbara.

vivaraṇa, (**1**) should mean *opening*; so Skt. and Pali; mg. uncertain in sarvāvaraṇa-vivaraṇa-paryutthāna-(q.v.)-vigataḥ Mvy 814, ep. of Bodhisattvas; Tib. sgrib pa (= **āvaraṇa**) daṅ chad pa (must = vivaraṇa) daṅ kun nas ldaṅ ba (= paryutthāna) thams cad (=sarva) daṅ bral ba (= vigata). I should like to render: *free from the opening out and overwhelming* (taking possession) *of the 'obscurations'* (sins); Das gives *to open* ... *to give out* among other mgs. of the confusing word(s) chad pa. But the repeated daṅ in Tib. suggests rather a three-member dvandva. Another meaning of chad pa is *punishment*, but it is hard to see how vivaraṇa could get that mg.; (**2**) (nt.?) a high number: Gv 105.25, = **varaṇa** Mvy 7852 (cited from Gv; not in Gv 133).

[**-vivarcika, see vicarcika.**]

vivarjanā (= Pkt. vivajjaṇā; Skt. only °na, nt.), *riddance, the getting rid* (*of*, abl.): °nā ca (read cā, m.c.; note mss. reading) asārarūpavanāt Mv i.248.3 (vs), *riddance from the worthless-form-jungle.*

vivarṇa, adj. (in this sense hardly recorded exc. in Wilson's Dict.; but cf. vivarṇa-tā pw 7.375), *base, evil, wicked*: duṣṭo °ṇo raudro dāruṇo sāhasiko Mv iii.361.13 (prose; of a wicked king). Cf. next two.

vivarṇaka, adj. or n. ag. (from next; Pali vivaṇṇaka, see below), *speaking* (*one who speaks*) *ill of* ...: bodhisattva-°kānāṃ Gv 228.19; follows (bodhicitta-)vichindikānām, see **vichindika.** Pali vivaṇṇaka in Vin. iv.143.19 said to be noun of action, *dispraise*, but (sikkhāpada-) vivaṇṇake pācittiyaṃ may mean *there is a pācittiya in the case of one who speaks ill of* ...; cf. idaṃ tasmiṃ pācittiyaṃ iv.130.17, *this is in him a p°*, SBE 13.46.

vivarṇayati (cf. prec. two; in mg. 1, opp. of Skt. saṃvarṇayati, = Pali vivaṇṇeti; in mg. 2 denom. from vi-varṇa, in Skt. mg.), (**1**) *speaks ill of, depreciates*: saṃvarṇitaḥ samyaktvaniyato rāśir, vivarṇito mithyātvaniyato rāśiḥ (see **rāśi**) LV 351.9; sarvabuddha-°ṇito hy ayaṃ upadeśaḥ, yad-uta kāmaniṣevaṇaṃ Śikṣ 281.12; (atra kiṃcit) saṃvarṇayitavyaṃ kiṃcid vivarṇayitavyam iti viditvā Divy 263.13; (**2**) *discolors*: upariṣṭād °ṇayet (sc. cloth for a monk's robe), nīlakardama-gomayaiḥ Laṅk 363.9 (vs); yācñābhitāpena °ṇitāni (*grown pale*, Speyer) ... arthimukhāni Jm 24.21 (vs).

vivarta (m.? to **vivartati** 2), with or sc. kalpa, (*period of*) *evolution* of the world, after a periodic destruction (**saṃvarta**); so Pali vivaṭṭa and saṃvaṭṭa (misdefined PTSD, which precisely inverts the mgs.; Childers is correct; see notably Vism. 419.29 ff. which is completely clear, and consistent with BHS); °ta-kalpaḥ Mvy 8280, saṃvarta-k° 8279; caturaśīti-saṃvartavivarta-sthito Mv i.63.6, (the Lord) *abides thru 84 periods of destruction and* (new) *evolution* (see passage s.v. **vivartati** 2); yāvat saṃvartakalpam api vivartakalpam api saṃvarta-vivartakalpam api anekāny api saṃvartavivartakalpāny anusmarati sma (sc. the Buddha) LV 345.11–12; similarly Mv i.229.1 ff.; ii.284.10 ff.; and substantially ii.133.1–2, where mss. are more confused, one (followed by Senart) anekāpi saṃvartakalpā vā anekāpi saṃvartā anekāpi vivartā anekāpi saṃvartavivartakalpā (the other ms. always -kalpā after vi° and saṃ°); saṃvarta (v.l. °taṃ) ca vivarta (v.l. °taṃ; so mss.) ca aśītiṃ tena karmaṇā (a virtuous act), durgatiṃ nopalabhate ... Mv i.268.8 (vs); saṃvartavivartaṃ ... prajānāti Bbh 253.14; saṃvarta-vivartakalpān avataranti (2d ed. correctly °rati) sma Gv 277.25; cf. AbhidhK. LaV-P. iii.181 ff. (et al., Index). In Mv i.63.13 vivarta-caryā is used only in an attempt to explain **avivarta-caryā**, q.v.

vivartati, °te, (**1**) (cf. Skt., BR vart- with vi- 2), *falls back, backslides*, esp. of a Bodhisattva, from one bhūmi to a lower one: Mv i.77.4; 79.9 ff., 80.1; 89.9 ff.; 90.6 ff.; 96.2 ff.; 110.5; 120.6 ff.; 127.2 ff.; contrary to Senart, note on i.77.4, there is no record of **saṃvartati** in a sense opposite to this (saṃvartante 77.5 is Senart's em. and his Index has no other ref.); (**2**) (cf. similar use in Skt., BR vart- with vi- 4) *evolves*, said of the periodic evolution afresh of the world after a period of dissolution; opp. **saṃvartati, °te** (1), *devolves, comes to dissolution*; Pali in same mgs. vivaṭṭati, saṃvaṭṭati: so bhagavāṃ caturaśītihi śrāvakasahasrehi (Senart adds sārdhaṃ) caturaśītisaṃvarta-vivarta-sthito; saṃvartamāne loke bhagavāñ caturaśītihi śrāvakasahasrehi sārdhaṃ ābhāsvaraṃ devanikāyaṃ gacchati, vivartamāne loke ihāgacchati iha dharmaṃ deśayati Mv i.63.5–8; (ayaṃ loko ...) saṃvartati, saṃvartamāne ca ... loke yobhūyena sattvā ābhāsvare devanikāye upapadyanti; bhavati ... sa samayo yad ayaṃ loko ... vivartati, vivartamāne ... loke saṃsthite lokasaṃniveśe (mss. °sthito °veśo, may be kept) anyatarā sattvā ... ābhāsvarāto devanikāyāto cyavitvā icchatvam (see **itthatva**) āgacchanti Mv i.338.14–18; saṃvartamāne khalu loke sarvaprathamaṃ pṛthivīpradeśo uddahyati vivartamāne ca ... loke sarvaprathamaṃ pṛthivīpradeśo saṃsthihati Mv ii.262.11–13; bhavati ... sa samayo yadāyaṃ lokaḥ saṃvartate (*is destroyed*; Bendall and Rouse, *comes together!*); tadeyaṃ mahāpṛthivī agninā vā dahyate ... Śikṣ 246.7; vivartamāne ... loke ... abhragaṇāḥ saṃtiṣṭhante ... 247.5; contrast, saṃvartamāne khalu punar loke 247.10. See **vivarta, vivartanī(ya).**

vivartana, nt., *chapter*, or *treatise*: (asti Mañjuśrīḥ tvadīya-) kalpa-visare (*in the abundance of thy books of rules?*) śabdagaṇanānirdeśaṃ nāma vivartanaṃ Mmk 253.4; in line 10 it is called a **dharmaparyāya.**

vivartanī (to **vivartati**, 2), *evolution, development*, opp. **saṃvartanī** (1) q.v.: AbhidhK. (vyākhyā) LaV-P. iii.181 note 3 (**bhājana-** and sattva-vi°), see Wogihara, Lex. 38.

vivartanīya, adj. or subst.? (= prec., or adj. of corresp. mg.), (*of*) *new evolution* of the world, after periodic destruction: °ya-kāla-samaye Mv i.52.6; for similar passage i.338.14 ff. (where vivartamāne loke replaces this phrase) see s.v. **vivartati** (2).

vivartiya, vivartya (cf. **vivartati** 1), *liable to turning back, to backsliding*, formed as pendant to **a-vi°**, q.v.: LV 392.2 no vivartyāḥ (together = **a-viv°**); Mv i.80.4 (prose) vivartiyāś ca avivartiyāś ca, as two classes of Bodhisattva in the 2d bhūmi (an early stage); in Gv 244.12 for (a)kṣobhyavivartyavīryatāṃ read with 2d ed. akṣobhyāv° (i. e. avivartya-).

vivardhayitar (n. ag. to Skt. vivardhayati), *increaser, one who causes to grow*: °tāraḥ bodhicittasya (kalyāṇamitrāṇi) Gv 463.2.

vivarya, nt., a high number: Mvy 7856 = Tib. (ḥ)khrul yas; = **viparya,** q.v.

vi-vahati, intrans. (with mg. of Skt. passive), *strays away, is distracted*: (te tejograstās tatra-)tatrāśu pratipadyante na °hanti na viceṣṭante akriyāyai Bbh 31.11.

vivācayati, (?) **vipācayati** (= Pali vipāceti), *grumbles, makes disapproving remarks*: °yanti Mvy 2643 (= Tib. kha zer ba, acc. to Das = mukhara, *loquacious*, but Lex. also *abusive*); Divy 492.17; MSV i.44.16; 236.13; °yati Mvy 9360, but here Mironov **vipācayati** (= Pali), and Tib. rnam par smod pa, *speaks abusively*; always the third of a series of near-synonyms, avadhyāyati (Skt.) and kṣipati (Skt.; in Divy **dhriyati,** in Mv perhaps **kṣīyati,** q.v., in a similar context) being the others; in Pali, ujjhāyati khīyati vipāceti. Orig. form not clear; if it was vipāc°, what etym.? Yet vivāc° looks like a lect. fac., and is not really a natural form (caus. to vi-vac-?); the occurrence of vipāc- in Mironov also makes one doubtful. Perhaps vipācayati was a bit of ancient slang: *gets* (one) *cooked = reviles.*

vivādaka, m. (to Skt. vivāda, °dayati; Pali id., *one who quarrels*), either *quarrelsome person* (as Pali), or (= Skt. °da plus -ka svārthe) *quarrel*: no bhuyo (m.c. for bhūyo) puravarasmi dehināṃ lobhadoṣakalahā vivādakā (several mss. °da-tā) LV 54.9 (vs), ... *no disputes due to greed or hatred, no quarrelers* (or *quarrels*).

vivādayati (not recorded in this sense), *rebukes, reviles*, or the like: Śikṣ 13.1 devatā uccagghanti vivādayanti (a Bodhisattva who fails in his duty).

[**vivādika-saṃjñā** ŚsP 1258.7, read **vikhāditaka°**, q.v.]

vivāha, (**1**) m. (= Pali id., see PTSD s.v.), *giving in marriage*, see s.v. **āvāha**; (**2**) m. or nt., a moderately high number, commonly about 100 **akṣobhya** (so LV): m., always in Mvy, 7722; 7848 (cited from Gv); 7960 (cited from LV); 8010; Sukh 31.1; Mmk 343.17 (read vi-vāhas); nt., LV 148.1; Gv 133.6 (105.24 gen. °hasya); Mmk 262.14.

vi-vipāta, adj. (vi plus vipāta, Skt. Gr., to Skt. vi-pat-, *depart, fall away, become separated*), *without quitting*: °tena (so with v.l. for Senart vinipātena) nāgarājena ... parikṣiptā (mss.; read °to? sc. the Buddha), parikṣipi hi mahatā paribhogena saptāhaṃ Mv iii.301.6. Senart (Index) app. takes Vinipāta as n. pr. of the nāga-king who 'encompassed' and protected the Buddha. But his name has just been given (line 4) as **Mucilinda**; no second nāga can be concerned; vinipātena makes no sense.

Vivṛtā, n. of a lokadhātu: Kv 90.5.

viveka, m., (**1**) (= Pali id., e. g. Vism. 140.17 ff.) *separation, aloofness* (from sin): rāgadveṣamoha-vivekakuśalamūlāś ca bhavanti Mv i.134.3 (prose); (**2**) (= Pali id.) *solitude, seclusion* (of life): ete ... vivekārāmā vivekābhiratāḥ; naite kulaputrā devamanuṣyān upaniśrāya viharanty asaṃsargacaryābhiratāḥ SP 309.10–11 (rightly Kern, wrongly Burnouf); sukho vivekas tuṣṭasya LV 380.16 (vs), Tib. dben pa; atyabhīkṣṇaṃ vivekaṃ sevanti Mv i.96.6, of backsliding Bodhisattvas, *they devote themselves too earnestly to solitude* (which violates the Bodhisattva ideal); vivekādayaḥ Mvy 2987 = Tib. dben paḥi rnam paḥi miṅ la, *names for varieties of solitude* (list includes prānta, araṇya, etc.); °kam anubṛṃhayet Ud xiii.6 = Pali Dhp. 75 °kam anubrūhaye; saṃgaṇikayāpi vivekagocaraḥ Śikṣ 202.20, *even with a crowd, he ranges in solitude.*

vivecayati (= Pali viveceti), *causes* (one) *to abandon* (abl.), *dissuades* (from): Vaideharājaṃ dānāto viveceti Mv iii.42.16 (prose), *dissuades from giving*; piśunavacanād °cayati Gv 155.16.

[**viveṣṭati,** read viceṣṭ°, *wallows, writhes* (so Skt.); on confusion of c and v, Senart, i, Introd. p. xii: uttheṣyaṃ (so with v.l. for utthehiṣyaṃ) ti patanti patitā mahīyaṃ viveṣṭanti (read vice°) Mv iii.83.15.]

viśada, adj. (in this sense not recorded elsewhere), *abundant, extensive*, syn. prabhūta: °dam, nt. Mvy 9565 (so Tib., rgya che ba, and Chin., *broad, far-reaching, abundant*); Bbh 379.19 prabhūtenotsadena viśadenānnapānena; contrast alpa, Bbh 122.6 (of gifts) alpād api viśadaṃ dadāti, *even for a slight (gift) he gives a great one*; Bbh 185.5 viśadam, Tib. rgya che ba; perhaps Bbh 4.21 viśadaṃ ca dānam anuprayacchati na hīnam (but here possibly *pure, distinguished*).

viśalyī-kṛta, ppp. (Skt. viśalya plus kṛ-), *made free from an arrow(-shot)*: (tatas tena) °kṛta upanāho (*a poultice*) datta uktaś ca Divy 583.18.

Viśākha, (**1**) n. of a deer-prince (= Pali Sākha, in the Nigrodha-Jātaka): Mv i.359.19 ff.; (**2**) n. of a son of **Mṛgāra**, who married **Viśākhā**: MSV ii.53.4.

Viśākhadeva, n. of a Bodhisattva: Gv 442.15.

Viśākhā, (**1**) n. of the 'woman-jewel' of King Śaṅkha: Dvy 61.18; (**2**) n. of Śākyamuni's leading female lay-disciple, called **Mṛgāramātar,** q.v. (= Pali Visākhā Migāramātā): Divy 77.28; 466.24; Av i.224.3; ii.9.7; Karmav 87.15; 97.3 (in 97.3 spelled **Viśākhyā**); MSV ii.53.16 ff. (her story in full, different in many ways from the Pali).

viśāta, also **visāta,** adj. or subst. nt. (neg. of **śāta,** q.v.; oftener **a-śāta,** q.v.), *unpleasant, offensive*: °tam, opp. to śātam, Mvy 1883; Dharmas 34 (here spelled sātam and visātam). Perhaps understood as n. in both cases, *the unpleasant, unpleasantness.*

Viśāṃpati, n. of an emperor, former incarnation of Mañjuśrī: Gv 254.10, 260.18, 20.

viśāra, m. or nt., a high number: Gv 106.1 (read viśāla?); not in parallels.

viśārada, also **viśālada,** q.v., adj. (doubtless specialized or developed mg. of Skt. id., but hardly used in Skt. in this sense; = Pali visā°; see also **śāradya**), *confident, sure of oneself, fearless* (Tib. regularly mi ḥjigs pa, *fearless*): Mvy 1820, in list of 'synonyms of abhaya'; regularly ep. of a Buddha or Bodhisattva; caturhi vaiśāradyehi °da, caturvaiśāradya-°da, and the like, see s.v. **vaiśāradya**; sometimes with near-synonyms, as anolīno SP 278.9; others (of Bu. or Bodhis.) SP 57.9; 59.2; Mv ii.302.17; in SP 70.6 (vs) ep. of Śāriputra (it may be significant that Buddhahood has just been predicted for him); so in LV 358.18 (vs) °dāḥ, of persons saved by the Buddha (next line says of them, mokṣyante ca laghuṃ sarve); but in LV 377.13 (prose) of monks whom Buddha is going to convert, sthavirā bhikṣavo bhaviṣyanti dāntā ... °radā bahuśrutā etc. (but not Buddhas!); LV 25.11, see **viśālada,** and cf. Divy 617.15 s.v. **vaiśāradya.** In a less technical sense, of monks, Karmav 105.6–10 (relating to standard monkish behavior, *with confidence*); see **vaiśāradya,** end.

viśāradya, = (and only m.c. for?) **vaiś°**: bhavān viśāradyabalaiḥ (v.l. vaiś°, unmetr.; best mss. viś°) samanvitaḥ LV 399.2 (vs), of the Bodhisattva.

viśārayati (unrecorded; caus. to Skt. viśīryate), *destroys*: viśāritā śalyā LV 351.6 (prose), so Lefm.; mss. °tā, °taḥ, or vibhāvitā, and śalya or mānaśalya; followed by mukto granthiḥ, a separate clause. The state of the Buddha after enlightenment is described.

viśālada, adj. = **viśārada**: of the young Bodhisattva, about to proclaim his supremacy among men, LV 93.16 (vs); of the Bodhisattva's mother, °dāyā(ḥ) LV 25.11 (prose).

Viśālanetra, n. of a Bodhisattva: Mvy 678.

Viśālaprabha, n. of a former Buddha: Mv i.139.14.

Viśālabuddhi, n. of a Bodhisattva: Gv 4.14.

viśālā = (Skt.) tṛṣṇā: Dharmasamuccaya (unpublished BHS work) 5.23 and 32, acc. to Renou, JA Jul.–

Sept. 1939, p. 336, n. 1; see s.v. **jālinī**. (Renou kindly informs me in a letter of May 16, 1945, that his reference to Abhidharmakośa, Index, was an error.)

Viśālākṣa, (1) n. of a disciple of Buddha: Mv i.183.1; (2) n. of a yakṣa: Māy 51.

vi-śikhin, *without fire*: (in a magic formula; ... devebhyo manuṣyebhyo gandharvebhyaḥ) śikhigrahād evā (!) viśikhigrahād evā (!) Ānandasyāgamanāya ... juhomi Divy 612.19; so printed; read surely śikhigrahā devā viśikhigrahā devā(ḥ); these are vocs. pl.; śikhi- = *fire*, viśikhi- = *fireless, without fire*; does graha mean *planet*? *cup*? *seizure*? or what? At any rate, some 'gods' are addressed.

viśiṣṭa, (1) m. or nt., a high number: m. Mvy 7735; nt. Mvy 7863, cited from Gv 133.11; = Tib. bstan (brtan) yas; in Gv 106.1 **vimṛṣṭa**(sya, gen.), by error (m for ś, graphic); (2) m., n. of a Bodhisattva: Gv 442.18.

Viśiṣṭacandra, n. of a Bodhisattva: Gv 442.25.

Viśiṣṭacāritra, n. of a Bodhisattva: SP 300.12; 387.4 f.; 390.11; 425.5; 487.3.

Viśuddha, n. of a Śuddhāvāsakāyika deity: Mmk 71.23; see s.v. **Śuddha**.

Viśuddhacāritra, n. of a Bodhisattva: SP 300.13.

Viśuddhacārin, n. of a Buddhist monk: Gv 47.9.

Viśuddhanandin, n. of a Bodhisattva: Gv 442.10.

Viśuddhanetrābhā, n. of a goddess of night: Gv 233.23.

Viśuddhabuddhi, n. of a Bodhisattva: Gv 4.13.

Viśuddhamati, (1) n. of a monk in Śākyamuni's order: Mv ii.293.17; 294.6; 397.5; (2) n. of a Bodhisattva: Gv 442.11.

Viśuddhaviṣayajyotirvikaraṇa(read °kiraṇa-?)**vidhvaṃsinī**, n. of a samādhi: Mmk 1.19.

Viśuddhasvaranirghoṣā, n. of a Bodhisattvadhāraṇī: Mvy 749.

Viśuddhinetra, n. of a Bodhisattva: Gv 3.1.

viśeṣa-gamana (nt.), = **viśeṣādhigama**, q.v.: °nākāraṃ (sc. śruta-praveśam) Śikṣ 191.2.

viśeṣa-gāmitā = prec.: Śikṣ 191.9; 316.5 ff.; KP 6.2, 11.

Viśeṣagāmin, n. of a former incarnation of Śākyamuni: LV 171.1.

viśeṣaṇa, m. (recorded only as nt.), *distinction, distinguishing trait*: (yasmāc ca jāter na) viśeṣaṇo 'sti tasmān na vai varṇacatuṣka eva Divy 630.11 (vs, printed as prose; °ṣaṇam asti would be unmetr.), *and since there is no distinction of birth, therefore the four castes simply do not exist.*

Viśeṣamati, (1) n. of one of sixteen **satpuruṣa** (q.v.): SP 3.12; (2) n. of one of the sons of the Buddha Candrasūryapradīpa: SP 19.4; (3) n. of a Bodhisattva: RP 2.1.

Viśeṣamitra, n. of a teacher: Mvy 3509.

viśeṣayati (see BR s.v. śiṣ- plus vi-, caus.; not quite the same mgs.), *tests, examines* (for proficiency): in LV 145.21 (prose) acc. to Tib. *vies, contends*, (śākyakumārā ... bodhisattvena) sārdhaṃ lipiṃ viśeṣayanti sma, Tib. yi ge ḥgran to, *vied, contended* (about) *writing*; but perhaps better, *tested* (skill in) *writing*, as in the next two; viśiṣyatāṃ tāvat kumāro lipijñāne, saṃkhyājñāne kumāro viśeṣayitavyo jijñāsyaś ca LV 146.8–9, *let it be granted that the prince is superior in knowledge of writing; let him be tested for proficiency and examined in numbers* (Tib. for the two gdves. khyad par ci yod ḥgran par bya-ḥo); yuddhena tāvat kumāro viśeṣayitavyo jijñāsyaś ca 152.8 (Tib. for gdves. khyad par ci yod pa ḥaṅ saḍ par bya-ḥo; sad pa = *try, test*).

viśeṣādhigama (m., = Pali visesā°, see Childers s.v. viseso), *'specific attainment'*, grasping one thought so intently that dhyāna is attained: asaṃprāpte °game (in a caramabhavika sattva, death is impossible then) Divy 174.1. In BHS also called **viśeṣa-gamana** and **-gāmitā**, qq.v.

Viśeṣodgata, n. of a Bodhisattva: Gv 3.25.

viśodha, nt., a high number: Gv 133.6; see s.v. **visoda**.

viśodhaka (= AMg. visohaya; Skt. viśodhayati plus -aka), *purifying, one who purifies*: °kāni ... kalyāṇamitrāṇy āvaraṇīyānām Gv 462.19; (uttarottara-) °ko 'yaṃ ... mārgo Laṅk 10.17; in su-vi° and dur-vi°, adj. Bhvr., like Pali dubbisodha (PTSD s.v. visodha), *easy* (*hard*) *to purify*; in view of su-**vijñāpaka** (q.v.), used in the same context, the lit. mg. seems to be *well* (*ill*) *taking* (i. e. subject to, controllable by) *a purifier* (were it not for the clear mg. of **vijñāpaka**, n. ag., we might interpret -viśodha plus -ka, *having good, or bad, purification*): (kaccid bhagavan sattvāḥ svākārāḥ suvijñāpakāḥ) suvineyāḥ suviśodhakā(ḥ)? mā haiva bhagavataḥ khedam utpādayanti? SP 301.2 (to a Buddha), *I hope, Lord, your creatures are of good character ('form'), easily instructed, ... easily purified, and do not cause you trouble?* the answer, line 10, repeats the epithets, ending (line 11) na ca me khedaṃ janayanti viśodhyamānāḥ, *and cause me no trouble in being purified*; note also the gdve. su-vineyāḥ, *easily disciplined*, in the context; it is impossible to understand **-vijñāpaka** and -viśodhaka here as karmadhārayas, *well instructing* and *well purifying*; in this way, therefore, we must also interpret: (sattvān ... svākārān) suviśodhakān durākārān durviśodhakān LV 400.1; (katamaḥ sattvaḥ śuddhaḥ svākāraḥ) suvineyaḥ suvijñāpakaḥ suviśodhako ... LV 403.5 (repeated in essence 9 and 404.8); Tib. seems to support this, go sla ba (= su-vijñāp°, *facile à instruire*, Foucaux), sbyaṅ sla ba (*facile à purifier*).

viśodhayitar, *one who purifies*: °tāraḥ prajñācakṣuṣo (kalyāṇamitrāṇi) Gv 463.1.

viśodheya, anomalous gdve. of Skt. viśodhayati (see § 34.24), *purifiable*: adrākṣīt sattvā durākārā durvineyā dur-viśodheyā adrākṣīt sattvā svākārāṃ suvineyāṃ su-viśodheyāṃ (v.l. °yā) Mv iii.318.2–3. Obviously influenced in form by -vineya preceding.

viśrambhika, adj. (AMg. vissambhiya; to Skt. °bha plus -ika), *trusting, confident*: SP 107.7, Kashgar rec. visra°, for ed. viśrabdho.

Viśravaṇa = Skt. Vai° (Pali Vessavaṇa), *Kubera*: °ṇam iva yakṣagaṇair Divy 621.24.

[**viśrātas** (gen. °taso), a high number: Gv 105.23 (= **visoda, viśodha**, qq.v.); but read with 2d ed. **visrotas**, or viś°.]

[**viśrāmayati**, as pw (s.v.) says, error for viśrāṇayati, *presents*, in LV 141.16 dārikābhyo viśrāmayiṣyati (so both edd., no v.l.).]

Viśrutaśrī, n. of a king, previous incarnation of Buddha: RP 25.4.

viśreṇayati, see next.

viśreṇī-kṛtvā, **°ṇī-bhūta**, also **niḥśreṇī-bhūta** (neg. cpd., vi- or niś- plus Skt. śreṇi, *association, company*), *having made* (outside things) *void of association* (with oneself), or, *having become void of association* (with them); **viśreṇayitvā** also replaces viśreṇīkṛtvā once, implying denom. viśreṇayati, to vi-śreṇi; the Pali is viseneti, SN iii.89.23 (ariyasāvako ...) pajahati na upādiyati, viseneti no usseneti (*dissociates from himself, gets rid of, does not accumulate or associate with himself*; object, the khandhas); in BHS only in forms of a vs (occurring also twice in Pali and once in the Dutreuil 'Prakrit Dhammapada', see LaV-P. on Ud xxxii.19, but none of these versions contain our word) which is found twice in Ud, xi.12 and xxxii.19, and once in Mv iii.422.14–15: yas tu puṇyaṃ ca pāpaṃ ca (Mv yo ca kāmāṃ ca pāpāṃ ca) prahāya (oldest ms. in Ud xi.12 vāhetvā, as bāh° in same vs in Pali, Dhp. 267; Mv (a)dhikṛtvā, read dhikkṛtvā?) brahmacaryavān, viśreṇīkṛtvā (so oldest ms. Ud xi.12, later ms. viśreṇayitvā,

Ud xxxii.19 viśreṇībhūtaś, Mv niḥśreṇībhūto) carati (Mv saprajño) sa vai sthero ti (so oldest ms. Ud xi.12, later ms. sthavira; Mv bhikṣū ti; Ud xxxii.19 bhikṣur nir-) ucyate (Mv vuccati), *whoever abandoning good* (Mv *desires*) *and evil, living in chastity, dissociated, he verily is called an elder* (*monk*).

viśva, *all*; this essentially Vedic word, occasionally used in Class. Skt., is also occasionally found here: mohitā viśva-kalpanaiḥ Laṅk 9.5 (vs); viśva-kamala-śara-kapāla-cāpa-dharām Sādh 460.5 (prose).

Viśvaḍākinī, n. of a yoginī: Sādh 460.5.

Viśvaṃtara, m., (**1**) epithet of Buddha: Mvy 32; (**2**) (= Pali Vessantara), n. of a prince, previous incarnation of the Buddha: Jm 52.9 ff.

Viśvapadmā, n. of a goddess: Sādh 76.2.

Viśvabhuj = next: °bhuk, n. sg., Mvy 89 = Tib. kun (*all*, = thams cad, see next) skyobs; Mmk 68.27; 397.12 (in list of '7 Buddhas'); contrast Mmk 426.9, next.

Viśvabhū, also, more rarely, °**bhuj** (= Pali Vessabhū), n. of a former Buddha, regularly third of the 'seven **Tathāgata**' (q.v. for refs.), immediate predecessor of **Krakucchanda**; Tib. on LV 5.15 (°bhuvā, instr.) thams cad (*all*) skyobs (*help*, which hardly renders either -bhū or -bhuj): Mv i.294.19; iii.240.7 f.; 243.15; 244.6; 246.8 (°bhuvasya, gen., mss.); 247.10; 249.5; Kv 24.14; Mmk 426.9 (prose; °bhuvā, instr.); Gv 206.12.

Viśvamātā, n. of a goddess (form of Tārā): Sādh 240.1, 14.

Viśvamitra (the Pali parallel, DN ii.257.1 has pl. Vessāmittā pañcasatā yakkhā . . .; the sg. Vessāmitto is a yakkha-leader DN iii.205.2), n. of a yakṣa: °traḥ pañcaśato viśvadevo (are these two epithets of V°, or other names?) maharddhikaḥ Mahāsamāj. Waldschmidt, Kl. Skt. Texte 4, 167.32. Cf. **Viśvāmitra**, the usual Skt. form.

Viśvavajrā, n. of a goddess: Sādh 76.3.

Viśvavarṇa, n. of a Bodhisattva: Gv 443.6.

Viśvāmitra, (**1**) n. of a teacher of writing in the school attended by the Bodhisattva: LV 124.9; 145.21; 146.2; Gv 447.20; 448.2, 9; (**2**) n. of a Bodhisattva: Gv 442.23; (**3**) n. of a ṛṣi (= Skt. id.?): Divy 321.4. Cf. **Viśvamitra**.

viṣakti (once in Skt., Schmidt, Nachträge; to Skt. vi-sañj-, viṣajjate, viṣakta), *attachment* (= next): kāya-°tiḥ kāyādhyavasānaṃ (and other synonyms) Av ii.191.7, *attachment to the body*.

viṣaktikā (= Pali visattikā) = prec.: tarataitāṃ °tikāṃ Ud iii.14 (= Pali Sn 333 visattikaṃ); (visaktikā) 15; (kālenottarate °tikām) xv.4 (= Pali Ud. vii.8); xvi.6; yasya jālinī °tikā tṛṣṇā xxix.64(55).

viṣaṭa, adj. (= Pkt. visaḍa, visaḍha, = Skt. viṣama, see Hem. 1.241; Deśīn. 7.62; and Sheth), *hard, difficult, oppressive*: pañca-viṣaṭa-bandhanāṃ kāraṇāṃ kārayanti (viz. in hell) Divy 376.12. (Etym.?)

viṣaṇṇa (ppp. of Skt. viṣīdati, in specialized mg.), *incapable, unskilled* (in, loc.): so 'haṃ tīrthikasādhāraṇāyāṃ ṛddhyāṃ viṣaṇṇaḥ Divy 44.18. (Text continues: tena vīryam āsthāya ṛddhim utpādya . . .)

viṣamatā, a high number: Gv 106.6. Precedes **samatā**, q.v., and seems to have been invented to match it; not in Gv 133.16 nor the Mvy version of this list.

viṣaya (= Skt.), *range, sphere*; on two somewhat dubious uses of the word in Laṅk 2.7 and 13 see s.vv. **pratyātma** and **ālayavijñāna**.

Viṣayatīrṇa, m., n. of a samādhi: Mvy 581; ŚsP 1421.21.

viṣūcita, adj. (a sort of denom. pple. to Skt. viṣūcikā), *afflicted with purging in both directions*: °taḥ kālagataḥ MSV ii.118.10; 144.13; °taḥ iii.137.5.

viṣkadya, ger. of Skt. Gr. vi-ṣkand- (Pāṇ. 8.3.73; not recorded in genuine literature), *moving rapidly, with quick motion, quickly passing* (from one stage to another), substantially = *quickly*: (bodhisattvāḥ . . . samādhi-)samāpattiś ca viṣkadya samāpadyante ŚsP 273.17.

viṣkambhaṇa, also written °**na**, and °**na-tā**, nt. (to next; = Pali vikkhambhana, of the nīvaraṇa), (**1**) *something that holds fast, immobilizes*, esp. a gag or prop holding the mouth open and immovable: Mv i.8.2; Divy 375.10 (see **viṣkambhate** 1); (vadana-)viṣkambhaṇa-kāṣṭham Jm 237.2, *the stick of wood which held* (*open*) *the* (lion's) *mouth*; (**2**) *blocking, suppression*, of nīvaraṇa and other evils: °nam Mvy 2551 = Tib. rnam par (= vi) gnon pa (*suppression*) or sel ba (*removal, blotting out*); nīvaraṇānāṃ viṣkambhana-tā Śikṣ 191.7; paryutthāna-vi° Śikṣ 50.8; Samādh p. 5 line 1 (see **paryutthāna**).

viṣkambhate, °**bhayati** (= Pali vikkhambheti; in Skt. essentially Vedic, replaced in Cl. by vi-ṣṭambh-; and only partly in these mgs.), (**1**) primarily, *makes fast, fixes firmly*: kim ity aham ato siṃhaviṣkambhitena (see this) viṣkambhayeyam (text viklambh- both times for viṣkambh-; or possibly for MIndic vikkhambh-?) ŚsP 110.19, *shall I then make* (sc. creatures) *firm with lion's firmness*?; used of holding the mouth open, as with a gag (cf. prec.), tato sānaṃ (sc. of the damned in hell) naraka-pālāḥ ayo-viṣkambhanebhi mukhaṃ viṣkambhayitvā Mv i.8.(2–)3; (tatas te, sc. yama-puruṣāḥ, taptāyoguḍā) mukhe (sc. of the damned) viṣkambhante (*prop, fix*), dahyante, teṣām oṣṭham (so read for text īṣṭam, cf. Divy 375.13) api dantāni viśīryante Kv 37.6; (ayomayena viṣkambhanena) mukha-dvāraṃ viṣkambhya Divy 375.(10–)11, 18 (also of the damned); (**2**) *blocks, suppresses*, esp. the hindrances (**nīvaraṇāni**; so also in Pali): (pañca nīvaraṇāni) viṣkambhitāni Mv i.148.1; (**3**) lit. *blocks, stops*, and so *completely fills* or *covers* (so Skt. viṣṭambhita, BR s.v. stabh with vi, caus., 2 b): Māyā ca devī . . . vividhābharaṇa-viṣkambhita-bhujā LV 41.8 (prose; only v.l. viṣkabhita), *her arms completely covered with various ornaments*; Tib. śin tu rgyan te, *being well ornamented*; Foucaux *couvert*, on Skt. and Tib.

viṣkambhita, see prec.; cf. **siṃha-vi°**.

viṣkambhin (cf. **viṣkambhayati** 2), *blocking, suppressing*, (**1**) in **Sarva-nīvaraṇa-viṣkambhin**, q.v.; (**2**) Viṣkambhin, n. of a Bodhisattva: Sādh 50.1.

viṣṭi, (m. or) f., °ṭiḥ Mvy 4397, *comet* acc. to Tib., ḥjug (mjug) phod; note mjug phod can, *having a tail*, acc. to Das *comet*; in a list of prodigies and omens.

viṣṭhapana, semi-Sktized form of **viṭhapana**, q.v. for the passage Gv 524.1 (text corruptly a-vi°).

viṣṭhā? in Divy 274.22, acc. to Index *rope* (i. e. *lasso*), but all that is clear is that it is some means of catching and holding: nedaṃ kenacid viṣṭhayā vā śiṭayā (see **śiṭā**) vā karkaṭakena vā gṛhītavyam. Possibly read ciṣṭhayā or ciṣṭayā = AMg. ciṭṭhā, with MIndic i for e, = Skt. ceṣṭā, *with movements* (of the hands, etc.); but this is naturally doubtful.

viṣṭhihati (see § 1.93; Chap. 43, s.v. sthā 7; = Skt. vi-tiṣṭhati, BR s.v. 3), *pauses, stops*: Mvy 6821 (Mironov wrongly viṣṭhirati) = Tib. ḥgyur, or thogs, or sdod, or ḥchad pa; nāntarā tiṣṭhati na viṣṭhihati Śikṣ 18.6 (prose; so read with ms., ed. wrongly em., Tib. cited as gcod pa, *pause*); kṛtvā asaṃgatam upeti a-viṣṭhihantā Dbh.g. 4(340).8.

Viṣṇu, (**1**) n. (i. e. prob. an element in the compound name) of a large group of kings: prabhanāmā sahasrāṇi viṣṇunāmā tathaiva ca Mmk 625.24 (vs), *thousands with names containing prabha, and also containing Viṣṇu*; in 26 a single one of them, perhaps referred to as named Viṣṇu, simply: teṣām apaścimo rājā viṣṇunāmā bhaviṣyati; (**2**) n. of a yakṣa leader: Māy 235.31.

Viṣṇudvīpa (Pali Veṭhadīpa), n. of a region; °**pīyaka**, adj., *of* that place: °pīyakā brāhmaṇā °pe MPS 51.12.

Viṣṇulā, n. of a rākṣasī: Māy 240.7.

visaṃyuta, ppp. (to Skt. [saṃ-]yu-; only at end of

anuṣṭubh lines, and doubtless m.c. for Skt. visaṃyukta), *disjoined, disconnected* (*from*, instr. or in cpd.): paryutthānair °tāḥ Laṅk 135.10; 321.14; vikalpena °tam 284.10; svalakṣaṇa-°tā 317.14.

visaṃyoga, m. (= Pali id.), *dissociation, severance*: °gaḥ Mvy 2568, among synonyms of nisṛjā, (religious) *abandonment* (of worldly things); (asmākaṃ devena sārdhaṃ nānābhāvo bhaviṣyati vinābhāvo viprayogo) °yoga iti viditvā Divy 323.29; (saṃyogāt) saṃskṛtaṃ pravartate, °gān na pravartate Dbh 52.16; (sarvakleśā-)tyanta-°gāt Bbh 26.18; kleśāvaraṇa-°gaṃ 74.5; grāhyagrāhaka-°gān na pravṛttir na nirvṛtiḥ Laṅk 351.8 (vs); °ga-phala, nt., one of the 5 **phala** (2, q.v.); in Sūtrāl. xvii.31 comm. of karuṇā, defined heṭhāpahatvena tadvipakṣavihiṃsāprahāṇād; of more general application Mvy 2277; Bbh 102.17, expl. in 24, āryāṣṭāṅgasya mārgasya kleśanirodho °gaphalam.

visaṃyojana, adj. (to Skt. vi-sam-yuj-; cf. prec.), (*one who* or) *that which detaches, unbinds, frees*: (dharmaparyāyaṃ ...) svacittadṛśyagocara-°janaṃ Laṅk 43.16. Cf. next.

visaṃyojanaka, adj., = prec.: (Buddhānāṃ ...) navasaṃyojana-°nakānāṃ Divy 95.22, *who free from the nine bonds* (see **saṃyojana**).

visaṃvādanatā, see **a-vi°**.

visaṃskāra (m.; cf. next; = Pali visaṃkhāra, to vi- plus sam-skṛ-), *dissolution, annihilation*: sarve te pārṣukā (read °śukā) bhagnā gṛhakūṭaṃ visaṃskṛtam, visaṃskāragate citte ihaiva kṣayam adhyagāḥ Ud xxxi.7 (= Pali Dhp. 154; Jāt. i.76.27 ff., with words cited).

visaṃskṛta, ppp. (= Pali visaṃkhita), *destroyed, fallen to nothing*; see prec.

visaṃsthita, adj. or ppp. (unrecorded in this mg.), *deformed, misshapen*: °taḥ Mvy 6669 = Tib. tshul mi sdug par ḥdug pa, *become of unpleasing form*; °ta-virūpa-rūpā(ḥ) LV 118.7 (prose); °taṃ bībhatsarūpaṃ 205.18; °ta-mukhāḥ 206.6, °ta-rūpāḥ 9; °ta-rūpa virūpāṃ (so divide) 308.7 (vs); °ta-śarīrāṇāṃ sattvānāṃ Gv 288.23 (prose).

visaṃjñāvati, or °**tī**, corruptly °**gatī** in LV 148.9, a high number: Mvy 7974, cited from LV (where all mss. and both edd. g for v) = Tib. rnam par brdaḥ śes ldan (ldan = *possessing*, -vant); so Tib. on LV; both edd. of Mvy °vatir (n. sg.); the true reading may have been °vatī; cf. s.v. **saṃjñā** (7).

vi-saṃjñin, adj. (= Pali visaññin), *of false views* or *unsound mind*: yair ādīpta suranarā viparīta-visaṃjñino viparyastāḥ LV 375.17 (vs).

visada, nt., a high number: Gv 133.16, cited in Mvy 7878 as **vimadam**, q.v., which is prob. to be read in Gv (graphic corruption). Seems not to occur in the similar list Gv 105 ff.

visandati (m.c. for Pali vissandati = Skt. viṣyandate), *flows forth*: pūrā mukhato visaṃdetsuḥ (so one ms., v.l. visaṃhetsu; Senart em. viṣyandensu; first syllable short) Mv i.220.20 (vs).

visaṃdhi (m.?), (**1**) acc. to Tib. *minor joint* (of the body): (asmākaṃ ...) saṃdhi-visaṃdhayaś ca duḥkhanti SP 100.12 (prose), *and our joints and minor joints* (so Tib., tshigs daṅ tshigs phreḥu) *ache*; (**2**) in SP 374.1 (vs) the same two words occur, and the mg. is not clear: (one who masters the SP) saṃdhiṃ visaṃdhiṃ ca vijānate 'sau (Tib. des ni mtshams daṅ tshigs [both mtshams and tshigs = saṃdhi] kyaṅ rab tu śes) sarveṣu dharmeṣu vilakṣaṇāni, prajānate artha niruktayaś ca yathā ca taṃ jānati bhāṣate tathā, perhaps *he understands each connection and (minor?) interconnection, of various sorts* (vilakṣaṇāni, prob. adj. with the two nouns) *in all states of existence* ...

visabhāga, adj. (= Pali id.; cf. **sabhāga**), *different, unlike, discordant, inappropriate, uncongenial*: te ca vilakṣaṇa te °gāḥ Samādh 19.16 (vs); see s.v. **udāra** for id. 22.26; °ga-sattvānunayāt Śikṣ 193.17, *thru attachment* (see **anunaya**) *to people of the wrong sort* (one may be dissuaded from the solitary life); (sarvasattvānāṃ) °ga-samavadhānabhayābhyanta-(read °ātyanta-)-vigamāya Śikṣ 296.9, *in order to complete divorce for all creatures from the fear of association with uncongenial (people)*; °ga-sarvasamavadhānabhayabhītānāṃ °ga-sarvasamavadhānabhayavinivartanatāyai Gv 264.16–17; a-visabhāga-varṇā 347.6, *I* (have come to be) *of no discordant external appearance* (foll. by avaivarta-varṇā, avikalpa-v°, anīla-v°, etc., long series of chiefly negative adj. ending in -varṇā); anyathā tu °gaṃ bhavati nirmāṇam ātmanaḥ Bbh 64.15, *but otherwise* (if it were not created in his own image) *the magic creation* (of a Bodhisattva) *will be one inappropriate to himself*; visabhāgāśaya (upāya), one of the six **upāya** (q.v.) of a Bodhisattva, viz. *that* (*method*) *in which the mental disposition* (of the B.) *is* (represented as being) *discordant* (with its real nature, in order to influence and help creatures; he may make it appear that he is angry and hostile towards the recalcitrant, tho he never is) Bbh 264.8, cf. 269.14, 17.

? **visampādayati** (unrecorded; v.l. vipādayati, Skt., reported only from Rājat., but since vipadyate is common in Skt. its caus. is likely to be the true reading here), *brings to disaster, ruins*: sa (sc. nāstikaḥ) ātmānam api (as well as others) °dayati Bbh 46.20.

visaṃbhavati (nonce-formation, pendant to saṃbhavati), *becomes non-existent, passes away*: (sarvadharmāḥ ...) na saṃbhavanti na visaṃbhavanti Śikṣ 263.13. *they do not come into being nor pass away* (Bendall and Rouse, strangely, *influence each other*).

visara, m. Mvy 7718, or nt., a high number, = Tib. ḥphro yas: °ram Mvy 7844 (cited from Gv); Gv 105.23; 133.5.

-visaraṇā, see **a-vi°**.

visarjayati (= Pali vissajjeti), *answers* (a question), *replies*: ko nv atra samarthaḥ syād etam arthaṃ °jayituṃ SP 7.8, ... *to reply to this matter*; etāṃ yo praśnāṃ °jeti tasya dhītā ca dīyati ... Mv iii.384.1, *whoever answers these questions, to him is given my daughter*; (anye praśnān) pṛcchanti anye °jayanti Divy 162.20; (yadi ... praśnān paripṛccheyur yān sa) ... na śaknuyād °jayitum Śikṣ 201.3, ... *which he could not answer*; (pṛṣṭā mayā pūrvakās tathāgatā ...) taiś cāpi visarjitaṃ Laṅk 16.11, similarly 19.15, *and they replied*; sa ca mayaivaṃ °jitas tūṣṇībhāvena prakrāntaḥ 179.5, *and being thus answered by me, he departed in silence*.

visarjayitar (= Pali vissajjetar; n. ag. to prec.), *one who answers* (questions): (praśnaprabhedakuśalaś ca bhavet praśnakoṭinayutaśatasahasrāṇāṃ) °jayitā SP 340.3.

visāta = **viśāta**, q.v.

? **visāriṇī**, in Divy 562.23 (prose) sa tābhyāṃ yāvat trir apy ukto visāriṇī kṛṣṇā nivāryamāṇā (so text, em., mss. °ṇau, intending °ṇo, which read) nāvatiṣṭhate, *he* (the king), *tho spoken to* (in admonition) *by those two* (ministers) *as many as three times, being held back* ... *did not remain* (in good conduct; he kept backsliding into evil ways). The words visāriṇī kṛṣṇā perhaps corruptly represent an abl. phrase, *from his evil course* (cf. **kṛṣṇa** 1). As they stand, they could apparently only be a strange parenthetical clause; *the corruption* (? visāriṇī, or viśār°?) *was black* (*dark, evil*). The Index to ed. renders kṛṣṇā by *tongue of fire*, which seems unacceptable; presumably it takes visā° as *spreading*; but even with the em. to nivāryamāṇā this hardly gives an intelligible result.

visikā, MIndic for **vṛṣikā**, q.v.: MSV iv.107.11; 108.8; 109.3.

visubhati (see **subhati**), *destroys*: anyam-anyaṃ ghātenti (mss. °tanti) anyam-anyaṃ visubhanti Mv i.27.8.

visṛta, see **a-vi°**.

visṛṣṭa, adj. (= Pali vissaṭṭha), *clear, distinct* (of voice, speech): visṛṣṭaś ca (of Buddha's voice, svara; in a list of epithets) Mv iii.343.1; °ṭena svareṇa . . . svādhyāyaṃ karontī 391.8, of a female ascetic.

visota, m., Mvy 7721, or **visoda,** nt., Mvy 7847, = Tib. (b)rgyud yas, a high number; in 7847 cited from Gv, which reads **viśodha** or **viśrātas,** corr. visrotas, qq.v.

vistara, (**1**) nt. = Skt. m., (great) *extent*: mohapaṭala-°raṃ bhinnaṃ (n. sg.) LV 373.12 (vs); (**2**) m. (special application of Skt.; Pali vitthāra similarly used), *the full text* (of a cliché, or well-known passage) is to be supplied, an indication of abbreviation: vistaraḥ Divy 428.11 (the full text meant is found in 132.20 ff.); usually instr. adv. vistareṇa, (*supply*) *in full*, Mv i.47.16; °ṇa kāryam Divy 377.1, *the text is to be done* (i. e. recited) *in full*; the text may be specifically named, °reṇa rākṣasīsūtraṃ (Divy chap. 8) sarvaṃ vādyam Divy 524.19–20; vistareṇa yāvat, (*read*) *in full* (the part here omitted) *as far as* . . . (the foll. words resume the text at a later point) Mv i.1.10; Divy 381.10; 394.5; 406.19; Bbh 230.1; cf. **peyāla,** similarly used, and **vistīrṇa**; (**3**) (= Skt. Lex. id.; Skt. viṣṭara, M. viṭṭhara), *seat*: netrāṇi cābharaṇa-vāhana-vistarāṃś ca dattvā . . . Mv i.83.16 (vs), (Buddhas) *having given away their eyes, and ornaments, vehicles, and seats*; (**4**) in Divy 84.4 (vs) gṛha-vistaraḥ should mean (or represent a word that means) *a poor, mean house* (see description 83.20 ff.): divyaṃ cāsya sudhābhaktam ayaṃ ca gṛha-vi°, suviruddham iti kṛtvā jāto me hṛdi saṃśayaḥ (mss. °yam), *heavenly is his nectar-food, and* (yet) *this is a miserable house* . . . I suspect a corruption. But MSV i.83.3 agrees. Perhaps, after all, *and* (merely) *this is the size of the house*(?).

vistarati, (**1**) (in Skt. only trans.; back-formation from caus. vistārayati?; but simple star- recorded once as intrans., see Schmidt, Nachträge), *becomes widespread, appears everywhere*: tadā vividhāni kalpavṛkṣā °ranti, cūtavṛkṣā (text cyūta°) °ranti Kv 17.12–13; (**2**) pass. vistīryate, *is set forth at length, is explained*: (nāvagacchāmi) °yatāṃ vacanam etad Divy 378.2, *I don't understand, explain this statement*; cf. **vistīraṇa.**

vistarīṃ-karoti, prob. read °rī-k° with pw 7.376, *spreads far and wide, distributes*: Bhagavad-dhātum ca °kariṣyati Divy 379.10.

vistārika (adj., = Pali vitthārika, *extensive*), °kaiḥ, adv., *extensively*: °kaiḥ puja (m.c. for pūjāṃ) karoti prasannacitto Gv 215.3 (vs); adj., -vistārikaṃ v.l. of most mss. for text -vaistārikaṃ LV 129.16; see **vaistārika.**

vistīraṇa (nt.; to vistīryate, see s.v. **vistarati** 2, plus -ana), *full explanation*: akalpāvikalpa-dharmanaya-°ṇa-cakraṃ LV 422.20, *the wheel that sets forth in detail the principles of the Doctrine*. . .

vistīrṇa, adj.-ppp., nt. °ṇam, (*supply*) *in full*, like vistaraḥ, °reṇa (see **vistara** 2) used to mark abbreviation of a fuller text: yadā dāni ekaṃ pārśvaṃ pakvaṃ bhavati, vistīrṇam, atha dvitīyena pārśvena Mv i.25.7. So I interpret the word; Senart's interpretation seems to me impossible; I admit, however, that I do not know the full text here abbreviated.

Vistīrṇabheda, n. of a former Buddha: LV 5.11. No v.l.; but Tib. ḥod, *light*, instead of °bheda (indicating rather °tejas, or °prabha, or the like).

Vistīrṇalalāṭā, n. of a kiṃnara maid: Kv 6.6.

Vistīrṇavatī, n. of a lokadhātu: SP 469.8, 10.

(**visthāpayati,** see **vithāpita.**)

[**visthita,** only bad writing for Skt. viṣṭhita, ppp. of vi plus sthā, BR s.v. 3, *stood still*: sarvā nadyaś ca °tāḥ LV 98.1 (vs); so Lefm. with ms. A; vv.ll. tiṣṭhatāḥ, tiṣṭhitāḥ; the latter could be a MIndic ppp. to pres. tiṣṭhati.]

visnapayati, visnā° (cf. AMg. viṇhāvaṇaka, *a bath in holy water*; no other form or deriv. of vi-snā- has been found outside of a Nirukta etym.), *bathes* (trans.): visnapī (aor.) nāyakaṃ LV 93.2 (vs); (paramasurabhigandhodaka-) kalaśair visnāpya Gv 381.20 (prose).

vispandita, nt. (= Pali vipphandita; orig. ppp. of Skt. vi-spand-), *twitching; motion*: °ta-mātra-parāyaṇaṃ mīnakulam avekṣya Jm 96.4, *perceiving the tribe of fish engaged in nothing more than twitching* (in a nearly dry pond); (teṣāṃ sattvānāṃ citta-)carita-°tāni jñāsyati SP 372.7.

vi-sparśati (vi plus Skt. spṛś-, § 28.40), *mishandles, maltreats*: (ye 'pi māṃ ākrośeyur) visparśeyus tāḍayeyuḥ . . . Śikṣ 182.11 (prose).

Visphūrjita, n. of a nāga: Mvy 3344.

Visphoṭaka, n. of a nāga: Mvy 3345.

vismāpanā (Skt. only nt. °na), *the causing astonishment*: Bbh 140.27, see s.v. **toṣaṇā.**

visrotas, see **viśrātas.**

[**visvāpana,** in KP 126.14, read (Skt.) vismāpana, (*causing*) *astonishment*; so Tib., ṅo mtshar; parasya °na-hetu kurvati.]

vihata, adj.-ppp., with karpāsa or kār°, lit. *broken, dissolved cotton*, i. e. prob. *cotton batting, cotton wool*: vihataṃ kārpāsaṃ (v.l. kar°) ubhayatrāśraye saṃstaritavyaṃ, tatra etāni aṇḍakāni . . . nikṣiptavyāni upari vihataṃ kārpāsam (mss. kar°) tam ete mātṛkārthaṃ poṣiṣyati Mv i.273.3–4 (vihataṃ is read only in the second occurrence in one ms., but the other readings prob. intend it).

vihanyita, quasi-MIndic ppp. or subst. (to Skt. vihanyate, *is distressed*), either *distressed*, or (subst.) *distress*: kiṃ ti (= te) °yitena Mv i.155.14 (vs); if ti (te) is instr., lit., *what use is there of you(r being) distressed*?; if gen., *what is the use of your distress*?

viharati, rarely °**te** (perh. m.c.), (= Pali id.) *lives, dwells, spends one's time*, in very general sense: usually = Tib. gnas (pa), e. g. Mvy 1478 ff.; sarve saddharmaguravo vyahārṣur (so read) viharanti ca, athāpi vihariṣyanti eṣa buddheṣu dharmatā Ud xxi.12, *all* (sc. Buddhas, past, present, and future) *lived, live, and will live showing respect for the Good Law; this is the nature of Buddhas* (= Pali AN ii.21.21–22, where the preceding prose makes the mg. clear; Chakravarti is unsatisfactory); Buddhavihāreṇa viharan Mvy 354, *living in the way of life of a B.*, = Tib. saṅs rgyas kyi gnas pas gnas pa; something like this is prob. meant by, vihārakuśalo dhīro tatra (viz. in the city of Ratanakholaka) viharate muniḥ Mv i.186.20 (vs), *the wise Sage* (Buddha) *dwells there, knowing the right way* (or *the way appropriate to him, the Buddha's way*) *to live* (Senart sees in vihāra-kuśalo a reference to the four **brahma-vihāra,** which I doubt; cf. Bbh 90.8 s.v. **vihāra** 2); buddha-vihāreṇa vatādya Tathāgato viharati, jina-vi° sarvajñatā-vi° mahānāga-vihāreṇa vatādya Tathāgato viharati, atītānāgatapratyutpannān vā tathāgatān . . . samanusmarati Sukh 3.11 ff., *the T. is dwelling in the Buddha-state* etc.; divyehi vihārehi āniñjehi vihārehi sāntatyehi vihārehi buddho buddha-vihārehi . . . (etc.) tehi tehi vihārehi viharati Mv i.34.11–14, . . . (Buddha) *dwells in* (various) *states* (*conditions* or *modes of life*); similarly ii.419.10–15; tadāpy ahaṃ bhagavan yadbhūyastvenānenaiva vihāreṇa viharāmi SP 60.8, *even then, Lord, I mostly live in this same state* (here, *of mind*); there follows a quotation of the speaker's thoughts; hence at least one Chin. translator renders *I think*, using the same character which elsewhere renders cintayati; Tib. seems to render mchi ba (*come, go, appear*): rtag par nam mchi ba deḥi tshe bcom ldan ḥdas ḥdi ltar; Senart (p. xxiii) renders a similar phrase *passe par les états d'esprit* in Mv iii.225.10–14 ekapiṇḍapātreṇāhaṃ ānanda traimāsaṃ niṣīdiṣyaṃ purimakānāṃ tathāgatānāṃ . . . vihārehi vihariṣyaṃ, . . . *I will dwell in the states of being* (*mind*?) *of the former Buddhas*, which he then does; (Mañjuśrīḥ . . .) imaṃ dharmaparyāyaṃ saṃprakāśayamānaḥ sukhasparśaṃ (v.l. sukhasaṃsparśaṃ) viharati SP 286.6, . . . *dwells in a happy condition*.

vihānyā (so also Mironov; app. to vi-han-), Mvy

7605, prob. *the being subject to damage, spoliation, or frustration*; Tib. rnam par ñams par byas pa, (*to be*) *made much damaged*; so essentially Chin.

vihāra, m. (Pali id.), in BHS chiefly in two mgs., both seemingly based on the meaning *dwelling* (to **viharati**, q.v.), (**1**) *dwelling place* of monks, esp. of a monkish community, *monastery*; so used also in Skt.: in this sense = Tib. gtsug lag khaṅ, *house of sciences*, because schools were associated with monasteries, Mvy 9096; 9152; (**2**) = Tib. gnas (pa), as for **viharati**, *state of being, stage* or *condition of existence*; sukhasparśa-vihāra-tā Mvy 6288; **brahma-vi°**, q.v.; see s.v. **viharati** for examples; others praviṣṭamānasya śubhair vihārair LV 7.2 (vs), prob. *being entered into* (instr. = loc.) *fair states*; mayā pramatta-vihārāye na samanvāhṛtaṃ (so read with mss.) Mv iii.355.1, *by me* (a devatā), *in a negligent state, it was not considered that*..., proved by vs version of same incident, mamedaṃ na viditaṃ pramattāye 356.5; ayaṃ (sc. Maitreya's dwelling, Vairocanavyūhālaṃkāragarbha) śūnyatānimit-tāpraṇihita-vihāra-vihāriṇām āvāsaḥ Gv 469.25, and long list of similar formulae, all with cpds. ending -vihāra-vihāriṇāṃ, *the abode of those who dwell in the state of*...; yat Tathāgataḥ tribhir... apratisamair vihāraiḥ tadba-hula-vihārī, āryeṇa vihāreṇa, divyena, brāhmeṇa; iyam asya vihāraparamatety ucyate. tatra śūnyatānimittā-praṇihita-vihārā (cf. Gv 469.25 above) nirodhasamāpatti-vihārāś cāryavihāra ity ucyate; catvāri dhyānāny ārupya-samāpattayaś ca divyo vihāra ity uc°; catvāry apramāṇāni (= **brahmavihāra**) brāhmo vi°... Bbh 90.7–13; twelve bodhisattva-vihāra, listed and explained at length in the 'vihāra-chapter (paṭala)' of Bbh, 317.5, 10 ff. (there is a 13th, the tāthāgato vi°, niruttaro vi°, 12–14), listed 15 ff., gotra-vi°, adhimukticaryā-vi°, pramudita-vi°, adhiśīla-vi°, etc. (the long chapter must be read to understand the terms which by themselves sound obscure); ten jñānapāramitā-vihāra, Gv 537.11 ff. (listed); in Bbh 332.20 ff. the standard 10 bodhisattva-**bhūmi** (q.v.) are called b°-vihārāḥ (line 23); cf. Sūtrāl. xx–xxi.14 comm., ekādaśa vihārā ekādaśa bhūmayaḥ (the 11th is the buddha-bhūmi); (**3**) prob. *walking* (as in Skt.), in two almost identical passages in Divy: padā vihāra 78.6 ff. and 467.2 ff., also in MSV i.75.21 ff. (printed as cpd.), and iii.140.9, 19, *walking, marching on foot* (refers to passing around a holy place to the right, Divy 78.5, 467.1); below, mālāvihāraḥ kṛtaḥ Divy 78.25 and 467.26, and ff., and MSV i.76.18 ff., *a garland-perambulation* (?), precise mg. not clear to me; it is obviously some form of homage to the holy spot, more elaborate than the depositing of loose flowers (mukta-puṣpāṇi Divy 78.18; 467.18).

-vihārika, adj. (= Pali id.) = **vihārin**: ekāgradhar-mamaitrī-°rikāḥ Kv 65.17 (prose).

vihārin, *dwelling, living* (not markedly different from some Skt. uses but with the flavor of BHS **vihāra, viharati**): -vimokṣa-vihārī LV 424.18; sarvadharmasamatā-°rī 425.10; others 426.3 ff.; 428.8 ff., and s.v. **vihāra** (2), e. g. Gv 469.25; Bbh 90.8 ff.; pratyakṣa-°riṇo hy ete bodhi-sattvā atra sthāne Dbh 7.8, *existing in visible presence.*

-vihu, may be MIndic for Skt. vidhu, *moon*, as in Pkt. (Sheth), or, perh. more likely, for Skt. vibhu, *lord*, in mokṣa-vihūnām (sc. bodhisattvānām) Mmk 167.17 (vs), *lords* (or *moons*) *of salvation.*

viheṭhaka, adj. (subst.; = Pali id.; to **viheṭhayati** plus -aka), *one who injures*; *injurious, doing harm, troubling*: SP 63.6 (of Māra); Mv i.321.21; Mvy 2961; Divy 322.6; 629.13; Mmk 249.8; Gv 214.11; 337.13; neg. a-vi° Mv i.358.2.

viheṭhana, nt., and **°nā** (= Pali °na; to **viheṭhayati**), *injury, hurting, doing harm, violating*: ājñā-°nam Mvy 8433; (a-)°na- LV 430.2 (in cpd.); °nā Mv i.271.6; Mvy 783; 2114; 5360; Śikṣ 49.8 (so read with ms.); Dbh 23.11; °nābhiprāya (with °na or °nā?) Divy 494.15, 16.

Viheṭhanī, (cf. prec. and next), n. of a rākṣasī: Māy 243.31.

viheṭhayati, °ṭheti, rarely **°ṭhati** (cf. **heṭhayati**; viheṭhakaḥ once in Skt., Mbh. Crit. ed. 1.69.8, but the root is clearly MIndic; = Pali viheṭheti; and see surrounding items), *injures, annoys, disturbs, treats ill*; tends to replace Skt. vi-hiṃs-, which is occasionally bracketed with it, so vihiṃsayati viheṭhayati Bbh 158.14; °ṭhayati Dbh 91.1; °yasi Divy 42.17 f.; °yanti LV 76.18; Mmk 401.12; viheṭhāma Mv iii.131.19; opt. °ṭheya Mv ii.178.7; °ṭhayet LV 403.7; Mmk 154.4; °ṭhaye Mv iii.322.16, 19; °yeyuḥ Suv 73.13; °yeta LV 338.10; impv. °ṭhaya Av i.229.8; pple. °yat- Divy 104.13; 105.19; fut. °ṭhayiṣyati etc. LV 404.11; Mv i.361.16; Av i.321.2; °yiṣye Divy 360.15; aor. viheṭhi LV 75.16 (vs); °ṭhetsuḥ Mv iii.359.19; ppp. °ṭhita Mv ii.215.16 (mss. °hiṭhita or °hesthita, dental sth); 225.17; iii.431.8; Divy 145.22; 329.17; neg. a-°ta SP 161.12; 286.7; Divy 104.17; 106.10; 494.9; gdve. °yitavya Mv i.360.11; 365.15; Divy 360.14.

viheṭhā (to prec.), *injury, doing harm*: °ṭhā-vihiṃsā- (in cpd.) Gv 169.6, and neg. a-vi° 8; °ṭhā, n. sg., LV 52.8; 277.3; 396.2; 411.11; acc. °ṭhām Mv ii.409.6; SP 402.1; Bbh 19.26; Suv 73.14 (so best ms., Nobel °ṭhaṃ, but I know of no stem viheṭha in prose); m.c. °ṭha (mss. °tha) LV 50.8 (vs); m.c. °ṭha-saṃjña (Bhvr. adj.) LV 400.19 and Mv iii.319.5, 6 (vss; Mv mss. very corrupt, Senart's em. not wholly sound; cf. Pali SN i.138.22–25, esp. 24).

-viheṭhika or **°kā**, in danta-°kā pi kriyanti Mv ii.473.12, some product of the ivory-worker's craft; v.l. °vihaṭhakā; neither form seems plausible or indeed interpretable; prob. corrupt. Prec. by danta-bhṛṅgārakā (pi kriyanti); foll. by danta-**pādamayā**(?)...

vīci (= Pali id., PTSD, cf. CPD s.v. [1]avīci; AbhidhK. LaV-P. iii.148, and esp. 149 line 1), *interval, interruption*: vīci-paribhojitāyāḥ MSV ii.88.19 (after kāla-pari°), *enjoyed at* (proper) *intervals.*

vījanaka, nt. (= Skt. °na, AMg. vīyaṇaga), *fan*: °kāni Mv ii.475.8; 477.5 (both prose).

vījanī (= Pali id.; cf. prec.), *fan*: °nīyo, n.-acc. pl., Mv i.222.7 (mss. °nīye) = ii.24.15 (vs); iii.380.12 (vs).

Vīṇaka, Mmk 232.10 (vs); **Vīṇātṛtīyaka**, Mmk 19.13 (prose); **Vīṇādvitīyaka**, Mmk 43.19 (prose); all nom. pl. m.; names or epithets of a class of minor godlings; presumably the same class, since the accompanying items in the lists where these are found are very similar (see s.v. **karoṭa-pāṇi**); presumably all mean something like *lute-bearers* (cf. gandharvas?), but I have no further information; especially -tṛtīyaka is puzzling.

[**Vīṇāravaghoṣa**, see **Vāṇā°**.]

vītaṃsa (m.; Pali id.; Skt. see below), *falcon*; sa hatas tv itaraṃ hanti °seneva pakṣiṇaḥ Ud xiv.2, *he however, himself destroyed, destroys others, as birds* (are killed) *by a falcon*; so, acc. to Chakravarti, Tib. (khra) and Chin.; same word in same vs in Pali Therag. 139, rendered PTSD and Mrs. Rhys Davids *decoy-bird*, which is less plausible; in Skt. only Lex. and once in Harṣac. (pw), said to mean *bird-net, snare*, or *any implement used in catching birds*, which here is impossible.

vītatha, adj. (m.c. for Skt. vi°), *false*: satya-vī°-pa-theṣu Gv 55.3 (vs).

vītarāga-bhūmi, f., n. of the 6th of 7 śrāvaka-**bhūmi**: Mvy 1146 (here v.l. vigata-rāga); ŚsP 1473.13 et alibi, see s.v. **bhūmi** 4.

Vītaśoka (= Pali °soka), n. of a brother of Aśoka: Divy 419.19 ff.; Vītaśokāvadāna = Divy xxviii, colophon 429.5 (story of how he was converted to Buddhism after originally being an adherent of heretics).

vīti-, for **vyati-**, q.v. (chiefly in Mv).

vītikāśeti (also spelled °seti, °sati, °śati; for *vy-ati-kāśayati), *lets light shine through*; with synonym vītiloketi, in: gopānasī(ye)-antarāṇi (and, pāṃśulikāntarāṇi)...

vītilokenti vītikāśenti (vītiloketsuḥ vītikāśetsuḥ, with minor variants) Mv ii.125.14 f.; 127.2 f.; 128.8 f.; 129.10 f.; in the parallel LV 254.11 f. virājante, vyavabhāsante.

vītikrama (m.; semi-MIndic, = Pali vītikkama, Skt. vyatikr°), *passing beyond*: (sarvasaṃskāra-)°maṃ prāpayiṣyāmīti bodhisattvo ... Mv ii.279.20.

vītigata, ppp. (= Skt. vyati°), *passed beyond*: sarvabhāva-bhava-°tā sma, eṣa nirvṛtim upema ihaiva Mv i.69.11 (vs).

vītinamati, °nāmayati, see **vyati°.**

vītipatati (= Pali id.; for **vyati°**), *flies past*: pakṣiṇo na °tanti Mv iii.317.8.

vītiloketi (for *vy-ati-lokayati), *lets light shine through*: in same passages with **vītikāśeti,** q.v.

vītivartati (= Skt. vyati°), *passes beyond*: jātiṃ ca jarāṃ ca °tanti (so read with mss., not caus.; Senart em. °tenti) Mv iii.270.15, *pass beyond birth and age*; ppp. °vṛtta (= Pali °vatta; the only form recorded in Pali), *passed beyond*: vedanā-°tā LV 214.6 (vs); dharmā ime karaka-vedaka-°tāḥ 340.4 (vs); gaṇanā-vītivṛttā SP 66.4 (prose), Kashgar rec. for text °ṇāṃ samatikrāntā, *beyond calculation*; bhavantu aṣṭākṣaṇa-vītivṛttāḥ Suv 41.13 (vs), cited Śikṣ 219.2 (Nobel strangely °vyativṛttāḥ, unmetr., and against all his mss.), *passed beyond the 8 akṣaṇa*, q.v.

vītisaṃkrama, m., or adj. (for *vyati°; no such cpd. recorded), *transcending, one who transcends*: sarvalokagati-°mā (voc., to Buddha) Gv 54.26 (vs), *O thou that transcendest all the courses (states of existence) of the world!*

vītisaṃcarati (for *vyati°, nowhere recorded), *passes out, is emitted* (of sounds): (tasya me, sc. bodhisattvasya ... karṇaśrotravivarāntarehi) uccaśabdo (v.l. °dā, better) mahāśabdo (v.l. °dā) vītisaṃcaretsuḥ Mv ii.124.12.

vītisārayati = **vyati°,** q.v.

vītihāra, always and only in Mv (= Pali id., cpd. with pada-) and (in other texts than Mv) **vyatihāra,** m., (**1**) cpd. with pada- or krama(tala)-, *a setting down of the foot, footstep*: pada-°reṇa ṛddhīye yena śuddhāvāsaṃ devanikāyaṃ tena prakrāmi Mv i.35.2, *with one step went by magic* ...; ekakṣaṇena pada-°hāreṇa rājagṛhād vaihāyasam abhyudgamya Mv i.55.2; Padumāvatīye pada-°hārāṇām ubhayato padumāni ... Mv iii.162.6, *lotuses* (appeared) *in the footprints of both the feet of P.*; hastapādaparityāgena mahāpratiṣṭhāna-kramatala-°hāreṇa Śikṣ 24.6, (a Bodhisattva) *by sacrificing his hands and feet* (to suppliants, and so) *with the step of the soles of his feet on a firm foundation*; yo dharmaśravaṇahetuko vā dharmadeśanāhetuko vāntaśa ekakrama-°hāro 'ntaśa eka-ucchvāsapraśvāso vā Śikṣ 42.4, *whatever* (motion), *be it only a single footstep or a single breath, is motivated towards hearing or preaching the Doctrine*; ekakrama-°hāraṃ vātikramya vācaṃ bhāṣate Śikṣ 173.17, *or who, stepping a single footstep* (i. e. at every step), *pronounces the words* (Homage to that Buddha); (ekaikena ca cittotpādena ... -paramāṇurajaḥsamān) pada-°hārān (1st ed. corruptly °vyativyāhārān, 2d ed. °vyavahārān) kramāmi, ekaikena ca pada-°hāreṇa (text °vyavahāreṇa) ... -paramāṇurajaḥsamāni buddhakṣetrāṇy atikramāmi Gv 217.13, *with each thought I step innumerable footsteps, and with each footstep I pass* ...; (**2**) *passage* (of time), only in comp. with kṣaṇa (-°hāreṇa), *in the passage of a single instant*: bodhisattvā ekakṣaṇa-°hāreṇāprameya ... buddhān paśyanti (21.3 satkurvanti) Sukh 20.8; 21.3; ekena (mss., Senart em. ettakena, but cf. Sukh) kṣaṇa-°hāreṇa Mv i.55.14; to be sure ettakena is read in the mss. in the same phrase Mv i.56.9; iii.425.16, 22; 450.16, and it can be interpreted, see **ettaka.**

vīmati, m.c. for **vimati,** q.v.

vīra, (**1**) m. (?), (= Pali vera, Skt. vaira, nt.; § 3.50), *enmity*: kṣāntīmatā (mss. kṣāntimmatā) vopasamanti vīrāḥ Mv iii.371.5 (same vs in Pali Jāt. v.143.2 verā); (**2**) n. of a yakṣa: Māy 44. See the foll. items, especially **vīra-kraya, -mūlya, -vikraya,** which exhibit a curious use of vīra, unknown to me elsewhere.

vīra-kraya (cf. **vīra-mūlya, -vikraya**), *a good price, an excellent bargain*: dadyāt paṇyaṃ tataḥ kṣipraṃ °krayeti sa ucyate Mmk 58.5 (vs); °yeṇa krītvā 291.14, and read so (?) for °ye krītvā 695.10; °ya-krītāṃ, -krītaṃ, 314.14; 706.5; 720.20; on 74.18 see **vīra-vikraya.**

Vīradattagṛhapatiparipṛcchā, n. of a work: Mvy 1407; called Vīradatta-pari° Śikṣ 34.16; 230.10.

Vīranandin, n. of a Buddha: Śikṣ 169.8.

Vīrabāhu, (**1**) n. of a kumbhāṇḍa: Mvy 3444; (**2**) n. of a yakṣa: Māy 65.

[**vīramaṇī** is cited PTSD s.v. veramaṇī as a BHS form for the latter, see **vairamaṇa, °ṇya.** But the only passage quoted is Jm 213(.7), where the text reads vīramāṇī, which has nothing to do with Pali veramaṇī. If vīramaṇī exists in BHS I have failed to note it.]

Vīramatī, (**1**) n. of a yakṣiṇī: Mmk 612.8; (**2**) (the same?) n. of a yoginī: Sādh 427.4.

vīra-mūlya (cf. **vīra-kraya** and next), *a good price*: yathepsitam tasya kurvīta °yaṃ samāsataḥ Mmk 553.21 (vs).

vīra-vikraya = **vīra-kraya,** *a good bargain (sale)*: sarvagandhānāṃ °ya-krītānāṃ Mmk 705.7; in view of this, prob. read in 74.18 ādau tāvad vīra-vikrayeṇa (text om. vīra; Lalou, Iconographie 53 n. 1 would read vīrakrayeṇa, but the two seem to be used interchangeably) sūtrakaṃ krītvā.

Vīrasena, (**1**) n. of a Buddha: Śikṣ 169.8; (**2**) n. of a Bodhisattva: Samādh p. 36 line 2.

vīrasenaka, nt. (cf. Skt. Lex. vīrasena, 'fruit of a certain tree', pw), *a kind of fruit*: Mv ii.475.14 (prose), in a list of fruits, see s.v. **drākṣā-latikā.**

vīriya-vant, adj. (cf. Pali viri°, Skt. vīrya°), *possessing heroism*: Mv ii.90.5 (prose).

Vīryavant(a), n. of a companion of **Puṇyavant(a),** q.v.: Mv iii.33.16 ff.

Vīryā, n. of a nāga maid: Kv 4.10.

vīryārabdhi (f.), = next, *acquisition of heroic energy*: (Tathāgata āgatāgatānām) sattvānāṃ ... °bdhi-mātratāṃ (*extent of acquisition of heroic energy*) vyavalokya SP 317.14 (so KN, no v.l.; otherwise WT, claiming support of Tib., which contains ḥgrus kyi; does this not represent ārabdhi?).

vīryārambha, m. (= Pali viriyā°), = prec.: anuttarāyāṃ samyaksaṃbodhāv apratibalāḥ smāprati-°bhāḥ sma SP 100.9.

vukka, nt. (unrecorded MIndic, if not error or misprint, for Skt. vṛkka; cf. Pali vakka), *kidney*: °kaṃ ŚsP 1430.20; 1431.10, in lists of parts of the body.

vukta, semi-MIndic = Skt. ukta: sugatasya vuktāḥ KP 14.14 (vs); vukto 126.4 (vs). See next.

vuccati, vucyati (= Pali vuccati, Skt. ucyate), *is said*, see § 2.51.

vutta, ppp., = Pali id., (**1**) = Skt. ukta, see § 2.51; (**2**) = Skt. upta, see § 2.53.

vuddhi, f. (= Pali id. or vuḍḍhi) = **vṛddhi,** q.v.: jaya-vuddhi (with mss.) ca se (sc. rājño) kṛtā Mv iii.24.6.

vusta, ppp. (= Pali vuttha, Epic Skt. uṣta), *dwelt*: vāsaṃ (so mss.) vusto Mv iii.433.2, § 2.54, 62.

vuhyati (= Skt. uhyate, Pali vuyhati), *is carried* etc., see § 2.52.

[**vūdagra,** false em., see § 2.55.]

vṛṃhayitar, see **bṛṃh°.**

vṛkṣa, nt. (Skt. only m., and so app. Pali rukkha), *tree*: imāni ca ratnavṛkṣāṇi SP 410.12 (prose); anyatamad vṛkṣam upaśritya Av i.100.16.

vṛkṣamūlika, m. (= Pali rukkhamūlika), *living*, or *meditating, at the root of a tree*, one of the 12 **dhūtaguṇa,** q.v.: Mvy 1135; Dharmas 63; AsP 387.7.

Vṛji (Skt. Gr.; = Pali Vajji), n. of a people and country, = **Vaji,** q.v.: Divy 201.4, 13; MSV i.224.13 ff.

Vṛjika, name assumed by **Kuśa** (2) as garland-maker: MSV i.103.9.

vṛttaka, (1) nt. (= Skt. vṛtta), *event, occurrence, story*: °kaṃ tat sarvaṃ vistareṇa samākhyātam Divy 439.8; cf. also **iti-vṛttaka**; (2) ifc. Bhvr., in vs, = Skt. vṛtta, *manner of life*: araṇya-vṛttakāś SP 272.3 (vs).

Vṛddha, n. of a disciple of Buddha (no v.l., and seems surely a noun, not adj.): Mv i.182.19 (Nīlakeśaṃ ca Vṛddhaṃ ca . . .).

vṛddhaka, f. °**ikā,** adj., *old* (perhaps pitying or contemptuous dim. -ka): Mv iii.283.10, 13 (prose), see s.v. **jīrṇaka.**

Vṛddhakāśyapa, n. of a great ṛṣi (distinguished from **Kāśyapa** [4?], who is listed just before): Māy 256.16.

vṛddhataraka, adj. or subst. (to compv. of Skt. vṛddha; specifying -ka § 22.39), (*one that is*) *older, rather old*: Bbh 254.6 (see **prativiśiṣṭataraka**); similarly Bbh 5.1 and esp. 161.11; perhaps *oldest* (monk, to take precedence over the others), MSV iii.123.2, 6.

Vṛddhadeva, n. of a former Buddha: Mv i.141.1.

(**vṛddha-śrāvaka,** acc. to pw *a Śivaitic mendicant monk*: Mv iii.412.8, see s.v. **guruputraka**; LV 380.12 caraka-parivrājaka-vṛd°-gautama- etc.)

vṛddhānta, m. (not noted in Pali), *elder's end* or *place*, in an assembly of monks; opp. **navānta,** q.v.: °taḥ Mvy 8743 = Tib. rgan rims (so also Das; but read rim?); usually °te, foll. by a form of sthā, Divy 43.26 (°te sthitāni); 85.21; 180.17; 306.17; 349.26 (°te praṇāmaṃ kṛtvā yāvan navāntaṃ gatvā . . .); 384.28; 400.13 (°te niṣasāda); 404.19; Av ii.87.5 (°te niṣādayitvā); Bbh 122.17 (see **upādāya,** 2b); MSV ii.84.7.

vṛddhi, (1) (undeclined form!), in phrase: diṣṭyā vṛddhi (cf. Skt. diṣṭyā vardhase), *congratulations!* (regularly to a king): mahārāja di° vṛ° Mv ii.113.5; deva di° (mss. dṛṣṭvā) vṛddhi devasya putro jātaḥ Divy 405.20; deva di° (mss. dṛṣṭvā) vṛ° Divy 425.2. Cf. also jaya-vuddhi, s.v. **vuddhi**; (2) n. of one of the eight deities of the bodhi-tree: LV 331.21 (°dhiḥ).

[**vṛddhika** Mv iii.324.3, if reading is correct, n. of a tree. But v.l. quoted as mṛddhīkā; prob. read mṛdvīkā, *vine*. Cf. Pali muddikā, AMg. muddiyā.]

Vṛndakaṭa, n. of a locality, or (acc. to v.l.) of a yakṣa: Māy 75.

vṛndi, or **vṛndī** (related to Skt. vṛnda, orig. *swelling, mass*, as m. in Suśr. *tumor*; = Pali, AMg. bondi; see Edgerton, JAOS 69.229, anticipated, as I learned too late, by Lüders, KZ 52.106–9, with relevant materials not included by me; cf. **voṇṭa**), *body* (orig. *solid mass* or the like): vaḍḍā (see **vaḍḍa**) ca vṛndi (in this pāda mss. lack 3 syllables; perh. read ca vidyate vṛndi, or, ca vṛndī, which in this position makes better meter than vṛndi, bhavati) prajñā ca te na vidyate Mv ii.249.19 (vs), so mss., *you have a big body, but you have no wit*; = Pali Jāt. ii.160.11 mahatī vata te bondi na ca paññā tadūpikā. Senart failed to note the parallel and emended the text badly.

vṛścī (for Skt. vṛścika; cf. AMg. vicchu beside vicchuka), *scorpion*, of the zodiacal sign: tulā kanyā tathā vṛścīś ca Mmk 152.7 (vs, hypermetric even with this shortened form! anuṣṭubh).

Vṛṣabha-jātaka, n. of a jātaka story: Mv iii.29.4 (colophon).

vṛṣabha-tā (cf. next two), *'bull-like quality'*, so *lordliness, majesty*, a quality esp. of Buddhas: imāṃ ca bhagavato °bhatāṃ śrutvā SP 199.3 (two Nep. mss. °bhitāṃ, Kashgar rec. °bhitaṃ); (tathāgatadharmacakra-) -pravartana-°bhatāṃ Dbh 73.16 (cf. Gv 6.2, under next); °bhatayā . . . adhitiṣṭhati 90.24.

vṛṣabhi-tā (to next, plus -tā; cf. **ātma-vṛṣ°**); = prec.; mss., esp. Kashgar rec. of SP, sometimes present a nt. vṛṣabhita, which is however never well supported and surely only a corruption; Bendall even emends Śikṣ ms. °tā to °ta, referring to Mv ii.277.8, but this is a Bhvr. adj., so that stem in -ta is normal (Māra speaks and refers to himself as mahā-vṛṣabhitaṃ, acc. sg., *having great majesty*, parallel with mahāpratāpaṃ, mahāvikramaṃ); otherwise all unambiguous passages show always °tā, at least in some mss.; usually a quality of a Buddha: siṃha-vṛṣabhitābhigarjitanirghoṣasvara LV 435.15 (of Buddha); (saṃprakāśayati) tathāgata-°tāṃ (so v.l., text °taṃ) SP 308.5; tathāgatena tathāgata-°bhitā tathāgataparākramaḥ kṛtaḥ 311.5; sarvabuddha-°bhitā 391.3; (buddha-)°bhitā-sukhena Śikṣ 214.1 (ms.), *by the bliss of the majesty of a Buddha*; buddha-°tām AsP 432.10; very common in Gv, e. g. (tathāgatadharmacakrapravartana-)-vikurvita-°bhitām 6.2 (cf. Dbh 73.16 under prec.); acintyaṃ tathāgata-buddha-°bhitādhiṣṭhānam 7.22; buddhavyūhān buddha-°bhitāṃ (so read with 2d ed. for 1st ed. °tān) 17.24; na sā °bhitā 19.7; acintyāṃ buddha-°bhitāṃ 21.1, etc.

vṛṣabhin (see prec.; cf. Pali āsabhiṃ vācaṃ, acc. sg. f., derived by PTSD from a stem āsabhin, which is doubtful; it seems more likely to represent Skt. ārṣabhī, f. to °bha), *'bull-like'* and so *lordly, majestic*, esp. of a Buddha or Bodhisattva: labhi tada dhanamaṇi dṛḍhabala vṛṣabhī (voc.) LV 166.14 (vs), *then thou didst get the rich jewel, O majestic one*; applied to Bodhisattvas, Dbh.g. 4(340).17 (°bhī, n. pl.); 39(65).24 (°bhī, n. sg.); also Samādh p. 42 lines 20, 21.

Vṛṣasena, n. of a king, descendant of Aśoka: Divy 433.23.

vṛṣikā, vṛsikā (or bṛ°; also **visikā**; = Skt. bṛsī, bṛsī, vṛ°; Pali bhisikā beside bhisi, bhisī), *cushion, bolster*: Mvy 8991, text vṛsikā, Index vṛṣ°; omitted in Mironov's text but vṛṣikā added in some mss. acc. to his note); cīvara-vṛṣikā (cf. Pali cīvara-bhisī, *a robe rolled or folded as a pillow*) Mvy 9005 (so text and Index; but Mironov °bṛsikā, no v.l.). (Divy vṛṣi-, foll. by **kocava-,** q.v., repeatedly.)

vṛṣṭāyate (denom. to Skt. vṛṣṭa or vṛṣṭi; cf. next), *rains*: deve °yamāne MSV i.36.8 (prose), *while it was raining*.

vṛṣṭita, denom. ppp. (to prec.), *rained upon*: yadvad vṛṣṭita candrasūryabhavanā, vāyur mṛdur vāyate LV 283.10 (vs), *since the dwellings . . . are rained upon*, (and) *a gentle wind blows*; Tib. (. . . gnas kyi) rgyun char.

vṛsikā, see **vṛṣ°.**

vṛhatphala, see **bṛh°.**

ve (= Pali id., Skt. vai), emphatic particle: tvaṃ ve dāso ti manyasi Mv ii.487.7 ff.

vega, nt. (Skt. m.), see **saṃvega.**

Vegajavā, n. of a kiṃnara maid: Kv 5.24.

Vegadhārin, n. of a Bodhisattva: Gv 442.22.

Vegarājamati, n. of a Buddha: Gv 284.16.

[**vegā,** seemingly f. for vega, m., *strong impulse*, but read only vegāḥ, m. pl., or vegaḥ, m. sg.: suvipulā mahā-karuṇāvegā (read °gāḥ and delete daṇḍa) saṃbabhūvur Gv 331.2; -yācanakatarpaṇānivartya-(so read, see **anivartya**; or with 2d ed. °**vivartya-**)-vīryavegā (read °gaḥ) prādurabhavat 3; cf. 20, below, mahāprītivegāḥ saṃjātāḥ, 21 cittodagratāvegaḥ prādurbhūto, etc.]

? **veṭhaka,** m. (? to next plus -aka; cf. Pali veṭha, -ka), *something that wraps, covers*: in a list of goldsmith's products, veṭhakā pi kriyanti Mv ii.470.8, pādāṅguli-(mss. °la-)-°kā pi kriyanti 11; both evidently either made of, or ornamented with, gold; the mss. actually read veṭakā in 11 and this or veṭṭ° in 8.

veṭhayati, veṭheti (= Pali veṭheti; § 3.2; MIndic form of Skt. veṣṭ-), *encloses, surrounds, envelops; invests* (a city): veṭhetha Mv ii.451.9 (mango trees, with cloths; mss. vedetha); veṭhitvā, ger., Mv ii.173.6 (a corpse, vastrehi); veṭhayitvā iii.390.8 (tāmrapātreṇa pārśvaṃ, i. e. tying a copper vessel to his side, to carry a lighted firebrand in); vārāṇasī veṭhitā (so read) Mv ii.82.14; nagaraṃ ... veṭhiyāna (ger.) ii.485.14; caus. ppp. veṭhāpitā ii.171.15 (puṣkariṇī, see s.v. **prativeṭhāpeti**).

[**veṇika,** in LV 275.11 (prose) aṣṭādaśa-veṇika-buddhadharma-, error or misprint for **āveṇika.**]

Veṇu, n. of one of the 4 devatās of the bodhivṛkṣa: LV 278.10.

veṇukāra, *reed-worker* (so Tib., smig ma mkhan; pw *flute-maker*): (na bodhisattvā hīnakuleṣūpapadyante) ... °ra-kule vā LV 20.3.

[**Veṇu-gulma** Divy 103.1, not a proper name; see 106.5.]

Veṇugrāmaka, m. (= Pali Beḷu(va)gāma(ka), Veḷ°), n. of a village: MPS 13.2 ff.

Veṇuvana, nt. (= Pali Veḷuvana), n. of a grove at Rājagṛha where Buddha often stayed: Mvy 4108; Mv i.255.4; iii.47.12; 60.2; 91.14; Divy 143.1; 262.7; 298.24; 301.17, etc.; Av i.78.5 etc.; in MSV iv.71.6 **Veluvana** (but elsewhere Veṇu°, e. g. iv.83.7).

vetanaka (nt., = Skt. °na), *wages*: saviśeṣaṃ te 'haṃ °kaṃ dāsyāmi SP 106.9 (prose), *I will give you extra wages*; dviguṇaṃ ca te °kaṃ pradāsye 113.14 (vs).

? **vetayika,** see **cetayika.**

vetāḍa (= Skt. vetāla), a kind of demon: Suv 104.4; 107.8 (most mss. °la both times); Mmk 17.3; 292.11; Dbh 45.23; Māy 220.18 etc.

? **vetālika,** m., perh. to be read (mss. corrupt) for text vaitālika, tālika, Mv iii.113.2; 442.8, in lists of entertainers; mg.? Skt. vait°, *panegyrist*, acc. to Monier Williams also *conjurer*. Cf. the obscure Pali vetāla, °lika.

vetra, nt. (= Pali vetta; it is not clear that the Skt. word is used in this sense; cf. Skt. vetralatā), *rope* (made of reeds or creepers?), used in fastening a ship: (tatas tair...) vahanasyaikaṃ vetraṃ chinnaṃ; paścād ... sarve varatrāś chinnāḥ Divy 230.3. See **śiṭā.**

vetradaṇḍika, m. (so to be read with pw 7.342 for caitra-daṇḍika), *staff-bearer, usher* (to a king): Mvy 3735 (both edd. caitra°, no v.l.; but Index to Kyoto ed. also cites vetra°). Tib. dbyig gu thogs pa, *staff-bearer*. Cf. AMg. vetta-daṇḍa.

Vetranadī, n. of a river: Divy 451.1 ff.; 456.19 ff.; = **Vetravatī** (= Pali Vettavatī ?) MSV i.146.3; 153.14.

Vetramūlaka, m., n. of a region (in the south): Gv 151.4, 17.

Vetravatī, see prec. but one.

vedaka, adj. (f. °ikā) and subst. m., (**1**) (cf. Pali id., PTSD; but the real Pali corresp. is vedagū, see below), *one who knows, full of knowledge, learned, wise* (ep. of Buddha or an arhat or monk): kiṃprāptinam āhu vedako ti Mv iii.397.12, and (vedāni vicārya...) sarvavedanām atītya vedako ti 20, = Pali Sn 528 (vedaguṃ, acc. sg.) and 529 (sabbaṃ vedam aticca vedagū so); Pali vedagū = *one that attains* (true, supreme) *knowledge*; on the forms cf. Mv iii.401.2 antako si duḥkhasya pārago si dharmāṇāṃ with Pali Sn 539 antagū si pāragū si dukkhassa; further, (snātako) snātakaparivāro vedako °ka-parivāro Mv iii.407.11; (śramaṇo pi) tvaṃ brāhmaṇo pi tvaṃ vedako pi tvaṃ tārako pi tvaṃ pārago pi tvaṃ 423.14; (**2**) (connected with **vedanā** etc.) *one who experiences, feels* (the results of action): °kaḥ Mvy 421; 4679; na ca kārako 'sti tatha naiva ca vedako 'sti LV 419.11 (vs), *there is no actor, and no experiencer either* (= normal Skt. bhoktar, contrasting with kartar); kāraka-vedaka-virahita Dbh 49.6; karaka-(q.v.)-vedaka-vītivṛttāḥ LV 340.4 (vs); kāṅkṣā hi yā syād iha vā pṛthag vā ihavedikā vā paravedikā vā Ud xxix.6, *desire* (? *doubt*) ... *whether relating to experience* (lit. *experiencing*) *in this life or in the beyond*; the verse is not complete and has not been found in Pali; mg. not wholly clear; vedako vedanād (q.v.) anyaḥ pṛthagbhūto na vidyate Śikṣ 233.11 (vs); vedakaḥ vedaka iti vyavahriyate sa ca ... nopalabhyate ŚsP 120.19 (prec. by same formula with kārāpakaḥ, and foll. by same with vedayitṛko **vedayitṛka,** q.v., iti ...).

Vedagaccha, n. of a mountain: Māy 254.5.

vedanā, rarely °**na** (Pali only °nā recorded, so usually in Skt. in this mg. but rarely °na), *feeling, sensation*: as in Pali there are three, e. g. Mvy 1913, listed 1914–6 as sukhāḥ, duḥkhāḥ, aduḥkhāsukhāḥ; these are correlated in Śikṣ 232.11 ff. with rāga (for sukha), dveṣa (also **doṣa,** for duḥkha), and moha (in regard to aduḥkhāsukha), all of course to be abandoned; sarva-°nāsu vītarāgo (mss. tīvra-rāgo; Senart em. with Pali Sn 529) Mv iii.397.19 (vs); vedanā is the 7th link in the **pratītyasamutpāda,** q.v. (cf. e. g. sparśena tisra anuvartati vedanā ca LV 420.2, vs, in pra°sam°); it is also the 2d of the 5 **skandha,** q.v. and the 2d of the 4 **smṛtyupasthāna,** q.v. (Śikṣ 232.6 ff. discusses it in this connection); as nt., vedako vedanād anyaḥ pṛthagbhūto na vidyate Śikṣ 233.11 (vs).

vedanā-bhinna, m., Mvy 9245, or °**bhinnaka**(-tva), MSV iii.67.11, *one oppressed by painful sensations*. Corresp. to Pali vedanaṭṭa.

vedayita (nt.; orig. MIndic ppp. of Skt., Pali, and BHS vedayate, Pali, BHS also vedeti), *sensation, feeling*: sarva-vedayitaiśvaryadhvaja-samādhi- Gv 172.11, n. of a samādhi; **saṃjñā-°yita-nirodha,** q.v.; in Mv iii.66.7 and 14, where Senart's text reads te ... dharmā jātā bhūtā saṃskṛtā vedayitā pratītya samutpannā, read **cetasikā** for veday°, as suggested by mss. in 14.

vedayitṛka, m. (cf. Skt. °yitar), *one who causes to feel* or *experience* (cf. **vedaka** 2, **vedanā,** etc.): ŚsP 120.21, see s.v. **vedaka,** which precedes this in an identical formula and is clearly meant to be distinguished from it by lacking the caus. force.

Vedalī, n. of a locality (in the south): Laṅk 286.12.

vedikā (= Pali id.), *railing*, especially one made of bars with interstices, or network, of the kind commonly surrounding Buddhist stūpas; in BHS around cities: °kā Mvy 5586 = Tib. lan kan (*railing*), and others; °kāyāḥ sphaṭikamayā sūcī ālambanam adhiṣṭhānam Divy 221.8 (cf. **sūcī**); (nagarī ... uccaistoraṇa-)-gavākṣa-vātāyana-°kā-pratimaṇḍitā Divy 315.9; *coping* on a roof,-pravṛddhod-dhṛta-vedikaṃ ca tṛṇacchadaṃ SP 83.2 (vs; so with WT and Kashgar rec.), *the thatched roof was old and had a cracked* (*yawning*, uddhṛta) *coping*; °kā-jāla, nt., *network of a railing*, °lam Mvy 5583 = Tib. lan kan gyi dra ba; rājadhānī saptahi °kā-jālehi parikṣiptā Mv i.194.18 = iii.227.5.

vedita (nt.; orig. ppp. of Skt. vedayate, and so = **vedayita,** both forms occurring in Pali, but vedita in PTSD recorded only as ppp.), *sensation, feeling*: in **saṃjñā-vedita-nirodha,** q.v.; also in Śikṣ 24.11 aparyātta-vedita-cittaḥ, of a Bodhisattva, *not having his sensations and mind overpowered* (by disturbing elements; wrongly Bendall and Rouse; see **aparyātta**).

? **vedyāramitāḥ,** Mmk 41.5, obscure to me, prob. corrupt: teṣām upariṣṭāt vedyā° bhagavatī Māmakī ālekhyāḥ sarvālaṃkāravibhūṣitāś ca tāḥ prasannamūrtayaḥ.

vedhati (= Pali id.; to Skt. vyath-, Chap. 43, s.v.; see also **vyadhati, pra-v°, saṃpra-v°**), *shakes* (intrans.), *trembles*: °ti LV 303.22 (vs); Divy 479.11; avedhat LV 352.2 (prose); 411.1; avedhanta Dbh 98.31 (prose); a-vedhamānāḥ SP 24.15; vedhe (aor.) Mv iii.334.2; 341.5; vedhita, ppp., SP 6.1; LV 355.9 (so with Foucaux, Notes 188, for text vedhino); Mvy 3007; Divy 250.22; 365.14; Samādh 19.6.

vedhanīya, gdve. (to Skt. vyadh; cf. Skt. vedhana etc.), *penetrable*: Śikṣ 42.15.

vedhya, nt., *target-shooting*: Mvy 4990 = Tib. dbug pa, *piercing*; in a list of martial arts; follows **chedya** and **bhedya,** qq.v., and perh. has -ya by their influence; followed by **dūra-vedhaḥ** and other cpds. of (Skt.) vedha, which occur (without vedhya) in similar lists Divy 100.12; 442.8.

vepiṇīyā, or (v.l.) vepilīyā, ? Divy 560.13; see s.v. **kṛti.**

Vebhaḍiṅga, see s.v. **Veruḍiṅga.**

Vemacitra, (1) n. of a mountain: Māy 253.33; **(2)** = **Vemacitrin**: °traḥ Divy 148.20; Mahāsamāj. Waldschmidt Kl. Skt. Texte 4, 179.13; Suv 162.12 (°traś, v.l. °triś); Svay 69.17 (daityendra); °treṇa, instr., v.l. of 3 mss. for °triṇā SP 5.3; **(3)** n. of a yakṣa: Māy 96.

Vemacitrin (also °**tra**, q.v., 2, and **Vaimacitra**; = Pali Vepacitti), n. of a prince of the asuras: °trī, n. sg., LV 241.3; Mv iii.138.2; 254.9; Divy 182.13; Av i.108.10; °trir, n. sg., Divy 126.8; °triṇā (v.l. °treṇa) SP 5.3; °citri-(stem) Mmk 655.11; 663.21.

vemātra, m., a high number: Mvy 7756 = Tib. gzhal saṅs; cf. **vimantra** (also **vaimātra**, which must be distinguished from this).

Veraṭṭhi(ka)putra, Veraḍhi-putra, Verati°, see s.v. **Saṃjayin.**

Veruḍiṅga, m. or nt., v.l. °ḍidga; in a majority of occurrences (Mv i.326.10 and 327.6–8) both mss. Vebha°, which has support in Pali Vebhaliṅga (v.l.) or Vehaliṅga (see this in DPPN; Veka° is also recorded); Senart, with Mv i.319.8, 9 only, Veru°; n. sg. °go i.319.8, °gaṃ 326.10: n. of the village, on the site of the later **Mārakaraṇḍa**, which was the home of **Ghaṭikāra**. The orig. form seems to have been Vebhaḍiṅga. For other forms, see **Vaibhiḍiṅgī.**

veruli = next, app. shortened form m.c.: dakṣiṇavartita-veruli-varṇaṃ Suv 46.10 (vs), guaranteed by meter; Tib. cited as vai-ḍū-rya.

veruliya, m. (nt.? cf. prec.; = AMg. id., Pali veḷuriya, Skt. vaiḍūrya), a gem, commonly rendered *cat's-eye*: °liyasya (both mss. ce-, one celurī°) maṇi Mv i.213.14 (printed here as prose, but a vs in corrupt form, so printed in repetition ii.16.18 which reads vaiḍūryasya); °liyasya ii.36.10 (vs); yathā ākāśe vimalo śuddho °yo maṇiḥ iii.216.14 (vs).

vela, m., a high number: Mvy 7760 velaḥ = Tib. dus rlabs; = **velu**, q.v., and cf. **velā** (2).

Velatiputra, see s.v. **Saṃjayin.**

velambaka (= AMg. °baga, °baya), = **viḍambaka**, q.v., *jester, buffoon*: in lists of various kinds of entertainers, incl. **ḍimbara, dvistvala, kumbhatūṇika, śobhika**, etc.: Mv iii.57.10 (read so for mss. valambaka, Senart valañjaka); 113.3; 141.18; 161.4; 442.9.

velā (1) (= Skt.) *time*; in adv. phrases in Mv, acc. sg., usually with MIndic shortening of ending to -aṃ (§ 9.17): rarely yāṃ velāṃ (Mv i.362.11), usually yaṃ velaṃ, *what time* = *when, since*, used as conj.: i.361.3; 362.2, 17, 20; ii.172.15; 173.18; 210.17; 211.4, 12; 242.13 etc.; iii.76.1; 145.5; 163.4; 291.8, 20 (twice, second time with correl. taṃ velaṃ, *at that time, then*); yaṃ velaṃ ... taṃ velaṃ, *when ... then*, also iii.287.11, resumed in 13 with yatra kāle ... tatra kāle; yatra ca velāṃ, *and at what time*, Mv ii.65.14; **(2)** a high number: Gv 106.9 (cf. **vela, velu 1**).

velā-cakra, nt., lit. *time-wheel*: Mvy 9157 = Tib. ña tshod (this combination not in Jä. or Das; ña = *full-moon day*; chu-tshod = *water-clock*) kyi ḥkhor lo; Chin. has several renderings, one being *sun-dial*; Jap. *instrument for measuring the shadow of the sun*; *time-wheel* (*sundial*?).

Velāma, (1) n. of a brahman who gave advice to **Piṇḍavaṃśa**: MSV i.64.19 ff. There is a curious resemblance between his advice to P., which the latter followed, and the reputation of Pali Velāma (see DPPN); **(2)** n. of a brahman who was a generous giver (doubtless = Pali id.): MSV i.98.12.

Velāmasūtra (= Pali id.), n. of a work (AN iv.392 ff.): Karmav 163.1. Tells story of Velāma, a previous birth of the Buddha (a generous giver). Also MSV i.98.15.

velāsikā, = **vai°**, q.v.

velu, (1) m., f., or nt., a high number: veluḥ Mvy 7889 = Tib. dus rlabs, cited from Gv 133.20 where velu (nt.); cf. **vela, velā** (2); **(2)** (= Pali id., *bamboo*, acc. to Childers also *flute*; Skt. veṇu, both mgs.), *bamboo*; *bamboo-stick*: so pi ... ikṣustambo mahanto velupramāṇo ikṣu saṃjāto Mv ii.421.18 (*of the size of a bamboo stick*); *flute*: velum Mv iii.82.5 (vs), acc. sg., in a list of musical instruments; so mss., Senart em. veṇuṃ; perhaps, read velusmiṃ (pi) in Mv ii.423.16 for Senart veluṣi (which Index derives from velu), mss. veruṣi, loc. sg., after dhanuṣi pi, in a list of arts learned by a prince, *in* (playing) *the flute*(?); in a very similar list ii.434.12 Senart reads dhanusmiṃ pi veṇusmiṃ pi, but for the latter, mss. cekasmiṃ, or cakasmiṃ, pi.

veluva, m., a high number: Mvy 7779; Gv 106.15.

Veluvana, see **Veṇu°.**

vella (m.; Deśīn. 7.94 id.), *hair*: kiṃ imo puruṣo evaṃ pratikūlo pīto pāṇḍuka-vello Mv ii.152.15; so read with mss., Senart em.

(**vellita**, adj., *curly*, of hair; so not only in Pali but also in Skt., BR; in Mv ii.44.12 Senart strangely em. the correct mss., vellitāgrakeśā, to vallitā°; see **vallita**, which should perhaps rather be em. to vellita.)

vevara, m., var. for **vivara** (2), m., a high number: Mvy 7782.

[**vevalaka**, read devalaka (Skt.) with 2d ed.: Gv 45.19.]

? **vevādika**, or °**aka**, some musical instrument: Mv ii.159.6 (so mss.; Senart em. vipañcikā); represents same orig. form as **vādiśa**, q.v.

Veśadhārin, n. of a Tathāgata: Gv 360.26.

veśya, (1) (nt.), *the occupation of a harlot* (Skt. veśyā, cf. Lex. veśya, defined *Hurenhaus*, BR): mama duhitā veśyaṃ vāhayati Divy 14.20, *plies the ...*; **(2)** adj. with dharma, acc. to Tib. groṅ paḥi, *of the village*, i. e. *common, vulgar*? (cf. **grāmya**): veśyāṃ dharmān samādāya bhikṣur bhavati na tāvatā Ud xxxii.18(19); same vs in Pali, Dhp. 266, vissaṃ (comm. visamaṃ, cf. Mv below, vissagandhaṃ vā kāyakammādikaṃ dhammaṃ; in Pali sg.); SN i.182.18 (text visaṃ, v.l. vissaṃ, dhammaṃ); Dutreuil B 26 viśpa, supporting the PTSD theory that the Pali word = Skt. viśva; in Mv iii.422.13 same vs has viṣamāṃ (hypermetr.), cf. Dhp. comm. above. Could veśya be a false Sktization of MIndic (AMg.) vesiya, from Skt. veṣa, *of garb* or *external appearance* (only)?

veṣaka (= Skt. veṣa), *guise, garb*: kiṃ muni-°kena bhavato LV 326.21 (vs), spoken by daughters of Māra to the Bodhisattva: *what is the use of a wretched ascetic's guise for you*? Prob. contemptuous dim.

[-**veṣin**, in **kāla-veṣin**, q.v.]

veṣṭaka, nt. (Skt. Lex. *turban*), acc. to Tib. seṅ ras, *white* (or, *thin*) (cotton) *cloth*: Mvy 5875. But Chin. *linen cloth* (no color word).

veṣṭanikā, see **pāda-ve°.**

veṣṭāpayati, see **veṣṭeti.**

veṣṭi, (1) (f.; so AMg. rāya-veṭṭhi, *labor for the king*; cf. § 3.59; = Skt. viṣṭi), *forced labor*: mā ... gṛhṇitva veṣṭiṃ pi ca kārayeyam SP 113.3 (vs), *and I might be seized and made to perform even forced labor* (§ 37.17); cf. **veṣṭeti**; **(2)** *work* (for, in comp.), *supervision, management* (of; cf. **veṣṭeti**): na kāyajīvitasāpekṣasya dharmaveṣṭiṃ vadāmi RP 35.7 (prose), *and I do not propose labor for* (*management of*?) *the Doctrine for one who is concerned about his body and life.*

Veṣṭitaka, n. of a yakṣa: Māy 50.

veṣṭeti, veṣṭāpayati (caus. of denom. to **veṣṭi**), *manages, supervises, looks after* (servants, domestic animals), lit. *makes work*: gṛhajanā veṣṭetavyā dāsīdāsakarmakarapauruṣeyā veṣṭetavyā ... hastyaśva-ajagaveḍakāni veṣṭāpayitavyāni rathayugyayānāni veṣṭāpayitavyāni Mv iii.177.15–178.1.

Veṣṭhila, n. of a householder: Gv 205.15 ff.

Vaikṛtika, n. of a yakṣa: Māy 72.

vaicikitsa, adj. (to Skt. vicikitsā plus -a; cf. Pali vecikicchin, in which -in seems to be due to influence of kaṃkhin which regularly precedes in Pali), *characterized by doubt*: (tyakto . . .) °tso tathā martyo Mmk 551.2 (vs).

? **vaicchetuka**, intended as n. of some people or rather their mode of writing, in ramaṭhābhaya-(text °ṭhabhaya-)°kā (sc. lipī, in list of scripts): Mv i.135.7.

Vaijayanta, m. (**1**) (= Skt. Lex. id., Pali Ve°), n. of Indra's palace: °taḥ prāsādaḥ Mvy 5498; Divy 395.11; °taṃ prāsādaṃ (acc.) Av i.90.3; sumerumūrdhne yatha °nto Mv ii.346.20 (vs); others, LV 212.1; 213.18; (**2**) n. of one of the udyāna of the Trāyastriṃśa gods: Mv i.32.4; (**3**) n. of a yakṣa: Māy 39.

vaijayanti (= Skt. °tī), *flag, banner*: -paṭākā-°ti- (in a long cpd.) LV 295.15 (prose; so all mss.; Calc. °tī).

vaijayantīka, ifc. Bhvr., in sa-°kā(ḥ), *provided with banners*: SP 338.9 (prose).

Vaiḍūryagarbha, n. of a former Buddha: Sukh 6.14.

Vaiḍūryanirbhāsa, n. of a former Buddha: Sukh 5.13.

Vaiḍūryaprabha, n. of a nāga: Mvy 3321.

Vaiḍūryaśikhara, n. of a former Buddha: Mv i.141.11.

[**vaiṇu**, in tuṇa-vaiṇu-ravaiḥ LV 173.9 (vs), perh. read veṇu with v.l. and Calc.; but perh. hyper-Skt.; only two inferior mss. veṇu.]

Vaiṇvāṭata (= Skt. Veṇv°, see Lévi p. 68), n. of a locality: Māy 22.

vaitara = next: °reṇa (Tib. mtho btsam pa ñid du) MSV ii.188.10.

vaitarika (nt.), = prec., acc. to Tib. *scorn, insult*: (te 'smāṃś codayiṣyanti smārayiṣyanti) alajjitena vā °keṇa (Tib. mtho btsam paḥi phir) vā MSV ii.188.4; iii.102.8, 19.

vaitānya (nt.; to Skt. vitāna, *dejected*, plus -ya), *dejection*: āpatita-°yaṃ (Bhvr. adj.) Jm 164.9 (prose).

vaituṅgakā, ? in pattra-°kā sthāpayitavyā MSV iv.79.4 (in latrines, along with earth and water).

vaitulya (nt.; equivalent to **vaipulya**; cf. Pali vetulla-, or °lya-, -vāda, -vādin, a heretical sect, by some identified with Mahāyāna, see DPPN s.v., n. 3; Kern, Versl. K. Akad. Afd. Lett., 4 Reeks, Deel viii, 312 ff.), (*work of*) *great extent*(?): sarva-mahāyānasūtra-°lya-paramāmṛta- Thomas ap. Hoernle MR 95.8; acc. to Kern's SP preface ix, in Kashgar rec. for vaipulya; see also 65.1 n. 1; Śikṣ 354.6 (cf. p. 415).

? **vaidarya** (nt.), acc. to Tib. (lhod) *slackness*: ye punas te kāśyapa vaidaryā (marg. corr. °rpyāt) asaṃyatā itaḥ śramaṇaguṇadharmād uddhurāḥ . . . Śikṣ 136.9, *who thru slackness are uncontrolled and rebellious against this*... Note says Cowell suggests vaidhuryād, which is implausible.

vaidalya, (**1**) (= Pali vedalla; see s.v. **vaipulya**), n. of a type of works included in the canon, see **Sarvavaidalyasaṃgraha**; cited by BR from Tāranātha as 'title of a work'; (**2**) n. of one of the 10 great mountains of the earth: Dbh 96.2 (v.l. **Vaipulya** 2), 15.

Vaidehaka parvata, n. of a mountain: (as cpd.) Mvy 4158; (two words) Śakrapraśnasūtra, Waldschmidt, Kl. Skt. Texte 4, 67.6.

Vaidehī (cf. next; acc. to Pali tradition not a gentile name), n. of Bimbisāra's queen: Divy 545.8.

Vaidehīputra (= Pali Vedehīputta; cf. prec.), ep. of Ajātaśatru: Av i.57.2 ff.

Vaidyarāja, n. of a future Buddha: Gv 358.14.

Vaidyottama, n. of a Bodhisattva: Gv 442.19.

vaināyika, adj. (Skt. Lex. [Buddh.! Trik.] *Buddhist*(*ic*); BR say error for vaināśika, but the word seems to be found in BHS; irregularly from **vināyaka**, q.v.), *Buddhistic, of the Buddha* or *Buddhism*: Gv 348.15 yathāvaināyikopanāyikavarṇā (see s.v. **upanāyika**).

vaināśa, nt. (Skt. vināśa plus -a), *state of being subject to destruction*: bhāvānāṃ nāsti vaināśaṃ Laṅk 209.11 (vs).

vaināśika, adj. or subst. m. (so in Skt., there applied only to Buddhists), *one who believes in cessation of existence, in destruction* (of entities): °ko yadāgatvā brūyād yady asti deśyatām Laṅk 360.1 (vs), *when a destructionist shall come and say, If it exists, show it*! This doctrine is reprobated in Laṅk (Suzuki misunderstands the term); katamo 'tra . . .°ko bhavati Laṅk 145.16; repeatedly in the sequel, e. g. buddhaśrāvakapratyekabuddha-°ko 146.3, 7, *one who believes in the cessation of existence of* . . .; (nāstyastitvābhimāniko) hi . . .°ko bhavati 146.14; (kalpākṣararahitāni prativikalpayan punar api) °ko bhavati 147.2.

vaineya (in mg. 1 = Pali veneyya; cf. **vineya**), (**1**) adj. or subst. m. = **vineya** 1, *one that is to be* (religiously) *trained*, or *converted*: °yā(ḥ) LV 437.11; °ya-sattvānāṃ Mv i.314.2; buddha-vai°, *to be converted by the B.*, Mv i.314.3; Divy 150.20; Av i.67.6; °ya-prābhṛta Divy 36.21 *a gift of a prospective convert*, see **prābhṛta**; na tu °yavatsānāṃ Buddho velām atikramet Divy 96.6 = Av i.17.6; °ya-jana Divy 96.9; °yāpekṣayā 49.8; 330.7; darśana-°yānāṃ sattvānāṃ śravaṇa-°yānāṃ etc. Gv 348.24 ff.; others, Divy 202.29 etc.; Av ii.176.3 f.; Kv 21.22 ff.; (**2**) subst. (nt.? not recorded in Pali; cf. **vineya** 2), *religious training*, esp. *conversion*: vaineya-vaśena, °vaśam upādāya, see s.v. **vaśa**; sattva-vaineya-kāraṇāt SP 228.8, *for the sake of conversion of creatures*; tasya ca vaineya-kālaṃ jñātvā Divy 330.10, *knowing it was time for his conversion*.

vaineyaka = °ya (1), in bauddha-vai°, see **bauddha**.

vaineyika = °ya (1): śrāvaka-vai°, *a prospective convert of śrāvakas*, Dbh 69.4, and so, pratyekabuddha-, bodhisattva-, tathāgata-vai° 5, 6; yathāśayeṣu sattveṣu yathā-°keṣu 90.15; (yathāparipakvāparipakva-) °ka-tāṃ ca . . . yathābhūtaṃ prajānāti 75.1.

vaipañcaka, m. (= **vipañcika**, q.v., and next two), *soothsayer*: LV 58.4 (two mss. vaipañcika, so!).

vaipañcanika, m. (= prec. and next; see s.v. **vipañcika**), *soothsayer*: etaṃ śruṇitva rājā vaipañcanikāṃ samāgatāṃ avaca (so read in all) Mv i.207.13 = ii.12.3, 17 (vs; mss. vipañc° in first two cases).

vaipañcika, m. (see under prec.), *soothsayer* (prec. by **naimittika**): Mvy 3794 = Tib. mtshan mkhan; LV 186.15 (prose; best ms. vaipañcanika, v.l. with Calc. °camika); 228.9 (prose); Divy 474.26 °kā(ḥ) by em., but corrupt mss. look more like °canikā(ḥ). Kern, IF. 31.196, derives this group from a 'misunderstood Pkt. *vepañjanika' to Pali veyyañjaniya, Jāt. iv.233.24, from vyañjana; improbably, in my opinion.

vaipākika, adj., subst. (Skt. vipāka plus -ika), *produced by maturation* (of actions): in Laṅk 283.4, 11 said of a class of Buddhas, contrasted with **nairmāṇika**, q.v.; in Laṅk 34.2 **vipāka**-stha is used as equivalent; in Laṅk 292.13 °kikād, *from* (*as a result of*) *maturation* (of actions), seemingly subst., one of four sources of **abhijñā**.

vaipākya (= Pali vepakka; abstr. from Skt. vipāka plus -ya, but only in Bhvr. cpds. in Pali and BHS), *ripening, maturation*, ifc. Bhvr., *resulting in* . . .: rājya-°yaṃ kuśalam Divy 372.3, *merit resulting in kingship*; (mahāpuruṣa-)lakṣaṇa-°yaṃ śīlam, adhicitta-°yaṃ, iṣṭagati-°yaṃ, sattvārtha-°yaṃ ca Bbh 185.14; (sarvaṃ ca sattvānāṃ āpāyikaṃ karma . . .) ātma-°yam icchati 368.2, *he wishes that every deed resulting in evil for* (all) *creatures should work out for himself*.

vaipulya, nt. (**1**) (also **vaitulya**, q.v., and see below; doubtless secondarily modified by confusion with Skt. vaipulya from vipula), (*work of*) *great extent*, or acc. to Burnouf, Intr. 62 f., *development*: as one of the 9 (Dharmas) or 12 (Mvy) types of works in the canon, Dharmas 62; Mvy 1276 (in this sense seems to correspond to Pali vedalla as one of the 9 aṅga of the canon, cf. **vaidalya**); °lya-sūtra, applied by SP and LV to their own texts and similar works, SP 1.3; 46.4; 98.3, 11; LV 7.9; see also **mahā-vai°**, and refs. s.v. **vaitulya**; (**2**) n. of a mountain: var. for **Vaidalya** (2), Dbh 96.2 (one of the ten great mountains of the earth; in Pali Vepulla is one of the mountains surrounding Rājagaha).

? **vaipuṣpita**, = **vipuṣpita**, which prob. read for this: tena °tam, *he smiled*, Divy 17.6.

vaibhāṣika, an adherent of the Buddhist school of this name: Mvy 5148.

Vaibhiḍiṅgī (loc. °gyāṃ) = **Vebhaḍiṅga**, see s.v. **Veruḍiṅga**, n. of the village of **Nandīpāla Ghaṭīkāra**: MSV i.217.11. Tib. cited as Beḥi-bhi-ḍiṅ-ga-na.

vaibhūtika, (adj. or) subst. nt. (to Skt. vibhūti plus -ika), *splendor, magnificence*: °kam (prob. subst.) Mvy 7480 = Tib. dbaṅ ḥbyor pa, *lordly wealth*; Chin. *self-sufficient; independent*; in Dharmas 109 prob. read aśeṣa-vaibhūtika-dhyāna for text °vaibhūṣita°. In Pali vebhūtika seems to have only evil connotations; see PTSD.

Vaimacitra = **Vemacitrin**, °tra (perh. mere corruption or hyper-Sktism): Thomas ap. Hoernle MR 105.9.

vaimatika, adj. (= Pali ve°; to **vimati**, q.v., plus -ika), *in doubt*: (bhikṣur aprabhāte prabhātasaṃjñī nagarendrakīlaṃ samatikrāmaty) āpadyate duṣkṛtām; aprabhāte °kaḥ (i. e. if *in doubt* about the time; similarly Pali vema°, e. g. Vin. iv.220.6; this Divy passage is clearly of Vinaya type), āpadyate duṣkṛtām Divy 544.12 (see 543.20 ff.), and similarly 14, 16; MSV i.274.3.

? **Vaimadyapura**, see **Madyapura**.

vaimātra, (**1**) m., a high number: Mvy 7750 = Tib. tshad myas (or tshad ḥdas); not to be confused with **vemātra**, q.v., a diff. number; (**2**) adj. (cf. under next), *various, heterogeneous*: only noted in reading of mss. Mv iii.320.16 parapuṅgalānāṃ indriyavīryaṃ vaimātrāṇāṃ (Senart em. °vīrya-vaimātratāṃ) . . . prajānanti, *the power of the faculties of other individuals, so miscellaneous as they are*; (**3**) nt. (= next), *variety, diversity*: °tram Mvy 7208 (prob. noun) = Tib. bye brag (*diversity*) or rim pa (*series, order in a line*). (Pali vematta could = this or °**trya**.)

vaimātra-tā (cf. prec.; = Pali vematta-tā) = **vimātra-tā**, q.v., and next: sattvānām indriyavīryaparāpara-°tāṃ jñātvā SP 123.7; (āyativipāka-)-°tāṃ . . . prajānanti Mv iii.321.5; indriya-°tā Mvy 1256 (Tib. rim pa, *series, order*, or rnam pa tha dad pa, *difference, variety*); sattvānāṃ citta-°tāṃ . . . prajānāti Dbh 74.1.

vaimātrya (nt.; Pali vematta) = °**tra** (3), **vimātrya**, °**tratā**: buddhakāya-°trya- Gv 126.4; paśya . . . prajñā-viśeṣaṃ prajñā-°tryaṃ Sukh 66.12; lokadhātu-°tryāvatāraṇāya Dbh 15.16; lokadhātuvibhakti-°trya-kovidaḥ 82.5.

Vaimānika, epithet (or possibly n.) of a yakṣa, prob. geographical adj., *of Vimāna* (but I know no such local name): Māy 76.

vaiyākaraṇa, or with Senart vaiyyā°, nt. (= Pali veyyā°), = **vyākaraṇa** (1) as a genre of canonical Buddhist literature: sūtrānta-(so read with mss. and Senart's note for text °te)-vaiyākaraṇābhigīto (mss. vai āk°, Senart vaiyyāk°) . . . 'haṃ Mv iii.122.21 (vs), *I, praised in sūtras and vai°* (of the canon).

vaiyāpatya (only Prāt), °**pṛtya** (always in Śikṣ ms., Bbh.; once seems intended in Av, ii.13.5, see Speyer's note), °**vṛtya** (other texts, incl. Av usually; = Pali veyyāvacca, AMg. veyāvacca; Skt. Lex. °pṛtya, Jain Skt. °vṛtya; Buddh. and Jain word; from Skt. vyāpṛta plus -ya, a for ṛ and v for p MIndic), nt., *work* (of duty or service to a superior), esp. to a Buddha or (often) to monks: vaiyāvṛtya dharmenānumodanā ca (so mss., to be kept, but meter suggests pronunciation vyāvṛtya!) mahājano prīti (so mss.) karoti puṇyaṃ Mv i.298.19 (vs), *service* (to a Buddha); dharma-°vṛtyaṃ Divy 54.16 (saṃghasya); 347.27; °vṛtyaṃ Av i.260.6; ii.96.7, 11 (here by a monk to other monks); °pṛtyaṃ Av ii.13.5; °vṛtya-karmaṇi Av ii.9.3; °pṛtyakarmaṇi Bbh 16.7; sattvānāṃ °pṛtya-kriyā (by Bodhisattvas) 29.25; °pṛtya (ms.) Śikṣ 50.15 f.; 55.6 ff.; °patya Prāt 494.8, 10; gṛhikarmānta-°pṛtya Śikṣ 114.3 ff., *work at duties of the sort that householders do* (i. e. not religious); °**ya-kara** (so also in Pali and AMg.), *one who does* (such) *work*, Karmav 57.12 (vs; °vṛtya-k° for a Buddha); Divy 347.2, 24 (prose; id.); a servant in a monastery; Mvy 8736 (°vṛtya°); Divy 54.19; Śikṣ 55.8 (°pṛtya°); Bbh 166.24 (id.); Prāt 494.9, 11, etc. (°patya°); wrongly written vaiyāvṛtta-k° MSV iv.136.9.

? **vaiyyākaraṇa**, see **vaiyā°**.

Vaira, n. of a slave (dāsa): Gv 185.24 ff.

Vairaṭika-putra, Vairaṭi-putra, Vairaṭī°, Vairaṭṭī°, Vairaḍī°, see s.v. **Saṃjayin.**

Vairaṭṭasiṃha, n. of a brahman of Nagarabindu, converted by Buddha: MSV i.221.11 ff. (Cf. Pali Belaṭṭhasīsa? but the stories are not the same.)

Vairaṇyā (= Pali Verañjā), n. of a city: MPS 31.56 ff. (cf. Pali Vin. iii.6.18–27; 7.3–17). Cf. **Vairambhya.**

vairamaṇa, m. (! nt.? = next two; Pali only veramaṇī, but AMg. veramaṇa, nt.), *abstention* (from sin): prāṇātipāta-°ṇo dharmaḥ, and so with the other 9 akuśala **karmapatha** (q.v.), Mv ii.99.5 ff.; prāṇātipāta-°ṇa- Śikṣ 176.8. See also **prativairamaṇa.**

vairamaṇī (= Pali ve°) = prec.: adhyācāra-°ṇyāṃ (so read, see **adhyācāra**) Bhīk 24b.5; 27b.4; 28a.1, 4; 28b.2. On an alleged **vīramaṇī** see s.v.

vairamaṇya (nt.) = prec. two: prāṇātipāta-°ṇyaṃ-(all mss.; must be part of cpd.; § 8.14) -parasattva-samādāyana-(q.v.)-tvād LV 429.8, *because he incites other creatures to abstention from taking life*; prāṇātipāta-°ṇya-(text as above)-guṇavarṇasaṃprakāśanatvād 9; adattādāna-°ṇyārthaṃ Av i.223.12. All prose.

vairambha, m. (**1**) (= Pali ver°; see also next; appears to be derived from *virambha, but no form or deriv. of vi-rabh- is recorded), n. or epithet of certain very violent winds: vairambha-vāyu-vikṣipta (so, as one word) iva pakṣī LV 333.12 (vs); °bha-vātena yathaiva pakṣī kṣipyanti . . . RP 36.4 (vs); °bha-vātābhihata-śakuntavat Śikṣ 246.11 (prose); in Mv i.168.18 (vs) read, nearly with mss., vairambhā pi (mss. ṣi) ca vāta naṃ (see s.v. **naṃ**) vikopenti (q.v.) na dehakaṃ (q.v.; Senart em. wrongly); (Vairambhe mahāsamudre) vairambhā nāma vāyavo vānti Divy 105.26; (**2**) n. of an ocean: Divy 102.29 (read °bhas for text °bhā); 105.25 (see above), 29; (**3**) = **Vairambhya**, or as pl. its people: °bheṣu MSV i.216.4; 217.4.

vairambhaka = prec. (1): °kā (api) vāyavo Divy 90.24; 103.24.

Vairambhya (also °**bha** 3, q.v.), nt., n. of a city: MSV i.24.9; 25.14 ff. Corresp. to Pali Verañjā. Its king, **Agnidatta** (a brahman), takes the place of Pali Verañja.

Vairambhya-sūtra, nt., an account of Buddha's stay in prec., said to occur in Catuṣkanipāta of the Ekottarikāgama: MSV i.45.19. In Pali AN iv.172 ff. (in Aṭṭhakanipāta) occurs a vaguely corresp. text., cf. also Vin. iii.1 ff.; Apadāna i.301.1–2.

Vairā, n. of a place: Māy 9 (see Lévi p. 61).

vairāgyika, f. °**kī**, adj. (Skt. vairāgya plus -ika; = JM. veraggia), *relating to (causing) disgust with the world*: saṃsāra-°gyikī dharmadeśanā Av i.206.16; 271.11; ii.84.8; 162.9.

vairāja, m., *turquoise*: Mvy 5982 (in a list of gems); so Tib. rdoḥi rgyal po ste gyu, *turquoise as the king of gems* (implying derivation from vi-rāj-).

Vairāṭaka, n. or epithet of a yakṣa: Māy 74; perh. geographical adj., *living in Virāṭa*.

Vairāmaka (cf. Skt. Vairāma, n. of a people, Mbh. Cr. ed. 2.47.10), n. of a locality: Māy 48.

vairika, m. (= Pali verika, Skt. vairin), *enemy*: kṣetra-°kā(ḥ), *rivals in regard to a field*, also vastu-°kā, vapra-°kā, Mv i.16.9 (prose), see s.v. **sāpatnaka**; susukhaṃ bata jīvāmo vairikeṣu tv avairikāḥ, vairikeṣu manuṣyeṣu viharāmo hy avairikā(ḥ) Ud xxx.47 (= Pali Dhp. 197, where verin(a), averin).

? **vairuddhya**, nt. (Skt. viruddha plus -ya), *contrariety, opposition*: °yam utpannam MSV ii.174.3, by em. (ms. vairukṣyam).

Vairūṭīputra, see **Saṃjayin**.

vairocana, (**1**) (= Pali vero°, Skt. viro°) *the sun*: °naṃ vā gaganasmiṃ sarvaraśmisamāgataṃ arcitvā ... Mv ii.304.9 (vs); °nasya jagato viśiṣṭā ābhā (Senart adds abhū) bhaviṣyati kiṃ tu adya Mv ii.316.9 (vs); this is prob. the mg. of the first member of many of the cpd. proper names which follow this entry; (**2**) (cf. Pali 2 Verocana in DPPN, n. of a certain jewel; AMg. vairoyaṇa, *fire*; and see **virocana** 1), a certain jewel (also **viro**°): °nāṃ maṇiratnāṃ grahetvā Mv ii.317.13 (vs); °na-maṇiratna- Gv 101.12 (prose; -padmagarbhāṇi); 159.1 (prose; -vitāna-vitataṃ); (**3**) n. of one (the first) of the five 'transcendent' Buddhas: Dharmas 3 (first of 'five Buddhas'); Mvy 82 (foll. by the other four of Dharmas 3, at the head of a list of names of Tathāgatas) = Tib. rnam par snaṅ mdzad; once replaced by **Kāyeśa**, q.v.; Sādh 16.9 etc. (same group of five); he is prob. identical with the Vairocana who occurs in Śākyamuni's place in the standard series of Buddhas (after Kāśyapa) Gv 298.6; the standard story of Śākyamuni's birth in the Lumbinī grove is told of Vai°, Gv 379.24 ff.; 381.5, with the usual personnel, Māyā, Gopā, etc.; mentioned with Gopā but not as her husband, 396.23; other refs., see s.v. **Māyā** (1); and cf. P. Mus, Barabudur, p. 584; a Tathāgata of this name mentioned in several earlier passages of Gv, e. g. 40.1; 277.23; 290.23, with what seems to be special respect, may be identified with the V. just described, and so prob. with the 'transcendent' Buddha; in Gv 82.12 the last of a list of Buddhas the first of which is Amitābha, but the others mostly unknown; (**4**) prob. not to be identified with the prec., n. of one or more former (in Mmk perhaps contemporary) Buddhas: LV 171.10 (vs; Lefm. **Virocana** (3), most mss. Vai°, metr. indifferent); Mmk 64.2; Gv 104.18; (**5**) n. of a future Buddha: Mv iii.330.15; (**6**) n. of a cakravartin, former incarnation of Maitreya: Mv i.59.2, 13; (**7**) n. of a **nīlakāyika** (q.v.) devaputra: LV 383.11; (**8**) n. of a samādhi: Mvy 536; ŚsP 1417.12.

Vairocanaketu, n. of a Bodhisattva: Gv 442.12.

Vairocanagarbha, (**1**) n. of a Bodhisattva: Gv 2.25; 80.26; Mmk 63.5; (**2**) n. of a palace: Gv 123.20; 124.2.

Vairocanagarbhamahāmegha, n. of a Tathāgata: Megh 296.15.

Vairocanatejaḥśrī, n. of a lokadhātu: Gv 267.21 ff.; = **Vairocana-śrī**, °**na-dhvaja-pradīpa-ś(i)rī**, qq.v.

Vairocanadhvaja, n. of a Bodhisattva: Gv 2.19.

Vairocanadhvajapradīpaś(i)rī, n. of a lokadhātu: Gv 284.4 (vs); see °**cana-tejaḥśrī**.

Vairocanapraṇidhānaketudhvaja, = °**cana-praṇidhijñānaketu**: Gv 30.11 (prose).

Vairocanapraṇidhānanābhiraśmiprabha, n. of a Bodhisattva: Gv 8.21; 24.12.

Vairocanapraṇidhigarbhā, n. of a lokadhātu: Gv 13.25.

Vairocanapraṇidhijñānaketu, n. of a Bodhisattva: Gv 13.26 (prose); = °**cana-praṇidhānaketudhvaja**.

Vairocanaprabhav(i)yūha, n. of a Buddha: Gv 257.12 (vs).

Vairocanaprabhaś(i)rī, n. of a Buddha: Gv 285.7 (vs).

Vairocanaratnapadmagarbhaśrīcūḍa, n. of a cakravartin: Gv 268.25; 269.9; called °śrīprabhācūḍa 280.23, 25, where he is said to have been a previous incarnation of Maitreya.

Vairocanaraśmipratimaṇḍitadhvajarāja, n. of a Bodhisattva: SP 470.6 (no v.l. in edd.; Kern's Transl. om. dhvaja, Burnouf's om. rāja).

Vairocanaraśmipratimaṇḍitā, n. of a lokadhātu: SP 423.4 ff.; 457.6.

Vairocanavyūhālaṃkāragarbha, n. of a storeyed palace occupied by Maitreya: Gv 456.13; 469.20, 22.

Vairocanaśrī, (**1**) n. of a Bodhisattva: Gv 4.3; (**2**) = **Vairocanatejaḥśrī**, q.v.: Gv 281.21.

Vairocanaśrīgarbha, n. of a Tathāgata: Gv 282.20 (2d ed. line 21).

Vairocanaśrīgarbharāja, n. of a Tathāgata: Gv 422.26.

Vairocanaśrītejorāja, n. of a Tathāgata: Gv 8.20.

Vairocanīya, adj., *of* (the Buddha) *Vairocana* (3): °nīyo viṣayo 'prameyaḥ Gv 324.3 (vs).

Vairocanottarajñānin, n. of a Bodhisattva: Gv 2.16.

vailāsikā, velā° (cf. Skt. vilāsinī, °nikā), *a concubine*: Jento ... °kāye putro Mv i.348.13; similarly 349.2, 14; taṃ yugyayānakavigata (so v.l., metr. required) ceṭīvelāsikāhi (v.l. °vailā°) ca upetaṃ ii.37.5 (vs); bhāryāyo anupravrajetsuḥ kaḥ punar vādo anyāye velāsikāye janatāye iii.223.2.

? **Vailmavegarudra** (pw Bailma°, connecting with Skt. bilma), n. of some heretical ascetic sect (prob. corrupt): (divasanirīkṣakā ... dīkṣante, read dīkṣyante) °rudreṣu nagnaśravaṇeṣu ca Kv 81.8.

vaivarṇa (Skt. vivarṇa plus -a), *paleness*: samāpatitabhayaviṣādasveda-°ṇa-dainyo Jm 173.3; perh. error for °ṇya.

vaivarṇika (nt.; abstract, cf. prec. and Skt. vaivarṇya; = Pali vevaṇṇiya, in °yam amhi ajjhūpagato AN v.87.30 = 210.8, so read with CPD s.v. ajjhupagata; also Jāt. iii.394.26, same mg.), *loss of* (normal) *appearance, alteration* (for the worse) *of aspect*: pravrajyā khalu vaivarṇikābhyupagatā Divy 424.1 (the mg. is that of Pali AN above, which pertains to a monk; Divy Index and PTSD wrongly *outcaste*).

vaiśāradya, nt. (**viśārada** plus -ya; = Pali vesārajja), *confidence in oneself, fearlessness*, almost always a quality of a Buddha or Bodhisattva, who usually has a standard list of four such (below): caturhi °dyehi viśārada Mv i.38.15; 335.14; iii.64.5; 138.13; same with suviśārada, i.50.4–5; 238.18; 239.11–12; catur-°dya-viśārada Divy 95.16; 264.30; Av ii.105.14; vaiśāradya-viśāradaḥ LV 438.7 (vs); catur-°dya-prāpta LV 403.1; 428.5; vaiśāradyaprāptā Divy 617.15, of the nun (2) **Prakṛti**; °dya-varapāramiprāptaḥ Mv i.115.7 (vs); vigatakathaṃkatho °dyaprāptaḥ kuśaleṣu dharmeṣu Mv iii.201.12; °dye 'pi chedaṃ (mss. °do) vikartuṃ pratibalāḥ 322.4; among qualities of a Buddha (or Bodhisattva), LV 160.15 (caturbhiś ca tathāgata-°dyaiḥ samanvāgatam); Mv i.237.10; iii.386.14 (vs, °dyehi saṃpannāṃ, but read with mss. °nno, vācaṃ bhāṣe tathāgato); iii.97.10; SP 29.11; 77.7; 81.3; 259.5; LV 275.10; Av i.7.5 etc. (in cliché, prediction of Buddhahood, caturbhir °dyais); Divy 126.13; 182.20; Bbh 89.5; sarvaśāstra-°dyena LV 431.5; (anabhibhūtapratijñā-)-°dyaprāptatvād 433.22; the usual four vai° of a Buddha, corresp. to Pali, listed Mvy 131–4: (1) sarva-dharmābhisaṃbodhi-vai°, *confidence of being perfectly enlightened as to all dharmas*; (2) sarvāśravakṣayajñāna-vai°, *of knowledge that all impurities are destroyed for him*; (3) antarāyikadharmānanyathātva-niścita-vyākaraṇa-vai°, *of having described precisely and correctly the obstructive conditions* (to religious life); (4) sarvasaṃpadadhigamāya nairyāṇikapratipattathātva-vai°, *of the correctness of his way of salvation for realization of all* (religious) *success*; more briefly Dharmas 77, accidentally omitting 3 (in 4 nairvāṇika°); in somewhat diff. language and transposing 3 and 4, Bbh 402.3–12; a wholly diff. list (unknown to Pali) of 4 vai° of Bodhisattvas, Mvy 781–5 (*une liste fort obscure*, Lévi, Sūtrāl. iii.3 note 3, who gives a transl. of a diff.

Chinese version); a still different list of four vai° (attained by a Bodhisattva, preliminary to enlightenment) in Mv ii.261.5 f. and 262.6 f.: kāya-vai°, vācā-, citta-, and pṛthu-vai°; they are not explained, and the last is dubious, see **pṛthu** (Senart assumes that it means Skt. pṛthak, but does not explain how that would help); ten vai° of a monk listed Karmav 105.6 (otherwise unknown; viśārado grāmaṃ praviśati, vi° grāmān niṣkrāmati, etc.).

Vaiśāradyaprāpta, n. of a contemporary or future Buddha: Sukh 71.5.

Vaiśāradyavajranārāyaṇasiṃha, n. of a Tathāgata: Gv 310.1.

Vaiśāla, adj. (= Pali Ve°), *of* (the city) *Vaiśālī*: Mahāsamāj., Waldschmidt, Kl. Skt. Texte 4, 177.2; applied to the nāga Takṣaka, who is called Vaiśāleya from ancient times (AV). Cf. next two; Skt. Vaiśālaka, °lika.

Vaiśāleyaka, adj. (= Skt. °leya, see under prec.), *of Vaiśālī*: °kā Lecchavayaḥ Mv i.257.19 (but v.l. °lakā).

Vaiśālya, pl. (cf. under prec. two), (people) *of Vaiśālī*: Mv i.257.7 (prose); (Skt.) °laka and °lika are both used in the context; MSV i.225.8.

vaiśāstya (nt.; perh. hyper-Skt. to deriv. of AMg. visaṭṭa = vikasita, *blooming; extensive*), *full bloom, state of full development*: dṛṣṭā te tathāgatapraṇidhi-°stya-vaiśeṣikatā Gv 524.7–8.

Vaiśyāyanī, the gotra of the nakṣatra Kṛttikā: Divy 639.9.

Vaiśramaṇa (cf. AMg. Vesamaṇa, the regular Pkt. form; not in Pali) = Vaiśravaṇa (Kubera): Māy 105 (as king of yakṣas); Gv 494.24 (as god of wealth); v.l. with Calc. at LV 302.6 (cited s.v. **mahārājan**).

Vaiśravaṇa (in mg. 1 = Skt. id., Pali Vessavaṇa, and see prec.), (**1**) one of the four **mahārāja(n)**, q.v., guardian of the north and lord of yakṣas; (**2**) n. of a nāga-king: Māy 247.19.

Vaiśravaṇarājan (text Vaiśrā°; v.l. Vaiśramaṇa°), n. of a former Buddha: Mv i.139.11.

Vaiśvānaragupta, n. of a former Buddha: Mv i.140.2.

Vaiśvānaranirghoṣa, n. of a Buddha in the north: Sukh 97.21.

vaiṣamika, m. (cf. Skt. vaiṣamya, nt., same mg.), *disturbance, upset, distress, illness*: dhātu-vaiṣamikāṃś ca . . . vyupaśamayati Bbh 63.5–6 (cited s.v. **aupakramika**). Note dhātu-vaiṣamya-jaṃ (duḥkham) Bbh 246.24.

vaiṣṭika, m. (Skt. viṣṭi or BHS **veṣṭi** plus -ika), *forced laborer*: (mā haivāham iha) °ko vā gṛhyeya SP 103.10 (prose; Kashgar rec. viṣṭīkārako).

vaisarpa, m. (= Skt. visarpa; cf. next), a disease like *erysipelas*: Mvy 9509 = Tib. me dbal.

vaisarpya (m. or nt.?), = prec.: Māy 238.6; 245.23; 248.31; 259.22.

vaistārika, f. °kī, adj. (not noun with Burnouf, Senart, Kern; to Skt. vistāra plus -ika; cf. **vistārika** = Pali vitthārika; also **mahāvaistāra**), (**1**) *wide, broad*, physically: Merum . . . atyartha-vaistārikaṃ (most mss. -vist°) LV 126.16 (vs); (**2**) *extensive*, of a religious course: °kaṃ ca me brahmacaryaṃ Divy 202.14; (**3**) *widespread, widely diffused*, or *distributed*: (sc. samyaksaṃbodhiḥ) yathā vipulā °rikī bhavet SP 484.6; of sacred texts, or the Buddha's doctrine, iyaṃ dharmanetrī (sc. the LV) °rikī bhaviṣyati LV 439.1; °kaṃ kṛtva śāsanaṃ Mv i.252.13 (vs; em.); (of śāsana) MSV i.61.20 f.; bhagavān . . .°ka-(em., mss. °ko)-śāsana-saṃjāto (mss. °te or °taṃ) Mv ii.190.16 (prose), *became of widely diffused doctrine*; kṣemaṃ (so v.l.; adj.) °kaṃ prāvacanaṃ iii.234.20, and °kaṃ . . . prāvacanaṃ 245.8; of maintainers of the doctrine, °kān dharmadharān kuruṣva Divy 379.28 (vs); of the bodily relics of a Buddha, śarīra °riku tasya cābhūt SP 26.8 (vs), *and his body was widely distributed* (as relics); śarīra (separate word) °rika tasya tāyinaḥ 69.2 (vs), *widely ditributed (will be) the body of that Holy One*; °kāś ca te dhātavaḥ kartavyāḥ 411.2 (prose), *and these relics are to be widely distributed*; yo me śarīradhātūn °kān kariṣyati Divy 368.27; 379.21; °kā dhātavo 381.9; °kā dhātu-dharāḥ (*possessors of the relics*) kṛtāś ca 388.4.

Vaihāya, acc. to all mss, Mv i.70.16 (parvatasya vaihāya-varasya, vs), kept by Senart, = Skt. Vaibhāra (or Vaihāra, once Mbh.), n. of a mountain outside Rājagṛha. In Pali and AMg. the only form recorded is Vebhāra. See Senart's note ad loc.; he assumes Prakritic y for r, but Geiger 46.3, Pischel 255 make the interchange of y and r seem doubtful. Could this form be influenced by vaihāyasa, etc. (by popular etymology)?

vaihāyasaṃ, adv. (to Skt. °sa, *air*; the adv. is very rare in Skt.; Pali vehāyasaṃ and vehāsaṃ common, and so BHS), *in* or *into the air* (Kern regularly renders *as a meteor*; note esp. SP 250.5, where two persons are concerned, and Kern is obliged to render vaihāyasaṃ as if it were dual, *as meteors*!): SP 239.2 (abhyudgamya °sam); 240.5 (°sam antarīkṣe sthitaṃ); 241.11 (°saṃ tiṣṭhet), 15 (mss. °se); 248.13, 14; 250.5 (°sam antarīkṣasthau); 331.5 (vs, °su, v.l. °sa, m.c.); Mv i.21.7 (°sam abhyudgacchanti); 55.2; 158.13 (°saṃ dvīpāto dvīpaṃ saṃkrāmati); ii.492.7; iii.27.11; 107.12, 13; 366.12; Divy 223.15 (°saṃ ratho gacchati); 252.16 (°saṃ saptatālān abhyudgataḥ); common. In Mv perhaps commoner is vaihāyasena, a regular instr. of Skt. °yasa, e. g. ii.96.3; °se, loc., also occurs, ii.404.20.

(**Vokkāṇa**, m. or nt., n. of a place: °nam anuprāptaḥ Divy 580.5; refers, no doubt, to the home of the people so named in Skt., see BR.)

? **voṇṭa**, m. (noted Skt. Lex., and Hem. Pkt. Gr. i.139, as = Skt. vṛnta, but no mg. of that word seems to fit here; rather prob. related to **vṛndi**, q.v.), prob. *insect-shell*: Mvy 5995, among śaṅkhādi-nāmāni; after kapardikā, before abhraka, khaṭikā; Tib. srin lkog, or sriṅ khog, neither of which is comprehensible to me; prob. read srin (*insect*) khog (*body*, or *trunk*; -can, applied to a tortoise); Chin. *shell of an insect* (such as a cricket); the Mongolian Mvy takes Tib. to mean *body, trunk, of insects* (or more generally, including amphibious animals and fish).

vopasamati (m.c., MIndic for Skt. *vy-upa-śam-; see § 3.71 and Chap. 43, s.v. śam 1), *is quieted, pacified*: °manti Mv iii.371.5 (vs), see s.v. **vīra** (1); Pali Jāt. v.143.2 ūpa°.

vosārayati (MIndic for vy-ava-sār°; cf. Pali vosāraṇiya, rare for osār°, AN i.99.13), = osārayati, see s.v. 1 **osarati**: MSV iii.14.5 (prose) evaṃ ca punar vosarayitavyaḥ; also 26.1.

vyaṃsaka, adj. (Skt. Lex. id.; AMg. vaṃsaya; to next), *deceitful, tricky*: (vañcito bhavati . . .) na ca . . . taṃ vyaṃsakaṃ pudgalaṃ codayati Bbh 126.4.

vyaṃsayati (Skt. in mgs. *disappoints; wards off*), *deceives*: māsi mayā kiṃcid vyaṃsitaḥ? tāta mahātmā tvaṃ kiṃ māṃ vyaṃsayiṣyasi Divy 305.13–14, *I haven't cheated you in anything, have I? Father, you are a noble man, would you cheat me?*; vyaṃsitam MSV ii.102.13.

vyakta, adj. (= Pali vyatta), *wise, learned, clever*: paṇḍito vyakto medhāvī SP 320.6; Divy 108.9; 110.5; Dbh 61.15; vyaktau paṇḍitau medhāvinau Divy 318.18; others Mvy 2898; SP 46.3; Mv i.205.7 = ii.9.3 vyaktāyāṃ (loc. f.); ii.37.11; LV 25.11 vyaktāyā(ḥ); 377.13; Divy 202.12. See also **avyakta**.

vyagra, adj. and subst. (opp. to Skt. and BHS **samagra**; = Pali vagga, with cpds. vaggārāma, vaggarata), (**1**) adj., *separate, in separate places*: (imāni . . . śikṣāpadāni) teṣu-teṣu sūtrānteṣu vyagrāṇi Bhagavatā ākhyātāni Bbh 180.14; (ṣaṇṇāṃ pāramitānāṃ teṣu-teṣu sūtrāntareṣu) (read °teṣu?) Bhagavatā vyagrāṇāṃ nirdiṣṭānāṃ Bbh 215.15; vyagrāḥ kurvanti sātisārā bhavanti MSV ii.196.4, *if they do it separate(ly), they are guilty of sin*; similarly ii.202.14, 17; **vyagreṇa,** adv. (= Pali vaggena), *separately, in a sectarian* or *divisive way*, MSV ii.202.9; vyagra-karman (= Pali vagga-kamma, Vin. i.318.9 ff.), *disunited action*, MSV ii.210.1 ff., defined (opp. samagra-k°); (**2**) subst. (nt.?), *separation, disunion*: na vyagrārāmo bhavati na vyagra-rato na vyagra-karaṇīṃ vācaṃ bhāṣate sadbhūtāṃ asadbhūtāṃ vā Dbh 24.4 (follows passage cited s.v. **anupradāna** 2), *he takes no pleasure or delight in schism* (here with implication of dissension in the order of monks), *he speaks no word causing division, be it true or false*; (ye sattvā akalyāṇamitraparigṛhītā bhavanti, teṣāṃ tebhyaḥ akalyāṇamitrebhyo) ... vyagra-karaṇīṃ vācaṃ bhāṣate Bbh 168.2, ... *he speaks words to cause their separation from those evil friends.*

vyañjana, nt. (= Pali id.; in Skt. defined BR, pw, *consonant* and *syllable*; possibly *sound* should be substituted for the latter, at least in some cases), (individual) *sound*; defined AbhidhK. LaV-P. ii.239 by *akṣara, phonème* (*varṇa*), *voyelle et consonne, par exemple a, ā, i, ī, etc.*; here and in °na-kāyaḥ (see **kāya** 2) Mvy 1997 contrasted with **nāman,** *word*, and **pada,** *sentence*; much more commonly in contrast with artha, *meaning*, and regularly in such a context with implication of the *'letter'* as against the *'spirit'* (artha, the real *meaning*) in a sense close to the Biblical usage: arthato vā °nato vā SP 200.6, *either in regard to the meaning* (*spirit*) *or the letter* (Pali also atthato vā °nato vā); in Sūtrāl. xviii.32, comm., vyañjanasya is equated with yathārutārthasya, see s.v. **ruta** (2); na vyañjanā (v.l. °naṃ) bhrasyati (= bhraś°) nāpi cārthā LV 444.8 (vs), *neither sound(s) nor sense is lost*; (saddharmaṃ ...) svarthaṃ suvyañjanaṃ LV 3.8, *having good meaning and good sound(s)*; arthena mahyaṃ kāriyaṃ kiṃ bhoti vyañjanaṃ subahukaṃ Mv iii.60.20 (vs; so mss., with varr.; corrupt, but prob. was an āryā line), *my concern is with the meaning, what is the use of abundant sound?*; artha-pratisaraṇa as against vyañjana-prati°, Mvy 1546, Bbh 175.16, see s.v. **pratisaraṇa** (1); na vyañjanābhisaṃskārārthī, saḥ arthārthī ... na vyañjanārthī Bbh 256.25; śāstuḥ śrāvakāṇāṃ cārthenārthaḥ padena padaṃ (*word*, or *sentence*? see s.v.) vyañjanena vyañjanaṃ saṃsyandate sameti yad utāgrapadaiḥ Av ii.142.16; 143.5–6; pada-vyañjanaṃ, dvandva or tatp.? seemingly tatp. in SP 475.3 (yadā ...) ito dharmaparyāyād antaśaḥ pada-°naṃ paribhraṣṭaṃ bhaviṣyati, *when from this religious text so much as a* (single) *sound* (or *letter*) *of a word* (or *sentence*?) *shall be lost*; in the others could more easily mean *words* (*sentences*?) and *sounds* (*letters*), yāni ... pada-vyañjanāni paribhraṣṭāni SP 235.6; na ca yathoddiṣṭaṃ pada-°naṃ paripūrṇaṃ karonti Mv i.90.3, *and they do not make perfect(ly) as intended the sounds of the words* (*sentences*? or, *words and sounds*, sc. of sacred texts). — See further s.v. **vāla-vya°.**

vyañjita-jña, adj. or subst. m., *understanding* (only by) *what has been fully expressed*: Bbh 295.15, with its opposite **udghaṭitajña,** q.v. Actually an etymologizing distortion of **vipañcitajña,** q.v.

***vyatikāśa(ya)ti,** see **vītikāśeti.**

***vyatinamati, vīti°,** *passes* (intrans.; a time-expression as subject): madhyantike vītinate (ppp.) Mv iii.185.16, *now that high noon has passed*; caus. **°nāmayati** (in Mv **vītināmeti** = Pali id.), *passes* (trans.; a time-expression as object, or subject of pass.) (saptāham ...) vyatināmitam LV 380.14, *a week was passed*; saptāhaṃ ... vītināmeti (301.1; 302.21 °mesi, aor.) Mv iii.300.14; 301.1; 302.21, *spent a week.*

vyatipatati (once in late Skt., Schmidt, Nachträge), see **vīti°.**

Vyatipātin (cf. prec.), pl., n. of a group of yakṣas: Māy 59.

vyatibhindati (cf. **samatibhi°**), *shatters*: yathā hy agāraṃ succhan(n)aṃ vṛṣṭir na °ti, evaṃ subhāvitaṃ cittaṃ rāgo na °ti Ud xxxi.17; similarly 18–22.

vyatirocate, *is very resplendent*: prajñayā °cante (so with v.l.) samyaksaṃbuddhaśrāvakā Ud xviii.11.

***vyatilokayati,** see **vītiloketi.**

***vyatisaṃkrama,** see **vīti°.**

***vyatisaṃcarati,** see **vīti°.**

vyatisārayati, vīti° (= Pali vītisāreti), *makes to pass, carries on* (speech, conversation), only noted in ger. (kathāṃ) vyatisārayitvā Mv iii.206.1; 208.13; 325.14; 443.19; °retvā iii.60.11; vītisārayitvā iii.47.18; in iii.394.14 Senart vyatisārayitvā, v.l. sāropayitvā, see **sārāyaṇīya**; in virtually same phrase, which is also found in Pali, (kathāṃ) vyatisārya Divy 70.11; 75.23; 156.20; 619.2; Av i.229.3; ii.140.4; Karmav 27.2; 29.18.

vyatihāra, m., used in all other texts for **vītihāra,** q.v., of Mv.

Vyatyasta, (**1**) m., n. of a lokadhātu (associated with Avamūrdha; lit. *inverted*): Mvy 3069 (°dhaḥ), Gv 126.2, and Dbh 15.14 (on all these see s.v. **Avamūrdha**); °ta-lipī, 'the script of (the lokadhātu) Vyatyasta', Mv i.135.6 (cf. Avamūrdha-lipi LV 125.22); (**2**) m,, n. of a samādhi: Mvy 534 (not in ŚsP); perh. read so for **vyāskandaka-** (-samāpatti), q.v.; (**3**) nt., a high number: Mvy 7861 (cited from Gv); Gv 106.1; 133.10; = Tib. bsko (bsgo) yas, see **vicasta**; (**4**) adj. or subst., m. or nt., designation of a kind of yoga practice: Mvy 798 (see s.v. **yamaka**).

vyadhati (also Pali vyadhati, 'in poetry' acc. to PTSD, beside the usual vedhati; compromise form between straight MIndic **vedhati,** q.v., and Skt. vyathati), *shakes, trembles*: °ti pravyadhati saṃpravyadhati Divy 46.7; ppp. °dhitaḥ pravyadhitaḥ saṃpravyadhitaḥ 327.9.

vyadhvan, loc. °ani (cf. RV vyadhvan-aḥ), *on the way, midway* (adv.; synonym of antarā, which precedes it in all the foll.): AsP 286.19; 287.18; 289.4 (see s.vv. **vyavasāda, saṃsīdana**).

vyantī-karoti, rarely **vyanti°** (cf. rare Vedic vyanta, *remote*; = Pali vyanti-k°; cf. next), *puts an end to*: °roti Mvy 7044; AsP 343.19, see s.v. **chorayati** (8); °kṛta Mvy 2550; 7043 (a-vya°); yāva sānaṃ taṃ pāpakaṃ karma °taṃ na bhavati Mv i.18.14; 20.(4–)5 (most mss. here vyanti°); 21.11 (here na om. in mss., Senart transp. before taṃ), *until that evil action of theirs is ended* (i. e. its effect exhausted); avidyāye prahīṇatvāt tṛṣṇāye °kṛtatvāt Mv iii.66.2, *because ignorance is got rid of and thirst ended.* Tib. usually renders by forms containing byaṅ ba(r), *purify*, which would be a possible rendering in Mv i.18.14, but surely cannot be the lit. mg.

vyantī-bhavati (cf. prec. and next; = Pali vyanti°), *comes to an end*: Mvy 7042 = Tib. mthar (*to an end*) byed pa, or byaṅ bar ḥgyur (*becomes purified*, see under prec.).

vyantī-bhāva, once **vyanti°,** m. (to prec.), *coming to an end, being finished*; always prec. by **pratiniḥsarga,** a near-synonym: Mvy 7667 (= Tib. byaṅ bar gyur pa, *being purified*, see under prec. but one); pratiniḥsargo vyanti-bhāva(ḥ) Pischel SBBA 1904 p. 815, fol. 164a; kāmānāṃ prahāṇam ākhyātaṃ pratiniḥsargo vyantī° Bhīk 24a.3.

vyapakṛṣṭa, ppp., adj. (also **vyavakṛṣṭa**; in this use corresp. to Pali vūpakaṭṭha; specialized use of ppp. of Skt. vy-apa-(ava-)kṛṣ-, cf. also Pali vapakassati, vava°; in mg. *withdrawn* used as in Skt., e. g. kāmehi or LV kāmebhyo vyapakṛṣṭakāyo Mv ii.123.11, LV 248.2, *with body withdrawn from lusts*), *solitary, secluded* (from the world), in a cliché (as in Pali, eko vūpakaṭṭho appamatto ātāpī pahittatto, with a form of viharati, said of an arahat); the following are always followed by a form of viharati, *dwells*: eko 'pramatto ātāpī prahitātmā (om. LV) vyapakṛṣṭo Mv ii.118.11–12; 120.3; LV 239.2; eko vyapakṛṣṭo (Saṃy. Āg. vyava°) 'pramatta ātāpi prahitātmā (Saṃy.

Āg. pravivikto for prahi°) Divy 37.10; MSV i.48.12 f.; Saṃy. Āg. 3r.4; in Divy 618.3–4 occurs a fem. form, expanded and partly corrupt, ekā vyapakṛṣṭā 'pramattā ātāpinī smṛtimatī saṃprajānā prahitāni (! read prahitātmanī?) viviktāni (! read viviktā ? cf. Saṃy. Āg. pravivikto) viharati sma. Mvy 7166 vyapakṛṣṭaḥ = Tib. ḥdu ḥdzi med pa, *noiseless*, or dben pa, *solitary*.

Vyapagatakhiladoṣa, n. of a former Buddha: Sukh 6.10.

Vyapagatakhilamalapratighoṣa, n. of a former Buddha: Sukh 5.17.

vyapatrāpin, f. °**ṇī** (to Skt. vy-apa-trap-), *modest*: hrīmā °piṇi dharmacāriṇī LV 28.13 (vs); °**pi-tā**, abstr., *modesty*, Samādh p. 5 line 13. Cf. next.

vyapatrāpya, nt. (as prec.; cf. **apatrāpya**), *shame, modesty, bashfulness*: lajjā-°pya-saṃlīna-cetās Divy 255.16, hrī-°pya-gṛhītā 23 (here the bashfulness of love); *shame* of an evil deed, (śikṣāvyatikrame) °pyam utpadyate Bbh 137.20; in this sense in cpd. hrī-°pya, °pyaṃ prāviṣkaroti Bbh 6.1; similarly 137.25 f.; 159.14; 180.2; 250.8 (katamad bodhisattvānāṃ hrī-vyapatrāpyaṃ); a distinction between hrī and vyapa° is made in Bbh 250.10–12, where both are glossed lajjā, but hrī is said to mean the feeling that a blameworthy act is unworthy of oneself, vyapatrāpya is the feeling caused thereby thru fear or respect of others. Is this anything more than a commentator's ad-hoc attempt at subtlety? In AbidhK. LaV-P. ii.172 hrī is defined in a way suggesting rather vyapatrāpya of Bbh.

vyapadahyati, see **vyava°**.

vyapadeśa, see **su-vya°**.

vyapadeśate (for °diśati, but prob. denom. to Skt. vyapadeśa), °śamānā, pres. pple. f., *saying*, or acc. to Chin. (Finot) *commanding*: tatra ced bhikṣuṇī °nā sthitā syād Prāt 525.9 (what she says follows this but BHS. has a lacuna; acc. to Chin., 'Give rice and curry to this monk!').

vyapalokayati (=, and prob. error for, **vyavalo°**), *investigates*: °kayanto vivṛtena manasā (then lacuna) Ud xxi.18.

vyapasaṃsarati, *spends incarnations*: (ṣaṭsu kāmāvacareṣu) deveṣu sattvā (?) °sṛtya (ger.) Divy 200.10.

[**vyabhicārād api** Laṅk 246.4, not *even in exceptional cases* (Suzuki), but *also because of transgression* (on the part of butchers, as suggested in lines 5–8).]

vyarpaṇā (= Pali vyappanā; cf. s.v. **arpaṇā**), *application* (*of mind*), *focussing* (*of attention*), so PTSD: Mvy 7429. (Tib. renders etymologically.)

vy-alaṃkaroti, *disadorns, deprives of adornment*: na vayaṃ kumāraṃ vyalaṃkariṣyāmaḥ, alaṃkariṣyāmo vayaṃ kumāraṃ LV 142.18 (prose).

vyavakiraṇā (Skt. °kirati plus -anā), *mixing, confusion*: Mvy 7544 = Tib. ḥdres pa.

vyavakīrṇa, ppp. of vy-ava-kṛ *scatter* (= Pali vokiṇṇa, but see below), *interrupted, broken up, halting* (of speech): na vyava° = **a-vyava°**, q.v., Śikṣ 126.1 na vyavakīrṇa-vacanaḥ, *his speech is not halting, broken*. In Skt., and acc. to PTSD in Pali (vokiṇṇa), the only meaning seems to be *filled, pervaded, thoroughly mixed* (with, instr.); in this sense also BHS, e. g. Dbh 53.21. But cf. Pali abbokiṇṇa, CPD.

vyavakṛṣṭa, *solitary, secluded*, = **vyapakṛṣṭa**, in the cliché cited s.v.: Saṃy. Āg. 3r.4.

[**vyavagata-** SP 316.9 prose, so KN without ms. authority; read vyapa°.]

vyavacāra, m. (to **vyavacārayati**), (**1**) *wandering* or *searching through* (localities): (Sudarśanaṃ bhikṣuṃ mārgayamāṇo) janapada-°reṣu nagara-°reṣu, etc. (long series of locs. like these) Gv 127.16 ff.; sarvasattvabhājana-(text °nā-)-loka-°reṣu (see s.v. **bhājana**) sarvasattvagati-°reṣu Gv 180.8; kiṃvyavacārā (asi) Gv 287.9, *what have been your wanderings, searchings* (or, *considerations*)?; (**2**) prob. (cf. the usual mg. of **vyavacārayati**) *consideration, pondering, intellectual mastery*: samādhi-samudraṃ ca samādhivyutthānaṃ ca samādhi-°raṃ ca . . . adrākṣīt Gv 148.23. See also **a-vyavacāra**; if my assumption of the neg. in that word is right, it would mean lit. *non-consideration*; otherwise, if we must assume **vyavacāra**, not a-vy°, it is hard to see how the mg. *contempt* (which seems inevitable) could be explained.

vyavacāraṇa (nt.) and °**ṇā** (to next), *consideration, intellectual mastery*: °ṇā AsP 303.4, see next; °ṇa, ye mahāprajñāmahāsāgara-°ṇa-nayaprayogā(ḥ) Gv 248.10; °ṇa or °ṇā, samantamukha-°ṇālokena samādhimukhena Gv 180.6.

vyavacārayati, °**te** (cf. Pali vocarita and prec. items), *considers well, ponders thoroughly, understands*: °yadhvam SP 189.9, see **vyavalokayati** (parallel with this); etad bodhisattvasya . . . prajñayā °yataḥ (gen. sg. pres. pple.) Bbh 317.23 (ms. cited as vyavakār°; Rahder, App. to Dbh 1.17 cites this as vyavacār°); °yati AsP 433.2, see s.v. **prativahati**; (paśyati śṛṇoti) °yati **avacarati pratividhyati** (qq.v.) Gv 252.20; °yitavyaḥ Mvy 7458 (foll. by upanidhyātavyaḥ) = Tib. rnam par dpyad par bya ba; sarvajñatānimnā saṃtatir (q.v.) vyavacāritā bhavati (*mental disposition tending to omniscience becomes intellectually assimilated, considered to the point of mastery*), yā . . . sarvajñatānimnayā saṃtatyā vyavacāraṇā iyaṃ sā Subhūte vyavacāraṇā AsP 303.2–4.

vyavacchedana (nt.; JM. voccheyaṇa; cf. Skt. vyavaccheda), *cutting off, getting rid* (of, in comp.): sarvagatisaṃkhyā-°nāya Dbh 15.11.

vyavadahyati (v.l. vyapa°), pass., *is consumed, burnt away*: (atha teṣāṃ . . .) tac chavimānsalohitaṃ °yati Mv i.18.13 (prose).

vyavadāna, nt. (= Pali vodāna; n. act. to next), *purification, cleansing*: vyavadānāvyavadānataḥ Laṅk 18.9, *according to purity and impurity*; °na-saṃnihita-puṇya-bala (so with mss.) Mv i.204.18 (vs), *with the power of merit accumulated through purification*; kleśa-(mss. kleśaṃ) °naṃ vetti Mv i.160.2 (vs), *he knows how to purify the depravities*, one of the 10 **bala** of a Tathāgata, oftener **saṃkleśa-°na-**, Mvy 126 (also in list of the 10 **bala**); MSV iii.142.12; Mv iii.321.6 (°naṃ . . . saṃprajānanti); Divy 616.23, in passage parallel to Mv iii.357.14 and Pali Vin. i.15.36–38, but only Divy has saṃkleśa-°naṃ; Pali lacks vodāna; in Mv kāmeṣu bhayaṃ okāraṃ saṃkileśaṃ (construe with kāmeṣu, as in Pali with kāmānaṃ), naiṣkramyānuśaṃsā (prob. separate!) °naṃ saṃprakāśayati, *he sets forth the . . . impurity found in desires, the blessing* (*advantage*) *of renunciation, and purification* (sc. of the saṃkileśa mentioned just before?); saṃkleśa-°na also LV 433.14 f.; these two form a standardly contrasting pair, saṃkleśāya na °nāya Av ii.188.9 (by em.); saṃkleśaṃ °naṃ paśyati Śikṣ 172.11; two extremes (anta), saṃkleśa and °na KP 59.(2–)3; (kathaṃ ca saṃkleśo bhavati kathaṃ) ca °naṃ Bbh 99.11; similarly 215.7; 388.8 (cf. 5); asaṃbhinnajñāna-°nāya Dbh 3.14.

vyavadāyate, °**ti** (= Pali vodāyati; cf. prec., and BR and pw s.v. 7 dā, but app. not used in the same mg.), *becomes purified*: (naite . . . dharmā udvijante, na) saṃkliśyante na °yante Śikṣ 263.15; similarly, na saṃkliśyate na °yate ŚsP 140.14; (na ca . . . saṃkliśyate na . . .) °yati AsP 399.15, 16. Cf. saṃkleśa contrasting with **vyavadāna**.

vyavadiśati (cf. Pali ppp. vodiṭṭha; perh. represents Skt. vyapa°), *recognizes* (as true), *names, establishes, defines*: (na . . . abhijānāmi . . . anyaṃ śāstāraṃ) vyavadiśitum anyatraiva tena bhagavatā . . . Mv iii.50.8.

[**vyavana**, Gv 472.19, is a corruption for a word meaning *deviation* (from), or the like, perh. *vyavakramaṇa = Pali vokkamana: na ca mahāyāna-vyavana-vihāriṇaḥ, text.]

[**vyavapariṇāma**, read with 2d ed. vyaya-pari°: Gv 243.20.]

(**vyavabhāsate**, *shines*; caus. *illumines* is Skt., BR 5.1658: [-āntarikāś ca, pārśukā] virājante °sante LV 254.11, 12.)

vyavalambin, adj. (a-vyava° once Ved., in not quite same mg.), *hanging down* (from, comp.): idaṃ tu kaṇṭha-°bi . . . -ābharaṇaṃ Divy 360.11.

vyavalokana, nt. (to next plus -ana; = Pali volokana), *looking closely at, examining carefully*: rājā . . . janapadān °nāya nirgataḥ Divy 435.22; sarvasattvacittacarita-°na-sūkṣmapraveśajñānaṃ Dbh 86.31; -vimokṣabhavana-°na-(-siṃhavijṛmbhitena) Gv 39.24; -anantakāya-°na-cakṣur-viśuddhyā 237.15, et al.; in LV 62.6 (Śakro . . .) śīrṣa-vyavalokanenānuvilokayati sma, app. *looked with a sideways turn* (*look*) *of the head* (to try to see better), so Tib. mgo byol nas bltas kyaṅ; cf. the Tib. def. of **vyavalokita** cited s.v.

vyavalokayati, rarely °**te** (= Pali voloketi; cf. prec. and next, also **vyapalo°**), *looks closely* (*at*), *examines carefully*, in physical or intellectual sense, the two being sometimes indistinguishable: °yata (Tib. ltos, impv.) mārṣā bodhisattvasya kāyaṃ LV 30.20, and °yata . . . daśadikṣu . . . bodhisattvān 21, *behold!* (physically); (Asita speaks) yan nv ahaṃ °yeyam iti, sa divyena cakṣuṣā . . . adrākṣīt LV 101.5; siṃhāvalokitaṃ mahāpuruṣāvalokitaṃ °yati sma LV 84.5, *gazed the gaze of a lion, of a Great Man*; but intellectually just below, (sarvasattvānāṃ ca citta-caritaṃ [ca, omit with ms. A] prajānāti sma, jñātvā) ca °yati sma LV 84.10, *reflected, considered* (quotation follows of question he asked himself); sa narakān °yitum ārabdho, na paśyati . . . Divy 83.4; (Buddhacakṣuṣā lokaṃ) °yanti 95.25; (Bhagavān . . .) nāgāvalokitena °yati 208.17; cāturdvīpikaṃ °yituṃ pravṛttaḥ, tatrāpi nādrākṣīt Av i.258.3; nānāvāsaṃ °yitavyaṃ Kv 96.8, *is to be* (physically) *inspected*; °yantu māṃ Buddhāḥ Suv 30.7, cited Śikṣ 162.15, (physically) *examine*; sarvadharmārthagatiṃ (Tib. don gyi = artha, in gen. relation to rim pa = gati, *series* or *method*) ca tathāgato °yati (Tib. gzigs, *see*, both phys. and intellectually) SP 121.7; anusaran °kayan pratipadya-mānaḥ Dbh 47.19, of Buddhas passing from 5th to 6th bhūmi; lokasya saṃbhavaṃ ca vibhavaṃ ca °yate 47.24 (same situation); (dharmāṇāṃ . . . hetuphalavyavasthā-naṃ . . .) °yati, °lokya kāmadhātāv eva sabhāge dhātāv . . . Bbh 397.28 (here app. intellectually); (puruṣaḥ . . . na) °yitavyaḥ Bhīk 24a.4, cited s.v. **upanidhyāyati** (could be both physical and intellectual); °yadhvaṃ bhikṣavo vyavacārayadhvaṃ, yad yuṣmākaṃ nirvāṇaṃ naiva nirvāṇam SP 189.9.

vyavalokita, nt. (orig. ppp. to prec.), *intense gaze, steady look*; acc. to Tib. repeatedly (on LV 191.17, 240.3) gyas gyon du lta ba, *looking to the right and left* (i. e., I presume, *all around*): (prāsādikenā)valokita-vyavalokitena LV 191.17; similarly 240.3; **vilokita**, q.v. 1, is elsewhere used in a like cliché; °kita-mātreṇa LV 31.6, *by a mere look* (cf. vyavalokayata 30.20, 21); bodhisattva-°kitaṃ Gv 18.4.

[**vyavasana-tā** KP 114.2 (prose), read prob. vyasana-, less likely vyavasāna- (Pali id., *determination*, but rare and doubtful, see PTSD): mitrakulabhekṣāka-(= °bhaikṣ°)-kulād vyavasanatā-grahaṇaṃ, one of two evils (mala) of a pravrajita. Tib. renders the whole cpd. by yoṅs su ḥdzin pa, *wholly grasping* or *taking*.]

vyavasarga (m.; Skt. Gr. id.; Ved. in diff. mg.; = Pali vavassagga, wrongly defined PTSD; AN i.36.20 vavassaggārammaṇaṃ karitvā, comm. ii.38.19 vavassaggo vuccati nibbānaṃ, which is perh. over-narrow but comes close to BHS), = (pari)tyāga, *abandonment, giving up* or *away*; Tib. on Mvy rnam par gtoṅ (or, spoṅ) ba, both *abandonment*: °ga-pariṇatam, adj. with ṛddhipādam (acc.), after virāga-niśritam, nirodha-niśritam, Mvy 975, and Dbh 39.1; °ga-rata Mvy 2846, among tyāgādayaḥ, also Śikṣ 24.6 (adj. with hastapādaparityāgena).

vyavasāda (m.? to Skt. vyavasīdati), *sinking down, falling*: vyadhvani vyavasādam āpatsyate AsP 286.19; 287.18.

vyavasta, adj.-ppp. = Skt. vyavasita (§ 3.112), *resolved, determined*: ko jīvitaṃ sumadhuraṃ tyajituṃ vyavastaḥ Divy 416.26 (vs; m.c., hyper-Skt.?).

vyavasthāna, nt. (= Pali vavatthāna; Skt. not in this sense), *respective determination, differentiation*: bhūmi-bhūmi-°na-kuśalena Dbh 20.28; tattvalakṣaṇaṃ °na-taḥ advayaprabhāvitaṃ veditavyaṃ Bbh 39.1; 260.13 (see s.v. **vipaśyanā**); catvārīmāṇi bodhisattvānāṃ prajñapti-°nāni 292.7, listed as dharma-pra°-°naṃ, satya-, yukti-, and yāna-, 11–13, explained 292.14–294.8; 397.27 (see s.v. **vyavalokayati**); (all inhabitants of Sukhāvatī are niyatāḥ samyaktve, see s.v. **rāśi**) nāsti tatra dvayo rāśyor vyavasthānaṃ prajñaptir vā yad idam aniyatasya vā mithyātvaniyatasya vā Sukh 44.15, *there is no differentiation or clear statement as regards the* (other) *two groups, namely* . . . (i. e. they are equally unqualified for S.).

vyavasthānaprajñapti, a high number: Mvy 7965, cited from LV 148.3.

vyavasthita (in this mg. Pali vavatthita, not recorded in Skt. in the ppp.), *separated, not in conjunction*: nakṣa-trāṇi °tāni MSV ii.82.12.

vyavahasati (cf. Skt. Gr. vyāvahāsī, BR), *laughs loudly*: hasati °sati ca Kv 64.6.

vyavahāra, m. (**1**) (much as in Skt., BR s.v. 8, cf. 7; *designation, term*, in BHS with implication of superficiality, lack of substance, e. g. ŚsP 1334.18 °ra-mātra = nāma-mātra 19), *manner of speech*: ārya-°ra (= Pali ariya-vohāra, see CPD), eight (as in Pali), Bbh 220.7, 11 (dṛṣṭe dṛṣṭavāditā, etc.); aṣṭau °ra-padāni Bbh 389.13, 16 (evaṃnāmā, evaṃjātyaḥ, etc.); ṣaḍ °ra-pada-caritāni 19 ff. (āhvānāya saṃketaḥ, etc.); saṃvṛti-°ra Sukh 42.11, see **saṃvṛti**; (**2**) *motion, gesture*: (hasta-) °reṇa (contemptuously) uddeṣṭum ārabdhaḥ MSV ii.190.9; so also hasta-vyavahārakeṇa ib. 188.12.

vyavahāraka = prec., q.v. (2).

vyavahārika (Skt. °ra plus °ika; in Skt. vyāva°, but even in Skt. vyava° need not be called 'erroneous' with BR), (**1**) *dealer, man of business*: (after a list of tradesmen of many kinds) ete cānye ca bahu-°kā sarve . . . Mv iii.113.11, and similarly 442.16; (**2**) (Pali vohārika, said to be a judicial officer), *one who is in charge of the affairs of* . . ., in paura-°kaḥ Mvy 3712 = Tib. groṅ gi bla, *in charge of town(s)*, a royal officer (cf. Kauṭ, Arth. Sham.[1] 20.13 paura-vyāvahārika).

[**vyaskandaka**, see **vyā°**.]

vyastikā(-kṛta), (*in*) *a posture with the hands joined at the back of the neck*: Mvy 8609 (Tib. = **udvyastikā**, q.v.)

vyākutsanā (neither this nor any form of vi-ā-kuts-seems to be recorded anywhere), *contempt, loathing*: kāmeṣu °nā utpadye Mv iii.440.9; 451.2 (both prose).

vyākaraṇa, nt. (to **vyākaroti**; in mg. 1 essentially like Skt. id.; Pali id. also in mg. 3), (**1**) *explanation, elucidation*, esp. of questions put: praśnasya °ṇena Laṅk 15.1; dharmaṃ paripṛcchakās, tasya ca °ṇena tuṣṭā(ḥ) . . . SP 288.12; sarvapraśna-°ṇa- LV 427.14; (rājā . . .) pṛcchati, te ca jñātvā vyākaronti, teṣāṃ vyākaraṇaṃ śrutvā . . . Mv i.274.5; °ṇe bhāṣyamāṇe iii.66.17; prob. in this sense, persons like the Bodhisattva are called °ṇa-sampannāḥ, *perfect in elucidation* (of religious problems), Mv ii.290.19 (in one of the reproaches hurled at Māra; cf. pratibhāna-sampannāḥ 18, just before); so also the Pratyekabuddhas who entered nirvāṇa to 'empty' the earth for the birth of Śākyamuni are said to have vyākaraṇāni vyākaritvā Mv i.357.9, 11, before entering nirvāṇa; in this case the vyākaraṇāni are the khaḍgaviṣāṇa gāthās appropriate to Pratyekabuddhas; there are four technical kinds of °ṇa, *answers to questions*, in Mvy 1657–61, **ekāṃśa-, vibhajya-, paripṛcchā-**, and **sthāpanīya-°ṇa**, qq.v.; as one of the 12 or 9 types of literature in the canon, °ṇam Mvy 1269; Dharmas 62, *explanation*, perh. more specifically *answers to questions*, = **vaiyākaraṇa**, Pali veyyākaraṇa (which acc. to MN comm. ii.106.13 means all the Abhidhamma, suttas without gāthās, and whatever else is not included in the other 8 divisions!); not *predictions* with Burnouf Intr. 54 ff. and Lévi on Sūtrāl. i.7; (**2**) vyākaraṇaḥ, m., Av ii.19.8 (see Speyer's note), if correct would be nom. ag., *expounder, elucidator*; parallels Divy 619.24; 620.19 vaiyākaraṇaḥ, in Skt. and perh. here *grammarian*; (**3**) (as in Pali, not Skt.) *prophecy, prediction*, recorded only of a prediction that someone will attain perfect enlightenment (tho the verb **vyākaroti** is not so restricted); in this sense very common, regularly with gen. of the person (or in comp.) and loc. of the goal: Śāriputrasyedaṃ °ṇam anuttarāyāṃ samyaksambodhau SP 69.6; similarly SP 70.12; 214.3, 4; 222.12, etc. etc.; megha-māṇavaka-°ṇaṃ Mv i.2.1; °ṇaṃ . . . labheyā Bhad 59, *may I get a prophecy*; apramāṇa-°ṇa-pratyeṣakaś Dbh 71.24; others, Suv 168.4 etc., common everywhere; exceptionally, with loc. of beneficiary, gen. of maker of the prophecy, vyākaraṇam asmi (mss. asmiṃ) dyutimatŏ Mv i.43.18, so read, *the Glorious One's prophecy about him*.

vyākaroti (and other, MIndic presents; also **viyā°**; in mg. 1 not only = Pali but also Skt., see BR s.v. 2, hence only a few exx. here; cf. **vyākaraṇa**), (**1**) *elucidates*, esp. a question: . . . paripṛccheyaṃ, yathā me bhagavāṃ vyākariṣyati . . . Mv i.57.3; 274.5 (see **vyākaraṇa** 1); bhagavān taṃ arthaṃ vyākare ii.93.21; vyākuruṣva . . . kuta eti (WT with K′ enti) ime śūrā SP 307.1–2 (vs); asminn arthe vyākriyamāṇe SP 36.2 and 37.1; ity eṣā pañcamī bhūmī (mss. °myāṃ!) vyākṛtā . . . Mv i.120.14 (vs); nāpi ye dharmāḥ vyākṛtās te avyākṛtā iti deśayāmi Mv i.173.10; (**2**) (= Pali id.) *prophesies, predicts*, in general: (naimittikair vaipañcikaiś ca) vyākṛtam abhūt: maṅgaladvāreṇa kumāro 'bhiniṣkramiṣyatīti LV 186.16; similarly 211.3; Mv i.197.9; so (sc. naimittikaḥ) 'pi tathaivāmṛtādhigamanam eva vyākṛtavān LV 268.5; (naimittikehi kumāro) vyākṛtaḥ, rājā cakravartī bhaviṣyati Mv ii.32.7; (naimittikena ca) horapāṭhakena ca vyākṛto, yena kāryeṇa devadatto kumāro abhiniṣkramati, taṃ kāryaṃ na prāpayiṣyati Mv iii.178.18; Vārāṇasyāṃ naimittikair (mss. nimi°) dvādaśavarṣikānāvṛṣṭir vyākṛtā Divy 131.20; rarely, pratyekabodhi is predicted, Vipaśyinā . . . sa sārthavāhaḥ pratyekabodhau vyākṛtaḥ Av i.138.1; (sā Bhagavatā) pratyekāyāṃ bodhau vyākṛtā Divy 70.6; much more commonly, in fact constantly in most texts, perfect enlightenment or Buddhahood is predicted, always by an earlier Buddha, who declares that the person mentioned will attain his goal, often in a particular age and world; this constitutes **vyākaraṇa** (3), and seems to come to be regarded as a regular, perhaps necessary, preliminary to Buddhahood in Mahāyāna; it always occurs long before the event, under a Buddha of the remote past, tho it may be the Buddha immediately preceding the one for whom the prediction is made; sometimes a group prediction is made, all to become Buddhas in turn and each one to predict the next, SP 209.5 (vs) paraṃparā eva tathānyam-anyaṃ te vyākariṣyanti . . .; SP 27.3 (vs) anyonya vyākarṣu (°kārṣu? § 32.74) tadāgrabodhaye; see also SP 269.4; the person predicted is always in the acc., or nom. in a passive expression; only seeming exceptions are SP 206.6–7 (prose) saced asmākam api bhagavān, yatheme 'nye . . . vyākṛtā, evam asmākam api tathāgataḥ pṛthak-pṛthag vyākuryāt (in Buddha's reply, line 9, ahaṃ . . . vaśībhūtaśatāny anantaraṃ vyākaromi), and 215.7–8 (prose) yad bhagavān asmākaṃ vyākuryād . . . (asmākam is acc., as clearly elsewhere even in the prose of SP, § 20.48); the goal is regularly loc., in prose commonly anuttarāyāṃ samyaksaṃbodhau (abbreviated an° sam° in my citations); rarely what look like dat. forms occur, SP 27.3 (above); 212.6 (vs) yaṃ vyākṛtā sma paramāgrabodhaye; LV 392.2 (vs) boḍhisattvā ye vyākṛtā bodhayi (m.c. for °ye); Mv i.239.6 (prose) anuttarāye samyaksaṃbodhaye, but below 17–18 -vyākṛto . . . anuttarāye (v.l. °yāṃ!) samyaksaṃbodhāye (so both mss., Senart em. °aye, but a loc. is surely intended); these rare -bodhaye forms may actually intend locs., see § 10.142; rather often, no goal is expressed in words at all, so that the verb vyākaroti itself means *predicts* (someone) *unto enlightenment* (examples below); or the goal may be stated in a following direct quotation, as in SP 116.8 (vs) te vyākriyante . . . bhaviṣyathā buddha . . ., *they are prophesied, 'you shall become Buddhas'*; typical examples, (Śrīgarbhaṃ nāma) bodhisattvaṃ . . . an° sam° vyākṛtya SP 21.12; yadāpi (sc. māṃ) vyākurvasi agrabodhau 63.4 (vs); . . . nāma bodhisattvaṃ . . . vyākṛtyān° sam° 67.2; vayaṃ bhagavatā . . . an° sam° vyākṛtāḥ 212.1–2; tān vyākaromī aham . . . tathāgatatve 221.14 (vs); catasraḥ parṣado vyākaromy an° sam° 224.7, similarly 10; nāhaṃ . . . vyākṛtā cān° sam° 268.9–10; (yāvad . . .) bodhisattvā na vyākṛtā bhaviṣyanti an° sam° LV 377.18; ātmasamatāye (em.; loc.) samāsataḥ svayaṃbhūsamatāye vyākārṣīt Mv i.3.6; samanantara-vyākṛto . . . anuttarāyāṃ (so mss.) samyaksaṃbuddhāya (v.l. °yā, prob. loc., §10.142) 40.5–6; 239.17–18, see above; no goal expressed (besides some cited above), vyākṛto hy eṣa Śāriputro SP 70.6 (vs); na tāvad asmān saṃbuddho vyākaroti 147.11 (vs); vyākṛtā yada bheṣyāmas 147.14 (vs); (yenāyaṃ bhagavān prathamata) evaṃ vyākṛtaḥ Mv i.1.14; no cāhaṃ (tehi) vyākṛto i.46.2, 3, 5; interesting theoretical statement, Bbh 290.4–10: ṣaḍbhir ākāraiḥ samāsataḥ tathāgatā bodhisattvam an° sam° vyākurvanti. katamaiḥ ṣaḍbhiḥ. gotrastham anutpāditacittaṃ; tathotpāditaṃ cittaṃ; saṃmukhāvasthitaṃ; viparokṣāvasthitaṃ; parimitaṃ kālam, iyatā kālenān° sam° abhisaṃbhotsyata iti; aparimitakālaṃ vyākaroti, na tu kālaniyamaṃ karoti.

-vyākulika, in gṛha-vyā° Mvy 9261, which seems to mean (a monk) *who is disturbed by longing thoughts of his* (former lay) *house*; Tib. khyim so (Das *homesick*); so Jap. seems to intend, and so 2d Chin. version; vyākulika would mean *disturbed, upset* (Skt. vyākula).

vyākṛti (f.; = **vyākaraṇa** 3), *prediction* of future enlightenment for a Bodhisattva: °tir Bbh 290.2 (vs).

vyākopayati = **vikop°**, *disturbs*: °pya, ger., MSV i.6.14.

[**vyāghatika**(-saṃjñā), corruption for **vyādhmātaka-**, q.v.]

Vyāghranakha, pl., n. of a brahmanical gotra: Divy 635.19.

Vyāghrapadya (= Pali Vyagghapajja), another name for the **Koliyas**, q.v. (also in Pali): Mv i.355.13, with etym. explanation, mss. corrupt; prob. intends, as in Pali, to say that their city was built on a tiger's track.

Vyāghrabala, n. of a yakṣa: Māy 61(?). The mss. read the line: yakṣau siṃhabalau yau tu Siṃhavyāghrabalābalau; see Lévi's note for the evidently puzzled translations; but at least one Chin. supports the theory that **Siṃhabala** and Vyāghrabala are the two names, ā in -balābalau being lengthened m.c.

[**Vyāghrī-jātaka**, name adopted in Senart's Introd. for Jāt. of which colophon Mv ii.72.15 reads śrīyaśodharāye vyāghrībhūtāye jātakaṃ (no v.l.).]

vyāḍa, (**1**) m. (Skt. Gr. id., and in mg. *wild beast* in Skt. literature; = normal Skt. vyāla, Pali vāḷa), *wild beast* and *serpent*: both given by Tib., ma ruṅs pa, gdug pa, also sbrul, for Mvy 6962; *serpent* in Mvy 4841, = Tib. klu, sbrul; vyāḍa-mṛga (= Skt. vyāla°, Pali vāḷamiga), *wild beast*, Mv ii.215.16 (siṃhena vyāghreṇa vā anyena vā vyāḍamṛgeṇa); 216.5; vaneṣu ca vyāḍamṛgākuleṣu Jm 122.18 (vs); (**2**) adj. (Skt. Lex. id., Skt. vyāla), *violent, troublesome*: MSV ii.8.13.

vyāḍa-yakṣa (for vyāla°, cf. prec.; but the cpd. is not otherwise recorded), prob. *serpent-yakṣa* (being concerned with financial matters, collection of duties): sa (śulkaśālikaḥ, q.v.) °kṣeṣūpapannaḥ Divy 275.28.

vyādhi, *disease* (normally m.), f. LV 351.11 (prose) avabuddhā sattva-vyādhiḥ, *the disease of creatures was well understood* (by the Buddha); yatra ca punar vyādhyā (gen.? or read °yāṃ, loc.?) vyupanāmyante KP 87.2, see s.v. **upanāmayati** (5), *and for whatever disease they* (medicines) *are given*; nt., Mv i.353.3 (prose) sarvaṃ ca kuṣṭha-vyādhiṃ visrutaṃ.

[**-vyādhika,** adj., *diseased*, assumed by Senart in pitta-°kena Mv iii.347.17 and °kasya 19; but mss. in 17 °vyādhitena, which is standard Skt., prob. read °vyādhitasya also in 19.]

vyādhi-prajñāyate, see **prajñāyate.**

vyādhmātaka, nt. (also **dhmātaka,** q.v.; corresponds to Pali uddhumātaka), *a corpse swollen (by putrefaction*; cf. ādhmāyati Bṛh.Ār.U.Mādhy. 3.2.12); -saṃjñā, *contemplation of the notion of such a corpse*, one of the **aśubha-bhāvanā,** q.v., or saṃjñā: Mvy 1159; Bhīk 27a.2; ŚsP 1258.6 (text corruptly vyāghatika-); 1431.19; Gv 157.15.

vyāpadyate, °ti (= Pali vyāpajjati; cf. next two), *is cross, malicious, shows ill will*: tataḥ kupyanti °dyanti abhiṣyandanti kopaṃ ca roṣaṃ ca apratyayaṃ ca āviṣkaronti Mv i.30.5; (kupyati) °dyate madguḥ etc. Av i.286.5, see s.v. **maṅku**; tatra nāmāhaṃ vyāpadye Śikṣ 188.13, *under these circumstances, forsooth, I am cross* (as I ought not to be; Transl. wrong); (na ca mayā pareṣāṃ svaparāddhānāṃ) api vyāpattavyaṃ 14, *and I must not be cross at others even when they are guilty of grave offenses.*

vyāpanna, adj. (ppp.; = Pali id., regularly with citta; cf. prec. and next, and see **a-vyāpanna**), *malicious*: °na-citta, *malicious-minded*, LV 35.2; Divy 301.24; 302.9; Gv 352.19.

vyāpāda, m. (= Pali id.; see prec. two), *malice*; one of the three mental akuśala karmāṇi (regularly listed after **abhidhyā** and before **mithyādṛṣṭi** or °**darśana**): Mv i.107.15; Mvy 1697; LV 31.17; Mv ii.99.11 (avidyā in 10 by error for abhidhyā); Bbh 224.1; Karmav 79.16; °da-citta, *malicious thoughts*, SP 379.1; 382.7; °da-vitarka, substantially the same, LV 71.9; Śikṣ 39.15; avyāpādo . . . vyāpādavitarkaprahāṇāya saṃvartate LV 32.22, *non-malice . . . leads to abandonment of malicious reflections*; opposite of maitrī Bbh 204.24; 368.21; vyāpādasyāvyāpādo niḥsaraṇaṃ maitrī Mvy 1597; asuras are vyāpādabahulā Mv i.30.2, sureṣu vyāpādena, *with* (or, *because of*) *malice towards the gods* id. 3–4; associated with other vices, often in lists of vices, esp. juxtaposed to krodha, SP 419.6; LV 52.14; 411.17; miscellaneous LV 35.2; 42.5; 178.13; 279.8; 280.5; 430.12; Śikṣ 14.3; Dbh 25.4; Bbh 145.9; 243.21; Sukh 25.13; ākīrṇa-vyāpāda, *with abundant malice*, RP 34.9; one of the 5 **nīvaraṇa,** q.v.

vyābādha (m.; written vyāvādha; see next, and **a-vyā°**), *injury*: Divy 424.4 vyāvādhe khalv api bhaiṣajyam asulabhaṃ, *and, as everybody knows, in case of injury also, medicaments are not easy to get.* The ed. queries the word, without reason.

vyābādhati, °te, °dhayate, also written vyāvādhati, and at least in mss. vyāvadhati, °te, **vyāvahati** (cf. **vyābādha, °dhika, a-vyā°**; = Pali vyābādheti, byā°), *oppresses, injures, violates, harms*: na kaṃcit sattvaṃ vyābādhati Mv i.207.2; ii.10.12 (here vyāpādayati; as Childers and PTSD point out, there is confusion between these two roots; cf. s.v. **avyābādha**); iii.341.10 (here mss. vyāvahati, Senart em. vyābādhati); with gen. of personal object, na ca tasya rāgo vyāvadhiṣyate SP 419.5 (v.l. vyāvādh°; WT vyābādh°); na teṣāṃ rāgo vyāvādhiṣyati SP 481.4 (v.l. vyāvah°; WT vyābādh°); with acc. object, na cāsya kāyaṃ vyābādhate sma LV 152.20; netrāṇi vyābādhayate mūrchāṃ ca saṃjanayati Divy 105.12 (prose).

? **vyābādhika**: Gv 451.7 dhanvāyitatvaṃ (read dhandhā°) vā vyābādhikaś cāvasādanaṃ (2d ed. °kaṃ vāva°) vā ajñānaṃ vā etc., in a list of imperfections. Perhaps read vyābādhikatvaṃ vā, *or state of having been injured* (cf. **vyābādha, °dhati**)?

vyāmaka, nt., n. of a medicinal plant: Suv 104.7. So mss.; Nobel em. jñāmakaṃ on the basis of some Tib. and Chin. versions. But cf. vyāma, *Costus speciosus oder arabicus*, Vār.Bṛ.S. 77.7 (pw).

vyāma-prabhā, sg. or pl. (= Pali byāmappabhā), and (adj. Bhvr.) °bha, (*having*) *a halo extending a fathom* (around the Buddha): °bhā niścaretsuḥ Mv ii.44.20; (Bhagavantaṃ . . .) °bhālaṃkṛtaṃ Divy 46.29; 72.9; Av i.3.7 etc. (mss. often vyoma°, see Speyer, ii.cix); vyāmaprabhojjvalamuñcitaraśmiṃ Suv 49.1 (vs; most mss. vyoma°); °bhayā . . . lokaṃ sphuritvā tiṣṭhanti Sukh 29.6; adj., (Śākyamuni . . .) °bho (mss. vyoma°) Mv i.111.6; (Bodhisattvasya . . .) °bha-tā LV 270.18 (some mss. vyoma°), *state of having . . .*

vyāmotsaṅga, m., acc. to Senart some part, or the whole, of the *covering* or *facade* of a city gate; but utsaṅga could only mean horizontal, not vertical, covering; more likely it refers to some hollow in or about the gate; it may have measured a *fathom* (vyāma) in width: teṣāṃ . . . dvārāṇāṃ dvinnāṃ varṇānāṃ °gā abhūṣi suvarṇasya ca rūpyasya ca Mv i.195.10.

(**vyāmohaka,** *deluding, confusing*, Skt., Schmidt, Nachträge; °ka-tvād Laṅk 185.2.)

? **vyāyāsayati** (Skt. āyāsayati), *maltreats*, em. of KN °yantaś at SP 84.10 (vs); WT em. vābādhayantaś (MIndic for vyā°) which is remoter from mss. (which differ greatly), but at least well-known in BHS, and means the same; object śvānān, in the dilapidated house; pple. agrees with kumbhāṇḍakā(ḥ) line 7.

vyāyukta, adj., *variegated in color*: °tāśvā °ta-rathā etc. Mv i.261.5–9, replacing nīla, pīta, and other colors in otherwise identical passages above. Mg. seems certain, tho unrecorded; BR cite vyāyujya, ger., with mg. *sich trennen, auseinandergehen.*

(**vyāroṣa,** = Pali °sa, but also in Skt., Schmidt, Nachträge, *anger*: Mvy 2110.)

vyārta, adj. (= Skt. ārta), *distressed, afflicted*: vaira-°to bhavati Divy 163.6.

[**vyālaka,** in Jm 165.17 acc. to Speyer *elephant*; Speyer was misled by Skt. Lex. id., *rogue-elephant*, which really means *rogue*, not primarily *elephant*. It could only mean either *savage beast* of some sort, or *serpent*, and in the Jm clearly the latter: khe toraṇa-vyālaka-vad babhāse, *shone like a serpent on a toraṇa up in the air.*]

vyāvadhati, °te, see **vyābādhati.**

vyāvartana (nt.; to Skt. vyāvartayati; not quite in this mg. in Skt.), *reverse, reversal*: dhyāna-°ne Bbh 210.24 = Tib. bzlog na, *in case of reversal of dh.*; ātmadṛṣṭi-°nakuśalānāṃ Laṅk 10.13, *able to produce* (desirable) *reversal of their own* (wrong) *views* (= **parāvṛtti,** next line; wrongly Suzuki).

vyāvahati, *displays, indulges in*: Mv iii.429.4 (na ca) bhūyo krodhaṃ vyāvahati (said of a nāga, tamed by Buddha). In Mv iii.341.10 mss. vyāvahati, Senart em. **vyābādhati,** q.v.; the like occurs as v.l. at SP 481.4 for KN vyāvādhiṣyati, WT vyābā°, see **vyābādhati.**

vyāvādha, vyāvādhati, see **vyābādha, vyābādhati.**

vyāsajati (cf. Skt. vyāsakta; mid. once in Skt., pw), *puts together, attaches*: ger., sa pāṇau vyāsajya mūrdhānam Divy 596.15 (vs), *putting his head in his hand*; gdve., yeṣu vyāsajya-cetā . . . Divy 587.3, *with mind capable of being attached.*

Vyāsaparipṛcchā, n. of a work: Mvy 1392.

? **vyāseka,** m. (cf. Pali vyāsiñcati, avyāseka), should mean *pollution, defilement*, which seems reasonably appropriate in the context: Mvy 7540. But Tib. ḥphyar ba, *hang up, elevate* (also *sift, winnow,* and *show, represent*); Chin. *hang*; Jap. merely translates Tib. and speculates etymologically, and futilely, ignoring the Pali. Cf. AbhidhK. LaV-P. vi.289 bahuvidhaviṣaya-vyāseka-visārin (of buddhi), *qui se dispersent naturellement, distraites par la variété des objets* (it is not clear to me how LaV-P. took vyāseka).

vyāskandaka-, a kind of **samāpatti,** q.v.: Mvy 1497 (Mironov **vya°**). Tib. renders by snrel zhi, which usually = **vyatyasta** (q.v. 2), and Mvy ed. suggests reading so; cf. **vyutkrāntaka.** It would seem to be, like the latter, a manner of skipping from one trance-state to a non-adjoining one. But Chin. has the equivalent of nāsaṃjñāyatana, which as Ting says seems 'an abbreviation' (the last part) of **naivasaṃjñānāsaṃjñāyatana.**

vyāharati, in regular mgs. of Skt. viharati (mg. 1 once in BhP. acc. to BR), (**1**) *dwells, rests, stays* (in enjoyment): prathamaṃ dhyānam upasaṃpadya vyāhārṣaṃ yāvac caturthadhyānam upasaṃpadya vyāhārṣaṃ LV 263.17–18; (Vārāṇasīṃ) gatvā ṛṣipatane mṛgadāve vyāhārṣuḥ 264.22 (all prose, no v.l.); (**2**) *spends* (time): saptarātraṃ vyāhārṣīd LV 370.8 (prose, no v.l.); note saptarātraṃ viharati 370.6. Read vyah° in all?

[**vyāhāra,** in nityo vyāhāreṇa Samādh 22.11, acc. to Régamey *eternal from the standpoint of common experience*; but surely it means (only) *in words, by verbal expression,* as the northern versions cited in R's note, p. 88, seem to me to suggest.]

vyutkaṇṭhaśa(ḥ), adv., lit. *with open throat* or *outstretched neck*: na °śa(ḥ) piṇḍapātaṃ paribhokṣyāmaḥ, LaVallée-Poussin, JRAS 1913.845.18; = **vyutkhaṇḍaśaḥ,** q.v.; corresp. to Pali avagaṇḍakārakaṃ Vin. iv.196.11 (*so as to fill the cheeks with food,* CPD).

vyutkrāntaka(-samāpatti), a kind of **samāpatti** (q.v.) which involves first passing through the four dhyāna and four ārūpya and back, then jumping from one to the next but one, etc.; see AbhidhK. LaV-P. viii.173 f.; lit. *passing over* or *that has passed over,* Tib. thod brgal (so LaV-P., Mvy wrongly thod rgyal): Mvy 1496.

vyutkhaṇḍaśaḥ = **vyutkaṇṭhaśaḥ,** q.v.: Prāt 532.11; acc. to Chin., *picking out the best morsels* (to Skt. khaṇḍa).

vyuttiṣṭhati, °te (in some of these senses = Pali vuṭṭhahati, vuṭṭhāti; none, seemingly, in Skt.), (**1**) *returns, comes back* (safe from a sea-voyage): (mahāsamudro bahvādīnavo . . ., bahavo) 'vataranty alpā °ṭhanti Divy 35.22 (cf. **vyutpadyati** 1); (**2**) *returns* (to normal life), *comes out* (from meditative seclusion): pratisaṃlayanād (q.v.) vyutthāya Av i.242.11; ii.69.6, etc., in the cliché of the Buddha about to preach; also (ekaikasmin sūcīpradeśe) aṣṭau vimokṣān samāpadyate ca vyuttiṣṭhate ca Av ii.69.2, *with each stitch of the needle he attained by meditation the 8 vimokṣa and* (from that meditation) *came back* (to his sewing), Speyer's note; (**3**) *recovers,* as from illness or weariness: tasmād glānyād (ms. glānād, twice) vyutthitas Av ii.87.11; 125.8; (**4**) *arises, sets out* on a journey; vyutthito bhavati, lit. *becomes arisen,* i. e. *makes ready and starts* (a journey): yad vyutthitā bhavatha (104.6 °to bhavasi) nopaveṣṭavyaṃ śīghram āgantavyam Av ii.103.9; 104.6.

vyutthāpana (nt., = Pali vuṭṭhāpana), *causing to get rid* (of): anyonyāpatti-°nād Prāt 486.12, *thru helping one another to get rid of sin*; so Pali Vin. iii.178.13 aññamañña-vuṭṭhāpana (sc. āpattito, comm., see CPD; Finot's note 1 on Prāt is wrong).

vyutpadyati, (**1**) *returns, comes back* (safe from a sea-voyage): (bahavo 'vataranti) svalpā °patsyanti Divy 41.27 (cliché as s.v. **vyuttiṣṭhati** 1); (**2**) *is averse,* lit. *turns away*: teṣāṃ tathā °dyatāṃ na lebhe tac caityaṃ . . . kārayitum Divy 243.22, *as they were thus averse* (unfriendly; Index *resist*), *he did not succeed in having that caitya built*; vyutpannā na vayaṃ rājño 447.23, *we are not averse to the king.*

vyudāhāra, m., perhaps *varied utterance, utterance in varied terms*(?), with ekodāhāra (see **udāhāra**) and **pṛthag-udāhāra,** q.v.: ŚsP 567.7 and 615.7 (text in the latter °haro), quoted s.v. **udāhāra.**

[**vyupadiṣṭa,** prob. error for Skt. vyapa°, *prescribed* (of medicine) but occurs several times: MSV ii.27.1, 4, 6, 10, 12; in same context ādiṣṭa, saṃdiṣṭa, in 16 vyapadiśāmi.]

vyupanāmayati (= **upanām°** 5), *gives* (medicinal herbs, medicines, for a disease): °nāmyante, pass., KP 87.3 (cited s.v. upanām° 5).

[**vyupapatti** (f.; see **upapatti**), *rebirth*: sarvabhavagati-°tti-parāṅmukho Divy 2.1. But Tib. °gati-cyuty-upap°; Bailey, JRAS 1950.168, top; confirmed MSV iv.160.2 (same story).]

vyupaparīkṣaṇa (nt.; to next, and cf. **upaparī°**), also **°ṇa-tā,** *thorough investigation or reflection* (upon, in comp.): gambhīrapratītyasamutpāda-°ṇa-vihāriṇaś ca Gv 472.11; tulanā-(q.v.)-°ṇatā ŚsP 615.11 (comp., acc. to text); °ṇatā (not in comp.) 1325.2.

vyupaparīkṣate, and by haplology **vyuparīkṣate,** once **°ti,** fut. °kṣiṣyati (= **upaparīkṣ°**), *investigates* or *reflects thoroughly,* on religious truths: sa evaṃ (i. e. in words just quoted) °kṣamāṇas Śikṣ 122.1, *he thus reflecting*; °kṣamāṇo Dbh 31.17; vyuparīkṣate Dbh.g. 28(54).16 (last syllable lacking in mss.; vyupaparī° would be hypermetrical here and in the two other Dbh.g. occurrences); vyuparīkṣamāṇo 29(55).11; also introducing a question, evaṃ vyupaparīkṣate, katamena . . . Dbh 32.7; vyuparīkṣate, katama hetu . . . Dbh.g. 11(347).20; or a problem, vyuparīkṣiṣyati (so mss., Nobel em. vyuparīkṣeta), yenāyaṃ . . . sūtrendrarājas . . . pracaret Suv 113.4 (prose), *he will ponder on how this* . . . (the proved occurrence thrice in Dbh.g. of the haplological form justifies Nobel in keeping it here in prose, with his mss., but I see no advantage in his em. of fut. to opt.). Cf. prec.

vyupaśama, m. (= Pali vūpasama; also rarely Skt. id., see BR; see next two; at least in some of the applications here listed, only Buddh.), (**1**) *calming, tranquillization* of the mind (citta): (parameṇa citta-)°mena Divy 516.13; citta-dama-°mena samanvāgataṃ Av i.101.3 (of a Buddha; see **vyupaśamana**); (**2**) *bringing to rest,* of the **saṃskāra**: teṣāṃ °maḥ sukhaṃ Av ii.198.10 = Mmk 579.12 (vs, = Pali DN ii.157.9); *stilling,* of desires: nirodho °mo 'staṃgamaḥ Bhīk 24a.4; of misery (duḥkha), Divy 587.7; Bbh 27.1; sarvasattvakleśasaṃtāpa-°mena Gv 386.14; of disease, vyādhi-°mārthaṃ Divy 109.26; vyādhīnāṃ °māya Bbh 209.21; glānya-°māya Śikṣ 37.5; (**3**) *tranquillity,* presumably of mind (as in 1): (a-vyupaśāntaḥ) a-vyupaśamārāmaḥ Bbh 169.4.

vyupaśamana (nt.; = Pali vūpa°) = **°śama,** (**1**) *tranquillization* of mind (see **°śama** 1): citta-dama-°nasamanvāgataṃ (of an arhant) Av ii.114.12; (**2**) *allaying, healing,* of disease (see **°śama** 2): vyādher °manārthaṃ SP 133.11. Both prose.

vyupaśānta, adj. (= Pali vūpasanta; cf. prec. two; orig. ppp. of Skt. vy-upa-śam-; not recorded in Skt. by BR, pw), *quieted, calmed, allayed, appeased*: a-°taḥ Bbh 169.3, see s.v. **vyupaśama**; -duḥkhaṃ °tam abhūt LV 86.13; duḥkhaṃ ca °taṃ Kv 48.9; te kalahaṃ kṛtvā °tāḥ Divy 171.9, *when they were appeased after quarreling*; in LV 205.11 (prose) aho vatāhaṃ vyupaśāntasya (so both edd., no v.l., prose) lokasya tantrākulajātasya (so mss.; see under this for the rest of the passage) etc., it seems that the meaning requires a neg., *of the world which is not tranquillized* etc.; so Foucaux, *qui n'est pas apaisé,* tho he has no note and apparently accepted the reading of the ed.; his Tib. ed. omits the passage. It seems to me that a-vyupa° must be read.

vyupaśānti, f., = **vyupaśamana** (2): MSV ii.137.4.

vyupasthāna, (nt.), *approach, coming* or *being near*: prajñā paramapraśama-°nā (Bhvr.) Bbh 212.15, *that is near to supreme tranquillity* (Tib. ñe bar gnas pa, *being near*).

vyūha, also spelled **viyūha** chiefly in vss, and cf. **vyūhā**; m., (**1**) (as in Skt. and Pali, *mass, heap*) *mass, large amount*: yā kāci rati-viyūhā divyā LV 36.16 (vs) = Tib. lha yi dgaḥ ba rnam maṅ ji sñed pa, *what large quantities of divine pleasures*; (**2**) in Mahāyāna works (not in Pali), *arrangement*, but with regular overtones of *marvelous, supernatural, magical arrangement*, esp. of Buddha-fields; Tib. bkod pa; Jä. *orderly arrangement*, but it is more than that; the related ḥgod pa is also rendered *decorate, adorn*, and vyūha implies *magnificence, splendor*, as well as supernatural qualities; it seems very close to Skt. vibhūti as used e. g. in Bh.G. ch. 10 (see note 3 on vs 7 of my transl.), and *supernal manifestation*, which I chose for vibhūti, would do for BHS vyūha; note LV 317.19 (prose) tāṃś ca vyūhān vibhūtiṃ dṛṣṭvā bodhisattvasya, Māraḥ . . ., *seeing the B.'s supernal manifestations and marvelous power (splendor), Māra* . . . The word is used in such titles as Sukhāvatī-vyūha, Gaṇḍa-vyūha, with this mg., and is a special favorite in SP and LV; the translations of Burnouf, Kern, and Foucaux fumble it for the most part; hence the above attempt to make it clear; it seems to me essentially simple, tho no one English word is appropriate: (nāsmābhir eṣu . . . buddha-)kṣetravyūheṣu vā bodhisattvavikrīḍiteṣu vā . . . spṛhotpāditā SP 101.2, *we conceived no desire for . . . these supernal manifestations* (or *arrangements*) *of the Buddha-fields* . . .; kṣetreṣu buddhāna śruṇitva vyūhān 117.2 (vs); Raśmiprabhāsasya viyūha bheṣyati 146.12 (vs), *the supernal manifestation of* (the future Buddha) *R. shall exist* (in his Buddha-field, just described; viyūha n. sg., not loc. with Burnouf and Kern); sarveṣa etādṛśakāś ca vyūhā . . . tatha buddhakṣetraṃ 209.1 (vs), *all* (the Buddhas just mentioned) *shall have just such supernal manifestations, and also (a) Buddha-field(s)*; (Ānanda, for whom Buddhahood has just been predicted) ātmanaś ca buddhakṣetraguṇa-vyūhāñ śrutvā 219.4, *hearing the supernal manifestations of excellent qualities in his own* (future) *Buddha-field*; sarvākāraguṇopetā (v.l. °to) buddhakṣetraguṇa-vyūhā (v.l. °ho) bhaviṣyanti (no v.l. recorded) 220.5; samāś caiṣāṃ buddhakṣetraguṇavyūhā bhaviṣyanti 221.10; (tathāgatādhiṣṭhānena tathāgata-)balādhānena tathāgatavikrīḍitena tathāgatavyūhena (*by the T.'s supernal manifestation*) tathāgatābhyudgatajñānena 426.7 (all the parallel words mean substantially *by the T.'s supernatural power*); bodhimaṇḍaparipālakair devaputrais tādṛśā vyūhā bodhimaṇḍa abhinirmitā (q.v.) abhūvan LV 278.5; tāṃś ca vyūhān dṛṣṭvā 7; ye ca kecin mahāvyūhāḥ (sc. buddha-)kṣetrakoṭiṣv anantakāḥ 280.17 (vs); Chap. 20 of LV is entitled Bodhimaṇḍa-vyūha-parivartaḥ; in it the word is frequent, e. g. ratnachattra-vyūhaḥ 291.11, *manifestation of a jewelled umbrella*; prabhā-v° 292.1, referring to the ekaratnajāla of 291.22, which prob. means *single-jewel-magic*, a magical manifestation of a brilliant jewel (or jewels); buddhakṣetraguṇa-vyūhās (as above) 292.12, displayed at the bodhimaṇḍa; tebhyaḥ sarva-vyūhebhya iyaṃ gāthā niścarati sma 292.14; sarvaguṇa-vyūhaṃ kūṭāgāraṃ 293.1; kasyāyam evaṃrūpaḥ kūṭāgāra-vyūhaḥ 293.3; etc.; at beginning of next chapter, referring back to chapter 20, ima evaṃrūpā vyūhā . . . bodhimaṇḍe 'bhisaṃskṛtā abhūvan 299.15; dṛṣṭā sa viyūha śobhanā (ed. so°) bodhimaṇḍasmi marūbhi (so m.c. for text maru°) yā kṛtā 364.20 (vs); (tataś ca) prabhāvyūhād imā gāthā niścaranti sma 411.19, *and from this manifestation of splendor* (of the Buddha) . . .; yā bodhimaṇḍi prakṛtā ca surair viyūhā, yā vā viyūha kṛta sarva(-?)jinātmajebhiḥ, sā sarva saṃsthita viyūha ti dharmacakre 416.5–7 (at the dharmacakrapravartana; sā suggests that viyūha may be f., see **vyūhā**); buddhakṣetra-vyūha- Mvy 859; ahaṃ (sc. buddha-)kṣetravyūhān niṣpādayiṣyāmi Vaj 38.6, and ff.; many others could be added; other cases of viyūha, § 3.104.

Vyūhamati, n. of a devaputra (Trāyastriṃśa): LV 203.16.

Vyūharāja, (**1**) n. of a Bodhisattva: SP 3.5; 425.5; LV 292.8; (**2**) n. of a samādhi: SP 424.6; Kv 83.11; (**3**) n. of a group of future Buddhas (predicted): ŚsP 310.13.

Vyūharājendrā, n. of a kiṃnara maid: Kv 6.8.

vyūhā, viyūhā, = **vyūha** (2): mahatyā rājavyūhayā Suv 79.13 (prose); about half the mss. mahatā °vyūhena; (mahatā rājānubhāvena mahatā rāja-ṛddhīye) mahatā (so 1 ms., v.l. °tāye, Senart em. °tīye) viyūhāye (no v.l.) mahatīye vibhūṣāye Mv ii.113.13 (prose); in similar list, mahatā viyūhāye (no v.l.) ii.156.17. I have elected to take as pl. m. the forms in LV 36.16 (vs), see under **vyūha** (1); the citation there is completed by manasā vicintitā śrīmān, without significant v.l.; Calc. śrīman, as if voc. sg., but if voc. it should be pl. (the Bodhisattva, still in heaven, addresses the Tuṣita gods); if acc. pl., it would imply that the preceding forms ending in -ā are also acc. pl., coordinate with phalam idaṃ (śṛṇu-r-asya . . .) of next line; all of which would be quite possible in BHS.

vyomaka, (**1**) nt., some kind of *ornament*: °kam Mvy 6052, in a list of ornaments; Tib. mkhaḥ rten, see below; (**2**) m. and nt., = Tib. mkhaḥ rten, rendered by Das *the firmament*; *sky supporting*; *a sort of ornament*. The mg. *ornament* has not been found except in Mvy 6052. Elsewhere the word clearly means *a tall palatial building*, often supernaturally or magically created; lit., I suppose, *reaching to the sky* (Skt. vyoman; Tib. would mean *sky-support*), and usually in the cpd. ratna-vy°, one *made of jewels*; (nagarasya śṛṅgāṭake) saptaratnavyomakopary asaṃkhyeyaratnamaye . . . bhadrāsane Gv 143.8; (ekaikasyāṃ rathyāyām ubhayor antayor viṃśati-) vyomaka-koṭīḥ sarvopakaraṇaparipūrṇaiḥ sthāpitā(ḥ) Gv 164.21 (for the benefit of all creatures); (mārgaḥ . . .) ubhayato nānāratnavyomakapaṅktiviracitavyūhaḥ(Bhvr.), tatra keṣucid ratnavyomakeṣu vividharatnaparipūrṇāni ratnabhājanāni sthāpitāny abhūvan yācanakasaṃghapratipādanakārthaṃ, keṣucid vyomakeṣu etc. Gv 403.15 ff., down to 404.7, in numerous repetitions always keṣucid vyomakeṣu (they all contained largesse for beggars); ratnavyomakāni saṃsthitāny abhūvan, sarveṣu ca ratnavyomaka-mūrdhneṣu koṭīśataṃ devaputrāṇām . . . avasthitam abhūt SP 405.4–5; ratnavyomakāni 410.12; sarvasya ca tālavṛkṣasya purato ratnavyomakaḥ saṃsthito 'bhūt, sarvasmiṃś ca ratnavyomake aśītyapsaraḥsahasrāṇi . . . sthitāny abhūvan LV 274.5–6; ratnavyomakāṃs tasmin . . . 'bhinirmimīte sma, tebhyaś ca ratnavyomakebhya iyaṃ gāthā niścacāra LV 293.13–14; teṣu kūṭāgāreṣu ratnavyomakeṣu (not ep. of kūṭā° as stated BR 6.1486; Tib. makes the two coordinate nouns, connected by daṅ) . . . bodhisattvavigrahān abhinirmimīte sma 294.13.

vyoṣita, adj., see **avyoṣita**.

(**vraṇa**, m. or nt., in Skt. *wound*, also *crack, flaw, defect, fault*: ātmānaṃ sa-vraṇaṃ jñātvā SP 39.1, *knowing themselves to be at fault, defective*, so Tib. raṅ gi skyon (usually = doṣa) śes te, *of self fault knowing*; (cetopraṇidhānaṃ . . . akalmāṣam) a-vraṇam Mv i.239.6, *pure and flawless*; nava-vraṇa-mukha, *the openings of the nine slits* of the body, as in Skt. navadvāra, cf. Pali Milp. 74.15 navadvāro mahāvaṇo, of the body: (kāyo . . .) navavraṇamukha-romakūpa-srāvī Śikṣ 230.11; prasravan . . . kāyaḥ . . . navavraṇamukhair 232.1.)

[**vraṇotsata, °tā**, Kashgar rec. v.l. on SP 94.7, see s.v. **vrāṇika**; corrupt.]

vrata-pada, (m. or) nt. (cf. Pali vata-pada, not recorded of this group), *point of religious practice*; five, viz. the five **śikṣāpada**, q.v.: MSV iii.128.10 ff.; in MSV iv.249.2 ff. the five vra°, as taught by Devadatta, are listed as āraṇyakatva, vṛkṣamūlikatva, traicīvarikatva, pāṃsukūlikatva (no fifth named; these are **dhūtaguṇa**).

Vratamaṇḍala, n. of a Buddha: Gv 284.24.

Vratasamudra, n. of a Buddha: Gv 257.22.

? **vrāṇika**, adj., *having wounds, wounded*: SP 94.7 (vs) te ... bhonti kalmāṣakā vrāṇika kaṇḍulāś ca. On the face of it, appears to be vṛddhi deriv. of Skt. vraṇa with suffix ika. But only one ms. is cited as reading vrā°; 4 Nep. mss. vra-; perhaps ka-extension of Skt. vraṇi(n), with ā for a m.c.? Kashgar rec., for this and the following, khuḍḍulakā vraṇotsatā, both words obscure and prob. corrupt.

Ś

Śaṃvara? see **saṃvara** (4).

Śakaṭamukha, n. of a nāga: Māy 222.1; (a nāga king) 247.19.

-śakaṭikā (lit. *little cart*), in aṅgāra-sthāpana-°kā, a (prob. movable) *vessel for holding coals*, for cooking: Mvy 9010 = Tib. (g)zhugs (*fire*) gliṅ (?); Das records zhugs liṅ = śakaṭikā, aṅgārasthāpana (so!), *burning embers*.

-śakalā, see **asthi-ś°**.

śakalika, m., °**likā** (= Skt. °la, Pali sakalikā), (**1**) *chip, small piece* (as of wood): °kaḥ Mvy 6702 = Tib. dum bu, or zhogs ma; parītta-śakalikāgniḥ (°ka- or °kā-) 6703 (here Tib. sbur ma, defined *chaff, husks*); (**2**) °**likā**, id.: śukti-śa°, MSV ii.55.17.

śakānī-lipi, a kind of writing (*of the Śakas*; cf. **yonānī**): LV 125.20; so read for Lefm. sakāri° with all his mss., Calc. śakāri°; but Tib. śa-ka-ni.

Śakuna, n. of a cakravartin king, father of **Kuśa** (2): MSV i.99.10; later called regularly **Mahāśakuni**, q.v.

śakuna-vidyā, *science of marks* (la ñe) or *omens* (ltas kyi), acc. to Tib.: Mvy 5058; Pali sakuṇa-vijjā, acc. to DN comm. i.93.29, sapakkhaka-apakkhaka-dipada-catuppadānaṃ rūtagatādivasena sakuṇañāṇaṃ; also śakuni-v° Divy 630.22 (see s.v. **śivā-vidyā**).

Śakuni, n. of a cakravartin (of the race of Mahāsaṃmata): Mvy 3564.

śakuni-vidyā, see **śakuna°**.

Śaketaka, n. of a nāga: Māy 221.28.

śakkita, ppp. (MIndic), to śakyati, see Chap. 43, s.v. śak (3).

śaktina-lipi, some kind of writing: Mv i.135.6. Senart suggests śakāri-l°, as in LV 125.20 (sak°), for which **śakānī** is the true reading; perh. read so in Mv.

śaktiśūla, m. or nt. (= Pali sattisūla), n. of a hell: °le (mss. °lena) mahānarake upapanno Mv iii.361.11; narakaṃ °laṃ ... prapanno 369.6 (vs).

śaktuka-, in comp. (= Skt. saktu, AMg. sattuga), *grits* or *meal*: yadi mamāntikāc chaktuka-bhikṣām (v.l. saktuka°) pratigṛhṇīyād ... Divy 67.10.

śakyā, indecl. (= Pali, Pkt. sakkā; from Skt. root-aor. or precative śakyāt, Pischel 465), *it is possible, one can* (with inf.): śakyā etam evaṃ kartuṃ, yathā ... Mv i.351.10; asmākaṃ punar naivaṃ śakyā mānsena kāryaṃ kartuṃ ii.213.9, *but for us it is impossible thus to do what needs doing with meat*; nāpi ca svayaṃkṛtānāṃ karmāṇāṃ phalaṃ (em.; if right, read phala m.c.) palāyituṃ śakyā 224.14 (vs); kiṃ śakyā kartuṃ 448.13, *what is it possible to do*? (or pass., *what can be done*?); same 456.2; 457.5; na śakyā ma eṣāṃ (so read) bhūyo tatra mahānasaṃ visarjayituṃ Mv i.363.14, *it is impossible for me, after this, to have her sent there to the kitchen*; na śakyā sarvam ākhyātuṃ iii.277.19 (or pass.); with passive force (influenced by śakya, adj.?), narakeṣu na mucyituṃ śakyā ii.223.13, *in hells one cannot be freed* (but, N.B., here the inf. is formed on the passive stem mucyate!). No certain case outside of Mv; śakyā kartuṃ candrādityau tamatimira ... LV 337.14 (vs) can better be taken as containing śakyā(ḥ), n. pl. (for dual); personal forms of adj. śakya in adjoining lines.

śakra, m. or nt., a high number: Gv 105.23; corrupt for **saṃkrama** (Gv 133.4), the place of which it occupies.

Śakrapraśna, pl., n. of a work: yathoktaṃ bhagavatā °neṣu Mv i.350.8 (a sentence is then quoted). Doubtless = Pali Sakkapañhasutta (DN xxi), as noted by Waldschmidt, Kl. Skt. Texte 4, 58; fragments from the BHS text (not named in them) are here printed; a few important words have been cited here.

Śakrabhānu, n. of a former Buddha: Mv i.138.4.

śakrābhilagna, lit. *fixed upon* (worn by) *Indra*, n. of a jewel: usually compounded or associated with a following maṇiratna (or merely ratna); acc. to Gv 498.22 Indra mastered the gods by its magic, °na-maṇiratnāvabaddhaḥ śakro devarājā sarvadevagaṇān abhibhavati; usually it has no direct connection with Indra but is merely a name of a particular gem; so in a list of names of gems Mvy 5960 °na-ratnam; Mv ii.310.21 °nehi maṇiratanehi samalaṃkṛtaṃ (bodhivṛkṣaṃ); Sukh 54.8 °namaṇiratna-vicitritaś (bodhivṛkṣaḥ); Gv 101.21 °na-maṇiratna-vitānair; LV 297.16 °na-maṇiratna kṣipanti (at the tree of bodhi, before the Bodhisattva).

Śaṃkara, (**1**) n. of a cakravartin: Mvy 3578; (**2**) n. of a yakṣa: Māy 95. See also **Śaṃkāra**.

śaṅkalā (see s.v. **saṃkala**, °**lā**), *chain*, as n. of a mudrā: Mmk 356.22; 370.2; instead of **saṅkalā**, (causal) *chain*, normal in Laṅk, śaṅkalāyāḥ Laṅk 203.7. See also **asthi-śaṅkalā**, where the question of relationship between the two is discussed.

Śaṃkāra, n. of a nāga king: Mvy 3255 (so also Mironov; cited in BR as **Śaṃkara**). (**śaṃkāra-**, Mmk 131.21, read **saṃkāra**, q.v.)

śaṅkāviṣā? apparently some sort of noxious animal or plant (perhaps corrupt): Māy 252.3 śaṅkāviṣā-viṣāt (in a list of poisons; after vṛścika-viṣāt, and before oṣadhiviṣāt).

śaṅkulya, m. (or °yā, f.?, prob. = Pali saṅkulya, or °yā, acc. pl. °yā, Jāt. vi.524.17), a kind of cake: °yā parpaṭā khādyā (nom.) ... Mmk 147.4 (vs).

śaṅkha (also written saṃkha, Mv), (**1**) m. (Pali saṅkha), n. of one of the four 'great treasures', (saṃkha) Mv iii.383.18, and of the 'king' who presides over it, Divy 61.4 (see s.v. **elapatra**); as a nāga, known in Skt.; Divy 61.4 mentions this Ś. in juxtaposition with (2) but the relation between them is not made clear; in Pali the two have no connexion, (1) being only a 'treasure' DN comm. i.284.8 f.; (**2**) (= Pali id., DPPN Saṅkha 3), n. of a future emperor: Divy 60.14 ff.; (**3**) n. of a rākṣasa, = **Śaṅkhanābha**: Divy 104.8.

Śaṅkhakuñjara, n. of a dog, reincarnation of **Taudeya** (q.v.): Karmav 22.2 ff.

śaṅkha-dhāmaka, m. (= Pali saṅkha-dhamaka), *conch-blower*: MSV iv.117.15.

Śaṅkhanābha, n. of a rākṣasa: Divy 102.28; 104.17, 19 (called **Śaṅkha** 104.8).

Śaṅkhanābhī, n. of a magic herb controlled by the prec.: Divy 102.28; 104.10, 14.

Śaṅkhamedhī (so with v.l. for Senart Saṅkha°), n. of a place outside of Benares: Mv iii.328.14.

śaṅkha-valaya-kāra, m. (Skt. śaṅkha-valaya, see pw, in its only recorded occurrence seems not helpful), *an artisan who works in shell and ivory*: Mv ii.473.8; he makes śaṅkha-gajadanta-mayāni ābharaṇāni, 9; specific products are then named, some app. made of shell, others of ivory; did he work in both materials separately, or in combinations of the two, shell inlaid with ivory or vice versa, or wood inlaid with both? Cf. **śaṅkhikā** (q.v.) dantakārakā.

śaṅkhaśilā (°**śirā**, once; = Pali saṅkhasilā, conjectured PTSD to mean *mother-of-pearl*, a pure guess), a sort of precious or semi-precious stone, mentioned in rigmarole lists of gems and precious metals, and almost always placed between vaiḍūrya and **pravāḍa** (°la): LV 276.21 (Tib. makes it two items, duṅ = *shell*, and man śel = *crystal, glass*); SP 102.2 (prose; Tib. as in LV); 111.7 (vs; here Tib. only man śel); Mv ii.472.1; Divy 115.3; 229.6; 291.9; Av i.184.5; 201.2, etc.; RP 40.8; Dbh 18.26; spelled °śirā, prob. by error, Gv 164.8.

śaṅkhasvara-samācāra, adj. m. (Pali saṅkassara, usually cpd. with samācāra, or sometimes ācāra; sometimes the Pali cpd. begins with asuci-; Pali comms., e. g. Pugg. comm. 207.5 ff., Dhp. comm. iii.485.1 ff., have various labored and implausible interpretations assuming connexion with saṅkā = Skt. śaṅkā, root śaṅk), *of vile conduct*; etym. and precise mg. unknown; follows kaṣambaka-jāta (see **kaś°**) in Mvy, MSV, and occurs in the same cliché in Pali, referring to wicked monks: Mvy 9140; MSV i.50.7; Śikṣ 64.5. Tib. on Mvy cited as lug pon (?) ltar (*like*) spyad pa (*conduct*); Mvy 9141 and 9142 (not in Mironov) are given as synonyms or variants, **khānta-samācāra** and **saṃkasu**(note k, not kh)**samācāra**; Tib. this time (on 9141) luṅ rul-ba (*rotten*, see s.v. kaśambaka-) lta-bur gyur-pa; Jap. rendering of 9142 contains the word *rotten*. Both Mvy 9141 and 9142 seem evident corruptions, and śaṅkha-svara- looks like an unhistoric (hyper-Skt.) form. The Tib. renderings are prob. also corrupt; at least the Tib. Dictt. give no clue to what they might mean. Perhaps luṅ (on Mvy 9141), and maybe even lug (on Mvy 9140), may be corrupt for duṅ = Skt. śaṅkha, *shell*.

śaṅkhika (Skt. Lex. śāṅkhika, cf. Schmidt, Nachträge), *worker in conch-shells* (not *blower of* them, the mg. attributed to AMg. saṅkhiya): (hairaṇyikā prāvārikā) °kā dantakārakā ... Mv iii.113.7 (in list of artisans and tradesmen).

Śaṅkhinī, n. of a rākṣasī: Māy 241.13.

Śaṅkhila, n. of a yakṣa leader: Māy 235.19.

śaṃgerī, or **saṃ°** (cf. AMg. saṃgellī, °lliā, *mass, collection*; Deśīn. 8.4 saṃgella, m., and saṃgollī, = samūha), *mass, heap, collection*: mandāravāna (or mānd°) bharitā kācit śaṃgeriyo (v.l. saṃ°) gṛhītvāna (or bharitvāna) Mv i.216.6 = ii.19.3 (vs), *one was loaded down carrying masses of m. flowers.*

? **śaṭa-** (perhaps to AMg. saḍaṇa, nt., *decaying*, saḍiya, *rotten*; cf. Nepali sarnu, *to rot, putrefy, decay; fall to pieces*; and many New Indic cognates, Turner, Nep. Dict.; or, possibly, related to Skt. chaṭā, *lump*; cf. Deśīn. 3.33 chaṃṭo = jala-chaṭā, *drop of water*?), in śaṭa-(or chaṭa-)siṅghāṇa, *foul* (or *dropping*? or, *consisting of a lump*?) *mucus*: Mmk 112.24 (vs) (dūrād āvasathād gatvā ...) visṛjec chaṭa-siṅghāṇaṃ mūtraprasravaṇaṃ tathā. Note that chaṭa- is an equally possible assumption for the form intended.

śaṭaḥ-, v.l. for **saṭhaḥ-**, q.v.

śaṭha, app. as abstr. = Skt. śāṭhya (otherwise only *rogue*, or adj. *tricky*), *trickiness*: śaṭha-nikṛti-paiśunyāni tu manuṣya-gahanāni Mv i.91.17 (vs, metr. defective).

[**śaṭhaka**, both edd. with no v.l. at SP 267.4, would = Skt. śaṭha, *tricky*; but prob. read **kakkhaṭa**, q.v.]

śaḍha, or **saḍha**, adj. (= AMg. saḍha, Skt. śaṭha), *deceitful*: sadārjavā mārdavāś (so read with v.l.) ca aśaḍhāś (all mss. exc. A asa°) ca LV 38.4 (vs); of Māra, dharṣitvā Namuci śaḍha sasainyaṃ (so read, all acc. sg.) 164.8 (vs; all mss. ḍh); na bhramate sabalaṃ śaḍha (so Lefm., best ms. sadhu, others madhu or sādhu; acc. sg., meaning Māra; ending was -u, prob. saḍhu; = Tib. gyo sgyu) dṛṣṭvā 308.14 (vs); see also s.v. **asadha.**

[**śaṇanā**, error for gaṇanā, RP 59.16; see s.v. **upaniṣad** (2).]

śaṇa-śāṭi, °**ṭī**, °**ṭikā** (cf. Pali sāṇa-sāṭaka, e.g. Vism. i.54.7 °ko viya dubbaṇṇo hoti, sc. puggalo, dussīlyatāya), *hempen cloth* or *rag*, as something cheap and poor: sana-(read śaṇa, see Note p. 706)-śāṭikā-nivāsitaḥ sphaṭitapāṇipāda etc. Divy 83.22; kārṣaśatāny ... sphuṭitapāṇipādāni śaṇaśāṭī-nivāsitāni 463.8; (of a wandering brahman pupil) śaṇa-śāṭiṃ (mss. śana-, sana-; Senart em. snāna-) ādāya Mv i.232.4 (prose). Cf. **śāṇaka.**

Śatagiri, n. of a yakṣa: Samādh p. 43 line 20; intends Śātā° or **Sātā°**, q.v.

śataghnī, assumed by Senart to mean *scorpion* (so Wilson and Apte, no ref. in the latter): (yehi ...) prāṇakānāṃ śīrṣāṇi piccitāni bhavanti, ahīnāṃ vṛścikānāṃ śataghnīnāṃ (Senart em.; mss. śatadānāṃ) Mv i.24.4 (prose); (na teṣu, v.l. teṣa, śatrū, v.l. śatrur, janayati, Senart em. °yanti, krodhaṃ) maṇiviṣāṇāṃ yathā śataghnīyo (Senart em.; mss. śatrusaṃghāḥ) i.276.19 (vs, metr. confused). Uncertain but not implausible.

Śatadhanu, n. of an ancient king: Mv ii.146.19.

Śatadharma, n. of a brother of Śāriputra: Mv iii.56.11.

śatana (nt.; cf. Skt. śātayati, śātana), *fall, ruin, decay*: occurs in cpds. seemingly corresponding closely to **ucchādana**, q.v.; esp. in a cliché, sarvasaṃskāragatīḥ (...) śatana-patana-**vikiraṇa**-(or **vikaraṇa-**, q.v.)-vidhvaṃsana-dharmatayā (*because they are characterized by* ...) parāhatya (once °hanya) Divy 180.23; 281.30; 551.16; Av i.50.14; 96.5–6; 348.3, et alibi; same cpd., ending -dharmā, ep. of kāyo, the body, Śikṣ 229.12; śatanapatana-dharmo (of the body) Suv 210.8; śatana-patanavikiraṇa-vidhvaṃsanādibhiḥ duḥkhopadhānair uparudhyamānaṃ Mmk 110.20–21. (In Divy 299.22 cyavana replaces śatana in the same cpd.; see s.v. **vikiraṇa** 1).

Śatanetrā, n. of a rākṣasī: Māy 243.28.

Śataparivārā, n. of a nāga maid: Kv 4.1.

śatapādikā (Skt. Lex. id.), *centipede*: Kashgar rec. SP 84.2, for text śatāpadī.

Śatapuṣpa, n. of a former Buddha: Mv iii.231.10.

Śatapuṣpā, n. of a 'gandharva maid': Kv 4.18.

Śatabāhu, (**1**) m., n. of a son of Māra, unfavorable to the Bodhisattva: LV 309.18; (**2**) m., n. of a yakṣa: Māy 22; (**3**) m., n. of a nāga king: Māy 246.23; (**4**) f. (n. sg. °hur), n. of a nāga maid: Kv 4.3; (**5**) f., n. of a rākṣasī: Māy 243.27.

Śatamukha, (**1**) n. of a kiṃnara king: Kv 3.5; (**2**) n. of a nāga: Kv 95.13.

Śataraśmi, n. of a palace occupied by **Sudīpā**: Mv i.201.10 ff.

śata-rasa, see **sata°**.

Śatavarga Āgama, *holy text of 100 chapters*: Karmav 46.11; 70.7; 157.13. See Lévi's notes ad loc. and p. 11 f. It seems to be, or to include, the Saṃyukta Āgama, but the precise mg. is doubtful; Lévi thinks possibly it may mean the total collection of Āgamas, or at least Saṃy. with Madhy.

Śataśīrṣa, n. of a nāga king: Kv 2.10.

Śataśīrṣā, n. of a rākṣasī: Māy 243.27.

śatasahasrapattra, nt., n. of a certain flower: Mvy 6189. Cf. sahasrapattram 6190 (= Skt., a kind of lotus).

Śatasahasramātar, n. of a former Buddha: °tā, n. sg., Mv i.141.1.

Śatasāhasrikāprajñāpāramitā, n. of a work (= ŚsP): Mvy 1326; see **Prajñāp°**.

Śatākarā, n. of a kiṃnara maid: Kv 6.11.

Śatākārā, n. of a 'gandharva maid': Kv 4.24.

śatākṣara, nt., *'the hundred syllables'* or *charm of 100 syllables*: (akṣiṇī nimīlya buddhabodhisattvālambana-cittaḥ)°ram aṣṭasahasraṃ (*8000 times*) japet Śikṣ 173.1. This is an antidote for sin (pāpapratipakṣasamudācāraḥ). Not in Pali, and not otherwise known to me.

(**śatāpadī,** m.c. for Skt. śata°, *centipede*: SP 84.2; 86.1, vss.)

Śatāyudhā, n. of a kiṃnara maid: Kv 6.23.

śatima, ord. num. (= Pali satima, PTSD; Geiger cites only satama, which Dictt. do not record; like **sahasrima,** analog. to forms like rare Skt. viṃśati-ma, see § 19.36), *hundredth*: °māṃ kala (m.c. for kalāṃ) nopayānti LV 341.6 (vs); °māṃ api kalā(ṃ) nopaiti sahasrimāṃ api ... KP 159.15 (prose).

śada (m. or nt.), *petal*, or some kind of leaf: (tṛṇa-kāṣṭha-śākhā-)parṇa-śadam MSV ii.75.1, five-member dvandva acc. to Tib., which renders parṇa by lo ma, *leaf*, and śada by ḥdab (printed ḥdap) ma, *petal*, also *leaf*. (Cf. Sk'. Lex. śada = phalamūlādi, BR s.v. 3?)

śaniścara (= AMg. saṇiccara, saṇicchara; cf. Skt. śanaiścara), *the planet Saturn*: Mmk 19.22; 158.9; 179.1. Cf. **śāniś°**.

[**Śantaś(i)rī, Śantābha,** prob. by error for **Śānt°**, qq.v.]

śantra (so also Mironov; in Kyoto ed. v.l. śattra), in akṣi-śantraḥ Mvy 8916, acc. to Tib. mig ḥdzer can, (having) *eyes with excrescences* (*styes*?); one Chin. rendering, at least, also means this.

Śabara(pāda), see **Siddhaśabara(-pāda)**.

Śabarī, n. of a yoginī: Sādh 443.16.

śabda, nt. (regularly m.; in Skt. nt. very rare and 'suspicious', pw), *sound*: vividhāni śabdāni bahūvidhāni SP 358.14 (vs; m. forms in lines 8, 12 above); śabdam udīritam (nom.) Av i.3.14 (prose).

(**śabdavedha,** Skt., *the art of hitting a target by sound*, see next: Divy 100.12; 442.8.)

(**śabdavedhi-tva,** occurs in Skt., Mbh. (Crit. ed.) i.123.21; LV 156.13, *the art of a śabdavedhin* = Pali sadda-vedhi(n), i. e. of an archer who can hit a target he doesn't see by the sound which it makes; illustrated in Mbh. i.123.12 ff. See prec. and s.v. **akṣaṇavedhin**.)

śabdāpayati, °**vayati** (Epic Skt. °payati, Rām., acc. to BR *calls, summons*; AMg. saddāvei; MIndic caus. to Skt. śabdayati, śabdāyati, or *śabdati, cf. Pali saṃsaddati), may usually be interpreted as true caus., *has summoned, causes to be called*, e. g.: śākuntikā °pitā Mv i.272.14; but sometimes can hardly mean anything other than *calls*, °payitum ārabdhaḥ, amba ambeti Divy 171.5, *began to call, mother! mother!*; °payati Divy 31.23 f. (in 26 śabdayati, same situation). See § 38.56, and for a (very incomplete) list of passages Chap. 43.

śabdita, denom. pple. (to Skt. śabdayati), *conjured up, created by a magic word*: nagaraṃ gandharvaśabditam, *a city conjured up by a gandharva* Laṅk 9.1 (vs).

? **śabdīsaka,** v.l. for **candīsaka,** q.v.: Mv ii.159.5.

śama, *cubit*? see **śama-sāmantakam**.

śamatha, often written sa°, m. (= Skt. Lex. id., Pali samatha), (**1**) *tranquillity, tranquillization*; esp. often assoc. with **vipaśyanā** or (less often) its syn. **vidarśanā,** see these two; when cpd. they form a dvandva, never a tatp. as suggested erroneously in PTSD (in every passage there quoted samatha and vipassanā are parallel and coordinate, usually not even cpd.); also often with dama-(tha): dama-śamatham ākāṅkṣamāṇā(ḥ) SP 80.9; dama-samathe LV 169.5 (vs); paramadama-samatha- 427.22; ātma-dama-(iii.52.18 °damatha-)-śamatha-pariṇirvāṇār-thaṃ Mv ii.157.5; iii.52.18; uttama-damatha(so Senart, but mss. dama)-śamatha-pāramitā- iii.64.6; śamatha-saṃbhāra LV 35.14; 427.21; śamatha-sukha-vyavasthitaḥ Laṅk 15.4; smara ... śamathaṃ LV 11.14; samatha-dhanu gṛhītvā LV 156.5 (vs), *taking the bow of ...*; samatha-nirvāṇa-puram anupravekṣyāmi Mv ii.148.6; *tranquillization* of the mind as a process, a course of practice, dvāda-śavarṣābhyastaḥ śamathaś (or sa°) cittasya Divy 47.3; 461.20; adhyātmaṃ (adv.) cetaḥśamathaṃ (riñcanti) MSV iii.11.18; sarva(iii.314.5 pūrva)-saṃskāra-samatho (so read in ii.285.20) or °tha- Mv ii.285.20; iii.314.5, *the tranquillizing of (all) the (former) saṃskāra*, cf. Pali sabbasaṃkhārasa-matho Vin. i.5.2; (**2**) (= Pali adhikaraṇa-sa°) adhikaraṇa-śamathā(ḥ), *settling, appeasement, of disputed questions*: Mvy 8630 (see **adhikaraṇa** 1).

Śamathaketu, n. of a Buddha: Gv 259.6.

Śamathaghoṣa, n. of a Buddha: Gv 285.18.

? **śama-ruci,** see **sama°**

śama-sāmantakam, nt. adj. or adv., acc. to Tib. khru gaṅ khor yug, and Chin., *a (full) cubit in circumference*: Mvy 9185. See **sāmantaka** (4); but how śama comes to mean *cubit*, or any measure of length, I cannot see. Corrupt?

Śamitaśatru, n. of a former Buddha: Mv i.140.1.

śamitāvin, sam°, (**1**) adj. (§ 22.51; = Pali sam°), *one who has become tranquil*, ep. of a Buddha: śamitāviṃ (acc.; mss. gamitāvi) prahāya puṇyapāpaṃ Mv i.316.5 (vs, text confused); samitāvi (nom.) prahāya (em.) puṇya-vipākaṃ iii.396.19 (vs, text confused); (**2**) Sam°, n. of a former Buddha, under whom Śākyamuni took the anuloma-**praṇidhāna** (q.v.): Mv i.1.10, and 48.17 ff. where the story is told at length; (**3**) Sam°, n. of (prob.) another former Buddha: Mv iii.239.3.

[**Śambara,** see **Saṃvara** (5).]

śamya, or (in LV always written) **sa°** (= Pali samma, here m.; for Skt. see below), a kind of cymbal, always in LV and often in Pali in cpd. with **tāḍa** (tāḷa), which usually follows but in LV 301.16 precedes this (PTSD wrongly makes sammatāḷa the n. of a single instrument; Pali comms., e. g. Jāt. vi.61.7–8, make it a dvandva, and samma occurs alone in Pali); Skt. has only śamyā-(-tāla, e. g. Mbh. Cr. ed. 2.4.31), which is known in BHS only in Mvy 5018; in Skt. often and in LV always, acc. to Lefm., written with p for y, but (cf. pw 6.208) Pali proves that y is right, p a graphic corruption; prob. identical with Skt. śamyā, *wedge*, from the shape of the instrument; the m. (or nt.) stem in -a is not recorded in Skt. but is the only one recorded in Pali as n. of a mus. instrument, and so (except for Mvy) in BHS; in LV only stem-form recorded in long dvandva cpds. of names of mus. instruments: LV 40.20; 163.6 (here Calc. samya); 206.14; 212.4 (here °tāḍāvacara-); -tāḍa-sampādīṃś ca (no v.l.) 301.16.

śamyāprāsa, m. (= Pali sammāpāsa, e. g. Sn 303; expl. comm. i.321.29 ff. as a form of the 'sātrāyāga', = Skt. sattra-yāga?, repeated at intervals of a *'wedge-throw'*; so Skt. id., cf. KŚS 15.9.12 śamyāprāsa-śamyāprāse, in a ritual sūtra), a kind of elaborate brahmanical sacrifice: so read for somaprāsa Mv ii.237.20, and śāmyapraśa (śāmyā°) Divy 634.7, 11, 17, 20; in list of brahmanical sacrifices (as in Pali Sn) cited s.v. **nirargaḍa,** q.v.

śaya (or **śayā**), m.c. for (Skt.) śayyā, § 2.89, *bed*: śayāto, abl., LV 230.11 (vs; śayyāto would be unmetr.).

śayantaka, adj. (a-extension of pres. pple. śayant-, plus -ka), *lying down*: tiṣṭhanto vā niṣaṇṇā vā śayantakā vā Mv iii.330.2 (prose).

[**śayavatī,** in LV 221.5 °tī osvāpitā devataiḥ, would if correct have to be fem. to a *śayavant, *in bed*, sc. strī from prec. strīsaṃghaḥ śayitas. But Tib. grags ldan, *famous*, which indicates that the true reading was **yaśa-vatī,** which Calc. reads; see this.]

śayā (abl. śayāto), m.c. for śayyā, see **śaya**; **śayāni,** loc., m.c. for śayane, *on the bed*: tubhya prekṣami śayāni suptikāṃ LV 236.3 (vs).

śayi (= Skt. śayyā, § 3.115), *bed*: mama śayi chorayitvā LV 230.18 (vs), *having abandoned my bed.*

śayita, nt. (unrecorded as subst.), *lying down*: Mv i.167.18, see s.v. **niṣaṇṇa.**

śayitaka, f. **°ikā,** adj. (= °ta plus specifying -ka, § 22.39), *one who has been asleep* or *gone to sleep*: yathā °ko puruṣo buddhyeyā, tathā vijṛmbhanto utthito Mv ii.219.2; perhaps also, sa teṣāṃ śayitakānāṃ (*who had gone to sleep*?) taṃ vihāram (mss. vicāram) antarhāpayitvā mahāsamudraṃ praviṣṭaḥ, te vālukāsthale śayitakās (*the ones that had* . . .) tiṣṭhanti Divy 329.12 f.; agramahiṣī °tikā MSV i.99.21.

śayin, adj. (to Skt. śete, śayate, °ti, plus -in), *lying*: śayanasyādṛśi chinna pāda caturo dharaṇītalesmiṃ chayī (acc. pl. m.) LV 194.15 (vs), *she saw the four feet of the bed cut off, lying on the floor*; so Tib., sa yi steṅ na ñal ba mthoṅ, *saw lying on the surface of the ground.*

Śara, n. of a yakṣa: MSV i.17.7.

Śara-kṣepaṇa(ṃ) jātaka, *'the Arrow-shot,'* n. of a Jātaka story: Mv ii.83.12 (colophon); not found in Pali Jāt.

śaraḍa, a high number: Gv 106.12; = **saraḍa,** q.v.

śaraṇa (Skt.), *refuge*: in the Buddhist formula of ordination, buddhaṃ śaraṇaṃ gacchāmi dharmaṃ ś° g° saṃghaṃ ś° g°, followed by other variations, cited in extenso Mv iii.268.8 ff.; cf. also Mv iii.310.7 ff., trīṇi śaraṇagamanāni (Pali saraṇagamana).

śaratka-, adj. (Skt. śarad plus -ka), *autumnal*, in śaratkāvāsa, m., *dwelling for autumn*: Mvy 5627. In the parallel forms graiṣmikā°, vārṣikā°, haimantikā°, the first elements are all adjectives.

Śaradharā, n. of a rākṣasī: May 241.33.

śarapatha, m., n. of a muhūrta: Divy 643.9; 644.14.

Śarabha, (**1**) (= Pali Sarabha) n. of a parivrājaka (see DPPN): Pischel, SBBA 1904 p. 816 fol. 167a ff.; (**2**) n. of a maharṣi: Māy 256.25.

Śarabhaṅga (= Pali Sara°; known also in Skt., Mbh., where however the stories of him are not identical with those of Buddhist sources), n. of a noted ascetic: Mv iii.362.11 ff.; belonged to the Kauṇḍinya gotra, 370.12; °ga-jātakam (text here Sara°; mss. Śarabha- or Sarabha-j°) 375.12 (colophon).

śarita, see **sarita** 3.

śarīragati, f., *bodily course* in the sense of attention to the 'call of nature': °gatyā gacchann evaṃ cittam utpādayati Śikṣ 348.14 (prose). Cf. Pali sarīra-kicca and AMg. sarīra-cintā.

Śarīraprahlādana, n. of a gandharva king: Kv 2.19.

śarkalā (= Skt. °rā), *sand*: LV 249.3 (prose, no v.l.).

[**śardūla,** LV 207.17; read with some mss. **gardūla,** q.v.]

Śarmila, n. of a yakṣa: Māy 91.

śalati, °te (Skt. Dhātup., *shake, go*), or **śalayati** (Pali sal°, *shake*), ppp. śalita, *shaken, stirred up*: pavanabala-°ta-salila-vega-vaśagayā nāvā Jm 89.23.

Śalabha, n. of a nāga king: Māy 246.22.

śalākā (specialized mgs. of Skt. id.; also **śilākā,** q.v.), (**1**) app. *stick* used in counting (so Burnouf; Kern, *magic wand*): (gaṇayeta yadī naraḥ) śalākāṃ gṛhya hastena paryantaṃ naiva so labhet SP 305.14 (vs), *if a man counted them, taking a counting-stick in his hand, he could never get to the end*; (**2**) (= Pali sal°) *lot*: see s.v. **cārayati** 1; acc. to Chin. and Jap. on Mvy 9204, *a bamboo stick*; (**3**) (= Pali sal°) *ticket* for food, used by Buddhist monks when entertainment was offered them: (Ānanda, bhikṣūn ārocaya, yo yuṣmākam utsahate śvaḥ Sūrpārakaṃ nagaraṃ gatvā) bhoktuṃ, so śalākāṃ gṛhṇātv iti Divy 44.4, and ff. Just before this, in 43.27, (tāni puṣpāṇi . . . Jetavane gatvā vṛddhānte) sthitāni, dhūpo 'bhrakūṭavad udakaṃ vaidūryaśalākāvat (for vaiḍ°), prob. *like a sliver of vaiḍūrya* (in color), with ordinary Skt. mg. of śalākā.

śalākāvṛtti, f. or nt. (MSV ms. śilākā°, always; MSV °vṛtti, nt. as adj. with or sc. durbhikṣam), lit. *stick-operation*, n. of a kind of *famine*: Divy 131.21 (see s.v. **cañcu**); 132.3 śalākāvṛttir nāma tasmin kāle manuṣyāḥ khalu vilebhyo dhānyaguḍakāni śalākayākṛṣya bahūdakasthālyāṃ kvāthayitvā pivanti; iyaṃ śalākāsaṃbaddhatvāc chalākāvṛttir ity ucyate; similarly MSV i.250.16 ff.; see line 8 with note.

śalākī-bhūta, *constituting a surgical probe* (Skt. śalākā, Pali salākā): °taṃ avidyākośapaṭalapariśodhanatayā Gv 495.12, . . . *because it purifies* (by probing and opening) *the covering of the sheath of ignorance.*

śalya (m. or nt.; = Pali salla, see below), *rope*, as something that holds fast together; *ship's cable, hawser*: kṣānti-soratya-(= sau°) -smṛti-śalya-baddhā(ḥ) KP 153.5, (*the 'ship of the Doctrine'*, dharmanāvā, line 2) *that is moored* (*made fast*) *by the ropes of* **kṣānti, sauratya** and **smṛti**; so Tib., bzod pa daṅ des pa daṅ dran pa ḥi sbyor kas (sbyor, *connection, joining, fastening*; instr.) legs par sbyar ba. Pali salla in a similar sense should be recognized in Therīg. 347 kāmā . . . sallabandhanā, *desires which bind with cables* (the usual meaning of salla, tho adopted in PTSD and Mrs. Rhys Davids' transl., clearly makes no sense); comm. 242.7 rāgādīnaṃ sallānaṃ bandhanato sallabandhanā (tatp., not dvandva; and if rāgādi could be called *arrows* or *spears*, kṣānti etc. of KP could not!).

śalyāhartar (= Skt. śalya-h°), *surgeon*: MSV ii. 45.2 ff.

śallayati (denom. from śalya, with MIndic ll for ly; § 2.16; AMg. sallai, *afflicts*), *attacks, injures*: sarpāṇi śallayituṃ (inf.) Mmk 462.19 (prose).

śava, adj. (= **chava,** q.v.), *base, vile*, in śava-bhūta, of persons, *those who are base*: bālair vikalpitā hy ete śavabhūtaiḥ kutārkikaiḥ MadhK 262.5, cited from Laṅk 167.17 = 276.8; in Laṅk all mss. the first time sarva- for śava, so also one ms. the second time, text with the others there vaśa- (or is this only a misprint for -śava-?); Suzuki *corpse*; śavabhūtā(ḥ) MadhK 448.9; (yūyam api, addressed by King Bimbisāra to heretics who proposed to contest with Buddha) śavā bhūtvā bhagavatā sārdham ṛddhiṃ prārdhadhve (see **prārdhate**) Divy 146.11, *do you also, base as you are, aspire to* (?) *magic power along with the Buddha?*

Śavalāśva, n. of a former Buddha: Mv i.140.12.

śaśa, or (v.l.) **śaśaka** (nt. or m.), a kind of gem: anye devā śaśehi (v.l. śaśakehi) maṇiratanehi samalaṃkṛtaṃ bodhivṛkṣaṃ saṃjānanti Mv ii.311.4 (prose). Unrecorded.

śaśaka-rajas, Divy 645.10, or **śaśa-rajas,** Mvy 8194; LV 149.5, lit. *hare-speck*, a very small unit of matter, seven of which = one **eḍaka-(avi-)rajas,** q.v. for discussion of the mg.

Śaśiketu, *moon-bannered*, (**1**) ep. of Śākyamuni: °to, voc., LV 167.21; (**2**) n. of the future Buddha which it is predicted **Subhūti** will become: SP 148.7 (supported by Tib. zla baḥi tog, against v.l. Yaśasketu).

Śaśitejas, n. of a nāga: Mvy 3361.

Śaśimaṇḍalābha, n. of a Buddha: Gv 256.16.

Śaśimukha, n. of a Buddha: Gv 284.10.

Śaśivaktra-devī, n. of a queen: Gv 259.21 (previous birth of **Pramuditanayanajagadvirocanā**).

Śaśivimala, n. of a former Buddha: Mv iii.236.16.

Śaśivimalagarbha, n. of a Bodhisattva: Dbh 2.7.

Śaśī, n. of an apsaras: Kv 3.18.

śastraka (= Pali satthaka; Skt. śastra plus -ka), nt., *knife*: Mvy 8975; MSV ii.142.8; m. pl., applied figuratively to certain 'winds' in the body, compared to *knives*: Śikṣ 248.12 (see s.v. **kṣuraka**).

śastrādhāraka, m. (corresp. to Pali satthahāraka,

Vin. iii.73.11; Skt. śastra-*ādhāraka; see s.v. **ādhārayati**), (lit. *knife-holder,*) *assassin*: Bhīk 25b.2 °kaṃ vāsya paryeṣeta, *or should try to find an assassin for him.*

? **Śākaprabandha** (text Śāku°; true form very doubtful), n. of a yakṣa: Samādh p. 43 line 21.

Śākiya (semi-MIndic for Skt. Śākya; Pali Sākiya) = Śākya, which occurs in standard Skt., tho perhaps only referring to the Buddha, and to his tribe in relation to him; the form in -iya is common in vss and in prose of Mv, e. g. i.351.14; see Senart's Index and § 3.103 for others.

Śākiyānī, *Śākyan woman* (or *princess*; used of Māyā): Mv ii.12.15 (vs). Cf. **Śākyayanī, Śākyāyanī, °nikā.**

Śākī, n. of a brahman woman, app. an ascetic, who entertained the Bodhisattva: atha bodhisattvo yenaiva Śākyā brāhmaṇyā āśramas tenopasaṃkrāmat; sā bodhisattvaṃ vāsena bhaktena copanimantrayate sma LV 238.5 (prose); see Weller 29. But Tib. lacks the name: bram ze rigs ldan (see below) kyi gnas, *the dwelling of a person of brahman family(?)*. Note that immediately after this, line 7, the Bodhisattva visits and is entertained by another brahman woman, named **Padmā** (this time so named in Tib.); the two statements are closely parallel. The Tib. rigs ldan could mean *noble*, or represent a Skt. n. pr. such as Kulikā.

śākunikāyinī (to Skt. śākunika; § 22.10), *female bird-butcher*: kim ahaṃ °nī? na mama prāṇātipātaḥ kalpate Divy 530.6, 8 (prose; on being ordered to kill and cook partridges).

Śākyaputrīya, f. °yā (= Pali Sakyaputtiya), *a follower of the Buddha*: pl., Divy 338.13; 382.4; 419.20 (śramaṇa-Śāk°); 420.7; abstr. °ya-tva, *discipleship of the B.*, Laṅk 253.13; neg. a-, *no disciple of the B.*, Mvy 9126 (follows abhikṣuḥ, aśramaṇaḥ); abhikṣuṇī . . . aśramaṇī a-°yā Bhīk 23b.4.

Śākyabuddhi, n. of a teacher: Mvy 3489.

Śākyamitra, n. of a teacher: Mvy 3503.

Śākyamuni (= Pali Sak°; see also **Śākyasiṃha**), (**1**) ep. of the historic Buddha, passim; as 7th of the 'seven Buddhas', beginning with **Vipaśyin,** Dharmas 6; in SP 185.3 he is one of two Buddhas in the northeast, yet is located asyāṃ sahāyāṃ lokadhātau; Gv 419.20, see also **Vairocana,** who is identified with Ś. esp. in Gv; (**2**) n. of a former Buddha under whom 'this' (historic) Ś. made a praṇidhāna and received a prediction of Buddhahood: Mv i.1.6; 47.13 ff.; in 57.8 thirty crores of Buddhas of this name were worshipped by, and predicted the Buddhahood of, (the historic) Ś. while he was cakravartin; in LV 172.5 also a former B. of this name, to whom the historic Ś. made a gift; (**3**) n. of (presumably) another past Buddha: Mv iii.238.10 ff.; (**4**) n. of still another past Buddha, in the same list as (3), next in line to a Buddha named Yaśottara: Mv iii.240.4; 243.9, 10; 245.11; 247.7; 248.14; (in the same list, 240.10, the historic Ś. also names himself;) (**5**) n. of a future Buddha, rebirth of a girl who made a praṇidhāna under the historic Ś. and for whom he predicted Buddhahood: Divy 90.5, 28; (**6**) n. of a future Buddha, rebirth of **Vaḍika,** similarly predicted by the historic Ś.: Av i.35.3.

Śākyayanī, °yinī = **Śākyāy°**, q.v.

Śākyavardha, nt., n. of a temple (devakula) at Kapilavastu: Divy 391.1.

Śākyasiṃha, 'lion of the Śākyas', chiefly in vss (so all the foll. except Mvy), (**1**) ep. of the historic **Śākyamuni** (1): Mvy 50; SP 27.13; 28.8; 147.3 etc.; LV 3.18; Mv ii.349.12 = iii.273.11; (**2**) ep. or alternative name of **Śākyamuni** (4): Mv iii.241.15; 244.2 (in mss.).

Śākyasūtra, n. of a work: Karmav 42.8.

Śākyāyanikā = next: pañcānāṃ °kā-śatānām Bhīk 9a.1 (prose).

Śākyāyanī, °yinī, Śākya°, and prec. (cf. also **Śākiyānī**; § 22.10), *Śākyan woman*; only noted in prose of Mv, always preceded by Śākyā or Śākya- in comp., *Śākyan men and women*, always pl.: Śākyāyanīyo (? mss. corrupt as to ending) Mv iii.90.19, °yinyaś ca (Śākya° in 101.18, 20, and v.l. 108.7; 112.20) 101.18, 20; 107.2; 108.7; 112.20.

śākhāntika, adj., *enclosed in branches*: Mv ii.254.2, of a fowler stalking birds, see s.v. **saṃpariveṭhita.** But the use of **-antika** seems strange; read śākuntika?

śāṭayati (= Pali sāṭeti; Skt. śātayati, and Dhātup. śaṭati; note Kalpanāmaṇḍitikā, Lüders Kl. Skt. Texte 2, pp. 43, 63, 177 **aśātikā,** q.v., na śātayati = Pali MN i.220.18 et al. na āsāṭikaṃ sāṭetā hoti), (**1**) *removes, does away with* (impurity), *cleanses*: sarvaṃ kaṣāyaṃ śāṭayati (= Tib. sel ba) Mvy 2423; (**2**) *torments, destroys*: śāṭeti gātrāṇi duḥkhārditasya Mv iii.385.17 (vs).

śāṭi (= Skt. śāṭī, śāṭa), (strip of) *cloth* (= next): śākaṃ ca śāṭiṃ (no v.l.; but WT śāṭīṃ with ms. K') ca punar dadāmi SP 114.8 (vs); **śaṇa-śāṭiṃ** (so read) Mv i.232.4 (prose), see s.v.

śāṭikā (Skt. Lex. id., Pali sā°) = prec.: pāṇḍarāye °kāye ochannaṃ Mv ii.85.1; **śaṇa-°kā,** q.v., Divy 83.22; (bhikṣuṇīnāṃ) codakaśāṭikām (ca uda°) MSV ii.84.11.

Śāṭhā (so Index and Mironov; text Śāthā), n. of a country or part of the world: Mvy 3055 (= Tib. gyo ldan, *crafty*).

śāṭhiya (= Skt. śāṭhya), *guile*: Gv 54.7 (vs; may be m.c.).

śāṇaka, nt., also m. or f., sg. or pl. (= AMg. sāṇaa, Skt. śāṇa, Pali sāṇa, *a coarse hempen cloth,* PTSD), (*wrapping-*)*cloth of hemp*: sā (a dead slave-woman) °kaiḥ pariveṣṭya śmaśānam apakṛṣya parityaktābhūt LV 265.20; °kam (n. sg. nt.) Mvy 9160; MSV ii.91.14; °kā (n. sg. f. or n. pl. m. or f.?) vā Bhīk 22b.4, in list of kinds of cloth. Cf. next, and **śaṇa-śāṭi.**

Śāṇakavāsin (cf. prec.), n. of a monk: Divy 349.9; written Śān° 350.25; 351.5.

śāta, or **sāta,** adj., or sometimes subst. nt. (= Pali sāta; Skt. Lex., and once in cpd. ati-śāta, BR; cf. **sātīyati**), *pleasant, agreeable,* or as n. *pleasantness, pleasure* (opp. **a-,** less often **vi-śāta**): Mvy 1882 śātam = Tib. phya le ba (*fine, smooth, refined, pleasant,* Das) or mñam pa (*level*); sātaṃ Dharmas 34; sukha-sāta-saṃgatā Mv i.97.3, 5; sāta-sukha-sahagatam Bbh 208.26; priyarūpa-śātarūpa-Śikṣ 223.9; AsP 333.5 (°sāta°); sāta-sita (= Pali id., same vs, Dhp. 341) *bound by pleasures* Ud iii.5; in Mv ii.480.6 Senart by em. tasyā ahaṃ na sātā (mss. mātā) bhaviṣyāmi, *towards her I shall not be agreeable,* i. e. *I shall be offended at her*; but perhaps the reading of mss. may be kept; Princess Sudarśanā speaks, referring to her attendants: *I shall not be a mother to her,* i. e. *I shall not cherish her.*

Śātāgiri, see **Sātā°.**

Śādvalā, n. of a town: MSV i.xviii.2.

Śānakavāsin, see **Śāṇ°.**

śāniścara, adj. (to **śaniścara** plus -a; = Skt. śānaiścara), *of Saturn*: etat °ra-kṣetraṃ Mmk 272.1.

Śānta, (**1**) perh n. of a disciple of Buddha: (in a list) **Nīlakeśaṃ** ca **Vṛddhaṃ** ca Śāntaṃ (? or adj. with prec.?) śāstraviśāradaṃ Mv i.182.19 (vs); (**2**) one of the (**śuddhāvāsakāyika**) gods who asked the Buddha to recite the LV: LV 7.6 (vs); 438.16 (prose, with **Praśānta,** q.v.; om. in some mss., but Tib. both, zhi ba daṅ rab tu zhi ba daṅ).

Śānta-ga, n. of a previous incarnation of Śākyamuni: LV 171.2 (vs); Tib. zhi ba (= śānta or °ti) bstod, which Foucaux renders *proclamant*; it means primarily *exalt, praise*; he notes a Tib. var. ston, *teaching*; implying gā(i), *sing?*

Śāntadhvaja, n. of a Buddha: Gv 259.6 (vs).

Śāntanirghoṣa, n. of a Buddha: Gv 258.16 (vs).

Śāntanirghoṣahāramati, n. of a lokadhātu: Gv 258.22 (vs).

Śāntapradīpameghaśirirāja, n. of a Buddha: Gv 259.6 (vs; text divides after °megha, as two names).

Śāntaprabharāja, n. of two Buddhas: Gv 257.24; 258.18 (both vss).

Śāntamati, (**1**) n. of a (trāyastriṃśa) devaputra: LV 203.11 (prose; so Lefm. with best mss., supported by Tib. zhi ba ḥi blo gros, most mss. Śāntasumati, so Foucaux even in transl. of Tib. which does not render su); 217.5 (no v.l.); (**2**) n. of a Bodhisattva: Mmk 63.4; 68.20; 559.2 ff.; (**3**) (same as 2? or even as 1?) n. of a personage addressed in the Tathāgataguhya-sūtra: in citations Śikṣ 159.8 ff.; 242.7.

Śāntamukha, n. of a dhāraṇī: Gv 66.13.

[**śāntara,** corrupt, in defective vs Mv i.164.15; Senart, yathecchakaṃ (mss. yate°) araṇa-samādhi śāntara (read śānta ca? cf. Pali santaṃ samādhiṃ araṇaṃ, CPD s.v. araṇa)... (lacuna) devanareṣu (mss. devacareṣu) arcita, addressed to the Buddha.]

Śāntarakṣita, n. of a teacher: Mvy 3492.

Śāntaraja(s), n. of a former Buddha: Mv i.141.15.

Śāntaraśmi, n. of a Bodhisattva: Gv 442.18.

Śāntarutasāgaravatī, n. of a night-goddess: Gv 281.2.

Śāntareṇu, n. of a former Buddha: Mv i.137.15.

Śāntaś(i)rī, n. of a Buddha: Gv 285.8 (vs; text Śanta°).

Śāntābha, n. of a Tathāgata: Gv 82.8 (prose; text Śa°).

Śāntidhvaja, n. of a Buddha: Gv 285.19.

Śāntiprabha, n. of a Bodhisattva: Gv 3.16.

Śāntiprabhagambhīrakūṭa, n. of a Tathāgata: Gv 309.15.

Śāntimatī, n. of a locality: Māy 52.

Śāntirāja, n. of a Buddha: Gv 284.9.

Śāntendrarāja, n. of a Bodhisattva: Gv 4.6.

śāma, also **sāma,** q.v., semi-MIndic for Skt. śyāma, *dark*; in **kāḍi-śāma,** and ms. for **śyāma-śavala,** qq.v.

śāmbali (this seems indicated by the various mss. readings, combined with the Skt. form; Senart sām° or śām°, and °lī; mss. always °li or °ri), *the silk-cotton tree*, Skt. śālmali, Pali simbali; cf. AMg. sambaliyā: °li-koṭarāto (°rato) Mv i.272.7; 273.13, 15.

śāmyaka, nt., n. of a medicinal herb: Suv 104.6 (vs). Perh. m.c. for śamyāka? But mss. sāmyakaṃ.

[**śāmyaprāśa,** Divy 634.7, 11, 17, 20, mostly by em., mss. generally śāmyāprāṇaṃ; read **śamyāprāsa,** q.v.]

śāyāpitaka, adj. (-ka extension of ppp. of MIndic caus. *sāyāpeti to Skt. śāyayati, caus. of śete), *caused to lie down to sleep*: (tayā dārako...) °tako 'bhūt MSV i.117.13. See § 38.61.

śāyita, ppp. of caus. of Skt. śī-, lit. *caused to sleep*: kaccid bhagavan sukhaṃ śāyita iti MSV iii.142.1, *I hope, Lord, you have had a good sleep?*

śāra, m. or nt. (= AMg. sāla; perh. read śāla?), either 'the 77th planet, named śāla', or (more probably) 'a celestial abode named śāla of the 8th Devaloka' (Ratnachandra, s.v. sāla, 7 and 8). In Mv i.231.4 (vs) read: ādityo (? next word uncertain; mss. vatavallo, which is metr. correct, or vadbalo) śāraṃ (or śālaṃ; mss. śāram) abhyudgato (mss. atyudgataṃ; em. Senart) yathākāśe, *like the sun when it has arisen in the sky up to the śāra* (*śāla*). (On *śāra, a kind of bird, see **sāra.**)

śāradaka, adj. (= Skt. śārada), *autumnal*: pad(u)ma(ṃ) °kaṃ Ud xviii.5, so oldest ms., later ms. °dikaṃ; °dika is Skt. (BR, from Hariv.; also Schmidt, Nachträge), as well as Pali (sāra°), which uses it in Dhp. 285 = Jāt. i.183.17, the same vs as Ud above (Chakravarti cites wrongly); also °dikaṃ (tiktālāmbu) Mv ii.126.4; 127.8; 128.13; 129.15; °dikena rogeṇa Av i.168.9; MSV i.1.9.

śāradya (= Pali [sometimes parisa-]sārajja; this, with Skt. Lex. śārada, *timid*, and Pali -sārada in vītasārada, is a back-formation from BHS **viśārada, vaiśāradya,** or their Pali equivalents), *timidity* (Tib. on Śikṣ cited as bag tsha ba), in parṣacchāradya(-bhaya), *timidity in an assembly*: (sarvasattvaparṣac-)°ya-bhaya-vigamāya Śikṣ 296.7; durgatibhayaṃ vā parṣac-°ya-bhayaṃ vā Dbh 13.1; sattvānāṃ parṣac-°ya-bhaya-vinivartanatāyai Gv 264.7; parṣac-°ya-bhayād Bbh 146.18; in Dharmas 71 (list of 5 bhayāni) text parṣadasādya-bhayam, read prob. parṣac-chāradya° (possibly parṣada- or pārṣada-śāradya-).

Śāradvata = next: Divy 395.1 (vs).

Śāradvatīputra (not in Pali) = **Śāriputra**: Divy 361.16; 395.3, 4; Av i.213.9; ii.154.6; Śikṣ 158.8; 287.6 (here text Sār°); Karmav 55.20; ŚsP 55.17 etc. (common here); Jm 115.22; acc. to Kern, SP Preface ix, in Kashgar rec. of SP (spelled Śar°, doubtless by error). Nearly all these prose.

Śārasamātulya (so, or Sāra°, mss.), n. of a disciple of Buddha: Mv i.182.20 (vs).

Śārikā = **Śārī**: MSV iv.21.5 ff.

Śāriputra (= Pali Sāriputta; also **Śāli°, Śāradvatī-p°, Śārisuta**), n. of one of Buddha's two chief disciples, the other being (**Mahā-)Maudgalyāyana**; orig. named **Upatiṣya,** q.v. for story of his conversion; once also called **Tiṣya,** q.v. (6): Mvy 1032; Mv i.45.7; iii.41.6; 57.16 ff.; 94.1 ff.; 102.13; 255.15; 268.5; 375.7; (Senart always Śāri°, but usually some, often all, of his mss. **Śāli°**;) SP 2.2; 29.2 ff.; 60.1 ff.; 264.17 ff.; LV 1.12; 443.13; Divy 153.5; 182.21; 268.6; 314.15 ff.; 330.6 ff.; 394.21 ff.; 486.25 ff.; 542.24 ff.; Av ii.69.7 etc.; Sukh 2.6; 92.5; Karmav 161.17. Why is he never called Mahā-Ś° in BHS or Pali, when Maudgalyāyana, Kātyāyana, Kāśyapa, and other disciples so often have the prefix Mahā-?

Śārisuta = prec. (only in vss): SP 31.9; 47.13; 48.9.

Śārī (= Pali Sārī), also **Śārikā,** q.v., n. of the mother of **Upatiṣya** (**Śāriputra**): Mv iii.56.9 f. (v.l. Śālī); Av ii.186.6.

Śārdūla, n. of a Bodhisattva: Gv 442.16.

Śārdūlakarṇa, n. of a son of the Mātaṅga chief Triśaṅku: Divy 619.27 ff.

Śārdūlakarṇāvadāna, nt., = Divy xxxiii; colophon 655.10.

śāla, see **śāra**; **śāla-** in cpds., see also **sāla-.**

Śālarāja (cf. also **Sālarāja, Śālarājendra,** and **Śālendrarāja**), perh. = Viṣṇu, as Lord of Śālagrāma(?): siṃhāsani saṃniṣaṇṇako Śālarājo va yathā virājate SP 455.6 (vs), said of Amitābha; Tib. literally, sa la ḥi rgyal po.

Śālarājendra (cf. under prec.), n. of a Tathāgata: Mmk 426.6; prob. for the commoner **Śālendrarāja** (both sometimes assoc. with **Saṃkusumitarāja** or °**rājendra** and **Ratnaketu**).

Śālasucitra, n. of a kumbhāṇḍa: Mvy 3442.

Śāliputra = **Śāri°**: Av i.241.7, and ms. ii.186.7; mss. of Mv also often Śāli°.

Śālistamba-sūtra, nt., n. of a work (= our Śāl): Śikṣ 219.10; = next.

Śālistambaka, nt., = prec.: Mvy 1402.

śālīna, adj., ep. of odana (= Pali sāl°, acc. to PTSD from sāli = Skt. śāli, *rice*; but all odana was normally composed of rice), *rich, fine* (porridge); perhaps from śālā; some Skt. uses of śālīna suggest this; Apte gives *householder* as a mg., and Wilson, ap. MW, *an opulent householder*; perh. lit. *of the hall*? 'pukka' in the modern Indian vernacular sense?: °nam odanaṃ bhuktvā... bhuñjānaḥ śuṣkakalmāṣān kaccin na paritapyase Divy 559.8 (vs); similarly Mv iii.271.10 (vs), and in Pali sālīnaṃ odanaṃ Miln. 16.28.

[**śāluka,** nt. (= Skt. Lex. id., Pali sāluka; Skt. śālūka), (edible) *lotus-root*: Mvy 6246, text; but Index with Mironov °ūka, which accordingly read.]

Śālendrarāja or °**jan** (see also **Sāl°**), (**1**) n. of a Tathāgata well-known in Mmk: 7.11; 63.27; spelled Sāl°, 130.3; 305.14; prob. the same as **Śālarājendra**; (**2**) n.

of (another?) Buddha: Samādh p. 7 lines 24 ff.; (**3**) n. of a future Buddha, rebirth predicted for King Śubhavyūha: SP 469.6.

Śālendraskandha, n. of a Bodhisattva: Gv 442.20.

śālmalī-vana (m. or nt.; cf. Pali satti-simbali-vana; AMg. simbalī, n. of a tree in hell; Skt. śālmali, 1 and 3 in pw), n. of a hell: saṃjīve 'sipattre (read asi°) ca tathaiva °vane ... vaset Mmk 115.1 (vs).

śāśvata-dṛṣṭi, f. (= Pali sassata-diṭṭhi), *the doctrine of eternality* (that the world etc. is eternal), *eternalism*: Bbh 67.22 (see s.v. **ekatya-śāśvatika**).

śāśvata-dṛṣṭika, m., *an adherent of eternalism* (see prec.): Bbh 67.22.

Śāśvatavajra, n. of an author: Sādh 211.11 etc.

śāśvatavādin, adj. (= Pali sassatavādi), *one who says things are eternal*: Bbh 67.23 (see s.v. **ekatya-śāśvatika**).

-śāśvatika, see **ekatya-śāś°**.

śāśvatoccheda-, *permanence and annihilation* (both denied to the world, see **aśāśvatam**): Laṅk 22.10 = 264.7 (others, see Suzuki's Index, and Studies).

Śāsanāda, n. of a mountain: Māy 254.11.

śāsaniya, adj., gdve. (§ 3.42), *to be instructed*: LV 363.13 (vs).

śāstar (Skt.), *teacher*: ep. of a Buddha, śāstā devamanuṣyāṇāṃ or (usually) devānāṃ ca manuṣyāṇāṃ ca, Mvy 11; in cliché describing stock characteristics of a B. (a few of many passages s.v. **puruṣadamyasārathi**); ṣaṭ °tāraḥ, *the six* (heretical) *teachers*, Mvy 3544 (with list of names, see s.v. **Pūraṇa Kāśyapa**); RP 35.8 (acc., ṣac-chāstṝṃs).

śāstāra-vādin, see **vādin** (2).

? **Śāstraviśārada**, (perh.) n. of a disciple of Buddha: Mv i.182.19 (but perh. more likely adj. with a preceding name).

śāstrāvarta, in LV 126.7 °tāṃ, acc. sg., sc. lipim, a kind of script. The true text prob. had śāstrāvartalipiṃ, as indicated by Tib. which adds yi ge = lipi; every other item in the list ends in -lipiṃ. Does it mean *writing* (designed) *for science*? Cf. **gaṇanāvarta-lipi**, which follows °tāṃ.

śikyakā (cf. Pali sikkā, Skt. śikya and Lex. śikyā), *loop*: jala-°kayāpi vidhyataḥ (dual; in play with women) MSV iii.16.9.

śikṣa, nt., for **śikṣā**, q.v.

śikṣaṇā (= Skt. °ṇa, nt., Pali sikkhaṇa), *disciplined observance* (with loc.): ekasyāṃ śikṣāyāṃ śikṣaṇāyām aśaktasyetaraśikṣānabhyāsād anāpattiḥ Śikṣ 11.7.

śikṣā (see also **śiṣyā**), (**1**) śi° tisraḥ (or, in Mvy 929, trīṇi śikṣāṇi), (*the three*) *instructions* (Pali sikkhā), viz. by the Vinaya (-piṭaka) in reference to moral conduct (adhiśīlam), by the Sūtra in reference to thought, intellect (adhicittam), by the Abhidharma in reference to wisdom, insight (adhiprajñam); correspondingly in Pali: see Sūtrāl. xi.1; xx.17; Mvy 929; Dharmas 140; śikṣāsu RP 30.11. The words adhiśīlam etc. were orig. adverbs (adhi governing the second member, *in a manner referring to* ...) and are still so used, e. g. Bbh 373.20–21 adhiśīlaṃ (and adhicittaṃ, adhiprajñaṃ) śikṣā; loc. forms are also used in the same way, as adhicitte ca āyogaḥ Ud xxxii.27(32) = Pali Dhp. 185 (same text). These forms may be turned into adjectives: adhiśīlo vihāro Bbh 335.1; sa vihāraḥ adhicitta ity ucyate Bbh 338.21 (this usage seems not recorded in Pali). Often the stems adhiśīla-, adhicitta-, adhiprajña- are used as prior members of cpds., in which case precise analysis becomes difficult; so Bbh 185.14; 333.2; 335.3; 338.24; 341.8; etc. But sometimes adhiprajñā-śikṣā is used as a cpd., Dharmas 140, the prior member being then evidently taken as stem of a noun. As nouns, adhiśīla, adhicitta, and adhiprajñā, like their Pali equivalents, are used Mvy 930–2; Bbh 317.2 (parallel with adhimuktiḥ), being then reinterpreted (with adhi = adhika) as *superior morality, intellect, wisdom*, see CPD s.vv. adhisīla, °citta, °paññā; (**2**) like Pali sikkhā (tho PTSD and Childers do not clearly recognize the fact), śikṣā also means *morality*, perhaps as a reflex of its use in the cpd. **śikṣā**(Pali sikkhā)-**pada**, q.v.: Bhīk 10a.1, after repetition of the five śikṣāpada the novice says, teṣām ... śikṣāyām anuśikṣe, *I* (*will*) *imitate them* (see **anuśikṣati**) *in moral conduct*.

śikṣā-dattaka, m. (no parallel noted in Pali), *one that has been given* (a penance, for a serious offense) *according to the rules* (see AbhidhK. LaV-P. iv.98, note 3; *pénitent*; Sūtrāl. xi.4, note 4, wrongly Lévi): Mvy 8723 = Tib. bslab pas byin pa; MSV ii.154.13, one of five persons not to be made kaṭhināstāraka; iii.67.9; 69.4 (in these follows caritamānāpya).

śikṣāpada, nt. (Skt. in Harṣac.; = Pali sikkhāpada, see also **śiṣyā°**), *moral commandment*; as in Pali, there are five incumbent on all Buddhists, referred to as binding on an upāsaka and listed Mv iii.268.10–13, in the form of promises made, yāvajjīvaṃ prāṇātipātāt (adattādānāt, kāmehi mithyācārāt, mṛṣāvādāt, surāmaireyamadyapramādasthānāt) prativiramiṣyaṃ; the second five bind only monks, śrāmaṇerasya śikṣāpadaṃ iii.268.16–17, here not listed but referred to, yāvaj (this means that the first four are understood) jātarūparajatapratigrahaṇa-śikṣāpadaṃ dhārayāmi 17; the first eight are listed Mvy 8693–8700 in the form of cpds. in -viratiḥ (6–8 being gandhamālyavilepanavarṇaka-[*rouge* etc.]-dhāraṇa-v°, uccaśayanamahāśayana-v°, vikālabhojana-v°); here omitted is nṛtyagītavāditā, which is separate in the Pali list but grouped with gandhamālyavilepana in AbhidhK. LaV-P. iv.47, altho this text proceeds to point out that the standard number ten is made up by separating these two (and adding the prohibition against gold etc., which curiously, in AbhidhK. as in Mvy, is left out of the formal list of eight); the order of the second group of five varies slightly in different lists; pañca śi° Mv i.211.14 = ii.15.13 (observed by the Bodhisattva's mother while carrying him); i.321.18; in Śikṣ 174.1 ff., besides the 'five' and 'ten' śi°, are mentioned larger numbers, ye ca bodhisattvasaṃvaraṃ caturthaṃ śataṃ (Tib. acc. to note *400*) śikṣāpadānāṃ dhārayanti, ye punar abhiniṣkrāntagṛhāvāsā bhikṣavaḥ (250 śi°) ... dhārayanti, and 500 which nuns keep; no number, Mv iii.52.2; 265.14 (buddhaprajñapti-śi°): Divy 51.8; 549.6.

śikṣāpayati (= Pali sikkhāpeti), caus. to Skt. śikṣati (Pali sikkhati), *teaches* (two accs.): °peti Mv iii.362.5; °pehi 4, kumāraśataṃ iṣvastrajñānaṃ °payiṣyāmi 1; ppp. lipiṃ °pito iii.394.9; all prose.

Śikṣāsamuccaya, n. of a work (Śikṣ): Śikṣ 16.1.

śikṣitaka, f. **°ikā** (Skt. °ita, endearing dim.), *learned, skilled*: -nṛtya-su-°tikāṃ, of a daughter of Māra: LV 323.7 (vs; text °sikṣ°).

Śikhaṇḍin, (**1**) n. of a devaputra, as whose son the horse Kaṇṭhaka was reborn in heaven: Mv ii.190.11; (**2**) n. of a brahman, kinsman of Trapuṣa and Bhallika in a former birth, reborn in Brahmaloka: LV 386.11, 20; (**3**) n. of a son of King Rudrāyaṇa: Divy 545.5; 556.5 ff.; Karmav 58.10; (**4**) n. of a yakṣa: Māy 49.

Śikharadhara, n. of a deity in the Tuṣita heaven: Mv i.174.1 (here also called a Bodhisattva); iii.345.16.

Śikharābha, see **Śikhalābha**.

śikhala (= Skt. śikhara), *peak*: śaila-śi° LV 338.20 (all mss.); Gv 379.20; see also **Vimalaśikhala** and next.

Śikhaladatta (Senart Śikhara°, with 1 inferior ms.; cf. **śikhala**), n. of a former Buddha: Mv i.141.14.

Śikhalābha, read Śikharābha with 2d ed., n. of a Buddha: Gv 257.3 (vs).

śikhā-bandha, m., (**1**) (= Pali sikhā°, DN i.7.21), a particular manner of *doing up the hair* (*top-knot*; in Pali, acc. to DN comm. i.89.3 ff., with ornamentation): °dhaṃ kṛtvā Mmk 38.19; (**2**) a particular technique of *wielding* (the bow), presumably involving the *top of the head*; mentioned with **muṣṭi-b°** and **pada-(pāda-)b°** as an art to be mastered by a prince: Mvy 4979; LV 156.12; Divy 442.7; Tib. on Mvy and LV thor tshugs (var. on Mvy tsugs), which seems to fit mg. 1 above, meaning apparently simply *doing up the hair in a spiral* (so Das) *on top of the head*. This cannot be the mg. in these BHS passages, which certainly refer to a manner of wielding the bow; see s.v. muṣṭi-b°.

Śikhin, (**1**) (= Pali Sikhi), n. of a former Buddha, in the standard list between **Vipaśyin** and **Viśvabhū** (**Viśvabhuj**): Mvy 88; LV 5.15; Mv iii.94.1 ff.; 240.7; 241.17; 243.15; 244.5; 246.6; 247.10; 249.3; Dharmas 6 (second of the '7 Tathāgatas'); Divy 333.5; Kv 15.13; Gv 206.12; Mmk 68.27; 397.11; 426.9; (**2**) n. of 62 former Buddhas of the same name who predicted each one the next (in same list as iii.240.7 etc. above): Mv iii.235.2 ff.; (**3**) n. of a Brahman: SP 4.9; called a Mahābrahman SP 175.1; LV 393.20 etc.; 397.12 etc.; (**4**) n. of a Bodhisattva: AsP 449.20.

śikhī, n. of a kind of magic: Divy 636.26 (vs, in a list of names of vidyā).

śiṭā, app. *rope*: tatra (sc. on coming to three mountain-peaks, parvataśṛṅgāṇi) tvayā vetra-śiṭāṃ baddhvātikramitavyam Divy 113.16, *there you must gird yourself with staff* (or does **vetra,** q.v., also mean *rope*, or the material used for one?) *and rope* (for mountain-climbing) *and pass over* (them); 274.23, see s.v. **viṣṭhā**; te hi śiṭā-karkaṭaka-prayogenābhiroḍhum ārabdhāḥ 281.2 (of thieves entering a house to steal jewels).

Śitīcūḍa (or with Senart Śiti°; mss. Śithī°), n. of a former Buddha: Mv i.138.3.

Śithilakuṇḍala, n. of a former Buddha: Mv i.139.6.

Śibighoṣā, n. of Śibi's capital city: Av i.183.14. Cf. **Śivaghoṣā.**

Śiramakuṭa, n. of a former Buddha: Mv i.141.16.

Śirasāhvaya, n. of a former Buddha: Mv iii.231.12; 232.15, 20.

[**śirasitāḥ,** mss. **°tā,** acc. to Index *exalted* (?) in Divy 126.22 (vs): (ṛddhyā khalv avabhartsitāḥ paramayā śrīgarvitās te vayaṃ) buddhyā khalv api nāmitāḥ °tāḥ prajñābhimānodayam, prāptārthena ... saṃvejitās te vayaṃ, etc.; addressed by Aśoka to Vītaśoka on his miraculous soaring into the air. I suspect that śirasi is a separate word; for tā of mss. read te, n. pl., with vayaṃ?]

Śiri- and **Śirī-,** often, semi-MIndic for **Śrī,** both alone and in cpds; examples § 3.108.

Śirikā = **Śrī,** q.v., 3 and 4.

(**śrī-**)**Śiri-jātaka** (v.l. Śirī°), n. of a jātaka (see **Śrī** 4): colophon, Mv ii.94.14. No correspondent in Pali Jāt.; the Siri-j., 284, is wholly different.

Śiriprabha (for Śrī°), n. of a deer (the Bodhisattva): Mv ii.234.15 ff.; colophon, śiriprabhasya mṛgarājasya jātakaṃ ii.237.16.

Śiribhadra, see **Śrībhadra**(1).

Śirījalarāja (for Śrī°), app. n. of a country or region: Gv 208.11 (vs).

Śirīmatī (for Śrī°), n. of a devakumārikā in the southern quarter: Mv iii.307.8. Cf. LV 389.7 **Śriyāmatī.**

(**śiro-veṣṭana,** nt. [= Skt. Lex., also Harṣac., Schmidt, Nachträge], *turban*: Mvy 5842.)

śilā (**1**) (= Pali silā, defined in PTSD *a precious stone, quartz!*; read prob. *crystal*), *crystal*: Mvy 5955, in a list of gems, = Tib. man śel; (**2**) a high number: Gv 106.10 (precedes **švelā**; seems to have no correspondent in Gv 133 and the list cited thence in Mvy).

śilākā = **śalākā,** q.v. in mg. (3): MSV i.30.3, 5, 6, 7; in mg. (2) or (3), ib. ii.120.6, 8, ms. śilākā, ed. em. śilākā (why?); in 8 ms. °kā-caryamāṇāyaṃ, read °kāyāṃ cār°, see **cārayati.**

śilākuṭṭa, *stonemason, stonecutter*: Mvy 3783 = Tib. rdo mkhan; in a list of words for artisans; in Skt. Lex. defined BR as an *instrument* for breaking stone (prob. a misunderstanding).

śilā-putra, m. (cf. **niśādā-putra,** and Skt. dṛṣat-putra; Skt. Lex. śilāputra, *grindstone*; Pali nisada-pota, Vism. 252.27, which ṭīkā quoted in transl. glosses with silā-puttako), acc. to Tib. *pestle*, perhaps also *upper millstone*, = niśādā-putra: Mvy 7517 = Tib. gtun (misprinted gtur) bu.

Śilāpura, n. of a town: Māy 29.

śiliṣṭa, ppp. (= Pali siliṭṭha, Skt. śliṣṭa), *holding closely* (to, loc.): pālāś catasro hayacaraṇe °ṭāḥ LV 233.14 (vs).

? **Śilukṣa,** n. of a place (adhiṣṭhāna, nigama) where Trapuṣa and Bhallika built a stūpa for the stones used by Buddha in washing a robe: Mv iii.310.15 (adhiṣṭhāna; here mss. śilujvaṃ, śilahvaṃ); 313.2 (śilukṣa-nāma-nigama); but in the next line, adyāpi gandhārarājye adhiṣṭhānaṃ śilā-nāmena jñāyati; cf. śilahvaṃ of one ms. above; I suspect that Śilāhvaya should be read, *having the name of Stone(s)*.

Śilpavant(a), n. of a companion of **Puṇyavant(a),** q.v.: Mv iii.33.17 ff.

Śilpābhijña, n. of a śreṣṭhin's son in Kapilavastu: Gv 448.10 etc.

śilpāyatana, see **āyatana** (1).

śilpika (once in Skt. as ep. of Śiva; = Pali sippika), *one skilled in the arts and crafts*: śobhano °ko ya imāni ... karoti Mv ii.463.6; 464.4.

Śivaghoṣā, n. of King Śivi's capital: MSV ii.132.12; = **Śibighoṣā.**

Śivadattamāla, n. of a former Buddha: Mv i.141.14.

śivapathikā (see also next; a popular etym. based on Pali sīvathikā, same mg.), *a place where dead bodies are thrown out*: yadā paśyati mṛtaśarīrāṇi °kāyām ... Śikṣ 211.9; similarly in the sequel repeatedly; yadā śmaśānagataḥ paśyati nānārūpāṇi °kāyām apaviddhāni ... (dead bodies) ŚsP 1431.17.

śivapathī (back formation, prob. m.c., § 22.24, from prec.) = prec.: yogān ārabhate citrāṃ gatvā śivapathīṃ śubhāṃ Laṅk 310.4 (vs).

Śivapura, n. of a town: °rāhāre Māy 28.

Śivabhadra, n. of a yakṣa: Māy 28.

śivamantra, nt., or °**trā** (= next), a high number: °trā Gv 106.9; °tram, nt., Gv 133.19, cited Mvy 7887 (Mironov śivamātraḥ) = Tib. gzhal (= mātra!) phul.

śivamātra, m., = prec., q.v.: Mvy 7758 = Tib. gzhal phul (var. yul).

Śivarāgra (! occurs six times and only in this form, but doubtless corrupt), n. of a brahman: Gv 454.8 to 455.8.

Śivālaka-sūtra, n. of a work: Karmav 56.3. Probably (with Lévi) = the Pali Siṅgālovāda-(vv.ll. Sigālovāda-, Siṅgālaka-)suttanta (DN 31; quotation corresponds approximately to DN iii.189.14 ff.).

śivā-vidyā, *'jackal-science'*, divination from cries of jackals: aṅgavidyā vā vastra-(read vastu-, see Pali below) vidyā vā śi° vā śakunividyā vā tvayādhītā Divy 630.22; cf. Pali DN i.9.7 aṅga-vijjā vatthu-v° khatta-(v.l. khetta-) v° siva-v° ... sakuṇa-v°; comm. i.93.19 sivavijjā ti susāne parivasitvā santikaraṇavijjā; sigālarūtavijjā ti pi vadanti (Divy proves the latter right, with its śivā; śiva, m., also *jackal* in Skt., tho rarer).

Śivi, n. of the well-known king (also spelled Śibi); besides versions in Av No. 34 and Jm No. 2, which resemble those of Skt. and Pali, a new version occurs in MSV ii.132.12 ff.; the king bleeds himself daily for six months to supply a prescription for a sick man.

śivika-dvāra, nt., acc. to Tib. (lho sgo) on 139.15, *south gate* (of a city): MSV iii.139.15 ff. (in 16, °raṃ rātryāṃ dvau yāmau vivṛtaṃ tiṣṭhati, pūrvakaṃ paścima-

kaṃ ceti, implying a double gate, both parts open); in iii.137.12 tad eva te °raṃ bhavanam, *that very same śi° is your home.* I cannot explain śivika; but for Tib., I should suspect relation to Pali sivikā-gabbha, Vin. ii.152.18, acc. to comm. = caturassa-g°, *rectangular*; but this is equally obscure. Could śivika, as if *auspicious*, be a euphemism for the unlucky south?

śiśava, adj. (once in Skt., BR; not recorded in MIndic), = śiśu, *youthful*: (kanyāḥ) ārjavāḥ śiśavā madhurā(ḥ) . . . RP 41.17.

Śiśumāragiri, see **Śuśu°**.

? **śiṣita,** quasi-ppp. to śiṣyate, or denom. ppp. to śiṣya, *instructed*: tatraiṣa śiṣita (so divide; all mss. but one with Calc. śikṣita; meter indecisive) santo lipiśālām upāgataḥ LV 126.18 (vs).

śiṣyaṇa or **°ṇā** (see next; = śikṣaṇa or °ṇā), *instruction*: lipiśālam āgatu suśikṣitu °ṇārthaṃ (so all mss.) LV 124.20 (vs).

śiṣyate, could be considered normal Skt. pass. to śās-, *is instructed, learns* (with acc.): (dārakasahasrāṇi . . .) lipiṃ °ante sma LV 127.4 (prose; all mss.; Calc. śikṣante). The prec. and foll. items show that, acc. to persistent tradition, LV (and esp. in this vicinity) uses forms in śiṣy- for Skt. and usual BHS śikṣ-; those which Weller notices he regards as mere corruptions for śikṣ- (41, line 1); but it is not impossible that the word śiṣya is concerned in some or all of them, even in this, which could be a denom. In śiṣyā(-pada), for śikṣā-, the influence of śiṣya could only have been exerted in secondary blending. These substitutions may also have phonetic aspects (ṣ for kh for kṣ, § 2.26).

śiṣyayati, °te (either caus. to **śiṣyate,** q.v., or denom. to śiṣya), *instructs* (= Skt. and BHS śikṣayati): °yiṣye kathaṃ hy enaṃ LV 126.20 (vs; all mss.); śikṣitaṃ °yiṣyāmi sarvalokaparāyaṇaṃ 127.2 (but here only ms. A reads so; other mss. with Calc. śikṣay°).

śiṣyā (see s.v. **śiṣyate**) = **śikṣā**: (**1**) *phonetics*: vyākaraṇe nirukte śiṣyāyāṃ (all mss.; Weller 41 line 1 would read śikṣ°) LV 156.19 (prose); (**2**) **śiṣyāpada** = **śikṣāpada**: pañca-°pada-samādattā, *devoted to the five commandments*, said of Māyā, LV 71.14 (prose; all mss.; not noted by Weller).

śiṣyāpayati, = **śikṣāpayati** (see s.v. **śiṣyate,** to which this may be caus.), *teaches* (with acc. of thing taught): (āsām . . .)-lipīnāṃ katamāṃ tvaṃ °yiṣyasi LV 126.12 (prose; all mss.; Weller 41 line 1 assumes śikṣ°).

śista-(vikiram, adv.), Prāt 534.1; Finot's note says 'Corr. śiṣṭa-', but surely text intends a Sktized form of Pali sittha = Skt. siktha, *lump of rice*; see **vikira,** and s.v. **pṛthakkārakam.**

śīta, nt. (= Pali sīta), *sail*: (śīghram) āropyantāṃ (mss. °pyatāṃ) śītāni Jm 94.8; pravitata-pāṇḍura-śīta-cārupakṣā (. . . sā naur) 10 (vs).

śītaka, adj. (AV °ikā, f.; = Pali sītaka; Skt. śīta), *cold*: °ko vāto upavāyati Mv i.25.1 (prose).

Śītaprabha, n. of a future Pratyekabuddha: Av i.147.14.

śītara = °la, adj., *cool*, implied in **°rī-karoti,** *cools*: (sarvadāhaṃ śamayati) sarvaṃ cāśrayaṃ °roti Gv 501.6.

śītalaka (AMg. sīyalaga; = Skt. śītala), (**1**) adj., *cool*: °ko vāto upavāyati Mv i.24.11 (prose); (**2**) (nt.) *coolness*: muhūrtaṃ °ke gamiṣyasi Mv iii.187.1 (prose).

Śītavatī, n. of a **rakṣā** (q.v.): Dharmas 5 (no v.l.). See **Mahāsitavatī,** which is the form always printed in Sādh; but some of its mss. several times are reported as reading °śīta°.

Śītavana, nt. (= Pali Sīta°), n. of a cemetery at Rājagṛha; in BHS always referred to as (mahā)śmaśāna: °naṃ śmaśānam abhinirharati Divy 264.16; °naṃ mahāśmaśānam 268.8, and ff.; Av ii.134.5 (°naṃ śmaśānaṃ nītvā), 10; 135.1; 182.7; MSV ii.42.20 f.; iii.139.11.

Śītā, n. of a devakumārikā in the West: LV 390.6 (Mv iii.308.9 corrupt, see **Śuklā**).

śīti, aphetic form for aśīti, *eighty*; at beginning of line, and proved correct by meter, tho some mss. write 'śīti (preceding line ends in -o): śīti caturottarā (mss., Senart °uttarā) tava vibhū (mss. add vā) vihārān ahaṃ demi Mv i.112.14 (vs).

śīti-bhāva, -bhūta, see **śītī°**.

śītībhavati (= Pali sīti°, always short i acc. to PTSD; Skt. has this and derivs. only in literal sense, except once in Jain Skt., pw), lit. *cools off*, but fig. *becomes calm* or *extinguished* (religiously): śamanti °vanti astaṃgacchanti Pischel SBBA 1904 p. 815 fol. 165a; °vati Mvy 2541 (follows vimucyate, among pariśuddha-paryāyāḥ). See next two.

śītībhāva, also **śīti°**, m. (= Pali sīti°; see under prec.), *the becoming 'cool' in a religious sense, i. e. calm, extinguished, emancipated*: ajarāmaraśītībhāva (all mss. °tī°) ity ucyate (Buddha) LV 425.13 (prose); but antaparama-śītibhāvopanayanatayā tīrthabhūtā bhavanti Gv 388.1 (prose), *they become like means of salvation because they lead to final supreme 'coolness'* (extinction, nirvāṇa); in LV 392.12 (prose) śītībhāvo is Lefm.'s em., mss. either śītibhāvo or śīto (om. bhāvo; the word is an ep. of dharma); in verses of LV, where meter determines the quantity, nirvāṇamārgam upayāsyati śītibhāvāṃ (! Calc. °vaṃ; v.l. in Lefm. only °vī) 48.15; yada lapsyate hy amṛtu (read with best mss. °ta-) sparśana śītibhāvaṃ 303.10; saṃsthitu sītibhāvaḥ (v.l. śī°) 125.3.

śītībhūta, or **śīti°** (= Pali sīti°; see prec. two), *'cooled', calmed, emancipated*; only noted as ep. of Buddha: śītī° (so read with Index and Mironov) Mvy 56; also LV 405.21 (vs), v.l. śīti°, same vs with śītirbhūto in oldest ms. Ud xxi.4 (read prob. śīti-bh°), and in Pali with sīti-bh° Vin. i.8.24; in this vs meter indifferent as to i or ī; so also in the vs Mv iii.401.14 where Senart śītībhūto, mss. °bhūta, v.l. śīti°.

Śītodaka, n. of a hell: Kv 18.14; doubtless read so for text Sitodaka, Kv 50.3.

śīrṣaka, (**1**) nt., *top* of a column: °kam Mvy 5576 = Tib. bre phul; (**2**) m., *helmet*: °kaḥ (so read with Mironov for text °kāḥ) Mvy 6076 = Tib. rmog, *helmet* (alternatively, ḥtshem bu, = ? should mean something *sewn*, perhaps a knitted head-cover); listed among arms and armor; (**3**) n. of a nāga king: Mvy 3283, but v.l. and Mironov **Cicchaka.**

śīrṣa-kaṭāhaka, see **kaṭāhaka.**

śīrṣan, nt. (= Pali sīsa), *panicle* of rice, *ear* of grain (= **vallarī** 2): śāli-śīrṣāṇi MSV ii.62.5–6.

[**śīrṣavana,** prob., with pw, corruption for śirīṣavana: (śakyate mayā) śīrṣavanasyaikaika- (or °kaikāni) pattrāṇi gaṇayituṃ Kv 20.6; 72.13; 92.4.]

śīrṣas (nt., blend of śīrṣan and śiras), *head*: implied by śīrṣopakarṣikā (see **apakarṣikā**), in kāścic chīrṣo°kayā . . . rudanti sma LV 227.9 (prose), *some wept with lowering of the head.*

Śīlabhadra, n. of a teacher: Mvy 3506.

Śīlavalka, Divy 632.22, or **°valkala,** 24, pl., n. of a brahmanical school (of the Chandogas).

Śīlaviśuddhanetra, n. of a devaputra, one of the 16 guardians of the bodhimaṇḍa: LV 277.15.

śīlavrata, nt.; **°ta-parāmarśa,** m. (= Pali sīlabbata-parāmāsa), (*attachment to*) *practices and observances* (other than those approved by Buddhists), or *attachment to good works* (*alone*, as means of salvation); one of the five **dṛṣṭi** is this °parāmarśa: Dharmas 68, Mvy 1959; paraphrased ahetv-amārga-taddṛṣṭi AbhidhK. LaV-P. v.15, and explained 18 (see also Childers s.v.); in Mv i.292.3 (vs) śīlavrata alone = °ta-parāmarśa: (satkāyadṛṣṭī-vicikitsitaṃ, mss. °tā, ca) śīlavrataṃ (mss. śīlaṃ vrataṃ) cāpi yad asti kiṃcit (*are got rid of*); these three, satkāyadṛṣṭir vicikitsā śīlavrataparāmarśaś ca Laṅk 117.15, constitute the three first **saṃyojanāni**, q.v.; śīla° is explained in Laṅk 119.2 ff. Elsewhere śīlavrata may be used in the ordinary good sense, as in Skt. and Pali.

Śīlākhya, Mmk 625.12, or **Śīlāhva**, 624.9; 625.19, n. of a king.

Śīvālī (Pali Sīvalī, Jāt. i.40.9), n. of one of the two leading female disciples of Maṅgala Buddha: Mv i.248.19 (prose); 252.8 (vs); mss. each time final -o for -ī; it could stand for -ā, which is a variant of the Pali name.

śu, onomat. (cf. Pali su), a sound made in eating: na śu-kārakaṃ piṇḍapātaṃ paribhokṣyāmaḥ Prāt 533.7; corresp. to **śuścu-**, and to Pali surusuru-kārakaṃ Vin. iv.197, last line.

Śuka, (**1**) n. of a brahmanical sage: Divy 632.14; Śuka-paṇḍita, 651.8; (**2**) n. of a (brahman) youth (māṇava, which Lévi seems to take as part of his name), son of **Taudeya**: Karmav 21.15 etc.; in Pali known as Subha; see DPPN and Lévi's note, loc. cit.

Śukamukha, n. of a yakṣa: Māy 90.

śukra-visarga, m., Prāt 479.5, or °**visṛṣṭi**, f. (Pali sukka-visaṭṭhi), Mvy 8369, *emission of semen*, a saṃghāvaśeṣa sin.

Śukrā, see **Śuklā**.

[**Śukrodana**, false em. at Mv iii.177.1, see **Śuklodana**.]

Śukla, pl., n. of a brahmanical school (of the Bahvṛcas): Divy 632.18.

Śuklaka, n. of two nāga kings: Māy 248.1.

śuklapakṣa (m.; = Pali sukkapakkha, Therīg. 358; comm. 244.4 sattānaṃ anavajjakoṭṭhāsa-, so read for text °koṭṭhāsaya-, *the blameless part of creatures*), *the 'white' or virtuous party or group, the righteous*: °kṣeṇāntike nirvāṇasyety ucyate Divy 38.4, preceded by pūrvavad yāvad, indicating abbreviation, cf. line 1 above, but a nom., śuklapakṣo, seems required; Burnouf, Introd. 252 n. 1, cites °pakṣe (which he interprets wrongly); *it is said that the virtuous group is near to nirvāṇa*; contrasting with kṛṣṇapakṣa (= Pali kaṇha-pakkha, headed by Māra), *the 'black' or evil party*: kṛṣṇapakṣa-parivarjana-śuklapakṣa-kuśalopacaya- LV 431.14; °kṣe, *in the alternative case of good (procedure)*, MSV iii.114.8. Cf. next.

śuklapākṣika, adj. (to prec. plus -ika), *belonging to the virtuous party*: °kā māraputrā(ḥ) LV 360.10 (prose), i. e. those favorable to the Bodhisattva.

śuklavidarśanā-bhūmi (ŚsP 1473.11 śuklavipaśyanā°), n. of the first of 7 śrāvaka **bhūmi** (see this, 4): Mvy 1141; ŚsP 1473.11; 1520.20; 1562.21.

Śuklā, (**1**) n. of a daughter of **Rohiṇa**: Av ii.15.12 ff.; (**2**) n. of a goddess or yakṣiṇī (= Pali Sukkā, DN ii.260.22): Mahāsamāj, Waldschmidt, Kl. Skt. Texte 4, 187.1; (**3**) ? n. of a devakumārikā in the western quarter: Mv iii.308.9; Senart Śukrā; mss. corrupt, śukla or śukra; seems to correspond to **Śītā**, q.v.

Śuklodana (Pali Sukko°), n. of a brother of Śuddhodana: Mv i.352.13; 355.19; iii.176.14 (father of Ānanda, Upadhāna, and Devadatta); Mvy 3600. In Mv iii.177.1, acc. to mss., another Śuklodana, also brother of Śuddhodana, is named (just after iii.176.14 above), as the father of Nandana and Nandika (v.l. Nandaka); Senart em. to Śukrodana, referring to Kern, Der Buddhismus 310, who alleges among Śuddhodana's brothers, besides Śuklodana, also 'Śukrodana or Śuklodana'. The source of Kern's statement is not clear to me; it would have to be a northern (Skt. or BHS) text; both forms would be Sukkodana in MIndic. In any case I think that Mv iii.177.1 has carelessly substituted a repetition of Śuklo° for Dhautodana of i.352.13 and 355.20 (or Droṇodana of Mvy 3601), the correct name of the fourth of the brothers, otherwise missing in this passage.

śuṅgībhūta, adj.-ppp. (to Skt. śuṅgā, rarely śuṅga, or a deriv. *śuṅgin, not recorded in this sense, plus bhavati), *become provided with a calyx*, i. e. *budded, in bud*: sarvapuṣpāṇi śuṅgībhūtāni (text su°) na puṣpanti sma LV 76.10; (yathā ... kovidārasya) °tasya veditavyaṃ, bahūnāṃ puṣpaśatasahasrāṇām āyadvāraṃ bhaviṣyatīti Gv 501.17.

śucika, adj. (= AMg. suiga; Skt. śuci), *clean*: saṃkāradhānaṃ śucikaṃ (m.c.?) karoti SP 114.4 (vs).

Śucigātra, n. of a former Buddha: Mv i.137.9.

Śucinetraratisaṃbhava, n. of a gandharva: Mvy 3383.

? **Śucipraroja** (? so all mss., Senart em. °roha, perhaps rightly), n. of a former Buddha: Mv i.141.1.

śuṇṭhika (to Skt. śuṇṭhi, -ī), v.l. śuṇṭhipācaka, *dealer in* or *cooker of dried ginger*: °kāḥ (in list of tradesmen) Mv iii.113.10. See also s.v. **suṇḍika.**

śuṇḍā-peya, see **śauṇḍā°**.

śuṇḍika, su°, or **śuṇṭhika** (= Pali soṇḍi-, in °pañcamāni aṅgāni Miln. 371.17; SN iv.177, last line), *the neck of a tortoise*: śuṇṭhika-(mss.; Senart em. śuṇḍikā-)-pañcamāni (mss. add ca) aṅgāni prasāretvā Mv ii.244.16 = Jm (App.) 241.2 (prose), of a tortoise; in a figure, of something wrinkled and rough, suṇḍika-kiliñja-sadṛśa-jihvām LV 305.12 (prose), *having a tongue* (rough) *as a turtle's neck or a mat*; Tib. ḥbar ḥbur can, which seems to mean *having unevennesses.*

Śuddha (cf. Skt. Śuddhāḥ, a class of gods, Mbh 13.1372; perhaps a Buddhistic term, cf. the adjoining Nirmāṇaratāḥ which recalls BHS **Nirmāṇarati**, q.v.), prob. = next (2) pl.: sg. Śuddha, Mmk 69.6, prob. as representative of the class; in Mmk 71.23 Śuddha and Viśuddha are names of two Śuddhāvāsakāyika gods.

śuddhaka, (**1**) adj. (= Skt. śuddha), *white*: Mvy 8397 °ka-kālakānām, see s.v. **kālaka** (1); (**2**) pl., n. of a class of gods (see **Śuddha**): Māhāsamāj., Waldschmidt, Kl. Skt. Texte 4, 187.7; (**3**) (= Skt. śuddha) *unmixed, simple, unqualified* (as in śuddha-prāyaścittika and -pāpattika, see s.v. **pātayantika**), opp. to qualified in various ways: MSV iii.67.6; 72.1.

Śuddhadanta, n. of a former Buddha: Mv i.141.3.

Śuddhapratibhāsa, m., n. of a samādhi: ŚsP 1419.9 (cited as **Śubha-pra°**, q.v., in Mvy).

Śuddharaśmiprabha, n. of a Buddha in the west: Sukh 97.16.

Śuddhavaṃśa, n. of a cakravartin: Mv i.154.2.

Śuddhasattva, n. of a former Buddha: Mv i.141.11.

Śuddhasāra, m., n. of a samādhi: Mvy 543; ŚsP 1418.6.

Śuddhā, n. of a princess, daughter of **Sujāta** Ikṣvāku: Mv i.348.12.

śuddhādhivāsa, a class of gods, = **śuddhāvāsa**: Buddhacarita i.20; iii.26.

śuddhādhyāśaya-bhūmi, see **śuddhyadhyāśaya°**.

śuddhāntika, adj. with **parivāsa** (= Pali suddhanta-parivāsa), a kind of probation imposed for concealed saṃghāvaśeṣa offenses when the period of concealment was unknown: MSV iii.72.11; 73.7. Acc. to the Pali Vin. comm., it lasted for a time equal to that elapsed since the offender's ordination (see SBE 17.417, note 1).

śuddhābha, n. of a god or class of gods: Mmk 19.9. (Nonce-invention? cf. **puṇyābha**; the two follow ābhāsvaraḥ prabhāsvaraḥ.)

? **śuddhāraṃ** (pithayitvā) Mmk 560.27 (prose), mg.? Possibly read dvāraṃ.

śuddhāvāsa, m. (= Pali su°; see also **śuddhādhivāsa** and **āvāsaśuddha**), (**1**) *pure abode*, said of a heaven, or five heavens, in which dwell the gods so-called: sā (sc. raśmiḥ) sarvā (!) śuddhāvāsān devabhavanāny (apposition) avabhāsya LV 3.14 (prose); °vāso devanikāyo Mv i.35.1; (**2**) much oftener, *having a pure abode*, the class, or rather five classes, of gods who dwell in (1); they constitute the highest of the rūpāvacara gods in the 4th (and highest) dhyānabhūmi; usually with (sometimes sc.) **deva**, q.v., or devaputra; oftener called **śuddhāvāsa-kāyika** Mv i.33.4; 150.10; 197.1; 264.1; 357.3 (they announce the approaching birth of the Bodhisattva); 366.9; ii.150.17; 152.11; 163.16, 17, 19; 195.4; 259.10; 361.1; in Mv i.208.14 sg., as if n. of their chief, °vāso 'pi devaputro, but note in repetition of the same passage ii.11.2 pl. °vāsā pi devā; °sā (sc. devāḥ) Mmk 19.12; -sa-deva- Gv 331.15.

śuddhāvāsakāyika (= Pali su°), adj. with (or rarely sc.) **deva** (q.v.), devaputra, or devatā, = **śuddhāvāsa** (2), *belonging to* (this) *class of gods*; occasionally sg. of an individual, named LV 267.9, or unnamed Mv i.35.9; 45.14; two, Mmk 64.6 (unnamed); generally pl., or in cpd. (to be understood as pl.), very common: LV 4.5; 44.12; 56.3; 187.18; 205.17; 332.21; 357.18; 396.16; 444.11; Mv i.33.4; 35.4, 8; 212.16; ii.257.9; 287.4; Av i.122.9; °kā devatā(ḥ) RP 37.11; 45.20.

Śuddhipanthaka, n. of a disciple of Buddha: Sukh 92.7. (Error for **Cūḍa-p**°?)

Śuddhodana (= Pali Su°), n. of a Śākyan 'king', Buddha's father: Mv i.352.13 ff., 355.19 ff. (his lineage and family); ii.2.18 ff.; etc.; LV 26.6 ff.; 39.21 ff.; 55.14 ff.; 76.9 ff.; 117.19 ff.; 184.17; 185.19 ff.; 198.2 ff.; 211.3; 228.5; 237.18; Mvy 3599; Divy 390.28 ff.; Av ii.111.8 ff.; Suv 200.1; 239.3; Gv 439.1 ff.

śuddhyadhyāśaya-bhūmi, the 2d of six bodhisattva-**bhūmi**: Bbh 84.24; or śuddhādhyā°, as 3d of seven b° bh°, 367.4.

śunakha, see **su**°.

śubha (**1**) m. pl. (= Pali subha, MN iii.102.30), a class of rūpāvacara gods of the 3d dhyānabhūmi, acc. to Mv only; as adj. with **deva**, q.v.: Mv ii.314.7; 319.5; 348.19; 360.17; (**2**) m. sg., n. of a king, former birth of the Buddha: RP 23.8; (**3**) adj. (in this sense unrecorded), *white* (opp. to kṛṣṇa, *black*), only in LV 197.1 (vs) kṛṣṇā śubhā (Tib. dkar, *white*) caturi prāṇaka pāda lehī (so read with v.l. for Lefm. lekhī), *four animals, black and white, licked his feet.* There can be no doubt of the mg.

śubhakṛtsna, m. pl. (= Pali subha-kiṇṇa or °kiṇha), one (usually the 3d) of the classes of rūpāvacara gods in the 3d dhyānabhūmi, with or sc. **deva**, q.v.: LV 150.8; 396.16; Mv ii.314.8; 319.5 (here mss. corruptly seem to point to °kasina, cf. Pali kasiṇa, for °kṛtsna); 349.1; 360.18; Mvy 2292 (here as an example of beings in the fourth **sattvāvāsa**, q.v.); 3096; Dharmas 128; Divy 68.15; 138.22; 327.5, 20; 367.13; Gv 249.13; Av i.5.3, etc.

Śubhagarbha, n. of a Bodhisattva: Mvy 667.

Śubhaṃkara, n. of an upāsaka: Sādh 42.9.

Śubhadatta (so mss.), n. of a former Buddha: Mv i.138.7 (Senart em. °danta; but this name occurs in KSS).

Śubhanātha, n. of a former Buddha: Mv i.138.6.

Śubhapāraṃgama, nt., n. of a city: Gv 205.15 ff.

Śubhapuṣpitaśuddhi, n. of a samādhi: Mvy 584; ŚsP 1422.6.

Śubhapratibhāsa, m., n. of a samādhi: Mvy 556 (= **Śuddha-pra**°, q.v.).

Śubhaprabha, n. of a kalpa: Gv 444.1.

Śubhamālā, n. of a 'gandharva maid': Kv 4.21.

Śubhamekhalā, n. of a goddess: Sādh 502.7.

Śubharatna, n. of a Bodhisattva: Gv 442.6.

śubha-varṇanīya, see **varṇanīya.**

Śubhavimalagarbha, n. of a Bodhisattva: Mvy 668.

Śubhavyūha, n. of an ancient king: SP 457.7 f.; previous incarnation of **Padmaśrī** (1) 470.3.

Śubhasu, n. of a mleccha king: °sus, n. sg., Mmk 621.24.

Śubhā, n. of a goddess: Sādh 502.10.

Śubhāṅga, n. of a Tuṣitakāyika god: LV 124.11.

Śubhesthitā (so 1 ms., v.l. Sudra°; Senart em. °ṣṭhitā), n. of a devakumārikā in the southern quarter: Mv iii.307.9; corresponds to **Suutthitā** of LV.

śumbhaka, see **su**°.

śuluka, m. (so Mironov; var. in both edd. su°), Mvy 5713 = Tib. tshva, *salt* (but see s.v. **cukra**).

śulkayati (Skt. Dhātup.; denom. to śulka), *taxes, imposes a tax-duty* (upon); in the first passage perhaps *pays a tax-duty*: (yaḥ kascit paṇyam) aśulkayitvā gamiṣyati Divy 276.2, but this may mean *whoever goes without* (the tax-collectors') *having imposed the tax*; so at least the other passages suggest: śulkaśālikena sārthaḥ śulkitaḥ 276.18; (nūnaṃ sārtho na nipunaṃ) śulkito, bhūyaḥ śulkayāma iti 21; (tair asau sārthaḥ punaḥ pratinivartya) śulkitaḥ, nāsti kiṃcid (so punctuate) aśulkitam 22, *was assessed, and there was nothing* (that had) *not* (been) *taxed.* Alternatively, the mg. in all passages may be *figures the taxable value, assesses*; such a term could be applied to either the wares or their owners.

(**śulkaśālā**, occurs in Kauṭ. Arth. Sham.[1] 109.19, *customs-house*: Divy 275.27; 276.17.)

śulkaśālika, m. (to prec. plus -ika; Skt. Gr. id.), *official in a customs house*: Divy 275.27; 276.18.

śulba or **śulva**, nt. or m. (Skt. Lex. id., acc. to BR back-formation from śulbāri, *sulphur*, but the latter is not explained; = M. suvva, said to be nt.), *copper*: tāmralohaṃ ca śulvaṃ (Senart's plausible em. for suptaṃ of mss.) ca Mv i.12.7 (vs); see also **śaulbika.**

śuve, also **suve**, adv. (§ 3.14; = Pali suve, sve, Skt., also BHS, **śvas**), *tomorrow*: Mv i.271.11; ii.451.6, 12; 453.12 and 13 (both suve); 462.18; iii.10.10 (v.l. suve); 15.10; 37.7; 290.6; 457.18; mostly in prose. See foll. items.

(**śuvetanā**,) **suvetanā** (mss. suce°), adv., shortened form (m.c.?) for **śuvetanāya**, °**ye**, *for the morrow*: adhivāsa . . . (mss. corrupt) bhagavāṃ °nā sārdhaṃ (read sārdha, m.c.) bhikṣusaṃghena Mv i.307.2 (vs).

śuvetanāni, suve°, adv. (mss. °ce° for °ve°; blend of **śuvetanā** or °**nāya** with **śuvedāni**, or directly with (**i**)**dāni**), *for the morrow*: suvetanāni ca niveśanaṃ bhaktena nimantresi (Senart em. °ti) Mv i.323.20, similarly 324.5 (here v.l. śu°).

śuvetanāya, °**nāye**, adv. (mss. always °ce° for °ve°, as in prec. items, qq.v.; cf. Pali svātanāya, adv., and Skt. śvastana, adj., here blended with **śuve**), *for the morrow*: bhagavāṃ . . . °nāya bhaktena upanimantrito Mv i.263.3; modulations of this phrase, °nāye i.263.7; iii.257.2; °nāya i.271.14.

śuvedāni, adv. (blend of **śuve**, or **śuvetanā**[**ya**, -**ye**], with [**i**]**dāni**), *for the morrow*; used like prec. items, qq.v.: °ni (one ms., only, śuce°) ca bhaktena nimantreti Mv i.307.7, similarly 11, where śuvedāni without v.l.

śuśukā (= Pali susukā), *alligator*: MSV i.v.15. Cf. next? Both loanwords of unknown, but possibly common, origin.

śuśumāra, m. (= Pali suṃsumāra, AMg. susumāra; Skt. śiśu-māra, surely by popular etymology; cf. prec.?), *crocodile*: Mv ii.246.8 ff. (repeatedly; one ms. always śiśu°); Divy 105.27 (so mss.); 231.5 (no v.l.); MSV i.v.15.

Śuśumāragiri, rarely °**māla**°, only once (172.9) Śiśu° (= Pali Suṃsu°), n. of a city, capital of the **Bhargas**: Divy 167.2; 168.6; 172.9 (Śiśu°); 182.23 (here Śuśumāla); 185.13 f., etc.

Śuśumāragirīya, Divy 178.23, usually °**yaka**, and chiefly pl., *inhabitant(s)* of the prec.: Divy 174.6; 178.25; 182.26 ff.; 184.2 ff.; 186.14, etc.

śuścu-, onomat., in śuścu-kārakaṃ, *making* this *sound* (in eating): Mvy 8578; corresp. to **śu-**(kārakaṃ), q.v. Chin. onomat., sound of sucking while eating soup.

? **śuśrūyati**, desid. of śru, see § 40.1.

śuśrūṣaṇā (= AMg. sussūsaṇā; blend of Skt. °ṣā and °ṣaṇa, nt.), *obedience*: guru-śu° RP 14.14 (prose), one of the four ājāneya-gati of a Bodhisattva, see s.v. **ājanya.**

śuṣkati (= Pali sukkhati; denom. to Skt. śuṣka),

gets dry: yāvad bodhivṛkṣaḥ śuṣkitum ārabdhaḥ Divy 397.27 (prose).

śuṣka-vartikā, perh. *'dry wick'*, a form of torture: °kāṃ vā vartyamānasya Śikṣ 182.4, *when he is being turned* (whirled) *in the 'dry wick'* (possibly *treated as a wick*, dipped in burning oil?); acc. to note in Transl., Tib. skam (*dry*?) rim bya ba lta dril tam, which is not clear to me.

śūka, nt., (**1**) in manaḥ-śūka (possibly for śoka, *grief*? so Skt. Lex.; or simply *mind-sting*), either *grief*, or *pangs of conscience*: (katham ahaṃ khedaṃ na smariṣyāmi ... yena mayā evaṃvidhaṃ) pāpakaṃ karma kṛtam? tataḥ sa tayābhihitaḥ: na te °kam asminn arthe utpādayitavyaṃ Divy 257.12; (**2**) fig. (an enemy's) *offensive power*: śatruś ca te 'grabala durbalabhagnaśūko Mv i.156.16 (vs), *your mighty enemy's 'sting' is powerless and broken.*

śūnyaka, adj. (Skt. Gr. id., AMg. sunnaya; = Skt. śūnya; pejorative force may be suspected, at least in some cases), *empty, vain*: AsP 346.9, see s.v. **asāraka**; °ka dharma nirātmaka sarve Samādh 19.30 (vs); saṃskāra nirīha °kāḥ LV 176.3 (vs); (kṣetrakoṭinayutāni bahūni) °kāni puruṣapravarehi Mv i.122.3 (vs), *empty* (in lit. sense) *of Buddhas*, containing none.

śūnyakalpa, m. (= Pali suññakappa acc. to Childers), *an 'empty' kalpa*, in which no Buddha appears: Dharmas 87.

śūnyatā (Pali suññatā; in Pali an adj. suññata seems to have developed, see s.v. **apraṇihita**, but not in BHS as far as I know), *emptiness, void, vacuité* (S. Lévi, La Vallée-Poussin): often associated with **ānimitta** (an°), and **apraṇihita**, q.v. for SP 101.1; 136.13; 137.2; LV 422.20; paribhāvitā śūnyata dīrgharātram SP 117.7 (vs), *we have meditated long on emptiness*; °tā-bhāvanatayā RP 10.7, *by the fact of realization of the emptiness* (of things); °tāsu satataṃ gatiṃgata 10.16 (vs); there are different lists of kinds of ś°; eighteen in Mvy 933–951, found frequently in the same order in ŚsP, notably in 1407.4 ff. where each is defined and explained at great length, and nearly the same list, but with three additions and one subtraction, making 20 in all, Dharmas 41; this list is: adhyātma-ś°, bahirdhā-, adhyātmabahirdhā-, śūnyatā-ś°, mahā-, paramārtha-, saṃskṛta-, asaṃskṛta-, atyanta-, anavarāgra-, anavakāra-, prakṛti-, sarvadharma-, svalakṣaṇa- (Dharmas omits sva), anupalambha- (not in Dharmas, which adds here alakṣaṇa-, bhāva-), abhāva-, svabhāva-, abhāvasvabhāva- (Dharmas adds parabhāva-); seven kinds listed and defined Laṅk 74.5 ff., lakṣaṇa-ś°, bhāvasvabhāva-, apracarita-, pracarita-, sarvadharmanirabhilāpya-, paramārthāryajñānamahā-, and itaretara-; in Sūtrāl xiv.34 only three kinds, abhāva-ś°, tathābhāvasya ś°, prakṛtyā (prakṛti-)ś° (defined in comm.).

śūnyāgāra (m. or nt.; = Pali suññāg°), *solitary abode, solitude*: in phrase bṛṃhayitā (see °**yitar**) °rāṇām Mvy 2437 (Tib. translates with wooden literalness).

Śūrakūṭa, n. of a former Buddha: Sukh 5.17.

śūraṃgama, (**1**) n. of a samādhi: LV 442.8; Laṅk 374.15; Mvy 812; the first of a list of four, Dharmas 136; the first of much longer lists, ŚsP 483.11; 825.18; 1267.10; 1412.8; 1415.2; Mvy 506 (cited from Prajñāpāramitā); (**2**) n. of a Bodhisattva: Mvy 701.

Śūraṃgamasamādhinirdeśa, n. of a work: Mvy 1356; called **Śūraṃgamasūtra** Śikṣ 8.19; **Śūraṃgamasamādhisūtra** Śikṣ 91.8; a fragment edited under this title by Thomas ap. Hoernle MR 126 f. (in the text itself, 127.5, called **Śūraṃgamamahāsūtra**).

śūrataraka, adj. (compv. of śūra plus -ka), *more heroic*: tasya ... bahutarakāś ca °rakāś ca dṛḍhapraharaṇatarakāś ca ... anye udārakatarakāḥ pratyarthikāḥ ... AsP 373.3.

Śūradatta, n. of a Buddha: Śikṣ 169.10.

Śūradhvaja, n. of a Buddha: Gv 285.12.

Śūrabala, n. of a devaputra, one of the 16 guardians of the bodhimaṇḍa: LV 277.13.

Śūrpa-grāmaka, m., n. of a Vṛji village: MPS 21.6.

Śūla, n. of a rākṣasa king: Mmk 18.2.

śṛgāra (cf. Hindi siyār) = Skt. śṛgāla, *jackal*: so all Nep. mss. for text °la with Kashgar rec. SP 83.10 and 86.12 (vss).

śṛṅkhalika, nt. (var. śṛṅga°, so Mironov with no v.l.; Skt. śṛṅkhala, °lā; Pali saṅkhalikā, and stem in comp. °la-; see also s.vv. **saṅkala**, °**lā**, °**likā**), *chain*: Mvy 9032 = Tib. lcags thag.

sṛṅgāpuṭa, nt.? (ep. of salt): asti āyuṣman mama °ṭaṃ lavaṇaṃ yāvajjīvam adhiṣṭhitam MSV i.xiii.9. (Or n. of a container for the salt?)

śekhayati, śekheti, also **se**° (AMg. sehai; denom. from Pali se(k)kha, AMg. seha, see **śaikṣa**), *trains, instructs*: devīṃ (mss. devī) ... gītavādyehi ca śekheti Mv iii.162.10; pass. sekhīyati (v.l. śe°; lekhāyaṃ pi, etc.) Mv ii.423.15; śekhīyanti 434.10; sekhiyanti iii.184.6; śekhita, ppp., iii.390.4; see also **śeṣita**.

śeyyā (= Pali seyyā, Skt. śayyā), *bed*: svakāṃ śeyyāṃ omūtremi (= Skt. avamūtrayāmi) Mv ii.428.2; śeyyam (so, acc.) api kalpayati iii.411.14 (prose); śeyyāsana, *bed and seat* (Pali se°) Mv iii.264.9; Ud xiii.15 (text śaiyy°). See also **seyyā(ka)**.

Śela (read Śaila? q.v.; = Pali Selā), n. of an ascetic (tāpasa; in Pali a brahman): Karmav 155.16 (the same as **Śaila**).

? **śelālaka**, m., so mss. Mv iii.443.3, in a list of artisans and tradesmen (Senart em. peśalaka, certainly wrongly); in corresp. list iii.113.16 pelalaka, kept by Senart (follows **kālapattrika**, q.v.); possibly *mason*, if identifiable with AMg. sellāra, id. (said to be from Skt. śilākāra). The next but one preceding is, both times, vardhaki-rūpakārakā(ḥ); *carpenters and sculptors (carvers)*.

śeṣapati, a certain royal officer: Mvy 3739 = Tib. gñer ba (misprinted gñer ba), *administrator*.

śeṣita, prob. read śekhita, ppp. to **śekhayati**, *instructed*: na mayā kumāro kahiṃci śilpe śeṣito atipremnena Mv ii.73.10, *I have not instructed the prince in any art from too great affection*; also id. 15.

śaikṣa, (**1**) m. (= Pali sek(k)ha; see Childers s.v.; cf. **śaiṣya** and **aśaikṣa**), *one who is undergoing training; a disciple* (in one of the first seven stages of religious discipline; the 8th is the aśaikṣa or arhant; list Dharmas 102); in mss. sometimes (erroneously?) written **śaiṣya** (by confusion with śiṣya), q.v.: Mvy 1733; 5238 (read with Mironov śaikṣābhinikūjitam); Ānanda was a śaikṣa, SP 2.8; śaikṣa-bhūmi, *stage of a ś°*, SP 70.13; Mv i.106.15 (mss. śaikṣā°); others Mv i.142.5; 158.7; 267.20; 292.7; iii.53.8; 200.15; Divy 399.24; dvandva cpd. śaikṣāśaikṣa, *śaikṣas and aśaikṣas*, SP 2.9; 71.1; 215.9; in LV 327.4 (vs) read (m.c.) śaikṣa-aśaikṣa- (as cpd.; mss. śaikṣaśaikṣa- or śaiṣyāśaiṣya-; Lefm. em. śaikṣya-aśaikṣya-!); LV 427.11; Mv i.120.1; Divy 261.5 (most mss. śaikṣa-ś°); 337.26; Av i.335.1; śaikṣa-aśaikṣa-(as cpd., m.c.) Bhad 9; śaikṣāśaikṣa-tā *state of ś. and aś.* Dbh 70.1; fem. śaikṣāśaikṣībhir bhikṣuṇībhiḥ Av i.269.7; separate words, śaikṣā aśaikṣa LV 46.5 (vs); (**2**) adj. (= Pali sekhiya), with dharma, *(rule) of good behavior*, orig. doubtless for learners, but applied to all monks; they are minor rules of etiquette, 75 in number in Pali, 113 in Prāt: °kṣadharmāḥ Mvy 8362; °kṣā dharmāḥ Prāt 527.6. Cf. also **naivaśaikṣanāśaikṣa**.

śaikṣaka, adj. (to prec., 1, plus -ka), *of śaikṣas*: Śikṣ 55.10 (prose) °kaṃ karma, *a duty pertaining to a ś°*.

śaithilika, adj. (from Skt. śithila; not recorded elsewhere), *lax, loose*: esp. with **bāhulika**, q.v. for LV 407.19; Mv ii.241.3; iii.329.3; and Śikṣ 64.4. Also Bbh 47.2 (na ca °ko bhavec chikṣāpadeṣu); 156.15 (śikṣāsu).

śaiyyā, see **śeyyā**.

Śairīṣaka (v.l. Śe°; = Pali Serīsaka), n. of a celestial palace (vimāna): Divy 399.18.

Śaila (see also **Śela, Saila,** and **Pūrva-śaila, Apara-ś°**), n. of a brahmanical ascetic (ṛṣi), **Kaineya**'s sister's son: MSV i.264.3 ff.

Śailagāthā, pl., n. of a (part of a) Buddhist work, doubtless = Pali Selasutta (Sn pp. 102–112, incl. vss 548–573): Divy 20.23; 35.1.

Śailabāhu, n. of a nāga king: Mvy 3302; Māy 247.7.

Śailarājaketu, n. of a former Buddha: Mv i.139.8.

Śailaśikharābhyudgatateja, n. of a Tathāgata: Gv 311.18 (prose).

Śailā (= Pali Selā), n. of an important nun, follower of Śākyamuni: Divy 552.18 ff.; 573.8 ff.

śailīka, adj. (cf. Whitney 1186c), (made) *of stone*: °kaṃ mṛnmayaṃ lohaṃ ... (of a monk's bowl) Laṅk 308.1 (vs, but metr. indifferent).

Śailendrarāja, n. of a Bodhisattva: Gv 4.5.

Śailendrarājasaṃghaṭṭanaghoṣa, n. of a Bodhisattva: Gv 3.22.

Śailendraśrīgarbharāja, n. of a Tathāgata: Gv 309.12.

śaileya, nt., a kind of medicinal plant or substance: pattra-°yaṃ (in a list) Suv 105.1 (vs); the word seems to be a dvandva; Tib. rdo dreg (acc. to Das, *pitch*; Skt. śaileya, *bitumen*) lo ma (*leaf*; but see Nobel p. 267 lines 1–2, where Chin. seems to make pattra a plant); in Skt. Lex. śaileya is said to mean *Anethum graveolens.*

śailodaka, nt., a kind of medicament: Mvy 5784 = Tib. (g)coṅ zhiḥi chu, acc. to Das *juice of the soma plant.*

Śaivala, (**1**) n. of a nāga king: Māy 247.30; (**2**) n. of a Buddhist elder: MSV i.191.1 ff.

śaiṣya, m. (= **śaikṣa,** q.v.; some mss. present this in other passages), *disciple in training*: LV 250.18 (prose, all mss.) śaiṣyeṇa vā aśaiṣyeṇa vā. Note **śiṣyate** and the foll. items; possibly, like them, this is derived from Skt. śiṣya plus -a.

śokāgāra (m. or nt.), *grief-house, hall of lamentation* (rendered *boudoir* [orig. *sulking room*, but its present-day mg. is not appropriate] by Feer on Av and by Divy Index, followed by pw 7.378): °raṃ praviśya kare kapolaṃ dattvā (once kṛtvā) cintāparo vyavasthitaḥ Av i.55.4; 375.11; ii.37.3; 53.11; 97.4; °raṃ praviśyāvasthitaḥ Divy 287.13, cf. 288.2–3 kasmāt tvaṃ ... kare kapolaṃ dattvā cintāparas tiṣṭhasi; for the cause of his grief see 287.8 ff.; MSV i.64.17.

śocita, nt. (not in Skt. as noun; Pali socita may be so interpreted, kiṃ socitena Therīg. 462), *grief*: iha ... śocita-paridevitāna paryantaṃ LV 372.21 (vs).

Śoṇa (semi-MIndic for Pali Soṇa, BHS **Śroṇa**), n. of a disciple of Śākyamuni: Karmav 59.8; merely referred to with Rāṣṭrapāla as examples of disciples who were ordained only with their parents' consent. Prob. = **Śroṇa Koṭīkarṇa.**

śoṇīta, m.c. for Skt. śoṇita, *blood*: LV 208.14 (vs); also AMg. soṇīya, Ācār. (Schubring) 39.10 (Smith, see § 1.38 fn. 15, p. 12).

Śoṇottara (prob. semi-MIndic for Śroṇ°, cf. **Śoṇa**; the name Soṇuttara corresponds in Pali, but there is no record of this personage there), n. of a Buddhist disciple who was a leper, because of a sin in a previous birth: Karmav 75.18.

śodhaka, adj. or n. ag. (in Skt., rare, *cleaning, purifying*; Pali so°), *purifying* (religiously), *correcting* (creatures); only in vss for **viśodhaka,** q.v.: sattvāḥ su-vineyāḥ su-°kāḥ SP 301.6; 302.5 (vss).

śodhayati (in Skt., and Pali sodheti, in the sense of *pays* a debt or tax), *clears up* or *away, attends to, accomplishes,* specifically *carries out* a sentence upon a criminal: (devasya badhyaghātakāḥ puruṣāḥ) sthāpayitavyā ye devasya badhyakaraṇīyaṃ °yiṣyanti Divy 374.11.

Śobha, n. of the king of **Śobhāvatī,** q.v.: Av ii.29.10; 100.12. In Pali also Sobha was king of Sobhavatī, but in the time of Koṇāgamana (**Kanakamuni**), not **Krakucchanda.**

(**śobhate,** *looks well on, is suitable to,* with gen. of person; subject, garments: etāni vastrāṇi tava śobhante, imāni mama LV 226.6, *those* (fine) *garments go well with you, these* (old, faded ones) *with me.* Hardly non-Skt.)

śobhanaka, adj. (Skt. °na plus -ka; in the first prob. endearing dim.), *beautiful*: (su-vasantake ...) su-śobhanake LV 321.21 (vs), see § 22.34; na raktacittasya hi mānuṣasya prajñāyate °kaṃ śarīram Śikṣ 79.4 (-ka m.c.?).

Śobhanasāgara, n. of a Bodhisattva: Gv 443.3.

śobhanā (otherwise °na, nt.), *beauty*: dṛṣṭā sa (m.c. for sā) viyūha-śobhanā (one word; Lefm. so°, but most mss. śo°) bodhimaṇḍasmi marubhi yā kṛtā LV 364.20 (vs); there are too many f. forms to question; perh. blend of śobhana with śobhā.

Śobhāvatī, n. of a city, residence of the former Buddha **Krakucchanda**: Av i.286.1; ii.29.9; 100.11; ruled by King **Śobha,** q.v.

śobhika (= Skt. śaubhika, on which see Lüders, SBAW 1916.698 ff.; Winternitz, ZDMG 74.118 ff.; and, most recently and conclusively, Meyer Kauṭ. Arth. p. 850; Pali sobhiya doubtless same mg., Jāt. vi.277.7, vs, māyākārā ca sobhiyā; comm. is wrong), *shadow-playman*; in lists of entertainers, Mv iii.113.3; 141.18; 255.12 (mss. here śobhita); 442.9; Śikṣ 330.16; MSV iv.242.16, 19 (text śobhita; is this hyper-Skt. for sobhiya? in 16 ūru- can hardly be correct).

Śobhita, (**1**) n. of a rich Śākyan youth: Av ii.98.13 ff.; (**2**) (= Pali Sobhita 8 in DPPN) n. of a Buddhist elder: MSV i.178.9.

? **-śollaka,** obscure, prob. corrupt: ekaliṅgaṃ gatvā liṅgopari dakṣiṇāyāṃ mūrtiṃ pādaṃ sthāpya vāla-śollakena bandhayet, muṣṭiṃ baddhvā tāvaj japed yāvad rāvo niścarati marāmīti, tṛtīye rāve muṣṭiḥ siddhā bhavati Mmk 704.14 ff. I do not understand the passage. AMg. has a word sollaga = Skt. śūlya(-ka), *meat roasted on a spit*, but I do not see how it could be applied here.

? **śaucaka,** nt. or m., *message* or *news of oneself*; so context suggests in: kisya dāni so mama tāto na kiṃcit śaucakaṃ preṣayati Mv iii.258.4; Senart em. śobhanaṃ, but this seems just as incomprehensible (understood as *good news*?).

Śauṭīraka, n. of a locality: Māy 26.

śauṇḍā-peya, also **śuṇḍā°,** Bhvr., lit. *having liquor as beverage, drinker of liquor*: (ye, to be supplied somewhere in what precedes) tena samayena Dīpavatīye rājadhānīye manuṣyā abhūṣi śauṇḍāpeyā (Senart em. śuṇḍā°), te tena tālapattranirghoṣeṇa ... paricāretsu (mss.) Mv i.194.16; cf. Pali DN ii.172.3–5 ye ... rājadhāniyā dhuttā ahesuṃ soṇḍa-pipāsā (comm. ii.617.11 surā soṇḍā, te yeva ... pātukāmatāvasena pipāsā), te tāsaṃ tālapantīnaṃ ... saddena paricāresuṃ. The same cliché occurs, more corruptly, Mv iii.227.3; 232.1; in both the word manuṣyā has somehow been transposed to between śauṇḍā (232.1 śuṇḍā) and peyā, while the verb abhūṣi is omitted; there can be no doubt, however, that the original text was substantially as above in all occurrences (except for the name of the city).

Śauṇḍinī, n. of a yoginī: Sādh 427.7.

Śauṇḍinya, pl., n. of a brahmanical gotra: Divy 635.17.

śaulbika, m. (Skt. Lex. id., from **śulba** or **śulva**) *coppersmith*: Mvy 3790 = Tib. zaṅs mkhan.

ścyota (m.; n. act. to ścyut-, Skt. Lex.), (lit. *dripping,*) fig. *hanging down*: suvarṇasūtrajāla-ścyote ... bhadrāsane Gv 123.21.

śmaśānika = **śmā°,** q.v.: AsP 387.7; Laṅk 248.8; 254.10 (all prose).

śmāśānika, m. (also **śma°,** q.v.; = Pali sosānika),

one who frequents cemeteries, one of the 12 **dhūtaguṇa**, q.v.: Mvy 1137: Dharmas 63; Śikṣ 135.1.

Śyāma, (1) also **Śyāmaka**, sometimes written with S for Ś, and m.c. a for ā; honorific -ś(i)rī sometimes added to the name(= Pali Sāma), n. of a brahman lad, former incarnation of Śākyamuni (story in full Mv ii.209–219 in prose, then in verse to 231.6: Śyāma Mv ii.213.1, 3, 11, 15; 220.11; 226.4 (read at end with mss. Śyāmasya; before it ca or va), 12; 228.4 (Syāma); 231.1; Karmav 55.17; Syamu (n. sg.) LV 166.3 (vs, a m.c.); Śyāmaśiri Mv ii.214.8, 16; 217.5, 6, 7; Śyāmaka Mv ii.210.12, 13; RP 22.1; Śyāmaka-śiri, often with v.l. °ka-ṛṣi, Mv ii.215.6, 7, 13, 15, 18; 216.2, 17, 20; 217.10; 218.1 etc.; (**2**) Syamu (acc. sg., a m.c.) ṛṣi LV 166.19 (vs), n. of an ascetic who demanded of the Bodhisattva in a former birth that he count the leaves on a tree, which he did.

Śyāma-jātaka (= Pali Sāma-j°), Karmav 55.17; 56.12; or **Śyāmaka-j°**, colophon, Mv ii.219.16; 231.6; the story of the prec. (1).

śyāma-śavala (Senart's em., mss. **śāma-**, semi-MIndic, or soma-, intending sāma-, MIndic), pl., *dogs*: (so pi agninā dagdho mahānarake) upapanno °lehi ahorātrāṇi khādyati Mv iii.361.15, *born in hell, is eaten by dogs* (? see below) *day and night*. This old Vedic dvandva cpd., there used of the dogs of Yama, is not otherwise clearly used in the mg. *dog*. The comm. to Hāla (Weber) vss 185 and 211 knows a vrata called śyāma-(also śāma, sāma-)-śavala (also -sa°), which has something to do with fire and water; whether it is to be equated with kukkura-vrata implied by BHS °**vratika**, q.v., seems doubtful; Weber assumes that it refers to the two dogs of Yama, but admits inability to explain the term. In Pali sāma and sabala are used as adj. with soṇa, *dog* (so correctly comm.) Jāt. vi.106.21, and as names of two dogs in the Lokantara hell Jāt. vi.247.16; barely possibly, the Mv may mean the word as a dvandva, two nn. pr.

Śyāmā (= Pali Sāmā), n. of a courtesan of Benares: Mv ii.168.11 ff.; colophon, śyāmāye jātakaṃ ii.177.3 (in Pali, Kaṇavera-jāt°, No. 318).

Śyāmāka, n. of a son of the minister Hiru(ka): Divy 575.25 ff.

Śyāmāka-jātaka, n. of a work: Karmav 50.6. No details about it furnished here; did it concern the prec.? App. not the Śyāma story, since there is reference to a praṇidhāna in it, which as Lévi notes does not occur in any known version of Śyāma.

Śyāmādevī, n. of a yoginī: Sādh 427.6.

Śyāmāvatī, (1) (= Pali Sāmā°), n. of a consort of King Udayana: Divy 529.15 ff.; (**2**) n. of a daughter of the minister **Bhiru(ka)**: Divy 575.25 ff.

Śyāmāvartā, n. of a yakṣiṇī (yakṣī, text): Mmk 573.15 (vs; printed °varta).

śyāmikā (Skt. *blackness, impurity*), *rust*: Mvy 7015 = Tib. gyaḥ; so Chin.

śraddadha, adj., see **duḥśraddadha.**

śraddahanā (semi-MIndic, = Pali saddahanā), *belief, believing, the having faith*: acc. to Kern, SP Preface p. ix, in Kashgar rec. of SP for Nep. śraddadhānatā.

śraddha, adj. (= **śrāddha**, q.v., and Pali saddha; Vedic śraddha, not Class. Skt.), *believing*: SP 36.10, mss. śraddhā or śraddhāḥ, KN em. śrāddhāḥ; WT śraddhā-prasannāḥ as cpd.; Av i.83.8 (ms., ed. em. śrā°).

śraddhayate (denom. to Skt. śraddhā; once pres. pple. śraddhayant in Skt., BR), *believes, trusts*: °yamānu jinān jinadharmān °yate cari buddhasutānām, bodhi anuttara °yamāno ... Śikṣ 2.16–17 (vss); ppp. °yita, yo yuṣmākaṃ °yitaḥ pratyayitaś ca Divy 437.1 (prose). Cf. Pali saddhāyita, *believed* (of speech), Pv. ii.8.5 °yitaṃ (comm. 109.10 saddhāyitabbaṃ).

Śraddhā, n. of a devakumārikā in the northern quarter, LV 391.4 = Mv iii.309.9; one of four daughters of Indra, Mv ii.57.18 ff., see **Āśā.**

śraddhā-deya, nt. (= Pali saddhādeyya, cf. DN comm. i.81.4, on DN i.6.10), *gift of faith, religious gift* (given by laymen in the right spirit to monks): °yaṃ (here food) ca parīttaṃ bhaviṣyati Śikṣ 129.11; Bhagavatā °ya-paribhoge parikīrtite 137.17, *when the Lord has described the* (conditions proper for) *consumption of religious gifts*, also 19, 138.2, 5, 6; °yaṃ vinipātayati (so Pali, Vin. i.298.2), *spoils, wastes* (by not properly using) *such a gift*; one of the four kinds of (bodhisattva-)-**khaḍuṅka** is he who °yaṃ vinipātayati cyutapratijñaś ca °yaṃ paribhuṅkte KP 9.4 f.; vayaṃ °yaṃ vinipātayitvā (by letting gift-food spoil rather than give it to visiting monks) iha pratyekanarakeṣūpapannāḥ Divy 336.27; (mā ...) °yaṃ vinipātayiṣyata (so read; mss. śraddadheyaṃ) 337.3; °yaṃ vinipātya 571.6; 572.18.

Śraddhābalādhāna, nt., n. of a work: Mvy 1397; °**dhānāvatāramudrā-sūtra**, assumed to be the same, Śikṣ 86.1; 87.4; 153.16; 311.7.

Śramaṇa, n. of a nāga: Mvy 3329; cf. **Śrāmaṇeraka** (2). (On śramaṇa for **śravaṇa** see the latter.)

śramaṇaka, clearly with pejorative force (so also Pali sam°), *wretched, contemptible*, or *objectionable* (Buddhist) *monk*: (sa ruṣito, yāvad brāhmaṇānāṃ na dīyate ...) tāvat tvayā tasmai muṇḍakāya śramaṇakāyāgrapiṇḍakaṃ dattam Divy 13.15; (amaṅgalo 'yaṃ muṇḍakaḥ) °ṇako mayā dṛṣṭa iti 39.27; kim anena °ṇakena mama mṛtipravṛttiḥ śrutā, yena me bhavanam āgacchatīti 185.17; yasyāhaṃ priyaḥ, so 'sya muṇḍakasya °ṇakasyopary ekaikāṃ pāṃśumuṣṭiṃ kṣipatv iti 574.2; muṇḍakāḥ śram° MSV 1.47.5.

Śramaṇamaṇḍala, n. of a region in the south: Gv 131.4.

Śramaṇavarṇapratirūpaka, nt., n. of a **pratyeka-**(q.v.)-naraka: Śikṣ 136.10.

śramaṇoddeśa, m. (= Pali samaṇuddesa, here seems only applied to novices, sāmaṇera), *a subordinate of a* (Buddhist) *monk*, but not always = **śrāmaṇera**: Ṛddhilamātā upāsikā **śramaṇoddeśikā** (see next) Cundaḥ °deśaḥ (see **Cunda**, who is called in Divy a śrāmaṇeraka of Śāriputra) Divy 160.6; in Av ii.69.4 ff. (where mss. regularly śravaṇ° for śramaṇ°, em. Speyer) applied to **Sumanas** (4), who had been given by his father as attendant to Aniruddha; but at the time when this ep. is applied to him he had not only been initiated but become an arhant, while still acting in the rôle of attendant to Aniruddha, who calls him putraka, ii.69.3.

śramaṇoddeśaka, f. °**ikā**, = prec.: °ikā applied to a laywoman in Divy 160.6; °aka-tvam MSV iii.67.10; spelled samanuddeśakatvaṃ (semi-MIndic) MSV iv.101.4.

(**śravaṇa**, written for **śramaṇa**, *monk*, even in Skt., see BR s.v. 4 śravaṇa; so AsP 323.19; 324.1; Śikṣ 128.11; RP 17.13; 34.12; Av ii.69.4, etc. Conversely, śravaṇāya (kāṅkṣitāḥ) should be read for śramaṇāya of all mss. LV 399.8, where Lefm. em. śamanāya; *desiring to hear*; confirmed by Tib. thos par. At the end of this line **vā**, q.v. (1), = iva.)

śravaṇāmukha, see **śrāvaṇāmukha.**

śrāddha, adj. (see also **śraddha, a-śr°**; in Skt. literature cited only from Hem. (Jain); = Pali saddha, *believing, having true faith*, and rarely in bad sense *credulous*, cf. **aśraddha**), *believing, having* (true) *faith*, sometimes with loc. of what is believed in: LV 238.21 yasmin śr° = Mv ii.118.9 and 119.16 yatra śr°; Divy 305.27; Av i.383.4 (also i.83.8 in text, but ms. śraddha); Sukh 99.11.

śrāmaṇa, nt. (Skt. Gr. id.; to śramaṇa plus -a; = **śrāmaṇya**), *monkhood*: (naiṣa ... mārgo nirvṛtaye ... na) °ṇāya na **brāhmaṇāya** (q.v., 2) na nirvāṇāya saṃvartate LV 245.13 (prose). Some mss. śramaṇāya, which here makes no sense. (In Divy 338.13 śrāmaṇāḥ, misprint for śra°.)

śrāmaṇaka, adj. (= Pali sām°; cf. **a-śrā°**, **śrāmaṇyaka**), *monkish, belonging to monks*: °kaṃ susukham anubhonti Samādh 19.28 (vs), *experience a monk's excellent joy*; asmākaṃ . . . na ca °kā guṇāḥ Śikṣ 47.3, *and we have not the qualities of monks* (i. e. which monks should have).

śrāmaṇera (= Pali sām°), *novice* in the Buddhist order: Mvy 8719; Divy 404.14; Mv iii.268.16 (mss. śra°); Prāt 519.4; SP 180.8; 183.5, etc. The BHS f. seems to be °**rikā**, see next.

śrāmaṇeraka, (**1**) with f. °**ikā** (not recorded in Pali) = prec.: m., Divy 153.6; 342.27 ff.; 345.10; 382.8 (all prose); f. °ikā Bhīk 11b.4–5; assoc. with m. °ṇera, as its f., Mvy 8720; Prāt 519.4; (**2**) m., n. of a nāga: Māy 221.24; cf. **Śramaṇa**.

śrāmaṇya (= Pali sāmañña, in both senses), (**1**) nt., *monkhood*: LV 88.18 (read śrāmaṇyena bhav° with v.l. in Foucaux, Notes, 113); Mv iii.331.5, 9; 389.3; Mvy 9128; 9133; Śikṣ 198.5; KP 127.9; Bbh 85.11; 182.25; Ud xi.4, 5; Bhīk 3a.1; (**2**) adj., *devoted to monks*; regularly with **mātṛjña, pitṛjña**, and **brāhmaṇya**; see s.v. **mātṛjña** for references.

śrāmaṇyaka, adj. (= **śrāmaṇaka**), *belonging to monks*: etaṃ °kaṃ dhanaṃ Mv ii.357.12 (vs), repeated in foll.

Śrāmaṇyaphalasūtra (= Pali Sāmaññaphalasutta, DN ch. 2), n. of a work: Karmav 49.23.

śrāvaka (so in Skt., and Pali sāvaka, in Skt. also of Jains and other sects), *a* (Buddhist) *disciple*, in Mahāyāna texts regularly used of followers of the Hīnayāna, passim: technical description, sarveṣāṃ arhatāṃ kṣīṇāśravāṇāṃ uṣitavratānāṃ samyagājñāsuvimuktacittānāṃ parikṣīṇabhavasaṃyojanānāṃ anuprāptasvakārthānāṃ Mv i.248.10 f., repeated below; a similar formula in Pali, Vin. i.183.24 etc.; stages and types of śr° Mvy 1008–1028; names of well-known śr° ib. 1029–1073; their qualities 1075–1126. PTSD says a sāvaka is 'never an Arahant', but see CPD s.v. araha(t) 2.

śrāvaka-bodhi, *the enlightenment of* (i. e. peculiar to) *śrāvakas* (contrasting with pratyeka-b°, anuttarā samyaksaṃbodhi): (bhagavān . . .) °dhiṃ vyākartukāmo bhavaty . . . Divy 69.4.

Śrāvakabhūmi, Bbh 185.10, acc. to note app. designation of a part of the **Yogācārabhūmi**.

śrāvaka-yāna, *the vehicle of the disciples*, = **Hīnayāna** (cf. **yāna**): Mvy 1252; SP 79.6; 80.7, etc.

śrāvaka-vinaya, n. of a work, presumably a Hīnayāna version of the **Vinaya**: Śikṣ 135.9; 168.2.

śrāvakīya, adj. (to °ka plus -īya, § 22.20), *of* **śrāvakas**, q.v.: (yāna, = **śrāvaka-yāna**) Laṅk 134.16 (vs; with tāthāgataṃ, pratyekaṃ); pratyeka-śrāvakīyābhyāṃ (sc. yānābhyāṃ) niṣkrāntā saptamī (sc. bhūmir) bhavet 375.6 (vs).

śrāvaṇa = **pariśrā°, parisrā°**, *strainer*: pātra-°ṇam (dvandva) ekānta upanikṣipya Divy 582.21; in 24 below pātra-pariśrāvaṇaṃ.

śrāvaṇā-mukha, and **śravaṇā°**, acc. to Speyer's Index rendered by Tib. on Av (°kheṣu) bsgrags laḥi gnas rnams su, (in) *place(s) for proclamation*: rathyāvīthīcatvaraśṛṅgāṭakeṣu śrāvaṇāmukheṣv anuśrāvya Av ii.182.6; nagare catvaraśṛṅgāṭake śravaṇāmukheṣu āha Mv iii.90.11; Mathurāyāṃ catvaraśṛṅgāṭakavīthī-mukha-śravaṇāmukheṣu ghaṇṭā ghoṣāpitā 390.19; since -mukha- after -vīthī in the last surely means *entrance*, possibly °ṇāmukha also means lit. *entrance to a* (place of) *proclamation*, but Tib. (above) has no word for *entrance*; mukha could also mean lit. *occasion, means* (of *proclaiming*, or *hearing*, śravaṇā = °ṇa); there is a Pkt. sāvaṇā, *causing to hear, making known*.

śrāvaṇya (nt.), either for **śrāmaṇya**, *monkhood* (cf. **śravaṇa** = śramaṇa), or from śravaṇa = śruti plus -ya, *sacred learning*, cf. śrāvakāṇāṃ (text °nāṃ) in prec. line: (śrāvakānāṃ tu yā śikṣā adhiśīlānupravartate,) adhicittaṃ ca yad (so text) jñānaṃ śrāvaṇya-phala-hetukam Mmk 447.12 (vs).

Śrāvastīyaka, adj., = next: °kāḥ brāhmaṇagṛhapatayo Divy 618.10.

Śrāvasteya, adj. (= Skt. Gr. id.), *of Śrāvastī*: °yā baṇijaḥ Divy 34.20; °yo baṇijo 172.8; °yaiḥ brāhmaṇagṛhapatibhiḥ 618.21.

Śrāvasteyaka, adj., = prec.: °kāḥ kṣatriyabrāhmaṇagṛhapatayaḥ Divy 618.27.

śrāvikā (prob. for sr°, root sru, caus.; but Mironov also śr°), *boil* (= gaṇḍaḥ, prec. in Mvy, and Tib. ḥbras): Mvy 9488.

śrāvitaka, m. (Skt. °ta plus specifying -ka), *one that has been caused to hear* (the gospel): tehī tadā °kehi sārdhaṃ kurvanti pūjāṃ dvipadottamānām SP 194.8 (vs). Cf. **saṃśrāvitaka**.

śriyā = śrī; may be Sktization of MIndic siriyā (AMg., at least as n. pr.), which may actually represent *śrīkā; cf. **striyā** = strī, and § 10.6: mahatīye śriyāye, *with great magnificence*, Mv iii.36.14; tejasā śriyāye jvalamānaṃ iii.379.9 (both prose; no v.l.); tejena lakṣmyā (most mss. °mī, may be kept) śriyayā (most mss., Nobel śriyā, unmetr.) jvalantaṃ Suv 149.2 (vs); (yā śrī Vaiśravaṇe . . .) yā cāsurendra-śriyā (n. sg.) . . . yā ca graheṣu (so most mss.; Lefm. kṛṣṇe ca yā ca) śriyā LV 130.19, 20. Cf. stem Mañjuśriya, § 10.4.

Śriyāmatī (= **Śirīmatī**, q.v.), of a devakumārikā in the southern quarter: LV 389.7. Cf. **Śrīmatī**.

Ś(i)rī, (**1**) n. of a devakumārikā in the northern quarter: Mv iii.309.9 = LV 391.4 (read Śirī in both); one of four daughters of Indra, Mv ii.57.2 ff., see **Āśā**; (**2**) n. of one of the 8 deities of the Bodhi-tree: LV 331.21; (**3**) n. of the mother of the Buddha **Maṅgala**: Śirī (n.) Mv i.249.17; also Śirikā i.252.6 (vs); (**4**) n. of a brahman's daughter, in the '**Śiri-jātaka**': Mv ii.89.19 ff. (Śirir, n., 89.19; Śirikāṃ 90.4, prose; Śiriye, g., 90.5; Śirī, n., 91.4; Śiri, n., 94.2, 9, 11, v.l. Śirī); (**5**) honorifically added at the end of proper names, as in Skt. only at the beginning (Sadbhāvaśrī, as n. of a goddess, Rājat. 3.353, is not analogous); noted only in Mv: Kolita-śirī Mv i.62.10; Rāhula-śiri i.128.13; iii.258.15 ff.; 260.9 ff.; **Śyāma-**(°**maka-**)-śiri, see the names; Kāśyapa-śirī (the former Buddha) iii.243.16.

śrīkaṇṭha, (**1**) n. of some tree or woody plant: (homaṃ cāṣṭasahasraṃ tu khadirendhanavahninā,) pālāśaṃ cāpi śrīkaṇṭhaṃ bilvodumbara cākṣakaṃ Mmk 136.2 (vs); (**2**) n. of a nāga king: Megh 306.8; Māy 246.21.

śrīkāra, m. or nt. (cf. Skt. Lex. śrīkara, nt., the *red lotus*, Trik., which uses Buddh. sources; also Apte), a kind of lotus flower: śrīkāra-padmaṃ juhuyāt, padmaśriya āgacchati Mmk 712.20 (prose).

Śrīkūṭa, n. of a former Buddha: Sukh 5.15; (the same? could also be a contemporary or future B.) 70.15.

śrīgarbha, m. (or semi-MIndic śirig°), (**1**) a kind of gem, reddish in color: śirigarbhapiñjalehi (padumehi) Mv ii.301.4; in 302.3 read, śirigarbha-piñjarehi (Senart with mss. -pañjarehi; so one ms., v.l. śiriṣa-g°, Senart em. wrongly śirīṣa-g°); śrīgarbha-ratnam Mvy 5961 = Tib. rin po che (= ratna) dpal gyi (= śrī) sñin po (= *heart, essence*); śirigarbhehi maṇiratnehi Mv ii.311.6; similarly 318.4; śrīgarbha-siṃhāsane LV 51.4 (here of a throne occupied by the Bodhisattva in the Tuṣita heaven); id. RP 2.7 (here on earth, on Gṛdhrakūṭa, near Rājagṛha); (**2**) n. of one or more Bodhisattvas: Mvy 666; Dbh 2.6; Gv 442.9; one that is predicted for Buddhahood under the name Vimalanetra, SP 21.11, 13; 26.5.

Śrīgarbhakūṭavinarditarāja, n. of a Tathāgata: Megh 310.2.

Śrīgarbhaprabhāsa, n. of a (particular) gem: Gv 413.16 (cf. **śrīgarbha**).

Śrīgarbhavatī, n. of a lokadhātu: Gv 217.7.

Śrīcintāmaṇidatta, n. of an author: Sādh 99.12.

Śrītejas (°**ja**), (**1**) n. of a former Buddha: LV 5.5; (**2**) n. of a king: Gv 427.3 (vs; °ja-, m.c.); (**3**) n. of a nāga: Mvy 3360; Megh 306.4 (prose, but °jaṃ, acc. sg.).

Śrīdhara, n. of an author: Sādh 328.9.

Śrīprabhā, n. of a girl, attendant on **Subhadrā** (1): Gv 52.2.

Śrī-(Śiri-)-prabhāsamati (so connect), n. of a Buddha: Gv 285.4 (vs).

Ś(i)rībala (printed °vala), n. of a king (previous birth of Śākyamuni): Samādh p. 59 line 25; p. 66 line 23.

Śrībhadra, (**1**) (Śiri°) n. of a Buddha: Gv 257.13 (vs); (**2**) n. of a nāga: Mvy 3352; of a nāga king, Māy 246.21.

Śrībhadrā, (**1**) n. of a female lay-disciple: Gv 51.16; (**2**) n. of a girl, attendant on **Subhadrā** (1): Gv 52.2.

Śrīmati, f., n. of a girl, associate (sister ?) of **Śrīsaṃbhava** (2): Gv 455.4 etc.; usually n. sg. °tiḥ etc., but °tī in list at the end 549.22, and acc. °tīm 466.11–12.

Śrīmatī, (**1**) see prec.; (**2**) n. of a daughter of Ghoṣila, married to Udayana: Divy 541.19 ff.; (**3**) n. of a member of (Bimbisāra's and) Ajātaśatru's harem: Av i.308.10 ff. See also **Śirīmatī, Śriyāmatī.**

Śrīmant, n. of a nāga king: Māy 246.20. Cf. next.

Śrīmanta (nom. °taḥ, MIndic for Śrīmant), n. of a mountain: Māy 253.31. Cf. prec.

Śrīmālā, n. of a queen: Laṅk 222.19; 223.4; see next.

Śrīmālāsiṃhanāda-sūtra, n. of a work: Śikṣ 42.12; prob. referred to as a **deśanāpāṭha** (q.v.) *referring to Queen Śrīmālā*, Laṅk 222.19.

Śrīvardhana, (**1**) n. of a nāga king: Māy 246.21; (**2**) n. of an officer in charge of elephants for King Prasenajit: MSV ii.66.15 ff.

śrīveṣṭa (Skt. Lex., and °ṭa-ka Suśr., *resin of a kind of pine*), some sort of edible substance: havi(ḥ ?) pūrṇa(ṃ?) śrīveṣṭa-madhuśira-(q.v.)-payo-pakva-bhakṣādyāṃ . . . niryātayet Mmk 48.8.

Śrīśāna, n. of a yakṣa: Māy 236.26.

Śrī-(Śiri-)-samudra, n. of a Buddha: Gv 256.6 (vs).

Śrīsaṃbhava [(**1**) = Samantaśrīsaṃbhava, n. of a Tathāgata: Gv 217.9; error, corrected 2d edition;] (**2**) n. of a boy, associate (brother ?) of **Śrīmati**: Gv 455.4 ff.

Śrī-(Śiri-)-sumeru, n. of a Buddha: Gv 284.8 (vs).

Śrīharihara, n. of an author: Sādh 110.8.

Srughnā, see **Sru°**.

śruṇana (nt.), dat.-inf. °nāya (to śruṇati = Skt. śṛṇoti), *for hearing, in order to hear*: yo gacchate . . . śruṇanāya (so LaV-P. JRAS 1911.1072, for text śravaṇāya, no v.l.) dharmaṃ imam evarūpam SP 252.10 (vs); WT keep śravaṇāya but cite their ms. K′ as śruṇārtha (which would be good metrically, but looks like a half-hearted 'correction' of śruṇanāya).

śruṇoti, °**ṇute**, etc., semi-MIndic for śṛṇoti etc., see Chap. 43, s.v. śru. Also śrūṇute, m.c., LV 74.9 (vs).

(**śruta**, subst. nt., as in Skt., *the* (here Buddhist) *holy word*; cf. next, where the same mg. appears, as also in Pali suta: (Rāvaṇaḥ) cinteti kim idaṃ ko 'yaṃ deśitaṃ kena vā śrutam Laṅk 8.16 (vs), after disappearance of the vision of Buddha instructing Mahāmati etc., *he thought: What was this* (sight)? *Who was this? Or by whom was the sacred word taught?* Suzuki leaves deśitaṃ out of his translation, which is unsatisfactory in other ways.)

śrutādhāra, adj. (Skt. śruta plus ādhāra, not used in this sense in Skt.; = Pali sutādhāra, Jāt. vi.287.3), *holding fast* (*retaining in their minds*) *the sacred word*: SP 337.1 adhyāśayena saṃpannāḥ śrutādhārāś ca ye narāḥ.

śrutāvin (śruta plus -ā-vin, § 22.51), used like Skt. śrutavant as periphrastic perf., *who have heard*: (ye . . .) śṛṇvanti dharmaṃ atha vā °vinaḥ SP 49.11 (vs), *who are hearing or have heard the Doctrine.*

Śrutodgrahaṇa, n. of a dhāraṇī: Gv 66.12.

śrūṇute, see **śruṇoti.**

1 **śreṇika**, adj. (cf. **a-śreṇika**), a (relatively) complimentary epithet of a wandering mendicant, always with parivrājakaḥ: ŚsP 615.12; 633.13; AsP 8.21; 9.10. But apparently not a Buddhist; his knowledge is 'limited', **prādeśika**, ŚsP 615.13, tho superior to that of the aśreṇika. Cf. Rahder, JAOS 70.126. One might guess that śreṇika meant 'members of a guild or (non-Buddhist) order of monks'; but śreṇi is not a normal expression for a religious order. In AMg. seḍhi (= Skt. śreṇi) is used of a certain stage of religious advancement among the Jains, and a-seḍhi-gaya (= Skt. *a-śreṇi-gata) means one who has not yet attained that stage; see Ratnach. s.vv. Could aśreṇika equal AMg. aseḍhigaya, and śreṇika, its opposite, one who has attained that stage? Two Jain terms used, and applied to Jain or other heterodox monks? This is only a guess, and prob. not likely.

2 **Śreṇika**, less commonly used for next: Mv i.257.15 (v.l. °ya); 258.3 (in 4 °ya); 286.17; 288.3; otherwise noted only in Mvy 3652, where it is not juxtaposed with **Bimbisāra**, q.v.

Śreṇiya (see also prec. and next; = Pali Seniya), another name of King **Bimbisāra**, regularly accompanied by the latter: Mv i.254.14; 256.14, 17, etc.; 289.16; ii.198.5 (mss. senişo); 207.16; iii.437.1 ff.

Śreṇya = prec., with **Bimbisāra**: Mv iii.437.9, 13, 16; 439.14, 15, 17; 440.2, 7, 9, 11, 12, 13; 442.1, 4; 443.9 (in same line Śreṇiya), 11, 16; 449.6, 10, 13; Divy 145.24 ff.; 269.21 (vs); Māgadha-śreṇya 269.19 (prose); 558.9; MSV i.264.7; regularly written Śraiṇya in **Bimbasārasūtra** (q.v.), 121, line 2 of text et passim.

Śreyaka (corresp. to Pali Seyyasaka, Vin. ii.7.17 ff.), n. of a sinful monk, subjected to the **nigarhaṇīya** karman: MSV iii.5.2; 11.15 ff.

śreyatara, compv. (to Skt. śreyas; = Pali seyyatara, 'usual form in post-canonical prose', Geiger 100.3, but not in PTSD), in mg. of Skt. superl., *best* (of more than two): yā yeva vo (10 sā eva no) °tarā . . . Mv ii.54.6, 10 (vss).

Śreyasī, n. of one of the 8 deities of the Bodhi-tree: LV 331.21.

śreṣṭhaka, adj. (= Skt. śreṣṭha; unrecorded unless in Skt. n. pr. Bhūri-śreṣṭhaka, v.l. for °ika), *best*: °kaṃ bhojanaṃ Divy 638.17 (prose).

Śreṣṭhamati, n. of a Bodhisattva: Gv 442.7.

śreṣṭhika (= AMg. seṭhiya, Pali seṭṭhi, Skt. śreṣṭhin), *guild-leader, capitalist*: Śikṣ 331.1 (vs; m.c.?).

Śreṣṭhin, n. of a householder of Śrāvastī: MSV ii.127.20; 139.6.

Śraiṇya, see **Śreṇya.**

Śroṇa or **Śroṇaka** (= Pali Soṇaka, Soṇ°), n. of a chaplain's son, friend of **Arindama** (acc. to Mv former incarnation of Śākyamuni; Pali, Jāt. 529, makes him a Paccekabuddha): Mv iii.450.6 ff. (Śroṇa 450.6, 12; °ka 15 etc.).

Śroṇa Koṭikarṇa (= Pali Soṇa Koṭikaṇṇa), n. of an important disciple of Śākyamuni: Mvy 1058 Śroṇakoṭī°, as cpd. (so also Mironov); Divy 3.8, 9, 12 Śroṇaḥ Koṭīkarṇaḥ (°ṇo); 3.26, also 17.9, and colophon 24.8, Koṭikarṇas, alone; both names separately 4.12 ff., repeatedly; Śroṇa alone 7.29 ff., repeatedly. See also **Śoṇa.**

Śroṇa-koṭi-(or **koṭī-**)-**viṃśa** (see also **Koṭiviṃśa**; = Pali Soṇa Koḷivisa), n. of a disciple of Buddha: (°koṭi°) Mv iii.40.19; (°koṭī°) Mvy 1055b (so also Mironov).

Śroṇāparānta, m. pl. (= Pali Sunāparanta or Suṇ° [so SN comm. ii.374 bottom]; associated with Pali Puṇṇa Thera), n. of a people, located in the south; the city **Kaliṅgavana**, q.v., was located there: Gv 192.15. See next.

Śroṇāparāntaka (= Pali Sunāparantaka, MN iii.268.10), m. pl., = prec., q.v.: Divy 38.7 ff. (associated with Pūrṇa 1); they are described as fierce and violent, 38.9 (as in Pali, l.c.).

śroṇi-kaṭāha, ŚsP 1433.21 °ham, or °kaṭāhaka, Śikṣ 211.13 °kam (citation of this same passage), m. or nt. (may be understood as acc. sg.), lit. *rump-pot* (see **kaṭāhaka**), = *pelvis bones* (seen in a **śivapathikā**, q.v.).

śroṇi-bhaṇḍikā, or °**bhaṇḍā** (so mss.; cf. **bhaṇḍikā**; see BR s.v. bhāṇḍa, 3c), *hip-ornament*, made by goldsmiths: °bhaṇḍikā or °bhaṇḍā (mss., Senart em. °bhāṇḍikā) pi kriyanti Mv ii.470.10 (prose).

śrota, m. or nt. (Sktization of MIndic sota, as in Pali, AMg., which historically represents Skt. śrotra; there is no Skt. śrotas, *ear*, which Weller 39 considers correct, except in the Lex. Trik.), *ear*; *faculty of hearing*: esp. śrotam avadadhata LV 409.10; (read) śrotam odhāya Mv i.10.8; avahita-śrotaḥ LV 442.1–2 and °tā Mv i.158.3 (on these and Pali equivalents see **avadadhati**); cakṣur anityam adhruvaṃ tatha śrota (best mss. śrotra) ghrāṇaṃ (etc.) LV 419.5 (vs); śrotābhāsam avagacchati Mv i.6.3, and others, see s.v. **ābhāsa,** *the range of hearing*; badhirās taṃ muhūrtaṃ śrotaṃ pratilabhante Mv iii.256.3, *got hearing*; viśuddha-śroto Mv ii.382.24 (vs), cited as °śrotro Śikṣ 304.7; śrotendriyeṇa . . . Mv ii.383.2.

śrotaāpatti, °**panna,** see **srota°**.

śrotā (f.! for *srotā = Skt. srotas), *opening, aperture,* of the ears or nose: yad asya karṇaśrotābhyāṃ tṛṇatūlakaṃ prakṣipya nāsāśrotābhyāṃ niṣkāsyate sma LV 257.8 (prose), and others, down to (mukhadvāreṇa prakṣipya) karṇanāsikā-śrotābhyo (here several mss. śrotrobhi, but above almost all °tābhyāṃ repeatedly) niṣkāsyate sma 11.

śrotāpatti, °**panna,** see **sro°**.

(**śroṣyam,** in RP 44.1 (vs) gītaṃ na śroṣyam api vādyarutaṃ na grāhyaṃ, is surely 1 sg. fut. of śru-, *I will not listen to the song*; not a gdve. from the Vedic śruṣ-, despite the parallel grāhyaṃ.)

Ślakṣṇa, m., n. of a mountain: Divy 103.2; 107.1–3; 113.5.

Ślakṣṇā, n. of a river: Divy 107.4, 6.

ślakṣṇita, denom. ppp. (to Skt. ślakṣṇa; cf. late Vedic °ṇayati and Pali o-saṇheti), *made slippery*: yāva sānaṃ °ṇitāni aṅgāni Mv i.7.12 (prose; em. but doubtless right).

ślāghate (in this mg. only Skt. Gr.), *wheedles, coaxes*: (putrapriyatām eva) manyamānena ślāghamānenaikavarṇāny ekayānāni dattāni SP 77.2 (prose), *coaxing* (his children).

[**ślīpāda,** m., *elephantiasis*: Mvy 9521; read (Skt.) ślīpada with Mironov and Bhīk 17a.2; cf. ślīpadin Mvy 8792.]

[**śleṣmika,** adj., = Skt. ślaiṣmika, (disease) *due to* (disturbance of) *phlegm*: kathaṃ cikitsā kartavyā vāte pitte śleṣmike tathā Suv 177.10 (vs), so Nobel. But the meter is bad, and I think we should read vātike paittike tathā for the 2d pāda, with best ms. except that it reads yettike for pai°. Diseases of phlegm were, in the orig. reading, mentioned in the 2d pāda of the next line, where, contrary to Nobel, I would read with 2 mss., incl. the best, kaphavyādhipraśāntaye (v.l. kaphaja-vyā[b]). The four pādas then present the same four topics, and in the same order, as in 179.7–10 below.]

Śvabhrapada, n. of a man (unknown elsewhere): Karmav 78.16 (v.l. sūtrapada).

śvas, adv. (usually *tomorrow* as in Skt.; cf. **śuve** etc.), *yesterday*: yathādya śvo vā parinirvṛtam anusmarāmi SP 157.7 (prose); adya śvo vā 158.8 (vs, corresp. to prec.); samanusmarāmī yatha adya śvo vā 219.9 (vs). Note that Skt. kalyam, *on the morrow*, also = *yesterday* acc. to a Lex.; and JM. kalla(ṃ) has both mgs., *yesterday* in Jacobi, Ausgew. Erz. 11.32; 54.8; *tomorrow*, 50.20; 60.29.

śvasana, *trunk* of an elephant; see **gaja-śv°**.

śvasā, n. sg., *mother-in-law*: Mvy 3894 = Tib. sgyug mo. Evidently for Skt. śvaśrū with ending modified by that of svasā (svasṛ), *sister*; MIndic forms of the two words resemble each other more closely, cf. Pkt. sussū with susā, *sister*. Mironov reads svasā in Mvy; but the mg. is certainly *mother-in-law*, as shown not only by Tib. but by the position of the word, after śvaśura.

Śvāsa, n. of a nāga, previous birth of **Dhṛtarāṣṭra** (**mahārājan**): MSV i.260.18 ff.

śvāsa-viṣa, m., *a snake whose breath is poisonous*: (ye ca dṛṣṭiviṣā) āśiviṣāḥ śvāsaviṣāś cāgnijvālān utsṛjanti sma LV 317.9 (prose).

? **śvāsopavāsaka,** or °**ika,** adj., should, I think, be read in Mv iii.71.16 (prose; Senart sopavāsika) and 83.11 (vs; Senart māsopa° with mss.). At least the cpd. must begin śvāsa°, and Senart's interpretation cannot be accepted. In description of wretched victims of ogresses, after imprisonment and torment: 71.16 (mss.) susvāsopavāsikānāṃ (v.l. sāsopa°) dīrghakeśanakhaśmaśrūṇāṃ (pūtikhaṇḍavasanānāṃ, em.) etc.; in 83.11 (vs) text with mss. māsopavāsikānāṃ (v.l. °vāsak°; read śvāsopa°) virūḍhanakhakeśaśmaśrūṇām (mss. virūha°). Our cpd. may mean *devoted to sighs, subject to sighs* (cf. upavāsa, *Obliegen, sich Hingeben*, Schmidt, in Samayamātṛkā 5.82 kalahopavāsair, vyasanopavāsair); or else *fasting from* (barely able to get) *the breath* (of life), cf. śvāsaśeṣa, Rājat., *with* (nothing but) *breath left*, BR s.v. śvāsa.

Śveta, n. of a Pratyekabuddha: Mmk 64.13.

Śvetaka (Skt. as adj., see **setaka**), n. of a nāga (cf. Skt. Śveta, id.): Mvy 3326; of two nāga-kings, Māy 247.15.

Śvetaketu (= Pali Setaketu), n. of a previous incarnation of Śākyamuni in the Tuṣita heaven: Mv i.337.14, 18; LV 10.16.

śveta-paṭa, nt., *a white cloth*; see s.v. **indra-paṭa.**

Śvetabhadra, n. of a nāga king: Mmk 18.12.

śvetavarṇā (most mss. sveta°), Divy 263.9, acc. to Index *an astrologer's instrument*, acc. to pw 7.379 *chalk*; what is clear is that it is something used in astrological calculation; see the passage, s.v. **gaṇitra.**

Śvetavalākā, n. of a town: Mv iii.394.4.

śvetāsthi, nt., with durbhikṣa, lit. *white-bone*, a kind of famine: Divy 131.21 (see s.v. **cañcu**); 24–132.3 śve° nāma durbhikṣaṃ tasmin kāle manuṣyā asthīny upasaṃhṛtya tāvat kvāthayanti yāvat tāny asthīni śvetāni saṃvṛttānīti tatas tat kvāthaṃ pivanti; idaṃ śvetāsthi durbhikṣam ity ucyate; similarly MSV i.250.13.

Śvetikā, n. of a city: Karmav 80.4; corresp. to Pali Setavyā, see Lévi's note. Home of **Padāśva,** q.v.

Śveturāṣṭra (! twice; both mss. have śvetu° both times), n. of a former Buddha: Mv iii.235.2.

śvelā, a high number: Gv 106.10. Cf. next.

śvelu, m. (or f.; v.l. śvailu, but Mironov śvelu), a high number: Mvy 7891 = Tib. zal zul, cf. prec. and **svela.** Cited from Gv, which reads **khelu,** q.v., in 133.21; the orig. form was possibly svelu.

Ṣ

ṣaṭkikā (Skt. ṣaṭka, Pali chakka, plus -i-kā), *set of six, hexad*: MSV iii.83.8.

ṣaṭpañcika, adj., *consisting of six or five*: °kayā vācā dharmadeśanāyāḥ Mvy 8426; refers to situation of Pali Vin. iv.22.17 (uttari-chappañca-vācāhi).

Ṣaṭpura, n. of a locality: Māy 47.

ṣaḍ-akṣarī, (**1**) n. of a magic formula of six syllables (om maṇi padme hūṃ, Kv 76.6): Kv 67.3 ff.; 74.15 etc.; 76.4 etc.; (**2**) n. of a rākṣasī: Māy 243.29.

Ṣaḍaṅga (misprinted Saḍ°), n. of a nāga king: Māy 246.19.

ṣaḍabhijña, adj. Bhvr., possessing the six **abhijñā**: SP 90.7; 129.10; 150.2; 155.2; 180.1; see s.v. **traividya.**

ṣaḍ-āśīti (= Pali chaḷāsīti), *86*; cf. **catur-āśīti**, and § 19.35: Mv iii.96.23 = 101.4 and 6 (vs, metr. indifferent).

ṣaḍi, as (stem-)form of Skt. ṣaṣ, *six*: LV 414.19: 420.1 (vss); see § 19.24.

ṣaḍvargika, m. pl., = °**vārg**°: Divy 329.19; Av ii.139.8; MSV ii.99.3; 199.13 ff.

ṣaḍvargīya, m. pl., = next: Divy 306.28; 307.6 ff.; 489.20 ff.

ṣaḍvārgika, m. pl. (= prec. two and Pali chabbaggiya), *members of the group of six (monks)*, see Childers and PTSD: Mvy 9255 = Tib. drug sde. Their names are given 9471–6: Nanda, Upananda, Punarvasu, Chanda, Aśvaka, Udāyin; the Pali list agrees only in part. Nanda and Upananda also belong to this group in Divy; see s.v. **Nandopananda.** In Pali they seem to be represented as followers of the Buddha, though very imperfect ones, often transgressing rules of propriety. In BHS, at least in Divy, they seem to be heretics from the Buddhist standpoint.

ṣaḍ-vālaka, m. or nt., n. given to the specially strong gate built by Śuddhodana to guard the Bodhisattva; *having six bars* (?); perh. read °vāra-ka, but even this does not seem closely paralleled in the required mg.: Śuddhodanena rājakumārasya ṣaḍvālako (no v.l.) nāma dvāro kārāpito pañcapuruṣaśatehi apāvurīyati Mv ii.157.19; tena (sc. yakṣeṇa) °ka-dvāram (here by em.; mss. paṭṭālaka-dvāram, or only ṣa-dvāram!) apāvṛtaṃ, ghoṣaṃ ca nigṛhītaṃ 161.3.

Ṣaḍviṣāṇapāta, n. of a former Buddha: Mv i.140.12.

ṣaṇṇa = Skt. ṣaṇḍa, *thicket*: nānādvijonnāditavṛkṣa-ṣaṇṇe (Bhvr.) vane viśokā muditā ramāmi Gv 408.4 (vs). See § 2.16.

ṣaṣṭikodana, (cheap) *porridge made of quick-ripening rice* (Skt. ṣaṣṭika, °kā): AsP 239.3, 4.

ṣaṣṭo (ṣaṣ- plus -tas), so read with v.l., as quasi-abl. to ṣaṣ-, *in relation to the six* (senses): ṣaṣṭo (Senart °ṭho) adhipatī rājā Mv iii.384.6 (vs), *he that is overlord in relation to the six* (senses) *is a* (true) *king*; answers the question of line 3, kiṃ adhipatī rājā (so mss.); corresp. Pali, Dhp. comm. iii.233.3, cha-dvārādhipatī rājā (also refers to the senses; dvāra is used in Pali of their *outlets*).

[**ṣaṣṭhī**, in Mv ii.21.2 (vs): (atra kiṃ kāraṇaṃ uktaṃ yaṃ sapta kramate kramān,) na ca aṣṭa na ca ṣaṣṭhī atra āgamanaṃ śṛṇu, . . . *why he takes seven steps, and not eight or* . . . (?) Senart em. ṣaṣṭi, *sixty*, which seems to be correct; see P. Mus, Barabudur 492, 480; Mv i.318.10 caṅkrama-ṣaṣṭiḥ, *a promenade of sixty paces*. The only alternative, so far as I see, would be the unattractive one of understanding the ordinal ṣaṣṭhī in the mg. of the cardinal, *six*; the sense would, to be sure, then be simple.]

S

sa-, inseparable prefix in 'pleonastic' positive use, as opp. of neg. (= Pali id., see Childers); **sace(t), saca, sacchambita, saśakya, sāntarabahis, santika** and **sā**° (°ke), see s.vv.: (lokapālān yakṣarākṣasa-)-gandharvabhujagagaṇa-saparivṛtān LV 209.19 (prose), *attended by crowds of* . . .; paribubhukṣitā (so Senart em., mss. paribhuk°) sma sapipāsitā (Senart em. saṃpi°, but no such cpd. is recorded) sma Mv i.8.2 (prose), *we are hungry, we are thirsty*; ayoguḍā hi agnismiṃ yathā-d-iva (so mss.) satāpitā (so mss.) Mv i.15.15 (vs); this could be interpreted as m.c. for saṃtāpitā(ḥ), which Senart reads (unmetr.) by em.; sa-pṛthagjanasevitaṃ (dharmaṃ) Mv i.33.13 (vs); sajaḍaḥ sajaḍataro bhavati Śikṣ 152.12 (prose), *he is stupid, very stupid*. Cf. **sajyotibhūta, satejobhūta,** which do not require similar interpretation. (In **sayyathīdaṃ, °thāpi,** etc., the pronoun sa, tad, is concerned.)

saṃyathīdaṃ = sayya°, q.v.: Māy 251.4. Cf. next.

saṃyadhāpi nāma = **tad (say-)yathāpi nāma,** see s.v. **yathāpi 2**, and cf. prec.

Saṃyamanī, Divy 60.15 (aśītivarṣasahasrāyuṣām manuṣyāṇām Śaṅkho nāma rājā bhaviṣyati) °nī-cakravartī (so text, as cpd., with capital S-, but Index °manin, *ruler*) caturantavijetā dhārmiko dharmarājā . . . May not °manī-cakravartin mean *emperor of* (residing in) Saṃyamanī (Yama's city)?

Saṃyuktaka (nt.) = next: Divy 333.10. Also occurs in names of sections of the Madhyamāgama; see e. g. **Samādhi-saṃy°.**

Saṃyuktāgama, m., n. of a section of the canon, = Pali SN: Mvy 1424.

saṃyoga (m., = Pali id.), *binding, attachment* (in bad sense): (iyaṃ dṛṣṭiḥ saṃrāgāya saṃvartate nāsaṃrāgāya saṃdveṣāya) nāsaṃdveṣaya saṃmohāya nāsaṃmohāya saṃyogāya nāsaṃ° Av ii.188.9.

saṃyojana, nt., once (Gv 387.3) °**nā** (= Pali °na, or saññojana, Pugg. 22.11 ff.), *fetter*, as binding to existence, to misery: parikṣīṇa-bhava-°na ity ucyate (Buddha) LV 425.21; without listing or number, °naiḥ Ud iii.6; (sg.) iv.29; xv.6 (pl. ?); xx.1; sāvaśeṣa-°na (kālaṃ kṛ-) Divy 302.21; 553.24; 555.27–8, (*to die*) *while having* (some) *fetters remaining*; °nam Mvy 2134, foll. by bandhana, anuśaya, paryutthāna, upakleśa, paryupasthāna (read with var. paryavasth°); cf. °na-bandhanānuśayopakleśa-paryavasthānānāṃ Bbh 202.20; na °nayā (*by any fetter*) bandhanānuśayaparyavasthāna-vaśagatāḥ Gv 387.3; there are 10, as in Pali (see PTSD, order slightly diff.), listed AbhidhK. LaV-P. v.84 and 87, in two groups (also in Pali), called **avarabhāgīya,** q.v. (viz. satkāyadṛṣṭi, śīlavrataparāmarśa, vicikitsā, kāmacchanda, vyāpāda), and **ūrdhvabhāgīya,** q.v. (viz. rūparāga, ārūpyarāga, auddhatya, māna, avidyā); the first three are also specially listed as three saṃyojana, e. g. Laṅk 117.14 (with vicikitsā as No. 2 and śīlavrata° as 3, as in Pali), for reasons explained AbhidhK. op. cit. 85–87; they are prob. meant by trīṇi °nāṃ (tyaktvā) Mv i.192.7 (vs); trayāṇāṃ °nānāṃ MSV ii.86.11; Divy 534.3; but Divy 533.28 may intend to name rāga, dveṣa, and moha as 3 saṃyojana (but there is prob. a lacuna in text, read as in MSV ii.87.1–2); Divy 533.24–25 also speaks of pañcānām avarabhāgīyānām °nānāṃ prahāṇād, without listing them; same MSV ii.87.7; further, Divy 95.22 knows nine saṃy° (see s.v. **visaṃyojanaka**), which no doubt refers to the nine listed AbhidhK. LaV-P. v. 81 f. (shortly before the place cited above), viz. anunaya, pratigha, māna, avidyā, dṛṣṭi, parāmarśa, vicikitsā, īrṣyā, mātsarya; cf. īrṣyā-mātsarya-°na-saṃprayuktā devamanuṣyā Mv i.350.8.

saṃrajanīya, adj. (= next), *pleasing, causing pleasure*: °ya-vastu-saṃrāgaṃ ca karoti (subject, tṛṣṇā) Dbh 50.7; °yāṃ vividhāṃ kathāṃ vyatisārya (in cliché recorded under next) Karmav 27.1. Should the latter, perhaps also the former, be emended to the usual saṃrañj°? (In Mvy 2941 text saṃrajanīyaḥ, evidently misprint; Index saṃrañj°, and so Mironov, no v.l.).

saṃrañjana, only f. °nī with kathā (= **sārāyaṇīya**, adj., q.v. for discussion; cf. also prec. and next), *pleasing, courteous, friendly*: °nīṃ (vividhāṃ) kathāṃ (vyatisārya, or another ger.) Divy 70.11 etc., see list of passages s.v. **saṃmodana.**

saṃrañjanīya, adj., = prec.: °yaḥ Mvy 2941 (so Index, and Mironov, text misprinted saṃraj°); (tathāgato...) °yāṃ kathāṃ pravartayati LV 416.14; with dharma, as Pali sārāṇīya (see **sārāyaṇīya**) with dhamma, °yaṃ dharmaṃ samādāya vartataḥ (3 dual) Divy 404.15 (the sequel shows that it consists of mutual attentions); °ya-dharmeṣv anuvartanatā Śikṣ 183.17, *conforming to sociable (companionable, pleasing, friendly) principles (of conduct).*

saṃrāgayati, °**geti** (cf. **ārāgayati**, q.v., which = Skt. ārādh°, as this resembles **saṃrādha(ya)ti**; see also **virāgayati**), primarily, *says pleasant things to*; so *thanks*: (Vāsavadattā dṛṣṭasatyā Upaguptaṃ, who had brought her to the truth) saṃrāgayanty uvāca: (there follows a vs, printed as prose) tavānubhāvāt pihitaḥ sughoro hy apāyamārgo ... nirvāṇamārgaś ca mayopalabdhaḥ Divy 355.22.

saṃrādhana (nt.; to next, n. act.), *felicitation*, or *thanks*: °na-vyagrakarāgradeśair Jm 214.21 (vs), (people) *with the ends of their arms (hands) occupied* (i. e. clapping) *in applause* (of either *felicitation* or *thanks*, at the recitation of sacred texts).

saṃrādha(ya)ti, °**dheti** (cf. **saṃrāgayati**), *felicitates*: te dāni rājānaṃ °dhenti (so, or °dhyanti, read °dhanti?, mss.; Senart em. to ārocenti, the reading of i.226.14): lābhā te mahārāja sulabdhā yasya te 'yaṃ mahāpuruṣo kule utpanno Mv ii.29.17, *these* (gods) *now congratulated the king*: *You have won great good fortune, O king, in that this Great Person* (the Bodhisattva) *has been born in your family*; in Mv ii.403.18 Senart reads: bodhisattvo Kālaṃ nāgarājānaṃ (his em. of these words seems necessary) saṃrāgeti (but mss. saṃrādhati, proved essentially right by ii.29.17): evam etaṃ ... mahānāga, adyāhaṃ ... abhisaṃbudhyiṣyaṃ (v.l. °buddhiṣyaṃ).

saṃlakṣaṇā (= Pali sallakkhaṇā), *discernment, consideration*: (cintā katamā? praviveke dharmanidhyānābhiratasya) arthābhyūhanā-°ṇāniścayaḥ Bbh 83.6, *determination, by deduction and consideration, of the meaning* (of dharma).

-saṃlagnikā (to Skt. saṃlagna plus -ka, fem.), (position of) *joining* or *holding together*: na hasta-saṃlagnikayā (antargṛhaṃ pravekṣyāmaḥ, °he niṣatsyāmaḥ) Prāt 531.15, 16 = LaVallée-Poussin, JRAS 1913.844, Stein ms. fragm. 1.1.35, 36; Mvy 8554 = Tib. lag pa mi sbrel, *not with joining of the hands.*

saṃlaptaka, m. (to ppp. of Skt. sam-lap-, plus -ka), *one with whom one holds friendly conversation*(?): Mvy 2712 = Tib. phebs par smra ba, acc. to Das *to ask to come, to invite*; Jä., *to salute*, also *to speak politely*; MSV ii.131.12 saṃlaptakena saṃlaptakasya (as with **ālaptaka**, q.v.); yathāsaṃlaptikayā, adv., *according as* (you have) *a close friend*, MPS 13.8.

[**saṃlambha**, only for **sālambha**, q.v., in Das, Tib. Dict.]

saṃlāpayati, *talks nonsense* or the like (unrecorded in depreciative mg.): °payan vadatīti (*if he says of a preacher, 'he babbles when he talks'*) dharmaṃ pratikṣipati Śikṣ 96.11.

saṃlikhi(n), adj., *given to severe austerities*: °khiś ca bhavaty alpabhāṇḍo 'lpapariṣkāraḥ Bbh 239.11 (prose); Tib. yo byad bsñuṅs pa, see **saṃlekha**; ed. note suggests saṃlekhī, but note AMg. saṃlihaṇa, nt. (n. act.), from the same base.

saṃlikhita, adj. or ppp. (not in Skt. or Pali; = AMg. saṃlihiya, ppp. to the noun saṃlehaṇā = Jain Skt. saṃlekhanā; see prec.; Pali has sallekha = **saṃlekha**, q.v., and °lekhitācāra), *strictly, severely controlled, restricted*: in a cliché describing brahmacaryaṃ, ekānta-saṃlikhitaṃ ... Mv ii.117.17; 140.2; iii.50.10; 214.16; 217.9; 218.5 etc.; of food, nātīsaṃlikhito bhavati Śikṣ 127.19, *he does not limit himself* (in food) *too much*; 128.1, see s.v. **kuśalapakṣa.**

saṃlīyanā (= Pali sallī°; Skt. °yate plus -anā), *timidity, disheartenment* (PTSD wrongly *stolidity*): viśāradaś cāhu tadā prahṛṣṭaḥ °nāṃ sarva vivarjayitvā SP 57.9 (vs); prakāśayet sūtram idaṃ hi loke na cāpi °na (m.c.) tasya kācit 282.4 (vs).

saṃluḍita, ppp.-adj. (Skt. °lulita and °loḍita), in a-saṃ°, *not disarranged* (of hair): (keśāḥ ...) °ḍitāḥ samasadṛśasthānasaṃsthitāḥ Gv 402.14; asaṃluḍitakeśa, v.l. in both edd. for asaṃlul°, Mvy 345 (an **anuvyañjana**).

[**saṃlūṣitā** SP 85.9 (vs), read jvālūṣitā with WT, = jvālā-uṣitā(ḥ).]

saṃlekha, m. (= Pali sallekha; cf. **saṃlikhi**, °**khita**, **sālekhika**), *severe frugality, austerity* (as to the necessities of life): °khaḥ Mvy 7012 = Tib. yo byad bsñuṅs pa; saṃlekha-caritā asme(?) SP 272.4 (vs), or with WT (and their ms.) saṃlekha-vṛtti-cāri sma; °khaṃ mā prabhāṣe tvaṃ Śikṣ 354.12 (vs); dhutaguṇa-°khe 'nuvartana-tā ŚsP 1462.21 (prose).

saṃlobhana or °**nā** (to Skt. sam-lubh- plus -ana), *enticement, seduction*: Māraduhitaro ... bodhisattvasya °nārtham ... abhāṣanta LV 321.17 (prose).

saṃvara, m. (= Pali id.; cf. **a-saṃvara** and **saṃvāra**), (**1**) *restraint, control, obligation, vow*: Mvy 1608 (text erron. saṃvāra); 1632; 7010 (in all these = Tib. sdom pa *restraint, obligation, vow*), 9363 (= Tib. sdom po or sdom ba); LV 159.8 (vs) śīlaguṇa-saṃvaru (n. sg.); 379.14 (prose) saṃvaram (acc.; sc. *from sin*, atyayato) āpadyate; similarly Divy 617.22, 24; Mv i.104.14 deśayanti dama-dāna-saṃvaraṃ (mss. °ra); samātta-saṃvarasya Śikṣ 15.1; prātimokṣa-saṃvara-, *the moral restraints imposed in the code called Prātimokṣa* (= Pali pātimokkhasaṃvara) Mv iii.51.17–52.1; Śikṣ 17.7 (not by this alone can a Bodhisattva attain enlightenment); Bbh 155.26; KP 134.2; Ud xxxii.27 prātimokṣe ca saṃvaraḥ; Mv iii.52.8 (akuśalā dharmāḥ ...) teṣāṃ saṃvarāya: 423.3 ff. cakṣuṣā (śrotreṇa, ghrāṇena, etc.) saṃvaro; śīlasaṃvara- Mv i.143.1; Dbh 96.15; Jm 15.5; saṃvara-śīla-, *morality consisting of s°*, Bbh 138.24; 152.19; KP 103.3 tatra na saṃvaro nāsaṃvaraḥ; Dbh.g. 52(78).30 °raṃ samupācaret; RP 28.12 (vs) śīlaprayoga saṃvarakriyā ca; LV 31.15, 16, 17 kāya-, vāk-, manaḥ-s° (see **saṃbara** 1); (**2**) *rule, prescription* (an extension or specialization of prec., found only in neg. **a-saṃvara**, q.v.); (**3**) (treated as nt. in Divy 111.3, n. sg. °raṃ; the only distinctive occurrence), *provisions* (of food): Divy 110.26 saṃvaraṃ cāropaya; 111.1, 3; Prāt 500.5 piṇḍapāta-saṃvaraṃ (acc.), *provisions for a meal*; (is this mg. also an extension of 1, *regulation, requirement*?); (**4**) n. of an asura: Suv 162.12 (acc. to

Nobel, Tib. seems to suggest reading Śaṃvara; cf. also **Sambara**); (**5**) n. of a hell: Kv 50.4 saṃbare (so printed) mahānarake (read śaṃbare?).

saṃvarṇana, nt., and °**ṇā** (= Pali saṃvaṇṇana; Skt. °ṇa once, BR, *description, narration*), *praise, laudation*: bodhisattva-°naṃ Gv 503.9 (prose); tathāgata-dharmasya . . . °nāṃ karoti SP 34.5 (prose); guṇa-°ṇaṃ nāma doṣāṇāṃ ca nigūhanam Jm 102.2 (vs); karoti °na (acc.; m.c.; could be nt. or f.) SP 220.14 (vs).

saṃvarta (m.? to **saṃvartati** 1), (period of) *devolution, destruction* of the world, with or sc. kalpa: °ta-kāla-samaye Mv i.52.4, by a somewhat doubtful em.; the parallel is vivartanīya-kāla° 6; passage is similar to Mv i.338.14 ff. (see s.v. **vivartati**), where saṃvartamāne . . . loke is read for this; for other passages see s.v. **vivarta.**

saṃvartaka, adj., (**1**) (to **saṃvartati** 1) *world-destroying*: °kā pi vātā Mv i.236.15 = 241.9; so Senart both times, with mss. in 241.9, while in 236.15 mss. °**tanā,** q.v.; (**2**) (to **saṃvartati** 2) *conducive, leading* (*to*, dat.): anarthāyāhitāya °kaṃ bhaviṣyati Laṅk 255.10 (prose).

saṃvartati, °**te** (**1**) (= Pali saṃvaṭṭati) *devolves, comes to destruction*, opp. **vivartati** 2, q.v. for passages; cf. **saṃvarta** and other prec. and foll. items; (**2**) (= Pali saṃvattati, not confused with saṃvaṭṭati), *tends, is conducive* (*to*, dat.): duḥkhakṣayāya °tati Mv i.246.13; abhedyāśayatāyai °tate LV 31.13, similarly 14 ff.; duḥkhāyāhitāya °tante Bbh 7.10; cittasthitaye °tate 188.6, etc.

saṃvartana, (**1**) adj., = **saṃvartaka** (1), q.v : °nā pi vātā, mss., Mv i.236.15 (vs; Senart °kā); (**2**) (to **saṃvartati** 2) subst., and perh. adj., (*the*) *conducing, leading* (*to*, in comp.): atyantasukhasarvajñatābhūmi-°nāya pariṇāmayati Śikṣ 215.5, *develops so as to conduce to . . .*; sarvabodhisattvasaṃbhāra-°na-cittā (Bhvr.) Gv 279.20 (here °na could be transl. as adj. or subst.).

-saṃvartanaka, f. °**ikā,** adj. (cf. prec. and Pali saṃvattanika), *conducive* (*to*, in comp.): upasama-(with mss., for °śama-)-saṃvartanikā (of the madhyamā pratipadā) Mv iii.331.8, 11, 15 (mss. °tikā for °nikā each time).

saṃvartanī, (**1**) (to **saṃvartati** 1; cf. **vivartanī**), (periodic) *destruction* (of the world): tejaḥ-saṃ° Mvy 8285, ap-saṃ° 8286, vāyu-saṃ° 8287; Tib. ḥjig pa, *destruction*; daśadiśaṃ (*in all directions, universal*) ca vāta-°nīṃ tejaḥ-°nīm ap-°nīm adhitiṣṭhati Dbh 91.27; tejaḥ-°nī prādurbhaviṣyati AsP 180.7, repeated below; kalpa-°nyāṃ, loc., Divy 231.14; **bhājana**-saṃ° AbhidhK. LaV-P. iii.181; (**2**) acc. to Tib. (ḥdu ba, *assembling*) and Foucaux, *assembling*: LV 19.10 na bodhisattva ādipravṛtte loke sattva-°nī-kālasamaye mātuḥ kukṣim avakrāmati, *not when the world has just begun to evolve, at the time of assembling of creatures*; this is a meaning which saṃvartanī also has, acc. to LaV-P., AbhidhK. iii.182 note; in LV, however, if we could assume a mistake of Tib., we might render *at the time of world-destruction*, as under 1, this being not identical with ādipravṛtte loke, but another time when the B. *does not enter his mother's womb*; (**3**) (to **saṃvartati** 2; cf. Pali saṃvattanika) *conducive* (*to*; prob. adj.): (dakṣiṇāṃ . . .) svarga-saṃvartanīṃ Divy 229.12, 502.12. See next.

saṃvartanīya, (primarily) adj. (but see below; § 22.20; cf. Pali saṃvattaniya, °ika; also prec. items), *conducive* (*to*, in a cpd., prec. by complement): dharmavyasana-°nīyena karmābhisaṃskāreṇa SP 312.10, *by performance of actions conducive to injury to the Doctrine*; (ānantaryāṇi) narakakarma-°nīyāni karmāṇi Divy 260.8, *deeds which conduce to deeds* (leading to) *hell*; niraya-°yaṃ karma Śikṣ 167.9; (karmāṇi) . . . apāya-°yāni Vaj 34.18; karma alpāyuḥ-°yaṃ Karmav 30.6, and long list of parallels in same ending; sarvajñatā-°yaṃ kuśalamūlam Gv 18.19; (Avalokiteśvarāya . . .) bahuparivāra-°nīyāya Kv 11.15 (*who is conducive to an ample retinue*, sc., for his worshippers?); (dānaṃ dadāti mahātyāgabhoga-vipāka-)-pratilābhasaṃvartanīyaṃ Divy 482.8, *conducive to attaining the fruition of . . .*, and long list of such terms, all ending -vipākapratilābha- (in line 9 lābha omitted by obvious error)-°nīyam, qualifying some kind of dānam; kiṃ asya dārakasya rājñaḥ °nīyāni karmāṇi na veti? paśyati, santi Divy 579.28, *has this boy deeds conducive* (? *conforming, suitable*) *to* (becoming) *a king or not ? he saw, he has*! (and the boy was made king); puṇyābhisaṃskāraṃ prasaved buddhajñāna-°nīyam SP 337.4; here construable as adj. with puṇyābhi°, but seems clearly subst. in (sa kulaputro vā kuladuhitā vā) prasaved buddhajñāna-°nīyam (*what is conducive to Buddha-knowledge*) aprameyam asaṃkhyeyam aparyantam SP 339.11; in absolute use, without indication of complement, °nīyaṃ kuśalamūlam upacinoti Av i.214.1, *he accumulates a root of merit conducive* (to the proper result); seems to be used both as subst. and absolutely, without complement, in Mv ii.111.17, (having lived in pleasure many years in the city of the kiṃnaras with their princess Manoharā,) sarvodyāneṣu °nīyaṃ (one ms. °nīye) anubhavitvā, *having experienced what was 'conducive' (conforming, suitable, to be expected?) in all the parks*, (he said to M.).

saṃvardhaka, m., °ikā (to Skt. saṃvardhayati plus -aka; one questionable occurrence in Skt., see pw), *one who fosters, rears*: sa te . . . kalyāṇamitra-janakas tathāgatakule °kaḥ Gv 528.14; (bodhisattvānāṃ) vīryapāramitā °dhikā Gv 526.4 (both prose); °dhikā (like a mother) also AbhidhK. LaV-P. iv.214.

Saṃvalitā, the verse-equivalent of **Suvalitaratiprabhāsaśrī,** q.v., in the prose story: °tākhyā duhitā Gv 428.4 (vs).

saṃvasana (nt.; to Skt. saṃvasati plus -ana; once in RV only), (*co-*)*habitation, dwelling together* (*with*, or *in*): dīrghordhva-°na-saṃbhavaṃ (adj., *originating in long dwelling in lofty surroundings*) kalyāṇamitropasaṃkramaṇam Gv 242.8; (aparanta-, read °rānta-)-kalpa-bodhisattvacaryā-°nena (*involving, leading to, dwelling* or *association with the course of bodhisattvas of future ages*) kalyāṇamitropasaṃkramaṇena 242.20; (sarvakalpabodhisattvacaryā-)-saṃvāsa-°na-mahāpraṇidhāna- 267.16, *great vow to dwell in association with . . .*; sarvatathāgata-viṣaya-saṃvasanena (adj., *that involves dwelling in the realms of all T.*) . . . °vihāreṇa 533.6.

-saṃvācaka, adj., and °**cikā,** subst. f., (to Skt. saṃ-vac- plus -aka, -ikā), in hasta-saṃ°, *'talking with the hands'*, by signs (by or to the deaf): °cakaḥ (presumably personal) Mvy 7685 = Tib. lag brdaḥ byed pa, *making hand signs* (follows **eḍamūka,** q.v.); °cikā, subst. (the process), badhirāṃ °cikayārthaṃ grāhayati Bbh 145.6, *by hand-conversation he makes the deaf understand the meaning.*

[**saṃvācya,** corrupt, Divy 70.1; acc. to Index *having lived among*, but read some synonym of gatvā 73.15; perh. saṃcarya? The two passages are pratically identical: (vinipātaṃ na) gamiṣyati, kiṃ tarhi (73.15 tu) devāṃś ca manuṣyāṃś ca saṃvācya (73.15 gatvā) saṃsṛtya (70.1 mss. saṃvṛtya) paścime bhave (73.15 om. pa° bhave) paścime nikete . . . pratyekabuddho bhaviṣyati. Mr. D. R. S. Bailey informs me that Tib. reads in 70.1 mtshams sbyar ciṅ ḥkhor nas, normally = pratisaṃdhiṃ gṛhītvā saṃsṛtya (preceded by loc.), and in 73.15 the same preceded by ñiṅ, for the two gerunds.]

saṃvāra-, = **saṃvara**: Mvy 1608; so also Mironov; see s.v. **tāpa.**

saṃvāsana (nt.), some kind of medical treatment, perh. *fumigation* (lit. *perfuming*): . . . (snapanaṃ) °sanaṃ saṃvardhanaṃ varṇapariśodhanaṃ balasaṃjananaṃ prajānāmi Gv 152.11.

-saṃvāsika (in Pali °saka, or °sa), see **a-, nānā-, samāna-, steya-saṃ°**; also = **samāna-saṃvāsika,** q.v.: ātmānaṃ saṃvāsikaṃ sthāpayati MSV ii.179.7.

-saṃvāsya, see **a-saṃ°.**

saṃvāhita (nt.; orig. ppp. of Skt. saṃvāhayati), one of the arts mastered by the Bodhisattva as prince: ... mālyagranthane °hite maṇirāge ... LV 156.16. Skt. saṃvāhana suggests *shampooing*; but acc. to Tib. rluṅ yab gyob pa, *waving of fans*.

saṃvidyate (= Pali saṃvijjati = Skt. vidyate; pw is not justified in saying 'esp. in questions and with neg.'), *is found, exists*; often virtually = asti: saṃvidyayanta (= °dyante, § 38.21) ima āsana LV 115.9 (vs); saṃvidyanta (read so, transposing daṇḍa before this) imāny ... atiriktāny āsanāni, saced ākāṅkṣasi, niṣīda 408.4; mātṛgrāmo 'saṃvidyamāna-guṇo 'pi 141.9, *even when no virtues exist* (in them); puṇyasaṃbhāro na °te Kv 52.20; ko 'smākaṃ upāyaḥ °te 53.18; sthānam etan na °te LV 215.19, *that's out of the question, that can't be*; with gen., like asti, = ... *has*: yasyā ete guṇāḥ °yante LV 139.19, *who possesses these qualities*; (prabhūtaṃ me ... koṣṭhāgāraṃ) °te SP 102.11, *I have abundant* ...; (na ca me) ... kiṃcit °te Kv 43.21; na cāsmākaṃ svāmī °te Kv 45.15, *and we have no husband*.

saṃvimaṭṭha, ppp. (= Skt. *saṃvimṛṣṭa, cf. Pali vimaṭṭha), *touched, mingled*: svarṇaṃ yathā musaragalvaya (Susa's em., mss. **musāragalva-**, q.v., unmetr.; °vaya would imply an instr. sg. fem., °vayā, but no such gender occurs for the word; perh. read °lvaka, with -ka svārthe) saṃvimaṭṭhaṃ (so read with Rahder; Susa's mss. °māṣṭhaṃ; Susa em. °mṛṣṭaṃ) Dbh.g. 22(358).19.

saṃviśvasta, ppp. (of Skt. *sam-vi-śvas-), *completely put at ease* or *trusting*: yadā jānetsuḥ tā rākṣasīyo, saṃviśvastā ime vāṇijakā asmābhir iti Mv iii.70.17.

saṃviheṭhayati (sam plus vihe°), *injures*: (nāgarājā ...) mahābalo taṃ (better than Senart's so; one ms. lacks the syllable, the other reads va) ca na °ṭhaye (v.l. °ṭhayo; Senart em. °ṭhyo, as if gerundive; jagatī meter) Mv ii.183.22 (vs), *and I will not injure him*.

saṃvṛta, ppp. (of Skt. sam-vṛ-), (**1**) of a door, *narrow* (so Burnouf, Chin., and Tib. dog; Kern, *shut*): idaṃ khalu niveśanam ekapraveśaṃ saṃvṛta-dvāram eva SP 73.3; (**2**) (= Pali saṃvuta) *restrained, controlled*: °ta āyatanaiḥ Mvy 399 = Tib. skye mched rnams bsdams pa (to sdom pa, used for **saṃvara**, q.v.), *controlled as to the senses* (**āyatana** 5); not *by the senses*; we might expect loc., but the instr. may be influenced by the surrounding phrases (visaṃyukto dhātubhiḥ, pracchinno granthaiḥ, vimuktaḥ paridāghaiḥ, etc.) where it seems more appropriate.

Saṃvṛtaskandha, n. of two former Buddhas: Mv iii.230.16; Gv 360.24 (in otherwise quite different lists).

saṃvṛti, f., (**1**) in the sense of **saṃvara** (1), noted only Sūtrāl. iv.4 śīla-°tiḥ; (**2**) (= Pali saṃmuti; see also **sāṃvṛta**), *convention, general (popular) acceptance* or *belief*; *'common sense'*; *conditioned, exoteric, dependent, limited truth* or *knowledge*, often in contrast with paramārtha (so also in Pali, e. g. Miln. 160.1 saṃmuti mahārāja esā, ahan-ti mamāti, na paramattho eso); Tib. regularly kun rdzob, *altogether void*; may have been etym. understood sometimes as *covering*, but I have found no clear evidence for this (which is Bendall and Rouse's rendering, e. g. p. 236, on Śikṣ 256.4, 5) and believe it misleading; Pali saṃmuti suggests the true etym. (root man); cf. under (3) below: yāḥ kāścana saṃvṛtayo hi loke, sarvā hi tā munir nopaiti Bbh 48.24 (vs, metr. deficient) = Pali Sn 897, reading sammutiyo; defined Bbh 49.(3–)5 as *verbal symbols* (**prajñapti** 4, q.v. for citation, as also for Śikṣ 257.7–8 where saṃvṛti = nāmadheya, saṃketa, prajñapti); (laukikānāṃ ... yasmin vastuni saṃketa-)-saṃvṛti-saṃstavanāgamapraviṣṭayā buddhyā darśanatulyatā bhavati, tad yathā pṛthivyāṃ, pṛthivy eveyaṃ nāgnir iti Bbh 37.9; saṃvṛtyā deśanā Laṅk 25.4; 33.5, *instruction according to 'common sense'*; °ti-jñānam Mvy 1237 (et al., see **jñāna**), *common-sense knowledge*, = Pali saṃmuti-ñāṇa, the fourth of four kinds of knowledge (as also in Mvy), DN iii.226, last line, expl. comm. iii.1020.15 ff. as any other kind of knowledge than the first three; asti saṃvṛtyā cakṣuḥ Śikṣ 357.11, *the eye exists* (only) *in terms of limited, exoteric* (common-sense) *truth*; similarly 358.19; saṃvṛti-vyavahāreṇa Sukh 42.11, *by conventional terminology* or *exoteric* (not fundamentally true) *manner of speaking*; saṃvṛti-paramārthataḥ Śikṣ 2.8, (*knowing*) *both as to exoteric and esoteric truth*; etāvac caitat jñeyam, yad uta saṃvṛtiḥ paramārthaś ca. tac ca Bhagavatā śūnyataḥ sudṛṣṭaṃ ... tatra saṃvṛtir lokapracāratas (*because it is*, or, *as that which is, current in the world*) Tathāgatena dṛṣṭā; yaḥ punaḥ paramārthaḥ so 'nabhilāpyaḥ Śikṣ 256.4; katham anadhiṣṭhānā saṃvṛtir yuktā, katham punar ayuktā? yathā sati (text 'sati) sthāṇau puruṣabhrāntiḥ; kasya punaḥ śūnyatāvādinaḥ paramārthataḥ sthāṇuḥ siddho, yadāśrayāt puruṣabhrāntiḥ syād? Śikṣ 264.3 (Bendall and Rouse completely wrong), *how may common-sense, which is without any sound basis, be right, and how on the other hand wrong? As, given a post, the delusion* (occurs) *that it is a man. But how, for one who believes in voidness, can in real* (*esoteric*) *truth the post be a fact, on the basis of which the delusion that it is a man might arise*?; saṃvṛti-satya, *common-sense truth*, contrasted with paramārtha-s°, Mvy 6545 (Tib. kun rdzob kyi bden pa); Dharmas 95 (dve satye); Bbh 292.18 (dvividhaṃ satyam; but 17 has just said, avitathārthena tāvad ekam eva satyaṃ, na dvitīyam asti; this, of course, is paramārtha-s°); Bhad 6[3]; the cpd. sammuti-sacca is cited from a late Pali text in Childers, and from Miln. 160(.1) by PTSD, but this last is an error (does the cpd. occur in older Pali?); saṃvṛti-saṃgha, MSV iii.116.19; 117.1, defined as one in which all members are **pṛthagjana-kalyāṇaka**, q.v., and in which (117.4) it is possible that a rite may be performed incorrectly in all innocence, hence *conditioned assembly* (of monks), where intentions are good but not necessarily results; (**3**) *consent* in the sense of a formal vote (of the saṃgha): yāni punas tāni (kulāni) śaikṣa-saṃvṛti-saṃmatāni ... Prāt 526.3, *families which have been held by formal declaration to be śaikṣa*; so Chin.; note association of saṃvṛti with saṃmata (etym.!); samagreṇa ca bhikṣuṇīsaṃghena avandanārha-saṃvṛtyā saṃmataḥ Bhīk 28b.4 *and* (an expelled monk) *who by the entire congregation of nuns has been judged by formal vote that he is unworthy to be saluted*; does Pali saṃmuti have this mg.? for such passages as Vin. iii.199.26 bhikkhu-saṃmutiyā the Dictt. and Transl. give *by permission of the* (order of) *monks*, which here at least is possible; this, rather than *vote* (but the saṃgha did in fact vote on the question!), may be the meaning in brahmacaryopasthāna-saṃvṛtiṃ yācitavyā Bhīk 17b.1, *she must be made to ask for permission* (or, *for a vote*, sc. that she be allowed) *to enter the religious life*; so, āryikā-saṃghāt °tiṃ yāce ib. 2, (the initiate says) *I ask* (this) *permission* (or *vote*) *from the assembly of venerable nuns*. Both Prat 526.3 and Bhīk 28b.4 associate saṃvṛti (Pali saṃmuti) with saṃmata, suggesting that °vṛti is hyper-Skt. for Pali °muti.

saṃvṛtta, ppp.-adj. (also, but erroneously, written saṃvṛta), *rounded*, in su-saṃvṛtta-skandha, *with well-rounded shoulders*, the 20th **lakṣaṇa** (q.v.): Mvy 249 (Tib. śin tu zlum pa, *well-rounded*), etc.; Pali sama-vatta-.

Saṃvṛttateja(s), n. of a former Buddha: Mv i.140.7.

[**saṃvega**, nt. (Skt. only m.), *perturbation*: mahāntaṃ saṃvegam (nom. sg.) utpannaṃ Mv ii.45.8; but mss. vegaṃ, Senart em.; vega, also, is only m. in Skt.]

Saṃvegadhāriṇī, n. of a kiṃnara maid: Kv 6.18.

saṃvejanīya, gdve. (= Pali id., to saṃvejeti, see next two), *to be shuddered at*: °yaṃ sthānam Divy 432.16; °yāṃ ... dharmyāṃ kathāṃ Jm 110.19.

saṃvejayitavya, gdve., = prec.: MSV iii.63.7.

saṃvejita, ppp. (= Pali id., to saṃvejeti; caus. not in Skt.), *agitated*: °ta-mānaso LV 209.11 (prose). Cf. prec. two.

-saṃvedin, adj. (to Skt. saṃveda, or to saṃvedayati or saṃvetti), *being aware of, experiencing*: Vītaśokasya ... vimuktiprītisukha-°naḥ Divy 424.26.

saṃvedhati (cf. **vedhati** and Skt. saṃ-vyath-; Pali ppp. saṃvedhita), *shakes (severely)*, intrans.: mahāpṛthivī ... vedhe saṃvedhe (so mss., Senart em. pravedhe; aor.) saṃpravedhe Mv iii.341.5; the mss. of Mv supported by (lokadhātuḥ ...) vedhati saṃvedhati saṃpravedhati Divy 479.11.

saṃvyavahārate (= Pali saṃvohār°; prob. denom. to Pali saṃvohāra, Skt. saṃvyavahāra), *carries on business*: baṇigdharmaṇā °ramāṇaḥ Divy 259.10 (cf. Pali AN ii.188.10). See next.

saṃvyavahārin, adj. (to Skt. °ra plus -in, or to prec.), *carrying on business*: (mahāsamudre) pota-°riṇa āsan Divy 499.3; 501.11 (here text °saṃhāriṇa, certainly corruption for °saṃvyava°), 14, 17.

saṃśabdita, ppp. (of Skt. °bdayati, used like Skt. śabdyate, *is named, is called by name*; Mbh. Calc. 1.3215 ayam ehīti saṃśabdya means *calling him by name with the words, Come, so-and-so!*; but, to be sure, the true reading is śabdena, Crit. ed. 1.71.30), *named, called by name*: yena nāmnā °taṃ bhavati buddhakṣetraṃ Bbh 59.27; (tathāgatagarbho, line 9) ālayavijñāna-°dito Laṅk 220.14, *as called by the name ālayavi°*; (cittacaittakalāpo) vikalpa-°ditaḥ pravartamānaḥ Laṅk 150.15, *(mind and the mass of mental things,) being called by* (that) *name thru false discrimination* ...

saṃśamaka, adj. (Skt. °mayati plus -aka), *allaying, pacifying* (plagues): upadravopasarga-°kāni mantrapadāni Bbh 20.10; -upadrava-°kānāṃ ... mantrāṇāṃ 209.19.

saṃśaya, nt. (regularly m.), *doubt*: dharma-°yaṃ (n. sg.) chinnaṃ Mv i.247.15.

[**saṃśayālu,** by Nobel's em., assumed to be adj. to saṃśaya, *doubtful*: Suv 215.11 (vs); better read, substantially with best ms., (sudurbalā, with ms. F?) matir iva saṃśayo 'tra me.]

saṃśīlika (cf. Skt. saṃśīlana, and śīlayati), *associate, companion*, in monkish life: tatra dvau bhikṣū °likau Av ii.150.1, and taṃ °lika-bhikṣuṃ 4; so Speyer's plausible em., ms. °śītika, which seems senseless; Tib. mdzaḥ, *friend*.

Saṃśuddha, n. of a Bodhisattva: Mmk 42.5.

? **saṃśṛkhalā,** or °**la** (if correct, related to Skt. śṛṅkhalā, °la, *chain*, with loss of nasal m.c.; some mss. °śṛṅkh°, many with Calc. om. saṃ, both unmetr.), *chain*, as an ornament: maṇihāramuktahārāṃ mukhapuṣpake (final short!) ardhacandra °lāḥ LV 201.19 (vs); text uncertain; Tib. (Foucaux) seṅ ge (*lion*) śiṅ lo (*tree-leaf*) ris (*form*); or does Tib. confusedly represent an attempt at transliteration?

saṃśoṣaka, adj. (to Skt. °ṣayati plus -aka), *drying up* (trans.), fig. *destroying* (misery): -duḥkha-°kaḥ Suv 65.2 (prose).

saṃśrāvitaka, m. = **śrāv°**, q.v.: ye cāpi °kā tadāsī te śrāvakā teṣa jināna sarve SP 195.1 (vs).

(**saṃśleṣayati,** prob. *an sich heranziehen*, as in Skt., BR s.v. śliṣ with sam, caus., 3: evaṃ ca taṃ bhartsiya (so read with v.l. and WT) tasmi kāle °yet taṃ punar eva paṇḍitaḥ SP 114.9 (vs), *and thus* (the father) *having scolded him* (the son) *at that time, he yet again would attach him to himself skillfully*; Burnouf *embrace*; Kern *conciliate*; Tib. rab tu dkris, a lit. rendering, *completely enwrap*.)

saṃsaktaka, adj. (to Skt. °kta plus -ka, perh. pej.), (*wretchedly* ?) *enmeshed, entangled*: vanagahanajāla-°kānām apy ahaṃ sattvānāṃ ... samyag-gamana-(text °namana-)-patha-darśayitrī bhavāmi Gv 226.25 (-227.3; prose).

saṃsati (MIndic for Skt. sraṃs°; only noted Lex. and Gr. in Pkt., not in Pali), *falls away*: na ca vīryāta (so read) saṃsati Mv ii.232.14, 18 (vs), *and he does not fall away from his heroic stand* (in practising austerities); missed by Senart.

saṃsarin, adj. (m.c. for Skt. °sārin), *involved in the round of rebirths*: saṃsāre bahukāla-saṃsarī (n. pl.; no v.l.) duḥkhamūle (read dukha°) LV 324.17 (vs).

saṃsādana (nt.; n. act. in -ana to Pali saṃsādeti, *leaves unanswered*, so not only AN iv.398.14 but also MN i.214.26 and AN i.288.20, which PTSD defines wrongly; opp. of vissajjeti, *answers* a question), *'letting drop', leaving unanswered* (a question): praśna-°nena Bbh 151.22.

saṃsādayati (caus. of saṃ-sad-), *fells, strikes down*: (sc. vanamṛgān) saṃsādya (ger.) ... vyāghrāḥ ... Jm 229.24 (vs).

Saṃsāra, n. of a householder's son of Śrāvastī: Av ii.161.13 ff.

saṃsārika, adj. (= AMg. saṃsāriya: MIndic, or possibly error, for Skt. sāṃ°), *relating to the round of rebirths*: -°ka-citta- Gv 466.19 (prose).

Saṃsārottaraṇa, n. of a future Pratyekabuddha: Av i.152.10.

saṃsīdana (nt.), or °**nā** (= Pali °na; formed like **utsīdana,** q.v.), *sinking*: Divy 229.23 (of a ship) jale °na-bhayam; Gv 188.11 sarvasaṃsārasaṃsīdanabhayāni (sc. sattvānām); Gv 279.15, understand a-saṃ°, (anivartya-cittā-)-saṃsīdanacittā, *with mind not characterized by sinking*; AsP 289.4 kā ... bodhisattvasyāntarā vyadhvani saṃsīdanā; 336.14 nāpy asya °nā bhavati.

Saṃsṛṣṭa, n. of a mountain: °ṭa-mahāsaṃsṛṣṭau, dual dvandva, Kv 91.13.

saṃskāra, m. (= Pali saṃkhāra; both mgs. clearly foreshadowed in Skt., but here technically specialized), **(1)** usually pl., *predisposition(s)*, the effect of past deeds and experience as conditioning a new state: the fourth of the **(upādāna-)skandha,** qq.v., and the second item in the **pratītya-samutpāda,** q.v. (arising from avidyā, and cause of vijñāna); all as in Pali; for a brief and illuminating statement see Lévi, Sūtrāl. v.8 note 1; Skt. uses the word in virtually the same mg., BR s.v. 5; saṃskāra-duḥkhatā, see **duḥkhatā**; saṃskārahetu dadate na ca saṃkramo 'sti, vijñānam udbhavati saṃkramaṇaṃ pratītya LV 419.19–20 (vss), *it* (sc. avidyā, in prec. line) *furnishes the cause for the predisposition(s) and so* (once avidyā is gone) *there is no transmigration*; **vijñāna** (the next link after saṃskāra) *arises* (only) *in dependence on transmigration*; **(2)** pl., *conditionings, conditioned states*, which means collectively the **dharma** (4) or *states of* (normal, sentient) *being*, cf. **saṃskṛta**: sarvasaṃskārā anityāḥ (as in Pali, CPD s.v. anicca) sarvasaṃskārā duḥkhā sarvadharmā anātmānaḥ Mv ii.285.18–19; kathaṃ ca bodhisattvaḥ sarva-°rāṃ anityataḥ samanupaśyati Bbh 277.16 (and ff.); viraktaḥ sarva-°reṣu sarva-°ra-vītikramaṃ prāpayiṣyāmi Mv ii.279.19; sarva-°rāṇām ... prahāṇāt prahāṇadhātur ity ucyate, sarva-°rāṇāṃ virāgād virāgadhātur ... Av ii.141.3 (see **dhātu** 4); jīvita-°rān adhiṣṭhāya āyuḥ-°rān utsraṣṭum ārabdhaḥ Divy 203.7, *mastering, holding firmly, the conditionings of his life, he set about to renounce the conditionings of long-life*, i. e. he determined not to enter nirvāṇa immediately, but to do so after three months, which would give him time to complete his necessary tasks; see AbhidhK. LaV-P. ii.122 ff. (the term of three months, 124; so also Pali); Pali DN ii.99.10 (after statement of his reasons) jīvita-saṃkhāraṃ adhiṭṭhāya vihareyyaṃ; comm. ii.547.5 ff. °raṃ ti, ettha jīvitam pi jīvitasaṅkhāro, yena jīvitaṃ saṅkharīyati, chijjamānaṃ ghaṭetvā ṭhapīyati; yo phalasamāpatti dhammo pi jīvitasaṅkhāro, so idha adhippeto; adhiṭṭhāyā ti adhitiṭṭhitvā pavattetvā jīvitā-(read °ta-?)-ṭhapanasamatthaṃ phalasamāpattiṃ samāpajjeyyan ti, ayam ettha saṅkhepattho; āyuḥsaṃskāra, *conditionings of long-life*, only as obj. of utsṛjati as Pali āyusaṃkhāra ('usually pl.', PTSD) of ossa(j)jati; °rān utsṛjati Mvy 6454; °ram (text with 2 mss., read °rāṃ = °rān with 4 mss.) utsṛjantānāṃ (sc. Buddhānāṃ; pūrvā koṭī na prajñāyate) Mv i.125.19 (vs; next line, nirvāyantānāṃ, mss. °vāpaya°, vīrāṇāṃ p° k° na pra°); bhava-saṃskāra = āyuḥ-saṃ°; bhava-°ram apotsṛjan muniḥ Divy 203.16 (vs), after samanantarotsṛṣṭesv āyuḥ-°reṣu 10, which follows 203.7 above; same vs (also following āyusaṃkhāraṃ ossajji) in Pali Ud. 64.29 bhavasaṃkhāraṃ avassajji muni; [in LV 262.18 (vs) text lābhaślokau ca saṃskārau (most mss. °ro), but read (Skt.) satkāro = Pali sakkāra, *honor*, with same vs in Pali Sn 438, supported by Tib. bkur sti = satkāra; cf. also lābha-satkāra-śloka Mvy 183.]

saṃskṛta, ppp. (Skt. id., Pali saṃkhata), in the special sense belonging to **saṃskāra** (2), *conditioned*; in nt. substantially = saṃskāra (2): dṛṣṭijālaṃ uddharī °tātaḥ LV 195.12 (vs), *thou hast* (wilt have) *removed the net of wrong views from the conditioned* (state of existence); similarly 196.2 (vs); see **anarthika** for LV 180.12; tāny etāni catvāry api °ta-lakṣaṇāny abhisamasya saṃskārāṇāṃ samāsato dvayāvasthā-prabhāvitāni Bbh 278.25; Gv 496.6, see s.v. **avacara**; the Buddha's doctrine (dharma) is a-saṃskṛtaḥ (*unconditioned*) ṣaḍviṣayasamatikrāntaḥ LV 392.13 (prose); prāpto mi dharmo hy amṛto 'saṃskṛtaḥ (read with v.l. asaṃ-, m.c.) 393.1 (vs); uncertain, kalpākoṭī saṃskṛtā me anantā, bodhīmārgo śodhito me praṇītaḥ LV 196.7 (vs), shortly after 196.2 (above), but here Tib. ḥkhor bar (= saṃskṛtā; this Tib. word regularly = saṃsāra! whereas saṃskṛta is ḥdus byas in LV 195.12 and 196.2, as regularly, Mvy 940, 2187 etc., cf. ḥdu byed = **saṃskāra**; Foucaux for Tib. ... *kalpas d'une vie émigrante*, for BHS ... *kalpas dans le monde de la transmigration*, following Tib., and suggesting em. to saṃsṛtā in his Notes 144, where he cites a v.l. saṃbhṛtā) bskal pa bye ba mthaḥ yas su, *during endless crores of kalpas in succession*? did saṃskṛtā here mean *conditioned* = *in the conditioned state of life*, as in line 2 above? or perhaps *complete(d)*?; applied to samādhi and the like as taught by the imperfect teacher Rudraka, °tānāṃ sāśravāṇāṃ ... dhyānasamādhi-samāpattīnāṃ LV 244.2, and °ta-samādhīnām (asāratām upadarśayeyam) 7, in contrast with the Bodhisattva's own samādhi (sva-samādhi-guṇaviśeṣodbhāvanārthaṃ, 6); in this context *conditioned* (by the sentient world), *not absolute*, as perhaps in LV 196.7 above.

saṃstaraka, m., or °**rika**, only in tṛṇa-saṃ° (= Pali tiṇa-saṃtharaka; cf. Skt. saṃstara), *mat* or *bed* (*of grass*): eṣa te duhitus °rakaḥ Divy 517.8; °rake (v.l. °rike) niṣaṇṇo Mv iii.272.18; °rakaṃ upaviśetsuḥ 269.1, 12; bhūmyāṃ °rike śayitavyaṃ 264.8, or ... śayati 265.1.

saṃstaraṇaka, adj., in tṛṇa-saṃ° (cf. prec. and Skt. saṃstaraṇa; Pali saṃtharaṇaka-vāta), *occupied with strewing* or *laying a* (*grass*) *bed*: adrākṣīn Mākandikaḥ ... Bhagavantaṃ °ṇakaṃ Divy 517.6 (prose).

saṃstavana (nt.; = Pali saṃthavana; Skt. saṃstava), *intimate acquaintance*, *familiarity*: Bbh 37.9, cited s.v. **saṃvṛti**.

(**saṃstuta**, m., = Skt. as adj., *intimate acquaintance*, e. g. SP 346.1 ... jñāter vā saṃmodikasya (so read, see s.v.) vānyasya vā saṃstutasya kasyacit; so interpret, with Kern, SP 3.1 bahubuddhaśatasahasrasaṃstutair (Bodhisattvaiḥ), *who had been intimate with many ... Buddhas*; Burnouf, *praised by* ...; cf. also next.)

saṃstutaka, m., and °**ikā** (= prec. plus, perhaps, specifying -ka), (*one who is*) *an intimate acquaintance*, *friend*: °takaḥ Mvy 2713 = Tib. smos (ḥ)drin, which prob. read for smon (ḥ)drin in both Jä. and Das; in a chapter headed mitrakāryam; MSV ii.131.12; fem., of daughters of Māra, sukhakāraṇa devanarāṇa su-saṃtutikāḥ (see this; v.l. °saṃstu°) LV 322.2 (vs), here prob. endearing dim. -ka; (dve dārake) anyonya-°tike kṣatriyadārikā brāhmaṇadārikā ca Divy 541.12 (prose); yathāsaṃstutikayā, adv., *according as* (you have) *an intimate*, MPS 13.8.

[**saṃstuva**, indicated by most mss. at Mv i.120.9, read prob. saṃstava; see s.v. **saṃbhuva**.]

saṃstūpa, m. (otherwise recorded only Gobh.GS. i.4.11, *Kehrichthaufen* acc. to comm., but Knauer reads sastūpaṃ and considers the word prob. corrupt; prob. related to stūpa in some way), *collection*, *conglomeration*: abhinnaḥ °paḥ (ep. of the Buddha's dharma) Mvy 1300, *a close-knit mass*, = Tib. mi mthun pa med ciṅ (= abhinna) ḥdus pa daṅ ldan pa.

saṃsthāgāra, m. (= Pali saṃthā°; the noun saṃsthā does not seem to occur in an appropriate mg.), *assembly hall*, *hall of meeting*: (Śākyānāṃ) °ram upasaṃkrāntāḥ Mv i.354.19; (Śuddhodano...) Śākyagaṇena sārdhaṃ °re niṣaṇṇo 'bhūt LV 136.11; in LV 141.17 ff. the girls who are candidates for marriage with the Bodhisattva assemble there, while (18) Bodhisattvaḥ °ram upasaṃkramya bhadrāsane nyaṣīdat; in 142.2, 9 yena °ro ... tenopasaṃkrāman (°mat; text in 2 tenopā°); °re MSV i.62.2 (upāsakas gathered in it); ii.186.12 (laymen of Kauśāmbī).

saṃsthāpana (nt.; cf. Skt. id.), *determination*, *definition*, *establishment* (of the Doctrine); Burnouf, *démonstration* (good!); Kern, *exhortation* (less likely): °naṃ kurvati Śākyasiṃho bhāṣiṣyate dharmasvabhāvamudrām SP 28.8 (vs). Tib. yaṅ dag ḥjog, *complete arrangement*.

saṃsthita, nt. (in Skt. as ppp., and cited once as n., *form*, in pw from Mbh. but prob. false reading; Crit ed. 5.168.2 pūrva-saṃsthitim, v.l. °tam; acc. to Sheth, Pkt. saṃṭhia, *form*), *condition*, *state of existence*: sukhenti sarvasattvānāṃ °tāni nareśvarāḥ Mv i.91.8 (vs), *make the conditions* (of life) *of all creatures happy*.

-saṃsthitaka, adj. (= Skt. °ta) ifc., *formed*, *fashioned*: prakṛtisvabhāva-sa° Mv iii.65.5 (prose). Cf. next.

-saṃsthitikā, Bhvr. adj. f. (Skt. saṃsthiti plus -ka, or f. to °ta plus -ka, cf. prec.; with endearing dim. connotation), in su-saṃ°, *of fair form*: vaya (daughters of Māra) ... su-saṃsthitikāḥ LV 322.1 (vs).

saṃsthihati (= **saṃtiṣṭhate**, q.v.

saṃspariśa (= Skt. °sparśa; cf. **spariśa** and AMg. saṃpharisaṇa), *touch*, *contact*: °śena yeṣām ārogatāṃ ... yānti Gv 414.4 (vs, m.c.).

saṃspṛśati (cf. Pkt. saṃphusiya, *wiped away*, clearly ppp. to this verb, altho it is not otherwise recorded in this mg. and Sheth derives the Pkt. from saṃmṛṣṭa, implausibly), *wipes away*, *removes* (?), or perh. (as in Skt.) *comes in contact with*, or (BR s.v. 6) *masters*, *gets the better of*: mitreṣu (6 putreṣu) ādīnavaṃ (read °va, with mss. in 6, both times) saṃspṛśanto eko care khaḍgaviṣāṇakalpo Mv i.359.2, 6 (vss); so mss., both times, surely to be kept (Senart em. saṃmṛśanto, perhaps because of Pali Sn 69 saṃmasitā; but the two verses are otherwise quite different); the preceding, closely parallel vss have vijugupsamāno (viji°, tu ju°); translate, *wiping away* (*removing*), or *coming in contact with*, or *overcoming*, *the evil* (that resides) *in friends* (*sons*), *one should* ...; the first seems most likely.

saṃsphārayati, *diffuses* (light): ger. saṃsphārya Sādh 33.2 (vs; raktaraśmīn); 68.9 (prose; raśmimeghān).

saṃsyandati, °**te** (Pali saṃsandati, caus. °deti, is similarly used, but Skt. only in lit. mg., *flows together*, *unites*), *agrees* (*congruere*, Speyer), with instr.: (arthenārthaḥ padena padaṃ vyañjanena vyañjanaṃ) °date sameti Av ii.142.17; 143.6; (bahujanena te, sc. dṛṣṭiḥ) ... (na, added by em.) °diṣyati 188.4 (em. supported by Tib.); dhātutaḥ sattvā(ḥ) °danta iti MSV ii.137.16, *creatures agree according to their dispositions* (see **dhātu** 4); caus. °dayati, *brings into association* (in, loc.), or *into agreement* (with, instr.): taṃ sarvaṃ prajñāpāramitāyāṃ °dayati, yāni ca laukikāni śilpasthāna-karmasthānāni tāni sarvāṇi prajñāpāramitām āgamya (q.v.) dharmatayā °dayati AsP 327.16, 18, *all that he unifies in the pra°*, *and ... these*, *owing to the pra°*, *he reconciles* (brings into agreement) *with the standard*.

saṃsyandana, nt. (to prec. plus -ana; Pali samsandanā), *agreement*: sūtrādi-°naṃ buddhavacanatve hetur Bcṭ. 285.17.

saṃsvinna, ppp. (of saṃ-svid-, cf. AMg. saṃseyai; Skt. caus. saṃsvedayati, *makes sweat*, and cf. saṃsveda-ja, BR), *moistened, softened* (by boiling): tāṃ pakvamātrā saṃsvinnā (all mss.; cf. prec. line pacyanti; Senart em. saṃkhinnā, which does not fit) khādenti (mss. °tā) sunakhā bahu Mv i.15.1 (vs).

saṃharati, in Mmk 57.1 (iha janmani, see **janman**) saṃhartavyaḥ, acc. to Lalou, Iconographie, 21, *cela doit être accepté*, which is certainly wrong; prob. *to be drawn back, withdrawn* (because of an evil omen); acc. to Tib. brtul par bya (zhiṅ), *perform expiation*.

saṃharṣaka, adj. or subst. m. (to Skt. caus. of saṃ-hṛṣ- plus -aka), *delighting, one who causes joy*: catasṛṇāṃ parṣadāṃ °kaḥ (WT saṃdarśakaḥ with one Nep. ms. of KN; Tib. does not support them) SP 200.4 (prose); °kaś cā akilāsi nityaṃ 204.10 (vs; no v.l.).

saṃharṣaṇā (n. act. in -anā, see prec.), *a gladdening*: (teṣāṃ ... vaṇijānāṃ) imāṃ saṃharṣaṇāṃ akārṣīt LV 387.11 (prose), *made the following gladdening of those merchants* (by gāthās now cited).

saṃharṣaṇīya, adj. (gdve. to Skt. saṃ-hṛṣ-, or to prec. plus -īya), *joyful*; adv. °yaṃ, *joyfully, in a way to cause joy*: (mahāpṛthivī...) °yaṃ ca kampe Mv i.206.16, or (same with) kampayati ii.10.10; iii.341.6, *the earth quaked in a joy-causing manner*.

saṃhāta (m.; = Skt. or BHS saṃghāta, as such in Skt. but not in mg. 2; § 2.35; not recorded in MIndic), (**1**) *mass, collection*: (Jīvakena vaidyarājena...) bhaiṣajyataru-saṃhāta-mayaṃ dārikārūpaṃ kṛtaṃ Śikṣ 159.9; sarvaratnayamaka-saṃhāto (Bhvr. adj., with kūṭāgāro 14) Gv 6.17; (**2**) in acchaṭā-°ta, = **acchaṭā-**(q.v.)-**saṃghāta**: ekācchaṭā-°ta-mātram api Śikṣ 214.11, *for a single snap of the fingers* (*jiffy, trice*).

saṃhārāpayitavya, gdve. (to caus. of *saṃhārayati, MIndic for saṃbhārayati, denom., *collects, gathers*; see § 38.57), *to be caused to be gathered*: (dhānyajātāni...) khalahāneṣu (q.v.) °tavyāni Mv iii.178.5 (prose).

[**saṃhārin**, Divy 501.11, error for **saṃvyavahārin**, q.v.]

sakara adj. = Skt. sakala, *all*: ... bhavet sakara iya mahī LV 122.17 (vs), *this whole earth would be...*; only one ms. with Calc. sakala.

sa-karaṇīya, adj. (= Pali id.), *with duties still to be performed*: aṣṭāham evābhūṣi śaikṣo °ṇīyo, navame (sc. *day*) yevājñām ārāgaye Mv iii.53.8; hence, *imperfect, failing in duties*, MSV iii.93.8.

sakāyikā or °**ka**, a kind of toy (not 'game'), in a list beginning (**akāyikā**, q.v.) sakāyikā (n. pl.) vitkoṭikā... Divy 475.19 (v.l. saṃkāyikā).

[**sakāri-lipi**, see **śakānī**.]

sakāśāt, postpos. with gen., used in any sense pertaining to the abl. case; see Speyer Skt. Synt. § 189, citing a Skt. case of mg. (1), none of mg. (2); (**1**) *than*: ayaṃ deva sarveṣāṃ sakāśād adhikataraṃ (*more than all*) pūjyate Divy 396.26; asti sthavira tvatsakāśād anyo vṛddhataraḥ 399.28, *is there any other older than you*?; (**2**) *because, on account* (*of*): mahārāja tac caityaṃ na labhe brāhmaṇāṇāṃ sakāśād (*on account of the brahmans*) yathābhipretaṃ kārayitum Divy 243.25.

sa-kiṃcana, adj. (= Pali id), see **kiṃcana**.

sakṛd-āgāmin, f. °**nī** (= Pali sakad-ā°), *'once-returning', destined to have only one more incarnation* (in this world, see Childers): Mvy 5133; 5134; f. °nyaḥ, n. pl., Divy 534.1; °mi-phalam Divy 17.23; 50.9, etc.; °mi-phalāni Av i.65.1; etc. See s.v. **srota-āpanna**.

-sakkati (= Pali id., Pkt. -sakkai, both apparently only in cpds.), in cpds. ava-(o-), pari-, perhaps anu- (see s.v. **anuśakya**), *moves, goes*. Derivation obscure; Pischel 302 from ṣvaṣk-; Andersen, Pali Reader s.v. osakkati, from sṛp (curiously, the mss. of Mv read avasappanti in i.23.10, see **avasakkati**).

-sakkin (to **-sakkati**, q.v.), *going, moving*: koḍa- (= kroḍa-, cited by WT as the reading of K′)-sakkino SP 95.3, *moving on the breast* (like reptiles).

saktuka, see **śaktuka**.

sakhāya, m. (= Skt. sakhi; analog. form based on acc. sg. Skt. sakhāy-am; cf. the stem sakhāra in Pali, Geiger 84; AMg. and general Pkt. sahāya is ambiguous; it could represent this as well as Skt. sahāya), *friend*: °yān dṛṣṭvā RP 39.10 (prose); su-sakhāya-(in 37.27 printed sa-sa°) Mmk 37.27 (-rakṣā ātmarakṣā ca kāryā); 38.4 (-sametena ... karmaṇā); susakhāyopetā apramattāḥ 47.14 (all these prose); sakhāyair lakṣaṇopetaiḥ 97.20 (vs).

sakhikā (= Pali id.; ka svārthe, or endearing dim., to Skt. sakhī), *friend* (fem.): līlāṃ niśāmayatha he °kā Mv i.203.13 = ii.7.9 (vs).

1 **sakhila**, adj. (= Pali id.; cf. **sākhilya** and 1 **akhila**), *soft, smooth*, once of (a garment of) cloth: sakhilā khu-d-ayaṃ ... karpāsānāṃ paṭapilotikasaṃghāṭī, mṛdukā-d-ayaṃ... (same words), masinā-d-ayaṃ..., sukhumā-d-ayaṃ..., tanukā-d-ayaṃ..., etc., Mv iii.53.17; this proves that the usual interpretation, *friendly*, cannot be right; it is of course based on the assumption of derivation from sakhi, but this is proved wrong by the Mv passage; otherwise recorded in Pali and BHS only of speech, esp. the Buddha's; in Pali regularly assoc. with saṇha = ślakṣṇa and mudu = mṛdu; sakhilo glossed muduvacano DN comm. i.287.3 ff., and all comms. agree essentially on this, as well as on sākhalya, sākhalla (= **sākhilya**), which is the opposite of pharusa(-vācā etc.), e. g. Dhs. 1343; DN comm. iii.981.15–22; sākhallena Jāt. iv.57.5, glossed maṭṭhavacanena (note that maṭṭha is also applied to fine cloth, -sāṭaka Vism. 284.13); the mg. therefore is *smooth*, and of speech *suave, mild, gentle*: Buddhasya sakhilā girā Mv i.314.12 (vs), repeated below; su-sakhila-ślakṣṇa-vākyo ii.395.5; sakhilā Mvy 495, in list of epithets of Buddha's speech, = Tib. chub pa (? acc. to Das *accomplished, perfected*; Chin. seems to mean *affecting the hearts of all creatures*); of other (pious) persons, sūrataḥ (mss. su°) sakhilo mṛduḥ Mv ii.371.8 (vs); su-sakhila-vācā iii.280.19 (vs, by em.); saṃmodako sakhilo ślakṣṇavāco (mss. °cā) iii.372.4 (vs). The etym. of the word is obscure; BHS **akhila** = paruṣa, *harsh* (of speech), suggests interpretation as sa-khila, but may of course be a case of popular etym.; no meaning of khila is known which would seem to fit.

2 **sa-khila**, *afflicted with hardness of heart* (**khila**, q.v.): RP 35.12 (vs; see **kiṃcana**).

sa-khurapravāra (°vāla), see **khurapra°**.

[**Sagara**? see **Sāgara** 1.]

saṃkakṣikā (= Pali saṃkacchikā, surely not *belt, waistcloth* with PTSD; acc. to SBE 20.351 *vest*), an article of clothing, perhaps a kind of *undershirt* or *shift*: Mvy 8936 = Tib. ṅul gzan, *sweat garment*; Chin. *a garment covering the armpits*; Bhīk 15a.2 (in a list of nun's garments) °kā adhiṣṭhātavyā (see **adhitiṣṭhati** 1); see also **āsevaka**, °**kā**.

saṃkacchana (nt.), perh. *rustling* or the like, some sound made by water: apskandha-saṃkacchananirnādārutena Gv 251.24 (prose). Etym.? Perh. corrupt.

saṃkaṭīkṛta, ppp. (to *°ṭī-karoti, to Skt. saṃkaṭa), *pressed into a narrow space* (of deer, by hunters), or *endangered*: tato rājñā caturaṅgeṇa balakāyena nirgatya tan mṛgayūthaṃ sarvaṃ °taṃ (by em., ms. om. saṃ) Av i.235.8.

saṃkaṭṭati (see s.v. **kaṭṭati**), *collects, picks up*: Mv i.302.15 (... mālyaṃ vātena apakarṣīyate.) tāye dāni taṃ mālyaṃ saṃkaṭṭitvā (so, or v.l. saṃghaṭṭitvā, mss.; Senart °kaḍḍh°).

saṃkathya, see **a-saṃ°**.

saṃkampana (nt.; Skt. saṃkampate plus -ana), *a*

shaking: gurubhāra-°nā (so as one word, Bhvr.) Mārasenā jitā LV 366.4 (vs); pṛthivī-°na- (*earthquake*)-nirnādaruteṇa Gv 251.25 (prose); (taṃ lokadhātum apramāṇaiḥ) °nanayaiḥ saṃkampya 272.11 (prose).

saṅkala and °**lā** (see also **śaṅkalā**; AMg. saṅkala, °lā, °liyā; surely connected with Skt. śṛṅkhalā, °la; on k:kh see s.v. **asthi-śakalā** etc.), *chain* (so Chin. acc. to Suzuki's Index; Tib. ḥbrel, ib., *joining, connexion*); the rendering *skeleton* or *heap of bones*, given by Suzuki for Laṅk 97.9 and 273.12, cannot be right, since only **asthi-sa°** has this mg.; on 97.9 Nanjio alleges support of Chin. and Tib. for mg. *skeleton*, but Suzuki's Index groups this with the other refs. under the same Tib. and Chin., as above: in Laṅk used of the *chain* or *concatenation* of mutual interrelationship: saṃketamātram ... anyonyāpekṣasaṃkalā Laṅk 202.15; janyam arthaṃ na caivāsti pṛthak pratyaya-saṃkalāt 203.1; usually fem. forms, °lā n. sg. 203.6, stem in comp. 203.3, 13; °lāyā(ḥ) 203.4, 5, 7 (śaṅk°), 9, °lām 12, etc.; kṣaṇabheda-saṃkalābaddhāḥ 374.6; saṃkalā-buddhi-(mss., text °buddha- on basis of Tib. saṅs rgyas, but this is prob. an error; orig. possibly baddha?)-bimbaṃ ca 273.12, cf., also in the vicinity of bimba, 97.9 pudgala-nairātmya-bhāva-svasāmānya-bimba-saṃkalā-nityaduḥkhāśubhalakṣaṇābhiniveśa-pūrvakam evam idam lakṣaṇaṃ nānyatheti paśyataḥ; in both these saṃkalā can only mean *chain*, (causal) *concatenation*; cakrapeyāla(q.v.)-saṅkalāt MSV ii.206.11, *from the chain of*...

saṃkalikā, (**1**) see **asthi-saṃ°**; (**2**) in Divy 43.9, text, yat tatra (after a palace decorated with sandalwood had been built) saṃkalikā cūrṇaṃ cāvaśiṣṭaṃ tat piṣṭvā tatraiva pralepo dattaḥ; Index saṃkalikā-cūrṇaṃ as one word, *shavings*; better two words as in text, perh. *sweepings and sandal-powder* (saṃkalikā, *heap*, sc. of sweepings?); perh. cf. Skt. Lex. saṃkara, see s.v. **saṃkāra**.

? **saṃkaliyati** (acc. to Senart MIndic pass. to Skt. saṃkalayati), *is gathered together, assembled, united*, of Buddha's teaching: the mss. are corrupt and the line uncertain, but in prec. line read with mss. te hi no upavadeyur anudagrā (*they would blame us as ignoble*); then, acc. to Senart, yadi na saṃkaliye (assumed to be 3 sg. opt.; mss. indicate °liya) śāsanaṃ śāstuḥ (these words also uncertain) Mv i.70.(2 and) 3.

-saṃkalībhūta, see **asthi-saṃ°**.

saṃkalpa, m., = **vikalpa**, *false discrimination*: nimittaṃ nāma saṃkalpaḥ (229.8 nāma-nimitta-saṃkalpāḥ) svabhāvadvayalakṣaṇam, samyagjñānaṃ hi tathatā (229.9 °naṃ tathātvaṃ ca) pariniṣpannalakṣaṇam Laṅk 68.3–4 = 229.8–9 (vss); saṃkalpa-kalpa-janitena ayonisena (bhavate avidya ...) LV 419.17(–18), vs; there is no noun for the two instr. adj. to agree with, unless we separate saṃkalpa (as instr., § 8.8), *by false discrimination produced by vain fancy, and superficial*, (*ignorance comes to be*); or understand manasikāreṇa as suggested by ayonisena? Tib. kun rtog (= saṃkalpa) rtog pas (*by kalpa*) bskyed paḥi tshul bzhin ma yin pas, which perhaps supports the second alternative, as it seems to make -janitena modify ayonisena. (In SP 97.13, vs, read anyonyasaṃkalpasagauravāś, as one word, *having respect for each other's purposes.*)

Saṃkaśya = **Sāṃkāśya**, q.v.

saṃkasu-samācāra, adj. m., *of vile conduct*; synonym of, or variant for, **śaṅkhasvara-samācāra**, q.v.: Mvy 9142 (not in Mironov).

[**saṃkāyikā**, v.l. for **sakā°**.]

saṃkāra, m. (= Skt. Lex. and Pali id.; note Skt. Lex. saṃkara, id., but in Caraka *dung*), (**1**) primarily, *dust, sweepings, refuse, rubbish*: Mvy 9313 = Tib. phyag dar; tayā dārikayā gṛhaṃ saṃmṛjya ... °raḥ choritaḥ Divy 585.4; °ra-kūṭa (Pali id.), *rubbish heap* (see 2 below), Divy 177.10 (tair hastapādeṣu gṛhītvā °kūṭe kṣipto), 11; saṃkārāvakare śukle (read so, or °kara-śukle, for text śaṃkārāpakare śuklaṃ) paṭe ... Mmk 131.21 (vs), *on a cloth pure in regard to sweepings and rubbish* (i. e. free from them); lumbinivanaṃ ... vyapagatatṛṇa-reṇu-(read khāṇu-? see next)-pattra-saṃkāraṃ Mv i.149.3 (vs); padminivanaṃ ... (read)apagata-tṛṇa-khāṇu-pattra-saṃkāraṃ i. 215.14 (so mss., except khāṇḍa for **khāṇu**, q.v.), and read so ii.18.10 lumbinivanaṃ ... (mss. °saṃkara, and again khāṇḍa for khāṇu); Senart em. saṃskāraṃ and saṃkhāraṃ, respectively, for saṃkāraṃ in the last two; (**2**) seems to mean more specifically *dung*, perh. in °ra-kūṭa (cf. 1 above), *dung-heap, privy*(?): so 'medhyasthāneṣv evābhiramate saṃkārakūṭe jambāle (mss. jā°) keśāṃl luñcati amedhyaṃ mukhe prakṣipati Av i.280.5 (? but jambāla simply *mud*, so perh. saṃkāra-k° *rubbish-heap*); and more especially in SP 105.12 ff., 109.2, 113.13 and 114.4 (but Tib. renders phyag dar thruout), where saṃkāra-dhāna (Pali id.) seems to mean *privy*: °naṃ śodhayitavyaṃ 105.12; similarly 106.1, 3; dharmān pratyavarān °dhānasadṛśān 109.2; °dhānam imu mahya pūtikam uccāraprasrāva-vināśitaṃ ca 113.13 (vs), especially clear, *stinking, foul with dung and urine*; 114.4 (vs); (**3**) perh. *impurity* in the sense of *pariahhood, outcaste state, expulsion from caste*: (vayaṃ tvāṃ) jñātimadhyād utkṣipāmaḥ, saṃkāraṃ pātayāmo Divy 273.2, 11; but mss. are not unanimous, and in same phrase 272.24 it is alleged that they read salokānāṃ (! kept in text) for saṃkāraṃ; quite uncertain. Cf. **saṃkirati**.

Saṃkārin, n. of a yakṣa: Māy 42.

saṃkārya, adj. or subst. nt.? (gdve. of **saṃ-kirati**?), acc. to Tib. (what is) *mixed up, to be mixed, a mixture*, or *confused, disordered* (ḥdres pa, ḥchod ba): °yam Mvy 5344.

Saṃkāśya = **Sāṃ°**, q.v.

saṃkirati (in this sense only pass., *is soiled*, in Skt. saṃkīryate, saṃkīrṇa, and Pali saṃkīyate, saṃkiṇṇa), *soils*: dharaṇirajaḥ kramavarā(n) na saṃkirati (in 224.17 mss. °varān apasaṃkramati, unmetr.) Mv i.151.6 = 224.17 (vs), *the earth-dust does not soil their fair feet.*

saṃkilikilāyate, °**ti** (to Skt. kilikilāyate, pw), *makes happy noises together* (with others): Śikṣ 76.11 (mātṛgrāmeṇa sārdhaṃ) saṃkrīḍataḥ saṃkilikilāyamānasya; similarly MSV iii.16.2; Bbh 169.5 and Bhīk 28a.3 (see s.v. **saṃcagghati**).

saṃkiliṣṭa, see **saṃkliśyati**; **saṃkileśa**, see **saṃkleśa.**

? **saṃkīyati**, in Mv iii.37.9, text, tām eva agragaṇikāṃ °yanto śayito, presumably understood as *went to bed thinking about that courtesan* (and enjoyed her in dreams all night). The form is very dubious; it cannot = Pali saṃkīyati which is pass. to **saṃkirati**, q.v., and not connected with Pali saṃkati, Skt. śaṅkate (PTSD connects it with both at once!), Chap. 43, s.v. śaṅk. If our form is right, I can only understand it as a MIndic passive to Skt. caus. śaṅkayati, *makes concerned*; it would then mean, *being made concerned with* ... There is a v.l. sakrīḍanto; read saṃkrīḍanto, *amusing himself* (in thoughts)?

saṃkuñcana, nt. (to next plus -ana), *drawing in, retraction*: Mvy 6737 = Tib. bskum pa.

saṃkuñcayati (cf. Skt. saṃkocayati and saṃkucati; forms in kuñc- recorded with simplex and other preverbs, not with sam-), *draws in, retracts*: saṃkuñcitaṃ vā bāhuṃ prasārayet prasāritaṃ vā saṃkuñcayed Av ii.91.9–10; Divy 162.3. See prec.

saṃkuṭṭakā (cf. Skt. kuṭṭ-, not recorded with sam-), *beating, pounding*, or (prob.) rather *an instrument* for doing this: Mvy 6849 = Tib. (b)rduṅ ba; Chin. *mallet*. (Tib. could be either n. act. or instrument.)

Saṃkusuma (cf. **Kusuma** 2, and next three), n. of a Buddha: Mmk 426.8 (prose); °māya ca Buddhāya 499.22 (vs, hypermetric by one syllable).

saṃkusumita, (1) adj. (= Pali id., cf. Skt. kusumita; orig. denom. pple.), *flowering, beflowered*: (Vaiśākhamāse ... varapravara-)-puṣpa-°te LV 54.20; (vṛkṣās ...) °tāḥ 85.17; °teṣu śāleṣu Mv i.220.7 = °tehi śālehi ii.22.8; sahakāravanāni °tāni iii.80.12; fig., mahyaṃ hṛdayaṃ prīti-°taṃ Mv iii.111.14; anantaguṇaratnajñāna-°ta-vimuktiphalasusaṃpannatvād LV 428.22; aparimitaraśmi-°taśarīraṃ Dbh 83.1; also Gv 210.14, and in proper names such as **Nakṣatrarāja-°tābhijña** etc.; **(2)** n. of the buddhakṣetra of **Saṃkusumitarāja**: Mmk 4.16.

Saṃkusumitagandhottamarāja, n. of a Tathāgata (distinguished from next, both in same line): Mmk 426.6.

Saṃkusumitarāja, Mmk 4.16; 28.2, etc., or (more often) °rājendra, Mmk 2.6 etc.; 63.24; 68.26; 71.18 etc.; 79.28; 426.5–6, n. of a Tathāgata.

saṃketa, m. (in Skt. *agreement*, esp. *rendezvous*, and *agreed sign* or *gesture*; in AMg. saṃkeya app. *gesture* in general), **(1)** perh. *gesture*, in next, q.v.; but it may mean *conventional term*; **(2)** *conventional designation*, with implication of unreality (see **saṃketika**): Mvy 2776, follows **vyavahāra,** q.v.; = Tib. brdaḥ, which may mean *gesture*; *token, symbol*; *explanation*; *word* (the last prob. here, with the above implication); (of the Tathāgatakāya) sāmānyaḥ °tena, °taḥ paramārthena Samādh 22.11, *universal by convention, a* (mere) *convention(al term) in very truth*; saṃketamātram evedam Laṅk 202.15 = 339.11; nāmasaṃjñā-saṃketābhiniveśena ... bālāś cittam anusaranti 225.6; dharma-°ta evāyaṃ (*this world*) ... °tāc ca pṛthagbhūto na jāto na nirudhyate 289.8–9 (vs); (āhvānāya) °to Bbh 389.20, see **vyavahāra**; perh. here Mv i.78.10 (vs), which is textually dubious, (pravartate tatha pariśeṣabhūmiṣu, mss. °śeṣāsu bhū°,) sāmānyasaṃketānāṃ nirūpaṇaṃ (mss. °ketāni rūpāṇāṃ); the reading of the mss. could be translated, *so there are in use in regard to the other stages* (of a Bodhisattva) *the common conventional expressions of their forms* (the meter is uncertain).

Saṃketarutapraveśa, n. of a samādhi: Mvy 597 (Tib. brda daṅ sgra-la ḥjug pa, prob. *penetration into gestures*, or perhaps *conventional terms?, and sounds*); ŚsP 1423.16. Cf. prec.

saṃketika, f. °kī (cf. Skt. sāṃketika; to **saṃketa** 2, q.v., plus -ika), *conventional, nominal, consisting of a mere verbal expression*: nāma-°kīṃ dharmāṇāṃ prajñaptim avabudhya ŚsP 378.22; nāma-°kī (so divide) dharmaprajñaptir avaboddhavyā 382.9; nāma-dharma-samketikī (text °takī) dharmaprajñaptir 549.22.

saṃkrama, (1) m. (cf. next two; to saṃ-kram- in mg. *transmigrate*, recorded for Pali saṃkamati), *passage from one existence to another, transmigration*: LV 419.19 (vs), see s.v. **saṃskāra** 1; sthāpita-°ma ity ucyate 428.17 (prose), *he* (Buddha) *is called the one who has arrested transmigration*; cyuti-°maḥ Mvy 2986; **(2)** m. or nt., a high number: m., Mvy 7717, = Tib. sbar yas; nt., Mvy 7843 (so read with v.l. and Mironov, text saṃgramaṃ) = Tib. id., cited from Gv 133.4 (in Gv 105.23 corruptly śakra).

saṃkramaka (see prec.; saṃ-kram- plus -aka), *one who transmigrates*: na samkramako 'sti kaścit (mss.) LV 420.10 (vs).

saṃkramaṇa (nt.; see prec. two; saṃ-kram- plus -ana), *transmigration*: LV 419.20 (vs), see s.v. **saṃskāra 1,**

saṃkramaṇaka, nt. (also m. or f.?), pl. °kāni Mvy 5585 = Tib. bsti khaṅ, *rest-house, private pavilion* (acc. to Das, *private house, sanctum*); Chin. *room* or *house for lying down*; Jap. *private* (*rest*) *room*; ūrdhvī (on a wall) ekā nibaddhā °ṇakā (mss. °ṇakāḥ) Divy 220.22; (in a city; gṛhāḥ kūṭāgārā) harmyāḥ prāsādā ... avalokanakā °ṇakā 221.29; prob. *pavilion* for rest or private amusement, which might or might not be on a wall or roof. (Divy Index *gallery*.)

saṃkrānti-dṛṣṭi (cf. BR s.v. saṃkrānti 3); *the view of the Saṃkrānti(-vādin) school*, acc. to Wassiljew, a branch of the Sautrāntikas, so named (257, transl. 284) because they taught the *transmigration* (saṃkrānti = **saṃkrama** 1) of the skandhas; mentioned as heretical in: °ṭi-vigatena pratiṣṭhāsamatābhinirvṛtti(misprinted °narvṛtti)-jñānena Gv 469.10.

saṃkrāmaṇī, n. of a kind of magic (vidyā): Divy 636.26.

saṃkliśyati, °te (= Pali saṃkilissati, ppp. saṃkiliṭṭha; Skt. in other mgs.; saṃkliṣṭa *obscured, soiled*, of a mirror, pw), *becomes soiled*: Divy 57.19 akliṣṭāni vāsāṃsi saṃkliśyanti; KP 99.2 (cittaṃ ...) upakleśe saṃkliśyate (cited Śikṣ 234.8, kleśair upakliśyate; read in KP upakleśaiḥ); AsP 203.1–2 na ca ... prajñāpāramitā kaṃcid dharmam ālīyate na kaṃcid dharmaṃ saṃkliśyate (text °ṣyate) na kaṃcid dharmaṃ parigṛhṇāti, ... *does not cling to any dharma* (condition of existence), *does not soil itself on ..., does not take to itself ...*; ppp. saṃkliṣṭa, *soiled, impure* Bbh 40.11 °ṭa-cittaḥ; Ud xi.3, of tapaḥ (oldest ms. has saṃkiliṣṭā, semi-MIndic, the epenthetic i supported by meter); Dbh 58.10 °ṭa-viśuddhāyāś ca (lokadhātor), *impurely* (*imperfectly*) *purified*, in contrast with ekāntapariśuddha, *completely purified*, line 11; 58.16 kleśacaryāsaṃkliṣṭā bodhisattvacaryā; Jm 98.21 su-saṃkliṣṭaṃ, of the mode of life of a crow; Gv 263.16 lokadhātūn saṃkliṣṭān, *soiled*, contrasted with pariśuddhān, same line; 534.23 saṃkliṣṭānāṃ sattvānāṃ viśuddhaye; neg. a-saṃ°, *not impure*, Mvy 167 °ṭāḥ sarvadharmāḥ; Mv i.134.7 °ṭa-pratibhānāś ca (of Bodhisattvas); Bbh 303.15 asaṃkliṣṭa-dāna-tā; 308.4 saṃkliṣṭaṃ varjayitvā asaṃkliṣṭaṃ dānaṃ dadāti; in contrast with **vyavadāyate, °ti,** q.v., Śikṣ 263.15; ŚsP 140.14; AsP 399.14, 15.

saṃkleśa, in Mv iii.357.13 (prose) **saṃkileśa,** m. (= Pali saṃkilesa; to prec.; in Skt. *suffering*, see below), *defilement, impurity*: esp. in contrast with **vyavadāna,** q.v. for Mvy 126; Mv iii.321.6; 357.13; Divy 616.23; LV 433.14 f.; Av ii.188.9; Śikṣ 172.11; KP 59.2; Bbh 99.10; 215.7; dhyānādīnāṃ samāsato dvau saṃkleśau; aprāpteṣu caiṣu prāptaye **vibandha-**(q.v.)°śaḥ ... prāpteṣu caiṣu tadbhūmikaṃ kleśa-paryavasthānam anuśayo vā Bbh 388.5–8; rāgadveṣamohādikāt sarvasaṃkleśāc Bbh 40.10; others Bbh 55.7; 83.14; Śikṣ 136.4; Laṅk 156.9 (where śuddhiḥ replaces vyavadānam in contrast, in a vs); manuṣyaduḥkhadāridrya-°śa-doṣāṃś ca prajānāti Dbh 58.22 (here °śa may have its normal Skt. mg., see above).

saṃkṣayati (unless error, can only be hyper-Skt., prob. for Pali saṃkhāyati, or the like, § 2.25, = Skt. saṃkhyāti), *reckons, figures*, in the sense of *reflects*: purohitaḥ °ti (there follows a private reflection) MSV i.27.7.

saṃkṣipa-vikṣipa, adj. (cf. Skt. vi-kṣip-, saṃ-kṣip-), prob. better taken as two separate words, lit. *narrow* and *wide, limited* and *extensive*; applied either to creatures (sattva) or to their thoughts (cittāni; so Foucaux); in either case meant together to include all: (yāvanta sattva nikhilena triyadhvayuktāḥ, cittāni caitasikasaṃjñi vitarkitāni,) hīnāḥ praṇīta tatha saṃksipa vikṣipā ye, (ekasmi cittaparivarti prajāni sarvān) LV 151.(12–)14(–15), vs, (*all creatures ... and their thoughts ...,*) *low and excellent, also limited* (*narrow*) *and broad, he* (the Bodhisattva) *knows all of them in a single instant* (*'turn of thought'*); Tib. rgya chuṅ yaṅs pa dag, *of limited extent and broad.*

Saṃkṣiptabuddhi, n. of a former Buddha: Mv i.138.13.

saṃkṣiptena, adv. (instr. of Skt. saṃkṣipta; = Pali saṃkhittena; Skt. uses saṃkṣepāt, see LV below), *in brief, in summary*: °tena pañcopādānaskandhā duḥkhā Mv iii.332.4 (in the first Noble Truth; Pali saṃkhittena, e. g. Vin. i.10.29, but LV 417.7 saṃkṣepāt, as in Skt.); ity ucyate °tena na punar vistareṇa Sukh 44.17; sādhu me Bhagavāṃs tathā °tena dharmaṃ deśayatu Divy 37.8; others Gv 465.16, 26; 496.15; et al.

saṃkṣūyate, pres. pple. °yamāno (mss. a few times saṃkṣu°, or saṃkṣa°), *attacking* (*trying to shake*?), or the like, of some hostile action by Māra against the Bodhisattva: Māro pāpīmāṃ duḥkhī . . . bodhisattvaṃ °yamāno . . . mahā-ūhasitaṃ ūhase Mv ii.268.12–269.19, twelve times. Senart's etym. (Vedic root sku-, skū-) is unconvincing. Is there connexion with AMg. (saṃ)chuhai, the etym. of which is disputed? Cf. Hindi chūnā, Nep. chunu, *touch, meddle with*; Turner, Nep. Dict. s.v. chunu discusses the difficult sept; Skt. kṣubh- may be directly or indirectly involved.

[**saṃkṣepaya** MSV iii.128.19 seems to be an error for an adv. form of Skt. saṃkṣepa; = Tib. mdor na, *in short*.]

saṃkha, see **śaṅkha**.

Saṅkhamedhī, see **Śaṅkha°**.

saṃkhya, nt., Mvy 7928 (cited from Gv), or **saṃkhyā**, f., Gv 106.19; 134.4, a high number.

saṃkhyāta, in steye-saṃkhyātam, prob. read so, as adv. (= Pali theyya-saṃkhātaṃ = theyyacitto avaharaṇacitto Vin. iii.46.34), *with intent to steal*: (yā punar bhikṣuṇī . . .) pareṣām adattaṃ steye saṃkhyātaṃ (printed as two words) ādadīta Bhīk 25a.2–3; steye °taḥ (as two words, so also Mironov) Mvy 5352 = Tib. rku bar bgraṅ ba, rendered by Das steyasaṃkhyātam, *to count as stealing*.

Saṃkhyā-lipi, a kind of script: LV 125.22; rendered literally by Tib. graṅs, *number*, but prob. a geographical name (cf. Kirfel, Kosm. 81, Saṃkhya, Saṃkhyāta, n. of a people); after **ugra-lipi**, before **anuloma-l°**.

saṃgaṇanā (in Skt. once in mg. *counting up, reckoning*; so SP 114.14; to next plus -anā), (perh. lit. *counting, census, roll-call*?) *assembly, gathering*: (kva idānīṃ) deśi (= deśe, loc., m.c.) dharmadhara (q.v.) -°nā syāt Mv i.70.11 (vs).

saṃgaṇayati, *counts*: (. . . manuṣyān gaṇayati,) saṃgaṇya (ger.) . . . sarva-. . . manuṣyāṇāṃ samaṃ bhaktaṃ prajñapayanti Divy 293.10.

saṃgaṇikā (= Pali id.; cf. prec.), *society, crowd, association*, as opp. of *solitude*, **viveka** (2), q.v.: °kām adhikṛtyāha Śikṣ 106.11 (prose), also, na tiṣṭhate °kāsu yogī 12 (vs); (various evils) bhavanty amī °kāsu sarve 16, karoti yaḥ °kām asārām 18 (vss); (vyāpādaṃ . . . vitarkayeyaṃ, nirviśeṣo bhaveyaṃ) saṃsarga-°kābhir etaiḥ sattvaiḥ 201.18, (*if I had evil thoughts*,) *I should be nowise different from these creatures with associational groupings*; 202.20, see s.v. **viveka** (2); °kayā cātināmayataḥ Bbh 156.18, *and of one who spends his time in society* (i. e. frivolously); °kayā kālam atināmayati 1.2.7; (guṇā araṇyavāsasya . . .) °kāṃ (so read, mss. corrupt but final nasal in both) vivarjayati Karmav 104.7; °kā-saṃsarga-middha-nivaraṇa-vigatena bhavitavyam Laṅk 49.7; °kā-varjanatā Śikṣ 119.6 and °kā-vivarjanam 191.10, both with **ekārāmatā**; °kārāma (Pali id.), *delight in society* (Tatp.), °rāma-parivarjitena °rāma-doṣa-darśinā bhavitavyaṃ Śikṣ 104.18; na °rāma-kathāyogānuyogam anuyuktā viharanti AsP 334.15; same oftener Bhvr., *one who delights in society*, ye ca °rāmā(ḥ) Mv ii.355.16 = iii.280.1; others Śikṣ 52.5; a-°rāmā(ḥ) SP 309.9, *not delighting* . . .; °kābhirataiḥ Divy 464.19; ratiṃ °kāsu ca Sādh 17.11.

saṃgata, adj. (ppp. of Skt. sam-gam-), in saṃgata-bhrū LV 107.9, prob. *with dense* (*thick*) *eyebrows*, one of the **anuvyañjana**; cf. Pali saṃgata = nibbivara, *without interstices*, Vv. comm. 275.27; corresp. to snigdha-bhrū of parallel texts.

saṃgati, f., (**1**) (cf. BR s.v. 4, *Stimmen, Passen*, with artha-; Pkt. saṃgai = aucitya, ucitatā, Sheth), *success, attainment* (of desirable goal): duḥśīlabhūtasya praṇaṣṭa °tiḥ RP 35.14 (vs); (**2**) (*continued*) *involvement in the saṃsāra, transmigration*, the opposite of release: mūḍhasya saṃgatir bhavati, jāyate na ca mucyate Laṅk 257.5, *of a deluded man there ensues involvement, he is* (*re-*)*born, and is not released*; prob. in this sense saṃgatiḥ 179.2, in a bare list of disapproved results; acc. to Suzuki, Tib. ḥdus pa (*coming together*); in this light interpret tri-saṃgati, for which acc. to Suzuki Tib. (gsum, *three*) phrad pa (*meeting together*), in: yadi . . . vijñānānāṃ tri-saṃgati-pratyaya-kriyāyogenotpattir abhaviṣyad Laṅk 41.6, and cf. 10; trisaṃgaty-utpādayogalakṣaṇaṃ vijñānam, asaṃgati-yogasvabhāvalakṣaṇaṃ jñānam 157.15–16 (so read acc. to Suzuki's transl., following Chin.); trisaṃgati-pratyaya-kriyāyogābhiniveśāya (Tib. °śāt acc. to Nanjio) saṃdhir vijñānānāṃ nairantaryāt pravṛttiyogenābhiniveśato bhavasaṃdhir bhavati 163.1; trisaṃgati-pratyaya-vyāvṛtter vijñānānāṃ vimokṣatrayānudarśanāt sarvasaṃdhayo na pravartante 163.3 (note the three **vimokṣa**, q.v., to which the three saṃgati, *involvements in the saṃsāra*, appear to be pendants and opposites); from this passage it appears that the 3 saṃgati, or their causes (pratyaya), are the three **saṃdhi** (q.v. 6), viz. rāga, dveṣa, and moha, 162.14–15; (Tathāgatagarbho . . . pravartate naṭavad gatisaṃkaṭa) ātmātmīya-varjitas, tadanavabodhāt trisaṃgati-pratyaya-kriyāyogaḥ pravartate 220.11. Cf. (tri-)**saṃtati** (1), the application of which is obscure.

? **saṃgandharāja** (unrecorded); if = Skt. Lex. gandharāja, could mean one of several flowers or flowering plants, or sandalwood: Gv 337.2 (vs), read (tad vajradaṇḍaṃ . . .) saṃgandharājojjvalakesarāḍhyaṃ, as one cpd.; sa-gan° would be metrically equally good, hence saṃ- could not be m.c. for sa- (but may corruptly represent sa-).

saṃgamantrā, a high number: Gv 106.7; corresp. to **gamantra**, q.v.

saṃgaveṣati (Skt. gav° with sam), *seeks*: āhāraṃ samagaveṣi (aor.) Mv ii.205.2 (vs).

saṃgāyati, lit. *'sings in unison'* = *is concordant*, avoids quarreling, opp. of vivadati: saṃgāyiṣyāma(ḥ) vayam . . . na vivadiṣyāmaḥ KP 142.4 (prose).

Saṃgīta-nipāta (cf. **Saṃgīti-paryāya**), n. of a section of the Madhyamāgama: MSV iii.107.5.

saṃgīti, f. (in Skt. as n. of a meter, otherwise only Lex., and once in Schmidt, Nachträge, *conversation*; in Pali comes nearer to BHS usage, see esp. Childers, but still acc. to Dictt. is not identical), (**1**) *singing* (so in Pali; perh. esp. *in unison, choral singing*?), *music* (esp. *vocal*): Mvy 5022 (after tūryam) = Tib. glu dbyaṅs; apsarasaḥ-. . . -saṃgīti . . . LV 10.22; apsara-saṃgīti-rutena Gv 252.5; divya-°tiṣu ratir na bhavati Gv 118.24; (Śuddhodana speaks to the prince's female attendants, mā sma kadācit) °tiṃ vichetsyatha LV 193.1, similarly 12; °ti-prāsāda, *music-hall*, LV 41.10 (Śuddhodanasya; = Tib. rol mo bya baḥi, *for making music*); Bodhisattva-°ti-prāsāda Gv 385.18–19 (the young prince's *music-hall* in Kapilavastu, named **Dharmadhātupratibhāsaprabha**); sama-, or samaṃ, saṃgīti, *chanting in unison*, (sc. Mahā-brahmāṇaḥ) ekasvareṇa sama-(v.l. samaṃ; is this also part of cpd. with next?)saṃgītyā taṃ bhagavantam ābhiḥ . . . gāthābhir adhyabhāṣanta SP 167.3; virtually same phrase 170.12; 173.13; 178.8; 271.6; 401.1; 402.3; some mss. sometimes reported saṃgītya, which must be an error; *with one voice, in united choral chanting, addressed* . . . *with these verses* (in 401.1 bhagavata imāni dhāraṇīmantrapadāni prayacchanti sma); (**2**) esp. in dharma-°ti, *recitation* or *pronouncement* of the true Doctrine: (mahāvimāne, in heaven . . . mahāvipuladharma-)-saṃgīti-(Tib. yaṅ dag par brjod pas, *by perfect speech, expression*)-sarvakāmarativegakleśachedane LV 11.5; saṃgītikuśalās tathāgatadharmāṇām SP 312.3, *skilled in proclaiming the Buddha's Doctrine* (Tib. as on LV 11.5); (after statement that a Bodhisattva will preach the Doctrine) bhavanti cāsya dharma-°tyāṃ sahāyakā(ḥ) SP 286.7, *and he will have assistants in proclaiming the Doctrine*, not, I think, in *assemblies* or a *synod*, with Burnouf and Kern; Tib. here (chos) yaṅ dag par ḥgro baḥi; for the last read bgro baḥi, see s.v. **Saṃgītiparyāya**; ḥgro = *go*, but bgro = *argue, discuss, deliberate, consider*; so Tib. *in discussion of the Doctrine*; (Mahākāśyapaḥ . . .) dharma-°tiṃ kartukāmaḥ Av ii.204.12 (after Buddha's nirvāṇa; but there is no mention of a *council*!), and so in the title of the story, saṃgītiḥ 197.1, *proclamation, public declaration* (sc. of the Doctrine); prob. here also, satyasaṃgītiḥ kulaputra dharmasaṃgītiḥ Śikṣ 12.8–9, cited from Dharmasaṃgīti-sūtra, *proclamation of the Doctrine is* (the same as) *proclamation of Truth* (Bendall and Rouse, *to be in concert with*...); (**3**) in Pali (see Childers) used of the *rehearsal* of sacred texts at one of the Councils of Buddhist monks, also of these *Councils* themselves, as *'rehearsals'*, and finally of the *collections* (esp. the four great nikāya = BHS āgama) of *texts rehearsed*. This meaning, or these meanings, seem related, at least possibly, to the following: saṃgīti-kāraḥ Mvy 2762, acc. to Tib. yaṅ dag par sdud par byed pa, *one who puts into a grand collection*, i. e. who helps to establish the canon; etymologically the word could mean *one who makes a proclamation* (of the Doctrine); rājabhāryā sarvabuddha-°tiṃ sarvabuddhadharmaguhyasthānāni ca saṃjānīte sma SP 464.3, Tib. saṅs rgyas thams cad kyis kun bstan pa = *what has been completely taught by all the Buddhas* (could be taken with 2, above, as well as here); (after Buddha's nirvāṇa, his disciples mantrayanti . . .) nirvṛtisamayakāle (Senart em. nirvṛtī-, m.c.; mss. °la-) saṃgītiṃ (Senart's em., corrupt mss. mostly samaṃgīti) Mv i.69.4 (vs), here possibly *common rehearsal* or *'council'*, but could also mean merely *proclamation*; (**4**) *rehearsal* = *study, conning, memorizing, learning*, of non-Buddhist religious texts: (a brahman lad) Uttareṇa tahiṃ (to the sage Asita) gatvā vedā adhītā; so dāni saṃgītiṃ kṛtvā pituḥ sakāśam āgato Mv iii.383.1, *he studied the Vedas; he now, after having made a complete rehearsal* (or *memorization*, of them), *came home to his father*; (tāni parivrājaka-)śāstrāṇi (as taught by Saṃjayin Vairaṭīputra) saṃgītī- (mss. °tiṃ) kṛtvā (*having rehearsed*, or *memorized*) Rājagṛhaṃ praviṣṭā Mv iii.59.18 (they had already lost faith in the value of these doctrines, line 14).

Saṃgīti-paryāya (Pali °pariyāya; cf. also **Saṃgītanipāta**), m., n. of a work: Mvy 1416; = Tib. ḥgro, or bgro, baḥi rnam graṅs; read bgro, *discuss* or the like, see saṃgīti (2), on SP 286.7; Takakusu, JPTS 1904–5, p. 99. Fragments of **Saṃgīti-sūtra**, Hoernle MR 16 ff.

saṃgūhayati, *conceals* (*completely*): °hayan, pres. pple., Mvy 6342.

saṃgṛhīta-grāhin, Mv i.133.13, see s.v. **saṃgraha.**

Saṃgṛhītapakva (mss.; Senart em. °pakṣa), n. of a former Buddha: Mv i.141.15.

saṃgerī, see **śaṃ°**.

saṃgopāyati (cf. Pali saṃgopeti), *protects, spares*: vadhyāṃś (Senart ba°, mss. badhyāś; cf. prec. line, vadham ākṣepayanti) ca na °yanti Mv i.96.8 (of backsliding Bodhisattvas), *and they do not protect* (show mercy to) *those subject to execution.*

saṃgranthana (nt.; nowhere in this sense), *literary composition*: na ca °na-kauśalaṃ mamāsti Śikṣ 1.11 (vs), *and I have no skill in* . . .

[**saṃgrama**, nt., read **saṃkrama**, q.v. (2).]

saṃgraha, m., as in Skt., BR s.v. 14, *das Heranziehen, für sich Gewinnen; freundliche, liebevolle Behandlung*; so interpret LV 205.8–9 a-saṃgraha-gṛhītasya, *afflicted with lack of friendly behavior* or *disposition*; LV 426.5 sattvasaṃgrahaprayukta, *given to attractive treatment of creatures*; Mv i.107.10 kevarūpeṇa saṃgraheṇa satvā saṃgṛhṇanti, *by what sort of attraction do* (Bodhisattvas) *attract creatures*?; cf. Mv i.133.13 saṃgṛhītagrāhiṇaś ca (bodhisattvāḥ), *they are characterized by holding those who have been attracted*, sc. by the **saṃgraha-vastu**, as Senart rightly saw, but he was wrong in taking saṃgṛhīta as a subst. = saṃgraha; other cases Mv i.133.17; 163.7. Note especially Gv 495.20 samantapāśa-jāla-bhūtaṃ (bodhicittaṃ), sarvavineyasattva-saṃgraha-karṣaṇatayā, *it is* . . . *a net* . . . *because it draws in by attraction* (by kindly behavior) *creatures* . . .; cf. LV 429.13 s.v. saṃgraha-vastu. Sometimes = saṃgraha-vastu, q.v.: SP 142.11 (vs) catvāraḥ saṃgrahā(ḥ).

? **saṃgrahaka-**, = (and prob. error for) **saṃgrāhaka,** *charioteer*, q.v.: °ka-rūpeṇa Gv 225.26 (without context), foll. by **sārthavāhakarūpeṇa.**

saṃgrahaṇī (= AMg. saṃgahaṇī), *summary, résumé*, in **Paryāya-sa°**, q.v.

saṃgraha-vastu, nt. (= Pali saṃgahavatthu), *article of attraction*, means by which a Buddha or (more often in BHS) a Bodhisattva *attracts*, draws to himself and to religious life, creatures. The literal mg. has been much disputed; it seems to me clarified by LV 429.13 where reference is made to the Buddha's *cleverness in drawing-in creatures* (sattvasaṃgrahakauśalyaṃ) *by the net* (-jālena) *of the 4 saṃgrahavastu*; with this cf. Gv 495.20, cited s.v. **saṃgraha.** As in Pali, there are four of these: dāna, **priya-vacana** (or the like), **artha-caryā** (or **-kriyā**), and **samānārthatā** (or **samānasukhaduḥkhatā**), qq.v.; they are listed LV 38.16–17; 160.6–7; 182.6; 429.12–13; Mv i.3.11–12; ii.395.8–9 (without use of the term saṃgraha-vastu); Mvy 924–928; Dharmas 19; Bbh 217.2–230.19, the inclusive term 227.5; 230.19; without lists of the 4 items, SP 259.5; LV 35.9; 437.15; Mvy 793; Divy 95.15; 264.29; Śikṣ 50.11; Av i.16.12; Gv 495.17 (in most of these the number *four* is specified). Sometimes replaced by **saṃgraha,** q.v., alone.

saṃgrāmayati, °meti (= Skt. Gr. °mayati, Pali °gāmeti; denom. to Skt. saṃgrāma), *fights*: (devehi trāyastriṃśehi) °menti Mv i.30.9; °mayanty eva Śikṣ 181.4; °mayataḥ (gen. sg. pres. pple.) 181.8; śatruṇā sārdhaṃ °mayet 254.1; °mayitum MSV i.95.13; all prose.

saṃgrāma-śīrṣa, m. or nt., or **°ṣā,** f. (cf. Skt. saṃgrāma-śiras, -mūrdhan, *battle-front, van, front line*, and Pali Dhp. comm. ii.227.1–2, gloss on saṃgāmaj-uttama, so saṃgāmajitānaṃ uttamo pavaro, saṃgāma-śīsa-yodho ti), lit. *battle-van, front line*, as one of a list of arts learned by a young prince, prob. *the art of leading*, or *fighting in the front line*: °śīrṣe Mv ii.423.17; °śīrṣāyāṃ ii.434.13 (all items in the list are locs.).

saṃgrāha (m.?; the only real Skt. literary occurrences are Mbh. 5.152.17 susaṃgrāhāḥ [so Crit. ed., for vulgate asaṃ°], *under good control*, of horses; and one passage in Schmidt, Nachträge, = *Griff am Messer*), *seizure, overwhelming* (and dangerous) *grasp* (?): LV 374.17 (vs) iha rāgamadana-makaraṃ tṛṣṇormijalaṃ kudṛṣṭi-saṃgrāhaṃ saṃsārasāgaram ahaṃ saṃtīrṇo, *I have here crossed the ocean of the saṃsāra, whose sea-monsters are passion and love, whose wave-water is thirst, whose overwhelming grasp is heresy* (? both *control* and *attachment* seem inappropriate here; I have thought of emending to -saṃgāhaṃ, *depths, profound abyss*, but this is not quotable); neg. a-saṃgrāha, *non-grasping, not* (wrongly) *clinging to*, Bbh 44.6, 7 asadbhūta-samāropāsaṃgrāha-vivarjito bhūtāpavādāsaṃgrāha-vivarjitaś (Wogihara, Index, renders by Chinese meaning *not wrong holding*).

saṃgrāhaka (= Pali saṃgāhaka, both mgs.), (**1**) adj., *attracting, drawing to oneself*: saṃgrahavastu-(q.v.)-sarvasattva-°kāḥ, one of the 18 āveṇika-bodhisattvadharmāḥ, Mvy 793; (**2**) *charioteer*: Mātalinā ca °kena Mv ii.49.11; Mātaliṃ °kam Jm 75.16; prob. read so for **saṃgrahaka-,** Gv 225.26. (Also Buddhac. iii.27.)

saṃghaṭati (Skt. id., not in this meaning), *strives, works, exerts oneself*: Mv ii.59.3 (āśāya kṣetrāṇi kṛṣanti karṣakā) saputradārā (mss. add pi, om. Senart) saṃghaṭanti ekadā (so mss., Senart em. ekato).

saṃghaṭana, °naka (nt.?; to prec.), *vigor, firmness*,

strength: Mv iii.13.5 nārāyaṇa-saṃghaṭano (mss. °tano, °ṭṭano) rājā ... *having the vigor* (prowess) *of N.*; in LV 229.13–14 text clearly corrupt, mss. on the whole seem to support the following reading, which corresponds to Tib. sred med kyi bu chen po ltar mkhregs pa daṅ sred med kyi by phyed ltar mkhregs pa ḥi rkyan de rnams de dag gis ma theg go: tāni (sc. the Bodhisattva's abandoned ornaments) mahānārāyaṇa-saṃghaṭanakāny ardhanārāyaṇa-saṃhananāni na śaknuvanti sma dhārayitum, *since these* (ornaments) *had the stoutness of Great N., the vigor of Half-N.* (see **Ardhanārāyaṇa**; so Tib.), *they* (the Śākyas) *could not lift them.* Tib. uses the same word, mkhregs pa, *hardness, firmness*, for both saṃghaṭanaka and saṃhanana (the latter is Skt.). Cf. LV 234.15 Nārāyaṇa-sthāmavan (Lefm. text narā°), which indicates that saṃghaṭana is a synonym of **sthāman.**

saṃghaṭita, ppp. (of saṃghaṭ(ay)ati, in unrecorded mg.), in SP 249.5 (prose) prob. *shrunken, shrivelled* (or possibly *drawn in, contracted*): (Prabhūtaratnas...) pariśuṣkagātraḥ saṃghaṭitakāyo yathāsamādhisamāpannas tathā saṃdṛśyate sma; Tib. skum, *drawn in, contracted*, also *paralyzed* (Das); prob. the cpd. (°kāyo) is near-synonym of pariśuṣkagātraḥ, the correctness of which is supported by Tib. kun bskams, *very dry*; but possibly referring to temporary contraction of limbs in samādhi-posture; perh. same mg., *contracted, limited* or the like, with neg. a-, substantially *free*, in LV 272.13 (prose), in series of epithets of Bodhisattva, ... askhalitagatir a-saṃghaṭita-gatir alīnagatir...; Tib. ḥdrud pa med paḥi, *not rubbed* or *dragged*, perh. based on a-saṃghaṭṭita which is read in Calc. but in none of Lefm.'s mss.

saṃghaṭṭaka, m. pl. (to Skt. saṃ-ghaṭṭate or °ṭṭayati plus -aka), *smashers*, n. given to the monsoon winds: (grīṣmāṇām) paścime māse °kā nāma vātā vāyanti Mv iii.411.15 (prose).

saṃghaṭṭati (cf. caus. Skt. °ṭṭayati, pw s.v. 4, and Pali id., Mahāvaṃsa 21.28, *sounds, makes resound*, trans.), *sounds* (intrans.), *gives forth sound*: (yāni ratanāni nagare nihitāni...) tāni pi saṃghaṭṭetsuḥ... Mv i.235.16 (vs), at Dīpaṃkara's entrance; similarly, peḍākaraṇḍagatāni (so read) ratanāni saṃghaṭṭanti 308.10 (prose).

saṃghata, adj. (= Skt. saṃhata, cf. Pischel 267; Pkt. saṃghaa), *compact*: nitya-ātmasukhasaṃjña-°taṃ (... mokṣadvāru vivarāhi) Gv 55.1 (vs).

saṃgha-bheda, m., *disuniting of the community of monks*, a saṃghāvaśeṣa sin: Mvy 8378; MSV iii.88.2; cf. Prāt 482.10 ff.; 483.3; Pali Vin. iii.172.31 ff.

Saṃgharakṣita (app. unconnected with Pali Saṃgharakkhita), n. of a man who became a disciple of Buddha: Divy 330.24 ff.; 346.19 ff. Cf. next.

Saṃgharakṣitāvadāna (cf. prec.), n. of Divy chap. xxiii: Divy 343.24 (colophon); Śikṣ 57.11, citing Divy 342.13 ff.

saṃgha-sāmagrī-dattaka, adj. (with bhikṣu), (a once suspended monk) *who has been given communion with the order*: MSV ii.195.1 ff. (see **sāmagrī** 2).

saṃghāṭa, m., and **°ṭā**, f., *vessel, jar* (of metal, for storing treasure); only in comp., preceded by loha- or lohī- (cf. **lohī**): catvāro loha-°ṭāḥ suvarṇasya pūrṇāḥ Divy 14.25; catasraḥ lohī-°ṭāḥ suvarṇapūrṇās 16.26; (hiraṇya-suvarṇasya) caturo lohasaṃghāṭān (acc. pl.), v.l. °ṭā(ḥ), Karmav 28.25 (Chin. *jar*); (catvāro) lohasaṃghāṭā(ḥ) MSV iii.135.12.

Saṃghāṭa-sūtra, n. of a work: Mvy 1386. The mg. of saṃghāṭa here is uncertain. There is a Pkt. (AMg. etc.) word saṃghāḍa, *pair, couple*; Tib. on Mvy seems to have had this in mind with its dge ḥdun (= saṃgha!) zuṅ (*pair*) gi mdo, *book of a pair of* (monastic) *assemblies*? One Chin. renders *collection* or *fusion* (cf. Skt. saṃghāta), the other transliterates the word and adds a term which otherwise renders **Arthavargīya**, q.v. Jap. cites the full title, Āryasaṃghāṭadharmaparyāya-sūtra.

saṃghāṭi, oftener **°ṭī** (see also **sāṃ°**; but both recorded in prose; = Pali °ṭi, AMg. °ḍi, °ḍī, also °ḍiya, nt.), *waist-cloth* of a monk (the other two garments are the antarvāsas and uttarāsaṅga, both Skt.; the three listed e.g. Mvy 8933–35; and cf. SBE 17.212, n. 2): Mvy 8933 = Tib. snam sbyar (Chin. = kāṣāya); °ṭī-pātra-cīvara-dhāraṇena LV 191.18; Mv i.301.6; iii.60.6; 182.13; °ṭī-paṭṭa(read paṭa?)-pātra-cīvara-dhāraṇe Śikṣ 120.14; °ṭī-paṭa-pātraṃ (so mss.) Mv ii.307.16 (vs); paṭa-pilotika (q.v.)-°ṭī iii.53.14, 16; 54.1 ff.; sometimes folded and used as a seat, caturguṇa-°ṭiṃ Mv i.318.15, *folded in four*, for sitting on; similarly prob. understand dvipuṭa-°ṭī Mvy 9187, tripuṭa° 9188; muṇḍaḥ saṃvṛttaḥ °ṭi-(or °ṭī-)-prāvṛtaḥ (also pl.) Divy 37.1; 159.9; 281.24; 558.20; muṇḍaḥ °ṭi-prāvṛto Av ii.119.5; muṇḍā °ṭī-prāvṛtā Bhīk 3a.2; °ṭī-pariveṣṭito muṇḍaśiraḥ KP 122.3 (prose); °ṭī-prāvṛtaḥ sadā Ud xiii.15 (= Pali Therag. 153 muṇḍo °ṭi-pāruto); read prob. muṇḍaḥ saṃghāṭiprāvṛtaḥ Mv iii.452.1 (vs; mss. muṇḍa saṃghāṭikodhana, or °nam; = Pali Jāt. v. 251.28 muṇḍo °ṭipāruto; read the first half-line in Mv with mss. kṛpaṇo vata tvaṃ bhikṣo); °ṭim (°ṭīm) ādāya Divy 154.17, 27; cīvaraṃ °ṭīm adhitiṣṭhāmi Bhīk 15a.1; (gaccha mahārājemāṃ) °ṭīṃ dhvajāgre baddhvā ... Av i.82.2; saṃghāṭikāṃ sādhayet ... (9) tasyopari saṃghāṭiṃ pratiṣṭhāpya Mmk 715.8–9 (prose).

saṃghāṭikā (cf. AMg. saṃghāḍiya, nt.) = prec., q.v.: Mmk 715.8 (prose).

saṃghāta, m. (= Pali id., DPPN; also Skt. id.), n. of a (hot) hell: Mvy 4922; Dharmas 121; Mv i.5.10; 9.8; 13.11, etc.; 21.1; 42.16; 337.5; ii.350.10 = iii.274.12; iii.454.7; Divy 67.21; 366.28; Gv 157.19; Av i.4.8 etc.; in Jm 196.9 the name is explained, those who go there are crushed by clashing mountains; similarly Pali (root han with sam).

saṃghāvaśeṣa, adj., m. with or sc. dharma, or f. with āpatti (= Pali saṃghādisesa, which Lévi, see below believes Pktic for *saṃghāti°), one of a group of 13 (so also Pali) monkish offenses requiring suspension, but not expulsion, from the order (contrast **pārājika, pātayantika**), perh. *permitting a remainder of* (association with) *the order* (Lévi, JA Nov.-Dec. 1912, 504); but acc. to SBE 20.35 n. 2, (*offences*) *which can be done away, but only by the saṃgha* (see **niravaśeṣa**): trayodaśa °ṣāḥ (sc. dharmāḥ) Mvy 8359 (the 13 items listed 8369–81); trayodaśa °ṣā dharmāḥ Prāt 479.3; listed and described in the following, each item called °ṣaḥ; °ṣām āpattim MSV iii.11.16 etc.

saṃghāvaśeṣaka, adj. from prec., with bhikṣu, *guilty of a saṃgh° sin*: MSV iii.94.16.

saṃghin (= Pali id.), *head of an order* or *assembly* of pupils, ep. of Rudraka Rāmaputra: read saṃghinaṃ and saṃghī in LV 243.19 and 20 for mss. and ed. saṃghe or saṃgha-, see s.v. **gaṇin.**

saṃghoṣa (unrecorded in this mg.), *sound, cry* (of animals): in Bhvr. cpd., nadiṃ vyāghragaṇasiṃhavāraṇa-°ṣāṃ Mv ii.105.14 (vs), *characterized by the cries of...*

saca (cf. Pali sacāca? Vin. i.88, last line, see comm. cited p. 372), *if*, = **sace(t)**: saca tvam īśvaro asyā Mv ii.406.1 (vs, but sa-ca not m.c.; no v.l.); saca (also not m.c.; Senart em. sacet) sumanasā (lacuna, two syllables) Alindā ramayāsi me iii.6.18 (vs); v.l. for **saci**, q.v., SP 448.5, 7, and ff. (vss). For sacāsya, saceha, sacaiva, see **sace(t).**

saci (or, v.l., **saca**, q.v.), *if*, m.c. for **sace(t)**: SP 448.5, 7, and ff.; Sukh 22.3, 7, 11 and ff.

sacet, sace, conj. (Pali sace; see also **saca, saci; sa-**, q.v., with cet, formed as pendant to no cet, Pali no-ce; so Childers and Andersen, Reader; otherwise, but to me unconvincingly, Geiger 105.2, Pischel 423), *if*; very common in most texts, prose as well as vss, and usually retaining in writing the final -t or -d: Mvy 5433; SP 47.13; 78.10; 97.3; 322.4 etc.; LV (common, usually printed sa cet by Lefm.) 101.12; 226.4; 408.4 (the only passage noted Weller, as not Skt.); Mv (common) ii.88.10; 141.3; 194.11; 272.16; 315.6, 7; iii.4.4; 20.7; 199.15; 204.2; 406.11; Divy 2.7; 88.22; 302.20; 559.23 etc.; Av i.14.10 etc.; RP 8.4; 48.15; Gv 138.19; Bbh 20.20 etc. (common); Vaj 21.3; Sukh 11.9, 12, 15 etc.; Karmav 26.12; Bhīk 3a.3; Laṅk 261.13 (rare in Laṅk; not in Index, no other case noted by me); sace not common, and in prose only in Mv, e. g. ii.158.13; 428.18; iii.54.14; sace, v.l. sacet, iii.187.7 (vs); see saci; saṃdhi forms in which either sace or saca might be understood, sacāsya (pron. asya) Mv i.323.21; iii.318.11 (both prose); saceha (-iha) SP 31.11 (vs); sacaiva, ms. K′ saceva, prob. containing evam rather than eva, SP 31.9; 204.6 (both vss); sacevam, v.l. sacaivam, Mv ii.409.15 (vs); exceptionally followed by verb in impv., sacen mama ... nayanaṃ gṛhītvā ... muñca, na tv evāhaṃ ... Divy 476.17–18, *if you take my eye and ...* (impv.) *let it go!* (if you like), *still I would not* ...; in a formula introducing a question, in most cases a double (alternative) question, saced (sacet, sacen) manyatha (twice both mss. and twice v.l. anyatha or °thā; both mss. manyatha only 340.2) bhikṣavaḥ Mv iii.337.11, 20; 338.5; 339.16; 340.2; in the corresp. passage in Pali, Vin. i.14.5, taṃ kiṃ maññatha bhikkhave, which is common also in BHS (kiṃ manyatha bhikṣavaḥ, or the like); does this Mv version have a different mg.? Perhaps *suppose, monks, you consider* (the following question)?

sa-caukṣa, see **saṃcaukṣa**.

sa-cchambita, adj. (**sa-**, q.v., plus ppp. of **chambati**, q.v.), *frightened*: ṛṣiṃ ... saṃtarjayetsuḥ °taṃ karetsuḥ Mv iii.194.17.

sajati, ppp. sajita, or saṃjita (cf. **utsajati**; = Pali sajati, cf. n. ag. saṃjitar, *creator*; MIndic for Skt. sṛjati), *sends forth, spreads abroad* (a false and slanderous report): (taṃ) sajitaṃ (so, or saṃjitaṃ, the two best mss.; 3 mss. sejitaṃ; one inferior ms. sevitaṃ, which Senart reads) Vasumate mahānagare Mv i.37.1; *this* (lying report just quoted) *was spread abroad in the city of V.*

sajjira, v.l. for **sarj(j)ara**, q.v.

sajjīva (= Pali sājīva, which represents this, i. e. sat-jīva, by the 'law of morae'), *good (moral) life*: bhava-sajjīva-tatve aparāmṛṣṭaśubhakarmāś ca bhavanti Mv i.134.6, *grâce à* (litt. *dans*) *la régularité de leur vie dans les existences* (qu'ils traversent), *ils ont une conduite pure et affranchie* (Senart). (But -tatve, -tattve, seems to me troublesome).

sajyotibhūta, adj. (= Pali sajoti°, which most mss. usually read in Mv), *aflame, on fire* (may be interpreted as sa-jyoti(s) plus -bhūta, rather than **sa-**, q.v., plus jyotibhūta): (parvatehi pīḍiyantā, mss. pīḍa°) ādīptasaṃprajvalita-sajyotibhūtehi Mv i.5.11, repeated with varr., esp. with °jvalita made a separate coordinate word, several times in the sequel and in i.18.9.

saṃcagghati (cf. **uccagghati**), *laughs together* (with others): Bbh 169.4 uccais saṃcagghati saṃkrīḍate saṃkilikilāyate; Bhīk 28a.3 avaśrutena puruṣeṇa sārdhaṃ saṃcagghet saṃkrīḍet saṃkilikilāyet.

saṃcaya (in this special sense peculiar to BHS; in Pali represented by ācaya, see CPD, PTSD s.v. apacaya), *accumulation* of evil karma, or of worldliness; opp. of **apacaya**, q.v.: (iyaṃ dṛṣṭiḥ ...) saṃcayāya nāpacayāya ... saṃvartate Av ii.188.9–10 (em., proved by the next); ... apacayāya na saṃcayāya ... saṃvartate 189.6. For Pali parallel see e. g. Vin. ii.259.5 apacayāya ... no ācayāya.

saṃcaritra, nt. (= Pali °tta; see also **sāṃ°**), *procuring, acting as go-between in liaisons*, one of the saṃghāvaśeṣa sins: Mvy 8373; cf. Prāt 480.6–7.

saṃcalatthā, var. for **calatthā**, q.v.

saṃcāraṇa, prob. *spying* (upon): (vyaktam ayaṃ ...) -śaṭhamadhuravacanaḥ pravṛtti-°ṇa-hetubhūtaḥ (*serving as a means for spying upon your activities*) kasyāpi pratyarthino rājño ... Jm 143.20 (prose); so Speyer seems to understand it, *to be informed of your actions*; pw 7.379, *das Ueberbringen* (einer Botschaft).

Saṃcāraṇī, n. of a yoginī: Dharmas 13.

saṃcāra-vyādhi, m. (cf. Skt. saṃcārin, *infectious*), *infectious disease*: Mvy 9526 = Tib. nad (*disease*) ḥgo ba (*infect*).

saṃcārikā (cf. **cārikā** and Skt. saṃcarati), (*religious*) *course of action*: ... kalpān bodhisattva-°kāṃ (1st ed. °kā) caranto na parikhidyante Gv 365.8.

saṃcārima, adj. (= AMg. id.; to Skt. saṃcāra plus -ima, § 22.15), *moving, movable*: asmākaṃ uṭajāni (em.) °māni, yena icchāma tena ... gacchāma Mv iii.147.16 (prose).

saṃcita, ppp. (of sam-ci), lit. *collected*: in °tātman, Bhvr., *who has 'collected' (disciplined, trained?) himself* (Senart, *meditated, 'qui se sont recueillis'*, doubtfully); naikakalpaśata-saṃcitātmanāṃ Mv i.64.1 (vs), of Buddhas.

Saṃcitora(s), n. of a former Buddha: Mv i.138.14 (n. sg. °raḥ).

saṃcintya, ger. of saṃ-cintayati (in same mg. Pali saṃcicca), used as adv., *intentionally, purposely*: Mvy 6470 = Tib. bsams pa zhiṅ; °tya vayaṃ bhikṣuṇībhir viheṭhitā Divy 494.9; °tya bhavopapattiṃ gṛhṇāti Bbh 414.7; yā ... bhikṣuṇī manuṣyaṃ ... °tya jīvitād vyaparopayec ... Bhīk 25b.2 (Pali parallel, Vin. iii.73.10).

saṃcetanā (= Pali id.), *thinking*; see **manaḥsaṃcetanāhāra.**

saṃcetanikāhāra, m., = **manaḥsaṃcetanāhāra**, q.v.: Dharmas 70. Cf. **sāṃcetanika.**

saṃcetanīya-tā, *condition of being made aware, notified*: Mvy 7536, 7537; Tib. sems (pa) las gyur pa.

Saṃcodaka, n. of a (trāyastriṃśa) devaputra: LV 204.7; 220.1. (As adj. or n. ag., ms. at Śikṣ 35.4; ed. em. **saṃbodhaka**, q.v.)

saṃcodayati (= **codayati**, q.v.; the cpd. not in Pali), *accuses* (of, instr.): (mā haiva tasya vaidyasya ... kurvataḥ) kaścin mṛṣāvādena °dayet SP 323.1 (prose), *if the physician did* (this), *might not some one accuse* (him) *of lying*? Two mss. codayet (om. saṃ); so the verse account reads, 326.6.

? **saṃcaukṣa**, adj., *completely pure*: tadgṛhaṃ °ṣaṃ kṛtvā ... dātavyam Suv 118.4–5 (prose); cf. caukṣam āsanaṃ prajñāpayitavyam 6; so Nobel, but most mss. sa- rather than saṃ-; perh. read sa-caukṣaṃ, *having purity*, i. e. *pure*? Or as s.v. **sa-**; caukṣa is recorded only as adj., not noun. Tib. śin tu gtsaṅ ma, *very pure*.

saṃchādana, f. °**nī**, adj. (to Skt. saṃchādayati plus -ana), *covering*: (jihvā ...) mukhamaṇḍala-°nī Gv 401.16; (sarvasattvaloka-)-°na-mahādharmachattramaṇḍalaḥ Gv 319.19.

saṃchedana, adj. (to Skt. sam-chid- plus -ana), **-tā**, subst., (*state of*) *destroying, cutting off, cutting down* or *to pieces*: varmabhūtam (cited Śikṣ 6.4 as dharma°, but surrounding comparisons are military) ayoniśomanaskāra-°natayā Gv 495.7; kuṭhārabhūtaṃ duḥkhavṛkṣa-°natayā 10.

-saṃjana (m.? or nt.? = Skt. and Pali saṃjanana), *producing, production*: Mv iii.77.10 (vs) romaharṣaṇa-saṃjanaṃ (Bhvr.), *which produces horripilation*; v.l. °saṃjananaṃ, but meter proves °saṃjanaṃ correct; Divy 467.3 (prose) avipratisāra-saṃjanārthaṃ, *to produce non-regret*, but in same phrase Divy 78.7 °saṃjananārthaṃ, which prob. read in 467.3 (haplography), with MSV i.76.2 (same text).

saṃjanaka, adj. or subst. (= AMg. saṃjaṇaa, °ṇaga; to Skt. saṃjanayati plus -aka), (*one who* or) *that which produces*: buddhotpāda-°kānāṃ sa (so divide) kuśalamūlānām antarāyaḥ Śikṣ 84.4, *this hindrance to the roots of merit which produce . . .*

saṃjanayitar (= Pali °netar; to °nayati), *one who creates, produces*: bodhicittasya °tāro Gv 463.2.

Saṃjaya, (**1**) (= Pali id.), n. of a king of the Śibis, father of Viśvaṃtara: Jm 52.3 ff.; (**2**) n. of a minister (amātya), former incarnation of the Buddha: Mv i.93.4 (gave his heart to a piśāca in exchange for recitation of a pious gāthā); (**3**) n. of a son of Kubera: Māy 230.21 (note that Saṃjaya is read by many mss. for **Saṃjñāya,** q.v., the yakṣa leader; so Burnouf, Introd. 532, citing from Suv).

Saṃjayantī, n. of the city of Bhīmaratha: Mv iii.364.4.

Saṃjayin Vairaṭīputra (the latter variously spelled, with e for ai, ṭṭ, ḍ, ḍh, or t for ṭ, i for ī, also °ika-putra, once even allegedly Vairūṭī°; = Pali Saṃjaya Belaṭṭhiputta), n. of one of the six famous heretical teachers of Buddha's day (see s.v. **Pūraṇa Kāśyapa**): usually named with the others, as in Mvy 3547 (Vairaḍīp°, but Mironov °ṭīp°); Divy 143.11 (Vairaṭṭīp°); Av i.231.4 (Vairūṭīp° acc. to Speyer's text, but Feer Vairaṭīp° with v.l.); Mv i.253.16 (mss. Saṃjayisya, or °yī, Velatiputrasya, or Veraḍhip°); 257.1 and iii.383.16 (mss. °yī Veraṭṭikaputra, v.l. in the latter Veraṅgikap°); mentioned without the others, as S. Vairaṭīp° Mv iii.59.9 (v.l. Veratip°); 59.11 (mss. Vairaṭikap°); 90.11 (Vairaṭip°); and as Saṃjayi(n) alone, without Vai°, iii.63.5 ff.

[**-saṃjāna-**, corrupt, represents a dat. sg. of a nom. act. meaning *production*, perh. -saṃjananāya?: jātijarāmaraṇamahāndhakārabhayapratipakṣāya kuśalamūla-saṃjānābhiyogaṃ (so text; °jananāyābhi°?) saṃvarṇayāmi Gv 318.8, *I recommend application to the production of roots of merit,* (a process) *which counteracts the dangers of birth* etc.]

saṃjānayati (= Skt. saṃjan°; § 38.15), *produces*: prītiprāmodyaṃ °yitvā (Senart em. saṃjan°) Mv i.238.1; mg. proved by prītiprāmodya-saṃjananārthaṃ i.238.8 (no v.l.); mahākaruṇāṃ saṃjānayya LV 137.19; mahādharmavarṣavegaṃ °nayiṣyanti LV 439.4; jñānālokaṃ ca °nayati Gv 502.23; all prose.

saṃjānāti, °nīte, pass. (or denom. to saṃjñā, *name*?) **saṃjñāyate**; caus. **saṃjñapayati, saṃjñāp°** (all mgs. seem to occur for Pali saṃjānāti, °nati, pass. saññāyati, Childers; nearest recorded Skt. seems to be saṃjajñe, *knew, understood*, once in Rām., BR jñā with sam, 7), (**1**) *knows* (*well*): (icchāmy etaṃ yasya dātavyaṃ yataś ca) grahītavyaṃ yac ca nidhātavyaṃ bhavet, sarvaṃ saṃjānīyāḥ SP 107.12, *I want that you should know about all this, to whom anything is to be given, from whom received, and what is to be stored*; similarly saṃjānīyād 108.2; Tib. for saṃjānīyāḥ, khyod kyis śes par (ḥdod do = icchāmi), *that you should know*; so for °yād, mchis par ḥtshal la; similarly jānāti in 108.12 = śes so; all these wrongly rendered in BR; (**2**) *knows = recognizes,* or *becomes aware of*: te pi anyam-anyaṃ saṃjānetsuḥ, anye pi kila iha bho sattvā upapannā Mv i.230.3, repeated 240.13, iii.334.11, 341.15; same passage, anyonyam evaṃ saṃjānanti SP 163.12; °nante LV 51.16, 410.20; (**3**) *holds, considers,* esp. falsely (cf. **saṃjñā, saṃjñin**): loka evaṃ saṃjānīte SP 316.2 (erroneous views are then stated); yad andhakāraṃ tat prakāśam iti saṃjānīṣe, yac ca prakāśaṃ tad andhakāram iti °nīṣe SP 135.4–5; (**4**) act., mid., *names, calls,* and pass. *is called, is named*: iti caike saṃjānanti (sc. māṃ) Laṅk 192.16; 193.3; māṃ janāḥ saṃjānanta udakacandra ivāpraviṣṭanirgatam 193.5; sarvatra ca śrāvaka iti saṃjñāyate sma SP 200.13, *and in all* (previous existences) *he has been called 'Disciple'* (of various Buddhas); adyāpi ca tāni ṛṣipadāny eva saṃjñāyante LV 18.19, *and even today they are still called 'the sage's traces'*; (adyāpi tat pāṃśukūlasīvanam) ity evaṃ saṃjñāyate sma LV 267.8; (**5**) caus., *makes known, declares*: tena (sa) yācanakaś (. . .) °jñapayitavyaḥ Śikṣ 20.4–5, 9, *he must declare to the suitor*; (rājā Padumāvatīṃ . . . bahuprakāraṃ) °jñāpeti Mv iii. 167.14 (foll. by direct quotation), *announced*(?), or, perh. better, *appeased, conciliated* (as in Skt.).

saṃjita, v.l. for sajita, see **sajati.**

saṃjīva, m. (nt. Mv i.16.8 acc. to Senart, but prob. corrupt, see P. Mus, La Lumière des six voies, 107, 111 f.; m. i.17.6), n. of a (hot) hell: attempt at etym. explanation of name, Mv i.17.6, see Mus, l.c. (orig. *coming to life again*); others, Mv i.5.3; 9.8 = iii.454.7; i.10.9 = iii.455.3; i.337.5; ii.350.8 = iii.274.10; Mvy 4920; Dharmas 121; Divy 67.21; 138.6; 366.28; 568.11; Av i.4.8; 10.8, etc.; Mmk 115.1; 635.22.

-saṃjña, ifc. Bhvr. = **saṃjñā,** q.v.

saṃjñapana, nt. (= AMg. saṇṇavaṇa; cf. next; to saṃjñapayati, caus. of **saṃjānāti,** plus -ana), *statement,* lit. *making known*: etac ca °nam upari doṣaparihārāyoktaṃ Śikṣ 20.9.

saṃjñapti, f. (= Pali saññatti, both mgs.; cf. **saṃjñāpti**), (**1**) *information, statement* (cf. **saṃjñapana**): tena sa yācanakaś catasṛbhiḥ °tibhiḥ saṃjñapayitavyaḥ Śikṣ 20.4; (**2**) *appeasement, mollification* (Skt. saṃjñapayati in this sense): saṃjñapyamānaś cāśu °tiṃ pratigṛhṇāti Bbh 8.1; mānābhigṛhītaḥ °tim anurūpaṃ (read °pāṃ?) nānuprayacchaty upekṣate, sāpattiko bhavati Bbh 170.23; also ff.

saṃjñā, ifc. Bhvr. **-saṃjña** (cf. Skt. id.; the Skt. mgs. *sign, signal,* and *name,* are also BHS; note esp. vaidya-saṃjñāṃ ghoṣayitvā Divy 109.21, *proclaiming the title of physician = saying that he was a physician*; Pali saññā is used in most of the mgs. listed below; Tib. regularly ḥdu śes, a mechanically literal rendering), (**1**) *awareness, consciousness,* as a generalized faculty, fundamentally as in Skt.: cf. visaṃjña, *unconscious* (in a swoon, or the like) = Skt. id., e. g. SP 104.8; technical uses, see **saṃjñā-vedayita-(vedita-)-nirodha, naivasaṃjñānāsaṃjñā-yatana (°nopaga)**; (**2**) not clearly distinguishable from prec., *notion, conception, idea,* of anything in the external world: the third of the five (**upādāna-)skandha** (as in Pali), see **upādāna** (sometimes rendered *perception*); when the Bodhisattva sat down at the bodhi-tree, he received (pratilabhati) at once five saṃjñā, *ideas* or *impressions,* viz. kṣema-s°, sukha-, śubha-, hita-, and (fifthly) adya cāhaṃ anuttarāṃ samyaksaṃbodhim abhisaṃbuddhiṣyati (so mss., Senart em. °ṣyaṃ ti) Mv ii.268.6–8, and similarly 404.17–19, where the fifth is substantially the same, the others being atīta-s°, kṣema-, sukha-, aśakya- (neither passage explains the first four); aśubha-saṃjñā (= Pali asubha-saññā), *conceptions of foul things* which must be meditated on by monks, see s.v. **aśubha-bhāvanā**; often prec. in comp. by other words specifying the emotional or intellectual content of the saṃjñā, (na ca) anitya-saṃjñā-bahulā viharanti Mv i.79.15, *and* (backsliders) *dwell not abounding in the notion of the impermanence* (of sentient existence, as they ought to); parikatha bhikṣu yadī na bhāra-saṃjñā LV 242.22 (vs), *speak, monk, if you are not conscious of a burden* (in doing as I ask), wrongly Foucaux on Skt. and Tib. (khur gyi ḥdu śes med na gsuṅs); in a neg., or impliedly or quasi-neg., expression, something like *the very idea, thought,* āhāra-saṃjñā ca na tatra bheṣyati anyatra dharme rati dhyānaprītiḥ (Nep. mss. jñāna°) SP 206.1 (vs), *and there will be no thought* or *idea of food, other than delight in the Doctrine and joy in meditation*; adhimāna-saṃjñāṃ ca vihāya sarvāṃ SP 287.8 (vs), *and abandoning every thought of pride*; sukhaṃ vinaśyatī teṣāṃ sukha-saṃjñā ca naśyati SP 177.5 (vs), . . . *and the very notion of happiness was lost*; tena ca mahatā duḥkhaskandhenābhyāhatā na duḥkhamanasikāra-saṃjñām utpādayanti SP 78.5, *and, afflicted with that great mass of misery, they do not conceive the idea of putting their minds on misery* (it does not occur to them to consider the question of misery seriously); (**3**) developing out of prec. (cf. āhāra-saṃjñā, SP 206.1 above, which might perhaps be rendered *interest in, inclination towards food*; and cf. AMg. saṇṇā = manovṛtti, *mental inclination*, Ratnach.), *interest in, purposeful thought about*: in Mv ii.147.12 (the Bodhisattva replies to his father's attempt to interest him in women; read with mss.) yasya tāta strīsaṃjñā bhaveyā so atra rajyeyā..., *father, whoever has 'ideas' about women, let him take pleasure in them*; the king replies, tava kīdṛśī saṃjñā bhavati 13, *what are your thoughts* or *ideas*?, to which the prince replies, mamātra viparītasaṃjñā bhavati 14, *I have the idea of the reverse*, i. e. (as the sequel explains), that things are the opposite of what they seem; here saṃjñā belongs to 2 above; cf. viparīta-saṃjñin SP 320.12, s.v. **saṃjñin** (3); (**4**) in BHS esp. *false notion, erroneous impression in the mind*: in LV 374.11–12 (vss, unmetr. in Lefm.; see his note and Foucaux's note on Calc. 485.7) read, iha hetudarśanād vai jitā mayā hetukās trayaḥ saṃjñāḥ, nityānitye saṃjñā sukhaduḥkha 'nātmani cātmani ca, ... *three false notions*, (viz.) *the notions about the permanent and impermanent, pleasure and pain, non-self and self*; saṃjñā-graheṇa (*by clinging to false notions*) bālā dṛṣṭi-viparyāsa niśritā LV 235.17 (vs); saṃjñākṛta-mātram (*a mere product of a false notion*) idaṃ kaṇṭhako vahatīti vādiśārdūlaṃ Mv i.157.10 (the gods held the horse's hoofs); saṃjñāsūtraṃ (*the cord of*...) uddharī saṃskṛtātaḥ LV 196.2 (vs); vitarkamālā saṃjñāsūtreṣu granthitā LV 372.3 (vs), *the garland of doubt, strung on the cords of*...; sattvānāṃ ... saṃjñā-vikalpa-caritānāṃ SP 318.13, *of creatures whose actions are characterized by false notions and vain imaginings*; mṛgīye ... taṃ prasrāvaṃ pānīya-saṃjñāya (instr., *under the mistaken impression that is was water*) pītaṃ Mv iii.143.17, so 153.12, °saṃjñāye 144.7; 154.9; bhagavaṃ (mss. °vāṃ) mṛgasaṃjñena mayā etaṃ iṣu kṣiptaṃ Mv ii.213.16, *under the mistaken impression of* (your being) *a deer* (cf. 5 below) *I shot this arrow*; krīḍāratiṃ ca janayec chubha-saṃjña-tāṃ ca LV 190.5 (vs), ... *and a state of having a false notion of* (its being) *fine* (also cf. 5); keṣa-cid ... vartati saṃjñā Samādh 19.24, *some have the false notion* ..., and so, keṣa-ci saṃjñā 25; (**5**) in comp. with a prec. noun or adj. (as in some cases under 4), the *notion* or *idea* or *impression, opinion*, that (something or someone) is (what the prior member of the cpd. means); esp. as object of utpādayati (cf. SP 78.5, under 2 above) or a synonym, *forms, conceives* such an *idea* or *opinion*; the object of the idea is generally loc., sometimes gen. with **antike**, q.v., rarely acc., sometimes not expressed (understood from context): (tato imā asmākaṃ striyaḥ sarvakālaṃ) paribhavetsuḥ, tṛṇasaṃjñā pi na (mss. recorded as ta) utpādayetsuḥ (so read) Mv iii.393.14, *then these our wives would always scorn us, would not even think we were worth a straw* (lit. *form a grass-blade-notion*, sc. of us); śrotavyaṃ (read °vya, m.c.) buddhavacanaṃ dullabha-saṃjñām upajanetvā Mv i.248.2 (vs), *one must listen to the word of a Buddha, realizing that it is hard to find*; (te ... durlabhaprādurbhāvāṃs) tathāgatān viditvāścaryasaṃjñām utpādayiṣyanti śoka-saṃjñām utpā° SP 320.1, ... *will conceive the notion of surprise and sorrow*, virtually = *will be surprised and grieved*; hīnasaṃjñā, *a low* (= *unfavorable*) *opinion*, (na tvayā ...) °jñotpādayitavyā SP 425.9, and with loc. of object, mā hīnasaṃjñām utpādayiṣyasi tathāgate ca bodhisattveṣu ca tasmiṃś ca buddhakṣetre 426.2; the opposite is viśiṣṭa-s°, LV 244.1–2, below; others with loc., śmaśāna-saṃjñāṃ (mss. °jño) janayate iṣṭikāsu Mv ii.384.22 (vs), *forms the idea about women that they are* (repulsive as) *cemeteries*; tāsu mātṛsaṃjñā upasthāpayitavyā bhaginī-saṃjñā duhitṛsaṃjñā Divy 115.5, *you must learn to think of them as if mothers, sisters, daughters*; kiṃīkṛta-(q.v., so read)-saṃjñā bhaveyur na ca tathāgate durlabha-saṃjñām utpādayeyuḥ SP 319.8, ... *and would not conceive the difficulty of finding a T.*; the object is in gen. with **antike** (q.v.), naiṣa mamāntike viśiṣṭasaṃjño (Bhvr.) bhaven LV 244.1–2, *he would not have a high opinion of me*; (sarvatathāgatānāṃ) cāntike pitṛsaṃjñām utpādayati sarvabodhisattvānāṃ cāntike śāstṛsaṃjñām utpā° SP 286.1; also SP 107.4–5 (see **antike**); object is acc., svabhavanāni śmaśāna-saṃjñām utpādayām āsuḥ LV 278.7, (gods etc.) *began to think of their own dwellings as cemeteries* (i. e. repulsive; = svāni vimānāni śmaśānānīva menire 280.20, vs); (**6**) (cf. Skt. mg. *sign, symbol*), *alphabetic sign, letter*: (yā) vā imā loke saṃjñā (mss. mostly sajñā, perh. representing a pronunciation like MIndic saññā, as in Pali?), brāhmī (etc., list of alphabets) Mv i.135.5; (**7**) a high number: Mvy 8034 = Tib. brdaḥ śes; cf. **mahā-saṃjñā, sarva-s°, visaṃjñāvatī.**

saṃjñānanā, *awareness*: Mvy 7566. Not to be read saṃjā° with pw 7 App.; confirmed by **vijñānanā**; see § 22.7.

[**saṃjñāpada**, see **saṃjñotpāda.**]

saṃjñāpti, f. (would seem to = **saṃjñapti**, Pali saññatti, but neither seems used in just this mg.), acc. to Tib. (gsol ba btab pa) *the making of a request* or *demand*: para-°ti-saṃcetanīyatā (q.v.) Mvy 7537.

saṃjñā-bhikṣu, m., *a monk in name alone*, or *by false notion*: Mvy 8750 (Tib. renders saṃjñā by miṅ, *name*).

Saṃjñāya (mss. mostly Saṃjaya, but Tib. yaṅ dag śes, supporting Nobel's reading), n. of a yakṣa prince or commander (senāpati): Suv 85.1; 91.16; 128.3 ff. (chap. XI, °ya-parivarta); 158.13 (here called janarṣabhaḥ, so read with best mss., others nararṣabhaḥ; Nobel's jinarṣabhaḥ, based on Tib., seems to me clearly wrong, cf. Nobel's note 14 above where N. corrects the same Tib. reading; context proves that a yakṣa, not a Buddha, is meant); 161.7.

saṃjñā-vedayita-(also °**vedita-**)**-nirodha**, m. (= Pali saññā-vedayitanirodha, the condition of the 8th vimokkha, and of the 9th samāpatti or anupubbavihāra), *suppression of consciousness and sensation*, an advanced stage of trance: (°vedita°) Mvy 1518, as condition of 8th **vimokṣa**; the ninth and highest of the **anupūrvavihāra-(-samāpatti)**, q.v.; also abbreviated **nirodha(-samāpatti)**, q.v.; (°vedita°) AbhidhK. LaV-P. ii.213, as a **samāpatti**; (°vedayita-)°dha-samāpattiyo ca spṛhayanti Mv i.127.5, one of the two reasons because of which Bodhisattvas ṣaṣṭhāyāṃ bhūmau vartamānāḥ saptamāyāṃ bhūmau vivartanti. This implies that it is an unworthy object of supreme religious ambition.

saṃjñita, (**1**) denom. ppp. to saṃjñā (Skt. id.), here (as Pali saññita) used with special sense corresp. to **saṃjñā** (4), *falsely termed*: arājyaṃ (mss. ār°) rājya-°taṃ Mv i.179.13 (vs); nityaṃ śāśvatadṛṣṭi-°taṃ jagad RP 55.11 (vs), *the world, falsely called 'eternal' according to the eternalist-heresy*; [(**2**) in Mv ii.103.10 Senart's em., (rājño vacanamātreṇa kumārasya gṛhaṃ yathā divyaṃ vimānaṃ tathā alaṃkṛtaṃ) sarva-saṃjñitaṃ (mss. sarva-saṅginaṃ or -saṃjñinaṃ); I do not understand the mss. readings or even the em. (supposed to mean *known to all*? but I find no such use of saṃjñita).]

saṃjñin, adj. (to **saṃjñā** plus -in; in all mgs., seemingly, in Pali saññin), (**1**) *conscious*, of living beings (so once in Skt., BR); (sattvāḥ ...) saṃjñino vāsaṃjñino vā Vaj 20.18; (**2**) *originating in, produced by*, **saṃjñā** in some sense (prob. 1, *consciousness*): cittāni caitasika-saṃjñi-vitarkitāni (so read as cpd.) LV 151.13 (vs), *thoughts, and the cogitations belonging to* (*arising from*) *thoughts and consciousness* (Tib. supports this construction, sems daṅ sems byuṅ ḥdu śes rnam par rtog pa daṅ, only two coordinate terms; caitasika and saṃjñi both adj. with vita°); (**3**) *having an idea, notion* (**saṃjñā** 2 and 5): evaṃsaṃjñin Mvy 1520, 1521, *having such an idea* (as stated in prec.);

kecid viparīta-°ñino bhaveyuḥ kecid aviparīta-°ñino SP 320.12, *some would have contrary notions, some not contrary* (to truth), see Mv ii.147.12–14, s.v. **saṃjñā** (3); parasparaṃ mātāpitṛsamjñino 'bhūvan LV 52.15 (here text erroneously °saṅgino, with v.l.); 411.18, *they thought of one another as mothers and fathers* (with respect and affection); (**4**) esp. (cf. **saṃjñā** 4) *having a false, wrong idea*: aprāpte prāptasaṃjñī (n. pl.) ca SP 272.2 (vs), *imagining that they have arrived when they have not*; aprāpte prāptasaṃjñino 'nadhigate 'dhigata-°ñinaḥ SP 38.14 f. (prose); aśaraṇe śaraṇa-°ñino 'maṅgalye maṅgala-°ñino LV 250.4; alene lena-°ñino (by em.) Mv i.7.7, *supposing that what is no refuge is a refuge*; alenā (Bhvr.) lena-°ñino (by em.) 11.15; kāmaguṇair (instr. for loc., cf. § 7.32) niguṇair (m.c. for nirg°) guṇasaṃjñinaḥ LV 206.20 (vs), *in regard to the worthless* (guṇa-less) **kāma-guṇa** (q.v.), *imagining that they are worthy* (are guṇas); prāptanirvāṇa-°ñinaḥ SP 142.3, *imagining that they have reached nirvāṇa*; nirvāṇa-°ñino SP 101.3 (same mg.); āgata-°ñinaś ca bhaveyur nistīrṇa-°ñinaś ca SP 188.7, *and would imagine falsely that they have arrived and are saved*; teṣu ca sāra-°ñino bhavanti LV 249.18, *and in regard to them falsely imagine that they are the chief thing*; bhaveṣu āsvāda-°ñino bhavanti Mv i.79.10, *cherishing the illusion of relish regarding states of being*; nāsty ātma-°ñino 'raṇyavāso nāsti para-°ñinaḥ Śikṣ 199.2, *forest life is not for one who has the false notions of self or other* (i. e. who sees a difference there).

saṃjñīkṛta, ppp. (to *saṃjñīkaroti; to Skt. saṃjñā, *name*; cf. Skt. saṃjñībhūtaka), *named, called*: satkāya-°taṃ LV 208.13 (vs), *termed the personality*.

saṃjñotpāda, m.c. °**pada** (cf. -saṃjñām utpādayati, see s.v. **saṃjñā** 5), *formation of ideas* or *conceptions, notions*: read in Mv i.215.6 = ii.18.3 (vs) sādhū ti nirāmiṣehi saṃjñotpadehi (mss. saṃjñāpad° or saṃjñotpād°, the latter unmetr.; Senart adopts the former) kṣapenti taṃ kālaṃ, *with cries of approval* (the divine guardians of the infant Bodhisattva and his mother) *pass the time in productions of ideas* (instigation of notions) *that are free from worldliness*.

? **saṭhaḥ-**, form and mg. obscure: LV 341.5 (vs) yajñā nirargaḍa ya yaṣṭa saṭhaḥ-kalībhiḥ, so Lefm. with best mss., AL; other mss. śaṭaḥ-; Calc. śataḥ (interpreted as = śata-); Calc. and 2 mss. (B) kalābhiḥ, H kalpabhiḥ. Have we to do with a form or relative of Skt. saṭā, śaṭā (also chaṭā), *mass, large amount*? The stem kalī, if correct, instead of kalā, *part*, is also suspicious. Tib. for the cpd. bsdoms kyaṅ ni, *even added together*. Foucaux, *énuméré dans ses parties*; his note cites a v.l. śaḍhaḥ kalābhiḥ. Prob. read -kalābhiḥ, preceded by a form meaning *all, complete*, or the like.

saḍha, see **śaḍha**.

satata-jvara, m., = **nitya-jvara**, q.v.: °raḥ Bhīk 17a.2.

Satataparigrahadharmakāṅkṣiṇī, n. of a kiṃnara maid: Kv 6.14.

satata-samita, adj. (once), °**tam**, also **satataṃ samitam**, adv. (Skt. satataṃ, adv.; Pali satataṃ samitaṃ, two words, as rarely in BHS; is Pali samitaṃ ever used without preceding satataṃ?; AMg. samiyaṃ, cited once after sayā = sadā), (**1**) adj., *eternal*; noted only in: eṣā (mss. eṣāṃ) ca Mahāmaudgalyāyana praṇidhi (mss. °dhiṃ) satatasamitā (one ms., of six, satataṃ sa°; one °mitāṃ, perh. with hiatus-bridging m) abhūṣi Mv i.61.2 (prose); (**2**) adv., *continually, constantly*; regularly as cpd. word, °ta-samitam, extremely common in BHS but not recorded elsewhere: SP 65.11; 102.8; 160.5; 201.10; 210.2; LV 44.16; 180.19; Mv i.144.14; iii.52.16; Mvy 7262; Suv 66.2; 70.4; 205.10 (vs); RP 40.17; 41.11; Śikṣ 9.16; 227.4; Mmk 320.3 (text satatta-sam°); Gv 50.22; Dbh 14.1; Bbh 4.19; Sukh 56.5; Laṅk 240.10; Śāl 72.10 (all but one of these prose); rarely, as in Pali, two words, satataṃ samitaṃ: Kv 13.5 ff.; 59.21; 64.20 (in some of these text prints sammitaṃ); LV 66.7 ff. (here vv.ll. satata-, cpd.); 72.12–13 (no v.l.).

Satatasamitābhiyukta (cf. prec.), n. of a Bodhisattva: SP 3.8; 354.1; 355.11; 357.7; 360.1; 366.5 etc.

[**sata-rasa**, adj., ep. of fine food; read prob. śata-rasa, *of a hundred flavors* (= Pali satarasa, of bhojana, PTSD s.v. sata); or possibly **śāta-**, q.v., or sāta-: puruṣaḥ °rasaṃ bhojanaṃ labdhvā hitavipākaṃ ... AsP 239.1; °rasaṃ bhojanam utsṛjya vivarjya taṃ ṣaṣṭikodanaṃ (q.v.; *cheap food*) paribhoktavyaṃ manyeta (foolishly) 4.]

[**Satāgiri**, see **Sā°**.]

satejobhūta, adj. (interpret like the synonym **sajyotibhūta**; cpd. satejas exists in the Veda), *aflame, on fire*: (ādīptāye bhūmiye saṃprajvalita-)-satejobhūtāye Mv i.8.1; similarly 3,4.

satkāya, m. (= Pali sakkāya), *real, existent, body; individuality, personality*: mā...imaṃ...satkāyaṃ kāyaṃ manyadhvam AsP 94.12, *don't think this existent (physical) body* (of Tathāgatas) *is their body* (but rather regard the **dharmakāya** as such); virtually = ātman, once at least in neutral or even favorable sense, prītibhakṣā bhaviṣyāmo satkāyenopaniḥśritāḥ (read °niśritāḥ) Ud xxx.50, *we shall feed on joy, relying on our selves* (alone, not dependent on anything outside); but commonly in unfavorable sense, of the personality to believe in which is a heresy (**dṛṣṭi**, see next); satkāyasaṃjñīkṛtaṃ (sc. śarīraṃ) LV 208.13 (vs), *formed thru the false notion of the personality*; nārāyaṇabhūtaṃ satkāya-dharma-nistāḍana-tayā Gv 495.6, ... *because it puts down the qualities of the individuality*. There seems little doubt of the etym. and fundamental meaning of this word (probably no one now agrees with Childers that it was orig. sva-kāya); and the scholastic fantasies of various schools listed by LaV-P. in AbhidhK. v.15–17 need not be recorded here, tho they evidently influenced Tib. and Chin. interpretations.

satkāya-dṛṣṭi, f. (= Pali sakkāya-diṭṭhi; cf. prec.), *the heretical belief in a real personality*: one of the 5 **dṛṣṭi**, Mvy 1955; Dharmas 68; paraphrased AbhidhK. LaV-P. v.15 by ātmātmīya(grāha), *belief in the self and what belongs to the self*; °dṛṣṭiś ca ghanāsya bhoti SP 97.1 (vs), *and* (this heresy) *becomes firm in him*, he holds firmly to it (wrongly Burnouf and Kern); viṃśati-śikhara-samudgataḥ satkāyadṛṣṭi-śailaḥ Mvy 4684 (the 20 erroneous views are listed 4685–4704); same phrase in acc., foll. by jñānavajreṇa bhittvā Divy 46.25; 52.24–25; 549.16; 554.20, et alibi; Kv 13.21; satkāyadṛṣṭi-vicikitsitā (mss., Senart em. °dṛṣṭī-, m.c., and °taṃ; may be pl. dvandva) ca, śīlavrataṃ (q.v.) ... Mv i.292.2 (vs); (trīṇi saṃyojanāni, yad uta) satkāyadṛṣṭir vicikitsā śīlavrataparāmarśaś ca Laṅk 117.15 (explanation of satkāyadṛṣṭi 17 ff.; two kinds, sahajā and parikalpitā); °dṛṣṭiḥ RP 48.2.

satkṛtya, adv. (orig. ger., *paying respect, respectfully*; = Pali sakkacca(ṃ), with suṇāti, see Childers, and °ca-kārin, PTSD), *carefully, thoroughly, zealously*: °ya-kārin Mvy 1793 = Tib. gus par (*with respect*) byed pa; śrotum ādāya (read śrotam odhāya = avadhāya) satkṛtya śṛṇotha mama bhāṣataḥ Mv i.10.8 (vs).

[**satta**, read **santa** SP 318.10 (prose); see § 18.12.]

Sattvagaganacittapratibhāsabimba, n. of a Tathāgata: Gv 422.6.

sattva-dhātu, see **dhātu** 6.

Sattvarājan, n. of a former Buddha: Mv i.136.17.

sattvavatī, (**1**) adj. (cf. Skt. āpanna-sattvā), *pregnant*: Divy 271.24; 272.5; (**2**) n. of a goddess: Mvy 4327; Sādh 160.3.

Sattvasaha, n. of a former Buddha: Mv i.138.9.

sattvasāra, m. (= Pali sattasāra, of Pratyekabuddhas MN iii.69.25), *best of creatures*, ep. of the Buddha or Bodhisattva: Mv ii.164.10; 204.5; 300.7; 414.19; iii.

110.20; 121.15; 356.10; of former Buddhas, pl., dṛṣṭā ti pūrvi sattvasāra gaṅgavālukopamā, kṛtā ti teṣa buddha-pūja apramey' acintiyā LV 171.5(-6), vss, *you saw of old Buddhas as* (many as) *the sands of the Ganges, and you paid them immeasurable, unthinkable homage such as is due to a Buddha* (wrongly Foucaux); LV 172.15 (vs).

sattvāvāsa, m. (= Pali sattāvāsa), *abode of beings.* Nine such are listed Mvy 2288-97 and in Pali DN iii.263.9 ff.; in both lists an example only (not an exhaustive enumeration) is cited under each 'abode'. The first includes all men and lower beings, and the kāmāvacara gods; the 2d, 3d, and 4th are the gods of the 1st, 2d, and 3d dhyānabhūmi (of the rūpāvacara gods); then in Mvy come as Nos. 5-8 incl. the 4 classes of arūpāvacara gods, and finally as an example of No. 9 the **asaṃjñisattva** (q.v.) gods; but this arrangement is certainly erroneous; DN iii.263.19 correctly puts the asaññasatta gods (who belong to the 4th dhyānabhūmi of rūpāvacara) in the 5th satt(v)āvāsa (the śuddhāvāsakāyika doubtless belong here too), while the four arūpāvacara classes constitute the 6th to 9th incl. In Mvy the first four are characterized respectively as nānātvakāyā nānātvasaṃjñinaḥ, nānātvakāyā ekatvasaṃjñinaḥ, ekatvakāyā nānātvasaṃjñinaḥ, ekatvakāyā ekatvasaṃjñinaḥ. Cf. AbhidhK. LaV-P. iii.22, n. 4.

Sattvottarajñānin, n. of a Bodhisattva: Gv 2.14.

satpuruṣa (cf. Skt. id., Pali sappurisa), lit. *worthy* or *true man*: Mvy 7358; sixteen s° listed SP 3.10, the chief being Bhadrapāla, who is the only one named in RP 2.3, where 16 are also referred to. They are evidently a lay category, and are mentioned immediately after a list of Bodhisattvas. According to Professor Paul Mus (oral communication, May, 1949), they are a kind of lay equivalent of the Bodhisattvas, who live the life of gṛhapatis; Prof. Mus finds a typical illustration of them in the figure of **Vimalakīrti** (q.v.), so well known in Chinese Buddhism. In BHS, V. is not listed so far as I know except once in a list of 16 Bodhisattvas. The term satpuruṣa may include monks: Mv i.37.4 (see s.v. **labhā, labhyam**).

Satyaṃvaca, see **Satyavaca(s)**.

satyaka, (**1**) adj. (unrecorded, exc. as n. pr.; = Skt. satya plus -ka, m.c.), *true*: sacet tava (read with v.l. sacaiva taṃ, m.c.) satyaka tāta sarvaṃ yad bhāṣitaṃ ... SP 88.9 (vs); (**2**) (= Pali Saccaka, a nigaṇṭha), n. of a contemporary of Buddha, described as a great debater (mahāvādin), with whom **Jayaprabha** is identified: Gv 358.26.

Satyaketu, n. of one or two former Buddhas: Mv i.137.10; LV 5.5.

Satyadarśin, n. of a former Buddha: LV 172.1.

? **satyadṛś-**, in Divy 34.29 satyadṛśaḥ (prob. abl. sg., like the prec. udānāt and pārāyaṇāt; one of 4 mss. satyasadṛṣṭaḥ), and (corruptly) satyadṛṣṭaḥ 20.23 (in almost identical context and prob. intending the same original text), app. n. of some (section of a) Buddhist work. Most of the other names in the list seem to be identifiable with parts of Pali Sn; I have found no equivalent for this term. After it come nom. pl. terms, (sthavi-ragāthāḥ) śailagāthā munigāthā arthavargīyāṇi (mss. °ni both times) ca sūtrāṇi.

Satyadharmavipulakīrti, n. of one or two former Buddhas: Mv i.136.13 (first of this list); LV 5.10 (before Tiṣya in list).

Satyanāma, n. of a former Buddha: Mv i.140.2.

Satyaprabha; n. of a former Buddha: Mv i.141.12.

Satyabhānu, n. of a former Buddha: Mv i.138.5.

Satyamugra (once RV as adj. with soma), pl., n. of a brahmanical school (of the Chandogas): Divy 632.24; 633.1.

Satyavaca(s), n. sg. °caḥ (Senart with v.l. Satyaṃvaca), n. of a former Buddha: Mv i.140.7.

satya-vacana and **satya-vākya**, nt., (see also **abhiyācanā**; = Pali sacca-vacana, more often sacca-kiriyā), *solemn statement of truth* as a means of magic control of events (cf. Burlingame, JRAS 1917.429 ff.): °vākyena Mv ii.97.9, 17, 20, °vacanena 19 (by this a kiṃnarī is bound); °vākya ii.218.4; 229.15; °vacana 218.15 ff., 229.17 ff. (by this an ascetic boy killed by a poisoned arrow is revived); °vacana Divy 473.19 ff. (by this a woman changes her sex); 571.5 ff.; SP 413.8, see **satyādhiṣṭhāna.** The 'Skt.' satyakriyā is cited in BR and pw only from a review of Hardy's Eastern Monachism in Ind. Stud. 3.119; if it actually occurs, even in BHS, I have failed to note it; is it perhaps a modern Sktization of the Pali saccakiriyā? See Burlingame, l. c. 433 f.

Satyavardhana, n. of a king, father of **Matisāra**: Mv iii.104.12; 105.1 ff.

satya-vākya, see **satya-vacana.**

Satyavādinī, n. of one of the eight deities of the bodhi-tree: LV 331.21.

satyādhiṣṭhāna (nt.; Pali saccādhiṭṭhāna, see below, is not used in this way in MN iii.245.19; DN iii.229.18), *truthful resolve*, viz. to apply **satyavacana,** q.v.: °naṃ karomi, yena satyena satyavacanena svaṃ mama bāhuṃ ... parityajya ... (9) tena satyena satyavacanenāyaṃ mama bāhur yathā paurāṇo bhavatv ... (11) samanantarakṛte 'smin satyādhiṣṭhāne ... SP 413.8-11 (his arm was restored). Could also perhaps be rendered, *(act of) taking one's stand on truth*, but see the prec. words, s.v. **adhiṣṭhāna** 2; as one of the four **adhiṣṭhāna** (q.v., 2) Mvy 1581 = Pali saccādhiṭṭhāna, rather *resolve to adhere to truth.*

Satyābharaṇa, n. of a former Buddha: Mv i.139.8.

satyābhiyācanā, see **abhiy°**.

? **Satyāvatāra**, by em., n. of a former Buddha: Mv i.139.10; see s.v. **Samīkṣitavadana.**

sadama, m., a high number: Mvy 7748 = Tib. rtag yas, rtog(s) yas; = **samatā**, q.v.

Sadānukāladarśinī, n. of a kiṃnara maid: Kv 6.14.

Sadānuvṛtti, n. of a kiṃnara maid: Kv 6.17.

Sadāparibhūta, n. of a Bodhisattva, the same otherwise called **Sadāprarudita**; acc. to SP and AsP began his career under the Buddha **Bhīṣmagarjita-(nirghoṣa-) svara(-rāja)**: SP 377.10 ff.; acc. to 381.13 f. a previous incarnation of Śākyamuni.

Sadāprarudita, n. of a Bodhisattva, the same called in SP **Sadāparibhūta,** q.v.: AsP 481.1 ff.; a section of this passage cited Śikṣ 37.14 ff.; named also Suv 120.4; Mmk 425.19.

sadāmatta, (**1**) m. pl. (= Pali id., but rare and usually not in corresponding lists), n. of a class of godlings (yakṣas, Mv i.30.8), associated with and functioning like **karoṭapāṇi** and **mālādhāra,** qq.v.; also °**taka** and **sadāmāda**, qq.v.: Mv i.30.8; Divy 218.9, 30 ff.; Mmk 19.13; 43.18; 232.10; Mahāsamāj. Waldschmidt Kl. Skt. Texte 4, 187.5; (**2**) nt.sg., n. of a mythical city (= Divy °**mattaka**, q.v.): Av i.201.6; 203.1; = Pali id., Jāt. i.363.11 = iii.207.2, in same vs as Av i.203.1; in Pali seems to be misinterpreted as a palace (pāsāda) by the comm. and transl. (the comm. in fact alleges that the word means lit. *silver*), but the full story as told in both Av and Divy (not found in the Jātakas which are truncated) shows that a city is meant.

sadāmattaka, (**1**) m. pl. = prec. (1): Divy 218.29; (**2**) nt. sg. = prec. (2): Divy 601.27 (prose); 603.6 (vs).

sadāmāda, m. (sg. in Kyoto ed., Index °mada; but Mironov sadāmādāḥ, pl.), = **sadāmatta** (**1**): Mvy 3152, following karoṭapāṇi and mālādhāra.

sadāramin, adj. (read as one cpd. word) = sadā-ārāmin (from Skt. ārāma plus -in), with a in penult m.c., *always taking delight* (in, loc.): tiryāṇa yonīṣu ca so sadāramī (so read) SP 97.2 (vs).

sadṛśaka, f. °**ikā** (cf. AMg. sarisaga, °saya; = Skt.

°śa, with -ka, perh. m.c.), *like, appropriate, suitable*: bhāryāṃ °śikāṃ Divy 559.16 (vs).

sadevaka, m. or nt., as subst., *the world of (men and) gods* (so Pali, Jāt. i.14.9, vs): bhagavāṃ ca anukampako kāruṇiko °kasya Mv i.256.12 (prose).

Saddharmaghoṣāmbaradīparāja, Gv 362.25 (vs), m.c. equivalent of **Dharmacakranirghoṣagaganameghapradīparāja**, q.v., n. of a Tathāgata.

Saddharmapuṇḍarīka, (**1**) n. of a work (our SP), expounded by Candrasūryapradīpa: SP 21.1, 6, 16, etc.; 181.5 etc.; Mvy 1335; Śikṣ 47.13; 92.8 (°ka-sūtra); 352.7; (**2**) n. of a samādhi: SP 424.2.

Saddharmasmṛtyupasthāna(**-sūtra**, 12.5), n. of a work: Śikṣ 12.5; 69.13; 125.4.

sadyaṃ, adv. (= Skt. sadyas, with analog. adaptation of ending; cf. Pkt. sajja, sajjaṃ; AMg. only sajja acc. to Ratnach.; Pali only sajju, sajjukaṃ Childers), *immediately, speedily* (wrongly Senart): tad eva paralokasmiṃ phalaṃ sadyaṃ ca hiṃsayā (gen.) Mv i.184.10 (vs); idaṃ te maraṇaṃ sadyaṃ yaṃ śraddhātaṃ (so mss.) samācara 187.6 (vs), *now your death (will occur) straightway; do whatever you like.*

sadyathāpi nāma, sadyathīdaṃ, ms. variants for **sayyath°**, q.v.

[**sana**, in a cpd. list of names of trees LV 11.2 (prose), -tinduka-sana-karṇikāra-(... vṛkṣopaśobhite); but Tib. asana, = Skt. id., which read (°tindukāsana°).]

Sanatkumāra (= Pali Sanaṃk°; doubtless in some sense to be identified with Skt. Sanatk°), n. or ep. of a (Mahā)brahman: Mv ii.197.5 (vs; °ra-pratimo kumāro, mss. °rā, dyutimān ayaṃ); iii.212.10 (vs; em., pṛcchāmi Brahmāṇaṃ °raṃ); 344.4 (vs; °ro, in 6 Brahmā).

sanandita, f. °**tā**, an ep. of the (or a, any) Bodhisattva's mother (in Senart's Index capitalized, as if n. pr.! but it is one of a long list of epithets, all loc. sg.): ... pramadottamāyāṃ °ditāyāṃ abhilakṣitāyāṃ (q.v., with mss.) ... Mv ii.9.1 (prose). The mg. is not clear; **sa-** (q.v.) plus Skt. nandita, *rejoiced, happy*? Or Bhvr. with sa- (as in Skt.) plus nandi(n)-tā, *who has the quality rejoicing* or *giving joy*?

santa = Skt. sant, see § 18.5 ff.

santaka, f. °**ikā** (= Pali id.; specialized use of prec. plus -ka), *belonging to* (gen. or comp.): bhaginyāḥ santikā preṣyadārikā Divy 174.4; Jyotiṣka-°ko maṇir 280.7; Manoharā-°kaṃ cūḍāmaṇim 446.18; MSV i.139.10; vihārasvāmi-°kaṃ śraddhādeyaṃ Divy 464.23; Śyāmāvatī devasya santakaṃ (= *Your Majesty's*) bhaktaṃ bhuṅkte 529.18.

saṃtati, f. (**1**) (like **saṃtāna**) *continuity* (Skt.), in Northern Buddhism applied to the *série personnelle* (Lévi, Sūtrāl. ix.5 and xi.53, notes) which causes the false appearance of a transmigrating personality or 'self': pudgalaḥ saṃtatiḥ skandhāḥ Laṅk 79.11, and the like 266.12; 282.5; °ti-kriyotpāda- 40.16; saṃtati-prabandha(q.v.)-76.4; 146.17; -prabandhana- (= prabandha, *continuation*? or as in Skt., *connexion*?) 235.11; (ajñānādi na vidyate,) tad-abhāve na vijñānaṃ saṃtatyā jāyate katham 371.13; tri-saṃtati (which Suzuki, Studies 407, could not interpret), may perhaps refer to the saṃtati of citta, manas, and mano-vijñāna (cf. citta-saṃtati under 2 below), all unreal, and mentioned immediately before the first mention of tri-saṃtati, viz.: (citta-mano-manovijñānasvabhāva-viveka-ratasya) trisaṃtati-vyavachinnadarśanasya Laṅk 9.18; (māyā-vetālayantrābhaṃ ...) trisaṃtati-vyavachinnaṃ jagat paśya vimucyate 96.1 = (°vetāḍa°) 265.14 (vs), *seeing the world as like a mirage ... and cut off from the triple continuity* (i. e. perceiving this to be unreal), *he is released*; trisaṃtati-vyavachinnaṃ ... bhavaṃ māyopamaṃ sadā 296.13; see (tri-)**saṃgati** (2) which might tempt to emendation but is prob. quite a different word; it = the 3 **saṃdhi** (q.v. 6); could trisaṃtati mean the same? (**2**) with or (usually) without preceding citta- in comp. (Pali has citta-saṃtati and -saṃtāna, but hardly in the same use, see refs. in PTSD), orig. developed from prec., *continuity of mind, frame of mind, mental disposition*: vismayāvarjita-citta-saṃtatir (Bhvr.) Divy 286.21; without citta, same mg., bhoktukāmāvarjita-°tiḥ Divy 171.4; Maitreyasya (sva-)saṃtatiḥ paripakvā Av ii.176.3; na cāvalīna-°tayo bhavanti (bodhisattvāḥ) udārasaṃtatikāś ca ... Śikṣ 309.17, *not of depressed disposition, with exalted d.*; tyāga-vāsitāṃ saṃtatiṃ karomi Gv 220.2; snigdha-°tir bhavati Karmav 91.2, *les moments de la pensée ont un glissement tout uni* (Lévi); nāmiṣaprakṣiptayā °tyā Śikṣ 128.7, see s.v. **āmiṣa**; ātmagrāha-patitayā °tyā Laṅk 177.14, *with your mentality fallen into* (erroneous) *acceptance of the soul*; antadvaya-patitayā °tyā 185.8; 209.4; dvayānta-patitayā °tyā 193.6; kudṛṣṭi-patitayā °tyā Laṅk 195.3; Dbh 17.26; vitathatā-patitayā °tyā Laṅk 232.1; svasaṃtatiṃ vyavalokayataḥ (*examining*) MSV ii.190.14, 21 ff.

-saṃtatika (-ka Bhvr.) = **saṃtati** (2), q.v. for citation: Śikṣ 309.17 (prose).

saṃtamasin, adj. (Skt. °sa plus -in), *afflicted by darkness* or *blindness*: mūḍho naras °masīva paśyati Divy 518.14 (vs).

saṃtāna, m. or nt., (**1**) = **saṃtati** 1, q.v.; figures underlying this in Laṅk 18.2, 3, continuity of fire with difference of individual flames, of vegetable growths unified by origin from one seed, agnijvālāyā eka-saṃtāna-patitāyā dṛṣṭo 'rciṣaś ca prativibhāgaḥ, ekabījaprasūtānāṃ yat-saṃtānānām api ...; saṃvidyante bhikṣavo yuṣmākaṃ saṃtāne kuśalamūlāni yāni mayā pūrvaṃ paripācitāni SP 211.12, *there are found in your personal-continuity-series roots of merit which were previously* (in former existences) *ripened by me* (or merely *mentality*, as in the following?); (**2**) = **saṃtati** (2), and cf. **sāṃtānika**, with or (usually) without citta-, *mental disposition, mentality* (Pali citta-saṃ°, seemingly not in this sense): sāsya bhajahe citta-°naṃ Mv iii.355.14 (vs), see § 31.20; same without citta, of which it is used as a virtual synonym, note esp. kṣubhita-cittair luḍita-saṃtānais Gv 338.3–4; also, (tathāgatajñānaṃ ...) parasattva-°neṣu vā pratiṣṭhāpayitum Gv 5.12; harṣa-utpadyana-saṃtānāni (so, cpd.) 48.5, *their mental conditions productive of joy*; mahākaruṇā-snehābhiṣyandita-°no (Bhvr.) 189.9, cf. mahākaruṇā-parisphuṭena °nena Śikṣ 28.7; dharmābhiṣyandita-prasanna-°nā (Bhvr.) Gv 333.3; similarly 469.21; svaśarīrānadhyavasita-°naḥ Śikṣ 23.12 (Bhvr.; *chain of thought*, Bendall and Rouse for saṃtāna); sarvajña-saṃtāna-nivāsinī (*mentality*) hi kāruṇyadhenur Divy 125.6; anekasattva-saṃtāna-kuśalamūlasamāropikāṃ dharmadeśanāṃ 130.14; mamāpi saṃtāne ye dharmāḥ praviśeyuḥ (*whatever religious principles may enter into my mentality, too*) te niṣkampaṃ tiṣṭhantu Divy 540.30; tasyāpi °ne 'kuśalamūlāni pratisaṃhṛtāni Av ii.87.10; kaṭhina-°nāś ca bhavanti Mv i.90.4–5, *and they become of harsh mental dispositions*; (**3**) nt., = Skt. saṃtānikā, *scum, top part of milk or ghee*: kṣīra-°naṃ vā sarpi-°naṃ vā Mv i.339.9; (**4**) m., n. of a 'medicinal tree': °no nāma mahābhaiṣajyavṛkṣas Gv 497.12; perh. to be identified with Skt. id. as name of a heavenly tree, BR s.v. 10.

saṃtāraka, m. (Skt. saṃtārayati plus -aka), *savior*: °ko (the Buddha) devamanuṣyakoṭīnām SP 152.9 (vs); (sattvāḥ ...) kuśala-°ka-virahitā(ḥ) Dbh 29.2 (prose).

saṃtāraṇa (nt.: cf. prec.; = Pali id.), *ferrying across*: yānapātraṃ ... sattva-°ṇāya Gv 351.1 (in literal mg.); (saṃsāranadīsrotasaḥ sarvasattva-)-°ṇāya 5 (fig.; so read).

santika, adj. (= Pali id., stem in comp.; cf. next; MIndic for **sāntika**, q.v.; **sa-**, q.v., plus Skt. antika, as adj. Gr. Lex.), *near*: evaṃrūpāḥ sattvāḥ nirvāṇa-°kā bhavanti Mv ii.287.14; santikāvacara (= Pali id.), *living near* (with gen.): bhagavato upasthāyakaṃ (acc. sg.) bhagavataḥ °raṃ bhagavato saṃmukhaṃ Mv iii.49.13. The form **sāntika,** tho very likely a secondary Sktization of this, seems to support the above theory of its origin; it is not connected with **santa(ka)** as has been held by some (e.g. Senart, see next).

santike, adv. (loc. of prec., q.v.; see also **sāntika**; = Pali id., Skt. antike), *near, in the presence* (of, gen.): bhagavato Kāśyapasya °ke Mv i.322.15 (same phrase with antike line 18; the two are precisely equivalent, and not of different origin as Senart i p. 395 and others have suggested); 323.1; sā me va (? em.) °ke ii.58.8; 59.10; bhikṣūṇa °ke 188.10 (vs); Śākyasiṃhasya °ke 194.11 (vs); °ke maraṇaṃ tava 238.7, *your death is near* (in same line LV 261.10 antike); bodhisattvasya °ke 238.14; mama °ke (v.l. sā°) iii.1.14; kasya °ke 193.13, (ṛṣisya) °ke 14; nirvāṇasyaiva °ke (later ms. sāntike) Ud xi.5; sugatāna °ke Sukh 54.1 (vs).

[**saṃtiraṇa,** read **saṃtīraṇa.**]

saṃtiṣṭhate, saṃsthihati, *turns into, assumes the form of*: LV 317.8 (te ca, sc. the weapons of Māra and his host, bodhisattvasyopari) prakṣiptāḥ puṣpavitāne (v.l. °tāna-, better) vimānāni saṃtiṣṭhante sma; similarly 317.10; Mv i.236.10 = 241.4 (vs), see s.v. **kañcuka.**

saṃtīraṇa, °**ṇā** (= Pali, both; cf. tīraṇa; to Pali tīreti with sam plus -ana; once written saṃtir°, doubtless by error), *judgment, function of judging*: °ṇa = viṣayopanidhyānapūrvakaṃ niścayākarṣaṇaṃ AbhidhK. LaV-P. viii.130 n. 4; i.81, *jugement précédé de la considération de l'objet*; āśayaḥ katamaḥ? dharmeṣu yā samyak-°ṇā kṣāntim (ed. prints this as cpd. with prec.) āgamya . . . Bbh 81.22; mithyādharmārtha-°ṇā-(v.l. °ṇa-)-pūrvikāṇi (v.l. °vakāṇi, prob. read so), Bhvr. adj., Bbh 253.7; saṃtiraṇa-(but read with v.l. saṃtīr°)-vikalpaḥ Dharmas 135 (one of three vikalpa), *false imagining due to judging.*

[**saṃtīrya,** error (or semi-MIndic?) for Skt. saṃstīrya, *having strewn*: (tasmin sakardame pṛthivīpradeśe) jaṭāṃ (mss. jaṭā, so read as acc. pl.?) saṃtīrya Bhagavataḥ purato Divy 252.2.]

(**su-**)**saṃtutikā,** adj., semi-MIndic or false Sktization (cf. Pali saṃthutika), f. to **saṃstutaka,** q.v.: LV 322.2 (vs; the best ms. reads saṃstu°).

Saṃtuṣita (= Pali °sita), n. of the chief of the Tuṣita gods (his official position esp. suggested by LV 363.21 °to devaputraḥ sārdhaṃ tuṣitakāyikair devair; also 302.6; 364.13): LV 44.10; 59.2; 241.2; 441.18; Mv i.208.13; 230.13; 263.20; ii.11.1; Mvy 3137; Mmk 45.8; 69.6; Bbh 343.5. Cases where a plurality (as if = tuṣitāḥ as a class) seems suggested are only apparent; see s.v. **Suyāma** for instances in Gv, Dbh.g., and RP.

-saṃtuṣitaka (ifc., adj. to °ta), *containing* (other gods and) Saṃtuṣita: (devapurālaye . . .) yāma-Suyāma-Saṃtuṣitake LV 327.18 (vs), *in the gods' city-dwelling which contains yāma* (gods), *Suyāma, and Saṃtuṣita* (see prec.).

saṃtṛṣita, adj.-ppp. (to sam plus tṛṣ-; unrecorded, unless in Pali Pv. iv.5.4, text saṃtāsito, comm. saṃtassito, v.l. saṃtasito; usually supposed to mean *frightened*, to tras-, but comm. gloss, kaṇṭha-oṭṭha-tālūnaṃ so saṃpattiyā suṭṭhu tasito; *thirsty* fits the context better; °tās° or °tass° could be m.c. for °tas°), *thirsty*: megho yathā °tāṃ vasuṃdharāṃ LV 399.10 (vs).

saṃtoṣaṇā (= Skt. °ṇa, nt.), *gratification*: sarvasattvasubhāṣita-°ṇāyai LV 35.19; (rājñā paramayā) °ṇayā saṃbhāṣita uktaś ca Divy 451.19.

saṃtrasin, adj. (no *saṃtrasa occurs; prob. really = Pali (a-)saṃtāsin, to Skt. saṃtrāsa plus -in, with a for ā m.c.), *frightened*: śabdeṣu na °sī na parapreksī LV 259.22 (vs).

Saṃtrāsanī, n. of a yoginī: Dharmas 13.

Saṃtha (Kātyāyana), = Pali Saṃdha (Kaccāyana, see DPPN s.v.), n. of a monk: Bbh 49.15 ff.

saṃthaṇā, or v.l. and Mironov sunthaṇā, *trousers* (Tib. dor ma, misprinted ror ma in ed., Tib. Index correctly): Mvy 5849, in list of garments.

saṃdaṃśikā (cf. Skt. saṃdaṃśa, °śaka), *bite* (of food), *nibble, mouthful*: LV 248.20, see s.v. **kāpotaka.**

(**saṃdarbhita,** ppp., in Skt., Deśīn. p. 1 line 2, and Schmidt, Nachträge, *put together, composed*: ŚsP 1534.7 kāmadhātuḥ . . . °taḥ, with implication of artificiality or even unreality, see s.v. **viṭhapayati.**)

saṃdarśaka, adj., f. °**ikā** (= Pali °dassaka; to Skt. °darśayati plus -aka), *showing, teaching*: sarvajñajñāna-°kaḥ SP 121.9; buddhajñāna-°kāḥ 183.7; buddhadharma-°kāni Gv 100.7; (prajñāpāramitā na kasyacit dharmasya . . .) °śikā AsP 203.10.

-saṃdarśana-tā (= Skt. °na), ifc., *the beholding* (? perh. caus., *revealing, teaching*?): °na-tāyai saṃvartate LV 36.3 (at end of cpd. listing main events of Buddha's life).

saṃdārayati (cf. Skt. dārayati; Pali saṃdālayitvā or °tvāna Sn 62, in the Khaggavisāṇa-sutta tho not in the same vs), *destroys*: °yitvā gṛhivyañjanāni Mv i.358.9 (vs, in Khaḍgaviṣāṇa gāthāḥ).

saṃdūṣaṇā (in Skt. only °ṇa, nt.), *defilement*, or *disgrace, vilification*: Gv 414.1 (vs), cited s.v. **jātivāda.**

saṃdṛśyati, *sees*: Gv 523.20–21 yathā māyākāro . . . sarvarūpagatāni sarvakriyāś ca saṃdṛśyati (by his magic power). Seems to be a nonce-formation analogical to saṃdṛśyante, regular passive, *they are seen*, which occurs three times in the text just before (lines 16, 18, 20); the meaning is confirmed by the following conclusion of the simile: evam eva sudhanaḥ . . . tāni sarvavyūhavikurvitāny adrākṣīt. To the pass. saṃdṛśyate, *is seen*, was formed an active saṃdṛśyati, *sees*. The same seems true once of **dṛśyati,** q.v.

saṃdṛṣṭika, adj., = **sāṃ°,** q.v.: *visible, actual, of the present* (life): Divy 426.10 °kam idaṃ phalam.

saṃdoṣa, nt. (! = Pali saṃdosa, to Skt. saṃduṣyati), *pollution*: mā . . . jāti-°ṣaṃ bhaviṣyatīti Mv i.351.3, 9.

saṃdveṣa (m.), *hatred*: °ṣāya nāsaṃdveṣāya (saṃvartate) Av ii.188.8, and similar passage Pischel, SBAW 1904.814, fol. 163a. Formed to Skt. dveṣa on the model of adjoining nouns in saṃ-, see s.v. **saṃyoga.**

saṃdhā (cf. the Skt. mg. *Absicht*, pw s.v. 3, and **saṃdhāya**), (*special, cryptic,*) *esoteric meaning*, the 'real' meaning of a Buddhist text or doctrine, opp. to its prima facie or superficial meaning; perh. always in comp. with a word for *speech, words*, or the like; but see also **saṃdhi** (5); see **ābhiprāyika,** which S. K. De, NIA 1.5, is right in relating to this; my note in JAOS 57.185 ff. is prob. misleading in regarding *complete meaning* as basic; Tib. regularly dgoṅs (te), *meaning, intention*, often preceded, sometimes replaced, by ldem po(r), *in a riddlesome way*; nevertheless the implication of the word is always *fundamental, 'real' meaning*, as is esp. shown by SP 60.12–13 (prose) yat punar bhagavann asmābhir anupasthiteṣu bodhisattveṣu saṃdhābhāṣyaṃ bhagavato 'jānamānais tvaramāṇaiḥ prathamabhāṣitaiva tathāgatasya dharmadeśanā śrutvodgṛhītā, *but in as much, Lord, as we, not knowing the Lord's words as He really intended them* (*esoterically, cryptically*, Tib. ldem por dgoṅs te bśad pa), *there being no bodhisattvas on hand, in our haste heard and accepted merely His prima-facie words*; so, saṃdhā-bhāṣya (Tib. usually as above) SP 29.7; 34.2, 10; 39.11; 70.5 (vs, Tib. ldem ṅag, omitting dgoṅs) and 8 (vs, Tib. as in 60.12–13 but om. ldem por); 273.14 and 337.2 (vss); saṃdhā-bhāṣita (Tib. generally as in 60.12–13) 125.2, 3 (see below; ldem por om. in 3); 199.2 (gsuṅs for bśad); 233.11 (parama-saṃdhā-bhāṣita-vivaraṇo hy ayaṃ dharmaparyāyas); 288.2; saṃdhā-vacanehi, °naṃ, SP 59.4 and 5 (here Tib. om. dgoṅs; in 4 ldem poḥi ṅag [= bśad or gsuṅs] rnams, *riddle-words*; in 5 ldem po ṅag); note Buddha's words in

SP 125.1 na sahasaiva sarvajñajñānaṃ saṃprakāśayāmi, *I do not reveal the Omniscient's knowledge all at once*, given as reason for his hearers' failure to understand saṃdhābhāṣitaṃ, since (3) ... durvijñeyaṃ ... tathāgatānāṃ ... saṃdhābhāṣitam. Note that this form seems to occur only in SP, while the ger. saṃdhāya is more widespread; saṃdhi, however, seems to be used, tho rarely, in the same sense, and once in Laṅk text has **saṃdhyā-bhāṣya,** q.v., clearly in this same mg., and prob. error for saṃdhā°.

Saṃdhāna, n. of a rich householder: Divy 540.7, 16.

saṃdhāya, ger. (to saṃ-dhā-, cf. **saṃdhā**), (**1**) (= Pali id.) *with reference to*, as quasi-postp. with prec. acc.: kiṃ saṃdhāya Bhagavān kathayati? Divy 241.22, (answer:) na ... pratyutpannaṃ saṃdhāya kathayāmy atītaṃ saṃdhāya ... 23–24; tat saṃdhāya kathayāmi 246.2; ādhyātmikaṃ rajaḥ saṃdhāyāha āhosvid vāhyam 491.16; (pravrajitān ...) mayā saṃdhāyoktaṃ MSV iii.123.12; idaṃ ca saṃdhāya ... abhihitaṃ Śikṣ 144.9; (bodhisattvabhūmayo, as expounded by other Buddhas ...) yāḥ saṃdhāyāham evaṃ vadāmi Dbh 5.6 (follows list of the ten names; possibly, but less likely, *summarizing which*, as in Mbh 14.1148, BR s.v. dhā with sam 1); (**2**) specialization of **saṃdhā**, with expressions of speaking, verbs or nouns, corresp. to **saṃdhā**, *using the (real, esoteric) meaning, the true (underlying, hidden, mystic) sense*; Tib. regularly (ldem por) dgoṅs te, *meaning* or *intending (in a riddlesome way)*; once in non-religious use, *(said) in riddles, cryptically*, MSV below; used as separate word or as part of a cpd.: tat sādhu bhagavān nirdiśatu yat saṃdhāya (Tib. dgoṅs te, cf. saṃdhā-bhāṣitaṃ 34.2) tathāgato gambhīrasya tathāgatadharmasya punaḥ-punaḥ saṃvarṇanāṃ karoti SP 34.4–5 (prose); saṃdhāya (could be instr. of saṃdhā, as may be meant by Tib. dgoṅs par) vakṣye ... 64.7 (vs); saṃdhāya (as prec.; Tib. ldem por dgoṅs te) ... bhāṣitaṃ 62.11 (vs); saṃdhāya (as prec.; Tib. dgoṅs ta, read te) yaṃ bhāṣitu 394.1 (vs); bhūta-°ya-vacanaṃ RP 8.11, *true esoteric gospel*; sarva-°ya-vacana- Bbh 56.18; 108.24; sūtrārtha-gati-°ya-bhāṣitāvabodhatayā Dbh 44.20; tathāgata-°ya-bhāṣitaṃ Bbh 174.15; kiṃ saṃdhāya (*according to what deeper sense*, Suzuki) Bhagavatā ... vāg bhāṣitā, aham eva sarvabuddhā ... Laṅk 141.2; caturvidhāṃ samatāṃ saṃdhāya (reply to prec.) 141.7, etc. (but these Laṅk cases may belong to 1 above, as do certainly 159.4 and prob. most in Laṅk); mātuḥ saṃdhāya bhāṣitaṃ vijñātam MSV ii.69.8, *you understood what your mother said in riddles* (here nonreligious).

[**saṃdhāyya,** read saṃdhāvya, MSV ii.86.13.]

saṃdhāra, m. (or nt.; to Skt. saṃdhārayati, in Gv 508.8 used specifically of the setting, bhājana, of a jewel *holding* the jewel), *holder*, of the setting (bhājana) of a jewel, metaphorically: sarvajñatācittotpāda-vajraṃ (*diamond*) na hīnādhimuktikeṣu sattvabhājaneṣu saṃdhāreṣu ... śobhate Gv 508.9.

saṃdhāraka, adj. or subst. m. (n. ag. to Skt. saṃdhārayati; cf. Pali id., Vism. 205.28, 31, seemingly in somewhat different mg.), *one who maintains, upholds*: śāsana-°kaḥ Divy 395.25, 26–27.

saṃdhāvaṇikā, or **°ka,** n. pl. °kā(ḥ), a kind of toy: Divy 475.19 (in a list). (Index °veṇikā.)

saṃdhāvati (= Pali id.), *'runs thru', spends* (time, in rebirths; the object may also be the creatures of the worlds in which rebirths take place), usually foll. by parallel and synonymous saṃsarati (Skt.): devāṃś ca manuṣyāṃś ca saṃdhāvya saṃsṛtya Divy 534.5; MSV ii.86.13 (text corruptly saṃdhāyya); ... kalpā saṃdhāvitā (em.) saṃsaritā Mv i.46.4; kalpāna śatasahasraṃ saṃdhāvitvāna (em.; in 55.8 mss. add saṃsaritvāna) ... i.55.8 = 56.14 (vs); the emendations are proved by suciraṃ dīrgham adhvānaṃ (*time*) saṃdhāvitvā saṃsaritvā i.244.19 (cf. Pali AN ii.1.6 dīgham addhānam saṃdhāvitaṃ saṃsaritaṃ).

saṃdhi, m., (in several mgs. substantially the same as in Skt.), (**1**) *joint* (= Skt.), as of the body, also *connexion* between entities, see s.v. **visaṃdhi**; *joint = junction, intermediate point* between one bodhisattva-bhūmi and the next, saṃdhi-cittaṃ Mv i.91.5, *the juncture-frame-of-mind*, of a Bodhisattva passing from one bhūmi to the next; bhūmi-saṃdhiṣu 97.17, prob. in this mg., but the verse is corrupt and obscure; (katamaṃ) saṃdhi-cittaṃ bhavati 110.16 (in passing from the 4th to the 5th bhūmi, similarly 18, and 127.15, 18); paryādānaṃ gacchanti, pātāla-saṃdhigatam iva vāri LV 207.14, *become exhausted like water when it reaches the boundary of the nether world*; (**2**) *crease, crack* (= Skt.): mānsi (māṃsi) nāsti saṃdhiḥ LV 49.22 (vs), *there is no crack, crease, in her flesh*; (**3**) acc. to Senart, (as in Skt. political science) *union, concord, conciliation*: sarvakāryeṣu saṃdhi-graha-saṃyojakāś ... rājakāryeṣu pada-saṃdhi-viduṣaś ca bhavanti (sc. bodhisattvāḥ) Mv i.133.15, *ils emploient les moyens d'union et de douceur* (graha) ... *ils savent (observer) un langage conciliant* (?); prob. also in the troublesome LV 431.11 ff., dīrgharātraṃ piśunavacanaparivarjana-bhedamantrāgrahaṇa-saṃdhisāmagrī-rocana-samagrāṇāṃ cedācittena (q.v.) piśunavacanavigarhaṇa-saṃdhisāmagrī-guṇavarṇaprakāśanaprayogatvāt suśukladanta ity ucyate, where it seems likely that saṃdhi-sāmagrī, *the totality of concord* (?), is the opposite of piśunavacana and bheda(mantra); (**4**) *intention* (see Senart's note ii.537): naiṣo kṣurapro saṃdhito (abl., *by intention*) āhato 'si mayā ajānantena Mv ii.222.17 (vs, so mss., meter impossible, but not improved by Senart's violent em.); saṃdhito is also read in mss. in the very similar line 7 above, where saṃdhīto would make the meter perfect and should prob. be read m.c. (rather than Senart's em. saṃdahito); possibly same mg. in LV 42.3 (vs) saṃdhi-pralāpam aśubhaṃ na samācariṣye, *I shall not commit any evil intentional (?) frivolity of speech*; Tib. for the cpd. kyal paḥi (read kaḥi? = *of frivolity of speech*) tshig (= *words*; but perh. read tshigs, *joint* etc., = saṃdhi? I do not understand the expression); this meaning is given for Skt. saṃdhā, see pw s.v. 3; (**5**) = **saṃdhā,** q.v., *esoteric meaning* (prob. developed out of prec.): na bhāṣate bhūtapadārtha-saṃdhiṃ SP 118.2 (vs), *he* (Buddha) *does not declare the real* (**bhūta**) *mystic meaning* (or *intent*) *of the sense of the words* (Tib. ldem dgoṅs, as for saṃdhā); tasya (sc. of what has been said by Buddhas) saṃdhiṃ vijānatha (impv.) Laṅk 283.9 (vs); also in **saṃdhi-nirmocana,** q.v.; (**6**) *connexion* with rebirth, (Suzuki) *'attachment* (to existence)', in a passage beginning Laṅk 160.8 ff. in which Buddha is asked to explain sarvadharma-saṃdhy-arthaparimocanārtham (9) *the meaning of attachment (connexion, binding) and of emancipation of all states of being*; in (sarvadharmāṇāṃ) saṃdhyasaṃdhi-lakṣaṇaṃ (11), asaṃdhi, *non-attachment*, replaces parimocana; in 162.9 ff. (same passage) sarvabhāvavikalpa-saṃdhi-vivikta-darśanān na saṃdhir nāsaṃdhilakṣaṇaṃ sarvadharmāṇāṃ, nātra kaścin Mahāmate badhyate (sc. by saṃdhi) na ca mucyate (by asaṃdhi), anyatra (*on the contrary*) vitathapatitayā buddhyā bandhamokṣau prajñāyete ... yad uta, sad-asatoḥ saṃdhy-anupalabdhitvāt sarvadharmāṇāṃ. (14) trayaḥ saṃdhayo bālānāṃ pṛthagjanānāṃ, *the three attachments of vulgar fools*, are (15) rāgo dveṣo mohaś ca, tṛṣṇā ca paunarbhavikī ... (16) yāṃ saṃdhāya (*being connected with which*) gati-saṃdhayaḥ (*the attachments to other destinies*, see **gati**) prajāyante. tatra saṃdhi-saṃdhānaṃ (read °nāṃ with v.l.; so implied by Suzuki transl.) (17) sattvānāṃ gatipañcakaṃ (*under these circumstances creatures who are attached to the attachments are subject to the five destinies*). saṃdher vyucchedān (abl.) ... na saṃdhir nāsaṃdhilakṣaṇaṃ prajñāyate (*after the cutting off of attachment there is no attachment, nor is any visible sign of detachment perceptible*); here follow the passages 163.1 ff., cited s.v. **saṃgati** 2, in which it appears that saṃdhi, esp. the three saṃdhayaḥ (above), are, or are correlated with, the three **saṃgati**, these two words being virtual synonyms in this use; after this, abhūtaparikalpo hi saṃdhi-lakṣaṇam ucyate 163.6 (vs), *for the mark of attachment (binding to rebirth) is false discrimination*; badhyante svavikalpena bālāḥ saṃdhy-avipaścitāḥ 163.9 (vs); vijñānaṃ pravartate 'nyagati-saṃdhau Laṅk 124.11–12, *the vi° 'continues to evolve in another path of existence'* (Suzuki, freely but in essence rightly); anyagati-saṃdhau also 140.3, and gati-saṃdhau 371.8.

saṃdhi-cchettar, m. (primarily, doubtless, = next, but here paradoxically used in a good sense, like **aśraddha** and **akṛtajña**, qq.v.; see **saṃdhi** 6), *one who cuts the bonds (of existence)*: aśraddhaś cākṛtajñaś ca °ttā ca yo naraḥ... (sa) vai tūttamapūruṣaḥ Ud xxix.33 (= Pali Dhp. 97, where saṃdhichedo; comm. vaṭṭasaṃdhiṃ saṃsārasaṃdhiṃ chetvā ṭhito).

saṃdhi-cchedaka, m. (Pali id. in similar sense; cf. prec., used in paradoxical and fig. mg.; to Skt. saṃdhi, see BR s.v. 2, l, with chedaka), *housebreaker, burglar*: Mvy 5361 = Tib. khyims ḥbugs pa; kulaghātakānāṃ °kānāṃ kilbiṣakāriṇāṃ Gv 157.2.

saṃdhi-nirmocana, nt., *setting forth, unfolding of the real truth, fundamental explanation*; this seems the only possible meaning in gambhīrārtha-saṃdhi-nirmocanatā Bbh 301.7; 303.19; 304.4; it is confirmed by Tib. and Chin. on Saṃdhi-nirmocanam Mvy 1359, n. of a work; Tib. dgoṅs pa (= saṃdhi, *esoteric meaning*) ṅes par ḥgrel pa (*real explanation*); Chin. *unfolding of the real truth*, or *explanation of the deep mystery*; cf. JAOS 57.185 ff. In a reply to this note, LaVallée-Poussin, HJAS 3.137 ff., properly corrects what I said about deśanānaya-nirmuktaṃ Laṅk 5.5 (see s.v. **deśanā**), but this does not, I think, affect my interpretation of saṃdhi-nirmocana.

saṃdhihati (= Skt. saṃ-dhā-; see § 28.44), *fits, joins* (arrows to a bow): °he, aor., Mv ii.221.20 (Senart em. saṃdahe).

saṃdhukṣita (nt.; see also **saṃdhūkṣita**; in Skt. as ppp., the n. act. being °kṣaṇa), (mental) *inflammation, excitement, longing* (follows **paridāha**): (yānīmāni krodhopanāhakhila-)-malavyāpādaparidāha-°kṣita-pratighādyāni tāni prahāya Dbh 25.4.

-saṃdhunakam, adj., *accompanied by shaking* (= **-avadhūnakam**, q.v.; cf. Pali saṃdhunāti): Mvy 8589 na hasta-saṃ°; 8590 na pātra-saṃ°; *not with waving of the hands, not with shaking of the bowl* (will we eat).

saṃdhūkṣaṇa-tā (Skt. only saṃ-dhukṣaṇa; cf. next), (mental) *inflammation, excitement*: anunayāsaṃdhūkṣaṇa-tāyai saṃvartate LV 32.7, *conduces to the state of not being inflamed by passion.*

saṃdhūkṣita, (prob.) ppp. (= Skt. saṃdhukṣ°, cf. prec., and **saṃdhukṣita**), *inflamed*: Kalpanāmaṇḍitikā, Lüders, Kl. Skt. Texte 2, p. 39; fragment 36 V 3 asakṛt-°ta-krodhaḥ.

saṃdhūmāyate (cpd. of Skt. dhūmāyate, denom.), *smokes, gives out smoke*: parvato dhūmāyate °yate Divy 107.7.

saṃdhūyate, °ti (pass. of Pali saṃdhunāti; cf. saṃdhūnoti, only RV), *is shaken*: śailāḥ saṃdhūyetsuḥ (mss. °petsuḥ, aor.) Mv ii.162.5, *the mountains were shaken.*

saṃdhovita, ppp. to Pali saṃdhovati, *cleansed, clean*: read °taṃ Mmk 60.7 (vs), as required by meter, for text saṃdhotaṃ; Lalou, Iconographie 27 n. 7, would read saṃdhitaṃ, but this fails to rectify the meter, and is disproved by Tib. which she quotes as dri med pa; this means not *sans défaut* but *free from filth*, and so supports my em.

saṃdhya, (substantivized) adj. nt. (from Skt. saṃdhyā; prob. semi-MIndic for Skt. sāṃdhya, adj., which is recorded only in mg. *of the evening twilight*, based on a commoner mg. of Skt. saṃdhyā), (*rite*) *pertaining to the three 'joints' of the day* (so saṃdhyā in Skt.), morning, noon, and evening: prathamaṃ saṃdhyam ucyate Mmk 94.17 (morning), madhyaṃ... 18–19 (noon), tṛtīyaṃ... 19 (evening); prathamaṃ °yam 99.5; tri-saṃdhyaṃ (*the 3 such rites*)... juhuyāt divasāny ekaviṃśati 106.24; tri-saṃdhyaṃ (adv.?) ṣaḍ lakṣāṇi japet 107.10; as adj., vaśyārthaṃ sarvabhūtānāṃ tri-saṃdhyaṃ japam iṣyate 144.13 (vs).

saṃdhyā-bhāṣya, = (and prob. error for) saṃdhābhāṣya (see s.v. **saṃdhā**), *esoteric, mystic language* (so, acc. to Suzuki, Tib., ldem po = saṃdhā): a-saṃdhyābhāṣya-kuśalaiḥ Laṅk 236.15, *by those not skilled in*...

saṃnahya, gdve. (of Skt. sam-nah-), *to be guided*: mahāsaṃnāha-°yaḥ (said of Bodhisattvas) ŚsP 1342.16 ff., the various kinds of (religious) saṃnāha explained 20 ff. Perhaps, however, saṃnaddha (the ppp.) should be read for saṃnahya, gdve.

saṃnāmana (nt.; to next plus -ana), *conquest*: kārvaṭikaṃ °nāya gacchāmi Divy 446.20; could be considered inf.

saṃnāmayati (Skt. id., not in this mg.; cf. prec.), *subdues, conquers*: na ca śakyate °yitum (Takṣaśilā) Divy 372.24; Takṣaśilānagaraṃ °yitum 407.28, and sa °yiṣyati 27; (naivam asau śakyaḥ) °yitum 446.1; kārvaṭikaḥ °yitavyo 447.6; kārvaṭikam ayuddhena °ya (impv.) 447.9; karvaṭakaḥ saṃnāmito 451.20; others, MSV ii.32.2.

saṃnidāhayati (seems to be caus. to *sam-ni-dahati, cf. Pali dahati, Chap. 43 s.v. dhā 3, = dadhāti), *collects, brings together*: (sarvasaṃghaṃ) °yanti MSV iv.87.8 (Tib. sdud par byed pa); ā analog. to pātayati : patati etc.

? **saṃnidhānin**, adj. (Skt. °na plus -in), in Divy 556.4 acc. to Index *social* (which is not clear to me), acc. to pw 7.380 'etwa *Güter sammelnd*' (cf. **saṃnidhi**), perh. rightly: (na mama pratirūpaṃ syād yad ahaṃ...) gṛhī agāram adhyāvaseyaṃ °dhānī kālaparibhogena vā kāmān (sc. in heaven, as had been suggested to him) paribhuñjīyaṃ. In accordance with the usual mg. of Skt. saṃnidhāna, perh. *staying in the neighborhood, living in the same vicinity* (as at present)?

saṃnidhi (gender? = Pali id., m. acc. to Childers; cf. Skt. nidhi), *store, hoard*: °dhi-kāraḥ Mvy 8416 = Tib. gsog ḥjog, *making a hoard, hoarding* (a sin); (nāhaṃ kriṇāmi nāpi vikriṇāmi) na cāpi me °dhi asti kiṃcit Mv ii.49.16 (vs; in same vs Pali Jāt. v.387.13 na... sannicayo ca atthi).

saṃnipāta, m. (also nt. in Mv; = Pali id.; Skt. id. not noted in this sense), *gathering, assembly* of people: so 'drākṣīd rājā ... mahājana-°taṃ vikrośantaṃ Divy 325.12; of bodhisattvas, parṣat-°taḥ... bodhisattvānāṃ Dbh 7.2; bodhisattva-°ta-maṇḍalamāḍe (q.v.) Mmk 1.4; usually of Buddhist disciples, śrāvaka; acc. to Divy 18.9 and 489.9 Buddhas hold two annual gatherings of disciples, (dharmatā khalu) yathā buddhānāṃ bhagavatāṃ śrāvakāṇāṃ dvau °tau bhavataḥ, viz. at the beginning of the rainy season and at the full moon of Kārttika; in Mv, as in Pali (DN ii.5.7 ff.; Jāt. i.30.4 ff.; 35.1 ff.), any Buddha is spoken of as holding three general assemblies, the number attending at each being generally stated, trayaḥ °pātā bhūtā (so most mss.), prathamo śrāvaka-°to ṣaṇṇavati koṭiyo abhūṣi, etc., Mv i.59.6; so also i.248.9 ff.; 251.7; iii.246.17 ff.; only one for each Buddha mentioned iii.233.19 = 237.21; (nt.,) (idaṃ) bhagavato prathamaṃ śrāvaka-°taṃ ardhatrayodaśa (em.) bhikṣuśatāni iii.432.6; more than three in Sukh, iyantataḥ (q.v.) sa prathama-°to 'bhūt 32.1, kaḥ punar vādo dvitīya-tṛtīyādīnāṃ śrāvaka-°tānām, evam anantāparyantas tasya bhagavataḥ śrāvakasaṃgho 4.

saṃniyojana (nt.; to Skt. sam-ni-yuj- plus -ana), *employment, putting into effect*: (sarvadharmasvabhāvārtha-) °nāya Gv 164.24.

saṃ-nir-jinati (cf. **nir-j°** and Skt. nir-jayati),

conquers: (tena hi te) pāpīmaṃ saṃnirjiniṣyāmi Mv ii.270.11.

saṃnirnāda (m.? see s.v. **nirnāda**), *sound, shout*: ekaghoṣa (v.l. eva gh°) ekasaṃnirnādo (v.l. °sa-nir°) LV 266.9 (prose). Skt. has saṃnināda, found also in BHS, Mv i.259.11 etc.

saṃnivāraka, adj. or n ag. (to Skt. saṃnivārayati plus -aka), *one who restrains* (from, abl.): (kalyāṇamitrāṇi ...) °kāni pramādasthānebhyo Gv 462.21, cited Śiks 35.4 as °kāḥ pramādasthānāt.

saṃnivāsayati (cf. **nivāsayati**; Pali nivāseti; no sam-ni-vas- recorded except in Mbh. Calc. 5.745 prāvārān saṃnivaste, for which Crit. ed. 5.26.7 prāvarān adhyavaste), *dresses oneself* (esp. perhaps in reference to an under-garment), *gets dressed*: kalyam eva °vāsya LV 240.1 (prose; in vs equivalent id. 11 nivāsayitvā); also with acc., *puts on* (clothes), kalpīyāni (sc. kāṣāyāṇi) ca °vāsya LV 271.18 (vs; in prose equivalent 267.11 nivāsya).

saṃniveśanā (Skt. and Pali °na, nt.; to Skt. °veśayati plus -anā; cf. AMg. saṃnivesaṇayā, for °na-tā?), *establishment*: (tasmiṃ kuśalamūle) °nā pratiṣṭhāpanā Bbh 30.18.

saṃniśraya (m.; in Skt. in general sense, *support, basis*), = **niśraya,** q.v., as one of the four technical *supports* of monkish life: Bbh 193.7 (= niśraya in 2 above).

saṃniśrita, adj.-ppp. (= Pali saṃnissita), (**1**) physically, *fixed, located, living in*: indrakīlo pṛthivī-°to Mv i.292.14, *fixed in the ground*; (mahāsamudre ...) °tāḥ Divy 230.23, *living in ...*; himavat-°tā iva tṛṇagulmauṣadhivanaspatayo Gv 465.8, *growing in ...*; (**2**) *devoted to* or *dependent on, supported by* (a person): mamaiṣa sārtho °to Divy 94.11 (Buddha speaks), similarly 101.10; śūra-°taḥ puruṣaḥ sarvaśatrubhyo na bibheti Gv 506.1; (**3**) *based, dependent on* (a quality, etc.): karma-sa° Mv i.102.2, see **viniśrita**; saṃskāra-°taṃ ... vijñānaṃ Dbh 48.26 (in **pratītyasamutpāda**); -adhimokṣe °taḥ Bbh 41.12; na ...-aiśvarya-°taṃ (dānaṃ) dadāti 121.24; catvāri smṛty-upasthānāni kāye (read kāya-?)-vedanācittadharma-°tānāṃ cikitsāḥ KP 95.1; neg. a-°ta-tā, *the not being dependent on* or *devoted to*, Gv 245.25 (saṃsāra-nirvāṇa-sukhāsaṃ°).

saṃniṣaṇṇaka, adj. (= Skt. °ṇa, with -ka svārthe; only in vss, possibly m.c.), *seated*: °ko SP 455.6, of Amitābha; °kāḥ Gv 34.9, 11, of Buddhas (in same context with **niṣaṇṇaka** 34.17).

saṃniṣedhati (= Skt. niṣe°), *forbids*: yukto 'si māṃ deva na °ṣeddhum Jm 119.21 (vs), *you ought not to forbid me, Sire.*

saṃniṣṭhāpana, nt., (*firm*) *determination*: MSV ii.161.15; °nāntika (kaṭhinoddhāra) 17; 162.10; 164.5; 165.2 etc. (= Pali saṃniṭṭhānantika).

sannīyate (analogical MIndic pass. for saṃjñāyate, § 37.3 n. 1, with nn for (ṃ)jñ, § 2.15, cf. Pischel 276), *is known*: (asmākaṃ pitā ... āhitāgnir ucchritayūpaḥ) °yate Karmav 27.27; Lévi thinks, naturally, of emending, but refrains wisely from doing so.

saṃnyasa, read (with Index, Tib. Index, and Mironov) **saṃnyāsa,** m. (in Skt. *complete exhaustion*, BR s.v. 3), a kind of disease: Mvy 9553 = Tib. rme bya (read rme ba, *spots, (birth-)marks on the skin*; so Chin., *moles, spots on the body*) or rmya-ba (*nausea*; acc. to Das also *degeneration, decay*).

[? **sapati,** text in Gv 335.2 viṣaṃ sapanti, see **vipaṃsayati.**]

[**sapātrī,** see **āśapātrī.**]

[**sapūrva-**(samādinna), adopted by Senart in Mv i.211.14 = ii.15.14 (prose), tāni (sc. śikṣāpadāni) ca sapūrva-(so one ms. in i.211.14, v.l. saṃpūrṇa-; in ii.15.14 one ms. pūrva-, the other omits this part of the cpd.)-samādinnāni bhavanti; Senart admits inability to suggest a reasonable interpretation; I would read saṃpūrṇa-, *and they were completely adopted* (by the Bodhisattva's mother). It is impossible to read pūrva- since the prec. sentence says that she adopted them when the B. entered her womb.]

[**sapṛṣṭhībhūto** Divy 326.9, read sa pṛ°, see **pṛṣṭhībhavati.**]

saptaka, nt. (in Skt. m.), *week*: °kāni Divy 99.20; 167.16; 441.17; MSV i.132.16 (all in same cliché).

Saptakuṭīraka, n. of a village: Laṅk 252.3.

saptakṛd-(or, in Divy, MSV, °**kṛtvo-**)-**bhava-parama,** adj. (Pali sattakkhattu-parama, without bhava), *destined to be reborn not more than seven times*, ep. of a **srotaāpanna**: Mvy 1010; MSV ii.86.12–13 (read °paramaḥ); Divy 534.4. (Edd. print saptakṛtvo as separate word.)

Saptaparṇa- (in comp.; = Pali Sattapaṇṇi, once at least with v.l. °ṇṇa, DN ii.116.21), n. of a cave at Rājagṛha: Mv i.70.15.

Saptamaithunasaṃyukta-sūtra, n. of a work: Śikṣ 76.7. (No such title seems to occur in the Pali SN.)

Saptaratnapadmavikrāntagāmin (vv.ll. °vikrāmin, so Burnouf, or °vikrama), n. of a future Buddha (= Rāhula, by prediction): SP 219.13; 220.2.

Saptaratnābhivṛṣṭa, n. of a former Buddha: Sukh 6.11.

Saptaśatikāprajñāpāramitā, n. of a work: Mvy 1391.

Saptaśīrṣaka, n. of a nāga king, apparently = **Avabhāsanaśikhin** (q.v.), who has the epithet saptaśīrṣa: Megh 302.14.

Saptasūryopadeśa, n. of a work: Karmav 36.11, = Pali Sattasuriyasutta, referring to AN iv.100 ff.; see Lévi's note.

Saptāmra and °**raka,** nt. (= Pali Sattamba, °baka), n. of a caitya in or near Vaiśālī: °ra-cetiya Mv i.300.5 ff.; °rakaṃ (caityaṃ) Divy 201.5, 13.

saptālāpaka, read °lopaka, see **ālopaka.**

Saptāśīviṣa-, usually in comp. with (**1**) -parvata, m. pl., n. of certain mountains: Divy 107.20–21; °viṣam (not in comp.; masc., hence mountain) atikramya 107.26; °parvatā (understand pause here? or adj. with nadī?) nadī (sc. Saptāśīviṣanadī?) bhavati paścimā 103.3 (in a list of mountains and rivers, commingled); (**2**) -nadī, f. pl., °nadyas, n. of rivers: Divy 107.22, and cf. 103.3 above. See **Āśīviṣā** and °**viṣa-nadī,** which suggest doubt whether sapta- is part of the name (*having seven venomous snakes*), or a separate numeral, giving the number of Āśīviṣa-mountains and rivers. But 107.26 above, if not corrupt, supports the former interpretation, being singular.

saptāha, nt. (as in Pali sattāha; in Skt. m., despite gender of ahan), *seven days, a week*: °ha trīṇi SP 54.13 (vs).

(**saptāhika,** = **sāptā°,** q.v., adj. to prec., *lasting a week* or *recurring weekly*: in Skt., Kauṭ. Arth. Sham.[1] 116.10 °kā meghā(ḥ), *clouds that rain for a week*; °kaṃ akāla-vardalaṃ Mv iii.301.1, *bad weather lasting a week*; of medicines, *to be used weekly* or (more likely) *for a week*, Mvy 9438; Bhīk 23b.1; in Pali sattāhakālika, Vin. iv.83.17; of fever, *recurring the seventh day*, Māy 220.20.)

sa-pratīśa or °**sa,** adj. (see s.v. **a-pratīśa**; = Pali sappaṭissa, °tissa), *respectful*: spelled with ś, Mvy 1776; Mv iii.372.5; Divy 333.16, 26; Śikṣ 189.10; KP 10.6; °śa-tā, *state of being* ..., Bhīk 31b.5; with s, Mv i.174.3; ii.287.6; LV 102.21, text su-pra°, read with v.l. sa-pra°; Divy 484.15, 20 (mss. s, ed. em. ś); Mmk 491.15; mss. vary, ś or s, Mv ii.258.9; iii.345.18; Divy 484.25; in Mv ii.200.19 Senart by em. sapatissa-, but with not even remote or partial support in mss., and resulting in incorrect meter; in LV 160.10 Lefm. sa-pratīkṣāḥ (which would accord with Senart's conjecture as to the etymology, see s.v. apratīśa), but no ms. supports the reading; they point rather to sapratīśāḥ, tho most are confused. Usually preceded by sa-gaurava (°**gārava**).

Saprabha, n. of a Buddha: Divy 480.25; associated with Maitreya in a former birth; the edd. are naturally su ʾicious, since he is mentioned as if he were a wellkno n personage; but their suggestions for emendation are not attractive.

saprema and **°maka,** adj. (and subst. m.? Skt. saprema once in mg. *taking delight* (in, loc.); otherwise unrecorded; Bhvr., sa plus Skt. preman), *friendly, friend*: °makaḥ Mvy 2714; MSV ii.53.8; 131.12; sapremān bhikṣūn anyāṃś ca sārdhavihāriṇaḥ prārabdho vaktum Divy 237.5, (anyaiś ca) °makair bhikṣubhir 7.

Sabala, n. of a nāga king: Māy 246.22.

sabhāga, (**1**) adj. (= Pali id., cf. **vi-sa°**; sa- plus Skt. bhāga, Bhvr.), lit. *of common lot*, so *like, equal, matching, belonging to the same category*, often with gen., *like to*...: ye devaputrāḥ bodhisattvasya (in the Tuṣita heaven) °gāḥ-samayānasaṃprasthitās LV 13.13 (Tib. skal ba mñam pa, *like portion*); similarly LV 71.2; tasya vidusya °ga-carīye Bhad 42, *to a course like (that of) this Wise One*; tasya ca prathamavijñānasya . . . anantarasabhāgā cittasaṃtatiḥ Śikṣ 253.5, *immediately* (or *in succession*) *similar to that former vijñāna*; also (instead of gen.) with instr. and saha, (kalyāṇamitraiḥ saha . . .) sabhāgakuśalamūlasaṃgrahaṇatayā Śikṣ 33.3, or prec. stem in comp., indriya-°gam indriyādhiṣṭhānaṃ Bbh 64.4; and without any formal expression of the thing resembled, sabhāga-mitra- Gv 110.19, *like* (perh. *congenial*) *friends*; °ga-hetuḥ Mvy 2265 (Tib. as on LV 13.13), *like, corresponding cause*, one of six hetavaḥ; Śāl 87.19 = Śikṣ 226.12 (et alibi, see LaV-P. note 11 ad loc.), read (with Tib., on this word as on LV 13.13) visadṛśāt sattvanikāyād dhi (some versions vi- for dhi) °gāḥ skandhā jātyantare 'bhinirvartante, *for in another birth there come into existence like* **skandha** (q.v.) *from a different category of creatures*; sabhāgaḥ Mvy 2126, and tat-sa° 2127, rendered in Tib. (deḥi = tat-) bsten pa daṅ bcas pa, which seems to mean *adhering* (to that; i. e. member of a class?); dṛṣṭir . . . °gakarmapratipattihetuḥ Jm 153.9, *one's creed is the cause of adoption of actions corresponding* (to it); in Bhvr. cpd. sabhāga-carita, *having similar conduct* (to someone else's, gen.), °tā bodhisattvasya LV 13.15; mama sabhāgacaritā bodhisattvāḥ Gv 104.11 (and similarly 9); similarly (with prec. gen.) Gv 528.18; (without gen.) sarva-°ga-caritabodhisattva- Dbh 83.17; (**2**) subst. m. (or nt.?), in nikāyasabhāgaḥ Mvy 1991 = Tib. rigs ḥthun pa, *what is common to a class* or *category*; so also Chin. appears to interpret, *common element in a class*; in AbhidhK. LaV-P. ii.195–6 nikāya-sabhāga is equated with the abstract **sabhāgatā** (*le 'genre'*, LaV-P.); nikāya-sabhāgasyāvedhaḥ Mvy 7004, here of *the common factor in the category* of living beings, sattva (AbhidhK., l. c.), see **āvedha**; in Śikṣ 176.9 (read) sa nikāya-sabhāge devamanuṣyāṇāṃ priyo bhavati nirātaṅko dīrghāyuṣka iti, *he, in the common quality of his class, becomes beloved of gods and men, free from care (suffering), long-lived.*

sabhāgatā (to prec., see esp. 2, plus -tā), *likeness, community*, (**1**) *the being one of a category* or *group* (specified usually by gen., or prec. part of cpd.): brahmaloka-°tāyāṃ copapanno mahābrahmā saṃvṛttaḥ Divy 122.16, *and being born as an inhabitant of the brahma-world, he became a Great Brahmā*; manuṣyāṇāṃ °tāyām upapannaḥ 194.30, = *born as a man*; 210.12, similar to 122.16; trayastriṃśānāṃ °tāyām upapadyeran Suv 193.6; ā caṇḍālānām ā śunāṃ °tāyām upapadyate Bbh 226.24, *he takes rebirth as low as a caṇḍāla or a dog* (to help creatures); devānāṃ °tāyopapatsyante SP 478.4 and (°syate) 11 (prose, °tāya here MIndic loc.); a kind of magic power (ṛddhi) of Bodhisattvas is °gatopasaṃkrānti Bbh 58.25, explained 61.17 ff., the (magical, illusory) assumption of the form of a being of some class (kṣatriya, brahman, householder, monk, or god of any class), taking on precisely all the class characteristics, only to vanish after delivering his religious message; instead of dependent gen. in the above construction with upa-pad-, the loc. occurs Suv 194.14 (deveṣu trayastriṃśeṣu °tāyām upapannāni); (**2**) also in looser sense, *resemblance, likeness* (to, prec. member of cpd.), (sarvakalyāṇa-)mitrasabhāgatāṃ (text here °prabhāgatāṃ) pratyalabhata Gv 342.10; bodhisattva-°tāḥ (acc. pl.) pratyalabhata 25, which are listed in the foll., smṛti-°tāṃ 26, *likeness* (to Bodhisattvas) *in respect of smṛti*, mati-°tāṃ 26, gati-°tāṃ 343.1, etc.; karma-°gatāye (instr.) sarve 'pi te svargam upenti sthānaṃ Mv i.299.1 (vs), *by reason of correspondence* (of this fate) *to their* (good) *deeds, they all go to heaven* (see s.v. **yenaiva**).

sabhāpati, ep. of Brahman; rationalization of **Sahāpati,** q.v.: MPS 31.76.

Sabhika (= Pali Sabhiya), n. of a man who became a disciple of Buddha: Mv iii.394.7 ff.

Sabhikā, n. of a goddess: Mahāsamāj., Waldschmidt, Kl. Skt. Texte 4, 185.13.

sa-bhikṣuka, adj. (= Pali sabhikkhuka; opp. a-bhi°, q.v.), *containing monks*: °ka āvāsaḥ MSV ii.96.18.

sabhojana, see **bhojana.**

(**sama,** adj., only as in Skt.; but see **sama-sama**; *level* (so Kern; Burnouf *unie*): buddhakṣetraṃ bhaviṣyati samaṃ ramaṇīyaṃ . . . SP 65.9; (vasudhā rājakule Kaṇṭhakasya pādehi) sama-nihatā rasati madhuraṃ . . . Mv i.157.5 (vs), *the earth, evenly struck by* (the horse) *Kaṇṭhaka's hoofs, made a pleasant sound*; Senart assumes sama = samanantara, *à peine frappée, dès qu'elle est frappée.*)

samagra, adj. (in this mg. not Skt. but = Pali samagga; opp. to **vyagra,** q.v.), (*united,*) *harmonious*: (yaḥ punar bhikṣuḥ) °grasya saṃghasya bhedāya parākramet Prāt 482.10, 13, *proceeds towards division of a harmonious assembly* (of monks); MSV iv.251.9 ff.

samagrībhūta, ppp. (to Skt. samagra- plus bhavati), *completely provided*: (pañcahi kāmaguṇehi) samarpitaḥ °bhūto Mv ii.170.14; sarvasukhopadhānena samupatiṣṭhamānāḥ te 'pi sarve °bhūtā(ḥ) . . . Kv 28.7.

samagrya (nt., = Skt. sāmagrya, Pali sāmaggiya; perh. short a only m.c.), *totality*; only in Bhvr. cpds., and only in vss: daśabalasamagryo 'cirād bhaviṣyasi LV 332.18 (meter obscure to me), *you will soon become* (a Buddha) *with the totality of the ten powers*; śāsanavaraṃ su-°yaṃ Mv i.71.19 (vs), *the excellent doctrine in its fair totality*; śāsanaṃ śṛṇuyu sarva-°yaṃ 72.1.

samaṅgi-tā (= Pali id.; to next plus -tā), *the being provided with* (comp.): pāpamitra-°gitāye (em.) pañcānantaryāṇi kṛtāni Mv i.243.18.

samaṅgin, adj., f. **°ginī** or (in vs) **°gī,** n. sg. (in diff. sense in late Vedic; = Pali id.), *provided* or *endowed with* (instr. or in comp.): °gī, n. sg. m., Mv i.71.16 (dhutadharma-); ii.179.9 (upavāsa-, *participating in a fast, fasting*); AsP 455.10 (bala-); Gv 386.5; n. sg. f., LV 56.20 (vs; dhyānasukha-°gī); n. pl. m., Mv i.266.9 (vs, dvātriṃśa-lakṣaṇa-); iii.140.19 (vs, pañcahi kāmaguṇehi; v.l. samanvagi, unmetr.; see **°gī-bhūta**); °gi, n. sg. m., Mv i.206.13 = ii.10.7 (vs, uttamalakṣaṇa-); °giṃ, acc. sg. m., Mv i.210.2 = ii.14.1 (vs, pravaralakṣaṇa-); °ginī, n. sg. f., Gv 172.4–5 (mātāpitṛ-); °ginīṃ, acc. sg. f., LV 228.5 (putreṇa, *provided with a son*); °gisya, gen. sg. m., Mv ii.178.16 (prose, mama upavāsa-, *while I am undertaking a fast, fasting*).

Samaṅginī, n. of one of the eight deities of the Bodhi-tree: LV 331.21 (prose).

Samaṅgira(s), n. of a maharṣi: Māy 256.22 (n. sg. °giro).

samaṅgībhūta, and (in vss, where it may be m.c.) **°gibhūta,** adj.-ppp. (**samaṅgin** with bhavati; = Pali samaṅgibhūta, recorded in Dictt. only with short i), *united* (with), *provided* (with), *enjoying the presence* (of; instr.):

(putrehi) °gībhūtā Mv iii.167.15 (here v.l. samanvagī-bh°) and 168.6 (prose), *united with children* (after separation); divyehi rūpehi (ii.187.22 kāmehi) °gibhūtā (or °taḥ; ii.187.22 v.l. samanvagībhūto) Mv i.299.3 and ii.187.22 (vs; meter requires samaṅgi-); in a cliché (corresp. to Pali pañcahi kāmaguṇehi samappito samaṅgibhūto, with inflectional varr.), prec. by pañca(hi) kāmaguṇehi samarpita(ḥ, or inflect. varr.), samaṅgībhūta Mv iii.162.9; 177.6; also Senart's text i.32.6, 8, where half the mss. samanvagi- or °gī-bh°, and i.31.6, 194.17, where they all read thus, except that one inferior ms. (out of six) in i.31.6 has samanvaṅgi°; the cliché is completed by forms of krīḍati ramati paricārayati, or equivalents; see s.v. **samanva(ṅ)-gībhūta.**

sama-jīvakā, Mvy 9453 = Tib. kha dum pa (acc. to Das *being in concert with, having agreed*); acc. to Jap. *a woman who has agreed with a man, before marriage, that they are to hold property in common.*

? **samajjitaka**, see **samarji°**.

samajñā (semi-MIndic for **samājñā**; § 3.34; cited by the Skt. Lex. Trik., Schmidt, Nachträge; = Pali samaññā), *name*: only in series (or cpd.) saṃjnā samajñā prajñapti(ḥ) vyavahāra(ḥ), ŚsP 905.2, 4, 7; AsP 177.22. Cf. **samanyā.**

samajya (nt.? app. = Pali samajja, for Skt. samāja, rarely samajyā, which Senart reads by em. in Mv; but the word can hardly have in Mv the mg. which the Pali has acc. to Hardy, Album Kern 61 ff., see **Giriyagra-samāja**), (festal or social) *gathering, meeting*: of a public debate, (brāhmaṇena evaṃ samayaṃ kṛtvā parivrājikāye daṇḍakaṃ [app. as a gauge] praśaktaṃ [read pras°, *was furnished, tendered*], parivrājikāpi) taṃ brāhmaṇaṃ samajya-pratyanubhāvārthaṃ uttaraṃ (mss. °ra-) pratyuddharehi (so mss.; read °reti, or °si, Senart °dhāreti) Mv iii.393.3, *and to that brahman the female ascetic, in order to participate in the public meeting, withheld (restrained, held back, moderated) her answer*, i. e. she deliberately refrained from doing her best in the debate.

samatā, a high number: Gv 106.6; 133.16; Mvy 7877 (cited from Gv) = Tib. rtogs yas; = **sadama**, q.v.

samatā-jñāna, one of the 5 **jñāna** (q.v.): Mvy 112 = Tib. mñam pa ñid kyi ye śes (lit. transl.); Dharmas 94.

Samatārthasaṃbhavā, n. of an earth-goddess: Gv 282.21 (2d ed. line 22).

? **samati**, prob. error for samiti, *assembly*, in Māy 226.15 na devo devasamatīye (read °samitīye, gen. sg.) sthānaṃ (lapsyate, supply from line 25); and so in a long list, deva being replaced by asura, maruta, etc. Always °samatīye in text!

(**samatikrama** = Pali °kkama, very rare in Skt., *the getting beyond* or *away from*: rūpasaṃjñānāṃ °māt Mvy 1492, 1514; duḥ-°maḥ, Bhvr., Mvy 6806; nirodhaṃ °mam, acc., referring to the third Noble Truth, Divy 164.13; etc. Cf. foll. items.)

samatikramaṇa, nt., = prec.: jāti-°ṇaṃ Mv ii.161.8 (prose, mss. °kramaṃ), maraṇa-°ṇaṃ 12 (v.l. jāti-°kramaṃ), upāyāsa-°ṇaṃ 13; -dṛṣṭi-°ṇa-cakraṃ LV 423.2; mārapatha-°ṇā (Bhvr., or adj.?) dharmāḥ KP 18.1, 4 (prose).

samatikrāma = °**krama**: saṃsāra-°maṃ kuryā iti Av i.300.3. Speyer would em. to °kramaṃ 'according to grammar', a reason which I fail to understand.

samatikrāmaṇa, nt. (to unrecorded caus. *samatikrāmayati, cf. next), (means of) *getting across* (trans.), *rescuing*: °ṇam samsāraviṣayād LV 423.13, of the dharmacakra.

samatikrāmayitar (cf. prec.), *one who gets across, rescues* (from, abl.): (kalyāṇamitrāṇi . . .) °tāro dṛṣṭikāntārād Gv 462.24.

samatibhindati (cf. **vyatibhi°**), *shatters*: yathā hy agāraṃ ducchan(n)aṃ vṛṣṭiḥ °ti, evaṃ hy abhāvitaṃ cittaṃ rāgaḥ °ti Ud xxxi.11; similarly 12–16.

sama-tīrthika, f. °**ikā**, adj. (var. °thaka, °tittika; Pali °titthika, var. °tittika, see below), *full to the brim*; in both Pali and BHS used (**1**) of rivers in flood (so most commonly in Pali, e. g. DN i.244.14, where text °tittikā, v.l. °titthikā, comm. ii.402.23 glosses samabharitā): (gaṅgā . . . suparipūrṇā) samatīrthakā (read with v.l. and Calc. °thikā) LV 407.2 (prose), Tib. mu daṅ mñam pa, *level with the borders (banks)*; (**2**) of bowls of food: samatīrthikāṃ (sc. pātrīṃ) pūriṣu bhojanena LV 387.3 (vs), Tib. zhal zas kyis ni (*with food*) kha da (*to the brim*) chad du (read tshad du? *to full measure*) bkaṅ (*filled*); na samatīrthikam Mvy 8565, (monks should) *not* (accept food) *up to the brim* (of the bowl); Tib. mu daṅ kha daṅ . . ., cf. above; var. °tittikam, which Mironov prints; Pali parallel, Vin. iv. 190.35, samatitthikaṃ piṇḍapātaṃ paṭiggahessāmi, *I shall accept almsfood* (only) *to the brim* (of the bowl, not heaped up higher). Acc. to Childers' informant, this is the true reading and interpretation; for others see PTSD s.v. The variant °tittika, tho found in both Pali and Mvy tradition, is prob. a corruption. The mg. of tīrtha here implied is an extension of Skt. usage, where it is used of what are now called *bathing ghats* in India; from this to *edge, bank*, of a river, was a short step; the cpd. samatīrthika was prob. used first of very full rivers, then by extension of food-bowls.

samatha, often written for **śamatha**, q.v.

Samadṛṣṭi, n. of a former Buddha: Mv i.137.7.

samadhikṛta, adj.-ppp. (= Pali adhikata), *irresolute, unsteady*: saced druta-°taṃ (*quickly made irresolute*) bhaviṣyati Divy 517.2, repeated in sequel.

? **samadhibhāṣati** (cf. **adhi-bh°**), *addresses*: pitaraṃ samadhyabhāṣati Mv ii.144.1 (vs); but the form is unmetrical, while the v.l. samabhāṣati is metrical and should prob. be adopted. Both are augmented presents; § 32.8.

[**samadhiṣṭha**, acc. to Lefm. LV 257.14 (prose) adj., *staying, presiding*; but read with v.l. and Calc. samadhiṣṭhāya, ger. (Tib. gnas śiṅ): te (sc. gods, etc.) rātriṃdivaṃ °ṣṭhā(ya) bodhisattvasya pūjāṃ kurvanti sma.]

samanantara-pratyaya, see **pratyaya** (1).

samanugāhyate (pass. to Pali °gāhati), *is examined, cross-questioned*, with synonym **samanuyujyate**, q.v.: Prāt 482.7.

samanugrāhaka, adj. or subst. m. (Skt. sam-anu-grah- plus -aka), *favoring, conferring (one who confers) favors*: lokajñaḥ vidhijñaḥ °kaḥ kāryāṇāṃ (text °yāvāṃ) vicakṣaṇaḥ . . . Mmk 93.23.

samanujñaka, adj. (cf. next; Pali samanuñña plus -ka), *giving consent, approving*: pūrva-°ko bhūtvā Prāt 504.4, *having first given his consent.*

samanujñā (= Pali °ññā; to Skt. sam-anu-jānāti), *approval, permission*: Mvy 6620.

samanuddeśaka-tva, semi-MIndic for **śramaṇoddе°**, q.v.

samanunayati (= Skt. anu-n°), *appeases*: (karuṇāyamānaḥ) samanuneṣyan (fut. pple.) Jm 188.8.

(a)samanupaśyana-tā (cf. Pali samanupassanā, f.), *(non-)consideration*: (yā ātmikānāṃ) dharmāṇām a-°tā ŚsP 1464.15.

samanupraveśana(-tā; cf. Skt. anu-pra-viś-; no sam-anu° recorded), *(complete) penetration*: Mmk 92.20, see s.v. **avisṛta.**

samanuprāpaṇa(-tā; to Skt. sam-anu-prāpnoti plus -ana), *attainment*: sarvajñajñānānukramaṇa-°tāyai Mmk 92.19.

samanubadhnāti, °**bandhati** (= Pali °bandhati), *follows*, usually in lit. and physical sense, often prec. by pṛṣṭhataḥ (-pṛṣṭhataḥ), or in Mv pṛṣṭhimena pṛṣṭhimaṃ or the like: (Sudhanaṃ . . .) gacchantaṃ pṛṣṭhataḥ °badhnāti sma Gv 389.11; °bandhe (so, or °bandho, mss., Senart em. °baddho) 'haṃ Mv iii.53.11; dharmeśvaraṃ °bandhayatāṃ LV 46.2 (vs), *let him follow* (here fig., in religion) *the Lord of Religion* (not caus., -ya- m.c.; v.l. °dhatāṃ, one ms., unmetr.); °bandhitavyā, gdve., Prāt 516.6; commoner is ppp. °baddha, usually with gen., rarely loc. or acc., of person: (Māraś ... bodhisattvasya ...) pṛṣṭhataḥ pṛṣṭhataḥ °ddho 'bhūt (to try to find some flaw in his defense) LV 260.18; similarly Mv ii.241.5, and others in Mv, see s.v. **pṛṣṭhima**; (Avalokiteśvarasya) ... Kv 43.7 (here in friendly wise); (all sorts of people) dharmabhāṇakasya ... °baddhā bhaviṣyanti SP 368.1; ṛṣabho ... gogaṇa-°ddho Mv iii.28.6; with loc., daśabale °ddhāḥ Mv i.115.12 (vs); acc., Bhagavantam eva pṛṣṭhataḥ pṛṣṭhataḥ °ddhā gacchanti Divy 68.24; Śāriputraṃ pṛṣṭhataḥ °ddhaḥ 331.6; no dependent case, Divy 137.28; 325.11; 615.3. See next.

samanubandha, m. (to prec.), *following after*: °dhaḥ Mvy 2167.

samanubudhyate (pass. of *sam-anu-budh-, otherwise unrecorded; Skt. anu-budh-), *is perfectly comprehended*: (sarvaṃ tam ekakṣaṇe) svayaṃbhūsamatāṃ °dhye (aor.) Mv i.4.10 (vs, printed as prose), ... *was comprehended unto* (so as to result in) *equality with the self-existent*; ppp. °buddhā LV 372.11 (buddhanarditānī, m.c. for °ni), °buddhaṃ 12 (-śatasahasraṃ dharmāna, so text; both vss).

samanumodana, nt. (to Pali °modati plus -ana), *approval*: (pareṣām) adattādānanivṛttānāṃ °nam Karmav 41.14, and paralābha-°nam 17.

samanuyujyate (pass. to Pali °yuñjati), *is examined, cross-questioned*: sā prathamā patnī °te, tvayā ... Av i.277.14, *that first wife was examined* (saying:) *Did you* ...?; °māno vā (a-°māno vā) Prāt 482.4; °mānasya samanugāhyamānasya (see this) 6–7, cf. Pali MN i.130.31–32 samanuyuñjiyamāno samanugāhiyamāno. The active is perhaps Skt. in this mg., cf. ger. samanuyujya (BR s.v. yuj with sam-anu); this ger. also MSV ii.145.3 bhikṣūn °jya, *questioning the monks*. Cf. **anuyukta** (2).

samanurakṣati, *guards, keeps carefully*: ātmānaṃ °kṣatā (pres. pple. instr.) Divy 104.13; 105.18.

samanuvicarati, *makes a tour of* (acc.): sa rājā dānaśālāḥ °caran ... Jm 7.15; upavanāni °caran ... 123.15.

[**samanuviṣṭavān**, read °śiṣṭavān (Skt.) (as suggested in note, p. 706), *governed*: °vān rājā Mūrdhātaḥ Pūrvavidehaṃ dvīpam Divy 214.21.]

samanuśāsana (nt.; to Skt. sam-anu-śās-), *instruction*: teṣām eva cānyeṣāṃ ca °nārthaṃ Bbh 151.7, pareṣāṃ ca hitakāmatayā °nārthaṃ 12.

samanusarati, *follows*: MSV iv.197.7.

(**samanusmarati**, °te, rare in Skt., = Pali samanussarati, *remembers*; common in BHS: SP 64.13; 102.9; Mv i.45.15; 228.16; 229.5; 245.20; ii.103.8; 104.2; 132.17; 153.11; 171.5; 190.1; 284.8; 313.13; iii.165.12; Divy 109.6; 196.24; 348.18; Jm 17.12, 14; Bbh 389.15; Sukh 3.14; 48.5; Laṅk 91.5, etc.)

Samanojñārutasiṃhadhvaja, var. for **Mano°**, q.v.: Mvy 3387.

Samanta, n. of a Bodhisattva: Mmk 576.15 (vs); prob. a short form (m.c.) for the well-known **Samantabhadra**, q.v.; in the same line **Mahāsthāma**, q.v., also prob. a short form.

Samanta-ābhaśiri, see **Samantābhaśrī**.

Samantakarṇa, n. of a rākṣasa king: Mmk 17.28.

Samantakusuma, (**1**) n. of a god: LV 370.3, 9; (**2**) n. of a Tathāgata: ŚsP 55.12.

Samantakusumārciḥpralambacūḍa, n. of a Bodhisattva: Gv 81.17.

samantagandha, (**1**) m., (in Mvy) or nt. (in Mv), a kind of flower: Mvy 6192 (°dhaḥ); Mv (n.-acc. only °āni) i.230.16; 267.1; ii.160.13; 286.17; iii.95.16; 99.15; (**2**) n. of a former Buddha: Mv i.138.12; (**3**) n. of a devaputra: SP 4.4.

Samantagandhavitāna, n. of a Tathāgata: Gv 81.2.

Samantagandhāvabhāsaśriya (dat. °śriyāya), n. of a Tathāgata: Mmk 27.27 (prose).

Samantagambhīraśrīvimalaprabhā, n. of a goddess of night: Gv 235.18; 237.4 ff., etc.

Samantaguṇamegha, n. of a Buddha: Gv 259.14.

Samantagupta, n. of a past Buddha: Mv i.58.11.

samanta-cakṣus, (**1**) adj., *of universal vision*, ep. of a Buddha (so also Pali samantacakkhu): °kṣuḥ SP 67.12 (vs); (**2**) n. of a former Buddha: Gv 104.19.

samantacandra, some sort of jewel: °drā maṇiratanāṃ grahetvā ... alaṃkaronti bhagavato bodhivṛkṣaṃ Mv ii.317.19 (vs); °drehi samalaṃkṛtaṃ bodhivṛkṣaṃ saṃjānanti Mv ii.310.13 (prose).

Samantacāritramati, n. of a Bodhisattva: Mvy 681.

Samantajñānacaryāvilamba, n. of a Tathāgata: Gv 422.19.

Samantajñānadhvajaśūra, n. of a Tathāgata: Gv 310.2.

Samantajñānaprabharāja, n. of a Buddha: Gv 256.19 (vs).

Samantajñānaprabhāsa, n. of a Tathāgata: Gv 312.8.

Samantajñānabhadramaṇḍala, n. of a Tathāgata: Gv 309.18.

Samantajñānamaṇḍalapratibhāsanirghoṣa, n. of a Tathāgata: Gv 15.18.

Samantajñānaratnārciḥpadmabhadrābhirāmanetraśrīcandrā, Gv 277.10; °jñānārcipadma° etc., 275.11; °jñānārciḥpadma° etc., 281.4, 5; all prose, = **Padmabhadrābhirāmanetraśrī**, q.v.

Samantajñānaratnārciśrīguṇaketurāja(n), n. of a Tathāgata: Gv 273.9; 276.24; 277.7 etc.

Samantajñānābhapravara, n. of a Tathāgata: Gv 310.23.

Samantajñānārci(ḥ)padma°, see above, °**jñānaratnārci(ḥ)-padma°**.

Samantajñānārci(ḥ)śrīguṇaketudhvaja, = °**jñānaratnārciśrī°**, Gv 270.21; and (with -rāja for -dhvaja) 281.12.

Samantajñānālokavikramasiṃha, n. of a Tathāgata: Gv 422.4.

Samantajyotigandhāvabhāsaśriya (dat. °śriyāya), n. of a Tathāgata: Mmk 28.12 (prose).

Samantata-bhadra, used m.c. in the vss of Bhad (42, 50, 55) instead of **Samantabhadra**, q.v., n. of a Bodhisattva. The regular name does not fit the meter of Bhad; this form was, I assume, interpreted as having the adv. samantata(s) as prior member.

Samantadarśananetra, n. of a Bodhisattva: Gv 3.1.

Samantadarśin (**1**) n. of a former Buddha: LV 171.15; (**2**) n. of a Tathāgata in the nadir: LV 294.19.

samantadigabhimukha (cf. **samantamukha**), a certain gem: Gv 219.17.

Samantadiśatejas, n. of a Buddha: Gv 259.17.

Samantadharmadvāravahanaśikharābha, n. of a Tathāgata: Gv 310.6.

Samantadharmadhātugaganapratibhāsamakuṭa, n. of a Bodhisattva: Gv 3.8.

Samantanetra, (**1**) n. of a Bodhisattva: Mvy 675; RP 1.11; Gv 3.3; (**2**) n. of a perfume-merchant: Gv 151.5, 24, etc.; (**3**) n. of an (imaginary?) Buddhist text (dharmaparyāya): Gv 65.26 ff.; in 66.26 called Samantanetra-tathāgatabodhisattvacaryāvabhāsadharmaparyāya.

Samantaprajñaptinirghoṣamegha, n. of a Tathāgata: Gv 311.13.

Samantaprajñābhadharmanagarapradīpa, n. of a Tathāgata: Gv 312.9.

Samantapratibhāsacūḍa, n. of a Tathāgata: Gv 310.9.

Samantaprabha, (**1**) n. of a Buddha: Gv 284.11, and see s.v. **Samantaprabhāsa**; (**2**) n. of a Bodhisattva:

Mvy 707; RP 1.12; (**3**) m., a kind of flower: Mvy 6191.

Samantaprabhatejas, n. of a Bodhisattva: Gv 2.22.

Samantaprabhaśrītejas, n. of a Bodhisattva: Gv 2.23.

Samantaprabhā, n. of an eleventh (Bodhisattva-) bhūmi, one of three added to the usual ten, acc. to Dharmas 65.

Samantaprabhāsa, reading of SP edd. in most occurrences for n. of a future Buddha, which it is predicted that Ājñāta Kauṇḍinya will become, SP 206.11, and also n. of 500 future Buddhas which 500 'great disciples' will become, 207.2. But the true reading in both places is prob. **Samantaprabha** (1), with Kashgar rec. In the same account, °prabha is read without v.l. in 207.9 and 208.10, guaranteed by meter; in 208.5 text reads prabhāsanāmasya (referring to the former case), but Kashgar rec. Samantaprabha-; in 209.4 text Samantaprabhāsasya, metr. very bad, Kashgar rec. and one Nep. ms. °prabhasya, better metrically (°prābhasya is required).

Samantaprāsādika, n. of a Bodhisattva: Mvy 680.

Samantabhadra, (**1**) (see also **Bhadra 1, Samanta, Samantata-bhadra**) n. of a celebrated Bodhisattva, sometimes one of eight (e. g. Dharmas 12) or sixteen (Mmk 40.13) Bodhisattvas; other cases: Mvy 648; SP 472.2 ff.; Suv 157.18; RP 1.10; Bhad, prose introduction (in vss **Samantata-bh°**); Kv 1.12; 63.18; 92.18; Mmk 62.21; 68.20, etc.; Gv 2.13; 33.1; 530.12, etc.; Sādh 8.2 etc.; (**2**) n. of one or more Tathāgatas: Mv iii.236.15; Laṅk 105.9; Sādh 12.4.

Samantabhadrā, n. of a goddess: Mvy 4289.

samantamukha, (**1**) (cf. **samantadigabhimukha**) a certain kind of gem: °kha-maṇiratna- Gv 101.14; (**2**) ep. of **Avalokiteśvara**: SP 456.5, 7 (°kha-parivarta, title of chap. 24 of SP); see the foll. entries; (**3**) n. of a city: Gv 151.5.

Samantamukhajñānabhadrameru, n. of a Tathāgata: Gv 309.13 (cf. **Samantamukha** 2).

Samantamukhajñānavirocanaghoṣa, n. of a Tathāgata: Gv 81.16. (Cf. prec.)

Samantamukhaviśuddhivyūha, m., n. of a samādhi: Gv 98.11. (Cf. prec. two.)

Samantamukhā, n. of a dhāraṇī: Gv 125.8. (Cf. prec. three.)

Samantaratnakiraṇamuktaprabha, n. of a gandharva: Mvy 3388.

Samantaratnakusumaprabhā, n. of a capital city (rājadhānī): Gv 307.11.

Samantaratnā, n. of a lokadhātu: Gv 380.24.

Samantarat(a)nārciś(i)rīguṇaketurāja, n. of a Buddha: Gv 284.7 (vs).

Samantaraśmi, n. of a Bodhisattva: RP 1.11; ŚsP 29.9.

sam-antara-hita, ppp. (to sam-antar(a)-dhā-; recorded only here and in Pali id., Jāt. i.29, last line, wrongly analyzed samanta-rahita in PTSD), (*completely*) *disappeared*: ... gṛhikalpaṃ sarvaṃ °taṃ Mv ii.234.4; similar context iii.65.4; 92.9; 329.11; 379.15; 430.16; 432.3 (on conversion to Buddhism, all traces of former way of life disappear).

Samantavighuṣṭakīrtidhvaja, n. of a Tathāgata: Gv 310.18.

Samantavilokitajñāna, n. of a Tathāgata: Gv 421.21.

Samantavilokitā, n. of a lokadhātu in the nadir: LV 294.19.

Samantavīryolkāvabhāsamegha, n. of a Tathāgata: Gv 311.19.

Samantaveda, pl., n. of a brahmanical school (of the Chandogas): Divy 632.24; 633.1.

Samantavairocanacandra, n. of a Tathāgata: Gv 422.2.

Samantavairocanamakuṭa, n. of a Bodhisattva: Gv 3.6.

Samantavairocanaśrīmerurāja, n. of a Tathāgata: Gv 13.25.

Samantavyūha, (**1**) nt., n. of a grove in **Samudravetāḍī**: Gv 99.11; 100.10; (**2**) m., n. of a parivarta (chapter) of the Prajñāpāramitā, acc. to Gv 124.26 f.

Samantaśrīkusumatejābha, n. of a Tathāgata: Gv 310.13.

Samantaśrītejas, n. of a Bodhisattva: Gv 2.22.

Samantaśrīvairocanaketu, n. of a Tathāgata: Gv 310.20.

Samantaśrīsamudrarāja, n. of a Bodhisattva: Gv 10.4, but read with 2d ed. °samudgatarāja; same called **Samantaśrīsamudgatatejorāja** in Gv 26.5.

Samantaśrīsaṃbhava, n. of a Tathāgata: Gv 217.8; see **Śrīsaṃbhava**.

Samantasattvatrāṇojaḥśrī (for °ṇaujaḥśrī), n. of a goddess of night: Gv 261.21 ff.; cited Śikṣ 149.7, corruptly, in instr., as Samantasattvaparitrāṇyojasaḥ striyā (!).

Samantasaṃpūrṇaśrīgarbhā, n. of a capital city (rājadhānī): Gv 296.18.

Samantasaṃbhavapradīpa, n. of a Buddha: Gv 258.9 (vs).

Samantasūcisuviśuddhajñānakusuma, n. of a Tathāgata: Gv 311.4.

Samantasūryāvabhāsaprabharāja, n. of a Tathāgata: Gv 309.21.

samantasthūlāvalokananayanābhirāma, m., a kind of flower: Mvy 6193.

Samantānuracitaśāntanirghoṣa, n. of a Tathāgata: Gv 422.7.

Samantābhaśrī, appearing in the form Samanta-ābha-śiri, m.c., n. of a Buddha-kṣetra: Gv 259.12 (vs) arvāg atas tadanu asti kṣetra samanta-ābhaśiri (1st ed. printed samanta ābhaśiri, separately) nāmni.

samantāloka, (**1**) m. or nt. (*having splendor*, āloka, *all around*), a kind of gem: Mv ii.310.17; (**2**) n. of a samādhi: Mvy 562; ŚsP 1420.2; (**3**) n. of a Bodhisattva: KP 150.1 ff. (prose).

Samantāvabhāsa, n. of a samādhi: ŚsP 1418.4; omitted in Mvy between 542 and 543.

Samantāvabhāsaketu, n. of a Bodhisattva: Gv 3.20.

Samantāvabhāsadharmaśrīghoṣa, n. of a Tathāgata: Gv 309.26.

Samantāvabhāsadhvaja, n. of a kalpa: Gv 296.10.

Samantāvabhāsavyūhaśrī, n. of a Tathāgata: Śikṣ 169.15.

Samantāvabhāsaśrī, n. of a Tathāgata: Mmk 7.10.

Samantāvabhāsaśrīgarbharāja, n. of a Tathāgata: Gv 9.9.

Samantāvabhāsodgata, n. of a Bodhisattva: Gv 4.1.

Samantāvaloka, n. of a Bodhisattva: Mmk 42.5.

Samantāvalokabuddhi, n. of a Bodhisattva: Gv 4.14.

Samantāvalokita, n. of a Bodhisattva: RP 1.11.

Samanteryāpatha, n. of a Bodhisattva: Mvy 679.

samanyā, false Skt. for Pali samaññā = **samājñā**, *name*: mss. at Mv i.351.14; Senart em. samājñā. This form, or a relative, may also have been intended by the mss. reading samanyite at Mv i.247.10 (vs), for which Senart em. samājñā (unmetr.). Cf. **samajñā**, and § 2.15.

samanvagībhūta (mss. of Mv), **samanvaṅgībhūta** (other texts), *provided* (with), *enjoying* (instr.): only (except two vv.ll. in Mv) in cliché pañcabhiḥ kāmaguṇāiḥ, or in Mv pañca(hi) kāmaguṇehi, samarpita(ḥ, etc.) °bhūta(ḥ, etc.), foll. by krīḍati ramati paricārayati, or other forms of these or equivalent verbs; = **samaṅgībhūta**, q.v., Pali samaṅgi°; on the Mv passages see samaṅgī°, which Senart always reads: samanvaṅgī° Mvy 7374; Divy 219.22 ff.; Śikṣ 166.8; AsP 488.11; MSV i.113.2. There seems no doubt that samaṅgī°, or °gi° (as app. always in Pali without v.l.), is the orig. form. In most Mv occurrences, some or all mss. read samanvagī° or °gi°; this may well have been the first change, and have actually existed in the language; it will have been analyzed as based on an adj. *sam-anvaga, equivalent to Pali anvaga (also anvagata), for anuga(ta), with intrusive -a- by anal. of augmented verb forms, see CPD; no doubt the common synonym **samanvāgata** also helped in this creation. This was later modified to samanvaṅgī° (found in a single ms. at Mv i.31.6), the only BHS form outside of Mv (in five texts); it was doubtless analyzed as sam-anv-aṅgī°, cf. Skt. aṅgīkaroti and derivs., as well as **sam-aṅgin**.

samanvāgata, adj.-ppp. (= Pali samannāgata), *provided, endowed, attended* (with, instr., or in comp.), very common: Mvy 7378; LV 9.17 (bodhyaṅgaratna-); 14.1 (mahāpuruṣalakṣaṇaiḥ; so, with °ṇehi, Mv i.226.15; 237.8; ii.29.18); LV 25.3 (catuṣṣaṣṭy-ākāraiḥ °taṃ ... kulaṃ; in corresp. Mv i.197.14; 198.10; ii.1.6; 2.6 ṣaṣṭīhi aṅgehi °taṃ); LV 160.21 (pañcābhijñābhiḥ); Mv i.128.3, 4 (-karmeṇa, sattvena); 193.14 (saptaratna-); 196.20 and ii.422.2 (varṇapuṣkalatāye, °tāya); i.211.7 = ii.15.6; i.237.9, 10; ii.99.13; 132.9 (kāyaduścaritena); 161.16 (yauvanena), 18 (ārogyena); 260.6 (sthāmena); 177.20 (aṣṭāṅga-); Kv 41.24 (puṇyaskandhena); 52.17 (samādhibhiḥ).

samanvāgama, m. (n. act., cf. prec.), *provision, accompaniment, the being accompanied* or *provided*: (yathāvat-samudāgama-hetu-parigrahād yathākāma)-samudācāra-vaśavartitā °gama ity ucyate Bbh 385.14, *the being in control of behavior as one wills, thru possession of ..., is called provision*; sa dharmas, tasya cotpādaḥ °gamaḥ (*accompaniment* or *provision*, the being provided with what naturally goes with it) sthitir jarā 'nityatā MadhK 148.3; guṇair viśiṣṭaiḥ °gamas Sūtrāl v.5, *the being provided with distinguished virtues* (not *réussite par* ..., Lévi); °gamāt AbhidhK. LaV-P. iv.181, n. 2, and 182, *par possession* (i. e. *thru being provided with* ..., e. g. abhidhyā, mithyādṛṣṭi).

? **sam-anvāsayati** (cf. Pali opt. anu-v-āseyyā, CPD s.v. anu-v-āsati), *attends* (?): eṣa te 'dya samanvāsayāmy aham Gv 487.10 (vs); but meter is wrong (syllable anv- should be short); prob. some corruption. I have also thought of reading samanvāśayāmy, *here today I wish* (prīti ... vipulām, in prec. line) *for thee*; cf. āśayan, *desiring*, Bhāg.P. 9.1.37 (BR 7.219), and Pali āsayānā, *desiring*, Jāt. iv. 291.22; but this does not correct the meter.

[**samanvāhara**, = °**hāra**, q.v., which prob. read: Bbh 155.7 (prose).]

samanvāharaṇa (to next) = **samanvāhāra**: MadhK 567.10 (in same passage Śikṣ 225.9 °hāra, q.v.).

samanvāharati, °te (in mg. 1 = Pali samannāharati), (**1**) (the only mg. discovered in Pali; PTSD also *to pay respect to, to honour*, but in the passages cited the mg. is simply *focus attention on, pay heed to*, e. g. Vin. i.180.20 °haranti, comm. 1081.15 f. punappunaṃ manasikaronti) *focuses the attention* (on), *pays heed* (to), *takes note* (of); complement, when expressed, generally acc., rarely gen.; sometimes the complement is a quotation of thought, so that the verb means *fixes one's mind on* (the thought ...), virtually *considers, realizes*, or with a future *makes up one's mind* (as follows), *decides*; with a question, *considers* (a problem); gen. complement, devate samanvāharāsya (*concentrate your attention on him*) yasya sakāśāt tāḍakaḥ kuñcikā ca gṛhītā; sā samanvāhartuṃ pravṛttā paśyati yāvat, kālagataḥ Divy 578.10; asmākaṃ (but this form is also used as acc.!) rājā na °rati Mv iii.162.17 (prose), *the king pays no heed to us* (his harem; note 163.8, similar situation, vayaṃ ca na °hariṣyati, where vayaṃ is acc.); mama saparivārasya na tathā °hariṣyanti Mv iii.424.14; (vyasanaprāpto 'ham) asmi na ca me (as acc.?) Bhagavān °rati Divy 613.2, foll. by, atha Bhagavān ... (3) Ānandaṃ °rati; asmākam api °harethāḥ Av i.211.2 (prose), *turn your thoughts to me too*; but much more often acc., °harati sma ... bodhisattvo Brahmāṇaṃ LV 69.19 (prose), *noticed, was aware of*, or *took notice of*; (Bodhisattvaḥ ...) sarvabuddhān °hṛtya (*having turned his attention to* ...) sarvabuddhebhyaś ca namaskāraṃ kṛtvā 209.14; (nagaraṃ, see s.v. **agocara**) Divy 51.1; °hara Jetavanaṃ 53.20, *concentrate* (your mind) *on the J.* (whereupon they immediately arrive there by magic); māṃ Bhagavān na °rati 154.9 (same phrase with me 613.2, above); °hartum ātmanaḥ pūrvajātīḥ pravṛttaḥ 240.27; °hara ... Rudrāyaṇaṃ 550.3, *turn your attention to R.*; divyena cakṣuṣā tān pretān °hartuṃ pravṛttaḥ Av i.258.2; asmān api °harethāḥ ii.66.9 (same with asmākam i.211.2, above); °harantu māṃ Buddhāḥ Suv 25.1; (Śrīr ... taṃ) gṛhaṃ °hariṣyati 117.2; °haratu māṃ Tathāgataḥ RP 48.16; (āścaryaṃ yan māṃ ete) °haranti Śikṣ 128.12, *it's a wonder that they notice me*; (bālapṛthagjanān ...) °harāpekṣasva Dbh 65.15, *pay heed and give consideration to* ...; passive expressions, sarvatathāgata-°hṛtaṃ (dharmacakraṃ) LV 415.16, *which has been the object of attention of all T.*; (Śakreṇa ...) °hṛto (v.l. °hṛtaṃ, better? *it*, rather than *he, was noted*) yathā rājā Kuśo ātmānaṃ ... māritukāmo Mv ii.492.2; so dāni Śakreṇa ... °hṛto iii.25.3; (people, bhojanāchādanena sarve, so read with mss. for Senart's em. sarvehi, ca utsavehi) °haritavyā 177.17, *are to be looked after, attended to, with* ...; vyavalokayantu māṃ buddhāḥ °hṛta-cetasā Suv 30.7 (*with minds attentive*, sc. to me); (buddhair ...) samanvāhriyate Śikṣ 351.5, *is noted, attended to*; °hṛtāḥ smaḥ Tathāgatena Gv 356.8; buddhāsamanvāhṛtair 529.10–11, *that have not been paid heed to by* (any) *Buddha*; absolute, no object expressed, te (ṛṣayaḥ, who have been invited) °haritvā (*taking note, paying heed*) ... ṛddhyā yajñavāṭaṃ gatāḥ Mv ii.96.3; °haritvā (*upon focussing their attention*) ṛṣīṇāṃ jñānaṃ pravartati iii.144.4; tatas te Buddhā bhagavanto °haranti mahābodhisattvāś ca Mmk 56.13, *the Buddhas* ... (who have just been invoked) *then pay attention, heed* (the call; Lalou, Iconographie 20, *viennent*, wrongly); samanvāharatāṃ, gen. pl. pres. pple., Bbh 155.7, see s.v. **samanvāhāra**; °haratv āyuṣmā(n) Bbh 181.6, *pay heed!*; sarvacetasā °hṛtya Mvy 7260; (ārya bhrātā te kṛcchra-)-saṃkaṭasaṃbādhaprāptaḥ, °hareti (°hara iti) Divy 42.7, *give* (the matter, or him) *your attention!* (the monk addressed then enters samādhi and saves his brother from a hurricane); a candidate for initiation into the order addresses his or her spiritual preceptor at the ceremony, samanvāhara (misprinted °hāra) ācārya Mvy 8701, *take note (of), pay heed (to me), Teacher!*; °hara ācāryike Bhīk 10b.3; and in taking the nun's robes, °hara upādhyāyike 15a.1; or (see above) the complement, that on which attention is focussed, may be a statement, usually attributed to the thoughts of the subject: °haradhvaṃ, tasya bhagavato dhātūnāṃ pūjāṃ kariṣyāma iti SP 412.7, *fix your minds on the thought, We will pay homage to the relics of that Lord*; but the quoted statement may also be a question, °harati sma bhikṣavas (voc.) Tathāgataḥ, kutrāsāv etarhīti, °haraṃś cājñāsīd, adya trīṇy ahāni kālagatasyeti LV 403.21–22, *the T. focused his mind on* (the question), *Where is he now? and doing so he knew, It is three days today since he died*; so dāni °harati, kahiṃ so rājā ... Mv ii.425.12; so dāni ṛṣi °harati, amukaṃ kālaṃ maye (= mayā) adhimātraṃ ... phalāni paribhuktāni ... iii.144.5, *the sage focused his mind on the thought, At that time I ate excessively, etc.*; mayā pramattavihārāye (see s.v. **vihāra** 2) na °hṛtam, evaṃ duṣkarakārakā bodhisattvā 355.1, *in my negligent state I did not focus on the thought that B's perform such difficult feats*; °harati, kim asau gāndhika utpannaḥ? Divy 350.26; occasionally, instead of a direct quotation, what the concentrated attention reveals is expressed by a clause with paśyati,

Pūrṇako °harati, paśyati Sthapakarṇikaṃ . . . saṃśaya-prāptaṃ Mv i.245.10, *P. focused his attention and saw that S. was in danger*; so °harati, paśyati taṃ . . . pravrajitaṃ ii.49.4; see also Divy 578.10 above; (**2**) (cf. SP 412.7 above, where before a future verb, samanvāharati could perhaps be rendered *determine, resolve, have a fixed intention*) ger. °hṛtya, *deliberately, with intention*: (a Bodhisattva never speaks falsely *even in sleep*, svapnāntaragato 'pi . . .) kaḥ punar vādaḥ °hṛtya Dbh 23.24, *how much less with deliberate intention!*; see also **a-samanvāharitvā, °hṛtya**; (**3**) also as specialization of mg. 1, *gives one's attention to*, so *prepares, makes ready, makes*: (bhagavato ca bhikṣu-saṃghasya ca mahantaṃ) maṇḍalamālaṃ samanvāhara Mv ii.274.18 (cf. line 13 maṇḍalamālaṃ taṃ māpayiṣyaṃ, and 275.1 where the order is carried out, and abhinir-miṇitvā is the term used); (divyo maṇḍalavāṭo) divyāsana-prajñaptir divya āhāraḥ samanvāhṛtaḥ Divy 288.16 (cf. maṇḍa-, read maṇḍala-, -vāṭaḥ kāritaḥ 286.15); see on these passages s.v. **maṇḍalamāḍa**.

samanvāhāra, m. (cf. also **a-sam°**; to prec.; = Pali samannāhāra), *focusing of attention, concentration* of the mind on something; = **manasikāra**, as in Pali, cf. MN i.190.21 tajjo samannāhāro, comm. ii.229.28 cakkhuṃ ca rūpe ca paṭicca . . . uppajjamāna-manasikāro; corresp. passage in Śikṣ 225.9 and MadhK 567.10 tajja-manasi-kāraḥ °hāra-(MadhK °**haraṇa**, q.v.)-kṛtyaṃ karoti, *the mental concentration thereby produced does the job of focusing the attention*; in MadhK 553.6 (Kār. xxvi.4) °hāram (acc.; in all these passages vijñāna is based on three things, the sense organ, its object, and the mental focusing or concentration); (-kāyapraṇāma-)-°hāreṇa kāyabalaṃ dṛḍhī-kurvāṇaḥ . . . (19) citta-manasikāraṃ gṛhṇan Gv 466.18, 19, and others in ff.; (teṣāṃ cānantaraṃ) samanvāhāras (text °haras, doubtless misprint) tasya bodhisattvasyāntike bhavati, samanvāharatāṃ (gen. pl. pres. pple.) ca jñāna-darśanaṃ pravartate Bbh 155.7.

samanvī, in Gv 254.11 (vs), app. a semi-MIndic contracted form for samanvitaḥ, *provided*: dvātriṃśalak-ṣaṇa-°vī so 'nuvyañjanai (read anu°?) racitagātraḥ; the meter is perfect in the first pāda, and may be partly responsible for this form, which I derive from a con-traction of a MIndic form resembling AMg. samaṇṇia (with Skt. nv restored); see § 3.118.

samanveṣaṇā (= Pali samannesanā), *search*: Mvy 7278.

Samapakṣa (v.l. °yakṣa), n. of a former Buddha: Mv i.140.11.

samapaiti (sam with Skt. apaiti, apa-eti), *departs completely*: (kāyadaurgandhyaṃ) °ti, saugandhyaṃ prā-durbhavati Karmav 100.13 (v.l., for sam°, jahāti, which looks like a lect. fac.).

[**Samabuddhi**, see s.v. **Sughoṣasamabuddhi**.]

samabhinayati, ppp. °nīta (sam with Skt. abhi-nī-), *conducts*, ppp. (was) *conducted*: (sā baddhā . . .) yajñavā-ṭaṃ °tā Mv ii.98.4.

samabhipraṇamati (sam with Skt. abhi°), *makes a profound bow*: ger. °ṇamya Jm 157.11 (taṃ mahākapiṃ; but here, and always, the acc. could also be construed with the main verb, and the ger. regarded as without complement); 201.18; 203.6; °ṇaman (n. sg. m. pres. pple.) Jm 161.14.

samabhiprasādayati (sam plus **abhiprasīdati**, Skt. °sādayati), *makes completely well-disposed*: ppp. °sādita Jm 26.16; 79.22.

samabhibhūta, ppp. (= AMg. °bhūa, Sheth; no sam-abhi-bhū- in Skt. or Pali; sam- with Skt. and Pali abhibhūta in mg. 1), (**1**) *conquered*: Jm 72.4; *surpassed, outdone*, Mv i.264.3; (**2**) (*overwhelmed*? and so) *overspread, covered* (with light, prabhayā): Sukh 63.6.

samabhirocate, *surpasses* (lit. outshines) *completely*: Śikṣ 43.2 (see s.v. **abhirocate**).

samabhivandati (cf. Skt. abhiv°), *accepts with respect* (a command or request): (mātur vacanaṃ kusu-mamālām) iva śirasā °vandya (ger.) . . . Divy 590.5.

samabhisarati (sam plus Skt. abhi-s°), *rushes up* (to): atha Saudāsaḥ . . . °sṛtyaiva Bodhisattvaṃ pādayoḥ sampariṣvajyovāca Jm 223.17, . . . *as soon as he had rushed up, embraced the B. at his feet and said.*

samabhyāhata, ppp. (= Pali samabbhā°), *smitten*: janmaduḥkhaiḥ °taṃ vyāhataṃ śatrubhiḥ LV 216.2 (vs).

samabhyudgacchati (sam with **abhyud°**), *arises, comes forth*: teṣv (sc. buddhakṣetreṣu) ayaṃ mamātma-bhāvavigrahastūpaḥ °gacchet SP 241.10; (cakraṃ . . . tasya mūrdhnaḥ) °gamya (ger.) . . . bhramitum ārabdham Divy 606.2.

samabhyupaiti (cf. Skt. °peya, subst. nt., in different mg.), *approaches*: (dharmarājāḥ . . .) iha madanugrahaṇāt °paintu Divy 399.9 (vs; metr. correct; °pa-yantu would be unmetr.).

Samamathita, n. of a former Buddha: Mv i.141.12.

samaya, (**1**) *time*, as in Skt.; app. nt. (Skt. only m.) in LV 210.2, see s.v. **ardharātri**; tena samayena (as in Pali), *at that time*, very common in phrase introducing a new episode, tena khalu punaḥ samayena (Pali tena kho pana sa°), *now, however, at that time* . . ., SP 19.11; LV 18.14; 238.14; Vaj 19.14; Mv i.35.14, etc. (in many pas-sages, incl. some of these, a voc. intervenes between punaḥ and sam°); (**2**) (Pali id.; not in Skt., not even in Vedic; AV 2.35.3 is to be taken otherwise, see Ludwig RV 3.302) *assembly, congregation, concourse* (of persons), = Skt. samiti: punar api devasamaye yadā satyāṃ prakāśayet Mv i.250.15 = 251.1 (vs); a rare usage, here and seemingly in Pali; (**3**) nt., a high number: Gv 133.9, cited in Mvy 7857 as **samarya**, q.v.; the corresp. form in Gv 105.26 seems to be **sāmpa** (prob. corrupt).

***samayati** (denom. from Skt. sama), see **sameti**.

samaya-vimukta, adj. (= Pali °vimutta), *released temporarily, occasionally, from time to time*: Mvy 1025 (opp. to **asamaya-vimukta**, q.v.). Pali also has nouns (a)samaya-vimutti, °vimo(k)kha. See Puggalap. p. 11 (§§ 1, 2); MN comm. ii.232.3 ff. (on MN i.197.27). There are eight states of 'temporary release', viz. the four dhyāna (or rūpāvacara-samāpatti), the four arūp(āvacar)-asamāpatti (so MN comm.). See also AbhidhK. LaV-P vi.251–2. (PTSD mistranslates the Pali.)

? **samayin** (acc. to Schmidt, Nachträge, *eine Verab-redung habend*, and m. 'eine Art Mönch'), possibly *doing what the occasion* (samaya) *requires*: kulejanmānunmādī samayī hevajradeśakaḥ Sādh 450.1 (vs). But I suspect a corruption; the meter is śloka, and as it stands, the first syllable of this word belongs to the first pāda, the rest of it to the second! I do not recall any parallel to this.

sama-ruci (or, with v.l. ii.14.11, śama°), *having even splendor*, or (śama°) *the splendor of tranquillity*, ep. of the Bodhisattva Dīpaṃkara Mv i.210.12 = (repeated of Śākyamuni) ii.14.11; also, in same context, ii.14.8, instead of amara-ruci (metr. inferior) i.210.9.

? **samarcitaka**, see **samarjitaka**.

samarjana? acc. to Lüders 45, 'wohl *Zusammen-biegen, Krümmen*, von sam-ṛj'; he then suggests that Pali sammiñjeti (our **saṃmiñjayati**, q.v.) stands for *sam-riñjayati for sam-ṛñjayati, which I think unlikely: in fragment 44 V 1 (p. 143) of Kalpanāmaṇḍitikā, Lüders, Kl. Skt. Texte 2: ārabhate śarīraṃ saṃtāpana (lacuna) . . . aṅgāvapāṭana-samarjana-vṛ(tt) . . . (lacuna). The mg. seems to be quite different from that of **saṃmiñjana**, °**jita**, qq.v.; here we seem to have to do with a form of (self-?)torture.

? **samarjitaka**, or samajji°, mss., Senart em. saṃ-marji°; none of these forms conveys a mg. to me; I suggest **samarcitaka**, *one that has been treated with respect, well-treated* (ppp. of Skt. sam-arc- plus -ka): (Yaśodharā is dissuading Rāhula from monastic life) tvaṃ . . . sukhocito rājakule saṃvṛddho tvaṃ ca putra °tako vīṇāvaṃśapaṇavamadhurāṃ śabdāṃ śruṇamāno kathaṃ te ratir bhaviṣyati (in ascetic life) Mv iii.264.13 (prose).

samarpita, adj.-ppp. (not in this mg. in Skt., but = Pali samappita), *affected, filled* (with feelings, pleasant or unpleasant, in comp.): te sukha-°tā bhaviṣyanti LV 85.5; kṣutpipāsā- (mss. always °sa)-°tānāṃ Mv iii.71.17, °tāni 75.4; *well provided*, °to kāmaguṇehi pañcabhiḥ SP 111.6.

samarya, m. Mvy 7729, or nt. id. 7857, a high number; in 7857 cited from Gv 133.9 which reads **samaya**, nt., q.v. (3).

samala (nt. or m., in Pali id., nt., wrongly given as °lā, f., in PTSD; cf. Vedic, also Bhag.P., śamala, and Skt. Lex. sa°), *filth*, or *sewer* (cf. DN comm. ii.597.2 samalaṃ nāma gūtha-niddhamana-panāḷi): nāstitā-dṛṣṭi-samale yasmād asmin nimajjati MadhK 496.2.

samavagāḍha, ppp. (of sam- with Skt. avag°; = AMg. samogāḍha), *plunged, entered* (into water): te . . . lavaṇajaladharaṃ °gāḍhā(ḥ) Mv iii.78.2.

(**samavatarati** = Pali samotarati; Skt. caus. °tārayati, and ppp. °tīrṇa, Schmidt, Nachträge; *goes down, descends* (into water): (mahāsamudre) vyavasitāḥ °taritum Divy 229.15.)

samavadhāya, ger. (of Vedic sam-ava-dhā-, rare and hardly in this mg.; Pali samodahati, hardly in this mg.), *setting down* (heavily): na sarvakāyaṃ °ya Mvy 8557, (*we will*) *not* (*sit down*) *plunking down the whole body* = Tib. lus thams cad kyis ljid gyis mi dbab, *we will not throw* (or *fall*) *down with the weight of the whole body.*

samavanamati, samonamati (= AMg. samoṇamai, pple. samoṇamanta, Sheth; sam- with Skt. avanamati, Pali onamati), *bends down* (upon, acc.): samonamantu nabhato jaladharā taṃ Mv i.215.18 = ii.18.14 (vs), *let clouds bend down from heaven upon it* (viz. the grove where the Bodhisattva was about to be born).

samavasaraṇa, nt. (to next with -ana; = Pali samosaraṇa; late Skt. once, acc. to comm. = nivāsa, Schmidt, Nachträge), also °**ṇa-tā** (*state, condition, of* . . .); written sometimes °**śaraṇa** (which has misled some interpreters into connecting it with Skt. śaraṇa), primarily *coming together, gathering, uniting, collection*: so regularly Tib. yaṅ dag par ḥdu ba, Mvy 527 (sarvadharma-°ṇasāgara-, *sea of gathering of all dh.*, cf. Gv 494.14 below); Mvy 617 and 618 (see **araṇa**); 5165 (here alternative Tib. gzhol ba, acc. to Das *coming down*, also *absorption in*, besides ḥdu ba); sahālokadhātu-°ṇāsu (Bhvr.) sarvalokadhātuparaṃparāsu Gv 396.2, *in all the series of world-systems that are joined with the sahā world-system*; (mahāsāgarabhūtaṃ, sc. bodhicittaṃ) sarvaguṇaratna-°ṇatayā 494.14, *it is like the great ocean, because it is a gathering of all the jewels of virtues*; sarvatraidhātukasvapna-°ṇajñānena 522.8, *by knowledge of the collection of dreams which constitute the whole triple universe*; since union with something may amount to *attainment of* it, *attainment* is often the best English rendering, esp. when a state or condition is what is *united with* or *attained*: (dharmavinayo . . .) nirvāṇa-°ṇaḥ (Bhvr.) SP 71.1, *characterized by attainment of nirvāṇa*; yāvad eva sattvāḥ sattvadhātau saṃgraha-°ṇaṃ gacchanti 346.10, . . . *arrive at attainment of* (or perh. *at coming together in*) *a unity* (saṃgraha); dharmadhātu-(q.v.)-°ṇa-cakraṃ LV 423.7; saptadhana-°ṇākāraṃ (sc. śrutaṃ, *holy learning*) Śikṣ 190.19 (written °śaraṇa, whence Transl. wrongly *protecting*; rather, *attaining*); (pañca-, so read)-dharmā bodhisattvasya piṭaka-°ṇatā Mmk 23.5 (°śar°), *conditions for acquisition* (= learning) *of the piṭakas*; °ṇaṃ saddharmanetrārakṣaṇārthaṃ ye (sc. mantravarāḥ, line 7) sādhayiṣyanti 74.9, *which will effect attainment* (not *sécurité*, Lalou Iconographie 52; written °śar°; sc. of religious learning), *the goal of which is the keeping of the Eye of the Good Law*; buddhakṣetravyūha-°ṇa- Gv 7.24; two bodhisattva-samādhi are named sarvakṣetrasamanta-°ṇādhiṣṭhāna Gv 37.12, *basis of complete attainment of all* (Buddha-) *fields*, and sarvajñānāvartābhimukha-°ṇa 38.3; -praveśa-°ṇa- Dbh 15.14, *attainment of entrance* (or *penetration*); tathāgatānāṃ kalpapraveśa-°ṇa-jñānāni, yad uta, (17) ekakalpāsaṃkhyeyakalpa-°ṇa-tā Dbh 87.16–17, and others in ff.

samavasarati, samosarati (= Pali samosarati; Jain Skt. in diff. mg.; cf. prec.), primarily *comes together, unites, associates*: kalpaṃ tābhi sahā samosṛto (*associated with them*) vihareyaṃ LV 325.14 (vs); śrota-samudra mamātiviśuddho yatra samosari śabda-śeṣāḥ (unmetr., read śabda aśeṣāḥ or -viśeṣāḥ?) Gv 231.1 (vs), . . . *in which all*, or *various, sounds have gathered together*; (dharmaśarīru . . .) yatra samosari loka aśeṣaḥ 235.26 (vs); (mārgū, § 8.21, . . .) yatra samosarī jina aśeṣā 258.20 (vs); sarvaguṇālaṃkāra-samavasṛtaṃ divasam 522.2, *joined* (*provided*) *with the ornament of all good qualities*; as with **samavasaraṇa**, sometimes to be rendered *get into, attain*, usually with acc., once loc.: praṇidhiṃ samavasaran Gv 99.24, cited Śikṣ 36.12, *attaining a solemn vow* ('earnest wish'); etc (sc. dharmāḥ) nītārthe (q.v.; loc.) samavasaranti Śikṣ 236.10, *they come to* (*have*), *attain to, the established meaning* (of the word), i. e. it is realized (by the Bodhisattvas) that states of being (dharma) are just what they are declared to be (unsubstantial, etc.); -ṣaḍgati-samavasṛta- Dbh 15.9; (read) yāvant' anāvaraṇa-satya samosaranti Dbh.g. 21(357).1, *attain to* (comprehension, realization of) *the Truths.*

samavasarga, m. (unrecorded; to Skt. samavasṛjati), °gaḥ Mvy 7603 = Tib. rgyun yaṅ dag par bcad pa, *continuous complete stopping* or *suppression* (in religious sense, like Skt. saṃnyāsa); Chin. also *continually stopping* or *cutting off flow.*

samavahanti (cf. AMg. samohaṇati, in different specialized mg.), *destroys, removes, abolishes*: °hanti Mvy 2421; utsṛṣṭaṃ °hanti 2596 (Mironov hanti, without samava-, but v.l. samava-).

samavaharati, samo° (unrecorded; Skt. subst. °hāra, *collection*), *collects*: ger. samoharitvāna dadanti pānaṃ Mv i.298.9; °haritva 22 (*having accumulated*, sc. merit).

Samaśarīra, n. of a Buddha: Samu-śarīru (n. sg.; § 8.13) Gv 285.10 (vs).

Samaśarīraś(i)ri, n. of a Buddha: °riḥ, n. sg., end of line, Gv 285.23 (vs); or is Sattvāśayaiḥ to be taken as cpd. with this?

sama-sama, adj. (āmreḍita of sama; = Pali id.), *quite equal* or *equivalent, exactly alike*: sarvadharmāḥ samāḥ sarve samāḥ samasamāḥ sadā SP 143.5 (vs); (nāsti me kaścid) āśayena sarvaloke samasamaḥ (*fully equal*), kutaḥ punar uttara ity . . . Dbh 13.10; Siddhārtha-kumārasya na kocit (but mss. kvacit, which may be kept, *anywhere*) samasamo tathā yuddhe vā . . . Mv ii.75.19; utsāhenāsya loke °mo na bhaviṣyati 430.17; 431.18 (se for asya); na koci (v.l. kvaciṇ, read °cit) puruṣo varṇarūpeṇa °mo bhaviṣyati 492.9; etasya varṇavīryeṇa (v.l. vara°) loke nāsti samāsamo (ā m.c.) ii.488.12 (vs); te rūpeṇa . . . samasamo na bhaviṣyati iii.25.5; nāsti te °maḥ kutottaro RP 6.13 (vs); sarvaṃ °maṃ bhavati nirviśiṣṭaṃ Bbh 93.26; °mā mātāpitara ācāryopādhyāyāḥ Karmav 59.5; (na caiṣāṃ) sarvajagati °mo 'sti jñānena Gv 470.25; indicating a repetition (like **peyālam**), satkareyā ity etaṃ samasamaṃ Mv ii.362.15, *this is just the same* (as in line 13, beginning satkareyā); samasamaṃ, adv., *at the very same time*: Rājagṛhe °maṃ . . . parvaṃ vartati Mv iii.57.6. See next.

samasamī-bhūta, ppp. (to prec. with bhavati), *become exactly like* (with instr.): (pāṃsunā) °tāni (so divide) Śikṣ 212.7.

samasūpika, adj. (cf. Pali °paka), (food) *having curry (sauce) equal* (to the rice in amount): na °kam (sc. pratigrahīṣyāmaḥ) Mvy 8566; in the Pali parallels, Vin. iv.190.24 and 192.4, there is no negative, and samasūpakaṃ must be taken to mean *having sauce in the right amount*, which acc. to the comm. 892.1 is one quarter of the rice.

samākampate (sam plus Skt. ā-kamp-), *trembles greatly*: (rājā...) samācakampe Jm 227.22 (vs).

Samākṣarākāra, m., ŚsP 1421.1, or °**kṣarāvakara**, Mvy 571, or with Mironov Mvy °**kṣarāvakāra**, m., n. of a samādhi. In another ŚsP list, 1413.15, the reading is °kṣarāvakāra as in Mironov.

samāgāḍha-tara, adj. compv. (cf. **āgāḍha-tara**), *very serious, severe*: °raṃ duḥkhaṃ Kv 25.13.

samāgṛhīta, ppp. (unrecorded; sam-ā-grah- rare and only Vedic), *collected, assembled*: °ta-puṇyāha-prasthāna-bhadrāṇāṃ... baṇijāṃ Divy 593.20.

-samācārin, adj. ifc. (Skt. °ra plus -in), *having, characterized by... conduct*: śuklakarma-°rī (n. sg. m.) Mmk 85.26.

(**samājñā**, *name*, a few times in late Vedic texts, = Pali samaññā; see s.vv. **samajñā, samanyā**.)

samātta, ppp. (= **samādatta**, q.v.; to **samādiyati**, Skt. sam-ā-dā-; = Pali samatta, acc. to Childers and PTSD = Skt. samāpta, but this is disproved by collocation with samādinna, AN ii.193.1, and (vatapadāni) samattāni samādinnāni Dhp. comm. i.264.21), *adopted, taken upon oneself*, esp. of religious and moral obligations: °tta-saṃvarasya (see **saṃvara**) Śikṣ 15.1; pareṣāṃ cāsamātte (v.l. °mādatte) tasmiṃ kuśale samādāpanāya varṇavāditā, samātte (v.l. samādatte) vā punaḥ saṃpraharṣaṇāya Bbh 30.15–16; śīlaṃ °ttaṃ rakṣati 137.26; (bodhisattva-śīla-saṃvara-)-samādānaṃ samāttam 155.6; samātta-śīlaḥ (Bhvr.) 183.23; cintāyāḥ su-samātta-tvāt 109.12; daśakuśalakarmapatha-°ttānāṃ sattvānāṃ Gv 268.24 (here the ppp. has active force, *who have adopted...*, see next).

samādatta, ppp. (= prec. and Pali, also BHS, **samādinna**; cf. the following items, and esp. **samādāya, samādiyati**), *adopted, taken on oneself*, of a moral or religious course; active in force: pañca **śiṣyāpada**-(q.v.)-samādattā LV 71.14, *having adopted the five moral precepts*, of Māyā; nāgarājā... upavāsaṃ °tto Mv ii.178.1, and mama... upavāsaṃ °ttasya 6, *having undertaken a fast*.

samādapaka, m. (or adj.; Pali id.; to °**dapeti**; = °**dāpaka**), *one who incites* (another) *to assume* or *take upon himself*: pravrajyā-°ko... bhūtakalyāṇamitra(ṃ)? KP 14.4 (prose!; em. °dāpako? cf. next).

samādapana, °**nā** (Pali id.; = °**dāpana**, °**nā**; cf. next), *incitement to assume, to take on oneself*: bodhayi citta-samādapanena (mss. °yanena; ed. prints citta as separate word) Śikṣ 337.2 (vs), *by incitement towards thoughts of enlightenment*; here °dap° may be m.c.; but, buddhayāna-°dapanāṃ na śṛṇvanti SP 43.8–9 is prose; WT em. to °dāpanāṃ, perh. rightly, since **samādapeti** occurs only in vss; cf. however prec.

samādapeti (only in vss, perh. m.c.; = Pali id.; cf. prec. two) = °**dāpayati**, q.v., *incites, inspires* (a person, acc.) to (a goal, when expressed acc. or loc.): pravrajya (acc.) ye cāpi samādapenti KP 14.13; °petī (mss. and WT) bahubodhisattvān acintiye 'nuttami (so read) buddhajñāne SP 23.6; various forms, always with object bahubodhisattvān, no goal expressed, SP 12.11; 56.4; 64.7; 323.9; 394.4. Pali (see Childers) uses dat. or loc. of goal; with samādetvā once acc. (and acc. of the person also). See also next.

[**samādayati**, prob. only erroneous reading for °**diyati** or °**dapeti**, qq.v.; (**1**) = °**diyati**, *assumes, takes on oneself* a religious duty: °dayitvā (sc. the moral and religious practices mentioned in the prec. line) Śikṣ 304.2 (vs), read °diyitvā, to °**diyati**, with same line Mv ii.382.14; in Mv i.145.8 (vs) mss. samodayāmi (prāṇehi ahiṃsa, so read, see v.l. ii.6.2, brahmacaryaṃ ca), for which samādayāmi might be read, but Senart properly reads samādiyāmi with same line i.202.5 and ii.6.2; (**2**) for the caus. **samādapeti**, °**dāpeti**, qq.v.: saṃbodhimārga (acc.) sada sattva (acc. pl.) °dayanti RP 15.6 (vs, read °dapenti, or possibly °dapanti with a for e), *they ever incite creatures to take up the way to enlightenment*; śīla samādayi (read °dapi, prob. aor., possibly ger.) yad bahusattvān Śikṣ 337.1 (vs), and so, vīrya samādayi (read °pi) yad bahusattvān 11 (vs); in SP 12.11 (vs) Nep. mss. samādayanto bahubodhisattvān, Kashgar rec. °dapenti, ed. em. °dapento; certainly °dap° is to be read.]

samādāna, nt. (once possibly m.; = Pali id.; to **samādiyati** etc.), (**1**) *assumption, taking upon oneself, undertaking*, of any course of action: sarveṣāṃ karmaṇāṃ karma-°nānāṃ Mv iii.321.3, *of all acts and undertakings of acts*; -karma-°na- LV 433.6, 7; sarvakarma-°na- Gv 463.24; rarely of evil courses, (mithyādṛṣṭi-karma-)°na-hetoḥ Mv ii.132.10; mithyādṛṣṭi-°nāt sattvā gacchanti durgatiṃ Ud xvi.4 (= Pali Dhp. 316); oftener of moral or religious undertakings, karmapatha- (q.v.) Mv ii.425.10 (mss.); vrata-°na Śikṣ 98.12; Mv iii.173.7, 20; bhagavāṃ... ātmano guṇa-°naṃ viditvā Mv iii.322.8; śīla- Bbh 137.18; śīlasaṃvara- 155.6 (see **samātta**); kuśala- 270.20; dharma-°neṣu Jm 143.23, *in the assumption of moral duties* (but catvāri dharma-°nāni Bbh 24.26 and ff. include both good and bad programs of behavior); sarvajagac-citta-samādānānantavarṇakāyanirmāṇasamudrameghān (acc., sc. apaśyat) Gv 247.4, seemingly ... *characterized by assumption of the mentality of the whole world*; cf. (jitvā ... rāgadveṣau) citta-°na-balena Jm 193.9, *by the power of assumption of* (the right) *mentality* (otherwise Speyer); (**2**) without specific expression of complement, *formal undertaking, vow* (since under 1 the *assumption* is usually of a moral or religious duty): eṣa me samādāno (but v.l., better, evaṃ me °naṃ), mama maraṇaṃ ihaiva bhaviṣyati Mv iii.131.13, *this is my vow, I shall die right here*; tena dāni °naṃ (below, lines 7, 20, it is called vrata-°naṃ) kṛtaṃ, na mayā adinnaṃ... paribhoktavyaṃ iii.173.5; tasyāsi (= °sīt) °naṃ Mv ii.221.1 (foll. by quotation of the vow); °nam Mvy 6482 = Tib. yaṅ dag par blaṅs pa, *completely taking on oneself*, or yi dam, *vow*; niyojayitāro bodhisattva-°nena Gv 462.26, *persons who make one possessed of the vow of bodhisattvas*; °naṃ kurvanti Śikṣ 12.3; °nāni... gṛhītāni 97.20; askhalita-°nam (Bhvr., acc. sg. m.) Jm 181.23, *not untrue to his vow*; dṛḍha-°na (both Karmadh. and Bhvr.; = Pali daḷha-°na, Jāt. i.233.17; Miln. 352.16), *a firm vow*, or *having...*, Mvy 2409, °naḥ, Bhvr., = Tib. yi dam la brtan pa; Mv ii.280.3–4; LV 181.14; 332.16; 429.4, 430.1; 431.1, etc.; (dṛḍhaṃ) °nam akarot LV 289.18.

[**samādānana**, dat. °nanāya, error for **samudānana**, q.v.: KP 25.1.]

samādānika, adj. (to °**dāna** plus -ika), (sc. a religious practice) *undertaken as a solemn vow*: Mvy 7478 °nikam.

samādāpaka, m. (adj.; to °**payati**; cf. °**dapaka**), *one who incites* (another) *to assume* or *take to himself*; also absolutely, *one who inspires* (another): tathāgatajñānadarśana-°paka evāham SP 40.11 (prose), *I am just the one who inspires* (people) *to the sight of T.-knowledge*; catasṛṇāṃ parṣadāṃ... °pakaḥ SP 200.4; tathāgatadarśana-°pakaḥ SP 466.8 (prose); °pakena bodhisattvena Bbh 154.12 (context indicates reference to assuming the śikṣāpadāni); mss. write °dāyaka sometimes, kept by Lefm. in LV 436.1 sarvabodhisattva-°dāyaka-samuttejaka-saṃpraharṣaka ity ucyate (surely °paka must be read, with Weller 39, see s.v. °**dāpayati** 4); teṣāṃ °dāpakaḥ (mss. °dāyakaḥ) Divy 142.5.

samādāpana, °nā, °natā (n. act. to **°dāpayati** with -ana; see also **°dapana, °nā**; also written erroneously **°dāyana**), *instigation* (of others) *to assume, take on themselves,* the goal most often preceding in comp.: prāṇātipāta-**vairamaṇya**(q.v.)-parasattva-°panatvād (so read for °yanatvād) LV 429.8; prativirati-°panā Bbh 223.18 and ff., also °panatā 20 and ff.; -kuśalacaryā-°pana- LV 431.8; -sarvasattva-samacitta-°pana- 431.19; parasattva-tathāgatadarśana-°pana- 432.6; -sattva-°pana- 432.8; pravrajyā-°panā Bbh 221.18; buddhajñāna-°panatā sarvasattveṣu KP 12.2 (*instigation towards Buddha-knowledge in reference to all beings,* i. e. instigation of them); buddhabimbadarśana-sattva-°panatayā Śikṣ 309.14–15; tathāgatajñānadarśana-°pana-hetunimittaṃ sattvānāṃ SP 40.3; without complement, yayā °panayā yena kalyāṇamitrasaṃcodanena Gv 512.18; °panā Sūtrāl. xvi.72 (comm.); goal in loc. (cf. **samādāpayati** 2), °na Bbh 30.16, see s.v. **samātta**; (sattvānāṃ . . .) samyaksaṃbodhau °pana-hetoḥ SP 77.12; arthe °panā Bbh 221.11 ff.

samādāpanikā (to °**dāpanā**, see prec., plus prob. pejorative -ka, f. -ikā), *instigation to religious duty,* in para-°, *on the part of others*: na para-°nikayā nāpi paraspardhayā (*not because of instigation by others, and not thru rivalry with others*) dhīro bodhisattvo veditavyaḥ Bbh 157.18. (These are unworthy motivations.)

samādāpayati, also (in vss, perh. m.c., but cf. °**dapaka,** °**dapana,** and Pali) °**dapeti,** q.v. (= Pali samādapeti, no °dāpeti recorded; primarily caus. to **samādiyati** in Pali and BHS), (**1**) *causes to assume, to take upon oneself,* usually a moral or religious duty: °yati Mvy 6833 = Tib. yaṅ dag par (= sam) ḥdzin (or byed) du ḥjug, *cause to take* or *to do*; personal object, if expressed, regularly acc.; impersonal object, that which the personal object is incited to take on himself, may be acc., (bodhisattvayānam eva) °yati SP 71.10 (prose), (the Buddha) *incites to take on the B.-vehicle only*; but much oftener (**2**) *incites* (to), with loc., which seems to imply weakening of the orig. lit. mg.: te codārāyāṃ buddhabodhau °pitāḥ SP 110.7; (aśrāddhaṃ . . . śraddhāsaṃpadi) °yati Divy 51.28 (and f.); Bbh 222.12 (and f.); dāne cainān °yati Bbh 4.23; parāṃs tatra kuśale °yati Bbh 270.21; mahājanakāyaṃ buddhānusmṛtau °paya Av i.82.3; this is the regular construction and is very common; sometimes the thing instigated (to) is not a religious or moral duty, as in Divy 57.17, (Śakra says to a king: yadi kaścic) cyavanadharmā devaputro bhaviṣyati, tat te putratve °payiṣyāmi, . . . *I will instigate him to become your son,* and so, (mayā tvaṃ Praṇādasya rājño putratve) °pito 59.5; (**3**) rarely with instr., *causes* or *urges to become endowed with* . . .: pañcahi śikṣāpadehi °paye (aor.) Mv i.321.18; rājānaṃ . . . bodhikarakair dharmaiḥ °yati Av i.69.12; (**4**) without formal expression of that to which one is *instigated*; may be rendered *inspires, excites,* but context always indicates a religious or moral purpose: tān sarvasattvān °payet SP 347.8; esp. in a cliché (also in Pali, e. g. DN ii.42.8 dhammiyā kathāya saṃdassesi samādapesi samuttejesi sampahaṃsesi), dharmyayā kathayā (or equivalent forms) saṃdarśayati samādāpayati samuttejayati saṃpraharṣayati (or with other forms of these verbs), *with a religious discourse showed* (expounded, explained to, instructed), *incited, inflamed, delighted,* Divy 80.18; 85.1; Av i.63.8; Bbh 106.22 ff.; LV 38.14 (text corrupt, read with v.l. saṃdarsya samādāpya etc.); 67.18; Mv i.309.2; 322.7; 329.14; iii.55.16; 143.6; 272.11, et passim; in SP 309.5 saṃ-darś- is omitted; (**5**) twice seems used in mg. of the simplex **samādiyati,** *assumes, takes on oneself* (duties): in Mv i.321.20 (after 18, Kāśyapo Jyotipālaṃ . . . pañcahi śikṣāpadehi samādāpaye, Jyotipāla replies: na) tāvad ahaṃ . . . sarvāṇi pañca śikṣāpadāni °payiṣyaṃ, *I shall not assume all the five observances*; cf. in the sequel, 322.5, eṣo 'haṃ . . . pañca śikṣāpadāni samādiyāmi, the expected form; and so in Suv 6.11 (yāvad) daśakuśalamūlakarmapathaṃ samādāpayet seems to mean *until he acquired (succeeded in assuming) the* . . .; subject is Śākyamuni in past existences; no personal object of the seemingly caus. verb, and the context does not seem to favor *until he induced creatures* (cf. sattvānāṃ, line 12) *to assume* . . .; Tib. also makes it non-caus., yaṅ dag par blaṅs par gyur, *come to be receiving,* or blaṅs te gnas par gyur, *receiving, come to remain (so).*

samādāpayitar (n. ag. to prec., q.v. 2; cf. Pali samādapetar), *one who incites* (to, loc.): °tāro 'rtheṣu Gv 463.6.

samādāya, ger. (= Pali id., as here assoc. with **samādiyati,** cf. **samādatta** etc.), *adopting, taking on oneself* (a religious or moral obligation): °ya vartate Mvy 1633; (daśakuśalāḥ) karmapathāḥ °ya vartitavyāḥ Divy 302.19; (daśa) kuśalāṃ karmapathāṃ °ya vartante Mv i.46.10; similarly ii.77.11; iii.450.8; the mss. of Mv seem to make a cpd. daśakuśalakarmapatha-samādāya-vartī (stem °tin), *living with adoption of the ten moral courses of action,* found (in some cases with slight corruptions) in mss. Mv i.49.3; 193.15; 283.18; 284.3–4; iii.419.1; akuśalān (mss. °lānāṃ, perh. read so, dependent on dharmā?) dharmā °ya vartetsuḥ Mv i.61.4; pañca śikṣāpadāni °ya vartate (or °ti) Mv i.211.14; ii.15.13; śīlaṃ °ya vartadhve Bbh 270.19; without expressed object, MSV i.50.2.

[**samādāyaka,** °**dāyana,** prob. erroneous readings for °**dāpaka,** °**dāpana.**]

samādinna, ppp. to next, q.v.

samādiyati (= Pali id.; see **samādatta,** °**dāna,** etc., and s.v. **ādiyati**), *takes on oneself, adopts, assumes* (morality)· °yāmi prāṇehi (or the like) ahiṃsa (so read m.c., cf. v.l. of C in ii.6.2) brahmacaryaṃ ca Mv i.145.8 (here mss. samodayāmi) = 202.5 = ii.6.2 (vs); bodhisattvo kiṃ kuśala (so with mss., m.c.) gaveṣayaṃ samādiyati, śuklaṃ kuśalaṃ dharmaṃ Mv ii.220.14(–15); śīlaṃ °diyitvā, ger., Mv i.128.9; °yitvā, without object (which is understood from brahmacārī in prec. line) pavanaṃ (q.v.) vrajitvā Mv ii.382.14 (vs); ppp. samādinnāni (śikṣāpadāni), *assumed, taken upon oneself* Mv i.211.14 = ii.15.14; also **samātta, samādatta,** qq.v. See also **samādayati.** Skt. samādadāti is used in substantially the same mg. (Mbh. Cr. ed. 5.47.100 samādadānaḥ pṛthagastramārgān, *assuming, taking to myself, various weapon-ways*), if not, perhaps, precisely with moral or religious objects.

samādhāna, nt., (**1**) acc. to Tib. lan gdab pa, *making answer, reply*: Mvy 4448; prob. in sense of refutation of an opponent's argument by way of *establishing* one's own view (cf. BR s.v. 5); in a section dealing with terms of logic and disputation, after parihāra = Tib. lan; (**2**) as in Skt. (misunderstood by Burnouf and Kern), *composing* or *concentrating the mind* or *attention*: sarvadharma-(here one ms., supported by Tib., inserts sarva sec. m. marginally, Kern SBE 21.250 n. 4)-sattva-°na-samādhi-sahasraikakṣaṇapratilābhinī SP 263.5, *in one moment she attained a thousand samādhis of concentration on all dharmas and (all) creatures*; so Tib. chos thams cad daṅ sems can thams cad la mñam par bzhag paḥi (cf. mñam par ḥjog go = samādhīyate Mvy 1589) tiṅ ṅe ḥdzin etc.

samādhi, *concentration, trance,* in Skt. and Pali recorded only as m.; acc. to Ratnach. only m. in AMg., but also f. in Pkt. acc. to Sheth; here f. and nt. occasionally: f., mahāvyūhāya (loc.) sthitaḥ samādhiye (loc.) LV 60.4 (vs; in prec. prose mahāvyūhasya samādher 59.20–21); etatpraveśo (v.l. °śā, so read?) yat samādhiḥ paramā jāyata iti Laṅk 21.4 (prose); -vipañcitāyāḥ (all mss., Régamey em. °citāt, which indeed occurs 19.5, 14) samādher (gen.) Samādh 19.1 (prose); samādhiya (certainly gen.) lābhī Samādh 19.27 (vs); also in **ceto-samādhi,** q.v., Mv iii.409.12; nt., tāni samādhīni Kv 51.7–8 (prose; line 2 above ete samādhayaḥ). As 8th step in the 8-fold

Path, samyak-sa°, see **mārga**. Sa° is 5-fold, ārya-pañcāṅgika-samādhi-saṃpannā(ḥ) Mv ii.292.9, of bodhisattvas; acc. to a Pali list (Childers s.v.) the 5 aṅga are pīti-pharaṇatā, sukha-phar°, ceto-phar°, āloka-phar°, and paccavekkhanānimittaṃ; see also s.v. **pañcāṅgika** (2). Four kinds of sa° Mvy 967–970: chanda-, citta-, vīrya-, mīmāṃsā-sa° (= Pali cha°, ci°, viriya-, vīmaṃsā-); another list of four kinds Dharmas 101, somewhat corrupt, cf. the adhimukticaryābhūmi-nāmāni Mvy 896–901, and Sūtrāl. xiv.24–26 with comm.; acc. to Dharmas āloka- (Mvy 898 °ka-labdha, read °lābha, Lévi on Sūtrāl.), vṛtāloka- (read vṛddhā°, cf. Mvy 899 āloka-vṛddhiḥ), ekādaśa-(read ekadeśa-)-pratiṣṭha- (cf. Mvy 900 tattvārthaikadeśānupraveśaḥ), and ānantarya-sa° (= Mvy 901, misprinted an°). There are a number of lists, some of them very long, of particular samādhis; over 100 in Mvy 505–623, from 'Prajñāpāramitā', e. g. ŚsP 1412.8 ff. (these are all included in this Dict.); a very different list AsP 490.8–492.6; nearly 70 (practised by Avalokiteśvara) Kv 51.9 ff.; list of 17, Kv 77.8 ff.; of 37, Kv 92.17 ff.; only four, **Śūraṃgama** (which occurs frequently), **Gaganagañja, Vimalaprabha,** and **Siṃhavikrīḍita,** Dharmas 136; 100 Bodhisattva-sa° Gv 36.22 ff. (this term occurs elsewhere in Gv and other works, e. g. Dbh 2.27, of named samādhis practised by Bodhisattvas). Few of the names in these and other lists recur, and most of them are not separately listed in this Dict.; they seem mostly to be ad hoc inventions of the respective authors. For samādhi in relation to **samāpatti** see the latter.

Samādhigarbha, n. of a Bodhisattva: Mvy 672.

[**samādhitaṃ** LV 129.4, error for samādhijaṃ in same passage LV 343.17–18, Mvy 1479, etc.]

Samādhimudrāvipulamakuṭaprajñāprabha, n. of a Tathāgata: Gv 311.20.

Samādhimervabhyudgatajñāna, n. of a Tathāgata: Gv 422.16.

Samādhirāja, m., n. of a work = our Samādh: Mvy 1332; Samādh 19.5; in Śikṣ called **Candrapradīpasūtra,** q.v. (The long list of Buddhas in Chap. 14, p. 56 line 32 – 58 line 19, is only partly excerpted, thru p. 57 line 25, in this Dict.; few of them occur elsewhere and the text of the Calcutta ed. is very corrupt.)

Samādhirājasupratiṣṭhita, m., n. of a samādhi: Mvy 518; ŚsP 1416.4.

Samādhi-saṃyuktaka, n. of a section of the Madhyamāgama: MSV ii.182.9 (see s.v. **Dīrghika**).

Samādhisamatā, f., or °ta, m., n. of a samādhi: °tā Mvy 615; ŚsP 1425.15 f.; °taḥ AdP Konow MASI 69,27.31 f., in same phrase, see **anuvikṣepa.**

Samādhihastyuttaraśrī, n. of a Tathāgata: ŚsP 39.17.

samādhyate (corresp. to Pali samādhiyati, functioning as pass. to samādahati = Skt. °dadhāti; perh. really denom. to **samādhi**; or is the BHS word a hyper-Sktism based on the Pali?), *is concentrated* (subject cittam, as also in Pali, DN i.73.23): °te kathaṃ cittaṃ Laṅk 24.17; kena (203.13 tadā) cittaṃ °te 33.8; 203.13 = 340.6; all vss.

Samādhyalaṃkṛta, m., n. of a lokadhātu: ŚsP 39.16.

samādhyāyika-tā, said to mean *acquisition* or *possession of samādhi* (so Foucaux; Burnouf, Lotus, 798; and app. Tib. tiṅ ṅe ḥdzin sgrub par): LV 34.6 (prose) prītisaṃbodhyaṅgaṃ dharmālokamukhaṃ °katāyai saṃvartate. So both edd., no v.l. But I do not understand the formation; if a cpd., the second member *āyika(-tā) does not seem plausible (*leading to*, as if from ā plus root i?); nor can I make a plausible analysis by assuming suffixation, starting with samādhi; perhaps primary formation from Skt. samādhyāyati, instead of °dhyāyaka-, *state of one that completely concentrates*?

samāna, adj. or pres. pple. (= Pali id., also AMg., JM. °ṇa, Pischel 561; = Skt. sant), *being*; like Skt. sant, often seems nearly superfluous: duḥkhaskandhena spṛṣṭāḥ °nā na duḥkhaṃ manasi kurvanti SP 72.15; sa utpannaḥ °naḥ paśyati 77.12; others, prose, 110.2; 216.8; 289.7; 290.11; LV 51.16; 89.9 (te cyutāḥ samānā avīcau ... prapatiṣyanti); 410.19; Mv i.311.19; 321.11; 362.6; ii.65.12 (tāṃ godhāṃ pakvāṃ °nāṃ dṛṣṭvā); 90.12; 96.13; 111.3; 119.4 (not samāna, *like*; evaṃdarśanaṃ ca °naṃ samānārthatāye [this samāna = *like*] sthāpayet); 242.11; 247.15; 276.19 ff.; 461.20; iii.49.12; 51.5 ff.; 198.9; 222.18; 302.4; 403.11; Divy 651.6 ff.; Suv 21.1; 91.11; 92.8; RP 34.11 (read pravrajitāḥ samānā, separate word); 41.12 (viṃśavarṣāḥ °nāḥ ṣoḍaśavarṣātikrāntāḥ kumārakāḥ, *youths of* [sc. up to?] *20 and more than 16 years of age*?); KP 106.7; Sukh 19.4; Karmav 65.3; 67.20; verses, SP 11.13; Mv i.163.4; Suv 47.9 (jāta-samāna-prabhāsitagātraṃ, *upon being born*, i. e. *as soon as born* ...); etc., common.

samānaka, adj. (= Skt. samāna plus -ka, perh. m.c.), *like*: pratiśrutkā-°kān SP 142.14 (vs).

samāna-saṃvāsika, adj. or subst. (= Pali °saka), *dwelling in communal life* (with other monks), opp. of **nānā-saṃv°,** q.v.: MSV ii.179.5 ff.

samānasukhaduḥkhatā (mss. confused and lack -tā), in Mv i.3.12 the fourth **saṃgraha-vastu,** instead of the usual **samānārthatā,** q.v. (end).

samānārthatā (in Pali samānattatā, as if *samānātmatā, is the 4th saṃgahavatthu), *equality*, (**1**) in general sense: LV 239.13 māṃ (sc. the Bodhisattva) °tayā saṃsthāpayati sma, *he* (Ārāḍa Kālāpa = °ma) *set me on terms of equality with himself*; in same incident Mv ii.119.4 samānārthatāye sthāpayet; (**2**) as one of the 4 **saṃgraha-vastu,** q.v., acc. to Bbh 225.21 ff. and Sūtrāl. xvi.72, (a Bodhisattva's) *adoption of the same* (religious) *aims for himself which he preaches to others*; in lists of the 4 saṃgraha-vastu occurs LV 38.17; 160.7; 182.6; 429.13; Mv ii.395.9; Mvy 928; Dharmas 19. But in Mv i.3.12 the 4th saṃgraha-vastu is given, instead, as **samāna-sukha-duḥkhatā** (mss. confused), i. e. *having the same joys and sorrows* (with others), or *sympathy*; this may have been the older interpretation, and seems to fit better the Pali equivalent (above), which is so interpreted DN comm. iii.928.10 ff. The definition in Bbh and Sūtrāl. may then be a late interpretation of pedantic Mahāyāna metaphysicians.

samāpatti, f., primarily (as in Skt.) *attainment* (to **samāpadyate,** Skt. and BHS); esp. used (as in Pali) of the *attainment* of the nine successive **anupūrvavihāra** (q.v. for list) or 'successive states induced by the ecstatic meditation' (Childers, who lists only eight, as sometimes in Pali; add as ninth [saññāvedayita-] nirodha-sam°); these states are also called **samādhi**; navānupūrvasamādhi-samāpattayaḥ Dharmas 82 clearly = *attainment of the nine successive samādhi*; so also Laṅk 100.9 samādhisamāpatty-adhiṣṭhānena, see **adhiṣṭhāna**; and in some other such cpds. But from this old association, in Pali and BHS alike, the *attainment* comes to mean the *state attained*, viz. one of the above nine (in Pali sometimes only eight, the nirodha-sa° being omitted) 'modes of abstract meditation' (Hardy ap. Childers), or *recueillements*, LaV-P. in AbhidhK, see esp. viii.182 n. 4 for a report of discordant Buddhist attempts to distinguish between **samādhi** and **samāpatti.** The fact seems to be that these two words are fundamentally and substantially identical in mg., and that the attempts to differentiate are scholastic pedantry. They are however used in dvandva cpds., sometimes with dhyāna too (note that the 4 **dhyāna** are included in the 9 samāpatti): dhyāna-samādhi-°ttīnāṃ LV 244.3, Tib. bsam gtan (dhyāna) daṅ tiṅ ṅe ḥdzin (samādhi) daṅ sñom par ḥjug pa, as a three-member dvandva. This is the regular Tib. rendering of samāpatti, *entering* (ḥjug pa) *into equanimity, evenness or calmness of mind* (sñom par). This Tib. expression is, however, not always parallel with tiṅ ṅe ḥdzin = samādhi, which may depend upon it, as in LV 3.11 where samādhiṃ samāpanno 'bhūt, containing the cognate ppp., is rendered tiṅ ṅe ḥdzin la sñoms par zhugs par gyur to, *arrived at equanimity-entrance into samādhi,* or *at entrance into equanimity* (leading) *to samādhi.* Mvy 1491–1502 contains eleven (in Mironov only ten, 1499 being omitted) miscellaneous and unsystematic *'names of* (various sorts of) *samāpatti'*; 1492–5 are brief statements of the ārūpyasamā° (see **ārūpya** for other citations); the others are **vyutkrāntaka-sa°**, **vyāskandaka-sa°**, (nava-)**anupūrvavihāra-sa°**, **samāpatti-skandhaḥ** (om. Mironov), **nirodha**-(more fully **saṃjñāvedayita-nirodha-**)**sa°**, **mahābhūtasamatāsādhanam,** and **asaṃjñā-sa°**, qq.v.; (bodhisattvasya ... sarvasamādhiparicayaviśeṣeṇa ca dhyānapramukhāni) sarvāṇi laukikāni lokottarāṇi samāpatti-śatāny āmukhībhavanti sma LV 244.21 (*attainments,* or more specifically *abstract meditations, trances, recueillements*? Tib. sñoms par ḥjug pa); in many other occurrences, like the last, I find it hard to draw a line between the two shades of mg.; (mārgo yas tvayā parigṛhītaḥ) samādhi-kauśala-samāpattyā Laṅk 11.1; sukhasamādhi-samāpatti-vihāras 12.7; (indriya-bala-bodhyaṅga-dhyāna-vimokṣa-)-samādhi-samāpattibhiś ca mahatīṃ ratiṃ pratyanubhaviṣyatha SP 80.2; dhyāna-vimokṣa-samādhi-samāpattīr (acc. pl.) 82.2; etc. See also next items.

samāpadana (nt.; to Skt. samā-pad plus -ana; cf. °**padyana**) = **samāpatti,** q.v.: (dhyānavyāvartane) punaḥ-°na-vaśitā-viśuddhyā viśuddhaṃ dhyānaṃ Bbh 210.25.

samāpadyate (in Skt. *attains*), *enters into* the state called technically **samāpatti**: yogināṃ caivaṃ bhavati, nirodhya vijñānāni saṃpatsyāmahe Laṅk 45.3; te cāniruddhair eva vijñānaiḥ °dyante ... 4. Cf. **samāpanna.**

samāpadyana, °**na-tā** (to prec. plus -ana; cf. °**padana**), *attainment,* in technical sense, = **samāpatti**: samādhimukha(Tib. sgo)-śatasahasra-°na-vyutthāna-kuśalā(ḥ) SP 312.2; māyopama-samādher abhīkṣṇa-°natā ŚsP 1458.6–7; katamo (= °mā?) bodhisattvasya ... abhīkṣṇa-°natā? (answer:) yad bodhisattvasya ... vipākajaḥ samādhiḥ ŚsP 1470.10–11.

samāpanna, ppp. (to °**padyate,** q.v.), *attained* (to **samāpatti,** in technical sense): (sc. Bhagavān) samādhiṃ samāpanno 'bhūd ... samanantara-°nnasya ... bhagavato ... SP 5.10, 11; °nnasyāpi yoginaḥ Laṅk 45.1.

samāpīḍayati (Skt. ā-pīḍ° with sam-), *torments*: pres. pass. pple., °ḍyamāna-hṛdayaś cintām āpede Jm 100.22.

samāpta, m., a high number: Mvy 8024 = Tib. legs byin (or phyin). Cf. **mahā-sam°.**

samāptalambha, nt., LV 148.6, cited thence as m., Mvy 7969, a high number, = Tib. rdzogs thob (Foucaux LV) or ḥthob (Mvy), *perfect acquiring.*

? **samāprabhāra** (!), m. or nt., (if reading is right) some kind of brahmanical sacrifice: Divy 634.7. The word is missing in line 11 and ff. where the list in which it occurs is several times repeated. Prob. corrupt.

samābṛṃhaṇa (nt., = **ābṛṃhaṇa,** q.v.), *extraction, plucking out, removal*: Gv 495.13 (cited s.v. **ābṛṃhaṇa**); Gv 491.22 (see **anuśalya-samā°**). Cf. also next.

samābṛṃhayitar (cf. prec.), *one who plucks out* (e. g. a thorn): Gv 462.23 °tāro duḥśalyānāṃ.

samāya, adv. °ya-tas (prob. m.c. for Skt. samayatas, but cf. Ved. samāyin, late Skt. samāya = saṃmukham āgata, Schmidt, Nachträge; and s.v. **samāsa**), *because of the* (arrival of the appropriate) *time*: iha te ciraṃ samāyata ... skandhā sopādānā jñānena mayā parijñātā(ḥ) LV 371.19(–20).

samāropaka, f. °**ikā,** adj. (to Skt. °ropayati plus -aka), (**1**) *causing to grow*: -kuśalamūla-°pikām dharmadeśanāṃ Divy 130.14; (**2**) *attributing, causing* (one) *to make a mental assumption or attribution* (cf. Skt. samāropa): (sā, sc. **prajñapti** 4, ... vastuni) °pikā cāpavādikā ca. tanmayasvabhāvavastugrāhikā °pikā, vastumātra-paramārthanāśagrāhikā 'pavādikā (*annulling*) saṃjñety ucyate Bbh 50.11 ff.

samārjana (nt.), °**na-tā** (to next with -ana), *acquisition*: Gv 342.18 (see **vibaddhana**); sarvajñatāsaṃbhāra-°na- 431.4 (both edd. misprinted sarmājana); sarvajñatā-saṃbhārakuśalamūlasaṃbhava-°natāyai saṃvartate 367.6.

samārjayati (ppp. °jitam once Mbh. 13.5551; AMg. samajjiya, ppp.), *acquires*: pres. pple. (puṇyaṃ) °yan Gv 367.3; sarvabodhyaṅgāni °yanti 493.4; ppp. sarvaśukla-su-°jita-varṇā Gv 347.19; (sc. dharmaḥ) kalpanayutaiḥ °jitu (n. sg. m.) jinena LV 412.11 (vs).

samāliṅga (m. or nt.; = Skt. °gana), *embrace*: kaṇṭhe °gaṃ kṛtvā Mv ii.172.4 (prose).

samāvartayati (not recorded in this sense), *gathers, collects, provides*: kāṣṭhāni samāvartayitvā Mv ii.78.15, *having gathered* (fire-)*wood*; (tasya ... nirmitaiḥ parṣadaḥ) samāvartayiṣyāmi, nirmitāṃś ca bhikṣubhikṣuṇyupāsakopāsikāḥ (acc. pl.) saṃpreṣayiṣyāmi dharmaśravaṇāya SP 235.2, *I will collect* (*provide, for him assemblies of auditors by means of nirmita,* sc. gods, see this), *and will send nirmita as monks, nuns, male and female lay-auditors, to hear the doctrine.*

samāsa (m.?), *time, occasion, juncture*: tasmin samāsi ... LV 415.21 (vs), certainly means *on this occasion*; so Tib. de tshe; Foucaux would em. to samāyi, see **samāya**; it is curious that, acc. to Sheth and Ratnach., AMg. samāsa = sāmāyika, a Jain religious exercise (see H. M. Johnson, Triṣaṣṭiśalākāpuruṣacaritra I p. 81 n. 122), which appears to be derived from samāya = Skt. samaya.

? **samāhita,** ppp. (to Skt. sam-ā-dhā-; recorded in BR only of persons, *concentrated* on an object), *that upon which one's mind is concentrated* (Senart, *la méditation*): moghaṃ (mss. mohaṃ) cāpi °taṃ Mv ii.50.20 (vs), *and vain is* ... But the corresp. Pali vs, Jāt. v.388.6, has samīhitaṃ, *what he desires,* which is likely to be the true reading.

[**samiñjayati,** °**jita,** wrong readings for **saṃmiñj°,** qq.v.]

samita-kāraka, m. (cf. Skt., also BHS, Divy 258.9, samitā, and AMg. samiā, *wheat flour*; AMg. samiya, 'flour, curds, etc., used in sacrifice', Ratnach.; Pkt. samia, 'a pastry made of wheat flour', Sheth), *maker of wheat-flour pastries*: °kā, pl., Mv iii.113.9; 442.14, in list of trades.

samitam, adv. (= Pali id., AMg. samiyaṃ), *constantly*; only following satata(ṃ), see **satata-samita.**

Samitāyus, n. of a Buddha: Gv 284.9.

Samitāvin, see **śami°.**

samidhā (extension of Skt. samidh; = Pali id.), *firewood*: °dhānām Divy 70.6 (mss., ed. em. samidhām); °dhā-hāraka- 487.14 ff.

samiya-, acc. to Senart MIndic for samyak-; *perfectly*: sarvaśaḥ samiya-mārdavānvitā Mv i.64.5 (vs); mss. unmetr. samīyā-. But the word may represent AMg. samiyā- (Skt. *śami-tā), *tranquillity,* which accords well with mārdava-; or a Pkt. form (AMg. samiya) of Skt. śamita, Pali samita, *calm,* as separate word (pl.; in either case final a m.c. for ā, as in Senart's interpretation).

samirita, ppp. or subst. (= Skt. samīrita, which one ms. and Calc. read; but cf. Pkt. and Skt. Lex. samira = Skt. samīra, *wind*), *blown, stirred,* or (subst.) *blowing, stirring*: anekakiṅkiṇijāla-°ritābhinādite (siṃhāsane) LV 30.11 (prose).

(**samīkaronti,** Skt. °oti, in a corrupt passage, which I cannot elucidate and which Senart also found impossible without radical em., Mv i.127.6 (mss.), should prob. be kept; *they* (unworthy Bodhisattvas) *equate* (themselves with their betters); Senart śamīkaro tti. But I cannot determine the rest of the sentence.)

samīkṣam, adv.-postpos. (unrecorded; cf. Skt. samīkṣā), *in the presence* (of, gen.): teṣām idaṃ sūtra bhaṇeḥ °kṣam SP 97.12 (vs), *in their presence you may speak this sūtra.* Or is it a gerund (§ 35.3)?

? **Samīkṣitavadana** (em.), n. of a former Buddha: Mv i.139.10. The mss. read Samīkṣitaḥ as one name, followed by Vadanasatyaṇḍatāraḥ; Senart em. °ta-vadanaḥ, and then **Satyāvatāraḥ**, which seems rather remote from the mss., but no good substitute occurs to me.

Samīkṣitārtha, n. of a former Buddha: Mv i.141.2.

samīkṣya-kārin, adj. (samīkṣya, ger.), *acting after consideration*: °rī asyā hi Mv i.277.10 (vs, metr. indiff.; Senart em. samīkṣā°).

? **samīhati** (in Pali may, it seems, mean *moves*, intrans.: ākāsamhi °ti Vv.5.1, comm. 35.15 ff. . . . carati gacchati), ppp. (vāyu-)samīhita, *stirred* (*by the wind*), based on act. (caus.?) mg. (°hayati?): °tā kisalayās LV 326.4 (vs). The mg. is certain, the reading less so; some mss. °samīritā; but the occurrence of māra-samīritāḥ in the prec. line suggests that this v.l. may have been only a lect. fac.; most and the best mss. are reported with °samīhitā.

samucchoṣaṇa (nt., cf. Skt. ucchoṣaṇa), *drying up, exhaustion*: pretanagara-°ṇa-karāya (of the Buddha) Kv 11.16 (prose).

samucchraya, m. (Pali samussaya; Skt. = *height, elevation*, also BHS, e. g. SP 150.10; 153.4; 159.9), (**1**) (Pali, Itiv. 34.15) *large quantity, mass*: mahādāna-°yaṃ kartuṃ Kv 29.22; (**2**) (= Pali, the usual mg.), *body*, esp. often *bodily existence*: svaśarīra-°yā (abl.) Mv ii.197.2 (vs), *from his own bodily frame*; virūpeṇa durvarṇena durdṛśena °yeṇa 491.20; sphuliṅgajālā va tato °ye (in hell; so read for text °yāḥ, cf. kāye in same vs Jāt. v.143.22) iii.369.5; °yaḥ Mvy 7220 = Tib. lus (*body*) or mtho ba (*height*); patanāntāḥ °yāḥ Divy 27.29; 100.18 (vss), *bodies end in ruin*; paryaṅka-baddhena °yena Gv 337.3 (in Gv 467.5, 9 read °raya for text °rāya); suvarṇavarṇaiḥ °yair SP 202.7; °yasya SP 43.12, see s.v. **paścimaka** (1); paścime °ye, *in the last incarnation*, Divy 70.2; 140.20; SP 144.4; 148.7; Av i.162.4; paścimake °ye SP 68.7 (vs); carimasmi °yasmin SP 222.2 (vs); dvitīye °ye SP 349.11, *in his next incarnation*; nirvāṇa-paryanti °ye 'smin SP 117.7 (vs), *in this bodily existence which ends in nirvāṇa* (said of Hīnayānists); °yi tattva niviṣṭāḥ LV 308.11 (vs); jahiyā (m.c., mss. jāhiya) °yaṃ Mv ii.63.14 (vs), *leaving the body* (Senart em. wrongly); Av i.162.4; ii.198.12 (nikṣepsyanti °yam); RP 25.11 (tyakta °yaḥ); 26.9; Śikṣ 277.13; Bbh 235.3 ff.; 253.21 (puruṣasya °yaṃ, acc.). Cf. next two, and **ucchraya.**

samucchrayaṇa (nt.; cf. Skt. samucchraya), *lifting up, elevation*: mahādharmadhvaja-°ṇaṃ (acc.) SP 16.11 (prose).

samucchrita, (**1**) ppp. (in this mg. = AMg. samucchiya = utpanna huā, *born*; in Skt. *raised, elevated, lofty*; so also BHS; duṣya-śata-samucchrita-patākaṃ Mv i.216.13 = ii.19.10, vs; prākāraiḥ . . . kiṅkiṇījāla-°tair RP 39.18), *produced* (by or in, in comp.): **parikalpa**-(q.v.)-sam° LV 174.8; (pakṣibhis) tat-°ritaiś ca krimibhir bhakṣyamāṇaṃ Divy 234.15, *being eaten by birds and worms produced by them*; vastrāṇi . . . nānādeśa-°tāni Divy 316.24, *produced in various countries*; (**2**) nt., = **samucchraya**, *body*: na ca maithunasaṃbhūtaṃ sugatasya °taṃ Mv i.170.1 (vs), *and the Buddha's body was not formed by sexual intercourse*; cf. Pali Dhp. 147 samussitaṃ, which certainly refers to the body; it is usually taken as adj., but could quite well be a noun, *body*.

[**samujyate**, Gv 24.17; read with 2d ed. samuhyate, *is collected*: yatra °te loko.]

? **samuñcita**, if correct, = Skt. samuccita (§ 3.4), *formed, made up*: (maulikuṇḍalam ca) nānāratna-°tam Kv 35.21.

samutkampin (cf. Skt. utkampin), *trembling greatly*: prītyā °pi-kapolaśobhā Jm 170.4 (vs).

samutkarṣika, adj. (= **sām°**, q.v.; to Skt. °ṣa plus -ika), *very eminent, excellent*: Mvy 7059 = Tib. yaṅ dag phul.

samutkīrtayati (cf. Skt. utkīr°), *proclaims, sets forth*: (iti daśa bhūmayo) °taye (aor., or with v.l. °tiye, aor. pass.) Mv i.161.7, *so the Ten Stages he has* (or, *they have been*) *set forth.*

Samutkhalī, or (v.l.; Tib. mu-khu-li) Samutkhulī (cf. also **Utkhalī**), n. of one of the four goddesses who attend the Bodhisattva in his mother's womb: LV 66.8. See s.v. **Sūtkhalin** (m.).

***samuttara**, *a crossing over* (cf. next), in an-a-samuttaro Mv i.14.10 (vs), *having no crossing over, that cannot be crossed over*, see under **an-a-**. Senart assumes that °tara is for °**tāra** (next), presumably m.c.; meter does indeed require a short penult. But neither °tara nor °tāra seems to be recorded except here and in the Divy passages, which are substantially repetitions of a single passage.

samuttāra, m. (cf. Skt. uttāra), *a crossing over*, *of rivers* (cf. prec.): Divy 451.9; (Vetranadyāṃ tīkṣṇaśastra-)-saṃpātayogena °raḥ 451.11; similarly 456.27; 457.1; all substantially one passage; nom. sg. °tāraḥ except in 451.9 where °tāraṃ of mss. and ed. is prob. an error for °tāraḥ.

samuttāraṇa (cf. **uttārayati**), *the carrying thru to the end*: (tatra ca . . . Sujātā . . . Bodhisattvasya duṣkaracaryāṃ) carata ādita eva Bodhisattvasya vratatapaḥsamuttāraṇārthaṃ (Tib. brtul zhugs, = vrata, daṅ dkaḥ thub, = tapas, ñams ḥog tu chud par bya ba daṅ) śarīrasyāpy āyatanahetoś ca pratidivasaṃ aṣṭaśataṃ brāhmaṇānāṃ bhojayati sma LV 265.12; the passage is not entirely clear to me in either Skt. or Tib.; Foucaux interprets uttāraṇa and its Tib. rendering as *interruption, departure from*; I render: *Now Sujātā, from the very beginning of the time when the B. was performing austerities, in order to bring the B.'s vows and penance to a successful conclusion, and also for the sake of support of the body* (whose body?), *fed every day 800 brahmans.* (And she made an earnest wish: 'Upon eating my food, may the B. attain supreme enlightenment'.)

samuttejaka, m. (adj., to next plus -aka), *one who inflames, incites*: LV 436.1–2, see **samādāpaka**; SP 200.4, after samādāpaka, q.v.

samuttejayati (= Pali °tejeti; cf. Skt. uttejayati and samuttejana), *inflames, incites* (to religious courses), regularly in a cliché with **samādāpayati**, q.v. for references, and other verbs; same cliché with omission of samādāp-, °jayitvā Mv i.261.18; 297.16. See prec. and next.

samuttejayitar (n. ag. to prec.), *one who inflames, incites*: (kalyāṇamitrāṇi) . . . °yitāraḥ pratipattiṣu Gv 463.7 (after **samādāpayitar**).

-samutthānaka, or °**ika**, adj. (or subst.; to Skt. °na; cf. Pali Atthasālinī 263.27 dvi-samuṭṭhāniko, *having two causes*), *(a thing) that causes* (or, if Bhvr., *is caused by*?): (manāpāsecana-)°nakā, or °nikā (so mss.; n. pl. nt.) Mv iii.66.5 (prose).

samutthāpaka, adj. (cf. Pali samuṭṭhā°; to Skt. °thāpayati plus -aka), *arousing, inciting*: °kaḥ Mvy 4683 = Tib. kun (text gun, corr. in Tib. Index) nas sloṅ ba po.

samutpuṭaka, presumably *a hollow bowl*, = **saṃpuṭa**, q.v.: LV 254.16, and acc. to Lefm. 15.

samudaya, m. (rarely nt. in Mv, ii.138.4; = Pali id.; cf. Skt. udaya; see also **samodaya**), *origin*: duḥkha-sam°, *origin of misery*, the second of the four Noble Truths, see s.v. **āryasatya**; also used alone, without duḥkha, in the same sense, Mvy 1221 ff.; 1312; Dharmas 21; Bbh 38.10. See also next.

samudayāstaṃgama, m., *arising and passing away* (of the skandhas): Mv iii.53.3 pañcasu upādānaskandheṣu samudayāstamgamān paśyī (in the foll. lines, 4 ff., samudaya and astamgama are used separately). Cf. (Skt.) **udaya,** and prec.

samudāgacchati, °**te** (= Pali id. in mg. 1; Skt. has not even ud-ā-ga°), (**1**) *arises, comes into being* or *sight, appears*: saptādityāḥ kalpasaṃvartanyāṃ °gamiṣyanti Divy 231.14, *at the destruction of an age seven suns will appear*; (jvaraparidāghanidānāḥ) sarvaśoka . . . upāyāsāḥ °gacchanti Dbh 48.20, *all miseries* (etc.) *arise*; abhivilokanā-pūrvaṃgamehi dharmehi (*conditions*) samudāgacchamānehi (loc. abs.) Mv ii.259.8, *as . . . were arising, appearing*; (tasya sarvacittotpāde) daśānāṃ bodhisattvapāramitānāṃ samudāgama-paripūriḥ °gacchati Dbh 56.28; ayam api mahāpṛthivī udakahradaṃ viya °gacchet (344.9 °gacchati) Mv i.339.7; 344.9, *this great earth, also, appeared* (arose, presented itself, in the beginning of an aeon), *as if a pool of water*; (**2**) in Śikṣ 11.9 there seems likely to be either a drastic abbreviation or a corruption: na cātra śithilena bhavitavyaṃ, na ca śeṣāsu (= śikṣāsu, *rules of morality*?) na samudāgacchati, *and* (yet) *in this case one must not be lax, and one does not fail to remain* (steadfast? or, *he does not fail to make a start, to practise*?) *in the others* (? transl. ignores the second negative). See **samudāgata** (ppp.) and °**gama(na)**.

samudāgata, ppp. (to prec.; cf. Pali id., and next), (**1**) *arisen* (after), *following upon* (in comp.): grīṣme vasanta-°ta-j(y)eṣṭhamāse (so, as one cpd.) LV 133.2 (vs), *in summer, in the month Jyaiṣṭha* (first summer month), *that comes after spring*; (**2**) *arrived, attained* (at or to a religious goal, esp. enlightenment); may be said of the person who attains the goal, in which case the goal (enlightenment) may be understood from the context and may lack formal expression; or of the goal attained: °taḥ Mvy 6844 = Tib. (as for °gamaḥ 6843) yaṅ dag par ḥgrub pa, or ḥthob pa, *completely accomplished* or *attained* (gender indicates personal application); anantakalpaiḥ °to 'si SP 161.6 (vs), *after endless ages you* (a Buddha) *have attained* (*arrived*, sc. at enlightenment, as context shows; not *arisen, appeared*; Tib. yaṅ dag bsgrubs); (eṣa buddho bhagavāṃ asaṃkhyehi kalpehi) °gato arhan samyaksaṃbuddho . . . Mv i.254.3 (as prec.); prajñāpāramitāyāṃ °taḥ Śikṣ 97.14; of the goal attained, pūrvajanma-°ta-kuśalacitta- Gv 250.24, *good thoughts attained in previous births*; dīrghakāla-°ta-buddhī Mv i.122.5 (vs), *having attained (to) buddhi thru a long time* (said of a Buddha); sarvabuddhadharma-°ta-buddheḥ LV 8.1 (prose), as prec.

samudāgama, m. (cf. prec. and Pali id., Jāt. i.2.3, where mg. is not clear), (**1**) *approach (to), arrival (at), attainment (of)*, a religious goal, esp. enlightenment, which is to be understood when no goal is specifically named: °maḥ Mvy 6843 (for Tib. see s.v. °**gata**); jñātvā °maṃ (mss. °ma-) saṃbodhau Mv i.3.6; paramo hi °ma īśvarāṇām i.135.15 (vs), *attainment* (of enlightenment); samyaksaṃbuddhānāṃ °maḥ so 'pi lokottaro 159.4 (prose); the seventh of seven mahattvāni of the mahāyāna (of bodhisattvas), Bbh 297.20 ff. (°ma-mahattvaṃ saivānuttarā samyaksaṃbodhiḥ; yasyātmabhāva-°masyānyaḥ ātmabhāva-°maḥ samo nāsti, kutaḥ punar uttari . . . ṣaṇ mahattvāni hetubhūtāni °gama-mahattvasya; tat punar ekaṃ °gama-mahattvaṃ phalasthānīyam eṣāṃ ṣaṇṇāṃ veditavyaṃ); Bbh 385.13; pratyekabuddhayāna-sam° Dbh 56.12; yo 'py ayaṃ . . . ṣaṭpāramitā-°mo Śikṣ 97.6; pāramitā-sam° (also) Dbh 17.15, and see Dbh 56.28 s.v. **samudāgacchati**; yathā puṇyajñāna-°gamāya saṃbhavati SP 132.2 (prose), *so that it results in attainment of* . . .; ye jñāna-pāramitā-caryā-prakāra-pravicaya-praveśa-saṃbhava-°gamā(ḥ) Gv 248.23; (**2**) SP 92.6 (vs) samudāgamas tṛṣṇa dukhasya saṃbhavaḥ could be rendered *craving is the origin, the source, of misery*; no v.l. is cited but WT em. to samudāgatā on the basis of Chin. renderings, which seem to agree with Tib., sred pa kun ḥbyuṅ las ni sdug bsṅal skye, app. *when craving has arisen, misery arises.* But more likely tṛṣṇa, m.c. for tṛṣṇā, is gen. (§ 9.67): *the origin of misery is the arising of craving*, which accords with Chin. and Tib.

samudāgamana (nt.; = prec.), *arrival* (at, a stage of religious development), *attainment* (of it): Dīpaṃkaro Meghasya . . . mahā-°naṃ ca jñātvā kuśalamūlasambhāraṃ ca cetopraṇidhānam jñātvā . . . Mv i.239.4.

samudācarati (once ger. °cārya, as if from *°cārayati; = Pali °carati; note that even Skt. uses the noun samudācāra in the mg. *address*), *addresses, speaks to* (with acc., once seemingly gen., of person, and usually inst. of the words used): LV 409.6 mā yūyaṃ bhikṣavas tathāgatam āyuṣmadvādena samudācariṣṭa (mss. °ṣṭaḥ, °ṣṭe); Mv i.84.5 (vs) (tān eva dṛṣtva [mss. dṛṣṭa] . . .) ślakṣṇābhi vāgbhir . . . samudācaranti; iii.49.2 and 9 kumāra(ka)-vādena samudācaritavyaṃ manyati, *thinks fit to address as 'boy'*; 182.(1–)2 (prose) (mā bhavanto āryasya upālisya) hīnajātyena samudācaratha (the gen. instead of acc. is curious; is it to be taken as dependent on hīnajātyena?); Divy 169.21 svāgatavādena samudācaritas; 520.8 mūtrapurīṣavādena samudācaritā(ḥ); 526.(7–)8 (svāgatavāda-samudācāreṇa) tāṃ samudācārya (if not a misprint or error, implies 'caus.' °cārayati; or denom. to samudācāra, in the same sentence?) kathayati; Av ii.44.8 bhikṣuṇyo dāsīvādena samudācīrṇāḥ; 132.10 āśīviṣavādena samudācaritāḥ.

samudācāra, m. (mgs. 1 and 2 as in Skt., mg. 3 Skt. Lex.), (**1**) *behavior, manner of conduct* (= Skt.); in Mv i.78.15 ff. list of 8 samudācāra of a Bodhisattva in the 1st bhūmi (tyāga, etc.); they resemble roughly the 10 bhūmipariśodhakā dharmāḥ of a Bodhisattva in the 1st bhūmi, Dbh 19.20 ff.; (**2**) *address* (= Skt.; see s.v. **samudācarati** for Divy 526.7); in Divy 485.6 possibly (*modes of*) *address*, part of the education of a brahman, see s.v. **autkara**; (**3**) *intention, purpose*: AsP 72.19, 22 (yadā) hi . . . asurāṇām evaṃrūpāḥ samudācārā utpatsyante, devāṃs . . . yodhayiṣyāma iti, etc.; (22) te samudācārāḥ punar evāntardhāsyanti.

samudācāraṇa (nt.; cf. prec.), *performance*: punaḥ-punaḥ °ṇāt Bbh 161.10, *from doing it again and again.*

samudācārika, adj. or subst. (to °cāra plus -ika), (*matter*) *of conduct*: evaṃrūpasya . . . kāya-°kasyāvakāśo na bhavati MSV ii.181.13; see also **ā-samud°**.

samudācārin (to °**carati,** q.v., plus -in), *addressing, speaking to*: paruṣavacana-°rī Divy 25.2, . . . *with harsh words.*

? **samudāna,** see next, and **samudānīya.**

samudānana, (nt.) and °**nā** (see §§ 3.43, 38.3; as if n. act. in -ana to *samudānati = °neti, °**nayati**; = **samudānayana**), *acquisition*, esp. of kuśalamūla: (sarvakuśalamūla-)°nanāya KP 19.5 (prose), Tib. yaṅ dag par sdud pa; °nanāyāś ca . . . kuśalāna mūlāna 19.11 (vs), Tib. yaṅ dag bsgrub phyir; read sarvakuśalamūlasamudānanāya (text samādānanāya) vīryaṃ 25.1 (prose), Tib. yaṅ dag par sgrub pa; kuśalamūla-°nanayā (prob. so, or °nanatayā, for text °natayā) atṛptatā 25.9 (prose); °nanāyā kuśalasya vīrya(ṃ) 27.8 (vs), Tib. yaṅ dag sgrub pa; v.l. for Mvy 7421 °nayanāya; in LV 441.5 (prose) text asaṅga-prajñā-°nayana-tayā, but most mss. °dānatayā or °dānatāyai, prob. read °dānanayā or °dānanatayā as in KP 25.9 (unless these two passages justify assumption of ***samudāna** = °dānana; cf. **samudānīya**?).

samudānaya (m.?), also °**ya-tā** (n. act. to °**nayati**; = Pali id., in su-°nayā, Bhvr., *easily acquired* or *accomplished*, Jāt. iii.313.24; not, of course, gdve. with PTSD), (**1**) *acquisition* or *collection*: sarvauṣadha-°yaṃ ca kartum Av i.169.14; vipulapuṇyasambhāra-°ya-cittā Gv 279.19; see under (2) for Gv 491.13; (prabhedārthābhiniścayajñāna-saṃsārabalaviśeṣa-)°ya-mahāvyūhaṃ ca nāma dharmamukham LV 182.12; in LV 353.22 (vs), text corruptly

°nayaṃ prabodhi, see Crit. App., read prob. samudānitāgrabodhiḥ (°nita- see under °**nayati**), metr. correct; (**2**) *preparation, making ready* (a ship; see s.v. **samudānayati** 5): mahādharma-nau-°nayatodyuktānāṃ mahādharmaratnapuṇya-°ya(*acquisition*, to 1)-kṛtavyavasāyānām Gv 491.12–13.

samudānayati, rarely °**te** (= Pali samudāneti; see prec. and foll. items; ppp. sometimes °nita and ger. °niya, §§ 3.43, 38.3; cf. Jacobi, San. § 25; M. Leumann, IF 57.211, 233 infra, and see **samudānana**; note also irregular °nīmahe Divy 92.9; in text of MSV sam-upā-nī- is often printed while Divy in the same passage has sam-ud-ā-nī, e. g. °nīya i.90.1, cf. Divy 90.1; misreading?), (**1**) *gathers, collects*: kṣīraṃ . . . gosahasrād (so with all mss.) . . . samudānayitvā LV 386.22 (vs); (gandhamālyaṃ) °nītaṃ Mv i.231.15; (gandhaṃ, mālyaṃ, puṣpaṃ, cūrṇaṃ) taṃ sarvaṃ samudānayatha Mv iii.266.5; kāṣṭhāni °nayata Divy 27.17; merchandise, for commerce, paṇyaṃ °nayatu Divy 34.14, or bhāṇḍaṃ 92.9 (yad vayaṃ . . . bhāṇḍaṃ samudānīmahe, *that we may assemble* . . ., see Chap. 43, s.v. nī 2); 228.23; (**2**) in part perhaps to (1), but at least in part better rendered *provides*: mahābhaiṣajyaṃ °nayitvā SP 321.4; bhaiṣyajyāni °netavyāni Divy 455.23, and similarly 457.6; °nitu . . . bhaiṣaju LV 414.16 (vs), Tib. bsgrubs; (sarvadharmabhaiṣajya-)°nītaḥ, mahāvaidyarājo LV 275.3–4, *having provided* (or *collected*; ppp. with active mg.) *all the medicaments of the Doctrine, he is the great King of Physicians* (punctuated badly in text); of food, for invited guests, nānnapānaṃ °nayet Śikṣ 12.14, *should not provide food and drink* (after inviting guests); °nīya (ger.) Divy 50.15; distinguished from sajjī-kar-, of food, praṇīta āhāraḥ sajjīkartavyaḥ prabhūtaś caiva °nayitavyo Divy 86.(14–)15, *you must make ready elegant food and provide it in abundance*; (**3**) either *collects* (to 1) or *acquires* (to 4); mahāpariṣā (acc., so mss.) °nayitvā Mv ii.419.1, (the Buddha) *having got* (or *collected*) *a large assembly* (of followers); bhogāḥ (*enjoyments*) °nītāḥ Divy 25.4; suvarṇalakṣaḥ °nīta(ḥ) 26.21; (**4**) *acquires*: prapañcaiḥ samudānitaṃ Laṅk 352.8 (vs; i may be m.c.; not to be em. to °nvitaṃ with Suzuki, Index), *acquired by vain fancies*; °nītaṃ **gotraṃ** (q.v., 3), *acquired* (in contrast with prakṛtisthaṃ, *innate*), Bbh 3.2, defined 5, yat pūrvakuśalamūlābhyāsāt pratilabdhaṃ; usually with religious ends, esp. enlightenment, as object: °niya (read °yā m.c.; ger.) jñānam idaṃ anuttaraṃ SP 145.11 (vs); bodhiṃ ca °nayiṣyati 148.6 (prose); buddhajñānaṃ °nayitavyaṃ 189.2 (prose); bodhisattvacaryāṃ °nayiṣyanti 221.5 (prose); asaṃkhyeyakalpa . . .°nītām anuttarāṃ samyaksaṃbodhiṃ 484.5 (prose); (read with Tib. and mostly with vv.ll.) saptāsaṃkhyeyeṣu kalpeṣu °nīta-sarvakuśalamūlasya dattasaptavidhadānasya LV 10.(4–)5 (prose); (read) samudānitāgrabodhiḥ 353.22 (vs); °nitaṃ maitrakṛpābhrajālaṃ 359.10 (vs); °nītva varāgrabodhim 361.9 (vs); bodhi (acc.) °niyā (ger.) 421.21 (vs; Tib. bsgrubs); bodhibalaṃ °nayamānaḥ Bhad 37; buddhadharmān °nayati Śikṣ 317.4; buddhadharmāḥ °nayitavyāḥ Gv 69.2; (-paripākaṃ . . .) °nayati Bbh 87.19; (buddhakṣetrapariśuddhiṃ, °tra-māhātmyaṃ, °trodāratāṃ) °nayan Sukh 25.10; (maunīndraṃ [pra]vacanaṃ) . . .°nītaṃ Divy 490.16, 18; dharma, the Doctrine, is referred to as duṣkaraśata-°nīta, *acquired by hundreds of hardships*, Jm 6.9, 12; 14.11; trikalpāsaṃkhyeya-°nītāṃ bodhiṃ °nīya Av i.7.3–4; valgusvaraṃ ca (read co, m.c., with v.l. and WT) madhuraṃ' pramuñca, °nitaṃ kalpa-sahasrakoṭibhiḥ SP 178.13 (vs), addressed to a Buddha, whose voice is to proclaim the gospel; puṇyaṃ °netvā (Senart em. °tvāna, m.c.) Mv iii.288.16; (**5**) *prepares, makes ready*, a boat (cf. **samudānaya** 2): maṅgala-potaṃ °naya (for an ocean voyage) Divy 110.26, and ff.; usually fig., dharma-nau, *the boat of the Doctrine*, °nāvaṃ °nayiṣyāmi KP 152.7, Tib. sbyar (which is used of a carriage, *ready* with harnessed horses) bar bya ḥo; °nāvaṃ samudānayitvanā LV 178.15 (vs), Tib. legs par sbyar byas la; °niyā dharmanāvaṃ LV 216.3; °nāva °nayanti RP 10.13 (vs); °nayitva . . . śivadharmanāvaṃ 14.10 (vs), śivadharmanāva °nayitāsmi (fut.) 44.18 (vs); dharmanāva °nayaty ayaṃ Gv 482.13 (vs), cited Śikṣ 102.7; mahādharmanau- . . . -puṇya-samudānīta-mahāsārthavāhasya caturogha-pāra-gāmitā-(so, almost, the best ms., and so Tib.; Lefm. °nā-)-bhiprāyasya LV 8.14–16, which acc. to Tib. means *great entrepreneur* (sārthavāha) *who by* . . . *and merit has made ready* (yaṅ dag par bsgrubs pa = samudānīta, with active force) *the great boat of Doctrine and purposes to go* (with it) *to the further shore of the quadruple flood.*

samudānayana, nt. (to °**nayati** plus -ana; cf. °**dānana**), *acquisition*: °nam Mvy 7211 = Tib. (b)sgrub pa, or sbyar ba; °nāya 7421 (v.l. °dānanāya; Mironov °dānayaṃ) = Tib. legs par sbyar ba, bsgrub pa, or bsdu (to sdud) pa; (sarva)kuśalamūladharma-°yana- LV 181.15; mahāyānaguṇa-°yana- 433.4; on 441.5 see **samudānana**; sarvabuddhadharma-°yana- Gv 467.12.

samudānīya, adj., quasi-gdve., perh. by haplology for °dānanīya, to *samudānati, from which **samudānana**, q.v.; or possibly to **samudāna** (if that stem is to be accepted with readings found in KP 25.9 and LV 441.5, s.v. **samudānana**), plus -īya, cf. § 22.20; *to be acquired* (cf. **samudānayati** 4), in duḥkha-°nīyā anuttarā (samyak)-saṃbodhiḥ Mv i.35.11; 57.1.

samudānetar (to **samudānayati**, 2), *one who provides*, with gen.: (miseries arise as caused by jvara-paridāgha,) teṣāṃ na kaścit °netā Dbh 48.21, *and no one provides them.*

samudāyāti (= **samudāgacchati**, q.v.), *appears, presents oneself*: jinasutāḥ . . . samudayāntv (a for ā m.c.) iha te 'dya kṛpābalāḥ Divy 399.16 (vs; cf. āyāntu, 19).

samudāhāra, m. (= Pali id.; to Skt. samudāharati, and cf. next), *speaking, conversation*; see s.v. **antarākathā**; anta-sam° MSV i.221.8.

samudāhāraka, adj. (cf. prec.; to Skt. °harati), *uttering, speaking*: LV 8.8; see s.v. **yathāvādi-tathākārin.**

samudita, in ālaya-samudita Mv iii.314.3, 4, see s.v. **ālaya** (2): *taking delight in* is certainly the mg. It is natural to think of em. to saṃmudita; but the corresp. Pali has in SN i.136.12 and 13 samudita, and this is a v.l. for saṃmudita of text in another parallel Vin. i.4.36 f. On the other hand, we find in Pali similar triple formulas containing -ārāma, -rata, and -saṃmudita in MN i.503.22; SN iv.389.10; 390.1–2. PTSD recognizes samudita, *excited* (allegedly from sam-ud-i, *'aroused'*), as well as saṃmudita *delighted*, and Childers cites, without reference, samuditamano (*elevated, excited*) udaggamano attamano, where the meaning seems clearly *rejoiced.* I have failed to note saṃmudita in BHS, or any other occurrence of samudita in this sense. Surely one of the two words is an ancient corruption of the other.

Samudgata, m., (**1**) n. of a samādhi: Mvy 521; ŚsP 1416.11; (**2**) n. of a maharṣi: Māy 256.23.

Samudgatarāja, n. of a Tathāgata: Mmk 7.10.

Samudgataśrī, n. of a Bodhisattva: Gv 4.3.

samudghaṭana (see s.v. °**ghāṭayati**), *removal, destruction*: (anuśayānāṃ . . .) ananyāryamārga-°na-tāṃ ca yathābhūtaṃ prajānāti Dbh 75.13 (*and the fact that the anu° find their abolition in*, or *by, the peerless Noble Path*).

samudghaṭita (cf. M. samugghaḍia, defined by *opened*), *freed*, in vimati-°ta LV 425.15, of Buddha; two mss. °ghāṭita, see °**ghāṭayati**; cf. **samudghāṭin**, and **samudghāta** etc.

samudghāṭa, m. (see °**ghāṭayati**), *removal, abolition* (= °**ghāta**): hetudṛṣṭi-°ṭo LV 33.6; sarvavāsanānusaṃdhi-°ṭam (acc.) 442.8.

samudghāṭana (nt.; to Skt. °ghāṭayati with -ana),

opening (of a stūpa): mahāratnastūpasya °ne SP 248.8 (prose).

samudghāṭayati, *removes, abolishes, destroys*: kleśānuśayāḥ °ṭayitavyāḥ Gv 458.11; cf. °**ghaṭana.** Skt. has udghaṭati, *opens* (intr.), and (sam-)udghāṭayati, *opens* (trans.); in this meaning BHS °**ghāṭana**; it seems that all the other related words (°**ghaṭana** etc. thru °**ghāṭin**) have the mg. appropriate to **samudghāta** and its sept, which is paralleled in Pali. In BHS, but only here so far as recorded, confusion has occurred between derivs. of (sam-ud-)ghaṭ- and han- (caus.).

-samudghāṭin (see prec.), *remover* (of), *liberator* (from): in **Vimati-°ṭin,** SP 19.4 (no v.l. in KN; but WT °ghātī with their ms. K′, and so BR cites the word, with Burnouf and Kern); cf. (vimati-)**samudghaṭita.**

samudghāta, m. (= Pali samugghāta; see also °**ghāṭa**), *removal, abolition, destruction*: Mvy 1601; 8355; kutsitadarśaneṣu doṣa-°ta-kuśalāḥ Mv i.134.1, (Bodhisattvas are) *clever in rooting out the errors in reprehensible* (heretical) *systems*; ālaya-°to Mv iii.200.11 (see **ālaya** 2; same cpd. in Pali °gghāto AN ii.34.24); anuśaya-°tāya (so read, Transl. 50 n. 1) Śikṣ 50.9; sarvamāna-°taṃ (acc.) 326.8; (anuśayānāṃ . . .) atyanta-°tād Laṅk 138.15.

samudghātana (nt.; Pkt. samugghāyaṇa = vināśa, Sheth), *plucking out, rooting out, destruction* (= prec.): sarvānuśayaśalya-°na-tayā Gv 494.23 (prose).

samudghātita, ppp. (= Pali samugghā°; to *samudghātayati, cf. °**ghāta,** °**ghātana**), *abolished, got rid of; freed from*: sarvamanyanā-°tasya bodhisattvavimokṣasya Gv 199.20; sarvālaya-°ta-cittatāyai 345.7.

samuddita, adj.-ppp., app. m.c. for Skt. samudita, § 2.82, *arisen, originated*: karma vastu-°tam MSV ii.209.23; °tāḥ iii.66.2 (vss). Cf. Pali samuddaya (if correct) = samudaya (PTSD), but note also vv.ll. and parallels cited Itiv. 16.4, note; also udraya, uddaya in PTSD; the Pali forms need further study.

samuddiśati = **uddiśati,** q.v., in mathematical sense: LV 147.1 (prose) °śanti.

samuddhānana, or (Mironov) samuddhanana, *rude behavior*: nt., Mvy 5194 = Tib. yoṅs su rgod byed. Cf. **uddhānana (uddhanana).**

Samudra, (**1**) n. of a Buddhist convert: Divy 376.19 ff.; (**2**) n. of another convert, in a vaguely similar story: Av ii.61.4 ff.; (**3**) n. of a nāga king: Māy 246.16.

Samudrakaccha, m., n. of a region in the south: Gv 456.12; 466.16.

samudraka-lekha(**-lekhaka**), m., see **sāmudrakalekhaka.**

Samudraputra, n. of a nāga king: Māy 246.16.

Samudrapratiṣṭhāna, nt., n. of a city: Gv 135.18; 136.16.

Samudrabuddhi, n. of a former Buddha: Mv i.137.5.

samudrayātrika, adj. (to Skt. °yātrā plus -ika), *seafaring*: °ko sārthavāho Mv iii.350.11; 351.1.

Samudravetāḍī (fem.), n. of a region (in the south): Gv 99.10; 100.9 (here misprinted °votā°); 110.11.

Samudrā, n. of a rākṣasī: Māy 241.31.

samudvartate (Skt. only ppp. °vṛtta and caus. °vartayati), *rises, swells* (of the sea): °tamānasyeva salilanidher Jm 92.13 (by em.).

samunmajjate (in Skt. only once, and in mg. *dive in*; but Skt. un-majj- oftener in the mg. of this word), *springs forth, dives out*: dharaṇīvivarebhyaḥ °jjante sma SP 298.7.

[**samupakaraṇa,** nt., in Mv ii.98.4, would mean *paraphernalia* = upakaraṇa; but surely read with v.l. sarvam upa°; the akṣara rva was lost in the ms. followed by Senart; rājñā Sucandrimeṇa yajñasya sa(rva)m upakaraṇaṃ sajjetvā . . .]

samupacarati, *performs*: Mv i.101.3, see s.v. **asthāna-tā.**

samupadarśayati, *displays, exhibits*: prātihāryāṇi °yati Kv 63.12.

samupanāmayati (= **upanām**° 5), *presents* (a necklace): (samyaksaṃbuddhasya ratnastūpe) °mayām āsa SP 446.10 (prose).

samupanikṣipati (= Skt. upani°), *deposits*: paramāṇurajaḥ °kṣipet SP 316.8 (Kashgar rec. om. sam); (rasās . . . tasya jihvendriye) °kṣiptā(ḥ) 366.10 (no v.l.); both prose.

samupapadyati (= **upapadyati,** °**te**), *is* (*re-*)*born*: narendrabhavane °dye or °dyi (aor.) Mv i.206.6 = ii.9.22 (vs); Senart reads samutpadye the first time, samupapadyi the second (both metr. possible, end of āryā vs); no ms. has t before p either time.

samupaśobhita, ppp. (= Pali id.; Skt. upa°), *adorned*: puṣpāvali-°taṃ Sukh 64.12 (prose).

samupahāsa (cf. Pkt. samuvahasia, ppp.), *ridicule* (as subst.); or °hāsam, ger. (§ 35.3), *ridiculing*: (tasyāḥ) °hāsam aṅgulīkartum ārabdhaḥ (. . . tayā . . . tasyāṅgulyo nipīḍitāḥ) MSV iv.233.21, *he began to 'make* (motions with his) *fingers' ridiculing her*(?).

samupādayati (m.c. for Skt. samutpā°, thru MIndic samuppā°, § 2.88, cf. Pali samuppajjati etc.), *causes* (a thought, cittam) *to arise, produces*: °dayetsuḥ (Nobel °dayitsuḥ) Suv 151.11; °danīyam Śikṣ 107.18.

samupādāya, quasi-postpos. (= **upādāya,** q.v., 2b), *from* (locally, with abl.): mūrdhnāto °ya yāvat pādeṣu Mv iii.148.18 (prose), *from head to foot*; same phrase with mūrdhāto upādāya . . . above, line 3.

[**sam-upā-nī-,** in MSV for **samudānayati,** q.v.]

samupāvartayati, *brings near*: °vartyamāneṣu . . . vicitreṣu yānaviśeṣeṣu Jm 8.11, *while various fine carriages were being brought up.*

samupāśrayati (Skt. only ppp. °śrita; not noted elsewhere), *resorts to* (acc.): dṛṣṭīṃ (*to heresy*) °yanti SP 204.4 (vs).

samupāhita, ppp. (cf. Skt. upāhita, *bewirkt, hervorgebracht*, BR 3.911), app. *established, festgesetzt*, said of a proposition or statement: yathā . . . ācāryāṇāṃ svayaṃ °hitaṃ Mv ii.12.9 (vs), *as is established* (doctrine) *of the teachers themselves*; text reads maya = mayā after yatha for mss. yathā; if this is right, *as I have established* (the doctrine) *of the teachers themselves* (viz. that the child conceived will become either an emperor or a Buddha). The mss. here read so; in the parallel i.207.19 they are hopelessly corrupt (one intends adrākṣīt taṃ for samupā°). Senart's em. samupāhitaṃ (i p. 519) has no support; the SP passage he refers to (KN 476.5–6) reads parisaṃharṣayiṣyāmi, with no v.l. that helps Senart. The earlier part of the line is shown by meter to be corrupt.

samula, m., a high number: Gv 133.24 (first sammulaḥ, by error, repeated twice as samula-), cited in Mvy 7902 as **sambala,** nt., q.v.; also samulaḥ Mvy 7773 = Tib. dpag ḥbyams (ḥphyam, ḥjal). Seems to have no correspondent in the list Gv 106.

samullāpa (m.; = Pali id., also AMg. °lāva), *conversation*: kathā-°pena ramati Mv ii.78.6, 8; parivrājikāhi sārdhaṃ °paṃ karoti iii.390.5.

samullokita, ppp. (cf. Skt. ullokita), *gazing up intently, very attentive*; in °ta-mukhaḥ, Bhvr., *with intent face* (of a hearer, towards the Buddha): Mvy 6452 = Tib. zhal du (b)ltas pa; see Das s.v. shal (i.e. zhal) ta.

samūlaka, f. °**ikā,** adj. (Pali adj., f. °ikā, Vin. ii.241. 35), (*a*) *well-grounded* (*charge, accusation*), opp. **amūlaka**: MSV iii.108.20 °kena kṛtena, etc.; 109.15 °likayā śīlavipattyā etc.

samūhata, ppp. (see **ūhata**; = Pali id.), *removed, destroyed*: Mv i.354.2 na cāsya rāgānuśayo samūhato; iii.92.1 yasya jālinī samūhatā (mss. °to) tṛṣṇā; 369.19 dṛṣṭvā ca rāṣṭrāṇi samūhatāni.

? **samūhati,** *raises*: āśvāsapraśvāsā uparudhvā (mss.

°ruddhā) ūrdhvaṃ śīrṣakapālaṃ vātā praharetsu samūhetsuḥ (v.l. samuttejetsuḥ) Mv ii.125.6; I believe this would have to be an anomalous denom. to **samūhata,** q.v., in the different meaning of *raised,* which is found also with **ūhata,** q.v.; or at least, this form, if correct, must have been influenced by that word. But it may be that we should read samūhanetsuḥ, to *samūhanati, on the basis of the Pali parallel MN i.243.23 vātā muddhānaṃ ūhananti (*raise*); the LV version is confused and doubtful, vāyur ūrdh(v)aṃ śiraḥkapālam (mss. °lām) upanihanti (v.l. upasaṃharati) 252.1, and āśvāsapraśvāsā ūrdh(v)aṃ śiraḥkapālam (v.l. °lā) upanighnanti (v.l. samuvaghnanti) 3–4; Senart implausibly connects the word with the noun samūha, detaching it from its evident direct object śīrṣakapālaṃ.

Samṛddhayajña, n. of a former Buddha: Mv i.139.12.

Samṛddharāṣṭra, n. of a former Buddha: Mv i.137.14.

sameti (for *samayati, denom. to Skt. sama?), *is like, resembles* (instr.): sameti so 'ntarikṣeṇa nānātvaṃ nāsya labhyate Samādh 22.14 (vs), *it* (the Buddha's body) *is like space, there is no differentiation found in it*; na sameti yad uta nānā-prajñaptyā MSV iii.122.9. (Both Skt., see BR 5.1137, and Pali use sam-eti with instr. in mg. *agrees with.* The use here recorded could possibly be derived from this, but seems more easily understood as above.)

? **samocaka,** nt., a (prob. corrupt) n. of a medicinal plant: Suv 105.2 (mss.); see **vaṃśarocanā.**

samodaya (m. ? once recorded as nt.), prob. *origin*; only in vss of Mmk and may be m.c. for **samudaya,** q.v., § 3.71, but see **samodita**: grahā ... dṛṣṭajātisamodayā(ḥ) Mmk 191.18; ādau tāvad bhavel liṅgam utpātānāṃ samodayam 195.23; nānābhāṣa-°yā(ḥ) 234.10; kulayoni-°yāḥ 403.16.

samodahana, m. (! so also Mironov, n. sg. °naḥ; cf. Pali odahana, and BHS **anvodahana**; to Pali sam-odahati, for sam-ava-dadhati = °dhāti), *completely attentive consideration*: Mvy 7473 °naḥ = Tib. legs par rab tu rtogs pa.

samodita, adj.-ppp., prob. *originated, arisen, come into being,* cf. **samudaya** and **samo°**; only in vss of Mmk, where it could be m.c., § 3.71, for samudita (which seems to occur in Pali in this mg., tho rarely); but Pali has samodita in prose, once at least in the mg. *assembled, united* (Vv. comm. 320.28), which samudita has in Skt.; this mg. would be possible in some of the Mmk passages (many of which are obscure and likely to be corrupt; they are here reproduced as printed): karma eṣa sadā vindyād vidhimuktā samoditā Mmk 180.4; tithayaś ca °tā 194.3; ulkāṃ liṅgair ebhiḥ °tām 200.18; yasmin deśe °tā 211.3; yatra sthite °tā 212.14; nānānāma-°tāḥ 214.21; yo yasya grahamukhyo vā kṣetrarāśisamoditā 222.8; mūlyasiddhiḥ °tā 263.11; mantratantraṃ °tam 320.24; teṣu siddhis tridhā yātā triprakārāḥ °tāḥ, uttamā madhyamā nīcā ... 342.17.

sam-o-namati, -sarati, -harati, see **sam-ava-.**

[**sampa,** see **śamya**;] **saṃpa** also = Skt. saṃpad, § 15.3.

saṃpaccate (MIndic for °cyate; Skt. has saṃpakva, saṃpācayati; otherwise no sam-pac- is recorded), *is tormented* (in hell): tatra (sc. mahānarake) bahūni prāṇasahasrāṇi °ccamānā (mss. saṃyacc°) saṃdarśitā Mv iii.43.3.

saṃpadā (= Pali id., Skt. saṃpad), *accomplishment; good luck, fortune, wealth*: bodhisattvasya abhiniṣkramaṇa-°dā Mv ii.164.16 (prose), *accomplishment of retirement* (n. sg.); same, 208.15 (prose); paramāye varṇa-°dāye saṃpannā 293.8 (prose), *blest with highest fortune of aspect*; cakravarti-°dā Divy 401.24 (prose), *fortune of a cakr°*; the rest in vss: durlabhā kṣaṇa-°dā SP 462.6, *hard to find is fortune of moment,* i. e. a fortunate or auspicious moment; te āśaya-°dāya (instr.) viśuddharūpāya (adj. with prec.) samanvitā bhūt SP 46.5, *they were endowed with a rich store of mental disposition that was pure in form* (otherwise Burnouf and Kern); na dānaguṇa-°dā (so with mss.; acc. sg. or pl.) Mv i.89.2.

Saṃpadin, °**di,** n. of a son of Kunāla and heir presumptive of Aśoka: °dī (nom.) nāma Divy 430.15; °dī r- (i. e. °dī or °dis), and °der (gen.), 433.22.

saṃpannaka, adj. (Skt. °na plus specifying -ka, § 22.39), *that has been acquired*: (idaṃ ca loptraṃ) ... °kam MSV ii.122.2.

saṃparāmārj-, or °**mṛj-** (cf. Skt. parā-mārj-, and **saṃparimārjati**), *wipes off*: aśru °mṛjya (ger.) Mmk 601.1 (vs; submetrical).

saṃparāya, m. (= Pali id., from Skt. and BHS **sāṃparāya**; see this), *future state, a life after death* (cf. **abhisaṃparāya**): gamanīyo saṃparāyo, *one has to go to a future life* (i. e. to die) Mv iii.217.10; 219.1; Bbh 221.20 saṃparāya-sukhito; 7.1 °ya-gurukaḥ; as in Pali often contrasted with dṛṣṭa dharma, Mv iii.211.15 = 212.2 dṛṣṭe (dṛṣṭa-) dharme hitārthaṃ vā saṃparāyasukhāya vā; similarly Divy 207.26; Bbh 198.9; Mvy 2982.

saṃparāyika, adj. (= Pali id., Skt. sāṃpa°; cf. **saṃparāya**), *of a life after death*: Ud iv.26 (Lévi JA 1912, Pt. 2, 269), contrasted with **dṛṣṭadhārmika.** But Chakravarti, Ud p. 48, assumes that sāṃpa° was read, as in Skt.; is Lévi's form a misprint? (There are rather numerous misprints in this text.) The Skt. (or Sktized) adj. **sāṃ°,** q.v., is otherwise well known in BHS: Ud v.22; Mvy 2981; 8355; Mv iii.212.6, 8, 9; Bbh 176.24, etc.

saṃparāhata, ppp. of (unrecorded) saṃ-parā-han-, *struck*: kaṃsapātrīye ... śilāpaṭṭe °hatāye Mv ii.282.11; pṛthivī °hatā (by the Bodhisattva) 412.7; both prose.

saṃparikartayati (cf. Pali samparikantati, and Skt. kṛntati, Epic kartati), *splits,* or *cuts off*: (govikartanena gāvīye śīrṣakapālaṃ dāleya ...) parikartaye saṃparikartaye Mv ii.125.5; so Senart em., mss. (saṃ)parivarttaye.

? **saṃparikālayati** (Skt. pari-kāl°), *drives, hunts* (birds, towards a snare): (śākuntiko ... taṃ mahāntaṃ yūthaṃ) yena te kālapāśā tena °kāleti (Senart's em.; mss. °kīreti, °kīleti) Mv ii.254.2.

saṃparitakṣṇoti, Divy 376.7, or **saṃpratakṣṇoti,** 375.27, *chops up, cuts to pieces*: (takṣṇuvanti saṃtakṣṇuvanti) °kṣṇuvanti (object, creatures in hell).

saṃparidīpayate (cf. Skt. pari-dīp-), *illumines completely* (fig.): bhagavān imam evārthaṃ ... °payamānas Suv 155.3 (prose).

saṃparipaśyati (Skt. pari-paś-), *perceives completely*: anityatāṃ °śyato (pres. pple.) me Divy 411.22 (vs).

saṃparipṛcchita, (MIndic) ppp. = Skt. saṃparipṛṣṭa, which precedes here, *completely questioned*: AsP 286.1 yena pūrvaṃ na saṃparipṛṣṭā bhavatīyaṃ prajñāpāramitā na saṃparipṛcchitā na saṃparipraśnīkṛtā ...; also in LV 147.5 (vs) prob. read (jñānasya śīghratā) ... saṃparipṛcchitā (text °atā).

saṃparipraśnīkṛta, ppp. (cf. **paripraśnīkaroti**), *questioned, interrogated*: AsP 286.2, see prec.

saṃparimārjati, °**mārjayati** (unrecorded; cf. **saṃparā°**, and Skt. pari-m°), *wipes, wipes off, cleanses*: keśehi (mss. jagahi!) pādatalāni (of Dīpaṃkara) °janto Mv i.238.13 (prose); mukhena ca keśena ca pādāni °jati (v.l. °jeti) ii.111.11 (prose); pāṇibhyāṃ mukhaṃ °jya (ger.) Divy 295.8; aśrūṇi °jya 296.23, 28, *wiping away*; (candrasūryau) ... pāṇinā °jayāmi Gv 70.16 (prose), prob. *clean, rub, polish* (hardly *wipe away*; in a list of deeds of magic).

saṃparivarta, prob. subst. m. (= Pali °vatta, acc. to PTSD adj.; cf. Skt. id., once, Schmidt, Nachträge; Skt. parivarta, and saṃparivartati), *rolling around*; in °varta-śāyin, *lying* (and) *rolling around* (lazily): rātriṃ divaṃ °ta-śāyī Ud xxix.13 = Pali (°vatta-sāyī) Dhp. 325

(comm. mañcādisu saṃparivattitvā), 'like a hog that has eaten his fill'. Cf. next.

saṃparivartana (nt., cf. Skt. parivartana, and see under prec.), *revolution, moving around* (said of movements of a horse): (vālāho 'śvarājaḥ...) āvartana-parivartana-saṃ°naṃ kṛtvā Kv 55.15.

saṃparivartayati (mg. 1 = Skt. parivartayati), (**1**) *interchanges, mixes*: so 'pi bhikṣur āsīl lābhī grāhikaḥ, tena mātsaryābhibhūtena lābhaḥ °titaḥ, yo vārṣikaḥ sa haimantikaḥ, pariṇāmitaḥ (*and vice versa*) Śikṣ 59.4; (**2**) *wrings* (the hands): hastau °yati mukhaṃ ca vibhaṇḍayati Divy 263.13, (°yasi) 15; mukhaṃ vibhaṇḍya hastān °vartya 575.24; (**3**) *rolls* (the eyes, in a fit): (akṣiṇi) °ti MSV i.285.17; (**4**) *upsets*: palyaṅkān (*cots*) api °yanti MSV iv.121.15.

saṃpariveṭhita, ppp. (to **pariveṭheti** with sam-), *all wrapped up*: (taṃ śākhāntikaṃ) vṛkṣaśākhehi °taṃ ... dṛṣṭvā Mv ii.254.3 (line 1 above, ātmānaṃ pariveṣṭayitvā).

? **saṃpaśyana** (nt.; Skt. saṃpaśyati plus -ana), dat. °nāya, quasi-inf., (*in order*) *to see*: devī āmrāṇi saṃpa-śyanāya (em., mss. so, or se, paś°) nirdhāvitā Mv ii.453.1.

saṃpiṇḍā (cf. Skt. saṃpiṇḍayati), *gathering, mass*: mahājanakāyasya °ḍā Mv ii.74.16, jana-°ḍā 18 (mg. clearly shown by mahāṃ janakāyasamāgamo in close parallel 75.7); (janakāyo) °ḍāye (instr., *in a mass, in a crowd*) kathaṃ pi (mss. vi) nirdhāvati 75.12.

saṃpidadhāti (cf. Skt. pi-dhā and sam-api-dhā), *shuts*: mukhadvāraṃ °dadhyāṃ Divy 232.19 (prose); cf. 16 pidhāsyāmi.

[**saṃpipāsati**, twice by Senart's em., assumed to be = pipāsati, *is thirsty*; on Mv i.8.2 see s.v. **sa-**; in i.28.9 read (kṣutpipāsāsamarpitā uccāraprasrāvakheṭasiṃhāṇikā-pubbarudhiraṃ) taṃ pi prārthenti (mss. taṃ pi nār°; Senart em. saṃpipāsanti), *even that they are eager for* (as food and drink, being so hungry and thirsty).]

saṃpīḍita, adj. (ppp.), *packed full, completely filled*: mahākaruṇā-saṃpīḍita-hṛdayo Kv 25.23.

saṃpuṭa, °**ṭaka**, in LV also **samutpuṭaka** (presumably = Skt. saṃpuṭa, °ṭaka, *a hollow bowl* or anything of that shape), (**1**) = Skt. añjali, as gesture of respect: kṛtakara-°ṭas Divy 380.1; cf. **saṃpuṭita**; (**2**) in °ṭa(ka)-jātam, *become like a hollow bowl* (?), in Mv and LV passage describing a plucked and withered gourd, to which the Bodhisattva's head after his austerities is compared; the general effect seems to be *shrivelled*: LV 254.15, 16 (tad yathā tiktakālābus taruṇo lūna āmlāno) bhavati saṃmlā-naḥ samutpuṭaka-jāta (no v.l. in Lefm., but Calc. and Weller's ms. saṃpuṭaka°) evam eva śira āmlānam abhūt saṃmlānaṃ samutpuṭaka-jātam (no v.l.; supported here by Calc. and Weller's ms.); corresp. Mv ii.126.4, 5 (say-yathāpi...) tiktālābu haritacchinnaṃ āmilātaṃ bhavati saṃmilātaṃ saṃpuṭajātam evam eva śīrṣakapālaṃ abhūṣi āmilātaṃ saṃmilātaṃ saṃpuṭajātam, repeated 127.8–9; 128.13–14; 129.16–17, sometimes spelled saṃpuṭaka°, and mss. often °pūṭa°, °ṭā°; but mg. is not certain; Tib. on LV (both times) rtsub rtsub por ḥgyur ro (gyur to), *becomes (became) very rough*; the Pali parallel, MN i.80.22–23 (also 246.1–2), has ... tittakālābu āmakacchinno vātātapena saṃpuṭito hoti sammilāto ... me sīsacchavi saṃpuṭitā hoti...; comm. ii.50.17 so hi vātātapena saṃphuṭati (v.l. saṃphusati) ceva milāyati ca, with a reading different from the text; (**3**) dual, in comp. with preceding kapāṭa, the two leaves or panels of a door or gate as forming, when opened, the two sides of a *container* (*'box'* or double *'bowl'*, as it were): (yathāpi ... mahānagaradvāreṣu mahākapāṭa-saṃpuṭāv argalavimuktau pravisāryate (mss.) SP 249.2, *as in a great city gate the half-boxes* (or *bowls, hemispheres*, possibly as being slightly concave?) *formed of the two great panels, when the bolt is removed, are moved apart*.

saṃpuṭita, denom. pple. (to **saṃpuṭa** q.v.; perh. cf. Pali saṃpuṭita, cited ibidem), *made into the shape of* (*a hollow bowl*, i. e.) *an añjali*: hastau °tau nityau Mmk 484.2 (vs; in description of a mudrā).

saṃpuraskaroti (= Pali sampurekkharoti, Skt. puras-k°), (**1**) *attends*: bhikṣugaṇa-°kṛtaḥ Mv i.66.19 (vs); (Bhagavān ... saptabhiś ca nikāyaiḥ) °kṛto Divy 159.16 (prose); (Bhagavantaṃ) °kṛtya MSV i.257.7; (**2**) *displays, employs, manifests*: karuṇāṃ °kṛtya (ger.) Bbh 16.24; sattvānukampām eva °kṛtya 198.4 (both prose).

saṃpuṣpita, adj., quasi-ppp. of denom. (= Pali sampupphita; Skt. puṣpita), *in full bloom*: LV 82.17 (of a tree, -nānāpuṣpa-saṃ°; prose); 92.1 and 97.13 (vs, of trees); 133.3 (of a summer month); Mv ii.191.17 (trees) and 203.10 (both vss); Divy 312.3 (prose, of trees); so also Av i.179.3; 225.9; 307.10; of a pond, RP 40.17 (prose); fig., of Bodhisattvas' minds, (bodhisattvāḥ...) puṣpa-bhūtā bhavanti sarvabuddhaguṇa-°ta-cittatayā Gv 388.3.

Saṃpūjita, n. of a former Buddha: LV 5.15 = Tib. yaṅ dag mchod; follows **Jitaśatru**, q.v. (in Mv **Supūjita** in the corresponding place).

Saṃpūrṇa, (**1**) = **Pūrṇa** 1, n. of a disciple of Śākyamuni: Av i.2.2 (here ms. Sa-p°); 3.1; (**2**) n. of a Buddha (possibly = **Pūrṇa** 5): Mmk 499.23 (vs).

Saṃpūrṇaśrīvaktrā, n. of a queen: Gv 269.9.

saṃprakampana (nt.; Skt. sam-pra-kamp- with -ana), *shaking, making to quake*: sarvalokadhātu-°naṃ bhavati Dbh 83.14; sarvabuddhakṣetra-°na-saṃkṣobhaṇa-Gv 246.26.

saṃprakaroti, *treats well, deals well with*, or, *honors, pays respect to* (acc.; Pali pakurute = sevati, object rājānaṃ, Sn. comm. 169.15): (na ... vyāpādo na ca vigrahaḥ,) anyonyaṃ saṃprakurvanti maitracittā sthitās tadā LV 280.6 (vs).

saṃprakāśaka, adj. or subst. m. (to Skt. saṃprakā-śayati plus -aka; the Skt. caus. verb is recorded only once in BR but may be commoner, cf. Skt. °kāśana; it is common in BHS, e. g. Mvy 2780; 6376; Mv iii.64.3; 357.14; 378.16; LV 254.17 °śyante, pass., etc.; the entire sept is unrecorded in MIndic), *making* (*one who makes*) *manifest, declaring*: -dharma-°kāḥ SP 29.12; °kaḥ LV 179.11. See next.

saṃprakāśana-tā and °**śanā** (= Skt. °śana, nt.; cf. prec.), *exposition, manifestation, declaration, setting forth*: dharmaparyāyasya °śanatāyai SP 270.11; 271.1; praṇidhānapāramitā-°śanatayā Gv 153.8; -guṇavarṇa-°śanatayā LV 430.12; prabhāva-°śanā Bbh 298.7; hīna-yāna-°śanā KP 11.4; all prose.

saṃprakirati (cf. ppp. Skt. a-saṃprakīrṇa, AMg. saṃpaiṇṇa; otherwise unrecorded; cf. Skt. prakirati), *scatters*: puṣpāṇi devā °re (aor.) tadā Mv iii.94.20 (vs), repeated ff.

-saṃprakṣālaka, adj. or n. ag., or n. act. (cf. Skt. °kṣāla and AMg. saṃpakkhālaga, in a different sense), *washing* (and then eating): LV 248.20, see s.v. **kāpotaka**; Tib. bkrus te za ba, *eating after having washed*.

saṃprakhyāna, nt. (cf. Skt. prakhyāna; see also **a-saṃ°**), *clarity*; *clarification* (in intellectual sense): Mvy 2671 = Tib. śin tu (*very much*) gsal ba (*to be bright, clear, evident, lucid*); or śin tu dran pa (*clear consciousness, mindfulness*; smar-); Bbh 384.9 (nirmāṇe pariṇāme) saṃ-prakhyāne (*clarification*) sarvālambaneṣu yā vaśavartitā, iyam ucyate sarvākārā ālambanapariśuddhiḥ. In AbhidhK. (La Vallée-Poussin vii.91, n. 2) = **asaṃmoṣa**, q.v.

saṃpragarjati, *roars loudly*; only after corresp. forms of (Skt.) garjati and pragarjati (subject being world-systems, lokādhātu, on solemn occasions): agarjat prā-garjat saṃprāgarjat LV 352.4; °jitaḥ Samādh 19.6; Mvy 3018.

saṃpragraha (m.? = Pali sampaggāha, glossed ukkhipanaṭṭhena cittaṃ sampaggaṇhātīti, Atthasālinī 372, cited note on Śikṣ 277.9), *exaltation* (so Tib., cited in Śikṣ as gzeṅs mtho ba): mahāvīryārambhavikrameṇa kāyacitta-

°haṃ janayan (Śikṣ saṃjanayamānaḥ) Gv 467.4, cited Śikṣ 277.9.

sampraghuṣṭa, ppp. (Skt. pra-gh°; cf. Pali sampaghosa), (**1**) *sounded*, of mus. instruments: tūryasahasraṃ °ṭaṃ Mv ii.308.14 (vs; v.l. praghuṣṭaṃ; metr. obscure); (**2**) *made resonant*: (jeṣṭha-māse...) -śukasārika-°ṭe LV 133.4 (vs); (**3**) *besung, praised*: bhuvi divi ca °ṭo jinu... LV 225.2 (vs).

sampracalati (cf. Skt. pra-cal-), (**1**) ppp., in (-saṃgīti)-sampracalite (sc. mahāvimāne), *stirred*, i. e. *made resonant* with song: LV 10.22 (Tib. glu dbyaṅs, = saṃgīti, len pa, *received, taken*); (**2**) otherwise noted only after corresp. forms of calati and pracalati, in same or similar passages to those of **sampragarjati**, q.v. (subject lokadhātu or pṛthivī), *shakes, quakes*: °lati Divy 158.8; °litaḥ, °litā, ppp., Mvy 3006; Samādh 19.6; Divy 250.22. In Mmk 74.6 sampracalitāḥ, ep. of certain mantras, is corrupt; read samaya- with some form of calita, as proved by Tib., cited Lalou Iconographie, 96.2, as dam chig (read dam tshig) gyos pa rnams kyi las (cf. samayaḥ Mvy 1438 = Tib. sṅags kyi skabs su dam tshig, perh. *conventional regulation in regard to the occasion of a mantra*). The prec. epithet in Mmk, printed samayagrastāḥ, is prob. to be read samayāgra-(sthāḥ?); Tib., l. c., dam chig (read tshig; = samaya) ñams pa (*height*).

sampracitrayati (cf. Skt. citrayati, also saṃ-citr°, Schmidt, Nachträge), *makes of variegated* or *nondescript color*: paṭaṃ vai °yet Laṅk 363.10 (vs), for monks' robes.

sampracchanna, adj.-ppp. (cf. Skt. pracchanna), *completely, properly clad*: (bhikṣūṃś ca samprāvṛtān) °nnān Divy 335.4.

sampracchedana, adj. or n. act. (to Skt. sam-pra-chid- plus -ana), *splitting, piercing*: (jñānam...) sarvaāvaraṇa-°naṃ Gv 56.2 (vs).

samprajanya, nt. (see also **a-saṃ**°; back-formation from MIndic, = Pali sampajañña, for *samprajānya from °**jāna**, q.v.), *consciousness, intelligence, mindfulness, clearheadedness, circumspection*; usually associated or compounded with its near-synonym smṛti (as in Pali with sati): described Śikṣ 120.11 ff. (following a description of smṛti 7 ff.); cpd. smṛti-saṃ° Śikṣ 120.5; 123.15; 190.14; 271.10; Bbh 139.22; Gv 410.3; closely associated with smṛti, Dharmas 119; Śikṣ 356.9; in Divy 654.27 and 655.3 read smṛtyā samprajanyenā 'pramādato yogaḥ karaṇīyaḥ (text has °janyetāpra°); not associated with smṛti, Gv 333.1 paramasamprajanyacāriṇī.

samprajāna, adj.-pres. pple. (thematization of Skt. °jānant), *conscious, mindful, thoughtful*; for instances see §§ 18.53 ff. Often follows **smṛta**, q.v. for a few exx.; so Pali sata sampajāna. Also samprajāna-(or °nan-)mṛṣāvādaḥ Mvy 9266 etc. (§ 18.53), *a deliberate lie*, = Pali sampajāna-musāvāda.

samprajñā (to Skt. sam-pra-jānāti; cf. prec.), *knowledge, intelligence*: su-°jñā-susamāhitaḥ LV 181.15 (prose; all mss.), *well intent on good intelligence*.

samprajvālana (nt.; to Skt. °jvālayati plus -ana), *a causing to shine forth*: (mahā-)dharmolkā-°naṃ (sc. kartum) SP 16.12 (prose).

sampratakṣṇoti, see **samparitakṣṇoti**.

sampratāḍana, nt. (cf. Skt. pratāḍayati; no *sampra-t° recorded), *beating* (of a drum): yac ca... dharmabherī-°naṃ AsP 137.2 (prose).

sampratigraha (m.? = Pali sampaṭiggaha, in Khud.p. comm. 100.2 vacana-saṃ°, *acceptance of something said*; wrongly defined PTSD), *acceptance*: vratisampratigrahāpadeśena Jm 37.24, *under pretext of acceptance* (of the proffered boon) *on the part of one* (viz. himself) *who had undertaken a vow*. (Speyer, Transl. 52 n. 2, follows Kern in emending vrati to vṛti, *boon*, = vara; but vṛti is known only in Skt. Lex. and seems unlikely to have been used in this prose passage; I see no difficulty in vrati-; pw 7.381 *gute Aufnahme, Vorliebe für Jmd*, not happily.) Cf. next.

sampratigrāhin, adj. or n. ag. (to Skt. sam-pratigrah- with -in; cf. prec.), *accepting, one who accepts*: taṃ nūnam agrasattvo hy agrāhuti-°hī LV 316.8 (vs), prob. *therefore surely the Supreme Being is accepting the supreme offering*. So Lefm. implies, by printing °huti-saṃ° as one word. In JAOS 57.22 I took the form as an aor. of °grāhayati (which is not recorded), in the mg. of °gṛhṇāti; this still seems to me possible, but I now prefer the interpretation given above.

sampraticchādana (nt.; cf. Skt. prati-cchādayati), *complete covering* or *shading*, as with a parasol (dharmacchattra, line 24): cittanagara-°na-prayuktena te... bhavitavyaṃ Gv 430.23.

samprati-jāta, adj. (= Pali sampati°), *just (now) born*: Mv i.220.9 = ii.22.10 (vs; °to Sugato); i.220.18, 19 = ii.23.3, 4 (vss); i.221.3, 4, 5 and ii.23.8, 10; 25.11 (prose); i.224.6 = ii.27.6 (vs).

sampratipūrṇa, adj.-ppp. (cf. Skt. pratipūrṇa), *completely filled* (with, in comp.): -bodhipakṣadharma-°ṇa- LV 9.5 (prose; no v.l.).

sampratimānayati (cf. Skt. pratimān°, and BHS id.), prob. *presents, bestows*, like **pratimānayati**, q.v.; with acc. of person and instr. of thing bestowed: (ātmānaṃ cānena dharmaśravaṇena) dharmāmṛtarasena saṃtarpayiṣyāmi °mānayiṣyāmi sampraharṣayiṣyāmi Suv 122.1, similarly 4; Tib. yaṅ dag par rim gro bgyi (*honor*, also *present, make offerings*, esp. to gods, saints, and priests).

sampratilabhate (cf. Skt. prati-l°), *attains*: sukhaṃ °te AsP 505.19 (prose).

? **samprativigacchati**, ppp. °**gata** (= **prativig**°, q.v.), (*is*) *scattered, dispersed, gone*: (yo 'sau) rūpayauvanamadaḥ saṃ°taḥ Av ii.25.10, ms.; Speyer em. sa prati°, with i.163.12, perh. rightly.

samprativedhaka, f. °**kī**, °**ikā**, °**ikī** (to Pali sampaṭivijjhati plus -aka, cf. Pali °vedha), *penetrating*; only in caturāryasatya-sampra°, cātur°, ep. of dharmadeśanā: °akī Divy 48.13; 52.23; 71.24; 75.24; 166.14; 310.27; °ikā Divy 199.2; 554.19; °ikī Divy 128.22 (v.l. °akī); 198.4; 462.10; 463.19; 580.12 (here satya is accidentally omitted in text); 617.3; Av i.64.13; 80.2, etc. (only this form seems to be noted in Av); MSV i.54.3 (cātur°), etc.

sampratīcchaka, adj. or n. ag. (to next plus -aka) = **sampratyeṣaka**, q.v.: -dharmamegha-°kā(ḥ) Gv 150.25.

sampratīcchati, °**te** (= Pali sampaṭi°, cf. Skt. pratī°; see also **sampratyeṣaka**, °**tyeṣaṇa**, °**tyeṣṭavya**), *receives*: °cchā (imperf.) LV 92.13 (vs); puṣpavarṣāṇi °cchanto Mv ii.152.10; sarvabodhisattva-°cchita-(ppp.)-jñānaḥ Mvy 366; °cchati Bbh 146.7; -dharmacakrāṇi °cchamānān Gv 534.13.

sampratīcchana (nt.), °**natā** (Pali sampaṭicchana; to prec. plus -ana-tā), *receipt, acceptance*: -dharmacakra-°cchanātṛptatāyai Gv 183.2; (-dharmamegha-)°na-saṃjñī 209.12; (-dharmamegha-)°natāyai 69.18; (id.)-natāsu 98.20; buddhadharma-°natāyai 189.26; etc.

sampratyayita, adj. (denom. pple. to Skt. sampratyaya; cf. Skt. pratyayita), *trusted, reliable*: °tasya vāntikāc chṛṇoti Bbh 13.25, *or hears from a trustworthy person*.

sampratyavekṣaṇa-tā (cf. **pratyave**°), *complete understanding, intellectual mastery*: dharma-°ṇatāyai saṃvartate LV 35.10 (prose).

sampratyeṣaka, adj. or n. ag. (to **sampratīcchati**, Skt. *sam-prati-iṣ-, plus -aka; cf. next two), *receiving, recipient*: -jñānāvavāda-°kaṃ (cittaṃ bodhisattvānāṃ) Dbh 11.23; tathāgatādhiṣṭhāna-°kaḥ (bodhisattvaḥ) 80.22; -dharmamegha-°kānāṃ bodhisattvānāṃ Gv 149.16.

sampratyeṣaṇa (nt.; as prec., q.v., with -ana), *reception*: tathāgatādhiṣṭhāna-°ṇa-taś ca Dbh 42.15; sarvameghavāri-°ṇātṛptitaś ca 97.12; -dharmamegha-°ṇāya

Gv 175.18; vimaladharmacakra-°ṇa-saṃdhāraṇa-kuśalānāṃ 261.18.

saṃpratyeṣṭavya (gdve. to **saṃpratīcchati,** q.v.), *to be received*: Gv 460.5 (see s.v. **abhisaṃbhinna**).

saṃpradarśana (nt.; to Skt. °darśayati plus -ana), *the making known, revealing, exhibiting*: sarvasattvakṣemagati-°na-prayogā (Bhvr.) Gv 304.18.

saṃpradālayati, °**leti** (= Pali saṃpadāleti), *splits, cuts* (off): (goghātako...) gāvīye śīrṣakapālaṃ dāleya °leya (opt.) Mv ii.125.4; śastreṇa aṅgam-aṅgāni chindetsuḥ °letsuḥ iii.258.15; °dālya (ger.)... kīlaṃ Mahāsamāj., Waldschmidt, Kl. Skt. Texte 4, 159, last line.

(? **saṃpranadahe,** LV 338.19, vs, seemingly 1 sg. fut. of Skt. saṃpraṇadati, but text very uncertain: § 31.20.)

saṃprapīta, ppp. (to *sam-pra-pibati), *eagerly drunk*, i. e. (fig.) *feasted upon*, with the eyes: padmānana-śrīśata-°taṃ... vaktram Divy 430.3 (vs).

saṃprapūra, adj. (= **prapūra,** q.v.), *full*: aṅgārakarṣū yatha °pūrā (so read) Mv ii.327.3 (vs); in 331.4 (vs) Senart aṅgārakarṣū paramā prapūrā, but the corrupt mss. may intend para(?) saṃprapūrā; tehi bhaveyā saha (so with mss. m.c. for **sahā,** q.v.) °pūrā 380.18 (vs); (rājadhānīṃ, by em....) nara-°pūrāṃ 389.16 (vs), *full of men.*

-saṃprabha, ifc. Bhvr. for saṃprabhā (root noun to Skt. sam-pra-bhā, *appear*), *appearance*: padma-pattrāṃśu-°bham... yogī... prapaśyate Laṅk 310.5 (vs), *something that has the appearance of*...

saṃprabhaṇati (to Skt. bhaṇati; unrecorded), *sounds* (trans., musical instruments; as if caus., lit. *makes to speak forth*): (yadā pramadaratanā...) turiyā...°bhaṇiṣu (aor.) LV 167.10 (vs); here could be m.c. for °bhāṇiṣu, as if to *-bhāṇayati. But cf. next.

saṃprabhaṇita, and °**bhāṇita** (nt.; orig. ppp. of prec.), *sound, resonance*: pañcāpsaraḥsahasrāṇi divyatūryasaṃgīti-°bhaṇitena bodhisattvamātaram upasaṃkramya LV 96.15 (prose); tūryasaṃgīti-°bhaṇitena mahatā gītavāditena 204.1 (prose; here could be adj. with °vāditena); tūryasahasra-°bhaṇite (so most mss.; read as one word, loc. abs., *in view of the sound of*...) pramadavaragaṇe (*and in view of the crowd of lovely houris*) LV 326.20 (vs); (koṭīśataṃ devaputrāṇāṃ tūryatāḍāvacara-)-saṃgīti-°bhaṇitenāvasthitam abhūt SP 405.6 (prose); -saṃgīti-°bhaṇitadharmasvabhāvopasaṃhitāni Gv 88.14 (prose); tāsāṃ madhyagataḥ Puṇyaraśmī rājakumāraḥ saṃgīti-°bhāṇitena RP 41.21 (prose), *and Prince P. moved in their midst to the sound of*...; (catvāro mahārājāḥ...) tūryatāḍāvacarasaṃgīti-°bhāṇitena (Lefm. °bhānitena)... pātrāṇi parigṛhya LV 383.19 (prose). Both °bha° and °bhā° seem well attested; the mg. must be the same.

saṃprabhāṣaṇa (nt.; to Skt. °bhāṣate plus -ana), *act of proclaiming*: sarvasūtrānta-°ṇa- Gv 222.9.

saṃprabhāsati (= Pali sampabhāsati), *shines*: Mv i.10.2 = iii.454.18 ekaiko (°ka) yojanaśataṃ ābhāye (i.10.2 corruptly ādāye) saṃprabhāsati (see s.v. **ādāye**).

saṃprabhīta, see **a-saṃ**°.

saṃpramathana, m. (*sam-pra-math-, cf. Pali sampamathita, plus -ana), *crusher*: mātā Mārabala-°nasya (sc. bodhisattvasya; so Senart em., mss. mālavara°) Mv i.149.9 (vs); kāyakali-°no nāma samādhiḥ Mvy 621.

saṃpramārjayati (Skt. only in mg. *washes*, but pramārj- in this mg. also), *strokes*: śīrṣaṃ °yanti sma Dbh 4.16 (prose).

saṃpramuñcana, adj. or n. act. (to Skt. °muñcati plus -ana; cf. **pramuñcana**), *sending forth*: (anantarucirapuṣpa-)-sumerumegha-°na-varṇā Gv 348.21.

saṃpramudita, adj.-ppp. (cf. Pali sampamodita), *delighted*: yadvac cāpsaragaṇāś ca °tā snigdhaṃ rutaṃ kurvate LV 283.5 (vs).

saṃpramuṣyate (pass. to sam-pra-muṣ-, otherwise not recorded as verb; cf. **a-saṃpramuṣita**), *is taken away* or *is lost*: Bbh 322.25 tad (sc. jñānam) api cā 'syai 'kadā saṃpramuṣyate; saṃpramoṣa-dharmo ca bhavati. [BR cite citta-saṃpramuṣita from Mvy; the ref. is doubtless to cittāsaṃpra° Mvy 803, see **asaṃpra**°.]

saṃpramoṣa(ṇa), see **a-saṃ**°.

saṃpraraṇati, *resounds greatly*, always after **praraṇati,** q.v. (same contexts): LV 318.21; 352.4; Dbh 98.32; Mvy 3015; Samādh 19.6.

saṃprarūḍha, ppp. (of *sam-pra-ruh-, unrecorded; = Skt. prarūḍha), *overgrown, covered* (with plants, comp.): hariṇatṛṇa-°ḍhaṃ Mv iii.79.18 (vs). Cf. next.

saṃpraroha (see prec.), *growth* (of plants): vasantakāle... saṃbhūtasasyoṣadhi-°he Gv 408.1 (vs).

saṃpravaṇa-tā, see **a-saṃ**°.

saṃpravarṇayate (cf. Pali ppp. saṃpavaṇṇita), *describes*: brahmacaryaṃ °yamānān Gv 86.3 (prose).

saṃpravartika, adj. (cf. Skt. °taka, °tin), *furthering, promoting*: sāvidyā kāraṇaṃ teṣāṃ cittānāṃ °tikam Laṅk 238.15 (vs).

saṃpravarṣaṇa (nt.?; to next plus -ana), *the act of raining down*: -kusumaugha-°ṇaṃ (Bhvr., acc.) Gv 435.1; -suvarṇacūrṇa-°ṇa- 511.11 (both prose).

saṃpravarṣati (cf. Skt. saṃpravṛṣṭa), *rains down* (trans.): °ṣi (aor.) divijaṃ kusumaṃ Mv i.146.9 = 203.10 = ii.7.6 (vs).

saṃpravāti (= Pali sampa°, Skt. pravāti), *blows fragrance*: puṣpitā vṛkṣā °vānti Mv iii.98.7 (vs).

saṃpravādayati (= Skt. pravād°; cf. Ved. and Gr. saṃpravadati), *makes to resound, sounds* (trans.), esp. of musical instruments; only in pass. and ppp.: °vādyanti, pres. pass. (mus. instr.), Mv i.308.12; °vādyetsu(ḥ), aor. pass., ii.160.19 (rutāni); iii.96.13; ppp. °dita, LV 85.16 (tūryāṇi °ditāni); 119.16 (nānātūrya-°ditena mārgeṇa, *way made resonant with*...); Mv ii.32.15 (°ditāni); so also Divy 357.16; 421.8; Sukh 77.2; Samādh 19.15 (tūryaśatebhyaḥ...°ditebhyo); RP 40.21 (°ditasya); also used as noun, see next.

saṃpravādita, nt. (orig. ppp. of prec., q.v.), *sound*: prabodhayanti ye 'grasattva (acc.) tūrya-°taiḥ LV 170.5 (vs); sārdhaṃ... nānātūryasaṃgīti-°tena 217.17 (prose); divyasaṃgīti-°tena 274.9; 366.14 (tathāgatasya pūjāṃ kṛtvā); -saṃgīti-°taiḥ pūjā karaṇīyā SP 232.3 (prose); śṛṇvantu te dundubhi-°taṃ Suv 23.13 (vs).

saṃpravāraṇa, nt. (to next plus -ana), *presentation*: (dharmadānena) sarvasattva-saṃtarpaṇaṃ dharmadāna-°raṇaṃ AsP 137.4.

saṃpravārayati (= Pali sampavāreti; cf. **pravārayati**), *presents, entertains*, with food: khādanīyaṃ bhojanīyaṃ dattvā °ritā(ḥ) Mv ii.423.4, *giving hard and soft food* (to them) *they were entertained*; otherwise noted only after parallel form of saṃtarpayati, which is preceded (in Divy and Av regularly by svahastaṃ, and everywhere) by khādanīya-(°yena)-bhojanīyena, or with addition of āsvādanīyena; so (khādanīyabhojanīy)āsvādanīyena saṃtarpya saṃpravārya LV 58.6; saṃtarpayitvā saṃpravārayitvā Mv i.38.8; iii.405.5; saṃtarpayati °vārayati (°vāreti) Mv iii.142.3, 14; Divy 65.6; 178.1; saṃtarpayet °vārayet Mv i.325.11; saṃtarpayi °vārayi (aor.) iii.257.10; saṃtarpya °vārya Divy 53.14; 65.8; Av i.64.11; saṃtarpitasya °vāritasya Śikṣ 208.2.

saṃpravutta, ppp. (semi-MIndic for Skt. saṃprokta; see **pravuccati**), *declared, said*: both edd. SP 129.10, 12 (vss); KN state that all Nep. mss. read saṃpravṛttā, which could be defended as a hyper-Sktism, but Kashgar rec. pravucyate (in 10 corruptly pramuc°); the mg. is confirmed by **129.14** and 130.4, close parallels, which read pravuccati (°te) or °cya°.

? **saṃpravṛtta,** see prec.

saṃpravedhati (= Pali sampa°; see s.v. **vedhati**; also **saṃpravyadhati**), *trembles, shakes extremely*; **usually**

after vedh° and pravedh°: LV 352.2; 411.1; Mv iii.256.7; 334.2; 341.5; Mvy 3009; Divy 250.23; 479.12; SP 6.1; 21.2; Samādh 19.6; Dbh 98.31.

saṃpraveśana (nt.; to Skt. saṃpraveśayati plus -ana), *the causing to enter*: tatrasthaḥ pālayan sattvān triyāna-°naiḥ Dbh.g. 54(80).18.

saṃpravyadhati = **saṃpravedhati**; see s.v. **vyadhati,** where citations (Divy only) are given.

saṃpraśaṃsā (cf. Skt. praśaṃsā), *laudation*: °sām abhyudīrayanti Sukh 48.14 (prose).

saṃpraśamana (cf. Skt. saṃpraśānta), *quieting, pacification, alleviation*: **sarvanirodhavirodha-°no** (q.v.) Mvy 606.

saṃpraśodhayati, *cleans up (thoroughly)*: hastapādau °dhya (ger.) MSV ii.129.17.

saṃprasava (m.? to Skt. sam-pra-sū-, cf. prasava), *birth*: °va-vikurvitāḥ sarvabodhisattvaguṇāś ca . . . śrūyate sma Gv 374.21 (! prose; cf. janma-vikurvitāni line 20–21).

saṃprasuptaka (= Skt. °supta), *sound asleep*: sarvanāriganī (loc.) °ke LV 236.1 (vs); -ka may be m.c.

saṃpraskandati (= Pali saṃpakkhandati, with loc. sotāpattiphale vā . . . arahatte vā °dati Miln. 35.27–29), lit. *leaps towards* or *into* (a religious state), *plunges into* or *strives towards, aspires to*: bodhisattvasya nirvāṇaśabdaṃ śrutvā nirvāṇasmiṃ eva manaṃ prasīde tiṣṭhe °nde (aor.) Mv ii.157.13.

saṃprasthāna, nt. (to Skt. sam-pra-sthā- plus -ana; unrecorded, except in Wilson's Dict.), *the setting out* (for), *starting* (towards; comp.): bodhisattvasya . . . prathamaṃ sarvajñatācittādhyāśaya-°naṃ pūrvaṃgamaṃ bhavati Gv 504.16.

saṃpraharṣaka, adj. (to Skt. °harṣayati plus -aka; Pali saṃpahaṃsana), *delighting, rejoicing* (trans.), assoc. with **samādāpaka, samuttejaka,** qq.v.: LV 436.2; SP 200.5.

saṃpraharṣaṇa, nt., **°ṇā,** f. (Skt. only °ṇa as adj., *geschlechtlich erregend*, pw; cf. Pali saṃpahaṃsana; to Skt. sam-pra-hṛṣ-, chiefly to caus. °harṣayati in mg.), *causing joy*, or *a thing that causes joy*: °ṇam Mvy 6831; °ṇāya Bbh 30.16, see s.v. **samātta,** *to cause them to delight* (in, loc.); kecit °ṇena paripākaṃ gacchanti Gv 541.7, *by something that causes joy*; (kāvyanāṭakākhyāna)-gāndharvetihāsa-°ṇāni Dbh 45.24, *things that cause joy, such as* . . .; sarvasattva-°ṇa-balaṃ Gv 246.26, *power of delighting all creatures*; fem., dānapati-°ṇāyām Jm 40.20, *in dealing with the joy* (or *causing of joy*?) *of generous givers.*

? **saṃprahārya(-jāta),** in Karmav 87.12 nityaṃ °jāto bhavati, one of the ten advantages derived from a gift of a bell (ghaṇṭāpradāna); Lévi, *on est toujours prêt au battement*(?); but his note cites Tib. rab tu dgaḥ bar ḥgyur ba, implying saṃpraharṣa-jāto, *characterized by joy*, which is prob. the true reading; text hardly interpretable.

saṃprāpaka, adj. (to caus. of Skt. sam-pra-āp-; = Pali saṃpāpaka), *causing to reach* or *attain* (this and related words, see next two items, seem to be always caus. in force in BHS and Pali): saddharmaṃ . . . nirvāṇa-°kaṃ LV 294.5 (vs); kalyāṇa-°kasya Suv 92.7 (prose).

saṃprāpaṇa (nt.) and **°ṇa-tā** (see prec.; contrary to PTSD, Pali saṃpāpana is caus. in Miln. 355.1 and 356.3), *the causing to reach* or *attain*: (-para-)sattva-°ṇa-kauśalyatvād LV 432.13 (prose); ekarutāt sarvaruta-°ṇa-svara(ḥ) (Bhvr.; Lefm. °na- with all mss. for °ṇa) 435.17; °ṇa- Mvy 785; -sarvajagat-°ṇatayā Gv 431.1, cited Śikṣ 123.8, *by causing all the world to attain* . . .; -ratnadvīpa-°ṇatāyai Gv 143.23, and °ṇatayā 463.19.

saṃprāpayitar, m. (see prec. two), *one who causes to attain* (with loc.): °tāraḥ sarvabuddhapādamūleṣu Gv 463.5.

saṃprāvṛta, adj., ppp. (= Pali saṃpāruta; Skt. prāvṛta), *completely clothed*: **bhikṣūṃś** ca °tān Divy 335.3; mss. sa-prā°, note suggests su-prā° with 336.5, but the foll. saṃpracchannān (q.v.) supports saṃ° (336.5 supracchannān).

saṃprekṣaṇa (nt.), **°ṇā** (to Skt. sam-pra-īkṣ- plus -ana), *the act of seeing, looking (upon), viewing*: °ṇena LV 309.4 (vs); °ṇa- 432.5 and 6 (prose); cakṣuḥ-°ṇām api na kṛtavān Av i.16.5 (prose), *didn't even give a look with the eyes.*

-saṃpremaka (cf. Skt. saṃpriya and preman), *a close friend*; implied by instr. sg. fem. adv. yathā-°mikayā MPS 13.8 (see s.vv. **saṃlaptaka, saṃstutaka**), *according as* (you have) . . .

saṃpreṣate (intending °khate? § 2.26, for °kṣate), *looks*: LV 206.2; Tib. bltas nas, *looking.*

saṃpreṣayati (like **preṣayati,** q.v.), with cittaṃ, *directs* the thought (with loc., *towards*): nirvāṇe ca cittaṃ °yati sma LV 180.10 (prose).

sambara, [(**1**) in kāya-, vāk-, manaḥ-s° Samādh p. 4 line 23, read **saṃvara,** q.v.;] (**2**) n. of a deity (cf. Skt. Śambara, n. of a demon?), associated (perh. identical?) with **Heruka**: Sādh 490.1 etc. See also s.v. **saṃvara** 4, 5.

Sambara-tantra (to prec., 2), n. of a work: Sādh 496.3.

sambala, nt., a high number: Mvy 7902 = Tib. dpag ḥbyam(s); cited from Gv, which (correctly) reads **samula,** m., q.v.

saṃbahula, adj., pl. only (= Pali id.), *many*; common in most texts, in prose as well as vss: SP 310.13; LV 4.13; 6.13; 160.3; 284.12; 379.19; Mv i.35.3, 8; 55.6, 10; 317.12; ii.31.9; 109.12; 257.8; 287.4; iii.323.5; Mvy 6267; 8362; Divy 91.13, 15; 93.3; 199.22; 351.3; 475.25; Jm 98.10; 203.15; Av i.73.1; 163.7; 346.10; Kv 1.6; Bbh 232.8; Sukh 2.14; Vaj 19.5, 11.

saṃbādha (in Skt., see pw 7 with App. and Schmidt, Nachträge, said to be limited to the *female privities*; in Pali those of both sexes, and so Tib. ḥdoms, mdoms), *the privities*: °dha-pradeśa Mvy 9329 = Tib. mdoms.

saṃbuddha, m. (= Pali id.; as if ppp. to **saṃbudhyate,** which however is rare in this mg.; prob. actually an intensive to Buddha, cf. **saṃbodhisattva, saṃbahula** etc.), *a perfectly enlightened one, a Buddha*: Mv i.77.9, 12; Suv 4.11; 11.8; 101.11 (all these vss); RP 47.19 (°dhò bhagavān, prose).

saṃbuddhi (= Pali id.; cf. prec. and next), *enlightenment*: anuttarāyāṃ (so mss.) samyaksaṃbuddhāya, or °yā, mss., Mv i.40.6; loc.; see § 10.142.

saṃbudhyate (in this specialized sense not recorded, even for Pali saṃbujjhati), *becomes perfectly enlightened, becomes a* (**saṃ**)**buddha,** q.v.: °dhyante kṛte yuge Laṅk 365.10 (vs).

saṃbodhaka (?) Śikṣ 35.4, or **°dhana,** Gv 462.20, adj. or n. ag. (to Skt. saṃbodhayati; °dhana, *awakening*, once in Skt., AMg. saṃbohaṇa), *one who makes aware, notifies, warns*: °dhanāni kalyāṇamitrāṇy akaraṇīyānāṃ Gv, cited Śikṣ as saṃcodakāḥ (mss., text em. saṃbo°) °mitrā akara°.

saṃbodhi (m. or f.; cf. prec. and foll. items; = Pali id.), *perfect enlightenment*: yāvat parama-°dhi-prāpto (so with mss.) Mv i.45.1 (prose), *until he attained* . . .; tathāgato . . . pūrve (em.) °dhim anabhisaṃbuddho Mv ii.136.14 (prose) and ff., *when he had not yet attained* . . .; °dhi-mārga RP 15.6 (vs); °dhi-prāptasya LV 35.9 (prose).

saṃbodhisattva (intens. to **bodhi**°; cf. prec. items), *one destined for supreme enlightenment, a Bodhisattva*; recorded only in vss: Mv i.92.10; LV 296.22; 297.8; 331.10; 343.8; Suv 41.10; Dbh.g. 14(350).14; Śikṣ 99.5 (to be kept with mss.; ed. em. sa bo°).

saṃbodhyaṅga, nt., = **bodhyaṅga,** q.v.

saṃbhakṣaṇa (nt.), *eating, devouring*: Gv 263.26 nānātiryagyonyupapannānāṃ sattvānāṃ anyonyasaṃbhakṣaṇa-bhaya-vinivartanatāyai; apparently *eating in common, feasting,* in cpd. ābhakṣaṇa-saṃ°, see s.v. **ābhakṣaṇa.**

Sambharāja (v.l. Sumbha°), n. of one of the ten krodha: Dharmas 11.

saṃbhavaka, adj. or n. ag., m.c. for saṃbhāvaka (to Skt. saṃbhāvayati plus -aka), *causing (one who causes) to come into being*: bhavate avidya napi saṃbhavako 'sya kaścit (mss.) LV 419.18 (vs), *ignorance comes to be, and there is no one who is its producer*; Tib. ḥbyuṅ byed.

Saṃbhavagiri, n. of a Buddha: Gv 258.26 (vs).

Saṃbhavā, n. of the world (lokadhātu) of the former Buddha Mahābhijñājñānābhibhū: SP 156.4.

saṃbhāra, m., *equipment* (as in Skt.); technically, sc. bodhi-saṃ° (cf. next, and in Pali Jāt. i.1 vs 5 anante bodhisaṃbhāre, not named), or °ro bodhisattvānāṃ Sūtrāl. xviii.38, *equipment for (those destined for) enlightenment*; consists of two things, puṇya and jñāna, acc. to Sūtrāl., Dharmas 117, and AbhidhK. LaV-P. vii.80–81; in LV 35.12 ff. four are named, each being a dharmālokamukha, viz. the above two plus śamatha and vidarśanā. See next.

[**saṃbhāraṇa** (nt.) = prec., q.v.: bodhisaṃbhāraṇaṃ (acc.) darśako Gv 528.15 (not named), *one who reveals the*...; but read with 2d ed. °saṃbhārāṇāṃ, gen. pl. of prec.]

saṃbhārikā (v.l. °īkā), a kind of musical instrument: °kāṃ (acc. sg.) Mv ii.159.5.

saṃbhāṣaṇa-tā, lit. *state of conversation*, in: tiryāṇa yonīṣu rutāni yāni anyonyasaṃbhāṣaṇatāṃ karonti SP 358.13 (vs), *the sounds which* (creatures) *in animal-existences make as mutual conversation*. Ed. says, 'read (°ṇa)-taḥ or -to, abl.', which seems unnecessary; apposition.

saṃbhinatti (Kashgar rec. saṃbhindati), *joins, associates with, comes to*: tathāgato ... asmān upekṣate (*neglects us*) na saṃbhinatti (*does not deal with us*; Tib. ma brtol) nācaṣṭe (*and does not tell us*; direct quotation of his words follows) SP 109.6 (prose). So essentially Burnouf, Kern, and BR; it is a strange use of sam-bhid, but I have been unable, despite much study, to find a more likely mg. The Tib. brtol is also not clear to me (said to mean *penetrate*; *reach, arrive, be present*).

saṃbhinna, adj., ppp. (= Pali id.; hardly in these mgs. in Skt.), *mixed* in sense of *confused*, see foll. items; **a-saṃbhinna,** (**1**) *unmixed, unadulterated, pure*: Gv 38.14 (jñāna); 45.8–9 (praṇidhāna, jñāna, sattvasaṃgrahaprayoga); SP 473.8 (tathatā, *unadulterated truth*); (**2**) *indistinguishable from, identical with* (instr.): sarvabuddhair asaṃbhinnaṃ sarvatathāgatair (dharmacakraṃ) LV 423.14 (so Tib., omitting sarvabuddhair, de bzhin gśegs pa thams cad daṅ dbyer med pa).

saṃbhinna-pralāpa, m. (cf. prec.; in Pali corresp. to sampha-ppalāpa, the prior member of which is obscure), *confused, senseless talk*; defined Śikṣ 74.1–2 (vss) pūrvottarābaddhapadaṃ nirarthakam asaṃgataṃ, abaddhaṃ ... proktaṃ; occurs exclusively, or nearly so, as one of the ten akuśala **karmapatha,** q.v.; **abaddha-pralāpa,** q.v., used once instead; Mvy 1694 = Tib. tshig bkyal ba, or ṅag ḥkhyal ba, *talking nonsense*; Mv ii.99.9; Divy 302.8; Gv 155.17; Śikṣ 73.15; 172.1; Dbh 24.18; Bbh 168.16; 304.17; Karmav 79.10. See next.

saṃbhinna-pralāpika, and **°pin,** adj. (to prec. plus -ika, -in), *talking confusedly, senselessly*: °pika Divy 301.24; °pin Bbh 168.19; Gv 352.18.

saṃbhinna-vyañjana, nt., or **°nā,** adj. or subst. (= Pali saṃbhinnā, Vin. ii.271.26; cf. **saṃbhinna**), *a hermaphrodite* of a special type, *whose sex organs are not clearly either male or female*: °nam Mvy 9514, °nā 8927, = Tib. gle (on 8927 also sle) gdams (also ḥdams, ḥthams) pa, cf. Das gle ḥdams ma (2) *hermaphrodite* (so Jap. on 9514; Chin. on 8927 *a male without a penis*); vyañjanaṃ (of the woman candidate for initation) pratyavekṣitavyam, mā avyañjanā ubhayavyañjanā saṃbhinna-°nā veti Bhīk 11a.4; mā (sc. asi) °nā 16a.5 (in the formal questioning of the initiate).

saṃbhuṇati (= Pali id.; see **abhi-saṃ°**), *gets, attains*: read na saṃbhuṇanti Mv i.41.6 with v.l. (most mss. na bhuṇanti, Senart em. nābhisaṃ°); (tṛṇāni na) °ṇanti i.328.2, repeated in 17 (where subject is bhikṣū, mss., misunderstood and em. by Senart); pakṣī pi kiṃnarāṇāṃ gatiṃ na °ṇanti ii.107.13–14, *even birds do not attain*...; on ii.130.9, 12, °ṇanti or abhisaṃ°, see s.v. **ettāvat-**; taṃ kuha nāma °ṇiṣyasi (mss. °ti) iii.264.14.

saṃbhuta (m.c. for Skt. °ūta), *originated* etc.: LV 419.9; Gv 255.12; Śikṣ 347.8 (all vss).

[**saṃbhuva,** or acc. to Senart saṃbhū (acc. sg. °bhuvaṃ), *association, social relations*: so Senart, with 2 mss., yogācārehi sārdhaṃ °vaṃ kurvanti Mv i.120.9 (prose). The mg. is certain, and Skt. saṃbhava has it; so however have Skt. saṃstava and Pali saṃthava, and the 4 other mss. point rather in this direction, suggesting a reading *saṃstuvaṃ. Prob. read saṃstavaṃ.]

saṃbhūta, m. Mvy 7794; or nt. 7923 (cited from Gv); Gv 106.18; 134.2–3, a high number.

saṃbhedana (adj. or subst.? to sam-bhid- plus -ana), *confusion, mixture, contamination*, or (adj.) *confusing* etc. (see **saṃbhinna**): asaṃbhinna-pāramiteyaṃ bhagavan sarvadharmāsaṃbhedanatām (a-saṃ°) upādāya AsP 206.11.

saṃbhoga-kāya, m., *'enjoyment-body'*: Mvy 117. Contrasts with **dharma-k°** and **nirmāṇa-k°**; see s.v. **kāya,** end. In Sūtral. ix.60 and 61 sāṃbhogyaḥ (or, comm., °gikaḥ) kāyaḥ; comm. on 60 says, °giko yena parṣanmaṇḍaleṣu dharmasaṃbhogaṃ karoti; Lévi, *passionnel*. Not in AbhidhK. Index. See Mus, Barabudur (II) 648 ff. (*corps communiel*; or, 650, *corps glorieux*; Mus finds it, not named, in SP). Perhaps saṃbhogo Laṅk 314.2 refers to this; cf. Suzuki, Studies, 145, and see **niṣyanda-buddha.**

saṃbhramaṇa (cf. Skt. sambhrama), *excitement*: MSV iv.247.20.

saṃmata, see **ratna-saṃ°**. (In Mv i.348.8 read with v.l. **Mahāsaṃmata,** q.v.)

saṃmataka, adj., f. **°ikā** (Skt. saṃmata with -ka, prob. specifying), (*one that has been*) *agreed upon*: MSV i.235.5 (kalpika-śālā ...) °tikā (sc. by the community of monks). The context is that of Pali Vin. i.240.3, where this word in acc. sg. is represented by sammutin (ti); cf. SBE 17.121 (the note 1 on p. 120 is wrong as to ussāvana, which = ussāpana; MSV i.235.4 ucchrīyamāṇāntikā, *whose confines* [anta-ka] *are being erected*).

Saṃmataraśmi, n. of a former Buddha: Mv i.139.12.

saṃmantrita (nt.; orig. ppp. of Skt. saṃmantrayati), *plan*: (sa tvaṃ) Śāriputra bodhisattva-°tritena bodhisattvarahasyeneha mama pravacana upapannaḥ; sa tvaṃ Śāriputra bodhisattvādhiṣṭhānena tat paurvakaṃ caryāpraṇidhānaṃ bodhisattva-°tritaṃ bodhisattvarahasyaṃ na samanusmarasi SP 64.12–14; *the bodhisattva-plan and bodhisattva-mystery* are connected, obviously, with the earlier caryā-praṇidhāna, and like it are Śāriputra's own (in a former birth), not Śākyamuni's; Burnouf and Kern misunderstand.

[**saṃmarjitaka,** see **samarji°**.]

[**saṃmā-pariṇāmāye,** with MIndic sammā for Skt. samyak, is only Senart's em. at Mv i.211.7, and is quite surely wrong; see s.v. **ṛtu-pariṇāma.**]

saṃmāyati (as in Skt. Dhātup., 4th class pres. to sam-mā-; not recorded otherwise), *is equal to* (instr.): gaṇikāvīthijanena °ti (so one ms. correctly; Senart em. wrongly) Mv ii.173.12, *it* (the crowd) *was equal* (in number) *to the people of the harlot's street*. Perhaps merely pass. of sam-mā-, with act. ending, lit. *is equated*; but māyet AsP 157.19 supports a māyati = Skt. māti, act.

saṃmiñjana (nt.; to next with -ana), *contraction, bending back* (of members of the body): na ca °na-prasāraṇam akarot LV 256.21, *and he* (the Bodhisattva, practising austerities) *made no contraction or extension* (of his members, presumably his arms, specifically).

saṃmiñjayati (= Pali °jeti, also written samiñjeti; connected with **un-minj-, ni-miñj-,** and prec. and next; in mss. and edd. also written samiñj-, but incorrectly, see below), *bends back, draws in, contracts,* parts of the body, esp. the arms; always assoc. with its opposite prasārayati (Skt.), *extends*: saṃmiñjitaṃ (vā) bāhuṃ (in Mv oftener °tāṃ ... bāhāṃ) prasāraye(t, once °yeya) prasāritaṃ (vā, or ca) bāhuṃ (the noun may be omitted; Mv oftener °tāṃ ... bāhāṃ) saṃmiñjaye(t) Mv i.55.1, 14; 56.8; iii.425.15, 22; 450.16; Mmk 3.26; Divy 473.6; Waldschmidt, Kl. Skt. Texte 4, 65.20 (Śakrapraśnasūtra, acc. to p. 5, ms. saṃmiñcita, but text prints saṃmiñj°); 157.18 (Mahāsamāj.); (yato care yato tiṣṭhe yato āse yato śaye, so Senart em.,) yato saṃmiñjaye kāyaṃ yato kāyaṃ prasāraye Mv iii.422.(16–)17 (so Senart, em., but prob. rightly), in a description of a bhikṣu, *whenever he draws in or extends* (any member of) *his body*. Leumann, Album Kern 393 f., adopts an earlier suggestion of Kern's and derives from sam-vṛj-. He rightly distinguishes this verb from Pali sam-iñjati (Dhp. 81, na samiñjanti paṇḍitā), *is moved, is perturbed*; cf. BHS **iñjate.** But when Leumann states that this sam-iñjati, in its Pali mg., is also found in BHS, I fear that he was speaking carelessly. The only cases of sam-iñj- which I have noted are shown by association with forms of prasār- to be false readings for saṃmiñj-; such cases also occur in Pali (PTSD). The only 'confusion' shown by BHS in this sept consists in the erroneous writing of samiñj- for saṃmiñj- (which Leumann also recognizes). Leumann's etym. seems to me at least more plausible than any other, including that of Lüders (s.v. **samarjana**). That double mm (or ṃm), not single m, is the only correct form is proved by un-miñj- and ni-miñj-, neither of which occurs in Pali; Leumann considers them (as he must according to his etymology) secondarily abstracted from saṃ-miñj-. I have found no trace of the sept elsewhere.

saṃmiñjita (also miswritten **samiñj°**), (**1**) ppp. to prec., q.v.; (**2**) subst. (presumably nt.) = **saṃmiñjana,** *bending back, retraction,* of parts of the body, esp. the arms; always assoc. with its opposite **prasārita,** q.v.: (parvahetukaṃ) saṃmiñjita-(text samiñj°)-prasārita-karma Bbh 97.21, *the action of retraction and extension is caused by the joints* (presumably refers to the arms); °te prasārite (along with other bodily movements), sc. saṃprajānacārī (so ms.) bhavati, Śikṣ 120.14, cited from 'Prajñāpāramitā', cf. very similar passage ŚsP 1429.1 containing °te prasārite; °ta-prasārita, with other bodily movements of monks or pratyekabuddhas, all described as prāsādika, *serene* (referring prob. especially to motions of the arms, but perhaps of other members too), Mv i.301.6; iii.60.6; 182.13; similarly Śikṣ 215.9; LV 191.17; °tena prasāritena (in virtually the same formula) LV 240.3.

[**saṃmitaṃ,** error in Kv for **samitaṃ,** q.v.]

saṃmiti, f. (cf. Skt. saṃmita; to sam-mā-; in this mg. recorded only in Pāṇ. 4.4.135 saṃmitau, for which Kāś. notes a var. samitau), *equality*: brahmalokaṃ tato yāti anyāṃ vā devasaṃmitim Mmk 140.22.

saṃmilāyati, and ppp. °**lāta** (see also **saṃmlāna;** to Skt. *sam-mlā-, unrecorded; Pali sammilāta), *withers* (intrans.): °yetsuḥ (opt.) Mv ii.178.8; °lāta ii.126.4, 5, etc., as under **āmilāta,** q.v.

saṃmukha, adj., ep. of gāthā, only in Mv (replaced elsewhere by °**kham,** adv., but once like it assoc. with **sārūpya,** q.v.), (spoken) *face to face* (not *passend, den Umständen angemessen,* pw 7.381, citing only passages with saṃmukham, adv.): bodhisattvaṃ ... saṃmukhābhiḥ sārūpyābhir gāthābhiḥ abhistave Mv ii.266.1; °khābhir gāthābhir abhistave iii.345.17; with omission also of the word gāthābhiḥ, bhagavantaṃ °khābhir adhyabhāṣe Mv i.174.2. Cf. °**kha-vinaya,** and °**kham,** °**khā(t).**

saṃmukham, adv. and postpos. (cf. prec.; used in Skt. in somewhat similar but, it seems, not quite identical ways), (**1**) adv., *in personal presence,* without dependent noun: replacing adj. **saṃmukha,** q.v., with gāthā, as in ābhiḥ sārūpyābhir gāthābhiḥ °kham (note position, which is very exceptional but significant, proving that saṃmukham has no dependent) abhiṣṭutya SP 162.8; bhagavantaṃ °kham ābhir gāthābhiḥ ... 161.4; 166.4, and similarly 166.12; 170.6; 172.15; LV 361.14; 362.19; 364.17; Mv iii.343.14 (read with mss.); Sukh 7.9; Bhagavatā (in Av Ānandena) sārdhaṃ °khaṃ ... kathāṃ vyatisārya Divy 70.10; 619.1; Karmav 29.17; Av i.229.2; saṃmukhaṃ me bhadanta Bhagavato 'ntikāc chrutaṃ °kham udgṛhītam Divy 206.28, *from the Lord in person I heard and received*; the position of saṃmukham in this Divy passage seems to prove that it is a pure adv., without dependent, also in bhagavato 'ntikāt °khaṃ śrutvā SP 69.7, and (with slight variations) 70.12; 100.2; 222.9; doubtless so interpret also śāstu saṃmukhaṃ śāṇaṃ pāṃśukūlaṃ pratigrahe Mv iii.54.15 (repetition 16), (Kāśyapa) *received from the Teacher* (prob. abl., śāstu) *face to face a robe* ...; (**2**) postpos. with gen., *in the presence (of)*: so prob. (cf. s.v. **saṃmukhā** 1) bhagavato saṃmukhaṃ pratiśrutvā °khaṃ pratigṛhītvā (so with 1 ms., Senart em. wrongly) Mv ii.257.15, *having heard and accepted it in the Lord's own presence* (but possibly *from the Lord, in his presence,* as in Divy 206.28 above); bahudharmaḥ śruto 'smābhir lokanāthasya saṃmukhaṃ SP 70.3 (vs); naigamajānapadānāṃ ca °khaṃ evaṃ saṃśrāvayet 108.8 (prose); me ... °kham 342.1 (vs), *in my presence*; (**3**) with a verb of giving, *to,* with loc. or gen.: dadanti dānāni ... jineṣu °kham SP 13.11 (vs), *they give gifts to the Jinas*; virtually same phrase with jināna °kham 13.14, and sugatāna °kham 13.16 (vss).

saṃmukha-vinaya, m. (= Pali saṃmukhāvi°, MN ii.247.10 ff., explained), *procedure in the presence of* (an assembly of all the monks in the chapter), one of the 7 **adhikaraṇaśamatha**: Mvy 8631. (In Pali saṃmukhā = BHS °khāt, see next.) In MSV ii.207.7 f. represented by saṃmukhakaraṇīyaṃ karma.

saṃmukhā(t), adv. (abl. of °kha; = Pali °khā), (**1**) *from (the presence of),* with gen. (cf. **saṃmukham,** 2): bhagavato °khā śrutvā °khā pragṛhītvā Mv i.319.6; śrutaṃ hi mayā mahābrahmaṇo °khād ... iii.217.8; 218.4 and (om. mahā) 17 (mss. always brāhm°); (**2**) *in the presence of,* with gen. (so also Pali, Miln. 28.6): evaṃ Bhagavāṃ Uruvilvā-kāśyapasya saṃmukhā (v.l. °khāt) trayo bhrātarāṃ ... vinayesi Mv iii.428.9; similarly 429.11 °kāśyapasya saṃmukhā (but here mss. pramukhā; Senart's note suggests reading in both places °Kāśyapa-pramukhā, *of whom K. was the chief*; there were, in fact, only three brothers, counting U.-K., and perhaps Senart's suggestion is right).

? **saṃmudita,** possibly to be read for samudita, *delighted,* in ālaya-sa° Mv iii.314.3, 4; but see s.v. **samudita.**

saṃmula, see **samula.**

saṃmūḍhaka, adj. or subst. m. (Skt. saṃmūḍha, plus -ka; in what mg.? svārthe?), *stupefied*: °kaś ca kālaṃ karoti Karmav 42.4 (prose); a preceding lacuna, and omission in Tib., make it hard to define the force of the suffix.

[**saṃmṛśati,** by em. Mv i.359.2, 6, *meditates on* (so Pali sammasati); but see s.v. **saṃspṛśati.**]

saṃmodate, °**dayati** (= Pali saṃmodati), *carries on a salutatory* or *greeting conversation with*; it involves inquiry into the health and well-being of the other person, cf. Pali MN comm. i.110.5 ff.: rarely with acc. of person, na tāḥ saṃmodayej jātu kauśalyaṃ sādhu pṛcchitum SP 280.1 (vs), *he should not engage at all in conversation with* *them to ask kindly after their welfare*; usually with instr. plus sārdhaṃ, devaiḥ sārdhaṃ ālapāmi saṃlapāmi saṃmode (1 sg. pres. mid.) Bhīk 26b.3, cf. in 4 devā api mayā sārdhaṃ ālapanti saṃlapanti pratisaṃmodante (see this; here prati clearly = *in return*, as in Pali, e. g. Miln. 25.4); the implication seems to be that despite the instr. with sārdhaṃ which regularly precedes, the verb saṃmodate, °dayati does not in itself involve *mutual* greetings, but only those of the subject to another person; also with cognate acc. (after instr. plus sārdhaṃ, or rarely saha) saṃmodanīyāṃ kathāṃ saṃmodayitvā, *having carried on* (such) *a salutatory conversation*, Mv iii.47.17; 60.11; 206.1; 208.12; 325.13; 394.13; 443.18, always followed by sārāyaṇīyāṃ kathāṃ vyatisārayitvā (or the like), see these words. In similar phrases kṛtvā, or another ger., may be substituted for saṃmodayitvā, see s.v. **saṃmodana.**

saṃmodana, f. °**nī,** adj. (to prec.; Pali °na as subst.), *salutatory, containing polite inquiries about the welfare* of the person addressed: vividha-°na-kathām upasaṃskṛtya (v.l. upasaṃhṛtya, but Mironov °skṛtya) Mvy 6272; vāk °nī Bbh 217.7, and in sequel; after instr. with sārdhaṃ (see under prec.), vividhāṃ °nīṃ kathāṃ kṛtvā LV 405.6; (after instr. with sārdhaṃ; most passages add saṃmukhaṃ) °nīṃ saṃrañjanīṃ vividhāṃ kathāṃ vyatisārya Divy 70.10; 75.22; 156.19; 619.1; Av i.229.2; ii.140.4; Karmav 29.17; same with upasaṃgṛhya for vyatisārya SP 261.6; with kṛtvā for vyati° and vividhāṃ before saṃmod° LV 409.1. See also next.

saṃmodanīya, adj. (= Pali id.), = prec.: °yaḥ Mvy 2942 (after saṃrañjanīyaḥ 2941); f. °yā, with kathā, Mv repeatedly, see s.v. **saṃmodate, °dayati.** In Karmav 27.1 text substitutes sukha-saṃbhāvanāyāṃ, which might be em. to °bhāvanāṃ, *causing pleasure*; but this is otherwise unrecorded in this cliché, and Lévi suggests in a note saṃmodanīyāṃ.

saṃmodika, adj. or subst. m. (cf. prec. items), (*one who is*) *on terms of friendly greetings* with another, *intimate, close friend*: °dikā priyamāṇā (n. pl.) Mv i.231.19; iii.57.4 (v.l. both times °ditā); °dikasya RP 31.8; (mātur vā pitur vā) jñāter vā °dikasya (so WT with K′ and v.l. in KN, who read °ditasya) vānyasya vā saṃstutasya kasyacit SP 346.1.

saṃmoṣa, saṃmoṣaṇa(-tā), see **a-saṃ°.**

saṃmlāna, ppp., = **saṃmilāta,** see **°lāyati**: LV 254.15, 16 (same passage as Mv ii.126.4, 5).

samya, see **śamya.**

samyak, (**1**) *right, proper*, in rāśiṃ samyak (for Skt. samyañcam; acc. m.) Mv i.175.16 (vs) = **samyaktvaniyata rāśi,** qq.v.; (**2**) (= Pali samma, which corresp. in use to Skt. saumya, falsely Sktized by confusion with Pali sammā, AMg. samma, = Skt. samyak), interj. of friendly address, *friend, comrade*: samyag Jyoti(ṣ)pāla Mv i.319.18; 320.1, 13, 19, etc., said by the potter Ghaṭikāra to his friend J.

samyaktva-niyata, see s.v. **rāśi.**

Samyaktvamithyātvasarvasaṃgrasana (see s.v. **rāśi**), m., n. of a samādhi: Mvy 605; ŚsP 1424.18 (in 16 misprinted °mithyatva°).

samyak-pradhāna, °prahāṇa, see the second members.

samyaksaṃbuddha, m. (= Pali sammā-saṃ°), *a perfectly enlightened one, a Buddha*: passim, e. g. Mvy 5; Mv i.80.4; 96.9, 12; Senart, i note 404, alleges that this stem is used for **samyaksaṃbodhi**; most of his instances are dubious or false (e. g. his two SP citations are read °buddhatvaṃ, not °buddhaṃ, in KN); but in Mv ii.311.8 the mss. are cited as reading °buddhāye (dat., = °bodhaye; prose).

samyaksaṃbodhi, f. (cf. prec.; = Pali sammā-saṃ°), *perfect enlightenment*, = (saṃ)bodhi: passim; (anuttarāṃ) °dhim abhisaṃbuddho Mv i.229.11, 13; ii.133.11; anuttarāye °bodhaye cittam utpādayiṣyāmi i.233.9, 12; °rāye °dhaye vyākārṣīt i.239.6; °tarāṃ °dhim abhisaṃbuddhe ii.285.3; °tarāṃ °dhim abhisaṃbhotsye Av i.171.15; °tarāyāṃ °dhau ... Mvy 6355 (abhisaṃbuddhaḥ); Divy 50.11 (cittāny utpāditāni).

? **samyag-avabodhi** (m. or f.; Pali and Skt. record only avabodha, m., not °dhi; no v.l. here in Kyoto ed. of Mvy; but Mironov °bodhaḥ without v.l.), *perfect enlightenment*: Mvy 2885 °dhiḥ.

samyag-ājñā, see s.v. **ājñā.**

samyagdṛṣṭi, (**1**) f. (= Pali sammādiṭṭhi), *true opinion, orthodox views*; as first stage in the noble eightfold path (mārga): Mvy 997; opp. of mithyādṛṣṭi, Mv ii.99.11; others, Mv ii.132.12; 284.2; (**2**) Bhvr., *one who holds right views* (= next): °ṭiḥ, n. sg., Dbh 25.7; °ṭayaḥ, pl., Divy 302.9.

samyagdṛṣṭika, adj. (Pali sammādiṭṭhika; = prec., 2), *holding right opinions*: Mv ii.132.12; 284.2.

[**samyag-namana-patha-** Gv 227.3, read samyaggamana°.]

samyag-vadamāna, m. (= Pali sammā-vad°, SN ii.221.22, 25), *one who speaks correctly, truthfully*: (sace ..., or evam eva ..., etc.) °nā vadetsuḥ Mv iii.54.14, 15, 17; 55.2.

[**sayathīme,** text in Śikṣ 290.11, corrected in Bendall and Rouse, Transl., 264 n. 2, to sa ya ime; cf. text 291.5.]

-sayyaka, see **manuṣya-raha-śayyāka.**

sayyathāpi (nāma), see s.v. **yathāpi** 2 and 3.

sayyathāpīdaṃ, once (Mv iii.283.8) for **yathāpīdaṃ,** see **yathāpi** 1.

sayyathīdaṃ, v.l. often **sadya°,** rarely **tadyathedaṃ** (Mv i.49.3 imāni sapta ratnāni abhunsuḥ tadyathedaṃ, cakraratnaṃ etc.), once **saṃyathīdaṃ,** q.v. (except this last, only noted in Mv; = Pali seyyathīdaṃ; cf. also **sayyathāpi** s.v. **yathāpi** 3; in Skt. tad yathā, which is also used in BHS, e. g. Mv i.261.15 tad yathā (*namely, to wit*) so 'pi mahājanakāyo, the persons composing the 'crowd' being listed in the preceding; Senart's note is inaccurate), *namely, to wit, viz.*: catvāri dvīpāni, sayyathīdaṃ (so most mss., Senart °idaṃ), jambudvīpaṃ pūrvavidehaṃ (etc.) Mv i.49.6; common in Mv, e. g. i.228.16; 249.11, 13; ii.116.4, 6, etc.; 132.17; 158.15 (v.l. sadya°, so in the next eight), 18; 280.16; 281.2, 8, 14; 282.2; 284.8; 285.3; iii.229.7; 232.5; 264.12; 331.18. Cf. **yad idam, yad uta.**

sara, nt. (Skt. Lex., m.; Pali id. in cpd. sīghasara, uddhaṃsara, Sn 3, 901), *going, course*: (te satpuruṣā ye ...) tathāgatacaṅkramaṇāni dharma-sarāṇi ca paśyanti Kv 13.15 (prose). In LV 329.5 (vs) kāmasarāhatāḥ, *struck with the arrows of love* (so Tib., ḥdod paḥi mdaḥ yis phog pa), sara (no v.l.) = Skt. śara.

saraṭa, m. (see under next), a high number: Mvy 7769 = Tib. brjod yas.

saraḍa, m. (= prec.; cited Mvy 7898 as **sarala,** nt., = Tib. brjod yas; in Gv 106.12, m. or nt., -śaraḍasya, gen.), a high number: Gv 133.23 (this seems prob. the orig. form).

sa-raṇa, adj. Bhvr. (see **raṇa,** and **a-raṇa**), *affected by impurity, passion, depravity*: Mvy 618; 2158; sabhayāḥ saraṇāḥ sādīnavāḥ sadoṣā(ḥ) LV 213.1 (prose). In SP 112.6 (vs) sa śuṣyate parasaraṇeṣu, *he withers in the houses of others* (so Tib. gzhan gyi khyim na), saraṇa = Skt. śaraṇa (rightly Burnouf; wrongly Kern).

sarati (= Pali id.; MIndic = Skt. smarati), *is mindful, thoughtful*: read, practically with mss., no rajyatī no saratī na thīnaṃ Mv iii.284.5 (vs; with other MIndicisms, **thīnaṃ,** and in prec. line **aññāya** q.v., or mss. **anyāya**), *he is not impassioned, is not mindful* (of worldly things), *has* (or, *there is*) *no torpor*; in Pali SN i.126.28 na kuppati na sarati ve (v.l. omits ve) na thīno (text thino); comm. i.187.23 f. dosena na kuppati rāgena na sarati mohena na thīno.

? **sarabū** (Pali id., Vin. ii.110.18; Jāt. ii.147.11; PTSD cites only °bhū), *lizard*: perhaps (as suggested in Senart's note) read sarabūṇāṃ vā (gen. pl.) Mv i.20.6; 23.2, before undurūṇāṃ vā, in a list of animals; mss. very confused; Senart's text em. kiṃpuruṣ(ak)āṇāṃ, supposed to mean *monkey* (which is unsupported and implausible).

Sarabhaṅga, see **Śara°**. The colophon Mv iii.375.12 reads Sarabhaṃgajātakam in Senart (v.l. Śara°).

sarala, nt., = (and cited from) **saraḍa**, q.v.

Saralaka (cf. Skt. sarala, *a pine tree*: Sarala, n. of a mountain, Kirfel, Kosm. 97), n. of a mountain: MSV ii.28.11; Tib. thaṅ śiṅ can gyi ri, *mount of pines*.

sarasarāyate, onomat. (cf. Pali sarasaraṃ, *a rustling sound*, karissāmi MN i.128.26; AMg. sarasara, m., a sound made by a snake, sarasarassai, *makes* such *a sound*), prob. *rustles*: °rāyamāṇa-mālā-samāyuktānāṃ (kumārīṇāṃ) Kv 30.13, *wearing rustling garlands* (acc. to pw *constantly moving to and fro*). May be MIndic for svara-svarā°; see s.v. **svarasvara**.

Sarasvatī, n. of a yakṣiṇī: Sādh 561.2; 562.5.

Saraha, n. of an author: (with honorific -pāda) Sādh 80.18; 83.4.

sa-rātrim, °tram, adv. (cf. sa-rātri, Pāṇ. 6.3.85; saratti = sahasā Deśīn. 8.2), *in the same night*, or perhaps better *while it was still night*: sa sārthaḥ °trim eva ... saṃprasthitaḥ Divy 5.25 (cf. 27 sa sārthas tāvad gato yāvat prabhātaṃ); sarātram eva MSV i.263.15; 264.5; iii.138.5.

Sarāpura, v.l. for **Sārapura**, q.v.

Sarāvatī, n. of a city and river: Divy 21.26, 27 (v.l. sarvā°, savārā°). Corresponds to Pali Sallavatī (or Saḷa°, Salala°, ? Salaḷa°), see Vin. i.197.23 with crit. app., and DPPN s.v. Salaḷavatī (a form which I do not know in the texts).

sarita (ppp. to Skt. sarati?), (**1**) adj., *fluent*, f. saritā, in a list of epithets of Buddha's voice or speech: Mvy 496; Sūtrāl. xii.9, comm.; Chin. *in constant flow* (Lévi, note to text, p. 80); Tib. on Mvy rgyun chags pa, *made continuous*; (**2**) adj., perhaps *passing constantly* or *rapidly away*, of worldly joys: Ud iii.5 saritāni vai snehitāni vai saumanasyāni bhavanti jantunaḥ (same word in Pali same vs, Dhp. 341; PTSD *gone, set in motion*; comm. anusaṭa, payāta; the former is doubtfully interpreted as *diffuse, extravagant*, CPD); (**3**) subst., m. or nt., *drinking-cup*: saritena (or **śar°**) Bhīk 29a.1, 5; see s.v. **kāyabandhana**; Tib. cited as phor bu, *drinking cup*, which renders BHS (and Skt.) sarakam Mvy 8956.

saritā (= Pali id., Skt. sarit), *river*: sa-nagara-nigama-saritā ... vasumatī Mv i.83.3; saritālayaṃ, *ocean*, Mmk 66.9; fig. applied to desire or greed (as in Pali, Sn 3 etc.; cf. **latā**), MSV iii.54.2; 57.16.

? **sarj(j)ara**, v.l. **sajjira**, some fragrant substance: °ra-gandham eva ca Sādh 411.10 (vs).

sarpiḥ-pradyotika, adv. °kaṃ (vā ... dīpyamānasya), *with lamps of butter* or the like: Śikṣ 182.2–3, after **taila-pradyotikaṃ** (q.v.) ..., in a list of tortures.

[**sarpisaro** LV 174.3 (vs), editorial error for sarpaśiro, *snake's head*, as in citation Śikṣ 204.13, and Tib. on LV sbrul gyi mgo.]

sarva (Skt.), *all*; adv. forms, esp. **sarveṇa** (noted by itself as adv. only in Mv i.90.6, all mss., Senart em. sarve te, wrongly), *altogether*; this is commonly emphasized by addition of a variety of other adv. forms in mg. *absolutely altogether, in the most complete way*: esp. **sarveṇa sarvam** (= Pali sabbena sabbaṃ) SP 321.8; LV 255.18; Mvy 6405; Mv ii.260.6, 7; 261.8; iii.223.6, 8; Divy 39.1; 105.7; 270.11; 502.22; Śikṣ 349.11; Mmk 400.5; 561.17; Dbh 39.26; Bbh 324.1; in Mv i.126.8 prob. read sarveṇa sarvaṃ (ed. with mss. sarva-)śūnyaṃ; **sarveṇa sarvaṃ sarvathā** SP 77.7; Bbh 11.19; **sarvathā sarvaṃ** (= Pali sabbathā sabbaṃ) Mvy 6406 (follows 6405, above); **sarveṇa sarvaṃ sarvathā sarvaṃ** Śikṣ 349.20; 350.7, 13; Laṅk 255.4; Suv 169.1, 6; AsP 25.13 et al.; **sarveṇa sarvaḥ** (read sarvaṃ) **sarvathā sarvaṃ sarvadā** Śikṣ 9.13, see note p. 395, which cites Bcp. as reading in the same passage sarveṇa sarvaṃ sarvathā, only. See also **sarvehi** and **sarvatratāye**.

Sarvaṃsaha (so read with most mss. for Senart Sarvasaha), n. of a former Buddha: Mv i.137.4.

sarvaka, adj. or subst. nt. (Skt. only Lex. and once in Vedic where -ka is pejorative), *all*, pl. *everything*: sarvakāni ujjhitvā Mv ii.112.1 (prose), *abandoning everything*; no special force of -ka perceptible.

sarva-karmika, adj. (-karman plus -ika), *effecting all works, universally efficacious*, said of mantras: Mmk 25.19; 74.6 (both prose).

sarvakālaka (see also **sārvakālika**), adj. with pudgala, *all-black, completely impure*, said of a delinquent monk who has gone thru five rites of purification, but all wrongly done: MSV iii.74.7; 77.6. If one or more of the five rites is done properly, the others wrongly, the delinquent remains impure and is called (successively) **yadbhūyaskālaka**, *mostly black*; **upārdhakālaka**, *half black*; **ekadeśakālaka**; and **pradeśakālaka**; if all are properly done, he is *pure*, **apagatakālaka**, q.v. In the virtual repetition, p. 78, **pradeśakālakaḥ** is accidentally omitted, but **ekadeśakālakaḥ** (line 13) has the definition given above to pradeśa-k° (only one of the five rites being done wrongly), which seems likely to be right. The ms. several times writes -kālika for -kālaka.

sarvakālajña, adj. (cf. Skt. kālajña; Pali kālaññu, ep. of Buddha, DN iii.134.24), *knowing all times* (past, present, and future); **-tā**, *quality of ...*: bodhimūlam upagamya cāprāptayāṃ °tāyām, *while this quality* (which comes with enlightenment) *has not yet been attained* (so 3 out of 6 mss.; Senart wrongly sarvākārajñatāyāṃ with v.l.), pañcacakṣusamanvāgatā (see **cakṣus**) bhavanti Mv i.158.1.

sarvakālika, adj. (= AMg. savvakāliya; to Skt. °kālaṃ, adv., Pali sabbakālaṃ, plus -ika), *perennial*: °kaś campakavṛkso Divy 325.24, 25; so, or *belonging to* (flowering or maturing in) *all seasons* (but not necessarily referring to the same plant), Mv ii.97.4 (°kāni, of flowers); 177.15 (puṣpaphalāni); 186.9 (vs) vanagulmā puṣpitā °kā; iii.69.12, 13 (puṣpāṇi).

Sarvagandhaprabhāsavatī, n. of a lokadhātu: Gv 81.4.

Sarvagandhārcimukhavajramaṇivicitra, n. of a Bodhisattva: Gv 442.13.

Sarvagātrajñānapratibhāsacandra, n. of a Tathāgata: Gv 421.14.

Sarvagāmin, n. of a wandering monk: Gv 179.4 ff.

Sarvaguṇaviśuddhigarbha, n. of a Bodhisattva: Dbh 2.20.

Sarvaguṇasaṃcayagata, m., n. of a samādhi: Mvy 582; ŚsP 1422.1.

Sarvaguṇālaṃkāravyūha, n. of a samādhi: SP 465.6

Sarvacakrā, n. of a goddess: Mvy 4292.

Sarvacaṇḍāla, n. of a son of Māra, unfavorable to the Bodhisattva: LV 314.3.

Sarvajagadduḥkhapraśāntyāśvāsanaghoṣa, n. of a Bodhisattva: Gv 3.24.

Sarvajagaddhitapraṇidhānacandra, n. of a future Tathāgata: Gv 358.12.

Sarvajagadrakṣāpraṇidhānavīryaprabhā, n. of a night-goddess: Gv 341.2 etc.

Sarvajjagābhimukharūpa, n. of a Buddha: Gv 285.9 (vs); m.c. (§ 2.80) for **Sarvajagadabhi°**; 2d ed. Sarvajagā°, unmetr.

sarvajña, *omniscient*, as ep. of a Buddha: Mvy 14 et al.

Sarvajñajñānaviśeṣābhiṣekavant, m., n. of a bodhisattva-samādhi: Dbh 82.20.

Sarvajñamitra, n. of a man, described as a Kashmirian scholar (mahāpaṇḍita) and devotee of Tārā: Sādh 223.17.

Sarvaṃjaya, n. of a future Buddha: Mv iii.330.12.

Sarvatathāgatadharmacakranirghoṣacūḍa, n. of a Bodhisattva: Gv 3.13.

Sarvatathāgataprabhāmaṇḍalapramuñcanamaṇiratnanigarjitacūḍa, n. of a Bodhisattva: Gv 3.11.

Sarvatathāgataprabhāmaṇḍalavairocanā, n. of a lokadhātu: Gv 14.24.

Sarvatathāgatavikurvitapratibhāsadhvajamaṇirājajālasaṃchāditacūḍa, n. of a Bodhisattva: Gv 3.12.

Sarvatathāgatasaṃtoṣaṇī, n. of a goddess: Mvy 4317.

Sarvatathāgatasiṃhāsanasaṃpratiṣṭhitamaṇimakuṭa, n. of a Bodhisattva: Gv 3.7.

Sarvatathāgatasuratasukhā, n. of a goddess: Mvy 4314.

Sarvatathāgatākarṣaṇī, n. of a goddess: Mvy 4315.

Sarvatathāgatānurāgaṇī, n. of a goddess: Mvy 4316.

? **sarvatraka,** adj. (cf. Pali sabbatthaka, *universal, in all places*, not in the BHS mg. in Jāt. i.172.1 or Dāṭh. 5.57; two other refs. in PTSD not found, app. erroneous), *capable of going everywhere*: vimānāni °kāni Mv ii.177.15 (prose); no v.l., but the mg. is suspiciously like that of Skt. sarvatra-ga, which perh. read, if the word really modifies the preceding vimānāni. However, the following words are sarvakālikāni puṣpaphalāni, and the position of our word suggests a corruption for Skt. sarvartukāni, *of all seasons*; equivalents of this word (see **sarvārtuka, sarvotuka**) precede **sarvakālika,** q.v., in Mv ii.97.4; iii.69.12, 13.

sarvatratāye, adv. (app. instr. of *sarvatra-tā; = Pali sabbattatāya or sabbatthatāya, see below), *altogether, in every way*: sarvehi (q.v.) °tāye sarvāvantaṃ lokaṃ spharitvopasaṃpadya viharati Mv iii.213.14, in a passage found repeatedly in Pali (PTSD s.v. sabbatthatā), e. g. DN i.251.2, analyzed Vism. 308.4 ff., where (as in DN and elsewhere) sabbattatāya is read; this is analyzed 308.29 as sabb-atta-(= ātma-)tāya: sabbadhi °tāya sabbāvantaṃ lokaṃ . . . pharitvā viharati; some texts read sabbatthatāya (as if based on sabbattha = sarvatra); there is no record in Pali Dictt. of any other occurrence of the word (on Kaccāyana-vutti's sabbathattā see CPD s.v. a-sabb° with ref.); but the BHS word occurs also in: śarvaśo °tāye jñātavyaṃ Mv i.229.9 = ii.133.10 = 285.2; (ye kecid) bhavā (mss. bhave) sarve hi (read **sarvehi,** q.v.?) °tāye saṃvartanti (prob. delete punctuation and add with mss. ye), sarve te bhavā anityā . . . ii.418.12.

Sarvatryadhvanāmacakranirghoṣacūḍa, n. of a Bodhisattva: Gv 3.14.

sarva-daṇḍa, m., acc. to Senart *subject to all punishment, completely criminal person*: °ḍehi vā duḥśīlehi vā . . . cīvarāṇi . . . paribhuñjitāni Mv i.19.3; other words in the uncertain passage are obscure and Senart em. violently.

Sarvadada, m. c. for **Sarvaṃdada,** q.v.

Sarvadaya (v.l. Sarvodaya), n. of a former Buddha: Mv iii.239.1.

sarvadarśi-tā, -tva (nt.; cf. next), *Buddhahood*: tena me bhavatu °śitā Mv i.48.4 = 81.21 (vs); svayaṃbhūsarvadarśitvam abhikāṅkṣanti paṇḍitāḥ i.88.13 (vs).

Sarvadarśin (acc. to Trik., Skt. Lex., *all-seeing* as ep. of a Buddha; cf. prec.), n. of two previous incarnations of Śākyamuni, the second called a king (nṛpa); in the same list, but their deeds are quite different: RP 24.8 and 15 (vss).

Sarvadiśapradīpaprabharāja, n. of a Buddha: Gv 257.21 (vs).

Sarvaduḥkhapraśamana, n. of a Tathāgata: Mmk 64.2.

[**Sarvadevagupta,** Senart's em. for **Gavādeva°,** q.v.]

Sarvadharmadhātutalabhedaketurāja, n. of a Bodhisattva: Gv 81.14.

Sarvadharmadhātusāgaranigarjitaghoṣa, n. of a Bodhisattva: Gv 3.23.

Sarvadharmadhātuspharaṇaghoṣa, n. of a Bodhisattva: Gv 3.22.

Sarvadharmanigarjitarāja, n. of two Tathāgatas: Gv 232.15; 360.15.

Sarvadharmanirnādachattramaṇḍalanirghoṣa, n. of a cakravartin king: Gv 325.9 ff., whence cited Śikṣ 154.2, 8.

Sarvadharmapadaprabheda, m., ŚsP 1420.21, or °prabhedana, m., Mvy 570, n. of a samādhi (in same list).

Sarvadharmaprabharāja, n. of a Buddha: Gv 257.13 (vs).

Sarvadharmapraveśamudrā, n. of a samādhi: Mvy 517; ŚsP 1416.2.

Sarvadharmabhāvanārambhasaṃbhavateja, n. of a Tathāgata: °jo (n. sg.) Gv 310.22.

Sarvadharmamudrā, n. of a samādhi: Mvy 512. (Not in ŚsP.)

Sarvadharmavīryavegadhvaja, n. of a Tathāgata: Gv 309.13.

Sarvadharmavaipulyasaṃgraha-sūtra, n. of a work: Śikṣ 95.11.

Sarvadharmasamatā, n. of a samādhi: Mvy 566; ŚsP 1420.11. See also **Sarvadharmasvabhāvasamatā°.**

Sarvadharmasamavasaraṇasāgaramudrā, n. of a samādhi: Mvy 527; ŚsP 1417.2 (here spelled °saraṇa°).

Sarvadharmasamādhiprabhaghoṣa, n. of a Tathāgata: Gv 312.2.

Sarvadharmasamudrābhyudgatavegarāja, n. of a Tathāgata: Gv 282.6.

Sarvadharmasāgaranirghoṣaprabharāja, n. of a Tathāgata: Gv 307.13 (prose); in vss called **Dharmaḥsamudraprabhagarjitaghoṣarāja** and **°garjitarājya,** qq.v.

Sarvadharmasāgaranirghoṣarāja, n. of a Tathāgata: Gv 296.23.

Sarvadharmasukhākrānta, m., n. of a samādhi: Śikṣ 181.10, 12.

Sarvadharmasvabhāvavicaya, m., n. of a samādhi: Dbh 82.13.

Sarvadharmasvabhāvasamatāvipañcita, n. of a samādhi: Samādh p. 4, lines 22, 23 (with corruptions); p. 6, line 27 etc. Cf. **Sarvadharmasamatā.**

Sarvadharmātikramaṇa, m., n. of a samādhi: Mvy 588; ŚsP 1422.15.

Sarvadharmāpravṛttinirdeśa, n. of a work: Mvy 1362; Śikṣ 6.16; 90.19; 99.3 (here vss of the usual BHS linguistic type).

Sarvadharmeśvararāja (text °dharmīś°), n. of a Bodhisattva: Mmk 40.16.

Sarvadharmodgata, n. of a samādhi: Mvy 511; ŚsP 1415.12.

Sarvadharmopapanna, m., n. of a samādhi: Gv 199.25.

Sarvanagararakṣāsaṃbhavatejaḥśrī, n. of a night-goddess: Gv 302.3 etc.

sarvanikṣepā, a high number, or method of calculation (gaṇanā): LV 148.17. See **sarvavikṣepatā.**

Sarvanirodhavirodhasaṃpraśamana, m., n. of a samādhi: Mvy 606; for variant forms see **Sarvarodha-.**

Sarvanīvaraṇaviṣkambhin (once, Dharmas 12, Sarvani°; in Kv always falsely printed Sarvaṇi°), n. of a Bodhisattva: Mvy 651; Dharmas 12 (cf. above); Mmk 40.13; 312.5; n. sg. °bhinaḥ (a-extension) Mmk 68.21; abbreviated to Sarvanīvaraṇa Mmk 62.12 (prose; but Tib.

renders Nīvaraṇaviṣkambhin, omitting sarva-, Lalou, Iconographie, 32); Kv 1.14; 8.12 etc. (see above).

Sarvaṃdada (cf. **-dada,** which see for use of this word as adj.), n. of a king, previous birth of Śākyamuni: m.c. Sarvadada RP 22.12 (cf. Finot p. vii, No. 7) °dadena nṛpeṇa satā me. In Mv iii.250.14 (vs) Senart assumes that Sarvaṃdada is also the name of a man, but nothing in the context indicates that it is anything but an adj., (an unnamed man) *who gave away everything*; the episode which is told in Mv shows no relation to the story alluded to in RP.

Sarvapaścimarocanaprabha (so read with 1 ms.), n. of a future Buddha: Mv iii.330.15.

Sarvapuṇyasamuccaya, n. of a samādhi: SP 424.5.

Sarvapraṇidhānasāgaranirghoṣamaṇirājacūḍa, n. of a Bodhisattva: Gv 3.10.

sarvaprathamam, adv. (= Pali sabbapaṭhamaṃ, Childers), *first of all*: Mv iii.56.18 (prose; mss. sarve pra°); LV 403.4, 6; 404.18 f.

[**Sarvaprabha,** see **Sarvapriya.**]

sarvaprabhāsasamuccaya, nt., n. of a gem (prob. mythical): Gv 498.10. Cf. **sarvamaṇiratnasamuccaya.**

Sarvapriya (so the only ms.; Senart em. Sarvaprabha; why?), n. of a future Buddha: Mv iii.330.9.

Sarvabandha, n. of a former Buddha: Mv i.137.2.

sarvabala, nt., a high number: LV 148.8, cited Mvy 7973.

Sarvabalavegavatī, n. of a lokadhātu: Gv 81.2.

Sarvabuddhakṣetrakāyasvabhāvasaṃdarśana, n. of a samādhi: Dbh 92.9.

Sarvabuddhanirmāṇapratibhāsacūḍa, n. of a Bodhisattva: Gv 3.9.

Sarvabuddhaviṣayāvatārajñānālokālaṃkāra, m., n. of a work: Mvy 1390.

Sarvabuddhasaṃbhūtagarbhamaṇimakuṭa, n. of a Bodhisattva: Gv 3.5.

Sarvabhadra, n. of a yakṣa: Māy 25.

Sarvabhūtaprasādana, or **°daka,** m., n. of a gem which reveals the nature of any disease: MSV ii.32.17 (°na); 33.5 (°ka); 35.16 (°ka).

sarvabhūtaruta, nt., °taṃ nāma śāstraṃ, *the science of* (understanding) *the cries of all creatures*: MSV ii.32.9.

sarvabhūtarutagrahaṇī, sc. lipi, a kind of script: LV 126.11; lit. *comprising* (or *grasping*) *the cries of all creatures*; Tib. renders literally; cf. prec. and **sarvarutasaṃgrahaṇī-lipi.**

sarvamaṇiratnasamuccaya, nt., n. of a (prob. mythical) gem: Gv 498.3. Cf. **sarvaprabhāsasamuccaya.**

Sarvamalāpagata, n. of a Bodhisattva: Mvy 688.

Sarvamahāpṛthivīrājamaṇiraśmipramuktā. n. of a lokadhātu: Gv 11.23(22) (2d ed. line 21).

Sarvamāramaṇḍalapramardanaghoṣa, n. of a Bodhisattva: Gv 3.23.

Sarvamāramaṇḍalavikiraṇajñānadhvaja, n. of a Bodhisattva: Gv 13.5; called °dhvajarāja 29.15.

Sarvamitra, (**1**) n. of a future Buddha: Mv iii.330.13; (**2**) n. of Aśoka's herald or official announcer (udghoṣaka): Divy 403.5; (**3**) (= Pali Sabbamitta) n. of a king in the Kumbha Jātaka: Jm 100.19 ff.

Sarvaratnarucirā, n. of a lokadhātu: Gv 81.10.

Sarvaratnavarṇasamantaprabhāsaśrī, n. of a lokadhātu: Gv 324.23.

Sarvaratnavicitravarṇamaṇikuṇḍala, n. of a Bodhisattva: Gv 442.5.

sarvarāja (cf. Skt. sarvarāj, rare), *emperor, universal king*: (tasya, sc. to Prince Puṇyaraśmi, son of King Arciṣmant, mātāpitṛbhyāṃ) koṭiḥ kanyānāṃ dattā, jñātisaṃghena koṭiḥ, naigamajānapadaiḥ koṭiḥ, sarvarājena koṭiḥ kanyānāṃ dattā abhūvan RP 41.15; it seems that sarvarāja must refer to a feudal superior of the prince's father, who was a rājan, 36.18.

Sarvarājendrā, n. of a mudrā: Kv 74.9, 18.

Sarvarutakauśalya, n. of a samādhi: SP 424.4.

sarvarutasaṃgrahaṇī-lipi, a kind of script: LV 126.9 (*comprising* or *grasping all cries* or *sounds*); Tib. translates literally; cf. **sarvabhūtarutagrahaṇī.**

Sarvarūpasaṃdarśana, m., n. of a samādhi: SP 405.14 ff.; 412.11; 435.9 ff.

Sarvarūpasaṃdarśanā, n. of the lokadhātu of the Buddha Meghadundubhisvararāja: SP 431.9. So both edd.; both Transl. Sarvabuddhasaṃ°, which is not cited from any ms. (the only v.l. omits rūpa, one ms.).

Sarvarodhavirodhasaṃpraśamana, m., Mvy Mironov 21.101, or **Sarvarodhapratirodhapraśamana** ŚsP 1424.19 or **Sarvarodhavirodhapraś°** ibid. 21, variants for **Sarvanirodhavirodhasaṃpraśamana,** q.v. The definition given in ŚsP contains the words rodha and virodha (not nirodha nor pratirodha).

Sarvalakṣaṇapratimaṇḍitaviśuddhiśrīgarbha, n. of a Bodhisattva: Dbh 2.15.

Sarvalokadhātūdgatamakuṭa, n. of a Bodhisattva: Gv 3.6.

Sarvalokadhātūpadravodvegapratyuttīrṇa, n. of a Buddha in a western lokadhātu: SP 184.13.

Sarvalokapriyadarśana, n. of a Litsavi (Licchavi) prince: Suv 14.10; 17.7. See also **Sarvasattvapriya°** (3).

Sarvalokabhayacchambhitatvavidhvaṃsanakara, n. of a Buddha in a northeastern lokadhātu: SP 185.2 (there are a number of variants in Kern's ed. and transl.; Burnouf °bhayāstambhitatvavidhvaṃs°).

Sarvalokahitaiṣiṇ, n. of a future Tathāgata: Gv 358.14.

sarvalokāgrabhūta, m. or nt., a kind of gem: Mv ii.310.20 (em.; mss. °lokagrasata).

Sarvavajradhara-mantra, n. of a charm: Śikṣ 140.13 (quoted in the following).

sarvavikṣepatā, = **sarvanikṣepā,** q.v.: Mvy 7985 (cited from LV); Tib. thams cad rnam par ḥbyed, which supports vi rather than ni, and is read also (with final ḥbyed pa) by Tib. on LV.

Sarvaviṣayāvabhāsālaṃkārapratibhānadarśanagarbha, n. of a Bodhisattva: Mvy 709.

Sarvavṛkṣapraphullanasukhasaṃvāsā, n. of a night-goddess: Gv 313.12 etc.

Sarvavaidalyasaṃgraha (cf. **vaidalya**), n. of a work: Mvy 1385.

Sarvavyādhicikitsaka, n. of a Bodhisattva: Mmk 40.15.

Sarvavyūharatisvabhāvanayasaṃdarśana, n. of a gandharva: Mvy 3390.

Sarvavyūhālaṃkārapratibhāsasaṃdarśanagarbha, n. of a Bodhisattva: Dbh 2.7.

Sarvaśilparāja, n. of a former Buddha: Mv i.141.13.

Sarvaśūra, n. of a Bodhisattva: Kv 1.15.

Sarvaśokāpagata, n. of a lokadhātu in the south: ŚsP 31.19.

Sarvaśvetā, n. of a mythical (magic) herb: Kv 55.14; 56.17; 58.6.

sarva-saṃjñā (see s.v. **saṃjñā** 7), a high number: Mvy 7975 = Tib. brdaḥ śes kun; cited from LV 148.10.

Sarvasattvakuśalamūlanigarjitasvara, n. of a Bodhisattva: Gv 4.10.

Sarvasattvacittacaritānugata, m., n. of a samādhi: Dbh 82.14.

Sarvasattvatrātar, n. of a Mahābrahman: SP 164.9.

Sarvasattvapāpajahana, m., n. of a samādhi: SP 464.2.

Sarvasattvapriyadarśana, (**1**) n. of a future Buddha (= Mahāprajāpatī Gautamī, as predicted): SP 269.1, 3; (**2**) n. of a Bodhisattva of old: SP 405.8 ff. (previous incarnation of Bhaiṣajyarāja); (**3**) n. of a Litsavi (Licchavi) prince (= **Sarvalokapriya°**): Suv 13.1, mss.; Nobel em.

to Sarvaloka° which Suv mss. read later; but his note shows that both forms occur in Chin.-Tib. versions of the story.

Sarvasattvāvabhāsateja, n. of a Tathāgata: °jo (n. sg.) Gv 310.14 (prose).

Sarvasattvojohārī (Burnouf °tvaujo°; Kern Transl. °tvoja°), n. of an ogress: SP 400.7.

? **sarva-santa**, adj. (**santa** = Skt. sant), *by all means real, sure to occur* (?): (a childless king reflects, mamātyayāt) svakulavaṃśacchede rāṣṭrāpahāraḥ sarvasantaḥ (ed. em. °taṃ), svāpateyam aputram iti Divy 439.30, *after my death, on the cutting off of my family line, plundering of the kingdom is bound to happen; my property lacks a son.*

Sarvasamādhisāgarāvabhāsasiṃha, n. of a Tathāgata: Gv 312.7.

Sarvasaha, see **Sarvaṃsaha.**

sarvasārasaṃgrahaṇī, sc. lipi, a kind of script: LV 126.11; lit. *comprising* (or *grasping*) *all essence*; Tib. renders literally.

Sarvasukhaduḥkhanirabhinandin, m., n. of a samādhi: Mvy 607; ŚsP 1424.9.

Sarvasvarāṅgarutaghoṣaś(i)rī, n. of a Buddha: Gv 285.22 (vs).

[**sarvākārajña-tā**, see s.v. **sarvakālajña.**]

Sarvākāraprabhākara, m., n. of a samādhi: Mvy 614; ŚsP 1425.12.

Sarvākāraraśmikusuma, m., n. of a samādhi: Dbh 82.12.

sarvākāravaropeta, (**1**) adj. (Skt. in elements, tho not recorded as cpd.; Pali sabbākāravarūpeta, of Buddha, Therag. 1046), *endowed with all excellent forms*: of Buddha's voice, Mvy 504; °tam, among synonyms for **anuttara**, 2533; etc.; in Gv several times misspelled sarvākārāvaro°, e.g. 418.7 (said of the cakra-ratna of a universal monarch) and 19 (of monasteries built by him); (**2**) m., n. of a samādhi: Mvy 602; ŚsP 1424.6.

Sarvākāśatalāsaṃbhedavijñaptimaṇiratnavibhūṣitacūḍa, n. of a Bodhisattva: Gv 3.11.

sarvānta, *the very end*; loc., *at* ..., with gen.: (teṣām eva devānāṃ) °te Divy 222.10.

Sarvābhibhū (in Pali sabbābhibhū is ep. of Buddha in Vin. i.8.17, but seems not to occur as n. pr.), (**1**) n. of a former Buddha, by whom Buddhahood was predicted for (the future) Śākyamuni: in Mv iii.240.1 ff. he was the next Buddha after Dīpaṃkara: LV 5.6; 171.20; Divy 226.16 ff.; Mv i.2.3; 36.6 ff.; iii.240.1; 241.13; 243.1, 2, 21; 244.16; 247.4; 248.6; (**2**) n. of three future Buddhas, in the same list, the second immediately following the first: Mv iii.330.12, 14.

? **sarvārtuka**, adj. (= Skt. sarvartuka; see also **sarvotuka**), *of all seasons*: °kāni (of flowers) Mv ii.97.4 (prose). So app. both mss. (one is specifically cited thus); but Senart ignores the form in notes and Index; may it be an editorial slip for the Skt. sarvar°?

Sarvārthadarśa, n. of a Tathāgata in the zenith: Sukh 98.18 (in JAOS 1880.185 printed Sarvādarśa).

Sarvārthadarśin, n. of a former Buddha: Mv iii.238.5.

Sarvārthanāman, n. of a Bodhisattva: SP 3.4.

Sarvārthasiddha, (**1**) personal name of Śākyamuni (in Mv and LV commoner than **Siddhārtha**; Pali seems to record only Siddhattha): LV 95.22 f. (so named by his father); 99.20; 104.9; 105.9 ff.; 111.4; 136.13; 360.16 et al.; Mv ii.26.15; 48.5; 73.6; 74.6 ff.; 75.18 (in next line Siddhārtha); iii.111.17; 176.2; 263.2; 377.16; Av ii.112.2; Karmav 71.21 (here applied to him as samyaksaṃbuddha); (**2**) m., n. of a bodhisattva-samādhi: Mvy 743.

sarvāvant, adj. (= Pali sabbāvant; not identical with sarvāvant, *containing everything*, BṛhU 4.3.10; Kern, SBE 21 p. xvii, is wrong), *entire*: SP 6.1 (°vac ca, v.l. °vantaṃ, MIndic n. sg. nt., buddhakṣetraṃ; prose); **72.7** (°vantaṃ, n. sg. nt., niveśanaṃ; prose); 315.1 (°vantaṃ bodhisattvagaṇaṃ), etc.; LV 4.14 (°vantaṃ Jetavanaṃ); 36.10; 67.2; 291.9; read (yaṃ jñeyaṃ ...) sarvāvantam (or m.c. sarvāvatam; an āryā vs, tho printed as prose) Mv i.4.9 (text sarvan tam, v.l. sarvāntaṃ); ii.313.17 (°vantā); 314.14 (°vatīṃ); 349.3 (°vatī ... lokadhātuḥ); iii.55.18 (°vantena kālena, em.); 213.14; 318.1 = LV 399.21 (°vantaṃ lokam); Mv iii.362.6 (°vantaṃ, em., iṣvastrajñānaṃ); Mvy 6328 (°vantaṃ, misprinted sarvāntaṃ, cf. Index); Divy 294.21; 298.21; 352.10; Suv 10.7; Śikṣ 269.13; Kv 99.8; Mmk 1.18; Sukh 77.6; Gv 169.14; Dbh 5.22. Common in most texts.

Sarvāvaraṇavikiraṇajñānavikrāmin, n. of a Bodhisattva: Gv 14.25; called °jñānavikrāntarāja 31.7.

Sarvāstivāda, see **Ārya-sarv°.**

sarveṇa, in adv. expressions, see **sarva.**

sarvehi, adv. (app. instr. pl. of sarva, but corresp. to Pali sabbadhi, of obscure ending), *altogether*: Mv iii.213.14, perhaps also ii.418.12, see **sarvatratāye.**

sarvotuka, or °**duka**, adj. (§ 3.92; semi-MIndic for Skt. sarvartuka; see **sarvārtuka**; = Pali sabbotuka, AMg. savvouya, savvottuya), *of all seasons*: °tukāni (mss. sarvodakāni; with puṣpāṇi) Mv iii.69.12, 13; (puṣpāṇi ...) sarvotuka-(so Senart em., 1 ms. °duka-, the other badly corrupted)-kālikāni iii.81.3 (vs). See also **sarvatraka.**

Sarvodaya, v.l. for **Sarvadaya**, q.v.

Sarvauṣadhi, n. of a magically endowed being (physician, vaidyarāja 36.6), a previous incarnation of Śākyamuni: Karmav 36.5 ff.

sarvauṣadhiniṣyandā, sc. lipi, a kind of script, (*having, bringing*) *issue* (result) *of all medicinal herbs*: LV 126.11 (Tib. renders literally; see s.v. **niṣyanda**).

sa-lila, adj. Bhvr. (m.c. for °līla), *graceful, charming*. Mv ii.142.8 (vs).

Salilagupta, n. of a former Buddha: Mv i.140.1.

Salīla, pl., n. of a brahmanical gotra: Divy 635.12.

Salīlagajagāmin (cf. **līḍa**), n. of a former Buddha: Mvy 100 = Tib. glaṅ po che ltar ḥgyiṅ (misprinted ḥgyin) zhiṅ bzhud pa, *departing while looking down (haughtily) like a great elephant*: LV 5.14 = Tib. ṅom bag (surely intending the word given by Jä. and Das as ṅo ḥbab, *with look cast down, bashful*) glaṅ poḥi ḥgros (*with walk of elephant*). Senart reads °gāmī by em. Mv i.139.2; but see **Savilambagāmin.**

[**salokānāṃ**, Divy 272.24, corruption; see s.v. **saṃkāra** (3).]

savara, (**1**) m., a high number: Mvy 7785 (Tib. mchog ldan); no v.l.; also as v.l. for mavaraḥ or maparaḥ Mvy 7707 (in earlier part of the same list); (**2**) nt., a high number (but much smaller than °raḥ Mvy 7785): °ram Mvy 7833 (corresponding in position to Mvy 7707, and rendered in the same way in Tib., ban bun, differing thus from Mvy 7785); for this a v.l. **mavaram**, q.v., is recorded, and it seems quite clear that s- is a graphic error for m-; Mvy 7833 is cited from Gv 133.2 which reads **maparam**, q.v.; in Gv 105.20 paramasya (gen.) is obviously another form of the same number, see **parama.**

savijñānaka, adj. (= Pali saviññāṇaka, also saviññāṇa), *conscious, living*: °ke kāye Divy 534.25, *in a living body* (*person*); cf. Pali AN i.132.23 saviññāṇake kāye.

Savilambagāmin, n. of a former Buddha: Mv i.139.2; so I would read for Senart's em. **Salīlagajagāmin**; most mss. Saciramba-gā° (one ms. Sari°, one good ms. Savi°). Cf. Skt. sa-vilambam, adv.

sa-vraṇa, see **vraṇa.**

sa-śakya, adj. (**sa-**, q.v., with śakya), *possible*: neha punaḥ saśakyaṃ labdhuṃ nareṇekṣurasaṃ pradhānam Śikṣ 110.19 (vs), *it is impossible for a man here to obtain the excellent juice of the sugarcane*. Cf. Pali sasakkaṃ, which needs further study; Childers, citing only from (the Lex.) Abhidhānappadīpikā, renders *certainly*; PTSD *as much as one can*; on MN i.415.36 sasakkaṃ na karaṇīyaṃ comm. iii.128.23 glosses ekaṃsen' eva (supporting Childers) na kātabbaṃ; on MN i.515.1 sasakkaṃ (brahmacariyaṃ na vaseyya), comm. iii.226.15 glosses ekaṃ satthe nipāto, prob. also intending the same (read ekaṃsatthe).

1 **saha-** (Skt.), indecl., as prior member of a cpd., or acc. to some also with a following separate abl., to be rendered *immediately upon* or *after*, or the like, of succession in time so close as to be spoken of as contemporaneous; (**1**) with foll. abl., as in Pali saha parinibbānā DN ii.156.35, taken as two words by ed. and Andersen, Reader, Glossary, *immediately after* (Buddha's) *nirvāṇa*; Senart, note on Mv i.24.10, and Weller 21, take such BHS forms as cpds., and I am inclined to follow them, largely because of the cases listed under (2); but saha seems to govern a prec. abl., in associative mg., in Ind. Spr. 1488 aiśvaryāt saha saṃbandhaṃ na kuryāt, *one should not make alliance with royalty*: saha-śravaṇād eva, *immediately upon hearing*, LV 62.12; 253.20; bodhisattvamātuḥ saha-darśanād eva 71.19–20; saha-pratilambhād 72.7, *as soon as they received it*; te dāni saṃmūrcchitvā saha-vedanā prapatanti Mv i.24.10 (but this might be taken as an ordinary Bhvr. of Skt. type, *with, accompanied by, pain*, n. pl. m.; Senart understands abl.); (**2**) certainly as prior member of cpds, followed by a noun, either an adverbial acc., dīpaṃkarasya saha-darśanaṃ LV 359.10 (vs), *immediately at the sight of D.*, or in further composition with another noun, tasyāś ca saha-nirgamana-kāle Śikṣ 72.10, *and at the very time when it comes forth*; oftener with a following ppp., (ekaḥ pradīpo ...) praveśyate, sa saha-praveśito (*as soon as it is put in*) ... tamondhakāraṃ vidhamayati Śikṣ 178.3; in loc. abs., te saha-pratiṣṭhāpite pāṇau LV 72.5, *they, as soon as* (Māyā's) *hand was placed* (on their heads) ...; sahodgate 'ruṇe Śikṣ 65.7, *immediately after sunrise*; a loc. abs. would be expected in the next, but instead a 'pendant' nom. is used, syntactically disconnected with what follows, sahapravartitaṃ cedaṃ ... dharmacakraṃ SP 179.14 (prose), *and as soon as this wheel of the Law was set in motion* ...

2 **saha,** m., = **sahā** (lokadhātu), q.v.; rare, but note that **lokadhātu** has both genders: sahe lokadhātāv Gv 317.22 (prose); in Kashgar fragments of SP, LaVallée Poussin JRAS 1911, 1074.13, 30, and 1075.5, and Lüders ap. Hoernle MR 151.12–13, imasmi (Lüders iha) sahe lokadhātau; all these phrases are omitted in printed text of SP 267.3, 11; 268.3; and 270.6. BR also cite sahapati from LV (Calc.), but for this Lefm. 44.11 sahāpati with all mss.; and sahalokadhātu from Mvy, but for this our Mvy (3066) and Mironov read sahā°.

Sahacittotpādadharmacakrapravartin, n. of a Bodhisattva who presented a wheel of the Law to the Buddha at Benares: LV 415.9.

sahajanmaka, °**mika** (to Skt. sahajanman, which in late Skt. = *brother*, Schmidt, Nachträge, plus -ka, -ika), *of like birth* or *origin*: (vayasyakaḥ) °mikaḥ (in 13 mss. °makaḥ) sahapāṃśukrīḍanakaḥ Divy 331.13, 15, 20, 25.

Sahajavilāsa, n. of an author: Sādh 384.9; 452.5.

sahadharma, adj. or subst. m. (= Pali sahadhamma, Nett., see below; and cf. next), *harmonizing, agreeing, in accord with the* (true) *Doctrine*: only in a cliché, substantially identical in Mv i.330.5; 331.5; 332.8; 333.1, 13; iii.334.16; 335.5; SP 179.2 (dharmacakraṃ ... apravartiyaṃ, or °tyaṃ, SP and some Mv °titaṃ, [kenacic] chramaṇena vā brāhmaṇena vā devena vā Māreṇa vā Brahmaṇā [some om. this] vānyena vā kenacit [some om. anyena or kenacit] punar loke) sahadharmeṇa; KN prints saha dharmeṇa as two words, wrongly; Tib. on SP chos daṅ mthun pas, *by one in harmony with the Doctrine* (instr.), immediately followed by (and clearly dependent on) ma bskor ba, *not set in motion*; the Pali equivalent cliché (e. g. Vin. i.12.1–3) regularly lacks any correspondent to sahadharma, but Nett. 169.14 ends a similar cliché (not concerning the dhammacakka) with (kenaci vā) lokasmiṃ sahadhammena (correctly printed as one word, but not in Pali Dictt.).

sahadhārmika, adj. (to prec., q.v., plus -ika; = Pali sahadhammika, which in the Dictt. is sometimes assigned this mg., sometimes defined *co-religionist*, a mg. which need, and prob. should, never be assumed in BHS, nor, I suspect, in Pali), *consonant with the* (true) *Doctrine*; m., of a person, *one who lives in consonance therewith* (the mg. *having the same doctrine* is given by Wogihara's Chin. renderings in Bbh Index but is never necessary and sometimes impossible): °ke dharmaśravaṇe Śikṣ 55.6; °keno (m.c. for °kena) vacanena 194.7 (vs), cf. Pali sahadhammiko vādānuvādo Vin. i.234.19–20, °ke vuccamāne Dhs. 1327; personal, yā ca °kasya darśanenābhipramodanā Bbh 30.11, *joy at sight of one who is true to the Doctrine*; °kaṃ ca dṛṣṭvā sumanā bhavati 184.26; (bodhisattvo vṛddhatarakaṃ guṇavantaṃ ...) °kaṃ dṛṣṭvā 161.12; °kasya bodhisattvasya kṛtapraṇidhānatayā 152.24, *because a Bodhisattva that is consistent with the doctrine has* (must necessarily have) *made an 'earnest wish' (vow for enlightenment)*; in the last the alleged meaning *co-religionist* is peculiarly impossible, but nevertheless given by Wogihara's Chin. (*of the same Doctrine*). On the Pali mg. see esp. Mahāniddesa 485.16 (a gloss on Sn 965) paradhammikā vuccanti satta sahadhammike ṭhapetvā ye keci Buddhe appasannā ... (also dhamme, saṃghe), te bhikkhū etc.; note that even the paradhammikā here are *monks*, but have no faith in the Buddha etc.; in contrast the sahadhammikā (of seven sorts; which seven?) are *in accord with the true doctrine*.

saha-pāṃśukrīḍanaka, m. (in Skt. °ḍana cited only as nt. n. act.; Skt. saha-pāṃśukrīḍita, = this, is found also in BHS, Mv iii.450.13), = **pāṃśukrīḍana,** *'dust-player', boyhood comrade*: Divy 331.13 ff.

sahaṃpati (= Pali id.; cf. **sahā-, sahāṃ-pati**), n. of Brahmā: Mv iii.381.11 (vs); °ti (em.), n. sg., without Brahmā.

saharṣya- (or acc. to Suzuki's Index harṣya-, taking sa- as associative prefix with entire cpd.), the first of the svara or notes of the musical scale: Laṅk 3.7 (first in a cpd., foll. by ṛṣabha, gāndhāra, etc.); kept in Suzuki's transl.; note in ed. suggests em. ṣaḍga (read ṣaḍja), and so Suzuki's Index for harṣya.

Sahalin, (**1**) (= Pali Sahaḷin, DN ii.259.22), n. of a deity: Mahāsamāj., Waldschmidt, Kl. Skt. Texte 4, 183.13; (**2**) n. of a king, ancestor of Aśoka: Divy 369.11.

sahavratā (corresponds to Pali sahavyatā; the origin of the latter is obscure, but the BHS form is prob. secondary to it, with hyper-Skt. adaptation to vrata, cf. Senart n. on Mv iii.223.5, p. 493), *association, state of being connected with*: regularly dat. -sahavratāyai, LV (also °tāye in Mv), in cpds., **ākiṃcanyāyatana-** (see this) LV 238.16 = Mv ii.118.3 (in Mv corruptly **āśaṅkitavya-,** q.v.); **naivasaṃjñānāsañjñāyatana-** (see this) LV 243.17; 403.11 = Mv ii.119.10; iii.322.12; brahmaloka- (and others) Mv iii.223.5, 6, 9, 11; cf. Pali DN ii.250.20 brahmaloka-sahavyatāya, same passage as Mv iii.223.5. The Tib. version of LV shows, confusedly, that it read as our text.

sahaśāyinī (cf. Pali sahaseyya, recorded only as m., *bedfellow* of another monk), *bedfellow* (f.); so I believe we must read (rather than sahasopinī with Senart, and mss. at Mv iii.86.19 only), deriving from root śī; (pra)suptāye °nīye (mss. sahasāpinīye) Mv iii.82.13 and 15 (vss); saha-śāyinībhiḥ (mss. saha-sāy°) 87.12 (vs); °nīye (here mss. hopelessly corrupt) śayitāye iii.74.18.

Sahasodgata, n. of a householder, hero of Divy Chap. xxi (colophon 314.10): Divy 309.27 ff.

[**sahasopinī,** see **sahaśāyinī.**]

sahasragarbha, a kind of jewel: Gv 124.5.

Sahasradātar, n. of a former Buddha: Mv i.140.13.

Sahasradharma, n. of a brother of Śāriputra: Mv iii.56.11.

Sahasrabhuja, n. of a gandharva king: Kv 2.18.

Sahasrayajña, n. of a king, previous incarnation of Śākyamuni: LV 170.17 (vs).

sahasrayodhin (= AMg. sahassajodhi), *one who can fight a thousand, a mighty warrior*; seems to be a rather technical term: (yato 'sya rājñā svapuruṣo) dattaḥ °yodhī Divy 243.26 (as guard); te brāhmaṇāḥ °dhinaḥ puruṣasyaivaṃ śrutvā bhītāḥ 244.5; tatra ca kriyamāṇe °dhinaḥ puruṣasyaivam utpannam 14; (stūpe sarvajātakṛtaniṣṭhite) °dhy abhyāgataḥ 245.8, and ff.; ahaṃ °dhī MSV i.104.11.

Sahasravarga (m.), n. of a section of the Dharmapada, quoted in 13 ff.; equivalent to the Sahassavagga of the Pali Dhp., vss 100 ff.: dharmapadeṣu °gaṃ bhāṣati Mv iii.434.12.

Sahasraśiri (m.c. = °śrī), n. of a kalpa: Gv 259.5 (vs).

Sahasrāvartā, n. of a goddess: Mvy 4294.

sahasrima, ord. num. (= Pali sahassima, SN ii.133.18, not in Dictt.; see under **śatima**), *thousandth*: KP 159.15 (cited s.v. śatima).

sahasrī (Pali sahassī, cited by Senart Mv i note 373, seems to be cited only with, or sc., lokadhātu or puthavī, see Childers, and app. is not used like our word; cf. **sāhasrī**), *a thousand*, perh. rather *a group of 1000*: sattva-sahasriyo (acc. pl.) Mv i.5.13 (here mss. all om. sattva); 6.4 (four mss. °sāh°), 7 (only 1 ms. °sāh°); anekāṃ brāhmaṇānāṃ sahasriyo samāgatāni (! acc. pl.) 310.1; jana-°riyo (n. pl.) ii.74.11; prāṇa-°riyo (n. pl.) 98.17; brāhmaṇa-°riyo (n. pl.) 103.11; devakoṭi-°riyo (n. pl.) 160.9. All prose.

sahā (also rarely 2 **saha**, m., q.v.; Skt. Lex. *earth*, but in lit. only BHS), name of the world-system in which we live; almost invariably with **lokadhātu,** but without it Mv ii.380.18 (vs) tehi bhaveyā saha (so mss., n. sg., m.c.) saṃprapūrā; Sahā nāmnā lokadhātuḥ Bbh 295.5; in the foll. either cpd. or (oftener) associated with lokadhātu: Mvy 3066; SP 185.3–4 (asyāṃ sahāyāṃ lokadhātau); 317.9 (id.); 244.4 (sahāṃ °tuṃ); Mv ii.319.12 (vs; sarvāṃ sahāṃ ... °tuṃ); Divy 293.19 (imāṃ sahā-lokadhātuṃ); Mmk 2.12; 229.25; Gv 8.23, etc.; 215.19 (sahāyā °dhātoḥ); Sukh 99.16. See **Sahā(ṃ)pati.**

sahāpati (also **sahaṃ°**, **sahāṃ°**, and **sabhāpati,** qq.v.; = Pali sahampati; cf. **sahā,** 2 **saha**), *lord of the sahā* (or *saha*) *lokadhātu,* ep. of Brahman, m., and almost invariably accompanied by a form of that word; in most texts sahāṃ° seems commoner, yet it may be only a false Sktization of Pali sahaṃ°, which could represent an orig. sahā- by the 'law of morae'; in the mss. of LV, Divy, and some other works, sahā° predominates: LV 44.11; 61.5; 63.1; 69.16; 70.1; 83.13; 274.18 (in some of these v.l. sahāṃ°); in 73.8; 130.20 most mss. sahāṃ°, but Lefm. sahā°; perh. Mv ii.63.11 (so one ms., Senart sahāṃ°, which the other ms. prob. intends); Divy 613.30; 652.13, 17; 655.6 (in the last three ed. sahāṃ°, against mss.); Av (Speyer always reads sahāṃ°; ms. sahā° in) i.305.14 f.; 311.17 f.; 317.15 (in prec. line sahāṃ°); 329.5 f.; 337.7 f.; 343.1 (in 2 sahāṃ°); ii.198.11; Suv 84.12 and 91.14 (all mss., both times; Nobel em. sahāṃ°); Bbh 75.4; 295.6.

sahāṃpati, (**1**) m., = prec., q.v.: SP 4.8; 69.8, and often (app. always sahāṃ°); Mvy 3116; Divy 638.25; Av i.273.9; 298.2; 317.14; 323.12 f.; 343.2; RP 2.3; Kv 2.6; Sukh 92.13; Mmk 19.9; 45.5; 69.7, etc. (always sahāṃ°, I believe); (**2**) m., n. of a gandharva king: Kv 2.18; (**3**) f., n. of a kiṃnara maid: °tir Kv 6.7. Cf. next.

[? **sahāṃpatīka**, n. sg. °ko, = prec.: Mv ii.136.4 (vs), by Senart's em.; mss. differ widely; if correct, -ī(ka) m.c.]

sahāya, in LV 387.9 (vs), if text is right must mean *accompanied* (by, with instr.): adhunāpy asau tāṃ ... saṃpūjayaty anyasuraiḥ sahāyaḥ, *even now he honors it, together with the other gods.* But this use of sahāya seems unparalleled, and Tib. makes it agree with anyasuraiḥ: lha gzhan grogs daṅ lhan cig mchod pa byed, *honors it together with the other companion gods*; this implies sahāyaiḥ, which is prob. the true reading, tho no v.l. is cited. Cf. however **sahīya,** Buddhac. x.26.

sahāyaka (see also next; in Skt. recorded only once at end of a Bhvr. cpd.; but Pali id. is well established, in prose; = Skt. sahāya plus -ka), *companion, comrade*: tau bhrātarau sārdha (so read; best mss. sārtha; m.c.) sahāyakais taiḥ LV 392.4 (vs); here -ka could be m.c., in any case svārthe as in Pali; MSV ii.176.17 (prose); but it is clearly pejorative in AsP 417.20 f. (prose) eṣa mama °kaḥ ... bahavo 'pi ... mamānye 'pi °kāḥ santi, na ca punas te mamābhiprāyaṃ paripūrayanti, ayaṃ tu mayā pratirūpaḥ sahāyo (NB!) labdhaḥ, *he is my despicable companion, and I have many others too, but they do not fulfil my purpose; however, here I have got a suitable companion* (sahāyaḥ).

sahāyika (could be from Skt. sahāyin plus -ka), = prec.: MSV ii.177.14 (so ms.); 185.1.

sahita, adj. (**1**) (= Pali id.) of speech, *connected, coherent, sensible*: Mvy 474 (°tā, of Buddha's speech); sahitaṃ ca bhūtaṃ (*true*) ca sadā prabhāṣate SP 373.4; sahitaṃ ... sumadhuraṃ ... abravīt Mv i.145.7 = 201.7 = ii.5.2 (Senart i.490 wrongly *kindly, agreeable*); MSV ii.174.2 (read) tavāsahitam, mama sahitam; (**2**) of hair and eyebrows, in sahita-bhrū LV 107.8 and sahita-keśa 12, both in list of **anuvyañjana** of the Buddha (Senart also reads sahita-keśa in Mv ii.44.10, but read with mss. **ahasita-keśa,** q.v.); Tib. LV both times mñam pa = *even,* which usually renders Skt. sama and has both mgs., *alike,* and *level, flat, smooth*; prob. therefore *with smooth* (orig. *connected,* so *close-growing*; perhaps *thick*?) *eyebrows* and *hair.* These terms seem to be substitutions for, and roughly equivalent to, ślakṣṇa-bhrū and -keśa of other texts (Nos. 65 and 76 of my list of anuvyañjana), both of which are lacking in LV. In Pali, Therīg. 254, sahita is used of a young woman's hair compared to a grove: kānanaṃ va sahitaṃ (comm. 210.7 ghanasaṃnivesaṃ uddham eva uṭṭhita-uddhadīghasākhaṃ upavanaṃ viya; in accordance with this Mrs. Rhys Davids renders *dense*).

sahitaka, adj. (= sahita, with -ka svārthe), *together, united*: (āgaccha deva adyaiva ... saṃghaṃ pariviṣiṣyāmaḥ) °takā (n. pl., for dual) Mv ii.275.13, *come, your Majesty, this very day we will serve the assembly of monks together.*

[**sahī,** LV 325.9 (vs), should be printed, sa hī (m.c. for hi): no rāgeṇa sa hī vasāmy ahaṃ na ca doṣaiḥ, Tib. ṅa ni ḥdod chags zhe sdaṅ lhan cig gnas pa ma yin te, *I* (emphatic) *am not dwelling with desire or hatred.* I assume sa ... ahaṃ = the common so 'ham of Skt. The only alternative would be to em. to sahā, m.c. for saha.]

sahīya, adj. (obscure, except for obvious connection with saha; suffix -īya, § 22.20 ? or hyper-Skt. for Pkt. sahijja, sahejja = sahāya? Against the latter, possibly, may be cited dependence of an instr. on sahīya in Buddhac.; see however s.v. **sahāya**), *associated, in company* (with), or as subst. *companion*: (sa gṛhapatiḥ ...) antarjana-°ya udyānabhūmiṃ nirgataḥ Divy 312.5; daṇḍa-°yaḥ (kumāraḥ) 446.3, 5, *accompanied by a punitive force*; devasahīyo Av i.365.15, *together with Your Majesty*; (tena gṛhapatinā ...) °yena 366.2; tena mahāraja-°yena ib. 6, *with ... in attendance, as companion* (so best ms. of Av all three times, Speyer's text sahāya always); sadbhiḥ sahīyā hi satāṃ samṛddhiḥ Buddhacarita x.26, *for the success of the good is associated with the good*; in MSV ii.73.4 read (hālāhalena viṣeṇa ca) sahīyena (ms. sahahīyena; ed. em. sahayogena), *by hālāhala and* (other) *poison combined.*

sahya, nt. (= Skt. Lex. id.), *health, welfare, fortune*:

Divy 258.16, see s.v. **asahya**, to which this is prob. a secondary back-formation.

sāṃyamanika, adj. (to Skt. saṃyamana; cf. Skt. sāṃyamana), *concerned with restraint* or *control*: °kaḥ Mvy 9419.

sāṃyogika, adj. (Skt. Gr. id.; to saṃyoga plus -ika), *arising from union* (Tib.): °kaḥ Mvy 7573 = Tib. sbyar ba las byuṅ ba; AdP, Konow MASI 69.23.6; nāsti °kaḥ svabhāvaḥ ŚsP 1411.11.

sāṃlekhika, see **sāle°**.

sāṃvarika (to **saṃvara**, 1, plus -ika), *one who observes the vows* (called saṃvara 1): Śikṣ 11.15 (saṃvaragrahaṇaṃ . . . °kasyāntikāt kartavyaṃ); 66.4, 5 (°kāḥ).

sāṃvṛta, adj. (to **saṃvṛti**, 2, plus -a), *exoteric, connected with exoteric existence*: °tānāṃ padārthānāṃ MadhK 10.12; 189.2; °tānāṃ cakṣurādīnāṃ 27.10; °tam etal lakṣaṇaṃ na pāramārthikam 85.6; tad evaiṣāṃ °taṃ svarūpam 261.6; °taṃ pratibimbākāram 591.1.

Sākali, or **°likā**, n. of the wife of **Mākandika**: °lir (n.) Divy 515.14; °like (voc.) 517.1 (vs).

Sāketā (= Skt. and Pali °ta, nt.), n. of a city (Oudh): MSV i.66.3; 67.4 ff. (°tām, °tāyām).

? **sākṣā-karoti** (for Skt. sākṣāt-k°, semi-MIndic; cf. AMg. sakkhaṃ, other Pkt. sakkhā = Skt. sākṣāt), *realizes*: dharmam (mss. °ma, °me) adhigami sākṣākari (aor.; but v.l. sākṣātk°) Mv ii.118.12. Cf. **sākṣī-k°**.

sākṣātkriyā (cf. prec. and next two), *realization*: nirodha-°kriyāyai LV 33.11; dharmasya prāptaye °kriyāyai LV 239.3; Mv ii.118.11; 120.3.

sākṣī-karoti (Sktization of Pali sacchi-karoti, which seems to be a modification of Skt. sākṣāt-k° blended with Skt. sākṣin; see prec. two and next), *realizes* (intellectually): taṃ dharmaṃ adhigami sākṣīkari (aor.; so Senart em.; mss. sākṣīkṛto or sākṣī, alone!) Mv ii.120.5; (pañca cābhijñā) °kṛtā iii.362.19; balavaśībhāvaṃ °karoti 409.2; dharmaṃ °karoti 412.13.

sākṣīkriyā (cf. prec.) = **sākṣātkriyā**, q.v.: KP 125.14 (dharmasya . . . °kriyāyai); 143.4.

sākhilya, nt. (to 1 **sakhila** plus -ya; cf. Pali sākhalya, °lla), *gentleness, mildness, softness* (of speech): °yamādhuryāśayatā (of a Bodhisattva) Dbh 37.11; °yam Mvy 6984 = Tib. bśes paḥi tshig, *friendly words* (a free rendering; this is the only use of a word meaning *friend* which I have found in comms. or transl. of 1 **sakhila** or sākhilya); Samādh p. 4, line 29; p. 61 line 15.

sākhilyaka, nt., = prec.: MSV iv.129.10, 20 (Tib. as on Mvy 6984).

Sāgara, (**1**) (see also **Upasāgara**, and cf. **Sāgaranāgarājaparipṛcchā**), n. of a nāga king, often mentioned in close association with **Anavatapta** 2; lives in the ocean, cf. samudramadhyāt sāgaranāgarājabhavanāt SP 261.3: Mvy 3238 = Tib. rgya mtsho, *ocean*; SP 4.11; 263.3, 14, etc.; LV 204.9; 219.9 (misprinted māgara); 270.6; 435.14; Suv 85.5; 91.19; 158.14; 162.8; Kv 68.5; Laṅk 2.3; 4.8; Mmk 18.12; 452.17, 21; in nearly all these identifiable by association with Anavatapta, or with the ocean; (**2**) n. of another nāga king, mentioned later in the same list: Mvy 3264; here Tib. dug can, *poisonous*, which suggests sa-gara; this word exists in Skt. as an adj. but seems not recorded as n. of a nāga; Mironov also sāgara; (**3**) n. of a former Buddha: LV 171.20; (**4**) nt., a high number, = 10 **mahāsamudra**: Mmk 343.22. (Skt. Lex. has sāgara, m., as a different high number.)

Sāgarakukṣi, n. of a nāga maid: Kv 4.8.

Sāgaragambhīrā, n. of a nāga maid: Kv 4.10.

Sāgaragarbha, (**1**) n. of a dhāraṇī: Gv 66.22; (**2**) n. of a samādhi: Dbh 82.12; (**3**) n. of a Buddha: Gv 258.26.

Sāgaraghoṣa, n. of a Bodhisattva: Gv 3.21.

Sāgaratīra, nt., n. of a 'region in Laṅkā' (**Laṅkāpatha**, q.v.): Gv 67.17; 68.3.

Sāgaradharapuruṣa, n. of a former Buddha: Mv i.137.12.

[**Sāgaradhvaja**, n. of a monk: Gv 83.20 ff.; but read **Sāradhvaja** with 2d ed. and Śikṣ 36.8.]

Sāgaranāgarājaparipṛcchā (cf. **Sāgara** 1), n. of a work: Mvy 1357; perhaps same as **Sāgaramati-(paripṛcchā-)sūtra**; doubtless same as **Bṛhat-sāg°** Śikṣ 309.13.

Sāgaranigarjitasvara, n. of a Bodhisattva: Gv 4.9.

Sāgaraputra, n. of a nāga king: Māy 246.17.

Sāgarabuddhi, n. of a monk, disciple of Śākyamuni: Gv 47.8, 17.

Sāgarabuddhidhārin, see **Sāgaravaradharabuddhivikrīḍitābhijña.**

Sāgaramati, (**1**) n. of a nāga king: Kv 2.14; here, acc. to Index, Śikṣ 12.13 etc., in numerous citations from next, q.v.; (**2**) n. of a Bodhisattva: Kv 1.17 (not the same as 1, who is mentioned on the next page).

Sāgaramati-sūtra (to prec., prob. 1), n. of a work: Śikṣ 12.12 and often, see Index; **°ti-paripṛcchā-sūtra**, doubtless the same, 313.6; perhaps the same as the **Sāgaranāgarājaparipṛcchā-sūtra**. In Śikṣ 43.5 ff are cited vss from it, with the linguistic aspects of most BHS vss.

Sāgaramukha, m. or nt., n. of a region or place, (dik-)**pratyuddeśa**, q.v., in the south: °kho Gv 62.13; °khaṃ (n. sg.) 63.5.

Sāgaramudrā, n. of a Bodhisattva-dhāraṇī: Mvy 752.

Sāgaramegha, n. of a monk: Gv 62.13 ff.; in Gv 2.7 (vs) referred to as **Sāgarāmbuda.**

Sāgaramerucandra, n. of a former Buddha: Sukh 6.4.

Sāgararāja, n. of a former Buddha: Mv i.138.11 (v.l. Sārarāja). Cf. **Sāgara** 3.

sāgara-lipi, a kind of script: LV 126.6 (so Tib., rgya mtshoḥi).

sāgaravati- (for °tī?), seemingly = sāgara, *ocean* (§ 22.50), in sarvadharma-°vati-garbheṇa Gv 39.9, n. of a 'bodhisattva-samādhi'.

Sāgaravaradharabuddhivikrīḍitābhijña (Kashgar rec. Sāgaravarabaddhavi°), n. of a future Buddha, predicted rebirth of Ānanda: SP 216.4 ff.; 220.4, 6 (prose); in 217.10 (vs) Sāgarabuddhidhārin Abhijñaprāpta (two words).

Sāgaravarabuddhivikrīḍitābhijña, n. of a former Buddha: Sukh 5.15.

Sāgaravyūhagarbha, (**1**) m., n. of a Bodhisattva: Dbh 2.19; (**2**) nt., n. of a magic gem: Gv 500.16.

Sāgaraśiri (m.c. for °śrī), n. of a Buddha: Gv 258.16 (vs).

Sāgarasamṛddhi, m., n. of a samādhi: Dbh 82.13.

Sāgarāmbuda, see **Sāgaramegha.**

sāṃkathya, nt. (to Skt. saṃkathā plus -ya; cited once from Caraka, pw; cf. Pali sākacchā, f., seemingly a blend of this word and saṃkathā), *conversation, talk, lecture*: Mvy 2808 (paurī-s°); Śikṣ 56.3 (°ya-maṇḍalaṃ viśodhayitavyaṃ, referring to hearers of religious discourse); Bbh 161.24; 218.25; Kv 15.8; 50.15; 66.5, 6; (mahā-)dharma-sā° SP 7.11; LV 11.7; Gv 72.25; 521.7; Dbh 79.23; Sukh 68.11; Kv 16.6; 43.3; 61.20; 66.4; (mahā-)dharmaśravaṇa-sā° SP 16.10; Śikṣ 151.18; Bbh 175.1.

Sāṃkāśya, Saṃ°, Saṃkaśya (mss. show still other variants; = Skt. Sāṃkāśya, Saṃ°, Pali Saṃkassa), also called **Devāvatāra** or **°taraṇa**, as being the name of the city (nagara) or country (janapada) where Buddha descended from the heaven of the Trāyastriṃśa (or Trayas°; °triṃśebhyo devebhyo Av, below) to earth by a supernatural ladder (see DPPN): MSV i.163.9; (bhagavān . . .) devebhyas trayastriṃśebhyo jambūdvīpaṃ Sāṃkāśye (in 13 ms. °śe) nagare Āpajjure (q.v.; no such name seems to occur in Pali, but the existence of a 'deer-park' at Saṃkassa is mentioned, DPPN) dāve udumbaramūla iti Av ii.94.8, 13; Sāṃkāśye nagare... (see s.v. **Devāvataraṇa**) Divy 150.22; °śye (here mss. Saṃkāśye) nagare 'vatīrṇo 'haṃ Divy 401.22; Saṃkaśye Mmk 88.14, see s.v. **Devāvatāra**; Śamkaśye (so text, read Saṃ°) tathā kṛtvā ṛddhir janapade tadā (so text; read ṛddhīr, ṛddhiṃ?) Mmk 582.24 (vs); this is followed by the two lines cited s.v. **Agnibhāṇḍa**, apparently referring to a devāvataraṇa of the Buddha which occurred at some other place than Sāṃkāśya.

sāṃkleśika, adj. (= Pali saṃkilesika; to **saṃkleśa** plus -ika), *sinful, impure*: LV 434.2; (āśravā vighātā paridāghā sajvarā) °kā(ḥ) Mv iii.338.3, 4, 9, 11; (akuśalair dharmaiḥ) °kaiḥ Av ii.107.3; same Bbh 182.27.

sāṅgana (written with °na, for °ṇa, see **aṅgaṇa**; = Pali id., sā°, acc. to CPD s.v. aṅgaṇa), *blemished*: Dbh 35.19.

sāṃghāṭi, °**ṭī** (= saṃ°), *monk's robe*: °ṭi-parītadehaḥ Av i.284.10 (vs); °ṭīm ādāya Divy 494.2 (prose; mss.; ed. em. saṃ°).

sāṃghāta, adj. (Skt. Gr.; Skt. saṃghāta plus -a), *due to* or *based on a conglomeration*: paramāṇu-°ta-tvāt MadhK 93.10.

sāṃghika, adj., f. °**kī** (= Pali saṃ°; to Skt. saṃgha plus -ika), *of* or *belonging to the congregation (order of monks)*: Divy 342.15 ff.; Av ii.86.2; RP 29.8 (vitta); Śikṣ 56.5 (sc. lābha? m.); 170.3 (dravya); Prāt 502.1 (lābha); Gv 228.21 (vastu); Kv 96.18 (°kī, bhūmi); 97.1 ff.; Bbh 162.5; 163.11; 166.19 etc.

sāṃcaritra, nt. (= **saṃc**°, q.v.), *procuring, acting as go-between in liaisons*: Bbh 117.13 na...°treṇa paradāram upasaṃhṛtya pareṣām anuprayacchati; °tra-samutthitāṃ (āpattim) MSV iii.87.18.

sāṃcetanika (= Pali saṃ°), *intentional*: (karma) °kaṃ Karmav 48.7, 17. Cf. **saṃcetanikāhāra**.

sāta, see **śāta**.

Sātagiri, see **Sātāgiri**.

sātatika, adj. (= Pali id.; to Skt. satata-m plus -ika), *lasting, constant*: Mmk 17.11; 82.20 (both of diseases); of persons, *constant, persevering* (in religion): Ud iv.3 (apramattāḥ °kāḥ) = Pali Dhp. 23. Cf. next.

sātatya (nt.; see also **sāṃtatya**; = Skt. id., which however seems not recorded in the religious sense, rather of *continuance* merely; cf. prec.; = Pali sātacca), *perseverance*, in a religious course: °tya-kārin Mvy 1794 (so Mironov; Kyoto ed. **sātantya-**); °tya-kāri-tā Bbh 81.21; °tya-kāriṇaḥ Ud iv.20 (= Pali Dhp. 293, sātaccakārino); °tya-karaṇīya Bbh 291.5 ff. (pañca sthānāni, bodhisattvasya, listed in ff.); °tya-prayoga Bbh 82.22, and °gi-tva 201.17; °tya-jāpināṃ Mmk 328.6 (vs).

[**sātantya**, error for **sātatya**, q.v.; or possibly intending **sāṃtatya**, q.v.]

Sātāgiri or **Śā**° (also **Śata**°, q.v. = Pali Sātāgira), n. of a yakṣa, contemporary of Buddha, regularly associated with **Haimavata** 2 (as in Pali with Hema°): Jm 115.25 (here without H°); (listed with gandharvas, along with Haim°) Suv 162.5 (Nobel Satā° with only one ms., on the basis of Tib. bde ba, but this, which usually = Skt. sukha, represents **śāta**, q.v., or sāta, not sat as Nobel assumes); Mahāsamāj., Waldschmidt, Kl. Skt. Texte 4, 167.1; Hoernle, MR 26.13 (Āṭānāṭiya-Sūtra); in Māy 87 printed Sāta°, prob. by misprint, as Sātā° occurs Māy 236.3 and 29 (Waldschmidt, op. cit. 175 n. 3).

sātisāra, see **atisāra**.

sātīyati, text, or **sādīyati**, Kashgar rec. (see below, and cf. **svādīyati**), in SP 277.8 (prose), *interests oneself in, shows attachment to, takes pleasure in*: (na ca śrāmaṇeraṃ) na ca śrāmaṇerīṃ na bhikṣuṃ na bhikṣuṇīṃ na kumārakaṃ na kumārikāṃ °yati, na ca taiḥ sārdhaṃ saṃstavaṃ karoti; Tib. mi sten, *not adhere, be attached, to*. Text and etym. uncertain; sātīyati could be denom. from sāta = **śāta**, q.v.; sādīyati prob. = Pali sādiyati, derived by Childers and PTSD from root svād, cf. **svādīyati**; both these forms could perhaps be caus. pass. of svād- as suggested PTSD, or svād° may (as I am inclined to guess) be only an unhistorical Sktization, the orig. being denom. sātīyati, with sādī° showing Prakritic d for t.

sātpauruṣya (Skt. satpuruṣa plus -ya), *state* or *quality of a noble man, satpuruṣa*: °ya-yuktaṃ Bbh 114.4; 137.4 (both em., but plausibly; one ms. sāpaur°).

-sātman, ifc., *giving oneself out as being..., claiming* or *pretending to be*: kuhanājihmabhāvena tāpasākumbhasātmanā Jm 186.16, ... *setting himself up as the foremost* (see **akumbha**) *of holy ascetics* (Speyer).

sādīyati, see **sātīyati**.

sādṛśa, adj., once perh. (**a-**)**sādiśa** (also °**śaka**, q.v.; = Pali sādisa; cf. AMg. sārikkha; once in Skt., ŚŚS, BR; = Skt. sadṛśa, with ā analog. to tādṛśa and the like; oftenest in vss, where meter might be involved, but also in prose of Mv, Divy), (**1**) *like*: maṇiratna-°śāḥ (putrā naranāyakānāṃ) SP 24.11 (vs); same word 98.3 (vs); asādiśā(ḥ) with MIndic i for ṛ, *matchless* (of Buddhas), Mv i.314.17 (vs), by Senart's plausible em., mss. madisāṃ, adiśā (meter requires long antepenult); keśā kācilindika-°śā(ḥ) ii.307.2 (vs); lokadhātu paramāṇu-°śāṃ (acc. pl.) Sukh 45.12 (vs), *like atoms* (in numbers); mano vidūṣa-°śam Laṅk 224.2 = 319.17 (vs); (**2**) *suitable, fitting*: tāye istriye °śaṃ tatra gṛhaṃ Mv iii.26.21 (prose); ... itihāsapañcamānāṃ sādṛśo vyākartā Divy 620.19 (prose).

sādṛśaka, adj. (= prec.; -ka m.c.?), *like*: tvaṃsādṛśakehi paṇḍitaiḥ SP 31.11 (vs).

sādya, adj. (?nt.; to Skt. sādayati, *presses down, depresses, overcomes*, etc.), prob. *heavy, weighed down, depressed* (follows sārdram, *wet*): °yam Mvy 7484 = Tib. ljid (lcid) gnon, *oppressed* (?*oppressive*) *with weight*; Chin. *subdue* or *be subdued*.

sādharma (nt.; to Skt. sadharma plus -a), = (if not error for) Skt. sādharmya, *likeness, resemblance*: Laṅk 110.9, 10; 276.1.

sādhu, m.c. **sādhū** and rarely **sādho**, indecl. (in Pali recognized by Childers and PTSD as mg. *please*; āyācane Pv comm. 232.9; with impv. or equivalent; I think they are right, but also that the same mg. applies in many Skt. cases, incl. most of those listed BR s.v. 5e), *please*, with impv. or equivalent: SP 34.4 (tat sādhu bhagavān nirdiśatu): 71.4; 164.13; 171.12; 180.12; 297.5, etc.; LV 6.16; 57.1; 78.15; 233.1, etc.; Mv i.254.18; ii.257.14; 258.14; 259.2; iii.91.4; 300.13, 19; Divy 335.27; Jm 110.2; 157.10; Av i.90.13, etc. (I see nothing un-Sanskritic in the use of sādhu Mv i.174.4 ff., and consequently no need for Senart's note); sādhū, sādho, m.c., §§ 3.21, 71.

sādhukam, adv. (= Pali id.; Skt. sādhu), *well, properly, effectively*: °kam uttiṣṭhāmīti gātrāṇy abhisaṃskurvann avakubjaḥ prāpataṃ LV 256.3 (prose).

Sādhuprabha, n. of a former Buddha: Mv i.140.7.

sādhumatī, (**1**) n. of the ninth bodhisattva-bhūmi: Mvy 894; Dharmas 64; Dbh 5.10 etc.; Bbh 354.7; Laṅk 15.5, etc.; (**2**) n. of a goddess: Mvy 4295.

Sādhurūpa, n. of a former Buddha: Mv i.138.3.

sānuka, m., n. of a muhūrta (in the first part of the night): Divy 643.24. Seems not to occur among Skt. lists of muhūrta names (see BR s.v. mu°). Cf. next.

sānu-kālam, adv., *at* (some specified, but to me unknown) *time*: gacchāmi sānukālaṃ tasya dārakasya bhaktaṃ nayāmi (said by the youth's mother); sā °lam gatvā ... Divy 88.2–3. One would be tempted to assume sānu = **sānuka** (prec., q.v.), *at the time of the sānu(ka) muhūrta*; but that muhūrta occurs in the first half of the night acc. to Divy 643.24, while this passage clearly refers to daytime.

sāṃtatya, adj. (cf. **sātatya**; but in Śikṣ, at least,

this word is clearly regarded as derived from saṃtati plus -ya), *continuous, constant*: divyehi vihārehi āniñjehi vihārehi °tyehi vihārehi buddho buddhavihārehi ... viharati Mv i.34.11; similarly ii.419.12 (v.l. sātatyehi); sāṃtatyavīryam Śikṣ 51.9, cf. saṃtaty-ārabdha-vīryasya 51.7.

sāntara, m., one of a list of kinds of monks who have no right to make valid objection to an action taken in the name of the saṃgha; perh. *schismatic*, or *having a weak point* (? cf. CPD s.v. ²antara, A 2): MSV ii.210.12 (context does not help).

sāntarottara, nt. (= Pali santaruttara), *the two inner garments* (antarvāsas and uttarāsaṅga, both Skt.) worn by monks, to accept more than which is a naiḥsargika pāyattika offense under the circumstances of the 7th nai° pāy° (cf. Pali Vin. iii.214.20): Mvy 8391; MSV ii.48.15 (Corr.). As adj., possibly read sāntarottara(paṭikā-) for sāntarocchada° Śikṣ 208.11; see s.v. **ucchada** (2). A monk is forbidden to wear only these two (and discard the **saṃghāṭī**): MSV ii.94.8 (cf. Vin. i.298.5).

sāntarbahi(s), adv. (cf. Pali santara-bāhira, adj.; **sa-**, q.v., plus antar plus bahis), *within and without*: te sāntarbahir (v.l. °hi) mṛgayante sma, sāntarbahir (v.l. °hi) mṛgayamānā na paśyanti sma LV 228.3 (prose).

sāṃtānika, adj. (to **saṃtāna,** 2, plus -ika; unrecorded in this mg.), *of the mental disposition*: sarvasattvānāṃ °ka-bhaya-praśamanāya Śikṣ 296.3; (duḥkhaprakṛtikā eveme) sarvasaṃskārāḥ sva-para-°kāḥ Bbh 189.23.

sāntika, in adv. forms °ke and °kāt (= Pali santike, °kā; see **santika, °ke,** of which this may well be a secondary Sktization; but it reveals the true origin of the MIndic form), *in* or *from the presence* (of, gen.): buddhasya °ke Karmav 161.2, 4; °ke, °kāt, acc. to Kern, Preface ix, Kashgar rec. of SP for Nep. antike, °kāt; so sāntikātu, v.l. of Kashgar rec. 119.3; for other such cases see **santike.**

sāṃdṛṣṭika, adj. (= Skt. Lex. id., Pali saṃdiṭṭhika; also **saṃ°,** q.v.), *visible, actual, perceptible*; *of the present* (*life*); opp. to **āgāmika**; syn. **akālika, ak°**: Mv ii.405.16 (see **āgāmika**); iii.195.11 °kaṃ ... idaṃ vipākaṃ; 200.10 dharmavinayaḥ sāṃdṛṣṭika akāliko; Mvy 1292 (of dharmaḥ) °kaḥ, followed in 1294 by ākālikaḥ; Karmav 58.1, 6 °kaḥ (phalavipākaḥ).

sāpateya (nt.; = Pali id., MIndic for Skt. svā°), *wealth*: bahudhana-°yā(ḥ) Mv ii.375.22 (vs), Bhvr.; so mss., Senart em. svā°.

sāpattika, adj. (= Pali id.; cf. **an-āp°**), *sinful*: °ko bhavati Śikṣ 15.6; 146.3; Bbh 160.24.

sāpatnaka (= Skt. °na), *son of a co-wife, rival*: (iha sapatnā ye; mss. sapatnīyeyo) vā bhonti °nakā vā vairinah kṣetra-vairikā vā vastu-vairikā vā vapra-vairikā vā pratirājāno vā ... anyamanyasmiṃ sāpatnāni cittāni upasthāpayitvā kālaṃ kurvanti Mv i.16.9 (prose).

sāparādhika, adj. (may be blend of **aparādhika,** q.v., and Skt. sāparādha; or **sa-,** q.v., plus **aparādhika**), *guilty of offense*: Śikṣ 62.20; 68.24.

sāptāhika, adj. (= **saptā°**; Pali sattāh°, Childers), *weekly*; *to be taken for one week*, of medicines: MSV i.ii.17 ff.; specifically of guḍa, id. i.248.20 f.

sābhisaṃskāra (sa-abhi°), *with proper preparation of mind*; *with fixed, determined mentality*: adj., chiefly in Divy (adverb °kāram 46.5; 365.1), said of the Buddha 158.5, or of his foot as he formally and solemnly sets it down, 46.13; 250.20; 364.26, resulting in earthquakes and miracles; but also applied to a king who is inviting a Buddha, 246.12, 248.10, so that it can hardly mean *with intent to do a miracle* (so Index); also sābhisaṃskāraparinirvāyī Mvy 1017, *entering nirvāṇa after proper mental preparation*; contrast anabhi° 1018; sābhisaṃskāraḥ sābhogo (q.v.) ... vihāraḥ (bodhisattvānām) Bbh 346.14; sābhisaṃskāreṇa, adv., Divy 250.24.

? **sābhīyati,** acc. to Tib. *delays in making*: (paropasthānaṃ) °yati, abhinandati Śikṣ 152.7 (so ms., ed. em. so 'bhiyāti, which is manifestly impossible); Tib. cited as gzhan gyi rim gro bya bar sdod ciṅ, *being slow to do honor to others*; abhinandati, doubtless, *he approves* (defends such behavior); this is a kind of Māra-karman, *evil behavior*. The word is obscure and may well be corrupt; I do not see any way of relating it to AMg. sāhī, *wicket-gate* (see Sheth), or Deśī sāhī, *way, road*.

sābhoga (sa-**ābhoga,** q.v.; opp. an-ābhoga, q.v.), *with, accompanied* or *characterized by, effort*; *not spontaneous*: Bbh 317.3; 346.14 bodhisattvānāṃ sābhisaṃskāraḥ (see this, and **abhisaṃskāra**) sābhogo nirnimitto vihāraḥ (contrasted with anābhogo ... vihāraḥ, see **anābhoga**); Dbh 67.11, 14, 18, see anābhoga.

sāma (= Pali id.; see also **śāma**) = Skt. śyāma, *dark*: iha ... vitarka-sāmo (em.; most mss. °samo, unmetr.; 2 mss. sabhūmau, prob. intending sadhūmo, see Foucaux, Notes, 194; sadhūma would be barely possible metrically; Tib. acc. to Foucaux *obscured by smoke*) mahāmadanavahniḥ LV 373.15 (vs), *here the great fire of passion, dark with ratiocination* (as with smoke) ...

sāmagrī (= Pali sāmaggī), (**1**) *concord*: saṃdhiṃ kuryāṃ °grīm MSV ii.190.18; 191.4–5 ff.; (**2**) *communion* (with the order of monks; withheld from those suspended): MSV ii.193.18; 194.7, (saṃgha-sā°) 8; °**grī-dattaka,** 195.5, = **saṃgha-sāmagrī-dattaka**; °**grī-poṣadha,** m., *participation in the poṣadha with the order*, 195.4 ff.; (**3**) *meeting* (of monks): sāmagrī-velāyāṃ punaḥ śayanāsanaprajñaptiḥ kartavyā MSV iii.98.5, *but at the time of a meeting he must arrange the seats.*

sāmato, adv. (to **sāma-m** plus -tas), *by, of oneself*: sarvadharmeṣu vaśavartī svayam eva sāmato (mss. syā° but Senart's em. seems certain) virakto bhavati Mv ii.144.19 (prose).

[**sāmanaka,** f. °**ikā,** read samānikā, to **samānaka,** *like, similar*: MSV iv.98.3.]

sāmantaka, adj. and subst. (unrecorded anywhere; cf. **pari-sā°**; Skt. and Pali sāmanta plus -ka), (**1**) adj., *neighboring, near*: °kehi pi me gocaragrāmehi Mv ii.131.4 (prose); °kaḥ pratiśatrurājā Suv 71.10 (and ff.); teṣu caṅkrameṣu °keṣu Kv 66.8; °kam, sc. dhyānam, Mvy 1485, (*recueillement*) *liminaire*, of which there are 8, one for each principal (maula) dhyāna and ārūpya, AbhidhK. LaV-P. viii.178 f.; (**2**) adj. or subst. nt. (?), (*something*) *connected with*, lit. *bordering on* (in comp.; cf. Pali MN i.95.28 kodhano hoti, kodha-sāmantaṃ vācaṃ nicchāretā): (yat tvaṃ ... prajñāpāramitā-pratisaṃyuktaṃ padaṃ vā) pada-°kaṃ vā nāśayer ... AsP 461.1, *if you should let get lost either a word, or something connected with a word* (i. e. a part of it, a letter or letters?) *belonging to the P.p.* (if it meant *something* [*physically*] *near a word* I cannot imagine what could be meant, except another word); bheda-sāmantakāḥ MSV iv.108.4, *spreaders of dissension*; (**3**) nt., *vicinity*: (tasyāḥ sarvaḥ kāyo dagdhaḥ) sthāpayitvā kukṣi-°kaṃ Divy 270.4, *her whole body was burnt, except the vicinity of her womb*; loc. °ke, *in the vicinity* (of), *near* (with prec. gen. or in comp.), rājño °ke Mv ii.447.13, *near the king*; maṇiratnasya °ke LV 17.3; Gṛdhrakūṭaparvata-°ke Av i.274.9; also instr. °kena, in comp., grīva-°kena mukha-°kena ca Gv 400.26–401.1, *in the vicinity of the throat and mouth*; Bhadraṃkara-°kena Divy 127.3–4, *round about Bh.*; Vaiśālī-°kena Divy 211.21, *near V.*; with gen., tadāsya (sc. ajagarasya) yojanaṃ °kena (*for a league round about him*) lālāsya spharitvā tiṣṭhati Divy 106.3; also in absolute use as adv., °kena śabdo visṛtaḥ Divy 34.18; 70.4; 84.24, *the word spread abroad in the vicinity*; in comp., yojanasahasra-°kena (vācaṃ niścārayati) 121.20, *for 1000 leagues round about*; others, mg. *near by, round about*, or *in the vicinity*, Divy 300.18; 464.2; 583.2; MSV i.36.11; (**4**) nt. (once m.) *circumference*: esp. in adv. forms, acc. **śama-°kam,** q.v., *a cubit in circumference*; instr. °kena, pañcahastapramāṇaṃ

°kena Kv 74.11; (purāṇa-)niṣīdana-saṃstara-°kāt Prāt 497.4, *from all sides* (Chin. *à chacun des quatre coins*) *of the old rug* (he must take pieces to put on the new one); uncertain is (vraṇa-)°kaḥ (m.!) Mvy 9330, Chin. (1) *scab* (*of a wound*), (2) *rim* or *circumference* (*of a wound*); Tib. cited as rmaḥi thaṅ (thoṅ) ḥkhor (kor), cf. thoṅ khor, *dense, thick; density* (Das), perh. *thick part* = *scab* as in Chin. (1); but for (śama-)sāmantakam Mvy 9185 (above) Tib. gaṅ khor, *circumference*; should this be adopted instead of thaṅ ḥkhor (kor)? It would correspond to Chin. (2).

sāmabhilaṣati (m.c. for Skt. sam°), *desires*: eta vimokṣa °ṣatyā (instr. sg. pres. pple. f.) Gv 258.15 (vs), *by* (me) *desiring*...

sāmam, indecl. pron. (= Pali sāmaṃ; in mg. = Skt. svayam; see **sāmato** and **svāmam**, **°ma**), *self, oneself*: na ... Ghaṭikāro kumbhakāro sāmaṃ (mss. somaṃ, so me) pṛthivīṃ khanati Mv i.326.19 (prose); sāmaṃ (mss. somaṃ) gṛhīto yatha kṛṣṇasarpo ii.81.7 (vs); tataḥ sāmaṃ (so 1 ms.; v.l. smenaṃ) ... ācikṣiṣyāmi iii.74.7 (prose); sāmaṃ (so 1 ms., v.l. somaṃ) ca ... lokam ... buddhacakṣuṣābhivilokayanto 317.19 (prose); in these the form seems fairly sure, tho by em. in the first two; much less clear are Senart's ems. in i.100.5 and 220.11 (here read cāsya with mss.).

sāmayika, m. or nt. (in this sense not otherwise recorded; the same are meant by pañca samayāḥ Mvy 8668), *seasonal period*; five are listed Mvy 9282–86, haimantikaḥ, grīṣmaḥ, vārṣikaḥ, mita-vārṣikaḥ, dīrgha-vārṣikaḥ; and Bhīk 22a.2–3 sāmayikā ārocayitavyāḥ: haimantikā graiṣmikā vārṣikā mita-v° dīrgha-vārṣikāś ca. tatra haimantikāś catvāro māsāḥ, graiṣmikāś catvāro māsāḥ, vārṣika eko māsaḥ, mita-vārṣika ekaṃ rātriṃdivasaṃ, dīrghavārṣikā ekarātronās trayo māsāḥ. This curious division is obviously monkish in basis, applying presumably in the Vinaya. Close parallel MSV iii.124.1 ff., sāmayikam, nt., and so nt. haimantikaṃ graiṣmikaṃ vārṣikaṃ mṛta-(! but Tib. thuṅ ṅu = *short*)-vārṣikaṃ dīrghavarṣikam; the extents are the same.

? **Sāmātaṭa**, f. °ṭī, adj., geographical, with vācā, (language) *of* (? some country or region; prob. corrupt): Mmk 332.7 (vs), see **Harikelika**.

? **sāmāyi** (-kāmaṃ?), obscure: LV 37.5 (vs) anyo-'nya-gama-(v.l. °gamana, which meter seems to require)-yuktā yathaiva sāmāyi kāmaṃ (Calc. °yi-kāmaṃ as one word) ca; Tib. seems to render the whole line: dper na ḥdus pa dag ni khri las su (Foucaux, *et, par exemple, les réunions sur des tapis*), phan tshun ḥgro bar sbyor bar byed daṅ mtshuṅs, app. *like one performing coition in moving back and forth* (in moving towards one another); so essentially Foucaux. Pali has adj. sāmāyika, seemingly based on samaya; is sāmāyi related to this? for samāyi, n. sg. of °yin, perh. with ā of first syllable m.c.? But the resulting sense is hardly satisfactory.

sāmiṣa, adj. (= Pali °sa; cf. **āmiṣa**), (**1**) *worldly*, opp. to **nir-āmiṣa** (1): Mvy 6751; (**2**) *fleshly, of the flesh, non-spiritual*, opp. to **nir-āmiṣa** (2): Mmk 286.3, 5, 7.

sāmīcī, **°ci** (= Pali id., mgs. 1 and 2; Skt. Lex. = vandanā; to weak stem of samyañc plus -a, f. ī, with vṛddhi), (**1**) *propriety of conduct, conformity to the ideal* (cf. Pali Vin. iv.142.20, = anudhammatā): °cī-pratipanna Mvy 1123 (Tib. mthun pa, *harmonize, be suitable, be wished for, desirable*); Sūtrāl. xiii.1, comm.; iyaṃ tatra °cī Prāt 488.3, *this is the proper procedure in this case* (so Chin.); bhikṣuṇī ... śikṣāsāmīcīṃ samāpannā Bhīk 24a.5, *having attained to propriety in the moral precepts*; (**2**) usually, *homage, respectful behavior, payment of respects*: Mvy 1768, among synonyms of mānanā, = Tib. ḥdud pa (and others); °cī-karaṇīyaḥ Mvy 1771 = Tib. phyag bya baḥi ḥos su gyur ba, *become worthy of having salutation made*; bodhisattvānāṃ °cīṃ kṛtvā Bbh 153.8 (here text °ciṃ); 154.19; 155.20 (here text °cī-kṛtvā); °cīṃ kārayitvā Bhīk 10a.4; °cī-karman (= Pali °cī-kamma), *payment of respects*, Bbh 239.23; 254.8; 378.9; Bhīk 6a.1; °cīm upadarśayantaṃ Bhīk 28b.5; in Divy 624.21 (vs, printed as prose) read labhate na ca sāmīcīṃ (ed. with mss. sāmītīṃ, note suggests samitiṃ, wrongly); (**3**) *consultation, arrangement, agreement*: MSV ii.103.2 °ciḥ (Tib. gros).

[**sāmītī**, Divy 624.21, see prec.]

sāmutkarṣika, adj., f. **°kī** (= **sam°**, q.v.; = Pali sāmukkaṃsika), *excellent, characterized by distinction*: °ko ... -dharmamukhāloko Dbh 5.15; °kī (dharmadeśanā) SP 60.11; Bbh 218.21; MSV iii.142.16; in Pali °kā (no °kī recorded) dhamma-desanā.

sāmudra, v.l. **°drika**, subst. (so BR) or adj., (*having to do with*) *chiromancy* (in Skt. as subst., and perh. so here): °dra-(v.l. °drika-)-jñānavidhijñaś ca naimittikas LV 268.4 (prose).

sāmudraka-lekhaka, m. (or adj.), Mvy 8898; v.l. samudraka-lekha, so Mironov (and °lekhaka, from Minayeff, pw 7.381, suggesting em. to sāmu°), *one who is marked with* (unfavorable) *bodily marks and lines* (in a list of bodily deformed persons); cf. Skt. samudra, and prec.; Tib. lag pa (*hand*) ḥjas te stebs (or ltebs) pa (= ?); Chin. *one who has a weak and crooked hand*; Jap. *one with unlucky lines on the hand*.

? **sāmpa**, m. or nt. (gen. °pasya), a high number: Gv 105.26. Prob. corruption for **samaya**, nt., of Gv 133.9, or **samarya** of Mvy.

(**sāṃparāya**, m., or nt., = Skt. id. = BHS and Pali **saṃparāya**, q.v. The definition in BR is not happy; *future life or state* is the mg. in Skt. The Sktized form occurs in BHS, e. g. Ud v.25 sāṃparāye, in contrast with dṛṣṭe dharme; and in Mv iii.214.17; 218.6; 222.9; in these gamanīyo (or °yaṃ) sāṃparāyaḥ (or °yaṃ, as if nt.) is read instead of **saṃparāyaḥ**, q.v., which occurs in the same phrase near by. See also **saṃparāyika** and next.)

(**sāṃparāyika**, adj. (Skt.), *of a future state*; see prec. and **saṃpar°**. The acc. nt. °kam is used as adv. SP 77.15, with dṛṣṭadhārmikaṃ, and 482.3 dṛṣṭadhārmikaṃ (noun) ca teṣāṃ sāṃparāyikaṃ (adv.) nivartiṣyati (or °tayiṣyati, medio-passive!), *and the worldly state will disappear for them in the future world*; misunderstood by Kern; Burnouf is free but correct in essence. However, WT omit sāṃp° with some mss. and Tib. Others, see **saṃ°** and **dṛṣṭa-dhārmika**.)

sāṃpreya, adj. (= Pali sappāya; etym. of both obscure; see **a-sāṃ°**, and CPD s.v. asappāya), (*suitable, fit, proper*, see **a-sāṃ°**;) esp. of food (so also in Pali), *wholesome*: Av i.255.1 °yam bhojanam; ii.110.2 °ya-bhojanena (Tib. phan pa, *beneficial, wholesome*); MSV ii.43.9 (Tib. ḥphrod pa); 45.17 (kriyā). Cf. **kula-sāṃ°**.

sāṃpreyaka, m., n. of a muhūrta (presumably *fit, suitable*, or *wholesome*, = **sāṃpreya**): Divy 643.23 °ko nāma muhūrtaḥ; 644.16.

sāṃbandhaka, nt. (to Skt. saṃbandha plus -ka; = Skt. °dhika), *an alliance by marriage*: (evaṃ) kṛtaṃ °kaṃ Av ii.37.9; evaṃ kṛte °ke 46.4; ms. both times sāvandhak°; Speyer em. sāṃbandhik°, because this occurs in Skt. and because 'the word must be a derivative from saṃbandhin, not saṃbandha'; I do not understand the second reason, and the first is irrelevant.

sāṃbali, for **śā°**, q.v.

Sāṃmitīya, m. pl., n. of a school (Hīnayāna, acc. to LaV-P., p. 148 note 1): MadhK 148.1.

sāmyaka, see **śā°**.

Sāyaṃgavendra (so all mss.; Senart em. Svāyaṃbhave°), n. of a former Buddha: Mv i.140.9.

sāyaṃprātika, adj. (Skt. Gr. id.; from Skt. sāyaṃ-prāta-r), *of, applicable to, evening and morning*: sakṛd eva daivasaṃ °kaṃ śālīṃ hareyaṃ Mv i.343.6 (prose).

sāra, m. (= Skt. śārī, śārikā, also written sā°), a

kind of bird, *maina*: sāra (all mss.; n. pl.) ivā ravanto LV 296.11 (vs).

Sāraka, n. of a hunter: Divy 437.12 ff.; MSV i.126.18 ff.

sāra-kalpa, m. (= Pali sārakappa, Childers and DPPN), a **kalpa** (q.v. 4) in which only one Buddha is born: Dharmas 87.

Sāraṅga, n. of a nāga king: Māy 246.20.

sārajyati, Senart's plausible em. for sārakṣyanti or °rakṣati (= Pali sārajjati, Skt. saṃrajyate; § 3.3), *is affectionately attached*: . . . puruṣā tatraiva °yanti tatraiva virajyanti (also em. for virakṣyanti) Mv iii.295.15; forms of rakṣ- make no sense.

Sārathi, n. of a former Buddha: LV 171.18.

sārathika (= °thi), *charioteer*: anurādhāyāṃ jāto bāṇijako bhavati °kaś ca Divy 646.24 (prose); app. -ka svārthe.

Sārathipura, n. of a town where the Buddha was entertained on the way to Benares to preach the first sermon: LV 406.20; Mv iii.328.4. (To be deleted in iii.327.19, with Senart, Introd. p. xxx, n. 1; in other respects Senart's summary on this page is inaccurate.)

Sāradhvaja, n. of a Buddhist monk: Śikṣ 36.8, and Gv 2d ed., for **Sāgaradhvaja,** Gv 99.19.

Sārapura (or Sarā°), n. of a locality: Māy 74.

sārambha (m., = Pali id.; for Skt. saṃrambha; § 3.3; see also **sālambha**), *quarrelsomeness*, or concretely, *quarrel, strife* (these seem to be clearly mgs. of the Pali word): prahīṇa-mada-māna-moha-sārambhaṃ (Bhvr.) Divy 425.24; cf. Pali Miln. 289.11 . . . sārambho māno atimāno mado . . . (in list of vices).

Sārarāja, v.l. for **Sāgararāja,** q.v.

Sāravatī, (**1**) n. of a samādhi: Mvy 610; ŚsP 1425.5; (**2**) in Gv 342.2 (prose) dharmakāya-bhedya-sāravatī-dhātu-niryātāṃ, said of a 'night-goddess', adept in religion. The word sāravatī seems to qualify dhātu closely, but what the combination means is not clear to me; *solid element* or the like? Cf. Gv 350.25 niḥsattvavatī-dhātu-jñāna-pratilabdho, said of a Bodhisattva, *who has attained to knowledge of the unsubstantial element(s)*, sc. of worldly existence; here too a fem. adj. stem qualifies dhātu in a cpd.

sārasi, m. or f. (= Skt. °sa or °sī), *crane*: °si-kāpotaka- (see this) LV 248.20 (prose; Calc. °thi).

sārāyaṇī, adj. f., = next (2), q.v.: °ṇīṃ (ms. °ṇī; v.l. unmetr. °ṇīyaṃ) kathāṃ kṛtvā Mv ii.199.9 (vs); the corresp. vs in Pali Sn 419 sārāṇiyaṃ.

sārāyaṇīya (on etym. see below), (**1**) nt., *hospitable entertainment*, esp. with food: °yaṃ karetsu (so mss., prec. by na) saṃbuddhasya punaḥ-punaḥ Mv i.304.5 (vs), (the villagers) *gave entertainment to the Perfectly Enlightened One again and again* (sc. with food, which they had previously refused him); ṛṣiṇā tasya lubdhakasya °ṇīyaṃ kṛtaṃ, yathā ṛṣidharmo phalodakam upanāmitaṃ Mv ii.96.17; (**2**) adj., f. °yā (= **saṃrañjana,** °**nīya, saṃrajanīya**; = Pali sārāṇīya, which Childers derives from the Skt. root smṛ, following standard Pali comms., e. g. MN comm. i.110.16 ff., ii.394.31 f., but this is certainly wrong; Kern, cited PTSD, rightly regards BHS saṃrañjana, °nīya, as the true original; all forms can be derived from this; saṃ- gave sā-, and for -rañja- was substituted first *-rāja-, both by § 3.3, then -rāya-, as in BHS, § 2.34; finally in Pali this -rāya- was contracted to the single syllable -rā-, Pischel 149, 150, cf. § 3.118, Geiger 20; the rare BHS saṃrajanīya, if not an error for saṃrañj°, may be derived from the unnasalized form of the same root raj), *courteous, pleasing, polite, friendly*: this form noted only in Mv iii.47.18 etc. (cited, with list of passages, s.v. **saṃmodate**; always °yāṃ kathāṃ); in iii.394.14, however, mss. sāropaṇīyāṃ instead (Senart em.), and one of them also reads sāropayitvā for the following vyatisārayitvā. For other parallels see the equivalent words cited above.

sārūpya, adj. (cf. next and **sāropya**; Skt. only nt. abstr. *similitude*; = Pali sāruppa), *suitable*: °pyābhir gāthābhiḥ (or equivalent), regularly foll. by verb of praising, *with suitable stanzas*: SP 161.4; 162.8; LV 357.19; 359.18; 360.12; 366.14; Laṅk 23.9; Mv ii.266.1; iii.379.20 (here mss. °pyehi gāthehi); 400.18 (°pyāhi gāthābhir); Suv 99.11 (so read with v.l. for Nobel °pābhir); Gv 253.3; na śramaṇasya sārūpyāṇi (pātrāṇi) LV 383.3, *not proper for a monk*; **pratisaṃlayana-** (see this)-sārūpya (so read) Mv ii.123.18, (places) *suitable for private meditation*.

sārūpyaka, adj., = prec., in **pratisaṃlayana-**sā° (v.l. °pya) Bbh 8.25 (prose).

[**Sārūpyavatī,** RP 25.2, read sā **Rūpāvatī** (see the latter).]

Sārocaya (?), m., n. of a kalpa: (text) sāroca yaś ca tada kalpas, tatra utpanna . . . Gv 258.14 (vs).

sāropya, adj., = **sārūpya,** q.v.; only in **pratisaṃlayana-**(q.v.)-sā°, of places: Mv iii.143.13; 200.17.

sārthaka, m. (= Pali satthaka; to Skt. sārtha plus -ka; Skt. only °ika), *merchant, trader*: Divy 173.7 (in next line °ika), 20.

Sārthavāha, (**1**) n. of a son of Māra (favorable to the Bodhisattva): Mv ii.327.17; 330.5; LV 44.11; 303.19; 304.7, 17; 305.4, 308.20; (**2**) n. of a Bodhisattva: Śikṣ 145.16, quoted from Dharmasaṃgīti; (**3**) n. of a yakṣa: Māy 26.

sārthavāhaka (= Skt. °vāha), *caravan leader*: °ka-rūpeṇa Gv 225.26 (prose; not dim.; after **saṃgrahaka-,** q.v., -rūpeṇa; no context).

sārdhaṃ-vihārika, and °**rin** (= Pali saddhiṃ-vih°; to Skt. sārdhaṃ cpd. with vihāra, plus -ika, -in), *a (co-) resident monk*, regularly however applied to those who are undergoing training, virtually *(fellow-)pupil*; sometimes with gen. of their preceptor, as: Ānandasya triṃśa °rikā śikṣāṃ pratyākhyāya . . . Mv iii.47.13; °ry-antevāsinaḥ sabrahmacāriṇaś ca Bbh 125.10; asya tatra pañca °ri-śatāni Divy 347.2; mahallena bhūtvā pañca °riṇāṃ *(of pupils)* śatāni upasthāpitāni Av ii.139.8; sārdha-(m.c. for sārdhaṃ-)-°riṇo RP 31.7 (vs); dvau °riṇau MSV ii.108.20.

sārdhaṃcara, adj. (= Pali saddhiṃcara), *going along with* (one): MSV ii.185.2.

sārvakālika, adj., *wholly black*, = **sarvakālaka,** q.v.: MSV iii.72.5, in an uddāna verse.

sārvayānika, f. °**kī,** adj., *applying to all vehicles* (**yāna,** in the technical Buddhist sense): prajñāpāramitā . . . °kī (one ms. sarva°) AsP 31.12.

Sāla (see also s.v. **Sālarāja**), n. of a former Buddha: Mv iii.236.13.

Sālabalā (cf. °bala BR 7.961), n. of a city: MSV i.66.3, 18.

sālabhañjaka, °**ikā,** (**1**) m. or nt., *breaking of the sāl-branch*, said of the Bodhisattva's mother in giving birth to him: °kaṃ ca kariṣyati Mv ii.18.9 (prose); (**2**) f., *breaking of sāl-branches*, n. of a festival: Av i.302.6, see s.v. **parvan.**

sālambha, m. (may be specialized use of **sārambha** = Pali id., which so far as I know is not recorded of physical fighting; in some LV mss. v.l. sār° occurs sometimes for this), app. *(contest of) wrestling*: °bhaḥ Mvy 4998 = Tib. gyad kyi ḥdzin staṅs, lit. *an athlete's style* (or *posture*) *of grasping*, Das = saṃgrāho mallasya, saṃlambha (! not recorded elsewhere; prob. Das's 'correction' for sāl°), *'the mode of seizing in wrestling'*: (in lists of arts) asi-dhanu(ṣ)-kalāpa-yuddha-sālambha- LV 4.21; 143.6; 144.8; in all these Tib. as on Mvy above, and so also for °bha-(dhanurvede) LV 156.9; that *wrestling* is meant seems confirmed by LV 152.10 ff., in which the Bodhisattva defeats the Śākya youths in what can only be *wrestling* (cf. esp. 152.18–20); our word occurs there several times, Śākyakumārāḥ sālambhāya sthitāḥ 152.11, *stood ready for wrestling*; similarly abhigatau °bhāya 12; °bhāyāgacchata 22; here, however, Tib. renders always by brgal ba (once preceded by stobs, *force*), a general word for *fight*.

Sālarāja (cf. **Sāla** and **Śālarāja**), n. of a former Buddha: Mv iii.237.9 f.

Sālibalā, n. of a city: MSV i.66.3, 20.

sālekhika, adj. (to **saṃlekha**, q.v., plus -ika; § 3.3), *relating to severe austerities*: kuryāḥ °kīṃ kathāṃ Śikṣ 354.14 (vs); ms. sāl°, ed. em. sāṃl°, which is cited p. 415 as reading of a ms. of Samādh containing the passage; but sāl° (cf. Pali sallekha) would be possible.

Sālendradhvajāgravatī (v.l. Śāl°), n. of a lokadhātu: Suv 172.4.

Sālendrarāja (see also Śāl°), (**1**) n. of a former Buddha: LV 171.22 (Calc. with most mss. Sār°, but Tib. with best ms. Sāl°); (**2**) n. of a Buddha in the zenith: Sukh 98.17.

Sālendrarājaś(i)rigarbha, n. of a Buddha: Gv 285.1 (vs).

sālohita, m. (= Pali id.; Skt. Gr. sa-lohita plus -a), *kinsman*: LV 118.1; 386.12 (pūrvajāti-sālohito); Mv i.27.7; 253.19; ii.154.15; iii.92.16; 180.17; 290.4; 303.14 ff.; Mvy 3910; Divy 111.6; 229.10; 502.10; Av i.139.7; Śikṣ 49.14; Gv 228.4; Bbh 132.16; 232.21. Mostly prose; often cpd. with prec. jñāti (and other words of this sphere).

sāvadāna, f. °**nā** and °**nī**, adj., °**nam**, adv. (= Pali sapadāna, rarely v.l. sā°, see CPD, s.v. apadāna, usually as in BHS of monks' begging rounds; acc. to Vism. 60.19–21 sa-apa-(= apetaṃ)-dāna (= avakhaṇḍanaṃ), avakhaṇḍa-virahitaṃ anugharan ti; true etym. uncertain), *in regular, systematic order*; chiefly of monks' begging rounds, *uninterrupted(ly)*, going from one house to the next in order: °naṃ (prob. adv.) Mvy 8567, Chin. acc. to Lévi on Karmav 21.14 *dans l'ordre de succession*, which is prob. intended by Tib. mthar chags; context proves application to begging rounds; taṃ grāmaṃ °naṃ piṇḍāya caritvā Mv i.301.9; brāhmaṇagrāme °naṃ piṇḍāya caranto 327.8; °nīṃ Vaiśālīṃ piṇḍāya caritvā Av i.8.7; °naṃ . . . piṇḍopacaraṇaṃ Karmav 21.14; (saṃtatyā piṇḍāya) cartavyaṃ °nacāriṇā ca bhavitavyaṃ Śikṣ 128.8; exceptionally of speech, sanidānavatīṃ vācaṃ bhāṣate kālena sāvadānāṃ Dbh 24.20 (*uninterrupted*? or *well-ordered, regulated*? but Tib. śin tu go ba, *well understanding*; one Chin. transl. *having stages* or *divisions*); Kondo's ed. cites one ms. as sāpa°.

sāvadya (nt.? Skt. as adj., rarely subst., only Hem. Pariś.; = Pali sāvajja), *what is sinful, sin*: in Bhvr. cpds., vigata-°dyāś ca bhavanti Mv i.134.9, *and they become free from sin*; sattvānām . . . uttaptakuśalamūlānām alpa-°dyānāṃ Gv 268.3, . . . *of little sin*.

sāvaśeṣa, adj. (= Pali sāvasesa), *not absolute, incomplete*, opp. of **niravaśeṣa**, q.v.; of a sin, *that can be atoned*: kṛtena (etc.) °ṣeṇa MSV iii.110.6 f.; 111.9 f.; 13 f.

sāvāsana, m.c. for sa-vāsana, Bhvr., see **vāsana**: LV 291.1; 294.6 (vss.)

sāśrava, see **āśrava**.

Sāhaṃjanī or °**nī** (°nin?; no distinctively fem. forms, such as oblique -īye, noted), n. of a hermitage locality (āśramapada) in the Himālayas, home of the ṛṣi **Gautama** (4): Mv ii.210.1; of the ṛṣi **Kāśyapa** (4), iii.143.12 °nī, n. sg.; 146.15 °nīṃ, acc. sg.; in 150.17 and 151.13 Senart prints °niṃ, but in the former 1 ms., in the latter both, read °nīṃ; 151.4 °nisya (v.l. °nīsya); also home of ṛṣi Kāśyapa (4) iii.362.12 ff.

sāhartavya, gdve. (semi-MIndic for Skt. saṃh°, § 3.3; cf. **abhisāhita**, and AMg. sāharaṇa = saṃh°), *to be collected*: ujjhita-coḍakā °vyā (v.l. sāhatavyā, for sāhi°?) Mv iii.264.11 (prose).

sāhasra (in Skt. as general adj.; cf. Pali sahassa, adj., ep. of a lokadhātu and of Brahmā as its ruler, sahasso . . . Brahmā sahassīlokadhātuṃ pharitvā MN iii.101.4–5), adj. with lokadhātu, or (Mv) subst., sc. lokadhātu, *consisting of 1000* (worlds); = **sāhasra-cūḍika**, q.v.: śakro (or, brahmā) . . . sāhasragatāna madhye Mv iii.119.12 (here by em.); 122.19; 123.2, *Indra* (*Brahmā*) *in the midst of inhabitants of* (a universe of) *1000 worlds*; °sra-lokadhātuṃ Dbh 72.25; °sro lokadhātuḥ Gv 75.2; °sre °dhātau ŚsP 26.8; contrasting with **dvisāhasra** and **trisāhasra-mahāsāhasra**. In Pali no form with ā in the first syllable is recorded. (Childers cites sāhassiko without reference, with definition suggesting no application to lokadhātu.)

sāhasra-cūḍika, m. (cf. Pali sahassī cūḷanikā lokadhātu), n. of a lokadhātu: Mvy 3042. Cf. repeatedly in AsP sāhasre cūḍike (or, cūḍikāyāṃ) lokadhātau, loc., the cpd. apparently divided into two words, sāhasre, always m., but cūḍikāyāṃ, f., in AsP 65.3; 66.2, and so v.l., one ms. out of six, 105.13, 16; 108.3, 5; but cūḍike text with 5 mss. in these four places, and elsewhere, e. g. 117.18, without v.l.; no reading with cūḍikāyāṃ has been noted except in the passages cited; (sahasrika)ś cyūḍiko (read cū°) lokadhātuḥ MPS 31.46. The form cūḍ° evidently means *small, minor*, and is related to Pali cūḷa, culla. Contrasted with **dvisāhasra** . . . and **trisāhasramahā-sāhasra** . . ., qq.v. In ŚsP 26.8 and elsewhere replaced by sāhasre lokadhātau, see **sāhasra**.

Sāhasrapramardanī, n. of a rakṣā (q.v.): Dharmas 5. Also **Mahā-sāh°**.

sāhasrika, adj. (not recorded in this mg.), *ruling a thousand* (worlds): °ko mahābrahmā Dbh 72.24; cf. brahmā °kādhipaḥ Dbh.g. 54(80).17.

sāhasrī (= AMg. sāhassī; cf. **sahasrī**), (*a group of*) *one thousand*: in Mv i.148.17 (vs) five of six mss. read viṃśa sahasriyo teṣāṃ, but meter seems to favor, with Senart, viṃśat sāh°. In some citations under **sahasrī**, in prose, some mss. read sāh°. Cf. **tri-sāhasrī**, but this seems to be adjectival (sc. lokadhātu).

sāhika, gen. pl. °kānāṃ, some kind of animal living in holes or caves: Mv i.20.6; 23.2; see s.v. **gutti**.

sāhoḍha, adj., m.c. for Skt. sahoḍha, *having stolen goods with him*: °ḍhā iva caurā(ḥ) LV 371.12 (vs).

1 **si** (or **sī**), syllable used in learning to write: Divy 486.2, 6 sīty ukte dham iti vismarati (of a stupid pupil). Prob. refers to the word siddham; the forgotten akṣara would strictly be ddham.

2 **si** = asi, *thou art*: §§ 4.7; 28.64.

Siṃha, (**1**) n. of a former Buddha: LV 171.21; Sukh 6.16; (**2**) n. of a future Buddha, to appear after **Maitreya** (q.v. on this passage): Mv ii.354.19 = iii.279.3; Gv 441.24; (**3**) n. of various other Buddhas: Gv 82.10; Sukh 70.12 and 13 (in same list; prob. the first is to be om. with one ms.); a Buddha in the nadir, Sukh 98.7; (**4**) n. of a Bodhisattva: SP 3.9; (**5**) (= Pali Sīha, 1 in DPPN) n. of a general, also called prince, in Vaiśālī: senāpati Mv i.288.5; 289.18; Av i.8.7 ff. and MSV i.236.10 ff. (in Vaiśālī); rājaputra, Karmav 92.5, 6, in Vaiśālī, with text agreeing with Pali AN iii.38 ff., dealing with Sīha senāpati; rājakumāra, cited from **Siṃhaparipṛcchā**, Śikṣ 5.15 (acc. to Bendall and Rouse, note in Transl., 'son of Ajātaśatru'; I do not know the basis for this); (**6**) n. of a merchant (= **Siṃhaka**): Divy 523.22; (**7**) n. of a yakṣa leader: Māy 235.18; (**8**) n. of a son of **Khaṇḍa** (2): MSV ii.4.5 ff.

Siṃhaka, n. of a merchant (= **Siṃha** 6): Divy 523.12.

Siṃhakalpā, n. of a town: Divy 523.9 ff.

Siṃhaketu, (**1**) n. of a Bodhisattva: LV 2.11; (**2**) n. of a former Buddha: LV 172.8; (**3**) n. of a king, father of **Maitrāyaṇī** (2): Gv 123.2.

Siṃhakeśarin, n. of a king: Divy 523.9; 526.4, 25.

Siṃhagāminī, n. of a 'gandharva maid': Kv 5.4.

Siṃhaghoṣa, n. of a Buddha in a southeastern lokadhātu: SP 184.8.

siṃha-candana, some variety of sandalwood: anye devā °nasya bodhivṛkṣaṃ saṃjānanti Mv ii.310.2.

Siṃhacandrā, n. of a nun: SP 383.1.

Siṃhajātaka (v.l. Siddha-j°), n. of a work: Karmav 44.21 (not identified; not Pali Jāt. 157).

Siṃhateja(s), n. of a former Buddha: °jaḥ, n. sg., Mv i.137.13.

Siṃhadatta, n. of a previous incarnation of Bindusāra: Mmk 613.13.

siṃha-dhvaja, (**1**) m. or nt., a kind of gem: Gv 511.4; (**2**) n. of a Buddha in a southeastern lokadhātu: SP 184.9; (**3**) n. of a former Buddha: Samādh p. 52 line 19.

Siṃhanandi(n), n. of a disciple of Buddha: Mv i.183.1.

Siṃhanāda, n. of a deity: Sādh 47.3 etc.

Siṃhanādanādin, n. of a Bodhisattva: Mvy 685.

siṃhanādin, (**1**) adj.-subst. m. (= Pali sīha° acc. to Childers, without ref.; PTSD only °nādika), *possessing* or *manifesting the* (religious) *'lion's roar'*: °nādinām agryaḥ (among Buddha's followers; of Piṇḍola-bharadvāja) Divy 399.30; cf. Pali AN i.23.24 (aggaṃ . . .) sīhanādikānaṃ yad-idaṃ Piṇḍola-bhāradvājo; (**2**) n. of a son of Māra (favorable to the Bodhisattva): LV 314.6.

siṃhapañjara, (**1**) nt. (= Pali sīha-p°), a kind of *window*: °re sthitā Mv ii.446.20; niryūha-°ra-gavākṣa-iii.69.17; 81.14; ratna-°rāṇi Gv 167.16; in 202.23 in cpd. containing niryūha and gavākṣa; (**2**) n. of a (perh. mythical) gem: °ra-maṇiratna-padmagarbhāṇi Gv 101.13.

Siṃhaparipṛcchā (see **Siṃha** 5), n. of a work: Mvy 1394; Śikṣ 5.13 f.; 53.5.

Siṃhapura, °rī, (**1**) °ra, n. of a city, in the Kiṃnarī Jātaka: Mv ii.95.5; 98.1 ff.; (**2**) °ra, n. of a city in the Kaliṅga country: Mv iii.432.14; (**3**) °rī, n. of the capital city (rājadhānī) of **Śākyamuni** (3), q.v.: Mv iii.238.11.

Siṃhapota, nt., n. of a city: Gv 147.12.

Siṃhabala, n. of a yakṣa: so prob. understand Māy 61, see s.v. **Vyāghrabala**.

Siṃhamati, (**1**) n. of a former Buddha: Sukh 6.17; (**2**) n. of a son of Māra (favorable to the Bodhisattva): LV 313.21.

siṃhamuktā, *'lion-pearl'*, a kind of gem: Gv 511.4.

siṃhamukha, (nt.), lit. *lion's mouth*, (**1**) *a spout* or *opening* thru which water was conducted into or out of a pond: aṣṭottaraṃ ca °kha-śataṃ yena gandhodakaṃ praviśati tasyāḥ . . . puṣkiriṇyāḥ (ms., ed. em. puṣka°), aṣṭaśatam eva °khānāṃ yena punar eva tad vāri nirvahati RP 40.15 f.; (**2**) an instrument of torture (cf. **ulkāmukha** 1 and Pali rāhumukha, MN i.87.13 with comm. ii.58.28): °khaṃ vā hriyamāṇasya Śiks 182.4.

Siṃhala, (**1**) also **°laka, °la-rāja**, n. of a son of the merchant **Siṃha** 6, and an incarnation of Śākyamuni: °la Divy 523.23 ff.; RP 23.14; °laka Divy 524.21 (prose; no perceptible mg. in -ka); °la-rāja Kv 52.21; (**2**) n. of a nāga king: Māy 247.37.

siṃha-latā, some kind of ornament, placed on trees and stūpas, and in groves (on their trees?); precise mg. can only be guessed (Müller on Sukh *'lion twists'*; Senart, Mv ii note 553, *'peut-être . . . des enroulements combinés de feuillage et de lions'*): Sukh 54.11 (among ornaments of Amitāyus's bodhi-tree); °tāhi . . . samalaṃkṛtaṃ bodhivṛkṣaṃ saṃjānetsuḥ Mv ii.311.13; siṃhalatāhi (or siṃho-, mss.; Senart em. siṃhī°, m.c.; better siṃhā° = siṃha°) sphuṭā bodhivṛkṣe (em., mss. sphuṭe °kṣo) Mv ii.317.8 (vs); (udyānaṃ . . . saṃchannaṃ . . .) °latā-jālaiḥ Gv 101.24; °latāḥ suruciravarṇasūtrā(ḥ) Śikṣ 302.2 (vs), in passage vaguely parallel to Mv ii.317.8; suruci° may be a parallel and independent ornament, rather than an ep. of siṃhalatā; here decorations of a stūpa.

Siṃhalarāja, see **Siṃhala** (1).

Siṃhavatsa, n. of a serpent king: Mvy 3432.

Siṃhavikrāntagāmin, n. of a Tathāgata: Gv 361.4.

Siṃhavikrīḍita, (**1**) n. of a Bodhisattva: Mvy 683; (prob. the same; not a Tathāgata with Index) Śikṣ 173.13, 18 (voc.; separate from foll. words); (**2**) n. of a samādhi: Mvy 509 (not in ŚsP); Dharmas 136.

siṃhavijṛmbhita, (**1**) (nt.?) *'lion's yawn'* of Bodhisattvas and mahāpuruṣas, fig. applied to their activities: Gv 224.11, parallel with **vikurvā** and vimokṣavikrīḍita; (**2**) nt., n. of a city: Gv 123.1, 18; (**3**) (m.) n. of a (Gv 33.26 tathāgata-, or Gv 34.26 buddha-)samādhi: Mvy 533 (not in ŚsP); Gv 33.22 ff.

Siṃhavijṛmbhitaprabha, n. of a Tathāgata: Gv 421.23.

Siṃhavijṛmbhitā, n. of a nun: Gv 192.16 ff.

Siṃhavinardita, (**1**) n. of a Buddha: Gv 259.9 (vs); (**2**) n. of a Bodhisattva: Gv 443.2.

siṃhaviṣkambhita (text °viklambhita, corruptly), nt., *lion-firmness, immovability*: °tena viṣkambhayeyam ŚsP 110.19, see **viṣkambhayati**; as n. of a samādhi, °taṃ samādhiṃ ŚsP 483.6 (text here also °viklambh°).

siṃhaśayyā (cf. Pali sīhaseyyā), *bed of state* (cf. siṃhāsana, **siṃhāṅgada**): upetya Bhagavataḥ (after his death) °yāṃ MPS 46.2 The Pali is traditionally supposed to refer to posture (lying on the right side); this seems unlikely in MPS (tho of course he is always represented in that posture). Cf. siṃhaśayyāyāṃ ib. 47.2.

Siṃhasāgarakūṭavinanditarāja, n. of a former Buddha: Sukh 6.3.

Siṃhasaudāsa, n. of a king: Laṅk 250.13.

Siṃhahanu, (**1**) (= Pali Sīhahanu), n. of a Śākyan king, father of Śuddhodana: Mvy 3598; Mv i.352.12 f.; 355.19 f.; ii.37.17; only the Bodhisattva proved able to wield his bow, Mv ii.76.4; LV 154.15; (**2**) n. of a Buddha in the east: Mv i.123.9; (**3**) n. of a disciple of Śākyamuni: Mv i.182.17; (**4**) n. of Māra's general (senāpati): LV 303.1.

siṃhāṅgada, or (v.l., and Senart) **sīhāṅgada**, see **sīha**, lit. *lion-bracelet*, perh. in sense of *superior, very fine bracelet*, cf. Pali sīha-kuṇḍala (worn in the ear, Sn. comm. 138.3): °dā, pl. (worn by Hrī) Mv ii.59.15 (vs).

siṃhāṇa, (m. or nt.; Skt. Lex. id.; cf. next), *snot*: °ṇa-lālā (mss.° mālā, °māro) Mv ii.326.6 (vs; lack of -ka m.c.?). Cf. also **siṅghāṇa**.

siṃhāṇaka, m. or nt., **°ṇikā**, f. (cf. prec., and Skt. siṅghāṇaka, Skt. and Pali siṅghāṇikā), *snot*: °ṇaka Divy 342.15; Māy 219.14 etc.; °kān (acc. pl., end of dvandva) LV 256.20; °kaṃ (n. sg., end of dvandva) Sukh 68.9; °ṇikā Mv i.28.8; all prose.

? **siṃhāsapīṭha** (°supīṭha ?), adj., only in first half of an anuṣṭubh vs, °pīṭho (or °pīṭhā) balavān: Mv ii.431.17 (here printed as prose, wrongly); 458.10; iii.7.2, 13; 13.9; so mss., with practically no variants except °sa° or °su°, °ṭhā or °ṭho; Senart has various emendations and suggested interpretations, doubting at last (iii n. 466) his suggestion of ii n. 568, -sapīṭha = sadṛśa, *(lion-)like*; except that the mg. must be in effect *strong*, or the like, I cannot interpret the word. It may be cpd. with the foll. balavān, and is doubtless corrupt. (Divide siṃhāsa-[= siṃhāsana-]-pīṭho?)

Siṃhoraska, n. of a former Buddha: Mv i.140.5.

sikthaka, nt. (= Skt. Lex. id., Pali sitthaka; Skt. siktha), *beeswax*: Mvy 7115 = Tib. (s)bra tshil (acc. to Jä. and Das spra tshil, *wax*).

siṅghāṇa, m. or nt. (= Skt. °ṇaka; see also **siṃhāṇa, °ṇaka**), *snot*: Mmk 112.24 (vs; lack of -ka perh. m.c.), see s.v. **śaṭa-**.

Sitaketu, n. of a Pratyekabuddha: Mmk 64.13; 111.10.

Sitatārā, n. of a form of Tārā: Sādh 213.4 etc.

sita-puṣpika, nt., acc. to BR *a kind of leprosy*: Mvy 9545 = Tib. śa mtshan; cf. śa tshan dmar po, *a tumor resembling a weal or a wart* (Jä.; dmar po = *red*); śa mtshan, *marks on the body* (Das); Chin. *dirty spots*.

Sitavatī, see **Mahā-si°** and **Śītavatī**.

Sitaviśālākṣa, n. of a Bodhisattva: Gv 442.7.

Sitaśrī, n. of a Bodhisattva: Gv 442.21.

Sitāṅga, n. of a Bodhisattva: Gv 442.1.

Sitātapatra, n. of one of the 8 Uṣṇīṣa-rājānaḥ (see **Uṣṇīṣa** 3): Mmk 41.11.

Sitāsitalocana, n. of a former Buddha: Mv i.140.5.

[**Sitodaka,** see **Śītodaka.**]

-sittha(ka), see **madhu-siktha(ka).**

siddhaka, adj.-ppp. (= Skt. and Pali siddha, *cooked*, the Pali word wrongly explained PTSD, plus specifying -ka), *that had been cooked, prepared*: yāni (foods) rājñā Kuśena siddhakāni Mv ii.478.16 (prose), *which were the ones that King Kuśa had prepared* (these were superlatively done); cf. siddhaṃ line 12, (kena . . . mamādya) āhāro siddho 18.

? **Siddha-jātaka,** see **Siṃha-j°.**

Siddhapātra, n. of one of the 16 guardian deities of the bodhimaṇḍa: LV 277.14.

Siddhayātra, n. of a yakṣa: Māy 60.

Siddhaśabara(-pāda), n. of an author: Sādh 387.16; adj. **Siddhaśabara-pādīya(-mata),** 456.13.

Siddhārtha, (**1**) (= Pali Siddhattha), personal name of Śākyamuni (Buddha; in Mv and LV more commonly **Sarvārthasiddha**): Mvy 49; 3603 (here in a list of 'cakravartin kings' but following the names of his Śākyan elders); Gv 439.2; Mv ii.75.19 (after Sarvārthasiddha, 18); iii.330.7 (mss.); LV 209.3; 226.17; 252.6; (**2**) n. of another, future Buddha: Mv iii.330.8; but I believe the passage is corrupt, and that actually Śākyamuni is here referred to a second time (as well as in line 7, see above); note that Maitreya is named next in line 8; (**3**) n. of a son of Māra (favorable to the Bodhisattva): LV 312.21; (**4**) n. of a yakṣa: Māy 69.

Siddhārthabuddhi, n. of an ancient Buddha: RP 36.16; 48.14 ff.

Siddhārthamati, n. of a Bodhisattva: LV 2.12.

Siddhārthā, n. of a devakumārikā in the eastern quarter: LV 388.9 = Mv iii.306.8.

Siddhaikavīra, n. of a form of Mañjuśrī: Sādh 137.1 etc.

Siddhottamā, n. of a goddess: Mvy 4296.

siddhya, sidhya, adj. (to Skt. siddha or siddhi plus -ya?), *leading to* or *concerning success*: siddhya-dravyāṇi vā sarvāṇi labhate Mmk 107.4 (prose; sc., as result of a magic rite); śiṣyagaṇaiḥ svakaiḥ parivṛto 'haṃ pūja jane sadātra cala sidhya RP 30.4 (vs); sidhya seems to be for °yā, n. sg. f., with pūja (= pūjā), tho it is very strange to find a for ā at the end of a line.

sindhava (m. or nt.; doubtless = **saindhava,** q.v.), a kind of musical instrument, prob. a sort of *drum*: (mṛdaṅgavādyeṣu āliṅgavādyeṣu) sindhavavādyeṣu paṇavavādyeṣu Mv iii.70.15 (prose).

Sindhu, n. of a nāga king: Mvy 3305; Māy 247.8.

sindhuvārita (m.; Pali and Skt. Lex. id.; Skt. °vāra, °vāraka, °vārikā; also sindu° in Skt. and Pali), a certain tree, *Vitex negundo*: Kalpanāmaṇḍitikā, Lüders, Kl. Skt. Texte 2, p. 45 (fragm. 23 V 2); °ta-gandharāja, a kind of perfume, Gv 153.14.

siyāti, *perhaps*, see **syāt.**

[**sī,** see **si.**]

sīṃhaka, some product of the jeweler's craft: °kā pi kriyanti Mv ii.473.12.

Sītā-nāgarāja, n. of a nāga king: Mvy 3306; Māy 247.8. Sītā is doubtless the river of that name; cf. s.vv. **Vakṣu** and **Pakṣu.**

sīphalā (v.l. si°), sc. lipi, a kind of writing: Mv i.135.7, between vaṅgā and tramidā (= drāviḍā); possibly error, or hyper-Skt., for Pali and AMg. sīhala = Skt. siṃhala, *Singhalese.*

sīma, nt.; also **sīman,** m. or f., or **sīmā,** f., a moderately high number: sīmaṃ Mvy 7836, cited from Gv 133.2; in Gv 105.20 gen. sattvāsīnasya, read sattva-sīmasya; sīmā, n. sg., Mvy 7710.

sīmātikrāntika, adj. (Pali °kkantika), with kaṭhinoddhāra, *due to* (a monk's) *having crossed the boundary* (of the vihāra): MSV ii.161.18; 163.4.

sīmābandha, m., (**1**) *drawing a strict line of* (moral) *demarcation* (between good and evil): °dhaḥ Mvy 6825; so Jap.; Tib. mtshams bcad pa; °dhaḥ kṛto bhavati (by Buddha, before he will enter nirvāṇa) Divy 150.21; (**2**) *drawing a* (*magic*) *boundary* ('magic circle', Bendall and Rouse, Śikṣ p. 136) as protection against evil: dṛṣṭyā manasā vā °dhaṃ karoti Śikṣ 139.10; °dhaṃ tataḥ kuryāt Suv 106.6, °dhaṃ samārabhet 7 (vss); similarly Māy 261.4; MSV i.286.17.

sīmāvati, presumably for °vatī, = Skt. sīmā, *boundary* (cf. § 22.50): sarvabuddhadarśana-°ti-krameṇa bodhisattva-samādhinā Gv 39.5 (prose), *march to the limit of all-Buddha-views* (? *insight*); in a list of bodhisattva-samādhis.

[**sīra,** n. pl. sīrāḥ, error for sītāḥ, *furrows*, to Skt. sītā: (sa yadaikaṃ) **halasīraṃ** (q.v.) kṛṣati tadā sapta sīrāḥ (read sītāḥ) kṛṣṭā bhavanti Divy 124.7, and similarly 134.7, *when he drew* (*plowed with*) *a single plow*(*-share*), *then seven furrows were plowed* (by magic power). Proved by Pali Vin. i.240.18–19 ekena naṅgalena kasantassa satta sītāyo gacchanti. Corruption due to preceding (hala-) sīraṃ.]

[**sīvaka,** em. for **sevaka** = **āsevaka,** q.v., *patch.*]

sīha, m. (= Pali, Pkt. id.; MIndic for siṃha), *lion*: Mv i.227.1 = ii.30.4 (vs); ii.59.15 (see **siṃhāṅgada**); v.l. siṃha in all; see also next, where no v.l. siṃha-.

Sīha-niṣadya (m.c. for °yā? see **niṣadyā**; cf. Pkt. Sīhanisijjā, acc. to Sheth n. of a Jain shrine on Mount Aṣṭāpada), lit. *lion's seat*, evidently referring to the top of a mountain or something located there; read in Mv ii.37.4 (vs) Sīhaniṣadya-niviṣṭaṃ (grasati . . . ādityaṃ), *the sun . . . when it has set on* (*behind*) *S.*

su, indecl. (= Pali id., for Skt. svid), particle used (in Pali) generally after interrog.: suvrataṃ kiṃ su kathaṃ ca dāntam (or da° with mss., MIndic) āhu Mv iii.395.7 (vs), = Pali Sn 513 sorata kena kathaṃ ca dantam āhu. (In LV 337.7 (vs) divide gṛhāṇa su Gautamam, but su here is a pronoun = Skt. taṃ, acc. sg. m.) Cf. **suda(ṃ) so, sva.**

Suutthitā, n. of a devakumārikā in the southern quarter: LV 389.8 (vs); corresp. to **Śubhesthitā** of Mv.

sukaniṣṭha, pl., a class of gods: Mmk 19.10 (prec. by **akaniṣṭhā,** foll. by **lokaniṣṭhā,** qq.v.).

Sukīrti, n. of a former Buddha: Mv i.136.14.

Sukukṣi, n. of a 'gandharva maid': Kv 4.20.

Sukuṇḍala, n. of a god (among the Śuddhāvāsakāyika): Kv 43.16.

Suketu, (**1**) n. of a Pratyekabuddha: Mmk 111.10; (**2**) n. of a Buddha: Mmk 130.4.

Sukeśa, n. of a Buddha: Mmk 499.21.

Sukrīḍā, n. of an apsaras: Kv 3.16.

sukha-divasa, see s.v. **sukharātri.**

Sukhaprabha, n. of a former Buddha: Mv i.139.10.

sukhama, adj. (MIndic for Skt. sūkṣma; cf. **sukhuma**; Pkt. id. and suhama, Sheth; §§ 2, 25; 3.45, 101), *fine, subtile*: SP 32.10, 13 (vss; see Corrigenda), no v.l., but WT sukhuma in both with K'; Mv iii.54.2 (prose)

sukharātri, °**trī** (very rare in Skt., and seemingly not in this mg., see BR; not recorded elsewhere), *a comfortable night*, also *a polite inquiry as to whether the night has been comfortable*: °triṃ sukhadivasaṃ pṛcchakā āgacchanti Mv i.214.1 = **ii.17.1** (prose), *come to ask whether he has spent a comfortable night or day*; in cpd. °trī-pṛcchikā(ḥ), n. pl. m., Mv iii.297.5, *persons who make such inquiries*; °trī dātavyā Mv iii.177.14, *the hope that he has spent a good night must be expressed* (in the morning, kalyato evotthitena).

sukhallikā (= Pali id.; cf. Deśīn. 8.36 suhellī, comm. sukham, suhallīty anye), *pleasure* (of worldly kinds): Mvy 7173 = Tib. bsod nams, *happiness*; generally in cpd. with foll. **anuyoga** (q.v.; as in Pali), or **āyoga** (q.v.): sukhallikānuyogam (LV 407.22 °kāyogam; KP sukhalikā°) anuyukta LV 264.20; 407.22; KP 105.9; kāmasukhallikāt-maklamathāntadvaya-(187.11 °klamathānuyoga-)-vivarjitatvāt Bbh 185.5; 187.11; kāmeṣu kāmasukhallikāyogo (same phrase in Pali, e. g. SN v.421.4 °ānuyogo, wrongly edited) LV 416.16; Mv iii.331.3 (here Senart em. °kāyogo, but mss. °kānuyogo [corruptly °gyo] as in Pali and elsewhere in BHS).

sukhasaṃvāsa, adj. Bhvr. (= Pali id.), *pleasant to associate with*: in Mv ii.423.19 replaces **sukhasaṃsparśa**, q.v., of ii.64.16, in closely similar list; after **surata, sūrata,** or **sauratya,** Mv ii.357.12; ii.355.21 = iii.280.6; Bbh 333.7 (°sāśayaḥ); Sukh 25.15; 61.7; Dbh 40.7.

sukhasaṃsparśa, adj. Bhvr. (= Pali sukhasamphassa, in Dhs. 648 in physical sense), *providing pleasant contacts*, either in physical or in social sense (the distinction being not always certain): physical, *pleasant to touch* (as certainly in Pali above), prob. Mvy 7154 = Tib. reg na bde ba; and °śa-vihāratā SP 301.1 (prose), following alpābādhatā mandaglānatā, hence prob. primarily physical, *state of dwelling in pleasant contacts*, tho it may also be partly social; certainly purely social, *agreeable to associate with*, in lists of complimentary epithets of princes Mv i.350.6; ii.64.16 (here between **nivāta** and **pūrvālāpin**, qq.v.; in ii.423.19 **sukhasaṃvāsa**, q.v.). See also next.

sukhasparśa = prec., q.v.: balaṃ ca sukhasparśa-vihāratāṃ ca Mvy 6288 = Tib. bde ba la reg par gnas (prob. physical), *state of dwelling with things that are pleasant to touch*: glānyād utthāsyati °śaṃ vihariṣyati (perh. *will enjoy good health*? or, *will live in pleasant conditions*?) MSV ii.85.2; sukhasparśaṃ (v.l. sukhasaṃsparśaṃ; adv.) viharati SP 286.6 (prose), prob. rather social, *dwells in pleasant* (social) *contacts*; alpātaṅkatāṃ laghutāṃ sukhasparśa-vihāritāṃ (so text; read °hāratāṃ?) ca Kv 18.8.

sukhākarā, ep. of **Sukhāvatī** (lokadhātu), *causing bliss* (m.c.? for sukha°): diśa paścima yatra °karā lokadhātu virajā Sukhāvatī SP 455.1 (vs).

sukhāpana (nt.; to next plus -ana; Ap. suhāvaṇaa, adj.), *the making happy*: °nārthaṃ SP 53.12; 54.3; Dbh.g. 22(358).10; °nārthāy(a) SP 92.12; all vss.

sukhāpayati, °te (caus. to Skt. sukhāyate, Pali °ti, *is happy*), *makes happy*: °paye (1 sg. pres., with mss.) Mv iii.355.8 (vs); °payitavyam Suv 79.6; °payitu-kāma 94.16; °pita 96.2 (all prose in Suv).

Sukhābhirati (m.), n. of a kalpa: Gv 258.24.

Sukhāvatī (cf. **sukhākarā**), with or sc. lokadhātu, the world of **Amitābha** or **Amitāyus**, from which **Avalokiteśvara** also comes (Kv 17.21 ff.; but in Kv also it is Amitābha's world, 21.8, cf. 18.7): Kv 13.22; 17.6, 22; SP 419.3; 455.1; Mvy 3067; Bhad 57; Gv 82.5; Śikṣ 175.5; Samādh p. 9 line 31; Mmk 610.7; 617.3; Laṅk 283.7; 286.15; Sukh 1.7; 28.10; 32.17 etc.

Sukhāvatīvyūha, n. of a work (our Sukh): Sukh 78.2; 100.4 (colophon).

Sukhāvaha, n. of two yakṣas: Māy 42; 65.

Sukhāvahā, n. of a devakumārikā in the southern quarter: LV 389.8 (= **Suvyākṛtā** of Mv).

sukhin (Skt.), *happy*; in phrase sukhī bhava(tu), *be* (*he*) *happy*! = *all right*! in formula of consent, followed by yasyedāni kālaṃ manyase, or the like; see s.v. **manyate.**

sukhila, adj. (sukha plus -ila, § 22.17; cf. **duḥkhila-tā**), *happy*: sukhilaṃ taṃ sukhitaṃ sadā viśokaṃ devā nānubhavanti darśanena Ud xxx.37; hāsya-lāsya-krīḍita-ramita-sukhila-madhuropacāraṃ (antaḥpuraṃ) LV 212.5 (prose); so all mss.; Calc. °sukhita°. Neither sukhila nor duḥkhila seems recorded outside of BHS.

[? **sukhiloma**, Sukh 25.17, °maḥ, in a description of a Bodhisattva; prob. misprint or corruption, but no em. occurs to me. Müller, transl., *tender*, with note suggesting 'for sukhulāma or (Pali) sukhumāla (i. e. sukumāra)', which is ingenious if bold. It may conceal a cpd. of **sukhila**, q.v.]

sukhuma, adj. (= Pali id., AMg. suhuma; cf. **sukhama** and § 3.114; MIndic for Skt. sūkṣma), *fine, subtile*: Mv ii.297.1 (prose, v.l. sūkṣma); 349.19 (vs, no v.l., metr. required); iii.314.1 (prose, no v.l.).

Sukhendriya, n. of a former Buddha: Mv iii.231.8 f.

sukhya, prob. nt. subst. (= AMg. sukkha, Skt. saukhya), *happiness*: yāvajjīva-°yaṃ kṛtaṃ ca bhaviṣyati Av ii.37.9.

Sugata (= Pali id.), *one that has attained bliss* (Tib. bde bar gśegs pa), ep. of a Buddha: Mvy 7 et passim; °ta-cīvara-gatam Mvy 8517, *attaining the size of the Buddha's robe*; it is a sin for a monk to have a robe of this size or larger, Vin. iv.173.21 ff.

Sugatacetanā, n. of a female lay-disciple: SP 383.2.

Sugatisaṃdarśanalokeśvara, n. of a deity: Sādh 88.14, 19.

Sugandhakāya, n. of a former Buddha: Mv i.141.11.

Sugandhamukha, (**1**) n. of a merchant's son living under the Buddha Vipaśyin; a previous birth of Śākyamuni: Kv 14.16; (**2**) n. of a group of Bodhisattvas: Kv 47.4.

Sugandharāyaṇa, pl., n. of a brahmanical gotra: Divy 635.21.

Sugandhi, n. of a youth of Kapilavastu who became an arhat: Av i.350.12 ff. (perh. cf. Pali Sugandha 3 in DPPN).

sugandhita, ppp. (to Skt. sugandhayati; perh. = AMg. sugandhiya, which acc. to Ratnach. = °dhika), *made fragrant*: °dhitāṅgo bhavati Mv ii.391.20 (vs).

Sugandhivastra, n. of a former Buddha: Mv i.138.10 (in Index cited Sugandhikavastra).

Sugātrā, n. of a female lay-disciple: Gv 51.15.

Suguptā, n. of a yakṣiṇī: Sādh 562.4.

Sugupti, n. of a former Buddha: Mv i.137.14.

Sugrīva, (**1**) n. of a future Buddha: Mv iii.330.11; (**2**) m., n. of a mountain in the south: Gv 58.17; 59.7 etc.

Sughora, n. of a rākṣasa king: Mmk 18.1.

sughoṣa, (**1**) (m.) a kind of musical instrument, = the commoner °**ṣaka**, q.v. (cf. AMg. sughosā, f., acc. to Ratnach. a certain *bell*, ghaṇṭā): °ṣaṃ (acc.) Mv ii.159.5; °ṣa- iii.70.15; v.l. in i.227.17 and iii.407.19; all prose; (**2**) n. of a former Buddha: LV 5.12; and acc. to Senart's em. Mv i.137.1, see **Sughoṣasamabuddhi.**

sughoṣaka, m., a kind of musical instrument, = prec. (1), q.v.: in Mv i.227.17 (prose) mss. sughoṣaṃ or °ṣakiṃ, read either °ṣaṃ or °ṣakaṃ (acc.); Senart em. °ṣakīṃ (no f. form noted in BHS); °sakaṃ, acc., Mv iii.165.7 (prose); °ṣakāṃ, acc. pl., LV 214.17 (vs); Mv ii.322.13 (vs); iii.407.19 (prose; v.l. °ṣaṃ); °ṣakā(ḥ), n. pl., Divy 221.24 (prose); Suv 40.1 (vs), cited Śikṣ 218.12; °ṣaka-, usually in long cpds. of names of musical instruments, LV 163.6; 177.14; 212.4; Divy 108.4; 315.11; 317.22; 320.6; 459.4 (mostly prose).

Sughoṣasamabuddhi, n. of a former Buddha: Mv i.137.1, acc. to mss.; Senart em. as two names, Sughoṣaḥ (see **sughoṣa** 2) and Samabuddhi; the reading of the mss. would mean *having a mentality* (as sweet and charming) *as the sughoṣa instrument.*

sucandra, (**1**) m. or nt., a kind of gem: Mv ii.310.13; (**2**) n. of a Bodhisattva: Mvy 731 *bis*; (**3**) n. of a king: Mmk 625.21; (**4**) n. of a householder in Bharukaccha: Gv 452.26; (**5**) n. of a kalpa: Gv 447.6; (**6**) n. of a samādhi: Mvy 508; ŚsP 1415.8.

Sucandradṛṣṭi, n. of a former Buddha: Mv i.137.5.

Sucandrima, n. of a king of Siṃhapura, in the Kiṃnarī Jātaka: Mv ii.95.5 ff.

Sucalā, n. of a rākṣasī: Māy 243.26.

Sucitra (Pali Sucitti), n. of an asura: Mahāsamāj., Waldschmidt, Kl. Skt. Texte 4, 179 line 2 from bottom.

sucitra-rājika, or (mss.) sucitri°, adj. Bhvr. (*sucitrin, or by Senart's em. °tra, plus Skt. rāji, plus -ka Bhvr.), *having very bright (clear?) lines*, said of the Buddha's hand: °kena (pāṇinā) Mv ii.282.5.

Sucintitārtha, n. of a son of Māra (favorable to the Bodhisattva): LV 314.14.

Sucintin, n. of a śreṣṭhin's son: Gv 51.22.

Sucīrṇadhvaja, n. of a kumbhāṇḍa: Mvy 3439.

Suceṣṭarūpa, n. of a former Buddha: LV 5.12.

Sujanaparivārā, n. of a 'gandharva maid': Kv 5.14.

Sujanaparisevitā, n. of a kiṃnara maid: Kv 6.6.

Sujanabhadra, n. of an author: Sādh 580.17.

sujāta, (**1**) in Mv i.188.3 (vs) seems to be an ep. of the Buddha (cf. Pali Sn 548 where it is one of a series of such): (śaraṇaṃ vādi-śārdūlaṃ, i. e. to the B., śreṣṭhī tatra upāgataḥ,) Sujāta-darśanatvaṃ ca śreṣṭhī paryadhigacchasi (aor.), ... *and the merchant attained the state of beholding the Well-born* (or, *of having the same views as...*; less likely, *of having agreeable views*, see next; Senart, *la connaissance des devoirs d'un bon fils*, which seems scarcely possible); (**2**) n. of two former Buddhas in the same list: Mv iii.231.6 f.; 235.10; (**3**) n. of a king, app. identified with Ikṣvāku, primeval king of Ayodhyā: Śākete (= Ayodhyāyāṃ) mahānagare °to nāma Ikṣvākurājā Mv i.348.10; (**4**) var. for **Suteja**, q.v.; (**5**) n. of a son and successor of King Kṛki(n): Divy 22.13; 23.4; Av i.338.8; (**6**) n. of a rich man of Śrāvastī: Divy 44.13; perh. the same as the seventh son of Anāthapiṇḍada, so named MSV iii.136.4 ff.; but Tib. rab sbyin = **Sudatta** (2), Bailey, JRAS 1950.180; (**7**) n. of one of the oxen of Trapuṣa and Bhallika: LV 381.7, 17.

sujāta-jāta, adj., in LV 77.16 (prose) *agreeable*, of sounds: °ta-śabdāś ca śrūyante sma, *and* (only) *agreeable sounds were heard*; so Tib., sgra skad sñan baḥi sgra dag kyaṅ; contrasting with ill-omened sounds (as of crows, jackals, etc.) just mentioned as abolished; here there can be no doubt of the mg. Cf. Pali Sn 548 paripuṇṇakāyo suruci sujāto cārudassano (of the Buddha). Perhaps in the same mg. sujātajātaḥ LV 112.12 (prose), in a list of epithets of Śākyamuni, *agreeable* (but Tib. here legs par skye bas skyes pa, quite literally, *born by a good birth*). Perh. also in LV 96.6; here, after the Bodhisattva's birth, (apsarases) bodhisattvamātaram upasaṃkramya sujātajāta-tām aklāntakāyatāṃ ca paripṛcchanti sma (Lefm. sujātajāte tām, but read with v.l. as above, and so in repetitions 8, 10, 12, 14); this, it seems, in view of the parallels, may well mean *approached ... and inquired as to her agreeable* (physical) *condition and state of having an unwearied body*, despite Tib. bltams pa legs par bltam mam, lit. *well-born born state*, which Foucaux, not unnaturally, takes to refer to successful parturition; yet the BHS (with -jāta, not jāti) hardly supports this.

Sujātabuddhi, n. of a former Buddha: Mv i.141.1.

Sujātā (**1**) (= Pali id., DPPN 6 Sujātā; contrary to DPPN, Pali sources, as Jāt. i.68.7 ff., Dhp. comm. i.86.1, agree with BHS as to the time when she presented food), n. of the daughter of a village chief (named Nandika in LV), who presented food to the Bodhisattva when he broke his fast after his long austerities: LV 265.6, 11, 19; 267.14 ff.; Mv ii.131.10; 200.17; 205.3 ff. (she had been the Bodhisattva's mother in 500 previous births); 206.19 (colophon, Sujātā-vyākaraṇaṃ samāptaṃ); 263.15 ff.; 300.12; for Divy equivalent see **Nandā** and **Nandabalā**; (**2**) n. of a nakṣatra(?): eko sujātāye (no v.l.) nakṣatre jātako Mv iii.303.7 (prose). Otherwise unrecorded; very probably a corruption.

Sujyeṣṭha, n. of a former Buddha: Mv i.136.15.

suṇḍika, see **śu°**.

suta, ppp. (= Pali id., MIndic for śruta), *heard*: sutā (so v.l., text śrutā; same vs Pali Jāt. v.138.12 sutā) Mv iii.367.6.

sutajīva, m. or nt. (= °vaka, Skt. Lex.; Skt. putraṃjīva, cf. Schmidt, Nachträge), n. of a plant: °vaṃ (acc.) Mmk 120.18 (vs).

Sutanu, n. of a Prajāpati: Māy 257.21.

Sutasoma (= Pali id., hero of Jāt. 537), n. of a previous incarnation of Śākyamuni: LV 170.19; RP 22.9; Jm 207.22 ff. (his story told here).

Sutāya (text), read prob. Sutāpa, n. of a piśāca: Mmk 18.5.

Sutīrtha, n. of a former Buddha: Mv i.141.9.

Suteja, n. of a prince, son of the king of Benares, in the **Godhā-Jātaka**: Mv ii.64.15 (v.l. Sujāta); 66.7 (both mss. Sujāta; but in all the rest both mss. Suteja); 66.8, 11; 67.8 ff. Not named in the Pali version of the story (Jāt. 333).

Sutejomaṇḍalaratiśrī, n. of a deity of the Lumbinī grove: Gv 365.5 etc. (2d ed. line 4–5 etc.).

suda, indecl. (m.c. for sudaṃ; cf. **svidaṃ**; § 3.117; = Pali sudaṃ, also suda, see Childers s.v. su; cf. **su**, Skt. svid), particle used in prohibitive clause: mā suda (mss. sudha, kuda) khu bhūmipāla kāmavitarko (mss. °kā) Mv ii.6.10 (vs).

Sudaṃṣṭra, n. of a prince (former incarnation of Buddha), = Viśvaṃtara: LV 167.21; RP 22.18; see refs. in Finot p. vii.

Sudaṃṣṭrā, n. of a kiṃnara maid: Kv 6.1.

sudatta, (**1**) adj., *well given, properly imposed*, of an ecclesiastical penance (opp. **durdatta**): MSV iii.64.1; (**2**) (= Pali id.) given name of **Anāthapiṇḍada**: MSV iii.134.6 ff.; 135.21–22; (**3**) n. of a lay-disciple: Gv 51.9.

Sudattā, n. of a yakṣiṇī: Sādh 561.1.

Sudanta, n. of a former Buddha: Mv i.141.3.

Sudaya, n. of a future Buddha: Mv iii.330.14.

sudarśa = next (1): Divy 68.17.

sudarśana, (**1**) m. pl. (Pali sudassi-n), n. of the 4th of the **śuddhāvāsa** (place, and class of gods), see **deva**: LV 150.11; Mv ii.314.9; 319.7; 360.22; Mvy 3105; Dharmas 128; Divy (in 68.17 **sudarśa**) 138.23; 367.14; 568.29; Mmk 19.11 (text Sudā°); Av i.5.4, etc.; (**2**) nt. (= Skt. Lex. id., Pali Sudassana), n. of the city of Indra, or of the trāyastriṃśa gods: Mv i.32.9, 13; 262.2, 3; Divy 218.7; 220.16; (**3**) m., n. of one of a group of seven mountains, forming with Sumeru (which they surround, Kirfel, Kosm. 186) a group of 8: Mv ii.300.18; Divy 217.8, 10; Mvy 4142; Dharmas 125: an unclassified mountain, Kv 91.17; Māy 253.31; (**4**) n. of various (?) former Buddhas: LV 5.9; Mv i.111.13; iii.235.17 ff.; (**5**) n. of two future Buddhas (in the same list): Mv iii.330.11, 14; (**6**) n. of a nāga-king who entertained the Buddha at Gayā, LV 406.18, or at Aparagayā, Mv iii.324.21; not the same as the nāgarāja Sudassana 25 in DPPN; is he the same as the nāgarājan Su° Mvy 3294, Māy 246.18?; (**7**) n. of a cakravartin-king (prob. the same as Pali Sudassana 31 in DPPN): Mvy 3569 (list starts with Mahāsaṃmata); (**8**) n. of a yakṣa (living at Campā): Māy 12; (**9**) n. of a monk: Gv 126.26 ff.; (**10**) m., n. of a medicament: °na-mahābhaiṣajyarājabhūtam Gv 494.22; °no nāma mahābhaiṣajyarājas 497.9–10.

Sudarśanaprītikara, n. of a kiṃnara: Mvy 3420.

Sudarśanā, (**1**) n. of a princess who married Kuśa: Mv ii.441.8 ff.; iii.9.4 ff.; 27.19; (**2**) n. of a 'gandharva maid': Kv 4.15; (**3**) n. of a courtesan: Gv 404.8 ff.; 428.4.

Sudānta, n. of a Bodhisattva: Mmk 42.5.

Sudāsa, n. of the father of Kalmāṣapāda: Jm 209.15 ff.

Sudīpā, n. of the wife of Arcimant and mother of Dīpaṃkara: Mv i.196.19 ff.

Sudurjayā (cf. **Durjayā**), n. of the 5th Bodhisattva bhūmi: Mvy 890; Dharmas 64; Dbh 5.9 etc.; Bbh 343.16.

Sudṛḍhajñānaraśmijālabimbaskandha, n. of a Tathāgata: Gv 422.8.

sudṛśa, m. pl. (= Pali sudassa), n. of the 3d of the **śuddhāvāsa** (place, and class of gods), see **deva**: LV 150.10; Mv ii.349.1; 360.22; Mvy 3104; Dharmas 128;

Divy 68.16; 138.23; 367.14; 568.29; Mmk 19.11; 69.6 (sg.); Av i.5.3 etc.

Sudeva (= Pali id.), n. of a leading disciple of the Buddha Maṅgala: Mv i.248.16; 252.7.

Sudhana, (**1**) n. of a prince, son of King **Dhana,** previous incarnation of the Bodhisattva, who marries **Manoharā** (cf. **Sudhanu**): Divy 441.20 ff.; MSV i.122.21; 132.18 ff.; colophon, Sudhanakumārāvadānam (Divy ch. 30) Divy 461.9; (**2**) n. of a śreṣṭhi-dāraka, chief character in Gv: Gv 2.3, 7; 51.21; 52.10, et passim; m.c. Sūdhana, 208.11; 215.14; in references to, or citations from, Gv, sometimes called Ārya-, Śikṣ 36.8; 95.6; 101.13 (here called Ācārya-, perh. error for Ārya-?); 122.14; 276.10; (**3**) n. of a Bodhisattva: Mmk 40.15 (one of 16 B.); 62.12 (one of 8); 111.8 (one of 10); 311.14, 18; 461.6; perh. the same (?), called Sudhana-kumāra and associated with Tārā, Sādh 37.9; Sudhana, with Vasudhārā, 46.11, with Tārā 64.17 etc.

Sudhanu (cf. **Sudhana** 1, who has the same rôle in the Divy version of the story), n. of a prince who marries **Manoharā** in the Kiṃnarī Jātaka: Mv ii.95.1 ff.

Sudharma (**1**) n. of a kiṃnara king: SP 4.14; (**2**) n. of a Mahābrahmā: SP 171.10; (**3**) n. of a Pratyekabuddha: Divy 200.12; (**4**) n. of a throne on which the Bodhisattva sits in the Tuṣita heaven: LV 13.12; 27.17.

Sudharmatīrtha, n. of a king: Gv 232.9.

Sudhāma, n. of a piśāca: Mmk 18.6.

Sudhāvadāta, m., n. of a mountain: Divy 107.27.

sunakha, also **śu°**, f. **°khī** (= Pali sunakha, °khī), *dog*: su° Mv i.15.1; ii.49.13; 52.6; śu° ii.409.9; iii.361.13; 369.12 (v.l. su°); sunakhī, *bitch*, ii.482.6; 483.15; iii.17.12; 18.18.

Sunanda, (**1**) n. of a devaputra: LV 4.12; 6.12; 438.16; Mv i.257.7; (**2**) n. of a cakravartin: Mv i.250.17; (**3**) n. of a nāga: Māy 222.2.

Sunandana, n. of a devaputra: LV 7.5 (vs; = **Sunanda** 1 of other lists).

Sunandā, n. of a yakṣiṇī: Sādh 562.4.

Sunaya, n. of a cakravartin: Mv i.154.1.

Sunidhyāna, n. of a former Buddha: Mv i.141.5.

Sunirmala, n. of a Bodhisattva: Mmk 42.5.

Sunirmāṇarati, instead of the usual **Sunirmita** (1), n. of the chief of the nirmāṇarati gods: Mvy 3135.

Sunirmita, (**1**) m. (= Pali Sunimmita, cf. DN i.219.4), n. of the chief of the **nirmāṇarati** (also called **nirmita**) gods: LV 44.10; 59.6; 302.6; 362.18; 363.19; 441.18; Mv i.208.13; 263.16; ii.11.1; iii.315.7; Divy 140.15; Mmk 45.8; 69.6; Bbh 345.22 (in Mvy **Sunirmāṇarati,** q.v.); most occurrences which seem to suggest use in pl., as of the class of nirmita (= nirmāṇarati) gods, are only apparent, see s.v. **Suyāma** for a number of cases in Gv, Dbh.g., and RP. However, I have noted two cases where the pl. seems unquestionable (unless we resort to emendation), and can only mean the class of which (the sg.) Sunirmita is chief: sunirmitāṃ devaputrāṃ paśyati ca svalaṃkṛtāṃ Mv ii.360.4 (vs); and, in a list of classes of gods, . . . sunirmitā paranirmitā śuddhāvāsā tuṣitā yāmā . . . Mmk 19.12 (prose). (But in LV 241.2, for Sunirmiteṣu, read with best ms. Sunirmito sa, supported by Tib.) Perhaps the fact that nirmita is used of the class, but less regularly than nirmāṇarati, led to occasional confusion with the name of its chieftain: (**2**) nt., n. of a buddhakṣetra: Mv i.123.6 (vs); located in the east.

Sunirmitadhvajapradīpa, n. of a (buddha-)kṣetra: Gv 259.4.

Sunirmitarūpa, n. of a former Buddha: Mv i.141.4.

Suniṣṭhita (?), n. of a buddhakṣetra: Mv i.124.7 (mss. vary confusingly).

Sunetra, (**1**) n. of a former Buddha (or several?): Mv i.137.12; ii.235.10; Mmk 64.1; 68.27; 130.3; 365.17; 499.23; (**2**) n. of a future Buddha: Mv ii.355.6 = iii.279.11; Gv 441.25; (**3**) n. of a previous incarnation of Śākyamuni: RP 23.16; Laṅk 141.5; (**4**) n. of a Bodhisattva: Gv 2.26; (**5**) (= Pali Sunetta, 4 in DPPN) n. of an ancient teacher: Karmav 37.1, 3; perhaps the same is meant by the maharṣi S. of Māy 257.3; (**6**) n. of a son of Māra, favorable to the Bodhisattva: LV 310.12; (**7**) n. of a śreṣṭhin's son: Gv 51.23; (**8**) n. of a rākṣasa prince, guardian of the Bodhisattvasaṃgītiprāsāda (see **saṃgīti** 1) in Kapilavastu: Gv 432.25; (**9**) n. of a yakṣa leader: Māy 235.11.

Sunetrā, (**1**) n. of a Śākyan woman, wife of Daṇḍapāṇi: Gv 420.19; (**2**) n. of a rākṣasī: Māy 240.23.

Sunetrādhipati, n. of a serpent king: Mvy 3429.

Sunemi, n. of a Pratyekabuddha: Mmk 64.13 (follows **Nemi,** q.v.).

sunthaṇā, var. for **saṃthaṇā,** q.v.

Sundara, (**1**) n. of a king: Mv i.249.16; 252.5; (**2**) n. of a prince (also °raka): Av i.189.10; 190.1 (both prose); (**3**) n. of a householder's son: Av ii.201.13 ff.; (**4**) n. of a nāga: Mvy 3312; (**5**) n. of a yakṣa: Māy 43.

sundaraka, (**1**) f. °ikā, adj. (= sundara with endearing -ka), *beautiful*: su-°rikāṃ LV 322.18 (vs), of a daughter of Māra; (**2**) n. of a prince (= **Sundara** 2): Av i.188.7 (prose).

Sundarananda (= Pali id.) = **Nanda** 1, a half-brother of Śākyamuni (so definitely stated Mv iii.176.13) who became his disciple; asked Yaśodharā to marry him after Śākyamuni's retirement, Mv ii.69.3; 72.7; referred to as a Śākyan youth, Mv ii.25.11; 74.17 ff.; LV 144.15 ff.; 154.2 ff.; as a Buddhist disciple, Mv i.75.1; iii.41.4; SP 2.7; Mvy 1057 (text Sundarī° or °ra°, but Mironov °ra° with no v.l.); Karmav 38.12; 85.9.

Sundaravarṇa, n. of a former Buddha: Mv i.136.15; LV 5.13.

Sundarā, n. of a female doorkeeper (dvārapālinī): Sādh 502.14.

Sundarikā, (**1**) (= Pali id. or Sundarī 3 in DPPN), n. of a wandering nun (pravrājikā): Laṅk 240.12 (prose); MSV i.212.8; (**2**) n. of a queen: Av i.188.6 ff.; (**3**) n. of a river (?): nadī-sundarikā-tīre MSV i.279.13 (vs; but in prose 266.3 called **Prabhadrikā**).

Sundarī, (**1**) n. of a village chief's daughter: LV 265.5; (**2**) n. of a goddess: Sādh 502.12.

? **sundhu,** or (most mss.) **sundha,** app. *blade* (or *point*?) of a sword: (kāma . . .) asi-su°-samāḥ LV 174.2 (vs), cited Śikṣ 204.12 as aśi-śūla°; Tib. ral gri (*sword*) gśog gnas (*cutting part*?) ḥdra (*like*).

[**supatīrtha,** ep. of rivers of Sukhāvatī: Sukh 39.3; read (Skt.) sūpa°, q.v. in BR.]

supana, acc. to Senart's note for more usual **supina,** q.v., = Skt. svapna: (kāyo . . .) ucchādana-(so read, Senart em. ācchā°)-parimardana-supana-(v.l. sū°)-bhedana-(etc.) . . . -dharmo Mv ii.278.1; same word ii.269.15 has svapna with no v.l.; yet supana may represent Skt. svapana, which Sheth assumes as basis for AMg. suvaṇa (not in Ratnach.); § 3.101.

su-parikarṣī-kṛtya, ger. (based on *su-parikarṣa, cf. Skt. parikarṣa, plus -karoti), *having made* (a field) *well plowed*: MSV ii.61.15.

Suparikīrtitanāmadheyaśrī, n. of a Tathāgata: Śikṣ 169.13.

Suparipūrṇajñānamukhavaktra, n. of a Tathāgata: Gv 422.13.

su-parītta (v.l. °parīta), see 2 **parītta.**

suparṇikā, in Divy 190.12 suparṇikā kuṭi (mss.; ed. kuṭir; perhaps kuṭī?), either (hut) *made of fair leaves, leafy,* or perhaps (hut) *made of the suparṇikā plant*; several plants are reported as called by that name in Skt. Lexx.; see pw. No adjective *suparṇaka is recorded.

Suparṇi(n), m. (Skt. Su-parṇa plus -in, Bhvr.; unrecorded otherwise), = Skt. Suparṇa, the garuḍa bird, 'king of birds': °ṇinā pakṣirājena Divy 344.16; Av ii.156.2;

°ṇī, n. sg., Divy 148.12; 182.5; Av i.108.4; Mmk 505.19 (vs, see s.v. **lampuṭa**); °ṇiḥ Mvy 4872; °ṇitaḥ, abl., Mahāsamāj., Waldschmidt, Kl. Skt. Texte 4, 179.4; in line 2 above, text suvaṇī, where meter requires long penult, read suvarṇī or suvaṇṇī (partly or wholly MIndic), see **Suvarṇin.**

Supaśyin, n. of a future Buddha: Mv iii.330.11.

Supātra, (**1**) (= Pali Supatta), n. of a crow king in the Kāka Jātaka (= Pali Supatta-j°, 292): Mv iii.125.14 ff.; (**2**) n. of one or two former Buddhas: Mv i.137.2; iii.234.7 ff.

Supāraga (in both mgs. = Pali Suppāraka; cf. **Sopāraka, Saupāraka**; as n. of a town = Skt. Śūrpāraka; BHS has a popular etym., see Kern's Crit. App. and Speyer's transl. 125 n. 2), n. of a city: Jm 88.12, and of a man (the Bodhisattva), Jm 88.11 ff.

Supārśva, n. of a former Buddha: Mv i.136.14.

Supārśvā, n. of a crow-queen, consort of **Supātra** (1), q.v.; in Pali called Suphassā = Susparśā: Mv iii.125.16 ff.

supiti (etc., Skt. svap-), *sleeps*, see Chap. 43, s.v. svap (2).

supina, m. (= Pali id., AMg. suviṇa; MIndic for Skt. svapna; §§ 3.111, 117; cf. **supana** and next), *sleep, dream*; only in vss (tho not always metr. required) except rarely in prose of Mv, but see also next, in Mmk: SP 293.9; 294.2, 3, 8; 295.1, 2 (note svapne 295.3, also vs), 10; LV 36.22 (read supina-kalpāḥ with most mss. for api na k°); 57.1, 3; 194.20; 302.21; 304.4; 324.9; Mv i.205.2 = ii.8.16 (read supine for Senart's em. °naṃ); i.207.14 = ii.12.4; ii.12.15, 18; 133.15, 19; 134.16; 135.13 (prose), 17; Samādh 19.26, 27; Suv 157.11; 250.3; Laṅk 287.14; Gv 214.12; 255.7, etc.; in Mmk 122.5, 7, 10, text svapne, meter requires supine.

Supināntalokamuni (see prec.; for Svapnā°), n. of a Buddha: Mmk 130.4 (prose).

[**supiya-,** LV 50.4 (vs), see s.v. **stuvati.**]

Supīlu, n. of a piśāca: Mmk 18.5.

Supuṣpa, n. of one or two former Buddhas: LV 5.12; Mmk 426.8; 499.21.

Supūjita, n. of a former Buddha: Mv i.136.16; follows **Jitaśatru,** q.v.; cf. **Saṃpūjita.**

Supūrṇa, n. of a yakṣa: Sādh 562.20.

Supūrṇika = **Pūrṇamukha** (2), q.v.

supeti (caus. to *supati, **supiti** = Pali supati, MIndic for Skt. svapiti, °pati), *puts to sleep*: (dhātrī) yā kumāraṃ ... udvarteti supeti Mv ii.423.7, and similarly 433.12 (both prose); supiya (ger.) LV 50.4 (but see **stuvati**).

supoṣa, adj. (= Pali suposa, also °tā; wrongly defined PTSD and SBE 13.153; synonym of subhara, as is clear in Pali from MN comm. i.96.30), *easily satisfied with food*: Śikṣ 202.19; °**ṣa-tā,** Mvy 2376; Śikṣ 119.8. Associated with **subhara-(tā).**

(**suptaka,** f. °**ikā,** cf. Skt. ardha-°ikā, BR; not recorded Pali or Pkt.; *asleep*: tubhya prekṣami śayāni (= śayane, m.c.) °kāṃ LV 236.3, vs.)

Supraṇihita, n. of a future Pratyekabuddha: Divy 70.3.

Supratāpa, n. of a former Buddha: Mv iii.230.11.

su-pratividdha (= Pali suppaṭi°, see below), *well-realized, penetrated*, presumably ep. of dharma, *religious truth*: dṛṣṭyā °dhaḥ Mvy 2416 = Tib. ... śin tu rtogs pa; °dhaḥ 2886 = Tib. legs par rtogs pa; cf. Pali AN ii.185.5 (dhammānaṃ ...) diṭṭhiyā suppaṭividdhānaṃ; comm. iii.170.8 = atthato ca kāraṇato ca paññāya suṭṭhu paṭividdhā paccakkhaṃ katā.

Supratiṣṭhā, f., n. of a lokadhātu: Gv 82.9.

Supratiṣṭhita, (**1**) n. of a former Buddha: Mv iii.230.12 f.; (**2**) n. of a devaputra, one of the 16 guardians of the bodhimaṇḍa: LV 277.13 (text °sthita); (**3**) n. of a yakṣa, companion of Chandaka: Mv ii.161.3; (**4**) n. of a samādhi: Mvy 563; ŚsP 1420.4; of a 'bodhisattva-samādhi', Mvy 738; Gv 122.16; (**5**) n. of a nāga: Mvy 3351; Māy 247.10; MSV i.240.9 ff.; (**6**) n. of a monk: Gv 67.18 ff.

Supratiṣṭhitacaraṇa, n. of a former Buddha: Mv i.140.8.

Supratiṣṭhitacāritra (Kashgar rec. Prati°), n. of a Bodhisattva: SP 300.14.

Supratiṣṭhitabuddhi, n. of a former Buddha: Mv i.139.10.

[**su-pratīsa,** Lefm. at LV 102.21, but read with v.l. sa-pratīsa or °**śa,** q.v.]

Suprathamā, n. of a devakumarikā in the southern quarter: LV 389.8 (corresp. to **Suprabhātā** of Mv).

su-pradharṣaka, adj. Bhvr., *subject to easy spoliation*: Bhīk 4a.3; see s.v. **sv-ādharṣaka.**

Suprabuddha, (**1**) n. of a Śākya prince, father of Māyā: LV 26.15 (but in Pali Suppabuddha was a brother of Māyā); (**2**) n. of a yakṣa: Māy 94.

Suprabuddhā, n. of a devakumārikā in the southern quarter: LV 389.8 (corresp. to **Suviśuddhā** of Mv).

Suprabha, (**1**) n. of a former Buddha: Mv i.112.17; (**2**) n. of a king of Benares, in the Godhā-jātaka: Mv ii.64.14; 66.7; (**3**) n. of another king: Gv 99.12; (**4**) n. of a śreṣṭhin's son: Gv 51.23; (**5**) n. of two kalpas: Gv 352.4; 446.26; (**6**) nt., n. of a city: Gv 160.15 ff.

Suprabhā, (**1**) n. of a daughter of a śreṣṭhin at Śrāvastī: Av ii.1.15; (**2**) n. of a female lay-disciple: Gv 51.15; (**3**) n. of a girl, attendant on **Subhadrā** (1): Gv 52.3.

Suprabhātā, n. of a devakumārikā in the southern quarter: Mv iii.307.9; corresp. to **Suprathamā** of LV.

Suprabhāyakā? (°bhāsvarā?), n. of a devakumārikā in the western quarter: Mv iii.308.8 (v.l. °bhāsvaraḥ, intending °rā).

Suprabhāsa, n. of a former Buddha: Mv i.59.1 ff.

suprabhāsa(-maṇi), m. or nt., a kind of gem: Mv ii.310.11.

Suprayāṇa, n. of a Bodhisattva: Gv 442.2.

Supriya, (**1**) n. of a cakravartin: Mv i.154.2; (**2**) n. of a gandharva: Av i.113.5; of a gandharva-king, Divy 202.29; cf. 3; (**3**) n. of a 'king of musicians' (gāndharvikarāja; cf. 2): Av i.93.7 ff.; (**4**) n. of a merchant's son: Divy 99.24 ff.; (**5**) n. of a younger son of Anāthapiṇḍada: Av ii.37.7.

Supriyā, (**1**) n. of a village chief's daughter: LV 265.4; (**2**) n. of a daughter of Anāthapiṇḍada: Av ii.7.10 ff.

Suprītyarati, n. of a former Buddha: Mv i.139.1.

supremaka, adj. (*su-prema-n plus -ka, Bhvr.), *intimately friendly*: asya °kā bhikṣavaḥ Av i.84.16 (prose).

Subaddhakakṣā, n. of a goddess: Mahāsamāj., Waldschmidt, Kl. Skt. Texte 4, 185.17.

Subandhu, n. of a legendary king of Benares, father of Ikṣvāku and grandfather of Kuśa: Mv ii.420.7 ff.

Subāhu, (**1**) (= Pali id.) n. of a disciple of Buddha (see s.v. **Yaśodeva**): LV 1.9; Mvy 1059; Sukh 2.4; (**2**) n. of a king of Hastināpura, in the Kiṃnarī Jātaka: Mv ii.94.19 ff.; (**3**) n. of a king of Mathurā: LV 21.22; (**4**) n. of a śreṣṭhin's son: Gv 51.23; (**5**) n. of a Bodhisattva: Samādh p. 36 line 2; (**6**) n. of a mountain: Māy 254.3.

Subāhuparipṛcchā, n. of a work: Mvy 1393.

Subāhuyukta, n. of a gandharva king: Kv 2.21.

Subuddhi (**1**) n. of a son of Māra (favorable to the Bodhisattva): LV 309.21; (**2**) n. of a śreṣṭhin's son: Gv 51.22.

subuddhivant (Skt. subuddhimant; cf. Ap. vuddhivanta; § 22.49), *having good intelligence*: LV 299.7.

Subrahma(n), (**1**) n. of a former Buddha: °maḥ Mv i.137.4; (**2**) n. of a purohita among the gods (= 3?): °mā LV 44.11; (**3**) (cf. Pali id., DPPN ?), n. of the leader of the brahmakāyika gods: LV 359.16; 360.7; (whether the same or not,) called devarāja LV 387.8 (acc. °mānam) a devaputra, employed as messenger by Brahmā Sahāpati, LV 61.15.

Subhaga, m., n. of a kalpa: Gv 446.24.

Subhagā, n. of a female doorkeeper (dvārapālinī): Sādh 502.14.

subhati (= Pali sumbhati, Ved. subh-, see BR; cf. **paṭi-, vi-su°**), *smites*: (āyasāsu ca droṇīṣu . . .) subhanti (mss. here sutanti) pratyamitrāṇi Mv i.14.2 (vs); line repeated with subh° 12; in 18.7 (prose) Senart em. subhassū (for subhasva) ti, but the em. is remote from the corrupt mss. and seems implausible.

Subhadra, (**1**) (= Pali Subhadda, 6 in DPPN) n. of a brahmanical ascetic, converted by the Buddha shortly before his death: Divy 152.22 ff.; 202.29; Av i.228.3 ff.; (**2**) n. of a householder: Divy 262.8 ff.; (**3**) n. of a nāga king: Māy 247.12.

Subhadrā, (**1**) n. of a householder's daughter: Gv 52.1; (**2**) n. of a yoginī: Sādh 427.6; (**3**) n. of a yakṣiṇī: Sādh 561.2; 562.4.

subhara, adj. (= Pali id.; Skt. has the opposite durbhara, see °**ra-tā**), *easily satisfied* (with food), said of monks: °raḥ supoṣaḥ Śikṣ 202.19; °**ra-tā,** with supoṣatā, Mvy 2377; Śikṣ 119.8.

Subhāṣitagaveṣin, n. of a prince: Av i.219.8 ff.

Subhikṣarāja, n. of a former Buddha: Mv i.141.8.

Subhikṣākānta (v.l. Subhikṣa°), n. of a former Buddha: Mv i.138.9.

Subhuja (misprinted Mu°), n. of a former Buddha: Mv i.137.13.

Subhūti, (**1**) n. of a Śākya of Devaḍaha, father of Māyā: Mv i.355.15; 356.5; ii.18.7; (**2**) (= Pali id., a thera) n. of a disciple of Buddha, a sthavira: Mvy 1035; SP 2.7; 100.1; 146.13; 148.5; 149.6; LV 1.17; Divy 361.19; Sukh 2.9; the Subhūti of Av chap. 91, ii.128.3 ff., has a story showing little resemblance to the Pali story of Subhūti, but both are entitled 'chief of disciples that are araṇāvihārin (see **araṇa**)', or in Pali araṇa°; Vaj 19.14 etc. 26.17; Su° is also first of dākṣiṇeya disciples, Karmav 161.18, as also in Pali of dakkhiṇeyya (in AN i.24.8–9 both titles are given him); the same as the Pali personage is doubtless meant also in KP 141.1 ff.; and Śikṣ 146.8 (from Dharmasaṃgīti-sūtra) and, all from the **Bhagavatī,** q.v., Śikṣ 202.8; 210.3 (= ŚsP 1430.5); 262.12; (**3**) n. of a Bodhisattva (cf. **Subhūmi**): Mmk 461.6; (**4**) n. of a kalpa: Gv 446.23.

Subhūma, n. of a yakṣa leader: Māy 236.9.

Subhūmi, n. of a Bodhisattva: Mmk 311.14; with **Sudhana** (3); perh. read **Subhūti** (3), who is also associated with **Sudhana** (3) in Mmk 461.6.

Subhūṣaṇabhūṣitā, n. of a kiṃnara maid: Kv 6.5.

Subhūṣaṇā, n. of a nāga maid: Kv 4.5.

Subhūṣitakhaṇḍa, n. of a former Buddha: Mv i.139.6.

Sumakuṭa, n. of a former Buddha: Mv i.137.3.

? **Sumata,** perh. to be read with mss. (twice) for **Sumana(s)** 2, q.v.

Sumati, (**1**) n. of a former Buddha: LV 172.6 (vs; m.c. sūmati); (**2**) n. of a Bodhisattva, with ep. kumārabhūta: Mvy 695; (**3**) n. of one of the sons of the Buddha Candrasūryapradīpa: SP 19.3; (**4**) n. of a brahman youth, previous incarnation of Śākyamuni under the Buddha Dīpaṃkara (= **Megha** of Mv, Sumedha of Pali): Divy 247.2 ff.; (**5**) n. of a lay-disciple: Gv 51.10; (**6**) n. of a śreṣṭhin's son: Gv 51.22; (**7**) n. of a king of serpents (mahoragendra): Gv 250.5; cf. **Sumatireṇu;** (**8**) f., n. of a merchant's wife, former incarnation of **Vasumitrā**: Gv 205.7.

Sumatibhadra, n. of an author: Sādh 592.7.

Sumatireṇu, n. of a serpent king (mahoragādhipati): Mvy 3426.

Sumana(s), (**1**) n. of a future Buddha: Gv 441.25; (**2**) n. of a śuddhāvāsakāyika god: Mv ii.257.8, 18 (in both mss. **Sumata**); 258.6, 19 (in all four n. sg. -o or -aś); (**3**) n. of one of the four devatās of the bodhivṛkṣa: °naḥ, n. sg., LV 278.10; (**4**) n. of a rich householder's son who was given by his father as attendant to **Aniruddha** and initiated by him: Av ii.68.6 ff.; (**5**) (perh. = Pali Sumana 8 in DPPN) n. of a Buddhist elder: MSV i.180.1 ff.

Sumanaska, n. of a park: Divy 621.12.

Sumanasoru, n. of a Buddha: Mmk 499.21 (vs) sumanasorave (metr. correct); a dat. is required.

Sumanāmukha, nt., n. of a city in the south: Gv 455.3; 529.3.

Sumanojñaghoṣa, n. of a former Buddha: LV 5.12.

Sumāgadhā, (**1**) n. of a daughter of Anāthapiṇḍada: Divy 402.1, 6; app. the same as Pali Subhaddā (either Mahā- or Cūla-subhaddā, qq.v., DPPN); (**2**) (= Pali id.) n. of a lake or pool: Pischel, SBBA 1904, p. 817, fol. 170 a.

Sumāgandhā, n. of a river: Kv 71.14. Error for Sumāgadhī (a river, Skt.), or **Sumāgadhā** (2, q.v.)?

[**sumātra,** m.; read with var. amātra, q.v.]

Sumānuṣa, n. of a nāga king: Māy 247.25.

Sumāla, n. of a cakravartin: Mv i.153.16.

Sumālinī, (**1**) n. of a 'gandharva maid' Kv 4.17; (**2**) n. of a goddess: Sādh 502.5.

Sumitra, n. of a king of Mithilā: LV 22.14, 18.

Sumitrarūpa, n. of a former Buddha: Mv i.138.5.

Sumitrā, n. of a rākṣasī: Māy 244.2.

Sumukā, n. of a pool near Veruḍiṅga (Vebha°): Mv i.320.10.

Sumukta, nt., n. of a locality of the Śākyas: Mv i.355.12.

Sumukha, (**1**) (= Pali id., 1 in DPPN), n. of a yakṣa: Māy 237.2; (**2**) n. of a nāga king: Māy 247.35; (**3**) n. of a kiṃnara king: Kv 3.1; (**4**) (= Pali id., 3 in DPPN) n. of a general of the haṃsa king Dhṛtarāṣṭra: Jm 128.4 ff.; (**5**) nt., n. of a city in the south: Gv 131.4.

Sumukhā, n. of a capital city (rājadhānī): Gv 205.3.

Sumekhalā, n. of a yakṣiṇī: Mmk 564.26; 566.11.

Sumedhā (= Pali id.), n. of a nun: Karmav 96.6.

Sumeru (cf. **Sumeruvatsa**), n. of a nāga king: Māy 246.23. As n. of a mountain (Pali id., oftener Sineru; also Meru), commoner than, but as in Skt. not distinguishable from, Meru (contrary to BR's statement); see Kirfel, Kosm. 15*, 16*, 182; it is located at the middle of the world (as in Skt.), and surrounded by seven concentric rings of mountain ranges, **Yugaṃdhara** etc. (Kirfel, op. cit. 186).

Sumerukalpa, (**1**) n. of a former Buddha: Sukh 5.10; (**2**) n. of a Buddha in the zenith: Sukh 98.19.

Sumerudhvajāyatanaśāntanetraśrī, n. of a Tathāgata: Gv 233.17.

Sumerupuṣpa (or possibly Merupuṣpa), n. of a former Buddha, acc. to Tib. orig. followed **Supuṣpa** in LV 5.12 (not in any BHS ms.); Ti ri rab (usually = Sumeru, once in Mvy 1388 = Meru which is otherwise lhun po) me tog (*flower*).

Sumeruvatsa (cf. **Sumeru**), n. of a serpent king (mahoragādhipati): Mvy 3434.

Sumeruś(i)rī, n. of a Buddha: Gv 284.12 (vs).

sumbhaka (once a ms. śu°), nt., a *bowl* of the sort used as *almsbowl* by Buddhist monks: the mg. is made clear by Mv iii.459.22 (vs) evaṃ te anvayiṣyāmi ādāya sumbhakaṃ tathā (so one ms., v.l. ādāya ca su°, Senart em. ādāya tava su°), = Pali Jāt. v.259.23 . . . pattam ādāya pacchato (pattam, *bowl,* = sumbhakam); otherwise found only as modifier of pātraṃ, in the cliché which tells how after ordination by the **ehibhikṣukā** formula, the signs of worldly life were magically replaced in the initiate(s) by monkish insignia: (. . . gṛhikalpaṃ sarvaṃ samantarahitaṃ, tricīvarā ca prādurbhūtā) sumbhakaṃ (mss., Senart here em. wrongly) ca pātraṃ prakṛtisvabhāvasaṃsthitā ca keśā, etc., Mv ii.234.5; substantially same formula (sometimes pl., °kā or °kāni ca pātrā or pātrāṇi), iii.65.5; 92.9; 180.15; 181.6; 329.12; 379.15 (one ms. śu°); 413.13; 423.9; 430.17. The word has not been found elsewhere; but cf. **sumbhalikā.**

Sumbhatārā, n. of a goddess (= **Sumbhā**?): Sādh 191.7.

Sumbharāja, v.l. for **Sambha°**, q.v.; cf. prec.(?)

? **sumbhalikā** (perh. related to **sumbhaka,** q.v.), *pot*(?): āśīviṣa-°likā dṛṣṭiviṣāvataṃsikā Sādh 249.2 (vs), ep. of **Jāṅgulī** (2), q.v.; the cpd. could mean *having a pot of serpent-venom,* see **āśīviṣa.**

Sumbhā, n. of a goddess (cf. prec. but two): Sādh 180.7 etc.

Suyakṣa, n. of a former Buddha: Mv i.139.5.

Suyāma (= Pali id.), n. of the head of the **yāma** (q.v.) gods: Suyāmadevaputrapramukhāḥ yāmā (so read with v.l. and Calc., supported by Tib., for Lefm. suyāmā) devāḥ LV 364.15; yāmādhipatiṃ ... ca suyāmaṃ Mv i.265.6 (so read for Senart Va-suyāmā, v.l. ca Suyāmā); note also LV 58.21; 302.6, in both of which the official position of S. is clear from the context; apparently the same, in general clearly a single individual, lord of his class, LV 44.10; 58.21; 241.1; 441.17; (formally not clear whether sg. or pl., but surely sg., LV 50.5; 327.18; 328.3;) Mv i.208.13; 230.13; 263.19; ii.11.1; iii.315.6; Mvy 3138; Mmk 69.5 (misprinted Sayāma); Bbh 340.14; cases where Su° seems to be pluralized, as if used for the class of yāma gods as a whole, are prob. only apparent; so daśa ca Suyāma-devarāja-sahasrāṇi Gv 118.22, compare the parallel daśa ca śakra-devendra-śatasahasrāṇi 119.1 (Śakra was certainly a single individual; similar phrases with Vaśavarti 117.21; Sunirmita 118.3; and Saṃtuṣita 118.15); cf. Gv 185.7; similarly in Gv 249.21 Suyāma-devarāja- is followed in 22 by parallel Śakra-devarāja- (and preceded by Vaśavarti- 17, Sunirmitá- 18, and Saṃtuṣita- 20, all names of the individual rulers of their classes); and likewise Gv 331.8. Accordingly we should interpret Suyāma patiḥ RP 52.18 and Suyāmādhipatir Dbh.g. 53(79).14 as *Suyāma the Lord* (of yāma gods). In the Dbh.g. passage we find, to be sure, as a parallel, trayastriṃśādhipo bhavet 53(79).8, which can only mean *lord of the Trayastriṃśa (class)*; but note Saṃtuṣitādhipo 22, Sunirmitādhipo 54(80).1, and Vaśavartīśvaro (*the Lord Vaśavartin*) bhavet 9 (in all these adhipo, īśvaro may be separate words, not necessarily parts of cpds.!) and esp. Brahmā sāhasrikādhipaḥ 17. So in the RP context we find (52.17, vs) Brahmāpi Śakra api lokapatiḥ bhavate ca Saṃtusita devapatiḥ (may be read as separate words!), (18) Paranirmito 'pi ca Suyāma patiḥ (this may also be two words!) ...

su-yutta, adj. (MIndic for su-yukta), *well joined:* °ta-saṃgītāḥ (of apsarases) Dbh.g. 42(68).10.

Suyodhana, (1) n. of a kiṃnara king: Kv 3.5; (2) n. of a rākṣasa king: Mmk 18.1.

Surakṣiṇī, n. of a goddess: Sādh 502.11.

surata, adj. (= **sūrata,** q.v.; meter prob. not concerned; su° noted either in prose or in metr. indifferent places in vss), *gentle, mild;* associated with kṣānti: Mv ii.368.2; 371.8; 355.21 = iii.280.6 (all vss; Senart always sū°, but mss. su° except one v.l. ii.355.21); with **sukha-saṃvāsa,** q.v., Sukh 25.15; 61.7 (both prose).

surati (f.; cf. AMg. surai, surati; Skt. and Pali surata), *sexual enjoyment, lust:* in Mv ii.63.4 (vs) read, nearly with mss., vipuṇya-mānā suratī-(mss. cited as °bhi, °bhir, a graphic corruption, cf. **saurabhya** for **sauratya**)-upadrutā, hirir nivāreti svacittam ātmano, *Modesty restrains women of unvirtuous conceit (caprice, jealousy?) who are afflicted with lust;* the Jāt. parallel, v.410.13–20, tho' only loose, is close enough to show that the author is speaking of Hrī restraining lustful women. Senart misunderstands and em. wildly.

Suranemin, n. of a maharṣi: Māy 257.4. Cf. **Asuranemin.**

Surabhicandana (? mss. °vandana), n. of a former Buddha: Mv i.140.13 (should the following rājā be compounded with this?).

Suraśmi, (1) n. of a former Buddha: LV 5.8; (2) n. of a prince: Gv 427.9, 15, 21; in 25 called **Suraśmiketu;** all vss.; (3) n. of a kalpa: Gv 360.21.

Suraśmiketu, see prec. (2).

Surasundarī, n. of a yakṣiṇī: Mmk 567.12; 571.23 (here text °daryāyā, read doubtless °daryā, gen., mantraḥ; prose).

Surā devī, n. of a devakumārikā in the northern quarter: Mv iii.309.8 = LV 391.3.

Surābhakṣī, n. of a yoginī: Sādh 427.5.

suriya (= Pali id., MIndic for Skt. sūrya), *sun:* read in LV 54.3 (vs) jihma sarva tuṣitālayo bhuto jambudvīpi suriyo (so best ms.; ed. puri yo) udāgataḥ, *the whole Tuṣita-abode has become darkened,* (since) *the sun* (= the Bodhisattva) *has arisen in Jambudvīpa;* candrasuriye LV 276.4 (vs); Suriyatejā Gv 259.7 (vs), see s.v. **Sūryatejas.**

Suruci, n. of a pratyekabuddha: MSV i.214.19 ff.

surucikā, acc. to Das, Tib. Dict., *belt, sash* (= śur bu, see s.v. **paṭṭikā** 2); acc. to Tib. cited on MSV = rgya caṅ, which Jä. defines as *a kind of girdle,* Das as ... *money-bag ... securely joined to the sash,* so that it seems to mean a part or appendage of a girdle or sash: MSV ii.89.11.

Surucirā, n. of the queen of King Subandhu: Mv ii.422.1.

Surūpa, (1) n. of a legendary king who gave son, wife, and himself to be eaten by an ogre in exchange for religious instruction: Mv i.92.13 (briefly told); Av i.188.1 ff. (at length; the demon is Śakra in disguise); (2) n. of another legendary king, with similar history: Mv i.94.2; (3) n. of a deer (the Bodhisattva) in the Surūpasya mṛgarājño Jātakam (colophon, ii.257.5): Mv ii.255.11 ff.; (4) n. of a yakṣa(?): Samādh p. 43 line 21.

Sureṇu, n. of a king (= **Reṇu;** follows **Diśāṃpati**): Mvy 3580.

Sureṇupuṣpadhvaja, n. of a kiṃnara: Mvy 3422.

Surendramālā, n. of a kiṃnara maid: Kv 6.20.

Surendrā, n. of a kiṃnara maid: Kv 6.20.

Surendrābhā, n. of a devakanyā: Gv 445.23 etc.

Sureśvaraprabha, n. of a king: Suv 174.9 ff.; 182.14 ff.

Sulakṣaṇa, n. of a former Buddha: Mv i.139.6.

su-laṃkṛtikā, see **alaṃkṛtaka,** and cf. **svālaṃkṛta.**

Sulabha, m., n. of a mountain: Gv 179.19, 23.

suluka, var. for **śu°**, q.v.

Sulocana, (1) n. of one or two former Buddhas: Mv i.137.12; LV 5.7; (2) n. of a Bodhisattva: Mmk 62.13.

Sulocanā, n. of a female lay-disciple: Gv 51.17.

suvacas, (1) adj. (= Pali suvaca, subbaca; not in this sense Skt. suvaca and Lex. °cas), *compliant, mild, gentle in speech:* agrakulīnā °cā (mss. sucavā) tyāgarucimārdavavatī (mss. °tā) ca Mv i.143.2 (vs); °cāḥ Mvy 2366 = Tib. bkaḥ blo bde ba, *of cheerful speech;* (2) n. of a 'gandharva maid': Kv 5.18.

? **Suvaṇṇin,** possibly to be read instead of **Suvarṇin** (for text Suvaṇī) = **Suparṇin,** q.v.

suvatthi, see **susvasti.**

Suvadana, n. of a former Buddha: Mv i.138.7.

suvarṇa, m., (1) (= AMg. suvaṇṇa, Skt. suparṇa; cf. **suvarṇin**), the garuḍa bird, 'king of birds': suvarṇarājāno suvarṇādhipatayo (in i.208.8 mss. suvarṇa-patayo) Mv i.208.8; 212.6 = ii.16.3; ii.164.3–4; others, Mv ii.91.13; iii.83.20; 84.5; Mmk 655.8 (pakṣiṇāṃ rājā); (2) n. of a former Buddha: Mv i.138.6.

Suvarṇakeśa, n. of a nāga: Mvy 3322. Cf. **Svarṇa°**

Suvarṇagarbha, (**1**) n. of a Bodhisattva: Mvy 664; Suv 120.4; (**2**) n. of a former Buddha: Sukh 6.13.

Suvarṇacārin, n. of a former Buddha: Mv i.138.9.

Suvarṇajambudhvajakāñcanābha, n. of a Tathāgata: Suv 169.3.

suvarṇa-dhovaka, in a list of artisans or craftsmen, *gold-washer*, i. e. some one employed in the goldsmith's trade (foll. by mauṣṭika, moṭṭ(h)ika, see **muṣṭika** 4): Mv iii.113.19; 443.6.

Suvarṇadhvaja (nt.), n. of a palace at **Aḍakavatī**: Suv 116.1.

Suvarṇapārśva (= Pali Suvaṇṇapassapabbata), n. of a mountain: Māy 253.28.

Suvarṇapuṣpa, n. of a predicted future Buddha: AsP 366.9.

Suvarṇapuṣpojjvalaraśmiketu, n. of a Tathāgata: Suv 120.1.

Suvarṇaprabha, (**1**) n. of a former Buddha: Sukh 5.13; (**2**) n. of a Māra: Gv 444.12.

Suvarṇaprabhāsa, see °**prabhāsottama**.

Suvarṇaprabhāsā, n. of the wife of the nāga king Kālika: LV 284.11.

Suvarṇaprabhāsitā, n. of a lokadhātu: Suv 168.6.

Suvarṇaprabhāsottama, nt., Mvy 1339, or m.(!), Mmk 109.28, and °ma-sūtra, Śikṣ 160.12, Mmk 38.13, = **Suvarṇabhāsottama**(sūtra).

Suvarṇaprastha, n. of a city: MSV i.66.3; 67.1, 3.

Suvarṇabhāsa = next: Śikṣ 216.6. Both the citation here and that in prec. but one are from Nobel's ed. 22.3 ff.

Suvarṇabhāsottama, (**1**) also -sūtra, n. of a work (our Suv); this form preferred by Nobel, p. xii, tho most Nep. mss. read usually Suvarṇaprabhās°; in vss also Svarṇa° occurs for Suvarṇa°; and sometimes, when modifying deśanā, the name becomes °ttamā, f.: Suv 2.1 (vs; Svarṇa°); 13.8; 14.2; 28.12 and 29.1 (vss; Svarṇa-°ttamā, with deśanā); etc. Note also **Svarṇaprabhāsa** Suv 53.18 (vs); (**2**) m., n. of a Bodhisattva: Suv 120.3 (most mss. Suvarṇaprabhās°).

Suvarṇabhujendra, n. of a king: Suv 45.4 (on the form or forms of the name see Nobel's note here).

Suvarṇamekhalā, n. of an apsaras: Kv 3.9.

Suvarṇaratnākarachattrakūṭa, n. of a Tathāgata: Suv 119.13; 168.8, 11; 241.2 ff.

Suvarṇaviṣāṇa, n. of a former Buddha: Mv i.139.12.

Suvarṇaśataraśmibhāsagarbha, n. of a Tathāgata: Suv 169.9.

Suvarṇaśṛṅga, n. of a mountain: Māy 254.2.

suvarṇa-saṃdhi (f. or nt., acc. to text), *a 'golden'* (i. e. advantageous) *alliance* (by marriage): °dhī ca (v.l. va) kṛtā putrapautrikā Mv ii.490.19 (prose), *and golden alliances* (with seven kings, by intermarriage) *were made for his sons and grandsons* (i. e. to hold for all future time); Senart here deletes suvarṇa; but in the repetition iii.24.11 he keeps it, reading °saṃdhīva (rather °dhī ca, with text above) putrapautrā (but here mss. °traṃ, as if °saṃdhi were nt.). The same incident is described both times.

Suvarṇasena, n. of a former Buddha: Mv i.139.1.

Suvarṇābha, n. of a rich man's son at Kapilavastu: Av i.346.4 ff.

Suvarṇāvabhāsa, n. of a peacock-king: Māy 222.30 etc.; MSV i.287.17.

Suvarṇāvabhāsā, n. of a 'gandharva maid': Kv 5.17.

Suvarṇin (semi-MIndic) = **Suparṇin**, q.v.: (sarva-)-nāgabhavanāny avabhāsya . . .°ṇi-bhayāny apanayanti Gv 119.15, see s.v. 1 **vālikā**; Mahāsamāj 179.2, read Suvarṇī or Suvaṇṇī, see s.v. **Suparṇin**, also **suvarṇa** 1.

Suvalitaratiprabhāsaśrī, n. of a courtesan's daughter: Gv 404.9 etc.; later, in vs, called **Saṃvalitā**, q.v.

Suvastra, n. of a cakravartin: Mv i.154.1.

Suvāsu (read Suvāstu?), n. of a river: Māy 253.7. In a list between Pañcālā and Prabhadrikā.

Suvikalpāṅga, n. of a former Buddha: Mv i.140.2.

Suvikrānta, n. of a former Buddha: Mv i.141.12.

Suvikrāntavikrāmin, (**1**) (v.l. °kramin, °krama) n. of a **satpuruṣa**, q.v.: SP 4.1; (**2**) n. of a work: Mvy 1347 (°mī, n. sg. m.); (**3**) n. of a Bodhisattva: ŚsP 6.17.

Suvikrāntaśrī, n. of a Buddha: Śikṣ 169.14.

Suvikrāmin, n. of a śreṣṭhin's son: Gv 51.22.

Suvicakṣaṇagātra, n. of a former Buddha: Mv i.139.11.

Suvicitra, m., n. of a lokadhātu: Gv 256.23.

Suvicintitārtha, n. of a former Buddha (rebirth of **Mahākaruṇācintin**): Samādh 8.17, 31.

[? **suvijātinā**, LV 9.6 (prose), at the end of a cpd. (so Tib., which begins a new word with the foll. vidyā), is a corruption for a gen. sg. form, prob. ending -jaṭino, as shown by Tib. ral pa can du (byas śiṅ), *having long hair*; for suvi we might conjecture śuci-, but Tib. has nothing that seems to correspond.]

? **Suvijṛmbhita** (mss. vary), n. of a former Buddha: Mv i.138.11.

Suvibhakta, n. of a Bodhisattva: Gv 442.10.

Suvibhaktavatī, n. of a samādhi: Sukh 20.7.

Suvimaladatta (mss.), n. of a former Buddha: Mv i.138.7 (Senart em. °danta; but cf. **Vimaladatta**).

Suvimāna, n. of a cakravartin: Mv i.153.16.

Suvilokitajñānaketu, n. of a Tathāgata: Gv 421.18.

Suvilokitanetra, n. of a Bodhisattva: Gv 3.2.

Suviśākha, n. of a Bodhisattva: Gv 442.13.

Suviśuddha, (**1**) n. of a former Buddha: Mv i.139.7; (**2**) m. or (°dhā) f., n. of a lokadhātu: SP 205.8 (vs; °dha n. sg., could be for °dhā m.c.).

Suviśuddhacandrābhā, n. of a 'goddess of night': Gv 232.19.

Suviśuddhajñānakusumāvabhāsa, n. of a Tathāgata: Gv 422.14.

suviśuddhadharmadhātu-jñāna, nt., one of the five **jñāna**, q.v.: Dharmas 94.

Suviśuddhā, n. of a devakumārikā in the southern quarter: Mv iii.307.9 (= Suprabuddhā of LV).

suviśodhaka, see **viśodhaka**.

Suvīrā, n. of a yoginī: Sādh 427.7.

Suvṛṣa, n. of a mleccha king: Mmk 621.24.

suve, and derivs., see **śuve**.

suvedha, adj., *having a good aim, hitting the mark*: Mv iii.285.8 (vs); the corresp. Pali, SN i.127.5, has anoko (v.l. aneko); the passage is corrupt in Mv.

suvyapadeśa-kṣema, adj., acc. to Senart something like *auspicious thru good* (physical) *signs* or *characteristics*, of the infant Bodhisattva: so vadati etha (in 2d and 3d occurrences, so avaca hanta) paśyatha °kṣemaṃ mama putraṃ Mv i.152.14 = 226.8 = ii.29.11 (vs, but meter imperfect, very possibly corrupt); spoken by Śuddhodana to gods pretending to be astrologers.

Suvyākṛtā, n. of a devakumārikā in the southern quarter: Mv iii.307.9 (≟ LV **Sukhāvahā**).

Suvyūhamukhā, n. of an apsaras: Kv 3.17.

Suvyūhā, n. of an apsaras: Kv 3.9.

Suvrata, n. of a śreṣṭhin's son: Gv 51.21.

Suśānta, n. of a Bodhisattva: Mmk 42.5.

su-śila, adj. (m.c. for °śīla), *of good behavior*: °lā LV 114.15 (vs).

Suśīla, n. of a śreṣṭhin's son: Gv 51.21.

Suśobhana, n. of a Bodhisattva (? or disciple): Mmk 311.16.

suśobhanaka, adj. (Skt. suśobhana plus endearing dim. -ka, § 22.34), *beautifully adorned*: LV 321.21 (vs), see s.v. **citritaka**.

suśaurya, a military art, mastered by the Bodhisattva as prince: (in a list) sthairya-sthāmni suśaurye bāhuvyāyāme . . . LV 156.11 (prose); several mss. read

°rya-, as cpd. with bāhu°, but Tib. renders as separate word, dpaḥ ba daṅ (normally = śaurya).

Suṣeṇa, (**1**) n. of a Bodhisattva: Mmk 576.18; (**2**) n. of a yakṣa: Māy 64; ((**3**) n. of a mountain: Māy 254.4; occurs in Skt., Kirfel 98, tho not in BR, pw.)

suṣṭhu, adj. (= AMg. suṭṭhu; Pali suṭṭhu and Skt. suṣṭhu only adv.; cf. next), *good, excellent*: suṣṭhuḥ Mvy 2531 (but Mironov suṣṭhu), among 'synonyms of anuttara'.

suṣṭhutā (= Pali suṭṭhutā; cf. prec.), *excellence*: saṃgha-°tāyai Mvy 8348.

Susaṃprasthita, (**1**) one of sixteen **satpuruṣa**, q.v.: SP 3.12 (Kern's Transl. Susaṃsthita with v.l., but Tib. śin tu yaṅ dag zhugs, supporting ed.); (**2**) n. of a Bodhisattva (possibly to be identified with 1?): Mvy 718; ŚsP 6.16.

Susaṃbhava, (**1**) n. of a king: Suv 146.10 ff.; previous incarnation of Śākyamuni, 152.12; °va-parivarta, n. of Chap. xiii of Suv, 145.8; (**2**) n. of a kalpa: Gv 258.3.

Susaṃbhavav(i)yūha, n. of a Buddha: Gv 259.15 (vs). The next word seems to be an ep. of this personage, not a separate name.

[**susāra(-galva, -galvārka)**, false reading for **musāra-**, q.v.]

Susārthavāha, (**1**) n. of a **satpuruṣa**, q.v.: SP 3.11; (**2**) n. of a Bodhisattva: Mvy 697; ŚsP 6.7 (to be identified with 1?).

Susīma, (**1**) (= Pali id.) n. of a devaputra: Mvy 3136; RP 2.4; (**2**) n. of a son of Bindusāra: Divy 369.14; 372.16 ff.

Susīmā, n. of a rākṣasī: Māy 240.22.

Susudhī (perh. corruption of name recorded in Pali as Sussondī? see Lévi's note), n. of the wife of a king of Benares: Karmav 78.16.

Susoma, n. of a former Buddha: Mv i.137.5.

Susthitamati, n. of a devaputra: RP 2.4; ŚsP 55.13 (here misprinted Susyita°).

susvasti, indecl. (false Sktization for Pali suvatthi = svasti; Senart i n. 590), *weal*: etena satyena °ti bhotu Mv i.291.3 (vs), repeated 8, 14, etc.; same vs in Pali KhP. vi.3 etena saccena suvatthi hotu. Meter requires short first syllable, as in Pali; su-svasti perh. only a textual corruption, due to a copyist who tried to make a 'correct' Skt. form out of the MIndic one.

Suharṣitaprabheśvarā, n. of a queen: Gv 381.3.

sū-, in comp. for Skt. su-, see § 3.22; usually m.c., but see **sūrata**.

sūka, perh. for Skt. śūka, *something sharp and stinging*: śaṅkha-sūke, dual dvandva, MSV ii.55.17, in list of things painful to step on.

sūkarikā (= Skt. and Pali °rī), *sow*: °kāyāḥ kukṣāv Divy 194.28; 195.14 (prose).

Sūkarikāvadāna, nt., title of Divy Chap. 14: Divy 196.15 (colophon); Śikṣ 177.10.

Sūkṣmatvac, n. of a future (predicted) Pratyekabuddha: Av i.142.20.

Sūkṣmavastra, n. of a former Buddha: Mv i.138.8.

sūcaka, m. (cf. Skt. sūcī, sūcikā; Pali sūcikā, both *needle* and *door-bolt*), (**1**) Mvy 5587 °kaḥ = Tib. gzuṅ(s) gzer, which means *bar*, orig. *peg* (in a wall; Das), not *railing, balustrade* (BR) but part of one, = **sūcikā**; (**2**) pl. °kāḥ, lit. *piercing, needling*, ep. of certain 'winds' in the body: Śikṣ 248.13 (see s.v. **kṣuraka**).

sūcanaka (= Skt. °na), *indicating, which indicates*: pratyātmavedyagati-°kaṃ deśehi . . . dharmanayaṃ Laṅk 3.12 (vs); -ka may be m.c.

sūcā (= Pkt. sūā, Sheth; cf. AMg. sūyā = asphuṭa śabdavacana, Ratnach.), *indication*: (śvā . . .) tvadbhāvasūcāṃ bhaṣitaiḥ karoti Jm 144.23 (vs); samṛddhi-sūcaiva tu hemamālikā 184.17 (vs).

-sūcika, ifc. Bhvr. (Skt. sūci plus -ka Bhvr.), *having . . . needles*: kuryād vajraṃ triśūcikam (so text) Mmk 140.15 (vs).

sūcikā (= **sūcī**, and cf. **sūcaka** 1), lit. *needle*, = *transverse bar* of a railing or balustrade: Mvy 5590 = Tib. śar bu, śar ba; sauvarṇasya pādakasya (q.v., 2) rūpyamayī °kā ālambanam adhiṣṭhānakaṃ cābhūṣi Mv i.194.20, similarly 195.1, 4; iii.227.7 ff.; Senart's note i.529 seems not quite right; each upright pillar (pāda, **pādaka**) in the railing had a crossbar (**sūcikā**) of a particular material as its *'support and prop'* (**ālambana** 3, **adhiṣṭhāna** 4, °**naka**).

sūcigṛha(ka), **sūcī°**, nt., = next: sūci-°ka-saṃpādanam Mvy 8511; sūcī-°kam 8972; sūcī-gṛham MSV i.281.18; Tib. khab ral.

sūcighara, **sūcī°** (nt.; = Pali sūcighara; cf. prec.), *needle-case*; Prāt 518.13 (sūcī°; cf. Pali Vin. iv.123.13); 523.7 (sūci°).

Sūciroma, (**1**) n. of a yakṣa (= Pali Sūciloma; cf. **Kharakarṇa**): Samādh p. 43 line 19; (**2**) n. of a gandharva: Suv 162.3; (**3**) °**roman**, n. of a nāga: Māy 221.28.

sūcī (= **sūcikā**), *transverse bar* of a railing or balustrade: Divy 221.8, see s.v. **vedikā**.

sūcī-gṛha(ka), °**ghara**, see **sūci°**.

sūcī-padaka, m., *'step with a needle'*, *stitch* (so app. Tib. khab kyis, *with a needle*, bsrubs, see Jä. s.v. srubs 2): dvau trayo vā °kā dātavyāḥ MSV ii.156.2.

? **Sūtkhalin**, m., n. of a devaputra, one of the 16 guardians of the Bodhimaṇḍa: LV 277.12, °lī Lefm. without v.l.; but Calc. (devaputra-) Mutkhalī, supported by Tib. mut-ka-li; this (esp. in view of preceding devaputra-which should be °traḥ or °tro) suggests Samutkhalin; see the fem. **Samutkhalī**.

sūtra, nt. (also **sūtrānta**, q.v.), (**1**) (= Pali sutta) *discourse*, as a type of Buddhist sacred text (**pravacana**), one of twelve, Mvy 1267, or nine, Dharmas 62; (**2**) also = **sūtra-piṭaka**, q.v. (= Pali sutta-piṭaka), *the (collection of) discourses*, one of the three grand divisions of the Buddhist canon: Mvy 1412; Divy 333.7; sūtravinayābhidharmeṇa Laṅk 290.8.

sūtradhara, m. (= Pali suttadhara, Childers), *a master of the* **sūtras** (q.v.), *one who controls them*: Mvy 5141.

sūtra-pada, (**1**) nt.? *a sūtra text*, or n. of some particular text (?): yathoktaṃ Bhagavatā °pade Mv ii.98.13 (there follows a vs, = Pali Dhp. comm. i.181.15 f., iii.30.19 f., 319.14 f.); (**2**) v.l. for **Śvabhrapada**, q.v.

sūtra-piṭaka (= **sūtra** 2), *discourse-basket*, as n. of part of the canon: bodhisattva-°kād Bbh 156.7; °ka- 8.

sūtrayati (Skt. id., not in this mg.), either *marks with a* (black) *cord* (see **kālasūtra**), or *reduces to threads, cuts into shreds* (sinners in hell): kālasūtreṇa (*by the hell k°*, or *by use of a black cord*, see s.v.) sūtritāṅgā(ḥ) Mv i.5.7 (prose); sūtrayitvāna teṣāṅgā (mss. tasyāṅgaṃ) vāsīhi paraśūhi ca i.12.16 (vs); this last does not suggest the mg. 'black cord'.

sūtrānta, m. (= Pali suttanta), a Buddhist **sūtra** (1) text: °ta-vaiyākaraṇābhigīto Mv iii.122.21 (vs), so virtually as mss., and as meter requires; °to LV 4.18, of the LV itself; Mvy 805; 1435 (°taḥ); Divy 274.14; Bbh 46.8 (°tān); etc., common; forms in -āṃ, before vowels even -ām, are (with Weller 23) to be understood as acc. pl. m., not acc. sg. f.; so, ya imām (!) evaṃ bhadrikāṃ sūtrāntāṃ pratikṣepsyanti LV 88.14 (prose); similarly 88.16.

sūtrāntaka, °**tika**, adj.-subst. m. (to prec. plus -ka, -ika; = Pali suttantika), *one versed in the sūtrānta*: °tako 'yaṃ sthaviro Divy 397.8; ifc., evam adhīta-catuḥ-°tikaṃ (acc. m.) Mmk 38.13, (one) *who has studied these four sūtrānta* (viz. the Prajñāpāramitā, Candrapradīpasamādhi, Gaṇḍavyūha, and Suvarṇaprabhāsottamasūtra).

sūdanā, f. (Skt. °na, nt.), *destruction*: kileśa-°nā (n. sg.) LV 53.15 (vs).

sūdayā (prob. cpd. of su- and udaya, Bhvr.), n. or ep. of a magic herb: °yā nāmauṣadhis, tayā... Divy 455.23.

Sūdhana, see **Sudhana**.

Sūna, n. of a locality: Māy 38.

sūpa, m. (= Skt. Lex. id.; AMg. sūva), *cook*: Mv ii.478.12, 17 (sūpa-mahattarakaṃ pṛcchati), 19, 20 (āgantuko sūpo); 479.1 (so sūpo) and ff.; iii.126.15 (tehi sūpehi ... niveditaṃ). All prose.

sūpaka (= prec. plus -ka; cf. Pali sūpika), *cook*: kena °kena mamādya āhāro siddho Mv ii.478.17 (prose).

sūpika, m. or nt. (= Skt. sūpa, Pali also sūpaka), *sauce* (on food): °kam Mvy 8566 (see **sama-°kam**); 8570; satkṛtya °kaṃ pratigrahiṣyāmaḥ Prāt 532.6 = La Vallée Poussin, JRAS 1913.845, Stein ms. fragm. 1.2.2 (here pratigṛhīṣ°); nānā-sūpika-rasopetasya bhaktasya MSV i.47.1.

Sūmati, m.c. for **Sumati** (1), q.v.

sūrata, adj. (also **surata**, q.v., and cf. **sauratya**; = Pali sūrata, oftener sorata; usually in vss, but sometimes prose, and sometimes where meter does not determine quantity of the ū; the word is no doubt orig. a cpd. of su- and rata, tho in a sense not known to Skt., except both su° and sū° in Skt. Lex.; Leumann's etym., ap. Wogihara, Lex. aus der Bbh., from sūnṛta, whence *sūrṇta, then sūrata, as if proto-IE., is absurd), *gentle, mild*, frequent as ep. of Buddha: Mvy 2360 = Tib. des pa, defined *fine, brave, noble, chaste*; this word is the regular Tib. for this and **sauratya**, but in Śikṣ 196.2 Tib. acc. to note in ed. dul, *gentle*; SP 46.3; LV 170.22; 178.19; 193.10; RP 10.14; 13.5; 37.17; KP 107.26; Gv 480.6; foll. by **sukhasaṃvāsa**, q.v., Mv ii.357.12; Dbh 40.7 (prose).

sūrī (unrecorded; cf. Pali, AMg. sūra, also Vedic id., *sun*), *sun* or *ray of light*: tāḥ sarvasūrīḥ (mss. surīḥ, surāḥ, meter demands sū-; refers to arciṣāṃ ... sahasrakoṭīḥ of prec. vs) punar etya tatra, mūrdhe ca astaṃ gami nāyakasya Sukh 51.15 (vs), *all those 'suns'* (Müller, Transl., *rays*; but note astaṃ-gami; prob. the text means to call them *suns*, by a bold figure) *returned there and 'set'* (went to rest) *on the head of the Guide*.

Sūrya, (**1**) n. of a prince of Mithilā: Mv iii.172.9 ff.; (**2**) n. of a Śākyan youth: Av i.381.1 ff.; (**3**) n. of a yakṣa: Māy 236.16 and 25.

Sūryakesaranirbhāsā, n. of a lokadhātu: Gv 81.16.

Sūryagarbha, (**1**) n. of a **satpuruṣa**, q.v.: SP 4.1; (**2**) n. of a Bodhisattva (same as 1 ?): Mvy 671; Kv 1.10; Gv 2.24; Dbh 2.6; (**3**) m., n. of a work: Mvy 1353 (a vaipulyasūtra); (**4**) a kind of gem (maṇirāja): Gv 90.4 (twice); nowhere recorded, perhaps nonce-formation based on aśmagarbha, which occurs in the prec. line (with thought of sūryakānta?).

Sūryagātrapravara, n. of a Tathāgata: Gv 405.4 ff.; 428.7 (vs).

Sūryagupta, n. of a former Buddha: Mv i.136.17.

(**Sūryatejas**) Sūriyatejā (n. sg.), n. of a Buddha: Gv 259.7 (vs).

Sūryadhvaja, n. of a Bodhisattva: Gv 2.19.

Sūryapratibhāsa, n. of a Bodhisattva: ŚsP 45.6.

Sūryapradīpa, n. of a samādhi: Mvy 552; Śikṣ 338.2; ŚsP 1419.5.

Sūryapradīpaketuśrī (°śiri, m.c.), n. of a Buddha: Gv 257.6 (vs).

Sūryaprabha, (**1**) n. of a Bodhisattva (in Mvy and Sādh follows **Candraprabha**): Mvy 690; Sādh 96.2; Gv 3.16; (**2**) n. of a nāga: Mvy 3323; Māy 246.24; (**3**) n. of a yakṣa: Māy 38.

Sūryaprabhatejas, or °**prabhā**°, n. of a 'Bodhisattva-samādhi': Mvy 742.

Sūryamaṇḍalapratibhāsottamaśrī, n. of a Tathāgata: ŚsP 45.3.

Sūryamitra, n. of a gandharva: Suv 162.3.

Sūryalocanā, n. of a 'gandharva maid': Kv 5.16.

Sūryavikramasamantapratibhāsa, n. of a Tathāgata: Gv 309.23.

sūryavikrānta, m. or nt., a kind of gem: Mv ii.310.15.

Sūryavidyutprabha, n. of a mountain-peak on Laṅkā: Laṅk 16.7.

Sūryānana, n. of a former Buddha: LV 172.6: Samādh p. 57 line 21.

sūryāvabhāsa, see **sūryobhāsa**.

Sūryāvarta, n. of a samādhi: SP 424.8.

Sūryāvartā, n. of a lokadhātu in the north: LV 292.7.

Sūryottarajñānin, n. of a Bodhisattva: Gv 2.15.

Sūryodana, n. of a former Buddha: Sukh 5.12.

Sūryodaya, n. of a kalpa: Gv 447.4.

sūryopaniṣad, m. pl., lit. *based on the sun*, or possibly *sun-like* (see s.v. **candropaniṣad**), a class of gods: °ṣado devāḥ Waldschmidt, Kl. Skt. Texte 4, 183.17; Pali DN ii.259.24 suriyassūpanisā devā.

sūryobhāsa (for sūryāvabhāsa), m. or nt., a kind of gem: Mv ii.310.14.

Sṛṣṭarūpa, n. of a former Buddha: Mv i.136.15.

seka (m.; Skt. id., in lit. sense), lit. *sprinkling*, so *augmentation* ('as of fire by oil', Bendall): ātmano bahumāno 'yaṃ stutinindādi-sekataḥ, vardhate nārakavaśāt (ms. °śa-) sekān narakavahnivat Śikṣ 265.15–16 (vss).

sekayati (denom. to seka; comm. on Hem. 4.96 cites Pkt. seai = siñcati, tho the sūtra ignores it), *sprinkles*: °yantī, pres. pple. n. sg. f., Sādh 246.14.

sekhayati, see **śekh**°.

setaka, adj. (= Pali id.; MIndic for śveta-ka, § 2.16), *clear, pellucid*, of water: nadīṃ ... setakāṃ (mss. siketāṃ, em. Senart) sūpatīrthāṃ (Skt.; so read with parallel LV 248.9, and Pali sūpatittha, see below; mss. corrupt, wrongly em. by Senart) śucisaṃpannatoyāṃ syandamānāṃ dṛṣṭvā Mv ii.123.20; the collocation setakā sūpatitthā, of a river or pool, occurs repeatedly in Pali, e. g. MN i.76.28; 167,5; 283, last line.

***se-ti**, for Skt. sīvyati, *sews*: gdve. setavya, MSV ii.50.13, 15; inf. setum, ib. 50.16; see § 28.50 and Chap. 43, s.v. sīv (2).

Senarāja, n. of a king: MSV i.xvii.12.

Senāṃjaya, °**yin**, n. of a monk living in Vāsavagrāma (2): MSV ii.199.2 ff. (°ya); °yin ib. 202.2.

Senāpati-grāma, °**maka**, m. (= Pali Senānī-nigama, or Senā-nigama), n. of a village near Uruvilvā: °ma Mv ii.123.16; iii.311.8; °maka LV 248.7; Mv iii.311.18; 415.11; 425.17.

Senika-guhā, n. of a cave at Rājagṛha: MSV iv.82.15.

seyyā, **-seyyāka** (= Pali id., for Skt. śayyā, § 3.97, and same plus -ka Bhvr.), *bed, sleeping-place*: tṛṇasaṃstarake seyyaṃ (v.l. śe°; Senart em. seyyāṃ) kalpesi Mv ii.234.10; -seyyāka, see s.v. **manuṣya-raha-śayyāka**. See also **śeyyā**.

sela, m., a high number (= **selā, selu**): Mvy 7766 = Tib. yad yod.

Selaka, n. of a (legendary?) knight to whom King Śreṇiya compares the Bodhisattva: udagro tvam asi rājñaḥ aśvāroho va °ko Mv ii.199.11 (vs); the Pali parallel passage, Sn 420–421, lacks any such words; AMg. knows a pious king Selaa, Selaga, assumed to represent Skt. *Sailaka (Ratnach.), but it seems doubtful whether he is the same person.

selā = next: Gv 106.11.

selu, m. or f., = **sela, selā**: seluḥ Mvy 7895 (Tib. yad yod), cited from Gv 133.22.

sevaka (Skt. Lex. said to mean *sack*), *patch*, = **āsevaka**, q.v.

sevanatā = Skt. sevana, *serving, service*: kṣāntyā sevanatā KP 20.3.

Saikata, n. of a Buddhist monk (who became insane): MSV i.ix.10, 16.

saindhava, m. (or nt., doubtless = **sindhava**, q.v.), a musical instrument, prob. a kind of *drum*: mṛdaṅgam āliṅga-saindhavāṃ paṇavāṃ Mv iii.82.3 (vs).

-sainyaka, in sa-s° (= Dutreuil sa-señaka, O 14, Bailey, BSOS 11.497; Skt. sainya plus -ka, Bhvr., or m.c.?), *soldier*: lokapālāḥ °kās LV 185.7 (vs); Māru °ku Bhad 53, *with his host*.

Saila (read **Śaila**?), n. of a yakṣa: Māy 2.

so, indecl. (= Pali sū; m.c. for **su**, q.v.) = Skt. svid: kiṃ so ... Mv iii.370.1 (vs); same vs Pali Jāt. v.141.10 kiṃ sū.

soḍhaukikā (etym. not clear), an attitude disapproved for monks on the begging round: Mvy 8553 na soḍhaukikayā; Tib. phrag pa mi sprad, *shoulders not brought together*; Chin. *shoulders not raised* or *not shaken*; Jap. = Tib. Not in Pali (Vin. iv.187–189).

soṇḍa, adj. (= Pali id., Skt. śauṇḍa, which is sometimes written śo°, but acc. to BR, pw, not with s-), *eager for, devoted to*, only noted in raṇa-s°, *eager for battle* (cf. Pali yuddha-s°): LV 43.19 (vs); 55.21 (vs), read raṇasoṇḍo (best ms. °soṇḍau, Lefm. °śauṇḍi, bad in meter and sense); 79.7 (Lefm. °sauṇḍān, best mss. °śo° or °so°). In LV 311.18 (vs) read māṃ soḍhum (cited by Lefm. soḍum!), with most and best mss., for taṃ soṇḍam.

sottara, adj. (= Pali sa-uttara; prob. formed as opposite to the commoner **anuttara**, q.v.), *having (a) superior(s)*, i. e. *inferior*: °rāṇi cittāni °rāṇi cittānīti yathābhūtaṃ prajānāti AsP 266.5; cf. anuttarāṇi etc., 266.13; close parallels in Pali, e. g. DN i.80.9.

sotpattika, adj., f. °**kī** (Bhvr., sa-utpatti plus ka), *with (its, etc.) origin*: °kaṃ śikṣāpadaṃ Bbh 219.5; °kīṃ sāvitrīṃ Divy 638.4.

? **sona**(= Pali sona, oftener soṇa; to Skt. śvan), *dog*: sonāhārīkṛtaṃ Mv i.129.9 (vs), *made food for dogs*, by Senart's ingenious but somewhat dubious em.; mss. corrupt, mostly sorā°.

sopadhi-śeṣa (= Pali sa-upādi-sesa, cf. under **upadhi**), *characterized by a remnant of upadhi = skandhas*, i. e. with normal life not fully extinct, ep. of nirvāṇa(-dhātu); opp. to **nir-upadhi°**, **an-upadhi°**, and see LaVallée-Poussin, AbhidhK. ii.284 n. 3 besides references under nirupa°; °śeṣa-nirvāṇam Mvy 1726.

[**sopavāsika**, see s.v. **śvāsopavāsaka**.]

sopādāna, see **upādāna** (2).

sopānamālā, lit. *ladder-garland*, acc. to pw (from Kern) *winding staircase*; Speyer *flowery ladder*; in any case fig., as leading to heaven: °māleva divo babhūva Jm 80.22 (vs; subject, the king's rule); -mahāsvarga-°mālāṃ RP 1.3 (vs, here said of the text of RP itself).

? **sopānīya**, nt. (perh. for *saupānīya, or su-pānīya), *plenty of good water* (?): (wherever the Buddha Śikhin went) tahiṃ tahiṃ °yaṃ bhoti aṣṭāṅga-saṃmitaṃ (mss. °mataṃ) Mv iii.94.5 (vs); note the closely parallel sumanodyānaṃ, *flower-park(s)*, in line 7, and see s.v. **aṣṭāṅga** (2), used regularly of water.

sopāyāsa, see **upāyāsa**.

Sopāraka (once in late Skt., pw; Sopāra, °raya; for Skt. Śūrpāraka; Divy v.l. Sūr°, Pali Suppāraka; see also **Supāraga, Saupāraka**), n. of a city and country: yadā Thapakarṇi gṛhapati °rakāto (so with mss.) ... mahāsamudram okasto Mv i.245.3. Sūrpāraka or Śūr° in Divy (24.10 ff.) is the home of this merchant and his brothers, including Pūrṇa; likewise Stavakarṇika belongs to Saupāraka in Av ii.166.6; Senart misunderstands and em. wrongly.

sopita, ppp. (to Pkt. sovai = suvai = Skt. svapiti, °ati; § 3.117; cf. **osopati**), *asleep*: °taṃ puravaraṃ Mv i.155.20 (vs).

Soma, n. of a yakṣa: Māy 236.17 and 25.

Somagupta, n. of the grandfather of the Buddha **Viraja** (2): Laṅk 364.16 (misunderstood by Suzuki).

Somachattra, n. of a former Buddha: Mv i.138.5.

Somadatta, n. of a previous incarnation of Kālodāyin: Mv iii.105.20 ff.

Somadarśana, n. of a nāga: Mvy 3365.

Somanadin, 2d ed. °nandin, n. of a lay-disciple: Gv 51.10.

[**somaprāsa**, Mv ii.237.20, read **śamyāprāsa**, q.v.]

Somabhuva, pl., n. of a brahmanical gotra: Divy 635.14.

Somaśrī, m., (**1**) n. of a lay-disciple: Gv 51.10; (**2**) (°śiri m.c.), n. of a kalpa: Gv 257.7 (vs).

Somā, (**1**) n. of a Śākyan girl (a brahman's daughter): Av ii.20.1 ff.; (**2**) n. of a rākṣasī: Māy 243.34.

somila or °**lā**, a kind of cloth-material, = **saumilakā**, °**likā**, q.v.: āmilā vā somilā (could be n. sg. f. or n. pl. m. or f.) vā kṛmivarṇā vā ... Bhīk 22b.4, in same list as Mvy 9175 etc.

sora = Skt. svara (§ 3.117), *voice, sound*: cakorasorāṃ (acc. pl.) karaviṅkanāditāṃ LV 214.18 (vs); meter requires long syllable so-; so Lefm. with 2 mss., ms. A °saurāṃ, others °svarāṃ, unmetr.

soratya, see **sauratya**.

sormika, adj. (= Skt. sormi, sa-ūrmi, plus -ka Bhvr.), *having waves*: Mvy 7036.

sovatthika, nt. (cf. Pali id., as adj., *auspicious, wealful*; MIndic, = **sauvastika**, q.v.), *benediction*: diśe (aor., mss. diśāṃ) °kaṃ divyaṃ maṅgalyaṃ cārthasādhakaṃ (mss. °dhikaṃ) Mv iii.305.10 (vs).

sostika (nt., = Skt. svastika, cf. Pkt. satthia; in other mgs., Pali sotthika; § 3.117), *the cross-legged posture in sitting*: niṣaṇṇa °kena LV 241.12 (vs). Despite variants in mss., this is the only true reading, and is supported by Tib. (skyil mo kruṅ), contrary to Foucaux's statement (Notes p. 156; there is in Tib.'s rendering of this line no equivalent of narendraḥ, which is read in Calc. and some mss.).

saukara = next, q.v.: SP 280.2 (vs).

saukarika (acc. to BR in Skt. only *boar-hunter*, and so AMg. soyariya acc. to Ratnach., but, acc. to Sheth, AMg. and other Pkt. soaria also *butcher*; the distinction was probably hardly made in India; from sūkara plus -ika; Pali only sūkarika), *pork-butcher*: Mvy 3760 = Tib. phag (ḥ)tshoṅ ba, *seller of, dealer in pork*; Divy 505.4, 11, 25; Bbh 302.9.

(**saugata**, also Skt., *Buddhist*; from **Sugata** plus -ka; *of, belonging to, the Buddha*: sattvā bhavantu °tāḥ Sādh 302.17 (vs); nagaro vā kva °taḥ, ... ratnaśobhāḥ kva °tāḥ Laṅk 8.17, 18 (vss; not nouns with Suzuki, who renders as if Sugata!); (labhate ...) kāyaṃ ... °taṃ Laṅk 374.17 (vs), *a Buddha's body*; labhadhvaṃ °tāṃ gatim Dbh.g. 55(81).17; dharmaṃ °taṃ cāryaṃ Mmk 435.8.)

saugandhikā (Skt. °dhika, nt., Lex. also °dhaka; Pali sogandhika, nt.; cf. next), a kind of water-lily: Mv i.308.5 (prose), in a cpd. list of water-plants.

saugandhī = prec.: indīvaraṃ ca °dhī puṇḍarīkam ... Mmk 132.12 (vs).

Sautrāntika, an adherent of the Buddhist school of this name: Mvy 5147.

Saudāsaka (so Tib. and Chin.), text **Saudāmaka**, n. of a nāga: Mahāsamāj. Waldschmidt, Kl. Skt. Texte 4, 177.5.

[? **sauparama**, adj., acc. to ed. (presumably from *suparama plus -a), *supreme*: sā sauparamā tathatā niruttarā ... Bbh 38.26 (prose). But prob. read sāsau (sā asau) paramā etc.]

Saupāraka (also spelled in mss. Saurp°, Śaurp°, Śaupārika; = **Supāraga, Sopāraka**, qq.v.), n. of a city: Av ii.166.6 ff.

Saubhadra (?), n. of a locality: Māy 73.

saubhāṣaṇika (and °**ṣiṇika**? see also **saubhāṣika**,

°sika), adj. (to *su-bhāṣaṇa = Skt. subhāṣita plus -ika), *functioning* (or, *that which functions*) *as fee for a noble* (holy, religious) *utterance*: tena rājñā °ṣaṇikasyārthe suvarṇapiṭako . . . paryaṭito, na ca tat subhāṣitam upalabhyate Av i.219.2, *the king sent around a basket of gold for the purpose of getting a noble utterance* (Speyer, *a sayer of beautiful religious sentences*), *and that utterance was not found*; read °ṣiṇika, or better °ṣaṇika, as in Av, for °sinika in Divy 116.18 (the mg. is made clear by 115.10 ff., yady api te, i.e. Supriya, subhāṣitasyārghamaṇiṃ prayaccheyus . . ., *if they should give you a jewel as reward for a noble utterance* . . .); Supriya later (116.13) preaches to kiṃnarīs, who give him many jewels (17), and (18) dharmadeśanāvarjitāś caikaṃ saubhāsinikaṃ (so text, read as above) ratnam anuprayacchanti, *being* (previously) *deprived of religious instruction, gave him a jewel as reward for his noble utterance*; so also in 117.15, tā api dharmadeśanāvarjitās, tā eva viśiṣṭataraṃ saubhāsinikaṃ (so text, read as above) . . . ratnam anuprayacchanti; and so also 118.19. See next.

saubhāsika, f. **°kī**, ep. of dakṣiṇā, read **saubhāṣika** or **saubhāṣaṇika**, q.v., *serving as reward for noble* (holy, religious) *utterances*: śramaṇabrāhmaṇebhyo dakṣiṇāṃ (*teacher's fee*) pratiṣṭhāpayituṃ mūrdhagāminīṃ (read ūrdhva-gā° with 229.11) saubhāsikīṃ (so text, read as above) . . . āyatyāṃ svargasaṃvartanīṃ Divy 502.(11–)12 (Index *splendid*); the closely parallel passage 229.12 has saubhāgyakarīṃ, *causing felicity*, instead of this word.

saumanasyaka, acc. to Senart nt. = °sya, *joy*; but I am not sure that it is not an adj., *joyous*: (ye, sc. Buddhas, sarvaguṇasaṃpannā lokānām anukampakā,) gṛhītā atyanta (so, or abhyanta, mss.; Senart °taṃ) teṣāṃ sāṃjalī saumanasyakā Mv i.182.(14–)15 (vs), *accepted* (may be) *on their part this very joyous salutation* (?).

Saumitrā, n. of a river: Māy 253.5; in a list between Carmaṇvatī and Viśvāmitrā.

saumilakā, or (v.l. Index, and Mironov) **°likā**, a kind of cloth-material, acc. to Tib. (beḥu phrug, v.l. phrag) and Chin. made of calf's skin or hair, = **somila** or **°lā** which replaces it in similar list in Bhīk: Mvy 9175.

? **saumeru**, adj. (irregular deriv. from Sumeru, = Skt. saumerava), *of Sumeru*: °ru mūrdhaḥ (! read mūrdhnaḥ, acc. pl.) prabhayā spharitvā Gv 336.26 (vs), *suffusing the peaks of S. with light*. Perhaps, however, we should read Sumeru-mūrdhnaḥ.

? **Saumbhavatsabāhu**, n. of a former Buddha: Mv i.139.9. As Senart notes, prob. corrupt; hardly to be derived from a cpd. of Śumbha-.

saumyaka, adj. (= Skt. saumya; -ka perh. m.c.?), *gentle*: °ko viśālākṣo Mv ii.220.10 (vs), in description of **Śyāma(ka)**.

sauratya, nt. (= Pali soracca; to **sūrata, su°**, plus -ya; also written soratya and erroneously **saurabhya**, q.v.), *gentleness, mildness*; regularly rendered by Tib. des pa, see **sūrata**: oftenest closely associated with kṣānti, Mvy 1115; SP 234.8 (all mss. °bhya, ed. em.); 236.9; Śikṣ 183.14; 326.12; KP 153.5 (sor°); Dbh 13.19; 37.11; Dbh.g. 51(77).20; Bbh 20.12; 143.27; Ud xix.2; with **sukhasaṃvāsa**, q.v., Bbh 333.6; without either of these words, Mvy 6597; Jm 41.3; Bbh 368.26 (a-sau°); Śikṣ 46.14 (dharma-sau°, *the gentleness of, according to, the law*; not *love for the law* with Bendall and Rouse).

[**saurabhya**, nt., false writing for **sauratya**, q.v., cf. Wogihara, Lex. 41 f.: with kṣānti, SP 234.8 (mss., ed. em.); LV 37.11; 181.13; 430.11 (ed. em.); Mv ii.354.1 = iii.278.5; ii.362.4; iii.195.12; Divy 39.12; 40.6; Sukh 60.16; Mmk 491.16; not with kṣānti, LV 127.20.]

Saurpārakīya, adj. (Sūrpāraka, Śūr°, plus -īya), of Śūrpāraka: °yo rājā Divy 31.14; °kīyā baṇijaḥ 34.11.

sauryodayikā (to Skt. sūryodaya plus -(i)ka), (something; context fails to make clear what) *relating to sunrise*: Mvy 7663 (so also Mironov; BR cite °ka, as adj.) = Tib. ñi ma śar ba; Chin. *sunrise*; Jap. makes it adj. but specifies no noun.

sauvarcalikā (°ka?), presumably = Skt. °cala, *a kind of salt*: °likāṣṭasahasrābhimantritāṃ kṛtvāñjitākṣaḥ sarvasattvāṃ vaśīkaroti Mmk 712.29 (a magic rite).

Sauvarcasa, pl., n. of a brahmanical school (of the Chandogas): Divy 637.27.

sauvarṇaka, f. **°ikā**, adj. (= Skt. °ṇa and next; to suvarṇa), *golden*: °ṇakasya hemajālasya Mv iii.227.15; °ṇakaṃ daṇḍakamaṇḍalu- Divy 246.18; °ṇikā Mv i.195.7 (kiṅkiṇikā); 196.6; all prose.

sauvarṇika, adj. (AMg. sovaṇṇiya; Childers cites Pali sovaṇṇika, only from Senart's Kacc.; to Skt. suvarṇa plus -ika; = prec.), *golden*: °kena hemajālena Mv i.196.5 (prose).

sauvastika, nt. (also **sovatthika**, q.v.; cf. Skt. Lex. °tika, m., *house-priest*; to Skt. svasti, Pali suvatthi, plus -(i)ka), *benediction*: °kam Mvy 2749 = Tib. bde legs brjod pa, *speaking welfare*.

Skanda, n. of an evil being: Mvy 4761 = Tib. skem byed, *a demon that causes drought*. It is possible, but far from certain, that this is to be identified with the Skt. god Skanda, who is said to cause diseases in children.

1 **skandha**, m. (= Pali khandha; in mg. 1 = Skt. Lex. id., recorded also in BR once from Bhāg.P. puṇya-s°, and once from Mbh. 12.449 = Crit. ed. 12.15.26, where however acc. to Nīl. it means personal *body*, deha), (**1**) *mass, large amount*, of *bulk* rather than quantity: lokadhātuṃ savāyu-skandhaṃ sapṛthivī-°dhaṃ sateja(ḥ)-°dhaṃ Gv 535.26 f., *the universe with its whole mass of air, earth, and fire*; agni-sk° (Pali aggi-kkh°), *a mass of fire*, Mvy 224; SP 72.6 (of a conflagration); 73.6; 438.8; LV 66.14; Mv i.13.14 (read with mss. °dha-nibhāntike); 95.14; ii.332.15; 393.23; iii.103.15; Jm 32.5; 193.1; Av i.331.13; arciskandha Gv 75.2, *a mass of flame* or *radiance*; āpa-skandha, *mass of water*, see s.v. **āpa**; in Divy 230.23 to 231.4 skandha seems to refer to three superimposed *masses of water* (udaka-sk° 231.1, 4, daka-sk° 231.1, see s.v. **daka**) in the ocean (they seem to be called bhūmi, *stage* or *story*, in 230.28 ff.); bhoga-°dham (avahāya, prahāya) Mv ii.161.6; iii.213.3, *abandoning a whole mass of enjoyments* (parallel with cpds. ending in -kāya, -varga, virtual synonyms of -skandha); puṇya-s°, *mass of merit*, SP 340.10; 351.12; Divy 197.19; Kv 20.14 (tathāgatānāṃ), etc.; for śīla-s° see 3 below; duḥkha-s°, *mass of misery*, of life as a whole, LV 347.21; 348.15; 420.4; Mv ii.285.12; iii.448.15; 449.3; (**2**) the five *agglomerations* which in Buddhism are the basis of (or substitute for) the 'personality', and which constitute the root of clinging to existence, hence more fully upādāna-s°, see **upādāna** (3), where the list is given, with examples; others, skandhānām udayaṃ (q.v.) vyayaṃ SP 69.16; maha-duḥkhaṃ pañca-skandhaṃ LV 191.7 (vs); °dhā pratītya samudeti hi duḥkham 419.13 (vs); vadhakāś ca skandhāḥ RP 44.15; etehi eva skandhehi parinirvāpayitavyaṃ Mv iii.263.13, virtually *with this present body* (or, at least, *existence, personality*; lit. *elements of separate existence*); for others see s.v. **dhātu** 1 and 4; (**3**) in a good sense, *religious agglomerations* or *concentrations*; rendered in PTSD *main portions* or *articles of the dhamma*: they may be, in Pali and BHS, three (śīla-s°, samādhi-s°, prajñā-s°, Sūtrāl. xx–xxi.22; in this sense prob. **Triskandha**[**-pathadeśika**], q.v.; same in Pali forms, each called ase(k)kha, q.v. in CPD, Itiv. 51.2 ff., where they constitute a group of three dhammā, imehi . . . °mehi samannāgato . . .), in Pali once four (dhammakkhandhā, DN iii.229.14 f., the above three plus vimutti-kkh°), but usually five, the above three plus vimukti-s° and vimuktijñānadarśana-s° (in Pali forms, e. g. as 5 dhamma-kkh° DN iii.279.15 ff., each called ase(k)kha SN i.99.30 ff. et al., CPD as above); these five listed as asama-sama-pañca-

skandhāḥ Mvy 103–108, as lokottara-pañca-sk° Dharmas 23; as *cinq skandhas purs* AbhidhK. LaV-P. i.48 (the first, śīla-s°, belongs to the rūpa-s° of the 5 upādāna-s°, the other four to the saṃskāra-s°); in DN comm. iii.1022.21 f. (on DN iii.229.14 f. above) khandha in these cpds. is rendered by guṇa; individual units in this group sometimes mentioned alone, śīlaskandhe ca acchidre ye bhikṣū supratiṣṭhitāḥ Mv ii.353.20 (prob. to be interpreted thus technically, yet cf. puṇya-skandha under 1 above); prajñā-skandhaṃ niveśeyaṃ Mv i.42.15 = 53.12 (vs), in parallel, i.337.4, replaced by prajñācakṣu, due to a misunderstanding (prob. of copyists, cf. bhavacakṣukaiḥ in same line); the true reading may be °skandho niveśeyaḥ with mss. in i.42.15; there is a passing allusion to 80,000 dharma-skandha in Av ii.155.8, prob. in substantially this mg.; (**4**) in another special (good) sense, related fundamentally to prec., there are three religious skandhas taught in the work called, for this reason, **Triskandhaka**, q.v.; in it, acc. to Śikṣ 290.2, trayaḥ skandhāḥ pāpadeśanā-puṇyānumodanā-buddhādhyeṣaṇā-(khyāḥ), puṇyarāśitvāt, *three agglomerations* (of religion), *called confession of sin, approval of* (gratification in) *good deeds, requesting a Buddha (for instruction)*, (called skandha) *because they constitute heaps* (rāśi = skandha) *of merit*. See **Skandha-māra.**

2 **Skandha** (perh. = **Skanda,** q.v.; often occurs as wrong reading for Skt. Skanda), n. of a class of evil powers: Māy 219.9 (text Skāndha); 220.16 etc. Cf. **Skandha-māra.**

Skandha-māra (= Pali Khandha-°), one of the four Māras, see s.v. **Māra.**

skandhākṣa, adj. or subst. m. (in Skt. once as n. of an attendant of Skanda; BR *Augen auf den Schultern habend*), (**1**) in Mvy 8837, in a list of deformities, acc. to Tib. *shoulder-eye*, phrag mig, which acc. to Das is applied to *a kind of spirits having eyes on their shoulders* (also *crab*); (**2**) n. of a yakṣa: Māy 81.

? **skandhopariṣvajānika,** corruption for some word meaning a garment for the shoulder(?): -ratnahāra-°nika-pṛṣṭhottaryāṇy . . . anyāni ca . . . vastrāṇi Kv 78.21.

skambhākṛta, also **kam°** (= Pali khambha-kata), *with arms akimbo*, lit. *prop-formed*: Mvy 8549 na skambhākṛtāḥ = Tib. dkur ma brtẹn (or, mi bsten), *not placed on the side*; cf. Prāt 530.12 (lacuna; Mvy text adopted); La Vallée Poussin JRAS 1913.843, Stein ms. fragm. 1.1.17, 18, kambhā° (semi-MIndic).

stana-dhātrī, or (in 16, text) **stanya-,** *wet-nurse*, = **kṣīra-dh°,** q.v.: Divy 475.13, 16.

stabdha, m., n. of some demoniac being, in a list of such: SP 401.5 (one ms. skabdho); WT state that Tib. reads reṅs pa, *stiff* (used in rendering forms of Skt. stabh, as e. g. stambha Mvy 7339).

stabdhika (read °aka? cf. Skt. stabdha), *stubborn*, in the sense of *fixedly devoted* (to, in comp.): udaka-°kā manuṣyāḥ Divy 19.25, *men are stubbornly attached to* (bathing in) *water*; cf. Pali Vin. i.196.2 manussā udaka-suddhikā (is the Divy form a bad Sktization for this?).

stambhanī (cf. Skt. °na), n. of a kind of magic: Divy 636.27.

stambhita, nt. (elsewhere only adj.), *paralysis* (from fear): bhayam abhūt °tam abhūd romaharṣaḥ MSV iii.140.1.

-stambhin, see **a-st°.**

stava, acc. to Tib. on Av ii.166.6 (see **Stavakarṇika**), cited by Feer in note to transl. as rgya skegs (= lākṣā), and acc. to Index to Divy, *lac* (in any case must be a cheap material): apareṇa stava-karṇikā Divy 26.27, *lac ear-ring*. See next.

Stavakarṇika, Av ii.166.6, or **°karṇin,** Divy 26.29; 45.16 etc. (also **Thapakarṇi, °ṇika, Sthapakarṇika,** qq.v.), nickname of a brother of Pūrṇa, lit. *lac-ear* (*-ring*), see s.v. **Trapukarṇin.**

stavati, stavayati, *praises*, = Pali thavati, Skt. stauti; see Chap. 43, s.v. stu (1).

Stavārha, n. of a future Pratyekabuddha: Divy 73.17.

? **-stāra,** see **phalaha-.**

? **Stimitarājan** (based on a single inferior ms. which reads Stimira-rājāḥ; other mss. Timi-rājan or, with metathesis, Miti°; stimita seems not recorded in Buddh. literature; very doubtful), n. of a former Buddha: Mv i.141.1.

stīna (= Pali thīna; § 3.115) = **styāna,** q.v.: -middhaṃ, v.l. of Kashgar rec. for SP 335.6 (vs).

stuti = Skt. stauti (which ms. reads, unmetr.), *praises*: Śikṣ 341.11 (vs). Possibly m.c. for *stoti, § 3.56; but may also be for stute, 3 sg. mid., or analog. to stumas, stuta, etc., with weak for strong stem, cf. § 28.64.

stuvati (AMg. thuvai, see Ratnach.) = Skt. stauti, *praises*: read prob. stuviya (ger.) yasavatī (acc.) jinasya mātā (acc.) LV 50.4 (vs); Lefm. supiya, v.l. suviya; acc. to Foucaux, Notes, p. 101, Tib. *having praised*. On apparent use of the same pres. form as passive, see § 37.35.

stūpa, m. (**1**) (rarely nt.; = Pali thūpa, AMg. thūbha, rarely thūva; Skt. Lex., in lit. only Buddh. and Jain), *relic-mound, tope*: Mvy 6999; SP 239.1 ff.; Mv ii.287.3; 363.16; Av i.119.7; °pa-bimbāni Kv 13.11; 36.19; °pa-bhedanam Mvy 2334, one of the **upānantarīya,** q.v.; °pa-bhedaka Kv 94.23; common everywhere; as nt., stūpaṃ kāritaṃ (n. sg.) Mv i.61.1; (**2**) (Pali, see next but one) *turret* or *pinnacle* of a building, in prākāraparikhādvāra-stūpābhinigūḍhaḥ Av ii.115 8, see Speyer's note.

stūpaka (m. or nt.; to prec. plus -ka, dim.), *little stūpa* (made by children in play): MSV i.1.21 ff.

stūpikā (dim. f. to **stupa** 2 plus -ka,-(i)kā), *small turret* or *pinnacle* on a house: read gṛhastūpikāvalīhī Mv ii.36.11 (vs), °hī m.c., otherwise with one ms., *with rows of house-pinnacles*; Senart em. wrongly; cf. Pali Jāt. vi.116.(28–)29 maṇimaya-kañcana-thūpikaṃ (Bhvr.), ep. of vihāram (acc.); in vs 117.6 pañcathūpaṃ (vimānaṃ), glossed pañcahi kūṭāgārehi samannāgataṃ; PTSD not happy in this sl.

? **stemita,** text Lefm. LV 230.9 (vs), could only = Skt. stimita (m.c.? cf. abstr. staimitya), *motionless*, i. e. *insensible, fainting*: (of Śuddhodana on hearing of his son's departure; in 7–8 dharaṇitale nirasto utkrośu kṛtvā . . .) so stemito (with only two inferior mss., others with Calc. stomito) hī jalaghaṭasaṃprasikto, āśvāsayantī bahuśata Śākiyānāṃ; Lefm. cites Tib. from Foucaux's transl. *sanglotait*, but this (ṅud mo phyuṅ) = utkrośu kṛtvā, and is put in prec. line; for line 9 Tib. de nas (*then*) de la (*on him*) bum paḥi chu blugs khrus byas nas (lit. *of-flask-water-pitcher-after-bathing*), with nothing that seems to render stemito; I can make nothing of stomito; de nas could point to ito, and I suspect a corruption in the first part of the word.

steya-saṃvāsika, m., and f. **°kā** (Pali theyya-saṃvāsaka), lit. *thief(-like) inhabitant*, one who tries to associate himself with a Buddhist monastic community without a right to it (see SBE 13.216 f. for a story which illustrates the mg.): °kaḥ Mvy 8756; MSV ii.204.10 (text steyā°); °kā Bhīk 16b.2.

stainyaka (m.; to Skt. stainya, nt., *theft*, or Lex., m., *thief*, plus -ka), *thief*: teṣāṃ mohapuruṣāṇāṃ dharma-°kānāṃ LV 88.5 (prose).

stomita, ppp. (= Pali thomita, to thometi = Skt. Dhātup. stomayati, denom. to stoma), *praised*: °taḥ Mvy 2614; stutaḥ °to varṇitaḥ praśasto Bhīk 24a.4; devaśatasahasra-stuta-°ta- (Lefm. staumita, wrongly)-varṇita-praśaṃsitasya LV 7.22 (prose). Most mss. stomito, for Lefm. **stemito,** q.v., in LV 230.9.

staupika, adj. and subst. (Skt. Lex., only Trik., = bauddha-dravya; to **stūpa** 1 plus -ika), *pertaining to a stūpa*; usually with parallel sāṃghika, and applied to *property* (dravya, vitta, vastu): Śikṣ 170.3; Bbh 166.20; RP 29.8; Gv 228.21; as subst., implying some such word, *what belongs to a stūpa*, Śikṣ 56.5; Bbh 163.11.

? **styayāntataḥ**, LV 3.22 (vs), uninterpretable; the preceding pāda is, yasyāpy avandhyāv iha darśana-śravā; then, after this word (the only v.l. is °takaḥ in Calc.; s- could possibly be the ending of -śravā, n. pl. for dual) śāntavimokṣapāragaḥ; Tib. faithfully renders all the rest but omits this completely. All the three other pādas of the vs begin with relative pronouns referring to the Bodhisattva; I have thought of reading here yo 'yaṃ tataḥ, which makes good sense but is remote from the mss.

styāna, nt., also (semi-MIndic) **stīna, thīna**, qq.v. (as noun rare in Skt.; = Pali thīna, AMg. thīṇa), *sluggishness, languor, torpor*: °nam Mvy 1981 = Tib. rmugs pa, *languor* (foll. by middham 1982); Dharmas 30, 69 (in 69 middham also occurs, not immediately following; this is a list of **upakleśa**); chiefly in cpd. **styāna-middha**, see next.

styāna-middha, nt. (= Pali thīna-m°; in Pali and BHS analyzed as **styāna** plus **middha**, dvandva, qq.v.; AMg. thīṇaddhi, thīṇagiddhi, Jain Skt. styānarddhi, styānagṛddhi; as suggested by me in NIA.2.607–610, all these forms go back to a cpd. *thīna-(m-)iddha or -iddhi, Skt. *styāna-ṛddhi, the m being orig. 'hiatus-bridging', *increase of languor*), *torpor and drowsiness*, esp. as one of the five **nīvaraṇa**, q.v., *hindrances* (to religious life); often in lists of (some or all) the **nīvaraṇa**, and almost always with definite implication that it is reprehensible; a rare exception is Gv 20.10 (tad yathāpi nāma puruṣo ... mahato janakāyasya) madhye styānamiddham avakrāmet (*would get sleepy*), sa suptaḥ svapnāntaragatas ... (note that **middha**, q.v., is sometimes used in this innocent sense); with nīvaraṇa or other evil qualities, Bbh 145.10; 173.1; 243.21; in Śikṣ 111.9 (vs; repeated several times below) read yaḥ styāna-middhe (for text yasmāna mi°) 'bhiratiṃ prayāti (these vss introduced in 111.5 by nidrārāmam adhikṛtyāhā); in Śikṣ 129.12 read styāna-middha for text mlāna°; also in Gv 447.17 (text °viddha); Sādh 365.12 (text °siddha); Mmk 23.27; SP 335.6 (vs; Kashgar rec. **stīna**-mi°); LV 139.9; 262.16 = Mv ii.240.5; RP 39.8; 45.19; 56.17; 57.1 ; styānamiddhe (so read with mss.) bahulāś ca bhavanti Mv i.79.16.

striyā, also **strīyā** (cf. **śriyā** = śrī; § 10.6; cf. **iṣṭiyā** = **iṣṭikā** = **iṣṭī**, and see s.v. **istrī**; may be Sktization of AMg. itthiyā, which may represent theoretical strīkā) = strī, *woman*: obl. sg. striyāya (gen., Mv ii.426.8; prob. instr., 428.3) and striyāye (prob. instr., Mv ii.426.8; iii.27.2; gen., ii.481.19 = iii.17.6; iii.27.4); striyāyā, gen., Mmk 54.1 (prose, before puruṣasya); 81.27 (prose, before v-); striyāyāṃ, loc., Mmk 562.25 (prose; text yasyā °yāṃ abhiśakto, read yasyāṃ ... abhirakto); striyās, n. pl., Mv iii.149.12 (prose, no v.l.); -striyāyo, acc. pl., iii.283.5 (prose); striyāhi iii.291.15 (prose).

striyāgāra, see **stryāgāra**.

strī (= Skt.), *woman*. 'Even now a woman never attains five stations (sthānāni): those of Brahman, Śakra, a mahārāja (= lokapāla), a cakravartin, and an avaivartika-bodhisattva' SP 264.11 ff.; in BHS often replaced by **mātṛgrāma**, and by **stryāgāra**.

strīkāgāra, see **stryāgāra**.

strīpoṣaka (= AMg. itthiposaya), *'keeper of women', whoremaster, pimp*: not to be associated with, SP 280.5; 480.9.

strī-maya, adj., (music) *made by women*: (rājā ...) °yena tūryeṇa vādyamānenodyānaṃ praviṣṭaḥ Av i.101.1. Speyer aptly compares Buddhacarita ii.29.

strīyā, strīyāgāra, see **striyā, stryāgāra**.

stry-āgāra (also spelled **striyā°, strīyā°, strīkā°, istriyā°**, and **istrigāra**; = Pali itthāgāra, ittha°), nt. sg. or m. (and nt.?) pl., *women-folk* (collectively), esp. used of inmates of a harem: n. sg. strīkāgāraṃ (v. l. strīyā°) Mv ii.424.20; istrigāra LV 213.19 (vs); istriyāgāraṃ (v.l. iṣṭiyo stryāg°) Mv ii.425.15; n. pl. istrigārāḥ (one ms. °rā) LV 138.4 (vs); °gārā LV 230.3 and (voc.?) 231.6 (vss); acc. pl. stryāgārān Sukh 67.15 (but reading uncertain); acc. sg. stryāgāram Mv ii.426.10 (v.l. striyā°); iii.1.6; 2.11; striyāgāraṃ Mv ii.426.7 (mss.); iii.1.4 (so read with v.l., ed. strīyā°, metrically inferior); gen. istrigārasya madhye LV 215.11 (vs); stem in comp. istrigāra-(madhye) LV 137.16 (vs); antaḥpura-stryāgāra- Gv 359.2; stryāgāra-parivṛta LV 14.9 (prose); Mv iii.437.19; Śikṣ 208.6; Bhvr. cpd. sa-stryāgāro Mv i.182.6, 12 (vss).

sthaṇḍila (nt.; cf. AMg. thaṇḍila, not quite in same mg.), acc. to Tib. (ḥdug gnas) *residence*: Madhuskandhasya devaputrasya °laṃ pradakṣiṇīkaroti MSV iii.140.4.

sthaṇḍilaka (in Skt. only ifc. Bhvr.; = Skt. °la), *bare open space*, for performance of a rite: kṛṣṇacaturdaśyāṃ gocarmamātraṃ °lakam upalipya Mmk 720.11 (prose).

sthaṇḍila-śayana (nt.; = Skt. °śayyā), *sleeping on the bare open ground*, as an ascetic practice: °naiś ca LV 249.4 (prose). See next.

sthaṇḍila-śāyikā, thaṇḍ° (= Pali thaṇḍila-sāyikā; cf. Skt. °śāyin, adj., *sleeping on the bare ground*), = prec.: Mv iii.412.16 = Divy 339.23 (vs; same vs in Pali Dhp. 141, with same word), in Mv written thaṇḍ° (MIndic).

sthaṇḍilya (m. or nt.; = Skt. °la; cf. AMg. thaṇḍilla, beside thaṇḍila; BR cite °lya as 'error' in Ch.Up. 5.2.8; Boehtlingk's ed. and that of AnSS. read there sthaṇḍile with no v.l.), = **sthaṇḍilaka**: mahodadhitaṭe ramye medhya-sthaṇḍilyam āśrite Mmk 476.28 (vs, but metr. indifferent as to °la or °lya).

Sthapakarṇika, also **Thapakarṇi(-ka)**, (and cf. **Stavakarṇin**, °ṇika) n. of a merchant figuring in the story of **Pūrṇa**(ka) 1: Sthapa°ṇikasya Mv i.245.5; °ṇikaṃ 10; Thapa°ṇi, n. sg., id. 3; °ṇikasya (v.l. Stha°) 11; all prose.

sthapayati, sthapeti, thapeti, rarely **ṭhapeti** (Pali only ṭhapeti, and AMg. and other Pkt. regularly ṭhavei etc.; Ap. thaviya, Jacobi, Bhav.), caus. to Skt. sthā, *places*, etc.: sthapemi SP 323.9 (vs); °peyaṃ, opt., 128.2 (vs); other forms, see Chap. 43, s.v. sthā (9). See also **sthāpayitvā**, in which the radical ā is always long in BHS.

[**sthapika**, app. error for **sthavika**, q.v., at Mvy 8951.]

sthavika, m., °**kā** (cf. Pali thavikā; MW cites Skt. Lex. sthavi, *sack, bag*, which is not in BR or pw), *receptacle, holder, bag*: pātra-sthavika (so Index, text °sthapika), = Pali pattatthavikā, *bag for carrying the begging-bowl*, Mvy 8951; kolāhala-sth° Mvy 9004, see s.v. **kolāhala**; °kā MSV ii.126.2; -bhaiṣajya-sthavikāś (could be m. or fem.), *medicine-bag(s)*, in a dvandva cpd., Divy 475.21. Tib. snod, *receptacle, that which holds anything* (Das); see **poṇika**, a synonym.

sthavira (cf. **thera, sthera**), (**1**) = Pali thera, *Buddhist elder*: Mvy 8733; Mv i.75.1; iii.268.6; sometimes in vss which suggest pronunciation as in MIndic (but, N.B., two shorts may replace a long), e. g. (in anuṣṭubh prior pādas) tataś ca Kāśyapa-sthaviraḥ Mv i.84.11, tataḥ Kātyāyanaḥ sthaviraḥ 17; common in most texts; (**2**) = **Sthaviraka** (2) (Pali Thera): Av ii.133.1; 136.7; 139.3; 140.3 (all prose), etc.; MSV i.194.1 ff. (also Sthavira-sthavira).

sthaviraka, (**1**) f. °ikā, adj. (Pali also theraka, °ikā; sthavira plus -ka; here perhaps pitying or contemptuous dim.), *old*: Mv iii.283.10, 13; see s.v. **jīrṇaka**; (**2**) n. of a disciple of Śākyamuni, hero of Av Chap. 92; also **Sthavira** (2): Av ii.136.1; 138.14; 139.5; 140.2 (all prose), etc.

sthavira-gāthā, pl., n. of a Buddhist work or part of one: Divy 35.1; = Pali Thera-gāthā? or, since most names in this list seem to refer to sections of Pali Sn, perhaps = Pali Sāriputta-sutta, aliter Therapañha-sutta (Sn 955–975); this seems to me more likely.

-sthāṇuka (to Skt. sthāṇu), in nagara-sthā°, *stump of a city, contemptible town*: °ke, °kaṃ (acc.) MPS 33.2, 3,

sthāna, nt. (in all these mgs. = Pali ṭhāna, but hardly Skt. sthāna except as indicated below), (**1**) *point, matter, subject*: (anyāṃ devāṃ) divyehi daśahi sthānehi abhibhavati, divyenāyuṣā (so with varṇena, sukhena, aiśvaryeṇa, parivāreṇa; rūpeṇa, divyehi śabdehi, gandhehi, rasehi, praṣṭavyehi) Mv i.337.15; similarly ii.190.13 (rūpehi for rūpeṇa, sparśehi for praṣṭavyehi); similarly Pali SN iv.275.2 (et alibi; here, dibbena āyunā, then vaṇṇena, sukhena, yasena, adhipateyyena; dibbehi rūpehi, saddehi, gandhehi, rasehi, phoṭṭhabbehi); in Mv iii.302.5, same with only pañcahi sthānehi, the first five above; five **vidyāsthāna,** see this, also called simply sthānāni, *points, subjects (of learning)*; the fifth of these is śilpa(karma)-sthānavidyā, cf. Divy 109.21 (kuśalā) Bodhisattvāḥ teṣu teṣu śilpasthānakarmasthāneṣu, ... *in various matters of arts and crafts*; also RP 41.13 sarvaśilpasthānakarma-sthāna-vidhijñāḥ; in Karmav 64.7 mātāpitaraḥ pañca sthānāni pratyanuśaṃsamānāḥ (*expecting five matters*) putram icchanti, some other group than the vidyā-sthānāni must be meant, perh. the five ānisaṃsā of a virtuous man as in Pali DN ii.86.1 ff.; durdṛśam imaṃ sthānaṃ (*hard to see thru is this subject*), yad ... pratītyasamutpādaḥ Mv iii.314.4; (paravipattiḥ) saṃvejanīyaṃ sthānaṃ Divy 432.16, *a matter that should be shuddered at*; anākhyātam idaṃ sthānam SP 230.8–9, *an article (of creed) not yet made known* (Kern); dharma-nigūḍha-sthānam 233.12, *secret article of the doctrine*; anyatamānyatamat sthānam adhyāpadya Bhīk 23b.4, *having violated one or another point (item*, of the code of conduct); 24a.1; evaṃrūpaṃ sthānaṃ nādhyāpatsyase 24b.5; asmin sthāne, *in (on) this point, subject, matter*, SP 317.3; 318.11 (tathāgataḥ khalv asmin sthāne, *on this subject*, 'saṃpramoṣadharmā; Kern here wrongly *in his position*); atra sthāne 323.4; (**2**) much as in Skt. (BR s.v. sthāna, 1 *w*), *underlying condition, occasion*, virtually *cause* (cf. Pali DN comm. i.77.32 ṭhānaṃ vuccati kāraṇaṃ): trayāṇāṃ sthānānāṃ saṃmukhībhāvāt (*as a result of the presence of three things, conditions*) putrā jāyante duhitaraś ca Divy 1.12, 15; (ṣaṇṇāṃ) sthānānām āścaryādbhuto loke prādurbhāvaḥ Av ii.55.2, *of six conditions* (or *causes*) *is a marvelous and miraculous appearance in the world* (they are then listed; the first is a Tathāgata, who in the story has just performed a miracle); na pramādasthānam asyopasaṃharati Bbh 15.24, *he does not produce for him an occasion for heedlessness*; kaukṛtya-sthānaṃ SP 287.2, see **kaukṛtya**; (**3**) *basis, cause*, so *organ, implement*: tenaikaṃ daṇḍasthānaṃ preṣitam Divy 531.11, *he sent out an instrument of punishment = a punitive force* or *expedition* (Index, *an army corps*; not plausible); similarly MSV ii.71.16; (**4**) in cpd. sthānāsthāna, (skandha-dhātv-āyatana-pratītyasamutpāda-)-sthānāsthāna- Bbh 4.8, either *possibilities* and *impossibilities* (see 5 below), or *sound and unsound propositions* or *conclusions* (*regarding* ...), and so in other cases, see s.v. **asthāna**; in Pali CPD s.v. aṭṭhāna, and PTSD s.v. ṭhāna(ṭṭhāna); (**5**) *occasion*, hence *possibility*: sthānam etad vidyati yaṃ (*it is quite possible that*) ete mama (acc.) jīvitāto vyaparopayitvā (°pitvā, mss.) ... Mv i.350.11; sthānam etaṃ vidyati yaṃ Sudarśanā upakrameṇa ātmānaṃ māreyā ii.448.12; sthānam etad vidyate yat ... Divy 109.14; 159.28; 175.27; 228.12; 273.16; 512.5; Gv 404.23, etc., common; (without yad) sthānaṃ (one ms. adds ca) me ... Sudarśanā paribhavati Mv ii.491.19 (so mss., which however are confused); with neg. (cf. Pali n' etaṃ ṭhānaṃ vijjati), referring to following, na etaṃ sthāna (so read with v.l., m.c.) vidyati, yatra ... Mv iii.46.2 (vs); but usually to preceding, nedaṃ sthānaṃ vidyate Vaj 34.8; Mmk 395.3; naitat sth° vi° Dbh 25.16; sthānam etan na saṃvidyate LV 215.19 (vs); iti naitat sthānaṃ vidyate SP 333.9.

sthāpana, nt. (cf. Pali ṭhapana, same mg.), *omission, avoidance*: MSV ii.176.8 adharmeṇa karmaṇā kopyena °nārheṇa (*which ought to be avoided*); so iii.73.16 etc.; poṣadha-°na, *omission, suspension, of the p°*, MSV iii. 108.11 ff. (list of valid and invalid reasons for it, as in Pali, Vin. ii.241.26 ff., pātimokkha-ṭhapanaṃ).

sthāpanīya-vyākaraṇa, nt. (cf. **ṭhapanīya-praśna-,** and Pali below), *elucidation* (response to a question, by saying that the matter is) *to be let alone, avoided*: Mvy 1661 (cf. **vyākaraṇa** 1). See Pali AN i.197.23 ṭhapanīyaṃ pañhaṃ, explained comm. ii.308.34 ff. taṃ jīvaṃ taṃ sarīraṃ ti ādīni puṭṭhena pana, avyākatam etaṃ bhagavatā ti ṭhapetabbo, esa pañho na vyākātabbo, ayaṃ ṭhapanīyo pañho.

sthāpayitvā, in vss rarely **sthāpetvā, sthāpya** (= Pali ṭhapetvā; cf. **sthapayati,** but in this form ā, never a; orig. ger. of Skt. caus. of sthā, *putting aside*, so in SP 79.1, and a transition case in SP 43.15, [asthānam etac ... yad bhikṣur ... saṃmukhībhūte tathāgata imaṃ dharmaṃ ...] na śraddadhyāt, sthāpayitvā parinirvṛtasya tathāgatasya, *it is impossible that ... in the T.'s presence a monk should not believe this doctrine, leaving aside the case when the T. has entered nirvāṇa*), *except*; usually followed by acc. object: sthāpetv' (Kashgar rec. sthāpya) upāyaṃ SP 91.8 (vs); the following all sthāpayitvā; Mvy 5458 (listed among indeclinables); followed by object acc., SP 66.12; LV 408.3; 442.12; Mv i.335.3; iii.181.3; 298.15; Divy 270.4; 394.25; 457.6; 506.4; Av ii.111.8; Suv 10.1; Dbh 59.17; Gv 136.26; 173.1, etc.; after object acc., (yaḥ svayam udāraṃ dharmābhisaṃskāram udārāṃ ca buddhakṣetrotpattiṃ) sthāpayitvāsya dharmaparyāyasya saṃprakāśanahetor ... upapanno veditavyas tathāgatadūtaḥ SP 226.10, *who himself must be regarded as a messenger of the T. born to make known this religious discourse*, (thus resembling a Buddha) *except for the exalted performance of the doctrine and the exalted birth in a Buddha-field* (which are functions of a Buddha alone; Burnouf rightly); tathāgataṃ °tvā LV 148.21 (prose); Mv ii.433.8 (putraṃ °tvā); Divy 544.9 (pratyayaṃ °tvā); Bbh 77.13; Sukh 2.12; followed by relative clause in lieu of object, °tvā ye tasyāṃ parṣadi saṃnipatitā abhūvan SP 244.14, *except those who* ...

sthāpitaka, adj. (Skt. °pita, ppp., plus specifying -ka, § 22.39; cf. AMg. ṭhaviyaga-bhoi), in pūrva-°ka, *that which has been previously placed*, as described before: Mmk 39.2 (°kaṃ cūrṇaṃ); 49.4; 50.23; 86.1; all prose.

sthāpetvā, sthāpya, see **sthāpayitvā.**

sthāma(n), nt., see also **thāma** (= Pali thāma; no s-stem forms like Pali thāmasā noted in BHS; recorded rarely in late Skt., see Renou, JA. 1939, 372 n. 1), *strength, power*; often assoc. with bala, vīrya: °ma Mvy 5152 = Tib. mthu (seems the common rendering) or stobs; LV 109.12 (vs, sthāmāsya = °ma-asya); 154.21 (acc.; so best mss., most mss. °maṃ); kāyasya °ma Divy 327.3; °mnā LV 155.15; Sukh 40.17; °mni LV 156.11; °ma-, stem in comp., SP 10.3; LV 86.15; 101.14; Divy 58.22; Bhvr., alpa-sthāma, *of little strength*, Divy 177.16; Av ii.135.4; acc. sg. °maṃ, used even in prose of such works as SP, LV, Suv: SP 53.16 (vs); 124.1 (yathā-°maṃ, adv., prose); 380.2–3 (prose, udārarddhibala-°maṃ pratijñāpratibhānabala-°maṃ prajñābala-°maṃ ca dṛṣṭvā); LV 153.3; 154.13; 264.2 (all prose); 234.7 (vs); Mv ii.91.6; 131.10; 205.1; 314.18; Suv 65.10; 70.7 (both these prose, but v.l. °ma); °mena, instr., Mv ii.74.12; 260.6 ff. and 261.8 ff. (here three sthāma, of body, speech, and thought, which pertain to Bodhisattvas only when they reach enlightenment, not before); -sthāma-tā SP 105.2.

sthāmavant (from **sthāma-n**), *powerful*: °vāṃś ca SP 340.1; °vantu, n. sg., LV 170.20 (vs); balasthāmavanto,

n. sg., Mv ii.182.7 (vs); sthāmavām, n. sg., Bbh 203.21; °vatā Av ii.107.1; see also Nārāyaṇa-sth°, s.v. **Nārāyaṇa** (1).

sthāla, nt., a kind of flower: Mvy 6185. Tib. transliterates.

sthālaka, m., nt., **sthālikā**, **°lika-** (?) (= Pali thālaka, °likā; Skt. sthāla, °lī, plus -ka, svārthe or dim.), (*little*) *pot*: °likā-mūlyena SP 106.10 (prose; all Nep. mss. but one °lika-, Kashgar rec. different); °likām, acc., Divy 123.22; 343.16; dīpa-sthālikā-(*lamp-pots*)-śata- RP 57.7; dīpa-sthālaka udvartavyaḥ MSV iii.97.12, *the lamp-pot is to be set up*; °likākāra, *pot-shaped*, Divy 338.9; 342.11; pānīya-sthālakam, (*small*) *water-pot*, Mvy 9029; Śikṣ 90.15 (prose); udaka-sthālakam (acc.) Mvy 8592, (monk's) *water-pot* (for drinking out of).

Sthālīsugandha, name assumed by **Kuśa** (2) as cook: MSV i.103.17.

Sthāvarā, n. of an earth-goddess, (mahā-)pṛthivīdevatā: LV 319.3, 9; Gv 220.19 ff. (dwelling at the bodhimaṇḍa, in Magadha-viṣaya).

Sthāvira, see **Ārya-s°**.

sthitaka, once (m.c.) **-āka**, fem. **°ikā** (Pali ṭhitaka, acc. to PTSD only in mg. 1), (**1**) *standing* (opp. to sitting or lying), *upright*: bodhisattvamātā sthitikā eva bodhisattvam samjaneti Mv ii.20.10 (prose), *gives birth . . . only in standing posture*; of images, sthitakā(ḥ) Mmk 68.23 (prose); sthitako no niṣaṇṇaḥ 111.5 (prose); (**2**) *standing* in the sense of *situated, located, abiding*: padminīye sthitako Mv ii.448.18 (prose), *standing* (*situated*) *in a pool*: ākāśadhātu-sthitakam (sc. cittam bodhisattvasya) Dbh 11.24 (prose); (**3**) *staying, remaining* (opp. to approaching or departing): tena bāhire nagarāto . . . sthitakena dūto preṣito Mv i.310.15 (prose), *he, staying outside the city, sent a messenger*; dūrato sthitakā Mv iii.30.7 (prose), *they* (n. pl. m.) *from afar, while staying* (there, and not approaching the water); (**4**) *lasting*, = **sthitika**, q.v., esp. **cira-sthitika**: a-cira-sthitāka (ā for a m.c., unless we should em. to -sthitīka, m.c. for sthitika!) Dbh.g. 11(347).1, *not long lasting*; perhaps here should be included, as fem. to sthitaka, sthitikā SP 53.7, see s.v. **sthitika.**

Sthitaniścitta, m., n. of a samādhi: Mvy 583; ŚsP 1422.4. Cf. **Niścitta**, and **Tathatāsthitaniścitta.**

Sthitabuddhidatta, n. of a former Buddha: LV 5.9.

sthita-lapa (v.l. sthita-raya), °pā (n. pl.), Mv i.134.10, of Bodhisattvas; foll. by **akāmakāmin**, q.v. Senart suggests taking sthita as *stopped*, virtually = sthāpita, a mg. which is not recorded for it in Pali, and in Skt. is supported, if at all, by Ind. Spr. 6986 na sthitaḥ, *you didn't stop.* If this somewhat dubious suggestion is accepted, I would assume **lapa**, q.v., in the mg. of **lapana**, and render *having abandoned boasting* (in the sense of **lapana**). Otherwise Senart.

sthitika, at end of Bhvr. cpds. for Skt. sthiti (Pali ṭhiti, -[ṭ]ṭhitika), see **kalpa-**, **cira-sthitika**; perhaps also fem. °ikā as separate word, *lasting*, in SP 53.7 (vs) sthitikā hi eṣā sada dharmanetrī; but this is perhaps rather fem. to **sthitaka** (4), q.v.

Sthitīmukha (? reading uncertain), n. of a place: Māy 5.

Sthiracakra, a name or epithet of Mañjuśrī: Sādh 89.7.

Sthiramati, n. of a teacher: Mvy 3484.

Sthirā, n. of a capital city (rājadhānī): Gv 170.13; 171.26 etc.

sthihati, *stands*, etc., = Skt. tiṣṭhati; see Chap. 43, s.v. sthā (7).

Sthūṇa, or **°na**, m. (**1**) also **Sthūnā** (dental n), f. (= Pali Thūṇa), n. of a brahman-village in the west: Mvy 4117 sthūṇopasthūṇau grāmau; Divy 22.1 (paścimena) Sthūṇopasthūṇakau brāhmaṇagrāmakau; Māy 1, 60 Sthūnāyām, loc.; (**2**) n. of a yakṣa at Sthūnā: Māy 60. (Pali does not record an equivalent of **Upasthūṇa**, q.v.)

sthūla, as ep. of bhūmi, *gross, material* (stage of life), in contrast with the ten Bodhisattva-bhūmayaḥ (just described in the text): asthānam . . . yadā sthūlāhi bhūmihi, tatpure adhigaccheyuḥ sarvajñatvam tathāgatāḥ Mv i.192.12(–13), vss; *it is impossible that T's should attain omniscience before that* (course of the ten bhūmi), *in gross* (worldly) *stages.* So Senart, plausibly.

sthūla-kambala, nt., *'coarse blanket'*, listed as a material unsuitable for monks' robes: MSV ii.52.10.

Sthūlakoṣṭhaka (= Pali Thullakoṭṭhika, °ṭṭhita, also °koṭṭha?), n. of a city, capital of King Koravya (Kau°): Av ii.118.5 ff.

Sthūlakoṣṭhakīya, adj., *of Sthūlakoṣṭhaka*: Av ii.118.5.

Sthūlanandā (= Pali Thullanandā), n. of a Buddhist nun: Mv iii.49.10 ff. (protests against Mahākāśyapa's disrespect to Ānanda, and is punished for it; cf. Pali SN ii.219.7 ff.); 55.19.

Sthūlabinduka (cf. Pali Thulla-phusitaka), n. of a rain-deity: Śikṣ 247.8; MSV iv.122.13.

sthūla-bhikṣa, adj. Bhvr., *giving abundant alms*, ep. of the family in which a Bodhisattva is born the last time: LV 24.5; Mv i.198.1; ii.1.12. Tib. on LV lag (*hand*) sbabs (or, spabs; see Foucaux's Transl. p. 28 n. 1) che ba (*great*).

sthera (= **sthavira**, cf. **thera**; Pali thera), *old*; *an elder*: sthero na tāvatā bhavati (pronounce bhoti) Ud xi.11 (required by meter; later v.l. sthaviro, unmetr); sthero ti ucyate xi.12 (later v.l. sthavira ucyate, where meter is preserved by omitting the MIndic ti = iti). The first of these corresp. to Pali Dhp. 260 na tena thero hoti, where meter requires either thaviro, or with vv.ll. bhavati, or so hoti.

[**sthairya-sthāman**, loc. °mni, LV 156.11 (prose), in a list of arts mastered by the Bodhisattva as prince; so Lefm., reportedly with all his mss.; Calc. sthairye sthāmni as separate words; the cpd. could possibly be a dvandva, but the surrounding items are chiefly single, not dvandvas; Tib. brtan pa (= sthairya) daṅ mthu daṅ, as if separate words (or possibly a dvandva).]

sthora or **sthorā**, acc. to Index and pw *cargo*, but acc. to Burrow, BSOS 7.514, sthorām is acc. pl. of **sthora**, *beast of burden*, = Niya Pkt. stora, *horse*, an Iranian loanword; only as object of forms of **lardayati**, q.v.: Divy 5.22, 23, 26; 334.18.

[**snāta-śāṭaka**, nt., read either snāna°, or with Mironov snātra° (see next), *bathrobe, bathing cloth*: °kam Mvy 8941 = Tib. khrus ras.]

snātra, nt. (Jain Skt. id., see pw; and cf. prec.), *bath*: śvo bhaktena jentāka-snātreṇa copanimantritaḥ Av i.286.8; this seems, as Speyer and Feer assume, to be the intention of the mss., tho they vary rather strangely; the cpd. is repeated 9, 10, written **jantāka°**, q.v.; and ii.205.1, where the reading of the mss. is not given; snātram Av i.71.1, title of chap. 13 (mss. snānta).

snāyaka, *in order to bathe* (§ 22.3): pāṇikhāta-nadī-°ko okasto Mv iii.313.7 (prose).

snigdhaka, adj. (cf. Pali ati-siniddhaka, acc. pl. °ke, *very loving friends*, Mahāvaṃsa 36.44, acc. to PTS ed., where Turnour read -sinehake, which is quoted by PTSD as well as Childers; cf. **snehaka** which replaces this word in Divy 38.24, 31; = Skt. snigdha; endearing dim. -ka?), *affectionate, gentle, kind*: (bhadrakā . . .) °kā vata Śroṇāparāntakā manuṣyā(ḥ) Divy 38.16 (prose).

Snigdhagātra, n. of a former Buddha: Mv i.141.8.

[**snedana**, in ŚsP 1461.9, doubtless misprint for svedana(-pacanāny), in the sense of *steaming, boiling*, as a kind of torture in hell; forms of svid are used in this sense in Pali and the ppp., at least, even in Skt.]

snehaka, adj. (cf. Pali ati-sinehaka, acc. to Turnour for -siniddhaka in Mahāvaṃsa 36.44, see **snigdhaka**; to Skt. sneha plus -ka, or snih- plus -aka), *affectionate*: Divy 38.24, 31, replacing **snigdhaka,** q.v., of parallel 38.16.

sneha-lābha, m., *an acquisition due to affection* (of the giver), *a loving gift* (on the part of laymen to monks): saṃghasya ca snehalābhe (mss. °bha) saṃpanna āgantukā bhikṣava āgatāḥ Divy 336.22.

snehita, adj. (denom. ppp. from sneha; = Pali sinehita, comm. taṇhāsinehamakkhita), *affected by lust, lusted after* (?): Ud iii.5 (see s.v. **sarita,** 2). Same in Pali, Dhp. 341.

spandana, (1) adj. (not in Skt.; = Pali phandana), *vacillating, volatile,* i. e. given to idle fancies (of mind): °naṃ capalaṃ cittaṃ Ud xxxi.8 (same vs Pali Dhp. 33, phandanaṃ); **(2)** nt. (= Pali phandana; Skt. id. but chiefly if not wholly of physical movement, and with no pejorative connotation), *vacillation, unsteadiness,* esp. of mind, *engaging in idle fancies* (cf. next); assoc. with **iñjana** (q.v. for citations), **manyanā, prapañca**: Gv 128.6; 253.14 (here text syandana).

spandita, also miswritten **syandita,** nt. (Skt. id., chiefly of physical movement, and not pejorative in connotation; = Pali phandita, which acc. to Mrs. Rhys Davids, Brethren, 344 note, may mean *vaporings, imaginings*), = prec. (2): Mvy 7219 = Tib. gyos pa, follows iñjitam (both edd. syanditam); (sarveñjita-manyanā-)syandita-(read spa°)-vikalpāpagato Dbh 64.14; with **vikalpa** and **prapañca,** sva-vikalpa-viparyāsaiḥ prapañca-°taiś ca vai Laṅk 312.12 (vs); vikalpa-°te (n. dual dvandva) gatau 356.9 (vs), seems to mean *vain fancy and vacillation* (of mind) *are* (concerned) *in the fate* (of creatures); I do not understand Suzuki's transl.

spariśa (cited without ref. in ŚKD, see BR s.v.; cf. **saṃ-sp°**; = AMg. pharisa; Pali only phassa), semi-MIndic for Skt. sparśa, *touch, contact*; metr. required: dṛśyanti bhogaṃ spariśaṃ samānaṃ Laṅk 268.14 (vs).

sparśa-kāya (m.; = Pali phassakāya, six in number, DN iii.243.23, cakkhu-samphasso, sota-, ghāna-, jivhā-, kāya-, and mano-), *the group of* (six) *contacts* (of the sense-organs with their objects): ābādhavipramukto 'si sparśa-(so all Nep. mss., Kashgar rec. °śaṃ, ed. wrongly em. °śaḥ)-kāye tavānagha SP 301.5 (vs), *are you free from trouble in your group-of-sensory-contacts?*

sparśanavant (= Skt. sparśavant), *pleasant to touch*: LV 287.15 °vatī (tṛṇamuṣṭi). See under **sparśa-vihāra-tā.**

sparśa-vihāra-tā (once by error °vihāri-tā; etym., see below), *state of comfort, agreeable condition*: SP 248.6; Bhīk 26a.3; in comp. with preceding sukha-, Kv 18.8 (here text erroneously °vihāri-tā); 89.13; oftener with sukhaṃ as separate and parallel near-synonym, Mv i.256.10; 323.20 (here sukha-tā); 324.5; Divy 156.14; Av i.326.1; ii.93.16. See **asparśavihāra**; and **phāsu, phāsa, (a)phāṣa(ka).** The Pali equivalent is (a)phāsu(ka), often with vihāra; and AMg. has phāsuya (-vihāra). Pischel 208 derives from *sparśuka; Skt. sparśavant, BHS **sparśana-vant,** *pleasant to touch,* suggest how the development of mg. might conceivably have taken place, but Pischel's form is unrecorded. In BHS sparśa- is the regular form in this cpd., but others occur, see above. It may be only a hyper-Sktism. The -u of the stem seems to be universally found in Pali and Pkt., and occurs in BHS, but never followed by -ka, a fact which is not helpful to Pischel's etymology. The Jain Skt. form is prāsuka, interpreted as *free from living creatures* (pra-asu; of a dwelling, vihāra, suitable for Jain monks); this looks like a fanciful hyper-Sktism. Various other etymologies have been suggested, see the Pali Dictt.; none are convincing. Note the use of phāsuṃ, phāṣaṃ as adverbs with viharati. The forms phāsa, phāṣa are recorded only in BHS.

[**sparśārgaḍa,** Mv ii.115.12, read sparśitārgaḍa, see s.v. **sparśita.**]

sparśāhāra, m. (= Pali phassāhāra), *touch-food,* ingested by contact (acc. to AbhidhK. iii.121, cf. also 95 f., 'contact' comes from association of sense-organ, object, and cognition), one of the four, or, in Dharmas, five, kinds of food (āhāra): Mvy 2285; Dharmas 70. See s.v. **kavalīkārāhāra.**

sparśita, ppp. (of caus. of Skt. spṛś-; in this mg. = Pali phassita, phussita), lit. *made to touch,* i. e. *closed,* of door-bolts: kūṭāgāre śayitvā tvaṃ nivāte (text nirvāte) sparśitārgaḍe (so read for text °tāgate), āsīno vṛkṣamūleṣu kaccin na paritapyase Divy 559.12(–13), *having slept in a secure tower with locked door-bolts, are you not tormented sitting at the roots of trees?*; the em. is proved by Pali MN i.76.5–6 kūṭāgāraṃ ... nivātaṃ phassitaggaḷaṃ (other parallel texts phussi°); and in Mv ii.115.12 read (kūṭāgārāṇi ...) nivātāni sparśitārgaḍāni (see Crit. App.; mss. sparśārga°).

sparṣṭavya, false Sktization, = **spraṣṭ°,** q.v.: Śikṣ 198.9. Influenced by sparśa etc.; perhaps intended by corrupt mss. Mv ii.391.16.

spaṣṭama, adj. (quasi-superl. to Skt. spaṣṭa, plus -ma, § 22.13, cf. Whitney 474, perh. anal. to one of the words there cited), *most clear, evident*: °māṃ viśvakārāṃ ... -sopānamālāṃ (q.v.) RP 1.2.

? **spuriti-**(śraddhayā), Dbh.g. 56(82).17 (prose, not vs), (anena cittena, katham amī sattvā evam udāradharmasya) lābhinaḥ spuriti-śraddhayā satkṛtya śrāvayiṣyanti (sc. this treatise, Dbh)...; Rahder queries spṛhita-; I have thought of sphūrti-; neither is satisfactory; perhaps something like Skt. jhaṭ-iti, or BHS **ṛg-(ṛṭ-, rig-)**-iti, *instantly* (as separate word).

spṛśana (nt.; = Pali phusana; MIndic to spṛśati plus -ana, for Skt. sparśana), *touch*: karatala-°nenā kampitā corvi sarvā LV 357.12 (vs).

spṛhaka, adj. (to Skt. spṛh- plus -aka), *envious,* with gen.: anyeṣāṃ °ko bhikṣuḥ Ud xiii.8 (same vs Pali Dhp. 365 pihayaṃ = spṛhayan).

(a-)spṛhaṇa-tā (Skt. spṛhaṇa), *the (not) desiring*: LV 34.18 (prose).

spṛhālu, adj. (= Pali pihālu; Skt. spṛhayālu, acc. to MW also Lex. spṛhālu, but I do not find this in BR, pw, or Schmidt), *covetous*: °lavaś ca bhavanti Mv i.79.13 (prose).

spraṣṭavya, nt. (in Mv sometimes has m. endings; also **praṣṭavya, sparṣṭavya,** qq.v.; = Pali phoṭṭhabba), orig. gdve. of Skt. spṛśati, used in BHS (and Pali) for Skt. sparśa, *contact,* as *object of the sense of touch* (the organ is regularly kāya, rather than tvac); regularly associated with the other sense objects, rūpa, śabda, gandha, rasa (all Skt.), sometimes also 2 **dharma** (q.v., 2) as object of manas: Mvy 1863 (°vyam, n. sg.); 2037 (°vyāyatanam); 2054 (°vya-dhātuḥ); Mv ii.391.16 (Senart em. spṛṣṭavyāṃ, acc. pl., read sparṣ° or spraṣ°, closer to mss.); iii.290.2 (°vyā, n. pl.); Av i.207.6 (°vyāni); Samādh 8.3; Śikṣ 128.5; 202.13 (kāyena °vyāni spṛṣṭvā); Gv 182.19; Bbh 37.12; 39.9 (°vyam, n. sg.); Laṅk 226.2; Sukh 26.8 et alibi; in Dharmas 38 list of eleven spraṣṭavyāni, viz. pṛthvy āpas tejo vāyuḥ ślakṣṇatvaṃ karkaśatvaṃ laghutvaṃ gurutvaṃ śītaṃ jighatsā pipāsā. (A curious hodge-podge!)

sphaṭā or **sphaṭa** (both Skt. Lex., also Skt. phaṭā, Pkt. phaḍā, and Skt. phaṭa, Deśī and Ap. phaḍa), *hood* of a snake: nāgarājānau saptasphaṭāvabhūṣitau Mmk 76.6.

sphaṭita, ppp., *torn, lacerated, cracked*: Divy 83.22 sphaṭita-pāṇi-pādo (same word 463.8 sphuṭita-pāṇi-pādāni and MSV i.82.13 sphuṭita°); Divy 304.7 sphaṭita-puruṣā (corrupt in final member? read -paruṣā?) rūkṣakeśā malinavastranivasanāḥ.

? **sphara,** in Gv 294.1 (prose) seems to be error for

spharita, ppp. to **spharati,** *suffused* or *pervaded*: na sphara-(read spharita-)-pūrvān spharāmi; in series of parallel sentences such as nāvatīrṇapūrvān avatarāmi, na dṛṣṭa-pūrvān paśyāmi, etc., all with ppp. forms cpd. with -pūrvān.

spharaṇa, nt. (= Pali, also BHS, **pharaṇa,** q.v.; to **(s)pharati**), *suffusion, pervasion,* primarily with light, fig. also with love, knowledge, etc.: Mvy 6491 spharaṇam = Tib. khyab pa, *suffusion,* as with light (or rgyas pa, *extensive*); Bbh 58.23 °ṇam, n. of a kind of ṛddhi, defined 59.17 ff. yathāpi tad gṛham apy ābhayā spharati ... lokadhātūn ābhayā spharati; chiefly used in the final of cpds., esp. Bhvr., often translatable by adj. forms, *pervading, suffusing*...; so a-sph° *having no pervasion, unpervadable,* LV 250.19 ākāśam aspharaṇam akaraṇam avikaraṇam tac ca (sc. dhyānam) sarvam spharati, *it pervades the unpervadable ... space*; LV 259.10 ākāśadhātu-spharaṇam (āsphānakam dhyānam); Mvy 816 (mahāmaitrī-...)-lokadhātu-spharaṇaḥ, *pervading the world-systems ... with supreme love*; Śikṣ 32.5–6 sarvadharmadhātv-eka-spharaṇāḥ, *having exclusive* (or *unitary*) *penetration of all dharmadhātu*; Śikṣ 270.16 yathā gaganam sarvabuddhakṣetra-spharaṇam evam sarvasattvamaitrīspharaṇam tad dānam dadāti, *pervading*...; Gv 37.3; 40.2; 93.10 (here 1st ed. misprinted rasphaṇa); 222.22–23 (here in a cpd. but a tatpuruṣa, as n., not Bhvr., see s.v. **anujava**); Dbh 2.2; 57.11 (jñāna-); 91.15 daśadikspharaṇam (as n., tatpur.) gacchati.

spharati, °te (also, in mg. 1, **pharati, phalati, sphurati**; = Pali pharati; cf. also **sphuṭa** (1); Skt. Gr., except for some forms based on 'caus.' sphārayati, as sometimes in BHS, maitryā sphāritvā Mv i.313.17 prose; karuṇāpareṇa cetasā ekām diśām sphāritvā, v.l. sphārayitvā, Senart em. spharitvā, iii.213.12), (**1**) *pervades, fills, suffuses,* esp. with radiance, or with love, compassion, or other moral emotions and qualities: for sphurati SP 264.1 (vs) a Kashgar fragment (Lüders ap. Hoernle MR 159, last line) reads spharati; °te trilokam (ābhāya) LV 196.21 (vs); °ti LV 250.20; ālokena vā ālokam na spharanti Mv i.230.2, *do not suffuse* (*spread abroad*?) *light with light,* and similarly 240.11–20 (in parallels iii.334.9; 341.14 sphuranti); spharati Śikṣ 187.7; 216.5; °ran Gv 10.14 ff.; °ritvanā 34.11 (vs); °ranti 43.6; °rāmi 254.21 (vs); (sarvā diśas...) spharitvā Bbh 263.10; (ābhayā) 332.4; neg. gdve. **a-spharaṇīya,** q.v.; (**2**) *spreads out* (intrans.): lālāsya spharitvā tiṣṭhati Divy 106.4; (**3**) *serves, is useful* (as in Pali): -bhaiṣajyārthāya °ti MSV i.iii.7, *serves as medicine*; 9 etc.

spharitra, nt., var. for **sphāritra,** q.v.

spharin, adj. (to **spharati** plus -in), *pervading, filling*: parṣāsu (read pariṣāsu, m.c.) ... dharmadhātu-°riṣu daśadiśaḥ (read °riṣū daśaddiśaḥ, m.c.) Gv 34.14 (vs).

sphārika (to Skt. Lex. sphara, cf. AMg. pharaya, *shield,* plus -ika), *shield-bearer* (a royal officer): Mvy 3734; so Tib. phub thogs pa.

sphāritra, nt. (Mironov sphar°, v.l. spār°, sic!), *oar*: Mvy 5894 = Tib. gru skya, *oar* (Das gives Skt. as sphāritra).

sphāla, m., *plowshare*: Mvy 5643 = Tib. thoṅ lcags; = Skt. phāla, of course by hyper-Sktism, certainly not by inheritance from IE., even tho the usually accepted etym. (Uhlenbeck, s.v.; Walde-Pokorny, 677*) assumes IE. initial s-.

sphālana (nt.; = Pali phālana; to next with -ana), *cleaving*; noted only as an (evidently martial) art, in list of arts learned by the young Bodhisattva: dālane sphālane LV 156.13; Tib. gśeg pa, *cleaving.*

sphālayati, °**leti** or (?) °**lati,** (= Pali phāleti, trans. and intrans., see below; Skt. Gr. sphalati, intrans., and in cpds. sphālay- as caus.-trans.), *bursts,* intrans. (possibly also trans.?): saptadhā mūrdhnam (n. sg.) sphāleyā (so mss., Senart em. sphal°) Mv iii.114.12 (prose), *the head would burst in seven pieces*; so in Pali, muddhā me sattadhā phāleyyā (one ms. phal°) Dhp. comm. i.17.20; sīsam pi no sattadhā phāleyyā (no v.l.) i.134.16. In Av i.339.9 (prose) Speyer reads by em. (niyatam devasya saptadhā mūrdhānam) sphālayāmi, *I will cause to burst*...; but the mss. clearly point to a 3 sg. verb (foll. by iti), which would have to be intrans., implying that mūrdhānam represents a n. sg. (cf. §§ 17.37, 39); so Feer translates, *la tête ... se fendra* ..., without stating the reading of his ms.; I suspect we should read sphāleyeti or sphālayatīti.

sphija, nt., *broom*: Mvy 9048 = Tib. thal phyags, *broom*; Chin. *broom for sweeping ashes.* Can this be related to Pali phiya, piya, *oar* (glossed dabbi-padara, lit. *spoon-board,* Sn. comm. 330.22)?

sphuṭa, (**1**) adj. (orig. no doubt MIndic form of ppp. of **spharati, sphurati,** and so orig. *suffused,* esp. with light; but has come to be used in very general sense; = Pali phuṭa; see also **phuṭa, sphūṭa, parisphuṭa,** °**sphūṭa, pratisphuṭa**), *full, filled,* usually with prec. instr., much less often in comp.: prītiprāmodyena SP 199.4, 485.8; stūpaiḥ sā lokadhātuḥ °ṭā bhaviṣyati 203.1, *full of stūpas*; yehi sphuṭo 205.10; (space in general, māra-senayā...) sphuṭam LV 307.15; sphuṭa ... yakṣād-yaiḥ 315.9 (vs); gaganam sphuṭam tair naranāyakebhiḥ 367.14 (vs); gaganam sphuṭa devasamghaiḥ 416.9 (vs); devatāhi Mv ii.333.9; tam (sc. mārgam) prāṇakehi °ṭam (mss. °ṭe) Mv i.270.13, (*the way*) *was filled with living things* (*insects*); (aghā) aghasphuṭā, *evil and filled with evil,* LV 51.(10–)11; 351.22; 410.14; pādapehi Mv ii.327.6; dhvaja-patākaiḥ ii.328.4; patākapaṭṭaiḥ ii.344.1; a person's body, lakṣaṇehi ii.327.7; 336.6; piṭakaiḥ, *with sores, pustules,* Av ii.167.1; gandhena Suv 7.6; sphuṭo 'bhavad Ānando bhikṣur Māreṇa pāpīyasā Divy 201.21, cf. 24, *completely occupied, possessed, by the Evil One*; maitryā, *suffused with love* (regularly by the Buddha), Mv iii.429.3; Av i.79.14; maitrāya with v.l. maitryāya Mv ii.350.15; avabhāsena (or in Mv obhāsena), *with radiance,* LV 300.10; Mv i.41.7; 230.2; 240.12; iii.334.10; 341.14; Divy 157.19; Suv 8.5; -jvālābhir SP 407.10; ābhayā SP 423.3; LV 277.11; prabhājālaiḥ LV 280.9; (yaśasā sarvā Śrāvastī) sphuṭā Av ii.20.7; in cpds., prīti-sphuṭāḥ SP 330.2 (vs); sarva-śarīram vikṛti-sphuṭam Av ii.173.10 (prose); (**2**) adj. or (prob.) subst. (nt.), in dvandva cpd. khaṇḍa-sphuṭa-, *ruined and broken* (*parts*), of a stūpa; here replaces BHS and Pali (khaṇḍa-)**phulla,** q.v. (cf. Skt. sphuṭati, *bursts open,* and, in the same context of Divy, sphuṭita or **sphuṭitaka,** q.v.): (stūpe) khaṇḍa-sphuṭa-pratisamskāra-(q.v.), *repair of*..., Divy 22.11, 18; 23.1, 3, 8, 10. This use of sphuṭa is doubtless secondary, due to influence of sphuṭati, sphuṭita(ka). Cf. **chutta.**

Sphuṭavikrama, n. of a former Buddha: Mv i.138.2.

sphuṭika, adj. (read °ṭaka?), = **sphuṭa,** *full, filled* (-ka perh. m.c.): te cāsya kṣetra sphuṭikā (v.l. sphuṭā, unmetr.; Tib. Chin. said to mean *full*) jina-aurasehi Dbh.g. 3(339).5, *filled with Bodhisattvas.*

sphuṭitaka, adj. and subst. nt. (= Skt. sphuṭita, ppp. of sphuṭ), *broken,* or (subst.) *break, broken place*: Divy 22.27 and 23.6, both cited s.v. **caṭita,** q.v.; cf. also **sphuṭa** 2.

sphutkāra (m.; prob. = Skt. phut-k°, and perh. error for that; note preceding -s), *hissing sound* (of a snake): (sarpān ...) hatvā pāṇitalaiḥ prayānti vivaśās sphutkāra-bhītāḥ punaḥ Divy 597.16 (vs).

sphurati, once **sphurayati** (= **spharati** 1 and 2; cf. also **sphuṭa**), (**1**) *suffuses, pervades, fills,* esp. with light, or with an emotion such as love: sphurati SP 264.1 (see spharati); ābhayā °ti 423.9; avabhāsena sphurayitvā LV 113.2 (prose); BR cite sphurayiṣyati from LV Calc., but Lefm. 145.3 reads sphuriṣyati (sarvanagaram daurgandhena); sphuri (aor.) jinavarakṣatrām (Lefm. em. °trā;

see **kṣatra**) LV 357.4; sphuranti Mv iii.334.9; 341.14, for spharanti of parallels, see spharati; triṃśadyojanāṃ sphuritvā Mv ii.410.6 (said of Māra's army; v.l. sphar°); sā maitreṇāṃśena (so with mss.) sphuritvā Divy 60.24, and so read in 61.12, see s.v. 1 **aṃśa**; the full expression is, sarvam imaṃ lokaṃ maitreṇāṃśena sphuritvā 66.18 (here Buddha is subject); sarvāṃ ca śrāvastīṃ sphuritvā Av i.24.4 (of incense); maitryā sphuran i.171.9; (**2**) *spreads* (trans.) *far and wide*, with acc. of the thing spread and loc. of the thing spread over or filled: dharmāmegha sphuritva sarvatribhave LV 294.4 (vs), *having spread abroad the cloud of the Law in all the triple world*; mahākaruṇāmeghaṃ (mss. °gha; one °ghā) sphuritvā LV 352.11 (prose).

? **Sphulantaśrī**, n. of a 'gandharva maid': Kv 5.11, perhaps error for sphurant-a-(pres. pple. to **sphurati**)-śrī.

sphūṭa, adj. (= **sphuṭa**; cf. **parisphūṭa**), *full*: mahatāvabhāsena sphūṭā abhūvan LV 86.20 (prose).

-sphoṭakam, adv. (cf. **sphoṭā**, **°ṭika**, and Skt. sphoṭa): na jihvā-°kam (sc. paribhokṣyāmaḥ) Mvy 8586 (a śaikṣa rule), (we will) *not* (eat) *making a smacking noise with the tongue*.

Sphoṭana, n. of a nāga king: Mvy 3277; Māy 246.26.

Sphoṭanī, n. of a rākṣasī: Māy 243.23.

sphoṭā (in this mg. Skt. sphoṭana, pw), *snap* of the fingers: mahā-sphoṭā-saṃghāta-śabdena SP 388.9 (prose), referring to, and synonymous with, acchaṭā-saṃghāta-śabda, just before, see **acchaṭā**.

sphoṭika, Mv iii.58.4, uncertain mg., see s.v. **tripuṣkara**.

-smaraṇika, adj. (to smaraṇa plus -ika), *charged with reminding* (of . . .): āpatti-°kena bhikṣuṇā MSV iv.124.15.

smi, seemingly = asmi, *I am*: Gv 231.5 (vs), see §§ 4.7; 28.64.

smitī-mukha, adj. Bhvr. (cf. late Skt. smiti, once, Schmidt, Nachträge; Skt. smitamukha), *with smiling face*: ep. of Māyā, °khā sā LV 28.12 (vs); Calc. smitā-m°, but all mss. reported smitī° except one smiti° (meter requires long).

smṛta, ppp. as adj. (= Pali sata, regularly followed by sampajāna), *mindful, in a state of full awareness* or *consciousness*, very common with following **saṃprajāna(nt)**: smṛtaḥ saṃprajānan Mvy 1480 (Tib. dran pa, = smṛti, . . . can, *possessing*); Av i.228.1; ii.197.13, etc.; smṛto saṃprajāno Mv i.206.4 = ii.9.20; i.218.10 = ii.20.11 etc.; smṛtāyāṃ saṃprajānāyāṃ Mv i.205.8 = ii.9.4 (of the Bodhisattva's mother). Sometimes replaced by **smṛtimant**, q.v.

smṛti, f. (= Pali sati; hardly distinguishable from some aspects of Skt. id.), *mindfulness*, (full) *consciousness* or *awareness*, esp. in samyak-s° = Pali sammā-sati, the 7th stage of the 8-fold Noble Path (**mārga**), in lists of its stages, such as Mvy 1003; Tib. dran pa, which seems to parallel the various aspects of Skt. and BHS smṛti. Cf. prec. and **smṛtimant**.

Smṛtiketurājaś(i)ri, n. of a Buddha: Gv 285.14 (vs).

[**smṛtimattaka**, see **smṛtimantaka**.]

smṛtimant, (**1**) adj., like Pali satimā (e. g. DN ii.313.6) bracketed with **saṃprajāna(nt)**, Pali sampajāna, replacing the commoner **smṛta**, q.v.: SP 68.5; °mān saṃprajānan LV 343.19 (prose); °māṃ su-saṃprajāno (mss. omit su) Mv i.206.12 = ii.10.6 (vs); (**2**) n. of a devaputra: Gv 445.24.

smṛtimantaka, adj. (to a-extension of prec. plus -ka svārthe), *gifted with memory* (of sacred texts): (in reply to a question, āgamāni kiṃ dhārayiṣyanti . . .) smṛtimantakā (so I read for text °mattakā; two other suggestions in note p. 708 seem implausible) hy ete dhārayiṣyanty (sc. āgamāni) Divy 333.21 (prose).

smṛtilabdhā, n. of a medicinal or magic herb: Gv 497.22.

smṛtivinaya, m. (= Pali sati-vi°, described MN ii.247.28 ff.), *procedure based on recollection* (on the part of a monk accused of sin; he denies recollection of the offense charged, and the chapter accepts his statement, cf. Childers s.v.), one of the **adhikaraṇa-śamatha**: Mvy 8632; MSV ii.207.11.

Smṛtiśrī, n. of a Buddha: Śikṣ 169.13.

Smṛtisamudramukha, n. of a Buddha: Gv 284.11.

smṛty-upasthāna, nt. (= Pali satipaṭṭhāna, which, as Childers says, represents sati-(u)pa° by MIndic saṃdhi), *application of mentality, of awareness* (*applications de mémoire*, LaV-P. AbhidhK. vi.153; see the foll. pages); Tib. dran pa (= smṛti) ñe bar bzhag pa (*application*); Chin. *place* or *location of smṛti*; normally there are (**1**) *four* such (same in Pali): listed Mvy 952–956 as kāya-, vedanā-, citta-, dharma-(*conditions of existence*)-smṛ°; so, with full discussion of each item, Śikṣ 228.9 ff. (the four terms 228.11; 232.6; 233.15; 236.5); the true nature of each term must be carefully reflected on; a fuller terminology, paralleled in Pali (kāyānupassanā- etc.), is kāye kāyānupaśyanā-smṛ° Bbh 259.21 (cf. 25 evam avaśiṣṭāni smṛ° °nāni); so, with °nudarśa- (v.l. °nudarśī, n. sg. of °śin, showing confusion with the KP formula, below) instead of °nupaśyanā- Dharmas 44; a slightly different formula (cf. Pali e. g. DN ii.290.12 ff.), kāye kāyānupaśyī viharati na ca kāye kāyānupaśyanāyām ātmyadṛṣṭyāṃ patati KP 95.2, and similarly with the other three in ff.; these four are listed first among the 37 **bodhipākṣika** (q.v., or the like) dharma, Dharmas 43; LV 8.5; 181.17 (here at end of list of bodhipakṣa-dharma is erroneously added ārya-satya, but several mss. correctly omit satya); 426.7; Divy 208.7; not in such a list, Śikṣ 105.13; (**2**) also *three*, more exactly **āveṇika** (q.v.) smṛ° of a Buddha: trīṇy āveṇikāni smṛ° Mvy 187, listed 188–190 as śuśrūṣamāṇeṣu (aśuśrū°, śuśrūṣamāṇāśuśrū°) samacittatā, i. e. Buddha is neither elated nor depressed when his audience is responsive, unresponsive, or partly both, cf. Bbh 403.10 ff., 15; mentioned but not listed Divy 182.20; Av i.7.5; and, without the word āveṇika, tribhiḥ smṛ° Divy 126.13 (that word is lacking also Bbh 403.10 ff.); smṛ° mentioned among āveṇika-buddha-dharma Bbh 230.14; (**3**) acc. to AbhidhK. LaV-P. vi.159 smṛ° is triple, svabhāva- (*en soi*; this is defined simply as = prajñā), saṃsarga- (*par connexion*), and ālambana- (*en qualité d'objet*); the two latter defined 160; this distinction I have not noted elsewhere.

sya, apparently particle of emphasis, = **asya**, q.v. for citations.

syanda, m. (cf. **niṣyanda**, virtually a synonym), *issue, outcome, result* (not *waste*, Bendall; it is only niṣphala-sya° that is *waste*; Tib. cited as sbyoṅ ba): sarvaniṣphala-°da-varjanāt Śikṣ 116.12; parārthaṃ . . . yaḥ syando na saṃvartate, sa niṣphalatvād varjayitavyaḥ 13; similarly 118.3 f.; cf. next.

syandana (nt.) = prec.: niṣphala-°na-varjanam Śikṣ 119.1; [also by error for **spandana**, q.v.]

syandanikā (in Skt., *rivulet*; on this and the Pali correspondent candanikā see Lévi's long note on Karmav below; acc. to Lévi, the Pali cand° is a deliberate, ironical distortion of syand°, by association with candana, *sandalwood*), (**1**) *drain, sewer*: SP 144.10 (prose) apagata-syandanikā-gūthoḍigallaṃ (ep. of Buddhakṣetra), *free from drains and cesspools*; Karmav 22.10–11 dāru-syandanikāyāṃ niṣaṇṇaḥ, *in a* (house-)*drain of wood*; (**2**) (= Skt. Lex. syandanī, syandinī), *saliva*: Māy 219.14; also **syandinikā**, id., Māy 237.25; 253.18 (in the last read syandinikāhārāḥ for text syandinihārāḥ).

syandamānikā (presumably to pres. mid. pple. of Skt. syand- plus -ikā; = Pali sanda°, defined in PTSD *chariot*; AMg. saṃdamāṇī, °ṇiyā, °ṇiā, *palanquin*, Ratnach.), a kind of *palanquin*: śivikā vā °nikā vā (in list of vehicles) Mv ii.434.7.

syandaraka, m., a kind of coverlet: Mvy 9182; v.l.

in Mironov syandu°; corresponds to Divy 19.22 **janduraka,** which is prob. a better reading; see this and s.v. **eraka.**

[**syandita,** false reading for **spand°**.]

syandinikā, see **syandanikā** (2).

syapeṭārikā, or **°ka** (n. pl. °kā(ḥ); probably corrupt at least in the first syllable), a kind of toy, in a list of them: vitkoṭikā °rikā agharikā Divy 475.19.

Syama, see **Śyāma.**

syāt, siyāti (as in Pali, AMg. siyā; in only Jain Skt., see BR), *perhaps*; common at end of Jātaka stories, usually: syāt khalu (punar) bhikṣavaḥ yuṣmākam (rarely omitted) evam asyā (or asyāt), *it may be, however, monks, that you may have the idea*..., Mv ii.64.2; 68.13; 72.4, 8, 10; 81.17; 83.7; 89.1, 3, 6; 94.5, 8; 113.16; 114.3; 176.15; 219.4; iii.76.18, and often in Mv; so in Mv i.45.1, 5, 8, 11, read siyāti (§ 29.41; Senart siyā ti) punar ... evam asya syāt; yasyeha pariśeṣaṃ syān (so mss. ii.3.7, in i.199.9 syā) nārīye (°yo) jīvitaṃ bhavet Mv i.199.9 = ii.3.7 (vs), *of what woman there may be perchance remaining in this world a life* (of ten months and seven days); Senart reads syā in both places and takes it for the pronoun asyāḥ, which seems to me impossible (§ 21.84).

Syāma(ka), see **Śyāma(ka).**

sraṃsanā (Skt. °na, nt., not quite in this sense), *relaxation* (of effort or activity): na °nāṃ karoti Śikṣ 279.7.

sraṃsanīya, adj. (to Skt. sraṃsana, see BR s.v. 2b, plus -īya), *loosening, relaxing* (medicines): (dravya) MSV ii.47.7 (here of things snuffed, against a cold).

Sragdharā, a name or form of Tārā: Sādh 223.23 ff.

sragmin, adj. (= Skt. sragvin), *garlanded*: sragmī, n. sg., Mmk 60.5; °miṇam, acc. sg., 134.26; °mibhiḥ 600.21.

Srajamālādhārin (v.l. Sragdha-mā°; v.l. °māla°), n. of a former Buddha: Mv i.139.12.

Srughnā, n. of a town (cf. Skt. Srughna, m.): Divy 74.17, 22 (written Śru°).

sruvaka, nt. (= Skt. sruva, m., plus -ka), *ladle*: Mvy 4348 = Tib. blug(s) gzar, said to be *a long ladle* used in offerings.

srota-āpatti, srotāpatti, often writen śrot°, so regularly in Mv, Divy, and mss. of Av (= Pali sotāpatti), *'entrance into the stream'*, *conversion* to Buddhism, the state of the **srota-āpanna,** the first of the four stages of Hīnayāna religious development, the others being the states of the **sakṛd-āgāmin, anāgāmin,** and **arhant**; esp. often in comp. with -phala, *the fruit* of this attainment; contracted form °tāpatti regular in Mv, prose as well as vss, in other texts rare in prose (Divy 17.21), used in vss where favored by meter (so, I believe, regularly in Laṅk, e. g. srota-āpatti-gati- 116.13, prose, srotāpatti-phalaṃ, mss. śro°, 65.9, vs); srota-āpatti-pratipannaḥ Mvy 5131; śrotāpatti-phala Mv i.175.1 (vs); 312.13 (prose); iii.254.11 (prose); 346.13 (vs); śrota-āpatti-phala Divy 46.26; 50.8, etc.; Av i.65.1 (ms., Speyer em. sro°) etc., common.

srota-āpanna, srotāpanna, also written śrot°, adj. or subst. (= Pali sotāp°), (*one*) *who has 'entered the stream'*, *been converted*; see under prec.; formal and orthographic variants as there stated: śrotāp° Mv i.103.13 (prose); srota-āp° Mvy 5132; Divy 534.4 (śro°); Laṅk 116.12; etc.

srotas, nt., a high number (between vivāha and ojas): Sukh 31.1.

srotā (= Skt. srotas), see **śrotā.**

srotāñjana, nt., in Mvy 5778, acc. to Tib. lig bu mig = *malachite* (which acc. to Das is said to cure headaches and pains in bones); occurs in a list of oṣadhi-nāmāni, some items of which, however, are mineral medicinal substances; Skt. Lex. sroto'ñjana = *antimony*; Pali sotañjanaṃ (Vin. i.203.14) in a list of kinds of añjana, used as eye-salve.

srotāpatti, °panna, see **srota-āp°**.

Sroto'nugata, m., n. of a samādhi: Mvy 532 (not in ŚsP).

? **sva,** inserted by Senart's em. in Mv iii.384.3 (vs), where mss. kiṃ (kim) adhipatī rājā, metr. deficient, Senart kiṃ sva, with next line kathaṃ sva; note says sva = svid or su; read both times svid or **su** (q.v.)? But cf. **khu-ssa.** Pali Dhp. comm. iii.231.21, same vs, kiṃ su ..., 22 kathaṃ su ...

? **svaka(m)** (cf. s.v. **svayaṃ**), (**1**) acc. to Senart = Skt. svayam, (*one*)*self*, in Mv iii.126.9, 10; the crow-king Supātra's minister speaks: (if I cannot fulfil the king's command, and steal food from the kitchen of the king of Benares) na puruṣakārakaṃ bhavati (here mss. punctuate) asmākaṃ, gacchāmi svakaṃ rājño Supātrasya niveditum (so Senart, but mss. °trasya kāke, or kāka-, niveditaṃ), mahārāja atra svakaṃ (so Senart em., mss. sekā) mahānasāto rājabhojanaṃ ānemi. The passage seems to me too uncertain to justify confidence in the em. (which might be explained as hyper-Skt. for svayaṃ, interpreted as having Pktic y for k, § 2.33). In the first line the orig. may have been svakaṃ ... niveditaṃ (with mss.); (**2**) in LV 237.16 (vs) Lefm. mahya saṃjñi svakam eva vartate, which might be rendered *my own self* (assuming svakam = ātmā) *is having the idea* (that you will become like the Highest of Men). But best mss. have saṃjñā for saṃjñi; meter will be satisfied by saṃjña, and we could interpret svaka-m-eva, with hiatus-bridging m; then, *my very own notion is* ... In SP 112.8 (vs) read prob. with Nep. mss. pitā svakasya, *his own father*; svakasya = Skt. svasya = ātmanaḥ.

Svaguṇaśākha, n. of a former Buddha: Mv i.138.14.

Svatejadīpta, n. of a former Buddha: Mv i.141.6.

svapnādhyāya (in Skt. as n. of a work; buf cf. also °ya-vid, *Traumdeuter*, Śaṃkara, pw), *the interpretation* ('reading') *of dreams*, in a list of arts learned by the Bodhisattva: °ye LV 156.17.

[***Svapnāntalokamuni,** see **Supinānta°**.]

svabhāva (Skt.), *nature*; used in Laṅk in several peculiar ways: (**1**) saptavidho bhāva-svabhāvo bhavati, yad uta, samudaya-svabhāvo bhava-sv° lakṣaṇa-sv° mahābhūta-sv° hetu-sv° pratyaya-sv° niṣpatti-sv° Laṅk 39.9–11; these are not explained here or elsewhere, and Suzuki has no explanation; (**2**) three svabhāva, mentioned Laṅk 132.4; 227.10; 348.10; and listed 67.2 ff. as **parikalpita, paratantra,** and **pariniṣpanna** (qq.v.) sva°; cf. Suzuki, Studies, 158 f.; in Mvy 1662–5 and Sūtrāl. xi.38–41 the term is **lakṣaṇa** (3) instead of svabhāva; Lévi renders *indice* (*imaginaire, du relatif*, and *absolu*). For other uses of the term in Laṅk see Suzuki ibid. 455 ff.

svabhāvaka, adj. (= Skt. °va plus -ka), usually ifc. Bhvr. and noted only in vss, perh. m.c.(?): avaktavyaṃ °kam Laṅk 369.11, *one must not speak of something that has self-nature* (analyze as Bhvr., sva plus bhāva, plus -ka?); otherwise = svabhāva ifc. Bhvr., vss, dharmān ... māyāsvapna-°kān SP 142.13; bhāvā ... a-°kāḥ Laṅk 273.8; gotraṃ vastu-°kam Laṅk 297.15.

svabhāsībhavati, read **svabhyāsī°** (to *sv-abhyāsa, *very near*; cf. **abhyāsībhavati**), *becomes very near* (to, loc.): °vati sarvākārajñatāyām ŚsP 682.4 (prose).

? **svayaṃ,** interpreted by Senart twice as prior member of cpds. in mg. *own*, = Skt. sva(ka), adj., for which saya, adj., is common in AMg.; I could hardly accept Senart's interpretation except on the assumption that the word is a form of that MIndic adj.; cf. conversely **svakam,** acc. to Senart = svayam. I can however not regard the interpretation as certain. In Mv i.284.4 (prose), kumāro brahmacārī svayam (perh. svaya- with m Hiatus-bridger?)-āśrame (mss. °maṃ) paryaṅkena niṣaṇṇo, svayam could be taken in its ordinary Skt. sense, (*the youth*) *himself*, rather than *in his own hermitage* with Senart. In i.302.6 (prose), Senart by em. svayaṃdhītā saṃveditā, *he spoke to his own daughter*; if it means this, I should read svayā, or (Skt.) svakā, or possibly svaya- (in comp.), dhītā; the mss. read svajanaṃ dhītā saṃviditā; could this (taking svajanaṃ as nom.) mean *his people* (and specifically) *his daughter was admonished*? Undoubtedly his daughter alone is actually addressed in the following, evaṃ tuvaṃ ...; and cf. svakā dhītā 304.8, in the verse version of the story; on the whole the mg. assumed by Senart is prob. to be accepted, but I question the form (= Skt. svayam).

svayaṃkārin, adj., *doing* (everything) *for oneself*; °**ri-tā**, *state of*...: °riṇā 'paropatāpinā na ca tenopasthānagurukeṇa bhavitavyaṃ Śikṣ 199.17, (a Bodhisattva living an ascetic life) *must wait on himself, not annoy others, and not be eager for service*; bodhisattvaḥ °ritāṃ pravrajyāyāḥ saṃdarśayituṃ tat pāṃśukūlaṃ Śakrasyādattvā svayam eva prakṣālayati sma LV 266.21.

svayam-ācāryaka, adj. Bhvr., *self-instructing*: pratibalā °kaṃ jñānaṃ paridīpayitum LV 377.14; see s.v. **ācāryaka** 2.

Svayaṃprabha, n. of a former Buddha: Mv iii.237.2.

svara-gupti, see **gupti**.

Svaraṅgaśūra, n. of a Bodhisattva: Gv 442.26. Read Svarāṅga°? See this, and °ga-ghoṣa.

Svaravivikta, n. of a dhāraṇī: Gv 66.18.

svarasvara (m.? prob. āmreḍita of Skt. svara, cf. **svarāsvara**; also **sarasarāyate** and Pali, AMg. sarasara, to which this could perh. be a hyper-Sktism, influenced by svara), *varied sound, noise of various sorts*: (a condemned criminal is led to execution) -kaṇṭheguṇena (so mss., see this) svarasvareṇa paṭahena vādyamānena Mv ii.168.9. (One might be tempted to take the form as an adj. with paṭaha, *rattling noisily*; but such a use of svara, or a MIndic equivalent, would seem to be unprecedented.)

svarāṅga (Skt. svara with **aṅga** 2, q.v.), *quality of voice* or *sound*: sarva-°ga-maṇḍalaparamapāramitāprāptatvāt sarva-°ga-maṇḍalaparamapāramitāprāpta ity ucyate LV 435.9–10, *He is called one who has attained the supreme Perfection of the circle of all qualities of voice, because he has* ... (of Buddha); sarva-°ga-samudrarutebhiḥ ... (sugatāṃ stavamī) Bhad 4, (*I praise the Buddhas*) *with the sounds of the ocean of all voice-qualities*; eka-°ga-samudrarutebhiḥ (as prec.), sarvajināna °ga-viśuddhiṃ (... otari) Bhad 30, *may I penetrate* (*comprehend*) *the purity of voice-qualities of all the Jinas, by the* ...

Svarāṅgaghoṣa, n. of a former Buddha: Samādh p. 56 line 32 f.; p. 65, line 15.

svarāsvara (cf. **svara-svara**, and § 23.12), *all kinds of sounds*: sarvasvarāsvara-susvarabuddhaṃ, brahmarutasvaragarjitaghoṣaṃ Suv 45.13(–14; vss); Tib. dbyaṅs rnams kun gyis = sarvasvarāsvara-.

Svarṇakeśa, n. of a gandharva: Suv 161.18. Cf. **Suvarṇa**°.

Svarṇaprabhāsa, and **Svarṇabhāsottama**, °**mā**, see **Suvarṇabhās**°.

Svalakṣaṇamaṇḍita, n. of a former Buddha: Mv i.138.2.

[**Svaśa**, as n. of a people living about Taxila: Svaśarājyaṃ Divy 372.11; surely graphic corruption for Skt. Khaśa, or **Khaṣa**, q.v., with Burnouf, Introd. 362 n. 2 and BR.]

Svaśarīraprabha, n. of a Buddha: Gv 284.24 (vs).

svasā (Skt. svasṛ; ā-stem, = AMg. sasā; not noted in Pali), *sister*: LV 341.19 (vs); Mv ii.189.13 (prose); see § 13.12.

svasti (nt.? cf. Skt. svastika), a (gold) ornament, presumably in the shape of a svastika: (tad yathā ...) suvarṇaṃ (so read with v.l. for °ṇa-) kaṭaka-rucaka-svasty-ādi-pariṇāmena pariṇāmyamānaṃ ... Laṅk 159.8 (prose), *just as gold, in being altered by change into a bracelet, necklace, svasti(ka), or the like* ...

Svastika, (**1**) (= Pali Sotthiya), n. of a grass-seller (**yāvasika**, q.v.; in Pali Jāt. i.70.31 tiṇahāraka) from whom the Bodhisattva begged grass for his seat at the bodhi-tree: LV 286.4 ff.; 287.1, 3, etc.; Mv ii.131.12 ff.; 264.6 ff.; 399.1, 4; 401.11; (**2**) n. of a yakṣa: Māy 46.

Svastikaṭaka, n. of a locality: Māy 46.

svastinā, adv. (instr., = Skt. svasti; Skt. Lex. id., only Trik., Schmidt, Nachträge; = Pali sotthinā), *happily, successfully*: °nā parimokṣyate Śikṣ 104.11; °nā parimoktukāmena 116.2 (both prose); ahaṃ °nā uttārayiṣyāmi (across the ocean) Mv iii.72.21 (prose); °nā jambudvīpaṃ gamanāya 73.5 (prose); °nā 88.2, 20; 89.20 (vss), et al.

svastyayati (denom. to Skt. svasti), *makes happy, rewards*: śilpinaṃ svastyayitvā tu saṃvibhāgārthavistaraiḥ Mmk 60.15 (vs).

svākāra, and m.c. svākara, see **-ākāra**.

Svāgata (= Pali Sāgata), n. of a disciple of the Buddha: Mvy 1067; SP 207.4; LV 2.3; Sukh 2.10; MSV i.185.1 ff.; long account of him Divy 169.22 ff., including several traits of the story of Pali Sāgata, e. g. his contest of magic with a nāga (**Aśvatīrthika**) 185.5 ff.; the Buddha's calling him foremost among experts in use of the fire-element (tejodhātu), 186.12, 19 ff.; and his falling a victim to intoxication, 190.4 ff.

svāgata-vant, adj., *having* (*being accorded*) *a welcome*: ṛṣiṇā ehi °vān iti ācaṣṭo svāgataṃ te etc. Mv ii.96.16, *come and welcome*!

Svācāra (su plus ā°), n. of a śreṣṭhin's son: Gv 51.22.

Svāti (perh. = Pali Sāti?), n. of a monk: Māy 219.28 et al.; MSV i.202.13 ff.; 285.10; 286.13; 287.7.

Svātikā (cf. Skt. svāti?), n. of a goddess: Mahāsamaj., Waldschmidt, Kl. Skt. Texte 4, 185.19.

Svātigiri, n. of a nāga maid: Kv 3.24.

Svātimukha, n. of a kiṃnara king: Kv 3.2.

Svātimukhā, n. of a nāga maid: Kv 3.21.

svādanīya (nt.) = **āsvādanīya**, q.v.; perh. *condiment*, or *savory* (food): LV 96.21 khādya-bhojya-svādanīya, both edd., no v.l.; 123.17 khādanīyabhojanīyasvādanīya, all mss. (only Calc. °nīyāsvādanīya).

svādīyati (see s.v. **sātīyati** for discussion; Pali sādiyati somehow related), *takes pleasure in* (acc.): (na gītaśabdā na nṛtyaravaśabdā na pramadāgaṇāṃ) rūpavantāṃ °yati Mv ii.145.3 (subject, the Bodhisattva as prince; mss. both times °śabde or °śabdo).

sv-ādharṣa-ka, adj. Bhvr., *subject to easy attack*: kulaṃ bahustrīkaṃ alpapuruṣaṃ °kaṃ bhavati, supradharṣakaṃ (q.v.) ... Bhīk 4a.3. Antonyms of Skt. durādharṣa, duṣpradharṣa; the nouns ādharṣa, pradharṣa are otherwise unrecorded. The corresponding Pali, Vin. ii. 256.17, has suppadhaṃsiya, but no equivalent of svādharṣaka.

svādhyāyati, rarely ***svādhyāti** (on the latter see §§ 28.54; 38.31; = Pali sajjhāyati; denom. to Skt. svādhyāya), *recites, rehearses, studies*; see Chap. 43 s.v. for forms and citations.

svādhyāyanikā, Divy 489.14; 491.10, 12; or °**yinikā**, 489.18, 23 ff.; 490.2; 492.10 (see s.v. **pariprcchanikā**, °**inikā**), *subject for study*.

Svāparṇa, pl., n. of a brahmanical gotra: Divy 635.12.

Svābha-devī, n. of a deity: Sādh 66.5.

svāmam, svāma (so even before a vowel, where also **svām'**; false Sktization of **sāmam**, q.v., by association with Skt. svayam, sva-), *self, oneself*: (read) bhavavibhava(m)karaṇo ṛjumārgo svām' anubuddhvā (with Tib.; mss. °baddhā) LV 169.19 (vs), Tib. ñid kyis (*by self*) khoṅ du chud byas te (*having made thoroughly understood*); svāma LV 236.17 (vs, n. sg., for °maṃ, m.c.); svām' upatīrya tāraya jagad 329.18 (vs), *having crossed yourself, bring the world across*; svāmaṃ (divided svā maṃ in Lefm.) 337.10 (vs); svāma-upasaṃpadā Mv i.2.15, and svām'-upa° 16 (prose), *ordination by oneself*; in Mv ii.38.6 (vs) mss. svāyaṃ, possibly m.c. for svayaṃ, Senart em. svāmaṃ.

svāmika (= Pali sāmika; in Skt. only ifc. Bhvr. for svāmin), *husband* (seemingly with no emotional tinge as a rule and mostly in prose; -ka svārthe): tvaṃ ca mama (244.9 me) °ko bhavesi (or bhaviṣyasi) Mv i.233.8; 244.9 (prose); others, ii.105.4; 246.16, 18; 247.3 (in this vicinity varies indifferently with svāmin; prose); 446.1; 485.20; iii.393.11; svāmika-svāmin, app. intensive repetition, used by a woman of her husband, °mi Mv ii.105.3 (vs), *my very lord and master*.

sv-ālaṃkṛta, adj. (m.c. for sv-a°), *well adorned*: LV 220.15; 221.17; 282.10 (all vss). Cf. **su-laṃkṛtikā.**

Svāśiṣa, or °**ṣā**, n. pl. or n. sg. f. °ṣā, n. of a goddess or class of deities: Mahāsamāj., Waldschmidt, Kl. Skt. Texte 4, 191.2 (Tib., p. 204 infra, indicates su plus āśis-).

[**svāsanaka**, see **ambāsanaka.**]

svidam (= **suda**, Pali suda(ṃ); Skt. svid), after āho in an alternative question, *or*...: āho svidaṃ neti Mv i.102.13, 14. Cf. also **su, so.**

svedana, see **snedana.**

svela, m. (v.l. svaila; Mironov svola, prob. by error, since all the surrounding terms end in -ela, as in the Kyoto ed.), a high number: Mvy 7763 = Tib. zal zul; cf. **śvelu.**

-ssa, see **khu-ssa.**

H

Haṃsakuśa, n. of a brother of Kuśa: Mv ii.433.17.

haṃsalakṣaṇa, m. or nt. (= AMg. haṃsalakkhaṇa, acc. to Sheth *white* or *pure*, acc. to Ratnach. *marked with the image of a haṃsa*; Ratnach. cites cpd. °khaṇa-paḍa-sāḍaga, which proves that it means a kind of cloth), *a kind of fine cloth*, prob. *haṃsa-like* in one of the senses indicated by Sheth above: SP 89.6 koṭambaka-haṃsalakṣaṇaiḥ, see s.v. **koṭambaka**; Chin. seems to render this word *bright, white*, and *clean* (three words), agreeing with Sheth; Gv 495.4 haṃsalakṣaṇa-vastra-bhūtaṃ sarvasaṃsāradoṣa-saṃsṛṣṭatayā (read with 2d ed. °doṣāsaṃ°), *it is like a pure white garment* (? *a haṃsalakṣaṇa garment*) *because it is not contaminated with all the bad qualities of the saṃsāra.*

hakkāra, m., rarely nt. (onomat.; cf. **hākkāra, hikkāra**; not related to AMg., JM. hakkai, hakkārai, on which see Edgerton, Indian Studies in honor of C. R. Lanman, 29), designates *a sound of joy, approbation, admiration, and esp. applause*; often foll. by **hikkāra**: janakāyasya hakkāra-hikkāra-bherīmṛdaṅgamarupaṇava-śaṅkhasaṃninādena Mv i.259.11; nearly the same phrase, ii.180.8; 444.1; iii.114.5 (mss. hakkāra-pikkāra°); 443.13 (mss. here hikkāra-pikkāra°); mahājanakāyena °ro (*applause*) mukto ii.75.4, similarly 15; 76.11 (°raṃ muktaṃ, n. sg., as if nt.), 13 (id.); °ra-sahasrāṇi (*applause*) ii.458.6; iii.116.7, 10, 11; °ro dinno iii.38.12; °raṃ (acc.) ca kṣipantānāṃ 57.18, *and (of them) clapping applause*; hakkāra-kilikilāni 312.13, of applause, cf. **hikkāra.**

[**haṃce**, 3 sg. opt., SP 111.4, represents a verb of *going*; WT añce, stating that their ms K′ reads aññe (Skt. añcati is almost restricted, in the mg. *goes*, to Gr. and Lex.); Kashgar rec. aṇvate (metr. equally good), which prob. read, see **aṇvati.**]

haḍa = (and prob. error for) **haḍi**, q.v.: haḍa-nigaḍa-bandhanair Kv 31.7.

haḍi (Skt. Lex. once, said to be m., BR; AMg. id., said to be f., Ratnach.), *fetter* made of wood; so Tib., confirmed by SP, below; always associated with, usually immediately followed by, nigaḍa, *iron shackles*: haḍi-nigaḍa LV 337.9 (vs) = Tib. śiṅ sgrog daṅ ni lcags sgrog, *wooden fetters and iron fetters*; dārvāyasmayair (so text, see this) haḍi-nigaḍa-bandhanair SP 440.4 (prose); dārumayair ayomayair haḍi-nigaḍair iha baddha bandhanaiḥ SP 450.1 (vs); haḍi-nigaḍa- Mv i.18.1 (so mss., Senart wrongly em. hasti-ni°); Divy 250.29; 365.4; 435.17; Gv 353.11 (see s.v. **kaṭaka**); haḍi-daṇḍa-bandha-nigaḍāś Gv 213.24 (vs). Cf. prec.

hatuna (Mironov, no v.l., for Mvy 7871), or **haduna**, Mvy 7871, v.l. **hanuna**, cited from Gv 133.14 which reads **hetuna**; all these nt., n. sg. °nam; or **haruṇa**, m., n. sg. °ṇaḥ Mvy 7743, and gen. °ṇasya Gv 106.4; a high number, rendered in Mvy both times by Tib. phyin phyod (var. once chod, once sbyod). Orig. form? most evidence for hatuna or haruṇa.

Hanuma(c)citra, n. of a mountain: Māy 253.34.

Hanumātīra, n. of a locality: Māy 34.

[**hantula**, see **hastala.**]

ham, interj., = next: MSV ii.27.11, expressing surprise.

hambho, also **hambhoḥ**, interj. (Pali hambho, acc. to PTSD 'expressing surprise or haughtiness'; AMg. id., merely saṃbodhanārthaka acc. to Ratnach.; Pali ambho, merely in attracting attention, but also in both pejorative and ameliorative implications, CPD), expressive of (**1**) mere emphatic address, vigorously calling attention, *hey there! look here! see here!* MSV ii.49.22; hambho ... yuktam idaṃ bhavataḥ Divy 383.4; hambhoḥ Puṣkarasārin svāgatam 621.26 (Divy prints haṃ bhoḥ as two words, perhaps rightly); hambho vaṇijaḥ (a question follows) Av ii.202.2; hambho (text as two words) tāta Suv 190.2 (to the speaker's grandfather); hambho Mahābrahma (mss. °me) Mv iii.215.1; (**2**) grief, *alas!* Mv iii.204.16 (said by a king on learning of the death of his valued purohita); (**3**) scornful incredulity: hambho (so read with mss.) na śraddadhāmy ahaṃ Mv ii.176.5 (vs), wrongly em. by Senart; same vs in Pali Jāt. iii.62.18 ambho na kira saddheyyaṃ.

Hayakarṇā, n. of a yoginī: Sādh 427.6.

Hayagrīva, n. of a deity, assoc. with Bhṛkuṭī: Sādh 37.10 et alibi.

[**hayana**, assumed by Senart's em. with Skt. Lex., Amarakośa, id. (v.l. ḍayana), *litter, palanquin*, in Mv i.109.1 (āryā vs) where mss. na-varehi, Senart hayana-va°, but yāna-va° is simpler and quite as good in both meter and sense; again in ii.171.10 (prose) Senart onaddha-hayane, but mss. -puṇya, -puṇyaṃ; in the corresp. incident in the Pali form of the same story, Jāt. iii.61.6, we find paṭicchanna-yāne; -yāne is at least as close to the mss. as Senart's -hayane, and might better be adopted.]

hari, m., (**1**) n. of a nāga king: May 246.32; (**2**) (m. or f.) a high number: Mvy 7868, cited from Gv 133.13; = **harisa**, v.l. hārisa, m., Mvy 7740; Tib. thiṅ yug in both Mvy citations; in Gv 106.3 represented by **harita.**

Harikelika, f. °**kā**, adj., with vācā, (language) *of* (some country, perh.) *Bengal* (? cf. Skt. Lex. Harikelīya, see BR): yā tu **Sāmātaṭī** (q.v.) vācā yā ca vācā °likā Mmk 332.7 (vs).

Harikeśī, n. of a piśācī: Māy 238.19.

Haricandrā, n. of a rakṣasī: Māy 243.11.

harita, nt., a high number: Gv 133.12, cited in Mvy as **haribha**, q.v.; in Gv 106.3 (m. or nt.) corresponds to **hari** (2), q.v., of Gv 133.13 and Mvy 7868; cf. also **hariva.**

harita-cārika, see s.v. **-cārika.**

Haripiṅgalā, n. of a piśāci: Māy 238.19.

haribha, nt., a high number: Mvy 7865, cited from

Gv where in 133.12 **haribham,** in 106.2 **paribheda**(sya); = **hariva,** m., Mvy 7737; Tib. in Mvy both times ḥphrog yas.

hariva, m., = prec., q.v.

harisa, m., a high number, = **hari** (2), q.v.: Mvy 7740 (v.l. **hārisa,** but Mironov only harisa).

Harisumeruś(i)rī, n. of a Buddha: Gv 285.14.

Harihariharivāhanodbhava, n. of a deity: Sādh 77.12, etc.

[**Harītī,** n. of a piśācī: Māy 238.19; prob. misprint or error for Hārītī.]

haruṇa, m. a high number: Mvy 7743; Gv 106.4; see s.v. **hatuna.**

[**hareṇḍa,** so wrongly mss. Mv ii.204.19 (vs), Senart °ṇḍā; but read hareṇu (or prob. °ṇū or °ṇuka, m.c.), which should be followed by -kalāya-kṛta-yūṣam upabhuñje; see LV 264.16 and Pali MN i.245.19–20.]

harmika, °**kā** (prob. hyper-Skt. to next = Pali hammiya, AMg. hammia = Skt. harmya; § 2.33), *room or apartment on the top of a building,* acc. to Tib. on LV bsil khaṅ, *cool room, summer-house;* Divy Index also *summer-house* (in Divy it is above the cupola of a stūpa): prāsādāś ca gavākṣa-harmika-(could be m.c. for °kā)-varā(ḥ) LV 293.16 (vs); tasyātinavāṇḍasyopari harmikā kṛtānupūrveṇa . . . Divy 244.12 (prose), here f. unless text is corrupt.

harmiya = prec., q.v.: prāsāda-°yaṃ Mv ii.36.4 (vs; metr. required).

Haryakṣa, n. of a disciple of Buddha: Mv i.75.15 (so Senart by em.)-

? **haryaṇī** (prob. corrupt), part of a cpd. listing various materials from which garments are made: aparāntaka-(q.v.)-phalaka-(*bark*?)-haryaṇī-kambala- . . . Divy 316.26.

harṣa, (**1**) nt. (= Skt. id., m. only), *joy:* -harṣaṃ (n. sg.) . . . utpadye Mv i.59.13 (prose); in SP 117.2 (vs) text harṣo pi . . . bhoti, with Kashgar rec., all Nep. mss. harṣaṃ pi; (**2**) m. (prob. = AMg. harisa, not in Ratnach., but acc. to Sheth = ābhūṣaṇa-viśeṣa), *necklace* (so Tib., mgul gdub, on Mvy and both LV passages): Mvy 6019 (harṣaḥ); kaṭakā harṣā mukuṭāni LV 121.9; harṣa-kaṭaka-keyūra- (etc.) 295.4; Divy 317.13, see s.v. **kaṭa** (2). All prose.

harṣaṇīya, adj. (prob. to Skt. harṣaṇa plus -īya, § 22.20), *pleasant, delightful;* of sounds: (śabdāḥ) LV 52.6; 411.8 (both prose); (iyaṃ mahāpṛthivī . . . kampe . . .) °yaṃ, adv., Mv i.206.17 (prose), *in a charming* (not frightening) *way.*

Harṣadatta, n. of a former Buddha: Mv i.137.15.

[**harṣya,** see **saharṣya.**]

Halaka, n. of a hunter: Divy 437.12 ff.; 442.15 ff. (in story of **Manoharā** the kiṃnarī; cf. **Mālaka**); in MSV i.126.18 ff. (as in one ms. of Divy, see 437.12, note) **Phalaka.**

Haladhara, n. of a former Buddha: Mv i.137.6.

hala-sīra (m. or nt.), *plow,* or perh. *plow-share* (so pw): Divy 124.7; 134.7; see s.v. **sīra.**

halita, nt., = next, q.v.

halibha, nt., a high number: Mvy 7867, cited from Gv, where in 133.12 **halitam,** in 106.2 **palimbha**(sya); also = **halibhu,** m. or f. (°bhuḥ, n. sg.) Mvy 7739; Tib. in Mvy both times rmoṅ yas, rmo yas.

halibhu, m. or f., = prec., q.v.

hava, havaca, see s.v. **havava.**

havala, nt., a high number: Mvy 7910 = Tib. ljab ljib; cited from Gv, and occurs in Gv 106.15 (°lasya) following hava(sya), see next, but both accidentally omitted in Gv 133.26, in the list which is the actual source of the Mvy list.

havava, var. **havaca** (so Mironov with v.l. havava in 246.85), in Gv **hava,** m., a high number: Mvy 7781; 7909, in both = Tib. bgraṅ yal (in 7909 var. °yas); in 7909 cited from Gv, which in 106.15 has -hava(sya, gen.) just before **-havala,** q.v. (omitted in Gv 133.26).

Hasanī, Divy 451.1, 456.19, or **Hasantī,** Divy 451.5, 9, 456.23, 27, n. of a river.

hasita, see **a-hasita-keśa.**

hasta, (**1**) nt. (= Skt. m.), *hand:* hastāni Mv i.18.2; haste (dual) 22.11 (both prose); (**2**) (m.; = Skt. hastaka, pw s.v. 1 f; Pali hattha), *handful:* sotpalahastena (read with v.l. utpala°; cf. 10 above, utpalahastakena) . . . vāhyamānau LV 381.18 (prose), *with a handful of lotuses being urged to drag* (the carts); (**3**) (m.; = Pali hattha; cf. **hastaka**) *fan,* see s.v. **mayūra-hasta(ka).**

hastaka, (**1**) (m.; = Pali hatthaka, cf. **hasta** 3) *fan,* see **mayūra-ha°**; (**2**) n. of a śreṣṭhin's son of Śrāvastī who became a disciple: Av ii.147.14 ff. (Pali, DPPN, has two disciples named Hatthaka, but neither seems to be this one.)

hastatva, nt. (= Pali hatthatta, Jāt. ii.383.9, with v.l. hatthattha, which is read without v.l. Jāt. i.244.10; iii.204.19; iv.420.17; 459.28, see below; v.346.9; vi.582.21; it cannot represent Skt. hasta-stha, with PTSD, being a nt. abstract, used only as obj. of a form of (ā)gacchati, barring an isolated *hatthattha-tā implied in °taṃ gato Jāt. v.349.6; CPD s.v. attha = Skt. artha refers to hatthattha, perh. implying analysis as *hastārtha; should we not read hatthatta always, with text in Jāt. ii.383.9, supported by the Mv version, below, of Jāt. iv.459.28?), *state of being in the hands* (= *power;* of, gen.): °tvam āgacche vaṇipakasya Mv ii.182.4, 9 (vs) = Pali Jāt. iv.459.28 hatthattham (read °ttam?) āgañchi vanibbakassa. Cf. **hastokta.**

hastadā, sc. lipi, a kind of writing: Mv i.135.7 (between **gulmalā** and **kasulā**).

hasta-pralehaka, see **pralehaka.**

hastala (= AMg. hatthala; to Skt. hasta, with -la, § 22.47), *thief:* haste (under the nakṣatra of that name) jātaś cauro bhavati hastalaḥ Divy 646.21; so I would read, or possibly hastulaḥ with 3 mss., for text hantulaḥ; hast- is made certain by haste.

hastasaṃvācaka, °**ikā,** see **saṃvāc°.**

hastāpatti, f., *sin of the hand,* perh. = striyā hastagrahaṇaṃ, which follows in line 1, *taking hold of a woman by hand:* °ttiḥ pañcavarge gurvī deśayitavyā Śikṣ 169.1; °ttiḥ, in list of sins, 3.

hastāvalehaka(m), see **-avalehakam.**

hastika, m., *toy-elephant:* Jm 63.10.

Hastikakṣya, nt. (cf. Skt. kakṣa, kakṣyā), n. of a Buddhist work: Mvy 1399 (Mironov v.l. °kakṣa); Laṅk 258.4 (vv.ll. °kakṣa, °kaccha), cited Śikṣ 133.4 (as °kakṣya). Tib. and Chin. interpretations of the name vary; Tib. for Laṅk glaṅ poḥi mtshan bciṅs, *binding of elephants;* other (Chin. and Jap.) versions render kakṣ(y)a by *part(s) under the forelegs;* Tib. on Mvy by rtsal, *skill, dexterity* (some Chin. versions *courage,* or *strength*).

Hastikaccha, n. of a nāga king: Mvy 3270; Māy 247.1.

Hastikarṇa, n. of a nāga: Mvy 3313.

Hastikaśīrṣa, n. of a son of King Sujāta Ikṣvāku: Mv i.348.12; 352.10; corresp. to Pali Hatthinika (with variants; refs. in DPPN); also n. of a descendant of his brother **Opura,** 352.12 (here mss. Hastinika-ś°).

hastigarbha, (**1**) m. or nt., a kind of gem: Mv ii.302.9; 310.9; (**2**) nt., a kind of fragrant black aloe-wood, or magic article made from it; °bhaṃ nāma kālāguru-ratnaṃ tena saha dhūpitamātraḥ . . . balakāyo vihāyase tiṣṭhati Gv 507.22.

hasti-grīvā, *the art of riding on an elephant's neck* (and so driving him); so Tib. (on LV and Mvy), glaṅ po cheḥi gñar zhon pa; in lists of arts: LV 156.10; Mvy 5002; Divy 442.5.

hastināga, m. (= Pali hatthi°, see PTSD s.v. nāga,

and Andersen's Reader, Glossary, *an excellent elephant*), acc. to pw (citing Divy) *ein fürstlicher Elephant*; this fits some BHS passages well enough, and may be meant in Pali Vv. comm. 37.8 hatthināga as gloss on nāga of text (this elephant was indeed a fine one); but it is not always clear that it means more than (any) *elephant* (they are all noble beasts); one suspects sometimes that hasti- may be prefixed to distinguish this from nāga, *serpent*: Mv ii.70.7; 74.12 ff.; Divy 74.2 ff.; 286.28 f.; 334.15 (read with mss.); 370.26. (In late Skt. Hastināgapura occurs as n. of a city, Schmidt, Nachträge; and acc. to Sheth, Pkt. Hatthiṇāgapura, or the like, = Hastināpura.)

Hastināpura, n. of a city in the Kiṃnarī Jātaka: Mv ii.94.19 ff. (hardly intended for the familiar Skt. city name, which is meant e. g. LV 22.6).

Hastinika-śīrṣa, see **Hastika-ś°**.

hastinikā (= Pali hatthinikā; Skt. °nī plus -ka svārthe, no dim. force), *she-elephant*: Mv iii.132.14; 137.5 (both prose); **Hastinikā-Jātaka**, in colophon of prose version, 133.5 (but Hastinī-j° 137.16, to verse version); in Pali called Māti (or Mātu)-posaka Jāt. (455).

Hasti-niyaṃsa (!), n. of a man: Mvy 3664 (Mironov id.) = Tib. glaṅ po ches ḥdul ba, *conquering* (! as if from ni-yam) *by elephants*. Is the second member actually connected with AMg. ṇiyaṃsai (Skt. nivaste), *puts on* (clothes, or, in Skt., a sword), ṇiyaṃsaṇa (Skt. nivasana), *garment, attire*?

[**hasti-madhya** (gen. °yasya), Divy 188.13, error for hasti-madya, *liquor for elephants*; cf. 190.7 hasti-madād, for which doubtless read likewise °madyād.]

hasti-vrata, *living like an elephant*, a kind of ascetic practice: LV 248.21 (prose), cited s.v. **kukkura-vratika**.

? **hastula**, see **hastala**.

hastokta, adj. (hasta-ukta; cf. Skt. hasta-stha), *declared to be in the hand* (= *power*); only °ktaṃ cakravartirājyam, referring to the imperium which the Bodhisattva renounced by retiring from the world: °ktaṃ (ca) °jyam apahāya Mv ii.68.20; 117.19; (Śuddhodana speaks of the glory which he would have shared if his son had not retired from the world,) asmākaṃ °ktaṃ °jyam abhaviṣyat iii.107.9. Cf. **hastatva**.

hahava, m. (corresp. to Pali ahaha, m.; see also **apapa**), n. of a (cold, Tib.) hell: Mvy 4932 (Tib. treats it as derived from an exclamation of grief); Divy 67.23; 138.7; Av i.4.9 etc.; Mmk 635.22. Cf. also **hāha, hāhava**, which however are mentioned with hot hells.

hākkāra = **hakkāra**, q.v., *sound of admiration* or *applause*: udānam udānayan °raṃ kurvan Gv 99.22 (prose), cited Śikṣ 36.11.

hāṭaka-prabhāsa, nt. (cf. hāṭaka 4 in BR), n. of a magic fluid: °saṃ nāma rasajātaṃ, tasyaikapalaṃ lohasahasraṃ cūrṇīkaroti, read with 2d ed. lohapalasahasraṃ svarṇī° Gv 502.5.

hāyate (= Pali hāyati; analogical pass. to Skt. hā), *wanes, declines, becomes deficient*: kiṃ hāyate tava Mv i.147.1 et al., *what is lacking to you*? Others, see Chap. 43, s.v. hā (2).

1 **-hāra**, v.l. -hāna (Senart reads -hāra and in his note compares muktā-hāra; to me the word seems dubious; one of the two mss. reads -hāna each time, but this also seems difficult), *clump, mass, thicket*, of reeds or the like; parallel with gahana: (vanagulmeṣu ca vanagahaneṣu ca) śara-hāreṣu ca naḍaka-hāreṣu ca kaṇṭaka-hāreṣu ca praviśitvā maranti Mv i.359.23; naḍagahaneṣu śara-hāreṣu ca kāśa-hāreṣu ca praviśiya maranti 361.5.

2 **-hāra**, f. **-hārī** (m. ifc., in Skt., BR, *carrying* etc.); expressing purpose, udakahārā gamiṣyāmo Mv iii.427.9, *we will go and fetch water* (also in Skt., BR s.v. udahāra, Daśak.); f., udakahārīyo, n. pl., *female water-carriers*, Mv ii.110.14; acc. adv., as ger., śāli-hāraṃ gamiṣyāmaḥ Mv i.343.8, 13, *let's go rice-gathering* (*to gather rice*), and others, § 35.4; see next, **-hāri, ojo-hāra**.

hāraka, m., (**1**) *porter, carrier* (in Skt. recorded only ifc., and so usually BHS): asati hārake (v.l. hartari) Prāt 497.12, *when no porter is available*; in same mg. bhāra-hāraka, (*load-*)*carrier*, Śikṣ 180.18; see **kāṣṭha-hāraka**; dhana-hārakaḥ, *to get wealth*, Divy 5.12, see s.v. **ṛṇadhara**, also **ojo-hāraka**; acc. adv., as ger. (§ 35.5), śāli-hārakaṃ gatasya Mv i.343.4, *gone rice-gathering*; (**2**) in Śikṣ 330.15 (vs) seems to denote a kind of entertainer: utkuṭa-śobhika-hāraka-nṛtyā māyakarāḥ . . . Perhaps corrupt.

Hārapradānajātaka, n. of a jātaka: (śrī-Yaśodharāye) °kaṃ Mv ii.68.19 (colophon).

Hārabhūṣita, n. of a former Buddha: Mv i.138.10.

Hāraśītalāṅga, n. of a former Buddha: Mv i.139.10.

hārāhāra, in °ra-kuśalāḥ Sukh 59.9, said of people born in Sukhāvatī, in long list of descriptive epithets; foll. by nayānaya-kuśalāḥ sthāna-(corruption of sthānāsthāna-? Müller's Transl., note)-kuśalāḥ; Müller, *clever in taking and refusing*; the foll. nayānaya- suggests Arthaśāstra (cf. Jāt. vi.581.22 hāra-hāriṇī, ep. of an army, senā, of uncertain mg., comm. haritabba-haraṇa-samatthā, not very plausibly), but *war-raids* (of all kinds? § 23.12) would not be appropriate to Sukhāvatī; prob. all these terms have rather an intellectual application (cf. **sthāna**); but the precise mg. escapes me.

-hāri, acc. adv. (udaka)-hāriṃ, as quasi-ger. expressing purpose, *to fetch water*: Mv ii.65.10, etc. (see § 35.6).

-hārika, adj., ifc. (to **-hāri**, prec., plus -ka? or error for **-hāraka**, q.v.?), in dhana-hārikaḥ Divy 100.28, *intending to get wealth*; see s.v. **ṛṇadhara**.

Hāritaka, m. pl. °kā(ḥ), n. of a class of gods or supernatural beings (yakṣas?): Mahāsamāj., Waldschmidt, Kl. Skt. Texte 4, 187.5; so more likely than as n. sg. f., n. of a yakṣiṇī (altho such names occur in prec. lines); follows Sadāmattā(ḥ), q.v.; in corresp. Pali (DN ii.260.24) Hāragajā; Pali knows Hārita as n. of a mahā-brahmā (DPPN).

Hāritī(-putra), see **Hārītī**.

[**hārisa**, m., var. for **harisa**, q.v.]

hārī (Skt. Lex. id.; perh. once in late Skt., see Schmidt), *pearl*: hārī strīviṣaye MSV ii.13.13, *a pearl among women*.

Hārītāyanī, n. of the gotra of the nakṣatra Ārdrā: Divy 639.16. Cf. Hāritayajña, as gotra of a nakṣatra, Weber, Die vedischen Nachrichten von den naxatra, 2.392.

Hārītī, n. of a deity (referred to as a yakṣiṇī, rākṣasī, or bhūta-mātar): SP 400.7 (Burnouf °ti; a rākṣasī); Māy 241.12 (rākṣasī); Suv 1.8; 85.4 (associated with yakṣas); 3.12 (bhūtamātā); 162.16 (id.); as yakṣiṇī Mmk 608.16; mahāyakṣiṇī Mmk 44.1; Sādh 103.9 etc.; in LV 202.10 yakṣas are called Hārītī-putra (so read, text Hāritī°, best ms. cited as Harītī°).

hālahala, m. or nt. (= Skt. halāhala, hālāhala), a kind of poison: viṣaṃ . . °laṃ (acc. sg.) Jm 219.21 (vs; a perh. m.c.).

Hālāhala, n. of a deity: Sādh 31.11 etc.

Hāsavatī, n. of a goddess: Mvy 4286.

hāsya-kāraka (cf. AMg. hāsakāraga), *jester*: °kā(ḥ) Mv iii.113.4, in list of entertainers.

hāha, Kv 18.13; 50.3; and **hāhava**, Kv 66.16; names of (a) hell(s), from the context seemingly hot; cf. **hahava** (a cold hell).

hāhā-kāra (m.; in Skt. and MIndic recorded only of grief, except once in pw said to be used in urging on horses; but Skt. Lex. cite hā also as indicative of joy, and there is one doubtful literary occurrence of hā-hā in this sense, BR s.v. 3 hā, end), *a sound of joy*: ati-r-iva udvilyaharṣā °raṃ udīretsuḥ Mv i.266.14; °ra-kilikilāprakṣveḍita-śabdaḥ Mvy 2800 (Tib. a-la-la, interj. of joy).

hāhādhara, n. of a cold hell: Dharmas 122. Replaces **huhuva** of other texts.

hiṃsatā, to be read with most mss. incl. the best for text hiṃsitā, *injuriousness*: kāma-chandu naiva tasya īrṣi naiva °tā LV 75.10 (vs); = hiṃsā, see § 22.43 (could also be derived, perhaps, from AMg. hiṃsa, adj., = Skt. hiṃsra, plus -tā; no *hiṃsin is recorded, and Skt. hiṃsa adj. only once in RV).

hikkāra, m. (onomat.; in Pali said to mean *hiccup*, cf. Pali and Skt. hikkā; here seems = **hakkāra** and associated with that), *a sound of applause, joy*, or the like: hikkārā (read °ra, m.c., n. pl.) tūryamiśrā samantato vartate (so with mss., m.c.) aho dharmaṃ Mv i.237.3 (vs); in ii.141.11 (vs) the corrupt mss. seem to indicate hikkāra-kilikilā (see s.v. **hakkāra**; otherwise Senart); dundubhi-śabdo hikkāranado ca ii.413.20 (vs, meter obscure); others see s.v. **hakkāra**.

hiṅgulaka (m. or nt.; = Pali id., Skt. °la), *vermilion*: MSV ii.142.9.

hiṇḍati (= Pali id.; Skt. Dhātup. hiṇḍate; for cpds. see Chap. 43), *wanders*: hiṇḍan (pres. pple.) LV 140.7 (prose; so text printed, but follows gatvā, perhaps understand āhiṇḍan).

hitaṃkara, adj. (= Skt. and Pali hitakara; only in vss, perh. m.c.), *beneficent*: °raḥ LV 359.9 (vs); °rāḥ Suv 159.9 (vs). Cf. next.

hitaṃkarin, adj., = prec.: °rī, n. sg., Suv 245.5 (vs).

Hitacaraṇasaṃkrama, n. of a kumbhāṇḍa: Mvy 3440.

Hiteṣin, Hitaiṣin (both spellings in mss.), n. of three former Buddhas in the same list: Mv iii.234.7; 236.11; 237.5.

hinihināyamānā, fem. pres. mid. pple., and **hinihinikā**, onomat.(?), applied to sandals: MSV iv.206.11; 207.11.

himantrā, a high number: °trāyā(ḥ), gen., Gv 106.8. Cf. **nahimantra** and **hemātra**.

Himaratī (read °vatī? but no such river-name is recorded), n. of a river: Kv 71.15.

himavac-candana, nt., n. of a specially fine variety of sandalwood (mahācandanaratnam): Gv 501.5.

Himavant, n. of a maharṣi: Māy 256.26.

Hiraṇyagarbha, n. of a king: Mmk 622.7.

Hiraṇyadhanyaśirika (v.l. °śirīka), n. of a former Buddha: Mv i.139.14 (prose).

Hiraṇyapāṇi, n. of a householder's son: Av ii.74.7 ff.

Hiraṇyavatī, once (m.c.?) °**vatyā** (cf. § 10.6), (= Pali Hiraññavatī; see s.v. **Āryavatī**), n. of a river, on the bank of which the Buddha entered nirvāṇa: Mmk 354.14; 580.9 (nadyāṃ °vatyāyāṃ, vs, perh. m.c. for °vatyāṃ); 595.4 (vs, °vatī-tīre); Māy 253.8 (in list of names); MPS 29.4.

hirā, *sand*, see **hirodaka**.

Hiri (= Pali id.), n. of a yakṣa leader: Māy 235.25.

Hirikeśa, n. of a yakṣa leader: Māy 235.25.

hirimanta-tā, for hrīmat-tā, *modesty*: Samādh p. 62 line 16 (vs). Meter proves the form.

Hirī, see **Hrī**.

Hiru, n. of a minister of Rudrāyaṇa, bracketed with **Bhiru(ka)**: Divy 545.5; 556.8, 13; 562.15; 570.26; 571.2; 576.21.

Hiruka, (**1**) m., = prec.: Divy 563.25; 564.10; 575.25 f.; 576.22; (**2**) nt., n. of a city founded by the prec.: Divy 576.22 f.

hirodaka (not ahiro°!), Divy 384.24, acc. to Note p. 709 hirā-udaka, *vein-water, blood*: but this is quite implausible. The phrase is hirodakasikatāpiṇḍair aṇḍakāṣṭhebhyo (see this) 'pi asārataratvaṃ kāyasyāvetya, *realizing that the body is more worthless even than eggshells*(?) *full of* (? so Burnouf, Introd. 376) *lumps of sand, water, and gravel*. (Burnouf, *pleines de boules de sable faites avec des larmes de serpent*.) The instr. -piṇḍair is apparently associative, with the following word; perhaps render *eggshells along with lumps* etc., *eggshells* (if Burnouf is right) being likewise symbolic of worthlessness, and also fragility. In Deśīn. 8.66 is noted hilā, *sand* (vālukā); hirā is prob. equivalent to this. It would fit with sikatā, and udaka could perhaps be used as a symbol of worthlessness.

? **hilima**, f. °**mā**, adj. with **jomā**, q.v.; mg. unknown; denotes a *good* kind of broth or liquid food: Divy 497.19 ff.

Hilliśāla, °**lin**, n. of a rich and miserly householder: Karmav 70.1 (°la-); 75.1 (°lī, n. sg.).

hiṣati (= **hīṣati**, q.v.), *neighs*: °ti LV 236.7 (vs); m.c. for hī° or Skt. he°? But hi° occurs as v.l. for hī° Mv ii.160.7 (prose).

hīna, nt. (rare in Skt. and not in this precise mg.), *the low*; hīnāya, with āvartati (mss. vartati; = Pali hīnāya āvattati, once vattati acc. to text Jāt. i.276.16), *returns to the low* = *gives up monkish life, returns to the world*: hīnāyāvartanti (mss. °yaṃ vart°) kāmehi Mv iii.47.14 (prose). Cf. **hīnāyāvarta**.

hīna-yāna (nt.), *the inferior vehicle*, i. e. that of the śrāvakas: Mvy 1253; depreciated, na °yānena nayanti buddhāḥ SP 46.14 (vs); others, see s.v. **yāna**.

hīnāyāvarta- (mss. hīnāya or hīnā-vartta-; see under **hīna**; Pali hīnāyāvatta), *one who 'returns to the low', quits monkish life for the world*: hīnāyāvartapravṛttā (by em.; mss. °vartta-pravṛtti) bhavanti Mv iii.47.16 (prose); in Pali, same incident, SN ii.217.29 hīnāyāvattā bhavanti.

[**Hīmavata**, error for **Haima**°, q.v.]

hīṣaṇa (nt.; to next plus -ana), *neighing* of a horse (both mss. in the first two instances, one in the third, bhīṣaṇa; em. Senart): uccena svareṇa hīṣitaṃ, mama °ṇa-śabdena . . . Mv ii.160.7; uccena svareṇa °ṇa-śabdaṃ kṛtaṃ 189.8; aśvarājasya °ṇa-śabdaṃ śrutvā iii.76.13. All prose.

hīṣati, hīṣyati (also **hiṣati**, q.v.; comm. on Hem. 4.258 hīsamaṇaṃ heṣitaṃ, and on Deśīn. 8.68 hīsamaṇaṃ heṣāravaḥ; cf. Skt. heṣati, hreṣ-), *neighs*: hīṣyanti (v.l. hreṣyanti) Mv i.308.6; hīṣitaṃ ii.160.7, *it was neighed* (v.l. hiṣ°); hīṣitvā iii.76.2, 12. All prose.

hu, and **hū**, m.c. (= AMg. id.), rarely for **khu** (q.v.) = Skt. khalu, *of course*, etc.: ma hū LV 141.3 (vs); mā hu 202.6 (vs). Prob. not contained in RP 58.18 (vs) **jāhu**, q.v.

huṃhuṃ-kāra, v.l. for **phuphu-kāra**, q.v.

Hutāsanī (read °śanī), n. of a rākṣasī: Māy 243.13.

huduhuduyati (onomat.; cf. Skt. huḍuk, Lex. hulahulī, and s.v. **huluhulu**), *roars*, of the sound of nāgas sending rain: Megh 304.18.

Huluka (Mironov Ulluka; v.l. in both edd. Uluka), n. of a nāga king: Mvy 3280.

Huluṭa (cf. prec. and next), n. of a nāga: MSV i.xvii.5.

Huluḍa, Hulura, vv.ll. for **Hullura**.

huluhulu, var. (in Calc. and Tib.) for **phuluphulu**, q.v.

Hullura (Mironov Hulluṇḍa, vv.ll. Hulluḍa, Huluḍa, Hulura; Kyoto ed. v.l. Huluḍa), n. of a nāga king: Mvy 3279; Kv 2.11 (confirms Hullura).

huvana, n. or epithet of some hostile (presumably magic or supernatural) power: Māy 237.27 huvanātaḥ (abl.). Follows Havanātaḥ, which I identify with Havana, used in the epic of a Rudra; followed by **unmardana**, q.v.

huhuṃ, interj. (= Pali id., or with v.l. huṃhuṃ; see Vin. comm. v.957.32) expression of haughtiness or irritability (Vin. comm. l.c. māna, kodha): huhun ti ca karoti (mss. corrupt; so Senart em.) Mv iii.325.3. Cf. **nihuhuṃka**. In iii.325.2–3 Senart reads by em. **huhuṃka-jātiko** (= Pali id., Vin. i.2.32), perhaps rightly, but mss. kuhako ti.

? **huhuṃka-jātika**, see prec.

huhuva, m., n. of a (cold) hell: Mvy 4933 (Tib. treats it as derived from an interjection expressing distress from cold, a-chu!); Divy 67.23; 138.7; Av i.4.9 etc. In Dharmas 122 replaced by **hāhādhara.**

hū, see **hu.**

hūṇa, hūna (-lipi), *Hun-script*, in list of modes of writing: hūna-lipi LV 126.1; -hūṇāpīrā (dvandva; sc. lipi) Mv i.135.6.

hūma, nt. (Mironov ḍūma; v.l. both edd. hama), a high number: Mvy 7711 = Tib. zam zim; also corresp. to **poma**, q.v.

hṛdi, stem in comp. for hṛd (= hṛdaya), *heart* (unrecorded otherwise; Speyer refers to BR s.v., but hṛdi is cited there only thrice from RV, and later Vedic scholars have almost unanimously agreed that these forms are locs. of hṛd; cf. § 15.14): hṛdi-maitryā sphuṭaṃ Av i.79.14 (prose), *suffused with heart-love*; bhāryāṃ priyāṃ hṛdi-sukhāṃś ca sutāṃ śirāṃsi (... dattvā) Mv i.83.15 (vs), *sons that rejoice the heart*; śravaṇa-hṛdi-nayana-subhagaiḥ 99.4 (vs), *pleasing to the ear, heart, and eye* (meter seems correct); manohṛdinandanaṃ 99.6 (vs), *rejoicing the mind and heart*. In the three Mv passages meter might be concerned; there is no real v.l.

? **hṛdimano**, obscure and prob. corrupt, in otherwise corrupt and metr. impossible line (first of an āryā): evam (mss.) ekaikasya vaśibhūtasya dhārenti hṛdimano (so 2 mss., 3 hṛmano, one hṛtmano) Mv i.116.9 (vs). The word could be n. pl. or gen. sg.; it is possible, but by no means evident, that it contains the stem **hṛdi** (prec.). Senart's note is not helpful.

heṭhaka, adj. (= Pali id.; to next plus -aka), *injurious*: °keṣu Ud xxx.48. See also **a-he°**.

heṭhati, heṭhayati (= Pali heṭheti; Skt. Gr. heṭhati; the root is not recorded in Pkt.), *injures, vexes, annoys*: °yanti na cānyonyaṃ LV 97.22 (vs); ma (= Skt. hiṃs-): (m.c.) heṭhatā (impv.) 123.5 (vs); heṭheti Mv iii.215.14 (vs); heṭhayitvā 369.8 (vs). Commoner is **vi-heṭh-**, q.v.

heṭhanā (= Pali id.; to prec. plus -anā), *injury*: prārthayāmi na jinasya °nām RP 9.14 (vs).

heṭhayitar (to **heṭhayati** plus -tar), *one who injures*: Mv iii.215.18 (vs) °tā na vidyati.

1 **heṭhā** (to **heṭha[ya]ti**), *injury, annoyance, vexation*: karonti ... heṭhāḥ (acc. pl.) LV 341.21 (vs); in Mv repeatedly in prose, always heṭhām, object of a form of utpādayati (in ii.236.13 utpādema for °dayema; in i.365.10 utpadyema, see § 38.24), Mv i.365.10; ii.236.13; 447.17; 448.7; 486.1; 489.3.

? 2 **heṭhā, heṭhe**, adv., = **heṣṭā, heṣṭe**, qq.v. (no forms with single ṭh are recorded in Pali or Pkt., and these are very rare and not very certain), *below, underneath*: heṭhā ca dharaṇī sarvā Mv ii.351.3 (vs), so Senart with 1 ms., but v.l. **heṣṭā**, which is read by both mss. and ed. in repetition of the line iii.275.5; tatra heṭhe (perh. to be read with 1 ms.; v.l. heto; Senart em. heṭhato, cf. **heṣṭato**) nihito nidhiḥ Mv ii.438.16 (prose).

? **heṭhya** (m. or nt.; cf. **heṭhā** and relatives), in a list of athletic and martial arts in which a prince is trained: chedye vā bhedye vā heṭhye (v.l. hāthe, with th) vā saṃgrāmaśīrṣāyāṃ vā ... Mv ii.434.13.

hetu, (**1**) (substantially = Skt. id.) *cause*; on relation to **pratyaya** (1) see this; normally m. as in Skt. and Pali (Childers), but mss. make it f. in Mv i.43.10 (vs), intending sarvābhi (°hi) hetūbhi upasthitāhi, where Senart em. sarvehi ... upasthitehi, in accord with repetition i.242.20 (where read upasthitehi instead of Senart's violent em.); six hetu, Mvy 2259–65 and AbhidhK. LaV-P. ii.245 (in different order), kāraṇa-h° (*raison d'être*, LaV-P.), saha-bhū- (*cause mutuelle*), vipāka- (*cause de rétribution*), saṃprayukta- (*cause associée*), sarvatraga- (*cause universelle*), sabhāga- (*cause pareille*); La V-P.'s note here, and the foll. pages of his transl., explain the terms at length; (**2**) hetu as adv. (= Pali id.; only noted ifc. in BHS but in Pali used alone with prec. gen.; acc. to Senart i note 536, an 'atténuation' of Skt. hetoḥ), *for the sake of, because of, in order to*: bodhihetur (*for the sake of enlightenment*, Tib. byaṅ chub don du; is -r 'Hiatus-bridger', § 4.62? or may -hetur be m.c. for -hetor, supporting Senart's theory? a nom. sg. is impossible here) aprameya tyaktu dustyajā tvayā LV 170.14 (vs); ārakṣahetu, *for the purpose of guarding, for a guard*, Mv i.204.6, 11 = ii.8.1, 6 (vss); parasya vismāpanahetu (so Tib., ṅo mtshar ...; text viśvāp°) KP 126.14 (vs), *to astonish another*; (**3**) a high number: hetuḥ Mvy 8018.

hetuka, adj. or subst. (cf. AMg. heuya, adj., *causal*), *causal*, or (= hetu) *cause*: °kās trayaḥ saṃjñā(ḥ) LV 374.11 (vs), *the three false notions which are causal*, or *causes* (= hetu); see s.v. **saṃjñā** 4.

hetudṛṣṭi, *rationalistic heresy*: °ṭi-samudghāṭo dharmālokamukhaṃ LV 33.6.

hetuna, nt., a high number: Gv 133.14, see s.v. **hatuna.**

Hetupadma, n. of a Tathāgata: Gv 310.16.

hetupratyaya, see s.v. **pratyaya** (1).

Hetumant(a), n. of a former Buddha: Mv iii.233.4 f. (acc. °taṃ, nom. °tas).

hetura, nt., a high number: Gv 133.9; = **hevara**, q.v.

hetu-śas (written °sas, °so; = Pali hetuso), *according to (the several) cause(s)*: -hetuso-vipākaso-jñāna- LV 433.6.

hetu-hila, nt., a high number: LV 148.4, cited Mvy 7966; = Tib. rgyu rig (Mvy adds ḥdzin), *cause-knowledge (-grasping)*.

hetv-indriya, nt., a high number: LV 148.5, cited Mvy 7968; = Tib. rgyu dbaṅ (lit. transl.).

? **Hemakroḍa** (em.; mss. Ahoma-, one Ahema-, and -kroḍha), n. of a former Buddha: Mv i.137.5 (prose).

hema-jāla (not noted as cpd. in Skt.; Pali id., defined as covering for gift-elephants, gift-chariots, a heavenly mansion or vimāna and the body of a possessor of one; AMg. °jālaga, *a kind of ornament*, Ratnach.), lit. *gold-net*, but seems to have acquired a special mg., which is not clear: in Mv i.171.8 (vs) one of the 60 qualities of a Buddha's voice is that it is hemajāla-tulya-ravā, *sounding like a...*; in Mv i.195.5 the *railing-networks* (vedikā-jāla, see **vedikā**) of Dīpavatī, and in 196.4 each of its city gates, are covered with two hemajāla, one of gold and the other of silver! (195.5) dvihi hemajālehi praticchannā abhūṣi suvarṇamayena ca °lena rūpyamayena ca; the next sentence, both times, says that the golden hemajāla had bells of silver, the silver one bells of gold; Senart supposes that hema- has come to mean *precious substance* in general, but I know of nothing else to support this; on the other hand, in Mv ii.453.17 the lit. mg. may well apply, elephants being described as hemajāla-praticchanna (misprinted hemalāla° in text), as in Pali AN iv.393.21 (°saṃchanna).

Hemajālapraticchannā, n. of a lokadhātu in the northeast: LV 294.8.

Hemajālaprabhu (Senart em. °prabha), n. of a former Buddha: Mv i.141.3.

Hemajālālaṃkṛta, n. of a Bodhisattva: LV 294.9 (he came from **Hemajālapraticchannā**).

hemantika, adj. (to hemanta plus -ika; = Pali id., Skt. hai°), *of or pertaining to winter*: °ko (sc. prāsāda, *palace*) Mv iii.405.13.

Hemaratha, n. of a former Buddha: Mv i.139.5.

Hemavarṇa, (**1**) n. of two former Buddhas in the same list: Mv i.136.15, and 137.1 (in the latter all mss. make Hemavarṇa a separate name; Senart reads Hemavarṇalambadāma as one name); also of a former Buddha in LV 5.6; (**2**) n. of a cakravartin: Mv i.153.16.

hemātra, m., a high number: Mvy 7755 = Tib. gar gzhal; cf. **nahimantra** and **himantrā.**

heri (cf. Pkt. heria, Skt. Lex. herika; late Skt. herika and heraka, Schmidt, Nachträge), *spy, secret listener, emissary*: heriḥ Mvy 3805 = Tib. ñam rna.

Heruka, n. of a deity: Sādh 146.4 et passim.

Herukī, n. of a goddess: Sādh 488.6 etc.

helā, (**1**) (perh. cf. JM. heḍā, defined by Hindi ghaṭā, samūha, Sheth) some sort of *container, basket* or the like: sa hiraṇya-suvarṇasya helāṃ pūrayitvā Av i.224.6; gṛhapatinā sā suvarṇa-helā brāhmaṇāya dattā 8; (**2**) a high number: Gv 106.12; no corresp. in Gv 133.22 or parallel lists.

heluka (m. or nt.), a high number: Gv 106.3; prob. a doublet for the next, for which the same line also has **loka** (read **aloka** or **āl°**), before this, and separated from it only by **indriya** which no other list contains; this, like **heluga** in Mvy 7741, is followed by **durbuda** (Mvy drabuddha), and then by **haruṇa** (in both alike).

heluga, m., a high number: Mvy 7741 = Tib. śugs ḥphyo, for which Das gives henuka as equiv.; corresp. to **aloka, āloka**, also to prec., qq.v.

heluta (m.), a high number: Gv 106.14; = next two.

heluya, m., a high number: Mvy 7778 = Tib. ḥod (or, ḥol) phyod, or ḥol chod; = prec. and next.

heluva, m., a high number: Gv 133.25; cited Mvy 7907 as **heluvuḥ** = Tib. ḥol phyod; = prec. two, qq.v.

Hevajra, (**1**) n. of a deity: Sādh 479.1; (**2**) (also °ra-tantra), n. of a tantric work: °ra-deśakaḥ Sādh 450.1; °ra-tantra-saṃbandhāṃ ... Kurukullāṃ 381.1.

hevara, m., Mvy 7731, or nt. id. 7859, a high number; Mvy 7859 is cited from Gv, which in 106.2 has **devala**, but in 133.9 **hetura**.

heṣṭa-, in comp., prob. only m.c. for **heṣṭā**, q.v.

heṣṭato (**heṣṭhato**), adv. and postpos. (= Pali heṭṭhato; see next), *below, underneath*; mss. regularly heṣṭato, rarely with ṣṭh; Senart inconsistently reads both, without regard to mss.: as adv., Mv iii.73.7, 329.6; with prec. gen., Mv ii.436.9; 437.17; 438.1 (śālarājānāṃ he°), 3.

heṣṭā, °**ṭhā**, adv. and prep. or postpos. with gen. (= Pali heṭṭhā, Skt. adhastāt; see prec. and foll. items; I find no difference in use between these various adverbial forms, all being potentially adv. and prep. or postpos.; Pali has heṭṭhā and heṭṭhato = **heṣṭato**, with the abl. suffix; AMg. has also heṭṭhi = **heṣṭi, heṣṭe**; cf. also 2 **heṭhā, heṭhe**; the BHS spelling with ṣṭ, rarely also ṣṭh, is hyper-Skt. for the MIndic forms), *below, underneath*: as adverb, Mv i.15.16 (vs) heṣṭā upari pārśvato (all adv.); 30.4 (prose) vayaṃ heṣṭā upari devā, *we are lower, the gods higher*; ii.29.19; 62.8; 304.16; 350.19; 378.21; iii.86.1 (mss.); 185.18 (vs, upari tapati, read tapat', ādityo heṣṭā tapati vālikā); Suv 59.2 (vs); in cpds., heṣṭāpaskandha, *the mass of water below*, LV 298.20; 339.14 (vss), cf. **heṣṭi** (so read) ... āpaskandho 368.19 (vs); heṣṭa-gāmī Suv 58.8 (vs; m.c. for heṣṭā-); with gen., usually preceding, Mv i.21.7 (prose) teṣāṃ heṣṭā; in Mv ii.92.13 (vs) Senart heṣṭā (mss. corrupt, heṣṭo, hastau) ca toyasya; iii.151.5 āśramapadasya heṣṭā; 350.10 nyagrodhasya heṣṭhā (v.l. heṣṭo); for SP 310.5 see **heṣṭe**.

heṣṭi, adv. (cf. prec.; AMg. heṭṭhi; in BHS very rare and doubtful, may be m.c. for **heṣṭe**), *below*: LV 73.21 (vs) read, mahāsahasralokadhātu heṣṭi (or, v.l., heṣṭa; Lefm. heṣvi, allegedly with most mss.) bhindayitvanā (so with v.l. for bhindiy°); heṣṭi (Lefm. em. hesti; some mss. hasti!) ... yāvataś cāpaskandho LV 368.19 (vs; see under **heṣṭā** in cpds.).

heṣṭima, rarely °**ṭhima**, adj. (= Pali heṭṭhima; to **heṣṭi**, etc., plus -(i)ma, § 22.13), *lower*, (what is) *below*: of the nadir, heṣṭimā diś(ā), SP 191.5 (vs; text, paścimā-heṣṭima-uttarasyāṃ, Kashgar rec. paścimāyottaraheṣṭimāyāṃ); 243.11 (prose; ed. adhastāyāṃ, Kashgar rec. heṣṭimāyāṃ, diśi); Mv i.124.7 (vs; °masmiṃ diśo bhāge); ii.163.6 °mā diśā; also of the body, °maṃ kāyaṃ, and °māto kāyāto (abl.), Mv iii.115.19, 20 (in these Senart °ṣṭhi°, v.l. °ṣṭi°); 410.5, 7, *the lower* (part of the) *body*.

heṣṭe, °**ṭhe**, (adv. and) postpos. with gen. (see prec. items; this is not recorded elsewhere, unless as heṭṭhi in AMg., but may be regarded as a loc. equivalent to Pkt. heṭṭhammi, Sheth), *below*: tasya heṣṭhe (v.l. haste; Senart em. heṣṭā) Mv ii.451.17; tasyaiva heṣṭe SP 55.1 (vs); kṣetrasya heṣṭe (so, or heṣṭhe, most mss.; KN heṣṭā; WT kṣetre 'sya heṣṭā, claiming support in Tib. zhiṅ ḥdiḥi ḥog na, which does not seem to me to support their em.) SP 310.5 (vs).

heṣṭena, adv. (may be regarded as instr. to Pkt. stem heṭṭha-, see under prec.; not recorded), *below*: yāvān avīci heṣṭena bhavāgraṃ copariṣṭataḥ SP 355.7 (vs).

heṣṭhato, etc., see **heṣṭato**, etc.

[**heṣvi**, see **heṣṭi**.]

[**hesti**, see **heṣṭi**.]

(**haimantika**, see s.v. **sāmayika**.)

Haimavata, (**1**) pl., n. of a school: Mvy 9092; (**2**) n. of a yakṣa (= Pali Hema°), regularly assoc. with **Sātāgiri**, q.v. (as in Pali with °gira): Mahāsamāj., Waldschmidt, Kl. Skt. Texte 4, 167.11 (pl.); Māy 87; 236.3 and 29 (Waldschmidt, ib. 175 n. 3); Samādh p. 43 line 20; (listed with Sātāgiri among gandharvas) Suv 162.5; in Hoernle, MR 26.14 (Āṭānāṭiya Sūtra), corruptly Hīmavata.

hairaṇyika (to hiraṇya plus -ika; Skt. °yaka; Pali heraññika and °aka), *goldsmith*: in lists of guilds, between sauvarṇika and prāvārika (*cloak-dealer*? or read prāvālika, *coral-dealer*? both Skt.), Mv iii.113.6 and 442.12; others, Divy 501.3 ff.; 590.26 ff.; Av i.199.1, 4, 6.

ho bhaṇe = **bho bhaṇe**, see **bhaṇe**.

hoti (= Pali id.), for Skt. bhavati, see Chap. 43, s.v. bhū (2). The pres. hoti is rare compared to bhoti; on the other hand, in futures of the hohiti (hohati) type, ho- is much commoner than bho-; and it is doubtful whether bhoṣyati (instead of bheṣyati) should be recognized at all as fut.

hora-pāṭhaka (= Pali horā-pā°, which perh. read here? Skt. horā is regular, hora- in comp. doubtful), *astrologer*: (naimittikena ca) °kena (v.l. °pāṭhena) ca vyākṛto Mv iii.178.18 (prose).

hyastanike, adv. (to Skt. hyastana plus -ika), *yesterday*: MSV ii.63.9.

[**hrada**, *pool*, only m.; not nt. Mv i.237.12 (prose), where interpret hrada-m-(hiatus-bridging)-iva accho anāvilo.]

? **hrāsi** (for hrāse, loc. of hrāsa, *diminution*?), is obscure to me; occurs five times in a series of śloka vss (in many of which both meter and sense are bad, as the text is printed) in Mmk, evidently dealing with astronomical portents: tato hrāsi madhyāhne (submetrical! as 4th syllable from end, -i could be m.c. for -e) aparāhne divākare Mmk 276.6; tamo (read tato with all the rest? or contrariwise, should they all be emended to tamo for tato?) hrāsi-gate bhānoḥ kṣmākampo yadi jāyate ib. 11; tato hrāsi yāme vai (submetrical) calite vasumatī tadā (! hypermetric) 277.1; tato hrāsi yāmānte (submetrical) dṛśyate karma dāruṇam 3; tato hrāsi-madhye tu (submetrical) ante yāme prajāyate 17.

hriyāpayati (caus. to next), *makes ashamed*: (tāś ca vinagnīkṛtya pratyavekṣante,) tā hriyāpayanti Bhīk 11a.5.

hriyāyati, hrī° (denom.? to hrī; cf. Pali hiriyati, hirī°, harāyati; Pkt. hiriāmi, Sheth), *is ashamed, embarrassed, shy*: pres. pple. n. sg. f., (Yaśodharā) hriyāyantī (v.l. °ti) kumāram (°rasya, 11) allīnā Mv ii.48.8 (v.l. hrīy°), 11; with gen., bhagavato ... (13 mama) hriyāyantī (v.l. hrī°) allīnā ib. 12, 13; tadāpi eṣā mama hrīyāyantī (v.l. hri°) 64.5; caus., see prec.

Hrī, (written) **Hirī** (so as common noun, examples § 3.108; Pali hirī, Skt. hrī), *Modesty* personified: as one of the four daughters of Indra (see **Āśā**), Mv ii.59.22 (vs);

as a devakumārikā in the northern quarter, Mv iii.309.9 = LV 391.4 (vs).

Hrīdeva, n. of a Tuṣita god: LV 183.16.

hrīyāyati, see **hriy°**.

hrīr-apatrāpya, nt. (doubtless represents an imperfect Sktization of the Pali cpd. hirottappa, hirotappa, which represents Pali hiri, hirī (Skt. hrī) plus Pali ottappa = BHS apatrāpya; in the Pali cpd. stem-final i has been lost before o-, leaving hir- which was Sktized as hrīr-; probably 'hiatus-bridging' r is also concerned, § 4.63; the form hry-apatrāpya is likewise recorded), see s.v. **apatrāpya.**

hretavya, adj.-gdve. (to Skt. hrī-; unrecorded; § 34.21), *shameful*: °yeṣu sthāneṣv āhrīkyaparyavasthānaṃ vinodayaty . . . Bbh 223.9.

Partial Index of Middle Indic Words

Here are included Middle Indic words referred to in the Dictionary, under the words cited, in so far as they might not be easy to locate without such a reference.

The great majority of Pali words cited, and many words from other Middle Indic languages, can be located by looking in the Dictionary under the words themselves, either in their Middle Indic forms, or in Sanskritized or semi-Sanskritized adaptations which will be obvious to anyone acquainted with Middle Indic phonology. Frequently representatives of both types will be found. Note that both must be searched for, if one wishes to know whether a given Middle Indic word exists in BHS; also that when a BHS word has a Pali correspondent, other Middle Indic correspondents are commonly *not* cited in this Dictionary. In the following Index, I have not included words of the type described in this paragraph.

Pali

Ardha-Māgadhī

Other Prakrit, Apabhraṃśa, and Deśī words

Addendum.

Page 294, 2d column, after line 8, insert:
nikubjayati (denom. to **nikubja**; Pali ni(k)kujjati), *turns upside down*: (khoraṃ) °yiṣyanti MSV iv. 52.16.